BDO's Orange Tax Guide 2011–12

BDO's Orange Tax Guide 2011–12

Covering
Value Added Tax, updated by Charles Barcroft
Stamp Taxes, updated by Roger Thomas, of Pump Court Tax Chambers, Barrister

LexisNexis®

Members of the LexisNexis Group worldwide

United Kingdom	LexisNexis, a Division of Reed Elsevier (UK) Ltd, Halsbury House, 35 Chancery Lane, London, WC2A 1EL, and London House, 20-22 East London Street, Edinburgh EH7 4BQ
Australia	LexisNexis Butterworths, Chatswood, New South Wales
Austria	LexisNexis Verlag ARD Orac GmbH & Co KG, Vienna
Benelux	LexisNexis Benelux, Amsterdam
Canada	LexisNexis Canada, Markham, Ontario
China	LexisNexis China, Beijing and Shanghai
France	LexisNexis SA, Paris
Germany	LexisNexis Deutschland GmbH, Munster
Hong Kong	LexisNexis Hong Kong, Hong Kong
India	LexisNexis India, New Delhi
Italy	Giuffrè Editore, Milan
Japan	LexisNexis Japan, Tokyo
Malaysia	Malayan Law Journal Sdn Bhd, Kuala Lumpur
New Zealand	LexisNexis NZ Ltd, Wellington
Poland	Wydawnictwo Prawnicze LexisNexis Sp, Warsaw
Singapore	LexisNexis Singapore, Singapore
South Africa	LexisNexis Butterworths, Durban
USA	LexisNexis, Dayton, Ohio

Published by LexisNexis

A CIP Catalogue record for this book is available from the British Library.

ISBN for this volume ISBN: 9781405757195

Printed and bound by CPI Group (UK) Ltd, Croydon, CR0 4YY

Visit LexisNexis at www.lexisnexis.co.uk

Foreword

Welcome to BDO's Orange Tax Guide 2011–12.

2011 saw another Finance Act, bringing with it a number of amendments and updates to fiscal legislation. The 2011–12 Yellow and Orange Tax Guides will help you navigate through this often complicated and difficult legislation.

BDO is delighted to be responsible for producing the Yellow and Orange Tax Guides. I hope that you will find them useful and informative. The vital role of the publishers, LexisNexis, in their timely production of these titles is very much appreciated.

Paul Eagland

Head of Taxation

BDO LLP

Preface

This annual is prepared by practitioners for practitioners and is of practical help to anyone involved in the day-to-day application of stamp duty, stamp duty reserve tax, stamp duty land tax and/or value added tax. It is essentially a brief explanation in plain words of the current tax statutes and statutory instruments in chronological order.

Commentary. Sections, paragraphs and regulations are explained, with references to case law, extra-statutory concessions, statements of practice, press releases and other useful information. Where appropriate the notes contain helpful tax planning suggestions and highlight practical danger areas that might otherwise be overlooked. We must emphasise that no commentary can replace study of the precise wording of the legislation.

Appendices. The appendices contain a unique easy-to-find collection of press releases, extra-statutory concessions, statements of practice and other useful information.

Indices. A single index for each tax covers both the commentary and the appendices. Indices are at the back of the book.

Currency. The law is stated as at August 2011 and covers the changes made by the Finance Act 2011, the many orders and regulations made by statutory instrument, recent case decisions and statements of practice.

Previous editions. This edition covers the legislation applicable in the year 2011–12 only, so readers should as usual **keep earlier editions** of the guide to deal with past years.

Other taxes. A similar treatment for income tax, corporation tax, capital gains tax, inheritance tax and national insurance contributions is in the twin publication BDO's Yellow Tax Guide.

Assistance. We gratefully acknowledge the help received in preparation of this work from Roger Thomas of Pump Court Tax Chambers as regards stamp taxes and Charles Barcroft as regards value added tax. I also wish to thank my colleagues at BDO for their efforts in our work on updating the book this year.

Improvements. If you would like to comment on our guide or suggest improvements, please email nigel.eastaway@bdo.co.uk. Alternatively, please write to: The Editor, BDO's Orange Tax Guide, 55 Baker Street, London W1U 7EU.

Nigel Eastaway

Editor

September 2011

Contents

Abbreviations

BTR	British Tax Review
CA	Contributions Agency
CCAB	Consultative Committee of Accountancy Bodies
COR	Contracted-out rate
DSS	Department of Social Security
EB	Earnings bracket
EU	European Union (European Community until 31 October 1993)
FA	Finance Act
FSA 1986	Financial Services Act 1986
ICAEW	Institute of Chartered Accountants in England and Wales
IHT	Inheritance Tax (formerly Capital Transfer Tax)
IHTA 1984	Inheritance Tax Act 1984
LEL	Lower earnings limit
PCTA 1968	Provisional Collection of Taxes Act 1968
PSO	Pension Schemes Office (formerly Superannuation Funds Office)
RR	Reduced rate
s	section
SA 1891	Stamp Act 1891
Sch	Schedule
SI	Statutory Instrument
SP	Statement of Practice
SR	Standard rate
SSAA	Social Security Administration Act
SSCBA	Social Security Contributions and Benefits Act
SSPA	Social Security Pensions Act
STC	Simon's Tax Cases
STI	Simon's Tax Intelligence
SWTI	Simon's Weekly Tax Intelligence
TA 1988	Income and Corporation Taxes Act 1988
TC	Tax Cases (HMSO)
TCGA 1992	Taxation of Chargeable Gains Act 1992
TMA 1970	Taxes Management Act 1970
UEL	Upper earnings limit
VATA 1994	Value Added Tax Act 1994

Part I Value Added Tax

Contents

1. UK Statutes

Contents

All references, in the style **V3.186** in this Part are to *De Voil: Indirect Tax Service.*

VAT and Duties Tribunal decisions unreported in the Value Added Tax Tribunal Reports (VATTR), now renamed the Value Added Tax and Duties Reports (V & DR), are cited by reference to the appellant's name and the tribunal's sequential numerical reference, eg *Nichols* (No 14521). The VAT and Duties Tribunal has now been replaced by the First-tier Tribunal and the Upper Tribunal. Decisions of the First-tier Tribunal are cited by reference to the Tax Chamber sequential decision number, eg *Masstech Limited* (TC 668). Decisions of the Upper Tribunal are cited by reference to *Simon's Tax Cases* (if reported) and to their neutral citation number in other cases, eg [2010] UKUT 175 (TCC).

Copies of tribunal decisions issued can be downloaded from the Tribunals Service web site (www.tribunals.gov.uk).

Orders, regulations and rules which amend or repeal existing statutory instruments are shown in the Contents list of SIs in italics in so far as they are were made since the last edition of this Guide went to press. They are not summarised or otherwise referred to in the text.

Orders dealing with the following matters are neither listed nor summarised in the text:

(1) commencement provisions;
(2) free zones designated under CEMA 1979 s 100A; and
(3) bodies entitled to refunds of VAT in respect of non-business activities under VATA 1994 s 33.

However, the effect of these orders is noted in the commentary on the statutory provisions to which they refer.

Finance Act 1997
Finance Act 1999
Access to Justice Act 1999
Crown Prosecution Service Inspectorate Act 2000
Finance Act 2000
Government Resources and Accounts Act 2000
Postal Services Act 2000
Finance Act 2002
Finance Act 2003
Income Tax (Trading and Other Income) Act 2005
Commissioners for Revenue and Customs Act 2005
Serious Organised Crime and Police Act 2005
Gambling Act 2005
Finance Act 2006
Finance Act 2007
Tribunals, Courts and Enforcement Act 2007
Finance Act 2008
Corporation Tax Act 2009
Finance Act 2009
Corporation Taxes Act 2010
Finance Act 2010
Finance (No 2) Act 2010
Finance (No 3) Act 2010
Finance Act 2011

Summary Jurisdiction (Process) Act 1881

1881 Chapter 24

4. Service of process of English court in Scotland and of Scotch court in England

If a process issued under the Summary Jurisdiction Acts by a court of summary jurisdiction in England is endorsed by a court of summary jurisdiction in Scotland, the process may be served and executed within the jurisdiction of the Scottish court in a like manner to the way in which it could be served and executed in the jurisdiction of the English court. A like procedure applies in the reverse situation (ie where the process is issued by a Scottish court of summary jurisdiction and endorsed by an English court of summary jurisdiction).

Partnership Act 1890

1890 Chapter 39

NATURE OF PARTNERSHIP

1. Definition of Partnership

Partnership is the relationship subsisting between partners carrying on a business in common with a view to profit. The relationship between two or more persons is a partnership if the facts establish that this is what it is. It is irrelevant whether or not this was intended by the persons concerned. For an example, see *Wild (a firm)* (No 18499), on appeal *Wild and another v Revenue and Customs Comrs* [2009] STC 566n.

The relationship between the members of any company or association is not a partnership if the company or association is:

- registered under the Companies Acts;
- registered under any Act of Parliament; or
- formed or incorporated by any other Act of Parliament, by letters patent or by Royal Charter.

RELATIONS OF PARTNERS TO PERSONS DEALING WITH THEM

14. Persons liable to "holding out"

A person (X) is liable to another person (Y) as a partner of a particular firm if:

- X has represented himself as a partner of the firm or knowingly suffered himself or be so represented; and
- Y has relied on the representation when giving credit to the firm. The reference to "giving credit" does not include the registration of individuals for VAT purposes as partners: see *Revenue and Customs Comrs v Pal and ors* [2008] STC 2442.

It is irrelevant whether the representation was made or communicated by X, or merely made with his knowledge.

Provisional Collection of Taxes Act 1968

1968 Chapter 2

1. Temporary statutory effect of House of Commons resolutions affecting . . . , value added tax (V1.131)

A House of Commons resolution varying VAT may contain a declaration that it is expedient for the change to have statutory effect. The resolution has this effect for seven months counted from the date on which the resolution takes effect or (in the absence of such a date) the date on which the resolution was passed. The resolution ceases to have statutory effect in specified circumstances (see s1(4)–(5B)) with the consequence that any money paid in accordance with the resolution must be repaid or made good, and any deduction is deemed to be unauthorised. Similar consequences follow if the resolution is enacted in a modified form. For the calculation of VAT repayable, see VATA 1994 s 90.

5. House of Commons resolution giving provisional effect to motions affecting taxation (V1.131)

A Budget resolution can be given immediate effect if the House of Commons so resolves; it lapses unless confirmed by the House within ten days.

Taxes Management Act 1970

1970 Chapter 9

PART I ADMINISTRATION

1. Responsibility for certain taxes

The Commissioners for Her Majesty's Revenue and Customs (HMRC) or the Board are responsible under the CRCA 2005 for the collection and management of income tax, corporation tax and capital gains tax.

PART V APPEALS AND OTHER PROCEEDINGS

General note For the application of this Part to certain appeals made under FA 2008 and FA 2009, see FA 2008 Sch 36 paras 32(5), 48(5), FA 2009 Sch 46 para 10(5) and FA 2009 Sch 49 para 4(2), 5(3).

APPEALS

47C. Meaning of tribunal

"Tribunal" means the First-tier Tribunal (see TCEA 2007 s 3) or, if determined by the Tribunal Procedure Rules (see TCEA 2007 s 22), the Upper Tribunal (see TCEA 2007 s 3).

48. Application to appeals and other proceedings

For the purposes of ss 49–58, "appeal" means any appeal under the Taxes Acts and a reference to notice of appeal given, or to be given, to HMRC is a reference to notice of appeal given, or to be given, under any provision of the Taxes Acts. However, this does not apply if the context requires otherwise.

Sections 49–58 apply to appeals and other proceedings as follows:

Proceedings	***Extent to which ss 49–59 apply***
Appeal under the Taxes Acts	
• Appeal against an assessment	Sections 49–59 apply
• Other appeals	Sections 49–59 apply with any necessary modifications, which include the omission of s 56
Proceedings (other than appeals) under the Taxes Acts subject to ss 49–58 other than ss 49A–49I	
• Applications under s 55	Sections 49–58 (other than ss 49A–49I) apply with any necessary modifications
• Other proceedings	Sections 49–58 (other than ss 49A–49I) apply with any necessary modifications, which include the omission of s 56

49. Late notice of appeal

Notice of appeal may be given to HMRC out of time if: (1) HMRC so agree; or (2) (if HMRC do not agree) the tribunal (see s 47C) gives permission.

HMRC are required to give their consent if: (1) the appellant requests HMRC to allow the notice of appeal to be given; (2) HMRC are satisfied that there was a reasonable excuse for not giving the notice in time; and (3) HMRC are satisfied that the appellant's request was made without unreasonable delay after the reasonable excuse ceased. The appellant's request must be made in writing.

49A. Appeal: HMRC review or determination by tribunal

The following options arise when a notice of appeal is given in writing under the Taxes Act to HMRC (see s 49):

(a) the appellant may notify HMRC that he requires HMRC to review the matter to which the appeal relates. For the consequences flowing from this option, see s 49B;

(b) HMRC may offer to review the matter to which the appeal relates. For the consequences flowing from this option, see s 49C; and

(c) the appellant may notify the appeal to the tribunal. For the consequences flowing from this option, see s 49D.

49B. Appellant requires review by HMRC

The appellant may notify HMRC that he requires HMRC to review the matter to which an appeal relates (see s 49A(2)(*a*)). If he does so, HMRC must review the matter in accordance with s 49E and notify the appellant of their views within the prescribed time limit (see s 49B(5)).

The appellant is not permitted to require a review if:

(a) he has already notified HMRC that he requires them to review the matter;

(b) HMRC have already offered to review the matter in accordance with s 49C; or

(c) he has already notified the appeal to the tribunal in accordance with s 49D.

49C. HMRC offer review

HMRC may set out their view of the matter to which an appeal relates and offer a review (see s 49A(2)(*b*)).

The appellant accepts HMRC's offer by notifying them in writing within the acceptance period (see s 49C(8)). If he does so, HMRC review the matter in accordance with s 49E. If not, HMRC's view of the matter is treated as if it were an agreement in writing for settlement of the matter in accordance with s 54(1)). The appellant is not permitted to resile from this settlement (cf s 54(2)). He may, however, notify the tribunal in accordance with s 49H.

HMRC is not permitted to offer a review if:

(a) HMRC have already offered to review the matter in accordance with this section;

(b) the appellant has already notified HMRC that he requires them to review the matter to which the appeal relates in accordance with s 49B; or

(c) the appellant has already notified the appeal to the tribunal in accordance with s 49D.

49D. Notifying appeal to the tribunal

The appellant may notify his appeal to the tribunal (see s 49(2)(*c*)). If he does so, the tribunal decides the matter to which the appeal relates.

The appellant is not permitted to notify his appeal to the tribunal if:

(a) following a review requested by the appellant, HMRC have notified him of their view of the matter to which the appeal relates;

(b) when offering a review, HMRC notified the appellant of their view of the matter to which the appeal relates; or

(c) the appellant has already notified the appeal to the tribunal in accordance with this section.

49E. Nature of review etc

A review under s 49B or 49C must be carried out in a manner, and to the extent, that HMRC consider appropriate. In particular, HMRC must have regard to the steps taken prior to the review by themselves and any person seeking to resolve the disagreement. The review must take account of any representations made by the appellant if they are given at a time which gives HMRC a reasonable opportunity to consider them. The review may conclude that HMRC's view of the matter is to be upheld, varied or cancelled.

HMRC must notify the appellant of their conclusions, and their reasons for them, within the prescribed period. This period may be varied by mutual agreement. If HMRC fail to notify the appellant by the end of the relevant period, HMRC's view of the matter is regarded as being upheld and HMRC must notify the appellant accordingly.

49F. Effect of conclusions of review

The result of a review under s 49B or 49C notified to the appellant under s 49E(6) (HMRC's view upheld, varied or cancelled) or (9) (HMRC's view deemed to be upheld) is treated as if it were an agreement in writing for settlement of the matter in accordance with s 54(1)) from which the appellant is not permitted to resile (cf s 54(2)). This does not apply if the appellant notifies the tribunal in accordance with s 49G.

49G. Notifying appeal to tribunal after review concluded

The appellant may notify the tribunal of the results of a review under s 49B or 49C (see s 49F) at any time with the post-review period (see s 49G(5)). A late notification requires the tribunal's permission.

49H. Notifying appeal to tribunal after review offered but not accepted

The appellant may notify the tribunal if he rejects HMRC's offer (see s 49C) to review the matter to which the appeal relates. He must do so within the acceptance period (see s 49H(5)). A late notification requires the tribunal's permission.

If the appellant notifies the tribunal, the matter is determined by the tribunal.

49I. Interpretation of sections 49A to 49H

The terms "matter in question" and "notification" are defined.

References to "the appellant" include a reference to his agent. However, specified notifications must be sent to the appellant. In these cases, a copy may be sent to his agent.

50. Procedure

As regards an appeal notified to the tribunal, the tribunal may decide that:

- the appellant has been overcharged by an assessment. If so, the assessment is reduced accordingly. The assessment otherwise stands good.
- the appellant has been undercharged by an assessment. If so, the assessment is increased accordingly.

In principle, the decision of the tribunal is final. However, this is subject to TCEA 2007 ss 9–14 and the Tribunal Procedure Rules (as to which see TCEA 2007 s 22).

54. Settling of appeals by agreement

HMRC and the taxpayer may reach agreement before the tribunal's determination of the appeal. Unless the appellant resiles from the agreement within 30 days, the agreement is treated as if it were a determination by the tribunal.

The agreement must be in writing or confirmed by notice in writing. An agreement involves an offer and an acceptance. If the inspector writes setting out figures for agreement, but his letter is ignored, there is no agreement and the appeal remains open even if the inspector amends the assessment: see *Schuldenfrei v Hilton* [1999] STC 821. For an example of rectification, see *R v Insp of Taxes, ex parte Bass Holdings Ltd; Richart v Bass Holdings Ltd* [1993] STC 122 (agreed computation where group relief mistakenly deducted twice). Contrast *Fox v Rothwell* [1995] STC (SCD) 336 (mistake but no agreement).

An appellant may give notice to HMRC that he does not intend to proceed with the appeal and this is effective unless HMRC within 30 days refuse to accept the withdrawal of the appeal: see *Beach v Willesden General Comrs & Others* [1982] STC 157. Appeals can be reinstated by the court: see *Sheppard (Trustees of the Woodland Trust) v IR Comrs* [1992] STC 460.

55. Recovery of tax not postponed

This section applies to an appeal to the tribunal against an assessment to tax.

The appellant may have grounds for believing that an assessment overcharges him to tax. If so, he may apply to HMRC for a determination of the amount of tax in respect of which payment should be postponed pending determination of the appeal. He does so by notice in writing within 30 days of the date when the assessment was issued. The notice must state the amount believed to be overcharged and the grounds for this belief. The appellant may refer the application to the tribunal if does not agree with the determination made. He must do so within 30 days of the date of the document notifying HMRC's decision regarding the amount to be postponed. The tribunal's decision is final and conclusive. The time for payment of the tax not postponed is specified (see s 55(6)(*a*)).

An application may be made beyond the 30-day limit if, following a subsequent change in circumstances, there are grounds for believing that the appellant has been over-charged by the assessment.

If no application for postponement is made, the tax charged by the assessment is due and payable as if there had been no appeal.

A party to the appeal may apply to the tribunal for a revised determination if he considers that circumstances have changed so that the previous determination was insufficient or excessive. The application may be made at any time before determination of the appeal. The tribunal's decision is final and conclusive. The time for payment of the tax not postponed is specified (see s 55(6)(*b*)).

An agreement between the parties (see s 55(10B)) regarding the amount of tax to be postponed may be made in writing. If not, the fact that an agreement has been made, and the terms of the agreement, must be confirmed by a notice in writing given by one party to the other.

For payment or repayment of tax on determination of the appeal, see s 55(9).

56. Payment of tax where there is a further appeal

On determination of an appeal against an assessment, tax is payable or repayable in accordance with the determination of the tribunal. This applies whether or not an appeal is made against that determination.

On determination of the further appeal by the Upper Tribunal or the court, tax is payable or repayable in accordance with the order or judgment given. Interest is added to the amount paid or repaid.

PART VI COLLECTION AND RECOVERY

General note For the application of this Part to the enforcement of certain penalties under FA 2008 and 2009, see FA 2008 Sch 36 paras 49(2), 51(2), FA 2009 Sch 46 para 11(2) and FA 2009 Sch 49 para 5(3).

60. Issue of demand notes and receipts

Collectors of taxes must issue a formal demand to the taxpayer's last known abode and must, if requested, issue a receipt.

DISTRAINT AND POINDING

61. Distraint by collectors

A collector may distrain taxpayer's goods and chattels for the payment of tax. The goods must be kept for five days and, if not redeemed plus costs, may be auctioned. A JP's warrant is needed for a collector to break into premises. See *Re Jet Support Centre Ltd; Brenner v R & Comrs* [2005] EWHC 1611 (Ch), [2005] SWTI 1315. The Treasury may make regulations regarding fees, costs and charges. For the regulations made, see Distraint by Collectors (Fees, Costs and Charges) Regulations 1994, SI 1994/236.

From a date to be appointed by Treasury Order, the Commissioners may recover amounts of tax due to them using the procedures in the Tribunals, Courts and Enforcement Act 2007: see FA 2008 s 127 and Sch 41. The 2007 Act applies only in England and Wales. From the appointed day, this section will therefore be confined to Northern Ireland.

63. Recovery of tax in Scotland

[This section applies to Scotland.]

63A. Sheriff officer's fees and outlays

[This section applies to Scotland.]

COURT PROCEEDINGS

65. Magistrates' courts

Any amount of £2,000 or less due and payable in respect of income tax, capital gains tax or corporation tax is recoverable summarily as a civil debt. Proceedings must be brought in the name of a collector within one year of the demand for payment.

In Northern Ireland, see s 65(4), (5). This section does not extend to Scotland: see s 67(2).

This section is prospectively repealed by FA 2008 Sch 43 para 12(*b*).

66. County courts

Proceedings may be taken in the county court to recover tax due and payable. The tax is recovered as a debt from the Crown.

In Northern Ireland, see s 66(3), (4). This section does not extend to Scotland: see s 67(2).

67. Inferior courts in Scotland

[This section applies to Scotland.]

68. High Court, etc

Proceedings may be taken in the High Court to recover tax. The tax is recovered as a debt from the Crown.

In Scotland, see s 68(2).

70A. Payments by cheque

A payment to HMRC made by cheque may be met on first presentation. If so, the relevant amount is treated as paid on the day when HMRC receive the cheque.

PART X PENALTIES, ETC

103A. Disapplication of sections 100 to 103 in the case of certain penalties

TMA 1970 ss 100–103 do not apply to penalties under FA 2007 Sch 24, FA 2008 Schs 36, 41 or FA 2009 Schs 55, 56.

PART XI MISCELLANEOUS AND SUPPLEMENTAL

General note For the application of ss 108, 114 and 115 to certain matters under FA 2008 and FA 2009, see FA 2008 Sch 36 para 56, FA 2009 Sch 46 para 13 and FA 2009 Sch 49 para 7.

COMPANIES

108. Responsibility of company officers

Everything required to be done by a company must be done by: (1) the company acting through the proper officer; or (2) (if a liquidator has been appointed) the person for the time being having authority to act on the company's behalf. A document may be served on a company by serving it on the proper officer.

The proper officer of a body corporate is the secretary or (if so appointed) the liquidator or administrator. In other cases, the proper officer is the treasurer.

DOCUMENTS

114. Want of form or errors not to invalidate assessments, etc

Minor defects do not invalidate an assessment or determination for tax purposes if the recipient is not misled by them (*Martin v IR Comrs* (1938) 22 TC 330; *Baylis v Gregory* [1986] STC 22; *Fleming v London Produce Co Ltd* (1968) 44 TC 582 and *Austin v Price* [2004] STC (SCD) 487).

115. Delivery and service of documents

A notice served under the Taxes Acts may be served on a person by delivering it to him or by leaving it at his usual or last known place of residence. A notice to be given, sent, served or delivered under the Taxes Acts may be served by post. Service to the last known place of business is not effective: *Re a debtor (No 1240/SD/91), ex parte the debtor v IR Comrs* [1992] STC 751.

PART XII GENERAL

119. Commencement and construction

This Act is related to the Taxes Acts which it governs.

120. Short title.

This Act may be cited as the Taxes Management Act 1970

Litigants in Person (Costs and Expenses) Act 1975

1975 Chapter 47

1. Costs or expenses recoverable

The First-tier Tribunal or Upper Tribunal may order that the costs of a litigant in person are to be paid by another party to the proceedings or in some other way. Subject to the rules of procedure, sums in respect of any work done, and any expenses and losses incurred by the litigant, may be allowed on taxation or other determination of those costs. The costs must be incurred in, or in connection with, the proceedings to which the order relates. For the rules of procedure relevant to VAT, see the Tribunal Procedure (First-tier Tribunal) (Tax Chamber) Rules 2009, SI 2009/273, and the Tribunal Procedure (Upper Tribunal) Rules 2008, SI 2008/2698.

2. Short title, commencement and extent

This Act may be cited as the Litigants in Person (Costs and Expenses) Act 1975. It extends to Northern Ireland.

Customs and Excise Management Act 1979

1979 Chapter 2

PART I PRELIMINARY

1. Interpretation

Various terms used in the Act are defined.

From 18 April 2005, "the Commissioners" means the Commissioners for Her Majesty's Revenue and Customs (HMRC) and an "assigned matter" means any matter in relation to which the Commissioners or HMRC officers have a power or duty. For the Commissioners, see CRCA 2005 s 1. For HMRC officers, see CRCA 2005 s 2. For VAT as an assigned matter, see VATA 1994 Sch 11 para 1.

5. Time of importation, exportation, etc (V3.307, V4.307)

Goods are considered, for customs and excise purposes, to have been imported when the ship enters the limits of a port, the aircraft lands or the goods cross the Irish land boundary. Whales and fresh fish, community transit goods and passengers' baggage brought by sea are not treated as imported until they enter the port of discharge.

Exportation occurs when goods are put on board a ship or aircraft or when they are cleared by the last Customs and Excise office on their way to the Irish land boundary.

Similar timing rules apply for goods imported and exported by pipe-line.

For postal packets, see Postal Packets (Customs and Excise) Regulations 1986, SI 1986/260 reg 5. For goods imported or exported through the Channel Tunnel, see Channel Tunnel (Customs and Excise) Order 1990, SI 1990/2167 art 5.

PART II ADMINISTRATION

APPOINTMENT AND DUTIES OF COMMISSIONERS, OFFICERS, ETC

8. Exercise of powers and performance of duties

The legislation may require an act or duty relating to an assigned matter to be performed by an officer. Another person can carry out the act or duty if the Commissioners so order. An order gives the person all the powers of an officer in relation to the act or duty. This applies whether or not the person is an officer. VAT is an assigned matter: see VATA 1994 Sch 11 para 1.

11. Assistance to be rendered by police, etc

Police officers, members of the armed forces and members of the coastguard have a duty to assist in enforcing the law relating to any assigned matter. VAT is an assigned matter: see VATA 1994 Sch 11 para 1.

However, this duty does not apply to the "former Inland Revenue matters" listed in CRCA 2005 Sch 1. A person can rely on a statement given by an HMRC officer that a matter is not a former Inland Revenue matter: see CRCA 2005 Sch 2 para 5(1).

PART III CUSTOMS AND EXCISE CONTROL AREAS

19. Appointment of ports, etc (V3.307, V4.251)

The Commissioners appoint customs ports by statutory instrument, and allocate within each customs port places where customs officers are to board or disembark from ships. See SI 1956/1796; SI 1980/482–486, 1367–1369, 1879–1882.

21. Control of movement of aircraft, etc into and out of the United Kingdom (V3.307)

The Secretary of State designates customs and excise airports where aircraft may land or depart. See orders made under Air Navigation Order 1989, SI 1989/2004 art 86. For the exercise of powers under this section, see F(No 2)A 1992 s 4.

31. Control of movement of goods to and from inland clearance depot, etc

The Commissioners may by regulation control the movement of goods between their place of importation and the place where they finally leave customs control, and between a place of examination and their place of exportation. See the Control of Movement of Goods Regulations 1984, SI 1984/1176.

Any person who fails to comply with the regulations is liable upon conviction by a magistrate to a maximum penalty of level 4 on the standard scale (see CEMA 1979 s 171) and the goods can be seized.

32. Penalty for carrying away officers

[Repealed.]

PART IV CONTROL OF IMPORTATION

INWARD ENTRY AND CLEARANCE

37A. Initial and supplementary entries (V3.308)

An authorised importer (or an authorised agent acting for an importer who is not authorised) may lodge an initial entry and provide security to obtain release of the goods. He must pay the duty and deliver a supplementary entry by a date fixed by the Commissioners. For entries, see Customs Controls on Importation of Goods Regulations 1991, SI 1991/2724 reg 5.

37B. Postponed entry (V3.308, V3.313)

An authorised importer (or an authorised agent acting for an importer who is not authorised) who lodges paperwork acceptable to Customs and Excise may take delivery of goods before an entry is made, or duty paid, if: (1) a record of the goods is maintained; and (2) arrangements are made for security of duty and custody of the goods. For entries, see Customs Controls on Importation of Goods Regulations 1991, SI 1991/2724 reg 5.

37C. Provisions supplementary to ss 37A and 37B (V3.308)

An authorised importer (or an authorised agent acting for an importer who is not authorised) is liable to prosecution if he contravenes any of the requirements imposed by ss 37A, 37B or directions made under s 37C(2). The prescribed penalty is a fine of level 4 on the standard scale (see s 171).

38B. Correction and cancellation of entry (V3.308)

An incorrect entry may be corrected or substituted with another at any time while the goods are in customs and excise charge, but not after clearance, notification that the goods are to be examined or discovery by an officer that the entry is incorrect. If the importer can satisfy the Commissioners that the entry was made by mistake or that the goods cannot be cleared for free circulation then the incorrect entry may be cancelled. For entries, see Customs Controls on Importation of Goods Regulations 1991, SI 1991/2724 reg 5.

41. Failure to comply with provisions as to entry

Failure to comply with any of the rules in connection with making entry for goods imported renders a person liable upon summary conviction to a penalty of level 2 on the standard scale (see s 171) and the goods may be forfeited. These penalties do not however apply if the entry can be corrected or cancelled under s 38B. For entries, see Customs Controls on Importation of Goods Regulations 1991, SI 1991/2724 reg 5.

42. Power to regulate unloading, removal, etc of imported goods

The Commissioners may make regulations to control vessels, aircraft and persons carrying goods arriving at a port, an airport or on the Northern Ireland land boundary, and to regulate the unloading, landing, movement and removal of goods. For the regulations made, see Aircraft (Customs and Excise) Regulations 1981, SI 1981/1259; Ship's Report, Importation and Exportation by Sea Regulations 1981, SI 1981/1260; Customs and Excise (Single Market etc) Regulations 1992, SI 1992/3095; Pleasure Craft (Arrival and Report) Regulations 1996, SI 1996/1406. For the control of vehicles arriving through the channel tunnel: see Channel Tunnel (Customs and Excise) Order, SI 1990/2167 art 4 and Sch para 6.

Failure to comply with these regulations renders the offender upon summary conviction to a penalty of level 3 on the standard scale (see s 171) and the relevant goods may be forfeited.

For appeals, see FA 1994 ss 7, 14–16 and Sch 5 para 2(3).

PROVISIONS AS TO DUTY ON IMPORTED GOODS

43. Duty on imported goods (V3.312)

Unless the law provides otherwise, imported goods may not be delivered out of customs and excise control until the duty, if any, is paid on making the entry.

The rate of customs duty payable is that in force when an entry is accepted or a s 78 declaration is made. The rate of customs duty payable on warehoused goods is ascertained in accordance with warehousing regulations. For warehousing regulations, see s 93. If no entry or declaration is made, the customs duty payable in relation to Community duty is that applicable when the goods entered the Community, and in relation to UK duties is that which applied when they were imported into the UK

If customs duty is payable because of a failure to comply with a condition or obligation under s 47 or 48, it is charged as if the entry had been accepted when the failure to comply occurred. Customs duties on debris from the destruction of goods are chargeable at the rate applicable when the goods were destroyed.

Goods brought into the UK as "merchandise in baggage" are subject to the same rate of duty as goods entered as cargo. The Commissioners determine the country of origin if the question arises, unless the question can be resolved by s 120 or by EC rules having the force of law. Where the entry of goods involves the use of a computer, the time of delivery of the entry is the time when the details on the entry are accepted by the computer.

Where there is a reduction in the rate of customs or excise duty between the time an entry or declaration is made and the time when the goods are cleared, the lower rate is chargeable unless clearance has been delayed by the importer. Where an application is made under s 38 for a sample of goods to be taken and the entry subsequently made excludes the sample quantity, the rate of duty chargeable on the sample is that which applied when the application to sample was made.

For corresponding provisions relating to excise duty, see F(No 2)A 1992 s 1.

44. Exclusion of section 43(1) for importers etc keeping standing deposits (V5.117, V5.118)

Importers or agents who keep a standing deposit with the Commissioners sufficient to cover any duty payable are not required to pay duty on making the entry.

45. Deferred payment of customs duty (V5.117)

The Commissioners may make regulations providing for the deferment of customs duty in specified cases. For the regulations made, see Customs Duties (Deferred Payment) Regulations 1976, SI 1976/1223; Customs and Excise (Deferred Payment) (RAF Airfields and Offshore Installations) (No 2) Regulations 1988, SI 1988/1898.

46. Goods to be warehoused without payment of duty (V3.332)

Imported goods, which may be entered for warehousing, may be warehoused duty free subject to any conditions imposed by the warehousing regulations. For warehousing regulations, see s 93.

47. Relief from payment of duty of goods entered for transit or transhipment (V3.333)

The Commissioners may allow goods entered for transit or transhipment to be removed without payment of duty, subject to any conditions they think appropriate.

For appeals, see FA 1994 ss 7, 14–16 and Sch 5 para 2(1)(*j*).

48. Relief from payment of duty of goods temporarily imported (V3.338)

Where the Commissioners are satisfied that goods have been imported temporarily and will be re-exported, the goods may be delivered duty free subject to such conditions as they think appropriate in accordance with regulations. See Temporary Importation (Commercial Vehicles and Aircraft) Regulations 1961, SI 1961/1523. For regulations revoked except insofar as they relate to goods imported before 1 January 1986, see Customs Duties (Temporary Importation) (Revocation) Regulations 1987, SI 1987/1781. Relief is now governed by Council Regulation (EEC) Nos 2913/92 and 2454/93.

For appeals, see FA 1994 ss 7, 14–16 and Sch 5 para 2(1)(*k*).

FORFEITURE, OFFENCES, ETC IN CONNECTION WITH IMPORTATION

49. Forfeiture of goods improperly imported

Goods which are imported without payment of customs or excise duty are liable to forfeiture. However, where prohibited or restricted goods are intended for re-exportation, entered for transit or transhipment, or warehoused for exportation or for use as stores, the Commissioners may allow the goods to be dealt with accordingly.

For goods on vehicles arriving through the channel tunnel, see Channel Tunnel (Customs and Excise) Order 1990, SI 1990/2167 art 4 and Sch para 7. For postal packets, see Postal Packets (Customs and Excise) Regulations 1986, SI 1986/260.

50. Penalty for improper importation of goods

Attempting to evade payment of duties or import restrictions renders a person liable to arrest. A person is liable upon summary conviction to a fine of up to three times the value of the goods or up to six months' imprisonment or both, or upon conviction on indictment to a fine of any amount or up to two years' imprisonment or to both. Sch 1 amends these penalties in relation to the importation of drugs as defined in the Misuse of Drugs Act 1971 s 3. For forgery the maximum term of imprisonment is 10 years.

Attempting to import goods concealed amongst goods of a different description renders the importer liable upon conviction to the greater of a penalty of three times the value of the goods or of level 3 on the standard scale (see s 171).

Offences and penalties specified in enactments that impose prohibitions or restrictions take priority over this section.

For offences relating to goods on vehicles arriving through the channel tunnel, see Channel Tunnel (Customs and Excise) Order 1990, SI 1990/2167 art 4 and Sch para 8.

PART VII CUSTOMS AND EXCISE CONTROL: SUPPLEMENTARY PROVISIONS

ADDITIONAL PROVISIONS AS TO INFORMATION

77. Information in relation to goods imported or exported

An officer may require any person concerned in the importation, exportation or carriage of goods which require an entry, or concerned in the carriage, unloading, landing or loading of goods which are being imported or exported, to produce any information relating to the goods and to allow an officer to inspect and make copies of any documents relating to the goods. Failure to comply renders a person upon summary conviction liable to a penalty of level 3 on the standard scale (see s 171).

If there is an export restriction, either on any goods to a particular destination or on particular goods to a particular destination, the Commissioners may require the exporter of such goods to make a declaration. If the Commissioners suspect that the declaration is untrue the goods may be detained and, if the declaration is untrue, forfeited. The exporter is liable to a penalty of the greater of three times the value of the goods or of level 3 on the standard scale (see s 171) unless he can demonstrate that he did not consent to or connive at the goods reaching a destination other than that stated and that he took all reasonable steps to secure that the ultimate destination was as stated.

For appeals, see FA 1994 ss 7, 14–16 and Sch 5 para 2(1)(*m*).

77A. Information powers

A person involved in the importation or exportation of goods must, on demand, furnish information or produce documents relating to goods for which an entry or specification is required.

An officer may require any person holding documents to produce them without prejudicing a lien on them and he may copy or take extracts from any document produced or if necessary remove any document for a reasonable period. Where a lien on the document is claimed, removal of the document will not break it.

A free copy of any document removed must be supplied by the officer when it is required for business purposes and expenses may be claimed from the Commissioners for replacing or repairing lost or damaged documents. A person failing to give information or provide a document is liable to a level 3 penalty on the standard scale (see s 171) upon summary conviction.

This section does not apply to goods of a class or description subject to customs duty: FA 1994 s 20(5). For enforcement powers in respect of those goods, see FA 1994 ss 20–27.

78. Customs and excise control of persons entering or leaving the United Kingdom (V3.345, V3.346)

Any person entering the UK, or arriving by air at his final destination in the UK, must declare any thing carried with him (in excess of the personal reliefs) which has been obtained outside the UK or duty free in the UK. He must answer any questions put to him with respect to any thing carried with him and may be required to produce such thing for examination. A person leaving the UK must similarly answer questions. Failure to declare any thing renders a person upon summary conviction to a penalty of the greater of three times the value of the thing not declared or produced or of level 3 on the standard scale (see s 171). Any thing found concealed or not declared or in breach of import or export prohibition or restriction is liable to forfeiture. For forfeiture, see s 139 and Sch 3. For the exercise of powers under this section, see F(No 2)A 1992 s 4.

79. Power to require evidence in support of information

Where the duty chargeable depends on any question of where the goods come from or where they were grown, manufactured or produced, then the Commissioners may require the importer of the goods to provide proof to support any statements made or provide evidence of the accuracy of any certificate or document. Failure to provide such evidence may result in the duty being charged without regard to the disputed statement or certificate.

For appeals, see FA 1994 ss 7, 14–16 and Sch 5 para 2(1)(*m*).

PART VIII WAREHOUSES AND QUEEN'S WAREHOUSES AND RELATED PROVISIONS ABOUT PIPE-LINES

92. Approval of warehouses (V3.138; V3.332; V5.141)

The Commissioners may approve a place of security known as an "excise warehouse". The following goods may be deposited, kept and secured therein in accordance with "warehousing regulations" (see s 93): (1) imported goods chargeable with excise duty; (2) goods for exportation; (3) goods for use as stores; (4) home manufactured or produced goods eligible for warehousing without payment of excise duty; (5) imported goods eligible for warehousing on drawback; and (6) home manufactured or produced goods eligible for warehousing on drawback. The substances specified in Hydrocarbon Oil Duties Act 1979 s 23B are treated as if they were chargeable with excise duty for the purposes of heads (1) and (4).

The Commissioners may approve a place of security known as a "customs warehouse". The following goods may be deposited, kept and secured therein in accordance with "warehousing regulations" (see s 93): (1) imported goods chargeable with customs duty or not otherwise in free circulation; (2) goods for exportation; (3) goods for use as stores; (4) goods for a purpose referred to in an EC regulation; and (5) goods on which any excise duty has been paid and which are eligible to be kept, without being warehoused, in a customs warehouse. The effect of this provision is confined to the charge to VAT on imported goods. See Customs Warehousing Regulations 1991, SI 1991/2725 reg 4.

A place of security may be approved as both an excise warehouse and a customs warehouse. The Commissioners may revoke or vary the terms of their approval at any time for reasonable cause.

Any person breaching conditions imposed under this section is liable to a civil penalty under FA 1994 s 9.

93. Regulation of warehouses and warehoused goods

"Warehousing regulations" are regulations made by the Commissioners regarding the deposit, keeping, securing and treatment of goods in a warehouse and the removal of goods therefrom. For the regulations made, see Excise Warehousing (Etc) Regulations 1988, SI 1988/809; Spirits (Rectifying, Compounding and Drawback) Regulations 1988, SI 1988/1760; Spirits Regulations 1991, SI 1991/2564; Customs Warehousing (Victualling) Regulations 1991, SI 1991/2726; Excise Goods (Holding, Movement, Warehousing and REDS) Regulations 1992, SI 1992/3135, Excise Duties (Deferred Payment) Regulations 1992, SI 1992/3152; Beer Regulations 1993, SI 1993/1228; Excise Goods (Drawback) Regulations 1995, SI 1995/1046; Beer (Amendment) Regulations 1995, SI 1995/3059; Warehousekeepers and Owners of Warehoused Goods Regulations 1999, SI 1999/1278; Excise Goods (Export Shops) Regulations 2000, SI 2000/645; Tobacco Products Regulations 2001, SI 2001/1712; Excise Goods (Accompanying Documents) Regulations 2002, SI 2002/501; Beer and Excise Warehousing (Amendment) Regulations 2002, SI 2002/1265; Excise Duty Points (Etc) (New Member States) Regulations 2004, SI 2004/1003; Excise Warehousing (Energy Products) Regulations 2004, SI 2004/2064; Biofuels and Other Fuel Substitutes (Payment of Excise Duties etc) Regulations 2004, SI 2004/2065; Denatured Alcohol Regulations 2005, SI 2005/1524; Duty Stamps Regulations 2006, SI 2006/202; Excise Duty Points (Etc) (New Member States) (Amendment) Regulations 2006, SI 2006/3159; Excise Warehousing (Etc) (Amendment) Regulations 2008, SI 2008/2832.

A person is liable to a penalty under FA 1994 s 9 if he fails to comply with warehousing regulations or with any condition, restriction or requirement imposed thereunder.

PART VIIIA FREE ZONES

100A. Designation of free zones (V3.331)

The Treasury may by statutory instrument designate areas of the UK as special free zones for customs purposes, and appoint a responsible authority to administer the area. Orders have been made designating Liverpool (SI 2001/2881, as amended by SI 2006/1834), Prestwick Airport (SI 2001/2882, as amended by SI 2006/1834), Southampton (SI 2001/2880, as amended by SI 2006/1834), Port of Sheerness (SI 2004/2742, as amended by SI 2006/1834) and Port of Tilbury (SI 2002/1418, as amended by SI 2006/1834).

100F. Powers of search (V3.331)

An officer may require answers to questions put to any person entering or leaving a free zone about any goods and require that those goods be produced for examination. An officer may search any vehicle entering or leaving a free zone and may also inspect all buildings and goods within a free zone.

PART X DUTIES AND DRAWBACKS—GENERAL PROVISIONS

General Provisions Relating to Imported Goods

119. Delivery of imported goods on giving of security for duty

Where the amount of duty payable is not certain at the time of importation of goods entered for home use, the Commissioners may allow delivery of the goods to the importer upon payment of a deposit. Delivery of the goods is allowed even where there is an incomplete entry. When the Commissioners have ascertained the amount of duty payable they will issue the importer with a notice, allow for any deposit and request further payment or repay any excess. Any dispute about the amount payable may be referred by the importer to arbitration only after it has been paid.

125. Valuation of goods for purposes of ad valorem duties (V3.314)

The Commissioners may make regulations requiring traders to provide information and documents required for valuation purposes.

See Import Duties (Valuation of Goods) Regulations 1935, SR & O 1935/689; Free Zone Regulations 1984, SI 1984/1177. Breach of these regulations is an offence tried summarily and punished by a fine of level 3 on the standard scale (see s 171).

Sub-sections (1) and (2) do not apply to VAT: VAT Regulations 1995, SI 1995/2518 reg 118(*c*)(ii).

PART XI DETENTION OF PERSONS, FORFEITURE AND LEGAL PROCEEDINGS

Forfeiture

139. Provisions as to detention, seizure and condemnation of goods, etc (V4.309)

A customs officer, police officer, coastguard or member of the armed forces may seize goods liable to forfeiture. Goods seized by someone other than a customs officer must be delivered, or seizure notified, to the nearest convenient customs and excise office. However, goods required in connection with non-customs proceedings may be retained by the police. Seized goods are dealt with in the manner directed by the Commissioners. Condemned and forfeited goods are disposed of in the manner directed by the Commissioners. For forfeiture and condemnation proceedings, see Sch 3. Failure to comply with the foregoing provisions, or Commissioners' directions made thereunder, is an offence tried summarily and punished by a fine of level 2 on the standard scale (see s 171).

GENERAL PROVISIONS AS TO LEGAL PROCEEDINGS

145. Institution of proceedings (V5.304)

In principle, only the Director of Revenue and Customs Prosecutions or the Commissioners can institute proceedings for an offence (see below) or for the condemnation of goods (see CEMA 1979 s 139 and Sch 3). Proceedings instituted by the Commissioners in England and Wales before a magistrate are commenced in the name of an HMRC officer. However, a law officer of the Crown may commence proceedings for an offence if he thinks fit, and do so in his own name. For the Director of Revenue and Customs Prosecutions, see CRCA 2005 s 34. For the Commissioners and HMRC officers, see CEMA 1979 s 1.

The court before which an arrested person is brought may try the offence even if the proceedings have not been instituted in accordance with the foregoing provisions.

This section applies to offences and criminal penalties in connection with VAT (see VATA 1994 s 72(12), (13)). For its application to free zone goods, see Free Zone Regulations 1991, SI 1991/2727 reg 7. For its application to Intrastat, see Statistics of Trade (Customs and Excise) Regulations 1992, SI 1992/2790 reg 13.

146. Service of process (V5.304)

A summons or other process issued for the purpose of proceedings may be served anywhere in the UK without further endorsement. It is served by delivering it to the person to whom it is addressed, leaving it at his last known address (the registered or principal office in the case of a company) or leaving it on board the vessel or aircraft on which he serves or has recently served.

This section applies to offences and criminal penalties in connection with VAT (see VATA 1994 s 72(12), (13)). For its application to free zone goods, see Free Zone Regulations 1991, SI 1991/2727 reg 7. For its application to Intrastat, see Statistics of Trade (Customs and Excise) Regulations 1992, SI 1992/2790 reg 13. For its modified application to the channel tunnel, see Channel Tunnel (Customs and Excise) Order, SI 1990/2167 art 4 and Sch para 22.

146A. Time limits for proceedings (V5.304)

Unless otherwise specified, proceedings must be commenced within three years (for a summary offence) or 20 years (for an indictable offence) from the date of the offence. However, summary proceedings must be commenced no later than six months after sufficient evidence to warrant the proceedings came to the knowledge of the prosecuting authority (as defined in CEMA 1979 s 146A(7)). The date when sufficient knowledge came to the authority's knowledge is proved by way of a certificate from the authority. For the Director of Revenue and Customs Prosecutions (the prosecuting authority in England and Wales), see CRCA 2005 ss 34–36.

This section applies to offences and criminal penalties in connection with VAT (see VATA 1994 s 72(12), (13)). For its application to free zone goods, see Free Zone Regulations 1991, SI 1991/2727 reg 7. For its application to Intrastat, see Statistics of Trade (Customs and Excise) Regulations 1992, SI 1992/2790 reg 13.

147. Proceedings for offences (V5.304, V5.308)

If a court in England and Wales has begun to consider the evidence, and any permitted representations, on an application for dismissal of a charge, it must not proceed to try the information summarily without the consent of the Attorney General (if the proceedings were instituted by him) or the Commissioners (in any other case). In the case of proceedings for an offence in England and Wales, the prosecutor may appeal to the Crown Court against any decision of a magistrates' court.

This section applies to offences and criminal penalties in connection with VAT (see VATA 1994 s 72(12), (13)). For its application to free zone goods, see Free Zone Regulations 1991,

SI 1991/2727 reg 7. For its application to Intrastat, see Statistics of Trade (Customs and Excise) Regulations 1992, SI 1992/2790 reg 13.

148. Place of trial for offences (V5.304)

Proceedings may begin in the court having jurisdiction at the place where:

- the person charged lives or is found;
- the goods, etc, were detained or seized; or
- the offence was committed.

If the offence was committed outside UK jurisdiction, the court having jurisdiction is the court for the place where the offender is found, or first brought, after commission of the offence.

This section applies to offences and criminal penalties in connection with VAT (see VATA 1994 s 72(12), (13)). For its application to free zone goods, see Free Zone Regulations 1991, SI 1991/2727 reg 7. For its application to Intrastat, see Statistics of Trade (Customs and Excise) Regulations 1992, SI 1992/2790 reg 13.

149. Non-payment of penalties, etc: maximum terms of imprisonment (V5.308)

A magistrates' court in England and Wales, or a court of summary jurisdiction in Scotland or Northern Ireland, may impose both a fine and a term of imprisonment. Failure to pay the fine results in a further period of imprisonment, but the aggregate of the periods of imprisonment must not exceed 15 months.

This section applies to offences and criminal penalties in connection with VAT (see VATA 1994 s 72(12), (13)).

150. Incidental provisions as to legal proceedings (V5.304, V5.307)

Where two or more persons are involved in an offence jointly, each person is liable for the full fine and the Commissioners may proceed against those persons jointly or severally. A court in England, Wales or Northern Ireland may mitigate any fine. The fact that security has been given for the payment of duty or for compliance with any condition is no defence in any proceedings for an offence or for condemnation. For the Commissioners, see CEMA 1979 s 1.

This section applies to offences and criminal penalties in connection with VAT (see VATA 1994 s 72(12), (13)). For its application to free zone goods, see Free Zone Regulations 1991, SI 1991/2727 reg 7. For its application to Intrastat, see Statistics of Trade (Customs and Excise) Regulations 1992, SI 1992/2790 reg 13.

151. Application of penalties

Compensation or costs paid to third parties are deducted from fines received or recovered and the balance is accounted for to the Commissioners. For the Commissioners, see CEMA 1979 s 1.

This section applies to offences and criminal penalties in connection with VAT (see VATA 1994 s 72(12), (13)). For its application to free zone goods, see Free Zone Regulations 1991, SI 1991/2727 reg 7. For its application to Intrastat, see Statistics of Trade (Customs and Excise) Regulations 1992, SI 1992/2790 reg 13.

152. Power of Commissioners to mitigate penalties, etc (V5.308)

The Commissioners may:

- compound an offence, whether or not proceedings have been instituted in respect of it (this does not apply to proceedings on indictment in Scotland);
- compound proceedings for the condemnation of anything as being forfeited; and
- restore anything forfeited or seized.

This section applies to offences and criminal penalties in connection with VAT (see VATA 1994 s 72(12), (13)). For its application to free zone goods, see Free Zone Regulations 1991,

SI 1991/2727 reg 7. For its application to Intrastat, see Statistics of Trade (Customs and Excise) Regulations 1992, SI 1992/2790 reg 13. For condemnation, seizure and forfeiture, see CEMA 1979 s 139 and Notice No 12A (April 2009). For the interpretation of an agreement between the parties, see *Empress Car Co (Abertillery) Ltd v C & E Comrs* (No 4832). For reviews and appeals, see FA 1994 ss 7, 13A–17 and Sch 5 para 2(1)(*r*).

154. Proof of certain other matters (V5.305)

A declaration of the following matters is sufficient evidence until the contrary is proved:

- the Commissioners instituted the proceedings;
- a person is a Commissioner, officer, constable or member of the armed forces or coastguard;
- a person has been appointed or authorised by the Commissioners to carry out a duty;
- the Commissioners are, or are not, satisfied regarding a matter;
- a ship is a British ship; and
- goods were destroyed to prevent seizure.

The burden of proof in respect of the following matters rests with the importer or exporter:

- the place from which goods have been brought; and
- whether or not VAT (see VATA 1994 s 70(12)) or duty has been paid, goods, etc, have been correctly described, goods have been lawfully imported, exported or delivered for loading, or goods are subject to a restriction on importation or exportation.

This section applies to offences and criminal penalties in connection with VAT (see VATA 1994 s 72(12), (13)). For its application to free zone goods, see Free Zone Regulations 1991, SI 1991/2727 reg 7. For its application to Intrastat, see Statistics of Trade (Customs and Excise) Regulations 1992, SI 1992/2790 reg 13. For its modified application to the channel tunnel, see Channel Tunnel (Customs and Excise) Order 1990, SI 1990/2167 art 4 and Sch para 23.

155. Persons who may conduct proceedings (V5.305)

An HMRC officer or person authorised by the Commissioners may conduct criminal proceedings relating to an assigned matter before a court of summary jurisdiction in Scotland or Northern Ireland. For the Commissioners and HMRC officers, see CEMA 1979 s 1.

VAT is an assigned matter (see VATA 1994 Sch 11 para 1). This section is nevertheless specifically applied to offences and criminal penalties in connection with VAT (see VATA 1994 s 72(12), (13)). For the application of this section to free zone goods, see Free Zone Regulations 1991, SI 1991/2727 reg 7(2). For its application to Intrastat, see Statistics of Trade (Customs and Excise) Regulations 1992, SI 1992/2790 reg 13.

PART XII GENERAL AND MISCELLANEOUS

General Powers, etc

159. Power to examine and take account of goods

An officer may examine and list goods which are imported, in a warehouse, in a free zone, in a ship or aircraft, to be used as stores, to be exported or subject to repayment of duty. He may open or unpack any container (or require it to be opened or unpacked) and search it or anything in it. Goods are examined at a place appointed by the Commissioners. In principle, the costs of examination and any handling expenses are the responsibilities of the proprietor of the goods (see s 1). However, the Commissioners are responsible for the expense of opening, unpacking or searching a container. For "container", see s 1.

Removing the goods from customs and excise charge before examination renders them liable to seizure and any person intending to defraud or to evade any restriction under any enactment may be arrested. On summary conviction a person is liable to a penalty of the greater of the prescribed sum (see s 171) or three times the value of the goods or to imprisonment for up to six months, or to both. On conviction on indictment a person is liable to an unlimited penalty, or to imprisonment for up to two years or to both. A person, approved by both the Commissioners and the proprietor, may be appointed to account for goods and that account accepted for any purpose.

The effect of this section is modified by Channel Tunnel (Customs and Excise) Order 1990, SI 1990/2167 art 4 and Sch para 24.

164. Power to search persons

An officer may detain a person ("the suspect") in order to exercise his powers of search if he has reasonable grounds for suspecting that the suspect is carrying prohibited, restricted or duty-evaded goods.

The officer may require a suspect to permit a search of any article which he has with him and to submit to a rub-down, strip or intimate search (as defined). The suspect has a right to have this requirement reviewed by a JP (in the case of a strip or intimate search) or by a superior officer (in the case of any personal search), and must be informed of this right before he is searched.

A rub-down or strip search must be carried out by a person of the same sex as the suspect. An intimate search must be carried out by a doctor or nurse.

The search powers may be exercised in relation to a suspect who is: (1) on board a ship or aircraft; (2) leaving a ship or aircraft; (3) entering or leaving the UK; (4) within the dock area of a port; (5) at a customs and excise airport; (6) in, entering or leaving an approved wharf, transit shed or free zone; or (7) crossing the land boundary with the Republic of Ireland. For suspects in, entering or leaving a customs approved area, see Channel Tunnel (Customs and Excise) Order 1990/2167 arts 3, 4 and Sch para 25.

A suspect detained for a search may be detained subsequently under Criminal Justice (Scotland) Act 1987 s 48(1) notwithstanding s 48(4) of that Act.

For the exercise of powers under this section, see F(No 2)A 1992 s 4.

GENERAL OFFENCES

167. Untrue declarations, etc (V5.304)

A person is guilty of an offence if:

- he makes, signs or delivers any document relating to an assigned matter that is untrue in a material particular; or
- in answer to a question, he makes a statement relating to an assigned matter that is untrue in any material particular.

The prescribed penalty for knowingly or recklessly making, signing or delivering the document, or making the statement, is an unlimited fine, two years' imprisonment or both (conviction on indictment), or a six months' imprisonment, a fine of level 4 on the standard scale (see CEMA 1979 s 171) or both (summary conviction). The term of six months is reduced to three months for offences relating to Intrastat: see Statistics of Trade (Customs and Excise) Regulations 1992, SI 1992/2790 reg 12. The person may be arrested. Any goods relating to the document or statement are liable to forfeiture.

In other cases (ie where the offence arises merely from the fact that the relevant document or statement is untrue), the prescribed penalty is a fine of level 4 on the standard scale (see s 171). The person is tried summarily.

For VAT as an assigned matter, see VATA 1994 Sch 11 para 1.

This section does not apply to a declaration, document or statement in respect of a former Inland Revenue matter: CRCA 2005 s 16 and Sch 2 para 6. For former Inland Revenue matters, see CRCA 2005 s 7 and Sch 1.

168. Counterfeiting documents, etc (V5.304)

A person is guilty of an offence if:

- he counterfeits or falsifies a document relevant to an assigned matter;
- he knowingly accepts, receives or uses such a document;
- he alters such a document after it has been officially issued; or
- he counterfeits any mark used by an officer for purposes relating to an assigned matter.

The prescribed penalty is an unlimited fine, two years' imprisonment or both (conviction on indictment), or six months' imprisonment, a fine of level 4 on the standard scale (see CEMA 1979 s 171) or both (summary conviction). The term of six months is reduced to three months for offences relating to Intrastat: see Statistics of Trade (Customs and Excise) Regulations 1992, SI 1992/2790 reg 12. The person may be arrested.

For VAT as an assigned matter, see VATA 1994 Sch 11 para 1.

This section does not apply to a declaration, document or statement in respect of a former Inland Revenue matter: CRCA 2005 s 16 and Sch 2 para 6. For former Inland Revenue matters, see CRCA 2005 s 7 and Sch 1.

171. General provisions as to offences and penalties (V5.306, V5.307)

A person is punished for each offence, contravention or failure for which he is convicted.

The "prescribed sum" (see ss 16, 159, 170A) in Magistrates' Courts Act 1980 s 32(9) is £5,000.

The "standard scale" in Criminal Justice Act 1982 s 37(2) as applied by Interpretation Act 1978 Sch 1 is as follows:

Level 1	£200	
Level 2	£500	(see ss 41, 139)
Level 3	£1,000	(see ss 42, 50, 77, 77A, 78, 92, 125; FA 1994 s 21)
Level 4	£2,500	(see ss 31, 37C, 167)
Level 5	£5,000	(see s 15)

Where a penalty for an offence relating to an assigned matter is fixed by reference to the value of any goods, the relevant value is their open market value at, or about, the time when the offence was committed.

Where a body corporate has committed an offence through a director, manager or secretary or anyone acting in such a capacity, that individual may also be prosecuted. However, this does not apply to an offence in respect of a former Inland Revenue matter: CRCA 2005 s 50(6) and Sch 4 para 28. For former Inland Revenue matters, see CRCA 2005 s 7 and Sch 1.

SCHEDULES

SCHEDULE 3 PROVISIONS RELATING TO FORFEITURE (SECTIONS 139, 143, 145)

Notice of seizure

1.—A person must be notified when goods are seized.

2.—Notice of seizure must be given in writing.

Notice of claim

3.—A person must give notice in writing within one month if he claims that seized goods are not liable to forfeiture.

4.—A notice must specify the claimant's name and address.

Condemnation

5.—Goods are forfeited if no notice is given within the specified one month period or if the notice does not contain the required particulars.

6.—The Commissioners institute proceedings if a valid notice is served.

7.—Forfeiture has effect from the date when liability to forfeiture arose.

Proceedings for condemnation by court

8.—Proceedings for forfeiture are civil proceedings. They may be instituted in the High Court or in a magistrates' court (or equivalent in Scotland and Northern Ireland).

9.—The magistrates' court (or equivalent) where proceedings are instituted is determined by the place where an offence was committed or tried, the claimant's residence (or his solicitor's office) or the goods were seized.

10.—The claimant must confirm that he owned the goods seized. He must give security for costs in High Court proceedings.

11.—A decision by a magistrate may be appealed to the Crown Court.

12.—Seized goods are held by the Commissioners pending the outcome of an appeal in condemnation proceedings.

Provisions as to proof

13.—The fact, form and manner of the seizure set out in the process is sufficient evidence thereof until the contrary is proved.

14.—Condemnation is proved by producing the order or certificate of condemnation or a certified copy thereof.

Special provisions as to certain claimants

15.—Special provisions apply in confirming ownership of goods owned by a body corporate, partnership or group of persons.

Power to deal with seizures before condemnation, etc

16.—The Commissioners may return goods to the claimant and sell or destroy living creatures and perishable goods.

17.—The Commissioners must account to the claimant if goods returned, sold or destroyed are not condemned as forfeit.

Customs and Excise Duties (General Reliefs) Act 1979

1979 Chapter 3

MISCELLANEOUS RELIEFS FROM CUSTOMS AND EXCISE DUTIES

7. Power to provide for reliefs from duty and value added tax in respect of imported legacies (V3.341)

The Commissioners may by order give exemption or relief from duty and VAT where a person imports goods as a legatee. Such an order may be in addition to EC reliefs.

See Customs and Excise Duties (Personal Reliefs for Goods Permanently Imported) Order 1992, SI 1992/3193 art 21.

8. Relief from customs or excise duty on trade samples, labels, etc (V3.342, V3.343)

Trade samples whether imported as such or taken from a parcel upon importation may enter the country free of customs or excise duties but subject to some conditions. Labels or similar goods may be imported free of customs or excise duty provided they are to be added to other goods which will be exported from the UK or the Isle of Man.

9. Relief from customs or excise duty on antiques, prizes, etc (V3.344)

Awards for meritorious achievement may be imported without payment of customs or excise duty.

PERSONAL RELIEFS

13. Power to provide, in relation to persons entering the United Kingdom, for reliefs from duty and value added tax and for simplified computation of duty and Tax (V3.345, V3.346)

The Commissioners may by order give exemption or relief from duty and VAT to persons entering the UK They may also by order provide for tax and VAT to be calculated at a global rate, but any person can elect that the true rates be used. The order may impose conditions which if not complied with may render the goods liable to forfeiture. Failure to notify non-compliance with a condition for relief prescribed by order may result in prosecution and forfeiture of the goods. For forfeiture, see CEMA 1979 s 139 and Sch 3. For the standard scale, see CEMA 1979 s 171. See Customs and Excise Duties (Personal Reliefs for Goods Permanently Imported) Order 1992, SI 1992/3193 arts 11–20; Travellers' Allowances Order 1994, SI 1994/955.

13A. Reliefs from duties and taxes for persons enjoying certain immunities and privileges (V3.347)

The Commissioners may make orders providing for the remission or repayment of customs duties (including agricultural levies), excise duties chargeable on goods, VAT and car tax on goods and services supplied to, or imported by, the persons specified in s 13B. The orders may not be construed as authorising the importation of prohibited or restricted goods. See Customs and Excise (Personal Reliefs for Special Visitors) Order 1992, SI 1992/3156.

13B. Persons to whom section 13A applies (V3.347)

Orders under s 13A may confer relief on: (1) international defence organisations; (2) the staff and dependants of such organisations; (3) military and civilian members of visiting forces, and their dependants; and (4) diplomatic missions.

13C. Offence where relieved goods used, etc, in breach of condition (V5.303)

A person is guilty of an offence if, with intent to evade payment of tax or duty and in contravention of a condition for relief, he acquires goods for his own or another person's use, allows goods to be used by another person, or disposes of goods to another person. Such a person may be arrested.

The offence may be tried summarily or on indictment. The maximum penalty on summary conviction is: (1) a fine of the greater of £5,000 (see CEMA 1979 s 171) or three times the value of the goods; (2) six months' imprisonment; or (3) both. The maximum penalty on indictment is: (1) an unlimited fine; (2) seven years' imprisonment; or (3) both. The goods are liable to forfeiture. For forfeiture, see CEMA 1979 s 139 and Sch 3.

Isle of Man Act 1979

1979 Chapter 58

1. Common duties (V1.217)

VAT, except insofar as it relates to gaming machines, is one of the common duties imposed by both the UK and the Isle of Man.

2. Isle of Man share of common duties (V1.262)

The VAT (net of collection expenses) collected by the Commissioners for goods consumed or used, and services supplied, in the Isle of Man must be paid to the Manx Treasury.

3. Recovery of common duties chargeable in Isle of Man (V1.271)

VAT not paid in the Isle of Man may be collected in the UK and may reduce any repayment the Commissioners should otherwise pay.

4. Enforcement of Isle of Man judgments for common duties (V1.271)

The Foreign Judgments (Reciprocal Enforcement) Act 1933 applies when a judgment made by the High Court of Justice of the Isle of Man relates to VAT or a penalty relating to VAT.

5. Offences relating to common duties etc (V1.217, V1.263)

These are reciprocal arrangements whereby persons in the Isle of Man may be summoned to court in the UK and vice versa.

6. Value added tax (V1.236)

The UK and the Isle of Man are to be treated for the purposes of VAT as one area so that VAT is only charged once on any transaction. An Order in Council provides the basis for determining where a person is registered, for imposing requirements applicable to both areas, for deciding who will be the representative member of a VAT group and for any supplementary or incidental matter. See VAT (Isle of Man) Orders 1982, SI 1982/1067, 1068.

10. Exchange of information

There is no restriction on the disclosure of information between the two customs and excise services.

11. Transfer of functions to Isle of Man authorities

An Order in Council transfers to an appropriate authority functions of the Commissioners and their officers and functions of the Lieutenant Governor of the Isle of Man or a deputy governor. See Isle of Man (Transfer of Functions) Order 1980, SI 1980/399.

12. Proof of Acts of Tynwald etc

In any proceedings in the UK which relate to a common duty any Act of Tynwald may be proved by producing a copy of the Act authenticated by a certificate purporting to be signed by or on behalf of the Attorney General for the Island.

The Bankers' Books Evidence Act 1879 may be used in respect of books and persons in the Isle of Man.

13. Amendments of customs and excise acts etc

[No longer relevant following the repeal of Sch 1 paras 1–35.]

14. Short title, interpretation, repeals, commencement and extent

The meaning of various terms and miscellaneous provisions are set out. Sections 6 and 11 are part of the law of the Isle of Man.

Supreme Court Act 1981

1981 Chapter 54

PART II JURISDICTION

COMMISSIONERS AND OFFICERS

35A. Power of High Court to award interest on debts and damages

The defendant is liable to pay simple interest to the plaintiff if there are proceedings (whenever instituted) before the High Court for the recovery of a debt and the defendant pays the whole debt to the plaintiff otherwise than in pursuance of a judgment in the proceedings.

Interest is paid on all or part of the debt at such rate as the court thinks fit or as the rules of court provide. Interest runs for all or part of the period between the date when the cause of action arose and the date of payment.

No interest is awarded for a period if, for whatever reason, interest on the debt already runs for that period.

For interest under this section in relation to delayed repayments of VAT credits, see *R (on the application of Elite Mobile plc) v C & E Comrs* [2005] STC 275; *R (on the application of Mobile Export 365 Ltd and another) v R & C Comrs* [2006] STC 1069.

Police and Criminal Evidence Act 1984

1984 Chapter 60

General Note From 1 December 2007, specified provisions of this Act apply in a modified form to HMRC investigations in England and Wales, and to persons detained there by HMRC officers, in accordance with Treasury directions. For the directions made, see PACE 1984 s 114. This commentary reflects the text of the Act as modified by the directions made. For interpretation and modifications of general application, see Police and Criminal Evidence Act 1984 (Application to Revenue and Customs) Order 2007, SI 2007/3175 arts 2, 3(2), 3(3), 5(1), 5(2), 13(2), 16, 19.

For corresponding provisions applicable in Northern Ireland from 1 December 2007, see Police and Criminal Evidence (Northern Ireland) Order 1989, SI 1989/1341 (NI 12) as most recently amended by FA 2007 ss 83, 84(3); Police and Criminal Evidence (Application to Revenue and Customs) Order (Northern Ireland) 2007, SR 2007/464; Finance Act 2007 (sections 82 to 84 and Schedule 23) (Commencement) Order 2007, SI 2007/3166.

For corresponding provisions applicable in Scotland from 1 December 2007, see Criminal Law (Consolidation) (Scotland) Act 1995, Criminal Procedure (Scotland) Act 1995 and Criminal Justice and Police Act 2001 as most recently amended by FA 2007 s 85 and Sch 23 paras 1–13; FA 2007 Sch 23 para 14; Finance Act 2007 (sections 82 to 84 and Schedule 23) (Commencement) Order 2007, SI 2007/3166.

For the cross-border exercise of powers, see Criminal Justice and Public Order Act 1994 as most recently amended by FA 2007 s 87.

PART II POWERS OF ENTRY, SEARCH AND SEIZURE

SEARCH WARRANTS

8. Power of justice of the peace to authorise entry and search of premises

An HMRC officer may apply for a warrant to enter and search one or more sets of specified premises (a "specific premises warrant") or any premises occupied or controlled by a specified person (an "all premises warrant"). The application is made to a justice of the peace. He issues a warrant if he is satisfied that there are reasonable grounds for believing that:

- an indictable offence has been committed;
- material on the premises is likely to be of substantial value to investigation of the offence and would be admissible in evidence at a trial for the offence. The material must not comprise items subject to legal privilege, excluded material or special procedure material. For access to excluded material and special procedure material, see s 9;
- any of the following conditions applies in relation to the relevant premises: (1) it is impractical to communicate with any person entitled to grant entry to the premises, or to the evidence; (2) entry to the premises would be refused without a warrant; (3) the search may be frustrated or prejudiced if an officer arriving at the premises is unable to gain immediate entry; and
- (in relation to an all premises warrant) it is not reasonably practical to specify all the premises which might need to be searched.

A warrant authorises an HMRC officer to enter and search premises. He may enter and search on more than one occasion if the warrant so allows. He may seize and retain anything authorised by the warrant.

Summary Jurisdiction (Process) Act 1881 s 4 applies to a warrant issued under this section.

9. Special provisions as to access

An HMRC officer must make an application under PACE 1984 Sch 1 if he wishes to obtain access to excluded material or special procedure material for the purposes of a criminal investigation.

In so far as a statute passed before 31 October 1984 allows applications in respect of this material, or for items subject to legal privilege, it ceases to have effect. For the meaning of excluded material and special procedure material in this context, see PACE 1984 s 14A.

Summary Jurisdiction (Process) Act 1881 s 4 and Petty Sessions (Ireland) Act 1851 s 29 apply to any process issued by a circuit judge under Sch 1.

14A. Exception for Revenue and Customs

As regards any statute passed before 31 October 1984 (see PACE 1984 s 9(2)), material in the possession of a person is neither excluded material nor special procedure material if:

- the person acquired or created it: (1) in the course of any trade, business, profession or other occupation; or (2) for the purpose of any paid or unpaid office; and
- the material relates to a matter in relation to which HMRC has functions.

14B. Revenue and Customs: restrictions on other powers to apply for production of documents

An HMRC officer may apply for the delivery of, or access to, documents under VATA 1994 Sch 11 para 11 only if the officer thinks that an application under PACE 1984 Sch 1 would not succeed because the material required does not consist of, or include, special procedure material.

15. Search warrants—safeguards

This section has effect in relation to warrants to enter and search premises issued to HMRC officers under any enactment. An entry on, or search of, premises under a warrant is unlawful unless it complies with PACE 1984 ss 15 and 16.

An HMRC officer applying for a warrant to enter and search premises must:

- state the ground on which he makes the application;
- state the enactment under which the warrant would be issued;
- (if he is applying for a warrant authorising entry and search on more than one occasion) state the ground on which is applying for the warrant and whether he is seeking either a warrant authorising an unlimited number of entries or a warrant authorising a maximum number of entries;
- (if the application relates to a specific premises warrant (see PACE 1984 s 8(1A)(*a*)) specify each set of premises he desires to enter and search;
- (if the application relates to an all premises warrant (see s 8(1A)(*b*)): (1) specify as many sets of premises as is reasonably practical; (2) specify the person who occupies or controls both the specified premises and any other premises for which entry and search is desired; (3) specify why it is necessary to search additional premises; and (4) specify why it is not reasonably practical to specify the additional premises; and
- identify, so far as is practical, the articles or persons sought.

The application is made ex parte. It must be supported by an information in writing. An HMRC officer is required to answer on oath any questions put to him by the justice of the peace or judge hearing the application.

In principle, a warrant authorises entry on one occasion only. A warrant authorising multiple entries must specify whether the number of authorised entries is either unlimited or limited to a specified maximum.

A warrant must specify the name of the applicant, the date on which it is issued and the enactment under which it is issued. It must also specify each set of premises to be searched (specific premises warrant) or the person in occupation or control of the specified premises and additional premises to be searched (all premises warrant). So far as is practical, the articles or persons sought must be identified.

Two copies are made of a specific premises warrant authorising entry on one occasion only. As many copies as may reasonably be required are made in other circumstances. Copies must be clearly certified as copies.

16. Execution of warrants

This section has effect in relation to warrants to enter and search premises issued to HMRC officers under any enactment. An entry on, or search of, premises under a warrant is unlawful unless it complies with ss 15 and 16: see s 15(1).

Entry and search under a warrant must take place no later than three months after the date of issue. The warrant may be executed by any HMRC officer. If the warrant authorises persons to accompany the officer executing it, those persons have the same powers as the officer to execute the warrant and seize anything to which the warrant relates. However, the officer must be present when they do so. The accompanying officers must act under his supervision.

An officer of higher officer grade must give written authorisation before:

- unspecified premises are entered and searched under an all premises warrant (see PACE 1984 s 8(1A)(*b*)); or
- premises are entered and searched for the second or any subsequent time under a warrant authorising multiple entries.

In principle, premises must be entered and searched at a reasonable hour. However, entry and search may take place at any time if the officer executing the warrant considers that this limitation may frustrate the purpose of the search.

If the occupier (or, in his absence, another person who appears to be in charge of the premises) is present when a warrant is executed, the officer must identify himself, produce the warrant and give the occupier or other person a copy. If not, the officer must leave a copy of the warrant in a prominent place on the premises.

The extent of the search is determined by the purpose for which the warrant was issued. Following the search, the warrant must be endorsed to indicate whether the articles or persons sought have been found and whether any other articles have been seized. If the warrant specifies two or more sets of premises, an endorsement must be made in respect of each set of premises.

A warrant must be returned once it has been executed (executed single premises warrant authorising entry on one occasion) or no later than three months from the date of issue (other cases). The warrant is returned to the designated officer for the local justice area (warrant issued by a justice of the peace) or the appropriate officer of the court (warrant issued by a judge). The designated officer or appropriate officer must retain the returned warrant for twelve months. He must allow the occupier of the premises to inspect the returned warrant on request.

Entry and Search Without Search Warrant

17. Entry for purpose of arrest etc

An HMRC officer may enter and search any premises for the purpose of arresting a person for an indictable offence. He may do so only if he has reasonable grounds for believing that the person sought is on the premises. If the premises consist of two or more dwellings, entry and search are confined to common areas and the dwelling where the person sought is believed to be.

18. Entry and search after arrest

An HMRC officer may enter and search any premises if:

- the premises are occupied or controlled by a person under arrest for any relevant indictable offence;

- the officer has reasonable grounds for suspecting that evidence (other than items subject to legal privilege) is to be found on the premises;
- the evidence relates to the relevant indictable offence (as defined in Police and Criminal Evidence Act 1984 (Application to Revenue and Customs) Order 2007, SI 2007/3175 art 2(1)) or to some other similar or connected indictable offence; and
- an officer of higher officer grade or above has given written authority. However, this condition is waived if the search is carried out before the arrested person is taken to an HMRC office, and the person's presence at a place other than an HMRC office was necessary for the effective investigation of the offence. In this case, an officer of higher officer grade or above must be informed as soon as practicable following the search.

The search must be confined to what is reasonably required in order to discover evidence relating to the relevant indictable offence, the similar offence or the connected offence. Any evidence falling within this description may be seized and retained unless it is covered by legal privilege.

A written record must be kept by the officer who either authorised the search or was informed of it. This record must show the grounds for the search and the nature of the evidence sought. It forms part of the custody record if, at the time the record was made, the person in occupation or control of the premises was in HMRC detention.

SEIZURE ETC

19. General power of seizure etc

An HMRC officer who is lawfully on any premises may exercise the following powers:

- he may seize anything found on the premises if he has reasonable grounds for believing that it has been obtained in consequence of the commission of an offence;
- he may seize anything found on the premises if he has reasonable grounds for believing that it is evidence in relation to an offence he is investigating or any other offence; and
- he may require any electronically stored information accessible from the premises to be produced in either a hard copy format or a format from which hard copies can be produced. He must have reasonable grounds for believing that the information is evidence in relation to an offence which he is investigating, evidence in relation to any other offence, or that the information has been obtained in consequence of the commission of an offence.

In each case, the officer must have reasonable grounds for believing that seizure is necessary in order to prevent concealment, loss, damage, alteration or destruction. In the case of seizure, the officer has no power to seize an item if he has reasonable grounds for believing that it is subject to legal privilege.

20. Extension of powers of seizure to computerised information

This section extends the powers of seizure (see PACE 1984 s 19) conferred by s 8(2) (warrant issued by justice of the peace), 18(2) (entry and search following arrest), Sch 1 para 13 (warrant issued by circuit judge) or any statute (whenever passed).

An HMRC officer who has lawfully entered premises can require electronically stored information accessible from those premises to be provided in either a hard copy format, or in a format from which hard copies can be produced.

21. Access and copying

An HMRC officer exercising a power of seizure is required to provide a record of seized material if so requested. The record must be provided within a reasonable time. The officer in charge of the investigation may allow supervised access to the seized material if so requested. He may allow a copy to be made or a photograph to be taken if so requested. An officer may provide a copy or photograph whether or not he has been so requested. There is no duty to do any of these things if the officer in charge has reasonable grounds for believing that this would prejudice: (1) the investigation of this or another offence; or (2) the criminal proceedings which may arise from either investigation.

22. Retention

Anything seized (see s 19) or taken away (see ss 19, 20) by an HMRC officer may be retained for so long as is necessary. In particular, anything seized for the purposes of a criminal investigation may be retained for use as evidence, for forensic examination or for investigation of an offence. However, this does not apply if a photograph or copy would be sufficient for the foregoing purpose(s). Similarly, anything may be retained in order to establish its lawful owner if there are reasonable grounds for believing that it has been obtained by committing a criminal offence.

However, anything seized on the following grounds must be returned when the relevant person is released from HMRC detention or custody of the court, or (if remaining in custody) is released on bail. The grounds are that the thing may have been used to cause physical injury, damage to property, interference with evidence or to escape from HMRC detention or lawful custody.

PART III ARREST

24. Arrest without warrant: officers of Revenue and Customs

An HMRC officer may arrest any person without a warrant if he has reasonable grounds for suspecting that an offence has been committed and that the person is guilty of it.

This provision does not limit an officer's power to arrest or detain persons under CEMA 1979 s 138(1), Criminal Justice (International Co-operation) Act 1990 s 20, Sch 3 para 4, or any other primary or secondary legislation for the time being in force: see Police and Criminal Evidence Act 1984 (Application to Revenue and Customs) Order 2007, SI 2007/3175 art 17.

28. Information to be given on arrest

An arrest by an HMRC officer is unlawful unless, at the time of his arrest or as soon as is practical thereafter, the arrested person is informed that he is under arrest and informed of the grounds for his arrest. This applies whether or not the grounds for arrest are obvious. However, this requirement is waived if the arrested person escapes before the information could be given to him.

29. Voluntary attendance at office of Revenue and Customs etc

A person may voluntarily attend an HMRC office, attend any other place where an officer is present, or accompany an officer to an HMRC office or other place without being arrested. Where this is so, the person is entitled to leave at will unless he is placed under arrest. If the officer decides to prevent the person from leaving, the officer is required to inform the person that he is under arrest.

30. Arrest elsewhere than at office of Revenue and Customs

A person may be arrested for an offence by an HMRC officer at a place other than an HMRC office. Where this is so, an officer must take the person to an HMRC office as soon as practicable after the arrest. The officer may delay doing so if this is necessary in order to carry out investigations and it is reasonable to carry out those investigations immediately. The reasons for the delay must be recorded when the arrested person first arrives at the HMRC office.

A person may be taken into custody by an officer after being arrested for an offence by a person other than an officer. Where this is so, the person must be taken to an HMRC office by an officer as soon as practicable after the arrest.

In principle, the arrested person must be taken to a designated HMRC office (as defined in PACE 1984 s 35(4)). However, the arrested person may be taken to any HMRC office if:

- the locality in which the officer is working is covered by an HMRC office which is not a designated HMRC office, and the officer considers that it will not be necessary to keep the arrested person in the HMRC office for more than six hours;
- the officer arrested the person without assistance from another officer, no other officer is available to assist him, and the officer considers that he will be unable to take the arrested person to a designated HMRC office without the arrested person injuring himself, the officer or some other person; or
- the officer has taken the person into custody from a person other than an HMRC officer without assistance from another officer, no other officer is available to assist him, and the officer considers that he will be unable to take the arrested person to a designated HMRC office without the arrested person injuring himself, the officer or some other person.

If the first office to which the arrested person is taken is not a designated HMRC office, the arrested person must either be taken to a designated HMRC office within six hours or released.

A person arrested by an officer at a place other than an HMRC office must be released without bail if, before arriving at an HMRC office, an officer is satisfied that there are no grounds for keeping the arrested person under arrest. The officer releasing the arrested person must record the fact that he has done so. This record must be made as soon as practicable after the release.

31. Arrest for further offence

A person arrested for an offence may, in consequence, be present an HMRC office. If it appears to an HMRC officer that, if released, the arrested person would be liable to re-arrest for some other offence, the arrested person must be arrested for that offence.

32. Search upon arrest

A person arrested at a place other than an HMRC office may be searched by an HMRC officer who has reasonable grounds for believing that the arrested person may present a danger to himself or others. The officer may seize and retain anything he finds if he has reasonable grounds for believing that the arrested person might use it to cause physical injury to himself or any other person.

The arrested person may also be searched for anything which might be used to assist his escape from lawful custody or anything which might be evidence relating to an offence. The officer must have reasonable grounds for believing that anything for which the arrested person may be searched may be concealed on him. The clothing that an arrested person can be required to remove in public is confined to an outer coat, jacket or gloves. However, his mouth can be searched. In principle, the officer may seize and retain anything he finds if he has reasonable grounds for believing that the arrested person might use it to escape, that it is evidence of an offence or that it has been obtained in consequence of the commission of an offence. However, he may neither seize nor retain an item subject to legal privilege.

If the arrested person has been arrested for an indictable offence, the officer may enter and search the premises in which the person was arrested and any premises he was in immediately before his arrest. If the premises comprise two or more separate dwellings, the search is limited to the dwelling in which he was arrested and common parts of the premises. The search is for evidence relating to the offence. The officer must have reasonable grounds for believing that such evidence is to be found on the premises.

PART IV DETENTION

34. Limitations on Revenue and Customs detention

Revenue and Customs detention of an arrested person is governed by PACE 1984 Part IV (ss 34–52). For Revenue and Customs detention, see Police and Criminal Evidence Act 1984 (Application to Revenue and Customs) Order 2007, SI 2007/3175 art 2(2)).

The custody officer (see PACE 1984 s 36(8)) must order the immediate release of a detained person if:

- he becomes aware that the grounds for detention have ceased to apply;
- he is unaware of any other grounds for continued detention;
- the person does not appear to have been unlawfully at large when he was arrested; and
- authority for the release has been given by the custody officer at the HMRC office (or last HMRC office) where detention was authorised.

35. Designated offices of Revenue and Customs

The HMRC offices used for detaining arrested persons are designated by the Director of Detention. Offices may be designated only if they provide enough accommodation for this purpose. The Director may designate additional offices and remove the designation of existing offices.

The term "designated office of Revenue and Customs" is defined.

36. Custody officers at designated office of Revenue and Customs etc

One or more custody officers must be appointed for each designated HMRC office (as defined in PACE 1984 s 35(4)). Custody officers are appointed by the Director of Detection or an HMRC officer directed by the Director. HMRC officers are eligible for appointment if they are of at lease officer grade.

A custody officer may carry out the following duties whether or not he is involved in the investigation of the offence for which the person was detained:

- perform any function assigned to custody officers by this Act or by a code of practice issued under this Act;
- carry out the duty imposed on custody officers by s 39; and
- do anything in connection with the identification of a suspect.

An officer of any grade can perform the functions of a custody officer if a custody officer is not readily available to perform them. However, an officer may not do so in relation to a detained person if he is involved in the investigation of the offence for which the person was detained.

An arrested person may be taken to an HMRC office which is not a designated HMRC office. As custody officers are not appointed for these offices, an officer must carry out the functions of a custody officer in relation to the arrested person. In principle, the functions are carried out by an officer who is not involved in the investigation of the offence for which the arrested person was detained. However, if no such officer is readily available, the functions are carried out by either the officer who took him to the HMRC office or by any other officer. If the officer who took the arrested person to the HMRC office is to carry out the functions of a custody officer, he must first inform an officer of higher officer grade or above who is attached to a designated HMRC office. This must be done as soon as practicable.

For the purposes of ss 34, 36(9) and 37 et seq, the term "custody officer" includes a person who, although not appointed as a custody officer, performs the functions of a custody officer.

37. Duties of custody officer before charge

A person arrested for an offence without a warrant, or under a warrant not endorsed for bail (as defined in PACE 1984 s 37(15)), may be taken to one or more HMRC offices following his arrest. The custody officer (see s 36(8)) at each office must decide whether there is sufficient evidence before him to charge an arrested person with the offence for which he was arrested. He may detain the arrested person for so long as is necessary in order to do so. The decision must be made as soon as practicable after the arrested person arrives at the HMRC office or (if arrested there) as soon as practicable after the arrest.

The custody officer may conclude that there is insufficient evidence to charge the arrested person. If so, the arrested person should, in principle, be released. However, the custody officer may authorise the arrested person to be kept in HMRC detention without charge if he has reasonable grounds for believing that that this is necessary in order to: (1) secure or preserve evidence relating to an offence for which the person has been arrested; or (2) obtain such evidence by questioning him.

If detention is authorised, the custody officer must: (1) inform the arrested person of the grounds for his detention; and (2) make a written record of those grounds in the presence of the arrested person. This must be done as soon as practicable. However, he is merely required to make a written record if: (1) the arrested person is incapable of understanding what is said to him, (2) he is violent or likely to become violent, or (3) he is in urgent need of medical attention.

The custody officer may conclude that there is sufficient evidence to charge the arrested person with the offence for which he was arrested. If so, the custody officer must decide whether the arrested person is to be:

- kept in HMRC detention for the purpose of enabling the Director of Revenue and Customs Prosecutions to decide whether or not there is sufficient evidence to charge the arrested person. The arrested person must be informed that he is being detained for this purpose;
- released. If, at the time of release, no decision has been taken whether or not to prosecute the arrested person, he must be informed of this; or
- charged. An HMRC officer does not have power to charge a person with an offence: see Police and Criminal Evidence Act 1984 (Application to Revenue and Customs) Order 2007, SI 2007/3175 art 4(*a*). This must be done by a police officer.

If the arrested person is not in a fit state to be released or charged, he may be kept in HMRC detention until he is.

39. Responsibilities in relation to persons detained

The custody officer (see PACE 1984 s 36(8)) at an HMRC office must ensure that detained persons are treated in accordance with the provisions of this Act and the codes of practice (see PACE 1984 s 60) relating to the treatment of detained persons. This duty passes to the HMRC officer investigating the offence for which the person was detained (if the custody officer transfers, or permits the transfer, of the detained person to this officer) or to the officer having charge of the detained person outside an HMRC office (if the custody officer transfers, or permits the transfer, of the detained person to this officer). The manner in which this duty has been discharged by the relevant officer must be reported to the custody officer if the detained person is subsequently returned to the custody of the custody officer. This must be done by the officer investigating the offence.

The custody officer at an HMRC office must ensure that all matters required to be recorded by this Act or the codes of practice are recorded in the custody records.

Directions relating to a detained person may be given by an officer of a higher grade than the custody officer. These directions may be at variance with a decision or action made, or proposed, by the custody officer. Where this is so, the custody officer must immediately refer the matter to an officer responsible for the HMRC office. This officer must be of senior officer grade or above.

40. Review of Revenue and Customs detention

The detention of detained persons must be reviewed periodically by a "review officer". As regards an arrested person who has not been charged, the review officer is an officer of higher officer grade or above who has not been directly involved in the investigation. As regards an arrested person who has been charged, the review officer is the custody officer.

The first review must be made no later than six hours after the detention was first authorised. The second review must be made no later than nine hours after the first. Subsequent reviews must take place at intervals of not more than nine hours. A review due at the end of a six or nine hour interval may be postponed if the prevailing circumstances make this impracticable. In particular, a review may be postponed if an interruption to the questioning of a detained person would prejudice the investigation, or if no review officer is readily available at the relevant time. A postponed review must be carried out as soon as practicable. The review officer must record the reasons for any postponement in the custody record.

The review officer must decide whether there is sufficient evidence before him to charge the detained person with the offence for which he was arrested. He may permit the continued detention of the arrested person for so long as is necessary in order to do so.

The review officer may conclude that there is insufficient evidence to charge the detained person. If so, the detained person should, in principle, be released. However, the review officer may authorise continued detention without charge if he has reasonable grounds for believing that this is necessary in order to: (1) secure or preserve evidence relating to an offence for which the person has been arrested; or (2) obtain such evidence by questioning him.

If continued detention is authorised, the review officer must: (1) inform the detained person of the grounds for his continued detention; and (2) make a written record of those grounds in the presence of the detained person. This must be done as soon as practicable. However, the review officer is merely required to make a written record if: (1) the arrested person is incapable of understanding what is said to him; (2) he is asleep; (3) he is violent or likely to become violent; or (4) he is in urgent need of medical attention.

If a detained person is not in a fit state to be charged (see PACE 1984 s 37(7)), the review officer is merely required to determine whether he is yet in a fit state.

Directions relating to a detained person may be given by an officer of a higher grade than the review officer. These directions may be at variance with a decision or action made, or proposed, by the review officer. Where this is so, the review officer must immediately refer the matter to an officer responsible for the HMRC office. This officer must be of senior officer grade or above.

A review officer must give the detained person (unless he is asleep) or his solicitor (if he is available at the time of the review) an opportunity to make representations about the detention before determining whether to authorise continued detention. These representations may be made orally or in writing. However, the review officer may refuse to hear oral representations from the detained person if he is unfit to make them by reason of his condition or behaviour.

41. Limits on period of detention without charge

In principle, a person may not be detained for more than 24 hours without being charged. This period commences on:

Event	*Time when 24-hour period commences*
1. Person arrested outside England and Wales	Earlier of: (*a*) arrival at the HMRC office in England and Wales at which the offence is being investigated (*b*) 24 hours after entering England and Wales
2. Person voluntarily attending an HMRC office and arrested there	Time of arrest
3. Person accompanying an HMRC office to an HMRC office and arrested there	Time of arrest

Event	*Time when 24-hour period commences*
4. Any other case	Arrival at the first HMRC office to which he is taken after arrest

As regards a person arrested for a further offence (see PACE 1984 s 31), the foregoing references to "arrest" are references to arrest for the offence for which he was originally charged.

A detained person may be removed to hospital because he is in need of medical treatment. Time spent on the journey there or back, or while at the hospital, is included in the 24-hour period only if, and to the extent, that the detained person is questioned by an HMRC officer for the purpose of obtaining evidence relating to an offence.

A detained person must be released at the end of the 24-hour period unless: (1) he has been charged; or (2) the 24-hour period has been extended under PACE 1984 s 42 or 43. A released person can be re-arrested without a warrant for the offence for which he was previously arrested only if new evidence justifying a further arrest comes to light after his release.

42. Authorisation of continued detention

The 24-hour detention period (see PACE 1984 s 41) can be extended by up to 36 hours by an HMRC officer of senior officer grade or above who is responsible for the HMRC office where the arrested person is being detained. The officer must have reasonable grounds for believing that:

- it is necessary to detain the arrested person without charge in order to secure or preserve evidence relating to the offence for which he was arrested, or to obtain such evidence by questioning him;
- the offence for which he was arrested is an indictable offence; and
- the investigation is being conducted diligently and expeditiously.

If the extension is for less than 36 hours, the officer can further extend the detention period so that the aggregate period of extension amounts to not more that 36 hours. He must have reasonable grounds for believing that the same conditions are met.

No extension may be granted if: (1) the 24-hour detention period has expired; or (2) the second review of the detention within the 24-hour period (see s 40(3)(*b*), (4), (5)) has not yet been carried out.

The officer must give the detained person, or his solicitor (if he is available), an opportunity to make representations before authorising an extension or further extension of the detention period. Representations may be made orally or in writing. However, the officer may refuse to hear oral representations from a detained person if he is unfit to make them by reason of his condition or behaviour.

An officer authorising an extension or further extension of the 24-hour detention period must inform the detained person of the grounds for his continued detention. He must record those grounds in the detained person's custody record.

At the time when an officer authorises an extension of the 24-hour detention period, the detained person may not have exercised his right to have someone informed of his arrest (see PACE 1984 s 56) or to have access to legal advice (see s 58). Where this is so, the officer must:

- inform the detained person of those rights;
- decide whether the detained person should be permitted to exercise them; and
- record in his custody record both the decision and (if permission is refused) the grounds for that decision.

A detained person must be released at the end of the extended or further extended detention period unless: (1) he has been charged with an offence; or (2) the extended or further extended detention period has been extended under s 43. A released person can be re-arrested without a warrant for the offence for which he was previously arrested only if new evidence justifying a further arrest comes to light after his release.

43. Warrants of further detention

An HMRC officer may apply to a magistrates' court for a warrant (known as a "warrant of further detention") authorising HMRC to keep a detained person in detention beyond the 36-hour period allowed by PACE 1984 s 42. The detained person must be brought before the court for the hearing.

The application must be made before the 36-hour period expires. However, if the court is unable to sit before the 36-hour period expires, but can sit within 42 hours, the application can be made before the 42-hour period expires. In these circumstances, the detained person may be detained until the hearing takes place. The fact that the detained person was detained for more than 36 hours must be noted in his custody record. The reason for this must be given. This is done by the custody officer.

The detained person is entitled to legal representation. If necessary, the hearing is adjourned to enable him to obtain representation. He may be kept in detention during the adjournment.

The application is made on oath. It must be supported by an information. The detained person must be furnished with a copy. The information must state:

- the nature of the offence for which the detained person has been arrested;
- the general nature of the evidence on which he was arrested;
- the inquiries made or proposed in relation to the offence; and
- why continued detention is necessary while further inquiries are made.

The court may issue a warrant only if it is satisfied that there are reasonable grounds for believing that:

- further detention is necessary to secure or preserve evidence relating to the offence for which the detained person was arrested;
- the offence is an indictable offence; and
- the investigation is being conducted diligently and expeditiously.

The court may not be so satisfied. If so, it must either refuse the application or adjourn the hearing to a later time within the 36-hour period. The detained person may be detained during an adjournment. An application made after expiration of the 36-hour period must be dismissed if the court considers that it would have been reasonable for HMRC to have made the application within that period. If an application is refused, the detained person must be charged forthwith or released. However, if the 24-hour period (see PACE 1984 s 41) or 36-hour period (see s 42) has not yet expired, the detained person may be detained until the relevant period has expired. A further application for a warrant may be made only if it is supported by evidence which has come to light since the refusal.

A warrant must:

- state the time of issue; and
- authorise the detained person to be detained for a stated period. This is a period which the court thinks fit having regard to the evidence before it. The period must not exceed 36 hours.

The detained person may be charged during the stated period. If not, he must be released when the period expires. If released, he may be re-arrested if new evidence justifying a further arrest comes to light following his release. In other circumstances, he may be re-arrested only with a warrant for the offence.

44. Extension of warrants of further detention

An HMRC officer may apply to a magistrates' court for an extension of a warrant of further detention (see PACE 1984 s 43). The detained person must be brought before the court for the hearing.

The detained person is entitled to legal representation. If necessary, the hearing is adjourned to enable him to obtain representation. He may be kept in detention during the adjournment.

The application is made on oath. It must be supported by an information. The detained person must be furnished with a copy. The information must state:

- the nature of the offence for which the detained person has been arrested;
- the general nature of the evidence on which he was arrested;
- the inquiries made or proposed in relation to the offence; and
- why continued detention is necessary while further inquiries are made.

The court may extend a warrant of further detention only if it is satisfied that there are reasonable grounds for believing that further detention is necessary to secure or preserve evidence relating to the offence for which the detained person was arrested, the offence is an indictable offence and the investigation is being conducted diligently and expeditiously. The warrant may be extended for such period (which must not exceed 36 hours) as the court thinks fit having regard to the evidence before it. The warrant must be endorsed accordingly. Once a warrant of further detention has been extended, it may be further extended under the same procedure.

If an application is refused, the detained person must be charged forthwith or released. However, if the warrant of further detention (as extended or further extended by an earlier application under this section) has not yet expired, the detained person may be detained until it does so.

50. Records of detention

The Commissioners must keep written records showing:

- the number of persons detained for more than 24 hours and subsequently released without charge;
- the number of applications for warrants of further detention and the results of those applications; and
- the following information regarding each warrant of further detention: (1) the period of further detention authorised; (2) the period for which the detained person was detained; and (3) whether the detained person was charged or released without charge.

Information about the foregoing matters must be set out in the Commissioners' annual report. The information must relate to the period in respect of which the report is made.

51. Savings

Nothing in Part IV affects a detained person's right to apply for a writ of habeas corpus or another prerogative remedy.

PART V QUESTIONING AND TREATMENT OF PERSONS BY REVENUE AND CUSTOMS

54. Searches of detained persons

The custody officer at an HMRC office must ascertain everything which a person has on him when he is brought to the office after being arrested or detained there under PACE 1984 s 37. The arrested or detained person may be searched for this purpose by an HMRC officer of the same sex. The things so ascertained may be recorded. They may also be seized and retained. In the case of an arrested person, the record may be made as part of his custody record.

A person in custody at an HMRC office, or detained elsewhere, may be searched at any time in order to ascertain whether he has with him anything which he could use to cause physical injury to himself or another person, to damage property, to interfere with evidence, or to assist him escape. The search must be carried out by an HMRC officer of the same sex. Anything found during the search may be seized and retained.

Clothes and personal effects may be seized and retained only if:

- the custody officer believes that the arrested or detained person may use them to cause physical injury to himself or another person, to damage property, to interfere with evidence, or to assist him escape; or
- the custody officer has reasonable grounds for believing that they may be evidence relating to the offence.

The arrested or detained person must be told the reason for the seizure. However, this does not apply if the person is violent, is likely to become violent or is incapable of understanding what is said to him.

An intimate search may not be conducted under this section. For intimate searches, see PACE 1984 s 55.

55. Intimate searches

An HMRC officer may authorise an intimate search of an arrested and detained person if he has reasonable grounds for believing that: (1) the person may have something concealed on him which could be used to cause physical injury to himself or others; (2) it might used for this purpose while in HMRC detention or in the custody of a court; and (3) it cannot be found without such a search. The search must be authorised by an officer of at least higher officer grade. This may be done orally or in writing, but an oral authorisation must be confirmed in writing as soon as practicable.

An intimate search is conducted by way of examination made by a registered medical practitioner or registered nurse. However, if this is considered impracticable, the search may be made by an HMRC officer of the same sex. The search must be carried out at an HMRC office, hospital, registered medical practitioner's surgery or some other place used for medical purposes. The custody record of the searched person must state which parts of the body were searched and why they were searched. This must be done as soon as practicable following the search.

Anything found during the search may be seized and retained by the custody officer if:

- he believes that the searched person may use it to cause physical injury to himself or another person, to damage property, to interfere with evidence, or to assist him escape; or
- he has reasonable grounds for believing that it may be evidence relating to the offence.

The searched person must be told the reason for the seizure. However, this does not apply if the person is violent, is likely to become violent or is incapable of understanding what is said to him.

56. Right to have someone informed when arrested

An arrested person may be held in custody in an HMRC office or other premises. Where this is so, he is entitled, on request, to have one person told that he has been arrested and detained. The person to be informed may be a friend, relative or other person known to the arrested person or likely to take an interest in his welfare. This person is to be informed as soon as practicable.

As regards a person detained for an indictable offence, delay is permitted in either of the following circumstances if this is authorised by an HMRC officer of at least higher officer grade:

- the officer has reasonable grounds for believing that telling the named person of the arrest will have any of the following consequences: (1) interference with, or harm to, evidence connected with the offence; (2) interference with, or physical injury to, other persons; (3) alerting other suspects who have not yet been arrested for the offence; or (4) hindering the recovery of any property obtained as a result of the offence; or

- the officer has reasonable grounds for believing that: (1) the detained person has benefited from his criminal conduct; and (2) recovery of the value of the property constituting the benefit will be hindered by telling the named person of the arrest. Whether a person has benefited from his criminal conduct is decided in accordance with Proceeds of Crime Act 2002 Part 2.

Delay may be authorised orally or in writing. If given orally, it must be confirmed in writing as soon as practicable. The detained person must be told the reason for the delay as soon as practicable. The reason must be noted on his custody record as soon as practicable. Delay ceases to be permitted, so that the person in custody must be allowed to exercise his right to have someone informed of his arrest and detention, on the earlier of: (1) 36 hours after the relevant time (as defined in s 41(2)); and (2) the time when the reason for authorising the delay ceases to subsist.

The rights conferred by this section are exercisable whenever the arrested or detained person is transferred to another place.

57. Additional rights of children and young persons

This section replaces Children and Young Persons Act 1933 s 34(2) with a new s 34(2)–(11).

58. Access to legal advice

A person arrested and held in custody in an HMRC office or elsewhere is entitled, if he so requests, to consult a solicitor privately at any time. In principle, the request, and the time when it was made, must be recorded in the custody record. However, this does not apply to a request made while a person is in court after being charged with an offence.

As regards a person detained for an indictable offence, delay is permitted in either of the following circumstances if this is authorised by an HMRC officer of at least senior officer grade:

- the officer has reasonable grounds for believing that telling the named person of the arrest will have any of the following consequences: (1) interference with, or harm to, evidence connected with the offence; (2) interference with, or physical injury to, other persons; (3) alerting other suspects who have not yet been arrested for the offence; or (4) hindering the recovery of any property obtained as a result of the offence; or
- the officer has reasonable grounds for believing that: (1) the detained person has benefited from his criminal conduct; and (2) recovery of the value of the property constituting the benefit will be hindered by the consultation with a solicitor. Whether a person has benefited from his criminal conduct is decided in accordance with Proceeds of Crime Act 2002 Part 2.

Delay may be authorised orally or in writing. If given orally, it must be confirmed in writing as soon as practicable. The detained person must be told the reason for the delay as soon as practicable. The reason must be noted on his custody record as soon as practicable. Delay ceases to be permitted, so that the person in custody must be allowed to consult a solicitor privately, on the earlier of: (1) 36 hours after the relevant time (as defined in PACE 1984 s 41(2)); and (2) the time when the reason for authorising the delay ceases to subsist.

62. Intimate samples

An HMRC officer of at least higher officer grade may authorise an intimate sample be taken from:

- a person in HMRC detention; or
- a person who, although not so detained, has given two or more non-intimate samples in the course of an investigation and, although the samples were suitable for the same means of analysis, they have proved insufficient.

The officer may give an authorisation only if:

- he has reasonable grounds for suspecting that the person has been involved in a recordable offence (see s 118(1)); and

- he has reasonable grounds for believing that the sample will tend to confirm or disprove this.

An authorisation may be given orally or in writing. If given orally, it must be confirmed in writing as soon as practicable. The person must be informed of the authorisation and the grounds for giving it (which must include the nature of the offence in which he is suspected of being involved). The person must consent to an intimate sample being taken. The consent must be given in writing. Before taking an intimate sample from a person at an HMRC office, an officer must inform the person that the sample may be the subject of a speculative search.

In practice, a sample of urine is provided by the person. A dental impression must be taken by a registered dentist. Any other sample must be taken by a registered medical practitioner or registered care professional.

The following information must be recorded as soon as practicable after an intimate sample has been taken:

- the authorisation by virtue of which the sample was taken;
- the grounds for giving the authorisation;
- the fact that the appropriate consent was given; and
- the fact that the person has been informed that the sample may be the subject of a speculative search.

If the person has been detained at an HMRC office, these matters must be recorded in his custody record.

A person may refuse consent to the taking of an intimate sample without good cause. Where this is so, a court, judge or jury may draw such inferences from the refusal as appear proper.

63. Other samples

In principle, a person must give written consent before a non-intimate sample is taken from him. However, no consent is required in the following circumstances if specified conditions are met:

- the person has been detained following his arrest for a recordable offence (see PACE 1984 s 118(1));
- he is being held in custody on the authority of a court;
- he has been charged with a recordable offence;
- he has been informed that he will be reported for a recordable offence;
- he has been convicted of a recordable offence after 9 April 1995. For prior convictions for sexual offences, see PACE 1984 s 63(9A);
- he has been detained following acquittal on grounds of insanity or a finding of unfitness to plead (see Criminal Evidence (Amendment) Act 1997 s 2).

The person must be told the reason for taking the sample and the nature of the offence of which he is suspected. This reason must be recorded as soon as practicable after the sample has been taken.

Before taking a non-intimate sample at an HMRC office, an officer must inform the person that the sample may be the subject of a speculative search. This applies whether or not consent has been given. The fact that the person has been so informed must be recorded as soon as practicable after the sample has been taken. In the case of a detained person, the fact that the person has been informed must be recorded in his custody record.

The power to take a non-intimate sample without consent is exercised by an HMRC officer. An electronic skin impression must be taken in the manner, and using the devices, approved by the Secretary of State.

64. Destruction of fingerprints and samples

Samples or impressions of footwear (hereafter "samples") taken from a person in connection with the investigation of an offence may be retained after they have fulfilled the purposes for which they were taken unless they are required to be destroyed under the provisions set out below.

Retained samples may only be used for purposes related to:

- the prevention or detection of crime;
- the investigation of an offence;
- the conduct of a prosecution;
- the identification of a deceased person; and
- the identification of the person from whom a body part came.

In principle, samples taken from a person in connection with the investigation of an offence must be destroyed as soon as they have fulfilled the purpose for which they were taken if that person is not suspected of having committed the offence. There are two exceptions.

First, a sample is not required to be destroyed if: (1) it was taken from a person (X) for the purposes of the investigation of an offence; (2) another person (Y) has been convicted of that offence; and (3) a sample was also taken from Y for the purposes of the investigation. If the sample taken from X is retained, neither the sample nor any information derived from it may be used in evidence against X or used for the purposes of the investigation of an offence.

Second, a sample is not required to be destroyed if the person from whom it was taken consents to its retention. The consent (whenever given) is irrevocable. It must be given in writing. If retained, the use made of the sample (or any information derived from it) is unrestricted.

When impressions of footwear are destroyed, any copies of those impressions must also be destroyed. The Director of Risk and Intelligence must, as soon as practicable, make access to the data impossible. A person has a right to witness destruction of the impressions or copies if he so requests. He can also request the Director for a certificate that access to the data is impossible. This must be issued within three months, counted from the day on which the request was made.

The power to take fingerprints arises under PACE 1984 ss 27, 61, 63A. These sections are not applied to HMRC by Police and Criminal Evidence Act 1984 (Application to Revenue and Customs) Order 2007, SI 2007/3175 art 3 and Sch 1. The foregoing commentary accordingly excludes provisions relating to the destruction of fingerprints.

PART VI CODES OF PRACTICE—GENERAL

66. Codes of practice

The Secretary of State is required to issue codes of practice in connection with:

- how HMRC officers exercise their statutory powers of searching a person without first arresting him, searching a vehicle without making an arrest, or arresting a person.
- the detention, treatment, questioning and identification of persons by HMRC officers;
- searches of premises by HMRC officers; and
- the seizure of property found on persons or premises by HMRC officers.

Codes of practice have been issued in respect of the following matters:

Code	*Matter*
Code A	Exercise of statutory powers to search a person or vehicle without first making an arrest
Code B	Powers to search premises and to seize and retain property found on premises and persons
Code C	Requirements for the detention, treatment and questioning of suspects not related to terrorism in custody
Code D	Main methods used to identify people in connection with the investigation of offences and the keeping of accurate and reliable criminal records

Code	*Matter*
Code E	Tape recording of interviews with suspects
Code F	Visual recording with sound of interviews with suspects
Code G	Powers of arrest under s 24 of this Act
Code H	Requirements for the detention, treatment and questioning of suspects related to terrorism in custody

For the codes of practice currently in force, see www.police.homeoffice.gov.uk/operational-policing/powers-pace-codes/pace-code-intro.

67. Codes of practice—supplementary

The Secretary of State may revise all or part of a code at any time. He must consult before doing so. A code (or revision) comes into operation on a day prescribed by statutory instrument.

HMRC officers charged with the duty of investigating offences must have regard to any relevant provision of a code in discharging that duty. Failure to do so does not of itself render officers liable to criminal or civil proceedings.

A code is admissible in evidence in all criminal and civil proceedings. If any provision of a code appears to be relevant to any question arising in the proceedings, it must be taken into account in determining that question.

PART VIII QUESTIONING AND TREATMENT OF PERSONS BY REVENUE AND CUSTOMS

CONVICTIONS AND ACQUITTALS

77. Confessions by mentally handicapped persons

The case against the accused at a trial may depend wholly or substantially on a confession made by him. The court must take the following measures if it is satisfied that the accused is mentally handicapped and that the confession was not made in the presence of an independent person:

- at a trial on indictment with a jury, the court must warn the jury that there is special need for caution before convicting the accused in reliance on the confession, and must explain that the need arises because of the foregoing circumstances;
- at a summary trial for an offence, the court must treat the case as one in which there is a special need for caution before convicting the accused on his confession; and
- at a trial on indictment without a jury, the court must treat the case as one in which there is a special need for caution before convicting the accused on his confession.

HMRC officers and other persons acting under the authority of the Commissioners are not "independent persons". Nor are police officers and persons employed for, or engaged on, police purposes (as defined in Police Act 1996 s 101(2)).

The term "mentally handicapped" is defined.

PART X REVENUE AND CUSTOMS—GENERAL

107. Officers of Revenue and Customs performing duties of higher rank

A provision of this Act or any other Act may provide that a power in respect of the investigation of offences or the treatment of persons in HMRC custody is exercisable only by (or with the authority of) an HMRC officer of at least senior officer grade. Where this is so, an officer of higher officer grade is treated as holding the grade of senior office if:

- he has been authorised by an officer above senior officer grade to exercise the power or give the authority for its exercise; or
- he is acting during the absence of an officer of senior officer grade who has authorised him to exercise the power, or give authority for its exercise, during the period of absence.

A provision of this Act or any other Act may provide that a power in respect of the investigation of offences or the treatment of persons in HMRC custody is exercisable only by (or with the authority of) an HMRC officer of at least higher officer grade. Where this is so, an officer of officer grade is treated as holding the grade of higher officer if he has been authorised by an officer of at least senior officer grade to exercise the power or give authority for its exercise.

PART XI MISCELLANEOUS

114. Application of Act to Revenue and Customs

The Treasury may direct that:

(a) any provision of this Act relating to investigations of offences conducted by the police, or to persons detained by the police, apply to investigations relating to assigned matters conducted by HMRC officers or persons detained by HMRC officers;

(b) in relation to investigations of offences conducted by HMRC officers, this Act has effect as if it included two additional sections (ss 14A, 14B);

(c) in relation to HMRC detention, Bail Act 1976 has effect as if references to a constable were references to an HMRC officer of a grade to be specified by order;

(d) an HMRC officer searching premises under a warrant has power to search persons found on the premises in circumstances to be specified by order; and

(e) an HMRC officer can exercise the powers and functions conferred by this Act only if he is acting with the authority of the Commissioners.

Directions are made by order. For the directions currently in force, see Police and Criminal Evidence Act 1984 (Application to Revenue and Customs) Order 2007, SI 2007/3175. These directions do not have effect in relation to the former Inland Revenue matters specified in CRCA 2005 s 54(4)(*b*), (*f*) or Sch 1 paras 3, 7, 10, 13–15, 19, 24–29: see FA 2007 s 84(3), (5); Finance Act 2007 (sections 82 to 84 and Schedule 23) (Commencement) Order 2007, SI 2007/3166.

If the Commissioners certify that an HMRC officer has authority to exercise a power or function under the 1984 Act, the certificate is conclusive evidence of that fact.

118. General interpretation

A "recordable offence" is an offence to which regulations under PACE 1984 s 27 apply. For the regulations made under s 27, see National Police Records (Recordable Offences) Regulations 2000, SI 2000/1139.

120. Extent

In principle, the application of this Act is confined to England and Wales. However, specified provisions extend to Scotland only (see PACE 1984 s 120(2)) or Northern Ireland only (see s 120(3)). Other specified provisions extend to England, Wales and Scotland (see s 120(4)) or to England, Wales, Scotland and Northern Ireland (see s 120(5)).

SCHEDULES

SCHEDULE 1 SPECIAL PROCEDURE

Making of orders by circuit judge

1.—A circuit judge may make an order (see PACE 1984 Sch 1 para 4) for production of, or access to, material in accordance with Sch 1 para 2 or 3. The application for such an order is made by an HMRC officer.

2.—A circuit judge may make an order for production of, or access to, material if he is satisfied that:

(a) there are reasonable grounds for believing that:
- an indictable offence has been committed;
- the material consists of, or includes, special procedure material (as defined in PACE 1984 s 14);
- the material does not also include excluded material (as defined in s 11);
- the material is on premises occupied or controlled by a person specified in the application;
- the material is likely to be of substantial value to the investigation; and
- the material is likely to be relevant evidence (as defined in s 8(4)).

(b) other methods of obtaining the material have been tried without success or (if not tried) have not been tried because it appeared that they were bound to fail; and

(c) it is in the public interest that the material should be produced or that access to it should be given. In determining whether or not the public interest is served, it is necessary to have regard to the benefit likely to accrue to the investigation and the circumstances under which the material is held.

3.—A circuit judge may make an order for production of, or access to, material if he is satisfied that:

(a) there are reasonable grounds for believing that:
- the material consists of, or includes excluded material (as defined in PACE 1984 s 11) or special procedure material (as defined in s 14), and
- the material is on premises occupied or controlled by a person specified in the application.

(b) prior to 8 November 2007, a search of the premises could have been authorised by a warrant issued under VATA 1994 Sch 11 para 11; and

(c) the issue of such a warrant would have been appropriate.

4–6.—An order is made in relation to the person who appears to the circuit judge to be in possession of the material to which the application (see PACE 1984 Sch 1 para 1) relates. The order may either:

(a) require the person to produce material to an HMRC officer for him to take away. Electronically stored material must be produced in a form in which it can be taken away. This may comprise either a visible and legible document, or a medium from which a visible and legible image can be produced. The material produced in either case is treated as if it were material seized by an HMRC officer so that PACE 1984 ss 21 (access and copying) and 22 (retention) apply; or

(b) require the person to give an HMRC officer access to material. An officer must be given access to electronically stored material in a visible and legible form.

The person must comply with the requirement within a specified period. This period may not be less than seven days, counted from the date of the order.

Notice of applications for orders

7.—An application for an order (see PACE 1984 Sch 1 para 1) is made inter partes.

8.—Notice of an application for an order (see PACE 1984 Sch 1 para 1) may be served on a person by any of the following methods:

- delivering it to him;
- leaving it at his proper address;
- sending it to him by post in a registered letter; or
- sending it to him by post by recorded delivery.

9, 10.—A notice of application may be served on a body corporate by serving it on the body's secretary, clerk or similar officer at the body's registered or principal office.

A notice of application may be served on a partnership by serving it on one of the partners at the firm's principal office.

In any other case, a notice of application is served at the person's last known address.

11.—A person served with notice of an application must not conceal, alter or dispose of the material without leave given by a judge or written permission given by an HMRC officer until: (1) he has complied with the order; or (2) the application has been dismissed or abandoned.

Issue of warrants by circuit judge

12.—A circuit judge may issue a warrant (known as an "all premises warrant") if he is satisfied that:

- the conditions in PACE 1984 Sch 1 para 2(*a*)–(*c*) or 3(*a*)–(*c*) are met;
- (in either case) any additional conditions in Sch 1 para 14 are met; or
- (in a case where the conditions in Sch 1 para 3(*a*)–(*c*) are met) an order for production or access (see Sch 1 para 4) has not been complied with.

An application for an all premises warrant is made by an HMRC officer. The warrant authorises an HMRC to enter and search:

- the premises specified in the order for production or access;
- all the premises occupied or controlled by the person specified in the order for production or access; and
- any sets of premises specified in the application for the all premises warrant.

12A.—A circuit judge must be satisfied on the following matters before issuing an all premises warrant:

(a) there are reasonable grounds for believing that it is necessary to search both premises specified in the application and premises which are not; and
(b) it is not reasonably practicable to specify all the premises which might need to be searched.

13.—An HMRC officer may seize and retain anything for which a search has been authorised.

14.—The additional conditions mentioned in Sch 1 para 12 are:

(a) it is not practicable to communicate with a person entitled to grant entry to the premises;
(b) (if it is practicable to communicate with a person entitled to grant entry) it is not practicable to communicate with a person entitled to grant access to the material;
(c) the material contains information subject to a restriction on disclosure, or an obligation of secrecy, and the information is likely to be disclosed unless a warrant is issued; and
(d) service of a notice of application for an order for production or access may seriously prejudice the investigation.

15.—Failure to comply with an order for production or access is dealt with in the same manner as contempt of the Crown Court.

Costs

16.—Costs in respect of the following matters are awarded at the judge's discretion:

- an application for a warrant; and

- anything done or to be done in relation to an order.

Interpretation

17.—The term "judge" is defined.

Agricultural Holdings Act 1986

1986 Chapter 5

PART 2 PROVISIONS AFFECTING TENANCY DURING ITS CONTINUANCE

VARIATION OF RENT

12. Arbitration of rent

The landlord or tenant of an agricultural holding may demand that the rent payable from the next termination date is referred to arbitration. He does so by means of a written notice served on the other party.

SCHEDULE

SCHEDULE 2 ARBITRATION OF RENT: PROVISIONS SUPPLEMENTARY TO SECTION 12 (SECTION 12)

Frequency of arbitrations under section 12

4.—A demand for arbitration (see s 12) is ineffective if the period between the following events is less than three years: (1) the date from which the previous increase or reduction of rent took effect; and (2) the next termination date. The exercise or revocation of an option to tax (which necessarily increases or reduces the amount payable) is disregarded for the purposes of head (1). So is a change in the rate of VAT.

For the option to tax, see VATA 1994 Sch 10.

Finance Act 1988

1988 Chapter 39

PART I CUSTOMS AND EXCISE

8. Disclosure of information as to imports

The Commissioners can disclose the names and addresses of persons receiving goods imported from third countries. This information can be disclosed to such persons as the Commissioners think fit and on such terms and conditions as the Commissioners think fit.

Finance Act 1989

1989 Chapter 26

PART III MISCELLANEOUS AND GENERAL

MISCELLANEOUS

182. Disclosure of information

A person commits an offence if he discloses, without lawful authority, any information concerning the tax affairs of a named person or a person whose identity can be deduced from the disclosure.

Finance (No 2) Act 1992

1992 Chapter 48

PART I CUSTOMS AND EXCISE, VALUE ADDED TAX AND CAR TAX

CHAPTER I CUSTOMS AND EXCISE

ABOLITION OF FISCAL FRONTIERS ETC

1. Powers to fix excise duty point

The time when the requirement to pay excise duty takes effect is referred to as the "excise duty point". The excise duty point and persons liable to pay excise duty are determined in accordance with regulations. For the regulations made, see in particular Excise Goods (Holding, Movement and Duty Point) Regulations 2010, SI 2010/593 regs 5–21. The amount of duty payable is determined by reference to the rate of duty in force at the excise duty point.

This section takes effect partly from 1 December 1992 and partly from 1 January 1993 and partly from 1 June 1993: see Finance (No 2) Act 1992 (Commencement No 2 and Transitional Provisions) Order 1992, SI 1992/2979; Finance (No 2) Act 1992 (Commencement No 4 and Transitional Provisions) Order 1992, SI 1992/3261; Finance (No 2) Act 1992 (Commencement No 5) Order 1992, SI 1993/1341.

4. Enforcement powers

As regards persons or things entering or leaving the UK, the Commissioners may not use their powers under CEMA 1979 ss 21, 26, 27, 28, 29, 34, 78 or 164 to prevent, restrict or delay movement between EU member states. However, they may do so for the purpose of: (1) finding out whether the persons or things are coming from or going to another EU member state; (2) collecting EU duties; or (3) enforcing EU or UK prohibitions or restrictions.

Charities Act 1993

1993 Chapter 10

10. Disclosure of information to Commission

Any relevant public authority (see s 10C(1)) may disclose information to the Charity Commission for the purpose of enabling the Commission to to discharge any of its functions. However, Revenue and Customs information (see CRCA s 18(1)) may be disclosed only if it relates to:

(a) a charity;
(b) an institution established for charitable, benevolent or philanthropic purposes;
(c) an institution for which a claim for exemption has been made under TA 1988 s 505(1);
(d) a subsidiary undertaking of a charity (as defined in s 10(3)); or
(e) a body managed or controlled wholly or mainly in England or Wales which is entered in the Scottish Charity Register.

10A. Disclosure of information by Commission

In principle, information received by the Charity Commission in connection with its functions may be disclosed to a relevant public authority (see s 10C(1), (2)). However, Revenue and Customs information (see CRCA 2005 s 18(1)) may only be disclosed with the consent of the HMRC Commissioners.

10B. Disclosure to and by principal regulators of exempt charities

Sections 10 and 10A apply in a modified form to information disclosed by a relevant public authority to the principal regulator of an exempt charity and vice versa. However, the Revenue and Customs information which may be disclosed by the principal regulator is confined to information relating to: (1) an exempt charity in respect of which the principal regulator exercises functions; or (2) a subsidiary undertaking of the exempt charity (as defined in s 10B(3)).

Finance Act 1994

1994 Chapter 9

PART I CUSTOMS AND EXCISE

CHAPTER III CUSTOMS: ENFORCEMENT POWERS

20. Interpretation, etc

The information gathering powers set out in FA 1994 ss 21–29 apply to any person carrying on a trade or business consisting of, or including, importing, exporting, producing, manufacturing, processing, buying, selling, dealing in, handling or storing customs goods, or financing or facilitating any of those activities. "Customs goods" are goods of a class or description subject to customs duties or EU agricultural levies, whether or not the goods are in fact so chargeable.

The existing powers in CEMA 1979 ss 75A, 75B, 75C, 77A, 77B and 77C cease to apply to customs goods.

21. Requirements about keeping records

Persons involved with customs goods must keep and preserve records in accordance with regulations. For the regulations made, see Customs Traders (Accounts and Records) Regulations 1995, SI 1995/1203 (not summarised). The duty to preserve records is discharged by preserving the information contained in them by means approved by the Commissioners. Failure to comply with a requirement imposed by this section is an offence which is tried summarily. The prescribed penalty is level 3 on the standard scale (see CEMA 1979 s 171).

22. Records and rules of evidence

Copies of documents are admissible as evidence in criminal and civil proceedings to the same extent as the records themselves. In Scotland, see s 22(2).

23. Furnishing of information and production of documents

Persons involved with customs goods must furnish information and produce documents when so required. An officer may take copies of documents produced, make extracts from them and, if necessary, remove them for a reasonable period.

24. Power of entry

An officer may enter and inspect premises, and inspect goods found there, if he has reasonable cause to believe that the premises are used by a person involved with customs goods and that customs goods are to be found there.

25. Order for production of documents

A justice of the peace may, on application by an officer, order documents to be produced and information furnished if there are reasonable grounds for believing that the documents or information may be required as evidence in criminal proceedings relating to customs duty or EC agricultural levy.

26. Procedure when documents are removed

An officer must, on request, give a receipt for documents removed under an order made by a justice of the peace. He must allow access to the documents and provide copies if so requested unless this would prejudice either the investigation or the criminal proceedings which might result from it.

27. Failure of officer to comply with requirements under section 26

An officer may be required to give a receipt, allow access to documents or provide copies of documents by an order made by a magistrate on application by way of complaint. Corresponding relief is given in Scotland and Northern Ireland.

Value Added Tax Act 1994

1994 Chapter 23

PART I THE CHARGE TO TAX

IMPOSITION AND RATE OF VAT

1. Value added tax (V1.101)

Supplies

VAT is charged on:

- a supply of goods or services made in the UK. For the charge to tax on supplies, see s 4. For supplies outside the scope of VAT, see ss 5(3) (transactions treated as neither a supply of goods nor a supply of services), 43 (supplies to a member of the same VAT group); and *Vereniging Happy Family Rustenburgerstraat v Inspecteur der Omzetbelasting* (case 289/86), *Mol v Inspecteur der Invoerrechten en Accijnzen* (case 269/86) [1989] 3 CMLR 729, ECJ (goods such as narcotics subject to a *total* ban).
- anything treated as a supply of goods or services in the UK. For the charge to tax on assets held at deregistration, see Sch 4 para 8. For the charge to tax on goods and services treated as being supplied by a person to himself, see ss 5(5) (goods used for business purposes without being supplied or incorporated in other goods), 5(6) (anything done for business purposes which would, if done for a consideration, be a supply of services), 18C(3) (services relating to goods subject to a warehousing or fiscal warehousing regime), 44 (business transferred as going concern to group member) and Sch 10 para 37 (use of building for something other than a relevant charitable or residential purpose).

In principle, VAT is a liability of the person making the supply. For the exceptions, see ss 8, 9A (reverse charge), 55 (gold), 55A (goods and services of a kind used in missing trader intra-Community fraud) and Sch 11 para 2(12) (goods sold under a power). Subject to the accounting rules, VAT becomes due at the time of supply. For the time of supply, see s 6.Acquisitions

Acquisitions

VAT is charged on an acquisition of goods from another EU member state made in the UK. For the charge to tax on acquisitions, see s 10. VAT is a liability of the person making the acquisition and (subject to the accounting rules) becomes due at the time of acquisition. For the accounting rules in relation to taxable persons, see s 25(1). For the time of acquisition, see s 12. For notifications and payments by non-taxable persons, see VAT Regulations, SI 1995/2518 regs 36 (excise goods) and 148 (new means of transport).

Importations

VAT is charged on goods imported into the UK from a third country (ie a country which is not an EU member state). However, no charge arises on: (1) the illegal importation of drugs *(Einberger v Hauptzollamt Freiburg (No 2)* (case 294/82) [1985] 1 CMLR 765, ECJ) or counterfeit money (*Witzemann v Hauptzollamt Munchen-Milte* (case C-343/89) [1993] STC 108, ECJ); and (2) goods seized on their introduction into the EU which are simultaneously or subsequently destroyed without having left the possession of customs authorities (Dansk Transport og Logistik v Skatteministeriet (case C-230/08) [2010] ECR I–0000, [2010] STC 1711, ECJ). VAT is charged and payable as if it were a customs duty, ie by reference to the legislation specified in s 16. The principle against double taxation does not appear to apply to goods imported from third countries: *Dullaghan v C & E Comrs* [2000] V & DR 189.

For the remission of VAT on supplies and importations in relation to visiting forces, defence contracts, US forces, American war graves and diplomats, see Notice No 48 (December 2010) paras 2.1–2.5.

The principle of preventing abusive practices

The principle of preventing abusive practices applies to VAT. In this context, an abusive practice exists if: (1) while meeting the formal requirements of the Sixth Directive and implementing national legislation, the relevant transactions result in a tax advantage contrary to the purpose of those provisions; and (2) the principal aim of the transactions, apparent from a number of objective factors, is to obtain a tax advantage. However, the principle does not apply where "the economic activity carried out may have some explanation other than the mere attainment of tax advantages": *Halifax plc and others v C & E Comrs* (case C-255/02) [2006] ECR I–1609, [2006] STC 919, ECJ at [74], [75] as clarified in *Ministero dell'Economia e delle Finanze v Part Service Srl (in liquidation)* (case C-425/06) [2008] ECR I–897, [2008] STC 3132, ECJ at [45]; see also *Ampliscientifica Srl and another v Ministero dell'Economia e delle Finanze, Agenzia delle Entrate* (case C-162/07) [2008] ECR I–4019, [2008] SWTI 1387, ECJ at [27], [28]; *R & C Comrs v Weald Leasing Ltd* (case C-103/09) [2010] ECR I–0000, [2011] STC 596, ECJ; *R & C Comrs v RBS Deutschland Holdings GmbH* (case C-277/09) [2010] ECR I–0000, [2011] STC 345, ECJ. The fact that an individual step in the scheme does not succeed does not preclude the application of this principle: see *R & C Comrs v Atrium Club Ltd* [2010] STC 1493.

Transactions involved in an abusive practice must be redefined so as to re-establish the situation that would otherwise have prevailed. The difference between the following amounts must be paid to, or repaid by, the tax authorities: (1) input tax deducted in relation to each transaction where the right to deduct has been exercised abusively; and (2) any output tax for which the taxable person was artificially liable under the scheme. The taxable person who, in the absence of an abusive practice, would have benefited from the first non-abusive transaction, is entitled to deduct the VAT on that transaction: *Halifax plc and others v C & E Comrs* (case C-255/02) [2006] ECR I–1609, [2006] STC 919, ECJ at [94]–[97]. For an example of redefinition, see *R & C Comrs v Atrium Club Ltd* [2010] STC 1493. For the manner in which payments or repayments are made by or to the relevant trader(s), see *R & C Comrs v Moorbury Ltd* [2010] UKUT 360 (TCC), [2010] STC 2715.

For examples of arrangements held to be abusive, see *WHA Ltd and another v R & C Comrs* [2007] STC 1695, CA; *R & C Comrs v Atrium Club Ltd* [2010] EWHC 970 (Ch), [2010] EWHC 970 (Ch), [2010] STC 1493; *R & C Comrs v Moorbury Ltd* [2010] UKUT 360 (TCC), [2010] STC 2715. For an example of arrangements that were not, see *Lower Mill Estate Ltd v C & E Comrs* [2010] UKUT 463 (TCC), [2011] STC 636.

For VAT schemes relating to the purchase of luxury yachts, see Revenue and Customs Brief 11/07, 7 February 2007; Revenue and Customs Brief 56/09.

2. Rate of tax (V3.101, V3.102)

VAT is charged on the value of the supply (see ss 19, 52, 53 and Sch 6), acquisition (see ss 20, 52 and Sch 7) or importation (see s 21) concerned.

The rate of VAT was increased from 17.5% to 20% from 4 January 2011: see F(No 2)A 2010 s 3. For the supplementary charge on supplies of goods and services which took place after 21 June 2010 and which spanned 4 January 2011, see F(No 2)A 2010 Sch 3.

The Treasury may by order increase or reduce the rate for up to 12 months by up to 25% of the existing rate. The minimum rate prescribed by Directive 2006/112/EC art 97(1) is 15%.

For the reduced rate of tax, see s 29A. For the zero rate, see s 30.

It is necessary to round an amount of VAT which includes a fraction of a penny. The rules and methods are determined by the member states. For the Community law principles to be observed, see *J D Wetherspoon plc v R & C Comrs* (case C-302/07) [2009] ECR I–1467,

[2009] STC 1022, ECJ (different principles apply to traders pricing in VAT-inclusive and VAT-exclusive prices). In the UK, see Notice No 700 (April 2002) paras 17.5, 17.5.1 and 17.6.

3. Taxable persons and registration (V3.123)

A taxable person is a person who is registered under Schs 1, 2, 3 or 3A or who is required to be so registered. The Commissioners keep a single register of registered taxable persons. Entries in the register are made and corrected in accordance with regulations. See VAT Regulations 1995, SI 1995/2518 regs 5, 7–9.

A taxable person is a person who *independently* carries on an economic activity: Directive 2006/112/EC art 9(1). For independence, see *Dimosio v Karageorgou* (joined cases C-78/02 to C-80/02) [2003] ECR I–13295, [2003] SWTI 1937, ECJ (employee); *J A van der Steen v Inspecteur van de Belastingdienst Utrecht-Gooi /kantoor Utrecht* (case C-355/06) [2007] ECR I–8863, [2008] STC 2379, ECJ (activities of individual being the sole shareholder, director and employee of a company); *Ministero dell'Economia e delle Finanze and another v FCE Bank plc* (case C-210/04) [2006] ECR I–2803, [2007] STC 165, ECJ (overseas branch) and commentary to s 45 (partnerships). For two or more persons treated as a single taxable person, see s 43 (groups of companies); Sch 1 para 2 (disaggregation direction).

A number of individuals (A, B, C and D) may hold themselves out as partners by completing and signing form VAT2. However, A, B, C and D must actually carry on a business in partnership if they are to constitute a taxable person: see *R & C Comrs v Pal and others* [2008] STC 2442. For "holding out", see the commentary to the Partnership Act 1890 s 14.

3A. Supply of electronic services in member states: special accounting scheme

This section introduces Sch 3B. The Treasury can amend Sch 3B by order.

SUPPLY OF GOODS OR SERVICES IN THE UNITED KINGDOM

4. Scope of VAT on taxable supplies (V3.101; V3.502)

VAT is charged on a supply of goods or services if: (1) it is made in the UK; (2) it is a taxable supply (ie a supply of goods or services made in the UK which is not an exempt supply); (3) it is made by a taxable person; and (4) it is made in the course or furtherance of business. For business, see s 94(1), (2). For supplies deemed to be made in the course or furtherance of business, see s 94(4)–(6). For a sale of capital assets not made in the course or furtherance of business, see *Trustees of the Mellerstain Trust v C & E Comrs* [1989] VATTR 223. For exempt supplies, see s 31. For taxable persons, see s 3. For the principle of preventing abusive practices, see s 1.

One or more transactions in a chain of supply may be tainted by VAT fraud. An untainted supply made by one trader in the chain does not cease to be made in the course or furtherance of business by reason of the fraudulent intentions of the other members of the chain or the fraudulent nature of other transactions in the chain of which the trader is unaware and has no means of knowing: *Optigen Ltd v C & E Comrs; Fulcrum Electronics Ltd v C & E Comrs; Bond House Systems Ltd v C & E Comrs* (joined cases C-354/03, C-355/03 and C-484/03) [2006] ECR I–483, [2006] STC 419, ECJ.

5. Meaning of "supply": alteration by Treasury order (V3.111, V3.118)

Nature of a supply

Generally, "supply" includes all forms of supply but excludes anything done without a consideration. However, the free gift or use of goods is treated as a supply despite the absence of consideration: see Sch 4 para 5; VAT (Supply of Services) Order 1993, SI 1993/1507. For nominal consideration, see *Hotel Scandic Gåsabäck AB v Riksskatteverket* (case C-412/03) [2005] ECR I–743, [2005] STC 1311, ECJ.

A supply must comprise a "supply of goods" or a "supply of services" if it is to fall within the scope of VAT. For the classification of supplies, see below. In determining whether a transaction is a supply of goods or services, it is irrelevant whether the transaction is carried out with the sole aim of obtaining a tax advantage: *Halifax plc and others v C & E Comrs* (case C-255/02) [2006] ECR I–1609, [2006] STC 919, ECJ; *University of Huddersfield Higher Education Corpn v C & E Comrs* (case C-223/03) [2006] ECR I–1751, [2006] STC 980, ECJ.

VAT is a general tax on the consumption of goods and services (Directive 67/227/EEC art 2). As such, there must be consumption as envisaged in the Community VAT system: see *Mohr v Finanzamt Bad Segeberg* (case C-215/94) [1996] STC 328 at [20], ECJ. Consumption is presumed if there is a supply of goods: see *Stewart and another (trading as GT Shooting) v C & E Comrs* [2002] STC 255 at [40], CA. For cases where this test was met, see *Parker Hale Ltd v C & E Comrs* [2000] STC 388, *Stewart and another (trading as GT Shooting) v C & E Comrs* [2002] STC 255, CA (compensation for hand guns surrendered for destruction). In other cases, it may be necessary to demonstrate that the trader has provided services to an identifiable consumer or any benefit capable of being regarded as a cost component of the activity of another person in the commercial chain: see *Landboden-Agrardienste GmbH & Co KG v Finanzamt Calau* (case C-37/95) [1998] STC 171 at [23], ECJ. For undertakings to restrict production not meeting this requirement, see *Mohr v Finanzamt Bad Segeberg* (case C-215/94) [1996] STC 328, ECJ (compensation to discontinue milk production); *Landboden-Agrardienste GmbH & Co KG v Finanzamt Calau* (case C-37/95) [1998] STC 171, ECJ (compensation to reduce potato production).

A transaction may amount to a supply despite the fact that it is carried out unlawfully. For examples, see *C & E Comrs v Oliver* [1980] STC 73 (void sale of stolen car); *Criminal proceedings against Goodwin* (case C-3/97) [1998] STC 699, ECJ (sale of counterfeit perfume infringing third party's rights); *Fischer v Finanzamt Donaueschingen* (case C-283/95) [1998] STC 708, ECJ (lawful game of chance carried out unlawfully); *R v Citrone* [1999] STC 29, CA (anabolic steroids supplied without a licence); *Staatssecretaris van Financiën v Coffeeshop siberië vof* (case C-158/98) [1999] STC 742, ECJ (space in cafe for sale of narcotic drugs); *C & E Comrs v Polok* [2002] STC 361 (escort agency). On the other hand, no supply takes place if the subject matter of the supply is unlawful. For examples, see *Vereniging Happy Family Rustenburgerstraat v Inspecteur der Omzetbelasting* (case 289/86), *Mol v Inspecteur der Invoerrechten en Accijnzen* (case 269/86) [1989] 3 CMLR 729, ECJ (drugs); cf *Witzemann v Hauptzollamt-München-Mitte* (case C-343/89) [1994] STC 108, ECJ (importation of counterfeit currency).

One or more transactions in a chain of supply may be tainted by VAT fraud. An untainted supply by one trader in the chain is unaffected by the fraudulent intentions of the other members of the chain or the fraudulent nature of other transactions in the chain of which the trader is unaware and has no means of knowing: *Optigen Ltd v C & E Comrs; Fulcrum Electronics Ltd v C & E Comrs; Bond House Systems Ltd v C & E Comrs* (joined cases C-354/03, C-355/03 and C-484/03) [2006] ECR I–483, [2006] STC 419, ECJ.

For dealing in foreign exchange, see *C & E Comrs v First National Bank of Chicago* (case C-172/96) [1998] STC 850, ECJ; *Republic National Bank of New York v C & E Comrs* [1992] VATTR 299; contrast *Willis Pension Trustees Ltd* (No 19183) (transactions to hedge exposure to adverse exchange rate fluctuations); Revenue and Customs Brief 5/07, 26 January 2007. For factoring, see *Finanzamt Groß-Gerau v MKG-Kraftfahrzeuge-Factory GmbH* (case C-305/01) [2003] STC 951, ECJ. For capital contributions when a partner is admitted to a partnership, see *KapHag Renditefonds 35 Spreecenter Berlin-Hellersdorf3 Tranche GbR v Finanzamt Charlottenburg* (case C-442/01) [2003] ECR I–6851, [2005] STC 1500, ECJ (no supply by incoming partner or partnership on cash contribution); Business Brief 21/04, 10 August 2004 (supply by incoming partner contributing assets). For the disposal of a partnership share, see Business Brief 30/04, 11 November 2004. For shares and other securities issued by a company, see *Kretztechnik AG v Finanzamt Linz* (case C-465/03) [2005] ECR I–4357, [2005] STC 1118, ECJ and Business Brief 21/05, 23 November 2005 (no supply by company); contrast *Trinity Mirror plc (formerly Mirror Group Newspapers Ltd) v C & E Comrs* [2001] STC 192, CA. For the transfer of land between partnerships with a common partner, see *Fengate Developments (a partnership) v C & E Comrs* [2005] STC 191, CA. For securities for money, see Business Brief 25/95, 20 November 1995. For MOT test charges, see Business Brief 21/96, 17 October 1996. For vehicle removal and recovery services outsourced by police authorities, see Business Brief 9/99, 21 April 1999 (not reproduced). For goods and services used by employees in the course of carrying out their duties, see *Co-operative Insurance Society Ltd v C & E Comrs* [1997] V & DR 65 (hotel accommodation on business trips); cf *Dean and Chapter of Hereford Cathedral v C & E Comrs* [1994] VATTR 159 (house occupied by employee in accordance with contract of employment). For non-compliance carbon credits and carbon offsetting services, see Revenue and Customs Brief 28/10, 15 June 2010.

Nature of consideration

The meaning of "consideration" is a matter of EU law: *Staatssecretaris van Financien v Cooperatiëve Vereniging "Cooperative Aardappelenbewaarplaats GA"* (case 154/80) [1981] 3 CMLR 337 at [9], ECJ. The essential element is a direct link between the relevant supply and whatever is alleged to have been the consideration for it: *Staatssecretaris van Financien v Cooperatiëve Vereniging "Cooperative Aardappelenbewaarplaats GA"* (case 154/80) [1981] 3 CMLR 337 at [12], ECJ; *Apple and Pear Development Council v C & E Comrs* (case 102/86) [1988] STC 221 at [11], [12], ECJ; *Naturally Yours Cosmetics Ltd v C & E Comrs* (case 230/87) [1988] STC 879 at [11], ECJ; *Tolsma v Inspecteur der Omzetbelasting Leuwarden* (case C-16/93) [1994] STC 509 at [13], ECJ; *C & E Comrs v Westmorland Motorway Services Ltd* [1998] STC 431 at 434. This link is provided by an agreement between the person making the supply and the person receiving it so that there is a reciprocal performance of obligations. It appears, however, that the agreement may be something less than a contract: see *Tolsma v Inspecteur der Omzetbelasting Leuwarden* (case C-16/93) [1994] STC 509 at [14], ECJ as interpreted in *C & E Comrs v Church Schools Foundation Ltd* [2001] STC 1661 at [31], CA. The obligations arising under the agreement do not have to be legally enforceable: *Town and Country Factors Ltd v C & E Comrs* (case C-498/99) [2002] STC 1263, ECJ (agreement binding in honour only). It is necessary to undertake a factual investigation in order to determine what the parties to the transaction thought they were agreeing to: *Peugeot Motor Company plc v C & E Comrs* [2003] STC 1438. For examples of cases where there was no direct link, see *Apple and Pear Development Council v C & E Comrs* (case 102/86) [1988] STC 221, ECJ; *Tolsma v Inspecteur der Omzetbelasting Leuwarden* (case C-16/93) [1994] STC 509, ECJ; *Commission v Finland* (case C-246/08) [2009] ECR I–10605, ECJ; *C & E Comrs v Littlewoods Organisation plc* [2001] STC 1568, CA; *C & E Comrs v Church Schools Foundation Ltd* [2001] STC 1661, CA.

An amount must be receivable by the supplier, or by a third party for and on behalf of the supplier. It may be given by the customer or a third party: see Directive 2006/112/EC art 73; *Keeping Newcastle Warm Ltd v C & E Comrs* (Case C-353/00) [2002] STC 943, ECJ; *Trafalgar Tours Ltd v C & E Comrs* [1990] STC 127, CA. For examples, see *C & E Comrs v Professional Footballers Association (Enterprises) Ltd* [1993] STC 86, HL; *Lord Advocate v Largs Golf Club* [1985] STC 226; *C & E Comrs v Telemed Ltd* [1992] STC 89; *Phillip Drakard Trading Ltd v C & E Comrs* [1992] STC 568 (goods transferred to third party who settles the hire purchase debt); *McDonald's Restaurants Ltd* (No 3884); *Seaton Sands Ltd* (No 13879); *Thorn plc v C & E Comrs* [1998] V & DR 383.

The supplier must be able to deal with the moneys as his own or receive some benefit from them: see *H J Glawe Spiel-und Unterhaltungsgeräte Aufstellungsgesellschaft mbH & Co KG v Finanzamt Hamburg-Barmbek-Uhlenhorst* (case C-38/93) [1994] STC 543, ECJ. For a case where the full amount received amounted to consideration, see *Town and County Factors Ltd v C & E Comrs* (case C-498/99) [2002] STC 1263, ECJ ("spot the ball" competition). For cases where part of the amount received did not, see *H J Glawe Spiel-und Unterhaltungsgeräte Aufstellungsgesellschaft mbH & Co KG v Finanzamt Hamburg-Barmbek-Uhlenhorst* (case C-38/93) [1994] STC 543, ECJ (gaming machine with reserve compartment); *C &*

E Comrs v Emap MacLaren Ltd [1997] STC 490 (sponsorship money paid in full to prizeman); *Patrick v C & E Comrs* [1994] VATTR 247 (hammer price divided between seller and auctioneer); *Nell Gwynn House Maintenance Fund Trustees v C & E Comrs* [1999] STC 79, HL (proportion of service charge attributable to wages and salaries).

For unused credits in a telephone box, see *New World Payphones* Ltd (No 15964). For a rent-free period as consideration, see *Port Erin Hotels Ltd* (No 5045); *Ridgeons Bulk Ltd v C & E Comrs* [1994] STC 427; Hansard, 17 December 1991; Business Brief 23/93, 26 July 1993. For the question whether face value vouchers are issued for a consideration, see *Kuwait Petroleum (GB) Ltd v C & E Comrs* (case C-48/97) [1999] STC 488, ECJ. For examples, contrast *Tesco plc* (No 17378) (consideration) and *Kuwait Petroleum (GB) Ltd v C & E Comrs* [2001] STC 62 (no consideration). For excess charges and penalty charges in car parks, see *Bristol City Council* (No 17665) and the Commissioners' revised policy set out in Revenue and Customs Brief 57/08, 8 December 2008 (nature of charge as consideration for supply or outside the scope of VAT governed by the contractual arrangements and all car park operators treated alike). For salary sacrifice, see VAT (Treatment of Transactions) Order 1992, SI 1992/630; *AstraZenica UK Ltd v R & C Comrs* (case C-40/09) [2010] ECR I–0000, [2010] STC 2298, ECJ (retail voucher); *Co-operative Insurance Society Ltd* (No 7109) (motor car); Business Brief 9/92, 19 June 1992; and Revenue and Customs Brief 27/11, 19 July 2011. For free banking, see *The Governor and Company of the Bank of Scotland* (No 13854). For interest-free bonds giving rights to purchase season tickets or match tickets, see *Arsenal Football Club plc v C & E Comrs* [1996] V & DR 5; *Rugby Football Union* (No 18075).

Whether or not consideration arises is determined at the time of supply in accordance with the contract made: see *Potters Lodge Restaurant* (No 905) and *NPD Co Ltd v C & E Comrs* [1988] VATTR 40 (restaurant service charge); *Warwick Masonic Rooms Ltd* (No 839) (unsolicited donation). The fact that the amount receivable is stolen does not prevent a consideration arising: *Benton v C & E Comrs* [1975] VATTR 138. The owner does not make a supply of goods for consideration if the goods are stolen: *British American Tobacco International Ltd and another v Belgian State* (case C-435/03) [2006] STC 158, ECJ (theft of warehoused tobacco).

For quantum, see s 19. For the tax adjustment made and documents to be issued when the consideration for a supply is varied, see VAT Regulations, SI 1995/2518 reg 38.

Distinction between supplies of goods and supplies of services

Whether a supply is of goods or services is determined in accordance with Sch 4 paras 1–6. For the dividing line between a supply of goods and a supply of services, see *Faaborg-Gelting Linien A/S v Finanzamt Flensburg* (case C-231/94) [1996] STC 774, ECJ (restaurant meal); *Levob Verzekeringen BV, OB Bank NV cs v Staatssecretaris van Financiën* (case C-41/04) [2005] ECR I–9433, [2006] STC 766, ECJ (customised computer software); *Graphic Procédé v Mimistère du budget, des comptes publics et de la function publique* (case C-88/09) [2010] ECR I–0000, [2010] STC 918, ECJ. For examples see *C & E Comrs v Jeffs* [1995] STC 759; *ADP Insulations (Group) Ltd v C & E Comrs* [1987] VATTR 36; *AZO-Maschinenfabrik Adolf Zimmerman GmbH v C & E Comrs* [1987] VATTR 25.

Anything done for a consideration which is not a supply of goods is a supply of services. This includes the grant, assignment or surrender of any right.

For examples of "anything done", see *Naturally Yours Cosmetics Ltd v C & E Comrs* (case 230/87) [1988] STC 879, ECJ (procuring a gathering at which goods were sold); *C & E Comrs v Tilling Management Services Ltd* [1979] STC 365 (procuring a group relief payment); *GUS Merchandise Corpn Ltd v C & E Comrs* [1981] STC 569, CA (agreeing to act as agent); *C & E Comrs v Diners Club Ltd* [1989] STC 407, CA (making payments under a credit card scheme); *C & E Comrs v High Street Vouchers Ltd* [1990] STC 575 (redemption of vouchers at a discount); *Tarmac Construction Ltd v C & E Comrs* [1981] VATTR 35 (services under contract of employment); *Gardner Lohmann Ltd v C & E Comrs* [1981] VATTR 76 (commodity option); *C & E Comrs v Battersea Leisure Ltd* [1992] STC 213, *Ridgeons Bulk Ltd v C & E Comrs* [1994] STC 427; *Gleneagles Hotel plc v C & E Comrs*

[1986] VATTR 196 (carrying out work to premises); *Medical Centre Developments Ltd* (No 15601) (entering into an agreement to grant an underlease); *Trinity Mirror plc (formerly Mirror Group Newspapers Ltd) v C & E Comrs* [2003] STC 518, *Neville Russell (a firm) v C & E Comrs* [1987] VATTR 194, *Hutchison, Lock & Monk* (No 5212), Business Brief 12/05, 15 June 2005 and contrast *Iliffe & Holloway v C & E Comrs* [1993] VATTR 439 (accepting a lease); *Landmark Cash and Carry Group Ltd v C & E Comrs* [1980] VATTR 1 (procuring discounts for members); *Portal (Linwood) Ltd* (No 3861) (right to remove materials after demolishing a building); *Cooper Chasney Ltd* (No 4898) (relinquish trade name); *Oxford Film Foundation* (No 5031) (publicity benefit to sponsor); *Leigh v C & E Comrs* [1990] VATTR 59 (fine for late return of video film); *Pottie* (No 5460) (ex gratia payment additional to consideration for supply already made); *Granada Group plc v C & E Comrs* [1991] VATTR 104 (free meal to driver bringing coach to motorway service station); *C & E Comrs v Bass plc* [1993] STC 42 (cancellation charge for reserved hotel accommodation); *Edinburgh Leisure* (No 18784) (payment by a local authority to cover any shortfall between income and operating costs). This does not include carrying out functions which a trader is obliged to carry out on his own behalf: *National Coal Board v C & E Comrs* [1982] STC 863; *British European Breeders Fund v C & E Comrs* [1985] VATTR 12. For goodwill, see Press Notice 790, 10 December 1982. For the variation of the terms of a lease, see The Law Society, 1 May 1991 (consideration when variation treated as surrender of old lease and grant of new lease). For transactions in commercial paper, see Business Brief 11/91, 9 August 1991. For retail consortia, see Business Brief 12/93, 22 April 1993.

For the assignment or surrender of rights, see *Lubbock Fine & Co v C & E Comrs* (case C-63/92) [1994] STC 101; *Central Capital Corpn Ltd* (No 13319); *Cantor Fitzgerald International Ltd* [1997] V & DR 233 (lease); *Croydon Hotel & Leisure Co Ltd v C & E Comrs* [1997] V & DR 254 (management agreement).

Treasury orders may set out what is to be treated as a supply of goods or of services or of neither. For transactions treated as supplies of goods, see VAT (Water) Order 1989, SI 1989/1114. For transactions treated as supplies of services, see VAT (Special Provisions) Order 1995, SI 1995/1268 art 6 (reconditioned goods); VAT (Tour Operators) Order 1987, SI 1987/1806 (goods and services amounting to a designated travel service).

For transactions treated as supplies of neither goods nor services, see VAT (Cars) Order 1992, SI 1992/3122 art 4 (motor cars); VAT (Special Provisions) Order 1995, SI 1995/1268 arts 4, 5, 8–10 (repossessed goods etc, business sold as going concern, assignment of finance agreements, used goods removed to the UK, services of agents and auctioneers relating to used goods); VAT (Treatment of Transactions) Order 1986, SI 1986/896 (pawned goods); VAT (Treatment of Transactions) Order 1992, SI 1992/630 (salary sacrifice where motor car provided to employee for private use); VAT (Supply of Temporarily Imported Goods) Order 1992, SI 1992/3130 (tax suspended goods); VAT (Treatment of Transactions) Order 1995, SI 1995/958 (sale of temporarily imported second-hand goods and works of art).

Orders may provide that business goods put to business use are not treated as a supply of services under Sch 4 para 5(4). No orders have been made to date.

Orders may provide that business assets removed from one EU member state to another are not treated as a supply of goods under Sch 4 para 6. See VAT (Removal of Goods) Order 1992, SI 1992/3111.

Services treated as being made in the course or furtherance of business

Treasury orders may treat particular transactions which, if done for a consideration, would be a supply of services as being supplied in the course or furtherance of the business. See VAT (Supply of Services) Order 1993, SI 1993/1507.

Self-supplies

Treasury orders may provide that goods used for business purposes are treated as being both supplied to and supplied by a trader. See VAT (Cars) Order 1992, SI 1992/3122 arts 5–7 (motor cars); VAT (Special Provisions) Order 1995, SI 1995/1268 art 11 (stationery). For other self-supplies, see s 18C (services relating to warehoused goods); s 44 (business transferred as going concern to group company); Sch 10 paras 1, 5, 6 (buildings and civil engineering works).

Treasury orders may provide that anything done for business purposes is treated as a supply of services made both to and by a trader. See VAT (Self-Supply of Construction Services) Order 1989, SI 1989/472.

Practical problems

The fact that money is received does not lead to the inevitable conclusion that there is a corresponding supply: see *Tolsma v Inspecteur der Omzetbelasting Leeuwarden* (case C-16/93) [1994] STC 509, ECJ (organ-grinder soliciting donations); *Mohr v Finanzamt Bad Segeberg* (case C-215/94) [1996] STC 328, ECJ (compensation for undertaking to cease milk production); *Landboden-Agrardienste GmbH & Co KG v Finanzamt Calau* (case C-37/95) [1998] STC 171, ECJ (compensation for undertaking to reduce potato production); *Warwick Masonic Rooms Ltd* (No 839) (unsolicited donation); *Hillingdon Legal Resources Centre Ltd v C & E Comrs* [1991] VATTR 39 (local authority grant); *Sleaford RFC* (No 9844) (match fees); *Iliffe & Holloway v C & E Comrs* [1993] VATTR 439 (mortgage capping agreement); *Vivat Holdings plc v C & E Comrs* [1995] V & DR 348 (payment by guarantor); *Turespaña* (No 14568) and contrast *Netherlands Board of Tourism* (No 12935) (grant from overseas government). For payments under out-of-court settlements, see *Reich* (No 9548) (payment in respect of supply denied to have been made); *Cooper Chasney Ltd v C & E Comrs* [1990] 2 CMLR 509 and *J E Greves & Son v C & E Comrs* [1993] VATTR 127 (supplies resulting from agreement between the parties); *Holiday Inns (UK) Ltd v C & E Comrs* [1993] VATTR 321; *Financial and General Print Ltd* (No 13795) (liquidated damages); Press Notice 82/87, 19 November 1987; The Law Society, 9 September 1992. For deposits retained on the cancellation of hotel bookings, see *Société thermale d'Eugénie-les-Bains v Ministère de l'Économie, des Finances et de l'Industrie* (case C-277/05) [2007] ECR I–6415, [2008] STC 2470, ECJ. For donations to universities, see Press Notice 84/88, 10 November 1988. For agricultural grants, see Press Notice 58/89, 9 August 1989 (UK grants for voluntary surrender of rights); Business Brief 28/99, 22 December 1999 (EU grant aid for processing dried fodder). For repairs to goods under warranty, see Press Notice 59/89, 10 August 1989. For mesne profits, see The Law Society, 14 October 1992. For payment of third party costs, see The Law Society, 28 October 1992. For recovered costs retained by debt collectors, see Business Brief 28/97, 12 December 1997. For apportionments of rent on freehold sale of tenanted property or assignment of lease, see The Law Society, 17 May 1991.

It may be necessary to determine the terms or nature of the transaction between the parties. For the general approach to analysing the arrangements adopted by the parties, see *Tesco plc v C & E Comrs* [2003] STC 1561, CA at [159]. For examples, see *C & E Comrs v Sai Jewellers* [1996] STC 269 (whether contracts were for exchange or refashioning of jewellery); *Hostgilt Ltd v Megahart Ltd* [1999] STC 141, *Wynn Realisations Ltd (in administration) v Vogue Holdings Inc* [1999] STC 524, CA, *Debenhams Retail plc v Sun Alliance and London Assurance Co Ltd* [2005] STC 1443, CA (whether agreed price inclusive or exclusive of VAT); *Debenhams Retail plc v R & C Comrs* [2005] STC 1155, CA (whether the contracts achieved their intended purposes); *C & E Comrs v Latchmere Properties Ltd* [2005] STC 731 (whether building contractor supplied services to landowner or they carried on a joint venture); *MBNA Europe Bank Ltd v R & C Comrs* [2006] STC 2089 (securitisation of credit card receivables); *Keydon Estates Ltd* (No 4471) (whether money received was share of partnership profit or consideration for supply of services fixed by reference to customer's profit on a transaction). For variations of commercial property leases, see The Law Society, 1 May 1991. For deposits relalting to sales of land on which dwellings are to be constructed, see Revenue and Customs Brief 36/09, 8 July 2009.

The contractual arrangements between the parties deal with their private law obligations. They may not (and need not) deal with the tax consequences. Thus, the correct VAT treatment does not necessarily flow from the contracts themselves. If not, the issue must be decided by the tribunal (see s 82) as a question of fact: see *C & E Comrs v Reed Personnel Services Ltd* [1995] STC 588 at 595. For an example, see *Don Bosco Onroerend Goed BV v Staatssecretaris van Financiën* (case C-461/08) [2009] ECR I–11079, [2010] STC 476, ECJ (sale of partly demolished building where demolition completed after the sale and at the vendor's expense). It is necessary to look at the whole circumstances in order to arrive at the proper characterisation of the supply: *R & C Comrs v Board of Governors of the Robert Gordon University* [2008] STC 1890. The starting point for deciding the relationship between the parties is the contract. Was it put into writing? If not wholly recorded in writing, was it supplemented orally? If this fails to provide the answer, what implications (if any) can be drawn from statute, custom, usage, previous dealings between the parties, etc and how their relations were conducted after the contract was made: *C & E Comrs v Music and Video Exchange Ltd* [1992] STC 220 at 222 and 223. The nature of a transaction is characterised at the time when the legal relationship is created: *Highland Council v R & C Comrs* [2008] STC 1280. The words used by the parties to describe the supply made do not necessarily reflect its true legal nature. For an example, see *HBOS plc v R & C Comrs* [2009] STC 486 (services of debt collector). For the characterisation of leisure facilities, see Revenue and Customs Brief 13/09, 20 March 2009.

It may be necessary to decide who supplies what and to whom where an intermediary (X) stands between the supposed supplier (S) and the known customer (C) in relation to such services as driving instruction, hairdressing and agency nursing. It is immaterial whether C is aware whether the services have been supplied by S or X: see *C & E Comrs v MacHenrys (Hairdressers) Ltd* [1993] STC 170 at 175; *Kieran Mullin Ltd v C & E Comrs* [2003] STC 274 at [32], [33].

X may be an employee or sub-contractor, so that in reality S makes a supply to C and X supplies his labour to S. For examples, see *Cronin v C & E Comrs* [1991] STC 333 and *TDA (School) Ltd* (No 4900) (driving school); *C & E Comrs v Jane Montgomery (Hair Stylists) Ltd* [1994] STC 256 (hairdresser); *Clark v C & E Comrs* [1996] STC 263 (bus service); *C & E Comrs v Reed Personnel Services Ltd* [1995] STC 588 and *Allied Medicare Nursing Services Ltd* (No 5485) (nurse). For employees, see s 94. For services provided by Independent Financial Advisor networks, see Business Brief 26/04, 17 September 2004.

Alternatively, X may be an independent contractor with the following consequences. First, X may supply the services to C and S may supply a service to C comprising arranging performance of the services. For the distinction between the supplies made by S and X, see *Nell Gwynn House Maintenance Fund Trustees v C & E Comrs* [1999] STC 79, HL. S may pay X and obtain reimbursement from C. For a supply by X to C against payment by S, see *Mölnlycke Ltd* (No 14641). For the quantum of the consideration received by S where he shares the amount received with X under an arrangement unknown to C, see *Joppa Enterprises Ltd v R & C Comrs* [2009] STC 1279 (entrance fee to sauna). For agents, disbursements by agents and the supplies deemed to be made to and by agents, see s 47. Secondly, X may supply services to C on his own account and S may supply services to X, eg *C & E Comrs v MacHenrys (Hairdressers) Ltd* [1993] STC 170 and *Kieran Mullin Ltd v C & E Comrs* [2003] STC 274 (hairstylist renting chair in salon); *Carless v C & E Comrs* [1993] STC 632 (taxi driver)); *Ringside Refreshments v C & E Comrs* [2004] STC 426 (supply of goods); *Spearmint Rhino Ventures (UK) Ltd v R & C Comrs* [2007] STC 1252 (women performing private dances, and providing companionship, for customers in a club) and contrast *Joppa Enterprises Ltd v R & C Comrs* [2009] STC 1279 (see above); *A1 Lifts Ltd v R & C Comrs* [2010] STC 214 (loft conversion. Thirdly, X may supply services to S but make no supply to C, eg *H Tempest Ltd v C & E Comrs* [1993] VATTR 482, *Lancashire County Council v C & E Comrs* [1996] V & DR 550 (school photographs).

For credit cards, see *C & E Comrs v Diners Club Ltd* [1989] STC 407, CA. For fuel cards, see *The Harpur Group Ltd v C & E Comrs* [1994] VATTR 180. For goods supplied through intermediaries, see *Philips Exports Ltd v C & E Comrs* [1990] STC 508 (property in goods vesting for an infinitely short time). For sub-sales of land, see *Kwik Save Group plc v C & E Comrs* [1994] VATTR 457 (shops sold by X to S conveyed direct to C). For contracts making provision for separate supplies by different persons to the same customer, see

Telewest Communications plc and another v C & E Comrs [2005] STC 481, CA; *Lower Mill Estate Ltd v R & C Comrs* [2010] UKUT 463 (TCC), [2011] STC 636. For employment bureaux, see Revenue and Customs Brief 8/09, 18 March 2009 (withdrawal of the staff hire concession). For charges to customers paying by credit card, see Business Brief 17/98, 7 August 1998. For works in default carried out by local authorities, see Business Brief 19/98, 15 September 1998.

It may be necessary to establish the true identity of one or more of the parties. For an example, see *Lancashire County Council v C & E Comrs* [1996] V & DR 550 (whether facilities supplied by school or local education authority).

6. Time of supply (V3.131)

VAT is chargeable (or not) in accordance with the legislation in force at the time of supply and is accounted for in the prescribed accounting period current at that time: see s 1 (2); VAT Regulations 1995, SI 1995/2518 regs 32 (3), 40 (*a*). The time of supply is therefore important in determining chargeability to VAT (eg when supplies become, or cease to be, exempt or outside the scope of VAT), the rate of VAT (eg when the rate of VAT changes or a supply becomes chargeable at a different rate) and accountability (ie whether VAT is accounted for in the current period or a later period). For the effect of these provisions on completed pre-registration supplies, see *B J Rice & Associates v C & E Comrs* [1996] STC 463, CA.

In principle, goods are supplied when they are removed or made available to the customer. See *West End Motors (Bodmin) Ltd* (No 1205); *Volvo Trucks (Great Britain) Ltd v C & E Comrs* [1988] VATTR 11. For land, see *Cumbernauld Development Corpn v C & E Comrs* [2002] STC 226; *Margrie Holdings Ltd v C & E Comrs* [1986] VATTR 213. However, goods sent out on approval or sale or return are supplied when they are accepted or, if sooner, 12 months after they were removed. For goods sent on approval or sale or return, see *R & C Comrs v Robertson's Electrical Ltd* [2007] STC 612; *Diaform Ltd* (No 11069); *The Littlewoods Organisation plc v C & E Comrs* [1997] V & DR 408.

In principle, services are supplied at the time when the services are performed. See *Trustees for the Greater World Association Trust v C & E Comrs* [1989] VATTR 91; *Mercantile Contracts Ltd* (No 4357); *Granton Marketing Ltd and Wentwalk Ltd (No 2) v C & E Comrs* [1999] V & DR 382.

The times indicated above are sometimes referred to as "basic tax points". They are overridden by the following tax points.

- If a VAT invoice is issued before the "basic tax point", the time of supply is the day when the invoice was issued. The supply is treated as taking place to the extent of the amount invoiced. An invoice is issued when it is sent or given to a customer: *C & E Comrs v Woolfold Motor Co Ltd* [1983] STC 715. It must contain all the information required to be shown on a tax invoice: *J D Fox Ltd v C & E Comrs* [1988] 2 CMLR 875. For self-billed invoices issued before the basic tax point, see Sch 11 para 2(3).
- If a payment is received before a basic tax point comprising the removal of goods, making goods available or performing a service, the time of supply is the day when the payment was received. The supply is treated as taking place to the extent of the amount received. The goods or services must be precisely identified when the payment is made, and all relevant information concerning their future delivery or future performance must be known, if VAT is to become chargeable by reference to a payment on account: *BUPA Hospitals Ltd and anor v C & E Comrs* (case C-419/02) [2006] ECR I–1685, [2006] STC 967, ECJ. A transfer of money need not involve a simultaneous transfer of future control of the money in order to amount to a payment: *C & E Comrs v Faith Construction Ltd* [1989] STC 539, CA. See also *Barratt Urban Construction (Northern) Ltd* (No 2723); *Barratt Construction Ltd v C & E Comrs* [1989] VATTR 204; *Thorn Materials Supply Ltd* (No 12914) (reversed on other grounds sub nom *C & E Comrs v Thorn Materials Supply Ltd* [1996] STC 1490, CA). A payment by cheque is received

when it is presented and met by the drawer's bank: *Rampling v C & E Comrs* [1986] VATTR 62. A payment by way of offset in an inter-company current account seems to be received when the accounting entry is made: see *Legal & Contractual Services Ltd v C & E Comrs* [1984] VATTR 85; *Schlumberger Inland Services Inc v C & E Comrs* [1985] VATTR 35, on appeal [1987] STC 228; *Pentex Oil Ltd* (No 7989). For an agreement closing out mutual transactions between two parties and establishing the net amount due from one party to the other, see *R & C Comrs v Enron Europe Ltd* [2006] STC 1339 (time of the supply made by each party to the other determined by reference to the date of the calculation made under the agreement). For payments made when the payer and payee are members of a VAT group, see *C & E Comrs v Thorn Materials Supply Ltd* [1998] STC 725, HL. For moneys held on behalf of the payer, see *Old Red Lion Restaurant* (No 1446) (stakeholder); *Ghaus* (No 4999), *Nigel Mansell Sports Cars Ltd v C & E Comrs* [1991] VATTR 491 (funds held in client account); and contrast *C & E Comrs v Richmond Theatre Management Ltd* [1995] STC 257, *Celtic plc v C & E Comrs* [1997] V & DR 111 (advance ticket sales). For payments appropriated for another purpose, see *C & E Comrs v British Telecommunications plc* [1996] STC 818, CA. For examples of payments on account, see *Purshotam M Pattni & Sons v C & E Comrs* [1987] STC 1; *C & E Comrs v Moonraker's Guest House Ltd* [1992] STC 544; *C & E Comrs v British Telecommunications plc* [1996] STC 818, CA; *C & E Comrs v Richmond Theatre Management Ltd* [1995] STC 257; *J D Fox Ltd v C & E Comrs* [1988] 2 CMLR 875; *Bethway & Moss Ltd v C & E Comrs* [1988] 3 CMLR 44; *Regalstar Enterprises v C & E Comrs* [1989] 1 CMLR 117.

- If a VAT invoice is issued no later than 14 days after the "basic tax point", the time of supply is the day when the invoice was issued. This rule does not apply if the supplier so elects. The 14-day period may be extended if the supplier so requests and the Commissioners so direct. A request may be made in respect of all supplies or specified classes of supply. For elections and requests where self-billed invoices are prepared, see Sch 11 para 2(4).
- If goods removed from the UK are acquired by a taxable person in another EU member state, the time of supply is the earlier of: (1) the fifteenth day of the month following that in which the removal took place; and (2) the day on which a VAT invoice is issued. This rule is over-ridden by VAT Regulations 1995, SI 1995/2518 reg 86 (5).

At the request of the taxable person the Commissioners may direct that the tax point is to be determined by the occurrence of some event which would be earlier than the physical time of supply mentioned above. The time of supply in such cases is either the beginning or end of a relevant working period as defined for that person.

Specific time of supply rules are specified:

- Self-supplies of motor cars and (where still relevant) stationery (see s 5(5)) are treated as taking place when the goods are first appropriated to business use.
- Free gifts of goods (see Sch 4 para 5(1)) are treated as supplied when the goods are transferred or disposed of so as to no longer form part of the business assets.
- The free use of business goods for private or non-business purposes (see Sch 4 para 5(4)) is treated as taking place when the goods are appropriated for such use. However, this rule is over-ridden by VAT Regulations 1995, SI 1995/2518 reg 81(1).

Additional specific time of supply rules are specified elsewhere. For goods subject to a warehousing regime, see s 18. For fiscally warehoused goods, see s 18B. For services performed in warehouses and fiscal warehouses, see s 18C. For supplies between members of a VAT group, see s 43. For supplies made to and by agents, see s 47. For supplies of gold, see s 55(4). For "designated travel services" supplied by a tour operator see VAT (Tour Operators) Order 1987, SI 1987/1086 art 4. For coin-operated machines, see Notice No 48

(December 2010) para 3.6. For practising barristers and advocates, see Notice No 700/44/02 para 2. For legal aid work, see Business Brief 4/00, 17 March 2000.

The Commissioners may make regulations varying the time of supply rules in specified circumstances. For the regulations made, see VAT Regulations 1995, SI 1995/2518 regs 81–95. These regulations are modified by the transitional rules set out in s 97A.

This section is modified by the transitional rules set out in s 97A.

The term "VAT invoice" is defined.

7. Place of supply of goods (V3.124)

A supply of goods is chargeable to VAT only if it is made in the UK: see s 1(1)(a). The place of supply of warehoused goods is determined under ss 18 and 18B. The place of supply of other goods is determined in accordance with the following provisions, although their effect is varied by s 14 in relation to certain overseas suppliers.

Goods in the UK are supplied in the UK if the supply does not involve their removal from the UK. Goods outside the UK are supplied abroad if their supply does not involve their removal to the UK.

Goods removed to the UK are supplied in the UK if: (1) the supplier is responsible for installing or assembling the goods at a place in the UK; (2) the goods are removed from another EU member state by a person registered under Schs 1, 2 or 3, or liable to registration under Schs 1 or 2, and supplied for a consideration (so that Sch 4 paras 5 (1) and 6 do not apply) to a person who is not a taxable person; or (3) the goods are imported from a third country by the supplier. Head (2) does not apply to new means of transport (see s 95). Goods removed to the UK in other circumstances are supplied abroad.

Goods removed from the UK are supplied abroad if: (1) the supplier is responsible for installing or assembling the goods at a place outside the UK; or (2) the goods are removed to another EU member state by a person who is a taxable person in another EU member state and liable to account for VAT on the supply under the VAT legislation of that member state. Head (2) does not apply to new means of transport. If the liability to account for overseas VAT in head (2) results from an option exercised in the UK, the supplier must have given, and not withdrawn, a notification under VAT Regulations 1995, SI 1995/2518 reg 98. Goods removed from the UK in other circumstances are supplied in the UK.

The foregoing rules may be varied by Treasury order. For the order made, see VAT (Place of Supply of Goods) Order 2004, SI 2004/3148. For the installation of undersea cables laid between two member states, see *Aktiebolaget NN v Skatteministeriet* (case C-111/05) [2007] ECR I–2697, [2008] STC 3203, ECJ.

7A. Place of supply of services

A supply of services is chargeable to VAT only if it is made in the UK: see s 1(1)(a). The place of supply of services is determined as follows:

- As regards designated travel services, the place of supply is determined in accordance with VAT (Tour Operators) Order 1987, SI 1987/1806 art 5(2). For designated travel services, see art 3 of the 1987 Order.
- As regards the services specified in Sch 4A, the place of supply is determined in accordance with that Schedule. Parts 1 and 2 of Sch 4A apply to services supplied to a customer who is a relevant business person. Parts 1 and 3 of Sch 4A apply to services supplied to a customer who is not.
- As regards other services (or a right to those services) supplied to a relevant business person, the services (or right) are supplied in the country in which the *customer* belongs. For the country in which the customer (ie a relevant business person) belongs, see s 9(1)–(4)
- In other cases, the services (or right) are supplied in the country in which the *supplier* belongs. For the relevant country in relation to a supplier who is a relevant business person, see s 9(2)–(4). For the relevant country in relation to a supplier who is not, see s 9(5), (6).

The supplier or customer is a relevant business person for the foregoing purposes if:

- he is a taxable person (as defined in Directive 2006/112/ art 9), or is registered (or identified) for VAT purposes in the UK, the Isle of Man or another EU member state; and
- (in relation to a customer) he receives the services wholly or partly for business purposes.

This section and Sch 4 may be modified by order. An order may be made on or after after 21 July 2009 (when FA 2009 received Royal Assent): see FA 2009 Sch 36 para 14(1). No order has been made to date. However, VAT (Tour Operators) Order 1987 art 5 is deemed to be such an order: see FA 2009 Sch 36 para 13(b). For transitional provisions in relation to orders, see s 97A.

This section was inserted by FA 2009 Sch 36 para 4 in relation to supplies made after 31 December 2009: see FA 2009 s 76 and Sch 36 para 14(3). For transitional provisions in relation to such supplies, see FA 2009 Sch 36 para 19. For a temporary administrative asesseement applicable from 15 March 2010 in relation to business to business supplies of freight transport services and services closely associated with freight transport, see Revenue and Customs Brief 13/10, 17 March 2010.

For an order in relation to the place of supply of services made under VATA 1994 s 7(11) prior to amendment by FA 2009 Sch 3 para 3(4), see VAT (Place of Supply of Services) Order 1992, SI 1992/3121. This has not been revoked.

For trading allowances in greenhouse gas emissions, see Business Brief 28/04, 26 October 2004. For the installation of undersea cables laid between two member states, see *Aktiebolaget NN v Skatteministeriet* (case C-111/05) [2007] ECR I–2697, [2008] STC 3203, ECJ. For the relocation abroad of telecommunication service providers, internet service providers and broadcasters, see Revenue and Customs Brief 58/09, 2 October 2009.

8. Reverse charge on supplies received from abroad (V3.231)

A person who belongs in a country other than the UK may make a supply of services which meets the following conditions:

- the place of supply of the services is inside the UK. For the place of supply of services, see s 7A.
- the recipient of the supply is a relevant business person (as defined in s 7A(4)) who belongs in the UK. For the country in which a relevant business person belongs, see s 9(2)–(4);
- the services do not fall within any of the descriptions in Sch 9. These descriptions may be altered by order. No order has been made to date.; and
- (if the services fall within Sch 4A paras 1–9) the recipient is registered for the purposes of VAT in the UK. For registration, see Schs 1–3A.

Where this is so, the actual supply made by the overseas supplier is disregarded and the UK recipient is deemed to make a taxable supply (as defined in s 4(2)) of services. This supply is deemed to be made in the UK and in the course or furtherance of a business carried on by the recipient.

For the value of the supply deemed to be made by the recipient, see Sch 6 para 8. The time of supply is prescribed by regulations. For the regulations made, see VAT Regulations 1995, SI 1995/2518 reg 82. These regulations are modified by the transitional rules set out in s 97A (see s 6(14A)).

For transitional provisions in relation to supplies deemed to have been made by the recipient after 31 December 2009, see FA 2009 Sch 36 para 19.

9. Place where supplier or recipient of services belongs (V3.124)

For the purposes of ss 7A, 8 and Sch 4A, the country in which a relevant business person (as defined in s 7A(4)) belongs is determined as follows:

- if the person has a business establishment, or some other fixed establishment, in only one country, he is treated as belonging in that country;
- if the person has a business establishment, or some other fixed establishment(s), in more than one country, the country in which he belongs is determined by reference to the location of the establishment most directly concerned with the supply; and
- in other cases an individual belongs in the country in which he has his usual place of residence and a body corporate belongs in the country in which it is legally constituted.

As regards other persons, the country in which an individual belongs is the country in which he has his usual place of residence, and the country in which a body corporate belongs in the country in which it is legally constituted.

An establishment is a "fixed establishment" if it has a sufficient minimum strength in the form of the permanent presence of the human and technical resources necessary for supplying specific services: *Berkholz v Finanzamt Hamburg-Mitte-Alstadt* (case 168/84) [1985] 3 CMLR 667, ECJ. For examples, see *ARO Lease BV v Inspecteur der Belastingdienst Grote Ondernemingen, Amsterdam* (case C-190/95) [1997] STC 1272, ECJ, *Lease Plan Luxembourg SA v Belgium* (case C-390/96) [1998] STC 628, ECJ *Cookies World Vertriebsgellschaft mbH v Finanzlandesdirektion für Triol* (case C-155/01) [2004] STC 1386, ECJ (car leasing business); *The Source Enterprise Ltd* (No 7881) (premises not continually staffed or attracting goodwill). A trader ("the agent") established in one member state may act as agent for another trader ("the supplier") established in a different member state. Where this is so, the supplier has a fixed establishment in the agent's member state if the agent has the human and technical resources characteristic of a fixed establishment and he acts as a mere auxiliary organ of the supplier: *C & E Comrs v DFDS A/S* (case C-260/95) [1997] STC 384, ECJ. Two establishments may contribute to the service performed. Where this is so, it is necessary to consider the significance of the contribution made by each establishment in order to decide from which establishment the service was supplied. See *C & E Comrs v Chinese Channel (Hong Kong) Ltd* [1998] STC 347.

For the relationship between the place of supply and the place of acquisition in relation to intra-EU movements of goods involving three parties, see *EMAG Handel Eder OHG v Finanzlandesdirecktion für Kärnten* (case C-245/04) [2006] ECR I–3227, [2007] STC 1461, ECJ and s 14.

For a supply received by an individual in his private capacity, see *Razzak & Mishari v C & E Comrs* [1997] V&DR 392 (temporary stay in the UK).

This section was substituted by FA 2009 Sch 36 para 6 in relation to supplies made after 31 December 2009: see FA 2009 s 76 and Sch 36 para 14(3). For transitional provisions, see FA 2009 Sch 36 para 19. For the interpretation of the legislation in force before 1 January 2010, see in particular *C & E Comrs v Chinese Channel (Hong Kong) Ltd* [1998] STC 347; *RAL (Channel Islands) Ltd (No 17914) refd RAL (Channel Islands) Ltd and others v C & E Comrs* (case C-452/03) [2005] ECR I–3947, [2005] STC 1025, ECJ; *R & C Comrs v Zurich Insurance Co* [2006] STC 1694, affd [2007] STC 1756, CA

9A. Reverse charge on gas, electricity, heat or cooling (V3.178)

The following consequences follow if "relevant goods" are supplied to a UK registered taxable person by a person who is outside the UK:

- the UK taxable person is deemed to make the supply in the UK at a time determined in accordance with VAT Regulations 1995, SI 1995/2518 reg 82A;
- the supply is deemed to be a taxable supply made in the course or furtherance of business;
- the UK taxable person is entitled to input tax credit in respect of the supply he is deemed to have made;
- the supply deemed to be made by the UK taxable person is disregarded when apportioning his input tax under the partial exemption rules, as to which see VAT Regulations 1995, SI 1995/2518 regs 101, 102; and

- (by implication) the supply made by the person outside the UK is disregarded so that he is neither liable to charge VAT (if he is a taxable person) nor liable to registration (in other cases) by reference to his supply.

"Relevant goods" comprise: (1) gas supplied through a natural gas system situated within the territory of an EU member state; (2) gas supplied through any network connected to such a system; (3) electricity; and (4) heat or cooling supplied through a network. For the persons who are "outside the UK", see VAT (Place of Supply of Goods) Order 2004, SI 2004/3148 art 14.

This section was amended by F(No 3)A 2010 s 20 in relation to supplies made after 31 December 2010.

ACQUISITION OF GOODS FROM MEMBER STATES

10. Scope of VAT on acquisitions from member states (V3.366)

VAT is charged on an acquisition of goods from an EU member state (defined in s 11) if: (1) the goods are acquired by a taxable person and conditions (*a*)–(*e*) are met; (2) the goods are subject to excise duty and conditions (*a*)–(*e*) are met; or (3) the goods comprise a new means of transport (defined in s 95) and conditions (*a*)–(*c*) are met. For acquisitions of new means of transport, see *X v Skatteverket* (case C-84/09) [2010] ECR I– 0000, [2011] STC 189, ECJ; *Criminal proceedings against R* (case C-285/09) [2010] ECR I–0000. [2011] STC 138, ECJ.

The stated conditions are that: (*a*) the acquisition is made in the UK (see s 13); (*b*) the acquisition is not made in pursuance of a taxable supply (ie the supplier's supply is made outside the UK); (*c*) the acquisition is not an exempt acquisition (see s 31); (*d*) the person acquiring the goods does so in the course or furtherance of a business (any person) or non-business activity (any incorporated or unincorporated body); (*e*) the supplier is a taxable person in another EU member state (see s 92) and supplies the goods in the course or furtherance of business. For activities amounting to a business, see s 94 (1)–(3).

For the text of an unpublished extra-statutory concession, see *Howard-Williams* (No 14474) (relief from payment of VAT on new means of transport acquired by certain persons moving their place of residence to the UK). For yachts removed from the EU country where they are supplied to the place where they are to be chartered without entering the UK, see Revenue and Customs Brief 20/11, 16 May 2011.

11. Meaning of acquisitions of goods from another member state (V3.367)

A supply of goods or a transaction treated as a supply of goods gives rise to an acquisition of goods from another EU member state if it involves removing the goods from one EU member state to another. See *Patterson* (No 13669) (whether linkage between supply and removal). It is irrelevant whether responsibility for transporting the goods lies with the supplier or his customer. A person is treated as supplying goods if he produces goods by applying a treatment or process to another person's goods: see Sch 4 para 2.

If the ownership of goods sent for treatment or process does not change, the supply is treated as a transaction giving rise to an acquisition by the person making it.

A transaction of a description specified by Treasury order is not treated as an acquisition. See VAT (Treatment of Transactions) (No 2) Order 1992, SI 1992/3132; VAT (Special Provisions) Order 1995, SI 1995/1268 art 7.

12. Time of acquisition (V3.388)

An acquisition is treated as taking place on the earlier of: (1) the fifteenth day of the month following that in which the goods are first removed under the transaction concerned; and (2) the date on which the supplier issues the invoice prescribed by VAT Regulations 1995, SI 1995/2518 reg 83. A different time may be prescribed by regulations in prescribed circumstances. For water, gas, power, heat, refrigeration and ventilation, see VAT Regulations 1995, SI 1995/2518 reg 87. The foregoing rules do not apply to warehoused and fiscally warehoused goods. For the time when such goods are acquired, see ss 18 and 18B. The foregoing rules are modified by s 14 in relation to certain supplies made by overseas suppliers.

13. Place of acquisition (V3.376)

Goods are treated as acquired in the UK if: (1) the goods are removed to the UK in pursuance of a transaction (see *Patterson* (No 13669)) without also being removed from the UK; or (2) the recipient makes use of his UK VAT registration number for the purposes of the acquisition. However, no acquisition is deemed to be made in the UK under head (2) if VAT is paid in another EU member state on the same acquisition under national legislation corresponding to head (1), and any UK VAT may be refunded in accordance with regulations if VAT is paid in both countries. No regulations have been made.

Example G (a German trader) orders goods from X (a UK trader). X does not have the requisite goods in stock. He places an order with F (a French trader) for delivery to G in Germany and uses his UK VAT registration number. An acquisition takes place in both the UK (head (2)) and Germany (German legislation corresponding to head (1)). X must account for VAT on the UK acquisition if he is unable to prove that German VAT has been paid on the German acquisition, but he can claim a refund if the proof subsequently becomes available. X does not make a UK acquisition, and does not therefore account for UK VAT, if he can prove that German VAT has been paid.

The Commissioners may make regulations in connection with specified matters. No regulations have been made.

The foregoing provisions do not apply to warehoused and fiscally warehoused goods. For the place where such goods are acquired, see ss 18 and 18B.

For the relationship between the place of supply and the place of acquisition in relation to intra-EU movements of goods involving three parties, see *EMAG Handel Eder OHG v Finanzlandesdirecktion für Kärnten* (case C-245/04) [2006] ECR I–3227, [2007] STC 1461, ECJ; *Euro Tyre Holding BV v Staatssecretaris van Financiën* (case C-430/09) [2010] ECR I–0000, [2011] STC 798, ECJ; and s 14.

14. Acquisitions from persons belonging in other member states (V3.364)

Relief is given if: (1) X makes a supply of goods to Y; (2) Y belongs in another EU member state (see below); (3) the goods are removed to the UK from another EU member state without being removed from the UK; (4) the supply and removal are for the purposes of a supply made by Y to Z; (5) Z is a registered taxable person; (6) neither supply involves removing the goods from the EU member state where Y is a taxable person, unless the goods are removed to the UK via that member state; (7) Z would make a taxable acquisition (see s 10 (2)) if the goods had been removed to the UK under Y's supply rather than the supply made by X to Y; and (8) Y furnishes invoices, documents and information in accordance with regulations. For notifications and invoices, see VAT Regulations 1995, SI 1995/2518 regs 11, 18. In these circumstances: (*a*) the supply made by X to Y is disregarded for VAT purposes (so that Y does not make an acquisition); (*b*) the supply made by Y to Z is deemed to involve a removal of goods to the UK from another EU member state (so that Y's supply is not made in the UK and Z is deemed to make an acquisition rather than receive a taxable supply); and (*c*) the position in (*b*) does not apply for the purposes of registration under Sch 3 (so that Z's acquisition is disregarded for determining liability to registration or cessation of liability to legislation under that Schedule).

A similar position applies under the law of the other EU member states in relation to goods removed to those member states. If Y is a registered taxable person in the UK, his position under UK law is simplified by providing that the supply by X to Y and by Y to Z are disregarded for VAT purposes, so that Y is neither charged to VAT on his acquisition nor liable to account for VAT on his supply. For invoices, see VAT Regulations 1995, SI 1995/2518 reg 17.

A supply is treated as involving a removal of goods to the UK but not being a taxable supply if: (1) X (a person belonging in another EU member state) makes a supply of goods to Y (a registered taxable person); (2) X (or his agent) installs or assembles the goods in the UK (so that the supply is deemed to be made in the UK under s 7 (3) (*a*)); (3) Y would make a taxable acquisition if X's supply was not a taxable supply and instead involved a removal of goods to the UK; and (4) X furnishes invoices, documents and information in accordance with regulations. For notifications and invoices, see VAT Regulations 1995, SI 1995/2518 regs 12, 19. The supply is not so treated for the purposes of Sch 3. The foregoing provisions have the result that: (*a*) X does not become liable to registration under Sch 1 as a result of the supply; (*b*) Y makes an acquisition on which he must account for VAT; and (*c*) Y's acquisition is disregarded in determining liability to registration and cessation of liability to legislation under Sch 3.

An acquisition under the foregoing provisions is normally made on the day when the relevant supplier issues an invoice prescribed by VAT Regulations 1995, SI 1995/2518 reg 83. For the exceptions, see ss 12 (3) and 18 (4).

A person belongs in another EU member state if: (1) he does not have a presence in the UK (cf s 9); (2) his usual place of residence is abroad; (3) he is neither registered nor liable to registration in the UK; (4) he does not have a tax representative (see s 48) in the UK; and (5) he is taxable in another EU member state (see s 92).

Importation of Goods from Outside the Member States

15. General provisions relating to imported goods (V3.302)

Goods are imported from a third country if: (1) they are removed from a third country to the UK, either directly or via another EU member state; (2) they enter the territory of the EU (see s 96 (3)) so as to come within customs supervision; and (3) the EU customs debt (if any) (see s 96 (3)) is incurred in the UK, whether immediately or on leaving duty suspension arrangements. Goods are not treated as imported until the EU customs debt (if any) has been incurred. For goods under inward processing arrangements declared for home use, see *Pezzullo Molini Pastifici Mangimifici SpA v Ministero delle Finanze* (case C-166/94) [1996] STC 1236, ECJ. The importer is the person required to discharge the EU customs debt (if any).

References to "importation" or "importer" in the customs legislation applied by s 16 are not construed in accordance with the foregoing provisions.

16. Application of customs enactments (V1.262, V1.263)

VAT on goods imported from third countries is charged in accordance with UK legislation applicable to customs and excise duties on imported goods (principally the Customs and Excise Acts 1979 as defined in CEMA 1979 s 1) and directly applicable EU legislation relating to EU customs duties. Any necessary exceptions and adaptations are to be prescribed by regulations. See VAT Regulations 1995, SI 1995/2518 regs 118–121.

Regulations under Postal Services Act 2000 s 105 may make special provision in relation to VAT. See Postal Packets (Customs and Excise) Regulations 1986, SI 1986/260.

For the relief given by concession on the importation of certain aircraft ground and security equipment, see Notice No 48 (December 2010) para 2.6.

17. Free zone regulations (V3.331)

This section applies to the VAT chargeable on goods imported from third countries. Goods chargeable with VAT may be moved into a free zone and remain as free zone goods without payment of VAT. The Commissioners may make regulations governing the movement of goods to and from free zones, the charge to VAT and related matters. See Free Zone Regulations 1991, SI 1991/2727; Free Zone Regulations 1984, SI 1984/1177.

The terms "free zone" and "free zone goods" are defined. For areas designated as a free zone, see CEMA 1979 s 100A.

GOODS SUBJECT TO A WAREHOUSING REGIME

18. Place and time of acquisition or supply (V3.138)

An acquisition or supply is deemed to be made outside the UK if:

- the goods enter EU territory from a third country (see s 96(3)(*a*));
- the time of acquisition (see s 12) or supply (see s 6) occurs while the goods are warehoused and before the "duty point"; and
- the goods have not been mixed with "dutiable goods" produced in the UK or acquired from another EU member state.

This provision may be disapplied by regulations. For the regulations made, see VAT Regulations 1995, SI 1995/2518 reg 145K. For the charge to VAT when a customs debt arises in respect of the goods: see s 15.

An acquisition or supply is deemed to be made outside the UK if: (1) the goods enter EU territory from a third country (see s 96(3)(*a*)); (2) the time of acquisition (see s 12) or supply (see s 6) occurs while the goods are warehoused and before the "duty point"; and (3) the goods have not been mixed with "dutiable goods" produced in the UK or acquired from another EU member state. This provision may be disapplied by regulations. No regulations have been made to date. The charge to VAT arises on such goods when a customs debt arises in respect of them: see s 15.

As regards "dutiable goods" acquired from another EU member state, the time of acquisition (see s 12) may occur while the goods are warehoused and before the "duty point". Special time and place of acquisition rules apply if the goods are supplied. If the time of supply occurs while the goods are warehoused and before the "duty point", the acquisition is deemed to be made outside the UK. If not, the acquisition is deemed to be made in the UK, and the time of acquisition is the earlier of the time when the goods are removed from warehouse and the "duty point". For the value of the acquisition, see Sch 7 para 2.

As regards "dutiable goods" produced in the UK, acquired from another EU member state and mixtures of such goods and other goods, the time of supply (see s 6) may occur while the goods are warehoused and before the "duty point". Special time of supply, place of supply and valuation rules apply. If the supply is followed by another supply, and the time of supply of the later supply also occurs while the goods are warehoused and before the "duty point", the earlier supply is deemed to be made outside the UK. If not, the earlier (or only) supply is deemed to be made in the UK; the time of supply is the earlier of the time when the goods are removed from warehouse and the "duty point".

Any tax payable must be paid at the time of supply or, in relation to a registered person approved for the purposes of duty deferment, the time prescribed in VAT Regulations 1995, SI 1995/2518 reg 43. The tax must be paid by the person who removes the goods or the person who is required to pay the excise duty, EU customs duty or EU agricultural levy concerned.

The terms "dutiable goods", "duty point", "material time" and "warehouse" are defined. As regards the "duty point" for goods subject to excise duty, the time when the requirement to pay duty takes effect is determined in accordance with F(No 2)A 1992 s 1(1) and Excise Goods (Holding, Movement and Duty Point) Regulations 2010, SI 2010/593.

18A. Fiscal warehousing (V3.384)

An approved person, referred to as a "fiscal warehousekeeper" (see s 18F (1)), is entitled to keep a "fiscal warehouse". A fiscal warehouse is a place in the UK notified to the Commissioners. A place may be so notified if it is controlled or occupied by a fiscal warehousekeeper and comprises something other than retail premises.

An application for approval as a fiscal warehousekeeper may be made by a registered person or by a body corporate included in a group registration (see s 43). A written application is made in the manner directed by the Commissioners. In considering an application, the Commissioners may take account of any matter which they consider relevant and, in particular, the applicant's record of compliance and ability to comply with VAT, customs duty and excise duty obligations under legislation of the EU, the UK or another EU member state.

An approved person ceases to be a fiscal warehousekeeper: (1) on ceasing to be a registered person or to be included in a group registration; (2) on notifying the Commissioners to that effect in writing; or (3) on the Commissioners withdrawing their approval by a written notice.

Approval as a fiscal warehousekeeper may be subject to conditions imposed by the Commissioners. These conditions may be supplemented, varied or revoked by way of a written notice.

Notification of a place as a fiscal warehouse is made in writing. The place becomes a fiscal warehouse from the date when the Commissioners receive the notification or, if later, the date specified in the notification. The place ceases to be a fiscal warehouse if: (1) it ceases to be controlled or occupied by the fiscal warehousekeeper; (2) the warehousekeeper notifies the Commissioners to that effect in writing; or (3) the Commissioners withdraw fiscal warehouse status from the premises by a written notice.

18B. Fiscally warehoused goods: relief (V3.384)

The place and time of supply or acquisition is varied in relation to goods of a description within Sch 5A upon which any import duties and VAT (in the case of imported goods) and excise duty (in the case of goods subject to such duty) have been paid or deferred. These goods are referred to as "eligible goods".

An acquisition of eligible goods is within these provisions if: (1) the goods are subject to a fiscal warehousing regime at the material time of acquisition and the person acquiring the goods keeps a certificate to this effect in the prescribed form (see VAT Regulations 1995, SI 1995/2518 reg 145B); or (2) the goods are placed in a fiscal warehousing regime after the material time of acquisition but before the material time of the supply (if any) which next follows, and the person making the acquisition prepares and keeps a certificate in the prescribed form that he will cause this condition to be met.

A supply of eligible goods under something other than a retail transaction is within these provisions if: (1) the goods are subject to a fiscal warehousing regime at the material time of supply; or (2) the goods are placed in a fiscal warehousing regime by the recipient of the supply after the material time of the supply made to him but before the material time of the supply (if any) which next follows, and the recipient of the supply gives his supplier a certificate in the prescribed form (see VAT Regulations 1995, SI 1995/2518 reg 145B) that he will cause this condition to be met.

A supply or acquisition within these provisions is treated as taking place outside the UK (so that it is not charged to VAT) if the material time for any subsequent supply takes place while the goods remain subject to the warehousing regime.

The supply or acquisition is treated as taking place in the UK if this condition is not met. The time of supply or acquisition is the time when the goods are removed from the fiscal warehousing regime. For the payment of tax on a supply, see s 18D.

VAT is chargeable on a supply or acquisition taxable at a positive rate made by a person who is not a taxable person if he would be a taxable person but for the fact that such supplies and acquisitions were disregarded for the purposes of determining liability to registration under Sch 1 para 1 (9), Sch 2 para 1 (7) and Sch 3 para 1 (6). For the payment of tax on an acquisition by a person who is not a taxable person, see s 18D.

For the circumstances in which goods are "subject to a warehousing regime", see s 18F (2). For the "material time" of a supply or acquisition, see s 18F (1).

18C. Warehouses and fiscal warehouses: services (V3.384)

"Specified services" comprise the services of keeping goods in a warehousing regime (see s 18F (3)) or fiscal warehousing regime (see s 18F (2)) and carrying out permitted operations on goods subject to such a regime.

A supply of specified services is zero-rated if:

(a) the service is supplied by a taxable person;
(b) it is wholly performed on, or in relation to, goods subject to a warehousing or fiscal warehousing regime;
(c) (if it comprises carrying out permitted operations) the recipient of the supply gives the supplier a certificate in the prescribed form (see VAT Regulations 1995, SI 1995/2518 reg 145C) that the service is wholly performed on goods subject to a warehousing or fiscal warehousing regime;
(d) the supply would be chargeable to VAT at a positive rate but for this relief; and
(e) the supplier issues an invoice in the prescribed form (see VAT Regulations 1995, SI 1995/2518 reg 145D) to the recipient of the supply.

A supply zero-rated under the foregoing provision is referred to as a "zero-rated supply of services". The recipient of a zero-rated supply of services is deemed to both make and receive an identical supply of services unless the goods to which the services relate are supplied and the material time for that supply occurs while the goods are subject to a warehousing or fiscal warehousing regime and after the material time for the zero-rated supply of services. For the "material time" for a supply of goods or services, see s 18F (1).

The time of the self-supply is the earlier of: (1) the time when the goods are removed from the warehousing or fiscal warehousing regime; and (2) the duty point (see s 18F (1)). For the circumstances in which goods are removed from a warehousing or fiscal warehousing regime, see s 18F (2) and (3).

The value of the self-supply is the same as the value of the zero-rated supply of services.

The self-supply is chargeable to VAT at a positive rate. VAT is chargeable on the self-supply whether or not the recipient of the zero-rated supply of services is a taxable person. For the payment of VAT, see s 18D.

For incorrect certificates given for the purposes of this section, see s 62.

18D. Removal from warehousing: accountability (V3.384)

Any VAT payable on a supply or acquisition under ss 18B (4), (5) or 18C (3) must be paid at the time when the supply or acquisition is treated as taking place (see ss 18B (4) and 18C (3) (*a*)) or a later time prescribed by regulations. For payment, see VAT Regulations 1995, SI 1995/2518 regs 40 (1) (*c*), (*d*) (accounting for VAT on a VAT return), 43 (payment under the excise duty deferment scheme) and 145J (payment on removal from a fiscal warehouse). VAT must be paid by the person removing the goods or by the person required to pay excise duty on the removal.

18E. Deficiency in fiscally warehoused goods (V3.384)

The Commissioners may require a fiscal warehousekeeper (see s 18F (1)) to pay VAT in respect of goods subject to a fiscal warehousing regime (see s 18F (2)) which are found to be missing or deficient. No payment is required if it is shown to the Commissioners' satisfaction that the absence or deficiency arises from natural waste or some other legitimate cause.

The amount payable is the VAT which would have been chargeable on a supply of the missing goods, or the amount of the deficiency, at their open market value immediately before the absence arose or the deficiency occurred.

It may not be possible to establish, to the Commissioners' satisfaction, the time when the absence arose or the deficiency occurred. If so, it is necessary to use the highest open market value for the relevant period or (if the rate of VAT changed during the relevant period and this produces a higher payment of VAT) the highest open market value for that part of the relevant period during which the highest rate of VAT prevailed. The "relevant period" for this purpose commences when the goods were placed in the fiscal warehousing regime and ends when the absence or deficiency came to the Commissioners' notice.

18F. Sections 18A to 18E: supplementary (V3.384)

Various words and phrases are defined.

An operation carried out on eligible goods (see s 18B (6)) may change their nature. If the resulting goods are also eligible goods ss 18B–18E apply as if the resulting goods were the original goods. If not ss 18B–18E apply as if the goods had been removed from a fiscal warehouse by the proprietor of the goods, so that a charge to VAT arises on an acquisition, supply or self-supply under ss 18B (4), (5) or 18C (3).

The Commissioners may make regulations in relation to fiscal warehouses. See also the power to make regulations under ss 18B (1), (2) and 18C (1). For the regulations made, see VAT Regulations 1995, SI 1995/2518 regs 145A–145J.

DETERMINATION OF VALUE

19. Value of supply of goods or services (V3.152, V3.161)

Consideration in money

The value of a supply made for a money consideration is such amount as, with the addition of VAT, equals the consideration, ie $^{100}/_{120}$ths ($^{5}/_{6}$ths) of the consideration (standard rated supply) or $^{100}/_{105}$ths ($^{20}/_{21}$sts) (reduced rate supply).

"Consideration" for this purpose is interpreted in accordance with Directive 2006/112/EC arts 73 and 78 (formerly Directive 77/388/EEC art 11A(1)(*a*) and (2)). It therefore includes:

- subsidies directly linked to the price of the supply (see Directive 2006/112/EC art 73). For subsidies, see *Office des Produits Wallons ASBL v Belgian State* (case C-184/00) [2003] STC 1100, ECJ; *Commission v Germany* (case C-144/02) [2004] ECE I–6985, ECJ; *Commission v Italy* (case C-381/01) [2004] ECR I–6845, ECJ; *Commission v Sweden* (case C-463/02) [2004] ECR I–7335, ECJ; *Commission v Finland* (case C-495/01) [2004] ECR I–6889, ECJ; *Hotel Scandic Gåsabäck AB v Riksskatteverket* (case C-412/03) [2005] ECR I–743, [2005] STC 1311, ECJ. For the vehicle scrappage scheme, see Revenue and Customs Brief 31/09, 14 May 2009;
- taxes, duties, levies and charges (see Directive 2006/112/EC art 78(*a*)). For stamp duty, see SP 11/91, 12 September 1991 and contrast *De Danske Bilimportører v Skatteministeriet* (case C-98/05) [2006] ECR I–4945, ECJ (Danish registration duty on new motor vehicles); and
- incidental expenses such as commission, packing, transport and insurance costs charged by the supplier to the customer (see Directive 2006/112/EC art 78(*b*)).

However, expenses of transport, for example, are not included in the consideration for the supply of the goods transported if the transport constitutes a separate supply. Thus, what is now Directive 2006/112/EC art 78 does not convert what would otherwise be two separate supplies into a single supply: *C & E Comrs v British Telecommunications plc* [1999] STC 798, HL. For examples of a single supply comprising delivered goods, see *C & E Comrs v British Telecommunications plc* [1999] STC 798, HL; *C & E Comrs v Plantiflor Ltd* [2002] STC 1132, HL.

For foreign exchange transactions for which no fee or commission is charged, see *C & E Comrs v First National Bank of Chicago* (case C-172/96) [1998] STC 850, ECJ.

Consideration in something other than money

In other cases, the value is such amount in money as, with the addition of VAT, is equivalent to the consideration. The monetary equivalent of a non-monetary consideration is determined by reference to a "subjective value": *Staatssecretaris van Financiën v Coöperatieve Aardappelenbewaarplaats GA* (case 154/80) [1981] ECR 445 at [13], ECJ. This is "the value for the purposes of the transaction". The distinction is between the value placed on the goods or services in the context of a particular transaction (which is relevant) and some "objective" value commanded in the open market (which is not): *C & E Comrs v Bugeja* [2001] STC 1568 at [101], CA. This maintains the neutrality of VAT by ensuring that it is not charged on a value exceeding the consideration actually received: *Staatssecretaris van Financiën v Coöperatieve Aardappelenbewaarplaats GA* (case 154/80) [1981] ECR 445 at [13], ECJ; *Elida Gibbs Ltd v C & E Comrs* (case C-317/94) [1996] STC 1387 at [28], ECJ. Monetary equivalents are ascertained in the same manner whether the non-monetary consideration takes the form of goods (eg as in *Lex Services plc v C & E Comrs* [2004] STC 73, HL) or services (eg as in *Naturally Yours Cosmetics Ltd v C & E Comrs* (case C-230/87) [1988] STC 879, ECJ): *C & E Comrs v Bugeja* [2001] STC 1568 at [100], CA).

If the parties have expressly or implicitly attributed a value to the non-monetary consideration, that determines the monetary equivalent: *C & E Comrs v Westmorland Motorway Services Ltd* [1998] STC 431 at 434, CA; *C & E Comrs v Littlewoods Organisation plc* [2001] STC 1568 at [30], CA. In exceptional circumstances, that may be nil. This was so in *C & E Comrs v Ping (Europe) Ltd* [2002] STC 1186, CA (surrender of golf clubs infringing the laws of golf). An attributed value is frequently ascertained from the relevant documentation: *Lex Services plc v C & E Comrs* [2001] STC 1568 at [80], CA affd [2004] STC 73, HL. For examples, see *Naturally Yours Cosmetics Ltd v C & E Comrs* (case C-230/87) [1988] STC 879, ECJ); *Rosgill Group Ltd v C & E Comrs* [1997] STC 811, CA; *C & E Comrs v Westmorland Motorway Services Ltd* [1998] STC 431, CA; *C & E Comrs v Bugeja* [2001] STC 1568, CA. If the documentation specifies different values for different circumstances, the relevant value is the one applicable in the circumstances that actually happen. The other values are irrelevant. For examples of alternative values, see *Rosgill Group Ltd v C & E Comrs* [1997] STC 811, CA (cash sum and cost to supplier irrelevant); *Lex Services plc v C & E Comrs* [2004] STC 73, HL ("true value" irrelevant).

If the parties have not attributed a value to the non-monetary consideration, the monetary equivalent is the price paid by the supplier for the goods or services supplied in return for the non-monetary consideration: *Empire Stores Ltd v C & E Comrs* (case C-33/93) [1994] STC 623 at [19], ECJ; *C & E Comrs v Westmorland Motorway Services Ltd* [1998] STC 431 at 434, CA; *C & E Comrs v Littlewoods Organisation plc* [2001] STC 1568 at [30], [31], CA. This is the only value that can be used: *C & E Comrs v Littlewoods Organisation plc* [2001] STC 1568 at [23], CA. Any delivery costs paid are added to this sum: *Bertelsmann AG v Finanzamt Wiedenbrück* (case C-380/99) [2001] STC 1153, ECJ.

Apportionment of consideration

A consideration must be apportioned where it relates to two or more supplies. The test applied in deciding whether an apportionment is appropriate was laid down by the Court of Justice in *Card Protection Plan Ltd v C & E Comrs* (case C-349/96) [1999] STC 270, ECJ at [26]–[32]. For recent statements of relevant principles, see *Byrom and others (trading as Salon 24) v R & C Comrs* [2006] STC 992 at [22]–[51]; *Tumble Tots (UK) Ltd v R & C Comrs* [2007] STC 1171 at [11]; *R & C Comrs v Bryce (t/a The Barn)* [2010] UKUT 26 (TCC), [2011] STC 903 at [23]. There is no advantage in refering to cases decided before the *Card Protection Plan* case and their citation is discouraged: *Dr Beynon and Partners v C & E Comrs* [2005] STC 55, HL.

It is necessary to have regard to all the circumstances of the transaction in order to identify its characteristic features: *Faaborg-Gelting Linien A/S v Finanzamt Flensburg* (case C-231/94) [1996] STC 774, ECJ. The line of reasoning in *C & E Comrs v FDR Ltd* [2000]

STC 672, CA, *College of Estate Management v C & E Comrs* [2005] STC 1597, HL and *Byrom and others (trading as Salon 24) v R & C Comrs* [2006] STC 992 suggests that there are three possible outcomes.

Firstly, two separate supplies, each of which is taxed or exempted from tax according to its nature. For an example, see *RLRE Tellmer Property sro v Finanční ředitelstvi v Ústí nad Labem* (case C-572/07) [2009] ECR I–4983, [2009] STC 2006, ECJ and Revenue and Customs Brief 67/09, 27 October 2009 (letting apartment and cleaning common parts of the building).

Secondly, one supply comprising a bundle of elements, of which one predominates, so that the single supply is taxed or exempted from tax according to the nature of the principal element. For examples, see *C & E Comrs v British Telecommunications plc* [1999] STC 758, HL (delivery of motor car subordinate to its sale); *Card Protection Plan Ltd v C & E Comrs* [2001] STC 174, HL (some peripheral parts of a package of services and some goods of trivial value subordinate to the main package of insurance services); *International Masters Publishers Ltd v R & C Comrs* [2007] STC 153, CA (binder containing CD and bound pages); *Ford Motor Company Ltd v R & C Comrs* [2008] STC 1016, CA (motor cars sold with "free" insurance and RAC membership).

Thirdly, a bundle of elements so closely linked that, objectively, they form a single indivisible economic supply which it would be artificial to split. Here, the elements must be considered as a whole when determining the nature of the supply made. In some cases, no single element may predominate over the others. For examples, see *C & E Comrs v FDR Ltd* [2000] STC 672, CA; *American Express Services Europe Ltd v R & C Comrs* [2010] STC 1023; *R & C Comrs v Bryce (t/a The Barn)* [2010] UKUT 26 (TCC), [2011] STC 903 (facilities for a children's party). In other cases, while there may be one predominant element, the others are not ancillary to it and the element itself cannot be regarded as a separate supply. For examples, see *Faaborg-Gelting Linien A/S v Finanzamt Flensburg* (case C-231/94) [1996] STC 774, ECJ (restaurant services a single supply of services although food was an indispensable element); *Dr Beynon and Partners v C & E Comrs* [2005] STC 55, HL (medical care requiring use of medication a single supply of services although the drugs were of central and indispensable importance); *College of Estate Management v C & E Comrs* [2005] STC 1597, HL (distance learning course a single supply of education although study material was the largest element); *Levob Verzekeringen BV, OB Bank NV cs v Staatssecretaris van Financiën* (case C-41/04) [2005] ECR I–9433, [2006] STC 766, ECJ (supply of standard software package and customising it to customer's requirements a single supply of services catergorised as the services of an engineer for place of supply purposes); *Byrom and others (trading as Salon 24) v R & C Comrs* [2006] STC 992 (various services supplied to masseuses, including licence to use room, a single supply of massage parlour services); *R & C Comrs v Denyer* [2008] STC 633 and *Holland (trading as the Studio Hair Company) v R & C Comrs, Vigdor Ltd v R & C Comrs* [2009] STC 150 (hairdressers' chair renting agreement); *R & C Comrs v David Baxendale Ltd* [2009] STC 2578, CA (weight loss programme comprising food packs and support services).

No single factor provides the sole test of whether an element of that which is provided comprises a distinct and independent supply or is merely incidental or ancillary to another principle supply: *C & E Comrs v British Telecommunications plc* [1999] STC 758, HL. Where ancillary goods or services are relevant to the analysis, describing them as "add-on" may be helpful. However, it must be borne in mind that they may be optional extras (eg in-flight catering provided by some, but not all, airlines), or goods or services which, although undoubtedly subsidiary, are for practical purposes indispensable (eg the ignition key of a motor car): *College of Estate Management v C & E Comrs* [2005] STC 1597, HL

It is normally necessary to have regard to the objective character of the transaction in question: *C & E Comrs v Cantor Fitzgerald International* (case C-108/99) [2001] STC 1453, ECJ. Thus, the question is: what does the customer get? It is not: why does the customer want it? See *College of Estate Management v C & E Comrs* [2005] STC 1471, CA; cf *British Railways Board v C & E Comrs* [1977] STC 221, CA.

The characterisation of a supply is a matter of law: *C & E Comrs v British Telecommunications plc* [1999] STC 758, HL. Thus, it is necessary to ascertain the essential features of the transaction in order to decide whether one supply, or two or more separate supplies, have been made: *Card Protection Plan Ltd v C & E Comrs* (case C-349/96) [1999] STC 270, ECJ. Every supply of a service is normally regarded as distinct and independent: *Card Protection Plan Ltd v C & E Comrs* (case C-349/96) [1999] STC 270, ECJ. Various tests assist in determining whether there is one supply or two or more separate supplies: (1) whether one element is an "integral" part of the other(s), or is "ancillary" or "incidental" to the others, or whether the elements are "physically and economically dissociable" (see *EC Commission v United Kingdom* (case C-353/85) [1988] STC 251, ECJ; *C & E Comrs v Wellington Private Hospital Ltd* [1977] STC 445, CA; *C & E Comrs v British Telecommunications plc* [1999] STC 758, HL); (2) a transaction should not be split if it comprises a single supply from an economic point of view (see *Card Protection Plan Ltd v C & E Comrs* (case C-349/96) [1999] STC 270, ECJ); and (3) the fact that a single price is charged is not decisive (see *Card Protection Plan Ltd v C & E Comrs* (case C-349/96) [1999] STC 270, ECJ).

A service is treated as ancillary if it is a means of better enjoying the principal service rather than constituting an aim in itself: *Card Protection Plan Ltd v C & E Comrs* (case C-349/96) [1999] STC 270, ECJ.

The fact that a court seeks to find the commercial reality of the situation does not mean that it should seek to apply VAT to the economic reality of the transaction. This may have nothing to do with the essential features of the agreement or the legal structure of the transaction: *Telewest Communications plc and another v C & E Comrs* [2005] STC 481, CA.

Supplies by different suppliers cannot be fused to make a single supply: *Nell Gwynn House Maintenance Fund Trustees v C & E Comrs* [1999] STC 79, HL; *Telewest Communications plc and anor v C & E Comrs* [2005] STC 481, CA. A money consideration cannot be apportioned between a donation element and a consideration element: *C & E Comrs v Tron Theatre Ltd* [1994] STC 177 (sponsorship payment providing negligible benefits). For the apportionment of membership subscriptions to non-profit-making bodies, see Notice No 48 (December 2010) para 3.35; Revenue and Customs Brief 6/09, 20 February 2009.

An apportionment must be carried out on a fair and reasonable basis: *Southend United Football Club v C & E Comrs* [1997] V & DR 202. For examples, see *Public and Commercial Services Union v C & E Comrs* [2004] STC 376 (matter remitted to a fresh tribunal); *River Barge Holidays Ltd* (No 572), *Rogers v C & E Comrs* [1984] VATTR 183 (cost method); *Jarmain v C & E Comrs* [1979] VATTR 41 (open market value method).

For recent UK cases illustrating the apportionment (or not) and characterisation of supplies, see in particular *Card Protection Plan Ltd v C & E Comrs* [2001] STC 174, HL (insurance); *C & E Comrs v British Telecommunications plc* [1999] STC 758, HL (car delivery charge); *Dr Beynon and Partners v C & E Comrs* [2005] STC 55, HL (drugs prescribed and administered by doctor); *College of Estate Management v C & E Comrs* [2005] STC 1597, HL (distance learning course); *C & E Comrs v FDR Ltd* [2000] STC 672, CA (credit card services); *C & E Comrs v Sinclair Collis Ltd* [1999] STC 701, CA (vending machine); *Co-operative Wholesale Society Ltd v C & E Comrs* [2000] STC 727, CA (funeral services); *Ford Motor Company Ltd v R & C Comrs* [2008] STC 1016, CA (sale of motor car with free insurance); *R & C Comrs v Weight Watchers (UK) Ltd* [2008] STC 2313, CA (weight loss service including provision of printed matter); *Appleby Bowers (a firm) v C & E Comrs* [2001] STC 185 (promotional services); *Byrom and others (trading as Salon 24) v R & C Comrs* [2006] STC 992 (use of room and other services in massage parlour); *Tumble Tots (UK) Ltd v R & C Comrs* [2007] STC 1171 (enrolment fee including insurance, a T-shirt and other goods); *Birkdale School, Sheffield v R & C Comrs* [2008] STC 2002 (school fee protection plan); *R & C Comrs v Axa UK plc* [2008] STC 2091 (administrative and support services for dentists). For the Commissioners' views, see Business Brief 2/01, 15 February 2001 (generally); Business Brief 20/03, 22 October 2003 (books and magazines packaged with another item); Business Brief 1/06, 19 January 2006 (company formation services). In the EU, see the commentary to Directive 2006/112/EC art 2 in Part 1B.

Separate payments forming a single consideration

For the aggregation of separate payments forming a single consideration, see *British Railways Board v C & E Comrs* [1977] STC 221, CA (student rail card and rail ticket); *Exeter Golf & Country Club Ltd v C & E Comrs* [1981] STC 211, CA (club subscription and benefit of interest free loan); *Patrick Eddery Ltd v C & E Comrs* [1986] VATTR 30 (jockey's retainer and riding fee); *Mothercare (UK) Ltd v C & E Comrs* [1993] VATTR 391 (discount card and subsequent purchases).

Set-off

The value of a supply by X to Y is unaffected if it is discharged partly by setting-off a debt owed by X to Y and partly by a cash payment by Y. For examples, see *Naturally Yours Cosmetics Ltd v C & E Comrs* (case 230/87) [1988] STC 879, ECJ; *Chaussures Bally SA v Belgium* (case C-18/92) [1997] STC 209, ECJ; *Davies v C & E Comrs* [1975] STC 28; *Theatres Consolidated Ltd v C & E Comrs* [1975] VATTR 13; *Smith & Williamson v C & E Comrs* [1976] VATTR 215. For reduced considerations which did not amount to set-off, see *National Coal Board v C & E Comrs* [1982] STC 863; *Goodfellow (a firm) v C & E Comrs* [1986] VATTR 119; *J Hopkins (Contractors) Ltd v C & E Comrs* [1989] VATTR 107; *Yorkshire Water plc v C & E Comrs* [1990] VATTR 118; *Co-operative Insurance Society Ltd v C & E Comrs* [1992] VATTR 44. For commissions taken into account when billing a customer, see ICAEW TR 787, 15 March 1990; The Law Society, 9 September 1992.

Price discounts and rebates

For price discounts and rebates, see Directive 2006/112/EC art 79(*b*) (formerly Directive 77/388/EEC art 11A(3)(*b*)); *C & E Comrs v Littlewoods Organisation plc* [2001] STC 1568, CA, *C & E Comrs v Euphony Communications Ltd* [2004] STC 301 (commission); *Co-operative Retail Services Ltd v C & E Comrs* [1992] VATTR 60 (co-operative society dividend); *Rosgill Group Ltd v C & E Comrs* [1995] V & DR 155 (party plan sales); *J E Beale plc* (No 15920) (discounts refunded to concessionaires under a storecard scheme); Business Brief 8/92, 15 June 1992 (staff discounts); Business Brief 16/97, 21 July 1997 (fleet buyer and dealer demonstrator bonuses given by car manufacturers and sole concessionaires); Business Brief 1/98, 7 January 1998 (fleet leasing bonuses given by car manufacturers and car dealers).

Business promotion schemes

For the Commissioners' views on business promotion schemes generally, see Notice No 700/7. For an extra-statutory concession, see Notice No 48 (December 2010) para 3.7 (minor promotional items supplied in linked supplies schemes). In relation to face value vouchers, see Sch 10A; VAT Information Sheets 3/03 (April 2002) and 8/03 (July 2003); Business Brief 4/03, 27 May 2003.

"Cash back" and "money-off" coupons may be issued without consideration. As regards the following schemes, the valuation of goods and services supplied by traders issuing and redeeming the coupons is dealt with under principles laid down by the EU Court of Justice:

- Cash back scheme promoted by a manufacturer. The consideration for the manufacturer's supply is the amount invoiced to the retailer less the amount refunded to the retailer's customer. The consideration for the retailer's supply is the amount received from the customer, ie the retail price. See *Elida Gibbs Ltd v C & E Comrs* (case C-317/94) [1996] STC 1387, ECJ and contrast *Total UK Ltd v R & C Comrs* [2008] STC 19, CA (face value voucher purchased from third party awarded to retailer's customer by manufacturer under a points scheme). For manufacturers' "cash back" payments, see Revenue and Customs Brief 8/07, 6 February 2007 (payments outside the direct supply chain); Revenue and Customs Brief 67/07, 9 November 2007 (supplier discounts, volume rebates and charges made by the customer when promoting the suppliers' products).
- Money-off scheme promoted by a manufacturer. The consideration for the manufacturer's supply is the amount invoiced to the retailer less the amount refunded to him. The consideration for the retailer's supply is the amount received

from the customer plus the amount received from the manufacturer. See *Elida Gibbs Ltd v C & E Comrs* (case C-317/94) [1996] STC 1387, ECJ; *EC Commission v Germany* (case C-427/98) [2003] STC 301, ECJ; *Yorkshire Co-operatives Ltd v C & E Comrs* (case C-398/99) [2003 STC 234, ECJ.

- Money-off scheme promoted by a retailer. The consideration for the retailer's supply is the amount received from the customer, ie the retail price less the face value of the coupon. See *Boots Co plc v C & E Comrs* (case C-126/88) [1990] STC 387, ECJ.
- "Free" gift schemes. For the charge to VAT on goods or services supplied as a "gift", see *Kuwait Petroleum (GB) Ltd v C & E Comrs* (case C-48/97) [1999] STC 488, ECJ and subsequently [2001] STC 62. See also *Total UK Ltd v R & C Comrs* [2008] STC 19, CA (consideration for the supply made comprising the price charged less the value of gift vouchers purchased from third parties awarded to retail customers under a points scheme).

Face value vouchers may be issued for a consideration. For the supply made by the issuer and any onward supply made by an intermediary, see Sch 10A. For the valuation of goods and services supplied by the trader who accepts the voucher in full or partial payment, see Sch 10A. For valuation under principles laid down by the EU Court of Justice where the trader is the person who issued the voucher, see *Argos Distributions Ltd v C & E Comrs* (case C-288/94) [1996] STC 1359, ECJ and Business Brief 25/96, 6 December 1996 (vouchers sold at a discount).

For loyalty schemes using points rather than vouchers, see in particular *Tesco plc v C & E Comrs* [2003] STC 1561, CA; *Total UK Ltd v R & C Comrs* [2008] STC 19, CA; *R & C Comrs v Loyalty Management UK Ltd* and; *Baxi Group Ltd v R & C Comrs* (joined cases C-53/09 and C-55/09) [2010] ECR I–0000, [2010] STC 2651, ECJ.

For schemes in the UK prior to the introduction of Sch 10A, see in particular *Hartwell plc v C & E Comrs* [2003] STC 396, CA (price reduction coupons); *Tesco plc v C & E Comrs* [2003] STC 1561, CA (points awarded by promoter and other traders); *Conoco Ltd v C & E Comrs* [1997] V & DR 47.

Disbursements

For disbursements, see Directive 2006/112/EC art 79(*c*) (formerly Directive 77/388/EEC art 9A(3)(*c*)). For the identification and treatment of agency disbursements, see s 47.

Exceptions

The foregoing rules have effect subject to Sch 6, and are displaced in relation to trading stamps (see s 52) and designated travel services (see s 53).

Open market value

Open market value is such amount in money as, with the addition of VAT, is equivalent to the consideration payable under an arm's length transaction. This definition is relevant to supplies valued in accordance with Sch 6 paras 1, 2.

20. Valuation of acquisitions from other member states (V3.390)

The value of an acquisition is the value of the transaction under which the goods were acquired. If the transaction is a taxable supply, it is valued in accordance with ss 19, 52, 53 and Sch 6, but the acquisition is not charged to tax: see s 10 (1) (*b*). This section is concerned with the valuation of acquisitions charged to tax and is therefore confined to transactions which are not taxable supplies. The following provisions apply to such transactions and have effect subject to Sch 7.

A transaction for a money consideration has a value equal to the consideration. A transaction wholly or partly for a non-money consideration has a value of such monetary amount as is equivalent to the consideration. A money consideration is apportioned if it relates to more than one transaction.

21. Value of imported goods (V3.322–V3.324)

The value of imported goods is the aggregate of:

- the value of the goods determined in accordance with EU customs rules;
- taxes, duties and charges (other than VAT) levied outside the UK;
- taxes, duties and levies (other than VAT) levied on importation into the UK;
- all incidental expenses up to the place in the UK mentioned in the import documentation or (in the absence of such documentation) the place in the UK where cargo is first transferred; and
- (if a further destination with the EU is known at the time of importation) all incidental expenses resulting from transporting the goods to the further destination.

A deduction is made for prompt payment discounts earned under the terms of the contract. For EU valuation rules, see Regulation (EEC) Nos 2913/92 and 2454/93. For the application of those rules in relation to goods imported from the Channel Islands, see *Dolland & Aitchison Ltd v C & E Comrs* (case C-491/04) [2006] ECR I–2129, [2006] SWTI 531, ECJ (single price for goods despatched from Jersey and services performed in the UK). For a simplified system of flat rates, see Business Brief 6/96, 30 April 1996.

The foregoing rules are modified in relation to the following goods:

(a) any work of art (see s 21(6), (6A), (6B);

(b) any antique, not being a work of art within (*a*) or a collection or collectors' piece within (*c*), which is more than 100 years old; and

(c) any collection or collectors' piece of zoological, botanical, mineralogical, anatomical, historical, archaeological, palaeontological, ethnographic, numismatic or philatelic (see s 21(6C)) interest. For collectors' pieces of historical or ethnographic interest, see *Pressland v C & E Comrs* [1995] V & DR 432.

The first modification applies where the goods listed above are sold by auction at a time when they are subject to the customs procedure for temporary importation with total relief from import duties (see Regulation (EEC) No 2913/92 arts 137–141). From 1 September 2006, any commission or premium payable to the autioneer in connection with the sale of the goods is excluded from their value.

The second modification reduces the value of the goods listed above. From 1 December 2008, the value of the goods is 33.34% of the value computed above. However, this modification does not apply if:

(a) the goods have previously been exported from the UK and the export and subsequent importation were effected to obtain relief under VAT (Imported Goods) Relief Order 1984, SI 1984/746, VAT (Small Non-commercial Consignments) Relief Order 1986, SI 1986/939, or VAT (Imported Gold) Relief Order 1992, SI 1992/3124; or

(b) the goods were exported from the UK less than twelve months before the relevant importation. For importation reliefs avoiding this condition, see Business Brief 3/00, 22 February 2000. For a concession confining this condition to cases of abuse, see Notice No 48 (December 2010) para 3.36.

22. Value of certain goods

[Repealed.]

23. Gaming machines (V3.264)

A supply of services is made to a person who gambles by means of a gaming machine. The consideration is the amount paid by him. In valuing supplies made for a period, the aggregate consideration for such supplies is deemed to be reduced by the aggregate amounts received by successful players in the period. There is no requirement for coins to be inserted in, or ejected from, the machine: *Feehan v C & E Comrs* [1995] STC 75. Under EU law, see *H J Glawe Spiel und Unterhaltungsgeräte Aufstellungsges mbH & Co KG v Finanzamt Hamburg-Barmbek-Uhhelhorst* (case C-38/93) [1994] STC 543, ECJ (coins entering reserve compartment).

Tokens inserted into a machine are deemed to be payment of an amount equal to that for which the token can be obtained. Tokens received by a successful player are deemed to be receipt of an amount equal to either the amount for which the token can be obtained (tokens of a kind used to use the machine) or the amount for which it can be exchanged (other tokens which can be exchanged for money).

"Gambling" comprises: (1) playing (see s 23(6)(*i*)) a game of chance (as defined in s 23(6)(*f*)) for a prize (see s 23(6)(*h*)); and (2) betting (cf Gambling Act 2005 s 19).

A "gaming machine" is a machine (see s 23(6)(*b*)) designed or adapted (see s 23(6)(*c*)) for use by individuals to gamble. A machine within this description is a gaming machine whether or not it can also be used for other purposes. However, a machine is not a gaming machine to the extent that it falls within one or more of the following descriptions:

- it is designed or adapted for betting on future real events. For "real", see Gambling Act 2005 s 353(1);
- it is designed or adapted for playing bingo (see s 23(6)(*g*)), and any game played is either charged to bingo duty under Betting and Gaming Duties Act 1981 s 17 or exempted from charge under Sch 3 paras 1–5 of that Act;
- it is designed or adapted for playing a real (see Gambling Act 2005 s 353(1)) game of chance (see s 23(6)(*f*)), and any game played is either charged to gaming duty under FA 1997 s 10(1) or exempted from charge under s 10(3) or (4) of that Act.

For electronic lottery terminals, see Revenue and Customs Brief 70/09, 18 November 2009.

Payment of VAT by Taxable Persons

24. Input tax and output tax (V3.402, V3.501)

Input tax

Input tax is: (1) VAT on goods or services supplied to a taxable person; (2) VAT on goods acquired from another EU member state by a taxable person; and (3) VAT paid or payable on goods imported from a third country by a taxable person. In each case, the goods or services must be for use in a business carried on or to be carried on by the taxable person.

The foregoing VAT is input tax only if, and to the extent, that the charge to VAT is evidenced and quantified by reference to the documents or other information specified in regulations. See VAT Regulations 1995, SI 1995/2518 reg 29; VAT (Input Tax) (Reimbursement by Employers of Employees' Business Use of Road Fuel) Regulations 2005, SI 2005//3290 reg 6. For the position under EU law, see Directive 2006/112/EC arts 178 (formerly Directive 77/388/EEC art 18(1)(a)); *Reisdorf v Finanzamt Köln-West* (case C-85/95) [1997] STC 180, ECJ. For a Statement of Practice regarding deduction of input tax without a valid VAT invoice, see Appendix 8.

VAT incurred before registration, or before the incorporation of a company, may be counted as input tax in accordance with regulations. See VAT Regulations 1995, SI 1995/2518 reg 111.

VAT incurred on services purchased after deregistration may be repaid by the Commissioners in accordance with regulations if the services were purchased for the purposes of the business carried on prior to deregistration. See VAT Regulations 1995, SI 1995/2518 reg 111.

Goods and services supplied to a person who is not a taxable person (eg an employee) may be treated as if they were supplied to another person (eg his employer) in accordance with a Treasury order. For the order made in respect of road fuel, see VAT (Input Tax) (Person Supplied) Order 1991, SI 1991/2306 (now revoked by SI 2005/3291); *Commission v United Kingdom* (case C-33/03) [2005] STC 582, ECJ. For modified provisions now in force, but made by regulation rather than by order, see VAT (Input Tax) (Reimbursement by Employers of Employees' Business Use of Road Fuel) Regulations 2005, SI 2005//3290.

Goods and services used for a business purpose

Goods or services are used for the purposes of a person's business if they are received in connection with his business activities for the purposes of being incorporated within his economic activities. See *C & E Comrs v Redrow Group plc* [1999] STC 161, HL. For an example, see *British Airways plc v C & E Comrs* [2000] V & DR 74, and contrast the earlier decision on similar facts in *British Airways plc v C & E Comrs* [1996] STC 1127 (food for passengers at airport restaurant). Goods or services purchased by a former member of a VAT group are not purchased for the purposes of its business if the goods or services are used for the purposes of making a supply to a member of the VAT group and the member paid for them before the former member left the group: *BUPA Purchasing Ltd v C & E Comrs* [2003] STC 1203; *R & C Comrs v Gracechurch Management Services Ltd* [2007] STC 795.

The test of purpose is subjective, but the credibility of evidence of intention can be tested against the standards and thinking of the ordinary businessman: *Ian Flockton Developments Ltd v C & E Comrs* [1987] STC 394. There must be a nexus between the expenditure and the business: see *C & E Comrs v Rosner* [1994] STC 228. For the relationship between these two cases, see *John Price Business Courses Ltd v C & E Comrs* [1995] V & DR 106; *Myatt & Leason (a firm) v C & E Comrs* [1995] V & DR 440. Promoting good industrial relations and motivating sub-contractors are business purposes: *RHM Bakeries (Northern) Ltd v C & E Comrs* [1979] STC 72; *Kelly (a firm) (No 2452)*. For accommodation occupied by an employee as a term of his contract, see *The Dean and Chapter of Hereford Cathedral v C & E Comrs* [1994] VATTR 159. For domestic accommodation used by directors, see below. For VAT on fuel for private motoring, see s 56.

No input tax arises if the goods or services are used for the purposes of somebody else's business (as, for example, in *Ashtree Holdings Ltd v C & E Comrs* [1979] STC 818; *Jackson (a firm) (No 1959)*) or for non-business purposes.

Whether or not a business is being carried on, or is to be carried on, is a matter of fact. For examples, see *Whitechapel Art Gallery v C & E Comrs* [1986] STC 156 (activity comprising free admission to premises); *H Lister (Slippers) Ltd (No 1747)* (racehorse owner making occasional bloodstock sales); *Chapman (a firm) (No 1209)* (temporary suspension of taxable supplies); *G B Turnbull Ltd v C & E Comrs* [1984] VATTR 247, *Cobb's Craft Service Station Ltd v C & E Comrs* [1976] VATTR 170 (no taxable supplies made in respect of planned business); *Purdue v C & E Comrs* [1994] VATTR 387 (no charge made for services provided). For activities lacking any business or economic character, see the commentary to s 4.

Goods and services used partly for business purposes and partly for other purposes

The goods or services may be used (or intended to be used) partly for business purposes and partly for other purposes. In principle, the VAT incurred is apportioned. For the manner of apportionment, see VAT Regulations 1995, SI 1995.2518 reg 102ZA. Only that part of the VAT referable to the business purpose is counted as input tax. The remainder (referred to as "non-business VAT") is counted as input only to the extent (if any) provided for by regulations. No regulations have been made to date.

However, a special rule is applied to the VAT incurred in respect of a "relevant asset" which is held for the purposes of a business carried on (or to be carried on) by a taxable person but which is used (or to be used) for the private purposes of himself or his staff. To the extent that the relevant asset is so used (or to be so used), it is never regarded as being used (or to be used) for the purposes of the business.

An asset is a relevant asset if it falls within one of the following descriptions: (1) an interest in land; (2) a building, a part of a building or any goods incorporated (or to be incorporated) in a building; (3) a civil engineering work, a part of a civil engineering work or any goods incorporated (or to be incorporated) in a civil engineering work; (4) a ship, boat or other vessel; or (5) an aircraft.

Evidence

VAT on purchases, acquisitions and importations is input tax only if and to the extent that the charge to VAT is evidenced and quantified by reference to the documents or other information specified in regulations. See VAT Regulations 1995, SI 1995/2518 reg 29; VAT (Input Tax) (Reimbursement by Employers of Employees' Business Use of Road Fuel) Regulations 2005, SI 2005//3290 reg 6. For the position under EU law, see Directive 2006/112/EC arts 178 (formerly Directive 77/388/EEC art 18(1)(a)); *Reisdorf v Finanzamt Köln-West* (case C-85/95) [1997] STC 180, ECJ. For a Statement of Practice regarding deduction of input tax without a valid VAT invoice, see Appendix 8.

Practical problems

For tax paid on imported goods, see *Mills Marketing Services Ltd* (No 4861). Tax erroneously charged on an exempt or zero-rated supply or supply outside the scope of tax is not input tax: *Genius Holding BV v Staatssecretaris van Financiën* (case 342/87) [1991] STC 239, ECJ; *Podium Investments Ltd v C & E Comrs* [1977] VATTR 121. See ICAEW (TAX 3/92), 13 February 1992. Tax paid (eg on a deposit) in respect of a supply which is not made (eg because the manufacturer ceases trading before making the goods ordered) is not input tax: *Howard* (No 1106); *Theotrue Holdings Ltd v C & E Comrs* [1983] VATTR 88. For VAT charged by traders not entitled to issue VAT invoices, see Notice No 48 (December 2010) para 3.9. A trader must have possession of, or control over, the goods so as to have the immediate facility for their use before the goods can be said to have been supplied to him: *W Puddifer (Jun) Ltd v C & E Comrs* [1996] V & DR 237. For input tax relating to activities carried on before registration, see *Investrand BV v Staatssecretaris van Financiën* (case C-435/05) [2007] ECR I–1315, [2008] STC 518, ECJ; *Charles-Greed* (No 7790); *Schemepanel Trading Ltd v C & E Comrs* [1996] STC 871. For sham transactions, see *R & C Comrs v Dempster (trading as Boulevard)* [2008] STC 2079.

A trader's purchase may form part of a chain of supply in which prior or subsequent transactions are tainted by VAT fraud. The trader is not entitled to input tax deduction in respect of his purchase if knew – or should have known – that, by his purchase, he was participating in a transaction connected with fraudulent evasion of VAT: *Axel Kittel v Belgian State; Belgian State v Recolta Recycling SPRL* (joined cases C-439/04 and C-440/04) [2006] ECR I–6161, [2008] STC 1537, ECJ. On the other hand, his right to deduct input tax is unaffected by this if he is unaware of the fraud and has no means of knowing of it: see *Optigen Ltd v C & E Comrs; Fulcrum Electronics Ltd v C & E Comrs; Bond House Systems Ltd v C & E Comrs* (joined cases C-354/03, C-355/03 and C-484/03) [2006] ECR I–483, [2006] STC 419, ECJ; For the application of these principles in the UK, see, in particular, *Mobilx Ltd (in administration) v R & C Comrs*, *Blue Sphere Global Ltd v R & C Comrs*, *Calltel Telecom Ltd and another v R & C Comrs (No 2)* [2010] STC 1436, CA. For examples, see *R (on the application of Just Fabulous (UK) Ltd) v R & C Comrs and related claims* [2009] STC 2123; *R & C Comrs v Livewire Telecom Ltd, R & C Comrs v Olympia Technology Ltd* [2009] STC 643; *Red 12 Trading Ltd v R & C Comrs* [2010] STC 589; *Megtian Ltd (in administration) v R & C Comrs* [2010] STC 840. For the nature of missing trader intra-Community ("MTIC") fraud – and its division into "acquisition fraud", "carousel fraud" and "contra trading fraud" – see, in particular, *R (on the application of Just Fabulous (UK) Ltd) v R & C Comrs and related claims* [2009] STC 2123 at [4]–[10] and the flow charts in Annexures 1, 2; *R & C Comrs v Livewire Telecom Ltd, R & C Comrs v Olympia Technology Ltd* [2009] STC 643 at [1].

Input tax arises only in respect of UK and Isle of Man VAT: see *British Iberian International Transport Ltd* (No 2101). For repayment of tax incurred in EU member states, see Directive 79/1072/EEC and Notice No 723. For repayment of VAT which is not input tax, see ss 33 (public authorities), 33A (museums and galleries), 35 (self-build projects), 39 (overseas traders), 27 (goods imported for private purposes), 41 (government departments).

A transaction may result in two or more persons receiving supplies of goods or services. It is necessary to identify one of those persons as the recipient of the supply. In principle, a supply is charged to VAT only if it is made for a consideration (see s 5(2)(*a*)). A supply is made for a consideration if there is a liability to pay for it. Thus, if X receives instructions from Y to supply services to Y and Z and Y is liable to pay X's charges, it is the service to Y which is made for a consideration and which carries the VAT charged by X. Z merely receives services for no consideration on which no VAT is chargeable. See *C & E Comrs v Redrow Group plc* [1999] STC 161, HL; Business Brief 27/99, 21 December 1999. The crucial factor is whether Y receives something from X in return for his payment to X: see *HMRC v Airtours Holidays Transport Ltd* [2010] UKUT 404 (TCC), [2011] STC 239. Contrast *Ashfield District Council v C & E Comrs* [2001] STC 1706 (home improvement grants paid by local authority). For examples, see *C & E Comrs v Plantiflor Ltd* [2002] STC 1132, HL; *WHA Ltd and another v C & E Comrs* [2004] STC 1081, CA; *P & O Ferries (Dover) Ltd v C & E Comrs* [1992] VATTR 221; *Crompton Enterprises Ltd v C & E Comrs* [1992] VATTR 321; *Kelly (a firm)* (No 2452); *Burntisland Golf House Club* (No 6340); *Thorp Architecture Ltd* (No 6955); *Property Enterprise Managers Ltd* (No 7711). For legal costs in civil and criminal proceedings in relation to directors, partners and sole traders, see *C & E Comrs v Rosner* [1994] STC 228; *Wallman Foods Ltd* (No 1411). In relation to employees contrast *R & C Comrs v Jeancharm Ltd (trading as Beaver International)* [2005] STC 918 (no deduction) and *P & O Ferries (Dover) Ltd v C & E Comrs* [1992] VATTR 221 (deduction allowed). For viability studies by investigating accountants, see Business Brief 6/95, 28 March 1995. For debt enforcement services provided by Under Sheriffs and Sheriffs' Officers, see Business Brief 6/00, 11 April 2000. For management and investment services by third parties in relation to funded pension schemes, see Business Brief 15/05, 9 August 2005 ("30/70 split" between employer and pension fund).

X does not make a supply to Z merely because Z pays X's charges. Similarly, X does not make a supply to Z merely because Z reimburses Y for the payment made by Y to X. The payment may amount to consideration for a supply made by Y to Z, but this is a different matter. For examples, see *Stirlings (Glasgow) Ltd v C & E Comrs* [1982] VATTR 116, *Co-operative Insurance Society Ltd v C & E Comrs* [1997] V & DR 65 (employee); *Berbrooke Fashions v C & E Comrs* [1977] VATTR 168 (sub-contractor); *Normal Motor Factors Ltd v C & E Comrs* [1978] VATTR 20 (customer); *Pollingfold Farms* (No 324) (associated business); *Culverpalm Ltd v C & E Comrs* [1984] VATTR 199 (agent); *Associated Concrete Repairs Ltd* (No 15963) (nominee); *Turner v C & E Comrs* [1992] STC 621 (other party's costs in legal proceedings); *C & E Comrs v Pennystar Ltd* [1996] STC 163 (financing supply made by one third party to another); Business Brief 17/93, 7 June 1993 (rent paid to someone other than immediate landlord). However, input tax is allowed if an agent contracts with a third party and assumes the obligation as principal when his principal repudiates liability: see *Scott* (No 6922). Also where the hirer is liable for repairs during the hire period: *Terry Cohn Ltd* (No 15962). For legal services in connection with insurance claims, see Press Notice 960, 31 December 1984. For the sale of repossessed property, see Business Brief 24/94, 8 December 1994. By concession, exact reimbursements to employees give rise to credit (see Notice No 700 (April 2002) section 12), but not round sum allowances: *BBC v C & E Comrs* [1974] VATTR 100. For supplies to employees, see *Leesportefeuille "Intiem" CV v Staatssecretaris van Financiën* (case 165/86) [1989] 2 CMLR 856, ECJ; *Commission v Kingdom of the Netherlands (UK intervening)* (case C-338/98) [2003] STC 1506, ECJ; *McLean Homes Midland Ltd* (No 5010).

Output tax

Output tax is: (1) VAT on supplies made by a taxable person; and (2) VAT on goods acquired from another EU member state by a taxable person. VAT under head (2) includes VAT which is also counted as input tax.

25. Payment by reference to accounting periods and credit for input tax against output tax (V3.402, V3.501)

A taxable person must account for and pay VAT on his supplies and acquisitions by reference to prescribed accounting periods in accordance with regulations. See VAT Regulations 1995, SI 1995/2518 regs 32, 39, 40, 50, 53–55, 57, 61–65.

At the end of each prescribed accounting period, a taxable person is entitled to credit for so much of his input tax as is allowable. He is entitled to deduct the credit from any output tax due from him. For the right to deduct, see *Belgium v Ghent Coal Terminal NV* (case C-37/95) [1998] STC 260, ECJ; *Gabalfrisa SL v Agencia Estatal de Administración Tributaria (AEAT)* (joined cases C-110/98 to C-147/98) [2002] STC 535, ECJ; *Finanzamt Goslar v Breitsohl* (case C-400/98) [2201] STC 355, ECJ. For the restriction of this right in relation to flat-rate traders, see s 26B(5). For the proportion of input tax that is allowable, see s 26.

A "VAT credit" arises if either: (1) no output tax is due at the end of the period; or (2) the input tax credit exceeds the amount of output tax due. The amount of the VAT credit is the amount of the input tax credit under head (1) or the amount of the excess under head (2). This amount is payable to the taxable person by the Commissioners. For payments directly to shipping agents and freight forwarders instead of to insolvent importers, see Notice No 48 (December 2010) para 3.13.

The right to payment of a VAT credit arises when the claim has been admitted or established: *R (on the application of UK Tradecorp Ltd) v C & E Comrs* [2005] STC 138. The Commissioners do not have a general power to withhold or delay payment: see *R v C & E Comrs ex parte Kay & Co Ltd* [1996] STC 1500. However, they can withhold payment if: (1) returns for one or more earlier periods are outstanding (see s 25(5)); or (2) the Commissioners dispute the amount claimed (see *Capital One Developments Ltd v C & E Comrs* [2002] STC 479). EU law obliges the Commissioners to investigate claims expeditiously and proportionately, and to pay claims promptly to the extent that they have been admitted, subject to exercising any right of set off: *R (on the application of UK Tradecorp Ltd) v C & E Comrs* [2005] STC 138. In principle, the tribunal (see s 82) has exclusive jurisdiction in relation to VAT credits. However, the Administrative Court has jurisdiction to decide whether a decision to withhold all or part of a VAT credit is unfair or disproportionate: see *Capital One Developments Ltd v C & E Comrs* [2002] STC 479; *R (on the application of UK Tradecorp Ltd) v C & E Comrs* [2005] STC 138.

All or part of an input tax credit may be held over to a subsequent period in accordance with regulations. See VAT Regulations 1995, SI 1995/2518 regs 25 (5) and 29 (3).

A deduction of input tax credit is made on a claim made in accordance with regulations. For the regulations made, see VAT Regulations 1995, SI 1995/1518 reg 29(1). The claim must be made at a time determined in accordance with regulations. For the regulations made, see VAT Regulations 1995, SI 1995/1518 reg 29. FA 2008 s 121(2) provides that the latter requirement does not apply to a claim for deduction made before 1 April 2009 if: (1) the input tax became chargeable in a prescribed accounting period ending before 1 May 1997; and (2) the claimant held the required evidence (see reg 29(2) of the 1995 Regulations) in a prescribed accounting period ending before that date. FA 2008 s 121(2) disapplies the three-year time limit in relation to claims for deduction made before 1 April 2009 if: (1) the input tax became chargeable in a prescribed accounting period ending before 1 May 1997; and (2) the claimant held the required evidence (see reg 29(2) of the 1995 Regulations) in a prescribed accounting period ending before that date.

Payment of a VAT credit is made on a claim made in accordance with regulations. A "claim" for these purposes seems to be a return furnished under VAT Regulations 1995, SI 1995/2518 reg 25 (1), (4). Payment of a VAT credit may be made subject to conditions if the taxable person has not made any taxable supplies in the period concerned or in any earlier period. For the vires of this provision, see *Hordern v C & E Comrs* [1992] VATTR 382 (conditions imposed on intending trader held to be unenforceable).

VAT on purchases, acquisitions and imports may be excluded from input tax credit by Treasury Order. See VAT (Tour Operators) Order 1987, SI 1987/1806 art 12; VAT (Input Tax) Order 1992, SI 1992/3222 arts 4–7. For expenditure in the nature of a luxury, amusement or entertainment, see s 84 (4), (11).

26. Input tax allowable under section 25 (V3.417)

A taxable person is entitled to credit for so much of his input tax for the period as is allowable by regulations as being attributable to:

(a) taxable supplies;
(b) supplies outside the UK which would be taxable supplies if made in the UK; or
(c) the supplies specified by VAT (Input Tax) (Specified Supplies) Order 1999, SI 1999/3121.

The Commissioners are required to make regulations for securing a fair and reasonable attribution of input tax to supplies within heads (*a*)–(*c*) above. For the regulations made, see VAT Regulations 1995, SI 1995/2518 regs 101–109. For the comprehensive nature of these regulations, see *C & E Comrs v University of Wales College Cardiff* [1995] STC 611.

For transitional relief in relation to major building projects in progress at 1 June 2004 following a change to the interpretation of the exemption conferred by Sch 9 Group 13 in the light of *C & E Comrs v The Zoological Society of London* (case C-267/00) [2002] STC 521, ECJ, see the extra-statutory concession in Business Brief 28/03, 10 December 2003, Annex A.

For the scope of head (*c*) in relation to issues of shares made outside the EU, see Business Brief 21/05, 23 November 2005; Business Brief 22/05, 2 December 2005.

26A. Disallowance of input tax where consideration not paid (V3.421)

A person who has become entitled to input tax credit in respect of a supply made to him (see s 25) ceases to be so entitled unless the consideration for the supply is paid within the later of: (1) six months after the time of supply (see s 6); or (2) six months after the due date for payment. He ceases to be entitled to credit for part of the input tax if part of the consideration is unpaid by the later of those two dates. Whether a payment of part-payment has been made is determined in accordance with regulations. All or part of the credit may be restored in accordance with regulations. For the regulations made, see VAT Regulations 1995, SI 1995/2518 regs 172F–172J.

This section has effect in relation to supplies made after 31 December 2002: see FA 2002 s 22, (Appointed Day) Order 2002, SI 2002/3028.

26AB. Adjustment of output tax in respect of supplies under section 55A (V3.231, V3.233)

The recipient of a supply is entitled to make an adjustment if:

- he has received a relevant supply (see s 55A(1)(*a*)) of goods to which s 55A applies (see s 55A(1)(*b*), (9));
- he is required to account to the Commissioners for the VAT due on the supply made by the supplier (see s 55A(6)); and
- he is not entitled to input tax credit in respect of that supply by virtue of s 26A.

The adjustment is made to the VAT that he is required to account for and pay. The amount of the adjustment is the credit for input tax to which he was not entitled by virtue of s 26A. Supplementary, incidental, consequential and transitional provisions are to be made by regulations. No regulations have been made to date.

This section has effect in relation to supplies made after 31 May 2007: see FA 2006 s 19(8); Finance Act 2006, section 19, (Appointed Day) Order 2007, SI 2007/1419 art 2.

26B. Flat-rate scheme

Regulations allow a taxable person to make an election whereby his liability to VAT in respect of his "relevant supplies" in any prescribed accounting period is the "appropriate percentage" of his "relevant turnover" for that period. A person is said to be participating in the flat-rate scheme if his liability to VAT is determined in this manner. For the regulations made, see VAT Regulations 1995, SI 1995/2518 regs 55A–55V. For the notice published by the Commissioners for the purposes of the scheme, see Notice No 733. For the legal effect of this notice, see VAT Regulations 1995, SI 1995/2518 regs 55G, 55S and 55T.

All supplies made by a person are "relevant supplies" unless regulations provide otherwise. For the exceptions, see VAT Regulations 1995, SI 1995/2518 reg 55C(2)–(5).

The "appropriate percentage" is the percentage specified by regulations for the category of business carried on by the person. For the percentages specified for each category of business, see the table in VAT Regulations 1995, SI 1995/2518 reg 55K. For selection of the percentage to be applied to all or part of relevant turnover for a prescribed accounting period, see VAT Regulations 1995, SI 1995/2518 regs 55H and 55J.

"Relevant turnover" is the aggregate of: (1) the value of both taxable and exempt relevant supplies; and (2) the VAT chargeable on taxable relevant supplies.

A person participating in the flat-rate scheme is not entitled to input tax credit unless regulations provide otherwise. For the exceptions, see VAT Regulations 1995, SI 1995/2518 regs 55E and 55F.

27. Goods imported for private purposes (V5.153)

A taxable person is not entitled to input tax credit in respect of VAT paid or payable on goods imported from a third country if the goods belong wholly or partly to another person and they are to be used wholly or partly for private purposes. However, the Commissioners may allow a claim where a double charge to VAT would otherwise result. For claims, see Notice No 702.

28. Payments on account of VAT (V5.110)

The Treasury may, by order, provide that a taxable person of a specified description is under a duty to make payments on account of tax for any prescribed accounting period which he may become liable to pay. See VAT (Payments on Account) Order 1993, SI 1993/2001. The Commissioners may give directions to a trader specifying the manner in which he is to make payments on account.

Where an order is made, the Commissioners may make regulations containing supplementary, incidental or consequential provisions. See VAT Regulations 1995, SI 1995/2518 Part VI (regs 44–48).

For national legislation requiring interim payments held to be contrary to EU legislation, see *Balocchi v Ministero delle Finanze* (case C-10/92) [1997] STC 640, ECJ.

29. Invoices provided by recipients of goods or services (V3.523)

If a self-billing invoice understates the VAT liability, the Commissioners may by notice to both the customer and the supplier elect to recover VAT from the customer instead of the supplier.

PART II RELIEFS, EXEMPTIONS AND REPAYMENTS

RELIEFS ETC GENERALLY AVAILABLE

29A. Reduced rate

A supply within Sch 7A is charged at the rate of 5%. So is: (1) an acquisition of goods from another EU member state if a supply of the goods would be within Sch 7A; and (2) an importation of goods within Sch 7A from a third country. Schedule 7A may be varied by Treasury order.

30. Zero-rating (V4.201, V4.202)

This section implements Directive 2006/112/EC art 169(*b*), (*c*) (exemption with refund in relation to specified supplies). It also maintains in force the exemptions with refund which the UK is permitted to retain in accordance with art 110 of the 2006 Directive. Exemption with refund is referred to in the UK as "zero-rating".

The precise effect of the UK legislation in relation to a particular zero-rated supply depends upon its legal basis under the 2006 Directive. It may therefore be necessary to research the legislative history of the relevant UK provision in order to determine its scope. Direct effect and the principle of consistent interpretation are relevant to the supplies specified in art 169(*b*), (*c*). For an example, see *R & C Comrs v EB Central Services Ltd* [2008] STC 2209, CA. A trader does not have any directly enforceable Community-law right in relation to zero-rating authorised under art 110. However, if a member state mistakenly interprets its national legislation so that zero-rated supplies are charged to tax, a trader making such supplies has a right to recover the sums mistakenly charged in respect of them: see *Marks and Spencer plc v C & E Comrs* (case C-309/06) [2008] ECR I–2283, [2008] STC 1408, ECJ, and subsequently [2009] STC 452, HL. For an example of zero-rating authorised by art 110, see *R & C Comrs v Stone* [2008] STC 2501.

No tax is charged on a supply of goods or services which is zero-rated, but the supply is in all other respects treated as a taxable supply. Thus, in principle, a taxable person is entitled to deduct input tax attributable to these supplies. (Directive 2006/112/EC approaches the question from the opposite direction. It provides that a taxable person is entitled to deduct VAT incurred in respect of specified exempt supplies, hence the description "exemption with refund".)

A supply of goods or services is zero-rated if the goods, services or supply are of a description for the time being specified in Sch 8. A person may produce goods by applying a treatment or process to another person's goods. If so, his supply of services is zero-rated if the resulting goods (or a hypothetical supply of them) are of a description for the time being specified in Sch 8. For free zone goods, see Notice No 48 (December 2010) para 3.14. For training services supplied in the UK to overseas governments, see Notice No 48 (December 2010) para 3.17. For supplies to diplomatic missions, international organisations, NATO forces, etc in EU countries, see Notice No 48 (December 2010) para 2.6.

No tax is chargeable on importations or acquisitions if the goods are of a description for the time being specified in Sch 8, unless provided otherwise in that schedule. See Sch 8 Groups 5 (Note 24), 6 (Note 3 applying Group 5 Note 24), 10 (Note 2) and 12 (Note 1).

Sch 8 may be varied by Treasury order. The order may also vary the refund scheme for do-it-yourself builders (see s 35(5)).

Goods exported to a third country by a charity are deemed to be supplied in the UK in the course or furtherance of a business carried on by the charity. Goods are "exported" if they are removed from the UK: *International Planned Parenthood Federation* (No 16922). This provision gives relief to non-business charities sending gifts of goods to third countries (eg disaster relief). The gift is deemed to be a supply (overriding s 5(2)(*a*)). As the supply is zero-rated (see Sch 8 Group 15 Item 3)—so as to be a taxable supply —and deemed to be made in the UK in the course or furtherance of business, it is within the scope of VAT (see s 4(1)). In consequence, the charity is liable or entitled to registration (see Sch 1 paras 1, 9(*a*)) and, if registered, entitled to deduction for input tax attributable to the exportation (see s 26(1), (2)(*a*)).

A supply of goods is zero-rated if the Commissioners are satisfied that they have been exported to a third country or shipped as stores or retail merchandise on a voyage or flight to an overseas destination. However, goods shipped as stores on a private voyage or flight are not zero-rated. Conditions may be specified in regulations or imposed by the Commissioners. No regulations have been made. For goods supplied at duty-free and tax-free shops, see Notice No 48 (December 2010) para 9.1. For marine fuel, see Notice No 48 (December 2010) para 9.2; *Staatssecretaris van Financiën v Velker International Oil Co Ltd NV* (case C-185/89) [1991] STC 640, ECJ; *Elmeka NE v Ipourgos Ikonomikon* (joined cases C-181/04 to C-183/04) [2006] ECR I–8167, ECJ.

Goods for export to a third country, removal to an EU member state, transfer from a fiscal warehousing regime to an equivalent regime in another EU member state, or for letting overseas may be zero-rated in accordance with regulations. See VAT Regulations 1995, SI 1995/2518 regs 127–155. For provisions having the force of law, see the parts of Notice Nos

703, 703/1/, 703/2, 704, 704/1, 705, 705A, 725 specified in Notice No 747. For a concession zero-rating sailaway boats supplied to UK residents, see Notice No 48 (December 2010) para 8.1; Notice No 703/2; *Shepherd v C & E Comrs* [1994] VATTR 47.

Goods zero-rated under the previous two paragraphs are liable to forfeiture if discovered in the UK after the alleged date of export or shipment or if conditions specified in regulations or imposed by the Commissioners have not been observed. VAT which would have been chargeable but for zero-rating is recoverable from the purchaser or person in possession of the goods. All or part of such VAT may be waived. For forfeiture, see Customs and Excise Management Act 1979 s 139 and Sch 3.

For the zero-rating of services relating to warehoused and fiscally warehoused goods, see s 18C. For terminal markets, see s 50. For goods exported in contravention of an export ban, see *Lange v Finanzamt Fürstenfeldbruck* (case C-111/92) [1997] STC 564, ECJ.

For the relationship between exemption and zero-rating, see *CGI Pension Trust Ltd* (No 15926).

31. Exempt supplies and acquisitions (V3.368; V4.101)

A supply of goods or services is exempt if it is of a description for the time being specified in Sch 9.

An exempt supply is not chargeable to VAT by virtue of s 4. An acquisition of goods from another EU member state is exempt if the goods are acquired under an exempt supply. Sch 9 may be varied by Treasury order.

32. Relief on supply of certain second-hand goods

[Repealed.]

33. Refunds of VAT in certain cases (V5.162)

Specified bodies may claim refund of VAT on goods and services used for non-business purposes. For claims, see Notice No 749. If analysis of business and non-business purchases is difficult, claims are made in respect of total VAT less VAT on business purchases. For apportionment of business and non-business use, see *Haringey London Borough Council v C & E Comrs* [1995] STC 830; Notice No 749. The fact that input tax includes VAT attributable to exempt supplies is disregarded if the proportion is insignificant. For "insignificant", see *Haringey London Borough Council v C & E Comrs* [1995] STC 830; Notice No 749. Input tax excluded from credit (see s 25 (7)) may not be claimed. See *R v C & E Comrs ex parte Greater Manchester Police* Authority [2001] STC 406, CA. For VAT incurred by voluntary aided schools, see Revenue and Customs Brief 53/09, 17 August 2009.

The specified bodies are listed in s 33 (3)(*a*)–(*j*) and the following orders made under s 33 (3) (*k*): SI 1973/2121; SI 1976/2028; SI 1985/1101; SI 1986/336, 532; SI 1989/1217; SI 1995/1978, 2999; SI 1997/2558; SI 1999/2076; SI 2000/1046; SI 2000/1515; SI 2000/1672; SI 2001/3453; SI 2006/1793, 2009/1177. For the criteria applied when specifying bodies, see *R v HM Treasury and another ex parte Service Authority for the National Crime Squad and others* [2000] STC 638.

For repayment supplement on refunds, see s 79.

33A. Refunds of VAT to museums and galleries

A body specified by order is entitled to a refund of VAT (other than VAT excluded from credit) incurred on purchases, acquisitions or importations taking place after 31 March 2001 (or a later date specified by order) if the relevant goods or services are used to provide free admission to a museum or gallery specified in the order. For the bodies, museums and galleries, and later dates specified, see VAT (Refund of Tax to Museums and Galleries) Order 2001, SI 2001/2879.

If the goods or services used to provide free admission cannot conveniently be distinguished, the amount refunded is such proportion of the whole VAT (other than that which is excluded from credit) incurred by the body as appears to the Commissioners to relate to providing free admission.

A claim must be made in the form and manner prescribed by the Commissioners within four years (or such shorter period as the Commissioners may determine) of the purchase, acquisition or importation.

For concessions which avoid the application of Sch 4 para 5(1), (4) (deemed supply of goods), VAT (Supply of Services) Order, SI 1993/1507 (deemed supply of services) and VAT Regulations, SI 1995/2518 reg 115 (adjustment under the capital goods scheme) when admission charges cease to be made, see Notice No 48 (December 2010) para 3.34.

33B. Refunds of VAT to Academies

The proprietor of an Academy (as defined in Education Act 1996 s 579) acting as such is entitled to a refund of VAT (other than VAT excluded from credit) incurred on non-business purchases, acquisitions and importations made after 31 March 2011 (see FA 2011 s 75(5)).

If the goods or services used for business and non-business purposes cannot conveniently be distinguished, the amount refunded is such proportion of the whole VAT (other than that which is excluded from credit) incurred by the proprietor as appears to the Commissioners to relate to the non-business activity.

A claim must be made in the form and manner prescribed by the Commissioners within four years (or such shorter period as the Commissioners may determine) of the purchase, acquisition or importation.

Claims may be made in respect of purchases, acquisitions and importations made after 31 March 2011: see FA 2011 s 75(5).

34. Capital goods (V5.166)

The Treasury may by order allow VAT to be deducted where plant or machinery is purchased but VAT cannot be credited under s 25. No orders have been made.

35. Refund of VAT to persons constructing certain buildings (V5.164)

A person may claim a refund of VAT chargeable on the purchase, acquisition or importation of goods if:

(a) he carries out any of the following works:
  (i) constructing a building designed as one or more dwellings (see Sch 8 Group 5 Notes 2, 3),
  (ii) constructing a building for use solely for a relevant residential purpose (see Sch 8 Group 5 Notes 4, 5),
  (iii) constructing a building for use solely for a relevant charitable purpose (see Sch 8 Group 5 Note 6),
  (iv) a residential conversion (see below); or
  (v) constructing a holiday home for non-business purposes (see *Jennings* (TC 362); Revenue and Customs Brief 29/10, 15 June 2010);

(b) he carries out the works lawfully and otherwise than in the course or furtherance of business; and

(c) the goods are building materials (see Sch 8 Group 5 Notes 22, 23) which are incorporated in the building or its site in the course of carrying out the works and VAT is chargeable on the supply (under UK law or the law of another EU member state), acquisition (under UK law) or importation (under UK law) concerned.

A houseboat is not a "building" for the purposes of head (*a*): *Parkinson* (No 17257).

A person may arrange for another person ("a contractor") to carry out all or part of a residential conversion (see below) carried out lawfully and otherwise than in the course or furtherance of business. He may claim a refund of VAT in respect of the work done by the contractor if: (1) the contractor's services are chargeable to VAT under UK law; and (2) the contractor's services comprise something other than the services of an architect, surveyor, consultant or supervisor.

A person carries out a "residential conversion" if he converts a non-residential building or a non-residential part of a building into:

(a) a building (or part) designed as one or more dwellings. If a building contains both a residential and a non-residential part, one or more additional dwellings must result from the conversion of the non-residential part (Sch 8 Group 5 Note 9). For a case where additional dwellings resulted, see *C & E Comrs v Jacobs* [2005] STC 1518, CA (conversion of boarding school); Business Brief 22/05, 2 December 2005. For cases where they did not, see *C & E Comrs v Blom-Cooper* [2003] STC 669, CA (public house with living accommodation converted into a house); *Claam Vale Ltd* (No 16869) (public house with living accommodation above split vertically to form two semi-detached houses). For three buildings converted to form a single dwelling, see *Moore* (No 15972);

(b) a building (or part) intended to be used solely for a relevant residential purpose.

A building or part is "non-residential" if it was neither designed nor adapted for use as one or more dwellings or for a relevant residential purpose. A building or part designed or adapted for use as one or more dwellings, or for a relevant residential purpose, is "non-residential" if it was more than ten years old when the conversion commenced and it had not been used as a dwelling or for a relevant residential purpose for ten years when the conversion commenced (Sch 8 Group 5 Note 7A as modified by s 35(4A)). A building or part is not "non-residential" if it comprises a garage occupied together with a dwelling: see Sch 8 Group 5 Note 8.

A claim for refund must be made in the form and manner, and within the time limit, prescribed by regulations. It must contain the information so prescribed. It must be accompanied by the documents specified by the Commissioners in accordance with regulations. For the regulations made, see VAT Regulations 1995, SI 1995/2518 regs 200, 201.

This section is interpreted in accordance with the Notes to Sch 8 Group 5. For the manner in which the Notes apply, see *C & E Comrs v Blom-Cooper* [2003] STC 669, CA; *R & C Comrs v Jacobs* [2005] STC 1518, CA. This section may be varied by an order made under s 30(4). For discretionary refunds to charitable organisations, see Press Notice 15/96, 13 March 1996.

36. Bad debts (V5.156)

A person is entitled to a refund if: (1) he supplied goods or services; (2) he has accounted for and paid tax on the supply (see *English Film Co Ltd* (No 1357)); (3) he has written off all or part of the consideration as a bad debt; (4) six months have elapsed from the time of supply; (5) the value of the supply does not exceed open market value; and (6) a claim is made. For claims in respect of mortgage debts, see Business Brief 24/94, 8 December 1994. For relief on the novation of domestic gas and electricity supply contracts, see the extra-statutory concession set out in Business Brief 20/04, 2 August 2004.

A claim is made in respect of the tax element of the outstanding amount. The "outstanding amount" is the consideration for the supply less the payments (if any) received by the claimant, or a person to whom the right to receive all or part of the consideration has been assigned, at the time of the claim. The outstanding amount must be written off in the claimant's accounts. For calculation of the outstanding amount written off, see VAT Regulations, SI 1995/2518 regs 170, 172(3), 172(4), 172A, 172B. For the manner in which the outstanding amount is written off, see VAT Regulations, SI 1995/2518 reg 172(2).

The outstanding amount is treated as a VAT-inclusive sum even if it comprises a VAT-only invoice or the unpaid VAT element of an invoice: see, for example, *A W Mawer & Co v C & E Comrs* [1986] VATTR 87 (VAT element) and *Caernarfonshire Fatstock Group Ltd* (No

5033). For the limited exception to this rule, see *Palmer* (No 11739) (delay by Commissioners in registering trader). There is no outstanding amount if shares are issued in full satisfaction of a debt: *A-Z Electrical* (No 10718); *AEG (UK) Ltd v C & E Comrs* [1993] VATTR 379.

The consideration for a supply is: (1) the money consideration (consideration consisting wholly of money); (2) the value of the supply plus the VAT charged thereon (consideration consisting wholly of something other than money); or (3) the money consideration plus the appropriate proportion of the figure in (2) (consideration consisting partly of money and partly of something other than money).

For the manner in which claims are made and the documents are to be prepared, retained and preserved, see VAT Regulations, SI 1995/2518 regs 166–169. For the repayment of refunds, see VAT Regulations, SI 1995/2518 reg 171.

For refunds in respect of supplies made before a company ceased to be included in a VAT group, see *Triad Timber Components Ltd v C & E Comrs* [1993] VATTR 384. For penalties, see ss 60 (civil), 72 (criminal). For appeals, see s 83(1)(*h*).

Import VAT paid by shipping agents and freight forwarders on behalf of their principals does not give rise to a claim for bad debt relief under this section. For repayments made by the Commissioners by extra-statutory concession, see Notice No 48 (December 2010) para 3.13; *Prestige Freight* (No 17614).

ACQUISITIONS

36A. Relief from VAT on acquisition if importation would attract relief (V3.398)

An order may provide that goods acquired from another EU member state are to be relieved from VAT in like manner to similar goods imported from a third country. For the order made, see VAT (Acquisitions) Relief Order 2002, SI 2002/1935.

The VAT otherwise chargeable must be paid if any condition imposed by the order has not been met. If a condition was breached, VAT is payable at the time of breach. If a condition was not complied with, VAT is payable at the latest time allowed for compliance.

IMPORTS, OVERSEAS BUSINESSES ETC

37. Relief from VAT on importation of goods (V3.316)

The Treasury may by order provide relief from VAT on imported goods to comply with international arrangements. See VAT (Imported Goods) Relief Order, SI 1984/746; VAT (Small Non-Commercial Consignments) Relief Order 1986, SI 1986/939; VAT (Imported Gold) Relief Order 1992, SI 1992/3124; VAT (Importation of Investment Gold) Relief Order 1999, SI 1999/3115; VAT (Imported Gas, Electricity, Heat and Cooling) Relief Order 2010, SI 2010/2924.

The Commissioners may remit or repay tax chargeable on imported goods in accordance with regulations where the goods are reimported or for re-export. See VAT Regulations 1995, SI 1995/2518 regs 123–126.

38. Importation of goods by taxable persons (V5.122)

The Commissioners by regulations may allow taxable persons to account for the VAT due on imported goods at the same time as they account for VAT on their supplies and acquisitions. See the VAT Regulations 1995, SI 1995/2518 reg 122.

39. Repayment of VAT to those in business overseas (V5.151, V5.152)

Persons carrying on a business in another EU member state, or in a third country, may claim repayment of VAT on supplies made to them in the UK and on goods imported by them into the UK from third countries which would be input tax if they were taxable persons in the UK. Claims are made in accordance with regulations. For the regulations made, see VAT Regulations 1995, SI 1995/2518 Parts XX (regs 173–184) and XXI (regs 185–187).

39A. Applications for forwarding of VAT repayment claims to other member states

Directive 2008/9/EC lays down detailed rules for refunding VAT incurred by a taxable person in another member state (see Directive 2006/112/EC art 170). From 1 January 2010, a taxable person established in member state X is required to send an electronic refund application to the relevant authority in member state X, which is required to forward it to the relevant authority in member state Y. The refund is made by the relevant authority in member state Y.

The Commissioners are required to make arrangements for forwarding refund applications by UK taxable persons to the tax authorities of other EU member states.

40. Refunds in relation to new means of transport supplied to other member states (V5.154)

A non-taxable person is entitled to a refund of VAT if he supplies a new means of transport (see s 95) and removes it to another EU member state. The amount refunded is the lower of: (1) the VAT paid on the original purchase, acquisition or importation; and (2) the VAT which would be chargeable on that value at the current rate of tax. Claims are made in accordance with regulations. For the regulations made, see VAT Regulations 1995, SI 1995/2518 Part XVII (regs 146–155).

PART III APPLICATION OF ACT IN PARTICULAR CASES

41. Application to the Crown (V5.161)

Taxable supplies made by the Crown are treated in the same manner as taxable supplies made by other taxable persons.

Goods or services supplied by a government department are treated as if they were supplied in the course or furtherance of business if the Treasury so directs. For the directions made, see Appendix 4.

Government departments may claim a refund of tax in respect of goods and services obtained otherwise than for the purposes of a business or deemed business if the Treasury so directs. The Commissioners may impose conditions concerning the keeping, preservation and production of records. For the directions made, see Appendix 5.

42. Local authorities (V2.108)

Local authorities are liable to be registered for VAT even if the value of their taxable supplies is below the registration limit.

43. Groups of companies (V2.190)

Two or more bodies corporate (eg, companies, limited liability partnerships, building societies and industrial and provident societies) may be treated as members of a group. Where this is so, they are often described as comprising a “VAT group”. One of the members of the VAT group is described as “the representative member”. For the formation, variation and termination of a VAT group, see ss 43A, 43AA, 43B and Sch 9A. For the appointment and variation of the representative member, see s 43A and Sch 9A. The following consequences arise from group treatment.

First, the businesses carried on by the group members are deemed to be carried on by a group member referred to as “the representative member”.

Secondly, intra-group supplies made by group members are disregarded for VAT purposes. Thus, if X and Y are members of a VAT group, X does not charge VAT on the supply and cannot become liable to registration because of it. However, the supply is not necessarily treated as non-existent or irrelevant for all other purposes: *C & E Comrs v Sveniska International plc* [1999] STC 406, HL (attribution of input tax incurred before joining the VAT group); *J P Morgan Trading and Finance v C & E Comrs* [1998] V & DR 161 (attribution of input tax incurred after leaving the VAT group). For a specific exception in relation to the exemption of sports supplies after 31 December 1999, see Sch 9 Group 10 Note 15. For prepaid supplies when a group member leaves the group, see *C & E Comrs v Thorn Materials Supply Ltd* [1998] STC 725, HL (goods); *BUPA Purchasing Ltd v C & E Comrs* [2004] STC 1203 (services).

This provision does not apply to services within Sch 5 paras 1–8 purchased by a group member belonging outside the UK at the time of purchase (see s 9 (4)) and resupplied (whether by that member or by a person to whom his business is directly or indirectly transferred as a going concern) to a group member who belongs in the UK at the time of resupply (see s 9 (4)) under a supply which would otherwise be a taxable supply of services within Sch 5. Where the services are not disregarded under this provision, the representative member is deemed to self-supply them. He must account for output tax accordingly and may be entitled to input tax credit for all or part of the VAT so accounted for.

No input tax is attributed to the supply deemed to be made when applying the partial exemption rules in VAT Regulations 1995, SI 1995/2518 regs 99–110. The resupplier and recipient are deemed to be connected persons (as defined in CTA 2010 s 1122) so that the Commissioners can make a valuation direction under Sch 6 para 1. The time of supply is determined in accordance with VAT Regulations 1995, SI 1995/2518 reg 82. The value of the supply is determined in accordance with Sch 6 para 1 (if a direction is made under that provision) and otherwise in accordance with Sch 6 para 8. The Commissioners may vary these provisions by regulations. No regulations have been made to date. However, for concessions relating to valuation and the time of supply, see Notice No 48 (December 2010) para 3.2. For a general statement of the Commissioners' approach to these provisions, see Business Brief 11/97, 9 May 1997.

Thirdly, the representative member is deemed to make all supplies to third parties, receive all supplies from third parties, acquire all goods from EU member states, import all goods from third countries and pay all VAT chargeable on acquisitions and importations. For orders under s 5 (5), (6) deeming self-supplies to be made by the representative member, see VAT (Self-Supply of Construction Services) Order 1989, SI 1989/472 (construction services); VAT (Cars) Order 1992, SI 1992/3122 (motor cars); VAT (Special Provisions) Order 1995, SI 1995/1268 (stationery). For fuel for private use, see s 56 (4). For self-supplies by developers, see Sch 10 para 5. Any liability to output tax or entitlement to input tax on these supplies, acquisitions or importations is determined by reference to the statutory description of the group member actually making or receiving them.

Fourthly, all members of the VAT group are jointly and severally liable for any VAT due from the representative member.

For the consequence of group treatment on transactions taking place before 27 November 1996, see *C & E Comrs v Kingfisher plc* [1994] STC 63; *C & E Comrs v Thorn Materials Supply Ltd* [1998] STC 725, HL; *C & E Comrs v Svenska International plc* [1999] STC 406, HL; *Midland Bank plc v C & E Comrs* [1991] VATTR 525; *Thorn EMI plc v C & E Comrs* [1993] VATTR 94; *Canary Wharf Ltd v C & E Comrs* [1996] V & DR 323; *J P Morgan Trading and Finance v C & E Comrs* [1998] V & DR 161. For the person assessed when a new representative member is appointed, see *Thorn plc v C & E Comrs* [1998] V & DR 80. For property transactions within VAT groups, see Press Notice 843, 23 June 1983; Sch 10 para 5 (6), (7). For bad debt relief when a company retires from a VAT group, see *Triad Timber Components Ltd v C & E Comrs* [1993] VATTR 384. For the capital goods scheme, see VAT Regulations 1995, SI 1995/2518 regs 114 (6), 115 (6).

This section is amended by FA 2009 Sch 36 paras 7, 14(2) in relation to supplies made after 31 December 2009: see FA 2009 s 76 and Sch 36 para 14(3). For transitional provisions, see FA 2009 Sch 36 para 19.

43A. Groups: eligibility (V2.190)

Two or more bodies corporate (eg, companies, limited liability partnerships, building societies and industrial and provident societies) established in the UK or having a fixed establishment in the UK are eligible to be treated as members of a group if one of them controls all the others or they are all controlled by an individual, partnership or another body corporate. For limited liability partnerships, see Business Brief 3/01, 20 February 2001.

A body corporate controls another body corporate if: (1) it controls that body's activities under statutory powers, or (2) it is the holding company (as defined by Companies Act 1985 s 736) of that body. Individuals and partnerships control a body corporate if (assuming they were a company) they would be the holding company of that body. See *Mannin Shipping Ltd v C & E Comrs* [1979] VATTR 83 (individual with casting vote owning 50% of equity share capital having control); *British Airways Board* (No 846) (whether company empowered by statute to control another company); *E Du Vergier & Co Ltd v C & E Comrs* [1973] VATTR 11 (whether individuals controlling company carrying on business in partnership).

43AA. Power to alter eligibility for grouping (V2.190)

The rules governing eligibility for membership of a VAT group (see s 43A) may be modified by Treasury order in relation to a specified class of person. For the order made, see VAT (Groups: Eligibility) Order 2004, SI 2004/1931.

43B. Groups: applications (V2.190)

The following applications can be made:

(a) For two or more eligible bodies corporate to form a new VAT group; or
(b) make any of the following changes to an existing VAT group:
  (i) another eligible body corporate to become a member of the VAT group,
  (ii) an existing member to leave the VAT group,
  (iii) a different member to be substituted as the representative member, or
  (iv) disband the VAT group (so that the members become liable or entitled to registration, or not, in accordance with their individual circumstances).

An application is made by a member of the VAT group (or prospective VAT group), or by the person who controls the bodies corporate. An application under (*a*) must appoint one of the prospective members as the representative member.

An application is deemed to be granted with effect from the day when the Commissioners receive it or from such earlier or later time as they allow. For retrospective effect under superseded legislation, see News Release 52/90, 17 July 1990; *Blue Boar Property & Investment Co Ltd v C & E Comrs* [1984] VATTR 12; *Legal & Contractual Services Ltd v C & E Comrs* [1984] VATTR 85.

The Commissioners can refuse an application under (*a*) or (*b*)(i) if they consider that the bodies corporate (in the former case) or the body corporate (in the latter case) are not eligible for membership of the prospective VAT group or VAT group respectively. The Commissioners can refuse any application under (*a*) or (*b*) if they consider this necessary to protect the revenue. For the Commissioners' right to delay an application under head (*b*)(ii), cf *C & E Comrs v Barclays Bank plc* [2001] STC 1558, CA under superseded legislation. For the exercise of this right, see Business Brief 20/02, 19 November 2002. For protection of the revenue, see *National Westminster Bank plc v C & E Comrs* [1999] V & DR 201; Business Brief 15/99, 12 July 1999. For the use of revenue protection powers against particular group structures, see Business Brief 1/01, 10 January 2001 (supplier and partly exempt customer run for benefit of independent third party); Business Brief 30/02, 19 November 2002 (contrived group structures).

The Commissioners must exercise their right of refusal within 90 days of receiving the application. If they do so, the application is treated as if it had never been granted. For the Commissioners' practice, see Business Brief 15/99, 12 July 1999. For appeals against a refusal, see ss 83(1)(*k*) and 84(4A).

Whether or not a body corporate is "eligible" for any of the foregoing purposes is determined in accordance with s 43A.

43C. Groups: termination of membership (V2.190)

The Commissioners can compulsorily remove a body corporate from a VAT group on revenue protection grounds. They may do this by serving a notice on the body corporate. The body corporate ceases to be a member of the VAT group from the date of the notice or a later date specified therein. For protection of the revenue, see *National Westminster Bank plc v C & E Comrs* [1999] V & DR 201; Business Brief 15/99, 12 July 1999 Business Brief 1/01, 10 January 2001; Business Brief 30/02, 19 November 2002. For appeals against a notice, see ss 83(1)(*ka*) and 84(4B), (4C).

The Commissioners can compulsorily remove a body corporate from a VAT group on grounds that it is not, or has ceased to be, eligible (as to which see s 43A). The Commissioners may do this by serving a notice on the body corporate. The body corporate ceases to be a member of the VAT group from a date specified in the notice. Subject to transitional provisions in FA 1999 Sch 2 para 6, this date may be no earlier than:

(a) the first date on which the Commissioners believe that the body was not eligible for membership of the VAT group; or

(b) the date on which they believe that the body ceased to be eligible for membership of the VAT group.

The Commissioners can specify a date later than the one mentioned in (*a*) or (*b*): cf *C & E Comrs v Barclays Bank plc* [2001] STC 1558, CA in relation to superseded legislation.

For appeals against a notice, see ss 83(1)(*ka*) and 84(4B), (4D).

43D. Supplies to groups (V2.190)

A body corporate is entitled to be a member of only one VAT group at any particular time. If it is already a member of one VAT group, it is ineligible to join another one. Any application to become a member of another VAT group is modified as follows:

- an application to join an existing VAT group is ineffective;
- an application to become a founder member of a new VAT group is ineffective as regards the body corporate; and
- an application to join an existing VAT group or become a founder member of a new VAT group is ineffective if another application to do either is still pending.

44. Supplies to groups (V3.246)

Where a registered trader transfers as a going concern to a company in a VAT group a business or part of a business together with assets the transfer of which would normally be treated as neither a supply of goods nor a supply of services, the transfer is treated as a supply both to and by the representative member of the group. This does not apply if the representative member of the group is entitled to credit for all of its input tax on supplies during the prescribed accounting period or any longer period in which the assets are transferred, or if the assets were obtained more than three years before the day on which they are transferred. Nor does it apply to the capital items defined in VAT Regulations 1995, SI 1995/2518 reg 113.

The transfer value has to be excluded from any calculation to determine the input tax allowable under the partial exemption rules to the representative member of the group.

The value of a supply made to or by the representative member is the price, net of VAT, between a buyer and a seller who have no relationship which could affect the price. An adjustment of tax payable may be allowed where the Commissioners are satisfied that the person transferring the assets did not receive full credit of input tax upon purchase of those assets (for example where the transferor was exempt).

These provisions apply only to assets chargeable at the standard rate.

45. Partnerships (V2.110)

A partnership is no more than a group of taxable persons trading jointly and having a joint liability for the tax liability arising from the partnership enterprise. The fact that a registration is made in the names of the partners, or in the firm name, does not create any legal or taxable personality separate from the individual partners: see *C & E Comrs v Evans* [1982] STC 342; *Scrace v R & C Comrs* [2007] STC 269.

A partnership may be registered in the firm name. A partnership is deemed to continue when a new partner is appointed or an existing partner retires. However, a retiring partner is deemed to be a continuing partner until his retirement is notified to the Commissioners and he has the same responsibilities for payment of tax and other duties as a continuing partner until this time. The other partners may claim from him only a just proportion of the VAT due for the prescribed accounting period in which he retires or is deemed to retire.

A number of individuals (A, B, C and D) may hold themselves out as partners by completing and signing form VAT2. However, A, B, C and D must actually carry on a business in partnership if they are to constitute a taxable person. If the partnership actually consists of A and B, an assessment made in the name of the firm, or in the names of A, B, C and D, is effective against A and B but ineffective against C and D: see *R & C Comrs v Pal and ors* [2008] STC 2442. For "holding out", see the commentary to Partnership Act 1890 s 14.

A notice addressed to a partnership in the firm name is deemed to be served on the partnership. For a change to the firm name, see *Scrace v R & C Comrs* [2007] STC 269 (assessment for periods before and after the change notified in the new name). A notice served or deemed to be served on a partnership is deemed to be served on a former partner if it relates to a period during which he was, or was deemed to be, a partner. See *C & E Comrs v Evans* [1982] STC 342; *Ahmed v C & E Comrs* [1988] VATTR 1; *Choudhury* (No 2490); *The Bengal Brasserie v C & E Comrs* [1991] VATTR 210; *Mumtaz Paan House v C & E Comrs* [1998] V & DR 52.

It may be necessary to decide whether one business is carried on in partnership or two separate businesses are carried on by sole traders. A tribunal (see s 82) should examine the substance and reality of the relationship and conclude that there are separate entities only if the so-called separate businesses are sufficiently at arm's length from each other and that they have normal commercial relationships with each other: *Burrell v C & E Comrs* [1997] STC 1413. However, relationships between husband and wife should not be expected to be wholly at arm's length or commercial: *Parker and Parker* (No 16350). For an example of partnership, see *Leonidas and Leonidas v C & E Comrs* [2000] V & DR 207. For examples of separate businesses, see *Staatssecretaris van Financiën v Heerma* (case C-23/98) [2001] STC 1437, ECJ (building leased by partner to partnership); *Newton (a firm)* (No 17222); *Parker and Parker* (No 16350); *James and James* (No 16988). For limited liability partnerships, see Business Brief 3/01, 20 February 2001.

46. Business carried on in divisions or by unincorporated bodies, personal representatives, etc (V2.190A)

A body corporate may be separately registered in the names of individual divisions.

A club, association or organisation may be registered in its own name. It is deemed to continue when new members join and existing members leave. An affiliated activity group may or may not be part of the club. For the test applied, see *Old Parkinsonians Association* (No 10908). For examples of separate entities, see *Watchet Indoor Bowling Club* (No 1026); *Cambuslang Athletic Club* (No 1592); *Old Parkinsonians Association* (No 10908). For a single entity, see *Belvedere and Calder Vale Sports Club* (No 931).

Regulations may: (1) identify who is responsible for doing anything required by the Act in relation to partnerships and unincorporated bodies; and (2) secure continuity of registration on the death, incapacity, insolvency etc of a taxable person. See VAT Regulations 1995, SI 1995/2518 regs 7–9. For flat-rate farmers, see VAT Regulations 1995, SI 1995/2518 reg 207.

47. Agents, etc (V3.221)

Goods are deemed to be both acquired and supplied by a taxable person as principal if: (1) the goods are acquired from another EU member state by a non-taxable-person; (2) the taxable person acts in relation to the acquisition; (3) the taxable person supplies the goods as agent for the non-taxable-person; and (4) the taxable person acts in his own name in relation to the supply.

Goods are deemed to be both imported and supplied by a taxable person as principal if: (1) the goods are imported from a third party by a taxable person; (2) the taxable person supplies the goods as agent for a non-taxable-person; and (3) the taxable person acts in his own name in relation to the supply.

A person is treated as a non-taxable person for these purposes if: (1) he is not resident in the UK; (2) his place, or principal place, of business is outside the UK; and (3) the fact that his agent, rather than himself, is treated as making the supply or acquisition means that he is not liable to registration, ie because the value of his other supplies and acquisitions (if any) are below the registration limits.

In other cases, goods deemed to be supplied to and by an agent if the goods are supplied through the agent who acts in his own name. For the vires of this provision, see *Express Medicare Ltd* (No 16969) (whatever the proper interpretation of Directive 2006/112/EC art 14(2)(*c*) (formerly Directive 77/388/EEC art 5(4)(*c*)), it cannot be reconciled with s 47(2A) without twisting the terminology to an unacceptable extent).

Where services are supplied through an agent acting in his own name the Commissioners may treat the supply as both to and from the agent. For the circumstances in which supplies may be so treated, see Notice No 700 (April 2002) paras 22.6 (taxable supply where supplier and customer are registered) and 24.1 (optional treatment for domestic supplies).

A trader acts in his own name if a third party does not know that he is acting for someone else: *Express Medicare Ltd* (No 16969). He may also do so where the agency relationship is known, but the identity of the principal is not disclosed: *Express Medicare Ltd* (No 16969). For an example, see *Bashir Mohamed Ltd* (No 16762) (sale by auction).

For the time of supply for the supplies made to and by the agent, see *Metropolitan Borough of Wirral v C & E Comrs* [1995] STC 597. For the Commissioners' revised policy on the valuation of international supplies and the treatment of agency services in connection with them, see Notice No 700 (April 2002) para 24.2.

For the identification of a person as an agent, see *C & E Comrs v Johnson* [1980] STC 624; *Potter v C & E Comrs* [1985] STC 45, CA; *Betterware Products Ltd v C & E Comrs* [1985] STC 648; *C & E Comrs v Paget* [1989] STC 773; *C & E Comrs v Music & Video Exchange Ltd* [1992] STC 220; *C & E Comrs v Reed Personnel Services Ltd* [1995] STC 588; *Cornhill Management Ltd v C & E Comrs* [1991] VATTR 1; *Durham Aged Mineworkers' Homes Association v C & E Comrs* [1994] STC 553; *Nordic Subscription Service UK Ltd* (No 10705); *Seagar Enterprises Ltd* (No 15432). For a contract conferring third party rights rather than creating an agency relationship, see *Mölnycke Ltd* (No 14641).

For agency disbursements, see *Nell Gwynn House Maintenance Fund Trustees v C & E Comrs* [1999] STC 79, HL; *C & E Comrs v Plantiflor Ltd* [2002] STC 1132, HL; *Rowe & Maw (a firm) v C & E Comrs* [1975] STC 340; Hamilton *v C & E Comrs* [1984] VATTR 95; Business Brief 28/97, 12 December 1997 (debt collection costs); Business Brief 28/93, 12 December 1997 (search fees). For motor cars purchased by non-franchised dealers through third parties, see Business Brief 4/98, 9 February 1998. For telegraphic transfer fees, see *Shuttleworth & Co v C & E Comrs* [1994] VATTR 355; Law Society, 18 November 1992. For the sale of repossessed property, see Business Brief 24/94, 8 December 1994.

48. Tax representatives (V2.106, V2.146)

The Commissioners may require a person to appoint a "tax representative" in the UK if:

- he is registered in the UK, liable to registration in the UK, or makes taxable supplies or acquisitions in the UK without being registered or liable to registration;
- he is not established in the UK and does not have a fixed establishment in the UK;
- he is established in a country or territory which is not an EU member state or part of an EU member state and which does not have mutual assistance provisions with the UK similar in scope to those provided by FA 2002 s 34 and Sch 39, FA 2003 s 197 and Regulation (EC) No 1798/2003; and
- (in the case of an individual) his usual place of residence is not in the UK.

However, this does not apply to a trader using the special accounting scheme for electronic services. This is so whether the trader is registered in the UK (under Sch 3B) or in another EU member state (under equivalent legislation): see Sch 3B paras 19 (generally) and 22(6) (in relation to the repayment scheme for third country traders).

A person may voluntarily appoint a tax representative with the Commissioners' agreement if he meets first, second and fourth conditions.

A tax representative is entitled to act on his principal's behalf. He must ensure that the duties imposed on his principal are discharged—by himself if necessary. He is personally liable for any failure to carry out these duties, and for anything done while acting on his principal's behalf, and may be prosecuted for a contravention in this respect. He may otherwise be prosecuted for his principal's actions on the grounds of consent, connivance or neglect.

A tax representative is not liable to be registered, but his particulars are included in the VAT Register in accordance with regulations. His appointment and retirement are governed by regulations. See VAT Regulations 1995, SI 1995/2518 reg 10. For penalties, see s 69 (1).

A person may be required to provide security if he fails to appoint a tax representative when directed to do so. Payment of any sum required by way of security can be enforced by distress or diligence in accordance with FA 1997 ss 51, 52.

49. Transfers of going concerns (V2.226)

Where all or part of a taxable person's business is transferred as a going concern, the transferor's turnover is treated as the transferee's turnover in deciding whether the transferee is liable to registration. As regards transfers under a contract made before 1 September 2007 (see FA 2007 s 100(1)), the duty to preserve records continues to be assumed by the transferee unless the Commissioners direct otherwise. Directions are made at the transferor's request. As regards transfers under a contract made after 31 August 2007, the duty to retain records is retained by the transferor unless there is also a transfer of registration (see below).

Regulations provide for continuity in cases where: (1) all or part of a business carried on by one taxable person is transferred to another as a going concern; and (2) the transferee takes the place of the transferor as the registered person. See VAT Regulations 1995, SI 1995/2518 reg 6. As regards transfers under a contract made before 1 September 2007 (see FA 2007 s 100(1)), the duty to preserve records is assumed by the transferee unless the Commissioners direct otherwise. Directions are made at the transferor's request. As regards transfers under a contract made after 31 August 2007, this applies only if regulations so provide. For the regulations made, see VAT Regulations 1995, SI 1995/2518 reg 6(3)(*f*). However, if the duty to preserve records is retained by the transferor, the transferee may require the transferor to provide information, supply copies of documents and make the records available for inspection.

As regards transfers under a contract made after 31 August 2007 (see FA 2007 s 100(1)), the Commissioners may disclose information about the business to the transferee to enable him to comply with his statutory duties.

50. Terminal markets (V4.208)

The Treasury may by order vary VAT provisions as regards dealings and dealers on terminal markers. In particular the order may zero-rate or exempt supplies of goods or services, register a body of persons representing dealers, disregard dealings by dealers so represented, and refund input tax. See VAT (Terminal Markets) Order 1973, SI 1973/173.

50A. Margin schemes (V3.531–V3.536)

A person may opt to charge VAT by reference to the profit margin of a supply in accordance with VAT (Cars) Order 1992, SI 1992/3122 art 8 and VAT (Special Provisions) Order 1995, SI 1995/1268 arts 12, 13.

A profit margin is the amount (if any) by which the sale price exceeds the purchase price.

51. Buildings and land (V4.111–V4.115)

This section introduces Sch 10. The Treasury may amend Sch 10 by order. For the making of orders, see s 97 (4).

51A. Co-owners etc of buildings and land (V2.117)

[Repealed.]

51B. Face-value vouchers

This section introduces Sch 10A.

52. Trading stamp schemes (V3.116)

The value of a supply or acquisition of goods under a trading stamp scheme may be modified by regulations. No regulations are currently in force.

53. Tour operators (V3.519)

The Treasury may, by order, modify the application of VATA 1994 in relation to goods and services supplied by tour operators. For the order made, see VAT (Tour Operators) Order 1987, SI 1987/1806.

"Tour operator" includes a travel agent operating as a principal and any other person providing services of any kind commonly provided by tour operators or travel agents for the benefit of travellers. See *C & E Comrs v Madgett and Baldwin* (joined cases C-308/96 and C-94/97) [1998] STC 1169, ECJ; *Béheersmaatschappij Van Ginkel Waddinxveen BV v Inspecteur der Omzetbelasting, Utrecht* (case C-163/91) [1996] STC 825, ECJ; *Minerva Kulturreisen GmbH v Finanzamt Freital* (case C-31/10) [2010] ECR I–0000, [2011] STC 532, ECJ; *Aer Lingus plc v C & E Comrs* [1992] VATTR 438; *Virgin Atlantic Airways Ltd v C & E Comrs* [1993] VATTR 136. Wholesale travel services are outside the scheme: *Independent Coach Travel (Wholesaling) Ltd v C & E Comrs* [1993] VATTR 357; *Norman Allen Group Travel Ltd v C & E Comrs* [1996] V & DR 405. So are exempt supplies comprising teaching English as a foreign language; Business Brief 27/99, 21 December 1999. For exemption, see Sch 9 Group 6 item 1 and note 1(*f*).

For the treatment of travel agents' commission for transport only sales on behalf of tour operators from 1 May 1996, see Business Brief 2/96, 9 February 1996.

54. Farmers etc (V2.191)

A person carrying on one or more designated activities may be certified in accordance with regulations. For designated activities, see VAT (Flat-rate Scheme for Farmers) (Designated Activities) Order 1992, SI 1992/3220. For activities outside this description, see *Finanzamt Rendsburg v Harbs* (case C-321/02) [2004] ECR I–7101, [2004] STC 340, ECJ (leasing part of the farm land, cattle and milk quota); *Finanzamt Arnsberg v Stadt Sundern* (case C-43/04) [2005] ECR I–4491, ECJ (grant of hunting licences). A designated activity is referred to as "the relevant part" of the certified person's business if it comprises all or part of his business. For certification, see VAT Regulations 1995, SI 1995/2518 Part XXIV (regs 202–211).

Supplies made by a certified person in the course of carrying on a designated activity are disregarded for registration and deregistration purposes in accordance with regulations. See VAT Regulations 1995, SI 1995/2518 reg 203 (2).

A customer is entitled to input tax credit (taxable person) or repayment (EU or third country trader) in accordance with regulations if he purchases goods or services from a certified person. See VAT Regulations 1995, SI 1995/2518 reg 209. A proportion of the consideration for the supply made by the certified person is treated as VAT for these purposes. The proportion specified is 1/26th of the consideration: see VAT (Flat-rate Scheme for Farmers) (Percentage Addition) Order 1992, SI 1992/3221. This is sometimes referred to as "flat-rate addition".

A certified person is required to keep, preserve and produce records in accordance with regulations. See VAT Regulations 1995, SI 1995/2518 regs 210, 211.

For appeals regarding certification and cancellation of certification, see s 83(1)(*m*). For civil penalties regarding invoices issued by certified persons, see s 67.

55. Customers to account for tax on supplies of gold etc (V5.143)

A trader ("Y") is deemed to make a taxable supply in the course or furtherance of business for registration purposes if: (1) X makes a positive rate supply of gold to Y; and (2) Y receives the supply for business purposes (eg resale). Y's deemed supply is not disregarded for registration purposes if X has disposed of a capital asset in making his supply.

A taxable person ("Y") must account for and pay VAT on a supply if X (another taxable person) makes a supply of gold to Y. The time of supply rules are modified for the purposes of the supply. Section 6 (4)–(10) is disregarded. The time of supply is therefore determined under ss 6 (1)–(3), (11)–(15), 18 (4) and VAT Regulations 1995, SI 1995/2518 Part XI (regs 81–95).

A supply of gold for the foregoing purposes comprises any of the following:

- (a) any supply of fine gold, gold grain of any purity, or gold coins of any purity;
- (b) any supply of goods containing gold sold for a price equivalent to the open market value of the gold content;
- (c) applying a treatment or process to another person's goods which produces gold, gold grain or gold coins within (*a*) above.

This definition may be extended by Treasury order to supplies of goods and services in relation to goods containing precious or semi-precious metal or stones. No orders have been made.

55A. Customers to account for tax on supplies of goods or services of a kind used in missing trader intra-community fraud (V3.321, V3.233)

This section introduces a "reverse charge" mechanism in respect of goods or services of a description specified in an order made by the Treasury (referred to as "goods or services to which this section applies") supplied by X (the supplier) to Y (the recipient) under a taxable supply chargeable at a positive rate. One supply within this description is referred to as a "relevant supply". Other supplies within this description are referred to as "corresponding supplies". A supply is not a relevant supply or corresponding supply if it is of a description specified in, or determined in accordance with, an order made by the Treasury. Such a supply is referred to as an "excepted supply". For the goods and services to which this section applies, see VAT (Section 55A) (Specified Goods and Services and Excepted Supplies) Order 2010, SI 2010/2239 arts 4–6. For excepted supplies, see arts 7 and 8 of the 2010 Order.

To the extent that the aggregate value of the relevant supply and any corresponding supplies made to Y (the recipient) in a calendar month exceeds £1,000 (referred to as "the disregarded amount") and those supplies are received by Y in connection with a business carried on by him, the supplies are treated for registration purposes as supplies made by Y in the course or furtherance of business. The supplies are not disregarded for registration purposes on the grounds that they are capital assets of Y's business (cf Sch 1 para 1(7)). In determining whether the disregarded amount has been exceeded, value is determined on the basis that no VAT was chargeable on the supply made by X. It follows that value, for this purpose, is the consideration for the supplies concerned.

The supply made by X (the supplier) is unaffected by the foregoing provisions. Thus, the supply is both made by X and treated as being made by Y.

If X and Y are both taxable persons at the time when X makes a relevant supply or corresponding supply to Y, Y is required to account for the VAT chargeable on the supply on X's behalf. Legislation relevant to the enforcement of any obligation to account for and pay VAT (referred to as "relevant enforcement provisions") applies for this purpose. For guidance, see Notice No 735; Revenue and Customs Brief 35/10, 20 August 2010.

The Treasury may increase the disregarded amount by order. No order has been made to date.

The Treasury may amend any provision of VATA 1994 by order for the purposes of this section. For the order made, see VAT (Administration, Collection and Enforcement) Order 2007, SI 2007/1421. No order may be made after 21 March 2009.

This section has effect in relation to supplies made after 31 May 2007: see FA 2006 s 19(8); Finance Act 2006, section 19, (Appointed Day) Order 2007, SI 2007/1419 art 2.

56. Fuel for private use (V3.266)

Fuel purchased, imported, acquired or manufactured by a taxable person is deemed to be supplied by him if:

- it is put in the fuel tank of: (*a*) a vehicle allocated to an employee by reason of his employment, or (*b*) a vehicle used by an employee, sole proprietor or partner without being allocated to him. For "allocation", see s 56(3)(*d*). For periods when a vehicle is not regarded as being allocated by reason of employment, see s 56(9). For "use" in this context, see s 53(1) and (3)(*c*);
- the vehicle (and therefore the fuel) is used wholly or partly for private purposes; and
- the consideration (if any) payable for the fuel consumed privately by the employee, sole proprietor or partner is less than the cost of the fuel or the cost (including excise duty) of its manufacture.

The time of supply is the time when the fuel is put in the fuel tank. The consideration actually paid or payable by an individual for the supply is disregarded. Instead, VAT is charged by reference to a notional consideration for all supplies made to him in a prescribed accounting period in respect of the vehicle concerned. The notional consideration (often described as the "scale charge") is determined by reference to the table in s 57. The amount relevant to the description of the vehicle and the length of the prescribed accounting period is treated as a VAT-inclusive sum.

VAT on fuel for private use is treated as input tax although the fuel is not to be used for the purposes of the business. No apportionment is therefore necessary under s 24 (5). However, the scale charge can be avoided by apportioning input tax on the basis of records showing business and private mileage: see Notice No 700/64. The scale charge applies in the absence of records. For examples, see *Kimber* (No 10469); *Phillips* (No 12184); *Mower* (No 17210). The scale charge can also be avoided by not claiming input tax on *any* road fuel: see Notice No 48 (December 2010) para 3.1.

Incidental private use of pool vehicles which are kept overnight on the employer's premises does not result in a scale charge.

For "vehicles", see Press Notice 24/87, 25 March 1987.

57. Determination of consideration for fuel supplied for private use (V3.266)

The consideration for supplies of fuel for private use in respect of any one vehicle in a prescribed accounting period (see s 56) is determined by reference to the following table:

Vehicle's CO_2 emissions figure	*12-month period*	*3-month period*	*1-month period*

(grams per kilometre driven)	£	£	£
120 or less	630.00	157.00	52.00
125	945.00	236.00	78.00
130	1,010.00	252.00	84.00
135	1,070.00	268.00	89.00
140	1,135.00	283.00	94.00
145	1,200.00	299.00	99.00
150	1,260.00	315.00	105.00
155	1,325.00	331.00	110.00
160	1,385.00	346.00	115.00
165	1,450.00	362.00	120.00
170	1,515.00	378.00	126.00
175	1,575.00	394.00	131.00
180	1,640.00	409.00	136.00
185	1,705.00	425.00	141.00
190	1,765.00	441.00	147.00
195	1,830.00	457.00	152.00
200	1,890.00	472.00	157.00
205	1,955.00	488.00	162.00
210	2,020.00	504.00	168.00
215	2,080.00	520.00	173.00
220	2,145.00	536.00	178.00
225 or more	2,205.00	551.00	183.00

If the CO_2 emission figure of a vehicle is specified in an EC Certificate of conformity (see s 57(9)) or a UK approval certificate (see s 57(9)), the vehicle's CO2 emission figure is determined in accordance with Notes 2–5 of Table A. In other cases, the vehicle's CO2 emission figure is:

- 140 (cylinder capacity 1–1,400 cc).
- 175 (cylinder capacity 1,401–2,000 cc).
- 225 or more (cylinder capacity exceeds 2,000 cc).

The Treasury may substitute a different table by order. The above table was substituted by VAT (Consideration for Fuel Provided for Private Use) Order 2011, SI 2011/898. It applies to prescribed accounting periods beginning after 30 April 2011.

Where an individual changes vehicles within a period and the vehicles are of the same description then the scale charge applicable is that of one vehicle used throughout the period. Where the descriptions of the cars used in a period differ, only one scale charge is applicable and that charge is the sum of the fractions on a time basis of the appropriate scale charges for each vehicle.

PART IV ADMINISTRATION, COLLECTION AND ENFORCEMENT

General Administrative Provisions

58. General provisions relating to the administration and collection of VAT

This section introduces Sch 11.

58A. Disclosure of avoidance schemes (V5.213, V5.358)

This section introduces Sch 11A. Schedule 11A came into force on 22 July 2004 as regards the power to make orders and regulations: see FA 2004 s 19(2)(*a*). Subject to this, s 58A and Sch 11A came into force on 1 August 2004: see FA 2004 s 19(2)(*b*); FA 2004 s 19(1) and Sch 2, (Appointed Day) Order 2004, SI 2004/1934.

58B. Payment by cheque

Regulations made under FA 2007 s 95(1) may provide that a payment by cheque is treated as made when the cheque clears, rather than when the cheque is received by the Commissioners, if: (1) the payment relates to the VAT shown as due on a VAT return; and (2) the cheque is received after the due date. The regulations may define when a cheque is cleared for this purpose. For the regulations made, see VAT Regulations 1995, SI 1995/2518 reg 40.

59. The default surcharge (V5.371–V5.376)

A person is liable to default surcharge if he is in "default" in respect of a prescribed accounting period ending within a "surcharge period" specified in, or extended by, a "surcharge liability notice" and some or all of the VAT due on his return for that period is paid late. He is surcharged with 2% (first default), 5% (second default), 10% (third default) or 15% (subsequent default) of the VAT paid late, subject to a minimum of £30, according to the number of previous defaults involving late payment occurring during the surcharge period.

A person is in "default" if: (1) the Commissioners do not receive a return by the due date or receive a late payment for some or all of the VAT due on a return received in time; and (2) the person is not required to make payments on account in respect of the prescribed accounting period concerned. For late payments, see *Starlite (Chandeliers) Ltd v C & E Comrs* [1999] V & DR 313 (no default where Commissioners allowed extension of time to pay without stating that liability to surcharge would be governed by statutory due date rather than extended date). For the Commissioners' power to vary the due date for furnishing returns and paying tax, see VAT Regulations, SI 1995/2518 regs 25(1)(*c*), 40(3). For the requirement to make payments on account, see s 28. For defaults in periods where payments on account are required, see s 59A. A late return attracts service of a surcharge liability notice whether or not VAT is paid late, but attracts surcharge (if applicable) only if VAT is also paid late. Late payment attracts both service of a surcharge liability notice and surcharge (if applicable) whether or not the return is late. For excepted defaults, see below.

The Commissioners may serve a "surcharge liability notice" if a person is in default in respect of a prescribed accounting period. The notice specifies a "surcharge period". This begins on the date of the notice. It ends on the first anniversary of the last day of the prescribed accounting period for which he is in default. A surcharge period is extended by service of a further surcharge liability notice if the person is in default for a prescribed accounting period ending at or before the end of the surcharge period. See *DOW Chemical Co Ltd v C & E Comrs* [1996] V & DR 52. A trader is not liable to surcharge if he proves, on the balance of probabilities, that he did not receive the surcharge liability notice served by the Commissioners: *C & E Comrs v Medway Draughting & Technical Services Ltd* [1989] STC 346; *Eidographics Ltd v C & E Comrs* [1991] VATTR 449.

A trader is not liable to surcharge if he satisfies the Commissioners or, on appeal, a tribunal (see s 82), that his return or remittance was despatched in reasonable time and manner to arrive no later than the due date. For successful appeals, see *Nazeing Glass Works Ltd* (No 2773) (entry in post book); *Granville Furniture Ltd* (No 3013) (firm recollection of witness). For unsuccessful appeals, see *Zilani Clothing* (No 2704) (cheque dated before due date); *Holmes* (No 2939) (standing instruction to post envelope in due time). It is insufficient to post a return or remittance *on* the due date: *Kings Portable Buildings Ltd* (No 2781). For due dates on a Sunday, see *Halstead Motor Co v C & E Comrs* [1995] VATTR 201. For payment by credit transfer, see *Barney & Freeman v C & E Comrs* [1990] VATTR 19.

A trader is not liable to surcharge if he satisfies the Commissioners or, on appeal, a tribunal (see s 82), that he has a reasonable excuse for despatching his return or remittance late. For successful appeals, see for example: *CMS Peripherals Ltd v R & C Comrs* [2008] STC 985 (manuscript entry on VAT return); *Silk Interiors Ltd* (No 2722) (Commissioners sent return to incorrect address); *Computer Presentations Ltd* (No 3039) (return mislaid when moving office); *T & H Collard Ltd* (No 2654) (trader believed that time limit had been extended); *Harrison* (No 3078) (return withheld for inspection at impending control visit); *Midas Publishing Services Ltd* (No 3227) (envelope mislaid during accident while driving to post office); *Snow & Rock Sports Ltd* (No 3223) (change of stagger group); *Appleyard Lees & Co* (No 2928) (misunderstanding regarding due date); *Corton Bashforth Screenprint Ltd* (No 3232) (clerical error in writing cheque); *Starlite (Chandeliers) Ltd v C & E Comrs* [1999] V & DR 313 (unconditional extension of time to pay VAT); *Renlon Ltd* (No 16987) (reliance on Commissioners' practice not to assess surcharge when credit transfer made on due date).

Delays resulting from an unforeseeable event at a material time normally amount to a reasonable excuse: see, for example, *Manchester Scaffolding Ltd* (No 2855) (sudden resignation of staff); *Wordsworth Trade Press Ltd* (No 2630) (illness); *Concours Motor Co Ltd* (No 3267) (computer breakdown); *Collyer* (No 2628) (fire). Delays resulting from foreseeable events do not amount to a reasonable excuse: see for example, *F & P Appointments Ltd* (No 2747) (holiday closedown); *Boston Copying Machines* (No 2648) (key staff on holiday or business trip); *Reid* (No 2963) (complex accounting system); *Photographic Applications Ltd* (No 2749) (end of financial year); *Warren* (No 2736) (pressure of work). Thus, an unexpected event may be reasonable in relation to one period but not in relation to the next period: see *Bowen v C & E Comrs* [1987] VATTR 255. Insufficiency of funds is not a reasonable excuse: see s 71 (1).

For the EU principle of proportionality, see *Bower v C & E Comrs* [1995] V & DR 294.

A surcharge liability notice is deemed not to have been served if, in relation to a default on which it depended, the trader satisfies the Commissioners that he despatched the return or remittance in reasonable time and manner to arrive no later than the due date or that he had a reasonable excuse for not doing so. In these circumstances, no surcharge arises in respect of the first default occurring within the surcharge period set out in the surcharge liability notice.

Where a penalty is imposed under s 69 for failing to comply with orders, rules and regulations, no default surcharge is payable.

For transitional provisions see Sch 13 para 14. For computer errors giving rise to assessments applying an incorrect rate of surcharge, see *Sullivan v C & E Comrs* [1995] V & DR 85; Information Sheet No 7/95, 10 April 1995. For the invalidity of assessments applying the incorrect rate, see *DOW Chemical Co Ltd v C & E Comrs* [1996] V & DR 52.

No deduction is allowed for income tax or corporation tax purposes in respect of a surcharge under this section: see ITTOIA 2005 ss 54, 272, 869; Corporation Tax Act 2009 s 1303.

59A. Default surcharge: payments on account (V5.371–V5.376)

A person required to make payments on account for a prescribed accounting period (see s 28) is in default if, on or before the due date, the Commissioners have not received:

(a) all or part of a payment on account due for the period; or
(b) a return for the period or (if the return has been received by the due date) all or part of the VAT shown thereon as payable.

The Commissioners may serve a "surcharge liability notice" if a person is in default for a prescribed accounting period. The notice must specify a "surcharge period". This begins on the date of the notice and ends on the first anniversary of the last day of the prescribed accounting period to which the default relates. If a default occurs in respect of a prescribed accounting period ending at or before the end of a surcharge period, the period is extended by service of another notice. The existing surcharge period and its extension are regarded as a single surcharge period.

A person is liable to default surcharge in respect of a prescribed accounting period if he is in default in respect of a prescribed accounting period ending within a surcharge period specified in, or extended by, a surcharge liability notice and the "aggregate value of his defaults" is more than nil. Default surcharge is an amount equal to 2%, 5%, 10% or 15% of the "aggregate value of his defaults" for the prescribed accounting period concerned (according to whether this is the first, second, third or later default in the surcharge period), subject to a minimum surcharge of £30.

The aggregate value of defaults for a prescribed accounting period is the aggregate of: (1) (as regards each payment on account giving rise to a default) the amount of the payment, or that part of it, which is received late; and (2) (as regards VAT paid after the due date for making the return) the amount received late in so far as it does not relate to payments on account.

A person is not liable to default surcharge if he satisfies the Commissioners or, on appeal, a tribunal (see s 82) that: (1) the time and method of despatch were such that it was reasonable to suppose that the payment or return concerned would be received by the Commissioners on or before the due date; or (2) there is a reasonable excuse (see s 70) for the payment or return not having been so despatched. The person is treated as if he were not in default for the prescribed accounting period concerned so that any surcharge liability notice served as a result of it is deemed not to have been served.

A default is left out of account if: (1) the default gives rise to a penalty under s 69 for a breach of regulations; or (2) the prescribed accounting period is specified in a direction made by the Commissioners.

A payment received on or before the due date is deemed to be received late if something remains to be done after the due date so as to enable the whole amount of the payment to become available to the Commissioners, eg where a post-dated cheque must be banked after the due date.

59B. Relationship between sections 59 and 59A (V5.371–V5.376)

A default occurs within a surcharge period for the purposes of ss 59 and 59A if the relevant surcharge liability notice was served under either section. However, the following questions are determined in accordance with the section under which the notice was served: (1) whether a surcharge period was begun or extended by the notice; and (2) whether the person was in default for an earlier prescribed period, if the previous default arose under the same section as the notice and the current default arose under the other section. If a surcharge liability notice was served under s 59A and the current default arises under s 59, an earlier default for the purposes of s 59 includes a default for a prescribed accounting period for which he was liable to make payments on account if the aggregate value of his defaults for that period exceeded nil.

60. VAT evasion: conduct involving dishonesty (V5.341)

This section was repealed by FA 2007 Sch 24 para 29(*d*) in accordance with the Finance Act 2007, Schedule 24 (Commencement and Transitional Provisions) Order 2008, SI 2008/568, art 2. For savings, see:

- art 4 of the 2008 Order (this section continues to have effect in relation to conduct involving dishonesty which does not relate to an inaccuracy in a document or a failure to notify HMRC of an under-assessment);
- the Finance Act 2008, Schedule 41 (Appointed Day and Transitional Provisions) Order 2009, SI 2009/511, art 4 (this section repealed in so far as it relates to conduct involving dishonesty giving rise to a penalty under FA 2008 Sch 41). Penalties under FA 2008 Sch 41 have effect in relation to relevant obligations arising after 31 March 2010 and to any unauthorised issue of an invoice taking place after that date: see art 3(*a*), (*b*) of the 2009 Order;
- the Finance Act 2008, Schedule 40 (Appointed Day, Transitional Provisions and Consequential Amendments) Order 2009, SI 2009/571, art 7 (this section continues to have effect in relation to conduct involving dishonesty unrelated to an inaccuracy in a document or a failure to notify HMRC of an under-assessment).

No deduction is allowed for income tax or corporation tax purposes in respect of penalties under this section: see ITTOIA 2005 ss 54, 272, 869; Corporation Tax Act 2009 s 1303.

61. VAT evasion: liability of directors etc (V5.341)

This section was repealed by FA 2007 Sch 24 para 29(*d*) in accordance with the Finance Act 2007, Schedule 24 (Commencement and Transitional Provisions) Order 2008, SI 2008/568, art 2. For savings, see:

- art 4 of the 2008 Order (this section continues to have effect in relation to conduct involving dishonesty which does not relate to an inaccuracy in a document or a failure to notify HMRC of an under-assessment);
- the Finance Act 2008, Schedule 41 (Appointed Day and Transitional Provisions) Order 2009, SI 2009/511, art 4 (this section repealed in so far as it relates to conduct involving dishonesty giving rise to a penalty under FA 2008 Sch 41). Penalties under FA 2008 Sch 41 have effect in relation to relevant obligations arising after 31 March 2010 and to any unauthorised issue of an invoice taking place after that date: see art 3(*a*), (*b*) of the 2009 Order;
- the Finance Act 2008, Schedule 40 (Appointed Day, Transitional Provisions and Consequential Amendments) Order 2009, SI 2009/571, art 7 (this section continues to have effect in relation to conduct involving dishonesty unrelated to an inaccuracy in a document or a failure to notify HMRC of an under-assessment).

62. Incorrect certificates as to zero-rating etc (V5.342)

A customer is liable to a penalty if he gives an incorrect certificate that:

(a) goods or services are wholly or partly chargeable at the lower rate under (see Sch 7A Group 6 Note 8);

(b) a building is intended to be used solely for a relevant residential purpose or relevant charitable purpose (see Sch 8 Group 5 Note 12(*b*) as applied by Sch 8 Group 6 Note 3 and Sch 9 Group 1 Note 3);

(c) goods will be placed in a fiscal warehousing regime (see s 18B(2)(*d*); or

(d) specified services have been performed (see s 18C(1)(*c*)).

The prescribed penalty is an amount equal to the tax under-charged, or not charged, on the supply. No liability to a penalty arises if either: (1) the recipient satisfies the Commissioners or, on appeal, the tribunal (see s 82). that he has a reasonable excuse for his conduct; or (2) he has been convicted of an offence in respect of it.

No deduction is allowed for income tax or corporation tax purposes in respect of penalties under this section: see ITTOIA 2005 ss 54, 272, 869; Corporation Tax Act 2009 s 1303.

63. Penalty for misdeclaration or neglect resulting in VAT loss for one accounting period equalling or exceeding certain amounts

[Repealed.]

64. Repeated misdeclarations

[Repealed.]

65. Inaccuracies in EU sales statements or in statements relating to section 55A (V5.346)

The Commissioners give a written warning if a material inaccuracy is discovered in an EU sales statement. If another material inaccuracy is discovered on a statement due before the second anniversary of the warning, the Commissioners give a written notice stating that future inaccuracies will attract a penalty. If another material inaccuracy arises on a statement due before the second anniversary of the notice, or the second anniversary of a previous statement which attracted a penalty, the trader concerned is liable to a penalty of £100.

An EU sales statement contains a material inaccuracy if the inclusion or omission of any information is misleading in any material respect. An inaccuracy is not regarded as material if: (1) the Commissioners or, on appeal, a tribunal (see s 82), are satisfied that there is a reasonable excuse for the inaccuracy; (2) full information regarding the inaccuracy is furnished when the trader's tax affairs are not under enquiry; or (3) the trader has been convicted of an offence in respect of it (eg under Statistics of Trade Act 1947 s 4 (3)).

A warning or notice is deemed not to have been issued if the inaccuracy is not regarded as material.

For the requirement to submit EU sales statements, see Sch 11 para 2.

As regards supplies made after 31 May 2007, this section applies in a like manner to material inaccuracies in reverse charge sales statements submitted by customers who are liable to account for VAT on the supplier's behalf. For the reverse charge, see s 55A(6). For reverse charge sales statements, see VAT Regulations 1995, SI 1995/2518, regs 23A–23C.

No deduction is allowed for income tax or corporation tax purposes in respect of penalties under this section: see ITTOIA 2005 ss 54, 272, 869; Corporation Tax Act 2009 s 1303.

66. Failure to submit EU sales statement or statement relating to section 55A (V5.355)

A trader is regarded as being in default if the Commissioners do not receive his EU sales statement by the due date. The Commissioners may service a notice on a trader in default. The notice gives information regarding the penalty regime and continues in force until the later of: (1) the first anniversary of service; and (2) expiration of a 12 month period in which no defaults have occurred.

A trader is not liable to a penalty if he remedies the default within 14 days after the notice is served. However, he is liable to a penalty for future defaults without further warning until the notice expires. The prescribed penalty is £5 (first default), £10 (second default) or £15 (subsequent default) for each day the default continues, subject to a maximum of £500, £1,000 or £1,500 respectively and a minimum of £50 in each case.

A trader is liable to a penalty if he fails to remedy the default within 14 days of service. The prescribed penalty is £5 for each day the default continues after the 14th day, subject to a maximum of £500 and a minimum of £50. He is liable to a penalty for future defaults without further warning until the notice expires. The prescribed penalty is £10 (next default) or £15 (subsequent default) for each day the default continues, subject to a maximum of £1,000 or £1,500 respectively and a minimum of £50 in each case.

A trader is not regarded as being in default if he satisfies the Commissioners or, on appeal, a tribunal (see s 82), that: (1) he submitted the statement in such time and manner that it was reasonable to suppose that it would be received by the due date; or (2) he has a reasonable excuse for not despatching the statement. For reasonable excuse, see s 71 (1). A trader is not liable to a penalty in these circumstances and any notice served in respect of the failure has no effect.

The daily penalties of £5, £10 and £15, and the minimum penalty of £50, may be varied by Treasury order. No orders have been made to date.

For the requirement to submit EU sales statements, see Sch 11 para 2.

As regards supplies made after 31 May 2007, this section applies in a like manner to the failure to submit a reverse charge sales statements by a customer liable to account for VAT on the supplier's behalf. For the reverse charge, see s 55A(6). For reverse charge sales statements, see VAT Regulations 1995, SI 1995/2518, reg 23C.

No deduction is allowed for income tax or corporation tax purposes in respect of penalties under this section: see ITTOIA 2005 ss 54, 272, 869; Corporation Tax Act 2009 s 1303.

67. Failures to notify and unauthorised issue of invoices (V5.347–V5.350)

This section is repealed from 1 April 2010: see FA 2008 s 123(2) and Sch 41 para 25(*f*); the Finance Act 2008, Schedule 41 (Appointed Day and Transitional Provisions) Order 2009, SI

2009/511, art 2. The repeal applies to obligations arising after 31 March 2010 and to invoices issued after that date: see art 3(*a*) and (*b*) of the 2009 Order. As regards the failure to notify an acquisition (see s 67(1)(*b*)), this section is repealed only in so far as it relates to conduct involving dishonesty which gives rise to a penalty under FA 2008 Sch 41: see art 4 of the 2009 Order. For corresponding penalties from 1 April 2010, see FA 2008 Sch 41 paras 1, 2. No deduction is allowed for income tax or corporation tax purposes in respect of penalties under this section: see ITTOIA 2005 ss 54, 272, 869; Corporation Tax Act 2009 s 1303.

67A. Breaches of controlled goods agreement
This section is inserted by Tribunals, Courts and Enforcement Act 2007 Sch 11 para 119 from a day to be appointed by order made under s 148(5) and repealed by FA 2008 Sch 43 para 4 from a day to be appointed by order made under s 129(4). No orders have been made to date.

No deduction is allowed for income tax or corporation tax purposes in respect of penalties under this section: see ITTOIA 2005 ss 54, 272, 869; Corporation Tax Act 2009 s 1303.

68. Breaches of walking possession agreements (V5.351)
Where a person has not paid an amount of VAT which is due and has had his goods and chattels distrained upon by a bailiff, the person may enter into a walking possession agreement whereby the sale of the goods and chattels is delayed and they remain in the custody of the person. The person must, however, acknowledge that the property specified in the agreement is under distraint and, except with the consent of the Commissioners who may impose conditions, the person is not allowed to remove the goods from the premises. For distraint, see FA 1997 s 51.

Infringement of the walking possession conditions render a person liable to a penalty of 50% of the tax due but no penalty is due if there is a reasonable excuse for the conduct. This section does not apply in Scotland.

This section is amended by TCEA 2007 Sch 13 para 120 from a day to be appointed under s 148(5). No order has been made to date. This section will cease to apply in England and Wales from the appointed day.

No deduction is allowed for income tax or corporation tax purposes in respect of penalties under this section: see ITTOIA 2005 ss 54, 272, 869; Corporation Tax Act 2009 s 1303.

69. Breaches of regulatory provisions (V5.352, V5.354)

A person is liable to a penalty if:

- he fails to notify matters affecting his continued liability or entitlement to registration;
- he fails to notify his appointment or retirement as a VAT representative;
- he fails to notify the Commissioners of the first occasion on which he makes a supply of goods in respect of which the customer, rather than himself, is required to account for and pay the VAT chargeable thereon. This provision applies to supplies made after 31 May 2007: see FA 2006 s 19(8); Finance Act 2006, section 19, (Appointed Day) Order 2007, SI 2007/1419 art 2. For the requirement to account, see s 55A(6). For the requirement to notify, see VAT Regulations 1995, SI 1995/2518 reg 23B;
- he fails to keep records, furnish information or produce documents (but see s 69A where the failure relates to gold transactions);
- he fails to comply with any orders, regulations or rules made under VATA 1994;
- he fails to comply with regulations relating to VAT made under the European Communities Act 1972; or
- he fails to comply with conditions attached to his authorisation as a fiscal warehousekeeper.

The prescribed penalty is £5, £10 or £15 for each day the failure continues according to whether this is the first, second or later failure within a two year period. The maximum penalty is £500, £1,000 or £1,500 respectively, and the minimum penalty is £50.

As regards a failure to produce documents in head (*c*), a penalty notice must properly and accurately specify the respect(s) in which the Commissioners say that a penalty has been incurred: *University Court of the University of Glasgow* (No 17744) (failure to specify which documents had not been produced).

A person is liable to a penalty if he fails to preserve records. The prescribed penalty is £500.

This section also allows the Commissioners to calculate manually a penalty for failure to furnish returns or pay tax. Where a failure to comply with the regulations consists of not rendering returns or not paying the VAT due on time then the following penalties may apply.

On the first occasion the penalty is the greater of £10 and 1/6 of 1% of the VAT due for each day of failure to comply. On the second occasion, within two years of the first, the penalty is the greater of £20 and 1/3 of 1% of the VAT due per day. On a third or subsequent occasion within two years of the first the penalty is the greater of £30 and 1/2 of 1% of the VAT due per day. The VAT due is taken as that declared on a VAT return for the period in question or the amount assessed by the Commissioners.

No penalty may be levied under this section where the Commissioners or a tribunal (see s 82) are satisfied that there is a reasonable excuse (see s 71) for the conduct or where the conduct has led to a conviction for an offence, to assessment of a penalty under ss 60, 63 or FA 2007 Sch 24 or assessment of default surcharge under s 59 or 59A.

A person is not liable to a penalty if:

- he satisfies the Commissioners or (on appeal) a tribunal (see s 82) that there is a reasonable excuse for the failure;
- he is assessed to a penalty for dishonest conduct (see s 60), misdeclaration (see s 63) or deliberate inaccuracy (see FA 2007 Sch 24) in respect of the failure;
- he is assessed to default surcharge (see ss 59, 59A) in respect of the failure; or
- he is convicted of an offence in respect of the failure.

The Treasury may increase the penalty due under this section by order. No orders have been made to date.

No deduction is allowed for income tax or corporation tax purposes in respect of penalties under this section: see ITTOIA 2005 ss 54, 272, 869; Corporation Tax Act 2009 s 1303.

69A. Breach of record-keeping requirements etc in relation to transactions in gold

A person is liable to a penalty under this section (and not s 69) if he fails to keep records or furnish information regarding gold transactions in accordance with VAT Regulations 1995, SI 1995/2518 regs 31A and 31B. The penalty may not exceed 17.5% of the value of the transactions concerned. This value is determined by the Commissioners. It must be notified to the person concerned.

Once the Commissioners have sufficient evidence of both the failure and the value of the transactions concerned, they must assess the penalty within two years.

A person is not liable to a penalty if:

- he satisfies the Commissioners or (on appeal) a tribunal (see s 82) that there is a reasonable excuse for the failure;
- he is assessed to a penalty for dishonest conduct (see s 60) or deliberate inaccuracy (see FA 2007 Sch 24) in respect of the failure; or
- he is convicted of an offence in respect of the failure.

No deduction is allowed for income tax or corporation tax purposes in respect of penalties under this section: see ITTOIA 2005 ss 54, 272, 869; Corporation Tax Act 2009 s 1303.

69B. Breach of record-keeping requirements imposed by directions

A person is liable to a penalty if he fails to keep records specified in a direction made under Sch 11 para 6A(1). The prescribed penalty is £200 for each day of default (maximum £6,000).

A person is liable to a penalty if he fails to preserve records specified in a direction made under Sch 11 para 6A(1) in accordance with a requirement imposed under Sch 11 para 6A(6). The prescribed penalty is £500.

The monetary value of the foregoing penalties may be varied by Treasury order.

No liability to either penalty arises if:

- the person concerned satisfies the Commissioners or (on appeal) a tribunal (see s 82) that there is a reasonable excuse for the failure;
- he is assessed to a penalty for dishonest conduct (see s 60 (repealed)) or deliberate inaccuracy (see FA 2007 Sch 24) in respect of the failure; or
- he is convicted of an offence in respect of the failure.

This section was inserted by FA 2006 s 21 with effect from 19 July 2006.

No deduction is allowed for income tax or corporation tax purposes in respect of penalties under this section: see ITTOIA 2005 ss 54, 272, 869; Corporation Tax Act 2009 s 1303.

70. Mitigation of penalties under sections 60, 63, 64 and 67 (V5.334)

A penalty under ss 60 (repealed), 62, 63 (repealed), 64 (repealed), 67 (repealed), 69A or Sch 11A para 10 may be reduced to such amount (including nil) as the Commissioners or, on appeal, a tribunal (see s 82), think proper. No account may be taken of inability to pay, absence of any loss to the revenue or exercise of good faith in reaching a decision. For the tribunal's approach, see *Jordan v C & E Comrs* [1994] VATTR 286 at 289, *Cohen v C & E Comrs* [1994] VATTR 290 at 294, 295 (late registration); *James Ashworth Waterfoot (Successors) Ltd v C & E Comrs* [1996] V & DR 66, *Smith & Byford Ltd v C & E Comrs* [1996] V & DR 386 (dishonest conduct). A reduction allowed by the Commissioners may be restored on appeal. For an example, see *Tanner* (No 15691).

71. Construction of sections 59 to 70 (V5.335)

A trader does not have a reasonable excuse merely because he has insufficient funds to pay the VAT due. See *Palco Industry Co Ltd v C & E Comrs* [1990] STC 594 (cheque dishonoured); *Gemini Publications Ltd* (No 2537) and *London Bridge Cycles* (No 2550) (post-dated cheques); *Artful Dodger (Kilmarnock) Ltd v Lord Advocate* [1993] STC 300 (repayment due to another person). However, the underlying cause of the insufficiency may give rise to reasonable excuse: see *C & E Comrs v Salevon Ltd* [1989] STC 907; *C & E Comrs v Steptoe* [1992] STC 757, CA; *Dollar Land (Feltham) Ltd v C & E Comrs* [1995] STC 414; *T E Davey Photo Service Ltd v C & E Comrs* [1997] STC 889n.

A trader does not have a reasonable excuse merely because he relied upon another person to perform a task or because the person was dilatory or inaccurate in performing the task. However, the reason for the dilatoriness or inaccuracy may give rise to reasonable excuse: see *Frank Galliers Ltd v C & E Comrs* [1993] STC 284. An employee is "another person": *Profile Security Services Ltd v C & E Comrs* [1996] STC 808. For ill health etc of a person relied on, see *Bowen v C & E Comrs* [1987] VATTR 255. For advice and opinions from third parties, see *C & E Comrs v Harris* [1989] STC 907; *Taylor and Beech (a firm)* (No 2337); *Noble* (No 2410); *Butler* (No 3067).

72. Offences (V5.311–V5.316)

The following conduct amounts to an offence:

	Penalty		
Conduct	*Summary conviction*	*Conviction on indictment*	*Authority*
1. Being knowingly concerned in the fraudulent evasion of VAT	(1) Fine of the greater of statutory maximum or three times the VAT, (2) six months' imprisonment, or (3) both	(1) Unlimited fine, (2) seven years' imprisonment, or (3) both	Para (1)

2. Taking steps with a view to the fraudulent evasion of VAT	(1) Fine of the greater of statutory maximum or three times the VAT, (2) six months' imprisonment, or (3) both	(1) Unlimited fine, (2) seven years' imprisonment, or (3) both	Para (1)
3. Producing, furnishing, sending or making use of any document which is false in a material particular with intent to deceive	(1) Fine of statutory maximum or VAT geared amount, (2) six months' imprisonment, or (3) both	(1) Unlimited fine, (2) seven years' imprisonment, or (3) both	Para (3)(*a*)
4. Furnishing any information which the person knows to be false in a material particular	(1) Fine of statutory maximum or VAT geared amount, (2) six months' imprisonment, or (3) both	(1) Unlimited fine, (2) seven years' imprisonment, or (3) both	Para (3)(*b*)
5. Making any statement which the person knows to be false in a material particular	(1) Fine of statutory maximum or VAT geared amount, (2) six months' imprisonment, or (3) both	(1) Unlimited fine, (2) seven years' imprisonment, or (3) both	Para (3)(*b*)
6. Recklessly making a statement which is false in a material particular	(1) Fine of statutory maximum or VAT geared amount, (2) six months' imprisonment, or (3) both	(1) Unlimited fine, (2) seven years' imprisonment, or (3) both	Para (3)(*b*)
7. Conduct which must have involved the commission of one or more of the foregoing offences	(1) Fine of the greater of statutory maximum or three times the VAT, (2) six months' imprisonment, or (3) both	(1) Unlimited fine, (2) seven years' imprisonment, or (3) both	Para (8)
8. Acquiring possession of VAT-evaded goods	Greater of (1) fine of level 5 on the standard scale, and (2) fine of three times the VAT		Para (10)
9. Dealing with VAT-evaded goods	Greater of (1) fine of level 5 on the standard scale, and (2) fine of three times the VAT		Para (10)
10. Accepting the supply of VAT-evaded services	Greater of (1) fine of level 5 on the standard scale, and (2) fine of three times the VAT		Para (10)
11. Receiving or supplying goods or services without providing security	Fine of level 5 on the standard scale		Para (11)

For the "statutory maximum" and levels on the "standard scale", see the commentary to CEMA 1979 s 171.

For "evasion" (heads 1 and 2), see *R v Dealy* [1995] STC 217, CA. For examples, see *R v Collier* [1997] SWTI 474, CA; *R v Hashash* [2008] STC 1158, CA. For conduct which must have involved the commission of an offence (head 7), see *R v McCarthy* [1981] STC 298, CA; *R v Asif* [1985] STI 317, CA; *R v Howard* [1990] STI 351, CA; *R v Ike* [1996] STC 391, CA; *R v Choudhury* [1996] STC 1163, CA.

For supplying goods or services without providing security (head 11), see *Chaudhry v C & E Comrs* [2008] STC 2357.

For cheating the public revenue, see *R v Mavji* [1986] STC 508, CA; *R v Redford* [1988] STC 845, CA; *R v Fisher* [1989] STI 269, CA; *R v Matthews* [2008] STC 1999, CA.

CEMA 1979 ss 145–155 apply to offences and penalties under this section. However, they do not apply to penalties under ss 60–70. For the circumstances in which the Commissioners prosecute rather than assess a penalty under s 60, see Notice No 700 (April 2002) para 27.4.3.

For confiscation proceedings under the Criminal Justice Act 1988, see *R v May* [2008] STC 852, HL; *R v Sangha* [2009] STC 570, CA; *Revenue and Customs Prosecutions Office v Pigott (Lamb, interested party)* [2010] STC 1190, CA. For confiscation proceedings under the Proceeds of Crime Act 2002, see *Revenue and Customs Prosecutions Office v Allad* [2009] STC 1568, CA; *Revenue and Customs Prosecutions Office v May* and others [2010] STC 1506, CA.

For the privilege against self-incrimination, see *R v K* [2009] STC 2553, CA.

Assessments of VAT and Other Payments Due

73. Failure to make returns etc (V5.131–V5.140)

Circumstances in which an assessment can be made

1. Failure to make returns, etc (s 73(1)). The Commissioners may assess a person if he fails to make returns, fails to keep documents and facilitate the verification of returns, or makes incomplete or incorrect returns. The assessment must be made to the Commissioners' best judgement. The VAT due must be notified to the person concerned. A person fails to keep documents if, for whatever reason, the documents are unavailable for inspection: see *Dafydd* (No 17652). A person fails to facilitate verification if he fails to maintain and present his records in a form that enables the accuracy of his VAT returns to be checked without undue effort: see *Dafydd* (No 17652).

2. Repayments, refunds and VAT credits (s 73(2), (3)). The Commissioners may assess the amount of a repayment, refund or VAT credit which has been paid or credited by mistake, without knowing the facts or in circumstances which later change. A VAT credit may be assessed, despite the cancellation of a person's registration, if the registration was cancelled on the grounds that he was neither liable nor entitled to registration at the time when he was registered. The amount is assessed for the prescribed accounting period to which the payment, repayment or refund relates. For the period concerned, see *C & E Comrs v Laura Ashley Ltd* [2004] STC 635; Business Brief 25/04, 14 September 2004. For the Commissioners' right to assess, see *Farm Facilities (Fork Lift) Ltd v C & E Comrs* [1987] VATTR 80; D J S Properties (No 12159). For the amount of an assessment, see *International Language Centres Ltd v C & E Comrs* [1982] VATTR 172; *Potter (a firm) v C & E Comrs* [1983] VATTR 108. For the assessment of statutory bodies in respect of refunds under s 33, see *West Devon Borough Council v C & E Comrs* [2001] STC 1282. For the Commissioners' right to sue without issuing an assessment, see *C & E Comrs v International Language Centres Ltd* [1986] STC 279.

3. Failure to account for goods (s 73(7)). A taxable person may be required to account for goods purchased, acquired or imported for his business. Failure to show that the goods are in stock or have been sold, removed abroad, lost or destroyed may lead the Commissioners to assess the amount of tax which would have been chargeable on those goods if they had been supplied.

4. Fiscal warehousekeepers (s 73(7A)). The Commissioners may assess a fiscal warehouse-keeper who fails to pay VAT on missing or deficient goods. The amount of VAT due must be assessed to the Commissioners' best judgment and notified to the fiscal warehousekeeper.

5. Goods withdrawn from warehouse (s 73(7B)). The Commissioners may assess the VAT due on goods removed from a warehouse or fiscal warehouse without payment of VAT. The amount of VAT due must be assessed to the Commissioners' best judgment and notified to the person liable for payment (eg the person removing the goods).

Making an assessment

There is a distinction between: (*a*) the decision to make an assessment; (*b*) making the assessment; and (*c*) notification of the assessment: *Don Pasquale (a firm) v C & E Comrs* [1990] STC 556 at 562, CA. However, the legislation neither draws a distinction between stages (*a*) and (*b*), nor needs to do so. Whether an assessment has been made is resolved objectively by reference to what has been done. If, on an objective analysis, the officer has made an assessment, there is no room for any further enquiry whether he decided to do what he did. Conversely, if the officer's actions did not amount to the making of an assessment, his state of mind is irrelevant: *Courts plc v C & E Comrs* [2005] STC 27, CA. For the difficulties that have arisen in determining when the tax has been assessed as opposed to notified, see for example *Babber v C & E Comrs* [1991] VATTR 268; *Harris* (No 11925); *Classicmoor Ltd v C & E Comrs* [1995] V & DR 1; *Pang and Kong* (No 17361); *Dashmore Clothing Ltd* (No 17776). For the Commissioners' practice, see Notice No 915. For assessments made in time but notified out of time, see *Mohammed* (No 10246).

The process for making an assessment is an internal matter for the Commissioners. Their processes and procedures should, as far as possible, be standardised. The steps followed in relation to a particular assessment, and the dates on which the various steps were taken, should be readily verifiable by contemporary documentary evidence: *Courts plc v C & E Comrs* [2005] STC 27, CA.

The date when an assessment is made is a matter of fact. An assessment is normally made when form VAT 641 has been signed off: *Courts plc v C & E Comrs* [2005] STC 27, CA. A letter may be sent to a trader prior to an assessment being made so as to enable him to query the preliminary calculations: Business Brief 5/96, 29 March 1996.

An assessment determines the net amount of VAT due from the trader in respect of a transaction or series of transactions. The Commissioners must supplement an assessment with a notification of reasons setting out the basis on which the assessment is made. This duty is grounded in public law, not statute. It is discharged by providing estimates of the output tax and input tax on which the assessment is based. The reasons for making the assessment do not form part of the assessment. The Commissioners may subsequently substitute different grounds to support the net amount (or a reduced net amount) of VAT assessed: *BUPA Purchasing Ltd and others v C & E Comrs (No 2)* [2008] STC 101, CA.

For the Commissioners' practice regarding the making and notification of assessments, see Notice No 915. For incorrect advice given by the Commissioners, see Revenue and Customs Brief 15/09, 30 March 2009. For VAT undercharged to customers on the basis of a misunderstanding, see Notice No 48 (December 2010) para 3.4. For supplies zero-rated on the basis of an incorrect declaration by the customer, see Notice No 48 (December 2010) para 3.11. For underpayments arising from a change to the legislation, see Business Brief 14/94, 6 July 1994. For underpayments arising from misunderstanding the proper tax treatment of hairdressing chair rentals, see Business Brief 22/97, 10 October 1997.

For assessments in respect of a backdated registration, see *Bjellica v C & E Comrs* [1995] STC 329, CA.

Global, protective and alternative assessments

The Commissioners may validly make a "global" assessment for two or more prescribed accounting periods: *S J Grange Ltd v C & E Comrs* [1979] STC 183, CA. They may do so whether or not separate assessments could be made for each prescribed accounting period concerned: *House v C & E Comrs* [1996] STC 154, CA. A trader is entitled to be informed in reasonably clear terms of the effect of an assessment: *International Language Centres Ltd v C & E Comrs* [1983] STC 394 at 398; *House v C & E Comrs* [1996] STC 154, CA. For a number of documents sent at the same time held to be a proper and adequate notification of the basis on which he was assessed, see *House v C & E Comrs* [1996] STC 154, CA. It is a question of fact whether there has been one global assessment or a number of assessments notified together and previous decisions are not binding: *C & E Comrs v Le Rififi Ltd* [1995] STC 103, CA. For documents treated as a global assessment, see *Don Pasquale (a firm) v C & E Comrs* [1990] STC 556; *House v C & E Comrs* [1996] STC 154, CA. For documents which have not, see *C & E Comrs v Le Rififi Ltd* [1995] STC 103, CA; *Georgalakis Partnership* (No 10083); *Strollmoor Ltd* (No 12765).

A "protective assessment" (ie an assessment made to protect the Commissioners' position in the event of a subsequent appeal being decided in their favour) is an assessment. The "protective" nature of the assessment does not render it void or unenforceable on the grounds of uncertainty. The epithet "protective" is directed to the reason for making it, not its content: *Courts plc v C & E Comrs* [2005] STC 27, CA.

The Commissioners can validly make "alternative assessments" provided the trader is made aware (or otherwise understands) that: (*a*) one of the assessments is not additional to the other; and (*b*) the later assessment does not replace the earlier one: *University Court of the University of Glasgow* [2003] STC 495; *Courts plc v C & E Comrs* [2004] STC 690, on appeal [2005] STC 27; *Westone Wholesale Ltd v R & C Comrs* [2008] STC 828.

Underdeclarations and overpayments for the same accounting period may be assessed together and notified as one assessment. See *Strollmoor Ltd* (No 12765).

Where a previous assessment has been paid without a proper return being submitted, a subsequent assessment may be for a sum greater than the Commissioners would otherwise have considered appropriate.

A person acting in a representative capacity (personal representative trustee in bankruptcy, receiver or liquidator) who fails to make a return or makes an incomplete return may be assessed in respect of the tax due from the person he represents.

Best judgment

As regards an assessment under head (1) above, the Commissioners must assess the amount of VAT due "to the best of their judgment". The context is a situation in which the trader's records may be incomplete so that a fully informed assessment is likely to be impractical. The word "best" recognises that an element of guesswork may be necessary. The phrase indicates that the assessment must be made to the best of the Commissioners' judgment on the information available: *C & E Comrs v Pegasus Birds Ltd* [2004] STC 1509, CA.

The Commissioners should fairly consider all material placed before them and reach a decision on that material that is reasonable and not arbitary. As long as there is some material on which they can reasonably act, the Commissioners are not required to carry out investigations that may (or may not) result in further material being placed before them. It is perfectly proper for the Commissioners to apply the results of a limited test period to the whole period of assessment: *Van Boeckel v C & E Comrs* [1981] STC 290.

The Court of Appeal has issued the following guidance to tribunals. A tribunal's primary task is to find the correct amount of tax from the material properly available to it, the burden resting on the trader. The tribunal should not allow itself to be diverted into an attack on the way in which the Commissioners exercised their judgment at the time of the assessment. If their judgment is challenged, the grounds must be clearly and fully stated before the hearing begins. Cross examination of an officer should not be allowed unless an allegation of dishonesty or other wrongdoing by him has been unequivocally stated, and fully particularised, before the hearing and a written response made by the Commissioners. The hearing should normally proceed on the issue of amount. Any submission on a failure of best judgment is normally best dealt with at the end of the hearing, but there may be a few cases where this can be dealt with shortly as a preliminary issue: *C & E Comrs v Pegasus Birds Ltd* [2004] STC 1509, CA.

It is exceptional for an assessment to be upset by a failure to exercise best judgment. The important issue is normally the amount of the assessment: *Rahman v C & E Comrs* [1998] STC 826. Thus, it is rarely justified to reject an assessment altogether on the ground that the guidance in the *Van Boekel* case has not been followed: *Rahman (trading as Khayam Restaurant) v C & E Comrs* [1998] STC 826; *Rahman (trading as Khayam Restaurant) v C & E Comrs (No 2)* [2003] STC 150, CA.

A tribunal (see s 82) should not treat an assessment as invalid merely because it disagrees with the manner in which judgment has been exercised. A stronger finding is required, eg that the assessment has been reached "dishonestly, vindictively or capriciously", that is is a "spurious estimate or guess in which all elements of judgment are missing", or that it is "wholly unreasonable": *Rahman v C & E Comrs* [1998] STC 826.

There are many reasons why an assessment may be determined at a fraction of the amount actually assessed. The relevant question is whether the mistake is consistent with an honest and genuine attempt to make a reasoned assessment of the VAT payable, or whether it is of such a nature that compels the conclusion that no officer seeking to exercise best judgment could have made it. Alternatively, there may be no explanation, in which case the proper inference may be that the assessment was, indeed, arbitrary: *Rahman (trading as Khayam Restaurant) v C & E Comrs (No 2)* [2003] STC 150, CA.

For cases on "best judgment", see in particular *Rahman (trading as Khayam Restaurant) v C & E Comrs (No 2)* [2003] STC 150, CA; *C & E Comrs v Pegasus Birds Ltd* [2004] STC 1509, CA; *Van Boeckel v C & E Comrs* [1981] STC 290; *Spillane v C & E Comrs* [1990] STC 212; *Georgiou v C & E Comrs* [1995] STC 1101 at 1116 as qualified on appeal [1996] STC 463 at 475, 476, CA; *Rahman v C & E Comrs* [1998] STC 826; *Murat v C & E Comrs* [1998] STC 923; *Ahmed v C & E Comrs* [1999] STC 468; *McNicholas Construction Co Ltd v C & E Comrs* [2000] STC 553; *Henderson (trading as Tony's Fish and Chip Shop) v C & E Comrs* [2001] STC 47; *Hossain v C & E Comrs* [2004] STC 1572. In the Upper Tribunal, see *Mithras (Wine Bars) Ltd v R & C Comrs* [2010] UKUT 115 (TCC), [2010] STC 1370. In the VAT and Duties Tribunals, see *Barber v C & E Comrs* [1992] VATTR 144; *Gauntlett v C & E Comrs* [1996] V & DR 138 at 143; *W H Smith Ltd v C & E Comrs* [2000] V & DR 1.

Time limits

Assessments under heads (1) and (2) above must be made no later than two years after the end of the prescribed accounting period concerned or (subject to the overriding time limits) more than one year after the facts sufficient to justify making the assessment come to the Commissioners' knowledge. The relevant prescribed accounting period under head (2) is the period in which the repayment, refund or VAT credit was paid or credited. The relevant prescribed accounting period for input tax is the period in which entitlement to credit is claimed: *C & E Comrs v Croydon Hotel & Leisure Co Ltd* [1996] STC 1105, CA (late deduction of input tax). The relevant prescribed accounting period for end-of-year adjustments under the tour operators' margin scheme is the period in which the adjustment should have been made: *R & C Comrs v Dunwood Travel Ltd* [2008] STCI 959, CA. For the time when facts come to the Commissioners' knowledge, see *Pegasus Birds Ltd v C & E Comrs* [2000] STC 91,CA (principles to be applied). For examples, see *Spillane v C & E Comrs* [1990] STC 212; *Mervyn Conn Organisation Ltd* (No 5205); *Joseph Samuel Developments v C & E Comrs* [1992] VATTR 1; *Winturn Ltd* (No 10699); *Strollmoor Ltd* (No 12765); *C & E Comrs v Post Office* [1995] STC 749; *Classicmoor Ltd v C & E Comrs* [1995] V & DR 1; *Lazard Brothers & Co Ltd* (No 13476).

For the application of these time limits to global assessments, see *S J Grange Ltd v C & E Comrs* [1979] STC 183, CA. For overriding provisions relating to time limits, see s 77.

Prescribed accounting period in respect of which an assessment is made

For the length and duration of prescribed accounting periods, see VAT Regulations, SI 1995/2518 reg 25. Any lack of clarity regarding the length and duration of a trader's first and subsequent prescribed periods may affect the validity of an assessment for the period(s) concerned. For an example, see *R & C Comrs v Raj Restaurant (a firm) and others* [2009] STC 729 (assessment invalid as made in respect of a period which did not constitute a prescribed accounting period).

Notification

For the notification of an assessment, see *House v C & E Comrs* [1996] STC 154, CA; *Cheeseman (trading as Well in Tune) v C & E Comrs* [2000] STC 1119; *Solomon's Kebab House* (No 13560).

A lenghty delay between making and notifying an assessment is undesirable. However, no unfairness should arise in practice as the Commissioners' policy is to treat the assessment as being made on the date when it is notified: *Courts plc v C & E Comrs* [2005] STC 27, CA.

Additional assessments

An additional assessment may be made if further facts are discovered in respect of an accounting period for which an assessment has already been made. However, the Commissioners are allowed only one bite at the same cherry: *Jeudwine v C & E Comrs* [1977] VATTR 115; *Barber v C & E Comrs* [1992] VATTR 144. If no further facts are discovered, the Commissioners must make a supplementary assessment under s 77(6): see *Roberts* (No 15759). In principle, an assessment quashed on appeal because it was not made to the Commissioners' best judgement can be replaced by a new assessment; so can an assessment upheld or varied on appeal. However, the doctrines of issue estoppel, cause of action estoppel and res judicata would invalidate the replacement assessment if it was based on issues decided against the Commissioners in the earlier appeal proceedings; judicial review is an adequate remedy to prevent this: see *Bennett v C & E Comrs (No 2)* [2001] STC 137 (replacement assessment validly made as it gave effect to the tribunal's decision). For the validity of replacement assessments, see *Heyfordian Travel Ltd v C & E Comrs* [1979] VATTR 139; *Scott* (No 517); *International Institute for Strategic Studies v C & E Comrs* [1992] VATTR 245; *Barber v C & E Comrs* [1992] VATTR 144; *Mohammed* (No 10246). For amended assessments, see *Fairbairn (a firm)* (No 12825).

Withdrawing or reducing an assessment

An assessment made and notified under this section may be withdrawn or reduced by the Commissioners. The amount assessed, or the amount to which it is reduced by the Commissioners or (on appeal) by a tribunal (see s 82), is deemed to be an amount due from the person assessed and is recoverable accordingly. In principle, the amount, or reduced amount, cannot be litigated (if no appeal has been made under s 83(1)(*p*)) or re-litigated (if the amount has been determined on appeal) in recovery proceedings: see *Bennett v C & E Comrs (No 2)* [2001] STC 137 and also the clarification of this judgment in *Westone Wholesale Ltd v R & C Comrs* [2008] STC 828 at [33].

However, the validity of the assessment can be litigated in the former case: see *Lord Advocate v Shanks* [1992] STC 928 (assessment out of time). For recovery of tax due, see Sch 11 para 5(1).

For the Commissioners' right to withdraw an assessment, see *Courts plc v C & E Comrs* [2004] STC 690, on appeal [2005] STC 27, CA; *Classicmoor Ltd v C & E Comrs* [1995] V & DR 1. A withdrawn assessment is a nullity. It may be replaced by another assessment for the same period and amount prepared on the same basis and within the same time limit: *Mohammed* (No 10246); *The Far East Restaurant v C & E Comrs* [1993] VATTR 226. For the Commissioners' power to reduce an assessment, see *Sitar Tandoori Restaurant v C & E Comrs* [1993] STC 582 at 586. The Commissioners are not required to exercise best judgment in exercising this power: *Elias Gale Racing v C & E Comrs* [1999] STC 66.

74. Interest on VAT etc recovered or recoverable by assessment (V5.161–V5.163)

An amount assessed under s 73 carries interest at the prescribed rate (see FA 1996 s 197) from the reckonable date until payment. However, one or more of the following conditions must be met in relation to an assessment made under s 73 (1):

(a) either a return has been made or an assessment notified (eg in the absence of a return) for the prescribed accounting period concerned;
(b) the period exceeds three months and commences at the effective date of registration; or
(c) the period commences at the date when the trader ceased to be exempted from registration.

If such an assessment is rendered unnecessary by payment of the amount concerned, the amount paid carries interest at the prescribed rate from the reckonable date until payment. See *P & O Ferries v C & E Comrs* [1991] 3 CMLR 683. For the amount of VAT on which interest runs where there have been two or more voluntary disclosures before the assessment is made, see *London Borough of Camden v C & E Comrs* [1993] VATTR 73; *Mackenzie* (No 11597); *SGS Holdings UK Ltd* (No 13018); *R Miller & N Miller Ltd* (No 13236).

Interest running more than three years before the date on which an amount is assessed or paid is disregarded, see *Shokar v C & E Comrs* [1998] V & DR 301.

VAT shown on, or included in the amount of, an invoice issued by an unauthorised person (as defined in FA 2008 Sch 41 para 2(3)) carries interest at the prescribed rate from the invoice date until payment.

The "reckonable date" is the seventh day after a payment, repayment or refund is authorised by the Commissioners (assessment under s 73 (2)) or the last day for furnishing a return for the prescribed accounting period concerned (other cases).

Interest is paid without deduction of income tax.

For the waiver of interest which does not represent commercial restitution, see Press Notice 34/94, 7 September 1994. The Commissioners' practice of waiving interest on voluntary disclosures (now known as error notifications) of amounts up to £2,000 (see Notice No 700/43 para 2.4) is withdrawn from 1 September 2008: see Revenue and Customs Brief 38/2008, 1 August 2008.

This section applies in a modified manner to assessments under ss 78A(1), 80(4A), 80B(1), 80B(1B), Sch 9A para 6(1) and FA 1996 s 49(1). See s 78A(6) (applied by ss 80(4C), 80B(1E), 80B(2) and FA 1997 s 49(4)) and Sch 9A para 6(9).

No deduction is allowed for income tax or corporation tax purposes in respect of interest under this section: see ITTOIA 2005 ss 54, 272, 869; Corporation Tax Act 2009 s 1303.

75. Assessment in cases of acquisitions of certain goods by non-taxable persons (V5.111)

A non-taxable person may be assessed if he fails to notify an EU acquisition, makes an incorrect notification, or fails to supply information required to verify the particulars notified. An assessment must be made to the Commissioners' best judgement. It must be notified to the person assessed or a person acting in a representative capacity, eg a personal representative, trustee in bankruptcy, receiver or liquidator.

An assessment must be made no later than two years after the notification (if any) is given or (subject to the overriding time limits in s 77) more than one year after information justifying the assessment becomes known to the Commissioners. A further assessment may be made if additional information becomes known to the Commissioners.

An assessment may be withdrawn or reduced. The amount assessed is otherwise deemed to be an amount of tax due and is recovered accordingly. For recovery, see Sch 11 para 5 (1).

76. Assessment of amounts due by way of penalty, interest or surcharge (V5.333, V5.336, V5.379)

The Commissioners may assess an amount due by way of penalty (see ss 60–69B and regulations made under FA 2002 s 135)), interest (see s 74) or default surcharge (see ss 59, 59A). No regulations relevant to VAT have been made to date under FA 2005 s 135. For the assessment of penalties under FA 2008 Sch 36 paras 39, 40, 40A and FA 2009 Sch 49 para 5, see FA 2008 Sch 36 para 46. For the assessment of penalties under FA 2008 Sch 41 paras 1, 2, see Sch 41 para 16. For the assessment of penalties under FA 2009 Sch 46 paras 4, 5, 7, see Sch 46 para 9.

This applies whether or not the conduct has already ceased. An assessment must be notified to the person concerned. For partnerships, see *Mumtaz Paan House v C & E Comrs* [1998] V & DR 52. For the distinction between assessment and notification, see *C & E Comrs v Bassimeh* [1997] STC 33, CA. For assessment and notification in respect of two or more prescribed accounting periods, see *C & E Comrs v Bassimeh* [1997] STC 33, CA; *Georgiou v C & E Comrs* [1996] STC 463, CA. The Commissioners have a discretion whether or not to assess: *C & E Comrs v Steptoe* [1992] STC 757 at 760, CA. This discretion is validly exercised by deciding that an assessment follows automatically unless a decision to the contrary is made in an individual case. The remedy against any improper exercise of this discretion is an appeal to the High Court by way of judicial review: *Dollar Land (Feltham) Ltd v C & E Comrs* [1995] STC 414.

Penalties, interest and surcharges are calculated by reference to a prescribed accounting period referred to as the relevant period. The relevant period for a s 60 penalty is the accounting period in which the VAT evaded should have been paid. Where a repayment is dishonestly obtained, the relevant period is the accounting period in which the payment was obtained. For a s 63 penalty the relevant period is the accounting period in which VAT was understated or where a greater repayment is made than is due the accounting period in which the overstatement occurred. For a penalty under regulations made under FA 2002 s 135, the relevant period is the prescribed accounting period in respect of which the contravention or failure occurred. For s 74 interest, the relevant period is the accounting period in which the tax or the amount assessed as tax was due. For a s 59 or 59A surcharge, the relevant period is the accounting period which creates the surcharge.

For the length and duration of prescribed accounting periods, see VAT Regulations, SI 1995/2518 reg 25. Any lack of clarity regarding the length and duration of a trader's first and subsequent prescribed periods may affect the validity of an assessment for the period(s) concerned. For an example, see *R & C Comrs v Raj Restaurant (a firm) and ors* [2009] STC 729 (penalty assessment invalid as made in respect of a period which did not constitute a prescribed accounting period).

Where a penalty, interest or surcharge is calculated by reference to tax which was not paid at the correct time and the tax or the supply which created the tax cannot be attributed to any one period, the penalty interest or surcharge is attributed to accounting periods by the Commissioners to the best of their judgement.

An assessment for tax can be combined with an assessment for penalty, interest or surcharge and notified as one assessment in specified circumstances. Where this is so, the penalty, interest or surcharge must be identified separately.

A daily penalty or interest on VAT underpaid can be calculated up to the date on the notice. If liability to the penalty or interest continues, a further notice of assessment may be raised. Where the relevant breach is corrected or tax paid within a time limit allowed by the Commissioners, the date of correction or payment is that on the notice detailing the failure.

An assessment for a penalty interest or surcharge may be reduced or withdrawn. However, an invalid assessment may not be reduced: see *DOW Chemical Co Ltd v C & E Comrs* [1996] V & DR 52 (default surcharge). The amount assessed is recoverable as if it was tax due. For recovery of tax due, see Sch 11 para 5.

An assessment may be validly notified to a personal representative, trustee in bankruptcy, interim or permanent trustee, receiver, liquidator or person acting in a representative capacity.

This section applies (with the omission of sub-ss (2)–(6)) to interest on assessments made under ss 78A(1), 80(4A), 80B(1), Sch 9A para 6(1) and FA 1997 s 49(1). See s 78A(7) (applied by ss 80(4C), 80B(2) and FA 1997 s 49(4)) and Sch 9A para 6(10). For the liability to interest, see s 74.

77. Assessments: time limits and supplementary assessments (V5.137, V5.139)

In principle, an assessment under VATA 1994 ss 73, 75 or 76 may not be made more than four years after the end of the prescribed accounting period, acquisition, importation or event concerned. As regards assessments under s 73(2), the relevant prescribed accounting period is the period in which the repayment, refund or VAT credit was paid or credited: see s 73(6A).

This general rule is subject to a number of exceptions.

First, a penalty mentioned in s 76(3) cannot be assessed more than two years after tax for the prescribed accounting period has been "finally determined" (as defined in *Sirpal Trading Co Ltd* (No 13288)).

Second, a penalty under ss 65 (inaccurate EC sales statement) or 66 (failure to submit an EC sales statement) cannot be assessed more than two years after the time when the Commissioners became aware of the material inaccuracy or default.

Third, an assessment may be made up to 20 years after the end of the prescribed accounting period, importation, acquisition or event concerned in any of the following situations:

(a) a person (or someone acting on his behalf) deliberately bringing about a loss of VAT. This includes a loss arising from a deliberate inaccuracy in a document given to HMRC;
(b) a person participating in a transaction knowing that it was part of arrangements intended to bring about a loss of VAT;
(c) failure to notify:
 (i) liability to registration under Sch 1, 2, 3 or 3A;
 (ii) a material change in the nature of the supplies made by a person exempted from registration under Sch 1 para 14;
 (iii) a taxable acquisition made by a person exempted from registration under Sch 3 para 8;
 (iv) an acquisition of goods subject to excise duty made by a non-taxable-person; or
 (v) an acquisition of a new means of transport made by a non-taxable-person; and
(d) failure to notify information about a notifiable scheme (see Sch 11A para 5) to which a person is a party. This comprises:
 (i) the reference number of a designated scheme; or
 (ii) prescribed information regarding a hallmarked scheme.

Fourth, a sum assessed by reason of some conduct by a deceased person during his lifetime may not be made more than three years after his death. A "sum" for this purpose includes an amount due by way of penalty, interest or surcharge.

The Commissioners may consider that an assessment understates the amount due from a trader. They can make an additional assessment under ss 73(6) or 75(2) if further evidence has come to light since the original assessment was made. In other cases, they must make a supplementary assessment under this section. The supplementary assessment is subject to the same conditions and time limits as the original assessment. For time limits, see *Roberts* (No 15759). For supplementary assessments generally, see *Bowden v C & E Comrs* [1987] VATTR 255; *Bill Hennessy Associates Ltd* (No 2656); *Bennett v C & E Comrs* [1997] V & DR 155, on appeal [1999] STC 248. This provision also applies to assessments made under ss 78A(1), 80(4A), 80B(1), Sch 9 para 6(1) and FA 1997 s 49(1), and to interest on such assessments: see s 78A(6), (7) (applied by ss 80(4C), 80B(2) and FA 1997 s 49(4)) and Sch 9A para 6(9), (10). For the liability to interest, see s 74.

LIABILITY FOR UNPAID VAT OF ANOTHER

77A. Joint and several liability of traders in supply chain where tax unpaid (V1.285, V3.233)

Two persons (X and Y) in a chain of supply are jointly and severally liable for an amount of unpaid VAT due from Y if X is served with a notice to that effect by the Commissioners. A notice may be served on X if:

(a) a taxable supply of goods or services was made to X;
(b) the goods or services fall within one or more specified descriptions (see s 77A(1)), which broadly comprise telephones, computers and electronic equipment for leisure, amusement or entertainment use; and
(c) at the time of supply, X knew, or had reasonable grounds to suspect, that all or part of the VAT payable in respect of any supply in the chain would go unpaid.

The notice must specify the amount of unpaid VAT. This is the lesser of: (1) the VAT chargeable on the supply made by Y; and (2) the aggregate of the VAT (if any) shown as due on any VAT return made by Y for the prescribed accounting period in question and any VAT assessed as due from him for that period.

Whether or not X had reasonable grounds for suspecting that VAT would go unpaid is decided by reference to the facts of the case. However, X is presumed to have reasonable grounds if he paid less than: (1) the open market value of the goods; or (2) the price payable on any previous supply of those goods. X can rebut this presumption by proving that the low price payable was unconnected with the failure to pay VAT.

A presumption of this nature must comply with the general principles of EU law and, in particular, the principles of legal certainty and proportionality. Thus, it must not be practically impossible, or excessively difficult, for X to rebut the presumption with evidence to the contrary. Whether the presumption complies with the general principles of EU law is a matter for the national court: see *Federation of Technological Industries and others v C & E Comrs* (case C-384/04) [2006] ECR I–4191, [2006] STC 1483, ECJ.

The descriptions of goods and services, and the circumstances in which a person is presumed to have reasonable grounds for suspicion, may be varied by order.

For the right of appeal against any liability arising under this provision, see s 83(1)(*ra*).

INTEREST, REPAYMENT SUPPLEMENTS ETC PAYABLE BY COMMISSIONERS

78. Interest in certain cases of official error (V5.196)

The Commissioners are liable to pay interest if one of the following events occurs due to an error on their part:

(a) a trader accounts for output tax which is not due;
(b) he fails to deduct input tax to which he is entitled (see *North East Media Development Trust Ltd* (No 13104));
(c) he pays an amount of VAT which is not due; or
(d) a payment due to him is delayed.

For "error", see *The Chartered Institute of Bankers* (No 15648). For examples see *CGI Pension Trust Ltd* (No 15926); *Freemans plc* (No 17019). As regards errors within heads (*a*)–(*c*), interest runs on that part of the claim (if any) which the Commissioners are required to satisfy. As regards head (*a*), this is the amount paid or repaid under s 80(2A), not the amount credited under s 80(1) or (1A). A payment in head (*d*) does not include a delayed payment of interest.

Interest is not payable on amounts giving rise to repayment supplement. For an example, see *Thi Leisure Two Partnership* (No 16876). For the relationship between repayment supplement, interest under this section and interest under Supreme Court Act 1981 s 35A, see *R (on the application of Elite Mobile plc) v C & E Comrs* [2005] STC 275.

Interest is calculated as simple interest: *National Council of YMCAs Inc v C & E Comrs* [1993] VATTR 299. For the rate of interest, see FA 1996 s 197. The rates are higher than those for default interest under s 74 because the interest is chargeable to income tax or corporation tax.

The period for which interest runs is referred to as "the applicable period".

In heads (*a*) or (*b*) above, interest runs from the date when the trader's payment for the prescribed accounting period concerned was received (payment return) or the date when the amount due to him for that period was authorised for payment or was set-off (repayment return). Interest ceases to run when the amount due to the trader regarding the error is authorised for payment or is set-off. For input tax, see *North East Media Development Trust Ltd v C & E Comrs* [1995] V & DR 240.

In head (*c*) above, interest runs from the date when the trader's payment was received to the date it was authorised for payment or was set-off.

In head (*d*) above, interest runs from the date when the payment would normally have been authorised or set-off to the date when it was actually authorised for payment or was set-off. A period is left out of account in determining the period for which interest runs if a delay in authorising payment or in set-off results from the claimant's conduct. Such conduct includes:

(a) unreasonable delay in claiming interest or the amount to which it relates;
(b) failing to provide information to the Commissioners; and
(c) making an incorrect claim.

The period left out of account in respect of a failure to provide information begins on the date when a reasonable request is made and ends on the date when the Commissioners could reasonably conclude that they have received a complete or sufficient answer or that no answer is necessary. A different period may be prescribed by regulations. No regulations have been made to date.

Claims for interest must be made in writing. A claim must be made no later than four years after the end of the applicable period to which it relates.

78A. Assessment for interest overpayments (V5.196)

If the Commissioners pay an amount of interest to which a person was not entitled, they may assess that amount to their best judgement and notify it to him. For interest, see s 78. For interest treated as if it were interest under s 78, and therefore assessed under this section, see VAT Regulations 1995, SI 1995/2518 regs 173W and 173X. For "best judgement", see s 73. For an example, see *Thi Leisure Two Partnership* (No 16876) (trader entitled to repayment supplement ordered to repay interest previously received on the same amount).

The assessment must be made no later than two years after the time when the Commissioners have sufficient evidence of facts to justify making the assessment. For "evidence of facts", see *C & E Comrs v DFS Furniture Co plc* [2004] STC 559, CA (excludes the coming into force of retrospective legislation and a judicial decision clarifying the law); Business Brief 25/04, 14 September 2004. The amount assessed is deemed to be VAT due and is recovered accordingly (see Sch 11 para 5(1)). The assessment may be withdrawn or reduced so as to extinguish all or part of the amount so recoverable. The Commissioners may make a supplementary assessment in accordance with s 77(6). An assessment may be validly notified to a personal representative, trustee in bankruptcy, interim or permanent trustee, receiver, liquidator or person acting in a representative capacity. These provisions apply equally to assessments under ss 80(4A), 80B(1) and FA 1997 s 49(1).

The amount assessed carries interest under s 74 in the same manner as VAT assessed under s 73. However, s 74(1) applies so that interest runs from the date when the assessment is notified (rather than from the reckonable date). The maximum period for which interest runs under s 74(1), (2) is a two-year period ending on the day when the interest assessment is made. However, this does not prevent one or more further assessments being made for later periods in accordance with s 76(7)(*b*). Interest is assessed in accordance with ss 76(1), (7)–(10) and 77(6). These provisions apply equally to assessments under ss 80 (4A), 80B (1) and FA 1997 s 49(1).

79. Repayment supplement in respect of certain delayed payments or refunds (V5.191, V5.192)

The amount of a VAT credit (to a taxable person under s 25(3)) or refund (to a statutory body under s 33, a museum or gallery under s 33A, or the proprietor of an Academy under s 33B) to which a person is entitled is increased by a supplement if:

(a) the return or claim is received by the Commissioners by the due date. See *C & E Comrs v W Timms & Son (Builders) Ltd* [1992] STC 374 (condition not met if return posted before due date physically received after due date) and *Refrigeration Spares (Manchester) Ltd* (No 17603) (extended time limit for furnishing returns under the credit transfer scheme (see commentary to VAT Regulations 1995, SI 1995/2518 reg 25));

(b) the written instruction directing the making of the payment or refund (see below) is issued (see below) more than 30 days after the later of:

  (i) the day following the last day of the prescribed accounting period to which the return or claim relates, and

  (ii) the day when the Commissioners received the return or claim; and

(c) the amount claimed does not exceed the amount actually due by more than £250 (if the amount due is £5,000 or less) or 5% of the amount due (in other cases).

The supplement is £50 (if the amount due is £1,000 or less) or 5% of the amount due (in other cases). Payment of supplement precludes payment of interest on the same amount: see s 78(2)(*a*); *Thi Leisure Two Partnership* (No 16876).

A "written instruction directing the making of the payment or refund" is a cheque or payable order. It is "issued" when the payee receives it: *Aston v C & E Comrs* [1991] VATTR 170.

The Commissioners may make regulations specifying periods to be disregarded in determining the 30-day limit. See VAT Regulations 1995, SI 1995/2518 regs 198, 199. The period referable to raising and answering an enquiry begins, for these purposes, when the Commissioners first consider it necessary to make the enquiry and ends when they decide not to make or pursue the enquiry or when they have received a complete answer to it. The relevant enquiry may be made of the taxpayer, another customs officer or any other person.

Repayment supplement is paid on the amount lawfully due to the trader. In the event of a dispute, this amount must be determined before supplement is calculated. See *British Steel Exports Ltd* (No 7562).

No liability to income tax or corporation tax arises in respect of repayment supplement: see ITTOIA 2005 s 777; Corporation Tax Act 2009 s 1286.

80. Recovery of overpaid VAT (V5.159)

Claims for credit and repayment

A person may claim a credit in either of the following situations:

- Where an amount that is not output tax has been accounted for as such for a prescribed accounting period. The claim must be made no later than four years (see below) after the end of the prescribed accounting period in which a voluntary disclosure was made (if the error was made in such a disclosure) or the prescribed accounting period concerned (in other cases).
- Where an amount that is not output tax has been assessed as such for a prescribed accounting period. The claim must be made no later than four years (see below) after the end of the prescribed accounting period in which a voluntary disclosure was made (if the assessment was made on the basis of an erroneous disclosure) or the prescribed accounting period in which the assessment was made (in other cases).

A claim is made in accordance with VAT Regulations 1995, SI 1995/2518 reg 37. Any sums due to the Commissioners may be set off against the credit and the balance (if any) is paid or repaid to him. However, the Commissioners have a defence against a claim if the claimant would be unjustly enriched by it. For unjust enrichment, see below.

A person may claim a repayment if he has paid an amount of VAT to the Commissioners that was not due to them. The amount must relate to a prescribed accounting period (so that it arises in respect of a return or assessment) and must comprise neither output tax (for which a credit can be claimed under the foregoing provisions) nor input tax. A claim would arise, for example, if a tax liability has been paid twice: see *Explanatory Notes: Finance Bill 2005* (HM Treasury, May 2005). The claim must be made no later than four years (see below) after the date on which the payment was made. A claim is made in accordance with VAT Regulations 1995, SI 1995/2518 reg 37. Claims for late deduction of input tax are made under VAT Regulations 1995, SI 1995/2518 reg 29: *University of Sussex v C & E Comrs* [2004] STC 1, CA. Errors in input tax claims are corrected in accordance with VAT Regulations 1995, SI 1995/2518 regs 34 or 35.

Payment of a claim does not prevent another claim in respect of the same period: *Hayward Gill & Associates Ltd v C & E Comrs* [1998] V & DR 352. For the amount of a claim, see *Sunningdale Golf Club v C & E Comrs* [1997] V & DR 79 (VAT charged on supplies exempted under EU law).

The Commissioners have no power to defer crediting or repaying a sum which they agree to be due: *R v C & E Comrs ex parte Kay & Co Ltd* [1996] STC 1500. For the rights of a former partner in relation to repayments made after his retirement, see *Hawthorn v Smallcorn* [1998] STC 591. For the right to repayment arising when an industrial and provident society transfers its engagements to another such society, see *Midlands Co-operative Society Ltd v R & C Comrs* [2008] STC 1803, CA; FA 2008 s 133. For repayment under an enforceable Community right, see *Marks and Spencer plc v C & E Comrs* (case C-309/06) [2008] STC 1409, ECJ and subsequently [2009] STC 452, HL. For the right to repayment following the redefinition of transactions amounting to an abuse of right, see *R & C Comrs v Moorbury Ltd* [2010] UKUT 360 (TCC), [2010] STC 2715. For examples of overpayment, see *R (on the application of British Telecommunications plc) v R & C Comrs* [2005] STC 1148; *R (on the application of Silicon Graphics Finance SA) v R & C Comrs* [2008] STC 1928; *Scottish Equitable plc* (No 19418), as to which see Revenue and Customs Brief 41/09, 17 July 2009 for the order made by the Court of Session on appeal.

For overcharged VAT resulting from a change to the legislation, see Business Brief 14/94, 6 July 1994; Business Brief 28/04, 26 October 2004.

Unjust enrichment

For "unjust enrichment" under EU law, see *Just v Ministry for Fiscal Affairs* (case C-68/79) [1980] ECR 501; *Amministrazione delle Finanze dello Stato v Denkavit Italiana* (case C-61/79) [1980] ECR 1205; *Amministrazione delle Finanze dello Stato v San Giorgio* (case C-118/82) [1983] ECR 395; *EC Commission v Italy* (case C-104/86) [1989] 3 CMLR 25, ECJ; *Les Fils de Jules Bianco SA v Directeur General des Douanes et Droits* (cases C-331/85, C-376/85 and C-378/85) [1989] 3 CMLR 36, ECJ; *Deville v Administration des Impots* (case 240/87) [1989] 3 CMLR 611, ECJ; *Société Comateb v Directeur général des Douanes et droits indirects* (joined cases C-192/95 to C-218/95) [1997] STC 1006, ECJ; *Weber's Wine World Handels-GmbH v Abgabenberufungskommission Wien* (case C-147/01) [2003] ECR I–11365, ECJ. Under UK law, see *C & E Comrs v National Westminster Bank plc* [2003] STC 1072; *Baines & Ernst Ltd v C & E Comrs* [2006] STC 2006, CA;. For cases decided under UK law before the enactment of ss 80(3A)–(3C) and 80A, see *C & E Comrs v McMaster Stores (Scotland) Ltd (in receivership)* [1995] STC 846; *Tayside Numbers Ltd v C & E Comrs* [1992] VATTR 406; *Lamdec Ltd v C & E Comrs* [1991] VATTR 296; *Creative Facility Ltd* (No 10891); *Computeach International Ltd v C & E Comrs* [1994] VATTR 237; *National and Provincial Building Society v C & E Comrs* [1996] V & DR 153; *Frampton (a firm)* (No 14065); *Marks and Spencer plc v C & E Comrs* [2000] STC 16, CA.

A statutory test applies for determining whether a trader would be unjustly enriched if all or part of his claim for credit relates to VAT which, for all practical purposes, has been borne by someone else. As regards an exempt supply erroneously treated as taxable, it is for the Commissioners to prove that all or part of the VAT has been passed on and, in the case of a partial passing on, the extent to which VAT has been passed on. It is necessary to determine what the trader would have charged during the claim period if his supplies had not been treated as taxable. It is then necessary to determine what the trader's financial position would have been in that hypothetical situation. This may involve assessing the level of the trader's sales in that situation. If the comparison shows that the claimant would have been better off if his supplies had not been treated as taxable, the Commissioners have no defence (or only a partial defence) to the claim on the basis of unjust enrichment. The assessment of the hypothetical comparative situation must be made on the basis of all available evidence of relevance or probative value. There is no scope for assumptions or for rules regarding the weight of one type of evidence as distinct from another. An economic analysis may be necessary in some, but not all, cases but the parties are entitled to adduce evidence based on an analysis of this kind: see *Baines & Ernst Ltd v C & E Comrs* [2006] STC 2006, CA at [13]–[16].

The amount to be repaid is restricted to the amount (if any) which appropriately compensates the trader for the loss or damage suffered by his business as a result of his misapplication of the legislation. The trader must demonstrate that loss or damage has arisen. He may do so by: (1) producing some material casting doubt on the inference of no economic loss that would otherwise be drawn, or (2) justifying his inability to produce the facts and figures that would establish his case: *Baines & Ernst Ltd v C & E Comrs* [2006] STC 653 (on appeal [2006] STC 2006, CA). He must quantify the loss requiring compensation. Past or future loss or damage is otherwise disregarded in determining whether he would be enriched, or enriched unjustly, by the repayment. For an example, see *RIBA Publications v C & E Comrs* [1999] V & DR 230. For unjust enrichment in relation to reimbursement arrangements, see s 80A.

Assessments

An amount credited by the Commissioners after 25 May 2005 may exceed the amount properly due. Where this is so, the Commissioners may assess the excess to their best judgement. They must notify the amount of the excess to the person who received the repayment. The assessment must be made no more than two years after the end of the prescribed accounting period in which the amount was credited or, if later, two years after the time when evidence comes to the Commissioners' knowledge. The evidence relates to facts which, in the Commissioners' opinion, justify the making of the assessment. The assessment is made in accordance with s 78A(3)–(8), and thus carries interest under s 74 (as modified by s 78A(6), (7)). For the detailed provisions, see the commentary to s 78A. For an example, see *C & E Comrs v DFS Furniture Co plc* [2004] STC 559, CA (assessment made out of time); Business Brief 25/04, 14 September 2004.

Commencement

This section (as amended by F(No 2)A 2005 s 3) applies to claims made after 25 May 2005: see F(No 2)A 2005 s 4(6). The amendments made by FA 2008 s 120(2)–(4) are deemed to have come into force on 19 March 2008: see s 120(5) of the 2008 Act. The amendment made by FA 2008 Sch 39 para 36 came into force on 1 April 2009: see FA 2008 s 118(2); the Finance Act 2008, Schedule 39 (Appointed Day, Transitional Provision and Savings) Order 2009, SI 2009/403, art 2. The three-year claim in force prior to 1 April 2009 did not apply to claims made before that date in respect of amounts relating to a prescribed accounting period ending before 4 December 1996: see FA 2008 s 121(1).

80A. Arrangements for reimbursing customers (V5.151–V5.166)

A trader may avoid being unjustly enriched (see s 80 (3)) by a credit under s 80 by entering into arrangements (referred to as "reimbursement arrangements") in accordance with regulations to pass on the amount claimed to those persons who have wholly or partly borne the VAT concerned. For the regulations made, see VAT Regulations 1995, SI 1995/2518 regs 43A–43H.

80B. Assessments of amounts due under section 80A arrangements (V5.151–V5.166)

A trader entering into reimbursement arrangements (see s 80A) may be required to make a payment to the Commissioners in respect of undistributed credits (see s 80) and interest (see s 78). For the circumstances in which the liability to make a payment arises, see VAT Regulations 1995, SI 1995/2518 reg 43D. The amount of the payment is the difference between the amount the trader is required to disburse under the arrangements and the amount he actually disburses. The Commissioners may assess this amount and notify it to the trader.

As the reimbursement arrangements in force on 26 May 2005 apply to amounts repaid (rather than credited) to the trader (see VAT Regulations 1995, SI 1995/2518 reg 43G(2)(*b*)), an assessment under the foregoing provision fails to take account of amounts set off against credits in determining the amount actually paid or repaid to the trader in accordance with s 80(2)(*a*). This deficiency is overcome by providing an alternative power of assessment from 26 May 2005. A person ceases to be entitled to so much of the gross credit (ie the credit before deduction of the amount set off) as exceeds the amount disbursed. To the extent that the trader is liable to make a payment to the Commissioners, he continues to be assessed under the existing power. As regards the excess, the Commissioners may assess this amount and notify it to the trader.

An assessment under either provision is made in accordance with s 78A(2)–(8), and thus carries interest under s 74 (as modified by s 78A(6), (7)). For the detailed provisions, see s 78A.

81. Interest given by way of credit and set-off credits (V5.196)

Any interest payable to a person is treated as if it were a VAT credit, ie it is paid to him by the Commissioners. However, he is not entitled to interest on the amount payable to him. For VAT credits, see s 25 (3).

An amount due to a person ("the credit") is set-off against any VAT, penalty, interest or surcharge due from him ("the debit"). The Commissioners may make a mistake as to whether (or to what extent) amounts are payable to or by a person and, in consequence, they may fail to assess, enforce or satisfy a sum due from him by way of VAT, penalty, interest or surcharge. Furthermore, the Commissioners may be out of time to take such action if they subsequently become liable to make a payment or repayment to the person as a consequence of the mistake. Where this is so, the time limits for recovery are disregarded in determining whether the sum due by way of VAT, penalty, interest or surcharge (ie the debit) is set-off against the amount of the payment or repayment (ie the credit).

A credit becoming due after application of an insolvency procedure is not set-off against either: (1) a debit arising before the insolvency commenced; or (2) a debit arising after the insolvency commenced if it relates to the business carried on before that time.

An insolvency commences in the circumstances set out below. It commences at the time stated:

	Circumstance	*Time*
(*a*)	(i) Bankruptcy order made	Time when bankruptcy order is made
	(ii) Winding up order made	Time when winding-up order is made
	(iii) An administrator is appointed to manage the affairs, business and property of another person under Insolvency Act 1986 Sch B1	Time when administration order is made

	(iv) Award of sequestration made	Time when award is made
(*b*)	The person is in administrative receivership (ie, there is a continuous period for which, disregarding any temporary vacancy, there is an administrative receiver (as defined by Insolvency Act 1986 s 29 (2)) of that person	Time when the person is put into administrative receivership
(*c*)	A corporation is being voluntarily wound-up	Time when corporation passes resolution for voluntary winding-up
(*d*)	A voluntary arrangement has been approved in accordance with Insolvency Act 1986 ss 1–7 (companies) or ss 252–263 (individuals)	Time when voluntary arrangement comes into force
(*e*)	Deed of arrangement has been registered in accordance with Deeds of Arrangement Act 1914 ss 5–8 and Deeds of Arrangement Rules 1925, SR & O 1925/795	Time when deed of arrangement takes effect
(*f*)	Person's estate becomes vested in his trustee under a trust deed as defined in Bankruptcy (Scotland) Act 1985 s 5(2)(*c*)	Time when estate is vested in trustee

In Northern Ireland, Insolvency (Northern Ireland) Order 1989, SI 1989/2405 applies in place of Insolvency Act 1986. The foregoing references should be read accordingly.

The application of an insolvency procedure is disregarded for the foregoing purposes if: (1) another insolvency procedure applies to a person at that time; or (2) it immediately follows when another insolvency procedure ceases to have effect.

PART V APPEALS

82. Appeal tribunals (V1.288)

In VATA 1994, "tribunal" means the First-tier Tribunal or, where so determined in accordance with Tribunal Procedure Rules, the Upper Tribunal. For the First-tier Tribunal and Upper Tribunal, see TCEA 2007 s 3. For the Rules of Procedure, see commentary to TCEA 2007 s 22.

83. Appeals (V5.404)

An appeal lies to a tribunal (see s 82) in respect of the following matters:

(*a*) the registration or deregistration of a person (see Schs 1–3B);

(*b*) the VAT chargeable on a supply (see *Odhams Leisure Group Ltd v C & E Comrs* [1992] STC 332; *Morrisons Central Garage Ltd* (No 907); *Grimsby & District Sunday Football League v C & E Comrs* [1982] VATTR 210), acquisition or importation. For the requirement to pay the VAT in dispute before an appeal can be entertained, see s 84(3). For appeals that do not lie to a tribunal under this head, see s 84(9);

(*c*) the amount of input tax credit (see s 26) to be deducted. This jurisdiction extends to: (1) repayments claimed by overseas traders (see VAT Regulations 1995, SI 1995/2518 regs 182, 195; *Jersey Telecoms* (No 13940)); and (2) disputed claims for repayment supplement (see *R (on the application of UK Tradecorp Ltd) v C & E Comrs* [2005] STC 138; *Richard Costain Ltd v C & E Comrs* [1988] VATTR 106; *Purple International Ltd* (No 18243)).

No right of appeal arises if the Commissioners delay repayment of all or part of a claim pending investigation without making a decision to refuse repayment: see *Touchwood Services Ltd v R & C Comrs* [2007] STC 1425; *R & C Comrs v Mobilix Ltd* [2008] STC 3071. For the limited jurisdiction of the Administrative Court, see *R (on the application of UK Tradecorp Ltd) v C & E Comrs* [2005] STC 138. For other circumstances in which the tribunal may not allow an appeal under this head, see s 84(4);

(*d*) a claim for refund of VAT on goods acquired both in the UK and another EU member state (see s 13 (5));

(*da*) a refusal of approval as a fiscal warehousekeeper, withdrawal of approval as a fiscal warehousekeeper, imposition of conditions for approval as a fiscal warehousekeeper or withdrawal of fiscal warehouse status from any premises (see s 18A);

(*e*) the proportion of input tax allowable (see s 26). The tribunal has a full appellate jurisdiction in relation to a decision by the Commissioners to terminate a trader's use of a special partial exemption method, or not to allow him to use a proposed special method: *Banbury Visionplus Ltd v R & C Comrs* [2006] STC 1568; *St Helen's School Northwood Ltd v R & C Comrs* [2007] STC 633; *DCM (Optical Holdings) Ltd v R & C Comrs* [2008] STC 1294. For circumstances in which the tribunal may not allow an appeal under this head, see s 84(4);

(*f*) a claim for refund of VAT on goods imported for private purposes (see s 27);

(*fza*) a refusal, or withdrawal, of authorisation to use the flat-rate scheme for small businesses (see s 26B), or the appropriate percentage (see s 26B(2)(*b*)) to be applied. For the matters on which the tribunal must be satisfied before allowing the appeal, see s 84(4ZA);

(*fa*) refusing to allow a trader to continue making payments on account by reference to his VAT liability for the previous month (see VAT (Payments on Account) Order 1993, SI 1993/2001 art 12A (4));

(*g*) the amount of a refund claimed in respect of goods used in self-build projects (see s 35; *Stott* (No 15622));

(*h*) a claim for refund of VAT on bad debts (see s 36);

(*ha*) refusal to make a repayment to a person carrying on business in another member state or in a third country (see s 39);

(*j*) the amount of a refund claimed in respect of a new means of transport supplied to another EU member state (see s 40);

(*k*) the refusal of an application to form, vary or disband a VAT group or change the representative member (see s 43B(5)). For the grounds on which the tribunal can allow an appeal, see s 84(4A);

(*ka*) the termination of a body corporate's membership of a VAT group on revenue protection grounds (see s 43C(1), (2)) or eligibility grounds (see s 43C(3), (4)). For the grounds on which the tribunal can allow an appeal, see s 84(4C), (4D). For the status of the notice pending outcome of the appeal, see s 84(4B);

(*l*) requiring a person to provide security for protection of the revenue (see *Mr Wishmore Ltd v C & E Comrs* [1988] STC 723; *C & E Comrs v Peachtree Enterprises Ltd* [1994] STC 747; *John Dee Ltd v C & E Comrs* [1995] STC 941, CA; *Gayton House Holdings Ltd v C & E Comrs* [1984] VATTR 111; *Colette Ltd v C & E Comrs* [1992] VATTR 240; *Lomond Services Ltd* (No 15451)) or because he has failed to appoint a VAT representative (see s 48(7) and Sch 11 para 4(1A), (2)). For the onus of proof on the Commissioners in relation to a requirement for security under Sch 11 para 4(2), see s 84(4E), (4F);

(*m*) refusing certification or cancellation of certification under the flat-rate farmers' scheme or the cancellation of certification (see s 54);

(*n*) liability to a penalty or surcharge under ss 59–69B. For the requirement to pay the VAT in dispute before an appeal can be entertained, see s 84(3);

(*o*) recovering all or part of a penalty for dishonest conduct from a named officer (see s 61 (5));

(*p*) the validity of an assessment (eg whether it is made to best judgement) or the amount of an assessment (see *Majid & Partners v C & E Comrs* [1999] STC 585) in respect of: (i) VAT underpaid by a trader or overpaid by the Commissioners in respect of a return (see s 73 (1), (2); *Murat v C & E Comrs* [1998] STC 923), (ii) VAT on goods not accounted for (see s 73 (7)), (iii) VAT on missing or deficient goods in a warehouse or fiscal warehouse (see s 73 (7A)), (iv) VAT on goods removed from a warehouse or fiscal warehouse (see s 73 (7B)), or (v) VAT undeclared or underpaid by a non-taxable-person in respect of acquisitions (see s 75). For the approach to be taken on appeal, see *Rahman (trading as Khayam Restaurant v C E Comrs (No 2)* [2003] STC 150 at [42]–[45], CA. For the requirement to pay the VAT in dispute before an appeal can be entertained, see s 84(3). For the circumstances in which the tribunal can allow an appeal, see s 84(4ZA). For penalties understated in an assessment, see s 84(5);

(*q*) the amount of any penalty, interest (see *London Borough of Camden v C & E Comrs* [1993] VATTR 73) or surcharge (see *Dollar Land (Feltham) Ltd v C & E Comrs* [1995] STC 414) assessed under s 76. For the requirement to pay the VAT in dispute before an appeal can be entertained, see s 84(3). For the tribunal's power to vary any penalty, interest or surcharge, see s 84(6);

(*r*) assessing VAT, penalties, interest or surcharge under the 20 year time limit (see s 77 (4));

(*ra*) any liability for another person's VAT arising from service of a joint and several liability notice (see s 77A). For the requirement to pay the VAT in dispute before an appeal can be entertained, see s 84(3);

(*s*) the Commissioners' liability to pay interest or the amount payable (see s 78);

(*sa*) an assessment, or the amount assessed, of interest overpaid to a person (see s 78A(1));

(*t*) a claim for credit of overpaid output tax (see s 80(1), (1A)), a claim for repayment of overpaid VAT (see s 80(1B)), and an assessment, or the amount assessed, of the amount overpaid on such claims (see s 80(4A)). For the extent of the tribunal's jurisdiction, see *C & E Comrs v National Westminster Bank plc* [2003] STC 1072 (complaint that unjust enrichment applied to claim by company but not to claims by competitors);

(*ta*) an assessment, or the amount assessed, of a repayment of overpaid output tax which is not passed on under disbursement arrangements (see s 80B (1), (1B));

(*u*) a direction or supplementary direction treating persons as a single taxable person (see Sch 1 para 2). For the grounds on which an appeal can be allowed, see s 84 (7);

(*v*) a direction relating to the valuation of goods or services supplied (see Sch 6 paras 1, 1A, 2);

(*w*) a direction relating to the valuation of acquisitions (see Sch 7 para 1);

(*wa*) a direction, or an assessment resulting from such a direction, made to counteract tax avoidance in relation to a group registration (see Sch 9A). For the circumstances in which an appeal can be allowed, see s 84(7A);

(*wb*) refusing to grant permission in relation to the option to tax land or refusing to exercise a power in relation to such an option (see Sch 10 Part 1). For the grounds on which the tribunal can allow an appeal, see s 84(7ZA);

(*x*) refusing to allow supplies to be valued under the retail schemes (see *J Boardmans (1980) Ltd v C & E Comrs* [1984] VATTR 118, affd [1986] STC 10) (see Sch 11 para 2 (6));

(*y*) refusing to approve use of the cash accounting scheme, or the termination of such authorisation (see Sch 11 para 2 (7));

(*z*) a requirement imposed on a trader in relation to self-billed invoices (see Sch 11 para 2B(2)) or electronic invoices (see Sch 11 para 3 (1));

(*zza*) a direction to keep specified records (see Sch 11 para 6A(1)). For the circumstances in which an appeal can be allowed, see s 84(7B);

(*za*) a direction for two or more persons to be treated as a single taxable person for the purpose of determining whether they are excluded from the duty to notify VAT avoidance schemes (see Sch 11A para 8);

(*zb*) liability to a penalty for failing to notify a VAT avoidance scheme (see Sch 11A para 10(1)), an assessment in respect of such a penalty (see Sch 11A para 12(1)), or the amount of such an assessment. For the requirement to pay the VAT in dispute before an appeal can be entertained, see s 84(3). For the tribunal's power to vary a penalty, see s 84(6A);

(*zc*) a decision about the mandatory electronic filing of returns (see regulations made under FA 2002 s 135). This includes a decision whether the requirement applies and a decision to impose a penalty. No regulations relevant to VAT have been made to date under s 135 of the 2002 Act. For the tribunal's power to vary a penalty, see s 84(6B);

(*zz*) [applies to money laundering.]

For the right of appeal in respect of other matters relevant to VAT, see:

Matter	*Authority for the appeal*
Requirement to make payments on account	VATA 1994 s 28(2AA)
Penalty for dishonest conduct apportioned to a named officer	VATA 1994 s 61(5) (repealed)
Special accounting scheme for electronic services	VATA 1994 Sch 3B para 20
A sum set-off against an assessment for interest, penalty or default surcharge	FA 1997 s 49(5)
Requirement to provide information or produce documents	FA 2008 Sch 36 paras 29–31
Penalty for failing to comply with an information notice, obstructing an inspection or providing inaccurate information	FA 2008 Sch 36 para 47
Penalty for failing to notify or improperly issuing an invoice	FA 2008 Sch 36 paras 17–19 and 22(5)(e)
Penalty for failure by senior accounting officer	FA 2009 Sch 47 para 10
Requirement to provide contact details for debtors	FA 2009 Sch 49 para 4
Penalty for failing to provide contact details for debtors	FA 2008 Sch 36 para 47 by virtue of FA 2009 Sch 49 para 5(3)

The words "with respect to" are wide enough to cover any legal question capable of being determinative of an issue between the parties falling within the matters listed above: see *Oxfam v R & C Comrs* [2010] STC 686 (jurisdiction in relation to issues of contract law and legitimate expectations in relation to a matter within s 83(1)(c)).

A reference to a "decision" in ss 83A–85 includes any matter listed in s 83(1). This applies whether or not the matter is described there as a decision.

For the manner in which HMRC enters into, handles and settles disputes, see Revenue and Customs Brief 44/07, 11 June 2007 and Appendix 11.

83A. Offer of review

HMRC may notify a decision to a person. If an appeal lies against the decision, HMRC must offer to review the decision. The offer is made by notice. The notice must be given to the person when he is notified of the decision. HMRC are not required to offer a review when notifying the outcome of a review (see s 83F(6)). For the matters in respect of which an appeal lies to a tribunal, see s 83. For the time limit for accepting an offer, see ss 83C(1)(*b*), 83D(1) and 83E. For the circumstances in which a person is not permitted to accept an offer, see s 83C(2). For the tribunal, see s 82.

83B. Right to require review

A person may have a right of appeal (see s 83) against a decision which has not been notified to him. If so, he may require HMRC to review that decision. He must do so within 30 days of becoming aware of the decision.

A person cannot require a review if he has already appealed to the tribunal. For the tribunal, see s 82. For appeals to the tribunal, see s 83G.

83C. Review by HMRC

HMRC must review a decision if their offer to review (see s 83A) is accepted by the relevant person, within 30 days. The 30-day period is counted from the date of the document notifying the offer. A person may not accept an offer if he has already appealed to the tribunal. If he does so, HMRC are not required to review the decision. For the tribunal, see s 82.

HMRC must review a decision if they are notified of a requirement to review (see s 83B). However, HMRC are not required to do so if the relevant person has already appealed to the tribunal.

83D. Extensions of time

If HMRC have offered to review a decision (see s 83A), they may extend the 30-day period for acceptance of the offer (see s 83C(1)(*b*)). They may do so at any time during that period. Similarly, if a person has a right to require a review (see s 83B(1), HMRC may extend the 30-day period for notifying the requirement (see s 83B(2)). They may do so at any time during that period. The relevant person must be notified in either case.

If an extension of time is given, the relevant period is extended to the end of 30 days from either: (1) the date of the notice; or (2) any other date set out in the notice or a further notice.

83E. Review out of time

A person offered a review (see s 83A) may not accept the offer within the period, or extended period, allowed (see ss 83C(1)(*b*) and 83D(3)). Similarly, a person requiring a review (see s 83B) may not notify this requirement within the period, or extended period, allowed (see ss 83B(2) and 83D(3)). HMRC are required to review the decision in either case if: (1) the person subsequently so requests in writing; (2) HMRC are satisfied that the relevant person had a reasonable excuse for failing to accept the offer, or require the review, in time; and (3) HMRC are satisfied that the request was made without unreasonable delay once the excuse ceased to apply. However, HMRC are not required to do so if the relevant person has already appealed to the tribunal (see s 82).

83F. Nature of review etc

The scope and depth of a review (see ss 83C and 83E) are determined by what the Commissioners consider to be appropriate in the circumstances. In particular, they must take into account how the decision was made and how the parties sought to resolve the disagreement prior to the review. For the conduct of reviews, see Revenue and Customs Brief 10/09, 16 March 2009.

The person offered a review (see s 83A) or requiring a review (see s 83B) may make representations. Representations are taken into account in the review only if HMRC are given a reasonable opportunity to consider them. They should therefore be made earlier rather than later in the review period (see below).

The review may conclude that the decision is to be confirmed, varied or cancelled. HMRC give the relevant person a "notice of conclusions". This notice sets out the conclusions of the review and HMRC's reasoning. It must be given no later than 45 days after: (1) the date when HMRC received the person's notice accepting the offer of a review (see s 83A); (2) the date when HMRC received the taxpayer's notice requiring a review (see s 83B); or (3) the date when HMRC decided to undertake a review following a request made out of time (see s 83E). The 45-day period may be varied by mutual agreement.

If HMRC fail to meet the foregoing deadline, the outcome of the review is deemed to be a conclusion that the decision should be upheld. HMRC must notify the relevant person accordingly.

83G. Bringing of appeals

As regards a decision in respect of which HMRC is required to offer a review (see s 83A), the time limit for bringing an appeal is 30 days. Time begins to run from the dates set out in the following table.

Circumstances	*Day from which time runs*	*Authority*
1. The offer is declined or no action is taken in respect of it	The later of: • the date of the document notifying the decision to which the appeal relates; and • the date of the notice (if any) extending the 30-day period	s 83G(1)(*a*)(i) and (*b*)
2. The offer is accepted in time	The date of the document notifying the conclusions of the review	s 83G(2) and (3)(*b*)
3. The offer is accepted out of time:		
• Reasonable excuse for the delay in accepting the offer	The date of the document notifying the conclusions of the review ("the conclusion date")	s 83G(4)(*b*)(i)
• No reasonable excuse or unreasonable delay after reasonable excuse ended	The date on which HMRC decide not to undertake a review	s 83G(4)(*b*)(ii)

No appeal may be made in head 3 until the day from which time runs, ie the conclusion date or the date on which HMRC decide not to undertake a review.

As regards a decision in respect of which HMRC is required to review a decision (see s 83B)), the time limit for bringing an appeal is 30 days. Time begins to run from the dates set out in the following table.

Circumstances	**Day from which time runs**	**Authority**
1. The right to require a review is exercised in time	The later of: • The date on which the person becomes aware of the decision; and • the date of the notice (if any) extending the 30-day period	s 83G(1)(*a*)(ii) and (*b*)
2. The right to require a review is exercised out of time		

Circumstances	Day from which time runs	Authority
• Reasonable excuse for the delay in exercising the right	The date of the document notifying the conclusions of the review ("the conclusion date")	s 83G(4)(*b*)(i)
• No reasonable excuse or unreasonable delay after reasonable excuse ended	The date on which HMRC decide not to undertake a review	s 83G(4)(*b*)(ii)

No appeal may be made in head 2 until the day from which time runs, ie the conclusion date or the date on which HMRC decide not to undertake a review.

84. Further provisions relating to appeals (V5.401)

The appeals listed below cannot be entertained unless one or other of the following requirements are met. The first requirement is that the relevant amount (see below) has been paid or deposited with HMRC. The second requirement is that HMRC are satisfied, or the tribunal (see s 82) decides, that the first requirement would cause the appellant to suffer hardship. An application is made to HMRC in the first instance. An application may be made to the tribunal if HMRC are not satisfied. The tribunal's decision is final. For hardship applications, see *Don Pasquale (a firm) v C & E Comrs* [1990] STC 556, CA (payment to be waived on all or none of the tax assessed); *Dapagem* (No 1072); *Western General Trading Ltd* (No 1551).

The appeals concerned are:

(1) An appeal against a decision in respect of a matter mentioned in s 83(1)(*b*), (*n*), (*p*), (*q*), (*ra*) or (*zb*). These decisions give rise to: (*a*) a liability to pay an amount of VAT (eg s 77A(2)); or (*b*) the assessment of an amount of VAT due (see s 73(1)), an amount as being VAT due (see s 73(2)), an amount deemed to be an amount of VAT due (see s 73(9)) or an amount recoverable as if it were VAT due (see s 76(9) and Sch 11A para 12(7)). "VAT" does not include an amount recoverable as if it were tax: *Widnell Group (a firm) v C & E Comrs* [1997] V & DR 145. This requirement "does not unfairly and improperly exclude access to justice": see *O'Brien v R & C Comrs* [2008] STC 487. It applies to an assessment in respect of input tax, but not a decision regarding input tax or the allowable proportion of input tax which does not involve an assessment: see *Safegold Fashions Ltd v C & E Comrs* [1992] VATTR 105; *Richard Haynes Associates* (No 12300). The amount to be paid or deposited is the amount determined by HMRC to be payable. For payment of this amount, see *Buckley* (No 297); *Mahoney* (No 318). For reallocation of payments made, see *Walker* (No 9973).

(2) An appeal against a recovery assessment, or the amount of such an assessment. A "recovery assessment" is an assessment made under ss 78A (1), 80 (4A), 80B (1) or FA 1997 s 49 (1): see s 78A (5) (applied by ss 80 (4C), 80B (2) and FA 1997 s 49 (4)). For the right of appeal against such assessments, see s 83(1)(*sa*), (*t*), (*ta*) and FA 1997 s 49 (5). The amount to be paid or deposited is the amount notified by the assessment.

In assessment appeals relating to the question whether goods have been used for business purposes, or whether the input tax is attributable to taxable supplies, a determination by HMRC in relation to something in the nature of a luxury, amusement or entertainment may be set aside only if it is unreasonable. For expenditure within this description, see *John Price Business Courses Ltd v C & E Comrs* [1995] V & DR 106; *Myatt & Leason (a firm) v C & E Comrs* [1995] V & DR 440. For expenditure outside this description, see *Ernst & Young v C & E Comrs* [1997] V & DR 183. A tribunal may consider new information only if it could not have been given to HMRC before the determination was made. For use of goods and services, and attribution of input tax, see VATA 1994 ss 24 (1), 26 (1), (2).

An appeal in relation to the flat-rate scheme (see s 83(1)(*fza*)) may be allowed only if the tribunal concludes that HMRC could not reasonably have been satisfied that there were grounds for: (1) a decision to refuse an application to use the scheme; (2) a decision to withdraw an authorisation to use the scheme; (3) a decision regarding the appropriate percentage to be used; or (4) an assessment based on a decision within (1)–(3). For the flat-rate scheme, see s 26B.

An appeal against the refusal of an application to form, vary or disband a VAT group or change the representative member (see s 83(1)(*k*)) on revenue protection grounds (see s 43B(5)(*c*)) may be allowed only if the tribunal concludes that HMRC could not reasonably have been satisfied that there were grounds for refusing the application. The application is held in abeyance until the appeal is determined. It is then given retrospective effect from the time specified in s 43B(4) if the appeal is allowed.

An appeal against the termination of a body corporate's membership of a VAT group (see s 83(1)(*ka*)) on revenue protection grounds (see s 43C(1), (2)) may be allowed only if the tribunal considers that HMRC could not reasonably have been satisfied that there were grounds for the termination. The termination has effect pending determination of the appeal. Membership of the VAT group is restored with retrospective effect if the appeal is allowed.

An appeal against the date from which a body corporate's membership of a VAT group is terminated (see s 83(1)(*ka*)) on eligibility grounds (see s 43C(3), (4)) may be allowed only if the tribunal considers that HMRC could not reasonably have been satisfied that the date was appropriate. The termination has effect pending determination of the appeal. Membership of the VAT group is restored with retrospective effect if the appeal is allowed.

An appeal against a requirement for security in respect of another person's tax (see Sch 11 para 4(2)) is allowed if HMRC fail to satisfy the tribunal that: (1) VAT has been evaded; (2) an attempt has been made to evade VAT; or (3) VAT is likely to be evaded unless security is given. Evasion, for this purpose, includes obtaining a VAT credit that is either excessive or not due.

A tribunal may make a direction increasing an understated assessment to the correct amount. That amount is deemed to have been notified to the appellant. For the manner in which a tribunal exercises its discretion to make a direction, see *Elias Gale Racing v C & E Comrs* [1999] STC 66. For an example, see *BUPA Purchasing Ltd and others v C & E Comrs (No 2)* [2008] STC 101, CA.

A tribunal may reduce a penalty, interest or surcharge assessment to the proper amount exigible, or to give effect to mitigation under s 70 (1), and may cancel a mitigation reduction allowed by HMRC under s 70 (2). It may not otherwise vary the amount of such an assessment.

In an appeal against a direction for persons to be regarded as a single taxable person, the tribunal may allow the appeal only if it considers that HMRC could not reasonably have been satisfied that there were grounds for making the direction. For the test applied, see *Chamberlain v C & E Comrs* [1989] STC 505; *South West Launderettes Ltd* (No 2608); *Mike Kiernan's Beer Tent Co Ltd* (No 17794).

In an appeal against an anti-avoidance direction in relation to a group registration or an assessment made as a consequence of it (see s 83(1)(*wa*)), the grounds on which a tribunal may allow the appeal include:

(a) the conditions for making a direction were met; and

(b) the tribunal is satisfied that the main purpose (or each of the main purposes) for a body's joining or leaving a group registration, or making the transaction concerned, was a genuine commercial purpose unconnected with the making of a supply within Sch 9A para 1 (3) giving rise to a tax advantage (see Sch 9A para 1 (4), (5)).

In an appeal against HMRC's refusal to grant permission or exercise a power in relation to the option to tax (see s 83(1)(*wb*)), the appeal may be allowed only if the tribunal concludes that HMRC could not reasonably have been satisfied that there were grounds for the refusal. The refusal has effect until the appeal is determined.

In an appeal against a direction to keep specified records (see s 83(1)(*zza*)), the tribunal may allow an appeal only if it considers that HMRC could not reasonably have been satisfied that there were grounds for making the direction.

A dispute regarding imported goods is normally dealt with by way of review and appeal under FA 1994 ss 14–16. However, an appeal lies direct to a tribunal under s 83(1)(*b*) if: (1) the dispute relates to the rate of VAT chargeable (ie the standard, reduced or zero rate); and (2) the review provisions of FA 1994 ss 14, 14A and 15 do not apply.

Where a decision of HMRC depended on an earlier decision which is not appealable under s 83, an appeal against the later decision only can be allowed if the Commissioners would have allowed an appeal against the earlier decision. See *XL (Stevenage) Ltd v C & E Comrs* [1981] VATTR 192; *Bardsley v C & E Comrs* [1984] VATTR 171; *London Borough of Camden v C & E Comrs* [1993] VATTR 73; *Brookes v C & E Comrs* [1994] VATTR 35; *Shepherd v C & E Comrs* [1994] VATTR 47; *C & E Comrs v Arnold* [1996] STC 1271; *Jersey Telecoms* (No 13940); *C & E Comrs v National Westminster Bank plc* [2003] STC 1072.

For the judicial review jurisdiction of the Upper Tribunal, see the Tribunal Procedure (Upper Tribunal) Rules 2008, SI 2008/2698, Part 4. For judicial review where an alternative remedy is available, see *R v C & E Comrs and London VAT Tribunal, ex parte Menzies* [1990] STC 263, CA; *R v London Value Added Tax and Duties Tribunal, ex parte Conoco Ltd* [1995] STC 468. For leave to appeal out of time against a tribunal decision, see *C & E Comrs v Facthaven Incentive Marketing Ltd* [1992] STC 839n. For leave to raise new points of law on appeal against a tribunal decision, see *Lenihan v C & E Comrs* [1992] STC 478.

A Treasury order may amend this section to take account of any order made under FA 2003 s 17(1)(*a*) rewriting Sch 10: see FA 2006 s 17(1)(*b*). No order has been made to date.

85. Settling appeals by agreement (V5.461)

The decision under appeal may be upheld, varied or discharged by agreement between the appellant and HMRC. For the essential elements of an agreement, see *R (on the application of DFS Furniture Co plc) v C & E Comrs* [2003] STC 1 at [42], CA. An oral agreement must be confirmed in writing by either party within 30 days. The same consequences follow as if a tribunal (see s 82) had determined the appeal at the date of the written agreement or written confirmation. For termination of the tribunal's jurisdiction, see *Abbey Life Japan Trust* (No 11205); *McGinty v C & E Comrs* [1995] V & DR 193.

The appellant may repudiate or resile from the agreement by giving written notice within 30 days of the written agreement or written confirmation. HMRC have no such right: see *Lamdec Ltd v C & E Comrs* [1991] VATTR 296.

The foregoing provisions apply where an appellant wishes to withdraw his appeal and HMRC do not object. The parties are deemed to have come to an agreement that the appeal should be upheld without variation. The agreement is deemed to be made when the appellant notifies HMRC that he does not wish to proceed with the appeal. HMRC may object by notifying the appellant in writing within 30 days that they are unwilling that the appeal should be treated as withdrawn. An appeal withdrawn under this provision cannot be reopened: *L'Arome International Ltd* (No 14419).

An agent may act on behalf of an appellant in making an agreement with HMRC, or in giving or receiving a notice or notification.

85A. Payment of tax on determination of appeal

The appellant may have paid or deposited an amount with HMRC as a condition of his appeal being entertained (see s 84). If the tribunal (see s 82) holds that all or part of this amount is not due, the amount not due must be repaid to the appellant with interest. For the rate of interest, see FA 1996 s 197.

HMRC may have withheld payment of all or part of a VAT credit claimed by the appellant. If the tribunal holds that all or part of this amount withheld is due to appellant, this amount must be paid to him. In so far as the amount does not qualify for repayment supplement (see s 79), it is paid with interest. For the rate of interest, see FA 1996 s 197.

In either case, interest is paid without deduction of income tax.

85B. Payment of tax where there is a further appeal

A party to an appeal ("the first appeal") may be dissatisfied with the tribunal's decision and appeal against it ("the second appeal"). The sum due to or by the appellant in accordance with the tribunal's decision on the first appeal must be paid notwithstanding the pending second appeal. If this sum is altered by the order made (tribunal) or judgment given (court) on the second appeal, the difference is paid to the appellant by HMRC, or vice versa, with such interest (if any) as the tribunal or court allows. If a sum is due to HMRC, HMRC must issue a notice to the appellant setting out the amount payable in accordance with the order or judgment. This amount must be paid within 30 days, counted from the date of the notice.

HMRC may be dissatisfied with the requirement to make a payment to the appellant. If so, they may make an application to the tribunal or court to which the second appeal is made. The tribunal or court may: (1) give permission for HMRC to withhold payment; or (2) require the appellant to provide adequate security before payment is made. The tribunal or court may do so if it considers this to be necessary for the protection of the revenue. For adequate security, see s 85B(8).

The appellant may be dissatisfied that he is required to make a payment to HMRC or that the sum he considers to be due from them continues to be withheld. If so, he may make an application to HMRC. HMRC may do one or more of the following things if they are satisfied that the payment, or the withholding of the payment, might reasonably be expected to result in "financial extremity": (1) decide how much (if any) of the sum under appeal should be paid to or by the appellant; (2) require the appellant to provide adequate security; or (3) stay the requirement to pay or repay. For adequate security, see s 85B(8).

The appellant may be dissatisfied with HMRC's response to his application. If so, he may make an application to the tribunal or court to which the second appeal is made. The court or tribunal may replace, vary or supplement HMRC's decision if it is satisfied that the payment, or the withholding of the payment, might reasonably be expected to result in "financial extremity". It may: (1) decide how much (if any) of the sum under appeal should be paid to or by the appellant; (2) require the appellant to provide adequate security; or (3) stay the requirement to pay or repay. For adequate security, see s 85B(8).

86. Appeals to the Court of Appeal

[Repealed.]

87. Enforcement of registered or recorded tribunal decisions etc

[Repealed.]

PART VI SUPPLEMENTARY PROVISIONS

CHANGE IN RATE OF VAT ETC AND DISCLOSURE OF INFORMATION

88. Supplies spanning change of rate, etc (V3.141)

A change in the rate of VAT, or a description of exempt, reduced-rate or zero-rated supplies, may occur between a basic tax point determined under s 4 (2), (3) and a tax point determined by reference to a payment or tax invoice under s 5 (1), (2), (3), (5). Where this is so, the supply is charged in accordance with the legislation in force at the basic tax point if an election is made to that effect. For corresponding elections where the time of supply is determined in accordance with regulations, see VAT Regulations 1995, SI 1995/2518 reg 95.

A change in the rate of VAT, or a description of exempt, reduced-rate or zero-rated acquisitions, may occur between the time when goods are first removed and the time when it is treated as taking place (see ss 12, 18). Where this is so, VAT is charged in accordance with the legislation in force when the goods are first removed if an election is made to that effect.

An invoice issued before an election has been made is corrected in accordance with regulations. See VAT Regulations 1995, SI 1995/2518 reg 15.

No election may be made if an invoice has been issued under self-billing arrangements or goods have been sold from the assets of a business in satisfaction of a debt.

89. Adjustment of contracts on changes in VAT (V3.151)

The consideration for a supply of goods or services specified in a lease or contract must be adjusted, unless the lease or contract specifies otherwise, to reflect a subsequent change in the rate of tax or the fact that tax has become, or ceased to be, chargeable on the supply as a result of a change in the legislation or the making of an option to tax land (as to which see Sch 10 Part 1). A lease "specifies otherwise" only if it refers specifically to VAT or to this section.

90. Failure of resolution under Provisional Collection of Taxes Act 1968 (V1.131)

The rate of VAT may be increased by a House of Commons resolution (see Provisional Collection of Taxes Act 1968 s 1). A person is entitled to a repayment in respect of a supply or acquisition if he has paid VAT at the increased rate and the resolution subsequently ceases to have statutory effect. VAT on the supply or acquisition is chargeable at the original rate if the resolution ceases to have effect before the VAT is paid. In either case, VAT at the original rate or increased rate is charged by reference to the same value determined in accordance with s 19(2) (supply) or 20(3) (acquisition). The VAT eligible for input tax credit or refund is determined by reference to the original rate.

For example, assume that VAT is increased from 20% to 25% by Budget resolution and that VAT is charged in accordance with the resolution on a supply with a value of £800. The VAT charged is £800 @ 25% = £200. If the Budget resolution fails, the VAT due is £800 @ 20% = £160. If the VAT was paid before the resolution ceased to have statutory effect, the VAT repayable is £200 – £160 = £40. The input tax credit or refund is £160. This applies whether or not the VAT was paid before the resolution ceased to have statutory effect and whether or not the supplier received a repayment.

91. Disclosure of information for statistical purposes (V1.270)

The Commissioners may disclose to the Department of Trade and Industry information for a central register of businesses or any statistical survey. The information which may be provided is the VAT numbers allocated, the names, addresses, status, trade classification and value of supplies. This information may be released provided it is in a form which does not identify any individual business.

Improper disclosure attracts on summary conviction a fine of up to £2,000 or on conviction on indictment up to two years' imprisonment and an unlimited fine.

Customs and Excise Management Act 1979 ss 145–155 apply to offences and penalties under this section: see s 72 (12).

INTERPRETATIVE PROVISIONS

92. Taxation under the laws of other member states etc (V1.272)

References to the law of another EU member state are references to national legislation giving effect to EU VAT legislation. The phrases "a person being taxable in another member state" and "goods being acquired by a person in another member state" are defined. The following matters may be determined in accordance with regulations: (1) proving the effect of the legislation of another EU member state and whether it corresponds to UK legislation: (2) identifying persons treated as taxable in another EU member state; and (3) identifying the proportion of any consideration treated as VAT charged under the law of another EU member state. No regulations have been made.

A certificate given by the Commissioners in relation to the following matters in civil or criminal proceedings is sufficient evidence of the fact stated until the contrary is proved: (1) whether a person is a taxable person in another EU member state; and (2) whether VAT payable under the law of another EU member state has been paid.

The Commissioners may use specified information powers under Sch 11 in order to comply with EU obligations, eg under Regulation (EC) No 1798/2003 (administrative co-operation).

93. Territories included in references to other member states etc (V1.213)

The territory of the EU and individual member states may be defined by regulations for VAT purposes. Customs legislation may be applied by regulations where territory is treated as being outside the EU. See VAT Regulations 1995, SI 1995/2518 regs 136–145.

94. Meaning of "business", etc (V2.202)

Business includes any trade, profession or vocation. The legislation "must so far as possible be construed so as to give effect to the Sixth Directive": *Institute of Chartered Accountants in England and Wales v C & E Comrs* [1999] STC 398 at 402, HL. Thus, the UK courts and the tribunal (see s 82) construe the term "business" by reference to the carrying out of an "economic activity" as defined in Directive 2006/112/EC art 9(1) second para (formerly Directive 77/388/EEC art 4(2)) and interpreted by the EU Court of Justice. The economic activity may be carried out in any place. The results or purpose of the economic activity are irrelevant: Directive 2006/112/EC art 9(1) first para (formerly Directive 77/388/EEC art 4(1)).

An economic activity is characterised, in particular, by a concern to maximise returns on capital investment: *Floridienne SA v Belgium* (case C-142/99) [2000] STC 1044 at [28], ECJ. Thus, independent notaries and bailiffs carry on an economic activity because their purpose is to cover their overheads and provide themselves with income: *Commission v Netherlands* (case C-235/85) [1987] ECR 1471, ECJ.

Early UK cases on the nature of a business were largely decided without reference to EU law: see in particular *C & E Comrs v Morrison's Academy Boarding Houses Association* [1978] STC 1; *National Water Council v C & E Comrs* [1979] STC 157; *Church of Scientology of California v C & E Comrs* [1979] STC 297; *C & E Comrs v Lord Fisher* [1981] STC 238; *C & E Comrs v Royal Exchange Theatre Trust* [1979] STC 728; *Greater London Red Cross Blood Transfusion Service v C & E Comrs* [1983] VATTR 241; *Singer & Friedlander Ltd v C & E Comrs* [1989] VATTR 27, [1989] 1 CMLR 814; *Westminster City Council v C & E Comrs* [1989] VATTR 71, [1990] 2 CMLR 81. For more recent authorities, see in particular *Institute of Chartered Accountants in England and Wales v C & E Comrs* [1999] STC 398, HL; *C & E Comrs v Yarburgh Children's Trust* [2002] STC 207; *C & E Comrs v St Paul's Community Project Ltd* [2005] STC 95; *C & E Comrs v Isle of Wight Council* [2005] STC 257; *Edinburgh Telford College v R & C Comrs* [2006] STC 1291; *Riverside Housing Association Ltd v R & C Comrs* [2006] STC 2072.

Although the results or purpose of an *economic activity* are irrelevant, results or purpose appear to be relevant in deciding whether an activity amounts to an economic activity in the first place. It is insufficient that money is paid and a benefit received. The activity must have an economic nature: *Institute of Chartered Accountants in England and Wales v C & E Comrs* [1999] STC 398 at 402, 404, HL. For examples of activities lacking an economic nature, see *Commission v France* (case C-50/87) [1988] ECR 4797 (lettings at low rent by local authority to associations with social objectives or undertakings establishing themselves in the locality); *Welcome Trust Ltd v C & E Comrs* (case C-155/94) [1996] STC 945, ECJ (management of investments); *Floridienne SA v Belgium* (case C-142/99) [2000] STC 1044, ECJ (holding company lending sums to subsidiaries to enable them to carry on their commercial activities with third parties). In the UK, see *Institute of Chartered Accountants in England and Wales v C & E Comrs* [1999] STC 398, HL (regulatory function); *C & E Comrs v Lord Fisher* [1981] STC 238 (pleasure and social enjoyment); *C & E Comrs v Yarburgh Children's Trust* [2002] STC 207 (lease to playgroup with a purpose of providing day care facilities for children); *C & E Comrs v St Paul's Community Project Ltd* [2005] STC 95 (day nursery). For the Commissioners' policy regarding non-profit making bodies, see Business Brief 2/05, 10 February 2005.

In determining whether an activity amounts to a business, it is irrelevant whether the sole economic objective is to obtain a tax advantage: *Halifax plc and others v C & E Comrs* (case C-255/02) [2006] ECR I–1609, [2006] STC 919, ECJ; *University of Huddersfield Higher Education Corpn v C & E Comrs* (case C-223/03) [2006] ECR I–1751, [2006] STC 980, ECJ.

One or more transactions in a chain of supply may be tainted by VAT fraud. An untainted supply made by one trader in the chain does not cease to be made in the course or furtherance of business by reason of the fraudulent intentions of the other members of the chain or the fraudulent nature of other transactions in the chain of which the trader is unaware or has no means of knowing: *Optigen Ltd v C & E Comrs; Fulcrum Electronics Ltd v C & E Comrs; Bond House Systems Ltd v C & E Comrs* (joined cases C-354/03, C-355/03 and C-484/03) [2006] ECR I–483, [2006] STC 419, ECJ.

For activities which do not give rise to supplies made for a consideration, see *Staatssecretaris van Financiën v Hong-Kong Trade Development Council* [1984] ECR 1277 (providing trade information without charge); *C & E Comrs v Apple and Pear Development Council* [1986] STC 192, HL (statutory levy); *Whitechapel Art Gallery v C & E Comrs* [1986] STC 156 (free admission to premises); Business Brief 23/93, 26 July 1993 (sale of property during rent-free period).

For activities kept afloat by charitable donations and subventions, see *Yoga for Health Foundation v C & E Comrs* [1983] VATTR 297, on appeal [1984] STC 630; *Holy Spirit Association for the Unification of World Christianity* (No 1777).

For activities carried on for pleasure and social enjoyment, see *C & E Comrs v Lord Fisher* [1981] STC 238 and contrast *Williams* (No 14240).

Anything done in connection with the termination of a business is done in the course or furtherance of business. For the winding up of a business, see *I/S Fini H v Skatteministeriet* (case C-32/03) [2005] ECR I–1599, [2005] STC 903, ECJ. For abandonment of an intention to carry on an economic activity, see *Intercommunale voor Zeewarerontzilting (in liquidation) v Belgian State* (case C-110/94) [1996] STC 569, ECJ.

Transferring all or part of a business as a going concern is a supply made in the course or furtherance of business. For transfers of going concerns, see s 49.

For specific provisions in relation to admission charges, clubs and offices, see below.

Specific activities

Admission charge. Admitting persons to premises for a consideration amounts to a business. For a testimonial match, see *Eric Taylor Deceased Testimonial Match Committee v C & E Comrs* [1975] VATTR 8. For admission by programme, contrast *Rochdale Hornets Football Co Ltd v C & E Comrs* [1975] VATTR 71 and *Jarmain v C & E Comrs* [1979] VATTR 41.

Club, association or organisation. The provision of facilities or advantages to members by a club, association, or organisation amounts to a business. For facilities or advantages, see *Eastbourne Town Radio Cars Association v C & E Comrs* [2001] STC 606, HL; *C & E Comrs v British Field Sports Society* [1998] STC 315, CA; *Carlton Lodge Club v C & E Comrs* [1974] STC 507; *Royal Highland and Agricultural Society of Scotland v C &*

E Comrs [1976] VATTR 38; *Cambuslang Athletic Club* (No 1592); *British Olympic Association v C & E Comrs* [1979] VATTR 122; *Royal Ulster Constabulary Athletic Association Ltd v C & E Comrs* [1989] VATTR 17; *Northampton Football Association* (No 12936); *Compassion in World Farming Ltd v C & E Comrs* [1997] V & DR 281. For the absence of benefit to members, see *Friends of the Ironbridge Gorge Museum v C & E Comrs* [1991] VATTR 97. For match fees, contrast *Belvedere & Calder Vale Sports Club* (No 931) and *Sleaford RFC* (No 9844). For external advertising activities carried out by a section of a political party, see *SPÖ Landesorganisation Kärnten v Finanzamt Klagenfurt* (case C-267/08) [2009] ECR I–9781, [2010] STC 287.

For subscriptions and other consideration, see *Lord Advocate v Largs Golf Club* [1985] STC 226 (payment by third party); *C & E Comrs v Automobile Association* [1974] STC 192 (apportionment); *C & E Comrs v Little Spain Club Ltd* [1979] STC 170 (special levy); *Exeter Golf & Country Club Ltd v C & E Comrs* [1981] STC 211, CA (interest free loan); *Dyrham Park Country Club v C & E Comrs* [1978] VATTR 244 (bond); *South Church Workmen's Club & Institute Ltd* (No 613) and *Oldbus Ltd* (No 5119) (shares).

Employee. For employees, see Directive 2006/112/EC art 10 (formerly Directive 77/388/EEC art 4(4)); *Dimosio v Karageorgou* (joined cases C-78/02 to C-80/02) [2003] ECR I–13295, [2003] SWTI 1937, ECJ. Contrast the position of office holders below. For the distinction between a contract of service and a contract for services, see *C & E Comrs v Hodges* [2000] STC 262; *New Way School of Motoring Ltd v C & E Comrs* [1979] VATTR 57; *Chalmers (a firm)* (No 1354); *Berbrooke Fashions v C & E Comrs* [1977] VATTR 168; *Headley Enterprises* (No 1295). Employments were held to exist in *Ricarby v C & E Comrs* [1973] VATTR 186; *Cant v C & E Comrs* [1976] VATTR 237; *Holland v C & E Comrs* [1978] VATTR 57; *Lean & Rose v C & E Comrs* [1974] VATTR 7; *Headline and Just Hair* (No 4089).

Exploitation of tangible and intangible property. For the exploitation of tangible and intangible property for the purpose of obtaining income therefrom on a continuing basis under Directive 2006/112/EC art 9(1) second para (formerly Directive 77/388/EEC art 4(2)), see *Rompelman v Minister van Financiën* (case 268/83) [1985] ECR 665, ECJ (right to future transfer of property); *van Tiem v Staatssecretaris van Financiën* (case C-186/89) [1993] STC 91, ECJ (grant of building rights); *C & E Comrs v Yarburgh Children's Trust* [2002] STC 207 (grant of lease by charity to playgroup not an economic activity); *Laurie (a firm)* (No 17219) (lease and leaseback arrangement entered into for tax avoidance purposes); *Enkler v Finanzamt Homburg* (case C-230/94) [1996] STC 1316, ECJ (hire of goods); *Polysar Investments Netherlands BV v Inspecteur der Invoerrechten en Accijnzen, Arnhem* (case C-60/90) [1993] STC 222, ECJ, *Sofitam SA v Ministre Chargé du Budget* (case C-333/91) [1997] STC 226, *Newmir plc v C & E Comrs* [1993] VATTR 55 (holding company); *Banque Bruxelles Lambert SA v Belgian State* (case C-8/03) [2004] ECR I–10157, [2004] STC 1643, ECJ (open-ended investment company); *NSPCC v C & E Comrs* [1992] VATTR 417, *The Wellcome Trust Ltd v C & E Comrs* (case C-155/94) [1996] STC 945, ECJ, *Harnas & Helm CV v Staatsecretais van Financiën* (case C-80/85) [1997] STC 384, ECJ, Business Brief 21/96, 17 October 1996 (investments in stocks and shares); *Adstock Ltd* (No 10034) (fishing rights). For cases relating to hirings decided under UK legislation, see *Three H Aircraft Hire v C & E Comrs* [1982] STC 653; *Coleman v C & E Comrs* [1976] VATTR 24; *Walker v C & E Comrs* [1976] VATTR 10; *Wilcox v C & E Comrs* [1978] VATTR 79. For the distinction between business and investment, see *Tarrakarn Ltd v C & E Comrs* [1996] V & DR 516.

Factoring. For factoring, see *Finanzamt Groß-Gerau v MKG-Kraftfahrzeuge-Factory GmbH* (case C-305/01) [2003] STC 951, ECJ.

Holding company. A holding company does not carry on a business merely because it acquires financial holdings in other undertakings. However, it may do so if it has direct or indirect involvement in management of its subsidiaries and makes taxable transactions, eg supplying administrative, financial, commercial or technical services to its subsidiaries: *Polysar Investments Netherlands BV v Inspecteur der Invoerrechten en Accijnzen, Arnhem* (case C-60/90) [1993] STC 222, ECJ; *Floridienne SA v Belgium* (case C-142/99) [2000] STC 1044, ECJ; *Cibo Participations SA v Directeur régional des impôts du Nord-Pas-de-Calais* (case C-16/00) [2002] STC 460, ECJ. For the disposal of shares in a subsidiary, see *Skatteverket v AB SKF* (case C-29/08) [2009] ECR I–10413; [2010] STC 419, ECJ.

Office holder. Where an office is held as part of a trade, profession or vocation (eg, a practising solicitor appointed as a director of a client company), remuneration for such services is part of the turnover of the business for VAT purposes. See *Hempsons (a firm) v C & E Comrs* [1977] VATTR 73; *Gardner v C & E Comrs* [1989] VATTR 132.

Partnership. For the admission of a new partner to a partnership, see *KapHag Renditefonds 35 Spreecenter Berlin-Hellersdorf3 Tranche GbR v Finanzamt Charlottenburg* (case C-442/01) [2003] ECR I–6851, [2005] STC 1500, ECJ.

Public authority. For the nature and business activities of public authorities under EU law, see the commentary to Directive 2006/112/EC art 13 in Part 1B. For the transposition of this provision into UK law, see *Glasgow City Council* (No 15491); *City of London Corporation* (No 17892); *Isle of Wight Council* (No 18557), on appeal sub nom *C & E Comrs v Isle of Wight Council* [2005] STC 257; cf *Commission v Ireland* (case C-554/07) [2009] ECR I–128. For the direct effect of this provision, see *C & E Comrs v Isle of Wight Council* [2005] STC 257; *Edinburgh Telford College v R & C Comrs* [2006] STC 1291. For the Commissioners' views, see Revenue and Customs Brief 27/08, 19 May 2008.

In the UK, see *C & E Comrs v Apple and Pear Development Council* [1986] STC 192, HL; *Institute of Chartered Accountants in England and Wales v C & E Comrs* [1999] STC 398, HL; *National Water Council v C & E Comrs* [1979] STC 157; *Haringey London Borough Council v C & E Comrs* [1995] STC 830; *West Devon Borough Council v C & E Comrs* [2001] STC 1282; *C & E Comrs v Isle of Wight Council* [2005] STC 257; *Edinburgh Telford College v R & C Comrs* [2006] STC 1291; *University of Southampton v R & C Comrs* [2006] STC 1389; *Cambridge University v R & C Comrs* [2009] STC 1288; *R & C Comrs v Isle of Wight Borough Council and others* [2008] STC 614, refd (case C-288/07) [2008] ECR I–7203, [2008] STC 2964, ECJ and subsequently [2009] STC 1098 (case remitted to the tribunal for rehearing); *The Radio Authority v C & E Comrs* [1992] VATTR 155; *The Arts Council of Great Britain v C & E Comrs* [1994] VATTR 313; *The City Council of Norwich* (No 11822); *Metropolitan Borough of* Wirral (No 14674); *Glasgow City Council* (No 15491) and Business Brief 19/98, 15 September 1998; *Rhonnda Cynon Taff County Borough Council v C & E Comrs* [2000] V & DR 150 and Business Brief 4/00, 17 March 2000; *Cardiff Community Housing Association Ltd v C & E Comrs* [2000] V & DR 346; *City of London Corporation* (No 17892); Business Brief 9/95, 18 May 1995 (supplies between local authorities); Business Brief 5/97, 5 March 1997 (building control fees). For overseas tourist offices, see *Netherlands Board of Tourism* (No 12935); *Austrian National Tourist Office* (No 15561); and contrast *Turespaña* (No 14568). For supplies by Financial Ombudsman Services Ltd, see Notice No 48 (December 2010) para 3.23. For supplies by the Financial Services Authority, see Notice No 48 (December 2010) para 3.42. For supplies by the Financial Services Compensation Scheme Ltd between 1 February 2001 and 30 November 2001, see Notice No 48 (December 2010) para 3.31.

Racehorses. For the activities of racehorse owners, see Notice No 700/67. For nominations sold by stallion syndicates, see Business Brief 13/00, 28 September 2000.

95. Meaning of "new means of transport" (V1.294)

The terms "means of transport" and "new" are defined. The time when a means of transport first enters into service is determined in accordance with regulations. See VAT Regulations 1995, SI 1995/2518 reg 147.

This section may be varied by Treasury order.

96. Other interpretative provisions

Words and phrases used in the Act are defined.

Following the merger of HM Customs and Excise and the Inland Revenue, "the Commissioners" means the Commissioners of HM Revenue and Customs: see CRCA 2005 s 50(1). The Commissioners are referred to as "HMRC" in recent legislation, and are now so defined in this section. For the Commissioners of HM Revenue and Customs, see CRCA 2005 s 1.

For "major interest", see *Isaac (a firm)* (No 14656) (rectification of lease to extend term beyond 21 years).

The following matters are determined in accordance with EU customs legislation: (1) whether goods have entered EU territory (see Regulation (EEC) No 2913/92 art 38 (OJ L302/1, 19.10.92)); (2) the time when a customs debt is incurred (see Regulation (EEC) Nos 2913/92 arts 201–206 (OJ L302/1, 19.10.92) and 2454/93 arts 859–867 (OJ L253/1, 11.10.93)); and (3) the person liable to discharge a customs debt (see Regulation (EEC) Nos 2913/92 arts 201–206 (OJ L302/1, 19.10.92) and 2454/93 arts 859–867 (OJ L253/1, 11.10.93)).

"Excise duty" is defined so as to include any increase or decrease made by Treasury order under Excise Duties (Surcharges or Rebates) Act 1979 s 1. For duties specified as excise duties, see FA 1994, s 14.

In Schs 7A (reduced rate), 8 (zero-rating) and 9 (exemption), the items in each group are interpreted in accordance with the notes to that group. The title of each group does not affect the interpretation of that group.

The exemption or zero-rating of an interest, right, licence or facility relating to land is often determined by reference to the description of the grant: see VATA 1994 Sch 8 Group 5 Item 1, Sch 8 Group 6 Item 1, Sch 9 Group 1 Item 1(*a*), (*c*), (*e*), (*h*)–(*n*), Sch 10 paras 5–11. However, a grant may give rise to one or more subsequent supplies. Where this is so, the subsequent supply is normally exempt or zero-rated if it falls within the same description at the time of supply. However, this does not apply if the subsequent supply relates to a grant of the fee simple in a new or partly completed building or civil engineering work. If the grant was excluded from exemption under VATA 1994 Sch 9 Group 1 Item 1(*a*), so is the subsequent supply. Thus, a subsequent supply may be excluded from exemption even though the building or civil engineering work is no longer new at the time of supply. For supplies made after 8 April 2003 arising from to a prior grant, see FA 2003 s 20(2); *RBS Property Developments Ltd* (No 17789).

SUPPLEMENTAL PROVISIONS

97. Orders, rules and regulations (V1.236)

Orders, regulations and rules are made by statutory instrument. Statutory instruments are subject to either the positive procedure (ie they must be laid before and approved by Parliament) or the negative procedure (ie they have effect unless annulled by Parliament).

Orders in respect of the following matters are subject to the positive procedure in the House of Commons. An order ceases to have effect 28 days after it is made unless it is approved. The matters are:

(a) free supply of services (s 5), place of supply of services (s 7A) and payments on account (s 28);

(b) reducing the de minimis limit for gifts of goods which are not treated as supplies of goods (Sch 4 para 5);

(c) increasing the rate of VAT (see s 2), excluding VAT from input tax credit (s 27), and varying the scope of the reduced rate, zero-rate or exemption (ss 29A, 30, 31);

(d) an order resulting in any bodies ceasing to be eligible to be members of a VAT group;

(e) variation of provisions relating to land and buildings (s 51);

(f) flat-rate addition and designated activities for the purposes of the flat-rate scheme for farmers;

(g) variation of the reverse charge for goods of a kind used in missing trader intra-community fraud (s 55A);

(h) a direction for open market value to apply (see Sch 6 para 1A); and
(i) additional circumstances in which the consideration for a credit voucher is not disregarded (see Sch 10A para 3);
(j) designation of a scheme or provision for the purposes of the notification rules relating to avoidance schemes (see Sch 11A paras 3, 4).

Any other order, and any regulation, is subject to the negative procedure in the House of Commons. However, this does not apply to:
(a) orders made in relation to repayment supplement (s 79);
(b) orders and regulations for which another procedure is specified; and
(c) orders and regulations appointing commencement dates or effective dates of repeal for the purposes of VATA 1994.

97A. Place of supply orders: transitional provision

An order made under s 7A (6) may change the place of supply in relation to services of a specified description made from a specified date (referred to as the "commencement date") so that the services are now treated as supplied in the UK. Where this is so, s 6 (14A) provides that the time of supply rules are modified by the rules set out below.

If the time of supply would otherwise be determined by reference to an invoice or document issued before the commencement date, the invoice or document is disregarded in determining the time of supply of services specified in the order.

If the time of supply would otherwise be determined by reference to a payment received by the supplier before the commencement date, any part of the payment relating to a period on or after the commencement date is deemed to have been received on that date.

If the time of supply would otherwise be determined by reference to a payment received by the supplier on or after the commencement date, any part of the payment relating to a period before the commencement date is deemed to have been received before that date.

In principle, a payment for services is deemed to relate to the time when the services are performed. However, an apportionment is made if services are performed over a period which straddles the commencement date. The proportion of the payment which relates to services performed before the commencement date is deemed to relate to a time before that date and the remainder to a time on or after that date. The apportionment must be made on a just and reasonable basis.

98. Service of notices (V5.371, V5.373)

Posting a notice, notification requirement or demand to the last or usual residence or place of business of a person, or his tax representative, is sufficient. But see *C & E Comrs v Medway Draughting & Technical Services Ltd* [1989] STC 346 in relation to surcharge liability notices.

99. Refund of VAT to Government of Northern Ireland (V1.215)

VAT incurred by the Government of Northern Ireland for non-business purposes is refunded by the Commissioners.

100. Savings and transitional provisions, consequential amendments and repeals

Schedule 13 makes savings and transitional provisions. Schedule 14 makes consequential amendments. Schedule 15 repeals the enactments and orders consolidated in this Act. Interpretation Act 1978 s 17 applies.

101. Commencement and extent

VATA 1994 came into force on 1 September 1994. The transitional provisions are no longer relevant.

VATA 1994 extends to Northern Ireland. It extends to the Isle of Man only as regards Sch 13 para 23 and Sch 14 para 7.

102. Short title

This Act is cited as Value Added Tax Act 1994.

SCHEDULES

SCHEDULE A1 CHARGE AT REDUCED RATE (SECTION 2)

This schedule has been repealed. For the goods and services charged to VAT at the reduced rate, see Sch 7A.

SCHEDULE 1 REGISTRATION IN RESPECT OF TAXABLE SUPPLIES (SECTION 3 (2))

Liability to be registered

1.—(V2.120–V2.122, V2.135, V2.136) A person is liable to registration if: (1) he makes taxable supplies and his taxable turnover for a one year period ending on the last day of any month exceeded £73,000; or (2) a business was transferred to him as a going concern and his taxable turnover for the one year period ending on the date of transfer exceeded £73,000. For taxable turnover where a business is transferred as a going concern, see s 49(1)(*a*). A person is not liable to registration if he satisfies the Commissioners that taxable turnover for next year will not exceed £71,000. The Commissioners must decide whether or not they are satisfied on the basis of the information available to them at the date when the registration is due to take effect under Sch 1 para 5 or 7: *Gray (trading as William Gray & Son) v C & E Comrs* [2000] STC 880. Taxable turnover is disregarded if: (1) it was made under a previous registration while the trader was liable or entitled to registration; and (2) the Commissioners were given all the information they needed to decide whether to cancel the previous registration.

A person is liable to registration if: (1) he makes taxable supplies and there are reasonable grounds for believing, at any time, that taxable turnover for the next 30 days will exceed £73,000 (see *XL (Stevenage) Ltd v C & E Comrs* [1981] VATTR 192); or (2) a business was transferred to him as a going concern and there are reasonable grounds for believing, at the date of transfer, that taxable turnover for the next 30 days will exceed £71,000. For the test applied under superseded legislation, see *Bennett v C & E Comrs* [1999] STC 248; *Optimum Personnel Evaluation (Operations) Ltd* (No 2334).

The following are disregarded when calculating turnover for registration purposes under Sch 1:

- sales of capital assets (other than standard rated interests, rights and licences in land). The following factors are taken into account in deciding whether goods are "capital assets": (*a*) whether they have a durable nature, (*b*) their value, (*c*) whether they are sold immediately or retained for a number of years, (*d*) whether the sales are unusual and make a drastic change in the turnover for one year, and (*e*) whether the sales reflect the actual size of the undertaking: *Harbig Leasing Two Ltd* (No 16845) (sale of motor cars acquired on transfer of part of a business as a going concern). For the exclusion of this provision in relation to goods of a kind used in missing trader intra-community fraud, see s 55A(4);
- the last supply of goods made before goods are removed from a fiscal warehouse (see s 18B(4)); and
- a self-supply of zero-rated services relating to goods in a fiscal warehouse (see s 18C(3)).

A trader using the special accounting scheme for electronic services is not required to be registered by virtue of the qualifying services (as defined in Sch 3B para 3) he supplies: see Sch 3B para 17. For the special accounting scheme, see Sch 3B.

1A.—Some traders hive off part of their business to separate ownership in order to avoid registration or exclude certain supplies from VAT. For example, a publican might arrange for his wife to supply the meals in his public house, or different persons might operate a launderette on certain weeks or days. The Commissioners may counter such arrangements by making a direction under Sch 1 para 2.

The purpose of such a direction is to prevent the maintenance or creation of an artificial separation of business activities carried on by two or more persons from resulting in an avoidance of VAT. In determining whether a separation is artificial, it is necessary to take into account the degree to which the persons are closely bound together by financial, economic and organisational links. For the tests applied, see *Mike Kiernan's Beer Tent Co Ltd* (No 17794).

2.—(V2.120) The Commissioners may make a direction for the purpose stated in Sch 1 para 1A. The effect of a direction is that named persons are treated as a single taxable person carrying on the activities of a described business. The single taxable person is liable to registration from the date of the direction or from such later date as may be specified therein. A direction is invalid if it specifies an earlier date: *Elder* (No 15882).

The Commissioners may make a direction if they are satisfied that:

(a) each named person makes (or has made) taxable supplies;

(b) the taxable supplies made by each person form only part of certain activities (ie the business described in the direction), additional activities being carried on concurrently or previously (or both) by the other named person(s); and

(c) a person carrying on the business described in the direction (ie the sum of the activities carried on by all of the named persons) would be liable to registration under para 1 above if all of the taxable supplies of that business were taken into account.

For the Commissioners' statement of practice, see Notice No 700/1 (May 2002) section 14. For examples of directions made before 19 March 1997, see *Chamberlain v C & E Comrs* [1989] STC 505; *Osman v C & E Comrs* [1989] STC 596, [1991] 3 CMLR 262; *Lyons v C & E Comrs* [1987] VATTR 187; *South West Launderettes Ltd* (No 2608); *Burrell (trading as The Firm) v C & E Comrs* [1997] STC 1413. For directions set aside, see *Grisdale v C & E Comrs* [1989] VATTR 162; *Myers (a firm)* (No 3951); *Thompson, Thompson and Giblin* (No 4196); *Knights* (No 5165); *Hundsdoerfer v C & E Comrs* [1990] VATTR 158; *Horsman v C & E Comrs* [1990] VATTR 151.

3.—(V2.151) A person ceases to be liable to registration under Sch 1 if he satisfies the Commissioners that: (1) he has ceased to make taxable supplies; or (2) the value of his taxable supplies does not exceed the registration limits in Sch 1 para 1.

4.—(V2.151) A registered trader ceases to be liable to registration at any time if he satisfies the Commissioners that his taxable turnover for the year then beginning will not exceed £71,000 and that he will neither cease making taxable supplies nor suspend making taxable supplies for more than 30 days during the one year period.

Sales of capital assets (other than standard rated interests, rights and licences in land) and direct sales relevant to registration under Sch 2 are disregarded when calculating turnover for deregistration purposes.

Notification of liability and registration

5.—(V2.135) A person liable to registration at the end of any month must notify his liability within 30 days. He is registered from: (1) the end of the next following month; or (2) a mutually agreed earlier date. For an invalid registration under head (1), see *Dyer v C & E Comrs* [2005] STC 715 (registration effective from a date earlier than the statutory date).

6.—(V2.136) A person liable to registration at any time must notify his liability within 30 days of that time. He is registered from that time.

7.—(V2.131) A person liable to registration at the date when a business is transferred to him as a going concern must notify his liability within 30 days of the date of transfer. He is registered from the date of transfer.

8.—If a person liable to registration at the end of any month is also liable to registration under another provision at the same time, he is registered under the other provision.

Entitlement to be registered

9.—(V2.144) A person who makes or intends to make taxable supplies is entitled to be registered if he so requests. See *Dewhirst* (No 13793). The registration takes effect from the date of his request or a mutually agreed earlier date. A registration will not be backdated more than three years: Business Brief 8/97, 25 March 1997. A body corporate cannot be registered under this provision if it is already included in a VAT group: *C & E Comrs v Eastwood Care Homes (Ilkeston) Ltd* [2001] STC 1629 (application for registration in respect of period prior to joining the group). For registration of property owners, see Press Notice 65/90, 25 September 1990; Business Brief 8/96, 17 May 1996. For registration of racehorse owners, see Notice No 700/67.

10.—(V2.146) A person is entitled to be registered if: (1) he makes or (if carrying on a business) intends to make either supplies outside the UK which would be taxable supplies if made within the UK or services specified in VAT (Input Tax) (Specified Supplies) Order 1999, SI 1999/3121; (2) his business establishment (or one of them) or his usual place of residence is in the UK; (3) he neither makes nor intends to make taxable supplies; and (4) he so requests. The registration takes effect from the date of his request or a mutually agreed earlier date. A registration will not be backdated more than three years: Business Brief 8/97, 25 March 1997.

A person is deemed to have a business establishment in the UK if he carries on a business through a branch or agency in the UK. The usual place of residence of a body corporate is the place where it is legally constituted.

Notification of end of liability or entitlement etc

11.—(V2.151) Within 30 days of ceasing to make taxable supplies, a registered person must notify the Commissioners of that fact so that the registration may be cancelled unless he is then liable or entitled to registration under Schs 2, 3 or 3A.

12.—(V2.152) A person registered under para 10 who ceases to make overseas supplies or who begins to make taxable supplies is required to give notice within 30 days unless, in the former case, he is then liable or entitled to registration under Schs 2, 3 or 3A.

Cancellation of registration

13.—(V2.151, V2.152) A person registered under Sch 1 para 9 or 10 is deregistered if he satisfies the Commissioners that he is not liable to registration under Sch 1 para 1 and (disregarding provisions preventing registration under more than one provision) he is not required to be registered under Sch 2, 3 or 3A. Deregistration must be requested. It is effective from the date of request or a mutually agreed later date.

A person registered under Sch 1 para 2 or 5–8 is deregistered if the Commissioners are satisfied that he meets one of the conditions in Sch 1 para 2 (5), 3 or 4 so that he has ceased to be liable to registration. A person registered under Sch 1 para 9 or 10 is deregistered if the Commissioners are satisfied that he no longer meets the conditions for registration under those provisions so that he has ceased to be entitled to registration. In either case, the Commissioners must be satisfied that (disregarding provisions preventing registration under more than one provision) he is neither liable nor entitled to registration under some other provision. Deregistration is effective from the date when he ceased to be liable or entitled to registration, or from a mutually agreed later date.

A person registered under Sch 1 para 2 or 5–10 is deregistered if the Commissioners are satisfied that he was neither liable nor entitled to registration under Sch 1 on the day from which he was registered. Deregistration is effective from that day.

For the deregistration of a person wishing to account for VAT under the special accounting scheme for electronic services, see Sch 3B para 18. For the special accounting scheme, see Sch 3B.

Exemption from registration

14.—(V2.139) Any person who makes zero-rated supplies may be exempted from registration if the Commissioners think fit. The test is whether exemption from registration is in the interests of the revenue: *Fong v C & E Comrs* [1978] VATTR 75. Any material change in the nature of supplies made, or the mix of taxable supplies, must be notified within 30 days.

Power to vary specified sums by order

15.— The registration and deregistration thresholds may be changed by Treasury order.

Supplementary

16.— The value of supplies for registration purposes is the consideration given. The value of supplies for deregistration purposes is the VAT-exclusive amount of consideration given.

17.—The Commissioners may by regulations prescribe the form and contents of any notification. See VAT Regulations 1995, SI 1995/2518 regs 5, 6 (2).

18.—A person is "registrable" if he is liable or entitled to registration under Sch 1 paras 1, 2, 9 or 10.

19.—"Supplies" means supplies made in the course or furtherance of a business.

SCHEDULE 2 REGISTRATION IN RESPECT OF SUPPLIES FROM OTHER MEMBER STATES (SECTION 3 (2))

Liability to be registered

1.—(V2.120–V2.122) An unregistered person who is not liable to registration under Sch 1 is liable to registration if:

(1) the cumulative value of his relevant supplies in a calendar year exceeds £70,000;
(2) he makes a relevant supply at a time when a place of supply option is in force; or
(3) he makes a supply of goods subject to excise duty.

For "relevant supplies" in heads (1) and (2), see Sch 2 para 10. A place of supply option in head (2) is an option exercised in another EU member state which treats a supply of goods removed from that member state as taking place outside that member state. A supply of goods subject to excise duty in head (3) must be made for a consideration to a non-taxable person and involve removal of the goods to the UK. The value of a relevant supply excludes VAT charged under the law of another EU member state. The last supply made before goods are removed from a fiscal warehouse (see s 18B (4)) is disregarded in determining liability to registration.

2.—(V2.151) A person ceases to be liable to registration if:

(1) the value of his relevant supplies for the past calendar year did not exceed £70,000;
(2) the corresponding value for the current calendar year is not expected to exceed £70,000;
(3) goods subject to excise duty have not, or will not, be supplied in either year; and
(4) any place of supply option made has expired.

For "relevant supplies", see Sch 2 para 10. For goods subject to excise duties and place of supply options, see Sch 2 para 1.

Notification of liability and registration

3.—(V2.126) Liability to registration must be notified within 30 days. Registration takes effect from the date when liability arose or a mutually agreed earlier date. For notifications, see Sch 2 para 9.

Request to be registered

4.—(V2.151, V2.152) A person may be registered if he so requests and satisfies the Commissioners that: (1) he intends to make relevant supplies from a specified date which are affected by a place of supply option made or to be made; or (2) he intends to make supplies of goods subject to excise duty from a specified date. The Commissioners may impose conditions. Registration takes effect from a mutually agreed date. A registration will not be backdated more than three years: Business Brief 8/97, 25 March 1997. A person is registered under Sch 1 paras 9 or 10, not under Sch 2, if he is entitled to registration under either of those provisions.

For "relevant supplies", see Sch 2 para 10. For place of supply options and supplies of goods subject to excise duty, see Sch 2 para 1.

Notification of matters affecting continuance of registration

5.—(V2.151, V2.152) A person registered under Sch 2 must notify the Commissioners within 30 days of ceasing to be liable or entitled to registration under Schs 1, 2, 3 or 3A.

A person registered under Sch 2A para 4 must notify the Commissioners within 30 days of exercising his place of supply option, making relevant supplies under his place of supply option or making a supply of goods subject to excise duty.

A person who has made a place of supply option must notify the Commissioners within 30 days of the option ceasing to have effect.

For place of supply options, see Sch 2 para 1. For persons ceasing to be liable to registration under Sch 2, see Sch 2 paras 1 (5) and 2. For notifications, see Sch 2 para 9.

Cancellation of registration

6.—(V2.130) The Commissioners may, on request, cancel a person's registration if he satisfies them that he is not liable to registration. The registration is cancelled from the date of the request or a mutually agreed later date. For the conditions to be met, see Sch 2 para 7 (1), (3).

The Commissioners may cancel a person's registration if they are satisfied that he was registered in error under Sch 2 para 1 or 4, ie because he was not liable to registration in the former case and did not have the required intention in the latter case. The registration may be cancelled from the day on which it took effect.

The Commissioners may cancel a registration under Sch 2 para 4 if they are satisfied that: (1) he has not made the supplies or option concerned by the specified date; or (2) he has contravened any registration condition imposed. The registration may be cancelled from the specified date, the date of contravention, or a mutually agreed later date in either case. For the conditions to be met, see Sch 2 para 7 (2), (3).

Conditions of cancellation

7.—(V2.130) If a person is liable to registration under Schs 1, 3 or 3A, he may not be deregistered on the ground that he is not liable to registration under Sch 2.

If a person is liable or entitled to registration under Schs 1, 3 or 3A, the Commissioners may not deregister him on the ground that the required intention for registration under Sch 2 para 4 has not been fulfilled or that conditions imposed under that provision have been breached.

If a place of supply option has been exercised, the registration may not be cancelled until the 1 January which is, or follows, the second anniversary of registration. For place of supply options, see Sch 2 para 1.

Power to vary specified sums by order

8.—The sum of £70,000 specified in Sch 2 paras 1 and 2 may be increased by Treasury order. No order has been made.

Supplementary

9.—Notifications are made in accordance with regulations. See VAT Regulations 1995, SI 1995/2518 reg 5.

10.—(V3.173) A supply is a "relevant supply" if: (1) it is a supply of goods made for a consideration in the course or furtherance of business to a non-taxable person in the UK in circumstances where the goods are removed to the UK from another EU member state and the supplier is responsible for delivery; (2) the supply does not involve installing or assembling the goods in the UK; (3) the supply is not an exempt supply; (4) the goods are not subject to excise duty; and (5) the goods do not comprise a new means of transport as defined in s 95.

SCHEDULE 3 REGISTRATION IN RESPECT OF ACQUISITIONS FROM OTHER MEMBER STATES (SECTION 3 (2))

Liability to be registered

1.—(V3.213) A person is required to register if: (1) the cumulative value of his relevant acquisitions in a calendar year, measured at the end of any month, has exceeded £73,000; or (2) the value of his relevant acquisitions, measured at any time, is likely to exceed £73,000 in the next 30 days. The value of a relevant acquisition excludes VAT charged under the law of another EU member state. An acquisition is disregarded for registration purposes if the goods have been fiscally warehoused and they are supplied after being removed from warehouse. For "relevant acquisitions", see Sch 3 para 11.

2.—(V3.213) A person ceases to be liable to be registered if: (1) the value of his relevant acquisitions for the past calendar year did not exceed £73,000; (2) the corresponding value for the current calendar year is not expected to exceed £73,000; and (3) the value of his relevant acquisitions in the next 30 days is not expected to exceed £73,000. For "relevant acquisitions", see Sch 3 para 11.

Notification of liability and registration

3.—(V3.213) Liability to registration under the historical limit must be notified within 30 days of the end of the month when liability is established and the registration takes effect from the end of the next month. Thus, if liability is established on 31.7.11, it must be notified by 30.8.11 and is effective from 1.9.11.

Liability to registration under the future limit must be notified before the end of the 30 day period and the registration takes effect from the beginning of that period. Thus, if relevant acquisitions for the period 1.8.11–30.8.11 are expected to exceed the registration limit, liability must be notified by 30.8.11 and is effective from 1.8.11.

An earlier effective date may be applied in either case by mutual agreement. For the historical and future limits, see Sch 3 para 1. For notifications, see Sch 3 para 10.

Entitlement to be registered etc

4.—(V3.213) A person is entitled to registration on request if he satisfies the Commissioners that: (1) he makes relevant acquisitions; or (2) he intends to make relevant acquisitions from a specified date. The Commissioners may impose conditions in the latter case. Registration takes effect from the date of request or a mutually agreed earlier date (former case) or a mutually agreed date (latter case). However, a registration will not be backdated more than three years: Business Brief 8/97, 25 March 1997. A person is registered under Sch 1 paras 9 or 10, not under Sch 3, if he is entitled to registration under either of those provisions. For "relevant acquisitions", see Sch 3 para 11.

Notification of matters affecting continuance of registration

5.—(V3.213) A registered person must notify the Commissioners within 30 days if he ceases to be liable or entitled to registration under Schs 1, 2, 3 or 3A or, having been voluntarily registered by reference to his intention to make relevant acquisitions, he ceases to have such an intention. Such a voluntarily registered person must notify the Commissioners within 30 days of making his first relevant acquisition. For "relevant acquisitions", see Sch 3 para 11. For notifications, see Sch 3 para 10.

Cancellation of registration

6.—(V3.213) A registered person may be deregistered on request if he satisfies the Commissioners that he is not liable to be registered under Sch 3 para 1. He is deregistered from the date of his request or a mutually agreed later date. Sch 3 para 7 (1) disapplies this provision if the Commissioners are satisfied that he is liable to registration under Schs 1 or 2 at that time. Sch 3 para 7 (3) provides that deregistration may not take effect before the 1 January which is, or follows, the second anniversary of registration if he was voluntarily registered under Sch 3 para 4, or he is not currently liable or entitled to registration under any other provision.

A registered person may be deregistered on request if: (1) he has ceased to be liable to be registered (ie he meets the test in Sch 3 para 2); or (2) he has ceased to make relevant acquisitions. He is deregistered from the date when he so ceased or a mutually agreed later date. Sch 3 para 7 (2) disapplies this provision if the Commissioners are satisfied that he is liable to registration under Schs 1 or 2, or entitled to registration under Schs 1, 2, 3 or 3A, at that time. Sch 3 para 7 (3) provides that deregistration may not take effect before the 1 January which is, or follows, the second anniversary of registration if he was voluntarily registered under Sch 3 para 4, or he is not currently liable or entitled to registration under any other provision.

The Commissioners may deregister a person if he was not liable to registration under Sch 3 para 1, he did not make relevant acquisitions, or he did not intend to make relevant acquisitions from a specified date, on the day on which he was registered. He is deregistered with effect from that day. For "relevant acquisitions", see Sch 3 para 11.

The Commissioners may deregister a person voluntarily registered by reference to his intention to make relevant acquisitions if they are satisfied that: (1) he is not liable to registration under Sch 3 para 1; and (2) he has either failed to make relevant acquisitions by the date specified in his request for registration, or breached any condition attached to his registration. He is deregistered from the specified date or date of contravention, or a mutually agreed later date. Sch 3 para 7 (2) disapplies this provision if the Commissioners are satisfied that he is liable or entitled to registration under Schs 1, 2 or 3A, or is entitled to registration under Sch 3 para 4 (1) (ie because he makes relevant acquisitions). For "relevant acquisitions", see Sch 3 para 11.

Conditions of cancellation

7.—(V3.213) The conditions for cancellation of registration are described under para 6 above.

Exemption from registration

8.—(V3.213) The Commissioners may, if they think fit, exempt a person from registration, if: (1) he so requests; and (2) he satisfies them that he acquires, or intends to acquire, goods of a description within Sch 8. An exempted person must notify the Commissioners within 30 days if he makes a relevant acquisition outside this description. Exemption from registration continues until the request is withdrawn or the Commissioners consider that it should no longer be acted upon. For "relevant acquisitions", see Sch 3 para 11.

Power to vary specified sums by order

9.—Any sum specified in Sch 3 may be increased by Treasury order.

Supplementary

10.—Notifications are made in accordance with regulations. See VAT Regulations 1995, SI 1995/2518 reg 5.

11.—An acquisition of goods from another EU member state (defined in s 11) is a "relevant acquisition" if: (1) it is a taxable acquisition of goods (defined in s 10 (2)); (2) the goods are not subject to excise duty; (3) the goods do not comprise a new means of transport (defined in s 95); (4) the supply made or deemed to be made by the supplier is not a taxable supply (defined in s 4 (2)); (5) the acquisition is treated as taking place in the UK (see s 13); and (6) the first removal of the goods under the transaction took place after 31 December 1992.

SCHEDULE 3A REGISTRATION IN RESPECT OF DISPOSALS OF ASSETS FOR WHICH A VAT REPAYMENT IS CLAIMED (SECTION 3 (2))

1.—An unregistered person is liable to registration at any time if he makes relevant supplies (see Sch 3A para 9) at that time or expects to make relevant supplies within 30 days of that time.

If a person's registration under Sch 1, 2 or 3 is cancelled with retrospective effect on the grounds that he was neither liable nor entitled to registration under those provisions when he was registered, he is regarded as an unregistered person for the purpose of determining whether he is liable to registration under Sch 3A.

A person ceases to be liable to registration if, but only if, he meets the conditions in Sch 3A para 2.

2.—A person ceases to be liable to registration under Sch 3A at any time if the Commissioners are satisfied that he has ceased to make relevant supplies (see Sch 3A para 9).

3.—A person liable to registration because he makes relevant supplies must notify the Commissioners within 30 days. He is registered from the day when he makes relevant supplies. For notifications, see para 8.

4.—A person liable to registration because be expects to make relevant supplies within 30 days must notify the Commissioners within 30 days. He is registered from the beginning of the 30 day period. For notifications, see para 8.

5.—A registered person must notify the Commissioners if he ceases to make, or intend making, relevant supplies at a time when he is neither liable nor entitled to registration under Schs 1, 2 or 3. He must do so within 30 days. For notifications, see para 8.

6.—The Commissioners may deregister a person if they are satisfied that he has ceased to make relevant supplies. He is deregistered from the day when he ceased, or a mutually agreed later date, if the Commissioners are satisfied that he is neither liable nor entitled to registration under Schs 1, 2 or 3 at that time. The fact that he is registered under one of those provisions is disregarded in determining whether he is so liable or entitled.

The Commissioners may deregister a person if they are satisfied that he was neither liable nor entitled to registration on the day when he was registered. He is deregistered from that day.

7.—A person is exempt from registration if some or all of his relevant supplies or intended relevant supplies are zero-rated. He must request exemption and satisfy the Commissioners that the condition for exemption is met. The Commissioners may accept the request if they think fit.

A person exempted from registration must notify the Commissioners of any material change in the nature of his supplies. He must do so within 30 days of the change (if the day can be identified) or within 30 days of the end of the quarter (see s 96(1)) in which the change took place (in other cases). For notifications, see para 8.

A person exempted from registration must notify the Commissioners of any alteration in the zero-rated proportion of his relevant supplies. He must do so within 30 days of the end of the quarter (see s 96(1)) in which the alteration took place. For notifications, see para 8.

A person is registered if he withdraws his request for exemption or the Commissioners consider that his request should no longer be acted upon. He is registered from the date of withdrawal or the date of the Commissioners' change of mind.

8.—Notifications must be made in accordance with regulations. No regulations have been made to date.

9.—A supply of goods (see Sch 4 para 5) is a "relevant supply" if:

(a) the supply is a taxable supply (see s 4(2));
(b) the goods are supplied in the course or furtherance of business and are assets of that business; and
(c) the person making the supply, his predecessor or one of his predecessors claims or receives a repayment under VAT Regulations, SI 1995/2518 regs 174 (if he is an EU trader) or 186 (if he is a third country trader) in respect of his purchase or importation of the goods.

A person ("X") is a predecessor of another person ("Y") in relation to a supply of goods if:

(a) X transferred all or part of his business to Y as a going concern;
(b) the assets transferred included those goods; and
(c) the transfer is treated as neither a supply of goods nor a supply of services (see VAT (Special Provisions) Order, SI 1995/1268 art 5) so as to be outside the scope of VAT.

If Y transfers all or part of his business as a going concern to another person ("Z") in similar circumstances, X is a predecessor of Z.

SCHEDULE 3B SUPPLY OF ELECTRONIC SERVICES IN MEMBER STATES: SPECIAL ACCOUNTING SCHEME (SECTION 3A)

PART I REGISTRATION

The register

1.—A person registered for the purposes of the special accounting scheme in the UK is registered in a single register kept by the Commissioners for the purposes of the scheme.

Persons who may be registered

2.—A person may be registered for the purposes of the special accounting scheme in the UK if:

(1) he makes or intends to make qualifying supplies in the course of business;
(2) he does not supply goods or services from a business establishment or other fixed establishment located anywhere in the EU;
(3) he is not registered for VAT purposes in the UK or elsewhere in the EU;
(4) he is not required to be registered for VAT purposes in the EU. Alternatively, if he is required to be registered for VAT purposes in the EU, this requirement arises solely from the fact that he makes or intends to make qualifying supplies;
(5) he is not registered for the purposes of the special accounting scheme in another EU member state.

Qualifying supplies

3.—The term "qualifying supply" is defined.

Registration request

4.—The Commissioners must register a person satisfying the conditions for registration (see Sch 3B para 2) if he so requests. The information to be set out in his request is stated. It must include a statement that he is not registered for VAT purposes in the UK, in another EU member state or in the Isle of Man. Requests are made electronically in accordance with regulations. No regulations have been made to date.

Date on which registration takes effect

5.—Registration takes effect from the date of a person's registration request or a mutually agreed date. However, no registration may take effect before 1 July 2003. Any earlier registration request is treated as if it had been made on that date.

Registration number

6.—A registered person is notified electronically of the registration number allocated to him.

Obligation to notify changes

7.—A registered person must notify the Commissioners electronically within 30 days if:

(a) any of the particulars in his registration request (see Sch 3B para 4(3)) change;
(b) he ceases to make or intend making qualifying supplies; or
(c) he ceases to satisfy any of conditions (2)–(5) specified in Sch 3B para 2.

Notifications are made in accordance with regulations. No regulations have been made to date.

Cancellation of registration

8.—A registration is cancelled in accordance with the following provisions:

	Circumstances	*Effective date of deregistration*
1	Person notifies the Commissioners that he has ceased to make, or intend making, qualifying supplies	The date when the notification is received or a mutually agreed date
2	The Commissioners otherwise determine that the person has ceased to make, or intend making, qualifying supplies	The date when the determination is made or such other date as the Commissioners direct
3	The person notifies the Commissioners that he has ceased to satisfy the conditions governing his entitlement to registration	The date when the notification is received or a mutually agreed date
4	The Commissioners otherwise determine that the person has ceased to satisfy the conditions governing his entitlement to registration	The date when the determination is made or such other date as the Commissioners direct
5	The Commissioners decide that the person has persistently failed to comply with obligations imposed by Sch 3B	The date when the determination is made or such other date as the Commissioners direct

Registration after cancellation for persistent default

9.—The term "persistent defaulter" is defined. The Commissioners are not required to re-register a persistent defaulter, but they have the power to do so.

PART II OBLIGATIONS FOLLOWING REGISTRATION, ETC

Liability for VAT

10.—A person is required to pay VAT if he makes a qualifying supply at a time when he is registered under Sch 3B. This VAT is calculated by reference to the rate of VAT in force in the UK (as regards qualifying supplies made in the UK) or by reference to the rate in force in another member state (as regards qualifying supplies made in that member state). This VAT is respectively regarded as being charged under the law of the UK or the member state concerned.

Obligation to submit special accounting returns

11.—A registered person is required to submit returns (referred to as "special accounting returns") in respect of accounting periods referred to as "reporting periods". A reporting period is a period of three months ending on 31 March, 30 June, 30 September or 31 December. A shorter period applies if the person is registered or deregistered part way through a reporting period:

Special accounting returns are submitted to the Controller of VAT Central Unit. They must specify:

(1) the person's registration number;

(2) the following information in respect of each member state in which he made qualifying supplies:

   (a) the total value of qualifying supplies,

   (b) the rate of VAT applicable, and

   (c) the total amount of VAT payable; and

(3) the aggregate of the total amounts of VAT payable in respect of each member state.

Further obligations with respect to special accounting returns

12.—Amounts shown in a special accounting return must be stated in sterling. Currency conversions are made by reference to exchange rates published by the European Central Bank on the last day of the reporting period.

Special accounting returns must be submitted electronically in accordance with regulations no later than 20 days after the end of the relevant reporting period. No regulations have been made to date.

Payment of VAT

13.—The total amount of VAT shown as due on a special accounting return must be paid to the Controller of VAT Central Unit in accordance with regulations at the time when the return is submitted. No regulations have been made to date. Payments must be made in sterling.

Obligations to keep and produce records

14.—A registered person must keep a record of his transactions. He must do so in a manner that enables the VAT payable to be verified. Records relating to transactions in a particular member state must be made available electronically to the tax authorities of that member state or to the Commissioners if, in either case, they so request. Records for a calendar year must be retained for ten complete calendar years thereafter.

Commissioners' power to request production of records

15.—If a person is registered for the purposes of the special accounting scheme in another member state, the Commissioners may request him to make his records available to them electronically. A request may be made in respect of qualifying supplies made in the UK.

PART III UNDERSTATEMENTS AND OVERSTATEMENTS OF UK VAT

Understatement or overstatement of UK VAT in special scheme return

16.—The Commissioners may consider that a person registered for the purposes of the special accounting scheme has submitted a special accounting return (if he is registered in the UK) or an equivalent return (if he is registered in another member state) which understates or overstates his liability to UK VAT. If so, they may give him a notice identifying the relevant return, specifying the amount of the understatement or overstatement and (in the case of an understatement) requesting payment within 30 days. The Commissioners must pay the amount of any overstatement.

In either case, a notice must be served no later than three years after the end of the reporting period or equivalent accounting period concerned.

PART IV APPLICATION OF PROVISIONS RELATING TO VAT

Registration under this act

17.—A person is not liable to registration under Schs 1–3A merely because he makes qualifying supplies.

De-registration

18.—A person making qualifying supplies may be registered under Sch 1. The Commissioners may, if he requests, cancel that registration if he satisfies them that he intends to apply for registration under the special accounting scheme in the UK (ie under Sch 3B) or in another member state. He is deregistered from the date of his request or from mutually agreed later date.

VAT representatives

19.—The Commissioners cannot direct a person to appoint a VAT representative if he is registered under the special accounting scheme in the UK (ie under Sch 3B) or in another member state. For VAT representatives, see s 48.

Appeals

20.—An appeal lies to a tribunal (see s 82) in respect of the following matters:

(a) the registration or deregistration of a person under Sch 3B;
(b) the Commissioner's decision to give a notice stating that a person has understated his liability to UK tax (see Sch 3B para 16(1));
(c) the amount of an underpayment or overpayment specified in a notice (see Sch 3B para 16(1) and (2)).

An appeal is subject to the same rights, duties and procedures as an appeal made under s 83(1).

Payments on account of non-UK VAT to other member states

21.—VAT collected under the special accounting scheme is not paid into the Consolidated Fund if it is payable to another EU member states in accordance with Regulation (EEC) 218/92.

The reference to Sch 11 para 1(2) is spent following substitution of a new Sch 11 para 1 by CRCA 2005 Sch 4 para 56.

Refund of UK VAT

22.—The repayment scheme for third country traders (see VAT Regulations 1995, SI 1995/2518 regs 185–197) applies in a modified form to persons registered for the purposes of the special accounting scheme in the UK or in another EU member state.

PART V SUPPLEMENTARY

Interpretation

23.—Various words and phrases are defined.

SCHEDULE 4 MATTERS TO BE TREATED AS SUPPLY OF GOODS OR SERVICES (SECTION 5)

1.—(V3.112, V3.113) Any transfer of the whole property in goods (ie transfer of ownership and all the rights associated with ownership) is a supply of goods. See *Staatssecretaris van Financiën v Shipping and Forwarding Enterprise Safe BV* (case C-320/88) [1991] STC 627, ECJ; *Auto Lease Holland BV v Bundesamt für Finanzen* (case C-185/01) [2005] STC 598, ECJ; *Philips Exports Ltd v C & E Comrs* [1990] STC 508; *Parker Hale Ltd v C & E Comrs* [2000] STC 388; Creditgrade *Ltd v C & E Comrs* [1991] VATTR 87; *The Post Office* (No 14075).

However, the transfer of any undivided share of the property or the transfer of the possession of goods is a supply of services. Thus, the hire of goods or the supply of the right to goods owned jointly with others is a supply of services. However, a supply of goods is made when all joint owners release their shares under a sale of goods: *Astor v C & E Comrs* [1981] VATTR 174.

Where the possession of goods is transferred under an agreement for the sale of goods, or under agreements which expressly intend that the property also will pass at some future time no later than when the goods are fully paid, then there is a supply of goods.

For "possession", see *Creditgrade Ltd v C & E Comrs* [1991] VATTR 87.

2.—(V3.112) [Repealed.]

3.—(V3.112) The supply of power, heat, refrigeration or other cooling, or ventilation is a supply of goods.

4.—(V3.112) The grant, assignment or surrender of a major interest (see s 96 (1)) in land is a supply of goods.

5.—(V3.211, V3.212) In principle, the transfer or disposal of goods belonging to a business, with or without consideration, is a supply of goods. This provision brings a free transfer of goods into charge to VAT by displacing s 5 (2). For "gifts" under a business promotion scheme, see *Kuwait Petroleum (GB) Ltd v C & E Comrs* (case C-48/97) [1999] STC 488, ECJ (goods exchanged for vouchers given to customers purchasing petrol). For examples, see *RHM Bakeries (Northern) Ltd v C & E Comrs* [1979] STC 72 (long service award); *C & E Comrs v West Herts College* [2001] STC 1245 (college prospectus); *Church of England Children's Society v R & C Comrs* [2005] STC 1644 (newsletter); *Terry's Supermarket* (No 631) (stock transferred to associated business). For the value of the supply made, see Sch 6 para 6.

There are two exceptions to this principle. First, a gift of goods is not a supply of goods if it is made in the course or furtherance of business and the cost (to the donor or, if he acquired the business as a going concern, to one or more of his predecessors) of acquiring or producing the goods was £50 or less. If other gifts within this description have been given to the same person in the previous twelve months, the aggregate cost of this gift and the previous gifts must also be £50 or less. For the nature of gifts, contrast *Mitrolone Ltd* (No 4301) and *Cartlidge* (No 7152) (inducements to prospective customers). For the "same person", see *EMI Group Ltd v Revenue and Customs Comrs* (case C-581/08) [2010] ECR I–0000, [2010] STC 2609, ECJ. The de minimis limit for gifts may be varied by order. No orders have been made to date. Second, the provision of a sample of goods to a person is not a supply of goods if it is made otherwise than for consideration. For the nature of a sample, see *EMI Group Ltd v Revenue and Customs Comrs* (case C-581/08) [2010] ECR I–0000, [2010] STC 2609, ECJ.

In principle, using land (see Sch 4 para 9(1)) or goods for private or non-business purposes is a supply of services whether or not there is a consideration. This brings a free use of goods and land into charge to VAT by displacing s 5(2)(b). However, no supply of services is made if the private or non-business use relates to: (1) an interest in land; (2) a building, a part of a building, or goods incorporated (or to be incorporated) in a building; (3) a civil engineering work, a part of a civil engineering work, or goods incorporated (or to be incorporated) in a civil engineering work; (4) a ship, boat or other vessel; or (5) an aircraft. For motor cars, see VAT (Cars) Order 1992, SI 1992/3122 art 4A. For free transport to employees, see *Julius Fillibeck Söhne Gmbh & Co KG v Finanzamt Neustadt* (case C-258/95) [1998] STC 513, ECJ. For hotel accommodation, contrast *Ibstock Building Products Ltd v C & E Comrs* [1987] VATTR 1 (supply made) and *Stormseal (UPVC) Window Co Ltd v C & E Comrs* [1989] VATTR 303 (no supply made). For meals provided without charge to staff and business contacts, see *Danfoss A/S and another v Skatteministeriet* (case C-371/07) [2008] ECR I–9549, [2009] STC 701, ECJ. For the value of the supply made, see Sch 6 para 7.

A transfer or use of goods without consideration gives rise to a supply of goods or services under the foregoing provisions only if the trader (or, if he acquired the business as a going concern, one or more of his predecessors) has or will become entitled to either:

(a) input tax credit for all or part of the VAT incurred on his purchase, acquisition or importation of the goods concerned; or

(b) a repayment of VAT under VAT Regulations, SI 1995/2518 reg 174 (if he is an EU trader) or 186 (if he is a third country trader).

For the charge to tax under Directive 2006/112/EC art 16 (formerly Directive 77/388/EEC art 5(6)) when goods have been wholly or partly included in business assets, or wholly excluded therefrom, see *Bakcsi v Finanzamt Fürstenfeldbruck* (case C-415/98) [2002] STC 802, ECJ. For the charge to tax under that provision when component parts have been incorporated in the goods after purchase, see *Finanzamt Burgdorf v Fischer; Finanzamt Düsseldorf-Mettmann v Brandenstein* (joined cases C-322/99 and C-323/99) [2001] STC 1356, ECJ. See also *Finanzamt München III v Mohsche* (case C-193/91) [1997] STC 195, ECJ (services relating to use and maintenance of the goods); *Kühne v Finanzamt München III* (case 50/88) [1990] STC 749, ECJ (purchase of the goods). Where a charge is made, see *Allied Lyons plc v C & E Comrs* [1994] VATTR 361 (motor car).

If a transfer or use of goods gives rise to a supply of goods or services under the foregoing provisions, the supply is deemed to be made in the course or furtherance of business. A sole trader makes a supply of goods or services under the foregoing provisions if he transfers the goods to himself personally or uses the goods personally.

For tax invoices in relation to supplies made without consideration, see VAT Regulations 1995, SI 1995/2518 reg 20. For tax certificates in respect of gifts of goods, see Notice No 700/35.

6.—(V3.213) A person makes a supply of goods if: (1) he removes goods forming part of the assets of his business from one EU member state to another; (2) the goods are removed under his directions; and (3) the goods are removed in the course or furtherance of business. This applies whether or not the removal takes place under a transaction made for a consideration. It does not apply to a removal from member state X to member state Y if: (1) the goods are removed from one part of member state X to another part via member state Y; or (3) the goods are removed from a third country to member state Y via member state X without a customs debt arising in member state X.

For removals which do not amount to a supply of goods, see s 5 (3); VAT (Removal of Goods) Order 1992, SI 1992/3111; VAT (Removal of Gas, Electricity, Heat and Cooling) Order 2010, SI 2010/2925.

7.—(V3.226) Where a trader's business goods are sold by another person to satisfy a debt owed by the trader, then the trader is deemed to supply those goods. For the sale of repossessed property, see Business Brief 24/94, 8 December 1994.

8.—(V3.261) When a trader deregisters, he is deemed to supply any business assets then held unless: (1) he transfers the business as a going concern; (2) his business is thereafter carried on by an executor, trustee, administrator, liquidator, etc; or (3) VAT on the deemed supply does not exceed £1,000. For certification under the flat-rate farmers scheme, see s 54.

Individual assets are not deemed to be supplied by a trader if:

(a) input tax credit was disallowed when he purchased, acquired or imported the goods;

(b) (if all or part of a business has been transferred to him as a going concern) the goods did not form part of the transfer; and;

(c) (if the goods were held on 1 April 1973) no relief was obtained for purchase tax paid when he purchased or imported the goods.

A trader is not entitled to input tax credit for the VAT accounted for if he subsequently re-registers: *Haugh* (No 15055).

The sum of £1,000 may be increased by Treasury order. For the value of the supply deemed to be made, see Sch 6 para 6.

9.—(V3.211) For the purposes of paras 5–8 above, "goods" includes land. Similarly, a "transfer", "disposition" or "sale" includes the grant, assignment or surrender of an interest in, right over or licence to occupy land.

For the purposes of Sch 4 para 5(1), a grant, assignment or surrender of an interest in, right over or licence to occupy land for a consideration is treated as either a supply of goods (major interest) or a supply of services (other interest). A grant, assignment or surrender without consideration is a supply of goods. For an ineffective declaration of trust, see *Veale (a firm)* (No 14637).

SCHEDULE 4A PLACE OF SUPPLY OF SERVICES: SPECIAL RULES (SECTION 7A)

PART 1 GENERAL EXCEPTIONS

Services relating to land

1.— The place of supply of specified services relating to land is determined by reference to the country in which the relevant land is situated. For the exchange of holiday usage rights in timeshare accommodation, see *RCI Europe v Revenue and Customs Comrs* (case C-37/08) [2009] ECR I–7533, [2009] STC 2407, ECJ; *Macdonald Resorts Ltd v Revenue and Customs Comrs* (case C-270/09) [2010] ECR I–0000, [2011] STC 412, ECJ.

Passenger transport

2.— The place of supply of passenger transport is the country in which the transport takes place. If the transport takes place in more than one country, a proportionate part of the journey takes place in each country.

"Passenger transport" includes:

- the transport of accompanied luggage and motor vehicles;
- a pleasure cruise (as defined in para 2(4)); and
- services provided as part of a pleasure cruise.

Hiring of means of transport

3.— The place of supply of a short-term hiring (as defined in para 3(2)) of a means of transport is the country in which the means of transport is put at the disposal of the person who hires it. However, if a means of transport made available in the UK is used and enjoyed partly in a third country (or vice versa), a proportionate part of the hire is made in each country.

Cultural, educational and entertainment services etc

4.— [Repealed.]

Restaurant and catering services: general

5.— In principle, the place of supply of restaurant and catering services is the country in which the services are physically carried out. For the exception, see para 6.

EC on-board restaurant and catering services

6.— The place of supply of restaurant and catering services provided on board a ship, aircraft or train during an intra-EC passenger transport operation (as defined in para 6(2), (4)) is the country in which the relevant point of departure (as defined in para 6(3)) is located. The outward and return stages are treated as separate passenger transport operations.

Hiring of goods

7.— In principle, the place of supply of a hire of goods is determined in accordance with s 7A(2). However, if the place of supply is the UK but the effective use and enjoyment of the hire takes place partly in a third country (or vice versa), a proportionate part of the service is supplied in each country.

This provision does not apply to the hire of a means of transport. For the short term hire of means of transport, see para 3.

Telecommunication and broadcasting services

8.— In principle, the place of supply of telecommunications services (as defined in para 8(2) or radio or television broadcasting services is determined in accordance with s 7A(2). However, if the place of supply is the UK but the effective use and enjoyment of the relevant service takes place partly in a third country (or vice versa), a proportionate part of the service is supplied in each country.

PART 2 EXCEPTIONS RELATING TO SUPPLIES MADE TO RELEVANT BUSINESS PERSON

Electronically-supplied services

9.— In principle, the place of supply of electronically supplied services (as defined in para 9(2), (3)) is determined in accordance with s 7A(2). However, if the place of supply is the UK but the effective use and enjoyment of the relevant service takes place partly in a third country (or vice versa), a proportionate part of the service is supplied in each country.

Admission to cultural, educational and entertainment activities etc

9A.— A supply of the following services to a relevant business person (as defined in s 7A(4)) is deemed to be made in the country in which the event in question actually take place:

(a) services in respect of admission to cultural, artistic, sporting, scientific, educational, entertainment or similar events (including fairs and exhibitions); and

(b) ancillary services relating to admission to the events in point (a).

This provision applies to services supplied after 31 December 2010.

PART 3 EXCEPTIONS RELATING TO SUPPLIES NOT MADE TO RELEVANT BUSINESS PERSON

Intermediaries

10.— The place of supply of specified intermediary services (see para 10(2)) is the same country as the supply to which the services relate.

Transport of goods: general

11.— This provision applies to services, comprising the transportation of goods, which are supplied to someone other than a relevant business person (as defined in s 7A(4)). In principle, the place of supply is the country in which the transportation takes place. However, if the transportation takes place in more than one country, a proportionate part of the transportation takes place in each country. For the exception, see para 12.

Intra-Community transport of goods

12.— This provision applies to services, comprising a transportation of goods beginning in one member state and ending in another, which are supplied to someone other than a relevant business person (as defined in s 7A(4)). The place of supply is the member state in which the transportation begins.

Ancillary transport services

13.— The place of supply of ancillary transport services (as defined in para 13(2)) supplied to a person who is not a relevant business person (as defined in s 7A(4)) is the place where the services are physically performed.

Long-term hiring of means of transport

13A.— [Applies to services supplied after 31 December 2012].

Valuation services

14.— The place of supply of the following services supplied to a person who is not a relevant business person (as defined in s 7A(4)) is the place where the services are physically performed:

- the valuation of goods; and
- the carrying out of work on goods.

Cultural, educational and entertainment services etc

14A.— A supply of the following services to a person who is not a relevant business person (as defined in s 7A(4)) is deemed to be made in the country in which the relevant activity takes place:

(a) services relating to cultural, artistic, sporting, scientific, educational, entertainment or similar activities (including fairs and exhibitions); and

(b) ancillary services relating to the activities in point (a). This includes services supplied by organisers of these activities.

This provision applies to services supplied after 31 December 2010.

Electronic services

15.— The place of supply of electronically supplied services (as defined in para 9(3), (4)) is the country in which the recipient belongs if:

- the supply is made by a person who belongs in a third country;
- the recipient is not a relevant business person (as defined in s 7A(4)); and
- the recipient belongs in a member state.

The Isle of Man is not a third country for this purpose. For the place where the supplier or recipient of services belongs, see s 9.

Other services provided to recipient belonging outside EC

16.— The place of supply of the following services is the country in which the recipient belongs if:

- the recipient is not a relevant business person (as defined in s 7A(4)); and
- he belongs in a third country.

The Isle of Man is not a third country for this purpose. For the place where the recipient of services belongs, see s 9. The services are:

(a) Transfers and assignments of copyright, patents, licences, trademarks and similar rights.

(b) Accepting an obligation to refrain from wholly or partly pursuing or exercising:
- any business activity or
- any copyright, patent, licence, trademark or similar right.

(c) Advertising services. For advertising services, see *EC Commission v France* (case C-68/92), *EC Commission v Luxembourg* (case C-69/92), *EC Commission v Spain* (case C-73/92) [1997] STC 700, ECJ; *Syndicat des Producteurs Indépendants (SPI) v Ministère de l'Economie, des Finances et de l'Industrie* (case C-108/00) [2001] STC 523, ECJ; *Lawrence* (No 13092); *International Trade and Exhibitions J/V Ltd v C & E Comrs* [1996] V & DR 165; *Austrian National Tourist Office* (No 15561); *John Village Automotive Ltd v C & E Comrs* [1998] V & DR 340; *Miller Freeman World-Wide plc* (No 15452).

(d) The following services, in so far as they do not relate to land:
- The services of consultants, engineers, consultancy bureaux, lawyers, accountants and similar services. See *Maatschap MJM Linthorst, KGP Pouwels and J Scheres cs v Inspecteur der Belastingdienst* (case C-187/95) [1997] STC 1287, ECJ (veterinary surgeon); *von Hoffmann v Finanzamt Trier* (case C-145/96) [1997] STC 1321, ECJ (arbitrator); *Banque Bruxelles Lambert SA v Belgian State* (case C-8/03) [2004] ECR I–10157, [2004] STC 1643, ECJ (consultancy services supplied to an open-ended investment company); *Levob Verzekeringen BV, OB Bank NV cs v Staatssecretaris van Financiën* (case C-41/04) [2005] ECR I–9433, [2006] STC 766, ECJ (supply and installation of customised computer software); *Commission v Germany* (case C-401/06) [2007] ECR I–10609,

[2008] STC 2906, ECJ (executor); *Kronospan Mielec sp zoo v Dyrektor Izby Skarbowej w Rzeszowie* (case C-222/09) [2010] ECR I–0000, [2011] STC 80, ECJ (research and development); *Hutchvision Hong Kong Ltd* (No 10509).

- Data processing and provision of information. See *Lawrence* (No 13092).

(e) Banking, financial, insurance and reinsurance services, but not the provision of safe deposit facilities. For financial services, see *Banque Bruxelles Lambert SA v Belgian State* (case C-8/03) [2004] ECR I–10157, [2004] STC 1643, ECJ (banking and financial services supplied to an open-ended investment company); *Swiss Re Germany Holding GmbH v Finanzamt München für Körperschaften* (case C-242/08) [2009] ECR I–10099, [2010] STC 189, ECJ (transfer of portfolio of life reinsurance contracts); *Culverpalm Ltd v C & E Comrs* [1984] VATTR 199; *Singer & Friedlander Ltd v C & E Comrs* [1989] VATTR 27, [1989] 1 CMLR 814; Business Brief 20/94, 18 November 1994.
For insurance and reinsurance services, see *Swiss Re Germany Holding GmbH v Finanzamt München für Körperschaften* (case C-242/08) [2009] ECR I–10099, [2010] STC 189, ECJ (transfer of portfolio of life reinsurance contracts).

(f) Providing:
- access to a natural gas system situated within the territory of an EU member state;
- access to any network connected a natural gas system situated within the territory of an EU member state;
- access to an electricity system;
- access to a network through which heat or cooling is supplied;
- transmission or distribution through any such system or network; and
- other directly linked services.

(g) The supply of staff. See *Strollmoor Ltd* (No 5454); *American Institute of Foreign Study (UK) Ltd* (No 13886).

(h) Hiring goods other than means of transport. For means of transport, see *Knut Hamann v Finanzamt Hamburg Eimsbüttel* (case 51/88) [1990] 2 CMLR 383, ECJ; *BPH Equipment Ltd* (No 13914).

(i) Telecommunications services (as defined in para 8(2)).

(j) Radio and television broadcasting services.

(k) Electronically supplied services (as defined in para 9(3), (4)).

SCHEDULE 5 SERVICES SUPPLIED WHERE RECEIVED (SECTION 8) (V3.193)

[Repealed]

SCHEDULE 5A GOODS ELIGIBLE TO BE FISCALLY WAREHOUSED (SECTION 18B)

The "eligible goods" to which a modified charge to tax applies (see s 18B) are listed.

SCHEDULE 6 VALUATION—SPECIAL CASES (SECTION 19)

1.—(V3.162) A supply is valued at open market value if the Commissioners so direct. A direction may be made if a taxable or exempt supply is made to a connected person (as defined in CTA 2010 s 1122) for a money consideration below open market value (see s 19(5)) and (in the case of a taxable supply) the recipient is partly exempt. A tribunal (see s 82) must determine whether the consideration for the supply is affected by the relationship between the parties: *RBS Leasing & Services (No 1) Ltd v C & E Comrs* [2000] V & DR 33.

A direction must be made no later than three years after the supply. It is given by written notice to the supplier. It may specify that similar supplies made from the date of the notice, or a specified later date, are to be valued on the same basis. No direction may be made in respect of food, beverages or accommodation valued in accordance with Sch 6 para 10.

A tribunal must decide whether the Commissioners were unreasonable in deciding to make a direction once they are satisfied that they have power to do so: *RBS Leasing & Services (No 1) Ltd v C & E Comrs* [2000] V & DR 33. For the test of reasonableness, see *John Dee Ltd v C & E Comrs* [1995] STC 941 at 952. For examples of directions upheld, see *Oughtred & Harrison Ltd v C & E Comrs* [1988] VATTR 140 (computer used by insurance subsidiary); *RBS Leasing & Services (No 1) Ltd v C & E Comrs* [2000] V & DR 33 (sale and leaseback of equipment to bank on nil cost of finance terms as part of corporation tax planning arrangements).

This provision derogates from Directive 2006/112/EC art 73 (formerly Directive 77/388/EEC art 11A(1)(*a*)). It is authorised under art 27(1)–(4) (see Authorisation, OJ L132/22, 21.5.87). The derogation was validly made and this provision falls within its scope: *RBS Leasing & Services (No 1) Ltd v C & E Comrs* [2000] V & DR 33. The authorisation is repealed with effect from 1 January 2008: see Directive 2006/69/EC art 2 and Annex II.

1A.—(V3.242) The Commissioners may direct that a supply is valued by reference to open market value if the following conditions are met:

- a taxable person makes a supply for a consideration to:
  - (a) one of his employees;
  - (b) a person who, under the terms of his employment, provides services to the taxable person; or
  - (c) a relative (as defined) of either.
  - (d) a relative (as defined) of either;
- the taxable person is a motor manufacturer (as defined) or motor dealer (as defined);
- the employee, person or relative is not a connected person (as defined in CTA 2010 s 1122) (so that no direction can be made under Sch 6 para 1);
- the supply comprises the private or non-business use of a motor car (as defined) or making a motor car available for non-business purposes (so that it is a supply of services by virtue of Sch 4 para 5(4));
- the motor car forms part of the taxable person's stock-in-trade (as defined);
- the value of the supply made by the taxable person is less than open market value.

A direction is a written notice given to the taxable person. It must be given no later than three years after the time of supply. It directs that the value of the supply is open market value. It may also direct that future supplies are similarly valued if they meet the foregoing conditions and take place after the day when the direction was given or the later date (if any) specified in the notice.

Various words and phrases are defined. These definitions can be amended by Treasury order. No orders have been made to date.

The provision applies to any use, or availability for use, on or after 1 January 2005: see FA 2004 s 22(5), (6); Finance Act 2004, section 22(2) (Appointed Day) Order 2004, SI 2004/3104, art 2. It derogates from Directive 2006/112/EC art 73 (formerly Directive 77/388/EEC art 11A(1)(*a*)). For the authorisation granted to the UK, see Decision 2004/736/EC. Although due to expire on 31 December 2009, this decision was repealed with effect from 1 January 2008: see Directive 2006/69/EC art 2 and Annex II.

2.—(V3.163) If a trader sells goods to non-taxable persons for resale to the public, the Commissioners may direct that the goods are to be valued at their retail open market value. The taxable person must intend that some or all of the goods are supplied for resale. The direction applies to those goods which are to be resold. See *Fine Art Developments plc v C & E Comrs* [1996] STC 246, HL. The information required for valuation purposes must be available or reasonably obtainable if the direction is to be valid: contrast *Fine Art Developments plc v C & E Comrs* [1996] STC 246, HL and *Beckbell Ltd v C & E Comrs* [1993] VATTR 212. For discounts for prompt payment, see *Gold Star Publications Ltd v C & E Comrs* [1992] STC 365. The vires of UK legislation was upheld in *Direct Cosmetics Ltd & Laughtons Photographs Ltd v C & E Comrs* (joined cases 138 and 139/86) [1988] STC

540, ECJ. For directions upheld, see *Direct Cosmetics Ltd* (No 3624); *Moore v C & E Comrs* [1989] VATTR 276; *Fine Arts Developments plc v C & E Comrs* [1996] STC 246, HL.

3.—(V5.141) The value of a supply (see s 19) is increased by the amount of any excise duty, EU customs duty or EU agricultural levy chargeable if: (1) the goods are charged to duty or levy on removal to the UK; or (2) the goods are supplied when warehoused and the supply is treated as being made in the UK (under s 18 (4)) at the duty point (defined in s 18 (6)).

4.—(V3.157) The value of goods or services is reduced by the amount of a cash discount offered for prompt payment, whether the discount is taken or not. See *Gold Star Publications Ltd v C & E Comrs* [1992] STC 365.

5.—[Repealed.]

6.—(V3.211, V3.213, V3.242, V3.243) The following supplies are valued at the current value of the same or similar goods, or at their cost of production, at the time of supply: (1) goods self-supplied by orders made under s 5 (5), ie motor cars and stationery; (2) goods transferred or disposed of without consideration under Sch 4 para 5 (1); (3) goods removed to another EU member state without consideration under Sch 4 para 6; (4) goods held at deregistration deemed to be supplied under Sch 4 para 8. For the valuation of goods in head (2) when component parts have been incorporated in them after purchase, see *Finanzamt Burgdorf v Fischer; Finanzamt Düsseldorf-Mettmann v Brandenstein* (joined cases C-322/99 and C-323/99) [2001] STC 1356, ECJ. For unsaleable stock under head (4), cf *McCormick v C & E Comrs* [1991] VATTR 196.

7.—(V3.212) The following services are valued at the full cost of providing them: (1) services performed without consideration brought within the scope of VAT by order made under s 5 (4) (but see VAT (Supply of Services) Order 1993, SI 1993/1507 arts 5, 7); (2) goods used for non-business purposes without consideration under Sch 4 para 5 (4). For the basis of valuation, see *Enkler v Finanzamt Homburg* (case C-230/94) [1996] STC 1316, ECJ; *Hausgemeinschaft Jörg und Stefanie Wollny v Finanzamt Landshut* (case C-72/05) [2006] ECR I–8297, [2008] STC 1618, ECJ; *Teknequip Ltd v C & E Comrs* [1987] STC 664.

Regulations may prescribe how "full cost" is to be determined in relation to non-business use within head (2). For the regulations made, see VAT Regulations 1995, SI 1995/2518 regs 116A–116M.

8.—(V3.231) Goods and services deemed to be supplied under the reverse charge provisions (see ss 8, 9A) are valued at an amount equal to the consideration (if the services were in fact supplied for a consideration in money) or the amount in money which is equivalent to that consideration (if all or part of the consideration is something other than money).

For the modified provision applicable to telecommunication services (see VATA 1994 Sch 5 para 7A) performed after 30 June 1997 in circumstances where part of the services are chargeable to VAT in another EU member state or where the services were performed over a period which commenced before 1 July 1997, see VAT (Reverse Charge) (Anti-avoidance) Order 1997, SI 1997/1523 art 7.

For the modified provision applicable where a right to use telecommunication services has been exercised with the result that the services are performed for a consideration which is lower than it would otherwise have been, see VAT (Reverse Charge) (Anti-avoidance) Order 1997, SI 1997/1523 art 8.

9.—(V3.166) Where accommodation is supplied in a hotel, boarding house or a similar establishment to an individual for a period exceeding four weeks, the value of the supply may be reduced so that VAT is charged only on the element attributable to facilities. The value of facilities cannot be less than 20%. See *Prior* (No 2157).

10.—(V3.166) An employer may provide food, beverages or accommodation for his employees. Where this is so, the value of any supply made or deemed to be made is the money paid (if a consideration is given wholly or partly in money) or nil (in other cases). This provision does not convert a transaction which is not a supply into one which is: *Co-operative Insurance Society Ltd v C & E Comrs* [1997] V & DR 65 (hotel accommodation booked by employer for use by employee on business trips not supplied to employee by employer). See *Goodfellow (a firm) v C & E Comrs* [1986] VATTR 119 (whether there was a consideration in money); *Glendale Social Club v C & E Comrs* [1994] VATTR 372 (whether committee members were employees).

11.—(V3.166, V3.393) Foreign currency amounts are converted into sterling at: (1) the market rate; (2) the rate specified in a notice (if the trader so opts); (3) the rate determined under a method specified in a notice (if the trader so opts); or (4) the rate determined under a method authorised by the Commissioners in relation to an individual trader. The relevant time for conversion is the time of supply. For provisions having the force of law, see Notice No 700 (April 2002) para 16.4.

12.—(V3.154) Regulations may be made which require payments made by third parties to a transaction to be included in the value of the supply. No regulations have been made to date.

13.—(V3.162, V3.163) The Commissioners may by written notice vary or withdraw a direction given under Sch 6 para 1 or 2.

SCHEDULE 7 VALUATION OF ACQUISITIONS FROM OTHER MEMBER STATES: SPECIAL CASES (SECTION 20)

1.—(V3.390, V3.391) A transaction giving rise to an acquisition may be made between connected persons (as defined in CTA 2010 s 1122) for a money consideration which is less than open market value. The transaction is valued at open market value if the person acquiring the goods is not entitled to credit for all of his input tax on the acquisition and the Commissioners so direct. Open market value is the money consideration which would be payable on an arm's length transaction. A direction is made by written notice to the person making the acquisition. It must be made within three years of the "relevant time" (see Sch 7 para 5) and may be varied or withdrawn by a subsequent direction. It may extend to future transactions.

2.—(V3.392) The value of an acquisition includes excise duty, EU customs duty and EU agricultural levy in the circumstances prescribed by regulations. See VAT Regulations 1995, SI 1995/2518 reg 97.

3.—(V3.390) A transfer, disposal or removal of goods forming part of the business assets is treated as a supply of goods under Sch 4 paras 5 (1) and 6 despite the absence of consideration. The value of a transfer, disposal or removal giving rise to an acquisition of goods from another EU member state is the current purchase price (excluding VAT) of identical or similar goods or, failing that, the current cost of producing the same goods.

4.—(V3.166, V3.393) Foreign currency amounts are converted to sterling at: (1) the market rate; (2) the rate specified in a notice (if the trader so opts); (3) the rate determined under a method specified in a notice (if the trader so opts); or (4) the rate determined under a method agreed between the Commissioners and an individual trader. Conversion is made by reference to the "relevant time" (see Sch 7 para 5). For provisions having the force of law, see Notice Nos 725, 728.

5.—The "relevant transaction" (Sch 7 paras 1 (1), 2 (1), 3 (1), 4 (1), (7)) is the supply giving rise to an acquisition. The "relevant time" (Sch 7 paras 1 (2), 4 (7)) is the time when the goods are first removed (acquisition by non-taxable person where consideration not determined periodically or from time to time or at the end of a period) or the time of acquisition (see s 12) (in other cases).

SCHEDULE 7A CHARGE AT REDUCED RATE (SECTION 29A)

PART I INDEX TO REDUCED-RATE SUPPLIES OF GOODS AND SERVICES

The titles of Groups 1–11 are set out in alphabetical order.

PART II THE GROUPS

GROUP 1—SUPPLIES OF DOMESTIC FUEL OR POWER

The following supplies are charged at the reduced rate.

Item 1

The following are charged at the reduced rate when supplied for domestic use (see Notes 5, 6, 7) or for non-business use by a charity:

(a) solid substances (eg coal and coke) held out for sale solely as fuel and combustible materials (excluding matches) for kindling fires;

(b) coal gas, water gas, producer gases and similar gases, but not road fuel gas (see Hydrocarbon Oil Duties Act 1979 s 5) chargeable with excise duty;

(c) gaseous hydrocarbons, including petroleum gases but not road fuel gas (see Hydrocarbon Oil Duties Act 1979 s 5) chargeable with excise duty;

(d) fuel oil (see Note 2(1)), gas oil (see Note 2(2)) or kerosene (see Note 2(3)). This includes rebated kerosene and heavy oil where the rebate is repaid in accordance with Hydrocarbon Oil Duties Act 1979 s 13AC (use for private flying) or 14E (private pleasure craft), but not hydrocarbon oil which is otherwise chargeable with excise duty without relief or rebate;

(e) electricity, heat or air-conditioning.

A supply partly for domestic use or non-business charitable use and partly for other use is charged at the reduced rate if at least 60% is supplied for domestic or non-business charitable use. An apportionment is made in other cases. For non-business use by a charity, see *Cambridge University v R & C Comrs* [2009] STC 1288 (university not acting as a public authority when providing higher education).

For coin meters, see *Mander Laundries Ltd v C & E Comrs* [1973] VATTR 136; *St Annes on Sea Lawn Tennis Club Ltd v C & E Comrs* [1977] VATTR 229; *Dyrham Park Country Club Ltd v C & E Comrs* [1978] VATTR 244; *High Wycombe Squash Club Ltd v C & E Comrs* [1976] VATTR 156. For accommodation with unmetered electricity, gas, etc, contrast *Hazelwood Caravans & Chalets Ltd v C & E Comrs* [1985] VATTR 179 (single supply of accommodation) and *Adams, Woskett & Partners* (No 9647), *Suffolk Heritage Housing Association Ltd* (No 13713) (separate supplies).

GROUP 2—INSTALLATION OF ENERGY-SAVING MATERIALS

The following supplies are charged at the reduced rate.

Items 1 and 2

The following are charged at the reduced rate:

(a) installing energy-saving materials (see Note 1) in residential accommodation (see Note 2) or in a building intended to be used solely for a relevant charitable purpose (see Note 3);

(b) energy saving materials (see Note 1) supplied by the person who installs them in residential accommodation (see Note 2) or in a building intended to be used solely for a relevant charitable purpose (see Note 3);

GROUP 3—GRANT-FUNDED INSTALLATION OF HEATING EQUIPMENT OR SECURITY GOODS OR CONNECTION OF GAS SUPPLY

The following supplies are charged at the reduced rate.

Item 1

Installing heating appliances (see Note 4). The supply must be made to a qualifying person (see Note 6). The goods must be installed in the sole or main residence of the qualifying person. The supply is taxed at the reduced rate only to the extent that the consideration is funded by a grant made under a relevant scheme (see Note 2). If the grant funds both the supply in question and another supply, a reasonable apportionment is made to determine the extent to which the consideration is funded by the grant.

Item 2

Heating appliances (see Note 4). The supply must be made to a qualifying person (see Note 6). The supply must be made by the person who installs the goods in the sole or main residence of the qualifying person. The supply is taxed at the reduced rate only to the extent that the consideration is funded by a grant made under a relevant scheme (see Note 2). If the grant funds both the supply in question and another supply, a reasonable apportionment is made to determine the extent to which the consideration is funded by the grant.

Item 3

Connecting or reconnecting a mains gas supply to the sole or main residence of a qualifying person (see Note 6). The supply must be made to a qualifying person (see Note 6). The supply is taxed at the reduced rate only to the extent that the consideration is funded by a grant made under a relevant scheme (see Note 2). If the grant funds both the supply in question and another supply, a reasonable apportionment is made to determine the extent to which the consideration is funded by the grant.

Item 4

Goods necessarily installed when connecting or reconnecting a mains gas supply. The supply must be made to a qualifying person (see Note 6). The supply must be made by the person who installs the goods in the sole or main residence of the qualifying person (see Note 6). The supply is taxed at the reduced rate only to the extent that the consideration is funded by a grant made under a relevant scheme (see Note 2). If the grant funds both the supply in question and another supply, a reasonable apportionment is made to determine the extent to which the consideration is funded by the grant.

Item 5

Installing, maintaining or repairing a central heating system (see Note 4A) in the sole or main residence of a qualifying person (see Note 6). The supply must be made to a qualifying person (see Note 6). The supply is taxed at the reduced rate only to the extent that the consideration is funded by a grant made under a relevant scheme (see Note 2). If the grant funds both the supply in question and another supply, a reasonable apportionment is made to determine the extent to which the consideration is funded by the grant.

Item 6

Goods necessarily installed when installing, maintaining or repairing a central heating system (see Note 4A). The supply must be made to a qualifying person (see Note 6). The supply must be made by the person who installs the goods in the sole or main residence of the qualifying person (see Note 6). The supply is taxed at the reduced rate only to the extent that the consideration is funded by a grant made under a relevant scheme (see Note 2). If the grant funds both the supply in question and another supply, a reasonable apportionment is made to determine the extent to which the consideration is funded by the grant.

Item 7

Leasing goods forming all or part of the central heating system (see Note 4A) installed in the sole or main residence of a qualifying person (see Note 6). The supply is taxed at the reduced rate only to the extent that the consideration is funded by a grant made under a relevant scheme (see Note 2). If the grant funds both the supply in question and another supply, a reasonable apportionment is made to determine the extent to which the consideration is funded by the grant.

Item 8

Goods forming all or part of the central heating system (see Note 4A) installed in the sole or main residence of a qualifying person (see Note 6). The goods must have been leased immediately before being supplied. The consideration for the leasing must have been wholly or partly funded by a grant made under a relevant scheme (see Note 2). The supply is taxed at the reduced rate only to the extent that:

(a) the consideration is funded by a grant made under a relevant scheme (see Note 2). If the grant funds both the supply in question and another supply, a reasonable apportionment is made to determine the extent to which the consideration is funded by the grant; or

(b) the consideration is a payment becoming due when the lease comes to an end.

Item 8A

Installing, maintaining or repairing a renewable source heating system (see Note 4B). The supply must be made to a qualifying person (see Note 6). The heating system must be situated in the qualifying person's sole or main residence. The supply is taxed at the reduced rate only to the extent that the consideration is funded by a grant made under a relevant scheme (see Note 2). If the grant funds both the supply in question and another supply, a reasonable apportionment is made to determine the extent to which the consideration is funded by the grant.

Item 8B

Goods necessary for the installation, maintenance or repair of a renewable source heating system (see Note 4B). The goods must be supplied to a qualifying person (see Note 6) by the person carrying out the installation, maintenance or repair. The heating system must be situated in the qualifying person's sole or main residence. The supply is taxed at the reduced rate only to the extent that the consideration is funded by a grant made under a relevant scheme (see Note 2). If the grant funds both the supply in question and another supply, a reasonable apportionment is made to determine the extent to which the consideration is funded by the grant.

Item 9

Installing qualifying security goods (see Note 5) in the sole or main residence of a qualifying person (see Note 6). The supply must be made to a qualifying person (see Note 6). The supply is taxed at the reduced rate only to the extent that the consideration is funded by a grant made under a relevant scheme (see Note 2). If the grant funds both the supply in question and another supply, a reasonable apportionment is made to determine the extent to which the consideration is funded by the grant.

Item 10

Qualifying security goods (see Note 5). The supply must be made to a qualifying person (see Note 6). The supply must be made by the person who installs the goods in the sole or main residence of a qualifying person (see Note 6). The supply is taxed at the reduced rate only to the extent that the consideration is funded by a grant made under a relevant scheme (see Note 2). If the grant funds both the supply in question and another supply, a reasonable apportionment is made to determine the extent to which the consideration is funded by the grant.

GROUP 4—WOMEN'S SANITARY PRODUCTS

The following supplies are charged at the reduced rate.

Item 1

Women's sanitary products (see Note 1).

GROUP 5—CHILDREN'S CAR SEATS

The following supplies are charged at the reduced rate.

Item 1

The following goods:

- a safety seat (see Note 2);
- a related base unit (see Note 2A) for a safety seat;
- a child's pushchair comprising a detachable safety seat (see Note 2) and related wheeled framework;
- a booster seat (see Note 4); and
- a booster cushion (see Note 5).

A child is a person aged under 14 years.

GROUP 6—RESIDENTIAL CONVERSIONS

The following supplies are charged at the reduced rate.

Item 1

The following supplies:

(a) qualifying services (see Note 11) supplied in the course of a changed number of dwellings conversion and relating to that conversion;

(b) qualifying services (see Note 11) supplied in the course of a house in multiple occupation conversion and relating to that conversion;

(c) qualifying services (see Note 11) supplied in the course of a special residential conversion and relating to that conversion. The supply must be made to the person who intends to use the converted premises for a relevant residential purpose. The person supplied must provide the supplier with a certificate in the prescribed form (see Note 8);

(d) garage works (see Note 9(2), (4)) carried out at the same time as a conversion in heads *(a)*–*(c)* where the resulting garage is intended to be occupied with the single household dwelling (see Note 4(1), (3), (4)), multiple occupancy dwelling (see Note 4(2), (3), (4)), institution or other accommodation resulting from the conversion.

A "changed number of dwellings conversion" takes place where:

(a) a building or part of a building comprising one or more single household dwellings (see Note 4(1), (3), (4)) is converted into a different number of single household dwellings;

(b) a building or part of a building comprising something other than a single household dwelling is converted into one or more single household dwellings.

A "house in multiple occupation conversion" takes place where a building or part of a building which does not contain any multiple occupancy dwellings (see Note 4(2), (3), (4)) is converted into one or more multiple occupancy dwellings which are not intended to be used for a relevant residential purpose (see Note 6) after the conversion.

A "special residential conversion" takes place where premises that have not been used for a relevant residential purpose (see Note 6) are converted with the intention of their being used for a relevant residential purpose after the conversion. If the intended relevant residential purpose is an institutional purpose (see Note 7(7)), the premises must be the sole premises occupied by the institution after the conversion. For "premises", see Note 7(1).

Any statutory planning consent or building control consent must have been granted.

Item 2

A supply of building materials (see Note 12) is charged at the reduced rate. The supply must be made by a person supplying qualifying services within Item 1. Those services must include incorporating the materials in the building concerned or its immediate site.

GROUP 7—RESIDENTIAL RENOVATIONS AND ALTERATIONS

The following supplies are charged at the reduced rate.

Item 1

The following supplies:

(a) qualifying services (see Note 5) supplied in the course of the renovation or alteration (see Note 2(1)) of a single household dwelling (see Note 2(4)) and relating to that renovation or alteration. One of the following conditions must be met:

(i) the dwelling was not lived in during the two years immediately before the relevant works (see Note 3(4)(*a*)) commenced, or

(ii) the relevant works (see Note 3(4)(*a*)) were commenced within one year of a major interest in the dwelling being granted or assigned (either alone or jointly with one or more other persons) to the person ("the occupier") who resides in it. The dwelling must not have been lived in, renovated or altered during the two years immediately preceding the grant or assignment. If the occupier began to live there after the major interest was granted or assigned, the dwelling must have remained empty until he did so;

(b) qualifying services (see Note 5) supplied in the course of the renovation or alteration (see Note 2(1)) of a multiple occupancy dwelling (see Note 2(4)) and relating to that renovation or alteration. It is a condition that the dwelling was not lived in during the two years immediately before the relevant works commenced;

(c) qualifying services (see Note 5) supplied in the course of the renovation or alteration (see Note 2(1)) of a building or part of a building which, when last lived in, was used for a relevant residential purpose (see Note 2(4)). The qualifying services must relate to that renovation or alteration. The following conditions must be met:

(i) the building or part was not lived in during the two years immediately before the relevant works commenced,

(ii) the building or part is intended to be used solely for a relevant residential purpose after the renovation or alteration, and

(iii) the recipient of the supply must give the supplier a certificate to that effect before the supply is made;

(d) qualifying services (see Note 5) supplied in the course of the renovation or alteration (see Note 2(1)) of all or part of a building which, when last lived in, formed part of a relevant residential unit (see Note 2(3)). The qualifying services must relate to that renovation or alteration. The following conditions must be met:

(i) neither the building (or part) nor any of the other buildings forming part of the relevant residential unit were lived in during the two years immediately before the relevant works commenced,

(ii) the building or part is intended to be used solely for a relevant residential purpose after the renovation or alteration, and

(iii) the recipient of the supply must give the supplier a certificate to that effect before the supply is made.

(e) qualifying services (see Note 5) supplied in the course of garage works (see Note 3A(2)) related (see Note 3A(3)) to a renovation or alteration in heads (*a*)–(*d*).

A number of buildings on the same site may be renovated or altered at the same time with the intention of using them together as a unit solely for a relevant residential purpose. Where this is so, each building is regarded for the purposes of head (*d*) as being intended for use for a relevant residential purpose if it would not otherwise be so regarded.

An apportionment is made where a supply of services includes both qualifying services and other services.

Item 2

A supply of building materials (see Note 6) is charged at the reduced rate. The supply must be made by a person supplying qualifying services within Item 1. Those services must include incorporating the materials in the building concerned or its immediate site.

GROUP 8—CONTRACEPTIVE PRODUCTS

The following supplies are charged at the reduced rate.

Item 1

The supply of any product designed for the purposes of human contraception, unless:

(a) the product is designed for the purpose of monitoring fertility; or

(b) the supply is made in connection with the provision of care, medical treatment or surgical treatment so as to be exempted from VAT under Sch 9 Group 7 Item 4.

GROUP 9—WELFARE ADVICE OR INFORMATION

The following supplies are charged at the reduced rate.

Item 1

The supply of:

(a) advice or information directly related to the physical or mental welfare of elderly, sick, distressed or disabled persons, or to the care or protection of children and young persons, which is neither provided solely for the benefit of a particular individual nor provided by reference to the personal circumstances of a particular individual;

(b) goods wholly, or almost wholly, for the purpose of conveying the advice or information.

The supply must be made either by a charity, or by a state-regulated welfare institution or agency. For "state regulated", see Sch 9 Group 7 Note 8.

A supply does not fall within Item 1 if it comprises goods or services of a description in Sch 9 Group 6 Items 1, 3 or 4 (ie education, research vocational training, examination services and closely related goods or services). Such a supply is exempted from VAT by those provisions if the charity, institution or agency is an eligible body (as defined in Sch 9 Group 6 Note 1) and chargeable at the standard rate in other circumstances.

GROUP 10—INSTALLATION OF MOBILITY AIDS FOR THE ELDERLY

The following supplies are charged at the reduced rate.

Item 1

Installing mobility aids (as defined in Note 1) in domestic accommodation (as defined in Note 2) for use by a person aged 60 or over at the time of supply.

Item 2

A supply of mobility aids by the person installing them under a supply falling within Item 1.

GROUP 11—SMOKING CESSATION PRODUCTS

The following supplies are charged at the reduced rate.

Item 1

A supply of pharmaceutical products designed to help people stop smoking tobacco. For the products concerned, see Revenue and Customs Brief 48/07, 26 June 2007.

SCHEDULE 8 ZERO-RATING (SECTION 30)

PART I INDEX TO ZERO-RATED SUPPLIES OF GOODS AND SERVICES

The titles of Groups 1–16 are set out in alphabetical order and cross-referenced to the corresponding Groups in VATA 1983 Sch 5 (repealed).

PART II THE GROUPS

GROUP 1—FOOD (V4.221, V4.226, V4.227)

Supplies of a description in General Items 1–4 are zero-rated unless they fall within the Excepted Items.

General Item 1

Food (see below) of a kind used for human consumption. Food is excluded from zero-rating (so as to be standard rated unless exempt from tax under Sch 9 Groups 6 and 7 (schools, hospitals, etc)) if:

(a) it is supplied in the course of catering. For the nature of a "supply in the course of catering", see *R & C Comrs v Compass Contract Services UK Ltd* [2006] STC 1999, CA; *C & E Comrs v Cope* [1981] STC 532; *C & E Comrs v Safeway Stores plc* [1997] STC 163; *Whitbread Group plc v C & E Comrs* [2005] STC 539; *DCA Industries Ltd v C & E Comrs* [1983] VATTR 317;

(b) it is supplied for consumption on the premises from which it is supplied. For food consumed in the grounds of a café, snack-bar, etc, see *Ivy Café Ltd* (No 288). For sales from kiosks, etc, see *R & C Comrs v Compass Contract Services UK Ltd* [2006] STC 1999, CA; *C & E Comrs v Cope* [1981] STC 532; *R v C & E Comrs ex parte Sims* [1988] STC 210; *Whitbread Group plc v C & E Comrs* [2005] STC 539; *DCA Industries Ltd v C & E Comrs* [1983] VATTR 317; *Armstrong v C & E Comrs* [1984] VATTR 53; *Crownlion (Seafood) Ltd v C & E Comrs* [1985] VATTR 188; *Bristol City Football Supporters Club v C & E Comrs* [1975] VATTR 93; *Mylo's of Reading (Catering and Ices) Ltd* (No 2538); *Ashby Catering Ltd* (No 4220); *Fresh Sea Foods Barry Ltd v C & E Comrs* [1991] VATTR 388; *St Benedict Trading Ltd v C & E Comrs* [1994] VATTR 376; *Travellers Fare Ltd* (No 13482). For mobile vans, see *James v C & E Comrs* [1977] VATTR 155; *Spragg v C & E Comrs* [1977] VATTR 162; *Cooper* (No 2665). For supplies of hot food made in the course of catering, see Revenue and Customs Brief 19/11, 1 April 2011;

(c) it is supplied for consumption *off* the premises from which it is supplied in the following circumstances: (i) it has been heated for the purposes of enabling it to be consumed at a temperature above ambient air temperature, and (ii) it is above that temperature at the time when it is provided to the customer. The supplier's intention in heating the food is paramount. An intention to sell the food above ambient air temperature does not necessarily imply an intention for the food to be consumed above that temperature: *John Pimblett & Sons Ltd v C & E Comrs* [1988] STC 358, CA; *Greenhalgh's Craft Bakery Ltd* (No 10955). For examples, see *Malik (trading as Hotline Foods) v C & E Comrs* [1998] STC 537; *Deliverance Ltd v R & C Comrs* [2011] UKUT 58 (TCC), [2011] STC 1049; *Redhead* (No 3201); *Lutron* (No 3686); *The Lewis's Group Ltd* (No 4931); *P & S Catering* (No 6382); *Stewarts Supermarkets Ltd* (No 13338); *Prêt à Manger (Europe) Ltd* (No 16246); *The Great American Bagel Factory Ltd* (No 17017); *Leach* (No 17767); Business Brief 9/05, 4 April 2005.

For "food", see Note 1. For examples, see *Soni v C & E Comrs* [1980] VATTR 9 (paan); *Marfleet Refining Co Ltd v C & E Comrs* [1974] VATTR 289 (cod liver oil); *Ayurueda Ltd* (No 3860) (herbal fruit concentrate); *C & E Comrs v Macphie & Co (Glenbervie) Ltd* [1992] STC 886 (soft bread roll concentrate); *Devro Ltd* (No 7570) (sausage casings); *Brewhurst Health Food Supplies* (No 8928) (laxative fruit cubes); *Hua* (No 13811) (herbal tea); *National Safety Associates of America (UK) Ltd* (No 14241) (fruit and vegetable tablets); *Arthro Vite Ltd* (No 14836) (powdered drink). For "normal and necessary packaging" of food, see *C & E Comrs v United Biscuits (UK) Ltd* [1992] STC 325. For fish used as bait, see *North Isles Shellfish Ltd v C & E Comrs* [1995] V & DR 415.

For door-to-door salesmen, see *Mowbray v C & E Comrs* [1986] VATTR 266; *Cooper* (No 2665); *Zeldaline Ltd v C & E Comrs* [1989] VATTR 191. For delivery of meals, see *Maheboob Refreshment House* (No 1539); *Levy* (No 1990); *C Chasney Ltd v C & E Comrs*

[1989] VATTR 152; *Lawson* (No 14903); *Leach* (No 17767). For electronic ordering, see *Emphasis Ltd v C & E Comrs* [1995] V & DR 419. For vending machines, see *Macklin Services (Vending) West Ltd v C & E Comrs* [1979] VATTR 31; *Streamline Taxis (Southampton) Ltd* (No 2016).

General Item 2

Animal feeding stuffs. Whether or not an edible substance is an animal feeding stuff is largely answered by the way in which it is sold or supplied: *Fluff Ltd (trading as Mag-it) v C & E Comrs* [2001] STC 674 (bait). For examples, see *Smith* (No 2954), *Marczak (a firm)* (No 13141) (grass-keep); *Chapman & Frearson Ltd* (No 4428) (product aiding digestion of silage).

General Item 3

Seeds etc producing plants yielding food suitable for humans or animals.

General Item 4

Live animals of a kind used as food (eg as meat), yielding food (eg milk) or producing food (eg honey). The food must be for human consumption.

For "live animals", see *C & E Comrs v Lawson-Tancred* [1988] STC 326; *Chalmers* (No 1433).

Excepted items

Goods within Items 1–4 are excluded from zero-rating if they fall within Excepted Items 1–7. However, this does not apply if the goods also fall within Items 1–7 of the Items Overriding the Exceptions. Excepted Items 1–7 broadly comprise frozen products, confectionery, alcoholic beverages, non-alcoholic beverages, savoury food products, animal foods and home brew kits.

For "ice cream, ice lollies, frozen yoghurt, water ices and similar frozen products", see *Meschia's Frozen Foods v C & E Comrs* [2001] STC 1 (common feature of products listed is being reduced to temperature below the freezing point of water); *Ross Young Holdings Ltd v C & E Comrs* [1996] V & DR 230 ("similar frozen products" includes both cream-based and ice-based products).

For "confectionery", see *R & C Comrs v Premier Foods Ltd* [2008] STC 176.

For "sweetened prepared food" see *Smith Kline Beecham plc v C & E Comrs* [1993] VATTR 219; *SiS (Science in Sport) Ltd* (No 17116).

For "cakes", see *Marks and Spencer plc* (No 4510); *United Biscuits (UK) Ltd* (No 6344).

For "biscuits", see *C & E Comrs v Ferrero UK Ltd* [1997] STC 881, CA.

For "beverages", see *Kalron Foods Ltd v R & C Comrs* [2007] STC 1100; *Bio-concepts Ltd* (No 11287); *McCormick (UK) plc* (No 15202); *SiS (Science in Sport) Ltd v C & E Comrs* [2000] V & DR 195. For "tea, maté, herbal teas and similar products", see *Orchid Drinks Co Ltd* (No 14222).

For "potato crisps, potato sticks, potato puffs and similar products", see *Procter & Gamble UK v R & C Comrs* [2009] STC 1990, CA.

For "savoury food products", see Business Brief 4/99, 15 February 1999 (not reproduced) (prawn crackers made from tapioca).

For the nature of "pet food", see *Popes Lane Pet Food Supplies Ltd v C & E Comrs* [1986] VATTR 221; *Normans Riding Poultry Farm Ltd v C & E Comrs* [1989] VATTR 124; *Norgate (a firm)* (No 5241); *Peters & Riddles* (No 12937).

Group 2—Sewerage Services and Water (V4.271)

The following supplies are zero-rated.

Item 1

The reception, disposal or treatment of foul water or sewerage, and emptying domestic cesspools, septic tanks, etc.

Item 2

The supply of water. The water must not be used in carrying on a relevant industrial activity (defined in the Note). Pure water (eg distilled and deionised water), bottled water and heated water are excluded from zero-rating. For water, see *Scott-Morley* (No 1097). For supplies made by a launderette, see *Mander Laundries Ltd v C & E Comrs* [1973] VATTR 136.

GROUP 3—BOOKS, ETC (V4.273)

In principle, the supplies (see Note 1(b)) in items 1–6 are zero-rated. However, a supply is excluded from zero-rating if it comprises either:

- Plans or drawings for industrial, architectural, engineering, commercial or similar purposes.
- A supply of goods connected with a supply of services made by another supplier where the two supplies, if made by a single supplier, would be treated as a single supply of services which is either: (1) charged to tax at the standard rate or reduced rate; or (2) exempt from tax.

Item 1

Books, booklets, brochures, pamphlets and leaflets. See *C & E Comrs v Colour Offset Ltd* [1995] STC 85 (book, booklet); *W F Graham (Northampton) Ltd* (No 908) (children's cut-out book); *Betty Foster (Fashion Sewing) Ltd v C & E Comrs* [1976] VATTR 229, *Schusman v C & E Comrs* [1994] VATTR 120, *Full Force Marketing Ltd* (No 15270) (brochures); *Pace Group (Communications) Ltd* (No 510) (pamphlets); *Cronsvale Ltd v C & E Comrs* [1983] VATTR 313, *Multiform Printing Ltd v C & E Comrs* [1996] V & DR 580 (leaflets). For examples, see *Evans & Marland Ltd v C & E Comrs* [1988] VATTR 125 (betting guide); *A E Walker Ltd v C & E Comrs* [1973] VATTR 8, *Butler & Tanner Ltd v C & E Comrs* [1974] VATTR 72 and *GUS Catalogue Order Ltd* (No 2958) (bound and unbound book signatures); *Odhams Leisure Group Ltd v C & E Comrs* [1992] STC 332 (children's pre-school teaching pack); *International Master Publishers Ltd* (No 8807) (binder and looseleaf pages).

For loose-leaf works, see Notice No 48 (December 2010) para 3.15. For goods used in connection with the collection of monetary donations, see Notice No 48 (December 2010) para 3.3. For knitting patterns, see Business Brief 5/91, 18 April 1991 (not reproduced). For plastic information cards, see *Infocard* (No 5732). For instruction manuals, see *John Harrison (Gatesby) Ltd* (No 5581). For market research reports etc, see *City Research Associates Ltd v C & E Comrs* [1984] VATTR 189. For diaries and address books, see *C & E Comrs v Colour Offset Ltd* [1995] STC 85.

Item 2

Newspapers, journals and periodicals. *See Geoffrey E Snushall (a firm) v C & E Comrs* [1982] STC 537 (monthly property guide); *Stillwell Darby & Co Ltd v C & E Comrs* [1973] VATTR 145 (theatre programme); *Rochdale Hornets Football Club Co Ltd v C & E Comrs* [1975] VATTR 71 (admission programme); *Evans & Marland Ltd v C & E Comrs* [1988] VATTR 125 (betting guide); *Emap Consumer Magazines Ltd* (No 13244), *European Publishing Consultants Ltd* (No 13841) (pictorial publication).

Item 3

Children's picture books and painting books. See *W F Graham (Northampton) Ltd* (No 908) (children's cut-out book).

Item 4

Printed, duplicated or manuscript music. For a product outside this description, see *Flip Cards (Marine) Ltd* (No 14483) (cards with a question on the front and answer on the back).

Item 5

Maps, charts and topographical plans. See *Brooks Histograph Ltd v C & E Comrs* [1984] VATTR 46.

Item 6

Covers, cases and other articles supplied with goods in Items 1–5. See *Odhams Leisure Group Ltd v C & E Comrs* [1992] STC 332.

GROUP 4—TALKING BOOKS FOR THE BLIND AND HANDICAPPED AND WIRELESS SETS FOR THE BLIND (V4.262)

The following supplies are zero-rated.

Item 1

The supply to the Royal National Institute for the Blind or other similar charities (whether by sale or lease) of equipment for recording, duplicating or playback of speech for the blind or severely handicapped is zero-rated.

Item 2

The supply to a charity of wireless receiving sets or equipment used to record and playback sound on tape cassettes lent free of charge to blind persons.

GROUP 5—CONSTRUCTION OF BUILDINGS, ETC (V4.233, V4.237, V4.238, V4.242)

The following supplies are zero-rated.

Item 1

The first grant of a major interest (see s 96(1)) in all or part of a building, dwelling or its site by a person constructing:

(a) a building designed as one or more dwellings (Item 1(*a*)(i)). The purchaser or tenant must be entitled to reside in the dwelling throughout the year and must not be prevented from doing so by the terms of a covenant, statutory planning consent or similar permission (Note 13(i)). The purchaser or tenant must not be prevented from using the dwelling as his principal private residence by the terms of a covenant, statutory planning consent or similar permission (Note 13(ii));

(b) a building to be used solely for a relevant residential purpose (Item 1(*a*)(ii)). The purchaser or tenant must provide the grantor with a certificate stating that the building is to be used solely for the purpose in question. This must be done before the grant is made (Note 12(*b*)). For the form and content of certificates, see Notice No 708;

(c) a building to be used solely for a relevant charitable purpose (Item (1)(*a*)(ii)). The purchaser or tenant must provide the grantor with a certificate stating that the building is to be used solely for the purpose in question. This must be done before the grant is made (Note 12(*b*)). For the form and content of certificates, see Notice No 708; or

(d) a garage to be occupied with a dwelling (Item 1(*a*)(i) and Note 3). The garage must be constructed at the same time as the dwelling (Note 3).

The first grant of a major interest (see s 96(1)) in all or part of a building, dwelling or its site by a person converting a non-residential building, or non-residential part of a building, into:

(a) a building designed as one or more dwellings (Item (1)(*b*)). The purchaser or tenant must be entitled to reside in the dwelling throughout the year and must not be prevented from doing so by the terms of a covenant, statutory planning consent or similar permission (Note 13(i)). The purchaser or tenant must not be prevented from using the dwelling as his principal private residence by the terms of a covenant, statutory planning consent or similar permission (Note 13(ii)). If the building contains both a residential part and a non-residential part, one or more additional dwellings must result from the conversion of the non-residential part (Note 9). For cases where additional dwellings did not result, see *C & E Comrs v Blom-Cooper* [2003] STC 669, CA (public house with living accommodation converted into one house); Claam *Vale Ltd* (No 16869) (public house with living accommodation above split vertically to form two semi-detached houses);

(b) a building intended to be used solely for a relevant residential purpose (Item 1(*b*)). The purchaser or tenant must provide the grantor with a certificate stating that the building is to be used solely for the purpose in question. This must be done before the grant is made (Note 12(*b*)). For the form and content of certificates, see Notice No 708; or

(c) a garage intended to be occupied with a dwelling (Item 1(*b*) and Note 3). The dwelling must result from the conversion of a non-residential building. The garage must be converted at the same time as the dwelling (Note 3).

In the case of a lease, the consideration for the grant comprises the premium payable (if there is one) or the first rent payable (in other cases). Thus all rents (premium) or the second and subsequent rent payments (no premium) are excluded from zero-rating (Note 14) so as to be exempt from tax. For the exemption, see Sch 9 Group 1.

Part of a building may be designed as one or more dwellings and part may not (eg retail shop with flat). Similarly, part of a building may be intended to be used for a relevant residential or charitable purpose, and part may not. A grant relating to both parts is apportioned to determine the extent to which the grant is zero-rated. (Note 10).

"Grant" includes an assignment or surrender (Note 1). For the person making a grant, see Sch 10 para 8 (co-owners, trustees and beneficiaries of a trust); *Monsell Youell Developments Ltd v C & E Comrs* [1978] VATTR 1; *Hulme Trust Educational Foundation v C & E Comrs* [1978] VATTR 179. As regards VAT groups, the "first" grant of a major interest is the first such grant made to a person outside the group: see Business Brief 11/03, 24 July 2003.

A "person constructing a building" is one who is constructing, or has constructed, a building: see *C & E Comrs v Link Housing Association Ltd* [1992] STC 718. For partly constructed buildings, see *Stapenhill Developments Ltd v C & E Comrs* [1984] VATTR 1.

For buildings intended to be used "solely" for a relevant charitable purpose, see Revenue and Customs Brief 39/09, 1 July 2009.

For grants which are not zero-rated under this Item, see Sch 8 Group 6 (protected buildings); Sch 9 Group 1 (exemption); Sch 10 para 1 (grants by purchaser or tenant using building for a relevant residential or charitable purpose). For the effect of an election to waive exemption made by the grantor, see Sch 10 para 2(2). For "independent living" units in the grounds of a residential care home, see Revenue and Customs Brief 66/07, 5 November 2007.

For input tax adjustments arising when a house builder temporarily lets a completed dwelling before selling it, see Business Brief 44/08, 15 September 2008. For the grant of a major interest in the completed dwelling to a connected person, who then lets the dwelling on short term tenancies, see Revenue and Customs Brief 54/08, 28 October 2008 (circumstances in which this is not considered to be an abusive practice).

Item 2

A supply of services made in the course of the construction of:

(a) a building designed as one or more dwellings (Item 2(*a*));

(b) a garage to be occupied with a dwelling (Item 2(*a*) and Note 3). The garage must be constructed at the same time as the dwelling (Note 3);

(c) a building to be used solely for a relevant residential purpose (Item 2(*a*)). The services must be supplied to the person intending to use the building for the relevant residential purpose (Note 12(*a*)). The customer must provide the supplier with a certificate stating that the building is to be used solely for a relevant residential purpose. This must be done before the supply is made. For the form and content of certificates, see Notice No 708 (Note 12(*b*));

(d) a building to be used solely for a relevant charitable purpose (Item 2(*a*)). The services must be supplied to the person intending to use the building for the relevant charitable purpose (Note 12(*a*)). The customer must provide the supplier with a certificate stating that the building is to be used solely for a relevant charitable purpose. This must be done before the supply is made. For the form and content of certificates, see Notice No 708 (Note 12(*b*)); or

(e) an annexe to an existing building which is capable of functioning independently from the existing building. All or part of the annexe must be for use for a relevant charitable purpose. The main or only entrance to the annexe must be in the annexe and it must not form the main or only entrance to the existing building (Item 2(*a*) and Notes 16(*c*), 17). The customer must provide the supplier with a certificate stating that the annexe is to be used solely for a relevant charitable purpose. This must be done before the supply is made. For the form and content of certificates, see Notice No 708 (Note 12(*b*)); or

(f) a civil engineering work necessary for development of a permanent park for residential caravans (Item 2(*b*)).

The services must comprise something other than the services of an architect, surveyor, consultant or supervisor. They must be related to the construction works concerned (Item 2). They must also comprise something other than: (1) a transfer of possession of goods (eg plant hire) which amounts to a supply of services; or (2) the use of business assets for non-business or private purposes (eg use of plant by director in do-it-yourself work to private residence) (Note 20). An apportionment is made if necessary to determine the extent to which the services are zero-rated (Note 11). Part of a building may be designed as one or more dwellings, and part may not. Similarly, part of a building may be intended for use for a relevant residential or charitable purpose, and part may not. A supply relating to both parts is apportioned to determine the extent to which the supply is zero-rated (Note 10). For apportionment in respect of communal areas in new buildings containing two or more dwellings, see Business Brief 11/03, 24 July 2003. For "civil engineering work", see *GKN Birwelco Ltd v C & E Comrs* [1983] VATTR 128; *UDF Ltd v C & E Comrs* [1981] VATTR 199. For civil engineering works carried out in conjunction with the construction of a building, see *C & E Comrs v Rannoch School Ltd* [1993] STC 389; *Lamberts Construction Ltd* (No 8882).

Part of a building may be designed as one or more dwellings, and part may not. Similarly, part of a building may be intended for use for a relevant residential or charitable purpose, and part may not. A supply relating to both parts is apportioned to determine the extent to which the supply is zero-rated (Note 10).

For "civil engineering work", see *GKN Birwelco Ltd v C & E Comrs* [1983] VATTR 128; *UDF Ltd v C & E Comrs* [1981] VATTR 199. For civil engineering works carried out in conjunction with the construction of a building, see *C & E Comrs v Rannoch School Ltd* [1993] STC 389; *Lamberts Construction Ltd* (No 8882).

For "residential caravan", see Note 19.

For site clearance and landscaping, see *Gazzard v C & E Comrs* (No 6029); *Rialto Homes plc v C & E Comrs* [1999] V & DR 477; Business Brief 7/00, 18 May 2000. For connection to gas or electricity mains supply, see Notice No 48 (December 2010) para 3.16.

For the test applied in deciding whether services are supplied "in the course of construction", see *C & E Comrs v St Mary's RC High School* [1996] STC 1091.

For the period during which a building is "in the course of construction", see *Lamberts Construction Ltd* (No 8882). For phased developments, see *Bruce v C & E Comrs* [1991] VATTR 280 and contrast *Whiteley v C & E Comrs* [1993] VATTR 248; *Brahma Kumaris World Spiritual University* (No 12946).

For the zero-rating of certain services excluded from zero-rating under this Item, see Item 3 below (conversion); Sch 8 Groups 6 (protected buildings) and 12 (supplies to charities and handicapped persons). For the reduced-rating of certain services similarly excluded, see Sch 7A Groups 6 (residential conversions) and 7 (renovation and alteration). For "independent living" units in the grounds of a residential care home, see Revenue and Customs Brief 66/07, 5 November 2007.

Item 3

A supply of services made in the course of converting a non-residential building, or a non-residential part of a building, into:

(a) a building (or part of a building) designed as one or more dwellings (Item 3(*a*)). If the building contains both a residential part and a non-residential part, one or more additional dwellings must result from the conversion (Note 9). For cases where additional dwellings did not result, see *C & E Comrs v Blom-Cooper* [2003] STC 669, CA (public house with living accommodation above converted into one house); Claam *Vale Ltd* (No 16869) (public house with living accommodation above split vertically to form two semi-detached houses);

(b) a building (or part of a building) to be used solely for a relevant residential purpose (Item 3(*b*)). The customer must provide the supplier with a certificate stating that the building or part is to be used solely for a relevant residential purpose. This must be done before the supply is made (Note 12(*b*)). For the form and content of the certificate, see Notice No 708; or

(c) a garage to be occupied with a dwelling (Item 3(*a*) and Note 3). The dwelling must result from the conversion of a non-residential building. The garage must be converted at the same time as the dwelling (Note 3).

The services must be supplied to a relevant housing association (as defined in Note 21). They must comprise something other than the services of an architect, surveyor, consultant or supervisor, a transfer of possession of goods (eg plant hire) which amounts to a supply of services, or the use of business assets for non-business or private purposes. They must also relate to the conversion (Item 3 and Note 20). An apportionment is made if necessary to determine the extent to which the services are zero-rated (Note 11).

Part of a building may be designed as one or more dwellings and part may not. Similarly, part of a building may be intended for use for a relevant residential purpose and part may not. A supply relating to both parts is apportioned to determine the extent to which the supply is zero-rated (Note 10).

Item 4

A supply of building materials made in conjunction with a supply of services zero-rated under Items 2 or 3 if the supplier incorporates the materials into the relevant building or site.

For "building materials", see Notes 22, 23. For "fitted furniture", see *C & E Comrs v McLean Homes Midlands Ltd* [1993] STC 335; *Edmond Homes Ltd* (No 11567); *Wade* (No 13164); *Moores Furniture Group Ltd* (No 15044); Business Brief 12/97, 5 June 1997. For goods prefabricated off-site, cf *C & E Comrs v Jeffs* [1995] STC 759. For roller blinds, see *John Price* (TC 1287); Revenue and Customs Brief 2/11, 25 January 2011.

Definitions common to more than one item

For "building", see *Walle v C & E Comrs* [1976] VATTR 101; *Smith* (No 5579). For contrasting views whether bed-sits amount to a dwelling, see *Look Ahead Housing Association* (No 16816) and *Amicus Group Ltd* (No 17693). For buildings "designed" as one or more dwellings, see Note 2; *Whiteley v C & E Comrs* [1993] VATTR 248; *Thompson* (No 15834). For buildings to be used solely for a "relevant residential purpose", see Note 4; *R (on the application of Greenwich Property Ltd) v C & E Comrs* [2001] STC 618 (concession for university student accommodation); *R & C Comrs v Fenwood Developments Ltd* [2006] STC 644 (mental home for women detained under the Mental Health Act 1983, but not receiving treatment, neither a hospital nor a prison); *Riverside School (Whassett) Ltd v C & E Comrs* [1995] V & DR 186; *Urdd Gobaith Cymru v C & E Comrs* [1997] V & DR 273;

Denman College v C & E Comrs [1998] V & DR 399; *General Healthcare Group Ltd* (No 17129). For groups of such buildings, see Note 5. For buildings to be used solely for a "relevant charitable purpose", see Note 6; *Jubilee Hall Recreation Centre Ltd v C & E Comrs, C & E Comrs v St Dunstan's Educational Foundation* [1999] STC 381, CA; *C & E Comrs v Yarburgh Children's Trust* [2002] STC 207; *C & E Comrs v St Paul's Community Project Ltd* [2005] STC 95; *Riverside Housing Association Ltd v R & C Comrs* [2006] STC 2072 (divisional headquarters for charitable housing association); Business Brief 2/05, 10 February 2005. For examples, see *Shinewater Association Football Club* (No 12938); *Ormiston Charitable Trust v C & E Comrs* [1995] V & DR 180; *Newtownbutler Playgroup Ltd* (No 13741); *Bennachie Leisure Centre Association* (No 14276); *Cardiff Community Housing Association Ltd v C & E Comrs* [2000] V & DR 346.

For the de minimis limit applied in deciding whether buildings are intended to be used "solely" for a relevant residential or relevant charitable purpose, see Revenue and Customs Brief 39/09, 1 July 2009.

For a "non-residential" building or part of a building, see Notes 7, 8 (in relation to Item 1(*b*)) and Notes 7A, 8 (in relation to Item 3). For the purposes of Notes 7, 7A, "dwelling" is given its ordinary meaning rather than the special meaning in Note 2: *Look Ahead Housing Association* (No 16816); *Calam Vale Ltd* (No 16869).

"Construction" is defined in exclusive terms. The conversion, reconstruction, alteration or enlargement of a civil engineering work does not amount to the construction of a civil engineering work (Note 15). The following works do not amount to the construction of a building: (1) converting, reconstructing or altering an existing building; (2) enlarging or extending an existing building (unless the enlargement or extension creates one or more additional dwellings); or (3) constructing an annexe to an existing building (subject to the exception noted under Item 2) (Notes 16, 17). For works within these descriptions, see *Shiri Guru Nanaka Sikh Temple* (No 14972).

An "existing building" ceases to be such only if: (1) it is completely demolished to ground level; or (2) a single facade (or double facade on a corner site) is retained to comply with the statutory planning consent or similar permission (Note 18). However, the structure may have ceased to be a building (so that it does not appear to be an "existing building") through damage, decay, etc prior to commencement of the relevant works. For the situation under superseded legislation, see *Gill* (No 4904); *Croxford* (No 5730); *C & E Comrs v Lewis* [1994] STC 739; *Jamieson* (No 10939). Furthermore, substantial works to an existing building (or what remains of it after partial demolition) may result in a new building rather than the conversion, reconstruction, alteration or enlargement of an existing building. For the situation under superseded legislation, see *C & E Comrs v Marchday Holdings Ltd* [1997] STC 272, CA; Business Brief 20/97, 24 September 1997.

For the tests applied in relation to Notes 15–17, see most recently *Cantrell and another (trading as Foxearth Lodge Nursing Home) v C & E Comrs* [2000] STC 100 at [4] and *Cantrell and another (trading as Foxearth Lodge Nursing Home) v C & E Comrs (No 2)* [2003] STC 486 at [11]. For the historical development of these tests under superseded legislation, see in particular *C & E Comrs v London Diocesan Fund* [1993] STC 369; *C & E Comrs v Marchday Holdings Ltd* [1997] STC 272, CA. For the relevance of planning permission, see *C & E Comrs v Perry* [1983] STC 383; *Marath Developments Ltd* (No 4213); *Waterways Services v C & E Comrs* [1990] VATTR 37; *Highacre Construction Ltd* (No 5772); *Whiteley v C & E Comrs* [1993] VATTR 248; *Brahma Kumares World Spiritual University* (No 12946). For "reconstruction", see *Wimpey Group Services Ltd v C & E Comrs* [1988] STC 625, CA; *Morton* (No 438); *Riches v C & E Comrs* [1994] VATTR 401. For "enlargement", see the guidelines summarised in Carrophill Ltd (No 10190). For "extension", see *Associated Nursing Services plc* (No 11203); *Siraj* (No 11742). For "annexe", see *Cantrell and another (trading as Foxearth Lodge Nursing Home) v C & E Comrs (No 2)* [2003] STC 486 (supplementary structure in the form of a room, a wing or a separate building).

GROUP 6—PROTECTED BUILDINGS (V4.235, V4.239)

The following supplies are zero-rated.

Item 1

The *first* grant of a major interest (see s 96 (1)) in all or part of a protected building or its site made by a person substantially reconstructing the building. For buildings subject to an immunity certificate issued under Planning (Listed Building and Conservation Areas) Act 1990 s 6 (2) treated as if they were listed buildings, see Press Notice 22/96, 22 April 1996. For substantial reconstruction, see below and *Barraclough* (No 2529). For the exemption of subsequent grants, see Sch 9 Group 1.

Where the grant relates to one or more dwellings, the purchaser or tenant must be entitled to reside in the dwelling throughout the year. He must not be prevented from doing so, or from using the dwelling as his principal private residence, by the terms of a covenant, statutory planning consent or similar permission (Note 3; Sch 8 Group 5 Note 13).

Where all or part of the building is intended to be used solely for a relevant residential purpose (see Sch 8 Group 5 Note 4) or a relevant charitable purpose (see Sch 8 Group 5 Note 6), the purchaser or tenant must provide the grantor with a certificate stating that the building is intended to be so used (Note 3; Sch 8 Group 5 Note 12 (*b*)). For the form and content of certificates, see Notice No 708. For the de minimis limit applied in deciding whether buildings are intended to be used "solely" for a relevant residential or relevant charitable purpose, see Revenue and Customs Brief 39/09, 1 July 2009.

Where the major interest is a lease or tenancy, the grant is zero-rated only to the extent that it is made for a consideration in the form of the premium (if a premium is payable) or the first payment of rent due (in other cases) (Note 3; Sch 8 Group 5 Note 14).

In carrying out the reconstruction, part of the building may have been designed to become, or remain as, one or more dwellings and part may not. Similarly, part may be intended to be used for a relevant residential or charitable purpose and part may not. A grant relating to both parts is apportioned to determine the extent to which the grant is zero-rated (Note 5).

For "grant" see Sch 8 Group 5 Note 1 (Note 3).

A protected building is regarded as substantially reconstructed if either of the following conditions is met:

(a) the works of reconstruction form 60% of the cost and are such that if supplied by a taxable person they would be zero-rated as approved alterations of a protected building; or

(b) the reconstructed building incorporates no more of the original building than the external walls, together with other external features of interest (Note 4).

Item 2

A supply of services in the course of an approved alteration of a protected building. The following services are excluded from zero-rating: (1) the services of an architect, surveyor, consultant or supervisor; (2) a transfer of possession of goods which amounts to a supply of services (see Sch 4 para 1 (1)); and (3) the use of business assets for non-business or private purposes (see Sch 4 para 5 (4)) (Item 1; Note 11).

Where all or part of the building is intended to be used solely for a relevant residential purpose (see Sch 8 Group 5 Note 4) or solely for a relevant charitable purpose (see Sch 8 Group 5 Note 5), the supply is zero-rated only if: (1) the services are supplied to the person intending to use the building for such purpose; and (2) he provides the supplier with a certificate stating that the building is intended to be used for such purpose (Note 3; Sch 8 Group 5 Note 12). For the form and content of certificates, see Notice No 708. For the de minimis limit applied in deciding whether buildings are intended to be used "solely" for a relevant residential or relevant charitable purpose, see Revenue and Customs Brief 39/09, 1 July 2009. This applies from 1 July 2009.

Part of the building may have been designed to become, or remain as, one or more dwellings and part may not. Similarly, part may be intended to be used for a relevant residential or charitable purpose and part may not. A supply relating to both parts is apportioned to determine the extent to which the supply is zero-rated (Note 5).

Where a service relates only partly to an approved alteration, an apportionment is made to determine the extent to which the supply is zero-rated (Note 9).

An approved alteration is work carried out to a building (being a listed building or scheduled monument) which is: (1) any alteration (in the case of an ecclesiastical building other than a vicarage, manse, etc) (see *Powell* (No 14520) (churchyard wall); (2) an alteration which would require listed building consent or scheduled monument consent but for the fact that the building is owned by the Crown, the Duchy of Cornwall or a government department; or (3) an alteration which requires, and has received, listed building consent or scheduled monument consent (see *Evans* (No 4415); *Gibbs* (No 5596); *Nicholls* (No 11115); *Walsingham College (Yorkshire Properties) Ltd v C & E Comrs* [1995] V & DR 141; *Wrencon Ltd* (No 13698); *Wells* (No 15169); *Alan Roper & Sons Ltd* (No 15260)) (Notes 6, 7, 8).

Constructing a separate building within the curtilage of a protected building does not amount to an approved alteration (Note 10). For "separate", see *C & E Comrs v Arbib* [1995] STC 490. For works carried out to an existing secondary building, see *C & E Comrs v Zielinski Baker & Partners Ltd* [2004] STC 456, HL. For works carried out to a garden, see *C & E Comrs v Tinsley* [2005] STC 1612.

An alteration does not include repair or maintenance, incidental alterations resulting from repairs, and maintenance work (Note 6). For examples, see *Wrencon Ltd* (No 13968) (repair or maintenance); *PCC of St Andrew's Church, Eakring* (No 15320) (not repair or maintenance).

For "alteration", see *C & E Comrs v Morrish* [1998] STC 954; contrast *Wrencon Ltd* (No 13968) (word construed by reference to relevant planning law) and *Evans* (No 4415) and later cases (word construed by reference to superseded legislation, as to which see *ACT Construction Ltd v C & E Comrs* [1982] STC 25, HL; *Viva Gas Appliances Ltd v C & E Comrs* [1983] STC 819, HL). For mains electrical wiring and lighting systems, see Business Brief 7/00, 18 May 2000. For "repair or maintenance", see *Wrencon Ltd* (No 13968). Under superseded legislation, see in particular *C & E Comrs v Windflower Housing Association* [1995] STC 860; *All Saints Tilsworth PCC v C & E Comrs* [1993] VATTR 315, *Browne* (No 11388); *Dodson Bros (Thatchers) Ltd v C & E Comrs* [1995] V & DR 514; cf *St Luke's Parochial Church Council v C & E Comrs* [1982] STC 856; *Home Protection Co v C & E Comrs* [1984] STC 278; *Sutton Housing Trust v C & E Comrs* [1984] STC 352. For incidental alterations, see *Wrencon Ltd* (No 13968). Under superseded legislation, see *Sharman v C & E Comrs* [1983] STC 809; *C & E Comrs v Morrison Dunbar Ltd* [1979] STC 406; *K & G Levell* (No 6202).

Item 3

A supply of building materials made in the course of an approved alteration if: (1) the supplier also supplies services zero-rated under Item 2; (2) the supplier incorporates the materials into the relevant building or site and his services in so doing are also zero-rated under Item 2; and (3) the goods and services are supplied to the same person.

For "building materials", see Sch 8 Group 5 Notes 22, 23 (Note 3).

Definition of "protected building"

A "protected building" is a listed building or scheduled monument within one of the following descriptions: (1) a building designed to remain as one or more dwellings (see Note 2) after the reconstruction or alteration; (2) a building designed to become one or more dwellings (see Note 2) after the reconstruction or alteration; (3) a building intended to be used solely for a relevant residential purpose (see Sch 8 Group 5 Note 4) after the reconstruction or alteration; and (4) a building intended to be used solely for a relevant charitable purpose (see Sch 8 Group 5 Note 5) after the reconstruction or alteration (Notes 1, 3). For a garage occpied together with a dwelling, see Note 2; *Grange Builders (Quainton) Ltd* (No 18905); Business Brief 11/05, 18 May 2005.

GROUP 7—INTERNATIONAL SERVICES (V4.246)

The following supplies are zero-rated.

Item 1

Carrying out work on goods within the EU is zero-rated if the goods are subsequently exported to a third country by the supplier (any recipient) or recipient (recipient belonging in a third country). For the place where the recipient belongs, see s 9.

Item 2

An agent's services for a disclosed, named principal are zero-rated if he arranges: (1) an export of goods to a third country; (2) a supply of services within Item 1; or (3) a supply of services made in a third country. For the place of supply of services, see s 7.

GROUP 8—TRANSPORT (V4.251)

The following supplies are zero-rated.

Item 1

The supply (including hire or charter), maintenance or repair of a qualifying ship (see Note A1(*a*)); *R & C Comrs v Stone* [2008] STC 2501; Revenue and Customs Brief 38/09, 8 July 2009). Charter services are excluded from zero-rating if they wholly comprise one or more of the following services performed in the UK: (1) transport of passengers; (2) accommodation; (3) entertainment; or (4) education. For passenger transport, see item 4. For "charter", see *Navicon SA v Administración del Estado* (case C-97/06) [2007] ECR I–8755, [2008] STC 2693, ECJ (contract for partial charter of vessel).

The modification or conversion of a qualifying ship if the ship continues to be such a ship following completion of the works. See Revenue and Customs Brief 38/09, 8 July 2009. For similar works prior to 1 January 1996, see *A & P Appledore (Falmouth) Ltd v C & E Comrs* [1992] VATTR 22; *Everett* (No 11736). For ship design services, see *Cholerton Ltd* (No 13387); Business Brief 5/99, 24 February 1999.

Item 1 is a derogation retained by the UK in accordance with Directive 2006/112/EC art 110 (formerly Directive 77/388/EEC art 28(2)(*a*) (first para)). It does not implement Directive 2006/112/EC art 148(*c*) (formerly Directive 77/388/EEC art 15(5)). It is not, therefore, required to be interpreted in conformity with art 148(*c*) of the 2006 Directive: see *R & C Comrs v Stone* [2008] STC 2501.

Item 2

The supply (including hire or charter), maintenance or repair of a qualifying aircraft (see Notes A1(*b*), B1 and C1). Charter services are excluded from zero-rating if they wholly comprise one or more of the following services performed in the UK: (1) transport of passengers; (2) accommodation; (3) entertainment; or (4) education. For passenger transport, see item 4.

The modification or conversion of a qualifying aircraft if the aircraft continues to be such an aircraft following completion of the works.

Item 2A

The supply (including hire) of parts and equipment installed or incorporated in the propulsion, navigation or communication systems, or the general structure, of a qualifying ship (see Note A1(*a*); *R & C Comrs v Stone* [2008] STC 2501; Revenue and Customs Brief 38/09, 8 July 2009) or a qualifying aircraft (see Note A1(*b*)). The parts and equipment must be of a kind ordinarily so installed or incorporated. Supplies to a government department are within this provision only if: (1) the parts or equipment are installed or incorporated in the course of a supply which is treated as being made in the course or furtherance of a business carried on by the department; or (2) the parts and equipment are for installation or incorporation in a ship or aircraft used to provide rescue or assistance at sea.

Item 2B

The supply (including hire) of life jackets, life rafts, smoke hoods and similar safety equipment for use in a qualifying ship (see Note A1(*a*); *R & C Comrs v Stone* [2008] STC 2501; Business Brief 35/04, 31 December 2004) or a qualifying aircraft (see Note A1(*b*)). Supplies to a government department are within this provision only if: (1) the goods are installed or incorporated in the course of a supply which is treated as being made in the course or furtherance of a business carried on by the department; or (2) the goods are for installation in a ship or aircraft used to provide rescue or assistance at sea.

Item 3

The following supplies made to a sea-rescue charity: (1) the supply (including hire) of sea rescue vessels, carriage equipment, tractors, winches and hauling equipment; (2) spare parts or accessories for the foregoing goods or for slipways; (3) sea rescue equipment for a sea rescue vessel; and (4) fuel for use in a lifeboat.

The following supplies made for a sea-rescue charity: (1) the repair or maintenance of sea rescue vessels, carriage equipment, tractors, winches and hauling equipment; and (2) the construction, alteration, repair or maintenance of slipways for launching and recovering sea rescue vessels.

The charity must give a certificate stating that the supply is zero-rated.

Item 4

Transport of passengers: (1) in a vehicle, ship or aircraft designed or adapted to carry ten or more passengers (see *R & C Comrs v Cirdan Sailing Trust* [2006] STC 185); (2) in a vehicle which would be capable of carrying ten or more passengers but for the fact that it is designed or adapted to carry one or more persons in a wheelchair (see Note 4D); (3) by a universal service provider (as defined in Note 4E); (4) on any scheduled flight; or (5) to or from a place in the UK (to the extent that the supply is made in the UK) (see *Virgin Atlantic Airways Ltd v C & E Comrs* [1995] STC 341; Business Brief 4/96, 13 March 1996).

"Transport" involves movement from one place to another for some purpose: see *C & E Comrs v Blackpool Pleasure Beach Co* [1974] STC 134 (ride on "Big Dipper"); *Quarry Tours Ltd v C & E Comrs* [1984] VATTR 238 (tour of slate cavern); *Faulkner (a firm)* (No 7597) (balloon flight); *C & E Comrs v Peninsular & Oriental Steam Navigation Co Ltd* [1996] STC 698 (holiday cruise); *Virgin Atlantic Airways Ltd* (No 13840) (river cruise); *Narogauge Ltd* (No 14680) (narrow-gauge railway in country park). For "vehicle", see *Llandudno Cabinlift Co Ltd v C & E Comrs* [1973] VATTR 1; *Quarry Tours Ltd v C & E Comrs* [1984] VATTR 238. For student travel cards, see *British Railways Board v C & E Comrs* [1977] STC 221, CA. For holiday and river cruises, see Business Brief 14/96, 15 July 1996.

The following passenger transport is excluded from zero-rating:

(a) passenger transport to, from or within any place in any vehicle if: (i) the transport is supplied by the person (or a connected person as defined in CTA 2010 s 1122) who supplies either a right of admission to the place or a right to use facilities at the place; and (ii) the place is either a place of entertainment, recreation or amusement, or a place of cultural, scientific, historical or similar interest;

(b) passenger transport between a car park (or adjacent land) and an airport passenger terminal (or adjacent land) if: (i) the transport is supplied by the car park operator (or a connected person as defined in CTA 2010 s 1122), and (ii) the means of transport is a mechanically propelled vehicle intended or adapted for use on the roads;

(c) passenger transport in an aircraft if the flight is advertised or held out to be for either of the following purposes and not primarily for the purpose of transporting passengers from one place to another; (i) providing entertainment, recreation or amusement, or (ii) providing the experience of flying, either generally or in that particular aircraft.

For apportionment, contrast *British Airways plc v C & E Comrs* [1990] STC 643, CA, *Quarry Tours Ltd v C & E Comrs* [1984] VATTR 238, *C & E Comrs v Peninsular & Oriental Steam Navigation Co Ltd* [1996] STC 356 (single service comprising transport); *Big Pit (Blaenafon) Trust* (No 6705), *Granada Group plc* (No 14803) (single service of something other than transport); and *River Barge Holidays Ltd* (No 572), *Virgin Atlantic Airways Ltd* (No 13840) (apportionment between transport and other services).

Item 5

Transporting freight to or from a third country. Cf *Baxter-Martin* (No 104); *Bevington* (No 282).

Item 6

The following services:

(a) handling a qualifying ship (see Note A1(*a*); *R & C Comrs v Stone* [2008] STC 2501; Business Brief 35/04, 31 December 2004) or qualifying aircraft (see Note A1(*b*)). The handling must take place:
   (i) in a port (see CEMA 1979 s 1(1)),
   (ii) in customs and excise airport (see CEMA 1979 s 21(7)), or
   (iii) overseas;

(b) handling or storing goods that have been carried in any ship or aircraft. The handling or storage must take place:
   (i) in a port,
   (ii) on land adjacent to a port,
   (iii) in a customs and excise airport, or
   (iv) in a transit shed (see CEMA 1979 s 1(1)).

   As regards goods that have been carried in aircraft, this provision is interpreted by reference to Directive 2006/112/EC art 148(*g*) (formerly Directive 77/388/EEC art 15(9)), as interpreted by the Court of Justice: see *R & C Comrs v EB Central Services Ltd* [2008] STC 2209, CA..

Item 6A

Air navigation services supplied in relation to a qualifying aircraft (see Note A1(*b*)). Air navigation services include information, directions and other facilities furnished, issued or provided in connection with the navigation or movement of aircraft and include the control of movement of vehicles in any part of an aerodrome used for the movement of aircraft (Note 6A; Civil Aviation Act 1982 s 105 (1)).

Item 7

Pilotage services.

Item 8

Salvage or towage services.

Item 9

The surveying or classification of a qualifying ship (see Note A1(*a*); Business Brief 35/04, 31 December 2004) or qualifying aircraft (see Note A1(*b*)) for the purposes of any register.

Item 10

Making arrangements for any of the following:

(a) the supply of a qualifying ship (see Note A1(*a*); Business Brief 35/04, 31 December 2004) or qualifying aircraft (see Note A1(*b*)), or space in such a ship or aircraft. For services outside this description, see *Société Internationale de Télécommunications Aéronautiques v C & E Comrs* [2004] STC 950;

(b) the supply of any service within Items 1, 2, 3–9 or 11;

(c) the supply of any goods within Items 2A or 2B or 3(*d*).

Item 11

The following services:

(a) handling or storing goods at, or transporting them to or from, the place of import or export.
This provision is interpreted by reference to Directive 2006/112/EC art 146(1)(*e*) (formerly Directive 77/388/EEC art 15(13), as interpreted by the Court of Justice. It follows that the services must be directly connected with the importation or exportation: *R & C Comrs v EB Central Services Ltd* [2008] STC 2209, CA;

(b) the following, when supplied to a person belonging overseas (see s 9(4)) for the purposes of his business:
 (i) handling any ship or aircraft in a port (as defined in CEMA 1979 s 1(1)), customs and excise airport (as defined in CEMA 1979 s 21(7)), or overseas,
 (ii) air navigation services (see under Item 6A above) supplied in relation to any aircraft,
 (iii) surveying or classifying any ship or aircraft for the purposes of any register, or
 (iv) arranging the supply of any ship or aircraft, or of space in any ship or aircraft.

Item 12

Supplying a designated travel service for enjoyment outside the EU. For designated travel services, see VAT (Tour Operators) Order 1987, SI 1987/1806 art 3.

Item 13

Transporting goods between: (1) an EU member state and the Azores or Madeira; (2) the Azores and Madeira.

GROUP 9—CARAVANS AND HOUSEBOATS (V4.275)

The following supplies are zero-rated.

Item 1

Caravans that cannot lawfully be towed on roads by a vehicle with an unladen weight below 2,030 kg. A caravan meets this test if it exceeds 7 metres in length and/or 2.55 metres in width: see Road Vehicles (Construction and Use) Regulations SI 1986/1078 reg 7(1) and 8(1). For the exclusion of removable contents, see para (*a*) of the Note to Group 9; *Telacre Beach Caravan Sales Ltd v C & E Comrs* (case C-251/05) [2006] ECR I–6269, [2006] STC 1671, ECJ.

Item 2

Houseboats not having a means of self-propulsion designed or adapted for use as places of permanent habitation. See Revenue and Customs Brief 38/09, 8 July 2009. For the exclusion of removable contents, see para (*a*) of the Note to Group 9; cf *Telacre Beach Caravan Sales Ltd v C & E Comrs* (case C-251/05) [2006] ECR I–6269, [2006] STC 1671, ECJ.

Item 3

The hire or loan of a caravan within item 1 or houseboat within item 2. However, a supply of accommodation in a caravan or houseboat is excluded from zero-rating. For the exclusion of a supply of accommodation, see para (*b*) of the Note to Group 9.

GROUP 10—GOLD (V4.277)

The supply of gold held in the UK by a Central Bank to another Central Bank or to a member of the London Gold Market or by such a member to a Central Bank is zero-rated. Gold coins and options are included.

GROUP 11—BANK NOTES (V4.279)

The issue of a bank note by a bank is zero-rated. For a supply outside this description, see *Royal Bank of Scotland plc v C & E Comrs* [2002] STC 575.

GROUP 12—DRUGS, MEDICINES, AIDS FOR THE HANDICAPPED, ETC (V4.281)

The following supplies are zero-rated.

Goods within this Group may not be acquired or imported without payment of VAT under VATA 1983 s 16 (3).

A person is "handicapped" for the purpose of this Group if he is chronically sick or disabled.

Item 1

The supply of any qualifying goods dispensed to an individual on the prescription of an appropriate practitioner (as defined in Note 2B). The qualifying goods must be for the individual's personal use. The prescription must be dispensed by a registered pharmacist (as defined in Note 2C) or dispensed in accordance with a requirement or authorisation under a relevant provision (as defined in Note 2D).

For a concession in relation to in-patients, residents and outpatients, see Notice No 48 (December 2010) para 3.30. For "dispensed" and "prescription", see *Bio Oil Research Ltd* (No 12252).

Item 1A

[Repealed.]

Item 2

The supply (or hire) of goods listed in paras (*a*)–(*i*) of Item 2 and paras (*a*)–(*c*) of Note 4 (but not hearing aids, dentures, spectacles or contact lenses) if: (1) the supply is made to a handicapped person for his domestic or personal use; or (2) the supply is made to a charity for the purpose of making the goods available, by sale or otherwise, to handicapped persons for their domestic or personal use.

As regards supplies made to a handicapped person, goods are not for domestic or personal use if the handicapped person is receiving medical treatment, surgical treatment or care as an in-patient, resident or out-patient of a "relevant institution" (see Note 5I) and either: (1) (if the supply is made by a body within Note 5H(*a*)–(*g*)) the goods comprise something other than goods within Note 4(*b*) or parts or accessories for them, or (2) (if the supply is made by someone else) the goods comprise goods within Item 2(*a*), parts and accessories for them, incontinence products or wound dressings (Notes 5B, 5C, 5D).

If the supply is made in accordance with any agreement, arrangement or understanding—whether or not legally enforceable—to which a body within Note 5H(*g*) (in the case of goods falling within Note 4(*b*)) or a body within Note 5H(*a*)–(*g*) (in other cases) is or has been a party, it is a condition that the body must be the supplier (Notes 5E(*a*), 5F(*a*)).

If the goods comprise goods within Note 4 (*b*), it is a condition that a body within Note 5H (*a*)–(*f*) has not directly or indirectly provided the whole of the consideration. In the case of any other goods, it is a condition that a body within Note 5H(*a*)–(*g*) has not directly or indirectly contributed to the consideration (Notes 5E (*b*) and 5F(*b*)).

For goods (other than spectacles or contact lenses) designed solely for use by a visually handicapped person and supplied at or below cost to a resident or out-patient of a relevant institution (see Note 5I) by a charity, see Notice No 48 (July 2009) para 3.24. The goods must fall within para (*g*) of Item 2.

"Clothing" in Note 4(*a*) includes incontinence products: Customs and Excise Manual, Vol V1 Part 7 Chapter 12 Section 4.36. For the retail sale of incontinence products, see Business Brief 12/01, 11 September 2001.

For "appliances" and "relief" in Item 2(*a*), see *British United Provident Association Ltd v C & E Comrs (No 2)* (No 12180), revsd on other grounds [1995] STC 628. For "severe abnormality or severe injury" therein, see *Neen Design Ltd* (No 11782) (chronic pain). Item 2(*a*) includes transcutaneous electrical nerve stimulators: *Neen Design Ltd* (No 11782); Business Brief 4/94, 21 February 1994 [not reproduced].

For "invalids" and beds "designed" for them in Item 2(*b*), see *Niagra Holdings Ltd v C & E Comrs* [1993] VATTR 503.

For motor vehicles in Item 2(*f*), see *Pantekoek* (No 17765) (vehicle must be adapted before, not after, purchase).

For other "equipment and appliances" in Item 2 (*g*), see *Princess Louise Scottish Hospital v C & E Comrs* [1983] VATTR 191; *Hobden* (No 1875); *Kirton Designs Ltd* (No 2374); *Tempur Pedic (UK) Ltd* (No 13744); *Foxer Industries* (No 13817); *Softley Ltd* (No 15034); *Morgan (a firm)* (No 15218); *Boys' and Girls' Welfare Society* (No 15274); Business Brief 20/97, 24 September 1997 (anti-allergen products). Goods are "solely" designed for use by handicapped persons if they are specifically designed for such persons. The fact that able-bodied people may also use them does not mean that they are not so designed: see *Ridgeon* (No 17749).

For apparatus similar to "renal haemodialysis units, oxygen concentrators and artificial respirators" in Note 4(*c*), see *Simmons* (No 6622).

Item 2A

The supply (or hire) of a qualifying motor vehicle (see Note 5L) to: (1) a handicapped person who usually uses a wheelchair; (2) a handicapped person who is usually carried on a stretcher; or (3) a charity which intends to sell, hire or loan the vehicle to a handicapped person in (1) or (2).

Item 3

Adapting goods to suit the purposes of a handicapped person. The supply must be made to a handicapped person.

Where goods are adapted prior to supply, an apportionment of value is required to find out how much should be zero-rated (Note 8).

Item 4

Adapting goods to suit the purposes of a handicapped person. The supply must be made to a charity. See *Boys' and Girls' Welfare Society* (No 15274).

Where goods are adapted prior to supply, an apportionment of value is required to find out how much should be zero-rated (Note 8).

Item 5

The repair or maintenance of any goods specified in items 2, 2A, 6, 18 or 19 supplied as described.

Item 6

The supply of goods in connection with a supply described in items 3, 4 or 5.

Item 7

Installing the equipment and appliances specified in Item 2 and parts or accessories for them. The supply must be made to a handicapped person or charity.

Item 8

Constructing ramps or widening doorways or passages within the private residence of a handicapped person. The supply must be made to a handicapped person. For "passages", see *Cannings-Knight* (No 11291).

Item 9

Constructing ramps or widening doorways or passages to enable a handicapped person to enter or move within a building. The supply must be made to a charity. For "passages", see *Cannings-Knight* (No 11291).

Item 10

The supply to a handicapped person of a service of providing, extending or adapting a bathroom, washroom or lavatory in a private residence where such provision is necessary by reason of his condition. Zero-rating is confined to building work: see *Strachan* (No 2165). For "washroom", see Note 5K.

Item 11

The supply to a charity of a service of providing, extending or adapting a bathroom, washroom or lavatory for use by handicapped persons in:

(a) residential accommodation; or
(b) a day centre where 20% or more of the users are handicapped persons.

For "residential accommodation", see Note 5J. For "washroom", see Note 5K. For examples, see *Mid Derbyshire Cheshire Home* (No 4512); *Brailsford* (No 13472); *Boys' and Girls' Welfare Society* (No 15274).

Item 12

The supply to a charity of a service of providing, extending or adapting a washroom or lavatory for use by handicapped persons in a building (or part) principally used by a charity for charitable purposes. For "washroom", see Note 4K.

Item 13

Goods supplied in connection with Items 8, 9, 10 or 11. It is irrelevant whether the supplier is registered or whether he supplies the services in Items 8–11: *Flather* (No 11960).

Item 14

The hire of a motor vehicle to a person in receipt of a disability living allowance (see Note 7) if: (1) the lessor's business predominantly comprises the provision of motor vehicles to such persons; (2) the hire period is three years or more; (3) the vehicle is unused when the hire period begins; and (4) all or part of the hire charge is paid by the Department of Social Security or the Ministry of Defence.

Item 15

The sale of a motor vehicle if: (1) it has been hired under a supply within Item 14; and (2) it is not otherwise supplied between the end of the hire period and the date of sale.

Item 16

The installation of a lift to facilitate movement between floors within the private residence of a handicapped person. See *Brian Perkins & Co Ltd* (No 3885).

Item 17

The supply of a lift to a charity providing a residence or day-centre for handicapped persons. For "day-centre", see *Union of Students of the University of Warwick v C & E Comrs* [1995] V & DR 519. For contracts to install a lift before 31 March 2005, see Business Brief 3/05, 21 February 2005.

Item 18

Goods supplied in connection with items 16 or 17.

Item 19

The supply to a handicapped person or to a charity of an alarm system.

Item 20

The supply of services performed by a control centre (see Note 9) responding to calls from an alarm as described in item 19.

GROUP 13—IMPORTS, EXPORTS ETC (V4.283)

Imports, acquisitions and exports are zero-rated under VATA 1994 s 30(2), (6) and regulations made under s 30(8). These provisions are supplemented by this Group. The following supplies are zero-rated.

Item 1

Imported goods if: (1) the supply is made before a customs entry is delivered; and (2) the contract requires the purchaser to deliver the customs entry.

Item 2

Goods or services supplied to or by an overseas authority participating in an international collaborative defence arrangement (see Note 1).

Item 3

The supply to an overseas authority, body or trader (see Notes 2–5) of jigs, patterns, templates, dies, punches and similar machine tools used in the UK solely to make goods for export to a third country. For the goods listed, see *Technicolor Ltd* (No 14871).

GROUP 14—TAX FREE SHOPS

[Repealed.]

GROUP 15—CHARITIES, ETC (V4.266)

The following supplies are zero-rated.

Item 1

The sale or hire of goods by a charity if:

(1) the goods comprise tangible moveable property (Note 1F);
(2) the goods were donated to the charity for sale, letting or export (Item 1);
(3) the sale or hire results from the goods having been made available to two or more specified persons or to the general public (Note 1(*a*));
(4) no arrangements were made by the parties to the sale or hire (or by the donor and one or more of those parties) before the goods were made available to specified persons or the general public (Note 1(*b*)); and
(5) apart from the periods when they are hired, the goods must be available for purchase, hire or export from the time when they are donated to the time when they are sold, exported or disposed of as waste and not used for any other purpose, or any additional purpose, during that period (Note 1B).

Goods are donated for letting if they are donated for letting, re-letting and subsequent sale, export or disposal as waste (Note 1A). A person is a "specified person" if he is either handicapped or entitled to one of the benefits listed in Note 1D (Note 1C). For goods unsuitable for sale, see Notice No 48 (December 2010) para 3.21. For land bequeathed to charities, see Business Brief 12/92, 29 July 1992. For donations, see *University of Wales College Newport* [1997] V & DR 417.

Item 1A

The sale or hire of goods by a taxable person if:

(1) the taxable person's profits are payable to a charity in accordance with a deed, written agreement or other provision (Item 1A; Note 1E);
(2) the goods comprise tangible moveable property (Note 1F);
(3) the goods were donated to the taxable person for sale, letting or export (Item 1A);
(4) the sale or hire results from the goods having been made available to two or more specified persons or to the general public (Note 1(*a*));
(5) no arrangements were made by the parties to the sale or hire (or by the donor and one or more of those parties) before the goods were made available to specified persons or the general public (Note 1(*b*)); and
(6) apart from the periods when they are hired, the goods must be available for purchase, hire or export from the time when they are donated to the time when they are sold, exported or disposed of as waste and not used for any other purpose, or any additional purpose, during that period (Note 1B).

Goods are donated for letting if they are donated for letting, re-letting and subsequent sale, export or disposal as waste (Note 1A). A person is a "specified person" if he is either handicapped or entitled to one of the benefits listed in Note 1D (Note 1C). For goods unsuitable for sale, see Notice No 48 (December 2010) para 3.21. For donations, see *University of Wales College Newport* [1997] V & DR 417.

Item 2

A donation of goods if:

- the goods comprise tangible moveable property (Note 1F); and
- the goods are donated for sale, letting or export by a charity or by a taxable person whose profits are payable to a charity in accordance with a deed, written agreement or other provision (Item 2; Note 1E).

Goods are donated for letting if they are donated for letting, re-letting and subsequent sale, export or disposal as waste (Note 1A). For donations, see *University of Wales College Newport v C & E Comrs* [1997] V & DR 417.

Item 3

The export of goods to a third country by a charity. Goods are "exported" if they are removed from the UK: *International Planned Parenthood Federation* (No 16922) (goods removed from an EU member state to a third country not an export).

The export is treated as a supply made in the UK in the course or furtherance of business if it would not otherwise be so (eg in the case of donated goods) (see s 30(5)) to facilitate zero-rating under Item 3.

Item 4

A supply of relevant goods (see below) for donation to a nominated eligible body (see below) purchased with funds provided by a charity or from voluntary contributions. "Supply" for this purpose includes the letting on hire of relevant goods (Note 9). If the eligible body falls within Note 4 (*f*), the goods must either be used in a relevant establishment (see below) or be used to provide domiciliary medical care (Notes 5A, 5B). A supply is excluded from zero-rating if the donee (being someone other than a charity) has contributed to the funds used to purchase or hire the goods (Notes 6, 9).

Item 5

A supply of relevant goods (see below) to an eligible body (see below) which pays for them with funds provided by a charity or from voluntary contributions. "Supply" for this purpose includes the letting on hire of relevant goods (Note 9). If the eligible body falls within Note 4 (*f*), the goods must either be used in a relevant establishment (see below) or be used to provide domiciliary medical care (Notes 5A, 5B). A supply is excluded from zero-rating if the eligible body (being someone other than a charity) has contributed to the funds use to purchase or hire the goods (Notes 7, 9).

A supply of relevant goods to an eligible body within Note 4 (*f*). "Supply" for this purpose includes the letting on hire of relevant goods (Note 9). The goods must be either used in a relevant establishment (see below) or used to provide domiciliary medical care (Notes 5A, 5B).

This item includes computer services by way of the provision of computer software solely for use in medical research, diagnosis or treatment (Note 10).

For the supply of relevant goods to either a charity whose sole purpose and function is to provide a range of care services to meet the personal needs (of which transport might form a part) of handicapped people or a charity which provides transport services predominantly to handicapped people, see Notice No 48 (December 2010) para 3.19.

Item 6

The repair or maintenance of relevant goods (see below) owned or hired by an eligible body (see below). If the eligible body falls within Note 4 (*f*), the goods must be used in either a relevant establishment (see below) or used to provide domiciliary medical care (Notes 5A, 5B). The supply must be paid for with funds provided by a charity or from voluntary contributions (Note 8 (*a*)). A supply is excluded from zero-rating if the eligible body (being someone other than a charity) has contributed to the funds used to repair or maintain the goods (Notes 8 (*b*), 9).

For the repair or maintenance of relevant goods owned or hired by a charity whose sole purpose and function is to provide a range of care services to meet the personal needs (of which transport might form a part) of handicapped people or a charity which provides transport services predominantly to handicapped people, see Notice No 48 (December 2010) para 3.19

Item 7

Goods supplied in connection with repair or maintenance zero-rated under Item 6. If the eligible body falls within Note 4 (*f*), the relevant goods must be used in either a relevant establishment (see below) or used to provide domiciliary medical care (Notes 5A, 5B). The supply must be paid for with funds provided by a charity or from voluntary contributions (Note 8 (*a*)). A supply is excluded from zero-rating if the eligible body (being someone other than a charity) has contributed to the funds used to purchase the goods supplied (Note 8 (*b*)).

For the supply of goods used in connection with the repair or maintenance of relevant goods owned or hired by a charity whose sole purpose and function is to provide a range of care services to meet the personal needs (of which transport might form a part) of handicapped people or a charity which provides transport services predominantly to handicapped people, see Notice No 48 (December 2010) para 3.19.

Item 8

The supply of a right to promulgate an advertisement by means of a medium of communication with the public if:

- the supply is made to a charity (Item 8);
- the legal or natural persons reached through the medium are not selected (whether by address, at random or otherwise) by or on behalf of the charity (Note 10A); and
- (if the charity has a website, whether hosted by itself or another person), the supply is not used to create or contribute to the charity's website (Note 10B).

For the zero-rating of pay-per-click charity advertisements, see Revenue and Customs Brief 25/10, 7 June 2010.

Item 8A

A supply consisting of the promulgation of an advertisement by means of a medium of communication with the public if:

- the supply is made to a charity (Item 8A);
- the legal or natural persons reached through the medium are not selected (whether by address, at random or otherwise) by or on behalf of the charity (Note 10A); and
- (if the charity has a web site, whether hosted by itself or another person), the supply is not used to create or contribute to the charity's web site (Note 10B).

For the zero-rating of pay-per-click charity advertisements, see Revenue and Customs Brief 25/10, 7 June 2010.

Item 8B

A supply of services comprising the design or production of an advertisement for promulgation by means of a medium of communication with the public if:

- the supply is made to a charity (Item 8B);
- (if the charity has a web site, whether hosted by itself or another person), the supply is not used to create or contribute to the charity's web site (Note 10B); and
- the supply is not used directly by the charity to design or produce an advertisement (Note 10C).

Item 8C

A supply of goods closely related to a supply within Item 8B if:

- the supply is made to a charity (Item 8C);
- (if the charity has a web site, whether hosted by itself or another person), the supply is not used to create or contribute to the charity's web site (Note 10B); and
- the supply is not used directly by the charity to design or produce an advertisement (Note 10C).

Item 9

The supply to a charity of a medicinal product solely for use in care, treatment or research. The charity must provide care for human beings or animals or engage in medical or veterinary research.

Item 10

The supply to a charity of a substance directly used for synthesis or testing in the course of medical or veterinary research.

Definitions

For "animals", see Note 2.

For "relevant goods", see Note 3. For "medical equipment" within Note 3(*a*), see *C & E Comrs v The David Lewis Centre* [1995] STC 485; Notice No 48 (December 2010) para 3.25 (concession in respect of resuscitation training models supplied to charities for first aid training). For examples of medical equipment, see *The Anglodent Co* (No 16891), *Medical and Dental Staff Training Ltd* (No 17031). For examples of goods outside this description, see *C & E Comrs v The David Lewis Centre* [1995] STC 485 (two-way observation window); *Clinical Computers Ltd v C & E Comrs* [1983] VATTR 121 (computer not programmed for medical purpose); *Lancer (UK) Ltd v* C & E Comrs [1986] VATTR 112 (washing machine). For accessories within Note 3(*c*), see *Royal Midland Counties Home for Disabled People v C & E Comrs* [2002] STC 395 (emergency generator an accessory). For examples of goods which are not accessories, see *Norwich Camera Centre Ltd* (No 11629) (chemicals and photographic paper for use with X-ray processing equipment); *Crown Treatment Centre* (No 15564) (photocopier). For motor vehicles within Note 3(*e*), see *C & E Comrs v Help the Aged* [1997] STC 406 (meaning of "permanently"); *Hansard*, 15 February 1996 (not reproduced) (Scott-Track Venturer).

For "eligible body", see Note 4. A body within Note 4(*f*) must provide care, medical treatment or surgical treatment in a relevant establishment and most of the persons receiving such care or treatment there must be handicapped persons (Note 4A). For "care", see *C & E Comrs v Help the Aged* [1997] STC 406; *Medical Care Foundation v C & E Comrs* [1991] VATTR 28. For "relevant establishment", see Note 4B. For "handicapped persons", see Note 5.

For "medicinal product", "medicinal purpose" and "administer", see Note 11.

For "substance" and "ingredient", see Note 12.

GROUP 16—CLOTHING AND FOOTWEAR (V4.287)

Supplies (see Note 5) of the following goods are zero-rated.

Item 1

Articles designed as clothing or footwear for young children (Item 1). This includes components for garments: *C & E Comrs v Ali Baba Tex Ltd* [1992] STC 590. The following are excluded from zero-rating:

- any article suitable for older persons (Item 1): see *Jeffrey Green & Co Ltd v C & E Comrs* [1974] VATTR 94; *Walter Stewart Ltd v C & E Comrs* [1974] VATTR 131; *Dauntgate Ltd* (No 11663); *Charles Owen & Co (BOW) Ltd v C & E Comrs* [1993] VATTR 514; *Benrose Ltd* (No 15783); *Smart Alec Ltd* (No 17832); and
- an article of clothing (other than headgear, gloves, buttons, belts, buckles and garments trimmed with fur skin) made wholly or partly of fur skin (see Note 3) (Note 2).

"Clothing" includes hats and other headgear (Note 1). For hats and other headgear, see *Cassidy* (No 5760). For "young children", see *H & M Hennes Ltd v C & E Comrs* [2005] STC 1749.

Item 2

Protective boots and helmets for industrial use. The goods must be manufactured to British Standards Institution or equivalent EU standards and be marked accordingly. (Item 2, Note 4). The services specified in Note 5 are not zero-rated if the goods are for use by the purchaser's employees (Note 5).

Item 3

Motor cycle helmets meeting the standards laid down in Motor Cycles (Protective Helmets) Regulations 1998, SI 1998/1807 as amended by SI 2000/1488 and pedal cycle helmets meeting UK or EU legal standards and marked accordingly (Item 3, Note 4A).

GROUP 17—EMISSIONS ALLOWANCES

[Repealed.]

SCHEDULE 9 EXEMPTIONS (SECTIONS 8 AND 31)

PART I INDEX TO EXEMPT SUPPLIES OF GOODS AND SERVICES

The titles of Groups 1–12 are set out in alphabetical order.

PART II THE GROUPS

GROUP 1—LAND (V4.111–V4.113)

General rule

The following are exempt: (1) the grant, assignment or surrender of an interest in land, a right over land or a licence to occupy land; (2) the supply made by the landlord when he accepts the surrender of an interest, right or licence and is paid by the tenant making the surrender (a "reverse surrender"); and (3) the grant, assignment or surrender of a personal right to call for, or be granted, an interest in or right over land in Scotland (Item 1 and Notes 1, 1A).

For the scope of Item 1 in relation to EU law and elections to waive exemption, see *Lubbock Fine & Co v C & E Comrs* (case C-63/92) [1994] STC 101, ECJ. For inducements to accept the assignment of a lease, see *C & E Comrs v Cantor Fitzgerald International* (case C-108/99) [2001] STC 1453, ECJ (supply comprising accepting the assignment for consideration not exempt from tax as a leasing or letting of land). For virtual assignments, see *Abbey National plc v C & E Comrs* [2006] STC 1961, CA; Business Brief 16/05, 18 August 2005. For inducements to enter into a lease, see *C & E Comrs v Mirror Group plc* (case C-409/98) [2001] STC 1453, ECJ and further hearing [2003] STC 518 (supply by anchor tenant receiving inducement not exempt from tax as a leasing or letting of land). For building land, see *Norbury Developments Ltd v C & E Comrs* (case C-136/97) [1999] STC 511, ECJ. For serviced building plots, see *Virtue (a firm)* (No 20259) and Revenue and Customs Brief 64/07, 17 October 2007. For land where demolition of a completed partly demolished building on the site was to be completed at the vendor's expense after the sale, see *Don Bosco Onroerend Goed BV v Staatssecretaris van Financiën* (case C-461/08) [2009] ECR I–11079, [2010] STC 476, ECJ. For the person making a grant, see Sch 10 para 8. For termination (rather than surrender) of a lease, see *Lloyds Bank plc* (No 14181). For options, see *C & E Comrs v Mirror Group plc* (case C-409/98) [2001] STC 1453, ECJ. For vending machines installed in premises, see *Sinclair Collis v C & E Comrs* (case C-275/01) [2003] STC 898, ECJ (supply not exempt from tax as a leasing or letting of land). For bridge tolls, see *EC Commission v United Kingdom* (case C-359/97) [2000] STC 777, ECJ; Business Brief 3/03, 28 March 2003. For the letting of buildings, see *Maierhofer v Finanzamt Augsburg-Land* (case C-315/00) [2003] STC 564, ECJ (prefabricated structures). For the letting of buildings constructed by the landlord on land owned by the tenant, see *Maierhofer v Finanzamt Augsburg-Land* (case C-315/00) [2003] STC 564, ECJ. For the private use of a dwelling forming part of the business assets of a taxable person, see *Seeling v Finanzamt Starnberg* (case C-269/00) [2003] STC 805, ECJ (use not a letting of immovable property and excluded from exemption). For the occupation of property in common with others, see *Belgian State v Temco Europe SA* (case C-284/03) [2004] ECR I–11237, [2005] STC 1451, ECJ. For land partly under water, see *Fonden Marselisborg Lystbådehavn v Skatteministeriet* (case C-428/02) [2005] ECR I–1527, [2006] STC 1467, ECJ. For apportionment of rents in serviced accommodation, see *Business Enterprises (UK) Ltd v C & E Comrs* [1988] VATTR 160. For service charges, see *Nell Gwynn House Maintenance Fund Trustees v C & E Comrs* [1999] STC 79, HL; Notice No 48 (December 2010) para 3.18; cf *Globe Equities Ltd v C & E Comrs* [1995] V & DR 472. For milk quotas, see Business Brief 17/94, 12 September 1994. For interests and rights, see *Trewby v C & E Comrs* [1976] STC 122; *Rochdale Hornets Football Club Co Ltd v C & E Comrs* [1975] VATTR 71.

For surrenders, see *Lubbock Fine & Co v C & E Comrs* (case C-63/92) [1994] STC 101, ECJ (payment by landlord to tenant so that supply made by tenant). For reverse surrenders, see *AA Insurance Services Ltd v C & E Comrs* [1999] V & DR 361 (payment by tenant to landlord so that supply made by landlord).

It appears that a licence must amount to a "letting of immovable property" within the meaning of Directive 2006/112/EC art 135(1)(*l*) (formerly Directive 77/388/EEC art 13B(*b*)) if it is to amount to a licence to occupy land. It must therefore confer, for an agreed period and for payment, the right to occupy property as if the licensee were the owner and to exclude any other person from enjoyment of such a right: see *Sinclair Collis v C & E Comrs* (case C-275/01) [2003] STC 898, ECJ at [25]. In the UK, see *C & E Comrs v Sinclair Collis Ltd* [2001] STC 989, HL; *Henley Picture House Ltd* (No 895); *Tameside Metropolitan Borough Council v C & E Comrs* [1979] VATTR 93; *South Glamorgan County Council* (No 1956); *Bullimore* (No 2626); *Abbotsley Golf & Squash Club Ltd v C & E Comrs* [1997] V & DR 355.

The right to exclusive use of a specific part of premises may include the right to use other parts of the premises in common with others and other services. The supply made cannot be classified as an exempt licence to occupy land if the trader needs to use both the specific part and the common part in order to carry on his business: *R & C Comrs v Denyer* [2008] STC 633 at [43]–[46]. For examples, see *Byrom (t/a Salon24) v R & C Comrs* [2006] STC 992 (massage parlour services supplied to a masseuse); *R & C Comrs v Denyer* [2008] STC 633 and *Holland (trading as The Studio Hair Company) v R & C Comrs, Vigdor Ltd v R & C Comrs* [2009] STC 150 (hairdressers' chair renting agreement).

For licences subsidiary to some other right which are not licences to occupy land, and therefore standard rated, see in particular *Trewby v C & E Comrs* [1976] STC 122 (admission charge); *British Airports Authority (No 3)* (No 147) (airport transfer desk); *South Glamorgan County Council* (No 1956) (swimming pool). For bridge tolls, see *EC Commission v United Kingdom* (case C-359/97) [2000] ECR I–6355, [2000] STC 777, ECJ; Business Brief 3/03, 28 March 2003. For commercially operated sports leagues, see Revenue and Customs Brief 4/11, 9 February 2011.For a licence where the use of the premises was dominant, see *Grovewood (1998) Ltd* (No 17125). For the Commissioners' views, see Notice No 742 (March 2002) para 2.5.

Exceptions to the general rule

The following grants are excluded from exemption and are chargeable to tax at the standard rate:

(a) the freehold of a building (subject to the following exceptions) or civil engineering work prior to completion or within three years after completion. However, the freehold of a dwelling is either zero-rated under Sch 8 Group 5 or 6; standard rated under para (*e*) below; or exempt from tax. The freehold of a building to be used solely for a relevant residential or relevant charitable purpose is either zero-rated under Sch 8 Group 5 or 6; or exempt from tax. For the de minimis limit applied in deciding whether buildings are intended to be used "solely" for a relevant residential or relevant charitable purpose, see Revenue and Customs Brief 39/09, 1 July 2009. This applies from 1 July 2009;

(b) a supply made pursuant to a tenancy, lease or licence if a developer's interest therein has been self-supplied *before* 1 March 1997 by virtue of the construction, reconstruction, enlargement or extension of a building or civil engineering work on the land which commenced after 31 December 1991. For the self-supply, see Sch 10 paras 5(1)(*b*) and 6(1) (which were repealed without being re-enacted by VAT (Buildings and Land) Order 2008, SI 2008/1146 art 2).
Although repealed by FA 2006 s 17(2) and art 4 of the 2008 Order, this provision (ie VATA 1994 Sch 9 Group 1 Item 1(*b*) and Note 7) continues to apply in relation to supplies made before 1 June 2020: see Sch 2 para 10(*b*) of the 2008 Order;

(c) rights to take game or fish, but not freehold grants where such rights are granted contemporaneously to the grantee. The consideration for a lease or licence is apportioned if it includes a valuable right to take game or fish. For "valuable", see Leaflet No 742/2/92 para 2.
A right to fish granted for a period of years to (say) an angling club does not amount to "the leasing or lettingof immovable property" for the purposes of Directive 2006/112/EC art 135(1)(*l*) (formerly Directive 77/388/EEC art 13B(*b*)) if the grantor reserves a personal right to continue fishing in the waters: see *Gabriele Walderdorff v Finanzamt Waldviertel* (case C-451/06) [2007] ECR I–10637, [2008] STC 3079, ECJ;

(d) sleeping and catering accommodation in a hotel, inn, boarding house etc or service flat (see *Swindon Masonic Association Ltd v C & E Comrs* [1978] VATTR 200; *McMurray, Governor of Allen Hall v C & E Comrs* [1973] VATTR 161; *Namecourt Ltd v C & E Comrs* [1984] VATTR 22; *Westminster City Council v C*

& E Comrs [1989] VATTR 71, [1990] 2 CMLR 81; *McGrath v C & E Comrs* [1992] STC 371; *Camilla Enterprises Ltd* (No 10426); *Packford* (No 11626); *International Student House* (No 14420); *Dinaro Ltd* (No 17148)); Business Brief 1/06, 19 January 2006;

(e) an interest, right or licence to occupy: (i) holiday accommodation, (ii) accommodation in a building, hut, caravan, houseboat or tent advertised or held out as holiday accommodation or as accommodation suitable for holiday use, other than accommodation within para (*c*) above; and (iii) a dwelling which the purchaser cannot lawfully occupy throughout the year or use as a principal private residence. For the vires of head (iii), see *Ashworth v C & E Comrs* [1994] VATTR 275. For beach huts, see *Poole Borough Council v C & E Comrs* [1992] VATTR 88. However, a supply is exempt if it relates to a building; it is made more than three years after the building was completed; and the consideration comprises either the sale price for a freehold grant or the premium for a lease or licence. A lease or licence is also excluded from exemption if the grantee is permitted to erect and occupy holiday accommodation on the land concerned. For licences to construct beach huts, see *Poole Borough Council v C & E Comrs* [1992] VATTR 88;

(f) seasonal caravan pitches and facilities in connection with them. This exclusion complies with Directive 2006/112/EC art 135(1)(*l*) and (2) (formerly Directive 77/388/EEC art 13B(*b*)): see *Colaingrove Ltd v C & E Comrs* [2004] STC 712, CA. For seasonal pitches, see Note 14; *R & C Comrs v Tallington Lakes Ltd* [2008] STC 2734 (consequences of local authority's failure to take enforcement action for breach of planning permission). For the storage of caravans, see *D H Commercials (Leasing) Ltd* (No 14115) (exclusion from exemption under this head applies to caravans available for human habitation);

(g) pitches for tents and camping facilities;

(h) facilities for parking a vehicle (see *Skatteministeriet v Henriksen* (case 173/88) [1990] STC 768, [1990] 3 CMLR 558, ECJ; *C & E Comrs v Trinity Factoring Services Ltd* [1994] STC 504; *C & E Comrs v Venuebest Ltd* [2003] STC 433);

(i) rights to fell and remove standing timber;

(j) housing or storing aircraft and mooring or storing vessels (see *Strand Ship Building Co Ltd* (No 1651); *Roberts v C & E Comrs* [1992] VATTR 30);

(k) rights to occupy accommodation at a place of entertainment (see *Southend United Football Club v C & E Comrs* [1997] V & DR 202);

(l) facilities for playing sport or taking part in physical recreation, unless the grant is for a continuous period exceeding 24 hours or a series of 10 or more sessions granted to a school, club, association etc (see *Queen's Park Football Club Ltd v C & E Comrs* [1988] VATTR 76 and Press Notice 72/88, 20 September 1988);

(m) an equitable right, option, right of pre-emption or personal right which enables the grantee to call for, or be granted, an interest in or right over land within para (*a*) or paras (*b*)–(*m*).

For the election to waive exemption in respect of grants otherwise exempt under this Group, see Sch 10 para 2.

GROUP 2—INSURANCE (V4.121–V4.124)

The following supplies are exempt.

Item 1

Insurance and reinsurance transactions.

For the nature of "insurance", see *Card Protection Plan Ltd v C & E Comrs* (case C-349/96) [1999] STC 270, ECJ; *Commission v Hellenic Republic* (case C-13/06) [2006] ECR I–11563, [2007] STC 194, ECJ; *Swiss Re Germany Holding GmbH v Finanzamt München für Körperschaften* (case C-242/08) [2009] ECR I–10099, [2010] STC 189, ECJ; cf *Co-operative Wholesale Society Ltd v C & E Comrs* [2000] STC 727, CA.

For reinsurance, see *Swiss Re Germany Holding GmbH v Finanzamt München für Körperschaften* (case C-242/08) [2009] ECR I–10099, [2010] STC 189, ECJ (transfer of portfolio of life reinsurance contracts).

As a matter of EU law, exemption is not confined to supplies made by persons authorised to conduct insurance business and by persons exempted from authorisation: *Card Protection Plan Ltd v C & E Comrs* (case C-349/96) [1999] STC 270, ECJ; *Card Protection Plan Ltd v C & E Comrs* [2001] STC 174, HL; Notice No 701/36 (March 2002) para 2.4. However, there must be a contractual relationship between the supplier and the insured: *Re Forsakringsaktiebolaget Skandia (publ)* (case C-240/99) [2001] STC 754, ECJ (management of insurance subsidiary not provision of insurance). For an example of the required relationship, see *Card Protection Plan Ltd v C & E Comrs* [2001] STC 174, HL (block insurance policy); see also the obiter remarks of Rix LJ (with whom Lloyd LJ agreed) in *Ford Motor Company Ltd v R & C Comrs* [2008] STC 1016, CA at [48]–[63] (free motor insurance provided on sale of motor car). For the management of personal pension schemes, see *Winterthur Life UK Ltd* (No 14935).

Item 2

[Repealed.]

Item 3

[Repealed.]

Item 4

The provision of any of the following services (see Item 4 and Note 1):

(a) bringing together the following persons with a view to the insurance or reinsurance of risks: (1) persons seeking insurance or reinsurance, and (2) persons who provide insurance or reinsurance;

(b) carrying out work preparatory to the conclusion of insurance or reinsurance contracts;

(c) providing assistance in the administration and performance of insurance or reinsurance contracts;

(d) collecting premiums.

The following conditions must be met:

- the services must be related to an insurance or reinsurance transaction. It is immaterial whether or not a contract is finally concluded (Item 4(*a*));
- the services must be provided by an insurance broker or insurance agent (Item 4). For the identification of a person as an "insurance broker" or "insurance agent", see *JCM Beheer BV v Staatssecretaris van Financiën* (case C-124/07) [2008] ECR I–2101, [2008] STC 3360, ECJ (indirect relationship with the parties to the insurance or reinsurance contract); *InsuranceWide.com Services Ltd v R & C Comrs, R & C Comrs v Trader Media Group Ltd* [2010] STC 1572, CA; Revenue and Customs Brief 31/10, 3 August 2010 (internet introductory services);
- the insurance broker or insurance agent must provide the services while acting in an intermediary capacity (Item 4(b)). For persons acting in an intermediary capacity, see *InsuranceWide.com Services Ltd v R & C Comrs, R & C Comrs v Trader Media Group Ltd* [2010] STC 1572, CA; Revenue and Customs Brief 31/10, 3 August 2010; Revenue and Customs Brief 31/10, 3 August 2010 (internet introductory services);
- (if insurance is provided in connection with a supply of goods or services) the relevant requirements (see Notes 4, 5) are met. For relevant requirements relating to disclosure of the premium and other charges in Note 5, see Notice No 701/36 (May 2002) para 11.3; *R Smith Glaziers (Dunfermline) Ltd v C & E Comrs* [2003] STC 419, HL (requirement does not comply with Directive 2006/112/EC (formerly Directive 77/388/EEC));

- the services are not excluded from exemption (ie under Notes 7–10).

The following services are excluded from exemption:

- market research, product design, advertising, promotional or similar services (Note 7(*a*));
- collecting, collating and providing information for use in connection with the services in (1) (Note 7(*b*));
- valuation or inspection services (Note 8);
- services supplied by loss adjusters, average adjusters, motor assessors, surveyors and other experts (other than handling and settling claims under an agency agreement) (Note 9);
- services supplied under an insurance or reinsurance contract in lieu of a contractual payment or indemnity, or in satisfaction of a claim (Note 10; see *WHA Ltd and another v C & E Comrs* [2003] STC 648);
- services supplied under arrangements made in connection with an insurance or reinsurance contract in lieu of a contractual payment or indemnity, or in satisfaction of a claim (Note 10; see *WHA Ltd and another v C & E Comrs* [2004] STC 1081, CA)).

Item 4 implements Directive 2006/112/EC art 135(1)(*a*) (formerly Directive 77/388/EEC art 13B(*a*)). This exempts services related to insurance and reinsurance transactions performed by insurance brokers and insurance agents. For cases decided under the directive rather than the text of Item 4, see *Century Life plc v C & E Comrs* [2001] STC 38, CA; *InsuranceWide.com Services Ltd v R & C Comrs, R & C Comrs v Trader Media Group Ltd* [2010] STC 1572, CA. For "related services", see *Staatssecretaris van Financiën v Arthur Andersen & Co Accountants cs* (case C-472/03) [2005] ECR I–1719, [2005] STC 508, ECJ (back office activities); *Century Life plc v C & E Comrs* [2001] STC 38, CA (personal pension policies reviewed by third party to identify whether redress necessary for misselling).

For call centres, see *Teletech UK Ltd* (No 18080); Business Brief 7/03, 30 June 2003. For internet services, see *InsuranceWide.com Services Ltd v R & C Comrs* [2010] STC 1572, CA.

GROUP 3—POSTAL SERVICES (V4.126)

For exemption under EU law, see Directive 2006/112/EC art 132(1)(*a*); *R (on the application of TNT Post UK Ltd) v R & C Comrs* (case C-357/07) [2009] ECR I–3025, [2009] STC 1438 (exemption confined to public and private operators providing all or part of the universal postal service).

The following supplies are exempt.

Item 1

The following services (referred to as "public postal services") supplied by a person (referred to as a "universal service provider") who provides a universal postal service (as defined in Postal Services Act 2000), or part of such a service, in the UK:

(a) Postal services (as defined in the 2000 Act) which the universal service provider is required to provide in the discharge of a duty imposed as a condition of a licence granted under the 2000 Act.

(b) Providing another person with access to the universal service provider's resources and systems for the purpose of discharging any duty to provide a universal postal service imposed as a condition of a licence under the 2000 Act.

The services in (a) and (b) are referred to as "public postal services". The price of the public postal services provided must be controlled by, or under, a licence under Part 2 of the 2000 Act. Public postal services are excluded from exemption if any of the other terms on which the services are provided have been freely negotiated.

Item 2

A supply of goods by a universal service provider. This supply must be incidental to an exempt supply of public postal services (see Item 1) made by him.

GROUP 4—BETTING, GAMING AND LOTTERIES (V4.131)

For the extent to which member states can impose limitations and conditions in relation to the exemption granted by Directive 2006/112/EC art 135(1)(*i*) (formerly Directive 77/388/EEC art 13B(*f*)), see *Finanzamt Gladbeck v Linneweber; Finanzamt Herne-West v Akritidis* (joined cases C-453/02 and C-462/02) [2005] ECR I–1131, [2008] STC 1069, ECJ. For services outside the scope of this exemption, see *United Utilities plc v C & E Comrs* (case C-89/05) [2006] ECR I–6813, [2006] STC 1423, ECJ (call centre providing communications and information technology) and contrast *Belgian State v Henfling and others (acting as trustees in the insolvency of Tiercé Franco-Belge SA)* (case C-464/10) [2011] ECR I–0000, ECJ (commission agent acting in his own name). For unlawful games of chance, see *Fischer v Finanzamt Donaueschingen* (case C-283/95) [1998] ECR I–3396, ECJ.

The following supplies are exempt.

Item 1

The provision of facilities for placing bets, or playing games of chance for a prize. For services held to be facilities for placing bets, see *Logic Ltd (No 13934)* (horse-racing betting game). For games of chance, see Notes 2, 3. For prize, see Note 4. For services held to be facilities for playing games of chance, see *J Seven Ltd v C & E Comrs* [1986] VATTR 42 (casino accommodation on cruise ship); *Grantham (a firm)* (No 853) (shooting gallery). For services that were not, see *C & E Comrs v Annabel's Casino Ltd* [1995] STC 225 (hiring chip sorting machines). For the inadvertent inclusion of pinball machines within the scope of this exemption between 6 December 2005 and 31 October 2006, see Business Brief 16/06, 12 October 2006.

The following are excluded from exemption:

- admission to the premises;
- facilities provided in return for a subscription;
- provision of a gaming machine (see *H J Glawe Spiel-und Unterhaltungsgeräte Aufstellungsgesellschaft mbH & Co KG v Finanzamt Hamburg-Barmbek-Uhlenhorst* (case C-38/93) [1994] STC 543, ECJ; *R v Ryan* [1994] STC 446, CA; *Feehan v C & E Comrs* [1995] STC 75; *McCann v C & E Comrs* [1987] VATTR 101; *R & C Comrs v The Rank Group* [2009] STC 2304. For the meaning of "gaming machine", see s 23(4)–(6); *Oasis Technologies (UK) Ltd* (TC 581); Revenue and Customs Brief 1/11, 19 January 2011.

For mechanised cash bingo, see *Rank Group plc* (No 20688), on appeal *R & C Comrs v The Rank Group plc* [2009] STC 2304; Revenue and Customs Brief 40/09, 14 July 2009; Revenue and Customs Brief 75/09, 8 December 2009 ("the bingo appeal"). For repayment claims arising from the bingo appeal, see Revenue and Customs Brief 40/09, 14 July 2009.

For fixed odds betting terminals, see *Rank Group Ltd* (No 20777), on appeal *R & C Comrs v The Rank Group plc* [2009] STC 2304 and subsequently *The Rank Group plc* (TC 301); ("the slots appeal"). For repayment claims in respect of the period 1 November 1998 to 5 December 2005 arising from the slots appeal, see Revenue and Customs Brief 40/09, 14 July 2009; Revenue and Customs Brief 11/10, 16 March 2010.

For bingo machines, see Revenue and Customs Brief 1/11, 19 January 2011.

Item 2

The granting of a right to take part in a lottery. See *Oasis Technologies (UK) Ltd* (TC 581); Revenue and Customs Brief 1/11, 19 January 2011.

GROUP 5—FINANCE (V4.136–V4.136J)

General note

Coins and banknotes. This Group does not include the supply of a coin or a banknote as a collectors' piece or as an investment article (Note 2).

Credit card, charge card and similar payment card operations. This Group includes the supply made by a person carrying on a credit card, charge card or similar payment card operation to a person who accepts a card in payment for goods or services (Note 4). For the basic features of credit card operations, see *C & E Comrs v Diners Club Ltd* [1989] STC 407, CA; *BAA plc* (No 17377) at [9], [10]. For affinity and co-branded credit cards, see *C & E Comrs v BAA plc* [2003] STC 35, CA. For fuel cards, see *The Harpur Group Ltd v C & E Comrs* [1994] VATTR 180. For check trading, see *Kingfisher plc v C & E Comrs* [2000] STC 992; Press Notice 1045, 21 October 1985.

Debt collection and factoring. For the exclusion of supplies from exemption, see Directive 2006/112/EC art 135(1)(*d*) (formerly Directive 77/388/EEC art 13B(*d*)(3)) as interpreted in *Finanzamt Groß-Gerau v MKG-Kraftfahrzeuge-Factory GmbH* (case C-305/01) [2003] STC 951, ECJ. For debt collection, see *R & C Comrs v Axa UK plc* (case C-175/09) [2010] ECR I–0000, [2010] STC 2825, ECJ (payment plan for dental care); Revenue and Customs Brief 54/10, 12 January 2010.

Individual savings accounts. For the Commissioners' views, see Business Brief 7/99, 23 March 1999 (not reproduced).

Outsourcing. For financial services provided by a third party on behalf of a financial institution, see *Sparekassernes Datacenter (SDC) v Skatteministeriet* (case C-2/95) [1997] STC 932, ECJ; *C & E Comrs v FDR Ltd* [2000] STC 672, CA; *C & E Comrs v Electronic Data Systems Ltd* [2003] STC 688, CA; *Nightfreight plc* (No 15479); *Prudential Assurance Co Ltd* (No 17030); *Abbey National plc* (No 17506).

Exemption. The supplies listed in Items 1–10 below are exempt. For UK cases decided (or primarily decided) under Directive 2006/112/EC art 135(1)(*b*)–(*g*) (formerly Directive 77/388/EEC art 13B(*d*)) rather than Group 5, see *C & E Comrs v BAA plc* [2003] STC 35, CA (affinity and co-branded credit cards); *C & E Comrs v Electronic Data Systems Ltd* [2003] STC 688, CA (loan centre supplying administrative services to a bank).

Item 1

The issue, transfer or receipt of, or any dealing with money or security for money or any note or order for the payment of money. For transfers, see Proceedings brought by *Nordea Pankki Suomi Oyj* (case C-350/10) [2011] ECR I–0000, ECJ and the cases cited therein. For the relevance of consideration, see Business Brief 25/95, 20 November 1995. For services included within this description, see *Kingfisher plc v C & E Comrs* [2000] STC 992 (vouchers sold on credit to customers); *R & C Comrs v Axa UK plc* [2008] STC 2091 (payment handling services); *British Hardware Federation v C & E Comrs* [1975] VATTR 172 (clearing house payment scheme); *Barclays Bank plc v C & E Comrs* [1988] VATTR 23 (credit checking service). This Item does not include: (1) anything included in Item 6 (Note 1); and (2) a supply of services which is preparatory to the carrying out of a transaction within Item 1 (Note 1A). For factoring and debt collection services, see the General Note.

For intermediary services, see Item 5. For the underwriting of an issue within this Item, see Item 5A. For excluded services, see *Nationwide Anglia Building Society v C & E Comrs* [1994] VATTR 30.

Item 2

The making of any advance or granting of any credit. This includes the supply of credit by a person, in connection with a supply of goods or services by him, for which a separate charge is made and disclosed to the recipient of the supply of goods or services (Note 3). For interest on payments deferred until delivery of goods or services, see *Muys' en De Winter's Bouw-en Aannemingsbedrijf BV v Staatssecretaris van Financiën* (case C-281/91) [1997] STC 665, ECJ.

For intermediary services, see Item 5. For services held to be intermediary services in relation to Item 2, see *C & E Comrs v BAA plc* [2002] STC 327.

Item 2A

The management of credit by the person granting it.

Item 3

The provision of instalment credit finance in a hire purchase, conditional sale, or credit sale agreement where a separate charge for finance is made and disclosed to the recipient of the supply of goods. See *Freight Transport Leasing Ltd v C & E Comrs* [1991] VATTR 142.

For intermediary services, see Item 5.

Item 4

The provision of administrative arrangements in connection with an item 3 supply if the consideration is specified in the agreement and is £10 or less. For the exemption of administration fees on conditional sale agreements, see *Wagon Finance Ltd* (No 16288); Business Brief 27/99, 21 December 1999. For option fees on hire purchase agreements outside the scope of exemption, see *General Motors Acceptance Corpn (UK) plc v C & E Comrs* [1999] V & VR 456 (fee for the right to secure ownership of the goods).

For intermediary services, see Item 5.

Item 5

Intermediary services (as defined below) provided by a person acting in an intermediary capacity (as defined below) in relation to a transaction within Items 1, 2, 3, 4 or 6.

A person provides "intermediary services" in relation to transactions within Items 1, 2, 3 or 4 if, with a view to the provision of those services, he (1) brings together actual or potential customers for those services and providers of those services, and (2) performs preparatory work (other than market research, product design, advertising, promotional or similar services, or the collection, collation and provision of information in connection with such activities) leading to the conclusion of contracts for those services (Notes 5, 5B). For intermediary services under this provision, see *C & E Comrs v BAA plc* [2003] STC 35, CA (affinity and co-branded credit cards) and, under superseded legislation, *C & E Comrs v Civil Service Motoring Association* [1998] STC 111, CA. For exemption under Directive 2006/112/EC art 135(1)(*b*) (formerly Directive 77/388/EEC art 13B(*d*)(1)) ("negotiation of credit") under the principle of direct effect, see *C & E Comrs v BAA plc* [2003] STC 35, CA (affinity and co-branded credit cards).

A person provides "intermediary services" in relation to transactions within Item 6 if, with a view to the provision of those services, he brings together actual or potential customers for those services and providers of those services (Notes 5, 5B).

A person acts in an "intermediary capacity" in relation to services within Items 1, 2, 3, 4 or 6 whenever he acts as an intermediary, or one of the intermediaries, between a person who provides those services and an actual or potential customer for those services. For intermediary services ("negotiation") within Directive 2006/112/EC art 135(1)(*b*)–(*f*) (formerly Directive 77/388/EEC art 13B(*d*)(1)–(5)), see *CSC Financial Services Ltd v C & E Comrs* (case C-235/00) [2002] STC 57, ECJ; *Volker Ludwig v Finanzamt Luckenwalde* (case C-453/05) [2007] ECR I–5083, [2008] STC 1640, ECJ. In the UK, see *C & E Comrs v BAA plc* [2003] STC 35, CA (affinity and co-branded credit cards); *Bookit Ltd v R & C Comrs* [2006] STC 1367, CA and *Scottish Exhibition Centre Ltd v R & C Comrs* [2008] STCI 967 (transfer of funds in connection with the advance booking of tickets); *HBOS plc v R & C Comrs* [2009] STC 486 (debt collection); cf *C & E Comrs v Civil Service Motoring Association* [1998] STC 111, CA under superseded legislation.

Item 5A

Underwriting: (1) an issue within Item 1, or (2) any transaction within Item 6.

Item 6

The issue, transfer or receipt of, or any dealing with, any security or secondary security being:

(a) shares, stock, bonds, notes (other than promissory notes), debentures, debenture stock or shares in an oil royalty; or

(b) any document relating to money, in any currency, which has been deposited with the issuer or some other person, being a document which recognises an obligation to pay a stated amount to bearer or to order, with or without interest, and being a document by the delivery of which, with or without endorsement, the right to receive that stated amount, with or without interest, is transferable; or

(c) any bill, note or other obligation of the Treasury or of a Government in any part of the world, being a document by the delivery of which, with or without endorsement, title is transferable, and not being an obligation which is or has been legal tender in any part of the world; or

(d) any letter of allotment or rights, any warrant conferring an option to acquire a security included in this item, any renounceable or scrip certificates, rights coupons, coupons representing dividends or interest on such a security, bond mandates or other documents conferring or containing evidence of title to or rights in respect of such a security; or

(e) units or other documents conferring rights under any trust established for the purpose, or having the effect of providing, for persons having funds available for investment, facilities for the participation by them as beneficiaries under the trust, in any profits or income arising from the acquisition, holding, management or disposal of any property whatsoever.

For transfers, see Proceedings brought by *Nordea Pankki Suomi Oyj* (case C-350/10) [2011] ECR I–0000, ECJ and the cases cited therein. For "dealing", see *Singer & Friedlander Ltd v C & E Comrs* [1989] VATTR 27, [1989] 1 CMLR 814 (arranging and underwriting new issue of shares not "dealing"); *Ivory & Sime Trustlink Ltd v C & E Comrs* [1998] STC 597 (initial charge for personal equity plan).

For intermediary services, see Item 5. For the underwriting of a transaction within this Item, see Item 5A.

Item 7

[Repealed.]

Item 8

The operation of any current, deposit or savings account.

The supply of coin or banknotes as collectors' items are excluded from this group. See *Milk Marketing Board* (No 3389).

Item 9

The management of:

(a) an authorised open-ended investment company (see Note 6);

(b) an authorised unit trust scheme (see Note 6);

(c) a Gibraltar collective investment scheme (see Note 6) which is not an umbrella scheme (see Note 6);

(d) a sub-fund (see Note 6) of any other Gibraltar collective investment scheme;

(e) an individually recognised overseas scheme (see Note 6) which is not an umbrella scheme;

(f) a sub-fund of any other individually recognised overseas scheme;

(g) a recognised collective investment scheme (see Note 6) authorised in a designated country or territory (see Note 6) which is not an umbrella scheme;

(h) a sub-fund of any other recognised collective investment scheme authorised in a designated country or territory;

(i) a recognised collective investment scheme constituted in another EEA state (see Notes 6, 6A) which is not an umbrella scheme; or

(j) a sub-fund of any other recognised collective investment scheme constituted in another EEA state.

For "management" and management services supplied by third parties, see *Abbey National plc and another v C & E Comrs* (case C-169/04) [2006] ECR I–4027, [2006] STC 1136, ECJ; Business Brief 10/03, 24 July 2003.

Item 10

The management of a closed-ended collective investment undertaking (see Note 6). For closed-ended investment funds, see *J P Morgan Fleming Claverhouse Investment Trust plc and another v R & C Comrs* (case C-363/05) [2007] ECR I–5517, [2008] STC 1180, ECJ. For "management" and management services supplied by third parties, see *Abbey National plc and another v C & E Comrs* (case C-169/04) [2006] ECR I–4027, [2006] STC 1136, ECJ; Business Brief 10/03, 24 July 2003.

GROUP 6—EDUCATION (V4.141)

The following supplies are exempt. However, a supply is excluded from exemption if: (1) it is supplied by a body which provides teaching of English as a foreign language; (2) the body would not otherwise be an eligible body; and (3) the supply consists of something other than the teaching of English as a foreign language. For the application of this exclusion, see *Pilgrims Language Courses Ltd v C & E Comrs* [1999] STC 874, CA. For education exempt under Item 1 as a single supply or exempt under Items 1 and 4 as separate supplies, see *Pilgrims Language Courses Ltd v C & E Comrs* [1999] STC 874, CA.

Item 1

The provision of education, research or vocational training by an eligible body. The education or vocational training may be supplied to anyone. The research must be supplied to another eligible body. For the secondment of teaching staff, see *Stichting Regionaal Opleidingen Centrum Noord-Kennemerland/West-Friesland (Horizon College) v Staatssecretaris van Financiën* (case C-434/05) [2007] ECR I–4793, [2008] STC 2145, ECJ. Contrast *R & C Comrs v Board of Governors of the Robert Gordon University* [2008] STC 1890 (supply of both staff and other resources)

Item 2

The supply of private tuition by an individual teacher acting independently of an employer. The tuition must be given in a subject ordinarily taught in a school or university.

Tuition must be provided by a teacher acting in an individual or private capacity. For tuition, see *Ingenieurbüro Eulitz GbR Thomas und Marion Eulitz v Finanzamt Dresden I* (case C-473/08) [2010] ECR I–0000, ECJ. Exemption does not apply to tuition provided by a teacher as an employee of a company or other organisation: *R & C Comrs v Empowerment Enterprises Ltd* [2008] STC 1835 (supply made by company, not the employed teacher); cf *Werner Haderer v Finanzamt Wilmersdorf* (case C-445/05) [2007] ECR I–4841, [2008] STC 2171, ECJ; *Ingenieurbüro Eulitz GbR Thomas und Marion Eulitz v Finanzamt Dresden I* (case C-473/08) [2010] ECR I–0000, ECJ.

Item 2 implements Directive 2006/112/EC art 132(1)(*j*) (formerly Directive 77/388/EEC art 13A(1)(*j*)). For art 132(1)(*j*) as interpreted by the Court of Justice, see Part 1B.

Item 3

The provision of examination services by anyone to (1) an eligible body; (2) a person receiving education or vocational training exempted under Items 1, 2, 5 or 5A; or (3) a person receiving education or vocational training provided otherwise than in the course or furtherance of a business.

The provision of examination services by an eligible body to anyone.

Item 4

A supply of goods or services made by an eligible body if: (1) the goods or services are closely related to education or vocational training provided by the body; (2) they do not comprise examination services; and (3) they are for direct use by the pupil, student or trainee receiving the education or vocational training.

A supply of goods or services (other than examination services) closely related to a supply of research made by one eligible body to another if either: (1) the supply is made by the body supplying the research; or (2) the supply is made by another eligible body to the body supplying the research.

Item 5

The following goods and services if, and to the extent that, the consideration is ultimately a charge to funds provided pursuant to arrangements made under Employment and Training Act 1973 s 2 (or equivalent provisions in Scotland and Northern Ireland): (1) the provision of vocational training; and (2) any goods or services essential thereto supplied by the person providing the vocational training and provided directly to the trainee. For vocational training, see Note 3; *Harrowgate & Business Development Centre Ltd* (No 15565).

Item 5A

The following goods and services if, and to the extent that, the consideration is ultimately a charge to funds provided by the Learning and Skills Council for England or the National Council for Education and Training for Wales under Learning and Skills Act 2000 Parts I or II: (1) the provision of education or training; and (2) any goods or services essential thereto supplied by the person providing the education or training and provided directly to the student or trainee.

Item 6

The provision of facilities by: (1) a youth club to its members; (2) an association of youth clubs to its members; or (3) an association of youth clubs to members of a youth club which is a member of that association. For "youth club", see Note 6 to Group 6. For "association of youth clubs" see *World Association of Girl Guides and Girl Scouts v C & E Comrs* [1984] VATTR 28.

Definitions common to more than one item

For "education", see *Phillips v C & E Comrs* [1992] VATTR 77 at 81–83 (not a static concept and not confined to formal instruction in a classroom); *North of England Zoological Society v C & E Comrs* [1999] STC 1027 at 1032, 1033 (course, class or lesson of instruction); *Oxford Open Learning (Systems) Ltd* (No 16890) at para 37 (instruction, tuition or schooling). For a supply of resources such as staff and use of equipment characterised as education, see *R & C Comrs v Board of Governors of the Robert Gordon University* [2008] STC 1890.

For "eligible body", see Note 1. For a "college, institution, school or hall" of a "UK university" (Note 1(*b*)), see *C & E Comrs v University of Leicester Students' Union* [2002] STC 147, CA (separate entity must be part of the university and supply education). For a body held to be a "college" (Note 1(*b*)), see *C & E Comrs v School of Finance and Management (London) Ltd* [2001] STC 1690 (commercial body providing tuition leading to degree granted by UK university under co-operation arrangement). For companies owned or controlled by a university, see Revenue and Customs Brief 9/10, 11 March 2010.

For "examination services", see Note 4.

For "vocational training", see Note 3.

GROUP 7—HEALTH AND WELFARE (V4.146)

The following supplies are exempt. For exemption under Directive 2006/112/EC art 132(1)(*b*), (*c*), (*g*) (formerly Directive 77/388/EEC art 13A(1)(*b*), (*c*), (*g*)), see *Ambulanter Pflegedienst Kugler GmbH v Finanzamt fur Korperschaften I in Berlin* (case C-141/00) [2002] ECR I-6833, ECJ; *Christoph-Domier-Stiftung für Klinische Psychologie v Finanzamt Gießen* (case C-45/01) [2003] ECR I–12911, [2005] STC 228, ECJ; *Finanzamt Leverkusen v Verigen Transplantation Service International AG* (case C-156/09) [2010] ECR I–0000, [2011] STC 255, ECJ. For the exemption of welfare services in the UK under directly applicable EU legislation, see *Yoga for Health Foundation v C & E Comrs* [1984] STC 630; *International Bible Students Association v C & E Comrs* [1988] STC 412; *Westminster City Council v C & E Comrs* [1989] VATTR 71, [1990] 2 CMLR 81; *Central YMCA* (No 12425); *Viewpoint Housing Association Ltd* (No 13148); and see now Items 9, 10.

For the provision of health professionals, nursing auxiliaries, care assistances and support workers by employment businesses, see Revenue and Customs Brief 12/10, 18 March 2010.

Item 1

The provision of medical care by a person registered or enrolled in one of the following registers.

Item	*Register*	*Authority*
1(*a*)	The following registers maintained by the General Medical Council:	Medical Act 1983 s 2 as amended by: SI 996/1591 and SI 2002/3135
	1. Register of medical practitioners. This is divided into the following lists: (*a*) the principal list; (*b*) the visiting overseas doctors list; and (*c*) the visiting EEA practitioners list. 2. Register of medical practitioners with limited registration.	
1(*b*)	The following registers maintained by the General Optical Council: 1. Register of optometrists. 2. Register of dispensing opticians. 3. Register of bodies corporate carrying on business as an optometrist, a dispensing optician or both.	Opticians Act 1989 ss 7 and 9
1(*c*)	The register maintained by the Health Professions Council. This is divided into the following parts: 1. Arts therapists: music, drama or art. 2. Chiropodists and podiatrists. 3. Clinical scientists. 4. Dietitians. 5. Biomedical scientists. 6. Occupational therapists. 7. Orthoptists.	Health Professions Order 2001, SI 2002/254 arts 5, 6 Health Professions (Parts of and Entries in the Register) Order in Council 2003, SI 2003/1571 Sch 1

	8. Paramedics.	
	9. Physiotherapists.	
	10. Prosthetists and orthotists.	
	11. Radiographers: diagnostic or therapeutic.	
	12. Speech and language therapists.	
	13. Operating department practitioners.	
	14. Practitioner psychologists.	
	15. Hearing aid dispensers	
1(*ca*)	The register maintained by the General Osteopathic Council.	Osteopaths Act 1993 s 2(3)
1(*cb*)	The register maintained by the General Chiropractic Council.	Chiropractors Act 1994 s 2(3)
1(*d*)	The register maintained by the Nursing and Midwifery Council. This is divided into the following parts:	Nursing and Midwifery Order 2001, SI 2002/253 arts 5(1), 6 Nurses and Midwives (Parts of and Entries in the Register) Order in Council 2004, SI 2004/1765 arts 2, 3 and Sch 1
	1. Nurses.	
	2. Midwives.	
	3. Specialist community public health nurses.	
1(*e*)	The following registers maintained by the Hearing Aid Council:	Hearing Aid Council Act 1968 s 2(1)
	1. Register of dispensers of hearing aids.	
	2. Register of persons employing dispensers of hearing aids.	

For the hire of goods in connection with such services, see Note 1 and contrast *Aslan Imaging Ltd v C & E Comrs* [1989] VATTR 54 and *Cleary (a firm)* (No 7305). For spectacles see *C & E Comrs v Leightons Ltd* [1995] STC 458; Business Brief 2/99, 13 January 1999 (not reproduced), Business Brief 4/99, 15 February 1999 (not reproduced) and Information Sheet 8/99, 22 June 1999 (apportionment of selling price). For hearing aids, see *Rowe* (No 17600). For services performed or supervised by the above persons, see Note 2; *Elder Home Care Ltd* (No 11185); *Land* (No 15547); Press Notice 23/96, 11 April 1996. For home care services, see written answer E-4062/96 (17 January 1997), OJ C217, 17 July 1997. For the zero-rating of drugs dispensed and administered by a medical practitioner, see Sch 8 Group 12 Item 1A; *Dr Beynon and Partners v C & E Comrs* [2005] STC 55, HL. For services as an expert witness, see *D v W (Österreichischer Bundesschatz intervening)* (case C-384/98) [2002] STC 1200, ECJ (paternity test by medical expert for the purposes of legal proceedings). For medico-legal services, see *Unterpertinger v Pensionsversicherungsanstalt der Arbeiter* (case C-212/01) [2003] ECR I–13859, [2005] STC 650, ECJ; *D'Ambrumenil v C & E Comrs* (case C-307/01) [2003] ECR I–13989, [2005] STC 650, ECJ. For beauty procedures using lasers and intense pulse light machines, see Business Brief 3/06, 9 March 2006.

Member states must comply with the objective pursued by Directive 2006/112/EC art 132(1)(*c*) (formerly Directive 77/388/EEC art 13A(1)(*c*)) (ie confining exemption to services provided by persons with the required professional qualifications) and the principle of fiscal neutrality when deciding which paramedical professions are to qualify for exemption: see *H A Solleveld v Staatssecretaris van Financiën; J E van den Hout-van Eijnsbergen v Staatssecretaris van Financiën* (joined cases C-443/04 and C-444/04) [2006] ECR I–3617, [2007] STC 71, ECJ.

Item 2

The provision of medical care or supply of dental prostheses by:

(a) a person registered in the dentists register maintained by the General Dental Council in accordance with Dentists Act 1984 s 14(1);

(b) a person registered in the dental care professionals register maintained under Dentists Act 1984 s 36B.

Item 2A

The supply of any services, or of dental prostheses, by a dental technician. For dental technicians, see *Bennett* (No 865). For dental prostheses supplied by someone other than a dentist or dental technician, see *VDP Dental Laboratory NV v Staatssecretaris van Financiën* (case C-401/05) [2006] ECR I–12121, [2007] STC 474, ECJ.

Item 3

The provision of medical care by a person registered in the register of pharmacists maintained by the Pharmaceutical Society of Great Britain under Pharmacists and Pharmacy Technicians Order 2007, SI 2007/289. This includes services wholly performed by a pharmaceutical chemist supplied by someone else. For the register in Northern Ireland, see Pharmacy (Northern Ireland) Order 1976.

Item 4

The provision of care or medical or surgical treatment and related goods in any hospital or state-regulated institution. For "care", see *C & E Comrs v Kingscrest Associates Ltd and another (trading as Kingscrest Residential Care Homes)* [2002] STC 490 ("care" must be medically or surgically related); *LuP GmbH v Finanzamt Bochum-Mitte* (case C-106/05) [2006] ECR I–5123, [2008] STC 1742, ECJ (medical tests performed outside a hospital or institution). For other care, see Item 9.

For the exemption of "closely related activities" under EU law, see Directive 2006/112/EC art 132(1)(*b*) (formerly Directive 77/388/EEC art 13A(1)(*b*)); *Diagnostikon & Therapeftikon Kentron Athino–Ygeia AE v Ipourgos Ikonomikon* (joined cases C-394/04 and C-395/04) [2006] STC 1349, ECJ (telephones and TV hire for in-patients, and beds and meals for persons accompanying them); *CopyGene A/S v Skatteministeriet* (case C-262/08) [2010] ECR I–0000, [2010] STC 1799, ECJ and *Future Health Technologies Ltd v R & C Comrs* (case C-86/09) [2010] ECR I–0000, [2010] STC 1836, ECJ (collection, testing and analysis of umbilical cord blood and storage of stem cells). In the UK, see *Nuffield Nursing Homes Trust v C & E Comrs* [1989] VATTR 62 (food and accommodation supplied to the mother of a child patient). For medical tests performed outside a hospital or institution, see Directive 2006/112/EC art 132(1)(*b*) (formerly Directive 77/388/EEC art 13A(1)(*b*)); *LuP GmbH v Finanzamt Bochum-Mitte* (case C-106/05) [2006] ECR I–5123, [2006] STC 1742, ECJ.

For goods supplied with services, contrast *Payton v C & E Comrs* [1974] VATTR 140 (goods supplied with hospital treatment) and *Coleman* (No 10512) (goods supplied with treatment not ordinarily regarded as hospital treatment). For drugs and surgically implanted prostheses, see *C & E Comrs v Wellington Private Hospital Ltd* [1997] STC 445, CA. For institutions that are "state-regulated", see Note 8. Relevant institutions for Item 4 include nursing homes, convalescent homes and clinics: *C & E Comrs v Kingscrest Associates Ltd and another (trading as Kingscrest Residential Care Homes)* [2002] STC 490.

Care, treatment and goods are exempt under this provision whether supplied by legal persons or natural persons: *Gregg v C & E Comrs* (case C-216/97) [1999] STC 934, ECJ.

Item 5

The provision of a deputy for a medical practitioner.

Item 6

The supply of human blood. For the transportation of blood, see *Belgian State v Nathalie De Fruytier* (case C-237/09) [2010] ECR I–0000, [2010] STC 1792, ECJ.

Item 7

The supply of products for therapeutic purposes, derived from human blood. For genetically engineered products, see *Baxter Healthcare Ltd* (No 14670).

Item 8

The supply of human organs or tissues for diagnostic or therapeutic purposes or medical research. For the transportation of human organs and samples, see *Belgian State v Nathalie De Fruytier* (case C-237/09) [2010] ECR I–0000, [2010] STC 1792, ECJ.

Item 9

Welfare services and related goods supplied by:

(a) a charity. For "charity", see *Kingscrest Associates Ltd and another v C & E Comrs* (case C-498/03) [2005] ECR I–4427, [2005] STC 1547, ECJ (term having its own independent meaning in EU law and not precluding bodies with a profit-making aim);

(b) a public body. For "public body", see Note 5; *Prospects Care Services Ltd v C & E Comrs* [1997] V & DR 209; or

(c) (as regards services in respect of which the institution is regulated) a state-regulated private welfare institution or agency. For "state regulated" in relation to a private welfare institution or agency, see Note 8; *Kingscrest Associates Ltd and another v C & E Comrs* (case C-498/03) [2005] ECR I–4427, [2005] STC 1547, ECJ (partnership registered under Care Standards Act 2000). For a trader who was not state-regulated, see *R & C Comrs v K & L Childcare Service Ltd* [2006] STC 18.

Accommodation and catering must be ancillary to the provision of care, treatment or instruction: see Note 7; *Viewpoint Housing Association Ltd* (No 13148); *Trustees for the MacMillan Cancer Trust v C & E Comrs* [1998] V & DR 289.

For "welfare services", see Note 6; *Viewpoint Housing Association Ltd* (No 13148), *Watford and District Old People's Housing Association Ltd* (No 15660), Business Brief 4/99, 15 February 1999 ("care"); *Parents and Children Together* (No 17283), now mitigated by Business Brief 21/01, 21 December 2001 (adoption services); Business Brief 1/03, 20 January 2003; Business Brief 5/05, 3 March 2005. A supply of staff does not amount to welfare services: *R & C Comrs v K & L Childcare Service Ltd* [2006] STC 18. For intermediaries, see *Staatssecretaris van Financiën v Stichting Kinderopvang Enschede* (case C-415/04) [2006] ECR I–1365, [2007] STC 294, ECJ.

Item 10

The supply of goods and services incidental to the provision of spiritual welfare by a religious community to a resident member in return for a consideration paid as a condition of membership. The supply must be made otherwise than for profit: cf *C & E Comrs v Bell Concord Educational Trust Ltd* [1989] STC 264, CA, *Phillips v C & E Comrs* [1992] VATTR 77 in relation to VATA 1983 Sch 6 Group 6 (repealed); Press Notice 30/89, 30 March 1989.

Item 11

The supply of transport services for sick or injured persons in specially designed vehicles.

GROUP 8—BURIAL AND CREMATION (V4.151)

The following supplies are exempt.

Item 1

The disposal of the remains of the dead. See *UFD Ltd v C & E Comrs* [1981] VATTR 199; *CJ Williams' Funeral Service of Telford v C & E Comrs* [1999] V & DR 318.

Item 2

The making of arrangements for or in connection with the disposal of the remains of the dead. For examples of services outside this description, see *Network Insurance Brokers Ltd v C & E Comrs* [1998] STC 742 (insurance broker); *Co-operative Wholesale Society Ltd v C & E Comrs* [1999] STC 1096 (making arrangements for a funeral service to be provided by an independent contractor).

GROUP 9—SUBSCRIPTIONS TO TRADE UNIONS, PROFESSIONAL AND OTHER PUBLIC INTEREST BODIES (V4.156)

Group 9 exempts the following supplies. For a case decided on the words of Directive 2006/112/EC art 132(1)(*m*), see *British Association for Shooting and Conservation Ltd v R & C Comrs* [2009] STC 1421.

Item 1

The supply of services and goods related to those services which are within the aims of the organisation in return for a membership subscription by:

(a) a trade union, ie an organisation whose main aim is to defend the collective interests of its members (being workers, employers, independent professionals or traders carrying on a particular economic activity) and to represent them vis-à-vis appropriate third parties: *Institute of the Motor Industry v C & E Comrs* (case C-149/97) [1998] STC 1219, ECJ. For a body outside this description, see *The Institute of the Motor Industry v C & E Comrs* [2000] V & DR 62 (main aim to promote standards of its members);

(b) a professional association. Membership must be wholly or mainly restricted to individuals seeking an appropriate professional qualification. For bodies within this provision, see *Allied Dancing Association Ltd v C & E Comrs* [1993] VATTR 405; *Institute of Chartered Shipbrokers* (No 15033). For a body outside this provision, see *Royal Photographic Society of Great Britain v C & E Comrs* [1978] VATTR 191);

(c) an association for the advancement of a branch of knowledge (for bodies within this provision, see *British Organic Farmers v C & E Comrs* [1988] VATTR 64; *The British Association for Counselling* (No 11855)) or for fostering professional expertise (for a body within this provision, see *Allied Dancing Association Ltd v C & E Comrs* [1993] VATTR 405). Membership must be wholly or mainly restricted to individuals whose professions or employments are directly concerned with the association's purposes (Note 4). For bodies outside this provision, see *Royal Photographic Society of Great Britain v C & E Comrs* [1978] VATTR 191; *The Bookmakers' Protection Association (Southern Area) Ltd v C & E Comrs* [1979] VATTR 215; *Bee Farmers Association* (No 1565); *The British Institute of Cleaning Science Ltd* (No 1981); *Committee of Directors of Polytechnics v C & E Comrs* [1992] STC 873; *The Association of Reflexologists* (No 13078); *The Institute of the Motor Industry v C & E Comrs* [1996] V & DR 492;

(d) an association lobbying the government on legislation and other public matters affecting members' business or professional interests. Membership must be wholly or mainly restricted to persons having business or professional interests directly connected with the association's purposes. For a body outside this provision, see *Bee Farmers Association* (No 1565);

(e) a body with objects in the public domain (see *English Speaking Union of the Commonwealth v C & E Comrs* [1980] VATTR 184) of a political (see *British Association for Shooting and Conservation Ltd v R & C Comrs* [2009] STC 1421), religious, patriotic, philosophical, philanthropic (see *Rotary International v C & E Comrs* [1991] VATTR 177) or civic (see *Expert Witness Institute v C & E Comrs* [2002] STC 42, CA; *British Association for Shooting and Conservation Ltd v R & C Comrs* [2009] STC 1421) nature.

For "profession", see *Carr v IR Comrs* [1944] 2 All ER 163, CA; Monopolies Commission Report on the Supply of Professional Services (1970). For activities which do not amount to a profession, see *The British Institute of Cleaning Science Ltd* (No 1981); *National Association of Funeral Directors* (No 1989); *Institute of Leisure and Amenity Management v C & E Comrs* [1988] STC 602; *The Institute of Employment Consultants Ltd* (No 2309); *Committee of Directors of Polytechnics v C & E Comrs* [1992] STC 873; *The Association of Payroll and Superannuation Administrators* (No 7009); *The British Association for Counselling* (No 11855); *The Institute of Legal Cashiers and Administrators* (No 12383); *The Association of Reflexologists* (No 13078); *The Institute of the Motor Industry v C & E Comrs* [1996] V & DR 492.

GROUP 10—SPORTS, SPORTS COMPETITIONS AND PHYSICAL EDUCATION (V4.161)

For the right of member states to impose conditions when applying Directive 2006/112/EC art 132(1)(*m*) (formerly Directive 77/388/EEC art 13A(1)(*m*)), see *EC Commission v Spain (supported by United Kingdom, intervener)* (case C-124/96) [1998] STC 1237, ECJ. For the conditions applied in the UK, see *Keswick Golf Club v C & E Comrs* [1998] V & DR 276.

Group 10 exempts the following supplies. For a case decided on the words of Directive 2006/112/EC art 132(1)(*m*), see *British Association for Shooting and Conservation Ltd v R & C Comrs* [2009] STC 1421. For the interpretation of art 132(1)(*m*) of the 2006 Directive, see *Canterbury Hockey Club and another v R & C Comrs* (case C-253/07) [2008] ECR I–7821, [2008] STC 3351. For the application of this interpretation, see Revenue and Customs Brief 15/10, 29 March 2010 (services supplied to bodies corporate and unincorporated associations).

Item 1

The payment of a right to enter a sports competition where the entry fees are allocated wholly to prizes. For an example of match fees outside the scope of this item, see *Wimborne RFC* (No 4547).

Item 2

The grant by a non-profit-making sporting body of the right to enter a sports competition. For an example of match fees outside the scope of this item, see *Wimborne RFC* (No 4547).

Item 3

Services (other than accommodation, catering and transport) supplied to an individual taking part in sport or physical education (see *Swansea Yacht & Sub Aqua Club v C & E Comrs* [1996] V & DR 89) by a non-profit making body which is not a local authority. If the body operates a membership scheme, the individual must be a member (see *Basingstoke and District Sports Trust Ltd v C & E Comrs* [1995] V & DR 405; Business Brief 3/96, 16 February 1996). His membership must last for three months or more. The services must be closely linked with the sport or physical education in which the individual is taking part and be essential to it. For situations where an individual does not take part in the main sporting activity, see *Royal Pigeon Racing Association* (No 14006) (pigeon racing). For non-refundable deposits taken when prospective members are entered on a waiting list, see *Milnathort Golf Club Ltd* (No 15816). For membership schemes allowing unlimited access to leisure facilities in a leisure centre, see Revenue and Customs Brief 37/10, 3 September 2010. For green fees, see *The Bridport and West Dorset Golf Club* (TC 1214) and Revenue and Customs Brief 30/11, 27 July 2011.

Non-profit-making bodies

For bodies that are "non-profit-making" for the purposes of Directive 2006/112/EC art 132(1)(*m*) (formerly Directive 77/388/EEC art 13A(1)(*m*)), see *Kennemer Golf & Country Club v Staatssecretaris van Financiën* (case C-174/00) [2002] STC 502, ECJ. For a body outside this description, see *Messenger Leisure Developments Ltd v R & C Comrs* [2005] STC 1078, CA; Business Brief 22/05, 2 December 2005.

In the UK, a non-profit-making body is referred to as an "eligible body" and defined by reference to Notes 2A–2C and 4–17. A body is a non-profit-making body (and therefore an eligible body) if it meets the following conditions:

(a) it is either precluded from distributing any profits it makes or allowed to distribute them only to a non-profit-making body (Note 2A(*a*)). A distribution of unapplied or undistributed profits is disregarded for this purpose if it is made to members on a winding-up or dissolution (Note 2C));

(b) its profits from supplies within Items 2 and 3 must be applied only for one or more of the following purposes (Notes 2A(*b*) and 2B):

  (i) the continuance or improvement of facilities made available in making supplies within Items 2 and 3,

  (ii) the continuance or improvement of facilities made available in connection with making supplies within Items 2 and 3,

  (iii) the purposes of a non-profit-making body;

(c) it is not subject to a commercial influence (see below) (Note 2A(*c*)).

A body is subject to a commercial influence if, but only if, one of the following conditions is met:

(a) the body received a relevant supply (see below) during the relevant period (see below) from a person who was associated (see below) with the body at the time when the supply was received (Note 4(*a*));

(b) the body paid an emolument (see Note 16) during the relevant period to a person who was associated with the body at the time when the emolument was paid (Note 4(*b*));

(c) an agreement (see Note 16) existed during the relevant period for the body to receive a relevant supply after the end of the relevant period from a person who was associated with the body during the relevant period while the agreement was in force (Note 4(*c*)(i));

(d) an agreement existed during the relevant period for the payment of an emolument by the body after the end of the relevant period to a person who was associated with the body during the relevant period while the agreement was in force (Note 4(*c*)(ii)).

As regards sports supplies (see Note 16) made after 31 December 2002, the relevant period is the period of three years ending with the making of the sports supply (Note 5(*b*)).

A supply is a "relevant supply" if it falls within one of the following descriptions (Notes 6, 7). The conditions relevant to each description are set out by reference to code letters.

	Description	*Conditions*
(*a*)	the grant of an interest in or right over land	A, B, C, D, E
(*b*)	the grant of a licence to occupy land	A, B, C, D, E
(*c*)	the grant of any personal right to call for or be granted an interest in or right over land in Scotland	A, B, C, D, E
(*d*)	a supply arising from a grant in (*a*), (*b*) or (*c*)	A, B, F, G
(*e*)	managing or administering the facilities provided by the body	A, B
(*f*)	goods or services supplied for an excessive consideration	A, B

A. The supply is not a relevant supply if, when the sports supply is made, the principal purpose of the body is confined to the provision of sporting or physical education facilities for use by the body's employees (see Note 16) (Note 7(*a*)).

B. The supply is not a relevant supply if it is made by a charity or local authority (Note 7(*b*)).

C. The supply is a relevant supply if the land is, or is expected to become, sports land (see Note 16) at any time during the relevant period (Note 6(*a*)–(*c*)).

D. The supply is not a relevant supply if the grant is made for a nominal consideration (Note 7(*c*)).

E. The supply is not a relevant supply if the grant is treated as a supply (see VATA 1994 Sch 4 paras 5, 9) merely because it is made for no consideration (Note 7(*e*)).

F. The supply is not a relevant supply if the grant was made before 1 April 1996 (Note 6(*d*)).

G. A supply arising from a grant in (*c*) is not a relevant supply if it is made for a nominal consideration (Note 7(*d*)).

A person is "associated" with the body if:

(a) the person was an officer (see Note 16), a shadow officer (see Note 16) during the relevant period (Note 8). However, if the person ceased to be an officer or shadow officer before 1 January 2000, he is associated with the body only if (Notes 10 and 11):
  - (i) the body received the supply under an agreement made between 14 January 1999 and 31 December 1999,
  - (ii) the body paid the emolument under an agreement made between 14 January 1999 and 31 December 1999,
  - (iii) the supply to be received after the end of the relevant period arises from an agreement made between 14 January 1999 and 31 December 1999, or
  - (iv) the emolument to be paid after the end of the relevant period arises from an agreement made between 14 January 1999 and 31 December 1999.

(b) the person was an intermediary (see below) for supplies to the body at any time during the relevant period (Note 8); or

(c) the person is connected (see Note 17) to a person in (*a*) or (*b*) (Note 9).

A person is an "intermediary" at all times in the relevant period if a supply (or an agreement for making a supply) was made at any time during the relevant period and the body would have been subject to commercial influence (see Note 13) if (Note 12):

(a) the supply were made (or intended to be made) to the body rather than to the person, and

(b) Note 7 is disregarded in determining whether that supply would be a relevant supply.

An intra-group supply is not disregarded (see s 43(1)(*a*)) for any of the foregoing purposes (Note 15).

GROUP 11—WORKS OF ART, ETC (V4.166)

Disposals of objects either to museums etc within IHTA 1984 Sch 3 or accepted in satisfaction of tax are exempt.

GROUP 12—FUND-RAISING EVENTS BY CHARITIES AND OTHER QUALIFYING BODIES (V4.171)

The following supplies are exempt.

Item 1

A supply of goods or services by a charity in connection with an event organised for charitable purposes. The event must be organised by a charity or jointly by two or more charities. The primary purpose of the event must be to raise money. This primary purpose must be publicised.

Item 2

A supply of goods or services by a qualifying body in connection with an event organised exclusively for the body's own benefit. The primary purpose of the event must be to raise money. This primary purpose must be publicised.

Item 3

A supply of goods or services by a charity or qualifying body in connection with an event organised exclusively for charitable purposes, exclusively for the body's own benefit or exclusively for a combination of charitable purposes and the body's own benefit. The event must be organised jointly by one or more of the charities and the qualifying body. The primary purpose of the event must be to raise money. This primary purpose must be publicised.

Exclusions

A charity or qualifying body may hold more than 15 events of the same kind in its financial year (or a proportionate number if the financial year is not twelve months) in circumstances where the events take place at the same location and involve the same charity or body. Where this is so, supplies in connection with those events during the financial year are exempt under Items 1–3 only if the gross takings of the event do not exceed £1,000 (Notes 4–6).

In principle, a supply in connection with an event is not exempt under Items 1–3 (Note 8(*a*)) if accommodation is:

- provided to a person by means of a supply;
- provided to a person in pursuance of arrangements made by the charity (or any of the charities) organising the event or a charity connected with any charity organising the event; or
- provided by a person under arrangements made by the qualifying body organising the event.

However, this does not apply to accommodation for one or two nights if the supply is outside the tour operators' margin scheme (Notes 8(*b*), 9). For the margin scheme, see s 53.

A supply in connection with an event is not exempt under Items 1–3 if exemption would distort competition to the disadvantage of a commercial enterprise carried on by a taxable person (Note 11).

Definitions

An "event" includes an event accessed wholly or partly by means of electronic communications or by communications by means of a telecommunications system (as defined in Telecommunications Act 1984 s 4(1), (2) by virtue of s 106(1)) (Note 1).

A "charity" includes a body corporate wholly owned by a charity if the profits from all of the body's activities are payable to a charity in accordance with a deed, written agreement or other provision (Note 2).

X (a charity) and Y (a body corporate paying profits to the charity which own it) are "connected" if X owns Y. Similarly, Y and Z (another body corporate paying profits to the charity which owns it) are "connected" if they are both owned by X (Note 10).

GROUP 13—CULTURAL SERVICES ETC (V4.176)

The following supplies are exempt.

Item 1

The supply of a right of admission to:

(a) a museum, gallery, art exhibition or zoo; or
(b) a theatrical, musical or choreographic performance of a cultural nature.

The supply must be made by a public body (see Note 1). It is excluded from exemption if it distorts competition so as to place commercial rivals at a disadvantage (Note 3). The performance in (*b*) must be exclusively provided by one or more public bodies or eligible bodies (see Note 2) or some combination of both (Note 4). For situations where exemption is financially disadvantageous, see Press Notice 33/96, 3 June 1996.

Item 2

The supply of a right of admission to:

(a) a museum, gallery, art exhibition or zoo; or
(b) a theatrical, musical or choreographic performance of a cultural nature.

The supply must be made by an eligible body. For "eligible body", see Note 2. For management and administration on a voluntary basis (Note 2(*c*)), contrast *C & E Comrs v Zoological Society of London* (case C-267/00) [2002] STC 521, ECJ (occasional or peripheral participation in decisions by paid staff) and *Bournemouth Symphony Orchestra v C & E Comrs* [2007] STC 198, CA (significant contribution by paid managing director). For persons having a direct or indirect financial interest in the body's activities, see *Bournemouth Symphony Orchestra v C & E Comrs* [2007] STC 198, CA (salary); *Longborough Festival Opera v R & C Comrs* [2006] STC 818, affd [2007] STC 198, CA (contracts and guarantees). For earlier examples, see *Glastonbury Abbey v C & E Comrs* [1996] V & DR 323; *Dean and Canons of Windsor* (No 15703).

Definition

For "museum", see *Dean and Canons of Windsor* (No 15703).

GROUP 14—SUPPLIES OF GOODS WHERE INPUT TAX CANNOT BE RECOVERED (V4.181)

The following supplies are exempt.

Item 1

A supply of goods if the following conditions are met:

(a) the person making the supply (referred to as "the relevant supplier"), or one of his predecessors, incurred VAT on his purchase, acquisition or importation of:
  (i) the goods supplied or on any goods comprised in them which were used in their production (Note 1); or
  (ii) if the supply comprises the grant of a major interest in land, his acquisition of the major interest or on the construction of a building or civil engineering work on the land (Note 2);

(b) the input tax is:
  (i) wholly attributed to exempt supplies (or would have been so attributed but for the fact that it is attributed to taxable supplies under the de minimis rules in VAT Regulations, SI 1995/2518 reg 106) and does not subsequently become wholly or partly attributable to taxable supplies in accordance with regs 107–109 or give rise to a deduction under the capital goods scheme (see reg 115(1)) Notes 3, 4);
  (ii) wholly excluded from credit on the grounds that it relates to goods and services used for business entertainment, goods other than building materials incorporated in a building or its site, or motor cars (see VAT (Input Tax) Order, SI 1992/3222, arts 7–9) (Notes 3, 5, 6); or
  (iii) incurred before the relevant supplier or his predecessor became registered or liable to registration or is attributable to that time (Notes 7, 8); and

(c) (if the supply falls within Sch 9 Group 1 Item 1 so as to be exempt from tax in the absence of an option to tax land) the relevant supplier has not made an option to tax land. For the option to tax, see Sch 10 Part 1.

The condition in (*b*) is not met if the relevant supplier or his predecessor (being a public body, overseas person or government department) is entitled to a refund of all or part of the VAT incurred under ss 33, 33A, 33B, 39 or 41 (Note 9).

The conditions in (*a*) and (*b*) are met if the goods have been self-supplied by the relevant supplier or his predecessor between the time when the goods were purchased, acquired or imported and the time when the supply takes place (Note 10).

A person ("X") is the predecessor of another person ("Y"). If X transfers all or part of his business as a going concern to Y, the goods or thing formed part of those assets, and the transfer was treated as neither a supply of goods nor a supply of services so as to be outside the scope of VAT in accordance with VAT (Special Provisions) Order, SI 1995/1268 art 5 (Notes 11, 12).

A body corporate ("X") is the predecessor of another body corporate ("Y") if:

(1) the goods or thing formed part of the assets of X when it became a member of the VAT group of which Y was the representative member at that time (Notes 11, 13(*a*));

(2) the goods or thing formed part of the assets of X, or any other member of the VAT group, when Y succeeded X as the representative member of the group (Notes 11, 13(*b*)); or

(3) the goods or thing formed part of the assets of Y at the time when Y ceased to be a member of the VAT group of which X was the representative member (Notes 11, 13(*c*)).

If Y meets either of the foregoing conditions in relation to another person or body corporate ("Z"), X is also a predecessor of Z (Note 11).

A "thing" is a major interest in land, a supply arising from the grant of the major interest, or goods used in the construction of a building or civil engineering work which becomes part of the land (Note 15).

The definitions of "grant" and "reverse surrender" in Sch 9 Group 1 Notes 1, 2 apply for the purposes of Group 14 (Note 16).

GROUP 15—INVESTMENT GOLD (V4.186)

The following supplies are exempt.

Item 1

The supply of investment gold (see Note 1).

Item 2

The grant, assignment or surrender of a right, interest or claim which confers a right to the transfer of the possession of investment gold (see Note 1). This does not include (Note 3):

(a) the grant of an option; or

(b) the assignment or surrender of a right under an option before the time when the option is exercised.

Item 3

The services supplied by an agent acting for a disclosed principal in effecting (or attempting to effect) a supply within Items 1 or 2 made to or by his principal.

Exclusions

A supply is not exempt if it is made by X (a member of the London Bullion Market Association) to Y (another member) or by X to Z (a non-member) (Note 4). For the zero-rating of these supplies, see VAT (Terminal Markets) Order 1973, SI 1973/173 arts 4 (supply by X to Y) and 5–7 (supply by X to Z).

SCHEDULE 9A ANTI-AVOIDANCE PROVISIONS: GROUPS (SECTION 43) (V2.190B)

Power to give directions

1.—The Commissioners may give a direction if:

(a) a body corporate has either joined or left a VAT group (see s 43) or entered into a transaction (a "relevant event");

(b) a taxable supply (an "undercharged supply") has been, will be or may be made so as to meet the following conditions:

 (i) VAT is not chargeable on the full value of the supply, ie the value on which VAT would be chargeable if the supplier and recipient were not members of the same VAT group at the time(s) of supply,

(ii) all or part of the supply is chargeable to VAT at a positive rate, and
(iii) one of the following events (a "tax advantage") arises from the supply:
— the supplier is entitled to deduct input tax on goods or services attributable to all or part of the supply,
— the supplier is entitled to deduct input tax on goods or services used in making the supply,
— an EU or third country trader is entitled to repayment of VAT charged on all or part of the supply;

(c) the supply in (*b*) meets the conditions therein because the event in (*a*) has taken place; and

(d) (if the transaction in (*a*) is a supply), the body corporate has entered into another transaction (which is also a supply) to which (*b*) and (*c*) apply.

In determining whether input tax is attributable to a supply for the purposes of head (*b*) (iii) above, A (a person who purchased an asset) is treated as the same person as X (the person to whom he supplies the asset on a transfer of all or part of his business as a going concern). Similarly, A, B, C and X are treated as the same person if the business (or part) is successively transferred from A to B, from B to C, and from C to X. In either case, the supply must have been treated as neither a supply of goods nor a supply of services in accordance with VAT (Special Provisions) Order 1995, SI 1995/1268 art 5 (1)–(3).

For the purposes of head (*b*) (iii) above, the supply of a right to goods or services and the supply of goods or services by virtue of such a right are regarded as separate parts of a single supply. A right for this purpose includes: (1) any right, option or priority with respect to the supply of goods or services; and (2) an interest deriving from any right to goods or services.

For restrictions on the power to make directions, see Sch 9A para 2. For the circumstances in which a direction may be made, see the statement of practice in Notice No 700/2.

Restrictions on giving directions

2.—The Commissioners may be satisfied that the relevant event (see Sch 9A para 1 (2)) had as its main purpose (or each of its main purposes) a genuine commercial purpose unconnected with the making of an undercharged supply giving rise to a tax advantage (see Sch 9A para 1(3)). If so, they cannot give a direction. However, they can give a direction if a body corporate is removed from a VAT group on revenue protection grounds (ie, by notice under s 43C(1)) or on eligibility grounds (ie, by notice under s 43C(3)).

For restrictions governed by the date on which the relevant event occurred, see Sch 9A para 4(2), (3)(*a*).

Form of directions under schedule

3.—The Commissioners may give a direction in relation to any supply of goods or services made by one body corporate to another. The direction requires it to be assumed that, to the extent described in the direction, the bodies are not members of the same VAT group so that the supply is not disregarded under s 43(1)(*a*).

The Commissioners may also give a direction relating to a particular body corporate. The direction requires it to be assumed that, for the period described in the direction, the body is not a member of a VAT group or particular VAT group, or is a member of a particular VAT group for which it is eligible to be a member. The direction may identify the representative member of the VAT group concerned.

VAT is chargeable in accordance with the assumptions contained in a direction, and must be accounted for and paid accordingly, from the time when the direction is given. An assessment giving effect to those assumptions is made under para 5 below in relation to the period (if any) before the time when the direction is given.

A direction may be varied by a further direction. A direction may be withdrawn by written notice at any time. The fact that the Commissioners have refused (or not refused) an application to form, vary or disband a VAT group, or change the representative member, does not prevent them making a direction requiring the opposite to be assumed. For applications and refusals, see s 43B.

Time limit on directions

4.—A direction may be given no later than six years after the later of:

(a) the relevant event (see para 1 above) giving rise to the direction; and

(b) the time when the entitlement to input tax credit or repayment of VAT (see Sch 9A para 1 (4)) arose in relation to the undercharged supply giving rise to a tax advantage.

A direction may be given by reference to a relevant event taking place after 28 November 1995. By implication, it may require assumptions to be made in relation to any time since 1 April 1973 (when VAT was first introduced).

Manner of giving directions

5.—A direction relating to a supply may be given either to the person who made it or to the representative member of the VAT group of which that person is a member at the time of supply.

A direction relating to a body corporate may be given either to the body concerned or to the representative member of the VAT group of which it is, was or is treated as being or having been, a member.

A direction is given by written notice. It must specify the relevant event (see Sch 9A para 1 (2)) by reference to which it is given.

Assessment in consequence of a direction

6.—The Commissioners may make an assessment if, as a result of a direction, a "relevant person" (see below) would have been liable for an amount of VAT ("unpaid tax") before the direction was given by applying the assumptions specified in the direction. Unpaid tax is assessed to the Commissioners' best judgment and notified to the relevant person concerned. The assessment may be incorporated in the same notice as the direction.

Unpaid tax is the aggregate of: (1) the amount by which output tax is increased and input tax credits are reduced for a prescribed accounting period ending before the direction was given; and (2) the amount by which a repayment of tax to an EU or third country trader is reduced.

The amount assessed must not exceed the amount which, to the Commissioners' best judgement, appears to be the "actual revenue loss". This is the amount of unpaid tax less the aggregate of every increased entitlement to input tax credit or repayment of tax which would have been due to anyone by applying the assumptions specified in the direction.

No assessment may be made if the direction is withdrawn. A supplementary assessment may be made in accordance with s 77 (6).

An assessment must be made no later than the first anniversary of the day on which the direction was given. The amount assessed (or any amount to which it is subsequently reduced) is treated as an amount of VAT due from the person assessed and is recovered accordingly (see Sch 11 para 5 (1)) from that person or from the representative member of the VAT group (if any) of which that person is a member. If two or more persons are liable for the same amount of unpaid tax, they are jointly and severally liable for that amount.

The unpaid tax assessed carried interest under s 74 in the same manner as VAT assessed under s 73. However, interest under s 74 (1) runs from the date when the VAT assessment is notified (rather than from the reckonable date). The maximum period for which interest runs under s 74 (1), (2) is a two year period ending on the day when the interest assessment is made. Interest is assessed in accordance with ss 76 (1), (7)–(10) and 77 (6). A further assessment of interest under s 76 (7) (*b*) may be made for an unlimited period.

A "relevant person" is:

(a) the person to whom a direction is given (see para 5 (1), (2) above);

(b) the representative member of the VAT group of which that person is a member, or is assumed to be a member by virtue of a direction, at the time when the assumption specified in the direction relates; or

(c) the body corporate assumed to be the representative member of the VAT group in (*b*) by virtue of a direction.

Interpretation of schedule etc

7.—Whether or not a body corporate is, or is eligible to become, a member of a VAT group is determined in accordance with ss 43–43C.

Any notice or notification required to be given to a person for the purposes of Sch 9A may be given to any receiver, liquidator or representative of that person.

SCHEDULE 10 BUILDINGS AND LAND (SECTION 51)

General note

This schedule was substituted with effect from 1 June 2008 by FA 2006 s 17(1)(*a*); VAT (Buildings and Land) Order 2008, SI 2008/1146. For amendments to the repealed Sch 10 para 8 repealed before they came into operation, see art 5 of the 2008 Order. For transitional provisions and savings, see Sch 2 of the 2008 Order. For the Commissioners' views and text having the force of law, see Notice No 742A.

PART 1 THE OPTION TO TAX LAND

Introduction

Overview of the option to tax

1.—(V3.248, V4.113) This paragraph gives an overview of paras 1–34.

The option to tax

Effect of the option to tax: exempt supplies become taxable

2.—(V4.115) A grant made in relation to land is not exempt from VAT under Sch 9 Group 1 if:

- a person has exercised the option to tax the land;
- the grant is made at a time when the option has effect; and
- the grant is made by either: (1) the person who exercised the option; or (2) (if the option was exercised by a body corporate) a relevant associate (as defined in Sch 10 para 3) of that person.

Meaning of "relevant associate"

3.—(V4.115) A body corporate (Y) is a relevant associate of body corporate which exercised the option to tax land (X) if any of the following conditions are met:

- X and Y were members of the same VAT group when the option first had effect;
- X and Y were members of the same VAT group at a later time and X had a relevant interest (as defined in Sch 10 para 3(6)) in the land or building at that time; or
- X and Y were members of the same VAT group at a time when X had a relevant interest (as defined in Sch 10 para 3(6)) in the land or building.

Y ceases to be a relevant associate of X in any of the following circumstances.

- the conditions specified in Sch 10 para 3(4) are met. Y ceases to be a relevant associate at the time when all of those conditions are first met;
- the conditions specified in a public notice are met. For the conditions, see Notice No 742A para 6.3.5. For the requirement to notify the Commissioners that the conditions have been met, see Sch 10 para 4(2), (3); or

- Y obtains the Commissioners' prior permission. For permissions, see Sch 10 para 4(4)–(8).

Permission for a body corporate to cease to be a relevant associate of the opter

4.—(V4.115) Y (a body corporate) meeting the conditions in Notice No 742A para 6.3.5 ceases to be a relevant associate of X (another body corporate) only if it notifies the Commissioners that those conditions have been met. The notification must be made on form VAT 1614B and contain the information requested on that form: see Sch 10 para 4(3); Notice No 742A para 6.3.6.

Y applies for prior permission to cease to be a relevant associate of X by completing form VAT 1614B and sending it to the relevant address stated thereon: see para 4(4); Notice No 742A para 6.3.8. Y ceases to be a relevant associate from the day on which the Commissioners give their permission or from an earlier or later day specified in the permission. The Commissioners may impose conditions. Failure to comply with those conditions may result in the permission becoming void.

Exclusions from effect of option to tax

Dwellings designed or adapted, and intended for use, as dwelling etc

5.—(V4.115) An option to tax has no effect in relation to any grant made in relation to a building or part of a building if: (1) the building or part is designed or adapted as one or more dwellings (as defined in Sch 8 Group 5 Note 2); and (2) the purchaser or tenant intends to use the building or part for this purpose.

An option to tax has no effect in relation to any grant made in relation to a building or part of a building if: (1) the building or part is designed or adapted solely for a relevant residential purpose (as defined in Sch 8 Group 5 Notes 4, 5); (2) the purchaser or tenant intends to use the building or part for this purpose; and (3) the purchaser or tenant gives the grantor a certificate to this effect. For the certificate to be given, see Sch 8 Group 5 Note 12(*b*). For "solely", see Revenue and Customs Brief 33/10, 29 July 2010.

Conversion of buildings for use as dwelling etc

6.—(V4.115) An option to tax has no effect in relation to any grant made by X (the grantor) to Y (the purchaser or tenant) in relation to a building or part of a building if any of the following conditions are met:

(1) Y intends to use the building or part as one or more dwellings. Y does not meet this condition if some other use is intended before use as one or more dwellings commences. However, intended use for minor or incidental purposes is disregarded;

(2) Y intends to use the building or part solely for a relevant residential purpose (as defined in Sch 8 Group 5 Notes 4, 5). For "solely", see Revenue and Customs Brief 33/10, 29 July 2010;

(3) Y intends to convert the building or part with a view to using it for a purpose in head (1) or (2); or

(4) Y intends to dispose of the whole of his interest in the building or part to another person ("Z") who, in turn, intends to dispose of the whole of his interest to another person who either: (*a*) intends to convert the building or part in accordance with head (3); or (*b*) dispose of the whole of his interest in accordance with this head. Z must give Y a certificate to this effect.

Y must certify his intention. This is done by completing form VAT 1614D: see para 6(10)(*b*); Notice No 742A para 3.4.2. Y must give this form to X within a specified period. For the specified period, see Sch 10 para 6(2)(*a*); Notice No 742A para 3.4.3. However, Y may give the form at a later time if X so agrees. This must be no later than the time when X makes the supply to which the grant gives rise.

Charities

7.—(V4.115) An option to tax has no effect in relation to any grant made by X (the grantor) to Y (the purchaser or tenant) in relation to a building or part of a building if:

- Y intends to use the building or part solely for a relevant charitable purpose (as defined in Sch 8 Group 5 Notes 6, 12). For "solely", see Revenue and Customs Brief 33/10, 29 July 2010;
- Y does not intend to use the building or part as an office; and
- Y gives X a certificate to this effect. For the certificate to be given, see Sch 8 Group 5 Note 12(*b*).

Residential caravans

8.—(V4.115) An option to tax has no effect in relation to any grant made in relation to a pitch for a caravan if:

- the caravan is a residential caravan; and
- the terms of a covenant, statutory planning consent or similar permission do not prevent the caravan being used as a residence for part of the year.

Residential houseboats

9.—(V4.115) An option to tax has no effect in relation to any grant of facilities for mooring, anchoring or berthing a houseboat (as defined in Sch 8 Group 9 Item 2) if:

- the houseboat is a residential houseboat; and
- the terms of a covenant, statutory planning consent or similar permission do not prevent the houseboat being used as a residence for part of the year.

Relevant housing associations

10.—(V4.115) An option to tax has no effect in relation to any grant made by X (the grantor) to a relevant housing association (as defined in Sch 10 para 10(3)) in respect of any land if:

- the association certifies that, after any necessary demolition work, the land will be used for the construction of one or more buildings. For garages in connection with buildings intended for use as one or more dwellings, see Sch 8 Group 5 Note 3;
- the association certifies that the building(s) are intended for use: (1) as one or more dwellings, or (2) solely for a relevant residential purpose (as defined in Sch 8 Group 5 Notes 4, 5);
- the association gives a certificate to this effect. The certificate is made on form VAT 1614G and must contain all the information requested on that form: see Sch 10 para 10(5); Notice No 742A para 3.6.2; and
- the certificate is given to X within a specified period. For the specified period, see Sch 10 para 10(2)(*a*); Notice No 742A para 3.4.3. However, the association may give the form at a later time if X so agrees. This must be no later than the time when X makes the supply to which the grant gives rise.

Grant to individual for construction of dwelling

11.—(V4.115) An option to tax has no effect in relation to any grant of land made to an individual if:

- the land is to be used for the construction of a building;
- the individual intends to use the building as a dwelling; and
- the individual does not construct the building in the course or furtherance of a business carried on by him.

Anti-avoidance

Developers of exempt land

12.—(V4.115) A supply is not a taxable supply as a result of an option to tax if:

(a) the person making the grant ("the grantor") giving rise to the supply is a developer of the land. For the circumstances in which a person is a "developer of the land", see Sch 10 para 13; and

(b) at the time when the grant was made, or treated as being made (see below), the grantor or a development financier (as defined in Sch 10 para 14) intended or expected that the land would immediately become exempt land, eventually become exempt land or continue for a period to be exempt land. This is referred to as the "exempt land test". For "exempt land", see Sch 10 paras 15, 16.

The grant and a supply arising from it may be made by different persons, eg where a landlord grants a lease and then assigns it to another person so that the periodic rents give rise to supplies made by the latter. For the purposes of head (*a*), the other person (in this case the assignee) is treated as if he were the grantor. He is deemed to have made the grant at the time when his first supply arising from the grant is made (eg when he first receives or invoices a periodic rent following the assignment).

This paragraph does not apply to a supply arising from: (1) a grant made before 26 November 1996; or (2) a grant made between 26 November 1996 and 29 November 1999 inclusive on terms forming part of the agreement which were fixed before 26 November 1996.

For grants made between 19 March 1997 and 9 March 1999 inclusive, see Sch 10 para 17.

Meaning of grants made by a developer

13.—The grantor is a "developer of the land" if:

- the grantor (see Sch 10 para 12) or a development financier (see Sch 10 para 14) intended or expected that the land, a building on the land or part of a building on the land would become a capital item (as to which see VAT Regulations 1995, SI 1995/2518 reg 113) for the purposes of the capital goods scheme in relation to either: (1) the grantor, or (2) a person (referred to as a "relevant transferee") to whom the land, building or part would be transferred in the course of a supply or in the course of a transfer of all or part of a business as a going concern.
- the grant is made before the end of the period of adjustment relevant to the land, building or part for the purposes of the capital goods scheme. This test is deemed to be met in cases where the grant and the supply arising from the grant are made by different persons, so that the person making the supply is treated as the grantor in accordance with Sch 10 para 12(6).

Meaning of "development financier"

14.—The term "development financier" is defined.

Meaning of "exempt land": basic definition

15.—(V4.115) Land is "exempt land" if the following conditions are met at any time during the adjustment period (as defined in para 15(4)) for the purposes of the capital goods scheme:

(a) the land is occupied by the grantor (see Sch 10 para 12), a development financier (see Sch 10 para 14) or a person connected with either. Occupation of the land at any time before the end of the relevant adjustment period by a development financier or a person connected with him is disregarded if:

- the development financier or connected person is neither the grantor nor a person connected with the grantor, and
- the building occupation conditions (as defined in para 15A) are met during the period of occupation.

For the circumstances in which a person is connected with another person, see CTA 2010 s 1122; and

(b) the land is not wholly, or substantially wholly, occupied by that person for eligible purposes.

Occupation of the land at any time before the end of the relevant adjustment period (as defined in para 15(4)) is disregarded if:

(a) the building occupation conditions (as defined in para 15A) are met at that time; or

(b) the land is occupied solely by reference to an automatic teller machine.

For "occupation", see para 16; *R & C Comrs Principal and Fellows of Newnham College in the University of Cambridge* [2008] STC 1225, HL; Revenue and Customs Brief 33/09, 8 June 2009. For the occupation of land for "eligible purposes", see para 16. For occupation which is "wholly" or "substantially wholly" for eligible purposes, see para 15(5); Notice No 742A para 13.10.1.

Meaning of "exempt land": the building occupation conditions

15A.—(V4.115) The "building occupation conditions" relevant to para 15(3A)(a) are met if:

(a) the grant consists of (or includes) the grant of a relevant interest in a building; and

(b) at the time in question, the person occupying the land neither:

   (i) occupies any part of the land which is not a building. Occupation of land is disregarded if it is used for parking, or falls within the curtilage of a building, and the occupation is ancillary to the occupation of a building; nor

   (ii) occupies more than the maximum allowable percentage (as defined in para 15A(4)) of any relevant building (as defined in para 15A(4)).

For occupation which is "wholly" or "substantially wholly" for eligible purposes, see para 15(5); Notice No 742A para 13.10.1. For "building", see para 18(4)–(7).

Meaning of "exempt land": eligible purposes

16.—(V4.115) A person "occupies" land if he occupies all or part of the land either alone or together with one or more other persons. A person is treated as occupying land for a particular purpose if he holds the land in order to use it for that purpose and does not occupy it for another purpose.

The following persons occupy land for "eligible purposes" if they meet the stated conditions at the relevant time:

- any taxable person meeting the following conditions: (1) he occupies the land for the purpose of making supplies in the course or furtherance of business; and (2) to the extent that VAT incurred by the taxable person is wholly attributable to those supplies, it gives rise to an entitlement to input tax credit;
- a body entitled to repayments of VAT in accordance with s 33. The body must not occupy the land for the purpose of carrying on a business;
- a government department (as defined in s 41(6)–(8));

A taxable person (X) may be regarded for VAT purposes as making the supplies actually made by another person (Y) who is not a taxable person. If Y occupies the land, X and Y are treated as a single taxable person for the purpose of deciding whether the land is occupied for an eligible purpose.

Paragraph 12: grants made on or after 19th March 1997 and before 10th March 1999

17.—(V4.115) A grant made between 19 March 1997 and 9 March 1999 inclusive is deemed to have been made on 10 March 1999 if the following conditions were met at the time when the grant was actually made:

- the grantor (see Sch 10 para 12) or a development financier (see Sch 10 para 14) intended or expected that the land, a building or part of a building on the land, or a building or part of a building to be constructed on the land would become a capital item (as to which see VAT Regulations 1995, SI 1995/2518 reg 113) for the purposes of the capital goods scheme in relation to: (1) the grantor, or (2) a person to whom the land, building or part has been transferred in the course of a supply or in the course of a transfer of all or part of a business as a going concern; and
- the land, building or part had not yet become a capital item.

Scope of the option, its duration, notification etc

Scope of the option

18.—(V4.115) An option to tax applies to the particular land specified in the option.

A building may be sited on the land. If so:

- the option may be exercised in relation to a building. If so, the option has effect in relation to the whole of the building and all the land within its curtilage;
- the option may be exercised in relation to part of the building. If so, the option has effect in relation to the whole of the building and all the land within its curtilage;
- the option may be exercised in relation to the land, but not in relation to the building or part of the building. If so, the option has effect in relation to: (1) the land, (2) any building which is constructed on the land, and (3) any building which is to be constructed on the land. In practice, the opter can exclude the building in (2) from the scope of the option by framing his option so as to exclude the land within the curtilage of the building. For the manner in which the opter can exclude the building in (3) from the scope of the option, see Sch 10 para 27.

The term "building" includes an enlarged building, an annexe to a building and a planned building. The following are treated as a single building:

- buildings linked internally. This does not apply if the internal link was created after the buildings were completed. For the time when a building is completed, see Sch 9 Group 1 Note 2;
- buildings linked by a covered walkway. This does not apply if: (1) construction of the walkway started after the buildings were completed, or (2) members of the general public have reasonable access to the walkway; and
- complexes consisting of a number of units grouped around a fully enclosed concourse.

The day from which the option has effect

19.—In principle, an option to tax has effect from: (1) the day on which it was exercised; or (2) the start of any later day specified in the option. However, when exercising the option, the opter may have intended to revoke it during the "cooling off" period (see Sch 10 para 23). If so, the option is treated as if it had never been exercised.

For the requirement to notify the option, see Sch 10 para 20. For the requirement to obtain prior permission before the option is exercised, see Sch 10 para 29(3). For the circumstances in which an option can be revoked, see Sch 10 paras 22(2), (3) and 23–25.

Requirement to notify the option

20.—(V4.115) An option has effect only if:

- it is notified to the Commissioners within 30 days or such longer period as the Commissioners may allow;
- the notification is given in the manner specified in a notice published by the Commissioners and contains the information so specified. For the Commissioners' views (which are not expressed as having the force of law), see Notice No 742A paras 4.2.2 and 4.2.3.

For the circumstances in which these requirements are waived, see Sch 10 para 29(3).

Real estate elections: elections to opt to tax land subsequently acquired

21.—An alternative to exercising the option to tax on a case by case basis is a global election (referred to as a "real estate election"). A real estate election applies to interests in, rights over and licences to occupy land and buildings acquired after the election is made. These interests, rights and licences are collectively referred to as "relevant interests".

The following consequences flow from an election:

- the person making the election deemed to exercise an option to tax in relation to any land or building in which he acquires a relevant interest after the election is made;
- he is not required to make any notification in respect of the option he is deemed to exercise;
- the option is deemed to be exercised on the day on which the acquisition is made; and

- the option is treated as if it had effect from the start of that day.

However, no option is deemed to have been exercised in relation to land or buildings if:

- the person making the election had exercised an option to tax in relation to the land or building and the option had effect before the relevant interest is acquired;
- the person making the election held a relevant interest in the land or building at the time when the election was made and continues to hold it when the later interest is acquired; or
- the person would have been required to obtain the Commissioners' prior permission if, in the absence of an election, he had wanted to exercise an option to tax in relation to the land or building with effect from the day on which the relevant interest is acquired.

The person making the election is treated as if he had exercised an option to tax in relation to the land or building in which the relevant interest is acquired. The deemed option is treated as if it had been exercised on the day when the interest is acquired. It has effect from the start of that day. It does not have to be notified.

An election has effect only if:

- it is notified to the Commissioners within 30 days or such longer period as the Commissioners may allow; and
- the notification is made on form VAT 1614, which must be accompanied by a list of properties setting out specified information: see Sch 10 paras 21(7), 22(10); Notice No 742A para 14.8.

The Commissioners may, at any time, require the person making the election to provide the information specified in a notice. The information must be provided within 30 days or such longer period as the Commissioners may allow. For the specified information, see Notice No 742A para 14.11. The Commissioners may revoke the election if the information is not so provided. The revocation applies to relevant interests acquired after the deadline for supplying the information has expired. This is the only situation in which an election can be revoked. The Commissioners' prior permission is required before another election can be made. The foregoing provisions apply in a modified form to elections made by a member of a VAT group.

The time at which a person acquires a relevant interest in any land or building is determined by reference to the time of the supply made by the vendor. The time of supply rules (see s 6 and the VAT Regulations 1995, SI 1995/2518) apply whether or not the vendor supplied the relevant interest on a transfer of all or part of his business as a going concern. If the transaction gives rise to more than one time of supply, the relevant time of supply is the earliest of them.

For "global options to tax" made before 1 June 2008, see Revenue and Customs Brief 24/08, 22 April 2008.

Real estate elections: supplementary

22.—An option to tax may have been exercised before the time when a real estate election is made. If so, the option is deemed to be revoked in either of the following circumstances:

- it was made in relation to any building, or to part of any building, in which the person making the election did not have a relevant interest (as defined in Sch 10 para 21(12)) at the time when the election was made. The revocation takes effect from the time when the election was made; or
- it was made in relation to land – without reference to any building or part of a building – in which the person making the election did not have a relevant interest (as defined in Sch 10 para 21(12)) at the time when the election was made. The revocation takes effect from the time when the election was made.

For anti-avoidance provisions in this connection, see Sch 10 para 26.

An option to tax exercised in relation to land – without reference to any building or part of a building – may be converted into separate options to tax if:

- the option was exercised before the time when a real estate election is made;
- the circumstances specified in a notice published by the Commissioners apply. For the specified circumstances, see Sch 10 para 22(6); Notice No 742A para 14.6; and
- a relevant interest (as defined in Sch 10 para 21(12)) is held in the land, or any part of it, at the time when the election is made.

The original option is converted into separate options to tax different parcels of land comprised in the land or part. These options are deemed to have been made by the person who made the election. They are deemed to have effect from the time when the election was made (for the purposes of Sch 10 para 3(2)) or from the time from which the original option had effect (in other cases). No "cooling off" period applies to the separate options. Thus, the options cannot be revoked under Sch 10 para 23. The notification of the real estate election (see Sch 10 para 21(7)) must identify the separate options and the different parcels of land.

The foregoing provisions apply in a modified form to elections made by a member of a VAT group.

Revocation of option: the "cooling off" period

23.—An option to tax may be revoked with effect from the day on which it was exercised if:

- this is done no later than six months after the option had effect;
- the taxpayer has not used the land since the option had effect;
- no tax has become chargeable as a result of the option;
- (if all or part of a business has been transferred as a going concern to or by the taxpayer since the option had effect) the grant of any land forming part of the assets of the business did not give rise to a supply treated as neither a supply of goods nor a supply of services. For the circumstances in which a supply is so treated, see VAT (Special Provisions) Order 1995, SI 1995/1268 art 5(1)–(3);
- the additional condition(s) specified in a notice are met. For the condition specified, see Sch 10 para 23(6)(*a*); Notice No 742A para 8.1.2; and
- the revocation is notified to the Commissioners on form VAT 1614C and contains the information requested thereon: see Sch 10 para 23(3); Notice No 742A para 8.1.3.

If the condition in Notice No 742A para 8.1.2 is not met, the taxpayer requires the Commissioners' prior permission before revoking his option. An application must be made no later than six months after the option had effect. An application is made on Form VAT 1614C: see Sch 10 para 23(5)(*b*); Notice No 742A para 8.1.5. The Commissioners may impose conditions. The Commissioners may treat the revocation as void if those conditions are broken: see Sch 10 para 23(5)(*e*); Notice No 742A para 8.1.2.

Revocation of option: lapse of 6 years since having a relevant interest

24.—An option is deemed to be revoked if a person does not have an interest in, right over or licence to occupy the relevant land or building throughout a continuous six-year period. The revocation has effect from the sixth anniversary of the later of:

- the day when the opter ceased to have the interest, right or concern; or
- the date from which the option had effect.

For anti-avoidance provisions, see Sch 10 para 26.

Revocation of option: lapse of more than 20 years since option had effect

25.—An option may be revoked at any time after the twentieth anniversary of the day from which it took effect if the conditions specified in a notice are met. Notice No 742A para 8.3.2 provides that the opter must meet either: (1) the condition in Box G para 1 of that paragraph; or (2) all of the conditions in Box G paras 2–5 of that paragraph. The revocation must be notified to the Commissioners on form VAT 1614J and contain the information requested thereon: see Sch 10 para 25(3); Notice No 742A para 8.3.3. If it subsequently transpires that the required condition(s) have not been met, the Commissioners may nevertheless regard the option as validly revoked. However, they are not required to do so.

If the condition(s) in Notice No 742A para 8.3.2 are not met, the opter must seek permission to revoke his option. Applications are made on form VAT 1614J and must contain the information requested thereon: see Sch 10 para 25(5); Notice No 742A para 8.3.5. For circumstances in which the Commissioners will refuse permission, see Notice No 742A para 8.3.6. The option is revoked from: (1) the day on which the Commissioners give permission; or (2) an earlier or later day or time specified in the permission. This day or time may be determined by reference to the happening of an event or the meeting of a condition. The Commissioners may impose conditions. They may treat the revocation as void if those conditions are broken.

Revocation of option under paragraph 22(2) or (3) or 24: anti-avoidance

26.—An option is not treated as being revoked under Sch 10 para 22(2), (3) if condition A or B is met. An option is not treated as being revoked under Sch 10 para 24 if condition A, B or C is met. Conditions B and C are relevant only if the opter is a body corporate.

Condition A is met if the opter (see Sch 10 para 26(7)), or a relevant associate (see Sch 10 para 3) of the opter, disposed of a relevant interest in the land or building (see Sch 10 para 26(7)) before the relevant time (see Sch 10 para 26(7)) and either of the following conditions is met at the relevant time:

- a supply is yet to take place for the purposes of the charge to VAT in respect of the disposal; or
- a supply would be yet to take place for the purposes of the charge to VAT in respect of the disposal if one or more conditions (eg the happening of an event or the doing of an act) were to be met.

Condition B is met if:

- the opter (being a body corporate) was a member of a VAT group (see ss 43A–43D) at any time before the relevant time;
- a relevant associate of the opter in relation to the land or building ceased to be a member of the same VAT group before the relevant time; and
- one of the following circumstances applied at the time when the relevant associate ceased to be a member of the VAT group:
  - (a) the relevant associate had an interest in the land or building,
  - (b) (if the relevant associate had disposed of an interest in the land or building) a supply was yet to take place for the purposes of the charge to VAT in respect of the disposal. This applies whether or not the supply depends upon one or more conditions (eg the happening of an event or the doing of an act) being met, or
  - (c) the relevant associate was connected with a person (being the opter, or a relevant associate of the opter in relation to the land or building), and that person had a relevant interest in the land or building.

Condition C is met if:

- the opter (being a body corporate) and a relevant associate are members of the same VAT group at the relevant time; and
- the relevant associate either holds a relevant interest in the land or building at the relevant time, or did so at any time during the previous six years.

Exclusion of new building from effect of an option

27.—A person may begin the construction of a building on land in respect of which he has exercised the option to tax. For "building", see Sch 10 para 18(4)–(6). For "construction", see Sch 8 Group 5 Notes 16, 18(*a*). For the time when construction begins, see Sch 10 para 27(7); Notice No 742A para 2.6.4.

The person may exclude the whole of the building and all of the land within its curtilage from the scope of the option if: (1) no land within the curtilage of the building falls within the curtilage of an existing building; and (2) he notifies the Commissioners of this exclusion. The notification must be made on form VAT 1614F. It must state the time from which the exclusion is to have effect and contain the other information specified on the form: see Sch 10 para 27(4); Notice No 742A para 2.6.3. The notification must be made within 30 days (or such longer period as the Commissioners may allow in an individual case) counted from the day from which the exclusion is to have effect.

The exclusion has effect from the earliest of the following times: (1) the first grant of an interest in the building or a part of the building; (2) first use of the building or a part of the building or (3) completion of the building. For the time when a building is completed, see Sch 9 Group 1 Note 2.

Pre-option grants: requirement for prior permission before exercise of option to tax

28.—The right to exercise an option to tax land from a particular day is restricted if, in the ten-year period ending on that day, a person has made, or formed the intention to make, an exempt supply arising from a grant in relation to the land. The person may exercise the option if he meets the conditions specified in Notice No 742A para 5.2: see Sch 10 para 28(2)(*a*). If not, he must obtain the Commissioners' written permission before exercising the option (see below). For applications for permission, see Sch 10 para 29. For the consequences of exercising the option without obtaining permission, see Sch 10 para 30.

The Commissioners must decide whether exercising the option would result in input tax being attributed on a fair and reasonable basis to supplies arising from a grant made in relation to the land. In doing so, they must have regard to all the circumstances of the case. In particular, they must have regard to: (1) the value of exempt supplies which are made or to be made before proposed effective date and arise from the grant; (2) the value of supplies which would be taxable as a result of the option; and (3) the amount of input tax incurred, or likely to be incurred, in relation to the land. The Commissioners are required to refuse permission if they are not satisfied that input tax would be attributed on a fair and reasonable basis.

Paragraph 28: application for prior permission

29.—An application for permission to exercise the option to tax is made on form VAT 1614H and must contain the information requested thereon: see Sch 10 para 29(1); Notice No 742A para 5.5. For the requirement to obtain permission, see Sch 10 para 28.

The consequence of permission being granted is that the applicant is treated as having exercised the option to tax the land with effect from: (1) the day on which the application was made; or (2) the start of any later day specified in the application.

The Commissioner may impose conditions when granting permission. The Commissioners may treat the application as void if those conditions are broken.

Paragraph 28: purported exercise where prior permission not obtained

30.—A person may purport to exercise an option to tax, and notify this to the Commissioners in accordance with Sch 10 para 20, in circumstances where he required the Commissioners' prior permission (see Sch 10 para 28) in order to do so. When this situation comes to light, the Commissioners have discretion to dispense with the requirement for prior permission. If they do so, the purported exercise of the option is treated as valid and it has effect from the day specified in Sch 10 para 19(1). For the circumstances in which the Commissioners may exercise their discretion, see Notice No 742A para 5.8.

Supplementary provisions

Timing of grant and supplies

31.—A grant may be made before the time when an option to tax has effect and may give rise to supplies which are treated as taking place after that time. Where this is so, the option operates in relation to those supplies as if the grant had been made at a time when the option has effect.

32.—Sch 8 Group 5 Note 10 applies for the purposes of Part 1.

Definitions in Schedule 8 or 9 that are applied for the purposes of this Schedule

33.—Various terms used in Part 1 are defined by reference to Sch 8 Group 5 and Sch 9 Group 1.

Other definitions etc

34.—The terms "notification" and "permission" are defined. Whether or not a person is connected with another person is decided in accordance with CTA 2010 s 1122. A company (as defined in CTA 2010 s 1121) is not connected with another company merely because both companies are under the control (as defined in CTA 2010 s 1122) of the Crown, a Minister of the Crown, a government department or a Northern Ireland department. References to a public notice are references to a notice published by the Commissioners.

PART 2 RESIDENTIAL AND CHARITABLE BUILDINGS: CHANGE OF USE ETC

Introductory

35.—(V2.248) Part 2 applies where one or more relevant zero-rated supplies relating to a building have been made to a person. If the person is a body corporate treated as a member of a VAT group (see ss 43A–43D), the term "person" applies to both the body corporate and any other member of the VAT group. The terms "relevant zero-rated supply", "relevant premises" and "relevant period" are defined.

Disposal of interest or change of use following relevant zero-rated supply

36.— A person (X") makes a self-supply (see para 37) if the following conditions are met during the relevant period (as defined in para 35(2)):

(1) A grant or other supply (eg construction services) has been made to X in relation to a building (or part of a building) (see para 35(1)).

(2) X intends to use the building (or part) solely for a relevant residential purpose (as defined in Sch 8 Group 5 Note 4) or a relevant charitable purpose (as defined in Sch 8 Group 5 Note 6) (see para 35(2)).

(3) The supply in (1) is zero-rated in accordance with Sch 8 Group 5 (see para 35(2)).

(4) Any of the following conditions is met during the ten year period beginning on the day when the building (or part) was completed (para 36(1)(a), (2)–(5)):

- (a) X disposes of his entire interest in the building (or part). This appears to encompass the following situations:
  - (i) X disposes of his entire interest in the building (or the part),
  - (ii) X disposes of part of that interest, or
  - (iii) (having previously disposed of part of that interest) X disposes of all or part of the remainder.
- (b) X retains his entire interest in the building (or part) but:
  - (i) begins to use the building (or part) for a different purpose,
  - (ii) begins to use an identifiable part of the building (or part) for a different purpose,
  - (iii) (having previously begun to use an identifiable part of the building (or part) for a different purpose) begins to use all of the remainder for that purpose, or
  - (iv) (having previously begun to use an identifiable part of the building (or part) for a different purpose) begins to use an identifiable part of the remainder for that purpose.
- (c) X retains his entire interest in the building (or part) and uses it partly for residential or charitable purposes and for partly for other purposes without allocating an identifiable part of the building (or part) to each purpose. The proportion of the building (or part) deemed to be used for each purpose is determined by reference to the proportion of use for each purpose.

(5) The consequence of the disposal or change of use is that the proportion of the building used for a relevant residential or charitable purpose is lower that it had been at any time since the beginning of the ten year period (para 36(1)(b)).

X may be a charity using all or part of the building (or part): (1) as a village hall; or (2) in providing social or recreational facilities for a local community. The building (or part) is treated as being used for a relevant charitable purpose whether or not the occupier is using the building (or part) for such a purpose.

Charge to VAT

37.— A disposal or change of use meeting the conditions in para 36 results in a self supply. The interest, right or licence in the building (or part) held by X immediately prior to the disposal or change of use is deemed to be: (1) supplied to him for the purposes of a business carried on by him; and (2) supplied by him in the course or furtherance of that business. The supply is charged to VAT at a positive rate.

The value of the first deemed supply is determined in accordance with the following formula:

$$R2 \times Y \times (120 - Z)/120$$

The value of the value of any subsequent supply is determined in accordance with the following formula:

$$(R2 - R1) \times Y \times (120 - Z)/120$$

Where:

R1 = The maximum proportion of the building (or part) disposed of or put to a different use;

R2 = The proportion of the building (or part) disposed of or put to a different use;

Y = The amount that yields an amount of VAT which, if the building (or part) had not been intended for use solely for a relevant residential or charitable purpose, would have been equal to: (1) the VAT which would have been chargeable on the relevant zero-rated supply; or (2) (if there was more than one supply) the aggregate amount of the VAT which would have been chargeable on the supplies;

Z = The number of whole months since the day on which the building (or part) was completed.

Supplies in relation to a building where part designed for residential or charitable use and part designed for other uses

38.—Sch 8 Group 5 Note 10 applies for the purposes of Sch 10 paras 36 and 37.

Definitions

39.—Various words and phrases used in Part 2 are defined.

PART 3 GENERAL

Benefit of consideration for grant accruing to a person other than the grantor

40.—The benefit of the consideration for the grant of an interest in, right over or licence to occupy land may accrue to someone other than the grantor. This person is referred to as "the beneficiary". The beneficiary is treated as if he were the person making the grant. Input tax attributable to the grant incurred by the grantor is treated as if it were input tax incurred by the beneficiary.

SCHEDULE 10A FACE-VALUE VOUCHERS (SECTION 51B) (V3.166)

Meaning of "face-value voucher" etc

1.—The terms "face value voucher" and "face value" are defined.

A stamp, token or voucher limited by time, rather than by a stated monetary amount, is not a face value voucher: see *Leisure Pass Group Ltd v R & C Comrs* [2008] STC 3340 (pass entitling the holder to enter any or all of a number of attractions without further payment during a specified period).

Nature of supply

2.—A person makes a supply of services if: (1) he issues a face value voucher (so as to be the "issuer"); or (2) he supplies a face value voucher issued by another person (so as to be an "intermediary"). For the Commissioners' views regarding phone cards, see Business Brief 29/03, 16 December 2003; Business Brief 18/04, 13 July 2004.

Treatment of credit vouchers

3.—The term "credit voucher" is defined.

If the consideration for a credit voucher exceeds face value, the consideration is deemed to be the excess. The consideration is disregarded in other cases. However, the foregoing treatment is disapplied if the person who accepts the voucher in payment or part-payment of a supply of goods or services fails to account for the VAT due thereon. In these circumstances, the consideration for the supply made by the issuer or intermediary appears to be the amount due. For an example, see *R & C Comrs v IDT Card Services Ireland Ltd* [2006] STC 1252, CA (no tax chargeable on issue or redemption of phone card due to different treatment of the transactions under UK and Irish VAT law). The foregoing treatment may also be disapplied in other circumstances by order. No order has been made to date.

Treatment of retail vouchers

4.—The term "retail voucher" is defined.

If the consideration for a retail voucher supplied by the issuer exceeds face value, the consideration is deemed to be the excess. The consideration is disregarded in other cases. However, the foregoing treatment is disapplied if a person other than the issuer accepts the voucher in payment or part-payment of a supply of goods or services and fails to account for the VAT due thereon. In these circumstances, the consideration for the supply made by the issuer appears to be the amount due. The consideration for the supply made by an intermediary appears to be the amount due in all cases.

For the charge to tax on a retail voucher supplied by an intermediary, see Sch 10A para 6.

Treatment of postage stamps

5.—If the consideration for a postage stamp exceeds face value, the consideration is deemed to be the excess. The consideration is disregarded in other cases.

Treatment of other kinds of face-value voucher

6.—The following face value vouchers are taxed or exempted from tax by reference to the tax position of the goods or services for which they are exchanged: (1) vouchers that are not credit vouchers, retailer vouchers or postage stamps; and (2) (by virtue of Sch 10A para 4(4)) retailer vouchers supplied by an intermediary. The tax position of goods or services is that they are either exempt from tax or charged to tax at the zero, reduced or standard rate. Thus, goods or services fall within one or other of four "rate categories". The tax position of the vouchers is summarised in the following table.

	Restrictions on use of the voucher	*Actual use of the voucher*	*Tax position of the voucher*
1	Voucher can be exchanged for goods or services in only one rate category	Voucher exchanged for goods or services in that rate category	The tax position of that rate category, ie exempt, zero-rate, reduced rate or standard rate
2	Voucher can be exchanged for goods or services in two or more rate categories	Voucher exchanged for goods or services in only one rate category	The tax position of that rate category, ie exempt, zero-rate, reduced rate or standard rate

	Restrictions on use of the voucher	*Actual use of the voucher*	*Tax position of the voucher*
3	Voucher can be exchanged for goods or services in two or more rate categories	Voucher exchanged for goods or services in two or more rate categories	The tax position of the rate categories of the goods or services purchased. The value of the supply in each rate category is determined on a fair and reasonable basis

Vouchers supplied free with other goods or services

7.—A face value voucher may be supplied with other goods or services to the same person in a composite transaction. It appears that the consideration is apportioned if: (1) the voucher is a postage stamp; or (2) the consideration for the goods or services would have been significantly different if no voucher had been supplied. The voucher is treated as if it had been supplied for no consideration in other cases.

Interpretation

8.—Various words and phrases are defined.

SCHEDULE 11 ADMINISTRATION, COLLECTION AND ENFORCEMENT (SECTION 58)

General

1.—(V1.262, V1.264) The Commissioners are responsible for the collection and management of VAT. For the Commissioners' duty of fairness, see *R (on the application of British Sky Broadcasting Group plc) v C & E Comrs* [2001] STC 437; *C & E Comrs v National Westminster Bank plc* [2003] 1072; *R (on the application of Sagemaster plc) v C & E Comrs* [2004] STC 813. For the principle of proportionality, see *R (on the application of UK Tradecorp Ltd) v C & E Comrs* [2005] STC 138. For the power to make interim payments, see *Capital One Developments v C & E Comrs* [2002] STC 479; *R (on the application of UK Tradecorp Ltd) v C & E Comrs* [2005] STC 138. For the Commissioners' right to bring an action for unlawful means conspiracy, see *R & C Comrs v Total Network SL* [2008] STC 644, HL (carousel fraud). For the civil investigation of serious fraud, see Business Brief 18/05, 16 September 2005 and Appendix 10. For amnesties, see *Commission v Italy* (case C-132/06) [2008] ECR I–5457, ECJ (general and indiscriminate renunciation of the tax authority's right of verification and recovery).

For rulings given by the Commissioners, see Notice 700/6 (obtaining rulings); Revenue and Customs Brief 15/09, 27 March 2009 (misdirection); When you can rely on information or advice provided by HM Revenue and Customs (HMRC) (HMRC guidance, reproduced in Appendix 19]). For examples of rulings given and misdirection in respect of them, see *F & I Services v C & E Comrs* [2001] STC 939, CA; *R (on the application of Software Solutions Partners Ltd) v C & E Comrs* [2007] SWTI 1399; *R (on the application of Corkdeck Ltd) vc R & C Comrs* [2009] STC 1681; *R (on the application of the Medical Protection Society Ltd) v R & C Comrs* [2010] STC 555. For non-statutory clearances, see Revenue and Customs Brief 20/08, 1 April 2008.

For the Commissioners' power to grant concessions, see *R (on the application of Wilkinson) v IR Comrs* [2006] STC 270, HL. For the Treasury's power to make orders giving effect to existing HMRC concessions, see FA 2008 s 160. For concessions relating to VAT, see Notice No 48 (December 2010), which is reproduced in Appendix 6; *R (on the application of Greenwich Property Ltd) v C & E Comrs* [2001] STC 616 (taxpayer entitled to rely on concession); *R (on the application of British Telecommunications plc) v R & C Comrs* [2005] STC 1148 and *R (on the application of Silicon Graphics Finance SA) v R & C Comrs* [2008] STC 1928 (simple duplication of output tax); *R (on the application of Accenture Services Ltd) v R & C Comrs and related application* [2009] STC 1503 (staff hire concession). For the tribunal's jurisdiction in relation to concessions, see the commentary to s 82.

The Commissioners have a general power to make administrative agreements with individual traders: *The Labour Party* (No 17034) (apportionment of input tax between business and non-business use). For specific powers, see for example VATA 1994 s 25 and VAT Regulations 1995, SI 1995/2518 regs 67 and, 102. For the variation of an agreement between the Commissioners and a trader, see R & C Comrs v Boots Co plc [2010] STC 637, CA. The Commissioners do not have a general power to withhold or delay payment of tax due to a trader: *R v C & E Comrs ex parte Kay & Co Ltd* [1996] STC 1500. Nor do they have a general power to pay interest: *R (on the application of UK Tradecorp Ltd) v C & E Comrs* [2005] STC 138; *R (on the application of Elite Mobile plc) v C & E Comrs* [2005] STC 275. For the specific powers in relation to interest, see ss 78 (official error) and 79 (repayment supplement); Supreme Court Act 1981 s 35.

For Business Briefs and Revenue and Customs Briefs of general application, see Appendix 1.For Business Briefs, see Business Brief 16/03, 19 August 2003; Business Brief 28/04, 26 October 2004. Business Briefs have now been replaced by Revenue and Customs Briefs.

For a list of notices and information sheets relating to VAT published by the Commissioners, see Appendix 2.

For the Commissioners' complaints procedure, see Notice No 1000. For the examination of complaints by the Adjudicator for the Inland Revenue and Customs & Excise, see the leaflet "How to Complain about HM Customs & Excise" published by the Adjudicator. For remedies under the general law, see *Swedish State v Sotckholm Lindöpark AB* (case C-150/99) [2001] STC 103, ECJ (failure to implement EU law); *R (on the application of British Sky Broadcasting Group plc) v C & E Comrs* [2001] STC 437 (abuse of power); *C & E Comrs and another v Federation of Technological Industries* (case C-384/04) [2006] ECR I–4191, [2006] STC 1483, ECJ (vires of UK legislation).

For the circumstances in which legislation can be given retrospective effect, see *Stichting "Goed Wonen" v Staatssecretaris van Financiën* (case C-376/02) [2005] ECR I–3445, [2006] STC 833, ECJ.

For the right of one taxpayer to bring proceedings against the Commissioners in respect of the tax affairs of another taxpayer, see *R (on the application of Freeserve.com plc) v C & E Comrs (America Online Inc, interested party)* [2004] STC 187.

Accounting for VAT and payment of VAT

2.—(V5.109) The Commissioners may make regulations in respect of the following matters:

Matter	***Authority***	***Regulations made (SI 1995/2518)***
Keeping accounts and making returns	Sch 11 para 2(1)	Regs 24–43 (accounting and returns) and 49–55 (annual accounting scheme)
Submission of statements relating to the intra-Community movement of goods	Sch 11 para 2(3), (3ZA)(*a*)	Regs 21–23 (EC sales statements)
Submission of statements relating to services in respect of which the customer is liable to a reverse charge in another member state	Sch 11 para 2(3), (3ZA)(*b*)	No regulations made to date
Submission of statements relating to reverse charge supplies (see s 55A(6))	Sch 11 para 2(3A)	Reg 23C (reverse charge sales statement)
Notification of commencing, recommencing or ceasing to make reverse charge supplies (see s 55A(6))	Sch 11 para 2(3B)	Reg 23B (notification of first relevant supply)

Matter	*Authority*	*Regulations made (SI 1995/2518)*
Notification of an acquisition of goods subject to excise duty by a non-taxable person	Sch 11 para 2(4), (5)	Reg 36
Notification of an acquisition of a new means of transport by a non-taxable person	Sch 11 para 2(4), (5)	Reg 148
Special provision for taxable supplies made by retailers	Sch 11 para 2(6)	Regs 66–75 (retail schemes)
Provision for VAT in respect of a supply to be accounted for and paid by reference to the time when the consideration is received	Sch 11 para 2(7)	Regs 56–65 (cash accounting scheme)
VAT in respect of supplies and acquisitions of dutiable goods to be accounted for and paid by reference to the duty point	Sch 11 para 2(8)	Regs 41(1)
Time when invoices are issued in respect of intra-Community removals of goods	Sch 11 para 2(9)	None
VAT chargeable in one prescribed accounting period treated as chargeable in another period	Sch 11 para 2(10)(*a*)	Reg 25(5)
Making entries in accounts and financial adjustments in respect of adjustments	Sch 11 para 2(10)(*b*)–(*e*)	Regs 34, 35, 38
Non-standard accounting periods	Sch 11 para 2(11)	Reg 25(1)
Accounting, payment and provision of information regarding goods sold under a power (see Sch 4 para 7)	Sch 11 para 2(12)	Reg 27

Amounts of less than £1 are to be treated as nil when due either to or from the Commissioners.

VAT invoices

2A.—Regulations may require taxable persons to provide VAT invoices. The regulations may specify the information to be shown on VAT invoices and the period within which the invoices must be provided. The regulations may also make provision for the provision, replacement or correction of invoices in connection with the supplementary charge: see FA 2009 Sch 3 para 22. For the supplementary charge, see FA 2009 Sch 3 para 1. For the regulations made, see VAT Regulations 1995, SI 1995/2518, regs A13–20.

Self-billed invoices

2B.—A "self-billed invoice" is a document prepared by a taxable person which purports to be a VAT invoice in respect of goods or services supplied to him by another taxable person. It is treated as the VAT invoice required to be provided by the supplier (see VAT Regulations 1995, SI 1995/2518 reg 13(1)) if the conditions specified in regulations are met. For the conditions specified, see VAT Regulations 1995, SI 1995/2518 reg 13(3A), (3D).

A self-billed invoice is not treated as a VAT invoice provided by the supplier for the purposes of s 6(4). Thus, if prepared before the basic tax point (see s 6(2), (3)), it is disregarded in determining the time of supply under that provision. For other circumstances in which a self-billed invoice is not treated as a VAT invoice provided by the supplier, see VAT Regulations 1995, SI 1995/2518 reg 13(3F).

A self-billed invoice is treated as a VAT invoice provided by the supplier for the purposes of s 6(5), (6) if additional conditions specified in regulations are met. Thus, a notice of election under s 6(5), or request under 6(6), may be given or made by the taxable person preparing the self-billed invoice.

Production of VAT invoices by computer

3.—Where information is stored on a computer and is transferred to another person electronically, tax invoices are regarded as issued even though no document is ever delivered.

Persons using electronic means to either supply or receive tax invoices must give one month's notice in writing to the Commissioners and comply with any requirements imposed by the Commissioners or specified in regulations. No regulations have been made to date.

Regulations may apply the foregoing provisions to invoices issued in respect of goods removed to or from another EU member state.

Power to require security and production of evidence

4.—(V5.186) The Commissioners may require a person to produce evidence relating to VAT before his input tax is allowed or repaid. The required evidence is specified by the Commissioners. It may comprise the documents listed in VAT Regulations 1995, SI 1995/2518 reg 29(2)(*a*)–(*f*) or the alternative evidence referred to in the proviso to reg 29(2). There is no right of appeal: see *Strangewood Ltd v C & E Comrs* [1988] VATTR 35.

The Commissioners may require a person to give security before paying any VAT credit (see s 25(3)) due to him. They may do so for the protection of the revenue. For the right of appeal, see s 83(1)(*l*).

The Commissioners may require a taxable person to give security, or further security, as a condition of making or receiving taxable supplies of goods or services. They may do so for the protection of the revenue. Security may be required in respect of VAT that is due, or may become due, from: (1) the taxable person; or (2) any earlier or later participant in a chain of supply that includes the taxable person. However, the Commissioners may only require security from X (the person liable for payment of the VAT) or Y (a person who is jointly and severally liable with X for the payment): see *Federation of Technological Industries and others v C & E Comrs* (case C-384/04) [2006] ECR I–4191, [2006] STC 1483, ECJ. Member states may provide that X (the person liable for payment) is a tax representative: see Directive 2006/112/EC art 204(1) (formerly Directive 77/388/EEC art 21(2)). For the Commissioners' power to require security from a tax representative, see s 48(7).

The Commissioners determine both the amount of the security and the manner in which it is given. "VAT" means the excess of output tax over input tax: see *Colette Ltd v C & E Comrs* [1992] VATTR 240. A taxable person is normally required to provide security for his own VAT if he has a past record of business failures leaving VAT debts. For examples, see *Mr Wishmore v C & E Comrs* [1988] STC 723; *C & E Comrs v Peachtree Enterprises Ltd* [1994] STC 747; *John Dee Ltd v C & E Comrs* [1995] STC 941, CA; *Giddian Ltd v C & E Comrs* [1984] VATTR 161; *Power Rod (UK) Ltd v C & E Comrs* [1983] VATTR 334; *Gayton House Holdings Ltd v C & E Comrs* [1984] VATTR 111; *Craig Security Services Ltd* (No 11484); *Northern Contract Services Group Ltd v C & E Comrs* [1994] VATTR 419; *Control Ltd* (No 16973). For security required on the sole ground that returns have been persistently furnished late, see *Longsight Cricket Club* (No 4064); *Compass Crane & Plant Hire Ltd* (No 13860); *Century Supplies Ltd* (No 14375); *Cameron* (No 15779). The normal amount of security is the estimated VAT due from four months' trading (monthly returns) or six months' trading (quarterly returns).

For the circumstances in which the Commissioners intend to require security for another person's VAT, and the amount required, see Notice No 700/52.

A trader should normally be given an opportunity to explain his conduct before security is required: see *Restorex Ltd* (No 15014). For the right of appeal, see s 83(1)(*l*). The Commissioners' statement of case should set out all the reasons for requiring security: see *Interseal 2000 Ltd* (No 4161). Making or receiving taxable supplies without providing security is a criminal offence: see s 72(11).

Recovery of VAT, etc

5.—(V5.171, V5.173) VAT due from any person is recoverable as a debt due to the Crown.

Where an invoice shows that tax was chargeable on a supply of goods or services, an amount equal to the tax is recoverable from the person who issued the invoice or, if tax is not separately shown, so much of this total of the invoice as represents tax on the supply. It is irrelevant whether the invoice is a tax invoice, the supply indicated actually takes place, that the amount shown as VAT or any amount calculated to be VAT is chargeable on the supply, or that the person issuing the invoice is a taxable person. If the sum concerned is VAT it is recovered as such. If not, it is recoverable as a debt due to the Crown. For recovery of tax on sham invoices, see *Sandell* (No 9665); Notice No 48 (December 2010) para 3.9. For invoices rendered to the state, see *Dimosio v Karageorgou* (cases C-78/02 to C-80/02) [2003] ECR I–13295, [2003] SWTI 1937, ECJ.

Duty to keep records

6.—(V5.201) Regulations may prescribe the records to be kept by: (1) taxable persons; and (2) other persons acquiring new means of transport and goods subject to excise duty. For the regulations made, see VAT Regulations 1995, SI 1995/2518, regs 31–33.

The Commissioners may require a person to preserve his records for a specified period. This must be done in writing. The specified period may not exceed six years.

The duty to preserve records is discharged by preserving the records (or the information contained in them) in any form and by any means. The Commissioners may impose conditions or grant exceptions. This must be done in writing.

Discharging the duty to preserve records in the foregoing manner does not imply that a statement contained in a document produced by a computer is admissible in evidence. In relation to Scotland, see Sch 11 para 6(6).

For penalties in respect of a failure to keep the prescribed records, see s 69(1)(*c*). For directions to keep additional records, see Sch 10 para 6A.

6A.—The Commissioners may make a direction requiring specified records to be kept in relation to specified goods and complied by reference to VAT invoices or any other matter. These records are additional to those required to be kept by virtue of Sch 11 para 6. The Commissioners may require them to be kept for a specified period, which may not exceed six years.

A direction applies to the taxable person named therein. It is made by written notice given to him. It must warn him of the penalties for non-compliance. It remains in force until replaced or revoked.

The prerequisite for making a direction is having reasonable grounds for believing that the specified records might assist in the identification of unpaid VAT in respect of taxable supplies made by the taxable person or any other person.

The duty to preserve records is discharged by preserving the records (or the information contained in them) in any form and by any means. The Commissioners may impose conditions or grant exceptions. This must be done in writing.

For penalties in respect of a failure to keep the records specified in a direction, see s 69B(1), (3).

Furnishing of information and production of documents

7.—(V5.234) The Commissioners may make regulations requiring taxable persons to notify details of changes in circumstances relating to either the persons or the business with the aim of keeping the VAT register up to date. For the regulations made, see VAT Regulations 1995, SI 1995/2518, reg 5. For penalties in respect of a failure to notify, see s 69.

Power to take samples

8.—(V5.240) An authorised person may take samples of the goods in the possession of a fiscal warehousekeeper (see s 18A), or of any person who supplies or acquires goods, with a view to determining how the goods or the materials of which they are made should be treated for the purposes of tax.

Samples are, for example, taken to decide whether or not an item is confectionery, or to decide whether an item of apparel is solely for children to wear.

A sample is disposed of and accounted for in such manner as the Commissioners direct.

Where an item is not returned in good condition within a reasonable time, compensation equal to the cost of the sample or such larger sum as the Commissioners decide may be paid to the person from whom the sample was taken.

Power to require opening of gaming machines

9.—(V5.238) An authorised person may at any reasonable time require a person operating a gaming machine to open the machine and to carry out any other operation necessary to calculate the value of supplies made in any period.

Entry and search of premises and persons

10.—[Repealed.]

Order for access to recorded information, etc

11.—(V5.236) A justice of the peace (or the equivalent in Scotland) may upon application by an officer of customs and excise make an order that access to recorded information is made available to an officer of customs and excise who may remove such information as he considers necessary on the grounds that the information may be required as evidence in connection with a VAT offence. Access must be given within seven days or such longer period as the order specifies. Where the information is stored in a computer the order may require the information be produced in a form which is visible, legible, and removable. This paragraph does not prejudice the furnishing of information and the entry and search of premises in paragraphs 8 and 10 above. For orders made under this provision, see *R v Epsom Justices ex parte Bell* [1989] STC 169; *R v City of London Magistrates, ex parte Asif* [1996] STC 611; *R v City of London Magistrates' Court ex parte Peters* [1997] STC 141.

For jurisdiction to make a costs order under Prosecution of Offences Act 1985 s 19 and Costs in Criminal Cases (General) Regulations 1986, SI 1986/1335 reg 3, see *C & E Comrs v City of London Magistrates' Court* [2000] STC 447.

Procedure where documents etc are removed

12.—(V5.233, V5.236) The occupier of premises or the person in charge of premises may request and must be given within a reasonable time a record of what has been removed.

If the officer in charge of an investigation has grounds to believe that the investigation of an offence may be prejudiced he is not required to grant access to or to supply a photograph of any document or thing removed under a warrant.

Otherwise, access under supervision to the thing or document may be granted, and copies made or photographs supplied within a reasonable time.

13.—(V5.233, V5.236) A magistrates' court in England and Wales (or the equivalent in Scotland or Northern Ireland) may order the officer of customs and excise to comply, in such manner and within such time as set out in the order, with the production of either a record of what was removed or give access to the thing or document.

Evidence by certificate, etc

14.—The Commissioners may issue a certificate that:

- a person was, or was not, registered for VAT at any date;
- any return has, or had not, been made at any date;
- an EU sales statement has not, or had not, been submitted at any date; or
- the acquisition of a new means of transport, or of goods subject to excise duty, has not been notified.

This certificate is sufficient evidence of the fact stated until the contrary is proved. A document is treated as a certificate until the contrary is proved.

Any VAT document given to the Commissioners may be photographed. The Commissioners may certify any document to be a photograph and may use the copy in civil or criminal proceedings to the same extent as the original. A document is treated as a certificate until the contrary is proved.

SCHEDULE 11A DISCLOSURE OF AVOIDANCE SCHEMES (SECTION 58A) (V5.213, V5.358)

Interpretation

1.—Various words and phrases are defined.

Obtaining a tax advantage

2.—A person obtains a "tax advantage" if:

- the net tax due for one of his prescribed accounting periods is less than it would otherwise be;
- he obtains a VAT credit (see s 25(3)) when he would not otherwise do so;
- he obtains a VAT credit earlier than would otherwise be the case;
- (if he recovers input tax as the recipient of a supply before the supplier has accounted for the output tax) the period between the two events is greater than it would otherwise be; or
- his non-deductible tax (see Sch 11A para 2A) for a prescribed accounting period is less than it would otherwise be.

Meaning of "non-deductible tax"

2A.—"Non-deductible tax" means:

- input tax excluded from credit (see s 25(7));
- VAT incurred on a purchase, acquisition or importation of goods or services which is not input tax; and
- VAT incurred on a purchase, acquisition or importation of goods or services which does not give rise to an entitlement to a refund (eg under s 33 or 33A).

Designation by order of avoidance schemes

3.—A scheme (see Sch 11A para 1) of a particular description may be designated (and thus be referred to as a "designated scheme") if:

(a) the Treasury considers that the scheme has been (or might be) entered into for the purpose of enabling someone to obtain a tax advantage (see Sch 11A para 2); and

(b) the Treasury considers it unlikely that anyone would enter into the scheme unless the main purpose, or one of the main purposes, of doing so was to enable someone to obtain a tax advantage.

A scheme is designated by Treasury order. A scheme may be designated even if the Treasury considers that, as a matter of law, no one can obtain a tax advantage from using it. The order allocates a reference number to each designated scheme. For the designated schemes and their reference numbers, see VAT (Disclosure of Avoidance Schemes) Order 2004, SI 2004/1933 Sch 1.

Designation by order of provisions included in or associated with avoidance schemes

4.—A provision (as defined) of a particular description may be designated if the Treasury considers that it is (or is likely to be) included in (or associated with) schemes (see Sch 11A para 1) entered into for the purpose of enabling someone to obtain a tax advantage (see Sch 11A para 2). A provision may be designated even if it is also relevant to schemes that are not entered into for this purpose.

A provision is designated by Treasury order. For the designated provisions, see VAT (Disclosure of Avoidance Schemes) Order 2004, SI 2004/1933 Sch 2.

Meaning of "notifiable scheme"

5.—A scheme (see Sch 11A para 1) is a "notifiable scheme" (and therefore gives rise to a duty to notify under Sch 11A para 6) if it is either:

(a) a designated scheme (see Sch 11A para 3); or

(b) any other scheme (see Sch 11A para 1) that includes (or is associated with) a designated provision (see Sch 11A para 4) and its main purpose (or one of its main purposes) is to enable someone to obtain a tax advantage (see Sch 11A para 2). A scheme within this description is hereafter referred to as a "hallmarked scheme".

Duty to notify Commissioners

6.—A duty to notify arises if any of the following consequences flows from being party to a notifiable scheme (see Sch 11A para 5):

(a) the VAT due to (or by) a taxable person disclosed in his VAT return for a prescribed accounting period is greater than (or less than) it would have been if he had not been a party to the scheme;

(b) the amount of a repayment claimed by him in respect of a previous prescribed accounting period is greater than it would have been if he had not been a party to the scheme; or

(c) the amount of his non-deductible tax (see Sch 11A para 2A) for a prescribed accounting period is less than it would have been if he had not been a party to the scheme.

If the taxable person is party to a designated scheme (see Sch 11A para 5(1)(*a*)), he must notify the scheme reference number (see Sch 11A para 3(3)) to the Commissioners in the time, form and manner prescribed by regulations. For the regulations made, see VAT (Disclosure of Avoidance Schemes) Regulations 2004, SI 2004/1929 regs 2, 3. However, no duty to notify arises if:

- the taxable person has already made a notification under this provision;
- he made a notification under the provisions relating to hallmarked schemes at the time when the scheme was not a designated scheme; or
- he is exempted from the duty to notify under Sch 11A para 7.

If the taxable person is party to a "hallmarked scheme" (see Sch 11A para 5(1)(*b*), (2), (3)), he must provide the Commissioners with certain information relating to the scheme. The information concerned, and the time, form and manner of its provision, is prescribed by regulations. For the regulations made, see VAT (Disclosure of Avoidance Schemes) Regulations 2004, SI 2004/1929 regs 2–4. However, no duty to notify arises if:

- the taxable person has previously made a voluntary notification under Sch 11A para 9 (and thereby obtained a scheme reference number from the Commissioners);
- another person has previously made a voluntary notification and given the scheme reference number to the taxable person;

- he has already made a notification under this provision; or
- he is exempted from the duty to notify under Sch 11A para 7.

Exemption from the duty to notify under paragraph 6

7.—A taxable person is exempted from the duty to notify information (see Sch 11A para 6) about a notifiable scheme (see Sch 11A para 5) if the aggregate value of his taxable and exempt supplies (determined on the basis that no VAT is chargeable on those supplies) is less than:

- £600,000 (in the case of a designated scheme) or £10 million (in the case of a "hallmarked scheme") in the period of twelve months ending immediately before the beginning of the relevant period (ie the prescribed accounting period in which the duty to notify arose); and
- the appropriate proportion of £600,000 (in the case of a designated scheme) or £10 million (in the case of a "hallmarked scheme") in the prescribed accounting period immediately preceding the relevant period. The appropriate proportion is a fraction of a year determined by reference to the length of the prescribed accounting period (eg $^1/_{12}$th for monthly periods and $^1/_4$th for three-monthly periods).

However, if the taxable person is a group undertaking (as defined in Companies Act s 259(5)) in relation to any other undertaking (as defined in Companies Act 1985 s 259(1)), the duty to notify is waived only if the other group undertakings all meet the foregoing turnover requirements. For similar restrictions where the taxable person in named in a disaggregation direction, see Sch 11A para 8.

The turnover limits specified above may be varied by Treasury order. No order has been made to date.

Power to exclude exemption

8.—The Commissioners can make a direction in order to prevent an avoidance of the duty to notify (see Sch 11A para 6) by maintaining or creating an artificial separation of business. In determining whether the separation of business activities is artificial for this purpose, it is necessary to have regard to the extent to which the separate persons carrying on the separated activities are closely bound to one another by financial, economic and organisational links.

The consequences of a direction are as follows:

- the persons named in the direction are treated as a single taxable person for the purposes of determining whether they are exempted from the duty to notify under Sch 11A para 7;
- the single taxable person is deemed to carry on the activities of a business described in the direction with effect from the date of the direction or the later date (if any) specified therein; and
- a named person is exempted from the requirement to notify only if the single taxable person would be so exempted.

A direction is served on each of the persons named in it. It remains in force until revoked or replaced by a further direction. The Commissioners must be satisfied on the following matters before they name a person in a direction:

- he makes (or has made) taxable or exempt supplies in the course of carrying on one or more activities;
- the activities form only part of a totality of activities;
- the other activities are carried on either concurrently, consecutively or both by one or more other persons; and
- if all the taxable and exempt supplies of the business described in the direction were taken into account, that business would not be exempted from the duty to notify by virtue of Sch 11A para 7.

Voluntary notification of avoidance scheme that is not [a] designated scheme

9.—Any person may, at any time, provide the Commissioners with prescribed information about a "designated provision scheme" (see Sch 11A para 5(1)(*b*), (2), (3)). Information is prescribed by regulations (see s 96 ("prescribed")). For the regulations made, see VAT (Disclosure of Avoidance Schemes) Regulations 2004, SI 2004/1929 regs 2–4.

On receiving this information, the Commissioners may allocate a scheme reference number and notify it to the informant.

Penalty for failure to notify use of a notifiable scheme

10.—A person is liable to a penalty if he fails to notify a notifiable scheme. For the duty to notify, see Sch 11A para 6. For the amount of the penalty, see Sch 11A para 11.

A person is not liable to a penalty if:

- he satisfies the Commissioners or, on appeal, a tribunal (see s 82), that there is a reasonable excuse for the failure;
- he is convicted of an offence in respect of the failure; or
- he is assessed to a penalty for dishonest conduct (see s 60) or deliberate inaccuracy (see FA 2007 Sch 24 paras 1, 1A) in respect of the failure.

Amount of penalty

11.—The penalty for failure to notify a notifiable scheme (see Sch 11A para 10) is:

- £5,000—if the failure relates to a "hallmarked scheme" (as to which see Sch 11A para 5(1)(*b*), (2), (3)).
- 15 per cent of the VAT saving (as defined)—if the failure relates to a designated scheme (as to which see Sch 11A para 5(1)(*a*)).

Penalty assessments

12.—The amount of a penalty for failing to notify a notifiable scheme (see Sch 11A para 11) may be assessed by the Commissioners and notified to the person liable. An assessment may be made whether or not a belated notification has been made.

The VAT saving arising from use of a designated scheme may not be readily attributable to specific prescribed accounting periods. If so, it may be allocated to specific periods in accordance with the Commissioners' best judgment.

The assessment must be made no later than two years from the time when sufficient facts to indicate a failure to notify came to the Commissioners' knowledge.

An assessment must specify:

(a) the amount of the penalty;
(b) the reasons for imposing the penalty;
(c) how the penalty was calculated; and
(d) the amount (if any) by which the penalty has been reduced by reference to mitigating circumstances. For the power to mitigate penalties, see s 70.

To the extent that assessments for a notification penalty and VAT relate to the same prescribed accounting period, they may be combined and notified as one assessment. However, the amount of the penalty must be separately identified. The VAT must be assessed under s 73(1), (2), (7), (7A) or (7B).

A penalty assessment may be withdrawn or reduced. The amount, or reduced amount, of the penalty is treated as VAT due. For the recovery of VAT due, see Sch 11 para 5.

An assessment notified on a person acting in a representative capacity (see s 76(10)) is deemed to be notified to the person in relation to whom the representative acts.

13.—Regulations may make different provision for different circumstances and may include transitional provisions or savings. For the power to make regulations, see Sch 11A paras 4, 9. For orders under Sch 11A paras 3, 4, see s 97(3), (4)(*g*).

SCHEDULE 12 CONSTITUTION AND PROCEDURE OF TRIBUNALS (SECTION 61)

General note

The VAT and duties tribunals (originally the value added tax tribunals) were abolished and their functions and members transferred to the First-tier Tribunal and Upper Tribunal with effect from 1 April 2009. This schedule was repealed accordingly by the Transfer of Tribunal Functions and Revenue and Customs Appeals Order 2009, SI 2009/56, Sch 2 para 228.

The Value Added Tax Rules 1986, SI 1986/590, which had effect under Sch 12 para 9, were revoked from 1 April 2009 by Sch 2 para 187(*c*) of the 2009 Order.

The Value Added Tax Tribunals Appeals Order 1986, SI 1986/2288, and the Value Added Tax Tribunals (Northern Ireland) Order 1994, SI 1994/1978, which had effect under s 86, were revoked from 1 April 2009 by Sch 2 para 187(*d*) and (*g*) of the 2009 Order.

For transitional provisions and savings in relation to appeals to the VAT and duties tribunals, appeals from the tribunals to the courts and transfers of staff, see Sch 3 paras 4 and 6–13 of the 2009 Order.

For the constitution and procedure of the First-tier Tribunal and Upper Tribunal, see TCEA 2007 ss 3 and 22.

SCHEDULE 13 TRANSITIONAL PROVISIONS AND SAVINGS (SECTION 100)

General provisions

1.—The continuity of VAT law is unaffected by the consolidation of legislation repealed by Sch 15. References to actions under VATA 1994 are construed as actions under the corresponding repealed provisions. Similarly, references to actions under the repealed provisions are construed as actions under the corresponding provisions of VATA 1994. Certain questions relating to supplies; acquisitions and importations made before 1 September 1994 are decided in accordance with the repealed provisions.

Validity of subordinate legislation

2.—VATA 1994 consolidates certain provisions originally enacted by statutory instrument (eg in relation to exemption and zero-rating). The validity of those provisions is unaffected by the consolidation.

Provisions related to the introduction of VAT

3.—A reimported vehicle is not charged to VAT if purchase tax was remitted on exportation.

Supply in accordance with pre-21.4.75 arrangements

4.—FA 1972 s 7 (6A) (repealed), now VATA 1994 s 6 (10), was introduced with effect from 21 April 1975 by F(No 2)A 1975 s 19 (1), (5) (repealed). Time of supply directions before that date continue to have effect.

President, chairmen etc of tribunals

5.—The appointment and remuneration of the President, chairmen and tribunal members is unaffected by the consolidation. For the abolition of the VAT and duties tribunals, see the general note to Sch 12.

Overseas suppliers accounting through their customers

6.—VATA 1983 s 32B (repealed) continues to apply to supplies made before 1 August 1993.

Supplies of fuel and power for domestic or charity use

7.—[Repealed.]

Zero-rated supplies of goods and services

8.—Transitional relief under FA 1989 s 13 (1) (repealed) continues to apply. A grant, assignment or other supply zero-rated in accordance with the transitional relief is not a "relevant zero-rated supply" for the purposes of Sch 10 Part 2.

Bad debt relief

9.—(V5.156) A claim for bad debt relief may not be made under s 36 if—

(a) the supply was made before 1 April 1989; or

(b) a claim has been made under VATA 1983 s 22 (repealed).

Supplies during construction of buildings and works

10.—[Repealed.]

Offences and penalties

11.—Continuing offences may be prosecuted under VATA 1994.

12–18.—(V5.344) Transitional provisions and original commencement dates relating to ss 58–81

Importation of goods

19.—The effect of Finance (No 2) Act 1992 (Commencement No 4 and Transitional Provisions) Order 1992, SI 1992/3261, is continued.

Assessments

20.—Transitional provisions relating to s 73.

Set-off of credits

21.—Transitional provisions relating to s 81.

VAT tribunals

22.—Transitional provisions relating to ss 83, 84. The VAT tribunals were renamed "the VAT and duties tribunals" from 1 July 1994. For the abolition of the VAT and duties tribunals, see the general note to Sch 12.

Isle of Man

23.—The validity of VAT (Isle of Man) Order 1982, SI 1982/1067 and VAT (Isle of Man) (No 2) Order 1982, SI 1982/1068 are unaffected by the amendment to Isle of Man Act 1979 s 6 made by Sch 14 para 7 (not reproduced).

Criminal Justice and Public Order Act 1994

1994 Chapter 33

General note In principle, ss 136–139 of this Act apply to officers of Revenue and Customs in the same manner as they apply to constables: see FA 2007 s 87(1). However, s 138(2), (6) are modified (see FA 2007 s 87(3)), references to "constables" and "police stations" are modified throughout (see s 87(2)) and a new s 136(9) is inserted (see FA 2007 s 87(6)) for this purpose. The following commentary reflects these modifications.

The terms "office of Revenue and Customs" and "designated office of Revenue and Customs" are defined in FA 2007 s 86(5).

PART X CROSS-BORDER ENFORCEMENT

136. Execution of warrants

A warrant issued in England, Wales or Northern Ireland for the arrest of a person charged with an offence may (without any endorsement) be executed in Scotland by any HMRC officer of the country of issue or of the country of execution. An officer executing the warrant may use reasonable force. He has the powers of search conferred by CJPOA 1994 s 139.

A warrant issued in Scotland or Northern Ireland for the arrest of a person charged with an offence may (without any endorsement) be executed in England or Wales by any officer of the country of issue or the country of execution. An officer executing a warrant issued in Scotland has the same powers and duties, and the person arrested the same rights, as they would have had if the warrant had been executed in Scotland. An officer executing a warrant issued in Northern Ireland may use reasonable force. He has the powers of search conferred by s 139.

A warrant issued in England, Wales or Scotland for the arrest of a person charged with an offence may (without any endorsement) be executed in Northern Ireland by any officer of the country of issue or of the country of execution as well as by any other persons within the directions in the warrant. An officer executing a warrant issued in England or Wales may use reasonable force. He has the powers of search conferred by s 139. An officer executing a warrant issued in Scotland has the same powers and duties, and the person arrested the same rights, as they would have had if the warrant had been executed in Scotland.

A person arrested in pursuance of a warrant must be taken, as soon as reasonably practicable, to any place to which he is committed by, or may be conveyed under, the warrant.

Any other person within the directions in a warrant executing that warrant under this section has the same powers and duties, and the person arrested the same rights, as they would have had if execution had been in the country of issue by the person within those directions.

In this section "judicial authority" means any justice of the peace or the judge of any court exercising jurisdiction in criminal proceedings. Any reference to a part of the United Kingdom in which a warrant may be executed includes a reference to the adjacent sea and other waters within the seaward limits of the territorial sea.

An officer may exercise a power under this section only in the exercise of a function relating to tax (including duties and tax credits): see FA 2007 s 87(4).

This section applies to a warrant of commitment and a warrant to arrest a witness issued by a judicial authority in England, Wales or Northern Ireland as it applies to a warrant for arrest.

This section applies to a warrant for committal, a warrant to imprison (or to apprehend and imprison) and a warrant to arrest a witness issued by a judicial authority in Scotland as it applies to a warrant for arrest.

This section applies as respects a warrant issued under Powers of Criminal Courts (Sentencing) Act 2000 Sch 1 para 3(2) as it applies to a warrant issued in England or Wales for the arrest of a person charged with an offence.

137. Cross-border powers of arrest etc

An HMRC officer in England and Wales may arrest a suspect in Scotland or Northern Ireland if: (1) it appears to the officer that it would have been lawful for him to have made the arrest if the suspect had been in England and Wales; (2) he has reasonable grounds for suspecting that an offence has been committed or attempted in England or Wales; and (3) he has reasonable grounds for suspecting that the suspected person is in Scotland or in Northern Ireland. He may make the arrest without a warrant. An officer arresting a person under this provision may use reasonable force. He has the powers of search conferred by CJPOA 1994 s 139.

An officer in Scotland can exercise the same powers of arrest or detention as it would be competent for him to exercise in Scotland if: (1) it appears to him that it would have been lawful for him to have exercised the powers had the suspected person been in Scotland; (2) he has reasonable grounds for suspecting that an offence has been committed or attempted in Scotland; and (3) he has reasonable grounds for suspecting that the suspect is in England, Wales or Northern Ireland. An officer arresting a person under this provision has the same powers and duties as he would have had if the arrest had been in Scotland. The person arrested has the same rights as he would have had if the arrest had been in Scotland. An officer detaining a person under this provision must act in accordance with the provisions applied by s 138(2) (as modified by s 138(6)).

An officer in Northern Ireland may arrest a suspect in England, Wales or Scotland if: (1) either (*a*) the suspected offence is an arrestable offence, or (*b*) (in the case of any other offence) it appears to him that service of a summons is impracticable or inappropriate for any of the reasons specified in s 138(3); (2) he has reasonable grounds for suspecting that an offence has been committed or attempted in Northern Ireland; and (3) he has reasonable grounds for suspecting that the suspect is in England, Wales or Scotland. He may make the arrest without a warrant. An officer arresting a person under this provision may use reasonable force. He has the powers of search conferred by s 139.

An officer who has arrested or detained a person under this section must, as soon as practicable:

(a) (if he arrested the person in Scotland) take the arrested person to either (i) the nearest convenient designated office of Revenue and Customs in England or Northern Ireland, or (ii) a designated office of Revenue and Customs in England, Wales or Northern Ireland in which the offence is being investigated;

(b) (if he arrested him in England or Wales) take the arrested person to either: (i) the nearest convenient office of Revenue and Customs in Scotland or (ii) a designated office of Revenue and Customs in England and Wales and Northern Ireland in which the offence is being investigated;

(c) (if he detained him in England or Wales) take the detained person to either: (i) the nearest convenient office of Revenue and Customs in Scotland, or (ii) the nearest convenient designated office of Revenue and Customs in England or Wales;

(d) (if he arrested him in Northern Ireland) to take the arrested person to either (i) the nearest convenient designated office of Revenue and Customs in England or Wales, or (ii) the nearest convenient designated office of Revenue and Customs in England and Wales in which the offence is being investigated, (iii) the nearest convenient office of Revenue and Customs in Scotland, or (iv) an office of Revenue and Customs within a sheriffdom in which the offence is being investigated;

(e) (if he detained him in Northern Ireland) to take the person detained to either (i) the nearest convenient office of Revenue and Customs in Scotland, or (ii) the nearest convenient designated office of Revenue and Customs in Northern Ireland.

The term "arrestable offence" is defined.

This section does not prejudice any power of arrest conferred apart from this section.

An officer may exercise a power under this section only in the exercise of a function relating to tax (including duties and tax credits): see CJPOA 1994 s 136(9) and FA 2007 s 87(4).

138. Powers of arrest etc: supplementary provisions

Where a person is detained under s 137(2), Criminal Law (Consolidation) (Scotland) Act 1995 ss 24(2)–(7), 25(1)–(4) (as modified by this section) and Criminal Procedure (Scotland) Act 1995 s 18 apply in the same manner as they apply to detention under Criminal Justice Act 1980 s 2. The modification referred to is that the reference to detention being terminated not more than six hours after it begins is construed as a reference to its being terminated not more than four hours after the person's arrival at the HMRC office to which he is taken under s 137(7)(*c*).

The reasons referred to in s 137(6)(*b*) are that:

(a) the name of the suspected person is unknown to, and cannot readily be ascertained by, the HMRC officer;

(b) the officer has reasonable grounds for doubting whether a name furnished by the suspected person as his name is his real name;

(c) either: (i) the suspect has failed to furnish a satisfactory address for service, or (ii) the officer has reasonable grounds for doubting whether an address furnished by the suspect is a satisfactory address for service. An address is satisfactory for this purpose if it appears to the officer that the suspect will be at it for a sufficiently long period for it to be possible to serve him with process, or that some other person specified by the suspect will accept service of process for the suspect at it;

(d) the officer has reasonable grounds for believing that arrest is necessary to prevent the suspected person (i) causing physical injury to himself or any other person, (ii) suffering physical injury, (iii) causing loss of or damage to property, (iv) committing an offence against public decency, or (v) causing an unlawful obstruction of a highway or road. However, head (iv) applies only where members of the public going about their normal business cannot reasonably be expected to avoid the person to be arrested; or

(e) the officer has reasonable grounds for believing that arrest is necessary to protect a child or other vulnerable person from the suspected person.

An officer may exercise a power under this section only in the exercise of a function relating to tax (including duties and tax credits): see CJPOA 1994 s 136(9) and FA 2007 s 87(4).

139. Search powers available on arrests under sections 136 and 137

An HMRC officer may exercise the following powers in relation to a person arrested under CJPOA 1994 s 136(1), 136(2)(*b*), 136(3)(*a*), 137(1) or 137(3).

First, the officer may search the person if he has reasonable grounds for believing that the person may present a danger to himself or others. The officer may seize and retain anything he finds if he has reasonable grounds for believing that the person searched might use it to cause physical injury to himself or to any other person.

Second, the officer may search the person for anything which he might use to assist him to escape from lawful custody or which might be evidence relating to an offence. He may seize and retain anything he finds, other than an item subject to legal privilege, if he has reasonable grounds for believing that (*a*) the person might use it to assist him to escape from lawful custody; or (*b*) that the thing is evidence of an offence, or has been obtained in consequence of the commission of an offence. However:

- a search is confined to what is reasonably required for the purpose of discovering any such thing or any such evidence;
- a person is not required to remove any of his clothing (other than an outer coat, jacket, headgear, gloves or footwear) in public, but his mouth may be searched;
- the officer must have reasonable grounds for believing that the person may have something concealed on him for which a search is permitted.

Thirdly, the officer may enter and search any premises for evidence relating to the offence for which the person was arrested. The person must have been on the premises when, or immediately before, he was arrested. The officer must have reasonable grounds for believing that there is evidence for which a search is permitted. If the premises consist of two or more separate dwellings, the power to search is limited to: (*a*) any dwelling in which the arrest took place or in which the person arrested was immediately before his arrest; and (*b*) any parts of the premises which the occupier of any such dwelling uses in common with the occupiers of any other dwellings comprised in the premises.

The terms "item subject to legal privilege", "premises" and "offshore installation" (which is relevant to the definition of "premises") are defined.

This section does not affect the power conferred by Terrorism Act 2000 s 43.

An officer may exercise a power under this section only in the exercise of a function relating to tax (including duties and tax credits): see CJPOA 1994 s 136(9) and FA 2007 s 87(4).

Finance Act 1996

1996 Chapter 8

PART VII MISCELLANEOUS AND SUPPLEMENTAL

MISCELLANEOUS: INDIRECT TAXATION

197. Setting of rates of interest (V5.196; V5.361–V5.365)

The rate of interest payable to or by the Commissioners (see VATA 1994 ss 74, 78) may be specified in regulations or determined in accordance with a scheme specified by regulations. For the scheme specified, see Air Passenger Duty and Other Indirect Taxes (Interest Rate) Regulations 1998, SI 1998/1461 regs 4–6. If the rate of interest changes in accordance with the scheme, the Commissioners must make an Order specifying the new rate of interest and the day from which it has effect.

The rates of interest applicable on 6 July 1998 were specified by Air Passenger Duty and Other Indirect Taxes (Interest Rate) Regulations 1998, SI 1998/1461 regs 4(1) and 5(1). The rates for the purposes of VATA 1994 ss 74 and 78 were 9.5% and 6% respectively. For the rates of interest previously in force, see Air Passenger Duty and Other Indirect Taxes (Interest Rate) Regulations 1998, SI 1998/1461 reg 8 Tables 3 and 7 respectively. The rates of interest substituted by Order since 6 July 1998 are as follows:

Order made	*Effective date*	*Rate applicable for VATA 1994 s 74 %*	*Rate applicable for VATA 1994 s 78 %*	*Authority*
18.12.98	6.1.99	8.50	5.00	News Release 31/98, 23.12.98
22.2.99	6.3.99	7.50	4.00	News Release 7/99, 3.3.99
20.1.00	6.2.00	8.50	5.00	News Release 6/00, 4.2.00
24.4.01	6.5.01	7.50	4.00	Business Brief 7/01, 4.5.01
23.10.01	6.11.01	6.50	3.00	Business Brief 15/01, 5.11.01
3.9.03	6.9.03	5.50	2.00	Business Brief 17/03, 11.9.03
3.12.03	5.12.03	6.50	3.00	Business Brief 25/03, 8.12.03
1.9.04	6.9.04	7.50	4.00	Business Brief 24/04, 8.9.04
Not identified	6.9.05	6.50	3.00	HMRC website
Not identified	6.9.06	7.50	4.00	HMRC website
Not identified	6.8.07	8.50	5.00	HMRC website
Not identified	6.1.08	7.50	4.00	HMRC website
Not identified	6.11.08	6.50	3.00	HMRC website

Order made	*Effective date*	*Rate applicable for VATA 1994 s 74 %*	*Rate applicable for VATA 1994 s 78 %*	*Authority*
Not identified	6.12.08	5.50	2.00	HMRC website
Not identified	6.1.09	4.50	1.00	HMRC website
Not identified	27.1.09	3.50	0.00	HMRC website
Not identified	24.3.09	2.50	0.00	HMRC website

This section has effect for periods beginning on 1 April 1997: see Finance Act 1996 section 197 (Appointed Day) Order 1997, SI 1997/1015 art 2.

Finance Act 1997

1997 Chapter 16

PART III VALUE ADDED TAX

37. Supplies to non-taxable persons etc (V4.115)

VATA 1994 Sch 10 paras 2(3A) (repealed) and 3(8A) (repealed) do not have effect in relation to any supply made after 26 November 1996.

PART IV PAYMENTS AND OVERPAYMENTS IN RESPECT OF INDIRECT TAXES

VALUE ADDED TAX

47. Repayments and assessments: time limits (V5.151–V5.166)

From 18 July 1997, an amount paid to the Commissioners in error is repayable by them only if it is claimed within three years (see VATA 1994 s 80(4)). This rule is modified if the person commenced appeal proceedings before 18 July 1996 and subsequently claimed repayment of: (1) the amount in dispute; or (2) a corresponding amount paid to the Commissioners before the earlier of 18 July 1996 and the time when proceedings were commenced. If the appeal is successful, the Commissioners are liable to repay the amount claimed. However, this liability does not extend to amounts paid to them more than three years before the time when proceedings were commenced.

The absence of transitional arrangements has given rise to a long line of litigation and attempts to remedy this deficiency on an extra-statutory basis: see, in particular, *Marks and Spencer plc v C & E Comrs* (case C-62/00) [2002] STC 1036, ECJ; Business Briefs 22/02 (5 August 2002) and 27/02 (7 October 2002); Revenue and Customs Brief 7/08, 20 February 2008. A statutory transitional period has now been provided: see FA 2008 s 121.

In so far as this section amends VATA 1994 s 77(1), (4), it is repealed by FA 2008 Sch 39 para 63(*c*) from 1 April 2010: see FA 2008 s 118(2), (3); the Finance Act 2008, Schedule 39 (Appointed Day, Transitional Provision and Savings) Order 2009, SI 2009/403, art 2(2).

49. Transitional provision for set-offs etc (V5.151–V5.166)

During the period 18 July 1996 to 3 December 1996 inclusive, the Commissioners may have offset a repayment of overpaid VAT due to a person ("the credit") against all or part of an amount of VAT, penalty, interest or surcharge to which he became liable before 4 December 1996 ("the debit"). All or part of the credit may cease to be repayable following the three-year time limit for repayments introduced by FA 1997 s 47. In consequence, all or part of the debit may not have been discharged by way of set-off. Where this is so, the Commissioners may assess the amount which has not been discharged to their best judgement. They must notify this amount to the person concerned.

The assessment is made in accordance with VATA 1994 s 78A(2)–(8), and thus carries interest under VATA 1994 s 74 (as modified by s 78A(6), (7)). For the detailed provisions, see VATA 1994 s 78A. An appeal lies to a tribunal against the assessment, or the amount of the assessment.

The person is not liable to penalties or surcharge in respect of his failure to pay the amount which has not been discharged.

An amount may be corrected or adjusted under VAT Regulations 1995, SI 1995/2518, regs 34, 38 only if it could be set-off under VATA 1994 s 81(3).

ENFORCEMENT OF PAYMENT

51. Enforcement by distress (V5.173)

The Commissioners may make regulations authorising distress to be levied on the goods or chattels of a person refusing or neglecting to pay an amount of VAT or an amount recoverable as if it were VAT. For the regulations made, see Distress for Customs and Excise Duties and Other Indirect Taxes Regulations 1997, SI 1997/1431. The regulations do not have effect in Scotland.

This section came into force on 1 July 1997: see Finance Act 1997 sections 52 and 53 (Appointed Day) Order 1997, SI 1997/1432.

Tribunals, Courts and Enforcement Act 2007 ss 62(3), 146, Sch 13 para 126, Sch 23 Part 3 insert a new s 51(A1), amend s 51(1) and repeal s 51(7) from a day to be appointed by order made under s 124(4) of the 2007 Act. No order has been made to date. The new s 51(A1) is repealed by FA 2008 Sch 43 para 6 from a day to be appointed by order made under FA 2008 s 129(4). No order has been made to date.

52. Enforcement by diligence (V5.173)

[Repealed.]

PART VIII MISCELLANEOUS AND SUPPLEMENTAL

OBTAINING INFORMATION

110. Obtaining information from social security authorities (V1.270)

The Social Security departments hold information relating to their social security functions. These functions include those relating to social security contributions, social security benefits, national insurance numbers and the jobseeker's allowance.

A person holding this information is entitled to supply it to the Commissioners for one or more of the following uses:

(a) the prevention, detection, investigation or prosecution of criminal offences within the Commissioners' jurisdiction;
(b) the prevention, detection or investigation of conduct subject to civil penalties;
(c) the assessment or determination of civil penalties;
(d) verifying information given to the Commissioners;
(e) amending or supplementing the information in (*d*); and
(f) use in legal or other proceedings relating to the matters in (*a*)–(*e*).

This section came into force on 2 July 1997: see Finance Act 1997 section 110 (Appointed Day) Order 1997, SI 1997/1603.

Finance Act 1999

1999 Chapter 16

PART II VALUE ADDED TAX

13. Gold (V5.143; V6.151)

The Commissioners' powers to make regulations are extended. For the regulations made, see the VAT (Amendment) (No 4) Regulations 1999, SI 1999/3114. These regulations amend the VAT Regulations 1995, SI 1995/2518. The provisions of VATA 1994 apply to those regulations, and to records kept in accordance with those regulations, in the same manner as they apply to regulations made under VATA 1994 Sch 11 para 6(1) and to records kept in accordance with those regulations.

HM Treasury's powers to make orders under VATA 1994 ss 31(2), 37(1) are extended. For the orders made, see the VAT (Importation of Investment Gold) Relief Order 1999, SI 1999/3115; and the VAT (Investment Gold) Order 1999, SI 1999/3116.

This section implemented Directive 98/80/EC (investment gold).

16. Groups of companies

This section introduces Sch 2.

PART VIII MISCELLANEOUS AND SUPPLEMENTAL

131. Economic and monetary union: taxes and duties

The Commissioners can incur expenditure in order to exercise their revenue functions if the UK moves to the third stage of economic and monetary union.

132. Power to provide for use of electronic communications

The Commissioners can make regulations to facilitate the delivery of information and making of payments by electronic means. For the regulations made, see the VAT Regulations 1995, SI 1995/2518, regs 25(4A)–(4L), 40(2A).

133. Use of electronic communications under other provisions

The Commissioners' existing power to make regulations regarding delivery of information and making of payments include the powers conferred by s 132.

SCHEDULES

SCHEDULE 2 VAT: GROUPS OF COMPANIES (SECTION 16)

Transitional provisions

6.—The terms "old law" and "new law" are defined.

Membership of a group formed under the old law is unaffected by the new law, but the relevant applications are deemed to have been made under the new law.

An application under the old law which is refused, or takes effect, after 29 July 1999 is deemed to be made under the new law but takes effect under the old law.

Membership of a VAT group cannot be terminated on eligibility grounds before 1 January 2000 if the application for membership, although made under the old law, is deemed to have been made under the new law.

An application received after 29 July 1999 is treated as an application under the new law.

Access to Justice Act 1999

1999 Chapter 22

PART I LEGAL SERVICES COMMISSION

COMMISSION

1. Legal Services Commission

The Legal Services Commission (referred to as "the Commission") is brought into being. It has functions relating to the Community Legal Service and the Criminal Defence Service.

5. Funding of services

The Legal Services Commission is required to establish and maintain a fund known as "the Community Legal Service Fund". Services forming part of the Community Legal Service are funded from the Community Legal Service Fund.

6. Services which may be funded

The Legal Services Commission is required to set priorities in funding services as part of the Community Legal Service. These priorities are set in accordance with any directions given by the Lord Chancellor and after taking into account the need for specified services.

The Commission is not permitted to fund any of the services specified in Sch 2. However, the Lord Chancellor may, by direction, require the Commission to fund any of those services in circumstances specified in the direction. The Lord Chancellor must either publish the direction or require the Commission to do so. For the directions made relevant to VAT, see Appendix 17.

The Lord Chancellor may authorise the Commission to fund services within Sch 2 in an individual case if the Commission so requests.

SCHEDULES

SCHEDULE 2 COMMUNITY LEGAL SERVICE: EXCLUDED SERVICES (SECTION 6)

The services which may not be funded as part of the Community Legal Service include services consisting of the provision of help (beyond the provision of general information about the law and the legal system and the availability of legal services) in relation to:

- matters of company or partnership law (see para 1(*g*)); and
- other matters arising out of the carrying on of a business (see para 1(*h*)).

Crown Prosecution Service Inspectorate Act 2000

2000 Chapter 10

1. Inspectorate

The Attorney General is required to appoint a person as Her Majesty's Chief Inspector of the Crown Prosecution Service. The Chief Inspector may appoint inspectors and other staff to assist him in the discharge of his functions.

2. Functions

The Chief Inspector is required to:

- inspect, or arrange inspection, of the operations of the Revenue and Customs Prosecutions Office;
- report on any matter concerning the operation of the Revenue and Customs Prosecutions Office referred to him by the Attorney General; and
- submit an annual report to the Attorney General on the operation of the Revenue and Customs Prosecutions Office.

3. Short title, commencement and extent

This Act came into force on 1 October 2000: see the Crown Prosecution Service Inspectorate Act 2000 (Commencement) Order 2000, SI 2000/2423 art 2. It was extended to include the Revenue and Customs Prosecutions Office from 18 April 2005 by the Commissioners for Revenue and Customs Act 2005 s 50(5) and Sch 4 para 77 and the Commissioners for Revenue and Customs Act 2005 (Commencement) Order 2005, SI 2005/1126 art 2(2)(*h*).

Finance Act 2000

2000 Chapter 17

PART VI MISCELLANEOUS AND SUPPLEMENTARY PROVISIONS

143. Power to provide incentives to use electronic communications (A4.101)

Incentives to use electronic communications are provided in accordance with regulations. Regulations are made in respect of the matters listed in Sch 38. No regulations are currently in force in relation to VAT. For regulations revoked with effect from 22 July 2004 by VAT (Amendment) (No 3) Regulations 2004, SI 2004/1675 reg 1(2), see VAT (Electronic Communications) (Incentives) Regulations 2001, SI 2001/759.

SCHEDULE

SCHEDULE 38 REGULATIONS FOR PROVIDING INCENTIVES FOR ELECTRONIC COMMUNICATIONS (SECTION 143(1)) (A4.101)

1.—Regulations may be made by the Commissioners for providing incentives to use electronic communications in relation to: (1) the delivery of information and making of payments (see FA 1999 s 132); (2) any other communications with the tax authorities; or (3) any other communication in connection with taxation matters.

2–7.—The matters in respect of which regulations can be made are stated.

8.—Various words and phrases are defined.

Government Resources and Accounts Act 2000

2000 Chapter 20

VALUE ADDED TAX

21. Supplies by government departments

Where government departments (as defined in VATA 1994 s 41) make taxable supplies of goods or services, the Treasury can make arrangements regarding:

(a) the treatment of receipts and payments in respect of VAT in accounts; and

(b) (in so far as there is a requirement to pay receipts into the Consolidated Fund) exempting receipts in respect of VAT from that requirement.

Postal Services Act 2000

2000 Chapter 26

PART VII MISCELLANEOUS AND SUPPLEMENTARY

INVIOLABILITY OF MAILS ETC

105. Applications of customs and excise enactments to certain postal packets

Customs and excise legislation applies to goods imported or exported by post in accordance with regulations. For the regulations made, see Postal Packets (Customs and Excise) Regulations 1986, SI 1986/260; Postal Packets (Revenue and Customs) Regulations 2007, SI 2007/2195.

Duties and other charges payable in respect of postal packets can be recovered as a civil debt. In recovery proceedings, a certificate by a postal operator is evidence that duties and other charges are payable.

The term "foreign postal packet" is defined.

Finance Act 2002

2002 Chapter 23

PART 6 MISCELLANEOUS AND SUPPLEMENTARY PROVISIONS

134. Recovery of taxes etc due in other member states

Schedule 39 sets out provisions relating to the recovery of tax, duties and levies in the UK following a request made by the appropriate authority of another EU member state in accordance with Directive 2008/55/EC (which is referred to as the "Mutual Assistance Recovery Directive").

The Commissioners of Customs and Excise can lawfully disclose information to:

(a) the Inland Revenue in connection with a request for enforcement made by the competent authority of another EU member state;

(b) the competent authority in another EU member state (if the Directive requires disclosure); and

(c) the competent authority of another EU member state in connection with a request made by the Commissioners for the enforcement of a debt in that member state in accordance with the Directive.

The Inland Revenue and (in relation to agricultural levies) the relevant Minister (as defined in European Communities Act 1972 s 6) can lawfully disclose information to the Commissioners of Customs and Excise in connection with a request for enforcement made by the competent authority of another EU member state.

This section and Sch 39 can be amended, replaced or repealed by regulations in order to give effect to any amending Directive or (by virtue of FA 2004 s 322(4)) any directive giving effect to Decision 1/2003 Title 1 Chapter 2 of the EC-Andorra Joint Committee (3 September 2003).

For the transfer of the functions of the Commissioners of Customs and Excise and the Commissioners of Inland Revenue to the HMRC Commissioners, see CRCA 2005 s 5.

Directive 2008/55/EC is repealed with effect from 1 January 2012: see Directive 2010/24/EU art 29. This section and Sch 39 are accordingly repealed with effect from that date by FA 2011 Sch 25 para 17. The 2008 Directive is replaced by the 2010 Directive. For implementation of the 2010 Directive in the UK, see FA 2011 s 87 and Sch 25.

135. Mandatory e-filing

HMRC is given power to make regulations requiring specified persons to use electronic communication to deliver specified information relating to a tax or duty for which HMRC is responsible. For the regulations made in relation to VAT, see VAT (Amendment) (No 4) Regulations 2009, SI 2009/2978. These regulations amended the VAT Regulations 1995, SI 1995/2518.

SCHEDULES

General note

For the repeal of this schedule from 1 January 2012, see the commentary to s 134.

SCHEDULE 39 RECOVERY OF TAXES ETC DUE IN OTHER MEMBER STATES (SECTION 134(1))

Introduction

1.—This Schedule applies to requests made by another EU member state for recovery of tax in the UK. These are referred to as "foreign claims".

Enforcement of claims in the United Kingdom

2.—The same laws, rules and procedures apply to the recovery of both foreign claims and corresponding UK debts.

Power to make supplementary provision by regulations

3.—The equivalence of UK and foreign claims is determined in accordance with regulations. Procedural and supplementary matters for implementing Directive 2008/55/EC are specified in regulations. For the regulations made, see Recovery of Duties and Taxes Etc Due in Other Member States (Corresponding UK Claims, Procedure and Supplementary) Regulations 2004, SI 2004/674.

Proceedings on contested claims

4.—In principle, no proceedings can be brought in the UK against a foreign claim if the claim is being litigated in the relevant member state. Regulations may permit otherwise. No regulations have been made to date.

Claims determined in taxpayer's favour

5.—No proceedings can be brought in the UK if the alleged debtor has obtained a final judgment in his favour in a court or tribunal in the member state concerned.

Other supplementary provisions

6.—(V1.271; V5.175) A request by an authority in another member state is assumed to have been duly made under Directive 2008/55/EC unless the contrary is proved. The sole ground for challenging liability to the foreign claim is that no proceedings can be brought for the reason set out in para 5.

Finance Act 2003

2003 Chapter 14

PART 3 TAXES AND DUTIES ON IMPORTATION AND EXPORTATION: PENALTIES (V3.311, V5.301. V5.331)

PRELIMINARY

24. Introductory

Part 3 (comprising ss 24–41) makes provision for civil penalties in relation to a "relevant tax or duty". The taxes and duties within that term include VAT chargeable on the importation of goods from a third country (see VATA 1994 s 1(1)(*c*)), which is referred to as "import VAT". The penalties comprise an evasion penalty (see s 25) and a contravention penalty (see s 26).

This section takes effect from 27 November 2003: see s 24(7); Finance Act 2003 (Appointed Day) Order 2003, SI 2003/2985.

THE PENALTIES

25. Penalty for evasion

A person is liable to a penalty if he engages in conduct for the purpose of evading import VAT and his conduct involves dishonesty. The prescribed penalty is an amount equal to the tax evaded or sought to be evaded. "Evasion" includes obtaining a repayment, relief, exemption or deferral of payment. No liability to a penalty arises if the person is convicted of an offence, served with notice of liability to a contravention penalty (see s 26) or liable to a penalty under the VAT legislation (eg the penalty for dishonest conduct under VATA 1994 s 60).

The evasion penalty to which a body corporate is liable can be wholly or partly apportioned to a "relevant officer" in accordance with s 28. An evasion penalty can be reduced by the Commissioners (on review) or by a tribunal (on appeal against a decision on review) in accordance with s 29. Liability to a penalty is notified by way of a demand notice, as to which see ss 30–31. For appeals and reviews, see ss 33–33F and 37. For the admissibility of certain statements and document in criminal and recovery proceedings, see s 38. For the service of notices, see s 39. For civil evasion penalty investigations, see Notice No 300 (December 2003).

This section takes effect from 27 November 2003: see s 24(7); Finance Act 2003 (Appointed Day) Order 2003, SI 2003/2985.

26. Penalty for contravention of relevant rule

A person of a description prescribed in regulations is liable to a penalty if: (1) he contravenes a duty, obligation, requirement or condition prescribed by regulations; (2) the duty etc relates to import VAT; and (3) the duty etc is imposed by Community customs rules (as defined in Regulation (EEC) No 2913/92 art 1). The prescribed penalty is an amount (which may not exceed £2,500) to be prescribed in regulations. For the regulations made, see Customs (Contravention of a Relevant Rule) Regulation 2003, SI 2003/3113.

For the circumstances in which a person is not liable to a penalty, see s 26. A contravention penalty can be reduced by the Commissioners (on review) or by a tribunal (on appeal against a decision on review) in accordance with s 29. Liability to a penalty is notified by way of a demand notice, as to which see ss 30–31. For reviews, see ss 33–35. For the right of appeal, see ss 36, 37. For the admissibility of certain statements and document in criminal and recovery proceedings, see s 38. For the service of notices, see s 39. For the calculation and notification of penalties, see Notice No 301 (December 2003).

This section takes effect from 27 November 2003: see s 24(7); Finance Act 2003 (Appointed Day) Order 2003, SI 2003/2985.

For corresponding provisions in relation to a "relevant export rule" of the Community Customs Code, see Export (Penalty) Regulations 2003, SI 2003/3102. These provisions have general application.

27. Exceptions from section 26

A person is not liable to a contravention penalty (see s 26) in respect of import VAT if:

(a) he satisfies the Commissioners or, on appeal, a tribunal that there is a reasonable excuse for his conduct;
(b) he is prosecuted for an offence;
(c) he is served with a notice of liability to an evasion penalty (see s 25); or
(d) he is liable to a penalty under VATA 1994 ss 62–69A.

This section takes effect from 27 November 2003: see s 24(7); Finance Act 2003 (Appointed Day) Order 2003, SI 2003/2985.

PART 9 MISCELLANEOUS AND SUPPLEMENTARY PROVISIONS

INTERNATIONAL MATTERS

197. Exchange of information between tax authorities of member states (V1.270; V5.234)

This section does not apply to VAT after 31 December 2003. Information in relation to VAT is now exchanged in accordance with Regulation (EC) No 1798/2003 as implemented by Regulation (EC) No 1925/2004.

Regulation (EC) No 1798/2003 is recast and replaced by Regulation (EU) No 904/2010 with effect from 1 January 2012. From that date, Regulation (EC) No 1925/2004 is read in accordance with art 61 and Annex III of the 2010 Regulation.

ADMINISTRATIVE MATTERS

204. Mandatory electronic payment

HMRC may make regulations requiring the taxes and duties for which they are responsible, to be paid electronically. For the regulations made in relation to VAT, see VAT (Amendment) (No 4) Regulations 2009, SI 2009/2978. These regulations amended the VAT Regulations 1995, SI 1995/2518.

205. Use of electronic means of payment under other provisions

Any power to make subordinate legislation (ie statutory instruments) relating to the making of payments in respect of a taxation or duty matter includes a power to require those payments to be made electronically.

Income Tax (Trading and Other Income) Act 2005

2005 Chapter 5

PART 2 TRADING INCOME

CHAPTER 4 TRADE PROFITS: RULES RESTRICTING DEDUCTIONS

PENALTIES, INTEREST AND VAT SURCHARGES

54. Penalties, interest and VAT surcharges

As regards VAT matters, no deduction is allowed for the following when calculating the profits of a trade:

- a penalty under VATA 1994 ss 60–70;
- interest under VATA 1994 s 74;
- a surcharge under VATA 1994 s 59;
- a penalty under FA 2007 Sch 24 paras 1, 1A, 2; or
- a penalty under FA 2008 Sch 41 ss 1, 2.

PART 3 PROPERTY INCOME

CHAPTER 3 PROFITS OF PROPERTY BUSINESSES: BASIC RULES

CALCULATION OF PROFITS

272. Profits of a property business: application of trading income rules

As regards VAT matters, no deduction is allowed for the following when calculating the profits of a property business, no deduction is allowed for:

- a penalty under VATA 1994 ss 60–70;
- interest under VATA 1994 s 74;
- a surcharge under VATA 1994 s 59;
- a penalty under FA 2007 Sch 24 paras 1, 1A, 2; or
- a penalty under FA 2008 Sch 41 ss 1, 2.

PART 6 EXEMPT INCOME

CHAPTER 9 OTHER INCOME

OTHER

777. VAT repayment supplements

No liability to income tax arises in respect of a repayment supplement paid under VATA 1994 s 79.

PART 10 GENERAL PROVISIONS

CHAPTER 2 GENERAL CALCULATION RULES ETC

PENALTIES, INTEREST AND VAT SURCHARGES

869. Penalties, interest and VAT surcharges: non-trades etc

As regards VAT matters, no deduction is allowed for the following when calculating the profits or other income charged to income tax (other than the profits of a trade or property business), no deduction is allowed for:

- a penalty under VATA 1994 ss 60–70;
- interest under VATA 1994 s 74;
- a surcharge under VATA 1994 s 59;
- a penalty under FA 2007 Sch 24 paras 1, 1A, 2; or
- a penalty under FA 2008 Sch 41 ss 1, 2.

For identical provisions in relation to the profits of a trade or property business, see ITTOIA 2005 ss 54 and 272 respectively.

Commissioners for Revenue and Customs Act 2005

2005 Chapter 11

COMMISSIONERS AND OFFICERS

1. The Commissioners

Commissioners for Her Majesty's Revenue and Customs ("the Commissioners") are appointed by Letters Patent. A Commissioner holds office in accordance with the terms and conditions of his appointment. Commissioners act on behalf of the Crown in exercising their functions.

2. Officers of Revenue and Customs

Staff (known as officers of Revenue and Customs, but hereafter referred to as "HMRC officers") are appointed by the Commissioners. An HMRC officer holds office in accordance with the terms of his appointment. He must comply with directions of the Commissioners. An HMRC officer may continue anything begun by another officer.

3. Declaration of confidentiality

Commissioners and HMRC officers must make a declaration acknowledging the obligation of confidentiality imposed by s 18.

4. "Her Majesty's Revenue and Customs"

Commissioners (see s 1) and HMRC officers (see s 2) are collectively referred to as Her Majesty's Revenue and Customs ("HMRC").

FUNCTIONS

5. Commissioners' initial functions

The Commissioners are responsible for:

- the collection of taxes, duties, national insurance contributions and other revenue formerly the responsibility of the Commissioners of Inland Revenue or the Commissioners of Customs and Excise;
- the payment and management of tax credits formerly the responsibility of the Commissioners of Inland Revenue; and
- all other functions (except those vested in the Revenue and Customs Prosecution Office under s 34) formerly the responsibility of the Commissioners of Inland Revenue or the Commissioners of Customs and Excise.

6. Officers' initial functions

Legislation in general confers specific functions on persons variously described as "an officer" (as defined in CEMA 1979 s 1(1)), "a person acting under the authority of the Commissioners of Customs and Excise", "an officer of the Commissioners of Customs and Excise", "a customs officer", "an officer of customs", "a customs and excise officer", "an officer of customs and excise" or "a collector of customs and excise". In principle, these functions now vest in an HMRC officer (as to which, see s 2). However, this does not apply to:

- the matters listed in Sch 1 (known as "former inland Revenue matters") (see ss 6(3), 7(4)); or

- the matters listed in s 35 for which the Revenue and Customs Prosecution Office is now responsible (see s 6(3)).

9. Ancillary powers

Except in relation to matters for which the Revenue and Customs Prosecution Office is now responsible (see s 35), the Commissioners (see s 1) may do:

- anything necessary or expedient when exercising their functions; and
- anything incidental or conducive to exercising their functions.

EXERCISE OF FUNCTIONS

11. Treasury directions

The Commissioners must comply with Treasury directions when exercising their functions.

16A. Charter of standards and values

The Commissioners are required to prepare a Charter. The Charter must state the standards of behaviour and values to which HMRC will aspire when dealing with people in the course of exercising their functions. For the text of the Charter, see Appendix 18.

The Commissioners must regularly review the Charter, publish revisions or revised versions when appropriate, and report annually on the extent to which HMRC have met the Charter standards and values.

INFORMATION

17. Use of information

Information acquired in connection with one function may be used in connection with another one unless this is prohibited or restricted by UK law or an agreement to which the UK (or the UK government) is a party.

18. Confidentiality

Revenue and Customs officials (as defined in s 18(4)(*a*)) are prohibited from disclosing information held by the Revenue and Customs (as defined in s 17(3)) in connection with a function of the Commissioners or an HMRC officer.

However, this does not prevent a disclosure being made in any of the following circumstances:

- it does not contravene any restriction imposed by the Commissioners;
- it is made in the public interest (under s 20);
- it is made to a prosecuting authority (under s 21);
- it is made for the purposes of civil proceedings;
- it is made for the purposes of a criminal investigation;
- it is made for the purposes of criminal proceedings;
- it is made under a court order;
- it is made for the purposes of an inspection (under s 27);
- it is made to the Independent Police Complaints Commission (under s 28); or
- it is made with the consent of the person(s) to whom the information relates.

19. Wrongful disclosure

A person commits an offence by disclosing information contrary to s 18(1) if:

- the information relates to a person;
- the information was acquired as a result of, or held in connection with, a function exercised by the Commissioners or an HMRC officer in respect of the person; or

- the identity of the person is specified in the disclosure or can be deduced from it.

The prescribed penalty is two years' imprisonment, a fine or both (conviction on indictment), or twelve months' imprisonment, a fine not exceeding the statutory maximum or both (summary conviction).

23. Freedom of information

Information is exempt information by virtue of Freedom of Information Act 2000 s 44(1)(*a*) if its disclosure would give rise to an offence under s 19.

PROCEEDINGS

24. Evidence

A document is treated as being issued or signed by the Commissioners (or with their authority) unless the contrary is proved. It is admissible in any legal proceedings.

A document certifying any of the following matters is treated as accurate unless the contrary is proved.

- a specified person was appointed as a Commissioner or HMRC officer on a specified date; and
- a function was delegated to a specified Commissioner, committee or person.

A certified copy of a document acquired by the Commissioners is admissible in any legal proceedings to the same extent as the document itself.

Documentary Evidence Act 1868 s 2 applies in a modified form.

25. Conduct of civil proceedings

An HMRC officer or person authorised by the Commissioners may conduct civil proceedings in a magistrates' court or in the sheriff court. An officer or authorised person may conduct county court proceedings for the recovery of amounts payable to the Commissioners. A solicitor employed by the Commissioners may act as a solicitor in connection with civil proceedings. A court must grant rights of audience for these purposes.

25A. Certificates of debt

An HMRC officer may provide a document certifying that, to the best of his knowledge and belief, a specified sum due to the Commissioners has not been paid. In principle, the document is sufficient evidence of that fact. However, other legislation may provide that it is conclusive evidence. The document is treated as a certificate until the contrary is proved.

26. Rewards

The Commissioners may pay rewards.

INSPECTION AND COMPLAINTS

27. Inspection

Regulations may confer functions on HM Inspectors of Constabulary (and their Scottish and Northern Ireland equivalents) in relation to the Commissioners and HMRC officers. For the regulations currently in force, see Revenue and Customs (Inspections) Regulations 2005, SI 2005/1133.

28. Complaints and misconduct: England and Wales. (A5.403)

Regulations may confer functions on the Independent Police Complaints Commission in relation to the Commissioners and HMRC officers. For the regulations currently in force, see Revenue and Customs (Complaints and Misconduct) Regulations 2010, SI 2010/1813.

OFFENCES

30. Impersonation

A person commits an offence if he pretends to be a Commissioner or HMRC officer with a view to obtaining admission to premises, information or any other benefit.

31. Obstruction

A person commits an offence if he obstructs an HMRC officer, a person acting on behalf of the Commissioners, a person acting on behalf of an HMRC officer or a person assisting an HMRC officer.

32. Assault

A person commits an offence if he assaults an HMRC officer.

33. Power of arrest

If so authorised by the Commissioners, an HMRC officer may arrest a person in connection with an offence under CRCA 2005 ss 30–32.

PROSECUTIONS

34. The Revenue and Customs Prosecution Office

The Attorney General must appoint an individual as Director of Revenue and Customs Prosecutions. He may appoint staff. The Director and his staff are collectively referred to as the Revenue and Customs Prosecutions Office.

35. Functions

The Director of Revenue and Customs Prosecutions may institute and conduct criminal proceedings in England and Wales relating to criminal investigations carried out by the Commissioners, an HMRC officer or a person acting on behalf of either.

The Director must:

- take over the conduct of criminal proceedings instituted in England and Wales by the Commissioners, an HMRC officer or a person acting on behalf of either; and
- provide such advice as he thinks appropriate regarding criminal investigations and criminal proceedings.

36. Functions: supplemental

The Director of Revenue and Customs Prosecutions discharges his functions under the superintendence of the Attorney General.

42. Inspection

This section extends the functions of the Chief Inspector of the Crown Prosecution Service. For the Chief Inspector and his functions in relation to the Revenue and Customs Prosecution Office, see Crown Prosecution Service Inspectorate Act 2000 ss 1 and 2.

GENERAL

50. Consequential amendments, etc

Insofar as appropriate, references to the Commissioners of Customs and Excise (however expressed) and customs and excise officers (however expressed) are treated as references to the Commissioners and HMRC officers respectively.

51. Interpretation

Various words and phrases are defined.

53. Commencement

This Act came into force in accordance with the Commissioners for Revenue and Customs Act 2005 (Commencement) Order 2005, SI 2005/1126. This provides that ss 5–8, 16, 35, 36, 50, 52, 54 and Schs 1, 2 (Part 1), 4, 5 came into force on 18 April 2005 and that the remaining provisions came into force at 5.45pm on 7 April 2005.

Serious Organised Crime and Police Act 2005

2005 Chapter 15

PART 1 THE SERIOUS ORGANISED CRIME AGENCY

CHAPTER 1 SOCA: ESTABLISHMENT AND ACTIVITIES

ESTABLISHMENT OF SOCA

1. Establishment of Serious Organised Crime Agency

The Serious Organised Crime Agency ("SOCA") is established. It replaced the National Criminal Intelligence Service ("NCIS") and the National Crime Squad ("NCS") with effect from 1 April 2006, see the NCIS and NCS (Abolition) Order 2006, SI 2006/540.

FUNCTIONS

2. Functions

SOCA's function is to prevent and detect serious organised crime and mitigate its consequences. In relation to conduct involving revenue fraud, SOCA's powers are subject to those of the Commissioners, who must agree to actions taken by the organisation in relation to the fraud. Revenue fraud is defined to include fraud relating to taxes, duties and National Insurance contributions.

3. Functions of SOCA as to information relating to crime

Information relevant to the prevention, detection or reduction of crime held by SOCA may be disseminated to police forces within the UK and equivalent bodies in Jersey, Guernsey and the Isle of Man.

USE AND DISCLOSURE OF INFORMATION

33. Disclosure of information by SOCA

Subject to the provisions of the Data Protection Act 1998, the Regulation of Investigatory Powers Act 2000 and certain other restrictions (see SOCPA 2005 s 35), SOCA may disclose information it has obtained for "permitted purposes". These include the prevention, detection, investigation or prosecution of criminal offences in the UK or overseas.

34. Disclosure of information to SOCA

A person disclosing information to SOCA does not breach any obligation of confidence or other restriction, subject to the provisions of the Data Protection Act 1998 and the Regulation of Investigatory Powers Act 2000.

Information may not be disclosed to SOCA on behalf of the Commissioners unless the Commissioners so authorise.

35. Restrictions on further disclosure

Information disclosed by SOCA must not be further disclosed except for a permitted purpose or a purpose connected with the reason for the disclosure to SOCA, and without SOCA's consent.

GENERAL DUTIES OF POLICE ETC

37. General duty of police etc to assist SOCA

It is the duty of every constable, HMRC officer and member of the armed forces or coastguard to assist SOCA in its functions in relation to serious organised crime.

PROSECUTIONS

40. Functions of Director of Revenue & Customs Prosecutions as to persons arrested for designated offence

Police and Criminal Evidence Act 1984 ss 37–37B are given effect in relation to a person arrested by SOCA following a designated offence, and references to the Director of Public Prosecutions are read as references to the Director of Revenue & Customs Prosecutions.

MISCELLANEOUS AND SUPPLEMENTARY

42. Interpretation of Chapter 1

Various terms are defined.

CHAPTER 2 SOCA: SPECIAL POWERS OF DESIGNATED STAFF

DESIGNATIONS

43. Designation of SOCA staff as persons having powers of constable etc

A staff member of SOCA may be designated as having the powers of a constable, an HMRC officer or an immigration officer by the Director General of SOCA.

44. Delegation of power to designate

The Director General may delegate his power to designate SOCA staff as having the powers set out in SOCPA 2005 s 43 to an employee of SOCA of a level specified in an order made by the Secretary of State.

45. Modification of withdrawal of designation

The designation made to a member of staff in accordance with SOCPA 2005 s 43 may be varied or withdrawn by the Director General of SOCA, or a person to whom the Director General has designated his powers under s 44 above.

POWERS EXERCISABLE

48. Person having customs powers

A designated person has the same customs powers as an HMRC officer and is authorised to exercise powers in relation to customs matters in the same way as an HMRC officer. "Customs matter" means any matter other than matters dealt with by the former Inland Revenue or any tax or duty not mentioned in CRCA 2005 Sch 1.

SUPPLEMENTARY

52. Modification of enactments

The Secretary of State may amend any enactment relating to designated persons or the exercise of their powers. The Commissioners must be consulted before any enactment conferring functions on the Commissioners or an HMRC officer.

PART 2 INVESTIGATIONS, PROSECUTIONS, PROCEEDINGS AND PROCEEDS OF CRIME

CHAPTER 1 INVESTIGATORY POWERS OF DPP ETC

INTRODUCTORY

60. Investigatory powers of DPP etc

Powers are conferred on the Director of Public Prosecutions, the Director of Revenue and Customs Prosecutions and the Lord Advocate in relation to the giving of certain notices. Various powers of delegation are also provided for.

61. Offences to which this Chapter applies

Various offences are specified. These include "lifestyle offences" under the Proceeds of Crime Act 2002, offences relating to money-laundering or fund-raising under the Terrorism Act 2000, VAT fraud and other offences under CEMA 1979.

DISCLOSURE NOTICES

62. Disclosure notices

A written disclosure notice requiring a person to answer questions, provide information or produce documents may be issued where it appears to the Investigating Authority that there are reasonable grounds for suspecting that an offence has been committed, and that the person has information or documents of substantial value to the investigation. A disclosure notice may be issued by a constable, an HMRC officer or to a designated member of SOCA, and must be counter-signed by the Investigating Authority.

CHAPTER 2 OFFENDERS ASSISTING INVESTIGATIONS AND PROSECUTIONS

71. Assistance by offender: immunity from prosecution

Where it is considered appropriate by a specified prosecutor, a person may be given immunity from prosecution through the means of a written immunity notice. The notice becomes void if the person fails to comply with any conditions contained therein. An immunity notice cannot be given in respect of cartel offences under Enterprise Act 2002 s 188.

Specified prosecutors are the Director of Public Prosecutions, the Director of Revenue and Customs Prosecutions, the Director of the Serious Fraud Office and the Director of Public Prosecutions for Northern Ireland.

CHAPTER 6 PROCEEDS OF CRIME

97. Confiscation orders by magistrates' courts

The Secretary of State may provide for confiscation orders to be issued by magistrates' courts where the amount does not exceed £10,000.

98. Civil recovery: freezing orders

New Proceeds of Crime Act 2002 ss 245A to 245D (Property Freezing Orders) and 255A to 255F (Prohibitory Property Orders (Scotland)) are inserted respectively after ss 245 and 255.

A property freezing order may be granted by the court where the enforcement authority may take proceedings for a recovery order in the High Court, and there is a good arguable case that the property to which the freezing order relates is, or includes, recoverable property or associated property. In the case of associated property, the enforcement authority must have taken all reasonable steps to identify the person holding it (s 245A).

The order may be varied or set aside by the court at any time (s 245B).

The power to vary a property freezing order includes the power to specify exclusions from the order, for example, to enable a person to meet reasonable living expenses or to carry on any trade, business, profession or occupation. In the case of exclusions made to enable legal expenses to be met, the court must ensure that the exclusion is limited to reasonable legal expenses which may be incurred (s 245C).

While a property freezing order has effect, the court may stay any action or other legal process in respect of the property under the order, and no distress may be levied against the property to which the order applies without leave of the court. In particular, if the frozen property is leased real estate, the landlord or other person to whom rent is payable is not able to exercise the right of forfeiture by peaceable re-entry in relation to the property in respect of the tenant's failure to pay rent, unless the court permits otherwise.

Equivalent provisions to those described above are given effect under Scottish law under the Prohibitory Property Orders (Scotland) legislation (ss 255A to 255F).

99. Civil recovery: interim receivers' expenses etc

The Proceeds of Crime Act 2002 is amended to permit the Director of the Assets Recovery Agency to apply proceeds realised under civil recovery proceedings in satisfaction of trustees' or interim receivers' remuneration and expenses.

100. Detention of seized cash: meaning of "48 hours"

It is clarified that, in calculating the 48-hour period mentioned in Proceeds of Crime Act 2002 s 295, no account is taken of Saturdays, Sundays or bank holidays under the Banking and Financial Dealings Act 1971, Christmas Day, Good Friday or court holidays in Scotland.

101. Appeal in proceedings for forfeiture of cash

An appeal may be made against an order for the forfeiture of cash (Proceeds of Crime Act 2002 s 298), or the decision not to grant such an order, within 30 days of the court's decision.

102. Money laundering: defence where overseas conduct is legal under local law

A person does not commit an offence under Proceeds of Crime Act 2002 ss 327 to 332 if he knows or believes on reasonable grounds that the relevant criminal conduct occurred in a particular country or territory outside the UK and the conduct was not, at the time, unlawful under local criminal law applicable to the country or territory, and is not a description prescribed by the Secretary of State.

103. Money laundering: threshold amounts

A deposit-taking body, such as a bank, does not commit a money laundering offence under Proceeds of Crime Act 2002 ss 327 to 329 if the value of the criminal property is below the threshold amount, calculated in accordance with new section 339A.

This provides that the threshold amount for acts done by a deposit-taking body is £250, or such higher amount as may be specified by an HMRC officer or a constable. Different threshold amounts may be specified for different acts done in relation to a single account. The £250 threshold may be varied by the Secretary of State.

104. Money laundering: disclosures to identify persons and property

An additional condition is introduced into Proceeds of Crime Act 2002 ss 330, 331 and 332, under which a person is treated as committing an offence if he knows or suspects, or has reasonable grounds for knowing or suspecting that a person is engaged in money laundering but fails to make the required disclosure.

In order for an offence to be committed under s 330, the person must:

(a) be able to identify the person engaged (or suspected to be engaged) in money laundering, or the whereabouts of the laundered property; or

(b) believe, or it would be reasonable to expect him to believe, that the information giving rise to the suspicion of money laundering will or may assist in the identification of the laundered property or the person engaged (or suspected to be engaged) in money laundering.

For an offence to be committed under either s 331 or 332, the person must:

(a) be able to identify the person engaged (or suspected to be engaged) in money laundering, or the whereabouts of the laundered property as a result of the disclosure made to him; or

(b) believe, or it would be reasonable to expect him to believe, that the information giving rise to the suspicion of money laundering will or may assist in the identification of the laundered property or the person engaged (or suspected to be engaged) in money laundering.

A "reasonable excuse" exemption applies under each of ss 330 to 332. A further exemption is available to professional legal advisers where the information giving rise to the suspicion of money laundering was made available under privileged circumstances.

105. Money laundering: form and manner of disclosures

An offence is committed if the person making disclosure under ss 330, 331, 332 or 338 does not do so in the form and manner prescribed by the Secretary of State, unless he has a reasonable excuse for not doing so. "Form" can include a request to the person making the disclosure to provide additional voluntary information. Where such a request is made, the form adopted must make it clear that there is no obligation to comply with the request for voluntary information. A person complying with a voluntary request is afforded the same protection in respect of a breach of any restriction on disclosure in the same way as a disclosure made under the statutory obligation.

106. Money laundering: miscellaneous amendments

A number of minor and miscellaneous amendments are made to the Proceeds of Crime Act 2002.

109. Minor and consequential amendments relating to Chapter 6

Minor and consequential amendments are made to Chapter 6.

PART 6 FINAL PROVISIONS

177. Interpretation

Various terms are defined.

178. Commencement

The Serious Organised Crime and Police Act 2005 comes into general affect on the date the Act was passed (7 April 2005). Certain parts of the Act are given effect on different dates.

179. Short title and extent

The Act may be cited as the Serious Organised Crime and Police Act 2005. Provisions regarding its territorial extent are set out.

SCHEDULES

SCHEDULE 6 MINOR AND CONSEQUENTIAL AMENDMENTS RELATING TO CHAPTER 6 OF PART 2 (SECTION 109)

A number of minor and consequential amendments are made.

Gambling Act 2005

2005 Chapter 19

PART I INTERPRETATION OF KEY CONCEPTS

6. Gaming & game of chance

"Gaming" means playing a game of chance for a prize.

A game is a "game of chance" if it involves elements of both chance and skill, an element of chance that can be eliminated by superlative skill, or is presented as involving an element of chance. A sport is not a game of chance.

A person "plays" a game of chance whether or not there are other participants in the game, and whether or not a computer generates images or data taken to represent the actions of other participants in the game.

A "prize" means money or money's worth. It includes both a prize provided by a person organising gaming and winnings of money staked. A person plays a game of chance for a prize if he acquires a chance of winning a prize, regardless of whether or not he risks losing anything at the game.

9. Betting: general

"Betting" means making or accepting a bet on one or other of the following:

- the outcome of a race, competition or other event or process. The fact that the race etc has already occurred or been completed, and one party knows the outcome, does not prevent the transaction being a bet;
- the likelihood of anything occurring or not occurring. The fact that the thing has already occurred, or failed to occur, and that one party is aware of this, does not prevent the transaction being a bet;
- whether anything is or is not true.

PART XVIII MISCELLANEOUS AND GENERAL

353. Interpretation (V4.131)

"Real", in relation to a game, event or process, means non-virtual.

Finance Act 2006

2006 Chapter 25

PART 2 VALUE ADDED TAX

LAND

17. Buildings and land

This section enables the Treasury to substitute a new VATA 1994 Sch 10 by order. For the order made, see VAT (Buildings and Land) Order 2008, SI 2008/1146.

PART 9 MISCELLANEOUS PROVISIONS

INTERNATIONAL TAX ARRANGEMENTS

173. International tax enforcement arrangements

An Order in Council may declare that specified arrangements relating to any of the following matters have effect:

(a) exchanging information relevant to the administration, enforcement or recovery of any tax or duty imposed under UK law or the law of some or all of the territories in relation to which the arrangements have been made;
(b) recovering debts relating to those taxes or duties; and
(c) serving documents relating to those taxes or duties.

For the orders made, see International Mutual Administrative Assistance in Tax Matters Order 2007, SI 2007/2126 and International Mutual Administrative Assistance in Tax Matters Order 2011, SI 2011/1079. These orders give effect to: (1) the Convention on Mutual Administrative Assistance in Tax Matters (Strasbourg, 25 January 1988), which was ratified by the UK on 24 January 2008; and (2) the Protocol amending the Convention on International Mutual Administrative Assistance in Tax Matters (Paris, 27 May 2010), which has yet to be ratified by the UK. The taxes coved by the Convention include VAT: see art 2(1)(b)(iii)(D) of the 1988 Convention..

Ministers and civil servants are permitted to disclose relevant information to the Commissioners and to authorised HMRC officials (see CRCA 2006 s 18). The Commissioners and officials are permitted to disclose relevant information to an authorised officer of a territory to which the arrangements apply. However, before doing so they must be satisfied that that territory observes rules of confidentiality equivalent to those applicable in the UK.

175. Arrangements under section 173: recovery of debts

The Treasury may make regulations providing for the recovery, in the UK, of foreign tax debts to which international tax enforcement arrangements (see FA 2006 s 173) apply. For the regulations made, see Recovery of Foreign Taxes Regulations 2007, SI 2007/3507.

Finance Act 2007

2007 Chapter 11

PART 6 INVESTIGATION, ADMINISTRATION ETC

INVESTIGATION ETC

82. Criminal investigations: powers of Revenue and Customs

This section amends Police and Criminal Evidence Act 1984 s 114 with effect from 7 November 2007: see s 84; Finance Act 2007 (Sections 82 to 84 and Schedule 23) (Commencement) Order 2007, SI 2007/3166 art 2(a).

83. Northern Ireland criminal investigations

This section amends Police and Criminal Evidence (Northern Ireland) Order 1989, SI 1989/1341 (NI 12) art 85 with effect from 7 November 2007: see s 84(5), (6); Finance Act 2007 (Sections 82 to 84 and Schedule 23) (Commencement) Order 2007, SI 2007/3166 art 2(b).

84. Sections 82 and 83: supplementary

This section introduces Sch 22. Schedule 22 has effect from 1 December 2007: see s 84(4), (5), (6); Finance Act 2007 (Sections 82 to 84 and Schedule 23) (Commencement) Order 2007, SI 2007/3166 art 3(a).

Sections 82 and 83 came into force on 7 November 2007: see s 84(5), (6); Finance Act 2007 (Sections 82 to 84 and Schedule 23) (Commencement) Order 2007, SI 2007/3166 art 2(a), (b).

The amendments made to CRCA 2005 are not relevant to VAT.

85. Criminal investigations: Scotland

This section introduces Sch 23.

86. Search warrants

This section inserts Police and Criminal Evidence Act 1984 s 8(7).

87. Cross-border exercise of powers

The police powers in Criminal Justice and Public Order Act 1994 ss 136–139 apply to HMRC officers in a modified form when exercising a function relating to tax. These powers relate to: (1) the execution of warrants; (2) arrest or detention; and (3) search powers following arrest.

OTHER ADMINISTRATION

93. Mandatory electronic filing of returns

This section amends FA 2002 s 135 and VATA 1994 ss 76, 83, 84.

94. Mandatory electronic payment

This section amends FA 2003 ss 204, 205.

95. Payment by cheque

The Commissioners may make regulations providing that a payment by cheque to HMRC is deemed to be made when the cheque clears. For the regulations made in relation to VAT, see VAT (Amendment) (No 4) Regulations 2009, SI 2009/2978. These regulations amend the VAT Regulations 1995, SI 1995/2518.

FA 2003 s 204 is amended and VATA 1994 s 58B inserted.

97. Penalties for errors

This section introduces Sch 24. Schedule 24 comes into force in accordance with an order made by statutory instrument. For commencement provisions, see the general note to the commentary on Sch 24.

PART 7 MISCELLANEOUS

VALUE ADDED TAX AND INSURANCE PREMIUM TAX

98. VAT: joint and several liability of traders in chain of supply where tax unpaid

This section amends VATA 1994 ss 77A and 94.

99. VAT: non-business use etc of business goods

This section amends: (1) VATA 1994 Sch 4 para 5 with effect from 1 September 2007; (2) VATA 1994 Sch 4 para 9 as regards surrenders made after 20 March 2007; and (3) VATA 1994 Sch 6 para 7 from 19 July 2007 (ie Royal Assent).

100. VAT: transfers of going concerns

This section amends VATA 1994 ss 49, 94, Sch 1 para 1 and Sch 4 para 8 in relation to contracts entered into after 31 August 2007.

SCHEDULES

SCHEDULE 22 AMENDMENTS AND REPEALS CONSEQUENTIAL ON EXTENSION OF HMRC POWERS (SECTION 84)

This schedule contains amendments and repeals consequential upon the extension of police powers to HMRC. As regards VAT, the schedule repealed VATA 1994 s 72(9) and Sch 11 para 10(3)–(6) with effect from 1 December 2007: see s 84(5), (6); Finance Act 2007 (Sections 82 to 84 and Schedule 23) (Commencement) Order 2007, SI 2007/3166 art 3(a).

SCHEDULE 23 EXTENSION OF HMRC POWERS: SCOTLAND (SECTION 85)

Police and Criminal Evidence Act 1984 has limited application to criminal investigations in Scotland. The relevant procedures are primarily determined in accordance with Scottish legislation. Schedule 23 amends this legislation to align it with the 1984 Act as amended by s 82. These amendments came into force on 1 December 2007: see Sch 23 para 14; Finance Act 2007 (Sections 82 to 84 and Schedule 23) (Commencement) Order 2007, SI 2007/3166 art 3(b).

SCHEDULE 24 PENALTIES FOR ERRORS (SECTION 97)

General Note This schedule introduces a new system of penalties together with provisions relating to assessment, suspension and appeal in relation to: (1) an error in the taxpayer's document (see paras 1, 1A), and (2) under-assessment by HMRC (see para 2). The commentary below describes the application of the new system to VAT. The new system also applies to aggregates levy, air passenger duty, alcoholic liquor duties, bingo duty, capital gains tax, climate change levy, construction industry deductions, corporation tax, gaming duty, general betting duty, hydrocarbon oil duties, income tax, inheritance tax, insurance premium tax, landfill tax, lottery duty, petroleum revenue tax, pool betting duty, remote gaming duty, stamp duty land tax, stamp duty reserve tax and tobacco products duty. For the VAT penalties superseded by the new system, see para 29(*a*).

This schedule came into force in accordance with s 97(2)–(4); Finance Act 2007, Schedule 24 (Commencement and Transitional Provisions) Order 2008, SI 2008/568 arts 2–4. The relevant dates are noted in the commentary to paras 1 and 2.

This schedule was amended by FA 2008 s 122 and Sch 40, which came into force on 1 April 2009: see Finance Act 2008, Schedule 40 (Appointed Day, Transitional Provisions and Consequential Amendments) Order 2009, SI 2009/571 art 2.

This schedule was further amended by FA 2009 s 108 and Sch 57. In the absence of any specific commencement provisions, these amendments came into force from 21 July 2009 (ie Royal Assent).

TMA 1970 ss 100–103 do not apply to a penalty under this schedule: see TMA 1970 s 103A(*a*).

PART 1 LIABILITY FOR PENALTY

Error in taxpayer's document

1.—A penalty is payable by a person if:

- he gives HMRC a document of a kind listed below;
- the document contains an inaccuracy;
- the inaccuracy amounts to (or leads to): (1) the understatement of a liability to tax, (2) a false or inflated statement of a loss, or (3) a false or inflated claim to repayment of tax;
- the inaccuracy on his part was either careless (see Sch 24 para 3(1)(*a*) and (2)) or deliberate (see para 3(1)(*b*) and (*c*)).

The documents referred to are:

- a VAT return (see VAT Regulations 1995, SI 1995/2518, reg 25(1)) relating to a prescribed accounting period commencing after 31 March 2008 for which a return is required to be made after 31 March 2009;
- a repayment claim by a third country trader (see VAT Regulations 1995, SI 1995/2518 Part XXI) relating to a year commencing after 30 June 2008;
- a repayment claim by a Community trader (see VAT Regulations 1995, SI 1995/2518 Part XX) relating to a year commencing after 31 December 2008;
- a return, statement or declaration made after 1 April 2009 in connection with a repayment claim unrelated to a tax period; and
- a document likely to be relied upon by HMRC to determine, without further enquiry, a question regarding any of the following matters where the liability to pay the tax arises after 31 March 2009: (1) his liability to tax, (2) payments made by him in relation to tax, (3) other payments made by him, or (4) payments, repayments or credits given to him.

The dates stated in relation to these documents were appointed by Finance Act 2007, Schedule 24 (Commencement and Transitional Provisions) Order 2008, SI 2008/568, art 2(*a*) and (*c*)–(*e*).

The person is liable to a penalty under this provision if the document containing a careless inaccuracy is given to HMRC on his behalf: see para 18(1). However, this does not apply if the person satisfies HMRC that he took reasonable care to avoid inaccuracy: see para 18(3).

For the liability of company officers to all or part of a penalty in respect of a deliberate inaccuracy, see para 19. For the liability of partners in relation to a partnership return, see para 20. For inaccuracies resulting in a person's conviction for an offence, see para 21.

For conduct involving dishonesty which does not relate to an inaccuracy in a document, see VATA 1994 ss 60 (repealed) 61 (repealed).

No deduction is allowed for income tax or corporation tax purposes in respect of penalties under this section: see ITTOIA 2005 ss 54, 272, 869; Corporation Tax Act 2009 s 1303.

Error in taxpayer's document attributable to another person

1A.—A penalty is payable by a person ("the taxpayer") if:

- another person ("the taxpayer's agent") gives HMRC any of the following documents: (1) a VAT return, (2) a return, statement or declaration in connection with a claim, or a document likely to be relied upon by HMRC to determine, without further enquiry, a question regarding (*a*) his liability to tax, (*b*) payments made by him in relation to tax, penalties or otherwise, or (*c*) payments, repayments or credits given to him;
- the document contains an inaccuracy;
- the inaccuracy amounts to (or leads to): (1) an understatement of a liability to tax, (2) a false or inflated statement of a loss, or (3) a false or inflated claim to repayment of tax;
- the inaccuracy arose from either: (1) the taxpayer deliberately supplying false information to his agent, or (2) the taxpayer deliberately withholding information from his agent; and
- the taxpayer intended that the document should contain the inaccuracy.

The same inaccuracy may give rise to penalties under both para 1 and para 1A. If so, the aggregate of the penalties payable is capped in accordance with para 12(4). For inaccuracies resulting in a person's conviction for an offence, see para 21.

This provision has effect from 1 April 2009: see FA 2008 s 122 and Sch 40 para 3; Finance Act 2008, Schedule 40 (Appointed Day, Transitional Provisions and Consequential Amendments) Order 2009, SI 2009/571, art 2.

No deduction is allowed for income tax or corporation tax purposes in respect of penalties under this section: see ITTOIA 2005 ss 54, 272, 869; Corporation Tax Act 2009 s 1303.

Under-assessment by HMRC

2.—A penalty is payable by a person if:

- an assessment is issued to him by HMRC;
- the assessment understates his liability to tax;
- the assessment relates to a tax period commencing after 31 March 2008 (see Finance Act 2007, Schedule 24 (Commencement and Transitional Provisions) Order 2008, SI 2008/568 art 2(*b*)); and
- he (or the person who acts on his behalf: see Sch 24 para 18(2)) fails to take reasonable steps to notify HMRC that there is an under-assessment before the end of a 30-day period beginning with the date of the assessment.

In deciding what steps were reasonable, HMRC must consider whether the person (or the person who acts on his behalf: see Sch 24 para 18(2)) knew or should have known about the under-assessment and what steps it would have been reasonable for him to take in order to notify HMRC.

The person is not liable to a penalty under this provision in respect of anything done or omitted by his agent if he satisfies HMRC that he took reasonable care to avoid unreasonable failure: see para 18(3). For failures resulting in a person's conviction for an offence, see para 21.

No deduction is allowed for income tax or corporation tax purposes in respect of penalties under this section: see ITTOIA 2005 ss 54, 272, 869; Corporation Tax Act 2009 s 1303.

Degrees of culpability

3.—An inaccuracy is "careless" for the purposes of Sch 24 para 1 if it results from a person's failure to take reasonable care. The relevant person is the person liable to the penalty or a person who acts on his behalf in relation to tax: see para 18(4).

A "deliberate" inaccuracy (see para 1) may or may not be concealed. The inaccuracy is "deliberate and concealed" if a person makes arrangements to conceal it, eg by submitting false evidence in support of an inaccurate figure. The inaccuracy is "deliberate but not concealed" if a person does not make such arrangements.

An inaccuracy which was neither careless nor deliberate at the time when a document was given to HMRC is treated as "careless" if the person who gave the document subsequently discovered the inaccuracy and failed to take reasonable steps to inform HMRC. This applies whether the person giving the document was the person liable to the penalty or a person who acted on his behalf in relation to tax: see para 18(5).

PART 2 AMOUNT OF PENALTY

Standard amount

4.—Penalties under Sch 24 paras 1, 1A and 2 are a percentage of "potential lost revenue" (as defined in paras 5–8). The relevant percentages are set out in the following table:

Provision	*Description*	*Percentage*
Para 1	Careless inaccuracy	30%
Para 1	Deliberate but not concealed inaccuracy	70%
Para 1	Deliberate and concealed inaccuracy	100%
Para 1A	Inaccuracy in document submitted by agent	100%
Para 2	Failure to notify under-assessment	30%

For reductions to these percentages to reflect the quality of a disclosure, see Sch 24 para 10. For reductions in respect of special circumstances, see Sch 24 para 11.

For the application of this provision to partnerships, see Sch 24 para 20.

Potential lost revenue: normal rule

5.—"Potential lost revenue" (see Sch 24 para 4) is defined as the additional amount due or payable in respect of tax as a result of correcting an inaccuracy. It includes amounts erroneously repaid and amounts that would have been repaid if the inaccuracy had not been corrected.

For the application of this provision to partnerships, see Sch 24 para 20.

Potential lost revenue: multiple errors

6.—Where there are multiple errors and the calculation of potential lost revenue (see Sch 24 para 5) depends on the order of correction, careless inaccuracies are corrected first, followed by deliberate but not concealed inaccuracies and then deliberate and concealed inaccuracies.

Any overstatement(s) of tax payable for the same tax period are taken into account if one or more understatements in one or more documents for the tax period attract a penalty. Overstatements are offset against understatements in the following order: those where the person is not liable to a penalty first, followed by careless understatements, followed by deliberate but not concealed understatements, followed by deliberate and concealed understatements.

In the case where another person's overpayment is available to offset against an understatement, it is not be taken into account when calculating the potential lost revenue unless there is an enactment that requires or permits a person's liability to be adjusted in this way.

For the application of this provision to partnerships, see Sch 24 para 20.

Potential lost revenue: losses

7.—[Not relevant to VAT.]

Potential lost revenue: delayed tax

8.—Where an inaccuracy resulted in an amount of tax being declared later than it should have been, the potential revenue lost is five per cent of the delayed tax for each year of the delay or proportion thereof.

For the application of this provision to partnerships, see Sch 24 para 20. For timing errors, see Revenue and Customs Brief 15/11, 6 April 2011.

Reductions for disclosure

9.—Disclosure is defined as telling HMRC about the conduct giving rise to the penalty, giving HMRC reasonable assistance in quantifying the inaccuracy or under-assessment and allowing access to records for the purpose of ensuring that the inaccuracy or under-assessment is fully corrected.

The disclosure is regarded as "unprompted" if the person has no reason to believe that HMRC has discovered, or is about to discover, the relevant conduct. The disclosure is regarded as "prompted" in other circumstances. The "quality" of a disclosure takes into account the timing, nature and extent of the disclosure.

For the application of this provision to partnerships, see Sch 24 para 20.

10.—In principle, conduct within Sch 24 paras 1, 1A and 2 gives rise to a penalty of 30 per cent, 70 per cent or 100 per cent of the potential lost revenue (see para 4). HMRC must reduce the penalty to a percentage reflecting the quality (see para 9(3)) of the disclosure. The minimum percentage to be applied is 15 per cent, 35 per cent or 50 per cent respectively in the case of a prompted disclosure and zero, 20 per cent and 30 per cent respectively in the case of an unprompted disclosure. The percentage actually applied in an individual case therefore falls within the relevant range set out in the following table.

Provision	***Description***	***Prompted*** %	***Unprompted*** %
Para 1	Careless inaccuracy	15–30	0–30
Para 1	Deliberate but not concealed inaccuracy	35–70	20–70
Para 1	Deliberate and concealed inaccuracy	50–100	30–100
Para 1A	Inaccuracy in document submitted by agent	50–100	30–100
Para 2	Failure to notify under-assessment	15–30	0–30

For the application of this provision to partnerships, see Sch 24 para 20.

Special reduction

11.—HMRC may reduce a penalty, stay a penalty or agree a compromise in relation to proceedings for a penalty if they think it right to do so because of special circumstances. "Special circumstances" for this purpose do not include: (1) a person's ability to pay, or (2) the fact that a potential loss of revenue from one person is balanced by a potential overpayment by another person.

For the application of this provision to partnerships, see Sch 24 para 20.

Interaction with other penalties and late payment surcharges

12.—A document relating to a tax period giving rise to a penalty under Sch 24 para 1 or 2 may also give rise to a penalty under some other provision or to a surcharge for late payment of tax. Where this is so, the penalty under para 1 or 2 is reduced by the other penalty and/or the surcharge. However, no reduction is made in respect of a penalty imposed by the Upper Tribunal under FA 2008 Sch 36 para 50(1) in respect of continued failure to comply with an information notice or deliberate obstruction of an HMRC officer in the course of an inspection: see FA 2008 Sch 36 para 50(6)(*b*).

A penalty may arise under Sch 24 paras 1 and 1A in respect of the same inaccuracy. Where this is so, the aggregate amount of the penalties must not exceed 100 per cent of the potential lost revenue.

For the application of this provision to partnerships, see Sch 24 para 20.

PART 3 PROCEDURE

Assessment

13.—Where a person becomes liable to a penalty under Sch 24 para 1, 1A or 2, HMRC must assess the penalty and notify the person concerned. The notice must state the tax period for which the penalty is assessed. The penalty must be paid no later than 30 days after the day on which the notification was issued.

The assessment is treated for procedural purposes as though it were a tax assessment (except in a matter expressly provided for). The assessment may be enforced in the same manner as a tax assessment. The assessment may be combined with a tax assessment.

An assessment relating to a penalty under Sch 24 para 1 or 1A must be made within 12 months of the end of the appeal period for the decision correcting the understatement or, where there is no assessment, the date on which the understatement is corrected. An assessment relating to a penalty under Sch 24 para 2 must be made within 12 months of the end of the appeal period for the decision correcting the understatement.

An appeal period is defined as the period during which an appeal could be brought or (if brought) the period during which the appeal has not been determined or withdrawn.

A supplementary penalty assessment may be made if an earlier assessment was insufficient because the potential lost revenue was underestimated.

For the application of this provision to partnerships, see Sch 24 para 20.

Suspension

14.—HMRC may suspend all or part of a penalty for a careless inaccuracy under Sch 24 para 1 if they think that compliance with a condition will help the person avoid becoming liable to future penalties. If HMRC do so, they must issue a notice to the person. This must specify what part of the penalty is suspended, the period of suspension (which may not exceed two years) and the conditions to be complied with by the person. A condition may specify an action to be taken and the period in which it must be taken. The suspended amount is cancelled at the end of the suspension period if the conditions have been met. If not, the suspended amount becomes payable.

For the application of this provision to partnerships, see Sch 24 para 20(5).

Appeal

15.—A person may appeal against the imposition of a penalty, the amount of a penalty, the decision not to suspend a penalty or the conditions imposed in relation to the suspension of a penalty.

For the application of this provision to partnerships, see FA 2007 Sch 24 para 20(6).

16.—An appeal under Part 3 is treated in the same way as an appeal against an assessment to the tax concerned. This does not require a person to pay a penalty before his appeal against the assessment has been determined. The right of appeal does not apply to any other matter expressly provided for by this Act.

17.—The tribunal may confirm or cancel HMRC's decision in relation to the imposition of a penalty. As regards the amount of the penalty, the tribunal may confirm HMRC's decision or substitute another decision in accordance with HMRC's powers. In the latter case, the tribunal can take special circumstances into account in accordance with Sch 24 para 11. In doing so, the tribunal may apply the same percentage penalty to a different starting point or (if it thinks HMRC's decision regarding the application of Sch 24 para 11 was flawed) to a different extent.

A tribunal can order HMRC to suspend a penalty if it considers that HMRC's decision not to do so was flawed. Similarly, a tribunal can order HMRC to vary the conditions for suspension if it considers that HMRC's decision in this respect was flawed.

Judicial review principles are applied in determining whether a decision is "flawed".

PART 4 MISCELLANEOUS

Agency

18.—This paragraph modifies the application of Sch 24 paras 1, 2 and 3 in cases where a person acts on the taxpayer's behalf in relation to tax. These modifications are reflected in the commentary to paras 1, 2 and 3.

Companies: officers' liability

19.—Where a penalty under Sch 24 para 1 is payable by a company for a deliberate inaccuracy attributable to an officer of the company, the officer as well as the company is liable to pay the penalty. HMRC may pursue the officer for all or part of the penalty. If they do so, the relevant proportion is set out in a written notice to the officer. HMRC pursue the company for the balance (if any).

An "officer" of a body corporate other than a limited liability partnership is a director (including shadow director), manager or secretary. An "officer" of a limited liability partnership is a member. In any other case an "officer" is a director, manager, secretary or any other person managing, or purporting to manage, any of the company affairs.

For the purposes of this paragraph, a "company" means any body corporate or unincorporated association. However, it does not include a partnership, local authority or a local authority association.

Partnerships

20.—Where a penalty is imposed under Sch 24 para 1, and the inaccuracy affects the amount payable by a partner of the person, the partner is also liable to a penalty. Sch 24 paras 4–13 and 19 apply. Sch 24 para 14 applies jointly to the person's and the partner's penalty. A person may appeal against a partner's penalty in accordance with Sch 24 para 15.

Double jeopardy

21.—A penalty under Sch 24 para 1, 1A or 2 may not be imposed on a person who has been convicted of an offence relating to the same inaccuracy.

PART 5 GENERAL

Interpretation

22–28.—In so far as they apply to VAT, these paragraphs define "HMRC" (Sch 24 para 23), "understating liability to VAT" (Sch 24 para 28(*d*)), "tax period" (Sch 24 para 28(*g*)), "giving a document to HMRC" (Sch 24 para 28(*h*), (*i*)), "making a return" or "doing anything in relation to a return" (Sch 24 para 28(*j*)) and "action" (Sch 24 para 28(*k*)). They also provide that an expression used in relation to VAT has the same meaning as in VATA 1994 (Sch 24 para 27).

Consequential amendments

29.—VATA 1994 ss 63 and 64 are repealed. The scope of VATA 1994 ss 60, 61 is confined to dishonesty which does not relate to an inaccuracy in a document or a failure to notify HMRC of an under-assessment made by HMRC, and are otherwise repealed: see Finance Act

2007, Schedule 24 (Commencement and Transitional Provisions) Order 2008, SI 2008/568, art 4; Finance Act 2008, Schedule 40 (Appointed Day, Transitional Provisions and Consequential Amendments) Order 2009, SI 2009/571, art 7.

30.—[Not relevant to VAT.]

31.—[Not relevant to VAT.]

Tribunals, Courts and Enforcement Act 2007

2007 Chapter 15

General note The following commentary is confined to the provisions of Part 1 relevant to VAT which are currently in force. For commencement provisions, see TCEA 2007 s 148.

PART 1 TRIBUNALS AND INQUIRIES

CHAPTER 1 TRIBUNAL JUDICIARY: INDEPENDENCE AND SENIOR PRESIDENT

2. Senior President of Tribunals

The Senior President of Tribunals is appointed by Her Majesty on the recommendation of the Lord Chancellor. In carrying out the functions of his office, the Senior President must have regard to:

- the need for tribunals to be accessible;
- the need for tribunal proceedings to be fair;
- the need for tribunal proceedings to be handled quickly and efficiently;
- the need for tribunal members to be experts in the law or subject-matter relevant to the cases they decide; and
- the need to develop innovative methods for resolving disputes.

This section introduces Sch 1. This deals with the appointment of the Senior President and other matters relating to his office.

This section came into force on 19 September 2007: see the Tribunals, Courts and Enforcement Act 2007 (Commencement No 1) Order 2007, SI 2007/2709, art 2(*a*).

CHAPTER 2 FIRST-TIER TRIBUNAL AND UPPER TRIBUNAL

ESTABLISHMENT

3. The First-tier Tribunal and the Upper Tribunal

This section establishes:

- the First-tier Tribunal. This consists of its judges and other members. Its purpose is to exercise the functions conferred on it. For the Tribunal's functions, see s 7; and
- the Upper Tribunal. This consists of its judges and other members. Its purpose is to exercise the functions conferred on it. It is a superior court of record. For the Tribunal's functions, see s 7. For the extent to which the Upper Tribunal is amenable to judicial review, see *R (on the application of Cart) v Upper Tribunal*; *R (on the application of MR (Parkistan) v Upper Tribunal (Immigration and Asylum Chamber) and anor* [2011] UKSC 28, [2011] SWTI 1943 (England and Wales); *Eba v Advocate General for Scotland* [2011] UKSC 29, [2011] SWTI 1941 (Scotland).

The Senior President of Tribunals (see s 2) presides over both tribunals.

This section came into force on 3 November 2008: see the Tribunals, Courts and Enforcement Act 2007 (Commencement No 6 and Transitional Provisions) Order 2008, SI 2008/2696, arts 2 and 5(*a*).

MEMBERS AND COMPOSITION OF TRIBUNALS

4. Judges and other members of the First-tier Tribunal

A person is a judge or member of the First-tier Tribunal if he falls within one of the descriptions listed.

This section introduces Sch 2. This deals with the appointment of judges and members and makes further provision in connection with them.

This section came into force on 1 April 2009: see the Tribunals, Courts and Enforcement Act 2007 (Commencement No 6 and Transitional Provisions) Order 2008, SI 2008/2696, arts 2 and 5(*a*).

5. Judges and other members of the Upper Tribunal

A person is a judge or member of the Upper Tribunal if he falls within one of the descriptions listed.

This section introduces Sch 3. This deals with the appointment of judges and members and makes further provision in connection with them.

This section came into force on 3 November 2008: see the Tribunals, Courts and Enforcement Act 2007 (Commencement No 6 and Transitional Provisions) Order 2008, SI 2008/2696, arts 2 and 5(*a*).

6. Certain judges who are also judges of the First-tier Tribunal and Upper Tribunal

A person is a judge of the First-tier Tribunal (see s 4(1)(*c*)) or the Upper Tribunal (see s 5(1)(*g*)) if he falls within one of the descriptions listed.

This section came into force on 1 April 2009: see the Tribunals, Courts and Enforcement Act 2007 (Commencement No 6 and Transitional Provisions) Order 2008, SI 2008/2696, arts 2 and 5(*a*).

7. Chambers: jurisdiction and Presidents

Orders may provide for the First-tier Tribunal and Upper Tribunal to be divided into chambers. Similarly, orders may allocate the functions of the tribunals between their respective chambers. For the order made under these provisions, see First-tier Tribunal and Upper Tribunal (Chambers) Order 2008, SI 2008/2684 (as amended by SI 2009/196, SI 2009/1021 and SI 2009/1590). The position from 1 September 2009 is summarised in the following table:

Chamber	*Established by*	*Functions listed in*
First-tier Tribunal		
• General Regulatory Chamber	SI 2010/2655 art 2(*a*)	SI 2010/2655 art 3
• Health, Education and Social Care Chamber	SI 2010/2655 art 2(*b*)	SI 2010/2655 art 4
• Immigration and Asylum Chamber	SI 2010/2655 art 2(*c*)	SI 2010/2655 art 5
• Social Entitlement Chamber	SI 2010/2655 art 2(*d*)	SI 2010/2655 art 6
• Tax Chamber	SI 2010/2655 art 2(*e*)	SI 2010/2655 art 7
• War Pensions and Armed Forces Compensation Chamber	SI 2010/2655 art 2(*f*)	SI 2010/2655 art 8
Upper Tribunal		
• Administrative Appeals Chamber	SI 2010/2655 art 9(*a*)	SI 2010/2655 art 10
• Immigration and Asylum Chamber of the Upper Tribunal	SI 2010/2655 art 9(*b*)	SI 2010/2655 art 11
• Lands Chamber	SI 2010/2655 art 9(*c*)	SI 2010/2655 art 12
• Tax and Chancery Chamber	SI 2010/2655 art 9(*d*)	SI 2010/2655 art 13

This section introduces TCEA 2007 Sch 4. This deals with: (1) Chamber Presidents, judges and other members; and (2) the composition of tribunals.

This section came into force partly on 19 September 2007 and partly on 3 November 2008: see the Tribunals, Courts and Enforcement Act 2007 (Commencement No 1) Order 2007, SI

2007/2709, art 2(*a*); the Tribunals, Courts and Enforcement Act 2007 (Commencement No 6 and Transitional Provisions) Order 2008, SI 2008/2696, arts 2 and 5(*a*).

8. Senior President of Tribunals: power to delegate

This section authorises the Senior President of Tribunals to delegate any of his functions to a judge or member of the First-tier Tribunal (see s 4), a judge or member of the Upper Tribunal (see s 4) or tribunal staff appointed by the Lord Chancellor for specified purposes (see s 40(1)).

This section came into force on 3 November 2008: see the Tribunals, Courts and Enforcement Act 2007 (Commencement No 6 and Transitional Provisions) Order 2008, SI 2008/2696, arts 2 and 5(*a*).

REVIEW OF DECISIONS AND APPEALS

9. Review of decision of First-tier Tribunal

The First-tier Tribunal may review a decision made by it on a matter in a case. It may do so on its own initiative or on an application by a party to the case. For the parties to a case, see s 11(2), (8). In the light of its review, the tribunal may: (1) correct accidental errors in the decision; (2) correct accidental errors in the record of the decision; (3) amend reasons given for the decision; or (4) set the decision aside. As regards head (4), the tribunal must either re-decide the matter or refer it to the Upper Tribunal. If re-decided, the tribunal's decision must fall within heads (1) or (2). If referred, the Upper Tribunal must re-decide the matter. It may correct, amend or set aside the decision in accordance with heads (1)–(4). A First-tier Tribunal or Upper Tribunal re-deciding a matter may make such findings of fact as it considers appropriate.

A First-tier Tribunal may not review a decision on a matter listed in s 11(5). This is referred to as an "excluded decision".

Having reviewed a decision, a First-tier Tribunal has no power to review that decision. Having decided not to review a decision, a First-tier Tribunal cannot change its mind.

Tribunal Procedure Rules (see s 22) may provide that: (1) the First-tier Tribunal may not review decisions of a specified description; (2) the First-tier Tribunal's power to review specified classes of decision is exercisable solely on the tribunal's own initiative or on specified grounds; and (3) an application of a specified description may be made solely on specified grounds. For the rules relating to the Tax Chamber, see the Tribunal Procedure (First-tier Tribunal) (Tax Chamber) Rules 2009, SI 2009/273, r 41.

This section came into force partly on 19 September 2007 and partly on 3 November 2008: see the Tribunals, Courts and Enforcement Act 2007 (Commencement No 1) Order 2007, SI 2007/2709, art 2(*a*); the Tribunals, Courts and Enforcement Act 2007 (Commencement No 6 and Transitional Provisions) Order 2008, SI 2008/2696, arts 2 and 5(*a*).

10. Review of decision of Upper Tribunal

The Upper Tribunal may review a decision made by it on a matter in a case. It may do so on its own initiative or on an application by a party to the case having a right of appeal to the Court of Appeal. For the parties having such a right of appeal, see s 13(2), (14). In the light of its review, the tribunal may: (1) correct accidental errors in the decision; (2) correct accidental errors in the record of the decision; (3) amend reasons given for the decision; or (4) set the decision aside. As regards head (4), the tribunal must re-decide the matter. In doing so, the tribunal may make such findings of fact as it considers appropriate. Its sole power in these circumstances is to make a correction within heads (1) and (2).

The Upper Tribunal may not review a decision on a matter listed in s 13(8). This is referred to as an "excluded decision". A decision to set aside the decision under review is not an excluded decision. This decision may have been a decision to set aside an earlier decision. If so, the earlier decision and the decision on review are treated as different decisions.

Having reviewed a decision, the Upper Tribunal has no power to review that decision. Having decided not to review a decision, the Upper Tribunal cannot change its mind.

Tribunal Procedure Rules (see s 22) may provide that: (1) the Upper Tribunal may not review decisions of a specified description; (2) the Upper Tribunal's power to review specified classes of decision is exercisable solely on the tribunal's own initiative or on specified grounds; and (3) an application of a specified description may be made solely on specified grounds. For the rules relating to the Tax and Chancery Chamber, see the Tribunal Procedure (Upper Tribunal) Rules 2008, SI 2008/2698, r 46.

This section came into force partly on 19 September 2007 and partly on 3 November 2008: see the Tribunals, Courts and Enforcement Act 2007 (Commencement No 1) Order 2007, SI 2007/2709, art 2(*a*); the Tribunals, Courts and Enforcement Act 2007 (Commencement No 6 and Transitional Provisions) Order 2008, SI 2008/2696, arts 2 and 5(*a*).

11. Right of appeal to Upper Tribunal

In principle, any party to a case has a right to appeal to the Upper Tribunal on any point of law arising from a decision made by the First-tier Tribunal. This right is circumscribed by the following provisions.

First, no right of appeal arises in respect of an "excluded decision". The decisions concerned are listed. They include a decision of the First-tier Tribunal falling within a description specified in an order made by the Lord Chancellor. The order currently in force is not relevant to VAT.

Second, the right of appeal may be exercised only with permission given by the First-tier Tribunal or the Upper Tribunal. An application must be made by the party concerned.

Third, an order may provide for a person to be treated as being, or not being, a party to a case. No order has been made to date.

This section came into force partly on 19 September 2007 and partly on 3 November 2008: see the Tribunals, Courts and Enforcement Act 2007 (Commencement No 1) Order 2007, SI 2007/2709, art 2(*a*); the Tribunals, Courts and Enforcement Act 2007 (Commencement No 6 and Transitional Provisions) Order 2008, SI 2008/2696, arts 2 and 5(*a*).

12. Proceedings on appeal to Upper Tribunal

In deciding an appeal from a decision of the First-tier Tribunal (see s 11), the Upper Tribunal may find that the decision involved the making of an error on a point of law. The Upper Tribunal may set aside the decision of the First-tier Tribunal, but is not required to do so. The Upper Tribunal has two options if it decides to set aside the decision.

First, it may remit the case to the First-tier Tribunal with directions for its reconsideration. The Upper Tribunal may direct that the re-hearing takes place before a differently constituted panel. It may also give procedural directions in connection with the re-hearing.

Second, it may re-make the decision. In doing so, the Upper Tribunal may make any decision that the First-tier Tribunal could make on a re-hearing. The Upper Tribunal may also make such findings of fact as it considers appropriate.

This section came into force on 3 November 2008: see the Tribunals, Courts and Enforcement Act 2007 (Commencement No 6 and Transitional Provisions) Order 2008, SI 2008/2696, arts 2 and 5(*a*).

13. Right of appeal to Court of Appeal etc

In principle, any party to a case has a right of appeal to the relevant appellate court on any point of law arising from a decision made by the Upper Tribunal. This right is circumscribed by the following provisions.

First, no right of appeal arises in respect of an "excluded decision". The decisions concerned are listed. They include a decision of the Upper Tribunal falling within a description specified in an order made by the Lord Chancellor. The order currently in force is not relevant to VAT.

Second, the right of appeal may be exercised only with permission given by the Upper Tribunal or the relevant appellate court. An order may provide that a proposed appeal to the Court of Appeal in England and Wales or the Court of Appeal in Northern Ireland must either: (1) raise some important point of principle or practice; or (2) give rise to some other compelling reason for the relevant appellant court to hear the appeal. For the order made, see Appeals from the Upper Tribunal to the Court of Appeal Order 2008, SI 2008/2834.

Third, an order may provide for a person to be treated as being, or not being, a party to a case. No order has been made to date.

An application must be made by the party concerned. An application may be made to the relevant appellate court only if permission has been refused by the Upper Tribunal. Before deciding an application, the Upper Tribunal must specify which court is to be the relevant appellant court in respect of the proposed appeal. This may be the Court of Appeal in England and Wales, the Court of Session or the Court of Appeal in Northern Ireland. The most appropriate court is specified.

This section came into force partly on 19 September 2007 and partly on 3 November 2008: see the Tribunals, Courts and Enforcement Act 2007 (Commencement No 1) Order 2007, SI 2007/2709, art 2(*a*); the Tribunals, Courts and Enforcement Act 2007 (Commencement No 6 and Transitional Provisions) Order 2008, SI 2008/2696, arts 2 and 5(*a*).

14. Proceedings on appeal to Court of Appeal etc

In deciding an appeal from a decision of the Upper Tribunal (see s 13), the relevant appellant court (see s 13(12)) may find that the decision involved the making of an error on a point of law. The relevant appellate court may set aside the decision of the Upper Tribunal, but is not required to do so. The relevant appellate court has two options if it decides to set aside the decision.

First, relevant appellate court may remit the case to the Upper Tribunal with directions for its reconsideration. The relevant appellate court may direct that the reconsideration takes place before a differently constituted panel. It may also give procedural directions in connection with the reconsideration.

If the decision of the Upper Tribunal was on appeal or reference from another tribunal or person, the relevant appellate court may remit the case (with directions) to either: (1) the Upper Tribunal; or (2) the tribunal or person below. If head (1) applies, the Upper Tribunal may, instead of reconsidering the case itself, remit the case to the other tribunal or person below with the directions given by the relevant appellate court for its reconsideration.

Second, relevant appellate court may re-make the decision. In doing so, the relevant appellate court may make any decision that the Upper Tribunal could make when re-making the decision. The relevant appellate court may also make such findings of fact as it considers appropriate.

This section came into force on 3 November 2008: see the Tribunals, Courts and Enforcement Act 2007 (Commencement No 6 and Transitional Provisions) Order 2008, SI 2008/2696, arts 2 and 5(*a*).

"JUDICIAL REVIEW"

15. Upper Tribunal's "judicial review" jurisdiction

The Upper Tribunal has power to grant any of the following kinds of relief in cases arising under the law of England and Wales: (1) a mandatory order; (2) a prohibiting order; (3) a quashing order; (4) a declaration; and (5) an injunction.

The Upper Tribunal may exercise these powers if: (1) the conditions in s 18 are met; or (2) (in other cases) the tribunal is authorised to proceed in accordance with s 19(3), (4).

The relief granted by the Upper Tribunal has the same effect as the corresponding relief granted by the High Court on an application for judicial review. It is enforceable in the same manner as the corresponding relief.

In deciding whether to grant a mandatory order, prohibiting order or quashing order, the Upper Tribunal must apply the principles used by the High Court in judicial review applications. In deciding whether to grant a declaration or injunction in cases arising under the law of England and Wales, the Upper Tribunal must apply the principles used by the High Court in deciding whether to grant relief under Supreme Court Act 1981 s 31(2).

For the application of these provisions in Northern Ireland, see s 15(1), (5)(*b*) and (6).

This section came into force on 3 November 2008: see the Tribunals, Courts and Enforcement Act 2007 (Commencement No 6 and Transitional Provisions) Order 2008, SI 2008/2696, arts 2 and 5(*a*).

16. Application for relief under section 15(1)

An application for an order, declaration or injunction under s 15(1) requires permission. This is obtained from the Upper Tribunal. Permission is refused if the tribunal considers that the applicant does not have a sufficient interest in the matter to which the application relates. Permission may be refused if two conditions are met. Any relief sought on the application may be refused if the same conditions are met. The first condition is that there has been undue delay in making the application. The second condition is that granting relief would be likely to cause substantial hardship to any person, would be likely to substantially prejudice the rights of any person or would be detrimental to good administration.

The applicant may appeal against the tribunal's decision to refuse relief. If the Court of Appeal grants permission, it may go on to decide the application for relief.

The Tribunal Procedure Rules (see s 22) may restrict the time limit for making applications. For the relevant time limits, see the Tribunal Procedure (Upper Tribunal) Rules 2008, SI 2008/2698, r 28.

An application may include a claim for damages, restitution or recovery of a sum due. The tribunal may make such an award if it is satisfied that this result would have followed from High Court proceedings begun at the time of the application. For enforcement purposes, the award is treated as if it had been made by the High Court.

This section came into force on 3 November 2008: see the Tribunals, Courts and Enforcement Act 2007 (Commencement No 6 and Transitional Provisions) Order 2008, SI 2008/2696, arts 2 and 5(*a*).

17. Quashing orders under section 15(1): supplementary provision

The Upper Tribunal may exercise either of the following additional powers if it makes a quashing order (see s 15(1)(*c*)).

First, the tribunal may remit the matter to the court, tribunal or authority that made the decision with a direction to reconsider the matter and reach a decision in accordance with the findings of the Upper Tribunal.

Second, the tribunal may substitute its own decision for the decision in question. The tribunal may do so only if: (1) the decision was made by a court or tribunal; (2) the decision is quashed on the ground that there has been an error of law; and (3) without the error, the court or tribunal could have reached only one decision. The substituted decision has effect as if it were a decision of the relevant court or tribunal; the Upper Tribunal may direct otherwise.

This section came into force on 3 November 2008: see the Tribunals, Courts and Enforcement Act 2007 (Commencement No 6 and Transitional Provisions) Order 2008, SI 2008/2696, arts 2 and 5(*a*).

18. Limits of jurisdiction under section 15(1)

An application to the Upper Tribunal may seek relief by way of an order, declaration or injunction (see s 15(1)) or permission to apply for such relief. The tribunal has the function of deciding the application if the following conditions are met:

(1) The application seeks no more than: (*a*) relief by way of an order, declaration or injunction (see s 15(1)); (*b*) permission to apply for relief under s 15(1); (*c*) an award of damages, restitution or recovery of a sum due (see s 16(6)); (*d*) interest; and/or (*e*) costs (see s 29).

(2) The application does not call into question anything done by the Crown Court.

(3) The application falls within a specified class. The class is specified in a direction given in accordance with Constitutional Reform Act 2005 Sch 2 Part 1 and the powers conferred by s 18(7).

(4) The judge presiding at the hearing of the application is either a judge of the High Court, a judge of the Court of Appeal in England and Wales, or such person as may be agreed from time to time by the Lord Chief Justice and the Senior President of Tribunals.

In other cases, the tribunal must make an order transferring the application to the High Court. The consequences of such an order are as follows: (1) the application is treated as if it had been made to the High Court; (2) the application is treated as if it sought things corresponding to those sought from the tribunal; and (3) any steps taken, permission given or orders made by the tribunal in relation to the application are treated as taken, given or made by the High Court. These provisions may be supplemented by rules of court.

For the application of these provisions in Scotland, see s 18(8). For the application of these provisions in Northern Ireland, see s 18(1)(*b*), (4)(*b*), (8), (12).

This section came into force partly on 19 September 2007 and partly on 3 November 2008: see the Tribunals, Courts and Enforcement Act 2007 (Commencement No 1) Order 2007, SI 2007/2709, art 2(*a*); the Tribunals, Courts and Enforcement Act 2007 (Commencement No 6 and Transitional Provisions) Order 2008, SI 2008/2696, arts 2 and 5(*a*).

19. Quashing orders under section 15(1): supplementary provision

This section inserts Supreme Court Act 1981 s 31A and Judicature (Northern Ireland) Act 1978 s 25A and makes consequential provisions.

This section came into force on 3 November 2008: see the Tribunals, Courts and Enforcement Act 2007 (Commencement No 6 and Transitional Provisions) Order 2008, SI 2008/2696, arts 2 and 5(*a*).

20. Transfer of judicial review applications from the Court of Session

[Applies to Scotland.]

21. Upper Tribunal's "judicial review" jurisdiction: Scotland

[Applies to Scotland.]

MISCELLANEOUS

22. Tribunal Procedure Rules

Rules governing the practice and procedure to be followed in the First-tier Tribunal and Upper Tribunal are made by the Tribunal Procedure Committee. These rules are called "Tribunal Procedure Rules". They are to be framed with a view to securing that:

- justice is done in proceedings before the First-tier Tribunal and Upper Tribunal;
- the system for deciding matters within the jurisdiction of the two tribunals is accessible and fair;
- proceedings are handled quickly and efficiently;
- the rules are both simple and simply expressed; and

- (where appropriate) responsibility for ensuring the quick and efficient handling of proceedings rests with members of the two tribunals.

This section introduces TCEA 2007 Sch 5. This deals with the content of the Tribunal Procedure Rules (see paras 1–19), membership of the Tribunal Procedure Committee (see paras 20–26), the making of rules (see paras 27–29), and the powers to amend legislation (see para 30). For the Tribunal Procedure Rules made, see the commentary to Sch 5 Part 3.

This section came into force on 19 September 2007: see the Tribunals, Courts and Enforcement Act 2007 (Commencement No 1) Order 2007, SI 2007/2709, art 2(*a*).

23. Practice directions

The Senior President of Tribunals (see s 2) may give directions regarding the practice and procedure of the First-tier Tribunal and the Upper Tribunal. He may vary or revoke those directions and may make different provisions for different purposes. In principle, the Lord Chancellor must approve directions before they are made.

A Chamber President (see s 7(4)) may give directions regarding the practice and procedure of the chamber over which he presides. He may vary or revoke those directions and may make different provisions for different purposes. In principle, the Senior President of Tribunals and the Lord Chancellor must approve directions before they are made.

Approval by the Lord Chancellor, or both the Senior President of Tribunals and the Lord Chancellor, is not required in respect of: (1) directions consisting of guidance about the application or interpretation of the law; (2) the making of decisions by members of the First-tier Tribunal or Upper Tribunal; or (3) criteria for determining which members of the First-tier Tribunal or Upper Tribunal may be chosen to decide particular categories of matter. However, the Lord Chancellor must be consulted before directions in head (3) are given.

The following practice directions have been given:

Date	***Title***	***Application***
30.10.08	Child, vulnerable adult and sensitive witnesses	First-tier Tribunal Upper Tribunal
30.10.08	Use of Welsh Language in tribunals in Wales	First-tier Tribunal Upper Tribunal
30.10.08	Transcripts of proceedings	Upper Tribunal
10.3.09	Categorisation of cases in the Tax Chamber (This direction supplements SI 2009/273 r 23(1))	First-tier Tribunal

This section came into force on 3 November 2008: see the Tribunals, Courts and Enforcement Act 2007 (Commencement No 6 and Transitional Provisions) Order 2008, SI 2008/2696, arts 2 and 5(*a*).

24. Mediation

The following principles must be taken into account when making Tribunal Procedure Rules (see s 22) or practice directions (see s 23) in relation to mediation:

- mediation is to take place only by agreement of the parties;
- the failure to mediate is not to affect the outcome of the proceedings; and
- the failure of mediation to resolve disputed matters is not to affect the outcome of the proceedings.

Practice directions may provide for members (see s 24(6)) to act as mediators in relation to disputed matters in a case subject to tribunal proceedings. The directions may provide that the member may so act even if he has been chosen to decide matters in the case.

The mediator may decide matters in the case only with the consent of the parties.

Staff (see s 40(1)) may act as mediators if their terms of appointment so allow.

This section came into force on 3 November 2008: see the Tribunals, Courts and Enforcement Act 2007 (Commencement No 6 and Transitional Provisions) Order 2008, SI 2008/2696, arts 2 and 5(*a*).

25. Supplementary powers of Upper Tribunal

The Upper Tribunal has the same powers, rights, privileges and authority as the High Court in relation to the following matters:

(a) the attendance and examination of witnesses;
(b) the production and inspection of documents; and
(c) all other matters incidental to the tribunal's functions.

This provision does not limit any power to make Tribunal Procedure Rules. It is not limited by anything other than an express limitation in Tribunal Procedure Rules.

A power, right or privilege or authority conferred in England and Wales is available for the purposes of proceedings in Scotland or Northern Ireland.

For the application of this provision in Scotland, see s 25(1)(*b*) and (4). For the application of this provision in Northern Ireland, see s 25(1)(*a*) and (4).

For the application of this section by the Tax and Chancery Chamber of the Upper Tribunal, see the Tribunal Procedure (Upper Tribunal) Rules 2008, SI 2008/2698, r 7(4).

This section came into force on 3 November 2008: see the Tribunals, Courts and Enforcement Act 2007 (Commencement No 6 and Transitional Provisions) Order 2008, SI 2008/2696, arts 2 and 5(*a*).

26. First-tier Tribunal and Upper Tribunal: sitting places

The First-tier Tribunal or Upper Tribunal in England and Wales may decide a case in Scotland or Northern Ireland. Equivalent provisions apply to tribunals in Scotland and Northern Ireland.

This section came into force on 3 November 2008: see the Tribunals, Courts and Enforcement Act 2007 (Commencement No 6 and Transitional Provisions) Order 2008, SI 2008/2696, arts 2 and 5(*a*).

27. Enforcement

A sum payable in pursuance of a decision of the First-tier Tribunal or Upper Tribunal is recoverable as if it were payable under an order of either a county court or the High Court. For equivalent provisions in Scotland and Northern Ireland, see s 27(2), (3).

An order may vary the foregoing provisions in relation to a sum of a specified description. No order has been made to date. The Tribunal Procedure Rules may vary those provisions in relation to a sum of a specified description.

The Tribunal Procedure Rules (see s 22) may make provision for determining where a decision is made for the purposes of this section.

This section does not apply to damages, restitution or recovery of a sum due awarded by the Upper tribunal under s 16(6). In relation to Scotland, see s 27(4)(*b*).

This section came into force partly on 19 September 2007 and partly on 1 April 2009: see the Tribunals, Courts and Enforcement Act 2007 (Commencement No 1) Order 2007, SI 2007/2709, art 2(*a*); the Tribunals, Courts and Enforcement Act 2007 (Commencement No 6 and Transitional Provisions) Order 2008, SI 2008/2696, arts 2 and 6(*a*).

28. Assessors

The First-tier Tribunal or Upper Tribunal may not have the necessary expertise in relation to a matter before it. It may obtain the assistance of person(s) appearing to have relevant knowledge or experience. It does so by way of a direction. The expert's remuneration is determined and paid by the Lord Chancellor.

The Lord Chancellor may establish panels of experts from which a tribunal may select experts. Tribunals are not required to select experts from these panels.

This section came into force on 3 November 2008: see the Tribunals, Courts and Enforcement Act 2007 (Commencement No 6 and Transitional Provisions) Order 2008, SI 2008/2696, arts 2 and 5(*a*).

29. Costs or expenses

The First-tier Tribunal and Upper Tribunal have discretion to award costs in relation to any proceedings. The relevant costs are costs of the proceedings and costs incidental to the proceedings. The tribunal has full power to determine by whom and to what extent the costs are to be paid. The tribunal may disallow all or part of any wasted costs (as defined in s 29(5)). Alternatively, the tribunal may order all or part of the wasted costs to be met by the legal or other representatives (as defined in s 29(6)) concerned. The amount disallowed or met by representatives is determined in accordance with the Tribunal Procedure Rules.

For costs in the Tax Chamber of the First-tier Tribunal, see the Tribunal Procedure (First-tier Tribunal) (Tax Chamber) Rules 2009, SI 2009/273, r 10. For costs in the Tax and Chancery Chamber of the Upper Tribunal, see the Tribunal Procedure (Upper Tribunal) Rules 2008, SI 2008/2698, r 10.

For the application of this section to Scotland, see s 29(7).

This section came into force on 3 November 2008: see the Tribunals, Courts and Enforcement Act 2007 (Commencement No 6 and Transitional Provisions) Order 2008, SI 2008/2696, arts 2 and 5(*a*).

CHAPTER 3 TRANSFER OF TRIBUNAL FUNCTIONS

30. Transfer of functions of certain tribunals

An order may provide for a function of a tribunal listed in Sch 6 Parts 1–4 (as extended by SI 2008/2833 art 2) to be transferred to the First-tier Tribunal or the Upper Tribunal. For the order made in relation to the VAT and duties tribunals, see the Transfer of Tribunal Functions and Revenue and Customs Appeals Order 2009, SI 2009/56, art 2(*c*) and 4.

This section came into force on 19 September 2007: see the Tribunals, Courts and Enforcement Act 2007 (Commencement No 1) Order 2007, SI 2007/2709, art 2(*a*).

31. Transfers under section 30: supplementary powers

An order may provide for the abolition of a tribunal following a transfer of its functions under s 30. For the order made in relation to the VAT and duties tribunals, see the Transfer of Tribunal Functions and Revenue and Customs Appeals Order 2009, SI 2009/56, arts 2(*c*) and 4.

An order may provide for a member of a tribunal to become: (1) a transferred-in judge or transferred-in other member of the First-tier Tribunal; or (2) a transferred-in judge, transferred-in deputy judge or transferred-in other member of the Upper Tribunal. For the order made in relation to the VAT and duties tribunals, see the Transfer of Tribunal Functions and Revenue and Customs Appeals Order 2009, SI 2009/56, art 5.

An order may make incidental, supplemental, transitional or consequential provisions. For the order made in relation to the VAT and duties tribunals, see the Transfer of Tribunal

Functions and Revenue and Customs Appeals Order 2009, SI 2009/56, art 6 and Schs 1–3. The procedural rules are revoked by Sch 2 para 187(*c*), (*d*) and (*g*) of the 2009 Order.

This section came into force on 19 September 2007: see the Tribunals, Courts and Enforcement Act 2007 (Commencement No 1) Order 2007, SI 2007/2709, art 2(*a*).

32. Power to provide for appeal to Upper Tribunal from tribunals in Wales

An order may make provision for appeals to the Upper Tribunal where a transfer of functions (see s 30) would leave a residual jurisdiction in Wales. For an order made, see the Transfer of Tribunal Functions Order 2008, SI 2008/2833.

This section came into force on 19 September 2007: see the Tribunals, Courts and Enforcement Act 2007 (Commencement No 1) Order 2007, SI 2007/2709, art 2(*a*).

33. Power to provide for appeal to Upper Tribunal from tribunals in Scotland

An order may make provision for appeals to the Upper Tribunal where a transfer of functions (see s 30) would leave a residual jurisdiction in Scotland without conferring the right of appeal which would apply in England in equivalent circumstances. For an order made, see the Transfer of Tribunal Functions Order 2008, SI 2008/2833.

This section came into force on 19 September 2007: see the Tribunals, Courts and Enforcement Act 2007 (Commencement No 1) Order 2007, SI 2007/270,9 art 2(*a*).

34. Power to provide for appeal to Upper Tribunal from tribunals in Northern Ireland

An order may make provision for appeals to the Upper Tribunal where a transfer of functions (see s 30) would leave a residual jurisdiction in Northern Ireland without conferring the right of appeal which would apply in England in equivalent circumstances. For an order made, see the Transfer of Tribunal Functions Order 2008, SI 2008/2833.

This section came into force on 19 September 2007: see the Tribunals, Courts and Enforcement Act 2007 (Commencement No 1) Order 2007, SI 2007/2709, art 2(*a*).

35. Transfer of Ministerial responsibilities for certain tribunals

An order may transfer a function relating to the operation of a tribunal listed in Sch 6 if the function is currently exercised solely or jointly by a Minister of the Crown. No order has been made to date.

This section came into force on 19 September 2007: see the Tribunals, Courts and Enforcement Act 2007 (Commencement No 1) Order 2007, SI 2007/2709,art 2(*a*).

36. Transfer of powers to make procedural rules for certain tribunals

An order may transfer any power to make procedural rules for a tribunal listed in Sch 6. The power may be transferred to the Lord Chancellor or the Tribunal Procedure Committee. No order has been made to date.

This section came into force on 19 September 2007: see the Tribunals, Courts and Enforcement Act 2007 (Commencement No 1) Order 2007, SI 2007/2709, art 2(*a*).

37. Power to amend lists of tribunals in Schedule 6

An order may vary the lists of tribunals in Sch 6. For an order made, see the Transfer of Tribunal Functions Order 2008, SI 2008/2833, art 2.

This section came into force on 19 September 2007: see the Tribunals, Courts and Enforcement Act 2007 (Commencement No 1) Order 2007, SI 2007/2709, art 2(*a*).

38. Orders under sections 30 to 36: supplementary

An order made under ss 30–36 may amend, repeal or revoke primary or secondary legislation.

Any power to extend an enactment to a territory outside the UK has effect as if it included a power to extend the enactment with or without an amendment or repeal made under ss 30–36. For powers in relation to the Isle of Man, see Isle of Man Act 1979 ss 6, 13.

This section came into force on 19 September 2007: see the Tribunals, Courts and Enforcement Act 2007 (Commencement No 1) Order 2007, SI 2007/2709, art 2(*a*).

CHAPTER 4 ADMINISTRATIVE MATTERS IN RESPECT OF CERTAIN TRIBUNALS

39. The general duty

The Lord Chancellor must ensure that:

- there is an efficient and effective system supporting the business carried on by the First-tier Tribunal and Upper Tribunal; and
- appropriate services are provided for those tribunals.

The Lord Chancellor must prepare an annual report setting out how he has discharged the foregoing duties in relation to those tribunals.

This section came into force on 19 September 2007: see the Tribunals, Courts and Enforcement Act 2007 (Commencement No 1) Order 2007, SI 2007/2709, art 2(*a*).

40. Tribunal staff and services

The Lord Chancellor may appoint staff for the purpose of discharging his general duty (see s 39) in relation to tribunals. He may also enter into contracts with third parties for the provision of non-judicial services if he makes an order for that purpose.

This section came into force on 19 September 2007: see the Tribunals, Courts and Enforcement Act 2007 (Commencement No 1) Order 2007, SI 2007/2709, art 2(*a*).

41. Provision of accommodation

The Lord Chancellor may provide, equip, maintain and manage tribunal buildings, offices and other accommodation for the purpose of discharging his general duty (see s 39). He may also enter into arrangements with third parties for this purpose.

This section came into force on 19 September 2007: see the Tribunals, Courts and Enforcement Act 2007 (Commencement No 1) Order 2007, SI 2007/2709, art 2(*a*).

42. Fees

An order may prescribe fees payable in respect of anything dealt with by the First-tier Tribunal or Upper Tribunal, eg in relation to scales or rates of fees, exemptions from fees, reductions in fees and remission of fees. No orders have been made to date in respect of the tribunals relevant to VAT. The Lord Chancellor must take reasonable steps to bring information about fees to the attention of persons likely to have to pay them.

This section came into force on 19 September 2007: see the Tribunals, Courts and Enforcement Act 2007 (Commencement No 1) Order 2007, SI 2007/2709, art 2(*a*).

43. Report by Senior President of Tribunals

The Senior President of Tribunals (see s 2) must prepare an annual report covering: (1) matters that he wishes to bring to the Lord Chancellor's attention; and (2) matters requested by the Lord Chancellor. Reports are presented to the Lord Chancellor. The Lord Chancellor is required to publish them.

This section came into force on 3 November 2008: see the Tribunals, Courts and Enforcement Act 2007 (Commencement No 6 and Transitional Provisions) Order 2008, SI 2008/2696, arts 2 and 5(*a*).

CHAPTER 5 OVERSIGHT OF ADMINISTRATIVE JUSTICE SYSTEM, TRIBUNALS AND INQUIRIES

44. The Administrative Justice and Tribunals Council

This section establishes the Administrative Justice and Tribunals Council. For membership and committees of the Council, see Sch 7 Part 1. For the Council's functions, see Sch 7 Part 2. For the requirement to consult the Council before making procedural rules for certain tribunals, see Sch 7 Part 3. For interpretative provisions, see Sch 7 Part 4.

This section came into force on 19 September 2007: see the Tribunals, Courts and Enforcement Act 2007 (Commencement No 1) Order 2007, SI 2007/2709, art 2(*a*).

45. Abolition of the Council on Tribunals

This section abolishes the Council on Tribunals and the Scottish Committee of the Council on Tribunals. Tribunals and Inquiries Act 1992 ss 1–4 are repealed accordingly. An order may transfer the property, rights and liabilities of these bodies to the Administrative Justice and Tribunals Council (as to which see s 44). No order has been made to date.

This section came into force partly on 19 September 2007 and partly on 1 November 2007: see the Tribunals, Courts and Enforcement Act 2007 (Commencement No 1) Order 2007, SI 2007/2709 arts 2(a) and 3(a).

CHAPTER 6 SUPPLEMENTARY

46. Delegation of functions by Lord Chief Justice etc

The Lord Chief Justice of England and Wales, the Lord President of the Court of Session and the Lord Chief Justice of Northern Ireland may nominate a judicial office holder to exercise any of their respective functions in relation to membership of the Tribunal Procedure Committee (as to which see s 22(2), (3) and Sch 5 Part 2).

This section came into force partly on 19 September 2007 and partly on 3 November 2008: see the Tribunals, Courts and Enforcement Act 2007 (Commencement No 1) Order 2007, SI 2007/2709 art 2(a); the Tribunals, Courts and Enforcement Act 2007 (Commencement No 6 and Transitional Provisions) Order 2008, SI 2008/2696, arts 2 and 5(*b*).

47. Co-operation in relation to judicial training: guidance and welfare

The Lord Chief Justice of England and Wales must co-operate with the Senior President of Tribunals (see s 2) in relation to the training, guidance and welfare of: (1) judiciary; and (2) judges and other members of the First-tier Tribunal and the Upper Tribunal.

For the application of this section in Scotland and Northern Ireland, see s 47(5).

This section came into force on 3 November 2008: see the Tribunals, Courts and Enforcement Act 2007 (Commencement No 6 and Transitional Provisions) Order 2008, SI 2008/2696, arts 2 and 5(*a*).

48. Consequential and other amendments, and transitional provisions

This section introduces Schs 8 and 9. Schedule 8 makes consequential amendments. Schedule 9 Part 1 (paras 1, 2) makes transitional arrangements in relation to membership of the Tribunal Procedure Committee (as to which see s 22(2) and Sch 5 Part 2).

For the extent to which Schs 8, 9 came into force on 3 November 2008 and 1 April 2009: see the Tribunals, Courts and Enforcement Act 2007 (Commencement No 6 and Transitional Provisions) Order 2008, SI 2008/2696, arts 2, 5(*c*), (*d*) and 6(*b*).

49. Orders and regulations under Part 1: supplementary and procedural provisions

The power to make orders and regulations under Part 1 is exercisable by statutory instrument.

PART 8 GENERAL

146. Repeals

This section introduces Sch 23. Part 1 deals with repeals relating to tribunals.

147. Extent

Parts 1 and 8 of this Act extend to England, Wales, Scotland and Northern Ireland.

148. Commencement

Part 1 comes into force in accordance with orders made by the Lord Chancellor. The relevant dates are noted in the commentary to each section.

149. Short title

This Act is cited as the Tribunals, Courts and Enforcement Act 2007.

SCHEDULES

SCHEDULE 1 SENIOR PRESIDENT OF TRIBUNALS (SECTION 2)

This schedule deals with the following matters:

- the manner in which the Lord Chancellor recommends a person for appointment as the Senior President of Tribunals (Part 1);
- selection of the Senior President of Tribunals by the Judicial Appointments Commission (Part 2);
- the tenure, removal, resignation and remuneration of the Senior President of Tribunals (Part 3); and
- functions of the Senior President of Tribunals in relation to: (1) making representations to Parliament; and (2) representing the views of tribunal members to Parliament (Part 4).

SCHEDULE 2 JUDGES AND OTHER MEMBERS OF THE FIRST-TIER TRIBUNAL (SECTION 4)

This schedule deals with the following matters:

- the appointment and removal of judges and other members of the First-tier Tribunal;
- the terms of their appointment;
- their remuneration, allowances and expenses;
- arrangements for their training, guidance and welfare; and
- the oaths taken by them on appointment or transfer.

A person is eligible for appointment as a member of the First-tier Tribunal if: (1) he is not a tribunal judge; and (2) he has the qualifications prescribed by order. For the order made, see the Qualification for Appointment of Members to the First-tier Tribunal and Upper Tribunal Order 2008, SI 2008/2692.

SCHEDULE 3 JUDGES AND OTHER MEMBERS OF THE UPPER TRIBUNAL (SECTION 5)

This schedule deals with the following matters:

- the appointment and removal of judges and other members of the Upper Tribunal;
- the terms of their appointment;
- their remuneration, allowances and expenses;
- arrangements for their training, guidance and welfare; and

- the oaths taken by them on appointment or transfer.

A person is eligible for appointment as a member of the Upper Tribunal if: (1) he is not a tribunal judge; and (2) he has the qualifications prescribed by order. For the order made, see the Qualification for Appointment of Members to the First-tier Tribunal and Upper Tribunal Order 2008, SI 2008/2692.

SCHEDULE 4 CHAMBERS AND CHAMBER PRESIDENTS: FURTHER PROVISION (SECTION 7)

This schedule deals with the following matters:

- Chamber Presidents, Deputy Chamber Presidents and Acting Chamber Presidents (paras 1–8);
- the assignment of Chamber Presidents, Deputy Presidents, judges and other members of the Upper Tribunal (paras 9–13); and
- the composition of tribunals (paras 14 and 15).

As regards matters falling to be decided by the First-tier Tribunal or Upper Tribunal, the Lord Chancellor must make provision for determining how many members of the tribunal are to decide the matter. This is done by order. The Lord Chancellor must consult the Senior President of Tribunals before making an order. For the order made, see First-tier Tribunal and Upper Tribunal (Composition of Tribunal) Order 2008, SI 2008/2835.

SCHEDULE 5 PROCEDURE IN FIRST-TIER TRIBUNAL AND UPPER TRIBUNAL (SECTION 22)

PART 1 TRIBUNAL PROCEDURE RULES

This Part (comprising paras 1–19) makes provision regarding the content of the Tribunal Procedure Rules.

PART 2 TRIBUNAL PROCEDURE COMMITTEE

This Part deals with the appointment and remuneration of members of the Tribunal Procedure Committee.

The following table lists the members of the committee and sets out the manner in which they are appointed (paras 20–24).

Members	***Appointed by***
The Senior President of Tribunals (see s 2 and Sch 1) or a person nominated by him	Sch 5 para 20(*a*)
Three persons having experience of tribunal practice or advising persons involved in tribunal proceedings	The Lord Chancellor
A person is nominated by the Administrative Justice and Tribunals Council (see s 44)	The Lord Chancellor
A First-tier Tribunal judge	The Lord Chief Justice of England and Wales
An Upper Tribunal judge	The Lord Chief Justice of England and Wales
A member of the First-tier or Upper Tribunal who is not a judge	The Lord Chief Justice of England and Wales
A person with experience in, and knowledge of, the Scottish legal system	The Lord President of the Court of Session (after consultation with the Lord Chancellor)

Members	*Appointed by*
One or more persons with experience in, and knowledge of, a particular issue or subject area	(At the request of the Senior President of Tribunals) the Lord Chief Justice of England and Wales, the Lord President of the Court of Session or the Lord Chief Justice of Northern Ireland

The foregoing provisions may be amended by order (para 25). The Lord Chancellor may reimburse the travelling and out-of-pocket expenses of the Committee members (para 26).

PART 3 MAKING OF TRIBUNAL PROCEDURE RULES BY TRIBUNAL PROCEDURE COMMITTEE

Tribunal Procedure Rules (as to which see Part 1) are made following consultation and (unless it is inexpedient to do so) a meeting of the Tribunal Procedure Committee (as to which see Part 2). The Rules must be signed by a majority of the Committee members. They must be submitted to the Lord Chancellor, who may allow or disallow the Rules so made. If he allows them, the Rules are contained in a statutory instrument and come into force on a day directed by the Lord Chancellor. The statutory instrument is subject to annulment by a resolution of either House of Parliament. If the Lord Chancellor disallows the Rules, he must give the Committee written reasons for doing so.

For the Rules relevant to VAT, see respectively the Tribunal Procedure (First-tier Tribunal) (Tax Chamber) Rules 2009, SI 2009/273 and the Tribunal Procedure (Upper Tribunal) Rules 2008, SI 2008/269.

The Lord Chancellor may think it expedient for the Rules to make provisions intended to achieve a specific purpose. If so, he may give the Committee a written notice to that effect. The Committee must make Rules designed to achieve the purpose.

PART 4 POWER TO AMEND LEGISLATION IN CONNECTION WITH TRIBUNAL PROCEDURE RULES

The Lord Chancellor may amend, repeal or revoke an enactment in order to facilitate the making of Tribunal Procedure Rules or as a consequence of the Rules made. He does so by order.

SCHEDULE 10 AMENDMENTS RELATING TO JUDICIAL APPOINTMENTS (SECTION 50)

As regards VAT, this schedule amends VATA 1994 Sch 12 paras 2(2) and 7(4).

Finance Act 2008

2008 Chapter 9

PART 7 ADMINISTRATION

CHAPTER 1 INFORMATION ETC

NEW INFORMATION POWERS

113. Information and inspection powers

This section introduces Sch 36. Schedule 36 came into force on 1 April 2009: see the Finance Act 2008, Schedule 36 (Appointed Day and Savings) Order 2009, SI 2009/404, art 2.

114. Computer records etc

HMRC have statutory powers to require persons to produce documents and permit HMRC officers to inspect, copy or remove them. The relevant legislation may also provide for penalties or offences in connection with the production or inspection of documents. References to a "document" in the relevant legislation are construed as references to anything in which information of any description has been recorded. Similarly, references to a "copy of a document" are construed as references to anything on to which the information recorded in the document has been copied.

A person authorised by the Commissioners to require documents to be produced, inspected, copied or removed may obtain access to any computer used in connection with those documents. He may inspect and check the operation of the computer and any associated apparatus or material used in connection with those documents. The authorised person may require reasonable assistance to be provided for those purposes.

A person is liable to a penalty if he obstructs the authorised person or fails to provide reasonable assistance within a reasonable time. The prescribed penalty is £300. For reasonable excuse, assessment of the penalty, appeal against liability to a penalty or the amount of a penalty, enforcement and double jeopardy, see Sch 36 paras 45–49 and 52.

This section replaces FA 1985 s 10, which is accordingly repealed.

OTHER MEASURES

115. Record-keeping

This section introduces Sch 37. The amendments made by Sch 37 came into force on 1 April 2009: see the Finance Act 2008, Schedule 37 (Appointed Day) Order 2009, SI 2009/402, art 2.

117. Power to open or unpack containers

This section amends CEMA 1979 ss 1(1), 159. An HMRC officer is permitted to open or unpack a container. He may search the container and anything in it.

CHAPTER 2 TIME LIMITS FOR CLAIMS AND ASSESSMENTS ETC

GENERAL

118. Time limits for assessments, claims etc

This section introduces Sch 39. The amendments made by Sch 39 come into force on a day to be appointed by order. For the order made, see the Finance Act 2008, Schedule 39 (Appointed Day, Transitional Provision and Savings) Order 2009, SI 2009/403, art 2.

VAT

120. Time limits for assessments of excess credits etc

This section amends VATA 1994 ss 73, 80 with effect from 19 March 2008.

121. Old VAT claims: extended time limits

The three-year time limit for claiming a credit or repayment of overpaid or overstated VAT (see VATA 1994 s 80(4), (4ZA)) does not apply to claims made before 1 April 2009 in respect of VAT paid or brought into account for prescribed accounting periods ending before 4 December 1996.

The three-year time limit for claiming input tax deduction (see VAT Regulations 1995, SI 1995/2518 reg 29(1A)) does not apply to claims made before 1 April 2009 in respect of prescribed accounting periods ending before 1 May 1997 if: (1) the input tax became chargeable in such an accounting period; and (2) the claimant held the required evidence (see reg 29(2)) in such an accounting period.

This section is deemed to have come into force on 19 March 2008.

CHAPTER 3 PENALTIES

122. Penalties for errors

This section introduces Sch 40. The amendments made by Sch 40 come into force on a day to be appointed by order. For the order made, see the Finance Act 2008, Schedule 40 (Appointed Day, Transitional Provisions and Consequential Amendments) Order 2009, SI 2009/571, art 2.

123. Penalties for failure to notify etc

This section introduces Sch 41. Schedule 41 comes into force from a day to be appointed by order. The appointed day is 1 April 2010: see the Finance Act 2008, Schedule 41 (Appointed Day and Transitional Provisions) Order 2009, SI 2009/511, art 2.

CHAPTER 4 APPEALS ETC

REVIEWS AND APPEALS ETC: GENERAL

124. HMRC decisions etc: review and appeals

HM Treasury may make orders in connection with reviews and appeals. For the order made, see the Transfer of Functions and Revenue and Customs Appeals Order 2009, SI 2009/56. For the amendment of VATA 1994 from 1 April 2009, see Sch 1 paras 216–229 of the 2009 Order.

CHAPTER 5 PAYMENT AND ENFORCEMENT

TAKING CONTROL OF GOODS ETC

127. Enforcement by taking control of goods: England and Wales

The Commissioners may recover a sum due to them by using the procedure in TCEA 2007 Sch 12. This section applies to England and Wales. It comes into force from a day appointed by order made under s 129. No order has been made to date.

128. Summary warrant: Scotland

The Commissioners may recover a sum due to them by way of a summary warrant granted by a sheriff. This section applies to Scotland. It came into force on 23 November 2009: see the Finance Act 2008, Section 128 and Part 2 of Schedule 43 (Appointed Day, Transitional Provision and Savings) Order 2009, SI 2009/3024 art 3.

129. Consequential provision and commencement

This section introduces Sch 43. Schedule 43 amends or repeals legislation affected by ss 127 and 128.

Sections 127, 128 and Sch 43 apply from a day to be appointed by order. For the orders made, see the commentary to those provisions.

SET-OFF

130. Set-off: England and Wales and Northern Ireland

The Commissioners may set a sum due to a person (referred to as a "credit") against a sum due from him (referred to as a "debit").

A credit is either: (1) a statutory sum payable by the Commissioners; or (2) the repayment of a sum paid to the Commissioners in respect of an actual, purported or anticipated liability arising by virtue of the legislation or a contract settlement.

A debit is a sum due to the Commissioners in accordance with the legislation or a contract settlement.

This section applies to England, Wales and Northern Ireland. It does not affect the Commissioners' other powers to set off amounts.

131. No set-off where insolvency procedure has been applied

Where an insolvency procedure has been applied to a person, the Commissioners cannot use the power (see s 130) to set a post-insolvency credit (as defined in s 131(3)) against a pre-insolvency debit (as defined in s 131(4)).

An insolvency procedure is applied to a person if:

- a bankruptcy order is made;
- a winding up order is made;
- an administrator (as defined in s 131(8)) is appointed in relation to the person;
- the person is put into administrative receivership. A person is treated as being in administrative receivership throughout any continuous period in which (disregarding any temporary vacancy in the office of receiver) there is an administrative receiver (as defined in s 131(8)) of the person;
- (in the case of a corporation) the person passes a resolution for voluntary winding up;
- a voluntary arrangement (as defined in s 131(8)) comes into force in relation to the person; or
- a deed of arrangement (as defined in s 131(8)) takes effect in relation to the person.

An insolvency procedure is not applied to a person if: (1) it is applied at a time when another insolvency procedure applies to the person, or (2) it immediately follows the cessation of another insolvency procedure.

This section applies to England, Wales and Northern Ireland.

132. VAT: requirement to set-off

This section amends VATA 1994 s 81.

133. Set-off etc where right to be paid a sum has been transferred

The right (see s 133(8)(*c*), (9)) to be paid a sum ("the transferred sum") by the Commissioners may be transferred (as defined in s 133(8)(*a*)) from one person ("the original creditor") to another person ("the current creditor"). The following consequences arise in the circumstances stated if the original creditor transfers his right to the transferred sum after 24 June 2008:

Circumstances	***Consequences***
The Commissioners would have had an obligation to set the transferred sum against a sum payable to them by the original creditor (see below) if he had retained the right	The Commissioners must set the transferred sum against a sum payable to them by the original creditor
The Commissioners would have had a power to set the transferred sum against any sum payable to them by the original creditor (see below) if he had retained the right	The Commissioners may set the transferred sum against a sum payable to them by the original creditor

The sum payable to the Commissioners must have arisen before the Commissioners discharged their obligation to pay the transferred sum to the current creditor. Subject to this restriction, it is irrelevant whether the sum first became due before or after the transfer.

The set-off discharges: (1) the Commissioners' obligations to the current creditor; and (2) the original creditor's obligations.

OTHER MEASURES

135. Interest on unpaid tax in cases of disaster etc of national significance

HM Treasury may make an order specifying a past or current disaster or emergency considered to be of national importance. For the order made, see Finance Act 2008 Section 135 (Disaster or Emergency) Order 2008, SI 2008/1936 (floods, caused by weather conditions, which occurred in the UK in June and July 2007).

The Commissioners may enter into an agreement (referred to as an "agreement for deferred payment") whereby payment of a relevant sum (defined in s 135(2)) may be deferred in a particular case by reason of a specified disaster or emergency. Where the Commissioners do so, no interest is chargeable on the amount deferred during a "relief period" and no liability to a surcharge arises on the deferred amount during that period.

The relief period begins on the date specified by order or, if the Commissioners so direct, a later date from which the agreement for deferred payment has effect. The date specified in relation to floods in June and July 2007 is 1 June 2007: see art 3 of the 2008 Order. The relief period ends on the earlier of: (1) the last day of the period of deferment specified in the agreement for deferment; and (2) the date on which the order is revoked. The Commissioners may extend, or further extend, the period of deferment by reason of circumstances arising from the disaster or emergency.

An agreement for deferred payment may provide for payment by instalments due on (or by) specified dates. If so, the period of deferment for each instalment ends on the date specified in relation to it. In principle, the relief period comes to an end if the taxpayer fails to pay an instalment by the agreed date. However, the Commissioners may extend the period of deferment in these circumstances.

Failure to enter into an agreement for deferred payment is not an absolute bar to relief. A notional agreement is deemed to apply if the Commissioners are satisfied that an agreement could have been made. The notional agreement is deemed to have been made on terms which, in the Commissioners' view, would have been agreed in the circumstances.

136. Fee for payment

Regulations may provide that a person must pay a fee when making a payment to the Commissioners (or to a person authorised by the Commissioners) using a method specified in the regulations. For the regulations made, see Taxes (Fees for Payment by Telephone) Regulations 2008, SI 2008/1948, and Taxes, etc (Fees for Payment by Internet) Regulations 2011, SI 2011/711.

137. County court proceedings

This section amends CRCA 2005 s 25.

138. Certificates of debt

This section introduces Sch 44 and inserts a new CRCA 2005 s 25A.

SUPPLEMENTARY

139. Interpretation of Chapter

Various words and phrases are defined.

PART 8 MISCELLANEOUS

OTHER MATTERS

160. Power to give statutory effect to concessions

R (on the application of Wilkinson) v IRC [1996] STC 270, HL indicates that HMRC's scope to make concessions is not as wide as had previously been thought. HMRC are reviewing their concessions accordingly.

This section allows the Treasury to make orders giving statutory effect to any concession made by HMRC (or the former HM Customs and Excise) before Royal Assent. In relation to a concession relevant to VAT, see the Enactment of Extra-Statutory Concessions Order 2009, SI 2009/730 art 17.

SCHEDULES

SCHEDULE 36 INFORMATION AND INSPECTION POWERS (SECTION 113)

General note This schedule came into force on 1 April 2009: see s 113(2), (3); Finance Act 2008, Schedule 36 (Appointed Day and Savings) Order 2009.

This schedule has been amended by: (1) FA 2009 s 95 and Sch 47 with effect from 21 July 2009; (2) FA 2009 s 96 and Sch 48 with effect from 1 April 2010 in accordance with Finance Act 2009, Section 96 and Schedule 48 (Appointed Day, Savings and Consequential Amendments) Order 2009, SI 2009/3054; and (3) FA 2011 s 86(2) and Sch 24 paras 5, 6 with effect from 19 July 2011.

This schedule is further amended by FA 2011 s 86(2) and Sch 24 paras 2–4 with effect from 1 April 2012.

The following commentary is confined to the provisions relevant to VAT in force from 19 July 2011.

TMA 1970 ss 100–103 do not apply to a penalty under this schedule: see TMA 1970 s 103A(*b*).

PART 1 POWERS TO OBTAIN INFORMATION AND DOCUMENTS

Power to obtain information and documents from taxpayer

1.—(A6.301A) An HMRC officer may require a taxpayer to provide information or produce documents reasonably required to check the taxpayer's tax position (see Sch 36 para 64). This is done by way of a written notice known as a "taxpayer notice" made under para 3.

Power to obtain information and documents from third party

2.—(A6.301A) An HMRC officer may require a person to provide information or produce documents reasonably required to check the tax position (see Sch 36 para 64) of another person ("the taxpayer"). This is done by way of a written notice known as a "third party notice". The taxpayer must be named unless the tribunal allows otherwise (see Sch 36 para 3(5)).

Approval etc of taxpayer notices and third party notices

3.—(A6.301A) A third party notice (see Sch 36 para 2) requires agreement by the taxpayer or approval by the tribunal before it is made. A taxpayer notice requires neither agreement nor approval, but an HMRC officer may nevertheless seek approval.

An HMRC officer may ask the tribunal to approve a taxpayer notice or third party notice. The application must be made by, or with the agreement of, an authorised HMRC officer (see Sch 36 para 59). The tribunal must be satisfied that the notice is justified by the circumstances.

In principle, the person to whom the notice is to be addressed must be notified of the application to the tribunal. The tribunal may waive this requirement if it is satisfied that this might prejudice the assessment or collection of tax. In the absence of a waiver, the tribunal may approve an application only if the following conditions have been met:

- the person to whom the notice is to be addressed has been told that the relevant information or documents are required;
- that person has been given reasonable opportunity to make representations to an HMRC officer;
- the tribunal has been given a summary of any representations made; and
- (in relation to a third party notice) the taxpayer has been given a summary of the reasons why an HMRC officer requires the information or documents.

The tribunal may disapply the requirement (see para 2(2)) to name the taxpayer in a third party notice. The tribunal must be satisfied that the officer has reasonable grounds for believing that naming the taxpayer might seriously prejudice the assessment or collection of tax. For "tax", see Sch 36 para 63.

Copying third party notice to taxpayer

4.—(A6.301A) In principle, a copy of a third party notice must be given to the taxpayer to whom it relates. However, a tribunal may disapply this requirement in relation to an application for approval (see Sch 36 para 3) made by, or with the approval of, an authorised HMRC officer (see Sch 36 para 59). The tribunal must be satisfied that the officer has reasonable grounds for believing that giving a copy of the notice to the taxpayer might prejudice the assessment or collection of tax. For "tax", see Sch 36 para 63.

Power to obtain information and documents about persons whose identity is not known

5.—(A6.301A) An authorised officer may require a person to provide information or produce documents reasonably required to check the UK tax position (see Sch 36 paras 5(5), 63) of an unknown person or class of unknown persons. This is done by way of a written notice approved by the tribunal.

An application for approval may be made without notifying the person to whom the written notice is to be addressed. The tribunal must be satisfied on the following matters before approving the written notice:

(a) the information or documents are reasonably required for the stated purpose; and
(b) there are reasonable grounds for believing that the person (or a member of the class of persons) has failed (or may fail) to comply with his UK tax obligations.

This paragraph is amended by FA 2011 Sch 24 para 2 with effect from 1 April 2012.

Notices

6.—(A6.301A) Notices under Sch 36 paras 1, 2 and 5 are collectively referred to as "information notices".

An information notice may specify or describe the information or documents to be provided or produced. An information notice approved by the tribunal must state that approval has been given.

A decision given by the tribunal under para 3, 4 or 5 is final.

Complying with notices

7.—(A0.301A) An information notice (see Sch 36 para 6(1)) must specify the time limit for compliance and describe the time, means and form (if any) for doing so. These requirements must be reasonable. A person is liable to a penalty if he fails to comply with a notice (see Sch 36 paras 39, 40).

Documents must be produced for inspection at either: (1) a mutually agreed place; or (2) a place (other than a dwelling) reasonably specified by an HMRC officer. Producing a document is not regarded as breaking any lien claimed on it.

Producing copies of documents

8.—(A0.301A) A requirement to produce a document is met by producing a copy unless the information notice (or a subsequent written request) specifies the original document. A written request must specify the time limit for compliance and describe the time and means (if any) for doing so. These requirements must be reasonable. The Commissioners may make regulations regarding the production of copies. No regulations have been made to date.

Restrictions and special cases

9.—Parts 4 (restrictions on powers) and 6 (special cases) of this schedule apply to information notices.

PART 2 POWERS TO INSPECT BUSINESSES ETC

Power to inspect business premises etc

10.—(A6.301A) An HMRC officer may enter a person's business premises (see Sch 36 para 10(3)) in order to inspect the premises and any business assets (see para 10(3), (4)) or business documents (see para 10(3)) on the premises. The inspection must be reasonably required to check a person's tax position.

This power does not permit the officer to enter or inspect any part of the premises used solely as a dwelling.

For restrictions on the power to inspect business documents, see para 28.

Power to inspect business premises etc of involved third parties

10A.—[Not relevant to VAT.]

Power to inspect premises used in connection with taxable supplies etc

11.—(A6.301A) An HMRC officer may enter premises if he has reason to believe that:

(a) the premises are used in connection with the making of taxable supplies (as defined in VATA 1994 s 4(2)) and that goods to be so supplied (or documents relating to those goods) are to be found on those premises;
(b) the premises are used in connection with taxable acquisitions (as defined in VATA 1994 s 10(2)) from other member states and that goods to be so acquired (or documents relating to those goods) are to be found on those premises; or
(c) the premises are either used as a fiscal warehouse (as defined in VATA 1994 s 18A(3)) or used in connection with a fiscal warehouse.

The officer may inspect the premises, any goods on the premises and any documents on the premises that appear to relate to: (1) taxable supplies of goods; or (2) acquisitions of goods under taxable acquisitions or warehousing. The officer may not enter or inspect any part of the premises used solely as a dwelling.

For restrictions on the power to inspect business documents, see para 28.

Carrying out inspections

12.—(A0.301A) An inspection under Sch 36 paras 10 or 11 must be carried out at one of the following times:

- a time agreed with the occupier of the premises;
- (if the occupier has been given at least seven days' notice) any reasonable time; or
- (if the inspection is either carried out by an authorised officer or sanctioned by an authorised officer) at any reasonable time. The officer must either: (1) give the occupier (or, in his absence, the person who appears to be in charge of the premises) a written notice stating the possible consequences of obstructing the inspection; or (2) (in other cases) leave such a notice in a prominent place on the premises. A written notice given with the approval of a First-tier Tribunal must state that it has been so approved. For approval by the tribunal, see Sch 36 para 13.

Powers to inspect property for valuation etc

12A.—[Not relevant to VAT.]

Carrying out inspections under paragraph 12A

12B.—[Not relevant to VAT.]

Approval of First-tier Tribunal

13.—(A0.301A) An HMRC officer may ask the tribunal to approve an inspection under Sch 36 para 10 or 11). The application must be made or sanctioned by an authorised officer. It may be made without notice. The tribunal must be satisfied that the inspection is justified. The tribunal's decision is final.

Restrictions and special cases

14.—(A0.301A) Parts 4 (restrictions on powers) and 6 (special cases) of this schedule apply to inspections. For the power to mark assets and record information, see Sch 36 para 17.

PART 3 FURTHER POWERS

Power to copy documents

15.—(A0.301A) An HMRC officer may copy, or make extracts from, any documents produced to him or inspected by, him.

Power to remove documents

16.—(A0.301A) If necessary, an HMRC officer may remove and retain the documents (see Sch 36 para 16(5)) to which he has been given access. Documents may be removed at a reasonable time and retained for a reasonable period. If requested, the officer must give a receipt and provide a copy of the removed documents. The officer does not break a lien by removing documents. If removed documents are lost or damaged, the Commissioners must compensate the owner for any expenses reasonably incurred by him in repairing or replacing them.

Power to mark assets and to record information

17.—(A0.301A) The powers conferred by Part 2 of this schedule include:

- the power to mark business assets (as defined in Sch 36 para 10(3)) to indicate that they have been inspected;
- the power to mark anything containing business assets to indicate that the assets have been inspected;
- the power to obtain and record information relating to the premises, assets and documents inspected.

PART 4 RESTRICTIONS ON POWERS

Documents not in person's possession or power

18.—(A6.301A) An information notice (see Sch 36 para 6(1)) may require a person to produce a document. He is required to do so only if the document is in his power or possession.

Types of information

19.—(A6.301A) An information notice (see Sch 36 para 6(1)) may require a person to provide or produce information or documents. He is not required to provide or produce the following information or documents:

- information relating to the conduct of a pending appeal;
- any part of a document containing information relating to the conduct of a pending appeal;
- personal records (see below). However, a person may be required to produce that part of a document which does not fall within this description;
- information contained in personal records (see below). However, a person may be required to provide that part of the information which does not fall within this description;
- journalistic material (see below) or information contained in journalistic material.

"Personal records" are defined by reference to Police and Criminal Evidence Act 1984 s 12. They comprise documentary or other records concerning an individual (whether living or dead) who can be identified from them, which relate to:

- his physical or mental health;
- spiritual counselling or assistance given, or to be given, to him; or
- counselling or assistance given, or to be given, to him for the purposes of his personal welfare by either: (1) a voluntary organisation; or (2) an individual who (by reason of his office or occupation) has responsibilities for his personal welfare or (by reason of an order of the court) has responsibilities for his supervision.

"Journalistic material" is defined by reference to Police and Criminal Evidence Act 1984 s 13. It means: (1) material created for the purposes of journalism held by the person who created it; (2) material acquired for the purposes of journalism held by the person who acquired it; and (3) material held by the person who received it from someone who intended that the former would use it for the purposes of journalism.

Old documents

20.—(A6.301A) An information notice (see Sch 36 para 6(1)) does not require a person to provide or produce a document wholly originated more than six years before the date of the notice. However, this does not apply if the notice is given by an authorised officer or sanctioned by him.

Taxpayer notices following tax return

21.—[Not relevant to VAT.]

Taxpayer notices following land transaction return

21A.—[Not relevant to VAT.]

Deceased persons

22.—(A0.301A) An information notice (see Sch 36 para 6(1)) relating to the tax affairs of a deceased person may not be given more than four years after the date of death.

Privileged communications between professional legal advisers and clients

23.—(A6.301A) An information notice (see Sch 36 para 6(1)) does not require a person to provide privileged information or produce any part of a document that is privileged. For privileged information and documents, see Sch 36 para 23(2). Disputes as to whether information or documents are privileged are determined in accordance with regulations. For the regulations made, see the Information Notice: Resolution of Disputes as to Privileged Communications Regulations 2009, SI 2009/1916.

Auditors

24.—(A6.301A, A6.310) An information notice (see Sch 36 para 6(1)) does not require an auditor to:

(a) provide information in connection with his statutory functions; or
(b) produce documents created by him (or on his behalf) relating to the performance of his statutory functions.

For the exceptions, see Sch 36 para 26.

Tax advisers

25.—(A6.301A, A6.310) An information notice (see Sch 36 para 6(1)) does not require a tax adviser (see para 25(3)) to:

(a) provide information about relevant communications (see para 25(3)); or
(b) produce documents owned by him and consisting of relevant communications.

For the exceptions, see para 26.

Auditors and tax advisers: supplementary

26.—(A6.301A, A6.310) Although an auditor or tax adviser served with an information notice is exempted from providing certain information and producing certain documents (see Sch 36 paras 24, 25), he is not exempted from providing:

- (as regards any information notice (see Sch 36 para 6(1)) an explanation of any information or document which, in the role as tax adviser, he assisted his client to prepare for HMRC;
- (as regards an information notice under Sch 36 para 5) information regarding the identity or address of the person (or his agent) to whom the notice relates; or
- a document (see Sch 36 para 27) containing the information specified in either of the foregoing heads.

However, he is not required to provide the explanation, information or document if he has already done so.

27.—(A0.301A) If an auditor or tax adviser is required to produce a document by virtue of Sch 36 para 26, the information notice requiring this has effect as if it required only the part (or parts) of the document containing the information to be produced.

Corresponding restrictions on inspection of business documents

28.—(A0.301A) An HMRC officer's powers to inspect documents (see Sch 36 para 10) are aligned with the provisions relating to information notices. If the occupier would not be required to produce a document in accordance with an information notice (see Sch 36 para 6(1)) by virtue of paras 18–27), an officer may not exercise his powers under Sch 36 Part 2 in order to inspect that document.

PART 5 APPEALS AGAINST INFORMATION NOTICES

Right to appeal against taxpayer notice

29.—(A6.301A) A taxpayer may appeal against:

- a taxpayer notice (see Sch 36 para 1) given to him. However, no appeal lies against a notice approved by the tribunal under Sch 36 para 3; or
- any requirement in the notice. However, no appeal lies against a requirement to provide information, or produce documents, forming part of the taxpayer's statutory records.

- any requirement in the notice (other than a requirement to provide information, or produce documents, forming part of the taxpayer's statutory records).

Right to appeal against third party notice

30.—(A6.301A) A taxpayer may appeal against:

- a third party notice (see Sch 36 para 2) given to him, on the ground that it would be unduly onerous to comply with the notice. However, no appeal lies against a notice approved by the tribunal under Sch 36 para 3; or
- any requirement in the notice, on the ground that it would be unduly onerous to comply with the requirement. However, no appeal lies against a requirement to provide information, or produce documents, forming part of the taxpayer's statutory records.

Right to appeal against notice given under paragraph 5

31.—(A0.301A) A taxpayer may appeal against:

- a notice under Sch 36 para 5 given to him, on the ground that it would be unduly onerous to comply with the notice; or
- any requirement in the notice, on the ground that it would be unduly onerous to comply with the requirement.

Procedure

32.—(A6.301A) Notice of appeal under Sch 36 paras 29–31 must be given in writing to the HMRC officer who issued the notice and state the grounds of appeal. This must be done no later than 30 days after the notice was given.

On appeal, the tribunal may confirm, vary or set aside the notice or requirement. The taxpayer must comply with a notice or requirement which is confirmed or varied. He must do so within: (1) the period specified by the tribunal (if the tribunal specifies a period), or (2) the period specified by an HMRC officer in writing following the decision (in other cases). The period specified in the latter case must be reasonable. The tribunal's decision is final.

The appeal is treated as if it were an appeal against an assessment to income tax. TMA 1970 Part 5 applies accordingly.

Special cases

33.—Part 6 (Sch 36 paras 34–38) applies to appeals against an information notice.

PART 6 SPECIAL CASES

Supply of goods or services etc

34.—(A0.301A) A taxpayer notice (see Sch 36 para 1) or third party notice (see Sch 36 para 2) may be confined to information or documents forming part of a person's statutory records relating to a supply, an acquisition or an importation in the course of carrying on a business. Where this is so:

- the notice does not require the agreement of the taxpayer or the approval of the tribunal;
- no right of appeal lies to the tribunal in respect of the notice or any requirement in the notice; and
- VATA 1994 ss 5, 11, 15 and Sch 4, together with any orders made under those provisions, apply for the purposes of this paragraph as if this paragraph were part of VATA 1994.

Involved third parties

34A.—[Not relevant to VAT.]

Registered pension schemes etc

34B.—[This provision does not appear to be relevant to VAT.]

Registered pension schemes etc: interpretation

34C.—[This provision does not appear to be relevant to VAT.]

Groups of undertakings

35.—(A0.301A) This paragraph modifies the application of Sch 36 paras 2, 3, 4, 5, 21, 21A and 30 in relation to an undertaking (see para Sch 36 33(7)) which is a parent undertaking (see Sch 36 para 33(7)) in relation to another undertaking (ie a subsidiary undertaking, as to which see Sch 36 para 33(7)).

Change of ownership of companies

36.—[Not relevant to VAT.]

Partnerships

37.—[Not relevant to VAT.]

Information in connection with herd basis election

37A.—[Not relevant to VAT.]

Information from persons liable to counteraction of tax advantage

37B.—[Not relevant to VAT.]

Application to the Crown

38.—(A0.301A) Parts 1–7, 9 and 10 apply to the Crown. However, they do not apply to Her Majesty in her private capacity (see Crown Proceedings Act 1947 s 38(3)).

PART 7 PENALTIES

Penalties for failure to comply or obstruction

39.—(A6.301A) A person is liable to a penalty if:

- he fails to comply with an information notice (see Sch 36 para 6(1)); or
- he deliberately obstructs an HMRC officer in the course of an inspection (see Sch 36 Part 2) which has been approved by the tribunal.

A person is also liable to a penalty if he breaches the duty to retain documents and keep them available for inspection (see Sch 36 paras 42, 43) by:

- concealing a document;
- destroying or otherwise disposing of a document; or
- arranging the concealment, destruction or disposal of a document.

The prescribed penalty in either case is £300.

For the circumstances in which no liability to a penalty arises, see Sch 36 paras 43 (extended time limit for compliance) and 44 (reasonable excuse).

Daily default penalties for failure to comply or obstruction

40.—(A6.301A) A person is liable to a penalty if the failure or obstruction in Sch 36 para 39 continues after the date on which a penalty is imposed under that provision.

The prescribed penalty is a sum not exceeding £60 for each subsequent day on which the conduct continues.

For the circumstances in which no liability to a penalty arises, see Sch 36 paras 43 (extended time limit for compliance) and 44 (reasonable excuse).

Penalties for inaccurate information and documents

40A.—(A0.301A) A person may provide inaccurate information, or produce a document containing an inaccuracy, when complying with an information notice (see Sch 36 para 6(1)).

He is liable to a penalty if: (1) the inaccuracy is careless (ie it is due to a failure to take reasonable care) or deliberate; or (2) he discovers the inaccuracy some time later and fails to take reasonable steps to inform HMRC.

The prescribed penalty is a sum not exceeding £3,000. If a document contains more than one inaccuracy, the person is liable to a penalty in respect of each inaccuracy.

This paragraph is amended by FA 2011 Sch 24 para 3 in relation to any inaccuracy in information provided or documents produced after 31 March 2012.

Power to change amount of penalties

41.—(A0.301A) Regulations may vary the sums prescribed in Sch 36 paras 39, 40 and 40A. No regulations have been made to date. The new sum does not apply to any conduct which commenced, or took place, before the date on which the regulations came into force.

Concealing, destroying etc documents following information notice

42.—(A0.301A) In principle, a person must not:

- conceal a document subject to an information notice (see Sch 36 para 6(1)) addressed to him;
- destroy or otherwise dispose of the document; or
- arrange for the concealment, destruction or disposal of the document.

However, he may do so once the document has been produced to an HMRC officer unless the officer has given (and not withdrawn) a written notification that the document must continue to be available for inspection. He may also do so if, having complied with the notice by producing a copy of the document (see Sch 36 para 8(1)), he acts more than six months later without the officer having requested the original document (see Sch 36 para 8(2)(*b*)) during the six months following production of the copy.

Concealing, destroying etc documents following informal notification

43.—(A0.301A) In principle, a person must not:

- conceal a document if an HMRC officer has informed him that the document is, or is likely to be, the subject of an information notice (see Sch 36 para 6(1)) addressed to him;
- destroy or otherwise dispose of the document if he has been so informed; or
- arrange for the concealment, destruction or disposal of the document if he has been so informed.

However, the person may do so if at least six months has expired since he was so informed or last so informed. Although the legislation states that he may also do so if an information notice requiring production of the document has been given, the person thereby becomes liable to the duty in Sch 36 para 42.

Failure to comply with time limit

44.—(A6.301A) A person's failure to do something within a limited period of time does not give rise to a penalty under Sch 36 paras 39 or 40 if the person did it within such further time (if any) as an HMRC officer may have allowed.

Reasonable excuse

45.—(A6.301A) A person is not liable to a penalty under Sch 36 paras 39 or 40 if he satisfies HMRC or (on appeal) the tribunal that there is a reasonable excuse for the relevant failure or obstruction of an HMRC officer.

An insufficiency of funds is capable of amounting to a reasonable excuse only if it is attributable to events outside the person's control.

Reliance on another person to do something is capable of amounting to a reasonable excuse only if the taxpayer took reasonable care to avoid the failure or obstruction.

Once a reasonable excuse has ceased, a person is treated as continuing to have a reasonable excuse if the failure is remedied, or the obstruction ceases, without unreasonable delay after the excuse ceased.

Assessment of penalty

46.—(A0.301A) A penalty under Sch 36 paras 39, 40 or 40A is assessed. HMRC must notify the assessed person.

A penalty under para 39 or 40 must be assessed within twelve months of the relevant date. As regards an information notice against which a person may appeal, this is the later of: (1) the date on which the person became liable to the penalty; (2) the end of the period allowed for appeal; and (3) (if notice of appeal is given) the date on which the appeal is determined or withdrawn. In any other case, it is the date on which the person became liable to the penalty.

A penalty under para 40A must be assessed within twelve months of the day on which the inaccuracy first came to the attention of an HMRC officer. This must be no later than six years after the day on which the person became liable to the penalty.

Right to appeal against penalty

47.—(A6.301A) A person may appeal against:

- a decision of an HMRC officer that a penalty is payable under Sch 36 paras 39, 40 or 40A; or
- the amount of such a penalty.

Procedure on appeal against penalty

48.—(A0.301A) Notice of appeal regarding a penalty under Sch 36 paras 39, 40 or 40A must be given to HMRC in writing no later than 30 days after the date on which the assessment (see para 46) was issued. The grounds for appeal must be stated.

As regards a decision that a penalty is payable (see para 47(*a*)), the tribunal may confirm or cancel the decision. As regards a decision relating to the amount of a penalty (see para 47(*b*)), the tribunal may confirm the decision or substitute another decision that the officer had power to make.

An appeal against a penalty under paras 39, 40 or 40A is treated in the same manner as an appeal against an assessment to income tax.

TMA 1970 Part 5 and paras 48, 49 of this schedule apply to appeals under Part 7 of this schedule.

Enforcement of penalty

49.—(A6.301A) In principle, a penalty under Sch 36 paras 39, 40 or 40A must be paid within 30 days, counted from the day on which the notice of assessment is issued. However, if notice of appeal is given (see Sch 36 para 47), the penalty must be paid within 30 days of the day on which the appeal is determined or withdrawn.

A penalty assessment (see Sch 36 para 46) is enforced in the same manner as an income tax assessment. For the enforcement of income tax assessments, see TMA 1970 Part 6.

Increased daily default penalty

49A.—(A6.301A) This paragraph is inserted by FA 2011 Sch 24 para 4. It has effect in relation to failures to comply with a notice under para 5 beginning after 31 March 2012.

49B.—(A6.301A) This paragraph is inserted by FA 2011 Sch 24 para 4. It has effect in relation to failures to comply with a notice under para 5 beginning after 31 March 2012.

49C.—(A6.301A) This paragraph is inserted by FA 2011 Sch 24 para 4. It has effect in relation to failures to comply with a notice under para 5 beginning after 31 March 2012.

Tax-related penalty

50.—(A6.301A) A failure or obstruction may continue after a penalty has been imposed under Sch 36 para 39. Where this is so, an HMRC officer may apply to the Upper Tribunal (see TCEA 2007 s 3) for an additional penalty to be imposed. He may do so if he has reason to believe that the failure or obstruction has resulted in a significant reduction in the tax paid or payable by the person.

The application must be made no later than twelve months after the relevant date (as defined in para 50(7)). As regards a failure or obstruction relating to an information notice against which a person may appeal, this is the later of: (1) the end of the period allowed for appeal; and (2) (if notice of appeal is given) the date on which the appeal is determined or withdrawn. In any other case it is the date on which the person became liable to the penalty.

The Upper Tribunal decides whether or not an additional penalty should be imposed and, if imposed, the amount of the penalty. In deciding the amount, the tribunal must have regard to the amount of tax which has not been paid or may not be paid. HMRC must notify the person accordingly.

The penalty is additional to the penalty or penalties imposed under Sch 36 paras 39 or 40. It is disregarded for the purposes of FA 2007 Sch 24 para 12(2) and Sch 41 para 15(1).

Enforcement of tax-related penalty

51.—(A6.301A) A tax-related penalty (see Sch 36 para 50) must be paid within 30 days of notification (see para 50(4)). The penalty is enforced in the same manner as an income tax assessment. For the enforcement of income tax assessments, see TMA 1970 Part 6.

Double jeopardy

52.—(A6.301A) A person is not liable to a penalty under Sch 36 paras 39, 40, 40A or 50 if he has been convicted of an offence in respect of the relevant conduct.

PART 8 OFFENCE

Concealing etc documents following information notice

53.—(A6.301A) A person may be required to produce a document in accordance with an information notice (see Sch 36 para 6(1)) approved by the tribunal in accordance with Sch 36 paras 3 or 5. He is guilty of an offence if:

- he conceals, destroys or otherwise disposes of the document; or
- he arranges for the concealment, destruction or disposal of the document.

In principle, a person is not guilty of an offence if the relevant conduct takes place after the document has been produced to an HMRC officer. However, the officer may have issued a notification in writing that the document must continue to be available for inspection. If so, the relevant conduct constitutes an offence if it takes place before the notification is withdrawn.

A person may have complied with an information notice by producing a copy of the relevant document (see Sch 36 para 8(1)). In principle, a person is not guilty of an offence if the relevant conduct takes place more than six months after the copy was produced. However, an HMRC officer may have requested the original document during this six-month period (see Sch 36 para 8(2)(*b*)). If so, relevant conduct in relation to the original document prior to its production constitutes an offence.

For the prescribed penalty, see Sch 36 para 55.

Concealing etc documents following informal notification

54.—(A6.301A) A person may be informed in writing by an HMRC officer that a document is, or is likely to be, the subject of an information notice (see Sch 36 para 6(1)) and that the officer intends to seek approval from a tribunal for the giving of the information notice (see Sch 36 paras 3, 5). The person is guilty of an offence if he subsequently:

- conceals, destroys or otherwise disposes of the document; or
- arranges the concealment, destruction or disposal of the document.

A person is not guilty of the offence if the relevant conduct takes place more than six months after he was informed, or last informed, by the officer.

A person is not guilty of the offence if the relevant conduct takes place after an information notice has been given to the person. However, the relevant conduct in these circumstances may constitute an offence under Sch 36 para 53.

For the prescribed penalty, see Sch 36 para 55.

Fine or imprisonment

55.—(A6.301A) A person guilty of an offence under Sch 36 paras 53 or 54 is liable to a penalty as follows:

- on summary conviction (ie by a magistrate in England and Wales): a fine not exceeding the statutory maximum.
- on indictment (ie by the Crown Court in England and Wales): two years' imprisonment, a fine or both.

As regards England and Wales, the "statutory maximum" is currently £5,000: see Interpretation Act 1979 Sch 1; Magistrates' Courts Act 1980 s 32(9) (as amended by Criminal Justice Act 1991 s 17(2)). In Scotland and Northern Ireland, see Criminal Procedure (Scotland) Act 1995 s 225(8) and Fines and Penalties (Northern Ireland) Order 1984 respectively by virtue of Interpretation Act 1979 Sch 1.

PART 9 MISCELLANEOUS PROVISIONS AND INTERPRETATION

Application of provisions of TMA 1970

56.—TMA 1970 ss 108, 114 and 115 apply for the purposes of this schedule as they apply for the purposes of the Taxes Acts (as defined in Sch 36 para 58).

Regulations under this Schedule

57.—Regulations under this schedule are made by statutory instrument.

General interpretation

58.—Various words and phrases are defined.

Authorised officer of Revenue and Customs

59.—The term "authorised officer of Revenue and Customs" is defined.

Business

60.—The phrase "carrying on a business" is defined. Regulations may provide that a specified activity, or an activity carried on by a specified class of person, is or is not to be treated as the carrying on of a business. No regulations have been made to date.

Chargeable period

61.—[Not relevant to VAT.]

Involved third parties

61A.—[Not relevant to VAT.]

Statutory records

62.—Information and documents form part of a person's statutory records only if they are required to be kept and preserved by virtue of VATA 1994 and any other enactment relating to VAT. They cease to form part of a person's statutory records when the period for preserving them has expired.

Tax

63.—The term "tax" is defined. It includes VAT and "relevant foreign tax".

VAT comprises: (1) VAT charged in accordance with VATA 1994; (2) VAT charged in accordance with the law of another member state; (3) amounts recoverable under VATA 1994 Sch 11 para 5(2) (VAT shown on invoices or included in the amount invoiced); and (4) Flat Rate Addition (as to which see VATA 1994 s 54(4) and VAT Regulations 1995, SI 1995/2518, art 209(1), (3)(*g*)).

"Relevant foreign tax" comprises VAT imposed under the law of a territory which is covered by international tax enforcement arrangements having effect under FA 2006 s 173. For the current arrangements, see International Mutual Administrative Assistance in Tax Matters Order 2007, SI 2007/2126. The reference to Directive 77/799/EEC does not apply to VAT: the 1977 Directive ceased to apply to VAT on 31 December 2003: see Directive 2003/93/EC arts 1(2), 3.

Tax position

64.—The "tax position" of a person is defined.

PART 10 CONSEQUENTIAL PROVISIONS

65–92.—The provisions amended or repealed as a consequence of this schedule are listed.

SCHEDULE 37 RECORD-KEEPING (SECTION 115)

General note As regards VAT, this schedule amends the record-keeping requirements in VATA 1994 Sch 11 paras 6, 6A and FA 1999 s 13(6). These amendments came into force on 1 April 2009: see FA 2008 s 115(2); the Finance Act 2008, Schedule 37 (Appointed Day) Order 2009, SI 2009/402.

SCHEDULE 39 TIME LIMITS FOR ASSESSMENTS, CLAIMS ETC (SECTION 118)

General note As regards VAT, this schedule amends VATA 1994 ss 33A, 77, 78, 80 and repeals FA 1997 s 47(1). These amendments came into force on 1 April 2010: see Sch 39 paras 32–36, 65; the Finance Act 2008, Schedule 39 (Appointed Day, Transitional Provision and Savings) Order 2009, SI 2009/403, art 2. For saving provisions, see arts 2–6 and 9 of the 2009 Order.

SCHEDULE 40 PENALTIES: AMENDMENTS OF SCHEDULE 24 TO FA 2007 (SECTION 122)

General note This schedule amends FA 2007 Sch 24 (Sch 40 paras 1–20) and makes consequential amendments which are not relevant to VAT (Sch 40 para 21).

This schedule came into force on 1 April 2009: see FA 2008 s 122(2); the Finance Act 2008, Schedule 40 (Appointed Day, Transitional Provisions and Consequential Amendments) Order 2009, SI 2009/571, art 2. For consequential amendments to VATA 1994, see Sch 2 paras 21–27 of the 2009 Order.

SCHEDULE 41 PENALTIES: FAILURE TO NOTIFY AND CERTAIN VAT AND EXCISE WRONGDOING (SECTION 123)

General note This schedule came into force on 1 April 2010: see FA 2008 s 123(2); the Finance Act 2008, Schedule 41 (Appointed Day and Transitional Provisions) Order 2009, SI 2009/511, art 2. The following commentary is confined to provisions relevant to VAT.

TMA 1970 ss 100–103 do not apply to a penalty under this schedule: see TMA 1970 s 103A(*c*).

Failure to notify etc

1.—A person is liable to a penalty if:

- he fails to notify liability to register under VATA 1994 Sch 1 paras 5–7, Sch 2 para 3, Sch 3 para 3 or Sch 3A paras 3, 4;
- (in the case of a person exempted from registration) he fails to notify a material change in the nature of supplies (see VATA 1994 Sch 1 para 14(2), (3)), an acquisition affecting exemption from registration (see VATA 1994 Sch 3 para 8(2)) or a relevant change in supplies (see Sch 3A para 7(2), (3)); or
- (in the case of a person who is not a taxable person) he fails to notify an acquisition of goods subject to excise duty or a new means of transport in accordance with VAT Regulations 1995, 1995/2518, regs 36, 148.

This penalty applies to obligations arising after 31 March 2010: see the Finance Act 2008, Schedule 41 (Appointed Day and Transitional Provisions) Order 2009, SI 2009/511, art 3(*a*). For the penalty in respect of obligations arising before 1 April 2010, see VATA 1994 s 67(1)(*a*) and (*b*).

Issue of invoice showing VAT by unauthorised person

2.—An unauthorised person (as defined in Sch 41 para 2(3)) is liable to a penalty if he issues an invoice showing: (1) an amount as being VAT; or (2) an amount as including an amount attributable to VAT.

A flat-rate farmer issuing an invoice showing an amount of flat-rate addition is liable to a penalty if the invoice fails to comply with VAT Regulations 1995, SI 1995/2518 reg 209(3).

A person issuing an invoice showing an amount of flat-rate addition is liable to a penalty if he was not certified for the purposes of the flat-rate scheme for farmers at the relevant time. For certification, see VAT Regulations 1995, SI 1995/2518, reg 203(1).

This penalty applies to invoices issued after 31 March 2010: see the Finance Act 2008, Schedule 41 (Appointed Day and Transitional Provisions) Order 2009, SI 2009/511, art 3(*b*). For the penalty in respect of invoices issued before 1 April 2010, see VATA 1994 ss 67(1)(*c*).

Putting product to use that attracts higher duty

3.—[Not relevant to VAT.]

Handling goods subject to unpaid excise duty

4.—[Not relevant to VAT.]

Degrees of culpability

5.—A deliberate failure to comply with an obligation in relation to VAT (see Sch 41 para 1) is "deliberate and concealed" if the relevant person makes arrangements to conceal the situation giving rise to the obligation. The failure is "deliberate but not concealed" if no such arrangements are made.

The conduct giving rise to a penalty under Sch 41 para 2 is "deliberate and concealed" if the relevant person makes arrangements to conceal the issuing of the invoice. The conduct is "deliberate but not concealed" if no such arrangements are made.

Amount of penalty: standard amount

6.—The penalties under Sch 41 paras 1 and 2 are 100% of the potential lost revenue if the conduct is deliberate and concealed (see Sch 41 para 5(1)(*a*), (2)(*a*)), 70% of the potential lost revenue if the conduct is deliberate but not concealed (see Sch 41 para 5(1)(*b*), (2)(*b*)), and 30% of the potential lost revenue in other cases.

For "potential lost revenue", see Sch 41 paras 7–11.

Potential lost revenue

7.—As regards a penalty under Sch 41 para 1, the potential lost revenue is:

- (for failure to notify an acquisition of goods subject to excise duty or a new means of transport) the VAT due on that acquisition;
- (in any other case) the VAT (if any) for which the person is liable (registered person or person liable to registration) or would have been liable (person exempted from registration) for the relevant period (as defined in Sch 41 para 7(7)). As regards conduct relating to an acquisition of goods from another member state or to goods treated as being supplied in the UK in accordance with VATA 1994 s 7(4), HMRC may be satisfied that VAT for the relevant period consists of (or includes) VAT paid in another member state. If so, the potential lost revenue is reduced accordingly.

8.—As regards a penalty under Sch 41 para 2, the potential lost revenue is the amount shown on the invoice as VAT or the amount to be taken as representing VAT.

9.—[Not relevant to VAT.]

10.—[Not relevant to VAT.]

11.—In principle, the fact that a potential loss of revenue is (or may be) balanced by a potential over-payment by another person is disregarded. However, this does not apply if an enactment requires or permits a person's tax liability to be adjusted by reference to that of the person liable to the penalty.

The term "relevant act or failure" is a failure to comply with a relevant obligation (see Sch 41 para 1) or the making of an unauthorised issued of an invoice showing VAT (see para 2).

Reductions for disclosure

12.—A penalty under Sch 41 paras 1 or 2 may be reduced by making a disclosure. The reduction is governed by the quality of the disclosure and whether it is prompted or unprompted (see Sch 41 para 13).

A relevant act or failure is disclosed by:

- telling HMRC about it;
- giving HMRC reasonable help in quantifying the unpaid tax; and
- allowing HMRC access to records for the purpose of checking how much tax is unpaid.

Disclosure of a relevant act or failure is "unprompted" if it is made at a time when the person has no reason to believe that HMRC have discovered, or are about to discover, the relevant act or failure. A disclosure in any other circumstances is treated as "prompted".

The "quality" of a disclosure is determined by reference to such matters as its timing, nature and extent.

13.—The penalties prescribed by Sch 41 para 6 are reduced to reflect the quality (see Sch 41 para 12(4)) of the disclosure and whether it was prompted (see Sch 41 para 12(3)(*b*)) or unprompted (see Sch 41 para 12(3)(*a*)) in accordance with the following table.

Conduct	***Penalty (% of potential lost revenue)***		
	Maximum	***Minimum***	
		Prompted	***Unprompted***
	%	%	%
Deliberate and concealed act or failure	100	50	30

Conduct	Penalty (% of potential lost revenue)		
	Maximum	Minimum	
		Prompted	Unprompted
	%	%	%
Deliberate but not concealed act or failure	70	35	20

Not deliberate:

Conduct	Penalty (% of potential lost revenue)		
	Maximum	Minimum	
		Prompted	Unprompted
	%	%	%
• HMRC become aware of the failure to comply (see para 1) less than 12 months after the tax became chargeable	30	10	0
• Other	30	20	10

Special reduction

14.—HMRC may reduce a penalty under Sch 41 paras 1 or 2, stay such a penalty or agree a compromise in relation to proceedings for such a penalty. HMRC may do so if they think this is warranted by special circumstances. Ability to pay and the fact that a potential loss of revenue from one taxpayer is balanced by a potential over-payment by another do not amount to special circumstances.

This provision applies to the portion of the penalty for which a company officer is liable: see Sch 41 para 22(1) and (5)(*a*).

Interaction with other penalties and late payment surcharges

15.—Conduct giving rise to a penalty under Sch 41 paras 1 or 2 may also give rise to: (1) a surcharge for late payment; or (2) a penalty under some other provision. Where this is so, the penalty under para 1 or 2 is reduced by the amount of the surcharge or other penalty. However, no reduction is made in respect of a penalty imposed by the Upper Tribunal under Sch 36 para 50(1) in respect of continued failure to comply with an information notice or deliberate obstruction of an HMRC officer in the course of an inspection: see Sch 36 para 50(6)(*b*).

For the Upper Tribunal, see TCEA 2007 s 3.

Assessment

16.—A penalty under Sch 41 paras 1 or 2 is assessed. HMRC must notify the assessed person. The notice of assessment must state the period in respect of which the penalty is assessed. The penalty must be paid within 30 days, counted from the day on which notice of assessment is issued.

For procedural purposes, a penalty assessment in respect of conduct within para 1 is treated in the say way as a tax assessment. The penalty assessment is enforced as if it were a tax assessment. The penalty may be combined with an assessment of tax. The penalty must be assessed no later than 12 months after expiration of either: (1) the period during which an appeal could be brought; or (2) the period during which an appeal which has been brought has not been determined or withdrawn.

For procedural purposes, a penalty assessment in respect of conduct within Sch 41 para 2 is treated in the same way as a demand for recovery. The penalty assessment is enforced as if it were such a demand. The penalty may be combined with such a demand. The penalty must be assessed no later than 12 months after the date on which the unpaid tax was ascertained.

If potential lost revenue is underestimated, so that a penalty is understated, HMRC can make a supplementary assessment.

For the application of this provision to the portion of the penalty for which a company officer is liable: see Sch 41 para 22(1) and 5(*c*), (*d*).

Appeal

17–19.—An appeal may be made against a decision by HMRC that a penalty is payable. Here, the tribunal may affirm or cancel the decision.

An appeal may also be made against a decision by HMRC regarding the amount of the penalty payable. Here, the tribunal may either affirm HMRC's decision or substitute another one that HMRC had power to make. In substituting its own decision, the tribunal may affirm HMRC's view of special circumstances (see Sch 41 para 14), so that the same percentage reduction is applied to a different starting point. Alternatively, the tribunal may substitute its own view of special circumstances. However, the tribunal may substitute its own view only if it considers that HMRC's decision was flawed in the light of judicial review principles.

An appeal is brought to the First-tier Tribunal. For procedural purposes, the appeal is treated in the same way as an appeal against an assessment to the tax concerned. For the First-tier Tribunal, see TCEA 2007 s 3.

For the application of this provision to the portion of the penalty for which a company officer is liable: see Sch 41 para 22(1) and 5(*e*).

Reasonable excuse

20.—No liability to a penalty arises under Sch 41 paras 1 or 2 if:

- the act or failure was not deliberate; and
- the taxpayer satisfies HMRC or (on appeal) the First-tier Tribunal that there is a reasonable excuse for the act or failure.

An insufficiency of funds is capable of being a reasonable excuse only if it is attributable to events outside the taxpayer's control.

Relying on another person is capable of being a reasonable excuse only if the taxpayer took reasonable care to avoid the relevant act or failure.

An act or failure may take place at a time when the taxpayer had a reasonable excuse and be remedied at a time when the reasonable excuse had ceased to apply. The taxpayer is treated as having a reasonable excuse if the act or failure has been remedied without unreasonable delay.

For the First-tier Tribunal, see TCEA 2007 s 3.

Agency

21.—A taxpayer is liable to a penalty under Sch 41 para 1 in respect of a failure by his agent unless he satisfies HMRC or (on appeal) the First-tier Tribunal that he took reasonable care to avoid the failure.

A taxpayer is liable to a penalty under Sch 41 para 2 in respect of a failure by his agent unless he satisfies HMRC or (on appeal) the First-tier Tribunal that he took reasonable care to avoid the failure.

For the First-tier Tribunal, see TCEA 2007 s 3.

Companies: officers' liability

22.—Liability to a penalty under Sch 41 paras 1 or 2 may arise from a deliberate act or failure attributable to an officer of a company. Where this is so, the officer is liable to pay the all or part of the penalty. The portion payable is specified in a written notice. The officer must pay this portion within 30 days, counted from the day on which the notice is given. Sch 41 paras 14, 16–19 and 23 are modified accordingly.

A "company" is defined as any body corporate or unincorporated association other than a partnership, a local authority or a local authority association. As regards a body corporate other than a limited liability partnership, an "officer" is a director, shadow director, manager or secretary. As regards a limited liability partnership, an "officer" is a member. In any other case, an "officer" is a director, manager, secretary or any other person managing or purporting to manage any of the company's affairs.

The term "P" is defined for the purposes of this schedule.

Double jeopardy

23.—A person is not liable to a penalty under Sch 41 paras 1 or 2 if he has been convicted of an offence in connection with the action or failure.

This provision applies to the portion of the penalty for which a company officer is liable: see Sch 41 para 22(1) and (5)(*f*).

Interpretation

24.—Various words and phrases are defined.

Consequent repeals

25.—Provisions repealed as a consequence of this schedule are listed. As regards VAT, VATA 1994 s 67 and, in consequence, a number of other provisions, are repealed (see para 25(*f*), (*g*), (*h*)(i) and (*k*)(i)).

SCHEDULE 43 TAKING CONTROL OF GOODS ETC: CONSEQUENTIAL PROVISION (SECTION 129)

General note Part 1 of this Schedule lists the legislation amended or repealed as a consequence of the enactment of s 127 (enforcement by taking control of goods in England and Wales). Part 2 lists the legislation amended or repealed as a consequence of the enactment of s 128 (summary warrants in Scotland).

This schedule takes effect from a day to be appointed by order made under s 129(4). No order has been made to date in respect of Part 1. Part 2 came into force on 23 November 2009 subject to transitional provisions and savings: see the Finance Act 2008, Section 128 and Part 2 of Schedule 43 (Appointed Day, Transitional Provision and Savings) Order 2009, SI 2009/3024 arts 3–5.

PART 1 CONSEQUENTIAL PROVISION: TAKING CONTROL OF GOODS

This Part repeals VATA 1994 s 67A and FA 1997 s 51(A1), which are prospectively inserted by TCEA 2007 Sch 11 paras 118, 126 (see Sch 43 paras 4, 6).

PART 2 CONSEQUENTIAL PROVISION: SUMMARY WARRANT

As regard VAT, this Part repealed FA 1997 s 52 with effect from 23 November 2009, subject to transitional provisions and savings: see Sch 43 para 15; the Finance Act 2008, Section 128 and Part 2 of Schedule 43 (Appointed Day, Transitional Provision and Savings) Order 2009, SI 2009/3024 arts 3–5.

SCHEDULE 44 CERTIFICATES OF DEBT: CONSEQUENTIAL PROVISION (SECTION 132)

This Schedule repeals VATA 1994 Sch 11 para 14(1)(*d*).

Corporation Tax Act 2009

2009 Chapter 4

PART 19 GENERAL EXEMPTIONS

MISCELLANEOUS

1286. VAT repayment supplements

No liability to corporation tax arises in respect of a sum paid by way of supplement under VATA 1994 s 79.

PART 20 GENERAL CALCULATION RULES

CHAPTER 1 RESTRICTION OF DEDUCTIONS

MISCELLANEOUS

1303. Penalties, interest and VAT surcharges

As regards VAT matters, no deduction is allowed for the following when calculating profits for corporation tax purposes:

- a penalty under VATA 1994 ss 60–70;
- interest under VATA 1994 s 74;
- a surcharge under VATA 1994 s 59;
- a penalty under FA 2007 Sch 24 paras 1, 1A, 2; or
- a penalty under FA 2008 Sch 41 paras 1, 2.

PART 21 OTHER GENERAL PROVISIONS

FINAL PROVISIONS

1328. Commencement

This Act came into force on 1 April 2009. For corporation tax purposes, it has effect for accounting periods ending after 31 March 2009. For income tax and capital gains tax purposes, it has effect for the tax year 2009–10 and subsequent tax years.

Finance Act 2009

2009 Chapter 10

PART 1 CHARGES, RATES, ALLOWANCES, ETC

VALUE ADDED TAX

9. Extension of reduced standard rate and anti-avoidance provision

The standard rate of VAT is increased from 15% to 17.5% from 1 January 2010. For the special accounting arrangements for businesses operating beyond midnight on 31 December 2009, see Revenue and Customs Brief 68/09, 5 November 2009.

This section introduces Sch 3.

PART 4 VALUE ADDED TAX

76. Place of supply of services

This section introduces Sch 36.

77. Repayment to those in business in other States

This section amends VATA 1994 ss 39, 83 and inserts a new s 39A.

78. Information relating to cross-border supplies of services to taxable recipients

This section amends VATA 1994 Sch 11 para 2.

79. Effect of VAT changes on arbitration of rent for agricultural holdings

This section amends Agricultural Holdings Act 1986 Sch 2 para 4. For the scope and interpretation of this provision (which is governed by this section), see the commentary to the 1986 Act.

PART 7 ADMINISTRATION

STANDARDS AND VALUES

92. HMRC Charter

HMRC must prepare a Charter by 31 December 2009. For the Charter, see CRCA 2005 s 16A. For the text, see Appendix 18.

93. Duties of senior accounting officers of qualifying companies

This section introduces Sch 46. Schedule 46 applies to financial years beginning on or after 21 July 2009 (ie Royal Assent).

94. Publishing details of deliberate tax defaulters

HMRC may publish information about a person if he becomes liable to one or more relevant penalties (see s 94(2)) following an investigation and the potential lost revenue (see s 94(3)) in relation the penalty or penalties exceeds £25,000. This sum maybe varied by order. No orders have been made to date.

in relation the penalty or penalties exceeds £25,000. This sum maybe varied by order. No orders have been made to date.

The information which may be published, the manner in which it may be published, and the earliest and latest times for publication are specified. No information may be published in specified circumstances.

This section came into force on 1 April 2010: see Finance Act 2009, Section 94 (Appointed Day) Order 2010 art 2.

INFORMATION ETC

95. Amendment of information and inspection powers

This section introduces Sch 47.

Incidental, supplementary, consequential, transitional or transitory provisions or savings in connection with FA 2008 Sch 36 (as amended by Schedule 47) may be made by order. For the order made, see Finance Act 2009, Schedule 47 (Consequential Amendments) Order 2009, SI 2009/2035.

96. Extension of information and inspection powers to further taxes

This section introduces Sch 48. The amendments made by Sch 48 came into force on 1 April 2010: see Finance Act 2009, Section 96 and Schedule 48 (Appointed Day, Savings and Consequential Amendments) Order 2009, SI 2009/3054 art 2.

97. Powers to obtain contact details for debtors

This section introduces Sch 49.

INTEREST

101. Late payment interest on sums due to HMRC

An amount due to HMRC (or set off against an amount payable by HMRC) carries interest (referred to as "late payment interest") at the prescribed rate (referred to as "the late payment interest rate") from a time (referred to as "the late payment interest start date") until the date of payment or set off. It is immaterial whether the late payment interest start date is a non-business day (as defined in the Bills of Exchange Act 1882 s 92). Late payment interest does not attract a liability to late payment interest. It is paid without deduction of income tax.

This section does not apply to an amount of a description specified by order. No order has been made to date.

This section introduces Sch 53. For the late payment interest start date, see Sch 53 paras 10–12.

This section comes into force on a day appointed by order under s 104(3). No order has been made to date.

This section is amended by F(No 3)A 2010 Sch 9 from a day to be appointed by order under F(No 3)A 2010 s 25. The amendments made to this section and the commencement order made to date do not appear to have any relevance to VAT.

102. Repayment interest on sums to be paid by HMRC

An amount payable by HMRC (see below) carries interest (referred to as "repayment interest") at the prescribed rate (referred to as "repayment interest rate") from a time (referred to as "the repayment interest start date") until the date of payment or set off. It is immaterial whether the repayment interest start date is a non-business day (as defined in the Bills of Exchange Act 1882 s 92). Repayment interest does not attract a right to repayment interest.

An amount payable by HMRC includes: (1) a payment on account repaid by HMRC; and (2) an amount set off against an amount owed to HMRC.

This section does not apply to: (1) an amount payable in consequence of an order or judgment of a court having power to award interest; (2) an amount of repayment interest; or (3) an amount of a description specified by order. No order has been made to date.

This section introduces Sch 54. For the repayment interest start date, see Sch 54 Part 1.

This section comes into force on a day appointed by order under s 104(3). No order relevant to VAT has been made to date.

This section is amended by F(No 3)A 2010 Sch 9 from a day to be appointed by order under F(No 3)A 2010 s 25. No order relevant to VAT has been made to date. The amendments made by F(No 3)A 2010 Sch 9 do not appear to have any relevance to VAT.

103. Rates of interest

The rates of late payment interest (see s 101) and repayment interest (see s 102) are prescribed by regulations. No regulations relevant to VAT have been made to date.

This section comes into force on a day appointed by order under s 104(3). No order has been made to date.

103A. Further provision as to late payment interest and repayment interest

This section is inserted by F(No 3)A 2010 Sch 9 from a day to be appointed by order under F(No 3)A 2010 s 25. No order has been made to date. This section introduces Sch 54A. Schedule 54A does not appear to have any relevance to VAT.

104. Supplementary

Various words and phrases are defined. Sections 101–103 come into force on a day appointed by order. No orders have been made to date.

This section is amended by F(No 3)A 2010 Sch 9 from a day to be appointed by order under F(No 3)A 2010 s 25. No order has been made to date. The amendments made by F(No 3)A 2010 Sch 9 do not appear to have any relevance to VAT.

PENALTIES

106. Penalties for failure to make returns etc

This section introduces Sch 55. In the absence of any specific commencement provision, this section came into force on 21 July 2009. Schedule 55 comes into force on days to be appointed by order.

Schedule 55 imposes penalties in respect of failures to make returns and other documents in respect of the direct taxes specified in Items 1–13 of the Table in Sch 55 para 1(5). The appointed day order made to date (SI 2011/702) relates to three of these Items.

Schedule 55 is amended by F(No 3)A 2010 Sch 10. In particular, Items 7A, 7B and 14–28 are added to the Table in Sch 55 para 1(5). These Items relate to VAT and other indirect taxes, duties and levies. The amendments come into force on a day to be appointed by order. No order has been made to date.

107. Penalties for failure to pay tax

This section introduces Sch 56. In the absence of any specific commencement provision, this section came into force on 21 July 2009. Schedule 56 comes into force on days to be appointed by order.

Schedule 56 imposes penalties for failure to pay specified amounts in relation to the direct taxes specified in Items 1–24 of the Table in Sch 56 para 1(5). The appointed day order made to date (SI 2010/466) relates to six of these Items.

Schedule 56 is amended by F(No 3)A 2011 Sch 11. In particular, Items 6A–6C, 11A–11M, 13A, 13B, 16A–16C, 17A are added, Item 20 is repealed and Items 23, 24 are amended. These Items relate to VAT and other indirect taxes, duties and levies. The amendments come into force on a day to be appointed by order. No order has been made to date.

108. Suspension of penalties during the currency of agreement for deferred payment

A person may request deferment if he is unable to pay an amount of VAT. He is not liable to default surcharge (see VATA 1994 ss 59(4), 59A(4)) in respect of that amount if: (1) an HMRC officer agrees that payment should be deferred for a period (referred to as the "deferral period"); and (2) liability to the surcharge would arise between the date of the request and the end of the deferral period. It follows that deferment may be granted whether the request is made before or after the due date for payment. However, liability to the surcharge is extinguished only if the request is made *before* the due date.

The agreement may be given subject to conditions. These conditions may include a requirement that part of the VAT is paid during the deferral period. The agreement may be varied at any time by a further agreement.

The person becomes liable to surcharge if: (1) he either fails to pay the outstanding VAT at the end of the deferral period or fails to comply with one or more of the conditions imposed by the agreement; and (2) an HMRC officer serves a notice specifying the amount of surcharge to which he would have been liable but for the deferral.

An order may remove VAT from the scope of this section or provide that it applies to a different penalty. No order has been made to date.

This section applies to agreements made after 23 November 2008.

109. Miscellaneous amendments

This section introduces Sch 57. In the absence of an specific commencement provision, this section and the amendments made by Sch 57 came into force on 21 July 2009.

MISCELLANEOUS

112. Customs and excise enforcement: movements between member states

This section amends F(No 2)A 1992 s 4. In the absence of an specific commencement provision, the amendments made by this section came into force on 21 July 2009.

PART 8 MISCELLANEOUS

GAMBLING

113. VAT exemption for gaming participation fees

This section amends VATA 1994 Sch 9 Group 4 with effect from 27 April 2009.

SCHEDULES

SCHEDULE 3 VAT: SUPPLEMENTARY CHARGE AND ORDERS CHANGING RATE (SECTION 9)

PART 1 SUPPLEMENTARY CHARGE TO VAT

The charge

1.—A supply of goods or services is subject to a supplementary charge if:

- the supply is treated as taking place after 24 November 2008;
- the supply spans 1 January 2010 (referred to as "the date of the VAT change"). For the circumstances in which the grant of a right to goods or services spans that date, see Sch 3 para 3. For the circumstances in which any other supply spans that date, see Sch 3 para 2;
- the supply is subject to VAT at the standard rate (see VATA 1995 s 2);
- the supply is not excepted from the supplementary charge. For the exceptions, see Sch 3 paras 12, 13 and 15; and
- the recipient of the supply is entitled to input tax credit, repayment or refund in respect of only part, or none, of the VAT chargeable on the supply.

Supply spanning the date of the VAT change

2.—This paragraph applies to a supply of goods or services which does *not* consist of the grant of a right to goods or services. The supply spans 1 January 2010 if the following conditions are met:

(1) the supply is treated as taking place before 1 January 2010 by virtue of:
  (a) the issue of a VAT invoice (see VATA 1994 s 6(4)); or
  (b) the receipt of a payment (see VATA 1994 s 6(4));
(2) the supplier (see Sch 3 para 5(2)) and the person to whom the supply is made are connected with each other at any time in the period beginning with the day on which the VAT invoice was issued or the payment made, and ending on 1 January 2010. This is referred to as "condition A";
(3) the aggregate of the following is more than £100,000:
  (a) the relevant consideration (see Sch 3 para 6(2)) for the supply;
  (b) the relevant consideration (see Sch 3 para 6(2)) for every related (see Sch 3 para 6(3), (4)) supply of goods or services spanning 1 January 2010; and
  (c) the relevant consideration (see Sch 3 para 6(2)) for every related (see Sch 3 para 6(3), (4)) grant of a right to goods or services spanning 1 January 2010.
  This is referred to as "condition B";
(4) a prepayment (see Sch 3 para 2(7)) in respect of the supply is financed (see Sch 3 para 7) by the supplier or by a person connected (see Sch 3 para 8) with the supplier. This is referred to as "condition C";
(5) the basic time of supply (see Sch 3 para 4) is after 31 December 2009;
(6) (if the supply is treated as taking place by virtue of the issue of a VAT invoice) full payment of the amount shown on the VAT invoice becomes due after 30 June 2010. This is referred to as "condition D"; and
(7) (if the supply is one of a series of supplies of the same, or substantially the same, goods or services) each of the supplies in the series was (or will) be made in the expectation that the affected supply would (or will) take place (see Sch 3 para 5(1)).

Head 3 is omitted and head 4 modified if the supply is treated as having taken place before 31 March 2009. See Sch 3 para 11.

For exemption from the supplementary charge in relation to the letting, hiring or rental of assets, see Sch 3 para 12. For exemption where "condition B" is met but conditions A, C and (where appropriate) D are not, see Sch 12 para 13. For exemption from the supplementary charge where the only condition met is "condition D", see VAT (Supplementary Charge) Order 2009, SI 2009/3127.

Grant of right spanning the date of the VAT change

3.—This paragraph applies to a supply of goods or services which consists of the grant of a right to goods or services (as defined in Sch 3 para 3(7)). The supply spans 1 January 2010 if the following conditions are met:

(1) the supply is treated as taking place before 1 January 2010;
(2) the goods or services are to be supplied at a discount or free of charge;

(3) the basic time of supply (see Sch 3 para 4(1)) for the supply of some or all of the goods or services is after 31 December 2009;

(4) the grantor (see Sch 3 para 5(2)) and the person to whom the right is granted are connected with each other at any time in the period beginning with the day on which the supply consisting of the grant of the right is treated as taking place, and ending on either 1 January 2010 or (if the right is wholly or partly exercised on a later date) the date (or the first date) on which the right was wholly or partly exercised. This is referred to as "condition A";

(5) the aggregate of the following is more than £100,000:

  (a) the relevant consideration (see Sch 3 para 6(2)) for the grant of the right,

  (b) the relevant consideration (see Sch 3 para 6(2)) for every related (see Sch 3 para 6(3), (4)) supply of goods or services spanning 1 January 2010, and

  (c) the relevant consideration (see Sch 3 para 6(2)) for every related (see Sch 3 para 6(3), (4)) grant of a right to goods or services spanning 1 January 2010.

  (d) This is referred to as "condition B";

(6) the payment (see Sch 3 para 2(7)) made in respect of the grant is financed (see Sch 3 para 7) by the grantor or by a person connected (see Sch 3 para 8) with the grantor. This is referred to as "condition C";

(7) (if the supply is one of a series of supplies of the same, or substantially the same, goods or services) each of the supplies in the series was (or will) be made in the expectation that the affected supply would (or will) take place (see Sch 3 para 5(1)).

Head 5 is omitted and head 6 modified if the supply is treated as having taken place before 31 March 2009. See Sch 3 para 11.

For exemption from the supplementary charge where condition B is met but conditions A and C are not, see Sch 12 para 13.

"Basic time of supply"

4.—This paragraph defines "the basic time of supply" for the purposes of Sch 3 paras 2 and 3.

Series of supplies

5.—The terms "supplier" and "grantor" are modified for the purposes of Sch 3 paras 2(3) and 3(3) where a supply or grant is one of a series relating to the same (or substantially the same) goods or services.

"Relevant consideration" and "related" supplies

6.—The terms "relevant consideration" and (in relation to a supply or grant) "related" are defined for the purposes of Sch 3 paras 2 and 3.

Financing

7.—The term "financed" is defined for the purposes of Sch 3 paras 2 and 3.

Connected persons

8.—CTA 2010 s 1122 applies for the purpose of determining whether two or more persons are "connected".

Receipt of payments

9.—The term "receipt of a payment" is defined.

Power to change relevant conditions

10.—Schedule 3 Part 3 (paras 16 and17) may be modified by order. No order has been made to date.

Supplies treated as taking place before 31 March 2009

11.—This paragraph modifies Sch 3 paras 2 and 3 in relation to supplies treated as taking place before 31 March 2009.

PART 2 EXCEPTIONS

Letting etc of assets

12.—No supplementary charge arises under Sch 3 para 2 if: (1) the supply arises from the letting, hiring or rental of assets; (2) the VAT invoice or payment relates to a period of twelve months or less; and (3) the invoice is issued or the payment is received in accordance with normal commercial practice (see Sch 3 para 14) in relation to the letting, hiring or rental of such assets.

Condition B cases involving normal commercial practice

13.—No supplementary charge arises under Sch 3 para 2 if: (1) "condition B" is met but conditions A, C and (where appropriate) D are not; and (2) the supply is made in accordance with normal commercial practice (see Sch 3 para 14).

No supplementary charge arises under Sch 3 para 3 if: (1) "condition B" is met but conditions A and C are not; and (2) the right is granted in accordance with normal commercial practice (see Sch 3 para 14).

Normal commercial practice

14.—The term "normal commercial practice" is defined.

Further exceptions

15.—An order may provide that no supplementary charge arises on supplies or grants of a specified description. For the order made, see VAT (Supplementary Charge) Order 2009, SI 2009/3127.

PART 3 LIABILITY AND AMOUNT

Liability

16.—A supplementary charge on a supply meeting the conditions in Sch 3 para 2 is a liability of the supplier. It becomes due on 1 January 2010.

A supplementary charge on a supply meeting the conditions in Sch 3 para 3 is a liability of the person who granted the right to goods or services ("the grantor"). It becomes due on the first occasion after 31 December 2009 on which the grant is exercised.

In either case, the person liable to the supplementary charge is the representative member of a VAT group if: (1) the supplier or grantor is not a taxable person on the due date; and (2) the supplier or grantor is a member of the VAT group at that time. For the formation, variation and termination of VAT groups, see VATA 1994 ss 43A–43D.

Amount

17.—In principle, the supplementary charge on a supply within Sch 3 para 2 or the grant of a right within Sch 3 para 3 is the difference between: (1) the amount of VAT chargeable using an assumed rate of 17.5%; and (2) the amount that would otherwise be chargeable.

However, the grant of a right may give rise to some supplies of goods or services with a basic time of supply (see below) falling before 1 January 2010 (period A) and to others with a basic time of supply (see below) falling after 31 December 2009 (period B). If so, the consideration for the grant is apportioned by reference to the goods or services supplied in each period. This is done on a just and reasonable basis. The supplementary charge on the grant is the difference between: (1) the amount of VAT chargeable on the proportion of the grant attributable to period B using an assumed rate of 17.5%; and (2) the amount that would otherwise be chargeable on that proportion.

The "basic time of supply" for the supplies listed in Sch 3 para 18 is determined in accordance with Sch 3 para 19.

PART 4 LISTED SUPPLIES

"Listed supply"

18.—A "listed supply" is a supply which is made for a consideration wholly or partly determined (or payable) periodically (or from time to time), and which is treated as taking place by virtue of a VAT invoice being issued or a payment being received. The supplies falling within this description are listed. This list may be varied by order. No order has been made to date.

"Basic time of supply": listed supplies

19.—In principle, the "basic time of supply" for a "listed supply" is the end of the period in which the VAT invoice was issued or the payment received. There are two exceptions.

First, the billing period for a listed supply may not coincide with the end of a prescribed accounting period. The "basic time of supply" for the part of the supply billed during the prescribed accounting period is the end of that period. The supply and the consideration for it must be apportioned between prescribed accounting periods on a just and reasonable basis.

Second, a VAT invoice may be issued, or a payment received, in respect of a premium for the grant of a tenancy or lease. The "basic time of supply" is the date of the grant.

PART 5 ADMINISTRATION AND INTERPRETATION

Person ceasing to be taxable person before supplementary charge due

20.—X (the person liable to pay the supplementary charge) may not be a taxable person on the due date (see Sch 3 para 16). If so, X must account for the supplementary charge as if it were VAT due for his final prescribed accounting period. If a supplementary charge is assessed, the amount assessed does not carry interest from a date earlier than the due date.

Adjustment of contracts following the VAT change

21.—A supplementary charge may arise in respect of a supply of goods or services arising from a contract made before 1 January 2010. The consideration for the supply is increased by the amount of the supplementary charge unless the contract provides otherwise.

Invoices

22.—The Commissioners may make regulations regarding the provision, replacement or correction of invoices for the supplementary charge. The regulations are made under VATA 1994 Sch 11 para 2A. No regulations have been made to date.

Orders under this Schedule

23.—An order made under Sch 3 is made by statutory instrument.

Interpretation: general

24.—Various words and phrases are defined.

PART 6 AMENDMENTS OF VATA 1994

25.—This paragraph amends VATA 1994 ss 2 and 97.

SCHEDULE 36 VAT: PLACE OF SUPPLY OF SERVICES ETC (SECTION 76)

General note The amendments made by this schedule apply to supplies made from the dates specified in Sch 36 paras 14, 16 and 18.

PART 1 AMENDMENTS COMING INTO FORCE IN 2010

Part 1 amends VATA 1994 ss 6, 7, 8, 43, 96, 97, 97A and the VAT (Tour Operators) Order 1987, SI 1987/1806, art 5; substitutes VATA 1994 s 9; inserts VATA 1994 s 7A and Sch 4A;

and repeals VATA 1994 Sch 5. In principle, these amendments apply to supplies made after 31 December 2009. However, there are two exceptions:

- The powers to make orders under the new VATA 1994 s 7A(6) may be exercised from 21 July 2009 (ie Royal Assent).
- The references to "a supply to which section 7A(2) applies" in the amended s 43 includes a supply of services of a description in VATA 1994 Sch 5 paras 1–8 made before 1 January 2010.

PART 2 AMENDMENTS COMING INTO FORCE IN 2011

Part 2 repeals the new VATA 1994 Sch 4A para 4 inserted by Part 1 and inserts new VATA 1994 Sch 4A paras 9A and 14A. These amendments apply to supplies made after 31 December 2010.

PART 3 AMENDMENTS COMING INTO FORCE IN 2013

The new VATA 1994 Sch 4A inserted by para 11 is amended. A new Sch 4A para 13A is inserted. It applies to supplies made after 31 December 2012.

PART 4 TRANSITIONAL PROVISIONS

19.—A supply of services is not treated as being made in the UK if:

- The services are treated as being supplied in another member state in accordance with the laws of that member state;
- the time of supply falls before the relevant commencement date (ie 1 January 2010, 1 January 2011 or 1 January 2013) in accordance with the laws of that member state;
- the services are treated as being supplied in the UK in accordance with VATA 1994 (as amended by Parts 1–3 of this Schedule); and
- the services would not have been so treated in accordance with the provisions of VATA 1994 in force before the relevant commencement date.

SCHEDULE 46 DUTIES OF SENIOR ACCOUNTING OFFICERS OF QUALIFYING COMPANIES (SECTION 93)

General note This schedule has effect in relation to financial years beginning on or after 21 July 2009 (ie the day on which this Act was passed): see s 93(2).

Main duty of senior accounting officer

1.—The senior accounting officer (see Sch 46 para 16) of a qualifying company (see Sch 46 para 15) must take reasonable steps to ensure that the company (see Sch 46 para 18(1)) establishes and maintains appropriate tax accounting arrangements (see Sch 46 para 14). In particular, he must take reasonable steps to monitor the accounting arrangements and identify any deficiencies in them.

Certificate for Commissioners

2.—The senior accounting officer (see Sch 46 para 16) must provide HMRC with a certificate for each financial year (see Sch 46 para 18(1)) of the company. The certificate must state whether the company had appropriate accounting arrangements (see Sch 46 para 14) throughout the year and, if it did not, provide an explanation of the deficiencies. The certificate must be provided in the form and manner specified by an HMRC officer. This must be done no later than the end of the period for filing (see Sch 46 para 18(1)) the company's accounts. A certificate may relate to more than one qualifying company.

Notifying Commissioners of name of senior accounting officer

3.—The name of the person (or each of the persons) acting as senior accounting officer at any time during a financial year (see Sch 46 para 18(1)) must be notified to HMRC. This must be done no later than the end of the period for filing (see Sch 46 para 18(1)) the company's accounts and in the form and manner specified by an HMRC officer. This period may be extended by an HMRC officer.

Penalty for failure to comply with main duty

4.—A senior accounting officer is liable to a penalty if he fails to comply with Sch 46 para 1. The prescribed penalty is £5,000. For the person liable to a penalty where there is a change of senior accounting officer during a financial year, see Sch 46 para 6.

Penalties for failure to provide certificate etc

5.—A senior accounting officer is liable to a penalty if fails to provide a certificate in accordance with Sch 46 para 2. Alternatively, he is liable to a penalty if the certificate provided contains a careless (see Sch 46 para 5(3), (4)) or deliberate inaccuracy. The prescribed penalty in either case is £5,000. For the person liable to a penalty where there is a change of senior accounting officer during a financial year, see Sch 46 para 6.

More than one senior accounting officer

6.—Two or more persons (X, Y and Z) may successively fill the role of senior accounting officer during a financial year. If so, the person liable to a penalty under Sch 46 paras 4 or 5 is determined as follows:

- as regards the requirement to keep and maintain appropriate tax accounting arrangements (see Sch 46 para 1) the person liable to a penalty under Sch 46 para 4 is Z;
- as regards a failure to provide a certificate (see Sch 46 para 2), the person liable to a penalty under Sch 46 para 5(1)(*a*) is Z;
- as regards a careless or deliberate inaccuracy in the certificate provided, the person liable to a penalty under Sch 46 para 5(1)(*b*) is the person who complied, or purported to comply, with the requirement to provide the certificate. This could be X, Y or Z.

Penalty for failure to notify Commissioners of name of senior accounting officer

7.—A qualifying company (see Sch 46 para 15) is liable to a penalty if the name of its senior accounting officer is not notified to HMRC. The prescribed penalty is £5,000. For the requirement to notify, see Sch 46 para 3.

Reasonable excuse

8.—No liability to a penalty arises under Sch 46 paras 4, 5 or 7 if the senior accounting officer or qualifying company satisfies HMRC or, on appeal, the First-tier Tribunal or Upper Tribunal that there is a reasonable excuse for the failure. For the First-tier Tribunal, see TCEA 2007 s 3. For the chambers into which the tribunals are divided, see TCEA 2007 s 7.

An insufficiency of funds is capable of being a reasonable excuse only if it is attributable to events outside the person's control.

If X relies on Y to do something, this is capable of being a reasonable excuse only if X took reasonable care to avoid the failure.

A person may have a reasonable excuse for a failure. If the excuse ceases to apply, the person is regarded as continuing to have a reasonable excuse if he remedies the failure without unreasonable delay.

Assessment of penalties

9.—HMRC may assess the penalty to which a senior accounting company or qualifying company is liable under Sch 46 paras 4, 5 or 7. HMRC are not required to do so. Any assessment must be made no later than: (1) six months after the failure or inaccuracy first came to the attention of an HMRC officer; or (2) six years after the end of the period for filing the company's accounts for the financial year concerned. It must be notified to the person liable to the penalty.

A person may be the senior accounting officer of two or more companies in the same group. The person is liable to only one penalty under either or both of Sch 46 paras 4 and 5 in respect of the same financial year.

A company (see Sch 46 para 18(1)) may be a member of a group at the end of a financial year (eg 31 December 2010). The company is not liable to a penalty under Sch 46 para 7 in respect of that financial year if another group company was so liable in respect of a co-terminus financial year (ie 31 December 2010) or for a financial year ending within that financial year (eg 30 September 2010).

Appeal

10.—A person may appeal against HMRC's decision that a penalty is payable by him. Notice of appeal must be given in writing to HMRC and state the grounds for appeal. This must be done no later than 30 days after the notice of assessment (see Sch 46 para 9) was issued. If an appeal is notified to the tribunal, the tribunal may confirm or cancel HMRC's decision.

TMA 1970 Part 5 (ss 44–58) applies to appeals against HMRC's decision in the same manner as they apply to appeals against an assessment to income tax. This application is subject to the provisions of Sch 46 paras 10(2)–(4) and 11.

Enforcement of penalties

11.—A penalty under Sch 46 paras 4, 5 or 7 must be paid within 30 days. The 30-day period is counted from: (1) the date on which the appeal is determined or withdrawn (if notice of appeal has been given); or (2) the date on which the notice of assessment (see Sch 46 para 9) was issued (in other cases).

The penalty may be enforced as if it were income tax charged in an assessment which is due and payable. For recovery of income tax, see TMA 1970 Part 6 (ss 60–70A).

Power to change amount of penalties

12.—The penalties prescribed in Sch 46 paras 4, 5 and 7 may varied by regulations. No regulations have been made to date.

Application of provisions of TMA 1970

13.—TMA 1970 ss 108, 114 and 115 apply to this Schedule in the same manner as they apply for the purposes of the Taxes Acts (as defined in TMA 1970 s 118(1)).

Meaning of "appropriate tax accounting arrangements"

14.—The term "appropriate tax accounting arrangements" is defined.

Meaning of "qualifying company"

15.—The term "qualifying company" is defined. Regulations may provide that companies of a specified description are excluded from this definition. No regulations have been made to date.

Meaning of "senior accounting officer"

16.—The term "senior accounting officer" is defined.

Regulations

17.—Regulations under Sch 46 paras 12 and 15 are made by statutory instrument.

Other definitions

18.—Various words and phrases are defined.

SCHEDULE 47 AMENDMENT OF INFORMATION AND INSPECTION POWERS (SECTION 95)

This schedule amends FA 2008 Sch 36. In the absence of specific commencement provisions, the amendments made by this schedule have effect from 21 July 2009 (ie Royal Assent). For consequential amendments (which are not directly relevant to VAT), see the Finance Act 2009, Schedule 47 (Consequential Amendments) Order 2009, SI 2009/2035.

SCHEDULE 48 EXTENSION OF INFORMATION AND INSPECTION POWERS (SECTION 96)

This schedule amends FA 2008 Sch 36. It came into force on 1 April 2010: see Finance Act 2009, Section 96 and Schedule 48 (Appointed Day, Savings and Consequential Amendments) Order 2009, SI 2009/3054 art 2.

SCHEDULE 49 POWERS TO OBTAIN CONTACT DETAILS FOR DEBTORS (SECTION 97)

General note In the absence of specific commencement provisions, this schedule has effect from 21 July 2009 (ie Royal Assent).

Requirement for contact details for debtor

1.—This Schedule applies to sums payable to HMRC where the following conditions are met:

(1) an HMRC officer reasonably requires the debtor's contact details in order to collect that sum;

(2) the officer has reasonable grounds for believing that a third party has those details; and

(3) the third party falls within one of the following descriptions:

(a) it is a company, local authority or local authority association, or

(b) (if the officer has reasonable grounds for believing that the third party obtained the details in the course of carrying on a business) the third party is someone other than:

(i) a charity which obtained the details in the course of providing services free of charge, or

(ii) a person other than a charity who obtained the details in the course of providing, on behalf of a charity, services which are free of charge to the recipient of those services.

Power to obtain details

2.—An HMRC officer may require a third party to provide a debtor's contact details. He does so by a notice in writing which names the debtor.

Complying with notices

3.—A third party served with a notice (see Sch 49 para 2) must provide the details within the period specified in the notice. He must do so in the form and manner specified in the notice.

Right to appeal

4.—A third party may appeal against a notice (see Sch 49 para 2), or any requirement specified in the notice, on the ground that compliance would be unduly onerous.

The notice of appeal must state the grounds of appeal. It must be given in writing to the HMRC officer who issued the notice. This must be done no later than 30 days after the officer's notice was given.

On appeal, the First-tier Tribunal may confirm, vary or set aside the notice or requirement. The taxpayer must comply with a notice or requirement which is confirmed or varied. He must do so within the period specified by the tribunal (if a period is specified) or within the period specified by an HMRC officer in writing following the decision (in other cases). The period specified in the latter case must be reasonable. The tribunal's decision is final.

The appeal is treated as if it were an appeal against an assessment to income tax. TMA 1970 Part 5 applies accordingly.

Penalty

5.—A third party is liable to a penalty if he fails to comply with a notice (see para 2). The prescribed penalty is £300. The penalty is assessed and enforced as if it were a penalty arising under FA 2008 Sch 36 para 39(1)(*a*). FA 2008 Sch 36 paras 44–49 and 52 apply for this purpose.

Power to change amount of penalty

6.—The penalty prescribed in Sch 49 para 5 may be varied by regulations. No regulations have been made to date.

Application of TMA 1970

7.—TMA 1970 ss 108, 114 and 115 apply to this schedule in the same manner as they apply for the purposes of the Taxes Acts (as defined in TMA 1970 s 118(1)).

General interpretation

8.—Various words and phrases are defined.

SCHEDULE 53 LATE PAYMENT INTEREST (SECTION 101)

General note Section 101 (and therefore this schedule) comes into force on a day appointed by order under s 104(3). No order has been made to date.

PART 2 SPECIAL PROVISION: LATE PAYMENT INTEREST START DATE

VAT due from persons not registered as required

10.—The date from which a person is registered may be later than the date from which he became liable to be registered. If an amount of VAT is due from him in respect of the period prior to his effective date of registration, the late payment interest date (see s 101(4)) in respect of that amount is the date which would have applied if he had been registered from the date when he became liable to registration.

Unauthorised VAT invoices

11.—An unauthorised person may issue an invoice showing either: (1) an amount of VAT; or (2) an amount which includes VAT. For the recovery of the VAT so shown or included, see VATA 1994 Sch 11 para 5. The late payment interest date (see s 101(4)) in respect of the VAT shown or included is the date which would have applied if the unauthorised person had been registered from the time when he first became liable to registration.

Death of taxpayer

12.—An executor or administrator may be unable to pay a tax debt due by the deceased until he has obtained probate or letters of administration. If the debt became due and payable after the date of death, the late payment start date is the later of: (1) the date that would have applied if the deceased were still alive; and (2) the day after the end of the period of 30 days beginning with the day on which probate or letters of administration were granted. Thus, if probate was granted on 1 January, the late payment date for the purposes of head (2) is 31 January.

SCHEDULE 54 REPAYMENT INTEREST (SECTION 102)

General note Section 102 (and therefore this schedule) comes into force on a day appointed by order under s 104(3). No order has been made to date.

PART 1 REPAYMENT INTEREST START DATE: GENERAL RULE

Introductory

1.—Part 1 sets out the general rule for determining "the repayment interest start date" for the purposes of s 102.

Repayment of amounts paid to HMRC

2–4.—If a payment has been made to HMRC in respect of an amount that is due and payable, the repayment interest start date is the date on which the payment was made.

If a payment has been made in connection with a liability to make a payment to HMRC, the repayment interest start date is the date on which the relevant amount becomes due and payable in respect of the liability. Thus, if a payment on account is made on 14 February in respect of an amount which will become due for payment on 31 July, the repayment interest start date is 31 July.

Payment of amounts on return or claim

5.—A return or claim may give rise to a repayment of tax which has not been paid to HMRC, eg where input tax exceeds output tax. The repayment interest start date is the later of: (1) the date (if any) on which the return or claim was required to be submitted; and (2) the date on which the return or claim was actually submitted.

SCHEDULE 55 PENALTY FOR FAILURE TO MAKE RETURNS (SECTION 106)

General note This schedule is amended by F(No 3)A 2010 Sch 10 to apply to VAT and other indirect taxes, duties and levies from a day to be appointed by order made under F(No 3)A 2010 s 26(2)–(7). No order has been made to date.

SCHEDULE 56 FAILURE TO MAKE PAYMENTS ON TIME (SECTION 107)

General note This schedule is amended by F(No 3)A 2010 Sch 11 to apply to VAT and other indirect taxes, duties and levies from a day to be appointed by order made under F(No 3)A 2010 s 27(3)–(7). No order has been made to date.

SCHEDULE 57 AMENDMENTS RELATING TO PENALTIES (SECTION 109)

General note This schedule amends FA 2007 Sch 24 and FA 2008 Schs 36, 40, 41. In the absence of any specific commencement provisions, these amendments came into force from 21 July 2009 (ie Royal Assent).

Corporation Taxes Act 2010

2010 Chapter 4

PART 24 CORPORATION TAX ACTS DEFINITIONS ETC

CHAPTER 1 DEFINITIONS

1122. "Connected" persons

Companies are connected if they are under common control. Two or more persons acting together to secure or exercise control of a company are connected with each other in relation to that Company: *Floor v Davies* [1978] STC 436; *IR Comrs v Harton Coal Co Ltd* (1960) 39 TC 174; *Steele v EVC International NV* [1996] STC 785. For HMRC's views, see Tax Bulletin, Issue 26, December 1996, p 372 (not reproduced).

An individual is connected with his spouse, brother or brother-in-law, sister or sister-in-law, parent or parent-in-law, grandparent or grandparent-in-law, son or son-in-law, daughter or daughter-in-law, grandson or grandson-in-law, grand-daughter or grand-daughter-in-law. Equivalent relationships apply if an individual has a civil partner.

A trustee of a settlement is connected with:

(a) a settlor;
(b) a person connected with a settlor, and
(c) a company connected with that settlement, ie:
   (i) a company which is (or would, if UK resident, be) a close company and its participators include the trustees; or
   (ii) it is controlled by such a company.

   Except in connection with bona fide commercial partnership arrangements, a partner is connected with his other partners and their spouses/civil partners or relatives. See also Statement of Practice D12 (not reproduced).

PART 25 DEFINITIONS FOR PURPOSES OF ACT AND FINAL PROVISIONS

FINAL PROVISIONS

1184. Commencement

This Act came into force on 1 April 2010. For corporation tax purposes, it has effect for accounting periods ending after 31 March 2010. For income tax and capital gains tax purposes, it has effect for the tax year 2010–11 and subsequent tax years.

Finance Act 2010

2010 Chapter 13

PART 2 ANTI-AVOIDANCE AND REVENUE PROTECTION

VALUE ADDED TAX AND INSURANCE PREMIUM TAX

50. Extension of reverse charge provisions to supplies of services

This section amends VATA 1994 s 55A and Sch 11 para 2(3B). In the absence of any specific commencement provision, this section came into force on 8 April 2010 (ie Royal Assent).

Finance (No 2) Act 2010

2010 Chapter 31

PART 1 RATES ETC

VALUE ADDED TAX

3. Rate of value added tax

The standard rate of VAT is increased from 17.5% to 20% from 4 January 2011.

This section introduces Sch 2.

SCHEDULES

SCHEDULE 2 VAT: SUPPLEMENTARY CHARGE TO VAT (SECTION 3)

PART 1 SUPPLEMENTARY CHARGE TO VAT

The charge

1.—A supply of goods or services is subject to a supplementary charge if:

- the supply is treated as taking place after 21 June 2010;
- the supply spans 4 January 2011 (referred to as "the date of the VAT change"). For the circumstances in which the grant of a right to goods or services spans that date, see Sch 2 para 3(1). For the circumstances in which any other supply spans that date, see Sch 2 para 2(1);
- the supply is subject to VAT at the standard rate (see VATA 1994 s 2);
- a relevant condition is met. For relevant conditions in relation to the grant of a right to goods or services spanning 4 January 2011, see Sch 2 para 3(2)–(6). For the circumstances in which any other supply spans that date, see Sch 2 para 2(2)–(8);
- the recipient of the supply is entitled to input tax credit, repayment or refund in respect of only part, or none, of the VAT chargeable on the supply; and
- the supply is not excepted from the supplementary charge. For the exceptions, see Sch 2 paras 11, 12, 13 and 15.

Supply spanning the date of the VAT change

2.—This paragraph applies to a supply of goods or services which does not consist of the grant of a right to goods or services. The supply spans 4 January 2011 if the following conditions are met:

(1) the supply is treated as taking place before 4 January 2011 by virtue of:
  (a) the issue of a VAT invoice (see VATA 1994 s 6(4)); or
  (b) the receipt of a payment (see VATA 1994 s 6(4));

(2) the supplier (see Sch 2 para 5(2)) and the person to whom the supply is made are connected with each other at any time in the period beginning with the day on which the VAT invoice was issued or the payment was received, and ending on 4 January 2011. This is referred to as "condition A";

(3) the aggregate of the following is more than £100,000:
  (a) the relevant consideration (see Sch 2 para 6(2)) for the supply;
  (b) the relevant consideration (see Sch 2 para 6(2)) for every related (see Sch 2 para 6(3), (4)) supply of goods or services spanning 4 January 2011; and
  (c) the relevant consideration (see Sch 2 para 6(2)) for every related (see Sch 2 para 6(3), (4)) grant of a right to goods or services spanning 4 January 2011.

This is referred to as "condition B";

(4) a prepayment (see Sch 2 para 2(7)) in respect of the supply is financed (see Sch 2 para 7) by the supplier or by a person connected (see Sch 2 para 8) with the supplier. This is referred to as "condition C";

(5) the basic time of supply (see Sch 2 para 4) is after 3 January 2011;

(6) (if the supply is treated as taking place by virtue of the issue of a VAT invoice) full payment of the amount shown on the invoice becomes due more than six months after the date on which the invoice was issued. This is referred to as "condition D"; and

(7) (if the supply is one of a series of supplies of the same, or substantially the same, goods or services) each of the supplies in the series was (or will) be made in the expectation that the affected supply would (or will) take place (see Sch 2 para 5(1)).

For exemption from the supplementary charge in relation to the letting, hiring or rental of assets, see Sch 2 para 11. For exemption where "condition B" is met but conditions A, C and (where appropriate) D are not, see Sch 2 para 12. For exemption where "condition D" is met but conditions A, B and C are not, see Sch 2 para 13.

Grant of right spanning the date of the VAT change

3.—This paragraph applies to a supply of goods or services which consists of the grant of a right to goods or services (as defined in Sch 2 para 3(7)). The supply spans 4 January 2011 if the following conditions are met:

(1) the supply is treated as taking place before 4 January 2011;

(2) the goods or services are to be supplied at a discount or free of charge;

(3) the basic time of supply (see Sch 2 para 4(1)) for the supply of some or all of the goods or services is after 3 January 2010;

(4) the grantor (see Sch 2 para 5(2)) and the person to whom the right is granted are connected with each other at any time in the period beginning with the day on which the supply consisting of the grant of the right is treated as taking place, and ending on either 4 January 2011 or (if the right is wholly or partly exercised on a later date) the date (or the first date) on which the right was wholly or partly exercised. This is referred to as "condition A";

(5) the aggregate of the following is more than £100,000:

  (a) the relevant consideration (see Sch 2 para 6(2)) for the grant of the right,

  (b) the relevant consideration (see Sch 2 para 6(2)) for every related (see Sch 2 para 6(3), (4)) supply of goods or services spanning 4 January 2011, and

  (c) the relevant consideration (see Sch 2 para 6(2)) for every related (see Sch 2 para 6(3), (4)) grant of a right to goods or services spanning 4 January 2011.

This is referred to as "condition B";

(6) the payment (see Sch 2 para 2(7)) made in respect of the grant is financed (see Sch 2 para 7) by the grantor or by a person connected (see Sch 2 para 8) with the grantor. This is referred to as "condition C";

(7) (if the supply is one of a series of supplies of the same, or substantially the same, goods or services) each of the supplies in the series was (or will) be made in the expectation that the affected supply would (or will) take place (see Sch 2 para 5(1)).

For exemption from the supplementary charge where condition B is met but conditions A and C are not, see Sch 2 para 12.

"Basic time of supply"

4.—This paragraph defines "the basic time of supply" for the purposes of Sch 2 paras 2 and 3.

Series of supplies

5.—The terms "supplier" and "grantor" are modified for the purposes of Sch 2 paras 2(3) and 3(3) where a supply or grant is one of a series relating to the same (or substantially the same) goods or services.

"Relevant consideration" and "related" supplies

6.—The terms "relevant consideration" and (in relation to a supply or grant) "related" are defined for the purposes of Sch 2 paras 2 and 3.

Financing

7.—The term "financed" is defined for the purposes of Sch 3 paras 2 and 3.

Connected persons

8.—CTA 2010 s 1122 applies for the purpose of determining whether two or more persons are "connected".

Receipt of payments

9.—The term "receipt of a payment" is defined.

Power to change relevant conditions

10.—Schedule 2 Part 1 (paras 1–10) may be modified by order. No order has been made to date.

PART 2 EXCEPTIONS

Letting etc of assets

11.—No supplementary charge arises under Sch 2 para 2 if: (1) the supply arises from the letting, hiring or rental of assets; (2) the VAT invoice or payment relates to a period of twelve months or less; and (3) the invoice is issued or the payment is received in accordance with normal commercial practice (see Sch 3 para 14) in relation to the letting, hiring or rental of such assets.

Condition B cases involving normal commercial practice

12.—No supplementary charge arises under Sch 2 para 2 if: (1) "condition B" is met but conditions A, C and (where appropriate) D are not; and (2) the supply is made in accordance with normal commercial practice (see Sch 2 para 14).

No supplementary charge arises under Sch 2 para 3 if: (1) "condition B" is met but conditions A and C are not; and (2) the right is granted in accordance with normal commercial practice (see Sch 2 para 14).

Condition D cases involving hire purchase, conditional sale or credit sale of goods

13.—No supplementary charge arises under Sch 2 para 2 if: (1) "condition D" is met but conditions A–C are not; (2) the VAT invoice relates to a supply of goods under a hire purchase, conditional sale or credit sale agreement; (3) the VAT invoice forms part of that agreement; (4) the VAT invoice is issued in accordance with normal commercial practice (see Sch 2 para 14); and (5) the intention and expectation is that the basic time of supply (see Sch 2 para 4(1)) of the goods will arise no more than six months after the date of the VAT invoice.

Normal commercial practice

14.—The term "normal commercial practice" is defined.

Further exceptions

15.—An order may provide that no supplementary charge arises on supplies or grants of a specified description. No order has been made to date.

PART 3 LIABILITY AND AMOUNT

Liability

16.—A supplementary charge on a supply meeting the conditions in Sch 2 para 2 is a liability of the supplier. It becomes due on 4 January 2011.

A supplementary charge on a supply meeting the conditions in Sch 2 para 3 is a liability of the person who granted the right to goods or services ("the grantor"). It becomes due on the first occasion after 3 January 2011 on which the grant is exercised.

In either case, the person liable to the supplementary charge is the representative member of a VAT group if: (1) the supplier or grantor is not a taxable person on the due date; and (2) the supplier or grantor is a member of the VAT group at that time. For the formation, variation and termination of VAT groups, see VATA 1994 ss 43A–43D.

Amount

17.—In principle, the supplementary charge on a supply within Sch 2 para 2 or the grant of a right within Sch 2 para 3 is the difference between: (1) the amount of VAT chargeable using an assumed rate of 20%; and (2) the amount that would otherwise be chargeable.

However, the grant of a right may give rise to some supplies of goods or services with a basic time of supply (see below) falling before 4 January 2011 (period A) and to others with a basic time of supply (see below) falling after 3 January 2011 (period B). If so, the consideration for the grant is apportioned by reference to the goods or services supplied in each period. This is done on a just and reasonable basis. The supplementary charge on the grant is the difference between: (1) the amount of VAT chargeable on the proportion of the grant attributable to period B using an assumed rate of 20%; and (2) the amount that would otherwise be chargeable on that proportion.

The "basic time of supply" for the supplies listed in Sch 2 para 18(2) is determined in accordance with Sch 2 para 19.

PART 4 LISTED SUPPLIES

"Listed supply"

18.—A "listed supply" is a supply which is made for a consideration wholly or partly determined (or payable) periodically (or from time to time), and which is treated as taking place by virtue of a VAT invoice being issued or a payment being received. The supplies falling within this description are listed. This list may be varied by order. No order has been made to date.

"Basic time of supply": listed supplies

19.—In principle, the "basic time of supply" for a "listed supply" is the end of the period to which a VAT invoice or payment relates. There are two exceptions.

First, the billing period for a listed supply may not coincide with the end of a prescribed accounting period. The "basic time of supply" for the part of the supply billed during the prescribed accounting period is the end of that period. The supply and the consideration for it must be apportioned between prescribed accounting periods on a just and reasonable basis.

Second, a VAT invoice may be issued, or a payment received, in respect of a premium for the grant of a tenancy or lease. The "basic time of supply" is the date of the grant.

PART 5 ADMINISTRATION AND INTERPRETATION

Person ceasing to be taxable person before supplementary charge due

20.—X (the person liable to pay the supplementary charge) may not be a taxable person on the due date (see Sch 2 para 16). If so, X must account for the supplementary charge as if it were VAT due for his final prescribed accounting period. If a supplementary charge is assessed, the amount assessed does not carry interest from a date earlier than the due date.

Adjustment of contracts following the VAT change

21.—A supplementary charge may arise in respect of a supply of goods or services arising from a contract made before 4 January 2011. The consideration for the supply is increased by the amount of the supplementary charge unless the contract provides otherwise.

Invoices

22.—The Commissioners may make regulations regarding the provision, replacement or correction of invoices for the supplementary charge. The regulations are made under VATA 1994 Sch 11 para 2A. No regulations have been made to date.

Orders under this Schedule

23.—An order under Sch 2 is made by statutory instrument.

Interpretation: general

24.—Various words and phrases are defined.

Finance (No 3) Act 2010

2010 Chapter 33

PART 2 OTHER TAXES AND DUTIES

VALUE ADDED TAX

19. Non-business use of business assets etc

This section introduces Sch 8.

20. Supplies of gas, heat or cooling

This section amends VATA 1994 s 9A and Sch 4 para 3 in relation to supplies made after 31 December 2010.

21. Supplies of aircraft etc

This section amends VATA 1994 Sch 8 Group 8 in relation to supplies, acquisitions and importations made after 31 December 2010.

22. Postal services etc

This section amends VATA 1994 s 96(1), Sch 8 Group 8 and Sch 9 Group 3 in relation to supplies made after 31 December 2010.

PART 3 ADMINISTRATION

25. Interest: corporation tax and petroleum revenue tax

This section introduces Sch 9. Schedule 9 amends FA 2009 ss 101, 102, 104 from a day to be appointed under sub-s (2). No order has been made to date

An order made under sub-s (4) may make incidental, supplemental, consequential, transitional, transitory or saving provisions in connection with the amendments made by Sch 9. No order has been made to date.

26. Penalties for failure to make returns etc

This section introduces Sch 10. Schedule 10 amends FA 2009 Sch 55 from a day to be appointed by order.

SCHEDULES

SCHEDULE 8 VALUE ADDED TAX: NON-BUSINESS USE OF BUSINESS ASSETS ETC (SECTION 19)

Input tax

1.— This paragraph amends VATA 1994 s 24. In the absence of any specific commencement provision, the amendments relating to s 24(5), (6) and (6A) came into force on 16 December 2010 (ie Royal Assent). The amendments relating to s 24(3), (5A), (5B), and (7) came into force on 1 January 2011 and apply to VAT incurred by a taxable person on or after that date. The circumstances in which VAT is "incurred" on an asset for this purpose are defined.

2.— This paragraph amends VATA 1994 s 26(4). In the absence of any specific commencement provision, the amendment came into force on 16 December 2010 (ie Royal Assent).

Non-business use of certain assets not to be treated as supply of services

3.— This paragraph inserts VATA 1994 Sch 4 para 5(4A) with effect from 1 January 2011.

Special provisions apply where VAT is incurred both before 1 January 2011 and after 31 December 2010 in respect of an asset of a description within the new VATA 1994 Sch 4 para 5(4A)(a)–(f). The VAT incurred after 31 December 2010 is not treated as referable to the trader's business if, and to the extent, that the asset is used (or to be used) for: (1) the trader's private use; (2) the private use of his staff; or (3) (more generally) the purposes other than those of the trader's business. The VAT incurred before 1 January 2011 is unaffected by this provision.

Output tax charge where credit attributable to purported paragraph 5(5) supply

4.— This paragraph deals with the consequences of the Commissioners' change of policy announced in Revenue and Customs Brief 2/10, 22 January 2010 following the judgment in *Vereniging Noordelijke Land-en Tuinbouw Organisatie v Staatssecretaris van Financiën* (case C-515/07) [2009] STC 935, ECJ.

A trader (or one or more of his predecessors) may have been allowed input tax credit (see VATA 1994 ss 25, 26) before 22 January 2010 on the basis that it is attributable something giving rise to a supply for the purposes of VATA 1994 Sch 4 para 5(4). If all or part of the input tax would have been disallowed on the basis that the thing done had not given rise to a supply (ie because the input tax was attributable to a non-economic use), the thing done continues to be give rise to a supply for the purposes of VATA 1994 Sch 4 para 5(4) unless the input tax credit has been reversed. If the input tax credit is reversed, the fact that the thing done is treated as giving rise to a supply for the purposes of VATA 1994 Sch 4 para 5(4) does not entitle the trader make a new claim for the reversed input tax credit. If the input tax credit has not been reversed, it is wholly or partly clawed back by way of the charge to VAT on the supplies which continue to be made in accordance with VATA 1994 Sch 4 para 5(4).

This paragraph is treated as if it had always had effect.

SCHEDULE 10 PENALTY FOR FAILURE TO MAKE RETURNS ETC (SECTION 26)

This Schedule brings VAT within the scope of FA 2009 Sch 55 from a day to be appointed by order made under s 26.

Finance Act 2011

2011 Chapter 11

PART 6 OTHER TAXES

VALUE ADDED TAX

74. Business samples

This section amends VATA 1994 Sch 4 para 5. In the absence of any specific commencement provision, the amendments came into force on 19 July 2011 (ie Royal Assent).

75. Zero-rating: splitting of supplies

This section amends VATA 1994 Sch 8 Group 3 in relation to supplies made on or after 19 July 2011 (ie Royal Assent): see FA 2011 s 75(4).

76. Academies

This section inserts VATA 1994 s 33B and amends ss 79, 90 and Sch 9 Group 14 . The amendments have effect in relation to supplies, acquisitions and importations made after 31 March 2011: see FA 2011 s 76(5).

77. Relief from VAT on imported goods of low value

This section amends VAT (Imported Goods) Relief Order 1984, SI 1984/746 Sch 2 Group 8 Item 8 in relation to goods imported after 31 October 2011: see FA 2011 s 77(3).

PART 7 ADMINISTRATION ETC

86. Data-gathering powers

This section introduces Schs 23 and 24.

87. Mutual assistance for recovery of taxes etc

This section introduces Sch 25. The Treasury may amend, replace or repeal Sch 25 by regulation in order to comply with: (1) any amendment or extension of Directive 2010/24/EU; and (2) any EU instrument replacing or supplementing that directive. The regulations are made by statutory instrument. No regulations have been made to date.

PART 8 MISCELLANEOUS PROVISIONS

88. Amendments of section 1 of the Provisional Collection of Taxes Act 1968

This section amends Provisional Collection of Taxes Act 1968 s 1 from a day to be appointed by order. Orders are made by statutory instrument.

93. Short title

This Act is cited as the Finance Act 2011.

SCHEDULES

SCHEDULE 23 DATA-GATHERING POWERS (SECTION 86(1))

General note This schedule 23 replaces a number of specialist information powers currently applicable to direct taxes with a modernised system applicable to the taxes specified in para 45(1). These taxes include VAT (as defined in para 45(3)) and relevant foreign tax (as defined in para 45(4)). This schedule comes into force on 1 April 2012 in accordance with para 65.

SCHEDULE 24 AMENDMENTS TO SCHEDULE 36 FA 2008 (SECTION 86(2))

General note This schedule amends or inserts FA 2008 Sch 36 paras 5, 40A, 49A, 49B, 49C, 50 and 61A. In the absence of any specific commencement provision, the amendment to FA 2008 Sch 36 para 61A came into force on 19 July 2011 (ie Royal Assent). The other amendments and insertions take effect in accordance with Sch 24 paras 2(5), 3(5), 4(2) and 5(4).

SCHEDULE 25 MUTUAL ASSISTANCE FOR RECOVERY OF TAXES ETC (SECTION 87)

General note Directive 2008/55/EC (mutual assistance for the recovery of claims to certain levies, duties, taxes and other measures) is repealed and replaced by Directive 2010/24/EU with effect from 1 January 2012 (see Directive 2010/24/EU art 29). The 2010 Directive came into force on 20 April 2010 and member states are required to implement it from 1 January 2012 (see Directive 2010/24/EU art 28(1)). The 2010 Directive applies to VAT (see Directive 2010/24/EU art 2(1)(a)).

This schedule gives effect to the 2010 Directive (paras 1–16). In the absence of specific commencement provisions, this schedule has effect from 19 July 2011. For the application of this schedule, see para 19.

The 2008 Directive is currently implemented by FA 2002 s 134 and Sch 39. This schedule repeals those provisions with effect from 1 January 2012, subject to savings (para 17).

MARD

1.— Directive 2010/24 is referred to in this schedule as "MARD".

HMRC functions

2.— Except in relation to excluded matters (as to which see para2(3), (4)), the Commissioners are the UK competent authority, and HMRC is the UK central liaison office, for the purposes of all matters under MARD.

Exchange of information

3.— A public authority is permitted to disclose information in order to comply with MARD or a MARD-related instrument. This over-rides any obligation of secrecy imposed by statute or in any other manner. However, this does not permit disclosure in relation to excluded matters (as to which see para2(3), (4)).

Onward disclosure of information received from HMRC

4, 5.— A person (ie a public authority or person listed in para 4(4)) commits an offence, and is liable to a penalty, if he discloses relevant information (as defined in para 4(2)) which he is not permitted to disclose. For the statutory defence, see para 5(1). For the prescribed penalty, see para 5(2).

Enforcement of foreign claims in the UK

6.— The relevant authority of another member state may request the relevant UK authority (as defined in para 7) to recover a claim. The claim is treated in the same manner as a corresponding UK claim (as defined in para 8) for the purposes of recovery proceedings or set-off in the UK. The claim may include interest and/or penalties.

The relevant UK authority

7.— The term "relevant UK authority" is defined.

Corresponding UK claim

8.— The term "corresponding UK claim" is defined.

Application of relevant enactments

9.— Regulations may make provision for the application, non-application or adaptation of any enactment or rule of law relating to corresponding UK claims. No regulations have been made to date.

Power to make further provision

10.— Regulations may make provision about procedural and other matters to give effect to MARD and MARD-related instruments, but not in relation to excluded matters (see para 2(3), (4)). No regulations have been made to date.

Contested claims

11.— Proceedings relevant to a person's liability on the claim must be suspended if the person shows that proceedings are either pending or about to be instituted in the member state in question and those proceedings are prosecuted or instituted with reasonable speed.

Claims determined in taxpayer's favour

12.— Any enforcement action taken in respect of the claim (see para 6(3)) must be discontinued if the claim has been dismissed in proceedings taken in the relevant member state and no appeal lies against that decision.

Liability to pay

13.— Liability to the claim may be questioned only if the circumstances in para 12 apply.

Presumption of validity

14.— A request made by an authority in another member state is taken to be duly made unless the contrary is proved.

Regulations

15.— Regulations are made by statutory instrument.

Interpretation

16.— Various words and phrases are defined.

Consequential amendments

17.— This paragraph repeals FA 2002 s 134 and Sch 39 with effect from 1 January 2012. However, those provisions remain in force – despite the repeal – insofar as they relate to excluded matters (as defined in para 2(3)) and any outstanding request made under Directive 2008/55/EC is treated as if it had been made under MARD.

18.— [Applies to mutual assistance under the customs union with Andorra.]

Application

19.— This schedule has effect in relation to the recovery of sums becoming due at any time.

2. UK Statutory Instruments

Contents

2000/1139 National Police Records (Recordable Offences) Regulations 2000
2001/2879 VAT (Refund of Tax to Museums and Galleries) Order 2001
2002/1502 VAT (Cars) (Amendment) Order 2002
2002/1503 VAT (Special Provisions) (Amendment) (No 2) Order 2002
2002/1935 VAT (Acquisitions) Relief Order 2002
2003/3102 Export (Penalty) Regulations 2003
2003/3113 Customs (Contravention of a Relevant Rule) Regulations 2003
2004/674 Recovery of Duties and Taxes Etc Due in Other Member States (Corresponding UK Claims, Procedure and Supplementary) Regulations 2004
2004/1002 Customs and Excise Duties (Travellers' Allowances and Personal Reliefs) (New Member States) Order 2004
2004/1929 VAT (Disclosure of Avoidance Schemes) Regulations 2004
2004/1931 VAT (Groups: Eligibility) Order 2004
2004/1933 VAT (Disclosure of Avoidance Schemes) Order 2004
2004/3148 VAT (Place of Supply of Goods) Order 2004
2005/3290 VAT (Input Tax) Reimbursement by Employers of Employees' Business Use of Road Fuel) Regulations 2005
2007/2195 Postal Packets (Revenue and Customs) Regulations 2007
2007/3175 Police and Criminal Evidence Act 1984 (Application to Revenue and Customs) Order 2007
2007/3507 Recovery of Foreign Taxes Regulations 2007
2007/3507 Recovery of Foreign Taxes Regulations 2007
2008/1146 VAT (Buildings and Land) Order 2008
2008/1936 Finance Act 2008 Section 135 (Disaster or Emergency) Order 2008
2008/1948 Taxes (Fees for Payment by Telephone) Regulations 2008
2008/2692 Qualification for Appointment of Members to the First-tier Tribunal and Upper Tribunal Order 2008
2008/2698 Tribunal Procedure (Upper Tribunal) Rules 2008
2008/2834 Appeals from the Upper Tribunal to the Court of Appeal Order 2008
2008/2835 First-tier Tribunal and Upper Tribunal (Composition of Tribunal) Order 2008
2009/56 Transfer of Tribunal Functions and Revenue and Customs Appeal Order 2008
2009/196 First-tier Tribunal and Upper Tribunal (Chambers) (Amendment) Order 2009
2009/273 Tribunal Procedure (First-tier Tribunal) (Tax Chamber) Rules 2009
2009/1916 Information Notice: Resolution of Disputes as to Privileged Communications Regulations 2009
2009/3127 VAT (Supplementary Charge) Order 2009
2010/593 Excise Goods (Holding, Movement and Duty Point) Regulations 2010
2010/1813 Revenue and Customs (Complaints and Misconduct) Regulations 2010
2010/1879 Taxes and Duties (Interest Rate) Regulations 2010
2010/2239 VAT (Section 55) (Specified Goods and Services and Excepted Supplies) Order 2010
2010/2240 VAT (Amendment) (No 2) Regulations 2010 (amending)
2010/2549 VAT (Emissions Allowances) Order 2010 (amending)
2010/2653 Tribunal Procedure (Amendment No 3) Rules 2010 (amending)
2010/2655 First-tier Tribunal and Upper Tribunal (Chambers) Order 2010
2010/2923 VAT (Place of Supply of Goods) (Amendment) Order 2010 (amending)
2010/2924 VAT (Imported Gas, Electricity, Heat and Cooling) Relief Order 2010
2010/2925 VAT (Removal of Gas, Electricity, Heat and Cooling) Order 2010
2010/2940 VAT (Amendment) (No 3) Regulations 2010 (amending)
2010/3017 VAT (Exceptions Relating to Supplies not Made to Relevant Business Person) Order 2010 (amending)
2010/3022 VAT (Amendment) (No 4) Regulations 2010 (amending)
2011/21 VAT (Payment on Account) (Amendment) Order 2011 (amending)
2011/86 VAT (Buildings and Land) Order 2011 (amending)
2011/254 VAT (Amendment) Regulations 2011 (amending)
2011/651 Tribunal Procedure (Amendment) Rules 2011 (amending)

2011/711 Taxes, etc (Fees for Payment by Internet) Regulations 2011
2011/897 VAT (Increase of Registration Limits) Order 2011 (amending))
2011/898 VAT (Consideration for Fuel Provided for Private Use) Order 2011 (amending)
2011/1043 Treaty of Lisbon (Changes in Terminology) Order 2011
2011/1071 VAT (Input Tax) (Amendment) Order 2011 (amending)

SI 1961/1523
TEMPORARY IMPORTATION (COMMERCIAL VEHICLES AND AIRCRAFT) REGULATIONS 1961

Note These regulations under Customs and Excise Act 1952 s 40 (repealed), now CEMA 1979 s 48, provide that the following goods may be imported without payment of duty: (1) road vehicles and aircraft designed for carrying goods or passengers (see regs 1–5); (2) spare parts and accessories to be incorporated in, or used with, such a road vehicle (see regs 6, 7); (3) spare parts and equipment to be incorporated in, or used with, such an aircraft (see reg 8(*a*)); and (4) aircraft, special tools, spare parts and equipment for use in the search for such an aircraft, or in its rescue, examination, repair or salvage (see reg 8(*b*)). Relief is subject to conditions, including conditions relating to re-exportation. For interpretation, see regs 9–11. The regulations came into operation on 14 August 1961 (see art 13).

SI 1973/173
THE VALUE ADDED TAX (TERMINAL MARKETS) ORDER 1973

Note This order under FA 1972 s 26, now VATA 1994 s 50, zero rates certain supplies of goods and services in the course of dealings on the terminal markets listed below which involve goods ordinarily dealt with on the markets. Supplies which are zero rated are fixtures transactions (including options) not resulting in a delivery of goods, provided they are supplied by or to a member of one of the markets; and sales of physical goods between members of one market (subject to certain conditions). The order also zero rates the services of any market member acting as a broker in connection with any of these supplies.

1. This order came into operation on 1 April 1973.

2. This order applies to the London Metal Exchange, the London Rubber Market, the London Cocoa Terminal Market, the London Coffee Terminal Market, the London Sugar Terminal Market, the London Vegetable Oil Terminal Market, the London Wool Terminal Market, the London Bullion Market, the London Meat Futures Market, the London Grain Futures Market, the London Soya Bean Meal Futures Market, the Liverpool Barley Futures Market, the International Petroleum Exchange of London, the London Potato Futures Market, the London Platinum and Palladium Market and the London Securities and Derivatives Exchange Limited (OMLX).

A "member of the market" is a member of the London Bullion Market Association (in relation to the London Bullion Market) and includes any person ordinarily engaged in dealings on the market (in other cases). The terms "investment gold" and "the Act" are defined.

3. The following supplies of goods or services in the course of dealings on the above markets are zero rated subject to the conditions below:

(a) a sale by or to a member of the market of any goods (other than investment gold) ordinarily dealt with on the market;

(b) a grant by or to a member of the market of the right to acquire any goods (other than investment gold) ordinarily dealt with on the market;

(c) agency services relating to a sale in (*a*), a grant in (*b*) or a supply within arts 4 or 5 where the sale, grant or supply is made in dealings between members of the market acting as agents.

The zero rating of such a sale is subject to the condition that the sale is either a sale which as a result of other dealings on the market does not lead to a delivery of the goods by the seller to the buyer, or a sale by or to a member of the market. In the latter case:

(i) if the market is The London Metal Exchange the transaction must be between members entitled to deal in the "open ring";

(ii) if the market is The London Cocoa Terminal Market, The London Coffee Terminal Market, The London Meat Futures Market, The International Petroleum Exchange of London, The London Potato Futures Market, The London Soya Bean Meal Futures Market, The London Sugar Terminal Market, The London Vegetable Oil Terminal Market or The London Wool Terminal Market the sale must be registered with the International Commodities Clearing House Limited;

(iii) if the market is the London Grain Futures Market, the sale must be registered in the clearing house of The Grain and Future Association Limited;

(iv) if the market is the Liverpool Barley Futures Market the sale must be registered at the clearing house of the Liverpool Corn Trade Association Limited.

The zero rating of the grant of a right to acquire such goods is subject to the condition that either the right is exercisable at a date later than that on which it is granted or any sale resulting from the exercise of the right would be a sale with respect to which the conditions in the previous paragraph are satisfied.

4. Supplies of investment gold between members of the London Bullion Market Association are zero-rated. These supplies are excluded from exemption by VATA 1994 Sch 9 Group 15 Note 4(*a*).

5. Supplies of investment gold between members of the London Bullion Market Association and taxable persons who are not members are excluded from exemption by VATA 1994 Sch 9 Group 15 Note 4(*b*). The customer is required to account for VAT in respect of the supply in accordance with VATA 1994 s 55(1)–(4). For the non-member's exemption from registration, see art 6. For record-keeping and accounting where the customer is the non-member, see art 7.

6. If a non-member becomes liable to registration under VATA 1994 Schs 1 or 3 solely in respect of a supply in art 5, he is not required to notify the Commissioners of his liability to registration.

7. If the customer required to account for VAT in art 5 is the non-member, the member is required to keep a record of the supplies, and pay the net VAT due, on the non-member's behalf. For the non-member's exemption from the requirement to keep records and submit VAT returns or EC sales lists, see VAT Regulations, SI 1995/2518 reg 33B.

SI 1976/1223
THE CUSTOMS DUTIES (DEFERRED PAYMENT) REGULATIONS 1976

Note These Regulations provide for deferment of customs duties payable on imported goods and on imported warehoused goods removed from warehouse; they also apply to agricultural levy and to VAT payable on imported goods (see VATA 1994 s 1 (4)) and on such goods removed from warehouse. The Regulations prescribe the period for which deferment is allowed and the action to be taken by those seeking deferment including the giving of security. Provision is also made for cases of over-or under-payment of duty. For the purposes of giving relief by repayment of duty, duty is deemed to have been paid at the time when deferment was permitted.

Citation and commencement

1. These Regulations come into operation on 1 September 1976.

Interpretation

2. Various words and phrases used in the Regulations are defined, the Interpretation Act 1889 applies and approvals granted by a Collector of Customs and Excise under the Customs Duties (Deferred Payments) Regulations 1972 remain valid.

Application

3. These Regulations apply where goods are chargeable with customs duty at the time a customs entry is made.

Approval

4. A person who wishes to be approved for duty deferment must apply to the Commissioners in such form and manner as they shall determine: in practice they require completion of form C1200. He must furnish security for payment of the amount of duty for which deferment is requested, by obtaining from a bank or insurance company a guarantee which is approved by the Commissioners, normally on form C1201.

If satisfied, the Commissioners will in writing permit the applicant to defer payment of an amount of duty not exceeding that for which security has been given.

The Regulations provide that the approval may be limited to deferments within named Collections but the Commissioners have extended this to cover entries at any port, airport or warehouse.

The Commissioners may, if they have reasonable cause, vary or revoke any approval granted under this regulation. Changes in the details given in the application, security given, or the arrangements for payment must be notified to the Commissioners forthwith.

Grant of deferment

5. If an approved person applies in the form and manner determined by the Commissioners, they will defer customs duty until payment day.

Payment

6. Payment of duty upon which deferment has been approved is due on the 15th day of the month following the month of importation, called payment day. The Commissioners will only accept a bank giro direct debit, for which they provide form C1202.

7. If at any time after entry has been made the Commissioners are satisfied that the full amount of duty has not been shown on the entry then, unless they allow otherwise, the balance is payable forthwith, deferment not being allowed. Where customs duty has been overpaid, the Commissioners repay the excess; however, the total amount has to be paid to the Commissioners on payment day.

8. Duty is regarded as having been paid at the time deferment is granted for the purposes of the Acts listed.

SI 1982/1067
THE VALUE ADDED TAX (ISLE OF MAN) ORDER 1982

Note This Order under Isle of Man Act 1979 s 6 modifies the law in various Acts relating to VAT in the UK to enable the UK and the Isle of Man to be treated as a single area for the purposes of VAT.

SI 1982/1068
THE VALUE ADDED TAX (ISLE OF MAN) (NO 2) ORDER 1982

Note This Order under Isle of Man Act 1979 s 6 modifies the law in various statutory instruments relating to VAT in the UK to enable the UK and the Isle of Man to be treated as a single area for the purposes of VAT.

SI 1984/746
THE VALUE ADDED TAX (IMPORTED GOODS) RELIEF ORDER 1984

Note This Order under VATA 1983 ss 19, 45, now VATA 1994 ss 37, 97, provides for relief from VAT chargeable on certain goods permanently imported in conjunction with activities such as commerce, scientific research, philanthropy, international relations, recreation and culture pursuits. Sch 2 is divided as follows:

Group 1	Capital Goods and Equipment on Transfer of Activities
Group 2	(Revoked)
Group 3	Promotion of Trade
Group 4	Goods for Testing, etc
Group 5	Health
Group 6	Charities, etc
Group 7	Printed Matter, etc
Group 8	Articles sent for Miscellaneous Purposes
Group 9	Works of Art and Collectors' Pieces
Group 10	Transport
Group 11	War graves, Funerals, etc

Items within these groups are interpreted in accordance with notes. Where goods are described by reference to a use or purpose, relief is given only if the goods are put to such use or the purpose is fulfilled.

Group 8 is amended by FA 2011 s 76 in relation to goods imported after 31 October 2011.

SI 1984/1176
THE CONTROL OF MOVEMENT OF GOODS REGULATIONS 1984

Note These regulations under CEMA 1979 s 31 lay down the procedure for the movement within the UK of (*a*) imported goods to be cleared from Customs control other than the port of importation; (*b*) goods in transit through the UK; (*c*) goods for exportation which are made available for customs examination before their movement to the port etc; and (*d*) goods moving between one free zone and another.

Citation and commencement

1. These Regulations came into operation on 6 August 1984.

Revocation

2. The Control of Movement of Goods Regulations 1981 are revoked.

Interpretation

3. Various words and phrases used in the Regulations are defined.

4. These Regulations do not apply where goods are moved under the Community transit procedure.

Restrictions on the movement of goods

5. Subject to reg 10 imported goods in the charge of customs and excise may not be moved from their place of importation without the authority of the proper officer of customs and excise.

6. Subject to reg 10 no goods shall be moved between a free zone and a place approved for clearance out of customs control or between free zones unless the movement is authorised by the proper officer.

7. Subject to regs 9 and 10 goods intended for export which are made available for inspection at an approved place by the proper officer may not be removed from such a place unless the movement is authorised by the proper officer of customs and excise.

8. Applications to move goods (regs 5, 6 and 7 above) shall be made in writing on documents obtained from and approved by the Commissioners.

Local export control

9. Where notice for movement of goods is given by an exporter to customs and excise and authority is neither given or refused by the date and time for the movement specified, the authority is deemed to have been given on the date immediately before the time so specified in the notice. Where the notice is for more than one movement of goods and the authority of the proper officer required under reg 7 is neither given nor refused and it is deemed to be given immediately before each movement commences.

Standing permission to remove

10. Where the Commissioners so permit, during a period specified by them, goods which are subject to the conditions as contemplated in regs 5, 6 and 7 may be moved without an application to the proper officer; and unless the proper officer previously gives or refuses his authority it shall be deemed to be given immediately before each movement commences.

Requirement for removal document

11. Before any removal commences the person in control of the goods is to be in possession of a removal document.

Specification of vehicles etc

12. The Commissioners may specify the type of vehicles in which any class or description of goods are to be removed and no person shall remove any goods where such a requirement has been imposed unless the vehicle or container complies with the specification or until such requirement has been relaxed.

Specification of routes

13. The Commissioners may specify the routes which goods may travel during a removal.

Security of goods, vehicles and containers

14. Before any goods are removed the vehicle or container carrying them shall be secured by such seals, locks or marks as Commissioners may specify. Seals, locks and marks shall be affixed by the proper officer or by such persons as the Commissioners may authorise.

15. No person may wilfully break, open or remove any seal, lock or mark fixed for any customs and excise purpose on any goods, vehicle or container unless so authorised by a proper officer or in accordance with special permission given by a Commissioner or in an emergency to safeguard the goods or to protect life or property.

Completion of removals, time limits and accidents

16. Save as the Commissioners may otherwise allow, the person in charge of goods being removed shall complete the removal by producing the goods and removal document to the proper officer at the approved place.

17. The person in charge of goods shall complete the removal within such a period as the Commissioners may specify.

18. If as a result of an accident a vehicle or container is delayed or diverted from a specified route the person in charge of the goods shall notify the local office of customs and excise of the circumstances.

SI 1984/1177
THE FREE ZONE REGULATIONS 1984

Note These regulations under CEMA 1979 ss 100B, 100C, 100D, 125 and VATA 1983 s 24, now CEMA 1979 s 125 and VATA 1994 s 19, prescribe the procedures governing the operation of free zones in the UK In relation to such zones the regulations (*a*) allow obligations for security to be placed on responsible authorities; (*b*) provide for the receipt of goods and where appropriate the discharge of existing procedures and establishment of EU status; (*c*) prescribe the scope of permitted operations and the related control requirements; (*d*) provide for the payment of customs duty and agricultural levy and for the delivery of goods from free zones; (*e*) define the control requirements placed upon free zone traders and responsible authorities; and (*f*) provide for the application of value added tax on delivery of any goods manufactured in free zones, whether or not made from imported components. The Regulations do not affect the control of goods in the course of movement to and from free zones.

PART I PRELIMINARY

Citation and commencement

1. These regulations came into operation on 6 August 1984.

Interpretation

2. Words and phrases used in these regulations are defined.

PART II SECURITY OF FREE ZONES

Security and recovery of expenditure by Commissioners

3. The Commissioners may by direction impose obligations on the responsible authority for a free zone to ensure the security of that free zone. Where that authority fails to comply with such a direction and the Commissioners incur any expense then that expense can be recovered by the Commissioners from the authority as a civil debt.

Residence in free zones not permitted

4. No person is allowed to take up residence within a free zone.

PART III GOODS CHARGEABLE WITH EXCISE DUTY

Excise goods which may become free zone goods without payment of excise duty

5. Goods chargeable with excise duty may be moved into a free zone without payment of duty and remain as free zone goods provided the Commissioners agree.

PART IV MOVEMENT OF GOODS INTO FREE ZONE

Goods to become free zone goods

6. Goods moved into a free zone shall not be free zone goods unless their details have been entered in a record kept by the occupier of the premises.

Acknowledgement of Community status of free zone goods

7. The proprietor of free zone goods may within seven days deliver to the proper officer a document and evidence to enable the officer to establish to his satisfaction that the goods are Community goods and if so satisfied the officer will endorse the document to provide a written acknowledgement of such Community status.

Goods from another customs procedure

8. Goods moved into a free zone will not be free zone goods until the proprietor of the goods has presented them to the proper officer and the other customs procedure has been discharged.

PART V OPERATIONS

Operations on free zone goods

9. Operations on free zone goods are subject to this Regulation.

Operations which combine non-free zone goods with free zone goods are prohibited.

The Commissioners may allow, subject to such conditions as they may impose, any operation on free zone goods which are Community goods. Other goods are subject to processing under customs control.

A person intending to carry out any operation shall inform the proper officer of his intention before commencing the process.

Free zone goods shall not be used or consumed in a free zone unless they are entered for home use.

Operations carried out on free zone goods which do not comply with Regulations shall cause the goods to be liable to forfeiture.

PART VI ENTRY, REMOVAL AND PAYMENT OF DUTY ETC

Procedure for entering free zone goods

10. Free zone goods shall be entered by the proprietor of the goods delivering to the proper officer an entry containing such particulars and accompanied by such documents as the Commissioners may direct.

Entry required before removal for home use etc

11. Subject to Regulation 12 before any free zone goods are removed from a free zone for home use or transfer to another customs procedure, the goods are to be entered for such purpose.

Removal without entry

12. The Commissioners may allow goods to be removed from the free zone for the purposes set out in Regulation 11 without the goods being entered, if such particulars as the Commissioners may direct are entered in a record kept by the proprietor of the goods.

Goods to be removed after entry etc

13. Goods which have been entered for home use etc having paid any tax due and with the approval of the proper officer are to be removed, forthwith, from the free zone.

Removal of goods for export etc

14. Any prohibition or restriction on the export of goods or on their shipment as stores shall apply to goods removed from a free zone for export or shipment as stores.

Restriction on removal of goods

15. No goods shall be removed from a free zone except with the authority of the proper officer.

Payment of duty before removal of goods

16. Save as the Commissioners may otherwise allow, no goods shall be removed from a free zone until any customs duty or agricultural levy has been paid.

Entry of goods which are to remain in a free zone

17. Free zone goods to be used or consumed in a free zone shall be entered for home use. Where the proprietor of free zone goods wishes to pay any customs duty or agricultural levy chargeable on the goods, the goods shall be entered for free circulation.

Payment of duty etc on goods to remain in a free zone after entry

18. Where goods are entered for consumption in a free zone, any customs duty and agricultural levy chargeable shall be paid at the time the entry is delivered.

Agricultural levy chargeable because of chargeable operation

19. Where agricultural levy is chargeable because of a chargeable operation, a schedule containing particulars of the goods and the operation must be given to the proper officer and any agricultural levy chargeable paid at the same time.

Customs duty etc deemed to have been paid

20. For the purposes of these Regulations, customs duty and agricultural levy are deemed to have been paid if the customs duties deferred payment system is in operation, or security has been given or the duty is otherwise accounted for.

Destruction of free zone goods

21. Free zone goods may be destroyed and no duty paid, subject to conditions imposed by the Commissioners, but duty will be payable on any resulting scrap or waste which is removed for use in the UK.

PART VII CONTROLS

Production of goods

22. Goods in a free zone are subject to inspection by the proper officer.

Segregation etc of goods

23. The proper officer may require goods to be segregated and marked or otherwise identified.

Keeping of records and provision of information

24. The occupier of any premises upon which free zone goods are kept or the responsible authority on his behalf shall keep such records relating to the goods as the Commissioners may direct. The records shall be kept in the free zone for such period as the Commissioners direct, not exceeding three years from the date the goods are removed from the free zone. A proper officer may examine any records relating to the goods and may take copies or make extracts from them or remove them for a reasonable time.

PART VIII CUSTOMS DUTY ETC CHARGEABLE ON FREE ZONE GOODS

Customs duty chargeable on free zone goods

25. The rate of customs duty or agricultural levy chargeable on free zone goods is that in force at the time of acceptance of the entry. The value for customs purposes of free zone goods is that accepted by the Commissioners at the time of acceptance of the entry of the goods for home use or free circulation. The amount of customs duty or agricultural levy chargeable on free zone goods which have been the subject of inward processing relief and which are entered for home use or free circulation is either the amount calculated in accordance with the Inward Processing Relief Regulations 1977 or that in force when the entry is accepted.

PART IX VALUE ADDED TAX

Tax charge on removal from free zone of manufactured goods

26. Revoked from 10 May 1988 so that, on delivery from a free zone of products manufactured in the free zone, import VAT is charged only on the value of any imported goods retained in these products.

Relief from import tax following supply to non-registered person

27. Where free zone goods have been supplied whilst in a free zone to a person who is not registered for VAT and he enters the goods for home use, the amount of tax payable directly to Customs and Excise is to be reduced by the amount of tax paid to the supplier of the goods.

SI 1986/260
THE POSTAL PACKETS (CUSTOMS AND EXCISE) REGULATIONS 1986

Note These regulations under POA 1953 s 16 set out the customs requirements relating to incoming and outgoing postal packets and to goods contained in them. Incoming and outgoing postal packets transmitted by letter-post are not required to have a separate, full customs declaration if they have a value below £270, and the category of person to whom a seizure notice may be issued is defined.

1. These regulations came into force on 1 March 1986.

2. The meanings of various words and phrases used in these Regulations are explained.

3. Postal Packets (Customs and Excise) Regulations 1975 are revoked.

4. These regulations apply to all postal packets other than postcards which are posted in the UK for transmission abroad or which are brought by post into the UK.

5. Various drafting modifications and exceptions to CEMA 1979 are listed. For references to entries, see Customs and Excise (Singles Market etc) Regulations 1992, SI 1992/3095 reg 10(1) and Sch 1 para 1.

5A. Customs Controls on Importation of Goods Regulations 1991, SI 1991/2724 reg 5 applies only where an entry is required to be made.

6. Dutiable goods for delivery in the UK or the Isle of Man must be brought into the UK in a letter, parcel, packet or other article transmissible by post conveyed by a universal service provider in connection with the provision of a universal postal service.

7. A customs declaration must accompany, or be affixed to, a postal packet (see reg 2) containing dutiable goods brought into the UK. The declaration must state the nature, quantity and value of the goods and any other particulars required by the Commissioners or the postal operator. In addition, the top portion of a prescribed green label must be affixed to the postal packet. If the value of the goods is £270 or less, these requirements are met by affixing a prescribed green label to the postal packet. The declaration thereon must be fully and correctly completed.

The Commissioners may relax the requirements relating to customs declarations by allowing a number of postal packets from the same person to the same address to be accompanied by a single declaration. A customs declaration may be enclosed in a postal packet sent by registered post.

For postal packets containing Community goods and postal packets posted abroad for delivery abroad, see reg 9.

8. A customs declaration must accompany, or be affixed to, a postal packet (see reg 2) containing dutiable goods posted in the UK for delivery abroad. The declaration must state the nature, quantity and value of the goods and any other particulars required by the Commissioners or the postal operator. In addition, the top portion of a prescribed green label must either be affixed to the postal packet or (if the overseas postal administration so requires) enclosed in it. If the value of the goods is £270 or less, these requirements are met by affixing a prescribed green label to the postal packet. The declaration thereon must be fully and correctly completed.

The Commissioners may relax the requirements relating to customs declarations by allowing a number of postal packets from the same person to the same address to be accompanied by a single declaration. A customs declaration may be enclosed in a postal packet sent by registered post if the sender so prefers.

For postal packets containing Community goods and postal packets posted abroad for delivery abroad, see reg 9.

9. A prescribed green label must be affixed to a mailbag if it contains postal packets containing dutiable goods brought into, or sent from, the UK.

Regulations 7, 8 and 9(1) do not apply to: (1) postal packets and mail bags containing Community goods posted within the EU for delivery in the UK or vice versa; and (2) postal packets and mail bags posted abroad for delivery abroad.

10. Every postal packet containing goods to be exported by post without payment of any duty must, upon removal to the post office, be accompanied by a shipping bill, declaration or other document containing such particulars as the Commissioners may require and have affixed to its outer cover a label saying "exported by post under customs and excise control".

11. The proper officer (see reg 2) of the postal operator is authorised to carry out the duties required in the Customs and Excise Acts to be performed by the importer or exporter of goods as the Commissioners may require.

12. The proper officer (see reg 2) of the postal operator must produce to the proper officer (see reg 2) of customs and excise postal packets arriving in the UK or about to be despatched from the UK and shall open them for customs examination if so required.

13. The proper officer (see reg 2) of the postal operator must, on accepting any packet to be exported, endorse a certificate of the posting of the packet on the appropriate document and give it to the sender.

14. If an officer of customs and excise requires a customs entry to be made in respect of any packet imported, such entry must be made within 28 days otherwise the postal operator must return the goods to the sender or deliver the goods to the proper officer of customs and excise or with the permission of the Commissioners and under the supervision of the proper officer, destroy them. Where goods have been delivered to the proper officer of customs and excise the goods may be deposited in a Queen's Warehouse.

15. The proper officer (see reg 2) of the postal operator may demand payment of any duty or other sum due to the Commissioners upon delivery of any postal packet. If payment is not made when demanded, then the postal operator may with the agreement of the Commissioners dispose of the goods contained in the packet as it sees fit. Where an amount demanded includes an amount other than duty which is not paid, the postal operator must deliver the packet to the proper officer of customs and excise.

16. Imported postal packets which do not contain a customs declaration or whose contents do not agree with the customs declaration are liable to forfeiture.

17. Where any postal packet contains goods which are liable to forfeiture the proper officer (see reg 2) of the postal operator must deliver the packet to the proper officer (see reg 2) of customs and excise.

18. These regulations do not authorise any importation or exportation of any article by post contrary to any provisions of the Postal Services Act 2000.

SI 1986/896
THE VALUE ADDED TAX (TREATMENT OF TRANSACTIONS) ORDER 1986

Note This Order under VATA 1983 s 3, now VATA 1994 s 5, removes from the scope of VAT disposals by pawnbrokers of goods to the person who pawned them within three months of the property and the goods passing to the pawnbroker under the Consumer Credit Act 1974 s 120(1)(*a*). Any such disposals would otherwise be a supply of goods and would be chargeable with VAT.

Citation and commencement

1. This Order came into operation 1 July 1986.

Interpretation

2. Phrases used in the Order are defined.

Treatment of transaction

3. The supply by a taxable person of goods, the property in which has passed to him by virtue of the Consumer Credit Act 1974 s 120 (1) (*a*) where the supply is to a person who pawned the goods in the first place, and where the supply is made not later than three months from the date when the taxable person acquired the property in the goods, is to be treated as neither a supply of goods nor supply of services and is therefore outside the scope of VAT.

SI 1986/939
THE VALUE ADDED TAX (SMALL NON-COMMERCIAL CONSIGNMENTS) RELIEF ORDER 1986

Note This Order under VATA 1983 s 19, now VATA 1994 s 37, replaces the VAT (Imported Goods) Relief Order 1980.

The Order increases the maximum quantity of spirits eligible for relief from one quarter bottle (not exceeding.25 litre) to 1 litre.

Citation and commencement

1. This Order came into operation on 1 July 1986.

Revocation

2. The Value Added Tax (Imported Goods) Relief Order 1980 and the 1985 Amendment Order are revoked.

Relief from value added tax

3. No VAT is payable on the importation of goods from a third country forming part of a small consignment of a non-commercial character. "Small consignment" means goods with a value not exceeding £40. A consignment must be from one private individual to another without any consideration in money and intended solely for the personal use of the consignee.

Conditions of relief

4. Goods must not be imported regularly.

Quantitative restriction on relief for certain goods

5. The quantities of tobacco products, alcoholic beverages and perfumes which may be imported in small non-commercial consignments are restricted.

Relief not applicable to travellers' baggage

6. Goods carried in the baggage of a person entering the UK are subject to different allowances.

SCHEDULE (ART 5)

(1) Tobacco products, 50 cigarettes or equivalent;
(2) Alcoholic beverages, 1 litre spirits or 2 litres still wine;
(3) Perfumes 50 grammes; toilet waters 250 millilitres.

SI 1987/1806
THE VALUE ADDED TAX (TOUR OPERATORS) ORDER 1987

Note This Order under VATA 1983 ss 3, 6, 16, 37A and 48, now VATA 1994 ss 5, 7, 30, 53 and 96, introduces the special scheme for tour operators. It implements Directive 2006/112/EC arts 306–310.

Citation and commencement

1. This Order came into force on 1 April 1988.

Supplies to which this order applies

2. This Order applies to goods or services supplied by a tour operator for the benefit of travellers. For similar supplies made in the context of another activity by traders who are not tour operators within the normal meaning of that term, see *C & E Comrs v Madgett and Baldwin* (joined cases C-308/96 and C-94/97) [1998] STC 1169, ECJ (hotelier); *Finanzamt Heidelberg v iSt Internationale Sprach- und Studienreisen GmbH* (case C-200/04) [2005] ECR I–8691, [2006] STC 52, ECJ (language tuition abroad). For "hotel billback" transactions, see Revenue and Customs Brief 21/10, 21 May 2010.

Meaning of "designated travel service"

3. The term "designated travel service" is defined. See *Aer Lingus plc v C & E Comrs* [1992] VATTR 438.

Time of supply

4. The time of supply rules in VATA 1994 s 6 do not apply to any supply comprising in whole or in part a designated travel service.

A tour operator may elect whether the time of supply is based on use or on payment, but once that choice has been made he may only use the method chosen.

Place of supply

5. In principle, a designated travel service is supplied in the EU member state where the tour operator has established his business. However, if the supply is made from a fixed establishment in another EU member state, the supply is made in that member state. A subsidiary company in another EU member state is a fixed establishment for this purpose if the subsidiary acts as a mere auxiliary organ of the tour operator and has the human and technical resources characteristic of a fixed establishment: see *C & E Comrs v DFDS A/S* [1997] STC 384, ECJ.

6. [Revoked.]

Value of a designated travel service

7. In principle, the value of a designated travel service is determined by reference to the difference between sums paid to and sums paid by the tour operator and sums paid by him. This is calculated in the manner specified by the Commissioners. For the manner specified, see Notice No 709/5. For the legal effect of this notice see Notice No 747 (reproduced in Appendix 3); *C & E Comrs v Simply Travel Ltd* [2002] STC 194; *Jenny Braden Holidays Ltd* (No 10892). For sums paid to the tour operator, see *C & E Comrs v First Choice Holidays plc* [2004] STC 1407, CA (package holiday sold at a discount by travel agent who accounts to tour operator for the full brochure price). For the treatment of overheads, see *Whittle (a firm) v C & E Comrs* [1994] VATTR 202; *The Devonshire Hotel (Torquay) Ltd* (No 14448). For the basis of valuing a service comprising both bought-in and in-house supplies, see *C & E Comrs v Madgett and Baldwin* (joined cases C-308/96 and C-94/97) [1998] STC 1169, ECJ. For the choice between the cost and market value methods of apportionment, see *My Travel plc v C & E Comrs* (case C-291/03) [2005] ECR I–8477, [2005] STC 1617, ECJ. For special rules, see arts 8, 9 and 9A.

8. The value of a supply between connected parties is deemed to be open market value if the Commissioners so direct by way of a notice to that effect given to the tour operator.

9. This provision sets out rules for dealing with input tax on goods and services acquired before 1 April 1988.

9A. All or part of the value of a designated travel service made by a tour operator is determined in accordance with VATA 1994 s 19 if:

- a taxable person supplied goods or services to a tour operator before 1 January 2010;

- the tour operator claimed input tax in respect of those goods or services;
- the tour operator supplied those goods or services to a taxable person after 31 December 2009 without materially altering or further processing them;
- the taxable person ordered the goods or services for use in his own business in the UK rather than for the purpose of re-supplying them.
- the supply made by the tour operator is either a designated travel service or part of a larger supply which is a designated travel service

10. [Revoked.]

11. [Revoked.]

Disallowance of input tax

12. Input tax on goods or services acquired by a tour operator for resupply as a designated travel service are excluded from credit under VATA 1994 ss 24–26.

Disqualification from membership of group of companies

13. A tour operator cannot be part of a group registration if any member of the group has an overseas establishment; or makes supplies outside the UK which would be taxable supplies of goods if made within the UK; or supplies goods or services which will become a designated travel service.

14. Supplies of designated travel services may be disregarded if the value of such supplies does not exceed 1% of all supplies made in one year and no supplies of accommodation or transport are made.

SI 1988/809
EXCISE WAREHOUSING (ETC) REGULATIONS 1988

Note These regulations under CEMA 1979 s 93 came into force on 1 June 1988. They make provision for: (1) the deposit, withdrawal and storage of warehoused goods and the operations which may be carried out on them (regs 10–19); (2) the keeping, preservation and production of records, and the furnishing of information (regs 20–25); (3) the charge to excise duty (regs 26–30); and (4) the ascertainment of duties on spirits, wine and made-wine (reg 31). Regulations 16 (4), (5) and 19(1)(*b*) do not apply for the purposes of VAT: see VAT Regulations 1995, SI 1995/2518 reg 119. For VAT and warehoused goods, see VATA 1994 s 18.

SI 1988/1898
THE CUSTOMS AND EXCISE (DEFERRED PAYMENT) (RAF AIRFIELDS AND OFFSHORE INSTALLATIONS) (NO 2) REGULATIONS 1988

Note These regulations permit deferment of customs and excise duties on dutiable goods imported in passengers' baggage, and prescribe the time limit for payment of deferred duties.

1. These regulations came into operation on 21 November 1988.

2. "The Act" means CEMA 1979.

3. Customs and excise duties payable on goods in passengers' baggage, or carried with him, are deferred if: (1) the passenger enters the UK from an offshore gas or oil installation or arrives at an RAF airfield; (2) he declares the goods in the prescribed form and manner; (3) he pays the deferred duties by the 15th day of the month following his arrival or such earlier date as the Commissioners may demand; and (4) the owner of the gas or oil installation provides adequate security.

4. The deferred duty is deemed to be paid when the goods are landed.

5. These regulations do not apply to persons approved for other duty deferment provisions.

6. Earlier regulations are revoked.

SI 1989/472
THE VALUE ADDED TAX (SELF-SUPPLY OF CONSTRUCTION SERVICES) ORDER 1989

Note This Order under VATA 1983 ss 3 and 29, now VATA 1994 ss 5 and 43, provides for a charge to tax by way of a self-supply where a person carries out specified construction, alteration or demolition works.

1. This Order came into operation on 1 April 1989.

2. "The Act" means VATA 1983 (now consolidated as VATA 1994).

3. A person is deemed to make a self-supply of services in the course or furtherance of his business if two conditions are met and he performs one of the specified services without consideration in the course or furtherance of his business and for the purpose of that business. The conditions are: (*a*) the value of the services is £100,000 or more; and (*b*) the services would be chargeable to tax at the standard rate if supplied by a third party.

The specified services are: (*a*) constructing a building; (*b*) increasing the floor area of a building by 10% or more; (*c*) constructing a civil engineering work; and (*d*) carrying out demolition work in connection with (*a*)–(*c*).

The supply is deemed to be made to the person for the purpose of his business.

To the extent that services are performed by a body corporate included in a group registration, the foregoing provisions apply as if all bodies included in the registration were one person and the supply is deemed to be made and received by the representative member.

4. The services are deemed to be supplied at their open market value. However, the value of services performed on or before 31 March 1989 is effectively treated as nil.

SI 1989/1114
THE VALUE ADDED TAX (WATER) ORDER 1989

Note This Order under VATA 1983 s 3, now VATA 1994 s 5, provides that all supplies of water (eg by a water company) are treated as supplies of goods in the same manner as gas, electricity and other forms of heat, power, refrigeration and ventilation.

1. This Order came into operation on 1 August 1989.

2. The supply of water is treated as a supply of goods (insofar as it is not otherwise such a supply) and not as a supply of services.

SI 1991/2724
CUSTOMS CONTROLS ON IMPORTATION OF GOODS REGULATIONS 1991

Note These regulations under ECA 1972 s 2 amend the text of CEMA 1979 and other provisions, and lay down rules supplementing the procedure for presentation, summary declaration and entry of goods, to take account of Regulation (EEC) No 4151/88 and implement Directive 79/695/EEC.

Citation and commencement

1. The regulations came into force on 1 January 1992.

Interpretation

2. Various terms used in the regulations are defined.

Entry

5. Goods must be entered within 45 days (sea cargo) or 20 days (other cases) after a summary declaration is lodged. The entry must be delivered to the proper officer after the goods have been presented at the proper office unless the Commissioners allow otherwise. Acceptance of an entry is signified in the manner directed by the Commissioners.

SI 1992/630
VALUE ADDED TAX (TREATMENT OF TRANSACTIONS) ORDER 1992

Note This Order under VATA 1983 s 3, now VATA 1994 s 5, provides that VAT is not chargeable if an employee makes a salary sacrifice in return for the right to use privately a motor car provided by his employer.

1. This Order came into operation on 1 April 1992.

2. An employer may give an employee a choice between a particular rate of remuneration or, in the alternative, a lower rate of remuneration and the right to private use of a motor car provided by the employer. If the employee chooses the latter alternative, provision of the right to use the motor car privately is outside the scope of VAT insofar as the consideration represents the remuneration forgone: cf. *Co-operative Insurance Society Ltd v C & E Comrs* [1992] VATTR 44. For clarification, see Business Brief Issue 9/92, 19 June 1992.

SI 1992/2790
STATISTICS OF TRADE (CUSTOMS AND EXCISE) REGULATIONS 1992

Note These regulations under ECA 1972 s 2 make provision for the collection of statistics relating to the trading of goods between EU member states under Intrastat, the data collection system established by Regulation (EC) No 638/2004 and implemented by Regulation (EC)

No 638/2004. Intrastat is administered in the UK in accordance with the EC regulations (which have direct effect) as supplemented by these regulations. For a commentary on the EC regulations, see Part 1B.

Citation, commencement and interpretation

1. These regulations came into force on 1 December 1992.

Various words and phrases are defined. Other words and expressions are defined by reference to CEMA 1979 s 1, Regulation (EC) No 638/2004 (referred to as the "establishing regulation") and Regulation (EC) No 1982/2004 (referred to as the "implementing regulation").

Application of Intrastat

2. As regards the UK's statistical territory, Intrastat is under the care and management of the Commissioners. The UK's statistical territory corresponds to the UK's customs territory: see Regulation (EC) No 638/2004 art 4(1).

Information collected on the value added tax return

3. The values of goods shown in Boxes 8 and 9 of a VAT return may be treated as simplified information for Intrastat purposes (see Regulation (EC) No 638/2004 art 10(1)). For VAT returns, see VAT Regulations 1995, SI 1995/2518 Sch, Form Nos 4, 5.

A person is not required to provide Intrastat information or provide supplementary declarations (see reg 4) concerning dispatches if their annual value is £250,000 or less. Similarly, he is not required to provide Intrastat information or provide supplementary declarations concerning arrivals if their annual value is £600,000 or less.

Supplementary declarations

4. A person responsible for providing Intrastat information must do so on the forms (known as "supplementary declarations") set out in the Schedule. There are separate forms for "arrivals" and "dispatches". Forms may be delivered by post or in person. The Commissioners may allow supplementary declarations to be delivered by electronic means. The form prescribed from time to time must be used where the Commissioners do so. Supplementary declarations must be delivered by the last day of the month following the end of the reference period concerned.

A person is not required to provide particulars relating to delivery terms on a supplementary declaration if the annual value of his arrivals or despatches does not exceed £16,000,000.

Administration of rules concerning specific goods and movements

4A. The Commissioners must give directions regarding the application of Regulation (EC) No 638/2004 arts 16, 17, 19, 20, 21, 22, 23, 24 and may give directions regarding arts 15, 18. Supplementary declarations (see reg 4) must comply with the directions made.

Duty to keep and retain records

5. A person registered in the register of intra-Community operators (see art 8 of the establishing regulation) must keep copies of his periodic declarations and the documents used to compile them. He must produce them when required, allow copies or extracts to be taken, and allow them to be removed. Records must be preserved for the period (maximum six years) required by the Commissioners. An authorised officer may enter the premises of a registered person or the person compiling his period declarations. For the register of intra-Community operators, see Regulation (EC) No 638/2004 art 8.

Offences and evidence

6. Failure to deliver a supplementary declaration is an offence tried summarily with a maximum penalty of level 4 on the standard scale (see CEMA 1979 s 171).

7. The text of an illegible document may be used in evidence in civil or criminal proceedings in place of the original.

8. Specified facts may be proved by certificate. Photocopies of documents are admissible as evidence.

Access to recorded information

9. An order given by a justice of the peace (in Scotland, justice) may require a person in possession of recorded information to make it available to an authorised person, and to allow him to copy or remove it. This applies to information stored in a computer.

10. An authorised person must give a receipt for removed documents on request. The owner must be allowed access to them and provided with copies of them on request unless this would hamper the investigation or proceedings resulting from it.

11. A magistrate may order access to documents or the provision of copies if this is refused by the investigating officer. An application for an order is made by way of complaint. Corresponding provisions apply in Scotland and Northern Ireland.

Supplementary

12. An offence under CEMA 1979 ss 167 (1), 168 (1) in connection with the Intrastat system carries a maximum prison sentence of three months (rather than six months) on summary conviction plus, or as an alternative to, the fines specified.

13. CEMA 1979 ss 145–148 and 150–154 apply for the purposes of these Regulations.

SCHEDULE

Forms C1500 (supplementary declaration for arrivals) and C1501 (supplementary declaration for dispatches) are set out.

SI 1992/3111
VALUE ADDED TAX (REMOVAL OF GOODS) ORDER 1992

Note This order under VATA 1983 s 3, now VATA 1994 s 5, sets out the circumstances in which movements of goods between EU member states are not treated as a supply under VATA 1983 Sch 2 para 5A, now VATA 1994 Sch 4 para 6.

1. This order came into force on 1 January 1993.

2. Various words and phrases are defined.

3. A person is deemed to be established in an EU member state if: (1) he has a business establishment or some other fixed establishment there; or (2) he carries on a business there through a branch or agency.

4. A removal of goods from one EU member state to another is not a supply of goods for the purposes of VATA 1994 Sch 4 para 6 if: (1) the supply involves installation or assembly so that the place of supply is governed by VATA 1994 s 7 (3) (see *Centrax Ltd v C & E Comrs* [1998] V & DR 369); (2) the goods are supplied to an unregistered person so that the place of supply is governed by VATA 1994 s 7 (4) or (5); (3) the goods are supplied on a ship, aircraft or train so that the place of supply is governed by VAT (Place of Supply of Goods) Order 1992, SI 1992/3283; (4) the goods are collected or delivered under a zero-rated supply; (5) the goods are removed for treatment or process by another person and subsequent return; (6) the goods are removed for the purpose of valuation by another person; (7) the goods are removed for work to be carried out on them by another person; (8) the goods are removed for use by the owner in making a supply of services and subsequent return; (9) the goods are removed for export to a third country within two years; (10) the goods are removed for subsequent removal to another EU member state within two years; (11) the goods are returned after treatment, process or use in (5) or (8), or are exported or removed in accordance with (9) or (10); or (12) the goods are returned after the valuation or work has been carried out in accordance with (6) or (7).

5. The removal in heads (5), (8), (9) or (10) is a supply of goods if the stated intention is not fulfilled. For accounting in these circumstances, see VAT Regulations 1995, SI 1995/2518 reg 42.

SI 1992/3121
VALUE ADDED TAX (PLACE OF SUPPLY OF SERVICES) ORDER 1992

Note This order under VATA 1983 s 6, now VATA 1994 s 7, sets out the place of supply rules for specified services.

PART I PRELIMINARY

Citation and commencement

1. This order came into force on 1 January 1993.

Interpretation

2. Various words and phrases are defined.

Revocation

3. VAT (Place of Supply) Order 1984, SI 1984/1684 is revoked.

PART II RULES FOR DETERMINING PLACE OF SUPPLY OF SERVICES

4. The place of supply is determined in accordance with the rules set out in VATA 1994 s 7. These rules are varied in accordance with arts 5–18 below.

Services relating to land

5. The following services are supplied where the land concerned is situated:

(a) the grant, assignment or surrender of (1) any interest in or right over land, (2) a personal right to call for or be granted any interest in or right over land, (3) a licence to occupy land, or (4) any other contractual right exercisable over or in relation to land. For fishing permits, see *Heger Rudi GmbH v Finanzamt Graz-Stadt* (case 166/05) [2006] ECR I–7749, [2008] STC 2679, ECJ;

(b) the construction, demolition, alteration, conversion, enlargement, reconstruction, repair or maintenance of a building or civil engineering work; and

(c) services of a kind provided by estate agents, auctioneers, architects, surveyors, engineers, etc, in relation to land.

Transport

6. Services are supplied in country X if they comprise transportation of goods or passengers between two points in country X. Services are supplied partly in country X and partly in country Y if they comprise transportation of goods or passengers between country X and Y.

For the proportion of the journey in each country, see art 7; Directive 2006/112/EC art 46 as interpreted in *Reisbüro Binder GmbH v Finanzamt Stuttgart-Körperschaften* (case C-116/96) [1998] STC 604, ECJ. For the exception to this rule, see art 10 below.

7. A journey is treated as being between two points in country X if the means of transport crosses international waters or airspace, or if it crosses another country without stopping, on such a journey, eg flight from Great Britain to Northern Ireland overflying the Irish Sea or the Republic of Ireland.

8. A pleasure cruise is treated as the transportation of passengers. Goods and services provided as part of a pleasure cruise are supplied in the same place as the transportation. Services of transporting the luggage or motor vehicle of a passenger are also supplied in the same place as the transportation. For the place of supply of transportation, see arts 6 and 10. For cruises beginning and ending in the EU but having an intermediate stop in a third country, see *Köhler v Finanzamt Düsseldorf Nord* (case C-58/04) [2005] ECR I–8218, [2006] STC 469, ECJ.

9. Loading, unloading, handling and similar services are supplied where the services are performed unless the recipient makes use of a non-UK VAT registration number. For the use of a non-UK VAT registration number, see art 14.

10. Services are supplied in country X if they comprise the transportation of goods from country X to country Y and both countries are EU member states. This does not apply if the recipient makes use of a non-UK VAT registration number. For the use of a non-UK VAT registration number, see art 14.

Services of intermediaries

11. The services of an intermediary are supplied in country X if he arranges the transportation of goods from country X to country Y and both countries are EU member states. This does not apply if the recipient makes use of a non-UK VAT registration number. For the use of a non-UK VAT registration number, see art 14.

12. An intermediary may arrange loading, unloading, handling or similar services in connection with the transportation of goods from country X to country Y. If both countries are EU member states, the intermediary's services are supplied in the country where the loading, unloading, etc takes place. This does not apply if the recipient makes use of a non-UK VAT registration number. For the use of a non-UK VAT registration number, see art 14.

13. An intermediary may arrange a supply by X to Y. The intermediary's services are supplied in the same place as X's supply. However, this does not apply if X's supply comprises any of: (1) loading, unloading, handling and similar services; (2) the transport of goods from one EU member state to another; or (3) services within VATA 1994 Sch 5 paras 1–8. Nor does it apply if the recipient makes use of a non-UK VAT registration number. For the use of a non-UK VAT registration number, see art 14. See *Staatssecretaris van Financiën v Lipjes* (case C-68/03) [2004] ECR I–5879, [2004] STC 1592, ECJ.

Use of customer's registration number

14. The recipient of a supply of services may use his VAT registration number for the purposes of any of the following supplies: (1) loading, unloading, handling and similar services (see art 9) in connection with the transportation of goods from one EU member state to another; (2) the transportation of goods from one EU member state to another (see art 10); (3) the services of intermediaries (see arts 11–13); (4) valuation of goods which are subsequently removed from the member state where the services were physically carried out; and (5) work carried out on goods which are subsequently removed from the member state where the services were physically carried out. Where he does so, the place of supply is the EU member state which issued the VAT registration number and the place of supply under arts 9–13, 15 is disregarded.

Services supplied where performed

15. The following services are supplied in the place where they are physically carried out: (1) cultural, artistic, sporting, scientific, educational or entertainment services; (2) services relating to exhibitions, conferences or meetings; (3) services ancillary to services within (1) or (2); (4) valuation of goods which subsequently remain in the member state where the services were physically carried out; and (5) work carried out on goods which subsequently remain in the member state where the services were physically carried out. This provision applies to suppliers moving between countries: see *British Sky Broadcasting Ltd v C & E Comrs* [1994] VATTR 1 (satellite TV broadcasts).

For entertainment services within head (1), see *RAL (Channel Islands) Ltd and others v C & E Comrs* (case C-452/03) [2005] ECR I–3947, [2005] STC 1025, ECJ (slot machines in an amusement arcade). For ancillary services within head (3), see *Dudda v Finanzamt Bergisch Gladbach* (case C-327/94) [1996] ECR I–4595, [1996] STC 1290, ECJ; *Sugar and Spice on Tour Catering* (No 17698). For organisational services within head (3), see *Ministre de l'Économie, des Finances at de l'Industrie v Gillian Beach Ltd* (case C-114/05) 2006] ECR I–2427, [2006] STC 1080, ECJ (services of organiser to exhibitors at boat show). For services within heads (4) and (5), see *Maatschap MJM Linthorst, KGP Pouwels and J Scheres CS v Inspecteur der Belastingdienst* (case C-167/95) [1997] ECR I–1195, [1997] STC 1287, ECJ.

Services supplied where received

16. Services within VATA 1994 Sch 5 paras 1–8 are supplied where the recipient belongs. For supplies to an intermediate supplier, see *Design Concepts SA v Flanders Expo SA* (case C-438/01) [2003] ECR I–5617, [2003] STC 912, ECJ; *Athesia Druck Srl v Ministero dell'Economia e delle Finanze and another* (case C-1/08) [2009] ECR I–1255, [2009] STC 1334, ECJ.

The recipient must belong in either a third country (but not the Isle of Man) or in a different EU member state to the supplier. In the latter case, the recipient must meet the following conditions: (1) he receives the supply for the purpose of his business (see *Banque Bruxelles Lambert SA v Belgian State* (case C-8/03) [2004] ECR I–10157, [2004] STC 1643, ECJ (supplies to open-ended investment company); *Kollektivavtalssiftelsen TRR Trygghetsrådet v Skatteverket* (case C-291/07) [2008] ECR I–8255, [2009] STC 526 (customer making both business and non-business supplies); *Diversified Agency Services Ltd v C & E Comrs* [1996] STC 398 (supplies to tourist board)); and (2) he does not make a reverse charge as a result of receiving the services. For the reverse charge, see VATA 1994 s 8. For the place where the recipient of a supply belongs, see VATA 1994 s 9.

16A. Electronically supplied services (see VATA 1994 Sch 5 para 7C) are supplied where the recipient belongs. The recipient must belong in an EU member state and receive the services for non-business purposes from a person who belongs in a third country. For the place where the supplier belongs, see VATA 1994 s 9.

Services supplied where enjoyed

17. To the extent that the effective use and enjoyment of the following services takes place in a third country, and they would otherwise be treated as supplied in the UK, they are not so treated and are therefore outside the scope of VAT. The supplies concerned are:

(a) the letting on hire of any means of transport;
(b) the letting on hire of goods other than means of transport (see VATA 1994 Sch 5 para 7), telecommunication services (see VATA 1994 Sch 5 para 7A) and radio and television broadcasting services (see VATA 1994 Sch 5 para 7B); and
(c) electronically supplied services (see VATA 1994 Sch 5 para 7C) received for business purposes.

But for this provision, the services in (*b*) and (*c*) could be treated as being supplied in the UK if the recipient of the supply belonged there (see art 16).

18. To the extent that the effective use and enjoyment of the following services takes place in the UK, and they would otherwise be treated as supplied in a third country, they are treated as being supplied in the UK. The supplies concerned are:

(a) the letting on hire of any means of transport;
(b) the letting on hire of goods other than means of transport (see VATA 1994 Sch 5 para 7), telecommunication services (see VATA 1994 Sch 5 para 7A) and radio and television broadcasting services (see VATA 1994 Sch 5 para 7B); and
(c) electronically supplied services (see VATA 1994 Sch 5 para 7C) received for business purposes.

But for this provision, the services in (*b*) and (*c*) could be treated as being supplied in a third country if the recipient of the supply belonged in a third country (see art 16).

19. [Revoked.]

20. [Revoked.]

21. If the place of supply of a service made by X to Y is in (say) the UK, the place of supply of a right to those services made by X to Y is also the UK. Y may make an onward supply of the right to Z. If so, the place of supply of the right made by Y to Z is the same as that of a notional supply of the service made by Y to Z. This applies whether or not the right is exercised. For a supply of phone cards amounting to a supply of services rather than the supply of a right to services, see *R & C Comrs v Arachchige* [2011] STC 33, CA.

For the foregoing purposes, a right to services includes any right, option or priority with respect to (1) the supply of services; and (2) the supply of an interest deriving from any right to services.

SI 1992/3122
VALUE ADDED TAX (CARS) ORDER 1992

Note This order under VATA 1983 ss 3, 18, 29, now VATA 1994 ss 5, 32, 43, revokes and re-enacts certain provisions of VAT (Cars) Order 1980, SI 1980/442 (as amended) with modifications arising from the new charge to VAT on acquisitions.

Citation and commencement

1. This order came into force on 1 January 1993.

Interpretation

2. Various words and phrases are defined.

A "motor car" is a motor vehicle of a kind normally used on public roads which has three or more wheels. It must be constructed or adapted solely or mainly for the carriage of passengers or have roofed accommodation to the rear of the driver's seat which is either fitted with side windows or constructed or adapted for the fitting of side windows. For the test applied, see *C & E Comrs v Jeynes* [1984] STC 30; *Withers of Winsford Ltd v C & E Comrs* [1988] STC 431. For the carriage of passengers, see *Chartcliffe Ltd v C & E Comrs* [1976] VATTR 165; *A L Yeoman Ltd* (No 4470). For car-derived vans and combination vans, see Business Brief 16/04, 9 June 2004. For examples, contrast *Compton* (No 10259) (adapted) and *Bolinge Hill Farm* (No 4217) (not adapted). For roofed accommodation see *John Beharrell Ltd v C & E Comrs* [1991] VATTR 497, applying *R v C & E Comrs ex parte Nissan (UK) Ltd* (1987) Times, 23 November, CA and contrast *County Telecommunications Systems Ltd* (No 10224).

The following vehicles are not a motor car:
(i) vehicles capable of carrying only one person;
(ii) vehicles capable of carrying twelve or more seated persons (see *Oddonetto* (No 5208); *W Hamilton & Son* (No 14812); Notice No 48 (December 2010) para 3.12);
(iii) vehicles of three tonnes or more unladen weight;

(iv) vehicles with a maximum gross weight of one tonne or more constructed to carry a payload;
(v) caravans, ambulances, prison vans;
(vi) vehicles constructed for a special purpose (see *Chartcliffe Ltd v C & E Comrs* [1976] VATTR 165; *Weatherproof Flat Roofing (Plymouth) Ltd* (No 1240); *Knapp* (No 778); *O'Dell (a firm)* (No 13802); *Appleby* (No 14580).

Revocation

3. The following orders are wholly or partly revoked: VAT (Cars) Order 1980, SI 1980/442; VAT (Cars) (Amendment) Order 1984, SI 1984/33; VAT (Cars) (Amendment) Order 1989, SI 1989/959; VAT (Cars) (Amendment) Order 1990, SI 1990/315; and VAT (Cars) (Amendment) Order 1992, SI 1992/627.

Treatment of transactions

4. The transactions set out in the following table are treated as neither a supply of goods nor a supply of services, so as to be outside the scope of VAT, subject to the conditions indicated by code letters.

	Transaction	*Conditions*
1.	Disposal of a used motor car repossessed under the terms of a finance agreement (as defined in art 2) (art 4(1)(*a*))	A, C, G, I
2.	Disposal of a used motor car by an insurer who has taken it in settlement of an insurance claim (art 4(1)(*b*))	B, C, G
3.	Disposal of a motor car for no consideration (art 4(1)(*c*))	G
4.	Services in connection with the supply of a used motor car provided by an agent acting in his own name (art 4(1)(*d*))	D, E
5.	Services in connection with the supply of a used motor car provided by an auctioneer acting in his own name (art 4(1)(*e*))	D, E
6.	The following services supplied by a taxable person who has hired, purchased, acquired or imported a motor car:	
	(*a*) Hiring the motor car to anyone for no consideration (art 4(1)(*f*) and (1C)(*a*))	G, H
	(*b*) Hiring the motor car to anyone for a consideration which is less than the money payable on an arm's length commercial transaction (art 4(1)(*f*) and (1C)(*a*))	G, H
	(*c*) Making the motor car available for private use by a sole proprietor, partner or any other person (art 4(1)(*f*) and (1C)(*b*))	F, G, H

The conditions indicated by code letters are as follows:

(A) The disposal must be made by the person who repossessed the motor car (art 4 (1) (*a*)). For goods surrendered to a hire purchase company, see *C & E Comrs v General Motors Acceptance Corpn (UK) plc* [2004] STC 577.

(B) The disposal must be made by the insurer (art 4 (1) (*b*)).

(C) The motor car must be disposed of in the same condition (art 4 (1) (*a*) and (*b*)).

(D) The services must be provided to the purchaser (agent or auctioneer) or to the vendor (auctioneer) (art 4 (1) (*d*) and (*e*)).

(E) The consideration for the services must be taken into account in calculating the purchase price (agent or auctioneer) or selling price (auctioneer) at which the agent or auctioneer is deemed to purchase or sell the motor car under the margin scheme described in art 8 below (art 4 (1) (*d*) and (*e*)).

(F) The motor car must be made available under an arrangement which does not amount to a letting on hire (art 7 (1C) (*b*)).

(G) Input tax on any previous purchase, acquisition or importation of the motor car must have been excluded from credit (art 4 (1A) and (1B)). For exclusion of input tax from credit, see VAT (Input Tax) Order 1992, SI 1992/3222 art 7(1).

(H) Input tax on any previous hire of the motor car must have been partly excluded from credit (art 4(1B)). For partial exclusion of input tax from credit, see VAT (Input Tax) Order 1992, SI 1992/3222 art 7(1) and (2H).

(I) No relief is given if VAT on the initial supply under the finance agreement has been (or may be) adjusted as a result of the repossession. This applies to motor cars delivered under a finance agreement after 31 August 2006 (art 4(1AA).

A transaction in (1) or (2) is a supply for the purpose of VATA 1994 s 11(1)(*a*).

4A. The private or non-business use of a motor car does not give rise to a supply of services under VATA 1994 Sch 4 para 5(4) if the use gives rise to a self-supply under art 5.

Self-supplies

5. A taxable person is deemed to supply a motor car in the course or furtherance of business (so as to give rise to a liability to account for output tax) if:

- he produced, purchased, acquired, imported or obtained the motor car in one of the circumstances set out below;
- he has not supplied the motor car in the course or furtherance of business; and
- he uses the motor car for a purpose which would prevent input tax credit arising on a motor car purchased for that purpose.

The motor car is also deemed to be supplied to the taxable person for the purpose of his business. The circumstances referred to in head (1) above are:

(a) he produced the motor car otherwise than by way of conversion;

(b) he produced the motor car by converting another vehicle and input tax on the purchase, acquisition or importation of that vehicle was not wholly excluded from credit;

(c) he purchased, acquired or imported the motor car and input tax on the purchase, acquisition or importation was not wholly excluded from credit;

(d) he obtained the motor car when all or part of a business was transferred to him as a going concern and the following conditions were met:

 (i) the transfer was treated as neither a supply of goods nor a supply of services so as to be outside the scope of VAT,

 (ii) the transferor, or one of his predecessors, produced, purchased, acquired or imported the motor car so that the circumstances in (*a*), (*b*) or (*c*) were met, and

 (iii) neither the transferor nor any of his predecessors self-supplied the motor car.

For the circumstances in which input tax is not wholly excluded from credit, see VAT (Input Tax) Order 1992, SI 1992/3222 art 7 (2).

For the time of supply, see VATA 1994 s 6(11). For the value of the supply, see VATA 1994 Sch 6 para 6.

6. [Revoked.]

6A. [Revoked.]

7. A self-supply made by a member of a VAT group (see VATA 1994 s 43) is deemed to be made by the representative member.

Relief for second-hand motor cars

8. A person supplying a used motor car may opt to account for output tax on the profit margin of the supply (as defined in VATA 1994 s 50A(4)) instead of by reference to its value (see VATA 1994 s 19 and Sch 6) if he complies with the conditions specified in a notice published by the Commissioners (see Notice No 718) and he took possession of the motor car in any of the following circumstances:

- no VAT was chargeable under UK or Isle of Man legislation (on the supply made to him eg because it was zero-rated (see *Peugeot Motor Co plc v C & E Comrs* [1998] V & DR 1) or because the vendor was not a taxable person). A car acquired from another EU member state does not fall within this description if VAT was charged on the acquisition: *Wood* (No 17256);

- VAT on the supply made to him was chargeable on the margin in accordance with UK legislation (ie this article) or corresponding legislation in the Isle of Man or an EU member state;
- (if the supply was made to him before 1 March 2000) VAT on the supply made to him was chargeable on the margin in accordance with VAT (Input Tax) Order 1992, SI 1992/3222 art 7 (4) (revoked) (ie because the vendor was not entitled to input tax credit when he took possession of the motor car);
- the supply made to him was treated as neither a supply of goods nor a supply of services by virtue of an order made under VATA 1994 s 5(3). However, if the supply made to him was so treated by virtue of VAT (Special Provisions) Order 1995, SI 1995/1268 art 5 (ie because all or part of a business was being transferred or because the motor car was subject to a hire purchase or conditional sale agreement), the option can be exercised only if the person who made that supply, or one of his predecessors in title, took possession of the motor car under a transaction within heads (1)–(3) above.

A person may not exercise his option in relation to:

(a) a supply which is a letting on hire;
(b) the supply of a motor car which he produced and which he has neither supplied nor self supplied (see art 5); or
(c) a supply for which he issues a VAT invoice or similar document.

For motor cars considered to be "used", see *Lincoln Street Motors (Birmingham) Ltd v C & E Comrs* [1981] VATTR 120; *Finglands Travel Agency Ltd* (No 1447).

The price at which a motor car is obtained or sold for the purpose of determining the profit margin is set out in the table below. Separate provisions apply to:

- a taxable person making the supply as a principal;
- a taxable person making the supply as an agent acting in his own name (as to which see VATA 1994 s 47); and
- an auctioneer (as defined in art 2 above) acting in his own name. For the auctioneers' scheme, see Notice No 718.

Person	*Price at which car obtained*	*Price at which car sold*
Principal	A	C
Agent or auctioneer	A	C + D
Auctioneers' scheme	B	E

The prices indicated by code letters are as follows:

(A) The consideration for the supply made to him (calculated in accordance with VATA 1994 s 19 and Sch 6) (supply made to him by third party or disposal of goods to himself by sole proprietor), the price at which his predecessor obtained the motor car (transaction treated as neither a supply of goods nor a supply of services in accordance with VAT (Special Provisions) Order 1995, SI 1995/1268 art 5) or the price he paid for the motor car (transaction treated as neither a supply of goods nor a supply of services in accordance with any other provision) (art 8 (5) (*a*) and (6)).
(B) Hammer price less commission payable to the auctioneer in connection with the sale (art 8 (7) (*a*)).
(C) Consideration for the supply made by the person, calculated in accordance with VATA 1994 s 19 and Sch 6 (art 8 (5) (*b*)).
(D) Consideration for services supplied to the purchaser of the motor car by the agent (art 8 (6)).
(E) Hammer price plus consideration for services chargeable to VAT supplied to the purchaser by the auctioneer in connection with the sale (art 8 (7) (*b*)).

SI 1992/3124
VALUE ADDED TAX (IMPORTED GOLD) RELIEF ORDER 1992

Note This order under VATA 1983 s 19, now VATA 1994 s 37, relieves Central Banks from liability to pay VAT on gold imported from third countries.

1. This order came into force on 1 January 1993.

2. The VAT chargeable on gold and gold coins imported by a Central Bank from a third country is not payable.

3. VAT (Imported Goods) Relief Order 1977, SI 1977/1790, is revoked.

SI 1992/3130
VALUE ADDED TAX (SUPPLY OF TEMPORARILY IMPORTED GOODS) ORDER 1992

Note This order under VATA 1983 s 3, now VATA 1994 s 5, provides that certain supplies of temporarily imported goods are outside the scope of VAT.

1. This order came into force on 1 January 1993.

2. A supply of goods is treated as neither a supply of goods nor a supply of services if: (1) the goods were temporarily imported into the UK and were granted total relief from customs duty in accordance with Regulation (EEC) No 3599/82 arts 7–23 (OJ L376/1, 31.12.82); (2) the goods remain eligible for relief; and (3) the supply is made to a person established in a third country.

SI 1992/3132
VALUE ADDED TAX (TREATMENT OF TRANSACTIONS) (NO 2) ORDER 1992

Note This order under VATA 1983 s 8A, now VATA 1994 s 11, provides that gold supplied to a Central Bank by an EC supplier does not give rise to an acquisition.

1. This order came into force on 1 January 1993.

2. A Central Bank does not make an acquisition when gold or gold coin is removed to the UK from another EU member state under a supply made to the Central Bank by a supplier in another EU member state.

SI 1992/3152
EXCISE DUTIES (DEFERRED PAYMENT) REGULATIONS 1992

Note These regulations under CEMA 1979 ss 93, 127A and other powers consolidate the provisions relating to the deferred payment of excise duties.

PART I PRELIMINARY

Citation, commencement and revocation

1. These regulations came into force on 1 January 1993.

Interpretation

2. Various words and phrases are defined.

Application

3. These regulations apply to excise duty on the following goods which would otherwise be payable after 31 December 1992: (1) wine; (2) made-wine; (3) cider; (4) spirits; (5) biofuels, (6) hydrocarbon oil; and (7) beer imported by a registered excise dealer and shipper.

PART II DEFERMENT OF EXCISE DUTY

Approved persons

4. A person must apply for approval if he wishes to be granted excise duty deferment. The Commissioners may limit approval to a maximum sum, or to goods at a specified place, and may vary or revoke approval for reasonable cause at any time. A person may be separately approved for different places.

Deferment

5. An approved person is granted deferment if he gives notice in the required manner. Duty is paid as follows:

Goods		*Period in which duty arises*	*Payment day*
1.	Beer imported by a registered excise dealer and shipper	Calendar month	25th day of next calendar month
2.	Goods other than beer imported by a registered excise dealer and shipper	Calendar month	15th day of next calendar month
3	Biofuels	15th day of one month to 14th day of next month	last business day of that next month
4.	Hydrocarbon oils delivered for home use	15th day of one month to 14th day of next month	last business day of that next month
5.	Any other case	15th day of one month to 14th day of next month	29th day (or last day in February) of that next month

Set-offs

6. Rebates and repayments arising under specified legislation are set-off against the payment due on payment day if a claim is submitted in the required manner.

Adjustments

7. If a claim for deferment mis-states the excise duty payable, the amount understated is payable immediately and the amount overstated is repaid.

PART III REQUIREMENTS TO BE OBSERVED

Security

8. An approved person must provide security.

Conditions

9. Approval or a grant of deferment may be made subject to conditions or requirements.

Change of circumstances

10. An applicant for approval or approved person must notify any material change of circumstances which affects his application, grant of deferment or security given.

PART IV RELATIONSHIP TO OTHER ENACTMENTS

Purposes for which excise duty is treated as paid

11. A deferment of excise duty is deemed to be a payment of duty for the purposes of specified legislation.

Savings for requirements of other regulations

12. A requirement or condition imposed by other regulations is modified insofar as it relates to the date for payment of duty, but not otherwise.

SI 1992/3156
CUSTOMS AND EXCISE (PERSONAL RELIEFS FOR SPECIAL VISITORS) ORDER 1992

Note This order under CED(GR)A 1979 s 13A confers relief from payment of customs duty, excise duty and VAT on certain purchases, acquisitions, importations and removals from warehouse by:

(a) Diplomats (as defined in art 14). The reliefs in arts 15 and 16 are subject to the conditions in arts 4, 10–13 and 17.

(b) Members of visiting forces, headquarters and international organisations (as defined in art 18). The reliefs in arts 19–21 are subject to the conditions in arts 6, 7, 10–13 and 22.

SI 1992/3193
CUSTOMS AND EXCISE DUTIES (PERSONAL RELIEFS FOR GOODS PERMANENTLY IMPORTED) ORDER 1992

Note This order under CED(GR)A 1979 ss 7, 13 confers relief from excise duty and VAT on personal property permanently imported into the UK from a third country if specified conditions are met. Separate reliefs are given for: (1) persons transferring their normal residence (arts 11, 12); (2) property imported on marriage (arts 13–15); (3) pupils and students (art 16); (4) honorary decorations, awards and goodwill gifts (arts 17–20); and (5) personal property acquired by inheritance (art 21). The order contains interpretation provisions (art 2), rules determining the place of normal residence (arts 3, 4) and conditions common to some or all reliefs (arts 5–12). The order came into force on 1 January 1993 (art 1) and replaces the reliefs previously given in revoked provisions (art 22). For extra-statutory concessions, see Notice No 48 (December 2010) paras 9.3–9.7.

References to Directive 77/388/EEC (the Sixth Directive) are construed in accordance with Customs and Excise Duties (Travellers' Allowances and Personal Reliefs) (New Member States) Order 2004/1002 art 6 and Relief for Legacies Imported from Third Countries (Application) Order 2006, SI 2006/3158 art 2. The Sixth Directive was repealed and replaced by Directive 2006/112/EC with effect from 1 January 2007.

SI 1992/3220
VALUE ADDED TAX (FLAT-RATE SCHEME FOR FARMERS) (DESIGNATED ACTIVITIES) ORDER 1992

Note This order under VATA 1983 s 37B, now VATA 1994 s 54, lists the agricultural goods and services counted as "designated activities" for the purposes of the flat-rate scheme for farmers.

1. This order came into force on 1 January 1993.

2. For the purposes of VATA 1994 s 54 (8), "designated activities" comprise the activities detailed in the Schedule under the following headings: (1) crop production; (2) stock farming; (3) forestry; (4) fisheries; (5) processing; and (6) services performed by a person carrying on activities within (1)–(5) using only his own and his employees labour and using equipment which is also used for carrying on his own activities within (1)–(5).

SI 1992/3221
VALUE ADDED TAX (FLAT-RATE SCHEME FOR FARMERS) (PERCENTAGE ADDITION) ORDER 1992

Note This order under VATA 1983 s 37B, now VATA 1994 s 54, specifies the rate of flat-rate addition for the purposes of the flat-rate scheme for farmers.

1. This order came into force on 1 January 1993.

2. The amount which may be included in the consideration for any supply for the purposes of VATA 1994 s 54 (3) is an amount equal to 4% of the sum which, with the addition of that amount, is equal to the consideration for the supply.

SI 1992/3222
VALUE ADDED TAX (INPUT TAX) ORDER 1992

Note This order under VATA 1983 s 14, now VATA 1994 s 25, revokes and re-enacts the provisions relating to disallowance of input tax credit previously contained in VAT (Cars) Order 1980, SI 1980/442 (as amended) and VAT (Special Provisions) Order 1981, SI 1981/1741 (as amended) with modifications arising from the new charge to VAT on acquisitions.

Citation and commencement

1. This order came into force on 1 January 1993.

Interpretation

2. Various words and phrases are defined. For cases relating to "motor cars", see the commentary to VAT (Cars) Order 1992, SI 1992/3122 art 2.

Revocation

3. VAT (Cars) Order 1980, SI 1980/442, VAT (Special Provisions) Order 1981, SI 1981/1741 and provisions amending those orders are wholly or partly revoked.

Disallowance of input tax

4. VAT incurred by a taxable person on the purchase, acquisition or importation of the following goods is excluded from credit in the circumstances indicated by code letters:

Goods	*Circumstances*
Works of art (defined in art 2)	A, B, C
Antiques (defined in art 2)	A, B
Collectors' items (defined in art 2)	A, B
Second-hand goods (defined in art 2)	A

The circumstances indicated by code letters are:

(A) VAT on the supply made to the taxable person was charged by reference to the profit margin in accordance with VAT (Cars) Order 1992, SI 1992/3122 art 8, VAT (Special Provisions) Order 1995, SI 1995/1268 art 12, or corresponding legislation in the Isle of Man or an EU member state (art 4(3)(*a*)).

(B) The taxable person imported the goods himself, and he has not elected to disapply an option exercised for the purposes of the margin scheme which has effect in relation to them (see VAT (Special Provisions) Order 1995, SI 1995/1268 art 12(4)(*b*), (8), (9)) (art 4(3)(*c*) and (4)).

(C) The taxable person purchased or acquired the work of art from its creator or his successor in title, and he has not elected to disapply an option exercised for the purposes of the margin scheme which has effect in relation to it (see VAT (Special Provisions) Order 1995, SI 1995/1268 art 12(4)(*b*), (8), (9)) (art 4(3)(*d*) and (4)).

5. In principle, VAT charged on any goods or services purchased, acquired or imported by a taxable person for the purposes of business entertainment (see below) is excluded from credit. However, this does not apply if: (1) the entertainment is provided for an overseas customer (as defined in reg 5(4)); and (2) the entertainment is of a kind and on a scale which, having regard to all the circumstances, is reasonable. For the circumstances in which a charge to tax may arise under VATA 1994 Sch 4 para 5 if input tax credit is claimed in respect of costs incurred in entertaining overseas customers, see Revenue and Customs Brief 44/10, 2 November 2010.

If input tax was excluded from credit when services were purchased for the purposes of business entertainment, the consideration for the subsequent supply of those services is deemed to be the amount by which the consideration for the supply exceeds the consideration for the purchase.

If input tax was excluded from credit when goods were purchased, acquired or imported for the purposes of business entertainment, the subsequent supply of those goods is exempt from VAT: see VATA 1994 Sch 9 Group 14.

"Business entertainment" means entertainment (including hospitality of any kind) provided in connection with the trader's business. It includes the entertainment of employees or (in the case of a body corporate) directors or managers if its provision is incidental to its provision of others (eg where a director entertains a customer), but not otherwise. However, VAT on goods and services used to entertain employees is not input tax, so that no deduction arises, if there is no business purpose in providing the entertainment: see VATA 1994 s 24 (1); *Ernst & Young v C & E Comrs* [1997] V & DR 183. Goods and services used solely to entertain partners may be disallowed on the same grounds. This was so in *KMPG (a firm) v C & E Comrs* [1997] V & DR 192. The presence of partners is discounted if it is incidental to, and part of, the entertainment of staff: *Ernst & Young v C & E Comrs* [1997] V & DR 183. Goods and services used to entertain guests of employees at staff functions are used for business entertainment, so that the input tax attributable thereto is disallowed, if the guests are admitted free (*KMPG (a firm) v C & E Comrs* [1997] V & DR 192) or for a charge which is so small that they are effectively admitted free of charge (*Ernst & Young v C & E Comrs* [1997] V & DR 183, where a charge of £15 for a meal and entertainment costing £82.50 was outside this description).

The vital characteristic of entertainment is that the recipient enjoys it free of charge: see *C & E Comrs v Shaklee International* [1981] STC 776, CA; *Celtic Football & Athletic Co Ltd v C & E Comrs* [1983] STC 470; *C & E Comrs v Kilroy Television Co Ltd* [1997] STC 901; *BMW (GB) Ltd v C & E Comrs* [1997] STC 824. This is so whether or not the provider of it obtains recompense from elsewhere: *BMW (GB) Ltd v C & E Comrs* [1997] STC 824. It is therefore necessary to identify the recipient where three parties are involved. For sponsored events, contrast *BMW (GB) Ltd v C & E Comrs* [1997] STC 824, *Evensis Ltd* (No 17218) (entertainment provided by organiser to guests) and *Webster Communications International Ltd v C & E Comrs* [1997] V & DR 173 (entertainment provided by sponsor to guests).

For examples of business entertainment, see *C & E Comrs v Shaklee International* [1981] STC 776, CA; *British Car Auctions Ltd v C & E Comrs* [1978] VATTR 56; *William Matthew Mechanical Services Ltd v C & E Comrs* [1982] VATTR 63; *Northern Clubs Federation Brewery Ltd* (No 8881); *BMW (GB) Ltd v C & E Comrs* [1997] STC 824; *Miller Freeman World-Wide plc* (No 15439). For examples of situations where no business entertainment took place, see *Celtic Football & Athletic Co Ltd v C & E Comrs* [1983] STC 470; *Football Association Ltd v C & E Comrs* [1985] VATTR 106; *W R Ltd* (No 6968); *Board of Trade, City of Chicago* (No 9114); *DPA (Market Research) Ltd* (No 14751); *Webster Communications International Ltd v C & E Comrs* [1997] V & DR 173; *C & E Comrs v Kilroy Television Co Ltd* [1997] STC 901.

For accommodation etc "supplied on", see *Ibstock Building Products Ltd v C & E Comrs* [1987] VATTR 1; *Northern Lawn Tennis Club v C & E Comrs* [1989] VATTR 1; cf *Institute of Purchasing and Supply v C & E Comrs* [1987] VATTR 207. For dual use, see *Thorn EMI plc v C & E Comrs* [1995] STC 674, CA. For concessions in relation to sporting bodies, see Notice No 48 (December 2010) para 3.10.

6. A taxable person may construct, or carry out works on, a building for the purpose of granting a freehold interest, or a lease for a term exceeding 21 years, in all or part of the building or its site under a supply zero-rated by VATA 1994 Sch 8 Groups 5 or 6. He may incorporate goods in the building or its site. If so, input tax in respect of the goods is excluded from credit unless the goods comprise building materials (as defined in art 2). For the vires of the predecessor of this provision, see *McCarthy & Stone plc v C & E Comrs* [1992] VATTR 198.

If input tax was excluded from credit when the goods were purchased, acquired or imported, the subsequent supply of the goods is exempt from VAT: see VATA 1994 Sch 9 Group 14.

7. In principle, all VAT charged on the purchase, acquisition or importation of a motor car (as defined in art 2 above), and one-half of the VAT charged on the hire of a motor car, is excluded from credit. As an exception to this principle, no VAT is excluded from credit in the following circumstances:

(a) the purchase, acquisition, importation or hire of a "qualifying motor car" (see below) by a taxable person who intends to use it *exclusively* (see below) for the purposes of his business or *primarily* for a "relevant purpose" (see below);

(b) the motor car is part of the stock in trade (as defined in art 2) of a motor manufacturer (as defined in art 2) or motor dealer (as defined in art 2);

(c) the hire of a motor car which is not a "qualifying motor car" (see below);

(d) the purchase of an *unused* (see below) motor car by a taxable person whose only taxable supplies are concerned with hiring motor cars to another taxable person whose business consists predominantly of hiring motor vehicles to handicapped persons under a supply zero-rated by VATA 1994 Sch 8 Group 12 Item 14;

(e) the hire of an *unused* (see below) motor car by a taxable person (whose business consists predominantly of hiring motor vehicles to handicapped persons under a supply zero-rated by VATA 1994 Sch 8 Group 12 Item 14) from another taxable person (whose only taxable supplies are concerned with hiring motor cars to such a person).

The exception in (*b*) does not apply to input tax deduction by Y if X hires the car to Y, Y hires on the car to Z, and the car is not a qualifying motor car solely by reason of the fact that Y hired on the car to Z before 1 August 1995. A motor car is a "qualifying motor car" in either of the following circumstances. First, input tax on any purchase, acquisition or importation of the car has never been wholly excluded from credit. However, the car is not treated as a qualifying motor car if it was purchased, acquired or imported after 31 July 1995 and supplied on hire before 1 August 1995 (eg under a prepayment scheme) by the person who purchased, acquired or imported it (see *C & E Comrs v BRS Automotive Ltd* [1998] STC 1210, CA). Second, a taxable person has made an election in respect of the car. An election can be made if:

(a) the car was first registered (ie in accordance with Vehicle Excise and Registration Act 1994 s 21) after 31 July 1995,
(b) the car was purchased, acquired or imported by the taxable person before 1 August 1995 and his input tax on the purchase, acquisition or importation was wholly excluded from credit, and
(c) the car was not supplied on hire by the taxable person before 1 August 1995.

A taxable person does not intend to use a motor car "exclusively" for the purposes of his business if he intends to:

- hire it to another person for no consideration;
- hire it to another person for a consideration which is less than the money payable on an arm's length commercial transaction (see *Crown & Cushion Hotel (Chipping Norton) Ltd v C & E Comrs* [2003] STC 1090; *Tamburello Ltd v C & E Comrs* [1996] V & DR 268); or
- make it available for private use, without hiring it, to a sole proprietor, partner or other person. A motor car may be made unavailable for private use by a director or employee by physical means (eg keeping the car in a locked compound outside business hours or requiring the keys to be surrendered) or by contractual means (eg a bona fide contract of employment prohibiting private use): *C & E Comrs v Elm Milk Ltd* [2006] STC 792, CA. For a case where there was no legally binding agreement or understanding, see *Thompson v C & E Comrs* [2005] STC 1777. In the case of a sole proprietor, availability for private use is a consequence of ownership. Thus, a motor car is available for private use by the proprietor unless he takes positive steps to prevent that use: *C & E Comrs v Upton (trading as Fagomatic)* [2002] STC 640, CA; *C & E Comrs v Skellett (t/a Vidcom Computer Services* [2004] STC 201; *Shaw v R & C Comrs* [2007] STC 1525. The same applies to partnerships: see *C & E Comrs v Robbins* [2005] STC 1103. For positive steps, see *Thompson* (No 14777) (insurance limited to business use); *Southern UK Breeders Ltd* (No 15303) (effect of MAFF licence). For private use, see *McLean Homes Midland Ltd* (No 5010).

A "relevant purpose" comprises:

- hiring the motor car with the services of a driver for carrying passengers;
- providing it for self-drive hire (as defined in art 7(3)(*b*) and see Business Brief 11/92, 21 July 1992); or
- using it to give driving instruction.

For the circumstances in which a motor car is considered to be "used", see *Lincoln Street Motors (Birmingham) Ltd v C & E Comrs* [1981] VATTR 120; *Finglands Travel Agency Ltd* (No 1447); Press Notice, 25 June 1992.

For VAT on delivery charges see *C & E Comrs v British Telecommunications plc* [1999] STC 758, HL and *Wimpey Construction UK Ltd v C & E Comrs* [1979] VATTR 174 (single supply comprising a motor car). For VAT on optional extras, contrast *Turmeau v C & E Comrs* (No 1135) (supply by vendor of motor car) and *Broadhead Peel & Co v C & E Comrs* [1984] VATTR 195 (supply by third party). For cars to be dismantled and parts sold as spares, see *Withers of Winsford v C & E Comrs* [1988] STC 431.

If input tax was excluded from credit when a motor car was purchased, acquired or imported, the subsequent supply of that car is exempt from VAT: see VATA 1994 Sch 9 Group 14.

SI 1993/1507
VALUE ADDED TAX (SUPPLY OF SERVICES) ORDER 1993

Note This order under VATA 1983 s 3, now VATA 1994 s 5, taxes private and non-business use of services received by a taxable person in circumstances where all or part of the VAT charged to him is deductible as input tax.

1. This order came into force on 1 August 1993.

2. "The Act" means VATA 1994.

3. The recipient of a supply of services is deemed to supply those services in the course or furtherance of business if: (1) he puts them to private use, (2) he uses them for a non-business purpose, or (3) he makes them available for use by another person. For an example of non-business use, see *Telecential Communications Ltd* (No 15361). For an example of use by another person, see *Tower Hamlets Housing Action Trust* (No 17308). For the circumstances in which VAT ceases to be chargeable on deemed supplies of a particular purchased service, see art 7.

This provision applies where there is no consideration for the use in heads (1)–(3) above (see VATA 1994 s 5(1)(*a*), (4); this order has effect under s 5(4)). For its disapplication where there is consideration for the use, see art 6(*a*). For its disapplication in other circumstances, see arts 6(*d*), 6A.

The foregoing supply does not count as business use for the purpose of determining whether the recipient is entitled to deduct all (see VATA 1994 s 24(1)) or part (see VATA 1994 s 24(5)) of the VAT charged to him as input tax. It follows that input tax cannot be fully recovered if private or non-business use is contemplated or inevitable at the time when a service is purchased. For the relief given if all or part of the VAT charged is irrecoverable, see art 6(*b*), (*c*).

3A. [Revoked.]

3B. [Revoked.]

4. A sole proprietor is deemed to make a supply of services under art 3 if he uses the services personally or makes them available for his personal use.

5. The value of the supply deemed to be made by the trader is a fair and reasonable proportion of the cost to him of the services. For services generally, see Business Brief 23/93, 26 July 1993. Where the trader's business was transferred to him as a going concern, see arts 8, 9.

6. No supply is deemed to be made if: (1) the services are used or made available for use in return for a consideration; (2) the VAT charged on purchase of the services was excluded from credit; or (3) the services comprise employee accommodation in a hotel, inn, boarding house or similar establishment. For the VAT charged under head (2) where the trader's business was transferred to him as a going concern, see arts 8, 9. If input tax is apportioned between business and non-business use, no supply is deemed to be made in respect of non-business use of that part of the services for which input tax was disallowed.

6A. No supply is deemed to be made if: (1) the services comprise hiring a motor car (as defined in VAT (Input Tax) Order 1992, SI 1992/3222 art 2); and (2) one half of the input tax was excluded from credit (see VAT (Input Tax) Order 1992, SI 1992/3222 art 7 (1), (2H)).

7. The trader's liability for output tax on successive supplies of the same service is limited to the input tax for which he receives credit. Thus, no supply is deemed to be made if the credit has been equalled or exceeded by output tax on one or more previous supplies, and the value of the supply is reduced accordingly in other cases. For the trader's input tax where the business was transferred to him as a going concern, see arts 8, 9.

8, 9. If Y transfers all or part of his business as a going concern to Z and the assets supplied by Y are treated as neither a supply of goods nor a supply of services (see VAT (Special Provisions) Order 1992, SI 1995/1268 art 5), Y and Z are treated as the same person for the purposes of determining: (1) the value of the supply made by Z under art 5; (2) whether Z was entitled to credit for all or part of the input tax incurred on his purchase of the services under art 6 (*b*); and (3) whether Z's liability for output tax has exceeded his entitlement to input tax credit under art 7.

If X transferred all or part of his business to Y in a like manner, X, Y and Z are treated as the same person for the same purposes. The same applies to any number of successive transfers.

SI 1993/2001
VALUE ADDED TAX (PAYMENTS ON ACCOUNT) ORDER 1993

Note This Order under VATA 1983 s 38C, now VATA 1994 s 55, makes provision for payments on account by taxable persons having a VAT liability in excess of £2 million a year.

Citation and commencement

1. This Order came into force on 2 September 1993.

Interpretation

2. Various words and phrases are defined.

Supplies to which section 55A of the Act applies (customers to account for tax on supplies of a kind used in missing trader intra-Community fraud)

2A. A taxable person purchasing mobile telephones or integrated circuits may be required to pay, on his supplier's behalf, the VAT chargeable on the supply made to him: see VATA 1994 s 55A; VAT (Section 55A) (Specified Goods and Services and Excepted Supplies) Order 2010, SI 2010/2239. In consequence, he may become liable to make payments on account, or his payments on account may be increased. If so, he may apply for these payments to be disregarded in determining: (1) his liability to make payments on account; or (2) the amount of his payments on account. If the application is accepted, the payments are disregarded for these purposes from the date notified by the Commissioners.

Revocation

3. VAT (Payments on Account) (No 2) Order 1992, SI 1992/1668 is revoked. This does not affect a taxable person's duty to make payments on account in accordance with that Order.

Payments on account

4. A taxable person is required to make payments on account in respect of prescribed accounting periods longer than one month if he meets the conditions in arts 5 or 6. Payments on account are required in respect of periods beginning after 31 March each year. Payments on account are also required in respect of periods beginning and ending between 2 March and 30 June inclusive each year. Payments on account are not required in respect of those prescribed accounting periods taken into account in determining whether a person is liable to make payments on account.

Persons to whom this order applies

5. Payments on account are required if total VAT payments for prescribed accounting periods ending within a one year period exceeded £2,000,000. This sum is increased to £2,300,000 with effect from 1 December 2011. The one-year period ends on the last day of a prescribed accounting period ending before 1 December in the previous year.

6. If art 5 does not apply, payments on account are required if total VAT payments for prescribed accounting periods ending within a one-year period exceed £2,300,000. The one year period ends on the last day of a prescribed accounting period ending after 30 November in the previous year.

Cessation of duty to make payments on account

7. A person ceases to have a duty to make payments on account if: (1) his total VAT payments for prescribed accounting periods ending within a one year period are less than £1,800,000; (2) the one year period ends later than the one year period taken into account in determining whether he is liable to make payments on account; (3) he makes a written application; and (4) the Commissioners give written approval. The duty ceases from the date of the written approval.

Time for payment

8. If prescribed accounting periods begin on the first day of a month and end on the last day of a month, payments on account must be made to VAT Central Unit no later than the last day of the month following the end of the first and second months included in each prescribed accounting period.

9. If a prescribed accounting period does *not* begin on the first day of a month and end on the last day of a month, payments on account must be made to VAT Central Unit no later than the last day of the month following the end of the first and second *complete* months included in each prescribed accounting period. However:

(i) If there is only one complete month, the first payment must be made by the last day of that month and the second payment must be made by the last day of the prescribed accounting period.

(ii) If there is an incomplete month followed by two complete months, payments must be made by the end of the first and second *complete* months.

(iii) If there is an incomplete month followed by two complete months and an incomplete month, payments must be made by the end of the first and second *complete* months.

10. [Revoked.]

Calculation of the payments on account

11. Where the duty to make payments on account is determined by a year ending before 1 December, each payment on account equals $^1/_{24}$ of the "total amount of VAT" which the taxable person was liable to pay in respect of the following "reference periods"—

Month in which prescribed accounting period begins	*Reference period*
April	1 October—30 September in the basic period
May	1 November—31 October in the basic period

June 1 December—30 November in the basic period

If a prescribed accounting period did not begin on the first day of a month or end on the last day of a month during the reference period, that period is deemed to comprise the prescribed accounting periods which related to the tax period references falling within the relevant one year period. The "total amount of VAT" excludes VAT on goods imported from third countries.

12. Where the duty to make payments on account is determined by a year ending after 30 November in the previous year, each payment on account equals $^1/_{24}$ of the "total amount of VAT" which the taxable person was liable to pay in respect of prescribed accounting periods ending within that one year period. The "total amount of VAT" excludes VAT on goods imported from third countries.

12A. A taxable person may elect to make payments on account by reference to his VAT liability (excluding VAT on goods imported from third countries) for the preceding month. An election must be notified to the Commissioners in writing. It must state the date from which it is to take effect. This must be at least 30 days after the date of notification.

A trader may revoke an election which has been in force for at least one year. It ceases to have effect from the day specified in a written notification to the Commissioners.

The Commissioners may revoke an election if they are satisfied that a trader has underpaid any payment on account due in accordance with the election. They do so by giving a written notification that the election ceases to have effect from a specified date. The trader must wait twelve months from the specified date before making another election.

13. Payments on account are reduced if: (1) the "total amount of VAT" which a taxable person is liable to pay for the prescribed accounting periods falling within any one year period is less than 80% of the "total amount of VAT" for the prescribed accounting periods taken into account in determining his liability to make payments on account; (2) the Commissioners are so satisfied (if the one year period has not yet ended); (3) he makes a written application; and (4) the Commissioners give written approval. Payments on account due after the date of the written approval are reduced to $^1/_{24}$ of the lower "total amount of VAT". The "total amount of VAT" excludes VAT on goods imported from third countries.

14. Payments on account are increased if: (1) the "total amount of VAT" which a taxable person is liable to pay for the prescribed accounting periods falling within any one year period exceeds the "total amount of VAT" used to calculate his current payments on account; (2) the one year period ends later than the one year period taken into account in determining whether he is liable to make payments on account; and (3) the excess is more than 20%. Payments on account are increased by $^1/_{24}$ of the excess beginning with the first payment due after the end of the one-year period. The "total amount of VAT" excludes VAT on goods imported from third countries.

15. Payments on account are reduced if: (1) they have been increased under art 14; (2) the "total amount of VAT" which a taxable person is liable to pay for the prescribed accounting periods falling within any one year period is less than 80% of the "total amount of VAT" used to calculate his current payments on account; (3) the Commissioners are so satisfied (if the one year period has not yet ended); (4) he makes a written application; and (5) the Commissioners give written approval. Payments on account due after the date of the written approval are reduced to $^1/_{24}$ of the lower "total amount of VAT". The "total amount of VAT" excludes VAT on goods imported from third countries.

Businesses carried on in divisions

16. The divisions of a body corporate registered in the names of its divisions are treated as if they were separate taxable persons in applying the foregoing provisions. Payments on account are calculated separately for each division. They must be remitted to VAT Central Unit separately by each division. For divisional registration, see VATA 1994 s 46 (1).

Groups of companies

17. Bodies corporate included in a group registration are treated as if they were one taxable person. The duty to make payments on account lies with the representative member, but each body corporate has a joint and several liability. For group registration, see VATA 1994 s 43.

SI 1994/236
DISTRAINT BY COLLECTORS (FEES, COSTS AND CHARGES) REGULATIONS 1994

Note These regulations were made under TMA 1970 s 61(6). As regards VAT, the regulations are relevant to distraint in respect of penalties assessed under FA 2008 Sch 36 para 39, 40, 40A or 50.

Citation and commencement

1. This Order came into force on 1 March 1994.

Interpretation

2. The terms "close possession" and "walking possession" are defined.

Ascertainment of fees, costs and charges

3. The fees chargeable on levying distress, and costs and charges thereafter, are specified in the schedule.

Deduction of fees, costs and charges by the collector

4. The collector must deduct fees, costs and charges from sums received in connection with the levying of distress.

Disputes as to fees, costs and charges

5. Disputed fees, costs and charges are taxed by a district judge in the county court. In Northern Ireland, see reg 5(3).

SCHEDULE (ART 3)

This schedule lists the fees, costs and charges for specified actions taken.

SI 1994/955
TRAVELLERS' ALLOWANCES ORDER 1994

Note This Order was made under Customs and Excise Duties (General Reliefs) Act 1979 s 13(1) and (3). It grants relief from excise duties and VAT in respect of goods contained in personal baggage brought into the UK by travellers from third countries. The following commentary is confined to VAT.

1. This Order came into force on 1 April 1994.

2, 3. A person is relieved from payment of VAT on goods brought into the UK if all of the following conditions are met:

- he arrives in the UK from a third country. This is a place outside VAT territory of the EU, as to which see Appendix 2 to Part 1B. A person does not arrive from a third country merely by passing through the territorial waters or air space of a third country on the journey to the UK;
- the goods are of a description and quantity specified in the Schedule;
- the goods are carried with, or accompanied by, the person. If his personal luggage was intended to accompany him, this condition is met if the baggage was consigned to the transport operator as personal luggage at the time of departure for the UK; and
- the goods are neither imported for a commercial purpose nor subsequently used for a commercial purpose. This condition is met, for example, if an occasional importation consists exclusively of: (*a*) goods intended as presents, or (*b*) goods for the personal or family use of the person importing them. Goods are liable to forfeiture if they are falsely declared at the time of importation (eg by walking through the "green channel" at a port or airport) or subsequently used for a commercial purpose (eg they are sold).

4. No relief is given to a person under the age of 17 in respect of tobacco products, alcohol or alcoholic beverages.

5. Customs Duty (Personal Reliefs) (No 1) Order 1968, SI 1968/1558 and amending orders are revoked.

SCHEDULE (ART 2)

This schedule lists the goods to which the relief applies and specifies the quantities in respect of which relief is given. The goods are classified by reference to: (1) goods other than fuel and goods in heads (2)–(5); (2) alcoholic beverages and alcohol other than beer and still wine; (3) beer; (4) still wine; and (5) tobacco products.

SI 1995/958
VALUE ADDED TAX (TREATMENT OF TRANSACTIONS) ORDER 1995

Note This Order under VATA 1994 s 5 relieves from VAT certain transactions relating to secondhand goods and works of art subject to temporary importation arrangements.

1. This Order came into force on 1 May 1995.

2. The term "work of art" is defined.

3. The following are treated as neither a supply of goods nor a supply of services: (1) the transfer of ownership on a sale by auction of second-hand goods imported from a third country for such a sale; (2) the transfer of ownership in works of art imported from a third country for exhibition for possible sale; and (3) the provision of services relating to a transfer of ownership of the goods in (1) or (2).

At the time of transfer, the goods in (1) and (2) must be subject to temporary importation arrangements with total exemption from import duty in accordance with Regulation (EEC) Nos 2913/92 arts 137–141, 144 (1) and 2454/93 art 682 (1) (*a*), (*c*), (2), (3).

By concession, head (2) includes certain works of art outside the definition in art 2 and certain antiques and collectors' items: see Notice No 48 (December 2010) para 3.26.

4. The relief in art 3 does not apply in the following circumstances:

- the goods comprise: (1) a work of art; (2) a collection or collector's piece of zoological, botanical, mineralogical, anatomical, historical, archaeological, palaeontological, ethnographic, numismatic or philatelic interest; or (3) an antique over 100 years old which does not fall within (1) or (2);
- the goods are sold by auction at a time when they are subject to the customs procedure for temporary importation with total relief from import duties (see Regulation (EEC) No 2913/92);
- arrangements made following the sale by auction result in a charge to VAT under VATA 1994 s 1(4) (importation of goods from a third country); and
- the arrangements are made by, or on behalf of, the purchaser.

SI 1995/1268
VALUE ADDED TAX (SPECIAL PROVISIONS) ORDER 1995

Note This Order under VATA 1994 ss 5 (3) and (5), 11 (4), 43 (2) and 50A revokes and re-enacts VAT (Horses and Ponies) Order 1983, SI 1983/1088 and VAT (Special Provisions) Order 1992, SI 1992/3129 (as amended) with modifications arising from the new margin scheme introduced by Directive 94/5/EC (OJ L60/17, 3.3.94) (which is incorrectly referred to as Directive 94/4/EC in the note to this order).

Citation and commencement

1. This order came into force on 1 June 1995.

Interpretation

2. Various words and phrases are defined. For "motor cars", see the cases listed under VAT (Cars) Order 1995, SI 1995/3122 art 2. For "second-hand goods", see *Förvaltnings AB Stenholmen v Riksskatteverket* (case C-320/02) [2004] ECR I–3509, [2004] STC 1041, ECJ (horses).

Revocations

3. The orders revoked by this order are listed.

Treatment of transactions

4. A disposal of the following goods is treated as neither a supply of goods nor a supply of services (so as to be outside the scope of VAT) if the conditions set out below are met:

(a) works of art, antiques, collectors' items and second-hand goods (as defined in art 2 above) disposed of by a person who repossessed them under the terms of a finance agreement (as defined in art 2 above);

(b) works of art, antiques, collectors' items and second-hand goods (as defined in art 2 above) disposed of by an insurer who took possession of them in settlement of an insurance claim;

(c) a boat disposed of by a mortgagee who took possession of it under the terms of a marine mortgage (as defined in art 2 above);

(d) an aircraft disposed of by a mortgagee who took possession of it under the terms of an aircraft mortgage (as defined in art 2 above).

The following conditions must be met:

- the goods are disposed of in the same condition (ie without repair or renovation);
- the person from whom the goods were obtained would not have charged VAT (eg because he is not a taxable person) or would have charged VAT on less than the full value (eg because he is entitled to use the margin scheme) if he had supplied the goods in the UK;

- (if the goods are re-imported) the goods were not zero-rated on the previous exportation;
- (if the goods are imported) the goods have borne VAT in the UK or the Isle of Man; and
- (as regards head (*a*) above) no relief is given if VAT on the initial supply under the finance agreement has been (or may be) adjusted as a result of the repossession. This applies to goods delivered under a finance agreement after 31 August 2006 (art 4(1A)).

5. A supply of business assets is treated as neither a supply of goods nor a supply of services so as to be outside the scope of VAT if: (1) the assets are supplied to the person to whom the vendor transfers all or part of his business as a going concern; (2) the purchaser intends to use the assets in the same kind of business; and (3) (if the vendor is a taxable person) the purchaser is a taxable person or becomes one as a result of the transfer. If part of a business is transferred, it must be capable of separate operation. For the relevant tests under EU law, contrast Directive 2006/112/EC art 19 as interpreted in *Zita Modes SARL v Administration de l'enregistrement et des domains* (case C-497/01) [2003] ECR I–14393, [2005] STC 1059, ECJ. The Commissioners consider that the UK legislation complies with that interpretation: see Business Brief 9/05, 4 April 2005.

The transferor must have power to transfer the business: see *Ryan & Townsend* (No 12806) (termination of licence to operate business). He must actually have carried it on: see *Kwik Save Group plc v C & E Comrs* [1994] VATTR 457 (concurrent purchase and resale of business). For purchasers acquiring legal title as nominee for a named beneficial owner, see the optional statement of practice in Notice No 700/9. For transfers between companies in the same VAT group, see Notice No 700/9.

For the meaning of "going concern" generally, see *C & E Comrs v Dearwood Ltd* [1986] STC 327; *C & E Comrs v Padglade Ltd* [1995] STC 602; *Kenmir Ltd v Frizzell* [1968] 1 All ER 414; Reference under *Electricity (Balmain Electric Light Co Purchase) Act 1950* [1957] SR (NSW) 100; *Spijkers v Gebroeders Benedik Abattoir CV (case 24/85)* [1986] 2 CMLR 296, ECJ; *Hartley Engineering Ltd v C & E Comrs* [1994] VATTR 453; *Kwik Save Group plc v C & E Comrs* [1994] VATTR 457; *Sawadee Restaurant* (No 15933). Contrast *Hardlife Ladder Co Ltd* (No 2715) (trader ceased manufacturing operations and seeking custom); *Thruxton Parachute Club Ltd* (No 1816) (business insolvent but not yet dead); *Montrose DIY Ltd* (No 2652) (purchaser able to carry on vendor's business without interruption). For the sale of land, see *The Golden Oak Partnership* (No 7212) (partly developed land); *Morland & Co plc v C & E Comrs* [1992] VATTR 411 (tied public houses); *Hordern v C & E Comrs* [1992] VATTR 382 (woodland); *Cashmore & Talbot* (No 9797); *Hallborough Properties Ltd* (No 10849) (tenanted properties sold by property developer); *DJS Properties* (No 12159) (sale and leaseback); Business Brief 23/93 (property sale during rent free period).

The supply may include a grant of land which would normally be chargeable to VAT at the standard rate because: (1) the transferor has exercised an option to tax in respect of the land; or (2) a new or partly completed commercial building or civil engineering work has been constructed on the land. Where this is so, the grant is treated as neither a supply of goods nor a supply of services if:

- the transferee has exercised an option to tax in respect of the land;
- the election has effect when a tax point first arises in respect of the grant, eg when a deposit is given (see *Higher Education Statistics Agency Ltd v C & E Comrs* [2000] STC 332). For tax points, see VATA 1994 s 6;
- the Commissioners have been notified of the election at that time (see VATA 1994 Sch 10 para 20); *Chalegrove Properties Ltd* (No 17151); Business Brief 11/2001, 21 August 2001). For the notification of elections, see VATA 1994 Sch 10 paras 20; and
- (from 18 March 2004) the transferee has notified the transferor at that time that his election would not be disapplied by virtue of VATA 1994 Sch 10 para 12 in relation to any subsequent supply of asset.

The transfer by an owner of goods which are the subject of hire purchase or conditional sale agreement to a bank or other financial institution is treated as neither a supply of goods nor a supply of services and is therefore outside the scope of VAT.

6. Exchanging a reconditioned article for an unserviceable article of a similar kind is treated as a supply of services if the supplier regularly offers a reconditioning facility in that manner.

7. A removal of goods to the UK is not treated as an acquisition of goods if:

- the goods are removed in pursuance of a supply to a taxable person;
- the supply is made by a person in another EU member state; and
- VAT on the supply is accounted for and paid in another EU member state by reference to the profit margin on the supply in accordance with legislation corresponding to arts 12 and 13 below or VAT (Cars) Order 1992, SI 1992/3122 art 8.

8. A removal of goods to the UK is treated as neither a supply of goods nor a supply of services (so as to be outside the scope of VAT) if:

- the goods are removed in pursuance of a supply to a person;
- the supply is made by a person in another EU member state; and
- VAT on the supply is accounted for and paid in another EU member state by reference to the profit margin on the supply in accordance with legislation corresponding to arts 12 and 13 below or VAT (Cars) Order 1992, SI 1992/3122 art 8.

9. A supply of services is treated as neither a supply of goods nor a supply of services (so as to be outside the scope of VAT) if:

- the services are provided by an agent acting in his own name to the purchaser of goods;
- the services are provided in connection with a supply of those goods; and
- the consideration for the supply of services is taken into account in calculating the price at which the agent obtained the goods.

For supplies deemed to be made by agents acting in their own names, see VATA 1994 s 47. For the valuation of such supplies of works of art, antiques, collectors' items and second-hand goods, see art 12 (6) below.

10. A supply of services is treated as neither a supply of goods nor a supply of services (so as to be outside the scope of VAT) if:

- the services are provided by an auctioneer acting in his own name to the vendor or purchaser of goods;
- the services are provided in connection with a supply of those goods; and
- the consideration for the supply of services is taken into account in calculating the price at which the auctioneer obtained or sold the goods.

For supplies deemed to be made by agents acting in their own names, see VATA 1994 s 47. For the valuation of such supplies of works of art, antiques, collectors' items and second-hand goods, see art 12 (7) below.

Goods put to private use or used, or made available for use, for non-business purposes

10A. The private or non-business use of goods or land does not amount to a supply of services for the purposes of VATA 1994 Sch 4 para 5(4) (as extended by Sch 4 para 9(1)) if the goods or land do not have an economic life at the time when they are used or made available for use. For the economic life of goods and land, see VAT Regulations 1995, SI 1995/2518 reg 116C.

Self-supply

11. [Revoked.]

Relief for certain goods

12. A person supplying works of art, antiques, collectors' items or second-hand goods (as defined in art 2 above) may opt to account for output tax on the profit margin of the supply (as defined in VATA 1994 s 50A(4)) instead of by reference to its value (see VATA 1994 s 19 and Sch 6) if he complies with the conditions specified in a notice published by the Commissioners (see Notice No 718) and he took possession of the goods under any of the following transactions:

(a) he took possession of the goods pursuant to:
  (i) a supply in respect of which no VAT was chargeable under UK or Isle of Man legislation (eg because the vendor was not a taxable person);
  (ii) a supply on which VAT was chargeable on the margin in accordance with UK legislation (ie this article) or corresponding legislation in the Isle of Man or an EU member state;
  (iii) a transaction treated as neither a supply of goods nor a supply of services (otherwise than by virtue of art 5) under the UK legislation or corresponding Isle of Man legislation;
  (iv) a transaction treated as neither a supply of goods nor a supply of services by virtue of art 5 (ie because all or part of a business was being transferred or because the goods were subject to a hire purchase or conditional sale agreement). However, the option can be exercised only if the person who made that supply, or one of his predecessors in title, took possession of the goods under a transaction within heads (i)–(iii) or (v); or
  (v) (if the goods are a work of art) the trader took possession of them under a supply by its creator or his successor in title, or under an acquisition from such a person;

(b) (if the goods are a work of art, antique or collectors' item) the trader imported the goods himself. An auctioneer falls within this description if he placed the goods in the customs procedure for temporary importation with total relief from import duties (see Regulation (EEC) No 2913/92 arts 137–141).

As regards works of art, antiques and collectors' items taken into possession under heads (*a*)(v) or (*b*), a taxable person may opt only if he does so in respect of all such purchases, acquisitions or importations and notifies the exercise of his option to the Commissioners in writing. The option applies to all supplies of such goods made during a specified period unless the taxable person elects to account for output tax on a particular supply by reference to its value. The period commences on the date of notification or such later date as may be specified therein and ends on the date when a written notification is given to the Commissioners, subject to a minimum duration of two years.

A trader may not exercise his option in relation to:

- a supply which is a letting on hire;
- a supply for which he issues a VAT invoice or similar document;
- the supply of an air gun, unless he is a firearms dealer registered under Firearms Act 1968 s 33; or
- a supply of goods which have been repossessed under the terms of a finance agreement, or taken into possession under the terms of an insurance policy, marine mortgage or aircraft mortgage, if the supply is chargeable to VAT because it is not disregarded under art 4.

The prices at which goods are obtained or sold for the purpose of determining the profit margin are set out in the table below. Separate provisions apply to:

- a taxable person acting as principal;
- a taxable person making the supply as an agent acting in his own name (as to which see VATA 1994 s 47); and
- an auctioneer (as defined in art 2 above) acting in his own name. For the auctioneers' scheme, see Notice No 718; Notice No 48 (December 2010) para 3.27 (extra-statutory class concession).

Person	*Price at which goods obtained*	*Price at which goods sold*

Principal	A	C
Agent or auctioneer	A	C + D
Auctioneers' scheme	B	E

The prices indicated by code letters are as follows:

(A) The consideration for the supply made to him (calculated in accordance with VATA 1994 s 19 and Sch 6) (supply made to him by third party or disposal of goods to himself by sole proprietor), the value of the acquisition plus the VAT chargeable thereon (work of art acquired from creator or successor in title), the value of the importation plus the VAT chargeable thereon (imported work of art, antique or collectors' item), the price at which his predecessor obtained the goods (transaction treated as neither a supply of goods nor a supply of services in accordance with VAT art 5) or the price he paid for the goods (transaction treated as neither a supply of goods nor a supply of services in accordance with any other provision) (art 12 (5) (*a*) and (6)).

(B) Hammer price less commission payable to the auctioneer in connection with the sale (art 12 (7) (*a*)).

(C) Consideration for the supply made by the person (art 12 (5) (*b*)).

(D) Consideration for services supplied to the purchaser of the goods by the agent or auctioneer (art 12 (6)).

(E) Hammer price plus consideration for services chargeable to VAT supplied to the purchaser by the auctioneer in connection with the sale (art 12 (7) (*b*)).

Global accounting

13. A taxable person may account for output tax by reference to the total profit margin on goods supplied by him during a prescribed accounting period instead of by reference to the profit margin on individual supplies if: (1) he has exercised an option under art 12 (1) in respect of those goods; and (2) he complies with such conditions as the Commissioners may direct by notice (as to which see Notice No 718) or otherwise.

This accounting method may not be used in relation to:

(a) motor vehicles;

(b) aircraft;

(c) boats and outboard motors;

(d) caravans and motor caravans;

(e) horses and ponies;

(f) goods purchased, acquired or imported for a VAT-inclusive amount exceeding £500.

The total profit margin for a prescribed accounting period is the amount (if any) by which the "total selling price" (defined in art 13 (4)) exceeds the "total purchase price" (defined in art 13 (5)). If the total purchase price exceeds the total selling price in a prescribed accounting period, the excess is carried forward and taken into account in calculating the total purchase price for the next period.

SI 1995/2518
THE VALUE ADDED TAX REGULATIONS 1995

Note These regulations are made under VATA 1994. They consolidate and revoke the 62 Regulations listed in Sch 2. The following are new: regs 43, 193, 196 and 197. The following make changes of substance: regs 14 (2), 16, 58 (2), 86, 115 (3), 136. Forms 1–5 in Sch 1 are revised.

PART I PRELIMINARY

Citation and commencement

1. These regulations came into force on 20 October 1995.

Interpretation—general

2. Various words and phrases are defined. For "datapost packet", see Notice No 48 (December 2010) para 3.33.

Revocations and savings

3. The Regulations specified in Sch 2 are revoked. Actions begun under the revoked Regulations may be continued under these Regulations. References to the revoked Regulations are construed as a reference to the corresponding provision of these Regulations.

Requirement, direction, demand or permission

4. The Commissioners may make a requirement, direction or demand, or give permission, by way of a notice in writing or by other means.

PART II REGISTRATION AND PROVISIONS FOR SPECIAL CASES

Registration and notification

5. Forms VAT 1, 1A, 1B and 1C are used to notify the Commissioners of a liability to registration. The forms include a declaration, signed by the person required to notify liability to registration, that all the information given is true and complete (see *Electric Tool Repair Ltd v C & E Comrs* [1986] VATTR 257). All partners in a partnership are required to sign form VAT 2, which details their names and addresses. For other registration forms, see regs 6 (transfer of a going concern) and 7 (partnership).

A registered person is required to notify the Commissioners in writing within 30 days if there is a change in the name, constitution or ownership of his business or any other event which may necessitate the variation or cancellation of his registration.

A registered person who is required to notify the Commissioners that he makes, intends to make, ceases to make or ceases to intend to make, supplies or acquisitions relevant to his registration must notify the relevant date in writing.

The Commissioners may make a general direction allowing the foregoing notifications to be made by specified electronic means. If they do so, notifications may be made in accordance with the direction in force at the relevant time provided the electronic system is functioning at the relevant deadline. The notification is deemed to have been made when an acknowledgement is generated by the electronic system. In the absence of an acknowledgement, no notification has been made.

A direction may modify the requirements relevant a particular class of notification.

Transfer of a going concern

6. A trader ("the transferor") registered under VATA 1994 Sch 1 may transfer all or part of his business as a going concern to another person ("the transferee"). The transferor and transferee can jointly apply for the transferor's registration number to be transferred to the transferee if:

- the transferor's registration under VATA 1994 Sch 1 is to be cancelled by virtue of the transfer and has not already been cancelled;
- the transferee is liable or entitled to registration under VATA 1994 Sch 1 para 1 or 9 by virtue of the transfer; and
- an application is made on form VAT 56.

If the application is accepted, the transferor's registration is cancelled from the date of the transfer and the transferee is registered with the number previously allocated to the transferor.

The following consequences flow from the transfer of a registration number:

(a) the transferee is liable to furnish returns or pay tax due at the date of transfer;
(b) the entitlement to deduction or repayment of input tax vests solely in the transferee;
(c) any right to payment of VAT credits is satisfied by payment to either the transferor or the transferee;
(d) the right to claim bad debt relief vests solely in the transferee;
(e) the transferee is liable to repay input tax (see reg 172D) claimed on unpaid bills for which the supplier has claimed bad debt relief; and
(f) (as regards contracts for a transfer of all or part of a business entered into after 31 August 2007) the transferee is required to preserve the transferor's records relating to the business (or part of the business) unless the Commissioners direct otherwise.

If the registration number is transferred after the end of the prescribed accounting period in which the business (or part of the business) is transferred, but backdated to the date when the business was transferred, any action taken by either the transferor or the transferee in making a return, accounting for and paying VAT, or claiming input tax is deemed to have been taken by the transferee. See *Ponsonby v C & E Comrs* [1988] STC 28; *Bjellica v C & E Comrs* [1993] STC 730; *Pets Place (UK) Ltd v C & E Comrs* [1996] V & DR 418.

Notice by partnership

7. Partners have a joint and several liability to give any notice required to be given by the partnership. A notice given by one partner discharges this requirement. In Scotland, the notice must be given and signed in the manner prescribed in the Partnership Act 1890 s 6.

Representation of club, association or organisation

8. Every officer, or (in default thereof) every committee member, or (in default thereof) every member, has a joint and several responsibility to do anything required to be done by a club, association or organisation. Action by an individual officer, committee member or member discharges this requirement.

Death, bankruptcy or incapacity of taxable person

9. Any person carrying on the business of a taxable person who has died, become bankrupt, is in liquidation or receivership, is under an administration order, or is otherwise incapacitated may be treated as the taxable person from the date of the incapacity. This does not include receivers appointed under the Law of Property Act 1925 by a mortgagee in respect of a fixed charge over a specific asset or assets: *Sargent v C & E Comrs* [1995] STC 398, CA. The person is treated as a registered taxable person for the purposes of VAT. He must notify the Commissioners within 21 days of the relevant event. The notification must be in writing, giving the date of the death or bankruptcy order, or the date and nature of the incapacity.

VAT representatives

10. A VAT representative must notify the Commissioners of his appointment on form VAT 1TR within 30 days and furnish evidence of his appointment. His name is entered in the VAT

Register (see VATA 1994 s 3 (3)) against the name of his principal. He must notify the Commissioners within 30 days in writing, giving full particulars, of: (1) any change in the name, constitution or ownership of his business; (2) ceasing to be his principal's tax representative; or (3) any other event which may necessitate variation of the VAT Register.

An appointment as tax representative is deemed to cease on the earliest of: (1) the date when the Commissioners receive notification of appointment or cessation under reg 5 (2); (2) the date when the Commissioners receive notification of the tax representative's retirement or his successor's appointment; or (3) the time when the tax representative dies, becomes insolvent, becomes incapacitated or (in the case of a company) goes into liquidation or receivership or becomes subject to an administration order.

Notification of intended section 14 (1) supplies by intermediate suppliers

11. A cross-border transaction may involve a supply by X to Y and by Y to Z. VATA 1994 s 14 (1) provides that the supply by X to Y is disregarded, and the supply by Y to Z is deemed to involve a removal of goods from an EU member state to the UK, in specified circumstances. Y must notify both Z and the Commissioners in writing. The notification must contain the particulars specified in reg 11 (2). It must be made no later than the date of the earliest invoice provided in connection with the supply. It must be sent to both an office designated by the Commissioners and Z. Separate notifications must be made in respect of each customer (Z) to whom such supplies are to be made. A notification made in respect of the first supply to a customer (Z) has effect in relation to later supplies made to Z while X belongs in another EU member state.

Notification of intended section 14 (2) supplies by persons belonging in other member states

12. A cross-border transaction may involve a supply by X to Y which results in the installation or assembly of goods in the UK VATA 1994 s 14 (2) provides that Y is deemed to make a taxable acquisition, and X is deemed not to have made a taxable supply, in specified circumstances. X must notify both Y and the Commissioners in writing. The notification must contain the information specified in reg 12 (2). It must be made no later than the date of the earliest invoice provided in connection with the supply. It must be sent to both an office designated by the Commissioners and Y. Separate notifications must be made in respect of each customer (Y) to whom such supplies are to be made. A notification made in respect of the first supply to a customer (Y) has effect in relation to later supplies made to Y while X belongs in another EU member state.

PART III VAT INVOICES AND OTHER INVOICING REQUIREMENTS

Interpretation of Part III

A13. Various words and phrases are defined.

Obligation to provide a VAT invoice

13. A registered taxable person must provide a VAT invoice if:

(a) he makes a taxable supply in the UK to a taxable person;
(b) he makes a supply of goods or services to a customer in another EU member state for the purpose of the customer's business. However, an invoice must be provided in respect of an exempt supply only if the other EU member state requires invoices to be issued in respect of exempt supplies;
(c) he receives a payment on account from a customer in another EU member state in respect of a supply made or intended to be made to that customer.

This requirement does not apply to supplies of specified services (see VATA 1994 s 18C(1)) for which a VAT invoice is properly issued in accordance with reg 145D(1). For electronic invoices, see reg 13A. For retailers' invoices, see reg 16. For face value vouchers issued to an intermediary, see Business Brief 4/03, 27 May 2003.

The following documents are treated as the VAT invoice required to be supplied under head (1) above:

- an invoice issued by an auctioneer or other person selling another person's goods under a power (see Sch 4 para 7). The invoice must show the particulars required to be shown on a VAT invoice (see reg 14(1));
- a document (referred to as a "self-billed invoice") prepared by the recipient of a supply. The document must be prepared under a "self-billing agreement". It must show the particulars required to be shown on a VAT invoice (see reg 14(1), (2)). It must relate to one or more supplies made by a taxable person in accordance with a "self-billing agreement" (see below) in respect of a supply made by a taxable person. It must comply with conditions set out in a notice or imposed in a particular case; and
- an authenticated receipt in respect of works carried out to a building or civil engineering work. The document must show the particulars required to be shown on a VAT invoice (see reg 14(1)). No VAT invoice or similar document must be issued in respect of the supply.

The foregoing documents must be provided no later than 30 days after the time of supply. The Commissioners may extend this period in accordance with general or special directions. See Notice No 700 (April 2002) para 16.2.3.

A document (equivalent to a "self-billed invoice") prepared by a customer in respect of goods or services supplied to him by a registered taxable person is treated as the VAT invoice required to be supplied under heads (2) and (3) above. The document must be prepared under a "self-billing agreement". It must show the particulars required to be shown on a VAT invoice (see reg 14(1), (2)). It must relate to one or more supplies made by a taxable person.

A "self-billing agreement" must authorise the customer to produce self-billed invoices for a specified period. This period must not exceed twelve months. It expires when the contract between the parties for the supply of goods or services comes to an end. The agreement must specify that the supplier will accept the self-billed invoices in lieu of VAT invoices prepared by himself and provide that the supplier will notify the customer if he ceases to be a taxable person or changes his registration number. For an invalid self-billing system under superseded legislation, see *UDL Construction plc (in administrative receivership and compulsory liquidation) v C & E Comrs* [1995] V & DR 396

A self-billed invoice does not create a tax point in relation to a grant or assignment of the fee simple in land for an undetermined consideration (see reg 84(2)), a lease treated as a supply of goods (see reg 85), water, gas, power, heat, refrigeration or ventilation (see reg 86), goods subject to a reservation of title (see reg 88), retention payments (see reg 89), continuous supplies of services (reg 90), royalties and similar payments (see reg 91), services of a barrister or advocate (see reg 92), works carried out to a building or civil engineering work (see reg 93) or supplies between connected persons or members of a group undertaking (see reg 94B).

This regulation does not apply to the supplies listed in reg 20.

Electronic invoicing

13A. A document provided by electronic transmission is treated as the VAT invoice required to be provided by the supplier (see reg 13(1)) if:

(a) both supplier and customer can guarantee the authenticity of the origin and integrity of the contents by specified means; and

(b) the customer (in the case of a self-billed invoice) or the supplier (in other cases) complies with any conditions imposed by the Commissioners. For self-billed invoices, see reg 13(3), (3A).

The means adopted for guaranteeing authenticity and origin must be preserved. The normal period of preservation is six years: see VATA 1994 Sch 11 para 6(3) and reg 31(1)(*c*).

13B. The Commissioners may require the recipient of a VAT invoice to provide an English translation of an invoice. They do so by notice in writing. The recipient must provide the translation within 30 days.

Contents of VAT invoice

14. From 1 October 2007, the following information must be shown on a VAT invoice issued to a taxable person or to a person in another EU member state:

	Taxable person	*Person in another EU member state*
(*a*)	A unique identifying number.	The same.
(*b*)	The time of supply.	The same.
(*c*)	The date of issue.	The same.
(*d*)	The supplier's name, address and VAT registration number.	The same. The VAT registration number must be prefixed by "GB".
(*e*)	The customer's name and address.	The same, plus the customer's registration number (if any) prefixed by the alphabetical code (see reg 2 (1)) of the EU member state in which he is registered.
(*g*)	A description sufficient to identify the goods or services supplied.	The same. The description of a new means of transport (see VATA 1994 s 95) must be sufficient to identify it as such.
(*h*)	The following information for each description of goods or services:	
	(i) the quantity of goods or extent of services,	The same.
	(ii) the rate of tax,	If a positive rate of VAT is chargeable, the rate of tax. If the supply is exempt or zero-rated, a statement to that effect.
	(iii) the amount payable (excluding VAT) expressed in any currency.	If a positive rate of VAT is chargeable, the amount payable (excluding VAT) expressed in sterling.
(*i*)	The gross total amount payable, excluding VAT, expressed in any currency.	The gross amount payable, excluding VAT.
(*j*)	The rate of any cash discount offered.	The same.
(*l*)	The total amount of VAT chargeable, expressed in sterling.	The same, if the supply is a taxable supply of goods.
(*m*)	The unit price.	The same.
(*n*)	(If the supply is made under a margin scheme (see ss 50A, 53)) a statement to that effect.	The same.
(*o*)	(If the customer is liable to pay the tax on one or more of the supplies invoiced) a statement to that effect.	The same.

The Commissioners may allow otherwise. For the requirement to include the unit price on VAT invoices, see Business Brief 27/03, 10 December 2003. For rounding of the VAT chargeable (see head (l) above), see *Fiscale eenheid Koninklijke Ahold NV v Staatssecretaris van Financiën* (case C-484/06) [2008] ECR I–5097, [2009] STC 45, ECJ; Notice No 700

(April 2002) para 17.5. For documents which do not show all of the required information, see *ABB Power Ltd v C & E Comrs* [1992] VATTR 491; *Libdale Ltd v C & E Comrs* [1993] VATTR 425. For retailers' invoices, see reg 16. For invoices in respect of intra-Community removals of goods, see regs 17–19.

A consignment note, delivery note or similar document containing all the above details but issued before the time of supply is not treated as a VAT invoice provided it is so endorsed.

Supplies of exempt or zero-rated goods or services must be distinguished from standard-rated supplies on a VAT invoice and separate gross amounts payable shown.

A VAT invoice relating wholly or partly to hiring a motor car (other than for self-drive hire) must state whether the motor car is a qualifying motor car (as defined in VAT (Input Tax) Order 1992, SI 1992/3222 art 7 (2A)).

As regards electronic invoices (see reg 13A) provided in batches to the same recipient, details common to each document may be stated only once for each batch file.

This regulation does not apply to the supplies listed in reg 20.

Change of rate, credit notes

15. A supplier must issue a credit note if: (1) the standard or reduced rate changes, or supplies become (or cease to be) exempt, zero-rated or reduced-rated; (2) a VAT invoice for a supply was issued before the change; and (3) the supply is the subject of an election under VATA 1994 s 88 which alters the date VAT is due. The credit note must be headed "credit note—change of VAT rate". It must be issued within 45 days of the change or such longer period as the Commissioners may allow. It must contain the following particulars:

(a) the identifying number and the date of issue of the credit note;
(b) the name, address and registration number of the supplier;
(c) the name and address of the person to whom the supply is made;
(d) the identifying number and date of issue of the VAT invoice;
(e) a description sufficient to identify the goods or services supplied; and
(f) the amount of VAT being credited.

This regulation does not apply to the supplies listed in reg 20.

Change of rate, supplementary charge invoices

15A. The person making a supply must provide the recipient with an invoice (referred to as a "supplementary charge invoice") if:

- a supplementary charge (see FA 2009 Sch 3 para 1 and F(No 2)A 2010 Sch 2) is due in respect of the supply;
- a VAT invoice has been issued in relation to the supply; and
- the invoice does not include the supplementary charge.

The supplementary charge invoice must be headed as such and contain the following information:

- the identifying number of the invoice;
- the date of issue;
- the amount of the supplementary charge;
- the name, address and registration number of the supplier;
- the name and address of the person to whom the supply is made; and
- the identifying number and date of the VAT invoice issued in respect of the supply.

Retailers' invoices

16. Retailers must provide VAT invoices for standard-rated supplies when asked by a customer who is a taxable person. If the consideration for the supply does not exceed £250, the invoice need only contain the following details:

(a) the name, address and registration number of the retailer;

(b) the time of the supply;
(c) a description sufficient to identify the goods or services supplied;
(d) the total amount payable including VAT; and
(e) the gross amount payable (including VAT), and the VAT rate applicable, for each rate of VAT.

Such less detailed VAT invoices must include only supplies which are subject to VAT. They must not be provided to a person in another EU member state.

This regulation does not apply to the supplies listed in reg 20.

Section 14 (6) supplies to persons belonging in other member states

17. A cross-border transaction may involve a supply by X to Y and by Y to Z. VATA 1994 s 14(6) provides that the purchase and sale by Y is disregarded in specified circumstances. Y is nevertheless required to provide Z with an invoice in respect of his supply. The invoice must comply with regs 13 and 14. Invoices issued before 1 October 2007 were required to bear the legend "VAT: EC Article 28 Simplification Invoice".

This regulation does not apply to the supplies listed in reg 20.

Section 14 (1) supplies by intermediate suppliers

18. A cross-border transaction may invoice a supply by X to Y and by Y to Z. VATA 1994 s 14 (1) provides that the supply by X to Y is disregarded, and the supply by Y to Z is deemed to involve a removal of goods from an EU member state to the UK, in specified circumstances. For the notification made by Y, see reg 11.

Y must provide Z with an invoice. This must:

(a) comply with law corresponding to reg 17 of the EU member state which issued the VAT registration number used by Y in connection with the supply made by X to Y;
(b) be provided no later than 15 days after the supply made by X to Y would have been treated as taking place under VATA 1994 s 6; and
(c) cover no less than the extent of the supply made by X to Y which would have been treated as taking place under VATA 1994 s 6 at the time when the invoice is provided.

Invoices issued before 1 October 2007 were required to bear the legend "VAT: EC Article 28 simplification invoice".

Once Y has provided Z with an invoice complying with requirements (*a*) and (*c*), he is not required to provide Z with a further invoice relating to the supply.

The invoice provided by Y is relevant in determining the time when Z is treated as making an acquisition of goods in accordance with VATA 1994 s 12 (1) (*b*) and reg 83. It is treated as a VAT invoice for the purposes of reg 18 if it complies only with requirement (*a*) above.

This regulation does not apply to the supplies listed in reg 20.

Section 14 (2) supplies by persons belonging in other member states

19. A cross-border transaction may involve a supply by X to Y which results in the installation or assembly of goods in the UK. VATA 1994 s 14 (2) provides that Y is deemed to make a taxable acquisition, and X is deemed not to have made a taxable supply, in specified circumstances. For the notification made by X, see reg 12.

X must provide Y with an invoice. This must:

(a) comply with the law corresponding to reg 14 of the EU member state where X belongs (as defined in VATA 1994 s 14 (5));
(b) be provided no later than 15 days after the supply made by X to Y would have been treated as taking place under VATA 1994 s 6; and

(c) cover no less than the extent of the supply made by X to Y which would have been treated as taking place under VATA 1994 s 6 at the time when the invoice is provided.

Invoices issued before 1 October 2007 were required to bear the legend "section 14 (2) VATA invoice".

Once X has provided Y with an invoice complying with requirements (*a*) and (*c*), he is not required to provide Y with a further invoice relating to the supply.

The invoice provided by X is relevant in determining the time when Y is treated as making an acquisition of goods in accordance with VATA 1994 s 12 (1) (*b*) and reg 83. It is treated as a VAT invoice for the purposes of reg 19 if it complies only with requirement (*a*) above.

This regulation does not apply to the supplies listed in reg 20.

General

20. Regulations 13–19 do not apply to the following supplies made in the UK:

(a) a zero-rated supply (see *Double Shield Windows Co Ltd* (No 1771)), unless the goods are acquired by a person in another EU member state;

(b) a supply of goods or services purchased for business entertainment, or of a motor car, where VAT is charged on the margin under VAT (Input Tax) Order 1992, SI 1992/3222 arts 5 (2) or 7 (4);

(c) a supply for no consideration on which VAT is chargeable, ie under VATA 1994 Sch 4 paras 5 and 6 (see Leaflet No 700/35/88, para 4 for tax certificates which may instead be provided to the recipient);

(d) goods supplied under the margin schemes for antiques, works of art, collectors' pieces and second-hand goods (see VATA 1994 s 32 (repealed) now replaced by VATA 1994 s 50A).

PART IV EC SALES STATEMENTS

Interpretation of Part IV

21. Various words and phrases are defined.

Submission of statements

22. A taxable person making a supply of goods (see reg 21) in any of the following circumstances must submit an EC Sales List (form VAT 101) to the Commissioners:

- the supply was made to a person who was registered in another member state (see reg 21) at the time of supply and the goods were despatched or transported to that (or another) member state;
- the supply is disregarded for VAT purposes in accordance with VATA 1994 s 14(6); or
- the supply was made to a person who was registered in another member state at the time of supply and was treated as a supply of goods in accordance with VATA 1994 Sch 4 para 6 (removal of business assets from another member state).

The supply is referred to as an "EU supply of goods". The EC Sales List ("ESL") must contain the prescribed information in respect of EU supplies of goods made in the return period (see below) and contain a declaration that the information provided is true and complete. For the text of the ESL, see Schedule 1, Form No 12.

In principle, an ESL must be submitted in respect of each calendar month in which an EU supply of goods is made. This general principle is subject to the following exceptions.

First, the taxable person may be deregistered during a calendar month. If so, the ESL is made up to the effective date of deregistration. However, this does not apply if the taxable person transferred his registration to another person in accordance with reg 6(1).

Secondly, the value of EU supplies of goods in each of four consecutive quarters may be £70,000 or less. If so, the taxable person may submit an ESL in respect of: (1) the next quarter (if the value of EU supplies of goods for that quarter is also £70,000 or less); or (2) (if the value of EU supplies of goods for the next quarter exceeds £70,000) the period beginning on the first day of the next quarter and ending on the last day of the month in which the value of EU supplies of goods for the quarter exceeded £70,000. For the consequences of deregistration during the next quarter in (1), see reg 22(4)(e)).

Thirdly, a taxable person may submit an ESL in respect of a one-year period in respect of which he does not made a supply of a new means of transport if the Commissioners are satisfied that either of the following conditions are met:

- at the end of any month, that : (1) the value of his taxable supplies was less than £95,500 in the one-year period then ending; and (2) the value of his supplies to persons registered in other member states was less than £11,000 in that period; or
- at any time, that there are reasonable grounds for believing that, in the one-year period beginning then or at any later time: (1) the value of his taxable supplies will not exceed £95,500; and (2) the value of his supplies to persons registered in other member states will not exceed £11,000.

Fourthly, a taxable person permitted to make VAT returns in respect of a period longer than three months in accordance with reg 25(1)(c) may submit an ESL in respect of an identical period in which he does not made a supply of a new means of transport if the Commissioners are satisfied that either of the following conditions are met:

- at the end of any month, that: (1) the value of his taxable supplies was less than £145,000 in the one-year period then ending; and (2) the value of his supplies to persons registered in other member states in that period was less than £11,000; or
- at any time, that there are reasonable grounds for believing that in the one-year period beginning then or at any later time: (1) the value of his taxable supplies will not exceed £145,000; and (2) the value of his supplies to persons registered in other member states will not exceed £11,000.

The sum of £70,000 in the second exception is the amount in force from 1 January 2010. It is referred to as the "first relevant figure". It is reduced to £35,000 from 1 January 2012 (see reg 21). Both amounts are VAT-exclusive.

The sum of £95,500 in the third exception is the amount in force from 1 April 2010. It is referred to as the "second relevant figure". It comprises the sum of: (1) the registration limit for the time being in force in accordance with VATA 1994 Sch 1 para 1(1)(a); and (2) £25,500 (see reg 21).

For ESLs in respect of goods (see above) and services (see reg 22A) in respect of periods ending on the same day, see reg 22B. For statements in respect of new means of transport, see reg 22C.

22A. A taxable person making a supply of services in any of the following circumstances must submit an EC Sales List (form VAT 101) to the Commissioners:

- the supply was made to a person in another member state; and
- the recipient of the supply is required to pay VAT on the supply in accordance with the national law of the member state giving effect to Directive 2006/112/EC art 196.

The supply is referred to as an "EU supply of services". The EC Sales List ("ESL") must contain the prescribed information in respect of EU supplies of services made in the return period (see below) and contain a declaration that the information provided is true and complete. For the text of the ESL, see Schedule 1, Form No 12.

In principle, an ESL must be submitted in respect of each month or quarter in which an EU supply of services is made. This general principle is subject to the following exceptions.

First, the taxable person may be deregistered during a month or quarter. If so, the ESL is made up to the effective date of deregistration. However, this does not apply if the taxable person transferred his registration to another person in accordance with reg 6(1).

Secondly, a taxable person permitted to make VAT returns in respect of a period longer than three months in accordance with reg 25(1)(c) may submit an ESL in respect of an identical period if: (1) he does not made a supply of a new means of transport in the period; and (2) the Commissioners are satisfied that either of the following conditions are met:

- at the end of any month, that: (1) the value of his taxable supplies was less than £145,000 in the one-year period then ending; and (2) the value of his supplies to persons registered in other member states in that period was less than £11,000; or
- at any time, that there are reasonable grounds for believing that: (1) the value of his taxable supplies in the one-year period beginning then, or at any later time, will not exceed £145,000; and (2) the value of his supplies in that period to persons registered in other member states will not exceed £11,000.

For ESLs in respect of goods (see reg 22) and services (see above) in respect of periods ending on the same day, see reg 22B. For statements in respect of new means of transport, see reg 22C.

22B. EC Sales Lists ("ESL") in respect of goods and/or services (see regs 22–22B) in respect of periods ending on the same date may be submitted on a single form. For the text of the relevant form, see Schedule 1, Form No 12.

ESLs must be submitted using one or other of the following methods:

- on paper. The ESL must be submitted not later than 21 days from the end of the period to which it relates; or
- online using an electronic portal provided by the Commissioners for that purpose. The ESL must be submitted not later than 21 days from the end of the period to which it relates.

22C. A taxable person making a supply of a new means of transport in any quarter must submit a statement (form VAT 411) to the Commissioners if:

- the supply was made to a person (referred to as "the acquirer") for the purposes of acquisition by him in another member state; and
- the acquirer is not registered in that member state at the time of acquisition.

The supply is referred to as a "NMT supply of goods". The statement must contain the prescribed information in respect of NMT supplies of goods made in the return period (see below) and contain a declaration that the information provided is true and complete. For the text of the statement, see Schedule 1, Form No 13.

In principle, the statement must be submitted within 42 days of the end of the period to which it relates.

The taxable person may be deregistered during a quarter. If so, the statement is normally made up to the effective date of deregistration. However, this does not apply if the taxable person transferred his registration to another person in accordance with reg 6(1).

Final statements

23. [Revoked.]

PART IVA REVERSE CHARGE SALES STATEMENTS

Interpretation of Part 1VA

23A. The terms "relevant supply" and "statement" are defined.

Notification of first relevant supply

23B. A person must notify the Commissioners when he makes his first relevant supply. He must do so within 30 days. He makes the notification by using the on-line portal provided by the Commissioners. The Commissioners may allow him to notify them by email if the portal is unavailable.

Submission of statements

23C. A taxable person must submit a "reverse charge sales statement" if he has made one or more relevant supplies in a prescribed accounting period. Statements must be submitted no later than the last day of the month following the end of the prescribed accounting period (see reg 25(1)). The statement must be submitted in the form and manner determined by the Commissioners. The statement must show:

- his registration number;
- the registration numbers of the customers to whom relevant supplies were made during the prescribed accounting period;
- the value of relevant supplies made to each customer. Separate totals are required for each month falling within the prescribed accounting period; and
- a declaration that the statement is true and complete.

A nil statement must be made in respect of a prescribed accounting period in which no relevant supplies were made. This statement must be submitted in the form and manner determined by the Commissioners. No statement is necessary if the taxable person has permanently ceased to make relevant supplies and informed the Commissioners accordingly (see reg 23D).

Notification of cessation and recommencement of relevant supplies

23D. A person must notify the Commissioners if:

(a) he permanently ceases to make relevant supplies; or
(b) (having done so) he subsequently recommences making relevant supplies.

He must do so within 30 days. Notification is given in the form and manner determined by the Commissioners.

PART IVB PROVISION OF INFORMATION RELATING TO ARRIVALS AND DESPATCHES

Interpretation of Part IVB

23E. Various words and phrases are defined.

23F. A taxable person required to provide information in relation to arrivals and despatches (see Regulation (EC) No 638/2004 art 7 and Statistics of Trade (Customs and Excise) Regulations 1992, SI 1992/2790 reg 3) must provide the following information regarding the arrivals and despatches to the Commissioners:

(a) his registration number;
(b) the reference period (ie the period applicable under Regulation (EC) No 638/2004 art 6(1) or the period directed by the Commissioners under Statistics of Trade (Customs and Excise) Regulations 1992, SI 1992/2790 reg 4(3));
(c) whether the information relates to arrival or despatch;
(d) the eight digit Combined Nomenclature code applicable to the commodity;
(e) the partner member state (as defined in Regulation (EC) Nos 638/2004, 1082/2004);
(f) the value of the goods (as defined in Regulation (EC) Nos 638/2004, 1082/2004);
(g) the quantity of the goods (as defined in Regulation (EC) Nos 638/2004, 1082/2004); and
(h) the nature of the transaction (as defined in Regulation (EC) Nos 638/2004, 1082/2004).

If the annual value of the taxable person's intra-Community trade exceeds £14,500,000 (see Statistics of Trade (Customs and Excise) Regulations 1992, SI 1992/2790 reg 4(2)), he must also provide the delivery terms (as defined in Regulation (EC) Nos 638/2004, 1082/2004) for the arrivals and despatches.

The foregoing information must be provided in the supplementary declaration (ie the relevant form set out in the Schedule to Statistics of Trade (Customs and Excise) Regulations 1992, SI 1992/2790) for the reference period in which information regarding the arrivals and despatches is provided for Intrastat purposes in accordance with Regulation (EC) Nos 638/2004, 1082/2004 and Statistics of Trade (Customs and Excise) Regulations 1992, SI 1992/2790.

PART V ACCOUNTING, PAYMENT AND RECORDS

Interpretation of Part V

24. Various words and phrases are defined.

Making of returns

25. A taxable person must make a return to the Controller no later than the last day of the month next following the end of the period to which it relates: see *Aikman v White* [1986] STC 1; *Hayman v Griffiths* [1987] STC 649; *Richard Costain Ltd v C & E Comrs* [1988] VATTR 111. The return must show: (1) the amount of VAT payable by or to him; (2) full information in respect of the other matters specified in the form; and (3) a declaration that the return is correct and complete. It must be signed by (or on behalf) of the taxable person. For the manner in which the return is made, see reg 25A.

Returns are made by reference to quarters (see VATA 1994 s 96 (1)) (unregistered persons) or three month periods notified in a registration certificate (registered persons). The first return starts on the effective date of registration. The Commissioners may vary the length of any return period: see *Spillane v C & E Comrs* [1990] STC 212; *Bjellica v C & E Comrs* [1995] STC 329, CA. The Commissioners may also vary the date by which any return must be rendered. For directions extending the due date, see reg 25A(20). For an ineffective direction, see *Leonidas and Leonidas v C & E Comrs* [2000] V & DR 207 (precise obligations unclear). Returns may be made monthly if the Commissioners so allow. Any lack of clarity regarding the length and duration of a trader's first and subsequent prescribed periods may affect the validity of an assessment for the period(s) concerned. For an example, see *R & C Comrs v Raj Restaurant (a firm) and others* [2009] STC 729 (assessments for VAT and penalties invalid). The Commissioners may nominate the address to which returns are sent. Traders must comply with any direction made by the Commissioners in this respect. For the penalties for non-compliance, see VATA 1994 s 69. For the alignment of the return periods of associated businesses, see *R (on the application of BMW AG and others) v R & C Comrs* [2009] STC 963, CA; Business Brief 12/05, 15 June 2005.

A person acting in a representative capacity for a taxable person (see reg 30) must make returns for the periods notified in the taxable person's registration certificate. The first return made in a representative capacity is for a period beginning on the day following the taxable person's death or incapacity.

A person is required to make a final return to the Controller if: (1) he ceases to be liable to registration under Schs 1, 2, 3 or 3A; or (2) he ceases to be entitled to registration under Sch 1 para 9 or 10. The return must contain: (1) full information in respect of the matters specified in the form; and (2) a declaration that the return is correct and complete. It must be signed by (or on behalf of) the taxable person. The return must be made within one month of: (1) the date from which the registration is cancelled (if the person is registered); or (2) the date from which the person ceases to be liable to registration (in other cases). For the manner in which the final return is made, see reg 25A.

The Commissioners may allow the VAT chargeable in one prescribed accounting period to be treated as chargeable in a specified later period. The VAT concerned is accounted for, paid or assessed by reference to the specified period. To be effective, the Commissioners' decision must be communicated to the trader. In particular, the relevant prescribed accounting period must be identified: *Inchcape Management Services Ltd v C & E Comrs* [1999] V & DR 397. For compensation on the surrender of handguns, see Business Brief 27/97, 21 November 1997.

25A. This provision specifies the manner in which a return (see reg 25(1)) or final return (see reg 25(4)) is made.

Specified person

In principle, a person registered for VAT purposes is a "specified person" if: (1) he is registered with effect from a date later than 31 March 2010; or (2) (if registered with effect from a date earlier than 1 April 2010) his VAT-exclusive turnover for the year ended 31 December 2009, or the year ending on any subsequent date, is £100,000 or more. The Commissioners are required to notify a person in writing if they consider him to be a specified person. He is not a specified person unless he has been so notified.

However, a person is not a specified person if: (1) the Commissioners are satisfied that he is a practising member of a religious society or order whose beliefs are incompatible with the use of electronic communications; or (2) an insolvency procedure in VATA 1994 s 81(4B) is applied to him at the time when he would otherwise be notified.

Electronic return system

A specified person is required to make a return (see reg 25(1)) or final return (see reg 25(4)) using electronic communications. This method of making returns is referred to as an "electronic return system".

The electronic system used to make returns must take a form approved by the Commissioners in a specific or general direction. An approved system must incorporate an electronic validation process. A direction may modify or dispense with any requirement of forms VAT 100 or VAT 193. It may also specify circumstances in which the electronic system may, or may not, be used and, in doing so, may specify different circumstances for different cases. A return is not made by an electronic return system if it is made by an unapproved system.

In the absence of proof to the contrary, the following consequences are presumed to result from using an approved electronic system: (1) (if this is successfully recorded by the relevant electronic validation process) a return has been made to the Controller; (2) the return was made at the time recorded by the validation process; and (3) the return was delivered by the person identified as such by any relevant feature of the electronic system.

The Commissioners may make a general or specific direction allowing additional time in which to make a return if any related payment is made solely by means of electronic communication. A direction may allow different times for different means of payment.

The Commissioners may make a general or specific direction allowing additional time in which to make a return for which no payment is required to be made.

Paper return system

A person who does not use an electronic return system is required to make a return or final return on form VAT 100 (return) or form VAT 193 (final return). For forms VAT 100 and VAT 193, see Sch 1 Form Nos 4 and 5 respectively. This method of making returns is referred to as a "paper return system".

The Commissioners may make a general or specific direction allowing additional time in which to make a return if any related payment is made solely by means of electronic communication. A direction may allow different times for different means of payment.

Penalties

A specified person is liable to a penalty if he fails to use an electronic return system to make a return or final return for a prescribed accounting period ending on or after 31 March 2011. The prescribed penalty is geared to turnover (calculated in accordance with reg 25A(19)) as follows:

Annual VAT-exclusive turnover	*Penalty*
£	£
100,000 and under	100
100,001 – 5,600,000	200
5,600,001 – 22,800,000	300
22,800,001 and above	400

In calculating annual VAT-exclusive turnover, the Commissioners must use any available figures which they determine to be fair and reasonable in the circumstances. These figures are taken to be the correct figure for the purposes of the calculation.

A person is not liable to a penalty if he has a reasonable excuse for the failure. For reasonable excuse, see VATA 1994 s 71(1)(b).

A person may appeal against the Commissioners' decision to impose a penalty on one or other of the following grounds: (1) he is not a specified person; (2) the amount of the penalty is incorrect; (3) he made the return using an electronic return system; or (4) he has a reasonable excuse. The appeal is made under VATA 1994 s 83(1)(zc).

Accounting for VAT on acquisition by reference to the value shown on an invoice

26. An acquisition may be deemed to be made when the supplier issues an invoice corresponding to a tax invoice issued under the law of another EU member state: see VATA 1994 s 12 (1) (*b*); reg 83. Where this is so, VAT is accounted for and paid in respect of so much of the value of the acquisition as is shown on that invoice.

Supplies under Schedule 4, paragraph 7

27. The goods of a taxable person (X) may be sold under a power by an auctioneer or other person (Y) in satisfaction of a debt due to Y. If so, Y must send a statement to the Commissioners within 21 days of the sale. The statement must show: (*a*) Y's name and address and, if registered, his registration number; (*b*) X's name, address and registration number; (*c*) the date of the sale; (*d*) the description and quantity of goods sold at each rate of VAT; and (*e*) the amount for which they were sold and the amount of VAT charged. Y must pay the amount of VAT charged and send to X a copy of the statement sent to the Controller. Goods sold under such arrangements are excluded from other VAT returns rendered by X and Y.

Estimation of output tax

28. The Commissioners may allow a person to estimate the output tax due in any period where they are satisfied that he cannot account for the exact amount of output tax chargeable in that period. The estimated amount must be adjusted and exactly accounted for in the next period or (if the exact amount is still unknown and incapable of being quantified) the next but one period.

Claims for input tax

29. In principle, a trader must claim input tax deduction on the VAT return for the prescribed accounting period in which the tax became chargeable. However, if he does not hold the document evidencing his claim (see below) in that period, he must claim deduction on his return for the first prescribed accounting period in which he holds the document. For input tax claimed late, see *University of Sussex v C & E Comrs* [2004] STC 1, CA (the Commissioners have only a narrow discretion to refuse a claim); *Terra Baubedarf-Handel GmbH v Finanzamt Osterholz-Scharmbeck I* (case C-152/02) [2004] ECR I–5583, [2005] STC525, ECJ.

The Commissioners may allow or direct otherwise. However, they must not allow deduction to be claimed more than four years after the due date for filing the return for the prescribed accounting period in which he was first entitled to make the claim. This date must not be earlier than 1 April 2006. For a direction made in relation to imported works of art, antiques and collectors' items, see Notice 718 (May 2003) para 18.3.

A trader must hold the following documents in respect of the transactions stated at the time when he claims deduction:

Transaction	*Document*
Supply from another taxable person	VAT invoice
Reverse charge (see VATA 1994 s 8(1))	The supplier's invoice
Importation of goods	Document showing specified particulars authenticated or issued by the proper officer
Goods removed from warehouse	Document showing specified particulars authenticated or issued by the proper officer
Acquisition of goods other than a new means of transport	Document showing specified particulars issued in accordance with the law of the EU member state from which the goods are removed
Acquisition of new means of transport	Document showing specified particulars issued in accordance with the law of the EU member state from which the goods are removed

The Commissioners may direct a trader to hold alternative evidence of the charge to VAT, eg because the trader holds an invalid VAT invoice. For the circumstances in which the Commissioners accept alternative evidence, see *VAT Strategy: Input Tax Deduction without a Valid VAT Invoice—Statement of Practice* (HMRC March 2007), which is reproduced in Appendix 8.

A taxable person is not entitled to deduct input tax more than once.

Persons acting in a representative capacity

30. Where any registered person dies or becomes incapacitated and control of the business assets passes to another person acting in a representative capacity that other person must make returns and pay tax to the extent of the assets over which he has control as if he were the registered person.

Records

31. A taxable person must keep the following records:

- his business and accounting records;
- his VAT account (see reg 31);
- copies of VAT invoices he issues;
- VAT invoices he receives;
- certificates relating to warehoused goods and warehousing services (see VATA 1994 ss 18B (1), (2) and 18C (1)) which he issues or receives;
- import, acquisition, removal and export documents;
- copies of the credit notes etc he issues;
- the credit notes etc he receives;
- a copy of any self-billing agreement (see reg 13(3B)–(3D)) to which he is a party;
- (if, as a customer, he is party to one or more self-billing agreements) the name, address and VAT registration number of each supplier with whom he has entered into an agreement; and
- documents specified in a notice published by the Commissioners.

A trader using the flat-rate scheme for small businesses (see regs 55A–55V) must keep the records specified in Notice No 733 para 6.4. For a joint statement of practice by HM Customs and Excise and the Inland Revenue regarding records, see Business Brief 27/03, 10 December 2003.

A non-taxable person acquiring excise duty goods or a new means of transport from another EU member state must keep the records prescribed in a notice published by the Commissioners.

31A. A person making an exempt supply of investment gold or exempt transaction resulting in the transfer of possession of investment gold must:

(1) issue an invoice in respect of the supply. For the information to be shown thereon, see Notice No 701/21;

(2) keep and maintain specified records relating to the supply, the recipient and other matters. For the records specified, see Notice No 701/21;

(3) give written notification to the Commissioners within 28 days of making the first such supply. For the information to be furnished, see Notice No 701/21;

(4) (in relation to taxable persons) a record of the exempt supplies made to another taxable person;

A person who does not trade in investment gold may sell investment gold to a person who does. Where this is so, the purchaser must issue an invoice on behalf of the seller and the seller must sign the declaration to be recorded thereon. For the information and declaration to be shown on the invoice, see Notice No 701/21.

The foregoing records and documents must be preserved for a minimum period of six years.

The foregoing requirements apply only if the value of the supply exceeds £5,000 or if the value of all such supplies made by him in the previous twelve months exceeds £10,000.

31B. A person making an exempt supply of investment gold or exempt transaction resulting in the transfer of possession of investment gold must retain the purchase invoice relating to that supply for a minimum period of six years.

31C. An authorised person may enter and inspect premises under the power conferred by VATA 1994 Sch 11 para 10(2) if he has reasonable cause to believe that the premises are being used to make exempt supplies of investment gold or exempt transactions resulting in the transfer of possession of investment gold.

The VAT account

32. A taxable person must keep and maintain a "VAT Account" in relation to each prescribed accounting period divided into a "VAT payable portion" and a "VAT allowable portion".

The following entries are made in the VAT payable portion:

- total output tax due on supplies and acquisitions for the period;
- total tax for which the taxable person is required to account and pay on behalf of the supplier. For the tax concerned, see VATA 1994 s 55A(6);
- corrections for output tax understated or overstated in prior periods (see regs 34, 35);
- adjustment to output tax on supplies made in prior periods where the consideration for the supply is varied (see regs 38, 38A); and
- adjustments to VAT payable for the period made in accordance with regulations. For the adjustments made, see regs 28 (adjustment to output tax estimated for a prior period) and 171 (2), (3) (repayment of bad debt relief); Notice Nos 727/4, 727/5 (annual adjustment under the standard retail schemes). Cf regs 40(1) (*b*), 122 (VAT on postal imports delivered under the postponed accounting system) and 43 (goods removed from a warehousing regime).

The following entries are made in the VAT allowable portion:

- input tax allowable for the period (see VATA 1994 s 26);
- corrections for input tax understated or overstated in prior periods (see regs 34, 35);
- adjustment to input tax on supplies received in prior periods where the consideration for the supply is varied (see reg 38); and

- adjustments to input tax allowable made in accordance with the VAT legislation. For the adjustments made, see regs 29 (3) (adjustment to input tax estimated for a prior period), 107 (annual partial exemption adjustment), 108 (amended attribution of input tax) and 115 (change in taxable use of a capital item). In practice, see also reg 166 (claim for bad debt relief); VATA 1994 s 33, Notice No 749 (refund of VAT incurred for non-business purposes by certain bodies).

"Input tax" includes VAT deductible in respect of acquisitions: see VATA 1994 s 26(1).

The register of temporary movement of goods to and from other member States

33. A taxable person must keep a register containing the following information regarding goods despatched to another EU member state, or received from another EU member state, which are to be returned within two years: (1) the date of despatch, receipt and return; (2) an identifying description; (3) a description of any process, work or operation carried out on the goods; (4) consideration for the supply of goods and for any process, work or operation carried out on them. These information requirements may be extended by a notice published by the Commissioners.

33A. Members of the London Bullion Market Association are not required to keep the records specified in regs 31, 31A, 32, 33 in relation to supplies of investment gold zero-rated under VAT (Terminal Markets) Order 1973, SI 1973/173 art 4.

33B. Investment gold transactions between members of the London Bullion Association and taxable persons who are not members are excluded from exemption by VATA 1994 Sch 9 Group 15 Item 4(*b*). The non-member is not required to keep records or submit VAT returns or EC sales lists under regs 21–43 in respect of these transactions. For registration, accounting and payment, see VAT (Terminal Markets) Order 1973, SI 1973/173 arts 5–7.

Correction of errors

34. A taxable person may correct his VAT Account if he discovers that input tax or output tax has been understated or overstated in one or more of the VAT returns he has submitted. Two conditions must be met.

First, the fourth anniversary of the last day of the prescribed accounting period in which the understatement or overstatement arose must expire during, or at the end of, the prescribed accounting period in which the correction is made. Thus, the latest period in which an understatement or overstatement for the prescribed accounting period ended 30 September 2009 may be corrected is normally the period ended 30 September 2013. However, if prescribed accounting periods have been changed so that the fourth anniversary falls within a three-month prescribed accounting period ending on (say) 31 October 2013, that is the latest period in which the correction may be made. Transitional arrangements apply in relation to understatements and overstatements for: (1) prescribed accounting periods beginning before 1 May 1997 (see reg 34(1B)); and (2) prescribed accounting periods for which the return was made, or required to be made, ended before 1 April 2006 (see reg 34(1C)).

Secondly, the net understatement or overstatement must not exceed:

- £10,000 (if the value of outputs for the period of discovery is less than £1,000,000);
- 1 per cent of the value of outputs for the period of discovery (if that value is between £1,000,000 and £5,000,000 exclusive); or
- £50,000 (in any other case).

The "value of outputs for the period of discovery" for this purpose is the sum required to be included in Box 6 of the taxable person's VAT return for the prescribed accounting period in which the understatement(s) and/or overstatement(s) were discovered.

The taxable person's VAT Account is corrected as follows:

- Output tax for the period of discovery is increased by the net amount of output tax understated in prior periods or decreased by the net amount of output tax overstated. Each entry is cross-referenced to the returns in which the errors were made and the documents to which they relate.

- Input tax for the period of discovery is increased by the net amount of input tax understated in prior periods or decreased by the net amount of input tax overstated. Each entry is cross-referenced to the returns in which the errors were made and the documents to which they relate.

The VAT Account must not be corrected if the net understatement or overstatement exceeds the relevant sum. For claims in respect of amounts erroneously accounted for as output tax, see VATA 1994 s 80. For voluntary disclosure in other circumstances, see Notice No 700/45.

35. Errors in accounting for VAT and errors made in any return must be corrected in such manner and within such time as the Commissioners may require. For the nature of an "error", see *Victoria and Albert Museum Trustees v C & E Comrs* [1996] STC 1016 (adopting a disadvantageous option for calculating tax not an error). For late deduction of input tax, see reg 29. For withdrawn claims for input tax deduction treated as errors for the purposes of this provision, see reg 116N.

For application of the "three-year cap" to deductions under reg 35, see FA 1997 s 47(8), (9); FA 2008 s 121.

Notification of acquisition of goods subject to excise duty by non-taxable persons and payment of VAT

36. A non-taxable person must notify the Commissioners of an acquisition of goods subject to excise duty. Notification must be given at the later of the time of acquisition (see VATA 1994 s 12) and the time when the goods arrive in the UK.

A notification must contain the following particulars: (1) the person's name and current address; (2) the time of acquisition; (3) the date when the goods arrived in the UK; (4) the value of the goods (see VATA 1994 s 20 and Sch 7) including any excise duty payable; (5) VAT due on the acquisition; and (6) a signed declaration that the information given is true and complete. The notification must be made in writing in the English language.

VAT must be paid at the time of notification and, in any event, not later than the last day for giving notification.

X's obligation to give notification and pay VAT is assumed by Y if control of X's assets passes to Y on X's death or incapacity. Y, in this situation, is a personal representative, trustee in bankruptcy, receiver, liquidator or other person acting in a representative capacity. Y's obligation to pay VAT is limited to the assets of which he assumes control.

Claims for, or repayment of, overstated or overpaid VAT

37. A claim for credit or repayment of overpaid tax (see VATA 1994 s 80) must be made in writing. The amount claimed and the method used to calculate it must be stated by reference to the documentary evidence (if any) held by the claimant. Form VAT 652 can be used. For documents which do or do not amount to a claim, see *R v C & E Comrs ex parte Building Societies Ombudsman Co Ltd* [1999] STC 974 at 988, 999.

Adjustments in the course of business

38. The person making a supply must adjust the VAT payable portion of his VAT Account if the consideration is varied after the end of the prescribed accounting period in which the supply was made and the variation is evidenced by a debit note, credit note or similar document. For acceptable documents, see *C & E Comrs v General Motors Acceptance Corpn (UK) plc* [2004] STC 577 (hire purchase transactions); *British Telecommunications plc* (No 14669) (requirement to issue credit note when consideration reduced). For credit notes and debit notes, see below.

Output tax for the period in which the variation takes place is increased (if the consideration is increased) or decreased (if the consideration is decreased). For output tax adjustments, see *Schmeink & Cofreth AG & Co KG v Finanzamt Borken* (case C-454/98) [2000] STC

810, ECJ; *Dimosio v Karageorou* (cases C-78/02 to C-80/02) [2003] ECR I–13295, [2003] SWTI 1937, ECJ (VAT improperly charged); *C & E Comrs v McMaster Stores (Scotland) Ltd (in receivership)* [1995] STC 846 (VAT erroneously charged on exempt supply).

If the recipient of a supply is required to account for and pay the VAT due on the supplier's behalf (see VATA 1994 s 55A(6)), entries are made in the recipient's VAT Account by reference to his prescribed accounting periods. For the adjustments made by both parties to the supply if the consideration is varied so that the recipient becomes, or ceases to be, liable to account for and pay the VAT due on the supplier's behalf, see reg 38A.

The person receiving a supply must adjust the tax allowable portion of his VAT Account. Input tax for the period in which the variation takes place is increased (if the consideration is increased) or decreased (if the consideration is decreased).

The period in which the supply was made or received is substituted for the period in which the variation took place if the person is insolvent.

The consideration for a supply is determined when the price payable has been agreed by the parties. This is the time when the contract is completed (eg under a fixed price contract), the time when an invoice is issued (eg when the customer accepts the price charged under a contract for an unascertained consideration) or the time when agreement is reached (eg when the customer disputes the amount invoiced under a contract for an unascertained consideration). The consideration shown on an invoice may be reduced by a credit note to reflect the agreed position: *Castle Associates Ltd* (No 3497). A credit note may also reduce the consideration shown on an invoice if it is made to correct a genuine mistake or overcharge, or give a proper credit: *British United Shoe Machinery Co Ltd v C & E Comrs* [1977] VATTR 187; *Securicor Granley Systems Ltd v C & E Comrs* [1990] VATTR 9. For the repossession or surrender of goods on hire purchase, see *C & E Comrs v General Motors Acceptance Corpn (UK) plc* [2004] STC 577. For discounts funded by travel agents, see Business Brief 21/98, 9 October 1998. For goods repossessed by a manufacturer when its customer went into administrative receivership, see *Brunel Motor Company Ltd (in administrative receivership) v R & C Comrs and another* [2009] STC 1146, CA (case remitted to tribunal).

A credit note must be addressed to the person to whom the relevant invoice was issued: *First County Garages Ltd* (No 14417). It cannot rewrite a completed contract. See, for example, *Mannesmann Demag Hamilton Ltd v C & E Comrs* [1983] VATTR 156 (repossessed machine); *M E Braine (Boatbuilders) Ltd* (No 3881) (boat taken over after repair); *Rickard* (No 3711) (payment for supply to be treated as loan); and contrast *C & E Comrs v General Motors Acceptance Corpn (UK) plc* [2004] STC 577(repossession or surrender of goods on hire purchase), *Kwik Fit (GB) Ltd v C & E Comrs* [1992] VATTR 427 (contractual right to return goods), *AEG (UK) Ltd v C & E Comrs* [1993] VATTR 379 (call-out charge refunded if appliance purchased). Nor can a credit note vary an agreed consideration: *British United Shoe Machinery Co Ltd v C & E Comrs* [1977] VATTR 187 (cancellation of charge for management services because it led to irrecoverable input tax in a recipient group company); *Peter Cripwell & Associates* (No 660) and many subsequent cases (cancellation of bad debt). For a valid credit note to cancel a charge for unauthorised services, see *Cobojo Ltd* (No 4055). For an invalid credit note, see *Senator Marketing Ltd* (No 5598) (supply made to third party at inflated price). For goods obtained by fraud, see Press Notice 761, 20 September 1982; Business Brief 19/96, 16 September 1996. For price discounts and rebates, see s 19.

For VAT mentioned in error on an invoice under EU law, see the commentary to Directive 2006/112/EC art 203.

If VAT is understated on a VAT invoice, the additional amount due is accounted for by either issuing a supplementary invoice or making a tax adjustment: see Notice No 700 (April 2002) para 19.10. For an invalid retrospective price increase, see *T S Harrison & Sons Ltd* (No 11043) (retained surplus contribution to pension fund). If VAT is overstated on a VAT invoice, the amount stated must be accounted for unless, or to the extent, that it is reduced by a credit note: see Notice No 700 (April 2002) para 19.10; cf Sch 11 para 5 and *Springfield China Ltd* (No 4546). For the customer's obligation to accept a credit note, see *Silvermere Golf and Equestrian Centre Ltd v C & E Comrs*, [1981] VATTR 106; *Highsize Ltd* (No 7098).

For the VAT Account entries, see reg 32(3), (4).

Adjustments were a supply becomes, or ceases to be, a supply to which section 55A(6) of the Act applies (customers to account for tax on supplies of goods or services of a kind used in missing trader intra-Community fraud)

38A. The customer may be liable to account for and pay the VAT due on specified goods and services purchased by him: see VATA 1994 s 55A and VAT (Section 55A) (Specified Goods and Excepted Supplies) Order 2010, SI 2010 2239. Both parties to the supply must make entries in their VAT Accounts if:

(a) as a result of an increase in the consideration for the supply, it becomes a supply in respect of which the recipient is required to account for and pay tax on the supplier's behalf (ie it ceases to be an excepted supply); or

(b) as a result of a decrease in the consideration, it ceases to be a supply in respect of which the recipient is required to account for and pay tax on the supplier's behalf (ie it becomes an excepted supply).

The necessary entries are made to reflect the changed situation. Entries are made for the prescribed accounting period in which the supply was made or received (insolvent person) or the period in which the increase or decrease was given effect (in other cases).

Calculation of returns

39. A VAT return is completed by entering: (1) the aggregate of entries in the tax payable portion of the VAT Account for the current period in Boxes 2 (acquisitions) and 1 (other); and (2) the aggregate of entries in the tax allowable portion of the VAT Account for the current period in Box 4. A VAT return is deemed to correct an earlier account return if a correction is made in accordance with regs 34 and 35 above. For VAT returns, see reg 25 (1), (4).

VAT to be accounted for on returns and payment of VAT

40. The following amounts due for a prescribed accounting period must be accounted for on the return for that period:

- output tax;
- VAT which the taxable person is required to pay on the supplier's behalf (see VATA 1994 s 55A(6));
- VAT accountable on postal importations delivered without payment of VAT (see reg 122);
- VAT payable on goods removed from a fiscal warehousing regime (where reg 145J(2) applies); and
- VAT payable on a self-supply of specified services (see VATA 1994 s 18C(3)) arising on an acquisition of excise goods which are held in an excise warehouse and which have not been supplied while warehoused.

The Commissioners may allow or direct otherwise. For a direction to account for output tax in the return for a specified prescribed accounting period, see *Cantors plc v C & E Comrs* [1993] VATTR 367.

VAT due for a prescribed accounting period must be paid by the due date for making the return for that period. For the due date, see regs 25 (1), (4) and 50(2)(b). The Commissioners may allow or direct otherwise. For the due date, see regs 25 (1), (4) and 50(*b*). For extensions of time to pay tax, see *Starlite (Chandeliers) Ltd v C & E Comrs* [1999] V & DR 313. For payments on account, see regs 50, 51 (annual accounting) and 40A (annual payments exceeding £2,000,000). For payment in euro, see Notice No 920.

A return (see reg 25(1)) or final return (see reg 25(4)) may be made, or required to be made, using an electronic return system (see reg 25A). Where this is so, the relevant payment (if any) must be made by electronic means acceptable to the Commissioners. A direction may extend the due date for payments made electronically. The direction may allow different times for different means of payment. The later payment does not of itself constitute a default for the purposes of default surcharge. For default surcharge, see VATA 1994 s 59.

A payment made to the Controller by cheque is deemed to be made on the second business day (as defined in reg 40(2D)) following (but not including) the day on which the cheque was received. This is the relevant time for determining whether a payment has been received by the due date for default surcharge purposes (see VATA 1994 s 59(1)).

40A. The Commissioners may have made a direction specifying the manner in which a trader is to make payments on account (see VATA 1994 s 28 (2A)). If so, the trader must pay any VAT due in respect of a return in the like manner.

Accounting etc by reference to the duty point, and prescribed accounting period in which VAT on certain supplies is to be treated as being chargeable

41. A supply or acquisition of warehoused goods made before the duty point is charged to VAT in the circumstances prescribed by VATA 1994 s 18 (4). The VAT arising is accounted for and paid by reference to the duty point or such later time as the Commissioners may allow. Whether or not the value of the supply or acquisition includes duty by virtue of VATA 1994 Sch 6 para 3 or Sch 7 para 2 is also determined by reference to the duty point or a later time allowed by the Commissioners. For "dutiable goods" and "duty point", see VATA 1994 s 18 (6).

Accounting for VAT on the removal of goods

42. VAT (Removal of Goods) Order 1992, SI 1992/3111 art 4 (*d*), (*f*), (*g*) provide that a removal of business goods from one EU member state to another is not treated as a supply of goods under VATA 1994 Sch 4 para 6 if the goods are removed for the purposes of processing, use in the course of supplying services, export to a third country or removal to yet another EU member state. A charge to tax arises if this intention is not fulfilled. The tax payable is shown as a positive entry in the VAT payable portion of the trader's VAT Account for the prescribed accounting period in which the intention is not fulfilled. The time of supply is thus irrelevant for accounting purposes. For the VAT Account, see reg 32.

For processing, see Business Brief 22/93, 14 July 1993.

Goods removed from warehousing regime

43. VATA 1994 s 18 (4) (*b*) specifies the time for payment of VAT in relation to warehoused goods subject to excise duty. VATA 1994 s 18D (2) specifies the time for payment of VAT in relation to a self-supply of specified services performed on, or in relation to, goods subject to a warehousing or fiscal warehousing regime in accordance with s 18C (3). The specified times are displaced in relation to a registered taxable person who has been approved for the purposes of the excise duty deferment system in respect of goods at a specified warehouse (see Excise Duties (Deferred Payment) Regulations 1992, SI 1992/3152 reg 4). Such a person may instead pay VAT on or before:

- the 15th day of the month following the month in which the goods were removed (hydrocarbon oil);
- the 15th day (wine, made wine, cider and spirits) or 25th day (beer) of the month following the month in which duty would otherwise be payable (goods imported by a registered excise dealer and shipper); or
- the 29th (or 28th) day of the month where the duty is otherwise payable during a period ending on the 14th day of that month (the period commences on the 15th day of the previous month) (beer, wine, made-wine, cider and spirits in other cases).

These provisions apply to goods relieved from payment of duty.

PART VA REIMBURSEMENT ARRANGEMENTS

Interpretation of Part VA

43A. Various words and phrases are defined.

Reimbursement arrangements—general

43B. Reimbursement arrangements made by a trader claiming credit in respect of overpaid VAT (see VATA 1994 s 80(1), (1A), (2)) are disregarded in determining whether he would be unjustly enriched by the repayment (see VATA 1994 s 80 (3)) unless they include the provisions described in reg 43C and are supported by the undertakings described in reg 43G.

Reimbursement arrangements—provisions to be included

43C. Reimbursement arrangements made by a trader claiming credit in respect of overpaid VAT (see VATA 1994 s 80) must include the following provisions in relation to that part of the repayment which is to be reimbursed to his customers:

(*a*) the trader will make reimbursements within 90 days of an amount being credited to him in respect of his claim;

(*b*) he will not deduct any fee or charge from the amounts to be reimbursed;

(*c*) he will make reimbursements only by cash or cheque;

(*d*) he will notify the Commissioners if any part of the credit has not been reimbursed when the 90 day-period expires;

(*da*) to the extent that any part of the credit paid or repaid to him has not been reimbursed when the 90-day period expires, he will repay that part to the Commissioners;

(*e*) to the extent that the credit (or part) paid or repaid to him carries interest, he will pass this on without deduction of any fee or charge within 90 days; and

(*f*) he will keep the records described in reg 43E and produce them in accordance with reg 43F.

Repayments to the Commissioners

43D. A notification under reg 43C(*c*) must be made no later than 14 days after expiration of the 90-day period. To the extent that the credit paid or repaid to the trader, and the interest (if any) thereon, has not been fully reimbursed when the 90-day period expires, the amount not reimbursed must be repaid, without prior demand, to the Commissioners within 14 days.

Records

43E. A record must be kept of the following matters:

(a) the names and addresses of the customers to whom reimbursements are to be made;

(b) the total amount reimbursed to each customer;

(c) the amount of interest included in the total in (*b*); and

(d) the date when each reimbursement was made.

Production of records

43F. The records in reg 43E must be produced if a signed and dated written notice is given to that effect. The notice must state the date, time and venue for production. A notice may be given before or after an amount has been credited by the Commissioners.

Undertakings

43G. The following undertakings must be given to the Commissioners in a signed and dated written document no later than the time when the credit is claimed:

(a) the names and addresses of the customers to be reimbursed can be identified;
(b) the amount credited will be wholly applied in reimbursing these customers by cash or cheque, without deduction, within 90 days;
(c) any interest received will be wholly applied in reimbursing these customers within 90 days;
(d) any breach of the undertakings in (*b*) or (*c*) will be notified to the Commissioners;
(e) any amounts received in respect of credit or interest will be repaid to the Commissioners if they have not been reimbursed to customers within 90 days;
(f) the prescribed records (see reg 43E) will be kept; and
(g) the prescribed records will be produced in accordance with any notice given under reg 43F.

Reimbursement arrangements made before 11 February 1998
43H. [Revoked.]

PART VI PAYMENTS ON ACCOUNT

Interpretation of Part VI

44. Various phrases are defined.

Payments on account
45. The Commissioners must notify the following information in writing to a taxable person having a duty to make payments on account (see VATA 1994 s 28):
(a) the amounts he is required to pay;
(b) how those amounts have been calculated; and
(c) the due dates for payment.

46. If payments on account for a prescribed accounting period exceed the VAT due for that period, the excess is set-off or repaid. For set-off, see VATA 1994 s 81.

46A. The Commissioners may have made a direction specifying the manner in which a trader is to make payments on account (see VATA 1994 s 28 (2A)). If so, any payment on account, or payment in respect of a return, made under reg 40A in accordance with a direction is deemed to have been made by the due date only if it is made sufficiently early for the relevant amount to be credited to the Commissioners' bank account on or before the due date.

47. A payment on account is recoverable in the same manner as VAT due if it is not paid by the due date. For "by the due date", see reg 46A (2). For recovery of VAT due, see VATA 1994 Sch 11 para 5 (1).

48. The provisions in regs 45–47 above are modified in their application to divisions of a body corporate required to make payments on account.

PART VII ANNUAL ACCOUNTING

Interpretation of Part VII
49. Various words and phrases are defined.

Annual accounting scheme

50. The Commissioners may authorise a taxable person to account for and pay VAT in accordance with regs 50 (2) (current accounting year) and 51 (transitional accounting period). A person so authorised is referred to as an "authorised person" (reg 49).

A "current accounting year" is a period of 12 months commencing on the date specified in the notification of authorisation or on an anniversary thereof (reg 49). An authorised person makes interim payments by credit transfer (as defined in reg 49) during a current accounting year and a final payment, together with a VAT return for the year, by the last working day (as defined in reg 49) of the *second* month following the end of the year. Interim payments comprise either: (1) the quarterly sum (as defined in reg 49) or the agreed quarterly sum (as defined in reg 49) made by the last working day of months 4, 7 and 10 of the current accounting year (if the authorised person and the Commissioners so agree); or (2) the monthly sum (as defined in reg 49) or the agreed monthly sum (as defined in reg 49) made by the last working day of months 4–12 inclusive of the current accounting year (in other cases).

51. A "transitional accounting period" is a period commencing on the first day of the prescribed accounting period in which a person is authorised (see reg 50 (1)) to use the annual accounting scheme. The period ends on the day immediately before the commencement of his first current accounting year (see reg 49).

An authorised person makes interim payments by credit transfer (as defined in reg 49) during a transitional accounting period of four months or more and a final payment, together with a VAT return for the period, by the last working day (as defined in reg 49) of the *second* month following the end of the period. Interim payments comprise either: (1) the quarterly sum (as defined in reg 49) made by the last working day of month 4 and (if applicable) months 7 and 10 of the period (if the authorised person and the Commissioners so agree); or (2) the monthly sum (as defined in reg 49) made by the last working day of month 4 and each successive month of the period (in other cases).

An authorised person must furnish a VAT return, and pay the VAT shown to be due thereon, in respect of a transitional accounting period of less than four months. This must be done by the last working day of the *first* month following the end of the period.

Admission to the scheme

52. A taxable person may apply for authorisation (see reg 50 (1)) if:

- he has reasonable grounds to believe that taxable turnover for the next 12 months will not exceed £1,350,000;
- he is not included in a VAT group (see s 43);
- he is not registered as a division of a body corporate (see s 46); and
- (if he has previously been authorised) he has not ceased to use the scheme in the previous 12 months.

The Commissioners may reject an application in order to protect the revenue.

For the address to which applications should be sent, see Business Brief 17/03, 11 September 2003.

53. An authorised person (as defined in reg 49) must account for VAT under the scheme until he ceases to be authorised.

An authorised person ceases to be authorised in accordance with the following provisions—

Circumstance (reg 53(2))		*Date when authorisation ceases (reg 55(1))*
(*a*)	Taxable turnover for a current accounting year or transitional accounting period exceeds £1,600,000	Day following the last day of the current accounting year or transitional accounting period
(*b*)	The Commissioners terminate the authorisation (see reg 54 (1))	Day on which the authorisation is terminated

(*c*)	The authorised person— (i) becomes insolvent and ceases to trade (other than to dispose of stocks and assets), (ii) ceases business or ceases to be registered, or (iii) dies, becomes bankrupt or becomes incapacitated	Day on which the event stated occurs
(*d*)	The authorised person voluntarily ceases to operate the scheme	Day when he gives written notification of his decision to cease using the scheme

54. The Commissioners may terminate a trader's authorisation (see reg 49) if—
(a) he made a false statement in relation to his application;
(b) he fails to furnish his VAT return by the due date;
(c) he fails to make a quarterly or monthly payment by the due date;
(d) he notifies the Commissioners that taxable turnover for a current accounting year or transitional accounting period is likely to exceed £1,600,000;
(e) the Commissioners have reasonable grounds for believing that taxable turnover for a current accounting year or transitional accounting period is likely to exceed £1,600,000;
(f) it is necessary to do so in order to protect the revenue;
(g) he has failed to pay all or part of the VAT declared on a return furnished prior to his authorisation; or
(h) he has failed to pay all or part of an assessment for VAT, penalties, default surcharge or interest made under VATA 1994 s 73 or 76.

An authorised person must give written notice of the event in head (*d*) within 30 days.

55. The dates from which an authorisation ceases are listed. (See under reg 53 above.)

An authorised person (or his representative) must make a return and final payment when his authorisation ceases. This is done in accordance with regs 50 (2) or 51 if the authorisation ceases at the end of a current accounting year or transitional accounting period. In other cases, the return and payment must be made within two months of the day on which the authorisation is terminated (event in reg 53 (2) (*b*)), the day on which a specified event occurs (event in reg 53 (2) (*c*)) or the date of the notification concerned (event in reg 53 (2) (*d*)). VAT must be accounted for and paid outside the scheme from the day following that on which the trader ceases to be authorised.

PART VIIA FLAT-RATE SCHEME FOR SMALL BUSINESSES

Interpretation of Part VIIA

55A. Various words and phrases are defined. A person (X) is associated with another person (Y) at any time if Y makes supplies in the course or furtherance of business and either: (1) X's business is under the dominant influence of Y (or vice versa); or (2) X and Y are closely bound to one another by financial, economic and organisational links.

Flat-rate scheme for small businesses

55B. A taxable person must apply to join the scheme. For the eligibility criteria, see reg 55L. If his application is accepted, he is authorised to use the scheme from the beginning of his next prescribed accounting period or from a mutually agreed earlier or later date. For retrospective authorisations, see HMRC's Flat Rate Scheme Guidance Manual para FRS3300; *R & C Comrs v Burke* [2009] EWHC 2587 (Ch), [2011] STC 625. The Commissioners can refuse an application in order to protect the revenue.

Authorisation to use the scheme involves accounting for and paying VAT on relevant supplies (see reg 55C). A person authorised to use the scheme (referred to as a "flat-rate trader") must continue to account for VAT in this manner until the date from which he ceases to be authorised (see reg 55Q(2)).

Relevant supplies and purchases

55C. A purchase, acquisition or importation by a flat-rate trader is known as a "relevant purchase". Goods and services purchased before, but paid for after, his authorisation took effect are relevant purchases.

In principle, all supplies made by a flat-rate trader are relevant supplies (VATA 1994 s 26B(2)(*a*)). This includes a supply made before his authorisation took effect if the payment was received afterwards. However, a supply of capital expenditure goods (as defined in reg 55A(1)) is not a relevant supply if he lawfully deducted input tax (see reg 55E(1)) in respect of his purchase, acquisition or importation of those goods.

A self-supply is neither a relevant purchase nor a relevant supply. Nor is a supply of the goods or services listed in VAT (Section 55A) (Goods and Excepted Supplies) Order 2010, SI 2010/2239 arts 5, 6) made to or by a flat-rate trader if the recipient is required to account for and pay the VAT due in accordance with VATA 1994 s 55A(6).

Method of accounting

55D. The output tax due from a flat-rate trader for a prescribed accounting period is the appropriate percentage (as defined in VATA 1994 s 26B(2)(*b*)) of his relevant turnover (as defined in VATA 1994 s 26B(2)(*c*)) for that period. For the calculation of relevant turnover, see reg 55G. For the appropriate percentage to be applied for all or part of a prescribed accounting period, see regs 55H, 55JB and 55K.

Input tax

55E. In principle, a flat-rate trader is not entitled to deduct input tax (see VATA 1994 s 26B(5)). By way of exception, he is entitled to do so in respect of:

- relevant purchases of capital expenditure goods (as defined in reg 55A(1)) with a VAT-inclusive cost exceeding £2,000; and
- purchases, acquisitions and importations that are not relevant purchases. However, this does not apply if credit is specifically disallowed. For the goods and services on which input tax is disallowed, see VATA 1994 s 25(7).

Capital expenditure goods are deemed to be used exclusively in making taxable supplies. Thus, input tax is not restricted under the partial exemption rules (see regs 99–110).

Exceptional claims for VAT relief

55F. In principle, a flat-rate trader is not entitled to deduct input tax (see VATA 1994 s 26B(5)). By way of exception, he is entitled to do so in respect of pre-registration and pre-incorporation purchases, acquisitions and importations in accordance with reg 111 if:

- he becomes a flat-rate trader at the time of registration; and
- the Commissioners authorise the claim.

The goods or services are deemed to be used exclusively in making taxable supplies. Thus, input tax is not restricted under the partial exemption rules (see regs 99–110).

Determining relevant turnover

55G. It is necessary to determine when supplies are treated as taking place for the purpose of ascertaining relevant turnover for a particular period. A flat-rate trader must use one of the following methods prescribed in Notice No 733:

(a) the basic turnover method (section 8 of the Notice);
(b) the cash based turnover method (section 9 of the Notice);

(c) the retailer's turnover method (section 10 of the Notice).

Appropriate percentage

55H. The appropriate percentage is the percentage (see table in reg 55K) applicable to the activity carried on by the flat-rate trader. This is determined as follows:

Event	*Appropriate percentage determined by reference to:*
Any relevant date (as defined in reg 55A(3)) coincides with the first day of a prescribed accounting period	The business reasonably expected (at the relevant date) to be carried on in the prescribed accounting period
The start date (see reg 55B(2)) falls part way through the prescribed accounting period	The business expected (at the start date) to be carried on in the remainder of the prescribed accounting period
Any other relevant date falls part way through the prescribed accounting period	As regards the remaining portion (see below) the business reasonably expected (at the relevant date) to be carried on in the prescribed accounting period
Any other case	Relevant turnover at the end of the previous prescribed accounting period

The "remaining portion" of a prescribed accounting period is the period starting on a relevant day and ending on the last day of the prescribed accounting period. If another relevant date subsequently occurs in the same prescribed accounting period, the existing remaining portion ends on the day before the latest relevant date. The new remaining portion starts on the new relevant date and ends on the last day of the prescribed accounting period. For example, if relevant days fall on 10 January and 20 February during a three month prescribed accounting period ending on 31 March, appropriate percentages are applied separately to the periods 1 January to 9 January, 10 January to 19 February and 20 February to 31 March.

Reduced appropriate percentage for newly registered period

55JB. Appropriate percentages (see the Table in reg 55K) are reduced by one percentage point during a flat-rate trader's "newly registered period" if:

- the trader's start date (see reg 55B(2)) falls before the first anniversary of his effective date of registration (referred to as his "EFR");
- the Commissioners received notification of (or otherwise became fully aware of) his liability to registration before that anniversary; and
- that anniversary (or, if earlier, his end date (see reg 55Q(2)) falls after 31 December 2004.

In principle, a trader's "newly registered period" begins on his start date (see reg 55B(2)) and ends on the day before the first anniversary of his "EFR". However, if the Commissioners became aware of his liability to registration after his start date, the trader's newly registered period begins on the day when the Commissioners received his notification of liability to registration or the day when they otherwise became fully aware of his liability to registration.

Category of business

55K. A flat-rate trader may expect to carry on two or more business activities during a period. If so, the business he is expected to carry on during this period is deemed to comprise the activity that he expects to be his main activity during the period. This is the activity that he expects to generate the largest proportion of relevant turnover during the period.

The categories of business, and the appropriate percentages applicable to them, in force from 4 January 2011 are set out in the Table.

Admission to the Scheme

55L. A taxable person can apply for authorisation to use the scheme if, at any time, he meets all of the following conditions:

- there are reasonable grounds for believing that the value of his taxable supplies (other than capital assets and services made under the reverse charge provisions (see VATA 1994 s 8)) for the twelve month period then beginning will not exceed £150,000;
- he is not a tour operator;
- he is not required to carry out adjustments under the capital goods scheme (see regs 112–116);
- he does not intend to account for output under the margin scheme for works of art, antiques, collectors' items, motor vehicles and second-hand goods (see VATA 1994 s 50A);
- he has not been convicted of an offence in connection with VAT in the previous twelve months;
- he has not made any payment to compound proceedings (see CEMA 1979 s 152) in respect of VAT in the previous twelve months;
- he has not been assessed to a penalty for dishonest conduct (see VATA 1994 s 60) in the previous twelve months;
- he has not ceased to operate the scheme in the previous twelve months;
- he is not eligible to be included in a VAT group (see VATA 1994 s 43A);
- he is not registered in the name of a division (see VATA 1994 s 46(1));
- he is not associated with another person (as defined in reg 55A(2)); and
- he has not been eligible to be included in a VAT group, registered in the name of a division or associated with another person in the previous two years.

The Commissioners can waive the condition in head (12) if they are satisfied that authorisation poses no risk to the revenue.

Withdrawal from the scheme

55M. A flat-rate trader ceases to be eligible to use the scheme in any of the following circumstances. The date specified in reg 55Q from which he ceases to be so authorised (known as the "end date") is also shown in respect of each circumstance. For the notification to be given in respect of heads (1)–(9), see reg 55N.

	Circumstance	*End date*
1.	His income (see reg 55M(3)–(5)) for the year ended on an anniversary of the start date exceeds £230,000. However, he does not cease to be eligible if the Commissioners are satisfied that his income for the coming year will not exceed £191,500.	(*a*) If the flat-rate trader uses the annual accounting scheme: the earlier of (i) the end of the prescribed accounting period in which the relevant anniversary occurs and (ii) the end of the month next following. (*b*) In all other cases: the end of the prescribed accounting period in which the relevant anniversary occurs.
2.	His income (see reg 55M(3)–(5)) for the next 30 days is expected to exceed £230,000.	The beginning of the 30 day period.
3.	He becomes a tour operator.	The date when the event occurs.
4.	He intends to acquire, construct or otherwise obtain a capital item (as defined in reg 112(2)) so as to fall within the capital goods scheme.	The date when the event occurs.
5.	He opts to account for output tax under the margin scheme for works of art, etc (see VATA 1994 s 50A).	The beginning of the prescribed accounting period for which he makes the election.

6.	He becomes eligible to become a member of a VAT group (see VATA 1994 s 43A).	The date when the event occurs.
7.	He becomes registered in the name of a division (see VATA 1994 s 46(1)).	The date when the event occurs.
8.	He becomes associated with another person (as defined in reg 55A(2)).	The date when the event occurs.
9.	He opts to withdraw from the scheme.	The date when his option is notified to the Commissioners or a mutually agreed earlier date.
10.	His authorisation is terminated (see reg 55P).	The date when the Commissioners issue a notice of termination, or the earlier or later date (if any) directed in the notification.

Notification

55N. A flat-rate trader must notify the Commissioners in writing within 30 days if:

- his appropriate percentage changes by reference to an anniversary of his start date (see reg 55H(2)(*a*)). The 30-day time limit runs from the first day of the prescribed accounting period;
- he begins to carry on a new business activity;
- he ceases to carry on an existing business activity; or
- he ceases to be eligible to use the scheme (see reg 55M(1)).

Termination by the Commissioners

55P. The Commissioners can terminate a flat-rate trader's authorisation at any time to protect the revenue. The Commissioners can also terminate an authorisation at any time if the application for authorisation contained a false statement.

Date of withdrawal from the scheme

55Q. The date from which a flat-rate trader ceases to be authorised to use the scheme is known as the "end date". For the end dates specified, see the table in reg 55M.

Self-Supply on withdrawal from scheme

55R. A flat-rate trader makes a self-supply of capital expenditure goods (as defined in reg 55A(1)) if:

(a) he continues to be a taxable person after he ceases to be authorised to use the scheme;

(b) he lawfully (ie under reg 55E) claimed input tax credit for the goods at a time when he was a flat-rate trader; and

(c) he did not make a supply of those goods whilst he was a flat-rate trader.

He is deemed to supply the goods in the course or furtherance of business (so that the supply is chargeable to tax). He is deemed to purchase the goods for the purpose of his business (so that the VAT concerned is input tax).

The supply and purchase are deemed to be made on the day after he ceased to be authorised to use the scheme. The value of the supply is open market value.

Adjustments in respect of stock on hand at withdrawal from the scheme

55S. A flat-rate trader is entitled to input tax credit in respect of stock on hand if:

(a) he continues to be a taxable person after he ceases to be authorised to use the scheme;

(b) he has stock on hand at that time for which he is not entitled to input tax credit (ie by virtue of VATA 1994 s 26B(5)); and
(c) the value of this stock exceeds the value of the stock held on the date from which his authorisation to use the scheme had effect and in respect of which he was entitled to input tax credit (ie in accordance with reg 55F in the case of a new registration and VATA 1994 s 24 in the case of an existing registration).

The amount of the input tax credit is determined in accordance with Notice No 733 (April 2002) para 7.11. This amount in deducted in the prescribed accounting period following that in which he ceased to be authorised.

Amendment by Notice

55T. The Commissioners can vary the methods prescribed in Notice No 733 (see regs 55G and 55S) by publishing an amendment to the notice or by publishing a new notice.

Reverse charges

55U. A flat-rate trader is not liable to the reverse charge. For the reverse charge, see VATA 1994 s 8.

Bad debt relief

55V. A flat-rate trader using the cash turnover method (see reg 55G) is entitled to claim a refund in respect of bad debts even though he has not accounted for and paid VAT on the supply (as required by VATA 1994 s 36(1)). The amount of the refund is X – (A × B) where:

X = the VAT chargeable on the relevant supply (see reg 55C).

A = the appropriate percentage (see reg 55H) current when the relevant supply was made.

B = the value of the relevant supply plus the VAT chargeable thereon.

A flat-rate trader using the basic turnover method or retailer's turnover method (see reg 55G) accounts for and pays VAT on the supply and therefore appears to be entitled to a refund in accordance with VATA 1994 s 36 and VAT Regulations 1995, SI 1995/2518 regs 165–172B. However, bad debt relief is claimed by reference to the VAT chargeable (VATA 1994 s 36(2)). As no VAT is "chargeable" on exempt and zero-rated supplies (VATA 1994 ss 4(1), 30(1)), it appears that no claim can be made in respect of them despite the fact that VAT has been accounted for at the appropriate percentage. Moreover, as VAT charged at the reduced rate (by reference to the value of the supply) is always less than VAT accounted for at the appropriate percentage (by reference to the value of the supply plus VAT thereon), a refund of the VAT chargeable is always less than the VAT accounted for.

PART VIII CASH ACCOUNTING

Interpretation of Part VIII

56. Various words and phrases are defined.

Cash accounting scheme

57. Subject to these regulations and the conditions described in Notice No 731, a taxable person may account for VAT in accordance with a scheme by which the operative date for output tax is the day on which payment is received and the operative date for input tax is the date on which payment is made or the date of any cheque, if later. For payments received, see *A-Z Electrical v C & E Comrs* [1993] VATTR 389 (shares issued in satisfaction of debt).

57A. A flat-rate trader (as defined in reg 55A) cannot use the cash accounting scheme to account for VAT in respect of his relevant supplies (as defined in VATA 1994 s 26B(2)(*a*)) or his relevant purchases (as defined in reg 55C). For the alternative scheme available, see reg 55G (cash turnover method).

Admission to the scheme

58. A trader is eligible to begin operating the scheme from the beginning of a prescribed accounting period if:

(a) he has reasonable grounds for believing that the value of his taxable supplies for the one year period then beginning will not exceed £1,350,000;

(b) he has made all returns which he is required to make and has either (i) paid all VAT, penalties, interest and surcharge due from him, or (ii) entered into an arrangement with the Commissioners to pay the outstanding amount by instalments; and

(c) he has not, in the previous year, been convicted of a VAT offence, accepted a compounded settlement for a VAT offence, been assessed to a penalty for dishonest conduct, or ceased to be entitled to continue operating the scheme.

The scheme does not apply to:

(a) lease purchase agreements;

(b) hire purchase agreements;

(c) conditional sale agreements;

(d) credit sale agreements;

(e) supplies for which a VAT invoice is issued if full payment is deferred for more than six months;

(f) supplies invoiced before the goods have been delivered or made available, or the services performed, unless the invoice relates to that part of the goods which have been delivered or made available or that part of the services which have been performed; or

(g) supplies of goods or services in respect of which the recipient is liable to account for and pay the VAT due on the supplier's behalf. For the supplies of goods and services, see VATA 1994 s 55A(6) and VAT (Section 55A) (Specified Goods and Excepted Supplies) Order 2010, SI 2010/2239.

A trader is not entitled to begin operating the scheme if, in order to protect the revenue, the Commissioners consider that he should not be so entitled. This enables the Commissioners to prevent a trader starting to operate the scheme if they know of his intentions in advance. For similar powers exercised after the trader has started to operate the scheme, see reg 64 (1)(*d*).

59. The Commissioners may vary the terms of the scheme by publishing either a fresh notice or a notice amending an existing notice. For the notice published, see Notice No 731.

60. A trader must withdraw from the scheme if the value of his taxable supplies for the one-year period ended on the last day of a prescribed accounting period exceeded £1,600,000. He must do so at the end of that prescribed accounting period. The Commissioners may allow or direct otherwise. For the accounting consequences, see reg 61.

A trader may withdraw from the scheme at the end of any prescribed accounting period. For the accounting consequences of ceasing to use the scheme at his own volition, see reg 61.

61. A trader must either "settle up" or "apply transitional arrangements" when he withdraws from the scheme (see reg 60(1), (2)). However, he cannot apply transitional arrangements if his taxable supplies for the three months prior to withdrawal exceeded £1,350,000.

A trader "settles up" by accounting for output tax, and deducting input tax, on "scheme supplies" unpaid at the date of withdrawal. This tax is accounted for on the return for the period in which the trader ceased to operate the scheme.

A trader "applies transitional arrangements" by continuing to operate the scheme in relation to unpaid "scheme supplies" for six months following withdrawal. He settles up at the end of the six-month period and accounts for the tax concerned on the return for the period that ends on, or straddles, the last day of the six-month period.

"Scheme supplies" are supplies made and received while operating the scheme in respect of which the trader is entitled to apply cash accounting. For excluded supplies, see regs 57 (supplies excluded by virtue of conditions described in a notice), 57A(*a*) (relevant supplies and relevant purchases under the flat-rate scheme for small businesses) and 58(2) (certain supplies subject to deferred credit terms.

62. An insolvent trader must account for VAT made and received up to the date of the insolvency which has not otherwise been accounted for, subject to any credit for input tax. He must do so within two months of the date of the insolvency.

63. A trader who ceases business or ceases to be registered must make a return accounting for, and pay, VAT due on all supplies made and received up to the date of cessation which has not otherwise been accounted for, subject to any adjustment for credit for input tax. He must do so within two months or such longer period as the Commissioners may allow.

A trader may transfer all or part of his business as a going concern. If he transfers his registration number (see reg 6 (1)), the transferee must use the scheme to account for and pay VAT on supplies made and received by the transferor prior to the date of transfer. If not, he must make a return accounting for, and pay, VAT due on all supplies made and received which has not otherwise been accounted for, subject to credit for input tax. He must do so within two months or such longer period as the Commissioners may allow.

Withdrawal from the scheme

64. A trader is not entitled to continue operating the scheme if:

- (a) he has been convicted of a VAT offence, or compounded proceedings for such an offence, while operating the scheme;
- (b) he has been assessed to a penalty for dishonest conduct while operating the scheme;
- (c) he has failed to leave the scheme because the value of his taxable supplies for a twelve month period exceeds £750,000 (see reg 60(1)); or
- (d) the Commissioners consider this to be necessary for the protection of the revenue.

A trader must "settle up" (to use the term in reg 64) when he ceases to be entitled to continue operating the scheme. He does so by accounting for output tax, and deducting input tax, on "scheme supplies" unpaid at the date of withdrawal. He accounts for this tax on the return for the prescribed accounting period in which he ceased to be entitled to operate the scheme.

Bad debt relief

64A. A trader is deemed to have accounted for and paid VAT on a supply for the purposes of bad debt relief (see VATA 1994 s 36(1)(*a*)) if he "settles up" when withdrawing from the scheme (see reg 61) or ceasing to be entitled to continue using the scheme (see reg 64). He is deemed to have accounted for and paid the VAT in the prescribed accounting period in which he ceased to operate the scheme.

Accounting

65. Tax is accounted for, with the exception of circumstances set out in regs 61–63 above, by reference to the prescribed accounting period in which payments are received or made. Receipted and dated invoices to substantiate output and input tax must be kept for a period of six years unless the Commissioners authorise a lesser period.

PART IX SUPPLIES BY RETAILERS

Interpretation of Part IX

66. Various words and phrases are defined.

Retail schemes

67. The Commissioners may, either by agreement with a retailer or by any method described in a notice, determine the method of valuing positive rated supplies made in any prescribed accounting period. The Commissioners may vary the terms by issuing a new notice, amending an existing notice or amending a method by agreement with a retailer.

The standard schemes specified in a notice are:

(1) The point of sale scheme: see Notice No 727/3. This can be used if tax exclusive turnover from retail supplies is less than £100 million. For the catering adaptation, see Notice No 727 (March 2002) section 8. For retail florists, see Notice No 727 (March 2002) section 10.

(2) The apportionment schemes: see Notice No 727/4. There are two schemes. Scheme 1 can be used if tax exclusive turnover from retail supplies is less than £1 million. Scheme 2 can be used if this turnover is less than £100 million. For the adjustment made by retail chemists, see Notice No 727 (March 2002) section 9. For retail florists, see Notice No 727 (March 2002) section 10.

(3) The direct calculation schemes: see Notice No 727/5. There are two schemes. Scheme 1 can be used if tax exclusive turnover from retail supplies is less than £1 million. Scheme 2 can be used if this turnover is less than £100 million. For the adjustment made by retail chemists, see Notice No 727 (March 2002) section 9. For retail florists, see Notice No 727 (March 2002) section 10.

For schemes agreed with a retailer (which are referred to as "bespoke schemes"), see Notice No 727/2; *GUS Merchandise Corpn Ltd v C & E Comrs (No 2)* [1995] STC 279, CA; *Tesco plc v C & E Comrs* [1994] VATTR 425. For the variation of such a scheme, see *R & C Comrs v Boots Co plc* [2010] STC 637, CA.

For the legal effect of Notice Nos 727, 727/3, 727/4 and 727/5, see Notice No 747 (reproduced in Appendix 3); *GUS Merchandise Corpn Ltd v C & E Comrs* [1980] STC 480. For VAT groups, see *C & E Comrs v Kingfisher plc* [1994] STC 63.

For the calculation of gross daily takings, see *Freemans plc v C & E Comrs* (case C-86/99) [2001] STC 960, ECJ; *GUS Merchandise Corpn Ltd v C & E Comrs (No 2)* [1995] STC 279, CA; *C & E Comrs v Primback Ltd* (case C-34/99) [2001] STC 803, ECJ; *Oxford, Swindon and Gloucester Co-operative Society Ltd v C & E Comrs* [1995] STC 583; *Courage Ltd* (No 8808). For the VAT treatment of the single use carrier bags charge (which comes into operation in Wales from 1 October 2011), see Revenue and Customs Brief 23/11, 21 June 2011. For the charge on carrier bags, see Single Use Carrier Bags Charge (Wales) Regulations 2010, SI 2010/2880. For changes in the rate of VAT generally, or in relation to particular goods or services, see Notice No 727 (March 2002) section 7; *R v C & E Comrs ex parte Littlewoods Home Shopping Group Ltd* [1998] STC 445, CA. For traders ceasing to be eligible to use a scheme, see *Piercy (a firm)* (No 12579).

68. The Commissioners may refuse to allow use of a method if:

(a) it does not produce a fair and reasonable result;

(b) it is necessary in order to protect the revenue; or

(c) the retailer could account for VAT by reference to VAT invoices or by using the cash accounting scheme.

69. A retailer may not use more than one method at a time unless a notice so permits or the Commissioners so allow. For mixtures of schemes, see Notice No 727 (March 2002) para 4.1.

69A. A retailer cannot use a retail scheme if he is authorised to account for and pay VAT in accordance with the flat-rate scheme for small businesses (see regs 55A–55V). For the alternative scheme available, see reg 55G (retailer's turnover method).

Notification of use of a scheme

70. [Revoked.]

Changing schemes

71. A method must be used for a minimum of one year unless: (1) the Commissioners allow otherwise; or (2) the trader ceases to be entitled to use a method (see reg 69A) because he has been authorised to account for VAT under the flat-rate scheme for small businesses.

A change of method is made on an anniversary of the first day of the prescribed accounting period in which he first used the method. For changes of scheme, see Notice No 727 (March 2002) section 4. For retrospective changes, see *Withers & Gibbs (a firm) v C & E Comrs* [1983] VATTR 323; *Patel* (No 936); *Vulgar v C & E Comrs* [1976] VATTR 197; *Bryan Markwell & Co Ltd* (No 4358); *L & P Flyer (a firm)* (No 14265); *L & J Lewis v C & E Comrs* [1996] V & DR 541; and contrast *Wadlewski (a firm)* (No 13340).

Ceasing to use scheme

72. A retailer must notify the Commissioners before he ceases to account for VAT by using a method. He may be required to pay VAT on a fair reasonable proportion of any sums due to him at the end of the last period in which a method is used. For the adjustments made when ceasing to use a scheme, see Notice No 727 (March 2002) section 6.

Supplies under Schedule 8 Group 1

73. [Revoked.]

Supplies under Schedule 8 Group 12

74. [Revoked.]

Change in VAT

75. A retailer must take the steps set out in a notice (see Notice No 727 (March 2002) section 7), or in an agreement with the Commissioners, if the rate of VAT changes or if supplies are moved from one tax category to another (ie taxable to exempt, exempt to taxable, or one rate to another).

PART X TRADING STAMPS

76–80. [Revoked.]

PART XI TIME OF SUPPLY AND TIME OF ACQUISITION

Goods for private use and free supplies of services

81. Where goods are put to non-business use but remain part of the assets of the business, the supply is deemed to be made on the last day of the accounting period in which they are used or continue to be used. The same time of supply applies to services specified in a Treasury Order made under VATA 1994 s 5 (4).

Services from outside the United Kingdom

82. This regulation applies to services subject to the reverse charge (see VATA 1994 s 8(1)). It also applies to intra-group services brought within the scope of VAT rather than being disregarded: see VATA 1994 s 43(2C)(c). For the modification of this regulation in relation to telecommunication services, see VAT (Reverse Charge) (Anti-avoidance) Order 1997, SI 1997/1523 art 4.

This regulation makes separate provision for:

- services supplied for a period where the consideration is either: (1) wholly or partly determined periodically or from time to time; or (2) wholly or partly payable periodically or from time to time; and
- other services.

For the meaning of "receipt of a payment", see reg 94A.

Services supplied for a period

This rule applies to services supplied for a period where the consideration is either: (1) wholly or partly determined periodically or from time to time; or (2) wholly or partly payable periodically or from time to time. In principle, the services are treated as separately and successively supplied at the end of the periods in respect of which, and to the extent that, payments are made or invoices are issued. This general rule is subject to the following exceptions.

The first exception (see reg 82(5)(b), (c)) applies to a payment made in any of the following circumstances: (1) it is made before the end of the period to which it relates; (2) it is made in respect of a period which is not identified; (3) it is made in respect of services performed before 1 January 2010; (4) it is made after the end of the period to which it relates; (5) it is made after the end of the period for which it is invoiced; or (6) it is made in respect of services from which the recipient received the benefit on or before the date of payment. The services are treated as being made at the time when the payment is made.

The second exception (see reg 82(6)) applies to a supply of services where all of the following conditions are met: (1) the supply commences before a calendar year and continues after it; (2) no invoice is issued in respect of that part of the services supplied in the calendar year; and (3) no payment is made in respect of the supply. To the extent that the recipient has received the benefit of the services supplied during the calendar year, the services are treated as being supplied on 31 December of that year.

The third exception (see reg 82(7)) applies to services supplied for a period which: (1) commenced on the day following the last day of the recipient's last complete prescribed accounting period in 2009; and (2) ended on 31 December 2009. Services supplied for a non-monetary consideration are treated as being supplied on 31 December 2009.

Other services

In principle, the services are treated as being made when they are performed. This general rule is subject to the following exceptions.

The first exception (see reg 82(5)(a), (c)) applies to a payment made in any of the following circumstances: (1) it is made before the services have been performed; (2) it is made in respect of services performed before 1 January 2010; (3) it is made after the period to which it relates; (4) it is made after the period in respect of which it has been invoiced; or (5) the recipient benefited from the services on or before the date of payment. The services are treated as being made at the time of payment. The services are treated as being made at the time of payment.

The second exception (see reg 82(7)) applies to services supplied for a period which: (1) commenced on the day following the last day of the recipient's last complete prescribed accounting period in 2009; and (2) ended on 31 December 2009. Services supplied for a non-monetary consideration are treated as being supplied on 31 December 2009.

Goods supplied by persons outside the United Kingdom

82A. Goods subject to a reverse charge are treated as being supplied on the day they are paid for (see reg 94A) (if the consideration is in money) or on the last day of the accounting period in which the goods are removed or made available (in other cases). For the reverse charge, see VATA 1994 s 9A (gas and electricity).

Time of acquisition

83. The invoice prescribed by VATA 1994 s 12 (1) (*b*) is an invoice issued by the supplier, or a self-billed invoice prepared by the customer, under the legislation of another EU member state equivalent to regs 13, 13A and 14.

Supplies of land—special cases

84. A landowner is deemed to make a supply of goods or services each time he receives a payment (see reg 94A) in respect of land compulsorily purchased if the total amount payable has not been determined when the freehold or leasehold interest is transferred.

Goods are treated as separately and successively supplied if a person (the grantor) grants or assigns a freehold interest for a consideration which includes (or comprises) an undetermined future payment. The grantor is deemed to make a supply for the present consideration (if any) at a time determined under VATA 1994 s 6(2), (4)–(6) or (10) and a later supply for the future consideration on the earlier of the date when he receives a payment (see reg 94A) or issues a VAT invoice. A self-billed invoice prepared by the purchaser or assignee is not regarded as being issued by the grantor for this purpose (see reg 13(3F)(*a*)). It does not, therefore, create a tax point.

However, a freehold interest in a new or partly completed building or civil engineering work is not treated as being separately and successively supplied if:

- the grant or assignment is excluded from exemption by VATA 1994 Sch 9 Group 1 Item 1(*a*);
- it is intended or expected that any of the persons specified in reg 84(4) will occupy the land at any time during the ten years following completion of the building or civil engineering work; and
- that occupation will be wholly, or substantially wholly, for a purpose that is not an eligible purpose.

For the time when a building or civil engineering work is completed, see VATA 1994 Sch 9 Group 1 Note 2. For the occupation of land wholly, or substantially wholly, for eligible purposes, see VATA 1994 Sch 10 paras 15, 16.

Leases treated as supplies of goods

85. Goods are treated as separately and successively supplied if: (1) the grant of a lease or tenancy is treated as a supply of goods; and (2) all or part of the consideration is payable periodically or from time to time. Each supply of goods is deemed to be supplied on the earlier of:

- the date when part of the consideration is received by the supplier (see reg 94A); and
- the date when the supplier issues a VAT invoice in respect of the grant. A self-billed invoice prepared by the tenant is not regarded as being issued by the supplier for this purpose (see reg 13(3F)(*b*)). It does not, therefore, create a tax point.

The supplier can issue a VAT invoice for a period of one year or less showing the following additional information: (1) the due date for each payment in the period; (2) the VAT-exclusive amount due on each date; (3) the rate of tax in force at the date of issue; and (4) the VAT due at that rate on each amount due. If he does so, each supply of goods is deemed to be supplied on the earlier of: (1) the due date for payment; and (2) the date when payment is received (see reg 94A). A self-billed invoice prepared by the tenant is not regarded as being issued by the supplier for this purpose (see reg 13(3F)(*c*)). It does not, therefore, create a tax point.

The invoice ceases to be treated as a VAT invoice in relation to any payment due and received after a change in the rate of VAT which affects the supply invoiced.

The time of supply specified above is overridden in certain circumstances. For the overriding rule, and the circumstances in which it applies, see reg 94.

Supplies of water, gas or any form of power, heat, refrigeration or other cooling, or ventilation

86. The following supplies are treated as taking place on the earlier of the date when a payment is received by the supplier (see reg 94A) or the date when he issues a tax invoice: (1) water (subject to specified exceptions); (2) coal gas, water gas, producer gases and similar gases; (3) petroleum gases and other gaseous hydrocarbons in a gaseous state; and (4) any form of power, heat, refrigeration or other cooling, or ventilation. A self-billed invoice prepared by the customer is not regarded as being issued by the supplier for this purpose (see reg 13(3F)(*d*)). It does not, therefore, create a tax point.

Water within (1) above, gas within (2) or (3) above and electricity within (4) above are treated as separately and successively supplied if all or part of the consideration is payable periodically or from time to time. Each supply of goods is deemed to be supplied on the earlier of: (1) the date when part of the consideration is received by the supplier (see reg 94A); and (2) the date when the supplier issues an invoice in respect of the supply. A self-billed invoice prepared by the customer is not regarded as being issued by the supplier for this purpose (see reg 13(3F)(*e*)). It does not, therefore, create a tax point.

The supplier can issue a VAT invoice for a period of one year or less showing the following additional information: (1) the due date for each payment under the agreement; (2) the VAT-exclusive amount due on each date; (3) the rate of VAT in force at the date of issue; and (4) the VAT due at that rate on each amount due. If he does so, each supply of goods is deemed to be supplied on the earlier of: (1) the due date for payment; and (2) the date when payment is received (see reg 94A). A self-billed invoice prepared by the customer is not regarded as being issued by the supplier for this purpose (see reg 13(3F)(*f*)). It does not, therefore, create a tax point.

The invoice ceases to be treated as a VAT invoice in relation to any payment due and received after a change in the rate of VAT which affects the supplies invoiced.

The time of supply specified above is overridden in certain circumstances. For the overriding rule, and the circumstances in which it applies, see reg 94.

The time of supply specified above does not apply to goods removed to another EU member state and charged to VAT by way of an acquisition made in that member state. In these circumstances, the time of supply is the date on which a VAT invoice is issued.

Acquisitions of water, gas or any form of power, heat, refrigeration or other cooling, or ventilation

87. All or part of the consideration for an acquisition of the following goods may be payable periodically or from time to time:

- water (subject to the exceptions specified in reg 86(1)(*a*));
- coal gas, water gas, producer gases and similar gases;
- petroleum gases and other gaseous hydrocarbons in a gaseous state; and
- any form of power, heat, refrigeration or ventilation.

Where this is so, the goods are deemed to be separately and successively acquired whenever an invoice is issued by the supplier, or a self-billed invoice is prepared by the customer, under the legislation of another EU member state equivalent to regs 13, 13A and 14.

Supplier's goods in possession of buyer

88. Goods may be supplied under an agreement whereby the property in the goods is retained by the vendor until the buyer appropriates them under an agreement which provides that all or part of the consideration is determined at that time. Where this is so, the time of supply is the earliest of:

- the date when the goods are appropriated by the buyer;
- the date when a VAT invoice is issued by the supplier. A self-billed invoice prepared by the customer is not regarded as being issued by the supplier for this purpose (see reg 13(3F)(*g*)). It does not, therefore, create a tax point; and
- the date when a payment is received by the supplier (see reg 94A).

The time of supply is determined by reference to the date when a VAT invoice is issued by the supplier, or a self-billed invoice is issued by the customer, if this is done within 14 days of appropriation.

The foregoing rules do not apply to the following supplies:

- goods supplied on sale or return or similar terms. For the time of supply, see VATA 1994 s 6(2)(*a*), (4), (5); and

- goods removed from another EU member state and charged to VAT by way of an acquisition made in that member state. For the time of supply, see VATA 1994 s 6(7), (8).

Retention payments

89. A supply is deemed to be separately and successively supplied if the contract allows the customer to retain part of the consideration pending full and satisfactory performance by the supplier. The supplier is deemed to make a supply for a consideration of the present sum payable at a time determined in accordance with VATA 1994 s 6(2)–(6), (10) or (13). He is deemed to make a later supply in respect of the sum retained at the earlier of:

- the date when a payment is received (see reg 94A); or
- the date when he issues a VAT invoice. A self-billed invoice prepared by the customer is not regarded as being issued by the supplier for this purpose (see reg 13(3F)(*h*)). It does not, therefore, create a tax point.

This provision does not apply to services, or services together with goods, supplied in the course of the construction, alteration, demolition, repair or maintenance of a building or civil engineering work. For the time of supply, see reg 93.

This provision does not apply to goods removed to another EU member state and charged to VAT by way of an acquisition made in that member state. For the time of supply, see VATA 1994 s 6 (7), (8), and reg 86 (5).

Continuous supplies of services

90. Services are treated as separately and successively supplied if all or part of the consideration is determined or payable periodically or from time to time. The time of supply is the earlier of the day when the supplier receives a payment (see reg 94A) and the day when he issues a VAT invoice. A self-billed invoice prepared by the customer is not regarded as being issued by the supplier for this purpose (see reg 13(3F)(*i*)). It does not, therefore, create a tax point.

This provision does not apply to services, or services together with goods, supplied in the course of the construction, alteration, demolition, repair or maintenance of a building or civil engineering work. For the time of supply, see reg 93. For overpayment of periodic payments, see *C & E Comrs v British Telecommunications plc* [1996] STC 818, CA. For payment by way of entry in an inter-company current account, see *Pentex Oil Ltd* (No 7989). For bad debts recovered in respect of pre-registration supplies, see *B J Rice & Associates v C & E Comrs* [1996] STC 463, CA.

If the agreement provides for successive payments, the supplier can issue a VAT invoice to cover a period not exceeding one year. A self-billed invoice prepared by the customer is not regarded as being issued by the supplier for this purpose (see reg 13(3F)(*j*)).

The invoice must set out the following additional particulars:

(a) the date on which each payment is to become due in the period;
(b) the amount payable (excluding VAT) on each date; and
(c) the rate of VAT in force at the time of the issue of the VAT invoice and the amount of VAT chargeable in accordance with that rate on each payment.

Each of the supplies is treated as taking place on the earlier of when a payment becomes due or is received (see reg 94A).

Where there is a change in the rate of VAT during the period covered by such a VAT invoice it ceases to be treated as a VAT invoice for any payment due and received after the change.

The foregoing provisions do not apply to relevant services if the period to which a payment relates ends before 1 July 1997 or if the services are deemed to be supplied on 1 July 1997 (see reg 90A).

"Relevant services" are telecommunication services (as defined in VATA 1994 Sch 5 para 7A) effectively used and enjoyed in the UK which are treated as supplied in the UK (see VAT (Place of Supply of Services) Order, SI 1992/3121, art 18).

The time of supply specified above is overridden in certain circumstances. For the overriding rule, and the circumstances in which it applies, see reg 94.

90A. Relevant services (as defined in reg 90(5)) are treated as supplied on 1 July 1997 if:
- (a) they are supplied for a period and all or part of the consideration is determined or payable periodically or from time to time;
- (b) the period covered by the payment in (*c*) ends after 30 June 1997; and
- (c) a payment was made in respect of the services before 1 July 1997.

90B. Where relevant services (as defined in reg 90 (5)) are treated as supplied after 30 June 1997 (see regs 90, 90A), the supply is treated as taking place only to the extent covered by the lower of:
- (a) the payment made; and
- (b) the part of the payment which is properly attributable to the part of the period which falls after 30 June 1997.

Royalties and similar payments

91. The whole consideration for a supply of services may not be ascertainable at the time the services were performed so that a series of payments may be made without there being a continuous supply of services. Where this is so, a supply is treated as taking place on the earlier of:
- the time a payment is received by the supplier (see reg 94A); and
- the time when he issues a VAT invoice. A self-billed invoice prepared by the customer is not regarded as being issued by the supplier for this purpose (see reg 13(3F)(*k*)). It does not, therefore, create a tax point.

Supplies of services by barristers and advocates

92. Services supplied by barristers (or advocates) acting as such are treated as taking place on the earliest of: (1) the time when the fee is received by the barrister (see reg 94A); (2) the time when the barrister issues a tax invoice; or (3) the day when the barrister ceases to practice as such. For deferment of payment when ceasing to practice, see Leaflet No 700/44.

Supplies in the construction industry

93. Services (or services together with goods) may be supplied in the course of the construction, alteration, demolition, repair or maintenance of a building or civil engineering work under a contract which provides for payment to be made periodically or from time to time. Where this is so, the services (or goods and services) are treated as separately and successively supplied at the earliest of the following times:
- (a) the time when the supplier receives a payment (see reg 94A);
- (b) the time when the supplier issues a VAT invoice. A self-billed invoice prepared by the customer is not regarded as being issued by the supplier for this purpose (see reg 13(3F)(*m*)). It does not, therefore, create a tax point; and
- (c) (to the extent that (*a*) or (*b*) do not apply):
  - (i) eighteen months after the date when the services were performed (supplies performed between 9 December 1997 and 8 June 1999), or
  - (ii) the day when the services were performed (services performed after 8 June 1999).

The tax point in (*c*) applies if, but only if, either of the following conditions are met:
- (a) it is intended or expected that "relevant land" (see below) will become or remain "exempt land" (see below). The relevant intention or expectation is that of the supplier or the person responsible for financing the supplier's costs (see below),
- (b) the supplier receives bought-in goods or services to which the tax point in (*c*) applies and uses them in making his supply. The tax point in (*b*) is disregarded for this purpose if the VAT invoice is unpaid.

Construction etc services relate to a building or civil engineering work. The site of the building or civil engineering work is referred to as "relevant land".

A person is responsible for financing the "supplier's costs" (see below) if he provides finance—or enters into any agreement, arrangement or understanding to provide finance—for those costs with the intention or expectation that the relevant land will become, or continue to be, "exempt land" (see below). A person "provides finance" if he loans funds, guarantees a loan, provides consideration for a share issue or transfers assets or value. The funds finance the supplier's costs whether they are used to pay for them or to discharge the liabilities of a person who provided funds to pay for them.

The "supplier's costs" comprise the costs of bought-in goods and services, together with internal costs (eg staff costs), in respect of the supply he makes.

Relevant land is "exempt land" if it is occupied (see below) for a purpose which is not wholly or mainly an "eligible purpose" (see below) by one of the following persons:

(a) the supplier,
(b) a person responsible for financing the supplier's costs, or
(c) a person connected (see below) with either.

A person cannot occupy land for an eligible purpose unless he is a taxable person. A non-taxable-person is treated as a taxable person for this purpose if his supplies are treated as being made by another person who is a taxable person, eg where the person is a member of a VAT group (see VATA 1994 s 43). In principle, a person occupies land for an eligible purpose to the extent that he does so for the purpose of making supplies in the course or furtherance of business which give rise to an entitlement to input tax credit. For the supplies concerned, see VATA 1994 s 26 (2). However, a body occupies land for an eligible purpose to the extent that the land is used for non-business purposes if the body is eligible for refunds under VATA 1994 s 33, and any land occupied by a government department (as defined in VATA 1994 s 41 (6)–(8)) is occupied for an eligible purpose.

A person is deemed to occupy land if he occupies it alone or jointly or in common with one or more other persons.

A person is connected with another person if he meets the criteria in TA 1988 s 839. However, a company (see TA 1988 s 839) is not connected with another company merely because both are under the control (see TA 1988 s 839) of the Crown, a Minister of the Crown, a government department or a Northern Ireland department.

This provision is confined to *actual* supplies made under a contract. It does not apply to services *deemed* to be supplied by agents under VATA 1994 s 47: *Metropolitan Borough of Wirral v C & E Comrs* [1995] STC 597.

General

94. Regulations 81–93 provide that a supply is treated as taking place each time that a payment is received (see reg 94A) or an invoice issued. Subject to the special provisions relating to certain telecommunication services (see reg 90B), the supply is treated as taking place only to the extent covered by the payment or invoice.

94A. A payment is deemed to be received for the purposes of regs 81–95 if it is received by a person to whom a right to receive the payment has been assigned.

94B. In principle, this regulation overrides the time of supply rules in regs 85, 86(1)–(4) and 90 in relation to supplies made in the following circumstances:

(a) the supplier, customer and (in relation to any leasing, letting, hiring or rental of assets) any superior lessor are connected with each other. A person is connected with another person if he meets the criteria in TA 1988 s 839. However, a company (see TA 1988 s 839) is not connected with another company merely because both are under the control (see TA 1988 s 839) of the Crown, a Minister of the Crown, a government department or a Northern Ireland department;
(b) one of those persons is an undertaking (as defined in Companies Act 2006 s 1161) in relation to which the other is a group undertaking (as defined in Companies Act 2006 s 1161). This condition is disregarded if both undertakings are members of the same VAT group (see VATA 1994 ss 43A–43C); and

(c) the supply is charged to VAT at either the standard rate or the reduced rate.

However, the time of supply rules are not overridden if:

- the supply is exempt from tax under VATA 1994 Sch 9 Group 1. Although this is specifically stated in relation to the time of supply rules in regs 85 and 90, it applies automatically because condition (*c*) is not met;
- an option for taxation of land (see VATA 1994 Sch 10 Part 1) has effect in relation to a supply that would otherwise be exempt from tax under VATA 1994 Sch 9 Group 1;
- the supplier can show that the customer is entitled to input tax credit for all of the VAT charged on the supply. For input tax credit, see VATA 1994 ss 25, 26.

The goods or services are treated as being separately and successively supplied on a specified date and thereafter at the end of each subsequent period of twelve months. The specified dates are determined as follows:

Circumstances	*Specified date*
The customer first received the benefit of the relevant goods or services before 2 October 2004	Twelve months after 1 October 2003
The customer first received the benefit of the relevant goods or services after 1 October 2004	Twelve months after the benefit was first received
The Commissioners are satisfied that each category of supply has been adequately identified	An earlier date for each category nominated by the supplier and notified to the Commissioners in writing

The supplier may issue a VAT invoice or receive a payment in respect of the supply within six months of the time of supply determined in accordance with these rules. If so, the supply is treated as taking place at the time when the invoice is issued or the payment is received, unless the supplier elects otherwise and notifies the Commissioners accordingly. The supply is treated as taking place to the extent that it has not already been treated as taking place under regs 85, 86(1)–(4), 90 or under any other provision. A period other than six months may be substituted if the supplier so requests and the Commissioners so allow. A self-billed invoice prepared by the customer is not regarded as being issued by the supplier for the foregoing purpose (see reg 13(3F)(*n*)). It does not, therefore, create a tax point.

The anniversary of a specified date may be changed with the Commissioners' approval in relation to some or all of the categories of supply made by the supplier. The end of the supplier's current period is established by reference to the new date.

Supplies spanning change of rate etc

95. The election available under VATA 1994 s 88 (2) when the rate of VAT changes is available also to supplies mentioned in regs 81, 82, 84, 85, 86 (1)–(4), 88–93 and 94B.

PART XII VALUATION OF ACQUISITIONS

Interpretation of Part XII

96. Various words and phrases are defined.

Valuation of acquisitions

97. Goods removed to the UK from another EU member state may be charged with: (1) excise duty; or (2) EU customs duty or agricultural levy having effect for transitional purposes in connection with the accession of a new EU member state. Where this is so, the value of the acquisition for VAT purposes is the aggregate of: (1) the value determined under VATA 1994 s 20 and Sch 7; plus (in so far as not already included) (2) the duty or levy payable. This does not apply to an acquisition of warehoused goods which is treated as taking place before the duty point. For the duty point, see VATA 1994 s 18 (6).

PART XIII PLACE OF SUPPLY

Distance sales from the United Kingdom

98. The place of supply of goods may be affected by an option made under the legislation of another EU member state giving effect to Directive 2006/112/EC art 34(4): see VATA 1994 s 7 (5) and Sch 2 para 1 (2). The making of an option must be notified to the Commissioners in writing at least 30 days before the first supply affected by the option is made. The notification must state the EU member state to which the goods have been or will be removed. Documentary evidence showing that the option has been notified to the authorities of that member state must be furnished to the Commissioners within 30 days of making the first supply affected by it. A notification may be withdrawn by written notice stating the date of withdrawal. This must be no earlier than 1 January which is, or follows, the second anniversary of the first supply affected by the option and 30 days after receipt of the notice of withdrawal. It must be no later than 30 days before the first supply affected by the withdrawal.

PART XIV INPUT TAX AND PARTIAL EXEMPTION

Interpretation of Part XIV and longer periods

99. Various words and phrases used in this Part of the Regulations are defined.

"Exempt input tax" is input tax incurred by a taxable person on goods or services used (or to be used) by him (or any successor (as defined in reg 107D) of his) in making: (1) exempt supplies; or (2) supplies outside the UK which would be exempt supplies if made in the UK. However, input tax is not exempt input tax if it is allowable under regs 101 (standard method), 102 (special method), 103 (supplies specified in an order made under VATA 1994 s 26(2)(*c*)), 103A (gold and services relating to gold) or 103B (financial services).

A "prescribed accounting period" is the period defined in reg 25. However, if a taxable person's first prescribed accounting period is six months or longer, the term refers to a "special accounting period" defined below.

A "special accounting period" is one of a succession of periods into which a prescribed accounting period is sub-divided. The length of the second and subsequent special accounting periods is determined by the length of the next prescribed accounting period which lasts three months or less. The first special accounting period runs from the effective date of registration to the day preceding the beginning of the second special accounting period. Thus, if the trader's first prescribed accounting period is 15.9.10–30.4.11 and the next period is for 1.5.10–31.7.11, the special accounting periods are 15.9.10–31.10.10, 1.11.10–31.1.11 and 1.2.11–30.4.11.

A "tax year" is a period of 12 calendar months commencing on 1 April, 1 May or 1 June. The Commissioners may approve or direct a different period or commencing date.

A "registration period" is a period commencing on a trader's effective date of registration and ending on the day before the commencement of his first tax year. For the effective date of registration, see VATA 1994 Schs 1, 2, 3 and 3A. For the commencement of the first tax year where the trader's prescribed accounting periods are changed, see *Dunn, Bryant, Lee & Franklin* (No 14788).

A "longer period" is applied to a trader if he incurs exempt input tax during his registration period or any tax year. In the former case, a longer period commences on the first day on which he incurs exempt input tax. In the latter case, a longer period normally commences on the first day of his tax year. However, it commences on the first day of the first prescribed accounting period in which he incurs exempt input tax if he did not incur exempt input tax during his immediately preceding tax year or registration period. Moreover, no longer period applies in these circumstances if he only incurs exempt input tax in the last prescribed accounting period of his tax year. A longer period ends on the last day of his registration period or tax year, or the day on which he ceases to be taxable. The Commissioners may approve a longer period which does not correspond with a tax year.

"Non-business VAT" is defined by reference to VATA 1994 s 24(5)(b).

100. Input tax is deductible under regs 101–111 only if the goods or services concerned are used or to be used in making supplies in the course or furtherance of business.

Attribution of input tax to taxable supplies

101. As regards taxable persons making supplies of investment gold, the input tax for a prescribed accounting period treated as allowable is determined in accordance with reg 103A. In other cases, input tax for a prescribed accounting period is provisionally attributed to taxable supplies in accordance with one or other of the following methods:

(1) the standard method (see below)

(2) (if the Commissioners so allow or direct) a special method, as to which see reg 102;

(3) (to the extent that the supplies specified in reg 103(a), (b)) are not attributed under the standard method or a special method) the method set out in reg 103; or

(4) (to the extent that the services specified in reg 103B(4), and related goods, are not attributed under the standard method) the method set out in reg 103B).

These attribution methods are separate: cf *C & E Comrs v Liverpool Institute for Performing Rights* [2001] UKHL/28, [2001] STC 891, HL.

The VAT incurred on a purchase, acquisition or importation is input tax only if the goods or services are used (or to be used) for business purposes: see VATA 1994 s 24(1). It follows that the attribution referred to above is concerned with: (1) VAT incurred on goods and services used wholly for business purposes; and (2) the business proportion of VAT incurred on goods and services used for mixed business and non-business purposes. The standard method (see below) makes explicit provision for the exclusion of VAT incurred wholly for non-business purposes (see rule 3 of the method). It does not specifically state that unattributed input tax (see rule 4 of the method) is confined to the business proportion of VAT incurred on goods and services used for both business and non-business purposes. However, it seems inevitable that this is so: cf *Securenta Göttinger Immobilienanlagen und Vermögensmanagement AG v Finanzamt Göttingen* (case C-437/06) [2008] ECR I–1597, [2008] STC 3473, ECJ. This position is specifically stated in Notice No 706 (December 2006) para 33.4. No specific apportionment method is prescribed. However, a trader's calculations "must be fair and reasonable" and he "must be able to justify them". An example of an apportionment method is set out in para 33.5 of the Notice. For the position under EU law, see the commentary to Directive 2006/112/EC art 173 in Part 1B.

The standard method

This method is used to make a provisionally attribute input tax to taxable supplies. For this purpose, "taxable supplies" includes supplies of a description within reg 103(a), (b). The method requires input tax to be analysed under the following heads:

(1) Input tax on goods and services exclusively used or to be used in making *taxable* supplies. This tax may be deducted.

(2) Input tax on goods and services exclusively used or to be used in making *exempt* supplies. This tax may *not* be deducted.

(3) Input tax on goods and services exclusively used or to be used in carrying on any activity other than the making of taxable supplies (eg a non-business activity). This tax may *not* be deducted. For the priority of apportionment under VATA 1994 s 24(5), see *BUPA Purchasing Ltd v C & E Comrs* [2003] STC 1203 (part of VAT incurred not treated as input tax so that there was no input tax to be excluded from deduction under this head).

(4) Input tax on goods and services used or to be used in making *both* taxable and exempt supplies. This is referred to as "residual input tax". It includes input tax on: (*a*) goods and services *linked* to both taxable and exempt supplies as in, for example, *Mayflower Theatre Trust Ltd v R & C Comrs* [2007] STC 1005, CA; (*b*) goods and services linked to transactions which do not amount to a supply of goods or services, where the costs have a direct and immediate link with the whole economic activity, as in, for example, *Abbey National plc v C & E Comrs* (case C-408/98) [2001] STC 297, ECJ (costs relating to part of business transferred as going concern)); and (*c*) goods and services which, although properly incurred in the course of the business, cannot be linked with any specific supply or transaction, eg audit and legal fees and the cost of the office carpet (see *C & E Comrs v Redrow Group plc* [1999] STC 161 at 169, HL).

Residual input tax in divided into two classes:

(a) Input tax attributable to: (i) supplies falling within VATA 1994 Sch 9 Group 5 Item 1 or 6, and (ii) supplies made from an establishment situated outside the UK. This input tax is attributed to taxable supplies on the basis of the extent to which the goods or services are used or to be used in making taxable supplies.

(b) The remainder. This is referred to as "relevant residual input tax". Relevant residual input tax is attributed to taxable supplies in accordance with one or other of three specified bases (referred to here as Basis 1, Basis 2 and Basis 3) and applied as follows:

(i) In principle, a taxable person is required to use Basis 1 if he does not have an immediately preceding longer period. However, he may instead use Basis 2.

(ii) In principle, a taxable person is required to use Basis 3 if he has an immediately preceding longer period. However, he may instead use Basis 1. If he does so, he must use this basis for all prescribed accounting periods falling within the same longer period.

For the circumstances in which the input tax in heads (2), (3) and (4)(b) is treated as being attributable to taxable supplies for the purposes of the provisional attribution, see regs 105A, 106 and 106ZA. In consequence, a taxable person is entitled to deduct all of his input tax for the relevant period.

For adjustment of the provisional attribution by reference to a longer period (as to which see reg 99(3)–(7)), see regs 107 and 107B; *C & E Comrs v University of Wales College Cardiff* [1995] STC 611 (provisional deduction stands if no adjustment at end of longer period).

For adjustment of the attribution in respect of a prescribed accounting period which does not form part of a longer period, see reg 107A.

For adjustments in respect of goods and services not put to their intended use, see regs 108 and 109.

For adjustments in respect of capital items, see regs 112–116.

Basis 1

Basis 1 apportions residual input tax by reference to the ratio of the value of taxable supplies made to the aggregate value of all supplies made. This ratio expressed as a percentage. If the percentage is not a whole number, it is rounded up to either the next whole number (if the residual input tax available for apportionment does not exceed £400,000 per month on average) or to two decimal places (in other cases).

The values of taxable and exempt supplies used to calculate residual input tax exclude:

(a) sums due on capital goods supplied. The characteristics of "capital goods" are their value and purpose relative to other goods used in the management and day-to-day running of the business and their accounting treatment: *C & E Comrs v JDL Ltd* [2002] STC 1 (motor dealer's demonstrator cars held to be capital goods). Goods are not capital goods if the trader sells them in the nature of a normal business activity: *Nordania Finas A/S and another v Skatteministeriet* (case C-98/07) [2008] ECR I–1281, [2008] STC 3314, ECJ (sale of vehicles by lessor at end of hire period). The Commissioners consider that the judgment in the *JDL Ltd* case has been over-turned by the *Nordania Finas* case: see Revenue and Customs Brief 43/10, 12 October 2010.

(b) sums due on financial transactions (whether or not exempt under VATA 1994 Sch 9 Group 5) or real estate transactions (as defined in reg 101(6)) which are incidental to one or more of the trader's business activities. For "incidental", see *Empresa de Desenvolvimento Mineiro SGPS SA (EDM) v Fazenda Pública (Ministério Público, intervener)* (case C-77/01) [2004] ECR I–4295, [2005] STC 65, ECJ; *NCC Construction Danmark A/S v Skatteministeriet* (case C-174/08) [2009] ECR I–10567, [2010] STC 532, ECJ. For interest, contrast *Régie Dauphinoise-Cabinet A Forest SARL v Ministre du Budget* (case C-304/94) [1996] STC 1176, ECJ (interest on clients' moneys) and *Floridienne SA v Belgian State* (case C-142/99) [2000] STC 1044, ECJ (interest on loan to subsidiary by holding company);

(c) the non-margin element of supplies under VAT (Input Tax) Order 1992, SI 1992/3222 arts 5 (2) (goods and services used for business entertainment) and 7 (4), (5) (motor cars) unless the goods were purchased, imported or acquired for the purpose of selling them;

(d) the value of any self-supply made;

(e) supplies falling within VATA 1994 Sch 9 Group 5 Item 1 or 6; and

(f) supplies made from an establishment situated outside the UK.

For the exclusion of dividends received, see *Sofitam SA v Ministre Chargé du Budget* (case C-333/91) [1997] STC 226, ECJ; *Floridienne SA v Belgian State* (case C-142/99) [2000] STC 1044, ECJ. For the exclusion of work in progress, see *António Jorge L^{da} v Fazenda Públicia* (case C-536/03) [2005] ECR I–4463, [2008] STC 2533. For input tax incurred in respect of non-taxable activities, see Business Brief 18/92, 16 December 1992.

Basis 2

Basis 2 apportions residual input tax by reference to the extent to which the goods or services are used or to be used in making taxable supplies.

Basis 3

Basis 3 apportions residual input tax by reference to the percentage recovery rate for the immediately preceding longer period. The "percentage recovery rate" is A expressed as a percentage of B. For this purpose, "A" is the amount of relevant residual input tax attributed to taxable supplies in accordance with reg 107(1)(*a*)–(*d*). "B" is the total amount of the residual input tax which fell to be so attributed. If the percentage is not a whole number, it is rounded up to either the next whole number (if the residual input tax available for apportionment does not exceed £400,000 per month on average) or to two decimal places (in other cases).

Attribution of input tax

The main principles of general application derived from the decided cases were summarised in *Mayflower Theatre Trust Ltd v R & C Comrs* [2007] STC 1005 at [9], [11] in the following terms:

- Input tax is directly attributable to a given output if it has a "direct and immediate link" with that output.

- That test has been formulated in different ways over the years, eg whether the input tax is a "cost component" of the output or whether the input is "essential to a particular output. However, these formulations have the same substance as the "direct and immediate link" test.
- Application of the "direct and immediate link" test is a matter of objective analysis as to how particular inputs are used. It is not dependent upon establishing what is the ultimate aim pursued by the taxable person. It requires more than mere commercial links between transactions or a "but for" approach.
- The test is not one of identifying the transaction with which the input has the most direct and immediate link. It is whether there is a sufficiently direct and immediate link with a taxable economic activity.
- The test is one of mixed fact and law. It is therefore amenable to review in the higher courts, albeit that the test is fact sensitive.
- An exempt transaction breaks the chain of attribution (see *Abbey National plc v C & E Comrs* (case C-408/98) [2001] STC 297, ECJ, per the A-G at [35]).

For the formulation and application of these tests, see in particular *BLP Group plc v C & E Comrs* (case C-4/94) [1995] STC 424, ECJ; *Midland Bank plc v C & E Comrs* (case C-98/98) [2000] STC 501, ECJ; *Abbey National plc v C & E Comrs* (case C-408/98) [2001] STC 297, ECJ (part of business transferred as going concern); *Royal & Sun Alliance Insurance Group plc v C & E Comrs* [2003] STC 832, HL (leased property empty between occupation and sub-letting); *C & E Comrs v Southern Primary Housing Association Ltd* [2004] STC 209, CA (overruling *C & E Comrs v Wiggett Construction Ltd* [2001] STC 933) (separate contracts for the sale of land and construction of buildings); *Dial-a-Phone Ltd v C & E Comrs* [2004] STC 987, CA (advertising costs of call centre marketing mobile phones and insurance); *Mayflower Theatre Trust Ltd v R & C Comrs* [2007] STC 1005 (attribution of theatre production costs to exempt ticket sales and sales of taxable programmes).

Input tax is attributed in accordance with the legislation in force at the time of supply. Contrast *Perna v C & E Comrs* [1990] VATTR 106 (input tax deducted late) and *St George's Home Co Ltd* (No 10213) (VAT incurred prior to registration); *Martin's Properties (Chelsea) Ltd* (No 14092) (change of legislation affecting supplies to which input tax is attributable); *BUPA Hospitals Ltd* (No 17588) (intention to order and sell prepaid goods after onward supply of such goods became exempt from tax).

For examples of attribution in relation to buildings refurbished for letting, see *Neuvale Ltd v C & E Comrs* [1989] STC 395, CA; *Sheffield Co-operative Society Ltd v C & E Comrs* [1987] VATTR 216; *Wigan Metropolitan Development Co (Investment) Ltd* (No 4993); *Clovelly Estate Co Ltd v C & E Comrs* [1991] VATTR 357; *Imperial War Museum v C & E Comrs* [1992] VATTR 346. In relation to pitches for mobile homes, see *C & E Comrs v Harpcombe Ltd* [1996] STC 726.

For costs in relation to an issue of shares or other securities, see *Kretztechnik AG v Finanzamt Linz* (case C-465/03) [2005] STC 1118, ECJ (shares); Business Brief 21/05, 23 November 2005; Business Brief 22/05, 2 December 2005. For costs in relation to the acquisition of a subsidiary, see *C & E Comrs v UBAF Bank Ltd* [1996] STC 372, CA. For costs in relation to an exchange of shares, see *Southampton Leisure Holdings plc* (No 17716); Business Brief 23/02, 20 August 2002. For costs in relation to the disposal of a holding of shares, see *BLP Group Ltd v C & E Comrs* (case C-4/94) [1995] STC 424, ECJ; *C & E Comrs v C H Beazer (Holdings) Ltd* [1989] STC 549; *Skatteverket v AB SKF* (case C-29/08) [2009] ECR I–10413, [2010] STC 419, ECJ. For holding companies, see *Polysar Investments Netherlands BV v Inspecteur der Invoerrechten en Accÿnzen* (case C-60/90) [1993] STC 222, ECJ; *Cibo Participations SA v Directeur régional des impô ts du Nord-Pas-de-Calais* (case C-16/00) [2002] STC 460, ECJ; Press Notice 59/93, 10 September 1993.

For the transfer of a business as a going concern, see *Abbey National plc v C & E Comrs* (case C-408/98) [2001] STC 297, ECJ, Business Brief 7/96, 3 May 1996 (costs); *Finanzamt Offenbach am Main-Land v Faxworld Vorgündungsgesellschaft Peter Hünninghausen und Wolfgang Klein GbR* (case C-137/02) [2004] ECR I–5547, [2005] STC 1192, ECJ (partnership formed to acquire assets for transfer to company).

For the fundraising costs of charities, see *Church of England Children's Society v R & C Comrs* [2005] STC 1644; Business Brief 19/05, 10 October 2005.

For legal costs, see *C & E Comrs v Deutsche Ruck UK Reinsurance Co Ltd* [1995] STC 495 (reinsurance contracts); *Midland Bank plc v C & E Comrs* (case C-98/98) [2000] STC 501, ECJ (misrepresentation made during provision of taxable supply).

For hire purchase transactions, see Revenue and Customs Brief 31/07, 30 March 2007.

For the costs of staging shows for which the theatre's admissions are exempt, see *Mayflower Theatre Trust Ltd v HMRC* [2007] STC 880, CA; *Garsington Opera Ltd* (TC 45); Revenue and Customs Brief 65/09, 14 October 2009.

For successive exempt and taxable grants of land (or vice versa), see *C & E Comrs v Briararch Ltd* [1992] STC 732; *Key* (No 15354); Revenue & Customs Brief 44/08, 15 September 2008.

For input tax incurred before the date from which an election to waive exemption has effect, see VATA 1994 Sch 10 para 2; *Royal & Sun Alliance Insurance Group plc v C & E Comrs* [2003] STC 832, HL (costs incurred in void period prior to letting); *Beaverbank Properties Ltd* (No 18099) (costs of abortive property project); Business Brief 14/04, 4 May 2004.

For goods and services used to make both disregarded intra-group supplies (see VATA 1994 s 41(1)(*a*)) and taxable supplies, see *J P Morgan Trading and Finance v C & E Comrs* [1998] V & DR 161.

For higher education institutions, see *University of Southampton v R & C Comrs* [2006] 1389 (publicly funded research).

For input tax on self-supplies and the reverse charge, see VATA 1994 ss 8(3), 44(6) and reg 104.

Use of other methods

102. The Commissioners may approve or direct the use of a bespoke method (known as a "special method") for attributing input tax to taxable supplies. The approval or direction is given in writing. A special method must identify the supplies to which input tax is attributed using the classification in VATA 1994 s 26(2). It may incorporate the attribution prescribed in reg 103. It may be used by a fully taxable person (as defined in reg 102ZA(5)) to apportion input tax incurred on goods and services used for both business and non-business purposes (see reg 102ZA(1)). It must be used for that purpose by a partly exempt person (see reg 102ZA(2). For the requirement to apportion input tax, see VATA 1994 s 24(5). The value of any supplies listed in reg 101(3)(*a*)–(*d*), wherever made, is excluded from an apportionment calculation. This overrides any contrary term of the approval or direction.

A request for approval of a special method must include a written declaration, signed by an authorised person, that the proposed method fairly and reasonably reflects the extent to which goods or services are used or to be used in making taxable supplies (as defined in reg 102(17)). For declarations, see Revenue and Customs Brief 23/07, 14 March 2007. The Commissioners may serve a notice on the trader if: (1) they consider that an incorrect declaration has been made; and (2) they are satisfied that use of the method gives rise to an over-deduction of input tax. The notice must give reasons and state the consequences. The effect of a notice is that reg 102B(1) applies in relation to: (1) prescribed accounting periods and longer periods commencing on or after the effective date of the method (as defined in reg 102(16)); and (2) (if a longer period straddles the effective date) that part of a longer period commencing at the beginning of the first prescribed accounting period commencing after the effective date. This applies unless or until use of the method is terminated by an approval or direction under reg 102(3). The Commissioners may either assess the VAT calculated under reg 102B(1) in respect of past periods or allow the trader to account for it in such manner, and within such time limit, as they may require. A notice under reg 102A takes priority over a notice under this provision.

A taxable person must continue to use a special method until the Commissioners approve or direct otherwise. An approval or direction may result in the taxable person using the standard method or a different special method. For the right of appeal against a decision by the Commissioners in relation to the use of a special method, see s 83(*e*). For examples of directions to cease using a special method set aside on appeal, see *Merchant Navy Officers Pension Fund Trustees Ltd* (No 14262) (direction to revert to using the standard method); *Dean and Chapter of the Cathedral Church of Christ* (No 15068) (direction to adopt a different special method). For the test applied, see *BMW (GB) Ltd* (No 14823).

A direction to use, or cease using, a special method takes effect from the date on which it was given or from a later date specified by the Commissioners. The date from which an approval takes effect is not specified. For retrospective approval of an application to use a different special method, see *Barrett (provisional liquidator for Rafidain Bank)* (No 11016).

An approval or direction has effect only if it is set out in a document identified as such. This document sets out the manner in which input tax is attributed to taxable supplies. For floor-area based methods, see *Banbury Visionplus Ltd v R & C Comrs* [2006] STC 1568; *Optika Ltd* (No 18627); Business Brief 34/04, 15 December 2004; *Vision Express (UK) Ltd v R & C Comrs* [2010] STC 742; *London Clubs Management Ltd v R & C Comrs* [2010] UKUT 365 (TCC), [2010] STC 2789. For time based methods, see *St Helen's School Northwood Ltd v R & C Comrs* [2007] STC 633. For hire purchase transactions, see Revenue and Customs Brief 31/07, 30 March 2007 and *R & C Comrs v Royal Bank of Scotland plc* [2008] STC 3301 (tribunal's decision quashed). For foreign exchange transactions, see *C & E Comrs v First National Bank of Chicago* (case C-172/96) [1998] STC 850, ECJ. For higher education institutions, see Business Brief 11/06, 7 August 2006. For special methods agreed with certain trade bodies, see the trade agreements noted in Appendix 7. For the London Clearing Banks special method, see *Barclays Bank plc v C & E Comrs* [1991] VATTR 115.

For the circumstances in which input tax attributable to exempt supplies is treated as being attributable to taxable supplies in a prescribed accounting period, see regs 105A(1)(a), 106(1)(a) and 106ZA. For the adjustment of amounts provisionally attributed in a prescribed accounting period by reference to a longer period, see regs 105A(1)(b), 106(1)(b), 106ZA, 107; *C & E Comrs v University of Wales College Cardiff* [1995] STC 611 (provisional deduction stands if no adjustment at end of longer period). For adjustments in other circumstances, see regs 108 and 109 (goods and services not put to intended use), and 112–116 (capital items). For the rounding of percentages resulting from a proportional calculation, see *Royal Bank of Scotland Group plc v R & C Comrs* (case C-488/07) [2008] ECR I–10409, [2009] STC 461, ECJ.

An ambiguous direction does not secure a fair and reasonable attribution (see VATA 1994 s 26 (3)) and is void ab initio: see *Kwik-Fit (GB) Ltd v C & E Comrs* [1998] STC 159.

The terms of a special method may fail to prescribe how all or part of the taxable person's input tax is to be attributed to taxable supplies, eg because it has not been updated to take account of changed circumstances. If so, the input tax concerned is attributed to taxable supplies in accordance with regs 103, 103A or 103B (if, or to the extent that, it falls within those provisions) and by reference to the extent to which the goods or services are used or to be used in making taxable supplies expressed as a proportion of the whole use or intended use (in other cases).

Paragraphs (1A)–(17) of this regulation apply to a special method used in connection with an apportionment of input tax incurred on goods and services used for both business and non-business purposes in accordance with reg 102ZA(1) or (2): see reg 102ZA(4)(a).

102ZA. A taxable person is required to apportion the input tax incurred in respect of goods or services used (or to be used) partly for business purposes and partly for non-business purposes: see VATA 1994 s 24(5). A fully taxable person (as defined in reg 102ZA(5)) is *entitled* to make the apportionment by using a special method. A partly exempt person is *required* to use a special method. For special methods, see reg 102. If a special method is used, regs 102(1A)–(17), 102A, 102B and 102C apply, regs 105A, 106 and 106ZA do not, and the definition of "exempt input tax" (see reg 99(1)(a)) is modified.

A person may be a fully taxable person at the time when the special method is approved. If he subsequently incurs exempt input tax, any adjustment of input tax under reg 103B(1) applies from the date on which the person first incurred exempt input tax. For the circumstances in which reg 103B applies, see regs 103A(1) (notice served by the Commissioners) and 103C(1) (notice served by the taxable person).

102A. A special method may not fairly and reasonably represent the extent to which a taxable person uses (or intends to use) goods or services in making taxable supplies (as defined in reg 102(17)). For an example, see *Vision Express (UK) Ltd v R & C Comrs* [2010] STC 742 (optician using floor-based special method). Where this is so, the Commissioners may serve a notice on him to that effect. The notice must set out the Commissioners' reasons for serving the notice. It must state the effect of the notice.

The notice requires the taxable person to make a tax adjustment in prescribed accounting periods commencing on or after the date of the notice and in longer periods ending on or after that date. In either case, a later date may be specified in the notice. If a longer period straddles the relevant date, the tax adjustment is confined to that part of the period commencing on or after the relevant date. The nature of the tax adjustment is set out in reg 102B.

A notice under this provision takes priority to a notice under reg 102(11) in relation to the period it covers: see reg 102(15).

For the circumstances in which the Commissioners expect to service notices, see Business Brief 27/03, 10 December 2003.

This regulation applies to a special method used in connection with an apportionment of input tax incurred on goods and services used for both business and non-business purposes in accordance with reg 102ZA(1) or (2): see reg 102ZA(4)(a).

102B. The Commissioners may serve a notice (under reg 102A) or approve a notice served by a taxable person (under reg 102C). Where this is so, the taxable person is required to calculate the difference between:

- the attribution made by him in the prescribed accounting period or longer period concerned; and
- an attribution for that period representing the extent to which the goods or services are used (or to be used) by him in making taxable supplies (as defined in reg 102(17)).

The amount of the difference for a prescribed accounting period must be accounted for on the taxable person's return for that period. The amount for a longer period must be accounted at the same time as the longer period adjustment for that period (see reg 107).

The taxable person must comply with the foregoing requirement until such time as use of his special method is terminated (see reg 102(3)). For the date from which the requirement runs, see regs 102A(2) (notice served by the Commissioners) and 102C(2) (notice served by the taxable person).

This regulation applies to a special method used in connection with an apportionment of input tax incurred on goods and services used for both business and non-business purposes in accordance with reg 102ZA(1) or (2): see reg 102ZA(4)(a).

102C. The special method used by a taxable person may not fairly and reasonably represent the extent to which he uses (or intends to use) goods or services in making taxable supplies (as defined in reg 102(17)). Where this is so, the taxable person may serve a notice on the Commissioners to that effect. The notice must set out his reasons in support of the notification.

If the Commissioners approve the notice, the taxable person is required to make a tax adjustment in prescribed accounting periods commencing on or after the date of the notice and in longer periods ending on or after that date. In either case, a later date may be specified in the notice. If a longer period straddles the relevant date, the tax adjustment is confined to that part of the period commencing on or after the relevant date. The nature of the tax adjustment is set out in reg 102B.

This regulation applies to a special method used in connection with an apportionment of input tax incurred on goods and services used for both business and non-business purposes in accordance with reg 102ZA(1) or (2): see reg 102ZA(4)(a).

Attribution of input tax to foreign and specified supplies

103. Input tax incurred by a taxable person is attributed to taxable supplies, so as to be allowable (see VATA 1994 s 26(1)), if the goods or services are used in making:

- supplies of goods or services outside the UK which would be taxable if made in the UK;
- services within VATA 1994 Sch 9 Group 2 Item 1 (insurance), wherever made, to a person who belongs in a third country or directly linked to the export of goods to a third country;
- services within VATA 1994 Sch 9 Group 5 Items 1, 2, 2A, 3, 4, 5A, 6 or 8 (financial services), wherever made, to a person who belongs in a third country or directly linked to the export of goods to a third country;
- intermediary services within VATA 1994 Sch 9 Group 2 Item 4 or Group 5 Item 5, wherever made, relating to the foregoing insurance and financial services.

The attribution is made in the standard method (see reg 101) or special method (see reg 102) calculation if the goods or services are wholly used (or to be used) in making those supplies. A separate calculation is necessary if the goods or services are partly used (or to be used) in making these supplies. The allowable proportion is the use (or intended use) in making these supplies expressed as a proportion of the whole use (or intended use).

For the circumstances in which input tax attributable to exempt supplies is treated as being attributable to taxable supplies in a prescribed accounting period or longer period, see regs 105A, 106, 106ZA.

Attribution of input tax to investment gold

103A. Input tax incurred by a taxable person in making supplies of a description in VATA 1994 Sch 9 Group 15 Items 1 or 2 (ie supplies specified in VAT (Input Tax) (Specified Supplies) Order 1999, SI 1999/3121 art 4) is allowable (see VATA 1994 s 26(1)) if the goods or services comprise:

(a) investment gold purchased or acquired by him (ie on a transaction within VATA 1994 Sch 9 Group 15 Item 1 or 2 where the supplier made an election to waive exemption under VAT (Investment Gold) Order 1999, SI 1999/3116 art 3 or where only one of the parties to the transaction was a member of the London Bullion Market Association so that the supply was excluded from exemption under VATA 1994 Sch 9 Group 15 Note 4(*b*) and the customer was required to account for the VAT chargeable under VAT (Terminal Markets) Order 1973, SI 1973/173 art 5);

(b) gold (other than investment gold) purchased, acquired or imported by him for transformation into investment gold; or

(c) services (comprising a change of form, weight or purity of gold) purchased by him.

A taxable person producing investment gold is entitled to credit for input tax on goods and services directly linked to the production process. A taxable person converting gold into investment gold is entitled to credit for input tax on goods and services directly linked to the conversion process.

Input tax is apportioned if the good or services were purchased, acquired or imported partly for making supplies of a description with VATA 1994 Sch 9 Group 15 Items 1 and 2 and partly for making other supplies. Input tax is attributed to the former supplies to the extent that the goods or services are used or to be used in making those supplies. This use is expressed as a proportion of the whole use or intended use.

For the circumstances in which input tax attributable to exempt supplies is treated as being attributable to taxable supplies in a prescribed accounting period or longer period, see regs 105A, 106, 106ZA.

Attribution of input tax incurred on services and related goods used to make financial supplies

103B. Input tax incurred by a taxable person in any prescribed accounting period is attributed to taxable supplies if the following conditions are met:

- the input tax is incurred in respect of a supply of specified services, and any related goods, made to him. Services are "specified services" if they are supplied by accountants, advertising agencies, bodies providing listing and registration services, financial advisers, lawyers, marketing consultants, persons who prepare and design documentation and persons providing services similar to those supplied by any the foregoing persons;
- the specified services and related goods are used (or to be used) in making both a relevant supply and one or more other supplies. A "relevant supply" is a supply of a description within VATA 1994 Sch 9 Group 5 Item 1 or 6 (financial services) made in the UK or another EU member state; and
- the relevant supply is incidental to one or more of the taxable person's business activities.

The input tax is allowable to the extent that the specified services or related goods are used (or to be used) in making taxable supplies expressed as a proportion of the whole use or intended use. A supply is a "taxable supply" for this purpose if it is:

- a taxable supply (as defined in VATA 1994 s 4);
- a supply of goods or services made outside the UK which would be a taxable supply if made in the UK;
- a supply of services within VATA 1994 Sch 9 Group 2 Item 1 (insurance), wherever made, supplied to a person who belongs in a third country or is directly linked to the export of goods to a third country;
- a supply of services within VATA 1994 Sch 9 Group 5 Items 1, 2, 2A, 3, 4, 5A, 6 or 8 (financial services), wherever made, supplied to a person who belongs in a third country or is directly linked to the export of goods to a third country; or
- an intermediary service within VATA 1994 Sch 9 Group 2 Item 4 or Group 5 Item 5, wherever made, relating to the foregoing insurance and financial services.

The attribution is made in the standard method calculation if the taxable person uses that method (see reg 101(8)(*a*)). A separate calculation is necessary in other cases.

For the circumstances in which input tax attributable to exempt supplies is treated as being attributable to taxable supplies in a prescribed accounting period or longer period, see regs 105A, 106, 106ZA.

Attribution of input tax on self-supplies

104. Input tax on a self-supply is not attributed to that supply. Compare VATA 1994 ss 8(3) and 44(6).

Treatment of input tax attributable to exempt supplies as being attributable to taxable supplies

105. [Revoked.]

105A. This provision applies a de minimis rule for input tax incurred in any prescribed accounting period or longer period. It applies to the difference between: (1) total input tax incurred in the relevant period; and (2) input tax incurred in the period on goods or services used or to be used exclusively in making taxable supplies and/or supplies of a description in reg 103(a) (foreign supplies) and 103(b) (specified supplies).

All input tax incurred in the period is treated as attributable to taxable supplies if: (1) the amount of the difference does not exceed £625 per month on average; and (2) as regards any supplies for the period which are not taxable supplies (referred to as "exempt supplies"), their value does not exceed 50% of the value of all supplies made in the period.

The attribution input tax for a prescribed accounting period reflects the use or intended use of the goods or services during the period concerned. The attribution of input tax for a longer period must reflect any subsequent change in that use or intention.

A taxable person entitled to attribute input tax for a longer period in accordance with this provision is entitled to attribute input tax in accordance with reg 106ZA for prescribed accounting periods falling within his immediately following longer period if the prescribed conditions are met.

This regulation does not apply to a special method used in connection with an apportionment of input tax incurred on goods and services used for both business and non-business purposes in accordance with reg 102ZA(1) or (2): see reg 102ZA(4)(b).

106. Relevant input tax for a prescribed accounting period is treated as being attributable to taxable supplies if: (1) it does not exceed £625 per month on average; and (2) it does not exceed 50% of total input tax for the period. Any input tax deducted as a consequence of this provision must be repaid to the Commissioners if an adjustment (see reg 107A) arises in respect of the prescribed accounting period. For the accounting entry, see reg 106A(4). This provision does not apply (regs 106(1) and 106A(1)), and reg 106A applies in its place, when making an adjustment under reg 107A.

The aggregate of (*a*) relevant input tax for a longer period and (*b*) the amount of any adjustment under reg 107B in respect of that period is treated as being attributable to taxable supplies if: (1) it does not exceed £625 per month (ie £7,500 per annum) on average; and (2) it does not exceed 50% of total input tax for the period. The fact that input tax was treated as being attributable to taxable supplies in a prescribed accounting period falling within the longer period is disregarded. No account is taken of adjustments under the capital goods scheme (see reg 115(1), (2)).

"Relevant input tax" is input tax attributed under regs 101 (standard method), 102 (special method), 103 (overseas supplies), 103A (gold), 103B (specified services) or 107 (adjustment for a longer period) to: (1) exempt supplies; or (2) supplies outside the UK which would be exempt if made in the UK. The following supplies do not fall within head (2):

- a supply of services within VATA 1994 Sch 9 Group 2 Item 1 (insurance) made to a person who belongs in a third country or is directly linked to the export of goods to a third country;
- a supply of services within VATA 1994 Sch 9 Group 5 Items 1, 2, 2A, 3, 4, 5A, 6 or 8 (financial services) made to a person who belongs in a third country or is directly linked to the export of goods to a third country;
- an intermediary service within VATA 1994 Sch 9 Group 2 Item 4 or Group 5 Item 5 relating to the foregoing insurance and financial services; and
- a supply within VATA 1994 Sch 9 Group 15 Items 1 or 2 (investment gold).

A taxable person entitled to attribute input tax for a longer period in accordance with this provision is entitled to attribute input tax in accordance with reg 106ZA for prescribed accounting periods falling within his immediately following longer period if the conditions prescribed therein are met.

This regulation does not apply to a special method used in connection with an apportionment of input tax incurred on goods and services used for both business and non-business purposes in accordance with reg 102ZA(1) or (2): see reg 102ZA(4)(b).

106ZA. A taxable person may treat input tax incurred in each prescribed accounting period within his current longer period as attributable to taxable supplies if:

- he was entitled to attribute his input tax to taxable supplies in his immediately preceding longer period (see reg 106ZA(2)) in accordance with regs 105A(1)(b) or 106(1)(b);
- he does not expect to incur more than £1,000,000 in his current longer period;

This is a simplification measure. A taxable person adopting it must use it for all prescribed accounting periods falling within his current longer period.

This regulation does not apply to a special method used in connection with an apportionment of input tax incurred on goods and services used for both business and non-business purposes in accordance with reg 102ZA(1) or (2): see reg 102ZA(4)(b).

106A. This provision applies in place of reg 106 to determine whether input tax is treated as being attributable to taxable supplies in cases where an adjustment arises under reg 107A. It is therefore relevant to prescribed accounting periods that do not form part of a longer period if input tax for the prescribed accounting period has been attributed under the standard method.

The aggregate of (*a*) the input tax specified below, and (*b*) the amount of any adjustment under reg 107A is treated as being attributable to taxable supplies if exceeds neither £625 per month (ie £1,875 per quarter or £7,500 per annum) on average nor 50% of total input tax for the period.

The input tax in head (*a*) is input tax attributed under regs 101 (standard method), 103 (overseas supplies), 103A (gold) and 103B (specified supplies) to: (1) exempt supplies; and (2) supplies outside the UK which would be exempt if made in the UK. However, this does not include input tax attributed, in either case, to any of the following supplies:

- a supply of services within VATA 1994 Sch 9 Group 2 Item 1 (insurance) made to a person who belongs in a third country or is directly linked to the export of goods to a third country;
- a supply of services within VATA 1994 Sch 9 Group 5 Items 1, 2, 2A, 3, 4, 5A, 6 or 8 (financial services) made to a person who belongs in a third country or is directly linked to the export of goods to a third country;
- an intermediary service within VATA 1994 Sch 9 Group 2 Item 4 or Group 5 Item 5 relating to the foregoing insurance and financial services; and
- a supply within VATA 1994 Sch 9 Group 15 Items 1 or 2 (investment gold).

If the input tax and adjustment are treated as being attributable to taxable supplies, it is necessary to calculate the difference between: (1) the total amount of the input tax for the period; and (2) the aggregate of (*a*) the amount of input tax deducted in the period, and (*b*) the amount of any adjustment under reg 107A. The amount of the difference is shown as an under-declaration in the trader's return for the first prescribed accounting period next following the period in respect of which the adjustment under reg 107A arises. However, the Commissioners may allow another return to be used for this purpose. Furthermore, if the trader's registration is cancelled at or before the end of the period in respect of which the adjustment arises under reg 107A, he must account for the amount of the difference on his final return.

The trader may have treated some input tax for the period as attributable to taxable supplies in accordance with reg 106(1). The input tax may cease to be so treated when the de minimis limit in reg 106A is used. Where this is so, the amount concerned represents an over-declaration of input tax. It must be included as such on the trader's return for the first prescribed accounting period next following the period in respect of which the adjustment in reg 107A arises. However, the Commissioners may allow another return to be used for this purpose. Furthermore, if trader's registration is cancelled at or before the end of the period in respect of which the adjustment arises under reg 107A, he must account for the amount of the difference on his final return.

Adjustment of attribution

107. A longer period is applied to a taxable person if he incurs exempt input tax (see regs 99(1)(*a*) and 102ZA(4)(*c*)) during a tax year (see reg 99(1)(*d*)) or registration period (see reg 99(1)(*e*)). For the duration of a longer period, see regs 99(4)–(7) and 102ZA(4)(*c*).

A taxable person must determine the amount of input tax attributable to taxable supplies in a longer period if:

- he has incurred exempt input tax (as defined in reg 99(1)(a)) so that a longer period is applicable to him;
- in one or more prescribed accounting periods he has:
  - (a) provisionally attributed an amount of input tax to taxable supplies in accordance with a method;
  - (b) treated an amount of input tax as attributable to taxable supplies in accordance with reg 105A(1)(a) (de minimis limit); or
  - (c) treated an amount of input tax as attributable to taxable supplies in accordance with reg 106ZA(1) (input tax for preceding longer period treated as attributable to taxable supplies); and
- the Commissioners have not dispensed with the requirement to make an adjustment.

The calculation proceeds as follows:

(1) The amount of input tax attributable to taxable supplies in the longer period is determined in accordance with the method used in the prescribed accounting periods falling within the longer period.

(2) If the standard method was used in those prescribed accounting periods, residual input tax (see reg 101(10)) is recalculated on the following basis:

- (a) if the taxable person did not have an immediately preceding longer period (so that he used the calculation in reg 101(2)(*d*) or (*e*) – referred to as Basis 1 and 2 respectively in the commentary to reg 101) the recalculation proceeds in accordance with Basis 2;
- (b) if the taxable person had an immediately preceding longer period (and used the calculation in reg 101(2)(*f*) – referred to as Basis 3 in the commentary to reg 101) the recalculation proceeds in accordance with Basis 1;
- (c) if the taxable person had an immediately preceding longer period and opted to use Basis 1 (see reg 101(2)(*d*) and (*g*)), the recalculation proceeds on the same basis; and
- (d) if all input tax was treated as being attributed to taxable supplies in one or more of the prescribed accounting periods (see regs 105A(1)(a) and 106ZA(1)), the recalculation proceeds in accordance with Basis 1 (if the taxable person had an immediately preceding longer period) or Basis 2 (f he did not).

(3) The relevant tests (see regs 105A and 106 as appropriate) are applied to determine whether all input tax in the longer period is treated as attributable to taxable supplies. The test in reg 106 is not applied when a special method is used to apportion input tax incurred on goods or services used for both business and non-business purposes. For the apportionment, see reg 102ZA(1).

(4) The amount due to or by the taxable person is the difference between:

- (a) the amount of input tax attributed to taxable supplies in accordance with heads (1)–(3); and
- (b) the aggregate amount of input tax deducted in the prescribed accounting periods comprised in the longer period.

(5) The amount in head (4) is normally increased or reduced by the amount of any adjustment under reg 107B (see reg 107B(2)(*b*)). For the exception, see reg 107B(3).

(6) The aggregate of the amounts in head (5) is included in one of the following returns as an over-deduction or under-deduction:

- (a) the return for the last prescribed accounting period of the longer period;
- (b) the return for the next prescribed accounting period; or
- (c) the return for such other prescribed accounting period as the Commissioners may allow.

For the entry made in the taxable person's VAT Account, see reg 32.

107A. A taxable person is required to make an adjustment if: (1) he has used the standard method (see reg 101) to attribute input tax for a prescribed accounting period to taxable supplies; (2) the prescribed accounting period does not form part of a longer period; and (3) there is a substantial difference (as defined in reg 107C) between (*a*) the attribution in (1), and (*b*) an attribution made by reference to the use made (or to be made) by the taxable person (or a successor (as defined in reg 107D) of his) in making taxable supplies. The taxable person must calculate the difference arising for the period. He must account for it on his return for the next period, the return for such other period as the Commissioners may allow or (if he is deregistered at or before the end of the period in which the difference arises) his final return.

For the circumstances in which a difference is treated as substantial, see reg 107C. For the circumstances in which a substantial difference is disregarded, see reg 107E. For the circumstances in which a substantial difference is treated as being attributable to taxable supplies, see reg 106A.

107B. There may be a substantial difference between: (1) the input tax attributed to taxable supplies in a longer period; and (2) an attribution representing the extent to which the goods or services were used by the taxable person or are to be used by him, or a successor of his, in making taxable supplies. If so, the taxable person must calculate the difference. The amount due to or by the taxable person is accounted for as part of his longer period adjustment (see reg 107).

This provision is confined to longer period adjustments made in accordance with reg 107(1)(*a*) or (*d*). It does not apply to attributions made under reg 101(8) or 107(1)(*b*), (*c*).

For the circumstances in which a difference is treated as substantial, see reg 107C. For the circumstances in which a substantial difference is disregarded, see reg 107E.

107C. A difference is substantial if it exceeds either £50,000 or the greater of:

(1) 50% of residual input tax for the prescribed accounting period (in the case of an adjustment under reg 107A) or longer period (in the case of an adjustment under reg 107B); and

(2) £25,000.

For residual input tax in relation to a prescribed accounting period, see reg 101(2)(*d*), In relation to a longer period, see reg 107F.

107D. A person (Y) is the successor of another person (X) if:

(a) X has transferred the assets of all or part of his business to Y as a going concern; and

(b) the transfer is treated as neither a supply of goods nor a supply of services.

This applies whether the assets are transferred directly to Y or indirectly via two or more transfers. For transfers treated as neither a supply of goods nor a supply of services, see VAT (Special Provisions) Order 1995, SI 1995/1268 art 5.

107E. No adjustment is made under regs 107A or 107B if the amount of residual input tax for the prescribed accounting period (in the case of reg 107A) or longer period (in the case of reg 107B) does not exceed:

(a) £25,000 (or a proportionate amount if the period is not 12 months) if the person (X) is a group undertaking (as defined in Companies Act 1985 s 259) in relation to one or more other undertakings (as defined in Companies Act 1985 s 259) (Y) and X and Y are not members of the same VAT group (see VATA 1994 ss 43A–43C);

(b) £50,000 (or a proportionate amount if the period is not 12 months) in any other case.

For residual input tax in relation to a prescribed accounting period, see reg 101(2)(*d*). In relation to a longer period, see reg 107F.

107F. References to "an apportionment under reg 101(2)(*d*)" in regs 107C and 107E in relation to a longer period include cases where the apportionment is made under reg 107(1)(*a*) or (*d*) using the calculation specified in reg 101(2)(*d*).

108. A taxable person is required to make a payment if:

(1) he deducts an amount of input tax because he intends to use the goods or services in making either taxable supplies or both taxable and exempt supplies;

(2) he uses, or forms the intention of using, the goods or services in making exempt supplies or both taxable and exempt supplies in the former case or exempt supplies in the latter case; and

(3) the use or intention occurs during a six year period commencing on the first day of the prescribed accounting period in which the deduction was made.

The taxable person must account for the tax which has ceased to be attributable to taxable supplies. He does so on the return for the prescribed accounting period in which the use or intention occurs. For examples, see *Cooper & Chapman (Builders) Ltd v C & E Comrs* [1993] STC 1 (input tax on individual flats repaid); *C & E Comrs v Briararch Ltd* [1992] STC 732 (part of input tax on whole building repaid); *C & E Comrs v Svenska International plc* [1999] STC 406, HL (joining VAT group before intended taxable supply made); *Tremerton Ltd v C & E Comrs* [1999] STC 1039 (services relating to exempt supply of land).

This provision does not apply if the intended supply—which is taxable under legislation in force at the time of purchase—subsequently becomes exempt following a change in the legislation: cf *Gulland Properties* (No 13955).

For "exempt supplies" and "method", see reg 110(5).

109. A taxable person is entitled to a repayment if:

(1) an amount of input tax cannot be deducted because he intends to use the goods or services in making either exempt supplies or both taxable and exempt supplies;

(2) he uses, or forms the intention of using, the goods or services in making taxable supplies or both taxable and exempt supplies in the former case or taxable supplies in the latter case; and

(3) the use or intention occurs during a six year period commencing on the first day of the prescribed accounting period in which deduction was not made.

The taxable person may claim repayment in such form and manner as the Commissioners may direct, giving such particulars as they may direct. The amount claimed is the input tax which has become attributable to taxable supplies. For claims, see Notice No 706; Revenue and Customs Brief 57/09, 4 September 2009.

This provision does not apply if the intended supply—which is exempt under the legislation in force at the time of purchase—subsequently becomes taxable following a change in the legislation: cf *Gulland Properties* (No 13955). For vacant property becoming subject to an election to waive exemption, see *Royal & Sun Alliance Insurance Group plc v C & E Comrs* [2003] STC 832, HL. For the assignment of building contracts, see *Community Housing Association Ltd v R & C Comrs* [2009] STC 1324.

For "exempt supplies" and "method", see reg 110(5).

110. The term "exempt supply" in regs 103B (where the term is not used), 108, 109, 110 and 112–116 includes a supply (other than a supply within VAT (Input Tax) (Specified Supplies) Order 1999, SI 1999/3121 arts 3 or 4) made outside the UK which would, if made in the UK, be an exempt supply. However, a supply within art 4 of the 1999 Order is counted as an exempt supply for the purpose of identifying the use or intended use of goods and services if the input tax attributed to it is disallowed under reg 103A.

The term "taxable supply" in regs 103B (where an identical definition is provided), 108, 109, 110 and 112–116 includes a supply made outside the UK which would, if made in the UK, be a taxable supply and a supply within VAT (Input Tax) (Specified Supplies) Order 1999, SI

1999/3121 art 3. A supply within art 4 of the 1999 Order is counted as a taxable supply for the purpose of identifying the use or intended use of goods and services if the input tax attributed to it is allowed under reg 103A.

The amounts payable or repayable under regs 108 and 109 are restricted if:

(a) there is a change of intended use so that regs 108 or 109 apply;

(b) the use or intended use of the goods or services includes making overseas supplies; and

(c) when the input tax was first attributed, the trader used either the standard method (see reg 101) or a special method which did not expressly provide for attribution of input tax attributable to overseas supplies (see reg 102).

The amount payable or repayable is restricted to:

$$\frac{\text{use or intended use in making taxable supplies}}{\text{whole use or intended use}} \times \text{amount in reg 108 or 109.}$$

Exceptional claims for VAT relief

111. A taxable person (a "relevant person") may incur VAT on goods or services purchased, acquired or imported before the date on which he became a taxable person. Where this is so, the Commissioners may authorise him to treat this VAT as if it were input tax.

A person (a "relevant person") may incur VAT on goods or services purchased, acquired or imported for the benefit of a body corporate, or in connection with its incorporation, before its incorporation. Where this is so, and the body corporate is a taxable person, the Commissioners may authorise it to treat this VAT as if it were input tax. The following conditions must be met:

(i) the relevant person must become a member, officer or employee of the body corporate and it must have fully reimbursed him for his expenditure;

(ii) the relevant person must not have been a taxable person at the time of purchase, acquisition or importation; and

(iii) he must have purchased, acquired or imported the goods or services for the purposes of a business to be carried on by the body corporate and not used them for any other purpose in the interim.

VAT cannot be treated as input tax in either case if it was incurred in respect of:

(a) goods or services supplied, or (unless the Commissioners allow otherwise) goods consumed, by the relevant person before the date from which the taxable person was, or was required to be, registered;

(b) (except in relation to a taxable person registered before 1 May 1997 who had not made any returns before that date) goods purchased, acquired or imported by the relevant person more than four years before the date from which the taxable person was, or was required to be, registered. This general rule is modified in the following circumstances:

 (i) the taxable person was registered before 1 May 1997 and he did not make any returns before that date (see reg 111(2A)),

 (ii) the relevant person was registered, or required to be registered, before 2 April 2009 (see reg 111(2C)), or

 (iii) the relevant person was registered, or required to be registered, between 2 April 2009 and 31 March 2010 inclusive (see reg 111(2D));

(c) services performed on goods to which (*a*) or (*b*) applies;

(d) services supplied to the relevant person more than six months before the date from which the taxable person was, or was required to be, registered; or

(e) capital items within reg 113.

No input tax may be reclaimed if the goods or services were to be used in making a supply which, under the legislation in force at the time of purchase, acquisition or importation, would have been an exempt supply: *C Jeffrey Black (Opticians) Ltd* (No 4072); *Douros* (No

12454); *Byrd* (No 12675); *Gulland Properties* (No 13955); *Jenkins* (No 14784). For traders who become registered as a result of an exercising the option to tax in respect of land, see Notice No 742A (June 2008) para 9.4; *R (on the application of Argyll House Developments Ltd) v R & C Comrs* [2009] STC 2698.

The taxable person must make a claim. If registered after 30 April 1997, the claim is made on the first return which he is required to make. If registered before 1 May 1997, the claim is made on the first return he makes. The Commissioners may allow otherwise. However, no claim may be made in respect of VAT incurred more than four years before the due date for furnishing the first return and no claim may be made if the first return was required to be made before 31 March 2006. For the due date, see reg 25.

The claim must be supported by invoices and other evidence if so required by the Commissioners.

A taxable person making a claim must compile and preserve:

(a) a stock account in respect of goods showing the particulars specified in reg 111(4)(*a*); and

(b) a list of services showing the particulars specified in reg 111(4)(*b*).

A person ceasing to be a taxable person may thereafter incur VAT on services supplied to him. He may claim repayment of VAT attributable to taxable supplies made by him in the course or furtherance of the business he carried on while registered or required to register. The claim must be made in the manner specified by the Commissioners and be supported by the evidence required by them. See Notice No 700/11.

In principle, the claim must be made no later than four years after the time of supply and in respect of services supplied after 31 March 2006. However, no time limit applies if the person ceased to be a taxable person before 1 May 1997 and the supply was made before that date.

PART XV ADJUSTMENTS TO THE DEDUCTION OF INPUT TAX ON CAPITAL ITEMS

Interpretation of Part XV

112. In the absence of a contrary intention, the definitions in regs 99, 110 apply. The terms "capital item", "interest" and "owner" are defined.

Capital items to which this Part applies

113. The capital goods scheme applies to capital expenditure of the type shown in column 2 incurred in respect of an item shown in column 1 where VAT has been incurred in respect of the expenditure and the value of that expenditure exceeds the sum in column 3:

	Item	*Capital expenditure*	*Minimum value*
(*a*)	Land	Expenditure relating to its acquisition	£250,000
(*b*)	All or part of a building	Expenditure relating to its acquisition, construction, refurbishment, fitting out, alteration or extension	£250,000
(*c*)	All or part of a civil engineering work	Expenditure relating to its acquisition, construction, refurbishment, fitting out, alteration or extension	£250,000
(*d*)	A computer or an item of computer equipment	Expenditure relating to its acquisition	£50,000

(*e*)	An aircraft	Expenditure relating to its acquisition, construction, refurbishment, fitting out, alteration or extension	£50,000
(*f*)	A ship, boat or other vessel	Expenditure relating to its acquisition, construction, refurbishment, fitting out, alteration or extension	£50,000

An item meeting these requirements is referred to as a "capital item" if the owner (see reg 112(2), (4), (5)) uses it in the course or furtherance of his business for a business purpose that does not wholly comprise resale: see reg 112(2).

Period of adjustment

114. In principle, the proportion (if any) of input tax deducted on a capital item is adjusted over a period of adjustment comprising ten successive intervals (in relation to land, buildings or civil engineering works, as to which see reg 113(2)(a)–(c)) or five successive intervals (in relation to computers, aircraft and vessels, as to which see reg 113(2)(d)–(f)) (reg 114(3)). However, the number of intervals is varied in the following circumstances:

(1) The owner's interest in the capital item is due to cease in, or before, the penultimate interval of the period of adjustment (reg 114(3A)). Here, the number of intervals is the higher of: (a) the number of complete years that the interest has to run (counted from the day on which the owner first used the capital item) plus one year; and (b) three intervals (reg 114(3A)). The relevant denominator in reg 115(1) is adjusted accordingly (reg 114(3C)).

(2) The owner's interest in the asset is deemed to be supplied in accordance with VATA 1994 Sch 10 para 37(1) and the numerator of the fraction in VATA 1994 Sch 10 para 37(3) is 36 or more. Here, the number of intervals is 1/12th of the numerator rounded up to the next whole number (reg 114(3B)). The relevant denominator in reg 115(1) is adjusted accordingly (reg 114(3C)).

(3) A person who registers for VAT owns a capital item on the day from which his registration takes effect. The number of intervals is reduced by the number of complete years between the date on which the owner first used the capital item and the date from which he was registered. His first post-registration interval is counted as a subsequent interval for the purposes of reg 115(1) (reg 114(3D)).

In principle, the first interval applied to a capital item commences on the day when the owner (as defined in reg 112(4)) first uses the capital item and ends on the last day of his current tax year (reg 114(4)); each subsequent interval corresponds with the owner's longer period (if he has one) or his tax year (if he does not) (reg 114(5)). However, special provisions apply in the following circumstances:

(1) The owner (being a registered taxable person) becomes a member of a VAT group. As regards the owner, each subsequent interval corresponds with the owner's longer period (if he has one) or his tax year (if he does not). As regards the VAT group, each subsequent interval (if any) ends on successive anniversaries of the day on which the owner became a member of the group (reg 114(5A)).

(2) The owner ceases to be a member of a VAT group. As regards the VAT group, the current interval ends on the day when the owner ceases to be a member of the group. As regards the former group member, each subsequent interval (if any) ends on successive anniversaries of the day on which the body corporate ceased to be a member of the group (reg 114(5A)),

(3) The owner transfers the capital item on the transfer of all or part of his business as a going concern under a supply which is outside the scope of VAT (see VAT (Special Provisions) Order 1995, SI 1995/1268 art 5). If the owner also transfers his registration number to the new owner, the interval straddling the transfer ends on the last day of the new owner's longer period (if he has one) or the last day of his tax year (if he does not) (reg 114(7)). If the owner does not transfer his

registration number: (a) his current interval ends on the day on which the transfer takes place; and (b) each subsequent interval (if any) of the new owner ends on successive anniversaries of the day on which the transfer took place (reg 114(5A)).

(4) The first and second intervals taken together may last less than twelve months. If there is no change in the extent to which the capital item is used in making taxable supplies, the two periods are treated as a single interval which ends on the last day of what would have been the second interval (reg 114(5B)),

Method of adjustment

115. The owner (see reg 112(4), (5)) is entitled to a deduction if his taxable use of a capital asset (as judged at the time when his original entitlement to input tax deduction was determined in accordance with regs 99–111) increases in a subsequent interval (reg 115(1)). He is liable to make a payment to the Commissioners in the reverse circumstances (reg 115(2)). In principle, the deduction or payment is calculated as follows:

$$\frac{\text{total input tax on the capital item}}{\text{number of intervals applied to the item}} \times \text{the adjustment percentage.}$$

The "total input on the capital item" is: (1) (in relation to any capital item) all VAT incurred by the owner on the capital item. This includes non-business VAT (as defined in VATA 1994 s 24(5)(b)) and VAT incurred prior to registration; and (2) (if the owner is deemed to make a supply under VATA 1994 Sch 10 para 37(1)) the VAT charged on that supply (see reg 115(5)).

The "number of intervals applied to the item" is ten (see reg 114(3)(a)), five (see reg 114(3)(b)) or the number determined in accordance with regs 114(3A), 114(3B) and 115(5A).

The "adjustment percentage" is the increase or decrease (expressed as a percentage) between: (1) his taxable use (or intended taxable use) of the capital asset (as judged at the time when his original entitlement to input tax deduction was determined (see regs 99–111)); and (2) his taxable use of the capital item (or the relevant part of it) in the current interval.

In principle:

(1) An adjustment is made by the person who is treated as the owner of the capital item immediately prior to the end of the relevant interval (reg 115(5B).

(2) A deduction or payment is included on a return for the second prescribed accounting period next following the interval to which the amount relates. This is referred to as a "specified return" (reg 115(8)). The Commissioners may allow another return to be used for this purpose (reg 115(6)). However, that return must relate to a prescribed accounting period commencing within four years of the end of the prescribed accounting period to which the specified return relates (reg 115(9)).

(3) A person may be required to make an adjustment after he has been deregistered. Where this is so, he must make the adjustment in his final return (reg 115(11)).

Special rules apply in the following circumstances.

First, the owner may supply all or part of his interest in the capital item prior to commencement of the last interval (reg 115(3)(a)). If the owner makes a taxable supply, the capital item (or part) is deemed to be wholly used in making taxable supplies in each of the subsequent intervals. If the owner makes an exempt supply, the capital item (or part) is not so treated (reg 115(3ZA)).

Second, the owner may be deemed to supply all or part of his interest in the capital item prior to commencement of the last interval (reg 115(3)(b)), eg if he deregisters without transferring his business to another taxable person (see VATA 1994 Sch 4 para 8(1)). If the deemed supply is a taxable supply, the capital item (or part) is deemed to be wholly used in making taxable supplies in each of the subsequent intervals. If the deemed supply is an exempt supply, the capital item (or part) is not so treated (reg 115(3ZA)).

Third, the VAT chargeable on the deemed supply in the second situation may be £1,000 or less so that no supply is deemed to be made (reg 115(3)(c)). This could arise by virtue of the value of the supply, or because it is exempt or chargeable at the zero rate. If the deemed supply would have been a taxable supply, the capital item (or part) is deemed to be wholly used in making taxable supplies in each of the subsequent intervals. If the deemed supply would have been an exempt supply, the capital item (or part) is not so treated (reg 115(3ZA)).

Fourth, the capital item may be irretrievably lost, stolen or totally destroyed (reg 115(4)).

As regards the first, second and third situations:

(1) The owner calculates the deduction or payment arising in respect of any remaining complete interval(s) (reg 115(3ZA)). If the aggregate of this sum, the initial input tax deduction and the adjustments made in respect of previous intervals ("input tax") exceeds the VAT chargeable on his supply of the capital item ("output tax"), the deduction or payment is restricted to the amount which results in input tax being equal to output tax (reg 115(3A), (3B)).

(2) An adjustment is made by the person who is treated as the owner of the capital item immediately prior to the end of the relevant event (reg 115(5B)).

(3) A deduction or payment is included on a return for the second prescribed accounting period next following the interval in which the supply or deemed supply took place. This is referred to as a "specified return" (reg 115(8)). The Commissioners may allow another return to be used for this purpose (reg 115(7)). However, that return must relate to a prescribed accounting period commencing within four years of the end of the prescribed accounting period to which the specified return relates.

(4) A person may be required to make an adjustment after he has been deregistered. Where this is so, he must make the adjustment in his final return (reg 115(11)).

As regards the fourth situation, no adjustment is made in respect of the subsequent intervals (reg 115(4)).

Ascertainment of taxable use of a capital item

116. The extent to which a capital item is used to make taxable supplies in a subsequent interval is determined by the reference to the partial exemption method used in that interval. The attribution of total input tax for subsequent intervals is determined in accordance with a method agreed with the Commissioners if the owner joins or leaves a VAT group, or transfers all or part of his business as a going concern, so that the accounting date of those intervals is changed (see reg 114 (5A)). The Commissioners may allow or direct otherwise in either case.

If the owner makes a zero-rated supply by reference to the premium or first rent payable under a lease or tenancy, any subsequent grant or assignment of that lease or tenancy is disregarded in determining the extent to which the building is used in making taxable supplies in a subsequent interval.

PART XVA GOODS USED FOR NON-BUSINESS PURPOSES DURING THEIR ECONOMIC LIFE

Application

116A. The value of a supply of services ("the relevant supply") consisting of the private or non-business use of business goods (see VATA 1994 Sch 4 para 5(4)) made for no consideration is the full cost to the taxable person of providing that service (see VATA 1994 Sch 6 para 7(*b*)). If the business goods have an economic life (see regs 116C, 116D, 116G, 116L) when used for private or non-business purposes, the value of the supply (or part of the supply) attributable to private or non-business use after 31 October 2007 is calculated in accordance with regs 116B–116N.

Interpretation of this Part

116B. The terms "full cost of the goods", "goods", and "predecessor" are defined. As regards goods which are relevant assets (as defined in VATA 1994 s 24(5B)), the "full cost of the goods" excludes any costs on which VAT was incurred after 31 December 2010.

Economic life of goods

116C. In principle, goods (see reg 116B) held or used for business purposes have an economic life of 120 months (land, a building or part of a building) or 60 months (all other goods) counted from the day when they were purchased, acquired or imported by the taxable person or one of his predecessors.

116D. An interest in land, a building or part of a building may have had less than 120 months to run at the time of purchase, acquisition or importation. If so, the economic life of the land, building or part is the number of months remaining at that time.

Value of a relevant supply

116E. The value of a relevant supply is determined by reference to the following formula:

$$\frac{A}{B} \times (C \times U\%)$$

For this purpose:

A is the part of the economic life of the goods (measured in months) which falls within the prescribed accounting period in which the relevant supply takes place.

B is the economic life of the goods (measured in months).

C is the full cost of the goods (see reg 116B).

U% is the proportion of private or non-business use expressed as a percentage.

116F. Goods (see reg 116B) may be used for business, private or non-business purposes in a prescribed period ("X"), not used for any purpose in one or more successive periods ("Y") and then used for private or non-business purposes in the next period ("Z"). If so, the numerator in the formula used for calculating the value of the supply (see reg 116E) in period Z is the period Y + A rather than period A.

Later increase in the full cost of goods

116G. A supply of goods or services may be made to a person (or one of his predecessors (see reg 116B)) in respect of goods (see reg 116B) held or used for business purposes so that all or part of the VAT incurred in respect of that supply is eligible for input tax credit (see VATA 1994 ss 25, 26) or repayment (see VATA 1994 s 39). The goods held or used for business purposes are deemed to have an additional economic life of 60 or 120 months (see reg 116C) commencing at the time when the goods or services were supplied.

Value of relevant supplies made during a new economic life

116H. A supply of goods or services made in relation to goods (see reg 116B) may result in: (1) an economic life in relation to the purchase, acquisition or importation of the goods; and (2) an economic life in relation to the subsequent supply of goods or services. The value of a relevant supply made during the economic life in head (2) is determined by reference to the formula in reg 116E subject to the following variations:

C is the increase in the full cost of the goods (see reg 116B) resulting from the supply of the goods or services giving rise to the new economic life.

U% is the proportion of private or non-business use (expressed as a percentage) during the part of the prescribed accounting period falling within the new economic life of the goods.

Value of relevant supplies of goods which have two or more economic lives

116I. A relevant supply may take place during a period common to: (1) the economic life of the goods; and (2) the economic life of the supply of goods or services made in relation to them. If so, the value of the supply is the aggregate of: (1) the value determined in accordance with reg 116E in relation to the goods; and (2) the value determined in accordance with reg 116H in relation to the goods and services.

Transitional provisions

116J–116M. Goods purchased, acquired or imported before 1 November 2007 may have been used for private or non-business purposes before that date by the person who held them on that date. If so, the economic life of the goods is deemed to commence on 1 November 2007. It lasts for the period of time determined in accordance with the following formula:

$$D \times \frac{(E - F)}{E}$$

For this purpose:

D is a period of 60 months, 120 months or a proportionate part of 120 months determined by reference to the nature of the goods in accordance with regs 116C, 116D.

E is the full cost of: (1) the goods having an economic life determined in accordance with reg 116E; or (2) the goods or services having an economic life determined in accordance with reg 116H.

F is a value determined by using the following formula:

$$\frac{G \times 100}{X\% \times 100}$$

Where:

G is the total value of relevant supplies made before 1 November 2007.

X% is the extent of private or non-business use before 1 November 2007. This is expressed as a percentage.

For the application of this provision, see Examples 5 and 6 in VAT Information Sheet 14/07 (November 2007) para 2.12.

116N. A person may have claimed input tax deduction in respect of incurred VAT on goods during the two-year period ending on 21 March 2007. He is entitled to withdraw all or part of this claim if:

(a) the goods have not been used since they were purchased, acquired or imported;

(b) the person intends, or expects, that the goods will be used for private or non-business purposes during their economic life;

(c) if only part of the claim is withdrawn, that part relates to his intended use of the goods for private or non-business purposes; and

(d) the claim is withdrawn before 1 February 2008.

The claim is treated as if it had been made in error. It is therefore withdrawn in accordance with reg 35. This does not give rise to any liability to penalties or interest.

PART XVI IMPORTATIONS, EXPORTATIONS AND REMOVALS

Interpretation of Part XVI

117. Various words and phrases are defined.

Enactments excepted

118. Alcoholic Liquor Duties Act 1979 ss 7 to 10, 22 (4), 42 and 43, Hydrocarbon Oil Duties Act 1979 ss 9 and 15 to 20AA, CEMA 1979 ss 43 (5), 125 (1), (2), 126, 127 (1) (*b*), Customs and Excise Duties (General Reliefs) Act 1979 (other than ss 8, 9 (*b*) and, by virtue of their subject matter ss 7, 13–13C), Isle of Man Act 1979 ss 8, 9, the Tobacco Products Duty Act 1979 s 2 (2) and FA 1999 ss 126, 127 do not apply for the purposes of the charge to VAT on imported goods.

Regulations excepted

119. Excise Warehousing (etc) Regulations 1988, SI 1988/809 regs 16 (4), (5) and 19 (1) (*b*) and Air Passenger Duty and Other Indirect Taxes (Interest Rate) Regulations 1998, SI 1998/1471 (in so far as it relates to customs duty payable to or by the Commissioners) do not apply for the purposes of the charge to VAT on imported goods.

Community legislation excepted

120. The following EU regulations (or the provisions stated) do not apply for the purposes of the charge to VAT on imported goods:

- Regulation (EEC) No 918/83 and implementing regulations made thereunder;
- Regulation (EEC) No 2658/87 (except Annex I, Section II, para A (2));
- Regulation (EEC) No 2913/92 arts 126–128, 137 (insofar as it relates to partial relief), 142, 145–160, 229 (*b*), 232(1)(*b*), (2), (3), and 241 (second and third sentences));
- Regulation (EEC) No 2454/93 arts 496–523 (to the extent applicable to outward processing and the drawback system of inward processing relief), 519 (compensatory interest), 536–544 (to the extent applicable to the drawback system of inward processing relief), 550 (to the extent applicable to the drawback system of inward processing relief), 585–592 (outward processing).

Adaptations

121. Regulations under CEMA 1979 s 125(3) may supplement VATA 1994 s 21 in relation to the valuation of imported goods for VAT purposes. Import VAT repaid in error is recoverable under FA 1999 s 129.

121A. Customs Duties (Deferred Payment) Regulations, SI 1976/1223 regs 4(1), (2), (3) and 8(*a*) are adapted in relation to any VAT chargeable on the importation of goods from third countries.

121B. Regulation (EEC) No 2913/92 arts 218(1) and 225 are adapted in relation to any VAT chargeable on the importation of goods from third countries.

121C. Regulation (EEC) No 2454/93 arts 244, 248(1), 257(3), 257(4), 258, 262(1) and 876a(1) are adapted in relation to any VAT chargeable on the importation of goods from third countries.

Adaptations and exceptions for the application of returned goods relief

121D. From 6 April 2006, the reliefs for certain reimported goods (see regs 124 (revoked), 125 (revoked)) are replaced by the relief for returned goods arising under Regulation (EEC) No 2913/92 arts 185–197 as implemented by Regulation (EEC) No 2454/93 arts 844–856 and 882 (see Part 1B), which cease to be disapplied for the purposes of the charge to VAT on imported goods (see reg 120(2)(*a*)(v) and (*b*)(iv) (revoked)). The texts of arts 3, 4 and 185–187 of the 1992 Regulation and arts 844, 848, 849 of the 1993 Regulation are adapted for this purpose.

Postal Importations by registered taxable persons in the course of business

122. Goods imported by post (other than by datapost packet) which do not exceed £2,000 in value, and are imported by a registered taxable person in the course of his business, may be delivered without payment of VAT provided that security for VAT has been given to the Commissioners and the VAT registration number is shown on the customs declaration accompanying the package. VAT is accounted for on the VAT return for the prescribed accounting period in which the goods were imported. For accounting, see reg 40 (*a*).

Temporary importations

123. VAT chargeable on goods imported from a third country is not payable if: (1) a taxable person makes a supply of goods which is to be zero-rated under regs 127–135; (2) the goods so imported are the subject of that supply; and (3) the Commissioners are satisfied the importer intends to remove the goods to another EU member state and is importing the goods in the course of such a zero-rated supply. The Commissioners may impose conditions and require the deposit of security. Relief continues to apply if the importer removes the goods to another EU member state within one month (or later if the Commissioners so allow) and makes the zero-rated supply.

Reimportation of certain goods by non-taxable persons

124. [Revoked.]

Reimportation of certain goods by taxable persons

125. [Revoked.]

Reimportation of goods exported for treatment or process

126. The VAT chargeable on reimportation of temporarily exported goods which were sent to a third country for repair, process, adaptation, making up or reworking is payable as if that work had been done in the UK provided that the Commissioners are satisfied that at the time of exportation the goods were intended to be reimported and ownership remained unchanged while the goods were in a third country.

Supplies to export houses

127. [Revoked.]

Export of freight containers

128. Supplying a freight container (as defined in reg 117 (2)) which is to be exported to a third country is, subject to conditions imposed by the Commissioners, zero-rated. For conditions, see Notice No 703/1.

Supplies to overseas persons

129. A supply of goods is zero-rated if the Commissioners are satisfied that: (1) they have been supplied to a non-resident, overseas trader or overseas authority (as defined in reg 117 (7)) who is not a taxable person; and (2) they were intended for export to a third country and have been so exported. The Commissioners may impose conditions. For conditions, see Notice Nos 703, 703/2. *Henry Moss of London Ltd v C & E Comrs* [1981] STC 139, CA; *Rayburn Trading Co Ltd* (No 2901); *Christopher Gibbs Ltd v C & E Comrs* [1992] VATTR 376. For goods sold to army units being posted abroad, see *Kingdom Sportswear Ltd v C & E Comrs* [1991] VATTR 55.

Supplies to persons departing from the member states

130. [Revoked.]

131. When the Commissioners are satisfied that goods (as defined in reg 117 (4)) have been supplied to a person who is an overseas visitor (as defined in reg 117 (7A)) and who, at the time of supply, intends to leave the EU within three months with the goods then, subject to conditions the Commissioners may impose and production of the goods to an officer in the EU member state from which the goods are finally exported to a third country, the supply is zero-rated. For conditions, see Notice Nos 704, 704/1. For forged proofs of export provided by customers, see *Netto Supermarkt GmbH & Co OHG v Finanzamt Malchin* (case C-271/06) [2008] ECR I–771, [2008] STC 3280, ECJ.

132. The Commissioners may allow an overseas visitor (as defined in reg 117 (8)), who intends to leave the EU within 15 months and stay away for at least six months, to purchase a motor vehicle for exportation from a manufacturer within 12 months of his departure free of VAT subject to such conditions as the Commissioners may impose. For conditions, see Notice Nos 705, 705A.

133. The Commissioners may allow any person, who intends to leave the EC within nine months and stay away for at least six months, to purchase a motor vehicle for exportation from a manufacturer within six months of his departure free of VAT subject to such conditions as the Commissioners may impose. For conditions, see Notice Nos 705, 705A.

Supplies to persons taxable in another member state

134. A supply of goods is zero-rated if the Commissioners are satisfied that: (1) the supply involves removing the goods from the UK; (2) the customer is a taxable person in another EU member state; (3) the goods are removed to another EU member state; and (4) VAT has not been charged under the secondhand goods scheme (see VATA 1994 s 50A). For "taxable person" in head (2), see *JP Commodities Ltd v R & C Comrs* [2008] STC 816. The Commissioners may impose conditions. For conditions, see Notice Nos 703, 703/1, 725; *C & E Comrs v Musashi Autoparts Europe Ltd (formerly TAP Manufacturing Ltd)* [2004] STC 220, CA (charge to interest when evidence of removal obtained out of time); *JP Commodities Ltd v R & C Comrs* [2008] STC 816 (validity of condition requiring the customer's VAT registration number to be shown on the supplier's sales invoice); *N2J Ltd v R & C Comrs* [2009] STC 2193; *Centrax Ltd v C & E Comrs* [1998] V & DR 369. In the Court of Justice, see *R (on the application of Teleos plc and others) v Customs and Excise Comrs* (case C-409/04) [2007] ECR I–7797, [2008] STC 706, ECJ (false consignment note provided by purchaser); *Albert Collée v Finanzamt Limburg an der Lahn* (case C-146/05) [2007] ECR I–7861, [2008] STC 757, ECJ (evidence of supply not produced in good time); *Twoh International BV v Staatssecretaris van Financiën* (Case C-184/05) [2007] ECR I–7897, [2008] STC 740, ECJ (member state not required to request information from tax authorities of destination member state alleged by supplier). For supplies where the customer's VAT registration is unavailable at the time of invoicing, see Business Brief 5/93, 3 February 1993.

Supplies of goods subject to excise duty to persons who are not taxable in another member state

135. A supply of goods subject to excise duty is zero-rated if: (1) the supply involves removing the goods from the UK to another EU member state; (2) the customer is not a taxable person in another EU member state; (3) the supply is not treated as made outside the UK by virtue of VATA 1994 s 7 (5), ie the supplier is not liable to account for output tax on the supply under the law of another EU member state in which he is a taxable person; (4) the goods have been removed to another EU member state in accordance with Excise Goods (Holding, Movement, Warehousing and REDS) Regulations 1992, SI 1992/3135 (now revoked and replaced by Excise Goods (Holding, Movement and Duty Point) Regulations 2010, SI 2010/593); and (5) VAT has not been charged under the second-hand goods scheme (see VATA 1994 s 50A). The Commissioners may impose conditions. For conditions, see Notice No 703.

Territories to be treated as excluded from or included in the territory of the Community and of the member states

136. The following territories do not form part of the territory of the EU for VAT purposes: (1) the Channel Islands; (2) Andorra; (3) San Marino; and (4) the Åland Islands.

137. The following territories do not form part of the territory of the EU for VAT purposes: (1) the Canary Islands; (2) the French overseas departments (ie Guadeloupe, Martinique,

Reunion, St Pierre and Miguelon, and French Guiana); and (3) Mount Athos. These territories do not form part of the territory of Spain, France and Greece respectively for the same purposes.

138. Transitional provisions are prescribed in relation to the accession of:

- Austria, Finland and Sweden (which became EU member states on 1 January 1995).
- The Czech Republic, Estonia, Cyprus, Latvia, Lithuania, Hungary, Malta, Poland, Slovenia and Slovakia (which became EU member states on 1 May 2004).
- Bulgaria and Romania (which became EU member states on 1 January 2007).

These countries are not treated as EU member states for specified purposes.

139. Monaco, the Isle of Man and (from 1 May 2004) the UK Sovereign Base Areas of Akrotiri and Dhekelia are treated as part of the territory of France, the UK and Cyprus respectively for VAT purposes. They are also treated as part of the territory of the EU for the same purposes.

Entry and exit formalities

140. Import and export formalities must be completed when goods are imported from, or exported to, the territories listed in regs 136 or 137. For formalities relating to goods entering EU customs territory, see Regulation (EEC) No 2913/92; Customs Controls on Importation of Goods Regulations 1991, SI 1991/2724. For formalities relating to goods exported to a place outside the EU customs territory, see Regulation (EEC) Nos 913/92 and 2454/93. For EU customs territory, see Regulation (EEC) No 2913/92 art 3.

Use of the internal Community transit procedure

141. The internal EU transit procedure applies if goods entering the UK from a territory in regs 136 or 137 are intended to be removed to: (1) an EU member state; or (2) a third country via another EU member state. For the internal transit procedure, see Regulation (EEC) Nos 2913/92 and 2454/93.

Customs and excise legislation to be applied

142. Goods imported from the territories listed in regs 136 or 137 are charged to VAT on importation under the same UK and EU legislation applicable to goods imported from third countries. For the legislation concerned, see VATA 1994 s 16 (1); regs 118–121 above.

143. The powers conferred by CEMA 1979 ss 21, 26–29, 34, 78, 164 and other enactments prescribed by Treasury Order may be exercised for the purposes of the charge to VAT on goods imported from the Canary Islands, the French overseas departments and Mount Athos. The restrictions imposed by F(No 2)A 1992 s 4 do not apply for this purpose.

144. Regulation (EEC) Nos 2913/92 and 2454/93 (insofar as they relate to goods exported to third countries) apply for the purpose of ensuring that zero-rating is correctly applied to goods exported to the territories listed in regs 136 or 137.

145. CEMA 1979 and statutory instruments made thereunder apply for the purpose of ensuring that zero-rating is correctly applied to goods exported to the territories listed in regs 136 or 137.

The powers conferred by CEMA 1979 ss 21, 26–29, 34, 78, 164 and other enactments prescribed by Treasury Order may be exercised in relation to goods despatched or transported to the Canary Islands, the French overseas departments and Mount Athos. The restrictions imposed by F(No 2)A 1992 s 4 do not apply for this purpose.

PART XVI(A) FISCAL AND OTHER WAREHOUSING REGIMES

Interpretation of Part XVI(A)

145A. Various words and phrases are defined.

Fiscal warehousing certificates

145B. The information to be shown on a certificate issued under VATA 1994 s 18B (1) (*d*) or (2)(*d*) is set out in Sch 1 Form No 17. As regards the former provision, an acquirer who is not a taxable person must keep the certificate for six years and produce it to a proper officer on request.

Certificates connected with services in fiscal or other warehousing regimes

145C. The information to be shown on a certificate issued under VATA 1994 s 18C (1) (*c*) is set out in Sch 1 Form No 18.

VAT invoices relating to services performed in fiscal or other warehousing regimes

145D. An invoice (referred to as a "VAT invoice") issued under VATA 1994 s 18C (1) (*e*) must state:

(a) an identifying number;
(b) the material time (as defined in reg 145A (1)) of the supply of services;
(c) the date when the invoice is issued;
(d) the supplier's name, address and registration number (as defined in reg 2 (1));
(e) the recipient's name and address;
(f) a description of the services which is sufficient to identify their nature;
(g) the extent of the services and VAT-exclusive amount payable expressed in sterling;
(h) the rate of any cash discount offered;
(i) the rate of VAT expressed as zero%; and
(j) a declaration that the conditions in VATA 1994 s 18C (1) (*a*)–(*e*) have been met.

The Commissioners may relax or waive these requirements. The invoice must be issued within 30 days of the material time of the supply. However, the Commissioners may extend this period by a general or special direction.

Fiscal warehousing regimes

145E. A fiscal warehousekeeper must make an entry in his fiscal warehousing record (see reg 145F) when eligible goods (as defined in reg 145A) enter his fiscal warehouse.

Eligible goods allocated to a fiscal warehousing regime in the fiscal warehousing record remain within that regime until they are recorded as having been transferred (see reg 145H (2)) or they are removed from the regime (see reg 145H (1)).

The fiscal warehousing record and stock control

145F. A fiscal warehousekeeper must keep a fiscal warehousing record. It may be maintained in any manner acceptable to the Commissioners. It must have the features set out in Sch 1A and comply with the requirements set out therein.

Events following a transfer or removal from a fiscal warehousing regime or (in the case of goods unallocated to the regime) a removal from the fiscal warehouse do not need to be recorded if they take place more than six years after the transfer or removal concerned.

If so requested by a proper officer, a fiscal warehousekeeper must:

(a) produce his fiscal warehouse record and allow it to be inspected or copied; and
(b) allow goods stored or deposited in his fiscal warehouse to be inspected.

Fiscal warehousing transfers in the United Kingdom

145G. Eligible goods (as defined in reg 145A) may be transferred from one fiscal warehousing regime ("X") to another ("Y") if the fiscal warehousekeeper of Y gives a written undertaking to the fiscal warehousekeeper of X that:

(a) he will record the entry in his warehousekeeping record;
(b) he will allocate the goods to his fiscal warehousing regime;
(c) he will deliver a certificate to the fiscal warehousekeeper of X within 30 days confirming that conditions (*a*) and (*b*) have been met; and

(d) he will retain a copy of the certificate in (*c*) as part of his fiscal warehousing record.

The fiscal warehousekeeper of Y must fulfil his undertaking. The transfer is not treated as a removal from X.

Removal of goods from a fiscal warehousing regime and transfers overseas

145H. Eligible goods (as defined in reg 145A (1)) are removed from a fiscal warehousing regime if:

(a) the time and date of removal is recorded in the fiscal warehousing record;
(b) the goods are moved outside the fiscal warehouse without being transferred in accordance with reg 145G; or
(c) the goods are sold by retail.

The person who causes the removal or movement, or who makes the retail sale, is referred to as "the person who removes or causes the removal of the relevant goods" so as to be liable for payment of VAT under reg 145J.

The following are treated as a transfer rather than a removal of goods. The conditions stated must be met.

	Circumstance	*Condition*
1.	Transfer of goods from one fiscal warehousing regime to another in accordance with reg 145G (1)	The fiscal warehousekeeper must receive a certificate (see reg 145G (3) (*c*)) within 30 days
2.	Transfer of goods to a regime which, under the law of another EU member state, corresponds to a fiscal warehousing regime	The fiscal warehousekeeper must receive a document evidencing completion of the transfer within 60 days
3.	Goods exported to a third country	The fiscal warehousekeeper must receive a document evidencing the export within 60 days
4.	Goods temporarily removed from the fiscal warehouse for repair, processing, treatment or other operations	The Commissioners' prior agreement must be obtained. Any conditions imposed by the Commissioners must be complied with

A fiscal warehousekeeper must make an adjusting entry in his fiscal warehousing record if he does not receive the required document within the period stated. The relevant goods are recorded as having been removed at the time when they left. The person removing the goods is identified as the person who gave the instructions leading to the removal. That person's name, address and registration number (as defined in reg 2 (1)) must be recorded and he must be informed that the document was not received in time.

145I. Eligible goods (as defined in reg 145A (1)) may be removed from a fiscal warehousing regime if, but only if, either:

(a) the Commissioners issue a removal document (see reg 145J (1)); or
(b) a registered person gives a written undertaking to account for any VAT payable on his VAT return (see reg 40 (1) (*c*)).

A fiscal warehousekeeper is jointly and severally liable for any VAT due if he fails to obtain a copy of the removal document or receive the written undertaking.

Payment on removal of goods from a fiscal warehousing regime

145J. VAT may be payable when eligible goods (as defined in reg 145A (1)) are removed from a fiscal warehousing regime. The Commissioners may accept payment from (or on behalf of) the person seeking to remove (or cause the removal) of the goods. They may issue a removal document to that person.

The Commissioners may refuse to issue a removal document until they are satisfied on the following matters:

(a) the value of the supply, the material time of supply (as defined in reg 145A (1)) and the registration status of the person who made the supply;

(b) the nature and quantity of the goods;

(c) the value of any relevant self-supply of specified services (see VATA 1994 s 18C); and

(d) the nature and material time of supply of the specified services giving rise to the self-supply in (*c*).

Payment on removal of goods from a fiscal warehousing regime

145K. A supply of warehoused goods is excluded from relief under VATA 1994 s 18(1) if:

- the supplier is a taxable person (or would be but for the fact that his supplies are treated as being made outside the UK by virtue of VATA 1994 s 18(1));
- all or part of his business consists of supplying goods to customers who are retailers, wholesalers who supply goods to retailers, or both;
- the supply is either a retail supply or a supply to a retailer; and
- the customer is not a taxable person.

PART XVII NEW MEANS OF TRANSPORT

Interpretation of Part XVII

146. Various words and phrases are defined.

First entry into service of a means of transport

147. For the purposes of VATA 1994 s 95 (3), a ship or aircraft first enters into service when it is either: (1) delivered or made available to its first purchaser or owner (whichever is earlier); or (2) taken into use for demonstration purposes by its manufacturer.

A motorised land vehicle first enters into service when: (1) it is first registered or liable to registration for road use in the EU member state where it was manufactured (whichever is earlier); (2) it is delivered or made available to its first purchaser or removed by its owner or first purchaser (whichever is earliest) (if not liable to registration for road use in the EU member state where it was manufactured); or (3) it is first taken into use for demonstration purposes by its manufacturer.

A means of transport is treated as having first entered into service when an invoice for its first supply is issued if the foregoing times cannot be established to the Commissioners' satisfaction.

Notification of acquisition of new means of transport by non-taxable persons and payment of VAT

148. A non-taxable person must notify the Commissioners if his acquisition of a new means of transport (defined in VATA 1994 s 95) is chargeable to VAT (see VATA 1994 s 10 (1)). Notification must be given within seven days of the later of: (1) the time of acquisition (see VATA 1994 s 12); and (2) the time when the goods arrive in the UK.

A notification must contain specified particulars. It must be made in writing in the English language. It is made by sending form VAT 415 to the designated office. For the designated office, see Notice No 728 (September 2008) para 3.2. VAT must be paid at the time of notification or within 30 days of receiving a written demand.

Refunds in relation to new means of transport

149. A claim for refund of VAT under VATA 1994 s 40 must be made in writing between 14 days and one month *before* the supply giving rise to the claim takes place.

150. Claims are made at an office designated by the Commissioners. For the designated office, see Notice No 728 (September 2008) para 3.2.

151. The information to be shown on a claim is specified.

152. The documents to be sent with a claim are specified.

153. The claimant or his agent must sign a declaration that the information set out in the claim and accompanying documents is true and complete.

154. The following documents must be submitted when the supply giving rise to the claim has been made: (1) a sales invoice or similar document identifying the new means of transport and showing the sale price; and (2) evidence that the new means of transport has been removed to another EU member state.

Supplies of new means of transport to persons departing to another member state

155. The Commissioners may permit a person to purchase a new means of transport (defined in VATA 1994 s 95) without payment of VAT if: (1) he is not a taxable person in another EU member state; (2) he intends to purchase a new means of transport in the UK and remove it to another EU member state within two months of the date of supply; and (3) he makes an application. The supply is zero-rated subject to conditions imposed by the Commissioners. For conditions, see Notice No 728.

PART XVIII BAD DEBT RELIEF (THE OLD SCHEME)

156–164. [Revoked.]

PART XIX BAD DEBT RELIEF (THE NEW SCHEME)

Interpretation of Part XIX

165. Words and phrases used in the regulations are defined.

Time within which a claim must be made

165A. A claim must be made within four years and six months of the later of: (1) the date when the consideration became payable; and (2) the date of the supply. The entitlement to a refund ceases if: (1) no claim is made within this period; or (2) the period ends before 1 October 2005. However, no time limit applies if the date from which the period runs falls before 1 May 1997.

The making of a claim to the Commissioners

166. A claim is made by including the correct amount of the refund in Box 4 of the claimant's VAT return for the prescribed accounting period in which the entitlement arose or, if the claim is still in time (see reg 165A), in any later return. The Commissioners may allow or direct otherwise. If the claimant is no longer required to make tax returns, a claim is made in the form and manner directed by the Commissioners.

Notice to purchaser of claim

166A. As regards supplies made before 1 January 2003, the claimant must give a written notice to any purchaser who is a taxable person. He must do so during the seven days following the day on which he made the claim. The information to be recorded is specified. For the action taken by the purchaser, see regs 172D, 172E.

Evidence required of the claimant in support of the claim

167. Before making a claim in respect of a supply, the claimant must hold: (1) a copy of any VAT invoice provided or, if there was no obligation to provide a tax invoice, a document showing the time, nature, purchaser and consideration; (2) written proof that output tax on the supply has been accounted for and paid; and (3) an entry in the Refunds for Bad Debts Account. The Commissioners may allow otherwise.

Records required to be kept by the claimant

168. The claimant must keep a single account known as the "Refunds for Bad Debts Account" which records the following information in respect of each claim made:

(a) the following information in respect of each supply:
   (i) the VAT chargeable,
   (ii) the period in which the VAT chargeable was accounted for and paid,
   (iii) the date and number of the invoice or (if none) alternative identifying details,
   (iv) any payment received in respect of the supply;
(b) the outstanding amount to which the claim relates;
(c) the amount of the claim;
(d) the prescribed accounting period in which the claim was made; and
(e) a copy of the notice required to be given to each purchaser (see reg 166A).

Preservation of documents and records and duty to produce

169. The documents, invoices and records required to be held must be retained until the fourth anniversary of the claim unless the Commissioners allow otherwise. The claimant must produce these items for inspection on demand and allow them to be removed.

Attribution of payments

170. A payment received in respect of two or more supplies is attributed to those supplies in chronological order. This method of attribution overrides any contractual basis agreed by the parties: see *Abbey National plc v C & E Comrs* [2006] STC 1. However, any payment allocated to a particular supply by the purchaser at the time of payment is attributed to that supply if the consideration for that supply is paid in full.

If all or part of a payment is attributable to two or more supplies made on the same date, the payment is attributed in ratio to the outstanding consideration for each supply.

For the attribution of payments under a hire purchase or conditional sale agreement, see reg 170A. For proceeds from the sale of repossessed goods, see Notice No 700/18.

Attribution of payments received under certain credit agreements

170A. A supply made under a hire purchase, conditional sale or credit sale agreement may comprise both a supply of goods and a supply of credit. If so, payments made under the agreement are attributed to each supply in accordance with one or other of two rules ("Rule 1" and "Rule 2") as follows:

Time when the supply of goods was made	*Rule used*
Before 1 September 2006	Rule 1
1 September 2006–31 August 2007 inclusive	Rule 1 or Rule 2
After 31 August 2007	Rule 2

Under Rule 1, the proportion of a payment attributed to interest is calculated by the following formula and the balance is attributed to goods:

$$\frac{\text{Interest due under the agreement}}{\text{Total amount payable under the agreement} - \text{the amount on which no interest is charged}}$$

Rule 2 falls into two parts:

First, as regards payments made on or before termination of the agreement, the proportion of a payment attributed to interest is calculated by the following formula and the balance is attributed to goods:

$$\frac{A-(B+C)}{(A+D)-(B+C+E+F+G)} \times \text{payment}$$

Where:

A = total interest due under the agreement.

B = any rebate of interest granted at termination.

C = any interest attributable to any unpaid instalments prior to the termination.

D = total amount due for the goods under the agreement.

E = the amount (if any) by which the amount in D is reduced as a consequence of the termination.

F = the amount included in D on which interest is not charged.

G = any part of the amount in D which is unpaid at the time of termination.

Second, the proportion of a payment made following termination is apportioned between goods and credit according to the proportion of the balances due at the time the payment is made.

Revenue and Customs Brief 14/07, 13 February 2007 explains Rule 2 in the following terms:

> "Previously, the legislation used a 'straight-line' methodology. The new legislation will, for the first time, reflect commercial practice. Thus, for suppliers, the numbers you feed into the calculation will be based upon whatever commercial method you use, for example an actuarial method or the 'Rule of 78'. The ultimate purpose of the calculation is to arrive at the amount outstanding in respect of the goods element, which is used for calculating the amount of bad debt relief. The new method will result in a figure which accurately reflects the commercial basis of apportionment adopted by suppliers."

If the agreement provides for a variable rate of interest, any variation made while the agreement is in force is disregarded for the purposes of attribution.

Repayment of a refund

171. All or part of a refund must be repaid to the Commissioners if a payment is subsequently received or attributed to a taxable supply on which the claim was based. The amount repaid is:

$$\frac{A}{B} \times \text{amount (or balance) of the refund}$$

Where:

A = the amount received or attributed.

B = the amount of the outstanding consideration or an amount equal to the negative entry made in the VAT allowable portion of the trader's VAT account.

Writing off debts

172. All or part of the consideration for a supply may be written off as a bad debt six months after the due date for payment. This is done by making an entry in the Refunds for Bad Debts Account (see reg 168).

The consideration written off is reduced by: (1) any amount owed to the purchaser which can be set-off; and (2) the value of any enforceable mortgage, charge, lien or other security held in relation to the purchaser.

Writing off debts—margin schemes

172A. The claimant may have exercised an option to charge VAT on the supply by reference to the profit margin (see VATA 1994 s 50A). Where this is so, the consideration written of in respect of the supply must not exceed:

(a) the profit margin, if:
  (i) no payment has been received in respect of the supply, or
  (ii) the payments received do not exceed the non-profit element; or
(b) the amount (if any) by which the consideration for the supply exceeds the payments received (if such payments exceed the non-profit element).

The "non-profit element" is consideration for the supply less the profit margin. For the "profit margin", see VATA 1994 s 50A(4).

Writing off debts—tour operators margin scheme

172B. The value of the supply may be determined in accordance with the tour operators margin scheme (see VATA 1994 s 53). Where this is so, the consideration written off in respect of the supply must not exceed:

(a) the profit margin, if:
  (i) no payment has been received in respect of the supply, or
  (ii) the payments received do not exceed the non-profit element; or
(b) the amount (if any) by which the consideration for the supply exceeds the payments received (if such payments exceed the non-profit element).

The terms "profit element" and "non-profit element" are defined.

PART XIXA REPAYMENT OF INPUT TAX WHERE CLAIM MADE UNDER PART XIX

Application

172ZC. Part XIXA applies to supplies made before 1 January 2003.

Interpretation of Part XIXA

172C. Part XIXA is interpreted in accordance with Part XIX. For definitions, see in particular reg 165.

Repayment of input tax

172D. The purchaser must make a negative entry in the VAT allowable portion of his VAT Account (see reg 32) if he has deducted all or part of the VAT charged to him on a supply and the supplier has claimed bad debt relief on the outstanding consideration. In practice, he will do so on receipt of a notice given by the supplier (see reg 166A). He does not make any adjustment under regs 34 or 35.

The negative entry is made for the prescribed accounting period in which the supplier made the claim. The amount of the entry is calculated by the following formula:

$$\frac{\text{Refund claimed by the supplier}}{\text{VAT chargeable on the supply}} \times \text{input tax deducted by the purchaser}$$

Restoration of an entitlement to credit for input tax

172E. The purchaser must make a positive entry in the VAT allowable portion of his VAT Account if:

(a) he has made an input tax repayment in accordance with reg 172D;
(b) he has made the return for the prescribed accounting period concerned and paid any VAT due from him for that period; and
(c) the supplier has repaid all or part of the bad debt relief claimed in respect of the supply in accordance with reg 171.

He does not make any adjustment under regs 34 or 35. The positive entry is made for the prescribed accounting period in which the supplier made the repayment. The amount of the entry is calculated by the following formula:

$$\frac{\text{Repayment made by the supplier}}{\text{Bad debt relief claimed by the supplier}} \times \text{input tax repayment made by the purchaser}$$

PART XIXB REPAYMENT OF INPUT TAX WHERE CONSIDERATION NOT PAID

Application

172F. Part XIXB applies to input tax credits claimed after 31 December 2002.

Interpretation

172G. The term "relevant period" is defined.

Repayment of input tax

172H. A person is required to make a negative entry in the VAT allowable portion of his VAT Account if he has claimed input tax deduction in respect of a supply made to him and all or part of the consideration for that supply is unpaid six months after the later of: (1) the date of supply; and (2) the date on which the consideration (or the unpaid part of it) became payable. The amount of the entry is:

$$\frac{\text{the unpaid amount of the consideration}}{\text{the total consideration for the supply}} \times \text{the amount of the deduction}$$

This entry does not give rise to an understatement, overstatement or error for the purposes of regs 34 or 35. No entry is made if the person uses the cash accounting scheme (as to which see regs 56–65).

Restoration of an entitlement to credit for input tax

172I. A clawback of input tax under reg 172H ("£x") is wholly or partly restored by way of a positive entry in the VAT allowable portion of a person's VAT Account if an amount ("£y") is subsequently paid to clear all or part of the unpaid consideration for the supply ("£z"). The amount of the entry is:

$$\frac{\pounds y}{\pounds z} \times \pounds x$$

This entry does not give rise to an understatement, overstatement or error for the purposes of regs 34 or 35.

Attribution of payments

172J. The attribution rules in regs 170 and 170A(5) are used to determine whether a payment relates to the consideration of any particular supply.

PART XIXC ADJUSTMENT OF OUTPUT TAX IN RESPECT OF SUPPLIES TO WHICH SECTION 55A(6) OF THE ACT APPLIES

172K. This Part sets out the mechanism for making adjustments under VATA 1994 s 26AB(2) in relation to supplies for which the customer is liable to account for and pay VAT on the supplier's behalf in accordance with VATA 1994 s 55A(6) ("reverse charge supplies").

Adjustment of output tax

172L. An adjustment under VATA 1994 s 26AB(2) is made by way of a negative entry in the VAT payable portion of the part of the trader's VAT account relating to the prescribed period in which he was required to make a negative entry in the VAT allowable portion in accordance with reg 172H(1), (2). The amount of the former entry is equal to the amount of the latter entry.

Readjustment of output tax

172M. Having made a negative entry in the VAT payable portion of his VAT account under reg 172L in relation to a reverse charge supply, a taxable person may subsequently make a positive entry in the VAT payable portion under reg 172I in respect of the same supply. If so, he must make a positive entry of the same amount in the VAT payable portion under this provision in respect of the same prescribed accounting period.

172N. The situations in regs 172L and 172M do not give rise to any adjustments under reg 34 or 35 (correction of errors).

PART XX REPAYMENTS TO COMMUNITY TRADERS

Interpretation of Part XX

173. Various words and phrases are defined.

Repayments of VAT

173A. The Commissioners are required to repay the VAT specified in reg 173B if:

- the VAT is incurred in the repayment period (see reg 173G) covered by a repayment application (see reg 173L);
- the claimant (see reg 173(1)) is a person to whom this Part applies (see reg 173E);
- the claimant makes a claim for repayment of the VAT in accordance with this Part; and
- the Commissioners are satisfied that the claimant is entitled to the repayment.

The repayment is made in accordance with this Part.

A trader may omit part of the VAT incurred in a repayment period from his repayment application. If so, the relevant amount can be included in a repayment application in respect of a later repayment period falling within the same repayment year (as defined in reg 173(1)).

173B. In principle, a repayment application may be made in respect of:

(a) the VAT charged on goods imported from a third country by the claimant. It is a condition that the VAT is ineligible for relief under some other provision; and

(b) the VAT charged on goods or services supplied to the claimant in the UK. It is a condition that the VAT would have been input tax if the claimant were a taxable person.

VAT charged on the following supplies and importations must be excluded from the repayment application:

- goods which the claimant has removed or intends to remove to another member state;
- goods which the claimant has exported or intends to export to a third country;
- goods or services which the claimant has used or intends to use for the purpose of any supply made by him in the UK. This does not apply if the supply is of a description in reg 173E(b)(i), (ii) or (iii);
- goods or services which, if made by a taxable person, would be excluded from credit under VATA 1994 s 25; and
- (if the claimant is a travel agent (as defined in reg 173B(3)) goods or services which are for the direct benefit of a traveller. This does not apply if the traveller is the travel agent or one of his employees.

173C. The amount of VAT incurred on goods and services in respect of which a repayment application may be made (see reg 173B) is restricted to the deductible proportion. This is the proportion of VAT which the claimant would be entitled to deduct if the VAT were chargeable in the claimant's member state. This proportion is determined in accordance with Directive 2006/112/EC arts 173, 174 and 175. For the commentary on these provisions, see Part 1B.

173D. The deductible proportion of VAT (see reg 173C) included in a repayment application may have been determined on a provisional basis in accordance with Directive 2006/112/EC art 175(2). If so, it is necessary to recalculate the deductible proportion by reference to the final proportion determined in accordance with Directive 2006/112/EC art 175(3). The difference between the two amounts is claimed (if the recalculated amount exceeds the amount originally claimed) or repaid (in the reverse situation).

A claim in relation to (say) 2010 is made by including the relevant amount in a repayment application made in the following repayment year (ie 2011). A repayment is made by either: (1) adjusting the amount claimed in a repayment application made in 2011; or (2) (if no repayment application is made in 2011) submitting a declaration. The declaration must be submitted via the electronic portal set up by the claimant's member state. This must be done before the end of 2011.

Persons to whom this Part applies

173E. In principle, a person is entitled to a repayment of VAT in accordance with Part XX if he meets the following conditions throughout a repayment period (see reg 173G): (1) he is established in another member state (see reg 173(2), (3)); and (2) he carries on business in another member state.

However, the person is not entitled to a repayment in respect of a repayment period if he meets any of the following criteria at any time during the period:

(a) he is established in the UK;

(b) (if he supplies goods or services in the UK) the goods or services comprise something other than: (1) specified freight transport services and/or services ancillary thereto; and (2) goods or services in respect of which the recipient is required to account for any pay the VAT chargeable in accordance with VATA 1994 ss 8 (services received from abroad), 9A (gas and electricity); or 14 (acquisitions of goods);

(c) (if he makes, or intends to make, any transactions in the member state in which he is established) he is entitled to deduct input tax in that member state in accordance with national legislation giving effect to Directive 2006/112/EC arts 168 or 169;

(d) (if he is a small enterprise) he makes or intends to make supplies which are exempt from VAT in accordance with national legislation giving effect to Directive 2006/112/EC arts 284–287; or

(e) (if he is a farmer) he makes or intends to make supplies covered by the flat-rate scheme for farmers in accordance with national legislation giving effect to Directive 2006/112/EC arts 954–305.

Time when VAT is incurred

173F. The time when input tax is incurred for the purposes of making a claim under Part XX (regs 173–184), is determined as follows:

Circumstances	*Time when incurred*
Importation of goods	Time when the VAT becomes chargeable
Supply of goods or services:	
• Time of supply at or before the time when the VAT invoice relating to it is issued	Time when the VAT invoice is issued

• Time of supply after the time when the VAT invoice relating to it is issued	Time when the supply is treated as made

Repayment period

173G. A repayment claim must be made in respect of one of the following periods:
- (a) a calendar year;
- (b) a period of three or more consecutive months falling wholly within the same calendar year; or
- (c) (if the period commences after 30 September) the period ending on the following 31 December.

Minimum total claim for a repayment period

173H. The repayment claimed must exceed £35 (repayment period comprising a calendar year), £395 (period of three or more consecutive months) or £35 (repayment period ending on 31 December).

Minimum total claim for a repayment period

173I. A repayment is claimed by way of a repayment application (see reg 173L–173O). The application must be completed in English, addressed to the UK and contain the information specified in reg 173L, 173M. It must be submitted via the electronic portal set up by the claimant's member state. For the time limit for doing so, see reg 173P(1).

173J. A claim may be made in respect of a supply or importation having a value of £200 or more (fuel) or £750 or more (other goods or services). If so, a copy of the relevant documentary evidence must be submitted at the same time, and in the same manner, as the claim. For the manner in which a claim is submitted, see reg 173I(c). For the relevant documentary evidence, see reg 29(2).

173K. The values relevant to reg 173J are specified.

Contents of a repayment application

173L. The information to be provided in a repayment application is specified.

173M. The information to provided in respect of each importation or supply is specified.

173N. The fraction relevant to reg 173M(g) is defined.

173O. A repayment application must describe the nature of the goods or services to which a claim relates (see reg 173M(h)). The nature of the goods or services listed reg 173O(2)(a)–(i) is described by reference to the relevant harmonised numerical code number specified therein (ie one of codes 1–9). The nature of any other goods or services (reg 173O(j)) is described as follows:

- If the goods or services fall within one of the harmonised numerical codes contained in the annex to Regulation (EC) No 1174/2009 and specified in reg 173O(4), their nature is described by reference to the relevant harmonised numerical code.
- If not, the goods or services are described by reference to both "code 10" and an explicit description.

Day by which a claim under this Part must be made

173P. A repayment application in respect of all or part of the calendar year 2009 must be submitted before 1 April 2011. A repayment application in respect of all or part of a subsequent calendar year must be submitted by 1 October of the following calendar year. An application is submitted only if its submission is successfully recorded by the validation process of the electronic portal. The time of submission is the time so recorded. The Commissioners must notify this time to the claimant. For the electronic portal, see reg 173I(c).

Notification of entitlement to repayment

173Q. If the Commissioners are satisfied that the claimant is entitled to repayment of the VAT claimed, they must notify him accordingly. If not, the Commissioners must notify the claimant of their reasons for rejecting all or part of the claim. Notifications must be given before the end of the "relevant period", as to which see the commentary to reg 173S. Failure to notify the claimant is treated as a refusal to repay the relevant amount. For repayments, see reg 173V. For appeals against the Commissioners' refusal to make a repayment, see VATA 1994 s 83(1)(ha).

Requests for further information or a document

173R. The Commissioners may request the claimant, a third party or the competent authority of another member state to provide information or produce a document. For their powers to do so, see FA 2008 Sch 36 paras 1, 2 and Regulation (EC) No 1798/2003. Requests must be given before the end of the "relevant period", as to which see the commentary to reg 173S. More than one request may be made.

Relevant period applicable to any VAT for which repayment is claimed

173S. The "relevant period" for the purposes of regs 173Q and 173R is a period of four months commencing on the day on which the Commissioners received the refund application. For the extension of this period in relation to requests for information and documents, see regs 173R(6), 173T and 173U.

In principle, the "relevant period" for the purposes of reg 173Q is a period of four months commencing on the day on which the Commissioners received the refund application. However, the "relevant period" is determined in accordance with reg 173T if a request for information or documents has been made. For the "relevant period" where such requests have been made or received on different occasions, see reg 173U.

In principle, the "relevant period" for the purposes of reg 173R is a period of four months commencing on the day on which the Commissioners received the refund application. However, the "relevant period" is determined in accordance with reg 173T if a request for information or documents has been made. For the "relevant period" where such requests have been made or received on different occasions, see reg 173U.

Extension of the relevant period by virtue of the making of a request for information or a document

173T. The Commissioners may request information or the production of a document in accordance with reg 173R before the end of the "relevant period" defined in reg 173S. If so, the "relevant period" ends: (1) six months after the day when the Commissioners received the repayment application (if the information or documents were received before the end of this period); (2) eight months after the day when the Commissioners received the repayment application (if the information or documents were received more than six months but less than eight months before the end of this period); or (3) two months after the Commissioners received the information or document (in other circumstances).

The Commissioners may receive the information or document(s) more than one month after the day on which the recipient received the request, or not at all. If so, the foregoing rules apply as if the Commissioners had received the information or document(s) one month after the recipient received the request.

Extension of a relevant period where more than one request for information or a document is made in relation to the same VAT

173U. Requests for information or documents may be made by the Commissioners (or received by the recipients) on different days. If so, the end of the "relevant period" is determined in accordance with reg 173T as if all the requests comprised a single request made on the day when the latest request was made and received on the day when the last request to be received was actually received.

Time when a repayment of VAT must be made

173V. The VAT to which a claimant is entitled must be paid to him no later than ten business days (as defined in reg 173V(2)) after the end of the "relevant period", as to which see regs 173S–173U.

Interest on late payments

173W. The claimant is entitled to interest on late repayments. Interest runs from the latest date for payment specified in reg 173V to the day on which the Commissioners authorise the repayment. The rate of interest is the rate in force from time to time in accordance with VATA 1994 s 78.

The claimant may fail to provide information or produce documents within one month of receiving the notice requiring him to do so. If so, no interest is paid in respect of that part of the claim to which the information or documents relate. This applies whether or not the information is subsequently provided or the documents are subsequently produced.

The claimant may fail to provide the documents required to be submitted with his repayment application, or may provide them late. If so, no interest is paid in respect of the period of failure. For the relevant documents, see reg 173J.

173X. The claimant may be paid interest (see reg 173W) to which he is not entitled. If so, the interest is treated as interest arising under VATA 1994 s 78. For the recovery of interest under that provision, see VATA 1994 s 78A.

174. [Revoked.]

175. [Revoked.]

176. [Revoked.]

177. [Revoked.]

178. [Revoked.]

179. [Revoked.]

Deduction of bank charges

180. The Commissioners may deduct bank charges from the amount repayable.

Treatment of claim

181. The Commissioners may assess a claimant under VATA 1994 s 73 (1) if they consider that his claim is incomplete or incorrect.

182. [Revoked.]

Incorrect claims

183. [Revoked.]

184. Amounts paid as the result of an incorrect claim may be deducted from repayments due on future claims.

PART XXI REPAYMENTS TO THIRD COUNTRY TRADERS

Interpretation of Part XXI

185. Various words and phrases are defined.

A person is treated as being established in any country if he has a business establishment, permanent address or usual place of residence there.

A person is treated as being established in a country if he carries out business through a branch or agency in that country. The usual place of residence of a body corporate is the place where it is legally constituted.

For "brass plate" companies, see *Planzer Luxembourg Sàrl v Bundeszentralamt für Steuern* (case C-73/06) [2007] ECR I–5655, [2008] STC 1113, ECJ.

Repayments of VAT

186. A trader is entitled to repayment of VAT charged in UK as if he were a taxable person in the UK.

A trader using the special accounting scheme for electronic services is entitled to repayment of VAT charged on goods imported into the UK and goods or services purchased in the UK in connection with the qualifying supplies made by him. This applies whether the trader is registered in the UK (under VATA 1994 Sch 3B) or in another EU member state (under equivalent legislation): see VATA 1994 Sch 3B para 22(2). For the special accounting scheme, see Directive 2006/112/EC arts 357–369 and VATA 1994 Sch 3B.

VAT representatives

187. The Commissioners may require a trader to appoint a VAT representative to act on his behalf.

This does not apply to traders using the special accounting scheme for electronic services. This is so whether the trader is registered in the UK (under VATA 1994 Sch 3B) or in another EU member state (under equivalent legislation): see VATA 1994 Sch 3B para 22(5). For the special accounting scheme, see Directive 2006/112/EC arts 357–369 and VATA 1994 Sch 3B.

Persons to whom this Part applies

188. Three conditions apply. Firstly, there is a requirement that a reciprocal arrangement for refunds is available to UK traders in the country to which the claimant belongs. Secondly, the claimant must not be established in an EU member state. Thirdly, the claimant must not make any supplies in the UK other than freight transport, services to which the reverse charge provisions apply and goods for which the person supplied is liable to pay VAT on the supply. For the reverse charge, see VATA 1994 s 8.

The first and third conditions do not apply to traders using the special accounting scheme for electronic services. This is so whether the trader is registered in the UK (under VATA 1994 Sch 3B) or in another EU member state (under equivalent legislation): see VATA 1994 Sch 3B para 22(3), (4). For the special accounting scheme, see Directive 2006/112/EC arts 357–369 and VATA 1994 Sch 3B.

Supplies and importations to which this Part applies

189. Repayments are confined to supplies and importations made after 30 June 1994 which are intended for neither use of the applicant in the UK nor export from the UK.

VAT which will not be repaid

190. No repayment is made in respect of:

- goods and services to which VAT (Input Tax) Order 1992, SI 1992/3222 regs 4–7 apply;
- (if the claimant is a travel agent (as defined in reg 190(2)) goods and services for the direct benefit of a traveller who is neither the travel agent nor his employee; or
- goods and services used or to be used in making supplies of a description within VAT (Input Tax) (Specified Supplies) Order 1999, SI 1999/3121.

Insofar as this provision gives effect to Directive 86/560/EEC art 4(2), it does not apply to traders using the special accounting scheme for electronic services. This is so whether the trader is registered in the UK (under VATA 1994 Sch 3B) or in another EU member state (under equivalent legislation): see VATA 1994 Sch 3B para 22(7). For the special accounting scheme, see Directive 2006/112/EC arts 357–369 and VATA 1994 Sch 3B.

Method of claiming

191. A claim for repayment is made on form VAT 65A (or an equivalent form). It must be accompanied by: (1) a certificate of status on form VAT 66A (or an equivalent form) issued by the official authority (as defined in reg 185 (1)) of the country where the claimant is established; and (2) the documents evidencing payment of VAT listed in reg 29 (2).

Time within which a claim must be made

192. VAT chargeable within a one-year period ended on 30 June in any year must be claimed by 31 December in that year. This time limit is mandatory: *Jack Camp Productions* (No 6261). Claims can be made for the year if the repayment due is £16 or more. Interim claims can be made for periods of three months or more (provided the repayment for the period is £130 or more) with a final claim for the remainder of the year (no minimum period, but the repayment for the period must be £16 or more).

Deduction of bank charges

193. The Commissioners may incur bank charges or costs when making a remittance to the country where the claimant is established. If so, they may deduct these amounts from the repayment due.

Treatment of claim

194. The Commissioners may assess a claimant under VATA 1994 s 73 (1) if they consider that his claim is incomplete or incorrect.

195. [Revoked.]

False, altered or incorrect claims

196. A claimant may furnish or send a false or altered document in support of a claim. If so, the Commissioners may refuse to pay the claim, or any subsequent claims, for a period of two years commencing with the date on which the claim to which the document relates was made.

197. An overpayment in respect of an incorrect claim may be deducted from a repayment in respect of a subsequent claim.

PART XXII REPAYMENT SUPPLEMENT

198, 199. The following periods are disregarded in relation to the matters stated in calculating the 30 day period in which the Commissioners are required to authorise a payment or refund:

Matter		*Period begins*	*Period ends*
(*a*)	Commissioners make reasonable inquiries regarding the tax return or claim concerned (see *Olive Tree Press Ltd* (No 5349)	Date when the Commissioners first raised the inquiry (see below)	Date when a complete answer to the inquiry is received (see below)
(*b*)	Commissioners correct errors or omissions in the tax return or claim	Date when the error or omission first came to the Commissioners' notice	Date when the error or omission is corrected

(*c*)(*i*)	Trader has failed to submit tax return(s) for prior period(s) (see *Richard Costain Ltd v C & E Comrs* [1988] VATTR 111)	Period of failure set out in a certificate issued by the Commissioners	
(*c*)(*ii*)	Trader has failed to produce documents or give security	Date when written notice of the requirement was served by the Commissioners	Date when the documents are produced or security given

For the manner in which the period in (*a*) is determined, see VATA 1994 s 79 (4); *Watford Timber Co Ltd* (No 14756); *Refrigeration Spares (Manchester) Ltd* (No 17603).

PART XXIII REFUNDS TO "DO-IT-YOURSELF" BUILDERS

Interpretation of Part XXIII

200. Various words and phrases are defined.

Method and time for making claim

201. A claim under VATA 1994 s 35 is made by furnishing the relevant form (see reg 201A) no later than three months after the relevant building is completed. For the time of completion, see *C & E Comrs v Arnold* [1996] STC 1271. For the addresses to which claims should be sent, see Business Brief 15/04, 28 May 2004.

The following documents must be furnished at the same time unless the Commissioners allow otherwise:

(a) a certificate of completion from the local authority or alternative evidence of completion acceptable to the Commissioners;

(b) invoices for each supply of goods incorporated in the building or its site on which VAT was paid;

(c) import documents for imported goods (if any) incorporated in the building or its site;

(d) documents showing that planning permission was granted; and

(e) a signed certificate from an architect or quantity surveyor that the goods were, or were likely to have been, incorporated in the building or its site.

201A. The relevant form for the purposes of reg 201 is either form VAT431NB or form VAT431C.

PART XXIV FLAT RATE SCHEME FOR FARMERS

Interpretation of Part XXIV

202. Various words and phrases are defined.

Flat-rate scheme

203. The Commissioners must certify a person for the purposes of the flat-rate farmers scheme if he meets the conditions in reg 204 below. Goods and services made by a certified person in the course or furtherance of a designated activity is disregarded for the purposes of registration and deregistration under VATA 1994 Sch 1. For designated activities, see VATA 1994 s 54 (7), (8); VAT (Flat-rate Scheme for Farmers) (Designated Activities) Order 1992, SI 1992/3220.

Admission to the scheme

204. A person is certified for the purpose of the flat-rate farmers scheme if: (1) he satisfies the Commissioners that he carries on a business involving one or more of the activities set out in VAT (Flat-rate Scheme for Farmers) (Designated Activities) Order 1992, SI 1992/3220 art 2, Sch; (2) he has not been convicted of an offence, compounded proceedings, or been assessed to a penalty for dishonest conduct in connection with VAT in the three years before his application for certification; (3) he applies for certification on form VAT 98; and (4) he satisfies the Commissioners that flat-rate addition charged to customers will not exceed input tax forgone by £3,000 or more in the one year period following certification.

Certification

205. A certificate issued by the Commissioners is effective from the date on which the application is received, an earlier date agreed by the Commissioners, or a day between 1 and 30 days after receipt requested by the trader. The effective day may be no earlier than 1 January 1993 or the day when the trader's registration under VATA 1994 Sch 1 or 3 is cancelled.

Cancellation of certificates

206. A certificate may be cancelled in the following circumstances. The effective date of cancellation in each case is as stated.

	Circumstances	*Effective date*
(*a*)	A statement made in relation to the application is false in a material particular	Date when the Commissioners discover that such a statement has been made
(*b*)	The trader is convicted of an offence in connection with VAT or makes a payment to compound such proceedings	Date of the conviction or date of payment
(*c*)	The trader is assessed to a penalty for dishonest conduct	30 days after notification of the assessment
(*d*)	The trader ceases to make designated activities	The date of cessation
(*e*)	Death, bankruptcy, liquidation, receivership or incapacity of the trader	Date of death, bankruptcy or incapacity
(*f*)	Trader becomes liable to registration under VATA 1994 Sch 1 or 3	Effective date of registration
(*g*)	Trader makes a written application for cancellation	An unspecified day not earlier than the first anniversary of certification or an earlier day agreed by the Commissioners
(*h*)	The trader makes a written application for registration under VATA 1994 Sch 1 or 3	As (*g*) above
(*i*)	The Commissioners consider cancellation is necessary to protect the revenue	Date when the Commissioners consider that a risk to the revenue arises
(*j*)	The Commissioners consider that grounds for cancellation arise under (*a*)–(*h*) above	The appropriate date under (*a*)–(*h*) above

Death, bankruptcy or incapacity of certified person

207. A person carrying on designated activities following the death, bankruptcy, liquidation, receivership or incapacity of a certified person is treated as a certified person from the date of death, bankruptcy, etc until some other person is certified in respect of the designated activities or the incapacity (if any) ceases. VATA 1994 s 46 (4), (5) apply to such a person. He must notify the Commissioners in writing within 30 days stating the date of death or nature of the incapacity and the date when it began.

Further certification

208. A person may be re-certified from the date of application (if he has not been registered under VATA 1994 Sch 1 or 3 since the cancellation of his previous certificate), the first anniversary of cancellation (if his previous certificate was cancelled following a penalty assessment for dishonest conduct) or the third anniversary of cancellation (in other cases).

Claims by taxable persons for amounts to be treated as credits for input tax

209. The consideration for a taxable supply made to a taxable person by a certified person is deemed to include flat-rate addition (see VATA 1994 s 54(4)) if the supply is made in the course or furtherance of the relevant part of his business (see VATA 1994 s 54(7)) at the time when he is not a taxable person.

Flat-rate addition is treated as input tax by the customer if he holds an invoice containing the following particulars issued by the certified person: (1) an identifying number; (2) the supplier's name, address and certificate number; (3) the customer's name and address; (4) the time of supply; (5) a description of the goods or services supplied; (6) the consideration for the supply; and (7) the amount of flat-rate addition. Input tax credit is claimed in the prescribed accounting period in which the invoice is issued.

Duty to keep records

210. A certified person must keep and preserve his business records, his accounting records and copies of invoices issued showing flat-rate addition. He must keep, preserve and produce records in accordance with any requirements notified to him by the Commissioners. Records must be kept and preserved for six years or such shorter period as the Commissioners may allow.

Production of Records

211. A certified person must produce documents for inspection if an authorised person so demands and allow him to copy such documents, make extracts from them, or remove them at a reasonable time and for a reasonable period. An authorised person must provide copies of uplifted documents without charge if they are reasonably required for the proper conduct of the trader's business. The Commissioners must compensate the owner for loss or damage to uplifted documents.

PART XXV DISTRESS AND DILIGENCE

A212. The term "job band" is defined.

Distress

212. [Revoked.]

Diligence

213. An application for a warrant may be made by a collector or officer of Job Band 7 or above. Lawful acts during a poinding or sale may be done by officers of like seniority.

SCHEDULE 1

This Schedule sets out the following forms:

No	*Title*	*Authority*	*Reference*
1.	Application for VAT registration	reg 5(1)	VAT 1
2.	Partnership details	reg 5(1)	VAT 2
3.	Application to use previous owner's VAT registration number following the transfer of a business as a going concern	reg 6(1)	VAT 68

4.	VAT return	reg 25(1)	VAT 100
5.	Final VAT return	regs 23, 25(4)	VAT 193
6.	Application for VAT registration—distance selling	reg 5(1)	VAT 1A
7.	Application for VAT registration—acquisitions	reg 5(1)	VAT 1B
7A.	VAT registration notification	reg 5(1)	VAT 1C
8.	Appointment of tax representative	reg 10	VAT 1TR
9.	Application by a business person not established in the Community for refund of value added tax	reg 191 (1)	VAT 65A
10.	Certificate of status of business person	reg 191 (1) (*b*)	VAT 66A
11A.	VAT refunds for DIY builders—claim form for new houses	reg 201 (*a*)	VAT 431NB
11B.	VAT refunds for DIY builders—claim form for conversions	reg 201 (*a*)	VAT 431C
12.	VAT EC Sales list	regs 21, 22, 23	VAT 101MAN
13.	New means of transport for removal from the UK to another member state of the European Community	regs 22(6), 23	VAT 411
14.	Flat rate scheme for agriculture—application for certification	reg 204(*c*)	VAT 98
15.	Application by a business person established in the Community for refund of value added tax	reg 178(1)(*a*)	VAT 65
16.	Certificate of status of taxable person	reg 178(1)(*b*)(i)	VAT 66
17.	Certificate required to secure relief from VAT on purchased or acquired goods intended to be placed in a fiscal warehousing regime	reg 145B	—
18.	Certificate required to secure zero-rating on services (other than the supply of warehousing) performed in a fiscal or other warehouse	reg 145C	—

SCHEDULE 1A

This Schedule sets out the features and requirements with which a fiscal warehousing record (see reg 145F) must comply.

SCHEDULE 2

This Schedule lists the statutory instruments revoked by reg 3 (1).

SI 1996/1255
VALUE ADDED TAX (FISCAL WAREHOUSING) (TREATMENT OF TRANSACTIONS) ORDER 1996

Note This Order under VATA 1994 s 5 (3) provides that the transfer of an undivided share in the property of goods is treated as a supply of goods rather than as a supply of services in specified circumstances.

1. This Order came into force on 1 June 1996.

2. Various words and phrases are defined.

3. A supply involving the transfer of an undivided share in the property in goods is treated as a supply of goods rather than as a supply of services if the goods are eligible goods (as defined in VATA 1994 s 18B (6)), the supply is not a retail transaction and either of the following conditions is met:

(a) the material time for the supply (as defined in VATA 1994 s 18F (1)) occurs while the goods are subject to a fiscal warehousing regime; or

(b) the transferee causes the goods to be placed in a fiscal warehousing regime after the material time for the supply he receives but before the material time for the next supply (if any) which involves the transfer of any property in the goods.

SI 1997/1431
DISTRESS FOR CUSTOMS AND EXCISE DUTIES AND OTHER INDIRECT TAXES REGULATIONS 1997

Note These regulations under FA 1997 s 51 (1)–(3) set out common provisions relating to distress applicable to all taxes and duties under the Commissioners' care and management. They replace separate regulations applicable to VAT, insurance premium tax and landfill tax. The regulations are described below only in so far as they relate to VAT.

Citation and commencement

1. These regulations come into force on 1 July 1997.

Interpretation

2. Various words and phrases are defined.

Revocations and transitional provisions

3. The revoked provisions are listed in Sch 3. The regulations apply to action taken under a warrant signed before 1 July 1997.

Levying distress

4. An officer (defined in reg 2 (1)) can levy distress if a person fails to pay VAT following a written demand. An officer can direct any authorised person (defined in reg 2 (1)) to levy distress. He does so by way of a signed warrant. Distress is levied by the authorised person. Alternatively, distress is levied under his direction and in his presence. Distress can be levied on goods and chattels located at any place.

Restrictions on levying distress

5. No distress can be levied in respect of VAT assessed under VATA 1994 s 73 until 30 days after the date of the assessment (see VAT Tribunal Rules 1986, SI 1986/590 r 4 (1)) or 21 days after the date notified by the Commissioners in a letter (see r 4 (2)).

Goods and chattels not subject to levy

6.s No distress can be levied on; (1) the goods listed in Sch 1 para 1 (*a*)–(*q*), if they are located in a dwelling house and are reasonably required for the domestic needs of anyone residing there; (2) the goods listed in Sch 1 para 2 (*a*), (*b*), if they are located in business premises.

Time for levying distress

7. A levy of distress must commence between 8am and 8pm or (if the hours of business fall wholly or partly outside that period) between those hours or during the hours of business. The levy can continue beyond 8pm or closing time until it is completed.

Costs

8. The person subject to distraint is responsible for the costs arising once a warrant has been signed. The costs are determined in accordance with the scale in Sch 2. An authorised person (see reg 2(1)) may retain costs from any amount received.

Sale

9. Goods and chattels may be sold if the VAT concerned and costs of the distraint are not paid within five days of a levy. The sale proceeds are applied in settlement of VAT and costs. Any surplus is paid to the owner.

Disputes as to costs

10. In the event of a dispute, costs are taxed by a district judge. Separate provisions apply in Northern Ireland.

SCHEDULE 1

This Schedule lists the goods and chattels which are not subject to levy (see reg 6).

SCHEDULE 2

This Schedule lists the scale costs for stated actions taken while levying distress (see reg 8).

SCHEDULE 3

This Schedule lists the provisions revoked by these regulations (see reg 3(1)).

SI 1997/1523
VALUE ADDED TAX (REVERSE CHARGE) (ANTI-AVOIDANCE) ORDER 1997

Note This order made under VATA 1994 s 8 (5), (7), (8) amends VATA 1994 Sch 5 to include telecommunication services in accordance with Decision 97/214/EEC (OJ L86/33, 28.3.97), makes provision for the performance of such services following the exercise of a right and varies the valuation and timing provisions relevant to such services.

Citation and commencement

1. This order applies to services performed after 30 June 1997.

Interpretation

2. Various words and phrases are defined.

Insertion of telecommunication services into Schedule 5 to the Act

3. Amends VATA 1994 Sch 5.

Modification of the effect of regulation 82 of the Regulations

4. A supply affected by VATA 1994 s 8 (1) or 43 (2A) is deemed to be supplied at the time specified in VAT Regulations, SI 1995/2518 reg 82. This timing provision applies to telecommunication services (see VATA 1994 Sch 5 para 7A) performed after 30 June 1997 if a payment was made in respect of them before 1 July 1997. It does not apply to telecommunication services performed before 1 July 1997, deemed to be performed before 1 July 1997 (see art 10) or wholly chargeable to VAT in another EU member state.

Treatment of a right to relevant telecommunication services

5. A right granted before 1 July 1997 may be exercised with the result that telecommunication services are performed after 30 June 1997 for a consideration which is lower than it would otherwise have been. Where this is so, the grant of the right and the performance of the services are treated as a single supply comprising two elements for the purposes of determining the time and extent to which the services are treated as being made. Any payment for the right is deemed to be a payment for the services for the purposes of art 4.

Rights not exercised before 1 July 1997

6. A payment is deemed to have been made when a right is exercised if:

(a) a right is exercised with the result that telecommunication services are performed for a consideration which is lower than it would otherwise have been;

(b) a right to telecommunication services (see VATA 1994 Sch 5 para 7A) is exercised after 30 June 1997;

(c) the right was granted for a consideration in money; and

(d) a payment was made in respect of the right before 1 July 1997.

Value of the relevant telecommunication services

7. The value of a supply deemed to be made under the reverse charge provisions (see VATA 1994 s 8) is determined by reference to "the consideration for which the services were in fact supplied to him" (see VATA 1994 Sch 6 para 8). The following provisions are substituted in relation to telecommunication services (see VATA 1994 Sch 5 para 7A) performed after 30 June 1997 in circumstances where part of the services are chargeable to VAT in another EU member state, or where the services were performed over a period which commenced before 1 July 1997.

If the consideration is a consideration in money, the value of the supply is the lower of:

(a) the total consideration minus the consideration for that part of the supply chargeable to VAT in another EU member state; and

(b) the proportion of the consideration which is properly attributable to the relevant period.

If the consideration consists wholly or partly of something other than money, the value of the supply is such amount in money as is equivalent to the lower of the amounts in (*a*) and (*b*) above.

Value of relevant telecommunication services supplied by virtue of a right

8. The value of a supply deemed to be made under the reverse charge provisions (see VATA 1994 s 8) is determined by reference to "the consideration for which the services were in fact supplied to him" (see VATA 1994 Sch 6 para 8, which applies in a modified form in the circumstances described in art 7). A deemed consideration is used for the purposes of the original and modified valuation provisions if a right to receive telecommunication services (see VATA 1994 Sch 5 para 7A) has been exercised with the result that the telecommunication services are performed for a consideration which is lower than it would otherwise have been.

The consideration for which the telecommunication services are in fact supplied is deemed to be the higher of:

(a) the consideration for which the services were in fact received; and

(b) the lower of:

 (i) the open market value of the telecommunication services which were in fact supplied (ie the amount which would have been payable for them if no right had been granted), and

 (ii) the aggregate of (A+B–C) where A is the consideration for which the telecommunication services were in fact supplied, B is the consideration for the right to the telecommunication services, and C is the open market value of the right to the telecommunication services (ie the amount which would have been payable for the right if the telecommunication services were to be supplied for the amount which would have been payable for them if no right had been granted).

Meaning of a right to relevant telecommunication services

9. A right to receive telecommunication services includes any right, option or priority with respect to a supply of telecommunication services and any interest deriving from any right to telecommunication services.

Time when relevant telecommunication services are treated as performed

10. All or part of the consideration for a supply of telecommunication services may be determined or payable periodically or from time to time. Where this is so, the time when the services are treated as being performed for the purposes of this order is the end of the period to which a payment, statement or invoice relates. The services are treated as being performed to the extent covered by the payment, statement or invoice.

SI 1998/1461
AIR PASSENGER DUTY AND OTHER INDIRECT TAXES (INTEREST RATE) REGULATIONS 1998

Note These regulations under FA 1996 s 197 specify the rates of interest applicable for the purposes of VATA 1994 ss 74 and 78. References to the rates of interest relevant to other duties and taxes are omitted.

Citation and commencement

1. These regulations came into force on 6 July 1998.

Interpretation

2. Various words and phrases are defined.

2A. [Revoked.]

3. The Air Passenger Duty and Other Indirect Taxes (Interest Rate) Regulations 1997 are revoked.

Applicable rate of interest payable to the Commissioners of Customs and Excise in connection with . . . VAT . . .

4. The "rate applicable under FA 1996 s 197" for the purposes of VATA 1994 s 74 on 1 April 2000 (when the 1998 Regulations were last amended) is stated. It has since been changed. For the rates in force before 6 July 1998, see reg 8. For the rates in force from time to time since that date, see the table in the commentary to FA 1996 s 197. From 1 April 2009, the "rate applicable under FA 1996 s 197" also applies for the purposes of VATA 1994 s 85A(3).

The rate of interest changes if the reference rate (defined in reg 2 (2)) differs from the established rate (defined in reg 2 (1)) on any future reference day (defined in reg 2 (1)). The new rate is 2.5% more than the reference rate. The new rate takes effect from the sixth day of the following month. The new rate is specified by order made by the Commissioners (see FA 1996 s 197 (5)). For the orders made to date, see FA 1996 s 197.

Applicable rate of interest payable by the Commissioners of Customs and Excise in connection with . . . VAT . . .

5. The "rate applicable under FA 1996 s 197" for the purposes of VATA 1994 s 78 on 1 April 2000 (when the 1998 Regulations were last amended) is stated. It has since been changed. For the rates in force before 6 July 1998, see reg 8. For the rates in force from time to time since that date, see the table in the commentary to FA 1996 s 197. From 1 April 2009, the "rate applicable under FA 1996 s 197" also applies for the purposes of VATA 1994 s 85A(2).

The rate of interest changes if the reference rate (defined in reg 2 (2)) differs from the established rate (defined in reg 2 (1)) on any future reference day (defined in reg 2 (1)). The new rate is the higher of: (1) 0.5%; and (2) 1% less than the reference rate. The new rate takes effect from the twelfth working day after the reference day. The new rate is specified by order made by the Commissioners (see FA 1996 s 197 (5)). For the orders made to date, see FA 1996 s 197.

Effect of a change in applicable rate

6. The new rate of interest applies to periods beginning on or after the operative day (as defined in reg 2 (1)). This applies whether interest begins to run from a day before, on or after that day.

7. The old rate of interest continues to have effect for periods immediately before the change.

Applicable rate of interest prior to the coming into force of these Regulations

8. The rates of interest in force before 6 July 1998 are listed. As regards VATA 1994 s 74, see Table 3. As regards VATA 1994 s 78, see Table 7.

Minimum amount of interest payable in connection with customs duty

9. [Applies to customs duty.]

SI 1999/3115
VAT (IMPORTATION OF INVESTMENT GOLD) RELIEF ORDER 1999

Note This order relieves imported investment gold from VAT.

1. These regulations came into force on 1 January 2000.

2. "Investment gold" is defined.

3. VAT is not chargeable on investment gold imported into the UK from a third country.

SI 1999/3116
VAT (INVESTMENT GOLD) ORDER 1999

Note This order implements Directive 98/80/EC. It makes provision for the exemption of investment gold, an election to waive exemption and a reverse charge under which the customer accounts for VAT.

Citation, commencement and interpretation

1. This order came into force on 1 January 2000. Various words and phrases are defined.

Exemption for investment gold

2. Inserts VATA 1994 Sch 9 Group 15.

Election to waive exemption

3. A taxable person who produces or transforms gold may make an election to waive exemption. The election has effect in relation to supplies of investment gold, and of rights to the possession of investment gold, made to a taxable person on or after the day when the election was made. Investment gold for this purpose is gold of a description within VATA 1994 Sch 9 Group 15 Note 1(*a*), (*b*) or (*c*). The consequence of an election is that the supply, grant, assignment or surrender is not exempt from tax under VATA 1994 Sch 9 Group 15 Items 1 or 2. The taxable person must comply with conditions specified by the Commissioners in a notice. An election is irrevocable.

A taxable person who supplies gold for industrial purposes in the normal course of his business may be permitted to make an election to waive exemption in accordance with a notice published by the Commissioners. The election has effect in relation to supplies of investment gold, and of rights to the possession of investment gold, made to a taxable person on or after the day when the election was made. Investment gold for this purpose is gold of a description within VATA 1994 Sch 9 Group 15 Note 1(*a*). The consequence of an election is that the supply, grant, assignment or surrender is not exempt from tax under VATA 1994 Sch 9 Group 15 Items 1 or 2. The taxable person must comply with conditions specified by the Commissioners in a notice. The Commissioners may withdraw permission to make the election if this is necessary to protect the revenue. The election ceases to have effect from the date specified in the notification made by the Commissioners. Subject to this, an election is irrevocable. The taxable person must comply with conditions specified by the Commissioners in a notice.

An agent acting for a disclosed principal may make an election to waive exemption. The election has effect in relation to services directly linked to a supply made by his principal which is excluded from exemption under VATA 1994 Sch 9 Group Items 1 or 2 by virtue of an election to waive exemption. The consequence of an election is that the agency services are not exempt from tax under VATA 1994 Sch 9 Group 15 Item 3. An election is irrevocable. By applying art 3(6), art 3(5) implies that an agent must comply with conditions specified by the Commissioners in a notice. However, art 3(6) applies only to a person making relevant supplies. A supply within VATA 1994 Sch 9 Group 15 Item 3 is not a relevant supply within the meaning of art 1(2).

Customers to account for tax on supplies of investment gold

4. A supply may be excluded from exemption under VATA 1994 Sch 9 Group 15 Items 1 and 2 by virtue of an election to waive exemption having effect under art 3. If so, the customer is required to account for VAT in accordance with VATA 1994 s 55(1)–(4).

SI 1999/3121
VAT (INPUT TAX) (SPECIFIED SUPPLIES) ORDER 1999

Note This order implements the right to deduct input tax set out in Directive 2006/112/EC arts 169(*c*), 354. It replaces VAT (Input Tax) (Specified Supplies) Order 1992, SI 1992/3123.

1. This order came into force on 1 January 2000.

2. Input tax is allowable in accordance with VATA 1994 s 26(1) if it is attributable to the supplies described in arts 3 and 4.

3. The following services:

(a) services supplied to a person who belongs in a third country. For the place where a person belongs, see VATA 1994 s 9. For the place of supply where shares are issued to a UK nominee acting for an overseas shareholder, see *Water Hall Group plc* (No 18007);

(b) services directly linked to the export of goods to a third country; and

(c) intermediary services exempt from tax under VATA 1994 Sch 9 Group 2 Item 4 or Group 5 Item 5 which relate to a transaction within (*a*) or (*b*) which is exempt from tax under VATA 1994 Sch 9 Group 2 or Group 5 Items 1–6, 8 or would be so exempt if it had been made in the UK.

4. Supplies exempt from tax under VATA 1994 Sch 9 Group 15 Items 1 or 2 and supplies which would be so exempt if they had been made in the UK.

5. VAT (Input Tax) (Specified Supplies) Order 1992, SI 1992/3123 is revoked.

SI 2000/1139
NATIONAL POLICE RECORDS (RECORDABLE OFFENCES) REGULATIONS 2000

Note These regulations are made under Police and Criminal Evidence Act 1984 s 27. They specify the offences recorded in national police records. These offences are known as "recordable offences": see s 118(1) of the 1984 Act.

1. The following may be recorded in national police records:

- convictions for any offence punishable with imprisonment;
- convictions for any offence specified in the Schedule to these regulations;
- cautions (as defined in Police Act 1997 Part V) in respect of the foregoing offences;
- reprimands given under Crime and Disorder Act 1998 s 65 in respect of the foregoing offences; and
- warnings given under Crime and Disorder Act 1998 s 65 in respect of the foregoing offences.

SI 2001/2879
VAT (REFUND OF TAX TO MUSEUMS AND GALLERIES) ORDER 2001

Note This order names the bodies entitled to claim refunds of VAT under VATA 1994 s 33A, the museums and galleries to which claims relate and (if later than 1 April 2002) the date from which claims can be made.

1. This order came into force on 1 September 2001.

2. The bodies listed in column 1 of the Schedule can claim refunds under VATA 1994 s 33A.

3. Claims can be made in respect of the museums and galleries listed in column 2 of the Schedule.

4. Claims are made in respect of purchases, acquisitions and importations made from the date specified in column 3 of the Schedule (if there is one) and from 1 April 2001 (in other cases).

SCHEDULE

This lists the bodies, museums and galleries, and dates referred to in arts 2–4.

SI 2002/1502
VAT (CARS) (AMENDMENT) ORDER 2002

Note This order amends the used goods scheme for motor cars (see VAT (Cars) Order 1992, SI 1992/3122 art 8).

1. This order came into force on 1 July 2002. The amendments to art 8 of the 1992 Order to not apply if the taxable person took possession of the motor car pursuant to:

(a) an assignment treated as neither a supply of goods nor a supply of services by virtue of VAT (Special Provisions) Order 1995, SI 1995/1268 art 5(4) (or equivalent Isle of Man legislation), if it took effect before 1 July 2002;

(b) a transaction forming part of a succession of two or transactions treated as neither a supply of goods nor a supply of services by virtue of any provision of art 5 of the 1995 Order (or equivalent Isle of Man legislation), one of which is an assignment, if the assignment took effect before 1 July 2002; or

(c) a transaction forming part of a succession of two or transactions treated as neither a supply of goods nor a supply of services by virtue of any provision of art 5 of the 1995 Order (or equivalent Isle of Man legislation), two or more of which are assignments, if any of the assignments took effect before 1 July 2002.

2. [Amends art 8 of the 1992 Order.]

SI 2002/1503
VAT (SPECIAL PROVISIONS) (AMENDMENT) ORDER 2002

Note This order amends the used goods scheme for goods other than motor cars (see VAT (Special Provisions) Order 1992, SI 1995/1268 art 12).

1. This order came into force on 1 July 2002. The amendments to art 12 of the 1995 Order to not apply if the taxable person took possession of the goods pursuant to:

(a) an assignment treated as neither a supply of goods nor a supply of services by virtue of art 5(4) of the 1995 Order (or equivalent Isle of Man legislation) if it took effect before 1 July 2002;

(b) a transaction forming part of a succession of two or transactions treated as neither a supply of goods nor a supply of services by virtue of any provision of art 5 of the 1995 Order (or equivalent Isle of Man legislation), one of which is an assignment, if the assignment took effect before 1 July 2002; or

(c) a transaction forming part of a succession of two or transactions treated as neither a supply of goods nor a supply of services by virtue of any provision of art 5 of the 1995 Order (or equivalent Isle of Man legislation), two or more of which are assignments, if any of the assignments took effect before 1 July 2002.

2. [Amends art 12 of the 1995 Order.]

SI 2002/1935
VAT (ACQUISITIONS) RELIEF ORDER 2002

Note This order relieves certain acquisitions from payment of VAT.

1. This order came into force on 15 August 2002.

2. No VAT is payable on an acquisition of goods from another EU member state if the goods fall within a description in VAT (Imported Goods) Relief Order 1984, SI 1984/746 art 4 or Sch 2.

3. The conditions in VAT (Imported Goods) Relief Order 1984, SI 1984/746 arts 6–8 apply for the purposes of the relief in art 2.

SI 2003/3102
EXPORT (PENALTY) REGULATIONS 2003

Note These regulations are made under European Communities Act 1972 s 2(2). They prescribe penalties for contravention of a relevant export rule (regs 3–5). The relevant export rules are set out in the Schedule. The regulations make provision for demand notices (regs 6–8), review of decisions (regs 9A–9E), appeals (regs 9, 9F, 13), and the service of notices (reg 14). For the calculation and notification of penalties, see Notice No 201 (December 2003).

SI 2003/3113
CUSTOMS (CONTRAVENTION OF A RELEVANT RULE) REGULATIONS 2003

Note These regulations prescribe the customs rules for which a contravention penalty applies under FA 2003 s 26.

1. These regulations came into force on 23 December 2003.

2. Various words and phrases are defined.

3. A person is liable to a penalty under FA 2003 s 26 if he contravenes a “relevant rule”. The schedule to these regulations specifies:

- the relevant rules and descriptions of relevant rules. These rules comprised defined provisions of EU customs rules and UK legislation;
- the person liable to the penalty; and
- the maximum penalty.

SCHEDULE

This lists the rules (column 1), persons (column 2) and penalties (column 3) referred to in reg 3.

SI 2004/674
RECOVERY OF DUTIES AND TAXES ETC DUE IN OTHER MEMBER STATES (CORRESPONDING UK CLAIMS, PROCEDURE AND SUPPLEMENTARY) REGULATIONS 2004

Note In conjunction with FA 2002 s 134 and Sch 39, these regulations implement Directive 76/308/EEC (mutual assistance in relation to recovery of duties and taxes between member states). For further implementing measures having direct effect in the UK, see Regulation (EC) No 1179/2008.

The 1976 Directive was repealed and replaced by Directive 2008/55/EC with effect from 30 June 2008. The 2008 Directive is repealed and replaced by Directive 2010/24/EU with effect from 1 January 2012.

PART 1 GENERAL

Citation and commencement

1. These regulations came into force on 1 April 2004.

Interpretation

2. Various words and phrases are defined.

PART 2 CORRESPONDING UK CLAIMS

Corresponding UK claims—Duties and Taxes

3. UK claims corresponding to foreign claims are set out in Sch 1.

PART 3 REQUESTS FOR ASSISTANCE

Requests for information

4. The relevant UK authority is not obliged to supply information requested by another EU member state if:

- the authority would be unable to obtain the information for the purposes of recovering a corresponding UK claim (as defined in reg 1(i));
- supplying the information would disclose a commercial, industrial or professional secret; or
- disclosing the information would: (1) prejudice the security of the UK; or (2) contravene UK law or public policy.

Requests for notification of instruments

5. [Repealed.]

Requests for recovery or precautionary measures

6. The relevant UK authority:

- must immediately inform the applicant authority when any enforcement action is taken on a request;
- must consult the applicant authority if it intends to allow the debtor time to pay the foreign claim or to pay it by instalments;
- is required to recover a foreign claim that would create serious economic or social difficulties in the UK only if this would be required under an enactment or rule of law relating to a corresponding UK claim.

Transfer of sums recovered

7. [Repealed.]

Contested recovery

8. UK legislation relating to proceedings for recovery or precautionary measures (as defined in reg 2(*r*)) applies equally to contested foreign claims.

Notice of inability to take action or proceedings upon a request for recovery of a contested claim

9. [Repealed.]

Notice of action contesting recovery

10. [Repealed.]

Reimbursement of sums recovered and compensation

11. The debtor may successfully contest a foreign claim or instrument permitting enforcement. If so, the applicant authority is liable for reimbursement of sums recovered or for compensation in accordance with UK law.

Reimbursement arrangements

12. [Repealed.]

Notice of cancellation or payment of a claim

13. [Repealed.]

Adjustment of a foreign claim

14. [Repealed.]

Minimum amount on requests for assistance

15. [Repealed.]

Limitation on requests for assistance

16. A request for assistance may be declined if the foreign claim is more than five years old.

Acceptance and transmission of communications

17. [Repealed.]

Communication of documents and information

18. [Repealed.]

Language requirements

19. The applicant authority must provide English translations of the documents provided.

Limitation

20. The limitation period for recovery of foreign claims is determined in accordance with UK law.

Notice of refusal of requests for assistance

21. [Repealed.]

PART 4 INTEREST

Adaptations

22. This regulation introduces Sch 2.

Interest enforced by the Board

23. [Applies to the former Inland Revenue.]

Interest enforced by the Commissioners

24. A foreign claim corresponding to any UK claim in respect of VAT carries interest under FA 1996 s 197.

PART 5 ENFORCEMENT OF CORRESPONDING CLAIMS

Evidence

25. [Applies to the former Inland Revenue.]

Enforcement in Scotland

26. [Applies to Scotland.]

SCHEDULE 1 CORRESPONDING CLAIMS

Part 1 provides that VAT (however described) charged in another EU member state in accordance with Directive 2006/112/EC corresponds to VAT charged in the UK in accordance with VATA 1994.

Part 2 is irrelevant to VAT, which now falls outside the scope of Directive 77/799/EEC (see Directive 2003/93/EC art 1(2), which deleted VAT and substituted taxes on insurance premiums).

SCHEDULE 2 ADAPTATIONS

VATA 1994 s 76 applies as if it reads: "An amount of VAT interest specified in a request concerning a person specified in regulation 4(2) of the Recovery of Duties and Taxes Etc Due to Other Member States (Corresponding UK Claims, Procedure and Supplementary) Regulations 2004 in relation to whom a request is made shall be recoverable as if it were VAT due from him". For "request", see Sch 2 para 1.

SI 2004/1002
CUSTOMS AND EXCISE (TRAVELLERS' ALLOWANCES AND PERSONAL RELIEFS) (NEW MEMBER STATES) ORDER 2004

Note This order affects the interpretation of two orders relevant to VAT. It is otherwise wholly concerned with excise duty.

Citation and commencement

1. This order came into effect on 1 May 2004.

1–5. [Relevant to excise duty.]

Interpretation of The Customs and Excise Duties (Personal Reliefs for Goods Permanently Imported) Order 1992 and The Travellers' Allowances Order 1994

6. References in the following orders to Directive 77/388/EEC (the Sixth Directive) are construed as references to that directive as amended, modified or otherwise affected by the Act of Accession (2003):

- Customs and Excise Duties (Personal Reliefs for Goods Permanently Imported) Order 1992, SI 1992/3193.
- Travellers' Allowances Order 1994, SI 1994/955.

Directive 77/388/EEC was repealed and replaced by Directive 2006/112/EC with effect from 1 January 2007.

SCHEDULE

[Relevant to excise duty.]

SI 2004/1929
VALUE ADDED TAX (DISCLOSURE OF AVOIDANCE SCHEMES) REGULATIONS 2004

Note These regulations specify the time limit for notifying VAT avoidance schemes, the form and manner of notification and the information to be notified.

Citation and commencement

1. These regulations came into effect on 1 August 2004.

Time of notification

2. As regards the duty to notify a notifiable scheme by reference to the VAT return made for a prescribed accounting period beginning after 31 July 2004, the relevant information must be notified to the Commissioners no later than 30 days after the end of the prescribed accounting period concerned.

As regards the duty to notify a notifiable scheme by reference to a repayment claim made in respect of a prescribed accounting period beginning after 31 July 2004, the relevant information must be notified to the Commissioners no later than 30 days after the claim is made.

For notifiable schemes, see VATA 1994 Sch 11A para 5. For the duty to notify, see VATA 1994 Sch 11A para 6. For the information to be notified, see VATA 1994 Sch 11A para 6(2) (designated scheme) and reg 4 below (hallmarked scheme).

Form and manner of notification

3. The information to be notified in respect of a notifiable scheme must be provided in the form and manner specified in a notice published by the Commissioners. For the notice published, see Notice 700/8/04; Business Brief 2/06, 27 February 2006.

Information to be notified

4. The following information must be provided when notifying a hallmarked scheme:

- A list of the designated provisions included in (or associated with) the scheme. For the designated provisions, see VAT (Disclosure of Avoidance Schemes) Order 2004, SI 2004/1933 art 3 and Sch 2.
- An explanation how the scheme gives rise to a tax advantage.
- An explanation how the involvement of the participants enables the tax advantage to arise.
- A list of UK, EU or foreign legislation relied upon to give rise to the tax advantage.

The same information must be provided when making a voluntary notification in respect of a hallmarked scheme. For voluntary notifications, see VATA 1994 Sch 11A para 9.

For the information to be provided when notifying a designated scheme, see VATA 1994 Sch 11A para 6(2).

SI 2004/1931
VAT (GROUPS: ELIGIBILITY) ORDER 2004

Note This order modifies the eligibility criteria for membership of a VAT group.

Citation and commencement

1. This order came into effect on 1 August 2004.

Modification regarding section 43A of the Value Added Tax Act 1994

2. In principle, any body corporate is eligible to become, or remain, a member of a VAT group if it meets the conditions in VATA 1994 s 43A. However, the body must also meet the following additional conditions if it is a "specified body" (as defined in art 3).

- it must satisfy the "benefits condition" (see art 5); and
- it must satisfy the "consolidated accounts condition" (see art 6).

Specified bodies

3. A body corporate is a "specified body" if it meets all of the following conditions.

First, it carries on a "relevant business activity" (as defined in art 4).

Second, it meets any of the following conditions at a time when the relevant business activity is being carried on.

- (in relation to a VAT group ABC or XABC controlled by X) it is not a wholly-owned subsidiary (see art 3(5)(*a*), (*b*)) of X;
- it is managed (directly or indirectly) by a third party (as defined in art 7(2)) in relation to relevant business activity; or
- it is the sole general partner of a limited partnership.

Third, it does *not* fall within any of the following descriptions.

- it controls (as defined in art 7(5)) all of the members of the VAT group (as defined in art 7(4)) (if it is not a member of the group) or all of the other members of the group (if it is a member of the group);
- another body corporate is empowered by statute to control (as defined in art 7(5)) its activities;
- its only activity is acting as the trustee of an occupational pension scheme (as defined in Pension Schemes Act 1993 s 1) established under a trust; and
- it is a charity.

Fourth, the VAT group (as defined in art 7(4)) meets either of the following conditions.

- the value of its supplies for the year then ending has exceeded £10 million; or

- there are reasonable grounds for believing that the value of its supplies in the year then beginning will exceed £10 million.

For the manner in which the Commissioners interpret art 3(2), see Business Brief 29/04, 11 November 2004.

Relevant business activities

4. As regards a body corporate that is *not* a member of the VAT group (as defined in art 7(4)), its business is a "relevant business activity" if:

- it involves making one or more supplies of goods or services to one or more members of the group;
- those supplies are not incidental to that business activity;
- at least one of those supplies is chargeable to VAT at a positive rate;
- the representative member is not entitled to input tax credit for all of the VAT chargeable on those supplies.

As regards a body corporate that *is* a member of the VAT group (as defined in art 7(4)), the foregoing tests are applied by reference to what would happen if the body were *not* a member of the group.

The benefits condition

5. The benefits condition (see art 2) is satisfied unless more than 50 per cent of the benefits of the relevant business activity (see art 4) accrue directly or indirectly to one or more third parties (as defined in art 7(2)). "Benefits", for this purpose, comprise the following.

- profits, whether or not they are distributed;
- charges for managing the business activity. These include charges for providing staff to manage the activity; and
- the amount (if any) by which any other charges made to the body corporate exceed the open market value of the goods or services concerned.

If there are no such benefits, the business activity is deemed to generate profits of £100. Thus, the benefits condition may continue to be met even if the relevant business activity gives rise to a loss.

The consolidated accounts condition

6. The consolidated accounts condition is satisfied if, in accordance with generally accepted accounting practice (as defined in art 6(3)), the accounts of the body corporate are required to be consolidated in the accounts of the person controlling the VAT group and are not required to be consolidated in the accounts of a third party (as defined in art 7(2)). This applies even if the accounts could be excluded from consolidation on the grounds of immateriality. It applies whether or not accounts are required to be prepared or are actually prepared.

Interpretation

7. The provisions of arts 4–6 are modified if the body corporate is the sole general partner of a limited partnership.

Various words and phrases are defined.

SI 2004/1933
VALUE ADDED TAX (DISCLOSURE OF AVOIDANCE SCHEMES) ORDER 2004

Note This order designates tax avoidance schemes and allocates reference numbers to them. It also designates provisions relevant to the identification of hallmarked schemes.

Citation and commencement

1. This order came into effect on 1 August 2004.

Interpretation

2. Various words and phrases are defined.

Designation of avoidance schemes and provisions included in or associated with avoidance schemes

3. Designated schemes are listed in Sch 1. Designated provisions are listed in Sch 2.

SCHEDULE 1

Designated schemes are listed and numbered by reference to the following headings.

1 First grant of a major interest in a building

2 Payment handling service

3 Value shifting

4 Leaseback agreement

5 Extended approval period

6 Groups: third party suppliers

7 Exempt education or vocational training by a non-profit making body

8 Taxable education or vocational training by a non-eligible body

9 Cross-border face value vouchers

10 Surrender of relevant lease

SCHEDULE 2

PART 1 PROVISIONS ASSOCIATED WITH SCHEMES

Confidentiality condition

1.—An agreement preventing or limiting disclosure of how the scheme gives rise to a tax advantage. For the circumstances in which a scheme falls within this description, see Business Brief 14/05, 27 July 2005.

The sharing of the tax advantage with another party to the scheme or with the promoter

2.—An agreement for sharing the tax saved with another party to the scheme or to the person promoting it.

Fee payable to a promoter which is in whole or in part contingent on tax savings from the scheme

3.—An agreement for fees to be contingent upon the scheme achieving a tax saving.

PART 2 PROVISIONS INCLUDED IN SCHEMES

Prepayment between connected parties

4.—Payments for goods or services before the basic tax point and payments for continuous supplies before the goods or services are provided where, in either case, the customer and supplier are connected persons.

Funding by loan, share subscription or subscription in securities

5.—Funding a supply of goods or services to a connected person by way of a loan or an issue of shares or securities.

Off-shore loops

6.—Supplying relevant services (as defined) for onward supply to a person belonging in the UK under an exempt or zero-rated supply or a supply made outside the UK.

Property transactions between connected persons

7.—Making a relevant grant (as defined) in circumstances where the grantor or grantee are both connected persons and partly exempt, and works have been (or will be) carried out on the land.

Issue of face value vouchers

8.—Issuing face value vouchers (as defined) for consideration. This does not apply if the vouchers are issued to a relevant person (as defined) and it is anticipated that 75% or more of the vouchers will be redeemed within three years of the date of issue.

SI 2004/3148
VALUE ADDED TAX (PLACE OF SUPPLY OF GOODS) ORDER 2004

Note This order under VATA 1994 ss 7, 9 varies the place of supply rules in relation to: (1) goods supplied on board ships, aircraft and trains engaged in the intra-Community transport of passengers; and (2) supplies of gas and electricity. As regards head (1), it re-enacts, with minor amendments, the provisions revoked by this order. As regards head (2), it implements, in part, Directive 2003/92/EC.

PART 1 PRELIMINARY

Citation and commencement

1. This order came into force on 1 January 2005. Part 3 applies to supplies made on or after that date.

Citation and commencement

2. This order varies the rules determining the place where goods are supplied.

Revocation

3. This order revokes VAT (Place of Supply of Goods) Order 1992, SI 1992/3283.

PART 2 GOODS SUPPLIED ON BOARD SHIPS, AIRCRAFT AND TRAINS

Interpretation of Part 2

4. Various words and phrases are defined.

5. Goods are deemed to be supplied at the point of departure if they are supplied on board a ship, aircraft or train transporting passengers between two member states without an intermediate stop in a third country. See *Peninsular and Oriental Steam Navigation Co v C & E Comrs* [2000] STC 488.

6. Goods are deemed to be supplied in a third country if they are supplied for immediate consumption on a ship, aircraft or train transporting passengers from one EU member state to another without an intermediate stop in a third country.

7. A journey involving a change in the means of transport is counted as two or more journeys. A return journey is counted as two journeys.

8. This order does not apply to goods supplied on a pleasure cruise. For the place of supply, see VAT (Place of Supply of Services) Order 1992, SI 1992/3121 art 8.

PART 3 SUPPLIES OF GAS, ELECTRICITY, HEAT OR COOLING

Interpretation of Part 3

9. Various words and phrases are defined. "Relevant goods" are (1) gas supplied through a natural gas system situated within the territory of an EU member state or any network connected to such a system; (2) electricity; and (3) heat or cooling supplied through a network.

10. The place of supply of relevant goods supplied to a dealer is:

- the place where the dealer has established his business;
- the place where the dealer has a fixed establishment; or
- (in the absence of either) the place where the dealer has his permanent address or usually resides.

11–13. The place of supply of relevant goods supplied to someone other than a dealer is the place where the goods are effectively used and consumed. The goods are effectively used and consumed for this purpose if: (1) the recipient supplies the goods as part of a single composite supply of other goods or services; or (2) (in the case of a supply to a member of a VAT group) the goods are effectively used and consumed by the member, or another member, of the VAT group.

In the case of partial consumption, the place of supply of the unconsumed goods is:

- the place where the recipient has established his business;
- the place where the recipient has a fixed establishment to which the goods are supplied; or
- (in the absence of either) the place where the recipient has his permanent address or usually resides.

14. For the purposes of VATA 1994 s 9A(1)(*a*), a person is "outside the UK" if:

- he has established his business outside the UK;
- he has a fixed establishment outside the UK; or
- (in the absence of either) his permanent address or usual place of residence is outside the UK.

SI 2005/3290
VAT (INPUT TAX) (REIMBURSEMENT BY EMPLOYERS OF EMPLOYEES' BUSINESS USE OF ROAD FUEL) REGULATIONS 2005

Note These regulations under VATA 1994 s 24(6)(*a*) enable an employer to deduct input tax in respect of road fuel purchased for business purposes by employees.

1. These regulations came into force on 1 January 2006.

2. A taxable person ("the employer") is entitled to input tax deduction under reg 5 if:

- the road fuel is delivered to his employee;
- the employee pays for the road fuel;
- the employee acts in his employer's name, and on his behalf, in respect of the delivery and payment;
- the road fuel is to be used by the employee wholly or partly for the purposes of his employer's business (see reg 7);
- the employer has agreed to reimburse the employee for the road fuel used wholly or partly for business purposes;
- the employer reimburses the employee; and
- the reimbursement is calculated in accordance with reg 3 (if all of the road fuel is used for the purposes of the employer's business) or reg 4 (if only part of the road fuel is so used).

3. The reimbursement is actual cost of the road fuel.

4. The reimbursement is either:

- an amount determined by reference to distance travelled on business journeys and the cylinder capacity of the vehicle in which the road fuel is used; or
- (if the employer will account for output tax on any private use (see VATA 1994 s 57)) the actual cost of the road fuel.

5. The amount of input tax deducted by the employer (see VATA 1994 s 24(1)) is calculated by reference to the amount reimbursed under reg 3 or 4.

6. A deduction is made under reg 5 only if the employer holds a VAT invoice. The invoice must contain the information listed in VAT Regulations 1995, SI 1995/2518 regs 14(1), (2) (normal VAT invoice) or 16(1) (retailers' invoice). In the former case, the employer must be identified as the recipient of the supply.

7. Road fuel is used for the employer's business only if the business use is to make onward taxable supplies.

SI 2007/2195
POSTAL PACKETS (REVENUE AND CUSTOMS) REGULATIONS 2007

Note These regulations apply to international movements of goods in postal packets.

Citation and commencement

1. These regulations came into force on 16 August 2007.

Application of customs and excise enactments to certain postal packets

2. Postal Services Act 2000 applies to all postal packets posted to or from the UK carried by a postal operator who, although not a universal service provider (as defined in Postal Services Act 2000 s 4(3)), provides postal services in connection with the provision of a universal postal service (as defined in s 4(1), (2) of the 2000 Act).

SI 2007/3175
POLICE AND CRIMINAL EVIDENCE ACT 1984 (APPLICATION TO REVENUE AND CUSTOMS) ORDER 2007

Note This Order is made under Police and Criminal Evidence Act 1984 s 114(2), (3). It applies to England and Wales.

Citation and commencement

1. This Order came into force on 1 December 2007.

Interpretation

2. Various words and phrases used in the Order are defined.

A person is in Revenue and Customs detention if he is detained at an HMRC office, or detained elsewhere in the charge of an HMRC officer, in any of the following circumstances: (1) he has been taken to an HMRC office after being arrested for an offence; (2) he is arrested at an HMRC office after attending the office voluntarily; or (3) he is arrested at an HMRC office after accompanying an HMRC officer to the office.

A detained person may be transferred between HMRC detention and police detention.

Application

3. The provisions of Police and Criminal Evidence Act 1984 ("PACE 1984") listed in Sch 1 (which deal with police investigations and persons detained by the police) apply to HMRC investigations and persons detained by HMRC officers with the following modifications:

- PACE 1984 has effect as if the words and phrases in Sch 2 Part I Column 1 were replaced by the words and phrases in column 2.
- PACE 1984 is interpreted as if the references to a constable of a rank specified in Sch 2 Part 2 Column 1 were references to an HMRC officer of at least the grade specified in Column 2.
- PACE 1984 is deemed to include new ss 14A, 14B (see arts 6, 7).
- The text of PACE 1984 ss 18(1), 35(1)–(3), 36(2), 41(2)(*b*), 50(1), 50(2), 64(5)(*b*), 77(3) (see arts 8–12, 14, 15) is amended.
- The application of PACE 1984 ss 8, 21, 24(2), 55, and Sch 1 para 12 is modified (see arts 5(3), 13, 17, 18).

The commentary to PACE 1984 has been drafted accordingly. The application of PACE 1984 generally is modified by arts 4, 5(1), 5(2), 13(2), 16–19.

Exceptions

4. PACE 1984 (as modified by art 3) does not confer any power on an HMRC officer to:

- Charge a person with any offence.
- Release a person on bail.
- Detain a person for an offence after he has been charged with at offence.

Seizure and retention of things found upon search

5. Where PACE 1984 (as modified by art 3) allows an HMRC officer to seize and retain any thing found during a lawful search of person or premises, he may do so even if the thing found is not evidence of an offence relating to an HMRC matter. Anything lawfully seized by a person under any legislation may be accepted and retained by an HMRC officer.

Excluded and special procedure material

6. [Inserts new PACE 1984 s 14A.]

Restriction on other powers to apply for production of documents

7. [Inserts new PACE 1984 s 14B.]

Modification of section 18 of the Act (entry and search after arrest)

8. [Substitutes new PACE 1984 s 18(1).]

Modification of section 35 of the Act (designated police stations)

9. [Substitutes new PACE 1984 s 35(1)–(3).]

Modification of section 36 of the Act (custody officers at police stations)

10. [Substitutes new PACE 1984 s 36(2).]

Modification of section 41 of the Act (limits on period of detention without charge)

11. [Substitutes new PACE 1984 s 41(2)(*b*).]

Modification of section 50 of the Act (records of detention)

12. [Substitutes new PACE 1984 s 50(1), (2).]

Modification of section 55 of the Act (intimate searches)

13. [Modifies the application of PACE 1984 s 55.]

The Commissioners' annual report must contain information about searches carried out under PACE 1984 s 55. The information must relate to the period covered by the report.

Modification of section 64 of the Act (destruction of fingerprints and samples)

14. [Substitutes new PACE 1984 s 64(5)(*b*), (6A).]

Modification of section 77 of the Act (definition of independent person)

15. [Amends PACE 1984 s 77(3).]

Use of reasonable force

16. An HMRC officer may, if necessary, use reasonable force when exercising a power which is not subject to the consent of another person.

Arrest without warrant

17. [Modifies the application of PACE 1984 s 24(2).]

Search of persons

18. [Modifies the application of PACE 1984 s 8 and Sch 1 para 12.]

Authorisation

19. HMRC officers may exercise powers and functions under PACE 1984 only if they are so authorised by the Commissioners. The authority may be general or specific.

Revocation

20. Police and Criminal Evidence Act 1984 (Application to Customs and Excise) Order 1985, SI 1985/1800 and amending instruments are revoked. The 1985 order applied only to assigned matters (as defined in CEMA 1979 s 1). VAT is an assigned matter by virtue of VATA 1994 Sch 11 para 1.

SCHEDULE 1

The provisions of PACE 1984 applicable to HMRC are listed.

SCHEDULE 2

Part 1 lists the words and phrases substituted for words and phrases used in PACE 1984. Part 2 lists the HMRC officer grades substituted for the police ranks used in PACE 1984.

SI 2007/3507
RECOVERY OF FOREIGN TAXES REGULATIONS 2007

Note These regulations are made under FA 2006 s 175.

Citation and commencement

1. This Order came into force on 3 January 2008.

Interpretation

2. Various words and phrases are defined

Relevant foreign tax claim

3. A claim for a relevant foreign tax debt by an overseas authority is treated as if it were a claim for UK income tax. The claim is enforced accordingly.

Requests for recovery

4. A request for recovery of relevant foreign tax must be made in writing. The request must include the information and documents agreed by HMRC and the overseas authority.

Procedure on receipt of request

5. The Commissioners must acknowledge the recovery request in writing.

Requests for recovery – further provisions

6. A recovery request is deemed to be duly made unless the contrary is proved. In principle, the taxpayer's liability to the foreign tax concerned cannot be questioned. For the exceptions, see regs 9, 10, 11.

Communication of information

7. Information received as part of the recovery request may be shared only with taxpayer, the authorities responsible for the recovery of the tax and the judicial authorities dealing with the recovery.

Adjustment of a foreign claim

8. Where the amount of foreign tax due from the taxpayer is decreased, the Commissioners may only recover the decreased amount. They must repay any excess to the taxpayer if it has already been collected from him but not yet paid to the overseas authority. Where the amount of foreign tax due from the taxpayer is increased, the additional amount is consolidated with the original request where possible. It is otherwise treated as a new request for recovery.

Cancellation or payment of a claim

9. HMRC must discontinue enforcement action if the overseas authority notifies them that the outstanding tax has been paid or the claim has been discontinued.

Disputed claims

10. HMRC must not take enforcement action to recover the foreign tax if proceedings relating to the liability are pending in the foreign territory.

Claims determined in taxpayer's favour

11. HMRC must not take enforcement action to recover the foreign tax (or part of it) if the taxpayer demonstrates that a final decision has been taken in his favour by a court, tribunal or other competent body in the foreign territory.

Limitation

12. The time limits for recovery of foreign tax are those applicable in the relevant foreign territory. Steps taken by HMRC to recover the debt may have the effect of suspending or interrupting the period of limitation applicable under the law of the foreign territory. If so, the steps taken by HMRC are treated as if they had been taken by the overseas authority in the foreign territory concerned.

Interest

13. Interest is charged by either HMRC or the overseas authority. In the former case, interest is charged in accordance with FA 1989 s 178. In the latter case, interest is charged in accordance with the law of the foreign territory. Interest is calculated up to and including the date of payment. In either case, interest is recovered in the same manner as interest charged under TMA 1970.

Evidence

14. A recognised instrument permitting enforcement of the foreign tax claim, together with a certificate from an HMRC officer stating that payment has not been made to HMRC, is treated as sufficient evidence that the amount claimed is unpaid.

Enforcement in Scotland

15. [Applies to Scotland.]

SI 2008/1146
VAT (BUILDINGS AND LAND) ORDER 2008

Note This Order is made under FA 2006 s 17(1)–(5). It repeals and replaces VATA 1994 Sch 10 (art 2) and makes corresponding amendments, repeals and revocations (arts 3, 5, 6 and Sch 1).

Citation, commencement and effect

1. This Order came into force on 1 June 2008. Article 4 has effect in relation to supplies made after 31 May 2020. For transitional provisions and savings in relation to art 4, see Sch 2.

Developmental tenancies, leases or licences

4. VATA 1994 Sch 9 Group 1 Item 1(*b*) and Note 7 are repealed in relation to supplies made after 31 May 2020.

Transitional provisions and savings

7. This article introduces Sch 2.

SCHEDULE 2

The following provisions have effect instead of Interpretation Act 1978 s 17(2):

- In so far as art 2 re-enacts VATA 1994 Sch 10 in a rewritten form, it does not affect the continuity of the law.
- Anything in force on 31 May 2008 which was done, or has effect as if done, under the superseded Sch 10 has effect as if it were done under the rewritten Sch 10.
- In so far as the context admits, references to the superseded Sch 10 in an enactment, instrument or document are read as if they were references to the rewritten Sch 10 and vice versa.

SI 2008/1936
FINANCE ACT 2008 SECTION 135 (DISASTER OR EMERGENCY) ORDER 2008

Note This Order is made under FA 2008 s 135.

Citation, commencement and interpretation

1. This order came into force on 13 August 2008.

Specification of disaster

2. The floods, caused by weather conditions, which occurred in the UK in June and July 2007 are a disaster for the purposes of FA 2008 s 135.

Specified date

3. The relief period (see FA 2008 s 135(4)(*a*)) commences on 1 June 2007.

SI 2008/1948
TAXES (FEES FOR PAYMENT BY TELEPHONE) REGULATIONS 2008

Note These regulations are made under FA 2008 s 136. They specify the fee payable for telephone payments made by credit card.

Citation and commencement

1. These regulations came into force on 13 August 2008.

Fee payable for telephone payments by credit card

2. A person making a payment to the Commissioners (or a person authorised by the Commissioners) must pay a fee equal to 0.91 per cent of the payment if he gives telephone authorisation for the payment to be made by credit card (as defined in reg 2(3)). The fee is payable in addition to the amount of payment. Thus, for example, a taxpayer must authorise payment of £10,091 in order to discharge a debt of £10,000.

SI 2008/2692
QUALIFICATIONS FOR APPOINTMENT OF MEMBERS TO THE FIRST-TIER TRIBUNAL AND UPPER TRIBUNAL ORDER 2008

Note This order sets out the qualifications or experience required by a person in order to be eligible for appointment as a member of the First-tier Tribunal or Upper Tribunal.

1. This order came into force on 3 November 2008.

2. A person other than a judge is eligible for appointment as a member of the First-tier Tribunal or Upper Tribunal if he meets any of the following criteria:

- he possesses one of the professional qualifications listed in art 2(2);
- he is experienced in dealing with the physical or mental needs of disabled persons (see art 2(3)); or
- he has substantial experience of the matters listed in art 2(4). These matters include tax matters and tax-related procedures.

SI 2008/2698
TRIBUNAL PROCEDURE (UPPER TRIBUNAL) RULES 2008

Note These Rules govern the practice and procedure to be followed in the Upper Tribunal. The following commentary is confined to the procedure relevant to VAT appeals.

PART 1 INTRODUCTION

Citation, commencement, application and interpretation

1. These Rules came into force on 3 November 2008. As regards VAT, they apply to proceedings before the Administrative Appeals Chamber and the Tax and Chancery Chamber.

Overriding objective and parties' obligation to co-operate with the Upper Tribunal

2. The overriding objective of the Rules is to enable the tribunal to deal with cases fairly and justly. This includes:

(a) dealing with cases in a manner proportionate to the importance of the case, the complexity of the issues, the anticipated costs and the resources of the parties;

(b) avoiding unnecessary formality and seeking flexibility in the proceedings;

(c) (so far as practicable) ensuring that the parties are able to participate fully in the proceedings;

(d) using any special expertise of the tribunal effectively; and

(e) (where compatible with proper consideration of the issues) avoiding delay.

The Upper Tribunal must seek to give effect to these principles when exercising powers conferred by these Rules or interpreting any rule or practice direction.

The parties must help the tribunal to further these principles. They must co-operate with the tribunal.

Alternative dispute resolution and arbitration

3. Where appropriate, the tribunal should draw attention to the availability of alternative procedures for resolving the dispute and, if the parties so wish, facilitate use of the procedure if this is compatible with the overriding objective (see r 2). Arbitration Act Part 1 does not apply to proceedings before the tribunal.

PART 2 GENERAL POWERS AND PROVISIONS

Delegation to staff

4. Tribunal staff (see TCEA 2007 s 40(1)) may, with the approval of the Senior President of Tribunals, carry out functions of a judicial nature that are permitted or required to be done by the tribunal.

Case management powers

5. In principle, the tribunal regulates its own procedure. The tribunal may give directions relating to the conduct or disposal of proceedings. In particular, it may exercise the specific powers specified.

Procedure for applying for and giving directions

6. The tribunal may give directions on an application made by one or more of the parties. Applications are made by written notice to the tribunal or orally during a hearing. The reason for making the application must be given. The tribunal may also give directions on its own initiative.

A written notice of a direction is normally sent to every party and to any other person affected by it. The direction can be challenged by applying for a direction amending, suspending or setting aside the first direction.

Failure to comply with rules etc

7. An irregularity may arise from a failure to comply with these Rules, a practice direction or a direction. This does not, of itself, void the proceedings or any step taken in them. The tribunal may take such action as it considers just in relation to a failure to comply.

A failure to comply with a requirement imposed by the First-tier Tribunal in respect of specified matters may be referred to the tribunal by the First-tier Tribunal. If so, the tribunal may exercise its supplementary powers (see TCEA 2007 s 25) in relation to the non-compliance as if it had itself imposed the requirement.

Striking out a party's case

8. A direction may warn an appellant or applicant that all or part of the proceedings would be struck out if he failed to comply. This consequence follows automatically if he fails to do so. The tribunal has an option to strike out the proceedings (or the relevant part of them) if the direction warned that this could happen. In either case, the appellant or applicant may apply for the proceedings (or the relevant part) to be reinstated. This must be done in writing. The application must be received no later than one month after the tribunal notified the appellant or applicant that the proceedings (or the relevant part) had been struck out.

A direction may warn a respondent or interested party that he will be barred from taking any further part in all or part of the proceedings if he failed to comply. This consequence follows automatically if he fails to do so. The tribunal has an option to bar the respondent or interested party from the proceedings (or the relevant part of them) if the direction warned that this *could* happen. In either case, the respondent or interested party may apply for the bar to be lifted. This must be done in writing. The application must be received no later than one month after the tribunal notified the respondent or interested party that the bar had been imposed.

The tribunal may not have jurisdiction in respect of all or part of the proceedings. The tribunal may transfer the proceedings to another tribunal in appropriate circumstances (see r 5(3)(*k*)). It must strike out the proceedings (or the relevant part), or bar the respondent or interested party from taking any further part in them, if it does not do so. However, the tribunal must give the appellant, applicant, respondent or interested party an opportunity to make representations before doing so.

The tribunal may strike out all or part of the proceedings if: (1) the appellant or applicant has failed to co-operate with the tribunal to such an extent that it cannot deal with the proceedings fairly and justly; or (2) the tribunal considers that the appellant or applicant's case (or the relevant part) has no reasonable prospect of success. The tribunal must give the appellant or applicant an opportunity to make representations before doing so in either case.

The tribunal may bar a respondent or interested party from taking any further part in all or part of the proceedings if: (1) he has failed to co-operate with the tribunal to such an extent that it cannot deal with the proceedings fairly and justly; or (2) the tribunal considers that the his case (or the relevant part) has no reasonable prospect of success. The tribunal must give him an opportunity to make representations before doing so in either case. Head (2) does not apply to: (*a*) appeals from the decision of another tribunal, and (*b*) judicial review proceedings.

The tribunal may not have jurisdiction in respect of all or part of the proceedings. The tribunal may transfer the proceedings to another court or tribunal in appropriate circumstances (see r 5(3)(*k*)). It must strike out the proceedings (or the relevant part), or bar the respondent or interested party from taking any further part in them, if it does not do so. However, the tribunal must give the relevant parties an opportunity to make representations before doing so.

The tribunal if not required to consider any response or other submission made by a respondent or interested party who is for the time being barred from taking any further part in the proceedings. The tribunal may summarily determine some or all of the issues against the respondent or interested party.

Substitution and addition of parties

9. The tribunal may give a direction adding, substituting or removing a party as an appellant, respondent or interested party. The tribunal may give such consequential directions as it considers appropriate.

Orders for costs

10. The tribunal may make an order in respect of costs in proceedings transferred by, or on appeal from, the Tax Chamber of the First-tier Tribunal. As regards proceedings transferred, referred or appealed from another tribunal, the tribunal may make an order for costs only if, and to the extent, that the other tribunal has power to make an order for costs in similar circumstances. In other proceedings, the tribunal's power to make an order in respect of costs is confined to: (1) judicial review proceedings; (2) applications for wasted costs (see TCEA 2007 s 29(4)); and (3) situations where the tribunal considers that a party to the proceedings (or his representative) has acted unreasonably in bringing, defending or conducting the proceedings.

The tribunal may make an order for costs on its own initiative or in response to an application. An application is made in writing to the tribunal. A schedule of the costs claimed must be annexed thereto. A copy of the application and schedule must be sent or delivered to the person against whom the proposed order should be made (who is referred to as "the paying party"). An application may be made at any time during the proceedings. It must be made no later than one month after the tribunal sends either: (1) a notice recording the decision which finally disposes of all issues in the proceedings; or (2) a notice of withdrawal (see r 17) ending the proceedings.

The tribunal must give the paying party an opportunity to make representations before it makes an order against him.

If the paying party is an individual, the tribunal must consider his financial means before making an order. However, the tribunal is not required to do so in relation to an order for wasted costs.

The amount of costs payable under an order may be: (1) summarily assessed by the tribunal; (2) agreed by the paying party and the recipient; or (3) (In the absence of such an agreement) assessed by reference to all or a specified part of the costs incurred by the recipient. As regards an order made under head (3), the paying party may apply for a detailed assessment of costs in accordance with r 10(9)(*a*). For equivalent provisions in Scotland and Northern Ireland, see r 10(9)(*b*) and (*c*) respectively.

Representatives

11. A party to the proceedings may appoint a representative. He is not required to be a legal representative (see r 11(9)). A written notice of the representative's name and address must be sent or delivered to the tribunal. The tribunal must send a copy to the other party or parties. Having received such a notice, the other party or parties must provide the representative with any documents required to be provided to his principal. The other party or parties may assume that the representative continues to act for his principal until they are notified otherwise in writing by the representative or his principal.

A representative may do anything (except sign a witness statement) required or permitted to be done by his principal.

A party to the proceedings may be accompanied at the hearing by someone other than an authorised representative. If the tribunal so permits, this person may act as a representative or otherwise assist in presenting the party's case at the hearing. However, the rights and duties of an appointed representative do not apply to him.

Calculating time

12. An act required to be done on or by a particular day must be done before 5pm on that day. If the specified time for doing an act does not end on a working day, the act is done in time if it is done on the next working day.

Sending and delivery of documents

13. Any document required to be provided to the tribunal must sent or delivered to the address specified for the proceedings using one of the specified means of delivery. It must normally be written in English or be accompanied by an English translation. However, a document or translation may be submitted in Welsh if the proceedings are in Wales or have a connection with Wales. If a party does not want a particular form of communication to be used, he should inform the tribunal and the other parties. Once he has done so, that form of communication must not be used. If a document is sent electronically, the recipient may request a hard copy. The address provided by a party or his representative for the service of documents may be assumed to be correct until a written notice to the contrary is received.

Use of documents and information

14. The tribunal may make an order prohibiting the disclosure or publication of: (1) specified documents relating to the proceedings; (2) specified information relating to the proceedings; or (3) (if the tribunal considers that a person's identity should be protected) any matter which may lead to his identification.

The tribunal may direct that certain documents or information may (or must) be disclosed to the tribunal on the basis that they will not be disclosed to other persons or specified other persons. A party applying for such a direction may withhold the relevant documents or information from the other parties until such time as the application has been granted or refused.

Evidence and submissions

15. The tribunal may give directions on specified matters relating to the issues on which it requires evidence or submissions. The tribunal may admit evidence which would not be admissible in a civil trial. It may exclude evidence in specified situations.

Summoning or citation of witnesses and orders to answer questions or produce documents

16. A tribunal may require any person to attend a hearing as a witness. The procedure for making and setting aside a witness summons is set out.

The tribunal may order any person to answer questions or produce relevant documents in his possession or control. The tribunal may do so on its own initiative or on the application of a party to the proceedings. However, its powers are limited to those available in the trial of an action in a court of law in the home country where the proceedings are to be determined.

Withdrawal

17. A party may withdraw all or part of his case. He normally does so by sending or delivering a notice of withdrawal to the tribunal before the hearing takes place or the proceedings are otherwise determined. However, a party may withdraw all or part of his case at a hearing. The notice of withdrawal takes effect if the tribunal so consents. The tribunal notifies the parties accordingly. By way of exception, the withdrawal of an application for permission to appeal does not require the tribunal's consent.

The party may subsequently apply for his case to be reinstated. The procedure for doing so is set out.

Appeal treated as abandoned or finally determined in an asylum case or an immigration case

17A. [Not relevant to VAT.]

Notice of funding of legal services

18. A party is granted funding by the Legal Services Commission. If so, he must send a copy of the funding notice as soon as practicable and notify every other party in writing that funding has been granted. Equivalent provisions apply in Scotland and Northern Ireland.

Confidentiality in child support or child trust fund cases

19. [Not relevant to VAT.]

Power to pay expenses and allowances

20. [Not relevant to VAT.]

Procedure for applying for a stay of a decision pending an appeal

20A. [This rule is relevant to the new types of cases to be dealt with by the tribunal from 1 September 2009. It does not appear to be relevant to VAT.]

PART 3 PROCEDURE FOR CASES IN THE UPPER TRIBUNAL

Applications to the Upper Tribunal for permission to appeal

21. A person may apply to the tribunal for permission to appeal against a decision of another tribunal if: (1) he has made an application for permission to the tribunal which made the relevant decision; and (2) that tribunal has refused the application or not admitted it. For applications to the Tax Chamber of the First-tier Tribunal, see Tribunal Procedure (First-tier Tribunal) (Tax Chamber) Rules 2009, SI 2009/273 r 39.

An application must be made in writing within the prescribed time limit (one month). It must provide: (1) the information listed; (2) a copy of the decision being challenged; (3) any separate written statement of the reasons for that decision; (4) the notice of refusal of permission to appeal or the notice of refusal to admit the application for permission to appeal; (5) (if the application is made late) an application for an extension of time to make the application (see r 5(3)(*a*)); (6) (if the other tribunal refused to admit an application for permission to appeal on the grounds that the application was made late) the reason why that application was made late; and (7) (if the other tribunal refused to admit an application for permission to appeal on the grounds that the application for a written statement of reasons was made late) the reason why that application was made late.

As regards head (5), the tribunal may admit the application only if it grants an extension of time. As regards heads (6) and (7), the tribunal may admit the application only if it is in the interests of justice to do so.

Decision in relation to permission to appeal

22. If the tribunal refuses permission to appeal, it must send written notice of the refusal, and the reasons for refusal, to the appellant.

If the tribunal gives permission to appeal, it must send the following to each party: (1) written notice of the appeal; and (2) the reasons for any limitations or conditions imposed. The application for permission to appeal stands as the notice of appeal. This is subject to any directions made by the tribunal. The tribunal must send each respondent a copy of: (1) the application for permission to appeal; and (2) any documents provided with it by the appellant. If the appellant and each respondent so consent, the tribunal may determine the appeal without obtaining any further response.

The tribunal may determine, without a hearing, an application for permission to appeal against a decision of the Tax Chamber of the First-tier Tribunal. If the tribunal refuses permission, or gives permission on limited grounds or subject to conditions, the appellant may apply for the decision to be reconsidered at a hearing. This application must be made in writing within the prescribed time limit (14 days).

Notice of appeal

23. This rule applies in the following circumstances:

(a) (if the tribunal so directs) a case is transferred or referred to the tribunal from the First-tier Tribunal (see rr 23(1)(*a*) and 26A(1)(*a*), (2)(*b*));

(b) if permission for a party to appeal to the tribunal has been given by another tribunal. For permission given by the Tax Chamber of the First-tier Tribunal, see the Tax Chamber of the First-tier Tribunal, see Tribunal Procedure (First-tier Tribunal) (Tax Chamber) Rules 2009, SI 2009/273 rr 39 and 40;

(c) (if the tribunal has given permission to appeal) the tribunal has directed that the application for permission does not stand as the notice of appeal. For applications otherwise standing as the notice of appeal, see r 22(2)(*b*).

In these circumstances, the appellant must provide a notice of appeal to the tribunal within the prescribed time limit (one month). The notice of appeal must provide the information listed in r 21(4)(*a*)–(*e*). The following documents must be annexed to it: (1) any written record of the decision being challenged; (2) any separate written statement of reasons for that decision; and (3) the notice of permission to appeal.

Permission for a party to appeal to the tribunal may be given by that tribunal. If the party's application for permission does not stand as the notice of appeal, the appellant must provide a notice of appeal to the tribunal within the prescribed time limit (one month). The notice of appeal must provide the information listed in r 21(4)(*a*)–(*e*) and the tribunal's case reference. The following documents must be annexed to the notice of appeal: (1) any written record of the decision being challenged; (2) any separate written statement of reasons for that decision; and (3) the notice of permission to appeal.

If a notice of appeal is provided late, it must include a request for an extension of time and the reason why the notice was not provided in time. The appeal may admit the notice of appeal only if grants and extension of time (see r 5(3)(*a*)).

The tribunal must send a copy of the notice of appeal and any accompanying documents to each respondent.

Response to the notice of appeal

24. Any response to the notice of appeal must be given to the tribunal in writing within the prescribed time limit (one month). It must state the information listed.

If the response is provided late, it must include a request for an extension of time and the reason why the response was not provided in time. The tribunal must send a copy of the response and any accompanying documents to the appellant and other parties.

Appellant's reply

25. The appellant may provide a reply to the response provided by the respondent (see r 24). If so, the response must be provided to the Upper Tribunal in writing within the prescribed time limit (one month). The tribunal must send a copy of the reply and any accompanying documents to each respondent.

References under the Forfeiture Act 1982

26. [Not relevant to VAT.]

Cases transferred or referred to the Upper Tribunal, applications made directly to the Upper Tribunal and proceedings without a notice to a respondent

26A. The Upper Tribunal must give directions as to the procedure to be followed in consideration and disposal of the proceedings in: (1) a case transferred or referred from the First-tier Tribunal; or (2) a case started by an application made directly to the tribunal. The direction determines the extent to which rr 21–26 apply to the proceedings. Any rules requiring documents to be provided to or by the respondent, or permitting him to participate in the proceedings, do not apply if the case or matter is to be determined without notice to the respondent or without his involvement.

Financial services cases

26B. [Not relevant to VAT.]

PART 4 JUDICIAL REVIEW PROCEEDINGS IN THE UPPER TRIBUNAL

Application of this Part to judicial review proceedings transferred to the Upper Tribunal

27. A court may transfer judicial review proceedings to the tribunal. If so, the tribunal must notify each party in writing and give directions regarding future conduct of the proceedings. The directions may modify or disapply rr 28–33 for the purposes of the proceedings.

For directions in relation to proceedings transferred from the Court of Session, see r 27(3).

Applications for permission to bring judicial review proceedings

28. A person seeking permission to bring judicial review proceedings before the tribunal must make a written application to the tribunal. This must be done promptly and within the prescribed time limit (normally three months). The application must state the information listed. It must be accompanied by the documents listed.

If the application is provided late, it must include a request for an extension of time and the reason why the application was not provided in time. The tribunal must send a copy of the application and any accompanying documents to the respondent and any interested parties named in it.

Acknowledgment of service

29. A respondent or interested party receiving a copy of an application for permission to bring judicial proceedings (see r 28(8)) must send or deliver an acknowledgment of service in writing to the tribunal within the prescribed time limit (21 days) if he wishes to take part in the proceedings. If he fails to do so, he may take part in the application for permission only if the tribunal so allows. He may, however, take part in the subsequent proceedings if the application is successful.

The acknowledgment of service must state the information listed.

Decision on permission or summary dismissal, and reconsideration of permission or summary dismissal at a hearing

30. For proceedings transferred from the Court of Session, see r 30(2) and (3)(*b*).

Responses

31. A person notified of permission being granted to bring judicial review proceedings may provide a response if he wishes to contest the application or support it on additional grounds. The response must be given in writing and sent or delivered to the tribunal within the prescribed time limit (35 days). It must provide detailed grounds for contesting or supporting the application.

Applicant seeking to rely on additional grounds

32. If permission has been given to bring judicial review proceedings on specified grounds, the applicant may not rely on any other grounds without the consent of the tribunal.

Right to make representations

33. Each party may: (1) submit evidence; (2) make representations at any hearing which they are entitled to attend; and (3) make written representations in relation to a decision to be made without a hearing. Evidence may not be submitted at the hearing of an application for permission.

The same applies to any other person if the tribunal gives permission.

PART 5 HEARINGS

Determination with or without a hearing

34. The tribunal may make any decision without a hearing. In deciding whether or not to hold a hearing and, if so, the form it should take, the tribunal must have regard to the views expressed by the parties.

Entitlement to attend a hearing

35. In principle, each party to the proceedings is entitled to attend a hearing. For the exclusion of persons from a hearing, see r 37(4).

Notice of hearings

36. The tribunal must give reasonable notice of: (1) the time and place of any hearing, adjourned hearing or postponed hearing; and (2) any changes to the time and place of any hearing. In principle, at least 14 days' notice must be given. However, shorter notice may be given if: (1) the parties so consent; or (2) the circumstances are urgent or exceptional.

As regards the hearing of an application for permission to bring judicial review proceedings, the minimum period of notice is two working days.

Special time limits for hearing an appeal in a fast-track case

36A. [Not relevant to VAT.]

Public and private hearings

37. In principle, all hearing must be held in public. This principle is subject to the following exceptions:

- the tribunal gives a direction that all or part of a hearing is to be held in private. The tribunal may determine who is entitled to attend;
- a person may be excluded if: (1) he is disrupting, or is likely to disrupt, the hearing; (2) his presence is likely to inhibit the giving of evidence or the making of submissions; (3) his exclusion is necessary to give effect to a direction prohibiting disclosure of information (see r 14(2)); (4) his attendance would defeat the purpose of the hearing; or (5) he is under the age of 18 years;
- a witness may be excluded until he gives evidence.

Hearing in a party's absence

38. A party may fail to attend a hearing. If so, the tribunal may proceed with the hearing in his absence if:

(a) the tribunal is satisfied that either: (1) the party has been notified of the hearing; or (2) reasonable steps have been taken to notify him of the hearing; and

(b) the tribunal considers that this is in the interests of justice.

PART 6 DECISIONS

Consent orders

39. The tribunal may make a consent order disposing of the proceedings and making such other appropriate provision as the parties have agreed. The tribunal is not required to hold a hearing.

Decisions

40. The tribunal may give a decision orally at a hearing.

Having made a decision which finally disposes of all issues in the proceedings, the tribunal must, as soon as practicable thereafter, provide:

- a decision notice stating the tribunal's decision. This requirement does not apply to harmful information withheld in accordance with r 14(11);
- information regarding any right of review or appeal, the time limit for exercising it and the manner in which it may be exercised. This requirement does not apply to a decision within Part 7; and
- written reasons for the tribunal's decision. This requirement does not apply if: (1) the parties so consent; or (2) the decision was made with the consent of the parties.

The tribunal may provide written reasons for a decision in other circumstances.

Special procedure for providing notice of a decision relating to an asylum case

40A. [Not relevant to VAT.]

PART 7 CORRECTING, SETTING ASIDE, REVIEWING AND APPEALING DECISIONS OF THE UPPER TRIBUNAL

Interpretation

41. The terms "appeal" and "review" are defined.

Clerical mistakes and accidental slips or omissions

42. The tribunal may correct any decision or record of a decision which contains a clerical mistake or an accidental slip or omission. It may do so at any time. The correction is made by: (1) notifying the amended decision or sending a copy of the amended record to the parties; and (2) amending any published information regarding the decision or record.

Setting aside a decision which disposes of proceedings

43. The tribunal may set aside all or part of a decision disposing of proceedings if the tribunal considers this to be necessary in the interests of justice. One or more of the specified conditions must be met. The tribunal may re-make the decision or part. A party may apply for this to be done. A written application must be made within the prescribed time limit (one month).

Application for permission to appeal

44. A person seeking permission to appeal to the relevant appellate court against a decision of the tribunal must make a written application to the tribunal. The application must be sent or delivered to the tribunal within the prescribed time limit (one month). If the time limit has expired, his application must include a request for an extension of time and set out the reason why the application was not provided in time. The application must identify the tribunal decision to which it relates, identify the alleged error(s) of law in the decision and state the result sought by the applicant.

Upper Tribunal's consideration of application for permission to appeal

45. An application for permission to appeal (see r 44) is dealt with as follows:

- the tribunal may review the decision in accordance with r 46. The tribunal may do so only if: (1) when making the decision, the tribunal overlooked a legislative authority or binding authority which could have had a material effect on the decision; or (2) since making the decision, a court has made a decision which is binding on the tribunal and which may have materially affected the tribunal's decision if made earlier. On review, the tribunal may decide to take no action in relation to all or part of the decision. If so, the tribunal must go on to decide whether to give permission to appeal in relation to the decision, or the part, on which it has decided to take no action.
- the tribunal may decide not to review the decision. In these circumstances, the tribunal must go on to decide whether to give permission to appeal against the decision.

The tribunal must send a record of its decision to the parties as soon as practicable. If the tribunal decides to refuse permission, the record must state the reasons for the refusal and indicate that the applicant is entitled to apply to the relevant appellate court for permission to appeal against the decision. If the tribunal decides to give permission to appeal on limited grounds, the record must state the reason for refusing permission on the other grounds and indicate that the applicant is entitled to apply to the relevant appellate court for permission to appeal against on the grounds for which permission has been refused.

The tribunal may refuse permission to appeal, give permission against only part of the decision or give permission to appeal on limited grounds. In any of these situations, the record of its decision must be accompanied by: (1) a statement of the reasons for refusing permission in relation to all or part of the application; and (2) a notification of the right to make an application to the tribunal for permission to appeal.

Review of a decision

46. For reviews generally, see TCEA 2007 s 10. The tribunal's jurisdiction to undertake a review of a decision is confined to the power conferred by r 40(1).

The tribunal must notify the parties of the outcome of a review and indicate any rights of appeal or review in relation to the outcome. This must be done in writing.

The tribunal may have decided to take an action in relation to a decision without having first given the relevant persons an opportunity to make representations. If so, this fact must be recorded on in the notification of outcome. The notification must indicate that the relevant persons may apply for the action to be set aside and for the decision to be reviewed again.

Review of a decision in proceedings under the Forfeiture Act 1982

47. [Not relevant to VAT.]

Power to treat an application as a different type of application

48. The tribunal may treat an application in respect of one of the following matters as an application against any of the other matters: (1) an application for a decision to be corrected, set aside or reviewed; and (2) an application for permission to appeal against a decision.

SCHEDULE 1 PROCEDURE AFTER THE NOTICE IN APPEAL AGAINST DECISIONS OF TRAFFIC COMMISSIONERS (RULE 24(1))

[Not relevant to VAT.]

SCHEDULE 2 ADDITIONAL PROCEDURE IN NATIONAL SECURITY CERTIFICATE CASES (RULE 26A(4))

[Not relevant to VAT.]

SCHEDULE 3 PROCEDURE IN FINANCIAL SERVICES CASES (RULE 26B)

[Not relevant to VAT.]

SI 2008/2834
APPEALS FROM THE UPPER TRIBUNAL TO THE COURT OF APPEAL ORDER 2008

Note This order sets out the grounds on which permission may be granted for an appeal from the Upper Tribunal to the Court of Appeal.

1. This order came into force on 3 November 2008.

2. The Upper Tribunal will not grant permission for an appeal to the Court of Appeal unless it considers that one of the following conditions is met: (1) the proposed appeal would raise some important point of principle or practice; or (2) there is some other compelling reason for the Court of Appeal to hear the appeal.

If the Upper Tribunal refuses permission, the Court of Appeal will not grant permission unless the same conditions are met.

Equivalent provisions apply in Northern Ireland.

SI 2008/2835
FIRST-TIER AND UPPER TRIBUNAL (COMPOSITION OF TRIBUNAL) ORDER 2008

Note This order makes provision for determining how many tribunal members are to decide a matter before the First-tier Tribunal or the Upper Tribunal, and how many of them are to be judges or other members.

Citation and commencement

1. This order came into force on 3 November 2008.

Number of members of the First-tier Tribunal

2. As regards a matter falling to be decided by the First-tier Tribunal, the number of members who are to decide the matter is determined by the Senior President of Tribunals. He must have regard to the need for members of tribunals to have particular expertise, skills or knowledge. If the matter was inherited from a tribunal whose functions have been transferred to the First-tier Tribunal, the Senior President must have regard to the rules of the earlier tribunal governing the number of members.

Number of members of the Upper Tribunal

3. A matter falling to be decided by the Upper Tribunal is normally decided by one member. However, the Senior President of Tribunals may determine that a matter is to be decided by two or three members.

Tribunal consisting of a single member

4. If a matter to be decided by a single member, that member is normally a judge. The Senior President of Tribunals may determine otherwise.

Tribunal consisting of two or more members

5–8. The following provisions apply if a matter is to be decided by two or more members:

- the division between judges and other members is determined by the Senior President of Tribunals;
- the Senior President of Tribunals must select one of the members to be chairman. He is referred to as the "presiding member";
- if the decision of the tribunal is not unanimous, the majority prevails; and
- if the votes are equally divided, the presiding member has a casting vote.

SI 2009/56
TRANSFER OF TRIBUNAL FUNCTIONS AND REVENUE AND CUSTOMS APPEALS ORDER 2009

Note This order abolishes four tax tribunals, transfers the functions and members of five tax tribunals and makes consequential amendments to the legislation relating to them.

Citation and commencement

1. This order came into force on 1 April 2009.

The existing tribunals

2. This lists the tribunals which are collectively referred to as the "existing tribunals". The only tribunals relevant to VAT are the VAT and duties tribunals, which were established under VATA 1994 Sch 12.

Transfer of functions, consequential and other amendments

3. Schedules 1 and 2 are introduced.

Abolition of existing tribunals

4. The VAT and duties tribunals are abolished.

Transfer of members of existing tribunals

5. A person holding an office in a VAT and duties tribunal on 31 March 2009 became a transferred-in judge or transferred-in other member of either or both the First-tier Tribunal and the Upper Tribunal on 1 April 2009.

Transitionals and savings

6. Schedule 3 is introduced.

SCHEDULE 1 CONSEQUENTIAL AMENDMENTS AND SUPPLEMENTARY PROVISIONS – PRIMARY LEGISLATION (ARTICLE 3)

This schedule makes consequential amendments to primary legislation flowing from: (1) establishment of the First-tier Tribunal and Upper Tribunal; and (2) abolition the VAT and duties tribunals.

SCHEDULE 2 CONSEQUENTIAL AMENDMENTS AND SUPPLEMENTARY PROVISIONS – SECONDARY LEGISLATION (ARTICLE 3)

This schedule makes consequential amendments to secondary legislation flowing from establishment of the First-tier Tribunal and Upper Tribunal (paras 1–186). It also repeals secondary legislation relating to the VAT and duties tribunals (art 187).

SCHEDULE 3 TRANSITIONAL AND SAVING PROVISIONS (ARTICLE 6)

General

1. Various words and phrases are defined.

Former VAT and duties tribunals matters (except VAT)

2, 3. [Not relevant to VAT.]

Former VAT and duties tribunals matters: VAT

4. The following consequences follow if HMRC notified a decision before 1 April 2009 against which an appeal lies to a VAT and duties tribunal and no notice of appeal has been served on the tribunal before that date:

- the following legislation continues to apply after 31 March 2009: VATA 1994, VAT Tribunal Rules 1986, SI 1986/590 and any other enactments applicable to the decision;
- those enactments apply subject to Tribunal Procedural Rules;
- any reference to an existing tribunal is treated as a reference to the First-tier Tribunal or, where determined in accordance with Tribunal Procedure Rules, the Upper Tribunal; and
- a time limit continues to apply if it started to run before 1 April 2009 and expires after 31 March 2009.

Matters formerly heard by existing tribunals (except VAT and duties tribunals)

5. [Not relevant to VAT.]

Current proceedings

6, 7. Any current proceedings (see para 1(2)) continue after 31 March 2009 before the First-tier Tribunal or (if so determined in accordance with Tribunal Procedure Rules) the Upper Tribunal. The following provisions apply to those proceedings:

- as regards hearings in progress immediately before 1 April 2009, the hearing must be continued with the same panel;
- the tribunal may give any direction to ensure that the proceedings are dealt with fairly and justly;
- any order or direction in force immediately before 1 April 2009 remains in force;
- a direction or order in force immediately before 1 April 2009 continues to apply; and
- an order for costs may be made only if, and to the extent, that an order could have been made before 1 April 2009.

Cases to be remitted by courts

8. A case remitted by a court after 31 March 2009 in relation to a VAT and duties tribunal must be remitted to the First-tier Tribunal or (if so determined in accordance with Tribunal Procedure Rules) the Upper Tribunal.

Directions of VAT and duties tribunals and courts: interest and payment

9. VATA 1994 s 84(8) continues to apply in relation to any decision of a VAT and duties tribunal made before 1 April 2009.

VATA 1994 s 85B does not apply in relation to an appeal from a decision of a VAT and duties tribunal, or a court, made before 1 April 2009.

10. VATA 1994 s 85B does not apply in relation to an appeal from a decision of a VAT and duties tribunal, or a court, made before 1 April 2009.

Decisions of existing tribunals: rights of appeal, reviews and irregularities

11. One of the following situations may apply immediately before 1 April in relation to a decision of a VAT and duties tribunal: (1) an appeal lies to a court from the decision; (2) an application has been (or may be) made to the tribunal seeking a review of that decision; or (3) the tribunal wishes to correct an irregularity. From 1 April 2009, those rights of appeal are governed by the rules applicable to an appeal against a decision of the First-tier Tribunal.

Existing tribunals: staff

12. Staff appointed to a VAT and duties tribunal before 1 April 2009 are treated from that date as if they had been appointed by the Lord Chancellor under TCEA 2007 s 40(1).

Transitional: general

13. If appropriate, references to a VAT and duties tribunal are to be taken as references to the First-tier Tribunal or (if so determined in accordance with Tribunal Procedure Rules) the Upper Tribunal.

SI 2009/196
FIRST-TIER TRIBUNAL AND UPPER TRIBUNAL (CHAMBERS) (AMENDMENT) ORDER 2008

Note This order amends the First-tier Tribunal and Upper Tribunal (Chambers) Order 2008, SI 2008/2684 and makes transitional provisions.

Citation and commencement

1. This order came into force on 1 April 2009.

Amendments to the First-tier Tribunal and Upper Tribunal (Chambers) Order 2008

2–8. [Repealed.]

Transitional provisions

9. As regards a decision of a VAT and duties tribunal, the reference to “the tribunal which made the decision challenged” in the Tribunal Procedure (Upper Tribunal) Rules 2008, SI 2008/2698 r 21(2)(*a*) is read as a reference to “the First-tier Tribunal”.

SI 2009/273
TRIBUNAL PROCEDURE (FIRST-TIER TRIBUNAL) (TAX CHAMBER) RULES 2009

Note These Rules govern the practice and procedure to be followed in the Tax Chamber of the First-tier Tribunal.

PART 1 INTRODUCTION

Citation, commencement, application and interpretation

1. These Rules came into force on 1 April 2009. They apply to proceedings allocated to the Tax Chamber of the First-tier Tribunal (hereafter "the tribunal"). Various words and phrases are defined.

Overriding objective and parties' obligation to co-operate with the Tribunal

2. The overriding objective of the Rules is to deal with cases fairly and justly. This includes:

(a) dealing with cases in a manner proportionate to the importance of the case, the complexity of the issues, the anticipated costs and the resources of the parties;
(b) avoiding unnecessary formality and seeking flexibility in the proceedings;
(c) (so far as practicable) ensuring that the parties are able to participate fully in the proceedings;
(d) using any special expertise of the tribunal effectively; and
(e) (where compatible with proper consideration of the issues) avoiding delay.

The tribunal must seek to give effect to these objectives when exercising powers conferred by these Rules or interpreting any rule or practice direction.

The parties must help the tribunal to further these principles. They must co-operate with the tribunal.

Alternative dispute resolution and arbitration

3. Where appropriate, the tribunal should draw attention to the availability of alternative procedures for resolving the dispute and, if the parties so wish, facilitate use of the procedure if this is compatible with the overriding objective (see r 2). Arbitration Act Part 1 does not apply to proceedings before the tribunal.

PART 2 GENERAL POWERS AND PROVISIONS

Delegation to staff

4. Tribunal staff (see TCEA 2007 s 40(1)) may, with the approval of the Senior President of Tribunals, carry out functions of a judicial nature which are permitted or required to be done by the tribunal. If a member of the tribunal staff does so in a particular case, a party may make a written application to the tribunal requiring the decision to be considered afresh by a judge. The application must be made no later than 14 days after the notice of the decision was sent.

Case management powers

5. In principle, the tribunal regulates its own procedure. The tribunal may give directions relating to the conduct or disposal of proceedings. In particular, it may exercise the specific powers specified.

Procedure for applying for and giving directions

6. The tribunal may give directions if one or more of the parties so apply. Applications are made by written notice to the tribunal or orally during a hearing. The reason for making the application must be given. The tribunal may also give directions on its own initiative.

A written notice of a direction is normally sent to every party and to any other person affected by it. The direction can be challenged by applying for a direction amending, suspending or setting aside the first direction.

Failure to comply with rules etc

7. An irregularity may arise from a failure to comply with these Rules, a practice direction or a direction. This does not, of itself, void the proceedings or any step taken in them. The tribunal may take such action as it considers just in relation to a failure to comply.

The tribunal may make a reference to the Upper Tribunal asking it to exercise its High Court powers (see TECA 2007 s 25) in relation to any of the failures listed.

Striking out a party's case

8. A direction may warn the appellant that all or part of the proceedings would be struck out if he failed to comply. This consequence follows automatically if he fails to do so. The tribunal has an option to strike out the proceedings (or the relevant part) if the direction warned that this could happen. In either case, the appellant may apply for the proceedings (or the relevant part) to be reinstated. This must be done in writing. The application must be received no later than 28 days after the tribunal notified the appellant that the proceedings (or the relevant part) had been struck out.

A direction may warn the respondent that he will be barred from taking any further part in all or part of the proceedings if he failed to comply. This consequence follows automatically if he fails to do so. The tribunal has an option to bar the respondent from proceedings (or the relevant part) if the direction warned that this *could* happen. In either case, the respondent may apply for the bar to be lifted. This must be done in writing. The application must be received no later than 28 days after the tribunal notified the respondent that the bar had been imposed.

The tribunal may not have jurisdiction in respect of all or part of the proceedings. The tribunal may transfer the proceedings to another tribunal in appropriate circumstances (see r 5(3)(k)). It must strike out the proceedings (or the relevant part), or bar the respondent from taking any further part in them, if it does not do so. However, the tribunal must give the appellant or respondent an opportunity to make representations before doing so.

The tribunal may strike out all or part of the proceedings if: (1) the appellant has failed to co-operate with the tribunal to such an extent that it cannot deal with the proceedings fairly and justly; or (2) the tribunal considers that the appellant's case (or the relevant part) has no reasonable prospect of success. The tribunal must give the appellant an opportunity to make representations before doing so in either case.

The tribunal may bar the respondent from taking any further part in all or part of the proceedings if: (1) the respondent has failed to co-operate with the tribunal to such an extent that it cannot deal with the proceedings fairly and justly; or (2) the tribunal considers that the respondent's case (or the relevant part) has no reasonable prospect of success. The tribunal must give the respondent an opportunity to make representations before doing so in either case.

The tribunal may not have jurisdiction in respect of all or part of the proceedings. The tribunal may transfer the proceedings to another tribunal in appropriate circumstances (see r 5(3)(*k*)). It must strike out the proceedings (or the relevant part), or bar the respondent from taking any further part in them, if it does not do so. However, the tribunal must give the relevant parties an opportunity to make representations before doing so.

Substitution and addition of parties

9. The tribunal may give a direction substituting a party if: (1) the wrong person has been named as a party; or (2) the substitution has become necessary because circumstances have changed since the proceedings began. The tribunal may give such consequential directions as it considers appropriate.

The tribunal may give a direction adding a person to the proceedings as a respondent. The tribunal may give such consequential directions as it considers appropriate.

A person may apply to be added as a party to the proceedings. If the tribunal refuses the application, it must consider whether to permit the applicant to provide submissions or evidence.

Orders for costs

10. The tribunal may make an order for wasted costs in accordance with TCEA 2007 s 29(4). The tribunal may also make an order for costs if the tribunal considers that a party to the proceedings (or his representative) has acted unreasonably in bringing, defending or conducting the proceedings.

In proceedings allocated as a complex case (see r 23)), the taxpayer (see r 10(8)) may request that the proceedings are excluded from potential liability for costs. The tribunal may make an order for costs if he fails to send or deliver a written notice to the tribunal within the prescribed time limit.

The tribunal may make an order for costs on its own initiative or in response to an application. An application is made in writing to the tribunal. A schedule of the costs claimed must be annexed thereto. A copy of the application and schedule must be sent or delivered to the person against whom the proposed order should be made (who is referred to as "the paying party"). An application may be made at any time during the proceedings. It must be made no later than 28 days after the tribunal sends either: (1) a notice recording the decision which finally disposes of all issues in the proceedings; or (2) a notice of withdrawal (see r 17) ending the proceedings.

Before making an order against the paying party, the tribunal must give him an opportunity to make representations. If that person is an individual, the tribunal must consider his financial means before making the order.

The amount of costs payable under an order may be: (1) summarily assessed by the tribunal; (2) agreed by the paying party and the recipient; or (3) (in the absence of such an agreement) assessed by reference to all or a specified part of the costs incurred by the recipient. As regards an order made under head (3), the paying party may apply for a detailed assessment of costs in accordance with r 10(7)(*a*). For equivalent provisions in Scotland and Northern Ireland, see r 10(7)(*b*) and (*c*) respectively.

Representatives

11. A party to the proceedings may appoint a representative. He is not required to be a legal representative (see r 11(7)). A written notice of the representative's name and address must be sent or delivered to the tribunal and the other party or parties. Having received such a notice, the other party or parties must provide the representative with any documents required to be provided to his principal. The other party or parties may assume that the representative continues to act for his principal until they are notified otherwise in writing by the representative or his principal.

A representative may do anything (except signing a witness statement) required or permitted to be done by his principal.

A party to the proceedings may be accompanied by another person at the hearing. If the tribunal so permits, this person may act as representative or otherwise assist in presenting the party's case at the hearing. However, the rights and duties of an appointed representative do not apply to him.

Calculating time

12. An act required to be done on or by a particular day must be done before 5pm on that day. If the specified time for doing an act does not end on a working day (see r 12(3)), the act is done in time if it is done on the next working day.

Sending and delivery of documents

13. Any document required to be provided to the tribunal must be sent or delivered to the address specified for the proceedings using one of the specified means of delivery. If a party does not want a particular form of communication to be used, he should inform the tribunal and the other parties. Once he has done so, that form of communication must not be used. If a document is sent electronically, the recipient may request a hard copy. The address provided by a party or his representative for the service of documents may be assumed to be correct until a written notice to the contrary is received.

Use of documents and information

14. The tribunal may make an order prohibiting the disclosure or publication of: (1) specified documents relating to the proceedings; (2) specified information relating to the proceedings; or (3) (if the tribunal considers that a person's identity should be protected) any matter which may lead to his identification.

Evidence and submissions

15. The tribunal may give directions on specified matters relating to the issues on which it requires evidence or submissions. The tribunal may admit evidence which would not be admissible in a civil trial. It may exclude evidence in specified situations.

Summoning or citation of witnesses and orders to answer questions or produce documents

16. A tribunal may require any person to attend a hearing as a witness. The procedure for making and setting aside a witness summons is set out.

The tribunal may order any person to answer questions or produce relevant documents in his possession or control. The tribunal may do so on its own initiative or on the application of a party to the proceedings. However, its powers are limited to those available in the trial of an action in a court of law in the home country where the proceedings are to be determined.

Withdrawal

17. A party may withdraw all or part of his case. He normally does so by sending or delivering a notice of withdrawal to the tribunal before the hearing takes place or the proceedings are otherwise determined. However, a party may withdraw all or part of his case at a hearing.

The party may subsequently apply for his case to be reinstated. The procedure for doing so is set out.

Lead cases

18. Appeals may have been made, and not decided, in two or more cases giving rise to common or related issues of fact or law. The tribunal may give a direction specifying one of the cases as a lead case (or two or more of them as lead cases) and stay proceedings in the other related case(s). If the tribunal does so, it must give directions providing for: (1) disposal of the related cases; or (2) the further steps to be taken in relation to them.

When the tribunal has decided the common or related issued in the lead case(s), it must send a copy of its decision to each party in the related case(s). The decision is binding on all of them. However, any of the parties to a related case may apply for a direction that the decision is not to apply to that case and is not to be binding on the parties to it. The time limit for doing so is set out.

The lead case(s) may be withdrawn or disposed of before the tribunal makes a decision in respect of the common or related issues. If so, the tribunal must decide whether one or more cases are to be heard as a leading case (or leading cases) and whether any direction affecting the related cases should be set aside or amended. It must give directions accordingly.

PART 3 APPEALS AND REFERENCES TO THE UPPER TRIBUNAL

CHAPTER 1 STARTING PROCEEDINGS AND ALLOCATION OF CASES TO CATEGORIES

Proceedings without a notice to a respondent

19. Rules relating to the provision of documents to or by a respondent and to his participation in the proceedings do not apply if the case or matter is to be determined without: (1) notice to the respondent; or (2) his involvement in the proceedings.

Starting appeal proceedings

20. An appellant starts proceedings by sending or delivering a notice of appeal to the tribunal. This must be done within any time limit specified in the relevant legislation. The information to be included in the notice of appeal is specified. The following documents must be annexed to the notice: (1) a copy of any written record of disputed decision; (2) a copy of any statement of reasons for that decision; and (3) (in the case of a late appeal) a request for an extension of time and a statement of the reason why the notice was not provided in time. For the additional information to be provided where the appeal can proceed only if prior payment of the disputed amount has been waived, see r 22. A late appeal can be admitted only if the tribunal gives permission.

When the tribunal receives a notice of appeal, it must give notice of the proceedings to the respondent.

Starting proceedings by originating application or reference

21. [Applies where an enactment provides for one or more persons to make an originating application or reference to the tribunal.]

Hardship applications

22. An enactment may provide that an appeal in respect of a disputed amount may proceed only with the consent of HMRC or the tribunal if the amount in dispute has not been paid. For an example, see VATA 1994 s 84(3).

When starting proceedings, the appellant must provide the following information with his notice of appeal (see r 20):

(a) a statement whether or not the appellant has paid the amount in dispute;
(b) (if the amount is unpaid) a statement as to the status or outcome of his application to HMRC for the appeal to proceed without payment; and
(c) (if HMRC have refused the application) an application for the tribunal for their consent for the appeal to proceed without payment. The reasons for making the application must be stated. If the appellant intends to produce or rely on any documents in support of his application, he must provide a list.

The tribunal must stay proceedings in respect of the appeal until the application for consent has been determined.

Allocation of cases to categories

23. An appeal, application or reference is allocated to one of the following categories:

(*a*)	Default Paper case. These cases are usually disposed of without a hearing.
(*b*)	Basic case. These cases are usually disposed of after a hearing. They usually involve a minimal exchange of documents before the hearing.

(*c*) Standard case. These cases are usually disposed of after a hearing. They are usually subject to more detailed case management.

(*d*) Complex case. A case may be allocated to this category only if the tribunal considers that it falls within one or more of the following descriptions:

- the case will require lengthy or complex evidence;
- the case will require a lengthy hearing;
- the case will involve a complex or important principle or issue; or
- the case will involve a large financial sum.

The tribunal allocates the case by giving a direction. It may re-allocate a case to a different category at any time by giving a further direction. It may do so on its own initiative or following an application by a party to the proceedings. The categorisation rules seek to ensure that an appeal receives the appropriate degree of case management and that it is heard by judges and members with the appropriate experience and competence. For the factors taken into account when categorising cases, see *Capital Air Services Ltd v R & C Comrs* [2010] UKUT 373 (TCC), [2010] STC 2726.

The following rules apply to a Complex case: rr 10(1)(*c*) (costs) and 28 (transfer to the Upper Tribunal).

CHAPTER 2 PROCEDURE AFTER ALLOCATION OF CASES TO CATEGORIES

24–28. The procedure to be followed following the allocation of a case (see r 23) is set out below.

DEFAULT PAPER CASE (RR 25, 26)

The respondent must send or deliver a statement of case to the tribunal, the appellant and any other respondent within the prescribed time limit (42 days). A statement of case must state the legislative provision under which the disputed decision was made and set out the respondent's position in relation to the case. The statement may also request that the case is held with or without a hearing. If the respondent fails to make a reply within the prescribed time limit, or an extended time limit (see r 5(3)(a)), the statement of case must include a request for an extension of time and state the reason why the statement of case was not provided in time.

The appellant may make a written reply to the respondent's statement of case. This may provide additional information which is relevant to the case. It may also request that the case is dealt with at a hearing. The reply must be sent or delivered to the tribunal within the prescribed time limit (30 days). A copy must be sent to each respondent at the same time. A late reply must include a request for an extension of time and state why the reply was not provided in time.

Following receipt of the appellant's reply, the tribunal normally proceed to determine the case without a hearing. However, the tribunal may hold a hearing in any case if it so directs. It must hold a hearing if the appellant has so requested.

If the appellant fails to make a reply within the prescribed time limit, the tribunal must normally proceed to determine the case without a hearing. However, it may direct otherwise.

BASIC CASE (R 24)

The respondent is not required to prepare a statement of case. The case proceeds directly to a hearing unless:

- the respondent intends to raise additional grounds for contesting the proceedings at a hearing. In these circumstances, the respondent must notify the appellant. He must do so as soon as reasonably practicable and provide sufficient detail to enable the appellant to respond to those grounds at the hearing; or
- the tribunal directs otherwise.

STANDARD CASE (RR 25, 27)

A respondent must send or deliver a statement of case to the tribunal, the appellant and any other respondent within the prescribed time limit (60 days). A statement of case must state the legislative provision under which the disputed decision was made and set out the respondent's position in relation to the case. The statement may also request that the case is held with or without a hearing. If the respondent fails to make a reply within the prescribed time limit, or an extended time limit (see r 5(3)(*a*)), the statement of case must include a request for an extension of time and state the reason why the statement of case was not provided in time.

Each party must send or deliver a list of documents to the tribunal and to each other party to the proceedings. This must be done with the prescribed time limit (42 days). Each list sets out the documents which the providing party intends to produce, or rely upon, in the proceedings and of which he has possession, the right of possession or the right to take copies.

COMPLEX CASE (RR 25, 27, 28)

A respondent must send or deliver a statement of case to the tribunal, the appellant and any other respondent within the prescribed time limit (60 days). A statement of case must state the legislative provision under which the disputed decision was made and set out the respondent's position in relation to the case. The statement may also request that the case is held with or without a hearing. If the respondent fails to make a reply within the prescribed time limit, or an extended time limit (see r 5(3)(*a*)), the statement of case must include a request for an extension of time and state the reason why the statement of case was not provided in time.

Each party must send or deliver a list of documents to the tribunal and to each other party to the proceedings. This must be done with the prescribed time limit (42 days). Each list sets out the documents which the providing party intends to produce, or rely upon, in the proceedings and of which he has possession, the right of possession or the right to take copies.

The tribunal may, with the consent of the parties, refer the case (or a preliminary issue) to the President of the Tax Chamber of the First-tier Tribunal with a request that the case or issue is considered for transfer to the Upper Tribunal. The President may, with the concurrence of the President of the Tax and Chancery Chamber of the Upper Tribunal, direct that the case or issue is transferred to, and determined by, the Upper Tribunal.

CHAPTER 3 HEARINGS

Determination with or without a hearing

29. In principle, the tribunal must hold a hearing before making a decision which disposes of all or part of the proceedings. This principle is subject to the following exceptions:

- each party has consented to the matter being decided without a hearing and the tribunal considers that it is able to so decide the matter; and
- (as regards a Default Paper case), the tribunal is required to proceed without a hearing (see r 26(6)).

Entitlement to attend a hearing

30. In principle, each party to the proceedings is entitled to attend a hearing. This principle is subject to the following exceptions:

(a) the case or matter is to be determined without notice to, or the involvement of, the respondent (see r 19); and
(b) the respondent is excluded from a private hearing (see r 32(4)).

Notice of hearings

31. The tribunal must give reasonable notice of: (1) the time and place of any hearing, adjourned hearing or postponed hearing; and (2) any changes to the time and place of any hearing. At least 14 days' notice must be given in relation to a hearing to consider disposal of the proceedings unless: (1) the parties consent to shorter notice; or (2) the circumstances are urgent or exceptional. Notice must be given to every party entitled to attend the hearing (see r 30).

Public and private hearings

32. In principle, all hearing must be held in public. This principle is subject to the following exceptions:

- the tribunal may give a direction that the hearing is to be held in private. The tribunal may do so if it considers that restricted access to the hearing is justified on one or other of the grounds specified. As far as possible, any published report of the tribunal's decision must exclude information given while the tribunal was sitting in private if disclosure would undermine the purpose of the direction;
- a person may be excluded if: (1) he is disrupting, or is likely to disrupt, the hearing; (2) his presence is likely to prejudice the evidence given by another person; (3) his attendance would defeat the purpose of the hearing, or he is under the age of 18 years; and
- a witness may be excluded until he gives evidence.

Hearing in a party's absence

33. A party may fail to attend a hearing. If so, the tribunal may proceed with the hearing in his absence if:
(a) the tribunal is satisfied that either: (1) the party has been notified of the hearing; or (2) reasonable steps have been taken to notify him of the hearing; and
(b) the tribunal considers that this is in the interests of justice.

CHAPTER 4 DECISIONS

Consent orders

34. The tribunal may make a consent order disposing of the proceedings and making such other appropriate provision as the parties have agreed. The tribunal is not required to hold a hearing. It is not required to provide reasons for the order.

Notice of decisions and reasons

35. The tribunal may give a decision orally at a hearing.

The tribunal must provide a decision notice to each party within a prescribed time of making a decision. The notice must state the tribunal's decision. It must notify the party of any right of appeal and the time limit for appealing.

The notice must either: (1) be accompanied by full written findings and reasons; (2) include a summary of the findings of fact and reasons for the decision; or (3) (if the parties dispense with the requirements in heads (1) and (2)) neither. If heads (2) or (3) apply, a party may subsequently apply for full written findings and reasons. He must do so before making an application for permission to appeal (see r 39).

PART 4 CORRECTING, SETTING ASIDE, REVIEWING AND APPEALING TRIBUNAL DECISIONS

Interpretation

36. The terms "appeal" and "review" are defined.

Clerical mistakes and accidental slips or omissions

37. The tribunal may correct a decision, direction or other document which contains a clerical mistake or an accidental slip or omission. It may do so at any time. The correction is made by: (1) sending the amended decision, direction or document to the parties; and (2) amending any published information regarding the decision, direction or document.

Setting aside a decision which disposes of proceedings

38. The tribunal may set aside all or part of a decision disposing of proceedings if the tribunal considers this to be necessary in the interests of justice. One or more of the specified conditions must be met. The tribunal may re-make the decision or part. A party may apply for this to be done. A written application must be made within the prescribed time limit (28 days). The tribunal's decision to set aside the decision or part must be notified to the parties in writing as soon as practicable.

Application for permission to appeal

39. A person seeking permission to appeal must make a written application to the tribunal. The application must be sent or delivered to the tribunal within the prescribed time limit (56 days). If the time limit has expired, his application must include a request for an extension of time and set out the reason why the application was not provided in time. The application must identify the tribunal decision to which it relates, identify the alleged error(s) in the decision and state the result sought by the applicant.

Tribunal's consideration of application for permission to appeal

40. On receiving an application for permission to appeal (see r 39), the tribunal must first consider whether to review the decision (see r 41). In doing so, the tribunal must consider the overriding objective of the tribunal rules (see r 2).

The tribunal may decide not to review the decision. Alternatively, the tribunal may decide to review the decision but take no action in relation to all or part of it. In these situations, the tribunal must go on to decide whether to give permission to appeal in relation to the decision or part which it has decided not to review. The tribunal must send a record of its decision to the parties as soon as practicable.

The tribunal may refuse permission to appeal, give permission against only part of the decision or give permission to appeal on limited grounds. In any of these situations, the record of its decision must be accompanied by: (1) a statement of the reasons for refusing permission in relation to all or part of the application; and (2) a notification of the right to make an application to the Upper Tribunal for permission to appeal.

Review of a decision

41. The tribunal's jurisdiction to undertake a review of a decision is confined to the power granted by r 40(1). The tribunal may undertake a review only if it is satisfied that there was an error of law in the decision. The tribunal must notify the parties of the outcome of the review only if it decides not to take any action.

Before taking any action in relation to a decision following a review, the tribunal must give the parties an opportunity to make representations in relation to the proposed action.

Power to treat an application as a different type of application

42. A party may make an application for: (1) for a decision to be corrected, set aside or reviewed; or (2) permission to appeal against a decision. An application in respect of one of these matters may be treated as an application in respect of another of these matters.

SI 2009/1916
INFORMATION NOTICE: RESOLUTION OF DISPUTES AS TO PRIVILEGED COMMUNICATIONS REGULATIONS 2009

Note These regulations set out the procedures for referring disputes to the First-tier Tribunal on the question of whether documents specified in an information notice are subject to legal professional privilege.

Citation and commencement

1. These regulations came into force on 7 August 2009.

Interpretation

2. Various words and phrases are defined.

Application of these Regulations

3. A person may be given an information notice during the course of correspondence or during an inspection of premises. A person is not required to produce any part of a document in respect of which a claim to legal professional privilege (or the equivalent in Scotland) could be maintained in legal proceedings: see FA 2008 Sch 36 para 23(1), (2). It follows that a dispute arises if a person claims legal professional privilege in respect of all or part of a document specified in an information notice. This dispute is unhelpfully described as "a dispute . . . as to whether a document is privileged". In reality, a claim for legal professional privilege gives rise to a dispute regarding the effectiveness of the information notice. This is confirmed by the headings to regs 5 and 6: "procedure where information notice . . . is in dispute". This dispute may, or may not, give rise to a dispute whether legal professional privilege actually applies to the document in question.

Requirement to provide information and produce documents not in dispute

4. These regulations do not affect: (1) the requirement to provide information which is not in dispute; (2) the requirement to produce a document which is not in dispute; and (3) the power to inspect premises.

Procedure where information notice given in correspondence is in dispute

5. The following procedure applies where a person is given an information notice during the course of correspondence:

- the taxpayer (see reg 2), third party (see reg 2) or person acting on their behalf (see reg 2) must prepare a list describing the nature and contents of each document in respect of which there is a dispute as to whether the document is privileged. No description is required if the description would itself give rise to a dispute over privilege. The list must be prepared by the date given in the information notice;
- the taxpayer, third party or person acting on their behalf must the serve the list on HMRC. This must be done within a reasonable time determined by mutual agreement. This must be no later than 20 working days after the date specified in the notice. Proof of service must be given to HMRC;
- HMRC must respond within 20 working days (see reg 2) of receiving the list. The response is made to the person who served the list. The response must indicate which documents are not considered to be privileged and which must accordingly be produced;
- the taxpayer, third party or person acting on their behalf must make an application to the First-tier Tribunal for the dispute to be considered and resolved. This must be done within a reasonable time determined by mutual agreement. This must be no later than 20 working days after the date by which HMRC was required to respond to the list served on them. Copies of the disputed documents must be enclosed with the application.

In practice, it appears that this procedure is followed only if a claim for legal professional privilege is made. It also appears that the claim must be made by the date given in the information notice (see FA 2008 Sch 36 para 7) in order to avoid a penalty for non-compliance with the notice (see FA 2008 Sch 36 para 39(1)(*a*)).

Procedure where information notice given during inspection of premises is in dispute

6. The following procedure applies where a person is given an information notice during an inspection of premises:

- on receiving the information notice, the taxpayer (see reg 2), third party (see reg 2) or person acting on their behalf (see reg 2) ("the relevant person") must indicate which of the documents specified in the information notice are in dispute. A document is "in dispute" if there is a dispute between HMRC and the relevant person as to whether the document is privileged (see reg 2);
- the relevant person must place the document(s) in an opaque container. The container is sealed, labelled and signed by him and countersigned by the HMRC officer carrying out the inspection. The officer is given custody of the container;
- the officer must deliver the container (with the seal intact) to the First-tier Tribunal within 42 working days of having taken custody of it. At the same time, he must serve an application for the tribunal to consider and resolve the dispute.

Compliance with information notice

7. A person who complies with the procedure in reg 5 or 6 is treated as having complied with an information notice until such time as the status of the document(s) is decided by the tribunal or the dispute is resolved by agreement (see reg 10).

Finding of the First-tier Tribunal

8. The First-tier Tribunal resolves the dispute (see reg 3) by confirming whether, and to what extent, a document is or is not privileged. It directs which part(s) of a document (if any) are to be disclosed. For application to the tribunal, see regs 5(5) and 6(5).

9. The First-tier Tribunal must prevent any inappropriate disclosure of the document (or any copy thereof) pending consideration of its status.

Resolution of disputes by agreement

10. A dispute (see reg 3) may be resolved at any time by agreement between HMRC and the relevant person. The agreement may be in writing or otherwise.

SI 2009/3127
VAT (SUPPLEMENTARY CHARGE) ORDER 2009

Note This order provides an exemption to the supplementary charge under FA 2009 Sch 3 para 1.

1. This order came into force on 31 December 2009.

2. No supplementary charge arises on a supply of goods spanning 1 January 2010 if:

(a) the only relevant condition met is condition D. For condition D, see FA 2009 Sch 3 para 2(8);

(b) the VAT invoice meets the following conditions:
- it relates to a supply of goods made under a hire purchase, conditional sale or credit sale agreement,
- it forms part of that agreement, and
- it is issued in accordance with the supplier's normal commercial practice for supplies made under such an agreement at a time when an increase in the VAT rate is not expected; and

(c) the intention and expectation is that the basic time of supply (as defined in FA 2009 Sch 3 para 4(1)) of the goods will take place no later than six months after the invoice date.

For the circumstances in which a supply of goods spans 1 January 2010, see FA 2009 Sch 3 para 2.

SI 2010/593
EXCISE GOODS (HOLDING, MOVEMENT AND DUTY POINT) REGULATIONS 2010

Note

These regulations are relevant to VAT in so far as they define the time when excise duty is payable. Parts 3–17 of the regulations are not summarised. They are modified by Channel Tunnel (Alcoholic Liquor and Tobacco Products) Order 2010, SI 2010/595 (not summarised) in their application to control zones.

PART 1 PRELIMINARY

Citation and commencement

2. As regards Part 2, these regulations came into force on 1 January 2010.

Interpretation

3. Various words and phrases are defined.

PART 2 EXCISE DUTY POINTS AND PAYMENT OF THE DUTY

[Goods released for consumption in the United Kingdom]

5–7. In principle, an excise duty point (as defined in F(No 2)A 1992 s 1) arises when:

(a) excise goods leave a duty suspension arrangement. For the time when excise goods leave a duty suspension arrangement, see reg 7(1). For the persons liable to pay the duty, see regs 8, 9;

(b) the excise duty on excise goods held outside a duty suspension arrangement has not been paid, relieved, remitted or deferred. For the persons liable to pay the duty, see reg 10;

(c) excise goods are produced outside a duty suspension arrangement. For the persons liable to pay the duty, see reg 11; or

(d) excise goods are charged with duty at importation (as defined in reg 6(2), (3)). This does not apply if the goods are immediately placed in a duty suspension arrangement. For the persons liable to pay the duty, see reg 12.

For the exceptions, see regs 7(2) and 21. The excise duty point is the time when the goods are released for consumption in the UK.

[Goods already released for consumption in another member state]

13–17. The excise duty point is defined in relation to:

- excise goods which have already been released for consumption in another member state and which are held for a commercial purpose (as defined in reg 13(3)–(5)): see reg 13(1). For the person liable to pay the duty, see reg 13(2). For the exception, see reg 13(6);
- goods chargeable with excise duty under Hydrocarbon Oil Duties Act 1979 or an order made under FA 1993 s 10, which are acquired by a private individual in another member state and are transported to the UK by, or on behalf of, that individual. For the person liable to pay the duty, see reg 14(2);

- chewing tobacco which is imported into the UK from another member state and not immediately placed under a duty suspension arrangement. For the person liable to pay the duty, see reg 15(b);
- excise goods imported under a distance selling arrangement. For the person liable to pay the duty, see reg 16(2), (3);
- situations where an irregularity (as defined in Directive 2008/118/EC art 38(4)) occurs in the course of a movement of excise goods already released for consumption. For the person liable to pay the duty, see reg 17(2)–(4).

For the exception, see reg 21.

[Contravention of conditions or requirements]

18, 19. The excise duty point is defined in relation to:

- excise goods relieved from payment of duty in respect of which there is a failure to comply with any condition. For the person liable to pay the duty, see reg 18(2);
- excise goods to which Parts 6, 8, 9 or 11 apply. For the person liable to pay the duty, see reg 19(7), (8).

Time of payment of the duty

20. In principle, duty must be paid at or before the excise duty point. However, the duty on goods subject to a duty deferment arrangement is paid at the time specified in the arrangement. Regulations, or the terms of a specific relief, may specify alternative arrangements.

SI 2010/1813
REVENUE AND CUSTOMS (COMPLAINTS AND MISCONDUCT) REGULATIONS 2010

Note These regulations confer functions on the Independent Police Complaints Commission in relation to the manner in which HMRC Commissioners and officers exercise their functions in, or in relation to, England and Wales. These regulations modify the application of the Police Reform Act 2002 and restate, in a modified form, the provisions relating to misconduct and handling of claims in the following legislation: (1) the Police Reform Act 2002; (2) the Police (Complaints and Misconduct) Regulations 2004, SI 2004/643; (3) the Independent Police Complaints Commission (Investigatory Powers) Order 2004, SI 2004/815; and (4) the Independent Police Complaints Commission (Staff Conduct) Regulations 2004, SI 2004/660.

These regulations revoke and replace Revenue and Customs (Complaints and Misconduct) Regulations 2005, SI 2005/3311 with effect from 5 August 2010.

SI 2010/1879
TAXES AND DUTIES (INTEREST RATE) REGULATIONS 2010

Note These regulations specify the rates of interest for the purposes of FA 2009 ss 101 and 102 in relation to sums payable to and by HMRC.

Citation and commencement

1. These regulations came into force on 31 August 2010.

Interpretation

2. Various words and phrases are defined.

Late payment interest rate

3. The initial rate of late payment interest (see FA 2009 s 101) is specified in reg 5. Thereafter, late payment interest is 2.5% above the official bank rate announced at the most recent meeting of the Bank of England Monetary Policy Committee. This rate applies from the thirteenth working day following the meeting. This is referred to as "the operative date".

Repayment interest rate

4. The initial rate of repayment interest (see FA 2009 s 102) is specified in reg 5. Thereafter, repayment interest is the higher of: (1) 0.5% per annum; and (2) 1% below the official bank rate announced at the most recent meeting of the Bank of England Monetary Policy Committee. This rate applies from the thirteenth working day following the meeting. This is referred to as "the operative date".

Initial rates of interest

5. The rates of late payment interest and repayment interest (see FA 2009 ss 101 and 102) on 31 August 2010 are determined in accordance with regs 3 and 4 by reference the official bank rate announced at the most recent meeting of the Bank of England Monetary Policy Committee on, or most recently before, the thirteenth working day before 31 August 2010.

The rates of late payment interest and repayment interest in force on 31 August 2010 were 3% and 0.5% respectively.

Effect of change in rates of interest

6. The initial rate of late payment interest or repayment interest may change. When it does so, the rates fixed under regs 3 and 4 apply to both interest running before the operative date and interest running from that date.

SI 2010/2239
VAT (SECTION 55A) (SPECIFIED GOODS AND SERVICES AND EXCEPTED SUPPLIES) ORDER 2010

Note This order is made under VATA 1994 s 55A. It applies a reverse charge to specified goods and services of a kind used in missing trader intra-Community fraud. It revokes and replaces the VAT (Section 55) (Specified Goods and Excepted Supplies) Order 2007, SI 2007/1417 in relation to supplies made after 31 October 2010.

Citation, commencement and effect

1. This order came into force on 1 November 2010. It applies to supplies made after 31 October 2010.

Revocation

2. VAT (Section 55A) (Specified Goods and Excepted Supplies) Order 2007, SI 2007/1417 is revoked.

Interpretation

3. Various words and phrases are defined.

The application of section 55A of the Act to specified goods and services

4. VATA 1994 s 55A applies to the goods and services specified in arts 5 and 6.

Specified goods

5. VATA 1994 s 55A applies to:

(a) mobile telephones; and
(b) integrated circuit devices (eg a central processing unit or microprocessor unit) which have not been integrated into an end user product.

Specified services

6. VATA 1994 s 55A applies to the transfer of:
(a) an allowance (as defined in Directive 2003/86/EC art 3);
(b) an emission reduction unit (as defined in Directive 2003/86/EC art 3) which can be used by an operator (as defined in Directive 2003/86/EC art 3) for compliance with the scheme established by Directive 2003/86/EC; and
(c) a certified emission reduction (as defined in Directive 2003/86/EC art 3) which can be used by an operator (as defined in Directive 2003/86/EC art 3) for compliance with the scheme established by Directive 2003/86/EC.

Excepted supplies

7, 8. VATA 1994 s 55A does not apply to a supply of the goods specified in art 5 if:
(a) the value of the supply is less than £5,000. However, VATA 1994 s 55A applies if two or more such supplies with aggregate value of £5,000 or more are separately itemised on the same VAT invoice (as defined in VATA 1994 s 6(15));
(b) the goods are supplied under the margin scheme for second-hand goods (as to which see VAT (Special Provisions) Order 1995, SI 1995/1268 art 12);
(c) (as regards a mobile telephone) at the time of purchase, the purchaser enters in to an agreement for the supply of an electronic communication service (other than a "pay and go" service) with a provider of such a service;
(d) there is no consideration for the supply, so that it is charged to VAT in accordance with VATA 1994 Sch 4 para 5(1).

SI 2010/2655
FIRST-TIER TRIBUNAL AND UPPER TRIBUNAL (CHAMBERS) ORDER 2010

Note This order organises the First-tier Tribunal and Upper Tribunal into chambers and makes provision for the allocation of First-tier Tribunal and Upper Tribunal functions between the chambers of those tribunals. It revokes and replaces the First-tier and Upper (Chambers) Order 2008, SI 2008/2684. This order is summarised only in so far as it is relevant to VAT.

Citation and commencement

1. This order came into force on 29 November 2010. The First-tier and Upper (Chambers) Order 2008, SI 2008/2684 is revoked.

First-tier Tribunal Chambers

2. The First-tier Tribunal is organised into the following chambers:
(a) the General Regulatory Chamber;
(b) the Health, Education and Social Care Chamber;
(c) the Immigration and Asylum Chamber;
(d) the Social Entitlement Chamber;
(e) the Tax Chamber; and
(f) the War Pensions and Armed Forces Compensation Chamber.

Functions of the General Regulatory Chamber

3. [Not relevant to VAT.]

Functions of the Health, Education and Social Care Chamber

4. [Not relevant to VAT.]

Functions of the Immigration and Asylum Chamber of the First-tier Tribunal

5. [Not relevant to VAT.]

Functions of the Social Entitlement Chamber

6. [Not relevant to VAT.]

Functions of the Tax Chamber

7. All functions relating to an appeal, application, reference or other proceedings in respect of a function of the HMRC Commissioners or an HMRC officer, or the general revenue functions of the Serious Organised Crime Agency, are assigned to the Tax Chamber. However, functions relating to these matters are not assigned to the Tax Chamber if they are assigned to the Social Entitlement Chamber (see art 6) or the Tax and Chancery Chamber of the Upper Tribunal (see art 13).

Functions of the War Pensions and Armed Forces Compensation Chamber

8. [Not relevant to VAT.]

Upper Tribunal Chambers

9. The Upper Tribunal is organised into the following chambers:

(a) the Administrative Appeals Chamber;
(b) the Immigration and Asylum Chamber of the Upper Tribunal;
(c) the Lands Chamber; and
(d) the Tax and Chancery Chamber.

Functions of the Administrative Appeals Chamber

10. All functions relating to the following matters are assigned to the Administrative Appeals Chamber:

(a) an appeal against a decision made by a First-tier Tribunal chamber which is not assigned to the Tax and Chancery Chamber in accordance with art 13(1)(*a*);
(b) an application to grant the "judicial review" jurisdiction (see TCEA 2007 ss 15(1) and 21(2)) which is not assigned to the Tax and Chancery Chamber in accordance with art 13(1)(*g*);
(c) specified matters which are not assigned to the Tax and Chancery Chamber in accordance with art 13(1)(*f*); and
(d) a determination or decision under the Forfeiture Act 1982 s 4.

Functions of the Immigration and Asylum Chamber of the Upper Tribunal

11. [Not relevant to VAT.]

Functions of the Lands Chamber

12. [Not relevant to VAT.]

Functions of the Tax and Chancery Chamber

13. All functions relating to the following matters are assigned to the Tax and Chancery Chamber:

(a) an appeal against a decision of the First-tier Tribunal made in the Tax Chamber;
(b) [not relevant to VAT];
(c) [not relevant to VAT];
(d) an application for an additional penalty to be imposed on a person (see FA 2008 Sch 36 para 50(1)(*d*));

(e) proceedings transferred from the Tax Chamber of the First-tier Tribunal in accordance with the Tribunal Procedure Rules;
(f) a matter referred to the Upper Tribunal by the Tax Chamber of the First-tier Tribunal under TCEA 2007 s 9(5)(*b*) (decision of the First-tier Tribunal to set aside a decision on review); and
(g) an application to grant the "judicial review" jurisdiction (see TCEA 2007 ss 15(1) and 21(2)) relating to:
   (i) a decision of the Tax Chamber of the First-tier Tribunal, or
   (ii) a function of the HMRC Commissioners or an HMRC officer which would not be allocated to the Social Entitlement Chamber in accordance with art 6.

Resolution of doubt or dispute as to chamber

14. Doubts or disputes may arise regarding the chamber in which a particular matter should be dealt with. If so, the matter is allocated to the chamber which the Senior President of Tribunals considers most appropriate.

Re-allocation of a case to another chamber

15. A Chamber President may re-allocate a case to another chamber within the same tribunal by giving a direction to that effect.

SI 2010/2924
VALUE ADDED TAX (IMPORTED GAS, ELECTRICITY, HEAT AND COOLING) RELIEF ORDER 2004

Note This order is made under VATA 1994 s 37(1). It implements Directive 2009/162/EU art 1(10)(c).

Citation, commencement and effect

1. This order came into force on 1 January 2011. It applies to goods imported on or after that date.

Revocation of the Value Added Tax (Imported Gas and Electricity) Relief Order 2004

2. The VAT (Imported Gas and Electricity) Relief Order 2004, SI 2004/3147 is revoked.

Relief from value added tax

3. No VAT is payable on:
- gas imported from a third country through a natural gas system;
- gas imported from a third country through a network connected to a natural gas system;
- gas imported from a third country and fed into a natural gas system, or any upstream pipeline network, from a vessel transporting the gas;
- electricity imported from a third country; or
- heat or cooling imported from a third country and supplied through a network.

SI 2010/2925
VALUE ADDED TAX (REMOVAL OF GAS, ELECTRICITY, HEAT AND COOLING) ORDER 2010

Note This order is made under VATA 1994 s 5(3). It implements Directive 2009/162/EU art 1(4).

Citation, commencement and effect

1. This order came into force on 1 January 2011. It applies to supplies made on or after that date.

Revocation of the Value Added Tax (Removal of Gas and Electricity) Order 2004

2. The VAT (Removal of Gas and Electricity) Order 2004, SI 2004/3150 is revoked.

The application of paragraph 6(1) of Schedule 4 of the Value Added Tax Act 1994

3. A removal does not amount to a supply of goods for the purposes of VATA 1994 Sch 4 para 6(1) if it comprises:

- a removal of gas through the natural gas system situated within the territory of an EU member state;
- a removal of gas through a network connected to a natural gas system situated within the territory of an EU member state;
- a removal of electricity; or
- a removal of heat or cooling supplied through a network.

SI 2011/711
TAXES, ETC (FEES FOR PAYMENT BY INTERNET) REGULATIONS 2011

Note These regulations are made under FA 2008 s 136. They revoke and replace Taxes (Fees for Payment by Internet) Regulations 2008, SI 2008/2991. They specify the fee payable for payments made by credit card over the internet.

Citation, commencement, effect and interpretation

1. These regulations came into force on 1 April 2011. They have effect in relation to any credit card payment made on or after 1 April 2011 which is authorised by the credit card issuer via the internet.

Fee payable where internet authorisation is given to make a payment by credit card

2. A person making a payment to the Commissioners (or to a person authorised by the Commissioners) by credit card (as defined in reg 2(3)) must pay a fee if the payment is authorised via the internet by the credit card issuer. The fee is equal to 1.4% of the payment. It payable in addition to the payment. Thus, for example, a taxpayer pays £10,140 in order to discharge a debt of £10,000.

Revocation

3. The Taxes (Fees for Payment by Internet) Regulations 2008, SI 2008/2991 are revoked.

SI 2011/1043
TREATY OF LISBON (CHANGES IN TERMINOLOGY) ORDER 2011

Note This order is made under European Communities Act 1972 and the European Union (Amendment) Act 2008 s 3(4), (5). It amends legislation to reflect changes in terminology and numbering arising out of the Treaty of Lisbon. The following summary is confined to provisions which are both relevant to VAT and applicable to the whole of the UK.

PART 1 CITATION AND COMMENCEMENT

Citation

1. This order is cited as the Treaty of Lisbon (Changes in Terminology) Order 2011.

Commencement

2. This order came into force on 22 April 2011.

PART 2 AMENDMENTS TO ACTS OF PARLIAMENT . . . AND CERTAIN STATUTORY INSTRUMENTS

Application

3. This Part applies to provisions contained in an Act of Parliament or an instrument made thereunder. The amendments made by this Part do not apply to the European Communities Act 1972 or the Interpretation Act 1978.

European Community – the European Union

4. In principle, the term "European Union" replaces "European Community", "European Communities" and "European Coal and Steel Community".

Article 310 of the Treaty of Amsterdam

5. The phrase "Article 217 of the Treaty on the Functioning of the European Union" replaces "Article 310 of the Treaty of Amsterdam amending the Treaty on European Union, the Treaties establishing the European Communities and certain related Acts".

"Community"

6. References to "Community" in various phrases is replaced by "EU".

Miscellaneous

7. Schedule 1 is introduced.

SCHEDULE 1 MISCELLANEOUS AMENDMENTS (ART 7)

This schedule amends CEMA 1979, the Free Zone Regulations 1984, SI 1984/1177 and the Statistics of Trade (Customs and Excise) Regulations 1992, SI 1992/2790.

3.
UK Legislation Appendices

Contents

APPENDIX 1. PRESS NOTICES ETC—HM REVENUE AND CUSTOMS AND OTHERS

This Appendix sets out information relevant to VAT derived from a wide variety of sources. Individual items are selected on the basis of their importance, current relevance and general interest. HM Revenue and Customs (formerly HM Customs and Excise) Press Notices and Business Briefs are normally excluded if their substance has been incorporated in a Notice or Information Sheet.

12 MARCH 1980. HANSARD COSTS

Mr Eggar asked the Chancellor of the Exchequer if he will indicate the policy of Her Majesty's Customs and Excise and the Inland Revenue with regard to costs in the High Court and superior courts of appeal.

Mr Peter Rees: The general rule in the appeal courts is that the losing party risks having to pay the other side's costs, and I do not think it would be right to treat tax cases differently as a matter of course. However, both revenue departments exercise their discretion on matters of costs, and are willing in appropriate circumstances, and in particular where it is they who are appealing against an adverse decision, to consider waiving their claims to costs or making other arrangements. Influential factors include the risk of financial hardship to the other party and whether the case is one of significant interest to taxpayers as a whole, turning on a point of law in need of clarification. If the revenue departments are to come to an arrangement of this nature, they would expect to do so in advance of the hearing and following an approach by the taxpayer involved.

HC Written Answer, Vol 980, col 572.

[VATA 1994 s 86]

20 SEPTEMBER 1982. PRESS NOTICE 761 VAT: GOODS OBTAINED BY FRAUD

VAT registered traders who have been defrauded of goods may, in certain circumstances be able to recover VAT which they have accounted for as output tax and submitted to Customs and Excise in respect of the transaction.

If the trader reports the fraud to the police and, as a result, a conviction is obtained, he should apply in writing to his local VAT office for authority to adjust his VAT account. The application should be supported by evidence of his complaint to the police and of the conviction for the offence. A verifiable description of the goods in question will also be required.

[*Note:* A conviction is no longer necessary: see Business Brief 19/96, 16 September 1996.]

[VATA 1994 s 5]

12 OCTOBER 1982. PRESS NOTICE 768 VAT: SUPPLIES THROUGH SUBSIDIARY COMPANIES WITHOUT ASSETS

Customs and Excise now require companies acting as principals, who are not at present accounting for VAT on supplies through the agency of subsidiary companies without assets ("shell" companies), to correct their VAT accounting in accordance with one of three methods:

(a) the provisions of [VATA 1994 s 47(3)] may be adopted. The supplies by the principal company may be treated as supplies to the shell company and as supplies by the shell company. This is explained in para 5(*a*) of Notice 710 [now Notice 700 (August 1991) Part IX]. The principal company must, of course, issue invoices to the shell company, possibly in the form of a monthly invoicing procedure;

(b) applying, where eligible, for a group registration to include both the principal and the shell companies;

(c) by the principal company invoicing its supplies directly to the customer.

The same principles apply if the principal company is receiving supplies through a shell company. Note that if procedure (*c*) is adopted the shell company may cease to make any taxable supplies and may no longer be liable to be registered.

Companies affected must correct their accounting as soon as practicable. The date may be agreed with the local VAT office.

10 DECEMBER 1982. PRESS NOTICE 790
VAT: SALES OF GOODWILL

From 1 January 1983 Customs and Excise will treat all sales of the goodwill of a business as taxable supplies except where they are specifically relieved by law.

Unidentifiable goodwill, valued as the residual difference between the business as a whole and the sum of its identifiable assets, is currently treated as outside the scope of VAT.

Normally goodwill is sold as part of the assets of a business transferred as a going concern. Such sales will be relieved from tax if the transfer meets the provisions of [the VAT (Special Provisions) Order 1995, SI 1995/1268, art 5 (1)]

NOTE

Sales of goodwill which can be specifically identified as an asset of the business have always been treated as taxable supplies of services (eg, use of a trade mark or trading name, lists of customers etc).

[VATA 1994 s 5]

21 OCTOBER 1985. PRESS NOTICE 1045
VAT: CHECK TRADING COMPANIES—CHARGES TO RETAILERS

Customs and Excise announce that from 1 December 1985 the charges made by check trading companies to participating retailers will be treated as exempt for VAT purposes and will therefore no longer be regarded as a promotional service which is taxable. This follows a similar change of liability in respect of charges made to retailers by credit card, charge card and similar payment card companies announced in the last Budget. The National Consumer Credit Federation has been advised of this ruling.

NOTE

Check trading is a means of buying goods on credit whereby a check trading company sells a trading check for a special amount to a customer who pays for the check on credit terms over a period of time. The customer then uses the check to purchase goods from a participating retailer. The check trading company retains a percentage of the sum due to the retailer when he presents the check to the company for redemption. It is this charge which is the subject of the revised liability ruling. The change brings the treatment of check trading companies into line with that of credit card companies in respect of the broadly similar services they supply to participating retailers. It will have the effect of reducing their recovery of input tax.

[VATA 1994 Sch 9 Group 5]

11 FEBRUARY 1986. PRESS NOTICE 1078
VAT: SUPPLIES BY CONFIRMING HOUSES

Customs and Excise advise that with effect from 1 March 1986, the following supplies by confirming houses will be regarded as exempt from VAT:

Supplies of services for which a confirming commission is charged.

Credit facilities granted in return for interest.

. . .

NOTE

Exemption for financial services, including the provision of credit facilities, is contained in [VATA 1994 Sch 9 Group 5] . . .

25 MARCH 1987. PRESS NOTICE 24/87
VAT: MOTORING EXPENSES

In answer to a Parliamentary question yesterday, the Minister of State, Treasury (the Hon Peter Brooke MP) explained that the scheme of VAT scale charges starting on 6 April 1987 will apply only to cars and not to other motor vehicles. The charges will apply whenever road fuel is supplied or apportioned by business for private journeys.

The definition of a road vehicle in [VATA 1994 s 56] is wide enough to include vans. However, the derogation for which application was made under Article 27 of the EC Sixth VAT Directive was confined to cars; the scale charge will not therefore apply when road fuel is supplied or apportioned by business for private journeys in vans and the present VAT treatment of such journeys will remain unchanged.

NOTE

. . .

[VATA 1994 s 56]

19 NOVEMBER 1987. PRESS NOTICE 82/87
VAT: SETTLEMENT OF DISPUTES

Customs and Excise have reviewed their policy on the VAT treatment of payments made under out-of-court settlements of disputes, after proceedings have been commenced by service of originating process (or appointment of an arbitrator).

They now take the view that, where such payments are in essence compensatory and do not relate directly to supplies of goods or services, they are outside the scope of VAT. This will be so even if the settlement is expressed in terms that the payment is consideration for the plaintiff's agreement to abandon his rights to bring legal proceedings. But payments will remain taxable if, and to the extent, that they are the consideration for specific taxable supplies by the plaintiff, eg where the dispute concerns payment for an earlier supply, or where the plaintiff grants future rights to exploit copyright material under the settlement.

These changes of policy may be applied from 19 November 1987.

NOTE

Customs and Excise had previously taken the view that all payments under out-of-court settlements were generally taxable. The revised VAT liability brings the VAT treatment of out-of-court settlements into line with the VAT treatment of payments under court orders.

[VATA 1994 s 5]

20 SEPTEMBER 1988. PRESS NOTICE 72/88
VAT: LETTING OF FACILITIES FOR SPORT AND PHYSICAL RECREATION

The Commissioners have decided not to appeal against a decision of the Edinburgh VAT Tribunal (*Queen's Park Football Club Ltd v C & E Comrs* [1988] VATTR 76) that the letting, for 24 hours or less, of an entire football stadium complete with spectating and other facilities, for the playing of a football fixture, was a standard-rated supply. The Commissioners had argued that such lettings were exempt when made to someone who used the premises for staging a sporting event to which there was a charge for admission because the essential nature of the supply was to concede control over the whole stadium to the licensee who would exploit the property for the purpose of the taxable business of admitting the public to a sporting spectacle.

Although as a matter of strict law the Edinburgh Tribunal's decision applies only to the facts of the Queen's Park Football Club case, the Commissioners now accept that similar supplies by owners of other sporting stadia (outdoor or indoor venues) will, from a current date, also be taxable at the standard rate rather than exempt where the letting concerned is for 24 hours or less.

The existing reliefs for the letting of sports and physical recreation facilities for continuous periods of use exceeding 24 hours, and for a series of lets are unaffected. These reliefs are explained in VAT Leaflet 742/1/86.

The relevant VAT law is in [VATA 1994 Sch 9 Group 1 Item 1 exception (*m*)].

[VATA 1994 Sch 9 Group 1]

10 NOVEMBER 1988. PRESS NOTICE 84/88
VAT AND DONATIONS TO UNIVERSITIES

FINANCIAL SUPPORT

The impression seems to have arisen that all payments made to universities by bodies in the private sector are liable to VAT, including sponsorship payments, donations and the endowment of chairs. This is not the case.

There has been no change in the policy or practice of the Commissioners. The underlying principles are quite straightforward. There is no VAT on unconditional gifts of money to universities. Nor does the mere acknowledgement of such support attract VAT, for example the naming of a university chair after the donor. VAT applies only where something is supplied for a consideration: the name given to a payment is not important—it is what happens in reality that determines the VAT position.

So, where a payment is conditional upon the university supplying clearly identifiable benefits in return (such as advertising, publicity or the making available of university sports facilities), there is a supply by the university which is liable to VAT in accordance with the normal rules.

The value for VAT in such cases is normally the whole amount received. But where both parties recognise that a donor intends a single payment both to cover services supplied by the university and to provide a gratuitous donation, only the payment for services is taxed, provided that:

(1) the amount attributed to the supply is realistic in relation to the benefits provided; and

(2) it is clear from any agreement that this amount can be distinguished from the donation element.

DONATED EQUIPMENT

Free gifts of equipment, with no strings attached, are liable to VAT based on their cost to the donor. This is an EC obligation. Where goods are given to universities with an obligation that the recipient must do something in return, the transaction is a form of barter. Each party to the agreement, if registered for VAT, has to account for tax on the open market value of the goods or services supplied.

The correct VAT treatment may vary according to the facts of individual cases and Customs and Excise are happy to advise taxpayers in specific instances.

NOTE

As a result of representations made on behalf of universities the Commissioners have recognised the need to explain more fully their policy in this area. Individual decisions have been seen as an implicit indication that all funding of universities will be subject to VAT. This is not the case. Most university funding is not subject to tax. Pure donations, ie financial contributions with "no strings attached", are not liable to VAT. But if the "donor" receives something in addition to the mere acknowledgement of his support, then the university is making a supply which is subject to VAT under the normal rules.

[VATA 1994 s 5]

30 MARCH 1989. PRESS NOTICE 30/89
VAT: SUPPLIES OF EDUCATION AND WELFARE MADE OTHERWISE THAN FOR PROFIT—BELL CONCORD JUDGMENT

The Court of Appeal ruled last month, in the case of the *Bell Concord Educational TrustLtd v C & E Comrs* [1989] STC 264, that an educational trust which was prohibited by its foundation document from distributing any surpluses and was bound to apply them to the furtherance of the aims of the organisation was operating otherwise than for profit, even though its supplies generated surpluses which were used for future developments or expansion. Its educational courses were consequently exempt from VAT under VATA 1983 Sch 6 Group 6 item 2 [repealed]. The Commissioners of Customs and Excise have examined the implications of this decision, and this news release outlines the changes in interpretation of the law which they propose to make.

The term "otherwise than for profit" is used in two separate places in the VAT exemption Schedule. Under Group 6, research and education provided by a body other than a university or school may be exempt from VAT only if it is provided otherwise than for profit. Group 7 items 9 and 10 exempt welfare services provided by charities, public bodies and religious communities otherwise than for profit. The phrase has been interpreted as meaning that providers should set their prices at a level which at maximum does no more than recover the full overhead-inclusive cost of supplying the service. The Court of Appeal judgment, however, requires that attention should be paid to the status of the body providing the education or welfare.

Customs and Excise will now accept that supplies are made "otherwise than for profit" if they are made by non-profit-making organisations in circumstances where any surpluses are applied solely to the furtherance of the educational or welfare activity which generated the surplus. Where, however, a non-profit-making organisation is set up to pursue more than one activity, eg the provision of education and the propagation of some other cause, the education would *not* be supplied otherwise than for profit if surpluses from the educational activity were applied to the maintenance or furtherance of the other activity. Similarly with welfare: if the surpluses from a welfare activity are not to be devoted to the same general area of welfare, the supply is not made otherwise than for profit, even if the surpluses are used for another charitable activity.

The existing criteria will continue to apply in other cases where the body supplying the education or welfare is not constituted on a non-profit making basis.

[*Note:* From 1 August 1994, it is no longer necessary for education to be provided "otherwise than for profit". Similarly, from 21 March 2002, it is no longer necessary for welfare services provided by a charity or public body to be so provided. This Press Notice therefore continues to be relevant only in relation to welfare services provided by a religious community.]

[VATA 1994 Sch 9 Group 7]

9 AUGUST 1989. PRESS NOTICE 58/89
VAT: TREATMENT OF CERTAIN AGRICULTURAL GRANT SCHEMES

Customs and Excise have been considering whether the voluntary surrender of right by landowners and farmers in return for the payment of certain grants should be liable to VAT at the standard rate, eg the surrender by a farmer of his milk quota in return for the payment of a grant by the Ministry of Agriculture, Fisheries and Food.

Customs have consulted other member states and the EC Commission. These discussions have not yet been finally concluded, and Treasury Ministers have therefore decided that VAT should not be applied in the meantime, and in any case not before 1 April 1991.

Customs' discussions have centred on grant payments to "outgoers" under the milk quota arrangements and the set-aside schemes but the same issues arise on other grant schemes.

The decision to suspend the application of VAT applies to these grant schemes and similar schemes, in particular those listed below:

Ministry of Agriculture, Fisheries and Food
Farm Woodland Schemes
Set Aside Scheme
Agriculture Act 1986, Section 18 (Environmentally Sensitive Areas)
Outgoers under the Milk (Cessation of Production) Act 1985

Department of the Environment
Nature Conservancy Council management agreements
Countryside Premium Scheme for Set Aside Land
Countryside Commission Community Forests Scheme

Forestry Commission
Woodland Grant Scheme
Farm Woodland Scheme

The application of VAT to the sale of milk quota between farmers is not affected by these discussions, and continues to be liable to VAT at the standard rate.

[VATA 1994 s 5]

10 AUGUST 1989. PRESS NOTICE 59/89
VAT: REPAIRS UNDER WARRANTY—CHANGE IN TREATMENT OF REPAIRS CARRIED OUT ON BEHALF OF OVERSEAS MANUFACTURERS

Following representations from interested parties, Customs and Excise have reviewed the VAT treatment of warranty work done by UK repairers on behalf of overseas manufacturers and suppliers of goods.

Customs consider that a UK repairer may now, in all cases, recover as input tax, subject to the normal rules, any VAT he incurs on expenditure related to repairs carried out on behalf of overseas manufacturers (eg purchase of spare parts).

Where a repair is done by a UK importer or UK distributor who has taken title to the goods, any payment from the overseas supplier to cover the repair costs is regarded as compensation and no VAT is due. But if the repair is carried out by a third party on behalf of an overseas manufacturer, any payment which the repairer receives is the consideration for his supply of services to the manufacturer on which he must account for VAT at the standard rate.

An overseas manufacturer who incurs VAT in these circumstances may be eligible for a refund of the tax under the EC Eighth or Thirteenth VAT Directive schemes.

Alternatively, if he has a business establishment in the UK he may be able to register for VAT and claim the tax back as input tax, subject to the normal rules. Repairers may, if they choose, apply these changes back-dated to 1 April 1987.

NOTES

When a manufacturer repairs defective goods under warranty, the repair is not a supply for VAT purposes since the original supply of the goods was costed to allow for it. However, overseas manufacturers rarely carry out warranty work themselves; their involvement is normally confined to meeting the cost of repairs, which are usually done by the UK importer or distributor of the goods as part of his after sales service to customers, or possibly by an independent third party who has been appointed as the manufacturer's authorised repairer in the UK

In the past Customs have regarded *all* payments by overseas manufacturers to repairers in respect of warranty work as compensation, and not the consideration for any supply of repair services. No VAT was therefore charged to the manufacturer. Prior to 1 April 1987 this treatment did not normally result in any restriction on the ability of repairers to recover the input tax on their purchases connected with repair work. However, since 1 April 1987 only the input tax related to taxable supplies has been recoverable. The ability of a UK importer or distributor to recover input tax has not been affected by the 1987 changes because he takes title to and resupplies the goods produced by the overseas manufacturer. But independent repairers could no longer recover the tax they incurred in carrying out the repairs.

However, Customs have been advised that their current treatment of payments received by independent repairers is incorrect. They now accept that such payments are the consideration for a taxable supply of repair services, and that VAT should therefore be charged to overseas manufacturers. Consequently independent repairers will also be entitled to recover the input tax related to their repair activities, subject to the normal rules.

Overseas businesses which make no taxable supplies in the UK and which have no business establishment here may be eligible for a refund of the VAT charged to them on warranty work under schemes introduced under the EC Eighth and Thirteenth VAT Directives. This is explained in greater detail in Notice 723: Refunds of VAT in the European Community and other countries. If the overseas business has an establishment in the UK, it cannot use a refund scheme but may at its own request register for VAT and claim as input tax any incurred in respect of its business overseas.

Note: this notice is printed as amended by Press Notice 67/89, 7 September 1989.

[VATA 1994 s 5]

15 MARCH 1990. ICAEW TR 787
VAT: INSURANCE SERVICES OF INTERMEDIARIES OTHER THAN BROKERS: APPLICATION TO PRACTISING ACCOUNTANTS

1. Practising accountants are frequently involved in arrangements resulting in clients taking out insurance. This will often be life assurance or pensions insurance business as part of personal financial planning, including provision for estate taxes. But other types of insurance can also be involved. Often this results in commissions (or shared commissions) being received by the accountant either from an insurer or from an insurance broker. In practice, most will be accounted for to the client, usually as an abatement of the fee.

. . .

8. As stated in para 1 above commissions received are often accounted for to the client. In this respect attention is drawn to para 6 of VAT Notes No 1 1988–89:

"6. Method of accounting for VAT on fees

Many traders when charging fees to their clients reduce the amount by taking into account commission they receive from third parties. For example, a financial adviser provides guidance on insurance to a client; the insurance company pays the adviser a commission and the adviser passes on the benefit to the client by charging a lower fee. In the past, traders have accounted for output tax on the full value of their supply before any deductions for commission. Customs and Excise have reviewed this ruling, and from now on you need only account for output tax on the fee shown on the invoice".

9. The fee note to the client may be set out in either of the following ways:

	Method A	*Method B*
	£	£
Fee	110	
Rebate equivalent to commission received	10	
Fee	100	
VAT @ 15%	15	
Total	115	
Fee net of £10 commission		100
VAT @ 15%		15
Total		115

Note: If method A is used it is important that the commission be described as a rebate.

[VATA 1994 s 19]

25 SEPTEMBER 1990. PRESS NOTICE 65/90
VAT REGISTRATION: INTENDING TRADERS—PROPERTY OWNERS AND DEVELOPERS—OBJECTIVE EVIDENCE REQUIREMENTS

Following representations from the accountancy profession and the trade, HM Customs and Excise have reviewed their objective evidence requirements in respect of property owners and developers who apply for VAT registration on the basis that they intend to make taxable supplies by way of business at a future date.

The evidential requirements will be relaxed with a view to reducing the burdens on business:

(a) applicants will now only be required to state the nature of their intended supplies in order that local VAT office staff can confirm the liability of such supplies; in appropriate cases this may involve notification of their election to waive exemption for the relevant building or planned building;

(b) applicants will also be asked to confirm that they have commenced preparatory activities and the amounts of VAT that they have incurred to date; and

(c) the minimum evidence of preparatory activity that will be accepted is that an applicant has commissioned a feasibility study for which a consideration has, or will be, charged.

Further information regarding other types of acceptable evidence of preparatory activity is available from local VAT offices.

Prior to the review applicants had to produce copy documentation to show that they held title to the respective land or buildings, that full or outline planning permission had also been obtained, and firm arrangements had been made for the disposal of the property.

NOTE

Under [VATA 1994 Sch 1 para 9 (*b*)] a person who is not liable to be registered but who can satisfy HM Customs and Excise that he is carrying on a business and intends to make taxable supplies in the course or furtherance of that business is entitled to be registered on an "intending trader basis".

Prior to the changes in property liability introduced in FA 1989, many supplies in the field of property ownership and development could only be exempt. In order to satisfy Customs that taxable supplies were likely to be made, an applicant had to provide objective evidence to show that title was held to the respective land or buildings, that full or outline planning permission had been obtained, and firm arrangements had been made as regards the disposal of property.

Customs have decided to relax the above criteria following representations. The minimum evidence of preparatory activity that will be accepted is that an applicant has commissioned a feasibility study for which a consideration has, or will be, charged. Other types of acceptable evidence of preparatory activity are:

(a) that the applicant holds title to land or buildings, or is currently negotiating to purchase, or holds an option to purchase;

(b) the applicant holds full or outline planning permission or is to apply for permission in the near future;

(c) the applicant has commissioned architect's services with a view to applying for planning permission or is to apply for permission, or legal or other professional services in connection with the intended sale or letting of the property;

(d) in respect of intended zero-rated sale or long lease of old people's homes, hospices and non-business charity buildings the applicant has obtained from his customers the certification required for zero-rating; and

(e) in respect of the intended zero-rated sale or long lease of substantially reconstructed protected buildings, the applicant has the listed building consent for conversion to residential use and, if necessary, the relevant certification from his customers.

Local VAT offices will now accept written statements from either the applicant or his professional adviser confirming that the above types of evidence are held. They will no longer have to produce copies of planning permission and legal documentation.

More information about the election to waive exemption in respect of property transactions is in Notice [No 742].

[VATA 1994 Sch 1 para 9]

17 MAY 1991. THE LAW SOCIETY
VAT AND APPORTIONMENT OF RENT

The Law Society has taken the view that apportionments of rent between vendor and purchaser do not form part of the sale consideration and are not subject to VAT because the apportionments are not consideration for any supply.

Following discussions with the Society's Revenue Law Committee, HM Customs and Excise have agreed (*Law Society's Gazette*, 8 May 1991) that, on completion of a sale of the landlord's interest in tenanted property or of an assignment of the tenant's interest in a lease, apportionments or "settlements" of the rent should be treated as outside the scope of VAT.

Where either the landlord or the tenant changes at a date within a rent quarter (and where the lease remains in place), any apportionment of the quarter's rent should be treated as falling outside the scope of VAT, notwithstanding that an election to tax the rent has been, or will be, made.

This agreement has no bearing on the liability of the actual consideration received for the sale or assignment. The VAT treatment of the consideration depends on the nature of the supply and the election to waive exemption.

[VATA 1994 s 5]

12 SEPTEMBER 1991. STATEMENT OF PRACTICE SP 11/91 STAMP DUTY AND VALUE ADDED TAX (VAT)—INTERACTION

1. This statement is a revised version of the statement about stamp duty and VAT issued on 22 July 1991, and replaces it.

INTRODUCTION

2. To comply with a judgment of the European Court of Justice in June 1988, standard rate UK VAT has been applied to non-residential construction with effect from 1 April 1989 (FA 1989 s 18 [repealed]). VAT is compulsory on sales of buildings treated as new for this purpose, which are mainly buildings under three years old that have been completed after March 1989. And owners of non-residential property were given the option from 1 August 1989 of charging VAT on sales of old buildings and on leases.

3. These new charges have prompted a number of enquiries about the relationship between stamp duty and VAT where both taxes arise on a sale or lease of commercial property or, occasionally, other assets.

. . .

NO VAT ON STAMP DUTY

14. It is sometimes suggested that stamp duty might itself attract a charge to VAT. This is not the case. The value for VAT depends on the amount (consideration) obtained by the supplier from the purchaser, less the included VAT itself. Stamp duty is paid by the purchaser/lessee of property direct to the Inland Revenue and not to the supplier; it does not therefore form part of the consideration for VAT purposes.

[VATA 1994 s 19]

17 DECEMBER 1991. HANSARD RENT-FREE PERIODS (VAT)

Mr Fraser asked the Chancellor of the Exchequer if he will review the decision of the Customs and Excise to treat rent free periods as benefit subject to VAT.

Mrs Gillian Shephard: It is long-standing Customs policy that rent-free periods are outside the scope of VAT unless services are performed in return by the tenant for the landlord. As this is uncommon, in practice only a few cases will lead to VAT being charged.

HC Written Answer, Vol 201, col 119.

[VATA 1994 s 5]

RETROSPECTION

The new order that came into effect from 1 April 1992 does not affect the legal position applying to cars provided for a salary sacrifice prior to that date. There remain, however, a number of VAT tribunal appeals outstanding on the Commissioners' interpretation of the law as it stood before that date.

In the most significant case so far decided, [*Co-operative Insurance Ltd v C & E Comrs* [1992] VATTR 44], the tribunal found against the Commissioners. It is our view that that case can be distinguished on its particular facts and does not necessarily provide conclusive guidance on the law as it then stood.

Nevertheless, in the interests of equity, the Commissioners have decided not to pursue the VAT due in those other appeals outstanding. Where traders have already paid VAT on salary sacrifice cars they should approach their local VAT office with their details and we will consider retrospective application of the change to them.

But where a direct charge has been made by an employer for the use of the car, whether through salary deduction or not, VAT will still have to be accounted for.

For further information please contact your local VAT office listed under Customs & Excise in the telephone book.

[VATA 1994 s 5]

29 JULY 1992. BUSINESS BRIEF 12/92
VAT ON EXPENSES OF SALE OF DWELLINGS BEQUEATHED TO CHARITIES

Customs and Excise have recently received a number of queries on the sale of bequeathed dwellings or land, and the circumstances under which charities may be treated as making zero rate supplies of bequeathed property in cases where the charities have never acquired legal title ([VATA 1994 Sch 8 Group 15 item 1]).

Following legal advice we have decided that buildings and land are not covered at all by the provisions of [Group 15 item 1], because they are not "goods which have been donated for sale".

Moreover in most cases the dwelling or land concerned would not have been a business asset of either the deceased person or the charity. Any supply of the property flowing from the bequest would normally be outside the scope of VAT, so a charity would not be able to claim input VAT on the expenses of the sale.

Any previous rulings given by the Department on bequeathed buildings and land, and [Group 15 item 1], are now cancelled, except where any charity can show it has relied on such a ruling to zero rate a supply taking place before 1 August 1992.

[VATA 1994 Sch 8 Group 15]

9 SEPTEMBER 1992. THE LAW SOCIETY
VAT AND COMMISSION

The question of the effect on the application of VAT to a bill for professional services rendered to a client on the receipt of commission from a third party has recently been the subject of correspondence between the VAT sub-committee of the Revenue Law Committee and HM Customs and Excise.

By way of background, before April 1988 the relevant rule was that where taxable persons (including solicitors) received commission from a third party in connection with making a supply to a client, VAT had to be calculated on the gross amount of the fee, with commission then being deducted to arrive at a net figure.

Customs announced a change of policy in VAT Notes No 1 1988/89 item 6 published in April 1988, so that VAT could be calculated on the net amount of the fee, following the setting off of the commission.

Customs then indicated that they considered solicitors were a special case because of r 10 of the solicitors practice rules which obliges solicitors to account for any commission they receive to their client (subject to a de minimis limit of £10), so solicitors should calculate VAT on the gross fee (ie a reversion to the pre-April 1988 practice). The Law Society argued that the effect of r 10 was not to put solicitors in a special position, and they should be treated equally as any other taxable persons who received commission which would then be passed on to clients.

Customs indicated to the Law Society on an informal basis that the Commissioners accepted that solicitors were not to be treated differently from other taxable persons, who would all be required to calculate VAT on the gross amount of the fee (ie the pre-April 1988 position).

A letter of confirmation from customs was then sent to the Law Society stating that the guidance in item 6 of VAT Notes No 1 1988/89 could no longer be regarded as sound, and it would be withdrawn as soon as possible.

The Revenue Law Committee wished to bring to the attention of Law Society members this development, and awaited a copy of a text from Customs in order that a notice in the *Gazette* could coincide with the general promulgation of the new approach to local VAT offices.

Pending receipt of the new guidelines, it was difficult to advise Law Society members in the absence of any authoritative guidance. In the meantime, members have been advi... committee, but by revised approach, not in the form of an official statement by the VAT ... article on the second edition of the way of guidance issued in other areas, for example, in an ... national conveyancing protocol (see (1991) *Law Society's Gazette*, 13 November) dealing with the solicitors' charges form and in an article on commissions generally by the standards and guidance committee (see (1991) *Law Society's Gazette*, 23 October).

The Law Society is minded to agree with the view currently taken by the Commissioners as being legally correct, but doubts have been expressed by other professional bodies, so the situation remains unresolved. Until agreement can be reached and revised guidance is published, Customs have advised that members could continue to rely upon the practice outlined in item 6 of the VAT Notes No 1 1988/89, namely to charge VAT after netting off any commission.

The Law Society's Gazette, 9 September 1992, p 16.

[VATA 1994 s 19]

9 SEPTEMBER 1992. THE LAW SOCIETY VAT: SETTLEMENT OF DISPUTES

A meeting with HM Customs and Excise was held on 23 October 1991 . . .

The Law Society said that the tribunal decision in *Cooper Chasney Ltd* (No 4898) had generated comment and correspondence within the VAT sub-committee of the Law Society's revenue law committee on the basis that it might be understood as throwing doubt on the guidance contained in Customs' press notice of 19 November 1987.

An approach was therefore made to Customs, which had replied that it did not consider the decision to be in conflict with the press notice. The Law Society, however, felt there were several aspects of the settlement of disputes where VAT treatment is not straightforward and that further clarification was necessary. It was important that solicitors should be applying the correct principles and assurance from Customs with a view to giving agreed guidance to the profession would be welcome.

Customs and Excise's original approach had been that giving up a right to sue somebody in return for payment was a taxable supply and it satisfied [VATA 1994 s 5 (2) (*b*)], which provides that anything which is not a supply of goods but is done for a consideration (including, if so done, the granting, assignment or surrender of any right) is a supply of services (if done in the course of furtherance of a business).

There had never been any question that if a payment by way of compensation was made pursuant to a court order, this was outside the scope. However, given that basic principle, and the uncertainty surrounding out-of-court settlements prior to the issue of the press notice, it had seemed that Customs was forcing taxpayers to go all the way through the courts and not to enter any settlement by way of compromise, in order to guarantee that any payment would not attract VAT. Customs had reviewed its policy in the light of the decision in the case of *Whites Metal Company* (No 2400) where the VAT tribunal had held that services were not supplied by a plaintiff to a defendant in reaching a settlement of an action in tort.

PRESS NOTICE 82/87

The press notice had been issued with the object of restricting its application to genuine disputes only. If a settlement agreement was worded in terms that the plaintiff was giving up rights to sue the defendant in exchange for a sum of money, this was not a supply. If the agreement not to sue and to settle out of court confirmed a previously agreed price, or confirmed a reduction to a previously agreed price, VAT would be adjusted, using the credit note mechanism, by reference to the price finally agreed. The situation when payment was made subject to a court order remained unchanged.

Since the press notice had been issued, very few cases had been brought to VAT headquarters. *Cooper Chasney* and *Edenroc* were notable exceptions. Customs believed that both these decisions were in accordance with the press notice. Local offices had been dealing with queries. However, it was the Law Society's view that the lack of cases which had been brought could indicate unawareness of the potential traps where elements of a settlement could attract a VAT liability.

Customs had considered when drafting the press notice, the particular example of royalties when there had been an inadvertent breach of copyright. If payment was partly to compensate for a past breach, and partly for permission to use in the future the material subject to copyright, there should be a reasonable apportionment. A distinction needed to be drawn. Payment by way of compensation in respect of a past transgression was outside the scope but payment in consideration of allowing the future use of the copyright material was in respect of a taxable supply.

In the Law Society's view, the facts of *Cooper Chasney* were perhaps more straightforward than difficulties which could be experienced in practice. In that case, the plaintiff had expressly allowed the defendant to use the name "Infolink" in the future (a name which the plaintiff had previously used in his business), but the terms of the settlement were that, in return for payment to the plaintiff by the defendant of an agreed sum, the plaintiff reverted to his own name (Cooper Chasney Ltd) and agreed to discontinue proceedings against the defendant. It was clear that the elements of the agreement went beyond breaches which were alleged to have occurred in the past and giving up a right to sue.

Customs said that in deciding what the payment in the settlement of a dispute was for, it looks carefully at the words used by the parties (as in *Cooper Chasney*, where an agreement had been entered into which had been set out in the decision) and taxes the parties accordingly.

The Law Society asked if Customs was happy that press notice 82/87 was correct and it confirmed it was satisfied with the general approach and did not think it should be extended, for example, on the basis of the decisions in *Neville Russell v C & E Comrs* [1987] VATTR 194 and *Gleneagles Hotel plc v C & E Comrs* [1986] VATTR 196, to indicate that anything done in exchange for consideration is a supply.

Customs did not consider that a person had an intrinsic right to sue so that by not suing, a person was not necessarily giving up any right. Customs thought the position could be analysed by saying that a person was really exercising an option not to enforce an alleged wrong, rather than giving up any right. The acceptance of an offer not to sue is taken because the reason for wanting to sue in the first place is settled on receipt of payment.

Customs agreed that if VAT was never mentioned in negotiating a settlement, the plaintiff could suddenly find that the amount of cash he or she received in settlement was reduced by VAT. There was a suggestion that this could be avoided by adding to the agreement for settlements the words "VAT will be added [to the agreed sum] if applicable". However, it would obviously be preferable to issue clear guidance to avoid the necessity of requiring such terms automatically to be added to settlement wordings.

The Law Society asked if Customs agreed that liquidated damages paid under contracts were also outside the scope and Customs confirmed this. Such cases would not involve litigation but were within the spirit of the press notice. If a contract contained provisions for damages in respect of a breach, this would generally be within the press notice, but if a plaintiff was giving up a separate right, for example, the right to receive notice, this could be a taxable supply.

Customs has agreed a "joint statement of practice" (JSP) with the principal leasing associations in order to avoid contractual arguments and any ambiguity over the correct VAT treatment of termination payments and rebates/refunds of rentals arising under equipment leases. The object of the JSP is to establish a common treatment which provides that:

1. all lease termination payments may be treated as being in respect of taxable supplies, ie of the right to terminate. Here the termination payment is usually calculated by reference to the amount of rental payments outstanding under the primary lease period; and

2. where, on expiry or termination of an equipment lease, the lessee receives from the lessor a rebate or refund of rentals, no adjustment for VAT previously charged need be made. However, credit notes should be endorsed "this is not a credit note for VAT purposes".

Importantly, the JSP does not override any contractual arrangements in force. If the lessors wish to revert to the terms of their original agreements, they may do so. For example, lease termination payments may arise on default by a lessee which are by way of liquidated damages and therefore outside the scope of VAT.

Taxpayers who were not within the major leasing associations could rely on this agreement but they would not necessarily be aware of it. It was confirmed that local VAT offices had knowledge of it.

The Law Society's letter to the solicitor's office at Customs of 18 June had listed examples of where it had sought Customs' guidance on specific issues. These were raised for discussion and the following answers given:

1. Customs confirmed that press notice 82/87 covered only payments made after proceedings had commenced. If it was clear that payments had been made before proceedings had been commenced, but such payments would not be within s 3 (2) (*b*), Customs would extend outside the scope treatment to such payments.

2. In the area of involuntary supplies (eg a dispute concerning right of light for which damages are awarded) Customs confirmed that only damages in respect of past infringements would be outside the scope. Where a settlement covered past infringements, and also permission to continue in the future the conduct which gave rise to those infringements, Customs would accept a reasonable apportionment.

The Law Society asked about the case where the court required a party to give up a right (eg a right of light or an intellectual property right) in exchange for a payment from the other party. Customs said that this was a difficult point which it would need to consider further. art 6 (1) of the Sixth Directive was relevant where it referred to "tolerating an act or situation" as a possible supply for VAT purposes.

Questions concerning rights of light can cause problems. Much depends on whether a payment is made in return for the right to take someone else's light or whether it is compensation for the loss of light subsequent to an adjacent building being constructed. It could be argued in exceptional circumstances that the court is deciding what level of consideration is due in return for the granting of the right. However, it is thought that in the majority of cases the payment will be damages imposed upon the payer by the court and therefore outside the scope of VAT. For example, in cases where the court decides that light may be taken and that compensation is payable this will be seen as outside the scope of VAT—there is no consensual element.

3. Where litigation has involved a supply on which VAT had already been accounted for (but the price was not paid) and the result is a reduction in the price paid for the supply, it may be necessary for a supplier to issue a credit note in order to recover part of the VAT which he or she had previously accounted for and not received. Customs confirmed that, in such a case, the credit note could be accepted as valid and it would prima facie be necessary for the recipient of the supply to repay to Customs the tax which he or she had already claimed back.

4. By way of clarification as to when damages were considered to be compensatory and when such payments would constitute consideration for taxable supplies, Customs offered the example of a local authority digging up a pavement in front of a parade of shops. Compensation for loss of trade suffered as a result of its action paid by the local authority to a shop-keeper would not be regarded as a taxable supply. However, if a shop-keeper was paid by the local authority to allow it to work on his or her land, the payment would be consideration for a taxable supply.

Customs said that it would want to consider in greater detail the question of warranty claims. For example, in a standard rated property transaction, where a warranty had understated the rent and the contract provided for a reduction in the purchase price in such a situation, the procedure set out in **3** above would apply and the vendor would have to issue a credit note to recover that part of the VAT previously accounted for.

The example of net assets of a business having been overstated in warranties given on sale was not so relevant since if it was a question of shares, it would be in the realm of exempt supplies anyway. Compensation in these circumstances would be regarded as outside the scope unless the agreement provided for a reduction in price.

5. Where the settlement involved cross supplies (other than the mere surrender of the right of action) tax would be payable by each party, without netting off, according to the nature of the supply. The situation may arise that there may be a consideration paid in return for a party agreeing to enter into an agreement. For example, in the property industry, reverse premiums may be paid to a potential tenant in consideration of the tenant agreeing to enter into a property lease or for agreeing to carry out building, refurbishment or demolition works, *viz Neville Russell* and *Battersea Leisure*.

If the supply under the agreement was, eg free services, VAT would not be due.

6. Customs confirmed that interest on damages is outside the scope of VAT. It has been confirmed in the European decision in *BAZ Bausystem AG v Finanzant München für Körperschaften* [1982] ECR 2527 that interest would not increase consideration for a supply.

If an international breach had occurred, the same basic principles should be followed. For example, [VATA 1994 Sch 5] should not apply to a cross border giving up of rights. Apparently, the Dutch and the Germans had had bilateral discussions and had confirmed that they would apply outside the scope treatment on the same basis as in the UK.

The Law Society's Gazette, 9 September 1992, p 32.

[VATA 1994 s 5]

14 OCTOBER 1992. THE LAW SOCIETY VAT—MESNE PROFITS

Following an enquiry from a member of the profession, the Revenue Law Committee has been in correspondence with Customs as to what extent VAT is relevant to an award of mesne profits.

The Commissioners of Customs and Excise agree that mesne profits are damages for trespass (*Bramwell v Bramwell* [1942] 1 All ER 137). Such damages can only be recovered in respect of a defendant's continued occupation of premises after that right of occupation has expired. As such, an award of mesne profits is not consideration for a supply.

Where a landlord has elected to waive exemption from VAT under the provisions of [VATA 1994 Sch 10 paras 2–4], and arrears of rent accrue, in respect of which the landlord sues the tenant, in addition to a claim for mesne profits, the landlord will clearly have made a taxable supply, and non-payment of the rent by the tenant would not affect the landlord's liability to account for tax on the grant of the lease (the supply) subject to any cash accounting considerations.

If the landlord is not on cash accounting, tax points for the period in respect of which he is claiming arrears of rent will already have been determined under [the VAT Regulations 1995, SI 1995/2518, reg 85 (1) (*b*) or (2) or 90 (1) (*b*) or (2)] as the case may require.

If the landlord is on cash accounting, payments received both pursuant to and by way of settlement of litigation will be viewed by the Commissioners as referable in the first instance to being in satisfaction of rent (ie consideration for the grant). Therefore, if the total amount of the settlement is equal to or less than the arrears of rent, the whole of the settlement will be viewed by the Commissioners as payment received by the landlord in respect of the grant.

The Law Society's Gazette, 14 October 1992, p 16.

[VATA 1994 s 5]

28 OCTOBER 1992. THE LAW SOCIETY VAT—PAYMENT OF THIRD PARTY COSTS

[An article was published in the *Law Society's Gazette* on 24 October 1990 entitled "Payment of another party's costs". The article has been agreed with Customs and Excise and set out the rules which apply when a solicitor's costs are paid by a person other than the person to whom the solicitor's services are supplied. Recent discussions between members of the VAT Sub-Committee of the Law Society's Revenue Law Committee and Customs and Excise have led to the agreement with Customs of new guidance, which is set out below.]

It should be noted that this guidance incorporates a change of practice by Customs and that in certain circumstances, set out below, VAT will be chargeable where this had previously been accepted not to be the case.

"THE INDEMNITY PRINCIPLE"

The October 1990 article stated that when a person other than the solicitor's own client is paying the solicitor's costs, the liability of the paying party is one of indemnity only, and thus in itself outside the scope of VAT. In fact, such payment will only be regarded as outside the scope in certain circumstances, for example, as follows—

(a) where following completion of litigation (or arbitration), one party is ordered to pay the other party's costs;

(b) where a party to a transaction undertakes to pay the other party's costs, and the matter does not proceed to completion, so the costs are "abortive".

However, there are other circumstances where the payment of costs by a third party is regarded as consideration for the supply for VAT purposes. One specific example of such a situation would be where a transaction obliges one party to be responsible for the costs of the other relating to that transaction, in which case payment will be regarded as part of the consideration for the supply (provided the transaction proceeds to completion).

It is worth restating the following general principles which apply when the payment is on an indemnity basis—

(a) the solicitor whose costs are to be paid should deliver a tax invoice to his own client. If his client is not a registered taxable person, it is permissible to deliver a VAT inclusive bill without distinguishing the VAT element, although this would not be common practice;

(b) if the solicitor's client is a registered fully taxable person, and the supply of legal services is obtained for the purpose of the client's business, the client will be entitled to an input tax credit in which case the indemnifying party need only pay the costs exclusive of VAT;

(c) if the solicitor's client is not a registered fully taxable person and cannot obtain input tax credit, the indemnifying party is liable to pay the costs and VAT as well. However, the indemnifying party cannot recover the VAT;

(d) where the solicitor's client is a partly exempt registered taxable person, para (*b*) above applies only to the extent that the client can obtain credit for input tax. Paragraph (*c*) applies to the balance;

(e) *in no circumstances may a tax invoice be issued by the client's solicitor to the paying party* who is not in law entitled to receive an input tax credit as the services have not been rendered to him. The paying party should therefore receive a note of the other party's costs in such terms that the note cannot be mistaken for a tax invoice issued to the paying party.

For solicitors' services in insurance cases, please refer to previous guidance on this subject which has been published in the *Law Society's Gazette* on 16 January 1985 and 15 January 1986.

"WHEN PAYMENT CONSTITUTES PART OF THE CONSIDERATION FOR THE SUPPLY"

It is clearly stated in Customs and Excise Notice 742B (Property ownership) para 15 that payment by a tenant of a landlord's costs incurred in respect of the grant of a lease or licence would be regarded as part of the consideration for the supply by the landlord to the tenant. The practical implications will depend on whether the landlord has elected to waive exemption from VAT in relation to the property. If no election to waive exemption has been made, the landlord would not be entitled to an input tax credit on his costs, so the tenant would be required to pay the gross costs including the VAT element: there will have been no taxable supply, so the tenant will not receive a VAT invoice and will be unable to recover as input tax the VAT he has paid to the landlord.

If the landlord has elected to waive exemption, so VAT is payable in respect of the rent or premium, the landlord can recover the VAT element of the costs, and the tenant will only be required to pay the net amount of the landlord's costs, but to that net amount, the landlord will add a VAT charge.

In effect, the amount paid by the tenant would be the same whether or not the landlord has elected to waive exemption, but only if the landlord has done so will the tenant receive a tax invoice from the landlord, and be able to recover the VAT element if the tenant is a registered taxable person.

CHANGE OF POLICY

It has recently become apparent that Customs will also regard payment of costs which have been incurred by a landlord in respect of the exercise by a tenant of an existing right under the lease or licence as constituting part of the consideration for the supply by the landlord to tenant (and thus potentially subject to VAT as described in the paragraph above headed "When payment constitutes part of the consideration for the supply"). This represents a change from the agreed guidance published on 24 October 1990, and it has been agreed that the effective date for the new regime will be 1 December 1992. It is accepted that if, under the terms of the lease, a landlord cannot unreasonably withhold his consent to the tenant's exercising a right, or where the tenant is permitted to exercise a right without the landlord's consent, but subject to payment by the tenant of the landlord's costs, this will be regarded as an existing right. However, where the landlord has absolute discretion as to whether consent is to be granted for the exercise of a right, payment of costs incurred by the landlord is regarded as consideration for a *separate* supply, on which the landlord will charge VAT unless the right sought to be exercised would constitute an exempt supply.

The contents of this article supersede the article which was published in the *Law Society's Gazette* on 11 July 1990, entitled "VAT and notices of assignment" which should now be disregarded.

The Law Society's Gazette, 28 October 1992.
[VATA 1994 s 5]

18 NOVEMBER 1992. THE LAW SOCIETY VAT AND TELEGRAPHIC TRANSFER FEES

Customs and Excise VAT Administration Directorate has set out its views on the treatment of telegraphic transfer fees charged in solicitors' bills in the following letter to the VAT sub-committee of the Law Society's Revenue Law Committee.

In response to our very useful meeting about VAT and solicitors' bills I am writing to confirm our long-held view that telegraphic transfer fees are not disbursements for VAT purposes and thus must be subjected to VAT when passed on to the client.

We understand that there have been uncertainties in this area in the past and I am happy to confirm that in those cases where VAT has not been charged on telegraphic transfer fees following incorrect advice from Customs and Excise staff, no action will be taken to recover VAT on past transactions. I have made arrangements for LVO staff to be notified about the contents of this letter.

The Law Society's Gazette, 18 November 1992.
[VATA 1994 s 47]

16 DECEMBER 1992. BUSINESS BRIEF 18/92 INPUT TAX INCURRED IN RESPECT OF OUTSIDE THE SCOPE TRANSACTIONS

With effect from 1 January 1993 certain supplies of services which are currently zero-rated will become outside the scope of the tax. Nevertheless in the majority of cases there will still be a right to input deduction.

. . .

OUTSIDE THE SCOPE VALUES

. . .

Having said that, we do not, in principle, see any objection to the values of outside the scope supplies continuing to be used in proportional calculations within special methods. The values of outside the scope supplies with a right to input tax deduction would be treated as "taxable" values; the value of outside the scope supplies with no right to input tax deduction would be treated as "exempt" values.

Partly exempt businesses which are currently using the standard method and include the currently zero-rated values in proportional calculations will be allowed to continue including those values when they become outside the scope on 1 January 1993. Their methods will, however, become special methods.

. . .

POSITION OF NON-UK BRANCHES

We currently require businesses which make supplies from an establishment outside the UK to identify the tax they incur in the UK in respect of those supplies. We do not allow the values of such supplies to be used in proportional calculations.

This is because it is normally impossible to accurately verify income received abroad and the mere fact that a UK business may have, for example, a branch abroad does not necessarily mean that it incurs tax in the UK in supporting that branch. Businesses engaged in this kind of activity will continue to identify the input tax incurred in the UK in support of supplies made from an establishment abroad as they do at present.

The situation is, of course, different in respect of those zero-rated supplies which will become outside the scope, because there exist identifiable and verifiable values which could be used in a proportional calculation.

[SI 1995/2518 reg 101]

3 FEBRUARY 1993. HANSARD
VAT—ARRANGEMENT FEES

Mr Mudie asked the Chancellor of the Exchequer what VAT liability is applied to arrangement fees charged by a bank to its customers in connection with a debt for equity exchange by that bank.

Sir John Cope: The VAT liability of arrangement fees charged by banks depends strictly on the terms of the contracts between the parties. Without further details, it is difficult to be precise about the liability. Arrangement fees charged by the banks in respect of loans or other forms of credit form part of the consideration for the loan, an exempt supply. Moreover, where a borrower issues shares in return for loan capital, any arrangement fee would also be exempt from VAT. In either case, any associated VAT incurred by the bank would not be recoverable.

HC Written Answer, 3 February 1993, Vol 218, col 186.

[VATA 1994 Sch 9 Group 5]

3 FEBRUARY 1993. HANSARD
VAT—NON-EXECUTIVE DIRECTOR'S SERVICES

Mr Mudie asked the Chancellor of the Exchequer what VAT treatment has been agreed between the British Bankers' Association and Customs and Excise with regard to the VAT treatment of supplies of non-executive director's services made by investing institutions to investee companies.

Sir John Cope: There has been no specific agreement concerning non-executive directors' fees. These fall to be treated in the same way as management fees which are included in the list of guidelines agreed between Customs and the British Bankers' Association (BBA). Where a director is appointed to the board of the UK investee company as a condition of a loan, any charges for the director's services are part of the consideration for the loan, an exempt supply. Alternatively, where the investor acquires shares and exercises the right to appoint a director, Customs take the view that there is no supply for VAT purposes, as any shares are supplied to the investing institution by the investee company. In either case, any associated VAT incurred by the investing institution would not be recoverable.

HC Written Answer, 3 February 1993, Vol 218, cols 185, 186.

[VATA 1994 Sch 9 Group 5]

3 FEBRUARY 1993. BUSINESS BRIEF 5/93
SUPPLIES OF GOODS TO OTHER EC COUNTRIES WHERE THE CUSTOMER'S VAT REGISTRATION NUMBER IS NOT AVAILABLE—STANDARD PROCEDURE

You can zero-rate the supply of goods removed to other EC countries provided you hold commercial evidence of removal and show the VAT registration number of your customer on the sales invoice. If you do not hold that number, you cannot zero-rate your supplies (but see the special procedure below for supplies before 28 February 1993) [not reproduced]. However, if you charge VAT to a customer in another EC country who subsequently provides a valid VAT registration number issued by that country you can issue a credit note for the amount of VAT charged and zero-rate the supply.

When you obtain the number, the tax exclusive value of the supply must be recorded on your EC sales list (ESL) as you will not have recorded this at the time of the original sale.

[SI 1995/2518 reg 134]

22 APRIL 1993. BUSINESS BRIEF 12/93
PAYMENTS TO A RETAIL CONSORTIUM

Retailers may join together to form a purchasing consortium for the purposes of negotiating lower prices for the goods they purchase.

The terms of agreement between different consortia and the suppliers of goods can vary, but a common feature is for the suppliers to make periodic payments to the [purchasing consortium]. The purpose of this brief is to confirm the correct VAT treatment of payments made by suppliers/manufacturers of goods to a purchasing consortium.

Payments made by a manufacturer or supplier to a consortium, are regarded as the consideration for a taxable supply of services, by the consortium, of introducing the manufacturer/supplier to a larger customer base. The purchasing consortium is therefore required to account for output tax at the standard rate on all such receipts.

This view was upheld at a VAT tribunal (*Landmark Cash and Carry Ltd* [1980] VATTR 1, London, November 1979), although it has since become apparent that some traders may have been treating these payments incorrectly. In particular, traders should note that the payments do not fall to be treated as contingent discounts under Notice 700 para 16 because the consortium does not purchase or take ownership of the goods.

[VATA 1994 s 5]

7 JUNE 1993. BUSINESS BRIEF 17/93
VAT ON RENT ARREARS

When a tenant is in default the landlord can, pursuant to the Law of Distress Amendment Act 1908 s 6, collect the arrears of rent from any sub-tenant. This is done by the service of a notice upon the sub-tenant which, until the arrears have been paid, transfers to the landlord the right to recover, receive and give a discharge for the rent. The sub-tenant can, in turn, reduce the rent payable to the defaulting tenant under the sub-lease by the amounts paid to the superior landlord.

There has been some confusion over the VAT treatment of the rental payments where an election to waive exemption (option to tax) has been exercised. Contrary to views which have been expressed, any deemed relationship between the superior landlord and the sub-tenant under the Law of Distress Amendment Act 1908 s 3 has no effect on the nature of the supplies for VAT purposes. By virtue of the lease the superior landlord continues to make a series of separate and successive supplies to the tenant; and by virtue of the sub-lease the tenant continues to make a series of separate and successive supplies to the sub-tenant.

If the superior landlord has elected to waive exemption of the property, any tax invoice should be issued to the tenant and not to the sub-tenant.

Any right to recover the VAT charged by the superior landlord rests with the tenant and not with the sub-tenant. The sub-tenant may only treat as his input tax any VAT charged by the tenant on rents payable under the sub-lease.

26 JULY 1993. BUSINESS BRIEF 23/93
VAT ON THE SALE OF RENT FREE PERIODS

Where a person grants a lease on a property and receives rental income he is regarded as carrying on a property rental business. In circumstances where a lease is subject to an initial rent free period there is some doubt whether a property rental business can be said to be carried on during this period.

However it is now accepted that if a building which is subject to a rent free period is sold during the rent free period, and no income has previously been received, the vendor can, nevertheless be regarded as carrying on a property rental business. It follows the sale may be treated as a transfer of a going concern, explained in VAT Leaflet 700/92—Transfer of a business as a going concern [VAT Leaflet 700/9/94].

[SI 1995/1268 art 5]

10 SEPTEMBER 1993. PRESS NOTICE 59/93
VAT RECOVERY BY HOLDING COMPANIES

In the light of business responses to a Customs & Excise consultative paper, only minor changes will be made from 1 October to the treatment of VAT on costs incurred by holding companies.

The position of the vast majority of holding companies with active trading subsidiaries will remain unchanged.

GENERAL APPROACH FOR THE FUTURE

Customs will continue to keep the VAT recovery by holding companies under review and will be monitoring developments in Europe, particularly emerging case law from the European Court of Justice.

They accept that any wider changes in the VAT treatment of holding companies would only occur as the result of the adoption of a uniform approach by all member states. If EC proposals on this subject were to be brought forward at any time in the future, Customs would consult with interested parties to allow them the opportunity to comment further.

MINOR CHANGES

Where holding companies are unregistered they cannot by definition recover tax.

But there are VAT registered holding companies who are neither active trading companies in their own right, nor are grouped with active trading subsidiaries making taxable supplies outside the VAT group, nor providing genuine management services to separate trading subsidiaries. Many are in effect investment vehicles with no active involvement in trading subsidiaries and are often grouped with a subsidiary supplying management services to them.

In the case of those types of holding companies, and those companies alone, when they incur costs on the following items they will not be able to recover the tax as it will not be regarded by Customs as relating to any taxable supply. These items are costs incurred in acquiring another company; disposing of a subsidiary; restructuring costs relating to the group or any subsidiary; and investment costs incurred on holdings held.

NOTE

In its simplest sense a holding company describes a company with shareholdings in one or more subsidiaries. But their structures and purpose are much more diverse, ranging from companies with minimal activities where shares are held in subsidiaries and dividends received, but no part is played in the management of the investment, to businesses fully integrated with trading subsidiaries and where the holding company is actively concerned with the supervision and management of the subsidiaries.

The basic functions of a holding company are to acquire and hold shares in subsidiaries, from which it receives dividends; defend itself and its subsidiaries from takeovers; and make disposals. From time to time it may invest, deposit or lend money, and issue or sell shares. Some of these activities are outside the scope of VAT, while others are exempt. A company which had no other activities would not be eligible for VAT registration and would not be able to recover any of the tax it incurred on purchases.

However, holding companies are liable to be registered for VAT, where they have taxable trading activities, supply management services to subsidiaries, or are included in a VAT group with trading subsidiaries.

A consultation paper was issued by Customs on 24 June. Most of the responses to the paper touched upon the importance of a level playing field across Europe so as not to erode the international competitiveness of British business or encourage holding companies to locate elsewhere.

[SI 1995/2518 reg 101]

6 JULY 1994. BUSINESS BRIEF 14/94
HOW CUSTOMS AND EXCISE PUBLICISE VAT LAW INTERPRETATION CHANGES

We sometimes change our view of what the VAT law means because of decisions made by the VAT tribunal, the courts, or as a result of internal reviews.

This statement explains how we will publicise such changes. It indicates how businesses and their advisors can keep abreast of the changes.

YOUR POSITION

VAT is a self-assessed tax, but we will ensure that you are kept informed of changes in the law and its interpretation. You should take steps to keep yourself up to date with these and how they affect your business.

OUR POSITION

We apply what we consider to be the correct interpretation of the law relating to VAT. However, we can be challenged at the VAT tribunal and in the courts. In addition we may reconsider our interpretation and change it.

We will take all reasonable action to publicise a change before it is implemented. Our Charter commitment to provide clear, accurate and timely information about VAT reinforces this intention.

TIMING OF CHANGES

Where, for whatever reason, interpretation of the law is changed, we are obliged to apply this change as quickly as possible. Delay will clearly be unfair if a change is beneficial to taxpayers.

If a change is to the advantage of the Exchequer it cannot be delayed unduly as we must collect the tax properly due. However, wherever possible we will give you time to prepare for it.

PUBLICITY FOR CHANGES

Our action will include consultation with relevant trade bodies and representative organisations. We will issue a News Release or Business Brief setting out details of the change and the justification for it. These go to a wide variety of media outlets and are available through a subscription service operated for us by the Central Office of Information.

We will also make an announcement in "VAT Notes", a broadsheet publication sent quarterly to all registered persons with their returns. Where appropriate this will include a cross reference to any other relevant publications. You are asked to read "VAT Notes" carefully and to implement any changes which affect your business.

At the earliest opportunity we will update our publications covering the subject affected by the change. These will not show dates earlier than that of the month in which they are published.

OVERPAYMENTS RESULTING FROM A CHANGE

If despite taking all reasonable steps to keep yourself informed, you were not aware of a change in interpretation of the law at the time it was made, and you overcharge VAT as a result, we will normally agree to you applying the change retrospectively. You will be entitled to adjust the VAT due, subject to the provisions concerning unjust enrichment (FA 1989 s 24) which precludes anyone securing a repayment of VAT overpaid which benefits them rather than the person to whom they have charged the VAT.

If it is established that the overpayment occurred because of a failure on our part to publicise the change adequately we will pay you interest on the amount involved.

UNDERPAYMENTS RESULTING FROM A CHANGE

If you do not implement a change at the correct time you could be liable for the VAT underpaid as a result.

However, if despite you taking all reasonable steps to keep informed about changes, a change is introduced of which you could not have been aware, we will require you to pay any extra VAT only from the date when it was reasonable for you to have known about it. This would normally be not later than the date of receipt by you of "VAT Notes" referring to the change. In these special circumstances any tax underpaid would qualify to be remitted on grounds of misunderstanding.

[VATA 1994 ss 73 and 80]

7 SEPTEMBER 1994. PRESS NOTICE 34/94
INTEREST ON VAT ASSESSMENTS

In general Customs will not in future seek to assess interest where it does not represent commercial restitution. The assessment is subject to an administrative discretion. This means that the decision to assess is made on the facts of any particular case. However, advice recently issued to local VAT offices will emphasise the role of interest as commercial restitution.

The change of emphasis is the first result of an ongoing internal review into the way the interest regime operates in practice. The change addresses concerns that interest should not be charged where there is no overall loss to the exchequer, and reflects Customs' wider commitment to keep burdens on business to a minimum.

NOTE

Interest on tax assessments and voluntary disclosures is charged under [VATA 1994 s 74]. The discretion to assess is contained in [VATA 1994 s 76]. The change of emphasis announced in this Press Release is a development of the [s 76] discretion. There has been no change to the underlying statutory basis for interest.

Although commercial restitution has always been the principal rationale for interest, the VAT mechanism means that in some cases interest has been charged where there is no overall loss to the exchequer. This might happen for example where the company fails to charge VAT but, had it done so, another company would have been able to claim that VAT as input tax.

[VATA 1994 s 74]

12 SEPTEMBER 1994. BUSINESS BRIEF 17/94 VAT ON MILK QUOTAS

Recent amendments to the Dairy Products Quotas Regulations allow the transfer of milk quotas without land in certain circumstances. This is a derogation from the general principle of quota attached to land. The supply or transfer of a milk quota without land qualifies as a supply of services, and is therefore standard-rated.

However, when the transfer of a milk quota is linked with a supply of land under one agreement, this is regarded as one supply for VAT purposes. It doesn't matter if the land is sold freehold or as a leasehold transfer. The VAT liability of the quota will be the same as the VAT liability for the land, even if separate identifiable sums are paid for the land and the quota, or if the invoice details are split between the land and the quota.

If a milk quota is transferred with a grazing licence there are two separate supplies, one of animal feeding stuffs, through the grazing licence which is zero-rated, and the other of the quota which is standard-rated.

[VATA 1994 Sch 9 Group 1]

18 NOVEMBER 1994. BUSINESS BRIEF 20/94 EXTENSION TO THE LIST OF FINANCIAL SERVICES

Customs are extending the list of unallocated precious metals which are treated as a taxable financial service for VAT purposes. This change will provide the same VAT treatment for all precious metals and may encourage overseas traders to obtain these services from UK suppliers.

From 1 December 1994 the sale of unallocated rhodium, ruthenium, osmium and iridium will be treated as being within the provisions of VATA 1994 Sch 5. The sale of unallocated goods gives the buyer the right to call for delivery, but not ownership of a specific parcel of goods.

The sale of any of these metals on an unallocated basis to businesses established elsewhere within the EC, or to any person established outside the EC will be outside the scope of UK VAT. However, the supplier will retain the right to recover the VAT on related costs.

The receipt of these services from a person outside the UK will come within the reverse charge provisions of VATA 1994 s 8.

PRESENT TREATMENT

Until now only unallocated gold, silver, platinum and palladium have been treated as a financial service. The sale of the other precious metals has to date been treated as supplied within the UK and therefore liable to UK VAT.

There is more information about the provisions of Sch 5 and the application of the reverse charge in Notice 741 "Place of supply of services".

[VATA 1994 Sch 5 para 5]

8 DECEMBER 1994. BUSINESS BRIEF 24/94 SALE OF PROPERTY UNDER A POWER OF SALE—RECOVERY OF VAT ON COSTS INCURRED BY MORTGAGE LENDERS

Customs & Excise have reconsidered the VAT treatment of costs incurred by mortgage lenders when selling property to realise their security in circumstances where a borrower has defaulted on a loan.

The Business Brief explains the reasons for this and sets out the arrangements which will apply for the future. It also sets out the position on payment of claims for past periods.

BACKGROUND

Business Brief 20/93 [30 June 1993] indicated that Customs were prepared to see lenders as agents of the borrower in arranging the sale of repossessed property, and hence allow them to claim bad debt relief (BDR), where appropriate, on the VAT incurred on selling costs.

However, Customs subsequently became aware that the order of attribution of the proceeds of sale under the Law of Property Act 1925 s 105 might override the Bad Debt Relief Regulations. This is because under s 105 the proceeds of sale are allocated first to costs such as those incurred in selling the property, which threw some considerable doubt over whether a bad debt was created on which relief could be claimed.

Doubts arose also about the status of lenders as agents and there was concern that some claims had included costs which went beyond the terms of the Business Brief. Customs therefore issued a further Business Brief 5/94 [1 March 1994] suspending the processing of claims, until such time as they could take legal advice and examine more fully the issues involved.

CURRENT POSITION

Having taken Counsel's advice, Customs are of the view that there is a good argument that in arranging the sale of repossessed property, mortgagees act under rights conferred by the mortgage agreement, and not as agents of the borrower. However, Customs believe they can rely on the wider interpretation of "agent" contained in the Sixth VAT Directive [Directive 77/388/EEC] in maintaining their current view on agency, as laid out in Business Brief 20/93. They face more difficulty with the Law of Property Act 1925 s 105, as it may override the order of attribution in the Bad Debt Relief Regulations, but again the matter is not free from doubt.

In the circumstances, Customs believe that the finely balanced nature of the legal advice allows some freedom of choice and they are re-introducing a form of easement.

NEW ARRANGEMENTS

General

The easement is strictly for the purposes of allowing a measure of relief for VAT on bad debts and depends crucially on Customs taking a relaxed view of the supply position. Lenders must not extend this treatment more widely in accounting for VAT within their businesses.

The new arrangements will apply to bad debt relief claims relating to supplies made on or after 1 July 1994. The overall aim is to provide relief to lenders where they suffer sticking tax on the costs of selling property in circumstances where borrowers have defaulted—in effect where the net proceeds of sale are reduced because the VAT element of the costs has not been recovered.

In principle, the easement covers costs incurred by lenders in arranging the sale of repossessed property and also to selling costs incurred when property is sold through a Law of Property Act receiver. It is emphasised that, with the single exception of build-out costs, the arrangements apply only to sale costs, and not to any incurred in relation to letting.

Although the Law of Property Act does not apply in Scotland, there are analogous provisions in the Conveyancing and Feudal Reform (Scotland) Act 1970 s 27. The arrangements therefore apply equally in Scotland.

Basic Principle

Under the new arrangements, lenders can be seen as agents of the borrower in relation to the costs of sale whether or not the mortgage deed specifies such a relationship. As an agent, the lender may treat the selling costs incurred as supplies made to them and by them under VATA 1994 s 47 (3). The order of attribution of the sale proceeds in the Bad Debt Relief Regulations can then be applied and bad debt relief claimed as appropriate in accordance with normal rules.

These new arrangements apply only to costs relating directly to the sale of property, which would ordinarily have been incurred by the borrower had he arranged the sale himself. Examples of such costs include charges for professional services connected with the sale eg legal and estate agency fees.

The easement does not include costs incurred on services provided to, and used by, the lender as principal, even though they may be charged on to the borrower under the mortgage deed. Examples of such costs include legal fees associated with taking possession, and locksmith's fees for securing the property. Costs incurred in pursuing claims against a valuer for negligence are also excluded.

Other Expenses

The position of certain other expenses incurred by lenders was discussed at recent meetings with trade representatives. Treatment of these under the new arrangements is outlined below.

Law of Property Act Receivers' Charges

Law of Property Act receivers' charges which relate specifically to the sale (not letting) of the property and any costs incurred by them in respect of the sale can be regarded as falling within the scope of the new arrangements, but only where the proceeds of sale received by lenders have been reduced by the VAT element of the charges. Where this happens, lenders may be regarded as acting as agents for the borrower in paying the costs.

This means that Customs are not prepared to apply this arrangement where the Law of Property Act receiver recovers the VAT incurred on behalf of a VAT registered borrower and this is reflected in the proceeds passed to the lender. This may occur, for example, where the Law of Property Act receiver has control of the borrower's VAT returns.

Build-Out Costs

These are expenses incurred on completion of a partly-completed building or major refurbishment of the property before sale. Customs' legal advice is that lenders incur such costs as principals and do not make any onward supplies to the borrower even though the costs are charged on under the terms of the mortgage deed. It was argued at the recent meetings with trade representatives that strict application of this line would create a hidden VAT charge in respect of buildings whose sale is zero-rated.

Customs are sympathetic to this view and are therefore prepared, very exceptionally, to treat the onward charge of the build-out costs as a supply by the lender as principal to the borrower, where the sale of the building by the borrower is the subject of a taxable supply or the transfer of a going concern for VAT purposes. In the case of build-out costs only, Customs are also prepared to see a supply where the property is the subject of a taxable let and output tax on the rents has been accounted for to Customs.

Customs are not prepared to see an onward supply (creating an entitlement to bad debt relief) when the sale of the building is exempt, where the VAT incurred on building costs would be sticking tax. Customs believe it would be quite wrong to allow recovery of tax by lenders in these circumstances. The arrangements will also not apply if the proceeds of sale or rent received by lenders reflect any input tax on build-out costs recovered by the borrower.

Repairs and Maintenance

Lenders can be seen as agents of the borrower in incurring these expenses and may use the VATA 1994 s 47 (3) invoicing procedure to qualify for bad debt relief.

In-House Services

If lenders use their own in-house estate agencies or solicitors to deal with the sale, they may, exceptionally, be regarded as making a supply of those services as principal to the borrower under the new arrangements. However lenders may adopt this treatment in order to claim bad debt relief only where output tax has been accounted for on the supply to the borrower in accordance with normal rules.

Records

There is no requirement on lenders to adopt the above arrangements but, if they wish to do so, the normal VAT invoicing and record keeping requirements must be followed for all supplies concerned.

Past Claims

The new arrangements outlined above are not being applied to claims in respect of supplies made on or before 30 June 1994. For past claims Customs are prepared to accept the wider application sought by lenders following Business Brief 20/93 and will allow relief in respect of all selling costs incurred before the above date, including build-out costs and Law of Property Act receivers' charges.

However, with the exception of build-out costs, those attributable to the letting out of property are excluded, as are those incurred by lenders in pursuing negligence claims against valuers. Customs do not accept that the latter are costs relating to the sale of property. In relation to in-house services, claims for past periods will be allowed only where a VAT charge to the borrower has been raised and output tax has been accounted for to Customs.

Any claims blocked as a result of Business Brief 5/94 will be released. Similarly, any claims held back by lenders because of the Business Brief may now be lodged in the normal way. Claimants are advised to contact their local VAT office to arrange the most suitable way to action their claims.

[VATA 1994 ss 24, 36, 47 and Sch 4 para 7]

28 MARCH 1995. BUSINESS BRIEF 6/95 VAT ON VIABILITY STUDIES

Both the trade and Customs have experienced difficulties in determining who receives the services of an investigating accountant and who is entitled to recover the VAT on those services.

Customs has therefore reviewed its policy and the following new arrangements have been agreed with the Society of Insolvency Practitioners, and will take effect from 1 May 1995.

CHANGES

From May 1, accountants who are engaged to conduct viability studies will be making supplies of their services to the person who has commissioned the work, instructed them, and who also receives the end product. The direction of the supply does not necessarily follow the direction of the payment for the services. The fact that the company may ultimately pay does not mean that the supply is received by the company. Accountants should issue invoices only to those persons to whom they are providing their services.

Where the company commissions the work and receives the report, the investigating accountant is making a supply to the company. The supply is received by the company for the purpose of its business and the company is entitled to recover the input tax subject to the normal rules. The accountant should therefore issue invoices to the company to allow this recovery. This will apply even if the bank or another third party receives a copy of the report. Acknowledgement of a separate duty of care to the bank by the accountant will not prejudice this supply route, or the ability of the company to recover the VAT on the costs of the viability study.

Where the bank commissions the work and receives the report, the investigating accountant is making a supply to the bank. The supply is received by the bank for the purpose of its business and the bank is entitled to recover the input tax subject to the normal rules. The accountant must issue invoices to the bank. This treatment will apply even if the company ultimately pays for the work, and receives copies of the report.

In some instances the bank receives one report and the company another. An example is where the bank requires a confidential security review as part of the investigation. The accountant might receive instructions only from the company, or separate instructions from both the company and the bank. In either case the accountant makes two separate supplies, one to the bank, and one to the company, and should issue two separate invoices.

Each supply is received for the purpose of the particular business, and both the bank and the company are entitled to recover the input tax invoiced to them subject to the normal rules.

If the company and bank issue joint instructions and both receive the same work product, the accountant's supply is made equally to both. The accountant should issue invoices to both the bank and the company, each for 50% of the cost, and both recipients may recover input tax subject to the normal rules.

There may be circumstances where the company commissions the work, but does not receive any report. In this case the accountant's supply is made to the company, but is not used by the company for the purpose of its business. Therefore neither the bank nor the company is entitled to recover any input tax.

[VATA 1994 s 24].

5 MAY 1995. BUSINESS BRIEF 8/95
BARTERS OF SERVICE

There is an increasing number of transactions which involve barters of services. In principle all barter transactions are subject to VAT.

A common example of such a barter transaction is the supply by a newspaper of advertising to a business, with the business supplying the newspaper with a service in return, instead of making a payment in money. This might be the provision of a right for the newspaper to offer its readers a discount on goods or services which are supplied by the business.

In barter transactions the supply by one party is also the consideration for the supply by the other party. Consideration which is not in money must be valued subjectively. Each party therefore must determine the monetary value of the supply it makes, normally by reference to the costs incurred in making the supply, and account for VAT accordingly. At the same time each will be able to recover as input tax the VAT it has been charged, subject to the normal rules.

In most cases the monetary values put on each supply will be identical, but there may be circumstances where each party to a transaction places a different value on the supply it makes. In this case each should account for the appropriate amount of VAT, which will again be recoverable as input tax by the other party, subject to the normal rules.

[VATA 1994 s 19]

18 MAY 1995. BUSINESS BRIEF 9/95
SERVICES SUPPLIED BETWEEN LOCAL AUTHORITIES

. . .

Since 1 July 1994 all supplies of goods between local authorities have to be treated as business supplies. This policy was adopted in the light of the [ruling from the EC Court of Justice in *Commune di Carpaneto Piacentimo v Ufficio Provinciale Imposta sul Valore Aggiunto di Piacenza* (case C-4/89) [1990] 3 CMLR 153, ECJ], and following a consultation exercise.

. . .

The treatment of services between local authorities [is] dealt with as set out in the following practice statement.

The supply of services made under a statutory obligation and not in competition with the private sector should be treated as non-business.

The supply of services not made under a statutory obligation and not in competition with the private sector should be treated as non-business, but may be taxed if both parties agree.

The supply of services made under a statutory obligation but in competition with the private sector should be treated as business and are subject to the appropriate rate of VAT.

The supply of any services which are in competition with the private sector on a significant scale, ie nationally, should be treated as business and are subject to the appropriate rate of VAT.

The supply of services that includes any supply of goods should be treated as business and are subject to the appropriate rate of VAT.

[VATA 1994 s 94]

20 NOVEMBER 1995. BUSINESS BRIEF 25/95
VAT TREATMENT OF TRANSACTIONS IN BILLS OF EXCHANGE AND OTHER SECURITIES FOR MONEY

Customs and Excise will now treat any issue of, or dealings in, securities for money falling under VATA 1994 Sch 9 Group 5 item 1 as a supply of services. This follows the change in policy concerning transactions in commercial paper (see Business Brief, Issue 11, 9 August 1991 [not reproduced]).

In addition to commercial paper, securities for money under item 1 include bills of exchange, trading coupons, eurocurrency paper, instruments and paper negotiable for cash, local authority bills and certain promissory notes.

In the past Customs' policy was to see a supply of services fall within item 1 only if the price paid for the security for money exceeded the indicated face value. If the security for money was sold below face value there was no consideration and therefore no supply.

We now take the view that the consideration for the supply by the drawer of the security is the price paid. This treatment also applies to any subsequent sale of the security, except at redemption when it is outside the scope. The service, the right to future receivables including interest where appropriate, falls to be treated as a supply under VATA 1994 s 5 (2) (*b*).

These supplies fall within VATA 1994 Sch 5 para 5. Since 1 January 1993, the place of supply of such services has been determined by the status and place of belonging of the customer on the following basis.

If the services are provided to a customer who belongs in the UK (including the Isle of Man) or to a non-business customer who belongs in another member state, the place of supply is the UK and the supply is exempt under VATA 1994 Sch 9 Group 5 item 1.

If the services are provided to a business customer who belongs in another member state or to any customer who belongs outside the EU, the place of supply is where the customer belongs and the supply is outside the scope of UK VAT.

From 1 January 1993 related input tax is recoverable when the supply is made to a person outside the EU, or if a security is issued in connection with the export of goods to a place outside the EU Such supplies before that date would have been exempt when supplied to persons in the EU, but zero-rated when made to third country counterparties.

Customs will normally require the exclusion of the values of supplies of item 1 securities for money from outputs-based proportional calculations, as their inclusion can distort the amount of residual input tax partly exempt business can recover.

Any businesses wishing to make retrospective adjustments to their partial exemption calculations may do so, but only if the necessary evidence is available to support any recalculation. Any claims will be subject to checking by the relevant local office.

[VATA 1994 s 5 and Sch 9 Group 5 Item 1]

9 FEBRUARY 1996. BUSINESS BRIEF 2/96
CHANGE IN TREATMENT OF TRAVEL AGENTS' COMMISSION

The VAT treatment of commission for transport only sales by travel agents on behalf of tour operators will change from 1 May 1996 following recent legislation changes.

Travel agents are currently allowed to zero-rate their service of arranging transport only sales, whether the transport is provided to the customer direct from the transport provider (eg an airline or ferry company) or through a tour operator. Tour operators include, for VAT purposes, seat only operators selling to the public.

ACTION REQUIRED

Travel agents arranging transport only sales will in future need to make a distinction between sales of transport direct from transport providers and transport sold through a tour operator, and then apply the appropriate VAT rate in accordance with the following guidelines.

1. The service of arranging a supply of passenger transport direct from a transport provider (eg an airline or ferry company) remains outside the scope of UK VAT or is zero-rated depending on the circumstances. In short, no UK VAT is chargeable.

2. The service of arranging a supply through a tour operator, who is buying in and reselling transport on its own, is to become standard-rated. Standard-rating already applies to the agents' services where the transport is provided as part of a tour operators package.

3. Exceptionally, a tour operator may be able to provide transport from his own resources, in which case he will be regarded as a transport provider. In these cases, which are likely to be rare, the travel agents services will remain outside the scope of UK VAT or be zero-rated.

4. Travel agents are advised that when issuing an invoice to a tour operator for a seat only sale, they should standard-rate their supply unless they have ascertained in advance that the tour operator is providing the seat only sale from his own resources, in which case no VAT is chargeable. The same liabilities apply if a travel agent is being self-billed by a tour operator.

IMPLEMENTATION DATE

Although the legislative changes affecting the liability of tour operators' suppliers are effective from 1 January 1996, Customs & Excise recognise that some travel agents may have initial practical difficulties in identifying affected supplies and adapting their systems. It has therefore been agreed between Customs & Excise and The Association of British Travel Agents (ABTA) to introduce the change of liability of travel agents' commission with effect from 1 May 1996.

In practice, this means that invoices issued by travel agents and self-billed invoices raised by tour operators on or after 1 May 1996 will be subject to the change in liability. VAT should therefore be charged on all such invoices unless it is ascertained in advance that the seat only supplies were made prior to 1 January 1996 or that the commission qualifies for zero-rating under the revised rules.

Traders are reminded that, following the issue of an invoice, any subsequent amendment to the price is liable to the same rate of VAT as the original invoice.

PRACTICAL EXAMPLES

1. Currently there is no VAT due on commission from an airline for arranging a flight. This will continue to be the case after 1 May 1996.

2. The commission from a UK based tour operator arranging a holiday package (transport and accommodation) in another EU state such as Greece is currently standard-rated. This will continue to be the case after 1 May 1996.

3. The commission from a UK based tour operator arranging a holiday package (transport and accommodation) in a country outside the EU such as the USA is standard-rated. This will continue to be the case after 1 May 1996.

4. Currently there is no VAT due on commission from a UK based tour operator for arranging the sale of a bought in flight. From 1 May 1996 there will be VAT due on the commission at the standard rate.

[VATA 1994 s 53]

16 FEBRUARY 1996. BUSINESS BRIEF 3/96
VAT EXEMPTION OF NON-PROFIT MAKING SPORTS CENTRES

Following a recent VAT Tribunal case [see *Basingstoke and District Sports Trust Ltd v C & E Comrs* [1995] V & DR 405] Customs & Excise are clarifying the VAT exemption for sporting services provided by non-profit making sports centres.

Exemption from VAT of certain sporting and physical education services supplied by non-profit making bodies was introduced on 1 April 1994, although in practice such bodies could backdate the exemption and claim a refund of VAT covering the period 1 January 1990–31 March 1994, if they wished.

Under the terms of the exemption a non-profit making body operating a membership scheme has to tax at the standard rate all services supplied to non-members. However any such body, which is not operating a membership scheme, has to exempt sporting and physical education services supplied to all individual participants, for example, where usage is entirely on a pay and play basis.

In considering the appeal by the *Basingstoke and District Sports Trust Ltd* against refusal by Customs & Excise of VAT exemption for non-members, the VAT Tribunal decided that the privilege cards, issued by the Trust and previously described as membership cards, did not amount to a membership scheme for the purposes of exemption. Consequently supplies by the Trust of qualifying services to all users of the Trust's sporting and physical recreation facilities (not just privilege card holders) are exempt from VAT.

In the light of the Tribunal decision and following discussion with sports representative bodies, Customs & Excise have issued the following clarification of the applicability of the exemption to sports centres operated by charitable trusts and like bodies.

> "Where a sports centre operated by a charitable trust or similar non-profit making body makes supplies of sporting and physical education services of a type which would normally qualify for exemption from VAT (see para 18 of VAT Notice 701/45/94 "Sport and physical education") and does not operate a full membership scheme (for example where members do not have voting rights or any form of control over the management of the centre), such services will be exempt from VAT. This relates only to supplies to individuals or groups of individuals using the centre and applies irrespective of whether users are called 'members' for the purposes of obtaining discount on use of the facilities."

Where such a sports centre operates a full membership scheme and limits its application to selected activities or locations, exemption of qualifying services will be limited to supplies to members, even if an activity is not used by members. For example where a centre provides a swimming pool and squash courts and the membership scheme is only for squash players, supplies to all users of the swimming pool, other than squash members, will continue to be standard-rated.

The position of sports centres operated by local and other public authorities, which are specifically excluded from exemption by VATA 1994 Sch 9 Group 10 Item 3 Note 3 is unaffected by this statement.

Sports centres whose supplies are affected by this clarification or who wish to take advantage of the repayment arrangements detailed in Annex A to VAT Notice 701/45/94 or require further information should contact their local VAT business advice centre listed under Customs & Excise in the telephone book.

[VATA 1994 Sch 9 Group 10 Item 3]

13 MARCH 1996. BUSINESS BRIEF 4/96
VAT TREATMENT OF AIRLINE PASSENGER PERKS

Customs & Excise have reached agreement with the airline industry on the VAT treatment of passenger perks offered by airlines.

Under the agreement passenger perks may be treated as part of a supply of air passenger transport provided certain criteria are met.

This agreement is to operate with immediate effect for an initial period of six months. It will then be subject to review and, if appropriate, extended for a further period.

ALLOWABLE PERKS

To be eligible—the perks must be included in the flight ticket price for the class of travel concerned, with no discount if the perk is not taken up; form an integral part of an international flight (as illustrated below); not be gifts of goods (except where currently permitted, for example in-flight catering, toiletries); and be restricted to one per customer, although the customer may be offered a choice of options.

The following perks are treated as an integral part of an international flight: limousine transport to or from the airport; or up to two days' car hire for a one way ticket (four days for a return ticket); or hotel or similar accommodation; or car parking at the airport. The accommodation should not be for more than one night's stay and there must be a direct connection with the zero-rated travel, eg where it is necessary to catch a connecting flight or it is required for the night prior to a take-off or on the night after landing.

When allowable perks are supplied to the passenger they will be treated as part of the zero-rated supply of passenger transport. One effect of this is that the provisions of allowable perks will not, in itself, render the airline liable to use the Tour Operators' Margin Scheme. Airlines would also be able to recover any related input tax, subject to the normal rules.

New options will not be automatically disallowed. However, individual prior approval must be obtained from local VAT offices to ensure that the services are incidental to and directly connected with the air travel.

PERKS WHICH ARE NOT ALLOWABLE

The following perks should be treated as separate supplies and taxed accordingly—restaurant meals, theatre trips and other entertainment provided during a trip or holiday, hotel accommodation and car hire other than as specified above. This list is not exhaustive.

The provision of perks which are not allowable may mean the airline is liable to use the Tour Operators' Margin Scheme. For further information see Notice 709/5 "Tour Operators' Margin Scheme".

BACKGROUND

The agreement has been reached following a decision in the High Court about certain optional extras provided to international passengers [see *Virgin Atlantic Airways Ltd v C & E Comrs*, *Canadian Airlines International Ltd v C & E Comrs* [1995] STC 341]. In those cases it was decided that optional extras supplied by those airlines should be treated as part of a single zero-rated supply of air transport where these are offered as part of the ticket price for air travel.

[VATA 1994 Sch 8 Group 8 Item 4]

13 MARCH 1996. PRESS NOTICE 15/96
CREATION OF DWELLINGS AND OTHER ACCOMMODATION BY CONVERSION

Since 21 July 1994 residential conversions have been effectively free of VAT by one of three methods—

— zero-rated on the grant of a major interest by a VAT registered company;
— the supply of zero-rated goods and services in the course of conversion to a Registered Housing Association;
— by refund of VAT to a non-business converter under the DIY VAT refund scheme.

This relief was introduced after public consultation and was intended to make the provision of new dwellings by the conversion of existing buildings by any organisation free of VAT.

There are a small number of charitable organisations who fall outside the above legal framework. This is usually because they are prevented by legal constraints from selling the converted property (even to an associated organisation) and being in business, do not qualify under the DIY scheme. The Commissioners of Customs & Excise, by the exercise of their discretionary powers under the Customs & Excise Management Act 1979, will consider refunds of VAT to these bodies.

Any charitable organisation who considers that it may benefit under this relief should write with full details to—Mr D Kelly, VAT Construction Branch, Customs & Excise, New Kings Beam House, 22 Upper Ground, London SE1 9PJ.

NOTES

The relief for conversions creating dwellings for the first time was announced, together with other changes, on 21 July 1994 [in Press Notice 31/94 (not reproduced)], and a public consultation was issued inviting comments. Responses resulted in a number of changes to the proposal including the inclusion of relevant residential buildings within the relief but did not identify the type of charities mentioned above.

This announcement recognises that a small number of organisations who provide accommodation for rent fail to benefit from the Government's policy that the provision of new accommodation by either construction or conversion should generally not be subject to VAT.

[VATA 1994 s 35]

29 MARCH 1996. BUSINESS BRIEF 5/96 VAT ASSESSMENT CHANGES

From 1 April 1996 a letter may be sent to traders facing a VAT assessment which will enable them to query the preliminary calculations prior to the assessment being made.

The change follows a Law Committee seminar at which this suggestion was made. A widespread consultation exercise has been carried out and the suggestion has been favourably received by both members of the Department and the trading community, including members of the Joint VAT Consultative Committee.

[VATA 1994 s 73]

11 APRIL 1996. PRESS NOTICE 23/96 VAT HEALTH EXEMPTIONS—DIRECT SUPERVISION

[VATA 1994 Sch 9 Group 7 Item 1 exempts the services of medical professionals enrolled on the statutory registers. Note 2 states that services may also be exempt when carried out by unqualified people, but only if they are under the direct supervision of qualified personnel. Customs & Excise have produced guidelines on what is meant by direct supervision. Guidance on the optical and homecare sectors has been issued to the relevant representative bodies for dissemination to members and is also available at local VAT offices. General guidance for other sectors is set out below.]

GENERAL GUIDELINES ON "DIRECT SUPERVISION"

If all the conditions below are met, Customs & Excise will accept that the services supplied qualify for VAT exemption, even though those services have not been supplied directly by qualified staff.

1. The supervisor *must* be an appropriately registered person.

2. Supervision cannot take place via a third party ie the supervisor must always be in a direct relationship with the unqualified staff.

3. The presence of the appropriately qualified supervisor must be required at appropriate times during the process and he or she must be responsible, contractually, for supervising the unqualified staff. Customs & Excise will not accept that direct supervision exists where a supervisor is introduced primarily to gain VAT exemption and in practice carries out little or no supervision.

4. The services performed by the unqualified staff must *require* supervision. Customs & Excise will not accept exemption for services performed by unqualified staff for which no supervision is required and will not accept that services which are not broadly of a medical or caring nature can gain exemption simply by the use of a qualified individual in a supervisory or managerial role.

5. The supervisor must be readily available for the whole of the time that the unqualified staff are working, and must be able to take appropriate action in an emergency. The supervisor need not always be the same individual—for example, a number of registered professionals working within an establishment can supervise different unqualified staff as demand dictates; a registered locum may be brought in to cover periods of holiday or similar; or a team of supervisors, all of whom are qualified as above, can rotate the supervision of particular staff amongst themselves to fit in with their other commitments.

6. The supervisor must see the client at the outset of treatment and at the outset of any new treatment required thereafter.

7. The supervisor must decide the treatment to be provided by the unqualified staff.

8. The supervisor must be able to demonstrate that they monitor the services of the unqualified staff.

9. The ratio of registered professionals to unqualified staff must be such that it enables requirement 5 to be fulfilled.

[VATA 1994 Sch 9 Group 7 Item 1]

22 APRIL 1996. PRESS NOTICE 22/96
BUILDINGS SUBJECT TO IMMUNITY CERTIFICATES—NEW VAT CONCESSION

A concession has been granted by Customs & Excise so that developers of certain buildings can benefit from VAT zero-rating. The buildings concerned are those which are currently the subject of a certificate granting immunity from listing as a protected building issued by the Secretary of State for National Heritage.

The operation of the certificate means that the buildings cannot be listed for a period of five years and owners are given an opportunity to work on them and preserve them for other uses without the additional burden of supplementary planning controls which apply to listed buildings. In certain cases the advantageous VAT treatment afforded to the reconstruction of listed buildings was not appreciated when application for immunity from listing was made.

The effect of this concession will be limited to those buildings to which immunity certificates currently apply and which, on the grant of a major interest (ie sale or long lease) following substantial reconstruction, are to be used solely for a non-business charitable purpose. They will be given, for VAT purposes, a status equivalent to protected buildings and on application the developer will be authorised to register for VAT.

This class concession is operational immediately. It only applies to cases where immunity certificates have already been granted. Following this announcement future applicants for such certificates will need to consider the VAT consequences before making an application.

NOTES

An immunity certificate is issued under the Planning (Listed Building and Conservation Areas) Act 1990 s 6 (2) and precludes the Local Planning Authority from serving a building preservation order on the building for a period of five years from the date of issue. The concession also applies to Northern Ireland where the Department of the Environment is empowered to issue such a certificate under the provisions of the Planning (Northern Ireland) Order 1991 art 43. There is no equivalent provision in Scotland.

The full text of the concession is—

> "For the purpose of VATA 1994 Sch 8 Group 6 item 1 a building which, following its substantial reconstruction, is intended to be used solely for a relevant charitable purpose may (notwithstanding the provisions of Group 6 note 1) be treated as if it were a listed building if at the time of the grant of the major interest there is in force in respect of it a certificate issued before 1 March 1996 by the Secretary of State under the Planning (Listed Building and Conservation Areas) Act 1990 s 6, or for Northern Ireland, issued by the Department of the Environment under the Planning (Northern Ireland) Order 1991 art 43."

Zero-rated construction work has, since 1989, been limited to dwellings, relevant residential buildings and relevant charitable buildings. Since 1 March 1995 a non-residential building converted to create a residential building for the first time has been eligible for VAT relief, but this change did not apply to charity buildings.

However, an existing VAT relief applies, on their disposal, to listed buildings which have been substantially reconstructed for certain purposes. This concession allows similar relief to those buildings currently the subject of an immunity certificate being converted for a non-business charity use.

Customs & Excise concessions are intended to have general application, but all the circumstances of any particular case must be taken into account in considering the concession.

For further information traders and their advisers should write to Construction Branch, VAT Policy Directorate, 4W, New King's Beam House, 22 Upper Ground, London SE1 9PJ.

[VATA 1994 Sch 8 Group 6 Item 1]

30 APRIL 1996. BUSINESS BRIEF 6/96
VAT: TAXABLE AMOUNT AT IMPORTATION—POST IMPLEMENTATION REVIEW

Customs & Excise are conducting a post implementation review of the changes to the rules governing the taxable amount at importation. These came into effect on 1 January and implement the requirements of European law in this area.

The measures require that all incidental expenses incurred up to the first destination of the goods in the UK should be included in the value for import VAT. Additionally, if a further destination in the UK or another member state is known at the time the goods are imported, any costs incurred in transporting the goods to that further place must also be included in the value.

Customs & Excise realise that the changes presented practical difficulties for many importers, freight forwarders and shipping agents, and have worked with a number of representative bodies to find reasonable ways of dealing with specific and general problems. In particular, a simplified system of flat rates was agreed, which may be used in instances where it is not possible to declare actual costs. These arrangements were introduced to help with transitional difficulties, and were subject to review after they had been operating for some time. Information on the changes and details of the simplified arrangements have been provided to members of the Joint VAT Consultative Committee and the Joint Customs Consultative Committee. The information is also available on the CHIEF Noticeboard system.

. . .

[VATA 1994 s 21]

3 MAY 1996. BUSINESS BRIEF 7/96
VAT ON COSTS OF ACQUIRING A BUSINESS AS A GOING CONCERN

With effect from 1 June 1996 when a business acquires assets by way of the transfer of a going concern and the assets are used exclusively to make taxable supplies, the VAT incurred on the cost of acquiring those assets should be attributed to those taxable supplies and can be recovered in full. Conversely if the assets of the acquired business are to be used exclusively to make exempt supplies, none of the input tax on the cost of acquiring those assets can be recovered. However, if the assets are to be used in making both taxable and exempt supplies, any input tax incurred is non attributable and must be apportioned in accordance with the agreed VAT partial exemption method.

This change follows a decision by the Court of Appeal (*C & E Comrs v UBAF Bank Limited* [1996] STC 372). The Court confirmed that where the assets of a business are acquired for use in the making of taxable supplies, the input tax incurred on the acquisition costs can be recovered in full. Previously such costs were treated as general business overhead costs.

This change does not affect the treatment of VAT on costs incurred by the transferor which should continue to be treated as a general business overhead, because the costs incurred are not used to make any supply.

IMPLEMENTATION OF THE CHANGE

Businesses which had previously treated the costs of acquiring a business by way of a transfer of a going concern as a general overhead for VAT purposes should, from 1 June 1996, attribute the cost directly as described above. Such businesses may also re-open past accounting periods.

Any business wishing to make such a claim for input tax recovery must apply the new treatment consistently, in all prescribed accounting periods and longer periods, from the date it starts to apply the change. In addition such businesses will need to produce the records necessary for the claims to be verified.

[SI 1995/2518 reg 101]

17 MAY 1996. BUSINESS BRIEF 8/96
VAT REGISTRATION AND PROPERTY DEVELOPMENT

The VAT (Building and Land Order) 1995 [SI 1995/279] has introduced the gradual abolition of the self supply charge. (Business Brief 7/95 [not reproduced]).

This means that any development where construction commenced on or after 1 March 1995 will not be liable to a taxable self supply charge. It is therefore no longer the case that a taxable supply will always be made of commercial property.

This will only be the case if the developer intends to make a taxable freehold sale of a new property or the developer has opted to tax the property and intends to let it. This change means it is essential that Customs & Excise establish the trader's intentions at an early stage.

[Press Notice 65/90, 25 September 1990], relaxed the evidential requirements necessary for securing intending trader registration. However, in view of this order, local VAT offices may require more detailed information before allowing intending trader registration. Notification of the option to tax is still required prior to registration being allowed.

[VATA 1994 Sch 1 para 9]

24 MAY 1996. BUSINESS BRIEF 9/96
VAT AND CHARITY ADVERTISING

Following a recent VAT tribunal decision concerning charity advertising (see *Royal Society for Encouragement of Arts, Manufacture and Commerce* (No 14007)), Customs & Excise will no longer accept that recruitment advertisements for paid staff are eligible for zero-rating even if they contain a "qualifying" message. This means that unless an advertisement's primary purpose is making known the objects of a charity, the reasons for the objects of a charity, or for raising money for the charity, it does not come within the scope of the relief.

This decision reverses the liability decision given in Business Brief 1/95 of 11 January 1995 [not reproduced] and is effective from 1 June 1996.

The Tribunal . . . Chairman stated that for an advertisement to come within the scope of zero-rating under VATA 1994 Sch 8 Group 15 item 8, its principal purpose must be for one of the purposes mentioned in the law.

Advertisements for volunteers (including advertisements for people to work overseas at local rates of pay plus travelling expenses, such as Voluntary Service Overseas) will continue to be regarded as qualifying for the relief. Other advertisements such as those for university courses, school open days held in order to attract potential pupils, conferences connected with the furtherance of the charity's objectives, church services, events held to raise funds for the charity, and requests for aid goods will also continue to qualify for relief.

These arrangements will help clarify the borderlines of the relief and do away with the requirement to consider qualifying messages and strap lines.

[VATA 1994 Sch 8 Group 15 Item 8]

3 JUNE 1996. PRESS NOTICE 33/96
EXEMPTION FROM VAT OF CULTURAL SERVICES

The Value Added Tax (Cultural Services) Order 1996 [SI 1996/1256], which takes effect from 1 June 1996, has introduced a new exemption from VAT for admission charges to certain cultural places and events.

Where exemption does not disadvantage competing commercial bodies, public authorities are able to exempt the right of admission to their museums, galleries, art exhibitions, zoos, together with theatrical, musical and choreographical performances of a cultural nature. In cases where exemption would be financially disadvantageous to a public body and the body wishes to continue to tax admission charges, it is Customs & Excise's current policy not to compel the body to exempt. For example disadvantage may arise where exemption would cause local authorities to forfeit the right to recover the VAT paid on building refurbishment and other capital projects.

. . .

[VATA 1994 Sch 9 Group 13 Item 1]

1 JULY 1996. BUSINESS BRIEF 13/96
VAT AND HAIRDRESSERS

The VAT and Duties Tribunal has now ruled in favour of Customs & Excise in the case of *Simon Harris Hair Design Ltd* [No 13939]. This decision clarifies both the VAT position of hairdressers and the advice given in Business Brief 16/94 issued on 25 July 1994 [not reproduced].

The Tribunal Chairman found that although the agreement between the owner of the salon and the stylist had two separate charges, it nevertheless amounted to a single supply taxable at the standard rate. The company had maintained that one of the charges was an exempt license to occupy land, which would have reduced their VAT liability.

Even though each stylist had an allocated space within the salon, a license to occupy that space could not be dissociated from the right to use other facilities of the salon such as junior staff, basins and dryers.

As a result of this ruling local VAT officers have been advised to assess for VAT in cases where it is clear that stylists working in open plan salons are using the facilities of the premises as a whole.

[VATA 1994 s 19]

15 JULY 1996. BUSINESS BRIEF 14/96
VAT TREATMENT OF HOLIDAY AND OTHER CRUISES

This Business Brief explains the implications of a recent High Court decision on the VAT treatment of holiday cruises and a decision by a VAT Tribunal on the VAT treatment of river cruises providing catering and entertainment.

HOLIDAY CRUISES

Business Brief 27/95 [not reproduced] contained details of the VAT Tribunal's decision of 14 July 1995 about the treatment of holiday cruises and agents' supplies in the case of *Peninsular and Oriental Steam Navigation Co Ltd* [No 13478].

The High Court upheld that decision [see [1996] STC 698] and Customs & Excise now accept that a holiday cruise of a kind provided by P & O may be treated as a single supply of passenger transport, and zero-rated (subject to the normal conditions) to the extent that it takes place within the UK. Therefore, the making of arrangements for the supply of such a cruise is also zero-rated.

RIVER CRUISES

A recent VAT Tribunal considered the VAT treatment of certain river cruises used for various functions including business entertainment, fashion shows and wedding receptions in the case of *Virgin Atlantic Airways Ltd* [No 13840]. The Tribunal decided that such cruises were mixed supplies consisting of zero-rated passenger transport and standard-rated catering.

Taken together, the two cases demonstrate the importance of looking closely at the facts of each case, to determine whether there is a single supply or mixed supplies, and the appropriate VAT rates.

WHO IS AFFECTED BY THESE DECISIONS

These decisions may affect all cruise operators whether supplying international and coastal holiday cruises or cruises on rivers and canals or other inland waterways, including disco, dinner, wedding reception and similar entertainment cruises. In all cases, the vessels must be designed or adapted to carry 12 or more passengers, including crew, otherwise any supplies in the UK will be automatically standard-rated. The decisions are also relevant to businesses making arrangements for such supplies. However, they do not affect cruises bought in and re-supplied under the tour operators' margin scheme.

PRACTICAL EFFECTS

For VAT liability purposes, a cruise may be treated as a single or multiple supply depending on the facts of the case. Each transaction should be examined objectively and as a matter of common-sense. The following principles should generally be applied.

Single zero-rated supplies. You will be making a single zero-rated supply of passenger transport when—the essential nature of the supply is passenger transport and the normal conditions for the relief are met; all the elements of the cruise are integral to the main supply and it would be neither realistic nor practicable to separate them; and the cruise is held out for sale at a single price with no specific charges or discounts for particular services taken or not taken up.

Mixed supplies. Separate supplies would normally arise when different elements of the cruise are the subject of separate negotiation and customer choice, separately identifiable obligations on the supplier, and separate charges; separate supplies are not integral to the main supply and could be omitted; and, it must be practicable, reasonable and realistic to separate the elements of the cruise.

Single standard-rated supplies. When a cruise contains only a minor transport element which is incidental to a standard-rated supply, you will be regarded as making a single standard-rated supply.

Making arrangements. The making of arrangements for the above supplies will be determined by the liability of the supply being arranged. The making of arrangements for a supply of zero-rated passenger transport may itself be zero-rated whereas the making of arrangements for a standard-rated supply will be standard-rated. If you make arrangements for both zero-rated and standard-rated supplies, a reasonable apportionment will be accepted.

When any of the elements of a trip are bought in from a third party and re-supplied to travellers, the provisions of the tour operators' margin scheme may apply (see Notice 709/5).
[VATA 1994 s 19 and Sch 8 Group 8 Item 4]

16 AUGUST 1996. BUSINESS BRIEF 17/96
THE RECOVERY OF INPUT TAX FOLLOWING AN ELECTION TO WAIVE EXEMPTION (OPTION TO TAX)

The High Court decision in the case of *R & R Pension Fund* [1996] STC 889 gave clear support to Customs & Excise's policy concerning the recovery of input tax in cases where an option to tax is made and the property in question has already been the subject of an exempt grant.

In such cases, where input tax has been incurred on the acquisition of a capital item, legislation introduced on 1 January 1992 removes what was a block on input tax recovery and allows the capital goods scheme to run its course.

Thus, where a building is a capital item falling within the scope of the capital goods scheme and an election to waive exemption (option to tax) is allowed after an exempt grant has been made, any adjustment to the input tax initially incurred must be made on an annual basis for the remaining intervals of the ten year adjustment period of capital goods scheme. Adjustments should start on the date when the building was first brought into use, in accordance with the normal operation of that scheme.

Before 1 January 1992 if a business made an exempt grant of a building on which it subsequently elected to waive exemption, the business was unable to recover input tax incurred in connection with that building where the input tax was incurred prior to the date of the election. Input tax recovery was blocked even if the building was a capital item falling within the scope of the capital goods scheme.

On 1 January 1992 the legislation was introduced with the primary purpose of removing the block for capital items to allow the capital goods scheme to run its course. Where a business made an exempt grant and then wished to elect to waive exemption, it was required to seek the permission of the Commissioners who would give such permission only if they were satisfied that there would be a fair and reasonable attribution of input tax to taxable supplies.

If the input tax was incurred on the acquisition of an item which was not a capital item for the purposes of the capital goods scheme, in principle there was no entitlement under the partial exemption legislation to deduct the pre-election input tax. However, the legislation gave the Commissioners discretion to provide administratively a fair and reasonable allowance of exempt input tax for taxable persons who could not benefit from capital goods scheme adjustments. This would be a one-off payment, following the granting of the election, which would be calculated on some agreed fair and reasonable basis.
[VATA 1994 Sch 10 para 3]

27 AUGUST 1996. BUSINESS BRIEF 18/96
RECOVERY OF TAX INCURRED ON REPAIRS, MAINTENANCE, RENOVATION ETC TO FARMHOUSES

Following a number of VAT tribunal decisions Customs & Excise have reviewed their approach to input tax claims made by sole proprietors and partnerships in relation to farmhouses. The following sets out guidelines which have been agreed with the National Farmers' Union.

However, it must be pointed out that this does not give an automatic entitlement to recover an amount of tax. Businesses should continue to consider their own particular circumstances, and use the guidelines below to assess the proportion of tax that is claimable.

THE GUIDELINES

In the case of a normal working farm where the VAT registered person is actively engaged in running it, 70% of tax incurred on repairs, maintenance and renovations, may be recovered as input tax. This position is in line with that adopted by VAT tribunals who have found that in those given circumstances the dominant purpose was to allow the farming business to be carried on, and allowed 70% of the tax to be claimed.

However, where the building work is more associated with an alteration, eg building an extension, the amount that may be recovered will depend on the purpose for the construction. If the circumstances are such that the dominant purpose is a business one then 70% can be claimed. But if the dominant purpose is a personal one we would expect the claim to be 40% or less, and in some cases, depending on the facts, none of the VAT incurred would be recoverable.

Where farming is not a full-time business and occupation for the VAT registered person, ie income is received from either full-time employment or other sources, the amount of tax that may be claimed will be considerably less. With these kind of cases VAT tribunals have accepted somewhere between 10% and 30% of tax incurred is claimable on the grounds that the dominant purpose is a personal one. Businesses should therefore assess their particular circumstances, and make claims within those parameters.

RETROSPECTIVE CLAIMS

Customs policy reflects the High Court judgment in the case of *The Victoria and Albert Museum Trustees v C & E Comrs* [1996] STC 1016. The museum wished to revisit past input tax claims on the grounds that it could have used a different and more favourable method to calculate its input tax. The court held there had been no error of law or fact, and consequently the museum were not permitted to revisit those earlier tax periods. The three year capping set out in News Release 42/96 [not reproduced] also has to be considered.

(a) Where a trader has claimed input tax of less than 70% without reference to Customs & Excise.
In this situation a retrospective claim is not allowable. The trader has assessed the input tax recovery position, and made a claim. There has been no error in law or fact to be corrected.

(b) Where a trader has claimed input tax based on an officer's decision, or has been assessed.
In this instance a retrospective claim may be made but any claim will be subject to the three year capping. Where the business self-assessed its input tax at less than 70%, a refund claim will be allowed to the extent of the percentage self-assessed.

LIMITED COMPANIES

Where the occupant of the farmhouse is a director of the company, or a person connected with the director of the company, different legislation applies. This means that only tax on supplies that are used for other than domestic purposes is claimable as input tax. If a room is used partly for business and partly for domestic purposes, VAT will only be recoverable to the extent of the business use and suitable records will need to be kept to justify the proportion of tax being claimed.

[VATA 1994 s 24]

16 SEPTEMBER 1996. BUSINESS BRIEF 19/96 GOODS OBTAINED BY FRAUD

Customs & Excise have relaxed the requirements to recover the VAT paid when the supplier has been the victim of a fraud.

Previously suppliers had to report the fraud to the police and a conviction had to be obtained. Customs & Excise are now relaxing the requirement for a conviction to have been obtained provided that they are satisfied that the goods were lost through fraud. However, it will still be necessary that the details were promptly reported to the police.

Details can also be found in para 3.14 (*f*) of Notice 700 "The VAT guide".

[VATA 1994 s 5]

17 OCTOBER 1996. BUSINESS BRIEF 21/96 VAT—MOT TEST CHARGES

Following a review of their policy on the VAT treatment of Ministry of Transport (MOT) tests, Customs & Excise are introducing changes to operate from 1 November 1996, which will simplify the law in this area.

We are also clarifying the conditions which must be met, if the MOT test fee charged by the test centre to an unapproved garage and recharged to the latter's customer, is to be treated as a disbursement.

THE REVISED POSITION

The charge for an MOT test provided direct by a test centre to its customers is outside the scope of VAT, provided it does not exceed the statutory maximum.

The discount given by a test centre to an unapproved garage will be treated as a normal trade discount and will no longer be seen as consideration for a taxable supply by the unapproved garage either to the test centre or its customer.

Any amount charged by an unapproved garage to its customer over and above the amount charged by the test centre is consideration for its own service of arranging the test as agent of the customer and is taxable at the standard rate. Where the unapproved garage shows the exact amount charged by the test centre separately on the invoice to the customer, and meets the other conditions of para 10.8 of the VAT Guide, it may treat this element as a disbursement and also outside the scope of VAT.

If the unapproved garage chooses not to treat the amount charged by the test centre as a disbursement, or otherwise does not satisfy all the conditions set out in para 10.8 of the VAT Guide, it must account for VAT on the full invoiced amount.

We carried out the review because we recently became aware that our policy is creating difficulties for the trade and our own staff alike. Previous policy was formulated at a time when it was customary for test centres to charge the statutory fee and charge a lower amount only where an unapproved garage delivered a customer's vehicle for testing.

However, many test centres now offer discounts to all customers. Depending on the contractual situation, we have seen the discount as consideration either for a supply by the unapproved garage to the test centre of introducing a customer, or for a supply by the unapproved garage to its customer of arranging for the MOT test to be done. This has been the main difficulty because neither the trade nor local VAT audit staff have any easy way of knowing how much the test centre might normally charge.

We also found there was confusion about the procedures to be adopted where the unapproved garages were treating the charges raised by the test centre as a disbursement on behalf of their customers.

[VATA 1994 s 5]

17 OCTOBER 1996. BUSINESS BRIEF 21/96
SHARE DEALING BY CHARITIES

A recent decision of the European Court of Justice in the case of the *Wellcome Trust* [1996] STC 945 has confirmed the Customs & Excise view that the buying and selling of shares by charities is outside the scope of VAT.

Concerns had been expressed by tax advisers and some financial organisations that this would have wider implications for financial trading. However, the court made it clear that its decision applies to charitable trusts. There will, therefore, be no changes affecting organisations other than charitable trusts as a result of this case.

VAT Notice 701/1/95 "Charities" can be amended by the removal of the Note at the end of para 10 (*d*).

[VATA 1994 s 94]

6 DECEMBER 1996. BUSINESS BRIEF 25/96
EUROPEAN COURT JUDGMENTS AFFECT BUSINESS PROMOTION SCHEMES

The European Court of Justice released two judgments, *Elida Gibbs Ltd* and *Argos Distributors Ltd* on 24 October which will affect Customs & Excise's policy on business promotion schemes. This business brief outlines the effects of the two cases and how businesses in a similar position can recover overpaid VAT as a result of the rulings.

ELIDA GIBBS LTD V C & E COMRS (CASE C-317/94) [1996] STC 1387, ECJ

. . .

Manufacturers—If you are a manufacturer and have been operating money-off coupon schemes or cashback schemes you may be eligible for a VAT refund. You will have to demonstrate that payments are made to the retailers and consumers in the transaction chain and that the payments relate directly to successfully redeemed coupons following a retail sale of the goods.

. . .

Retailers—Customs & Excise do not consider that this decision alters the amount of tax due from retailers participating in money-off coupon or cashback schemes. Following from the court's reasoning in establishing the value of Elida Gibb's supplies, it is clear that for the retailers' position to remain fiscally neutral, no adjustments should be made to the value of either their inputs or their outputs.

. . .

It is clear from the judgment that retailers must account for output tax in respect of payments from manufacturers as well as the money paid by customers. However, if a VAT registered customer requests a tax invoice in respect of purchases made using money-off vouchers, this should be based on only the amount paid by the customer. This achieves fiscal neutrality as required by the judgment.

There is a similar case to that of Elida Gibbs, involving Conoco Ltd, awaiting a hearing date at the ECJ. In the long term, the VAT position of manufacturers' money-off and cashback schemes will have to be viewed in the light of both of these cases. Businesses using money-off and cashback schemes should be aware that Customs & Excise will further review its position once the *Conoco* case has been concluded.

ARGOS DISTRIBUTORS LTD V C & E COMRS (CASE C-288/94) [1996] STC 1359, ECJ

. . .

If, as part of your business, you supply goods or services in return for face value vouchers that have been previously sold by you and you will not be reimbursed by a third party, you will be able to claim a repayment of VAT if you can satisfy all the following conditions.

You must have accounted for VAT on the full face value of the vouchers in the past. You must be able to demonstrate that vouchers included in your claim were sold at less than face value. You must be able to substantiate the sale price of the vouchers at the time of their redemption.

. . .

A key element in the *Argos* decision was that the supplier had to be able to show the price at which vouchers had been sold at the time they were redeemed for goods. When the customer is a VAT registered business, the VAT invoice must therefore show the VAT due upon the actual sale price of the redeemed vouchers.

Businesses presently unable to meet these requirements will be allowed the period between the issue of this business brief and 30 June 1997 to modify their accounting arrangements so that—

(a) the price at which vouchers were sold can be identified at the time of their redemption; and

(b) accurate VAT invoices can be issued at the time of redemption.

After that date, where these conditions remain unfulfilled, VAT will have to be accounted for upon the full face-value of the vouchers as before.

Businesses should also note that where vouchers are redeemed by VAT registered businesses and VAT invoices issued as above, these must be accounted for outside any retail scheme being used; if a retail scheme based on expected selling prices is used these must be adjusted to reflect discounts given in respect of all redeemed vouchers sold below face value.

Next year Customs & Excise intend to review the arrangements under which VAT is not charged on face value vouchers at point of sale. Businesses will be consulted on the review.

[VATA 1994 s 19]

19 DECEMBER 1996. BUSINESS BRIEF 26/96
CHANGE IN VAT LIABILITY OF MEDICO-LEGAL SERVICES

Customs & Excise have recently changed the liability of certain services provided by doctors from exempt to taxable when made to third parties. To give doctors time to adjust, the ruling will be effective from 20 January 1997 although they may treat their supplies as taxable before then if they wish.

Customs & Excise were recently faced with a legal challenge on the liability of medico-legal services and have now agreed that certain services, which are predominantly legal rather than medical, are taxable.

The services of a registered medical practitioner using the knowledge, skills, judgment and experience acquired in the course of his professional training are exempt. The services do not have to be solely medical in nature nor do they have to be provided solely to the patient to gain exemption. Thus, the services of a GP acting as a GP are exempt; but a doctor could not exempt his supplies of a taxi service.

Taxable services are those in the medico-legal field where the doctor plays an integral role in the legal work and which are usually carried out to satisfy the needs of third parties—such as insurers and solicitors. These are—arbitration, mediation and conciliation services; investigating the validity of claims against parties such as insurers; considering medical reports and other evidence in order to resolve disputes; and work, other than just medical reports, for lawyers and insurers in preparing reports for the resolution of disputes following personal injury.

The change does not apply to any other services outside the general heading of "medico-legal" work which a doctor may make. However, this does not mean that all services a doctor makes to an insurance company become taxable; tax should be charged only on those services where the doctor is engaged primarily for work in the legal process.

Please note however, that exemption continues to apply to services provided by doctors which arise out of the normal doctor/patient relationship and to services which, although they may be for the information needs of a third party, are predominantly medical and not legal in nature, such as medical reports for employers and for life assurance policies and the provision of expert medical advice.

Indications are that doctors in general will not be greatly affected by this change as there are only a few doctors engaged in such practice in the UK. Those who do make these supplies however, will from 20 January 1997 be entitled or required to register for tax if they are not already registered, and recover related input tax (subject to the normal rules). Doctors who wish to go back and treat their supplies as taxable in order to recover input tax will be entitled to do so provided that their entitlement to input tax deduction is established and provided they account for output tax on the supplies. Statutory interest will be payable on claims for input tax and requests should be made in writing to local offices in the usual way.

Following an agreement with the Revenue we have undertaken to advise traders seeking a refund of tax that the payment may be subject to income or corporation tax. Traders should therefore notify their inspector of taxes of the amount of VAT repaid to them, as well as the amount of any interest they may receive.

Note. A guidance note is available at local VAT business advice centres (see Business Brief 2/97, 7 February 1997 (not reproduced)).

[VATA 1994 Sch 9 Group 7 Item 1]

5 MARCH 1997. BUSINESS BRIEF 5/97
VAT ON BUILDING REGULATION FEES IN ENGLAND AND WALES

From 13 January the possibility of competition exists across the whole range of building control work and VAT is therefore chargeable at the standard rate on all building control fees as from that date.

New approved inspectors have been authorised by the Department of the Environment to provide building regulation services for commercial and mixed developments, as well as the residential and mixed developments for which NHBC (Building Control Services) Ltd was already authorised.

The revised liability rulings apply to building regulation applications received on or after 13 January 1997. Applications received prior to this date should be treated as non-business by local authorities irrespective of when the work is actually carried out or invoices issued. This is because a local authority monopoly existed at the time the application was made and there is, therefore, no competition in respect of the supply of these particular services.

We can also confirm that repayments of VAT paid in error in the past on building regulation fees will continue to be made. These are not caught by the three year capping provisions.

This supplements and amends the guidance contained in Business Briefs 23/95 [24 October 1995—not reproduced] and 26/95 [11 December 1995—not reproduced].

[VATA 1994 s 94]

25 MARCH 1997. BUSINESS BRIEF 8/97
VAT—RETROSPECTIVE VOLUNTARY REGISTRATION

. . .

All businesses applying for retrospective voluntary registration and whose applications are received on or after 1 April 1997 will be restricted to a registration date no earlier than three years before the current date.

. . .

[VATA 1994 Sch 1 paras 9, 10; Sch 2 para 4; Sch 3 para 4]

9 MAY 1997. BUSINESS BRIEF 11/97
GROUP SUPPLIES USING AN OVERSEAS MEMBER—FA 1997 S 41

Since 26 November 1996 there has been a tax charge for the representative member of a VAT group, where certain supplies are purchased by an overseas member of a VAT group and used for making supplies to a UK member of the VAT group. Supplies affected are those set out in VATA 1994 Sch 5 and include the assignment of copyright, advertising services, data processing and legal services, amongst others.

This business brief sets out . . . a general statement of Customs & Excise's approach to the new measure . . . The general statement of Customs & Excise's approach covers some questions raised by trade bodies over the past months.

. . .

GENERAL STATEMENT OF CUSTOMS & EXCISE'S APPROACH TO CLAUSE 41

Since its introduction, Customs & Excise have received some recurring questions on how they will implement s 41 in practice. Set out below are guidelines covering a variety of specific situations.

EVIDENCE FOR REDUCED VALUE

Under the first ESCC, the value for calculating the s 41 charge may be reduced to the value of the Sch 5 services purchased by the overseas group member, if the group can provide evidence in the UK of the value of those services. Copies of invoices from the external supplier to the overseas group member will be acceptable evidence of the value of a bought-in service.

Alternatively, businesses may be able to agree with their local VAT assurance officer that different evidence is adequate. For example, where the overseas group member buys in services and applies a fixed mark-up, documentary evidence of this would normally satisfy a local officer that the value of the bought-in service was equal to the value of the onward supply less the mark-up.

Copy invoices or mark-up agreements are likely to be meaningful only where a service is bought-in by an overseas group member for the exclusive use of a UK group member. In many cases, an invoice to an overseas group member may not relate exclusively to an onward supply to a UK group member. Or, an overseas group member may not code its costs according to the recipient of any intended onward supply at the time when those costs are incurred. It may calculate the value of its onward supply to each of its associated companies by uplifting its total costs, and then allocating shares to associated companies in accordance with a predetermined formula.

In these cases it will be necessary for the VAT group to calculate a fair and reasonable value for the s 41 charge. The evidence required to support the reduced value would depend on the method of calculating it. However, in most cases the following evidence will be satisfactory—a summary statement of the overseas member's costs; and an outline of the basis on which the overseas member calculates its charge; and a record of the method for reducing the s 41 charge to an amount based on the bought-in supplies.

Customs & Excise do not expect a group to estimate the costs that should be allocated to a supply where services have been bought in by the overseas member and supplied to the UK member in substantially the same state. In this case we expect the value to be accurate, and to be supported by documentary evidence.

EVIDENCE NOT AVAILABLE

Taxpayers who are not in a position to demonstrate a reduced value must account for VAT with reference to the full value of the intra-group supply. This does not require groups to provide Customs & Excise with evidence of reduced values prior to filling in their VAT Returns. Rather, they must be in a position to substantiate the value later, if asked.

DE MINIMIS LEVELS

Section 41 is triggered when an overseas member of a VAT group receives a Sch 5 service, and uses this service for making a supply to another group member. If the bought-in supply forms a cost component of the onward supply, then the measure is triggered. However, a legal provision will not be applied to circumstances which the Courts consider to be de minimis.

An example of this for s 41 might be where a company seconds staff to a fellow group member, and takes external legal advice on contractual arrangements. By far the greater part of the onward charge would relate to staff salaries. In such circumstances, Customs & Excise will take the view that the extent to which a supply is bought in and used for making an onward supply is de minimis, with the result that no tax charge arises.

As a rule of thumb, bought-in supplies are de minimis if their value is less than 5% of the value of the supplies from the overseas group member to the UK group member. However, Customs & Excise will not apply this rule mechanistically, either if they suspect that supplies or values have been manipulated in order to meet the 5% test, or if they feel that, despite the fact that the 5% test is not met, the s 41 charge would be insignificant. The extent to which VAT on the s 41 charge could be recovered under the group's partial exemption method, along with the amount of the charge in the context of the group's size, will be considered when deciding whether or not a potential s 41 charge is de minimis.

Evidence to show that the value of the bought-in Sch 5 service is very small in the context of the overall supply will vary from case to case. In the example of supply of staff, the group would generally only be required to provide a copy of the agreement under which the staff were seconded. This should show that the supply was a supply of staff from a fellow group company. It should also be possible to see that the value of the supply was consistent with the number of staff seconded, so that any recharge of bought-in Sch 5 services must be very small in the context of the overall supply.

TAXABLE, OR NEARLY FULLY TAXABLE GROUPS

Section 41 is principally an anti-avoidance measure aimed at the exempt sector, but it does not exclude fully taxable groups. Most groups affected by the measure will have some element of exemption, and it was not feasible to draft a specific threshold for s 41 which would be proof against manipulation. Fully taxable groups should account for any s 41 charge.

However, a fully taxable group is not expected to go to great lengths to demonstrate that its s 41 supplies are de minimis or to justify any apportionment of supplies from overseas members between services falling within Sch 5 and other supplies. In the unlikely event that Customs and Excise disagreed with the view taken by the group on these points, an assessment may be raised, but no interest or penalties would apply.

Groups which are almost fully taxable will have to account for the s 41 charge in the same way as any other partly exempt group. They will be able to negotiate what evidence is required to reduce the value of their charge. Also, such groups can expect their local assurance officer to take into account the extent to which VAT on the charge could be recovered under the group's partial exemption method, along with the amount of the charge in the context of the group's size.

Some groups may even wish to propose a change to their partial exemption method, so that the s 41 charge can be treated in a straightforward way for partial exemption purposes. In most cases it is expected that the s 41 charges will be dealt with unproblematically within the terms of existing partial exemption methods.

INTERIM PAYMENTS

Where interim payments are made in respect of supplies subject to s 41, then VAT must be accounted for on each payment. If the group is not able to calculate the reduced value of the s 41 charge by the time it has to account for VAT, it should account for VAT from month to month on a best estimate, making an appropriate adjustment at the end of the year.

PENALTIES AND INTEREST

Groups who fail to comply with s 41 may incur a misdeclaration penalty—subject to normal rules. However, the Commissioners accept that taxpayers may need time to understand the measure, to communicate the effects to staff and to gather relevant information. For this reason misdeclaration penalties relating to s 41 errors will only be assessed in exceptional circumstances before 1 January 1998.

Interest is currently charged on assessments as commercial restitution to the Exchequer. However, as many taxpayers will only know precisely how to account for the s 41 charge as a result of this Business Brief, interest on assessments based on s 41 errors will only be charged from the start of a trader's prescribed accounting period following the date of this Business Brief.

Note. For the concessions set out in this Business Brief, see Notice No 48 (September 1997) paras 2.2 and 2.3 reproduced in Appendix 6.

[VATA 1994 s 43]

5 JUNE 1997. BUSINESS BRIEF 12/97
FITTED FURNITURE IN NEW BUILDINGS

Legislation is now in place to ensure that people who buy, rent or have constructed for them a new zero-rated building which includes "incorporated" furniture do not gain a tax advantage over others who buy, rent or have constructed for them a similar building and then separately purchase furniture upon which VAT is chargeable.

Previous Business Briefs 13/93 [29 April 1993] and 3/94 [15 February 1994] outlined Customs & Excise's policy on what is regarded as furniture. These took into consideration the High Court decision in *C & E Comrs v McLean Homes (Midlands) Limited* [1993] STC 335 and the VAT tribunal decision in *Edmond Homes Limited* [No 11567]. More recently the VAT tribunal decision of *Stuart Henry Wade* [No 13164] provided further comment on when a supply of fitted furniture takes place.

This case confirmed Customs & Excise's view that a standard-rated supply of fitted furniture takes place when furniture, such as commonly supplied by specialist retailers or manufacturers, is designed to be, and actually is, fixed to the wall of the room.

Customs & Excise are anxious to minimise disputes in this complex area. Set out below is a restatement and expansion of previous information.

BASIC POSITION

Suppliers of zero-rated construction services can generally also zero-rate the supply of building materials incorporated into a qualifying building or its site. However, "finished and prefabricated furniture, other than furniture designed to be fitted in kitchens" and "materials for the construction of fitted furniture, other than kitchen furniture" are specifically excluded from the definition of building materials. Therefore their supply is always standard-rated, even if supplied with zero-rated services.

A person making a zero-rated grant of a major interest in a property is specifically blocked from recovering input tax on items of "finished and prefabricated furniture" or the "materials for the construction of fitted furniture" which are incorporated in any part of the building or its site. Again these restrictions do not apply to items of kitchen furniture.

The service of incorporating finished, prefabricated and fitted furniture into qualifying buildings is zero-rated when supplied in the course of construction of that building, and is subject to a correct zero-rating certificate for relevant residential or charitable buildings. See Section 3 of Notice 708 "Buildings and Construction" for further information on certificates. A fair and reasonable apportionment can be made between the service and goods element of any supply.

Building materials which are not finished or prefabricated furniture, or materials for the construction of fitted furniture, or any other statutory exclusion such as electrical and gas appliances or carpets, and which are incorporated into a qualifying building, can be zero-rated when they are supplied with zero-rated incorporation services. Similarly, subject to the normal rules, the developer is not blocked from recovering input tax on the purchase of the materials used.

FREE STANDING ITEMS OF FURNITURE

Free standing items of furniture are not items that are incorporated into a building. They are not building materials and their supply to the developer would always be standard-rated. The developer can recover input tax, which relates to a separate onward standard-rated supply of that item of furniture. Output tax must be accounted for by the developer.

WHAT IS FURNITURE?

Furniture is not defined in law. Tribunals and the High Court have indicated that whether an item is furniture is very much a matter of impression, but have indicated that the function of furniture includes, "convenient places to hang things or to store things; as decoration for a house; and to provide areas for the preparation of food, or for work of various kinds associated with domestic, social or working life". This is not an exhaustive list.

Items of furniture include the items listed below. The supply of these goods is always standard-rated whether or not they form part of a range of matching units—beds, chairs, bookcases, sideboards, dining tables, cupboards (but see below), dressing tables, bedside cabinets, chests of drawers, linen chests, etc. Developers cannot recover input tax on these goods when they are incorporated into a zero-rated building.

Items which are not furniture include the items listed below. The supply of these goods can be zero-rated when supplied with zero-rated construction services—cupboards such as airing or under-stair storage cupboards or other similar basic storage facilities which are formed by becoming part of the fabric of the building; baths, WCs, wash hand basins, etc; items which provide storage capacity as an incidental result of their primary function. Such items include shelves formed as a result of constructing simple box work over pipes. Developers are not prevented from recovering input tax on the purchase of these goods or materials for their construction.

BEDROOM WARDROBES

The tribunal case of *Stuart Henry Wade* on bedroom furniture made distinctions between the types of wardrobes being supplied to Mr Wade and those supplied by McLean Homes (Midlands) Limited. The tribunal chairman considered that the wardrobes supplied to Mr Wade were elaborate items of furniture which were fitted into the rooms of Mr Wade's house, whereas those supplied by McLean Homes (Midlands) Limited were much more simple units fitted into alcoves or annexes of bedrooms.

Customs & Excise accept simple bedroom wardrobes installed on their own as not being furniture. Other more elaborate wardrobes—however fitted—are furniture. Customs & Excise also regard simple bedroom wardrobes which are installed as part of a larger installation of furniture in the room—typically as part of a matching range—as being furniture.

A simple bedroom wardrobe would have the following characteristics—

It would enclose a space bordered by the walls, ceiling and floor. Units whose design includes, for example, an element to bridge over a bed or create a dressing table, are regarded as furniture. The sides and back would be formed by using three walls of the room or two walls and a stub wall. For these purposes, the wardrobe could be fitted across the whole of the end of a room. The installation of a cupboard in the corner of a room where one side is a closing end panel is regarded as furniture. On opening the wardrobe you should see the walls of the building.

These would normally be either bare or painted plaster. Wardrobes which contain internal panelling, typically as part of a modular or carcass system, are regarded as furniture. The wardrobe should feature no more than a single shelf running the full length of the wardrobe, a rail for hanging clothes and a closing door or doors. Wardrobes with internal divisions, drawers, shoe racks or other features are regarded as furniture.

VANITY UNITS

Where wash hand basins installed in bathrooms and cloakrooms are supported by basin units rather than pedestals, the basin unit is not regarded as furniture. The unit will typically be a box like structure entirely below the line of the top of the basin and contain a shelf and a covering door or doors—the only storage space being directly beneath the basin itself. More elaborate vanity units, typically with other storage space constructed on either or both sides of the basin, are furniture; as are wall units such as bathroom cabinets.

[VATA 1994 Sch 8 Group 5 Item 4]

21 JULY 1997. BUSINESS BRIEF 16/97
VAT CHANGES FOR BONUSES GIVEN BY CAR MANUFACTURERS TO DEALERS OR FLEET BUYERS

Fleet buyer bonuses are given by manufacturers or sole concessionaires to customers who make bulk purchases of their vehicles. Dealer demonstrator bonuses are payments made, or credits allowed, by car manufacturers or sole concessionaries to dealers, when the dealer agrees to adopt the car as a demonstrator vehicle.

In the past it has been common practice to treat the bonuses as the payment for a supply of services by dealers and customers, so VAT was due from the dealer or customer on this supply.

Following the decision by the European Court of Justice in [*Elida Gibbs Ltd v C & E Comrs* (case C-317/94) [1996] STC 1387, ECJ], which established that discounts can be given by a supplier for his goods to someone other than his direct customer, we now accept that these bonus payments will normally be treated as discounts by manufacturers and sole concessionaires which reduce the value of their supplies. Values should also be adjusted by dealers in their second hand stock books.

In many cases the net effect of this change will not alter the net tax due. However, if businesses believe that they have overpaid VAT in the past three years they should contact their local VAT business advice centre listed under Customs & Excise in the telephone book.

[VATA 1994 s 19]

24 SEPTEMBER 1997. BUSINESS BRIEF 20/97 VAT CONSTRUCTION CHANGES

On 20 May the House of Lords refused the Commissioners leave to appeal against the Court of Appeal's decision in [*C & E Comrs v Marchday Holdings Ltd* [1997] STC 272, CA].

The purpose of this business brief is to explain what effect the company's successful legal challenge has on the Commissioners' VAT construction policy. It also describes the action to take to obtain a refund of VAT in other cases where the *Marchday* decision applies.

. . .

REVISED POLICY ON SUPPLIES MADE PRIOR TO 1 MARCH 1995

In the light of the Court of Appeal's decision, the Commissioners accept that VAT may have been charged incorrectly on some supplies made prior to 1 March 1995 changes. This includes both supplies of construction services, and certain disposals of qualifying buildings. The details of the redevelopment undertaken by Marchday is only one example of works that could not be described as being carried out on an existing building. It is impossible to give extensive examples of all such works, as each case is unique. The Commissioners will therefore consider claims for refunds of VAT from any trader, who considers that the Court of Appeal's findings in *Marchday* can be applied to supplies they have made prior to 1 March 1995.

CLAIMS FOR REFUNDS

. . .

Claims for refund should be made in to local VAT offices, using the voluntary disclosure procedure Form VAT 642 available from them.

To enable the Commissioners to verify claims they should be accompanied with all available supporting evidence. Examples would be any photographs, plans or drawings showing the building both before work started and on completion; copies of the planning application and permission, together with any other relevant documentation; a brief description of the work carried out on the building; a breakdown of how the amount claimed was quantified; details of the dates when the overpayment of VAT was made to Customs & Excise; and any other information thought to support the claim.

If you were the recipient of a supply which you believe comes under the terms of this Business Brief, you will have to ask your supplier to consider making a refund to you. Refunds in these circumstances are a commercial matter between the supplier and his or her customer.

[VATA 1994 Sch 8 Group 5 Note 18]

24 SEPTEMBER 1997. BUSINESS BRIEF 20/97 VACUUM CLEANERS, AIR PURIFICATION AND SIMILAR ANTI-ALLERGEN PRODUCTS

Customs & Excise have undertaken and have completed a review of the VAT liability of vacuum cleaners, air purification products and similar allergy relief products. The review concluded that such products are standard-rated and not zero-rated under provisions relating to equipment "designed solely" for disabled people (Business Briefs 16/96 [not reproduced] and 17/96 [not reproduced].)

Since 26 August 1996, all supplies of such products have been liable to VAT at the standard rate irrespective of to whom they are supplied.

This confirmation will help to provide certainty for suppliers and customers alike, and will prevent considerable distortion in the trade, particularly for vacuum cleaner suppliers. Previously VAT treatment of these products had been inconsistent.

[VATA 1994 Sch 8 Group 12 Item 2]

10 OCTOBER 1997. BUSINESS BRIEF 22/97 HAIRDRESSER CHAIR RENTALS

VAT Notice 742 ("Land & Property") December 1995 confirmed at para 2.7 that in most cases the liability of hairdresser chair rentals is standard-rated. The availability of the Notice was advertised in VAT Notes 1 which were issued from April 1996.

Prior to the issue of this notice we are aware that there was some uncertainty over the VAT treatment of chair rentals. Accordingly, where businesses have not taxed chair rentals due to a genuine misunderstanding, as opposed to any tax avoidance scheme, then Customs & Excise will not raise additional assessments for accounting periods prior to April 1996. The same criteria will be applied to new VAT registrations.

We would stress that in circumstances where the trader was aware of the VAT liability of chair rentals and did not act on information received from either Customs & Excise, their accountant or any other source additional assessments and belated registrations will be raised.

[VATA 1994 s 73]

12 DECEMBER 1997. BUSINESS BRIEF 28/97 VAT TREATMENT OF DEBT COLLECTION REVISED

After consulting with the trade Customs & Excise have agreed to changes to provide greater clarity and certainty to the VAT treatment of debt collection, with effect from 1 April 1998.

However, nothing in this agreement restricts the freedom of debt collectors to negotiate and agree with their clients as to how sums collected from the debtors are to be allocated between the principal debt, Court fees and solicitors scale charges.

BACKGROUND

Up to now, collectors have regarded the services of the solicitor engaged to pursue the debt as being supplied to them, and have recovered the VAT charged by the solicitor as their input tax. At the same time, however, collectors have not accounted for any output tax on amounts they retain which they have collected from debtors in respect of costs (ie those awarded by the Court to the creditor to cover Court fees and solicitors' charges).

Customs & Excise looked at these arrangements and concluded that the correct VAT treatment is not being applied. Court fees and solicitors scale charges are awarded by the Court, to the creditor, and are outside the scope of VAT. However, Customs & Excise consider that where the creditor allows these monies to be retained by the collector, their nature changes to that of simply being payments made by the creditor to the collector.

There are arguments either way for seeing collectors as agents of the creditor or as acting in their own right in pursuing legal recovery of debts, and the true position in any particular case may depend on the precise arrangements in place. However, whatever the position, where the collector retains monies belonging to the creditor, Customs & Excise consider that those monies can only be one of two things, either consideration for the collectors supply of services to the creditor, or reimbursement of payments made by the collector on the creditor's behalf.

COLLECTORS WHO ACT AS AGENTS

Court fees—Customs & Excise agree that amounts paid by collectors to solicitors in respect of Court fees may be treated as disbursements made on behalf of the creditor. Any amount recovered from debtors in respect of such fees and retained by collectors may then be regarded as reimbursement of the amount disbursed and outside the scope of VAT.

Legal fees—In respect of VAT charged by solicitors for their services, there are only two options open to collectors—

They may choose not to recover the VAT as input tax, and simply treat the charges as disbursements in accordance with para 10.8 of Notice 700 "The VAT guide". In this case, where the agreement with the creditor provides that the collector bears the cost of solicitors' services but may retain, as reimbursement of his costs, any amounts recovered from the debtor in respect of solicitors' scale charges awarded by the court, such amounts may be treated as outside the scope of VAT.

Alternatively they may choose to recover the VAT as input tax, subject to the normal rules, but recharge the fees plus VAT to the creditor under the terms of VATA 1994 s 47(3). Under this option, the scale charges retained represent payment of the fees recharged.

COLLECTORS WHO ACT AS PRINCIPALS

If, in the particular circumstances of any case, the collector considers that he is acting as a principal, any VAT charged by the solicitor may be recovered as input tax, subject to the normal rules. However, any amounts recovered from the debtor both in respect of Court fees and/or solicitors' scale charges and retained by the collector can only represent consideration for his supply of services to the creditor. Output tax must be accounted for on all such amounts in the normal way. This treatment will not apply to assignments of debts for which the next paragraph applies.

ASSIGNED DEBTS

An equitable or legal assignment of the debt to the collector, whether in whole or in part, is an exempt supply of services to the collector. Collection of both equitably or legally assigned debts by the person to whom they are assigned is outside the scope of VAT.

[VATA 1994 ss 5, 47]

12 DECEMBER 1997. BUSINESS BRIEF 28/97 VAT AND SEARCH AGENCIES

Following a review Customs & Excise have clarified the circumstances where search fees charged to an agency and passed on to its customer may be treated as a disbursement, and outside the scope of VAT.

With effect from 1 February 1998, Customs & Excise will regard the fiche or document, obtained from a source such as Companies House, as a piece of information rather than a tangible object, and the following VAT rules will apply.

The recharge of a search fee to the customer for the provision of a fiche or document may be treated as a disbursement and outside the scope of VAT, provided the information is passed on by the agency without analysis or comment, and all the conditions outlined in para 10.8 of Notice 700 "The VAT guide" are met.

Where the agency carries out a process on the fiche or document itself, provided it has not used the data to inform an opinion or report, it may treat the recharge of the search fee as a disbursement and also outside the scope of VAT.

An example would be where the agency obtains a search but its customer does not have facility to read a fiche, and the agency simply converts the fiche into readable hard copy and passes it on to the customer, without comment or analysis. The same would apply where the agency provides typewritten extracts of a fiche or document, again without analysis or comment.

If the agency analyses, comments on, or produces a report on a fiche or document, or otherwise uses the information obtained on a search to produce a report, it may not treat the search fee as a disbursement and outside the scope of VAT when recharged to the customer. In this example, the agency could not provide the customer with the required information without utilising the content of the fiche or document. The search fee, therefore, is a component part of the agency's costs in providing its services to the customer, and is taxable at the standard rate.

[VATA 1994 s 47]

19 DECEMBER 1997. BUSINESS BRIEF 30/97 STATEMENT OF PRACTICE ON A BUDGET CHANGE TO THE CAPITAL GOODS SCHEME

1 INTRODUCTION

1.1 Changes to the capital goods scheme announced at the time of the July 1997 budget included a test to be applied on the disposal of a capital item by the owner during the adjustment period. The test compares the total amount of input tax deducted or deductible on a capital item with the amount of output tax due on the disposal of that item. For the purposes of this Statement of Practice and the examples annexed, this test will be known as "the disposal test".

1.2 The policy objective underlying the disposal test is to ensure that partly exempt businesses such as banks, building societies, insurance companies, educational establishments, sports clubs, providers of private health care and the like, do not obtain an unjustified tax advantage by being able to recover the input tax they incur on land or property which is to be used for exempt purposes.

1.3 The change was announced as part of a package of anti-avoidance measures in the 1997 Budget. It was introduced by the Value Added Tax (Amendment) (No 3) Regulations, SI 1997/1614 and came into force with effect from 3 July 1997.

1.4 It is not intended that the disposal test should be applied to bona fide commercial transactions. The legislation gives Customs & Excise the power to exclude individual transactions and this power will be used either generally or specifically in cases that do not appear to Customs & Excise to involve unjustified tax advantage. So, for example, given the policy objective, the disposal test will not be applied to sales of computer equipment.

1.5 The purpose of this Statement of Practice is to clarify Customs & Excise policy in this area. It does not qualify the relevant legislation, nor does it affect a taxpayer's right of appeal to an independent VAT tribunal.

2 BACKGROUND

2.1 Generally, businesses making taxable supplies can recover VAT on goods and services they buy in for their business (input tax). Businesses making exempt supplies cannot normally recover their input tax. Businesses which make both taxable and exempt supplies can recover input tax to the extent that the goods and services on which it is incurred are used to make taxable supplies.

2.2 The capital goods scheme recognises that certain major capital assets (capital items) are not consumed immediately but are used by businesses over a number of years. It is designed to be fair to both businesses and the Exchequer. The scheme applies to—

— certain land and buildings where the VAT bearing costs of purchase or development (acquisition) amount to £250,000 or more, with an adjustment period of 10 intervals;
— items of computer equipment of a value of £50,000 or more, with an adjustment period of 5 intervals.

2.3 An interval normally equates with the partial exemption tax year. In the first interval the owner deducts input tax incurred on a capital item to the extent that the item is used or to be used in making taxable supplies. He must then review his use of the item over the relevant adjustment period. In each subsequent interval, if the extent of taxable use differs from that which governed the initial recovery of input tax, the owner must make an adjustment. The adjustment is calculated by comparing the percentage of taxable use in the subsequent interval with the initial recovery percentage.

2.4 For example, input tax is deducted in full when a property is acquired, because it is being used exclusively in making taxable supplies. In a subsequent interval the use to which it is put changes from fully taxable to fully exempt. The owner must pay back 1/10th of the input tax originally claimed. If the owner continues to use the property for exempt purposes, similar adjustments will have to be made (and amounts paid back) at the end of each interval for the remainder of the adjustment period.

2.5 The legal basis of the scheme is Part XV of the Value Added Tax Regulations [SI 1995/2518] (regs 112–116). Further information about the scheme can be found in VAT Leaflet 706/2/90 "Capital goods scheme—input tax on computers, land and buildings for use in your business".

3 DISPOSAL OF A CAPITAL ITEM

3.1 The period of adjustment is brought to an end by the outright disposal of the capital item during the adjustment period. In effect, on termination the item is treated as if it were used for the remainder of the adjustment period in making the supply which gives rise to the termination. So, where the capital item is sold and the sale is a taxable supply, the item is treated as being used in all remaining complete intervals for the making of taxable supplies. The owner must make a final adjustment in respect of all remaining intervals to reflect this.

3.2 Prior to 3 July 1997 businesses could acquire a new commercial building as a capital item and recover all of the input tax by putting the item to taxable use in the first interval. At the beginning of interval 2, the owner could make a very substantial exempt supply (say a 999 year lease—which is not an outright disposal because the freehold interest remains) and then immediately sell the freehold of the building—that sale being a compulsory taxable supply. Because there was an exempt lease, the value of the freehold sale was very low and there was output tax only on that very low value. The taxable sale of the capital item ensured the recovery of a high proportion of the input tax incurred while very little output tax was paid. The building then ceased to be a capital item. This results in an unjustified tax advantage and is the sort of arrangement that the new rule is designed to counter.

4 THE INTRODUCTION OF A TEST ON DISPOSAL

4.1 With effect from 3 July 1997 where the owner of a capital item disposes of it and the total input tax deducted is greater than the output tax due on the supply of the item, the owner is required to make an adjustment so that the input tax recoverable does not exceed the output tax chargeable on the supply of the item. The input tax recoverable is the aggregate of—
— the initial deduction of input tax incurred on the purchase or development of the item;
— any adjustments made previously in respect of the item under the scheme; and
— any adjustment that would otherwise be required due to the disposal of the item.

5 APPLICATION OF THE PROVISION

5.1 In principle the disposal test is wide ranging and impacts on many disposals of capital items. In practice it will only be applied where the owner of a capital item would otherwise gain an unjustified tax advantage, and then the tax charge will be limited to an adjustment amount that would ensure no unjustified tax advantage arises. The legislation includes a "save as the Commissioners otherwise allow" provision to enable Customs & Excise to exclude individual transcriptions. This power will be used to exclude the application of the disposal test in cases that do not appear to Customs & Excise to involve unjustified tax advantage. It will not be applied—

— to sales of computer equipment;
— where an owner disposes of an item at a loss due to market conditions (such as a general downturn in property prices);
— where the value of the item has depreciated;
— where the value of the item is reduced for other legitimate reasons (such as accepting a lower price to effect a quick sale);
— where the amount of output tax on disposal is less than the total input tax claimed only due to a reduction in the VAT rate;
— where the item is used only for taxable (including zero-rated) purposes throughout the adjustment period (which includes the final disposal).

5.2 Where there is no unjustified tax advantage a business should not apply the disposal test and in such circumstances it is not necessary to apply to Customs & Excise for a specific ruling. A business need only apply the disposal test where it has entered into arrangements for tax mitigation affecting the particular capital item or its disposal. In cases of doubt or difficulty businesses should contact the local VAT office. Examples of where the disposal test should and should not be applied are set out in the annex.

5.3 Where there is an unjustified tax advantage businesses will need to work out the amount of tax to be adjusted. To do this, they will need to calculate the net tax advantage and then work out how much of the net tax advantage is unjustified. The net tax advantage is the overall benefit derived from the avoidance device. Normally the benefit is that the owner is able to secure the amount of input tax that would still be subject to adjustment under the scheme, were it not for the sale of the capital item. In order to achieve this benefit a taxable supply is made. The net tax advantage would therefore be the amount of input tax secured by the sale less any output tax due on the sale. Some form of apportionment needs to be applied to work out how much of the net tax advantage is unjustified.

Normally this could be achieved by using the ratio that the value of the final taxable sale bears to the value of both the exempt supply and the final taxable sale (see example 4 in the annex).

5.4 If Customs & Excise consider that the disposal of a capital item has resulted in an unjustified tax advantage to the owner the provision will be vigorously enforced. Implementation of the provision is to be closely monitored. For the next two years, where the provision is enforced and a business requests a review of that decision, any review will be carried out by the Partial Exemption Branch, Commercial Division, VAT Policy Directorate.

5.5 This Statement of Practice may be changed or disapplied if used for the purposes of avoidance of tax.

ANNEX 1—EXAMPLES

Example 1

A business acquires the freehold of a newly constructed commercial property for £2 million plus VAT on 1 June 1995. The business immediately occupies the building for its own business purposes. The business is partly exempt with a recovery rate of 50% and is therefore only able to deduct half of the input tax incurred under the normal partial exemption rules.

The business continues to use the building for taxable and exempt purposes for the remainder of the tax year ending on 30 April 1996 (the end of the first interval) and for the following tax year (the second interval) there is a small capital goods scheme adjustment made in respect of the second interval because the overall recovery rate increases.

During the third interval, on 1 August 1997, the business disposes of the property by way of a taxable supply (sold within three years of completion of the construction of the building) for £2 million plus VAT. As a consequence the business is required to carry out a final adjustment and is able to deduct 7/10ths of the input tax previously restricted. The disposal test does not affect the recovery of the 7/10ths because the output tax on disposal is greater than the input tax claimed in the adjustment period.

Example 2

A business completes the construction of a £20 million office block, the whole cost of which had borne VAT, on 1 June 1995 and immediately occupies the building for its own business purposes. The business is partly exempt with a recovery rate of 50% and is therefore only able to deduct half of the input tax incurred.

The business continues to use the building for taxable and exempt purposes for the remainder of the tax year ending on 30 April 1996 (the end of the first interval) and for the following tax year (the second interval). There is a small capital goods scheme adjustment made in respect of the second interval because the overall recovery rate increased.

During the third interval, on 1 August 1997, following a downturn in property prices, the business disposes of the property by way of a taxable supply (sold within three years of completion of construction of the building) for its open market value of £16 million plus VAT. As a consequence the business is required to carry out a final adjustment and is able to deduct 7/10ths of the input tax previously restricted. Since the output tax on disposal is less than the input tax claimed in the adjustment period, the disposal test applies. However, the owner is not required to pay any amount back to Customs & Excise because the building was sold at an open market price and not to obtain an unjustified tax advantage.

Example 3

A business acquires the 20-year leasehold interest in an office block for a premium of £10 million plus VAT (the previous owner having opted to tax) on 1 June 1995. The business immediately occupies the building for its own business purposes. The business is partly exempt with a recovery rate of 65% and is therefore only able to deduct that proportion of the input tax incurred.

The business continues to use the building for taxable and exempt purposes for the remainder of the tax year ending on 31 March 1996 (the end of the first interval) and for the following six tax years (the second to the seventh intervals). There are some small capital goods scheme adjustments made in respect of the later intervals because the overall recovery rate increases or decreases as the case may be.

During the eighth interval, on 1 August 2003, following an expansion in their business, the business relocates to new premises and sells the remaining 12 years leasehold interest in the existing office block to a third party as an exempt supply (not having opted) at an open market price. As a consequence the business is required to carry out a final adjustment in respect of the ninth and tenth intervals and pay back 2/10ths of the input tax previously recovered in the first interval. In addition, since the output tax on disposal is less than the input tax claimed in the adjustment period, the disposal test applies. However, the owner is not required to pay any amount back to Customs & Excise because the building was sold at an open market price and there was no attempt to obtain an unjustified tax advantage. The capital goods scheme adjustments have adequately reflected the exempt use to which the property will be put for the remaining two complete intervals.

Example 4

On 1 June 1997 a developer completes a £25 million commercial development, the whole cost of which had borne VAT (£4,375,000). The developer opts to tax the building and leases it out on a two year lease to a third party tenant at a market rent plus VAT. The developer is therefore able to deduct all the input tax incurred on the development under the normal partial exemption rules.

The business continues to let the building on a taxable lease for the remainder of the tax year ending on 31 March 1998 (the end of the first interval) and for the following tax year (the second interval). A capital goods scheme adjustment is therefore not required for the second interval.

On 1 June 1999 (part way through the third interval) the developer grants a 99 year lease at a premium of £24 million and a peppercorn rent to its wholly owned subsidiary. The subsidiary is wholly exempt. FA 1997 s 37 (VATA 1994 Sch 10 para 2 (3AA)) operates so as to disapply the developer's option to tax so that the premium is not subject to VAT. At the end of the third interval there is therefore an adjustment in respect of $^1/_{10}$th (£437,500) of the initial input tax incurred and a proportion of $^1/_{10}$th (because there was some taxable use in the first part of the third interval) is paid back to Customs & Excise (assuming a recovery rate of 50%—£218,750).

On 1 May 2000 the developer sells the freehold, subject to the 99 year lease for £250,000 plus VAT, to the wholly owned subsidiary (a compulsory taxable supply). The sale effectively ends the fourth interval. Since the building is used for exempt purposes up to the sale there is an adjustment in respect of $^1/_{10}$th of the initial input tax incurred. It is a full $^1/_{10}$th that is restricted because the item is only used for exempt purposes up to the disposal of the item.

As a consequence of the low value taxable disposal, since there is no change in the extent of taxable use the business is not required to carry out a final adjustment. But since the output tax on disposal is less than the input tax claimed in the adjustment period, the disposal test applies. In this instance there is an unjustified tax advantage because the high value exempt grant in the third interval enables a low value taxable sale of the freehold. At the same time the taxable sale enables full recovery of input tax in respect of the remaining six intervals (the fifth to the tenth) while only $^1/_{10}$th of the input tax is restricted (in the fourth interval) to reflect the exempt grant—

Interval	*Input tax claim*	*Output tax declared*	*Difference*
1	4,375,000		4,375,000
2			4,375,000
3	(218,750)		4,156,250
4	(437,500)	(43,750)	3,762,500
5–10			3,762,500

In principle £3,762,500 would be due. But the net tax advantage is that the owner is able to secure the amount of input tax that would still be subject to adjustment under the scheme (intervals 5–10), were it not for the sale of the capital item and in order to achieve this benefit a taxable supply is made.

The amount of input tax involved is $^6/_{10}$ths of £4,375,000–£2,625,000. The amount of output tax involved is £43,750. The net tax advantage is therefore £2,581,250.

Some form of fair and reasonable apportionment needs to be applied to work out how much of the net tax advantage is unjustified. This could be achieved by using the ratio that the value of the final taxable sale bears to the value of both the exempt supply and the final taxable sale—

$$\frac{250{,}000}{24{,}250{,}000} \text{ or } \frac{1}{97} \times £\,2{,}581{,}250 = £\,26{,}611 \text{ taxable use}$$

£2,554,639 exempt use.

Thus, in practice the disposal test would be applied, but the amount due to Customs & Excise would be the value of the unjustified tax advantage—£2,554,639.

[SI 1995/2518 reg 115]

7 JANUARY 1998. BUSINESS BRIEF 1/98
VAT CHANGES TO FLEET LEASING BONUSES

This business brief explains a change in Customs & Excise's approach to the treatment of "fleet leasing bonus" payments—also known as fleet support payments.

BACKGROUND

A "fleet leasing bonus" is a payment made by a car manufacturer or dealer to a business who has leased a number of vehicles previously sold by the manufacturer or dealer to intermediaries. In the past it has been common practice to treat the bonus payment as the consideration for a supply of services by the customer, so VAT was due from the customer on this supply.

REVISED POSITION

Following the European Court of Justice judgment in [*Elida Gibbs Ltd v C & E Comrs* (case C-317/94) [1996] STC 1387], which established that discounts can be given by a supplier for his goods to someone other than his direct customer, we now accept that fleet leasing bonus payments will normally be treated as discounts. This interpretation follows that applied to bonus payments given by car manufacturers to businesses that buy fleets, detailed in Business Brief 16/97 [21 July 1997].

This change means that businesses that have received such payments will, in many cases, have overpaid VAT. Treating the payment as a discount rather than as the consideration for a supply of services will mean that no output tax can be due from the customer. However, as a discount the payment will also reduce the input tax recovered by the customer (if any) on the lease payments. For example where 50% of the VAT incurred on the lease payments has been recovered, the bonus payment will reduce the VAT originally claimed by $^{7}/_{47}$ × (50% × gross bonus payment).

If businesses believe that they have overpaid VAT in the past three years they should contact their local VAT business advice centre listed under Customs & Excise in the telephone book.

[VATA 1994 s 19]

9 FEBRUARY 1998. BUSINESS BRIEF 4/98
VAT—TREATMENT OF "PREMIUM", "NEARLY NEW" AND "PERSONAL IMPORT" CARS

The administrative concession allowing non franchised dealers input tax recovery on cars supplied to a third party (Press Notice 748) will be withdrawn with effect from 1 April 1998.

BACKGROUND

Press Notice 748 explained a special VAT treatment which allows unfranchised car dealers to recover input tax on cars which they obtain anonymously through third parties. For example, getting an employee to buy a car in their name from another dealer.

Following changes in 1995 to the UK VAT law on supplies of goods through agents, we have reviewed our position and concluded there is no longer any legal basis for continuing with the administrative concession. From 1 April 1998 the normal rules for supplies of goods through agents will apply. This means that if, on buying goods from a third party, an intermediary issues an invoice in his own name for the onward supply of the goods to a customer, the intermediary will be seen as both receiving and making a supply. When, in this situation, the intermediary decides not to disclose the identity of the customer to the third party he is acting as an "undisclosed agent".

NEW ARRANGEMENTS

From 1 April 1998 non franchised dealers will only be able to treat tax as input tax if it is incurred on a supply made directly to them. Therefore if they purchase cars which are invoiced to them, either directly from a manufacturer or from another dealer then tax will be recoverable.

However where non franchised dealers purchase their cars through "undisclosed agents" they will now only be able to recover VAT on the agent's supply of the car to them if the agent is VAT registered and has issued a proper tax invoice.

Intermediaries who act as undisclosed agents for non franchised dealers are entitled to be registered provided they are in business for VAT purposes. When considering whether an agent's activities constitute "business" we must take into account the five "business tests" applied in the case of [*C & E Comrs v Lord Fisher* [1981] STC 238]. As these tests require us to look at both the value and frequency of intended supplies, it is unlikely that we will see an intention to sell a single car as constituting "business" and thus allow VAT registration.

It should be noted that undisclosed agents will suffer a block on the input tax they incur on the purchase of the car if they make it available for private use. This is likely to occur if there is a gap between the purchase of the car and it being supplied to the non franchised dealer. [VATA 1994 s 47]

7 AUGUST 1998. BUSINESS BRIEF 17/98
CHARGES MADE TO CUSTOMERS PAYING BY CREDIT CARD

Customs and Excise have received a number of enquiries about the VAT treatment of charges made by businesses for payment by credit card.

If the charge for payment by credit card is made by the supplier of the goods or services being bought, Customs view this as a further payment for the purchase. VAT would be payable on the charge at the same rate as on the goods or services.

However, if the charge is made by an agent acting for the supplier of the goods or services, for example a travel agent acting on behalf of a tour company, then Customs consider that the charge is for a separate supply of exempt services, ie accepting payment in the form of a credit card.

This policy will be applied from today. If a trader wishes to submit a voluntary disclosure it will be subject to the usual unjust enrichment rules. Partial exemption rules which have not been applied correctly in respect of these supplies will also be corrected from today.

[VATA 1994 s 5]

15 SEPTEMBER 1998. BUSINESS BRIEF 19/98
LOCAL AUTHORITIES—WORKS IN DEFAULT

In the case of [*Glasgow City Council* (No 15491)] the Edinburgh VAT and duties tribunal ruled on the liability of works in default and the subsequent recovery of costs under the Housing (Scotland) Act 1987 ss 108, 109.

This Act requires local authorities in Scotland to serve a repair notice to the owner of a property that they consider is in disrepair. If the owner does not comply with the notice the council is empowered to arrange for the work to be carried out and recover the cost of the work from the owner. The tribunal decided that, in these specific circumstances there was no supply for VAT purposes by the Council.

The decision only applies to works in default carried out by Scottish local authorities under ss 108, 109 of the Act. However Customs are taking this opportunity to clarify their guidance on the treatment of all types of default works throughout the UK.

VAT LIABILITY OF WORKS IN DEFAULT

Local authorities are empowered, by specific legislative provisions, to issue notices requiring that works are carried out in a number of situations. The recipient of the notice may or may not comply.

When the recipient of the notice agrees to the work being carried out and arranges the work with either a contractor or with the authority then the supply of the contractor's services is to the recipient of the notice. If the authority arranges the contractor's supplies on the recipient's behalf they may treat these supplies as being to the authority and by the authority under VATA 1994 s 47(3).

If the recipient of the notice refuses to comply the authority may exercise its statutory powers, have the work carried out and recover the cost of the works from the recipient. In these circumstances the authority is not making a supply for VAT purposes.

RECOVERY OF VAT

Only when the supply of the works is to the local authority—as in the *Glasgow City Council* case—may it recover the VAT charged by the contractor. Where the authority makes an onward taxable supply in the course of furtherance of business, the VAT incurred will be recoverable as input tax under VATA 1994 s 25. Where the authority does not make a taxable supply but imposes the works under its statutory powers, as described above, VAT recovery will be under VATA 1994 s 33.

[VATA 1994 s 5]

9 OCTOBER 1998. BUSINESS BRIEF 21/98
TOUR OPERATORS' MARGIN SCHEME—TREATMENT OF DISCOUNTS FUNDED BY TRAVEL AGENTS

Customs and Excise have examined the VAT treatment of discounts funded by travel agents, on package holidays provided by tour operators. Typically these arise when a travel agent sells a package on behalf of a tour operator for a lower price than that advertised in the tour operator's brochure.

It has been common practice in the industry that when a travel agent sells a holiday in this way, the brochure price of the holiday, less the full contracted value of the travel agent's commission, is passed from the travel agent to the tour operator. The tour operator accounts for the full brochure price of the holiday under the tour operators' margin scheme. The travel agent accounts for output tax on the full value of his commission, and this is deducted as input tax by the tour operator. However, because the traveller pays a price lower than that advertised in the brochure, queries have arisen about the correct VAT treatment of this reduction in price. Customs' view, supported by advice from Counsel, is that the practice outlined above leaves the VAT position unchanged, and no adjustment to the VAT accounts of either the tour operator or the travel agent is necessary in respect of the discount to the traveller. This is because the supply by the tour operator to the traveller is made at the full value of the brochure price, and it is the tour operator, not the travel agent, who accounts for the VAT on the supply of the holiday. The tour operator is unaffected by a discount given by the travel agent. The supply by the travel agent is to the tour operator, not to the traveller, and is also unaffected. The full price of the holiday is indeed paid: part of it directly by the traveller, and part of it (the "discount") funded by the travel agent. The effect of this trade practice is that the tour operator receives payment in full. It would be incorrect if VAT were declared by the tour operator on an amount lower than received.

Claims for refunds of VAT in respect of adjustments for discounts in the circumstances described above will not therefore be accepted by Customs from either tour operators or travel agents.

[VATA 1994 s 5]

15 FEBRUARY 1999. BUSINESS BRIEF 4/99
ROUTINE DOMESTIC TASKS PROVIDED BY CHARITIES

This Business Brief explains Customs' position after their review of whether home help services supplied on a not-for-profit basis by charities or public bodies are VAT exempt welfare services (see Business Brief 24/98 [2 December 1998—not reproduced]).

REVISED INTERPRETATION

Customs now accept that routine domestic tasks are exempt from VAT where an assessment of recipients' needs has been carried out which shows that there is a risk to the recipient's physical or mental health or welfare because they are unable to carry out those tasks safely or adequately, or without significant pain or discomfort, for themselves.

ASSESSMENT OF NEEDS

A VAT Tribunal stated [see *Watford and District Old People's Housing Association Ltd* (No 15660)] that domestic tasks, when looked at on their own, cannot be construed as welfare. However, looking beyond the service, ie at the level of the recipient's needs, such services may be considered as welfare. It follows that some form of assessment of recipients' needs is required to determine whether a domestic task qualifies for exemption.

The assessment procedure required is uncomplicated, and will often be consistent with the assessments currently being carried out by charities. Assessments must be carried out by the charity itself, social services, a GP, a nurse or another care organisation and assessors should have received appropriate training or experience (they do not need to be medically trained). The assessment should consider whether the recipient can carry out each proposed task safely or adequately or without significant pain or discomfort. Exemption will only extend to those tasks which have been the subject of assessment.

ROUTINE DOMESTIC TASKS

It is not possible to list all the tasks which are routine domestic tasks. The guiding principle is whether the task is one the majority of the population would expect to carry out themselves and which is needed to keep a household going. For example, housework and shopping are clearly routine domestic tasks.

FURTHER DETAILS

Customs are producing a VAT Information Sheet for charities who provide home help services and their advisers, which gives full details of Customs' revised interpretation. [See Information Sheet 6/99.]

[VATA 1994 Sch 9 Group 7 Note 6(a)]

24 FEBRUARY 1999. BUSINESS BRIEF 5/99
VAT: SHIP DESIGN SERVICES

This business brief gives Customs' position regarding ship design services. In June 1995, a Tribunal [see *Cholerton Ltd* (No 13387)] held that, in certain circumstances, design services were integral to the modification of a ship, despite the fact that Cholerton did not carry out the modification services. The design services were found to be zero-rated.

At the time, Customs accepted the decision and have since allowed businesses supplying design services in identical circumstances to zero-rate their supplies. However, we have now reviewed our policy. We consider that the Tribunal failed to take into account that Cholerton was contracted to supply only design services and therefore made no supply of modification services to which the design services could be integral.

Accordingly, with effect from 1 July 1999, Customs will treat design services supplied in the UK as integral to the supply, modification or conversion of a qualifying ship only where a supplier specifically contracts with a customer to design and supply, modify or convert a qualifying ship. In other circumstances, design services will be standard-rated and deductible, subject to the normal rules.

[VATA 1994 Sch 8 Group 8 Item 1]

31 MARCH 1999. BUSINESS BRIEF 8/99
VAT: THE THREE YEAR CAP AND PARTIAL EXEMPTION

This Business Brief clarifies Customs' policy about how the three year cap affects businesses' partial exemption position, illustrated by a number of examples.

BACKGROUND

The purpose of the three year cap is to provide certainty and stability for both the Exchequer and the taxpayer. The provisions are not intended to have any impact on the normal system of deduction and adjustments to deduction as set out in the VAT Regulations.

Any trader or business currently operating the partial exemption rules correctly will not be affected by the three year cap. This also applies to businesses which discover a mistake and make the necessary correction within the three year time limit. In other words, the three year cap only affects businesses who do not claim the input tax to which they were entitled or claim input tax to which they were not entitled, and fail to correct this within 3 years.

In addition, if a business fails to make an initial deduction of input tax (or gets the initial deduction wrong) and the error falls in a period which is more than three years old, the error cannot be corrected in the partial exemption annual adjustment even if the adjustment itself is not capped. However, even though the unclaimed amount of input tax cannot be reclaimed because it is capped, the annual adjustment itself should be based on the true amounts of input and output tax.

EXAMPLES

The effects of the three year cap are illustrated in the following examples:

(i) A partly exempt business (makes both exempt and taxable supplies) fails to use a partial exemption method and does not claim any input tax for a number of years. After an audit, the business submits a refund claim, in which the first quarter of the third tax year is "capped" (ie more than three years old) but the annual adjustment period itself is not "capped" (it falls within the three year period). Can the input tax in that period be recovered in the annual adjustment?

No – The trader, by failing to recover input tax in the relevant period, has failed to exercise the right to deduct. The trader is not able to claim this "capped" amount in the annual adjustment.

(ii) A partly exempt business calculates deductible input tax in accordance with his partial exemption method. In the first two quarters he fails the de minimis limits and so correctly restricts his exempt input tax. In the second two quarters he is able to benefit from the de minimis limits and so correctly recovers all his input tax in those quarters. At the end of the year he is able to benefit from the de minimis rules for the year as a whole but does not apply them. If he discovers this mistake within three years from the last day of the annual adjustment quarter is he able to correct it?

Yes – The partly exempt trader has correctly applied the de minimis rules to each quarter. Since it is at the time of the annual adjustment that the de minimis rules are applied to all the input tax incurred in the previous four quarters, it is at that time that any exempt input tax previously restricted may be recovered.

However, where a trader was entitled to apply the de minimis rules to a particular period but did not do so, and that period was "capped", any affected input tax falling in that period may not be recovered in the final de minimis calculation at the time of the annual adjustment (which itself is not "capped"). This is because the trader failed to exercise the right to deduct within the three year period.

(iii) A business with an agreed partial exemption method mistakenly treats taxable input tax as exempt. Can this input tax be recovered at the time of the annual adjustment if the input tax is proper to a period which is "capped" (but the annual adjustment is not "capped")?

No – We would not allow the trader to recover the exempt input tax at the time of the annual adjustment. The trader has mistakenly treated taxable input tax as exempt, and so he has failed to recover it.

Similarly, if the trader had incorrectly claimed exempt input tax and the input tax was proper to a period which was "capped", we would be unable to recover it under the assessment provisions in that period or the period of the annual adjustment (even if it was not "capped").

Customs are aware that, because of the complexity of the three year cap, we have agreed some claims and settled them as if the annual adjustment can be used to override the cap, effectively giving some claimants a repayment to which they were not entitled. We do not propose to revisit any of these claims, but all future claims will be treated on a proper basis.

[SI 1995/2518 regs 34, 35]

2 JULY 1999. BUSINESS BRIEF 14/99
VAT: MOBILE PHONES PROVIDED TO EMPLOYEES

This Business Brief explains Customs and Excise revised policy on the VAT treatment of mobile phones provided by businesses to employees.

BACKGROUND

In the 1999 Budget the Chancellor announced his intention to abolish the Inland Revenue scale charge which taxed the benefit in kind of mobile phones provided to employees. This has prompted a number of organisations to ask for similar proposals for VAT purposes. EC law would not permit the UK to stop charging VAT on the private use of business assets such as mobile phones. However Customs has reviewed its policy to ensure businesses can continue to account for VAT in a simple and flexible way.

VAT ON THE COST OF PROVIDING AND CONNECTING A MOBILE PHONE

Where a business provides its employees with mobile phones for business use then, regardless of whether it allows private use, it can treat as input tax all the VAT it incurs on purchasing a phone and on standing charges for keeping it connected to the network providing the charges do not contain any element for calls.

VAT ON MOBILE PHONE CALL CHARGES

If a business does not allow its employees to make private calls, all of the VAT incurred on the call charges is input tax. Customs will accept this is the case where a business has imposed clear rules prohibiting private use and enforces them. However we realise that in practice businesses with such a policy often tolerate a small amount of private calls. We are prepared to treat such minimal use as being insignificant for VAT purposes and it will not prevent a business treating all the tax it incurs on calls as input tax.

If a business charges its employees for any private calls they make, then it may treat the VAT incurred on the calls as input tax, but must account for output tax on the amounts it charges.

If a business allows its employees to make private calls without charge, then it must apportion the VAT incurred on the call charges. It is not appropriate for businesses to adopt an alternative treatment of accounting for output tax on the private use.

Businesses can choose any apportionment method that suits their individual circumstances providing the method chosen produces a fair and reasonable result. For example businesses could analyse a sample of bills taken over a reasonable period of time and use the same ratio for future VAT recovery on mobile phone bills.

Where the phone package allows the business to make a certain quantity of calls for a fixed monthly payment and there is no separate standing charge, then it must apportion the VAT on the total charge for the package. Similarly, where the contract is for the purchase of the phone and the advance purchase of a set amount of call time for a single charge, the apportionment will also apply to the whole charge.

[VATA 1994 s 24]

12 JULY 1999. BUSINESS BRIEF 15/99
VAT GROUPS—PROTECTION OF THE REVENUE

In the 1999 Budget, changes to the VAT grouping rules were announced. This included a new revenue protection power. This Business Brief sets out our approach to this new power, and to our use of existing revenue protection powers contained in the grouping legislation.

. . .

THE MEANING OF "FOR THE PROTECTION OF THE REVENUE"

Even though some of the revenue protection powers for groups are new, the concept of refusing group applications for the protection of the revenue is not. Until the Budget changes are enacted, the relevant legislation is set out in s 43(4) and (5A) of the Value Added Tax Act 1994. The meaning of "protection of the revenue" in this context was recently discussed in the VAT & Duties Tribunal in the case of *National Westminster Bank plc v C & E Comrs* (No 15514).

Paragraph 72 of the decision says that:

> "the protection in question under s 43(5A) may be against any loss of revenue which is not de minimis whether or not it follows from the normal operation of grouping. It certainly covers an artificial avoidance scheme but it also covers a straightforward case which would not be characterised as avoidance or abusive".

In future, we will not normally use our revenue protection powers when we consider that the revenue loss follows from the normal operation of grouping. By this, we mean the "revenue loss" which occurs because VAT is eliminated on the value added by a group member, when a supply takes place between two group members. This includes the loss arising from supplies between group members being disregarded, where the recipient of the supply would not normally be able to deduct that VAT because it makes exempt supplies. We would normally consider such revenue loss, the same as if the VAT group members were all one company, to be a natural result of grouping.

Where we consider that there seems likely to be a revenue loss that goes beyond the accepted result of grouping, we will feel entitled to use our revenue protection powers. When deciding in any particular case whether to refuse a VAT group application, or to expel a company from a VAT group, we will bear in mind the decision in *National Westminster Bank*. Paragraph 74 of that decision says:

> "the phrase 'necessary for the protection of the revenue' must be considered as a totality and involves a balancing exercise in which the Commissioners must weigh the effect on the Appellant of refusal of grouping against the loss of revenue likely to result from grouping".

WEIGHING THE LIKELY REVENUE LOSS AGAINST THE ADMINISTRATIVE COST OF USING OUR POWERS

When considering whether or not to use our revenue protection powers, we will aim to follow this approach. If we have concerns that the revenue loss does go beyond the accepted consequence of VAT grouping, we will ask for relevant information about the administrative savings that grouping brings in the particular circumstances, and an estimate of the revenue impact of grouping. We will normally ask you to comment on the impact on your business of any refusal or removal on our part. For example, you may incur extra costs in having to submit an extra VAT return, or in having to account for VAT on supplies between group members. The extent of these costs will depend on how your accounting systems are set up.

We will weigh any likely abnormal revenue loss against the administrative cost to you of our refusal or removal. When that revenue cost significantly outweighs the administrative cost we will consider invoking our powers.

DECISIONS AND APPEALS

We will make a judgement based on the information that you provide, and any other information that we have. If you fail to provide the information that we ask for, we will endeavour to come to a balanced decision based on the information that we already have to hand. But if you consistently fail to provide information or records which we might reasonably request in the course of our enquiries, that may be treated as sufficient grounds for exercising our revenue protection powers.

Any decision on whether to exercise our revenue protection powers will take into account the scheme of VAT as a whole. Our internal guidance will make it clear to local VAT assurance officers in what circumstances they must have headquarters' agreement before using the revenue protection powers.

If we invoke our revenue protection powers, we will write to you explaining why. If you disagree with our view, you can appeal to the VAT & Duties Tribunal who can rule on whether our decision was reasonable in the circumstances.

[VATA 1994 s 43B]

7 SEPTEMBER 1999. BUSINESS BRIEF 20/99
INTRASTAT: RECOGNITION BY H M CUSTOMS AND EXCISE OF PARTICULAR PROBLEMS WITH THE TIMELINES OF SUPPLEMENTARY DECLARATIONS FOR ARRIVALS

The majority of businesses have no difficulty in submitting their dispatches supplementary declarations (SDs) to arrive with Customs by the due date (ten working days after the end of the reference period). However, the submission of timely arrivals SDs has often caused problems because the information required to complete the SDs is not always available in time.

Recent dialogue between the Customs' Intrastat Penalty Regime and a number of businesses has resulted in an agreed joint statement being produced by Customs and the Joint Customs Consultative Committee (JCCC) recognising the problems which can cause difficulty with the timeliness of arrivals SDs.

The text of the agreement is as follows:

> "Where a company furnishes some of its Arrivals data late and where the TSO is satisfied, taking into account the company's representations and the views of local HMC&E staff that:
>
> - the company has made every effort to capture and supply data on time
> - supplementary declarations are normally made on time

- the bulk of the data for a particular period has been furnished but it is nevertheless inevitable that some data cannot be provided on time for reasons which can include data capture systems already in place
- additional data is provided in the normal way as soon as it becomes possible

then

TSO will not pursue enforcement action in respect of the lateness of the additional data so long as there has been no significant distortion of the overall statistics. TSO will always provide notification where penalty action is contemplated."

Customs recognises that problems exist with arrivals data and, provided that a company is normally compliant and makes every effort to capture and submit data as soon as possible, we will adopt a reasonable approach to such difficulties.

If you would like any further information about this please Email us on <tmb.tso.hmce@gtnet.gov.uk>.

17 NOVEMBER 1999. BUSINESS BRIEF 23/99 VAT APPEALS

BACKGROUND

This Business Brief sets out Customs' position on applications for "strike out" and dismissal of appeals following the Tribunal's decision in *Coleman* (No 15906). Customs can apply for an appeal not to proceed to a full hearing (a "strike out" or dismissal) if certain conditions have not been met by the appellants. *Coleman* was the lead case in an applications hearing involving four appellants which looked at these conditions.

. . .

CUSTOMS' POSITION

Customs have decided not to appeal against the Tribunal's decision. Customs are considering whether to suggest an amendment to the pre-conditions which caused the Tribunal concern. In the meantime Customs will not apply for appeals to be struck out solely because returns and payments are outstanding for VAT periods not under dispute. However, Customs will continue to make applications for strike out or dismissal in appropriate cases where a return has not been rendered for a VAT period subject to a disputed assessment, or where the tax in dispute has not been paid . . .

[VATA 1994 s 84]

21 DECEMBER 1999. BUSINESS BRIEF 27/99 VAT: ADMINISTRATION FEES IN CONNECTION WITH CREDIT DEALS

Customs recently lost a tribunal case [see *Wagon Finance Ltd* (No 16288)] on the liability of administration fees in connected credit transactions (eg hire purchase and conditional sale). Having taken further advice, Customs have decided not to appeal against this decision. Such administration fees are therefore exempt from VAT.

. . .

Traders may submit voluntary disclosures for fees incorrectly treated as taxable, subject of course to the normal rules on capping and unjust enrichment. However, one of the arguments put to the Tribunal was that the trader did little work in connection with the taxable supply of the goods. All their work was in relation to the exempt supply of credit. It follows from this that, apart from the costs of the goods themselves, there may be little or no cost in making the taxable supply. Claimants, other than those operating Partial Exemption (PE) methods based on the Finance and Leasing Association (FLA) agreement (which provides for flat rate recovery of 15% of residual input tax allocated to instalment credit finance activities) will almost certainly have to recalculate their deductible input tax by reference to their PE method.

Customs and the FLA are currently in discussion on the agreed 15% method. The outcome of these discussions will be published as soon as possible.

[VATA 1994 Sch 9 Group 5 Item 3]

21 DECEMBER 1999. BUSINESS BRIEF 27/99
TOUR OPERATORS' MARGIN SCHEME (TOMS) AND THE VAT EXEMPTION FOR TEACHING ENGLISH AS A FOREIGN LANGUAGE (EFL)

. . .

Business Brief 18/99 [18 August 1999] explained that, as a result of *Pilgrims Language Courses Ltd v C & E Comrs* [1999] STC 874, CA, Customs accepted that all elements integral to, or closely related to, the supply of a course in the teaching of EFL, held out for sale as such by a commercial provider, were covered by the exemption for the teaching itself. The implications of the judgment for the TOMS were not at that stage clear.

Customs now accept that supplies made by EFL providers which fall within the education exemption are not within the TOMS. This applies whether EFL providers are making supplies from their own resources, or by buying and selling packages of tuition and other services. TOMS does not therefore apply to bought-in services such as transport, catering, accommodation or excursions where these are integral to, or closely related to, a supply of exempt EFL tuition.

This ruling is retrospective, subject to the normal capping and unjust enrichment provisions.

[VATA 1994 s 53]

21 DECEMBER 1999. BUSINESS BRIEF 27/99
VAT: REDROW GROUP PLC—HOUSE OF LORDS DECISION

This Business Brief explains Customs' interpretation of the House of Lords judgment in *C & E Comrs v Redrow Group plc* [1999] STC 161, HL, and sets out the policy we intend to adopt in cases where the *Redrow* decision is being relied upon . . .

Our view is that the decision only applies where the circumstances are similar to the Redrow case. That is, where there is a claim to input tax credit by a taxable person who has commissioned the goods or services and contracted with the supplier for them. The claim would then be allowed to the extent that the goods or services provided by the supplier on which input tax is incurred are used by the taxable person in making taxable supplies.

Specifically, Customs do not consider that the Redrow decision supports a broad principle of "anyone that pays for a supply is its recipient and can deduct the tax on it" or, alternatively, that "anyone who pays must always be receiving a supply of something in return for the payment". For example, we consider that it has no relevance to circumstances where a third party is simply meeting the costs of another. Neither do we accept that a taxable person must have paid for a supply in order to be entitled to recover the input tax.

Finally, Customs consider that the broad principles and precedent governing input tax deduction are not affected by the *Redrow* decision.

[VATA 1994 s 24]

22 DECEMBER 1999. BUSINESS BRIEF 28/99
REVISED VAT ARRANGEMENTS FOR THE LLOYD'S MARKET

This Business Brief explains Customs and Excise's revised policy on the VAT arrangements for the Lloyd's insurance market affecting Lloyd's names, syndicates, managing agents and member's agents.

The current Lloyd's VAT arrangements have, since 1985, embraced the major aspects of VAT within the Lloyd's insurance market. Significant changes have occurred in the market over the past few years. Therefore Customs, in conjunction with Lloyd's, have reviewed the arrangements. In addition, recent rulings in the VAT Tribunal and the European Court of Justice have resulted in a requirement for Customs to review the registration position of syndicates. This has taken place alongside a review of the VAT procedures. A joint meeting with Lloyd's was held in July 1999 at which the new arrangements were described to the Lloyd's market.

REGISTRATION

With effect from 1 January 2000 Lloyd's syndicates underwriting in the 2000 year of account with a requirement to be registered for VAT, or those who choose to be registered voluntarily, must do so in their own right. They can no longer conduct their VAT affairs through the VAT registration of their managing agent. Syndicates should apply for VAT registration on Form VAT1 available from The Insurance Helpdesk, Thomas Paine House, Angel Square, Torrens Street, London EC1V 1TA.

PARTIAL EXEMPTION

The review of the Lloyd's partial exemption method has resulted in the withdrawal of the central arrangements with effect from 1 January 2000. The old central arrangement is replaced with a framework document which details the minimum requirements of any Lloyd's partial exemption method. All Lloyd's VAT registrations, for example syndicates, managing agents etc will need to negotiate new partial exemption methods that reflect their individual circumstances with their local VAT office, in line with the new framework.

MEMBERS AGENTS

The services provided by Members Agents to Lloyd's names are not regarded as falling within Item 4 of Group 2 to Schedule 9 of the VAT Act 1994. The services are therefore standard-rated for VAT. Although these supplies have been properly standard-rated since 1997, we have agreed as part of the implementation of the new Lloyd's VAT arrangements not to demand VAT in respect of supplies where the tax point is before 1 January 2001. Subject to the normal rules some supplies to members outside the UK may be outside the scope of VAT with input tax recovery.

FURTHER ADVICE

Registration forms and copies of the partial exemption framework are available from the Insurance Helpdesk, Thomas Paine House, Angel Square, Torrens Street, London EC1V 1TA. The telephone number is 0645 742541.

22 DECEMBER 1999. BUSINESS BRIEF 28/99
VAT: TREATMENT OF EC GRANT AID FOR THE PROCESSING OF DRIED FODDER

The purpose of this business brief is to notify a change to the VAT treatment of EC grants paid by the Intervention Board to processors of dried animal fodder.

DETAILS OF CHANGE

Until now the UK has not treated such payments as consideration for supplies by processors, but has regarded them as outside the scope of VAT. However, following an approach by the European Commission, the UK has agreed that these particular payments will be treated as falling within the scope of the tax. This does not involve a change in UK policy in relation to other EC grants.

ACTION FOR DRIED FODDER PROCESSORS

Since supplies of animal fodder are zero-rated no VAT is due on these grants. But processors who supply dried fodder must include the value of grants received in the total value of sales in box 6 of their VAT returns. This also applies to grants received where a business processes the grass of a third party and returns it to them after drying (although Customs understand that this does not happen at present in the UK). However, where the grants relate to fodder for the processors' own use, there is no supply by the processor for VAT purposes, and grants should continue to be treated as outside the scope of VAT. This change will take effect from 1 January 2000.

[VATA 1994 s 5]

22 FEBRUARY 2000. BUSINESS BRIEF 3/2000
IMPORTED WORKS OF ART, ANTIQUES AND COLLECTORS' ITEMS

With the change in the rate of import VAT on works of art, antiques and collectors' items in July 1999, an anti-avoidance measure was introduced to prevent the artificial movement of such items by people seeking to gain a tax advantage from the reduced rate of import VAT. This means that only qualifying imported goods, which have not been exported from the UK in the previous 12 months, are eligible for the 5% effective reduced rate of import VAT.

In practice, however, works of art and similar goods are sent outside the UK for various legitimate commercial reasons, and often return within 12 months. For instance, goods may be sent for exhibition, prior to auction in the UK, or sent on a sale or return basis and returned unsold. The anti-avoidance provision was not intended to disrupt businesses engaged legitimately in such activities and, in many cases, there are specific reliefs which override the "12 month" rule.

GOODS HELD IN TEMPORARY IMPORTATION (TI) ARRANGEMENTS

Goods which are held under a TI regime are not regarded, for VAT purposes, as having been "imported" into the UK. For VAT, goods are not treated as imported until the customs duty debt is incurred (for instance, on removal from TI to home use). Consequently, goods which are removed from TI and sent outside the EU are not considered to have been exported for VAT purposes, and therefore will not be caught by the "12 month" rule. This covers, for example, goods held under TI, intended for sale by auction in the UK, but sent to third countries for exhibition prior to auction.

GOODS NOT HELD IN TI ARRANGEMENTS

For goods sent outside the Member States "on approval", or for goods exported for sale by auction, but which fail to sell and have to be returned to the UK within 12 months, "returned goods relief" may apply. Regulation 125 of the VAT Regulations 1995 allows such goods to be relieved from VAT at importation where they remain the property of the taxable person who exported them. Provided all the conditions of the relief are satisfied such goods qualify for full relief from VAT on importation, and will not be affected by the "12 month" rule.

For goods exported from the UK for repair or restoration work and returned to the UK within 12 months, "outward processing relief" may apply. Regulation 126 of the VAT Regulations

1995 allows the original value of the goods (ie. the value at export) to be relieved from VAT at importation, where they have been sent outside the EU for process or repair and are subsequently returned without a change of ownership. Provided all the conditions of the relief are satisfied such goods will not be affected by the "12 month" rule. However, VAT at the standard rate is due on the price charged for the repair or restoration.

For goods which are exported from the EU, sold, and imported back into the UK within 12 months, there are no VAT reliefs available. Consequently they will normally attract VAT at 17.5% on importation. However, Customs have agreed that, if goods were exported from the UK prior to the introduction of the new rules on 28 July 1999, businesses should not be disadvantaged. Where businesses would not have known about the "12 month" rule at the time of exportation, then, where appropriate, goods will still qualify for import VAT at the 5% rate, following importation into the UK within the 12 month limit.

[VATA 1994 s 21]

17 MARCH 2000. BUSINESS BRIEF 4/2000
VAT: NEW ARRANGEMENTS FOR LEGAL AID WORK

This Business Brief explains the VAT treatment of payments received by solicitors under revised procedures introduced by the Legal Aid Board.

BACKGROUND

On 1 January 2000 the Legal Aid Board introduced new payment arrangements for solicitors undertaking certain types of work for clients eligible for legal aid. This is mainly for the provision of initial legal advice and is governed by the contractual arrangements of the legal aid scheme. Any further legally aided work for the same client remains subject to existing Legal Aid Board billing and payment procedures.

ACTION FOR SOLICITORS

Under the new arrangements, solicitors will receive regular monthly payments based on their anticipated level of legal aid work over the coming year. Customs anticipate that these payments will generally be received in advance of a supply being made to the client. On this basis, the date payment is received will be regarded as the tax point. VAT on the full amount received will therefore be due at that time, unless the solicitor can demonstrate that an element of the payment will not be subject to VAT, for example, because it includes non-taxable disbursements. Solicitors accounting for VAT on the full amount at the time of receipt who subsequently find that an element was not taxable, may adjust the amount of VAT previously accounted for accordingly.

[VATA 1994 s 6]

17 MARCH 2000. BUSINESS BRIEF 4/2000
VAT AND CEMETERIES

This Business Brief explains Customs' position following the Tribunal decision in *Rhonnda Cynon Taff County Borough Council* [No 16496].

. . .

NEW POSITION

Customs has concluded that the decision only applies to the provision and maintenance of local authority operated cemeteries. This includes the grant of a right to an exclusive burial, the right to place and maintain a tombstone, the keeping and storage of the plans and records of burials, general maintenance, and any actions intended to remove dangerous obstructions, eg collapsed vaults or broken headstones.

Local authority cemeteries may also offer further services, such as the provision of books of remembrance and the erection of headstones for which a charge is made. As the provision of these services is not covered by the special legal regime applicable to cemeteries, they remain business activities of the local authority.

CREMATORIA

Some local authorities also provide crematoria. While crematoria are governed by special legal provisions, similar to those which apply to cemeteries, the higher incidence of privately owned crematoria means that a distortion of competition would result if local authorities were allowed to treat these activities as non-business. Where local authorities operate sites which contain both cemeteries and crematoria and they have exceeded the partial exemption de minimis limits, a business/non-business apportionment will have be made between the activities.

[VATA 1994 s 94]

11 APRIL 2000. BUSINESS BRIEF 6/2000 DEBT ENFORCEMENT SERVICES PROVIDED BY UNDER SHERIFFS AND SHERIFFS' OFFICERS

This Business Brief explains changes with effect from 1 April 2000 to the VAT treatment of services provided by Under Sheriffs and Sheriffs' Officers in enforcing judgement debts.

BACKGROUND

Customs previously regarded services provided by Under Sheriffs and Sheriffs' Officers in enforcing High Court judgement debts and those of the county court transferred to the High Court for enforcement as supplies to the High Sheriffs. As the High Sheriffs are not in business for VAT purposes, the tax on these services was not recoverable by them.

NEW VAT TREATMENT

Following an approach by the Under Sheriffs Association, and with the agreement of the Sheriffs' Officers' Association, Customs are now prepared to treat these debt enforcement services as supplies by Under Sheriffs to creditors. This means that, from 1 April 2000, where such creditors are registered for VAT, they will be able to recover tax charged by Under Sheriffs and Sheriffs' Officers, subject to the normal rules.

Therefore, while Under Sheriffs and Sheriffs' Officers may collect fees for their enforcement services from debtors, they should issue VAT invoices only to creditors in all cases. Any documents issued to debtors should make it clear that they are not VAT invoices.

[VATA 1994 s 24]

18 MAY 2000. BUSINESS BRIEF 7/2000 APPROVED ALTERATIONS TO PROTECTED BUILDINGS

This Business Brief sets out Customs' policy on the issue of whether or not mains electrical wiring and lighting systems are part of the fabric of a protected building.

. . .

CUSTOMS' NEW POLICY

Customs have changed their policy and now accept that mains electrical wiring and lighting systems are part of the fabric of a building when determining whether work qualifies for zero-rating. However, only mains electrical wiring and lighting systems that are either on, or in, the structure of the building itself will be considered to be part of the fabric of the building. Those parts of systems that extend beyond the structure of a building into its grounds will not, such as wiring to floodlights located in the grounds of churches. Electrical appliances that are attached to and serviced by the mains supply are not considered to be part of the mains wiring system.

The change of policy means that works to existing mains electrical wiring and lighting systems can now be considered for relief in the same way as works to, say, a wall. . . .

Customs continue to maintain that zero-rating is not available for works to the fabric of a building that are:

— works of repair or maintenance;
— or incidental alterations which result from the carrying out of works of repair or maintenance;-or alterations where the de minimis rule is applicable.

The fact that work is a one-off, large or exceptional item of expenditure does not change the inherent character of the work and is not relevant when determining whether it qualifies for zero-rating as an approved alteration. This approach is consistent with the Court of Appeal's judgement in *C & E Comrs v Sutton Housing Trust* [1984] STC 352, CA.

[VATA 1994 Sch 8 Group 6 Item 2]

18 MAY 2000. BUSINESS BRIEF 7/2000
SUPPLIES OF SOFT LANDSCAPING

This Business Brief sets out Customs' policy on the extent to which supplies of soft landscaping may be zero-rated following the Tribunal's decision in *Rialto Homes plc* (No 16340).

. . . .

CUSTOMS' NEW POLICY

Customs now accept that, as well as turfing, it is possible for other types of planting carried out as part of a soft landscaping scheme to be zero-rated as a supply made in the course of the construction. Where applicable, zero-rating will apply to both the labour element and the plants supplied with those services by the contractor.

For planting supplies to be made in the course of the construction the following conditions must be met.

1. There must be a temporal link between the work and the construction of the building. This means that the work must be carried out at the same time as, or immediately after the construction of the building.

2. The landscaping work must be connected with the construction of the building in that it produces in its result a "whole with it". This concept comes from the High Court judgement in St. Mary's RC School where the Court thought the issue was a matter of degree. For reasons of administrative ease, Customs will accept that all planting carried out within the plot of a house will meet this condition to the extent that it is detailed on a landscaping scheme approved by a planning authority under the terms of a planning consent condition. Work carried out outside the plot of a specific house will not meet this condition.

Customs continue to maintain that the following are examples of soft landscaping supplies which do not meet the conditions and remain standard-rated.

— Screening planted along road-side verges.
— Work within the plot of a specific house that is not on a landscaping scheme approved by a planning authority under the terms of a planning consent condition.
— Work performed after completion of the construction such as the replacement of trees and shrubs which die, or become damaged or diseased.

The above principles will also apply to planting made within the sites of buildings intended for use solely for a relevant residential or relevant charitable purpose.

. . . .

[VATA 1994 Sch 8 Group 5 Item 2]

23 MAY 2000. PRESS NOTICE 21/2000
GET AN EXTRA WEEK TO PAY YOUR VAT

1. For VAT returns with a due date on or after 31 May 2000 use of electronic means of payment will be made simpler. Qualifying businesses will automatically receive the seven calendar day extension for the submission and payment of VAT returns, on a return by return basis. Businesses will no longer have to request this concession and, as the extension will be applied automatically, they will not be advised whether or not they have been given it.

2. The small number of businesses in the Payment on Account and Annual Accounting schemes cannot use this concession. Virtually all businesses in the Payment on Account scheme pay VAT electronically, and those in the Annual Accounting Scheme already get extra time to pay their VAT.

3. The automatic application of the concession on a return-by-return basis gives businesses the freedom to change payment methods without having to notify Customs. However if a business changes back to paying by cheque it will not have the extra week to make that payment.

4. If the VAT return and electronic payment are not received on or before the seventh calendar day following the normal due date, businesses may be liable to default surcharge, the penalty regime for late payment.

5. Any VAT liabilities can be paid by an electronic method; however, the 7 extra calendar days apply only to VAT return payments and not to other VAT payments such as assessments or underdeclarations.

[SI 1995/2518 regs 25, 40]

28 SEPTEMBER 2000. BUSINESS BRIEF 13/2000
BLOODSTOCK—SALE OF ADDITIONAL NOMINATIONS BY STALLION SYNDICATES

This business brief explains changes to the VAT treatment of additional nominations sold by stallion syndicates. The changes will take effect from 1 November 2000.

BACKGROUND

When a colt is to become a stallion standing at stud, it is often syndicated, usually into 40 shares. Each share entitles its owner to one nomination. This lets the owner nominate one mare to be covered by the stallion each breeding season. Each syndicate appoints a secretary, usually a bloodstock agency or a firm of solicitors, to deal with its financial and practical arrangements.

Until recently any additional nominations over and above the initial 40 have been sold through the secretary and the income has been distributed to the members. As the sums involved were low and likely to be below the VAT registration threshold, Customs accepted that these supplies could be treated as not subject to VAT. However, as stallions are now managing up to 100 coverings in a season, this VAT treatment is no longer appropriate.

NEW VAT TREATMENT

From 1 November 2000 the sale of additional stallion nominations will be treated as supplies in the course of business by the syndicates, which will render them liable to VAT registration.

However, the bloodstock industry has said that the syndicates do not wish to be registered as partnerships. Customs are therefore prepared to treat syndicate secretaries as agents acting in their own names, but on behalf of the syndicates.

The accounting arrangements which follow have been discussed and agreed with the British Horseracing Board.

Secretaries will raise an invoice in their own name when the supply of an additional nomination is made. Where a secretary's turnover exceeds or is expected to exceed the current VAT registration threshold, the invoice should bear the secretary's own VAT registration number. It should be for the full value of the nomination plus VAT.

When secretaries pass money on to the syndicate members, the members will raise an invoice to the secretary for their share. This will be an invoice bearing the appropriate VAT if the member is registered. Any VAT charged may be treated as input VAT by the secretary.

Any money passed to members will count towards the calculation of their taxable turnover for VAT registration purposes.

The tax point for the supply by the member to the secretary will be the same as that of the supply by the secretary to the purchaser of the nomination.

The stud farm will raise a VAT invoice to the secretary for the keep of the stallion and the secretary will raise a VAT invoice to the stud for the nominations given in return for the keep.

Any input tax incurred by the secretary on behalf of the syndicate may be recovered by the secretary. The secretary will pass these charges on in full to the members of the syndicate and raise a VAT invoice charging output tax on the onward supply.

Where a syndicate does not wish to use these arrangements, it will be required to register for VAT in its own right if its turnover exceeds or is expected to exceed the current VAT registration threshold.

[VATA 1994 s 94]

10 JANUARY 2001. BUSINESS BRIEF 1/2001
VAT GROUPS—PROTECTION OF THE REVENUE

This business brief is a follow up to Business Brief 15/99 [12 July 1999] and announces Customs' intention to use its revenue protection powers in relation to VAT grouping.

We are aware that some businesses have adopted structures that enable them to include a supplier and a customer from different organisations in a single VAT group. Typically this is achieved by ensuring that the holding/subsidiary company relationship necessary for VAT grouping is in place between supplier and customer, even though the supplier is in reality run by and for the benefit of an independent third party and that third party provides almost all the investment in the supplier. By adopting these structures, partly exempt customers are able to obtain goods or services without incurring irrecoverable input tax.

We consider that such contrived structures result in revenue loss that goes beyond the normal consequences of grouping since—

- they distort the VAT grouping rules, which aim to put a group into the same VAT position as a single company and a single company would not normally have a division which was financed and run by outsiders, for their benefit;
- they introduce distortions of competition between third party service providers who are independent and those who join one of these contrived VAT group structures;
- similarly they give unfair advantages to partly exempt customers in these group structures, particularly over smaller competitors and new entrants to the market;
- they often require special arrangements to ensure that the supplying company reports its VAT figures through the VAT group (normally it would be included in

the third party organisation and accounting systems). This is contrary to the rationale for grouping, which is to reduce burdens for business, not relieve tax.

In accordance with the procedures outlined in Business Brief 15/99, Customs will be writing to companies who appear to be involved in contrived structures to seek further information about the structure and the transactions between the group members, with the aim of deciding whether relevant suppliers should be removed from the VAT group on revenue protection grounds. Similar procedures will be adopted for any application from a supplier to join a VAT group, where membership is dependent on the use of a contrived structure, with the aim of deciding whether the application should be rejected on the grounds of revenue protection.

[VATA 1994 s 43B]

15 FEBRUARY 2001. BUSINESS BRIEF 2/2001
EUROPEAN COURT RULING CLARIFIES WHETHER TRANSACTIONS ARE SINGLE OR MULTIPLE SUPPLIES FOR VAT

This business brief sets out Customs' policy as to whether a transaction consists of a single composite supply or two or more independent supplies for VAT purposes. This follows the judgments of the European Court (ECJ) and (on 31 January 2001) the House of Lords in the case of *Card Protection Plan* [[1999] STC 270, ECJ, [2001] STC 174, HL], as to whether a transaction consists of a single composite supply or two or more independent supplies.

While indicating that, having regard to the diversity of commercial operations, it is not possible to give exhaustive guidance on how to approach the problem correctly in all cases, the ECJ did lay down a number of tests to be applied.

THE ECJ TESTS

As its starting point, the ECJ relies on its earlier judgment in *Faaborg-Gelting Linien* [[1996] STC 774], where it held that, where the transaction in question comprises a bundle of features and acts, regard must first be had to all the circumstances in which that transaction takes place.

At the same time, two fundamental principles must be taken into account. Every supply must be regarded as distinct and independent, and a supply which comprises a single supply from an economic point of view should not be artificially split, so as to distort the functioning of the VAT system. With all this in mind, the essential features of the transaction must be ascertained in order to determine whether the customer, being a typical customer, is being provided with several distinct principal supplies or with a single supply.

The Court goes on to say that there is a single supply in particular where one or more elements are to be regarded as constituting the principal service, while one or more elements, by contrast, are to be regarded as ancillary services which share the tax treatment of the principal service. It indicates that a service must be regarded as ancillary to a principal service if it does not constitute for customers an aim in itself, but a means of better enjoying the principal service.

The charging of a single price is not decisive. A service provided to customers that consists of several elements for a single price may suggest there is a single service. But if the circumstances of the transaction indicate that customers intended to purchase two distinct services to which two different tax liabilities apply then the single price would need to be apportioned.

Customs consider that the tests laid down by the Court will be appropriate in the great majority of cases, and will apply to transactions, whether the individual elements are of goods or services or a combination of both. Customs also consider that (as held in the House of Lords *British Telecommunications plc* case [[1999] STC 758]) no single factor will provide the sole test, and therefore the ECJ tests should be applied as a package.

Customs believe that applying the ECJ tests may produce a different result from the outcome of some earlier UK litigation cases. Where traders have previously relied on earlier UK litigation (or on rulings, trade agreements or statements of practice based on that litigation) to determine whether they are making a single composite supply or two or more independent supplies, they should, by 1 June 2001, apply the ECJ tests to determine whether there is a single supply or multiple supplies.

This advance notification of the need to apply the ECJ tests is to allow these traders time to review the position and to make any changes to their accounting systems. (Traders who have not previously relied on some earlier litigation to determine whether there is a single or multiple supply should currently be applying the ECJ tests.)

Where a trader has previously relied on the outcome of previous UK litigation (or on a ruling, trade agreement or statement of practice based on that litigation) and the application of the ECJ tests would have given a different result, Customs will not require the ECJ tests to be applied to supplies made before 1 June 2001. However Customs reserve the right to review past periods in any case where the relevant supplies are considered to have formed part of a tax avoidance arrangement.

Where application of the ECJ tests would lead to a reduction in VAT payable, traders can of course choose to apply those tests in previous periods but repayment of any VAT claimed will be subject to the three-year cap on repayments and to the unjust enrichment rules.

Proposed Concession

[For the extra-statutory concession currently in force, see Notice No 48 (March 2002) para 3.35.]

[VATA 1994 s. 19]

20 FEBRUARY 2001. BUSINESS BRIEF 3/2001
VAT POSITION OF LIMITED LIABILITY PARTNERSHIPS

This business brief is to help businesses who are considering forming limited liability partnerships (LLPs) and outlines Customs' views on the VAT position of such partnerships. The contents of this business brief have been agreed with the Association of Partnership Practitioners and other interested parties.

WHAT IS A LIMITED LIABILITY PARTNERSHIP?

The Limited Liability Partnership Act 2000 received Royal Assent on 20 July 2000. LLPs can be formed with effect from 6 April 2001.

An LLP will have a legal status distinct from its members, and will be able to enter into contracts in its own right. This means that individual members of the LLP will be protected from debts or liabilities arising from negligence, wrongful acts or misconduct of another member, employee or agent of the LLP.

LIMITED LIABILITY PARTNERSHIPS AND VAT

The members of the LLP must prepare an incorporation document for the Registrar of Companies who, on acceptance, will issue a certificate of incorporation. This means that the LLP will be a corporate body, and that it, rather than the members, will be the legal entity for VAT purposes. The LLP itself then becomes liable for VAT registration, subject to the normal registration rules.

As with unlimited partnerships this does not normally mean that the members will be seen as supplying their services to the LLPs and they therefore will not normally have to register for VAT.

VAT LIABILITY IF AN EXISTING PARTNERSHIP CHANGES TO A LIMITED LIABILITY PARTNERSHIP

As the legal entity has changed from that of a partnership to a corporate body, the LLP may have to apply for VAT registration, subject to the normal rules. The normal transfer of a going concern rules will then also apply, including those relating to any option to tax. If the general partnership ceases to exist, it may be possible for the VAT number to be transferred to the LLP (Notice 700/9, "Transfer of a going concern", gives full details).

MEMBERSHIP OF A VAT GROUP

An LLP will be able to join a VAT group provided it meets the control conditions in VATA 1994 s 43A. This section allows two or more corporate bodies to apply for VAT grouping if each is established or has a fixed establishment in the UK and one of them controls the others; or one person controls all of them; or two or more individuals carrying on a business in partnership control all of them.

A corporate body is "controlled" by its "holding company". Individuals can fulfil the definition of a "holding company" without actually being a corporate body themselves. So, for VAT grouping purposes, individuals can "control" a corporate body. The terms "control" and "holding company" are defined in the Companies Act 1985 s 736.

Thus, if the LLP fulfils these control conditions with a number of subsidiary companies, it may form a VAT group with them. It is also possible that a group could be formed by two or more eligible companies and an LLP, where those eligible companies are controlling partners in the LLP.

Customs will also see the third of the above control conditions, ie two or more individuals carrying on a business in partnership control all of them, being met when the members of an LLP control all of the corporate bodies to be grouped.

[VATA 1994 ss 43C, 45]

2 JULY 2001. BUSINESS BRIEF 8/2001
OPTING TO TAX BUILDINGS TO BE CONVERTED TO DWELLINGS

This Business Brief is about how Customs and Excise will implement [the decision in *SEH Holdings Ltd v Customs and Excise Comrs* [2000] V & DR 324] on how the option to tax buildings applies to buildings which will be converted into dwellings.

. . . .

AUCTION SALES

Customs are aware that there may be particular problems at auctions because the vendor is not normally aware of the purchaser prior to the auction day. The vendor may have difficulty in finding out what the purchaser intends to do with the building, at the time he has to decide whether to charge VAT or not if he has opted to tax the building. Similarly a purchaser who intends to convert a non-residential property into dwellings, and sell them zero-rated, may also find it difficult to agree with the vendor in writing, prior to the auction date, that the option to tax should still apply to the sale of the building.

Customs are currently reviewing this area of policy and will include the problems of auction sales. In the meantime we suggest that the purchaser should discuss any problem he is facing with the vendor or his representatives prior to the completion date so that they can agree to apply the correct VAT liability.

Customs recognise that in applying the decision strictly, there may be certain circumstances when the VAT charged becomes an additional cost and that this may discourage some developers from converting commercial property into dwellings. Consequently any business, which needs further advice on applying the decision, should contact their Local VAT Office.

[VATA 1994 Sch 10 para 2]

11 SEPTEMBER 2001. BUSINESS BRIEF 12/2001
VAT AND THE RETAIL SALE OF INCONTINENCE PRODUCTS

This Business Brief announces easier arrangements for zero-rating incontinence products purchased through retail outlets by entitled people. The changes take effect from 1 October 2001.

BACKGROUND

People who are incontinent and live in their own homes are entitled to buy incontinence products at the VAT zero rate. A condition of the zero-rating is that retailers obtain a declaration from the purchaser confirming that they are eligible for VAT relief.

Some retailers find it difficult and expensive to adapt systems to meet the needs of customers who are eligible to buy these goods at the VAT zero rate. Equally, many incontinent people are unaware that they are eligible for VAT relief, or are simply reluctant to draw attention to their condition.

Customs, after consultation with manufacturers, retailers and representative bodies, are now introducing easier arrangements in order to improve access to the VAT zero-rate by people who are eligible.

NEW VAT TREATMENT FOR RETAIL SALES FROM 1 OCTOBER 2001

The main change is that eligible incontinence products, for retail sale, may be zero-rated on the shelf. In practice, this means that an incontinent person may purchase incontinence products at any till and receive automatic zero-rating.

There will no longer be a requirement for the customer to provide a written declaration to the retailer confirming they are eligible for VAT relief. Due to the specialist nature of these products, Customs believe that only entitled people are likely to buy them.

INTERNET AND MAIL ORDER SALES

Supplies of eligible incontinence products over the Internet or by mail order also qualify for VAT relief providing they are made to individuals and not institutions.

RESTRICTIONS

Customs will expect retailers, Internet and mail order suppliers to have a signed declaration, or other supporting evidence that the supply is to an incontinent individual and not to an institution such as a nursing home, for customers who buy more than:

- 200 disposable pads, or
- 50 washable pads, or
- 5 collecting devices, or
- 10 pairs of waterproof or leak-proof underwear.

GOODS THAT QUALIFY FOR ZERO RATING ON THE SHELF

Disposable and washable incontinence pads including pads that are incorporated in briefs, underwear designed for use by an incontinent person (ie underwear that is waterproof or leak-proof), and collecting devices.

NURSING HOMES/NATIONAL HEALTH SERVICE

These new measures do not change the VAT liability of incontinence products. Consequently, they do not affect the VAT position of nursing homes, hospitals or the NHS who continue to remain ineligible for VAT relief on the purchase of incontinence products.

. . .

[VATA 1994 Sch 8 Group 12 Note 4(*a*)]

21 DECEMBER 2001. BUSINESS BRIEF 21/2001 VAT AND ADOPTION SERVICES

This Business Brief article sets out a change to Customs' policy on the VAT treatment of home study assessments carried out in connection with inter-country adoption applications.

BACKGROUND

Those wishing to adopt a child from overseas are required to undergo a home study assessment of suitability, carried out by an approved adoption agency or a Local Authority. These assessments have been subject to VAT at the standard rate.

Services in connection with domestic adoption applications are exempt from VAT.

POLICY CHANGE

Customs have decided that there should be equal treatment for VAT of pre-adoption assessment services carried out in connection with domestic and inter-country adoptions. From 1 January 2002 therefore, any charge made by a charitable adoption agency for a home study assessment in connection with an inter- country adoption application will also be exempt from VAT, provided that the assessment is supplied on an "otherwise than for profit" basis.

PRACTICAL IMPLICATIONS

This change in policy should only affect the small number of charitable adoption agencies that are approved to carry out assessments of prospective adopters in respect of inter-country adoptions. There are no other changes to the existing VAT treatment of services in connection with adoption applications.

Services provided by a charitable adoption agency in connection with domestic adoptions remain exempt from VAT, where the supply is made otherwise than for profit. This includes the provision of pre-adoption training, advice and guidance; the assessment of prospective adopters; as well as the actual placement of a child.

Services provided by a Local Authority in connection with adoption remain non-business activities. They are not subject to VAT when carried out as part of the Local Authority's statutory responsibility.

All supplies in connection with any adoption that are not made either by a charity on a not for profit basis or by a Local Authority remain standard-rated.

[VATA 1994 Sch 9 Group 7 Note 6]

12 FEBRUARY 2002. BUSINESS BRIEF 3/2002 SINGLE AND MULTIPLE SUPPLIES: SALE OF SPECTACLES AND CONTACT LENSES

Business Brief 2/2001 set out Customs' policy as to whether a transaction consists of a single supply or two or more independent supplies for VAT purposes. The policy, which followed judgements of the European Court and House of Lords in the case of Card Protection Plan, has since been confirmed in a number of cases in the courts and VAT tribunal.

This Business Brief provides further clarification of Customs policy in this area, following the decision of the VAT Tribunal in the cases of *Southport Vision Plus* (No 17502) and *Leightons Ltd and Eye-Tech Ltd* (No 17498). These cases concerned the sale of spectacles and contact lenses by dispensing opticians. The Tribunal found in favour of the appellants that this should be regarded as two separate supplies—one of standard-rated goods and the other of exempt dispensing services. The supply of dispensed spectacles and contact lenses therefore continues to be treated in the same way as since 1995. The sight test and supplies of dispensing services independent of the supply of spectacles or contact lenses continue to be exempt. The treatment of dispensed hearing aids, which is similar to that of dispensed spectacles and contact lenses, also remains unchanged.

Customs and Excise are not appealing this ruling. However, we wish to clarify our views on two aspects of the Tribunal's reasoning.

THE PROPORTION OF COST

The Tribunal took into account the existing agreement between Customs and opticians that dispensing services are a relatively high percentage of the total price of dispensed spectacles and contact lenses. *Card Protection Plan* established the principle that a single price is not a decisive indicator that there is a single supply. In the light of the Tribunal decision, Customs accept that if a distinct service element represents 50% or more of the price of a bundle of goods and services, it will be a strong indicator that this service is not ancillary to a principal supply of any other goods or services in that bundle and that the consideration may need to be apportioned accordingly.

However, Customs also believe that this should not be allowed to open scope for avoidance. It will therefore not accept such an argument where it believes that there has been manipulation of values. It will continue to challenge the apportionment and any attempt to use manipulated values in a way that might distort a decision about whether a transaction is a single supply or multiple supplies.

ANCILLARY ELEMENTS

One of the tests established in *Card Protection Plan* is that a service should be regarded as ancillary to a principal supply if it does not constitute an aim in itself but a means of better enjoying the principal service supplied. In the opticians cases, the Tribunal concluded that the dispensing service cannot be regarded as a means of "better enjoying" the optical appliance, which, in the Tribunal's view, could not be enjoyed at all without the dispensing service.

If taken too widely, that line of reasoning would imply that a service would only be regarded as ancillary where it was, in effect, an optional part of the package. Customs continue to believe that the primary test remains what the customer thinks they are buying. A service can be regarded as an ancillary part of a single supply even where it is a compulsory part of the transaction.

[VATA 1994 s 19]

20 AUGUST 2002. BUSINESS BRIEF 23/2002
VAT: ATTRIBUTION OF INPUT TAX INCURRED ON PROFESSIONAL SERVICES WHEN A COMPANY ACQUIRES SHARES IN ANOTHER COMPANY IN EXCHANGE FOR SHARES IN ITSELF

BACKGROUND

This Business Brief article sets out Custom's policy following the decision in *Southampton Leisure Holdings plc* (No 17716).

The appeal was concerned with the attribution of input tax incurred on certain professional services by the business, when it issued shares to the shareholders of Southampton Football Club Limited in exchange for their shares. Customs' view was that the services were used exclusively for the purposes of an exempt issue of shares, whereas the taxpayer's view was that the services were used in making both taxable and exempt supplies.

TRIBUNAL'S DECISION

The tribunal partly allowed the appeal. Whilst it supported Customs' view that the services relating to the public relations exercise was exclusively related to the issue of shares, the tribunal found that supplies of services, which included certain tasks namely:

- acting as financial advisor,
- the drafting of service contracts for the directors,
- the due diligence review of the target company's affairs,
- the investigation of title and/or the valuation of that company's property, and
- coordinating the transaction,

were not used exclusively in making the exempt supply of the issue of shares. As a result, the tax incurred on those supplies should be treated as residual input tax.

Customs have decided not to appeal the tribunal's decision.

IMPLICATIONS

Customs now accept that any taxed supplies of professional services, which include any of the above tasks in the circumstances of a merger and acquisition or management buy-out, has to some extent a direct and immediate link with the whole of the taxpayer's business. The tax incurred is residual input tax and is attributable to taxable supplies by reference to that person's partial exemption method. However, where a taxed supply of professional services is partly used in making an issue of shares to a person belonging outside the European Union, then the deductible proportion of tax is to be determined on a "use" basis under VAT Regulations 1995, SI 1995/2518 reg 103(2).

WHAT THE DECISION DOES NOT AFFECT

Customs take the view that the decision has no application where shares are issued for subscription. For example, an initial public offer or rights issue. In these instances, the taxed professional services relating to the offer are used exclusively for the purposes of the exempt supply of an issue of shares. But Customs do accept that any services providing general advice on the means of capital raising (provided it is just that) is part of the business' overheads and that the tax incurred on any such services should be treated as residual input tax. In most offers the decision to issue shares is taken at the outset and the question of any general advice simply does not arise.

CLAIMS

Customs will, subject to the normal capping rules, accept claims for overpaid tax. This will largely arise where a business, in the course of a merger or acquisition or management buy-out activity, has wholly attributed to exempt supplies and so treated as irrecoverable an amount of input tax incurred on a supply of professional services, but which following the tribunal's approach in *Southampton Leisure* ought to have been attributed to both taxable and exempt supplies. The amount of overpaid tax being the deductible proportion of (what is now accepted to be) residual input tax.

[SI 1995/2518 reg 103]

19 NOVEMBER 2002. BUSINESS BRIEF 30/2002
VAT: POLICY STATEMENT ON THE TREATMENT OF APPLICATIONS TO LEAVE A VAT GROUP

This Business Brief is issued as a result of recent representations to Customs following the Court of Appeal decision in the case of *Customs and Excise v Barclays Bank PLC* [2001] EWCA Civ 1513, [2001] STC 1558. This article clarifies how Customs and Excise intend to deal with applications for a company to leave a VAT group.

The Court of Appeal ruled in October 2001 that Customs were not obliged to exclude a company from a VAT group as soon as the company ceased to be controlled by the group holding company. As a result of this ruling, Customs were able to prevent the company leaving the VAT group before FA 1995 s 25 came into effect on 1 March 1995. The Finance Act 1995 introduced an "exit charge" for companies leaving a VAT group in certain circumstances and would have applied in this case, increasing the amount of VAT due from Barclays.

Businesses and tax advisers are concerned that keeping a company in a VAT group after the company has been sold to a third party may cause commercial difficulties. In practice, it would be rare for Customs to set a later date for cases. Normally Customs policy will be to agree the date requested by the selling group. Customs will set a later date only if VAT avoidance is involved or is likely to arise through obtaining an earlier date.

Applications to leave a VAT group should continue to be made to Customs in the normal way as set out in Notice No 700/2, indicating the date that the company wishes to leave the VAT group.

[VATA 1994 s 43B]

19 NOVEMBER 2002. BUSINESS BRIEF 30/2002
VAT: VAT GROUPS—PROTECTION OF THE REVENUE

This article provides businesses with further guidance about VAT grouping structures. Customs will not use their revenue protection powers to challenge acceptable grouping structures.

VAT GROUPING RULES

The VAT grouping rules are a business facilitation measure. They allow members of a VAT group to disregard, for VAT purposes, any supplies between group members, with only one VAT return then being required for the whole VAT group. As a result, a company which decides to set up subsidiaries to carry on parts of its business will be treated for VAT purposes in the same way as if it had decided to carry on the business through branches of a single company.

Two companies can join a VAT group provided both are established (or have a fixed establishment) in the UK and both meet the control criteria, ie one of them controls the other, or they are both controlled by one person, or by two or more individuals carrying on business in a partnership.

Full details of the VAT grouping rules are in Notice No 700/2.

REVENUE PROTECTION POWERS

The VAT grouping legislation gives Customs the power to prevent a company joining a VAT group and to remove an existing member from a VAT group where this is considered necessary for the protection of the revenue. (Business Briefs 15/99 and 1/2001 provide more information about these powers.) One aim of these revenue protection powers is to prevent a company from using contrived structures which seek to extend the benefits of VAT grouping to supplies from what is, in effect, a third party supplier.

One example of a contrived structure which Customs have and will continue to challenge is the so-called A-B share scheme. This involves the setting up of a company where the VAT group holding company (the customer) will have "A" shares and a third party supplier, eg of IT services, will have "B" shares. Typically, while the "A" shares may attract some dividend, the "B" shares will entitle the third party supplier to all or the majority of the profits. The holding company will have the right to appoint the majority of the board of directors of the company, thus meeting the control criteria for eligibility to VAT grouping. The result is contrary to the VAT system and enables partly exempt VAT groups to avoid paying VAT on bought-in services.

ACCEPTABLE GROUPING STRUCTURES

As a general principle, Customs consider that the VAT grouping of two corporate bodies (A and B) is acceptable where A's corporate group either receives or has the ability to control 50% or more of the "economic benefits" of running B's business, provided that the determination of the "economic benefits" is not manipulated to divert benefits to a third party through, for example, high management charges, special dividend payments or other charges, payments or arrangements.

Customs will consider challenging any grouping structure which does not meet this general principle, unless the amount of VAT revenue at stake is nil or too low to justify action.

Examples of normal commercial structures which Customs consider acceptable and therefore would not be challenged are set out below. These are provided for guidance only. In all grouping cases, Customs will apply the principles set out above when determining whether to challenge any particular grouping scheme.

EXAMPLE 1—VAT GROUPING DOES NOT AFFECT THE NET VAT REVENUE TO A SIGNIFICANT EXTENT

A jointly owned supplier S is VAT grouped with one of its owners C, to whom it provides various taxable services. In the absence of VAT grouping, C would be able to recover all or substantially all the VAT it would pay on S's services. Customs would not take action under Business Brief 01/01 because such action would not be necessary for the protection of the revenue. The position would be similar if all of S's services to C were exempt or zero-rated.

EXAMPLE 2—50:50 JOINT VENTURES

JV is jointly owned by companies P and Q, and has issued "A" shares to P and "B" shares to Q. It is VAT grouped with P by the "A" shares giving P a slim majority of the voting rights at general meetings. In reality, P and Q share approximately equally in the investment in JV and receive similar shares of its profits. JV is not a subsidiary of either P or Q for UK group accounts purposes. Customs would normally see such grouping as acceptable subject to the caveat under the general rule above that there were no arrangements for Q to obtain significantly more than 50% of the benefits from running JV's business, eg by levying management charges tailored to remove most of JV's profits.

[VATA 1994 ss 43B, 43C]

20 JANUARY 2003. BUSINESS BRIEF 01/03
VAT: EXEMPTION FOR WELFARE SERVICES PROVIDED BY STATE-REGULATED PRIVATE WELFARE AGENCIES

This Business Brief article outlines a change to the VAT treatment of commercially provided welfare services, which will accompany the implementation of a statutory regime of regulation and registration by health and social services administrations across the UK. It also provides details of a concession that will allow exemption for welfare services from 31 January 2003.

HOME CARE SERVICES—BUSINESS BRIEF 3/2000

In Business Brief 3/2000, [22 February 2000, not reproduced] Customs announced their intention to introduce a VAT concession for home care services, alongside the Department of Trade and Industry's changes to regulations governing the conduct of employment agencies and employment businesses and the rights of work-seekers using them. The concession would have allowed businesses providing home care services to charge VAT only on their commission, and not on that part of their charge relating to the salaries and associated costs of home care workers.

The changes announced below cancel the planned concession, and replace it with a more comprehensive relief, which will allow the whole charge for welfare services (including home care) supplied by domiciliary care and other state-regulated agencies to be exempt from VAT.

NEW VAT TREATMENT

At present, welfare services are only exempt when supplied by public bodies; charities; or establishments, such as residential care homes, that are state-regulated private welfare institutions. The Government will shortly, subject to Parliamentary approval, also exempt from VAT welfare services supplied by state-regulated private welfare agencies.

State-regulated private welfare agencies are those agencies that are registered with and/or regulated by: the National Care Standards Commission; the Scottish Commission for the Regulation of Care; the Care Standards Inspectorate for Wales; or the Northern Ireland Health and Personal Social Services Regulation and Improvement Authority. This may include: domiciliary care agencies; independent fostering agencies; voluntary adoption agencies and nursing agencies. In Scotland, this may also include child care agencies and housing support services.

All welfare services provided by state-regulated private welfare agencies will be exempt. Welfare services are those directly connected with the provision of care, treatment or instruction designed to promote the physical or mental welfare of elderly, sick, distressed or disabled persons; or the care and protection of schildren and young persons.

In the case of commercial domiciliary care agencies, exemption will apply to all care services (including routine domestic tasks) provided to elderly, sick or disabled persons, where the recipient of the service cannot perform the task safely or adequately, or without significant pain or discomfort. Home care services provided by local authorities and charities are already exempt from VAT, and are therefore not affected by these changes. (See News Release 107/02 [30 December 2002, not reproduced]).

In the case of commercial independent fostering agencies and non-charitable voluntary adoption agencies, exemption will apply to any service directly connected with the care and protection of children and young people. This includes the placement of children with foster carers and the assessment of prospective adopters for domestic and inter-country adoption. Any allowances received by an agency for the care of a child will also be exempt from VAT. There will be no change to the liability of services provided by charitable fostering or adoption agencies. Welfare services supplied by these charitable providers are already exempt from VAT.

Care services provided by registered nurses are already exempt from VAT under separate provisions. This change will not therefore alter the VAT treatment of care services provided by agencies providing nursing services.

ARRANGEMENT SERVICES

Some businesses, such as employment agencies, do not provide welfare services themselves, but make arrangements for the provision of welfare services by a third party (such as a self-employed home care provider). The VAT liability of a service of making arrangements for welfare provision is not affected by these changes, and VAT will continue to be chargeable on arrangement and introduction fees or commissions charged by businesses that do not themselves supply welfare services.

TIMING

For those agencies already registered with, and/or regulated by, the appropriate regulatory body, the change will take effect [from 31 January 2003, ie the date when VAT (Health and Welfare) Order 2003 came into force].

For other agencies, statutory exemption will take effect from the first date on which they are registered with, and/or regulated by, the appropriate regulatory body. However, any agency that is not yet registered or regulated, either because the regulations providing for the mechanics of such registration or regulation are not yet in force, or because its application for registration is being processed, may exempt its welfare services from 31 January 2003 under the VAT concession detailed below.

WELFARE SERVICES AND VAT REGISTRATION

We anticipate that as a result of the changes announced in this Business Brief, many VAT registered businesses that are, or will be, required to register with the regulatory body and to implement the relevant care standards, will no longer have to remain VAT registered.

Any state-regulated welfare agency that wishes to remain VAT registered will be required to demonstrate that, in addition to its exempt welfare services, it is also making, or intends to make, taxable supplies.

THE EXTRA STATUTORY CONCESSION—BACKGROUND

The extra statutory concession reproduced below will be available from 31 January 2003. This concession will enable a consistent VAT treatment for welfare services across the UK during the phased introduction of the registration and regulatory regimes to which the exemption is linked.

The concession provides that any welfare provider that is not a state-regulated private welfare agency but will become one once the regulatory register opens, or any business that is in the process of registering with the appropriate regulatory body, may treat the welfare services it provides as exempt from VAT.

This concession will be available only where a business can demonstrate a reasonable expectation that it will be required to register at the appropriate time, and will cease to apply when the business registers with the regulatory body or if its application for registration with that body is refused.

Customs may withdraw or restrict the application of this concession if they have reasonable cause to believe that it is being abused.

Use of this concession is voluntary, and until they register with the appropriate regulatory body, commercial providers of welfare services may choose to continue taxing their supplies. However, once a business registers with the regulatory body, and thereby becomes a state-regulated private welfare agency, all of the welfare services it provides will be exempt.

THE EXTRA STATUTORY CONCESSION—VAT: EXEMPTION FOR SUPPLIES OF WELFARE SERVICES BY PRIVATE WELFARE AGENCIES PENDING REGISTRATION

[For the text of the concession, see Notice No 48 (December 2010) para 3.37, which is reproduced in Appendix 6]

[VATA 1994 Sch 9 Group 7 Item 9]

20 JANUARY 2003. BUSINESS BRIEF 01/03
AMENDMENT TO VAT INFORMATION SHEET 2/00

This Business Brief article highlights an amendment to the evidential requirements for zero-rating the supply of goods to businesses in other EC Member States. The change is effective from 1 January 2003.

The current evidential requirements are contained in Notice No 703 and VAT Information Sheet 2/00.

Customs aim to manage controls over exports and removals from the United Kingdom in a balanced way, seeking to safeguard the revenue while at the same time facilitating trade. To assist this, and work towards the aim of relieving burdens on business, Customs are amending Section 3 of VAT Information Sheet 2/00, concerning "Evidence of Export or Removal". The amendment is in paragraph 3(b) and changes the current sentence from "This information must include the following . . . " to "This information should include the following . . . "

The paragraph will now read, "Information held must provide information identifying the date and route of the movement and the mode of transport involved. The information should include the following . . . ". The items of information are then listed.

From 1 January 2003 businesses only need to obtain sufficient information from the list to prove that the goods have been physically removed from the UK. It will not be necessary to obtain every item on the list.

This clarification should relieve administrative burdens placed upon businesses by reducing the amount of information they will be required to obtain and hold, in order to meet the evidential requirements for supplies to businesses in other Member States.

In accordance with the normal VAT rules in such circumstances the basic requirement is that businesses hold reasonable evidence to corroborate the physical removal of the goods from the United Kingdom, thus enjoying the benefit of zero-rating the supply of the goods.

[VATA 1994 s 30]

28 MARCH 2003. BUSINESS BRIEF 03/03
VAT: THE INTRODUCTION OF VAT ON PRIVATELY OPERATED TOLLS

WHAT HAS HAPPENED?

As announced in news release 108/02, from 1 February 2003 the toll charges payable to use certain bridges, tunnels and roads became subject to 17.5% VAT. This follows a ruling by the European Court of Justice in *EC Commission v United Kingdom* (case C-359/97) [2000] STC 777 that while tolls payable to use bridges operated by public authorities are outside the scope of VAT, other tolls are subject to VAT at the standard rate.

WHAT TYPES OF TOLL CHARGE ARE AFFECTED BY THIS RULING?

Under EC VAT legislation, central and local government bodies are not engaged in a business for VAT purposes when they do something in the capacity of a public authority. Government bodies do this when they act under a legal regime that is only applicable to the public sector, as opposed to legal regimes that can equally apply to the business or voluntary sectors.

The European Court of Justice ruled that, in certain circumstances, central and local government bodies act as public authorities when they operate tolled bridges, tunnels or roads. These tolls therefore remain outside the scope of VAT. Individual tolls included in this category, whose operators have not been individually contacted by Customs about the changes covered by this Business Brief, are as follows:

- Cleddau Bridge
- Dartford Crossing
- Erskine Bridge
- Forth Road Bridge
- Humber Bridge
- Itchen Bridge
- Mersey Tunnel
- Tamar Bridge
- Tay Bridge
- Tyne Tunnel

Where a central or local government body operates a congestion-charging scheme under public statute, these congestion charges are also outside the scope of VAT.

The Court held that in any other circumstances than those described above, a toll charge is consideration for a standard-rated supply.

Customs has therefore written to the operators of regulated tolls affected by this ruling to inform them that, from 1 February 2003, their toll charges are subject to VAT, and alerting them to the arrangements which have been put in place by the Department of Transport and Scottish Executive to manage the impact of these changes.

Any operator in any doubt about the VAT status of their toll charges, or any body which is in the process of introducing a toll or similar charge, is invited to contact the National Advice Service.

HOW DOES THIS AFFECT VAT REGISTERED BUSINESSES USING TOLLED ROADS?

From 1 February 2003, VAT registered businesses will be able to recover the VAT charged on tolls if they are entitled to do so under the normal rules. Businesses are advised to enquire about the VAT status of toll charges when they pay them.

It will not be necessary to obtain a VAT invoice to support any claim for input tax on a toll paid at the toll booth for a single or return journey costing up to £25. Otherwise, it will be necessary to obtain a VAT invoice or other proof or payment as appropriate.

[VATA 1994 Sch 9 Group 1 Item 1]

27 MAY 2003. BUSINESS BRIEF 4/03
VAT: FACE VALUE VOUCHERS—INVOICING

VAT Information Sheet 3/03 gives guidance on the VAT treatment of face value vouchers (such as telephone cards and gift vouchers) following changes introduced in the Budget 2003.

This article gives further clarification on the invoicing arrangements between the issuers of face value vouchers and any intermediate suppliers.

Issuers of face value vouchers, which are not credit vouchers, who redeem them for goods or services will need to issue a full VAT invoice if the vouchers are sold to an intermediate supplier. As the issuer who redeems the voucher does not need to account for VAT until the voucher is redeemed, it is suggested that the invoice is annotated with the following wording, "the issuer of the voucher will account for output tax under the face value voucher provisions in Schedule 10A VAT Act 1994".

Intermediate suppliers of face value vouchers, which are not credit vouchers, must account for VAT on the sale of the vouchers at the time the vouchers are sold. They will need to issue a full VAT invoice to any further intermediate supplier in the supply chain. They will be entitled to reclaim input tax on the purchase of the vouchers, and the evidence for this will be the VAT invoice they receive from their supplier.

Where it is known that the voucher has been redeemed for zero-rated, reduced rated or exempt goods or services, or those outside the scope of VAT, a subsequent adjustment may be made by an intermediate supplier to reflect the liability of those goods or services.

Where the intermediate supplier knows in advance that the voucher can be redeemed for zero-rated, reduced rated or exempt goods or services, or those outside the scope of VAT, the intermediate supplier may use a percentage split from the outset and avoid the need to make later adjustments.

Information regarding any split in liability can only be provided by the issuer who redeems the voucher. In order to avoid the need to track individual vouchers redeemers can base adjustment figures on retail scheme percentages or other overarching calculations, providing the result is fair and reasonable.

If the redeemer chooses to make this information available to intermediate suppliers they may include the percentage split on any VAT invoice they issue to an intermediate supplier. This split should be quoted on any further VAT invoices issued by intermediate suppliers in the supply chain.

[SI 1995/2518 reg 13]

30 JUNE 2003. BUSINESS BRIEF 7/03
VAT: EXEMPTION OF CALL CENTRE SERVICES IN THE INSURANCE SECTOR

Following a recent VAT and Duties Tribunal decision [*TeleTech UK Ltd* (No 18080)], this article explains Customs' revised policy on the VAT treatment of call centre services where the call centre is attempting to sell insurance by cold calling and is able to put the insurer "on risk" at the point of sale.

THE TRIBUNAL DECISION

The appeal involved TeleTech, a company providing call centre and IT support services to a wide range of clients. The decision related to the services supplied to an insurance company. TeleTech cold called people using contact lists provided by the insurer and attempted to sell them health insurance products. The products were very straightforward and the telephone operatives were selected mainly for their expertise in call handling and selling. Only a small percentage of calls led to sales and TeleTech was paid on a flat fee rather than commission basis.

Customs ruled that TeleTech's services fell outside the exemption for insurance related services, arguing that TeleTech's services were principally of an advertising/promotional nature. The Tribunal allowed TeleTech's appeal on the grounds that TeleTech was selling or trying to sell insurance policies as agents. The decisive factor being that, where calls led to sales, TeleTech was able to put the insurer on risk and the customer on cover. The Tribunal Chairman also observed that the manner of remuneration (ie whether by flat fee or commission) had no bearing on the VAT treatment.

REVISED VAT TREATMENT

As a result of this decision, Customs now accept that call centre services, such as those supplied by TeleTech, are VAT exempt insurance related services where the call centre is able to put the insurer on risk at the point of sale without referral back to the insurer.

Due to the unique nature of the insurance exemption, Customs see this decision as applying only to call centre services supplied in connection with insurance. Customs do not see the decision as having any implications for cases concerning the VAT liability of call centre services supplied to other sectors.

[. . .]

[VATA 1994 Sch 9 Group 2 Note 2]

24 JULY 2003. BUSINESS BRIEF 10/03
VAT: CHANGES TO FINANCE EXEMPTIONS

This Business Brief explains changes being made [by VAT (Finance) Order 2003, SI 2003/1568 and VAT (Finance) (No 2) Order 2003, SI 2003/1569] to the finance exemptions [VATA 1994 Sch 9 Group 5]. The changes follow Customs' defeat in the Court of Appeal decision in the case of *C & E Comrs v FDR Ltd* [2000] STC 672, CA, a case concerning credit management, and the Tribunal decisions in the cases of *Prudential Assurance Co Ltd* (No 17030) and *Abbey National plc* (No 17506), concerning the VAT liability of sub-contracted investment management.

It updates Business Briefs 10/2000 [not reproduced] and 10/2001 [not reproduced] in respect of credit management and cancels the first items of Business Brief 06/2001 [not reproduced] in respect of sub-contracted investment management provided to an authorised unit trust.

The new legislation applies to supplies made on or after 1 August 2003. However, taxpayers have had the benefit of the decisions since the dates of the judgments, which were 13 July 2000 for *FDR*, 16 January 2001 for *Prudential* and 19 December 2001 for *Abbey National*.

[. . .]

WHAT CONSTITUTES "MANAGEMENT"?

The operator of an [authorised unit trust] or [trust-based scheme] or the [authorised corporate director] of an [open-ended investment company] has overall responsibility for managing the portfolios of their client. This management service is made up of a variety of elements including: monitoring the performance of the scheme property; making investment decisions; dealing with the paperwork and book-keeping; offering advice on the growth of the portfolio; contracting with dealers to buy and sell assets on behalf of their client. This service is exempt from VAT.

In some cases, this service is contracted out to a third party or a sub-fund manager. Where the whole management function is delegated, and the sub-contracted fund manager makes a single supply of management to the operator or ACD, their supply will be exempt. However, if only particular elements are provided by the sub-contracted manager, the VAT liability may vary, eg advice, advertising and data processing supplied by the sub-contractor will continue to be standard-rated.

Investment/portfolio management for any investment vehicle other than a UK based [authorised unit trust, trust-based scheme or open-ended investment company] remains taxable.

[. . .]

[Note: for an update to this guidance, see Business Brief 7/06, 27 June 2006]

[VATA 1994 Sch 9 Group 5 Items 9, 10]

24 JULY 2003. BUSINESS BRIEF 11/03
VAT: BUILDING AND CONSTRUCTION—GRANTS OF A MAJOR INTEREST BY MEMBERS OF VAT GROUPS

The first grant of a major interest in a new dwelling, communal residential building or charitable building is zero-rated. "Grant of a major interest" means a freehold sale or a long lease in a building. This Business Brief article clarifies Customs' policy in relation to grants of major interest in zero-rated buildings by VAT groups in the rare situation when a group member makes more than one grant of a major interest in a building, the first of which is to another group member.

Where a major interest in a building is granted by one member of a VAT group to another, the grant should not be considered to be the "first grant of a major interest" in that building by that group member for the purpose of zero-rating.

In effect this means that the first grant of a major interest to a person outside the group can be zero-rated, regardless of the previous activity within the VAT group, so long as the group member making the grant is a person constructing (or converting) the building and it meets all the other criteria.

[VATA 1994 Sch 8 Group 5 Item 1]

24 JULY 2003. BUSINESS BRIEF 11/03
VAT: TREATMENT OF COMMUNAL AREAS IN BLOCKS OF FLATS

This Business Brief article announces Customs' new policy on communal areas in new buildings containing two or more dwellings. Typically these buildings are blocks of flats, which consist of individual dwellings and areas for the use of all residents, such as a lounge, laundry and refuse area. The first sale of each flat is zero-rated and the buyer also acquires a right to use the communal areas.

Where the communal areas are only used by residents and their guests, Customs accept that the construction of the whole building is zero-rated. Where the communal areas are partly used by others, for example if they contain leisure or gym facilities, whether or not for a charge, then the construction of the communal areas is standard-rated.

Where a building contains both a non-residential part and a dwelling, such as a shop with a flat above, zero-rating continues to apply only to the extent that the building is designed as a dwelling.

[VATA 1994 Sch 8 Group 5 Note 10]

24 JULY 2003. BUSINESS BRIEF 11/03
VAT: SCHOOLS RUN BY LOCAL AUTHORITIES

The VAT and Duties Tribunal has found in the case of *City of London Corporation* (No 17892) that the Corporation is not in business when running three fee-paying schools. This Business Brief article explains Customs' position following that decision.

BACKGROUND

Local government bodies do not act in a business capacity when they engage in activities as public authorities, provided that this does not lead to any significant distortion of competition. Such activities, which can include the provision of education, are outside the scope of VAT. Local authorities recover the VAT incurred in connection with their non-business activities under a scheme in section 33 of the VAT Act 1994. On the other hand, if a local authority provides education in the course of business the supply would, subject to the normal rules, be exempt and the authority would not be able to recover the related input tax.

THE TRIBUNAL'S DECISION

The Tribunal found that the Corporation was not engaged in a business activity when running the three fee-paying schools in question. It held that the schools were established under special legal provisions, which placed a duty on the appellant, as a public body, to maintain them. The Tribunal also held that, in this particular case, treating the activity in this way would not lead to significant distortions of competition.

The Tribunal went on to express doubt whether the UK has implemented a relevant part of EC legislation in its national VAT legislation. The second indent of Article 4(5) Sixth VAT

Directive provides that central and local government bodies must be treated as being engaged in business activities in relation to their statutory functions, where to do otherwise would lead to significant distortions of competition.

CUSTOMS' RESPONSE TO THE TRIBUNAL'S RULING

Customs consider that this case turned on its own, unusual, facts. Customs accept the decision that the Corporation engages as a public authority when it runs the three schools in question, and that this special treatment for VAT purposes will not lead to significant distortions of competition in this particular case. However, Customs do not accept the Tribunal's comments concerning the implementation of Article 4(5) into UK VAT Law. This matter has been considered in the past by both the High Court and Tribunal, and the conclusion has been that the provision is fully implemented in UK Law.

[VATA 1994 s 94]

7 AUGUST 2003. BUSINESS BRIEF 14/03
VAT: ANTI-AVOIDANCE VISITING PROGRAMME

This article announces the start of a national VAT anti-avoidance visiting programme. This programme is designed to identify and challenge avoidance schemes and is part of the VAT Compliance Strategy announced in the Pre-Budget Report in November 2002. The visit programme will run in tandem with Customs normal anti-avoidance work.

. . .

Customs are to begin a rolling programme of visits designed to identify and challenge avoidance schemes which businesses have put in place. Businesses will be selected for inclusion in the programme using a stratified sample primarily focused on larger businesses. Initial contact will normally be made by either the National Business Manager for the business, the allocated officer, or directly by anti-avoidance staff. During the visit Customs staff will examine the business as a whole by questioning senior staff (such as the financial director or equivalent), and inspecting records such as annual accounts and VAT summaries in order to identify the presence of any avoidance schemes. For larger businesses, because of their size and complexity, staff will concentrate on selected parts of the business and its related purchases.

Regardless of the size of the business, Customs anticipate that the process as a whole will require relatively little time on the part of the business—although, of course, those cases where avoidance schemes are identified and challenged are likely to be more time consuming.

Data from the visits will feed back into the national figures for the amount of VAT at risk from avoidance.

[VATA 1994 Sch 11 para 10]

12 AUGUST 2003. BUSINESS BRIEF 15/03
VAT: NEW VAT NOTICE AND STATEMENTS OF PRACTICE FOR ANTI-FRAUD MEASURES ANNOUNCED AT THE BUDGET

In this year's Budget, the Government introduced legislation to help tackle VAT fraud in the computer, mobile phone, alcohol and road fuel trade sectors. Consultation papers were published alongside draft statements of practice for both measures—joint and several liability for unpaid VAT and new rules on deducting input tax with an invalid invoice.

. . .

GUIDANCE

. . . [A] Statement of Practice explaining the new input tax rules [is] now available. [The revised statement dated March 2007 is reproduced in Appendix 9].

VERIFICATION OF VAT NUMBERS

As a result of the consultation exercise, Customs has set up a designated team specifically for businesses in the computer, mobile phone, alcohol and road fuel trade sectors. The team can confirm whether a business' VAT registration details are current, valid and match the information held by Customs.

The team does not offer a service of approving transactions nor, if they confirm that the details provided are correct, can this be viewed as authorisation for the trader to do business with that VAT registration. Any decision to trade is a commercial decision for the individual business and Customs cannot tell businesses whether or not to undertake any specific transaction.

To check the validity of another trader's VAT registration telephone 01737 734 then 516, 577, 612 or 761 during normal office hours.

If you are not in these four trade sectors, VAT registration details can still be checked by telephoning the National Advice Service on 0845 010 9000.

[VATA 1994 s 24]

19 AUGUST 2003. BUSINESS BRIEF 16/03 HOW CUSTOMS AND EXCISE WILL ANNOUNCE CHANGES USING BUSINESS BRIEFS

PURPOSE

The main purpose of Business Briefs is to announce policy changes resulting from legislation, litigation or internal policy reviews. . . .

ISSUING OF BUSINESS BRIEFS

Business Briefs will normally be issued when:

- new legislation is introduced. Legislation announced in the Budget, however, will generally be covered by Budget Notices;
- with the exception of minor amendments, whenever there is a change in Customs and Excise policy. On occasion, where changes only affect a small number of people in a particular trade sector, we may just notify the relevant trade bodies;
- court decisions are announced that result in a change in Customs' previously published policy;
- Customs intend to appeal a decision of the High Court or above. In this event the Business Brief will advise taxpayers on Customs' view of the options available to traders who might be affected by the decision which is to be appealed; or
- requested by a significant number of taxpayers. Rulings on particular cases should be sought from the National Advice Service (NAS).

PUBLICATION OF BUSINESS BRIEFS

Business Briefs are published on both the Customs and Excise and Government News Network websites, and are also issued in printed form to subscribers to the Government News Network. They are issued to national and regional media and specific trade media as appropriate.

VAT policy changes which have been announced in a Business Brief will also be included in the next edition of "VAT Notes", a publication sent to each VAT registered person with their VAT return. Business Brief 14/94 explained Customs' policy on any overpayments or underpayments of VAT which may occur when changes notified in "VAT Notes" are not implemented by a trader. That policy statement continues to apply . . .

TIMING OF BUSINESS BRIEFS

Customs will seek to issue Business Briefs resulting from court decisions as soon as possible following the decision, however, there may be occasions when the need to seek legal advice, or consult with business, delays the issue of a Business Brief.

When there is a change in the law or in policy then Customs would expect to issue it in advance of the change coming into force, except where there is a need for a change to apply from the date of announcement.

CONTENT OF BUSINESS BRIEFS

Business Briefs necessarily reflect Customs' views on the implications for taxpayers of court decisions, new legislation and other policy changes but Customs acknowledge that alternative interpretations are often possible. Business Briefs will clearly state that they reflect Customs' interpretation of the law by including the statement: *The views expressed in this Business Brief are those of HM Customs and Excise.*

Business Briefs will continue to be reviewed by legal specialists where necessary but not on every occasion.

. . .

[VATA 1994 Sch 11 para 1]

19 AUGUST 2003. BUSINESS BRIEF 16/03
VAT: OPTION TO TAX LAND AND PROPERTY—CHANGE OF OFFICE ADDRESS FOR NOTIFICATION OF AN OPTION

Supplies of land and buildings are normally exempt from VAT. However, businesses can opt to tax these supplies. Once the decision to opt has been taken, Customs and Excise must be notified in writing within 30 days for the option to be valid.

Following an internal review of VAT procedures, the work of processing notifications of options to tax is being transferred from local offices to a centralised Option To Tax Unit. The unit will deal with all notifications of options to tax including cases requiring permission from Customs & Excise.

With effect from 18 August 2003, all notifications of and queries relating to Option to Tax should be made:

- in writing to Option To Tax, UK Central Office, Portcullis House, 21 India Street, Glasgow, GL2 4PZ;
- by fax to 0141 308 3367;
- by telephone to 0141 308 3548/3599 (Monday to Thursday 09.00 to 17.00 and Friday 09.00 to 16.30); or
- by E-Mail to optiontotaxnationalunit@hmce.gsi.gov.uk.

Some businesses become liable to be registered for VAT purposes as a result of electing to waive exemption. In such cases, and in order to streamline procedures, the application to register for VAT and the notification of the option to tax should be submitted together to the appropriate VAT Registration Unit, which is determined by a businesses postcode.

The correct VAT Registration Unit for your business postcode can be found by accessing the Customs website or by telephoning the National Advice service on 0845 010 9000.

. . .

[VATA 1994 Sch 10 para 2]

11 SEPTEMBER 2003. BUSINESS BRIEF 17/03
VAT: APPLICATIONS TO USE THE ANNUAL ACCOUNTING SCHEME

Following an internal review of VAT procedures, the processing of applications to use the Annual Accounting Scheme has been transferred from local VAT offices to the Customs National Registration Service.

With effect from 1 September 2003, applications should be sent to the National Registration Service, Deansgate, 62–70 Tettenhall Road, Wolverhampton WV1 4TZ.

. . .

[SI 1995/2618 reg 52]

22 OCTOBER 2003. BUSINESS BRIEF 20/03
VAT: CLARIFICATION OF SINGLE OR MULTIPLE SUPPLY RELATING TO BOOKS AND MAGAZINES PACKAGED TOGETHER WITH ANOTHER ITEM

This Business Brief provides guidelines, in the light of the Card Protection Plan case, on how to deal with books or magazines that are packaged together with another item.

It supplements the advice given in Business Brief 2/01 and VAT Information Sheet 2/01 which, following the Card Protection Plan case, set out Customs policy on whether a transaction consists of a single composite supply or two or more independent supplies for VAT purposes.

It is not possible to give exhaustive guidance to cover every eventuality, and the advice given here is intended as a general guideline only.

MULTIPLE SUPPLY

Employing the tests outlined in VAT Information Sheet 2/01, it is Customs view that in most cases books or magazines which are packaged together with another item are likely to represent a multiple supply of the two elements.

Extra Statutory Concession 3.7, "VAT on minor promotional items supplied in linked supplies schemes" may be applied where a multiple supply exists.

SINGLE COMPOSITE SUPPLY

However, in the following circumstances there is likely to be a single composite supply:

(1) Children's books packaged with a tape or CD where there is audible interaction between the operation of the tape/CD and the book would be a single zero-rated supply. Examples of audible interaction are:
   - a noise to indicate the turning of a page; or
   - an instruction to operate the tape/CD on specific pages of the book; or
   - exercises on the tape/CD which require the book to proceed.

(2) Educational books with a tape/CD where there is clear interaction between the book and the tape/CD would be a single zero-rated supply. The tape/CD must:
   - be clearly subservient to the written material;
   - have negligible independent use without the book; and
   - not be available for sale separately.

(3) An educational tape/CD incorporating a booklet, where the booklet is simply an instructional manual explaining how to use the tape/CD, would be a single standard-rated supply.

[VATA 1994 s 19]

27 NOVEMBER 2003. BUSINESS BRIEF 23/03 VAT: INVOICING CHANGES

All EU based businesses will be affected by changes being made to the requirements for VAT invoicing, which come into force on 1 January 2004. This Business Brief article explains what the changes will mean for UK businesses.

. . .

The requirement to include unit price on an invoice [see VAT Regulations, SI 1995/2518 reg 14(1)(*m*)] applies to countable goods or services. For services the countable element might be, for example, an hourly rate or a price for standard services. If the supply cannot be broken down into countable elements, then the total tax exclusive price will be the unit price.

Customs will apply a light touch for a transitional period of twelve months, so invoices in the old format (ie without a unit price) will continue to be acceptable until 31 December 2004. This will also give businesses time to adjust to the revised procedures for self-billing and electronic transmission and storage of VAT invoices.

. . .

[SI 1995/2518 reg 14]

10 DECEMBER 2003. BUSINESS BRIEF 27/03 VAT: CHANGES TO THE VAT FLAT RATE SCHEME

. . .

One of the common criticisms of [the flat-rat scheme ("FRS")] is that the potential accounting simplifications for VAT are reduced by the need to retain detailed records for direct tax purposes. Inland Revenue and Customs and Excise have agreed a joint statement clarifying the accounting requirements for both Departments. The full text of the statement [is set out below].

JOINT STATEMENT BY CUSTOMS AND INLAND REVENUE ON RECORD KEEPING AND THE FRS

The optional VAT Flat Rate Scheme for small businesses was launched in Budget 2002. Some commentators on the scheme have suggested that conflicting requirements of the two revenue Departments complicate the scheme and reduce the compliance cost benefits. Some of those criticisms arise from a misunderstanding of the revenue requirements and this statement clarifies those requirements.

1 Accounts

No additional analysis is required to prepare accounts that are satisfactory for Inland Revenue purposes.

The main bookkeeping advantage of the VAT Flat Rate Scheme is that each purchase need no longer be analysed into Gross, VAT and Net figures when entered into the books of the business. This of course would be undone if at the end of each year the Gross, VAT and Net figures still have to be extracted for the preparation of annual accounts acceptable to Inland Revenue. The Inland Revenue confirms that for businesses who are using the VAT Flat Rate Scheme, it is expected that accounts will be prepared using gross receipts less flat rate VAT percentage for turnover and that expenses will include the irrecoverable input VAT.

This is similar in form to accounts prepared by non VAT registered businesses who cannot recover VAT they are charged.

2 Records

The standard of records for Inland Revenue purposes is the same as that for HM Customs and Excise.

Another of the key benefits of the scheme is that it removes the need to check the deductibility of VAT on purchases and even their liability to VAT. For both Customs and Inland Revenue, there is still a requirement to keep a record of sales and purchases. But for businesses using the VAT Flat Rate Scheme, that record does not have to analyse Gross, VAT and Net separately. The revenue Departments are not prescriptive about the way in which records are kept and for the simplest business it may be as little as a file of invoices issued and received in date order with a summary of totals. Clearly most businesses will do more than the minimum. In any case, the requirements of Revenue and Customs are that the records (whether tax exclusive or tax inclusive) are orderly and easy to follow.

3 VAT "profits"

Any VAT advantage gained by using the Flat Rate Scheme will form a part of taxable profits. Any VAT loss incurred by using the scheme will constitute an expense that reduces profit and therefore reduces direct tax.

The scheme is about lowering the cost to small business of complying with the VAT regulations. There is no requirement to keep a separate account of the "VAT profit" or "VAT loss" arising from use of the scheme.

By its very nature a scheme based on flat rates for trade sectors leads to almost all businesses who use it paying a different amount of VAT from that they would pay if they were still using the normal system. Those who pay less VAT will have increased profits that are in principle taxable. Those who pay more VAT will have increased costs that in principle will reduce direct tax on profits. It is important to remember that even those who pay more VAT under the Flat Rate Scheme may find the additional VAT is compensated for by the administrative savings made by all businesses who use the scheme. Each business will have to decide if being on the scheme will benefit them.

[SI 1995/2518 reg 31]

10 DECEMBER 2003. BUSINESS BRIEF 27/03
VAT—PARTIAL EXEMPTION—SPECIAL METHOD OVERRIDE NOTICE

This Business Brief article describes the effect of the Special Method Override Notice announced in today's Pre-Budget Report and which comes into force from 1 January 2004.

. . .

SITUATIONS COVERED BY THE NEW NOTICE

A Notice is intended to be a temporary measure and Customs expect its use to be rare. Customs will only issue or approve a Notice where:

- they have clear evidence that the current special method does not fairly and reasonably reflect the principle of use; and
- they are satisfied that preparing a replacement method will not conclude quickly and that Customs or business would otherwise lose out.

[Customs will serve a Notice only when:

- they have clear evidence that the current special method does not fairly and reasonably reflect the principle of use;
- they are satisfied that preparing a replacement method will not conclude quickly and that Customs or business would otherwise lose out; and
- they have decided that direction of a special method is not appropriate.]

SERVING AND APPROVING A NOTICE

A Notice must specify:

- that it is a special method override notice;

- the current or future date from which it takes effect; and
- the reasons why the current special method does not meet the principle of use.

When Customs serve a Notice they will also explain its practical effect, for example what a business must do to comply. When Customs approve a Notice served by a business, they will do so in writing as soon as possible and ideally within 30 days of receipt. Decisions on serving a Notice will be taken by a central team.

COMPLYING WITH A NOTICE

To comply with a Notice a business must for each VAT return period (including any year end adjustment):

- determine the amount of deductible VAT using its current special method;
- determine the amount of deductible VAT in accordance with the principle of use; and
- account for any difference between these amounts as a Notice correction.

In most cases the reasons given by Customs or business in the Notice will provide a basis for determining the Notice correction. However, a business must still consider its whole method and determine whether there are any other aspects that would otherwise give an unfair result. The Notice correction must therefore ensure that each time a VAT return is prepared, the amount of VAT deducted fairly and reasonably reflects the extent that costs and purchases are used or will be used in making taxable supplies (the principle of use).

If a business does not make corrections to the amount of VAT deducted, and Customs conclude that a Notice correction should have been made, then Customs will make the correction by way of VAT assessment.

RIGHT OF APPEAL

A business can appeal to the VAT and Duties Tribunal against:

- Customs' decision to serve a Notice;
- Customs' decision not to approve a Notice; and
- any VAT assessments made under a Notice.

[*Note*: text in square brackets reflects the Commissioners' revised policy notified in Business Brief 7/05, 17 March 2005 (not reproduced). It applies to notices taking effect in relation to VAT periods beginning on or after 1 April 2005.]
[SI 1995/2518 reg 102A]

10 DECEMBER 2003. BUSINESS BRIEF 28/03
VAT: CULTURAL EXEMPTION—CHANGES FOLLOWING LONDON ZOO EUROPEAN COURT OF JUSTICE DECISION

This Business Brief sets out Customs' new policy on qualifying as an eligible body for the purposes of exempting the right of admission to certain cultural activities. It follows the judgment in the European Court of Justice (ECJ) in *C & E Comrs v The Zoological Society of London* (case C-267/00) [2002] STC 521, ECJ ("London Zoo"), which ruled on the UK's interpretation of the words "managed and administered on an essentially voluntary basis" in EC VAT law.

It explains what businesses affected by the change need to do.

BACKGROUND

Under UK VAT law, the right of admission to museums, galleries, art exhibitions, zoos, theatrical, musical or choreographic performances of a cultural nature are exempt from VAT when supplied by an "eligible body". To be an eligible body, an organisation must:

(a) be precluded from distributing, and not distribute, any profit it makes;

(b) apply any profits arising from the right of admission to the above cultural activities to the continuance or improvement of the facilities made available by means of the supplies; and

(c) be managed and administered on a voluntary basis by persons who have no direct or indirect financial interest in its activities.

. . .

CUSTOMS' REVISED POLICY

To qualify as an eligible body for the purposes of the cultural exemption, a body must meet *all* the conditions listed above at (*a*) to (*c*). However, for determining whether a body is managed and administered on a voluntary basis, Customs now accepts that 'voluntary' in UK law means 'essentially voluntary', and that consideration need only be given to those persons who take the decisions of last resort concerning the policy of a body, particularly in the financial area, and carry out the higher supervisory tasks. Persons who are remunerated for carrying out purely executory tasks (ie those who implement, rather than take high level decisions) will not cause the cultural body to fail the test of being managed and administered on an essentially voluntary basis.

Customs further accept that small or token payments made to people who manage and administer will not disqualify a body from exemption.

. . .

ANNEX A

Extra Statutory Concession
VAT: Transitional relief for major cultural building projects

Following the ECJ's decision in the case of the Zoological Society of London (C-267/00), Customs has reviewed its policy in respect of the cultural bodies which qualify for exemption as eligible bodies under VATA 1994 Sch 9 Group 13 Item 2. As a result, certain supplies (admission charges) which have been treated as taxable will be treated as exempt. The policy change will be implemented with effect from 1 June 2004.

In these circumstances, Customs has decided that it is appropriate to provide some limited relief against the unforeseen adverse VAT effects of exemption on input tax claims in relation to major cultural building projects whilst at the same time ensuring that account is taken of any equally unforeseen VAT savings resulting from exemption.

Major building projects in progress at 1 June 2004

(1) This concession only applies in the case of major building projects which are in progress at 1 June 2004 and have been costed and funded on the basis that any input tax incurred on them will be recoverable.

(2) From 1 June 2004 to 31 May 2007, taxpayers may deduct input tax incurred on such a project which cannot otherwise be deducted as if their supplies (admission charges) were still treated as taxable but only to the extent that this deduction exceeds any net claim made or to be made and/or benefit obtained or to be obtained resulting from the application of exemption for any periods which end prior to 1 June 2004 or span that date.

(3) In all cases, before a taxpayer recovers any input tax under this concession, he must submit his calculations to the Commissioners and obtain their written approval.

(4) If any of the input tax deducted under (2) above is also subsequently recoverable as a result of a taxpayer's longer period adjustment for partial exemption, he must make a further adjustment to cancel this out on the same VAT return as the longer period adjustment to prevent a double deduction

(5) This concession allows additional input tax recovery for certain construction services over and above the actual taxable use of the asset. Therefore, where a claim is made under this concession, adjustments for subsequent intervals 2-10 under the Capital Items Scheme as required by SI 1995/2518 (Regulations 112 to 116) can only be made if the actual use made of the asset is outside the range between the percentage which was initially correctly reclaimable under the partial exemption rules and the percentage which has been effectively recovered including all adjustments under this concession. Where an adjustment falls to be made because the usage in any subsequent interval is outside the range defined above, it can only be made to the extent that the usage falls outside this range.

(6) For the purposes of this concession, building projects are "in progress" at 1 June 2004 where:

- construction services have been contracted for before 10 December 2003; or
- grant funding has been formally approved before 10 December 2003; or
- there is documentary evidence that negotiations were at an advanced stage before 10 December 2003 and construction work has commenced as at 1 June 2004.

(7) A "major building project" means any building project covered by the Capital Items Scheme. However, consideration will also be given to similar smaller projects which would have qualified for treatment under the Capital Items Scheme had their total value exceeded £250,000 VAT bearing value.

(8) The Commissioners may withdraw or restrict the application of this concession if they have reasonable cause to believe that it is being abused.

[VATA 1994 s 26]

16 DECEMBER 2003. BUSINESS BRIEF 29/03
VAT: SALES OF PHONE CARDS

This Business Brief article sets out the views of Customs on the VAT treatment of phone cards where they have been supplied to a UK distributor by an issuer in another member state.

It has been suggested to Customs that arrangements of this type could lead to less VAT being payable on telecommunication services supplied in the EU compared to the VAT due where the phone card is issued by a UK company. However, Customs do not accept that there are any circumstances in which telecommunications services consumed within the EU can be VAT free. Where specific arrangements are put in place in an attempt to obtain a VAT free status or reduce the amount of VAT that is properly due, Customs view this as avoidance. Customs will challenge any attempted use of avoidance arrangements of this type.

The guidance below explains Customs' view of the correct method of accounting for VAT where phone cards have been supplied to a UK distributor by an issuer in another Member State. It supplements the advice given in Information Sheet 12/03 which gave general guidance on the VAT treatment of Face Value Vouchers following the changes introduced in Budget 2003. . . .

PHONE CARDS

Phone cards are regarded as face value vouchers for VAT purposes. A phone card is usually issued by a telecommunications company and is ultimately used by the final customer to obtain telephone services. In some cases the card is not sold directly to the final customer but is purchased from the issuer by another business (the distributor) for onward sale to retail or business customers.

Although a phone card is a face value voucher, because it is normally used to obtain telephone services, the supply of the phone card is treated as being governed by the rules relating to telecommunications services. In particular this means that the place of supply rules for telecommunications services apply.

VAT TREATMENT OF SUPPLIES OF PHONE CARDS RECEIVED BY A UK DISTRIBUTOR FROM AN ISSUER BELONGING IN ANOTHER MEMBER STATE

Where a UK distributor (that is a business that belongs in the UK) purchases a phone card for business purposes from an issuer that belongs in another member state, because the supply by the issuer is regarded as a supply of telecommunications services, it falls within VATA 1994 Sch 5 para 7A (Article 9(2)(*e*) of the Sixth VAT Directive). Because the supply is received for business purposes, VAT is to be accounted for by the UK distributor under the reverse charge provisions in section 8 of the Act (Article 21(1)(*b*) of the Directive). The UK distributor is also entitled to reclaim the VAT as input tax, subject to the normal rules.

VAT TREATMENT OF SUPPLIES MADE BY A UK DISTRIBUTOR

When the UK distributor makes an onward supply of the card, the circumstances which apply mean that the distributor is normally considered to be acting on its own behalf and not on behalf of the issuer. The distributor buys the card at a certain price and then sells it on at a higher (or, if it chooses, lower) price in the same way that it (the distributor) buys and sells items from other suppliers and sells them on. The distributor also receives the consideration for that supply and is the entity to which the customer would look first in the event of any dissatisfaction. Because a distributor acts on its own behalf, it is a principal for VAT purposes. This determines the way in which the distributor must account for VAT; as a principal, it is responsible for accounting for all VAT due on its onward sale of phone cards.

UK VAT is therefore due on the whole amount that the UK distributor charges to its customers for cards used to access telecommunication services within the European Union (EU), irrespective of whether the customer is a business that belongs in the UK or a private consumer.

ACCOUNTING FOR VAT

A phone card is *a retailer voucher* if, as is usually the case, it can be redeemed by the person who issued it. The issuer accounts for his part of the VAT when the card is redeemed rather than at the time of the initial sale of the card, and the liability of the supply is subject to the use to which it is put. As above, a UK distributor who purchases a phone card from such an issuer is normally regarded as acting as a principal when it sells on the card. Where telecommunications services are consumed within the EU, VAT is due on the full amount for which the card is sold. Again, the UK distributor is entitled to recover the VAT on its purchase as input tax, subject to the normal rules.

PHONE CARDS SOLD AS CREDIT VOUCHERS

A phone card is *a credit voucher* if it cannot be redeemed by the person who issued it. The consideration for any supply of a credit voucher is disregarded for VAT purposes under the provisions of VATA 1994 Sch 10A para 3(2). However, paragraph 3(2) is subject to paragraph 3(3) of the same Schedule which provides that the consideration is only disregarded in circumstances where VAT is accounted for in full by the person from whom the goods or services are obtained by the use of such a voucher.

Certain schemes involving phone cards have been suggested to Customs based on arrangements which are said to constitute credit voucher arrangements. Customs' view is that, even if a phone card can be viewed as a credit voucher, the consideration for its supply is not disregarded in circumstances where no VAT will be accounted for on the subsequent supply of telecommunications services.

[VATA 1994 Sch 10A para 2]

4 MAY 2004. BUSINESS BRIEF 14/04
VAT—PARTIAL EXEMPTION: ATTRIBUTING INPUT TAX TO INTENDED SUPPLIES OF PROPERTY

This Business Brief article reports a change in policy on evidence of an intention to make taxable supplies of property. It also clarifies policy on attributing input tax to intended supplies of property and when subsequent adjustments need to be made. This takes account of the decision of the VAT and Duties Tribunal in *Beaverbank Properties Ltd* (No 18099) (*Beaverbank*) and of the House of Lords in the case of *Royal & Sun Alliance Group plc v C & E Comrs* [2003] STC 832, HL (*RSA*).

This Business Brief withdraws VAT Information Sheet 08/01 regarding the attribution of input tax on speculative supplies of property.

BACKGROUND

A taxpayer can deduct VAT on costs attributed to taxable supplies that it intends to make in future. Equally, if the intention is to make exempt supplies, then attributed VAT cannot normally be deducted.

Where an intention changes *before costs are used* the original VAT attribution may need to be adjusted. If the intention changes from exempt to taxable, then a taxpayer may be entitled to claim the VAT previously attributed to the exempt supply. This is known as a payback claim. Conversely, if the intention changes from taxable to exempt then VAT previously deducted may need to be repaid. This is known as a clawback adjustment. Further information is available in VAT Notice 706 "Partial Exemption".

Certain supplies of land and property that are exempt can be made taxable by making and notifying an option to tax (option). Doing so can allow VAT on costs to be deducted where it otherwise could not. Further information is available in VAT Notice 742A "Opting to tax land and buildings".

EVIDENCE OF AN INTENTION TO MAKE TAXABLE SUPPLIES OF PROPERTY

Some land and property supplies are always taxable whereas other supplies are exempt unless an effective option is in place. Prior to the *Beaverbank* case Customs maintained that, where an option was needed to make supplies taxable, then a taxpayer could only have an intention to make taxable supplies once an option was in place.

Customs now accept that a taxpayer can have an *intention* to make taxable supplies before an option is in place, even though the taxable supplies cannot occur until after the option is made. However, clear documentary evidence of taxable intention is essential.

Suitable evidence includes documents involving third parties that consistently show a firm commitment to make taxable supplies. For example, a document accepting a bank loan on the basis that taxable supplies will be made. However, in most cases, the best evidence of taxable intention remains an effective option to tax.

A firm commitment to make taxable supplies is essential before there can be a taxable intention where the normal liability of planned supplies is exempt. In particular, where property is to be let and the taxpayer is keeping his options open as to whether to opt or not, a taxable intention does not exist.

Customs recognise that property developers often look at many sites in connection with a taxable project and that it may be onerous to immediately opt them all. As projects progress through acquiring an interest in the land and doing necessary work to active marketing, the weight of evidence needed to substantiate a continuing taxable intention without an option will increase. At the same time any commercial reasons to put off opting will decrease. Where a taxpayer is actively marketing a property Customs view the lack of an option as strong evidence that the taxpayer is merely keeping his options open as to whether to opt and that a taxable intention does not exist.

CHANGES OF INTENTION

VAT on costs related to subletting property must be attributed to planned exempt supplies unless there is absolutely no doubt that only taxable supplies will be made. VAT incurred on rents paid (and on other day-to-day costs) that have been attributed to exempt supplies cannot be adjusted once an option is put in place. This is because a payback claim can only be made if costs are put to an alternative taxable use. Costs such as rent for expired periods are not available for use in making taxable supplies because they have effectively been used-up in trying to make exempt supplies.

VAT on costs incurred prior to the option that are not used-up before the option is made will be available for adjustment assuming all other conditions are met. Equally, VAT on day-to-day costs incurred following the making of an effective option can be attributed to taxable supplies.

SPECULATIVE SUPPLIES OF PROPERTY (UNCLEAR INTENTION)

Some land and property businesses incur VAT on costs without knowing what supplies will be made. For example, costs related to acquiring land for property development when it is not yet clear what type of project, if any, will take place. In these situations it is not possible for VAT to be directly attributed to either taxable or exempt supplies.

Provided the costs are incurred for business purposes, the VAT can be treated as residual VAT relating to the business as a whole. Residual VAT can be deducted to the extent allowed by the taxpayer's partial exemption method.

If a project is aborted, and costs incurred wasted, no adjustments are made to the deduction of VAT on those costs. But, if a project is firmed-up or costs are used in different projects in which taxable or exempt intentions are known, then payback or clawback may apply.

IMPACT OF RSA

Following the comments of Lord Hoffmann in *RSA* there has been speculation that the lack of a clear intention of what supplies would eventually be made in speculative property projects prevents the later application of payback or clawback. Customs view the apportionment of residual input tax incurred in speculative projects under partial exemption methods as attribution to taxable and exempt intentions and thus view the input tax as eligible for later adjustment if all other conditions are met.

. . .

[SI 1995/2518 reg 101]

28 MAY 2004. BUSINESS BRIEF 15/04
VAT—CHANGE IN DIY CLAIM HANDLING ARRANGEMENTS UNDER DIY BUILDERS AND CONVERTERS SCHEME

There has recently been a reorganisation of Customs' processing centres dealing with claims for VAT submitted under the provisions of the above scheme.

With effect from 1 April 2004 all claims submitted under this scheme will be processed by the Birmingham Business Centre. Their address is: HM Customs and Excise, 2 Broadway, Broad Street, Five Ways, Birmingham, West Midlands B15 1BG, Tel: 0121 697 4000, Fax: 0121 697 4002.

. . .

[SI 1995/2518 reg 201]

9 JUNE 2004. BUSINESS BRIEF 16/04
VAT—DEFINITION OF A MOTOR CAR

This Business Brief clarifies Customs' interpretation of the definition of a motor car as contained in the Value Added Tax (Cars) Order 1992, SI 1992/3122.

BACKGROUND

The UK operates a "block" on the deduction of input tax on the purchase of a vehicle that is defined in VAT legislation as a motor car. As a result of this block, most businesses that purchase motor cars are unable to recover the VAT they have incurred. In broad terms, the purpose of the block is to prevent recovery of input tax on vehicles whose physical attributes make them suitable for private motoring. It is important, therefore, for business to know the status of their vehicles under the terms of the legislation, as this will affect the deductibility of VAT on their purchase.

The clarification is necessary in the light of recent developments in the car-derived van market, which have resulted in the manufacture of vehicles that have blurred the distinction between cars and vans. This means that these vehicles are difficult to categorise in relation to the definition of motorcars in VAT legislation.

In response, Customs have issued new guidance, produced in consultation with manufacturers, which clarifies our treatment of car-derived vans and highlights the correct interpretation of the legal definition when considering combination vans. This guidance is available on request from the Customs' National Advice Service on 0845 010 9000.

VEHICLES AFFECTED AND THEIR VAT TREATMENT

The vehicles affected are certain car-derived vans and the combination van.

CAR-DERIVED VANS

Many car-derived vans pose no problem with regard to our current definition of a motor car, in that they are clearly vans or non-motor cars for VAT purposes eg they have no rear seats, metal side panels to the rear of the front seats, a load area which is highly unsuitable for carrying passengers etc.

However a number of models, where the vehicle starts off life as a car and is subsequently altered, cannot be so clearly defined. It is these vehicles which are the focus of this brief.

On the exterior, these vehicles look like a motor car but their interior has been altered to give the appearance and functionality of a van. The rear seats and seat belts along with their mountings have been completely removed and the rear area of the shell is fitted with a new floor panel to create a load area. In addition, the side "windows" to the rear of the driver's seat are fitted with immovable opaque panels.

Customs will *not* view such a "car-derived" vehicle as a motorcar for VAT purposes, if:

- the technical criteria specified in Customs guidance are met by the manufacturer. The criteria relate to how any alterations to the vehicle have been effected, and
- the adaptations give the vehicle the functionality of a commercial vehicle. As such, the removal of a bench seat or similar from what is essentially a two-seater car would not automatically satisfy Customs' requirements, and
- the space that remains behind the front row of seats is highly unsuitable for carrying passengers.

It may be difficult for businesses to satisfy themselves fully that all of the technical criteria have been met. At present, Customs, in partnership with the manufacturers, are developing a list of car-derived vans on which VAT can be deducted, subject to the normal rules. This list will be available shortly on the Customs' website. In the meantime, if businesses are in any doubt, they should obtain confirmation in writing from the vendor that the vehicle meets the technical criteria.

Customs consulted the manufacturers on the technical criterion in September 2003. As such, if businesses have bought such a car-derived van prior to 1 October 2003, it is unlikely that it will satisfy all of the technical criteria set out in Customs' guidance.

However, where the vehicle has the appearance of a car-derived van as defined above, in such circumstances, Customs will allow that vehicle to be treated as a non-motor car for VAT purposes, and the VAT incurred can be recovered, subject to the normal rules.

COMBINATION VANS

While these vehicles have the appearance of vans, they are designed to be fitted with or include additional seats behind the front row of seats to enable the carriage of passengers.

Such vehicles are motor cars for VAT purposes except in the case of:

- larger vehicles which have a payload of more than one tonne (these vehicles are automatically excluded from becoming motor cars by the one tonne payload test contained in legislation); and
- those vehicles where the dedicated load area (ie that load area which is completely unaffected by the additional seating) is of a sufficient size compared to the passenger area to make the carriage of goods the predominant use of the vehicle.

If businesses have previously bought a combination van, which does not fall within the exceptions above, it is a motor car under VAT legislation. If businesses have recovered the VAT incurred on the purchase, they must make an adjustment to correct this overclaim.

[SI 1992/3122 art 2]

13 JULY 2004. BUSINESS BRIEF 18/04
VAT—SALES OF PHONE CARDS

This Business Brief article sets out the action Customs will be taking to deal with tax avoidance schemes relating to sales of phone cards as outlined in Business Brief 29/03, 16 December 2003, available on Customs' website.

Business Brief 29/03 set out Customs' view of both the VAT treatment of phone cards, specifically the treatment of supplies of phone cards received by a UK distributor from an issuer belonging in another member state, and the VAT treatment of supplies made by that UK distributor. In particular, it drew attention to the treatment of phone cards issued as credit vouchers and emphasised that the consideration for such vouchers is only disregarded where VAT has been accounted for correctly by the person from whom goods or services are obtained by the use of the voucher.

Customs are aware that, in an attempt to obtain a VAT free status or reduce the amount of VAT that is properly due, some businesses have adopted arrangements that do not follow the guidance on credit vouchers in Business Brief 29/03. One consequence of such avoidance arrangements is that the incorrect tax treatment will be applied each time a phone card is sold, whether by an issuer, distributor or retailer.

To ensure the correct tax treatment is applied, Customs need to be satisfied that the correct amount of VAT is accounted for in relation to each sale of the phone card. Businesses may therefore wish to check with their suppliers that VAT has been correctly accounted for on the vouchers supplied to them. Those businesses which have not already received an assurance of this from their suppliers may therefore wish to contact them to seek assurance that VAT has been, or will be, properly accounted for in line with Customs' existing guidance.

Customs are inviting businesses affected by avoidance arrangements to submit voluntary disclosures. To allow businesses time to prepare these disclosures, Customs will suspend enforcement of the guidance in Business Brief 29/03 for a period of 21 days from the date of this Business Brief.

. . .

[VATA 1994 Sch 10A para 2]

2 AUGUST 2004. BUSINESS BRIEF 20/04
VAT—GAS AND ELECTRICITY SUPPLIERS: NEW EXTRA STATUTORY CONCESSION FOR BAD DEBTS

This Business Brief article outlines a new Extra Statutory Concession, enabling suppliers of gas and electricity to obtain relief from VAT on debts owed by domestic customers, after the suppliers have accepted the transfer of a domestic customer and their debt from another supply company.

BACKGROUND

The VAT Bad Debt Relief scheme enables VAT registered businesses to recover some or all of the VAT they have declared and paid in respect of their supplies, where their customer has failed to pay. Under the terms of the scheme, the person who makes the supply is the only person entitled to claim VAT bad debt relief.

This concession supports Government policy to allow greater flexibility for domestic fuel and power consumers by enabling them to change suppliers even if they have a debt.

CHANGES

The ESC applies where a domestic customer who is in debt to one supplier changes supplier, and the debt is transferred to the new supplier. The new supplier may claim bad debt relief on any part of the debt that remains outstanding six months after the date of transfer.

TIMING

The ESC takes effect today, Monday 2 August 2004.

THE EXTRA-STATUTORY CONCESSION

1. Where a contract for the supply of gas or electricity is substituted by a new contract ("novation") as a result of a domestic consumer transferring from one supplier to another, then, by concession, the new supplier may claim bad debt relief on a supply of gas or electricity made by the former supplier to that consumer, provided that all of the conditions in paragraph 2 below are satisfied.

2. The conditions referred to in paragraph 1 above are:

(a) the whole or any part of the consideration for the supply is outstanding at the time of the novation;

(b) the whole of the debt is transferred to the new supplier;

(c) at the time of the novation, the former supplier (if he has not already done so) accounts for VAT on the supply at the appropriate rate or, if he has already received a refund upon a claim for bad debt relief in relation to that supply, repays to the Commissioners the amount of that refund;

(d) the claim is not made until six months after payment for the novation and takes account of any payments made by the customer after the date of the novation;

(e) both the former supplier and the new supplier have evidence of:

(i) the value of the debt (including the VAT amount) that has been transferred; and

(ii) the date of payment for the novation,

(f) the new supplier has a copy of the document issued by him to the consumer to recover the debt (not required if a pre-payment meter is in use).

3. In this concession:

"domestic consumer" means a person to whom fuel or power is supplied for domestic use.

"domestic use" has the same meaning as in VATA 1994 Sch 7A Group 1.

"gas" means gas that is conveyed through pipes to premises by a licensed gas transporter.

"licensed gas transporter" means any person authorised by a licence under the Gas Act 1986 s 7 [as amended] to supply gas through pipes to any premises.

4. This concession does not apply in circumstances where its application would give rise to tax avoidance.

[VATA 1994 s 36]

10 AUGUST 2004. BUSINESS BRIEF 21/04
VAT—VAT POSITION OF SHARE ISSUES AND PARTNERSHIP CONTRIBUTIONS FOLLOWING THE ECJ DECISION IN KAPHAG RENDITEFONDS

This Business Brief clarifies Customs' position on two issues arising from the decision of the European Court of Justice in the German case of *KapHag Renditefonds 35 Spreecenter Berlin-Hellersdorf3 Tranche GbR v Finanzamt Charlottenburg* (case C-442/01) [2003] ECR I–6851:

(A) Whether the issue of shares constitutes a supply for VAT purposes; and
(B) The VAT position of contributions to partnerships.

The case of *KapHag* concerned the admission of a new partner into a partnership on payment of a capital contribution. The European Court held that no supply was being made by either the individual partners or the partnership to the incoming partner in return for the capital contribution.

A. WHETHER THE ISSUE OF SHARES CONSTITUTES A SUPPLY

[This section has been overtaken by the judgment in *Kretztechnik AG v Finanzamt Linz* (case C-465/03) [2005] SWTI 1020, ECJ, which was announced in Business Brief 12/05, 15 June 2005 (not reproduced).]

B. CONTRIBUTIONS TO PARTNERSHIPS

Partnerships to which this section applies include "normal" partnerships of individuals or corporate bodies, limited partnerships whose members are individuals or corporate bodies, overseas limited partnerships that are registered as "normal" partnerships or corporate bodies and limited liability partnerships.

BACKGROUND

In *KapHag*, the incoming partner was contributing cash in return for admission into the partnership but it will often be the case that the contribution is in the form of other assets. For example, a new partner's contribution may comprise land or interests in land. The European Court's decision tacitly accepted the Advocate-General's Opinion that the same principles would apply whether the contribution consisted of cash or other assets. Whatever the nature of the assets comprising the contribution, there is no reciprocal supply from the partnership. However, where the assets are not cash, the making of the partnership contribution may have other VAT consequences.

The Advocate-General was satisfied that there was "no doubt that the new partner is effecting an act of disposal of his assets, for which the admission to the partnership is not the consideration" (para 33 of the Opinion). Such a disposal can therefore have VAT consequences when the partner contributing the assets is a VAT registered person. These consequences will vary depending on the nature of the assets being contributed.

KapHag establishes that nothing is provided by the partnership in return for the assets contributed, therefore any such disposal by the incoming partner is made for no consideration. The VAT Act provides that certain things are subject to VAT even when they are provided or done for no consideration. Customs' view is that all those provisions will still apply where there is no consideration when there is a contribution to partnership assets. A VAT registered person may therefore have to account for tax if he contributes assets to the partnership in the circumstances described in the Act. The VAT consequences can be considered under several main heads:

(i) contribution to partnership comprising services;
(ii) contribution to partnership comprising goods other than land;
(iii) contribution to partnership comprising land or interests in land;
(iv) whether contribution to partnership can constitute the transfer of a going concern;
(v) how the partnership can reclaim the output tax accounted for by an incoming partner on his contribution as its input tax;
(vi) capital Goods Scheme consequences; and
(vii) transfer of assets out of a partnership.

(i) Contribution to partnership comprising services

A partnership contribution may comprise services rather than goods—examples of this could be a trademark or trading logo or the use of an asset the ownership of which is retained by the incoming partner. Two legislative provisions set out the circumstances in which such a contribution may be regarded as a taxable supply: VATA 1994 Sch 4 para 5(4) and VAT (Supply of Services) Order 1993, SI 1993/1507.

A supply can arise under VATA 1994 Sch 4 para 5(4) where a taxable person applies business goods to private use or makes them available for purposes other than those of his business. The taxable person or his predecessor must have been entitled to input tax under VATA 1994 ss 25 and 26 on the supply of those goods (or anything comprised in them) to him.

The Supply of Services Order similarly provides that a supply arises where a taxable person applies bought-in services to private or non-business use for no consideration where he has been entitled to input tax credit under ss 25 and 26. The value of such a supply cannot exceed the taxable person's input tax entitlement.

Where the above criteria are satisfied, a VAT registered incoming partner will have to account for tax on the supply of services that he is regarded as making in the disposal of the services from his existing business. The partnership may be able to recover this as its input tax where the contributed services are to be used for its business. The procedure for doing this is described at (v) below.

(ii) Contribution to partnership comprising goods other than land

If a partnership contribution comprises goods other than land that a taxable person (the transferor) held as assets, then a deemed supply will be generated as a result of VATA 1994 Sch 4 para 5(1). This deemed supply does not require there to be consideration when the goods are transferred. It does however only apply where the taxable person disposing of the goods, or their predecessor, if for example they obtained the goods by way of a TOGC, was entitled to full or partial credit for the VAT charged when the goods were supplied to him. Where such a deemed supply arises, the incoming partner will have to account for VAT. The partnership may be able to recover this as its input tax where the contributed assets are to be used for its business. The procedure for doing this is described at (v) below.

(iii) Contribution to partnership comprising land or interests in land

The VAT treatment of land or interests in land also depends upon whether the incoming partner or his predecessor was entitled to deduct input tax in relation to the property that he is contributing to the partnership. For example, if he had opted to tax the property, or it was inherently taxable like new freehold commercial property, there may be a deemed supply as described at (ii) above. The incoming partner will then have to account for VAT on this supply. As with other contributed goods, the partnership may be entitled to recover this as input tax where the property is to be used for the partnership's business. The procedure for doing this is described at (v) below.

Please note all submitted notifications of an option to tax need to be signed by "an authorised signatory" as described in para 7.1 of VAT Notice 742A—"Opting to tax Land & Buildings" available online at—www.hmce.gov.uk/forms/notices/742a.htm.

(iv) Whether contribution to partnership can constitute the transfer of a going concern

It is possible that when assets are transferred by way of a partnership contribution that this could qualify to be treated as a transfer of a going concern (VATA 1994 s 49 and VAT (Special Provisions) Order 1995, SI 1995/1268 art 5). If the contribution meets the conditions to be treated as a transfer of a going concern no VAT will be due from the transferor.

(v) How the partnership can reclaim the output tax accounted for by an incoming partner on his contribution as its input tax

When an incoming partner contributes goods and/or services (on which VAT is due as described above) and the partnership uses them for its business purposes, the partnership can recover the VAT as input tax subject to the normal rules. The incoming partner cannot issue a tax invoice, but in order to provide the partnership with acceptable evidence to support a claim for recovery of input tax, he may use his normal invoicing documentation overwritten with the following statement:

> "Certificate for Tax on Partnership Contribution
>
> No payment is necessary for these goods/services. Output tax has been accounted for on the supply."

The incoming partner must show full details of the goods and/or services on the documentation and the amount of VAT shown must be the amount of output tax accounted for to Customs & Excise.

(vi) Capital Goods Scheme consequences

Where the capital contribution is in the form of an interest in land or a computer, it may be an existing capital item of the incoming partner under the Capital Goods Scheme (CGS). If the transfer to the partnership constitutes a supply which is a disposal of an existing CGS item, then this will wind up the existing CGS item and a disposal adjustment may be due. If the transfer constitutes a TOGC then this will end the current interval for the incoming partner and the partnership will then be responsible for making adjustments for any remaining intervals.

As transfers of assets capital contributions will always constitute either a supply or a TOGC, any existing CGS items will always either be subject to a disposal adjustment or continuing CGS adjustments.

Even if the asset transferred as a capital contribution is not a CGS item in the hands of the incoming partner, it may create a new CGS item for the partnership when its transfer constitutes a supply. If this happens the partnership will need to make adjustments in subsequent intervals in the normal way.

The CGS is further explained in VAT Notice 706/2 "Capital Goods Scheme" available online at www.hmce.gov.uk/forms/notices/706-2.htm.

(vii) Transfer of assets out of a partnership

KapHag was only concerned with assets moving into a partnership in the form of a partnership contribution. It did not cover the reverse situation, where partnership assets are paid out to an outgoing partner or otherwise disposed of by the partnership for no consideration. Where a transfer of assets out of a partnership for no consideration occurs, one of the following sets of circumstances will apply.

(a) If the incoming partner accounted for output tax when he contributed the assets to the partnership and the partnership was entitled to recover all or part of this as its input tax, there will be a subsequent supply by the partnership when the same assets are transferred out unless the transfer out now satisfies the TOGC criteria.

(b) If no output tax was accounted for when the assets were contributed to the partnership because they constituted a TOGC, the transfer out of the same assets will be a deemed supply upon which the partnership will have to account for tax unless the TOGC criteria are again satisfied.

(c) The partnership may be transferring out more assets than those originally contributed to it. Although the original contribution to the partnership may not have been a TOGC, the subsequent transfer out may now satisfy the TOGC criteria. If it does, no VAT will be due from the partnership.

(d) The original contribution to the partnership may have been a TOGC but the partnership may now be transferring out less of the assets than were originally contributed. Unless the assets being transferred out still meet the TOGC criteria in their own right, there may be a deemed supply upon which the partnership will have to account for the appropriate tax. As explained at (ii) and (iii) above, the entitlement of the partnership or its predecessor to deduct input tax in relation to the items that are the subject of the transfer out will determine whether or not there is a supply.

APPLICATION OF VATA 1994 S 45

In the past, there was uncertainty as to whether it was VATA 1994 s 45(1) that led to there being no supply from a partnership to an incoming partner. That section provides for the registration of partnerships in the following terms:

"45(1) The registration under this Act of persons—

(*a*) carrying on a business in partnership, or

(*b*) carrying on in partnership any other activities in the course or furtherance of which they acquire goods from other member States,

may be in the name of the firm; and no account shall be taken, in determining for any purpose of this Act whether goods or services are supplied to or by such persons or are acquired by such persons from another member State, of any change in the partnership."

Partnerships in England and Wales have no legal identity. A new partner joining a partnership, or old one leaving it, would result in a new partnership rather than change the composition of the existing one. Without VATA 1994 s 45(1), deregistration and registration would be necessary every time a partner joined or left. The purpose of VATA 1994 s 45(1) is to ensure continuity by providing that a business carried on in a firm's name is treated as a continuing business irrespective of changes in its composition. The situation addressed by s 45(1) is therefore entirely different to that considered in *KapHag*.

[VATA 1994 s 5]

14 SEPTEMBER 2004. BUSINESS BRIEF 25/04
VAT—CUSTOMS' POLICY ON ASSESSMENTS FOLLOWING THE JUDGMENTS OF THE HIGH COURT IN C & E V LAURA ASHLEY AND THE COURT OF APPEAL IN DFS FURNITURE COMPANY V C & E

This Business Brief clarifies Customs' policy on assessments following recent court judgments in *C & E Comrs v Laura Ashley Ltd* [2004] STC 635 and *C & E Comrs v DFS Furniture Co plc* [2004] STC 559, CA. Taxpayers are not asked to take any action as a consequence of this Business Brief.

GENERAL

The recent judgments in *Laura Ashley*, in the High Court, and *DFS*, in the Court of Appeal, are concerned with the validity of VAT recovery assessments, ie assessments made to recover money paid, repaid or credited to taxpayers in error. The judgments raised several points that Customs regarded as "unsettled" and so we petitioned the House of Lords to hear a further appeal in the *DFS* case to clarify the position for the benefit of Customs and taxpayers alike. That petition was unsuccessful and so the *DFS* litigation is now at an end.

In dealing with the validity of recovery assessments, the court judgments, by implication, raise an issue of a more general nature about the effect of a finding that any assessment raised by Customs is invalid. It is Customs' view that the proper course for a taxpayer to take if the taxpayer has been assessed and believes the assessment to be incorrect for any reason is to ask Customs to review the decision and, if still unsatisfied, to make a timely appeal to the VAT & Duties Tribunal.

Where an underdeclaration of tax has been correctly established but the related assessment, which has been paid but not appealed, is subsequently acknowledged to be technically flawed, for example where it was made for the wrong accounting period, Customs will not withdraw the assessment. There will not be any reason to do so. In addition, and subject always to the VAT appeal provisions, no repayment of money paid against a technically flawed but otherwise correct assessment will be made.

This general policy in no way alters Customs' obligation and commitment to make every effort to ensure that assessments for arrears of tax are correct in all respects.

THE LAURA ASHLEY AND DFS JUDGMENTS

The effect of these judgments, taken together, is that:

(a) assessment time limits cannot begin to run from the date of a court judgment, or its delivery; but there is continuing uncertainty about:

(b) whether an assessment to recover money repaid or credited to a taxpayer as a result of a mistake of law is properly made under VATA 1994 s 80(4A) or s 73(2);

(c) whether, for a recovery assessment, time limits can run from the date a repayment is made; and

(d) which prescribed accounting period should be assessed when a recovery assessment is made under s 73(2).

CUSTOMS FUTURE PRACTICE

1 Assessments time limits running from a court judgment

The law as currently interpreted by the courts in *DFS Furniture Co plc v C & E Comrs* [2004] STC 559, CA is that a court judgment, or its delivery, is not a fact for the purposes of the "evidence of facts" time limit rules for making assessments. Customs now accept the *DFS* judgment on this point and will make no more assessments that rely solely on a court judgment as evidence of facts.

Where past recovery assessments have relied on a court judgment, it is probable that the repayment being recovered was made following a mistake of law. Any tax paid on the recovery assessment was properly due on remedy of the mistake of law.

Some appeals challenging the validity of recovery assessments have been lodged and stood over behind *DFS*. These appeals will now be reviewed by Customs and the appellants informed of the outcome as soon as possible.

2 Assessments made to recover money repaid or credited following a mistake of law

The judgment in *DFS Furniture Co plc v C & E Comrs* [2004] STC 559, CA includes obiter dicta remarks which might be taken as suggesting that amounts repaid under VATA 1994 s 80(1) following a mistake of law were only properly recoverable by assessment made under VATA 1994 s 73(2), subject to the time limits in s 73(6)(*a*). Customs do not accept this approach.

For the time being, Customs will continue to make assessments under VATA 1994 s 80(4A) for recovery of amounts repaid under s 80(1). However, to protect the Exchequer in the event that the Court of Appeal in *DFS* is right, we will also assess in the alternative under s 73(2).

Whether past assessments were made under VATA 1994 s 80(4A) or s 73(2) it was appropriate for Customs to recover amounts repaid that ought not to have been repaid.

3 Recovery assessments time limits running from the date the incorrect repayment was made

The Court of Appeal in *DFS Furniture Co plc v C & E Comrs* [2004] STC 559, CA appears to have taken the view that repayment is not itself a fact for the purposes of the "evidence of facts" time limit rules for making assessments.

Customs do not think that many, if any, recovery assessments will have been made that rely on the fact of repayment to satisfy the evidence of facts time limit rules. Where at the time of considering a repayment claim Customs are already out of time to make a recovery assessment, we will take account of the obiter dicta remarks in *DFS Furniture Co plc* v C & E *Comrs* [2004] STC 559, CA and not repay unless the claimant signs an undertaking to return any payment with interest in the event that the underlying issue is finally determined in Customs' favour.

4 The period to assess under s 73(2)

There are now three apparently conflicting judgments of the courts concerning the period Customs should assess when a recovery assessment is made under VATA 1994 s 73(2).

Customs have taken the period to assess as the period for which a return was made that contained the incorrect claim; or, following the judgment of the Court of Appeal in *C & E Comrs v Croydon Hotel and Leisure Co Ltd* [1996] STC 1105, CA, the period in which a voluntary disclosure containing the incorrect claim was made. On this basis, the time limits applying to incorrect returns and to incorrect voluntary disclosures are consistent.

The judgment of the High Court in *C & E Comrs v Laura Ashley Ltd* [2004] STC 635 was that the period to assess should have been the period to which the relevant tax related, ie the assessment made under VATA 1994 s 73(2) to recover a repayment or credit wrongly given following a voluntary disclosure of an error in an earlier period should have been made for that earlier period.

Finally, the Court of Appeal in *DFS Furniture Co plc v C & E Comrs* [2004] STC 559, CA took the view that, in similar but not identical circumstances, the period to assess was the period current when the repayment was made.

Until these apparently conflicting judgments are resolved, Customs may in future need to protect tax in certain cases by making assessments in the alternative or by means of enforceable undertakings.

Where, following a court judgment against Customs on, for example, a liability point, Customs are appealing to have that judgment reversed, we would normally meet the claim of another taxpayer in a similar position and raise a recovery assessment to protect the revenue in the expectation that Customs' appeal will succeed. The *Laura Ashley* judgment may mean that such a protective assessment for an earlier period would be out of time under existing assessment time limit rules. In those circumstances, Customs will not pay a claim unless the claimant signs an undertaking to return any payment with interest in the event that the matter is finally determined in Customs' favour.

For the past, no corrective action is required, as any taxpayer who paid a recovery assessment made under VATA 1994 s 73(2) will have paid an amount that was properly due.

[VATA 1994 ss 73, 78A, 80]

17 SEPTEMBER 2004. BUSINESS BRIEF 26/04
VAT—TREATMENT OF SERVICES SUPPLIED BY INDEPENDENT FINANCIAL ADVISOR (IFA) NETWORKS

This Business Brief article clarifies the VAT treatment of services supplied by Independent Financial Advisor (IFA) networks and their appointed representatives (ARs).

BACKGROUND

Customs are aware there has recently been some concern over the VAT treatment of services supplied under arrangements that allow IFA firms, authorised to carry out regulated activities under the Financial Services and Markets Act 2000 (FSMA), to operate as networks for non-authorised financial advisers. Under these arrangements, the authorised IFA firm takes regulatory responsibility for non-regulated advisers, known as appointed representatives, enabling the ARs to carry out regulated activities without the need to be authorised directly by the Financial Services Authority (FSA).

Currently, "regulated activities" means the selling of investment products. This will extend to the selling of mortgages from 31 October 2004 and to general insurance sales in January 2005. This Business Brief only applies to regulated activities provided under IFA network arrangements.

These network arrangements are permitted under FSMA 2000 s 39 and are subject to strict regulatory rules. These rules are outlined in Chapter 12 of the Supervision Manual of the FSA Handbook and, in particular, the following should apply—

- the network appoints the ARs and trains them to operate in accordance with FSA requirements;
- in all dealings with the client, the ARs make it clear, both orally and on any paperwork, that they are acting on behalf of the network;
- the network has the contractual relationship with the financial product providers and at all times the AR acts on the network's behalf;
- the network maintains a high level of control over the ARs, carrying out regular checks and audits and imposing sanctions where appropriate;
- the network accepts responsibility for the actions of the ARs and handles all customer complaints made against the AR;
- the network meets the regulatory requirement relating to professional indemnity insurance to cover any claims resulting from the activities of the ARs and is legally liable for any sanctions imposed under the FSMA; and
- all fees or commissions for regulated activities are paid by the clients or product providers to the network and these form part of the income of the network for accounting and direct tax purposes.

VAT TREATMENT

When networks operate in this way, a "sub-agency" or "sub-contract" arrangement in effect exists between the network and the ARs. The network acts as principal, making supplies of financial intermediary services to the financial product providers and supplies of advice and/or financial intermediary services to the clients. The networks effectively sub-contract their functions to the ARs who interact directly with the client and the product providers in the provision of individual supplies on behalf of the network.

This means that—

- All payment (whether by fee or commission) received by the network from the product providers or clients for the supplies of regulated financial intermediary services provided via the ARs is the network's VAT exempt income, and the onward payment made to the ARs is consideration for the AR's VAT exempt intermediary services supplied to the network.
- Fees, whether paid directly to the network or via the ARs, in respect of regulated advice only services which fall outside the exemptions for intermediary services are the network's standard rated income. Any onward payment made by the network to the ARs is consideration for the provision of those services by the ARs

to the network on which VAT will be due if the AR is registered or required to be registered for VAT (ie its taxable income, including those onward payments, is above the VAT registration threshold).

- Any optional services supplied by the network to its ARs for additional consideration (such as specific compliance or IT services) will be separate supplies and the relevant VAT liability will apply.
- Any non-regulated services provided by ARs may fall outside the network arrangements altogether and, if so, will be made directly by the ARs to the client/product provider.

A different VAT treatment will apply to supplies made by networks that do not operate in the way outlined above (for example, firms, which on first appearance look like networks, but are set up to provide marketing and/or compliance support services to directly authorised IFA firms). In the event of any doubt, businesses are advised to contact Customs immediately on the number shown below.

[VATA 1994 s 4]

26 OCTOBER 2004. BUSINESS BRIEF 28/04 VAT—PLACE OF SUPPLY OF TRADING ALLOWANCES IN GREENHOUSE GAS EMISSIONS

This Business Brief article announces Customs' policy in determining the place of supply of emissions allowances when traded across borders. This follows extensive discussions in Europe on the EU Emissions Trading Scheme (EU ETS) and ensures consistency with other member states, removing the possibility for double or no taxation.

BACKGROUND

The EU ETS sets out the rules for a scheme in greenhouse gas emission allowance trading within the Community. It is likely to come into force on 1 January 2005. However, in advance of that date all member states have agreed the rules for determining the place of supply of those allowances for VAT purposes. Whilst the UK initially considered that the place of supply of such supplies would come under the "basic rule" (ie taxed in the country where the supplier is based), we have now agreed, as the result of representations made by businesses and discussions with other member states, that for cross-border supplies of allowances, the place of supply should be the place where the customer belongs. This approach aligns our place of supply treatment with other member states and therefore avoids instances of double taxation.

PLACE OF SUPPLY RULES

This only affects supplies of allowances when they are traded across borders; there is no change to the place of supply of supplies within a country (which continue to be taxed where the supplier is based, subject to the normal rules).

For supplies across borders, emissions trading in allowances will be treated as supplied where received (falling within VATA 1994 Sch 5 and Directive 77/388/EEC art 9(2)(*e*)).

The place of supply of brokers' services needs to be determined separately. As the place of supply for cross-border transactions in allowances is where they are received, the broker's supply will take place where that broker's customer belongs, regardless of where the actual emissions allowances are sold. According to the normal rules, a broker is regarded as such when sufficient intermediation is performed.

Introduction is not sufficient—where the service is one of mere introduction, the supply will be seen in accordance with the basic rule ie where the introducer belongs.

EFFECTIVE DATE

This policy will be implemented from the date of this Business Brief. However, suppliers may continue to treat their supplies as basic rule for contracts entered into before this date.

[VATA 1994 s 9]

11 NOVEMBER 2004. BUSINESS BRIEF 29/04
VAT—CLARIFICATION OF THE VALUE ADDED TAX (GROUPS—ELIGIBILITY) ORDER 2004

This Business Brief provides clarification of the Order, which came into force on 1 August 2004. The Order lays down additional tests that certain bodies corporate must satisfy in order to be members of a VAT group. These new tests only apply to VAT groups with turnover over £10 million in the last year, or expected turnover over £10 million in the coming year (the "de minimis" test). To avoid uncertainty about how to determine expected turnover for the VAT group, Article 3(2) of the Order assumes that the group includes the body that is applying for membership.

During Parliamentary debate on the Order, concern was expressed that Article 3(2) might require inclusion of the turnover of all bodies corporate not in the VAT group, including third parties who have nothing to do with the VAT group. This would make it impossible for any VAT group to ever satisfy the "de minimis" test. Customs do not agree with this reading and consider that, in context, it is clear that Article 3(2) refers only to the body that is applying to join the group. This is how Customs will apply the legislation in practice.

[SI 2004/1931 art 3]

19 NOVEMBER 2004. BUSINESS BRIEF 30/04
VAT AND PARTNERSHIP "SHARES"

BACKGROUND

Business Brief 21/04 clarified Customs' policy on share issues and partnership contributions following the European Court of Justice (ECJ) decision in *KapHag Renditefonds 35 Spreecenter Berlin-Hellersdorf3 Tranche GbR v Finanzamt Charlottenburg* (case C-442/01) [2003] ECR I–6851. That Business Brief did not deal with the VAT position of transfers of partnership interests ("shares"). This Business Brief explains the VAT treatment of transactions involving the transfer of a partner's "share".

IS THE DISPOSAL OF A "SHARE" IN A PARTNERSHIP A SUPPLY?

KapHag established that a partnership entity or the existing partners are making no supply when a new partner is admitted in return for making a capital contribution. The question arises whether the subsequent disposal by the partner of that "share" in the partnership is a supply for VAT purposes. It is important to bear in mind that this "share" is distinct from the assets that were contributed by the partner when they joined the partnership. Therefore, even though the selling price of the "share" may be determined by the value of those assets, they are not the subject of the later sale, which has its own liability for VAT purposes.

Although the ECJ has not considered this type of transaction with respect to partnership "shares", there have been a number of cases where it has given a decision in respect of transactions involving shares in companies. The cases of *Polysar Investments Netherlands BV v Inspecteur der Invoerrechten en Accijnzen, Arnhem* (case C-60/90) [1993] STC 222, *Harnas & Helm CV v Staatssecretaris van Financiën* (case C-80/95), *Wellcome Trust Ltd v C & E Comrs* (case C-155/94) [1996] STC 945 and *Régie Dauphinoise-Cabinet A Forest SARL v Ministre du Budget* (case C-306/94) [1996] STC 1176 have established that the mere acquisition and holding of shares in a company is not to be regarded as an economic activity. However, it has stated that transactions in shares or interests in companies and associations may constitute economic activity in three situations:

(a) where the transactions constitute the direct, permanent and necessary extension of an economic activity;

(b) where the transactions are effected in order to secure a direct or indirect involvement in the management of a company in which the holding is acquired;
(c) where the transactions are effected as part of a commercial share-dealing activity.

Customs considers that the same principles apply to transactions involving partnership "shares". This means that in some circumstances the disposal of a partnership "share" will not constitute a supply and in others it will.

Circumstances in which the disposal of a partnership "share" will not constitute a supply

This list is not exhaustive. The most common situations in which the disposal of a partnership "share" by a partner will not be a supply are likely to be:

1. **The "share" is disposed of for no consideration.** A "share" in a partnership comprises services rather than goods. When services are transferred, assigned or otherwise disposed of for no consideration, they do not constitute any supply for VAT purposes.
2. **The "share" being sold was acquired simply as an investment.** Where a partner has acquired his "share" merely to secure a share in any future profits and has had no involvement in running the partnership, the subsequent sale or assignment of that "share" for consideration will not be an economic activity. This will not constitute any supply for VAT purposes.

Circumstances in which the disposal of a partnership "share" will constitute a supply

Again, this list is not exhaustive. The most common situations in which the disposal of a partnership "share" by a partner will be a supply are likely to be:

1. **Where the partnership "share" was acquired and disposed of as a direct extension of the partner's economic activities.** Where a partner is a taxable person in their own right, the partnership "share" may have been acquired in the course or furtherance of their own economic activities. If that is the case, the subsequent transfer or assignment of that "share" for a consideration will also be economic activity of that taxable person. For example, the partner may have a business asset to be sold and, rather than selling the asset directly, may have contributed that asset into a partnership and sold the resultant partnership "share" instead. The sale of that partnership "share" will constitute a supply for VAT purposes.

2. **Where the partnership "share" was acquired in order to obtain an active role in the business of the partnership.** Where a partner is a taxable person in their own right and had acquired the partnership "share" in order to actively participate in, or control, the business of the partnership, then the sale of that "share" can be economic activity on the partner's part.

The sale of the "share" will constitute a supply for VAT purposes.

3. **Where the partnership "share" was acquired as part of a commercial partnership "share-dealing" activity.** A partner who is a taxable person may have a business of dealing in partnership "shares". This will be economic activity on the partner's part. Sales or assignments of the partnership "shares" that were acquired in the course of this activity that are for a consideration will constitute supplies for VAT purposes.

For the avoidance of any doubt, you should note that supplies of partnership "shares" in the above circumstances cannot be disregarded by virtue of VATA 1994 s 45(1). As Business Brief 21/04, 10 August 2004 explained, the purpose of s 45(1) is to ensure continuity by providing that changes in the composition of a partnership do not create the need for a partnership to deregister and re-register for VAT every time the partners change. It also makes it unnecessary to take account of any changes in the composition of the partnership when determining what supplies have been made or received by the partnership business. The section has no effect upon any supply that one of the partners may be making as a taxable person in their own right.

LIABILITY OF SUPPLIES OF PARTNERSHIP SHARES

In those circumstances where the disposal of a partnership "share" is a supply, that supply will be an exempt financial service.

TREATMENT OF VAT ON ASSOCIATED PURCHASES

Where the disposal of an existing partnership "share" is not a supply, the VAT incurred in connection with the disposal will normally not be input tax. Where the disposal is a supply, the related VAT will be input tax, but recovery will normally be fully restricted under the partial exemption rules as the supply is exempt. This is subject to the de minimis provisions (see VAT Notice 706 "Partial Exemption").

APPLICATION TO PAST TRANSACTIONS

This Business Brief clarifies existing policy and the above principles will be applied to all future transactions. Where a past transaction has been treated differently from the above and resulted in an underdeclaration Customs will take no further action. If a past transaction has been treated differently and resulted in an overdeclaration, businesses may use the voluntary disclosure procedure to reclaim the VAT. Any such claims will be subject to the "three-year capping rules" and rules relating to the payment of statutory interest.

[VATA 1994 s 5]

15 DECEMBER 2004. BUSINESS BRIEF 34/04
VAT—PARTIAL EXEMPTION: FLOOR-AREAS BASED SPECIAL METHODS IN THE RETAIL SECTOR

This Business Brief article sets out Customs' view on the use of floor-area based calculations in partial exemption special methods (special methods), particularly in the retail sector. No other businesses are affected.

This brief deals with questions put to Customs following the Tribunal's decision in the case of *Optika Ltd* (No 18627) ("Optika"). There is no change of Customs' policy. Further information on partial exemption is available in Notice 706 "Partial Exemption".

BACKGROUND

Optika, a retail optician, appealed against Customs' rejection of their proposed floor-area based special method. The Tribunal agreed with Customs because, in Optika's case, a floor-area based special method did not give a fair and reasonable result. A method is likely to be fair and reasonable if it:

- can be operated by the business;
- can be checked by Customs; and
- produces a fair result.

In the right circumstances, floor-area based methods will meet all these conditions and Customs will approve them.

FLOOR-AREA BASED SPECIAL METHODS

Floor-area based special methods are likely to be acceptable when:

- most of the business's VAT bearing costs relate to their premises; and
- most of the floor-area of those premises is used for either wholly taxable or wholly exempt activities, with only minor areas relating to both.

FLOOR-AREA IN THE RETAIL SECTOR—THE IMPACT OF OPTIKA

Floor-area based special methods are seldom fair and reasonable for retailers. The following features from the *Optika* case illustrate this.

- NOTIONAL SPLITS OF "MIXED USE" AREAS: Few areas of Optika's premises were exclusively used for taxable or exempt activities. Optika's proposals therefore required notional splits of mixed-use floor-areas in order to create any workable calculation. Methods that require significant notional splits are unacceptable due to the inherent uncertainties in making and checking them.
- WEIGHTING OF FLOOR AREAS: The method proposed by Optika required a weighting of floor areas with those at the front of the premises having far greater impact on the amount of tax deductible. Optika argued this reflected a system of weightings (known as zoning) commonly used by landlords to calculate rental charges. However, just because zoning is used to calculate an overall rent, this does not mean that more is charged for some areas than for others. Each rental is a single supply covering the entire premises.
- USE OF RETAIL AREAS: Optika's proposals assumed that the use made of the retail area and the shop front related to their taxable products. However the shop front attracted customers to purchase all of their products and much of the selling of exempt products took place in the retail area. Consequently the shop front and retail area are related to both taxable and exempt sales. Because the proposals were based on a mistaken assumption, they were unacceptable.

Many retailers share some or all of these features, either generally or in specific floor-area based special method proposals. Where this occurs floor-area based special methods will not be approved.

FLOOR-AREA IN THE RETAIL SECTOR—GENERAL

The sale of exempt products is often an important and consistent part of the trading activities of retailers, making a significant contribution to profits. For example when finance or insurance is standardly offered and actively marketed on goods being sold. Many retailers advertise and sell both taxable and exempt products in a large proportion of their premises. Where these factors are present, floor-area is unlikely to prove capable of providing a good basis for a special method.

Customs will refuse to approve any method that includes one or more of the features confirmed as unacceptable in the *Optika* case. Customs will seek to amend or replace any such existing methods that come to light. Businesses who feel that their current special method might not be fair and reasonable, based on the content of this brief, should contact their local VAT office or Customs' National Advice Service.

[SI 1994/2158 reg 102]

19 JANUARY 2005. BUSINESS BRIEF 1/05
VAT—TRIBUNAL DECISION IN EDINBURGH LEISURE, SOUTH LANARKSHIRE LEISURE AND RENFREWSHIRE LEISURE

The VAT and Duties Tribunal has found in favour of the appellants in the joined appeals of *Edinburgh Leisure, South Lanarkshire Leisure and Renfrewshire Leisure* (No 18784). This Business Brief article explains Customs' position following that decision.

. . .

THE COMMISSIONERS' VIEWS

Customs shall not be appealing the Tribunal's decision and we accept that, on the facts of the case, the payments from the local authorities to the appellants constituted consideration for a supply, that of agreeing to take over the provision of leisure services previously supplied by the local authority.

However, Customs' interpretation of the relevant legislation is that it does not impose an obligation on local authorities to provide leisure facilities themselves, only that they must ensure that there is adequate provision within their area.

Additionally, in Customs' view the relevant legislation does not require local authorities to enter into contracts with parties to discharge this duty. The legislation gives local authorities flexibility in how they meet the obligation to ensure the adequate provision of leisure, including the award of grants or loans.

Consequently, whilst Customs recognise that local authorities may wish to ensure that leisure facilities are widely available to all, including the more socially and economically disadvantaged, in all cases the terms of the payment and the direct benefit received by the funding body must be considered.

GUIDANCE AND MEMORANDUM OF UNDERSTANDING (MOU) WITH CIPFA

A long standing Memorandum of Understanding between Customs and the Chartered Institute of Public Finance and Accountancy (CIPFA) sets out the various scenarios relating to the provision of leisure services and their VAT consequences. It also offers guidance on situations similar to those considered by the Tribunal. It explains that VAT treatment generally depends on the circumstances in which the payments are made—in some cases they are simply grants and therefore outside the scope, whilst in others they are consideration for a supply. Customs are considering whether the MoU requires amendment or clarification in the light of this Tribunal decision.

[VATA 1994 s 5]

10 FEBRUARY 2005. BUSINESS BRIEF 2/05
VAT—SUPPLIES OF NURSERY AND CRECHE FACILITIES BY A CHARITY

This Business Brief article is issued to clarify Customs' position on the business status of supplies of nursery and creche facilities where those supplies are made by a charity. This issue first arose as a result of the High Court case of *C & E Comrs v Yarburgh Children's Trust* [2002] STC 207 (see Business Brief 4/03, 27 May 2003) and has recently been tested again in the High Court case of *C & E Comrs v St Paul's Community Project Ltd* [2005] STC 95.

In the earlier case of *Yarburgh*, the Court decided that the charity was not making supplies by way of business. Despite that decision, Customs' position remained that the provision of nursery and creche facilities in such circumstances was a business activity for VAT purposes. However, in the more recent case of *St Paul's*, the Court's decision has again gone in favour of the charity. The Court found that the intrinsic nature of the enterprise was not the carrying on of a business, identifying the distinguishing features as the social concern for the welfare of disadvantaged children, lack of commerciality in setting fees and the overall intention simply to cover costs.

Customs do not agree that these features point to the activities being non-business because we consider that the charity is making supplies of services for consideration in much the same way as a commercial nursery. However, taking into account all the circumstances in this case, Customs have decided not to appeal further.

This means Customs will now accept that the provision of nursery and creche facilities by charities, along the same lines as those in *Yarburgh Children's Trust* and *St Paul's Community Project Ltd*, is not a business activity for VAT purposes.

BACKGROUND

Both Yarburgh Children's Trust and St Paul's Community Project Ltd are charities which undertake to provide nursery and creche facilities for pre-school age children as part of their charitable objectives. Both organisations charge fees for their services, which are set at a level designed to ensure that they merely cover their costs. They both undertook construction of new nursery premises. Such supplies would normally be subject to VAT but there are provisions in UK law which allow construction work to be zero-rated where buildings are used by a charity otherwise than in the course of business. Zero-rating can be beneficial to charities, if they undertake exempt activities and the amount of VAT they recover would be heavily restricted. Customs denied zero-rating on the grounds that these charities were making business supplies. The High Court has taken the opposing view that neither charity is in business for VAT purposes.

CUSTOMS' POLICY

It remains Customs' long standing policy that a business activity is possible even in the absence of a profit motive. Customs believe that this approach is consistent with UK and EC legislation and is supported by a number of decisions of the UK and European Courts. Many charities with activities not motivated by profit and whose fees are subsidised by public funds or donations benefit from such activities being business for VAT purposes, because they are able to recover VAT incurred in relation to those activities. It would not be beneficial for the charity sector as a whole if charitable activities were all regarded as non-business, as it would deny them recovery of input tax. In cases that are not broadly in line with St Paul's or Yarburgh, Customs shall continue to apply the business test, in order to determine whether the supplies concerned are being made by way of business.

WHAT CONSTITUTES A BUSINESS ACTIVITY FOR VAT PURPOSES?

As neither UK nor EC legislation has provided an exhaustive definition or test for determining if an activity is business, the meaning of business and economic activity has emerged from a body of case law. This has given rise to the business test, which consists of six elements or indicators that the Courts have seen as being characteristic of a business. These are not a checklist and a business may have some, but not all, of the features indicated. Instead they are a set of tools designed to help compare activities where there is some uncertainty about their nature with features of activities that are clearly business. In most cases, it will be clear that an activity is business but, where difficulties arise, Customs will apply this business test. The elements of this test were set out in Business Brief 4/03 and are reproduced below.

- Is the activity a serious undertaking earnestly pursued? (This considers whether the activity is carried on for business or daily work rather than pleasure or daily enjoyment.)
- Is the activity an occupation or function that is actively pursued with reasonable or recognisable continuity? (When considering this test one should consider how frequently the supplies will be made.)
- Does the activity have a certain measure of substance in terms of the quarterly or annual value of taxable supplies made?
- Is the activity conducted in a regular manner and on sound and recognised business principles?
- Is the activity predominately concerned with the making of taxable supplies for a consideration? (This has in many instances been seen as the most important and arguably the most problematic indicator. In the appeal of The Institute of Chartered Accountants England & Wales, the House of Lords found that the test must be read as asking "what is the real nature of the activity" ie is the real nature of the activity the making of taxable supplies for consideration or is it something else?)
- Are the taxable supplies that are being made of a kind which, subject to differences of detail, are commonly made by those who seek to profit from them?

[VATA 1994 s 94 and Sch 8 Group 5 Note 6]

21 FEBRUARY 2005. BUSINESS BRIEF 3/05
VAT—CLARIFICATION OF THE LIABILITY OF THE SUPPLY OF LIFTS TO EDUCATIONAL INSTITUTIONS

This Business Brief sets out Customs' policy on the VAT treatment of lifts installed in educational institutions.

BACKGROUND

Educational institutions which have charitable status, such as grant-maintained schools and universities, can receive the supply and installation of lifts to facilitate the movement of disabled staff and pupils between floors in certain buildings at the zero rate of VAT. For such supplies to qualify for zero-rating, the building must be used by the educational institution for the provision of a permanent or temporary residence or a day-centre for disabled people. The relevant legislation is VATA 1994 Sch 8 Group 12 Items 17 and 18.

As a consequence of comments made by the High Court in 1997 in *C & E Comrs v Help the Aged* [1997] STC 406, Customs formed the view that educational institutions could be regarded as day-centres providing care for disabled people and therefore the installation of lifts in their non-residential buildings could be zero-rated under the above provisions, providing all other conditions were met.

Customs subsequently reconsidered our understanding of the comments made by the High Court, which concerned the interpretation of a different piece of legislation, and decided our original view of them was incorrect. Whilst having a duty of care, especially to disabled people, educational institutions, generally, do not provide care in a day-centre and the High Court's comments did not suggest that they do. Customs' policy therefore reverted to the scope of the zero-rating being limited to the supply of lifts installed in residential accommodation.

However, as a concession, where an educational institution could demonstrate that they had made a decision to proceed with the purchase and installation of a lift in non-residential accommodation before 1 January 2004, on the basis of our former policy, then zero-rating would apply. Additionally, Customs agreed that any lifts zero-rated in this way could also benefit from the zero-rating of their future repair and maintenance under the provisions of VATA 1994 Sch 8 Group 12 Item 5.

Unfortunately, the changes in policy were not widely publicised at the time and we have recently been made aware that not all those concerned were aware of them. Customs have therefore decided to publicise the change of policy by means of this Business Brief. Customs have also decided to extend the transitional arrangements so that where a contract for the installation of a lift in non-residential accommodation has been entered into before 31 March 2005; we accept that the supply can be zero-rated providing all other conditions have been met. Where the installation of a lift has been zero-rated under these arrangements, subsequent supplies of repair and maintenance of that lift can also be zero-rated.

Where a contract for the installation of a lift in non-residential accommodation is entered into after that date the supply of installation services and any subsequent supplies of repair and maintenance will be standard-rated.

. . .

This Business Brief does not apply to lift installations in those buildings where an educational institution provides permanent or temporary residence, which remains zero-rated, provided all other conditions are met.

[VATA 1994 Sch 8 Group 12 Item 5]

3 MARCH 2005. BUSINESS BRIEF 5/05
VAT—PRIVATE WELFARE AGENCIES: EFFECTIVE DATE OF STATE-REGULATION

This Business Brief item announces a change in Customs' policy concerning the date from which commercial providers of welfare services (such as domiciliary care agencies and independent fostering agencies) are "state-regulated" and thereby required to exempt their services. It supplements the announcement of exemption for welfare services provided by state regulated private welfare agencies in Business Brief 01/03, 20 January 2003, and cancels the item on VAT exemption and independent fostering agencies published in Business Brief 03/03, 28 March 2003.

This announcement does not have any impact upon any supplies made by local authorities, charitable bodies or residential institutions, such as homes for children or the elderly.

. . .

WHEN IS A WELFARE PROVIDER "STATE-REGULATED"?

The question of when a welfare agency is "state-regulated", and thereby required to exempt welfare supplies, has been reviewed. Customs now accept that a welfare provider is not "state-regulated" until its registration has been approved by the relevant national body for the regulation and/or inspection of care. A welfare provider is not "state-regulated" for the purposes of the VAT exemption, and therefore not required to exempt welfare services, during the period of time in which this registration application is being considered and processed.

. . .

[VATA 1994 Sch 9 Group 7 Item 9(*b*)]

4 APRIL 2005. BUSINESS BRIEF 9/05
VAT—HOT TAKE-AWAY FOOD

This Business Brief clarifies Customs policy on the treatment of hot take-away food in light of recent VAT Tribunal decisions. It includes some minor amendments to policy, and replaces the guidance previously published in Business Brief 26/02, 2 October 2002.

Most food is zero-rated for VAT purposes. But hot take-away food and drink is standard-rated, whether sold from a traditional take-away, supermarket or any other outlet. Standard rating applies where the supplier's main intention in heating the food is to enable it to be consumed hot or warm (regardless of whether, in practice, the food is always consumed hot or warm). Standard rating applies irrespective of the customer's intention, the place of consumption or whether the food is collected or delivered.

CAN HOT FOOD BE ZERO-RATED?

You can only zero-rate hot food if your main purpose in heating the food is other than to enable it to be consumed hot or warm. For example, newly baked bread is often warm when sold, but is not normally heated for the purpose of enabling it to be consumed hot or warm. In some cases suppliers have stated that they have other reasons for heating food and supplying it hot or warm. Supplies in such cases may qualify for zero-rating, but only where the circumstances (ie the nature of the product and the way in which it is stored, displayed, advertised, packaged and supplied) support the contention that the supplier's main purpose is other than to enable the food to be consumed hot. For example, items like chips, hot dogs, burgers and baked potatoes are always standard rated when sold hot because they are clearly intended to be eaten hot.

HOW DO I KNOW IF I CAN ZERO-RATE HOT FOOD?

You can only zero-rate hot food if your main reason for heating the food is other than to enable it to be consumed hot or warm. Any such claims must be consistent with the circumstances under which the hot food is supplied (see below). It is important to consider all of your reasons for heating the food before deciding on the VAT liability of your supplies. Often you may have more than one purpose in heating the food, in which case you must decide which is the dominant purpose.

On the basis of Tribunal and court findings, Customs consider the following to be relevant indicators.

- Type of outlet—if advertised as a take-away food outlet, supplies of hot food will be standard-rated.
- What happens to the food between the time it is cooked or heated and the time it is handed to the customer—if efforts are made to keep it hot, this may be an indicator for standard rating, whereas if it is left to cool naturally for a period of time this may be an indicator for zero-rating.
- Type of packaging used—if food is packaged to retain heat, this would be an indicator for standard rating. However, the reverse does not necessarily apply, since food intended for immediate consumption will often be sold in packaging that is not heat retentive.
- Availability of condiments, napkins and utensils—this would be an indicator for standard rating.
- The way in which the food is advertised and promoted, including in-store signage and any wording shown on packaging.
- Food hygiene regulations—Customs accept that in some cases food may be kept hot partly for the purpose of complying with food hygiene regulations. However, the requirement to comply with these regulations will often not be an aim in itself for the supplier, but merely a consequence of supplying food for consumption whilst hot or warm. If this is the case, then the supplies will be standard rated.
- Palatability—if an item is generally accepted to be unpalatable when cold, this would be an indicator for standard rating. However, the reverse does not necessarily apply—the fact that an item remains palatable when cold does not preclude the possibility that it has been heated for the purpose of enabling it to be consumed hot.

[VATA 1994 Sch 8 Group 1]

4 APRIL 2005. BUSINESS BRIEF 9/05
VAT—TRANSFER OF GOING CONCERN (TOGC): UK IMPLEMENTATION OF THE EUROPEAN COURT OF JUSTICE (ECJ) JUDGMENT IN THE CASE OF ZITA MODES SARL

This Business Brief article explains Customs' position following the ECJ judgment of 27 November 2003 in the case of *Zita Modes Sarl v Administration de l'enregistrement et des domains* (case C-497/01) [2003] SWTI 2225 ("Zita Modes").

. . .

CUSTOMS' POSITION

Customs' view is that UK legislation is in line with the *Zita Modes* decision. Therefore, no legislative changes will be made in response to this decision. Customs are considering whether changes to our guidance are needed to ensure the legislation is interpreted consistently with the ECJ decision in *Zita Modes*.

Customs will continue to consider changes to guidance and, where necessary, our legislation to prevent distortion of competition and combat avoidance.

. . .

[SI 1995/1268 art 5]

18 MAY 2005. BUSINESS BRIEF 11/05
ZERO RATING FOR PROTECTED BUILDINGS—DEFINITION OF GARAGE

This Business Brief article sets out HM Revenue & Customs' (HMRC) revised policy on what constitutes a "garage" for the purpose of the zero ratings relating to listed buildings which are dwellings.

It follows a decision of the VAT & Duties Tribunal in the case of *Grange Builders (Quainton) Ltd* (No 18905).

. . .

HM REVENUE & CUSTOMS' REVISED POLICY

HMRC now accept that, provided a garage is in use as a garage before the alteration or reconstruction takes place and continues to be used as one afterwards, it is not necessary for the garage to have been constructed as a garage (ie as an enclosure for the storage of motor vehicles). It can also have been constructed as something different eg a barn. The other criteria for zero rating must still be met; these are—

- listing (the garage must be listed, either in its own right or through the deeming provisions of planning law);
- occupation (the garage must be occupied together with the dwelling); and
- time of construction (the garage must have been either constructed at the same time as the listed dwelling or, where the dwelling has been substantially reconstructed, at the same time as that reconstruction).

. . .

[VATA 1994 Sch 8 Group 6 Note 2]

15 JUNE 2005. BUSINESS BRIEF 12/05
VAT—ALIGNING VAT ACCOUNTING PERIODS

This Business Brief article explains and further publicises HM Revenue & Customs' existing policy on the use of the power to align VAT accounting periods.

BACKGROUND

HM Revenue & Customs continue to be concerned about situations in which businesses "stagger" their VAT accounting periods in order to gain an unjustified and unintended cash flow benefit at the expense of the revenue.

One familiar example is the routing of export sales through a subsidiary which is outside the VAT group, or main VAT registration. In these cases, the export company has zero rated outputs and makes monthly repayment claims. By contrast, output tax on the supply to the subsidiary is standard rated and only brought to account by the parent or other associated company once a quarter. There is, accordingly, a cashflow benefit to the corporate group.

HM REVENUE & CUSTOMS' POLICY ON ALIGNMENT

HM Revenue & Customs have a discretionary power in VAT Regulations 1995, SI 1995/2518 reg 25 to align VAT periods between the associated businesses, thereby removing the cash flow benefit. They may exercise that power by either withdrawing existing permission for monthly periods or by directing a variation to accounting periods. HM Revenue & Customs intend to continue to exercise this power where there is little or no commercial rationale for the VAT period "stagger" between the associated businesses besides obtaining the cash flow advantage. They may do so, notwithstanding that the usual policy for businesses expecting to make regular claims for repayment of VAT in other factual situations is to allow monthly returns.

There is no intention to use these powers except in cases where a significant cash flow advantage arises and there is a need to protect the revenue.

HM REVENUE & CUSTOMS' USE OF THE REGULATION 25 POWERS

There is no right of appeal to the VAT and Duties Tribunal against the use of the regulation 25 powers. However, the use of the power is subject to judicial review and new guidance shortly to be issued to staff will emphasise the need for exercise of the powers to be proportionate and to take into account all relevant information. That guidance will be available soon through the normal channels.

[SI 1995/2518 reg 25]

15 JUNE 2005. BUSINESS BRIEF 12/05
VAT—LANDLORD INDUCEMENTS TO TENANTS ENTERING LEASES

This Business Brief article provides revised guidance on the VAT status of inducement payments by landlords to tenants. It replaces earlier guidance in Business Brief 4/03, dated 27 May 2003.

BUSINESS BRIEF 4/03

Business Brief 4/03 set out Customs' policy following the European Court of Justice (ECJ) and High Court decisions in the case of *Trinity Mirror plc v C & E Comrs* (case C-409/98) [2001] STC 1453, ECJ and *Trinity Mirror plc (formerly Mirror Group plc) v C & E Comrs* [2003] STC 518.

In paragraph 26 of the ECJ's judgment, it was held that a "tenant who undertakes, even in return for a payment from the landlord, solely to become a tenant and pay the rent does not, so far as that action is concerned, make a supply of services to the landlord". The High Court subsequently held that paragraph 26 of the ECJ judgment is narrowly drawn, and Business Brief 4/03 sought to give guidance on that.

In line with the High Court ruling, Business Brief 4/03 advised that "a prospective tenant receiving an inducement payment would make a taxable supply by affording the landlord the advantage of being bound by the lease obligations the tenant has to fulfil." In effect, this meant any such obligations other than to pay the rent (eg to redecorate the demised area every five years) would be sufficient to make the inducement payment consideration for a taxable supply.

CHANGE OF POLICY

Following representations from and detailed discussions with various bodies, HM Revenue & Customs now accept that lease obligations, to which tenants are normally bound, do not constitute supplies for which inducement payments on entering leases are consideration.

HM Revenue & Customs believe that the majority of such payments are therefore likely to be outside the scope of VAT as they are no more than inducements to tenants to take leases and to observe the obligations in them. There will be a taxable supply only where a payment is linked to benefits a tenant provides outside normal lease terms. However, merely putting such a benefit as an obligation in a lease will not mean it ceases to be a taxable transaction.

It is considered that this change of policy now effectively puts inducement payments on a similar VAT footing to rent free periods, in being mainly outside the scope of VAT and only a taxable consideration when directly linked to a specific benefit supplied by a tenant to a landlord.

Examples of *taxable* benefits by tenants that may be supplied in return for such inducements are:

- Carrying out building works to improve the property by undertaking necessary repairs or upgrading the property.
- Carrying out fitting-out or refurbishment works for which the landlord has responsibility and is paying the tenant to undertake.

ACTING AS ANCHOR TENANT

HM Revenue & Customs accept that this is a difficult area where the undertakings of landlords and tenants can change a number of times in the course of negotiating a tenancy. HM Revenue & Customs will therefore seek as much documentation as possible before reaching a decision. HM Revenue & Customs will not assume that there has been a supply and agree that less specific indicators do not determine the issue. For example, publicity indicating that Company X is to take a lease in a development does not, in itself, determine that the company is an anchor tenant.

Equally, undertakings to use improved materials as part of continuous repairs under a tenant repairing lease would not constitute a taxable benefit to the landlord under the first example above.

. . .

[VATA 1994 s 5]

4 JULY 2005. BUSINESS BRIEF 13/05
VAT: BELATED NOTIFICATION OF AN OPTION TO TAX LAND AND BUILDINGS—CLARIFICATION OF HM REVENUE & CUSTOMS' POLICY

This Business Brief clarifies HM Revenue & Customs' (HMRC) policy in relation to the exercise of their discretion to accept a belated notification of an option to tax land and buildings. In particular, it explains the distinction between a belated notification and a retrospective or backdated option. This clarification is given following a rise in the number of attempts to notify options to tax that are retrospective or backdated.

WHO IS AFFECTED?

All those who seek acknowledgement of a decision to opt to tax (sometimes known as an election to waive exemption) outside the 30-day time limit.

BACKGROUND

There are two distinct stages in the process of opting to tax. The first is making the decision to opt, the 'election'. The second is notifying HMRC of that decision, in writing, within 30 days of the date that the decision was made.

Of course, HMRC must be satisfied that the trader was legally entitled to opt to tax. If a trader has made previous exempt supplies of the property, they may require our prior written permission to opt to tax. If permission is required, the trader cannot make a valid election until our permission has been received. The circumstances when permission is required are detailed in VAT Notice 742A Opting to tax land and buildings, Section 5.

RETROSPECTIVE OR BACKDATED OPTIONS

The option has effect from the day on which the election is made or any later day specified in the election. This means that no option to tax can take effect from a date prior to the date on which the trader decided to make the election. This would be a backdated or retrospective option and HMRC has no discretion under the law to accept or acknowledge that it is valid.

BELATED NOTIFICATION OF AN OPTION

However, HMRC has discretion to accept a notification of an option to tax later than the prescribed time limit of 30 days after the decision to opt was made. The discretion is designed to cover situations where a trader has genuinely made the decision to opt to tax, but has failed to notify it to HMRC in time. Before considering whether to exercise this discretion, we would need to be satisfied that the decision was made on the date stated in the written notification.

EXERCISING THE DISCRETION

HMRC will usually accept a belated notification if a trader provides evidence, such as the minutes of a Board or management meeting, or correspondence referring to the decision.

However, we accept that this is sometimes not available, so in its absence we would normally accept a statement from the responsible person, plus evidence that

- all the relevant facts have been given;
- output tax has been properly charged and accounted for from the date of the supposed election; and
- input tax recovery in respect of the land or building is consistent with the trader having made taxable supplies of it.

There may be other circumstances where we would accept a belated notification, but this would depend on the individual circumstances of the case.

Conversely, HMRC may not accept that a decision to opt was taken, even when the above conditions are met, if for example —

- there has been correspondence concerning or investigation into the liability of supplies of the property in question since the supposed date of the option, and no mention of the option to tax was made;
- the trader or his representative has previously put forward an alternative explanation for the charging of output tax (for example, that the supply was not of land and buildings, or was of a sports facility).

Moreover, HMRC reserves the right to refuse to accept the belated notification if to do so would produce an unfair result, or if the exercise of the discretion was sought in connection with a tax avoidance scheme.

[VATA 1994 Sch 10 paras 2, 3]

27 JULY 2005. BUSINESS BRIEF 14/05
VAT—DISCLOSURE OF VAT AVOIDANCE SCHEMES—CHANGES TO THE RULES

. . .

This Business Brief . . . clarifies the application of the existing "confidentiality" hallmark.

. . .

CLARIFICATION OF THE CONFIDENTIALITY HALLMARK

One of the existing hallmarks is that a confidentiality condition prohibits or limits a person from giving others details of how a scheme gives a tax advantage. It is standard practice for advisers to include a "general confidentiality condition" within their terms of engagement, prohibiting the client from passing on advice to third parties.

Professional advisers have raised concerns that a literal interpretation of the legislation would result in any tax advice that was subject to such a general confidentiality condition falling within the hallmark.

The confidentiality hallmark is aimed at confidentiality conditions that are intended to protect the competitive advantage of a promoter or creator of the scheme over other promoters. That competitive advantage is most likely to arise from the promoter being aware of an opportunity to profit from innovative tax avoidance ideas so that he would want to keep his tax scheme secret from other persons. Such conditions are usually imposed by a promoter on a potential user before explaining the workings of the scheme.

Consistent with this, HMRC's interpretation of the legislation is that a confidentiality condition does not fall within the hallmark if it is simply a general confidentiality condition that is imposed in relation to all advice, not merely the scheme in question.

Subject to this, HMRC consider that a scheme will fall within the confidentiality hallmark if either:

- a specific condition of confidentiality is imposed that prohibits or limits a person from revealing details of how a particular scheme gives rise to a tax advantage;

- a general confidentiality condition is introduced specifically in order to prohibit or limit a person from revealing details of how a particular scheme gives rise to a tax advantage;
- a client is required to undertake (either in writing or verbally) not to reveal details of how a particular scheme gives rise to a tax advantage; or
- an adviser specifically draws a client's attention to a pre-existing general confidentiality condition when introducing a scheme to the client, in order to prohibit or limit the client from revealing details of how that particular scheme gives rise to a tax advantage.

VAT Notice 700/8 (August 2004), "Disclosure of VAT Avoidance Schemes", is being updated and will be reissued shortly.

[SI 2004/1933 Sch 2 para 1]

9 AUGUST 2005. BUSINESS BRIEF 15/05
VAT: RECOVERY OF INPUT TAX BY EMPLOYERS IN RESPECT OF FUNDED PENSION SCHEMES—THE 30/70 SPLIT

This Business Brief clarifies the rules relating to recovery of input tax by employers who provide funded pension schemes for their staff and, in particular, sets out the correct application of the rule commonly known as the 30/70 split. This is to address increasing HM Revenue & Customs (HMRC) concerns that businesses are applying the 30/70 split more generously than is intended and recovering input tax to which they are not entitled. The new arrangements will come into effect from [1 January 2006].

BACKGROUND

An employer usually establishes a funded pension scheme under a trust deed and, in consequence, the business activities of the fund are separate from those of the employer. Where trustees of a pension fund are carrying on taxable business activities, they are liable or entitled to register for VAT, although they normally have to restrict their input tax deduction because they usually make mainly exempt supplies. HMRC accepts that employers establish pension schemes for business purposes and that VAT on expenditure relating to management, or what can also be termed administration, of the pension scheme is their input tax. Correct attribution of the services between employer and trustees is essential – just as it is in any situation where both exempt and taxable supplies are made.

VAT Notice 700/17 "Funded Pension Schemes", paragraph 2.8 states that where third parties, such as fund managers, are appointed to manage the scheme, their charges will usually cover both management services to the employer as well as investment services proper to the trust. Where such third parties issue only one invoice for both supplies, HMRC has generally accepted that the employer can treat 30 per cent of the VAT charged as his input tax, with the remaining 70 per cent being proper to the fund (this is commonly known as the 30/70 split).

The 30/70 split has been in operation for many years and was intended as a facilitation measure in days before the present level of computerisation, when it would have been more difficult to determine separate values for these supplies. However, an HMRC review has shown that, where separate invoices are issued for management services and for services in respect of fund activities, the 30/70 split has also become a frequently used method of attribution. This happens even where the work could easily be separated out and invoices issued based on the actual values of the respective services. In some cases, the 30/70 split is even being used where fund managers are providing no pension scheme administration services whatsoever to the employer, but are providing services that relate wholly to exploitation of the fund's assets. Also, where the third party does undertake work of an administrative nature because of, among other things, increased computerisation, it is often a much less significant component of the whole activity than in the past.

HMRC does not wish to withdraw an arrangement which is a helpful business facilitation. However, where employers administer the scheme themselves, or engage specialist pension scheme administrators and in addition separately engage fund managers to provide investment services only, it is clearly inappropriate to attribute 30 per cent of the fund managers' charges to the management of the pension scheme. HMRC considers that, in most cases nowadays, fund managers and other professionals are easily able to distinguish the nature of their services and issue separate invoices to employers and trustees, reflecting the actual values of the services provided to each.

NEW ARRANGEMENTS WITH EFFECT FROM [1 JANUARY 2006]

Third parties providing both investment and administration services who are able to determine the actual values of each must provide separate invoices to trustees and employers showing the actual value of services provided. Where third parties are genuinely unable to determine separate values for investment and administration services, HMRC will continue to accept use of the 30/70 split, but only where the third parties are administering the pension scheme fully or providing the bulk of the administration of the scheme.

In all other cases, employers will have to agree a fair and reasonable apportionment with HMRC that is robust, transparent and able to be tested. Where employers consider that the administration work done amounts to more than 30 per cent of the total services provided, they will also have to agree an apportionment with HMRC, but our current enquiries have indicated that the administration element is more often well below 30 per cent.

WHAT DOES THIS MEAN FOR EMPLOYERS?

HMRC will not challenge use of the 30/70 split for invoices received for periods up to and including [31 December 2005]. After this date, if HMRC considers that employers have over-recovered input tax, an assessment will be raised to recover this. This means, of course, that any tax over-claimed by employers is proper to the trustees of the fund and may be recovered by them, subject to the normal rules. Any such assessments can be appealed, again subject to the normal rules.

WHAT DOES THIS MEAN FOR THOSE PROVIDING SERVICES IN CONNECTION WITH PENSION SCHEMES?

Third parties will need to consider carefully the nature and values of the services they provide and, where possible, issue separate invoices showing the actual value of services provided to trustees on investment work and to employers on administering the scheme. If this is not done, HMRC will want to check with them why they are unable to do so.

[Note: The start date was put back from 1 October 2005 to 1 January 2006 by Business Brief 16/05, 18 August 2005 (not reproduced)]

[VATA 1994 s 24]

18 AUGUST 2005. BUSINESS BRIEF 16/05
VAT RULING—ABBEY NATIONAL PLC—VIRTUAL ASSIGNMENTS

This Business Brief article provides guidance on how to treat supplies of virtually assigned property and the use of VATA 1994 Sch 10 para 8, following the High Court case of *Abbey National plc v C & E Comrs* [2006] STC 852.

. . .

BACKGROUND

(a) Virtual assignment of property

. . . [Abbey National plc ("Abbey")] were successful in their appeal that a virtual assignment of the relevant properties back to them by a third party was a supply equivalent to "a leasing and letting of immoveable property".

The Court of Appeal has given HMRC leave to appeal against this decision of the High Court. [Note: the appeal was allowed in *Abbey National plc v R & C Comrs* [2006] STC 1961, CA.]

(b) VATA 1994 Schedule 10, paragraph 8

. . . The view of the Court was that as the agreement between Abbey and the third party incorporated a clear and unambiguous declaration of trust, whereby the rents paid by the sub-tenants accrued in full for the benefit of the third party, VATA 1994 Sch 10 para 8 applied and thus the third party should be treated as making the supplies to Abbey's sub-tenants. . . .

HMRC has not appealed against this aspect of the High Court's decision.

THE WAY FORWARD

(i) Virtual assignments

In HMRC's view, under a virtual assignment agreement (ie where the interest in the property has been assigned to a third party without the landlord's consent and is then purported to be assigned back by the third party) the third party's assignment is not an exempt supply of an interest in land, but a taxable supply of management and agency services. As a result, the third party provider should continue to account for VAT on the taxable supply.

. . .

(ii) Schedule 10, paragraph 8

Where a legal transfer of an interest in a property is contemplated and:

- the benefit of all of the consideration received from sub-leases accrues to a third party and
- that consideration is held in a trust for the benefit of the third party,

then VATA 1994 Sch 10 para 8 applies. The third party will be deemed to have made the supply to the sub-lessees as the benefit of the consideration from those sub-leases accrues to the third party. Such a deemed supply will be exempt, unless an option to tax has been exercised by the third party.

Equally, by virtue of VATA 1994 Sch 10 para 8(*b*), any input tax attributable to the original grant made by the legal owner becomes the input tax of the third party from the time the deemed supply to the sub-lessee is made. The legal owner must not, in these circumstances, claim any of the input tax directly attributable to the legal grant made to the sub-lessee. Thus, where the legal owner remains in occupation of part of the building for the purpose of his business, and

- is still required to make taxable payments to the landlord, or
- carry out repairs to the property,

the third party will only be entitled to recover a portion of the VAT that is directly attributable to the deemed supply made by the third party to the sub-lessee. This is subject to the third party having exercised an option to tax. The legal owner will still be entitled to recover any appropriate input tax incurred in the course of any taxable supplies made by him in relation to any continued occupation of the building, or part of a building, of which he is a legal owner.

[VATA 1994 Sch 9 Group 1]

16 SEPTEMBER 2005. BUSINESS BRIEF 18/05
NEW CIVIL INVESTIGATION OF FRAUD PROCEDURES

Both HM Customs and Excise and the Inland Revenue had procedures for tackling suspected serious tax fraud using civil powers. The former Inland Revenue's Hansard procedures and all former Customs & Excise Civil Evasion procedures are being replaced with a new single Civil Investigations of Fraud procedure for HMRC. (The only exception is the Customs Duties Civil Evasion Penalties applied to travellers at port and airport controls).

1 SEPTEMBER 2005 START AND NEW CODE OF PRACTICE 9 (2005)

The new Civil Investigation of Fraud procedure came into effect on 1st September 2005 for new cases with a new Code of Practice 9 (2005)

Existing cases will be worked to a conclusion under the old Hansard procedures (Code of Practice 9), New Approach or C&E Notice 730.

Initially, the new procedure will only be used by officers serving in HMRC Special Civil Investigations. Use by other specialist teams within HMRC is under consideration.

. . .

[Note: A new edition of Code of Practice 9 was published in 2009. For documents relevant to investigations, see Appendix 10]

[VATA 1994 Sch 11 para 1]

10 OCTOBER 2005. BUSINESS BRIEF 19/05
VAT: HIGH COURT DECISION: CHURCH OF ENGLAND CHILDREN'S SOCIETY

This Business Brief outlines the decision of the High Court in *Church of England Children's Society v R & C Comrs* [2005] STC 1644 in favour of the charity, and how HM Revenue & Customs intend to apply the decision. HMRC have decided not to appeal.

. . .

FUNDRAISING COSTS

Where funds are raised solely for a restricted charitable purpose involving wholly non-business activities, the VAT incurred on raising those funds is not input tax and is not recoverable.

Conversely, where the funds raised are used wholly to support the making of business supplies, all of the VAT incurred on fundraising costs can be treated as input tax. The recovery of this input tax will depend upon whether these business supplies are taxable or exempt. Where fundraising input tax is wholly attributable to the making of taxable supplies by the charity, it can be recovered in full, subject to the normal rules. On the other hand, where fundraising input tax is wholly attributable to the making of exempt supplies by the charity, none of it will be recoverable, subject to the partial exemption de-minimis limits.

So where a charity which has non-business and business activities incurs VAT on fundraising costs and the funds raised support various activities of the charity, the VAT incurred can only be recoverable input tax to the extent that the funds raised will support taxable business supplies. In practice this means that VAT incurred on fundraising costs must first be subject to an initial business/non-business apportionment to determine how much of the VAT incurred may be treated as input tax. Then, in circumstances where the charity has exempt business activities, this input tax is further subject to the partial exemption rules.

In some cases, a charity's existing business/non-business apportionment method and partial exemption method will produce a fair and reasonable basis by which input tax can be recovered. However, where this is not the case, HMRC will consider proposals for alternative methods. If exceptional circumstances exist, HMRC may allow alternative methods to be applied retrospectively, provided it is fair and reasonable for the charity as a whole.

DEEMED SUPPLIES

The High Court decision has confirmed that input tax relating to a deemed supply is recoverable where the deemed supply is taxable.

However, in order for there to be a deemed supply, the gifted goods must first be business assets. This means that a charity purchasing or acquiring goods in order to give them away in the furtherance of its non-business charitable purposes would not be able to recover the VAT incurred on the purchase or acquisition of those goods.

Following changes to the rules on gifts of business assets with effect from 1 October 2003, there is no longer a deemed supply where the total cost of production of newsletters provided to any donor does not exceed £50 in a twelve month period.

Where input tax is incurred on business assets that are given away, but those gifts are not deemed supplies, the attribution of the input tax will be based on the business reasons behind making the gifts. Where input tax is incurred on business assets that are given away, and some of those gifts are deemed supplies whereas others are not, the attribution of the input tax will take both the deemed supplies and the underlying purpose behind making the gifts into account.

Examples

- If a religious charity incurs VAT producing and distributing bibles that it gifts to local hotels for use by guests, the VAT is not input tax and is not recoverable even if the bibles exceed the £50 cost rules that apply to deemed supplies. This is because giving away bibles is not a business activity and VAT incurred cannot therefore be input tax. However, if the charity produced bibles for gifts and for sale, then VAT incurred would be partly input tax.
- If the charity produces religious newsletters that advertise its business activities, VAT incurred will be input tax because of the advertisements. Furthermore, if the newsletters satisfy the deemed supply rules, then the input tax will be fully recoverable even if the charity's business activities are heavily exempt.

[VATA 1994 s 24]

23 NOVEMBER 2005. BUSINESS BRIEF 21/05
VAT: FURTHER CLARIFICATION OF THE VAT POSITION OF SHARE ISSUES FOLLOWING THE ECJ DECISION IN KRETZTECHNIK

Business Brief 12/05, 15 June 2005 [not reproduced] explained HM Revenue and Customs' position on the VAT treatment of share issues and subsequent input tax recovery, following the decision in *Kretztechnik AG v Finanzamt Linz* (case C-465/03) [2005] STC 1118, ECJ. This Business Brief article contains additional guidance, with specific implementation dates underlined.

REVISED TREATMENT OF SHARE ISSUE TRANSACTIONS

Business Brief 12/05 advised that companies making a new issue of shares to raise capital for their business, in circumstances identical to those in the *Kretztechnik* case, were not making any supply but were entitled to treat the VAT on the costs of the issue as input tax. Companies that make both taxable and exempt supplies should recover a proportion of the input tax in accordance with their partial exemption method that applied at the time of the issue.

The following guidance explains the VAT position of share transactions where the circumstances differ from those in *Kretztechnik*.

TRANSACTIONS INVOLVING ISSUES OF OTHER TYPES OF SHARES

Businesses may issue shares of different types. For example, there may be an issue of preference shares, a special rights issue, a bonus issue or issue of scrip dividends. *Kretztechnik* principles are applicable to all such share issues and these are now to be regarded as non-supplies for VAT purposes.

TRANSACTIONS INVOLVING ISSUES BY DIFFERENT TYPES OF COMPANIES

Kretztechnik was a public limited company but the body issuing shares could be another type of company, a private company for example. Provided that the issuer's motivation is, like Kretztechnik's, the raising of capital, issues of shares by these other types of company will also be non-supplies for VAT purposes.

TRANSACTIONS INVOLVING THE ISSUE OF FINANCIAL INSTRUMENTS OR SECURITIES OTHER THAN SHARES

The issue of other types of security, such as bonds, debentures or loan notes, should also be treated as non-supplies when the purpose of the issue is to raise capital for the issuer's business. The input tax consequences will be the same as for an issue of shares. Similarly, the issue of shares or units in collective investment funds such as open-ended investment companies or authorised unit trusts will not be supplies for VAT purposes.

SHARES AND OTHER SECURITIES ISSUED IN OTHER SITUATIONS

An issue of shares or other securities may be one of several transactions that take place in the context of wider arrangements. For example, they may be issued in order to effect a company takeover or as part of a company restructuring through merger or demerger. When the issue does take place as part of such wider arrangements, it should still be regarded as a non-supply for VAT purposes.

. . .

TRANSFERS OF EXISTING SHARES

Transfers of existing shares for a consideration will continue to be exempt supplies provided that the supplies occur in the course of business activity. In such cases, the input tax that relates to the transfer will be exempt input tax and only recoverable to the extent that the shares have been sold to purchasers outside the EU.

LIABILITY CONSEQUENCES

There are no changes to the exemption for financial services arising from the judgment. Transactions that are no longer supplies, such as issues of shares, will no longer have a corresponding VAT liability such as exemption. However, intermediary and underwriting services in relation to such transactions will continue to be exempt.

CONSEQUENCES FOR THE VAT (INPUT TAX) (SPECIFIED SUPPLIES) ORDER 1999

Input tax on issues of shares made outside the EU

Prior to *Kretztechnik*, issues of shares and other securities to customers belonging outside the EU were treated as specified supplies. This meant that the input tax on related costs could be recovered. From the date of publication of this Business Brief this treatment will no longer apply unless:

(a) you have chosen to apply the *Kretztechnik* treatment to other issues before that date or

(b) you are making a claim for retrospective recovery of input tax.

The changes announced in paragraph 2 of Business Brief 32/04 will still apply to other incidental financial transactions not affected by *Kretztechnik.*

Input tax incurred by intermediaries in share issues

The changes in this paragraph are effective only from 1 January 2006.

Previously, intermediaries could treat the following transactions as specified supplies:

(a) arranging an issue of shares or other securities on behalf of an issuer belonging outside the EU

(b) arranging an issue of shares or other securities on behalf of an issuer (wherever they belonged) to recipients outside the EU.

This meant that the input tax on related costs could be recovered whether or not the intermediary's customer belonged outside the EU, provided the issue was made to someone belonging outside the EU. This was because this underlying issue of shares was treated as a supply for VAT purposes.

Following *Kretztechnik*, the situation has changed and, from 1 January 2006, only the services described at (*a*) above will be treated as specified supplies. This is because the underlying issue of shares by the intermediary's customer to the non-EU purchaser is no longer a supply. However, intermediary services to their own customers, as long as they belong outside the EU, is still a specified supply under the Specified Supplies Order.

There is no change to the position of intermediaries who arrange supplies of existing shares or other securities.

Impact of Kretztechnik upon the Water Hall Group decision

In *Water Hall Group plc*, a VAT Tribunal found that, when shares were issued to a UK company acting as nominee for purchasers belonging outside the EU, the input tax relating to those shares could not be reclaimed by the issuer because the supply was to the UK nominee rather than the non-EU purchasers. In Business Brief 02/05, 10 February 2005 [not reproduced], HMRC announced that businesses should apply the *Water Hall* decision to issues of shares in the same circumstances. The situation would then be reviewed following release of the *Kretztechnik* decision.

This review has now been completed. HMRC's conclusion is that *Water Hall* no longer has any application. In *Kretztechnik*, an issue of shares was found not to be a supply for VAT purposes, so the question of who is making or receiving the supply no longer arises. We consider that transactions involving sales of existing shares are fundamentally different from share issues because they are capable of constituting supplies. Such transactions were not considered in *Water Hall* and that decision does not therefore apply to them. Supplies of existing shares are to be regarded as being made to or by the person who actually makes the purchase or sale of the shares. Where the actual purchaser is not known to the seller, the place of belonging of a nominee account for the purchaser, if known, may be used to determine the place of supply. If neither is known, you should treat the supply as made in the UK or refer to the special rules in paragraph 9.2 of Public Notice 701/49 "Finance and Securities".

[Note: For issues of shares and other securities made outside the EU, see Business Brief 22/05, 2 December 2005.]

[VATA 1994 ss 5, 26]

2 DECEMBER 2005. BUSINESS BRIEF 22/05
VAT: JUDGEMENT OF THE COURT OF APPEAL IN THE CASE OF IVOR JACOBS ([2005] EWCA CIV 930)

This Business Brief article sets out HM Revenue & Customs' (HMRC) revised policy on the recovery of VAT by those using the "VAT refunds for DIY builders and converters" scheme in cases where a mixed use building (used for non-residential and residential use) is converted into dwellings in light of the judgement of the Court of Appeal in the case of *C & E Comrs v Jacobs* [2005] STC 1518, CA.

. . .

HM REVENUE & CUSTOMS' REVISED POLICY

HMRC now accept that, for the purposes of the DIY Refund Scheme, the conversion of a building that contains both a residential part and a non-residential part comes within the scope of the Scheme so long as the conversion results in an additional dwelling being created. It is no longer necessary for the additional dwelling to be created exclusively from the non-residential part. However, VAT recovery is restricted to the conversion of the non-residential part.

BUILDERS AND DEVELOPERS

HMRC do not consider that the Court of Appeal decision has any impact in similar situations where a building, which is part residential/part non-residential, is being converted into a number of dwellings and the number of dwellings present post-conversion is greater than the number of dwellings present pre-conversion.

VATA 1994 Sch 8 Group 5 Items 1(*b*) and 3(*a*) restrict the zero-rating to the dwelling(s) deriving from the conversion of the non-residential part. Our policy remains that the zero rate will not apply to any dwelling(s) deriving (whether in whole or in part) from the conversion of the residential part.

VAT TREATMENT OF PAST SUPPLIES

DIY house builders, who have converted property that was part residential/part non-residential and have increased the number of dwellings in the building overall, are invited to submit claims for VAT incurred on eligible expenditure in converting the non-residential part of the building into a part of the resulting dwellings.

HMRC will only entertain claims in respect of such conversions completed no later than three years prior to the date of this Business Brief.

[VATA 1994 s 35]

2 DECEMBER 2005. BUSINESS BRIEF 22/05
FURTHER CLARIFICATION ON THE VAT POSITION OF SHARE ISSUES MADE TO CUSTOMERS OUTSIDE THE EU

We have had one or two enquiries on Business Brief 21/05, 23 November 2005 which explained HM Revenue and Customs' position on share issues following the decision in *Kretztechnik AG v Finanzamt Linz* (case C-465/03) [2005] STC 1118, ECJ. This item clarifies the situation regarding issues of shares and other securities made outside the EU.

INPUT TAX ON ISSUES OF SHARES MADE OUTSIDE THE EU

Prior to *Kretztechnik*, issues of shares and other securities to customers belonging outside the EU were treated as specified supplies. This meant that the input tax on related costs could be recovered under the VAT (Input Tax) (Specified Supplies) Order 1999, SI 1999/3121. From 29 November 2005, this treatment will no longer apply to new shares and securities issued outside the EU as they are no longer supplies, although input tax will still be recoverable on the related costs provided the issue is made for the purposes of a fully taxable business. If the issue is made for the purposes of a partly exempt business, then a proportion of the input tax will be recoverable under the business' normal partial exemption method.

The changes announced in paragraph 2 of Business Brief 32/04, 2 December 2004 [not reproduced] will still apply to other incidental financial transactions not affected by *Kretztechnik*.

[VATA 1994 s 26]

2 DECEMBER 2005. BUSINESS BRIEF 22/05
MESSENGER LEISURE DEVELOPMENTS LIMITED—REFUSAL OF LEAVE TO APPEAL TO THE HOUSE OF LORDS

The House of Lords has refused the taxpayer leave to appeal in the case of *Messenger Leisure Developments Ltd v R & C Comrs* [2005] STC 1078, CA. The case concerns the VAT treatment of supplies of sporting services and confirms HMRC's view that VAT exemption for sporting services cannot be claimed by companies that are not genuine non-profit making bodies.

. . .

IMPLICATIONS OF THE CASE

The House of Lords' refusal to grant leave to appeal means that the Court of Appeal's decision represents the final determination of the issues in the *MLD* case. Plainly, the Court of Appeal's decision should now determine any other case involving a company which is a member of a commercial group.

HMRC take the view that the *MLD* precedent is also highly relevant to a number of other cases. The EC law, as set out in the case of *Kennemer Golf and Country Club v Staatssecretaris van Financiën* (case C-174/00) [2002] STC 502, ECJ, is clear. Companies which are set up in a commercial context, with the aim of benefiting from the VAT exemption, do not qualify as non-profit-making bodies, even if their constitution precludes them from distributing profit.

It is normally clear that a company is operating in a commercial context if it is a subsidiary within a commercial group. However, there are in addition many examples where a purported non-profit making company operates in a commercial context, without being a subsidiary of another company.

In *MLD* the main witness's evidence, to the effect that he was not interested in extracting profit from the business, was not challenged, and did not need to be, given the existence of the commercial group. It goes without saying that, in any case not involving a subsidiary within a commercial group, any claims to the effect that commercial parties were not intended to benefit from the arrangements in question will not be accepted by HMRC without challenge.

BUSINESSES AFFECTED BY THE MLD DECISION

In HMRC's view it is now clear that any company which is precluded from distributing profit, but whose function is nevertheless to create VAT exemption in the context of a wider commercial undertaking, is not a non-profit making body for VAT purposes. It follows that such a company is not entitled to claim the VAT exemption which is directed at such bodies.

Any such company, which HMRC has already decided is not a non-profit making body, should now consider its position in light of the fact that the *MLD* case has been finally determined in HMRC's favour, and the EC law is clear.

Any such company, which has not so far been subject to such a decision from HMRC, should now contact the National Advice Service on 0845 010 9000 in order to regularise its position. Co-operation from taxpayers is taken into account when deciding the level of any penalty for failing to declare VAT or to notify a liability to register for VAT.

[VATA 1994 Sch 9 Group 10]

19 JANUARY 2006. BUSINESS BRIEF 1/06
VAT: COMPANY FORMATION SERVICES WITH ANCILLARY PRINTED MATTER—CLARIFICATION OF TREATMENT POST CPP

The Commissioners are aware that traders providing company formation services may be incorrectly treating some supplies as separate zero-rated supplies of printed matter and standard-rated services.

This Business Brief article clarifies HMRC guidance previously issued [see Business Brief 02/2001, 16 February 2001 and VAT Information Sheet 02/01]. HMRC confirms its view, in the light of the *Card Protection Plan* case [see *Card Protection Plan Ltd v C & E Comrs* (case C-349/96) [1999] STC 270, ECJ; *Card Protection Plan Ltd* v *C & E Comrs* [2001] STC 174, HL], on the correct treatment of these supplies. It aims to ensure that all traders providing such services treat them correctly for VAT purposes.

Furthermore there may be cases where traders have attempted to secure a competitive advantage over traders that have been treating the supplies correctly by using this incorrect treatment as a basis for value shifting by invoicing a breakdown of the package price.

. . .

TREATMENT OF COMPANY FORMATION SERVICE PACKAGES INCLUDING ANCILLARY PRINTED MATTER

HMRC's view is that where there is a single advertised price for a company formation package that includes some printed matter (for example a number of copies of the printed and perhaps bound Memorandum & Articles of Association), there is a single standard-rated supply of company formation services. This supply is the principal supply to which the supply of printed matter is ancillary.

The supply of the service by a registration agent of preparing and lodging the original Memorandum and Articles of Association with the Registrar of Companies is wholly standard-rated. In this situation, one or more copies of documents, such as the Certificates of Incorporation and the Memorandum and Articles of Association may be provided. Where these are provided in hard copy form (as opposed to digital format), the question arises as to whether there is a single supply of company registration services to which the supply of printed matter is ancillary, or separate supplies of zero-rated printed matter and standard-rated services.

The judgement [of the Court of Justice in the *Card Protection Plan* case] set out a number of relevant criteria, namely:

- Where a transaction comprises a number of features or acts, regard must be had to all the circumstances in which it takes place.
- Where a supply is a single supply from an economic point of view, it should not be artificially split so as to distort the functioning of the VAT system.
- There is a single supply, in particular, in cases where one or more elements of a transaction are to be regarded as constituting the principal service, with other elements being ancillary to that principal service.
- While the charging of a single price is not decisive, the fact that several elements are supplied for a single price may indicate a single supply.

Therefore where a customer acquiring a registered company also receives hard copy documents as part of a fixed-price package, he would normally be seen as receiving a single supply of company formation services rather than separate supplies of company registration services and printed matter.

Where additional copies of documentation are offered as an option for additional payment, there may be either a single supply or multiple supplies.

. . .

[VATA 1994 s 19]

19 JANUARY 2006. BUSINESS BRIEF 1/06
VAT: HOTEL CONFERENCE/FUNCTION FACILITIES—REVISED INTERPRETATION OF LAW ON VAT TREATMENT

This Business Brief article announces changes in HM Revenue & Customs' interpretation of the law on the VAT treatment of hotel conference/function facilities. This change will be incorporated in an update to VAT Notice 709/3, Hotels and Holiday Accommodation, to be issued in due course.

The change being made affects the liability of supplies of rooms by hotels that are to be used for meetings, conferences and similar functions. There is no change to the treatment of supplies of rooms where the primary use will be for the purpose of supplies of catering, such as dinner/dances, wedding receptions, etc. Supplies of rooms for such purposes are always taxable supplies.

BACKGROUND

Hotels and other establishments often provide rooms for meetings, conferences and similar functions organised by third parties. It is usual for them to make inclusive charges depending on the requirements of individual delegates. It is the general practice for hotels and similar providers to charge organisers on a delegate or attendee basis (referred to as the "delegate rate"), ie the charge will be determined according to the number of delegates requiring:

- Use of conference room only.
- Use of conference room plus meal(s) ("8-hour conference delegate rate").
- Use of conference room plus meals and overnight sleeping accommodation ("24-hour conference delegate rate").

The supply of a conference/function room on its own in these circumstances is exempt from VAT (unless an option to tax has been made). Where, in addition to the use of the conference/function room, a meal is provided to delegates and an inclusive charge made (the 8-hour delegate rate), each element is treated as a separate supply, so whilst the conference room continues to be exempt from VAT (unless an option to tax has been made), the part of the consideration relating to the provision of food is taxable (unless the provision of refreshments is minimal, such as tea and biscuits). However; where the 24-hour conference delegate rate has been applied and an inclusive charge made, HMRC has until now seen the charge as consideration for a single taxable supply of use of the entire hotel's facilities including conference/function facilities, sleeping accommodation and food.

REVISED INTERPRETATION OF THE LAW

Where a room is provided for a meeting, conference or similar function organised by a third party (but not where the primary purpose is for a supply of catering—see above), HMRC now accepts that the provision of conference/function room hire, meals and sleeping accommodation under the 24 hour delegate rate, even where made in return for an inclusive charge, should be treated as separate supplies. These will be taxable supplies, with the exception of the conference/function room hire, which will be an exempt supply, unless the hotel has opted to tax its supplies. In cases where a single consideration is paid for supplies having different liabilities, for example where a charge for room hire is made under the 24-hour delegate rate by a hotel which has not opted to tax its room hire, a fair and reasonable apportionment of the consideration must be made. There is no change to the treatment of 8-hour delegate charges.

Where hotels organise and run conferences or similar events themselves and charge for entry to delegates, their supplies are always taxable supplies.

MAKING CLAIMS OR ADJUSTMENTS

Hotels that have made an option to tax will be unaffected by the change and should continue to charge tax on their supplies. For other hotels and businesses, the change described above should be implemented from the date of this Business Brief and there is no requirement to make adjustments in respect of supplies made prior to this date. However, where hotels or other establishments wish to make a claim to HMRC for a repayment of output tax incorrectly paid, they may do so . . . .

FUTURE VAT IMPLICATIONS FOR HOTELS AND SIMILAR PROVIDERS

You should treat supplies in the way described above. Some hotels will now be making exempt supplies as a result of these changes. The input tax that they incur will, as a result, be subject to partial exemption rules and some restriction on the amount they can reclaim may follow. Details can be found in VAT Notice 706, Partial Exemption. If hotels prefer, they can continue to treat their supplies as taxable (and thereby be entitled to continue claiming their input tax in full) by opting to tax. Details about how to do this are given in VAT Notice 742A, Opting to tax land and buildings. Hotels that have already made exempt supplies of the meeting room may require permission for an option to tax and they will find further details in Section 5 of Notice 742A.

[VATA 1994 Sch 9 Group 1 Item 1(*d*)]

27 FEBRUARY 2006. BUSINESS BRIEF 2/06
VAT AVOIDANCE DISCLOSURES UNIT—CHANGE OF ADDRESS

A revised edition of VAT Notice 700/8 "Disclosures of VAT avoidance schemes", which will be published soon, will prescribe that postal disclosures of notifiable schemes must be sent to the following address:

VAT Avoidance Disclosures Unit
Anti-Avoidance Group (Intelligence)
HM Revenue & Customs
1st Floor
22 Kingsway
London WC2B 6NR

To allow businesses a reasonable period of time to adjust their processes to meet this change, disclosures made to the current postal address will be continue to be accepted as validly made where the relevant affected accounting period starts before or during February 2006.

Disclosures can continue to be made by email to: vat.avoidance.disclosures.bst@hmrc.gsi.gov.uk

[SI 2004/1929 reg 3]

9 MARCH 2006. BUSINESS BRIEF 3/06
VAT: BEAUTY PROCEDURES PERFORMED USING CLASS 3B OR 4 LASERS AND/OR INTENSE PULSE LIGHT (IPL) MACHINES—CLARIFICATION OF LIABILITY

HMRC have become aware that some businesses providing beauty procedures using class 3B or 4 lasers and/or IPL machines may be incorrectly treating their supplies as VAT-exempt health services rather than standard rated supplies of beauty treatment. This Business Brief article is issued to assist those businesses to determine the correct liability of these services.

BACKGROUND

Following the establishment of the Healthcare Commission under the Care Standards Act 2000, certain procedures using prescribed techniques or prescribed technologies became regulated for the first time. Among these were the use of class 3B and 4 lasers and IPL machines.

This has led to establishments such as beauty salons, where class 3B and 4 lasers and/or IPL machines are used (for instance, for removing unwanted hair), being classified as independent hospitals for the purposes of the Care Standards legislation.

TREATMENT OF SUPPLIES MADE USING CLASS 3B AND 4 LASERS AND/OR IPL MACHINES

Where the procedure utilising this equipment is supplied as part of a treatment programme drawn up by a registered health professional following the diagnosis of a medical condition, this treatment is exempt from VAT. But where it is carried out for a cosmetic reason rather than as an element of medical or surgical treatment, this service is taxable at the standard rate of VAT.

ACTION REQUIRED BY BUSINESSES MAKING NON-MEDICAL SUPPLIES USING CLASS 3B AND 4 LASERS AND/OR IPL MACHINES

Businesses to which this Business Brief applies must review their VAT treatment of these supplies and ensure that any necessary changes are implemented.

. . .

[VATA 1994 Sch 9 Group 7 Item 1]

27 JUNE 2006. BUSINESS BRIEF 07/06
VAT—EXEMPTION FOR THE MANAGEMENT OF AUTHORISED COLLECTIVE INVESTMENT SCHEMES

This Business Brief article announces changes to HMRC's policy concerning the VAT exemption for the management of authorised collective investment schemes, following the judgment of the European Court of Justice (ECJ) in *Abbey National plc and another v R & C Comrs* (case C-169/04) [2006] STC 1136, ECJ on 4 May 2006.

It updates the section of Business Brief 10/03, 24 July 2003 headed "What constitutes 'management'?" and the changes apply from 1 October 2006.

. . .

HMRC accept that, to benefit from the exemption, it is not necessary that a third party provider of fund administration services performs all of the administration functions required by regulations such as those listed in Directive 85/611/EEC Annex II (and applicable to UK funds under Financial Services Authority sourcebook rules). It is, however, necessary that the services must, viewed broadly, form a distinct whole fulfilling in effect the specific essential functions of management. In other words, the service must be recognisable in its own right as a service of fund administration.

Just because a particular operation (such as each of those listed in Annex II) is a requirement of regulations it does not necessarily mean that it is exempt if provided in isolation. For example, legal services such as advice or drafting may be required to ensure that certain documents, eg a trust deed or fund prospectus, are valid and comply with the regulations, but this does not mean that the legal service is one of exempt fund administration. Similarly, an external audit of accounts does not of itself assume the characteristics of a fund administration service.

To be exempt, it is necessary for the service to be distinct as a fund administration service. This "distinctiveness" is normally attained by the bundling, into a single supply, of numerous operations that are typical of the administrative management of eg an open-ended investment company ("OEIC"). In deciding whether the overall service is distinct as fund administration, both the number of specific operations and their individual characteristics need to be taken into account.

For example, the daily valuation of assets is of particular importance and relevance to OEICs and authorised unit trusts ("AUTs") in determining the price of shares or units and so this, together with related accounting and reporting functions would be sufficiently distinctive as a fund administration service. However, a service such as "price feeding" of information consisting of the market value of individual stocks, provided to the person carrying out the fund asset valuation, is not in itself a fund administration service.

As a further example, the maintenance of a register of shareholders does not, in isolation, represent a fund administration service. However, if the service is combined with the issue and redemption of the units or shares and collating the number of shares in issue for the purpose of establishing the daily price of the units, such a package takes on the distinct characteristics of fund administration and will be exempt.

HMRC are satisfied that the bundle of services provided by the Bank of New York in the *Abbey* case is exempt. This consisted of computing the amount of income and the price of units or shares, the valuation of assets, accounting, the preparation of statements for the distribution of income, the provision of information and documentation for periodic accounts, income forecasts and tax returns, as well as data processing, record-keeping and customer inquiries.

There are a number of businesses which provide specialist fund administration services in respect of AUTs and OEICs. In many cases, these services comprise a package of functions which, together, will satisfy the criteria for the exemption.

However, as with some of the examples above, certain services or bundles of services cannot be viewed as a distinct service of fund administration. For instance, the legal services referred to above might be described as "specific to, and essential for", the management of the fund but they are not fund administration services.

If the criteria for exemption are satisfied, it should also be noted that a person providing such a package of services will generally be viewed as making a single exempt supply of fund administration services in respect of each fund where the manager has delegated the administrative functions. The fact that each element may be priced separately on a rate card does not affect this.

In summary, HMRC accept that, in accordance with the judgment, services which, viewed broadly, are distinct as fund administration services, and are specific to and essential for the management of AUTs or OEICs are exempt.

[VATA 1994 Sch 9 Group 5 Items 9, 10]

7 AUGUST 2006. BUSINESS BRIEF 11/06
VAT: PARTIAL EXEMPTION—HIGHER EDUCATION SECTOR VARIABLE TUITION FEES

This Business Brief article concerns the potential detrimental impact of Variable Tuition Fees (VTFs) on the Partial Exemption (PE) methods of Higher Education Institutions (HEIs). Specialist PE terms are explained in HMRC Notice 706: Partial Exemption.

BACKGROUND

Many HEIs use a PE special method in which input tax on their overhead costs is apportioned by reference to the value of their taxable and exempt supplies. Such a values-based method is easy to operate, responsive to normal business change, and generally works well provided the value of supplies is proportionate to the consumption of VAT-bearing, overhead costs.

The supply of VAT-exempt education by a HEI is heavily subsidised by grant income. This means that the charge to the student, which is the value of the supply for VAT purposes, is often below cost. Unless an adjustment is made to reflect the subsidy, a values-based method will misallocate overhead input tax so will not be fair and reasonable. HMRC believes the easiest way to correct for the subsidy is for the HEI to include its teaching support grant in its method as if it were part of the value of its supplies.

VARIABLE TUITION FEES

The introduction of VTFs from 1 August 2006 increases the value of exempt education. This is because VTFs are charged to students even if a third party subsequently pays them. However, as HMRC understands is often the case, HEIs will return part of the VTFs to students as bursaries rather than use them solely for additional expenditure. If this happens, a values-based method might misallocate overhead input tax to the detriment of the HEI.

CORRECTING AN UNFAIR METHOD

HMRC will approve any PE method that is fair and reasonable for the HEI as a whole. HMRC is firmly of the view that a values-based method works well for a HEI provided sensible adjustments are made to correct for subsidies and receipts that are disbursed rather than expended (thereby reflecting the fact that a grant-subsidised HEI will normally price its supplies so as to cover its costs). But, in order to be acceptable, an adjustment must be clearly justified, transparent and objectively determined – an arbitrary adjustment can never be accepted. Where a HEI returns part of the VTF as a statutory bursary under its Access Agreement with the Office for Fair Access, this may provide a suitable basis for adjustment.

WHAT SHOULD HEIS DO

If you consider that your PE method is no longer fair and reasonable because of the introduction of VTFs, you are invited to contact your local VAT Office with proposals for a new method (this applies even where HMRC has directed your special method). Alternatively, you may wish to serve a Special Method Override Notice (Notice) on HMRC to correct your method as an interim solution until a new method is approved.

[SI 1995/2518 reg 102]

12 OCTOBER 2006. BUSINESS BRIEF 16/06
CHANGES TO VAT LAW IN LIGHT OF THE GAMBLING ACT

. . .

Two new Treasury Orders [VAT (Betting, Gaming and Lotteries) Order 2006, SI 2006/2685 and VAT (Gaming Machines) Order 2006, SI 2006/2686] are being laid before Parliament today that will come into effect on 1 November 2006. The new Orders continue to update VAT law in light of the Gambling Act, and will:

. . .

- restore the application of VAT to pinball machines;
- ensure that any game of chance which is not played for a prize does not fall within the exemption.

PINBALL MACHINES AND OTHER GAMES OF CHANCE NOT PLAYED FOR A PRIZE

The takings from pinball machines had inadvertently been brought within the scope of the exemption by [VAT (Betting, Gaming and Lotteries) Order 2005, SI 2005/3328 ("the PBR Order")], when the Gambling Act concept of gaming was imported into VAT legislation dealing with gaming machines. VAT exemption is currently available for the provision of facilities for playing a game of chance, whether or not for a prize. Gaming machines are excluded from the scope of this exemption. Before the PBR order was introduced, pinball machines were taxed as gaming machines as it was not a requirement for a gaming machine to offer a prize. However, the PBR order applied section 6(1) of the Gambling Act 2005, which provides that gaming is playing a game of chance for a prize, to the definition of gaming machines. Although this meant that pinball machines were excluded from the definition of gaming machines, as they do not offer prizes, they still qualified for VAT exemption as the provisions of facilities for playing a game of chance. In future, only a game of chance played for a prize, whether or not played on a machine, will qualify for exemption in any event. "Prize" will be defined so as to exclude the opportunity to play the game again ("free plays").

Consequently, traders who have been accounting for VAT on pinball machines takings in the period from 6 December 2005 to 31 October 2006 may make a claim to HMRC for a repayment of output tax incorrectly paid, subject to the conditions set out below . . . :

- all claims must take into account input tax that has been claimed, but which, while pinball machine takings were exempt, did not relate to taxable supplies;
- businesses must be able to produce evidence that they accounted for VAT in the circumstances described above, and must be able to substantiate the amount claimed.

Any claim should be for all prescribed accounting periods in which the liability error occurred.

Should a claim not take into account all errors or all affected accounting periods, then HMRC will seek to set-off amounts owed to us for these periods against amounts claimed in other periods.

. . .

[VATA 1994 Sch 9 Group 4 Item 1]

19 OCTOBER 2006. BUSINESS BRIEF 17/06
VAT: DISPOSABLE BARBECUES

HM Revenue & Customs (HMRC) have been asked to clarify the VAT treatment of the sale of disposable barbecues. Some retailers have been treating such sales as reduced rate or mixed rate supplies (part standard-rated; part reduced-rated). The correct VAT treatment is that the sale of disposable barbecues is a single standard-rated supply, subject to VAT at 17.50%.

. . .

22 DECEMBER 2006. BUSINESS BRIEF 23/06
VAT: FIRST GRANT OF A MAJOR INTEREST IN RESIDENTIAL PROPERTY—ATTRIBUTION OF INPUT TAX AND THE CAPITAL GOODS SCHEME

This Business Brief article confirms and explains HMRC policy regarding input tax incurred on the construction of residential property where the developer sells a long leasehold interest separately from the freehold interest.

BACKGROUND

The first grant of a major interest (freehold sale or lease exceeding 21 years) in residential property by its developer is zero-rated, under VATA 1994 Sch 8 Group 5. However, all subsequent grants in the property are VAT exempt. VAT on costs relating to zero-rated supplies is fully recoverable whereas VAT relating to exempt supplies is not normally recoverable.

Detailed rules on the liability of supplies of buildings are in Notice 708 Buildings and construction, on partial exemption in Notice 706 Partial exemption and on the capital goods scheme in Notice 706/2 Capital Goods Scheme.

ATTRIBUTION OF INPUT TAX

When a residential property is constructed or results from the conversion of a non-residential property and the developer makes a first grant of a major interest in that property, any input tax incurred is recoverable in full. This is because the input tax is wholly attributed to that taxable first grant.

This is the case even where the value of the first grant does not represent full equity in the property, such as in shared ownership schemes run by housing associations.

APPLICATION OF THE CAPITAL GOODS SCHEME (CGS)

Regulations 112(2) and 113 of the VAT Regulations 1995, SI 1995/2518, set out when a building will be a capital item for the purposes of the CGS.

If a developer constructs a residential property and the first grant of a major interest in the building is a long lease, he is using the building for a business purpose other than solely for the purpose of selling the building. As a result, the developer will have to treat the building as a capital item. The input tax incurred on the construction of the building and wholly attributed to the zero-rated long lease will have to be adjusted through the CGS should a subsequent exempt grant be made of the building.

If a developer constructs a residential property and the first grant of a major interest is the sale of the freehold, the developer is using the building solely for the purpose of selling the building and will not have to treat the building as a capital item.

EXAMPLES

There are essentially three ways a developer might grant all the leases and the reversionary interest in the freehold of a residential property (typically a block of flats):

(a) All flats sold followed by the freehold – The sale of each individual flat will be zero-rated as first grant of a major interest. While the developer will hold a capital item, when the freehold is sold, we consider that this will only be exempt to the extent that it relates to those areas of the building that were previously the subject of the zero-rated grants of individual flats. Most of the sale of the freehold will be zero-rated because it relates to the common parts that have not been subject to any previous supply.
These circumstances are part of the sale of new dwellings for which the zero-rating was designed. Furthermore any CGS adjustments would be negligible. Accordingly there is no need for CGS adjustments in this example.

(b) Freehold sold before any flats are sold – The sale of the freehold will be a zero-rated grant and since no leases had been granted, would not be a capital item (by virtue of Reg 112(2), VAT Regulations 1995). Since the freehold is zero-rated, all input tax incurred on the construction costs will be fully deductible.
As the new freeholder, the purchaser will normally make any exempt grants of leases to buyers of flats. Even where the consideration for such sales accrues to the developer, so that VAT law treats the developer as the person supplying the flat, this will not impact on the initial deduction of input tax by the developer. It may, however, have implications for any input tax incurred on selling costs.

(c) Freehold sold after some flats have been sold – The flats sold before the freehold has been supplied will each be a zero-rated first grant of a major interest. While the developer will hold a capital item, when the freehold is sold, we consider that this will only be exempt to the extent that it relates to those areas of the building that were previously the subject of the zero-rated grants of individual flats. Most of the supply of the freehold will be zero-rated relating to the common parts and unsold flats that haven't been subject to any previous supply. As per example (*a*) above, no CGS adjustments are needed.
If, under the agreement for sale, the developer has retained the right to receive the monies from the sale of the remaining unsold flats, the considerations set out in example (*b*) above apply.

OTHER RESIDENTIAL PROPERTY

The first grant of a major interest in a relevant residential property (for example a care home) is zero-rated. Under Reg 116(3), VAT Regulations 1995, in determining any CGS adjustments in subsequent years, the developer disregards any exempt supply arising directly from that grant (including all rents due under that lease). Even though the developer holds a capital item, providing he makes no exempt supplies other than those arising from that zero-rated grant, he will retain full deduction of the input tax on the construction of the development.

However, if the developer makes a new grant, like selling the freehold, this is the second grant in the building and will be exempt. In this situation CGS adjustments are likely to be required and CGS calculations must be carried out.

[SI 1995/2518 reg 115]

26 JANUARY 2007. REVENUE & CUSTOMS BRIEF 5/07 VAT—FURTHER CLARIFICATION OF THE TREATMENT OF FOREIGN EXCHANGE TRANSACTIONS (FOREX) AND TRANSACTIONS IN OTHER FINANCIAL INSTRUMENTS

Business Brief 21/05 explained HMRC's position following the tribunal decision in *Willis Pension Fund Trustees Limited* (No 19183) ("*Willis*") and the implications of the decision for other businesses conducting forex transactions. The Tribunal found that the forex transactions Willis entered into were not supplies for VAT purposes.

This Brief article sets out HMRC's view on when forex transactions are supplies for VAT purposes and the implications this has for VAT recovery. It also outlines HMRC's view on any wider application of the decision to transactions in other financial instruments.

DETERMINING IF YOUR FOREX TRANSACTIONS ARE SUPPLIES FOR VAT PURPOSES

The Tribunal decision in *Willis* applied to a very specific set of circumstances and, whilst some general principles can be drawn from the decision, care needs to be taken when seeking to give it wider application. The European Court of Justice ("ECJ") judgment in *C & E Comrs v First National Bank of Chicago* (case 172/96) [1998] STC 850, ECJ ("FNBC") is the leading authority on the VAT treatment of forex transactions.

In *Willis*, forex deals were entered into for the purposes of "hedging". This is a term that is variously defined, but "hedging" is about reducing exposure to risk of loss resulting from fluctuations in some commodity or financial market. What is relevant for VAT purposes is whether any underlying trade is performed to achieve that objective. "Hedging" is not in itself a test for determining whether or not there is a supply for VAT purposes.

In general, forex transactions are supplies for VAT purposes if you adopt a spread position over a period of time when buying and selling currency. This applies whether this is being done for your own account, in support of other areas of your business, or to reduce any exposure position in forex that you hold. A spread position means a difference between a bid price and a sell price from which you would expect to derive a profit. These forex transactions would include both 'spot' and 'forward' transactions, as envisaged by the *FNBC* judgment.

Most businesses actively involved in forex trading should readily be able to identify whether their forex transactions fall under the *FNBC* principle of adopting a spread position. If uncertainties remain, you should consider whether, in selling a currency, you are in a position to set the selling price. If so, you are able to determine the consideration you receive by setting a spread, even if only mimicking market movements, and your forex transactions are likely to be supplies for VAT purposes.

Where your forex transactions are supplies, the consideration will be the net result of all your forex transactions over a period of time and would be exempt under VATA 1994 Sch 9 Group 5 Item 1. Any forex transactions, for which you charge an attributable fee or commission, would also be exempt supplies under Item 1.

The following are examples of circumstances when it is unlikely that your forex transactions would be seen as supplies for VAT purposes:

- a business simply exchanging one currency for another to realise foreign earnings into sterling, for example, or to acquire currency to settle liabilities incurred outside the UK, is unlikely to be seen as making supplies for VAT purposes provided such transactions are not part of a wider economic activity being carried out for an identifiable consideration;
- a business entering into forward forex deals in order to limit its exposure to forex fluctuations in respect of future obligations is unlikely to be seen as making supplies for VAT purposes provided such transactions are not part of a wider economic activity being carried out for an identifiable consideration.

Businesses with a corporate treasury operation active in the financial markets may need to look carefully at their forex transactions. If no spread position is being taken and no profit being actively sought, it is unlikely that any forex transactions would be regarded as supplies. However, a number of larger businesses have corporate treasury operations that are much more pro-active, either externally or internally, within their commercial groups. For example, a business might typically run a "forex desk" in a similar manner to any other financial institution or market maker more traditionally associated with forex dealing. Such businesses are likely to be taking a spread position and would be making supplies. All their forex transactions, whether spot or forward and whether proprietary or in support of other activities or areas of the business, should be treated as forex supplies.

Intermediaries acting in relation to a forex transaction can exempt their intermediary services under Sch 9 Group 5 Item 5. This applies whether or not the underlying forex transaction is a supply for VAT purposes.

HOW YOUR INPUT TAX RECOVERY WILL BE AFFECTED

The normal input tax recovery rules will apply. Businesses making exempt financial supplies cannot normally recover the VAT attributable to those supplies unless the recipient of those supplies is located outside the EU (in which case recovery is allowed under the VAT (Input Tax) (Specified Supplies) Order 1999, SI 1999/3121). Businesses involved in forex transactions which are not seen as supplies for VAT purposes are able to recover the VAT attributable to those transactions as residual input tax, subject to the partial exemption method used. However, there is no right of recovery under the Specified Supplies Order for such transactions.

Supplies by financial intermediaries can attract recovery under the Specified Supplies Order if the recipient of the intermediaries' supply is based outside the EU, or if the underlying forex transaction is itself a supply which is made outside the EU. There is no right of recovery under the Specified Supplies Order, however, where the recipient of an intermediary's supply is based in the UK or elsewhere in the EU but the underlying transaction is not a supply for VAT purposes. Intermediaries arranging non-EU forex transactions will therefore need to determine whether the underlying transaction is a supply.

Businesses may wish to seek clarification on their present partial exemption methods, and some methods may need to be revised. There are provisions for excluding, in certain circumstances, incidental financial transactions from values-based calculations in partial exemption methods and the provisions of the VAT Regulations 1995, SI 1995/2518 reg 106 allows for de minimis levels of exempt input tax to be treated as attributable to taxable supplies. For further information on this, please refer to VAT Notice 706, Partial Exemption. Whilst HMRC would wish to avoid disproportionate changes, any proposed changes will need to result in a fair and reasonable method.

WIDER APPLICATION IN RESPECT OF TRANSACTIONS IN OTHER FINANCIAL INSTRUMENTS

The *Willis* Tribunal made reference in its decision to interest rate swaps. It suggested that, in its view, there would only be a supply when it was possible to identify the consideration being obtained by a party entering into the contract.

There would appear to be nothing arising directly out of *Willis* that indicates a shortfall in HMRC's current approach to the VAT treatment of other financial instruments and it is, therefore, not intended to revise existing published policy. HMRC do, however, recognise that there may be particular circumstances where *Willis* principles could apply to transactions in other financial instrument transactions and HMRC would consider such cases on an individual basis.

[VATA 1994 s 5]

1 FEBRUARY 2007. REVENUE & CUSTOMS BRIEF 7/07 VAT—CASH BINGO: ACCOUNTING FOR VAT ON PARTICIPATION AND SESSION FEES

This briefing is about participation and session fees paid by cash bingo players. It clarifies HM Revenue & Customs' policy on how to calculate those fees for VAT purposes.

BACKGROUND

Participation and session fees charged for taking part in bingo played for cash prizes on premises licensed or registered under Part II of the Gaming Act 1968 (sometimes termed "mainstage" cash bingo) are consideration for standard-rated supplies. Stake money – the amount risked by the player, all of which must be returned as winnings – is not payment for a supply and so is outside the scope of VAT.

Where participation and session fees and stake money are received together in one composite amount charged to players, bingo promoters must work out how much of the payment is stake and how much is the participation and session fee in order to determine how much VAT is due. Section 3.2 of Notice 701/27 Bingo explains how to do this.

We have received enquiries from some bingo promoters performing the VAT calculation on a game-by-game basis, asking whether they are acting correctly and these have prompted the issue of this clarification.

CALCULATING THE VAT DUE

When a player pays to participate in all or part of a bingo session, the supply made by the promoter is the right to participate in the number of games during that session for which they have received payment. As a player cannot participate in further sessions unless they make further payment, the supply to the player is completed when the session ends. In these circumstances the amount of VAT due on participation and session charges should properly be calculated on a session-by-session basis by deducting the stake money arising in each individual session from the total amount (less any admission fees) paid by players to participate in that same session. Where money from other sources is added to the stake money received in the session in order to meet guaranteed prizes, that additional money cannot be used to reduce the value for VAT of the participation and session charges paid for taking part in that session.

Where a player pays to take part in an additional game ("flyer") that does not form part of the session charge, this is a separate supply of the right to participate in that further game. The VAT due on fees charged for participating in additional games should be calculated on a game-by-game basis.

Where a promoter provides facilities for participating in linked games or a national game, in which players located at more than one venue all participate in the same game, charges received at all the promoter's participating venues should be aggregated in order to calculate the amount of VAT due on par fees relating to the linked game or national game.

Promoters should not perform a single calculation for the whole of each VAT return period, aggregating stake money and receipts taken for all bingo played during that time.

Notice 701/27 Bingo will be updated.

. . .

[VATA 1994 Sch 9 Group 4 Note 1(b)]

6 FEBRUARY 2007. REVENUE & CUSTOMS BRIEF 8/07 VAT: MANUFACTURERS' "CASH BACK" PAYMENTS

This Revenue & Customs Brief article explains the VAT treatment of 'cash backs' and what businesses should do if they pay or receive 'cash backs', or have paid or received them in the past.

BACKGROUND

The term "cash back" refers to a payment usually made by a manufacturer directly (or via a recovery agency) to the customer of a wholesaler or retailer – mostly in recognition of the volume of purchases. Similar payments may also be made under manufacturers' discount schemes, or may be referred to as volume bonuses or described in similar terms. Such payments occur outside the direct supply chain and as a result credit notes should not be used.

HM Revenue & Customs (HMRC) has become aware that some businesses have been accounting for "cash back" payments incorrectly. Some manufacturers have reduced their output tax, some have not. Some have made retrospective claims for overpaid output tax, but the recipients of those 'cash backs' have not necessarily reduced their input tax.

VAT TREATMENT

The treatment of payments of this nature was laid down by the European Court of Justice (ECJ) in two cases: *Elida Gibbs Ltd v C & E Comrs* (C-317/94) [1996] STC 1387 and *EC Commission v Germany* (case C-427/98) [2003] STC 301. HMRC's policy is set out in VAT Notice 700/7 Business Promotion Schemes Section 7.5, which states that manufacturers are entitled to reduce the output tax on their sales in respect of the "cash backs", provided that they charged and accounted for VAT on their original supply.

If you are VAT-registered and you receive a "cash back" that relates to a taxable supply, this reduces the taxable value of your purchase, and you must reduce your input tax in the proportion in which you claimed it.

WAY FORWARD

. . .

From 1 March 2007, businesses should correctly make the necessary adjustments as outlined above. Businesses providing "cash backs" are entitled to reduce their output tax provided that they charged and accounted for VAT on their original supply.

If you are VAT-registered and you receive a "cash back", this reduces the taxable value of your purchase, and you must reduce your input tax accordingly. HMRC will assess for over-claimed input tax where these adjustments are not made.

Any "cash back" payment from manufacturer to customer, that does not affect the wholesaler, does not require the wholesaler to make any VAT adjustment.

CROSS BORDER "CASH BACKS"

Where "cash backs" are paid between businesses in different EU member states (MS), no VAT adjustments should be made. This means in practice:

- where a UK manufacturer pays a "cash back" to a recipient in another MS, the manufacturer cannot reduce his output tax;

- where a UK recipient receives a "cash back" from a manufacturer in another MS, no input tax deduction is required by the recipient.

CHANGE OF LIABILITY IN THE SUPPLY CHAIN

Where the VAT liability of the goods changes in the supply chain (eg where a charity buys certain goods zero-rated from the wholesaler which were standard-rated for VAT when supplied by the manufacturer), manufacturers cannot reduce their output tax in relation to the "cash back" paid to the charity. Where the "cash back" relates to goods that were supplied VAT-free to a business receiving the "cash back", no adjustments should be made.

Note. This Brief has now been re-issued as Revenue & Customs Brief 78/09, 12 January 2010. The text is unchanged.

[VATA 1994 s 19]

7 FEBRUARY 2007. REVENUE & CUSTOMS BRIEF 11/07 VAT SCHEMES FOR LUXURY YACHTS

We are aware that various advisors are promoting VAT schemes through which private individuals incur little or no VAT on the purchase of pleasure craft (both sailing and motor vessels), particularly at the top end of the market.

The purpose of this Brief is to describe the key features of the schemes and to announce that we have serious concerns about the validity of the VAT treatment which is claimed for the schemes.

Under the schemes, the user acquires a new vessel which purportedly has "VAT paid" status while, in reality, paying no VAT (or a minimal amount of VAT).

The schemes fall broadly into two categories – cross-border leasing and artificial chartering to the private funder. Both categories share the following common features:

- They involve a contrived leasing or chartering arrangement of a vessel which is predominantly for the recreational use of an individual.
- The individual provides the funds that are used to pay for the vessel either directly or indirectly (maybe by lending money to an intermediary).
- Registered title to the vessel is held by a special purpose entity (otherwise known as a special purpose vehicle or "SPV") which is controlled (directly or indirectly) either by the individual or by the scheme provider. This SPV may be simply a shell company – also known as a "brass plate" company, bought off the shelf and with nominee directors standing in front of whoever really benefits.
- The SPV purports to use the vessel in a chartering or leasing business. It does not incur VAT (either through a zero-rated export if the SPV is outside the EU, or otherwise by recovering as input tax any VAT charged on the supply).
- The vessel is chartered or leased to the individual. No VAT (or only a minimal amount of VAT) is charged on the lease or charter payments.

Where there is evidence to suggest that a vessel has been supplied through one of these schemes we shall carry out a full investigation of the facts surrounding the supply and take any necessary action.

Note. This Brief has now been re-issued as Revenue & Customs Brief 79/09, 12 January 2010. The text is unchanged. For more recent guidance taking account of the relevant case law, see Revenue and Customs Brief 56/09, 26 August 2009.

[VATA 1994 s 1]

14 MARCH 2007. REVENUE & CUSTOMS BRIEF 23/07 VAT: PARTIAL EXEMPTION SPECIAL METHOD APPROVALS

This article provides further guidance on preparing and submitting the new Declaration that is required for all partial exemption special method applications that are approved on or after

1 April 2007. This article should be read in conjunction with the guidance at: [http://www.hmrc.gov.uk/ria/vat-partial-amendments-qa.pdf (Q&A guidance on VAT partial exemption measure announced at PBR 2006)]. Further guidance on partial exemption is in Public Notice 706.

BACKGROUND

With effect from 1 April, HMRC will only approve a special method if the business has declared it to be fair and reasonable. The Declaration requires a reasonable person to take reasonable steps to ensure the proposed method is fair. If HMRC approves a method but subsequently discovers the person signing the Declaration did not act reasonably, it could override the method and require the business to recover VAT in accordance with the principle of use. This will improve equity between businesses and lessen the risk of unfair methods enabling HMRC to offer speedier approval increasing business certainty and reducing administrative costs.

HOW SHOULD THE DECLARATION BE MADE?

The Declaration can be made by completing the template in Annex A. It should clearly identify the business, the method to which it relates, and the signatory.

WHEN SHOULD THE DECLARATION BE MADE?

In most cases, the Declaration would accompany the special method proposal inviting HMRC to give approval. HMRC will review the method and unless problems are found, transpose it onto a special method letter adding standard clauses, glossary terms and routine references to ensure clarity, before returning it to the business. Provided the business is content that the method reflects its proposal, it can adopt it as agreed without further correspondence. There is no longer a requirement for the business to sign and return a copy of its finalised method, further saving administrative cost.

In some cases, the business will wish to discuss its draft special method before making a firm proposal to ensure it accords with guidance and partial exemption principles. In these cases, the Declaration should not be made until the special method has been fully developed, otherwise a new Declaration will be required before approval can be given. Similarly, if HMRC consider that a proposed method cannot be approved, despite the accompanying Declaration, it will discuss with the business giving reasons and invite a new proposal and Declaration.

ANNEX A
PARTIAL EXEMPTION—SPECIAL METHOD DECLARATION

Name of Business: . . .

Address: . . .

VAT Registration Number: . . .

This Declaration is in accordance with paragraphs (9) and (10) of regulation 102 of the VAT Regulations 1995.

As

- [the taxable person (ie where the signatory is a sole proprietor)] [1]
- [the person authorised by the taxable person to sign this declaration on its behalf] [1]

, I hereby declare that to the best of my knowledge and belief, the proposed special method [state precisely where the method is set out] fairly and reasonably represents the extent to which goods or services are used or to be used in making taxable supplies.

I also confirm that I have taken reasonable steps to ensure that I am in possession of all relevant information before making this declaration.

Name (print): . . .

Signed: . . .

Position (print): . . .

Date: . . .

---

1 Please delete as appropriate.

[SI 1995/2518 reg 102]

28 MARCH 2007. REVENUE & CUSTOMS BRIEF 30/07 OUTCOME OF HALIFAX CASE

In February 2006 the European Court of Justice (ECJ) gave its decision in *Halifax plc and others v C & E Comrs* (case C-255/02) [2006] STC 919, ECJ (the *Halifax* case).

That decision was in response to questions referred by the VAT & Duties Tribunal in London. The next step was for the Tribunal to make its final decision in the case, in light of the ECJ's guidance.

However, on 8 March 2007 the taxpayer withdrew its appeal in the case. Accordingly, the case is now settled in favour of HMRC. There will be no further Tribunal hearing or decision.

In similar cases, many of which were stood over pending the outcome of the ECJ reference in *Halifax*, HMRC expect taxpayers either to withdraw their appeals or to proceed to a full hearing, so that the Tribunal can decide whether VAT is due.
[VATA 1994 s 1]

30 MARCH 2007. REVENUE & CUSTOMS BRIEF 31/07 VAT: PARTIAL EXEMPTION VAT RECOVERY ON OVERHEAD COSTS RELATING TO SUPPLIES OF HIRE PURCHASE

This article explains HMRC's policy on attributing VAT on overhead costs to supplies made under hire-purchase (HP) agreements. It affects businesses that make supplies under HP agreements to consumers, but does not apply to those who arrange such supplies and receive a commission. HMRC is aware that policy is not being applied consistently, so this article confirms the policy to be applied from 1 April 2007. This article also refers to the Tribunal decision in *Royal Bank of Scotland Group plc* (No 19983) regarding VAT recovery and HP agreements.

BACKGROUND TO VAT RECOVERY

An HP transaction involves the supply of goods on credit terms. Provided the charge for credit is clearly identified to the customer, an HP transaction is treated as two supplies for VAT purposes, comprising:

- a supply of goods which is subject to VAT; and
- a supply of credit which is exempt from VAT.

Businesses making both taxable and exempt supplies must apply a partial exemption method to apportion VAT on overhead costs (such as lighting and heating) to recover that VAT to the extent that the costs are "used" for making taxable supplies.

The European Court of Justice (ECJ) has established the principles that apply to the recovery of input tax and the Court of Appeal in *Dial-a-Phone v C & E Comrs* [2004] STC 987, CA confirmed that these principles also applied in UK law.

Costs are therefore "used" to make taxable supplies of goods or services within the meaning of the partial exemption regulations, if they:

- have a direct and immediate link with the taxable transaction (see *BLP Group Ltd v C & E Comrs* (case C-4/94) [1995] STC 424, ECJ);
- are borne directly by the cost components of a taxable transaction (see *Midland Bank plc v C & E Comrs* (case C-98/98) [2000] STC 501, ECJ);
- are costs of the various components of the price (see *Rompelman v Mimister van Financiën* (case C-268/83) [1985] ECR 655).

These are different aspects of a single test to determine whether VAT is recoverable.

In applying these ECJ principles, HMRC's view is that in order for costs to be a cost component of a taxable transaction, the costs should normally be reflected in the selling price of the taxable transaction. In other words, there is an objective test for determining VAT recovery, in that VAT on costs is not recoverable unless the costs are reflected in the selling price of the taxable supply.

VAT RECOVERY FOR HP TRANSACTIONS

Normally it is clear when VAT on costs is recoverable. This is because goods and services are either sold independently, each priced to reflect the costs incurred, or if they are supplied together, the price of each item reflects both direct costs and overheads.

In most HP transactions, the goods are resold at cost without any margin to cover overhead costs. As there is no margin on the HP goods, the cost of the overheads will normally be built into the price of the supply of credit. In this scenario, HMRC's view is that the overheads are purely cost components of the exempt supply. Otherwise the business would continually enjoy net VAT refunds despite:

- making no zero-rated or reduced rate supplies; and
- charging a total consideration under the HP agreement that fully recovers its costs and an element of profit.

Where overheads are used to make both HP transactions and other supplies on which VAT is charged (such as taxable purchase option fees or sales of repossessed goods), then some VAT on overhead costs is recoverable. In this scenario the partial exemption method should reflect the extent to which the overhead costs are a cost component of the prices of the supplies in question.

EXISTING METHODS

Businesses using special methods will need to review them to ensure that they are fair and reasonable in accordance with the above principles. If an existing method is not fair and reasonable, the business concerned should contact HMRC to discuss a new method going forward. In approving new methods, or reviewing existing methods, HMRC will ensure that methods fairly attribute VAT to taxable supplies taking account of this article.

HP businesses using the standard method will need to consider the standard method override provisions and, if necessary, apply for a special method. In doing this the above principles for HP transactions will need to be taken into account. Further guidance is available in VAT Notice 706 Partial exemption.

ROYAL BANK OF SCOTLAND

In February, the Scottish Tribunal released its decision in *Royal Bank of Scotland Group plc* (No 19983) (RBS) regarding VAT recovery and HP transactions. RBS appealed HM-RC's refusal to approve a replacement partial exemption method in which HP transactions would be treated as two transactions, one taxable and one exempt such that 50% of the VAT on related overhead costs would be recoverable. The Tribunal found for RBS. HMRC has lodged an appeal to the Court of Session. The cost component point was not tested because the appeal predated this Revenue and Customs Brief.

Note. This Brief has now been re-issued as Revenue & Customs Brief 82/09, 12 January 2010.

[SI 1995/2518 reg 101]

11 JUNE 2007. REVENUE & CUSTOMS BRIEF 44/07 LITIGATION AND SETTLEMENTS STRATEGY (LSS)

The Litigation and Settlements Strategy (LSS) [see Appendix 11] is relevant to all aspects of how HMRC enters into, handles and settles disputes about any of our taxes, duties or credits. It sets out principles for bringing tax disputes to a conclusion, whether by agreement with the taxpayer, or by litigation, ie statutory appeal to an independent body, including the General or Special Commissioners, the VAT Tribunal, or the courts.

The aim of the LSS is to ensure that we conduct disputes in a way that is professional, effective and that supports HMRC's objectives to close the tax gap and provide customers with a clear understanding of the law.

The central themes of the LSS are:

- Seek non-confrontational solutions where possible.
- Focus on issues that will best serve HMRC's goal of tax gap reduction.
- Choose cases for their wider impact, as well as for their own value.
- Where we have a strong case we should seek full value from settlement, or take the matter to litigation.
- Do not pursue weak arguments.
- Team-work cases with colleagues, including those in other parts of HMRC.

. . .

[VATA 1994 s 83]

14 JUNE 2007. REVENUE & CUSTOMS BRIEF 45/07 VAT: PARTIAL EXEMPTION—VAT DEDUCTION BY THEATRES ON PRODUCTION COSTS

HMRC has revised its policy on input tax recovery on the costs of staging shows (production costs) for which the theatre's admissions are VAT exempt. It follows the judgment of the Court of Appeal in the case of *Mayflower Theatre Trust Ltd v HMRC* [2007] STC 880, CA (MTT). It replaces the first article in Business Brief 12/06 [not reproduced], which is now withdrawn. Further information on partial exemption can be found in Public Notice 706.

. . .

THE NEW HMRC POLICY

Theatres which receive single supplies of production services from touring companies, that include material essential for the printing of programmes, may treat the input tax as residual. This applies even where that programme material is a minor part of the contract.

Theatres that stage their own shows may receive supplies such as costumes or scenery. These supplies will not be residual. This is because the costs have a direct and immediate link with admissions and not with the printing of programmes even though costumes and scenery might be visible in subsequent programme photographs.

IMPACT ON THEATRES

The vast majority of theatres use the partial exemption standard method to apportion residual input tax between taxable and exempt supplies. This works well provided VAT bearing costs are used in proportion to the value of supplies made. However, residual production services are used almost entirely for exempt admissions with only a minimal link to taxable programmes. The Court of Appeal recognised that this led to an over-recovery of input tax.

Since 18 April 2002, if the standard method results in an over (or under) recovery of input tax which is classed as "substantial" then the recovery must be re-calculated in accordance with the "actual use" of the costs in question. This is known as the Standard Method Override (SMO). Further information on the SMO, including the definition of "substantial" can be found in the public notice.

Major theatres which buy in large numbers of shows are the ones most likely to trigger the SMO and thus need to undertake a "use-based" calculation for their costs.

A "use-based" calculation is any calculation that fairly reflects how costs are used. As production services only have a direct and immediate link with box office sales and programme sales, a fair calculation could be:

$$\text{Recoverable input tax on production services} = \frac{\text{Value of programme sales}}{\text{Value of programme sales plus value of box office sales}} \times \text{Input tax incurred on production services}$$

Theatres operating the standard method which regularly receive production services that are residual may wish to seek approval for a special method to avoid the risk of triggering the SMO.

. . .

[SI 1995/2518 reg 101]

26 JUNE 2007. REVENUE & CUSTOMS BRIEF 48/07
VAT: INTRODUCTION OF A REDUCED RATE FOR THE SUPPLY OF SMOKING CESSATION PRODUCTS

With effect from 1 July 2007, the supply of smoking cessation products will be eligible for the reduced rate of VAT (5%).

. . .

The reduced rate will apply to non-prescribed sales of nicotine patches, nicotine gums, nicotine inhalators, lozenges and other pharmaceutical products held out for sale for the primary purpose of helping people to stop smoking.

The supply of smoking cessation products on a prescription by a medical practitioner will continue to be zero rated.

[VATA 1994 Sch 7A Group 11]

13 AUGUST 2007. REVENUE & CUSTOMS BRIEF 55/07
REVISED TREATMENT OF VAT INCURRED ON HOME COMPUTERS MADE AVAILABLE BY EMPLOYERS TO THEIR EMPLOYEES

This Revenue and Customs Brief sets out HMRC's revised policy on the VAT treatment of computers made available by employers for use in their employee's homes; this follows withdrawal of the tax exemption which allowed employers to loan computer equipment to their employees tax-free.

BACKGROUND

In April 1999 the Government introduced a direct tax exemption which enabled employers to loan a computer to their employees tax-free. The objective was to help increase access to computers and help employees increase their IT literacy skills. In January 2004 the Government launched the Home Computer Initiative ("HCI") which encouraged employers and employees to take advantage of the exemption and sought to make it as straightforward as possible for employers to lend computer equipment to their employees.

At that time the former HM Customs and Excise considered that, while there would undoubtedly be some private use of the computer—usually requiring some restriction on VAT recovery—in the circumstances of the HCI there would be wider benefits to the business and so the VAT treatment should mirror the approach taken for direct tax. Consequently, as long as there was some business use, any VAT incurred, could be deducted in full without any adjustment for private use.

Following a review of the HCI the direct tax exemption was withdrawn with effect from 6 April 2006. Consequently HMRC have now reviewed the VAT position.

HMRC'S REVISED POLICY

HMRC's policy to allow full VAT recovery without any adjustment for private use, in circumstances where there is any business use, is withdrawn from the date of this Revenue and Customs Brief.

With immediate effect businesses must consider why the computer is being provided to the employee to determine the level of VAT that can be claimed. Businesses will only be able to claim full VAT recovery without any requirement to account for VAT on any private use (subject of course to any restriction in respect of exempt supplies) where the provision of a computer is necessary for the employee to carry out the duties of his employment. In these circumstances HMRC's view is that it is unlikely that any private use will be significant when compared with the business need for providing the computer in the first place. This mirrors the approach taken for direct tax concerning exemptions for work related benefits in kind where there is no significant private use.

Where a business cannot demonstrate that it is necessary to provide an employee with a computer in order to carry out the duties of his employment then only a portion of the VAT incurred will be recoverable as input tax. HMRC will accept any method of apportioning the VAT incurred as long as the result fairly and reasonably reflects the extent of business use. In order to minimise your administrative burdens you may be able to agree a set percentage with HMRC based on a representative period.

TRANSITIONAL PROVISIONS

Where a business continues to provide a computer under an existing HCI agreement full VAT recovery can continue until the agreement (normally three years) has expired. For further information on these transitional provisions please refer to direct tax guidance EIM2699.

WHAT IF THE BUSINESS IS NOT THE RECIPIENT OF THE SUPPLY?

Please note that it is a basic principle of the VAT system that VAT can only be recovered as input tax where the supply is to the taxable person or business. So, in circumstances where the supply of the computer is to the employee the business cannot recover the VAT incurred on that supply as input tax.

Note. This Brief has now been re-issued as Revenue & Customs Brief 82/09, 12 January 2010.

[VATA 1994 s 24]

17 OCTOBER 2007. REVENUE & CUSTOMS BRIEF 67/07
VAT: CHANGES IN THE VAT TREATMENT OF SERVICED BUILDING PLOTS

HM Revenue & Customs (HMRC) is announcing a change in the liability treatment of serviced building plots.

A serviced building plot is bare land in respect of which civil engineering works have been carried out to provide access to essential services such as gas, electricity, water, main drainage, street lighting and sewerage. Until now, we have treated the supply of a serviced building plot by the landowner to a developer as consisting of two supplies – an exempt supply of land and a standard-rated supply of civil engineering.

A recent VAT Tribunal decision in Virtue (a firm) (No 20259) held that the sale of a 'plot of land within a serviced site' (the Tribunal's description, in preference to the term serviced plot) constituted a single exempt supply of land.

The Tribunal also held that, in this case, the supply of the civil engineering works to the landowner was zero-rated because it had been made in the course of the construction of a 'building designed as a dwelling'.

The supply of civil engineering works is normally standard-rated.

REVISED POSITION

We now accept that, with immediate effect, the supply of a serviced building plot of land is a single exempt supply of land by the landowner.

The supply of civil engineering works to the landowner to provide access to essential services will continue to be standard–rated in most cases. However, where the landowner can demonstrate that these services are being received in the course of construction of a building designed as dwellings, or buildings intended for use solely for a relevant residential or a relevant charitable purpose, they can be zero-rated.

We would normally expect all the following to be met to demonstrate that zero-rating is appropriate:

- the landowner holds sufficient planning consent to demonstrate that the civil engineering works were received in the course of construction of a building designed as dwellings, or buildings intended for use solely for a relevant residential or a relevant charitable purpose;
- the civil engineering is closely connected with or facilitates the construction of buildings;
- the construction of the buildings will follow on closely after the completion of the civil engineering works.

The extent to which the above conditions have been met will be a matter of fact and degree. We would need to be satisfied that at the time the civil engineering is supplied, any potential purchaser of a serviced plot can only construct a qualifying building on the plot. In addition, it must be clear that the landowner has a firm intention to sell the serviced plots once the civil engineering is complete and that any purchaser is ready to begin actual construction of the buildings as soon as possible.

IMPACT ON LANDOWNERS COMMERCIAL HOUSEBUILDERS AND DIY HOUSEBUILDERS

. . .

New policy following the finding by the Tribunal:

- landowners will now be making an exempt supply of land and will not be able to register for VAT unless they have other taxable activities;
- if the supply of the civil engineering works to them is standard-rated, they will not be able to recover this VAT and it will become a cost to the landowner;
- developers and DIY housebuilders will now not be charged VAT by landowners in this situation.

Note. This Brief has been re-issued as Revenue & Customs Brief 88/09, 12 January 2010. The text is unchanged.

[VATA 1994 Sch 9 Group 1]

5 NOVEMBER 2007. REVENUE & CUSTOMS BRIEF 66/07
VAT: TREATMENT OF THE CONSTRUCTION OF HOUSES OR FLATS IN THE GROUNDS OF EXISTING CARE HOMES, NURSING HOMES OR SIMILAR BUILDINGS

This brief sets out HMRC's policy on the VAT treatment of the construction, and first major interest grant of, "independent living" units within the curtilage or grounds of residential care homes. (A "first major interest grant" is defined as the freehold sale or a lease in excess of 21 years (20 years in Scotland).)

In order for services of the construction, or first major interest grant, of such units to qualify for zero-rating, they must qualify either as buildings "designed as dwellings" or as buildings "intended for use solely for a relevant residential purpose", within the meaning of the these terms as defined in VATA 1994.

Although "independent living" units generally have all of the physical characteristics of a "dwelling", the units only qualify for zero-rating if they meet all the conditions laid down in VATA 1994 Sch 8 Group 5 Note 2. Where such units have a stipulation in their planning permission that they cannot be used separately from the care homes, of which they form a part, the construction of such units is ineligible for the zero rate, as is the first grant of a major interest in such units.

We have also been asked to consider whether the new units form a building (or buildings) that are "intended for use solely for a relevant residential purpose" thus qualifying the construction of the units for the zero rate.

In our view, the units do not qualify for the zero rate because, if personal care is provided to the occupants of the units, it is either not provided as a zero-rated home or institution would provide personal care or, if it is, it is provided as part of an existing home or institution.

Finally, we consider that such a unit would not qualify for zero-rating as "an institution which is the sole or main residence of at least 90 per cent of its residents", because the units are not institutions.

Note. This Brief has now been re-issued as Revenue & Customs Brief 89/09, 12 January 2010.

[VATA 1994 Sch 8 Group 5 Notes 2, 4]

9 NOVEMBER 2007. REVENUE & CUSTOMS BRIEF 67/07
VAT: REBATES AND CREDIT NOTES RELATING TO CUSTOMER DISCOUNTS AND ASSOCIATED PAYMENTS

This Revenue & Customs Brief article explains the VAT treatment of rebates, credit notes and similar transactions relating to business promotions between suppliers and their customers.

BACKGROUND

Revenue & Customs Brief 8/07 explains the VAT treatment of manufacturers' cash back payments. That brief covers payments that occur outside the direct supply chain. This brief explains the correct VAT treatment for supplier discounts, volume rebates and charges made by the customer when promoting the suppliers' products.

The table below outlines the differing forms that these transactions take and their VAT treatment.

With effect from 1 January 2008, you are required to apply the correct VAT treatment as outlined. We do not wish to create any unnecessary business cash flow problems where there is little or no revenue at risk. Therefore, no retrospective action will be taken on transactions occurring before that date.

CUSTOMER DISCOUNTS – A GLOSSARY OF TERMS

Type	Principles	VAT position
Over-rider	% discount paid to the customer monthly/quarterly/annually Customer usually invoices manufacturer Pence per case rebate	Follows liability of goods
Long-term retro	Pence per case rebate Customer invoices manufacturer Volumes expressed in cases	Follows liability of goods
Business protection deals	One-off lump sum Usually paid annually Customer invoices manufacturer Protects the business with the customer	Taxable
Third party rebate or end-user rebates	Rebate paid to customer for supplies to one of their customers or paid to customer of manufacturers' customer National account manager will often supply volumes/wholesaler reports Based on pence per case or percentage Customer invoices manufacturer	See Revenue & Customs Brief 08/07
Short-term retro	Pence per case either bought during the period or sold during the period Given to customer either as multisave or price promotion Customer invoices manufacturer	Follows liability of goods
Price promotions	Off invoice discounts No action by customer	Follows liability of goods
Multisave	Based on triggers (EPOS systems) and redemption rate Includes BOGOF, three for price of two, two for £1.50 etc Customer invoices manufacturer on basis of volume sold	Follows liability of goods
Lump sums	One-off payment to secure best spot in store eg gondola ends and ends of shelves Usually attached to a promotion (STR, PP, MSV)	Taxable
Agreements and advertising allowances	Like business protection deals Applies in main to smaller outlets Customer invoices manufacturer	Taxable
Consumer marketing	Often in-store Supplier invoices manufacturer	Taxable

EPOS – BOGOF – Buy One Get One Free Electronic Point of Sale

Note. This Brief has been re-issued as Revenue & Customs Brief 90/09, 12 January 2010. The text is unchanged.

[VATA 1994 s 19]

19 NOVEMBER 2007. REVENUE & CUSTOMS BRIEF 69/07 VAT: THE DECISION OF THE TRIBUNAL IN INSURANCEWIDE.COM SERVICES LTD

This Revenue & Customs Brief concerns the VAT treatment of insurance introductory services following the VAT tribunal decision in *InsuranceWide.com Services Ltd* (2007) VAT decision 20394 ("InsuranceWide"). The tribunal found that certain internet services provided to insurers and brokers in connection with the arranging of insurance policies do not fall within the exemption for insurance related services provided by insurance brokers and agents and are liable to VAT at the standard rate.

. . .

IMPLICATIONS OF THE DECISION

The decision in *InsuranceWide* confirms HMRC's current published policy in this area (see in particular paragraph 10.5 of Notice 701/36, Insurance) and, as such, does not have implications for any of the insurance-related services that HMRC currently see as falling within the VAT exemption.

Whilst certain services provided via the internet were found to be liable to VAT, HMRC do not see the decision as applying to all internet services and accept that, where the necessary criteria are met, some internet services can fall within the VAT exemption and it is the arrangements between the parties and the nature of the services themselves that determines the VAT liability and not the means by which those services are delivered.

HMRC see the decision as applying, in particular, to advertising/promotional type services such as internet "click through" services and mail-shot and leaflet distribution services where the provider does little more than put one party in touch with the other and plays no part in any interaction between the parties once that introduction has been made. Such services are specifically excluded from the VAT exemption and are taxable regardless of whether (as with InsuranceWide's co-branded websites) the products are promoted in the name of the provider of the service, the provider is an insurance agent or broker by profession, or whether payment is made by fee or commission.

In circumstances (which would include certain "affinity" arrangements) where the provider is clearly acting as an agent of an insurer or insurers and is playing a more active role in arranging the policies than mere introduction—for example, negotiating terms and conditions of the insurance contacts, assisting with forms/queries and actively recommending/endorsing the insurance product(s)—VAT exemption continues to apply.

[VATA 1994 Sch 9 Group 2 Item 4]

1 APRIL 2008. REVENUE & CUSTOMS BRIEF 20/08 EXTENSION OF NON-STATUTORY CLEARANCES SERVICE FOR HM REVENUE AND CUSTOMS (HMRC) BUSINESS CUSTOMERS

. . . A non-statutory clearance is written confirmation of our view of the application of tax law to a specific transaction or event.

At Pre-Budget Report 2007, we announced an extension of the non-statutory clearances we provide to all our business customers from April 2008.

CHANGES AFFECTING BUSINESS

From 1 April 2008 clearances will be provided across all business taxes regardless of the age of the legislation, where there is material uncertainty. . . .

We will aim to respond to clearance applications within 28 calendar days, though in complex cases this may take longer.

In addition, as part of the extended clearances service from 1 April 2008, we will publish new guidance on clearances for our business customers, bringing together and updating existing guidance so as to provide a consistent and clear framework for clearance applications across HMRC. The guidance for businesses is available on the HMRC website (http://www.hmrc.gov.uk/cap/links-dec07.htm).

WHO DO I CONTACT?

Large Business Service (LBS) customers should continue to send their clearance applications to their Client Relationship Manager (CRM).

All other business customers, and those acting on behalf of a business, should send their applications to: HMRC Clearances Team, Alexander House, 21 Victoria Avenue, Southend-on-Sea Essex SS99 1BD; Email: mailto:hmrc.southendteam@hmrc.gsi.gov.uk.

OTHER GUIDANCE ON INFORMATION AND ADVICE

. . . Notice 700/6 VAT rulings will remain in place for our customers who are not covered by the new clearances process to provide guidance on how to seek information and advice from HMRC. We will be reviewing these documents over the next year to provide more consistent guidance on the information and advice available to our customers.

[VATA 1994 Sch 11 para 1]

22 APRIL 2008. REVENUE & CUSTOMS BRIEF 24/08 VAT: LAND AND BUILDINGS—NEW SCHEDULE 10 OF THE VAT ACT 1994 INCLUDING CHANGES TO THE OPTION TO TAX

This Brief announces the introduction of a new VATA 1994 Sch 10 that becomes effective from the 1 June 2008 following the announcement in Budget Note 79 at Budget 2008.

. . .

OTHER CHANGES

At present, a small number of taxpayers, typically large taxpayers, have what has become known as a global option to tax. This option to tax is effectively an option on the whole of the UK, and is typically expressed as follows:

> "I opt to tax the whole of the UK" or more commonly "I opt to tax all the land I currently own and all that I acquire in the future".

While there is no problem with retaining these global options, HM Revenue & Customs (HMRC) has in some cases, by concession, allowed the cooling off period to apply to each property as it is acquired. Under the normal rules, the cooling off period can only apply to the option to tax itself and so should expire three months after the option was made (this will be extended to six months from 1 June 2008). Because of the introduction of the new real estate election, this concession will be withdrawn with effect from 31 July 2009. This should allow sufficient time for those with a global option to decide whether to retain it without a cooling-off period in future, or to convert their global option into a new real estate election.

Note. This Brief has now been re-issued as Revenue & Customs Brief 95/09, 12 January 2010.

[VATA 1994 Sch 10]

19 MAY 2008. REVENUE & CUSTOMS BRIEF 27/08 INTERPRETATION OF ARTICLE 13 OF THE PRINCIPAL VAT DIRECTIVE— "BODIES GOVERNED BY PUBLIC LAW" AND "SPECIAL LEGAL REGIME"

HM Revenue and Customs has reconsidered its interpretation of the terms "bodies governed by public law" and "special legal regime" in the context of article 13(1) of the Principal VAT Directive (Directive 2006/112/EC) ("article 13(1)") as well as the application of this provision.

Our current interpretation is based on the decisions in the Court of Session's judgment in *Edinburgh Telford College v R & C Comrs* [2006] STC 1291 ("ETC"), the High Court's judgment in *Riverside Housing Association v R & C Comrs* [2006] STC 2072 ("Riverside") and the decision of the VAT and Duties Tribunal in *The Chancellors, Masters and Scholars of the University of Cambridge* (2008) VAT decision 20610 ("Cambridge University").

This Revenue & Customs Brief explains HMRCs' current thinking on the matter. While the Brief is of immediate interest to further education ("FE") and higher education ("FE") providers, it may be relevant to other bodies as well.

. . .

BODY GOVERNED BY PUBLIC LAW

In the light of the decision in *Riverside*, HMRC has concluded that the term "body governed by public law" in article 13(1) is narrow in application. HMRC consider that a body will only satisfy this criterion if it is a public sector body which forms a part of the UK's public administration, such as a government department, a local authority or a non-departmental public body. Article 13(1) is not intended to enable other bodies to claim special treatment merely because they have delegated powers, are regulated in some way by the State, are funded by public money or are subject to certain specific rules in the pursuit of their activities.

This view has recently been endorsed by the VAT and Duties Tribunal in the *Cambridge University* case.

Accordingly HMRC no longer accept that the generality of FE and HE providers are bodies governed by public law as defined in article 13(1).

A number of FE and HE bodies have sought to rely on article 13(1) to support an argument for entitlement to zero-rating under VATA 1994 Sch 8 Group 5 and/or reduced rating under Sch 7A. FE and HE bodies should be aware that HMRC does not agree that such bodies can assume that they fall within this provision: rather it is necessary to examine the facts of each case separately.

Further, HMRC is of the view that, even were a body to come within article 13(1) in respect of a particular activity, that would serve only to take supplies in respect of that activity outside the scope of VAT and would not affect the liability of supplies made to that body.

Note. This Brief has now been re-issued as Revenue & Customs Brief 96/09, 12 January 2010.

[VATA 1994 s 94]

1 AUGUST 2008. REVENUE & CUSTOMS BRIEF 38/08 VAT: DEFAULT INTEREST AND NET ERRORS OF LESS THAN £2,000

The current practice, described in paragraph 2.4 of Notice 700/43 (Default Interest) and note 4 on form VAT 652, of not charging default interest on net errors of £2,000 or less separately notified to HMRC, will continue until the end of August 2008. However, following the decision in *R (on the application of Wilkinson) v IR Comrs* [2006] STC 270, HL, this practice is not considered lawful and will be withdrawn with effect from 1 September 2008. This means therefore that all error notifications (previously known as voluntary disclosures) requiring an assessment may be subject to a default interest charge, irrespective of the amount involved. However, as before, de minimis net errors can continue to be corrected on a VAT return and will not attract interest.

[VATA 1994 s 74]

15 SEPTEMBER 2008. REVENUE & CUSTOMS BRIEF 44/08 VAT: PARTIAL EXEMPTION—VAT ADJUSTMENTS WHEN HOUSE BUILDERS LET THEIR DWELLINGS BEFORE SELLING THEM

We have published an Information Sheet 07/08 which provides guidance, including worked examples, on the VAT implications when house builders decide to temporarily let their dwellings before selling them.

This Information Sheet is in response to recent enquiries from the house building sector and takes account of the High Court decision in the joined cases of *C & E Comrs v Briararch Ltd, C & E Comrs v Curtis Henderson Ltd* [1992] STC 732 which arose in the early 1990s. The key points to which the Information Sheet refers are:

- if you temporarily let a dwelling before selling it, you may affect the VAT you can recover on your costs
- many house builders who temporarily let a dwelling will not be affected but you need to check this to avoid making VAT mistakes
- there is an easy way to check if you are affected by applying what we describe here as a "simple check for de minimis"

If you fail this check, you may have to:

- adjust the VAT previously recovered on your submitted VAT returns
- restrict the VAT to be recovered on your current and future VAT returns
- both adjust your past VAT recovery and restrict your future VAT recovery.

If you need to adjust VAT previously recovered, exceptionally and if you prefer, you may be able to do this without contacting us.

[VATA 1994 Sch 8 Group 1 Item 1; SI 1995/2518 reg 101]

28 OCTOBER 2008. REVENUE & CUSTOMS BRIEF 54/08 VAT—NEW ZERO-RATED DWELLINGS—WHETHER ARRANGEMENTS ARE ABUSIVE

1. This brief is for house builders who have built or are building new dwellings with the intention, when they are completed, of selling either the freehold interest or a long lease of over 21 years (at least 20 years in Scotland) in each of the properties.

2. Several such house builders have sought guidance on whether HM Revenue & Customs (HMRC) considers certain transactions involving the supply of new dwellings to be abusive. This brief identifies those situations that HMRC considers not to be abusive.

BACKGROUND

3. The first grant of a major interest (freehold sale or a long lease of over 21 years (at least 20 years in Scotland)) of a new dwelling is zero rated. This allows the house builder to recover all the input tax they have incurred in connection with the development (subject to the normal rules about blocked input tax) and to sell the dwelling without adding VAT.

4. In the current economic climate, many house builders have found that they are unable to sell new dwellings. For most, this leaves them with the choice of leaving them empty until they find a buyer, or renting them out in the short term while they wait for the housing market to recover in order to sell them.

5. Revenue & Customs Brief 44/08 and Information Sheet 07/08 (both published on 15 September 2008) provide guidance for house builders renting out new dwellings on short term lets while retaining the intention to sell a major interest in the dwellings when the markets recover. As those documents explain, short term lets of this kind can sometimes give rise to adjustments of input tax previously recovered.

APPROACH MADE

6. HMRC have been asked about the possibility that house builders might, in advance of any short term lets, make the first grant of a major interest in the completed dwellings to a connected person, who would not be a member of a VAT group with the house builder. This zero-rated sale might remove the need for the kind of adjustments explained in Information Sheet 07/08. The suggestion put to HMRC is that the connected person would then rent out the properties until such a time as they could be sold. The rentals would be exempt and not give rise to input tax deduction on ongoing costs including the costs of the eventual sale (for example estate agency and legal costs). However, deduction of the VAT associated with the original construction would have been secured. We have been asked whether we would see this arrangement as abusive from a VAT point of view. This brief does not attempt to address any other tax consequences that might flow from such transactions or any commercial or legal issues.

IS THIS INTENDED STRUCTURE ABUSIVE?

7. For a scheme to be abusive, it must (as well as having the essential aim of saving VAT) produce a result contrary to the purpose of the VAT legislation. HMRC believe that Parliament intended that the construction of new dwellings should be relieved from VAT. The first grant mechanism introduced by Parliament does achieve this but it relies on the assumption that there will always be a grant of a major interest around the time the dwelling is complete, so ensuring deduction of VAT on all appropriate costs.

8. In HMRC's view, the arrangement set out in paragraph 6 above does not produce a result contrary to the purpose of the legislation, but rather ensures that a transaction of the kind Parliament envisaged will actually take place at the appropriate time. That view rests on the assumption that the purpose of the zero rating provisions associated with new dwellings is to relieve fully from VAT the provision of precisely that – new dwellings. That means that all the costs (save on blocked goods such as washing machines, carpets etc – see Section 13 of Notice 708 Buildings and Construction for more details) associated with producing a new house should either not carry VAT, or carry VAT that is deductible in full.

9. However, whilst we believe it is the policy objective that new dwellings should be zero rated, that does not extend to other goods or services that might be packaged up with the supply of a dwelling. HMRC consider it abusive when a major interest is granted with an essential aim of deducting VAT on costs such as repair, maintenance and refurbishment of dwellings (other than for remedying defects in the original construction) the relief of those kinds of costs not falling within the policy objective as we see it. These types of arrangements are likely to be challenged.

SUMMARY

10. In short, HMRC agree that the arrangement outlined in paragraph 6 above is one that they would not see as abusive and so would not seek to challenge. However, if the VAT deducted goes beyond the VAT that would normally be deducted in relation to the supply of the new dwelling (for example VAT on costs such as repairs, maintenance or refurbishment, which is not normally deductible) such arrangements are likely to be challenged as abusive.

Note. This Brief has now been re-issued as Revenue & Customs Brief 101/09, 12 January 2010.

[VATA 1994 Sch 8 Group 5 Item 1]

8 DECEMBER 2008. REVENUE & CUSTOMS BRIEF 57/08
VAT—EXCESS CHARGES IN NON-LOCAL AUTHORITY CAR PARKS

This Revenue & Customs Brief explains our revised policy on VAT on excess charges and other penalties levied in non-local authority car parks and what you should do if you have incorrectly accounted for VAT on such charges. Certain excess charges which have to date been regarded as further consideration for a taxable supply of parking are now regarded as outside the scope of VAT.

BACKGROUND

Business Brief 19/02, 19 July 2002 [not reproduced] explained our policy on the VAT treatment of excess charges in off-street car parks following the tribunal case of *Bristol City Council* (No 17665) ("*BCC*"). The Tribunal had concluded that excess charges levied by the Council in its off-street car parks were outside the scope of VAT because they were levied pursuant to the Road Traffic Regulation Act 1984 and were not part of the contract entered into between the driver and the council. We accepted that the decision would also apply to other local authorities operating off-street car parks under the same statutory framework.

However, where off-street car parks were not operated by local authorities, we considered that excess charges would normally be subject to VAT because they arose under the terms of the contract between the driver and car park operator. This followed the rationale adopted by the Tribunal in the case of *J G Leigh t/a Moor Lane Video* (No 5098), which concerned additional charges for videos held by customers beyond the agreed period of hire.

REVISED POLICY

We have recently reconsidered that policy in the light of new legal advice and have concluded that, in the case of *BCC*, the Tribunal's decision was founded as much upon the contractual relationship as the statutory regime. Therefore, we now accept that there is a difference between the situation where the contract under which parking is supplied allows for an extension of the original terms, for which additional consideration will be payable, and the situation where the driver is not permitted to extend the original terms and a penalty for breach of contract ensues if this in fact happens. Thus, where a car park operator makes an offer of parking under clear terms and conditions, setting punitive fines for their breach, the fines constitute penalties for breaching the contract, rather than additional consideration for using the facilities. Consequently, they are outside the scope of VAT. Since the same contractual relationships arise between drivers and local authority car park operators as arise between drivers and other car park operators, we have also concluded that the VAT treatment of excess charges will be the same for **all** car park operators.

EXCESS CHARGES NOT SUBJECT TO VAT

The penalty charges that will no longer be subject to VAT are those that are levied where a driver is in breach of the terms of the contract with the car park operator. The commonest situations where a driver may be in breach of the contract are:

- no parking ticket on display
- underpayment
- overstaying purchased parking time
- returning within a specified time
- parking outside marked bays
- parking in bays set aside for disabled drivers or parents with children

EXCESS CHARGES SUBJECT TO VAT

Where the terms and conditions make it clear that the driver can continue to use the facilities after a set period upon payment of a further amount without being in breach of the contract – for example, no charge for an initial three hours parking but £70 if that period is exceeded – then the payment will be consideration for use of the facilities and subject to VAT.

EXCESS CHARGES RETAINED BY CONTRACTORS

Some parking site owners contract out the management and operation of their parking sites and allow the contractor to retain all or part of the penalties collected. Any such payments retained by the contractor will constitute further consideration for their services supplied to the parking site owner and are subject to VAT.

[VATA 1994 s 5]

20 FEBRUARY 2009. REVENUE & CUSTOMS BRIEF 06/09 CLAIMS FOR RETROSPECTIVE APPLICATION OF EXTRA-STATUTORY CONCESSION (ESC) 3.35

[Notice No 48 para 3.35 (see Appendix 6)] permits non-profit making membership bodies that supply a single package of benefits to their members to apportion their subscriptions to reflect the value and VAT liability of the individual benefits, without regard to whether there is one principal benefit.

A practical example is where the principal benefit of a membership subscription is standard-rated, but there are ancillary benefits which, if supplied in their own right, would be zero-rated and/or exempt. In such a case, the body may apportion the subscription to reflect the different elements, rather than treating the whole subscription as standard-rated.

HM Revenue & Customs (HMRC) is aware that some bodies have been using the ESC to rework previously submitted VAT returns, and have submitted claims for "overpaid" VAT. In our view, the ESC may not be used to make retrospective adjustments, as such returns were correct in law. HMRC will therefore reject any such claims.

In some cases the claims have alleged 100 per cent zero rating, due to the principal benefit being zero-rated. Such cases will be given due consideration by HMRC, provided the claim is based on the application of the law, as opposed to retrospective use of the ESC.

[VATA 1994 s 19; Apendix 6]

16 MARCH 2009. REVENUE & CUSTOMS BRIEF 10/09 TRIBUNALS REFORM—CHANGES TO THE TAX APPEALS SYSTEM AND NEW INTERNAL REVIEW PROCESS

SUMMARY

This Revenue & Customs Brief outlines the new tax appeals system and HMRC's new internal review process, due to be implemented from 1 April 2009.

INTRODUCTION

From 1 April 2009 there will be a major change to the current system of tax tribunals. To coincide with this, HMRC is changing the way it handles disagreements about tax. The new review process will help provide a more consistent approach to the way we seek to resolve disputes with those who disagree with appealable tax decisions made by HMRC.

[. . .]

INTERNAL REVIEW

To coincide with tribunal reform, our customers will be entitled to request an internal review of appealable tax decisions. This new legal right to a review will replace reconsiderations and mandatory reviews in indirect taxes (mandatory reviews will remain for decisions about the restoration of seized goods).

Reviews will be optional and will be done by a trained review officer, who has not previously been involved with that decision, who will be able to offer a balanced and objective view. In the vast majority of cases the review officer will be outside the immediate line management chain of the decision maker.

We must complete reviews within 45 days (unless another period is agreed with the customer). If customers do not want a review, or if they do not agree with the result of the review, they can appeal to the tribunal for a decision.

[VATA 1994 s 83F]

18 MARCH 2009. REVENUE & CUSTOMS BRIEF 08/09 [VAT: STAFF HIRE CONCESSION]

As announced at Budget 2008 the VAT Staff Hire Concession, which applies to supplies of staff by employment bureaux, is to be withdrawn from 1 April 2009. This brief is intended to remind affected businesses of its withdrawal and to set out the VAT treatment that should be applied from 1 April. VAT Information Sheet 03/09 issued on 19 March 2009 contains more detailed guidance.

The concession is set out in Part A of the Statement of Practice in Notice 700/34 Staff and in Business Brief 02/04. It enables businesses making supplies of their own staff to exclude from the value of their supply the remuneration element and any PAYE (Pay As You Earn), National Insurance Contributions, pension contributions and similar payments relating to the worker provided such payments are made directly to the worker by the hirer, or a payroll company separate from the employment business supplying the staff. Such employment businesses have thus charged VAT solely on their profit margin and not on the full value of their supply.

Parts B and C of the Statement of Practice in Notice 700/34 Staff are unaffected and will not be withdrawn on 1 April 2009.

Business Brief 10/04 allowed employment bureaux that did not fall within the conditions of the Staff Hire Concession, because they made supplies of staff using self-employed workers, to choose whether to act as agents or principals for VAT purposes until the review of the Staff Hire Concession was completed. As announced at Budget 2008, this concession will also be withdrawn from 1 April 2009.

From 1 April 2009, in line with normal VAT principles, businesses making supplies of staff must charge and account for VAT on the full value of their supply. The correct VAT treatment following withdrawal is as follows:

If you act as a principal (eg employment business) in making a supply of staff using either:

- your own employees (which includes a director of your company) engaged under a contract of services
- self-employed workers who make their supplies to you under a contract for services

then VAT will be due on the full value of the supply (not just the profit margin).

If you act as an agent in providing introductory services of finding employment for workers or workers for your client and the workers enter into a direct contractual relationship with the client, who pays them, then VAT is due on your intermediary service only (based on your commission received). Such supplies are unaffected by the Staff Hire Concession and so will be unaffected by its withdrawal.

If you are making a supply of services other than staff, for example, supplies of care services, then your supply may qualify for exemption from VAT. See Notice 701/57 Health professionals for more information and the qualifying criteria. If your supply is of services other than staff it is unaffected by the Staff Hire Concession and so will be unaffected by its withdrawal.

[. . .]

ACCOUNTING PROCEDURES AROUND 1 APRIL 2009

The normal time of supply (tax point) rules will apply. However, in respect of supplies spanning 1 April 2009, the Staff Hire Concession will be available to the extent that the service is performed prior to 1 April 2009. For example, if you raise an invoice or receive a payment on Friday 3 April, the concession will by then have been withdrawn. But you may, if you wish, account for VAT on the basis of the value of the services actually performed before and after the withdrawal of the concession, ie you may apportion the consideration for the services between:

- those services performed before 1 April, in respect of which the Staff Hire Concession is available
- those services performed on or after 1 April, in respect of which the Staff Hire Concession will no longer be available

[VATA 1994 s 5]

27 MARCH 2009. REVENUE & CUSTOMS BRIEF 15/09 EXTRA STATUTORY CONCESSION (ESC) 3.5—MISDIRECTION

ESC 3.5 Misdirection [see Notice No 48 para 3.5] gave the view of HM Revenue & Customs (HMRC) of the circumstances in which they would regard themselves as bound by incorrect advice given to customers in respect of Value Added Tax (VAT) [. . .].

HMRC are required by law to collect all the taxes, duties and levies under their care, but they have a limited degree of discretion in specific circumstances. In recent years, there have been a number of cases before the courts which have defined the circumstances in which HMRC can regard themselves as bound by incorrect advice. More information is available on the Internet. ESC 3.5 Misdirection is therefore no longer necessary because it has been overtaken by other published guidance.

HMRC will not accept any further claims under this ESC from 1 April 2009. Customers who think they have received incorrect advice from HMRC in respect of VAT [. . .] should see the guidance [reproduced in Appendix 19] for further help, or contact the National Advice Service on Tel 0845 010 9000. There will be no change in service to our customers, as they will still be able to ask us to consider their case if they feel they have been wrongly advised by HMRC.

This does not affect customers who think they have over declared tax, as such cases will continue to be considered under the relevant sections of the Value Added Tax Act 1994, and Finance Acts 1994 and 1997.

[VATA 1994 Sch 11 para 1.]

14 MAY 2009. REVENUE & CUSTOMS BRIEF 31/09 TAX IMPLICATIONS OF THE VEHICLE SCRAPPAGE SCHEME

The government announced at Budget 2009 the introduction of a temporary vehicle scrappage scheme. It is a voluntary scheme which will be administered by participating motor manufacturers and dealers, along with the Department for Business, Enterprise and Regulatory Reform (BERR). Information about it can be found on the BERR website and at Directgov – Motoring. You may also contact BERR's enquiry unit on Tel 020 7215 5000, or email the BERR Automotive Unit with "scrappage" entered in the subject heading.

A. VAT AND DIRECT TAX PROFITS IMPLICATIONS

Vehicles supplied under the scheme will be subject to the normal VAT and direct tax rules. The purpose of this brief is to explain how those rules apply to the £1,000 subsidy payable by BERR on qualifying supplies made under their scheme, plus the £1,000 discount paid by the manufacturer.

Manufacturers

If you are a manufacturer participating in the scheme you will be providing a £1,000 subsidy to the final consumer (over and above any other subsidy or discount you might provide), even though you have no direct contractual relationship with them. You may treat the VAT on your contribution as a discount to the output tax you have paid to HMRC on your sale of the car. You may therefore reduce your output tax by the appropriate VAT amount (which on a gross payment of £1,000 and the current standard rate of VAT of 15 per cent means £130.43). Any such adjustment should be made in the period in which it takes effect in the business records of the manufacturer. This treatment is in accordance with the decision of the European Court of Justice in *Elida Gibbs Ltd v C & E Comrs* (case C-317/94) [1996] STC 1387, ECJ and *EC Commission v Germany* (case C-427/98) [2003] STC 301, ECJ. Guidance on the VAT treatment of such payments by manufacturers was given previously in Revenue and Customs Brief 08/07

You must not reduce your output tax in respect of BERR's £1,000 contribution. Under the terms of the scheme, BERR will pay you £1,000, but you must pass it on to the dealer within 14 days who, in turn, is obliged to ensure that the final consumer receives the benefit of that sum. You are thus acting as a conduit, receiving and passing on BERR's third party payment to the dealer. The £1,000 subsidy provided by BERR is not a discount on the value of your supply, and so you should make no adjustment in respect of that payment.

For direct tax purposes BERR's £1,000 contribution has no overall effect on the trading profits of the manufacturer. The corresponding £1,000 payable by the manufacturer to the dealer will be an allowable deduction for the purposes of computing the profits of the manufacturing trade.

Dealers

If you are a dealer participating in the Scheme and the manufacturer uses the arrangements above, the cost of the new vehicle received by you is unaffected, and you should make no adjustments to the VAT you pay to the manufacturer, or claim from HMRC as input tax. As explained above, the manufacturer is not providing a £1,000 (or greater) discount to you as part of the Scheme – they are providing it to your customer. Your selling price for the vehicle has not changed and you must not reduce your output tax. Whatever your final VAT-inclusive ("On The Road") selling price of the new vehicle is, under the Scheme your customer pays £2,000 less, with the balance of the consideration being made up of the two £1,000 subsidies. Under the Scheme, it is important that it is clear to your customer that they are paying £2,000 less than would otherwise be the case – see Directgov – Motoring.

The effect of the Scheme on the dealer is neutral for the purposes of computing trading profits. The £2,000 reduction in the sale proceeds received from the customer is matched by the £2,000 trade receipt received in the form of the subsidies paid to the dealer under the scheme.

Customers

Customers buying a new vehicle under the scheme will pay £2,000 less for the vehicle, since BERR will be paying £1,000, and the vehicle manufacturer will be paying £1,000 towards the cost of the purchase. The subsidies will be settled between the manufacturer, dealer and BERR so you will not physically be paid these amounts.

If you are VAT-registered and buy a new car or van under the scheme, you may need to reduce your input tax in respect of the manufacturer's discount. However, you only need to consider this if you are entitled to claim VAT on the purchase of a vehicle – for example, on certain commercial vehicles, or a car that is intended to be used primarily as a taxi; driving instruction car, or self-drive hire (but see paragraph 3.1 of VAT Notice 700/64 (Motoring Expenses). If, under the normal VAT rules, you are entitled to reclaim the VAT you are charged on the purchase of a new vehicle and you buy one under the Scheme, you must reduce the input tax you claim in proportion to the manufacturer's discount. This is because, at the beginning of the chain of transactions culminating in your purchasing the vehicle, the manufacturer will have reduced its output tax. Therefore, since the manufacturer contributes £1,000 and the standard rate of VAT is 15 per cent, you must reduce your input tax by £130.43. You will not receive an amended invoice or credit note. This is the normal VAT treatment for business customers receiving such manufacturer's discounts – see Revenue and Customs Brief 08/07

B. CAPITAL ALLOWANCES

[. . . .]

[VATA 1994 a 19]

8 JUNE 2009. REVENUE & CUSTOMS BRIEF 33/09
VAT: CLARIFICATION OF HMRC'S POLICY FOLLOWING THE HOUSE OF LORDS JUDGMENT IN NEWNHAM COLLEGE

This Revenue and Customs Brief announces HM Revenue and Customs' (HMRC) revised interpretation of the law following the judgment of the House of Lords in the case of *The Principal and Fellows of Newnham College in the University of Cambridge v R & C Comrs* [2008] STC 1225, HL. It also provides guidance for those businesses affected by the judgment.

THE ISSUE

The case before the House of Lords concerned whether Newnham was "in occupation" of the college library. If they were, their option to tax the library would be disapplied and their occupation would be for the purpose of making supplies of exempt education. Consequently, the VAT incurred on the rebuilding and refurbishment of the library would be irrecoverable. The House of Lords upheld the judgment of the Court of Appeal and found in Newnham's favour. They concluded that Newnham was not in occupation and, as a result, that their option to tax was not disapplied.

HMRC'S REVISED INTERPRETATION OF LAW

HMRC now accept that physical presence alone is not the correct test of occupation for the purposes of what is now VATA 1994 Sch 10 paras 12–17 (the "anti-avoidance test"). Following the House of Lords judgment, a person is considered to be "in occupation" if, in addition to physical presence which occupation normally entails, they have the right to occupy the property as if they are the owner and to exclude others from enjoyment of such a right. This means a person must have actual possession of the land along with a degree of permanence and control. Such a right will normally result from the grant of a legal interest or licence to occupy. Occupation could also, however, be by agreement or de facto and it is therefore necessary to take account of the day to day arrangements, particularly where these differ from the contractual terms. An exclusive right of occupation is not a requirement; an agreement might, for example, allow for joint occupation. Equally, it is not necessary for a person to be utilising all of the land for all of the time for them to be considered as occupying it.

A person whose interest in land is subject to an inferior interest, such as to prevent him from having rights of occupation for the time being, is not "in occupation" for the purposes of the anti-avoidance test until the inferior interest expires. It should be noted, however, that an important feature of the test is that it is forward looking and takes account of the intended or expected occupation of the building at any time during the Capital Goods Scheme (CGS) adjustment period. As a result, a person who has granted an inferior interest but intends during that adjustment period to occupy the land himself would intend to be 'in occupation' for the purposes of the anti-avoidance test and so must consider whether his intended occupation was for eligible purposes.

However, a person can ignore the following types of occupation for the purposes of the test:

(1) Occupation which is purely for the purpose of making his rental supplies under the grant, since those are the very supplies whose liability he is trying to determine by applying the test. For example:
  (a) occupation by the grantor between the date of the grant and the start of occupation by the tenant which is for the purpose of undertaking refurbishment or repairs,
  (b) occupation by maintenance, security or reception staff (or similar), unless it is for the purpose of providing ongoing services separate from the letting itself.

(2) Occupation at a future date, but within the CGS adjustment period, which is solely for the purpose of re-letting the property or making a fresh grant.

PRACTICAL IMPLICATIONS

Businesses that were wrongly denied input tax recovery may submit claims to their local Business Advice Centre. [. . .]

[VATA 1994 Sch 10 para 15]

1 JULY 2009. REVENUE & CUSTOMS BRIEF 39/09
VAT: CHANGES TO THE APPLICATION OF THE ZERO-RATE TO NEW BUILDINGS USED FOR A RELEVANT CHARITABLE OR RESIDENTIAL USE

This Brief announces a change in HM Revenue & Customs (HMRC) interpretation of the legal provisions that apply the zero rate to new buildings used for a relevant charitable purpose [. . .].

[. . .] HMRC now recognise that the term "solely", as used in the phrase "solely for a relevant residential or relevant charitable purpose", can incorporate an appropriate de minimis margin. And in order to avoid unnecessary disputes in marginal cases, HMRC will accept that this statutory condition is satisfied if the relevant use of the building by the charity is 95 per cent or more.

A person can now rely on this revised interpretation of "solely" that is, 95 per cent or more, to determine whether a building will be eligible for the zero rate or not.

[. . .] Any method may be used to calculate the qualifying use of the building, so long as it is fair and reasonable. Prior approval from HMRC for any method of calculation is not required. [For fair and reasonable methods, see VAT Information Sheet 13/10 (21 June 2010) (not reproduced)].

If a building is zero rated as a result of applying this new interpretation, there will be a change of use charge if it ceases to be eligible within ten years of the buildings completion.

[. . .]

The meaning of the term "solely" will depend on the legal context in which it occurs and on the nature of the underlying transactions to which any particular piece of legislation is directed. The revised interpretation described above applies only to the construction of the phrase "solely for a relevant residential or relevant charitable purpose" as used in the context of VATA 1994 Sch 8 Groups 5 and 6, Sch 9 Group 1 and Sch 10 Part 2.

Notes. (1) This Brief also announced the withdrawal of the concession in Notice No 48 para 3.29 from 1 July 2010. (2) For transitional arrangements between 1 July 2009 and 30 June 2010, see VAT Information Sheet 8/09 (July 2009) paras 1–4 (not reproduced). (3) Charities which made use of the concession prior to 1 July 2010 must meet the conditions specified in Revenue and Customs Brief 26/10, 21 June 2010 before 1 January 2011. (4) For the application of the 95 per cent rule in relation to exclusion of the option to tax on buildings to be used for a relevant residential or relevant charitable purpose, see Revenue and Customs Brief 33/10, 29 July 2010.

[VATA 1994 Sch 8 Groups 5, 6; Sch 9 Group 1; Sch 10 paras 5–7]

8 JULY 2009. REVENUE & CUSTOMS BRIEF 36/09
VAT: THE VAT TREATMENT OF DEPOSITS RELATING TO SALES OF LAND ON WHICH DWELLINGS ARE TO BE CONSTRUCTED

This Revenue & Customs Brief clarifies HM Revenue and Customs' (HMRC) view on how deposits paid in relation to sales of land, and in particular sales by developers to registered social landlords (RSLs), should be treated.

BACKGROUND

Where development land is sold to RSLs, it is normal for a deposit to be paid at the time of exchange of contracts when construction has not commenced and the land is bare land. In many cases this deposit will be held by a stakeholder and will not create a tax point for VAT purposes until it is released to the vendor (or vendor's agent), normally at the time of completion. Completion of the sale will in most cases occur at a time when construction of the dwellings has commenced and progressed beyond what is commonly known as the "golden brick", that is, beyond foundation level. This means the supply can normally be zero-rated.

It has, however, become increasingly common for the deposit to be made available to the vendor at the time of exchange when the land is still bare land. This has raised questions about the VAT treatment of the deposit, and in particular, whether it can be treated as part payment for the future zero-rated supply.

HMRC'S INTERPRETATION OF THE CORRECT VAT TREATMENT

HMRC takes the view that where the deposit is released to the vendor and it is clear from the contract or agreement that what will be supplied at completion, or the time of the grant, will be partly completed dwellings (beyond "golden brick"), the deposit is part payment for the grant/supply that will occur at that time. It follows that the VAT liability of the deposit is determined by the anticipated nature of the supply and that zero-rating will be appropriate if it is intended that the conditions for zero-rating will be satisfied at the time of completion. For example, there must be a clear intention that the vendor will have commenced construction of the dwellings at that time and acquired "person constructing" status.

It is possible that the state of the land at completion will differ from that which was anticipated and where this is the case it will be necessary to revisit the VAT treatment of the deposit. It is not possible to give more detailed guidance as the position will depend upon the facts and contractual terms applicable in the particular case. Where taxpayers are uncertain about the correct treatment they should refer to the National Advice Service by phoning 0845 010 9000.

[VATA 1994 s 5]

8 JULY 2009. REVENUE & CUSTOMS BRIEF 38/09
VAT—"DUTCH BARGES" AND SIMILAR VESSELS DESIGNED FOR AND USED AS PERMANENT RESIDENTIAL ACCOMMODATION BY OWNERS

WHO NEEDS TO READ THIS?

Businesses making supplies of:

- vessels to be used for permanent residential living by the owner
- certain goods and services to the owners of vessels used for permanent residential living by the owner

This brief also withdraws Section 4 of Business Brief 35/04 VAT—clarification of the VAT liability of ships supplied to customers who intend to use them as residential accommodation.

BACKGROUND

"Qualifying ships"—are zero-rated for VAT purposes. A "qualifying ship" is defined as a ship which is not less than 15 gross tons and is neither designed nor adapted for use for recreation or pleasure. The law is set out in VATA 1994 Sch 8 Group 8 Item 1 and Note A1(*a*).

"Houseboats"—are covered by a separate zero-rate. For VAT purposes, "houseboats" are boats designed as living accommodation that do not have, and cannot be fitted with, a means of propulsion. If a boat can be fitted with a means of propulsion, it is not a "houseboat" The law is set out in VATA 1994 Sch 8 Group 9 Item 2.

HM REVENUE & CUSTOMS (HMRC) POLICY

In the light of the High Court decision in the case of *R & C Comrs v Stone* [2008] STC 2501, HMRC are changing their long-standing policy on the liability of vessels used as residential accommodation, excluding houseboats, for VAT purposes. This case concerned the VAT liability of the supply of "Dutch barges" acquired for the purpose of being used as a permanent residence.

The High Court decided that the supply of the vessel was entitled to zero-rating under the terms of UK law, because it was designed to be lived in as a permanent home and, therefore, not designed for use as recreation or pleasure.

HMRC consider that many of these and similar vessels, although designed for use as a permanent residence, can also be designed for use as recreation or pleasure and are perfectly capable of being so used. It was never the intention that UK legislation should provide for the supply of such vessels to benefit from zero-rating but, following Tribunal and Court decisions over time, HMRC have found it increasingly difficult to apply a consistent and coherent policy around the borderlines in this area.

HMRC do not rule out a wider review of policy and legislation in this area. However, in the meantime, we have decided to treat Dutch barges and similar vessels that are designed and supplied for use as the permanent residence of the customer as qualifying ships and eligible for zero-rating. As vessels of less than 15 gross tons can never be zero-rated regardless of their design, the majority of narrow boats designed for permanent residential use will not meet this requirement and their supply will continue to be standard-rated.

As a result of this policy change some supplies of goods and services to the owners of such vessels may also be zero-rated by suppliers.

These include:

- repairs and maintenance of the vessel itself; this does not extend to the domestic equipment and fittings on board
- modification or conversion of the vessel itself provided that it remains a qualifying ship after modification or conversion; this does not extend to domestic equipment and fittings

- parts and equipment ordinarily installed or incorporated in the propulsion, navigation, communications or structure of a ship; this does not extend to domestic equipment and fittings

Further details can be found in Notice 744C.

EVIDENCE OF INTENTION

In keeping with normal rules, suppliers will have to hold evidence to satisfy HMRC that the supply is entitled to zero-rating. This may be in the form of contractual or other documentary evidence. HMRC would also advise suppliers to obtain a declaration from their customers that the vessel is to be designed for use as a permanent residence and intended for such use. We would suggest that suppliers use the format set out for the Undertaking of Use in Notice 744C, adapted as necessary where the supply is one of the vessel itself. Customers should be aware that HMRC have powers to impose penalties where false documentation is used to obtain a tax advantage.

[VATA 1994 Sch 8 Group 8 Items 1, 2A and Group 9 Item 2]

13 JULY 2009. REVENUE & CUSTOMS BRIEF 40/09
VAT: THE DECISION OF THE HIGH COURT IN RESPECT OF RANK (MECHANISED CASH BINGO AND GAMING MACHINES)

The High Court issued its decision in this case [see *R & C Comrs v The Rank Group* [2009] SWTI 1884, [2009] EWHC (Ch) 1244], [2009] STC 2304 on 8 June 2009 – the judgment being in Rank's favour. It confirmed that there had been a breach of fiscal neutrality in the tax treatment of the supply of mechanised cash bingo (MCB). This means that participation fees for playing MCB should have been exempt from VAT and businesses can now submit claims to HM Revenue & Customs (HMRC) for repayment of any output tax wrongly accounted for, subject to the guidelines below.

In relation to gaming machines, the High Court judgment relates to an appeal against an interim ruling of the VAT and Duties Tribunal. As the Tribunal has not yet ruled in respect of Rank's full appeal, HMRC will not at this time consider any claims relating to this issue.

BACKGROUND

Rank, which operates Mecca bingo halls, claimed there had been inconsistencies in the way VAT had been applied to the participation fees customers paid to play MCB and to the takings of gaming machines.

Last year the VAT and Duties Tribunal ruled there had been a breach of fiscal neutrality in the case of MCB as some participation fees were taxed while others were exempt. (Fiscal neutrality means that similar supplies must be treated the same for tax purposes to avoid any distortion of competition). The High Court has agreed with the Tribunal's decision that all participation fees for MCB should have been exempt from VAT.

The VAT Tribunal also issued an interim decision regarding the way HMRC taxed gaming machines, stating there had been a breach of fiscal neutrality in some cases and over a short period of time before the law was changed in December 2005.

IMPLICATIONS OF THIS JUDGMENT

HMRC will now consider claims for output tax wrongly accounted for by bingo operators on MCB participation fees.

As bingo duty is charged on the VAT-exclusive value of participation fees, this judgment will have an effect on bingo duty declarations although HMRC is still considering the precise implications. However, HMRC will now enforce those bingo duty assessments already made. Further assessments to bingo duty may be made as appropriate.

As the gaming machine case is continuing, with a [tribunal] hearing later this year, HMRC will not credit any claims on this issue.

Note. For the tribunal decision, see Revenue & Customs Brief 11/10, 16 March 2010.

[VATA 1994 Sch 9 Group 4 Item 1]

17 JULY 2009. REVENUE & CUSTOMS BRIEF 41/09 THREE-YEAR CAP FOR VAT CLAIMS—R & C COMRS V SCOTTISH EQUITABLE PLC (UNREPORTED)—ORDER OF THE INNER HOUSE OF THE COURT OF SESSION

THE JUDGMENT OF THE INNER HOUSE

In an Order handed down on 2 July, the court overturned the 2006 decision of the VAT and Duties Tribunal [see *Scottish Equitable plc* (No 19418)] that the introduction of the three-year time limit without a transitional period in 1996 meant that it had never been lawfully enacted.

The Inner House held that the Tribunal was wrong to decide that the absence of transitional provisions, that enabled claims to be made under the old time limits before the new time limit took effect, meant that the provisions were void. The court stressed that it was well recognised that national legislation which breaches Community law is not void and noted that the Tribunal had failed to recognise the difference between rights to claim that accrued before the enactment of the three-year cap and those that accrued afterwards.

The Inner House followed the judgment of the House of Lords in *Fleming (t/a Bodycraft) v R & C Comrs* [2008] STC 324, HL in which the Law Lords held that the three-year time limit should be disapplied in relation to rights to claims that had accrued before its enactment and that that disapplication should continue until the expiry of an adequate, prospective transitional period.

There will be no application for leave to appeal to the House of Lords.

CURRENT CASE LAW ON TIME LIMITS

There are a number of judgments of the European Court of Justice (including *Marks & Spencer plc v C& E Comrs* (case C-62/00) [2002] STC 1036) confirming that the imposition of reasonable time limits does not breach principles of Community law and that they are necessary to provide legal certainty for both the citizen and the state.

The judgment of the House of Lords in *Fleming* (referred to above) led to the enactment of FA 2008 s 121. This provided businesses with a prospective transitional period of twelve months, ending on 31 March 2009, in which claims could be made for accounting periods ending before the introduction of the new time limits.

The Inner House in *Scottish Equitable* has taken the same view as the High Court in *Local Authorities Mutual Investment Trust v C & E Comrs* [2004] STC 246, which held that VAT claims for accounting periods ending after the enactment of the new time limit were properly capped.

STATUS OF VAT TIME LIMITS

All VAT claims are now capped at four years, or back to 1 April 2006, whichever is the shorter – see VATA 1994 s 80(4) as amended by the Finance Act 2008, Schedule 39 (Appointed Day, Savings and Transitional Provisions) Order 2009, SI 2009/403 arts 2 and 6 (output tax claims) and regulation 29(1A) of the VAT Regulations 1995, SI 1995/2518 reg 29(1A) as amended by the VAT (Amendment) Regulations 2009, SI 2009/586 reg 3.

APPEALS ON-HOLD BEHIND THIS LITIGATION

A significant number of appeals to the First-tier Tribunal (Tax Chamber) are on-hold, pending the outcome of this litigation. Appellants will need to consider, in the light of the recent order, whether they wish to withdraw their appeal or proceed to a full hearing. HM Revenue & Customs are now taking steps to have these appeals restored to the Tribunal list so that, where necessary, a hearing date can be fixed.

[VATA 1994 s 80]

17 AUGUST 2009. REVENUE & CUSTOMS BRIEF 53/09
VAT – RECOVERY BY LOCAL AUTHORITIES UNDER SECTION 33 VAT ACT 1994 IN RESPECT OF VOLUNTARY AIDED SCHOOLS

This Revenue and Customs Brief explains our revised policy on VAT recovery by local authorities on expenditure relating to capital works at voluntary aided schools.

[. . .]

REVISED POLICY

A local authority is allowed to contribute funding to a governing body to help it meet the cost of its responsibilities. We have to date accepted that local authorities can recover the VAT incurred on expenditure which is the responsibility of the governing bodies but which the authority funds. This is explained in Notice No 701/30 para 15.5 and 'V1-14: Government and public bodies' and 'V1-07 chapter 21; Education'.

We have reviewed this policy, and we now realise that it goes beyond what s 33 actually permits. Section 33 is confined to VAT incurred by local authorities etc on the goods and services that they purchase, not on the goods and services that another legal entity purchases. Therefore, with effect from 1 September 2009, with respect to projects initiated after this date, VAT may no longer be recovered by local authorities in these circumstances, as the supplies are not made to them (whether or not paid for from the delegated budget). We will consider, on their individual facts, cases where a project initiated after 1 September 2009 was funded on the basis of the previous policy.

A local authority may, however, continue to recover VAT on expenditure at a voluntary aided school for which the local authority is statutorily responsible, or where the local authority, rather than the governing body, procures a supply of works and pays for that supply from its own funds (for further details please refer to Notice No 749 para 7.1). In such cases HMRC accept that the local authority receives the supply in connection with its non business activities.

[. . .]

[VATA 1994 s 33]

26 AUGUST 2009. REVENUE & CUSTOMS BRIEF 56/09
VAT TREATMENT OF YACHT CHARTERING OR LEASING ACTIVITIES

1. BACKGROUND AND AIM

In Revenue & Customs Brief 11/07 [7 February 2007] we announced our concerns relating to VAT schemes through which private individuals incur little or no VAT on the purchase of pleasure craft. We have since investigated a number of such schemes which typically involve artificial leasing or chartering structures.

There are also, of course, many bona-fide businesses who charter and lease pleasure craft. The aim of this Brief is to clarify our view of the VAT treatment applying to the purchase and use of pleasure craft and, in particular, the chartering and leasing of pleasure craft. We also set out our approach to artificial structures such as those described in Revenue & Customs Brief 11/07.

The term 'pleasure craft' is used to describe motor and sailing yachts which are designed for recreational use. This guidance takes into account relevant case law including the ECJ's judgement in the case of *Halifax plc and others v C & E Comrs* (case C-255/02) [2006] STC 919 (the Halifax case).

2. VAT REGISTRATION

Persons who are in business and are either making or intending to make taxable supplies, relevant EC acquisitions, distance sales or supplies of certain assets may be liable or entitled to register for VAT.

'Business' is defined in VATA 1994 s 94(1) as including any trade, profession or vocation. This definition is not designed to be exhaustive and the VAT meaning of business has emerged through the judgements of UK courts and the ECJ. Although the Principal VAT Directive refers to 'economic activity' rather than 'business' our domestic legislation must be interpreted so it conforms with the Directive. Consequently 'business' and 'economic activity' must be seen as having the same meaning.

A person carrying out yacht chartering or leasing is therefore only entitled to VAT registration (and the related entitlement to deduct input VAT) where the chartering or leasing is carried out in the course of an economic activity. We may ask for evidence to show that an economic activity is being pursued, either before registration is allowed or during subsequent verification.

The ECJ case of *Enkler v Finanzamt Homburg* (case C-230/94) [1996] STC 1316 shows that, where an asset is suitable for both business and for private purposes, then the Tax Authority has to consider all the circumstances in which it is used to determine whether it is actually used in the course of a business. The actual length of the period for which the vessel is hired, the number of customers and the amount of earnings are factors which, forming part of the circumstances of the case as a whole, may be taken into account, together with others. In addition the actual use should be compared with the circumstances in which the corresponding economic activity is usually carried out.

During any verification of entitlement to VAT registration we will look for evidence that a chartering or leasing activity has sufficient substance and continuity to meet the criteria set by the ECJ in *Enkler*. We will also consider the evidence in relation to the 'business test' that emerged from the case of *C & E Comrs v Lord Fisher* [1981] STC 238, and the earlier case of *C & E Comrs v Morrison's Academy Boarding Houses Association* [1978] STC1. The full circumstances in which the vessel is used will be considered and the onus will be on the registered person (or the applicant) to provide sufficient evidence to support a contention that the vessel is used in an economic activity.

3. VAT TREATMENT OF PRIVATE (NON-BUSINESS) USE OF A PLEASURE CRAFT

We are aware that the purchase of a pleasure craft is typically funded by a high net worth individual who agrees the specification with the supplier and who will use the vessel himself for some or all of the time that it is in service.

Such an individual may have legal ownership of the vessel in his own name or he may arrange for legal ownership to be held by a company (or other entity) which he may control, directly or indirectly.

When an individual has legal ownership of the vessel in his own name

If an individual has legal ownership of the vessel in his own name and uses it wholly for his own private use then there is no economic activity and he is not entitled to register for VAT.

Mixed business and private use

If an individual has legal ownership of the vessel in his own name and charters the vessel to others with sufficient continuity and substance to comprise an economic activity as well as using it himself then the vessel will be used partly for business and partly for private use.

If he is registered for VAT because of the business use he will incur VAT on goods (the vessel) that are intended for both business and private purposes.

He has a choice as to how to treat these goods for VAT purposes:

- He may treat them as a part business, part non-business asset, in which case the VAT incurred is only deductible to the extent that it relates to the taxable business activities [VATA 1994 s 24(5)].
- He may treat them as a wholly business asset, the 'Lennartz' approach, in which case the VAT incurred is treated as input tax and is deductible in full, subject to any partial exemption ('PE') restriction. However, VAT must then be accounted for when the goods are used for private purposes. Where a taxable person adopts the 'Lennartz' approach he must do so at the time the input tax is incurred.

If the asset is subsequently sold within the UK, VAT will be due on that 'portion' of the asset that is treated as business (in the circumstances described above) and on the whole of the asset (in the circumstances described above).

Further information on the application of the 'Lennartz mechanism' is given in VAT Information Sheet 14/07.

When an individual arranges for legal ownership to be held by a company (or other entity)

The nature of the entity which owns a vessel does not, in itself, affect the VAT treatment of the vessel.

However, we are aware that structures involving a company (or an entity such as a limited liability partnership) have been used by individuals to obtain a VAT advantage. Put simply, this arises where an individual who has funded the purchase of a pleasure craft arranges for legal ownership of that vessel to be held by a company (or other entity) which registers for VAT as a chartering or leasing business and recovers VAT incurred on the purchase and operation of the vessel.

The individual's own use of the vessel is covered by charter or lease agreements issued to him in the name of the company. As a result it is claimed that there is no private use of the vessel.

We will consider the entitlement of such a company (or other entity) to VAT registration by applying the approach set out above to identify whether the chartering or leasing comprises an 'economic activity'.

The connection between the company and the user of the vessel does not in itself prevent the chartering or leasing being an economic activity. On the other hand, merely issuing charter agreements to the individual in the name of the company is not, alone, sufficient to create an economic activity. The full circumstances in which the vessel is used will be considered, as explained above.

We may also consider whether the structure amounts to an abusive practice by applying the tests identified by the ECJ in the *Halifax* case. More information on this aspect is given below.

4. APPLICATION OF THE PRINCIPLE OF PROHIBITING ABUSIVE PRACTICES

In recent years there have been significant developments in the case law of the ECJ concerning the application to VAT of the principle of prohibiting abusive practices. Of particular relevance are the ECJ's judgements in the *Halifax* case and in the case of *Ministero dell'Economia e delle Finanze v Part Service Srl (in liquidation)* (case C-425/06) [2008] STC 3132.

From these cases it is clear that the principle of prohibiting abusive practices 'applies to the sphere of VAT' (*Halifax*, para 70). This means it applies to all aspects of VAT and not just the right to recover input tax. This was further demonstrated in the *Part Service* case which concerned avoidance of output tax.

The tests to establish whether an abuse exists are as follows:

> 'For it to be found that an abusive practice exists, it is necessary, first, that the transactions concerned, notwithstanding formal application of the conditions laid down by the relevant provisions of the Sixth Directive [now the Principal VAT Directive] and of national legislation transposing it, result in the accrual of a tax advantage the grant of which would be contrary to the purpose of those provisions. Second, it must also be apparent from a number of objective factors that the essential aim of the transactions concerned is to obtain a tax advantage.' (*Halifax*, para 86).

With regard to the first test ('contrary to purpose'), if the objective facts show that the economic reality underlying the structure is that an individual has purchased a pleasure craft for his own recreational use then, if no VAT is borne by that individual in relation to the purchase and use of the pleasure craft, that result may be contrary to article 1(2) of the Principal VAT Directive.

With regard to the second test, 'essential aim' is determined by considering 'the real substance and significance of the transactions concerned' taking account of 'the purely artificial nature of those transactions and the links of a legal, economic and/or personal nature between the operators involved in the scheme for reduction of the tax burden' (*Halifax*, para 81).

It is important to note that 'essential aim' is not a sole purpose test. There can be a finding of an abusive practice when the accrual of a tax advantage constitutes the principal aim of the transaction or transactions at issue (*Part Service*, paras 45 and 62).

The essential aim of the transactions concerned is determined from the objective facts of the case rather than the subjective aim or intention of the parties engaged in those transactions. It is an 'objective' test which does not rely on establishing what the parties say their intention was (or what their subjective intention is found to have been). Instead, the essential aim is established by taking account of all the evidence and the commercial realities to determine what, viewed objectively, is the principal aim of the transactions viewed as a whole.

Where an abusive practice is found to exist then:

> 'It follows that transactions involved in an abusive practice must be redefined so as to re-establish the situation that would have prevailed in the absence of the transactions constituting the abusive practice.' (*Halifax*, para 94).

If we conclude that a structure meets the tests for an abusive practice then we will consider appropriate action to restore the situation that would have existed in the absence of the abusive transactions. This might include issuing assessments to disallow input tax and/or deregistration of the entity concerned. Such assessments might also give rise to interest charges and penalties.

5. POSSIBLE INDICATORS OF AN ABUSIVE PRACTICE

The existence of one or more of the following features might indicate an abusive structure (the list is not exhaustive – the indicators are illustrative of the points that we might take into account, together with others):

- The main user of a pleasure craft is the ultimate owner of the chartering or leasing entity.

- The main user of a pleasure craft funded the purchase of the vessel (directly or indirectly).
- The person who funded the purchase of a pleasure craft (directly or indirectly) uses the vessel for prolonged periods in the peak chartering season.
- The chartering of a pleasure craft to third parties would not, alone, be of sufficient continuity and substance to comprise an economic activity.
- The chartering or leasing entity shows significant ongoing losses in its financial statements.
- Charter fees or lease instalments due from the main user of a pleasure craft are paper transactions only (for example being offset against loans).
- Charter fees or lease instalments are below open market value.
- The terms of a lease differ significantly from normal commercial practice (for example, the duration of the lease is unusually long).

[VATA 1994 s 1]

4 SEPTEMBER 2009. REVENUE & CUSTOMS BRIEF 57/09 VAT: PARTIAL EXEMPTION – POLICY IN RESPECT OF PAYBACK CLAIMS IN THE LIGHT OF THE HIGH COURT DECISION IN CHA

This Revenue and Customs Brief confirms HM Revenue & Customs ("HMRC") policy on the VAT partial exemption 'payback' rules following the High Court decision in the case of *Community Housing Association Ltd v R & C Comrs* [2009] STC 1324 ("CHA"). It uses a number of specialist terms which are explained more fully in Notice No 706.

PAYBACK POLICY

VAT Regulations 1995, SI 1995/2518, reg 109, 'payback' allows a business to recoup input tax on costs that are incurred to make exempt supplies, but are instead used wholly or partly to make taxable supplies. Payback also applies to costs incurred for both taxable and exempt purposes, but actually used to make wholly taxable supplies. A payback claim cannot be made unless:

- the costs in question were not used as originally intended
- the change of use arises after the end of the partial exemption longer period (if there is one)
- the change of use results in taxable supplies or both taxable and exempt supplies if the original intention had been to make a wholly exempt supply

[. . .]

HMRC CONCLUSION

Supply covers a wide range of circumstances but there are some basic requirements that must apply before a supply can exist. The recipient of the supply must receive some benefit, he must provide some consideration and the consideration must be paid in return for the benefit.

Any business making a supply will incur costs in doing so. These are the cost components of the supply. Conclusions on what the cost components of any supply are will flow from an analysis of the nature of that supply. The mere raising of invoices and passing of funds between companies does not automatically create supplies. Careful analysis may be called for, especially if the companies are close associates.

[SI 1995/2518 reg 109]

2 OCTOBER 2009. REVENUE & CUSTOMS BRIEF 58/09 VAT: RELOCATION OF TELECOMMUNICATION SERVICE PROVIDERS INTERNET SERVICE PROVIDERS AND BROADCASTERS

[. . .]

HMRC are aware that some businesses within the telecommunications, Internet service provision and broadcasting sectors have implemented arrangements that claim to move the place of supply of their services from the UK to another Member State in order to take advantage of more favourable VAT rates.

The place of supply of telecommunications, Internet service provision and broadcasting services when provided to non-business customers in the EU is the place where the supplier is established. Some suppliers to the UK market claim to have reorganised their businesses so that the place of supply is no longer in the UK but another Member State.

HMRC accepts that businesses have the freedom to choose where to locate and to enjoy any resultant benefits.

However, HMRC will carefully examine all such arrangements. Where HMRC considers that there are sufficient human and technical resources in the UK to form a fixed establishment from which the services are supplied, or where the entity purporting to make the supplies does not have a sufficient presence in the other Member State to be established there, HMRC will mount a robust challenge.

[VATA 1994 s 7A]

14 OCTOBER 2009. REVENUE & CUSTOMS BRIEF 65/09 VAT: PARTIAL EXEMPTION – VAT DEDUCTION BY THEATRES ON PRODUCTION COSTS

HMRC has revised its policy on input tax recovery on the costs of staging shows (production costs) for which the theatre's admissions are VAT exempt. It follows the tribunal decision in *Garsington Opera Limited* (TC 45). [. . .]

REVISED POLICY

It is an established principle of partial exemption that input tax is residual if the costs are 'used or intended to be used' to make both taxable and exempt supplies. Costs are used if they have a direct and immediate link to supplies. Production costs will always be directly and immediately linked to exempt admissions to the show. Production costs only become partly deductible (residual) if there is a firm intention to make taxable as well as exempt supplies when the costs are incurred. Production costs are not 'overhead costs' which are treated as residual because they relate to the organisation as a whole. Production costs only become residual if they relate to specific taxable supplies as well as exempt admissions. Examples of when production costs relate to taxable supplies include if a theatre has contracted to or intends to:

- Secure sponsorship – the sponsorship must relate to an event or a clearly defined run of events over a clearly defined time. Putting on the shows must be a condition of the sponsorship so that production costs become cost components of the sponsorship income. The intention may be evidenced by way of clear financial commitment.
- Tour the production – once again the intention may be evidenced by way of clear financial commitment.
- Record the show for later sale on CD or other media.

Production costs remain residual if an intention to make taxable supplies is frustrated. For example if production costs were treated as residual because of an intention to tour the show, the costs remain residual if the intended tour is later cancelled.

The intention to make taxable supplies must be a genuine intention. The mere aspiration or hope of making a taxable supply is insufficient to secure residual status. For example supplies of intellectual property or props/equipment created in a production are not sufficient to create a direct & immediate link in the absence of a firm intention at the time the costs were incurred that these costs would be used to make these supplies after their use in the show's run in the theatre.

Furthermore, residual status is not secured if the link to taxable supplies is indirect. For example, production costs do not become residual simply because the production is photographed for inclusion in the show programme which is a taxable supply. Likewise, the inclusion of synopses, lists of performers or performer profiles in a programme does not demonstrate that costs are directly and immediately linked to making the taxable supplies.

THE COURT OF APPEAL DECISION IN MAYFLOWER

In the similar case of *Mayflower Theatre Trust Ltd v R & C Comrs* [2006] EWCA Civ 116, [2007] STC 880, CA a direct and immediate link to programme sales was found in relation to 'bought in' shows. This was because copyright information necessary for the programmes was obtained as part of the single supply of production services received from the touring company thus creating the direct and immediate link. If an individual actor or designer provides copyright information to a theatre/opera putting together a show 'in house' as part of a single supply of their services this cost will also be residual. However it will not make other costs incurred residual.

The *Mayflower* decision also made clear that securing general corporate sponsorship does not make production costs residual even if the sponsorship package includes the provision of seats at performances. Likewise, catering supplies which arise as a consequence of admission do not make production costs residual.

IMPACT ON THEATRES

The vast majority of theatres use the partial exemption standard method to apportion residual input tax between taxable and exempt supplies. This works well provided VAT bearing costs are used in proportion to the value of supplies made. The standard method can work less well when significant residual costs do not relate to all of the taxable and exempt supplies made by the business.

Since 18 April 2002, if the standard method results in an over (or under) recovery of input tax which is classed as 'substantial' then the recovery must be re-calculated in accordance with the 'actual use' of the costs in question. This is known as the Standard Method Override (SMO). Further information on the SMO, including the definition of 'substantial' can be found in the public notice and Information Sheet 04/02.

Where production costs are residual because of direct and immediate links to specific taxable supplies such as sponsorship or touring performances and those taxable supplies are small in comparison to the total taxable supplies of the theatre the SMO might be triggered and a 'use-based' calculation required. In the case of theatres, the total taxable supplies may include substantial amounts of catering and refreshments for which the production is not a direct cost.

A 'use-based' calculation is any calculation that fairly reflects how costs are used in making supplies. Calculations should be as simple as is possible whilst achieving a fair result. A fair calculation could be:

$$\begin{array}{c}\text{Recoverable input tax}\\\text{on production costs}\\\text{incurred in the tax year}\end{array} = \frac{A}{A+B} \times C$$

Where:

A = Value of supplies in the year (such as sponsorship or touring) with a direct and immediate link from the production costs of any show.

B = Value of all box office sales in the year; and

C = Residual input tax incurred on production costs in the tax year.

Theatres operating the standard method where the SMO is likely to be triggered on a regular basis may wish to seek approval for a special method.

[. . .]

[SI 1995/2518 reg 101]

27 OCTOBER 2009. REVENUE & CUSTOMS BRIEF 67/09 VAT – LIABILITY OF PROPERTY SERVICE CHARGES FOLLOWING THE EUROPEAN COURT OF JUSTICE CASE OF RLRE TELLMER (C-572/07)

This Revenue & Customs Brief sets out HM Revenue & Customs' (HMRC) view of the judgment of the European Court of Justice ('ECJ') in the case of *RLRE Tellmer Property sro v Finančni ředitelství v Ustí nad Labem* (case C-572/07) [2009] STC 2006 ('Tellmer') and confirms that the UK's current VAT treatment of service charges is unchanged following this decision.

[. . .]

IMPACT OF TELLMER

It is clear from the decision of the ECJ that Tellmer itself provided both the property leasing and the cleaning services to the tenants. However, the tenants had the choice of making an independent contract with a third party to provide the cleaning services. In the particular circumstances the court did not consider that the cleaning services were ancillary to the property letting and, as a result, concluded that they constituted a separate supply.

On this basis, since the UK only treats leasing of property and related service charges as a single supply, where the services are provided by the lessor (or his agent) as a condition under the lease agreement, HMRC considers that the findings in *Tellmer* are consistent with existing UK policy.

[VATA 1994 s 19]

5 NOVEMBER 2009. REVENUE & CUSTOMS BRIEF 68/09 VAT: RETURN OF STANDARD RATE TO 17.5 PER CENT ON 1 JANUARY 2010 – MEASURES TO HELP BUSINESS

[. . .]

On 1 December 2008 the standard rate of VAT was temporarily reduced to 15 per cent. It reverts to 17.5 per cent on 1 January 2010. HMRC recognises that the date of the change may cause problems for certain businesses at a particularly busy time of year so we have introduced two measures to help business to implement the change. These are:

- special accounting arrangements for businesses operating beyond midnight on 31 December 2009;
- the 'light touch' to be operated by HMRC audit staff in dealing with errors arising out of the rate change.

Further details on each of these are provided below.

1. SPECIAL ACCOUNTING ARRANGEMENTS FOR BUSINESSES OPERATING BEYOND MIDNIGHT ON 31 DECEMBER 2009

Retailers

The temporary reduction of the standard rate of VAT to 15 per cent ends on 31 December 2009. As is normal with changes to the VAT rate, the return to 17.5 per cent will be effective from midnight on 31 December. However, HMRC recognises that making the necessary changes to account for VAT at 17.5 per cent may cause particular problems for certain businesses operating after midnight at what can be a particularly busy time of year. For example, it would not be practical for a pub, club, restaurant or hotel hosting a New Year's Eve celebration to stop serving customers at midnight in order to adjust their tills to account for VAT at 17.5 per cent and to amend their prices accordingly.

In order to assist businesses in this position HMRC will allow them to account for VAT at 15 per cent on takings received up to the earlier of:

- the end of trading of the 31 December session or
- 6am on the morning of 1 January 2010.

This treatment is subject to the following conditions:

- It is restricted to those businesses open at midnight on 31 December 2009 that account for VAT at the point of sale such as businesses on a retail scheme – pubs, shops, restaurants etc. It will not apply to:
  - mail order or on-line retailers;
  - businesses that account for VAT on the basis of VAT invoices issued; or
  - pre-payments for supplies of goods or services to be provided after 6am on 1 January 2010.
- It will not apply to sales made through coin operated or similar machines (vending, amusement or gaming machines etc). In these cases businesses must follow the normal rate change rules as set out in section 10.1 of the detailed rate change guidance [http://www.hmrc.gov.uk/vat/forms-rates/rates-rise-guidance.pdf] and account for VAT based on the date that the machine is used or by apportionment if the machine does not record the date of usage.
- It will not apply to transactions made after midnight on 31 December that would have been caught by the rate change anti-forestalling legislation (Finance Act 2009, Schedule 3) had they been made before midnight. Any such supplies will be liable to VAT at 17.5 per cent. Further guidance on the anti-forestalling legislation [http://www.hmrc.gov.uk/vat/forms-rates/anti-forestall-guidance.pdf] is available.
- HMRC may withdraw or restrict the application of this treatment in individual cases.

Telecommunications Providers

As the hours around midnight on New Year's Eve are traditionally the busiest time of year for voice calls and text messages, it may similarly be difficult for telecommunications service providers to change their accounting and billing systems to take account of the change in the rate. HMRC will therefore allow VAT to be charged at 15 per cent on charges for voice calls and text messages that take place and are billed up to 6am on 1 January 2010.

2. THE LIGHT TOUCH

The following guidance has been given to HMRC VAT audit staff about the approach to adopt in relation to errors discovered in relation to the rate change:-

[. . .]

- HMRC wants to encourage and assist businesses as they make the changes necessary to deal with the change in the standard rate.
- If a business discovers that it has made material mistakes, it should correct them through the normal error correction process.
- HMRC will however be operating a 'light touch' in terms of errors made in the first VAT return after the change (where the error relates to a change of rate issue). This means that in our audit plans we will not target change of rate errors that are unlikely to lead to any material net revenue loss. And if we find errors which relate to a change of rate issue we will not seek an adjustment unless we have reason to suppose that there is an overall revenue loss.
- For example, consider a fully taxable business which supplies standard-rated goods to a fully taxable customer and incorrectly charges 15 per cent rather than 17.5 per cent. As the detailed guidance makes clear, the customer should treat only 15 per cent of the tax exclusive (net) price as input tax. If the customer does this

there will be no overall loss of tax. When auditing the supplier, HMRC will assume that the purchaser has followed the accounting documents unless there is good reason to suppose otherwise.

- However, if the supply is or may be to a customer who is not able to recover VAT in full, then there is likely to be an overall loss of tax and HMRC will seek to adjust (issue an assessment) in the normal way.
- In situations where HMRC do need to adjust (and issue an assessment) we will take into account the difficulties the business has faced in adjusting to the change in considering whether penalties apply.

[. . .]

[VATA 1994 s 2; FA 2009 s 9]

18 NOVEMBER 2009. REVENUE & CUSTOMS BRIEF 70/09 [AMUSEMENT MACHINES]

This Revenue & Customs Brief outlines HM Revenue & Customs (HMRC) policy in relation to amusement machines known as 'electronic lottery terminals' and their liability to VAT and Amusement Machine Licence Duty (AMLD).

BACKGROUND

HMRC is aware that certain gaming machines are being marketed as 'electronic lottery terminals'. The manufacturers argue that the product constitutes a lottery that is exempt from VAT and lottery duty, and outside the scope of AMLD. HMRC does not accept this as these 'electronic lottery terminals' are completely different from the lottery ticket dispensers or vending machines typically found in members' clubs.

GUIDANCE

Certain machines being marketed as 'electronic lottery terminals' are gaming machines as they fall within the definitions of a gaming machine set out in VATA 1994 s 23 and Betting and Gaming Duties Act 1981 s 25.

IMPLICATIONS

Gaming machine income is standard-rated for VAT purposes, and depending on stake and prize limits, gaming machines are liable to AMLD.

WHAT YOU NEED TO DO

You must account for VAT on any income you receive from an 'electronic lottery terminal' and if you provide an 'electronic lottery terminal' on any premises you must hold a valid AMLD licence before you make the machine available for play unless the machine falls within any of the exemptions.

[. . .]

[VATA 1994 s 23]

8 DECEMBER 2009. REVENUE & CUSTOMS BRIEF 75/09 VAT AND BINGO DUTY: UPDATE ON IMPLICATIONS OF RANK LITIGATION IN RESPECT OF BINGO

Revenue & Customs Brief 40/09 was issued on [14 July 2009] following the High Court decision in the case of *R & C Comrs v Rank Group plc* [2009] STC 2304. This confirmed that participation fees for playing mechanised cash bingo (MCB) should have been exempt from VAT following the High Court's decision that there had been a breach of fiscal neutrality in the VAT treatment of this type of bingo.

Businesses were therefore invited to submit claims to HMRC for repayment of any VAT accounted for in respect of MCB and these are being dealt with. Revenue & Customs Brief 55/09 explained the effect these claims would have on businesses' liability to bingo duty.

Since then HMRC has received representations that the High Court judgment applies more widely to other forms of bingo played under the same sections of the Gaming Act as MCB. Having considered this carefully, HMRC accepts that the judgment has a wider application to other forms of bingo participation games. Claims for VAT accounted for on participation fees for other types of bingo, in addition to MCB, will now be considered, subject to the guidelines below. This means that the advice about bingo duty in Revenue and Customs Brief 55/09, 20 August 2009 [not reproduced] now applies in relation to all bingo participation fees.

However, the *Rank* litigation continues, with the Court of Appeal due to hear HMRC's appeal in April 2010. If HMRC is successful either then or at a future date in a higher court, then any repayments made to businesses as a result of the High Court decision will need to be repaid, including interest.

Businesses may therefore prefer to wait until the final outcome of the litigation is known although protective claims can be lodged.

[. . .]

[VATA 1994 Sch 9 Group 4]

22 JANUARY 2010. REVENUE & CUSTOMS BRIEF 2/10
VAT: LENNARTZ ACCOUNTING – NEW POLICY FOLLOWING ECJ CASE

INTRODUCTION

Last year, the ECJ in the case of *Vereniging Noordelijke Land-en Tuinbouw Organisatie v Staatssecretaris van Financiën* (case C-515/07) [2009] STC 935 ("VNLTO") considered whether or not Lennartz accounting can be used by a taxpayer who engages in activities that are not within the scope of VAT. As a result of this judgment, it is now clear that EU VAT legislation does not give, and has never given, a right to use Lennartz accounting in circumstances such as those of the VNLTO case.

WHO SHOULD READ THIS?

This Brief brings UK VAT policy in line with this judgment and should be read by anyone currently using, or intending to use, Lennartz accounting. It means that Lennartz accounting will only be available in the specific, limited circumstances set out below.

HMRC's policy on Lennartz accounting as set out in Information Sheet 14/07 now has only limited application and should be read in conjunction with this Brief.

BACKGROUND

Guidance inInformation Sheet 14/07 states that, where a taxable person incurs VAT on the cost of goods intended solely for business purposes, there is an entitlement to deduct the input tax incurred to the extent that it is used for making taxable supplies (or other supplies carrying a right to input tax deduction under VATA 1994 s 26). See Information Sheet 14/07 para 2.4 for the types of goods this policy applies to.

If goods are used for both business and private/non-business purposes, there is a choice about how to treat them for VAT purposes, which must be made at the time they are acquired, namely:

- as a wholly non-business or private asset, in which case the VAT is not deductible;

- as a part business, part non-business asset, in which case the VAT incurred is only deductible to the extent that it relates to the taxable business activities (VATA 1994 24(5)); or
- as a wholly business asset (the 'Lennartz' approach) in which case the VAT incurred is treated as input tax and is deductible in full, subject to any partial exemption restriction; however, output tax must then be declared in so far as the goods are used for private/non-business purposes.

Lennartz accounting is not therefore available in cases where goods (including services used to create goods) are used wholly for business purposes.

ECJ DECISION

The case before the ECJ concerned an association – VNLTO – that promotes the interests of the agricultural sector. Its members, who are traders in that sector, pay a membership subscription to it, the greater part of which goes towards activities designed to promote their general interests. In addition to promoting those interests, VNLTO provides a number of individual services to its members for which it charges a fee.

Even though the activities of promoting members' interests are not subject to VAT, the ECJ held that this did not mean they were non-business activities. The ECJ stated that 'business' in the context of Lennartz accounting extends beyond economic activities giving rise to supplies within the scope of VAT. It also includes use for any activity that forms part of the wider purpose of the taxable person's undertaking or enterprise, even those activities that are not economic activities (such as those outside the scope of VAT), and that are not normally regarded as 'business' for UK VAT purposes.

IMPLICATIONS

From 22 January 2010, Lennartz accounting will only be available where:

(a) the goods are used in part for making supplies in the course of an economic activity that give a right to input VAT deduction (broadly, taxable supplies, supplies that would be taxable if made in the UK, or certain financial and insurance supplies to non-EC customers); **and**

(b) they are also used in part for the private purposes of the trader or his staff, or, exceptionally, for other uses which are wholly outside the purposes of the taxpayer's enterprise or undertaking.

From that date, where Lennartz accounting is not available, and goods are used (or to be used) for both economic activities and non-economic business activities, subject to the transitional provisions outlined below, the VAT incurred must be apportioned between these different activities on the basis of use (or intended use). The VAT attributed to the economic activities is input tax and is recoverable to the extent that the economic activities give rise to supplies with a right to input VAT deduction. The VAT attributed to the non-economic business activities is not input tax and cannot be recovered.

TAXPAYERS WITH ASSETS SUBJECT TO EXISTING LENNARTZ ACCOUNTING ARRANGEMENTS

Taxpayers for whom Lennartz accounting has, strictly speaking, never been available would normally be expected to unravel the mechanism and adjust both any input tax claimed and any output tax accounted for accordingly.

However, HMRC is committed to easing the administrative and financial burden on taxpayers who have already embarked on, and continue to operate, Lennartz accounting under HMRC's old policy.

Consequently, where a taxpayer has applied Lennartz accounting on the basis of HMRC's pre-VNLTO understanding of the law, the taxpayer may opt to continue using Lennartz accounting in respect of the assets concerned.

Taxpayers exercising this option must honour the full, ongoing commitment to account for output tax imposed under Lennartz accounting and HMRC will take action if a taxpayer fails to do so.

Those taxpayers who do not exercise this option must unravel the Lennartz accounting mechanism by adjusting both their output tax and corresponding input tax. They should write to their Client Relationship Manager within HMRC or the HMRC Written Enquiries Section at Alexander House, Victoria Avenue, Southend. SS99 1BD to discuss and agree a fair way of doing so. HMRC will not accept one-sided claims for repayment of the output tax only.

TAXPAYERS WHO HAVE COMMITTED TO PROJECTS ANTICIPATING THE AVAILABILITY OF LENNARTZ ACCOUNTING

Taxpayers who are not permitted to use Lennartz accounting must apportion VAT incurred for both economic and non-economic activities on the basis of use and intended use from the date of this announcement.

However, HMRC will consider claims from taxpayers who have already entered into binding commitments for projects on the understanding that Lennartz accounting will be available. Taxpayers should contact HMRC at the addresses above.

FLEMING CLAIMS

Some taxpayers (following the House of Lords' judgments in the cases of *Fleming (trading as Bodycraft) v R & C Comrs, Condé Nast Publications Ltd v R & C Comrs* [2008] STC, HL) have submitted "Fleming" claims for Lennartz treatment for assets where VAT was incurred in accounting periods ending before 1 May 1997. No decisions on these claims were taken pending the issuing of this announcement. These claims will now be reviewed and, where appropriate, rejected if the taxpayer had not taken up the option to use Lennartz accounting at the time the input tax was incurred (where this was available) and/or where the VNLTO decision means that the claimants were not entitled to use Lennartz accounting as there was no EU law right to do so.

[VATA 1994 s 24]

11 MARCH 2010. REVENUE & CUSTOMS BRIEF 9/10 VAT STATUS OF UNIVERSITY TRADING SUBSIDIARY COMPANIES

This Revenue & Customs Brief announces our revised policy with regard to the supply of education by a university subsidiary trading company. VAT Information Sheet 03/10 provides further detail.

SUMMARY

Following developments in VAT case law and in methods by which education is delivered by universities, we have reviewed our policy on the treatment of supplies of education delivered by companies that are owned or controlled by a university. This review has identified a need for a change in policy, and as a result the VAT liability of supplies of education will change in certain circumstances. The new policy applies to supplies made on or after the date of this Brief subject to transitional arrangements (see below).

WHO SHOULD READ THIS?

This Brief should be read by any university owned company that delivers education and any university owning such a company.

Background

Supplies of education are exempt from VAT when provided by a UK university and any college, institution, school or hall of a university (VATA 1994 Sch 9, Group 6, Note 1(b)). Following the review, we have concluded that, in many cases where a university trading company provides education, they are acting as a 'college, institution, school or hall of a university.' As a consequence it is an 'eligible body' for the purposes of VATA 1994 Sch 9 Group 6. This means that any education or training provided by the university subsidiary trading company is an exempt supply of education. Please see VAT Information Sheet 03/10 for further detail.

Implications

This policy change is limited to those companies that

- are owned/controlled by a university
- provide university level education leading to a qualification awarded by a university or a nationally recognised body
- have close academic links with their parent university; for example, where students on the company's courses are registered/enrolled with the parent university, subject to its rules and regulations and awarded qualifications by it

Please see VAT Information Sheet 03/10 for further detail.

Once a university subsidiary company is regarded as an eligible body within Note (1)(b):

(a) All supplies of education and vocational training provided by that company are exempt from VAT.

(b) Any supplies which fall within VATA 1994 Sch 9 Group 6 should be treated as an exempt supply. (For example supplies of goods which are closely related to the supply of education under item 4.)

Other supplies, in particular consultancy services, provided by a subsidiary company of a university remain subject to VAT at the standard rate.

Transitional arrangements

The policy change comes into effect formally from the date of this Brief. An affected company may also apply it with retrospective effect and make the relevant adjustments to its VAT accounting, subject to the statutory time limits.

However we recognise that many university companies have budgeted on the basis that their supplies would be taxed. Therefore, as a transitional measure, affected companies may continue to apply the old policy (that is taxation at the standard rate) to supplies, which are to be delivered before 1 August 2010.

If a tax point is created for courses (including closely related supplies) to be delivered both before and after 1 August 2010, only that part of the supply which comprises courses which are delivered before 1 August 2010 may be subjected to the previous policy that is taxed.

This transitional measure will not apply if used for tax avoidance purposes, including any attempts to forestall the impact of the policy change. In addition, any pre-invoicing and/or prepayments which have been made in anticipation of the issue of this Brief and which do not comprise the normal commercial practice of the company that is the company is attempting to create a tax point in anticipation of this formal announcement of the policy change will be considered to be tax avoidance and we will apply the policy change to any supplies covered by such pre-invoicing and/or prepayments delivered after 1 August 2010.

CAPITAL GOODS SCHEME

VAT Information Sheet 03/10 gives guidance on what, if any, impact this change of policy will have on capital items used by university owned or controlled companies in delivering university education.

[VATA 1994 Sch 9 Group 6]

16 MARCH 2010. REVENUE & CUSTOMS BRIEF 11/10 VAT: THE DECISION OF THE VAT TRIBUNAL IN RESPECT OF RANK (GAMING MACHINES) ISSUED DECEMBER 2009

Revenue & Customs Brief 40/09, 14 July 2009 advised of a High Court decision in the case of *R & C Comrs v Rank Group plc* [2009] STC 2304, confirming there had been a breach of fiscal neutrality in the tax treatment of the supply of Mechanised Cash Bingo (MCB) and gaming machines.

In respect of gaming machines, as the judgment related to an appeal against an interim ruling of the VAT Tribunal [*Rank Group Ltd* (No 20777)], we advised that no claims for output tax wrongly accounted for would be considered until the Tribunal issued a final ruling in respect of Rank.

The First Tier Tribunal issued this in December 2009 [*The Rank Group plc* (TC 301)], finding that Fixed Odds Betting Terminals (FOBTs) were similar to, and in competition with, taxable gaming machines. We are appealing against this decision to the Upper Tribunal. Additionally, the Court of Appeal is due to hear the appeal against the earlier findings of both the VAT Tribunal and the High Court.

We intend, on the basis of the findings of both the VAT Tribunal and the High Court (and subject to the appeals), to consider those claims already received in respect of VAT paid on gaming machine takings.

[. . .]

IMPLICATIONS OF THIS JUDGMENT

As FOBTs came into commercial use in the United Kingdom in November 1998, this date agreed by the Tribunal, we will now consider existing claims submitted within required time limits for repayment of VAT paid on gaming machine takings for the period from 1 November 1998 to 5 December 2005.

Claims that have previously been rejected (for whatever reason) and which are not under appeal will not be considered. No new claims for the repayment of VAT paid for the period between 1 November 1998 and 5 December 2005 can be made.

The aim is to process all existing claims, where satisfactory evidence to support the claim has been provided, by 31 March 2011.

MAKING CLAIMS OR ADJUSTMENTS

Where a business has already made a claim to us for output tax wrongly accounted for in respect of gaming machines, this will be considered although further evidence may be requested.

All claims will be subject to the time limit in VATA 1994 s 80(4) – three years where the claim was made before 1 April 2009 or, where the claim was made on or after that date, four years or back to accounting periods ending on or after 1 April 2006 whichever is the shorter.

Protective assessments will also be issued under VATA 1994 s 80(4A) in order to allow us to recover any payments made should any appeals be successful.

There may be direct tax implications where amounts of over-declared output tax are repaid to businesses and your attention is drawn to Revenue & Customs Brief 14/09 issued previously.

Note. This Brief notes that "the law was changed from 5 December 2005 and from that date the treatment of comparator machines, FOBTs and gaming machines has been the same (and subject to VAT)". This appears to be a reference to VATA 1994 s 23(2), (3), which were amended by FA 2006 s 16(3), (4) in relation to anything done after that date. Hence the limition of claims to the period ending on that date.

[VATA 1994 Sch 9 Group 4 Item 1]

18 MARCH 2010. REVENUE & CUSTOMS BRIEF 12/10 VAT – PROVISION OF HEALTH PROFESSIONALS, NURSING AUXILIARIES, CARE ASSISTANTS AND SUPPORT WORKERS BY EMPLOYMENT BUSINESSES – CLARIFICATION OF POLICY

BACKGROUND

This brief aims to clarify our policy on the VAT treatment of supplies of health professionals, nursing auxiliaries, care assistants and support workers by employment businesses.

DEFINITIONS

The Employment Agencies Act 1973 defines an 'employment business' as a 'business (whether or not carried on with a view to profit and whether or not carried on in conjunction with any other business) of supplying persons in the employment of the person carrying on the business, to act for, and under the control of, other persons in any capacity'. 'Employment' is construed widely to include engagement on a contract of employment or a contract for services.

'Health professional' is an individual enrolled or registered on the appropriate statutory register including any and all of the following:

- Dentist or Dental Care Professional – an individual registered with the General Dental Council
- Doctor – an individual registered with the General Medical Council
- Nurse, midwife or community public health nurse – an individual registered with the Nursing & Midwifery Council
- Individuals registered by the Health Professions Council – including:
  - Arts Therapist
  - Biomedical Scientist
  - Chiropodist/Podiatrist
  - Clinical Scientist
  - Dietician
  - Occupational Therapist
  - Operating Department Practitioner
  - Orthoptist
  - Paramedic
  - Physiotherapist
  - Psychologist
  - Prosthetist/Orthotist
  - Radiographer
  - Speech & Language Therapist.

'Nursing auxiliary' – an individual who is not enrolled on any register of medical or health professionals but whose duties must include the provision of medical, as well as personal, care to patients.

'Care assistant' is an individual who is not enrolled on any register of medical or health professionals but who provides both medical and personal care to the recipient.

'Support worker' is an individual providing personal care and support services that may or may not be directly connected with the welfare of the recipient.

'Medical care' – in the context of what is provided by nursing auxiliaries and care assistants, includes monitoring the health of patients, for example, by taking blood pressure and temperatures, as well as administering drugs to patients under the direct supervision of a health professional.

'Personal care' – includes washing and dressing, feeding, helping people to mobilise, bed making, toileting etc., but does not include medical care.

EMPLOYMENT BUSINESSES IN THE HEALTH AND WELFARE SECTOR: BASIC VAT POSITION

Staff supplied by an employment business may be either employees of that business, or self-employed and engaged by an employment business. In both cases the workers' services are provided to the employment business, which in turn makes a supply of that worker to the client. If the worker comes under the direction and control of the client, this is a supply of staff. The employment business must therefore account for VAT when appropriate on the full charge to the client as in these circumstances it is acting as the 'principal'.

However, if the employment business maintains the direction and control of its staff to make a supply of welfare or medical services directly to the final consumer, we would see it as providing health or welfare services rather than merely a supply of staff. In these circumstances, subject to relevant criteria, we would see the business as making an exempt supply of welfare or health services – see Notice Nos 701/2 (Welfare) and 701/57 (Health Professionals) and the section headed 'Supplies of Contracted out Welfare Services' below.

SUPPLIES OF REGISTERED HEALTH PROFESSIONALS (OTHER THAN NURSES, MIDWIVES AND COMMUNITY PUBLIC HEALTH NURSES)

When an employment business supplies registered health professionals as a principal to a third party, where the health professional is working under the control and guidance of the third party, it is making a taxable supply of staff to that third party – not an exempt supply of healthcare or welfare services. It is the third party which is responsible for providing healthcare to the final patient, rather than the business supplying the staff which has no such responsibility.

A taxable supply of staff is made even where the employment business is responsible for ensuring that the workers it provides are properly trained and qualified when they work under the control of the third party.

SUPPLIES OF LOCUM GPS

Where an employment business supplies a locum GP to a practice, the employment business' only responsibility is to make a taxable supply of staff to the practice, not exempt healthcare to the final patient.

SUPPLIES OF NURSES, NURSING AUXILIARIES AND CARE ASSISTANTS BY STATE REGULATED AGENCIES

The nursing agencies' concession [as amended by Revenue & Customs Brief 40/10, 22 September 2010]

By concession (HMRC regularly reviews these), nursing agencies (or employment businesses that provide nurses and midwives, as well as other health professionals) may exempt the supply of nursing staff and nursing auxiliaries supplied as a principal to a third party, if the supply is of:

- a person registered in the register of qualified nurses and midwives maintained under article 5 of the Nursing and Midwifery Order 2001
- an unregistered nursing auxiliary who is 'directly supervised' by one of the above, or
- an unregistered nursing auxiliary, whose services are supplied to a hospital (NHS or private), hospice, care home with nursing under item 4 of Group 7, Schedule 9 VAT Act 1994 and form part of the care made to the patient.

The institution to which staff are supplied may be operated by a local authority, NHS body, charity or other organisation operating in the public or private sector.

From 1 October 2010, to qualify for the concession, the employment business must be registered with one of the following organisations:

- Care Quality Commission (or for supplies on or after 1 October 2010 would have been required to be registered with the Quality Care Commission prior to that date)
- Scottish Commission for the Regulation of Care
- Care Standards Inspectorate for Wales, or
- Northern Ireland Health and Personal Social Services Regulation and Improvement Authority.

For the supply of nursing auxiliaries or care assistants to benefit from the concession, they must undertake some direct form of medical care, such as administering drugs or taking blood pressures, for the final patient. The concession does not apply to supplies of general care assistants who are:

- only involved in providing personal care such as catering, washing or dressing the patients
- working in care homes without nursing where they do not require supervision by health professionals to provide their services.

However, where a state-regulated domiciliary care agency supplies the services of its care assistants directly to the final patient, we would see the agency as making an exempt supply of welfare services – see Notice No 701/2 (Welfare) and the section headed 'Supplies of contracted-out welfare services' below.

SUPPLIES OF CONTRACTED-OUT WELFARE SERVICES

As is clear from above, employment businesses in the welfare sector make a taxable supply of staff to third parties, such as local authorities, if the third party is legally responsible for the onward supply of providing care to the final recipient. This is subject to the nursing agencies' concession. The mere fact that an employment business is state-regulated does not mean that its supplies of staff are exempt if they are not covered by the nursing agencies concession.

However, when state-regulated welfare providers provide welfare services to the final consumer, these services remain exempt even if they are contracted and paid for by a local authority or other third party. For example, a local authority may contract out the provision of domiciliary care services for the elderly or disabled to a state-regulated domiciliary care agency. Although the local authority rather than the final consumer may pay the domiciliary care agency charities for the care services, for VAT purposes the care agency has still made an exempt supply of welfare services rather than staff to the local authority. This is because the care agency's staff will still be working directly to the agency itself throughout the provision of the services rather than to the local authority.

Exemption would also apply to cases where a local authority or other body subcontracts the provision of adult placement schemes. Under these schemes a 'worker' provides personal care and/or support services to adults living with them or living in their own homes. Currently scheme providers need to be registered with the Care Quality Commission.

Sometimes local authorities make payments directly to people who have been assessed as needing help from social services, and who would like to arrange and pay for their own care and support services instead of receiving them directly from the local council. These arrangements are called direct payment schemes, and any welfare services provided to the recipient by a charity or state-regulated private institution or agency are again exempt from VAT.

THE WORDING OF TERMS AND CONDITIONS OF AGREEMENTS

We are aware that some employment businesses state in their contract terms that their staff are still working under their control and direction rather than the third party to which their staff are being supplied. If that is the case you are no longer acting as an 'employment business' within the definition of the Employment Act 1976. You are reminded that the VAT liability of a supply is not determined conclusively by the terms of any contract or other documentation alone. If the wording of a contract does not reflect any changes in the way that the business actually operates in practice, the VAT liability of a taxable supply of staff will not change.

[VATA 1994 Sch 9 Group 7]

17 MARCH 2010. REVENUE & CUSTOMS BRIEF 13/10 VAT – PLACE OF SUPPLY OF FREIGHT TRANSPORT AND ASSOCIATED SERVICES – USED AND ENJOYED OUTSIDE THE EU

This Revenue & Customs Brief announces a temporary administrative easement in relation to business to business (B2B) supplies of freight transport (or services closely associated with freight transport) which are physically performed wholly outside the EU.

WHO NEEDS TO READ THIS?

UK based businesses making or receiving supplies of freight transport (or services closely associated with freight transport) where the services are physically performed wholly outside the EU.

BACKGROUND

Until 1 January 2010, the place of supply of freight transport and associated services was the country where the activity physically took place, to the extent that it took place there. That meant that supplies physically performed outside the EU were outside the scope of VAT. Transportation related to imports to and exports from the EU could have a place of supply both within and outside the EU and, to the extent they were performed within the EU, the VAT liability was at zero rate.

From 1 January 2010, business to business (B2B) supplies of freight transport and associated services became subject to the new B2B general rule for place of supply of services – where the business customer belongs – regardless of the place of physical performance. This means that, where the customer is in the UK, the place of supply is the UK even if the supply physically takes place wholly outside the EU. As zero rating only applies to supplies in connection with EU imports and exports, the liability of supplies wholly outside the EU is standard-rated. That means that either the UK-based customer must perform a reverse charge for the supply (if the supplier is outside the UK) or the supplier needs to account for UK VAT on the supply.

HM REVENUE & CUSTOMS (HMRC) POLICY

We have become aware (via UK businesses and charities) that this change has had a real impact, either in terms of increasing administrative burdens (with no revenue impact for the UK) or, in some cases, resulting in a real VAT cost. We recognise that this change in law has produced an unintended anomaly in the treatment of supplies wholly enjoyed outside the EU, which may also be taxed locally in the place of performance.

With immediate effect, where a supply of freight transport (or services closely associated with freight transport) would be treated as supplied in the UK, it will not be treated as supplied in the UK if the use and enjoyment of the services is outside the EU. This administrative easement is being introduced as a temporary measure to allow time for consideration of a more permanent legislative solution.

PAST SUPPLIES AND CLAIMS

This treatment applies from 15 March 2010; it is not retrospective.

[VATA 1994 s 7A]

29 MARCH 2010. REVENUE & CUSTOMS BRIEF 15/10
VAT – CHANGES TO THE TREATMENT OF CERTAIN SPORTS RELATED SERVICES FOLLOWING THE ECJ JUDGMENT IN CANTERBURY HOCKEY CLUB (C-253/07)

THE ISSUE

Changes to the VAT exemption for sports related services are being introduced from 1 September 2010. This will primarily affect affiliation fees charged by sports governing bodies to member clubs but the VAT treatment of other sports-related supplies may also be affected.

BACKGROUND

Certain services closely linked with and essential to sport or physical education are VAT exempt when supplied by an eligible body (that is, essentially non-profit making bodies not subject to commercial influence) to an individual taking part in sport.

In respect of affiliation fees charged by sports governing bodies to their member sports clubs, we have previously restricted the exemption to fees calculated on a per person basis (provided the services were closely linked to sport). Affiliation fees calculated by other methods, for example, on the basis of the club size or the number of teams fielded, were standard rated for VAT.

However, the ECJ in the case of *Canterbury Hockey Club and another v R & C Comrs* (case C-253/07) [2008] STC 3351 found that the exemption applies more widely. It has ruled that in the context of persons taking part in sport, the exemption includes services supplied to corporate persons and to unincorporated associations, provided that the supplies are closely linked and essential to sport, that they are supplied by non-profit making organisations and the true beneficiaries are individuals taking part in sport.

IMPLICATIONS

The ECJ ruling means that some supplies which were standard rated, for example because they were supplied to a corporate body or unincorporated association, may now be exempt from VAT if the services are closely linked and essential to sport and the true beneficiaries are individuals taking part in sport.

From 1 September 2010, eligible bodies meeting the conditions for exemption outlined in VAT Notice 701/45 Sport must exempt supplies where the true beneficiaries are persons taking part in sport, even if the supply is not made direct to an individual and irrespective of how the fee is calculated. Supplies made to commercial profit-making organisations do not meet the true beneficiary test and will not fall within the exemption for supplies of services closely linked and essential to sport.

Where the affiliation fee confers a number of benefits, which individually would be liable to different VAT treatment, the advice in Notice No 701/5 (March 2002) section 4 will help determine whether there is a single or multiple supply. Where the conditions of Extra Statutory Concession 3.35 (apportionment of membership subscriptions to certain non-profit making bodies) are met governing bodies may continue to take advantage of the option to apportion their affiliation fees between the rates of VAT applicable to the individual elements. The ECJ gave some examples of services that do not fall within the exemption, including advice about marketing and the obtaining of sponsors. These will be liable to the standard rate of VAT when ESC 3.35 is applied unless relief is available under another part of the VAT Act.

This policy change may also affect some other supplies closely linked and essential to sport by eligible bodies to corporate persons and unincorporated associations where the true beneficiary is a person taking part in sport. An example could be the letting of sports facilities to a club for the direct use of its members. In these circumstances, the supply is exempt if the club is non-profit making. Otherwise it will be taxable.

MAKING CLAIMS OR ADJUSTMENTS

The changes described above must be implemented from 1 September 2010 and there is no requirement to make adjustments in respect of supplies made prior to this date. However, any organisations wishing to implement the judgment before 1 September 2010 (and start exempting affected fees from an earlier date) are entitled to do so.

[. . .]

[VATA 1994 Sch 9 Group 10]

21 MAY 2010. REVENUE & CUSTOMS BRIEF 21/10
TOUR OPERATORS' MARGIN SCHEME AND THE TREATMENT OF 'HOTEL BILLBACK' TRANSACTIONS

Following changes to the Tour Operators' Margin Scheme ("TOMS") from 1 January 2010, this Revenue & Customs Brief sets out details of an agreement with representative bodies of the business travel sector about invoicing for supplies under the arrangement known as 'hotel billback'.

TOMS is a special VAT accounting scheme applying to certain designated travel supplies such as accommodation and transport that are bought in and sold on by businesses. Under the scheme, businesses are unable to recover VAT charged on their purchases but account for VAT on their supplies only on their margin. This means that invoices for these supplies cannot show the VAT element, which becomes sticking tax to business customers.

Under the 'hotel billback' arrangement, hotel booking agents book accommodation on behalf of their business client. The hotel issues a VAT invoice for the accommodation to the booking agents, who recover the VAT charged and then issue a VAT invoice to the business traveller, charging VAT on both the accommodation and their commission.

Without specific provisions in place, the VAT on such supplies should have been accounted for under the TOMS. Until the end of 2009, UK legislation provided for businesses making supplies of travel services to opt out of TOMS where the supplies were made to business customers for their own consumption, thus allowing the business customers to recover VAT on these supplies (subject to normal rules). However, with effect from 1 January 2010, a number of changes were introduced to the TOMS including withdrawal of the business to business opt out, to comply with EU law.

This means that hotel booking agents who receive invoices in their own name for hotel accommodation and recover the VAT charged must now account for VAT on their onward supplies under the TOMS and, in turn, their business customers will incur sticking tax.

However, it is entirely open to hotel booking agents to act in a disclosed capacity, with the hotels supplying accommodation direct to their business clients, rather than buy in and supply the accommodation themselves. Following separate approaches by the Hotel Booking Agents Association and the Guild of Travel Management Companies, we have agreed the arrangements detailed below where agents operate in this way. These arrangements are available generally to all business travel agents that wish to adopt them.

The agreed arrangements are:

- Invoices from hotels will be addressed c/o the hotel booking agent for payment. (This is to indicate that the invoice has been issued to the hotel booking agent in its capacity as an agent.)
- The booking field on the hotel invoice will identify the hotel guest, their employer and will ideally carry a unique reference number. (Until hotels can address their

invoices directly to their business customers, it may be necessary for hotel booking agents to enter an employer identification number on the invoice.)

- The hotel booking agent will arrange for payment of the invoice(s) but will not recover the input tax thereon.
- The hotel booking agent will send the customer a payment request/statement of the expenditure incurred by the hotel booking agent on its behalf, separately identifying the value of its supplies, VAT, etc.
- The payment request/statement should say something along the lines of 'The VAT shown is your input tax which can be reclaimed subject to the normal rules'.
- The customer will use the payment request/statement as a basis for their input tax reclaim.
- The hotel booking agent will retain the original hotel invoices and these will be made available if evidence of entitlement is required by VAT staff.
- The hotel booking agent will send a VAT invoice for its own services, plus the VAT. This may be consolidated with the statement of hotel charges, or it can be a separate document.
- The hotel booking agent will charge its client the exact amount charged by the billback supplier, as a disbursement.

[SI 1987/1806 art 2]

7 JUNE 2010. REVENUE & CUSTOMS BRIEF 25/10
VAT: PAY-PER-CLICK CHARITY ADVERTISEMENTS

This Brief explains HM Revenue & Customs (HMRC) revised policy on the VAT treatment of pay-per-click (PPC) charity advertising on sponsored links and other associated services.

BACKGROUND

PPC is used by organisations on search engines such as Google to encourage searchers to click on the organisation's link in priority to any other links on the results page following a search. The organisation pays the search engine provider an agreed amount each time their website is accessed through the sponsored link.

Supplies of advertisements for charities, when placed on a third party's website, and their design and production costs, attract the zero-rate of VAT under VATA 1994 Sch 8 Group 15 Items 8–8C.

HMRC have until now taken the view that a PPC-sponsored link is not an advertisement itself but simply a means of access to the charity's website. As such, HMRC considered the costs of providing PPC were excluded from zero-rating by VATA 1994 Sch 8 Group 15 Note 10B which excludes zero-rating on the costs of providing a charity's website.

Following representations from charities that zero-rating should apply to PPC charity advertisements, we have reviewed our approach and concluded we should revise the VAT treatment of PPC advertising supplied to charities.

REVISED POLICY

HMRC now accept that PPC-sponsored links appearing on search engine websites are advertisements for the purpose of Item 8 and 8A, and qualify for zero-rating when supplied to a charity. It follows that the supply of copyright and design services associated with such sponsored links fall within the zero-rating.

However, HMRC still maintain that services supplied by copywriters and designers for the purpose of search engine optimisation (structuring a website so that it contains as many keywords as possible) do not qualify for relief. HMRC consider that these services entail the optimisation of the charity's own website, and so are specifically excluded from Item 8 by Note 10B to Group 15.

The listing of a charity in the results of a search engine ('natural hits') does not constitute the promulgation of an advertisement for the purpose of Item 8 since the charity's name appears automatically, regardless of any action taken by or on behalf of a charity, and merely highlights text from the charity's own website.

[. . .]

[VATA 1994 Sch 8 Group 15]

21 JUNE 2010. REVENUE & CUSTOMS BRIEF 26/10
VAT: CHANGES TO THE APPLICATION OF THE ZERO RATE TO NEW BUILDINGS INTENDED TO BE USED FOR A RELEVANT CHARITABLE PURPOSE

In Revenue & Customs Brief 39/09 [1 July 2009], we announced the 'charitable buildings' concession (ESC 3.29) would be withdrawn on 1 July 2010.

[. . .] Any charity wishing to make use of the concession before 1 July 2010 must issue the necessary certificate before that date (late certificates will not be permitted) and by 1 January 2011, either:

- the building must have been constructed to a point above foundation level; or
- the charity must be in occupation of the building if it is being acquired or leased

If you fail to issue the certificate in time or do not meet these conditions, you will not be eligible to use ESC 3.29 to secure zero-rating for your building.

However, charities, and those who use buildings solely for a relevant residential purpose, may still acquire or construct new buildings zero-rated for VAT providing they are able to demonstrate that the building concerned is intended to be used 95 per cent or more for a relevant residential or relevant charitable purpose. Any method can be used to measure qualifying use, provided that it is fair.

[. . .] guidance to assist charities in identifying methods that they could consider using [. . .] can be found in VAT Information Sheet 13/10.

[Notice No 48 (December 2010) para 3.29 (see Appendix 1)]

15 JUNE 2010. REVENUE & CUSTOMS BRIEF 28/10
VAT: LIABILITY OF NON-COMPLIANCE CARBON CREDITS AND CARBON OFFSETTING SERVICES

[. . .]

SCOPE

This Brief covers the VAT treatment of supplies of carbon credits and services provided by carbon offset providers. For the purposes of this brief, 'carbon offset providers' offer advice and/or the facility to reduce an individual's 'carbon footprint'.

CARBON CREDITS

Carbon credits fall into two categories:

- compliance market credits, which derive from the Kyoto Protocol and the EU Emissions Trading System ('EUETS')
- non-compliance credits, of which the most common example is the Verified Emission Reduction (VER)

The important distinction, for VAT purposes, between compliance market credits and VERs is that the former are capable of consumption of the type envisaged by the VAT system, and the latter are not. As VAT is a tax on consumption, this means that compliance market credits are subject to VAT, whilst VERs are outside the scope of VAT.

COMPLIANCE MARKET CREDITS

Compliance market credits are recognised under statutory 'cap and trade' regimes. Polluting businesses which are subject to these regimes must hold, or obtain on the open market, and then 'retire' sufficient emissions credits to cover their emissions. If they do not, then they will suffer financial penalties. The credits are consumed to enable businesses to engage in economic activity without penalty, and to meet their Kyoto commitments.

Kyoto and the EUETS provide for exacting verification and regulatory processes, which mean that both parties to a compliance market transaction are able to attribute a subjective value to the credit units. The credits are widely traded on national and international markets.

The motive of an individual paying for a credit does not matter, nor does it matter what is done with it. Thus if a private individual buys a compliance market credit, the supply of the credit to the individual is still taxable (even though the individual is not subject to any regime) because the credit is capable of consumption.

Examples of compliance market credits include Emission Reduction Units (ERUs), Certified Emission Reductions (CERs) and EU Allowances (EUAs).

VERIFIED EMISSION REDUCTIONS

A Verified Emission Reduction (VER) is essentially a promise that carbon has been or may be reduced somewhere in the world. There may be a general benefit to the reputation of a business (good PR/marketing/corporate responsibility) in paying for a VER, but no particular service is rendered which can be identified as a cost component of the business. There is therefore no consumption. No service is being provided to an identifiable consumer and no benefit is being provided which is capable of forming a cost component of the activity of another person in the commercial chain.

Payment for a VER might produce a general social benefit, it might produce a specified result, or it might give rise to a legal relationship with reciprocal obligations. However, a taxable person's income is relevant for VAT purposes only if it constitutes the consideration for a supply of goods or services to a consumer. The mere fact that something is or may be done in exchange for a payment is insufficient to bring such a transaction within the VAT system. The public at large cannot constitute a specific recipient of the kind which must exist in order to give rise to a transaction chargeable to VAT.

Further, and in marked contrast to the situation with compliance market credits, we have seen no evidence of the existence of a genuine secondary trading market in VERs.

CARBON OFFSET SERVICES

There are a growing number of businesses providing carbon offsetting services. The range of services offered varies widely, but the VAT treatment of any individual transaction will depend on the particular arrangements. Because arrangements vary so widely, it is not considered practicable to provide anything beyond general advice in this brief.

In many situations, when a member of the public makes a payment to a carbon offset provider, there is no supply for VAT purposes. This is because there is no identifiable, direct benefit being received by the member of the public in return for their money.

Examples would be where a carbon offset provider makes a commitment that funds paid across by members of the public will be used to fund overseas projects, wind farms, development of environmentally friendly energy generation projects etc. without making any supply of direct benefit to the person making the payment. In such scenarios, the payment by the member of the public is outside the scope of VAT.

A common arrangement is where an airline offers its passengers the facility to offset the carbon emissions generated by their flights, perhaps via a third party carbon offset provider.

Generally the passenger pays across an amount, calculated to be the cost of offsetting the resulting emissions, but receives no identifiable, direct benefit in return. There are a number of possible variants, including:

- the passenger has no choice, being obliged to pay the offsetting charge – the airline is making a single zero-rated supply of transport services
- the offsetting facility is optional, but a separate administration charge is made to the customer for providing the service – the admin charge is standard-rated, but the amount paid to offset provision is outside the scope of VAT
- the offsetting service is optional, there is no administrative charge, and the entire payment goes to offset provision – the payment is outside the scope of VAT

In other situations, a carbon offset provider might make taxable supplies of carbon credits (supplies of compliance market credits are currently zero-rated), or of the purchase and 'retirement' of compliance market credits (standard-rated), or of general advice on how an individual or a business can improve its energy efficiency (standard-rated).

INPUT TAX RECOVERY

Whether you are an offset provider, or simply a business incurring VAT in order to offset your own carbon emissions, you must follow the usual rules to determine whether any VAT incurred is input tax and the extent to which it is recoverable.

[VATA 1994 s 5]

15 JUNE 2010. REVENUE & CUSTOMS BRIEF 29/10 VAT: DIY HOUSEBUILDERS AND CONVERTERS VAT REFUND SCHEME – TREATMENT OF HOLIDAY HOMES

This Brief announces a change to the treatment of claims received by HM Revenue & Customs (HMRC) under the provisions of the above Scheme in respect of holiday homes.

THE EFFECT OF THE CHANGE

Following a decision of the VAT Tribunal, HMRC now accept that the DIY Housebuilders and Converters Scheme applies to the construction of new holiday homes and to the conversion of non-residential buildings into holiday homes. Any refund of VAT is subject to the conditions of the Scheme being met.

Guidance for the Scheme is attached to application forms as follows:

- VAT 431NB: VAT refunds for DIY housebuilders (new houses)
- VAT 431C: VAT refunds for DIY housebuilders (conversions)

[. . .]

BACKGROUND

[. . .]

HMRC have never applied the DIY Housebuilders Scheme to holiday homes since their supply by a developer attracts VAT at the standard rate. However, a recent decision of the VAT Tribunal (*Jennings* (TC362) has found that the existing legislation does allow the same recovery of VAT on building materials for holiday homes that have been constructed by the individual for a non-business purpose.

As a consequence of this decision, HMRC now accept that claims, for VAT incurred on building materials, may also be made for holiday homes that meet the necessary criteria.

HMRC will also allow claims for a VAT refund on building materials and, where appropriate, services of conversion, where the work has involved the conversion of a previously non-residential building into a home.

HOW TO CLAIM

If you have not submitted a claim before in respect of your holiday home, then you may do so now providing the certificate of completion was issued within the last four years and three months from the date of this Brief. If your certificate of completion is older than this then HMRC regret that your claim is out of time.

If you have, at any time, submitted a claim in relation to a holiday home which was refused in full or in part, for that reason, then you may now resubmit that claim if you wish.

If you are making a claim, please ensure you use the correct form as identified above.

The guidance to the forms is in the process of being amended to reflect this change in policy but the forms themselves will not require alteration.

Exceptionally, where you have submitted a claim in the past, HMRC will accept the original claim form. All claim forms should be accompanied by:

- planning permission
- certificate of completion
- building plans
- all original VAT invoices, bills and credit notes

Please note that a claim cannot be considered unless the above evidence is provided.

Resubmitted claims should be sent, along with a covering note quoting this Brief, to: HMRC DIY Claims Unit, Two Broadway, Broad Street, Five Ways, Birmingham B15 1BG.

[VATA 1994 s 35]

29 JULY 2010. REVENUE & CUSTOMS BRIEF 33/10
VAT: CHANGES TO THE EXCLUSION OF THE OPTION TO TAX ON SUPPLIES OF BUILDINGS TO BE USED SOLELY FOR A RELEVANT RESIDENTIAL OR RELEVANT CHARITABLE PURPOSE, (PARAGRAPHS 5, 6 AND 7 OF SCHEDULE 10 TO THE VAT ACT 1994 REFER)

In Revenue & Customs Brief 39/09 [1 July 2009, not reproduced], HM Revenue & Customs (HMRC) announced changes to the application of the zero rate to new buildings and that, following a review, the phrase 'solely for a relevant residential or relevant charitable purpose' could incorporate a de minimis margin.

In order to avoid unnecessary disputes in marginal cases, HMRC accept that this statutory condition is satisfied for new buildings where the relevant use of the building by the charity or relevant residential user is 95 per cent or more. In light of this review, HMRC announced the withdrawal of Extra Statutory Concession (ESC) 3.29 and two related concessions as we considered them to be no longer necessary or appropriate.

However, ESC 3.29 also allowed charities to exclude the option to tax on supplies of buildings to them (other than parts used as an office) if they were solely used for a relevant charitable purpose. For consistency, HMRC accept that, where the customer and supplier agree, the option to tax can be excluded on supplies of a building or part of a building that is to be used 95 per cent or more for a relevant purpose in the following situations:

- where a building or part of a building (other than used as an office) will be used by a charity solely for a relevant charitable purpose (VATA 1994 Sch 10 para 7 refers)
- where a grant is made in a building or part of a building designed solely for a relevant residential purpose (VATA 1994 Sch 10 para 5 refers)
- where a grant in a building or part of a building is made to a person who intends to use the building solely for a relevant residential purpose (VATA 1994 Sch 10 para 6 refers).

[VATA 1994 Sch 10 paras 5, 6, 7]

3 AUGUST 2010. REVENUE & CUSTOMS BRIEF 31/10 HM REVENUE & CUSTOMS POSITION FOLLOWING THE COURT OF APPEAL JUDGMENT IN INSURANCEWIDE AND TRADER MEDIA GROUP

This Brief explains HM Revenue & Customs (HMRC) position following the Court of Appeal judgment in *Insurancewide.com Services Ltd v R & C Comrs; R & C Comrs v Trader Media Group Ltd* [2010] STC 1572, CA.

[. . .]

HMRC'S POSITION

[. . .] HMRC now accept that insurance introductory services will be exempt from VAT when a provider is doing much more than acting as a 'mere conduit' through which a potential customer is passed to a provider. This can be demonstrated by all of the following four conditions being met:

(1) The services are provided by someone engaged in the business of putting insurance companies in touch with potential clients or more generally acting as intermediaries between the two parties (although this may not necessarily be their principal business activity).

(2) The business provides the means (that is, by way of an internet 'click through' or some other form of introduction) by which a person seeking insurance is introduced to a provider of insurance or to another intermediary in a chain leading to an insurance provider.

(3) That introduction takes place at the time a customer is seeking to enter into an insurance contract (although in some instances an insurance contract may not actually go on to be finally concluded).

(4) The introducer also plays a proactive part in putting in place the arrangements under which that introduction is effected.

For the purposes of condition 4 above, evidence that the introducer has been proactive in putting in place the arrangements under which the introduction is effected could, for example, take the form of some or all of the following:

- active endorsement of the insurer or the insurance product
- involvement in the selection of the insurance products and/or providers
- involvement in the process under which the insurance contract is entered into, even though the intermediation of the contact itself is undertaken by a 3rd party (for example, by having input into what questions should be asked of the prospective insured or the design of the 3rd party's website)
- negotiating a special rate for the insurance product/s on behalf of its customers or membership base
- some form of assessment of the customer's requirements so that they are directed to the most appropriate insurer for them

Previous case law has told HMRC that the means by which a business is remunerated for its services, that is, whether by fee or commission or some other means, is not determinative of the liability. Whilst remuneration based on successful take-up may indicate an introduction has taken place it is not enough in itself to determine exemption and it is always important to consider what is actually being done rather than how it is paid for.

Although the judgment specifically concerned insurance intermediary services, it does also provide some general guidance on the application of the exemption to finance intermediary services. It must be borne in mind, however, that the UK and EU law covering the exemption for finance intermediary services is different from that for insurance intermediary services. For example, for most finance intermediary services to be exempt, UK law requires businesses to be both bringing together a prospective customer with a product provider with a view to entering a contract for the provision of financial services and carrying out work preparatory to the conclusion of those contracts.

[. . .]

[VATA 1994 Sch 9 Group 2]

20 AUGUST 2010. REVENUE & CUSTOMS BRIEF 35/10
VAT: PROPOSED REVERSE CHARGE ACCOUNTING FOR BUSINESSES TRADING IN EMISSIONS ALLOWANCES

INTRODUCTION

Budget Note 49 (24 March 2010) announced the introduction of legislation for a reverse charge with effect from 1 November 2010.

The purpose of this Brief is to share the draft legislation and provide guidance on how the reverse charge for emissions allowances will operate.

[. . .]

THE REVERSE CHARGE MECHANISM

Under the reverse charge accounting mechanism, it is the responsibility of the customer, rather than the supplier, to account to HM Revenue & Customs (HMRC) for VAT on supplies of the specified emission allowances. As is the case with the mobile telephone and computer chip reverse charge it will only apply to business to business transactions in the UK. However, there are two key differences between these measures, which are:

- there is no 'de minimis' rule excluding supplies under £5,000 so the reverse charge applies to all specified supplies of emission allowances
- businesses will not be required to complete a Reverse Charge Sales List

COMPLETION OF THE VAT RETURN

Suppliers of goods under reverse charge accounting must *not* enter in box 1 of the VAT Return any output tax on sales to which the reverse charge applies, but must enter the value of such sales in box 6.

Customers must enter in box 1 of the VAT Return the output tax on purchases to which the reverse charge applies, but must *not* enter the value of such purchases in box 6. They must reclaim the input tax on their reverse charge purchases in box 4 of the VAT Return and include the value of the purchases in box 7, in the normal way.

INVOICING

When making a sale to which reverse charge accounting applies, suppliers must:

- show all the information normally required to be shown on a VAT invoice
- annotate the invoice to make it clear that the reverse charge applies and that the customer is required to account for the VAT

The amount of VAT due under the reverse charge rules must be clearly stated on the invoice but should *not* be included in the amount shown as total VAT charged. The precise wording is not prescribed in law and discussions with business have highlighted the need to keep the annotation short. Either of the following would be acceptable:

- customer to pay output tax of £X to HMRC
- UK customer to pay O/T of £X to HMRC

Alternatively, any of the following would also be acceptable, provided that the amount of tax is shown elsewhere on the invoice (but not in box for total output tax charged):

- VAT Act 1994 Section 55A applies
- s 55A VATA 94 applies
- customer to account for the VAT to HMRC
- reverse charge supply – customer to pay the VAT to HMRC
- customer to pay VAT to HMRC
- UK customer to pay VAT to HMRC

Detailed guidance on the reverse charge mechanism can be found in Notice No 735.

[. . .]

Note. The relevant legislation was enacted by FA 2010 s 50 and VAT (Section 55A) (Specified Goods and Services and Excepted Supplies) Order 2010, SI 2010/2239.

[VATA 1994 s 55A]

3 SEPTEMBER 2010. REVENUE & CUSTOMS BRIEF 37/10 VAT: LEISURE TRUSTS PROVIDING ALL INCLUSIVE MEMBERSHIP SCHEMES

THE ISSUE

With effect from 1 April 2009 HM Revenue & Customs (HMRC) amended its interpretation of the law and therefore its guidance on the VAT treatment of membership schemes allowing unlimited access to leisure facilities in a leisure centre. Businesses that will be most affected are community leisure centres that are run by non-profit making trusts. Supplies made by commercial organisations are not affected and remain taxable at the standard rate.

[. . .]

BACKGROUND

Supplies of services closely linked with and essential to sport or physical education, in which an individual takes part, are exempt from VAT when supplied by an 'eligible body' (essentially a non-profit making body not subject to commercial influence) as set out in VATA 1994 Sch 9 Group 10 (Sport, Sports Competitions and Physical Education). Prior to 1 April 2009 HMRC's view was that where a scheme offered, over a period, unlimited use of a variety of both taxable and exempt facilities, typically in return for a monthly or annual payment, there was generally a single supply of the standard-rated right to use the facilities. However, following representations from the leisure industry and taking into account the comments made in the Court of Appeal in *R & C Comrs v Weight Watchers (UK) Ltd* [2008] STC 2313, CA about the typical consumer, we no longer see the supply as a right to use the services but as being the supply of underlying services.

The *Weight Watchers* case indicated that it is appropriate to look at the transaction from the viewpoint of the typical consumer, rather than the supplier. The extent of the linkage between the relevant transactions must be considered from an economic point of view; the question then is whether it would be artificial to split the transaction into separate supplies. If it would be artificial, then there will be a single supply and the predominant element from the viewpoint of the typical consumer, will determine whether the supply is exempt or standard-rated.

REVISED APPROACH

VAT liability depends on the nature of the supply which has to be decided at the time the all inclusive fee is paid. Where the supply is a single supply that would be artificial to split there can only be one overarching liability. In most cases, the typical consumer who purchases an all inclusive package will have access to a range of facilities at the leisure centre. Usually most of these facilities would, if supplied individually, be exempt as 'services closely linked with and essential to sport or physical education in which the individual is taking part', (for example use of the swimming pool, showers, changing rooms). Therefore, in cases where the predominant reason for purchasing an all inclusive package is to use the range of available sports facilities, the single supply is exempt.

In some instances packages may include facilities that would be standard-rated if supplied on their own, for example, sauna facilities. However, providing that the predominant reason that the typical consumer purchases the package is to use the (exempt) sports services, the supply of the package is still exempt.

If the predominant reason a typical consumer purchases an all inclusive package is to make use of standard-rated facilities the single supply is standard-rated.

EFFECTS OF THE CHANGE

The effect of this change is that since 1 April 2009 non-profit making bodies, including leisure trusts which were previously charging VAT on their all inclusive packages, will in the majority of cases have to treat them as exempt. If businesses make both exempt and taxable supplies they will be partly exempt and will have to apply the partial exemption rules to determine how much of the Input Tax incurred on their costs can be deducted.

[. . .]

CAPITAL GOODS SCHEME (CGS) ITEMS; THE EFFECT OF THE CHANGE

[. . .]

After affected bodies begin treating their supplies as exempt there will be an apparent change of use from taxable to exempt. However, the policy change represents what the true liability always was, assuming that sports providers have not changed the way they operate. The CGS adjusts the true amount that was initially claimable ignoring any errors that may have occurred whether they can be corrected or not. Therefore, no significant CGS adjustments are likely provided that the way sports facilities are supplied has not changed since any capital expenditure was incurred. If you are concerned that the CGS may significantly affect you then please contact your local VAT Office.

If sports providers acquired a CGS building asset as part of a TOGC then the CGS may require adjustments if the previous owner deducted and was properly entitled to deduct Input Tax on the item. This is likely if the previous owner was a Local Authority.

[. . .]

[VATA 1994 Sch 9 Group 10 Item 3]

12 OCTOBER 2010. REVENUE & CUSTOMS BRIEF 43/10
VAT: 'ITALIAN REPUBLIC' CLAIMS FOR OVERPAID VAT – PARTIAL EXEMPTION IMPLICATIONS OF THE ECJ DECISION IN *NORDANIA FINANS*

This Brief gives information concerning a review by HM Revenue & Customs (HMRC) of the proper treatment of claims submitted as a result of *EC Commission v Italian Republic* (case C-45/95) [1997] STC 1062, ECJ.

[. . .]

BACKGROUND – CLAIMING VAT EXEMPTION AND PARTIAL EXEMPTION

When UK law says a supply is taxable but European law says it is exempt taxpayers are entitled to claim exemption. However such claims must take into account the effect of the additional exempt supplies on the taxpayer's ability to deduct input tax (partial exemption).

The effect of partial exemption on motor sector businesses depends on whether cars owned by and used in the business for a limited time (such as demonstrators) can be treated for partial exemption purposes as capital goods used in the business. This is because the sale values of any such goods must be excluded from partial exemption calculations.

Until 2001 it was HM Customs and Excise's policy that demonstrator cars should not be classified as capital goods and therefore should be included in partial exemption calculations. This resulted in Italian Republic claims being reduced to take account of the partial exemption impact.

In 2001 however, the High Court ruled in *C & E Comrs v JDL Ltd* [2002] STC 1 that demonstrator cars were capital goods used in a car dealer's business. It was therefore accepted that, other things being equal, 'Italian Republic' claims for over-declared output tax need not take partial exemption into account. A number of claims have been repaid by HMRC on that basis.

THE ECJ DECISION IN NORDANIA FINANS

In March 2008 the ECJ delivered its decision in the case of *Nordania Finans A/S and anor v Skatteministeriet* (case C-98/07) [2008] STC 3314, ECJ. This case concerned whether cars bought for leasing followed by sale were capital goods used in the business. Nordania's business model was to buy cars, lease them for a fixed period of eighteen months and then sell them at auction. Through these two ways of exploiting their assets they realised sufficient funds to cover their direct costs and overheads. The ECJ ruled that the exclusion of the sales, when the sales were an integral part of their business model, would distort Nordania's partial exemption calculations. The sales should therefore not be seen as sales of capital goods used in Nordania's business.

After due consideration, HMRC has concluded that Nordania has over-turned *C & E Comrs v JDL Ltd* [2002] STC 1. The sale of cars that were bought to be used in a motor sector taxpayer's business for a limited time and then sold is an integral part of that taxpayer's business. As such, based on Nordania, it would distort partial exemption calculations to exclude the sale, and the cars cannot be viewed as capital goods used in the business. As a result any claim for over-declared output tax arising from the 'Italian Republic' case must take the impact of partial exemption on deductible input tax into account.

[. . .]

[SI 1995/2518 reg 101]

2 NOVEMBER 2010. REVENUE & CUSTOMS BRIEF 44/10
VAT: CHANGE IN THE TAX TREATMENT OF BUSINESS ENTERTAINMENT OF OVERSEAS CUSTOMERS

HM Revenue & Customs (HMRC) has reviewed its policy on the treatment of business entertainment provided to overseas customers in the light of the European Courts of Justice (ECJ) judgment in the joined case of *Danfoss A/S and anor v Skatteministeriet* (case C-371/07) [2009] STC 701, ECJ.

[. . .]

WHAT VAT CAN BE RECOVERED IN RESPECT OF ENTERTAINMENT?

HMRC now takes the view that VAT incurred on the entertainment of overseas customers may be recovered under the terms of EU law. However, in some circumstances an output tax charge to reflect private use arises and cancels out any deductible input tax. Where that is the case, there is no benefit in making a claim, so in considering whether to claim you should also consider whether there is a charge to output tax.

PRIVATE USE CHARGE

The charge that taxes private use is intended to ensure that the taxable person, his/her staff and others do not achieve an advantage over private individuals simply because the taxable person is registered for VAT and can recover VAT incurred on costs. The ECJ has addressed the question of the applicability of such a charge and it is clear from two particular decisions that the circumstances under which an individual can benefit privately from a business expense without a private use charge arising should be very narrowly defined. The two cases – *Julius Fillibeck Söhne GmbH & Co KG v Finanzamt Neustadt* (case C-258/95) [1997] ECR 1–5577 and *Danfoss A/S and anor v Skatteministeriet* (case C-371/07) [2008] ECR I–9549, [2009] STC 701, ECJ – introduce separate tests that should be applied to private use of business expenditure; these are set out in more detail below. As no advantage arises if the VAT is not recovered by the taxable person there is no need to consider the applicability of the private use charge unless you intend to recover the VAT paid.

In the *Fillibeck Söhne* case an employer provided transport to his staff to get them from their homes to a construction site. As commuting expenditure is private, the Court was asked to consider whether having recovered tax on the cost of the transport it was appropriate to apply a charge to reflect the private use by the employees. The Court's starting point was that a charge applied in principle but they considered the particular facts of the case and concluded that because it was practically impossible for the employees to get to the site on their own a private use charge should not be applied. From this judgment we must therefore consider whether it is necessary for the taxable person to provide goods or services that are enjoyed privately in order for him to make his taxable supplies; this is **the necessity test**.

The joined case of *Danfoss* and *AstraZeneca* involved the provision of free meals to both employees and business contacts. In the context of the business having recovered VAT on the meals, the ECJ was asked to consider whether it was appropriate to apply a private use charge. The Court concluded that where the meals were provided for a strict business purpose no such charge should arise. In reaching this conclusion they carefully considered the circumstances of the free meals. In particular the lack of choice by the recipient of what, when and where to eat, the relatively basic nature of the fare and crucially the fact that the meals were provided to ensure the smooth running of business meetings; this is **the strict business purpose test**.

These cases set out the circumstances where it is and is not appropriate to apply a private use charge to a benefit provided by the business. HMRC considers that unless there is a necessity for the business to provide entertainment or there is a strict business purpose behind it, such as the facilitation of a meeting, it is appropriate to apply a private use charge to entertainment provided to overseas customers.

If you conclude that the entertainment you provide should trigger such a private use charge, HMRC suggests that you treat the VAT incurred as non-deductible instead, rather than claiming a deduction and offsetting this with an output tax charge. This approach is consistent with the view that VAT incurred on the entertainment of overseas customers should only be recovered where it is clearly used for the making of taxable supplies as well as being reasonable in scale and character.

We set out below a number of scenarios that should assist in deciding the correct VAT treatment of any expenditure that you have incurred on entertaining overseas customers.

MEETINGS IN YOUR OFFICE

HMRC considers that where you entertain overseas customers in your staff canteen or similar, and the entertainment is provided to facilitate a business meeting, then the VAT on such expenditure will be recoverable and no charge to reflect the private use will arise; we take the view that any private benefit derived by your overseas customer is accessory to the needs of your business. This approach satisfies the basic input tax recovery test by establishing a link between the expense and the taxable supplies that your business makes. It is also consistent with the approach adopted by the ECJ in assessing the applicability of any private use charge in that this expense has a strict business purpose.

EXTERNAL MEETINGS/EVENTS

Where you cannot host meetings in the office because, for example, you have a large number of attendees or you have no in-house facilities, then you can still use the principles set out above to determine if your input tax is recoverable or there is a charge to output tax under the private use charge. The provision of basic refreshments at, for example, a training event or a meeting will be treated as if it were supplied by your own in-house canteen. However, where the provision goes beyond merely providing basic food and refreshment to facilitate the smooth running of the event, then you should not recover any input tax or, failing that, account for output tax under the private use charge.

CORPORATE HOSPITALITY EVENTS

Many businesses offer their customers or potential customers general entertainment and hospitality, for example, golf days, track days, trips to sporting events, evening meals, trips to night clubs. HMRC will generally not allow deduction of VAT in respect of these events or will require you to account for output tax, as such events are unlikely to have a strict business purpose and be necessary for the business to make its supplies.

[SI 1992/3222 art 5]

12 JANUARY 2011. REVENUE & CUSTOMS BRIEF 54/10 THE EUROPEAN COURT OF JUSTICE (ECJ) JUDGMENT IN AXA UK PLC

This brief explains the HM Revenue & Customs (HMRC) position following the ECJ judgment in *R & C Comrs v AXA UK plc* (case C-175/09) [2010] STC 2825. The case concerned the application of the VAT exemption in Directive 2006/112/EC art 135(1)(d) for:

- transactions, including negotiation, concerning deposit and current accounts, payments, transfers, debts, cheques and other negotiable instruments, but excluding debt collection'
- the Court found that the services in AXA were specifically excluded from the exemption as 'debt collection' and were therefore liable to VAT at the standard rate.

[. . .]

THE HMRC POSITION

The ECJ judgment in AXA now specifically defines what 'debt collection' means for the purposes of the exclusions to the VAT exemption. The ECJ says in paragraph 34 of its judgment that:

- ' . . . it is irrelevant that such service is supplied at the time when the debts concerned become due . . . '
- it then goes onto say that the words 'debt collection' in art 135(1)(d)
- ' . . . cover the collection of debts of any nature, without limiting their application to debts which were not paid on their due date.' and also cover ' . . . debts which have not yet become due and which will be paid on the due date.'

Following the *AXA* judgment, therefore, 'debt collection' cannot be seen as applying solely to the service of chasing and recovering overdue payments on behalf of the creditor and all services principally concerned with collecting payments from the person owing them for the benefit of the entity to which those payments are owed (regardless of whether those payments are received before, on, or after their due date) fall within the exclusion to the exemption and are consequently liable to VAT at the standard rate.

Supplies which involve the collection of payments as a minor or ancillary function but which are principally concerned with other payment related transactions that fall within the art 135(1) exemptions, for example the movement and settlement of payments between bank accounts, will not be affected by the *AXA* judgment and will continue to fall within the VAT exemption.

WHAT THIS MEANS FOR BUSINESSES

All payment related services falling within the definition of 'debt collection' as outlined by the ECJ in the *AXA* judgment are now liable to VAT at the standard rate. If this applies to payment related services supplied by your business and your business has previously received a ruling from HMRC that those services fall within the VAT exemption (or it has previously been treating its services as exempt in line with HMRC's published policy in this area) then VAT must be applied to those services from the date of this brief.

[VATA 1994 Sch 9 Group 5 Item 1]

19 JANUARY 2011. REVENUE & CUSTOMS BRIEF 1/11
VAT AND AMLD: HMRC'S TREATMENT OF ELECTRONIC LOTTERY MACHINES AND BINGO MACHINES

This Brief explains HM Revenue & Customs' (HMRC's) position following the Tribunal decision in *Oasis Technologies (UK) Ltd* (TC 581). It also explains the treatment of electronic bingo machines.

1. LOTTERY MACHINES

[. . .]

The Tribunal released its decision on 1 July 2010. It held that the Oasis ELTVM is a gaming machine within VATA 1994 Sch 9 Group 4 Note 1(d) and that it also grants the right to participate in a lottery within VATA 1994 Sch 9 Group 4 Item 2. It ruled that the supplies made are exempt from VAT.

HMRC'S POSITION

In light of the conclusions of the Tribunal HMRC accept that a machine, whose operation is the same as that of the Oasis ELTVM, shall be treated as granting the right to participate in a lottery. The income thereof is VAT exempt.

The VAT exemption will apply to a machine having all of the following characteristics:

- the machine must provide a game of chance
- the tickets must be randomly distributed
- the player, operator or manufacturer must not be able to influence the order in which a ticket is revealed
- the result of the lottery must not be determined or influenced by means of the machine, and
- where groups of tickets have been pre-loaded into a machine, the machine may randomly select a new group when the current one is completed.

[. . .]

[VATA 1994 Sch 9 Group 4]

2. BINGO MACHINES

HMRC is aware that a number of manufacturers in the gaming industry have recently developed machines which are used to play an electronic version of bingo.

Where a machine meets the characteristics of bingo machines listed in guidance published by the Gambling Commission in June 2009 ('Key characteristics of bingo'), although some of the criteria are for regulatory purposes only, HMRC will accept that for VAT and gambling duties taxation the machine is designed or adapted for playing bingo.

The supply made thereof is exempt from VAT under VATA 1994 Sch 9 Group 4 Item 1.

The supply made thereof is exempt from VAT under VATA 1994 Sch 9 Group 4 Item 1.

[. . .]

[VATA 1994 Sch 9 Group 4 Items 1, 2]

25 JANUARY 2011. REVENUE & CUSTOMS BRIEF 2/11
VAT: HM REVENUE AND CUSTOMS' POSITION FOLLOWING THE FIRST TIER TRIBUNAL DECISION IN THE CASE OF JOHN PRICE

This Brief explains HM Revenue & Customs' (HMRC) policy following the First Tier Tribunal decision in the case of *John Price* (TC 1287).

The Tribunal agreed with the appellant that roller blinds were 'building materials' as defined by Note 22 to Group 5 of Schedule 8 to the VAT Act 1994. As a result, the appellant was entitled to treat the VAT incurred on the purchase of the blinds as recoverable from HMRC under the provisions of the DIY Housebuilders and Converters VAT Refund Scheme (VATA 1994 s.35).

HMRC'S POSITION

HMRC's view remains unchanged in that roller blinds (and other 'window furniture') are not 'building materials' as defined and will not be changing its policy. The Tribunal chairman did not hear any evidence on the point of what is and what is not a 'building material' for VAT purposes but reached his conclusion as a matter of judicial notice, that is, as a common sense fact.

Given the small amount of VAT at stake in this particular case, HMRC will not be appealing this decision further.

[. . .]

[VATA 1994 Sch 8 Group 5 Note 22]

9 FEBRUARY 2011. REVENUE & CUSTOMS BRIEF 4/11 [COMMERCIALLY OPERATED SPORTS LEAGUES]

This brief confirms HMRC's view of the VAT treatment of commercially operated sports leagues. It has been issued in response to enquiries from a number of organisations that run football leagues. The brief reflects what HMRC's policy has always been. It does not represent a change of policy.

BACKGROUND

There are a number of commercial organisations that run football and other sports leagues ('sports league providers'). Typically, a sports league provider will do most or all of the following:

- organise a league
- allocate fixtures to teams in the league
- provide pitches for teams to play on (some league providers own pitches, others rent them from other parties)
- provide referees
- determine results
- keep and publish scores and league tables
- award trophies to winning teams

Payments for such supplies are collected in a variety of ways. For example, the sports league provider may charge a one off 'admin fee' to teams plus a 'match fee' for each game that is played.

VAT LIABILITY

Some sports league providers have suggested that they are making supplies of land of a kind that are exempt under VATA 1994 Sch 9 Group 1 (they rely on Note 16 to Group 1 which allows a series of lets of sports pitches to be exempt, subject to certain conditions). They consider that the essential nature of their supplies is one of pitch hire.

HMRC disagrees with this analysis. We consider that the supplies made by sports league providers consist of a bundle of elements, which are integral to each other, but that it cannot be said that there is one principal element to which all others are ancillary. In these circumstances, it is necessary to establish the character of the overarching supply to determine whether it falls within the exemption. In HMRC's view, the overarching supply is of participation in a sports league, not a supply of land.

It is therefore HMRC's view that the supplies made by commercial sports league providers are liable to the standard rate of VAT.

However, supplies made by certain non-profit making bodies may fall within the Group 10 sports exemption. For details of the conditions that must be met for the Group 10 exemption to apply, please see Notice No 701/45.

[. . .]

[VATA 1994 Sch 9 Group 1]

6 APRIL 2011. REVENUE & CUSTOMS BRIEF 15/11 PENALTIES: CHANGE TO HMRC'S VIEW OF THE OPERATION OF THE DELAYED TAX PROVISIONS FOR INACCURACY PENALTIES

INTRODUCTION

The purpose of this brief is to explain a change in how HM Revenue & Customs (HMRC) views the operation of the 'delayed tax' provision of the new penalties for inaccuracies, introduced in FA 2007 Sch 24 para 8.

[. . .]

BACKGROUND

Under FA 2007, new penalties were introduced for inaccuracies on returns or other documents. Under these penalties, if a return contains an inaccuracy that relates to a timing error which is automatically reversed in a subsequent tax period, the penalty is not calculated on the full amount of tax underpaid in the first period, but on a reduced amount to take account of the timing error.

For example, if someone reclaims £100,000 VAT on a purchase in period 1 when it should have been reclaimed in period 2, they claim £100,000 too much in the first period but £100,000 too little in the second. Any penalty for the overclaim in period 1 is not calculated on the £100,000 but on a reduced amount to take account of the automatic reversal of the inaccuracy in period 2.

CURRENT POSITION

HMRC's approach to date has been that in order for the penalty to be calculated in this way, the customer had to have submitted both the return containing the initial inaccuracy, and the one containing the automatic reversal of the inaccuracy in a later period. This means that in some cases HMRC has charged a penalty on the full amount because they acted to correct the inaccuracy on the first return before the second return could be submitted, thereby preventing the inaccuracy from being reversed.

REVISED POSITION

HMRC is changing its approach for cases where HMRC intervened to correct the inaccuracy before the second return was received, preventing the inaccuracy from being reversed. When HMRC are satisfied that, but for their intervention, the inaccuracy would have been automatically corrected in a subsequent return, customers will receive the reduced penalty based on the rules for delayed tax. HMRC will shortly update our guidance to reflect this.

[. . .]

[FA 2007 Sch 24 para 8]

25 MARCH 2011. REVENUE & CUSTOMS BRIEF 16/11
VAT: REVERSE CHARGES WITHIN VAT GROUPS – LEGISLATING A VAT GROUPING EXTRA STATUTORY CONCESSION (ESC 3.2.2)

1. INTRODUCTION

HM Revenue & Customs (HMRC) have a published Extra Statutory Concession (ESC) covering how a tax charge applicable to VAT groups should be calculated[: see Notice No 48 (December 2010) para 3.2.2 ("ESC 3.2.2")]. HMRC is reviewing all its ESCs following R (on the application of Wilkinson) v IR Comrs [2006] STC 270, HL. ESC 3.2.2 is not 'Wilkinson' compliant. The Government intends to legislate to give statutory effect to ESC 3.2.2. This Brief sets out how the ESC should be applied in the interim.

[. . .]

3. BACKGROUND

A VAT group comprises two or more corporate bodies under common control within a single VAT registration. A VAT group can contain members that are established overseas provided that they are also established in the UK. Transactions between members of a VAT group are normally disregarded for VAT purposes.

In the mid-1990s a VAT avoidance scheme allowed partly exempt VAT groups to avoid paying VAT on certain services they bought in. The services involved were those where the VAT is accounted for by the customer. Services used in the UK would be bought by a VAT group member abroad so that UK VAT would not be charged (the supply being made outside the UK and thus outside the scope of UK VAT). The services would then be routed to the UK user via an intra-VAT group charge. As intra-VAT group charges were ignored for VAT purposes no VAT was chargeable at that point either. The net result was VAT-free services.

In the mid-1990s a VAT avoidance scheme allowed partly exempt VAT groups to avoid paying VAT on certain services they bought in. The services involved were those where the VAT is accounted for by the customer. Services used in the UK would be bought by a VAT group member abroad so that UK VAT would not be charged (the supply being made outside the UK and thus outside the scope of UK VAT). The services would then be routed to the UK user via an intra-VAT group charge. As intra-VAT group charges were ignored for VAT purposes no VAT was chargeable at that point either. The net result was VAT-free services.

- the supply incorporated services bought by the overseas member that would be treated as supplied here if bought by the UK members ('reverse charge services')
- and the supply was taxable and itself would have been treated as supplied in the UK

The legislation applied the tax charge to the whole intra-group transaction whereas the avoidance scheme only related to services bought in from third parties.

[. . .]

6. HOW ESC 3.2.2 SHOULD BE APPLIED UNTIL IT IS LEGISLATED

Where a group makes use of this ESC, it should be applied in a way that maintains its intended effect. To achieve this, the reference to Schedule 5 should be read as a reference to the new general rule for supplies to businesses, in VATA 1994 s 7A(2)(a). The ESC will continue to allow VAT groups to value the tax charge by reference to the services the overseas member has bought in that would now be treated as subject to UK VAT if the UK group member bought them direct. Evidence of the value of the services bought in, and that they have not been undervalued, will still be needed.

7. LEGISLATING ESC 3.2.2

The Government will commence a technical consultation with stakeholders in May 2011.

The Government will commence a technical consultation with stakeholders in May 2011.

1 APRIL 2011. REVENUE & CUSTOMS BRIEF 19/11 VAT TREATMENT OF SUPPLIES OF HOT FOOD MADE IN THE COURSE OF CATERING

BACKGROUND

The ECJ ruled [in *Finanzamt Burgdorf v Manfred Bog; CinemaxX Entertainment GmbH & Co KG v Finanzamt Hamburg-Barmbek-Uhlenhorst; Lothar Lohmeyer v Finanzamt Minden; Fleischerei Nier GmbH & Co KG v Finanzamt Detmold* (joined cases C-479/09, C-499/09, C-501/09 and C-502/09) [2011] STC 1221, ECJ] that the supply of food or meals freshly prepared for immediate consumption from snack stalls, mobile snack bars or in cinema foyers is a supply of goods within the meaning of Directive 77/388/EEC art 5 if a qualitative examination of the entire transaction shows that the elements of supply of services preceding and accompanying the supply of the food are not predominant. This is unlike the activities of a party catering service which are supplies of services within the meaning of 77/388/EEC art 6 except in cases in which a party catering service does no more than deliver standard meals without any additional elements of supply of services.

Furthermore, the ECJ has held that the term 'foodstuffs' in Directive 77/388/EEC Annex H category 1 as amended by Directive 92/111/EEC (now Directive 2006/112/EC Annex III category 1), must be interpreted as also covering food and meals which have been prepared for immediate consumption by boiling, grilling, roasting, baking or other means.

The significance of the decision for German taxpayers is that certain supplies of hot food may now be eligible for the reduced rate.

HM REVENUE & CUSTOM'S (HMRC) POSITION

The UK treats most basic supplies of foodstuffs as zero rated but along with other specified items there is a specific exclusion from the zero-rate for supplies made in the course of catering. The Law (VATA 1994 Sch 8 Group 1 Note 3) goes further to specifically legislate for certain supplies of food that are for consumption on and off premises including the supply of hot food.

Directive 2006/112/EC art 110 allows the UK to retain its zero-rate for food as long as there are clearly defined social reasons and the supplies are for the benefit of the final consumer. There can be no extension to the zero-rate provisions and the Courts have determined that exemptions (including zero rating) must be construed strictly, but exceptions from the exemption (including Note 3) should not be construed restrictively.

The zero rating provisions form a specific legal framework and subject to the conditions of the derogation the UK has discretion as to what supplies fall within those provisions. Since the UK has specifically legislated to exclude supplies of hot food it is clear that the intention was not to include such supplies within the zero-rate.

CONCLUSION

HMRC considers that the ECJ judgment has no implications for the UK treatment of supplies of hot food and businesses should continue to treat their supplies in accordance with published guidance.

[VATA 1994 Sch 8 Group 1]

16 MAY 2011. REVENUE & CUSTOMS BRIEF 20/11 ACCOUNTING FOR ACQUISITION VAT ON INTRA-EU SUPPLIES – CHANGES TO THE 'FALLBACK' PROVISIONS

INTRODUCTION

This brief announces a change in VAT treatment where a business uses a UK VAT registration number (other than for triangulation purposes – see below) to secure zero-rating of goods sent from one EU Member State to another, without arriving in the UK.

Under what is often referred to as the 'fallback' provision, use of a UK VAT registration number in these circumstances makes the customer liable to account for acquisition VAT in the UK. Significantly this does not cancel any liability to account for acquisition VAT in the Member State to which the goods are sent ('the Member State of arrival'). However, the UK VAT can be adjusted if VAT is accounted for correctly in the Member State of arrival.

The fallback rule is explained in Notice No 725 para 7.7 (The Single Market). The change follows the judgement of the Court of Justice of the European Union ("CJEU") in *Staatssecretaris van Financiën v X; Staatssecretaris van Financiën v fiscale eenheid Facet BV/Facet Trading BV* (joined cases C-536/08 and C-539/08) [2010] STC 1221, ECJ.

THE CJEU DECISION

The issue before the CJEU arose from two similar cases. In each, supplies of computer goods were sourced from Member States other than the Netherlands and sent direct to customers located elsewhere in the EU. Dutch VAT registration numbers were used to secure zero-rating of the intra-EU supplies. The CJEU was asked to consider whether there was a right to deduct the acquisition VAT each of the taxpayers was required to account for under the Dutch equivalent of the fallback provision, as input tax.

In its decision the CJEU held that there could be no right to deduct acquisition VAT where it falls due under the fallback arrangements as the goods did not actually enter the Member State. In arriving at its decision the Court noted that if there were a right to deduct in these circumstances, it could jeopardise the operation of the normal rules as it would remove the incentive for the acquisition to be taxed in the Member State of arrival.

EFFECT OF THE DECISION

The decision provides a welcome clarification of what was previously an uncertain position. The liability to account for acquisition VAT where a UK VAT registration number is used in the course of an intra-EU supply of goods not involving removal to the UK remains unchanged. However, it is now clear that there is no right to recover the acquisition VAT as input tax. The only basis on which the UK VAT may be adjusted is where it can be demonstrated that acquisition VAT has been accounted for in the Member State of arrival.

TRIANGULATION SIMPLIFIED PROCEDURE

Use of a UK VAT registration number as part of the triangulation simplification arrangements (see Notice No 725 section 13) is unaffected.

IMPACT ON ACQUISITIONS OF YACHTS IN THE UK

In 1997 Customs & Excise agreed to arrangements under which a UK VAT registered business could account for acquisition VAT in the UK on a yacht purchased from a supplier in another Member State without the yacht arriving in the UK. This was announced in Business Brief 12/97, 5 June 1997 [. . .] which also permitted input tax deduction subject to the normal rules.

Following the CJEU decision the UK acquirer may now no longer recover the UK acquisition VAT as input tax. For this reason the agreement will cease to have effect and so is to be withdrawn from 1 June 2011. After that date UK acquisition VAT accounted for on a yacht that does not arrive in the UK will no longer be recoverable as input tax. However, as a transitional measure, any UK VAT registered business who, before 1 June 2011, entered into a contract for the purchase of a yacht and who intended to adopt the procedure as agreed in Business Brief 12/97, may continue to rely on those arrangements (including recovery of the acquisition VAT as input tax, subject to the normal rules) when the yacht is eventually delivered. But this is subject their holding satisfactory evidence of the contract and the date that it was agreed.

[. . .]

[VATA 1994 s 10]

21 JUNE 2011. REVENUE & CUSTOMS BRIEF 23/11 VAT: INTRODUCTION OF LEVY ON 'SINGLE-USE' CARRIER BAGS IN WALES

1. INTRODUCTION

The Welsh Assembly Government is to introduce a compulsory charge on 'single-use' carrier bags which retailers must charge to customers in Wales, with effect from 1 October 2011.

This is not a HM Revenue & Customs measure, but it has implications for VAT and Direct Tax. This brief explains the basics of the charge and the tax implications.

2. WHO NEEDS TO READ THIS?

All retailers within Wales, and any retailers outside Wales who deliver goods to customers in Wales using 'single-use' carrier bags.

3. BACKGROUND

The Welsh Assembly Government is to introduce a compulsory charge (initially to be set at a minimum of 5 pence) on single-use carrier bags which retailers in Wales must charge to their customers. Retailers outside Wales who deliver goods to customers in Wales using single-use carrier bags will also have to make the charge.

The relevant legislation will be effective from 1 October 2011 and full details of how the charge is to operate is contained in the draft guidance available from the Welsh Assembly Government website [. . .].

4. VAT IMPLICATIONS

The charge is consideration for the bag and is taxable at the standard rate of VAT. In order that customers pay the same amount regardless of the VAT status of the business, the stated minimum charge (initially 5 pence) is the minimum total to be charged by non-VAT-registered businesses. The stated minimum charge will be deemed to include VAT when charged by a VAT-registered business.

Thus, for the avoidance of doubt, A VAT-registered business would charge 4.17 pence plus VAT.

Retail Scheme users should ensure that this is properly accounted through their scheme where applicable.

[. . .]

Note. For the charge on carrier bags, see The Single User Carrier Bags Charge (Wales) Regulations 2010, SI 2010/2880 (W.238) as amended by The Single User Carrier Bags Charge (Wales) (Amendment) Regulations 2011, SI 2011/2184 (W.236).

[SI 1995/2518 reg 67]

7 JULY 2011. REVENUE & CUSTOMS BRIEF 24/11 WITHDRAWAL OF BUSINESS BRIEF 28/04 ITEM 2 ISSUED 25 OCTOBER 2004

VAT - CORRECTING LIABILITY ERRORS MADE BY HMRC

[. . .]

Revenue & Customs Brief 15/09 (27 March 2009) confirmed that HMRC is bound by incorrect advice only in the circumstances explained in *When you can rely on information provided by HM Revenue & Customs (HMRC)* [reproduced in Appendix 19]. [. . .]

Taxpayers will usually only be required to apply the new interpretation of the law from a current or future date that HMRC will announce when advising on the correct interpretation.

If, following HMRC's announcement of its new interpretation of the law, a business nevertheless chooses to correct historical errors, HMRC will accept the corrections providing all of the following conditions are met:

- all past errors are corrected
- the neutrality of the tax is respected
- the business is no better off and the Exchequer no worse off than they would have been if the mistaken interpretation had not been made

As explained in Business Brief 28/04 (not reproduced), taxpayers will not usually be required to register in respect of previous supplies they had treated as exempt based on HMRC's interpretation of the law at the time of supply.

For example, a court rules that supplies previously regarded by HMRC as exempt were, and had always been, liable to VAT. HMRC would not usually require businesses affected by such rulings to register for VAT in relation to taxable supplies they made prior to the court decision. Businesses that choose to register for periods prior to the binding court decision on liability must satisfy the normal rules for VAT registration. They must also apply correct accounting procedures, including those for exempt supplies and associated input tax restrictions. They must also be able to submit supporting calculations and evidence any input tax deductions.

[VATA 1994 Sch 1 para 1]

28 JULY 2011. REVENUE & CUSTOMS BRIEF 28/11 VAT: CHANGES TO THE TREATMENT OF CERTAIN SUPPLIES MADE BY EMPLOYERS UNDER SALARY SACRIFICE ARRANGEMENTS FOLLOWING THE CJEU JUDGMENT IN CASE C-40/09

1.1 BACKGROUND

Astra Zeneca operated a flexible remuneration package scheme under which employees could opt to take part of their remuneration in the form of goods and/or services rather than as salary. The case before the Court of Justice of the European Union (CJEU) [*Astra Zenica v R & C Comrs* (case C-40/09) [2010] STC 2298, ECJ] concerned the correct VAT treatment of high street shopping vouchers provided to employees as one of the options of the scheme.

The Court found that the provision of vouchers amounted to a supply of services effected for consideration. As a consequence, whilst Astra Zeneca was able to recover VAT incurred on acquiring the vouchers, output tax was due on the consideration received from its employees.

Although this case was concerned with the supply of vouchers to employees, the principles considered by the Court are of general application and will apply to other supplies of goods and services to employees.

1.2 THE UK POSITION ON THE PROVISION OF GOODS AND SERVICES VIA SALARY SACRIFICE OR DEDUCTIONS FROM SALARY

Following earlier decisions by the UK courts, HM Revenue & Customs' (HMRC) policy was to make a distinction between the VAT treatment of supplies of goods and services to employees by a deduction from salary, and those provided under a salary sacrifice arrangement.

1.2.1 DEDUCTION FROM SALARY

This occurs where an amount is deducted from an employee's pay in return for a supply of goods or services by the employer. Output tax has always been and continues to be due on the amount deducted from salary. Input tax is recoverable in accordance with the normal rules.

1.2.2 SALARY SACRIFICE

For VAT purposes 'salary sacrifice' has a very narrow and specific meaning. It describes an arrangement such as in [*Co-operative Insurance Society* (No 7109)] where an employee opts to receive services and forgoes part of their salary in return. The employee enters into a new employment contract or has their existing contract amended to reflect the new arrangement which they are tied into.

In relation to such schemes HMRC have, to date, accepted that the reduction in the salary did not constitute consideration for the benefits received and output tax was not due. Employers were able to recover the related VAT as input tax, subject to the normal rules.

In relation to such schemes HMRC have, to date, accepted that the reduction in the salary did not constitute consideration for the benefits received and output tax was not due. Employers were able to recover the related VAT as input tax, subject to the normal rules.

1.3 THE JUDGMENT OF THE CJEU

The Court considered whether the provision of the vouchers was a supply for a consideration. It found that there was a direct link between the provision of the retail vouchers by the company to its employees and the part of the cash remuneration which the employees gave up.

As far as arrangements involving deductions from salaries are concerned, the judgment supports HMRC's existing policy that these are consideration for a supply for VAT purposes.

However, HMRC considers that the rationale used by the CJEU goes wider than deductions from salary, and as a consequence of this there is no longer a distinction between deductions from salary and a salary sacrifice. Therefore, the amount of salary foregone is consideration for supplies of the benefits whether provided under a salary sacrifice or by a deduction from salary.

It is clear that the principles applied by the CJEU are not confined to vouchers, but are equally applicable to many other situations where employers offer benefits to their staff. Where the benefit is subject to VAT, output tax will be due from, and input VAT recoverable by the employer in accordance with the normal rules.

1.4 IMPLEMENTATION: REVISED VAT TREATMENT OF SALARY SACRIFICE

Businesses providing benefits under arrangements, which qualify as salary sacrifice schemes for VAT purposes, must account for output VAT on these supplies, where they are subject to VAT. In order to allow businesses time to make the necessary adjustments, HMRC will not require output tax to be accounted for on taxable benefits provided under salary sacrifice schemes, until 1 January 2012.

See the annex for details of how this change of practice will apply in particular circumstances.

2. VALUATION

In most cases the value of the benefit for VAT purposes will be the same as the amount of salary deducted or the amount foregone under a salary sacrifice arrangement. Where this is less than the true value (for example where employers supply the benefits at below what it cost to buy them in), the value should be based on the cost to the employer.

[. . .]

4. EFFECT OF THE CJEU JUDGMENT IN PARTICULAR CIRCUMSTANCES

4.1 CYCLE TO WORK SCHEME

Under the Cycle to Work Scheme employers purchase bicycles and safety equipment and provide them to employees. Where this has been done under a salary sacrifice arrangement, the effect of the judgment is that employers must account for output tax based on the value of the salary foregone by the employee in exchange for the hire or loan of a bicycle.

Affected businesses should apply this treatment from 1 January 2012. Employers can continue to recover VAT on the purchase of the bicycle and associated equipment.

Employers who have provided bicycles under deduction from salary arrangements are unaffected by the judgment as payments received from employees have always been subject to VAT and will continue to be so.

VAT remains due when a bicycle is disposed of and its value should normally be based on the price of an identical or similar item, taking into account the age and condition etc.

We are aware that valuing bicycles has caused difficulties for Scheme operators and therefore, to reduce administration burdens, the table used to value bicycles for direct tax purposes may be used. This table provides valuations for bicycles based on the age and original price. Any bicycles that fall outside of the table (such as antique or specialist bicycles) should be valued using the normal VAT valuation rules. If businesses choose to use lower values, they may be challenged in which case evidence will be required to support the valuation.

4.2 FACE VALUE VOUCHERS

HMRC's published policy in relation to the provision of face value vouchers by employers to employees aligns with the judgment of the CJEU. In the case of supplies made under a deduction from salary arrangement input tax is recoverable but output tax must be declared. Where such vouchers have previously been provided under a salary sacrifice arrangement (as defined above) then input tax was claimable, subject to the normal rules, but output tax was due to the extent of the input tax claimed.

4.3 CHILDCARE VOUCHERS

Childcare vouchers are not directly affected by the judgment as they are not subject to VAT.

However, employers that incur administrative fees from their voucher provider have, to date, been permitted to recover VAT on those fees as a general business overhead. However, because the fees are directly attributable to the exempt supply of vouchers the normal partial exemption rules must be applied with the result that the VAT incurred may no longer be fully recoverable.

Affected businesses should apply this treatment from 1 January 2012.

4.4 FOOD AND CATERING PROVIDED BY EMPLOYERS

Employers may provide their staff with free or subsidised meals, snacks or drinks. Where employees pay for the meal etc, the normal VAT liability will apply.

If employees make no payment, VAT is not due (provided the benefit is available to all staff).

The judgment does not affect the VAT treatment where employees pay for their meals etc by a deduction from salary as VAT remains due.

However, from 1 January 2012 where employees pay for meals etc under a salary sacrifice arrangement, employers must account for VAT on the value of the supplies unless they are zero-rated. Subject to the normal rules, the employer can continue to recover the VAT incurred on related purchases.

HMRC are aware, that historically some employers have set up what they purport to be salary sacrifice arrangements to avoid VAT that is due on the consideration provided by employees for their meals, for example using electronic payments cards which record the value of consideration that is available to purchase meals. HMRC will continue to challenge such arrangements.

4.5 BENEFITS PROVIDED TO ALL EMPLOYEES FOR NO DEDUCTION OR REDUCTION FROM SALARY

The judgment only applies where an employee provides consideration in exchange for benefits. Where an employer provides, for example, a workplace gym which all employees may use for no deduction or reduction from their salary that will not fall within the scope of the judgment. Businesses may continue to recover VAT incurred on providing such facilities as a business overhead subject to the normal rules.

Separate charges to use facilities etc remain within the scope of VAT.

4.6 MOTOR CARS

Most businesses are prevented from recovering VAT in full on the purchase and leasing of company motor cars. The input tax block on cars (100 per cent on purchases and 50 per cent on leasing) means that employers do not account for output tax when cars are made available to employees. Where VAT recovery is restricted and output VAT is not due the judgment has no direct impact.

Where an employer suffers no input tax restriction, output tax remains due.

[VATA 1994 s 5]

27 JULY 2011. REVENUE & CUSTOMS BRIEF 30/11 VAT: HMRC'S POSITION FOLLOWING THE FIRST-TIER TRIBUNAL DECISION IN THE CASE OF THE BRIDPORT AND WEST DORSET GOLF CLUB LIMITED

This brief explains HM Revenue & Customs' (HMRC's) position following the First-Tier Tribunal decision in the case of The Bridport and West Dorset Golf Club (TC 1214). The appeal concerned the VAT liability of green fees charged by the golf club to non-members.

BACKGROUND

Bridport and West Dorset Golf Club is a non-profit making members' golf club. The issue before the tribunal was whether the charges, known as green fees, made by the club to visiting non-members in return for the right to play golf are exempt from VAT or, as HMRC maintained, standard rated.

Under VATA 1994 Schedule 9 Group 10 Item 3, supplies by non-profit making bodies of services closely linked and essential to sport to individuals taking part in sport are exempt from VAT. However, where the body operates a membership scheme, any supplies to individuals who are not members are excluded from the exemption and subject to VAT.

The tribunal concluded that by restricting the exemption to supplies made to members, the UK law was acting contrary to the purpose of the exemption in the Principal VAT Directive (or, in other words, had failed to "correctly implement its terms"). It was not persuaded by HMRC's argument that the exclusion applied to non-members was justified on grounds that it reduced distortion of competition. As a result, it agreed with the golf club that supplies to non-members of green fees were exempt from VAT.

HMRC'S POSITION

HMRC believes that the tribunal has erred in interpreting EU law and remains of the view that where clubs that run membership schemes make charges to non-members for the use of certain sporting facilities, such as green fees, the charges are standard rated. They have, as a result, sought permission to appeal to the Upper Tier Tribunal.

Decisions of the First-Tier Tribunal are binding only on the parties to the decision. Consequently, we do not propose to pay other claims already submitted and we are not inviting new claims in the wake of this decision. Any claims that are submitted will be rejected.

HMRC consider that businesses should continue to follow the guidance in Notice 701/45 Sport and standard-rate these types of supplies made to non-members of a membership club. Should any golf clubs decide to exempt their green fees on the basis of the First-Tier Tribunal's decision, HMRC will assess the underdeclared tax and enforce the assessments. Penalties may also be applicable in such cases.

[VATA 1994 Sch 9 Group 10 Item 3]

APPENDIX 2. VAT NOTICES AND INFORMATION SHEETS

The following lists are derived from the electronic version of Notice No 999 . The English language editions of notices have been listed in so far as they relate wholly or partly to VAT. Subsidiary notices have been given a suffix indicating the year of publication. Information sheets relating to VAT have been divided into separate lists for those of general interest and those relating to electronically supplied services. For notices, codes of practice and factsheets relating to investigations and compliance checks, see Appendix 10. Notices and information sheets can be viewed on-line or downloaded from the HMRC website (www.hmrc.gov.uk). Printed versions can be obtained from the National Advice Service (telephone: 0845 010 9000).

Main notice	*Subsidiary notices*	*Title*
12A		**What you can do if things are seized by HMRC**
48		**Extra-statutory concessions**
60		**Intrastat— general guide**
101		**Deferring duty, VAT and other charges**
143		**A guide for international post users**
160		**Compliance checks into indirect tax matters**
161		**Investigation into traders with suspected serious indirect tax irregularities**
179		**Motor and heating fuels: general information and accounting for excise duty and VAT**
197		**Excise goods: receipt into and removal from an excise warehouse of excise goods**
199		**Imported goods: customs procedures and customs debt**
232		**Customs warehousing**
236		**Customs: importing returned goods free of duty and tax**
252		**Valuation of imported goods for customs purposes, VAT and trade statistics**
266		**Rejected imports: repayment or remission of duty and VAT**
275		**Export procedures**
300		**Civil evasion penalty investigations—statement of practice**
301		**Civil penalties for contraventions of customs law**
317		**Imports by charities free of duty and VAT**
334		**Free zones**
340		**Importing scientific instruments free of duty and VAT**
341		**Importing donated medical equipment free of duty and VAT**
342		**Importing miscellaneous documents and other related articles free of duty and VAT**
343		**Importing capital goods free of duty and VAT**
361		**Importing museum and gallery exhibits free of duty and VAT**
362		**Imported antiques**
364		**Importing decorations and awards free of duty and VAT**

Main notice	*Subsidiary notices*	*Title*
365		**Importing animals for scientific research free of duty and VAT**
366		**Importing biological and chemical substances for research free of duty and VAT**
367		**Importing commercial samples of negligible value free of duty and VAT**
368		**Importing inherited goods free of duty and VAT**
369		**Importing blood grouping, tissue typing and therapeutic substances duty and VAT free**
371		**Importing goods for disabled people free of duty and VAT**
373		**Importing visual and auditory materials free of duty and VAT**
374		**Importing goods for test free of duty and VAT**
431		**Visiting forces**
700		**The VAT guide**
	700/1/10	Should I be registered for VAT?
	700/2/04	Group and divisional registration
	700/6/09	VAT rulings
	700/7/02	Business promotion schemes
	700/8/06	Disclosure of VAT avoidance schemes
	700/9/08	Transfer of a business as a going concern
	700/11/10	Cancelling your registration
	700/12/02	Filling in your return
	700/14/04	Video cassette films: rental and part-exchange
	700/15/02	The ins and outs of VAT
	700/17/02	Funded pension schemes
	700/18/02	Relief from VAT on bad debts
	700/21/07	Keeping VAT records
	700/24/03	Postage and delivery charges
	700/25/02	Taxis and private hire cars
	700/34/05	Staff
	700/35/97	Business gifts and samples
	700/41/11	Late registration penalty
	700/42/11	Misdeclaration penalty and repeated misdeclaration
	700/43/10	Default interest
	700/44/07	Barristers and advocates
	700/45/11	How to correct VAT errors and make adjustments or claims
	700/46/02	Agricultural flat rate scheme
	700/47/93	Confidentiality in VAT matters (tax advisers)—statement of practice
	700/50/11	Default surcharge
	700/52/10	Notice of requirement to give security to Customs and Excise
	700/56/06	Insolvency
	700/57/04	Administrative agreements entered into with trade bodies

Main notice	***Subsidiary notices***	***Title***
	700/58/10	Treatment of VAT repayment returns and VAT repayment supplement
	700/60/09	Payments on account
	700/62/03	Self-billing
	700/63/07	Electronic invoicing
	700/64/07	Motoring expenses
	700/65/02	Business entertainment
	700/67/02	Registration scheme for racehorse owners
(701)	701/1/04	Charities
	701/2/11	Welfare
	701/5/02	Clubs and associations
	701/6/03	Charity funded equipment for medical, veterinary etc uses
	701/7/02	VAT reliefs for disabled people
	701/8/03	Postage stamps and philatelic supplies
	701/9/02	Derivatives and terminal markets
	701/10/10	Zero-rating of books etc
	701/12/02	Disposal of antiques, works of art etc from historic houses
	701/13/04	Gaming and amusement machines
	701/14/02	Food
	701/15/02	Animals and animal food
	701/16/02	Water and sewerage services
	701/18/11	Women's sanitary protection products
	701/19/10	Fuel and power
	701/20/04	Caravans and houseboats
	701/21/02	Gold
	701/21A/11	Investment gold coins
	701/22/02	Tools for the manufacture of goods for export
	701/23/11	Protective equipment
	701/26/04	Betting and gaming
	701/27/07	Bingo
	701/28/03	Lotteries
	701/29/11	Betting, gaming and lotteries
	701/30/11	Education and vocational training
	701/31/07	Health institutions
	701/32/06	Burial, cremation and the commemoration of the dead
	701/35/11	Youth clubs
	701/36/02	Insurance
	701/38/03	Seeds and plants
	701/40/02	Food processing services
	701/41/02	Sponsorship
	701/45/02	Sport
	701/47/03	Culture
	701/48/02	Corporate purchasing cards
	701/49/09	Finance

Main notice	*Subsidiary notices*	*Title*
	701/57/07	Health professionals
	701/58/02	Charity advertising and goods connected with collecting donations
	701/59/02	Motor vehicles for disabled people
702		**Imports**
	702/7/10	Import VAT relief for goods supplied onward to another country in the EC
	702/8/11	Fiscal warehousing
	702/9/05	VAT: import customs procedures
	702/10/09	VAT: tax warehousing
703		**VAT export of goods from the United Kingdom**
	703/1/10	Supply of freight containers for export or removal from the United Kingdom
	703/2/11	Sailaway boats supplied for export outside the EC
	703/3/02	Sailaway boat scheme
704		**VAT retail exports**
	704/1/04	VAT refunds for travellers departing from the European Community
705		**Buyer's guide to personal exports of motor vehicles to destinations outside [the] EU**
705A		**VAT: supplies of vehicles under the personal export scheme for removal from [the] EC**
706		**Partial exemption**
	706/2/02	Capital goods scheme
708		**Buildings and construction**
	708/6/06	Energy-saving materials
(709)	709/1/07	Catering and takeaway food
	709/3/02	Hotels and holiday accommodation
	709/5/09	Tour operators' margin scheme
	709/6/02	Travel agents and tour operators
714		**Zero-rating young children's clothing and footwear**
718		**The VAT margin scheme and global accounting**
	718/1/11	The VAT margin scheme on second-hand cars and other vehicles
	718/2/11	The VAT auctioneers' scheme
719		**VAT refunds for "do-it-yourself" builders and converters**
723		**Refunds of VAT in the EC for EC and non-EC business [to 31 December 2009]**
723A		**Refunds of VAT in the European Community for EC and non-EC business [from 1 January 2010]**
725		**The single market**
726		**Joint and several liability for unpaid VAT**
727		**Retail schemes**
	727/2/11	Bespoke retail schemes
	727/3/11	Retail schemes: how to work the point of sale scheme
	727/4/11	Retail schemes: how to work the apportionment schemes

Main notice	*Subsidiary notices*	*Title*
	727/5/11	Retail schemes: how to work the direct calculations schemes
728		**New means of transport**
730		**Civil penalty investigations [commencing before 1 September 2005]: statement of practice**
731		**Cash accounting**
732		**Annual accounting**
733		**Flat rate scheme for small businesses**
735		**VAT reverse charge for mobile phones and computer chips**
741		**Place of supply of services (before I January 2010)**
741A		**Place of supply of services [from 1 January 2010]**
742		**Land and property**
	742/3/05	Scottish land law terms
742A		**Opting to tax land and buildings**
744A		**Passenger transport**
744B		**Freight transport and associated services**
744C		**Ships, aircraft and associated services**
747		**VAT notices having the force of law**
749		**Local authorities and similar bodies**
910		**How we use the information we collect: our code of practice**
915		**Assessments and time limits: statement of practice**
920		**The single currency**
930		**What if I don't pay?**
951		**Freedom of Information Act 2000**
989		**Visits by Customs and Excise officers**
998		**VAT refund scheme for national museums and galleries**
Factsheet		**Complaints and putting things right**
02/CD/010		Flying abroad? Bringing back cigarettes or alcohol? Don't be taken for a smuggler
02/CD/013		Entering the UK from another EU country: Customs rules fact and fiction
02/CD/22		Transporting excise goods in the United Kingdom
02/CD/26		The Joint Shadow Economy Teams—tackling the shadow economy
Misc 5		Help for your business in the construction industry
Misc 176		Help for your business in the catering and hospitality trade
CWL4		Fund-raising events: exemption for charities and other qualifying bodies
SIVA 1		Simplified import VAT accounting (SIVA)

Information sheets: general

Reference	*Title*
3/96	Tour operators' margin scheme—practical implementation of the "airline charter option" following the changes which came into effect on 1 January 1996
4/96	Tour operators' margin scheme—practical implementation of the "agency option" following the changes which came into effect on 1 January 1996
1/97	Tour operators' margin scheme—practical implications of the "trader to trader (wholesale) option" following the changes which came into effect on 1 January 1996
3/98	Local authorities and NHS—joint stores depots
5/98	Local authorities—supplies to new unitary authorities under local government reorganisation (transitional arrangements)
6/98	Local authority pension funds—VAT treatment and administrative concession
8/98	Charities: supply, repair and maintenance of relevant goods (including adapted motor vehicles)
2/99	Local authorities: agreement of section 33 recovery methods
3/99	New Deal Programme
6/99	Charities: liability of routine domestic tasks
8/99	Opticians: apportionment of charges for supplies of spectacles and dispensing
9/99	Imported works of art, antiques and collectors' pieces: changes to the reduced rate of VAT
12/99	VAT on business cars: changes to take effect on 1 December 1999
2/00	Exports and removals: conditions for zero-rating
3/00	Supplies through undisclosed agents: revised VAT treatment
2/01	Single or multiple supplies—how to decide
4/02	Budget 2002: VAT: partial exemption—standard method over-ride
6/03	Tribunal decision on VAT treatment of repossessed and voluntarily returned cars
11/03	Electronic point of sale (EPOS) systems
12/03	Face value vouchers
14/03	New time of supply rules for on-going supplies
5/04	Claims made in the light of GMAC High Court decision: VAT treatment of returned cars and other goods
7/04	Eligibility rules for VAT grouping
9/04	Partial exemption—fair recovery of costs of incidental financial supplies
6/05	Business travel agents
8/05	Recovery of VAT by businesses on fuel purchased by employees on their behalf
3/06	Dispensing doctors and VAT registration
5/06	VAT: supplies of goods under finance agreements
11/06	VAT: guidance on the VAT treatment of certain Islamic products

Information sheets: general

Reference	*Title*
12/06	VAT: further information for dispensing doctors
5/07	VAT: further information for health professionals affected by the changes to the exemption for medical services
8/07	VAT: reverse charge for purchases and sales of mobile phones and computer chips
10/07	Changes to VAT invoicing with effect from October 2007
11/07	Accounting for VAT on standard-rated prescription products
12/07	Transfer of a going concern (TOGC): changes to VAT record keeping requirements
14/07	HMRC guidance—assets used partly for non-business purposes
15/07	VAT: supply of parts and equipment for qualifying ships and aircraft
4/08	Supplies of government grant funded research
7/08	VAT: partial exemption—VAT adjustments when house builders let their dwellings before selling them
3/09	Withdrawal of the VAT staff hire concession on 1 April 2009
4/09	Partial exemption: changes to the standard method
7/09	VAT: private use charge for motor manufacturers' company cars, dealer demonstrators and daily rental cars
8/09	Changes to the zero-rate for buildings used for a relevant charitable use
03/10	VAT status of university trading companies: new guidelines
04/10	VAT: partial exemption—changes to the de minimis rules
13/10	Calculating qualifying use for a charitable or a communal residential building
21/10	Place of supply of natural gas and electricity (also heat and cooling)
4/11	Change in use provisions
5/11	Dispensing doctors (Scotland) and VAT registration
6/11	Implementing the VAT Technical Directive and changes to the partial exemption and capital goods scheme rules
8/11	VAT: Motor manufacturer's company cars, dealer demonstrators, daily rental cars
9/11	VAT refund scheme for academies

Information sheets: electronically supplied services

Reference	*Title*
1/03	Electronically supplied services and broadcasting services: new EU place of supply rules
4/03	Electronically supplied services: a guide to interpretation
5/03	Electronically supplied services: evidence of customer location and status

Information sheets: electronically supplied services

Reference	*Title*
7/03	Electronically supplied services: special scheme for non-EU businesses
10/03	Electronically supplied services: supplementary information on the special scheme for non-EU businesses
13/03	Electronically supplied services: VAT on e-services (VoeS) special scheme for non-EU businesses—currency exchange rates for reporting period ending 30 September 2003
1/04	Electronically supplied services: special scheme for non-EU businesses—currency exchange rates for reporting period ending 31 December 2003
3/04	Electronically supplied services: EU enlargement
4/04	Electronically supplied services: special scheme for non-EU businesses—currency exchange rates for reporting period ending 31 March 2004
6/04	Electronically supplied services: special scheme for non-EU businesses—currency exchange rates for reporting period ending 30 June 2004
8/04	Electronically supplied services: special scheme for non-EU businesses—currency exchange rates for reporting period ending 30 September 2004
11/04	Electronically supplied services: special scheme for non-EU businesses—currency exchange rates for reporting period ending 31 December 2004
1/05	Electronically supplied services: special scheme for non-EU businesses—currency exchange rates for reporting period ending 31 March 2005
2/05	Electronically supplied services: special scheme for non-EU businesses—changes to Greece VAT rate
3/05	Electronically supplied services: special scheme for non-EU businesses—currency exchange rates for reporting period ending 30 June 2005
4/05	Electronically supplied services: special scheme for non-EU businesses—change to Portugal VAT rate
5/05	Electronically supplied services: special scheme for non-EU businesses—currency exchange rates for reporting period ending 30 September 2005
1/06	Electronically supplied services: special scheme for non-EU businesses—currency exchange rates for reporting period ending 30 December 2005
2/06	Electronically supplied services: special scheme for non-EU businesses—change to Hungary VAT rate
8/06	Electronically supplied services: special scheme for non-EU businesses—currency exchange rates for reporting period ending 31 March 2006
9/06	Electronically supplied services: special scheme for non-EU businesses—currency exchange rates for reporting period ending 30 June 2006
10/06	Electronically supplied services: special scheme for non-EU businesses
1/07	Electronically supplied services: special scheme for non-EU businesses—currency exchange rates for reporting period ending December 2006

Information sheets: electronically supplied services

Reference	*Title*
2/07	Electronically supplied services: special scheme for non-EU businesses—to publish the VAT rates for Bulgaria and Romania
3/07	Electronically supplied services: special scheme for non-EU businesses—changes to Germany VAT rate
4/07	Electronically supplied services: special scheme for non-EU businesses—EU enlargement 1 January 2007
7/07	Electronically supplied services: special scheme for non-EU businesses
9/07	Electronically supplied services: special scheme for non-EU businesses
13/07	Electronically supplied services: special scheme for non-EU businesses—currency exchange rates for reporting period ending September 2007
1/08	Electronically supplied services: special scheme for non-EU businesses—currency exchange rates for reporting period ending December 2007
2/08	Electronically supplied services: special scheme for non-EU businesses—currency exchange rates for reporting period ending March 2008
5/08	Electronically supplied services: currency exchange rates to June 2008
6/08	Electronically supplied services: special scheme for non-EU businesses—changes to Portugal VAT rate
9/08	Electronically supplied services: special scheme for non-EU businesses—exchange rates for period ending September 2008
11/08	Electronically supplied services: special scheme for non-EU businesses—changes to VAT rates
12/08	Electronically supplied services: special scheme for non-EU businesses —Latvia
1/09	Electronically supplied services: special scheme for non-EU businesses—changes
2/09	Electronically supplied services: special scheme for non-EU businesses—exchange rates for period ending December 2008
5/09	Electronically supplied services: special scheme for non-EU businesses—exchange rates for period ending March 2009
9/09	Electronically supplied services: special scheme for non-EU businesses—exchange rates for period ending June 2009
10/09	Electronically supplied services: special scheme for non-EU businesses—changes
11/09	Electronically supplied services: special scheme for non-EU businesses—changes
13/09	Electronically supplied services: special scheme for non-EU businesses—changes
15/09	Special scheme for non-EU businesses—exchange rates for period ending September 2009
16/09	Special scheme for non-EU businesses – change to UK VAT rate from 1 January 2010

Information sheets: electronically supplied services

Reference	*Title*
17/09	Electronically supplied services: special scheme for non-EU businesses— changes
1/10	Special scheme for non-EU businesses—exchange rates for period ending December 2009
5/10	Electronically supplied services: special scheme for non-EU businesses (Greece)
6/10	Electronically supplied services: special scheme for non-EU businesses (Czech Republic)
9/10	Special scheme for non-EU businesses—exchange rates for period ending March 2010
11/10	Electronically supplied services: special scheme for non-EU businesses—Spain
14/10	Electronically supplied services: special scheme for non-EU businesses—Finland
15/10	Electronically supplied services: special scheme for non-EU businesses—change to Greece VAT rates with effect from 1 July 2010
16/10	Electronically supplied services: special scheme for non-EU businesses—change to Romania VAT rates with effect from 1 July 2010
17/10	Special scheme for non-EU businesses—exchange rates for period ending June 2010
18/10	Change to the Portuguese VAT rate from 1 July 2010
19/10	Special scheme for non-EU businesses—exchange rates for period ending September 2010
20/10	Special scheme for non-EU businesses—change to UK VAT rate from 4 January 2011
22/10	Change to the Polish VAT rate from 1 January 2011
23/10	Change to the Portuguese VAT rate from 1 January 2011
1/11	Change to the VAT rate in Latvia from 1 January 2011
2/11	Special scheme for non-EU businesses—exchange rates for period ending December 2010
3/11	Change to the Slovak VAT rate from 1 January 2011
7/11	Special scheme for non-EU businesses—exchange rates for period ending March 2011
10/11	Special scheme for non-EU businesses—exchange rates for period ending June 2011

APPENDIX 3. VAT NOTICES HAVING THE FORCE OF LAW (NOTICE NO 747)

Various provisions of the VAT legislation authorise the Commissioners to determine the detailed requirements of VAT by way of a public notice. These requirements have the force of law as tertiary legislation. The following table lists the relevant parts of public notices concerned and notes the relevant statutory authority. The information shown is derived from Notice No 747 (June 2003) Section 2.

Notice	*Part having the force of law and its purpose*	*Enabling powers*
Notice 700:	Para 7.7: values expressed in foreign currency	VATA 1994 Sch 6 para 11
The VAT Guide		
Notice 701/21:	Para 3.1: notification	VATA 1994 ss 26 and 31
Gold	Paras 4.3–4.5: further notification requirements	VAT Regulations 1995, SI 1995/2518 reg 31A
	Para 4.6: invoicing requirements	VAT (Investment Gold) Order 1999, SI 1999/3116
	Para 6.2–6.4: further invoicing requirements	
	Paras 7.1–7.7: record keeping requirements	
Notice 701/21A:	Section 3: list of investment gold coins	VATA 1994 Sch 9 Group 15
Investment gold coins		VAT Regulations 1995, SI 1995/2518 reg 31A
		VAT (Investment Gold) Order 1999, SI 1999/3116
Notice 701/36:	Para 11.3.1: requirement to keep records	VATA 1994 Sch 9 Group 2 Note 4(*c*)(iii)
Insurance	Para 11.3.2: relevant VAT invoice to be used when supplying goods or services under a VAT margin scheme	VATA 1994 Sch 11 para 6(1)
		VAT Regulations 1995, SI 1995/2518 regs 31(1) and 31(2)
Notice 701/48:	Para 3.3: Line Item Detail (LID) invoices	VATA 1994 Sch 11 para 2
Corporate purchasing cards	Para 3.4: the Summary VAT invoice	VAT Regulations 1995, SI 1995/2518 regs 13 and 14
Notice 703:	Principally paras 2.2 and 8.4, but specific conditions relating to the zero-rating of particular types of supplies of goods for export outside the EC, or removal to another EC Member State, are contained throughout the Notice	VATA 1994 ss 30(6), 30(8) and 30(10)
Exports and removals of goods from the United Kingdom		VAT Regulations 1995, SI 1995/2518 regs 127, 129 and 134

Notice	*Part having the force of law and its purpose*	*Enabling powers*
Notice 703/1:	Para 4 and 5 contain the conditions which must be met in full in order to zero-rate supplies (by way of sale) of freight containers for export outside the EC or for removal to another EC Member State	VATA 1994 ss 30(6), 30(8) and 30(10)
Supply of freight containers for export or removal from the United Kingdom		VAT Regulations 1995, SI 1995/2518 regs 128 and 134
Notice 703/2:	Principally Section 3, which sets out the conditions to be complied with, but other paragraphs outline additional conditions which must be met	VATA 1994 s 30(8)
Sail away boats supplied for export outside the European Community		VAT Regulations 1995, SI 1995/2518 reg 129
Notice 704:	Principally para 1.1, but the notice expands on the conditions for the retailer to supply goods that can be zero-rated to entitled customers	VATA 1994 s 30(8)
Retail exports		VAT Regulations 1995, SI 1995/2518 regs 130 and 131
Notice 704/1:	Principally para 1.2, but the notice expands on the conditions for travellers departing from the European Community and how they may be able to get a refund on some goods bought by using the Retail Export Scheme	VATA 1994 s 30(8)
VAT refunds for travellers departing from the European Community		VAT Regulations 1995, SI 1995/2518 regs 130 and 131
Notice 705:	Principally the conditions set out on page 2. Other conditions and procedures to be followed by the purchaser are set out elsewhere in the Notice	VATA 1994 s 30(8)
VAT: Personal exports of motor vehicles to destinations outside the European Community from 1 January 1993		VAT Regulations 1995, SI 1995/2518 regs 132 and 133
Notice 705A:	Principally the conditions set out in Appendix B. Other conditions and procedures to be followed by the supplier are set out elsewhere in the Notice	VATA 1994 s 30(8)

Notice	*Part having the force of law and its purpose*	*Enabling powers*
VAT: Supplies of vehicles under the Personal Export Scheme for removal from the European Community		VAT Regulations 1995, SI 1995/2518 regs 132 and 133
Notice 708:	Para 18.1: Certificate for developers and building contractors in respect of relevant residential and relevant charitable buildings	VATA 1994 Sch 7A Group 6 para 8(2)(*b*)
Buildings and construction		VATA 1994 Sch 7A Group 7 para 4A(1)(*b*)
		VATA 1994 Sch 8 Group 5 Note 12(*b*)
Notice 709/5:	The notice provides that certain goods and services which would otherwise be covered by the Margin Scheme are excluded, and specifies the method of calculation for the Margin Scheme	VATA 1994, s 53
Tour operators' margin scheme		VAT (Tour Operators) Order 1987, SI 1987/1806 arts 3 and 7 (as amended)
Notice 718:	The whole of Section 3 (Records and Accounts)	VATA 1994 s 50A
Margin Schemes for secondhand goods, works of art, antiques and collectors' items	In Section 6 (Global Accounting): paras 6.2 (all apart from final sentence),	VAT (Cars) Order 1992, SI 1992/3122 (as amended)
	6.3, 6.4 (final sentence), 6.5 (all apart from final sub-para), 6.6 (all apart from final sentence), 6.7, 6.9	VAT (Special Provisions) Order 1995, SI 1995/1268 (as amended)
		VAT (Input Tax) Order 1992, SI 1992/3222 (as amended)
	In Section 7 (The Auctioneers' Scheme—basic principles): the final sentence of para 7.3	
	In Section 8 (The Auctioneers' Scheme—records and accounts): paras 8.1 and 8.2	
	In Section 22 (Horses and ponies): the final sub-para of para 22.7	
Notice 725:	Para 3.1: Can I zero-rate a supply of goods to a VAT registered customer in another Member State?	VATA 1994 s 30(8)
VAT: The Single Market	Para 5.5: Values expressed in a foreign currency	VATA 1994 Sch 7 para 4
Notice 727:	In Section 2: paras 2.1, 2.2 and 2.4	VATA 1994 Sch 11 para 2(6)

Notice	*Part having the force of law and its purpose*	*Enabling powers*
VAT: Retail schemes	In Section 3: paras 3.4, 3.7, 3.9 and 3.12	
	In Section 4: paras 4.1, 4.2 and 4.4	
	In Section 5: para 5.1	
	In Section 6: paras 6.1 and 6.2	
	In Section 8: paras 8.3, 8.5, 8.6, 8.7 and 8.8	
	In Section 9: paras 9.4 and 9.5	VAT Regulations 1995, SI 1995/2518 Part IX (regs 66–75)
Notice 727/3:	In Section 2 (General rules): para 2.3–2.5	VATA 1994 Sch 11 para 2(6) VAT Regulations 1995, SI 1995/2518 (regs 66–75)
Retail schemes: How to work the Point of Sale scheme	In Section 3 (The Point of Sale Scheme): paras 3.2–3.4	
	In Section 4 (Mechanics of the Point of Sale Scheme): para 4.2	
	In Section 5 (Daily Gross Takings (DGT) checklist): paras 5.1–5.5	
	The whole of Section 6 (Special transactions)	
	In Section 7 (Business promotions): paras 7.2–7.6	
Notice 727/4:	In Section 2 (General rules): paras 2.3–2.5	VATA 1994 Sch 11 para 2(6)
Retail schemes: How to work the Apportionment Schemes	In Section 3 (Basic principles of Apportionment Schemes 1 and 2): paras 3.2–3.6	VAT Regulations 1995, SI 1995/2518 Part IX (regs 66–75)
	In Section 4 (Mechanics of Apportionment Scheme 1): paras 4.2–4.3	
	In Section 5 (Mechanics of Apportionment Scheme 2): paragraphs 5.2–5.4	
	In Section 6 (Daily Gross Takings (DGT) checklist): paras 6.1–6.5	
	The whole of Section 7 (Special transactions)	
	The whole of Section 8 (Business promotions)	
Notice 727/5:	In Section 2 (General rules): paras 2.3–2.5	VATA 1994 Sch 11 para 2(6)
Retail schemes: How to work the Direct Calculation schemes	In Section 3 (Basic Principles of Direct Calculation Schemes 1 and 2): paras 3.1–3.7	VAT Regulations 1995, SI 1995/2518 Part IX (regs 66–75)
	In Section 4 (Mechanics of the Direct Calculation Schemes (1 and 2)): paras 4.2–4.5	

Notice	***Part having the force of law and its purpose***	***Enabling powers***
	In Section 5 (Daily Gross Takings (DGT) checklist): paras 5.1–5.5	
	The whole of Section 6 (Special transactions)	
	The whole of Section 7 (Business promotions)	
Notice 728:	Para 6.1: What happens when I buy an NMT in the UK for removal to another Member State?	VATA 1994 s 30(8) and Sch 7 para 4(2)
New means of transport	Para 3.6: Rate of exchange used to calculate the value of an NMT	VAT Regulations 1995, SI 1995/2518 reg 155
	Other conditions and procedures to be complied with are set out elsewhere in the Notice	
Notice 731:	In Section 2 (Basics of cash accounting): paras 2.1 (final sub-para), 2.3 (first sub-para) and 2.5 (final sub-para)	VATA 1994 s 25(1) and Sch 11 para 2(7)
Cash accounting	In Section 3 (Records and accounting for VAT): paras 3.2.2 (first sub-para), 3.3 (final sub-para), 3.4.1 (final sub-para), 3.4.2 (final sub-para)	VAT Regulations 1995, SI 1995/2518 regs 56–65 (as amended)
	In Section 4 (Special rules for particular transactions): paras 4.2 (first sub-para), 4.3 (first sub-para), 4.5 (first sub-para), 4.7 (second sub-para) and 4.8 (final sub-para)	
	In Section 5 (Leaving the cash accounting scheme): paras 5.3 (first line, second sub-para), 5.6 (final sub-para), 5.7.2 (first sub-para), 5.9 (final sub-para)	

APPENDIX 4.

BUSINESS ACTIVITIES OF GOVERNMENT DEPARTMENTS—HM TREASURY DIRECTION (29 OCTOBER 2008)

This Appendix sets out the text of the Direction published in the *London Gazette*, 10 November 2008.

HM TREASURY DIRECTION

Treasury Directions dated 29 October 2008 under section 41(2), (5) and (6) of the Value Added Tax Act 1994 (c 23) as to the supply of goods or services by Government departments.

The Treasury, in exercise of the powers conferred on them by section 41(2), (5) and (6) of the Value Added Tax Act 1994, hereby direct as follows:

(1) These Directions shall come into force on 29 October 2008.

(2) In these Directions—
"the Act" means the Value Added Tax Act 1994.
"Government department" has the same meaning as in section 41(6) of the Act and includes part of a Government department designated for the purposes of that section by paragraph (3) below.
"List 1" and "List 2" mean Lists 1 and 2 respectively in these Directions.

(3) Where an entry in List 1 mentions a part of a Government department, that part is hereby designated for the purposes of section 41(6) of the Act.

(4) A supply by a Government department which is mentioned in List 1 of any goods or services of a description in List 2 shall be treated for the purposes of the Act as a supply in the course or furtherance of a business carried on by that department.

(5) The Treasury Directions made under section 41(2), (5) and (6) of the Value Added Tax Act 1994 on 23 May 2002 are revoked.

D Watts and T Cunningham

Two of the Lords Commissioners of Her Majesty's Treasury

LIST 1
HM REVENUE AND CUSTOMS—TREASURY (TAXING) DIRECTIONS: GOVERNMENT DEPARTMENTS

Advisory, Conciliation and Arbitration Service

Department of Agriculture and Rural Development

Army Base Repair Organisation

Cabinet Office

CADW (Welsh Historic Monuments)

Central Office of Information

Charity Commission

Crown Office Scotland

Crown Prosecution Service

Department of Culture, Arts and Leisure

Department for Culture, Media and Sport

Communities Scotland

Revenue and Customs

Ministry of Defence

Defence Aviation Repair Agency

Defence Science and Technology Laboratory

Driver and Vehicle Testing Agency for Northern Ireland

Department for Education and Skills

Department of Employment and Learning

Department for Enterprise, Trade and Investment

Department of the Environment

Department for Environment, Food and Rural Affairs

ESTYN (HM Inspectorate for Education and Training in Wales)

Export Credits Guarantee Department

Office of Fair Trading

Department of Finance and Personnel

Fire Authority for Northern Ireland

Fire Service College

Office of the First Minister and Deputy First Minister

Food Standards Agency

Foreign and Commonwealth Office

Forensic Science Northern Ireland

Forensic Science Service

Forestry Commission

Office of Gas and Electricity Markets

General Register Office for Scotland

Government Actuary's Department

Government Car and Dispatch Agency

Office of Government Commerce

Government Communications Bureau

Government Communications Centre

Government Communications Headquarters

Department of Health

Health Authorities (including Primary Care Groups, Local Health Groups (Wales) and Community Health Councils, Special Health Authorities, Special Health Boards (Scotland), Area Health Boards (Scotland), National Health Service Trusts, Primary Care Trusts, The Common Services Agency (Scotland), Dental Practice Board).

Health and Safety Executive

Department of Health, Social Services and Public Safety

Historic Scotland

Home Office

Hydrographic Office

Department for International Development

Land Registry

Lord Chancellor's Department

Meteorological Office

National Investment and Loans Office

Office for National Statistics

National Archives of Scotland

National Assembly for Wales

Northern Ireland Assembly

Northern Ireland Court Service

Northern Ireland Education and Library Boards

Northern Ireland Housing Executive

Northern Ireland Office

Office of the Ombudsman

OGC buying.solutions

Ordnance Survey

Ordnance Survey of Northern Ireland

Privy Council Office

Public Record Office

Public Record Office of Northern Ireland

Office for the Regulation of Electricity and Gas

Office of the Rail Regulator

Department for Regional Development

Registers of Scotland

Royal Mint

Royal Parks

Scotland Office

Scottish Executive

Scottish Parliamentary Corporate Body

Scottish Prison Service

Office of the Secretary of State for Wales

Security Service

Security Services Group

Serious Fraud Office

Department for Social Development

Office for Standards in Education (England)

Office of Telecommunications

Department of Trade and Industry

Department for Transport, Local Government and the Regions

Department for Transport, Local Government and the Regions – Queen Elizabeth II Conference Centre

Treasury

Treasury Solicitor's Department

Office of Water Services

Department for Work and Pensions

LIST 2
HM REVENUE AND CUSTOMS—TREASURY (TAXING) DIRECTIONS: BUSINESS ACTIVITIES—GOODS AND SERVICES

Accommodation, including property acquisition and disposal and any related services

Administration services

Admission to premises and to events, eg entertainments, air displays etc

Advertising or publicity services

Archives

Attendance of staff at court or any similar place

Bankruptcies and insolvency services

Broadcasting services

Catering, including supplies from vending machines

Car leasing

Community tradeable emissions allowances in return for payment pursuant to FA 2007 s 16 where such allowances could also be obtained from the private sector

Computer services or goods

Concessions for catering or other services

Conferences, exhibitions and any related facilities or services

Construction, alteration, demolition, repair or maintenance work, civil engineering work, any related services or goods

Contract or procurement services

Copying or supply of any reproductions or of any documents

Copyright, patents or licences to manufacture

Delivery or distribution services

Drainage work

Electronic transfer of data

Export of goods and related services

Filming, replay or recording services

Financial and any related services

Fishing licences or permits

Fire service assistance

Freight transport

Fuel and power

Government car service

Grant, assignment or surrender of any interest in or right over land, or of any licence to do anything in relation to land

Grant of a right to inspect records

Goods, including goods manufactured within a Government department and sold to its staff and to other customers, stores, surplus or other equipment

Grave maintenance

Grounds maintenance

Hairdressing

Heating

Hire of vehicles, machinery or equipment, with or without operator or crew

Hydrographic, cartographic and similar services

Information or statistical services

Inspection services

Laboratory services including analysis and testing of any substance

Laundry services

Licensing, certification, authorisation or the granting of any rights other than rights over land

Manufacturing, assembling and other services

Medical services

Membership subscriptions

Meteorological and related services

Mineral or prospecting rights

Mortuary services

Nursery and day-care facilities

Occupational health services

Passenger transport

Payroll and pension administration services

Pest or animal control

Photocopying services

Photographic services

Port, airport or harbour services and related goods

Postal, packing or distribution services

Professional services, including those of any manager, adviser, expert, specialist or consultant

Publications

Radio or communication services

Recruitment services

Research, testing, experimentation, sampling or other related laboratory services

Repair or maintenance of machinery, equipment or other goods

Searches

Secondment of staff where such services could also be obtained from the private sector

Secretarial services

Security services and related goods

Shipping services

Slaughter, rendering and diposal of animals

Social services

Statistical services, including the collection, preparation and processing of data

Storage facilities and related services

Telecommunications

Training, tuition or education and any related services or goods

Transfer of milk quota leases

Translation services

Tree planting and afforestation

Vehicle conversions

Vehicle servicing and maintenance

Verification of particulars of births, marriages or deaths

Waste disposal

Water

Weighbridge services

APPENDIX 5.

REFUND OF VAT TO GOVERNMENT DEPARTMENTS—HM TREASURY DIRECTION (2 DECEMBER 2002)

This Appendix sets out the text of the Direction published in the *London Gazette*, 10 January 2003 (as corrected, 15 January 2003).

HM TREASURY DIRECTION

The Treasury direction dated 2 December 2002 under section 41(3) of the Value Added Tax Act 1994 as to the refund to Government departments of tax charged on the supply of goods or services or on the acquisition or importation of goods by them otherwise than for the purpose of any business carried on by them or on a supply in the course or furtherance of a business.

The Treasury, in exercise of the powers conferred on them by section 41(3) of the Value Added Tax Act 1994, hereby direct as follows.

(1) This direction shall come into operation on 2 December 2002.

(2) Subject as provided in paragraph 3, a Government department listed as belonging to a category of departments listed in List 1 of this direction may claim and be paid a refund of the tax charged on:

- (a) the supply to it of any services of a description in List 2;
- (b) the supply to it of leased accommodation for more than 21 years as part of the supply to it of any services of a description in List 2; or
- (c) the supply to it or acquisition from another member state of importation from outside the member states by it of goods closely related to the supply to it of any services of a description in List 2.

(3) A tax refund as described in paragraph 2 will only be paid if:

- (a) either the supply of those services or goods is not for the purpose of:
  - (i) any business carried on by the department; or
  - (ii) any supply by the department which, by virtue of directions made under section 41(2) and (5) of the Value Added Tax Act 1994, is treated as a supply in the course or furtherance of a business; and
- (b) the department complies with the requirements of the Commissioners of Customs and Excise both as to the time, form and manner of making the claim and also on the keeping, preservation and production of records relating to the supply, acquisition or importation in question.

(4) The Treasury direction dated 7 August 2000 is hereby revoked.

Two of the Lords Commissioners of Her Majesty's Treasury.

Philip Woolas and *Jim Fitzpatrick*.

LIST 1
ELIGIBLE DEPARTMENTS

Advisory, Conciliation and Arbitration Service

Cabinet Office

CADW

Charity Commission

Centre for Management and Policy Studies Civil Service College

Communities Scotland

Crown Office (Scotland)

Crown Prosecution Service

Department for Culture, Media and Sport

HM Customs and Excise

Ministry of Defence

Defence Science and Technology Laboratory

Department for Education and Skills

Employment Service/Jobcentre Plus

Department for the Environment, Food and Rural Affairs

Estyn

Food Standards Agency

Foreign and Commonwealth Office

Forestry Commission

Forest Research

Government Actuary's Department

Government Car and Dispatch Agency

Government Communications Bureau

HM Government Communications Centre

Government Communications Headquarters

Care Trusts, Community Health Councils, Strategic Health Authorities, Health Authorities, Special Health Authorities, Special Health Boards (Scotland), National Health Service Trusts, Area Health Boards (Scotland), Primary Care Trusts, the Common Services Agency (Scotland), the Welsh Common Services Agency

Health and Safety Commission/Executive

Dental Practice Board

Department of Health

Historic Scotland

Home Office

Inland Revenue

Department for International Development

National Investment and Loans Office

Land Registry

Lord Chancellor's Department

National Savings

National Archives of Scotland

National Assembly for Wales

Northern Ireland Court Service

Northern Ireland Office

Office for Standards in Education (England)

Office of the Deputy Prime Minister

Office of the Deputy Prime Minister—Queen Elizabeth II Conference Centre

Office of Gas and Electricity Markets

Office of Fair Trading

Office for National Statistics

Office of the Rail Regulator

Office of Telecommunications

Office of the Secretary of State for Wales

Office of Water Services

Postal Services Commission

Privy Council Office

Public Record Office

General Register Office for Scotland

Registers of Scotland

Royal Parks

Department of Trade and Industry

Department for Transport

HM Treasury

Secret Intelligence Service

Security Service

Scotland Office

Scottish Executive

Scottish Parliamentary Corporate Body

Scottish Prison Service

Serious Fraud Office

Treasury Solicitor's Department

Department for Work and Pensions

Welsh European Office

LIST 2
ELIGIBLE SERVICES

1. Accounting, invoicing and related services
2. Administration of the following:
   - — Career development loans
   - — Certificates of Experience
   - — Government support payments to the Railway Industry Pension Funds

— Grants and awards
— Services supplied under the Companies Acts and the Patent and Trademark Acts
— Teachers' Superannuation Scheme
— Vehicle Excise Duty refunds
— Winter fuel payment scheme
— Inherited State Earnings Related Pension Scheme
— Student Loan Scheme
— Fast Track Teaching Programme

3. Administration and collection of toll charges
4. Aerial photographic surveys and aerial surveillance
5. Agricultural services of the kind normally carried out by the Farming and Rural Conservation Agency
6. Alteration, repair and maintenance of road schemes, except (*a*) any works carried out pursuant to an agreement made under section 278 of the Highways Act 1980, or (*b*) works involving contruction on land not already used for road schemes
7. Broadcast monitoring services
8. Cartographic services
9. Cash in transit services
10. Catering
11. Ceremonial services
12. Childcare services
13. Collection, delivery and distribution services
14. Computer Services supplied to the specification of the recipient, including the provision of a fully managed and serviced computer infrastructure
15. Conference and exhibition services
16. Debt collection
17. Departmental staff records and payroll systems including administration and payment of pensions
18. Employment advisory services as directed by the Race Relations Act 1976
19. Engineering and related process services
20. Enviromental protection services of the kind normally carried out for the Department of the Environment, Food and Rural Affairs
21. Estate management services
22. Export intelligence services
23. Filming, audio-visual and production services
24. Health promotion activities
25. Hire of reprographic equipment including repair and maintenance
26. Hire of vehicles including repair and maintenance
27. Insolvency services
28. Interpretation and translation services
29. Issue of documents to, and control of, bingo halls and off-course bookmakers
30. Issue of documents under Wireless and Telegraphy Act
31. Laboratory services
32. Laundry services
33. Library services
34. Maintenance and care of livestock and fauna in connection with the Royal Parks
35. Maintenance, non-structural repair and cleaning of buildings

36. Maintenance and repair of civil engineering works
37. Maintenance, repair and cleaning of equipment, plant, vehicles and vessels
38. Maintenance and repair of statues, monuments and works of art
39. Medical and social surveys
40. Messenger, portering and reception services
41. Nursing services
42. Office removals
43. Operation and maintenance of static test facilities, engineering and support services and test range industrial support and security/safety services including those acquired for the purposes of research and development
44. Operation and maintenance of stores depots
45. Operation of hospitals, health care establishments and health care facilities and the provision of any related services
46. Operation of prisons, detention centres and remand centres, including medical services
47. Passenger transport services
48. Pest control services
49. Photographic, reprographic, graphics and design services
50. Preparation and despatch of forms
51. Press cutting services
52. Professional services, including those of any manager, advisor, expert, specialist or consultant
53. Provision under a PFI agreement of accommodation for office or other governmental use, together with management or other services in connection with that accommodation
54. Publicity services
55. Purchasing and procurement services
56. Radio services
57. Recruitment and relocation of staff and other related services
58. Research, testing, inspection, certification and approval work for the Health and Safety Executive
59. Scientific work of the kind normally carried out for the Department of the Environment, Food and Rural Affairs and the Food Standards Agency
60. Security Services
61. Services of printing, copying, reproducing or mailing any documents or publications, including typesetting services
62. Share Registry Survey
63. Storage, distribution and goods disposal services
64. Surveying, certification and registration in connection with ships and relevant record-keeping and verification, issue of certification, cards, discharge books and campaign medals to seamen
65. Training, tuition or education
66. Transport research of the kind normally carried out for the Department for Transport
67. Travel services, excluding hotel accommodation and fares
68. Travel and transport surveys, including traffic census counts
69. Typing, secretarial, telephonist and clerical services including agency staff
70. Waste disposal services
71. Welfare services

72. Careers guidance, mentoring and counselling to help people into work as part of the New Deal and ONE service
73. Services relating to Action Teams for Jobs and Employment Zones
74. Original research undertaken in order to gain knowledge and understanding
75. Inspection of woodland sites for approval of felling licence applications and of timber imports/imports using timber packing to prevent entry of foreign tree pests and diseases

APPENDIX 6.

EXTRA-STATUTORY CONCESSIONS (NOTICE NO 48)

Notice No 48 (December 2010) sets out the text of extra-statutory concessions relating to VAT, customs duty, excise duty, insurance premium tax, landfill tax and climate change levy. This notice replaces Notice No 48 (July 2009). It has a number of shortcomings.

First, despite what is said in para 1.1 (second para), this notice has not been rewritten. It does no more than make minor changes to the text of the July 2009 edition and note the obsolescence of concessions since the March 2002 edition. The concessions in section 10 expired prior to publication of the March 2002 edition.

Secondly, despite what is said in para 1.1 (first para), it does not give details of *all* extra-statutory concessions in force at the time of going to print. Indeed, *Extra-statutory Concessions – Technical Consultation on Draft Legislation* (HMRC, 3 November 2008 para 1.1 suggests that Notice No 48 is not intended to be comprehensive. The position was stated more plainly in *Withdrawal of extra statutory concessions* (HMRC Technical Note, 13 December 2010) para 1.1. This states that "the term 'extra-statutory concession' refers to any stated concession from the statutory tax treatment. It is not limited to concessions published in . . . the former HM Customs and Excise booklet Notice 48". Thus, for example, the notice does not include:

- the concession for bad debts incurred by gas and electricity suppliers published in Business Brief 20/04, 2 August 2004;
- the zero-rating allowed in respect of items dispensed by a pharmacist against a nurse's prescription (see Notice No 701/57 (January 2007) para 9.4.1). This is recognised as an extra-statutory concession in *Extra-statutory Concessions – Second Technical Consultation on Draft Legislation* (HMRC, 15 July 2009) p 41;
- the VAT recovery on assets acquired prior to registration (see Notice No 742A (June 2010) para 9.4). This is described as an extra-statutory concession in Revenue and Customs Brief 53/10. 31 December 2010 (which confines recovery to traders registered before 1 January 2011);
- the concessions in respect of the recharge of non-domestic business rates, water rates and sewerage rates at caravan sites in Notice No 701/20 paras 4.3 and 4.4. These concessions are being withdrawn with effect from 1 January 2012: see *Withdrawal of extra statutory concessions* (HMRC Technical Note, 13 December 2010) Chapter 2;
- the zero-rating of motor vehicles adapted after initial supply (see HMRC Guidance V1–7, Chapter 12 para 29.6). This concession is being withdrawn with effect from 1 January 2012: see *Withdrawal of extra statutory concessions* (HMRC Technical Note, 13 December 2010) Chapter 2; or
- the zero-rating of parts and accessories for boats supplied for disabled people. This concession is being withdrawn with effect from 1 January 2012: see *Withdrawal of extra statutory concessions* (HMRC Technical Note, 13 December 2010) Chapter 2.

Third, the notice retains, without comment, a number of concessions which appear to have expired or been given statutory effect. The relevant concessions have been reproduced but noted accordingly.

Fourth, a number of concessions are due to expire from a known future date. The relevant concessions have been noted accordingly.

Fifth, a number of concessions included in the July 2009 edition have since been withdrawn. These concessions are noted as "obsolete" in accordance with the text of the notice. If identified, the document notifying withdrawal has been noted.

Sixth, the notice contains a significant number of typographical errors. Obvious typographical errors have been corrected. The relevant amendments have been enclosed in square brackets and an explanation given in the notes wherever this has appeared helpful.

The following text is confined to concessions relevant to VAT. Statutory references have been changed to reflect the house style of this work.

TEXT OF THE CONCESSIONS RELATING TO VAT

2 International Field

2.1 VAT, excise and customs duties: Goods and services

Duty (which includes all import and excise duties) and VAT are remitted or refunded in accordance with agreements with the authorities concerned on:

- goods and services imported by or supplied to visiting forces and their instrumentalities, for the official use of the force, or their instrumentalities
- goods and services imported by or supplied to NATO military headquarters, organisations or agencies, for their official use
- United States and Canadian Government expenditure on mutual defence or mutual aid contracts, and
- temporary importations of equipment required by contractors for fulfilling NATO infrastructure contracts or in connection with the provision and maintenance of US forces defence facilities in the United Kingdom.

[VATA 1994 s 1]

2.2 VAT, excise and customs duties: UK-manufactured alcoholic liquor and tobacco products purchased by diplomats

Duty and VAT are remitted on alcoholic liquor and tobacco products of UK manufacture imported by, or supplied to, diplomatic representatives of foreign states in the United Kingdom who are entitled to similar privileges in respect of imported products of foreign manufacture under the Diplomatic Privileges Act 1964.

[VATA 1994 s 1]

2.3 VAT, excise and customs duties: United States Air Force

Relief from VAT and/or excise duty is allowed, in accordance with conditions agreed with the United States Air Force, on:

- charges for admission to air shows and open days, and
- goods sold by US forces organisations during air shows and open days to persons not entitled to receive/consume them unless customs charges have been paid.

[VATA 1994 s 1]

2.4 VAT and customs duty: Gifts

Duty and VAT are remitted on gifts (whether imported or purchased in the United Kingdom) from United States forces to charitable organisations.

[VATA 1994 s 1]

2.5 VAT: American war graves

In order to place inland purchases on the same footing as imported goods, VAT is remitted on the supply of goods and services to the American Battle Monuments Commission for the maintenance of the American Military Cemetery and Memorial at Maddingley, Cambridge and Brookwood, Surrey.

[VATA 1994 s 1]

2.6 VAT: Supplies to diplomatic missions, international organisations, NATO forces etc in other EC countries

A VAT registered trader can zero-rate supplies of goods (other than new means of transport), or services made to entitled persons and bodies resident or situated in other EC countries provided:

- the goods or services are for either the official use of the entitled bodies or for the personal use of entitled members etc thereof[;]
- the supplier obtains from the customer an application for exemption from VAT under Directive 77/388/EEC art 15(10) (or, if not available, a written order/certificate confirming eligibility under that Article)[;]
- in the case of goods, they are removed to another EC country; and
- the supplier obtains and keeps proof of removal of the goods to another EC country within three months of the time of supply. This should be the commercial proof of export or removal normally acceptable for VAT zero-rating purposes.

[*Note*: Directive 77/388/EEC art 15(1) has been repealed and replaced by Directive 2006/112/EC art 151.]

[VATA 1994 s 30]

2.7 VAT and customs duty: Certain aircraft ground and security equipment

The Convention on International Civil Aviation (Chicago Convention) allows relief from duty and VAT for certain ground and security equipment imported into the territory of one Contracting State by an airline of another Contracting State operating an international service. The United Kingdom is a signatory to the Chicago Convention.

Additionally, the United Kingdom has concluded a number of Air Service Agreements which allow, on a reciprocal basis, the various reliefs detailed in the Convention, including the one mentioned above.

We have become aware that end-use relief may be being claimed erroneously in these cases. Aircraft ground and security equipment does not qualify for end-use relief. We are in the process of drawing up a new procedure to enable the relief to be correctly claimed.

In the interim period an extra-statutory concession has been agreed to allow relief for ground and security equipment to be claimed. The following list details those goods which qualify for relief and who is eligible to claim it.

2.7.1 Qualifying goods

The following ground and security equipment for aircraft:

(a) Repair, maintenance and servicing equipment:
- material for airframes, engines and instruments
- specialised aircraft repair kits
- starter batteries and carts
- maintenance platforms and steps
- test equipment for aircraft, aircraft engines, and instruments
- aircraft engine heaters and coolers, and
- ground radio equipment.

(b) Passenger-handling equipment:
- passenger-loading steps
- specialised passenger-weighing devices, and
- specialised catering equipment.

(c) Cargo-loading equipment:
- vehicles for moving or loading of baggage, cargo, equipment or supplies
- specialised cargo-loading devices, and
- specialised cargo-weighing devices.

(d) Component parts for incorporation into ground equipment including the items listed above.

(e) Security equipment:
- weapon-detecting devices
- explosives-detecting devices, and
- intrusion detecting devices.

(f) Component parts for incorporation into security equipment.

Claims for relief of duty and VAT under this concession should be addressed to the Entry Processing Unit where the goods will be cleared with a copy of this advice.

[VATA 1994 s 16]

2.8 Relief from UK excise duty on alcoholic drinks supplied duty-paid in another Member State for consumption on Eurostar trains which are in UK territory

[Applies to excise duty.]

3 Value Added Tax Concessions Designed to Remove Inequities or Anomalies in Administration

3.1 VAT: VAT on purchase of road fuel

VATA 1994 s 56 (formerly FA 1986 s 9) requires payment of a scale charge when road fuel purchased by a business is used for private journeys. However, where a registered person claims no input tax on purchases of road fuel, whether for business or private journeys, the VAT scale charge will not apply.

[VATA 1994 s 56]

3.2 VAT: Group supplies using an overseas member: anticipation of legislative changes

With effect from 26 November 1996, a resolution under the Provisional Collection of Taxes Act has created a new tax charge for the representative member of a [VAT] group, where supplies of a type set out in VATA 1994 Sch 5 are purchased by an overseas group member and used for making Sch 5 supplies to a UK group member. This new tax charge was made permanent when FA 1997 was passed on 19 March 1997. The new tax charge is given effect by FA 1997 s 41, which inserts the new rules into VATA 1994 s 43 at paras (2A)–(2E).

Committee Stage amendments to what became s 41 reduced the impact of the new tax charge in certain specified circumstances with effect from 19 March 1997, the date when FA 1997 was passed. The impact will be further reduced when Regulations are made under s 41. This concession will allow groups to account for VAT with effect from 26 November 1996 as though the amendments and Regulations had been in force from that date. The concession falls into two parts.

3.2.1 First part of concession

First, a tax charge under s 41 is triggered where an overseas member of a VAT group has been supplied with services falling within any of VATA 1994 Sch 5 paras 1–8 (services to be treated as supplied where received). By concession, no tax charge will be triggered by any such services which are exempt from VAT because they fall within one of the descriptions in Sch 9 of the Act. This concession applies to supplies made between 26 November and 19 March 1997. After that date the concession is not needed, because it has been given legal effect by the passing of the Finance Act.

3.2.2 Second part of concession

Second, the amount of the tax charge under s 41 is calculated with reference to the value of the supply by the overseas member to the UK member. By concession, the value for calculating the tax charge may be reduced to the value of the Sch 5 services purchased by the overseas group member, provided that the group is in a position to provide evidence in the UK of the value of those services, and that those services have not been undervalued. This concession will be given legal effect when Regulations are made under s 41.

[*Note*: The first part of the concession appears to be obsolete. As regards the second part of the concession, VATA 1994 Sch 5 was repealed with effect from 1 January 2010. For the manner in which the second part is now applied in order to maintain its intended effect, see Revenue & Customs Brief 16/11, 25 March 2011. For the power to make regulations, see VATA 1994 s 43(2C) as inserted by FA 1977 s 41(1). No regulations have been made to date.]

[VATA 1994 s 43]

3.3 VAT: Zero-rating of supplies of certain goods used in connection with collection of monetary donations

This concession applies to supplies to a charity of the following goods:

(a) lapel stickers or attachments designed to be worn on the lapel, which are of no intrinsic value, low cost to the charity and are given as a token in acknowledgement of a donation
(b) component parts of items described in (*a*) above when supplied for self assembly
(c) any form of receptacle which:
- is manufactured specifically for the purpose of collecting donated money
- is used solely for collecting money for charity
- is, or will be, clearly marked as collecting for a named charity, and
- can be secured by lock or tamper evident seal

(d) bucket lids, designed to fit buckets and provide a secure seal, for use solely in connection with collecting money for charity
(e) pre-printed letters the primary purpose of which is to appeal for money for charity (not necessarily including the addressees' particulars)
(f) envelopes used in conjunction with letters described in (*e*) above for forwarding donations, provided that they are over-printed with an appeal request related to that contained in the letter
(g) outer envelopes used in conjunction with letters described in (*e*) above, provided that they are over-printed with an appeal request related to that contained in the letter
(h) pre-printed collecting envelopes appealing for money (of the type used by the welfare charities and which are usually hand delivered to domestic premises), and
(i) stewardship envelopes used for planned giving which, as a minimum requirement, are pre-printed with the name of the relevant place of worship or other charity.

Where this concession applies, the supply may be treated as if it were a zero-rated supply.

This concession applies from 1 April 2000.

The Commissioners may withdraw or restrict the application of this concession if they have reasonable cause to believe it is being abused.

[VATA 1994 Sch 8 Group 3 Item 1]

3.4 VAT: Misunderstanding by a VAT trader

VAT undercharged by a registered trader on account of a bona fide misunderstanding may be remitted provided all the following conditions are fulfilled:

(a) there is no reason to believe that the tax has been knowingly evaded
(b) there is no evidence of negligence
(c) the misunderstanding does not concern an aspect of the tax clearly covered in the guidance published by HM Revenue & Customs or in specific instructions to the trader concerned, and
(d) the tax due was not charged, could not now reasonably be expected to be charged to customers, and will not be charged.

Where, at the time the misunderstanding comes to light, there are unfulfilled firm orders from customers, for which the price quoted has been based mistakenly on the assumption that no

VAT, or less VAT than properly due, would be chargeable, VAT undercharged may be remitted in respect of these orders providing conditions (*a*)–(*d*) above are met.

[*Note*: This concession is being withdrawn with effect from 1 January 2012 on the grounds that "it is not reasonable to allow remission of tax when the error is caused by the taxpayer": see Withdrawal of extra statutory concessions (HMRC Technical Note, 13 December 2010) Chapter 2.

[VATA 1994 s 73 and Sch 11 para 1]

3.5 VAT: Misdirection

[Obsolete.]

[*Note*: This concession was withdrawn with effect from 1 April 2009 by Revenue & Customs Brief 15/09, 27 March 2009. For reliance on information or advice provided by HMRC, see Appendix 19.]

3.6 VAT: Coin-operated machines

The tax point for supplies made from coin-operated machines is the date the machine is used. As an accounting convenience, however, operators may delay accounting for VAT until the takings are removed from a machine.

For all other purposes the normal tax point rules apply. Therefore in the event of a theft of takings from a machine, VAT must still be accounted for in full on any supplies that have been made from the machine.

[VATA 1994 s 6]

3.7 VAT: VAT on minor promotional items supplied in linked supplies schemes

These are schemes in which a minor article is linked, although not necessarily physically linked, with a main article (of either goods or services) and sold with it at a single price. The price paid should normally be apportioned to reflect any difference where the items are liable to VAT at different rates.

However, if the minor article:

(a) is not charged to the customer at a separate price

(b) costs the supplier no more than 20% of the total cost of the combined supply (excluding VAT), and

(c) costs the supplier no more than:

- £1 (excluding VAT) if included with goods intended for retail sale, or
- £5 (excluding VAT) otherwise

the supplier may account for VAT on the minor article at the same rate as the main article—that is, no apportionment is necessary.

[VATA 1994 s 19]

3.8 VAT: Use of margin scheme for vehicle sales when incomplete records have been kept

[Obsolete.]

[*Notes*: This concession was withdrawn with effect from 1 April 2010. For HMRC's announcement of their intention to do so, see *Withdrawal of Extra-Statutory Concessions* (HMRC Technical Note, 23 April 2009) Chapter 2.]

[SI 1992/3122 art 8]

3.9 VAT: Recoveries under VATA 1994 Sch 11 para 5

Where an amount is shown or represented as VAT on an invoice issued by a person who is neither registered nor required to be registered for VAT at the time when the invoice is issued, the provisions of VATA 1994 Sch 11 para 5 (formerly VATA 1983 Sch 7 para 6) enable the Commissioners to require that person to pay an equivalent amount to them. The Act does not provide any relief in respect of related VAT incurred by such a person. On the grounds of equity, a person making such a payment may be permitted to deduct from it the amount of VAT incurred on supplies to him of goods and services that were directly attributable to any invoiced supply in respect of which such payment is required.

Where such a person has made a supply to a taxable person and, on the invoice, showed or represented an amount as VAT, the recipient of the supply has no logical entitlement to treat that amount as his input tax. If it is clear that the taxable person who received the supply has treated such an amount as input tax in good faith, action to recover the amount so deducted may be remitted on grounds of equity.

[VATA 1994 s 24 and Sch 11 para 5; SI 1995/2518 reg 29]

3.10 VAT: VAT on necessary meals and accommodation provided by recognised representative sporting bodies to amateur sports persons chosen to represent that body in a competition

VAT (Input Tax) Order 1992 (SI 1992/3222) (formerly VAT (Special Provisions) Order 1981 (SI 1981/1741) as amended by the VAT (Special Provisions) (Amendment) Order 1988 (SI 1988/1124)) prevents input tax deduction where goods or services have been provided for the purposes of business entertainment except where this entertainment is of an employee. The effect of this provision is to produce different treatment as between, for example, professional football teams and amateur football teams. This is because the professional players are employees of their clubs and input tax is deductible, while the amateur players are, by definition, not employees and input tax is blocked. This distinction between amateur and professional sportsmen has led to inequity in the VAT treatment of certain amateur representative bodies who are registered for VAT and account for output tax on "gate money" in the same way as professional clubs, but cannot recover VAT on some of their genuine business expenses.

With the overwhelming number of clubs this has provided no problem as members' subscriptions are regarded as being payment, in part, for any accommodation or meals that they may receive when playing for that club. However, problems have been encountered with certain bodies that choose, from affiliated clubs, individual amateur sports persons to represent their country or county. These persons so selected are not full subscribing members of the representational body. They pay a very small nominal subscription, or no subscription at all so the provision in Notice 700/65—entertainment of members of clubs, associations etc—cannot apply. To remove this inequity of treatment as between professional and amateur bodies, it has been agreed that input tax necessarily incurred on the provision of accommodation and meals for team members selected by such representative bodies may be deductible as input tax. This concession not only applies to selected players but also to the committee members of the body who are to be treated as "persons engaged in the management of a company and deemed to be employees of that company". The concession does not cover alcoholic drinks and tobacco (including cigarettes and cigars) provided for consumption by players and committee members.

[SI 1992/3222 art 5]

3.11 VAT: Incorrect customer declaration

Where a customer provides an incorrect declaration claiming eligibility for zero-rating under Groups 2, 4, 5, 6, 8, 12 or 15 of VATA 1994 Sch 8, or eligibility for a reduced rate under Group 1 of Sch 7A for the qualifying use of fuel and power, and where a supplier, despite having taken all reasonable steps to check the validity of the declaration, nonetheless fails to identify the inaccuracy and in good faith makes the supplies concerned at the zero rate, or a reduced rate, HM Revenue & Customs will not seek to recover the tax due from the supplier.

[VATA 1994 s 73]

3.12 VAT: Buses with special facilities for carrying disabled persons

[. . .]

[*Notes*: The text of this concession has been omitted. The concession was given legislative effect from 6 April 2009 by the VAT (Input Tax) (Amendment) Order 2009, SI 2009/217, art 2.]

3.13 VAT: Repayment of import VAT to shipping [agents] and freight forwarders

Import VAT may be paid directly to shipping agents and freight forwarders where importers go into liquidation, or where an administrator or administrative receiver has been appointed who certifies that, in his or her opinion, ordinary unsecured creditors would receive nothing in a liquidation, leaving the agents unable to recover VAT paid on their behalf. The importers must have gone into a formal state of insolvency or receivership within six months of the date of lodgement of the Customs entry, and the goods must have remained under the agents' control throughout their stay in the UK and have been re-exported unused from the European Community.

[*Notes*: The word "agents" in square brackets has been substituted for "against" in conformity with the title of the concession as previously published in Notice No 48 (March 2002) para 3.13.]

[VATA 1994 s 25]

3.14 VAT: Zero-rating of certain supplies of free zone goods

From 1 August 1991 the supply of goods subject to import VAT which are free zone goods in the UK may be zero-rated on condition that there is an agreement between the supplier and the customer that the customer will clear the goods for removal from the zone and will take responsibility for payment of the import VAT.

[VATA 1994 s 30]

3.15 VAT: Printed matter published in instalments

Books are zero-rated for VAT under VATA 1994 Sch 8 Group 3 item 1 (formerly VATA 1983 Sch 5 Group 3 item 1). However, there is a specialist area of the market known as continuity publishing or part-works where the product is supplied in parts over varying periods but builds up into a greater whole, ie a loose-leaf book. Unless such items, when viewed independently, are books etc at the time of supply, they are not entitled to zero-rating under the present law.

From 1 February 1993 by way of concession, if, at the time of supply, an article is or was [not] by itself regarded as a book, including a loose-leaf book, qualifying for zero-rating under VATA 1994 Sch 8 Group 3 item 1, but is or was a part of a larger finite work which itself would fall under Sch 8 Group 3 item 1 as a book, then the individual component parts may also be zero-rated where they are or were being supplied either direct by the publisher or through a distribution chain to the final consumer.

From 26 October 1993 by way of further concession in relation to card-based boxed continuity series publications, such publications, even though not bound or held together other than in or by their container, and having all the other characteristics of a book, will for VAT purposes be treated as a book.

[*Note*: The word "not" in squared brackets substituted for the word "no" in the Notice.]

[VATA 1994 Sch 8 Group 3 item 1]

3.16 VAT: Connection to the gas or electricity mains supply

Connection to the gas or electricity mains supply, which would have been [a] zero-rated supply before 1 April 1994 by virtue of VATA 1983 Sch 5 Group 7, may continue to be treated as a zero-rated supply provided that:

(a) it is the first connection to the gas or electricity mains supply (as the case may be) of:
- a building, or part of a building, which consists of a dwelling or number of dwellings
- a building, or part of a building, used solely for a relevant residential purpose (within the meaning of note 4 to Group 7)
- a building, or part of a building, used by a charity otherwise than in the course or furtherance of a business
- a residential caravan (that is to say a caravan on a site in respect of which there is no covenant, statutory planning consent or similar permission precluding occupation throughout the year), or
- a houseboat (within the meaning of [note 6 to Group 7]), and

(b) the person receiving the supply does not do so for the purpose of any business carried on by him.

[*Notes*: (1) The word "a" in square brackets appears to have been omitted from the notice in error. (2) The words "note 6 to Group 7" in square brackets have been substituted for "Group 6 to Note 7", which is clearly incorrect. (3) This concession is being withdrawn with effect from 1 January 2012 on the grounds that "there are no legal vires in EU law which would permit this ESC to be introduced in UK legislation": see Withdrawal of extra statutory concessions (HMRC Technical Note, 13 December 2010) Chapter 2.]

[VATA 1994 Sch 8 Group 5 item 2]

3.17 VAT: Zero-rating of supplies of training for foreign governments

From 1 October 1993 the services of training (not being services comprised in any Group of VATA 1994 Sch 9 (formerly VATA 1983 Sch 6), supplied to a foreign government in furtherance of its sovereign activities (and not its business activities), is liable to VAT at the zero rate provided the supplier retains a statement in writing from that government (or its accredited representative), that the trainees are employed in furtherance of its sovereign activities.

[VATA 1994 s 30]

3.18 VAT: Exemption for all domestic service charges

The concession exempts from 1 April 1994 all mandatory service charges or similar charges paid by the occupants of residential property towards the upkeep of the dwellings or block of flats in which they reside and towards the provision of a warden, caretakers, and people performing a similar function for those occupants. The concession does not exempt service charges paid in respect of holiday accommodation as defined in VATA 1994 Sch 9 Group 1 [Item] 1(*e*) and Notes 11–13 (formerly VATA 1983 Sch 6 Group 1 [Item] 1(*d*) and Notes 10, 10A and 10B).

[VATA 1994 Sch 9 Group 1]

3.19 VAT: Supplies of "relevant goods" to charities

Where "relevant goods" of a kind described in VATA 1994 Sch 8 Group 15 Note 3 are supplied to a charity:

(a) whose sole purpose and function is to provide a range of care services to meet the personal needs of handicapped people (of which transport might form a part), or

(b) which provides transport services predominantly to handicapped people,

then by concession, the supply of those goods will be zero-rated, as will the repair and maintenance of those goods and the supply of any further goods in connection with that repair and maintenance.

"Handicapped" means chronically sick or disabled.

In order to be eligible for this concession, a charity must demonstrate that it meets the requirements of sub-paragraphs (*a*) or (*b*) above by way of:

- its charitable aims and objectives
- its publicity and advertising material
- any documents which it has issued for the purpose of obtaining funding from a third party such as a local authority
- its day-to-day operations, and
- any other evidence that may be relevant.

[VATA 1994 Sch 8 Group 15 items 5–7]

3.20 VAT: Disapplication of Repayment of Input Tax (VATA 1994 s 36(4A) and the VAT Regulations 1995, SI 1995/2518 (as amended by the VAT (Amendment) Regulations 1997, SI 1997/1086)

1 Subject to paragraphs 3 and 4 below, VATA 1994 s 36(4A) will not apply to any person where:

(a) an insolvency procedure has commenced in relation to that person under VATA 1994 s 81(4B), (4C) and (5)

(b) the claimant's notification of his claim for bad debt relief in accordance with the VAT Regulations 1995, SI 1995/2518 reg 166A, is received after the insolvency procedure has commenced, and

(c) each relevant supply upon which the claim for bad debt relief is based, was made prior to the commencement of the insolvency procedure.

2. Paragraph 1 above applies whether or not the business of the person who is the subject of the insolvency procedure continues to be carried on.

3. Paragraph 1 above does not apply unless the Commissioners have received notification on Form VAT 769 "Notification of Insolvency details", or such other notification as the Commissioners may require, in respect of the insolvency procedure referred to in that paragraph.

4. Paragraph 1 above does not apply in circumstances where its application would give rise to tax avoidance.

The insolvency procedures to which the extra-statutory concession applies

The insolvency procedures included in VATA 1994 s 81 for the purposes of this concession are:

- bankruptcy
- compulsory liquidation (winding up)
- creditors' voluntary liquidation (voluntary winding up)
- members' voluntary liquidation (voluntary winding up)
- administrative receivership
- administrative order
- individual voluntary arrangement
- company voluntary arrangement
- Scottish trust deed, and
- deed of arrangement.

After further consultations with representatives of insolvency practitioners and colleagues within Customs who deal with insolvency policy, it has been agreed that the application of this concession should be extended to a number of other types of insolvencies that are not included in the strict application of VATA 1994 s 81. Accordingly this concession will apply to the following types of insolvency that are not included in section 81.

- Partnership Voluntary Arrangement.
  (Insolvent Partnerships Order 1994).
  (Insolvent Partnerships Order (Northern Ireland) 1995).
- Partnership Liquidation.
  (Insolvent Partnerships Order 1994).

(Insolvent Partnerships Order (Northern Ireland) 1995).

- Partnership Administration Order.
  (Insolvent Partnerships Order 1994).
  (Insolvent Partnerships Order (Northern Ireland) 1995).
- Sequestration.
  (Bankruptcy (Scotland) Act 1985).
  (Bankruptcy (Scotland) Act 1993).
- County Court Administration Order.
  (County Court Act 1984).
- Scheme of Arrangement.
  (Companies Act 1985).
- Deceased Persons Administration Order.
  (Administration of Insolvent Estates of Deceased Persons Order 1986).
  (Administration of Insolvent Estates of Deceased Persons Order (Northern Ireland) 1991).

Application of extra-statutory concession

The effective date for the application of the concession will be the date of the Customs claim in the insolvency. This will be the relevant date of the insolvency and the insolvency meeting date (if applicable).

In Administration Order cases the effective date will be the date of the Administration Order.

Where there is a subsequent insolvency the concession will also apply to that subsequent insolvency.

If an insolvency arrangement fails[,] the insolvency is annulled and the requirement to account for clawback will be reinstated.

The concession will only apply to a provisional liquidation if it is followed by a permanent liquidation. In these circumstances the clawback concession will take effect from the date of the provisional liquidation.

[VATA 1994 s 36]

3.21 VAT: Sales of poor quality goods

By concession, the supply by a charity of any goods which have been donated for sale or the supply of such goods by a taxable person who is covenanted by deed to give all the profits of that supply to a charity, shall be treated as zero-rated, provided that:

(a) the supply is a sale of goods donated to that charity or taxable person; but
(b) the goods, although of a kind which the charity or taxable person makes available to the general public for purchase (whether in a shop or elsewhere) are by reason of their poor quality not fit to be so made available.

[VATA 1994 Sch 8 Group 15 items 1, 1A]

3.22 VAT: Valuation of the refurbishment or fitting out of a building for the purposes of the capital goods scheme

3.22.1 Part I: Introduction

VAT Regulations 1995, SI 1995/2518 reg 113(*h*) defines as a capital item (ie an item subject to adjustment under the capital goods scheme):

> "a building which the owner refurbishes or fits out where the value of capital expenditure on the taxable supplies of services and of goods affixed to the building, other than any that are zero-rated, made or to be made to the owner for or in connection with the refurbishment or fitting-out in question on or after 3rd July 1997 is not less than £250,000."

Some businesses have difficulty in identifying "goods affixed" for the purposes of determining the value of the capital item under this regulation and this concession allows them to include in the calculation the value of capital expenditure on goods which may not have been affixed to the building.

3.22.2 Part II: The concession

A taxable person seeking to determine the value of a capital item under regulation 113(*h*) can include any additional amount of capital expenditure, over and above that incurred on supplies of services and of goods affixed to the building, incurred for or in connection with the refurbishment or fitting out in question.

3.22.3 Part III: Conditions

(1) This concession applies with effect from 1 January 2000

(2) a taxable person taking advantage of this concession must keep a record of the value of the capital item and of the supplies on the basis of which the value was determined, and

(3) a taxable person who had determined the value of a capital item in accordance with this concession must apply the capital goods scheme to the VAT incurred on all the expenditure included in the calculation of the item's value.

3.22.4 Part IV: Warnings and definitions

The Commissioners may withdraw or restrict the application of any part of this concession if they consider that it is being used to avoid tax.

Where expenditure on goods which are not affixed to the building is included in the value of a capital item the requirement to apply the capital goods scheme to the VAT incurred on that expenditure means that adjustments will have to continue to be made even if those goods have been disposed of, unless they are disposed of as part of the disposal of the whole interest in the building when a final adjustment (unless the disposal is made in the last adjustment period applicable to the capital item) must be made in the normal way.

[*Note*: A new VAT Regulations 1995, SI 1995/2518 reg 113 was substituted with effect from 1 January 2011 by SI 2010/3022.]

[SI 1995/2518 reg 113]

3.23 VAT: Supplies by Financial Ombudsman Services Ltd to ombudsman authorities

This concession provides that payments from eight ombudsman authorities for the performance by the Financial Ombudsman Services Ltd (FOS) of the complaint handling duties of the authorities shall not be treated as consideration for any supply in the course of furtherance of any business by FOS.

The payment of any amount at any time by the:

- Office of the Building Societies Ombudsman (OBSO)
- Office of the Banking Ombudsman (OBO)
- Insurance Ombudsman Bureau (IOB)
- Personal Assurance Arbitration Service (PASS)
- PIA Ombudsman Bureau (PIAOB)
- Office of the Investment Ombudsman Bureau (OIOB)
- SFA Complaints Bureau and Arbitration Service (SFACBAS)
- FSA Independent Investigator (FSAII)

to Financial Ombudsman Services Ltd (FOS) for the supply of services by FOS in connection with the ombudsman and complaint handling scheme duties by OBSO, OBO, IOB, PAAS, PIAOB, OIOB, SFACBAS and FSAII (as the case may be) between 1 April 2000 and 1 October 2000 shall not be treated as consideration for any supply in the course of any business carried on by FOS.

[*Note*: This concession appears to have expired.]

[VATA 1994 s 94]

3.24 VAT: Charities who provide care in an institution and also supply goods to disabled persons resident in their own and other institutions

1. This concession applies in relation to a supply of goods which, apart from VATA 1994 Sch 8 Group 12 Note 5B, would fall within paragraph (*g*) of item 2 of that Group, where:

- (a) the goods are goods other than spectacles or contact lenses, and are designed solely for use by a visually handicapped person
- (b) the goods are supplied by a charity at or below cost
- (c) the recipient of the supply is a resident or is attending the premises of a relevant institution as defined in Note 5I to the said Group 12, and
- (d) the charity is not actively engaged in supplying goods within paragraph (*a*) above solely to handicapped persons who are resident in or attending the premises of a relevant institution as defined by Note 5I to the said Group 12 operated, managed or controlled by the charity.

2. Where this concession applies, the supply of the goods may be treated as if it were a zero-rated supply.

3. The Commissioners may withdraw or restrict the application of this concession if they have reasonable cause to believe that it is being abused.

[VATA 1994 Sch 8 Group 12 item 2]

3.25 VAT: Resuscitation training models supplied to charities and other eligible bodies for use in first aid training

1. The concession shall operate to include in VATA 1994 Sch 8 Group 15 Note 3, the following:

- (a) human resuscitation training models acquired for use in first aid training in either or both cardiopulmonary resuscitation and defibrillation techniques, and
- (b) parts and accessories for use in or with the goods described in paragraph (*a*) above, where the parts and accessories are for use in the training of either or both cardiopulmonary resuscitation and defibrillation techniques.

2. In this concession resuscitation training model means a model which includes a head and torso designed for use in the training of cardiopulmonary resuscitation or defibrillation techniques.

3. In this concession cardiopulmonary resuscitation means a combination of expired air ventilation and chest compression.

4. The Commissioners may withdraw or restrict the application of this concession if they have reasonable cause to believe that it is being abused.

[VATA 1994 Sch 8 Group 15 Note 3(*a*)]

3.26 VAT: Works of art, antiques and collectors' items

The Value Added Tax (Treatment of Transactions) Order 1995, SI 1995/958 relieves from VAT certain transactions by treating them as neither a supply of goods nor a supply of services. This Order may also be applied, in the same way that it applies to works of art, to the following goods:

- (a) all works of art falling within paragraph (*a*) of Annex I to Council Directive 77/388/EEC (inserted by Council Directive 94/5/EC) which do not already fall within the said order;
- (b) collectors' items falling within paragraph (*b*) of the said Annex I; and
- (c) antiques falling within paragraph (*c*) of the said Annex I.

[*Note*: Directive 77/388/EEC Annex I has been repealed and replaced by Directive 2006/112/EC Annex IX.]

[SI 1995/958 art 3]

3.27 VAT: Use of the Auctioneers' Scheme for sales of goods at auction on behalf of non-taxable persons

From 1 January 1999, an auctioneer selling, on behalf of a third party vendor who is a non-taxable person, goods which have been grown, made or produced (including bloodstock or livestock reared from birth) by that person, may enter the goods into the auctioneers' scheme provided he holds a certificate from the vendor which includes:

(a) vendor's full name and address
(b) description of goods and date of sale
(c) declaration that the vendor is not registered nor required to be registered for VAT
(d) signature of vendor and date, and
(e) signature of auctioneer and date

and all other conditions of the scheme must be met. The completed certificate must be retained with the relevant records for VAT purposes. An example of an acceptable certificate is set out below:

AUCTIONEERS' SCHEME FOR SECOND-HAND GOODS, WORKS OF ART, ANTIQUES AND COLLECTORS' ITEMS

Extra-statutory concession number xx

Vendor's Certificate for goods grown, made or produced and sold at auction on behalf of non-taxable persons

I (full name)

of (address)

declare that I am not registered or required to be registered for VAT and that the goods detailed below are to be sold at auction on my behalf by (auctioneer's name)

Description of goods

Date of sale (to be completed by auctioneer)

Signature of vendor

Signature of auctioneer

Date

[SI 1995/1268 art 12]

3.28 VAT: Supplies by Financial Services Authority to self-regulating organisations

The payment of any amount at any time by the Investment Management Regulatory Organisation (IMRO), the Personal Investment Authority ([PIA]) or the Securities and Futures Authority (SFA) to the Financial Services Authority (FSA) for the supply by the FSA in the carrying out of the regulatory functions of IMRO, PIA or SFA (as the case may be) between 1 April 1998 and the coming in to effect of the Financial Services and Markets Act 2000 and similar payments by the Registrar of Friendly Societies (RFS) and the Insurance Directorate of HM Treasury (ID) for the supply by FSA in the carrying out of regulatory functions of RFS or ID (as the case may be) between 1 January 1999 and the coming into effect of the Financial Services and Markets Act 2000 shall not be treated as consideration for any supply in the course or furtherance of any business carried on by FSA.

[*Notes:* (1) The acronym in square brackets has been substituted for "FSA". (2) The Financial Services and Markets Act 2000 came into force on 1 December 2001. It accordingly appears that this concession has expired.]

[VATA 1994 s 94]

3.29 VAT: Charitable buildings

[. . .]

Notes: (1) This concession was withdrawn from 1 July 2010: see the notes to Revenue and Customs Brief 39/09, 1 July 2009 (not reproduced). (2) For transitional arrangements between 1 July 2009 and 30 June 2010, see VAT Information Sheet 8/09 (July 2009) paras 1–4 (not reproduced). (3) Charities which made use of the concession before 1 July 2010 were required to meet specified conditions before 1 January 2011. For the conditions, see Revenue and Customs Brief 26/10, 21 June 2010 in Appendix 1.

3.30 VAT: Retail pharmacists

(1) This concession applies in relation to a supply of goods which, apart from VATA 1994 Sch 8 Group 12 Note 5A, would fall within item 1 of that Group, when:

(a) the goods supplied are dispensed to an individual for his/her personal use while he/she is an inpatient or resident or while [he]/she is attending a relevant institution which is a hospital or nursing home

(b) the goods are ordered in accordance with National Health Service Act 1977 s 41, National Health Service (Scotland) Act 1978 s 27 or Health and Personal Social Services (Northern Ireland) Order 1972 art 63

(c) the goods are dispensed in accordance with the National Health Service (Pharmaceutical Services) Regulations 1992, the National Health Service (Pharmaceutical Services) (Scotland) Regulations 1995 Sch 1 or the Pharmaceutical Services Regulations (Northern Ireland) 1997, and

(d) the person dispensing the goods is paid for doing so by:

- the Prescription Pricing Authority
- the Prescription Information and Pricing Services Division of the Welsh Health Common Services Authority
- the Pharmacy Practice Division of the Common Services Agency, or
- the Central Services Agency.

(2) Where this concession applies, the supply may be treated as if it were a zero-rated supply.

(3) The Commissioners may withdraw or restrict the application of the concession if they have reasonable cause to believe that it is being abused.

[VATA 1994 Sch 8 Group 12 item 1]

3.31 VAT: Supplies by the Financial Services Compensation Scheme Ltd (FSCS) to compensation scheme authorities

The payment of any amount at any time by the Investors Compensation Scheme (ICS), the Deposit Protection Scheme (DPS), the Building Societies Investor Protection Scheme (BSIPS), the Policyholders Protection Scheme (PPS), the Friendly Societies Protection Scheme (FSPS), and the Section 43 Scheme (S43S) for the supply of services by FSCS in carrying out the compensatory scheme functions of ICS, DPS, BSIPS, PPS, FSPS, and S43S (as the case may be) between 1 February 2001 and the coming into effect of the Financial Services and Markets Act 2000 shall not be treated as consideration for any supply in the course of any business carried on by FSCS.

[*Note:* (1) The acronym in square brackets has been substituted for "FSA". (2) The Financial Services and Markets Act 2000 came into force on 1 December 2001. It accordingly appears that this concession has expired.]

[VATA 1994 s 94]

3.32 VAT: Electronic face value vouchers

1. Under VATA 1994 Sch 6 para 5, where a right to receive goods or services for an amount stated on any token, stamp or voucher is granted for a consideration, the consideration shall be disregarded for the purposes of the Act except to the extent (if any) that it exceeds that amount.

2. The paragraph currently only has application in relation to face value vouchers or similar devices which have a physical form, such as paper vouchers.

3. From 8 March 2001 by way of concession the paragraph shall also apply to face value vouchers or similar devices in electronic form provided that they operate in the same way as their physical counterparts.

4. Paragraph 3 above does not apply in circumstances where its application would give rise to tax avoidance.

[*Note*: VATA 1994 Sch 5 para 5 was repealed by FA 2003 ss 19, 216, Sch 1 para 3 and Sch 43 Part 2 as regards stamps, tokens and vouchers issued after 8 April 2003. As regards stamps, tokens and vouchers issued from 9 April 2003, VATA 1994 Sch 10A para 1(1) provides that it is immaterial whether they take a physical or electronic form. It accordingly appears that this concession has expired.]

3.33 VAT: Supplies previously made by the Post Office

The Postal Services Act 2000 replaced each reference to "the Post Office" within VAT legislation with a reference to "the Post Office Company". This concession maintains the scope of existing VAT reliefs following a restructuring of the Post Office corporation immediately prior to the transfer of the property, rights and liabilities of the corporation to the Post Office Company.

This concession extends the reference to the 'the Post Office Company' to include a reference to any wholly owned subsidiary of the Post Office Company providing the public postal service, for the purposes of:

(a) the VAT exemption provided for postal services in VATA 1994 Sch 9 Group 3 Items 1 and 2, and
(b) the zero rating of transport services provided for in VATA 1994 Sch 8 Group 8 Item 4(*b*), and
(c) the interpretation of "datapost packet" provided for in the Value Added Tax Regulations 1995, SI 1995/2518 reg 2(1).

Any reference in this concession to a wholly owned subsidiary shall be construed in accordance with section 736 of the Companies Act 1985.

[*Note:* VATA 1994 Sch 8 Item 4 was amended and a new Sch 9 Group 3 substituted by F(No 3)A 2010 s 22. References to the Post Office Company have been replaced by references to a universal service provider. It accordingly appears that this concession has expired.]

[VATA 1994 Sch 8 Group 8 Item 4(*b*) and Sch 9 Group 3 Items 1, 2; SI 1995/2518 reg 2.]

3.34 VAT: Tax reclaimed by museums and galleries covered by VATA 1994 S 33A

1. Scope of this extra-statutory concession

1.1 The Government is committed to free public access to the main national museums and galleries. Ordinarily, when a museum or gallery moves from charging taxable entrance charges to free admission, it loses its entitlement to recover the VAT incurred on the related goods and services it purchases. This is because admitting the public free of charge is not a business activity and thus there is no entitlement to recover input tax in relation to it. The purpose of the scheme in VATA 1994 s 33A is to refund this irrecoverable VAT to the bodies listed in an Order made under section 33A(9). The entitlement to such refunds will commence from the date the Order takes effect in relation to the museum or gallery listed in it.

1.2 When a person recovers input tax on goods or services and subsequently transfers or uses them for a non-business purpose, a supply of the goods or services is deemed to have been made under VATA 1994 Sch 4 paras 5(1) or 5(4) (goods), or under the Value Added Tax (Supply of Services) Order 1993, SI 1993/1507 art 3 (services).

1.3 Furthermore, where input tax had been recovered in relation to a capital item as defined in the VAT Regulations 1995, SI 1995/2518 reg 113, a move from taxable admission charges to non-business free access can have an effect on the proportion of taxable as opposed to exempt use of the capital item. This would result in adjustments of the input tax recovered under the normal operation of the capital goods scheme.

1.4 This extra-statutory concession aims to ensure that the museums and galleries specified in an Order made under VATA 1994 s 33A(9) are not required to repay input tax, properly recovered at the time on goods and services used in connection with taxable supplies of admitting the public for payment, solely on account of the move to free admission.

1.5 The concession will not be extended to any situation where it appears to the Commissioners that its use will assist in avoiding VAT, and where it appears to them that the concession has been so used it will be treated as never having applied.

2. Operation of this extra-statutory concession

2.1 Each of the following descriptions of transactions shall be treated as neither a supply of goods nor a supply of services, namely:

(a) goods which after purchase are subsequently put to a non-business use giving rise otherwise to a supply under VATA 1994 Sch 4 paras 5(1) or 5(4); and

(b) services which after purchase are subsequently put to a non-business use giving rise otherwise to a supply under the Value Added Tax (Supply of Services) Order 1993, SI 1993/1507 art 3.

This is providing in each case, that the change in use of the goods and services arose solely as a direct result of a body listed in an Order made under VATA 1994 s 33A(9) using the goods or services for the purpose of offering free rights of admission to the museum or gallery to which the Order specifies.

2.2 This paragraph applies to adjustments to the deduction of input tax on capital items under the VAT Regulations 1995, SI 1995/2518 Part XV. Adjustment will not be required in so far as a change in use of a capital item relates to free admission with related refunds of VAT under VATA 1994 s 33A. Otherwise, adjustments are not affected. Where this paragraph applies, the owner of a capital item shall in each subsequent interval adjust the total input tax on the capital item and the extent of taxable use of the capital item for the purposes of Part XV as follows:

(a) the total input tax on the capital item shall be deemed to be the proportion that would have been input tax if admissions which have subsequently become free had been free at the time the VAT was incurred; and

(b) the extent of taxable use of the capital item at the time the original entitlement to deduction was determined shall be deemed to be the extent of taxable use at that time if admissions which have subsequently become free had been free at that time.

3. Dates when this extra-statutory concession has effect

3.1 This extra-statutory concession takes effect for each museum or gallery specified in an Order made under VATA 1994 s 33A(9) on the day appointed in the Order for that museum or gallery, whether or not the day appointed was before the date of publication of this concession.

[*Notes:* For the order made under VATA 1994 s 33A, see the VAT (Refund of Tax to Museums and Galleries) Order 2001, SI 2001/2879, which came into force on 1 September 2001. (2) VAT Regulations 1995, SI 1995/2518, reg 113 replaced with effect from 1 January 2011 by SI 2010/3022.]

[VATA 1994 s 33A]

3.35 VAT: Apportionment of certain membership subscriptions to non-profit making bodies

Where a membership body supplies, in return for its membership subscription, a principal benefit, together with one or more ancillary benefits, it will normally have to treat the subscription as being in return for that principal benefit. This means that the body will have to ignore the liability to the VAT of the ancillary benefits and account for VAT on the whole subscription based on the liability to VAT of that principal benefit.

However bodies that are non-profit making and supply a mixture of zero-rated, exempt and/or standard-rated benefits to their members in return for their subscriptions, may apportion such subscriptions to reflect the value and VAT liability of those individual benefits, without regard to whether there is one principal benefit. This concession may not be used for the purpose of tax avoidance.

[*Notes:* HMRC take the view that this concession may not be used to rework previously submitted VAT returns: see Revenue & Customs Brief 6/09, 20 February 2009.]

[VATA 1994 s 19]

3.36 VAT: Imported works of art, antiques etc

[. . .]

[*Notes*: This concession is not reproduced. It was given statutory effect from 6 April 2009 by the Enactment of Extra-Statutory Concessions Order 2009, SI 2009/730, art 17. It accordingly appears to have expired. The concession was originally published in Business Brief 10/2002, 15 April 2002.]

3.37 VAT: Exemption for supplies of welfare services by private welfare agencies pending registration

[Obsolete.]

[*Notes:* (1) This concession was withdrawn with effect from 9 December 2010. (2) It was originally published in Business Brief 1/2003, 20 January 2003 and incorporated into Notice No 48 (March 2002) as para 3.37 by Update 3 (March 2003).

[VATA 1994 Sch 9 Group 7 Note 6]

8 Facilitation of Exports

8.1 VAT: Sailaway boats

Under VAT Regulations, SI 1995/2518 reg 129, the supply of a sailaway boat to an overseas resident outside the VAT territory of the Member States may be zero-rated provided the boat is exported to a place outside the Member States within six months of the date of delivery, and the supplier obtains satisfactory proof of its eventual export.

As a concession and to prevent loss of UK trade, the supply of a boat to a UK resident may also be zero-rated provided:

(a) the supplier has evidence that the UK resident intends to keep the boat outside the VAT territory of the Member States for a continuous period of at least 12 months;
(b) the boat is exported, within two months of the date of delivery, to a place outside the VAT territory of the Member States;
(c) the boat is not used for any commercial purposes between the time of supply and exportation; and
(d) the supplier obtains and holds satisfactory evidence of export of the boat directly to a place outside the VAT territory of the Member States on copy three of the form C88 (Single Administrative Document).

The above conditions apply to boats supplied both to UK residents who intend to keep them abroad and to UK residents intending to emigrate.

[*Note*: This concession is being withdrawn with effect from 1 January 2012 on the grounds that "there are no legal vires in EU law which would permit this ESC to be introduced in UK legislation": see *Withdrawal of extra statutory concessions* (HMRC Technical Note, 13 December 2010) Chapter 2).]

[VATA 1994 s 30]

9 Non-Commercial Transactions

9.1 VAT: VAT on goods supplied at duty-free and tax-free shops

The supplier of goods which are liable to VAT and which are supplied to intending passengers at duty-free and tax-free shops approved by the Commissioners may, for those goods which are exported directly to a place outside the VAT territory of the Member States, be regarded as the exporter and zero-rate the supply.

[VATA 1994 s 30]

9.2 VAT: Marine fuel

Commercial vessels engaged on voyages within UK territorial waters (or within the limits of a port), may receive certain types of marine fuel VAT free providing the conditions set out in Notice 703 VAT: Exports and removals of goods from the United Kingdom are met.

This relief extends only to those supplies of fuel which were zero-rated prior to 1 July 1990 under VATA 1983 Sch 5 Group 7 Item 4. It does not apply to petrol, DERV or lubricating oil.

[VATA 1994 s 30]

9.3 VAT and excise duties: Personal reliefs for goods permanently imported from third countries

Where property (including motor vehicles) which has been purchased in accordance with the terms of Directive 77/388/EEC art 15(10) and which otherwise qualifies for relief from payment of customs charges under the [Customs and Excise Duties] (Personal Reliefs for Goods Permanently Imported) Order 1992, SI 1992/3193 art 11, relief is not to be refused solely by reason of art 11(2) of that Order.

[*Notes*: (1) The words in square brackets have been substituted for "HM Revenue & Customs" to correct the title of the 1992 Order. (2) Directive 77/388/EEC art 15(10) has been repealed and replaced by Directive 2006/112/EC art 151.]

[SI 1992/3193]

9.4 VAT and excise duties: Personal reliefs for goods permanently imported from third countries

Where property (including motor vehicles) which has been purchased by members of UK forces (or by the civilian staff accompanying them) in countries outside the area of the European Community and which otherwise qualifies for relief from payment of customs charges under the Customs and Excise Duties (Personal Reliefs for Goods Permanently Imported) Order 1992, SI 1992/3193 art 11, relief is not to be refused solely by reason of art 11(2) of that Order.

[*Note*: The words in square brackets have been substituted for "HM Revenue & Customs" to correct the title of the 1992 Order.

[SI 1992/3193]

9.5 VAT and excise duties: Personal reliefs for goods permanently imported from third countries

Where property (including motor vehicles) which has been purchased under a UK export scheme by members of the UK diplomatic service, by members of UK forces or by the civilian staff accompanying them or by members of international organisations and which otherwise qualifies for relief from payment of customs charges under the [Customs and Excise] Duties (Personal Reliefs for Goods Permanently Imported) Order 1992,SI 1992/3193 art 11, relief is not to be refused solely by reason of art 11(2) of that Order.

[*Note*: The words in square brackets have been substituted for "HM Revenue & Customs" to correct the title of the 1992 Order.

[SI 1992/3193]

9.6 VAT and excise duties: Personal reliefs for goods permanently imported from third countries

Where personal belongings otherwise qualify for relief under the [Customs and Excise] Duties (Personal Reliefs for Goods Permanently Imported) Order 1992, SI 1992/3193 art 11 save only that the property has not been possessed and used for the specified period, then just as relief can be granted from customs duties as "special cases justified by the circumstances" under Council Regulation (EEC) No 918/83 art 3, similar consideration shall apply in respect of VAT and excise duties and relief may be granted accordingly.

[*Note*: The words in square brackets have been substituted for "HM Revenue & Customs" to correct the title of the 1992 Order.

[SI 1992/3193]

9.7 VAT and excise duties: Personal reliefs for goods permanently imported from third countries

Where personal belongings otherwise qualify for relief under [Customs and Excise] Duties (Personal Reliefs for Goods Permanently Imported) Order 1992, SI 1992/3193 art 11 save only that property is declared for relief outside the specific periods, then just as relief can be granted from customs duties as special cases under art 6, or under art 9 of Council Regulation (EEC) No 918/83, similar consideration shall apply in respect of VAT and excise duties and relief may be granted accordingly.

[*Note*: The words in square brackets have been substituted for "HM Revenue & Customs" to correct the title of the 1992 Order.

[SI 1992/3193]

APPENDIX 7. ADMINISTRATIVE AGREEMENTS WITH TRADE BODIES

The Commissioners have published information regarding the following administrative agreements made with trade bodies. These agreements permit members of the trade bodies to use procedures which take into account their individual circumstances to meet their obligations under VAT law. The agreements apply only to areas where the Commissioners can exercise discretion, and they convey no direct financial advantage or relief from the legal requirements of the tax.

Agreements Reproduced in Notice No 700/57/04

	Trade body	Subject matter	Remarks
1.	London Bullion Market Association	Supplies of bullion	
2.	The Brewers' Society	Deduction of input tax in respect of tenanted estate	
3.	Association of British Factors and Discounters	Partial exemption	
4.	Finance Houses Association Ltd	Partial exemption	Cancelled with effect from 31 January 2000
5.	Association of British Insurers	Recovery of input tax incurred in UK in connection with supplies by branches outside the European Community	
6.	Association of Investment Trust Companies	Partial exemption	
7.	The British Printing Industries Federation	Apportionment of subsidy publishing supplies	
8.	Marine, aviation and transport insurance underwriters who are members of a particular trade organisation	Claims related input tax and associated imported services	
9.	Association of British Insurers, Lloyd's of London, the Institute of London Underwriters, the British Insurance and Investment Association	Coding supplies of marine, aviation and transport insurance services	
10.	National Caravan Council Limited, British Holiday and Home Park Association Limited	Method of valuing removable contents sold with zero-rated caravans	The agreement has been amended
11.	Association of Unit Trust and Investment Managers	VAT liability of charges made in connection with Personal Equity Plans (PEPs)	The agreement has been amended
12.	British Bankers' Association	VAT liability of electronic banking/cash management services	
13.	British Vehicle Rental and Leasing Association	Car leasing and repairs and maintenance services	Effective from 1 August 1995
14.	Society of Motor Manufacturers and Traders	Calculating output tax on the self-supply of a motor vehicle	Effective from 1 August 1992

Trade body		Subject matter	Remarks
15.	Gaming Board for Great Britain and the British Casino Association	Competitions in card rooms	Revised with effect from 1 September 2001
16.	British Phonographic Industry	VAT liability of promotional items given free of charge	Dated March 1998
17.	Thoroughbred Breeders Association	Arrangements under which racehorse owners may register for VAT and the procedures that must be followed	Dated March 1993
18.	British Horseracing Board	Revised arrangements under which racehorse owners may register for VAT and the procedures that must be followed	Dated January 1998
19.	British Horseracing Board and Thoroughbred Breeders Association	Racehorses applied permanently to personal or other non-business use	
20.	British Horseracing Board and Thoroughbred Breeders Association	Keeping of stallions at stud	
21.	British Horseracing Board and Thoroughbred Breeders Association	Racehorses and time limits for exportation	
22.	Meat and Livestock Commission	VAT treatment of levies collected (invoices) from 1 October 1990 by the Commission from operators of slaughterhouses and exporters of live animals	
23.	Society of Motor Manufacturers and Traders Ltd	How the one tonne payload test will be applied in practice to double cab pick-ups	Announced in Business Brief 10/00, 8 August 2000
24.	Society of Motor Manufacturers and Traders Ltd	A simplified method by which motor manufacturers, importers and wholesale distributors may calculate the VAT due on the private use of stock in trade cars provided to directors and employees free of charge	Announced in Business Brief 10/00, 8 August 2000. For amendments, see Update 1 (April 2005)
25.	Retail Motor Industry Federation	A simplified method by which retail motor dealers may calculate the VAT due on the private use of demonstrator cars provided to directors and employees free of charge	Announced in Business Brief 10/00, 8 August 2000. For amendments, see Update 1 (April 2005)

Trade body		Subject matter	Remarks
26.	British Vehicle Rental and Leasing Association	A simplified method which daily rental companies my use to calculate the VAT due on the incidental private use of their hire fleets	

OTHER AGREEMENTS

Trade/professional body		Subject matter	Remarks
1.	Representatives of racecourses	Recovery of input tax	Announced in Business Brief 18/93, 17 June 1993
2.	Contract Caterers Forum of the British Hospitality Association	Framework within which the contract catering industry operates and accounts for VAT	Announced in Business Brief 9/99, 21 April 1999
3.	Chartered Institute of Public Finance and Accountancy	VAT treatment of contracted out local authority leisure services	Text of memorandum of understanding published in Revenue and Customs Brief 28/07, 22 March 2007 (now re-issued as Revenue and Customs Brief 80/09, 12 January 2010)

APPENDIX 8.

INPUT TAX DEDUCTION WITHOUT A VALID VAT INVOICE—STATEMENT OF PRACTICE (MARCH 2007)

The publication of this statement of practice was originally announced in Revenue & Customs Brief 36/07, 10 April 2007. Publication was also announced, in identical terms, in Revenue & Customs Brief 83/09, 12 January 2010.

1. This Statement of Practice explains and clarifies HMRC's policy in respect of claims for input tax supported by invalid VAT invoices. It also explains why amendments were made to VATA 1994 s 24(6)(*a*) and Sch 11 para 4(1) and regulation 29(2) of the Value Added Tax Regulations 1995 to introduce new measures. These changes were effective from **16 April 2003** and apply to supplies made on or after this date. The statement of practice was first issued in July 2003 and has now been revised to provide clearer guidance and the updated legal position. This guidance does not apply to situations where HMRC may deny recovery of input tax for other reasons such as "abuse" of the right to deduct.

WHY WERE CHANGES NEEDED?

2. These changes were made to address the increasing threat to VAT receipts by the use of invalid VAT invoices and are part of the Government's strategy to address fraud, avoidance and non-compliance in the VAT system. They are a proportionate and necessary response to a systematic and widespread attack on the VAT system, where the use of invalid VAT invoices is becoming an increasing pressure on revenue receipts, particularly in those business sectors involved in the supply of the goods listed at Appendix 3. In addition to the revenue loss, this has led to distortion of competition.

3. For the vast majority of business there will be no change, and for businesses trading within the targeted sectors the measure will only impact if you have an invalid invoice. If you are a VAT registered business, and you have been issued with an invoice that is invalid, you should be able to return to your supplier and ask them for a valid VAT invoice that complies with the legislation. If for some reason you cannot, this Statement of Practice sets out whether or not you may be entitled to input tax recovery. In most cases, provided businesses continue to undertake normal commercial checks to ensure their supplier and the supplies they receive are "bona fide" prior to doing any trade, it is likely they will be able to satisfy HMRC that the input tax is deductible.

THE "RIGHT TO DEDUCT" PRINCIPLES

4. The basic principle of EU and UK law underlying input tax recovery is that of neutrality. In practice, this means that any business that makes taxable supplies has the right to deduct the VAT incurred on goods or services that form a cost component of those supplies. EU and UK law also provides for rules governing the exercise of the right to deduct VAT. These fundamental VAT principles governing the recovery of VAT are not being changed.

5. A business has incurred input tax if the following conditions are met:

- there has actually been a supply of goods or services;
- that supply takes place in the UK;
- it is taxable at a positive rate of VAT;
- the supplier is a taxable person, ie someone either registered for VAT in the UK, or required to be registered;
- the supply is made to the person claiming the deduction;
- the recipient is a taxable person at the time the tax was incurred; and
- the recipient intends to use the goods or services for his business purposes.

6. If you are a taxable person, in order to exercise your basic right to deduct input tax, you must hold **a valid VAT invoice**. Without a valid VAT invoice, there is no right to deduct input tax. However, in the absence of such an invoice, you may still be able to make claims for input tax, but these claims are subject to HMRC's discretion. This of course assumes that a taxable supply has taken place. Where HMRC question the fact that an underlying supply has taken place, these provisions do not apply.

WHAT LEGISLATIVE CHANGES HAVE BEEN MADE?

7. The change to VATA 1994 s 24(6)(*a*) permits HMRC to consider evidence other than that contained in documents when exercising their discretion (Sch 11 para 4(1) is merely a consequential amendment to this change). Before this change, regulation 29(2) permitted HMRC to accept alternative **documentary** evidence to support input tax deduction without a valid VAT invoice. The amendment to regulation 29(2) simply permits HMRC, in applying their discretion, to consider evidence other than just documents.

WHAT CONSTITUTES A VALID VAT INVOICE?

8. A valid VAT invoice is one that meets the full legal requirements as set out in regulations 13 and 14 of the Value Added Tax Regulations 1995 (SI 1995/2518). The contents of a valid VAT invoice should show the following information (as set out in regulation 14(1)):

(a) an identifying number;
(b) the time of the supply;
(c) the date of the issue of the document;
(d) the name, address and registration number of the supplier;
(e) the name and address of the person to whom the goods or services are supplied;
(f) [Omitted by SI 2003/3220, reg 7(a)];
(g) a description sufficient to identify the goods or services supplied;
(h) for each description, the quantity of the goods or the extent of the services, and the rate of VAT and the amount payable, excluding VAT, expressed in any currency;
(i) the gross total amount payable, excluding VAT, expressed in any currency;
(j) the rate of any cash discount offered;
(k) [Omitted by SI 2003/3220, reg 7(*a*)];
(l) the total amount of VAT chargeable, expressed in sterling;
(m) the Unit Price.

A self-billed invoice is not a valid invoice unless the recipient meets the conditions for self-billing in Reg 13(3A) and (3B). The conditions for self-billing are also set out in Notice 700/62 – Self Billing.

9. A taxable person may issue either a less detailed tax invoice where the charge made for an individual supply is £250 or less including VAT, or a modified tax invoice with the agreement of customer. If this is the case, not all of the above information is required. Information about less detailed and modified tax invoices can be found in Section 16.6 of Public Notice 700 (The VAT Guide). Copies can be obtained from the National Advice Service on 0845 010 9000 or downloaded from HMRC's web site at www.hmce.gov.uk.

WHAT IS AN INVALID VAT INVOICE?

10. An invoice that falls short of any of the requirements laid down in Reg 14(1) of SI 1995/2518 is an invalid invoice-see Paragraph 8 above. This includes situations where some or all of the details do not relate to the person/business that made the supply or the details shown are those of a company that has gone into liquidation **or is missing at the time the supply is made.**

WHAT DO I DO IF I HAVE AN INVALID VAT INVOICE?

11. The simplest thing is to ask your supplier to issue a valid VAT invoice (suppliers are legally obliged to do this). If a taxable supply has taken place but a revised invoice cannot be obtained HMRC may apply their discretion to allow recovery of input tax.

HOW DO I KNOW I HAVE AN INVALID VAT INVOICE?

12. The first step is to ensure that you hold an invoice that contains all the right information. It is difficult to spot an invalid invoice where a false name, address or VAT number has been used. HMRC have established a team who can confirm that supplied VAT registration details are current, valid and match information held by HMRC. This is **not** authorisation of a transaction with that VAT registration, but can help, along with other checks to verify the legitimacy of your supplier. Such information can be obtained by telephoning 01737 734 then 516, 577, 612 or 761.

INVALID INVOICE AND HMRC'S DISCRETION

[13.] A proper exercise of HMRC's discretion can only be undertaken when there is sufficient evidence to satisfy the Commissioners that a supply has taken place.

Where a supply has taken place, but the invoice to support this is invalid, the Commissioners may exercise their discretion and allow a claim for input tax credit.

[14.] For Supplies/transactions involving goods stated in Appendix 3 HMRC will need to be satisfied that:

- The supply as stated on the invoice did take place.
- There is other evidence to show that the supply/transaction occurred.
- The supply made is in furtherance of the trader's business.
- The trader has undertaken normal commercial checks to establish the bona fide of the supply and supplier.
- Normal commercial arrangements are in place – this can include payment arrangements and how the relationship between the supplier/buyer was established.

WHAT DO I DO IF MY CHECKS INDICATE THAT A FRAUD EXISTS?

15. If your checks indicate that there may be a fraud you should consider whether you wish to continue with the transaction. You may also wish to inform HMRC Confidential on 0800 595 000.

I HAVE AN INVALID VAT INVOICE; CAN I STILL RECOVER INPUT TAX?

16. Not automatically. However, HMRC may apply their discretion and still allow recovery.

HOW WILL HMRC APPLY THEIR DISCRETION?

17. For supplies of goods not listed at Appendix 3, claimants will need to be able to answer most of the questions at Appendix 2 satisfactorily. In most cases, this will be little more than providing alternative evidence to show that the supply of goods or services has been made (this has always been HMRC's policy).

18. For supplies of goods listed at Appendix 3, claimants will be expected to be able to answer questions relating to the supply in question including all or nearly all of the questions at Appendix 2. In addition, they are likely to be asked further questions by HMRC in order to test whether they took reasonable care in respect of transactions to ensure that their supplier and the supply were "bona fide".

19. As long as the claimant can provide satisfactory answers to the questions at Appendix 2 and to any additional questions that may be asked, input tax deduction will be permitted.

20. Decisions on when to disallow VAT claims will only be made after an independent central review of the case has been carried out.

CAN I APPEAL AGAINST HMRC'S DECISION?

21. If HMRC refuse to allow deduction of input tax under this Statement of Practice, unsuccessful claimants can first ask for a reconsideration of the decision. Should that be unsuccessful, they will then be able to appeal against HMRC's decision to the VAT & Duties Tribunal.

APPENDIX 1

Decision Flowchart

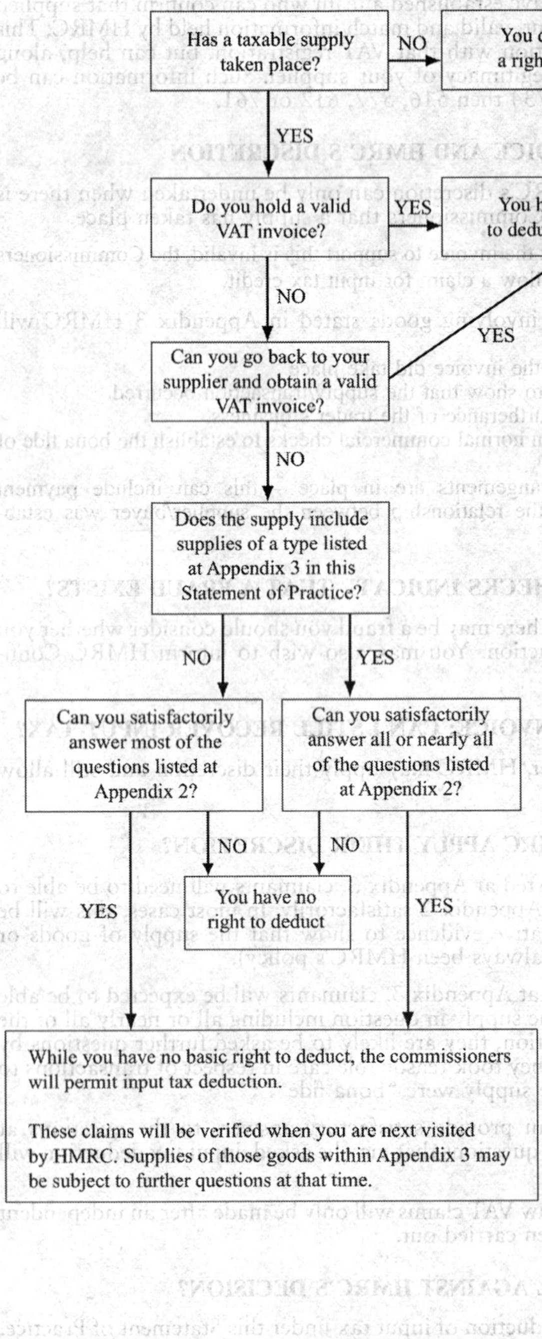

APPENDIX 2

Questions* to determine whether there is a right to deduct in the absence of a valid VAT invoice

(1) Do you have alternative documentary evidence other than an invoice (eg supplier statement)?
(2) Do you have evidence of receipt of a taxable supply on which VAT has been charged?
(3) Do you have evidence of payment?
(4) Do you have evidence of how the goods/services have been consumed within your business or their onward supply?
(5) How did you know that the supplier existed?
(6) How was your relationship with the supplier established? For example:
- How was contact made?
- Do you know where the supplier operates from (have you been there)?
- How do you contact them?
- How do you know they can supply the goods or services?
- If goods, how do you know the goods are not stolen?
- How do you return faulty supplies?

* This list is not exhaustive and additional questions may be asked in individual circumstances.

APPENDIX 3

Supplies of goods subject to widespread fraud and abuse

(a) **Computers and any other equipment**, including parts, accessories and software, made or adapted for use in connection with computers or computer systems.
(b) **Telephones and any other equipment**, including parts and accessories, made or adapted for use in connection with telephones or telecommunications.
(c) **Alcohol –** those alcoholic liquors liable to excise duty, which are defined by section 1 of the Alcoholic Liquor Duties Act 1979 or in any regulations made under that Act (eg spirits, wines and fortified wines, made-wines, beer, cider and perry).
(d) **Oils** – all oils that are held out for sale as road fuel.

APPENDIX 9. GRANT SCHEMES FOR LISTED PLACES OF WORSHIP AND MEMORIALS

BACKGROUND

In the March 2001 Budget, the Chancellor announced the introduction of an interim grant scheme for eligible repairs and maintenance to listed places of worship carried out on or after 1 March 2001. This scheme returned, in grant aid, the difference between the VAT actually incurred at the standard rate (17.5%) and the VAT that would have been incurred if the works had been charged at the reduced rate (5%). In the March 2004 Budget, the scheme was extended to cover the full amount of VAT incurred on eligible works carried out on or after 1 April 2004.

The scheme was due to continue until the earlier of: (1) 31 March 2006, and (2) an amendment to Directive 2006/112/EC (formerly Directive 77/388/EEC) introducing a permanent reduced rate of 5% for repairs and maintenance to listed places of worship. The reduced rate provisions of the 2006 Directive were amended by Directive 2009/47/EC. However, no provision was made for a permanent reduced rate for repairs and maintenance to listed places of worship. The scheme is currently due to continue until 31f March 2011.

In the March 2005 Budget, the Chancellor announced the introduction of an interim grant scheme to cover VAT costs incurred by charities in the construction, renovation and maintenance of memorials. This scheme is also currently due to continue until 2011.

LISTED PLACES OF WORSHIP

The listed places of worship grant scheme is administered by the Department for Culture, Media and Sport. For information about the scheme, and an application form, see www.lpwscheme.org.uk. The contact address is: Listed Places of Worship Grant Scheme, PO Box 609, Newport, South Wales NP10 8QD; telephone: 0845 601 5945.

In summary, a claim may be made if all the following conditions are met.

(1) The building is solely or mainly used as a place of public religious worship.
(2) The building meets one of the following conditions:
   - it is used for public religious services at least six times a year;
   - it belongs to a monastery, nunnery or other similar establishment; or
   - it is owned or vested in a designated organisation that looks after redundant churches. A list of designated organisations can be obtained from the contact address.
(3) The building is a listed building.
(4) The works were carried out by a contractor on or after 1 April 2001.
(5) The contractor was registered for VAT purposes at the relevant time.
(6) The works comprise repair or maintenance to the fabric of the building.
(7) The claimant holds an original VAT invoice or an original receipted invoice.
(8) The value of the works (excluding VAT) is £1,000 or more.

MEMORIALS

The memorial grant scheme is administered by the Department for Culture, Media and Sport. For information about the scheme, and an application form, see www.memorialgrant.org.uk. The contact address is: Memorials Grant Scheme, PO Box 609, Newport, South Wales NP10 8QD; telephone: 0845 600 6430.

In summary, a claim may be made in respect of costs incurred by a charity (including a religious group exempted from registration as a charity) after 15 March 2005 in respect of the construction, renovation or maintenance of a memorial in the UK or overseas. The following conditions must be met.

(1) The memorial must be a structure.

(2) The memorial must bear an inscription or plaque commemorating a person, animal or event.

(3) Members of the public must have access to the memorial for at least 30 hours per week.

APPENDIX 10.

INVESTIGATIONS AND COMPLIANCE CHECKS

INVESTIGATIONS

An investigation into a taxpayer's affairs may relate wholly or partly to VAT. The procedure followed by HMRC in differing circumstances is set out in the following notices:

Notice	*Title*	*Circumstances*
160 (November 2010)	Compliance checks into indirect tax matters	HMRC has reason to believe that dishonest conduct or deliberate behaviour has occurred
161 (January 2009)	Investigation into traders with suspected serious indirect tax irregularities (Missing Trader Intra-Community Fraud)	HMRC suspect that there are serious tax irregularities due to conduct involving dishonesty where knowing involvement in MTIC fraud is suspected
COP8 (November 2010)	Code of Practice: Specialist investigations (fraud and avoidance)	(1) Investigations carried on by the Fraud and Avoidance section of the Specialist Investigations directorate of HMRC where the civil investigation of fraud procedures (see COP9) are not used (2) Investigations carried out by another part of HMRC where the enquiry is being directed and coordinated by Specialist Investigations
COP9 (July 2011)	Code of Practice: Civil investigation of fraud	HMRC suspect serious tax fraud

COMPLIANCE CHECKS

FA 2007, FA 2008 and FA 2009 align and modernise the manner in which HMRC administers both direct and indirect taxes. For a summary of the legislation and the extent to which it has been brought into force, see *Implementation of the Review of HMRC Powers and Related Work* (HMRC Notice, 18 January 2011).

HMRC issue factsheets to taxpayers at different stages during a compliance check: see Revenue & Customs Brief 36/10 (31 August 2010). The factsheets are listed below.

Reference	*Title*
CC/FS1	General information
CC/FS2	Request for information and documents
CC/FS3	Visits – Pre-arranged
CC/FS4	Visits – Unannounced
CC/FS5	Visits – Unannounced – Tribunal approval

CC/FS6	What happens when we find something wrong
CC/FS7	Penalties for errors in returns or documents
CC/FS8(T)	Help and advice (for TEEL cases only)
CC/FS9	Human Rights Act
CC/FS10	Suspending penalties for careless errors in returns or documents
CC/FS11	Information about the failure to notify penalty
CC/FS12	Information about VAT and Excise wrong-doing penalties
CC/FS13	Publishing details of deliberate defaulters
HMRC1	HMRC decisions – what to do if you disagree

APPENDIX 11. LITIGATION AND SETTLEMENT STRATEGY

The Litigation and Settlements Strategy (LSS) sets out the principles within which HMRC handles all disputes about taxes, duties or credits. It applies to disputes which are subject to civil law procedures. It applies whether the disputes are resolved by agreement or through litigation.

LITIGATION AND SETTLEMENT STRATEGY (JULY 2011)

SCOPE AND PURPOSE

1. HMRC's Litigation and Settlement Strategy (LSS) is the framework within which HMRC seeks to resolve tax disputes through civil procedures:

(a) consistently with the law, whether by agreement with the customer or through litigation; and

(b) consistently with HMRC's customer-centric business strategy objectives of maximising revenue flows, whilst at the same time reducing costs and improving customer experience.

2. This document refreshes the previous LSS guidance published in 2007.

3. The LSS is designed to facilitate resolution of disputes in relation to a wide range of taxes, duties and associated payments and the term *tax* should therefore be interpreted accordingly.

4. *Dispute* is interpreted as covering all situations in which HMRC and the customer or their agent have a difference in view over what is the *right tax at the right time*, whether in the context of an enquiry into a return, an audit, pre-return work (whether undertaken on a pre- or post- transaction basis), or challenges to HMRC's legal interpretation brought by the customer. The definition of *dispute* includes a disagreement with a customer on tax liabilities with respect to a particular issue in a return, transaction or arrangement, but not a disagreement with a customer over several, unrelated issues.

5. *Litigation* refers to the resolution of a dispute through a statutory appeal to an independent body, including the Tribunals and the Courts, a common law claim to the Courts or an application for Judicial Review. It does not cover statutory internal reviews, litigation to recover debts, HMRC employment or commercial litigation.

6. The LSS applies to all tax disputes resolved through civil procedures and to all decisions taken by HMRC in relation to such disputes, at whatever level.

- Specific disputes governance arrangements within HMRC are there to give effect to the principles of the LSS in particular cases or for particular issues.

MINIMISING THE SCOPE FOR DISPUTES

7. A key part of HMRC's overall customer strategy is to help reduce the likelihood of situations arising which may give rise to a dispute.

- Disputes are costly for both HMRC and its customers and therefore HMRC is committed to supporting its customers to get their tax right without the need for a dispute.
- There are many strands of existing HMRC activity which play a significant part in helping to minimise disputes (e.g. well-framed legislation; guidance; rulings and clearances processes; HMRC's risk based approach to compliance work; relationship management for large and complex customers; etc).

ENGAGING IN DISPUTES

8. HMRC seeks to secure the best practicable return for the Exchequer, and to do that it must apply the law fairly and even-handedly. Entering into, or taking forward, disputes can contribute to maximising overall revenue flows in a fair and even-handed way.

- The objective of maximising revenue flows involves considering not only the tax at stake in the dispute itself but also – in circumstances where a precedent may be set, or where HMRC is seeking to influence customer behaviour – potential tax liabilities of the same or other customers.
- In general, HMRC will not take up a tax dispute unless the overall revenue flows potentially involved justify doing so.

HANDLING DISPUTES

9. HMRC will seek to handle disputes non-confrontationally and by working collaboratively with the customer wherever possible. In the majority of cases, this is likely to be the most effective and efficient approach.

- A collaborative approach requires all parties to be open, transparent, and focused on resolving the dispute.
- Working non-confrontationally can offer benefits in terms of effective and efficient dispute resolution in all civil cases, including where disputes are ultimately resolved through litigation.
- HMRC will foster a non-confrontational approach with the customer, but will not be deterred from efficient and effective dispute resolution by other means if collaboration is not forthcoming.
- HMRC will seek to articulate clearly the point(s) in dispute and timescales for reaching key decision points will be set and adhered to wherever possible.

10. Where there are good grounds to believe that evasion is involved, HMRC will consider whether a criminal investigation is appropriate.

11. In any dispute, HMRC will seek to establish and understand the relevant facts as quickly and efficiently as possible.

- A non-confrontational approach is likely to help identify and establish relevant facts. For example, HMRC will aim early on to articulate the basis of its enquiries – in terms of tax risks perceived. Wherever possible, HMRC will also seek to clarify and confirm its understanding of the relevant facts with the customer.
- Where needed, however, HMRC will make use of its statutory information powers in order to obtain the relevant facts and documents quickly and efficiently.

12. In complex cases, once sufficient facts have been established, taking early specialist advice, refreshed as appropriate to make sure it is current, can bring important efficiency savings. However no single piece of advice is necessarily decisive in determining HMRC's position.

13. HMRC will seek to work with the customer to understand fully the relevant facts and law, sharing and testing the strengths and weaknesses of HMRC's own arguments, and fully understanding and testing the strengths and weaknesses of the customer's arguments, before reaching a considered view on the strength of its case.

- HMRC will always seek to ensure that respective arguments are fully shared. This will however not normally require the exchange of copies of Counsel's or other legal opinions, as opposed to the substance of the arguments supported by such opinions, and HMRC would not normally expect legal professional privilege to be waived in respect of confidential legal advice.

14. HMRC will always consider whether something which initially appears to be an *all or nothing* issue is genuinely all or nothing or is in fact a case where there is a range of possible figures for tax due.

15. HMRC will aim to work disputes to the same professional standard whether or not the disputes are ultimately resolved by agreement or through litigation. Furthermore, HMRC will not usually persist with a tax dispute unless the revenue flows potentially involved justify doing so and HMRC has a case which it believes would be successful in litigation.

RESOLVING DISPUTES

16. Tax disputes must, in all cases, be resolved in accordance with the law.

- HMRC must be satisfied that both the substance of any decision leading to dispute resolution and the way that resolution is put into effect are fully in accordance with the law.

- Where there is more than one dispute between a customer and HMRC, each dispute must be considered and resolved on its own merits, not as part of any overall *package deal*. As a matter of process, however, it may be that a number of disputes will be resolved at the same time (each on their own merits), for example as part of a process of bringing a customer's tax affairs up to date.
- In certain cases Alternative Dispute Resolution can help support the resolution of disputes either by facilitating agreement between the parties or by helping the parties to prepare for litigation.

17. Tax disputes may be resolved either by agreement or through litigation, depending on which is likely to secure the right tax most efficiently. Where there is a range of possible figures for tax due, the terms on which HMRC will settle by agreement will also take into account which outcome secures the right tax most efficiently.

- In considering how to secure the right tax most efficiently, HMRC's objectives of maximising revenue flows and reducing costs will have regard to future as well as immediate revenue flows, costs and the deterrent effect on customer compliance.
- In considering settlement terms for one dispute, HMRC will take account of the potential read across to other open or prospective disputes as well as the impact which settling the dispute could have in releasing HMRC resources to work on other disputes.
- In order to ensure that overall current and future revenue flows and HMRC costs are not prejudiced, the terms on which disputes are resolved will take into account their likely impact on customer behaviour both generally and in relation to the customer concerned, including any question of avoidance, evasion, or a failure to take reasonable care.
- In most cases, resolution by agreement is likely to offer the most effective and efficient outcome. However, HMRC will not compromise on its view of the law to secure agreement, and in that context there will be cases where litigation offers the most effective and efficient means of resolving disputes. In such circumstances, HMRC will seek to reach resolution of the dispute by litigation as quickly as possible.
- Where there is a range of possible figures for tax due, HMRC will not settle by an agreement for an amount which is less than it would reasonably expect to obtain from litigation.

18. In relation to a dispute which is genuinely of an all or nothing nature:

- Where HMRC believes that it is likely to succeed in litigation and that litigation would be both effective and efficient, it will not reach an out of court settlement for less than 100% of the tax, interest and penalties (where appropriate) at stake. It therefore follows that, if the customer is unwilling to concede in such cases, HMRC will seek to resolve the dispute by litigation as quickly and efficiently as possible.
- Where HMRC believes that it is unlikely to succeed in litigation it will, in the majority of cases, concede the issue. In such cases, HMRC will not attempt to *split the difference* between its own and the customer's view of tax, interest and penalties (where appropriate) at stake. Taking a case to litigation where HMRC believes it is unlikely to succeed would need to be justified by the particular circumstances, such as a very large amount of tax at stake (in the case itself or from immediate precedent value where a large number of customers is affected), or a fundamental point of principle or behaviour at issue.

19. A decision to litigate (whether it relates to an all or nothing issue or not) does not mean that HMRC will stop taking steps to ensure an efficient and effective resolution to the dispute.

- A decision to litigate should be implemented expeditiously and opportunities for collaboration should continue where it could help reduce the costs or uncertainty of litigation for both parties.
- HMRC will continue to be open to considering the impact of any new information and / or analysis which may be put forward by the customer.

APPENDIX 12. REVIEW OF HMRC DECISIONS

From 1 April 2009, VATA 1994 ss 83A–83G make provision for the review of HMRC decisions as an alternative, or precursor, to an appeal to the First-tier Tribunal. Reviews may be offered by HMRC or required by a taxpayer in relation to decisions giving rise to a right of appeal under VATA 1994 s 83. This Appendix sets out an edited text of the guidance published by HMRC at http://www.hmrc.gov.uk/dealing with/appeals/indirecttax.htm.

Information notices and penalties in connection with them (see FA 2008 Sch 36) do not give rise to a right of right of appeal under VATA 1994 s 83. For HMRC guidance on the "direct tax" procedures applicable to them, see Appendix 13.

WHAT TO DO IF YOU DON'T AGREE WITH AN HMRC DECISION – INDIRECT TAX

[INTRODUCTION]

Your dealings with HM Revenue & Customs (HMRC) will normally be routine. But there may be occasions when you disagree with a decision made by HMRC. If this happens, you may be able to challenge the decision.

You may be able to resolve the matter by sending further information to the officer who sent you the decision you disagree with.

If not you can ask for either of the following:

- a review of HMRC's decision
- your appeal to be heard by an independent tribunal

This guide explains what you can do if you don't agree with [a VAT decision] made on or after 1 April 2009 [. . .]. It explains how and when you can ask for an HMRC review and how you can appeal to the tribunal.

[. . .]

The "direct tax" procedures apply if the decision you disagree with:

- about notices requiring you to send HMRC information or documents
- a penalty for failing to comply with one of these notices

[. . .]

HOW TO HAVE AN HMRC DECISION REVIEWED

When HMRC tells you about a decision that you can appeal against they will also offer you an opportunity to have the decision reviewed by an officer who wasn't previously involved in the original decision.

You will need to reply to this offer in writing – and send it to the address given in the decision letter – within 30 days of HMRC's decision.

There are also some circumstances in which you can ask for a review of a decision that was not sent to you but which directly affects what you have to pay to HMRC. Where this applies, you need to ask for a review within 30 days of finding out about the decision.

INFORMATION YOU WILL NEED TO PROVIDE WHEN ACCEPTING A REVIEW OFFER

HMRC will need the following information from you:

- your (or your business) name

- your reference number (as shown on the decision letter)
- the decision or assessment you disagree with
- an explanation of what you disagree with and why
- what you think are the correct figures and how you've calculated them (where applicable)

LATE ACCEPTANCE OF A REVIEW OFFER

If you do not write to HMRC accepting the offer until after the 30-day period has passed, HMRC will still carry out a review if you have a reasonable excuse why your acceptance was late.

You will need to give HMRC an explanation of why your acceptance was sent in after the 30-day period and show that you replied as soon as you could.

If HMRC does not think your explanation is reasonable they will write and tell you why. HMRC's decision about whether or not to conduct a review requested late is final. However, you may still appeal to the tribunal against the decision that HMRC have refused to review late. You have 30 days from the date of the refusal in which to do this, if you wish.

For more information about appealing to the tribunal, see the section below: "Appealing to the tribunal".

WHAT HAPPENS DURING THE REVIEW AND HOW LONG DOES IT TAKE?

HMRC will appoint an officer, who has not previously been involved with the decision you disagree with, to carry out a review of the decision. You can put your case in writing to the review officer.

The review will usually be completed within 45 days. In some instances it may take longer and HMRC will get in touch and ask you to agree a longer period. If HMRC does not write to you telling you the outcome of the review within the review period you can appeal to the tribunal.

When the review has been completed the review officer will write and tell you their decision.

If HMRC does not complete their review within the 45 days (or longer agreed period) they will usually ask you whether you will agree to an extension so that they can finish the review. If no extension is agreed, they will write to you explaining that the review is upheld. You will then have 30 days to send your appeal to the tribunal, if you wish to do so.

IF YOU DON'T AGREE WITH THE REVIEW CONCLUSIONS

If you disagree with the decision reached by the review officer you can appeal to the tribunal. You need to do this within 30 days of the review conclusion letter (or the letter telling you that the review conclusion is treated as upholding the original decision). The tribunal can alter the decision if it thinks it is wrong. For more information about appealing to the tribunal see the section below: "Appealing to the tribunal".

IF YOU DON'T REPLY TO THE REVIEW CONCLUSIONS

If you don't reply to the letter telling you the decision reached by the review officer, or appeal to the tribunal, within 30 days, HMRC will assume that you agree with them. They will then amend the decision in line with the outcome of the review and, where relevant, will amend the amount of tax or penalty you or your business has to pay.

APPEALING TO THE TRIBUNAL

If you want a tribunal to consider your appeal or application you must send it to the tribunal within 30 days of:

- the date on the decision letter (if you do not want a review)

- the date on the review conclusion letter (or the letter telling you that the review conclusion is treated as upholding the original decision)
- the date HMRC refused to do a review which was requested late

You can do this either by writing to the tribunal or completing the tribunal appeal form.

However you can't ask for a review by HMRC if you have already appealed to the tribunal, or appeal to the tribunal if you have already asked for a review by HMRC.

You can ask for your appeal to be considered by the tribunal without having a review first (except for certain decisions which are linked to a restoration decision). For more information about "linked decision" see HMRC's guidance "What to do if you disagree with a Customs decision about the return of seized goods" [www.hmrc.gov.uk/dealingwith/appeals/restorati on.htm].

PROBLEMS PAYING THE AMOUNT UNDER DISPUTE

The tribunal will not usually hear your appeal unless the tax due as a result of the decision you disagree with has been paid.

But if you believe that paying the amount you wish to appeal against would cause you hardship you can ask HMRC not to collect the payment due until the appeal has been considered by the tribunal. You will need to:

- write to the officer who made the original decision
- explain how paying this amount before the appeal hearing would cause you hardship

HMRC will write and tell you whether or not they agree with delaying the payment. If they do not, you can also refer this to the tribunal.

GETTING SOMEONE TO ACT ON YOUR BEHALF

You don't have to deal with HMRC personally. An accountant or other adviser can act on your behalf.

WHAT TO DO IF YOU WANT TO PROVIDE FURTHER INFORMATION

If at any time, you have further information that you think might affect HMRC's decision you should send it to the officer who sent you the decision letter. You can continue to discuss your affairs with this officer even if you have asked for a review or appealed to the tribunal.

APPENDIX 13. APPEALS UNDER THE DIRECT TAX PROCEDURE

Appeals against information notices and penalties in connection with them (see FA 2008 Sch 36) do not give rise to a right of appeal under VATA 1994 s 83. It is necessary to appeal against them by way of a notice of appeal given to HMRC. The provisions of TMA 1970 Part 5 apply to these appeals (see FA 2008 Sch 36 paras 32, 48). This is referred to as the "direct tax procedure".

This Appendix sets out the text of guidance on the direct tax procedure published by HMRC at http://www.hmrc.gov.uk/dealingwith/appeals/directtax.htm.

HOW TO APPEAL AGAINST AN HMRC DECISION – DIRECT TAX

[INTRODUCTION]

Your dealings with HM Revenue & Customs (HMRC) will normally be routine. But there may be occasions when you disagree with a decision made by HMRC. If this happens, you may be able to challenge the decision by appealing.

In most cases your appeal will be settled by reaching an agreement with HMRC. But if you can't agree, you can ask for either of the following:

- a review by HMRC
- your appeal to be heard by an independent tribunal.

This guide explains how to appeal against a "direct tax" decision from 1 April 2009 (please see the section below listing all direct taxes). It also explains what options are available to you after you have appealed, if you and HMRC can't agree.

LIST OF "DIRECT TAXES"

The process described below applies to what HMRC calls "direct taxes" in this guidance. The following is a list of direct taxes for the purposes of this guidance:

- Income Tax (including Self Assessment and tax collected by employers under PAYE)
- Corporation Tax
- Capital Gains Tax
- National Insurance contributions
- deductions under the Construction Industry Scheme (CIS)
- statutory payments, eg Statutory Sick Pay, Statutory Maternity Pay, etc
- Inheritance Tax
- Petroleum Revenue Tax
- student loan repayments
- Stamp Taxes (Stamp Duty, Stamp Duty Land Tax and Stamp Duty Reserve Tax)

The "direct tax" procedures apply if the decision you disagree with:

- about notices requiring you to send HMRC information or documents on a VAT matter
- a penalty for failing to comply with one of these notices

If the decision you don't agree with relates to a tax not in this list, you might want to check the process for what HMRC call "indirect taxes".

HOW AND WHEN TO MAKE YOUR APPEAL TO HMRC

When HMRC write to you with a decision they will also tell you:

- if you have a right to appeal
- how to appeal

- what time limits apply
- where to send the appeal

You must send your appeal to HMRC in writing, normally within 30 days of the date of decision you disagree with.

You can either use an appeal form (which you may have been sent with the decision letter) or you can appeal by letter.

INFORMATION YOU WILL NEED TO PROVIDE WITH YOUR APPEAL

HMRC will need the following information from you:

- your (or your business) name
- your reference number (as shown on the decision letter)
- the decision(s) or assessment(s) you are appealing against
- an explanation of what you disagree with and why
- what you think are the correct figures and how you've calculated them (where relevant)

WHAT TO DO IF YOU HAVE MISSED THE DEADLINE FOR YOUR APPEAL

Appeals sent to HMRC after the 30-day appeal period has passed may be accepted if you have a reasonable excuse why the appeal was late.

You will need to give HMRC an explanation of why your appeal has been sent in after the 30-day appeal period and show that you appealed as soon as you could.

If HMRC does not accept your late appeal, they will tell you. You can then apply to the tribunal to accept your late appeal. For more information about applications to the tribunal see the section below: "Appealing to the tribunal".

POSTPONING PAYMENT OF SOME OR ALL OF THE TAX DUE

If you have sent an appeal to HMRC you can apply to postpone paying the amount of tax you think you are being overcharged as a result of the decision.

Interest will still accrue on the postponed amount until the appeal is settled.

You can avoid interest accruing by paying the amount due. If the decision is changed and HMRC owes you money then you will be repaid the difference.

To apply to postpone the tax payment you will need to write to HMRC at the address shown on the decision letter and tell them:

- why you think the amount you (or your business) have been asked to pay is too much, and by how much
- what amount you propose to pay while your appeal is being settled

HMRC will write to you and tell you whether or not they agree with postponing the tax payment due or they may suggest an alternative amount should be postponed. If they don't agree you can ask the tribunal to decide the matter.

APPEALS SETTLED BY AGREEMENT WITH HMRC

Most appeals are settled by agreement with HMRC.

HMRC will consider your reasons for appealing and may agree with you whether, and how, the decision should be amended. HMRC will confirm the agreement in writing and you will have 30 days within which to tell HMRC if you change your mind.

They will then amend the amount of tax or penalty you or your business has to pay.

IF YOUR APPEAL CAN'T BE SETTLED BY AGREEMENT

If your appeal can't be settled by agreement HMRC may offer you a review.

Alternatively, at any time after sending your appeal to HMRC you can either:

- ask HMRC to review their decision
- ask the tribunal to consider your appeal

If you choose to have a review of HMRC's decision you can still ask the tribunal to consider your appeal, once the review has finished. But you cannot do both at the same time.

HOW TO HAVE AN HMRC DECISION REVIEWED

HMRC aims to settle most appeals by agreement. In some cases, after considering your reasons for appealing and discussing your reasons with you, HMRC may still be unable to agree with you.

Where this happens they will write to you and explain why they don't agree with you. They will also offer you a review of their decision by another officer not previously involved in the original decision.

If HMRC offers you a review you should write to them at the address on the letter, telling them whether you accept the offer. You need to do this within 30 days of the offer being made.

Even if HMRC hasn't offered you a review, you can write to the officer who made the original decision and ask for a review. If you do this HMRC will write to you explaining their view of the matter under appeal. Usually they have 30 days to do this. The review will not start until after this has happened.

LATE ACCEPTANCE OF A REVIEW OFFER

If HMRC offer you a review but you do not write to HMRC accepting the offer until after the 30-day period has passed, HMRC will still carry out a review if you have a reasonable excuse why your acceptance was late.

You will need to give HMRC an explanation of why your acceptance was sent in after the 30-day period and show that you replied as soon as you could.

If HMRC does not think your explanation is reasonable they will write and tell you why. You may then send your appeal to the tribunal, and ask the tribunal to accept your appeal late, if you wish. For more information about appealing to the tribunal see the section below: "Appealing to the tribunal".

WHAT HAPPENS DURING THE REVIEW AND HOW LONG DOES IT TAKE?

HMRC will appoint an officer, who has not previously been involved with the decision you are appealing against, to carry out a review of the decision. You can put your case to the review officer. This is usually done in writing but other arrangements can be made.

The review will usually be completed within 45 days. In some cases it may take longer and HMRC will get in touch and ask you to agree to a longer period. If HMRC do not write to you telling you the outcome of the review within the review period you can send your appeal to the tribunal.

When the review has been completed the review officer will write and tell you their decision.

If HMRC does not complete their review within the 45 days (or longer agreed period) they will usually ask you whether you will agree to an extension so that they can finish the review. If no extension is agreed, they will write to you explaining that the review is upheld. You will then have 30 days to send your appeal to the tribunal, if you wish to do so.

IF YOU DON'T AGREE WITH THE REVIEW CONCLUSIONS

If you disagree with the decision reached by the review officer you can ask for your appeal to be heard by an independent tribunal. You need to do this within 30 days of the review conclusion letter (or the letter telling you that the review conclusion is treated as upholding the original decision). The tribunal can alter the decision if it thinks it is wrong. For more information about appealing to the tribunal see the section below, "Appealing to the tribunal".

IF YOU DON'T REPLY TO THE REVIEW CONCLUSIONS

If you don't reply to the letter telling you the decision reached by the review officer, or send your appeal to the tribunal, within 30 days, HMRC will assume that you agree with them. They will then amend the decision in line with the outcome of the review and, where relevant, will amend the amount of tax or penalty you or your business has to pay.

APPEALING TO THE TRIBUNAL

If you want a tribunal to consider your appeal or application you must send it to the tribunal. If you have not been offered a review you can do this at any time after sending your appeal to HMRC. However if you have:

- been offered a review, and do not want one, you must send your appeal to the tribunal within 30 days of date of the letter offering the review
- had a review and HMRC have written to you telling you their review conclusion (or to tell you that the review conclusion is treated as upholding the original decision) you must send your appeal to the tribunal within 30 days of date of that letter

You can do this either by writing to the tribunal or completing the tribunal appeal form.

You can only ask for your appeal to be considered by the tribunal if you have already sent an appeal to HMRC. You do not have to have a review as well.

However you can't ask for a review by HMRC if you have already appealed to the tribunal, or appeal to the tribunal if you have already asked for a review by HMRC.

GETTING SOMEONE TO APPEAL OR ASK FOR A REVIEW FOR YOU

You don't have to appeal or ask for a review personally. An accountant or other adviser can do this on your behalf.

WHAT TO DO IF YOU WANT TO PROVIDE FURTHER INFORMATION

If at any time, you have further information that you think might affect HMRC's decision, you should send it to the officer who sent you the decision letter. You can continue to discuss your affairs with this officer even if you have asked for a review or appealed to the tribunal.

APPENDIX 14. APPEALS TO THE FIRST-TIER TRIBUNAL

The Tax Chamber of the First-tier Tribunal has published a booklet on how to make an appeal. This Appendix sets out the text of this booklet in so far as it applies to VAT.

MAKING AN APPEAL (AUGUST 2010)

1. THE TRIBUNALS SERVICE

The Tribunals Service is part of the Ministry of Justice and provides administrative support for the Tribunals' judiciary who hear cases and decide appeals. The tax appeals system was created on 1 April 2009, and this provides for tax appeals to be heard in a First-tier Tax Chamber, with a right of appeal with permission to the Upper Tribunal. The tax appeals system is totally independent of Her Majesty's Revenue and Customs (HMRC).

2. ABOUT THIS BOOKLET

This booklet is designed to provide you with useful information about how to appeal against a decision of HMRC and how to make your appeal to the Tax Chamber of the First-tier Tribunal.

We explain what decisions can be appealed against and how you may bring a case before the tax tribunal. This booklet aims to give you the essential information you need to make your appeal, though it cannot cover all circumstances.

3. WHAT IS THE TAX TRIBUNAL?

The First-tier Tribunal is divided into several Chambers, one of which is the Tax Chamber. Throughout this booklet this Tax Chamber is referred to as the tax tribunal. The tax tribunal hears the full range of appeals against HMRC decisions in relation to direct and indirect tax cases (explained in **paragraph 4** below). It has a single set of procedural rules giving it the flexibility to deal with the whole range of tax matters from the straightforward to the complex.

The tax tribunal is completely independent of HMRC, and cases are heard by Judges and other Members who are qualified to hear cases. **Annex A** provides a list of the types of tax appeal the tribunal can deal with.

4. APPEAL RIGHTS

You can appeal only where the law gives you a right of appeal. Not every HMRC decision on a tax matter carries a right of appeal. When you do have a right of appeal the official letter from HMRC giving the decision will make this clear. The tribunal will determine, in doubtful cases, if it has the jurisdiction (which means the power) to deal with the dispute or not.

The main areas that the tribunal deals with are tax assessments and penalties. A list of the more common tax decisions made by HMRC that can be appealed to the tribunal can be found at **Annex A**. This is not a complete list and appeals against tax credit decisions are dealt with in the Social Entitlement Chamber and not by the tax tribunal.

Direct tax refers to tax that is usually levied directly off an organisation or an individual person, such as income tax or corporation tax. Indirect tax refers to tax that is usually levied on goods or services rather than on an individual or organisations, such as VAT or Customs Duties.

5. THE TRIBUNAL'S POWERS

In deciding whether to appeal or not, you need to know what the tribunal can and can't do for you. The tribunal does not have unlimited powers. It can only do what the law gives it the power to do. Sometimes, if it accepts that your appeal is valid, it can replace the decision you are appealing against with the decision it thinks should have been made. In other cases it can only direct HMRC to reconsider their decision. If it does not accept that your appeal is valid it will uphold the decision you are appealing against.

6. DECIDING WHETHER TO APPEAL

Before making your appeal, you should know that the tribunal *cannot*:

- *Change the law.* It has to apply the law as it stands, even if that leads to an outcome that you think is unfair
- *Deal with administrative complaints about the conduct of HMRC officials.* (If you are unhappy with the way HMRC have dealt with your tax affairs, please refer to their guidance on how to complain on the HMRC website http://www.hmrc.gov.uk/dealingwith/complain.htm.)

We cannot advise you whether you have a case or whether you are likely to win or lose your appeal nor can we tell you if you should appeal or not. HMRC, in their decision letter, will have told you whether you have a right of appeal to the tribunal.

Many people who make an appeal choose to get professional advice and support with it.

If you do decide to get advice, please do so at the earliest opportunity – when you are thinking about appealing. Please do not leave it until your appeal is well under way as we may not be able to put your appeal on hold whilst you are seeking representation. If you face a delay in getting advice please keep an eye on the time-limit for appealing.

In indirect tax appeals, the tax tribunal cannot hear an appeal that relates to disputed tax unless either you have paid or deposited the tax in dispute, or the Tribunal (or HMRC) have waived that requirement.

In direct tax, the payment of the tax in dispute is usually postponed pending the outcome of the appeal, and this is not an issue.

7. HARDSHIP CASES – APPLYING FOR YOUR APPEAL TO BE HEARD WITHOUT PAYMENT OF THE DISPUTED TAX

This relates to indirect tax only. The tribunal cannot hear an appeal which relates to disputed tax unless either you have paid or deposited the tax in dispute, or the Tribunal (or HMRC) have waived that requirement. If paying or depositing the disputed tax would cause you financial hardship, you should first write to HMRC asking them to waive the requirement. It is essential that you demonstrate your financial position to them so that they can consider the matter fully. If HMRC do not agree to waive the requirement, you may apply to the tribunal to consider the matter. If HMRC oppose your hardship request, we will arrange a tribunal hearing to decide whether or not to allow it.

To make an application for hardship to the tribunal after receiving HMRC's decision on the matter, you should complete the relevant section on the Notice of Appeal Form and send it to us.

8. WILL I BE EXPECTED TO PAY TO GO TO TRIBUNAL?

What follows applies to appeals and applications started since 1 April 2009.

In most tax cases each side will pay their own costs. Your own costs in preparing your appeal will depend on the difficulty of your case and whether you decide to handle your appeal yourself or instruct a tax adviser such as a barrister, solicitor or accountant.

However, in certain circumstances, the Tribunal may order one side to pay costs to the other. Those circumstances can include the case where one side has behaved unreasonably in the way they have carried out the case. Costs awards in those circumstances are quite rare.

There is a special rule that additionally applies to cases categorised by the tribunal as "complex", where the winning party can ask for the losing party to pay its costs. However, you can choose to opt out of this rule, so that each party pays their own costs except where one side has behaved unreasonably. If your appeal is categorised as complex, you will be notified of this as soon as it has been categorised and given information about the implications, including your right to opt out of the "complex" costs rule.

For appeals started before 1 April 2009 the Tribunal has discretion to order that they continue to be covered by the rules which applied before April 1 2009. These old rules are as follows: the General Commissioner Rules (where no one was liable to pay the other side's costs), the Special Commissioner Rules (where costs could only be awarded for wholly unreasonable conduct) and the VAT and Duties Tribunal's Rules (where costs could always be awarded at the tribunal's discretion). Costs can only be awarded under the new rules for such appeals if they could have been awarded under the old rules.

Community Legal Advice and other help

Free legal assistance is not available in most tax appeals, see www.communitylegaladvice.org.uk. However, if you are on a low income, you may be able to get free help, for example from:

- a qualified lawyer or accountant (although most will wish to charge a fee)
- a Citizens Advice Bureau
- TaxAid at http://www.taxaid.org.uk
- TOP – TaxHelp for Older People at http://www.taxvol.org.uk which provides help to those over 60.

Any of the above are also able to refer your case to the Bar Pro Bono Unit. This is a charity which provides free legal assistance from volunteer barristers, see www.barprobono.org.uk. You cannot apply directly to the Unit, but if your adviser refers the case, and it is accepted, a barrister will act for you before the Tribunal. It is strongly recommended that you make contact with an adviser in good time before the date of your appeal, as it may otherwise be impossible to provide support. Because of resource constraints, the organisations listed above cannot guarantee that free legal help will be provided.

9. WHAT SHOULD I DO FIRST?

Before you can make your appeal, you must first have an appeal-able written decision from HMRC with which you disagree. HMRC will have informed you of your options if you disagree with a decision.

You should consider your options seriously before appealing, including asking HMRC to look again at the decision as many disagreements can be settled by discussion or correspondence with HMRC without you actually having to go to a tribunal. HMRC are able to offer a formal internal review of your decision by a reviewer who will have had no previous involvement with your dispute. If you do not wish to engage these processes you can still appeal directly to the tribunal.

10. TIME LIMIT FOR APPEALING

You will normally have 30 days to appeal a disputed HMRC decision. If you make use of HMRC's review process you will have 30 days to appeal from the date they tell you the outcome. The time limit runs from both the original decision and any decision following review. The letter you receive from HMRC, both the original decision and any decision following review, will confirm the time you have for appealing.

If you are making your appeal outside the time limit, you must give reasons to the tribunal in writing.

11. WHERE DO I OBTAIN A NOTICE OF APPEAL?

Appeals to the tax tribunal must be made in writing. When you decide to make your appeal to the tax tribunal, you are strongly advised to complete a Notice of Appeal form and send it to the address at the bottom of the form.

You can download the Notice of Appeal form from our website at http://www.tribunals.gov.uk. If you do not have access to the Internet, please phone us on **0845 223 8080** and we will send you a copy.

12. COMPLETING THE NOTICE OF APPEAL

The Notice of Appeal form is an important document as the details contained in this form will be used to process your appeal to a tribunal hearing, and to ensure we convene a panel that is appropriate for determining your case. It helps the tribunal to consider your case fairly and also helps us contact you with information about how your appeal is progressing.

A separate information sheet with guidance notes on completing the Notice of Appeal is available on our website and will be sent to you with the Notice of Appeal if you ask us to send you one. Please phone us on 0845 223 8080 to request this.

The completed Notices of Appeal should be sent to: Tribunals Service, Tax, 2nd Floor, 54 Hagley Road, Birmingham B16 8PE. Telephone: **0845 223 8080**.

If you prefer to complete the Notice of Appeal electronically, you can send it to us at: taxappeals@tribunals.gsi.gov.uk.

The tribunal will acknowledge receipt of your appeal in writing. You will be given a Tribunal Service Reference Number which you should quote whenever you contact us. At this stage, we will also notify HMRC of your appeal.

13. CASE CATEGORISATION

When you appeal to the tax tribunal, it will put your appeal in one of four categories: Default Paper, Basic, Standard or Complex. Which of the four categories your appeal is allocated to is dependent on the nature and complexity of your appeal.

When we acknowledge your appeal, we will tell you in writing which category your appeal has been allocated, and how your appeal will proceed. We will keep you or your representative informed of progress throughout your appeal. Please note, however, that if you have a representative, we will only send correspondence to them. If you disagree with the way your case has been categorised you should contact the tribunal.

Default Paper cases, by their nature, are generally decided by the tribunal after reading the Notice of Appeal and the other written material provided by you and HMRC. Default Paper cases are dealt with without a hearing, though you may ask for your appeal to be decided at a hearing. If you or HMRC request a hearing or it is decided there should be a hearing by the tribunal, you will be expected to attend. HMRC will also send a representative to the hearing.

Basic category appeals are dealt with at informal hearings (see **paragraph 14** below).

The vast majority of appeals within the Standard and Complex categories will be registered at our Tribunals Service Centre in Birmingham but will then be passed to other Tax tribunal offices in London, Manchester and Edinburgh. We will advise you in writing if we transfer your appeal.

Tax appeals are heard at a number of venues across the UK and we will, where possible, arrange for your appeal to be heard at a venue reasonably close to where you live or work. Sometimes, however, due to the size or complexity of an appeal, we may not be able to do this but we will let you know as soon as possible.

There may be occasions during the appeal process when judicial direction on your appeal will be sought. If this is required, we will inform you of the directions and any associated time limits which may apply. In more complex cases, you may be asked to attend a hearing at which a Judge will make directions.

14. STATEMENT OF CASE AND NEXT STEPS

The next step will usually be for the tribunal to request a statement of case from HMRC, except in relation to basic category cases. A statement of case is a written statement of

HMRC's position on your case. It will normally contain information such as the legislation under which the appealed decision was made, HMRC's position on the case and any other relevant information associated with the appeal.

Default Paper category (where there is no hearing)

A case categorised as default paper is generally decided when the tribunal has read the Notice of Appeal and other written material provided by you and HMRC. When we have notified HMRC that you have made an appeal against a decision which falls into this category, HMRC have 42 days to provide a statement of case to the tribunal. When the statement of case has been prepared, HMRC will send a copy to you.

You may provide a written response to the statement of case within 30 days of it being sent to you. You should send your response, if you wish to make one, to us and send a copy to HMRC. Please remember to quote your Tribunals Service reference number when writing to us and your HMRC reference number when corresponding with them. Unless you have asked for an oral hearing, the case will be decided by the tribunal when you have provided your response, or if you do not provide one, when the 30–day time limit has expired. The tribunal will send you its response as soon as possible after considering your case.

Basic Category (where there is an informal hearing)

The tribunal does not normally require a statement of case to be produced by HMRC for cases categorised as Basic. If your case is categorised in this way it will be listed for a hearing. You are expected to attend the hearing, when you will be given the opportunity to put forward your case, show the Tribunal any relevant documents you have and, if you wish, call witnesses. HMRC will also attend, and they may put their case, produce documents and call witnesses at the hearing. The hearing will be informal, and the tribunal will usually tell you what it has decided at the end of the hearing.

Standard and Complex categories

When we have notified HMRC that you have made an appeal against a decision in the Standard and Complex categories, HMRC have 60 days to provide a statement of case to the tribunal. The statement of case will contain similar information to that described above for the default paper category, though the facts and issues are likely to be much more complex. As with default paper cases, when HMRC have prepared the statement of case they will send a copy to you.

You will normally have 42 days from receipt of the statement of case from HMRC in which to provide to the tribunal and HMRC a list of the documents which you will rely on at the tribunal hearing. HMRC also have to provide a list of documents and copy their list to you. The tribunal may also make any other direction at this time as to what may be required of you, and may determine that your case requires more intensive case management. You will have the opportunity to express your views on how your case should be managed.

15. WHEN AND WHERE WILL MY APPEAL BE HEARD?

Hearings in the tax tribunal take place at a network of venues across the UK and we will arrange your appeal, where possible, at a venue which is local to you.

If your appeal is categorised as Basic, Standard or Complex, you should attend your hearing. For more information about the process of informing you of your hearing, please see **paragraph 16** below.

16. NOTIFICATION OF HEARING

If your appeal is to be decided at a hearing, we will write to you notifying you of the date, time and venue of your hearing. We will give you at least 14 days notice of a hearing, unless both you and HMRC agree to a shorter period. However, we will usually give at least a month's notice.

You should tell us immediately in writing if the date we set for your tribunal hearing is not convenient and give the reasons why you cannot attend. We will then write to you to tell you whether your postponement request has been granted or not. For appeals in the Standard and Complex categories, we will ask you in advance about dates which are inconvenient for you. In these cases, the tribunal will be less willing to agree to a postponement, though it will do so for good reason, such as sudden illness.

Appellants in the Basic category appeals will usually be asked to attend at either 10:00 or 14:00 on the day of the hearing. In the Standard and Complex categories you will be given a set time to attend and the case may last a number of days.

The time to arrive at the venue is given in your notice of hearing letter, and it is the latest time by which you should arrive at the tribunal venue. If you are likely to be late for your hearing, please telephone us and we will relay a message to the tribunal.

For further information of what can happen at your hearing, please refer to the booklet "At your hearing".

17. WITHDRAWALS OF APPEALS

You can withdraw your appeal at any time. Should you wish to withdraw your appeal, you should write to us immediately. If HMRC decide to concede the matter in dispute, they will write to both the tribunal and you.

ANNEX A: WHAT TYPE OF APPEALS DOES THE TAX TRIBUNAL DEAL WITH?

The tax tribunal deals with appeals against decisions about tax made by HMRC. These include [value added tax (VAT)].

APPENDIX 15. APPEAL HEARINGS

The Tax Chamber of the First-tier Tribunal has published a booklet on procedure at a tribunal hearing. This appendix sets out the text of the booklet.

AT YOUR HEARING (APRIL 2010)

1. ABOUT THIS BOOKLET

This booklet is designed to provide you with useful information about your tribunal hearing once you have received the notification of hearing date letter.

This booklet cannot deal with every set of circumstance or eventuality. Its aim is to provide you with information about what to expect at a hearing and what you need to do to prepare beforehand.

Please note that if your appeal is in the Default Paper category, the information provided in this booklet does not apply. For a description of the four procedural categories, please refer to our booklet "Making an appeal".

If you have any questions about your hearing which are not covered in this booklet, please phone us on 0845 223 8080. Textphone users can contact us via Typetalk on 1800108452238080.

2. WHAT DOCUMENTS WILL I NEED TO BRING WITH ME?

Essentially, you should bring evidence to the hearing which proves the facts of your case and also the legal grounds.

The proceedings for cases categorised as Basic are informal. You should attach the documents you intend to rely on with the Notice of Appeal form and bring them also to the hearing to make your case. HMRC will notify you in writing and in advance if they wish to raise new grounds contesting your case that they have not raised before.

In Standard and Complex categories, once you have received the statement of case from HMRC, you must supply us and them with a list of the documents you will be producing which you will rely on at the tribunal hearing. You must remember to bring these documents to the hearing. In addition to this, any document which you intend to refer to in support of your case should be available at the hearing. Examples may include invoices, books of accounts, bank statements, contracts or export documents etc.

If you are in doubt about whether a document will be needed, your best course is to bring it with you. You should not assume that the hearing will be adjourned to another occasion to enable the documents to be produced.

You should also bring with you the statement of case from HMRC together with any response you made.

3. WHO CAN BE PRESENT AT THE TRIBUNAL HEARING

The tribunal panel

The composition of a tribunal panel depends on the complexity of your appeal. The exact composition of the panel will depend on the needs of your case.

Tribunal clerk

When you arrive at the Tribunal venue you will be met by the clerk to the tribunal. The clerk will show you into a waiting-room and give you an indication of when your appeal will begin.

The clerk will deal with any last minute enquiries about the arrangements for the hearing. The clerk will also be present from time to time in the Tribunal room during the hearing in case the Tribunal needs administrative assistance and will help ensure that special needs are met.

HMRC representative

HMRC are also entitled to send a representative to take part in your appeal. You cannot ask for the HMRC representative to be excluded.

Your representative

A representative is someone who helps you deal with the correspondence and represent you at any hearing. If you have appointed a representative or somebody to act on your behalf and have provided us with their details, they are also entitled to attend the hearing.

You should attend the tribunal hearing. However, if you are unable to attend but have a representative the appeal may still proceed in your absence.

You may also bring with you to the hearing to support you a friend or family member or a business associate.

Witnesses

If you need the evidence of a witness to prove your case, it is normally up to you to arrange for the witness to attend to give evidence. If a witness is reluctant to attend, the Tribunal has power to compel attendance by means of a witness summons. If you think the evidence of a witness is necessary but it is not likely to be disputed by HMRC, you can ask your witness to prepare a witness statement in writing and then send it to them. A witness statement must be in writing and signed and dated by the witness themselves.

For appeals in the Basic category, the rules of giving evidence are informal. At the hearing of a Standard or Complex case, witnesses usually give evidence on oath or affirmation. After being examined (questioned) by the party calling them, the witness may be cross-examined by the other party, re-examined by you and perhaps questioned also by the Tribunal.

HMRC may also, if it chooses, bring a witness.

Public hearings

Hearings before the Tax Tribunals are normally open to the public. However, any party to the proceedings can ask for a hearing, or part of a hearing, to be held in private in certain circumstances. If you wish for your hearing to be conducted in private, you should write to us with reasons why. The fact that your financial affairs are personal is not enough; there must be a special reason such as it is in the interests of public order or national security or not do so would prejudice the interests of justice. Should you wish for your hearing to be heard in private, you should write to us as soon as possible. The Tribunal will make the final decision on this

4. BURDEN OF PROOF

In most appeals the "burden of proof" is upon you. This means it is up to you to show why the disputed assessment, penalty or decision is wrong. In most Penalty Cases the burden of proof is on HMRC, who must satisfy the Tribunal that the penalty is due.

You will need to put evidence before the Tribunal which will establish the facts, figures and dates etc. If you need to call witnesses or produce documents, it is up to you to make sure that they are all available at the hearing (see above).

5. WHAT WILL HAPPEN AT THE HEARING?

Procedures differ depending on the nature and complexity of the appeal. Generally, however, hearings for cases categorised as Basic will be conducted in an informal atmosphere while appeals in the Standard and Complex categories will tend to be conducted more formally.

Normally, you or your representative will be asked to present your case first, explaining why you think HMRC's decision is wrong and support your argument with documentary evidence and/or the spoken evidence of your witnesses. You will need to explain what is already agreed, what is in dispute, what evidence you are putting forward and the basic points you are making. It is essential for each party, in the course of presenting the case, to bring out all the relevant facts.

The HMRC representative will then be asked to present HMRC's case, again explaining it in detail and offering evidence to support the original decision. While a party is presenting their case the other party will be allowed to question the other or to respond to points raised by the other although if the Tribunal feels the questions are not relevant or if they have accepted the point they may ask you to stop or move on. The Tribunal may ask questions of you and/or your representative, HMRC representative(s) and any witnesses.

6. THE DECISION

A Tribunal which hears appeals categorised as Basic will normally announce its decision on the day of the hearing and will later provide a written decision with brief reasons.

In Standard and Complex cases, the Tribunal may announce its decision there and then but will usually reserve it to be given in writing later, normally within 28 days.

If your appeal is dealt with in the Default Paper category, a decision in writing will be posted to you as soon as possible after the appeal has been considered by the Tribunal on the papers.

7. WHAT CAN I DO IF I LOSE MY APPEAL?

If you are unhappy with the decision which the Tribunal reached, you will usually have a further right of appeal. When you receive the Tribunal's written decision notice it will contain information about how you can appeal to the Upper Tribunal on a point of law against a decision given by the First-tier Tribunal.

You can also ask the Tribunal to reconsider its decision on the grounds of a procedural irregularity, if you think there was one. For instance, a document relating to proceedings was not sent or received by a party or somebody related to the hearing was not present. When you write to us, you will need to identify the irregularity which you think occurred.

Full information on your further appeal rights will be provided to you with the decision notice.

APPENDIX 16. APPEALS—PRACTICE DIRECTIONS

This Appendix sets out the text of Directions made by the Lord Chief Justice of England and Wales and Practice Directions made by the Senior President of Tribunals.

[UNDATED]. DIRECTION—CLASSES OF CASES SPECIFIED UNDER SECTION 18(6) OF THE TRIBUNALS, COURTS AND ENFORCEMENT ACT 2007

It is ordered as follows–

1. The following direction takes effect in relation to an application made to the High Court or Upper Tribunal on or after 3 November 2008 that seeks relief of a kind mentioned in section 14(1) of the Tribunals, Courts and Enforcement Act 2007 (the 2007 Act).

2. The Lord Chief Justice hereby directs that the following classes of case are specified for the purposes of section 18(6) of the 2007 Act–

(a) Any decision of the First-tier Tribunal on an appeal made in the exercise of a right conferred by the Criminal Injuries Compensation Scheme in compliance with section 5(1) of the Criminal Injuries Compensation Act 1995 (appeals against decisions on review); and

(b) Any decision of the First-tier Tribunal made under Tribunal Procedure Rules or section 9 of the 2007 Act where there is no right of appeal to the Upper Tribunal and that decision is not an excluded decision within paragraph (*b*), (*c*), or (*f*) of section 11(5) of the 2007 Act.

3. This Direction does not have effect where an application seeks (whether or not alone) a declaration of incompatibility under section 4 of the Human Rights Act 1998.

4. This Direction is made by the Lord Chief Justice with the agreement of the Lord Chancellor. It is made in the exercise of powers conferred by section 18(6) of the 2007 Act and in accordance with Part 1 of Schedule 2 to the Constitutional Reform Act 2005.

30 OCTOBER 2008. PRACTICE DIRECTION—CHILD, VULNERABLE ADULT AND SENSITIVE WITNESSES (FIRST-TIER TRIBUNAL AND UPPER TRIBUNAL)

1. In this Practice Direction:

(a) "child" means a person who has not attained the age of 18;

(b) "vulnerable adult" has the same meaning as in the Safeguarding Vulnerable Groups Act 2006;

(c) "sensitive witness" means an adult witness where the quality of evidence given by the witness is likely to be diminished by reason of fear or distress on the part of the witness in connection with giving evidence in the case.

CIRCUMSTANCES UNDER WHICH A CHILD, VULNERABLE ADULT OR SENSITIVE WITNESS MAY GIVE EVIDENCE

2. A child, vulnerable adult or sensitive witness will only be required to attend as a witness and give evidence at a hearing where the Tribunal determines that the evidence is necessary to enable the fair hearing of the case and their welfare would not be prejudiced by doing so.

3. In determining whether it is necessary for a child, vulnerable adult or sensitive witness to give evidence to enable the fair hearing of a case the Tribunal should have regard to all the available evidence and any representations made by the parties.

4. In determining whether the welfare of the child, vulnerable adult or sensitive witness would be prejudiced it may be appropriate for the Tribunal to invite submissions from interested persons, such as a child's parents.

5. The Tribunal may decline to issue a witness summons under the Tribunal Procedure Rules or to permit a child, vulnerable adult or sensitive witness to give evidence where it is satisfied that the evidence is not necessary to enable the fair hearing of the case and must decline to do so where the witness's welfare would be prejudiced by them giving evidence.

MANNER IN WHICH EVIDENCE IS GIVEN

6. The Tribunal must consider how to facilitate the giving of any evidence by a child, vulnerable adult or sensitive witness.

7. It may be appropriate for the Tribunal to direct that the evidence should be given by telephone, video link or other means directed by the Tribunal, or to direct that a person be appointed for the purpose of the hearing who has the appropriate skills or experience in facilitating the giving of evidence by a child, vulnerable adult or sensitive witness.

8. This Practice Direction is made by the Senior President of Tribunals with the agreement of the Lord Chancellor. It is made in the exercise of powers conferred by the Tribunals, Courts and Enforcement Act 2007.

30 OCTOBER 2008. PRACTICE DIRECTION—USE OF THE WELSH LANGUAGE IN TRIBUNALS IN WALES (FIRST-TIER TRIBUNAL AND UPPER TRIBUNAL)

GENERAL

1. The purpose of this Practice Direction is to reflect the principle of the Welsh Language Act 1993 that in the administration of justice in Wales, the English and Welsh languages should be treated on a basis of equality.

2. In this Practice Direction "Welsh case" means a case which is before the Tribunal in which all "individual parties" are resident in Wales or which has been classified as a Welsh case by the Tribunal. An "individual party" is a party other than a Government Department or Agency. Where not all of the "individual parties" are resident in Wales the Tribunal will decide whether the case should be classified as a Welsh case or not.

USE OF THE WELSH LANGUAGE

3. In a Welsh case the Welsh language may be used by any party or witnesses or in any document placed before the Tribunal or (subject to the listing provisions below) at any hearing.

LISTING

4. Unless it is not reasonably practicable to do so a party, or their representative, must inform the Tribunal 21 days before any hearing in a Welsh case that the Welsh language will be used by the party, their representative, any witness to be called by that party or in any document to be produced by the party.

5. Where the proceedings are on appeal to the Upper Tribunal and the Welsh language was used in the Tribunal below, the Tribunal Manager must make arrangements for the continued use of the Welsh language in the proceedings before the Upper Tribunal.

6. Where practicable, a hearing in which the Welsh language is to be used must be listed before a Welsh speaking Tribunal and, where translation facilities are needed, at a venue with simultaneous translation facilities.

INTERPRETERS

7. Whenever an interpreter is needed to translate evidence from English into Welsh or from Welsh into English, the Tribunal Manager in whose tribunal the case is to be heard must ensure that the attendance is secured of an interpreter whose name is included in the list of approved interpreters.

WITNESSES

8. When a witness in a case in which the Welsh language may be used is required to give evidence on oath or affirmation the Tribunal must inform the witness that they may be sworn or affirm in Welsh or English as they wish.

9. This Practice Direction is made by the Senior President of Tribunals with the agreement of the Lord Chancellor. It is made in the exercise of powers conferred by the Tribunals, Courts and Enforcement Act 2007.

30 OCTOBER 2008. PRACTICE DIRECTION–TRANSCRIPTS OF PROCEEDINGS (UPPER TRIBUNAL)

1. At any hearing where the proceedings are recorded such recordings must be preserved by the Tribunal for six months from the date of the hearing to which the recording relates, and any party to the proceedings may, within that period, apply in writing for a transcript and a transcript must be supplied to that party.

2. If a transcript is supplied to a party under paragraph 1, that party must pay for the production and supply of the transcript unless they have applied in writing for, and the Tribunal has given, a direction that the transcript be produced and supplied at public expense.

3. The Tribunal may direct a transcript be supplied at public expense if satisfied that:

(a) a recording of the relevant proceedings is in existence; and

(b) the party making the application;

   (i) has applied, or intends to apply, for permission to challenge the Upper Tribunal's decision in another court and has reasonable grounds for bringing or intending to challenge that decision; or

   (ii) has been granted permission to challenge the Upper Tribunal's decision and has brought, or intends to bring, such proceedings; or

   (iii) is a respondent to any such challenge to a decision of the Upper Tribunal in another court; and

(c) the transcript is necessary for the purpose of challenging the Upper Tribunal's decision; and

(d) the party's financial circumstances are such that that party cannot afford to pay for the transcript from their own income or funds.

4. Any transcript of proceedings directed to be supplied at public expense must be restricted to that part of the proceedings necessary for the purposes of any such challenge.

5. For the purposes of considering an application for a transcript at public expense, the Tribunal may give directions, for example, requiring the party to disclose details of their financial circumstances.

6. This Practice Direction is made by the Senior President of Tribunals with the agreement of the Lord Chancellor. It is made in the exercise of powers conferred by the Tribunals, Courts and Enforcement Act 2007.

27 JULY 2010. PRACTICE DIRECTION—CATEGORISATION OF CASES IN THE TAX CHAMBER (FIRST-TIER TRIBUNAL)

1. This Practice Direction applies to cases in the Tax Chamber of the First-tier Tribunal, and paragraphs 2 and 3 supplement rule 23(1) of the Tribunal Procedure (First-tier Tribunal) (Tax Chamber) Rules 2009 relating to the allocation of cases to categories.

2. Default Paper cases

[Not relevant to VAT.]

3. Basic cases

When the Tribunal receives a notice of appeal, application notice or notice of reference in one of the following types of cases, the Tribunal must allocate the case to the Basic category unless the case is of a type listed in paragraph 2, or the Tribunal considers that there is a reason why it is appropriate to allocate the case to a different category.

(a) Appeals—
- (i) against penalties for late filing and late payment, including daily penalties[1];
- (ii) against penalties under paragraph 15 of Schedule 24 of the Finance Act 2007 except:
  - appeals against penalties for deliberate action (whether concealed or not);
  - cases where an appeal is also brought against the assessment of the tax to which the penalty relates; and
  - indirect cases
- (iii) on the basis of reasonable excuse against penalties in relation to indirect taxes[2];
- (iv) [not relevant to VAT]; and
- (v) against information notices[3].

(b) Applications—
- (i) for permission to make a late appeal;
- (ii) [not relevant to VAT]; and
- (iii) [not relevant to VAT].

4. In proceedings without notice to a respondent under the following enactments the Tribunal must consider whether to give a direction under rule 32 that a hearing, or part of it, be held in private:
- (a) [not relevant to VAT];
- (b) [not relevant to VAT];
- (c) [not relevant to VAT];
- (d) [not relevant to VAT]; and
- (e) paragraphs 3, 4, 5, 13 of Schedule 36 to the Finance Act 2008 (from the day those provisions come into force).

5. This Practice Direction is made by the Senior President of Tribunals with the agreement of the Lord Chancellor. It is made in the exercise of powers conferred by section 23 of the Tribunals, Courts and Enforcement Act 2007.

[Footnotes]

(1) This includes penalties imposed under [. . .] sections 59 and 59A of the Value Added Tax Act 1994 [. . .].

(2) This includes appeals under sections 59(7), 62(3), 65(3), 66(7), 67(8), 68(4), 69(8) and 70 of the Value Added Tax Act 1994 [. . .] and regulations 4 and 5 of the Export (Penalty) Regulations 2003.

(3) This includes appeals under [. . .] paragraphs 45 and 47 of Schedule 36 to the Finance Act 2008.

APPENDIX 17. TRIBUNAL FUNDING

This appendix sets out the text of the directions referred to in the commentary to the Access to Justice Act 1999 s 6. The direction currently in force is the 2008 Authorisation. However, the 2005 Direction continues to have transitional effect in accordance with para 4 of the 2008 Authorisation.

The directions are reproduced in so far as they are relevant to VAT. Paragraph headings have been omitted. The omitted text relates to the Care Standards Tribunal and the General and Special Commissioners of Income Tax.

SECRETARY OF STATE'S DIRECTION (OCTOBER 2005)

1. This is a direction by the Secretary of State under section 6(8) of the Access to Justice Act 1999 ("the Act"). It authorises the Legal Services Commission ("the Commission") to fund in specified circumstances services generally excluded from the scope of the Community Legal Service Fund by Schedule 2 of the Act.

2. References in this direction to services which the Commission may fund are to the levels of service defined in those terms in the Commission's Funding Code ("the Code").

3. All applications under this direction remain subject to the relevant regulations under the Act and all relevant criteria in the Code.

4. [. . .]

5. The Secretary of State authorises the Commission to fund Legal Help, Help at Court and Legal Representation in all proceedings before . . . the VAT and Duties tribunal in the circumstances specified below.

6. The circumstances are where:

(a) it is in the interests of justice for the client to be legally represented and therefore, that Legal Help, Help at Court and Legal Representation be granted; and

(b) the proceedings concern penalties which the courts have declared to be criminal in ECHR terms or where an appellant reasonably seeks to argue that the penalties under consideration by the tribunal are criminal in ECHR terms.

7. Appeals from the above tribunals [. . .] to the High Court, the Court of Appeal and the House of Lords may also be funded in the same specified circumstances.

8. For the avoidance of doubt, the Secretary of State authorises funding for cases which fall within sections 4–7 of the Direction and arise out of the running of a business.

9. Only organisations authorised to do so by contract with the Legal Services Commission may provide Legal Help, Help at Court and Legal Representation under this Direction.

SECRETARY OF STATE'S AUTHORISATION (OCTOBER 2008)

1. This is an authorisation by the Secretary of State under section 6(8) of the Access to Justice Act 1999 ("the Act"). It authorises the Legal Services Commission ("the Commission") to fund in specified circumstances services generally excluded from the scope of the Community Legal Service Fund by Schedule 2 of the Act ("the Schedule").

2. This authorisation comes into force on 3rd November 2008.

3. References in this authorisation to services which the Commission may fund are to the levels of service defined in those terms in the Commission's Funding Code ("the Code").

4. This Authorisation replaces the Secretary of State's Direction on Tribunal Representation dated 31 October 2005 insofar as the functions referred to in that Direction are transferred by the Transfer of Tribunals Functions Order 2008. This Authorisation does not affect the 2005 Direction in relation to proceedings before the [...] VAT and Duties Tribunal, or onward appeals from such proceedings.

5. All applications under this authorisation remain subject to the relevant regulations under the Act and all relevant criteria and procedures in the Code.

6. Only organisations authorised to do so by contract with the Commission may provide Legal Help, Help at Court and Legal Representation under this Authorisation.

7. This Authorisation only applies to proceedings arising under the law of England and Wales. It does not apply to proceedings arising under the law of Northern Ireland or Scotland, or to proceedings transferred to the First-tier Tribunal or Upper Tribunal from the High Court in Northern Ireland or from the Court of Session.

8. Subject to paragraphs 9 and 10, the Lord Chancellor authorises the Commission to fund Legal Representation in the types of proceedings described at paragraphs 11–14 which would otherwise be excluded services under paragraph 2 of the Schedule.

9. [Not relevant to VAT.]

10. Services that would otherwise be excluded under paragraph 1 of the Schedule including Legal Help, Help at Court and Legal Representation, are authorised in the types of proceedings described at paragraph 13 (Judicial Review) and in any onward appeals to the High Court, Court of Appeal, and House of Lords. However, services in such proceedings which would be excluded under paragraph 1(*h*) of the Schedule (business cases) are only authorised where the proceedings or potential proceedings concern:

(a) serious wrongdoing,
(b) abuse of position or power, or
(c) significant breach of human rights by a public authority.

11. [Not relevant to VAT.]

12. [Not relevant to VAT.]

13. [Judicial Review Proceedings]

(a) Proceedings which are brought before the Upper Tribunal (wholly or primarily) to exercise its "judicial review" jurisdiction under section 15 of [TCEA 2007]; or
(b) Judicial review applications transferred to the Upper Tribunal from the High Court under section 31A of the Supreme Court Act 1981.

14. [Not relevant to VAT.]

APPENDIX 18. YOUR CHARTER

HMRC announced the publication of *Your Charter* in a press release dated 12 November 2009. The charter sets out what individuals, businesses and other groups dealing with HMRC can expect from the department and what the department expects from them. The text of the charter is set out below.

Our role

We make sure that the money is available to fund the UK's public services by collecting taxes and duties as laid down by Parliament. We help families and individuals with targeted financial support.

We want to give you a service that is even-handed, accurate and based on mutual trust and respect. We also want to make it as easy as we can for you to get things right.

To find out more about our Vision go to www.hmrc.gov.uk/governance/vision.htm
This Charter explains what you can expect from us and what we expect from you.

Your rights

1. Respect you

We recognise that you might be concerned about how we will deal with you.

We will:

- treat you with courtesy and consideration;
- listen to your concerns;
- answer your questions in a way you can understand;
- try to understand your circumstances;
- make you aware of your rights, including your right to appeal our decisions;
- tell you how to exercise your right to appeal against our decisions.

2. Help and support you to get things right

We want to give you as much certainty as we can that you are paying or claiming the right amount.

We will:

- provide information that helps you understand what you have to do and when you have to do it;
- provide information that clearly explains the taxes, duties, exemptions, allowances, reliefs and tax credits that we are responsible for;
- process the information you give us as quickly and accurately as we can;
- put mistakes right as soon as we can.

3. Treat you as honest

We know that the great majority of people want to get things right. Unless we have a good reason not to.

We will:

- presume you are telling us the truth;
- accept that you will pay what you owe and only claim what you are entitled to;
- explain why we need to ask you questions and why we have decided to check your records;
- only question what you tell us if we have good reason to.

4. Treat you even-handedly

We will be even-handed in the way we deal with you. We will take into account your circumstances and provide a consistent service. If you need help we will also give you the appropriate support so you can meet your obligations.

We will:

- act within the law and our published guidance;
- help you understand your legal rights;
- explain what you can do if you disagree with our decisions or want to make a complaint;
- provide you with information in a way that meets your particular needs;
- consider any financial difficulties you may be having.

5. Be professional and act with integrity

Whenever you deal with us we will take responsibility for our actions and behave in a professional way.

We will:

- act with integrity;
- make sure that you are dealt with by people who have the right level of expertise;
- make decisions in accordance with the law and published guidance and explain them clearly to you;
- respond to your enquiries and resolve any problems as soon as we can;
- let you know how appeals, investigations or complaints are progressing.

6. Tackle people who deliberately break the rules and challenge those who bend the rules

The great majority of people are honest and get things right. We want to protect them from the effects of people deliberately breaking the rules. We will also challenge those who engage in avoidance, deliberately bending the rules. We will treat genuine mistakes, acting without reasonable care and deliberately misleading actions differently from each other.

We will:

- identify people who are not paying what they owe or claiming more than they should;
- recover the money they owe and charge interest and penalties where appropriate;
- distinguish between legitimately trying to pay the lowest amount and bending the rules through tax avoidance;
- use our powers reasonably.

7. Protect your information and respect your privacy

We recognise we have privileged access to your information. We will only ask you for information we need to do our jobs. We will protect that information.

We will:

- protect information we obtain, receive or hold about you;
- explain why we need information, if you ask us to;
- only allow our staff to see information when they need it to do their job;
- give you the information we hold about you when you ask for it, as long as the law lets us;
- only share or release information about you when the law lets us and we need to;
- respect your legal rights when we visit premises.

8. Accept that someone else can represent you

You may want someone else to deal with us on your behalf. To protect your privacy, we will only deal with them if they have been authorised to represent you.

We will:

- respect your representative's right to act for you and deal with them appropriately.

You should always check that your representative has the right experience and knowledge to help you.

9. Do all we can to keep the cost of dealing with us as low as possible

We aim to take up as little of your time and money as we can.

We will:

- try to make our services straightforward and easy to access;
- make it as cheap as we can for you to contact us;
- explain clearly what we need from you;
- do our best to give you complete, accurate and consistent advice;
- do our best to get things right first time.

Your obligations

1. Be honest

We need you to be honest with us. If someone else acts for you, we expect them to be honest too.

We expect you to:

- be truthful, open and act within the law;
- give us accurate information;
- give us all the relevant facts;
- tell us as soon as you can if you think you have made a mistake.

2. Respect our staff

Our staff will respect you and we ask you to show them respect too. If someone else acts for you, we expect the same respect from them.

We expect you to:

- be polite;
- accept that we will not tolerate rude or abusive behaviour.

3. Take care to get things right

We need you to take responsibility for getting things right, even if you have authorised someone to act on your behalf.

We expect you to:

- take reasonable care when you complete tax returns and fill out forms;
- send us tax returns and forms on time;
- make payments on time;
- respond in good time if we ask you to do something;
- talk to us if there is anything that you are not sure about or if you are having difficulty meeting your obligations;
- tell us if you have any particular needs so we can take them into account;
- tell us about any changes in your circumstances that will affect your payments or claims;
- keep adequate records that support what you tell us and hold them for as long as the law says you need to.

APPENDIX 19. INFORMATION OR ADVICE PROVIDED BY HMRC

HMRC have published the following guidance at http://www.hmrc.gov.uk/pdfs/info-hmrc.htm under the title When you can rely on information or advice provided by HM Revenue and Customs (HMRC).

Who this guidance is for

This guidance is relevant to all customers who receive information or advice from HMRC. It applies to advice we provide relevant to all taxes we collect and payments we administer.

Information or advice you receive from HMRC applies:

- to the applicant (even where the application has been made by the applicant's adviser
- to the particular transaction that was the subject of the request for advice

Or

- as stated in the information where it takes the form of Guidance or Public Notices

There is no general right of appeal against advice or information we provide except where rights of appeal are set out in statute. The information and advice we provide is aimed at helping you to understand your obligations, liabilities, entitlements or the consequences of your transactions. You are not required to act on the basis of our advice for example when completing a return or paying tax.

General principles

We aim to provide information and advice that will give certainty to our customers as to the tax consequences of their transactions, their obligations or liabilities and entitlements. Our starting point is therefore that you should be able to rely on any information or advice we provide. However for information or advice you have received to be considered binding on HMRC, when contacting HMRC you must set out all the relevant facts and draw attention to all the issues. This has been described by the courts as the need for the applicant to place all his cards face up on the table. We expect you to interpret this relatively broadly, for example, by providing information on related transactions where relevant.

Under our existing powers of 'collection and management' (Section 5 of the Commissioners for Revenue and Customs Act 2005), the principles of administrative law and the Courts will ultimately determine if we are bound by advice we have given. The underlying principle is that HMRC has a duty to collect the correct amount of tax as required by statute. In the vast majority of cases advice we give will be correct in law and therefore binding on HMRC. However there are some circumstances in which our primary duty to collect tax according to the statute may mean that we can no longer be bound by advice we have given.

For example, this may occur in the following circumstances:

- for pre-transaction advice, where the nature of the transaction changes in a way that has a material impact on the transaction as a whole
- where you provided incorrect or incomplete information when you requested advice from HMRC
- when a Court or Tribunal judgment changes the prevailing interpretation of the law on which the advice was based and your liability to tax for that period has not been finalised, for example, where you have not yet submitted your return or, if you have submitted your return, where the opportunity to amend that return remains. Advice will be based on the prevailing understanding of the law at the time it is given. Where the Courts change the prevailing interpretation of the law, subject to the principle of legitimate expectation, we are required to collect the correct amount of tax as required by the new interpretation of the law
- when the statutory law relevant to the transaction for which the advice was given changes. If this change is retrospective, we will not be bound by any advice we have previously given. This situation occurs very infrequently. If the new statute

is enacted pre-transaction and is prospective, any earlier advice relating to the transaction will not be considered to be binding. HMRC has a duty to collect the correct amount of tax as required by statute at the time the transaction takes place. It remains your responsibility to take account of changes in the law.

Where HMRC provides incorrect information or advice

There may be a small number of cases where we provide information or advice that is incorrect in law. Where this happens, we will be bound by such advice provided that it is clear, unequivocal and explicit and you can demonstrate that:

- you reasonably relied on the advice
- where appropriate, you made full disclosure of all the relevant facts
- the application of the statute would result in your financial detriment

Where this is the case, to apply the statute may be so unfair that it could amount to an abuse of power. But, where we have given incorrect information or advice, our primary duty will always remain to collect the correct amount of tax as required by the law and therefore there will be some circumstances where we will not be bound by the advice we have given.

Where we provide you with erroneous advice that is binding on us and subsequently notify you that it is incorrect, the established legal position is that you will only be required to start accounting for tax on the correct basis from the date of notification. All cases will be subject to any statutory time limits.

Misunderstanding

There may be certain circumstances where you have misunderstood the law and applied the wrong tax treatment when carrying out a transaction or providing information or payment to HMRC. In these circumstances, the wrong amount of tax has been collected. As HMRC has a duty to collect the correct amount of tax as required by law, the situation must be rectified for the past and for the future in order to ensure that the law is applied correctly. However, in rectifying the situation, HMRC will be bound by considerations of public law for example to treat taxpayers fairly.

For any cases of misunderstanding concerning VAT or IPT, please see extra statutory concession 3.4 Misunderstanding (Notice 48 Extra statutory concessions).

Note. The concession in Notice No 48 (December 2010) para 3.4 is being withdrawn with effect from 1 January 2012 on the grounds that "it is not reasonable to allow remission of tax when the error is caused by the taxpayer": see *Withdrawal of extra statutory concessions* (HMRC Technical Note, 13 December 2010) Chapter 2.

4.
EU Founding Treaties

Contents

CITATION OF THE FOUNDING TREATIES

The Treaty on European Union is referred to in this Part as "the EU Treaty". Provisions of the EU Treaty are cited in the form "TEU art 000".

The Treaty on the Functioning of the European Union is referred to in this Part as "the Functioning Treaty". Provisions of the Functioning Treaty are cited in the form "TFEU art 000".

The Treaty Amending the Treaty on European Union and the Treaty Establishing the European Community is referred to in this Part as "the Reform Treaty".

The EU Treaty and the Functioning Treaty are collectively referred to as "the treaties" in accordance with TEU art 1.

TREATY ON EUROPEAN UNION (MAASTRICHT, 7 FEBRUARY 1992)

General note This treaty (referred to as "the EU Treaty") entered into force on 1 November 1993 in accordance with art R(2). A new numbering system was introduced following the Treaty of Amsterdam (2 October 1997).

This treaty is amended by the Treaty Amending the Treaty on European Union and the Treaty Establishing the European Community (Lisbon, 13 December 2007) ("the Reform Treaty"), which came into force on 1 December 2009. For a consolidated version of the EU Treaty as amended by the Reform Treaty and subsequent rectifications, see OJ C83/13, 30.3.10.

The "ex" articles refer to articles of the Treaty in the numbering system introduced following the Treaty of Amsterdam.

TITLE I—COMMON PROVISIONS

Article 1
(ex art 1)

A European Union ("the EU") is established. It replaces and succeeds the European Community. Member states confer competences on the EU to attain common objectives. The EU is founded on this treaty and the Treaty on the Functioning of the European Union ("the Functioning Treaty"). These treaties are collectively referred to as "the treaties". They have the same legal value.

Article 2

The EU is founded on values respecting human dignity, freedom, democracy, equality, the rule of law and respect for human rights.

Article 3
(ex art 2)

The EU is required to establish: (1) an internal market, and (2) an economic and monetary union ("EMU"). The currency of the EMU is the euro.

Article 4

Member states retain competences which have not been conferred on the EU. The EU must respect the equality of the member states, their national identities and their essential state functions. The EU and member states must assist each other in carrying out tasks flowing from the treaties (see art 1). Member states must: (1) take appropriate measures to comply with obligations arising from the treaties or resulting from the acts of EU institutions; (2) facilitate achievement of the EU's tasks, and (3) refrain from taking measures which could jeopardise attainment of the EU's objectives.

Article 5
(ex art 5)

The limits of the EU's competences are governed by the principle of conferral (ie acting only within the limits of the competences conferred by the treaties (see art 1)). The use of EU competences is governed by the principles of subsidiarity and proportionality, as to which see Protocol No 2 on the application of the principles of subsidiarity and proportionality.

Article 6
(ex art 6)

The Charter of Fundamental Rights of the European Union (Nice, 7 December 2000) has the same legal value as the treaties (see art 1). For the text of the Charter (as adapted at Strasbourg on 12 December 2007), see OJC83/389, 30.2.10.

The EU must accede to the European Convention for the Protection of Human Rights and Fundamental Freedoms (Rome, 4 November 1950).

The EU must respect fundamental rights as general principles of Community law. "Fundamental rights" for this purpose are:

- Rights guaranteed by the European Convention for the Protection of Human Rights and Fundamental Freedoms (Rome, 4 November 1950).
- Rights resulting from the constitutional traditions common to the member states.

TITLE III—PROVISIONS ON THE INSTITUTIONS

Article 13

The EU institutions comprise: (1) the European Parliament (see art 14); (2) the European Council (see art 15); (3) the Council (see art 16); (4) the European Commission (see art 17); (5) the Court of Justice of the European Union (see art 19); (6) the European Central Bank; and (7) the Court of Auditors.

Article 19

The Court of Justice must ensure that the law is observed in the interpretation and application of the treaties (see art 1).

TITLE VI—FINAL PROVISIONS

Article 47

The EU has legal personality.

Article 51

The Protocols (see OJ C83/201, 30.3.10) and Annexes (see OJ OJ C83/329, 30.3.10) to the treaties (see art 1) form an integral part of those treaties.

Article 52

This treaty applies to Austria, Belgium, Bulgaria, Cyprus, the Czech Republic, Denmark, Estonia, Finland, France, Germany, Greece, Hungary, Italy, Ireland, Latvia, Lithuania, Luxembourg, Malta, the Netherlands, Poland, Portugal, Romania, Slovenia, Slovakia, Spain, Sweden and the UK.

For the territorial scope of the treaties (see art 1), see TFEU art 355.

TREATY ON THE FUNCTIONING OF THE EUROPEAN UNION (ROME, 25 MARCH 1957)

General note The original title of this treaty was the Treaty Establishing the European Economic Community ("the EEC Treaty"). The title was changed to the Treaty Establishing the European Community ("the EC Treaty") by art G(1) of the Treaty on European Union (Maastricht, 7 February 1992). A new numbering system was introduced following the Treaty of Amsterdam (2 October 1997).

This treaty was amended and renamed the Treaty on the Functioning of the European Union by the Treaty Amending the Treaty on European Union ("the Functioning Treaty") and the Treaty Establishing the European Community (Lisbon, 13 December 2007) ("the Reform Treaty"), which came into force on 1 December 2009. For a consolidated version of this treaty as amended by the Reform Treaty and subsequent rectifications, see OJ C83/47, 30.3.10.

The "ex" articles shown refer to the numbering system introduced by the Treaty of Amsterdam.

PART TWO—NON-DISCRIMINATION AND CITIZENSHIP OF THE UNION

TITLE II—PROVISIONS HAVING GENERAL APPLICATION

Article 18
(ex art 12)

Any discrimination on the grounds of nationality is prohibited. The Council may adopt rules designed to prohibit such discrimination. For specific provisions prohibiting discrimination in relation to indirect taxes, see arts 90 and 91.

PART THREE—POLICIES AND INTERNAL ACTIONS OF THE UNION

TITLE 1—THE INTERNAL MARKET

Article 26
(ex art 14)

The internal market comprises an area without internal frontiers that ensures the free movement of goods, persons, services and capital.

TITLE II—FREE MOVEMENT OF GOODS

Article 28
(ex art 23)

1. The Community is based upon a customs union. It covers all trade in goods. It involves the prohibition of customs duties and charges having equivalent effect on import and export between member states. It involves the adoption of a common customs tariff in the relations between member states and third countries.

2. Articles 25 and 28–31 apply to:

- Products originating in member states.
- Products from third countries in free circulation (see art 29) in member states.

Article 29
(ex art 24)

Products from third countries are said to be in "free circulation" in a member state if:

- Import formalities have been complied with.
- Any customs duties (or charges having equivalent effect) payable on them have been levied in the member state.
- The products have not benefited from total or partial drawback of those duties or charges.

CHAPTER 1—THE CUSTOMS UNION

Article 30
(ex art 25)

The following are prohibited between member states:

- Customs duties on imports and exports.
- Charges having equivalent effect.
- Customs duties of a fiscal nature.

CHAPTER 3—PROHIBITION OF QUANTITATIVE RESTRICTIONS BETWEEN MEMBER STATES

Article 34
(ex art 28)

The following are prohibited between member states:

- Quantitative restrictions on imports.
- All measures having equivalent effect.

Article 35
(ex art 29)

The following are prohibited between member states:

- Quantitative restrictions on exports.
- All measures having equivalent effect.

Article 36
(ex art 30)

The provisions of arts 34 and 35 do not preclude prohibitions or restrictions on imports, exports or goods in transit if they are justified on the following grounds:

- Public morality, public policy or public security.
- The protection of health and life of humans, animals or plants.
- The protection of national treasures possessing artistic, historic or archaeological value.
- The protection of industrial and commercial property.

TITLE VII—COMMON RULES ON COMPETITION, TAXATION AND APPROXIMATION OF LAWS

CHAPTER 1—RULES ON COMPETITION

Section 2—Aid granted by States

Article 107
(ex art 87)

In principle, aid is incompatible with the internal market if:

- It is granted by a member state or through state resources. For circumstances where this test was not met, see *Sandra Puffer v Unabhängiger Finanzsenat, Außenstelle Linz* (case C-460/07) [2009] ECR I–3251, [2009] STC 1693 (national measures transposing what is now Directive 2006/112/EC art 168(*a*)).
- It distorts, or threatens to distort, competition by favouring certain undertakings or the production of certain goods.
- It affects trade between member states.

This treaty may provide otherwise. Aid of specified descriptions is, or is considered to be, compatible with the common market.

CHAPTER 2—TAX PROVISIONS

Article 110
(ex art 90)

Member states may not impose internal taxation on the products of other member states if:

- It exceeds the internal taxation imposed on similar domestic products.
- It affords indirect protection to other products.

Article 111
(ex art 91)

Any repayment of internal taxation in respect of products exported to the territory of another member state must not exceed the internal taxation imposed on those products.

Article 112
(ex art 92)

This article does not apply to turnover taxes.

Article 113
(ex art 93)

The Council must adopt provisions for the harmonisation of legislation concerning turnover taxes to the extent necessary to: (1) ensure the establishment and functioning of the internal market; and (2) avoid distortion of competition. The Council must act unanimously in so doing.

For the directives adopted by the Council in relation to VAT, see Directives 91/680/EEC art 2, 92/77/EEC (repealed) and 92/111/EEC (repealed). For the internal market, see art 26.

PART SIX—INSTITUTIONAL AND FINANCIAL PROVISIONS

TITLE 1 – PROVISIONS GOVERNING THE INSTITUTIONS

CHAPTER 1—THE INSTITUTIONS

Section 5—The Court of Justice of the European Union

Article 258
(ex art 226)

The Commission must deliver a reasoned opinion if it considers that a member state has failed to fulfil an obligation under the treaties (see TEU art 1). The Commission lays down a period within which the member state must comply with the opinion. The Commission can bring the matter before the Court of Justice if the member state fails to do so.

For proceedings against the UK in relation to VAT, see:

- *Commission v United Kingdom* (case C-353/85) [1988] ECR 817, [1988] STC 251 (goods supplied in the exercise of a medical or paramedical profession).
- *Commission v United Kingdom* (case C-416/85) [1988] ECR 3127, [1988] STC 456 (zero-rating).
- *Commission v United Kingdom* (case C-359/97) [2000] ECR I-6355, [2000] STC 777 (road tolls).
- *Commission v United Kingdom* (case C-33/03) [2005] ECR I–1865, [2005] STC 582 (road fuel).
- *Commission v United Kingdom* (case C-349/03) [2005] ECR I–7321, [2005] STC 1944 (mutual assistance in relation to Gibraltar).
- *Commission v United Kingdom* (case C-305/03) [2007] ECR I–1213, [2007] STC 1211 (goods temporarily imported for sale at auction).
- *Commission v United Kingdom* (case C-582/08) [2010] ECR I–0000, [2010] STC 2364 (repayments to third country traders).

Article 259
(ex art 227)

A member state may bring an action before the Court of Justice if it considers that another member state has failed to fulfil an obligation under the treaties. The procedure for doing so is specified.

Art 260
(ex art 228)

The Court of Justice may, in proceedings under arts 258 or 259, hold that a member state has failed to fulfil an obligation under the treaties. The member state must take the necessary measures to comply with the judgment. The Commission may bring a case before the Court of Justice if it considers that the member state has failed to do so.

For examples, see:

- *Commission v Kingdom of Belgium* (case C-391/85) [1988] ECR 579, [1989] 2 CMLR 972.
- *Commission v Italian Republic* (case C-262/91) [1992] ECR I–5269.

Article 267
(ex art 234)

The Court of Justice has jurisdiction to give preliminary rulings concerning, inter alia, the interpretation of: (1) the treaties, and (2) the acts of the Community institutions, eg directives. A national court or tribunal may refer such a question to the Court of Justice for a ruling. It may do so if a ruling is necessary to enable the court or tribunal to give judgment. It must do so if there is no judicial remedy under national law against a decision of the court or tribunal concerned.

The Court of Justice takes account of a number of factors in determining whether a body making a reference is a "court or tribunal".

(1) whether the body is established by law;
(2) whether it is permanent;
(3) whether its procedure is inter partes;
(4) whether it applies rules of law; and
(5) whether it is independent: see *Dorsch Consult Ingenieurgesellschaft mbH v Bundesbaugesellschaft Berlin mbH(case C-54/96)* [1997] ECR I–4961 at [23].

For an example, see *Nidera Handelscompagnie BV v Valstybiné mokesčiu inspekcija prie Lietuvos Respublikos finansu ministerijos (case C-385/09)* [2010] ECR I–0000 (Tax Disputes Commission (Lithuania)).

Proceedings under this provision are based on a clear separation of functions between the national court and the Court of Justice. It is for the national court to determine, in the light of the particular circumstances of the case, both: (1) the need for a preliminary ruling in order to deliver judgment; and (2) the relevance of the questions it submits to the Court of Justice. Any assessment of the facts in the case is a matter for the national court. Thus, in principle, the Court of Justice is, bound to give a ruling where the questions submitted concern the interpretation of Community law. The Court of Justice may reject a request only where it is quite obvious that: (1) the interpretation sought bears no relation to the actual facts of the main action; (2) the interpretation sought is hypothetical, or (3) the Court does not have before it the factual or legal material necessary to give a useful answer to the questions submitted. Any assessment of the facts in the case is a matter for the national court. However, in order to give the national court a useful answer, the Court of Justice may provide the national court with all the guidance that it deems necessary. See, most recently, *Magoora sp zoo o v Dyrektor Izby Skarbowej w Krakowie* (case C-414/07) [2008] ECR I–10921 at [22], [23], [33].

CHAPTER 2—LEGAL ACTS OF THE UNION, ADOPTION PROCEDURES AND OTHER PROVISIONS

Section 1—The Legal Acts of the Union

Article 288
(ex art 249)

A regulation has general application. It is binding in its entirety. It is directly applicable in all member states.

A directive is binding, as to the results to be achieved, upon each member state to which it is addressed. However, the national authorities have a choice of form and methods. For the transposition of directives into national law, see Commission Recommendation 2005/309/EC (OJ L98/47, 16.4.05). The settled case law of the Court of Justice regarding the transposition of directives into national law (see *Finanzamt Düsseldorf-Süd v SALIX Grundstücks-Vermietungsgellschaft mbH & Co Objekt Offenbach KG* (case C-102/08) [2009] ECR I–4983, [2009] STC 1607 at [40]–[44]) is briefly summarised as follows:

- The provisions of a directive do not have to be incorporated formally, and verbatim, in express, specific national legislation. A general legal context may be adequate if this guarantees the full application of the directive in a sufficiently clear and precise manner.
- Where a directive is intended to create rights for individuals, it is particularly important that the persons concerned can ascertain the full extent of their rights and rely on them, if necessary, before the national courts.
- The provisions of a directive must be implemented with unquestionable legal certainty and with the requisite specificity, precision and clarity.
- Mere administrative practices, by their nature, are alterable at will and are not given the appropriate publicity. They do not constitute the proper fulfilment of obligations under the Functioning Treaty.
- Whether or not the foregoing conditions have been met is a matter for the national court. On a reference, the Court of Justice may nevertheless provide the national court with all the guidance that it deems necessary.

A decision is binding in its entirety upon those to whom it is addressed.

Section 2—Procedures for the Adoption of Acts and Other Provisions

Article 297
(ex art 254)

Council and Commission regulations are published in the Official Journal of the European Union. So are Council and Commission directives addressed to all member states. These regulations and directives enter into force on the date specified in them (if a date is specified) or on the twentieth day following publication (in other cases).

PART SEVEN—GENERAL AND FINAL PROVISIONS

Article 349
(ex art 299(2) second, third and fourth paras)

The Council must adopt specific measures laying down the conditions for applying the treaties to the following territories (which are collectively referred to as "the outermost regions"): Guadeloupe, French Guiana, Martinique, Réunion, Saint-Barthélemy, Saint-Martin, the Azores, Maderia and the Canary Islands. Saint-Barthélemy ceases to be included in this list with effect from 1 January 2012: see Decision 2010/718/EU art 2(1).

Article 355
(ex arts 299(2) (first para) and 299(3)–(6))

This article defines the territory to which the EU Treaty applies. Different definitions apply in relation to VAT, customs duty and excise duty. For the VAT territory of the EU, see Directive 2006/112/EC arts 5–8. For the customs territory, see Regulation (EEC) No 2913/92 art 3 (the Community Customs Code). For the excise territory, see Directive 92/12/EEC art 2. For a table comparing the definition in this article with the VAT and customs territories, see Appendix 2.

1. This treaties apply to Guadeloupe, French Guiana, Martinique, Réunion, Saint-Barthélemy, Saint-Martin, the Azores, Maderia and the Canary Islands. Saint-Barthélemy ceases to be included in this list with effect from 1 January 2012: see Decision 2010/718/EU art 2(2).

2. The special arrangements for association (see Part Four) apply to the overseas countries and territories listed in Annex II (which includes Saint-Barthélemy from 1 January 2012: see Decision 2010/718/EU art 2(3)). The treaties do not apply to an overseas country or territory having special relations with the UK if it is excluded from this list.

3. The treaties apply to the European territories for whose external relations a member state is responsible. In practice, this provision is confined to Gibraltar. For the Channel Islands, the Isle of Man and the UK Sovereign Base Areas of Akrotiri and Dhekelia in Cyprus, see para 5.

4. The treaties apply to the Aland Islands in accordance with Protocol No 2 to the Fourth Accession Treaty (1994).

5. The treaties apply to the Channel Islands and the Isle of Man only to the extent set out in Protocol No 3 to the First Accession Treaty (1972). The treaties apply to the UK Sovereign Base Areas of Akrotiri and Dhekelia in Cyprus only to the extent set out in Protocol No 3 to the Fifth Accession Treaty (2003). The treaties apply do not apply to the Faeroe Islands.

TREATY AMENDING THE TREATY ON EUROPEAN UNION AND THE TREATY ESTABLISHING THE EUROPEAN COMMUNITY (LISBON, 13 DECEMBER 2007)

General note This Treaty (referred to as "the Reform Treaty") amends, rearranges and renumbers the Treaty Establishing the European Community (Rome, 25 March 1957) (which is renamed the Treaty on the Functioning of the European Union ("the Functioning Treaty")) and the Treaty on European Union (Maastricht, 7 February 1992) ("the EU Treaty"). Following deposit of the last instrument of ratification on 13 November 2009, this treaty came into force on 1 December 2009 in accordance with art 6.

For the text of the treaty, see OJ C306, 17.12.07. For corrigenda by way of process-verbal of rectification signed at Rome on 27 November 2009 and 23 March 2010, see OJ C290/1, 30.11.09 and OJ C83/389, 30.3.10.

5.
EU Accession Treaties

Contents

FIRST ACCESSION TREATY (BRUSSELS, 22 JANUARY 1972)

General note Denmark, Ireland and the UK became member states with effect from 1 January 1973.

The Act of Accession (1972) provides that:

- Acts of the Community (now EU) institutions on the harmonisation of legislation of the member states concerning turnover taxes do not apply to Gibraltar unless the Council unanimously provides otherwise (art 28).
- Directives notified to the original member states before 1 January 1992 were deemed to be addressed to the new member states from that date (art 149).
- The new member states were required to give effect to those directives from 1 January 1973 unless an alternative time limit was specified in relation to a particular provision (art 152).
- The UK was permitted to defer giving effect to Directive 67/227/227 (the First Directive), Directive 67/228/EEC (the Second Directive) and Directive 69/463/EEC (the Third Directive) until 1 July 1973 (Annex XI Part VI points 1, 2, 4).

Protocol No 3 on the Channel Islands and the Isle of Man provides that Community (now EU) rules on customs matters and quantitative restrictions apply to the Channel Islands and the Isle of Man in the same manner as they apply to the UK (art 1).

Part I VAT

SECOND ACCESSION TREATY (ATHENS, 28 MAY 1979)

General note Greece became a member state with effect from 1 January 1981.

The Act of Accession (1979) provides that:

- Directive 68/228EEC (the Second Directive), 77/388/EEC (the Sixth Directive) and Directive 69/169/EEC apply to Greece in accordance with the conditions laid down in Annex VIII Part II (art 128).
- Directives notified to the original member states before 1 January 1981 were deemed to be addressed to Greece from that date (art 145).
- Greece was required to give effect to those directives from 1 January 1981 unless an alternative time limit was specified in relation to a particular provision (art 145).
- Greece was permitted to defer giving effect to Directive 67/227/227 (the First Directive), Directive 67/228/EEC (the Second Directive) and Directive 69/463/EEC (the Third Directive) until 1 January 1984 (Annex XII Part II). This date was subsequently extended to 1 January 1966 by Directive 83/648/EEC (the Fifteenth Directive) and further extended to 1 January 1987 by Directive 86/247/EEC (the Twenty-first Directive).

The joint declaration concerning Mount Athos provides that the Community (now EU) will ensure that the special status granted to Mount Athos, as guaranteed by art 105 of the Hellenic constitution, is taken into account in the application and subsequent preparation of Community (now EU) law and, in particular, in relation to customs franchise privileges, tax exemptions and the right of establishment.

THIRD ACCESSION TREATY (MADRID, 12 JUNE 1985)

General note Portugal and Spain became member states with effect from 1 January 1986.

The Act of Accession (1985) provides that:

- Community (now EU) law applies to the Canary Islands, Ceuta and Melilla subject to specified derogations. In particular, the conditions relating to the free movement of goods and customs legislation apply in accordance with Protocol No 2 (art 25(1), (2)). In relation to the Canary Islands, see also Reg (EEC) No 1911/91 art 4(1) (the territory of the Canary Islands remains outside the field of application of the common VAT system).
- The Council may, at the request of Spain, include the Canary Islands, Ceuta and Melilla in the customs territory of the Community (now EU) (art 25(4)). Spain made a request in respect of the Canary Islands on 7 March 1990. For the progressive introduction of the Common Customs Tariff, see Reg (EEC) No 1911/91 art 6.
- Directives notified to the original member states before 1 January 1986 are deemed to be addressed to the new member states from that date (art 395).
- The new member states were required to give effect to those directives from 1 January 1986 unless an alternative time limit was specified in relation to a particular provision (art 395).
- Portugal was permitted to defer giving effect to Directive 67/227/227 (the First Directive), Directive 67/228/EEC (the Second Directive), Directive 69/463/EEC (the Third Directive), Directive 79/1072/EEC (the Eighth Directive), Directive 81/181/EEC and Directive 84/386/EEC (the Tenth Directive) until 1 January 1989 (Annex XXXVI Part II).

The joint declaration concerning the introduction of the common system of VAT in Portugal provided that Portugal was treated as a third country for the purposes of the foregoing VAT directives until 1 January 1989.

FOURTH ACCESSION TREATY (CORFU, 24 JUNE 1994)

General note Austria, Finland and Sweden became member states with effect from 1 January 1995.

The Act of Accession (1994) provides that:

- Acts of the Community (now EU) institutions on the harmonisation of legislation of the member states concerning turnover taxes do not apply to the Aland islands unless the Council unanimously provides otherwise (art 28).
- Directives made before 1 January 1995 are treated as if they were addressed to the new member states (art 166).
- The VAT directives are amended in accordance with Annex I Part XIII Section B (art 29).
- The new member states were required to give effect to those directives from 1 January 1995 unless an alternative time limit was specified in relation to a particular provision (art 168).
- Directive 77/388/EEC (the Sixth Directive) applies to the new member states in accordance with the conditions laid down in Annex XV Part IX point 2 (art 151).

Protocol No 2 on the Aland islands provides that the Treaties apply to those islands subject to specified derogations. In particular, the territory of the Aland islands is excluded from the territorial application of Community (now EU) provisions in the field of harmonisation of the laws of the member states on turnover taxes (art 2(a)).

FIFTH ACCESSION TREATY (ATHENS, 16 APRIL 2003)

General note The Czech Republic, Estonia, Cyprus, Latvia, Lithuania, Hungary, Malta, Poland, Slovenia and Slovakia became member states with effect from 1 May 2004 (see Notice Concerning the Entry into Force of the Treaty of Accession (OJ C104/20, 30.4.04)).

The Act of Accession (2003) provides that:

- Directives and decisions made before 1 May 2004 have effect as if they were addressed to the new member states (art 53).
- The VAT directives are amended in accordance with Annex II Chapter 9 (art 20).
- XIV) (art 54).
- Directive 77/388/EEC (the Sixth Directive) applies to the new member states in accordance with the provisions laid down in Annex V Chapter 5 point 1 (Czech Republic), Annex VI Chapter 7 point 1 (Estonia), Annex VII Chapter 7 point 1 (Cyprus), Annex VIII Chapter 7 point 1 (Latvia), Annex IX Chapter 8 point 1 (Lithuania), Annex X Chapter 7 point 1 (Hungary), Annex XI Chapter 7 (Malta), Annex XII Chapter 9 point 1 (Poland), Annex XIII Chapter 6 point 1 (Slovenia) and Annex XIV Chapter 7 point 1 (Slovakia) (art 24). The text of the directive has not been amended to reflect these provisions.

Protocol No 3 on the Sovereign Base Areas of the UK in Cyprus amends primary and secondary EU legislation to include the Sovereign Base Areas in the Community (now EU) customs territory and VAT territory.

Protocol No 10 on Cyprus provides for suspension of the (now EU) Community acquis in those areas of Cyprus in which the government does not exercise effective control (art 1(1)). Referenda held on 24 April 2004 failed to end the de facto partition of Cyprus with the consequence that the Community (now EU) acquis does not apply to the northern (Turkish) area (see the conclusions adopted by the Council at its 2576th meeting, Luxembourg, 26 April 2004). The Council was accordingly required to define the terms under which the provisions of EU law apply to the line between the areas over which the Government of Cyprus does and does not exercise effective control (art 2(2)). For the provisions currently in force, see Regulation (EC) No 866/2004 (as amended by Regulation (EC) Nos 293/2005, 601/2005, 1283/2005 and 587/2008).

SIXTH ACCESSION TREATY (LUXEMBOURG, 25 APRIL 2005)

General note Bulgaria and Romania became member states of the European Union on 1 January 2007: see Notice Concerning the Entry into Force of the Treaty (OJ C321/1, 29.12.06).

The following provisions of the Protocol concerning the conditions and arrangements for admission of the Republic of Bulgaria and Romania to the European Union (OJ L157/29, 21.6.05) are relevant to VAT:

- Article 16 and Annex III point 4 (adaptations to acts adopted by the institutions).
- Article 20, Annex VI point 6(1) (Bulgaria) and Annex VII point 7(1) (Romania) (transitional measures).

For the text of the treaty, see OJ L157/11, 21.6.05.

Part I VAT

6. EU Regulations

Contents

REGULATION (EEC) NO 2658/87
TARIFF AND STATISTICAL NOMENCLATURE AND THE COMMON CUSTOMS TARIFF

General note VAT Regulations 1995, SI 1995/2518 reg 120(3) provides that this regulation applies to the charge to VAT on imported goods only in so far as it relates to goods admitted into territorial waters for the following purposes:

- Incorporating them into drilling or production platforms for the purposes of the construction, repair, maintenance, alteration or fitting out of such platforms.
- Linking drilling or production platforms to the mainland of the UK.
- Fuelling and provisioning drilling or production platforms: see VATA 1994 s 16(1)(b) VAT Regulations 1995, SI 1995/2518 reg 120(3)).

For the suspension of customs duties in relation to drilling and production platforms, see Annex I, Part One, Section IIA.

REGULATION (EEC) NO 2913/92
THE COMMUNITY CUSTOMS CODE

General note This regulation applies to the charge to VAT on imported goods in the UK unless it is specifically excluded or varied: see VATA 1994 s 16(1)(*b*). For exclusions and variations, see VAT Regulations 1995, SI 1995/2518 regs 120(2)(*a*) and 121B respectively. Articles 1–4 apply in the UK and arts 2 and 3 are summarised. The commentary on arts 5–253 is largely confined to noting whether, or to what extent, those articles apply in the UK.

This regulation is repealed and replaced by Regulation (EC) No 450/2008 (the Modernised Customs Code) in accordance with art 188 of the 2008 Regulation. This will be take place no earlier than 24 June 2009 and no later than 24 June 2013.

This regulation is implemented by Regulation (EEC) No 2454/93.

TITLE I—GENERAL PROVISIONS

Chapter 1 – Scope and Basic Definitions

Article 1

Customs rules comprise:

- The Code established by this Regulation.
- Implementing measures adopted at Community level. For implementing measures adopted by the EU, see Regulation (EEC) 2454/94.
- Implementing measures adopted by the member states.

Article 2

In principle, Community customs rules apply throughout the customs territory of the Community defined in art 3. However, this general rule is modified as follows:

- In accordance with international conventions.
- In accordance with customary practices of a limited geographic and economic scope. Thus, for example, the customs status of the Vatican State is governed by the Italian-Vatican customs agreement of 30 June 1930. However, the Vatican State does not thereby form part of the customs territory of the Community: see the Court of Auditors Special Report No 2/93 para 6.19 (OJ C347/1, 27.12.93).
- In accordance with autonomous Community measures. Thus, for example, the Community has entered into a customs union with Andorra (as to which see Decision 90/680/EEC (OJ L374/13, 31.12.90)) and with the Republic of San Marino (as to which see Decision 90/680/EEC and the interim agreement annexed thereto (OJ L359/13, 9.12.92)).

Article 3

This article defines the customs territory of the Community. Unlike the VAT and excise territories of the Community, the definition makes no reference to EC Treaty art 299 (now TEU art 52 and TFEU art 355). Gibraltar does not form part of the territory of the UK and is not, therefore included in the customs territory of the Community. The French overseas departments (Guadeloupe, Martinique, Reunion and Guiana) "are an integral part of the Community, and all the customs rules of the Community apply": Court of Auditors Special Report No 2/93 para 6.4 (OJ C347/1, 27.12.93).

This article takes account of the customs union between France and the Principality of Monaco (as to which see the Customs Convention of 18 May 1963) and the special position of the UK Sovereign Bases Areas of Akrotiri and Dhekelia in Cyprus (as to which see Protocol No 3 to the Act of Accession (2003)). It also takes account of the manner in which the EC Treaty (now the Functioning Treaty) applies to the Channel Islands and the Isle of Man in accordance with Protocol No 2 to the Act of Accession (1972). The UK and the Isle of Man are in customs union (as to which see the Customs Agreement 1979 (Cmnd 7747)). The Community aquis is currently suspended in relation to the northern (Turkish) part of Cyprus in accordance with Protocol No 10 to the Act of Accession (2003).

For the customs unions with Andorra and San Marino, see Table 3 in Appendix 2.

For the purposes of applying arts 185–187 and Regulation (EEC) No 2454/93 arts 844–856 and 882 to VAT in the UK, the description of the customs territory of the Community in this article is regarded as a description of the VAT territory (see VAT Regulations 1995, SI 1995/2518 reg 121D(9)(*a*)). For the VAT territory, see VAT Regulations 1995, SI 1995/2518 reg 121D(2) and Appendix 2.

1, 2. The customs territory of the Community comprises:

Member state	Territories included	Territories excluded
Austria	Territory of Austria	None
Belgium	Territory of Belgium	None
Bulgaria	Territory of Bulgaria	None
Cyprus	1. Territory of Cyprus 2. UK Sovereign Base Areas	None (but see note above regarding the Turkish zone)
Czech Republic	Territory of the Czech Republic	None
Denmark	Territory of Denmark	1. Faeroe Islands 2. Greenland
Estonia	Territory of Estonia	None
Finland	Territory of Finland	None
France	1. Territory of France 2. Monaco	1. Saint Pierre et Miquelon 2. Mayotte 3. Overseas territories
Germany	Territory of Germany	1. Island of Heligoland 2. Territory of Busingen
Greece	Territory of Greece	None
Hungary	Territory of Hungary	None
Ireland	Territory of Ireland	None
Italy	Territory of Italy	1. Livigno 2. Campione d'Italia 3. National waters of Lake Lugano
Latvia	Territory of Latvia	None

Lithuania	Territory of Lithuania	None
Luxembourg	Territory of Luxembourg	None
Malta	Territory of Malta	None
Netherlands	Territory of the Netherlands in Europe	None
Poland	Territory of Poland	None
Portugal	Territory of Portugal	None
Romania	Territory of Romania	None
Slovakia	Territory of Slovakia	None
Slovenia	Territory of Slovenia	None
Spain	Territory of Spain	1. Ceuta 2. Melilla
Sweden	Territory of Sweden	None
UK	1. Territory of the UK 2. The Channel Islands 3. The Isle of Man	None

3. The customs territory of the Community includes territorial waters, inland maritime waters and airspace of the member states.

Article 4

Various terms are defined.

As regards the charge to VAT on the importation of goods into the UK, the following definitions (which are relevant to arts 185–187 and Regulation (EEC) No 2454/93 arts 844–856 and 882) are applied in a modified manner:

- The reference to "released for free circulation" in the definition of "Community goods" (point 7, second indent) is regarded as including a reference to the completion of the formalities referred to in Directive 77/388/EEC art 33a(1)(*a*) as amended to 6 April 2006 (VAT Regulations 1995, SI 1995/2518 reg 121D(9)(*b*)(i), (10)).
- The definition of "import duties" (point 10) is regarded as defining instead VAT charged on the importation of goods from places outside the member states in accordance with VATA 1994 (VAT Regulations 1995, SI 1995/2518 reg 121D(9)(*d*)(i)).

Directive 77/388/EEC art 33(1)(*a*) was repealed and replaced by Directive 2006/112/EC art 275 with effect from 1 January 2007.

Chapter 2—Sundry General Provisions Relating in Particular to the Rights and Obligations of Persons with Regard to Customs Rules

Articles 5–19

These articles apply (so far as relevant) in relation to any VAT chargeable on the importation of goods from places outside the member states in the same manner as they apply to any duty of customs and excise or Community customs duties: see VATA 1994 s 16(1).

Part I VAT

TITLE II—FACTORS ON THE BASIS OF WHICH IMPORT DUTIES OR EXPORT DUTIES AND THE OTHER MEASURES PRESCRIBED IN RESPECT OF TRADE IN GOODS ARE APPLIED

Articles 20–36

These articles apply (so far as relevant) in relation to any VAT chargeable on the importation of goods from places outside the member states in the same manner as they apply to any duty of customs and excise or Community customs duties: see VATA 1994 s 16(1).

TITLE III—PROVISIONS APPLICABLE TO GOODS BROUGHT INTO THE CUSTOMS TERRITORY OF THE COMMUNITY UNTIL THEY ARE ASSIGNED A CUSTOMS APPROVED TREATMENT OR USE

Articles 37–57

These articles apply (so far as relevant) in relation to any VAT chargeable on the importation of goods from places outside the member states in the same manner as they apply to any duty of customs and excise or Community customs duties: see VATA 1994 s 16(1).

TITLE IV—CUSTOMS-APPROVED TREATMENT OR USE

CHAPTER 1—GENERAL

Article 58

This article applies (so far as relevant) in relation to any VAT chargeable on the importation of goods from places outside the member states in the same manner as it applies to any duty of customs and excise or Community customs duties: see VATA 1994 s 16(1).

CHAPTER 2—CUSTOMS PROCEDURES

SECTION 1—PLACING GOODS UNDER A CUSTOMS PROCEDURE

Articles 59–78

These articles apply (so far as relevant) in relation to any VAT chargeable on the importation of goods from places outside the member states in the same manner as they apply to any duty of customs and excise or Community customs duties: see VATA 1994 s 16(1).

SECTION 2—RELEASE FOR FREE CIRCULATION

Articles 79—83

These articles apply (so far as relevant) in relation to any VAT chargeable on the importation of goods from places outside the member states in the same manner as they apply to any duty of customs and excise or Community customs duties: see VATA 1994 s 16(1).

SECTION 3—SUSPENSIVE ARRANGEMENTS AND CUSTOMS PROCEDURES WITH ECONOMIC IMPACT

A—Provisions common to several procedures

Articles 84–90

These articles apply (so far as relevant) in relation to any VAT chargeable on the importation of goods from places outside the member states in the same manner as they apply to any duty of customs and excise or Community customs duties: see VATA 1994 s 16(1).

B—External transit

Articles 91–97

These articles apply (so far as relevant) in relation to any VAT chargeable on the importation of goods from places outside the member states in the same manner as they apply to any duty of customs and excise or Community customs duties: see VATA 1994 s 16(1).

C—Customs warehouses

Articles 98–113

These articles apply (so far as relevant) in relation to any VAT chargeable on the importation of goods from places outside the member states in the same manner as they apply to any duty of customs and excise or Community customs duties: see VATA 1994 s 16(1).

D—Inward processing

Articles 114–129

In principle, these articles apply (so far as relevant) in relation to any VAT chargeable on the importation of goods from places outside the member states in the same manner as they apply to any duty of customs and excise or Community customs duties: see VATA 1994 s 16(1). However, arts 126–128 do not apply in the UK: see VAT Regulations 1995, SI 1995/2518 reg 120(2)(i).

E—Processing under customs control

Articles 130–136

These articles apply (so far as relevant) in relation to any VAT chargeable on the importation of goods from places outside the member states in the same manner as they apply to any duty of customs and excise or Community customs duties: see VATA 1994 s 16(1).

F—Temporary importation

Articles 137–144

In principle, these articles apply (so far as relevant) in relation to any VAT chargeable on the importation of goods from places outside the member states in the same manner as they apply to any duty of customs and excise or Community customs duties: see VATA 1994 s 16(1). However, arts 137 and 142 do not apply: see VAT Regulations 1995, SI 1995/2518 reg 120(2)(i).

G—Outward processing

Articles 145–160

These articles do not apply to the charge to VAT on imported goods in the UK: see VATA 1994 s 16(1)(*b*) and VAT Regulations 1995, SI 1995/2518 reg 120(2)(iv).

SECTION 4—EXPORT

Articles 161 and 162

These articles apply (so far as relevant) in relation to any VAT chargeable on the importation of goods from places outside the member states in the same manner as they apply to any duty of customs and excise or Community customs duties: see VATA 1994 s 16(1).

SECTION 5—INTERNAL TRANSIT

Articles 163–165

These articles apply (so far as relevant) in relation to any VAT chargeable on the importation of goods from places outside the member states in the same manner as they apply to any duty of customs and excise or Community customs duties: see VATA 1994 s 16(1).

CHAPTER 3—OTHER TYPES OF CUSTOMS-APPROVED TREATMENT OR USE

Articles 166–182

These articles relate to free zones and free warehouses (Section 1) and re-exportation, destruction and abandonment (Section 2). They apply (so far as relevant) in relation to any VAT chargeable on the importation of goods from places outside the member states in the same manner as they apply to any duty of customs and excise or Community customs duties: see VATA 1994 s 16(1).

TITLE V—GOODS LEAVING THE CUSTOMS TERRITORY OF THE COMMUNITY

Article 183

This article applies (so far as relevant) in relation to any VAT chargeable on the importation of goods from places outside the member states in the same manner as it applies to any duty of customs and excise or Community customs duties: see VATA 1994 s 16(1).

TITLE VI—PRIVILEGED OPERATIONS

CHAPTER 1—RELIEFS FROM CUSTOMS DUTY

Article 184

This article applies (so far as relevant) in relation to any VAT chargeable on the importation of goods from places outside the member states in the same manner as it applies to any duty of customs and excise or Community customs duties: see VATA 1994 s 16(1).

CHAPTER 2—RETURNED GOODS

Article 185

In principle, this article applies (so far as relevant) in relation to any VAT chargeable on the importation of goods from places outside the member states in the same manner as it applies to any duty of customs and excise or Community customs duties: see VATA 1994 s 16(1).

However:

- This article is regarded as applying only in the case, and to the extent, of a reimportation to the UK by the person who originally exported or re-exported the relevant Community goods or compensating products from the VAT territory of the Community (see VAT Regulations 1995, SI 1995/2518 reg 121D(2)(*a*)). For the "VAT territory of the Community", see VAT Regulations 1995, SI 1995/2518 reg 121D(2), (10) and Appendix 2.
- This article does not apply to VAT in the circumstances described in VAT Regulations 1995, SI 1995/2518 reg 121D(7), (8) (see reg 121D(6)(*a*)).
- For the purposes of arts 185–187 and Regulation (EEC) No 2454/93 arts 844–856 and 882, a reference to "released for free circulation" in para 1 of this article is regarded as including a reference to the completion of the formalities referred to in Directive 77/388/EEC art 33a(1)(*a*) as amended to 6 April 2006 (see VAT Regulations 1995, SI 1995/2518 reg 121D(9)(*b*)(i), (10)).
- For the purposes of arts 185–187 and Regulation (EEC) No 2454/93 arts 844–856 and 882, a reference to "import duty" and "duty" in para 1 (second para, second indent) is regarded as a reference to VAT charged on the importation of goods from places outside the member states in accordance with VATA 1994 (see VAT Regulations 1995, SI 1995/2518 reg 121D(9)(*d*)(ii)).

Directive 77/388/EEC art 33(1)(*a*) was repealed and replaced by Directive 2006/112/EC art 275 with effect from 1 January 2007.

Article 186

In principle, this article applies (so far as relevant) in relation to any VAT chargeable on the importation of goods from places outside the member states in the same manner as it applies to any duty of customs and excise or Community customs duties: see VATA 1994 s 16(1).

However:

- This article is regarded as applying only in the case, and to the extent, of a reimportation to the UK by the person who originally exported or re-exported the relevant Community goods or compensating products from the VAT territory of the Community (see VAT Regulations 1995, SI 1995/2518 reg 121D(2)(*a*)). For the "VAT territory of the Community", see VAT Regulations 1995, SI 1995/2518 reg 121D(2), (10) and Appendix 2.
- The article does not apply to VAT in the circumstances described in VAT Regulations 1995, SI 1995/2518 reg 121D(7), (8) (reg 121D(6)(*a*)).
- The amount of relief mentioned is regarded as reduced by the amount of any unpaid VAT (see VAT Regulations 1995, SI 1995/2518 reg 121D(3)). For "VAT" and "unpaid", see VAT Regulations 1995, SI 1995/2518 reg 121D(5)(*a*), (*b*), (*d*), (10).

Article 187

In principle, this article applies (so far as relevant) in relation to any VAT chargeable on the importation of goods from places outside the member states in the same manner as it applies to any duty of customs and excise or Community customs duties: see VATA 1994 s 16(1).

However:

- This article is regarded as applying only in the case, and to the extent, of a reimportation to the UK by the person who originally exported or re-exported the relevant Community goods or compensating products from the VAT territory of the Community (see VAT Regulations 1995, reg 121D(2)(a)). For the "VAT territory of the Community", see VAT Regulations 1995, SI 1995/2518 reg 121D(2), (10) and Appendix 2.
- The article does not apply to VAT in the circumstances described in VAT Regulations 1995, SI 1995/2518 reg 121D(7), (8) (see reg 121D(6)(*a*)).
- The amount legally owed is regarded as reduced by the amount of any paid VAT (see VAT Regulations 1995, SI 1995/2518 reg 121D(4)). For "VAT" and "paid", see VAT Regulations 1995, SI 1995/2518 reg 121D(5)(*a*), (*c*), (*d*), (10).
- For the purposes of arts 185–187 and Regulation (EEC) No 2454/93 arts 844–856 and 882, a reference to "import duty" or "duty" is regarded as a reference to VAT charged on the importation of goods from places outside the member states in accordance with VATA 1994 (see VAT Regulations 1995, SI 1995/2518 reg 121D(9)(*d*)(ii)).

CHAPTER 3—PRODUCTS OF SEA-FISHING AND OTHER PRODUCTS TAKEN FROM THE SEA

Article 188

This article applies (so far as relevant) in relation to any VAT chargeable on the importation of goods from places outside the member states in the same manner as it applies to any duty of customs and excise or Community customs duties: see VATA 1994 s 16(1).

TITLE VII—CUSTOMS DEBT

Articles 189–234

These articles relate to:

- Security to cover customs debt (Chapter 1: arts 189–200).

Part I VAT

- Incurring a customs debt (Chapter 2: arts 201–216).
- Recovery of the amount of the customs debt (Chapter 3: arts 217–232).
- Extinction of customs debt (Chapter 4: arts 233 and 234).
- Repayment and remission of duty (Chapter 5: arts 235–242).

In principle, these articles apply (so far as relevant) in relation to any VAT chargeable on the importation of goods from places outside the member states in the same manner as they apply to any duty of customs and excise or Community customs duties: see VATA 1994 s 16(1). However, the following articles do not apply:

- Art 229(*b*) (see VAT Regulations 1995, SI 1995/2518 reg 120(2)(vi)).
- Art 232(1)(*b*), (2) and (3) (see VAT Regulations 1995, SI 1995/2518 reg 120(2)(vii)).
- Art 241 (second and third sentences) (VAT Regulations 1995, SI 1995/2518 reg 120(2)(vi)).

Articles 218(1) and 225 are varied in their application to VAT in accordance with VAT Regulations 1995, SI 1995/2518 reg 121B.

TITLE VIII—APPEALS

Articles 243–246

These articles apply (so far as relevant) in relation to any VAT chargeable on the importation of goods from places outside the member states in the same manner as they apply to any duty of customs and excise or Community customs duties: see VATA 1994 s 16(1).

TITLE IX—FINAL PROVISIONS

Articles 247–253

These articles relate to:

- The Customs Code Committee (Chapter 1: arts 247–249).
- The legal effects in a member state of measures taken, documents issued and findings made in another member state (Chapter 2: art 250).
- Repeals, amendments to earlier legislation and commencement (Chapter 3: arts 251–253).

These articles apply (so far as relevant) in relation to any VAT chargeable on the importation of goods from places outside the member states in the same manner as they apply to any duty of customs and excise or Community customs duties: see VATA 1994 s 16(1).

REGULATION (EEC) NO 2454/93
IMPLEMENTATION OF THE COMMUNITY CUSTOMS CODE

General note This regulation lays down provisions for the implementation of the Community Customs Code (see Regulation (EEC) No 2913/92). It applies to the charge to VAT on imported goods in the UK unless it is specifically excluded or varied: see VATA 1994 s 16(1)(*b*). For exclusions and variations, see VAT Regulations 1995, SI 1995/2518 regs 120(2)(*b*), 121C and 121D.

Prior to 6 April 2006, the relief from VAT on the reimportation of certain goods was conferred by VAT Regulations 1995, SI 1995/2518 regs 124, 125. Thereafter, relief is conferred by Regulation (EEC) No 2913/92 arts 185–187, as implemented by arts 844–856 of this Regulation. Articles 844–856 are modified by VAT Regulations 1995, SI 1995/2518 reg 121D. Article 882 (which, with arts 878–881, implements Regulation (EEC) No 2913/92 arts 185–187 (repayment and remission of duty)) is modified by the same provision.

Articles 844–856 and 882 are regarded as applying only in the case, and to the extent, of a reimportation to the UK by the person who originally exported or re-exported the relevant Community goods or compensating products from the VAT territory of the Community (see VAT Regulations 1995, SI 1995/2518 reg 121D(2)(*b*)). However, reg 121D(6)(*b*) provides that these articles do not apply to VAT in the circumstances described in reg 121D(7), (8). For the "VAT territory of the Community", see VAT Regulations 1995, SI 1995/2518 reg 121D(2) and Appendix 2. The application of the following articles is modified.

Article 844

For the purposes of arts 185–187 and Regulation (EEC) No 2454/93 arts 844–856 and 882:

- A reference to "entered" and "declared" for "release for free circulation" in (or for the purposes of) para 4 of this article is regarded as including a reference to the completion of the formalities referred to in Directive 77/388/EEC art 33a(1)(*a*) as amended to 6 April 2006 (see VAT Regulations 1995, SI 1995/2518 reg 121D(9)(*b*)(ii), (10)).
- A reference to "customs export formalities" in para 1 of this article is regarded as a reference to completion of the formalities referred to in Directive 77/388/EEC art 33a(2)(*a*) as amended to 6 April 2006 (or to a declaration under those formalities) (see VAT Regulations 1995, SI 1995/2518 reg 121D(9)(*c*)(i), (10)).
- A reference to "customs formalities relating to their exportation" in para 4 of this article is regarded as including a reference to the completion of the formalities referred to in Directive 77/388/EEC art 33a(1)(*a*) as amended to 6 April 2006 (see VAT Regulations 1995, SI 1995/2518 reg 121D(9)(*c*)(iii), (10)).

Directive 77/388/EEC art 33(1)(*a*) was repealed and replaced by Directive 2006/112/EC art 275 with effect from 1 January 2007.

Article 848

For the purposes of arts 185–187 and Regulation (EEC) No 2454/93 arts 844–856 and 882:

- A reference to "export declaration" in para 1 of this article is regarded as including a reference to the completion of the formalities referred to in Directive 77/388/EEC art 33a(1)(*a*) as amended to 6 April 2006 (see VAT Regulations 1995, SI 1995/2518 reg 121D(9)(*c*)(ii), (10)).
- A reference to "customs formalities relating to their exportation" in para 1 of this article is regarded as including a reference to the completion of the formalities referred to in Directive 77/388/EEC art 33a(1)(*a*) as amended to 6 April 2006 (see VAT Regulations 1995, SI 1995/2518 reg 121D(9)(*c*)(iii), (10)).

Directive 77/388/EEC art 33(1)(*a*) was repealed and replaced by Directive 2006/112/EC art 275 with effect from 1 January 2007.

Article 849

For the purposes of arts 185–187 and Regulation (EEC) No 2454/93 arts 844–856 and 882:

- A reference to "customs formalities relating to their exportation" in para 1 of this article is regarded as including a reference to the completion of the formalities referred to in Directive 77/388/EEC art 33a(1)(*a*) as amended to 6 April 2006 (see VAT Regulations 1995, SI 1995/2518 reg 121D(9)(*c*)(iii), (10)).
- A reference to "customs export formalities" in paras 1–3 of this article is regarded as a reference to completion of the formalities referred to in Directive 77/388/EEC art 33a(2)(*a*) as amended to 6 April 2006 (or to a declaration under those formalities) (see VAT Regulations 1995, SI 1995/2518 reg 121D(9)(*c*)(i), (10)).
- A reference to "entered" and "declared" for "release for free circulation" in (or for the purposes of) paras 1 or 5 of this article is regarded as including a reference to the completion of the formalities referred to in Directive 77/388/EEC art 33a(1)(*a*) as amended to 6 April 2006 (see VAT Regulations 1995, SI 1995/2518 reg 121D(9)(*b*)(ii), (10)).

Directive 77/388/EEC art 33(1)(*a*) was repealed and replaced by Directive 2006/112/EC art 275 with effect from 1 January 2007.

REGULATION (EC) NO 1798/2003
ADMINISTRATIVE COOPERATION IN THE FIELD OF VALUE ADDED TAX

General note This regulation (as amended by Regulation (EC) Nos 885/2004, 1791/2006, 143/2008 art 1 and 37/2009) sets out:

- the conditions under which the administrative authorities in the member states cooperate with the Commission and each other to ensure compliance with VAT legislation relating to supplies of goods and services, acquisitions of goods and importations of goods from 1 January 2010.
- the rules and procedures for the electronic exchange of information relating to the special scheme for electronically supplied services made to non-taxable persons by non-established taxable persons (see Directive 2006/112/EC arts 357–369) from 1 January 2010.

Detailed rules for implementing arts 18, 35 and 37 are set out in Regulation (EC) Nos 1925/2004 and 1174/2009.

This regulation entered into force on 1 January 2004 (art 48). It is recast, repealed and replaced by Regulation (EU) No 904/2010 with effect from 1 January 2012. However, the following provisions continue to have effect after that date:

- The effect of art 2(1) is maintained until the list of competent authorities referred to in art 3 of the 2010 Regulation has been published.
- Articles 22–27 (with the exception of art 27(4)) remain applicable until 31 December 2012.

From 1 January 2012, references to this regulation are construed as references to Regulation (EU) No 904/2010 in accordance with the correlation table in Annex III to the 2010 Regulation: see art 61 (third para) of the 2010 Regulation.

CHAPTER 1—GENERAL PROVISIONS

Article 2

For the purposes of this regulation, the "competent authority of a member state" means:

Member state	**Competent authority**
Austria	Bundesminister für Finanzen
Belgium	Le minister des finances De Minister van financiën
Bulgaria	Изпълнителният директор на Националната агенция за приходите
Cyprus	Υπουργός Οικονομικών ή εξουσιοδοτημένος αντιπρόσωπος του
Czech Republic	Ministerstvo finance
Denmark	Skatteministeren
Estonia	Maksuamet
Finland	Valtiovarainministeriö Finansministeriet
France	le ministre de l'économie, des finances et de l'industrie
Germany	Bundesministerium der Finanzen
Greece	Υπουργειο Οικονομίας και Οικονομικων

Member state	Competent authority
Hungary	Adó- és Pénzügyi Ellenőrzési Hivatal Központi Kapcsolattartó Irodája
Ireland	The Revenue Commissioners
Italy	il Capo del Dipartimento delle Politiche Fiscali
Latvia	Valsts ie ēmumu dienests
Lithuania	Valstybin mokesči inspekcija prie Finans ministerijos
Luxembourg	L'Administration de l'Enregistrement et des Domaines
Malta	Dipartiment tat-Taxxa fuq il-Valur Mi jud fil-Ministeru tal-Finanzi u Affarijiet Ekonomiċi
Netherlands	De minister van Financiën
Poland	Minister Finansów
Portugal	O Ministro das Finanças
Romania	Agentia Naţională de Administrare Fiscală
Slovakia	Ministerstvo financií
Slovenia	Ministrstvo za finance
Spain	El Secretario de Estado de Hacienda
Sweden	Chefen för Finansdepartementet
UK	The Commissioners of Customs and Excise (now the Commissioners of Revenue and Customs)

CHAPTER V—STORAGE AND EXCHANGE OF INFORMATION SPECIFIC TO INTRA-COMMUNITY TRANSACTIONS

Article 22

Each member state must maintain an electronic database for storing and processing information collected in accordance with Directive 2006/112/EC arts 262–271 (recapitulative statements), keep the database up to date and ensure that it is complete and accurate.

Article 23

A member state (X) must provide the following information to another member state (Y): (1) VAT identification numbers issued by member state Y; and (2) the total value of all intra-Community supplies of goods and services made by all operators identified for the purposes of VAT in member state X to persons holding a VAT identification number. Values are expressed in the currency of member state X.

Article 24

The competent authority of a member state (X) may consider it necessary to obtain the following information for the control of intra-Community acquisitions of goods or intra-Community supplies of services in its territory and to prevent a breach of VAT legislation: (1) the VAT identification numbers of the persons who made intra-Community acquisitions of goods or intra-Community supplies of services in another member state (Y); and (2) the total value of supplies made by each person in member state Y to a person identified for VAT in member state X. Member state X must: (1) obtain the information directly and without delay; or (2) have direct access to it by electronic means.

Article 25

A member state required to grant access to information under arts 23 and 24 must do so no later than one month after the end of the period to which the information relates. However, information regarding recapitulative statements (see art 22) must be provided no later than one month after the end of the period in which it was collected.

Article 26

The competent authorities of member states must comply with art 41 when storing information in an electronic database and exchanging information by electronic means for the purposes of arts 22–25.

Article 27

Member states must maintain an electronic register of the persons to whom they have issued a VAT identification number. A member state may obtain: (1) confirmation of the validity of the VAT identification number under which a person has effected or received an intra-Community supply of goods or services; and (2) the name and address of the person to whom the number was issued.

REGULATION (EC) NO 638/2004
COMMUNITY STATISTICS RELATING TO THE TRADING OF GOODS BETWEEN MEMBER STATES

General note This regulation (as amended by Regulation (EC) No 222/2009) establishes a system ("Intrastat") for collecting data required to compile the statistics on intra-Community removals of goods required following the abolition of internal frontiers, and the consequent abolition of physical checks on cross-border movements of goods, from 1 January 1993. It is implemented by Regulation (EC) No 1982/2004.

This regulation repeals and replaces Regulation (EEC) No 3330/91 (as amended by Regulation (EEC) No 3046/92 art 22 and Regulation (EC) No 1182/99, Regulation (EC) No 1624/2000 and Regulation (EC) No 1822/2003) with effect from 1 January 2005. In consequence, references to the 1991 Regulation are now construed as references to this Regulation (art 15(2)).

REGULATION (EC) NO 1925/2004
DETAILED RULES FOR IMPLEMENTING CERTAIN PROVISIONS OF REGULATION (EC) NO 1798/2003

General note This regulation (as amended by Regulation (EC) No 1792/2006) lays down detailed rules for implementing Regulation (EC) No 1798/2003 arts 18, 35 and 37 (art 1) regarding administrative cooperation in the field of VAT. It entered into force on the twentieth day following 5 November 2004.

Regulation (EC) No 1798/2003 is repealed, recast and replaced by Regulation (EU) No 904/2010 with effect from 1 January 2012. From that date, references to arts 18, 35 and 37 of the 2003 Regulation are construed as references to arts 14(1) (first para), 49 and 51(1) of the 2010 Regulation: see art 61 (third para) of the 2010 Regulation and Annex III thereto.

REGULATION (EC) NO 1982/2004
IMPLEMENTING REGULATION (EC) NO 638/2004

General note This regulation implements Regulation (EC) No 638/2004 (art 1) regarding Intrastat. It repealed and replaced Regulation (EEC) No 2590/92 and Regulation (EC) No 1901/2000 (as amended by Regulation (EC) No 2150/2001, Regulation (EC) No 1835/2002, Regulation (EC) No 2207/2003 and the Act of Accession (2003)) (art 27) with effect from 1 January 2005 (art 28). It was amended by Regulation (EC) No 1915/2005 with effect from 1 January 2006 and by Regulation (EU) Nos 91/2010 and 96/2010 with effect from 1 January 2010.

REGULATION (EC) NO 1777/2005
IMPLEMENTING MEASURES FOR DIRECTIVE 77/388/EEC

General note

This regulation implemented Directive 77/388/EEC (now Directive 2006/11/EC). It was repealed and replaced by Regulation (EU) No 282/2011 with effect from 1 July 2011.

REGULATION (EC) NO 143/2008
AMENDING REGULATION (EC) NO 1798/2003

General note This regulation amended Regulation (EC) No 1798/2003 with effect from 1 January 2010 (art 1). It prospectively amends the 2003 Regulation with effect from 1 January 2015 (art 2). The 2003 Regulation is repealed with effect from 1 January 2012 by Regulation (EU) No 904/2010 art 61. It follows that the prospective amendments to the 2003 Regulation will not come into effect.

REGULATION (EC) NO 450/2008
THE COMMUNITY CUSTOMS CODE (MODERNISED CUSTOMS CODE)

General note This regulation repeals and replaces Regulations (EEC) Nos 3925/91, 2913/92 (the Community Customs Code) and Regulation (EC) No 1207/2001 in accordance with the following timetable:

- Article 188(1) provides that the articles listed therein have effect from 24 June 2008. These articles set out powers to make provisions implementing this regulation.
- Article 188(3) provides that art 30(1) applies from 1 January 2011.
- Article 188(2) provides that the remaining articles apply once the implementing provisions have effect. This must be no earlier than 24 June 2009 and no later than 24 June 2013.

References to the repealed regulations are construed as references to this regulation. These references are read in accordance with the correlation tables set out in the Annex (see art 186 (second para)).

REGULATION (EC) NO 1179/2008
DETAILED RULES FOR IMPLEMENTING CERTAIN PROVISIONS OF DIRECTIVE 2008/55/EC

General note This regulation repeals and replaces Directive 2002/94/EC with effect from 1 January 2009. It lays down detailed rules for implementing arts 4(2), 4(4), 5(2), 5(3), 7, 8, 9, 11, 12(1), 12(2), 14, 18(3) and 24 of Directive 2008/55/EC in relation to claims for the recovery of certain levies, duties, taxes and other measures.

REGULATION (EC) NO 1174/2009
RULES FOR THE IMPLEMENTATION OF ARTICLES 34A AND 37 OF COUNCIL REGULATION (EC) NO 1798/2003 AS REGARDS REFUNDS OF VALUE ADDED TAX UNDER COUNCIL DIRECTIVE 2008/9/EC

General note This regulation lays down rules for implementing Regulation (EC) No 1798/2003 arts 34a and 37 (see arts 1–3). These rules apply to information requests by a member state in relation to VAT refunds claimed by traders established in another member state. For refunds to such traders, see Directive 2008/9/EC.

This regulation came into force on 1 January 2010 (see art 4).

Regulation (EC) No 1798/2003 is repealed, recast and replaced by Regulation (EU) No 904/2010 with effect from 1 January 2012. From that date, references to arts 34a and 37 of the 2003 Regulation are construed as references to arts 48 and 51(1) the 2010 Regulation: see art 61 (third para) of the 2010 Regulation and Annex III thereto.

REGULATION (EC) NO 1186/2009
COMMUNITY SYSTEM OF RELIEFS FROM CUSTOMS DUTY

General note This regulation codifies and replaces Regulation (EEC) No 918/83 with effect from 1 January 2010. The 1983 Regulation is excepted from the Community legislation applicable to the charge to VAT on imported goods: see VAT Regulations 1995, SI 1995/2518 reg 120(1). However, art 60 of the 1983 Regulation, which is re-enacted as art 53 of this Regulation, is relevant to the relief conferred by Directive 2009/132/EC art 36 (formerly Directive 83/181/EEC art 35).

TITLE II— RELIEF FROM IMPORT DUTY

CHAPTER XII— LABORATORY ANIMALS AND BIOLOGICAL OR CHEMICAL SUBSTANCES INTENDED FOR RESEARCH

Article 53

1, 3. Relief from import duties is granted in respect of:

- Animals specially prepared for laboratory use.
- Biological or chemical substances imported exclusively for non-commercial purposes. The substances must be included in a list drawn up in accordance with Regulation (EEC) No 2913/92 art 247a.

2. The relief in para 1 is limited to animals and biological substances intended for either:

- Public establishments (or departments of public establishments) principally engaged in education or scientific research.
- Private establishments which are principally engaged in education or scientific research and which are authorised by the competent authorities to receive such articles duty free.

REGULATION (EU) NO 904/2010 ADMINISTRATIVE COOPERATION AND COMBATING FRAUD IN THE FIELD OF VALUE ADDED TAX

General note This regulation recasts and replaces Regulation (EC) No 1798/2003. It sets out:

- The conditions under which the competent authorities in the member states cooperate with the Commission and each other in order to ensure compliance with the VAT legislation (see art 1(1) (first para)).
- The conditions under which the competent authorities are required to assist in the protection of VAT revenue in all the member states (see art 1(2)).
- The rules and procedures under which the member states cooperate, exchange information that may help effect a correct assessment of VAT, monitor the correct application of VAT (in particular, in relation to intra-Community transactions) and combat fraud (see art 1(1) (second para)).
- The rules and procedures for member states to collect and exchange information by electronic means (see art 1(1) (second para).
- The rules and procedures for the electronic exchange of information relating to the special scheme for electronically supplied services made to non-taxable persons by non-established taxable persons (see Directive 2006/112/EC arts 357–369) (see art 1(4)).

Chapter X (Eurofisc) applies from 1 November 2010. The remaining provisions come into force with effect from the following dates:

- Articles 17 – 21 and 24 (storage and exchange of information) apply from 1 January 2013.
- Articles 38 – 42 (special schemes in Directive 2006/112/EC Title XII Chapter 5) apply between 1 January 2012 and 31 December 2014.
- Articles 43 – 47 apply from 1 January 2015.
- The remaining articles apply from 1 January 2012.

Detailed rules for implementing arts 14(1) (first para), 49 and 51(1) of this regulation are set out in Regulation (EC) No 1925/2004.

CHAPTER X—EUROFISC

Article 33

This chapter establishes a network (referred to as "Eurofisc") for the exchange of targeted information between member states. The purpose of Eurofisc is to promote and facilitate multilateral cooperation in the fight against VAT fraud. For organisational and operational details for the functioning of the network, see the Council Statement on Eurofisc, OJ C275/4, 12.10.10.

Article 34

Member states are required to choose the working fields in which they intend to participate. Having done so, they are required to actively participate in the multilateral exchange of targeted information between all participating member states. Information communicated or collected is subject to the confidentiality requirements set out in art 55.

Article 35

The Commission is required to provide Eurofisc with technical and logistical support. It does not have accesses to the information exchanged.

Article 36

Each member state is required to appoint one or more "Eurofisc liaison officials" to carry out the activities listed in art 33(2). A liaison official is responsible only to his national administration. He is referred to as a "participating Eurofisc liaison official" if he participates in a particular Eurofisc working field. The participating liaison officials of the member states working in a particular working field are required to designate one of their number as a coordinator, who is referred to as a Eurofisc working field coordinator. The duties of the coordinator are defined.

Article 37

Eurofisc working field coordinators are required to prepare an annual report on the activities of all working fields. The report is submitted to the Standing Committee on Administrative Cooperation, as to which see art 58(1).

REGULATION (EU) NO 282/2011 IMPLEMENTING MEASURES FOR DIRECTIVE 2006/112/EC ON THE COMMON SYSTEM OF VALUE ADDED TAX

General note This regulation recasts, repeals and replaces Regulation (EC) No 1777/2005. It came into force on 12 April 2011 and applies from the dates specified in art 65. The "ex" references indicate the corresponding provision (if any) in the 2005 Regulation.

Preamble

Directive 2006/112/EC contains some rules that are subject to interpretation by the member states. Divergences in national VAT systems have arisen, or may arise, that are incompatible with the proper functioning of the internal market. The implementing provisions of this regulation contain specific rules designed to bring about uniform treatment throughout the Community in specific circumstances. They are not conclusive for other cases. In view of their formulation, they are to be applied restrictively.

CHAPTER I—SUBJECT MATTER

Article 1 (ex art 1)

This Regulation lays down measures for implementing Directive 2006/112/EC Titles I–V and VII–XII.

CHAPTER II—SCOPE (TITLE I OF DIRECTIVE 2006/112/EC)

Article 2

The following movements of new means of transport by a non-taxable person do not result in an intra-Community acquisition for the purposes of Directive 2006/112/EC art 2(1)(b):

- Transfer on a change of residence. This relief does not apply if the means of transport qualified for the exemption in Directive 2006/112/EC art 138(2)(a) at the time of supply.
- Return to the member state in which the new means of transport was initially supplied to the non-taxable person. The initial supply must have been exempted from VAT under Directive 2006/112/EC art 138(2)(a) at the time of supply.

Article 3

In principle, a supply of the services listed in 2006/112/EC art 59 is outside the scope of VAT if the supplier demonstrates that the place of supply is outside the EU. For this purpose, the place of supply is determined in accordance with Directive 2006/112/EC art 59a (if it applies) or arts 16–18 below (if it does not).

From 1 January 2013, the relief applies to the services in 2006/112/EC art 56(2) (first para) (as amended with effect from that date by Directive 2008/8/EC art 4).

From 1 January 2015, the relief applies to the services in 2006/112/EC art 58 (as substituted with effect from that date by Directive 2008/8/EC art 5(1)).

Article 4

Intra-Community acquisitions of goods are relieved from VAT in accordance with Directive 2006/112/EC art 3 even if a VAT identification number has been attributed to the taxable person in respect of: (1) services received for which he is liable to pay VAT; or (2) services supplied by him in another member state on which VAT is payable solely by the recipient. However, the taxable person is deemed to have exercised the option in art 3(3) of the 2006 Directive (so that the general scheme in art 2(1)(b)(i) of the 2006 Directive applies) if he communicates his VAT identification number to the person who supplied the goods.

Part I VAT

CHAPTER III—TAXABLE PERSONS (TITLE III OF DIRECTIVE 2006/112/EC)

Article 5 (ex art 2)

An European Economic Interest Grouping is a taxable person within the meaning of Directive 2006/112/EC art 9(1), if it supplies goods or services for consideration to its members or to third parties.

CHAPTER IV—TAXABLE TRANSACTIONS (ARTICLES 24 TO 29 OF DIRECTIVE 2006/112/EC)

Article 6

1. Services are "restaurant and catering services" if: (1) they consist of the supply of (a) prepared or unprepared food, (b) beverages or (c) both; (2) the food and/or beverages are supplied for human consumption; (3) the food and/or beverages are accompanied by sufficient support services allowing the food and/or beverages to be consumed immediately; and (4) the food and/or beverages are only one component of a single supply in which the services predominate.

The services are "restaurant services" if the food and/or beverages are supplied on the supplier's premises. The services are "catering services" if the supply is made off the supplier's premises.

2. It is immaterial whether or not transport services are provided. However, a supply does not comprise "restaurant services" or "catering services" if the food and/or beverages are supplied without any other support services.

Article 7 (ex arts 11 and 12)

The term "electronically supplied services" includes: (1) services reliant on information technology which, by virtue of their nature, are delivered automatically, or with minimal human intervention, via the Internet or an electronic network; and (2) the services listed in art 7(2). The goods and services listed in art 7(3) are not electronically supplied services.

Article 8 (ex art 3(2))

Assembling a machine from parts provided by the customer is a supply of services within the meaning of 2006/112/EC art 24(1).

Article 9 (ex art 3(1))

The sale of an option is a supply of services within the meaning of Directive 2006/112/EC art 24(1) if the transaction falls within the scope of Directive 2006/112/EC art 135(1)(f). The supply is distinct from the underlying transactions to which the services relate.

CHAPTER V—PLACE OF TAXABLE TRANSACTIONS

SECTION 1 CONCEPTS

Article 10

1. For the purposes of Directive 2006/112/EC arts 44 and 45, the place where a taxable person has established his business is the place where the central administrative functions of the business are carried out.

2. In determining where these functions are carried out, it is necessary to take into account: (1) the place where essential decisions concerning the general management of the business are taken; (2) the place where the registered office of the business is located; and (3) the place where management meets. Any doubt is resolved by giving precedence to point (2).

3. A postal address does not, of itself, constitute the place where a business has been established.

Article 11

For the purposes of Directive 2006/112/EC arts 44, 45 and 192a, a "fixed establishment" is any establishment (other than the place where a person has established his business) which is characterised by: (1) a sufficient degree of permanence; and (2) a suitable structure in terms of human and technical resources which enables the establishment provide the services it supplies. The fact that a taxable person has a VAT identification number does not in itself imply that he has a fixed establishment.

The same definition applies for the purposes of Directive 2006/112/EC art 58 until 31 December 2014.

From 1 January 2013, the same definition applies for the purposes of Directive 2006/112/EC art 56(2) (second para) (as substituted by Directive 2008/8/EC art 4 with effect from that date).

Article 12

For the purposes of Directive 2006/112/EC, the "permanent address" of a natural person is either: (1) the address entered in the population or similar register; or (2) the address indicated by him to the relevant tax authorities. This applies whether or not the person is a taxable person. These criteria do not apply if there is evidence that the relevant address does not reflect reality.

Article 13

For the purposes of Directive 2006/112/EC, the place where a natural person " usually resides" is the place where he usually lives as a result of personal or occupational ties. This applies whether or not the person is a taxable person.

A natural person may have no occupational ties, or have occupational ties in different countries. If so, his usual place of residence is determined by reference to personal ties showing close links between the person and a place where he is living.

SECTION 2 PLACE OF SUPPLY OF GOODS (ARTICLES 31 TO 39 OF DIRECTIVE 2006/112/EC)

Article 14 (ex art 22)

The value of goods (other than goods chargeable to excise duty) despatched or transported to another member state during a calendar year may exceed the turnover limit specified in Directive 2006/112/EC art 34(2). Where this is so, the place of supply of goods supplied prior to exceeding the limit is determined under that provision. The place of supply of the following supplies is determined under Directive 2006/112/EC art 33:

- The supply that results in the threshold being exceeded.
- All subsequent supplies in the same calendar year.
- All supplies in the subsequent calendar year.

Two conditions must be met:

- The supplier has not exercised the option in Directive 2006/112/EC art 34(4).
- The supplier did not exceed the threshold during the previous calendar year.

Article 15

For the purposes of Directive 2006/112/EC art 37, the section of a passenger transport operation effected within the EU is determined by the journey of the means of transport rather than the journey competed by each of the passengers.

SECTION 3 PLACE OF INTRA-COMMUNITY ACQUISITIONS OF GOODS (ARTICLES 40, 41 AND 42 OF DIRECTIVE 2006/112/EC)

Article 16 (ex art 21)

Where the despatch or transport of an intra-Community acquisition of goods (see Directive 2006/112/EC art 20) ends in a member state, the acquisition must be taxed in that member state. This applies whether or not the goods are charged to VAT by the member state in which the despatch or transport began. The member state in which the despatch or transport began applies its own domestic rules when responding to a request by the supplier to correct the VAT shown on his invoice.

SECTION 4 PLACE OF SUPPLY OF SERVICES (ARTICLES 43 TO 59 OF DIRECTIVE 2006/112/EC)

SUBSECTION 1 STATUS OF THE CUSTOMER

Article 17

1. The place of supply of services may depend on whether the customer is a taxable or non-taxable person. If so, the status of the customer is determined in accordance with Directive 2006/112/EC arts 9–13 and 43.

2. A non-taxabe person is treated as a taxable person if he is identified for VAT purposes, or required to be so identified, because: (1) his intra-Community acquisitions of goods are subject to VAT; or (2) he has exercised the option to tax those operations in accordance with Directive 2006/112/EC art 43.

Article 18

(a) (If the customer has communicated his individual VAT identification number to the supplier) the supplier confirms the validity of the customer's name, address and identification number in accordance with Regulation (EC) No 904/10 art 31.

(b) (If the customer has not yet received an individual VAT identification number, but informs the supplier that he has applied for one) the supplier: (i) obtains any other proof demonstrating that the customer is a taxable person or non-taxable legal person required to be identified for VAT purposes; and (ii) takes reasonable steps to verify the accuracy of the information given to him. He does this by carrying out normal commercial security checks such as those relating to identity or payment.

2. As regards a customer established in the EU, the supplier may, in the absence of a VAT identification number for the customer, regard the customer as a non-taxable person. However, the supplier may not do so if he has information to the contrary.

3. As regards a customer established outside the EU, the supplier may, in the absence of information to the contrary, regard the customer as a taxable person in either of the following circumstances:

(a) He obtains a certificate from the customer confirming that the customer is engaged in economic activities in order to enable him to obtain a refund of VAT under Directive 86/560/EEC. The certificate is issued by the customer's competent tax authorities.

(b) (In the absence of a certificate) the supplier: (i) holds the VAT number or similar number by which the customer is identified in the country in which he is established or, in the absence of any such number, any other proof demonstrating that the customer is a taxable person; and (ii) takes reasonable steps to verify the accuracy of the information given to him. He does this by carrying out normal commercial security checks, eg checks relating to identity or payment.
1. As regards a customer established within the EU, the supplier may, in the absence of information to the contrary, regard the customer as a taxable person in either of the following circumstances:

SUBSECTION 2 CAPACITY OF THE CUSTOMER

Article 19

For the purposes of applying Directive 2006/112/EC arts 44 and 45 (place of supply of services), the following persons are regarded as non-taxable persons when receiving services exclusively for private use or for use by their staff: (1) a taxable person; and (2) a non-taxable legal person who is deemed to be a taxable person. On this basis, the place of supply is determined in accordance with Directive 2006/112/EC art 45.

However, the supplier may regard the services as being supplied for the customer's business use (so that his services are supplied to a taxable person "acting as such") if the customer has provided his individual VAT identification number in relation to the transaction. On this basis, the place of supply is determined in accordance with Directive 2006/112/EC art 44. However, the supplier may not so regard the services if he has information to the contrary, eg where the nature of the services indicates that they are not for business use. In these circumstances, the place of supply is determined in accordance with Directive 2006/112/EC art 45.

A service may be intended for both private/staff use and business use. Where this is so, the place of supply is exclusively determined in accordance with Directive 2006/112/EC art 44 unless this give rise to an abusive practice.

SUBSECTION 3 LOCATION OF THE CUSTOMER

Article 20

A supply of services to either of the following persons may fall within the scope of Directive 2006/112/EC art 44: (1) a taxable person; or (2) a non-taxable legal person deemed to be a taxable person. If the taxable person is established in a single country, the services are taxable in that country. If, in the absence of a place of establishment or fixed establishment, the taxable person has his permanent residence and usually resides in a single country, the services are taxable in that country.

The supplier is required to establish the relevant country on the basis of information provided by the customer. This information may include the customer's VAT identification number in the member state where he is established. The supplier is required to verify the information provided. He does this by carrying out normal commercial security measures, eg by using measures relating to identity or payment checks.

Article 21

A supply of services to one of the following persons may fall within the scope of Directive 2006/112/EC art 44: (1) a taxable person; or (2) a non-taxable legal person deemed to be a taxable person. If the taxable person is established in more than one country, the supply is taxable in the country where the taxable person has established his business. There are two exceptions to this rule.

First, if the service is provided to a fixed establishment located in another place and the services are used for the needs of that establishment, the supply is taxable at the place where the establishment is located.

Second, if the taxable person does not have a place of establishment or fixed establishment, the supply is taxable at the taxable person's permanent address or usual residence.

Article 22

1. The supplier is required to identify the location of the customer's fixed establishment to which the service is provided. This is done by using one the following methods. These methods are applied in the order given.

First, the supplier examines the nature of his service and the use made of it.

Second, the supplier pays particular attention to whether the contract, the order form and the customer's VAT identification number in order to identify a fixed establishment as the customer and whether that fixed establishment is the entity paying for the service.

Third, the supplier may legitimately consider that the services has been supplied at the place where the customer has established his business.

Services covered by Directive 2006/112/EC art 44 may be supplied to a taxable person under a contract covering one or more services used in an unidentifiable and non-quantifiable manner. In these circumstances, the supplier may legitimately consider that the services have been supplied at the place where the customer has established his business.

2. This article is applied without prejudice to the customer's obligations.

Article 23

1. [This paragraph applies from 1 January 2013.]

2. The place where a supply of services is taxable may be determined by reference to the place where the customer is established or the place where he has his permanent address or usually resides (see Directive 2006/112/EC art arts 58 and 59). Where this is so, the supplier is required to establish that place based on factual information provided by the customer. He must verify that information by normal commercial security measures, eg by reference to measures relating to identity or payment checks.

Article 24

1. [This paragraph applies from 1 January 2013.]

2. Services of a description in Directive 2006/112/EC arts 58 and 59 may be supplied to: (1) a non-taxable person who is established in more than one country; or (2) a non-taxable person

who has his permanent address in one country and his usual residence in another. In determining the place of supply, priority is given to the place which best ensures that the services are taxed in the country where consumption actually takes place,

SUBSECTION 4–COMMON PROVISION REGARDING DETERMINATION OF THE STATUS, THE CAPACITY AND THE LOCATION OF THE CUSTOMER

Article 25

The circumstances taken into account when applying the rules governing the place of supply of services are those existing at the time of the chargeable event. The place of supply so determined is unaffected by any subsequent changes to the customer's use of the service unless this constitutes an abusive practice.

SUBSECTION 5–SUPPLY OF SERVICES GOVERNED BY THE GENERAL RULES

Article 26 (ex art 7)

The general place of supply rule in Directive 2006/112/EC art 44 applies to the assignment of television broadcasting rights by a body to a taxable person.

Article 27 (ex art 8)

The general place of supply rule in Directive 2006/112/EC art 44 applies to a supply of services consisting of applying for, or receiving, refunds under Directive 2008/9/EC.

Article 28 (ex art 4)

Services supplied in the framework of organising a funeral may constitute a single service for VAT purposes. Where this is so, the general place of supply rules in 2006/112/EC arts 44 and 45 apply.

Article 29 (ex art 6)

In principle, the general place of supply rules in Directive 2006/112/EC arts 44 and 45 apply to a supply of services consisting of the translation of texts. For an exception, see art 41 below.

SUBSECTION 6– SUPPLY OF SERVICES BY INTERMEDIARIES

Article 30 (ex art 9)

The place of supply rule in Directive 2006/112/EC art 46 covers: (1) the services of an intermediary acting in the name, and on behalf of, the recipient of the service procured; and (2) the services performed by an intermediary acting in the name, and on behalf of, the provider of the services performed.

Article 31

An intermediary may act in the name, and on behalf of, another person in connection with the provision of hotel and similar accommodation. The place of supply of the intermediary's service is determined in accordance with Directive 2006/112/EC art 44 (if his services are supplied to a taxable person acting as such or to a non-taxable legal person deemed to be a taxable person) or art 46 (if his services are supplied to a non-taxable person).

SUBSECTION 7–SUPPLY OF CULTURAL, ARTISTIC, SPORTING, SCIENTIFIC, EDUCATIONAL, ENTERTAINMENT, AND SIMILAR SERVICES

Article 32

1. For the purposes of the place of supply rule in Directive 2006/112/EC art 53, "admission" includes services having the essential characteristic of granting the right of admission to an

event in exchange for a ticket or payment. A "payment" for this purpose includes payment in the form of a subscription, season ticket or periodic fee.

2. A right of admission for the purposes of para 1 includes, in particular, the right of admission to: (1) shows, theatrical performances, circus performances, fairs, amusement parks, concerts, exhibitions and similar cultural events; (2) sporting events such as matches or competitions; and (3) educational and scientific events such as conferences and seminars.

3. The use of facilities (eg gymnastics halls and suchlike) in exchange for the payment of a fee does not fall within para 1.

Article 33

For the purposes of the place of supply rule in Directive 2006/112/EC art 53, "ancillary services" include services which are: (1) directly related to admission to cultural, artistic, sporting, scientific, educational, entertainment or similar events; and (2) supplied separately for a consideration to a person attending an event. Such services include, in particular, the use of cloakrooms or sanitary facilities. They do not include mere intermediary services relating to the sale of tickets.

Subsection 8–Supply of ancillary transport services and valuations of and work on movable property

Article 34 (ex art 5)

In principle, the place of supply rule in Directive 2006/112/EC art 54 applies to the services of a taxable person comprising no more than assembling a machine from parts provided by the customer, where the customer is a non-taxable person. However, this does not apply if the goods being assembled become part of immovable property.

Subsection 9–Supply of restaurant and catering services on board means of transport

Article 35

For the purposes of the place of supply rule in Directive 2006/112/EC art 55, the section of a passenger transport operation effected within the Community is determined by reference to the journey of the means of transport, not the journey completed by each of its passengers.

Article 36

Restaurant services and catering services may be supplied during the section of a passenger transport operation effected within the Community. Where this is so, the place of supply is determined in accordance with Directive 2006/112/EC art 57.

Restaurant services and catering services supplied outside such a section may be supplied in the territory of a member state, third country or third territory. Where this is so, the place of supply is determined in accordance with Directive 2006/112/EC art 55.

Article 37

Restaurant services and catering services may be carried out during the section of a passenger transport operation effected within the Community and partly outside such a section but within the territory of a member state. Where this is so, the place of supply is wholly determined by reference to the place of supply rules applicable to the point in the journey when the restaurant or catering services commenced.

Subsection 10–Hiring of means of transport

Article 38 (ex art 10)

For the purposes of Directive 2006/112/EC arts 56 and 59(g), "means of transport" includes:

(a) Vehicles (whether or not motorised).
(b) The vehicles listed in art 38(2).
(c) Other equipment and devices designed to transport persons or objects from one place to another. The equipment and devices may be pulled, drawn or pushed by vehicles. They are normally designed to be used for transport and are actually capable of being so used.

The following are not considered to be means of transport:
(a) Vehicles which are permanently immobilised.
(b) Containers.

Article 39

1. For the purposes of Directive 2006/112/EC art 56(2), the duration of "continuous possession or use" is determined by reference to the contract made by the parties to the hiring. This determination is a presumption. It may be rebutted by any means in fact or law in order to establish the actual duration of the continuous possession or use. The fact that the contractual period of short-tern hire has been exceeded on grounds of force majeure is disregarded.

2. A hiring of one and the same means of transport may be covered by consecutive contracts between the same parties. Where this is so, the duration of the hiring is the period of continuous possession or use provided for under the contracts as a whole. A contract and its extension(s) are treated as consecutive contracts.

A long-term contract may be preceded by one or more short-term contracts. Where this is so, the duration of the short-term contract(s) is not called into question unless there is an abusive practice.

3. Consecutive contracts between the same parties for different means of transport are not consecutive contracts for the purposes of para 2 unless there is an abusive practice.

Article 40

For the purposes of Directive 2006/112/EC art 56(1), the place where a means of transport is "actually put at the disposal of the customer" is the place where the customer (or a third party acting on his behalf) takes physical possession of it.

SUBSECTION 11–SUPPLY OF SERVICES TO NON-TAXABLE PERSONS OUTSIDE THE COMMUNITY

Article 41 (ex art 6)

A service comprising the translation of texts may be supplied to a non-taxable person established outside the EU. Where this is so, the place of supply is determined in accordance with Directive 2006/112/EC art 59(c).

CHAPTER VI—TAXABLE AMOUNT (TITLE VII OF DIRECTIVE 2006/112/EC)

Article 42 (ex art 13)

For the purposes of Directive 2006/112/EC arts 73–80, an amount constitutes an integral part of the taxable amount for a supply of goods or services if:

- The supplier, as a condition of accepting payment by credit or debit card, requires the customer to pay an amount to himself or another undertaking.
- The total price payable by the customer is unaffected by the means of payment.

CHAPTER VII—RATES

Article 43

For the purposes of Directive 2006/112/EC Annex III point 12, "provision of holiday accommodation" includes the hiring out of tents, caravans or mobile homes if: (1) the tents, caravans or mobile homes are installed on camping sites; and (2) they are used as accommodation.

CHAPTER VIII—EXEMPTIONS

Section 1 Exemptions for certain activities in the public interest (Articles 132, 133 and 134 of Directive 2006/112/EC)

Article 44 (ex art 14)

For the purposes of Directive 2006/112/EC art 132(1)(i), "vocational training or retraining" includes:

- Instruction relating directly to a trade or profession.
- Instruction to impart or update knowledge for vocational purposes.

The duration of the course is irrelevant.

Section 2 Exemptions for other activities (Articles 135, 136 and 137 of Directive 2006/112/EC)

Article 45 (ex art 15)

The exemption conferred by Directive 2006/112/EC art 135(1)(e) does not apply to platinum nobles.

Section 3 Exemptions on importation (Articles 143, 144 and 145 of Directive 2006/112/EC)

Article 46

The exemption conferred by Directive 2006/112/EC art 144 applies to transport services connected with the importation of movable property carried out as part of a change of residence.

Section 4 Exemptions on exportation (Articles 146 and 147 of Directive 2006/112/EC)

Article 47 (ex art 16)

For the purposes of Directive 2006/112/EC art 146(1)(b), "means of transport for private use" includes means of transport used for non-business purposes by persons other than natural persons, eg bodies governed by public law (as to which see Directive 2006/112/EC art 13) and associations.

Article 48 (ex art 17)

In principle, the exemption conferred by Directive 2006/112/EC art 146(1)(b) applies to goods carried in the personal baggage of travellers only if the value (including VAT) exceeds EUR 175 or the equivalent in national currency (see Directive 2006/112/EC art 147(1) (first para)). However, members states are permitted to exempt goods with a value below this threshold (see Directive 2006/112/EC art 147(1) (second para)).

It is necessary to determine whether national threshold has been exceed in order to determine whether the exemption in art 146(1)(b) applies to goods carried in passengers' baggage. The

Part I VAT

calculation is based on the invoice value of the goods. The aggregate value of several goods may be used only if all those goods are included in the same invoice issued to the same customer by the same supplier.

Section 5 Exemptions relating to certain transactions treated as exports (Articles 151 and 152 of Directive 2006/112/EC)

Article 49

The exemption conferred by Directive 2006/112/EC art 151 also applies to electronic services provided by a taxable person to whom the special scheme for electronically supplied services applies. For the special scheme, see Directive 2006/112/EC arts 357–369.

Article 50

For the purposes of the exemptions conferred by Directive 2006/112/EC arts 143(1)(g) and 151(1)(b), a body which is to be set up as a European Research Infrastructure Consortium ("ERIC") is recognised as an "international body" only if it meets specified conditions. Exemption applies only if the ERIC is recognised as an international body by the host member state.

Article 51

The exemption certificate set out in Annex II is used to confirm that a supply of goods or services made in one member state to a recipient who is established in another member state qualifies for exemption under Directive 2006/112/EC art 151.

CHAPTER IX—DEDUCTIONS
(TITLE X OF DIRECTIVE 2006/112/EC)

Article 52 (ex art 18)

For the purposes of Directive 2006/112/EC art 178(e), the term "import document" includes an electronic version of an import document if:

- The importing member state has introduced an electronic system for completing customs formalities.
- The relevant input tax deduction can be verified by reference to the electronic version.

CHAPTER X—OBLIGATIONS OF TAXABLE PERSONS AND CERTAIN NON-TAXABLE PERSONS
(TITLE IX OF DIRECTIVE 2006/112/EC)

Section 1 Persons liable to pay the VAT (Articles 192a to 205 of Directive 2006/112/EC)

Article 53

1. For the purposes of Directive 2006/112/EC art 192a, a "fixed establishment" of the taxable person is taken into consideration only if it has a sufficient degree of permanence and a suitable structure in terms of human and technical resources enabling it to make the supply of goods or services in which it intervenes.

2. A taxable person may have a fixed establishment within the territory of the member state where the VAT is due. The fixed establishment intervenes in a supply of goods or services for the purposes of 2006/112/EC art 192a(b) only if the technical and human resources of the establishment are utilised in making the supply of goods or services in respect of which the

VAT is due. The establishment does not intervene in the supply if it merely provides administrative support such as accounting, invoicing and debt collection. However, in the absence of proof to the contrary, the establishment is regarded in intervening in the supply if the invoice in respect of it is issued under the VAT identification number of the member state in which the establishment is located.

Article 54

A taxable person may have established his place of business in the territory of the member state where the VAT is due. Directive 2006/112/EC art 192a does not apply to a supply of goods or services made in that member state. This applies whether or not the place of business intervenes in the supply.

Section 2 Miscellaneous provisions (Articles 272 and 273 of Directive 2006/112/EC)

Article 55

A taxable person to whom a VAT identification number has been attributed may, when acting as such, receive goods or services in respect of which the supplier is required to make a recapitulative statement in accordance with Directive 2006/112/EC art 262. Where this is so, he is required to communicate his VAT identification number to the supplier. A similar requirement applies to non-taxable legal persons identified for VAT purposes.

A taxable person receiving goods is not required to notify his VAT identification number to the supplier if: (1) he falls within one or other of the descriptions in Directive 2006/112/EC art 3(1)(a); (2) he is entitled to non-taxation of his intra-Community acquisitions of goods in accordance with art 4 above; and (3) his VAT identification number was attributed to him in accordance with Directive 2006/112/EC art 214(1)(d) or (e).

CHAPTER XI—SPECIAL SCHEMES

Section 1 Special scheme for investment gold (Articles 344 to 356 of Directive 2006/112/EC)

Article 56 (ex art 19(1))

The "weights accepted by the bullion markets" referred to in Directive 2006/112/EC art 344(1)(1) include the traded units and weights set out in Annex III.

Article 57 (ex art 19(2))

The "price" and "open market value" referred to in Directive 2006/112/EC art 344(1) point 2, are determined annually on 1 April.

Section 2 Special scheme for non-established taxable persons supplying electronic services to non-taxable persons (Articles 357 to 369 of Directive 2006/112/EC)

Article 58 (ex art 20(1))

A non-established taxable person supplying electronic services to non-taxable persons is excluded from the special scheme (as to which see Directive 2006/112/EC arts 357–369) if, in the course of a calendar quarter, he meets one or more of the criteria for exclusion laid down in Directive 2006/112/EC art 363. He may be excluded with effect from the time when the criterion was met or any later time in the same quarter. He must submit a return for the quarter in respect of the electronic services supplied prior to the date of his exclusion. This requirement does not affect his liability (if any) to be identified for VAT purposes in a member state under the normal rules.

Article 59 (ex art 20(3) (first para))

Each calendar quarter (see Directive 2006/112/EC art 364) is a separate return period.

Article 60 (ex art 20(3) (second para))

Any errors discovered after a return has been submitted must be corrected by amending that return rather than by adjusting a subsequent return.

Article 61 (ex art 20(4))

The exact amount of VAT must be reported on a VAT return (see Directive 2006/112/EC arts 364–366) and remitted (see Directive 2006/112/EC art 367). Rounding to the nearest monetary unit is not permitted.

Article 62 (ex art 20(2))

A non-established taxable person is entitled to a repayment if a quarterly return submitted in accordance with Directive 2006/112/EC art 364 overstates the amount due. Repayments are made by the member state(s) of consumption if the amount paid by the taxable person has been distributed to those member states by the member state of identification.

Article 63 (ex art 20(3) (third para))

Any payment made in respect of a return is specific to that return. Any underpayment or overpayment may not be off set against a payment or repayment in respect of another return or adjusted on a subsequent return.

CHAPTER XII—FINAL PROVISIONS

Article 64

Regulation (EC) No 1777/2005 is repealed. References to the 2005 Regulation are construed as references to this regulation in accordance with the correlation table in Annex IV.

Article 65 (ex art 23)

This regulation enters into force on 12 April 2011. It applies in accordance with the following provisions:

- Articles 3(a), 11(2)(b), 23(1) and 24(1) apply from 1 January 2013.
- Article 3(b) applies from 1 January 2015.
- Article 11(2)(c) applies for the period 1 July 2011 to 31 December 2014.
- The remaining provisions apply from 1 July 2011.

This regulation is binding in its entirety and directly applicable in all member states.

Annex I—Article 7 of this Regulation

This is the list referred to in art 7(2)(f). It supplements the broad headings set out in Directive 2006/112/EC Annex II.

Annex II—Article 51 of this Regulation

This is VAT and/or excise duty exemption certificate specified in art 51.

Annex III—Article 56 of this Regulation

This is the list referred to in art 56. It sets out "weights accepted by the bullion markets" in relation to the kilogram, gram, ounce, tael and tola.

Annex IV—Correlation table

This sets out a destination table for the provisions of Regulation (EC) No 1777/2005, which is repealed by art 64.

7.
EU Directives

Contents

DIRECTIVE 86/560/EEC ARRANGEMENTS FOR THE REFUND OF VALUE ADDED TAX TO TAXABLE PERSONS NOT ESTABLISHED IN COMMUNITY TERRITORY (THE THIRTEENTH DIRECTIVE)

General note This directive does not apply to goods which are, or may be, exempted under Directive 2006/112/EC art 138 when the goods are despatched or transported by, or on behalf of, the person acquiring the goods: see Directive 2006/112/EC art 171(4).

Article 1

1. A "taxable person not established in the territory of the Community" is a taxable person (see Directive 77/388/EEC art 4(1), now Directive 2006/112/EC art 9(1)) who meets the following conditions during the period of claim (as to which see art 3(1)):

- His business is not in the territory of the Community.
  The term "business" refers to the place where: (1) the essential decisions concerning the general management of the company are adopted; and (2) the functions of its central administration are carried out: *Planzer Luxembourg Sàrl v Bundeszentralamt für Steuern* (case C-73/06) [2007] ECR I–5655, [2008] STC 1113 at [60].
  The most important factors taken into account in determining a company's place of buiness are: (1) the location of its registered office; (2) the place of its central administration; (3) the place where its directors meet; and (4) the place where the general policy of the company is determined. Other factors include: (1) the place of residence of the main directors; (2) the place where general meetings are held; (3) the place where administrative and accounting documents are kept; and (4) the place where the company's financial transactions (particularly its banking transactions) take place. A fictitious presence (eg a "letter box" or "brass plate" company) is not a place of business for the purposes of this directive: *Planzer Luxembourg Sàrl v Bundeszentralamt für Steuern* (case C-73/06) [2007] ECR I–5655, [2008] STC 1113 at [61], [62].
- He does not have a fixed establishment in the territory of the Community from which his business transactions are effected.
  The term "fixed establishment" implies a minimum degree of stability derived from the permanent presence of both the human and technical resources necessary for the provision of given services. It thus requires a sufficient degree of permanence and, in terms of human and technical resources, a structure adequate to supply the services in question on an independent basis. A fixed installation does not constitute a fixed establishment if it is used only for preparatory or auxillary activities, eg recruiting staff or purchasing the technical means needed for carrying out the undertaking's tasks: *Planzer Luxembourg Sàrl v Bundeszentralamt für Steuern* (case C-73/06) [2007] ECR I–5655, [2008] STC 1113 at [54], [56].
  As regards transport activities in particular, the term "fixed establishment" implies at least: (1) an office in which contracts may be drawn up and daily management decisions taken; and (2) a place where the relevant vehicles are stored. Registering vehicles in a member state is not an indicator of a fixed establishment in that member state: *Planzer Luxembourg Sàrl v Bundeszentralamt für Steuern* (case C-73/06) [2007] ECR I–5655, [2008] STC 1113 at [55].
- (If he has neither a business nor a fixed establishment) neither his permanent address nor his usual place of residence is in the territory of the Community.
- (Subject to specified exceptions) he has not supplied any goods or services in the member state from which the refund is claimed.

Whilst one and the same place may be both the place of "business" and a "fixed establishment", the two concepts are independent: *Planzer Luxembourg Sàrl v Bundeszentralamt für Steuern* (case C-73/06) [2007] ECR I–5655, [2008] STC 1113 at [58].

For "permanent address", see Regulation (EU) No 282/2011 art 12. For the place where a person usually resides, see Regulation (EU) No 282/2011 art 13.

Part I VAT

2. The "territory of the Community" is the VAT territory of the Community (as to which see Directive 2006/112/EC arts 5, 6 and Appendix 2).

Article 2

1. A member state must refund VAT to a taxable person if:

- He is not established in the VAT territory of the Community (see art 1(2)). This does not apply to third country traders using the special scheme for electronic services: see Directive 77/388/EEC art 26cB(7).
- The conditions laid down have been met.
- The VAT has been charged in respect of: (1) services supplied to him by taxable person(s) in the territory of the country, (2) movable property supplied to him by taxable person(s) in the territory of the country, or (3) goods imported into the country.
- The goods and services are used for the purposes of specified transactions.

The specified transactions are:

- The transactions referred to in Directive 77/388/EEC art 17(3)(*a*), now Directive 2006/112/EEC art 169(*a*) (transactions relating to economic activities carried out in another country if the VAT would be deductible had the activities been performed in the territory of the country).
- The transactions referred to in Directive 77/388/EEC art 17(3)(*b*), now Directive 2006/112/EEC art 169(*b*) (specified exempt transactions).
- Services provided in circumstances where tax is payable by the recipient of the supply in accordance with Directive 77/388/EEC art 21(1)(*b*), now 2006/112/EEC art 196.

For the omission of transactions referred to in Directive 77/388/EEC art 17(3)(c), now Directive 2006/112/EC art 169(c), from the list of specified transactions, see *Commission v United Kingdom* (case C-582/08) [2010] ECR I–0000, [2010] STC 2364.

2. Member states may confine refunds to claimants established in countries with reciprocal refund arrangements. This does not apply to third country traders using the special scheme for electronic services: see Directive 2006/112/EC art 368.

3. Member states may require claimants to appoint a tax representative. This does not apply to third country traders using the special scheme for electronic services: see Directive 2006/112/EC art 368.

Article 3

1. A taxable person qualifies for a refund if he submits an application. Member states must determine the arrangements for submitting applications, making refunds and verifying eligibility to refunds. Claimants must make a written declaration that they have not carried out any transaction during the claim period that nullifies his status as a person not established in the territory of the Community (see art 1).

2. The conditions imposed by member states must be no less strict than those imposed in relation to refunds under Directive 2008/9/EC (formerly Directive 79/1072/EEC).

Article 4

1. Eligibility for refunds is determined in accordance with national legislation giving effect to Directive 77/388EEC (now Directive 2006/112/EC arts 167, 173, 176, 177).

2. Member states may exclude certain expenditure from refund or make refunds subject to additional conditions. This does not apply to third country traders using the special scheme for electronic services: see Directive 2006/112/EC art 368.

3. This directive does not apply to supplies of goods exported to a third country exempted from tax under Directive 77/388/EEC art 15(2) (now Directive 2006/112 art 147).

Article 5

Member states were required to implement this directive no later than 1 January 1988.

Article 6

The Commission was required to submit a report on the application of this directive by 1 January 1991.

Article 7

[Spent.]

Article 8

This directive is addressed to the member states.

DIRECTIVE 2006/79/EC SMALL NON-COMMERCIAL CONSIGNMENTS IMPORTED FROM THIRD COUNTRIES

General note This directive codifies Directive 78/1035/EEC and the amendments made thereto. It applies to both VAT and excise duties. Excise duties are outside the scope of this work and references to them have been omitted.

Article 1

1. Goods in small consignments of a non-commercial character sent from a third country to a member state are exempt from VAT on importation if both sender and recipient are private persons.

2. The phrase "small consignments of a non-commercial character" is defined.

Article 2

1. The exemption in art 1 applies, subject to specified quantitative limits, to tobacco products, alcohol and alcoholic beverages, perfumes, toilet waters, coffee, coffee extracts and essences, tea and tea extracts and essences.

2. Members states can reduce the quantities in para 1 or abolish exemption altogether.

Article 3

If the quantity of goods contained in a consignment exceeds the limits in art 2, the goods are excluded from exemption in their entirety.

Article 4

National currency equivalents of the euro amount in art 1(2)(*c*) (ie EUR45) are updated annually on 1 January by reference to the rates of exchange on the first working day of October.

Article 5

Member states are required to provide the Commission with the text of the main national provisions transposing this directive.

Article 6

Directive 78/1035/EEC is repealed.

Article 7

This directive enters into force on 6 November 2006.

Article 8

This directive is addressed to the member states.

DIRECTIVE 2006/112/EC
THE COMMON SYSTEM OF VALUE ADDED TAX

General note This directive (as last amended by Directive 2010/88/EU) sets out the structure of the common system of VAT adopted by the EU in 1967. It replaces Directives 67/227/EEC (the First Directive) (as last amended by Directive 77/388/EEC) and 77/388/EEC (the Sixth Directive) (as last amended by Directive 2006/98/EC), which are accordingly repealed by art 411. It also includes the substance of a number of provisions relating to VAT included in the Acts of Accession and Protocols annexed to the First, Second, Third, Fourth, Fifth and Sixth Accession Treaties.

The repealed and related provisions have been "recast" as they apply during the "transitional period", ie the period beginning on 1 January 1993 (abolition of fiscal frontiers). Thus, the text of the Sixth Directive has been recast as temporarily amended, in particular, by arts 28cE and 28f–28j. The structure and wording have been changed to "ensure that the provisions are presented in a clear and rational manner, consistent with the principle of better regulation" and a small number of substantive amendments inherent to the recasting exercise have been made.

References to the repealed directives are construed as references to this directive. They are read in accordance with the destination table in Annex XII (see art 411(2)).Text reflected in the commentary **The commentary** reflects the text of the directive in force on 31 July 2011. Although the amendments made by Directive 2010/45/EU came into effect on 11 August 2010, member states are required to enact implementing legislation by 31 December 2012 and apply it from 1 January 2013. These amendments have been reflected in the commentary. An asterisk has been added to the relevant article numbers to indicate that the commentary underpins national legislation which is yet to be enacted. For a commentary on the text of these articles in force on 31 July 2010, see the 2010–11 edition of this work. For a list of the articles concerned, see the commentary to Directive 2010/45/EU.

In principle, the derivation of each article is stated with an "ex" reference in the following commentary. References to an article are references to an article in the Sixth Directive as it applies during the transitional period. Other references are cited in full. These references are derived from the destination table in Annex XII but set out in a condensed format. To avoid confusion, "ex" references have been omitted in relation to articles inserted or substituted by an amending directive.Prospective amendments **This directive is** amended with effect from 1 January 2013 and 1 January 2015 by Directive 2008/8/EC. For a list of the articles concerned, see the commentary to that directive. These changes will be reflected in the commentary to this directive in future editions.

Article 192a of this directive expires on 30 June 2015: see Directive 2010/23/EU arts 1 and 4

TITLE I—SUBJECT MATTER AND SCOPE

Article 1
(ex Directive 67/277/EEC art 1 (first para) and art 2)

1. This directive establishes the common system of VAT.

2. The principle of the common system of VAT involves applying a general tax on the consumption of goods and services. This tax is exactly proportional to the price of the goods and services regardless of the number of transactions taking place in the production and distribution process before the stage at which tax is charged.

For examples of transactions which did not give rise to consumption, and did not therefore amount to supplies of goods or services, see *Mohr v Finanzamt Bad Segeberg* (case C-215/94) [1996] ECR I–959, [1996] STC 328 (undertaking to discontinue milk production); *Landboden-Agrardienste GmbH & Co KG v Finanzamt Calau* (case C-384/95) [1997] ECR I–7387, [1998] STC 171 (reduction in annual potato production).

On each transaction, VAT is calculated on the price of the goods or services at the rate applicable to such goods or services.

In the absence of specific Community legislation, it is for member states to decide on the rules and methods of rounding amounts of VAT. In doing so, member states must observe the principles underpinning the common system of VAT and, in particular, the principles of fiscal neutrality and proportionality: see *Fiscale eenheid Koninklijke Ahold NV v Staatssecretaris van Financiën* (case C-484/06) [2008] ECR I–5097, [2009] STC 45 at [24] and [27]–[32]. Traders supplying goods and services at VAT-exclusive prices and traders supplying goods and services at VAT-inclusive prices are in different situations. In the former case, the VAT charged to the customer and the VAT paid to the tax authority are the same regardless of the rounding method applied. Rounding is necessary in order to invoice a price which the customer is capable of paying. This is not so in the latter case. Thus, while systematic rounding down at a lower level than the VAT return would collect the amount of VAT actually due from the customer, the trader would benefit because the VAT paid to the tax authority would be not be exactly proportional to his VAT-inclusive turnover for the tax period: *J D Wetherspoon plc v R & C Comrs* (case C-302/07) [2009] ECR I–1467, [2009] STC 1022 at [60]–[63]. Member states are not obliged to permit taxable persons to round down the amount of tax per item: *Fiscale eenheid Koninklijke Ahold NV v Staatssecretaris van Financiën* (case C-484/06) [2008] ECR I–5097, [2009] STC 45 at [43]. Traders selling at VAT-inclusive prices cannot invoke the principle of fiscal neutrality to claim the right to round down at line level or basket level: *J D Wetherspoon plc v R & C Comrs* (case C-302/07) [2009] ECR I–1467, [2009] STC 1022 at [64].

VAT is chargeable after deduction of the amount of VAT borne directly by the various cost components.

The fundamental principle underlaying the VAT system is that VAT applies to each transaction by way of production or distribution after deduction has been made of the VAT levied directly on transactions relating to inputs: *BP Supergas Anonimos Etairia Geniki Emporiki-Viomichaniki kai Antiprossopeion v Greece* (case C-62/93) [1995] ECR I–1883, [1995] STC 805 at [16].

The deduction system is meant to relieve the trader entirely of the burden of VAT payable or paid in the course of all his economic activities. The common system of VAT therefore ensures that all economic activities subject to VAT are taxed in a wholly neutral way, whatever their purpose or results: *Rompleman and Rompelman-Van Deelen v Minister van Financiën* (case 268/83) [1985] ECR 655, [1985] 3 CMLR 202 at [19]. For the deduction system, see arts 167–192.

The common system of VAT is applied up to and including the retail stage. It does not prevent member states imposing administrative penalties on persons liable to VAT: *K-1 sp zoo v Dyrektor Izby Skarbowej w Bydgoszczy* (case C-502/07) [2009] ECR I–161 at [21].

Article 2
(ex arts 2, 28a(1)(a) (first para), 28a(1)(b), 28a(1)(c), 28a(2), 33(2))

1. The following transactions are subject to VAT:

(a) A supply of goods (as defined in art 14(1)) made for consideration within the territory of a member state by a taxable person (as defined in art 9) acting as such. For transactions treated as a supply of goods, see arts 16–18. For transactions not treated as a supply of goods, see art 19.

Part I VAT

A new share issue does not constitute a supply of goods for consideration. This is so whether or not such a transaction is carried out in connection with the admission of a company to a stock exchange: *Kretztechnik AG v Finanzamt Linz* (case C-465/03) [2005] ECR I–4357, [2005] STC 1118 at [25]–[28].

The theft of goods does not constitute a supply of goods for consideration and cannot, therefore, be subject to VAT. It is irrelevant whether the goods are subject to excise duty: *British American Tobacco International Ltd and another v Belgian State* (case C-435/03) [2005] ECR I–7077, [2006] STC 158 at [42]. For the disappearance of excise stamps, see *Heintz Landewyck SARL v Staatssecretaris van Financiën* (case C-494/04) [2006] ECR I–5381.

For simplification measures retained by the UK in relation to futures transactions on terminal markets and supplies of warehoused goods, see Appendix 1.

(b) An intra-Community acquisition of goods (as defined in art 20) made for consideration within the territory of a member state (as defined in art 5(2)) falling within any of the following descriptions:

(i) An acquisition by taxable person acting as such or a non-taxable legal person, where:

- The vendor is a taxable person acting as such.
- The vendor is not eligible for exemption under the special scheme for small enterprises (see arts 282–292).
- The place of the vendor's supply is not determined in accordance with arts 33, 38.

For acquisitions excluded from the charge to VAT under this head, see arts 3(1), 4.

(ii) An acquisition of a new means of transport (as defined in para 2) by any of the following persons:

- A taxable person whose other acquisitions are not subject to VAT by virtue of art 3(1).
- A non-taxable legal person whose other acquisitions are not subject to VAT by virtue of art 3(1).
- Any other non-taxable person.

For the circumstances in which no acquisition arises under this provision, see Regulation (EU) No 282/2011 art 2.

(iii) An acquisition of products subject to excise duty (as defined in para 3) made by a taxable person or non-taxable legal person in the following circumstances:

- The excise duty is chargeable within the territory of the member state (see art 5(2)) pursuant to Directive 92/12/EEC. The 1992 Directive is repealed and replaced by Directive 2008/118/EC with effect from 1 April 2010. From that date, references to the 1992 Directive are construed as references to the 2008 Directive in accordance with art 47(2) of the 2008 Directive.
- The other acquisitions of the taxable person or non-taxable legal person are not subject to VAT by virtue of art 3(1).

Prior to 1 January 1993, goods removed from one member state to another were charged to tax as an importation of goods. For double taxation in relation to removals by one private person to another under this charge, see: (1) *Gaston Schul, Douane Expéditeur BV v Inspecteur der Invoerrechten en Accijnzen* (case 15/81) [1982] ECR 1409, [1982] 3 CMLR 229; (2) *Staatssecretaris van Financiën v Gaston Schul Expediteur BV* (case 47/84) [1985] ECR 1491, [1986] 1 CMLR 559; (3) *Bergeres-Becque v Chef de Service Interregional des Douanes* (case 39/85) [1986] ECR 259, [1986] 2 CMLR 143; (4) *Commission v Spain* (case C-31/89) [1990] ECR I–2139; (5) *Commission v Kingdom of Spain* (case C-119/89) [1991] ECR I–641, [1993] STC 150; (6) *Commission v Hellenic Republic* (case C-159/89) [1991] ECR I–691, [1993] STC 160; (7) *Commission v Italian Republic* (case C-120/88) [1991] ECR I–621, [1993] STC 136.

(c) A supply of supply of services (as defined in art 24(1)) made for consideration within the territory of a member state (as defined in art 5(2)) by a taxable person (as defined in art 9(1)) acting as such. For transactions treated as a supply of services, see arts 26–28. For transactions not treated as a supply of goods or services, see art 29.

A partnership does not make a supply of services for consideration when in admits a new partner who makes a cash contribution to the partnership: *KapHag Renditefonds 35 Spreecenter Berlin-Hellersdorf3 Tranche GbR v Finanzamt Charlottenburg* (case C-442/01) [2003] ECR I–6851, [2005] STC 1500.

A new share issue does not constitute a supply of services for consideration. This is so whether or not such a transaction is carried out in connection with the admission of a company to a stock exchange: *Kretztechnik AG v Finanzamt Linz* (case C-465/03) [2005] ECR I–4357, [2005] STC 1118 at [25]–[28].

(d) An importation of goods (as defined in art 30).

The chargeable event is constituted by the mere entry of the goods into the territory of a member state. It is irrelevant whether or not there is a transaction. If there is one, it is irrelevant whether it is carried out for valuable consideration or free of charge, or carried out by a taxable person or a private person: *Gaston Schul, Douane Expéditeur BV v Inspecteur der Invoerrechten en Accijnzen* (case 15/81) [1982] ECR 1409, [1982] 3 CMLR 229 at [14].

Goods unlawfully brought into EU customs territory may be seized and destroyed by the tax or customs authorities. A chargeable event occurs if the goods were seized *after* their unlawful introduction into the EU customs territory (ie when they have gone beyond the area in which the first customs office inside that territory is situated). This applies even if the goods have been placed under a customs warehousing procedure. The VAT chargeable is recoverable by the competent authorities in the member state situated at the external EU border at which the goods were unlawfully introduced into EU customs territory. This applies even if the goods were subsequently transported to the member state where they were discovered and seized. However, no chargeable event occurs if the goods were seized at the time when they entered EU territory: *Dansk Transport og Logistik v Skatteministeriet* (case C-230/08) [2010] ECR I–0000, [2010] STC 1711.

It is necessary to draw a distinction between the charge to tax on supplies of goods and services and the charge to tax on imported goods, as they are based on different economic and legal considerations: *Einberger v Hauptzollamt Freiburg* (*No* 2) (case 294/82) [1984] ECR 1177, [1985] 1 CMLR 765 at [9].

2. [Definition of "new means of transport"]

The vessels, aircraft and motorised land vehicles regarded as "means of transport" are defined.

Motorised land vehicles are regarded as "new" if: (1) they are supplied within six months of first entering into service, or (2) they have not travelled more than 6,000 kilometres.

Vessels are regarded as "new" if: (1) they are supplied within three months of first entering into service, or (2) they have not sailed for more than 100 hours.

Aircraft are regarded as "new" if: (1) they are supplied within three months of entering into service, or (2) they have not flown more than 40 hours.

Member states must lay down the conditions for establishing these facts. Whether or not a means of transport is new is determined by reference to the time when the right to dispose of it as owner was transferred from the vendor to the purchaser: see X v Skatteverket (case C-84/09) [2010] ECR I– 0000, [2011] STC 189 at [53]–[57].

3. [Definition of "products subject to excise duty"]

The term "products subject to excise duty" means: (1) energy products (other than gas supplied through a natural gas distribution system situated within EU territory or any network

Part I VAT

connected to such a system); (2) alcohol and alcoholic beverages; and (3) manufactured tobacco. These terms are defined by reference to current Community legislation. The relevant definitions are set out in the following table:

	Product	*Legislation where product defined*
(1)	Energy products	Directive 2003/96/EC art 2(1)
(2)	Alcohol and alcoholic beverages:	
	Beer	Directive 92/83/EEC art 2
	Wine	Directive 92/83/EEC art 8
	Fermented beverages other than wine and beer	Directive 92/83/EEC art 12
	Intermediate products	Directive 92/83/EEC art 17
	Ethyl alcohol	Directive 92/83/EEC art 20
(3)	Manufactured tobacco	
	Cigarettes	Directive 95/59/EC art 4
	Cigars and cigarillos	Directive 95/59/EC arts 3, 7
	Smoking tobacco	Directive 95/59/EC art 5

Supplies of goods and services

The terms "supply of goods" (defined in art 14(1)) and "supply of services" (defined in art 24(1)) are objective in nature. They apply without regard to the purpose or results of the transactions concerned. An obligation on the tax authorities to carry out inquiries to determine the intention of the taxable person would be contrary to the objectives of the common system of VAT of ensuring legal certainty and facilitating the application of VAT by having regard, save in exceptional cases, to the objective character of the transaction in question: *Halifax plc and others v Customs and Excise Comrs* (case C-255/02) [2006] ECR I–1609, [2006] STC 919 at [56], [57].

Transactions constitute supplies of goods or supplies of services provided they satisfy the objective criteria on which those concepts are based. This is so even if they are carried out with the sole aim of obtaining a tax advantage without any other economic objective: *Halifax plc and others v Customs and Excise Comrs* (case C-255/02) [2006] ECR I–1609, [2006] STC 919 at [60].

Those criteria are not satisfied where tax is evaded, eg by means of untrue tax returns or the issue of improper invoices: *Halifax plc and others v Customs and Excise Comrs* (case C-255/02) [2006] ECR I–1609, [2006] STC 919 at [59]. For the recovery of input tax where the transactions from which the right to deduct derived constitute an abusive practice, see the commentary to art 167.

Transactions which are not themselves vitiated by VAT fraud constitute supplies of goods or services effected by a taxable where they fulfil the objective criteria on which the definition of that term is based. The intention of another trader involved in the same chain of supply is irrelevant if the taxable person had no knowledge, and no means of knowledge, of it. So is the possible fraudulent nature of another transaction in the chain, whether prior or subsequent to the transaction carried out by the taxable person, if the taxable person had no knowledge, and no means of knowledge, of it: *Optigen Ltd and others v Customs and Excise Comrs* (joined cases C-354/03, C-355/03 and C-484/03) [2006] ECR I–483, [2006] STC 419.

Consideration

Taxable transactions presuppose the existence of a transaction between the parties in which a price or consideration is stipulated: *Commission v Finland* (case C-246/08) [2009] ECR I–10605 at [43]. It follows that a supply of services is effected for "consideration", and hence taxable, only if there is a legal relationship between the provider of the service and the recipient in which there is reciprocal performance, the remuneration received by the provider of the service constituting the value actually given in return for the service supplied to the recipient: *Tolsma v Inspecteur der Omzetbelasting Leeuwarden* (case C-16/93) [1994] ECR I–743, [1994] STC 509 at [14]. The concept of a supply of services for consideration therefore presupposes that there is a direct link between the service provided and the consideration received: *Apple and Pear Development Council v Customs and Excise Comrs* (case 102/86) [1988] ECR 1443, [1988] STC 221 at [12].

An agreement between the supplier and recipient amounts to a "legal relationship" even if, under national law, the agreement is not enforceable: *Town and County Factors Ltd v Customs and Excise Comrs* (case C-498/99) [2002] ECR I–7173, [2002] STC 1263 at [21]–[23].

It is irrelevant whether the price paid is higher or lower than the cost price: *Hotel Scandic Gåsabäck AB v Riksskatteverket* (case C-412/03) [2005] ECR I–743, [2005] STC 1311 at [22]. Any evasion, avoidance or abuse arising from a symbolic payment must be dealt with by way of a derogation under art 27: *Hotel Scandic Gåsabäck AB v Riksskatteverket* (case C-412/03) [2005] ECR I–743, [2005] STC 1311 at [26].

For the nature of a deposit in relation to the reservation of hotel accommodation, see *Société thermale d'Eugénie-les-Bains v Ministère de l'Économie, des Finances et de l'Industrie* (case C-277/05) [2007] ECR I–6415, [2008] STC 2479 at [21]–[31]. If the hotelier retains the deposit when the reservation is cancelled, this does not amount to consideration for a supply made by the hotelier. Similarly, if the hotelier makes a payment to the guest when he fails to provide the reserved accommodation, this does not amount to consideration for a supply made by the guest: *Société thermale d'Eugénie-les-Bains v Ministère de l'Économie, des Finances et de l'Industrie* (case C-277/05) [2007] ECR I–6415, [2008] STC 2470.

For examples of supplies made for consideration, see: (1) *Customs and Excise Comrs v First National Bank of Chicago* (case C-172/96) [1998] ECR I–4387, [1998] STC 850 (foreign exchange transactions, even when performed without commission or direct fees); (2) *Kennemer Golf & Country Club v Staatssecretaris van Financiën* (case C-174/00) [2002] ECR I–3293, [2002] STC 502 (annual subscription to an association making sports facilities and associated advantages available to members on a permanent basis so that members who do not use – or regularly use – the facilities must still pay the subscription); (3) *Town and County Factors Ltd v Customs and Excise Comrs* (case C-498/99) [2002] ECR I–7173, [2002] STC 1263 ("spot the ball" competition where the organiser's obligations were binding in honour only); (4) *Finanzamt Groß-Gerau v MKG-Kraftfahrzeuge-Factoring GmbH* (case C-305/01) [2003] ECR I–6729, [2003] STC 951 (purchasing debts owed to a trader without enjoying a right of recourse against the trader if debtors default); (5) *AstraZeneca UK Ltd v R & C Comrs* (case C-40/09) [2010] ECR I–0000, [2010] STC 2298 (providing retail vouchers to employees in exchange for their giving up part of their cash remuneration).

For examples of payments made or work done which did not amount to consideration, see: (1) *Apple and Pear Development Council v Customs and Excise Comrs* (case 102/86) [1988] ECR 1443, [1988] STC 221 (imposition of annual charge for the purpose of meeting administrative and other expenses incurred by a statutory body in the exercise of its statutory functions); (2) *Tolsma v Inspecteur der Omzetbelasting Leeuwarden* (case C-16/93) [1994] ECR I–743, [1994] STC 509 (musician performing on the public highway and soliciting donations from passers-by); (3) *Julius Fillibeck Söhne GmbH & Co KG v Finanzamt Neustadt* (case C-258/95) [1997] ECR I–5577, [1998] STC 513 (employer providing employees with free transport from home to place of work where there was no real connection with either the work performed or the wages received); (4) *Commission v Finland* (case C-246/08) [2009] ECR I–10605 (payment to public legal aid office where proportion of scale fee payable determined by reference to the income and assets of the person receiving legal services).

The territory of a member state

A member state clearly has jurisdiction to charge VAT on supplies and acquisitions made within its territory. For the "territory of a member state", see art 5(2). For the place where goods and services are supplied, see arts 31–59.

Member states are entitled to extend the scope of their tax legislation beyond their normal territorial limits, so long as they do not encroach on the jurisdiction of other states: *Trans Tirreno Express Spa v Ufficio Provinciale IVA, Sassari* (case 283/84) [1986] ECR 231, [1986] 2 CMLR 100 at [20]. Thus, member states are entitled to tax services provided on board sea-going ships over which they have jusrisdiction. A member state may tax such services even if they are provided outside the member state's territorial jurisdiction: *Berkholz v Finanzamt Hamburg-Mitte-Altstadt* (case 168/84) [1985] ECR 2251, [1985] 3 CMLR 667 at [16]. Contrast *Aktiebolaget NN v Skatteverket* (case C-111/05) [2007] ECR I–2697, [2008] STC 3203 in relation to the supply and laying of a fibre-optic cable linking two member states, where the transaction was not subject to VAT in so far as it was carried out in the exclusive economic zone, on the continental shelf and at sea.

Taxable person acting as such

The term "taxable person acting as such" is objective in nature and applies without regard to the purpose or results of the transactions concerned: *Optigen Ltd and others v Customs and Excise Comrs* (joined cases C-354/03, C-355/03 and C-484/03) [2006] ECR I–483, [2006] STC 419 at [44].

A taxable person "acts as such" when he carries out transactions in the course of his taxable activity: *Optigen Ltd and others v Customs and Excise Comrs* (joined cases C-354/03, C-355/03 and C-484/03) [2006] ECR I–483, [2006] STC 419 at [42]. Thus, a transaction performed by a taxable person in a private capacity is not subject to VAT: *Finanzamt Uelzen v Armbrecht* (case C-291/92) [1995] ECR I–2775, [1995] STC 997 at [17], [18]. A taxable person may act in a private capacity in relation to a capital item used wholly or partly for business purposes if he decides to retain the item, or a proportion of the item, within his private assets. For the allocation of assets in this manner, see the commentary to art 17(1).

Although deliveries for export are themselves exempt from tax whether carried out by taxable persons or private persons, only taxable persons are authorised to exercise the right to deduct. As a result, only goods delivered for export by taxable persons, or on their behalf, may be exempted from all VAT applied in the country of exploitation. Goods delivered for export by private persons remain liable to VAT to the extent proportionate to their value at the time of export: *Gaston Schul, Douane Expéditeur BV v Inspecteur der Invoerrechten en Accijnzen* (case 15/81) [1982] ECR 1409, [1982] 3 CMLR 229 at [15].

One supply or two

Where a transaction comprises a bundle of features and acts, regard must be had to all the circumstances in which the transaction in question takes place in order to determine: (1) if there were two or more distinct supplies or one single supply; and (2) in the latter case, whether that single supply is to be regarded as a supply of services: *Levob Verzekeringen BV, OB Bank NV cs v Staatssecretaris van Financiën* (case C-41/04) [2005] ECR I–9433, [2006] STC 766 at [19].

As regards the first question, every transaction is normally regarded as distinct and independent. A supply which comprises a single supply from an economic point of view should not be artificially split. The essential features of the transaction must be ascertained in order to determine whether the taxable person is making several distinct principal supplies to the customer, or a single supply: *Aktiebolaget NN v Skatteverket* (case C-111/05) [2007] ECR I–2697, [2008] STC 3203 at [22]. In particular, there is a single supply where:

- One or more elements are to be regarded as constituting the principal supply, while one or more elements are to be regarded, by contrast, as ancillary supplies which share the same tax treatment of the principal service: *Levob Verzekeringen BV, OB Bank NV cs v Staatssecretaris van Financiën* (case C-41/04) [2005] ECR I–9433,

[2006] STC 766 at [21]. A service must be regarded as ancillary to a principal service if, for customers, it constitutes a means of better enjoying the principal supply rather than an aim in itself. The fact that a single price is charged is not decisive: *Card Protection Plan Ltd v Customs and Excise Comrs* (case C-349/96) [1999] ECR I–973, [1999] STC 270 at [30], [31]. Nor is the fact that the value of materials exceeds the value of work done, or vice versa: *Aktiebolaget NN v Skatteverket* (case C-111/05) [2007] ECR I–2697, [2008] STC 3203 at [37].

- Two or more elements or acts supplied by a taxable person to his customer, being a typical customer, are so closely linked that they form, objectively, a single indivisible economic supply which it would be artificial to split: *Levob Verzekeringen BV, OB Bank NV cs v Staatssecretaris van Financiën* (case C-41/04) [2005] ECR I–9433, [2006] STC 766 at [20]–[22].

As regards the second question, it is vital to identify the predominant elements of the supply: *Levob Verzekeringen BV, OB Bank NV cs v Staatssecretaris van Financiën* (case C-41/04) [2005] ECR I–9433, [2006] STC 766 at [27]. This is determined from the point of view of the typical consumer: *Levob Verzekeringen BV, OB Bank NV cs v Staatssecretaris van Financiën* (case C-41/04) [2005] ECR I–9433, [2006] STC 766 at [22]. It is also necessary to have regard to both the qualitative and quantitative importance of the goods elements and service elements: *Finanzamt Burgdorf v Manfred Bog*; *CinemaxX Entertainment GmbH & Co KG v Finanzamt Hamburg-Barmbek-Uhlenhorst*; *Lothar Lohmeyer v Finanzamt Minden*; *Fleischerei Nier GmbH & Co KG v Finanzamt Detmold* (joined cases C-497/09 C-499/09 C-501/09 C-502/09 [2011] ECR I–0000, [2011] STC 1221 at [62]. The marketing of goods is always accompanied by a minimal supply of services, eg displaying the products on shelves or issuing an invoice. In assessing the part played by services, it is necessary to disregard services which necessarily accompany the marketing: see *Ottmar Hermann* (in his capacity as liquidator of *Volkswirt Weinschänken GmbH) v Stadt Frankfurt am Main* (case C-491/03) [2005] ECR I–2025 at [22]. Characterising the single supply as goods or services may give different answers in different cases. In relation to reprographics, see *Graphic Procédé v Ministère du budget, des comptes publics et de la function publique* (case C-88/09) [2010] ECR I–1049, [2010] STC 918. The question was left to the national court in *Card Protection Plan Ltd v Customs and Excise Comrs* (case C-349/96) [1999] ECR I–973, [1999] STC 270.

For examples of a single supply, see: (1) *Faaborg-Gelting Linien A/S v Finanzamt Flensburg* (case C-231/94) [1996] ECR I–2395, [1996] STC 774 at [14] (restaurant transactions characterised by a cluster of features and acts, of which the provision of food is only one component and in which services largely predominate); (2) *Levob Verzekeringen BV, OB Bank NV cs v Staatssecretaris van Financiën* (case C-41/04) [2005] ECR I–9433, [2006] STC 766 (granting a non-transferable licence of unlimited duration to use standard computer software, customising this software on the customer's computer and providing staff training, all of which were separately invoiced); (3) *Aktiebolaget NN v Skatteverket* (case C-111/05) [2007] ECR I–2697, [2008] STC 3203 (supply and installation of fibre-optic cable); (4) *Revenue and Customs Comrs v Axa UK plc* (case C-175/09) [2010] ECR I–0000, [2010] STC 2825 (payment plans for dental care); (5) *Everything Everywhere Ltd (formerly T-Mobile (UK) Ltd) v Revenue and Customs Comrs* (case C-276/09) [2010] ECR I–0000, [2011] STC 316 (additional charge invoiced where certain methods of payment used for mobile telephone service); (6) *Finanzamt Burgdorf v Manfred Bog; CinemaxX Entertainment GmbH & Co KG v Finanzamt Hamburg-Barmbek-Uhlenhorst; Lothar Lohmeyer v Finanzamt Minden; Fleischerei Nier GmbH & Co KG v Finanzamt Detmold* (joined cases C-497/09 C-499/09 C-501/09 C-502/09 [2011] ECR I–0000, [2011] STC 1221 at [68], [70], [71], [80] (food or meals freshly prepared for immediate consumption from snack stalls or mobile snack bars or in cinema foyers; and a party catering service doing more than merely delivering standard meals).

For an example of separate supplies, see *RLRE Tellmer Property sro v Finanční ředitelstvi v Ústí nad Labem* (case C-572/07) [2009] ECR I–4983, [2009] STC 2006 (cleaning common parts of building invoiced separately from rent of apartments).

Abuse

An abusive practice exists if: (1) although meeting the formal requirements of this directive and of national legislation transposing it, the transactions concerned result in the accrual of a tax advantage; (2) the advantage is contrary to the purpose of the directive and national legislation; and (3) the essential aim of the transactions, apparent from a number of objective factors, is to obtain a tax advantage. The prohibition of abuse is not relevant where the economic activity carried out may have some explanation other than the mere attainment of a tax advantage: *Halifax plc and others v Customs and Excise Comrs* (case C-255/02) [2006] ECR I–1609, [2006] STC 919 at [74], [75], [86]. Attaining a tax advantage may be the principal aim of the transaction(s). It does not have to be the sole aim: *Ministero dell'Economia e delle Finanze v Part Service Srl (in liquidation)* (case C-425/06), [2008] ECR I–897, [2008] STC 2132 at [45], [62]. Whether the relevant transactions constitute an abusive practice is a matter for the national court: *Revenue and Customs Comrs v Weald Leasing Ltd* (case C-103/09) [2010] ECR I–0000, [2011] STC 596 at [49].

The transactions involved in an abusive practice must be redefined so as to re-establish the situation that would have prevailed in the absence of the transactions constituting that practice: *Halifax plc and others v Customs and Excise Comrs* (case C-255/02) [2006] ECR I–1609, [2006] STC 919 at [94], [98]. Redefining the relevant transactions is a matter for the national court. This redefinition must go no further than is necessary for the charging of VAT and the prevention of tax avoidance (referred to as "tax evasion" by the court): *Revenue and Customs Comrs v Weald Leasing Ltd* (case C-103/09) [2010] ECR I–0000, [2011] STC 596 at [50], [52].

In *Ministero dell'Economia e delle Finanze v Part Service Srl (in liquidation)* (case C-425/06), [2008] ECR I–897, [2008] STC 3132, the question of abuse arose in relation to the leasing of motor cars. The arrangements adopted gave rise to: (1) supplies of a financing element (divided into a credit service, an insurance service and a brokerage service) by one group company; and (2) a service of renting the vehicle by another group company. Whether those transactions amounted to an abusive practice is a matter for the national court (paras [54], [55]). In assessing this, the national court must:

- Verify whether the result sought is a tax advantage, the granting of which would be contrary to one or more of the objectives of this directive. In doing so, the national court can take into account that the anticipated result is the accrual of a tax advantage linked to exemption of the financing element. As the leasing of vehicles under leasing contracts is normally subject to VAT, the result sought appeared to be contrary to the objective of art 73, ie the taxation of everything which constitutes consideration received or to be received from the customer (see paras [58]–[61]).
- If so, verify whether the tax advantage constituted the principal aim of the contractual approach adopted. The national court may take account of "the purely artificial nature of the transactions and the links of a legal, economic and/or personal nature between the operators involved, those aspects being such as to demonstrate that the accrual of a tax advantage constitutes the principal aim pursued, nothwithstanding the possible existence, in addition, of economic objectives arising from, for example, marketing, organisation or guarantee considerations" (see paras [58], [62]).

For the vires of national legislation preventing the national court from taking account of Community rules of law relating to abusive practices in the field of VAT, see *Amministrazione dell'Economia e delle Finanze and another v Fallimento Olimpiclub Srl* (case C-2/08) [2009] ECR I–7501 (national law laying down the principle of res judicata).

A tax advantage may arise if a trader leases an asset rather than purchasing it. The tax advantage is not contrary to the purpose of this directive, and the national provisions transposing it, if: (1) the terms of the leasing contract (in particular, the terms relating to the level of rentals) have been made on an arm's length basis; and (2) the involvement of an intermediate third party (ie the leasing company) does not preclude the application of this directive and the national provisions transposing it. The fact that the trader does not engage in leasing transactions in the context of his normal commercial operations is irrelevant. Whether the condition in (2) is met is a matter for the national court. see *Revenue and Customs Comrs v Weald Leasing Ltd* (case C-103/09) [2010] ECR I–0000, [2011] STC 596 at [45].

The principle of prohibiting abusive practices does not preclude the right to deduct VAT in circumstances where: (1) a company ("X") (which is established in member state A) elects to have its subsidiary ("Y"), (which is established in member state B), carry out transactions for the leasing of goods to a third company ("Z") (which is established in member state A); (2) X does so in order to avoid a situation in which VAT is payable on the consideration for those transactions; and (3) member state A categorises the supplies as rental services carried out in Member state B whereas member state B categorises the rental services as supplies of goods carried out in member state A: *Revenue and Customs Comrs v RBS Deutschland Holdings GmbH* (case C-277/09) [2010] ECR I–0000, [2011] STC 345.

Illegality

The purpose of this directive is to achieve widespread harmonisation in the area of VAT. It is based on the principle of neutrality. This principle precludes a generalised differentiation between lawful and unlawful transactions. However, an exception is made where, because of the special characteristics of certain products, all competition between a lawful economic sector and an unlawful sector is precluded: *Lange v Finanzamt Fürstenfeldbruck* (case C-111/92) [1993] ECR I–4677 at [16]. Three situations can be distinguished.

First, some goods are subject to an absolute prohibition on importation. No charge to VAT arises on the unlawful importation of these goods. For an example, see *Witzmann v Hauptzollamt München-Mitte* (case C-343/89) [1990] ECR I–4477, [1993] STC 108 (importation of counterfeit currency).

Secondly, some goods may be lawfully imported or supplied within strictly controlled economic channels, eg narcotic drugs for use for medical or scientific purposes. A charge to VAT arises in respect of goods imported or supplied within those channels. No charge to VAT arises if the goods are imported or supplied outside those channels. For examples of supplies and importations outside the scope of VAT, see: (1) *Einberger v Hauptzollamt Freiburg* (*No 2*) (case 294/82) [1984] ECR 1177, [1985] 1 CMLR 765 (unlawful importation of morphine); (2) *Mol v Inspecteur der Invoerrechten en Accijnzen* (case 269/86) [1988] ECR 3627, [1989] 3 CMLR 729 (supply of amphetamines); (3) *Vereniging Happy Family Rustenburgerstraat v Inspecteur der Omzetbelasting* (case 289/86) [1988] ECR 3655, [1989] 3 CMLR 729 (supply of hemp based drugs). A supply does not cease to be unlawful for this purpose merely because the national authorities give a lower priority to bringing proceedings against a certain type of trade in drugs: *Vereniging Happy Family Rustenburgerstraat v Inspecteur der Omzetbelasting* (case 289/86) [1988] ECR 3655, [1989] 3 CMLR 729 at [29].

Thirdly, in other cases, the mere fact that conduct amounts to an offence is not sufficient to justify exemption from VAT: *Staatssecretaris van Financiën v Coffeeshop Siberië vof* (case C-158/98) [1999] ECR I–3971, [1999] STC 742 at [21]. For examples of illegal activities chargeable to VAT, see: (1) *Lange v Finanzamt Fürstenfeldbruck* (case C-111/92) [1993] ECR I–4677 (prohibition on export of goods to certain destinations); (2) *Criminal proceedings against Goodwin and another* (case C-3/97) [1998] ECR I–3257, [1998] STC 699 (counterfeit products, where prohibition is linked to their detrimental impact on the rights of third parties); (3) *Fischer v Finanzamt Donaueschingen* (case C-283/95) [1998] ECR I–3369, [1998] STC 708 at [23] (game similar to roulette organised without official authorisation); (4) *Staatssecretaris van Financiën v Coffeeshop Siberië vof* (case C-158/98) [1999] ECR I–3971, [1999] STC 742 (making a table available to a third party for the sale of cannabis); (5) *Finnish State v Tullihallitus Kaupo Salumets* (case C-455/98) [2000] ECR I–4993 (contraband importation of ethyl alcohol).

Transactions which are not themselves vitiated by VAT fraud constitute supplies of goods or services effected by a taxable person where they fulfil the objective criteria on which the

Part I VAT

definition of that term is based. The intention of another trader involved in the same chain of supply is irrelevant if the taxable person had no knowledge, and no means of knowledge, of it. So is the possible fraudulent nature of another transaction in the chain, whether prior or subsequent to the transaction carried out by the taxable person, if the taxable person had no knowledge, and no means of knowledge, of it: *Optigen Ltd and others v Customs and Excise Comrs* (joined cases C-354/03, C-355/03 and C-484/03) [2006] ECR I–483, [2006] STC 419.

Article 3
(ex art 28a(1)(a) (second and third paras), 28a(1a))

1(*a*). An acquisition of goods is not charged to VAT by virtue of art 2(1)(*b*)(i) if a supply of those goods within the territory of the member state (see art 5(2)) would be exempt from VAT under arts 148 or 151.

1(*b*), 2. An acquisition of goods is not charged to VAT by virtue of art 2(1)(*b*)(i) if:

- It is made by any of the following persons: (1) a taxable person for the purpose of an agricultural, forestry or fisheries business subject to the common flat-rate scheme for farmers (see arts 295–305); (2) a taxable person who is not entitled to deduct VAT in respect of the goods or services he supplies; and (3) a non taxable person.
- The goods comprise neither a new means of transport nor goods subject to excise duty.
- The acquisition is not relieved from VAT under para 1(*a*) or art 4.
- The value of acquisitions for the current calendar year does not exceed the threshold described below.
- The value of acquisitions for the previous calendar year did not exceed the threshold described below.

The threshold is determined by the member states. It must be not less than EUR 10,000 (or the equivalent in national currency). It consists of the total amount (exclusive of VAT due or paid in the member state from which the goods were despatched or transported) of acquisitions under this head. For conversion rates, see art 399.

For the option to tax acquisitions under this provision, see para 3. For the retention of non-taxation under this provision, see Regulation (EU) No 282/2011 art 4.

3. Member states must allow acquisitions within para 1(*b*) to be charged to VAT under art 2(1)(*b*)(i) if a taxable person or non-taxable legal person so elects. An election lasts for two calendar years. The detailed rules for making an election are laid down by the member states.

Article 4
(ex arts 26aD(b) and 28o(1)(g))

The following intra-Community acquisitions of goods are not charged to VAT:

(a) An acquisition of second-hand goods, works of art, collectors' items or antiques (as defined in art 311(1)–(4)) in the following circumstances:
  - The vendor is a taxable dealer (as defined in art 311(5)) acting as such.
  - VAT has been charged in the member state in which transport or despatch of the goods began.
  - VAT has been charged under the margin scheme for taxable dealers (see arts 312–325).

(b) An acquisition of second-hand means of transport (as defined in art 327(3)) in the following circumstances:
  - The vendor is a taxable dealer acting as such.
  - VAT has been charged in the member state in which the despatch or transport began.
  - This VAT has been charged under the transitional arrangements for second-hand means of transport (see arts 326–322).

(c) An acquisition of second-hand goods, works of art, collectors' items or antiques in the following circumstances:
- The vendor is an organiser of sales by public auction (as defined in art 311(6)) acting as such.
- VAT has been charged in the member state in which transport or despatch of the goods began.
- VAT has been charged under the margin scheme for sales by public auction (see arts 333–341).

TITLE II—TERRITORIAL APPLICATION

Article 5
(ex art 3(1))

The following definitions apply for the purpose of applying this directive:

(1) The "territory of the Community" is the territories of the member states (see point 2). "Community" has the same meaning.

(2) The "territory of a member state" is the territory to which the EC Treaty (now the Functioning Treaty) applies in respect of each member state. This is now defined in TFEU 355. The extent of this territory is modified by excluding "third territories" (see point 3). The territory of coastal states extends to their territorial sea and to the bed and subsoil of that territorial sea: *Aktiebolaget NN v Skatteverket* (case C-111/05) [2007] ECR I–2697, [2008] STC 3203.

"Member state" has the same meaning.The member states currently comprise Austria, Belgium, Bulgaria, Cyprus, the Czech Republic, Denmark, Estonia, Finland, France, Germany, Greece, Hungry, Ireland, Italy, Latvia, Lithuania, Luxembourg, Malta, the Netherlands, Poland, Portugal, Romania, Slovakia, Slovenia, Spain, Sweden and the UK.

It is for each member state to establish the breadth of its territorial sea. This may not exceed twelve nautical miles: see *Aktiebolaget NN v Skatteverket* (case C-111/05) [2007] ECR I–2697, [2008] STC 3203 at [56]–[58], applying United Nations Convention on the Law of the Sea (Montego Bay, 10 December 1982) art 3.

For the sovereignty of coastal states over the exclusive economic zone and the continental shelf, see *Aktiebolaget NN v Skatteverket* (case C-111/05) [2007] ECR I–2697, [2008] STC 3203 at [59], [60].

The term "territory of a member state" defines the territory to which the VAT legislation of a member state applies. The extent of this territory is not always the same as: (1) the territory to which the Functioniong Treaty applies; and (2) the customs territory of the Community (as defined in Regulation (EEC) No 2913/92 art 3). The relationship between the three areas is compared in Appendix 2.

(3) A "third territory" is a territory listed in art 6 below.

(4) A "third country" is any state or territory to which the Functioning Treaty does not apply. For the countries and territories concerned, see the TFEU art 355(2), (5) (the Faroe Islands and certain overseas territories having special relations with the UK).

For countries and territories which are not treated as third countries, see art 7(1).

Article 6
(ex art 3(3); EC Treaty art 299(5), (6)(c); Act of Accession (1972), Protocol No 3; Act of Accession (1994), Protocol No 2)

1. The following territories form part of the customs territory of the Community (as defined in Regulation (EEC) No 2913/92 art 3). This directive does not apply to them:

(a) As regards Greece: Mount Athos.

(b) As regards Spain: the Canary Islands.

Part I VAT

(c) As regards France: the overseas departments.
(d) As regards Finland: the Åland Islands.
(e) As regards the UK: the Channel Islands.

2. The following territories do not form part of the customs territory of the Community (as defined in Regulation (EEC) No 2913/92 art 3). This directive does not apply to them:

- As regards Germany: the Island of Heligoland and the territory of Büsingen.
- As regards Spain: Ceuta and Melilla.
- As regards Italy: Livigno, Campione d'Italia and the Italian waters of Lake Lugano.

Article 7
(ex art 3(4))

1. Monaco (an independent principality), the Isle of Man (which does not form part of the UK) and the UK Sovereign Base Areas of Akrotiri and Dhekelia are not treated as "third countries" for VAT purposes.

2. Member states must treat transactions originating in Monaco, the Isle of Man and the UK Soverign Base Areas of Akrotiri and Dhekelia as transactions originating in France, the UK and Cyprus respectively. Similarly, they must treat transactions intended for Monaco, the Isle of Man and the UK Soverign Base Areas of Akrotiri and Dhekelia as transactions intended for France, the UK and Cyprus respectively.

Article 8
(ex art 3(5))

The Commission must present appropriate proposals to the Council if it considers that the provisions in arts 6 and 7 are no longer justified, particularly in terms of fair competition or own resources.

TITLE III—TAXABLE PERSONS

Article 9
(ex arts 4(1), (2) and 28a(4) (first para))

1. A person is a "taxable person" if he independently (see art 10) carries out any of the following activities (referred to as "economic activities") in any place:

- All the activities of producers, traders and persons supplying services. This includes mining activities, agricultural activities and the activities of the professions. Thus, VAT has a very wide scope. It covers all stages of production, distribution and the provision of services: *WM van Tiem v Staatssecretaris van Financiën* (case C-186/89) [1990] ECR I–4363, [1993] STC 91 at [17].
  The foregoing activites are generally categorised as economic if they are permanent and carried out in return for remuneration which is received by the person carrying out the activity. It is for the national court to determine whether both of these criteria have been met: *Landesanstalt für Landwirtschaft v Franz Götz* (case C-408/06) [2007] ECR I–11295 at [18], [20]–[22].
  The concept of "economic activity" does not include activities carried out on an occasional basis: *Enkler v Finanzamt Homburg* (case C-230/94) [1996] ECR I–4517, [1996] STC 1316 at [21]. For an exception, see para 2 below.
  The concept of "economic activity" does not include an activity consisting exclusively in providing services for no direct consideration. In these circumstances, the person providing the service is assimilated to a final consumer because he is at the final stage of the production and distribution chain: *Staatssecretaris van Financiën v Hong Kong Trade Development Council* (case 89/81) [1982] ECR 1277, [1983] 1 CMLR 73 at [10] (organisation promoting trade with Hong Kong). The purpose or results of the activity are irrelevant.

- The exploitation of tangible or intangible property for the purpose of obtaining income therefrom on a continuing basis.

  The term "exploitation" refers to all transactions, whatever their legal form, by which it is sought to obtain income from the goods in question on a continuing basis: *WM van Tiem v Staatssecretaris van Financiën* (case C-186/89) [1990] ECR I–4363, [1993] STC 91 at [18]. It is necessary to evaluate all the specific circumstances of a given case in order to determine whether the purpose of the activity in question is to obtain income on a continuing basis. One relevant factor is the nature of the goods concerned: *Enkler v Finanzamt Homburg* (case C-230/94) [1996] ECR I–4517, [1996] STC 1316 at [24], [27] (motor caravan).

  For examples of exploitation in relation to holding companies, see: (1) *Polysar Investments Netherlands BV v Inspecteur der Invoerrechten en Accijnjen, Arnham* (case C-60/90) [1991] ECR I–3111, [1993] STC 222, *Cibo Participations SA v Directeur régional des impôts du Nord-Pas-de-Calais* (case C-16/00) [2001] ECR 6663, [2002] STC 460 (acquisition of financial holdings in other undertakings, where this is accompanied by direct or indirect involvement in the management of the companies concerned, ie making taxable supplies to subsidiaries such as administrative, financial, commercial and technical services); (2) *Flordienne SA and another v Belgian State* (case C-142/99) [2000] ECR I–9567, [2000] STC 1044, *Empresa de Desenvolvimento Mineiro SGPS SA (EDM) v Fazenda Pública (Ministério Público, intervener)* (case C-77/01) [2004] ECR I–4295, [2005] STC 65 (holding company making capital available to its subsidiaries if this is carried out otherwise than on an occasional basis, it is not confined to management of an investment portfolio and it is carried out with a business or commercial purpose characterised, in particular, by a concern to maximise returns on capital investment); (3) *Skatteverket v AB SKF* (case C-29/08) [2009] ECR I–10413, [2010] STC 419 (disposal of all shares in a wholly-owned subsidiary and the remaining shareholding in a controlled company which was previously wholly owned where first, it had supplied taxable services to those companies and secondly, insofar as the disposal of shares is equivalent to the transfer of all or part of the assets of an undertaking, the member state has not exercised the option to exclude such transfers from the scope of VAT (ie under art 19 and, presumably, under art 29)).

  For examples of exploitation in other circumstances, see: (1) *WM van Tiem v Staatssecretaris van Financiën* (case C-186/89) [1990] ECR I–4363, [1993] STC 91 (grant of building right by owner of immovable property); (2) *Enkler v Finanzamt Homburg* (case C-230/94) [1996] ECR I–4517, [1996] STC 1316 (hiring out tangible property); (3) *Finanzamt Groß-Gerau v MKG-Kraftfahrzeuge-Factoring GmbH* (case C-305/01) [2003] ECR I–6729, [2003] STC 951 (factoring); (4) *Banque Bruxelles Lambert SA (BBL) v Belgian State* (case C-8/03) [2004] ECR I–10157, [2004] STC 1643 (collective investment, in transferable securities, of capital raised from the public).

  For examples of transactions that do not amount to exploitation, see: (1) *Polysar Investments Netherlands BV v Inspecteur der Invoerrechten en Accijnjen, Arnham* (case C-60/90) [1991] ECR I–3111, [1993] STC 222, *Cibo Participations SA v Directeur régional des impôts du Nord-Pas-de-Calais* (case C-16/00) [2001] ECR 6663, [2002] STC 460, *Welthgrove BV v Secretary of State for Finances* (case C-102/00) [2001] ECR I–5679 (receiving dividends); (2) *Wellcome Trust Ltd v Customs and Excise Comrs* (case C-155/94) [1996] ECR I–3013, [1996] STC 945 (purchase and sale of shares by a trustee in the course of managing the assets of a charitable trust); (3) *Harnas & Helm CV v Staatssecretaris van Financiën* (case C-80/95) [1997] ECR I–745, [1997] STC 364 (mere acquisition of ownership in, and the holding of, bonds where this is not subservient to any other business activity); (4) *Flordienne SA and another v Belgian State* (case C-142/99) [2000] ECR I–9567, [2000] STC 1044 (holding company merely reinvesting dividends received from subsidiaries by making loans to those subsidiaries); (5) *KapHag Renditefonds 35 Spreecenter Berlin-Hellersdorf3 Tranche GbR v Finan-*

zamt Charlottenburg (case C-442/01) [2003] ECR I–6851, [2005] STC 1500 (admission of new partner to a partnership); (6) *Hutchison 3G UK Ltd and others v Customs and Excise Comrs* (case C-369/04) [2007] ECR I–5247, [2008] STC 218, *T-Mobile Austria GmbH and others v Austria* (case C-284/04) [2007] ECR I–5189, [2008] STC 184 (allocation of licences to use defined parts of the radio-frequency spectrum reserved for telecommunications services); (7) *SPÖ Landesorganisation Kärnten v Finanzamt Klagenfurt* (case C-267/08) [2009] ECR I–9781, [2010] STC 287 (external advertising activities carried out by a section of a political party).

The scope of the term "economic activities" is very wide. It is objective in character, ie the activity is considered per se and without regard to its purpose or results. It is neutral in character, so that it is irrelevant whether the activities are conferred and regulated by law in the public interest: *Commission v Netherlands* (case C-235/85) [1987] ECR 1471, [1988] 2 CMLR 921 at [8], [10].

The question whether a given transaction has been carried out for the sole purpose of obtaining a tax advantage is entirely irrelevant in determining whether the transaction constitutes an economic activity. The test is whether the transaction satisfies the objective criteria on which the concept of an economic activity is based. Those criteria are not satisfied where tax is evaded: *Halifax plc and others v Customs and Excise Comrs* (case C-255/02) [2006] ECR I–1609, [2006] STC 919 at [58], [59]; *University of Huddersfield Higher Education Corpn v Customs and Excise Comrs* (case C-223/03) [2006] ECR I–1751, [2006] STC 980 at [50], [51].

Transactions which are not themselves vitiated by VAT fraud constitute an economic activity where they fulfil the objective criteria on which the definition of that term is based. The intention of another trader involved in the same chain of supply is irrelevant if the taxable person had no knowledge, and no means of knowledge, of it. So is the possible fraudulent nature of another transaction in the chain, whether prior or subsequent to the transaction carried out by the taxable person, if the taxable person had no knowledge, and no means of knowledge, of it: *Optigen Ltd and others v Customs and Excise Comrs* (joined cases C-354/03, C-355/03 and C-484/03) [2006] ECR I–483, [2006] STC 419.

For activities held to be economic activities, see: (1) *Commission v France* (case C-276/97) [2000] ECR I–6251, *Commission v Ireland* (case C-358/97) [2000] ECR I–6301, *Commission v United Kingdom* (case C-359/97) [2000] ECR I–6355, [2000] STC 777, *Commission v Kingdom of the Netherlands* (case C-408/97) [2000] ECR I–6417, *Commission v Hellenic Republic* (case C-260/98) [2000] ECR I–6537 (tolls); (2) *Finanzamt Offenbach am Main-Land v Faxworld Vorgündungsgesellschaft Peter Hünninghausen und Wolfgang Klein GbR* (case C-137/02) [2004] ECR I–5547, [2005] STC 1192 (partnership established for the sole purpose of founding a capital company); (3) *Finanzamt Bergisch Gladbach v HE* (case C-25/03) [2005] ECR I–3123, [2007] STC 128 (house purchased or built by person in order to live in it with his family, where one room is used as an office for carrying on an economic activity and that part of the building is allocated to the assets of his business). See also the examples of exploitation of property above.

Economic activities may consist of several consecutive transactions. Preparatory acts forming part of those transactions must themselves be treated as constituting an economic activity. It is unnecessary to distinguish the various legal forms taken by such preparatory acts. The principle that VAT should be neutral as regards the tax burden on a business requires that the first investment expenditure incurred for the purposes of, and with a view to, commencing a business must be regarded as an economic activity: *Rompleman and Rompelman-Van Deelen v Minister van Financiën* (case 268/83) [1985] ECR 655, [1985] 3 CMLR 202 at [22], [23].

This provision does not preclude tax authorities from requiring objective evidence in support of the declared intention to commence the economic activities which will give rise to taxable transactions: *Intercommunale voor Zeewaterontzilting (in liquidation) v Belgian State* (case C-110/94) [1996] ECR I–857, [1996] STC 569 at [23].

Once a tax authority has accepted that the taxpayer has the status of a taxable person, carrying out a study into the technical and economic aspects of the envisaged activity is regarded as an economic activity. This is so even if the purpose of the study is to investigate the degree to which the envisaged activity will be profitable. Although the status of taxable person can be withdrawn retrospectively in cases of fraud or abuse, it cannot be withdrawn retroactively on the ground that the result of the study is a decision not to move to the operational phase, so that the envisaged economic activity does not give rise to taxable transactions: *Intercommunale voor Zeewaterontzilting (in liquidation) v Belgian State* (case C-110/94) [1996] ECR I–857, [1996] STC 569 at [18], [24], [25] (company put into liquidation).

A person who has ceased an economic activity continues to be regarded as a taxable person if, because the lease of the business premises contains a non-termination clause, he continues to pay rent and charges on the business premises until the lease expires: *I/S Fini H v Skatteministeriet* (case C-32/03) [2005] ECR I–1599, [2005] STC 903.

In principle, bodies governed by public law are taxable persons if they meet the foregoing criteria. For the exemption from such status in respect of activities forming part of their specific duties as public authorities, see art 13. A private individual is not covered by this exemption merely because his activity consists of carrying out acts falling within the prerogatives of a public authority: *Commission v Netherlands* (case C-235/85) [1987] ECR 1471, [1988] 2 CMLR 921 at [21]. For examples, see: (1) *Commission v Netherlands* (case C-235/85) [1987] ECR 1471, [1988] 2 CMLR 921 (notaries and bailiffs); (2) *Ayuntamiento de Sevilla v Recaudadores de las Zonas Primera y Segunda* (case C-202/90) [1991] ECR I–4247, [1993] STC 659 (tax collectors not bound by a contract of employment to the local authority); (3) *Commission v Ireland* (case C-358/97) [2000] ECR I–6301, *Commission v United Kingdom* (case C-359/97) [2000] ECR I–6355, [2000] STC 777 and cf *Commission v France* (case C-276/97) [2000] ECR I–6251 (tolls).

The fact that a holding company belongs to a world-wide group which, in the main, outwardly appears under a single name, is irrelevant in determining whether the company is a taxable person: *Polysar Investments Netherlands BV v Inspecteur der Invoerrechten en Accijnjen, Arnham* (case C-60/90) [1991] ECR I–3111, [1993] STC 222 at [16].

For European Economic Interest Groupings treated as a taxable person for the purposes of this provision, see Regulation (EU) No 282/2011 art 5.

2. A person who occasionally supplies new means of transport in the following circumstances is regarded as a taxable person:

- The new means of transport is delivered to, or collected by, the customer.
- The delivery or collection involves removing the new means of transport from the territory of a member state (see art 5(2)) to a place elsewhere within the Community (see art 5(1)).

Article 10
(ex art 4(4) (first para))

A person does not carry on an activity "independently" for the purposes of art 9(1) if he is bound to an employer by:

- A contract of employment.
- Any other legal ties creating the relationship of employer and employee as regards working conditions, remuneration and the employer's liability.

Where a person's sole economic activity consists in the letting of an item of tangible property to a company or partnership of which he is a member, that letting is regarded as an independent activity: *Staatssecretaris van Financiën v Heerma* (case C-23/98) [2000] ECR I–419, [2001] STC 1437.

Contracts entered into by a company may be wholly carried out by an individual pursuant to a contract of employment. The individual is not a taxable person even if he is the sole shareholder, sole manager and sole member of staff: *J A van der Steen v Inspecteur van de Belastingdienst Utrecht-Gooi/kantoor Utrecht* (case C-355/06) [2007] ECR I–8863, [2008] STC 2379.

A fixed establishment which is not a legal entity distinct from the company of which it forms a part is not a person carrying on an activity "independently": see *Ministero dell'Economia e delle Finanze and another v FCE Bank plc* (case C-210/04) [2006] ECR I–2803, [2007] STC 165.

Article 11
(ex art 4(4) (second para))

Member states may treat persons as a single taxable person if:

- The persons are established in the territory of the member state (as defined in art 5(2)).
- The persons, although legally independent, are closely bound together by financial, economic and organisational links.

The consequences of implementing this provision are that: (1) the closely linked persons are neither treated as separate taxable persons nor permitted to submit separate tax declarations; and (2) the single taxable person is identified by a single VAT number. It is for the national court to decide whether the national legislation meets these criteria: *Ampliscientifica Srl and another v Ministero dell'Economia e delle Finanze, Agenzia delle Entrate* (case C-162/07) [2008] ECR I–4109, [2008] SWTI 1387.

Member states must consult the VAT Committee (see art 398) before implementing this provision. For a scheme implemented without consultation, see *Ampliscientifica Srl and another v Ministero dell'Economia e delle Finanze, Agenzia delle Entrate* (case C-162/07) [2008] ECR I–4109, [2008] SWTI 1387.

Member states may adopt anti-evasion or anti-avoidance measures when implementing this provision.

Article 12
(ex art 4(3))

1–3. Member states may treat a person as a taxable person if he carries out a transaction relating to an activity (see art 9(1)) on an occasional basis. In particular, member states may do so in relation to:

(a) The supply of all or part of a building (ie any structure fixed to or in the ground) and the land on which it stands. The supply must be made before the building is first occupied. Member states may lay down detailed rules for applying this provision to conversions of buildings. They may determine what is meant by "the land on which a building stands". They may apply criteria other than first occupation.

(b) The supply of any improved or unimproved land (referred to as "building land") defined by the member states. Member states must have regard to the objective pursued by art 135(1)(k) when framing a definition. This objective is to confine exemption to land which has not been built on and which is not intended to support a building. Thus, the Court of Justice is not required to specify the degree of improvement that land must exhibit in order to be classified as "building land": see *Gemeente Emmen v Belastingdienst Grote Ondernemingen* (case C-468/93) [1996] ECR I–1721, [1996] STC 496 at [25], 26].

For the option to tax in relation to land and buildings, see arts 137 and 391; *Finanzamt Goslar v Breitsohl* (case C-400/98) [2000] ECR I–4321, [2001] STC 355.

Article 13
(ex art 4(5))

1, 2. This article applies to "bodies governed by public law". This term includes states, regional government authorities and local government authorities. It also includes individuals: *Ufficio Distrettuale delle Imposte Dirette di Fiorenzuola d'Arda v Comune di Carpaneto Piacentino; Ufficio Provinciale Imposta sul Valore Aggiunto di Piacenza v Comune di Rivergaro* (joined cases 231/87 and 129/88) [1989] ECR 3233, [1991] STC 205 at [31].

A body governed by public law may rely on this provision for the purpose of opposing the application of a national provision making it subject to VAT in respect of an activity in which it engages as a public authority, which is not listed in Annex I and whose treatment as non-taxable is not liable to give rise to significant distortions of competition: *Ufficio Distrettuale delle Imposte Dirette di Fiorenzuola d'Arda v Comune di Carpaneto Piacentino; Ufficio Provinciale Imposta sul Valore Aggiunto di Piacenza v Comune di Rivergaro* (joined cases 231/87 and 129/88) [1989] ECR 3233, [1991] STC 205 at [33].

Exemption from treatment as a taxable person (para 1, first sub-para)

In principle, a body governed by public law (see below) is not a taxable person in respect of its activities or transactions as a public authority. This applies even if the body collects dues, fees, contributions or payments in connection with those activities or transactions.

A body governed by public law engages in activities as a "public authority" if it does so under the special legal regime applicable to public authorities. It does not do so if it acts under the legal conditions applicable to private traders: *Ufficio Distrettuale delle Imposte Dirette di Fiorenzuola d'Arda v Comune di Carpaneto Piacentino; Ufficio Provinciale Imposta sul Valore Aggiunto di Piacenza v Comune di Rivergaro* (joined cases 231/87 and 129/88) [1989] ECR 3233, [1991] STC 205 at [19]. An activity is pursued under the special regime applicable to public authorities if it involves the use of public powers: *Fazenda Pública v Câmara Municipal do Porto (Ministério Público, third party)* (case C-446/98) [2000] ECR I–11435, [2001] STC 560 at [22], [24] (letting spaces for parking vehicles involving use of powers such as authorising or restricting parking on the public highway or penalising people who exceed the authorised parking time).

It is for member states to choose the appropriate legislative technique for transposing this provision into national law. Member states may, for example, merely incorporate the form of words used in this directive, or an equivalent expression, into national law or draw up a list of activities in respect of which bodies governed by public law are not to be regarded as taxable persons: *Ufficio Distrettuale delle Imposte Dirette di Fiorenzuola d'Arda v Comune di Carpaneto Piacentino*; *Ufficio Provinciale Imposta sul Valore Aggiunto di Piacenza v Comune di Rivergaro* (joined cases 231/87 and 129/88) [1989] ECR 3233, [1991] STC 205 at [18], [19]. It is for the national court to classify activities in the light of the foregoing criteria: *Ufficio Distrettuale delle Imposte Dirette di Fiorenzuola d'Arda v Comune di Carpaneto Piacentino*; *Ufficio Provinciale Imposta sul Valore Aggiunto di Piacenza v Comune di Rivergaro* (joined cases 231/87 and 129/88) [1989] ECR 3233, [1991] STC 205 at [12].

This provision must be strictly interpreted: see *Commission v Ireland* (case C-554/07) [2009] ECR I–128 at [42].

Distortion of competition (para 1, second sub-para)

Activities carried on under the legal regime applicable to public authorities may be carried on both by bodies governed by public law and, in competition with them, by private individuals. In these circumstances, member states are required to ensure that bodies governed by public law are treated as taxable persons in respect of those activities if their treatment as a non-taxable person could lead to significant distortions of competition: this provision as explained in *Ufficio Distrettuale delle Imposte Dirette di Fiorenzuola d'Arda v Comune di Carpaneto Piacentino; Ufficio Provinciale Imposta sul Valore Aggiunto di Piacenza v Comune di Rivergaro* (joined cases 231/87 and 129/88) [1989] ECR 3233, [1991] STC 205 at [24].

Member states are not required to transpose the foregoing criterion literally into their national law, or to lay down precise quantitive limits for such treatment: *Ufficio Distrettuale delle Imposte Dirette di Fiorenzuola d'Arda v Comune di Carpaneto Piacentino; Ufficio Provinciale Imposta sul Valore Aggiunto di Piacenza v Comune di Rivergaro* (joined cases 231/87 and 129/88) [1989] ECR 3233, [1991] STC 205 at [23]. They may, for example, entrust an administrative body with the task of specifying the situations in which an activity is regarded as bringing about significant distortions of competition, and of applying those criteria to individual cases, provided the body's decisions are reviewable by the national courts: *Fazenda Pública v Câmara Municipal do Porto* (*Ministério Público, third party*) (case C-446/98) [2000] ECR I–11435, [2001] STC 560 at [32].

This provision implies a prior finding on the question whether the relevant activity has an economic nature: see *T-Mobile Austria GmbH and others v Austria* (case C-284/04) [2007] ECR I–5189, [2008] STC 184 at [48]. For an example of activities having an economic nature, see *Landesanstalt für Landwirtschaft v Franz Götz* (case C-408/06) [2007] ECR I–11295 (milk quota sales point). For an example of activities that did not, see *T-Mobile Austria GmbH and others v Austria* (case C-284/04) [2007] ECR I–5189, [2008] STC 184 (allocation of licences to use defined parts of the radio-frequency spectrum reserved for telecommunications services).

Significant distortions of competition are evaluated by reference to the relevant activity as such. This evaluation does not relate to any local market in particular: *R & C Comrs v Isle of Wight Council and others (*case C-288/07) [2008] ECR I–7203, [2008] STC 2964, [2009] STC 1096 at [40]–[53]. For a situation where there was no competition, see *Landesanstalt für Landwirtschaft v Franz Götz* (case C-408/06) [2007] ECR I–11295 (milk quota sales point).

In determining whether treatment as a non-taxable person could lead to competition, it is necessary to consider both actual competition and potential competition. However, the possibility of a private operator entering the relevant market must be real, not purely hypothetical. Thus, it must be based on fact, objective evidence or an analysis of the market: see *R & C Comrs v Isle of Wight Council and others* (case C-288/07) [2008] ECR I–7203, [2008] STC 2964 at [63]–65].

The distortion of competition may be to the detriment of either the bodies governed by public law or their private competitors: see *Finanzamt Düsseldorf-Süd v SALIX Grundstücks-Vermietungsgellschaft mbH & Co Objekt Offenbach KG* (case C-102/08) [2009] ECR I–4629, [2009] STC 1607 at [76].

A private person in competition with a body governed by public law is entitled to rely on this provision in proceedings against the national tax authorities in relation to an allegation that a body governed by public law is treated as a non-taxable person for VAT purposes, or undertaxed, in respect of the activities it engages in as a public authority: *Finanzamt Eisleben v Feuerbestattungsverein Halle eV* (*Lutherstadt Eisleben, joined party*) (case C-430/04) [2006] ECR I–4999, [2006] STC 2043.

Activities listed in Annex D (para 1, third sub-para)

A body governed by public law is a taxable person if, and in so far as, it carries on specified activities (listed in Annex I) to a material (ie non-negligible) extent. Member states are free to exclude the activities listed in Annex I from the scope of compulsory tax liability in so far as they are negligible, but are not required to do so: *Ufficio Distrettuale delle Imposte Dirette di Fiorenzuola d'Arda v Comune di Carpaneto Piacentino; Ufficio Provinciale Imposta sul Valore Aggiunto di Piacenza v Comune di Rivergaro* (joined cases 231/87 and 129/88) [1989] ECR 3233, [1991] STC 205 at [27].

A body governed by public law is always a taxable person in respect of its non-negligible Annex I activities. Negligible scale is taken into account in determining whether a body governed by public law is a taxable person only if a member state has enacted national legislation to that effect. This legislation must be restricted to Annex I supplies: *Ufficio Distrettuale delle Imposte Dirette di Fiorenzuola d'Arda v Comune di Carpaneto Piacentino; Ufficio Provinciale Imposta sul Valore Aggiunto di Piacenza v Comune di Rivergaro* (joined cases 231/87 and129/88) [1989] ECR 3233, [1991] STC 205 at [28]; *Fazenda Pública v Câmara Municipal do Porto* (*Ministério Público, third party*) (case C-446/98) [2000] ECR I–11435, [2001] STC 560 at [28].

Member states may entrust an administrative body with the task of specifying the situations in which an activity is regarded as being negligible, and of applying those criteria to individual cases, provided the body's decisions are reviewable by the national courts: *Fazenda Pública v Câmara Municipal do Porto* (*Ministério Público, third party*) (case C-446/98) [2000] ECR I–11435, [2001] STC 560 at [32].

Exemption (para 2)

Member states may provide that bodies governed by public law carry on an activity as a public authority, so that they are not regarded as a taxable person in respect of it, if the activity is exempt from tax under arts 132, 135, 136, 371, 374–377, 378(2), 379(2) or 380–390. Member states may so provide even if the activities are performed in a similar manner to those of a private trader: *Finanzamt Augsburg-Stadt v Marktgemeinde Welden* (case C-247/95) [1997] ECR I–779, [1997] STC 531.

Member states adopting this option must do so by an express provision. This may be done by: (1) incorporating the form of words used in art 13(2) (or an equivalent expression); (2) drawing up a list of those activities considered to be activities of a public authority; or (3) authorising an executive authority to draw up such a list. The decisions of an executive authority in point (3) must have unquestionable binding force; they must also be specific, precise and clear, and be reviewable by the national courts: see *Finanzamt Düsseldorf-Süd v SALIX Grundstücks-Vermietungsgellschaft mbH & Co Objekt Offenbach KG* (case C-102/08) [2009] ECR I–4629, [2009] STC 1607 at [55]–[58].

This provision is irrelevant in relation to a particular activity carried on by a body governed by public law if: (1) the body acts as a public authority; and (2) the activity does not distort competition: *Fazenda Pública v Câmara Municipal do Porto* (*Ministério Público, third party*) (case C-446/98) [2000] ECR I–11435, [2001] STC 560 at [45]

TITLE IV—TAXABLE TRANSACTIONS

CHAPTER 1—SUPPLY OF GOODS

Article 14
(ex art 5(1), (4), (5))

1. A "supply of goods" is the transfer of the right to dispose of tangible property as owner.

The term "supply of goods" covers any transfer of tangible property by one party which empowers the other party actually to dispose of it as if he were the owner of the property. This is so even if there is no transfer of legal ownership of the property: *Staatssecretaris van Financiën v Shipping and Forwarding Enterprise Safe BV* (case C-320/88) [1990] ECR I–285, [1991] STC 627 at [7]–[9].

The term is objective in nature and applies without regard to the purpose or results of the transactions concerned: *Halifax plc and others v Customs and Excise Comrs* (case C-255/02) [2006] ECR I–1609, [2006] STC 919 at [56]. For the application of this principle to chains of transactions tainted by fraud or avoidance, see the commentary to art 2.

The term does not refer to the transfer of ownership in accordance with the procedures prescribed by the applicable national law: *Staatssecretaris van Financiën v Shipping and Forwarding Enterprise Safe BV* (case C-320/88) [1990] ECR I–285, [1991] STC 627 at [7]. For examples of cases where the national courts had applied national law, see: (1) *Staatssecretaris van Financiën v Shipping and Forwarding Enterprise Safe BV* (case C-320/88) [1990] ECR I–285, [1991] STC 627; (2) *Finanzamt Uelzen v Armbrecht* (case C-291/92) [1995] ECR I–2775, [1995] STC 997; (3) *Finanzamt Bergisch Gladbach v HE* (case C-25/03) [2005] ECR I–3123, [2007] STC 128; (4) *Auto Lease Holland BV v Bundesamt für Finanzen* (case C-185/01) [2003] ECR I–1317, [2005] STC 598.

A thief merely obtains possession of goods. He does not, therefore, dispose of stolen goods under the same conditions as their owner. A theft is not, therefore regarded as a "transfer" from the victim to the thief: *British American Tobacco International Ltd and another v Belgian State* (case C-435/03) [2005] ECR I–7077, [2006] STC 158 at [36].

It may be necessary to identify the person to whom the "right" was transferred. For an example, see *Auto Lease Holland BV v Bundesamt für Finanzen* (case C-185/01) [2003] ECR I–1317, [2005] STC 598 (whether right to dispose of road fuel as owner transferred to the lessor of a motor vehicle (who paid for the fuel and billed the lessee) or to the lessee (who used the fuel)).

A transfer of the right to dispose of tangible property does not necessarily cease to be classified as a supply of goods merely because it has been installed or assembled – with or without a trial run – by or on behalf of the supplier. Moreover, no distinction is drawn between different methods of installation. Thus, movable property is not necessarily classified as "works of construction" for the purposes of para 3 merely because the property is installed in such a way as to be incorporated in the ground: *Aktiebolaget NN v Skatteverket* (case C-111/05) [2007] ECR I–2697, [2008] STC 3203 at [35] (supply and installation of fibre-optic cable). For "tangible property", see art 15.

A supply consisting of both goods (or several goods) and various service elements may comprise a single transaction which must be classified as either a supply of goods or a supply of services in accordance with the principles summarised in the commentary to art 2 under the heading "one supply or two". For examples of a single transaction classified as a supply of goods, see: (1) *Aktiebolaget NN v Skatteverket* (case C-111/05) [2007] ECR I–2697, [2008] STC 3203 (supply and installation of fibre-optic cable); (2) *Finanzamt Burgdorf v Manfred Bog; CinemaxX Entertainment GmbH & Co KG v Finanzamt Hamburg-Barmbek-Uhlenhorst; Lothar Lohmeyer v Finanzamt Minden; Fleischerei Nier GmbH & Co KG v Finanzamt Detmold* (joined cases C-497/09 C-499/09 C-501/09 C-502/09 [2011] ECR I–0000, [2011] STC 1221 (in relation to (a) the supply of food or meals freshly prepared for immediate consumption from snack stalls or mobile snack bars, or in cinema foyers, and (b) party catering services, where the caterer does no more than deliver standard meals without any additional services or where the supply of food represents the predominant element of the transaction).

It is for the national court to apply this provision, as interpreted by the Court, to an individual case: *Staatssecretaris van Financiën v Shipping and Forwarding Enterprise Safe BV* (case C-320/88) [1990] ECR I–285, [1991] STC 627 at [11], [13].

2. The following are treated as a supply of goods:

- The transfer of the ownership of property against payment of compensation, where the transfer takes place: (1) by order made by a public authority, (2) by order in the name of a public authority, or (3) in pursuance of the law.
- The actual handing over of goods pursuant to a contract for the hire of goods for a certain period. The contract must provide that, in the normal course of events, ownership will pass no later than the date when the final instalment is paid.
- The actual handing over of goods pursuant to a contract for the sale of goods on deferred terms. The contract must provide that, in the normal course of events, ownership will pass no later than the date when the final instalment is paid.
- The transfer of goods pursuant to a contract under which commission is payable on purchase or sale. For an example of a transaction within this description, see *Commission v United Kingdom* (case C-305/03) [2006] ECR I–1213, [2007] STC 1211 at [31] (sale by auction).

3. Member states can treat the handing over of certain works of construction as supplies of goods.

Article 15
(ex art 5(2), (3))

1. Electricity, gas, heat, cooling energy and the like are treated as if they were tangible property.

2. Member states can treat the following as tangible property:

(a) Certain interests in immovable property.

(b) Rights in rem giving the holder a right of user over immovable property. This option enables the creation of a right of user over immovable property to be treated as a "transfer" for the purpose of para 1: *WM van Tiem v Staatssecretaris van Financiën* (case C-186/89) [1990] ECR I–4363, [1993] STC 91 at [23].

(c) Shares, or interests equivalent to shares, giving the holder de jure or de facto rights of ownership or possession over all or part of immovable property.

Member states may lay down conditions. However, any conditions imposed must not alter the nature of the choice afforded: *Stichting "Goed Wonen"* (formerly *Woningbouwvereniging "Goed Wonen") v Staatssecretaris van Financiën* (case C-326/99) [2001] ECR I–6831, [2003] STC 1137 at [34].

Article 16
(ex art 5(6))

The following are treated as supplies made for consideration where VAT on the goods in question (see below), or on component parts (see below) of them, was wholly or partly deductible:

- The application by a taxable person of goods forming part of his business assets for his private purposes.
- The application by a taxable person of goods forming part of his business assets for the private purposes of his staff.
- The disposal, free of charge, of goods forming part of his business assets. However, a disposal is not treated as a supply made for consideration if it comprises either:
  (i) The gift of a sample. The nature of a sample was considered in *EMI Group Ltd v Revenue and Customs Comrs* (case C581/08) [2010] ECR I–0000, [2010] STC 2609 in relation to recorded music. A "sample" is a specimen of a product. It is intended to promote sales of the product. It allows the characteristics and qualities of the product to be assessed without resulting in final consumption (other than final consumption which is inherent in such promotional transactions) (see paras [22], [25]). It may be gifted in the form in which it is offered for sale (see paras [26]–[29]). The recipient of a sample given for promotional purposes may be someone other than a potential or actual buyer (see paras [30], [31]). More than one sample of the same product may be given if this is justified by the nature of the product and the use made of the samples by the recipient (see paras [32]–[40]). The tax status of the recipient is irrelevant (see para 53]).
  (ii) A gift of small value for the purposes of the taxable person's business. Member states may fix a monetary limit for gifts made to the same person in the course of a twelve-month period or for gifts forming part of a series or succession of gifts. However, member states may not apply a presumption that goods distributed to different employees of the same employer are to be treated as gifts made to the same person: *EMI Group Ltd v Revenue and Customs Comrs* (case C581/08) [2010] ECR I–0000, [2010] STC 2609 at [42]–44] and [46]–49].

  These exceptions are construed narrowly so as to avoid undermining the charge to tax. However, this construction must not deprive the exceptions of their effectiveness: see *EMI Group Ltd v Revenue and Customs Comrs* (case C581/08) [2010] ECR I–0000, [2010] STC 2609 at [20].

  Where gifts are not of small value, they are treated as supplies made for consideration whether or not they are made for business purposes: *Kuwait Petroleum (GB) Ltd v Customs and Excise Comrs* (case C-48/97) [1999] ECR I–2323, [1999] STC 488 at [22] (business promotion scheme under which vouchers issued with petrol sales were exchanged for goods or services).

Part I VAT

- The application of goods forming part of his business assets for purposes other than those of his business.

The "VAT on the goods in question" refers solely to tax on the initial purchase or manufacture of the goods: *Finanzamt Burgdorf v Fischer; Finanzamt Düsseldorf-Mettmann v Brandenstein* (joined cases C-322/99 and C-323/99) [2001] ECR I–4049, [2001] STC 1356 at [53]. Thus, a subsequent application or disposal is not treated as a supply for consideration merely because VAT was deducted in respect of expenses (eg repairs) incurred subsequent to the initial purchase or manufacture: *Bakcsi v Finanzamt Fürstenfeldbruck* (case C-415/98) [2001] ECR I–1831, [2001] STC 802 at [33].

Goods are "component parts" if: (1) they are tangible physical objects; (2) they have been incorporated into those goods; (3) they have definitively lost their physical and economic distinctiveness as a result of being incorporated into the relevant goods; and (4) they have given rise to a lasting increase in the value of the relevant goods which has not been entirely consumed at the time when those goods are applied or disposed of. It follows that the following do not amount to "component parts": (*a*) goods which retain their physical and economic distinctiveness; (*b*) goods which merely contribute to maintaining the value of the relevant goods; and (*c*) supplies of services. As regards head (*c*), if a mixed supply of goods and services is categorised as a supply of services, the overall supply of services necessarily includes ancillary and minor supplies of goods: *Finanzamt Burgdorf v Fischer; Finanzamt Düsseldorf-Mettmann v Brandenstein* (joined cases C-322/99 and C-323/99) [2001] ECR I–4049, [2001] STC 1356 at [55], [59], [63]–[70].

Goods on which VAT is deductible may form component parts of other goods which, when acquired, did not give rise to input tax deduction. Where this is so, the charge under this provision is confined to the component parts: *Finanzamt Burgdorf v Fischer; Finanzamt Düsseldorf-Mettmann v Brandenstein* (joined cases C-322/99 and C-323/99) [2001] ECR I–4049, [2001] STC 1356.

A taxable person may choose to include only part of an item of property in his business assets. If he does so, the part excluded does not form part of his business assets. As such, no right to deduct input tax arises in respect of the excluded part (see commentary to art 167), and any application or disposal of it is outside the scope of VAT: *Finanzamt Uelzen v Armbrecht* (case C-291/92) [1995] ECR I–2775, [1995] STC 997 at [28].

For examples of transactions in respect of property excluded from business assets, see: (1) *De Jong v Staatssecretaris van Financiën* (case C-20/91) [1992] ECR I–2847 (building contractor acting as a taxable person constructing a dwelling for his own occupation on land owned by him but excluded from business assets); (2) *Finanzamt Burgdorf v Fischer; Finanzamt Düsseldorf-Mettmann v Brandenstein* (joined cases C-322/99 and C-323/99) [2001] ECR I–4049, [2001] STC 1356, *Bakcsi v Finanzamt Fürstenfeldbruck* (case C-415/98) [2001] ECR I–1831, [2001] STC 802 (application or disposal of motor cars purchased from private individuals).

The purpose of this provision is to ensure equal treatment between: (1) a taxable person who applies business assets for private purposes; and (2) an ordinary consumer who purchases goods of the same type: *De Jong v Staatssecretaris van Financiën* (case C-20/91) [1992] ECR I–2847 at [15].

No charge to tax arises under this head if consideration has been given for the private or non-business use: *Hotel Scandic Gåsabäck AB v Riksskatteverket* (case C-412/03) [2005] ECR I–743, [2005] STC 1311 at [24] (staff meals provided for a consideration below cost price).

For the valuation of supplies under this provision, see art 74 and, in relaltion to the UK, Decision 2006/659/EC (fuel for private use in motor cars).

Article 17*
(ex art 28a(5) (first para))

1. A taxable person may transfer goods forming part of his business assets from one place to another. This is treated as a supply of goods for consideration if:

- The goods comprise tangible movable property.
- The transfer is made for business purposes.
- The goods are collected or delivered by, or on behalf of, the taxable person.
- The goods are moved from the territory of a member state (see art 5(2)) to a place elsewhere in the Community (see art 5(1)).

2. A transfer from member state X to member state Y is disregarded if it is made for the purposes of any of the following transactions:

(a) A supply of the goods made by the taxable person in member state Y. The conditions in art 33 must be met.

(b) A supply of the goods by the taxable person in member state Y, where they are to be installed or assembled by, or on behalf of, the supplier. The conditions in art 36 must be met.

(c) A supply of goods by the taxable person on board a ship, aircraft or train in the course of a passenger transport operation. The conditions in art 37 must be met.

(d) The following, if made in accordance with the conditions in arts 38 and 39:
- a supply of gas through a natural gas system situated with EU territory or through any network connected to such a system,
- a supply of electricity, and
- a supply of heat or cooling energy through heating or cooling networks.

(e) A supply of the goods by the taxable person in member state X. The conditions in arts 138, 146, 147, 148, 151 or 152 must be met.

(f) A supply of services performed for the taxable person. The service must comprise work either: (1) valuation of the goods in question; or (2) work on those goods. The work must be physically carried out in member state Y. On completion of the work, the goods must be returned to the taxable person in member state X.

(g) Temporary use of the goods in member state Y for the purposes of a supply of services by the taxable person, who is established in member state X.

(h) Temporary use of the goods in member state Y for a period not exceeding 24 months, if an importation of the same goods into member state Y with a view to their temporary use would be covered by the arrangements for temporary importation with full exemption from import duties.

3. If any of the conditions governing eligibility under para 2 ceases to be met, the goods are regarded as having been transferred to member state Y so that para 1 applies. This transfer is deemed to take place when the condition ceases to be met.

Article 18
(ex art 5(7))

Member states may treat the following as supplies made for consideration:

(a) The application of goods for the purposes of the taxable person's business where:
- the goods were produced, constructed, extracted, processed, purchased or imported in the course of the taxable person's business; and
- the VAT on such goods would not have been wholly deductible if they had been acquired from another taxable person. For the right to deduct input tax, see art 167.

(b) The application of goods by a taxable person for the purposes of a non-taxable activity if the VAT on such goods became wholly or partly deductible on:
- Their acquisition.
- Their application for the purposes of his business in accordance with point (*a*).

(c) The retention of goods by a taxable person or his successors when he ceases to carry on a taxable economic activity if:
- VAT on such goods became wholly or partly deductible on their acquisition, or on their application for the purposes of his business in accordance with point (*a*).

- The retention does not arise from a transfer of assets within art 19 (a transfer of all or part of the assets which is not treated as a supply of goods).

For the valuation of supplies in heads (*a*)–(*c*), see art 74.

Article 19
(ex art 5(8))

Member states may consider that no supply of goods takes place if a taxable person transfers all or part of his assets to another person. This applies whether or not there is a consideration for the transfer and whether or not the transfer takes place as a contribution to a company.

This "no supply" rule applies to any transfer of a business or an independent part of an undertaking. The transfer includes both tangible and intangible elements which, together, constitute an undertaking or part of an undertaking capable of carrying on an independent economic activity. However, the transferee must intend to operate the business (or the part of the undertaking) transferred. An intention to liquidate the activity immediately and sell the stock (if any) is insufficient: *Zita Modes SARL v Administration de l'enregistrement et des domains* (case C-497/01) [2003] ECR I–14393, [2005] STC 1059 at [40], [44].

The recipient is treated as the successor to the transferor. This does not constitute a condition for applying the "no supply" rule. It is merely a result of the fact that no supply is considered to have taken place: *Zita Modes SARL v Administration de l'enregistrement et des domains* (case C-497/01) [2003] ECR I–14393, [2005] STC 1059 at [43].

Member states may adopt measures to prevent distortion of competition in cases where the recipient is not wholly liable to tax. They may also introduce anti-avoidance or anti-evasion measures. However, these are the only circumstances in which the "no supply" rule may be limited. It follows that member states adopting a "no supply" rule must apply it to any transfer of all or part of the assets. The rule cannot be limited to a restricted class of transfers: *Zita Modes SARL v Administration de l'enregistrement et des domains* (case C-497/01) [2003] ECR I–14393, [2005] STC 1059 at [30], [31].

The recipient is "not wholly liable to tax" if he is not a taxable person or if he acts as a taxable person only in relation to part of his activities": *Zita Modes SARL v Administration de l'enregistrement et des domains* (case C-497/01) [2003] ECR I–14393, [2005] STC 1059 at [30].

CHAPTER 2—INTRA-COMMUNITY ACQUISITION OF GOODS

Article 20
(ex art 28a(3))

An acquisition of the right, as owner, to dispose of movable tangible property is an "intra-Community acquisition of goods" if the following conditions are met:

(1) The goods are despatched or transported from one member state ("X") to another member state ("Y").
(2) The goods are despatched or transported to the person acquiring the goods.
(3) The goods are despatched or transported by, or on behalf of, the vendor or the person acquiring the goods.

The despatch or transport may arise from a supply of goods in member state X. This supply is exempt from tax if the conditions in art 138 are met. The intra-Community acquisition is effected only when: (1) the right to dispose of the goods as owner has been transferred to the purchaser; (2) the supplier establishes that those goods have been despatched or transported to another member state; and (3) the goods have physically left the territory of the member state of supply as a result of the despatch or transport: see *R (on the application of Teleos plc and others) v Customs and Excise Comrs* (case C-409/04) [2007] ECR I–7797, [2008] STC

706, The legislation does not require transport of the goods to be commenced or completed within any specific period. In principle, it is merely necessary to establish: (1) a temporal and material link between the supply of the goods and their transportation, and (2) continuity in the course of the transaction. However, as regards new means of transport, it is necessary to make an overall assessment of all the objective circumstances, and of the purchaser's intentions, on the basis of objective evidence which enables the envisaged member state of final use to be identified: see *X v Skatteverket* (case C-84/09) [2010] ECR I- 0000, [2011] STC 189 at [29], [33], [42]–[51]. For the charge to tax on the acquisition made in member state Y, see art 2(1)(b).

Goods acquired by a non-taxable legal person may be despatched or transported from a third territory (see art 5(3)) or third country (see art 5(4)) to member state X and then despatched or transported to member state Y. For the purposes of condition (1), the goods are regarded as having been despatched or transported from member state X. In consequence, the non-taxable person makes an acquisition in member state Y if conditions (2) and (3) are also met. The non-taxable person may be designated or regarded as the person liable to pay VAT in respect of the importation into member state X (see art 201). If so, he is entitled to a refund of the VAT paid on importation. However, he must establish that VAT has also been charged in respect of his acquisition in member state Y.

Article 21
(ex art 28a(6) (first para))

A taxable person may use goods for the purposes of his business. This is treated as an intra-Community acquisition of goods for consideration if:

- The goods were despatched or transported from another member state by, or on behalf of, the taxable person.
- The goods were either: (1) produced, extracted, processed, purchased or acquired in that member state; or (2) imported into that member state by the taxable person for the purposes of his business.

Article 22
(ex art 28a(6) (second para))

An appropriation of goods by the armed forces of a NATO member state is treated as an intra-Community acquisition of goods for consideration if:

- The goods were appropriated for the use of those armed forces or the civilian staff accompanying them.
- When purchased, the goods were not subject to the general rules governing taxation on the domestic market of a member state.
- An importation of the goods would not be eligible for exemption under art 143(1)(*h*).

Article 23
(ex art 28a(7))

Member states must take measures to ensure that a transaction – which would have been classified as a supply of goods if it had it been carried out within their territory by a taxable person acting as such – is classified as an intra-Community acquisition of goods.

CHAPTER 3—SUPPLY OF SERVICES

Article 24
(ex arts 6(1) (first para) and 9(2)(e) (tenth indent, second sentence))

1. A transaction is a supply of services if it does not constitute a supply of goods. For transactions constituting a supply of goods, see arts 14–19.

The term "supply of services" is objective in nature and applies without regard to the purpose or results of the transactions concerned: *Halifax plc and others v Customs and Excise Comrs* (case C-255/02) [2006] ECR I–1609, [2006] STC 919 at [56]. For the application of this principle to chains of transactions tainted by fraud or avoidance, see the commentary to art 2.

A supply consisting of both goods (or several goods) and various service elements may comprise a single transaction which must be classified as either a supply of goods or a supply of services in accordance with the principles summarised in the commentary to art 2 under the heading "one supply or two". For examples of a single transaction classified as a supply of services, see: (1) *Faaborg-Gelting Linien A/S v Finanzamt Flensburg* (case C-231/94) [1996] ECR I–2395, [1996] STC 774 (restaurant transactions); (2) *Levob Verzekeringen BV, OB Bank NV cs v Staatssecretaris van Financiën* (case C-41/04) [2005] ECR I–9433, [2006] STC 766 (granting a non-transferable licence of unlimited duration to use standard computer software, customising this software on the customer's computer and providing staff training, all of which were separately invoiced); (3) *Finanzamt Burgdorf v Manfred Bog; CinemaxX Entertainment GmbH & Co KG v Finanzamt Hamburg-Barmbek-Uhlenhorst; Lothar Lohmeyer v Finanzamt Minden; Fleischerei Nier GmbH & Co KG v Finanzamt Detmold* (joined cases C-497/09 C-499/09 C-501/09 C-502/09 [2011] ECR I–0000, [2011] STC 1221 (party catering service).

An undertaking given by a farmer to reduce potato production does not constitute a supply of services: it does not give rise to any consumption; there is no identifiable consumer; and there is no benefit capable of being regarded as a cost component of another person's activity in the commercial chain. Thus, compensation received in respect of the undertaking is outside the scope of VAT: *Landboden-Agrardienste GmbH & Co KG v Finanzamt Calau* (case C-384/95) [1997] ECR I–7387, [1998] STC 171 at [23]–[25]. A similar position arises in relation to an undertaking to cease milk production: see *Mohr v Finanzamt Bad Segeberg* (case C-215/94) [1996] ECR I–959, [1996] STC 328 at [20]–[23].

A taxable person (eg a tenant) does not make a supply of services merely because he pays, or undertakes to pay, the consideration due (eg rent) in respect of a supply of services (eg a letting of immovable property). However, a future tenant makes a supply of services for consideration if a landlord – taking the view that the presence of an anchor tenant in the building contained in the leased premises would attract other tenants – were to make a payment for the future tenant's undertaking to transfer his business to the building concerned: *Customs and Excise Comrs v Mirror Group plc* (case C-409/98) [2001] ECR I–7175, [2001] STC 1453 at [27].

For guarantees, see *Skandinaviska Enskilda Banken AB Momsgrupp v Skatteverket* (case C-540/09) [2011] ECR I–0000, [2011] STC 1125 at [18].

For the application of this provision, see Regulation (EU) No 282/2011 arts 8(machine assembled from parts provided by customer) and 9 (sale of option).

2. The term "telecommunications" is defined. For the place of supply of telecommunications services, see art 56(1)(*i*).

Article 25
(ex art 6(1) (second para))

A supply of services may include:

(a) An assignment of intangible property, whether or not it is the subject of a document establishing title.

(b) An obligation to refrain from an act, or to tolerate an act or situation.
For the cancellation of hotel reservations, see *Société thermale d'Eugénie-les-Bains v Ministère de l'Économie, des Finances et de l'Industrie* (case C-277/05) [2007] ECR I–6415, [2008] STC 2470 (deposit retained by hotelier does not amount to consideration for a supply made by the hotelier).

(c) Performing a service in pursuance of: (1) an order made by, or in the name of, a public authority, or (2) the law.

Article 26
(ex art 6(2))

1. The following are treated as supplies of services for consideration:

(a) The use of goods forming part of the assets of a business for:

- The private use of the taxable person.
- The private use of his staff.
- Non-business purposes.

VAT must have been wholly or partly deductible when the goods were acquired. This requirement avoids double taxation, which would be contrary to the principle of fiscal neutrality: *Finanzamt München III v Mohsche* (case 193/91) [1993] ECR I–2615, [1997] STC 19 at [9].

Input tax is not "wholly or partly deductible" if the asset was purchased from a non-taxable person: *Kühne v Finanzamt München III* (case 50/88) [1989] ECR 1925, [1990] STC 749 at [11].

Input tax is apportioned if goods are purchased partly for the purposes of an economic activity and partly for the purposes of a non-economic activity (see the commentary to art 173). Where an apportionment falls to be made, the non-business use does not give rise to a supply of services under this provision: see *Vereniging Noordelijke Land-en Tuinbouw Organisatie* (case C-515/07) [2009] ECR I–839, [2009] STC 935 at [34]–[38]. In effect, the non-business use is dealt with by way of a disallowance of input tax rather than by way of a charge to tax under this provision.

The purpose of this provision is to ensure equal treatment between taxable persons and final consumers: *Enkler v Finanzamt Homburg* (case C-230/94) [1996] ECR I–4517, [1996] STC 1316 at [35]. It is designed to prevent the non-taxation of business goods for private purposes and of services provided free of charge by a taxable person for private purposes: *Julius Fillibeck Söhne GmbH & Co KG v Finanzamt Neustadt* (case C-258/95) [1997] ECR I–5577, [1998] STC 513 at [25].

The phrase "use of goods" must be interpreted strictly. It is confined to use of the goods themselves: *Finanzamt München III v Mohsche* (case 193/91) [1993] ECR I–2615, [1997] STC 19 at [14]. Accordingly, services supplied by third parties for the purpose of maintaining or using goods are not covered by this provision if the taxable person is unable to deduct the input tax paid: *Enkler v Finanzamt Homburg* (case C-230/94) [1996] ECR I–4517, [1996] STC 1316 at [34].

The private use of immovable property is excluded from exemption under art 135(1)(l): *Seeling v Finanzamt Starnberg* (case C-269/00) [2003] ECR I–4101, [2003] STC 805.

A taxable person may rely on this provision before the courts of a member state in so far as it precludes: (1) taxation of the private use of business goods where the VAT on those goods was not wholly deductible; or (2) taxation of the private use of business goods from which VAT has already been deducted in so far as that use includes services which the taxable person received without deduction of input tax from third parties for the maintenance or use of the goods: *Kühne v Finanzamt München III* (case 50/88) [1989] ECR 1925, [1990] STC 749 at [27]; *Finanzamt München III v Mohsche* (case 193/91) [1993] ECR I–2615, [1997] STC 19 at [19].

Decision 2007/884/EC authorises the UK to derogate from this provision by providing that the private use of a leased or hired motor car does not amount to a supply of services for consideration for the purposes of that provision.

(b) Supplies of services carried out free of charge by the taxable person for:

- His own private use.
- The private use of his staff.
- Non-business purposes.

This provision prevents a taxable person or members of his staff from obtaining, free of tax, services provided by the taxable person for which a private individual would had to have paid: *Hotel Scandic Gåsabäck AB v Riksskatteverket* (case C-412/03) [2005] ECR I–743, [2005] STC 1311 at [23].

Part I VAT

No charge to tax arises under this head if consideration has been given for the private or non-business use: *Hotel Scandic Gåsabäck AB v Riksskatteverket* (case C-412/03) [2005] ECR I–743, [2005] STC 1311 at [24] (staff meals provided for a consideration below cost price).

Paragraphs (*a*) and (*b*) treat certain transactions (for which no consideration is actually received by the taxable person) as supplies of services effected for consideration. The purpose of these provisions is to ensure equal treatment between: (1) a taxable person who applies goods or services for his own private use or for that of his staff; and (2) a final consumer who acquires goods or services of the same type.

In principle, transport between home and workplace in a company vehicle provided free of charge for employees by an employer serves the employees' private purposes and thus serves purposes other than those of the business. However, this does not apply if, having regard to certain circumstances (eg difficulty of finding other suitable means of transport and changes in the place of work), the requirements of the business make it necessary for the employer to provide transport for employees. In this case, the supply of transport services is not effected for purposes other than those of the business. The same principle applies if, instead of transporting employees in his own vehicles, the employer commissions one of his employees to provide the transport using his own private vehicle: *Julius Fillibeck Söhne GmbH & Co KG v Finanzamt Neustadt* (case C-258/95) [1997] ECR I–5577, [1998] STC 513 at [34], [37].

The provision of canteen meals free of charge may be classified as an application for private use. However, a charge to VAT arises only if the provision of those meals is for non-business purposes. Free canteen meals for business contacts are not charged to VAT if they are provided in the course of a meeting held on company premises and objective evidence indicates that they are provided for strictly business-related purposes. In principle, free canteen meals for company staff are charged to VAT. However, no charge arises if the needs of the company (eg ensuring that work meetings run smoothly and without interruption) require that meals are provided: *Danfoss A/S and another v Skatteministeriet* (case C-371/07) [2008] ECR I–9549, [2009] STC 701 at [50], [53]–[63].

For the valuation of supplies in heads (*a*) and (*b*), see art 26.

2. Member states may derogate from the provisions in para 1(*a*) and (*b*) if this does not lead to distortion of competition.

As an exception to harmonisation, this power is defined strictly. Member states may refrain from treating certain supplies or uses as services supplied for consideration, eg in order to simplify administrative procedures relating to the collection of VAT: *Charles and another v Staatssecretaris van Financiën* (case C-434/03) [2005] ECR I–7037, [2006] STC 1429 at [26], [27]. However, member states may not: (1) provide for chargeable events which are not referred to in paras (*a*) or (*b*): *Cookies World Vertriebsgellschaft mbH v Finanzlandesdirektion für Triol* (case C-155/01) [2003] ECR I–8785, [2004] STC 1386 at [59]; (2) deny full and immediate deduction of input tax to traders who allocate mixed use goods wholly to business assets (see commentary to para (*a*) above): *Charles and another v Staatssecretaris van Financiën* (case C-434/03) [2005] ECR I–7037, [2006] STC 1429 at [28]; or (3) waive the charge in respect of the private or non-business use (see para (*a*) above) if the trader has been able to deduct in full the VAT incurred on his acquisition of the goods: *Charles and another v Staatssecretaris van Financiën* (case C-434/03) [2005] ECR I–7037, [2006] STC 1429 at [29]. For a detailed treatment of the relationship between arts 26(1)(*a*) and 168(*a*), see *Sandra Puffer v Unabhängiger Finanzsenat, Außenstelle Linz* (case C-460/07) [2009] ECR I–3251, [2009] STC 1693 at [39]–[62].

For the input tax consequences of changes to the proportion of business use of immovable property and goods specified by the member states, see art 168a(1) (second para) and (2). These provisions derogate from the provisions of this article.

Article 27
(ex art 6(3))

Member states may treat a service supplied by a taxable person for the purposes of his business as a supply of services if VAT on such a service would not be wholly deductible if it had been supplied by another taxable person. This may be done to prevent distortion of competition. It is subject to consultation with the VAT Committee (see art 398). For the right to deduct input tax, see art 167.

For the valuation of these supplies, see art 77.

Article 28
(ex art 6(4))

A taxable person acting in his own name, but on behalf of another person, may take part in a supply of services. If so, he is deemed both to receive and to supply those services.

This provision is not confined to taxable supplies of services. Thus, if a bookmaker (the principal) carries on his business through an agent who acts in his own name, the bookmaker makes a supply of betting services to the agent. The agent is deemed to receive betting services from the bookmaker and make a supply of betting services to the client (who makes the bet): *Belgian State v Henfling and others (acting as trustees in the insolvency of Tiercé Franco-Belge SA)* (case C-464/10) [2011] ECR I–0000 at [32]–[35] (agent acting in own name in accepting bets from clients and paying out winnings to them). For the exemption of betting services, see art 135(1)(i).

Article 29
(ex art 6(5))

Member states may consider that no supply of services takes place if a taxable person transfers all or part of his assets to another person. This applies whether or not there is a consideration for the transfer and whether or not the transfer takes place as a contribution to a company. The recipient is treated as the successor to the transferor. Member states may take measures to prevent distortion of competition in cases where the recipient is not wholly liable to tax.

For the right to deduct VAT incurred in connection with a transfer of assets, see the commentary to art 167.

CHAPTER 4—IMPORTATION OF GOODS

Article 30
(ex art 7(1))

As regards the UK, an "importation of goods" takes place if one or other of the following conditions is met:

- Goods which are not in free circulation enter the territory of the UK to which the EU Treaty applies.
- Goods in free circulation enter the territory of the UK to which the EU Treaty applies from a third territory forming part of the EU customs territory. The third territories concerned are listed in art 6(1).

  Goods entering the UK from the Channel Islands fall within this provision. The Channel Islands form part of the EU customs territory (see Regulation (EEC) No 2913/92 art 3; Protocol No 3 art 1 to the First Accession Treaty). They are also listed in art 6(1)(e). As such, they fall within the definition of "third territory" in art 5(3)).

  Goods entering the UK from the Isle of Man do not. Although the Isle of Man forms part of the EU customs territory (see Regulation (EEC) No 2913/92 art 3; Protocol No 3 art 1 to the First Accession Treaty), it is not listed in art 6 and is consequently outside the definition of "third territory" in art 5(3).

Goods are regarded as not having been imported into the EU if: (1) the goods are seized by the local customs or tax authorities on their introduiction into EU territory; and (2) the goods are simultaneously or subsequently destroyed by those authorities: *Dansk Transport og Logistik v Skatteministeriet* (case C-230/08) [2010] ECR I–0000, [2010] STC 1711.

The EU Treaty applies to the European territories for whose external relations the UK is responsible (see TFEU art 355(3)). These territories comprise the Channel Islands, Gibraltar, the Isle of Man and the Soverign Base Areas of Akrotiri and Dhekelia.

VAT does not apply to the Channel Islands (see art 6(1)(e)) and Gibraltar (see the Act of Accession (1972), art 28). The Isle of Man and the Soverign Base Areas are not regarded as third countries for VAT purposes (see art 7(1)). However, the UK is required to take the measures necessary to ensure that transactions intended for the Isle of Man are treated as transactions intended for the UK and that transactions intended for the Sovereign Base Areas are treated as transactions intended for Cyprus (see art 7(2)).

The EU Treaty does not apply to the following UK overseas countries and territories: Anguilla, Cayman Islands, Falkland Islands, South Georgia and the Sandwich Islands, Montserrat, Pitcairn, Saint Helena and Dependencies, British Antarctica Territory, British Indian Ocean Territory, Turks and Caicos Islands, British Virgin Islands, and Bermuda (see TFEU art 355(2) and Annex II).

For free circulation, see TFEU art 29.

TITLE V—PLACE OF TAXABLE TRANSACTIONS

CHAPTER 1—PLACE OF SUPPLY OF GOODS

SECTION 1—SUPPLY OF GOODS WITHOUT TRANSPORT

Article 31
(ex art 8(1)(b))

Where goods are not despatched or transported, the place of supply is the place where the goods are located when the supply takes place.

SECTION 2—SUPPLY OF GOODS WITH TRANSPORT

Article 32
(ex art 8(1)(a) (first sentence))

Where goods are despatched or transported by the supplier, the person to whom the goods are supplied or a third party, the place of supply is the place where the goods are located at the time when the despatch or transport begins.

However, if the despatch or transport begins in a third territory (as defined in art 5(3)) or third country (as defined in art 5(4)), the place of supply is the member state into which the goods are imported. This applies in relation to: (1) a supply made by the importer designated or recognised under art 201 as liable for payment of VAT; and (2) any subsequent supply.

A supply of goods by X to Y and an onward supply by Y to Z may give rise to a single intra-Community despatch, or single intra-Community transport, of the goods. If so, the single intra-Community movement of goods can be ascribed to only one of the two supplies. The place of that supply is deemed to be the member state of the departure of the despatch or transport (see art 31). As the other supply does not involve despatch or transport, the place of that supply is deemed to be the location of the goods when the supply takes place (see above). Thus, if the first of the two supplies (ie the supply by X to Y) is the one involving intra-Community despatch or transport, the second supply (ie the supply by Y to Z) is deemed to occur in the member state of arrival. Similarly, if the second of the two supplies (ie the supply by Y to Z) is the one involving intra-Community despatch or transport, the first supply (ie the supply by X to Y) is deemed to occur in the member state of that despatch or transport: *EMAG Handel Eder OHG v Finanzlandesdirecktion für Kärnten* (case C-245/04) [2006] ECR I–3227, [2007] STC 1461 (goods, which were in Italy or the Netherlands when supplied by X, despatched or transported to Z (or Z's customers) in Austria – in accordance with instructions given by Z to Y – by a forwarding agent engaged by Y).

For a derogation from this provision, see art 33.

Article 33
(ex art 28bB(1))

1. This provision applies in place of art 32 where goods are despatched or transported from member state X to member state Y by, or on behalf of, the supplier and the following conditions are met:

- The supply of goods is carried out for: (1) a taxable person or non-taxable legal person whose intra-Community acquisitions of goods are not chargeable to VAT by virtue of art 3(1); or (2) any other non-taxable person.
- The goods supplied are neither: (1) a new means of transport; nor (2) goods supplied after assembly or installation, with or without a trial run, by or on behalf of the supplier.

The place of supply of the despatched or transported goods is deemed to be the place where the goods are located when the despatch or transport to the customer ends.

For a derogation from this provision, see art 34 and Regulation (EU) No 282/2011 art 14.

2. The supplied goods are regarded as having been despatched or transported from the member state of importation if they were: (1) despatched or transported from a third territory (see art 5(3)) or third country (see art 5(4)); and (2) imported by the supplier into a member state other than the one in which despatch or transport to the customer ends.

Article 34
(ex art 28bB(2), (3))

1. The place of supply of goods not subject to excise duty is not determined in accordance with art 33 if the total value (excluding VAT) of goods despatched or transported to the same member state, being the member state in which despatch or transport of the goods ends, does not exceed:

- EUR 100,000 (or the equivalent in national currency) in the current calendar year.
- EUR 100,000 (or the equivalent in national currency) in the previous calendar year.

For the conversion of currency, see art 399.

For the place of supply where the relevant threshold is exceeded during a calendar year, see Regulation (EU) No 282/2011 art 14.

2. These thresholds may be reduced from EUR 100,000 to EUR 35,000 (or the equivalent in national currency) if the member state fears that the higher threshold would lead to a serious distortion of competition. A member state exercising this option must notify the relevant public authorities in the member state in which despatch or transport of the goods begins.

3. The Commission must prepare a report on the operation of the EUR 35,000 threshold and make any appropriate proposals.

4. The member state in which the despatch or transport begins must allow taxable persons to opt for the place of supply to be determined in accordance with art 33 rather than para 1. An option must remain in force for two calendar years. The detailed rules for exercising it are prescribed by the member states.

Article 35
(ex arts 26aD(c), 28o(1)(h))

Articles 33 and 34 do not apply to supplies of the following goods:

- Antiques (as defined in art 331(1)(4) and Annex IX Part C).

- Collectors' items (as defined in art 331(1)(3) and Annex IX Part B).
- Second-hand goods (as defined in art 331(1)(1)).
- Second-hand means of transport (as defined in art 327(3)) subject to VAT in accordance with the relevant special arrangements.
- Works of art (as defined in art 331(1)(2) and Annex IX Part A).

Article 36
(ex art 8(1)(a) (second and third sentences))

Where goods despatched or transported by the supplier, the person to whom the goods are supplied or a third party are installed or assembled, with or without a trial run, by or on behalf of the supplier, the place of supply is the place where the goods are installed or assembled (see below).

If the installation or assembly is carried out in another member state, that state must take any necessary steps to avoid double taxation in that state.

The "installation" of goods in the territory of one member state may continue into the territory of another member state, eg where a fibre-optic cable links two member states. Where this is so, each member state has the right to tax that part of the goods installed in its territory. The price is apportioned by reference to the length of the cable in each member state. The cable may cross international waters when linking two coastal member states. If so, the transaction is outside the scope of VAT in so far as it is carried out in the exclusive economic zone, on the continental shelf and at sea. For the purposes of apportionment in these circumstances, the territory of a member state extends to the limit of its territorial sea: *Aktiebolaget NN v Skatteverket* (case C-111/05) [2007] ECR I–2697, [2008] STC 3203.

SECTION 3—SUPPLY OF GOODS ON BOARD SHIPS, AIRCRAFT OR TRAINS

Article 37
(ex art 8(1)(c))

1. Where goods are supplied on board a passenger-carrying ship, aircraft or train, the place of supply in relation to the section of the journey within the Community is determined by reference to the "point of departure". For "the section of the journey within the Community", see para 2 and Regulation (EU) No 282/2011 art 15.

2. The section of the journey within the Community is measured as follows.

Suppose that the first scheduled point of passenger embarkation within the Community is at A. This is the first pick-up point in the Community (if the journey starts in the Community) or the first scheduled stopover in the Community involving passenger embarkation (if the journey starts outside the Community). Also suppose that the last scheduled point of disembarkation within the Community is X. This is either the place where the journey terminates or the last scheduled point of disembarkation before the journey continues outside the Community with a stopover at Y (a place outside the Community).

On this basis:

- Assume that the journey from A continues wholly within the Community or, if it leaves and re-enters the Community, it does so without a stopover, and that last scheduled point of disembarkation within the Community is X. The journey within the Community starts at A and ends at X. The "point of departure" is A. The place of supply for goods supplied during the journey A–X is therefore A.
- Assume that the journey from A continues outside the Community making a stopover at B (a place outside the Community), re-enters the Community making a stopover at C (a place in the Community, being the first scheduled point of passenger embarkation within the Community after the stopover at B) and that the last scheduled point of disembarkation within the Community is X. The journey within the Community starts at C and ends at X. The "point of departure" is C. The place of supply for goods supplied during the journey C–X is therefore C.

A ship entering port makes a stopover for the foregoing purposes if passengers may leave the ship, even for a short period, during the stay: *Köhler v Finanzamt Düsseldorf Nord* (case C-58/04) [2005] ECR I–8129, [2006] STC 469.

3. The Commission is required to submit a report to the Council on the place of taxation of:

- Goods supplied for consumption on board ships, aircraft or trains.
- Services (including restaurant services) provided for passengers on board ships, aircraft or trains.

If necessary, the report must be accompanied by appropriate proposals. Pending adoption of these proposals, member states may apply (or continue to apply) exemption with deduction to goods supplied for consumption on board ships, aircraft or trains where the place of supply is determined in accordance with para 1.

SECTION 4—SUPPLIES OF GAS THROUGH A NATURAL GAS SYSTEM, OF ELECTRICITY AND OF HEAT OR COOLING ENERGY THROUGH HEATING AND COOLING NETWORKS

Article 38
(ex art 8(1)(d))

1. As regards a supply of any of the following products to a taxable dealer, the place of supply is the place where the taxable dealer has established his business, the place where he has a fixed establishment for which the goods are supplied, or (in the absence of either) the place where he has his permanent address or usually resides:

- The supply of gas through a natural gas system situated within EU territory or any network connected to such a system.
- The supply of electricity.
- The supply of heat or cooling energy through heating or cooling networks.

For "permanent address", see Regulation (EU) No 282/2011 art 12. For the place where a person usually resides, see Regulation (EU) No 282/2011 art 13.

2. A "taxable dealer" is a taxable person whose principal activity in relation to purchases of gas, electricity, heat or cooling energy is reselling those products and whose consumption of those products is negligible.

Article 39
(ex art 8(1)(e))

The goods listed in art 38(1) may be supplied to a person who is not a taxable dealer (as defined in art 39(2)). Where this is so, the place of supply is the place where the customer effectively uses and consumes the goods.

The customer may not consume all or part of the gas, electricity, heat or cooling energy. Where this is so, the unconsumed goods are deemed to be used and consumed at the place where the customer has established his business, the place where he has a fixed establishment for which the goods are supplied, or (in the absence of either) the place where he has his permanent address or usually resides.

For "permanent address", see Regulation (EU) No 282/2011 art 12. For the place where a person usually resides, see Regulation (EU) No 282/2011 art 13.

CHAPTER 2—PLACE OF AN INTRA-COMMUNITY ACQUISITION OF GOODS

General note

The purpose of this Chapter is to transfer tax revenue to the member state in which final consumption of the goods supplied takes place: *EMAG Handel Eder OHG v Finanzlandesdirektion für Karnten* (case C-245/04) [2006] ECR I–3227, [2007] STC 1461 at [40]. For the application of this chapter, see Regulation (EU) No 282/2011 art 16.

Article 40
(ex art 28bA(1))

The place of an intra-Community acquisition of goods is the place where the despatch or transport of the goods to the person acquiring them ends.

The purpose of this provision is to transfer tax revenue to the member state in which the final consumption takes place. It does not determine which person effected the intra-Community supply: *Euro Tyre Holding BV v Staatssecretaris van Financiën* (case C-430/09) [2010] ECR I–0000, [2011] STC 798 at [43].

Article 41
(ex art 28bA(2) (first and second paras))

An intra-Community acquisition of goods within art 2(1)(*b*)(i) takes place in the territory of the member state which issued the VAT identification number used by the person acquiring the goods to make the acquisition. However, this does not apply if the person acquiring the goods establishes that VAT has been applied to the acquisition under art 40. For the disapplication of this provision, see art 42.

If the same intra-Community acquisition of goods has been charged to tax under both this provision and art 40, the taxable amount of the acquisition charged to tax under this provision is reduced accordingly.

Article 42
(ex art 28bA(2) (third para))

Article 41 (first para) is disapplied if the following conditions are met:

- The person acquiring the goods establishes that he made the intra-Community acquisition for the purposes of a subsequent supply.
- The place of this supply is the member state where the despatch or transport of the goods to him ended.
- The customer is the person liable for payment of the tax due on the supply in that member state in accordance with art 197.
- The person acquiring the goods has complied with his obligation to submit a recapitulative statement (see art 265).

In these circumstances, VAT is deemed to have been applied to the intra-Community acquisition in accordance with art 40.

CHAPTER 3—PLACE OF SUPPLY OF SERVICES

General note Chapter 3 is designed to secure the rational delimitation of the respective areas covered by national VAT rules by determining, in a uniform manner, the place where services are deemed to be provided for tax purposes: *Berkholz v Finanzamt Hamburg-Mitte-Altstadt* (case 168/84) [1985] ECR 2251, [1985] 3 CMLR 667 at [14].

Section 3 sets out a number of specific instances of places where certain services are deemed to be supplied. Section 2 lays down the general rule on the matter. The object of these provisions is to avoid: (1) conflicts of jurisdiction which may result in double taxation; and (2) non-taxation: *Berkholz v Finanzamt Hamburg-Mitte-Altstadt* (case 168/84) [1985] ECR 2251, [1985] 3 CMLR 667 at [14].

Section 2 does not take precedence over Section 3. In every situation, the question arising is whether it is covered by one of the instances mentioned in Section 3. If not, it falls within the scope of Section 2: *Dudda v Finanzamt Bergisch Gladbach* (case C-327/94) [1996] ECR I–4595, [1996] STC 1290 at [21].

For a situation where the place of supply was determined by reference to Section 2 rather than art 52 (as effective prior to 1 January 2010) in order to avoid conflicts of jurisdiction between member states, see *Commission v French Republic* (case C-429/97) [2001] ECR I–637, [2001] STC 156 (waste disposal).

Chapter 3 (comprising arts 43–59) was replaced by a new Chapter 3 (comprising arts 43–59b) with effect from 1 January 2010 by Directive 2008/8/EC art 2(1).

SECTION 1—DEFINITIONS

Article 43
(ex art 9(1))

In applying the rules relating to the place of supply of services, the rules identifying a person as a taxable person (see arts 9–13) are extended as follows:

- A taxable person may carry out activities or transactions which are not considered to be taxable supplies of goods or services. If so, he is regarded as a taxable person in respect of all services supplied to him.
- A non-taxable legal person may be identified for VAT purposes. If so, he is regarded as a taxable person.

For the identification of a customer as a taxable person or non-taxable person, see Regulation (EU) No 282/2011 art 17. For the circumstances in which the supplier may regard a customer as such a person, see Regulation (EU) No 282/2011 art 18. For the circumstances in which a person is regarded as a non-taxable person, see Regulation (EU) No 282/2011 art 19. For the time at which the place of supply is determined, see Regulation (EU) No 282/2011 art 25.

SECTION 2—GENERAL RULES

General note For cases decided under the general rule in force prior to 1 January 2010, see: (1) *Berkholz v Finanzamt Hamburg-Mitte-Altstadt* (case 168/84) [1985] ECR 2251, [1985] 3 CMLR 667 (installation of gaming machines on board a sea-going ship where the machines were maintained intermittently); (2) *Faaborg-Gelting Linien A/S v Finanzamt Flensburg* (case C-231/94) [1996] ECR I–2395, [1996] STC 774 (restaurant services on ferry service between Denmark and Germany); (3) *ARO Lease BV v Inspecteur der Belastingdienst Grote Ondernemingen, Amsterdam* (case C-190/95) [1997] ECR I–4383, [1997] STC 1272 and *Lease Plan Luxembourg SA v Belgium* (case C-390/96) [1998] ECR I–2553, [1998] STC 628 (leasing company with neither its own staff nor a structure with a sufficient degree of permanence in a member state to provide a framework in which agreements can be drawn up, and management decisions taken, so as to enable the services in question to be supplied on an independent basis).

Article 44
(ex art 9(1))

In principle, services supplied to a person ("X") acting as a taxable person (see art 43) are supplied at the place where X has established his business. However:

- X may have a fixed establishment in another place. If the services are provided to that establishment, the place of supply is the place where the establishment is located.
- X may have neither a fixed establishment nor a place where he has established his business. If so, the place of supply is the place where X has his permanent address or usually resides.

Member states may adopt the rules in art 59a(*a*), (*b*) in order to avoid double taxation, non-taxation or distortion of competition: see art 59a.

For the application of this article to the assignment of television broadcasting rights in respect of football matches, see Regulation (EU) No 282/2011 art 26.

For the application of this article to services consisting of applying for, or receiving, refunds of VAT under Directive 2008/9/EC, see Regulation (EU) No 282/2011 art 27.

For the application of this article to services made in the framework of organising a funeral, see Regulation (EU) No 282/2011 art 28.

For the application of this article to services comprising the translation of texts, see Regulation (EU) No 282/2011 art 29.

For the application of this article to the services of intermediaries in respect of the provision of accommodation, see Regulation (EU) No 282/2011 art 31(a).

For the place where a person has established his business, see Regulation (EU) No 282/2011 art 10. For "fixed establishment", see Regulation (EU) No 282/2011 art 11. For "permanent address", see Regulation (EU) No 282/2011 art 12. For the place where a person usually resides, see Regulation (EU) No 282/2011 art 13. For the location of a customer, see Regulation (EU) No 282/2011 arts 20–22.

Article 45

In principle, services supplied to a non-taxable person are supplied at the place where the supplier ("X") has established his business. However:

- X may have a fixed establishment in another place. If the services are provided to that establishment, the place of supply is the place where the establishment is located.
- X may have neither a fixed establishment nor a place where he has established his business. If so, the place of supply is the place where X has his permanent address or usually resides.

It appears that services are not deemed to be supplied from an establishment other than the place where the supplier has established his business unless that establishment is of a certain minimum size and both the human and technical resources necessary for the provision of the services are permanently present: cf *Berkholz v Finanzamt Hamburg-Mitte-Altstadt* (case 168/84) [1985] ECR 2251, [1985] 3 CMLR 667 at [18].

For the application of this article to services made in the framework of organising a funeral, see Regulation (EU) No 282/2011 art 28.

For the application of this article to services comprising the translation of texts, see Regulation (EU) No 282/2011 art 29.

For "fixed establishment", see Regulation (EU) No 282/2011 art 11. For "permanent address", see Regulation (EU) No 282/2011 art 12. For the place where a person usually resides, see Regulation (EU) No 282/2011 art 13.

Member states may adopt the rules in art 59a(*a*), (*b*) in order to avoid double taxation, non-taxation or distortion of competition: see art 59a.

SECTION 3—PARTICULAR PROVISIONS

General note This section is a rule of conflict which determines the place of taxation and, consequently, delimits the powers of the member states: *Ministre de l'Économie, des Finances et de l'Industrie v Gillian Beach Ltd* (case C-114/05) [2006] ECR I–2427, [2006] STC 1080 at [20]. Its overall purpose is to establish a special system for services provided between taxable persons where the cost of the services is included in the price of the goods: *Dudda v Finanzamt Bergisch Gladbach* (case C-327/94) [1996] ECR I–4595, [1996] STC 1290 at [23].

Subsection 1—Supply of services by intermediaries

Article 46

This article prescribes the place of supply rule for services rendered to a non-taxable person by an intermediary who acts in the name of another person, and on his behalf, in so doing. The place of supply is the place where the underlying transaction is supplied. The place of supply of the underlying transaction is determined in accordance with this directive.

For the application of this article to the services of intermediaries acting in the name and on behalf of the recipient of the service procured, see Regulation (EU) No 282/2011 art 30.

For the application of this article to the services performed by intermediaries acting in the name and on behalf of the recipient of the service procured, see Regulation (EU) No 282/2011 art 30.

For the application of this article to the services of intermediaries in respect of the provision of accommodation, see Regulation (EU) No 282/2011 art 31(b).

For a case decided under the place of supply rule in force prior to 1 January 2010, see: *Staatssecretaris van Financiën v Lipjes* (case C-68/03) [2004] ECR I–5879, [2004] STC 1592.

Subsection 2—Supply of services connected with immovable property

Article 47

The place of supply of services connected with immovable property is the place where the property is located. For this purpose, "services connected with immovable property" include:

- The services of estate agents and experts.
- The provision of accommodation in the hotel sector or in sectors having a similar function, eg holiday camps or sites developed for use as camping sites.
- The granting of rights to use immovable property.
- Services for preparing and co-ordinating construction works, eg the services of architects and firms providing on-site supervision.

One of the essential characteristics of "immovable property" is that it is attached to a specific part of the earth's surface. A piece of land which is permanently delimited can be classified as immovable proverty, even if it is under water: *Heger Rudi GmbH v Finanzamt Graz-Stadt* (case C-166/05) [2006] ECR I–7749, [2008] STC 2679 at [20]. For an example of immovable property, see *Heger Rudi GmbH v Finanzamt Graz-Stadt* (case C-166/05) [2006] ECR I–7749, [2008] STC 2679 at [21] (stretches of water to which fishing permits relate).

Services fall within this provision only if they have a sufficiently direct connection with immovable property: *Heger Rudi GmbH v Finanzamt Graz-Stadt* (case C-166/05) [2006] ECR I–7749, [2008] STC 2679 at [24]. For examples of services having such a connection, see: (1) *Heger Rudi GmbH v Finanzamt Graz-Stadt* (case C-166/05) [2006] ECR I–7749, [2008] STC 2679 (transmission of the right to fish by means of a transfer of fishing permits for valuable consideration); (2) *RCI Europe v R & C Comrs* (case C-37/08) [2009] ECR I–7533, [2009] STC 2407 (exchange of timeshare usage rights in overseas holiday accommodation).

For services supplied to each party on the exchange of timeshare usage rights in overseas holiday accommodation, see *RCI Europe v R & C Comrs* (case C-37/08) [2009] ECR I–7533, [2009] STC 2407 (place of supply governed by the location of the property in which the transferor relinquishes usage rights). For the rights acquired under a points scheme converted into hotel accommodation or temporary use of a property, see *Macdonald Resorts Ltd v Revenue and Customs Comrs* (case C-270/09) [2010] ECR I–0000, [2011] STC 412 (scheme operator's services performed at the place where the hotel or property is situated).

Subsection 3—Supply of transport

Article 48

The place of supply of passenger transport is the place where the transport takes place. This is proportionate to the distances covered.

As regards cross-frontier passenger transport on an all-inclusive basis, the requirement for the place of supply to be determined by "having regard to the distances covered" has the consequence that:

(1) a supply of transport services is deemed to be supplied in each member state; and

(2) the consideration for the supply deemed to be made in each member state is determined by apportioning the all-inclusive price on a pro rata basis by reference to the distances covered in each member state: *Reisebüro Binder GmbH v Finanzamt Stuttgart-Körperschaften* (case C-116/96) [1997] ECR I–6103, [1998] STC 604 at [14]–[18].

The only obligation placed on member states in relation to "transport services" is to tax services carried out within their territorial limits: *Commission v French Republic* (case C-30/89) [1990] ECR I–691 at [15].

Transport services between two points within the national territory of a member state may involve crossing international waters or air space without a stop in another member state. A member state may bring the whole journey within the charge to VAT: *Trans Tirreno Express Spa v Ufficio Provinciale IVA, Sassari* (case 283/84) [1986] ECR 231, [1986] 2 CMLR 100 (transport of goods and passengers between mainland Italy and Sardinia). However, it is not obliged to do so. A member state may confine the charge to VAT to those parts of the journey falling within its national territory and exclude the part(s) in international waters or air space: *Commission v French Republic* (case C-30/89) [1990] ECR I–691 at [17], [18] (air and sea transport between mainland France and Corsica). A similar situation applies in relation to sea voyages where the vessel does not put in at a foreign port: *Commission v Hellenic Republic* (case C-331/94) [1996] ECR I–2675, [1996] STC 1168 (round trips beginning and ending in the same member state).

Article 49

The place of supply of the transport of goods (other than an intra-Community transport of goods) to a non-taxable person is the place where the transport takes place. This is proportionate to the distances covered.

It appears that the requirement for the place of supply to be determined by "having regard to the distances covered" has the consequence that:

(1) a supply of transport services is deemed to be supplied in each member state; and
(2) the consideration for the supply deemed to be made in each member state is determined by apportioning the all-inclusive price on a pro rata basis by reference to the distances covered in each member state: cf *Reisebüro Binder GmbH v Finanzamt Stuttgart-Körperschaften* (case C-116/96) [1997] ECR I–6103, [1998] STC 604 at [14]–[18] in relaltion to passenger transport.

The only obligation placed on member states in relation to "transport services" is to tax services carried out within their territorial limits: *Commission v French Republic* (case C-30/89) [1990] ECR I–691 at [15].

Transport services between two points within the national territory of a member state may involve crossing international waters or air space without a stop in another member state. A member state may bring the whole journey within the charge to VAT: *Trans Tirreno Express Spa v Ufficio Provinciale IVA, Sassari* (case 283/84) [1986] ECR 231, [1986] 2 CMLR 100 (transport of goods and passengers between mainland Italy and Sardinia). However, it is not obliged to do so. A member state may confine the charge to VAT to those parts of the journey falling within its national territory and exclude the part(s) in international waters or air space: *Commission v French Republic* (case C-30/89) [1990] ECR I–691 at [17], [18] (air and sea transport between mainland France and Corsica). A similar situation applies in relation to sea voyages where the vessel does not put in at a foreign port: *Commission v Hellenic Republic* (case C-331/94) [1996] ECR I–2675, [1996] STC 1168 (round trips beginning and ending in the same member state).

For the place of supply of intra-Community transport of goods, see art 50.

Article 50

The place of supply of an intra-Community transport of goods (as defined in art 51 (first para)) to a non-taxable person is the place of departure (as defined in art 51). For an intra-Community transport of goods taking place over waters which do not form part of EU territory, see art 52.

Article 51

An "intra-Community transport of goods" is a transportation of goods from a place of departure in the territory of one member state to a place of arrival in the territory of another member state..

The "place of departure" for this purpose is the place where transportation of the goods actually begins, irrespective of the distance covered, in order to reach the place where the goods are located.

The "place of arrival" is the place where transport of the goods actually ends.

Article 52

Member states are not required to apply VAT to any part of an intra-Community transport of goods to non-taxable persons taking place over waters which do not form part of EU territory. For the extent of EC territory, see art 5.

Subsection 4—Supply of cultural, artistic, sporting, scientific, educational, entertainment and similar services, ancillary transport services valuations of and work on movable tangible property

Article 53

As regards supplies made to a taxable person, the place of supply of the following services is the place where those events actually take place:

- Admission to cultural, artistic, sporting, scientific, educational, entertainment or similar events (eg fairs and exhibitions).
- Ancillary services related to the admission.

For the terms "artistic", "sporting" and "entertainment", cf *Dudda v Finanzamt Bergisch Gladbach* (case C-327/94) [1996] ECR I–4595, [1996] STC 1290 at [25]; *Ministre de l'Économie, des Finances et de l'Industrie v Gillian Beach Ltd* (case C-114/05) [2006] ECR I–2427, [2006] STC 1080 at [19]; *RAL (Channel Islands) Ltd and others v Customs and Excise Comrs* (case C-452/03) [2005] ECR I–3947, [2005] STC 1025 at [32], [33].

For the application of this article to services of which the essential characteristics are the granting of the right of admission to an event, see Regulation (EU) No 282/2011 art 32.

For ancillary services, see Regulation (EU) No 282/2011 art 33.

Article 54

1. As regards supplies made to a non-taxable person, the place of supply of the following services is the place where the activities actually take place:

- Services relating to cultural, artistic, sporting, scientific, educational, entertainment or similar activities (eg fairs and exhibitions).
- Ancillary services relating to cultural, artistic, sporting, scientific, educational, entertainment or similar activities (eg fairs and exhibitions).
- Services of the organisers of cultural, artistic, sporting, scientific, educational, entertainment or similar activities.

No particular artistic or sporting level is required for an activity to fall within the terms "artistic", "sporting" and "entertainment": *Dudda v Finanzamt Bergisch Gladbach* (case C-327/94) [1996] ECR I–4595, [1996] STC 1290 at [25]; *Ministre de l'Économie, des Finances et de l'Industrie v Gillian Beach Ltd* (case C-114/05) [2006] ECR I–2427, [2006] STC 1080 at [19]. Indeed, "entertainment" and similar activities do not require any artistic input by the supplier. An activity falls within that description if the principal objective pursued by the supplier is the entertainment of his customers: *RAL (Channel Islands) Ltd and others v Customs and Excise Comrs* (case C-452/03) [2005] ECR I–3947, [2005] STC 1025 at [32], [33]. For an example of entertainment services, see *RAL (Channel Islands) Ltd and others v Customs and Excise Comrs* (case C-452/03) [2005] ECR I–3947, [2005] STC 1025 (provision of slot gaming machines in entertainment arcades).

"Similar activities" is a Community concept which must be interpreted uniformly in order to avoid instances of double taxation or non-taxation. An activity is regarded as "similar" if: (1) it includes features that are also present in the other categories of activity listed; and (2) in the light of the objective of this provision, those features provide justification for its application to those activities. The relevant features are: (1) the complex nature of the services concerned; (2) the services are provided for a number of different recipients in a variety of capacities; (3) the services are usually provided for specific events; and (4) it is generally easy to identify where the services are physically carried out: *Ministre de l'Économie, des Finances et de l'Industrie v Gillian Beach Ltd* (case C-114/05) [2006] ECR I–2427, [2006] STC 1080 at [18]– [24].

Services which do not constitute an artistic or entertainment activity are regarded as "ancillary services" if they are a prerequisite for its performance: *Dudda v Finanzamt Bergisch Gladbach* (case C-327/94) [1996] ECR I–4595, [1996] STC 1290 at [27]. For an example of ancillary services, see *Dudda v Finanzamt Bergisch Gladbach* (case C-327/94) [1996] ECR I–4595, [1996] STC 1290 (sound engineer).

2. As regards supplies made to a non-taxable person the place of supply of the following services is the place where the services are physically carried out:

- Ancillary transport activities, eg loading, unloading, handling and similar activities.
- Valuations of movable tangible property.

  The term "valuations" signifies examination of the physical condition or investigation of the authenticity of a good with a view to estimating its value, quantifying the work to be carried out or the extent of the damage sustained: *Maatschap M J M Linthorst, K G P Pouwels and J Scheres cs v Inspecteur der Belastingdienst/Ondenemingen Roermond* (case C-167/95) [1997] ECR I–1195, [1997] STC 1287 at [13]. For an example of services which do not comprise valuation, see *Maatschap M J M Linthorst, K G P Pouwels and J Scheres cs v Inspecteur der Belastingdienst/Ondenemingen Roermond* (case C-167/95) [1997] ECR I–1195, [1997] STC 1287 at [14] (veterinary surgeon).
- Work on tangible movable property.

  The phrase "work on movable tangible property" suggests purely physical action which, by its nature, is neither scientific nor intellectual: *Maatschap M J M Linthorst, K G P Pouwels and J Scheres cs v Inspecteur der Belastingdienst/Ondenemingen Roermond* (case C-167/95) [1997] ECR I–1195, [1997] STC 1287 at [16]. For an example of services which do not comprise work on movable tangible property, see *Maatschap M J M Linthorst, K G P Pouwels and J Scheres cs v Inspecteur der Belastingdienst/ Ondenemingen Roermond* (case C-167/95) [1997] ECR I–1195, [1997] STC 1287 at [18] (veterinary surgeon). For waste disposal, see *Commission v French Republic* (case C-429/97) [2001] ECR I–637, [2001] STC 156 (place of supply determined under art 9(1) in order to avoid conflicts of jurisdiction between member states).

  For assembling a machine from parts supplied by the customer, see Regulation (EU) No 282/2011 arts 32.

Subsection 5—Supply of restaurant and catering services

Article 55

In principle, the place of supply of restaurant and catering services is the place where the services are physically carried out. For "restaurant and catering services" see Regulation (EU) No 282/2011 art 6. For the exception to this rule, see art 57.

For the application of this article to restaurant and catering services supplied outside a section of a passenger transport operation effected within the Community, but on the territory of a member state, third country or third territory, see Regulation (EU) No 282/2011 art 36 (second para).

Subsection 6—Hiring of means of transport

Article 56

The place of supply of a short-term hiring of a means of transport is the place where the means of transport is actually put at the disposal of the customer. A hiring is "short-term" for this purpose if it involves continuous possession or use of the means of transport for no more than 90 days (in the case of vessels) or 30 days (in other cases).

For "means of transport", see Regulation (EU) No 282/2011 art 38. For the duration of a continuous possession or use of a means of transport, see Regulation (EU) No 282/2011 art 39. For the place where a means of transport is actually put at the disposal of the customer, see Regulation (EU) No 282/2011 art 40.

Member states may adopt the rules in art 59a(*a*), (*b*) in order to avoid double taxation, non-taxation or distortion of competition: see art 59a.

Subsection 7—Supply of restaurant and catering services for consumption on board ships, aircraft or trains

Article 57

The place of supply of restaurant and catering services is the point of departure of the passenger transport operation if the services are physically carried out on board a ship, aircraft or train during the section of a passenger transport operation effected within the Community. Three situations may be distinguished.

First, a passenger transport operation may be wholly confined to the territory of member state A. If so, the section of the passenger transport operation effected within the Community is the journey between: (1) the first scheduled point of embarkation; and (2) the last scheduled point of disembarkation. The point of departure is the first scheduled point of embarkation within the Community. As this is located in country A, all restaurant and catering services physically carried out on the journey are supplied in member state A.

Second, a passenger transport operation may begin in member state A and terminate in member state B. If so, the section of the passenger transport operation effected within the Community is the journey between: (1) the first scheduled point of embarkation in member state A; and (2) the last scheduled point of disembarkation in the member state B. The point of departure is first scheduled point of embarkation within the Community. As this is located in country A, all restaurant and catering services physically carried out on the journey are supplied in member state A.

Third, a passenger transport operation beginning in member state A and terminating in member state B may cross into, and stop in, a third country during the journey. If so, there are two separate sections of "a passenger transport operation effected within the Community": The first section ends at the last scheduled point of disembarkation within the Community before a stopover outside the Community. The second section begins at the first scheduled point of embarkation within the Community after a stopover outside the Community. Thus:

- The first section is the journey between: (1) the first scheduled point of embarkation in member state A; and (2) the last scheduled point of disembarkation in member state A. As the point of departure is located in country A, all restaurant and catering services physically carried out on this section are supplied in member state A.
- The second section is the journey between: (1) the first scheduled point of embarkation in member state B; and (2) the last scheduled point of disembarkation in member state B. As the point of departure is located in member state B, all restaurant and catering services physically carried out on this section are supplied in member state B.

In the case of a return trip, the return leg is regarded as a separate transport operation.

For the scope of this article, see Regulation (EU) No 282/2011 art 36 (first para).

For restaurant and catering services supplied outside a section of a passenger transport operation effected within the Community, but on the territory of a member state, third country or third territory, see the commentary to art 55.

For restaurant and catering services carried out within the Community partly during a section of a passenger transport effected within the Community and partly outside such a section but on the territory of a member state, see Regulation (EU) No 282/2011 art 37.

For "restaurant and catering services", see Regulation (EU) No 282/2011 art 6. For a "passenger transport operation effected within the Community", see Regulation (EU) No 282/2011 art 35.

Subsection 8—Supply of electronic services to non-taxable persons

Article 58

A taxable person may supply electronically supplied services to a non-taxable person. The place of supply is the place where the non-taxable person is established, the place where he has his permanent address, or the place where he usually resides if:

- The taxable person has established his business outside the Community, has a fixed establishment outside the Community from which the service is supplied, or (in the absence of such a place of business or fixed establishment) either has his permanent address outside the Community or usually resides outside the Community.
- The non-taxable person is established in a member state, has his permanent address in a member state, or usually resides in a member state.

The fact that the supplier and customer communicate via electronic mail does not of itself mean that the service supplied is an electronically supplied service.

For "electronically supplied services", see Anex II and Regulation (EU) No 282/2011 reg 7. For "permanent address", see Regulation (EU) No 282/2011 art 12. For the place where a person usually resides, see Regulation (EU) No 282/2011 art 13. For the manner in which the place where a non-taxable person is established, see Regulation (EU) No 282/2011 arts 23(2) and 24(2).

Subsection 9—Supply of services to non-taxable persons outside the Community

Article 59

This article prescribes the place of supply in relation to the following services:

(a) Transfers and assignments of copyrights, patents, licences, trademarks and similar rights. For the place of supply of an assignment of television broadcasting rights in respect of football matches, see Regulation (EU) No 282/2011 art 26.

(b) Advertising services.

The term "advertising services" is a Community concept. It must be interpreted uniformly in order to avoid double taxation or non-taxation resulting from conflicting interpretations. It necessarily entails the dissemination of a message intended to inform consumers of the existence of a product or service, and its qualities, with a view to increasing sales. It also includes: (1) a promotional activity involving the dissemination of such a message; and (2) any activity forming an inseparable part of an advertising campaign which thereby contributes to conveying the advertising message: *Commission v French Republic* (case C-68/92) [1993] ECR I–5881, [1997] STC 684 at [14], [16]–[19]. For examples of advertising services, see: (1) *Commission v French Republic* (case C-68/92) [1993] ECR I–5881, [1997] STC 684; (2) *Commission v Kingdom of Spain* (case C-73/92) [1993] ECR I–5997, [1997] STC 700; (3) *Commission v Grand Duchy of Luxembourg* (case C-69/92) [1993] ECR I–5907, [1997] STC 712.

The relevant factor is the nature of the services in question. Thus, this provision applies to both: (1) services supplied directly to the advertiser; and (2) services supplied to an intermediary who invoices them to the advertiser: *Syndicat des Producteurs Indépendants (SPI) v Ministère de l'Économie, des Finances et de l'Industrie* (case C-108/00) [2001] ECR I–2361, [2001] STC 523 at [19], [21]. It is irrelevant whether the advertiser produces goods or services in which the cost of the advertising services may be included: *Design Concepts SA v Flanders Expo SA* (case C-438/01) [2003] ECR I–5617, [2003] STC 912 at [28]. For examples of advertising services supplied to intermediaries, see: (1) *Syndicat des Producteurs Indépendants (SPI) v Ministère de l'Économie, des Finances et de l'Industrie* (case C-108/00) [2001] ECR I–2361, [2001] STC 523; (2) *Design Concepts SA v Flanders Expo SA* (case C-438/01) [2003] ECR I–5617, [2003] STC 912; (3) *Athesia Druck Srl v Ministero dell'Economia e delle Finanze and another* (case C-1/08) [2009] ECR I–1255, [2009] STC 1334.

(c) Services of consultants, engineers, consultancy firms, lawyers, accountants and other similar services, as well as data processing and the supplying of information. The only common feature of the disparate activities listed in this provision is that they all come under the heading of liberal professions: *Maatschap M J M Linthorst, K G P Pouwels and J Scheres cs v Inspecteur der Belastingdienst/Ondenemingen Roermond* (case C-167/95) [1997] ECR I–1195, [1997] STC 1287 at [20]. However, this provision refers to services, not professions. It is therefore necessary to consider whether the services at issue are among those principally and habitually carried out as part of the professions listed: *Bernd von Hoffmann v Finanzamt Trier* (case C-145/96) [1997] ECR I–4857, [1997] STC 1321 at [16]. For an example of the services of "engineers" and similar services, see (1) *Levob Verzekeringen BV, OB Bank NV cs v Staatssecretaris van Financiën* (case C-41/04) [2005] ECR I–9433, [2006] STC 766 at [38]–[40] (customising standard software); (2) *Kronospan Mielec sp zoo v Dyrektor Izby Skarbowej w Rzeszowie* (case C-222/09) [2010] ECR I–0000, [2011] STC 80 (research and development work relating to the environment and technology).

For an example of services which fall outside the concepts of "consultants" and "consultancy bureaux", see *Maatschap M J M Linthorst, K G P Pouwels and J Scheres cs v Inspecteur der Belastingdienst/Ondenemingen Roermond* (case C-167/95) [1997] ECR I–1195, [1997] STC 1287 at [14] (veterinary surgeon).

For examples of services which fall outside the concept of a "lawyer", see *Bernd von Hoffmann v Finanzamt Trier* (case C-145/96) [1997] ECR I–4857, [1997] STC 1321 (arbitrator); *Commission v Germany* (case C-401/06) [2007] ECR I–10609, [2008] STC 2906 (executor of a will).

The expression "other similar services" does not refer to some common feature of the disparate activities mentioned. It refers to services similar to those of each of those activities. A service is regarded as "similar" to one of those activities if both serve the same purpose: Bernd *von Hoffmann v Finanzamt Trier* (case C-145/96) [1997] ECR I–4857, [1997] STC 1321 at [20], [21]. For examples of services which are not "similar" services, see: (1) *Maatschap M J M Linthorst, K G P Pouwels and J Scheres cs v Inspecteur der Belastingdienst/Ondenemingen Roermond* (case C-167/95) [1997] ECR I–1195, [1997] STC 1287 at [14] (veterinary surgeon); (2) *Bernd von Hoffmann v Finanzamt Trier* (case C-145/96) [1997] ECR I–4857, [1997] STC 1321 (arbitrator).

For the application of this provision to services consisting of the translation of text supplied to a non-taxable person established outside the Community, see Regulation (EU) No 282/2011 art 41.

(d) Obligations to refrain from pursuing or exercising (in whole or in part): (1) a business activity; or (2) a right referred to in this article.

(e) Banking, financial, insurance and reinsurance transactions with the exception of the hire of safes.

For an example of services which do not amount to a "banking transaction", see *Swiss Re Germany Holding GmbH v Finanzamt München für Körperschaften* (case C-242/08) [2009] ECR I–10099, [2010] STC 189 at [30] (transfer of a portfolio of reinsurance contracts).

The terms "insurance transactions" and "reinsurance transactions" in this provision and in art 135(1)(a) are interpreted uniformily in order to avoid double taxation or non-taxation: *Swiss Re Germany Holding GmbH v Finanzamt München für Körperschaften* (case C-242/08) [2009] ECR I–10099, [2010] STC 189 at [31], [32].

An insurance transaction involves an insurer undertaking, in return for prior payment of a premium, to provide the insured, in the event of the materialisation of the risk covered, with the service agreed when the contract was concluded: *Swiss Re Germany Holding GmbH v Finanzamt München für Körperschaften* (case C-242/08) [2009] ECR I–10099, [2010] STC 189 at [34] For an example of services which do not amount to an insurance transaction, see *Swiss Re Germany Holding GmbH v Finanzamt München für Körperschaften* (case C-242/08) [2009] ECR I–10099, [2010] STC 189 (transfer of a portfolio of reinsurance contracts). See also art 135(a).

A reinsurance transaction is a tranaction whereby an insurer concludes a contract in which it undertakes to assume, in return for payment of a premium and within the confines of that contract, the debts resulting, for another insurer, from its undertakings in the insurance contracts which it concluded with its own policyholders: *Swiss Re Germany Holding GmbH v Finanzamt München für Körperschaften* (case C-242/08) [2009] ECR I–10099, [2010] STC 189 at [38] For an example of services which do not amount to a reinsurance transaction, see *Swiss Re Germany Holding GmbH v Finanzamt München für Körperschaften* (case C-242/08) [2009] ECR I–10099, [2010] STC 189 (transfer of a portfolio of reinsurance contracts). See also art 135(a).

For services supplied to an open-ended investment company, see *Banque Bruxelles Lambert SA (BBL) v Belgian State* (case C-8/03) [2004] ECR I–10157, [2004] STC 1643.

(f) The supply of staff.

(g) Hiring movable tangible property that does not comprise a means of transport. For the place of supply of a hiring out of means of transport, see art 56. For "means of transport", see Regulation (EU) No 282/2011 art 38.

(h) The provision of:

- access to a natural gas system situated within EU territory;
- access to any network connected to such a system;
- access to the electricity system;
- access to heating or cooling networks;
- transmission or distribution through these systems or networks; and
- other services directly linked thereto.

(i) Telecommunications services (as defined in art 24(2)).

For the circumstances in which the place of supply is determined in accordance with art 59a(*b*) rather than in accordance with this provision, see art 59b.

(j) Radio and television broadcasting services.

(k) Electronically supplied services. For the scope of this description, see Annex II and Regulation (EU) No 282/2011 reg 7. The fact that the supplier and customer communicate via electronic mail does not of itself mean that the service supplied is an electronically supplied service..

The foregoing services must be supplied to a non-taxable person within one of the following descriptions:

- He is established outside the Community (as defined in art 5(1)).
- He has his permanent address outside the Community.
- He usually resides outside the Community.

For persons carrying on both an economic activity and an activity outside the scope of this directive, cf *Kollektivavtalssiftelsen TRR Trygghetsrådet v Skatteverket* (case C-291/07) [2008] ECR I–8255, [2009] STC 526 (taxable person receiving consultancy services used for non-business purposes).

In principle, the place of supply is:

- The place (if any) where the customer has established his business.
- The place (if any) where the customer has a fixed establishment to which the service is supplied.
- (In other cases) the place where the customer has his permanent address or usually resides.

However, subject to an exception in relation to electronically supplied services (see point (k) above), member states may adopt the rules in art 59a(*a*), (*b*) in order to avoid double taxation, non-taxation or distortion of competition: see art 59a. Member states must apply the rule in art 59a(*b*) in relation to telecommunication services (see point (*i*) above) and radio and television services (see point (j) above) supplied in specified circumstances: see art 59b.

For "permanent address", see Regulation (EU) No 282/2011 art 12. For the place where a person usually resides, see Regulation (EU) No 282/2011 art 13. For the manner in which the place where a non-taxable person is established, see Regulation (EU) No 282/2011 arts 23(2) and 24(2).

Subsection 10—Prevention of double taxation or non-taxation

Article 59a

Member states may adopt a different place of supply in order to avoid double taxation, non-taxation or the distortion of competition. In principle, they may do so in relation to any or all of the following services:

- The services listed in arts 44, 45, 56 and 59.
- The hiring out of means of transport.

However, this option does not apply in relation to electronically supplied services (see art 59(k)) rendered to a non-taxable person who is not established within the Community. For the mandatory requirement in respect of telecommunications services (see art 59(i)) and radio and television services (see art 59(j)) in specified circumstances, see art 59b.

If a member states applies this option, the place of supply is determined as follows:

	Circumstances	*Place of supply under arts 44, 45, 56 or 57*	*Substituted place of supply*
(*a*)	Effective use and enjoyment of the services takes place outside the Community	Within the territory of the member state	Outside the Community
(*b*)	Effective use and enjoyment of the services takes place within the territory of the country	Outside the Community	Within the territory of the member state

As regards advertising services, the country within which the effective use and enjoyment of the services takes place is the country from which the advertising material is disseminated: *Athesia Druck Srl v Ministero dell'Economia e delle Finanze and another* (case C-1/08) [2009] ECR I–1255, [2009] STC 1334 at [29].

Article 59b

Member states must apply the place of supply rule in art 59a(*b*) to telecommunications services (see art 59(i) and radio and television broadcasting services (see art 59(j)) if:

- The services are supplied by a taxable person who has: (1) established his business outside the Community; (2) has a fixed establishment outside the Community from which the service is supplied; or (3) (in other cases) has his permanent address or usually resides outside the Community.
- The services are supplied to a non-taxable person who is established in a member state, has his permanent address in a member state, or usually resides in a member state.

For "permanent address", see Regulation (EU) No 282/2011 art 12. For the place where a person usually resides, see Regulation (EU) No 282/2011 art 13.

CHAPTER 4—PLACE OF IMPORTATION OF GOODS

Article 60
(ex art 7(2))

In principle, when goods enter the territory of a member state (see art 5(2)) from a third country (see art 5(4)), the place of importation is that member state. For the exceptions, see art 61.

Article 61
(ex art 7(3))

Goods may enter the Community from a third country and be placed under one of the arrangements listed below, rather than being placed in free circulation, and may subsequently cease to be covered by those arrangements. Where this is so, the place of importation is determined by reference to the location of the goods when the relevant arrangement ceases to apply.

The arrangements referred to are as follows:

- The arrangements or situations listed in art 156.
- Temporary importation arrangements with total exemption from import duty.
- External transit arrangements. For the member state in which goods cease to be covered by these arrangements, see *Liberexim BV v Staatssecretaris van Financiën* (case C-371/99) [2002] ECR I–6227 (goods placed on the Community market after a number of irregularities had been committed in various member states).

Similarly, goods in free circulation on entry into the Community may be placed under one of the arrangements or situations listed in arts 276, 277 and may subsequently cease to be covered by those arrangements or situations. Where this is so, the place of importation is determined by reference to the location of the goods when the relevant arrangement or situation ceases to apply.

TITLE VI—CHARGEABLE EVENT AND CHARGEABILITY OF VAT

General note This Title confers rights on which individuals may rely in national courts in order to oppose incompatible national rules: *Balocchi v Ministero delle Finanze dello Stato* (case C-10/92) [1993] ECR I–5105, [1997] STC 640 at [35].

CHAPTER 1—GENERAL PROVISIONS

Article 62
(ex art 10(1))

The following definitions apply for the purposes of this directive:

(1) A "chargeable event" takes place when the legal conditions necessary for tax to become chargeable are fulfilled.

(2) VAT becomes "chargeable" when the tax authority becomes legally entitled to claim it from the person liable to pay. This applies whether or not the time of payment has been deferred.

CHAPTER 2—SUPPLY OF GOODS OR SERVICES

Article 63
(ex art 10(2) (first para, first sentence))

The chargeable event occurs when goods or services are supplied. VAT becomes chargeable at the same time.

For the power to derogate from this provision, see art 66.

Article 64*
(ex art 10(2) (first para, second and third sentences))

1. A supply of goods or services giving rise to successive statements of account or successive payments is regarded as being completed on expiry of the periods to which the statements of account or payments relate.

However, this provision does not apply to a supply of goods consisting of: (1) the hire of goods for a certain period; or (2) the sale of goods on deferred terms (as to which see art 14(2)(*b*)). For other circumstances in which this provision does not apply, see art 67 (second para).

For the power to derogate from this provision, see para 2 and art 66.

2. Goods may be despatched or transported from member state X to member state Y under a continuous supply which is exempt from VAT under art 138. If the period of supply spans two or more calendar months, the supply is regarded as being completed on the expiry of each calendar month until the supply comes to an end.

Goods may be transferred from member state X to member state Y by a taxable person for the purposes of his business under a continuous supply which is exempt from VAT. If the period of supply spans two or more calendar months, the supply is regarded as being completed on the expiry of each calendar month until the supply comes to an end. For the circumstances in which the transfer amounts to a supply of goods, see art 17. For the exemption, see art 138(2)(c).

Services supplied continuously over a period of more than one year are regarded as being completed on the expiry of each calendar year until such time as the supply of services comes to an end if:

- VAT on the supply is payable by the customer in accordance with art 196.
- The supply does not give rise to statements on account or payments during that period.

In other cases, member state may provide that a continuous supply of goods or services is deemed to be completed at intervals of one year or less. For circumstances in which this provision does not apply, see art 67 (second para).

Article 65
(ex art 10(2) (second para))

Where a payment on account is to be made before the goods or services are supplied, VAT becomes chargeable on receipt of the payment by reference to the amount received. For the circumstances in which this provision does not apply, see art 67 (second para).

For the power to derogate from this provision, see art 66.

Article 66*
(ex art 10(2) (third para))

Member states may derogate from arts 63–65 by providing that, in relation to certain transactions or certain categories of taxable person, that VAT become chargeable at one of the following times:

(a) No later than the time when an invoice is issued.

(b) No later than the time when a payment is received.
This provision is construed strictly. The following conditions must be met: (1) all relevant information regarding future delivery of the goods, or future performance of the services, must already be known; and (2) the goods or services must have been precisely identified at the time when the payment is made. Thus, payments on account of supplies of goods or services that have not yet been clearly identified are not subject to VAT: *BUPA Hospitals Ltd and another v Customs and Excise Comrs* (case C-419/02) [2006] ECR I–1685, [2006] STC 967 at [45], [48], [50].

(c) (Where an invoice is not issued, or it is issued late) within a specified time. The specified time must be no later than expiry of the time limit for the issue of invoices fixed by the member states in accordance with art 222 (second para). A member state may not have fixed a time limit for the issue of invoices. Where this is so, VAT becomes chargeable within a specified period from the date of the chargeable event.

Member states are not required to lay down a "specified period", even where the price has not yet been received. Nor are they required to lay down detailed rules for documenting and recording the completion of a service and the payment for it: *Ufficio IVA di Trapani v Italittica SpA* (case C-144/94) [1995] ECR I–3653 [1995] STC 1059 at [24], [28].

This provision does not apply to: (1) a supply of services where the VAT is payable by the customer in accordance with art 196; (2) an exempt supply of goods despatched or transported from one member state to another; and (3) an exempt transfer of goods from one member state to another by a taxable person for the purposes of his business. For exemption in respect of heads (2) and (3), see art 138.

It appears that member states may apply this derogation to all transactions, or to all transactions by certain categories of taxable person: *Ufficio IVA di Trapani v Italittica SpA* (case C-144/94) [1995] ECR I–3653 [1995] STC 1059 (tax chargeable by reference to the time when the price is received prescribed in relation to all supplies of services).

Article 67*
(ex art 28d(4))

The following provisions apply to: (1) an exempt supply of goods despatched or transported from one member state to another; and (2) an exempt transfer of goods from one member state to another by a taxable person for the purposes of his business. For exemption in respect of these supplies and transfers, see art 138.

First, if an invoice has been issued in respect of the supply or transfer, VAT becomes chargeable when the invoice is issued. However, if no invoice has been issued by the fifteenth day of the month following that in which the chargeable event occurs, VAT becomes chargeable on that day.

Second, the following provisions of this directive do not apply to the supply or transfer: arts 64(1), 64(2) (third para) and 65.

CHAPTER 3—INTRA-COMMUNITY ACQUISITION OF GOODS

Article 68
(ex art 28d(1))

The chargeable event occurs when an intra-Community acquisition of goods is made. This is the time when a supply of similar goods within the territory of the member state is regarded as being made.

Article 69*
(ex art 28d(2), (3))

This provision applies to an intra-Community acquisition of goods. If an invoice has been issued in respect of the acquisition, VAT becomes chargeable when the invoice is issued. However, if no invoice has been issued by the fifteenth day of the month following that in which the chargeable event occurs, VAT becomes chargeable on that day.

CHAPTER 4—IMPORTATION OF GOODS

Article 70
(ex art 10(3) (first para, first sentence))

The chargeable event occurs when the goods are imported. VAT becomes chargeable at the same time.

Article 71
(ex art 10(3) (first para, second sentence) and 10(3) (second para))

1, 2. This article prescribes the time when the chargeable event takes place, and the time when VAT becomes chargeable, in the following circumstances:

Circumstances	*Time*
• Goods are placed under one of the arrangements or situations listed in arts 156, 276, 277 on entry into the Community	Time when the goods cease to be covered by the relevant arrangement or situation
• Imported goods subject to customs duties, agricultural levies or charges having equivalent effect established under a common policy	Time when the chargeable event for those duties occurs, and the duties become chargeable
• Other imported goods	Time applicable under the provisions in force governing customs duties as regards the occurrence of the chargeable event and the moment when duty becomes chargeable

TITLE VII—TAXABLE AMOUNT

General note For the interpretation of this Title in relation to payments accepted by credit cards and debit cards, see Regulation (EU) No 282/2011 art 42.

Chapter 1 is incorrectly titled “Chapter 4—Importation of goods” in the text of this directive.

CHAPTER 1—DEFINITION

Article 72
(ex art 11A(7))

For the purposes of this directive, “open market value” is the full amount that a customer at the marketing stage at which the supply takes place would have to pay – to a supplier at arm’s length within the territory of the member state (as defined in art 5(2)) at the time of supply under conditions of fair competition – in order to obtain the relevant goods or services.

In the absence of a comparable supply, “open market value” is:

- As regards goods, an amount (determined at the time of supply) that is not less than the purchase price of the goods, the purchase price of similar goods, or (in the absence of a purchase price) the cost price.
- As regards services, not less than the full cost incurred by the taxable person in providing them.

CHAPTER 2—SUPPLY OF GOODS OR SERVICES

General note For modifications to the rules in this Chapter, see arts 308 (supplies under the special scheme for travel agents) and 315, 336 (supplies under the special scheme for second-hand goods, works of art, collectors’ items and antiques).

Chapter 2 confers rights on individuals on which they may rely before national courts: *BP Supergas Anonimos Etairia Geniki Emporiki-Viomichaniki kai Antiprossopeion v Greece* (case C-62/93) [1995] ECR I–1883, [1995] STC 805 at [35].

For examples of national legislation amounting to an unauthorised derogation from the provisions arts 73, 78, 79, see: (1) *Commission v Kingdom of Belgium* (case 324/82) [1984] ECR 1861, [1985] 1 CMLR 364; (2) *Direct Cosmetics Ltd v Customs and Excise Comrs* (case 5/84) [1985] ECR 617, [1985] STC 479; (3) *"K" Line Air Service Europe BV v Eulaerts NV and Belgian State* (case C-131/91) [1992] ECR I–4513, [1996] STC 597; (4) *BP Supergas Anonimos Etairia Geniki Emporiki-Viomichaniki kai Antiprossopeion v Greece* (case C-62/93) [1995] ECR I–1883, [1995] STC 805.

For examples of national legislation which did not, see: (1) *Commission v Kingdom of the Netherlands* (case 16/84) [1985] ECR 2355, [1986] 1 CMLR 336; (2) *Commission v Ireland* (case 17/84) [1985] ECR 2375, [1986] 1 CMLR 33; (3) *Direct Cosmetics Ltd v Customs and Excise Comrs; Laughtons Photographs Ltd v Customs and Excise Comrs* (Joined cases 138/86 and 139/86) [1988] ECR 3937, [1988] STC 540.

For derogations currently in force in relation to the UK, see:

- Authorisation (10 December 1986). This authorises the UK to apportion supplies of long-stay hotel accommodation between an exempt supply (comprising a letting of immoveable property) and other services on a flat-rate basis.
- Decision 89/534/EEC. This authorises the UK to substitute open market value in relation to supplies made through unregistered sellers.

For a simplification measure retained by the UK in relation to the taxable amount of supplies by retailers, see Appendix 1

Article 73
(ex art 11A(1)(a))

In principle, the taxable amount for a supply of goods or services is everything which constitutes the consideration which has been, or is to be, obtained by the supplier from the customer or a third party. This includes subsidies directly linked to the price of the supply. For the inclusion of charges for accepting payment by credit card or debit card, see Regulation (EU) No 282/2011 reg 42.

For examples of "everything which constitutes the consideration", see: (1) *Commission v French Republic* (case C-404/99) [2001] ECR I–2667 (restaurant services charges form part of the taxable amount even if shared out in full between staff members having direct contact with customers); (2) *Keeping Newcastle Warm Ltd v Customs and Excise Comrs* (case C-353/00) [2002] ECR I–5418, [2002] STC 943 (payment by grant-making body in respect of energy advice given to eligible householders).

To be regarded as consideration for a supply of goods or services, a "subsidy" must be paid for the specific purpose of enabling the subsidised body to provide particular goods or services. It is insufficient for a subsidy to do no more than affect the cost of the goods or services supplied by covering part of the subsidised body's running costs. Purchasers of the goods or services must benefit from the subsidy granted to the subsidised body. Thus, the price payable by purchasers must be fixed in such a way as to diminish in proportion to the subsidy granted and thereby consititute an element determining the price demanded by the subsidised body. Payment of the subsidy must allow the subsidised body to sell the goods or services at a price lower than it would otherwise have to demand. The consideration represented by the subsidy must, at the very least, be identifiable. It is not necessary for there to be an exact correlation between the subsidy and the diminuition in price. It is sufficient for the relationship to be significant: *Office des Produits Wallons ASBL v Belgian State* (case C-184/00) [2001] ECR I–9115, [2001] STC 1100 at [12]–[14], [17].

For subsidies that did not meet these tests, see: (1) *Commission v Italy* (case C-381/01) [2004] ECR I–6845; (2) *Commission v Finland* (case C-495/01) [2004] ECR I–6889; (3) *Commission v Germany* (case C-144/02) [2004] ECR I–6985; (4) *Commission v Sweden* (case C-463/02) [2004] ECR I–7335. For subsidies linked to transactions that did not amount to a supply, see *Mohr v Finanzamt Bad Segeberg* (case C-215/94) [1996] ECR I–959, [1996]

STC 328 (undertaking to discontinue milk production); *Landboden-Agrardienste GmbH & Co KG v Finanzamt Calau* (case C-384/95) [1997] ECR I–7387, [1998] STC 171 (reduction in annual potato production).

Consideration is a subjective value, ie the value actually received and not a value estimated according to objective criteria. It must also be capable of being expressed in money: *Julius Fillibeck Söhne GmbH & Co KG v Finanzamt Neustadt* (case C-258/95) [1997] ECR I–5577, [1998] STC 513 at [13], [14] and the cases cited therein. For an example of a provision of services for which there was no definite subjective value, see *Staatssecretaris van Financiën v Coöperatiëve Aardappelenbewaarplaats GA* (case 154/80) [1981] ECR 445, [1981] 3 CMLR 337 (cooperative waiving storage charges).

There must be a direct link between the goods supplied and the "consideration" received: *Naturally Yours Cosmetics v Customs and Excise Comrs* (case 230/87) [1988] ECR 6365, [1988] STC 879 at [11], [12]. It follows that the determining factor is the existence of an agreement between the parties for reciprocal performance, the payment received by one being the real and effective counter-value for the goods furnished to the other: *Chaussures Bally SA v Belgian State* (case C-18/92) [1993] ECR I–2871, [1997] STC 209 at [15].

That the basis of assessment is the consideration actually received is one of the fundamental principles of the Sixth Directive. The corollary is that the tax authorities may not, in any circumstances, charge an amount of VAT exceeding the tax paid by the taxable person: *Goldsmiths (Jewellers) Ltd v Customs and Excise Comrs* (case C-330/95) [1997] ECR I–3801, [1997] STC 1073 at [15].

The "consideration actually received" is the remuneration which the trader can actually take for himself: *H J Glawe Spiel-und Unterhaltungsgeräte Aufstellungsgesellschaft mbH & Co KG v Finanzamt Hamburg-Barmbek-Uhlenhorst* (case C-38/93) [1994] ECR 1-1679, [1994] STC 543 at [9]. This remuneration is the amount due (if the amount is freely at the trader's disposal) or a net amount after deduction of outgoings (in other cases). Contrast *Town and County Factors Ltd v Customs and Excise Comrs* (case C-498/99) [2002] ECR 1–7173, [2002] STC 1263 (entry fee to prize competition) and *H J Glawe Spiel-und Unterhaltungs-geräte Aufstellungsgesellschaft mbH & Co KG v Finanzamt Hamburg-Barmbek-Uhlenhorst* (case C-38/93) [1994] ECR 1-1679, [1994] STC 543 (gaming machine where a statutory percentage of the takings was withheld for prizes).

It is inappropriate to draw general conclusions from the taxation of gambling transactions in order to apply them to the taxation of ordinary supplies of goods: *Freemans plc v Customs and Excise Comrs* (case C-86/99) [2001] ECR I–4167, [2001] STC 960 at [30]. It is therefore necessary to distinguish situations where the consideration for a supply made by X to Y is discharged by a "third party" ("Z"). X may receive a smaller sum that the price agreed with the Y. This deduction may comprise the consideration for a supply made by Z to X. This deduction is disregarded in determining the taxable amount of the supply made by X. The taxable amount of this supply is therefore the price agreed with Y, not the amount received from Z. For examples, see: (1) *Chaussures Bally SA v Belgian State* (case C-18/92) [1993] ECR I–2871, [1997] STC 209 (credit card transaction); (2) *Primback Ltd v Customs and Excise Comrs* (case C-34/99) [2001] ECR I–3833, [2001] STC 803 (sale on "intrest-free credit" where interest on a loan made by Z to Y was deducted from the consideration for the supply made by X to Y remitted by Z to X).

The "consideration actually received" may comprise the overall result of the trader's transactions over a given period of time: *Customs and Excise Comrs v First National Bank of Chicago* (case C-172/96) [1998] ECR I–4387, [1998] STC 850 at [47]. For an example, see *Customs and Excise Comrs v First National Bank of Chicago* (case C-172/96) [1998] ECR I–4387, [1998] STC 850 (foreign exchange transactions where no fee or commission is charged on individual transactions).

In practice, a "subjective value" capable of being expressed in money normally comprises a sum of money agreed between the parties. The agreement may specify a specific sum. If so,

Part I VAT

subjective value (and therefore the taxable amount) is the sum so specified. However, it may be necessary to take account of money sums passing in different directions. This is so, for example, in relation to "money off" coupons where the costs of the promotion were borne by the manufacturer. Here, the taxable amount of the goods supplied by the retailer is the aggregate of: (1) cash received from the customer (ie the difference between the retail price of the goods and the face value of the coupon surrendered by the customer); and (2) cash received from the manufacturer (ie an amount equal to face value of the coupons accepted from customers and surrendered to the manufacturer): *Boots Co plc v Customs and Excise Comrs* (case C-126/88) [1990] ECR I–1235, [1990] STC 387. The taxable amount of the goods supplied by the manufacturer is the difference between: (1) the sale price paid by the wholesaler; and (2) the cash paid to retailers in respect of the coupons surrendered by them: *Elida Gibbs Ltd v Customs and Excise Comrs* (case C-317/94) [1996] ECR I–5339, [1996] STC 1387 at [28], [29]. A similar situation arises in respect of "cash back" coupons where the costs of the promotion are borne by the manufacturer. The taxable amount of the goods supplied by the manufacturer is the difference between: (1) the sale price paid by the wholesaler; and (2) the cash refunded to consumers in respect of the coupons surrendered by them: *Elida Gibbs Ltd v Customs and Excise Comrs* (case C-317/94) [1996] ECR I–5339, [1996] STC 1387 at [28], [29]. The VAT charged by manufacturers to wholesalers is not disturbed in respect of either "money off" or "cash back" coupons: *Elida Gibbs Ltd v Customs and Excise Comrs* (case C-317/94) [1996] ECR I–5339, [1996] STC 1387 at [33]. The foregoing position was confirmed in *Commission v Germany* (*United Kingdom intervening*) (case C-427/98) [2002] ECR I–8315, [2003] STC 301; *Yorkshire Co-operatives Ltd v Customs and Excise Comrs* (case C-398/99) [2003] ECR I–427, [2003] STC 234. For "money off" coupons where the costs of the promotion are borne by the retailer, see para 3 below.

The overall agreement between the parties may specify separate sums from which the agreed sum can be calculated. For example, a trader ("X") may supply goods or services to another person ("Y") for a money consideration below the normal price as an inducement for Y to perform some service. It is necessary to ascertain the subjective value of the supplies made by X and Y. As regards the supply made by Y, this is the difference between: (1) the normal price; and (2) the money consideration paid. As regards the supply made by X, this is the normal price, ie the aggregate of: (1) the money consideration paid by Y; and (2) the subjective value of the service performed by Y: *Naturally Yours Cosmetics v Customs and Excise Comrs* (case 230/87) [1988] ECR 6365, [1988] STC 879 at [17], [18] (inducement for Y to procure another person to arrange a gathering at which goods supplied by X are sold to members of the public at the normal price). For the taxable amount in foreign exchange transactions, see *Customs and Excise Comrs v First National Bank of Chicago* (case C-172/96) [1998] ECR I–4387, [1998] STC 850.

All or part of the consideration for a supply of goods or services may be discharged by tendering a face value voucher. For example, a consideration of £56 maybe discharged by tendering one or more vouchers with a face value of £50 and cash of £6. Face value vouchers sold by X (the issuer) may be used in payment or part payment for goods or services purchased from X, from Y (one or more other traders) or from either X or Y according to the terms of the scheme. As regards vouchers which can be used only in connection with purchases from X, it is necessary to determine the subjective value of the vouchers tendered. This is the sum of money received when the voucher was issued, ie £50 (if the voucher was sold at face value) or £47.50 (if it was sold at a 5% discount): *Argos Distributors Ltd v Customs and Excise Comrs* (case C-288/94) [1996] ECR I–5311, [1996] STC 1359 at [18]–[23]. For "money-off" vouchers, see the commentary to art 79. For customer loyalty reward schemes, see *Revenue and Customs Comrs v Loyalty Management UK Ltd and Baxi Group Ltd* (joined cases C-53/09 and C-55/09) [2010] ECR I–0000, [2010] STC 2651.

A different approach is necessary if a sum of money is neither specified nor capable of calculation by reference to other sums. For example, a mail order trader ("X") may supply an article without extra charge to a person ("Y") who introduces himself or another person as a potential new customer. There is a direct link between the supply of the article and the introduction of a potential customer because no article is supplied unless an introduction is made. Subjective value is the value which X – the recipient of the service – attributes to the service provided by Y. This corresponds to the amount which X is prepared to spend for that purpose. If the article is not be listed in X's catalogue, value is the price paid by X for the article: *Empire Stores Ltd v Customs and Excise Comrs* (case C-33/93) [1994] ECR I–2329, [1994] STC 623 at [16]–[20]. If the costs of delivery are borne by X, value is the aggregate of the price paid by X and the costs of delivery paid by him: *Bertelsmann AG v Finanzamt Wiedebbrück* (case C-380/99) [2001] ECR I–5163, [2001] STC 1153.

The general rule set out above gives way to the special rules set out arts 74–76. In relation to the special scheme for travel agents, see art 308.

Article 74
(ex art 11A(1)(b))

The taxable amount of the following supplies is: (1) the purchase price of the goods or of similar goods; or (2). (in the absence of a purchase price) the cost price determined at the time of supply. For the inclusion of charges for accepting payment by credit card or debit card, see Regulation (EU) No 282/2011 reg 42.

The supplies referred to are:

- Application of goods for private or non-business purposes (see art 16).
- Disposal of business goods free of charge (see art 16).
- Application of goods for business purposes (see art 18(*a*)).
- Application of goods for non-taxable transactions (see art 18(*b*)).
- Goods retained when a taxable person or his successors cease to carry on an economic activity (see art 18(*c*)).

For derogations granted to the UK, see:

- Decision 2006/659/EC. This authorises the UK to apply a scale charge in respect of fuel for private use in motor cars.
- Decision 89/466/EEC. This authorises the UK to apply open market value in respect of the use of buildings.

Article 75
(ex art 11A(1)(c))

The taxable amount of the following supplies is the full cost to the taxable person of providing the services:

- Use of business goods for private or non-business purposes (see art 26(1)(*a*)).
- Free supplies of services for private or non-business purposes (see art 26(1)(*b*)).

For the inclusion of charges for accepting payment by credit card or debit card, see Regulation (EU) No 282/2011 reg 42.

For an example of the taxable amount in relation to an application of goods for private purposes, see *De Jong v Staatssecretaris van Financiën* (case C-20/91) [1992] ECR I–2847, [1995] STC 727 (building contractor acting in his business capacity to construct a dwelling for his own occupation on land held by him in a private capacity).

For an example of the taxable amount in relation to a building wholly allocated to business assets where the relevant input tax was deducted in full and the building was used partly for business purposes and partly for private purposes, see *Haugemeinschaft Jörg und Stefanie Wollny v Finanzgericht Landshut* (case C-72/05) [2006] ECR I–8297, [2008] STC 1618 (fixed proportions of the building used respectively as a dwelling and as an office).

For an example of the taxable amount in relation to a motor vehicle used partly for business purposes and partly for private purposes where no input tax was deductible on the purchase of the vehicle because the seller was a non-taxable person, see *Kühne v Finanzamt München III* (case 50/88) [1989] ECR 1925, [1990] STC 749 (taxable amount calculated by reference to expenses incurred on maintenance and use of the goods in respect of which input tax was deductible).

For an example of the taxable amount in relation to a motor caravan used partly for business purposes and partly for private purposes where input tax was deductible in respect of both purchase of the vehicle and the running expenses incurred in respect of it, see *Enkler v Finanzamt Homburg* (case C-230/94) [1996] ECR I–4517, [1996] STC 1316 (apportionment by reference to the ratio between the total duration of actual use and the duration of actual use for non-business purposes).

Article 76
(ex art 28e(2))

As regards a transfer of assets to another member state treated as a supply of goods by virtue of art 17(1), the taxable amount is either: (1) the purchase price of the goods, or of similar goods, at the time of transfer; or (2) (in the absence of a purchase price) the cost price determined at the time of transfer. For the inclusion of charges for accepting payment by credit card or debit card, see Regulation (EU) No 282/2011 reg 42.

Article 77
(ex art 11A(1)(d))

The taxable amount of services provided by a taxable person for the purposes of his own undertaking (see art 27) is open market value. For the inclusion of charges for accepting payment by credit card or debit card, see Regulation (EU) No 282/2011 reg 42.

Article 78
(ex art 11A(2))

The taxable amount includes:

(a) Taxes, duties, levies and charges, excluding the VAT itself.
Taxes, duties, levies and charges form part of the taxable amount only if they are directly linked to the supply: *De Danske Bilimportører v Skatteministeriet* (case C-98/05) [2006] ECR I–4945 at [17]. For an example of a duty directly linked in this manner, see *Lidl & Companhia v Fazenda Pública* (case C-106/10) [2011] ECR I–0000 (tax on the manufacture, assembly, admission or import of vehicles). For an example of a duty which was not, see *De Danske Bilimportører v Skatteministeriet* (case C-98/05) [2006] ECR I–4945 (duty on registration of motor vehicles).

(b) Incidental expenses charged to the customer by the supplier, eg commission, packing, transport and insurance costs. Member states may consider expenses covered by a separate agreement to be incidental expenses.
"Incidental expenses" do not include interest awarded by a judicial decision: *BAZ Bausystem AG v Finanzamt München für Köperschaften* (case 222/81) [1982] ECR 2527, [1982] 3 CMLR 688 (action for recovery of debt in respect of services supplied).

For the inclusion of charges for accepting payment by credit card or debit card, see Regulation (EU) No 282/2011 reg 42.

Article 79
(ex art 11A(3))

The taxable amount does not include:

(a) Price reductions by way of discount for early payment.

(b) Price discounts and rebates allowed to the customer and accounted for at the time of supply.
Customers receive a discount if, at the time of supply, they pay a reduced price. They receive a rebate if the seller refunds part of the price already paid: *Freemans plc v Customs and Excise Comrs* (case C-86/99) [2001] ECR I–4167, [2001] STC 960 at [22], [23].

The grant of a price discount or rebate presupposes that goods or services are supplied for consideration. The terms indicate a partial reduction of the total price agreed. The reality of a 100% reduction is that goods are changing hands free of charge, so that the transaction falls within the scope of this provision: *Kuwait Petroleum (GB) Ltd v Customs and Excise Comrs* (case C-48/97) [1999] ECR I–2323, [1999] STC 488 at [16].

For an example of a price discount, see *Boots Co plc v Customs and Excise Comrs* (case C-126/88) [1990] ECR I–1235, [1990] STC 387 ("money off" coupons where the costs of the promotion were borne by the retailer). Here, the taxable amount of the goods supplied by the retailer was the cash received from the customer, ie the difference between the retail price of the goods and the face value of the coupon surrendered by the customer who purchased them. For "money off" coupons where the costs of the promotion are borne by the manufacturer, see art 73. For discounts credited to mail order agents by reference to payments made by them for goods ordered, see *Freemans plc v Customs and Excise Comrs* (case C-86/99) [2001] ECR I–4167, [2001] STC 960. For an example of a situation where there was no price discount or rebate, see *Kuwait Petroleum (GB) Ltd v Customs and Excise Comrs* (case C-48/97) [1999] ECR I–2323, [1999] STC 488 (reduction covering the whole cost of supplying redemption goods under a business promotion scheme).

(c) Amounts received by a taxable person as a reimbursement of expenses paid out in the name, and for the account, of the purchaser or customer. These amounts must be entered in a suspense account in his books. The taxable person must furnish proof of the actual amount of the expenditure. Any tax charged on these transactions is not deductible.

For an example of a payment regarded as a reimbursement, see *De Danske Bilimportører v Skatteministeriet* (case C-98/05) [2006] ECR I–4945 (duty on registration of motor vehicles). For an example of a payment that was not, see *Lidl & Companhia v Fazenda Pública* (case C-106/10) [2011] ECR I–0000 (tax on the manufacture, assembly, admission or import of vehicles).

For the inclusion of charges for accepting payment by credit card or debit card, see Regulation (EU) No 282/2011 reg 42.

Article 80
(ex art 11A(6))

1. A supply of goods or services may involve family or other close personal ties, management ties, ownership ties, membership ties, financial ties, or legal ties (including the relationship between an employer on one hand and an employee, a member of an employee's family or any other closely connected person on the other hand). Where this is so, member states may prevent tax avoidance or evasion by providing that the taxable amount of the supply is determined by reference to open market value. Member states may do so in any of the following situations:

(a) (If the recipient does not have a full right of deduction under arts 167–171 and 173–177) the consideration is lower than open market value.

(b) (If the supplier does not have a full right of deduction under arts 167–171 and 173–177) the consideration for the supply is lower than open market value and the supply is exempted under arts 132, 135, 136 or 371. (The exemptions in arts 375, 376, 377, 378(2), 379(2) and 380–390b do not apply to the UK).

(c) (If the supplier does not have a full right of deduction under arts 167–171 and 173–177) the consideration is higher than open market value.

For the inclusion of charges for accepting payment by credit card or debit card, see Regulation (EU) No 282/2011 reg 42.

2. Member states may exercise this option in relation to a defined class of suppliers or recipients.

3. Member states must inform the VAT Committee (see art 398) of any new national measure adopted.

Article 81
(ex art 11A(4))

Member states may derogate from arts 73, 74, 76, 78 and 79 in relation to works of art (as defined in Annex IX Part A) supplied by the following persons:

- A person who created the work of art.
- A successor in title to the person who created the work of art.
- A person ("X") who imported the work of art. X must be a taxable person (other than a taxable dealer) who supplies works of art on an occasional basis.
- A person ("X") to whom the work of art was supplied by another person ("Y"). X must be a taxable person (other than a taxable dealer) who supplies works of art on an occasional basis. Y must be either the person who created the work of art or his successor in title.
- A person ("X") who was entitled to full deduction of the input tax he incurred when he obtained the work of art. X must be a taxable person (other than a taxable dealer) who supplies works of art on an occasional basis.

A member state may do so if:

- It did not apply a reduced rate on 1 January 1993. The UK meets this condition.
- It taxes imported works of art at a fractional rate in accordance with the option provided for in art 89.

The taxable amount comprises a fraction of the amount determined in accordance with arts 73, 74, 76, 78 and 79. This fraction is determined in such a way that the VAT due is equal to at least 5% of the amount determined in accordance arts 73, 74, 76, 78 and 79.

Article 82
(ex art 11A(5))

Member states may provide that the taxable amount of a supply includes the value of investment gold (as defined in art 346) provided by the customer which, by being used as a basis for working, loses its VAT exempt investment gold status when the relevant goods or services are supplied. The value of the investment gold is its open market value (see art 72) at the time when the goods or services are supplied.

CHAPTER 3—INTRA-COMMUNITY ACQUISITION OF GOODS

Article 83
(ex art 28e(1) (first para))

The taxable amount of an intra-Community acquisition of goods is determined in the same manner as a supply of like goods. For the taxable amount in relation to supplies, see arts 73–82. For products subject to excise duty, see also art 84.

As regards transactions treated as an intra-Community acquisition of goods in accordance with arts 21, 22, the taxable amount is either: (1) the purchase price of the goods, or of similar goods, determined at the time of the supply; or (2) (in the absence of a purchase price) the cost price, determined at the time of the supply.

Article 84
(ex art 28e(1) (second para))

Member states must take the measures necessary to ensure that the excise duty payable by the person making an intra-Community acquisition of products subject to excise duty is included in the taxable amount. This requirement follows from art 78(*a*) as applied by art 83.

The taxable amount is reduced if the excise duty paid in the member state of departure is subsequently refunded to the person making the acquisition.

CHAPTER 4—IMPORTATION OF GOODS

General note This chapter confers rights on individuals on which they may rely before national courts: *BP Supergas Anonimos Etairia Geniki Emporiki-Viomichaniki kai Antiprossopeion v Greece* (case C62/93) [1995] ECR I–1883, [1995] STC 805 at [35].

Article 85
(ex art 11B(1))

The taxable amount of imported goods is their value for customs purposes. This is determined in accordance with the Community provisions in force.

Article 86
(ex art 11B(3))

In so far as not already included, the taxable amount of imported goods includes:

- Taxes, duties, levies and other charges due outside the importing member state.
- Taxes, duties, levies and other charges due by reason of importation, excluding the VAT to be levied.
- Incidental expenses (eg commission, packing, transport and insurance) incurred up to the first place of destination within the territory of the importing member state. This is the place mentioned on the consignment note or any other document by means of which the goods are imported into the importing member state or, in the absence of such an indication, the place of the first transfer of cargo in the importing member state.
- Incidental expenses (eg commission, packing, transport and insurance) resulting from transport to another place of destination within the territory of the Community if that place is known when the chargeable event occurs.

Article 87
(ex art 11B(4))

The taxable amount of imported goods does not include:

(a) Price reductions by way of discount for early payment.
(b) Price discounts and rebates granted to the customer and obtained by him at the time of importation.

Article 88
(ex art 11B(5))

Special provisions apply to the re-importation of goods meeting the following conditions:

- They were temporarily exported from the Community.
- They were repaired, processed, adapted, made up or reworked while outside the Community.

Member states must take steps to ensure that the goods are treated for VAT purposes in the same manner as they would have been treated if the foregoing operations had been carried out within their territory. For the territory of a member state, see art 5(2).

Article 89
(ex art 11B(6))

Member states may provide that the taxable amount of imported works of art, collectors' items and antiques (as defined in Annex IX) is an amount equal to a fraction of the amount determined in accordance with arts 85–87. This fraction is determined in such a way that the VAT due on the importation is equal to at least 5% of the amount so determined in accordance with those provisions.

Member states may exercise this option if they did not apply a reduced rate of VAT at 1 January 1993. The UK meets this condition.

CHAPTER 5—MISCELLANEOUS PROVISIONS

Article 90
(ex art 11C(1))

1. The taxable amount is reduced in the case of:

- Cancellation.
- Refusal.
- Total or partial non-payment.
- Price reduction after the supply has taken place.

The taxable amount is reduced under conditions determined by the member states.

This provision applies whether or not there has been a subsequent modification of the contractual relations between the parties. In principle, it requires member states to reduce the taxable amount if, following conclusion of a transaction, the supplier does not receive all or part of the consideration payable in respect of it: *Freemans plc v Customs and Excise Comrs* (case C-86/99) [2001] ECR I–4167, [2001] STC 960 at [33].

2. Member states may derogate from para 1 in the case of total or partial non-payment. However, the power to derogate is based on the notion that non-payment of consideration may be difficult to establish or may be only temporary. Member states must justify its use: *Goldsmiths (Jewellers) Ltd v Customs and Excise Comrs* (case C-330/95) [1997] ECR I–3801, [1997] STC 1073 at [18]. For an example of unjustified use of this derogation, see *Goldsmiths (Jewellers) Ltd v Customs and Excise Comrs* (case C-330/95) [1997] ECR I–3801, [1997] STC 1073 (national rules confining reduction in taxable amount to considerations expressed in money and excluding considerations in kind).

Article 91*
(ex art 11C(2))

The information for determining the taxable amount may be expressed in a foreign currency. Where this is so, the exchange rate is determined as follows.

As regards imported goods, the rate of exchange is determined in accordance with Community provisions governing the calculation of value for customs purposes. One of the following methods is used in other cases:

- The latest selling rate recorded, at the time when VAT becomes chargeable, on the most representative exchange markets of the member state concerned.
- A rate determined by reference to those markets in accordance with the rules prescribed by that member state.
- The latest exchange rate published by the European Central Bank at the time when the tax becomes chargeable. Conversion between currencies other than the euro are made by using the euro exchange rate of each currency. Member states may require taxable person to notify the exercise of this option.
- (At the option of a member state in relation to some transactions or certain categories of taxable person) the exchange rate determined in accordance with Community provisions in force governing the calculation of value for customs purposes.

Article 92 (ex art 11C(3))

Member states may exclude returnable packing costs from the taxable amount and take the necessary measures to ensure that this amount is adjusted if the packing is not returned. Alternatively, member states may include these costs in the taxable amount and take the necessary measures to ensure that this amount is adjusted if the packing is returned.

TITLE VIII—RATES

CHAPTER 1—APPLICATION OF RATES

Article 93
(ex arts 12(1), 28e(3))

In principle, VAT is charged at the rate in force at the time of the chargeable event. However, VAT is charged at the rate in force at the time when tax becomes chargeable in the following circumstances:

(a) In relation to a supply of goods or services, in the cases referred to in arts 65, 66.
(b) In relation to an intra-Community acquisition of goods.
(c) In relation to an importation of goods, in the cases referred to in art 71(1) (second para) and 71(2).

Article 94
(ex art arts 12(5), 28e(4))

1. The same VAT rate must be applied to like goods whether they are acquired under an intra-Community acquisition of goods or supplied within the territory of the member state.

2. In principle, like goods must be charged at the same rate of VAT whether they are supplied within the territory of the member state (as defined in art 5(2)) or imported. For the exception, see para 103(1).

Article 95
(ex art 12(2))

As regards the cases referred to in arts 65 and 66, member states may, when rates are changed, effect adjustments to take account of the rate applicable at the time when the goods or services were supplied.

Member states may also adopt all appropriate transitional measures.

CHAPTER 2—STRUCTURE AND LEVEL OF RATES

SECTION 1—STANDARD RATE

Article 96
(ex art 12(3)(a) (first para, first sentence))

Member states must apply a standard rate of VAT. The rate is fixed by each member state as a percentage of the taxable amount. The same rate is applied to both supplies of goods and supplies of services.

Article 97
(ex art 12(3)(a) (first para, second sentence) and 12(3)(a) (second para))

Member states must apply a standard rate of 15% or more during the period 1 January 2011 to 31 December 2015.

SECTION 1—REDUCED RATES

Article 98
(ex art 12(3)(a) (third para, first sentence), 12(3)(a) (third para, part of second sentence), 12(3)(a) (fourth para) and Annex H (first para))

1. Member states may apply either one or two reduced rates.

The option to apply one or two reduced rates is an exception to the principle that the standard rate applies, and must be interpreted strictly: *Commission v Kingdom of Spain* (case C-83/99) [2001] ECR I–445 at [18], [19].

Part I VAT

Whether or not to apply reduced rates is a matter for individual member states to decide. However, member states must respect the principle of neutrality in exercising that power: *Commission v Germany* (case C-109/02) [2003] ECR I–12691, [2006] STC 1587 at [19], [20]. For examples of reduced rates meeting this principle, see: (1) *Commission v French Republic* (*Republic of Finland intervening*) (case C-481/98) [2001] ECR I–3369, [2001] STC 919 (distinction between medicinal products according to whether or not they are reimbursable under the social security system); (2) *Commission v French Republic* (case C-384/01) [2003] ECR I–4395 (reduced rate confined to standing charge for supply of energy). For an example of reduced rates which did not, see *Commission v Germany* (case C-109/02) [2003] ECR I–12691, [2006] STC 1587 (distinction between soloists according to whether or not they work for an organiser).

2. Reduced rates may be applied to any of the goods and services specified in Annex III. However, they may not be applied to electronically supplied services. For "electronically supplied services", see Annex II and Regulation (EU) No 282/2011 reg 7.

Annex III is divided into 21 categories. Member states are not required to apply all aspects of a particular category. Provided a member state observes the principle of fiscal neutrality, it may apply a reduced rate which is limited to "concrete and specific aspects" of a particular category: *Commission v French Republic* (case C-94/09) [2010] ECR I– 0000 at [29], [30]. For examples of selective reduced rates, see: (1) *Finanzamt Oschatz v Zweckverband zur Trinkwasserversorgung und Abwasserbeseitgung Torgau-Westelbien* [2008] ECR I–1817, [2009] STC 1 (water supplies); (2) *Commission v French Republic* (case C-94/09) [2010] ECR I– 0000 (undertakers).

3. Member states may use the Combined Nomenclature to establish the precise coverage of the goods and services listed in Annex III.

Article 99
(ex art 12(3)(a) (third para, part of second sentence) and 12(4) (first para))

1. Reduced rates are fixed as a percentage of the taxable amount. The minimum rate is 5%.

2. Each reduced rate must be fixed in such a manner that the resulting output tax normally exceeds deductible input tax.

Article 100
(ex art 12(4) (second para))

From 1994, the Council must review the scope of the reduced rates every two years. The Commission must prepare reports for this purpose. The Council may decide to amend Annex III. TFEU art 113 requires this decision to be unanimous.

Article 101
(ex art 12(4) (third para))

The Commission is required to prepare a report assessing the impact of applying reduced rates to locally supplied services. The deadline is 30 June 2007.

Section 3—Particular provisions

Article 102
(ex art 12(3)(b))

Member states may apply a reduced rate to supplies of natural gas, electricity and district heating. They must inform the Commission before doing so.

Article 103
(ex art 12(3)(c))

1. Member states may provide that their reduced rate, or one of their reduced rates, applies to imported works of art, collectors' items and antiques (as defined in Annex III).

2. Where they do so, member states may also apply the reduced rate to supplies of works of art (as defined in art 26a(*a*)(*a*)) made in any of the following circumstances:

- Supplies made by the person who created the work of art or by one of his successors in title.
- Supplies made on an occasional basis by a taxable person (other than a taxable dealer), if the taxable person himself imported the works of art.
- Supplies made on an occasional basis by a taxable person (other than a taxable dealer), if the person who created the work of art or one of his successors in title supplied the works of art to the taxable person.
- Supplies made on an occasional basis by a taxable person (other than a taxable dealer), if the works of art have entitled the taxable person to full deduction of VAT.

Article 104
(ex Act of Accession (1994), Annex XV(IX) point 2(b))

[Applies to Austria.]

Article 104a

[Applies to Cyprus.]

Article 105
(ex art 12(6))

[Applies to Portugal.]

CHAPTER 3—TEMPORARY PROVISIONS FOR PARTICULAR LABOUR-INTENSIVE SERVICES

Article 106
(ex art 28(6) (first para))

[Repealed.]

Article 107
(ex art 28(6) (second and third paras))

[Repealed.]

Article 108
(ex art 28(6) (fourth para))

[Repealed.]

CHAPTER 4—SPECIAL PROVISIONS APPLYING UNTIL THE ADOPTION OF DEFINITIVE ARRANGEMENTS

Article 109
(ex art 28(2) (introductory sentence))

This chapter applies pending the introduction of definitive arrangements. For the definitive arrangements, see art 402.

Article 110
(ex art 28(2)(a) (first para))

Member states may maintain exemptions with deduction of VAT paid at the preceding stage if:

- They were in force on 1 January 1991.
- They comply with Community law.

Although a single supply is normally subject to a single rate of VAT, case law does not preclude some elements of that supply being taxed separately where this is necessary to comply with the conditions of this provision: *Talacre Beach Caravan Sales Ltd v Customs and Excise Comrs* (case C-251/05) [2006] ECR I–6269, [2006] STC 1671 at [24]–[27].

- They were introduced for clearly defined social reasons and for the benefit of the final consumer.

In principle, the identification of "social reasons" is a matter of political choice for member states. This choice is subject to supervision at the Community level only in so far as, by distorting that concept, it leads to measures which, because of their effects and their true objectives, lie outside its scope: *Commission v United Kingdom* (case 416/85) [1988] ECR 3127, [1988] STC 456 at [14].

The "final consumer" is the person who acquires the goods or services for personal use, as opposed to an economic activity, and thus bears the tax. Goods or services are for the "benefit" of the final consumer (as so defined) if: (1) they are provided at a stage higher in the production or distribution chain; and (2) that stage is sufficiently close to the consumer to be of advantage to him: *Commission v United Kingdom* (case 416/85) [1988] ECR 3127, [1988] STC 456 at [17].

For examples of exemptions with refund (known as "zero-rating" in the UK and Ireland) which failed to meet this test, see: (1) *Commission v United Kingdom* (case 416/85) [1988] ECR 3127, [1988] STC 456; (2) *Commission v Ireland* (case 415/85) [1988] ECR 3097, [1988] 3 CMLR 189.

Maintenance of a national exemption with refund in respect of specified supplies does not give traders making such supplies a directly enforceable Community-law right to have those supplies taxed at a zero rate of VAT. However, the principles governing the common system of VAT (including the principle of fiscal neutrality) apply and they may be relied on by a taxable person against a national provision, or the application of such a provision, which fails to have regard to those principles. Thus, if a member state misinterprets its national legislation so that supplies benefiting from the zero rate are taxed at the standard rate, a trader making such supplies has a right to recover the sums mistakenly charged in respect of them. Refusal to make a repayment on the ground of unjust enrichment does not of itself infringe the principles of equal treatment and fiscal neutrality. However, traders who are not necessarily in competition with each other, but are nevertheless in a similar position in other respects, must be treated alike. This applies whether or not the trader has suffered any loss or disadvantage by virtue of the wrongly levied tax. The remedy for unequal treatment is a matter for the national court. However, the court must act in compliance with Community law. In particular, the court must comply with the principle of equal treatment and the principle of ensuring that the remedies it grants are not contrary to Community law: *Marks & Spencer plc v Customs and Excise Comrs* (case C-309/06) [2008] ECR I–2283, [2008] STC 1408 at [28], [34], [35]. [54], [57], [64].

Identical provisions apply to reduced rates. However, the UK did not apply reduced rates at 1 January 1991. The identical provisions are not, therefore, relevant to the UK. For reduced rates, see *Commission v French Republic* (*Republic of Finland intervening*) (case C-481/98) [2001] ECR I–3369, [2001] STC 919.

Article 111
(ex Act of Accession (1994), Annex XV(IX) points 2(l), (z))

[Applies to Finland, Malta and Sweden.]

Article 112
(ex art 28(2)(a) (third para))

[Applies to Ireland.]

Article 113
(ex art 28(2)(b))

Member states may apply the reduced rate (or one of the reduced rates) provided for in art 99 to goods and services other than those specified in Annex III if:

- Exemptions with deduction at the preceding stage were applied to those goods and services at 1 January 1991.
- The exemptions with deduction were applied in accordance with Community law.

Identical provisions apply to goods and services which were charged to tax at reduced rates on 1 January 1991. However, the UK did not apply reduced rates at that date. The identical provisions are not, therefore, relevant to the UK.

Article 114
(ex art 28(2)(c))

[Not relevant to the UK.]

Article 115
(ex art 28(2)(d))

[Not relevant to the UK.]

Article 116
(ex art 28(2)(k))

[Repealed.]

Article 117
(ex art 28(2)(j); Act of Accession (1994), Annex XV(IX) point 2(f))

[Applies to Austria.]

Article 118
(ex art 28(2)(e))

[Not relevant to the UK.]

Article 119
(ex Act of Accession (1994), Annex XV(IX) point 2(g))

[Applies to Austria.]

Article 120
(ex art 28(2)(f))

[Applies to Greece.]

Article 121
(ex art 28(2)(h))

[Not relevant to the UK.]

Article 122
(ex art 28(2)(i))

Member states may apply a reduced rate of tax to the following supplies:

- Live plants and other floricultural products (including bulbs, roots and the like, cut flowers and ornamental foliage).
- Wood for use as firewood.

CHAPTER 5—TEMPORARY PROVISIONS

Article 123
(ex Act of Accession (2003), Annex V(5) point 1(a))

[Applies to the Czech Republic.]

Article 124
(ex Act of Accession (2003), Annex VI(7) point 1(a))

[Repealed.]

Article 125
(ex Act of Accession (2003), Annex VII(7) point 1)

[Applies to Cyprus.]

Article 126
(ex Act of Accession (2003), Annex X(7) point 1(a))

[Repealed.]

Article 127
(ex Act of Accession (2003), Annex XII(7) point 1)

[Repealed.]

Article 128
(ex Act of Accession (2003), Annex XII(7) point 1(a))

[Applies to Poland.]

Article 129
(ex Act of Accession (2003), Annex XIII(9) point 1(a))

[Applies to Slovenia.]

Article 130
(ex Act of Accession (2003), Annex XIV(7) (first para))

[Repealed.]

TITLE IX—EXEMPTIONS

General note This Title sets out the general rules in relation to supplies, intra-Community acquisitions of goods and importations. For the special rules in relation to investment gold, see arts 346–351. For derogations available to states which were members of the Community on 1 January 1978, see arts 370, 371. For the effect of exemption on the status of bodies governed by public law, see art 13(2).

Exemptions constitute independent concepts of Community law. Their purpose is to avoid divergencies in the application of the VAT system from one member state to another. They have their own independent meaning in Community law: *Stichting Uitvoering Financiële Acties v Staatssecretaris van Financiën* (case 348/87) [1989] ECR 1737, [1991] 2 CMLR 429 at [11], [13]. That is also true of the specific conditions laid down for the application of those exemptions and, in particular, conditions concerning the status or identity of the economic agent performing the services covered by the exemption: *Bulthuis-Griffioen v Inspector der Omzetbelastiong* (case C-453/93) [1995] ECR I–2341, [1995] STC 954 at [18]. Exemptions are therefore given a Community definition: *Commission v Ireland* (case C-358/97) [2000] ECR I–6301 at [51].

Exemptions must be placed in the general context of the common system of VAT introduced by this directive: *Commission v Netherlands* (case 235/85) [1987] ECR 1471 at [18]. That system is based, in particular, on two principles. First, each supply of goods and services made for consideration by a taxable person is subject to VAT. Secondly, in accordance with the principle of fiscal neutrality, economic operators carrying out the same transactions may not be treated differently in relation to the levying of VAT: *Climber Air A/S v Skatteministeriet* (case C-382/02) [2004] ECR I–8379, [2005] STC 547 at [24].

Exemptions are construed strictly since they constitute exceptions to the general principle that VAT is levied on all goods and services supplied for consideration by a taxable person: *Stichting Uitvoering Financiële Acties v Staatssecretaris van Financiën* (case 348/87) [1989] ECR 1737, [1991] 2 CMLR 429 at [13]. That does not mean that the terms used to specify exemptions should be construed in such a way as to deprive them of their intended effect: *Belgian State v Temco Europe SA* (case C-284/03) [2004] ECR I–11237, [2005] STC 1451 at [17]. For an example, see *Navicon SA v Administración del Estado* (case C-97/06) [2007] ECR I–8755, [2008] STC 2693 at [32]. Neither the objectives of an exemption nor the principle of fiscal neutrality can compel a broad interpretation of an unambiguous provision so as to bring about a result that was clearly unintended: *VDP Dental Laboratory NV v Staatssecretaris van Financiën* (case C-401/05) [2006] ECR I–12121, [2007] STC 474 at [36].

A member state fails to fulfil its obligations under art 3 if it extends the scope of an exemption by administrative circular: see *Commission v French Republic* (case C-60/96) [1997] ECR I–3827, [1999] STC 480.

Member states must exempt the transactions listed in Chapters 2–9. They have discretion to exempt the transactions listed in Chapter 10. A member state cannot rely on its failure to implement national legislation giving effect to an exemption in order to deny relief to a taxpayer who falls within the scope of an exemption and who has not charged VAT to his customer: *Becker v Finanzamt Munster-Innenstadt* (case 8/81) [1982] ECR 53, [1982] 1 CMLR 499 at [49]; *Weissberber v Finanzamt Neustadt an der Weinstraße* (case 207/87) [1988] ECR 4433, [1991] STC 589 at [15].

Part I VAT

CHAPTER 1—GENERAL PROVISIONS

Article 131
(ex introductory sentences to arts 13A(1), 14(1), 15, 28cA, 28cB; art 28cD (second para))

The exemptions provided for in Chapters 2–9 apply without prejudice to other Community provisions.

Member states must lay down conditions for the purpose of:

- Ensuring the correct and straightforward application of the exemptions.
- Preventing any possible evasion, avoidance or abuse.

These conditions imposed by member states do not in any way affect the definition of the subject-matter or the exemption conferred: *Becker v Finanzamt Munster-Innenstadt* (case 8/81) [1982] ECR 53, [1982] 1 CMLR 499 at [32]. Thus, a member state cannot lay down conditions whereby a transaction which is to be exempted is treated as one which is outside the scope of VAT: *Commission v Italian Republic* (case C-45/95) [1997] ECR I–3605, [1997] STC 1062.

A member state cannot rely on its failure to lay down conditions in order to deny a legitimately claimed exemption: *Becker v Finanzamt Munster-Innenstadt* (case 8/81) [1982] ECR 53, [1982] 1 CMLR 499 at [33], [34].

Member states must comply with the general principles of law forming part of the Community legal order when laying down conditions in relation to intra-Community supplies of goods. These principles include, in particular, the principles of legal certainty and proportionality. National measures must not be used in such a way as to undermine the neutrality of VAT. As regards legal certainty, taxable persons must know the precise extent of their tax obligations before concluding a transaction. As regards proportionality, while it is legitimate for national measures to seek to preserve the rights of the public exchequer as effectively as possible, these measures must go no further than is necessary for that purpose: *R (on the application of Teleos plc and others) v Customs and Excise Comrs* [2007] ECR I–7797, [2008] STC 706 at [45], [46], [48], [53].

As regards intra-Community supplies of goods, the competent authorities of the member state of supply are precluded from requiring a supplier to account for VAT on goods if: (1) he has submitted evidence establishing, at first sight, his right to exemption; (2) he acted in good faith in so doing; (3) the evidence is subsequently found to be false; (4) it is not established that the supplier was involved in the evasion of tax; and (5) the supplier took every reasonable measure in his power to ensure that his supply did not lead to such evasion: *R (on the application of Teleos plc and others) v Customs and Excise Comrs* [2007] ECR I–7797, [2008] STC 706. As regards exports of goods to third countries, see *Netto Supermarkt GmbH & Co OHG v Finanzamt Malchin* (case C-271/06) [2008] ECR I–771, [2008] STC 3280 at [21]–[27]. Similarly, the competent authorities are precluded from refusing to allow an intra-Community supply – which actually took place – to be exempt from VAT solely on the ground that the evidence of such a supply was not produced in good time: *Albert Collée v Finanzamt Limburg an der Lahn* (case C-146/05) [2007] ECR I–7861, [2007] STC 757. However, the member state of departure may refuse to allow exemption if, at the time of the intra-Community supply, the supplier concealed the identity of the true purchaser in order to enable the latter to evade payment of VAT in the member state of destination: *Criminal proceedings against R* (case C-285/09) [2010] ECR I–0000, [2011] STC 138.

CHAPTER 2—EXEMPTION FOR CERTAIN ACTIVITIES IN THE PUBLIC INTEREST

General note The purpose of this Chapter is to exempt from VAT certain activities which are in the public interest. However, it does not provide exemption for every activity performed in the public interest – only for those which are listed and described in great detail: *Commission v Federal Republic of Germany* (case 107/84) [1985] ECR 2655, [1986] 2 CMLR 177 at [17].

The heading "exemptions for certain activities in the public interest" does not, of itself, restrict the the scope of the exemptions conferred: *Criminal proceedings against Hoffmann* (case C-144/00) [2003] ECR I–2921, [2004] STC 740 at [40].

Article 132
(ex art 13A(1)(a)–(q))

1. Member states must exempt the following transactions:

(a) Services, and goods incidental thereto, supplied by public postal services.

A public or private operator is a "public postal service" if he undertakes to provide all or part of a universal postal service (as defined in Directive 97/67/EC art 3) in a member state: *R (on the application of TNT Post UK Ltd) v R & C Comrs* (case C-357/07) [2009] ECR I–3025, [2009] STC 1438; cf *Commission v Federal Republic of Germany* (case 107/84) [1985] ECR 2655, [1986] 2 CMLR 177 at [16]. For the 1997 Directive, see OJ L14/14, 21.1.98.

Exemption is confined to the services and incidental goods supplied by a public postal service in its capacity as the universal service provider. Thus, it does not apply to services and incidental goods for which the terms have been individually negotiated: *R (on the application of TNT Post UK Ltd) v R & C Comrs* (case C-357/07) [2009] ECR I–3025, [2009] STC 1438 at [44]–[49].

Passenger transport and telecommunication services are excluded from exemption under this head.

(b) Hospital care, medical care and closely related activities supplied by hospitals, centres for medical treatment or diagnosis and other duly recognised establishments of a similar nature.

These services "encompass a whole range of medical care normally provided on a non-profit-making basis in establishments pursuing social purposes such as the protection of human health": *Commission v United Kingdom* (case 353/85) [1988] ECR 817, [1988] STC 251 at [32]. For the direct effect of this provision, see *Christoph-Domier-Stiftung für Klinische Psychologie v Finanzamt Gießen* (case C-45/01) [2003] ECR I–12911, [2005] STC 228.

The care and activities must be either undertaken by bodies governed by public law or (subject to any conditions imposed by member states in accordance with art 133) undertaken under social conditions comparable to those applicable to bodies governed by public law. The absence of national law imposing conditions under art 133 does not affect the possibility that an establishment may be recognised for the purposes of this exemption: *Christoph-Domier-Stiftung für Klinische Psychologie v Finanzamt Gießen* (case C-45/01) [2003] ECR I–12911, [2005] STC 228 at [64]–[67].

"Medical care" comprises the diagnosis, treatment and, in so far as possible, the cure of diseases or health disorders: *Ambulanter Pflegedienst Kugler GmbH v Finanzamt fur Korperschaften I in Berlin* (case C-141/00) [2002] I–6833, [2002] SWTI 1277 at [51]. Although "medical care" must have a therapeutic aim, it does not necessarily follow that the therapeutic purpose of a service must be confined within an especially narrow compass. Thus, medical services provided for a prophylactic purpose may benefit from exemption, even if the patient is not suffering from any disease or health disorder. Accordingly, medical services may benefit from exemption if they are effected for the purpose of protecting, maintaining or restoring human health: *LuP GmbH v Finanzamt Bochum-Mitte* (case C-106/05) [2006] ECR I–5123, [2008] STC 1742 at [29].

The concept of "activities closely related to hospital and medical care" does not envisage services unrelated to hospital care for the patients receiving those services or to any medical care they may be receiving. Thus, services must be ancillary to the principal service supplied, ie the hospital or medical care received by the patients in question: *Christoph-Domier-Stiftung für Klinische Psychologie v Finanzamt Gießen* (case C-45/01) [2003] ECR I–12911, [2005] STC 228 at [33], [35] (psychotherapeutic treatment in out-patient facility closely related to hospital or medical care when ancillary to the principal service, but not when the treatment constitutes an end in itself).

A service is ancillary to the principal service where it constitutes a means of enhancing the enjoyment or benefit of the principal service supplied rather than constituting an end in itself: *Diagnostikon & Therapeftikon Kentro Athinon–Igeia AE v Ypourgos Ikonomikon* (joined cases C-394/04 and C-395/04) [2006] ECR I–10373, [2006] STC 1349 at [19]. Thus, supplying telephone services and hiring televisions to in-patients do not, as a general rule, amount to activities closely related to hospital and medical care; nor does the supply of beds and meals for people accompanying in-patients. It can be otherwise only if: (1) those supplies are essential to achieve the therapeutic objectives sought by the hospital and medical care provided, and (2) their basic purpose is not to obtain additional income by carrying out transactions in direct competition with commercial enterprises: *Diagnostikon & Therapeftikon Kentro Athinon–Igeia AE v Ypourgos Ikonomikon* (joined cases C-394/04 and C-395/04) [2006] ECR I–10373, [2006] STC 1349.

The term "other duly recognised establishments of a similar nature" includes natural persons running a business: *Gregg v Customs & Excise Comrs* (case C-216/97) [1999] ECR I–4947, [1999] STC 934 (partnership).

The requirement for "recognition" does not presuppose a formal recognition procedure. Furthermore, recognition does not necessarily derive from national tax laws. If national rules contain restrictions which exceed the limits of discretion allowed to member states, national courts must determine whether a taxable person must nonetheless be regarded as an "other duly recognised establishment" for the purposes of this exemption. This must be done in the light of all the relevant facts. These include the public interest of the activities, the fact that other taxable persons carrying on the same activities have similar recognition and the fact that the costs incurred for the treatment may be largely met by health insurance schemes or other social security bodies: *Christoph-Domier-Stiftung für Klinische Psychologie v Finanzamt Gießen* (case C-45/01) [2003] ECR I–12911, [2005] STC 228 at [72], [73], [76]. In relation to similar services, the conditions for recognition must be the same for all categories of establishment governed by private law: *LuP GmbH v Finanzamt Bochum-Mitte* (case C-106/05) [2006] ECR I–5123, [2008] STC 1742 at [50].

For medical tests having as their purpose the observation and examination of patients for prophylactic purposes carried out by a laboratory governed by private law outside a centre for treatment on prescription from general practitioners, see *LuP GmbH v Finanzamt Bochum-Mitte* (case C-106/05) [2006] ECR I–5123, [2008] STC 1742; cf *Commission v French Republic* (case C-76/99) [2001] ECR I–249 (fixed allowance for the transmission of samples for the purpose of medical analysis).

For services that do no more than ensure that a particular resource will be available for medical treatment in the uncertain event that it becomes necessary, see *CopyGene A/S v Skatteministeriet* (case C-262/08) [2010] ECR I–0000, [2010] STC 1799 and *Future Health Technologies Ltd v Revenue and Customs Comrs* (case C-86/09) [2010] ECR I–0000, [2010] STC 1836 (collection, transportation, analysis and storage of umbilical cord blood).

For goods and services excluded from exemption under this head, see art 134.

(c) The provision of medical care in the exercise of the medical and paramedical professions. The relevant medical and paramedical professions are defined by the member states. For the direct effect of this provision, see *Christoph-Domier-Stiftung für Klinische Psychologie v Finanzamt Gießen* (case C-45/01) [2003] ECR I–12911, [2005] STC 228.

"Medical care" comprises the diagnosis, treatment and, in so far as possible, the cure of diseases or health disorders: *Finanzamt Leverkusen v Verigen Transplantation Service International AG* (case C-156/09) [2010] ECR I– 0000, [2011] STC 255 at [24]. Although "the provision of medical care" must have a therapeutic aim, it does not necessarily follow that the therapeutic purpose of a service must be confined within an especially narrow compass. Thus, medical services provided for a prophylactic purpose may benefit from exemption, even if the patient is not suffering from any disease or health disorder. Accordingly, medical services may benefit from exemption if they are provided for the purpose of protecting, maintaining or restoring human health: *LuP GmbH v Finanzamt Bochum-Mitte* (case C-106/05) [2006] ECR I–5123, [2008] STC 1742 at [29]. The determining factor is the purpose of the medical service. A service is excluded from exemption if its principal purpose is the provision of advice to a third party taking a decision with legal consequences: *Unterpertinger v Pensionsversicherungsanstalt der Arbeiter* (case C-212/01) [2003] ECR I–13859, [2005] STC 650 at [42]; *D'Ambrumenil v Customs & Excise Comrs* (case C-307/01) [2003] ECR I–13989, [2005] STC 650 at [60].

For examples of exempt medical care, see (1) *Ambulanter Pflegedienst Kugler GmbH v Finanzamt fur Korperschaften I in Berlin* (case C-141/00) [2002] I–6833, [2002] SWTI 1277 (care, other than general care and domestic help, provided by qualified nursing staff); (2) *D'Ambrumenil v Customs & Excise Comrs* (case C-307/01) [2003] ECR I–13989, [2005] STC 650 (conducting medical examinations, taking samples to test for the presence of viruses, infections or other diseases, and certifying medical fitness where, in each case, the principal purpose was to protect the health of the person concerned); (3) *LuP GmbH v Finanzamt Bochum-Mitte* (case C-106/05) [2006] ECR I–5123, [2008] STC 1742 (medical tests prescribed by general practitioners); (4) *Finanzamt Leverkusen v Verigen Transplantation Service International AG* (case C-156/09) [2010] ECR I–0000, [2011] STC 255 (removal of joint cartilage cells from cartilage material taken from a human being and the subsequent multiplication of those cells for reimplantation for therapeutic purposes).

Exemption extends to "minor provisions of goods which are strictly necessary at the time when the care is provided", but not to medicines and other goods: *Commission v United Kingdom* (case 353/85) [1988] ECR 817, [1988] STC 251 at [33].

Exemption does not depend upon the legal form of the taxable person supplying the medical or paramedical services: *Ambulanter Pflegedienst Kugler GmbH v Finanzamt fur Korperschaften I in Berlin* (case C-141/00) [2002] I–6833, [2002] SWTI 1277 at [31]. For examples, see (1) *Ambulanter Pflegedienst Kugler GmbH v Finanzamt fur Korperschaften I in Berlin* (case C-141/00) [2002] I–6833, [2002] SWTI 1277 (services provided by limited liability company); (2) *Christoph-Domier-Stiftung für Klinische Psychologie v Finanzamt Gießen* (case C-45/01) [2003] ECR I–12911, [2005] STC 228 (services provided by foundation governed by private law).

It is unnecessary for every aspect of therapeutic care to be provided by medical staff: *Finanzamt Leverkusen v Verigen Transplantation Service International AG* (case C-156/09) [2010] ECR I– 0000, [2011] STC 255 at [28] (services were carried out by laboratory staff who where not qualified medical practitioners).

Medical care is "provided outside hospitals and similar establishments and within the framework of a confidential relationship between the patient and the person providing the care, a relationship which is normally established in the consulting room of that person": *Commission v United Kingdom* (case 353/85) [1988] ECR 817, [1988] STC 251 at [33]. It can also be provided at the patient's home or elsewhere outside a hospital or similar establishment: *Ambulanter Pflegedienst Kugler GmbH v Finanzamt fur Korperschaften I in Berlin* (case C-141/00) [2002] I–6833, [2002] SWTI 1277 at [36].

It is for each member state to define, in its own domestic law, the paramedical professions to which exemption applies. In exercising their discretion to define a particular profession, member states may prescribe both the qualifications required to carry on that profession and the medical care falling within its scope. Member states must have regard to the objective of the exemption (ie to ensure that it is confined to medical care provided by practitioners with the required professional qualifications) and to the principle of fiscal neutrality (so that similar services in competition with each other are not treated differently). It is for national courts to decide whether national legislation exceeds the limits of the discretion granted to member states: *H A Solleveld and J E van den Hout-van Eijnsbergen v Staatssecretaris van Financiën* (joined cases C-443/04 and C-444/04) [2006] ECR I–3617, [2007] STC 71.

For examples of services outside the scope of the exemption, see: (1) *D v W* (*Österreichischer Bundesschatz intervening*) (case C-384/98) [2000] ECR I–6795, [2002] STC 1200 (establishing the genetic affinity of individuals through biological tests); (2) *Ambulanter Pflegedienst Kugler GmbH v Finanzamt fur Korperschaften I in Berlin* (case C-141/00) [2002] I–6833, [2002] SWTI 1277 at [40] (provision of general care and domestic help); (3) *Unterpertinger v Pensionsversicherungsanstalt der Arbeiter* (case C-212/01) [2003] ECR I–13859, [2005] STC 650 (doctor making an expert report on a person's state of health in order to support or exclude a claim for disability pension); (4) *D'Ambrumenil v Customs & Excise Comrs* (case C-307/01) [2003] ECR I–13989, [2005] STC 650 (medical certificates, examinations and reports as described in para 69 of the judgment).

(d) Supplies of human organs, blood and milk. This description has an autonomous and uniform interpretation specific to EU law: *Belgian State v Nathalie De Fruytier* (case C-237/09) [2010] ECR I–0000, [2010] STC 1792 at [22].

For an example of services outside the scope of exemption, see *Belgian State v Nathalie De Fruytier* (case C-237/09) [2010] ECR I–0000, [2010] STC 1792 (transporting human organs and samples).

(e) Services supplied by dental technicians in their professional capacity. Dental prostheses supplied by dentists and dental technicians.

Part I VAT

Dental prostheses are not exempted by this provision if they are supplied by someone other than a dentist or dental technician: *VDP Dental Laboratory NV v Staatssecretaris van Financiën* (case C-401/05) [2006] ECR I–12121, [2007] STC 474 (supply by intermediary who acquired the prostheses from a dental technician).

(f) Services supplied by an independent group of persons for the purpose of rendering services to its members which are directly necessary for the exercise of their activity. The independent group must do no more than claim from each member an exact reimbursement of his share of the joint expenses. The activities of the independent group must be either exempt from VAT or not subject to VAT.

The needs of the members may vary from one tax period to another with the consequence that, in any given period, the independent group may supply certain services to all, some or only one of the members. Similarly, the needs of the members may differ so that the services supplied to each of them are not necessarily the same. The services are exempt even if they are supplied only to one or several of the members: *Stichting Centraal Begeleidingsorgaan voor de Intercollegiale Toetsing v Staatssecretaris van Financiën* (case C-407/07) [2008] ECR I–9615, [2009] STC 869 at [34], [35], [42].

This exemption does not apply if it is likely to distort competition. This would be so if there is a genuine risk that exempting the independent group's services may, by itself, give rise to distortions of competition either immediately or in the future. National legislation may grant temporary exemption in cases where there is some doubt regarding the future risk, but exemption may be renewed only for so long as the independent group satisfies the conditions for exemption: *Assurandør-Societet (acting on behalf of Taksatorringen) v Skatteministeriet* (case C-8/01) [2003] ECR I–13711, [2006] STC 1842.

For an example of services outside the scope of this exemption, see *Stichting Uitvoering Financiële Acties v Staatssecretaris van Financiën* (case 348/87) [1989] ECR 1737, [1991] 2 CMLR 429 (one foundation supplying services exclusively to another foundation, neither foundation being a member of the other).

(g) The supply of goods and services closely linked to welfare and social security work. This includes goods and services supplied by old people's homes. The supply must be made by either: (1) a body governed by public law; or (2) (subject to any conditions imposed by member states in accordance with art 133) a body recognised by the relevant member state as being devoted to social wellbeing.

A natural person is not a "body" for the purpose of head (1) and his supplies are therefore outside the scope of this exemption: *Bulthuis-Griffioen v Inspector der Omzetbelastiong* (case C-453/93) [1995] ECR I–2341, [1995] STC 954.

Goods and services are "closely linked" if they are essential to the exempted service: *Staatssecretaris van Financiën v Stichting Kinderopvang Enschede* (case C-415/04) [2006] ECR I–1385, [2007] STC 294 at [25]. For an example of goods and services "closely linked" to welfare and social security work, see *Ambulanter Pflegedienst Kugler GmbH v Finanzamt fur Korperschaften I in Berlin* (case C-141/00) [2002] I–6833, [2002] SWTI 1277 at [44] (general care and domestic help by an out-patient care service to those in a state of physical or economic dependence). For intermediary services between carers and parents in relation to child care, see *Staatssecretaris van Financiën v Stichting Kinderopvang Enschede* (case C-415/04) [2006] ECR I–1385, [2007] STC 294.

For goods and services excluded from exemption under this head, see art 134.

(h) The supply of goods and services closely linked to the protection of children and young persons. The supply must be made by either a body governed by public law or (subject to any conditions imposed by member states in accordance with art 13A(2)(*a*)) by another organisation recognised by the relevant member state as being devoted to social wellbeing.

For "closely linked", see para (*g*) above. For intermediary services between carers and parents in relation to child care, see *Staatssecretaris van Financiën v Stichting Kinderopvang Enschede* (case C-415/04) [2006] ECR I–1385, [2007] STC 294.

For goods and services excluded from exemption under this head, see art 134.

(i) Children's or young people's education, school or university education, vocational training or retraining, and goods and services closely related to any of the foregoing. The supply must be made either: (1) by a body governed by public law having education, training or retraining as their aim, or (2) (subject to any conditions imposed by member states in accordance with art 133) by an organisation having similar objects. Organisations having similar objects are defined by the member states.

"Education" consists of a combination of elements, of which the transfer of knowledge and skills between teachers and students is particularly important. Educational activity also includes elements making up the organisational framework of the establishment concerned: *Ingenieurbüro Eulitz GbR Thomas und Marion Eulitz* (case C-473/08) [2010] ECR I–907 at [30].

An educational establishment does not supply "education, vocational training or retraining" by seconding a teacher to another educational establishment for teaching duties under the direction of that establishment. However, its supply may amount to services "closely related" to such services: *Stichting Regionaal Opleidingen Centrum Noord-Kennemerland/West-Friesland (Horizon College) v Staatssecretaris van Financiën* (case C-434/05) [2007] ECR I–4793, [2008] STC 2145.

Research projects undertaken for consideration by state universities are not "closely related" to university education: *Commission v Federal Republic of Germany* (case C-287/00) [2001] ECR I–5811, [2002] STC 982 at [49].

For goods and services excluded from exemption under this head, see art 134. For the scope of vocational training or retraining services, see Regulation (EU) No 282/2011 reg 44.

(j) Tuition given privately by teachers. The tuition must cover school or university education.

It appears that "tuition" includes private lessons given to an individual, or to two or more individuals at the same time, where there is a link between the actual content of the tuition and the teacher's qualifications: *Werner Haderer v Finanzamt Wilmersdorf* (case C-445/05) [2007] ECR I–4841, [2008] STC 2171 at [31].

Tuition is given "privately" if the teacher provides it on his own account and at his own risk. Whether or not a teacher meets this test is a matter for the national court: *Werner Haderer v Finanzamt Wilmersdorf* (case C-445/05) [2007] ECR I–4841, [2008] STC 2171 at [35]. For examples, see (1) *Werner Haderer v Finanzamt Wilmersdorf* (case C-445/05) [2007] ECR I–4841, [2008] STC 2171 (freelance teacher at an adult education institute); (2) *Ingenieurbüro Eulitz GbR Thomas und Marion Eulitz* (case C-473/08) [2010] ECR I–907 (partner of an engineering consultancy teaching at an education institute).

"School or university education" is not confined to education leading to examinations for the purpose of obtaining qualifications, or to education providing training for the purpose of carrying on a professional or trade activity. It also includes activities, other than those that are purely recreational, which are taught in schools or universities in order to develop knowledge and skills: *Werner Haderer v Finanzamt Wilmersdorf* (case C-445/05) [2007] ECR I–4841, [2008] STC 2171 at [26].

Teaching work performed in an education institute does not necessarily comprise "school or university education". However, it may fall within this provision if it includes the transfer of knowledge and skills between a teacher and pupils or students in the context of training for the purpose of carrying out, or continuing, a professional activity. Work other than teaching in the strict sense (eg acting as an examiner) amounts to tuition only to the extent that it can be regarded as being carried out in the context of the transfer of knowledge and skills between a teacher and pupils or students: *Ingenieurbüro Eulitz GbR Thomas und Marion Eulitz* (case C-473/08) [2010] ECR I–907 at [33], [35], [37].

(k) Certain supplies of staff by religious or philosophical institutions with a view to spiritual welfare. Staff must be supplied for the purpose of hospital and medical care within (*b*), welfare and social security work within (*g*), protection of children and young persons within (*h*), or education, training and retraining within (*i*).

(l) The supply of services and of goods linked closely thereto by non-profit-making organisations. The services and goods must be for the benefit of members and be provided in return for a subscription. The subscription must be fixed in accordance with the rules. The organisation must have aims of a political, trade union, religious, patriotic, philosophical, philanthropic or civic nature. It must meet any conditions imposed by member states in accordance with art 133. Exemption does not apply if it is likely to cause distortion of competition.

For "non-profit-making", cf *Kennemer Golf & Country Club v Staatssecretaris van Financiën* (case C-174/00) [2002] ECR I–3293, [2002] STC 502 at [35].

A "trade union" is an organisation whose main object is to defend the collective interests of its members – whether they are workers, employers, independent professionals or traders carrying on a particular activity – and to represent them vis-à-vis the appropriate third parties, including public authorities: *Institute of the Motor Industry v Customs and Excise Comrs* (case C-149/97) [1998] ECR I–7053, [1998] STC 1219 at [20].

For goods and services excluded from exemption, see art 134.

(m) Certain services closely linked to sport or physical education supplied to persons taking part in sport or physical education. The services must be supplied by a non-profit-making organisation. The organisation must meet the conditions (if any) imposed by member states in accordance with art 134.

When confining exemption to "certain" services, a member state may not make the exemption subject to conditions other than those laid down in arts 133: see *Commission v Kingdom of Spain* (*supported by United Kingdom, Intervener*) (case C-124/96) [1998] ECR I–2501, [1998] STC 1237 at [18].

In the context of persons taking part in sport, exemption extends to services supplied to corporate persons and to unincorporated associations if: (1) the services are closely linked and essential to sport; (2) they are supplied by a non-profit-making organisation; and (3) the true beneficiaries of the services are persons taking part in sport. It is for the national court to establish whether these conditions are met: see *Canterbury Hockey Club and another v R & C Comrs* (case C-253/07) [2008] ECR I–7821, [2008] STC 3351 at [35].

It is necessary to take account of all the organisation's activities in deciding whether it is "non-profit-making": *Kennemer Golf & Country Club v Staatssecretaris van Financiën* (case C-174/00) [2002] ECR I–3293, [2002] STC 502 at [22]. An organisation may be categorised as "non-profit-making" even if it seeks to achieve surpluses which it then uses for the purposes of the provision of its services: *Kennemer Golf & Country Club v Staatssecretaris van Financiën* (case C-174/00) [2002] ECR I–3293, [2002] STC 502 at [35].

For examples of conditions that unlawfully altered the scope of the exemption, see: (1) *Commission v Kingdom of Spain* (*supported by United Kingdom, Intervener*) (case C-124/96) [1998] ECR I–2501, [1998] STC 1237 (exemption confined to entry fees below a specific price); (2) *Canterbury Hockey Club and another v R & C Comrs* (case C-253/07) [2008] ECR I–7821, [2008] STC 3351 (exemption confined to services supplied to individuals).

For goods and services excluded from exemption, see art 134.

(n) Certain cultural services and goods closely linked thereto. The goods or services must be supplied by either: (1) a body governed by public law, or (2) any other cultural bodies recognised by the member state concerned.

Any restriction on this exemption must be imposed by reference to art 133: see *Criminal proceedings against Hoffmann* (case C-144/00) [2003] ECR I–2921, [2004] STC 740 at [39]. The reference to "certain" cultural services must be read accordingly.

The term "other cultural bodies recognised by the member state concerned" does not exclude soloists performing individually: *Criminal proceedings against Hoffmann* (case C-144/00) [2003] ECR I–2921, [2004] STC 740

For goods and services excluded from exemption under this head, see art 134.

(o) Goods and services supplied by an organisation in connection with fund raising events organised exclusively for its own benefit. The activities of the organisation must be exempted under (*b*), (*g*), (*h*), (*i*), (*l*), (*m*) or (*n*) above. Exemption does not apply if it is likely to cause distortion of competition. For restrictions imposed by member states, see para 2.

(p) The supply, by duly authorised bodies, of transport services for sick or injured persons in vehicles specially designed for such transport.

(q) The non-commercial activities of public radio and television bodies.

2. As regards point (*o*) of para 1, member states may introduce any necessary restrictions, eg in relation to the number of events held or the amount of the receipts giving entitlement to exemption.

Article 133
(ex art 13A(2)(a))

As regards exemptions under art 132(*b*), (*g*), (*h*), (*i*), (*l*), (*m*) and (*n*), member states may impose one or more of the following conditions on bodies that are not governed by public law:

(a) The body must not systematically aim to make a profit. However, any profits nevertheless arising must not be distributed; they must be assigned to the continuance or improvement of the services supplied.

For the interpretation of this condition in its application to art 132(*b*), (*g*), (*h*), (*i*) and (*n*) (which do not require the supply to be made by a "non-profit-making" body), see *Kennemer Golf & Country Club v Staatssecretaris van Financiën* (case C-174/00) [2002] ECR I–3293, [2002] STC 502 at [35]; *Kingcrest Associaties Ltd and another v Customs and Excise Comrs* (case C-498/03) [2005] ECR I–4427, [2005] STC 1547 at [38]–[40].

(b) The body must be managed and administered on an essentially voluntary basis by persons having no direct or indirect interest, whether personally or through intermediaries, in the results of the activities concerned.

Whether a body is "managed and administered on an essentially voluntary basis" is determined by reference to: (1) members of the body who, in accordance with the constitution, are designated to direct it at the highest level, and (2) other persons who, without being so designated, in fact direct it inasmuch as they take decisions of last resort concerning policy (especially in the financial area) and carry out the higher supervisory tasks: *Customs and Excise Comrs v Zoological Society of London* (case C-267/00) [2001] ECR I–3353, [2002] STC 521 at [23].

In determining whether a body is managed and administered "on an essentially voluantary basis", it is necessary to refer to both (1) the composition, in terms of membership, of (*a*) the directing organs, or (*b*) the persons who actually direct without being designated by the constitution; and (2) the reward which the latter may receive (whether habitually or by way of exception) from the body concerned: *Customs and Excise Comrs v Zoological Society of London* (case C-267/00) [2001] ECR I–3353, [2002] STC 521 at [26].

(c) The bodies must: (1) charge prices approved by the public authorities, (2) charge prices which do not exceed such approved prices, or (3) (in respect of services not subject to approval) charge prices lower than those charged for similar services by commercial enterprises subject to VAT.

(d) Exemption must not be likely to create distortions of competition so as to place commercial enterprises liable to VAT at a disadvantage.

Article 134
(ex art 13A(2)(b))

Member states must not grant exemption under art 132(*b*), (*g*), (*h*), (*i*), (*l*), (*m*) and (*n*) if:

(a) The supply is not essential to the transaction exempted.

(b) (If the transactions are in direct competition with those of commercial enterprises liable for VAT) the basic purpose of the supply is to obtain additional income for the organisation.

CHAPTER 3—EXEMPTIONS FOR OTHER ACTIVITIES

Article 135
(ex art 13B(a), (b), (d)–(h))

1. Member states must exempt the following:

(a) Insurance and reinsurance transactions. Related services performed by insurance brokers and insurance agents.

The essentials of an insurance transaction are that the insurer undertakes, in return for prior payment of a premium, to provide the insured, in the event of materialisation of the risk covered, with the service agreed when the contract was concluded. It is not essential for the agreed service to comprise payment of a sum of money. It may also take the form of providing assistance in cash or kind of the types listed in the annex to Directive 73/239/EEC: *Card Protection Plan Ltd v Customs and Excise Comrs* (case C-349/96) [1999] ECR I–973, [1999] STC 270 at [17], [18].

The expression "insurance transactions" is broad enough in principle to include the provision of insurance cover by a taxable person who is not himself an insurer but, in the context of a block policy, procures such cover for his customers by making use of the supplies of an insurer who assumes the risk insured: *Card Protection Plan Ltd v Customs and Excise Comrs* (case C-349/96) [1999] ECR I–973, [1999] STC 270 at [22]. For an example of services amounting to an insurance transaction, see *Commission v Greece* (case C-13/06) [2006] ECR I–11563, [2007] STC 194 (road assistance in the event of a breakdown).

For examples of services that do not amount to insurance transactions, see: (1) *Re Försäkringsaktiebolaget Skandia* (*publ*) (case C-240/99) [2001] ECR I–1951, [2001] STC 754 (commitment assumed by X — an insurance company – to carry out, in return for remuneration at market rates, the business activities of Y – another insurance company, being a 100% subsidiary of X, which continues to conclude insurance contracts in its own name); (2) *Assurandør-Societet* (*acting on behalf of Taksatorringen*) *v Skatteministeriet* (case C-8/01) [2003] ECR I–13711, [2006] STC 1842 (motor vehicle damage assessments carried out, on behalf of its members, by an association whose members are insurance companies); (3) *Staatssecretaris van Financiën v Arthur Andersen & Co Accountants cs* (case C-472/03) [2005] ECR I–1719, [2005] STC 508 ("back office" services, consisting of rendering services, for payment, to an insurance company); (4) *Swiss Re Germany Holding GmbH v Finanzamt München für Körperschaften* (case C-242/08) [2009] ECR I–10099, [2010] STC 189 (transfer of a portfolio of reinsurance contracts).

Member states may not restrict the scope of the exemption for insurance transactions exclusively to supplies by insurers who are authorised by national law to pursue the activity of insurer: *Card Protection Plan Ltd v Customs and Excise Comrs* (case C-349/96) [1999] ECR I–973, [1999] STC 270 at [36].

A reinsurance transaction is a tranaction whereby an insurer concludes a contract in which it undertakes to assume, in return for payment of a premium and within the confines of that contract, the debts resulting, for another insurer, from its undertakings in the insurance contracts which it concluded with its own policy-holders: *Swiss Re Germany Holding GmbH v Finanzamt München für Körperschaften* (case C-242/08) [2009] ECR I–10099, [2010] STC 189 at [38] For an example of services which do not amount to a reinsurance transaction, see *Swiss Re Germany Holding GmbH v Finanzamt München für Körperschaften* (case C-242/08) [2009] ECR I–10099, [2010] STC 189 (transfer of a portfolio of reinsurance contracts).

Recognition of a person as an "insurance broker or agent" presupposes an examination of what the activities in question comprise. An essential aspect of the work of an "insurance agent" is the finding of prospects and their introduction to the insurer: *Staatssecretaris van Financiën v Arthur Andersen & Co Accountants cs* (case C-472/03) [2005] ECR I–1719, [2005] STC 508 at [32], [36].

Traders must have freedom to choose the form of organisation which best suits them from a strictly commercial point of view. The activity of an insurance broker or agent may be broken down into separate services which may comprise related services performed by insurance brokers and insurance agents. The absence of a direct relationship with the insurer is immaterial if an indirect contractual relationship is present: *JCM Beheer BV v Staatssecretaris van Financiën* (case C-124/07) [2008] ECR I–2101, [2008] STC 3360 at [26]–[28].

For an example activities which were "unquestionably the characteristic activities of an insurance broker or agent", see *JCM Beheer BV v Staatssecretaris van Financiën* (case C-124/07) [2008] ECR I–2101, [2008] STC 3360 (indirect relationship with the parties to the insurance contracts as sub-agent of an insurance broker or agent having a direct relationship with one of those parties).

For an example of services that were not "related services" of a kind performed by insurance brokers or insurance agents, see: (1) *Assurandør-Societet* (*acting on behalf of Taksatorringen*) *v Skatteministeriet* (case C-8/01) [2003] ECR I–13711, [2006] STC 1842 (motor vehicle damage assessments carried out, on behalf of its members, by an association whose members are insurance companies); (2) *Staatssecretaris van Financiën v Arthur Andersen & Co Accountants cs* (case C-472/03) [2005] ECR I–1719, [2005] STC 508 ("back office" services, consisting of rendering services, for payment, to an insurance company).

For the right to deduct input tax on goods and services used for the purposes of transactions exempted under this head, see art 169(*c*). This exemption is, therefore, an exemption with refund.

(b) The following supplies in connection with credit:

- Granting credit. In principle, a supplier makes an exempt grant of credit when he authorises his customer to defer payment of the price in return for payment of interest. However, this does not apply if payment is merely deferred until delivery. In this situation, the interest constitutes part of the consideration for the supply of goods or services concerned: *Muys' en De Winter's Bouw-en Aannemingsbedrijf BV v Staatssecretaris van Financiën* (case C-281/91) [1993] ECR I–5405, [1997] STC 665.
- Negotiating credit. If a taxable person contributes to the conclusion of a credit agreement, his services are not excluded from exemption under this head merely because: (a) he does not have direct contact with one of the parties to the agreement, and (b) he does not have a contractual link with either or both of the parties to the agreement: *Volker Ludwig v Finanzamt Luckenwalde* (case C-453/05) [2007] ECR I–5083, [2008] STC 1640 (sub-agent).

  A taxable person may analyse the financial situation of clients canvassed by him with a view to obtaining credit for them. His overall service may fall within this head if the negotiation of credit is the principal service to which the provision of financial advice is ancillary: *Volker Ludwig v Finanzamt Luckenwalde* (case C-453/05) [2007] ECR I–5083, [2008] STC 1640.

  For the direct effect of this provision in the absence of national implementing legislation, see *Becker v Finanzamt Munster-Innenstadt* (case 8/81) [1982] ECR 53, [1982] 1 CMLR 499; *R A Grendel GmbH v*

Part I VAT

Finanzamt für Köperschaften, Hamburg (case 255/81) [1982] ECR 2301, [1983] 1 CMLR 379; *Kloppenburg v Finanzamt Leer* (case 70/83) [1984] ECR 1075, [1985] 1 CMLR 205; *Weissberber v Finanzamt Neustadt an der Weinstraße* (case 207/87) [1988] ECR 4433, [1991] STC 589.

- The management of credit by the person granting it.

The assumption of an obligation to renovate a building does not fall within the scope of this provision: *Velvet & Steel Immobilien und Handels GmbH* (case C-455/05) [2007] ECR I–3225, [2008] STC 922.

For the right to deduct input tax on goods and services used for the purposes of transactions exempted under this head, see art 169(*c*). This exemption is, therefore, an exemption with refund.

(c) The following supplies in connection with securities for money:

- Negotiating credit guarantees or any other security for money.
- Dealing in credit guarantees or any other security for money. For an example of a transaction which did not amount to dealing within this description, see *Swiss Re Germany Holding GmbH v Finanzamt München für Körperschaften* (case C-242/08) [2009] ECR I–10099, [2010] STC 189 (transfer of a portfolio of reinsurance contracts).
- The management of credit guarantees by the person who granted the credit.

These transactions are defined in terms of the nature of the services provided and not in terms of the person supplying or receiving the service. The services provided must, viewed broadly, form a distinct whole, fulfilling in effect the specific, essential functions of a transaction of the relevant description. It is immaterial whether the service is carried out by a bank or other financial institution. However, it must relate, as a whole, to the sphere of financial transactions: *Swiss Re Germany Holding GmbH v Finanzamt München für Körperschaften* (case C-242/08) [2009] ECR I–10099, [2010] STC 189 at [44]–[46].

For the right to deduct input tax on goods and services used for the purposes of transactions exempted under this head, see art 169(*c*). This exemption is, therefore, an exemption with refund.

(d) Transactions (including negotiation) concerning:

- Deposit and current accounts.
- Payments. Transactions under this head include operations carried out by a data-handling centre if those operations are distinct in character and are specific to, and essential for, the exempt transactions: *Sparekassernes Datacenter (SDC) v Skatteministeriet* (case C-2/95) [1997] ECR I–3017, [1997] STC 932.
- Transfers. Transactions under this head include operations carried out by a data-handling centre if those operations are distinct in character and are specific to, and essential for, the exempt transactions: *Sparekassernes Datacenter (SDC) v Skatteministeriet* (case C-2/95) [1997] ECR I–3017, [1997] STC 932. For an example of services which do not amount to a transfer, see Proceedings brought by *Nordea Pankki Suomi Oyj* (case C-350/10) [2011] ECR 1–0000 (electronic messaging services for financial institutions).
- Debts. For an example of a transaction which did not concern debts, see *Swiss Re Germany Holding GmbH v Finanzamt München für Körperschaften* (case C-242/08) [2009] ECR I–10099, [2010] STC 189 (transfer of a portfolio of reinsurance contracts).
- Cheques.
- Other negotiable instruments.

These transactions are defined in terms of the nature of the services provided and not in terms of the person supplying or receiving the service. The services provided must, viewed broadly, form a distinct whole, fulfilling in effect the specific, essential functions of a transaction of the relevant description. It is immaterial whether the service is carried out by a bank or other financial institution. However, it must relate, as a whole, to the sphere of financial transactions: *Swiss Re Germany Holding GmbH v Finanzamt München für Körperschaften* (case C-242/08) [2009] ECR I–10099, [2010] STC 189 at [44]–[46].

Exemption is not subject to the condition that the transactions are effected wholly or partly by certain electronic means or manually. Exemption is not subject to the condition that the service is provided by an institution having a legal relationship with the end customer. Exemption is not precluded merely because a transaction effected by a third party appears, to the end customer, to be a service provided by a bank. Making financial information available to banks and other users is not exempted under this head. A transaction is not excluded from exemption under this head merely because it is invoiced by a third party. See *Sparekassernes Datacenter (SDC) v Skatteministeriet* (case C-2/95) [1997] ECR I–3017, [1997] STC 932.

Debt collection is specifically excluded from exemption. The essential aim of factoring is the recovery and collection of debts owed by a third party. It is therefore regarded as a variant of the more general concept of debt collection, whatever the manner in which it is carried out: *Finanzamt Groß-Gerau v MKG-Kraftfahrzeuge-Factoring GmbH* (case C-305/01) [2003] ECR I–6729, [2003] STC 951 at [77], [78]. For an example of debt collection, see *Revenue and Customs Comrs v Axa UK plc* (case C-175/09) [2010] ECR I–0000, [2010] STC 2825 (payment plans for dental care).

For the right to deduct input tax on goods and services used for the purposes of transactions exempted under this head, see art 169(*c*). This exemption is, therefore, an exemption with refund.

(e) Transactions (including negotiation) concerning currency, bank notes (other than bank notes which are not normally used as legal tender) and coins (other than gold, silver or other metal coins which are not normally used as legal tender and coins of numismatic interest) used as legal tender. For platinum nobles, see Regulation (EU) No 282/2011 reg 45.

For the right to deduct input tax on goods and services used for the purposes of transactions exempted under this head, see art 169(*c*). This exemption is, therefore, an exemption with refund.

(f) Transactions (including negotiation) in shares, interests in companies or associations, debentures and other securities. This includes transactions carried out by a data-handling centre if they are separate in character and are specific to, and essential for, the exempt transactions: *Sparekassernes Datacenter (SDC) v Skatteministeriet* (case C-2/95) [1997] ECR I–3017, [1997] STC 932.

Exemption is not subject to the condition that the transactions are effected by a certain type of institution, by a certain type of legal person, or wholly or partly by certain electronic means or manually. Exemption is not subject to the condition that the service is provided by an institution having a legal relationship with the end customer. Exemption is not precluded merely because a transaction effected by a third party appears, to the end customer, to be a service provided by a bank. Making financial information available to banks and other users is not exempted under this head. A transaction is not excluded from exemption under this head merely because it is invoiced by a third party. See *Sparekassernes Datacenter (SDC) v Skatteministeriet* (case C-2/95) [1997] ECR I–3017, [1997] STC 932.

Transactions in "securities" are transactions liable to create, alter or extinguish parties' rights and obligations inrespect of securities: *CSC Financial Services Ltd v Customs and Excise Comrs* (case C-235/00) [2001] ECR I–10237, [2002] STC 57 at [33]. This includes services supplied for consideration by a credit institution, in the form of an underwriting guarantee to a company wishing to issue shares, under which the credit institution undertakes to acquire any shares which are not subscribed within the period for share subscription: *Skandinaviska Enskilda Banken AB Momsgrupp v Skatteverket* (case C-540/09) [2011] ECR I–0000, [2000] STC 1125.

For examples of services which amount to a transaction in shares etc, see: (1) *Skatteverket v AB SKF* (case C-29/08) [2009] ECR I–10413, [2010] STC 419 (sale of shares in subsidiary by a holding company); (2) *Skandinaviska Enskilda Banken AB Momsgrupp v Skatteverket* (case C-540/09) [2011] ECR I–0000, [2000] STC 1125 (underwriting guarantee to a company wishing to issue shares, under which the credit institution undertakes to acquire any shares which are not subscribed within the period for share subscription). For an example of services which do not amount to a transaction in shares etc, see Proceedings brought by *Nordea Pankki Suomi Oyj* (case C-350/10) [2011] ECR 1–0000 (electronic messaging services for financial institutions).

For the purposes of this exemption, "negotiation" refers to the activity of an intermediary who does not occupy the position of any party to a contract relating to a financial product, and whose activity amounts to something other than the provision of contractual services typically undertaken by the parties to such contracts. Negotiation is a service rendered to, and remunerated by a contractual party as a distinct act of mediation. It may consist, among other things, in pointing out suitable opportunities for the conclusion of such a contract, making contact with another party or negotiating (in the name of, and on behalf of, a client) the detail of the payments to be made by either side. The purpose of the negotiation is therefore to do all that is necessary in order for two parties to enter into a contract, without the negotiator having any interest of his own in the terms of the contract: *CSC Financial Services Ltd v Customs and Excise Comrs* (case C-235/00) [2001] ECR I–10237, [2002] STC 57 at [39].

For an example of services that do not amount to "negotiation", see *CSC Financial Services Ltd v Customs and Excise Comrs* (case C-235/00) [2001] ECR I–10237, [2002] STC 57 (services limited to providing information about a financial product and, as the case may be, receiving and processing applications for subscription, without issuing them).

The following transactions are specifically excluded from exemption:

- Management and safe-keeping.
- Transactions in documents establishing title to goods.
- Transactions in interests in immovable property (see art 15(2)(*a*)).
- Transactions in rights in rem giving the holder a right of user over immovable property (see art 15(2)(*b*)).
- Transactions in shares or interest equivalent to shares giving the holder de jure or de facto rights of ownership or possession over immovable property (see art 15(2)(*c*)).

For the right to deduct input tax on goods and services used for the purposes of transactions exempted under this head, see art 169(*c*). This exemption is, therefore, an exemption with refund.

(g) Management of special investment funds.

The "special investment funds" to which the management must relate are those defined by the member states. In defining the funds concerned, member states must respect the objective pursued by the exemption (ie to facilitate investment in securities for investors through investment undertakings) and the principle of fiscal neutrality (which includes the principle of elimination of distorition in competition as a result of differing treatment for VAT purposes): *J P Morgan Fleming Claverhouse Investment Trust plc and another v R & C Comrs* (case C-363/05) [2007] ECR I–5517, [2087] STC 1180 at [41]–[47].

A "special investment fund" is an undertaking for collective investment. Its legal form is irrelevant. It may therefore be constituted under the law of contract or trust law, or under statute: *Abbey National plc and another v Customs & Excise Comrs*

Finanze – Ufficio IVA di Milano v CO.GE.P Srl (case C-174/06) [2007] ECR I–9359, [2008] STC 2744 (concession to use areas of state maritime property); (4) *Macdonald Resorts Ltd v Revenue and Customs Comrs* (case C-270/09) [2010] ECR I– 0000, [2011] STC 412 (conversion of rights acquired under a timeshare points scheme into a right to temporarily use a property).

For examples of transactions that do not amount to a letting, see (1) *Commission v Ireland* (case C-358/97) [2000] ECR I–6301 and *Commission v United Kingdom* (case C-359/97) [2000] ECR I–6355, [2000] STC 777 (road and bridge tolls); (2) *Swedish State v Stockholm Lindöpark AB* (case C-150/99) [2001] ECR I–493, [2001] STC 103 (golf course); (3) *Customs and Excise Comrs v Mirror Group plc* (case C-409/98) [2001] ECR I–7175, [2001] STC 1453 (reverse premium paid to anchor tenant as inducement to enter into a lease); (4) *Customs and Excise Comrs v Cantor Fitzgerald International* (case C-108/99) [2001] ECR I–7257, [2001] STC 1453 (reverse premium paid to new tenant on assignment of lease by existing tenant); (5) *Seeling v Finanzamt Starnberg* (case C-269/00) [2003] ECR I–4101, [2003] STC 805 (the supply of services deemed to be made under art 6(2)(*a*) in respect of the private use of a dwelling in a building by a taxable person who has treated the entirety of building as part of the assets of his business); (6) *Sinclair Collis Ltd v Customs and Excise Comrs* (case C-275/01) [2003] ECR I–5965, [2003] STC 898 (grant of the right to install, operate and maintain vending machine on the premises); (7) *Gabriele Walderdorff v Finanzamt Waldviertel* (case C-451/06) [2007] ECR I–10637, [2008] STC 3079 (grant in respect of area of water confined to right to fish and landlord retaining right to continue fishing with one guest); (8) *RLRE Tellmer Property sro v Finanční ředitelstvi v Ústí nad Labem* (case C-572/07) [2009] ECR I–4983, [2009] STC 2006 (cleaning of common parts of building invoiced separately from rent of apartments).

"Immovable property" is property that is neither mobile nor easily moved. There is no need for the property to be inseverably fixed to, or in, the ground. The terms of the lease are irrelevant in determining whether the property is movable or immovable: *Maierhofer v Finanzamt Augsburg-Land* (case C-315/00) [2003] ECR I–563, [2003] STC 564 at [32], [33]. The fact that land is partly under water does not prevent it from being categorised as immovable property that can be leased or let: *Fonden Marselisborg Lystbådehavn v Skatteministeriet* (case C-428/02) [2005] ECR I–1527, [2006] STC 1467 at [34]. For examples of immovable property, see: (1) *Maierhofer v Finanzamt Augsburg-Land* (case C-315/00) [2003] ECR I–563, [2003] STC 564 (buildings with a concrete base erected on concrete foundations sunk into the ground requiring 80 man-days to be dismantled for subsequent re-use); (2) *Fonden Marselisborg Lystbådehavn v Skatteministeriet* (case C-428/02) [2005] ECR I–1527, [2006] STC 1467 (water-based mooring berths). For an example of movable property, see *Commission v French Republic* (case C-60/96) [1997] ECR I–3827, [1999] STC 480 (mobile property such as caravans and mobile homes and easily moved property such as tents and light-framed leisure dwellings).

2. The following transactions are excluded from exemption under para 1(*l*):

(a) The provision of accommodation (as defined in the laws of the member states) in the hotel sector, or in sectors with a similar function. This includes: (1) accommodation in holiday camps, and (2) accommodation on sites developed for use as camping sites. For "accommodation in sectors with a similar function to the hotel sector", see *Blasi v Finanzamt München I* (case C-346/95) [1998] ECR I–481, [1998] STC 336 (exclusion from exemption of short-term accommodation under German law).

(b) The letting of premises and sites for parking vehicles. The phrase "premises and sites for parking vehicles" covers the letting of all places designed to be used for parking vehicles, including closed garages. However, lettings of closed garages are not excluded from exemption under this head if they are closely linked to lettings of immovable property for another purpose, which are themselves exempt from

VAT. It is for the national court to establish whether lettings meet this criterion: *Skatteministeriet v Henriksen* (case 173/88) [1989] ECR 2763, [1990] STC 768 at [17], [18]. The term "vehicles" covers all means of transport, including boats: *Fonden Marselisborg Lystbådehavn v Skatteministeriet* (case C-428/02) [2005] ECR I–1527, [2006] STC 1467 at [44].
- (c) Lettings of permanently installed equipment and machinery.
- (d) Hire of safes.

The exclusions in (*a*)–(*d*) represent an exception to the exemption laid down for the letting and leasing of immovable property. The consequence is that the transactions concerned become subject to the general rule that that VAT is charged on all taxable transactions. It follows that the exclusions cannot be interpreted strictly: *Fonden Marselisborg Lystbådehavn v Skatteministeriet* (case C-428/02) [2005] ECR I–1527, [2006] STC 1467 at [43].

Member states may apply further exclusions to the scope of the exemption in para 1(*l*). Although member states are free to limit the scope of the exemption by providing additional exclusions, they may not exempt transactions that are excluded from exemption: *Skatteministeriet v Henriksen* (case 173/88) [1989] ECR 2763, [1990] STC 768 at [21]. Thus, they cannot tax the consideration paid by one party to the other in connection with the surrender of the lease where the rent paid under the lease is exempt from VAT: *Lubbock Fine & Co v Customs and Excise Comrs* (case C-63/92) [1993] ECR I–6665, [1994] STC 101. On the other hand, member states may introduce a general rule charging all lettings of immovable property to tax and, by way of exception, exempt only lettings of immovable property for use as dwellings: *Miguel Amengual Far v Juan Amengual Far* (case C-12/98) [2000] ECR I–527, [2002] STC 382.

Article 136
(ex art 13B(c))

Member states must exempt the following transactions:
- (a) A supply of goods used wholly for an activity exempted under arts 132, 135 or 371 if those goods have not given rise to deductibility. The exemptions in arts 375–390b do not apply to the UK.
- (b) A supply of goods on the acquisition or application of which VAT was not deductible pursuant to art 176. For a transaction which did not amount to a supply of goods, see *Swiss Re Germany Holding GmbH v Finanzamt München für Körperschaften* (case C-242/08) [2009] ECR I–10099, [2010] STC 189 (transfer of a portfolio of reinsurance contracts). For the resale of motor vehicles originally purchased secondhand from non-taxable-persons, see *Jyske Finans A/S v Skatteministeriet* (case C-280/04) [2005] ECR I–10683, [2006] STC 1744.

Article 137
(ex art 13C)

1. Member states may allow taxpayers a right of option for taxation in respect of the following transactions:
- (a) Financial services within art 135(1)(*b*)–(*g*).
- (b) The supply of a building (or part of a building) and the land on which it stands. This does not apply to a supply made before first occupation.
- (c) The supply of land which has not been built on. This does not apply to a supply of improved or unimproved land defined as such by the relevant member state.
- (d) The leasing or letting of immovable property.

2. Member states must lay down detailed rules governing exercise of the option in para 1. They may restrict the scope of this right of option.

Member states may allow persons benefiting from one of the foregoing exemptions to waive the exemption in all cases, or within certain limits, or subject to certain detailed rules. In drawing a distinction by reference to types of transactions or groups of taxable persons, member states must observe the general objectives and principles of the Sixth Directive. In particular, they must observe the principle of fiscal neutrality and the requirement of correct, straightforward and uniform application of the exemptions provided for: *Turn-und Sportunion Waldburg v Finanzlandesdirektion für Oberösterreich* (case C-246/04) [2006] ECR I–589, [2006] STC 1506 (restriction of the right of option in relation to letting or leasing by sports clubs).

Member states merely have the right to allow, to a greater or lesser degree, persons entitled to those exemptions to opt for taxation themselves if they consider that it is in their interests to do so: *Becker v Finanzamt Munster-Innenstadt* (case 8/81) [1982] ECR 53, [1982] 1 CMLR 499 at [39].

This provision allows member states to grant a right of option to their taxable persons. It also allows them to restrict the scope of that right or to withdraw it. Any expectations a taxable person may have regarding the opportunities for deduction arising from exercising the option do not arise from this directive: *Gemeente Leusden v Staatssecretaris van Financiën; Holin Groep BV cs v Staatssecretaris van Financiën* (joined cases C-487/01 and C-7/02) [2004] ECR I–5337, [2007] STC 776 at [66]–[69].

To the extent that national legislation has not been brought into force prior to repeal, it is for the national court to determine whether the principle of protection of legitimate expectations or the principle of legal certainty has been breached: *Belgocodex SA v Belgian State* (case C-381/97) [1998] ECR I–8153, [2000] STC 351.

Member states are not precluded from adopting legislation making full deduction of input tax conditional upon non-retrospective prior approval by the tax authorities: *Administration de l'enregistrement et des domains, État du grand-duché de Luxembourg v Vermietungsgesellschaft Object Kirchberg SARL* (case C-269/03) [2004] ECR I–8067, [2005] STC 1345.

CHAPTER 4—EXEMPTIONS FOR INTRA-COMMUNITY TRANSACTIONS

General note National legislation must provide for the possibility of correcting any tax improperly invoiced where the person who issued the invoice shows that he acted in good faith. However, good faith is not a requirement if that person has, in sufficient time, wholly eliminated the risk of any loss in tax revenues. These rules apply equally to an account adjustment made for the purpose of obtaining an exemption in respect of an intra-Community supply: *Albert Collée v Finanzamt Limburg an der Lahn* (case C-146/05) [2007] ECR I–7861, [2087] STC 757 at [35].

SECTION 1—EXEMPTIONS RELATED TO THE SUPPLY OF GOODS

Article 138
(ex art 28cA(a) (first para), 28cA(b), 28cA(c) (first para), 28cA(d))

1. A member state must exempt a supply of goods if the following conditions are met:

- The goods are despatched or transported to a destination outside its territory (see art 5(2)).
- The destination is within the Community (see art 5(1)).
- The goods are despatched or transported by, or on behalf, of: (1) the vendor, or (2) the person acquiring the goods.
- The goods are despatched or transported for either: (1) another taxable person; or (2) a non-taxable legal person acting as such in another member state. The precise formulation of this condition, and its meaning, are unclear. In the UK, VAT Regulations 1995, SI 1995/2518 reg 134 proceeds on the basis that the goods must be supplied to a person in (1) or (2).
- The supply is not excluded from exemption under art 139(1), (3).

No VAT is payable on a supply which meets the foregoing conditions, even if the taxable person has failed to comply with some of the substantive requirements, unless that non-compliance would effectively prevent the production of conclusive evidence that the substantive requirements have been satisfied: *Albert Collée v Finanzamt Limburg an der Lahn* (case C- 146/05) [2007] ECR I–7861, [2008] STC 757 at [30], [31]. It is for the national court to determine whether the conditions have been met: *Transport Service NV v Belgian State* (case C-395/02) [2004] ECR I–1991 at [19].

The legislation does not require transport of the goods to be commenced or completed within any specific period. It is merely necessary to establish: (1) a temporal and material link between the supply of the goods and their transportation, and (2) continuity in the course of the transaction. See *X v Skatteverket* (case C-84/09) [2010] ECR I– 0000, [2011] STC 189 at [29], [33].

Tax authorities principally rely on evidence provided by taxable persons and statements made by them. The burden of proving entitlement to exemption lies with the supplier. If the supplier is unable to provide the required evidence, the member state of despatch is not required to request the necessary information from the authorities of the destination member state alleged by the supplier: *Twoh International BV v Staatssecretaris van Financiën* (case C-184/05) [2007] ECR I–7897, [2008] STC 740.

As regards an intra-Community supply of goods which actually take place, the supplier may – at the time of supply – conceal the identity of the true purchaser in order to enable the latter to evade payment of VAT in the member state of destination. In these circumstances, the member state of departure may refuse to allow exemption in respect of the supply: *Criminal proceedings against R* (case C-285/09) [2010] ECR I–0000, [2011] STC 138.

The following conditions must be met: (1) the right to dispose of the goods as owner has been transferred to the person acquiring the goods; (2) the supplier establishes that those goods have been despatched or transported to another member state; and (3) as a result of the despatch or transport, the goods have physically left the territory of the member state of supply: *Euro Tyre Holding BV v Staatssecretaris van Financiën* (case C-430/09) [2010] ECR I–0000, [2011] STC 798 at [29].

The application of these conditions becomes complex where a single intra-Community despatch or transport involves both: (1) a supply by X (a taxable person in member state A) to Y (a taxable person in member state B); and (2) a supply by Y to either Z1 (a taxable person in member state B) or Z2 (a taxable person in member state C). It is necessary to determine whether the despatch of transport should be ascribed to the supply made to Y, Z1 or Z2. The despatch or transport can be ascribed to only one of these supplies: *EMAG Handel Eder OHG v Finanzlandesdirecktion für Kärnten* (case C-245/04) [2006] ECR I–3227, [2007] STC 1461 at [45].

As regards the first condition, the collection of the goods from X's warehouse by Y's representative is regarded as a transfer of the right to dispose of the goods as owner from X to Y. However, this alone is insufficient to demonstrate that the supply by X to Y constitutes an intra-Community supply because Y may have transferred (to Z1 or Z2) his right to dispose of the goods as owner before the intra-Community transport commenced in member state A (so that the intra-Community supply is made by Y). See *Euro Tyre Holding BV v Staatssecretaris van Financiën* (case C-430/09) [2010] ECR I–0000, [2011] STC 798 at [32], [33].

As regards the second condition, X has no first-hand evidence that the goods have left member state A if the goods are collected from his premises by Y (or Y's representative). In these circumstances, X necessarily relies on the information provided by Y. He is entitled to rely on: (1) Y's expressed intention to transport the goods to member state B or member state C; and (2) the fact that he has been provided with Y's VAT identification number in member state B. However, X must act in good faith and take every reasonable measure in his power to ensure that his supply does not lead to participation in tax fraud. See *Euro Tyre Holding BV v Staatssecretaris van Financiën* (case C-430/09) [2010] ECR I–0000, [2011] STC 798 at [34]–[38].

As regards the third condition, the address at which the transport of the goods ends seems to be relevant in determining whether the goods have left member state A. However, it seems to be irrelevant in determining whether the transport is effected in the context of the first or second supply See *Euro Tyre Holding BV v Staatssecretaris van Financiën* (case C-430/09) [2010] ECR I–0000, [2011] STC 798 at [42] (goods not transported to Y's address). The following consequences arise if Y fails to despatch or transport the goods from member state A. First, X is liable for VAT on his supply if, following the transfer of his right to dispose of the goods: (1) Y informs him that the goods are to be sold to Z1 or Z2; (2) the sale is to take place before the goods leave member state A; and (3) X fails to send a rectifying invoice charging VAT to Y. Secondly, if X has fulfilled his obligations relating to evidence, it is Y who is liable for the VAT due in member state A. Whether or not X has fulfilled his obligations relating to evidence and diligence is a matter for the national court. The court makes its assessment on the basis of the conditions laid down by national law. See *Euro Tyre Holding BV v Staatssecretaris van Financiën* (case C-430/09) [2010] ECR I–0000, [2011] STC 798 at [36], [39].

The person holding the right to dispose of the goods during the intra-Community transport could be X, Y, Z1 or Z2. In principle, it is irrelevant who holds this right during the intra-Community transport. However, the fact that the transport is effected by (or on behalf of) the owner may nevertheless play a role in deciding whether the transport is ascribed to the first or second supply. It is not decisive where the transport is effected by (or on behalf of) Y. See *Euro Tyre Holding BV v Staatssecretaris van Financiën* (case C-430/09) [2010] ECR I–0000, [2011] STC 798 at [40], [41] (Z1's involvement in the transport not a factor supporting the conclusion that the transport must be ascribed to the supply by Y to Z1).

For examples of a single intra-Community despatch or transport involving two separate supplies, see: (1) *EMAG Handel Eder OHG v Finanzlandesdirecktion für Kärnten* (case C-245/04) [2006] ECR I–3227, [2007] STC 1461; (2) *Euro Tyre Holding BV v Staatssecretaris van Financiën* (case C-430/09) [2010] ECR I–0000, [2011] STC 798. For the place of supply of each supply, see the commentary to art 32.

For conditions imposed by member states, see art 131.

2. A member state must also exempt the following transactions:

(a) The supply of a new means of transport. The following conditions must be met:
- The new means of transport is despatched or transported to the customer at a destination outside the territory of the member state.
- That destination is within the Community.
- The new means of transport was despatched or transported by: (1) the vendor, (2) the person acquiring the goods, or (3) a person acting on behalf of either of those persons.
- The supply is made on behalf of: (1) a taxable person whose acquisitions of goods are not charged to VAT under art 3(1); (2) a non-taxable legal person whose acquisitions of goods are not charged to VAT by virtue of art 3(1); or (3) any other non-taxable person.

(b) The supply of products subject to excise duty. The following conditions must be met:
- The products are despatched or transported to the customer at a destination outside the territory of the member state.
- That destination is within the Community.
- The products are despatched or transported by: (1) the vendor, (2) the person acquiring the goods, or (3) a person acting on behalf of either of those persons.
- The despatch or transport is carried out in accordance with Directive 92/12/EEC arts 7(4), (5) or 16. The 1992 Directive is repealed and replaced by Directive 2008/118/EC with effect from 1 April 2010. From that date, references to the 1992 Directive are construed as references to the 2008 Directive in accordance with art 47(2) of the 2008 Directive.
- The supply is made on behalf of a taxable person, or non-taxable legal person.

- If the taxable person or non-legal person makes intra-Community acquisitions of goods other than products subject to excise duty, his acquisitions of those goods are not charged to VAT by virtue of art 3(1).

For supplies excluded from exemption under this provision, see art 139(2), (3).

(c) A transfer of goods to another member state. The following conditions must be met:

- The transfer amounts to a supply of goods. For transfers of goods amounting to a supply of goods, see art 17.
- The transfer would be exempted under paras 1, 2(*a*) or 2(*b*) if it had been made on behalf of another taxable person.

For supplies excluded from exemption under this provision, see art 139(3).

Article 139
(ex arts 28cA(a) (second para), 28cA(c) (second para), 28o(1)(h))

1. The exemption in art 138(1) does not apply if:

- The goods are supplied by a taxable person exempt from tax under the special scheme for small enterprises (see art 283).
- The supply is made to a taxable person, or non-taxable legal person, whose intra-Community acquisitions of goods are not charged to VAT under art 3(1).

2. The exemption in art 138(2)(*b*) does not apply if the products subject to excise duty are supplied by a taxable person exempt from tax under the special scheme for small enterprises (see art 283).

3. The exemptions in art 138(1), (2)(*a*), (2)(*c*) do not apply to goods charged to VAT in accordance with the margin schemes for taxable dealers (see arts 312–325) and sales by public auctions (see arts 333–341).

The exemptions in art 138(1), (2)(*c*) do not apply to second-hand means of transport charged to VAT in accordance with the transitional arrangements for second-hand means of transport (see arts 326–332).

SECTION 2—EXEMPTIONS FOR INTRA-COMMUNITY ACQUISITIONS OF GOODS

Article 140
(ex art 28cB)

Member states must exempt the following transactions:

(a) An intra-Community acquisition of goods (as defined in art 28(3)), if a supply of those goods by a taxable person would, in all circumstances, be exempt within the territory of the member state (as defined in art 5(2)).

(b) An intra-Community acquisition of goods (as defined in art 28(3)), if an importation of those goods would, in all circumstances, be exempt under art 143(1)(*a*), (*b*), (*c*) or (*e*)–(*l*).

(c) An intra-Community acquisition of goods (as defined in art 28(3)), if the person acquiring the goods would, in all circumstances, be entitled to full reimbursement of the VAT incurred by him under art 2(1)(*b*). For the reimbursement arrangements, see arts 170, 171; Directive 2008/9/EC (formerly Directive 79/1072/EEC) (EC traders); and Directive 86/560/EEC (third country traders).

Article 141
(ex art 28cE(3))

A member state ("member state A") must take specific measures to ensure that VAT is not charged on an intra-Community acquisition of goods within its territory in the following circumstances:

- The acquisition in member state A is made by a taxable person ("X").
- X is not established in member state A. However, he is identified for VAT purposes in another member state ("member state B").

- The acquisition is made by X for the purpose of supplying the goods in member state A to another person ("Y").
- Y is a taxable person, or non-taxable legal person, who is identified for VAT purposes in member state A.
- The goods acquired by X are directly despatched or transported to Y from a member state other than the one in which X is identified for VAT purposes ("member state C").
- Y is designated as the person liable for the VAT due on the supply made by X in accordance with art 197.

SECTION 3—EXEMPTIONS FOR CERTAIN TRANSPORT SERVICES

Article 142
(ex art 28cC)

Member states must exempt the following supplies:

- An intra-Community transport of goods to or from the islands making up the autonomous regions of the Azores and Madeira.
- The transport of goods between those islands.

CHAPTER 5—EXEMPTIONS ON IMPORTATION

General note Member states do not enjoy a complete discretion in implementing the exemptions under this provision. Member states must observe the fundamental objectives of the harmonisation of VAT such as, in particular, facilitating the free movement of goods and persons, and preventing cases of double taxation: *Ministere Publique and Ministere des Finances v Profant* (case 249/84) [1985] ECR 3237, [1986] 2 CMLR 378 at [25].

Article 143
(ex arts 14(1)(a), (d), (e), (g), (h), (j), (k) and 28c(d) (first para))

1. Member states must exempt the following transactions:

(a) A final importation of goods if, in all circumstances, a supply of those goods by a taxable person would be exempted within the territory of the member state. For the territory of a member state, see art 5(2).

(b) A final importation of goods governed by:
- As regards international travel, Directive 2007/74/EC (replacing Directive 69/169/EEC);
- As regards the scope of art 143(b), (c), Directive 2009/132/EC (replacing Directive 83/181/EEC);
- As regards small non-commercial consignments, Directive 2006/79/EC (replacing Directive 78/1035/EEC).

(c) A final importation of goods in free circulation from a third territory forming part of the Community customs territory (ie one of the territories listed in art 6(1)), if the goods would have been entitled to exemption under point (*b*) if they had been imported within the meaning of art 30 (first para).

(d) An importation of goods, if:
- The goods are despatched or transported from a third country (see art 5(4)) or third territory (see art 5(3)) to a place in a member state.
- The goods are removed to another member state.
- The supply made by the importer is exempt under art 138.

The importer is the person liable for payment of the VAT due on importation in accordance with art 201. For the conditions to be met, see para 2 below.

(e) A reimportation of goods if: (1) the goods are reimported by the person who previously exported them; (2) the goods are in the same state as that in which they were exported; and (3) the goods are exempt from customs duties.

(f) Goods imported under diplomatic and consular arrangements. The goods must be exempt from customs duties.

(g) Goods imported by: (1) the European Community; (2) the European Atomic Energy Community; (3) the European Central Bank; and (4) (subject to specified conditions) a body set up by the Communities if the Protocol on the Privileges and Immunities of the European Communities (8 April 1965) applies to it. For a consolidated version of the Protocol in force from 1 December 2009, see OJ C83/266, 30.3.10.

(h) Goods imported by: (1) an international body (other than a body specified in (fa) above) recognised as such by the public authorities of the host member state; and (2) a member of such a body. The goods must be within the limits laid down by: (1) the relevant international convention establishing the organisation; or (2) the relevant headquarters agreement. The goods must meet the conditions laid down by the convention or agreement.
For the recognition of European Research Infrastructure Consortium as an international body and the application of this provision to an ERIC which has been so recognised, see Regulation (EU) No 282/2011 reg 50.

(i) (As regards a member state which is a member of NATO) goods imported into the territory of the member state by the armed forces of another NATO member. The armed forces must take part in the common defence effort. Exemption extends to: (1) goods for the use of such forces; (2) goods for the use of the civilian staff accompanying them; and (3) goods for supplying their messes or canteens.

(j) Goods imported by UK forces stationed in Cyprus. Exemption extends to: (1) goods for the use of those forces; (2) goods for the use of the civilian staff accompanying them; and (3) goods for supplying their messes or canteens.

(k) The catch of a sea fishing undertaking imported into a port prior to supply. The catch may have undergone preservation for marketing but must not have been processed.

(l) Importation of gold by a central bank.

(m) Importation of: (1) gas through a natural gas distribution system or any network connected to such a system; (2) gas fed in from a vessel transporting gas into a natural gas system or any upstream pipeline network; or (3) electricity; or (4) heat or cooling energy through a heating or cooling network.

2. Imported goods may be supplied after the importation has taken place. If the supply is exempt under art 138(1) or 138(2)(c), the exemption on importation conferred by para 1(d) above is subject to a special rule. The exemption applies only if the information provided to the competent authorities of the member state of importation at the time of importation includes:

(a) The VAT identification number of the importer (or his tax representative) issued in the member state of importation.

(b) Either:
- as regards a supply exempted under art 138(1), the VAT identification of the customer issued by another member state, or
- as regards a transfer in accordance with art 138(2)(c), the importer's VAT identification number issued by the member state in which the despatch or transport ends.

(c) Evidence of the intention to transport or despatch the goods from the member state of importation to another member state. Member states may relax the requirement for this evidence to be provided at the time of importation. They may instead require the evidence to be provided only if it is requested.

Article 144
(ex art 14(1)(i))

Member states must exempt supplies of services relating to the importation of goods. Exemption applies if the value of the services is included in the taxable amount in accordance with art 86(1)(*b*).

For the application of this article to transport services connected with the importation of movable property carried out as part of a change of residence, see Regulation (EU) No 282/2011 reg 46.

For the right to deduct input tax on goods and services used for the purposes of transactions exempted under this provision, see art 169(*b*). These exemptions are therefore exemptions with refund.

Article 145
(ex art 14(2))

1. The Commission is required to make proposals for restricting the scope of the exemptions in arts 143, 144 and to lay down detailed rules for their implementation. The Commission is required to do so "where appropriate" and "as soon as possible".

2. Member states may:

- Maintain their own national provisions until these rules come into force.
- Adapt their national provisions to minimise distortion of competition and prevent non-taxation or double taxation within the Community.
- Use whatever administrative procedures they consider most appropriate to achieve exemption.

3. Member states must notify the Commission of: (1) the national measures currently in force, in so far as they have not already been notified; and (2) any measures they adopt under para 2. The Commission must inform the other member states of these measures.

CHAPTER 6—EXEMPTIONS ON EXPORTATION

Article 146
(ex art 15(1), 15(2) (first para), 15(3), 15(12), 15(13))

For the right to deduct input tax on goods and services used for the purposes of transactions exempted under this article, see art 169(*b*). These exemptions are, therefore, exemptions with refund.

Member states must exempt the following transactions:

(a) A supply of goods despatched or transported to a destination outside the Community (as defined in art 5(1)). The goods must be despatched or transported by, or on behalf, of the vendor.
No distinction is drawn between lawful and unlawful exports when applying this provision. However, member states may impose penalties for contravention of national legislation requiring export permits for exports to specified third countries: *Lange v Finanzamt Fürstenfeldbruck* (case C-111/92) [1993] ECR I-4677, [1997] STC 564 at [19]–[24]. For an example of unlawful exports, see *Lange v Finanzamt Fürstenfeldbruck* (case C-111/92) [1993] ECR I-4677, [1997] STC 564 (computer hardware and software covered by export permit for export to country X diverted to country Y, which was covered by a national embargo).

(b) A supply of goods despatched or transported to a destination outside the VAT territory of the Community (as defined in art 5(1)). The goods must be despatched or transported by, or on behalf of, a customer who is not established within the territory of the relevant member state (as defined in art 5(2)).
The supply is not exempt if the goods are transported by the customer himself for the purpose of equipping, fuelling or provisioning a pleasure boat, private aircraft or any other means of transport for private use. For means of transport for private use, see Regulation (EU) No 282/2011 art 47.
For the conditions to be met if the goods are carried in the personal luggage of a traveller, see art 147(1).

(c) Member states must exempt goods supplied to approved bodies which export them from the VAT territory of the Community (see art 3) as part of their humanitarian, charitable or teaching activities outside the Community. For the implementation of this exemption, see para 2.

(d) A supply of services consisting of work on movable property. The property must be acquired or imported for the purpose of undergoing such work within the Community (as defined in art 5(1)). The property must be despatched or transported out of Community by: (1) the person providing the services; (2) the customer (if he is not established within "their respective territory"); or (3) a third party on behalf of either of them.
It is unclear what is meant by the phrase "their respective territory". The text of Directive 77/388/EEC art 15(3) used the phrase "the territory of the country".

(e) Member states must exempt the supply of services directly connected with the importation or exportation of goods covered by arts 61 or 157(1)(*a*). "Services" for this purpose includes transport and ancillary transactions but excludes services exempted by arts 132, 135.

2. The exemption in para 1(*c*) may be implemented by means of a refund of the relevant VAT.

Article 147
(ex art 15(2))

The following conditions must be met for exemption under art 146(1)(*b*) if the relevant goods are carried in the personal luggage of a traveller:

- The traveller must not be established within the Community.
  A traveller falls within this description if his permanent address or habitual residence is not situated within the Community (as defined in art 5(1)). A "permanent address or habitual residence" for this purpose is the place entered as such in a passport, identity card or other document recognised as an identity document by the member state in which the supply takes place.
- The goods must be transported outside the Community before the end of the third month following the month in which the supply takes place.
- The total value of the supply (including VAT) is more than EUR 175 or the equivalent in national currency. However, member states may exempt a supply with a total value of less than this amount.
  The currency equivalent for a calendar year is fixed by reference to the conversion rate obtaining on the first working day of October in the previous year.
  For the requirement to use invoice value when determining whether or not the threshold set by a member state has been exceeded, see Regulation (EU) No 282/2011 art 48.
- Proof of exportation must be furnished by means of the invoice (or other document in lieu thereof) endorsed by the customs office at the place where the goods left the Community.
  A supply may fail to meet this condition because the purchaser has provided a forged document. A member state may grant exemption in these circumstances if, despite exercising due commercial care, the supplier was unable to detect the forgery: *Netto Supermarkt GmbH & Co OHG v Finanzamt Malchin* (case C-271/06) [2008] ECR I–771, [2008] STC 3280.

Member states must provide the Commission with a specimen of the stamps it uses for endorsing invoices. The Commission must transmit this information to the tax authorities of the other member states.

For the right to deduct input tax on goods and services used for the purposes of transactions exempted under this article, see art 169(*b*). These exemptions are, therefore, exemptions with refund.

CHAPTER 7—EXEMPTIONS RELATED TO INTERNATIONAL TRANSPORT

Article 148
(ex art 15(4) (first para), 15(5)–(9))

Member states must exempt the following transactions:

(a) The supply of goods for fuelling and provisioning of vessels used for navigation on the high seas for:

- The carriage of passengers for reward (see *Elmeka NE v Ipourgos Ikonomikon* (joined cases C-181/04, C-182/04 and C-183/04) [2006] ECR I–8167 at [16]).
- Commercial, industrial or fishing activities (see *Elmeka NE v Ipourgos Ikonomikon* (joined cases C-181/04, C-182/04 and C-183/04) [2006] ECR I–8167 at [16]).
- Rescue or assistance at sea.

Member states must also exempt the supply of goods for fuelling (but not provisioning) vessels used for inshore fishing.

Exemption is confined to goods supplied to the operator of a vessel who will use the goods for fuelling and provisioning. Exemption applies whether or not the goods are actually loaded on board a vessel at the time when they are supplied to the operator: *Staatssecretaris van Financiën v Velker International Oil Co Ltd NV* (case C-185/89) [1990] ECR I–2561, [1991] STC 640 at [22], [27], [30]. For an example, see *Staatssecretaris van Financiën v Velker International Oil Co Ltd NV* (case C-185/89) [1990] ECR I–2561, [1991] STC 640 (bunker oil stored in rented tanks before being loaded on to a vessel).

For the power to limit the scope of this exemption, see art 150(2).

(b) The supply of goods for fuelling and provisioning fighting ships (as specified in the combined nomenclature (CN) code 8906 10 00) leaving the territory of the relevant member state and bound for ports or anchorages outside that territory. For the territory of a member state, see art 5(2).

For the power to limit the scope of this exemption, see art 150(2).

(c) The supply, modification, repair, maintenance, chartering and hiring of vessels used for navigation on the high seas for:

- The carriage of passengers for reward.
- Commercial, industrial or fishing activities.
- Rescue or assistance at sea.
- Inshore fishing.

Exemption also applies to the supply, hiring, repair and maintenance of equipment incorporated in, or used in, those vessels. "Equipment" for this purpose includes fishing equipment.

"Chartering" includes both full chartering and partial chartering of vessels used for navigation on the high seas. A chartering contract differs from a contract for the carriage of goods. As regards partial charters, it is for the national court to determine whether the relevant transaction should be considered as chartering (which is exempted by this provision) or a supply of services for the carriage of goods (which is exempted under art 146(*e*)). In doing so, the court must take account of: (1) the terms of the contract concluded between the parties, and (2) the specific nature and content of the service provided: *Navicon SA v Administración del Estado* (case C-97/06) [2007] ECR I–8755, [2008] STC 2693 at [33], [37], [38].

This provision does not apply to services consisting of making a vessel available for reward, and with a crew, to natural persons for the purposes of leisure travel on the high seas: *Etat du Grand-Duché de Luxembourg, Administration de l'Enregistrement et des Domaines v Feltgen (Administrator in the bankruptcy of Banco Charter Company SA) and another* (case C-116/10) [2010] ECR I–0000, [2011] STC 994 (yacht).

For the exemption of other services in relation to these vessels and to their cargoes, see point (*d*).

(d) A supply of services (other than a supply of services specified in point (*c*)) to meet the direct needs of vessels or their cargoes. The vessels must be used for navigation on the high seas for:

- The carriage of passengers for reward.

Part I VAT

- Commercial, industrial or fishing activities.
- Rescue or assistance at sea.
- Inshore fishing.

Services must be directly connected with the needs of the vessels or their cargoes, ie they must be necessary for the operation of those vessels: *Berkholz v Finanzamt Hamburg-Mitte-Altstadt* (case 168/84) [1985] ECR 2251, [1985] 3 CMLR 667 at [21]. For an example of services outside this description, see *Berkholz v Finanzamt Hamburg-Mitte-Altstadt* (case 168/84) [1985] ECR 2251, [1985] 3 CMLR 66 (installation of gaming machines to entertain passengers).

Exemption is confined to services supplied directly to the shipowner for the direct needs of sea-going vessels: *Elmeka NE v Ipourgos Ikonomikon* (joined cases C-181/04, C-182/04 and C-183/04) [2006] ECR I–8167 at [25].

Member states may limit the extent of the exemptions conferred by para 8 until such time as Community fiscal rules come into force. For Community fiscal rules, see the introductory paragraphs to this article.

(e) The supply of goods for fuelling and provisioning aircraft used by airlines operating for reward chiefly on international routes.

The test for exemption is whether an airline operates "chiefly" on international routes. If it does so, exemption applies in relation to both domestic and international flights. The term "airlines operating for reward chiefly on international routes" has a Community meaning and must be interpreted strictly. Airlines fall within this description if their operations on non-international routes are considerably less extensive than their international activities. It is for national courts to assess the extent of international business. In doing so, they may take account of all information indicating the relative importance of the type of operations concerned. In particular, they may takes account of turnover: *Climber Air A/S v Skatteministeriet* (case C-382/02) [2004] ECR I–8379, [2005] STC 547 at [28], [37], [39], [40].

(f) The supply, modification, repair, maintenance, chartering and hiring of aircraft used by airlines operating for reward chiefly on international routes.

Exemption also applies to the supply, hiring, repair and maintenance of equipment incorporated in, or used in, those aircraft.

For "airlines operating . . . chiefly on international routes", see the commentary to point (*e*).

(g) a supply of services (other than those specified in point (*f*)) to meet the direct needs of: (1) aircraft used by airlines operating for reward chiefly on international routes; or (2) their cargoes.

For "airlines operating . . . chiefly on international routes", see the commentary to point (*e*).

For the right to deduct input tax on goods and services used for the purposes of transactions exempted under this article, see art 169(*b*).These exemptions are, therefore, exemptions with refund.

Article 149
(ex art 15(15))

15. [Applies to Portugal.]

Article 150
(ex art 15(4) (second para))

1. The Commission is required to present proposals designed to restrict the scope of the exemptions in art 148 and to lay down detailed rules for their implementation. The Commission is required to present these proposals "where appropriate" and "as soon as possible".

2. Until such time as these rules come into force, member states may limit the scope of the exemptions conferred by art 148(*a*) and (*b*).

Chapter 8—Exemptions relating to certain transactions treated as exports

Article 151
(ex art 15(10))

1. Member states must exempt:

(a) A supply of goods and services under diplomatic and consular arrangements.

(b) A supply of goods to: (1) the European Community; (2) the European Atomic Energy Community; (3) the European Central Bank; or (4) (subject to specified conditions) a body set up by the Communities if the Protocol on the Privileges and Immunities of the European Communities (8 April 1965) applies to it. For a consolidated version of the Protocol in force from 1 December 2009, see OJ C83/266, 30.3.10.

(c) A supply of goods and services to: (1) an international body (other than a body in (b) above) recognised as such by the public authorities of the host member state; and (2) members of such bodies. Exemption applies within the limits, and under the conditions, laid down by: (1) the relevant international convention establishing the body; or (2) the relevant headquarters agreement.

For the recognition of European Research Infrastructure Consortium as an international body and the application of this provision to an ERIC which has been so recognised, see Regulation (EU) No 282/2011 reg 50.

(d) A supply of goods and services within a member state. The member state must be a member of NATO. The goods or services must be intended for: (1) the use of the forces of another NATO member or the civilian staff accompanying them; or (2) supplying their messes or canteens. The supply must be made when the NATO forces take part in the common defence effort.

(e) A supply of goods and services to another member state. The goods or services must be intended for the forces of any member state (other than the forces of the member state of destination). The member state must be a member of NATO. The goods or services must be intended for: (1) the use of the forces of another NATO member or the civilian staff accompanying them; or (2) supplying their messes or canteens. The supply must be made when the NATO forces take part in the common defence effort.

(f) A supply of goods or services to UK armed forces stationed in Cyprus for: (1) the use of those forces or the civilian staff accompanying them; or (2) supplying their messes or canteens. This provision appears to be new. It was not reflected in Directive 77/388/EEC art 15(10).

Pending the adoption of common rules, the foregoing exemptions are subject to limitations laid down by the host member state.

For the application of this article to electronic services, see Regulation (EU) No 282/2011 reg 42.

For certificates serving to confirm that a transaction qualifies for exemption, see Regulation (EU) No 282/2011 reg 51 and Annex II.

For the right to deduct input tax on goods and services used for the purposes of transactions exempted under these provisions, see art 169(*b*). These exemptions are therefore exemptions with refund.

2. The exemptions for goods in para 1 may be granted by way of a refund of VAT if the goods are not despatched or transported out of the member state in which the supply takes place. The exemptions for services may be also given by means of a refund of tax.

Article 152
(ex art 15(11))

Member states must exempt supplies of gold to central banks.

For the right to deduct input tax on goods and services used for the purposes of transactions exempted by this provision, see art 169(*b*). These exemptions are, therefore exemptions with refund.

CHAPTER 9—EXEMPTIONS FOR THE SUPPLY OF SERVICES BY INTERMEDIARIES

Article 153
(ex art 15(14))

Member states must exempt services supplied by brokers and other intermediaries acting in the name, and for the account, of another person. The services must form part of either: (1) a transaction specified in Chapters 6–8; or (2) a transaction carried out outside the Community (as defined in art 5(1)).

In principle, this exemption does not apply to travel agents who supply services in the name, and for the account, of a traveller if they supply services which are carried out in another member state. For an exception, see art 309.

For the right to deduct input tax on goods and services used for the purposes of transactions exempted under this article, see art 169(*b*). The foregoing exemption is therefore an exemption with refund.

CHAPTER 10—EXEMPTIONS FOR TRANSACTIONS RELATING TO INTERNATIONAL TRADE

SECTION 1—CUSTOMS WAREHOUSES, WAREHOUSES OTHER THAN CUSTOMS WAREHOUSES AND SIMILAR ARRANGEMENTS

Article 154
(ex art 16(1)B (first para, point (e)), 16(1)B (second para, first indent), 16(1)B (second para, second indent, first sentence))

"Warehouses other than customs warehouses" means:

- As regards products subject to excise duty, the places defined as tax warehouses in Directive 92/12/EEC art 4(*b*). The 1992 Directive is repealed and replaced by Directive 2008/118/EC with effect from 1 April 2010. From that date, references to the 1992 Directive are construed as references to the 2008 Directive in accordance with art 47(2) of the 2008 Directive.
- As regards products not subject to excise duty, the places defined as such by the member states.

Article 155
(ex art 16(1) (first para))

Member states may take special measures designed to exempt some or all of the transactions specified in Section 1. Member states must consult the VAT Committee (see art 398) before doing so. The measures must not be aimed at final use or consumption. The amount of VAT charged when the relevant arrangement or situation ceases to apply must correspond to the amount of VAT that would have been charged had each transaction been taxed within the territory of the member state.

Article 156
(ex art 16(1)B (first para, points (a)–(d)) and 16(1)B (second para))

1. Member states may exempt a supply of goods in the following circumstances:

(a) The goods will be presented to customs and, where applicable, placed in temporary storage.

(b) The goods will be placed in a free zone or free warehouse.

(c) The goods will be placed under customs warehousing arrangements or inward processing arrangements.

(d) The goods will be admitted into territorial waters for one of the following purposes:

- To be incorporated into a drilling or production platform.
- For the construction, repair, maintenance, alteration or fitting-out of a drilling or production platform.

- To link a drilling or production platform to the mainland.

(e) The goods will be admitted into territorial waters for fuelling and provisioning a drilling or production platform.

For the right to deduct input tax on goods and services used for the purposes of transactions exempted under this head, see art 169(*b*). This exemption is, therefore, an exemption with refund.

2. The places referred to in para 1 are defined by reference to Community customs provisions in force.

Article 157
(ex art 16(1)A, 16(1)B (first para, point (e))

1. Member states may exempt the following transactions:

(a) An importation of goods intended to be placed under warehousing arrangements other than customs warehousing.

(b) A supply of goods intended to be placed under warehousing arrangements other than customs warehousing within the territory of the relevant member state. For the right to deduct input tax in respect of these goods, see art 169(*b*). This exemption is, therefore, an exemption with refund.

For "warehousing arrangements other than customs warehousing", see art 154.

2. Member states may not provide for warehousing arrangements other than customs warehousing in relation to goods if: (1) the goods are not subject to excise duty; and (2) the goods are intended to be supplied at the retail stage. For derogations from this provision, see art 158.

Article 158
(ex arts 16(1)B (first para, point (e)) 16(1)B (third para, second, third and fourth indents), 28k(1) (second para, point (a) and 28k(5))

1. Member states may provide for warehousing arrangements other than customs warehousing in relation to:

(a) Goods intended for tax free shops (as defined in para 3). For the measures to be taken by member states, see para 2.

(b) Goods for sale to travellers on board a ship or aircraft with a place of arrival outside the Community (as defined in art 5(1)).

(c) Goods intended for taxable persons to enable them to make supplies exempted from VAT under art 151.

For the right to deduct input tax on goods and services used for the purposes of transactions exempted under this head, see art 169(*b*). This exemption is, therefore, an exemption with refund.

2. A member state exercising the option in respect of tax free shops (see para 1(*a*)) must take the necessary measures to: (1) ensure the correct and straightforward application of the exemption; and (2) prevent any evasion, avoidance or abuse.

3. A "tax free shop" is an establishment situated within a port or airport fulfilling the conditions laid down by the competent public authorities.

Article 159
(ex art 16(1)C)

Member states may exempt supplies of services relating to the goods referred to in arts 156, 157(1)(*b*) or 158.

For the right to deduct input tax on goods and services used for the purposes of transactions exempted under this head, see art 169(*b*). This exemption is, therefore, an exemption with refund.

Article 160
(ex art 16(1)D)

1. Member states may exempt the following transactions:

(a) A supply of goods or services carried out in one of the locations referred to in art 156(1). The supply must be made while the goods are subject to one of the specified arrangements in the territory of the member state.

(b) A supply of goods or services carried out in one of the locations referred to in arts 157(1)(*b*) or 158. The supply must be made while the goods are subject to one of the specified arrangements in the territory of the member state.

For the right to deduct input tax on goods and services used for the purposes of transactions exempted under this head, see art 169(*b*). This exemption is, therefore, an exemption with refund.

2. A member state exercising the option in para 1(*a*) in respect of transactions effected in customs warehouses must take the necessary measures to provide that warehousing arrangements other than customs warehousing may be applied to the same transactions if: (1) they relate to goods listed in Annex V; and (2) they are carried out in warehouses other than customs warehouses.

Article 161
(ex art 16(1)E)

Member states may exempt the following transactions:

- A supply of goods referred to in art 30 (first para) if they are still subject to: (1) arrangements for temporary importation with total exemption from import duty; or (2) external transit arrangements.
- A supply of goods referred to in art 30 (second para) if they are still subject to the internal Community transit procedure referred to in art 276.
- Services relating to either of the foregoing supplies.

For the right to deduct input tax on goods and services used for the purposes of transactions exempted under this head, see art 169(*b*). This exemption is therefore an exemption with refund.

Article 162
(ex art 16(1a))

Member states must avoid discrimination between:

- An intra-Community acquisition of goods intended to be placed under one of the arrangements or situations referred to in arts 156, 157(1)(*b*) or 158.
- A supply of goods carried out within the territory of the member state under the same conditions.

Article 163
(ex art 16(1) third para)

The member state of importation must take the necessary measures to prevent double taxation where goods cease to be covered by the arrangements or situations referred to in Section 1 and thereby give rise to importation for the purposes of art 61.

SECTION 2—TRANSACTIONS EXEMPTED WITH A VIEW TO EXPORT AND IN THE FRAMEWORK OF TRADE BETWEEN THE MEMBER STATES

Article 164
(ex art 16(2) (first and second paras))

1. Member states may opt to exempt the following transactions:

- Intra-Community acquisitions of goods made by a taxable person intending to export them as they are or after processing.

- Imports for a taxable person intending to export them as they are or after processing.
- Supplies of goods to a taxable person intending to export them as they are or after processing.
- Supplies of services linked to his export business.

Exemption applies on transactions up to an amount equal to the value of exports made by a taxable person in the preceding twelve months. Member states must consult the VAT Committee (see art 398) before implementing this option.

For the right to deduct input tax on goods and services used for the purposes of transactions exempted under this head, see art 169(*b*). This exemption is therefore an exemption with refund.

2. Member states exercising the option in para 1 must also apply the exemption to supplies exempted under art 138 (intra-Community transactions) carried out by the taxable person up to an amount equal to the value of supplies made by him under the same conditions in the preceding twelve months. Member states must consult the VAT Committee (see art 398) before implementing this requirement.

Article 165
(ex art 16(2) (third para))

Member states may set a common maximum amount for transactions exempted under art 164.

SECTION 3—PROVISIONS COMMON TO SECTIONS 1 AND 2

Article 166
(ex art 16(3))

The Commission is required to present proposals concerning common arrangements for applying VAT to the transactions exempted by Sections 1 and 2. It must do so where appropriate and as soon as possible.

TITLE X—DEDUCTIONS

CHAPTER 1—ORIGIN AND SCOPE OF THE RIGHT OF DEDUCTION

Article 167
(ex art 17(1))

The right to deduct arises at the time when the deductible tax becomes chargeable (as defined in art 62(2)).

The right to deduct

The right to deduct is a fundamental principle of the common system of VAT: *Garage Molenheide BVBA and others v Belgian State* (joined cases C-286/94, C-340/95, C-401/95 and C-47/96) [1997] ECR I–7281, [1988] STC 126 at [47]. The deduction system is meant to relieve the trader entirely of the burden of the VAT payable or paid in the course of all his economic activities, whatever their purpose or results, provided that they are themselves subject in principle to VAT: *Kretztechnik AG v Finanzamt Linz* (case C-465/03) [2005] ECR I–4357, [2005] STC 1118 at [34].

The right to deduct must be applied in such a way that its scope corresponds, as far as possible, to the sphere of the taxable person's taxable activity: *Sofitam SA (formerly Satam SA) v Ministre chargé du Budget* (case 333/91) [1993] ECR I–3513, [1997] STC 226 at [11].

The use to which the goods are put, or intended to be put, is irrelevant to the question whether the right to deduct has arisen in respect of them. Use or proposed use merely determines the extent of the initial deduction and the extent of any adjustments in following periods: *Lennartz v Finanzamt München III* (case C-97/90) [1991] ECR I–3795, [1995] STC 514 at [15].

The right to deduct is determined by the capacity in which a person acts at the time when the deductible tax becomes chargeable. Thus, if a taxable person acting as such uses goods for the purposes of his taxable transactions, he is entitled to deduct the VAT due or paid in respect of those goods. Conversely, no right to deduct arises if he uses the goods for his private consumption: *Lennartz v Finanzamt München III* (case C-97/90) [1991] ECR I–3795, [1995] STC 514 at [8], [9].

A person who acquires goods for the purposes of an economic activity does so as a taxable person, even if the goods are not used immediately for those economic activities: *Lennartz v Finanzamt München III* (case C-97/90) [1991] ECR I–3795, [1995] STC 514 at [14], [15].

Where a marital community, which does not have legal personality and does not itself carry out an economic activity, places an order for a capital item, the co-owners forming that community are regarded as recipients of the transaction: *Finanzamt Bergisch Gladbach v HE* (case C-25/03) [2005] ECR I–3123, [2007] STC 128 at [58]. If part of the item is used exclusively for business purposes by one of the co-owning spouces, he is entitled to deduct all the input tax attributable to that part, insofar as the amount deducted does not exceed the limits of his interest in the item: *Finanzamt Bergisch Gladbach v HE* (case C-25/03) [2005] ECR I–3123, [2007] STC 128 at [74] (spouce with 25% share of building, 12% of which used by him exclusively for business purposes, entitled to deduct 12% of the VAT charged to the co-owners).

For exceptions to the right to deduct, see arts 302 (common flat-rate scheme for farmers), 310 (special scheme for travel agents), 322, 323, 331 (special arrangements for second-hand goods, works of art, collectors' items and antiques).

Decision 2009/938/EU authorises the UK to derogate from art 167 by postponing the right to deduct until the time of payment as regards taxable persons authorised to account for VAT under the cash accounting scheme.

Option to include only part of an asset as a business asset

Traders have a choice where a capital item is used for both business and private purposes: *Finanzamt Bergisch Gladbach v HE* (case C-25/03) [2005] ECR I–3123, [2007] STC 128 at [46].

Firstly, the trader can allocate the item wholly to the assets of his business. Whether a taxable person has acquired goods for the purposes of his economic activity is a question of fact to be determined in the light of all the circumstances of the case. These include the nature of the goods concerned and the period between acquisition and use for the purposes of the economic activity: *Lennartz v Finanzamt München III* (case C-97/90) [1991] ECR I–3795, [1995] STC 514 at [21]. If a trader adops this option, the VAT incurred is, in principle, immediately deductible in full. The private or non-business use is treated as a supply of services for consideration (see art 26(*a*)) valued on the basis of the cost of providing the service (see art 75): *Charles and another v Staatssecretaris van Financiën* (case C-434/03) [2005] ECR I–7037, [2006] STC 1429 at [24], [25]. For examples, see (1) *Lennartz v Finanzamt München III* (case C-97/90) [1991] ECR I–3795, [1995] STC 514; (2) *Bakcsi v Finanzamt Fürstenfeldbruck* (case C-415/98) [2001] ECR I–1831, [2001] STC 802; (3) *Seeling v Finanzamt Starnberg* (case C-269/00) [2003] ECR I–4101, [2003] STC 805; (4) *Charles and another v Staatssecretaris van Financiën* (case C-434/03) [2005] ECR I–7037, [2006] STC 1429 (holiday bungalow for letting and private use).

Secondly, he can retain the item wholly within his private assets. In this situation, the item is entirely excluded from the system of VAT.

Thirdly, he can integrate the item into his business only to the extent to which it is actually used for business purposes. Here, the taxpayer acts, to the extent to which the item was used for business purposes, as a taxable person in acquiring the item and, to that extent, it is regarded as being used for the purposes of his taxable transactions: *Finanzamt Bergisch Gladbach v HE* (case C-25/03) [2005] ECR I–3123, [2007] STC 128 at [47]. This directive does not preclude a taxable person who wishes to retain part of an item of property amongst his private assets from excluding it from the VAT system. Thus, a taxable person may choose whether or not to intergrate into his business part of an asset which is given over to private use. Apportionment between the part allocated to the taxable person's business activities and the part retained for private use are based on the proportions of private and business use in the year of acquisition and not on a geographical division. The taxable person must, throughout the period of ownership, demonstrate an intention to retain part of the property amongst his private assets. The part of the property excluded from business assets is not taken into account when applying art 168(*a*): *Finanzamt Uelzen v Armbrecht* (case C-291/92) [1995] ECR I–2775, [1995] STC 997 at [19], [20], [21], [29].

For a detailed treatment of the relationship between arts 26(1)(*a*) and 168(*a*), see *Sandra Puffer v Unabhängiger Finanzsenat, Außenstelle Linz* (case C-460/07) [2009] ECR I–3251, [2009] STC 1693 at [39]–[62].

Intending traders

A person who has the intention, confirmed by objective evidence, to commence independently an economic activity is regarded as a taxable person when he incurs the first investment expenditure for those purposes. Acting in that capacity, therefore, he has the immediate right to deduct the VAT paid or payable on investment expenditure incurred for the purposes of the taxable transactions without having to wait for the actual exploitation of his business to begin. It follows that the right to deduct does not depend upon the tax authority's formal recognition of the person's status as a taxable person. The only effect of formal recognition is that – save in situations of fraud or abuse – his stautus as a taxable person cannot be withdrawn with retrospective effect without infringing the principles of the protection of legitimate expectations and legal certainty. In the absence of fraud or abuse, the right to deduct, once it has arisen, is retained even if the tax authority is aware, from the time of the first tax assessment, that the envisaged economic activity will not be taken up: *Finanzamt Goslar v Breitsohl* (case C-400/98) [2000] ECR I–4321, [2001] STC 355 at [34], [38], [41]. For status as a taxable person, see the commentary to art 9.

Member states are not entitled to limit an intending trader's right to deduct by making it conditional upon the fulfilment of certain requirements (eg the submission of an express request to that effect before the tax concerned becomes due and compliance with a time limit of one year between that submission and the actual commencement of taxable transactions) and penalising infringement of those requirements by forfeiture of the right to deduct or deferment of the exercise of that right until the time at which taxable transactions actually begin to be carried out on a regular basis: *Gabalfrisa SL v Agencia Estatal de Administración Tributaria* (joined cases C-110/98 to 147/98) [2000] ECR I–1577, [2002] STC 535. On the other hand, member states are entitled to demand objective evidence to support a declared intention to commence economic activities giving rise to taxable supplies: *Finanzamt Goslar v Breitsohl* (case C-400/98) [2000] ECR I–4321, [2001] STC 355 at [34].

Derogations from the right to deduct

Any limitation on the right of deduction affects the level of the tax burden and must be applied in a similar manner in all member states. Consequently, derogations are permitted only in cases expressly provided for in the directive: *BP Soupergaz Anonimos Etairia Geniki Emporiki-Viomichaniki Kai Antiprossopeion v Greece* (case C-62/93) [1995] ECR I–1883, [1995] STC 805 at [18]. For derogations granted to member states, see art 176 (retention of national legislation restricting the right to deduct), art 177 (restriction on right to deduct for cyclical economic reasons) and arts 394, 395 (simplification measures and prevention of tax evasion or avoidance). For specific circumstances in which the right to deduct does not apply, see arts 79(*c*) (disbursements), 310 (travel agents), 322, 323 (second-hand goods, works of art, collectors' items and antiques), and 368 (electronic services).

For examples of unauthorised derogations, see: (1) *Commission v French Republic* (case 50/87) [1988] ECR 4797, [1989] 1 CMLR 505 (limitation on deduction where the proceeds from letting immovable property are less than one-fifteenth of its value); (2) *Lennartz v Finanzamt München III* (case C-97/90) [1991] ECR I–3795, [1995] STC 514 (business use falls below a specified threshold); (3) *BP Soupergaz Anonimos Etairia Geniki Emporiki-Viomichaniki Kai Antiprossopeion v Greece* (case C-62/93) [1995] ECR I–1883, [1995] STC 805 (traders in the petroleum sector exempted from the obligation to submit returns and thereby denied the right to deduct input tax); (4) *Commission v Kingdom of the Netherlands* (case C-338/98) [2001] ECR I–8265, [2003] STC 1506 (deduction representing part of an allowance paid to an employee for business use of a private car); (5) *Commission v Spain* (case C-204/03) [2005] ECR I–8389, [2006] STC 1087, *Commission v France* (*Spain intervening*) (case C-243/03) [2005] ECR I–8411, [2006] STC 1098; (6) *PARAT Automotive Cabrio Textiltetőket Gyártó Kft v Adó- és Pénzügyi Ellenőrzési Hivatal Hatósági Főosztály Észak-magyarországi Kihelyezett Hatósági Osztály* (case C-74/08) [2009] ECR I–3459 (special rule limiting the right to deduct VAT on purchases of goods and services financed by subsidies); (7) *Uszodaépítő Kft v APEH Központi Hivatal Hatósági Főosztály* (case C-392/09) [2010] ECR I–0000 (retrospective legislation affecting invoices evidencing the right to deduct).

Transactions tainted by fraud

A trader's purchases may form part of a chain of supply in which prior or subsequent transactions are tainted by VAT fraud. His right to deduct input tax is unaffected by this if he is unaware of the fraud or has no means of knowing of it: *Optigen Ltd and others v Customs and Excise Comrs* (joined cases C-354/03, C-355/03 and C-484/03) [2006] ECR I–483, [2006] STC 419 at [52]. It is irrelevant whether the VAT payable on the prior or subsequent sales of the goods concerned has, or has not, been paid to the Treasury: *Axel Kittel v Belgian State; Belgian State v Recolta Recycling SPRL* (joined cases C-439/04 and C-440/04) [2006] ECR I–6161, [2008] STC 1537 at [49].

A taxable person who knew or should have known that, by his purchase, he was taking part in a transaction connected with fraudulent evasion of VAT is regarded as a participant in that fraud. This is so irrespective of whether or not he profited by resale of the goods. It is for the national court to ascertain, having regard to objective factors, whether the trader participated in a transaction connected with the fraudulent evasion of VAT. The court may refuse entitlement to the right to deduct if it finds that he did: *Axel Kittel v Belgian State; Belgian State v Recolta Recycling SPRL* (joined cases C-439/04 and C-440/04) [2006] ECR I–6161, [2008] STC 1537 at [56], [59].

By contrast, a trader is entitled to rely on the legality of his purchase if he has taken every precaution which could reasonably be required of him to ensure that his transactions are not connected with fraud. He does not lose the right to deduct by virtue of a national law providing that the contract of sale is void if he did not, and could not, know that the relevant transaction was connected with a fraud committed by the seller: *Axel Kittel v Belgian State; Belgian State v Recolta Recycling SPRL* (joined cases C-439/04 and C-440/04) [2006] ECR I–6161, [2008] STC 1537 at [51], [52] (civil law provision rendering the contract incurably void as contrary to public policy by reason of unlawful basis of the contract attributable to the seller).

Abuse

A taxable person is precluded from deducting input tax where the transactions from which that right derives constitute an abusive practice: *Halifax plc and others v Customs and Excise Comrs* (case C-255/02) [2006] ECR I–1609, [2006] STC 919 at [85]. An abusive practice exists if: (1) although meeting the formal requirements of this directive and of national legislation transposing it, the transactions concerned result in the accrual of a tax advantage; (2) the advantage is contrary to the purpose of the directive and national legislation; and (3) the principal aim of the transactions, apparent from a number of objective factors, is to obtain a tax advantage: *Halifax plc and others v Customs and Excise Comrs* (case C-255/02) [2006] ECR I–1609, [2006] STC 919 at [74], [75], [86] as clarified in *Ministero dell'Economia e delle Finanze v Part Service Srl (in liquidation)* (case C-425/06), [2008] ECR I–897, [2008] STC 3132 at [45].

Transactions involved in an abusive practice must be redefined so as to re-establish the situation that would have prevailed in the absence of those transactions. The tax authorities are entitled to demand, with retroactive effect, repayment of the amounts deducted in relation to each transaction whenever they find that the right to deduct has been exercised abusively. However, they must subtract therefrom any tax charged on an output transaction for which the trader was artificially liable under the tax reduction scheme and, if appropriate, they must reimburse the excess. Similarly, the tax authorities must allow a trader who, in the absence of transactions constituting an abusive practice, would have benefited from the first non-abusive tranaction, to deduct the VAT on that input transaction: *Halifax plc and others v Customs and Excise Comrs* (case C-255/02) [2006] ECR I–1609, [2006] STC 919 at [94]–[97].

Time when the right to deduct arises

The right to deduct arises when the relevant goods or services are acquired by a taxable person acting as such: *Lennartz v Finanzamt München III* (case C-97/90) [1991] ECR I–3795, [1995] STC 514 at [15]. For the time when the right to deduct is exercised, see arts 179, 180.

Decision 97/375/EC authorises the UK to derogate from art 17(1) by providing that small enterprises using an optional scheme must postpone the right of deduction until tax has been paid to the supplier.

Retention and adjustment of the the tax deducted

Once it has arisen, the right to deduct is retained in the absence of fraud or abuse, although adjustments may be made in accordance with the conditions laid down in art 20: *Halifax plc and others v Customs and Excise Comrs* (case C-255/02) [2006] ECR I–1609, [2006] STC 919 at [84].

The right to deduct is retained even if the planned economic activity has not given rise to taxable transactions: *Intercommunale voor Zeewaterontzilting (in liquidation) v Belgian State* (case C-110/94) [1996] ECR I–857, [1996] STC 569 at [20]. It is also retained if, due to circumstances beyond his control, the taxable person is unable to use the goods or services for the purpose of carrying out taxable transactions: *Belgian State v Ghent Coal Terminal NV* (case C-37/95) [1998] ECR I–1, [1998] STC 260 at [22].

For examples of circumstances beyond the trader's control, see: (1) *Belgian State v Ghent Coal Terminal NV* (case C-37/95) [1998] ECR I–1, [1998] STC 260 (exchange of land neither foreseen nor planned); (2) *Grundstückgemeinschaft Schloßstraße GbR v Finanzamt Paderborn* (case C-396/98) [2000] ECR I–4279 (legislative amendment withdrawing the right to opt for taxation taking effect between (*a*) purchase of the relevant goods and services, and (*b*) commencement of the relevant activities) and contrast *Stichting "Goed Wonen" v Staatssecretaris van Financiën* (case C-376/02) [2005] ECR I–3445, [2006] STC 833 (retroactive legislation to counter contrived financial arrangements).

The tax authority is entitled to claim repayment of the sums deducted if the deductions were made on the basis of false declarations: *Intercommunale voor Zeewaterontzilting (in liquidation) v Belgian State* (case C-110/94) [1996] ECR I–857, [1996] STC 569 at [24]. Similarly, a finding of abusive practice renders undue all or part of the input tax deducted and thereby leads to an obligation to repay. It does not, however, lead to a penalty: *Halifax plc and others v Customs and Excise Comrs* (case C-255/02) [2006] ECR I–1609, [2006] STC 919 at [93].

A claim by the tax authority is unjustified if, due to circumstances beyond his control, the taxable person is unable to use the goods or services for the purpose of making taxable transactions: *Belgian State v Ghent Coal Terminal NV* (case C-37/95) [1998] ECR I–1, [1998] STC 260 at [20].

Direct effect

This provision confers rights on individuals on which they may rely before a national court: *BP Soupergaz Anonimos Etairia Geniki Emporiki-Viomichaniki Kai Antiprossopeion v Greece* (case C-62/93) [1995] ECR I–1883, [1995] STC 805 at [36].

Article 167a*

Member states may introduce an optional scheme for taxable persons making supplies on which VAT becomes chargeable solely by reference to the time when payment is received. If a taxable person uses the scheme, his right to deduct input tax on the goods or services supplied to him is postponed until he has paid the VAT thereon to his supplier.

The following rules apply to the optional scheme adopted by a member state:

- The member state must set a threshold for taxable persons using the scheme within their territory. This threshold is based on a taxable person's annual turnover. Annual turnover is calculated in accordance with art 288.
- The threshold must not exceed EUR 500,000 (or the equivalent in national currency).
- A member state may increase the threshold to a maximun of EUR 2,000,000 (or the equivalent in national currency) after consulting the VAT Committee. However, no consultation is necessary if the threshold applied by a member state on 31 December 2012 exceeded EUR 500,000 (or the equivalent in national currency). For the threshold applied by the UK, see VAT Regulations 1995/2518 reg 58.
- The member state must inform the VAT Committee of national measures adopted in connection with postponement of the right to deduct.

The UK currently applies an optional scheme in accordance with Decision 2009/938/EU. The 2009 Decision expires no later than 31 December 2012.

Article 168
(ex art 17(2))

In so far as the goods and services are used for the purposes of the taxed transactions of a taxable person, a taxable person is entitled to deduct:

(a) VAT due or paid in respect of goods or services supplied or to be supplied to him by another taxable person.

X (a taxable person) is entitled to deduct VAT if, under an agreement with Y (X's employee) and Z (another taxable person): (1) Z supplies goods to Y at X's expense; (2) Y uses the goods exclusively for the purpose of X's business; and (3) X receives invoices from Z showing the VAT chargeable in respect of the goods: *Leesportefeuille "Intiem" CV v Staatssecretaris van Financiën* (case 165/86) [1988] ECR 1471, [1989] 2 CMLR 856. Contrast *Commission v Kingdom of the Netherlands* (case C-338/98) [2001] ECR I–8265, [2003] STC 1506 (deduction of part of an allowance paid to an employee for business use of a private car amounting to an unauthorised derogation); *Commission v United Kingdom* (case C-33/03) [2005] ECR I–1865, [2005] STC 582 (deduction in respect of cost of road fuel reimbursed to employees).

Where a marital community, which does not have legal personality and does not itself carry out an economic activity, places an order for a capital item, the co-owners forming that community are regarded as recipients of the transaction: *Finanzamt Bergisch Gladbach v HE* (case C-25/03) [2005] ECR I–3123, [2007] STC 128 at [58]. For the right to deduct by one co-owner, see commentary to art 167.

(b) VAT due in respect of transactions treated as supplies of goods or services by virtue of arts 18(*a*) and 27.

(c) VAT due in respect of intra-Community acquisitions by virtue of art 2(1)(*b*)(i). For an exception, see *Staatssecretaris van Financiën v X and another* (joined cases C-536/08 and C-539/08) [2010] ECR I–0000, [2010] STC 1701.

(d) VAT due on transactions treated as intra-Community acquisitions in accordance with arts 21, 22.
(e) VAT due or paid in respect of imported goods.

This VAT is deducted from the VAT which the taxable person is liable to pay. The deduction is made in the member state in which the transactions are carried out.

In principle, the goods or services in question must have a direct and immediate link with one or more taxable transactions made by the taxable person: *Midland Bank plc v Customs and Excise Comrs* (case C-98/98) [2000] ECR I–4177, [2000] STC 501 at [23], [24]. For exceptions, see *Intercommunale voor Zeewaterontzilting (in liquidation) v Belgian State* (case C-110/94) [1996] ECR I–857, [1996] STC 569 (envisaged economic activity does not give rise to taxable transactions); *Belgian State v Ghent Coal Terminal NV* (case C-37/95) [1998] ECR I–1, [1998] STC 260 (unable to use goods or services to make taxable transactions due to circumstances beyond the trader's control).

The right to deduct VAT charged on the acquisition of input goods or services presupposes that the expenditure incurred in acquiring them was a component of the cost of the output tax transactions that gave rise to the right to deduct: *Kretztechnik AG v Finanzamt Linz* (case C-465/03) [2005] ECR I–4357, [2005] STC 1118 at [35]. Consequently, those cost components must generally have arisen before the taxable person carried out the taxable transactions to which they relate: *Abbey National plc v Customs and Excise Comrs* (case C-408/98) [2001] ECR I–1361, [2001] STC 297 at [28]. For an example of expenditure that did not amount to a cost component, see: (1) *Midland Bank plc v Customs and Excise Comrs* (case C-98/98) [2000] ECR I–4177, [2000] STC 501 (costs of litigation arising from services previously supplied in connection with a company takeover); (2) *Investrad BV v Staatssecretaris van Financiën* (case C-435/05) [2007] ECR I–1315, [2008] STC 518 (litigation pursued by a holding company at a time when it carried on an economic activity, but relating to shares sold before the economic activity commenced, where there was no direct and immediate link between the expenditure and the economic activity).

The VAT incurred may relate to a transaction that does not amount to a supply of goods or services. These costs form part of the trader's overheads. As such, they are component parts of the price of his products and therefore have a direct and immediate link with the whole of the trader's economic activity: see *Kretztechnik AG v Finanzamt Linz* (case C-465/03) [2005] ECR I–4357, [2005] STC 1118 at [36]. It follows that the VAT incurred is fully deductible if the trader's activity is solely concerned with making taxable supplies (as in *Kretztechnik AG v Finanzamt Linz* (case C-465/03) [2005] ECR I–4357, [2005] STC 1118 (costs in connection with an issue of shares)) and partly deductible if he makes both transactions in respect of which VAT is deductible and transactions in respect of which it is not (as in *Abbey National plc v Customs and Excise Comrs* (case C-408/98) [2001] ECR I–1361, [2001] STC 297 (sale of part of a business as a going concern)). However, a partnership established for the sole purpose of founding a capital company is entitled to deduct input tax where its only transaction is to effect, by a formal act for consideration, a transfer of the goods and services acquired to the company: *Finanzamt Offenbach am Main-Land v Faxworld Vorgündungsgesellschaft Peter Hünninghausen und Wolfgang Klein GbR* (case C-137/02) [2004] ECR I–5547, [2005] STC 1192.

There is a right to deduct input tax on services purchased for the purposes of a disposal of shares if there is a direct and immediate link between the services and the overall economic activities of the taxable person. It is for the national court to determine whether the costs incurred are likely to be incorporated in the price of the shares sold or whether they form part of the cost components of transactions within the scope of the taxable person's economic activities: *Skatteverket v AB SKF* (case C-29/08) [2009] ECR I–10413, [2010] STC 419 (disposal of all shares in a wholly-owned subsidiary and the remaining shareholding in a controlled company by a holding company which had supplied taxable services to those companies);

The ultimate aim pursued by the taxable person is irrelevant: *BLP Group plc v Customs and Excise Comrs* (case C-4/94) [1995] ECR I–983, [1995] STC 424 at [19].

It is for the national court to apply the test of "direct and immediate link" to the facts of each case before it: *Midland Bank plc v Customs and Excise Comrs* (case C-98/98) [2000] ECR I–4177, [2000] STC 501 at [25], [33].

The right to deduct is confined to VAT which is actually due. Thus, no right to deduct arises in respect of VAT shown on an invoice if this exceeds the amount legally due, or if the transaction is not subject to VAT: *Genius Holding BV v Staatssecretaris van Financiën* (case C-342/87) [1989] ECR 4227, [1991] STC 239 at [13], [15].

This provision confers rights on individuals on which they may rely before a national court: *BP Soupergaz Anonimos Etairia Geniki Emporiki-Viomichaniki Kai Antiprossopeion v Greece* (case C-62/93) [1995] ECR I–1883, [1995] STC 805 at [36].

Decision 2007/884/EC authorises the UK to derogate from art 168 by restricting the right to deduct input tax in respect of leased or hired motor cars to 50% of the VAT charged.

Article 168a

1. A proportionate deduction is made in respect of expenditure on immovable property forming part of the business assets of a taxable person if the property is used for both: (1) the purposes of the taxable person's business; and (2) his private use, the private use of his staff or, more generally, for purposes other than those of his business. The deductible proportion of VAT is determined by reference to business use of the property. The principles set out in arts 167, 168, 169 and 193 apply to the VAT determined in this manner.

Changes in the proportion of business use are taken into account in accordance with the principles set out in arts 184–192. This provision derogates from art 26. Thus, if a taxable person has made a proportionate deduction in respect of immovable property (under this para) or other goods (under para 2), he adjusts his input tax if the proportion of business use changes rather than becoming liable for output tax on a supply deemed to be made under art 26.

2. Member states may apply the rules in para 1 to other goods forming part of the business assets.

Article 169
(ex art 17(3))

A taxable person is also entitled to deduct the VAT listed in art 168(*a*)–(*e*) in so far as the relevant goods or services are used for the purposes of:

(a) Transactions relating to economic activities (as defined in art 9(1) (second para)) carried out in another member state. It is a condition that VAT on the goods or services would have been deductible if the transactions had been carried out in the territory of the member state of deduction.

For the application of this provision to telecommunication services, see *EGN BV–Filiale Italiana v Agenzia delle Entrate–Ufficio di Roma 2* (case C-377/08) [2009] ECR I–5685, [2009] STC 2544. A trader established in Italy made supplies to customers in Italy and Ireland. The place of supply is the place where the customer is established (see art 56). The trader therefore made supplies in both Italy and Ireland. As input tax was deductible in respect of the supplies made to Italian customers, it was also deductible in respect of supplies made to Irish customers

The principle of prohibiting abusive practices does not preclude the right to deduct VAT in circumstances where: (1) a company ("X") (which is established in member state A) elects to have its subsidiary ("Y") (which is established in member state B) carry out transactions for the leasing of goods to a third company ("Z") (which is established in member state A); (2) X does so in order to avoid a situation in which VAT is payable on the sums paid as consideration for those transactions; and (3) member state A categorises the supplies as rental services carried out in Member state B whereas member state B categorises the rental services as supplies of goods carried out in member state A: *Revenue and Customs Comrs v RBS Deutschland Holdings GmbH* (case C-277/09) [2010] ECR I–0000, [2011] STC 345.

(b) Transactions exempted under arts 138, 142 or 144, 156–149, 151, 152, 153 or 156, 157(1)(*b*), 158–161 or 164.
(c) Transactions exempted under art 135(1)(*a*)–(*f*) where: (1) the customer is established outside the Community; or (2) the transactions are relate directly to goods which are to be exported from the Community.

This list is extended by arts 354 (investment gold), 355 (production or transformation of gold), and 172 (new means of transport). For exemptions with refund, see arts 110, 111.

Decision 2007/884/EC authorises the UK to derogate from arts 168 and 169 by restricting the right to deduct input tax in respect of leased or hired motor cars to 50% of the VAT charged.

Article 170
(ex art 17(3))

A taxable person may not be established in the member state in which he purchases goods and services or imports goods. He is entitled to obtain a refund of that VAT in so far as the goods and services are used for the purposes of:
(a) Transactions referred to in art 169.
(b) Transactions for which the tax is solely payable by the customer in accordance with arts 194–197 or 199.

For the place where a taxable person is established, see art 171, Directive 86/560/EEC art 1 and Directive 2008/9/EC arts 2(1), 3.

Article 171
(ex art 17(4))

1. A taxable person purchasing goods or services, or importing goods, subject to VAT in a member state is entitled to a refund in that member state if the following conditions are met:
- He is not established in that member state. This condition is met if his only supplies of goods and services in the member state are made to a person designated as the person liable to pay tax in accordance with arts 194–197 or 199.
- He is established in another member state.

The refund is made in accordance with Directive 2008/9/EC.

2. A taxable person purchasing goods or services, or importing goods, subject to VAT in a member state is entitled to a refund in that member state if he is not established in the territory of the Community (as defined in art 5(1)). This condition is met if his only supplies of goods and services in the member state are to a person designated as the person liable to pay tax in accordance with arts 194–197 or 199.

The refund is made in accordance with Directive 86/560/EEC. This directive is adapted in its application to traders using the special scheme for electronic services: see art 368.

3. No refund is made in respect of:
- VAT incorrectly invoiced.
- VAT invoiced in respect of goods exempted by arts 138 or 146(1)(b).

Article 171a

Member states may exclude taxable persons from the refund procedure in Directives 86/560/EEC or 2008/9/EC and instead allow them to deduct VAT in accordance with art 168.

Article 172
(ex art 28a(4) (second and third paras))

1. A person is entitled to deduct VAT if:
- He is regarded as a taxable person because he supplies new means of transport on an occasional basis (see art 9(2)).
- The supplies meet the conditions for exemption in art 138(1), (2)(*a*).

The right to deduct arises in the member state in which the supply takes place. Deduction arises in respect of: (1) VAT included in the purchase price of the new means of transport; (2) VAT paid in respect of its importation; or (3) VAT paid in respect of the intra-Community acquisition of it. The deduction must not exceed the amount of VAT for which the person would be liable if the supply were not exempt. The right to deduct arises at the time when the new means of transport is supplied. It must be exercised at that time.

2. The detailed rules for implementing this provision are made by the member states.

CHAPTER 2—PROPORTIONAL DEDUCTION

Article 173
(ex art 17(5))

General note

A taxable person is entitled to deduct VAT on goods and services used for the purposes of his taxable transactions (see art 168). It follows that no right to deduction arises in connection with: (1) goods and services used for the purposes of his exempt transactions; and (2) goods and services used for the purposes of his non-economic activities (if any).

Article 173 sets out rules relating to input tax on expenditure connected exclusively with economic activities. These rules distinguish between economic activities which are taxed (and thus give rise to the right to deduct) and those which are exempt (and do not give rise to such a right): *Securenta Göttinger Immobilienanlagen und Vermögensmanagement AG v Finanzamt Göttingen* (case C-437/06) [2008] ECR I–1597, [2008] STC 3473 at [33]. These rules are described under the next heading.

If a taxable person carries on both economic activities and non-economic activities, he must clearly apportion his input tax between the two activities before applying the rules in art 173 to the former. This directive does not prescribe any methods or criteria to be used for this purpose: *Securenta Göttinger Immobilienanlagen und Vermögensmanagement AG v Finanzamt Göttingen* (case C-437/06) [2008] ECR I–1597, [2008] STC 3473 at [33]. Apportionment is therefore governed by the case law of the Court of Justice. This is considered under the second heading.

Expenditure incurred by a holding company in connection with the acquisition of a subsidiary forms part of its general costs. In principle, therefore, it has a direct and immediate link with its business as a whole. Thus, a holding company carrying out both transactions in respect of which VAT is deductible, and transactions in respect of which it is not, may deduct the proportion of the input tax attributable to the former transactions: *Cibo Participations SA v Directeur régional des impôts du Nord-Pas-de-Calais* (case C-16/00) [2001] ECR 6663, [2002] STC 460 at [32]–[35].

A holding company may or may not carry on an economic activity (see the commentary to art 9(1)). It may therefore find it necessary to use either or both forms of apportionment. Public authorities, charities and other organisations may find themselves in a similar situation.

Apportionment between taxable and exempt economic transactions (art 173)

A proportion of VAT is deductible if the goods and services are to be used for both: (1) transactions in respect of which VAT is deductible, and (2) transactions in respect of which VAT is not deductible. Deduction is restricted to the proportion attributable to the former transactions.

In principle, the deductible proportion is determined in accordance with arts 174, 175 for all transactions carried out by the taxable person. However, member states may:

(a) Authorise a taxable person to determine a proportion for each sector of his business. The authorisation must require the taxable person to keep separate accounts for each sector.

(b) Require the taxable person to determine a proportion for each sector of his business and keep separate accounts for each sector of his business.
(c) Authorise or require a taxable person to make the deduction on the basis of the use made of all or part of the goods and services.
(d) Authorise or require a taxable person to make the deduction in accordance with the general rule as regards goods and services used for both: (1) transactions in respect of which VAT is deductible, and (2) transactions in respect of which VAT is not deductible.
(e) (Where the non-deductible VAT is insignificant) provide that the non-deductible amount is treated as nil.

Apportionment between economic and non-economic activities (case law)

This directive does not include rules for apportioning input tax between expenditure relating to economic activities and expenditure relating to non-economic activities. In those circumstances, the methods and criteria used to make the necessary calculations are a matter for the member states. When exercising their discretion, member states must have regard to the aims and broad logic of the directive. In particular, they must comply with the principle of fiscal neutrality on which the common system of VAT is based. Thus, member states must provide for a method of calculation which objectively reflects the part of the input expenditure actually to be attributed to the two types of activity. Member states may apply any one or more of: (1) an investment formula, (2) a transaction formula, or (3) any other appropriate formula: *Securenta Göttinger Immobilienanlagen und Vermögensmanagement AG v Finanzamt Göttingen* (case C-437/06) [2008] ECR I–1597, [2008] STC 3473 at [33]–[39].

Article 174
(ex art 19(1) (first para), (2))

This article makes provision for an apportionment of input tax where goods or services are used for both: (1) taxable transactions in respect of which VAT is deductible, and (2) transactions in respect of which tax is not deductible. It sets out the manner in which the apportionment is made. It has no application to a taxable person if all his supplies are transactions in respect of which VAT is deductible. A member state infringes this directive if it applies this article to such a person: *Commission v Spain* (case C-204/03) [2005] ECR I–8389, [2006] STC 1087 at [25]–[28].

For examples of limitations on the right to deduct which are not permitted by this article, see: (1) *Commission v Spain* (case C-204/03) [2005] ECR I–8389, [2006] STC 1087 (special rule limiting the right of all taxable persons to deduct VAT on the purchase of subsidised goods and services); (2) *Commission v France* (*Spain intervening*) (case C-243/03) [2005] ECR I–8411, [2006] STC 1098 (subsidies on capital goods where depreciation on the subsidised element is not reflected in the price of supplies made).

1. The deductible proportion of input tax (see art 173) is determined by reference to the following fraction:

$$\frac{A}{A+B+C}$$

Where:

A = Turnover (excluding VAT) per year attributable to transactions in respect of which VAT is deductible in accordance with arts 168, 169.

B = Turnover (excluding VAT) per year attributable to transactions in respect of which VAT is not deductible.

C = (If member states so decide) the amount of any subsidies which are not directly linked to the price of supplies of goods or services. (Directly linked subsidies are included in the taxable amount in accordance with art 73, and are thus included in A or B).

Transactions outside the scope of VAT must be excluded from the calculation of the deductible proportion: and *Empresa de Desenvolvimento Mineiro SGPS SA (EDM) v Fazenda Pública (Ministério Público, intervener)* (case C-77/01) [2004] ECR I–4295, [2005] STC 65 at [54], [73]. For examples of incomings to be excluded from the denominator (ie "A + B + C"), see: (1) *Sofitam SA (formerly Satam SA) v Ministre chargé du Budget* (case 333/91) [1993] ECR I–3513, [1997] STC 226 at [14], [15] (dividends received by holding company not involved in the management of its subsidiaries); (2) *Flordienne SA and another v Belgian State* (case C-142/99) [2000] ECR I–9567, [2000] STC 1044 (dividends received by holding company which is a taxable person in respect of other activities and which supplies management services to those subsidiaries); (3) *Flordienne SA and another v Belgian State* (case C-142/99) [2000] ECR I–9567, [2000] STC 1044 (interest paid by subsidiary to holding company where loans made by the latter to the former do not constitute an economic activity of the latter); (4) *António Jorge Lda v Fazenda Pública* (case C-536/03) [2005] ECR I–4463, [2008] STC 2533 (the value of work in progress in the course of civil construction activity, where that value does not correspond to (*a*) the supply of goods, or the provision of services, which has already been effected, (*b*) statements of account of work, or (*c*) the receipt of payments on account).

2. The following amounts are excluded from the fraction in para 1:

(a) Turnover attributable to supplies of capital goods used by the taxable person for the purposes of his business.

This description does not include capital goods sold in the nature of a normal business activity: *Nordania Finas A/S and another v Skatteministeriet* (case C-98/07) [2008] ECR I–1281, [2008] STC 3314 at [25]. For an example, see *Nordania Finas A/S and another v Skatteministeriet* (case C-98/07) [2008] ECR I–1281, [2008] STC 3314 (vehicles purchased for leasing to third parties and sold on termination of the leasing contracts).

For the circumstances in which this exclusion does not apply, see para 3.

(b) Incidental real estate and financial transactions.

For an example of real estate transactions which were not "incidental", see *NCC Construction Danmark A/S v Skatteministeriet* (case C-174/08) [2009] ECR I–10567, [2010] STC 532 (buildings constructed for its own account by a building business).

For an example of financial transactions which were not "incidental", see *Régie Dauphinoise—Cabinet A Forest SARL v Ministre du Budget* (case C-306/94) [1997] ECR I–3695, [1996] STC 1176 (interest realised by a company managing immovable property on treasury placements, made on its own account, of funds received from the owners or lessees).

(c) Turnover attributable to financial services specified in art 135(1)(*b*)–(*g*). This applies to the extent that these services are incidental transactions.

The scale of the income generated by the financial services may be an indication that they should not be treated as incidental. However, it is not decisive. Thus, income is not necessarily precluded from being treated as incidental merely because it exceeds the income generated by the main activity: and *Empresa de Desenvolvimento Mineiro SGPS SA (EDM) v Fazenda Pública (Ministério Público, intervener)* (case C-77/01) [2004] ECR I–4295, [2005] STC 65 at [77], [78].

An economic activity cannot be classified as "incidental" for the purposes of heads (b) and (c) above if: (1) it constitutes the direct, permanent and necessary extension of the business; or (2) it entails a significant use of goods and services subject to VAT (see *NCC Construction Danmark A/S v Skatteministeriet* (case C-174/08) [2009] ECR I–10567, [2010] STC 532 at [31]).

3. A member state may include disposals of capital goods in the calculation of the deductible proportion if it exercises the option to dispense with an adjustment in respect of capital goods. For the adjustment in respect of capital goods, see art 187. For the option to dispense with an adjustment, see art 191.

Article 175
(ex art 19(1) (second para), 19(3))

1. The deductible proportion is determined on an annual basis. It is fixed as a percentage and rounded up to a figure not exceeding the next whole number.

This rounding rule applies to a calculation of the deductible proportion in accordance with art 174. Member states are not obliged to apply it to a calculation of the deductible proportion made in accordance with a special method adopted under art 173(2)(*a*)–(*d*): *Royal Bank of Scotland Group plc v R & C Comrs* (case C-488/07) [2008] ECR I–10409, [2009] STC 461.

2. The provisional proportion for a year is calculated in accordance with one of the following methods:

- By reference to the preceding year's transactions.
- By reference to a provisional estimate made by the taxable person from his own forecasts. This method is used if: (1) there were no transactions in the previous year, or (2) the amount of those transactions was insignificant. The estimate is made under supervision of the tax authorities.
- In accordance with national rules in force at the relevant date. The relevant date is 1 January 1979 (member states at that date) or the date of accession (new member states).

3. Deductions made on the basis of a provisional proportion must be adjusted when the final proportion is fixed during the following year.

CHAPTER 3—RESTRICTIONS ON THE RIGHT OF DEDUCTION

Article 176
(ex art 17(6))

The Council, acting unanimously on a proposal from the Commission, must decide what expenditure is not deductible. The Commission's most recent proposal (see COM (1998) 377 final) has been withdrawn: see OJ C64/9, 17.3.06. Pending the adoption of common rules, member states may retain all the exclusions provided for under their national laws at the relevant time. This applies despite the fact that the Council did not meet the four-year deadline for introducting common rules envisaged by Directive 77/388/EEC art 17(6) (repealed): *Royscot Leasing Ltd and others v Customs and Excise Comrs* (case C-305/97) [1999] ECR I–6671, [1999] STC 998. The relevant time is 1 January 1979 (for member states at that date) or the later dates of accession (for new member states): see *Oasis East sp zoo v Minister Finansów* (case C-395/09) [2010] ECR I–0000 at [26].

The expression "all the exclusions" comprises exclusions related to expenditure which is strictly business expenditure: *Commission v French Republic* (*supported by United Kingdom, intervener*) (case C-43/96) [1998] ECR I–3903, [1998] STC 805 at [18]. Thus, for example, member states are authorised to retain national rules denying a right of deduction to means of transport constituting the very tool of the taxable person's trade and motor vehicles which are incapable of being use privately: *Royscot Leasing Ltd and others v Customs and Excise Comrs* (case C-305/97) [1999] ECR I–6671, [1999] STC 998.

However, the expression presupposes that the exclusions were lawful: *Royscot Leasing Ltd and others v Customs and Excise Comrs* (case C-305/97) [1999] ECR I–6671, [1999] STC 998 at [21]. As regards exclusions in force on 1 January 1979, Directive 67/228/EEC art 11(4) (repealed) did not confer an unfettered discretion to exclude all, or almost all, goods and services from the right to deduction. Moreover, Directive 77/388/EEC art 17(6) (repealed) did not permit member states to maintain a restriction which applies in a general manner. It follows that national legislation must adequately define the nature of: (1) the excluded goods or services, or (2) the excluded purpose for which any goods or services are to be used: *X Holding BV v Staatssecretaris van Financiën; Oracle Nederland BV v Inspecteur van de Belastingdienst Utrecht-Gooi* (joined cases C-538/08 and C-33/09) [2010] ECR I–0000, [2010] STC 1221 at [42]–[44]. For exclusions which met this test, see *X Holding BV v Staatssecretaris van Financiën; Oracle Nederland BV v Inspecteur van de Belastingdienst Utrecht-Gooi* (joined cases C-538/08 and C-33/09) [2010] ECR I–0000, [2010] STC 1221 (private transport, food, drink, accommodation and opportunities for recreation provided for staff and gifts). For exclusions which did not, see: (1) *Charles and another v Staatssecretaris van Financiën* (case C-434/03) [2005] ECR I–7037, [2006] STC 1429 at [35] (all goods used for private purposes); (2) *PARAT Automotive Cabrio Textiltetőket Gyártó Kft v Adó- és Pénzügyi Ellenőrzési Hivatal Hatósági Főosztály Észak-magyarországi Kihelyezett Hatósági Osztály* (case C-74/08) [2009] ECR I–3459 (machinery subsidised by public funds); (3) *Oasis East sp zoo v Minister Finansów* (case C-395/09) [2010] ECR I–0000 (services imported from specified overseas countries and territories); (4) *Bogusław Juliusz Dankowski v Dyrektor Izby Skarbowej w Łodzi* (case C-438/09) [2010] ECR I–0000 (VAT paid by X (a taxable person) to Y (a taxable person who has not complied with the requirement to register for VAT purposes) in respect of supplies made by Y to X).

The term "national laws" includes both: (1) legislative acts, and (2) administrative measures and practices of public authorities. Thus, the scope of the exclusion in force at the relevant time is determined in accordance with the law as actually applied in the member state at that time: *Metropol Treuhand WirtschaftstreuhandgmbH v Finanzlandesdirektion für Steiermark* (case C-409/99) [2002] ECR I–81 at [49]–[51] (consistent practice of public authorities on the basis of a ministerial circular).

A member state is entitled to reduce the scope of the exclusion in force at the relevant time: *Commission v French Republic* (case C-40/00) [2001] ECR I–4539, [2003] STC 390 at [22] (total exclusion from deduction for private cars amended to allow deduction in respect of cars used exclusively for driving instruction). Legislation introduced for this purpose is lawful even if, in exceptional circumstances, it results in an extension of the exclusion: *X Holding BV v Staatssecretaris van Financiën; Oracle Nederland BV v Inspecteur van de Belastingdienst Utrecht-Gooi* (joined cases C-538/08 and C-33/09) [2010] ECR I–0000, [2010] STC 1221 (flat-rate scheme).

Having reduced the scope of an exclusion, a member state is not entitled to reverse the reduction, whether wholly or partly, at some later date: *Commission v French Republic* (case C-40/00) [2001] ECR I–4539, [2003] STC 390 at [18], [19]. For examples, see: (1) *Commission v French Republic* (case C-40/00) [2001] ECR I–4539, [2003] STC 390 (no right to deduct in respect of diesel fuel at relevant date replaced by right to partial deduction which was subsequently abolished); (2) *Danfoss A/S and another v Skatteministeriet* (case C-371/07) [2008] ECR I–9549, [2009] STC 701 (enforcement of exclusion on right to deduct in respect of free canteen meals where deduction allowed in accordance with an administrative practice in force at the relevant time).

A member state is not entitled to increase the scope of the exclusion in force at the relevant time: *Commission v French Republic* (case C-40/00) [2001] ECR I–4539, [2003] STC 390 at [17]. For an example, see *Cookies World Vertriebsgellschaft mbH v Finanzlandesdirektion für Triol* (case C-155/01) [2003] ECR I–8785, [2004] STC 1386 (national legislation entering into force five days after the relevant time, ie the date of accession to the EU).

The repeal and replacement of national legislation with effect from the relevant time does not in itself give rise to the presumption that the member state has stopped applying exclusions on the right to deduct. Nor does it automatically lead to the conclusion that there has been an infringement of the standstill provisions if the new national provisions do not extend the old ones: see *Magoora sp zoo o v Dyrektor Izby Skarbowej w Krakowie* (case C-414/07) [2008] ECR I–10921 at [41].

A provision is covered by the derogation in this article if: (1) it is, in substance, identical to the previous legislation; or (2) it is limited to reducing or eliminating an obstacle to the exercise of Community rights and freedoms in the earlier legislation. On the other hand, legislation is not treated as legisltaiton existing at the relevant time if: (1) it is based on an approach which differs from that of the previous law; and (2) it establishes new procedures. It is irrelevant whether the previous legislation was amended on the basis of a correct or incorrect interpretation of Community law. Whether an amendment to a national provision also affects another national provision depends upon whether those provisions are interdependent or autonomous. This is a matter for the national court to determine: *Sandra Puffer v Unabhängiger Finanzsenat, Außenstelle Linz* (case C-460/07) [2009] ECR I–3251, [2009] STC 1693 at [87], [93]–[98].

VAT is not deductible on expenditure which is not strictly business expenditure, eg expenditure on luxuries, amusements or entertainment.

Article 177
(ex art 17(7))

For cyclical economic reasons, member states may wholly or partly exclude some or all capital goods or other goods from the system of deductions. Measures must be limited in time and may not be of a structural nature: *Metropol Treuhand WirtschaftstreuhandgmbH v Finanzlandesdirektion für Steiermark* (case C-409/99) [2002] ECR I–81 at [67]. For an example of a structural measure, see *Stradasfalti Srl v Agenzia Entrate Ufficio Trento* (case C-228/05) [2006] ECR I–8391, [2007] STC 508 (measure systematically renewed so as to remain in force for more than 25 years).

Member states must consult the VAT Committee (see art 398) before implementing this option. Consultation is a condition precedent to the adoption of any measure on the basis of this provision: *Metropol Treuhand WirtschaftstreuhandgmbH v Finanzlandesdirektion für Steiermark* (case C-409/99) [2002] ECR I–81 at [61]–[63]. It involves: (1) informing the VAT Committee of an intention to adopt a national measure derogating from the general system of deducting VAT, and (2) providing the Committee with sufficient information to enable it to examine the measure in the full knowledge of the facts. However, no obligation is laid down regarding the result of the consultation. Thus, the Committee may take a favourable or unfavourable view of the national measure, or merely take note of it: *Stradasfalti Srl v Agenzia Entrate Ufficio Trento* (case C-228/05) [2006] ECR I–8391, [2007] STC 508 at [30]–[32].

In the absence of consultation, member states cannot rely on national legislation, to the detriment of a taxable person, restricting the right to deduct: *Metropol Treuhand WirtschaftstreuhandgmbH v Finanzlandesdirektion für Steiermark* (case C-409/99) [2002] ECR I–81 at [64]–[65]. For examples, see: (1) *Cookies World Vertriebsgellschaft mbH v Finanzlandesdirektion für Triol* (case C-155/01) [2003] ECR I–8785, [2004] STC 1386; and (2) *Stradasfalti Srl v Agenzia Entrate Ufficio Trento* (case C-228/05) [2006] ECR I–8391, [2007] STC 508.

To maintain identical conditions of competition, member states may, instead of refusing deduction, tax goods in such a way that the tax does not exceed the VAT that would have been charged on the acquisition of similar goods. Member states may do so in relation to:

- Goods manufactured by a taxable person himself.
- Goods purchased within the Community by a taxable person.
- Goods imported into the Community by a taxable person.

CHAPTER 4—RULES GOVERNING EXERCISE OF THE RIGHT OF DEDUCTION

Article 178*
(ex art 18(1))

A taxable person must meet the following conditions in order to exercise his right of deduction:

	Circumstances	*Conditions*
(*a*)	Deduction in respect of goods or services supplied or to be supplied by another taxable person (see art 168(*a*))	Hold an invoice drawn up in accordance with Title XI, Chapter 3, Sections 3–6 (arts 220–240)
(*b*)	Deduction in respect of transactions treated as supplies of goods or services (see art 168(*b*))	Comply with the formalities laid down by each member state
(*c*)	Deductions in respect of intra-Community acquisition of goods (see art 168 (*c*))	1. Set out all the information needed to calculate the amount of VAT due on his intra-Community acquisitions of goods. This information must be set out in his tax return (see art 250) 2. Hold an invoice drawn up in accordance with Title XI, Chapter 3, Sections 3–5 (arts 220–261)
(*d*)	Deduction in respect of transactions treated as intra-Community acquisitions of goods (see art 168(*d*))	Comply with the formalities laid down by each member state
(*e*)	Deduction in respect of imported goods (see art 168(*e*))	Hold an import document identifying him as the consignee or importer and either stating the amount of VAT due or enabling that amount to be calculated. For electronic versions of import documents, see Regulation (EU) No 282/2011 art 52.
(*f*)	Payment of tax as a customer in relation to goods or services supplied by a person who is not established in the member state (see arts 194–197)	Comply with the formalities laid down by each member state

As regards the invoices in head (a), member states may not make the exercise of the right to deduct dependent on compliance with conditions relating to the content of invoices which are not expressly laid down by the provisions stated: *Pannon Gép Centrum Kft v APEH Központi Hivatal Hatósági Főosztály Dél-dunántúli Kihelyezett Hatósági Osztály* (case C-368/09) [2010] ECR I–0000, [2010] STC 2400 at [41].

The imposition and extent of the "formalities laid down by each member state" in head (*f*) must not exceed what is strictly necessary for the purposes of verifying the correct application of the reverse charge procedure concerned. Where the tax administration has the information necessary to establish that the taxable person is liable to VAT as recipient of the relevant supply, it cannot impose additional conditions which may have the effect of rendering the right to deduct ineffective for practical purposes: *Finanzamt Gummersbach v Brokemühl* (case C-90/02) [2004] ECR I–3303, [2005] STC 934 at [50]–[52]. For examples of conditions having this consequence, see (1) *Finanzamt Gummersbach v Brokemühl* (case C-90/02) [2004] ECR I–3303, [2005] STC 934 (requirement for the taxable person to hold an invoice drawn up in conformity with art 226); (2) *Ecotrade SpA v Agenzia delle Entrate Ufficio di Genoa 3* (joined cases C-95/07 and C-96/07) [2008] ECR I–3457, [2008] STC 2626 (failure to apply the reverse charge resulting in collection of unpaid output tax but denial of input tax deduction because the time limit for deducting input tax had expired).

For national legislation which did not comply with this provision, see: *Commission v Kingdom of the Netherlands* (case C-338/98) [2001] ECR I–8265, [2003] STC 1506 and *Commission v United Kingdom* (case C-33/03) [2005] ECR I–1865, [2005] STC 582 (no requirement to hold an invoice in relation to deduction for part of a car allowance paid to employees).

For proof of the right to deduct once that right has been exercised, see the commentary to art 273.

Article 179
(ex art 18(2))

In principle, this article provides that the right to deduct must be exercised for the tax period in which the right arose: *Ecotrade SpA v Agenzia delle Entrate Ufficio di Genoa 3* (joined cases C-95/07 and C-96/07) [2008] ECR I–3457, [2008] STC 2626 at [41]. For the time when the right to deduct arises, see art 167. However, in order to exercise the right to deduct, a taxable person must hold the document, or comply with the formalities, specified in art 178. Both conditions must be met before the right to deduct can be exercised: *Terra Baubedarf-Handel GmbH v Finanzamt Osterholz-Scharmbeck* (case C-152/02) [2004] ECR I–5583, [2005] STC 525 at [31]–[38].

Deduction is effected by subtracting X from Y, where X is the total amount of VAT arising for a given period in respect of which the right to deduct has been exercised, and Y is the total amount of VAT due for the same period. For deduction in a later period, see art 180.

As regards taxable persons who carry out occasional transactions (as defined in art 12), member states may require the right to deduct to be exercised only at the time of the supply.

Article 180
(ex art 18(3))

A taxable person holding the evidence to support deduction (see art 178) may fail to exercise the right to deduct (see art 179) during the tax period in which the right to deduct arose (see art 167). Member states may authorise him to make a deduction. For conditions and rules in this respect see art 182.

If art 178 does not provide the means for exercising a right to deduct, member states cannot rely on this provision to provide such means if the right to deduct conferred by national legislation does not comply with arts 168, 169: *Commission v Kingdom of the Netherlands* (case C-338/98) [2001] ECR I–8265, [2003] STC 1506 (national legislation allowing deduction of part of a car allowance paid to employees).

Article 181*
(ex art 18(3a) (part))

A taxable person may not hold an invoice drawn up in accordance with Title XI, Chapter 3, Sections 3–5 (arts 220–261) in respect of an intra-Community acquisition of goods. A member state may waive the requirements of art 168(c) and authorise him to make a deduction. For conditions and rules in this respect see art 182.

Article 182
(ex art 18(3), (3a) (part))

Member states must determine the conditions, and lay down rules, for making a deduction under arts 180 and 181.

Member states may impose a time limit for exercising the right to deduct. A taxpayer forfeits his right to deduct at the end of the limitation period. This penalises a taxable person who has been insufficiently diligent to claim deduction at the proper time. However, this consequence is not incompatible with the common system of VAT in so far as: (1) the limitation period applies in the same way to analogous rights in tax matters founded on domestic law and to those founded on Community law; and (2) it does not render the right to deduct virtually impossible or excessively difficult. A two-year time limit does not render the right to deduct virtually impossible or excessively difficult. This is so even if the tax authority has a longer period in which to demand recovery of unpid VAT: *Ecotrade SpA v Agenzia delle Entrate Ufficio di Genoa 3* (joined cases C-95/07 and C-96/07) [2008] ECR I–3457, [2008] STC 2626 at [45]–[54].

Article 183
(ex art 18(4))

The amount of deductions for a given tax period may exceed the amount of VAT due. Where this is so, member states may either: (1) make a refund, or (2) carry the excess forward to the following period. However, member states may refuse to refund or carry forward an excess which is insignificant.

Refund and carry forward are not mutually exclusive. Thus, for example, the excess may initially be carried forward and subsequently refunded. Moreover, the excess may be set-off against a debt due to the state by the trader. Furthermore, member states may – in some circumstances at any rate – carry forward the excess for more than one period: see *Enel Maritsa Iztok 3 AD v Direktor 'Obzhalvane i upravlenie na izpainenieto' NAP* (case C-107/10) [2011] ECR I–0000 at [47], [49], [66] (excess due to trader with monthly tax periods carried forward for three periods).

In principle, member states are not precluded from retaining refundable amounts of VAT where: (1) there are grounds for the presumption of tax evasion; or (2) there is a disputed VAT debt which is not apparent from the taxable person's returns. In doing so, however, member states must observe the principle of proportionality and go no further than is necessary to preserve the rights of the Treasury. It is for the national court to decide whether or not the relevant national measures, and the manner in which they are applied, are proportionate. The national court should disapply, or refrain from construing, national measures (or a particular construction of them) if the relevant measure or construction constitutes a bar to effective judicial review. Moreover, in the event of the retention being lifted, the amount retained should carry interest from the date on which it would have been repaid in the normal course of events: *Garage Molenheide BVBA and others v Belgian State* (joined cases C-286/94, C-340/95, C-401/95, C-47/96) [1997] ECR I–7281, [1998] STC 126 at [41], [44]–[49], [64].

National conditions for repayment of excess VAT are not proportionate to the objective of combating tax evasion and avoidance if: (1) they are more onerous for one category of taxable persons because of a presumed risk of evasion, and (2) they do not make any provision for the taxable person to demonstrate the absence of tax evasion or avoidance in order to take advantage of less restrictive conditions: *Alicja Sosnowska v Dyrektor Izby Skarbowej we Wroclawiu Ośrodek Zamiejscowy w Walbrzychu* (case C-25/07) [2008] ECR I–5129 at [24].

Member states have a certain freedom of manoeuvre in determining the conditions for refunding VAT credits. However, the "conditions" determined by member states must not undermine the principle of neutrality. Taxable persons must be able to recover the entirety of the credit in appropriate conditions. It follows that: (1) refunds must be made within a reasonable period of time; and (2) refunds must be made by payment in liquid funds or equivalent means, in a manner that does not entail any financial risk for taxable persons: *Commission v Italian Republic* (case C-78/00) [2001] ECR I–8195 at [32]–[34]. A limitation period of three years in which to apply for a refund meets the first test: *Alstom Power Hydro v Valsts ienēmumu dienests* (case C-472/08) [2010] ECR I–623, [2010] STC 777. For refund systems that did not meet the second test, see (1) *Commission v Italian Republic* (case C-78/00) [2001] ECR I–8195 (VAT credits discharged by issuing government bonds); (2) *Enel Maritsa Iztok 3 AD v Direktor 'Obzhalvane i upravlenie na izpainenieto' NAP* (case C-107/10) [2011] ECR I–0000 (interest on refund, which was delayed by commencement of tax investigation, running from the date when the investigation was completed rather than the earlier statutory date for making the refund); (3) *Commission v Hungary* (case C-274/10) [2011] ECR I–0000 (input tax deduction deferred until the supplier has been paid).

CHAPTER 5—ADJUSTMENT OF DEDUCTIONS

Article 184
(ex art 20(1)(a))

The initial deduction is adjusted if it is higher or lower than the amount to which the taxable person was entitled. For the manner in which the adjustment is made, see art 186.

Article 185
(ex art 20(1)(b))

1. In particular, the initial deduction is adjusted (see art 184) if, after the VAT return is made, some change occurs in the factors used to determine the amount to be deducted, eg if purchases are cancelled or price reductions are obtained.

For the application of this provision to post-acquisition purchases of goods (other than component parts) and services on which input tax was deducted, see *Finanzamt Burgdorf v Fischer; Finanzamt Düsseldorf-Mettmann v Brandenstein* (joined cases C-322/99 and C-323/99) [2001] ECR I–4049, [2001] STC 1356 at [88]–[95].

2. However, no adjustment is made in any of the following circumstances:

- Total or partial non-payment of a transaction. However, member states may provide otherwise.
- The destruction, loss or theft of property, if it is duly proved or confirmed. However, member states may provide otherwise in respect of theft.
- The application of goods for the purpose of: (1) making gifts of small value, or (2) giving samples for the purposes of the taxable person's business. An application of this kind is not treated as a supply made for consideration (see art 16) and is therefore outside the scope of VAT (see art 2(1)(*a*)).

Article 186
(ex art 20(1) (introductory sentence))

Adjustments to the initial deduction (see arts 184, 185) are made in accordance with detailed rules laid down by the member states.

Article 187
(ex art 20(2))

Adjustments in respect of capital goods are spread over five years.

In principle, the five-year period comprises the year in which the goods were acquired or manufactured and the following four years. However, member states may instead base the adjustment on a period of five full years starting from the time at which the goods were first used. They may also extend the five-year period in relation to immovable property acquired as capital goods. The maximum permitted period for these goods is 20 years.

The annual adjustment is confined to one-fifth of the VAT charged on the goods. The adjustment is based on the degree to which the deduction entitlement for the year in which the goods were acquired or manufactured varies in subsequent years.

This provision does not create any right to deduct. It merely establishes the procedure for calculating adjustments to the initial deduction: *Lennartz v Finanzamt München III* (case C-97/90) [1991] ECR I–3795, [1995] STC 514 at [12]. Its purpose is to ensure the accuracy of deductions and hence neutrality of the tax burden: *Proceedings brought by Uudenkaupungin kaupunki* (case C-184/04) [2006] ECR I–3039, [2008] STC 2329 at [26].

Application of the deduction mechanism depends upon the existence of a right to deduct: *Proceedings brought by Uudenkaupungin kaupunki* (case C-184/04) [2006] ECR I–3039, [2008] STC 2329 at [37]. The right to deduct arises if, at the time of acquisition, a person acquires capital goods in his capacity as a taxable person and allocates them to his economic activity: *Lennartz v Finanzamt München III* (case C-97/90) [1991] ECR I–3795, [1995] STC

514 at [17]. It follows that no right to deduct, and therefore no right to a subsequent adjustment, arises if the capital goods are acquired by: (1) a non-taxable person; or (2) a taxable person who allocates the goods to his private assets. Thus, if a person within either of these descriptions sells the goods during the period of adjustment, he cannot make an adjustment in order to deduct the VAT incurred when the goods were acquired. This is so even if the person acts as a taxable person in relation to a sale of the goods: see *Waterschap Zeeuws Vlaanderen v Staatssecretaris van Financiën* (case C-378/02) [2005] STC 1298 (body governed by public law constructing sewage treatment plant as a public authority – ie as a non-taxable person – not entitled to an adjustment when, following a change to the national legislation, it sold the plant in the capacity of a taxable person).

If a right to deduct arises, it does not necessarily follow that a deduction is actually made. Thus, for example, no deduction may be made if the goods are immediately used for the purposes of making exempt supplies. However, as there is a right to deduct, there is also a right to make an adjustment if circumstances change. For an example, see *Proceedings brought by Uudenkaupungin kaupunki* (case C-184/04) [2006] ECR I–3039, [2008] STC 2329 (option to tax exercised seven months after a renovated building had been let).

Where capital goods are allocated partly to business assets and partly to private assets, so that only part of the VAT incurred on acquiring the goods is deductible, the adjustments made under this provision are confined to the input tax deducted in respect of the part of the property assigned to business assets: *Finanzamt Uelzen v Armbrecht* (case C-291/92) [1995] ECR I–2775, [1995] STC 997 at [32], [33].

An adjustment may arise under this provision if a member state withdraws the right to opt for taxation of lettings of immovable property (see art 13C). Neither this directive nor the principles of the protection of legitimate expectations and legal certainty preclude a withdrawal of the option having this consequence: *Gemeente Leusden v Staatssecretaris van Financiën; Holin Groep BV cs v Staatssecretaris van Financiën* (joined cases C-487/01 and C-7/02) [2004] ECR I–5337, [2007] STC 776.

Article 188
(ex art 20(3))

Capital goods may be supplied during the period of adjustment. Where this is so, the goods are regarded as being applied for business use between the time of their supply and the end of the period of adjustment. The taxable person's business activities are presumed to be fully taxed (if the supply of the capital goods is taxed) and fully exempt (if the supply is exempt). A single adjustment is made in respect of the unexpired part of the period of adjustment.

The owner may "transfer his right to dispose of the [capital goods] as owner" (see art 5(1)) by two separate but inextricably linked supplies, one of which is taxable and the other exempt. If so, the capital goods are regarded as having being used, until the expiry of the period of adjustment, in business activities which are presumed to be partly taxable and partly exempt in proportion to the respective values of the two transactions: *Centralan Property Ltd v Customs and Excise Comrs* (case C-63/04) [2005] ECR I–11087, [2006] STC 1542 (grant of 999 year lease to X followed by transfer of freehold reversion to Y three days later).

Member states may waive the requirement for adjustment in the case of an exempt supply if: (1) the purchaser is a taxable person, and (2) he uses the goods solely for transactions in respect of which VAT is deductible.

Article 189
(ex art 20(4) (first para))

Member states take the following measures in relation to capital goods (see arts 187, 188):

(a) They may define the concept of capital goods.
(b) They may specify the amount of VAT to be taken into account for adjustment.
(c) They may adopt any measures needed to avoid an unjustified advantage arising from the adjustment.

(d) They may permit administrative simplifications.

Article 190
(ex art 20(4) (second para))

Member states may apply arts 187, 188, 189 and 191 to services having similar characteristics to capital goods.

Article 191
(ex art 20(5))

A member state may refrain from applying the capital goods scheme adjustment (see arts 187, 188) if: (1) the practical effect of the adjustment would be insignificant; (2) no distortion of competition would arise; and (3) the member state consults the VAT Committee (see art 398) before doing so.

The member state must have regard to the following factors:

- The overall tax effect in the member state concerned.
- The need for due administrative simplification.

Article 192
(ex art 20(6))

Member states may introduce measures to secure tax neutrality where a taxable person changes from the normal method of taxation to a special scheme or vice versa. For the special schemes, see arts 282–292 (small enterprises), 295–305 (farmers), 306–310 (travel agents), 311–343 (second-hand goods, works of art, collectors' items and antiques), 344–356 (investment gold) and 357–369 (electronic services).

TITLE XI—OBLIGATIONS OF TAXABLE PERSONS AND CERTAIN NON-TAXABLE PERSONS

CHAPTER 1—OBLIGATION TO PAY

SECTION 1—PERSONS LIABLE FOR PAYMENT OF VAT TO THE TAX AUTHORITIES

Article 192a

For the purposes of this section, a taxable person may have a fixed establishment in the territory of the member state where tax is due. If so, he is regarded, for the purposes of this section, as a taxable person who is not established in that member state if:

- He makes a taxable supply of goods or services within the territory of that member state.
- None of the supplier's establishments within the territory of the member state intervenes in the supply.

For the circumstances in which an establishment is regarded as a fixed establishment, see Regulation (EU) No 282/2011 art 53(1).

For the circumstances in which a fixed establishment does not intervene in a supply of goods or services, see Regulation (EU) No 282/2011 art 53(2).

For the circumstances in which this article does not apply to a taxable person who has established his place of business in the territory of the member state in which the VAT is due, see Regulation (EU) No 282/2011 art 54.

Article 193
(ex art 21(1)(a))

In principle, VAT is payable by any taxable person carrying out a taxable supply of goods or services. For the exceptions, see arts 194–199 and 202.

Article 194
(ex art 21(1)(a))

1. As regards a taxable supply of goods or services carried out by a taxable person who is not established in the member state in which the VAT is due, member states may provide that the person liable for payment of the VAT is the person to whom the goods or services were supplied.

2. Member states applying this provision must lay down the conditions for implementing it.

Article 195
(ex art 21(1)(f))

As regards goods supplied in the circumstances specified in arts 38 or 39 by a taxable person who is not established within the member state, the person liable for payment of the VAT is the person to whom the goods were supplied if he is identified for VAT purposes in the member state in which the tax is due.

Article 196

A taxable person who is not established in the territory of the member state may supply intermediary services (see art 44) to: (1) a taxable person; or (2) a non-taxable legal person identified for VAT purposes. Where this is so, VAT is payable by the person to whom the supply is made.

Article 197
(ex art 21(1)(c))

1. As regards a supply of goods carried out in accordance with the conditions laid down in art 141, the person liable for payment of the VAT is the person to whom the goods are supplied if: (1) that person is either another taxable person, or a non-taxable legal person, identified for VAT purposes in the member state in which the supply is carried out; and (2) the invoice, which is issued by the taxable person not established in the member state of the person to whom the goods are supplied; and (3) the invoice is drawn up in accordance with Chapter 3, sections 3–5 (arts 220–237).

2. Member states may derogate from para 1 if a tax representative has been appointed as the person liable for payment of the VAT in accordance with art 204.

Article 198
(ex arts 28b(f) (first sentence) and 28b(g)(2)(b))

1. As regards specific transactions relating to investment gold between X (a taxable person who is a member of a regulated gold bullion market) and Y (another taxable person who is not a member of that market) taxed in accordance with art 352, the person liable for payment of VAT is the customer.

If the customer is Y, and he is required to be identified for VAT purposes in the member state in which the tax is due solely in respect of the transactions referred to in art 352, X is required to fulfil Y's tax obligations on Y's behalf in accordance with the law of that member state.

2. Member states may designate the customer as the person liable for payment of VAT in respect of the following goods:

- Gold material or semi-manufactured products of a purity of 325 thousandths or greater.
- Investment gold (as defined in art 344(1)).

Member states may do so where the supply is made by a taxable person exercising one of the options under arts 348–350.

3. Member states must lay down the procedures for implementing paras 1 and 2. They may impose conditions.

Article 199
(ex art 21(2)(c))

1. As regards a supply of any of the following goods and services made to a taxable person, member states may provide that the person liable for payment of VAT is the customer:

(a) Construction works (including repair, cleaning, maintenance, alteration and demolition services in relation to immovable property; the handing over of construction works treated as a supply of goods under art 14(3);

(b) A supply of staff engaged in the activities covered by point (*a*).

(c) Immovable property within art 135(1)(*j*) or (*k*) in respect of which the supplier has opted for taxation (see art 137).

(d) Used material (whether or not it can be used in the same state), scrap, industrial waste, non-industrial waste, recyclable waste, part processed waste, and some or all of the goods and services listed in Annex VI.

(e) Goods provided as security by X (a taxable person) to Y (another taxable person), where Y's supply takes place in the execution of that security.

(f) Goods supplied following cessation of a reservation of ownership to an assignee and the exercising of this right by the assignee.

(g) Immovable property sold by a judgment debtor in a compulsory sale procedure.

2. Member states applying the option in para 1 may specify: (1) the supplies of goods and services covered; and (2) the caterories of suppliers or recipients to whom these measures may apply.

3. Member states may take the following measures for the purposes of para 1:

(a) As regards a customer who "also" carries out activities or transactions that are not considered to be taxable supplies of goods or services in accordance with art 2, provide that he is treated as a taxable person in respect of the supplies within para 1(*a*)–(*g*) which he receives. The word "also" suggests that the customer carries on both an economic activity (so that he is a taxable person by virtue of art 9(1)) and some other activity.

(b) As regards a non-taxable body governed by public law, provide that the body is treated as a taxable person in respect of the supplies within para 1(*a*)–(*g*) which it receives.

4. Member states must inform the VAT Committee (see art 398) of national legislative measures adopted under para 1. However, this is not required if the national measures were authorised by the Council under Directive 77/388/EEC art 27(1), (4) before 13 August 2006.

Article 199a

1. Member states may provide that the person liable for payment of VAT is the taxable person to whom any of the following supplies are made:

(a) The transfer of allowances to emit greenhouse gases (as defined in Directive 2003/87/EC art 3). The allowances must be transferable in accordance with art 12 of the 2003 Directive.

(b) The transfer of other units. The units must be of a kind that may be used by operators for compliance with the 2003 Directive.

Member states applying this option must do so for a minimum period of two years. They may not apply the option after 30 June 2015.

2. Member states applying the mechanism in para 1 must inform the Commission and provide specified information.

3. Member states applying the mechanism in para 1 must submit a report to the Commission by 30 June 2014.

4. A member state must submit a report to the Commission by 30 June 2014 if it detects a shift in the trends of fraudulent activity in relation to the allowances and units (see para 1) in its territory.

Article 200
(ex art 21(1)(e))

As regards a taxable intra-Community acquisition of goods, the person liable for payment of VAT is the person making the acquisition.

Article 201
(ex art 21(4))

As regards importations, the person liable for payment of VAT is the person designated or recognised as liable for payment by the member state of importation.

Article 202
(ex art 16(1) (second para))

As regards goods ceasing to be covered by the arrangements or situations listed in arts 156–158, 160 and 161, the person liable for payment of VAT is the person whose action results in this consequence.

Article 203
(ex art 21(1)(d))

As regards an entry for VAT on an invoice, the person liable for payment of VAT is the person who makes the entry.

The VAT is due to the member state to which the VAT relates. This applies whether or not the transaction is taxable in that member state. Identification of the relevant member state is a matter for the national court. The national court must take all the relevant circumstances into account. These include the rate of VAT charged, the currency in which the amount due is expressed, the language in which the invoice was drawn up, the content and context of the invoice, the place of establishment of the issuer and recipient of the invoice, and the behaviour of the parties: *Staatssecretaris van Financiën v Stadeco BV* (case C-566/07) [2009] ECR I–5295, [2009] STC 1622 at [31]–[33].

A person may issue an invoice mentioning VAT in circumstances where no VAT is due. For example, a person may issue invoices to customers on the basis that he independently carries out an economic activity (so as to be a taxable person under art 9(1)), whereas the true legal relationship is one of employer and employee: see *Dimosio v Karageorgou* (cases C-78/02 to C-80/02) [2003] ECR I–13295, [2003] SWTI 1937. Similarly, a person may issue an invoice for goods that are never delivered or services that are never performed: see *Schmeink & Cofreth AG & Co KG v Finanzamt Borken; Strobel v Finanzamt Esslingen* (case C-454/98) [2000] ECR I–6973, [2000] STC 810. Although an amount shown on an invoice issued in these circumstances is described as VAT, this amount cannot be classified as VAT: *Dimosio v Karageorgou* (cases C-78/02 to C-80/02) [2003] ECR I–13295, [2003] SWTI 1937 at [51]. No right to deduct (see art 167) arises in respect of it, and the recipient must make an adjustment (see art 184) if he has deducted input tax: *Genius Holding BV v Staatssecretaris van Financiën* (case C-342/87) [1989] ECR 4227, [1991] STC 239 at [13]–[17].

However, the directive does not make express provision for any adjustment to be made by the supplier in respect of undue VAT mentioned in error on an invoice he has issued: *Dimosio v Karageorgou* (cases C-78/02 to C-80/02) [2003] ECR I–13295, [2003] SWTI 1937 at [49]. It follows that, for so long as lacuna has not been filled by the Community legislature, it is for the member states to provide a solution in that regard: *Schmeink & Cofreth AG & Co KG v Finanzamt Borken; Strobel v Finanzamt Esslingen* (case C-454/98) [2000] ECR I–6973, [2000] STC 810 at [48], [49]. In order to ensure that the principle of the neutrality of VAT is applied, it is for member states to provide in their internal legal systems for the possibility of correcting any tax improperly invoiced where the person who issued the invoice shows that he acted in good faith: *Genius Holding BV v Staatssecretaris van Financiën* (case C-342/87) [1999] ECR 4227, [1991] STC 239 at [18]. However, an adjustment is not conditional on the issuer's good faith if, in sufficient time, he has eliminated the risk of any loss to tax revenues, eg by retrieving and destroying the invoice before the recipient makes an input tax deduction or by accounting to the tax authorities for the undue tax shown: *Schmeink & Cofreth AG & Co KG v Finanzamt Borken; Strobel v Finanzamt Esslingen* (case C-454/98) [2000] ECR I–6973, [2000] STC 810 at [57]–[61], [63].

Correction of an invoice may lead to a refund of the VAT incorrectly charged. That refund is not dependent upon the discretion of the tax authorities. The measures adopted by a member state must go no further than ensuring the correct levying and collection of tax and for the prevention of fraud. They may not be used in a way which undermines the neutrality of VAT. If reimbursement becomes impossible or excessively difficult, it may be necessary for a member state to enact detailed procedural rules. In principle, correcting an invoice or issuing a credit note eliminates the risk of revenue loss because the customer is clearly informed that no VAT is due and that he is not, therefore, entitled to a deduction. Member states may make this a condition for refund if the trader has not completely eliminated any risk to the revenue in sufficient time. Whether or not the supplier has so eliminated the risk is a matter for the national court: *Staatssecretaris van Financiën v Stadeco BV* (case C-566/07) [2009] ECR I–5295, [2009] STC 1622 at [38]–[51].

Community law does not prevent member states treating the issuing of bogus invoices improperly mentioning VAT as attempted tax evasion and imposing penalties accordingly: *Schmeink & Cofreth AG & Co KG v Finanzamt Borken; Strobel v Finanzamt Esslingen* (case C-454/98) [2000] ECR I–6973, [2000] STC 810 at [62].

Article 204
(ex arts 21(2)(a), (b) and 26cB(10))

As regards taxable persons liable for payment of VAT in accordance with arts 193–197 or 199 who are not established in the member state in which the VAT is due, member states may allow those persons to appoint a tax representative as the person liable for payment of the VAT. This option is subject to the conditions and procedures laid down by each member state.

As regards a taxable transaction carried out by a taxable person who is not established in the member state in which the VAT is due, member states may take measures to provide that the person liable for payment of VAT is a person appointed by the non-established taxable person if no legal instrument relating to mutual assistance exists with the country in which the taxable person is established or has his seat. However, member states may not apply this option to a non-established taxable person within the meaning of art 358(1) if he has opted for the special scheme for electronically supplied services (as to which see arts 359–369).

A "legal instrument relating to mutual assistance" is an instrument similar in scope to that provided for in Directive 76/308/EEC and Regulation (EC) No 1798/2003.

Article 205
(ex art 21(3))

As regards the situations referred to in arts 193–200 and 202–204, member states may provide that the person liable for payment of VAT and a third party are to be held jointly and severally liable for payment of VAT.

However, member states must comply with the general principles of Community law when doing so. As regards the principle of proportionality, while it is legitimate to seek to preserve the rights of the public exchequer as effectively as possible, the national measures must go no further than is necessary for that purpose. The measures may provide that a third party may be made jointly and serverally liable if, at the time of supply, he knew (or had reasonable grounds for suspecting) that the VAT payable on that supply (or on any previous or subsequent supply) would go unpaid. The measures may also rely on presumptions in this regard. However, rebutting those presumptions with evidence to the contrary must not be made practically impossible or excessively difficult. Traders must be able to rely on the legality of the chain of transactions of which their transaction forms a part if they take every reasonable precaution to ensure that the chain does not include a transaction vitiated by VAT fraud. It is for the national court to determine whether national legislation complies with the principles of Community law: *Customs and Excise Comrs and Attorney General v Federation of Technological Industries and others* (case C-384/04) [2006] ECR I–4191, [2006] STC 1483 at [26], [28]–[30], [32]–[34].

SECTION 2—PAYMENT ARRANGEMENTS

Article 206
(ex art 22(5))

A taxable person liable for payment of VAT must pay the net amount of the VAT when submitting his VAT return. For the VAT return, see art 250.

However, member states may set a different date for payment. They may also require interim payments.

As the accounts for an accounting period may not have been finalised at the time when an interim payment becomes due, member states may provide that the interim payment is calculated by reference to the corresponding period in the previous year. As turnover for the corresponding period may exceed turnover for the current period, member states may allow taxable persons to calculate the interim payment by reference to estimated turnover for the current period and waive a surcharge if an estimate made in good faith proves too low: *Balocchi v Ministero delle Finanze dello Stato* (case C-10/92) [1993] ECR I–5105, [1997] STC 640 at [26]. For a national system of interim payments which contravened paras 4 and 5, see *Balocchi v Ministero delle Finanze dello Stato* (case C-10/92) [1993] ECR I–5105, [1997] STC 640 (requirement to pay 65% of the tax due for a period which had not expired, and thereby amounting to an advance payment of the amount due under para 4(*b*) rather than a payment on account).

Individuals may rely rely on this provision in national courts in order to oppose national rules which are incompatible with it: *Balocchi v Ministero delle Finanze dello Stato* (case C-10/92) [1993] ECR I–5105, [1997] STC 640 at [35].

For returns submitted by third country traders using the special scheme for electronic services, see art 367.

Article 207
(ex art 22(7))

A member states must take the measures necessary to ensure that the following persons meet the payment obligations set out in arts 206–211:

- A person liable to pay the tax instead of a taxable person who is not established within the territory of the member state. For the persons concerned, see arts 194–197 and 199.
- A person jointly and severally liable for tax. For joint and several liablility, see art 205.

Article 208
(ex art 26bF (second sentence))

A member state may designate the customer as the person liable for payment of VAT in accordance with arts 198(1) (investment gold) or 198(2) (gold material, semi-manufactured products or investment gold). If so, the member state must take the measures necessary to ensure that the customer meets the payment obligations set out in arts 206–211.

For "investment gold", see art 344(1).

Article 209
(ex art 22(10))

As regards non-taxable legal persons who are liable for payment of VAT due in respect of intra-Community acquisitions of goods, a member state must take the measures necessary to ensure that those persons meet the payment obligations set out in arts 206–211. For the charge to VAT, see art 2(1)(*b*)(i). For the obligation to pay the VAT chargeable, see art 200.

Article 210
(ex art 22(11))

Member states must adopt arrangements for payment of VAT in respect of the following intra-Community acquisitions of goods:

- New means of transport. For the charge to VAT, see art 2(1)(*b*)(ii). For the obligation to pay the VAT chargeable, see art 200.
- Products subject to excise duty. For the charge to VAT, see art 2(1)(*b*)(iii). For the obligation to pay the VAT chargeable, see art 200.

Article 211
(ex art 23))

Member states must lay down detailed rules for payment in respect of imported goods.

In particular, member states may provide that the VAT payable on imported goods is mentioned on a tax return (see art 250) rather than being paid at the time of importation. This may apply to goods (or certain categories of goods) imported by taxable persons or by persons liable to payment of VAT. For persons liable to pay VAT on importation, see art 201, 202.

Member states can prescribe different periods for payment in respect of: (1) VAT on imported goods; and (2) VAT arising under the internal system: *Dansk Denkavit Aps v Ministeriet for Skatter og Afgifter* (case 42/83) [1984] ECR 2649, [1985] 3 CMLR 729.

Article 212
(ex art 22(9)(c))

Member states may waive payment of VAT by taxable persons where the amount due is insignificant.

CHAPTER 2—IDENTIFICATION

Article 213
(ex art 22(1)(a), (b))

1. A taxable person must state when his activity as a taxable person commences, changes or ceases. Member states must allow, and may require, taxable persons to make such statements by electronic means in accordance with conditions which they lay down.

This provision does not allow member states to defer a taxable person's right to deduct input tax, or to deprive him of that right, if he fails to submit a declaration: *Gabalfrisa SL v Agencia Estatal de Administración Tributaria* (joined cases C-110/98 to 147/98) [2000] ECR I–1577, [2002] STC 535 at [51]. However, member states are entitled to lay down a reasonable time limit for compliance and impose an administrative penalty in the event of non-compliance: see *Nidera Handelscompagnie BV v Valstybinė mokesčiu inspekcija prie Lietuvos Respublikos finansu ministerijos* (case C-385/09) [2010] ECR I–0000 at [52].

2. A taxable person or non-taxable legal person may make an intra-Community acquisition of goods which is outside the scope of VAT, ie it does not meet the conditions in art 2(1)(*b*). The person must inform the relevant authorities that he has made such an acquisition if the conditions are subsequently fulfilled.

Article 214
(ex art 22(1)(c))

Member states must identify the following persons by means of an individual number:

Part I VAT

- A taxable person who supplies of goods or services within the territory of the member state in respect of which VAT is deductible. However, member states are not required to identify: (1) the taxable persons referred to in art 9(2) (persons supplying new means of transport on an occasional basis), (2) certain taxable persons carrying out transactions referred to in art 12 (land and buildings) on an occasional basis; or (3) taxable persons who supply goods or services in circumstances whereby the tax concerned is payable solely by the customer or the person for whom the goods or services are intended (see arts 194–197 and 199).
- A taxable person or non-taxable legal person who makes intra-Community acquisitions of goods subject to VAT in accordance with art 2(1)(*b*).
- A taxable person or non-taxable legal person who exercises the option of making their intra-Community acquisitions subject to VAT. For the option, see art 3(3)
- A taxable person who makes intra-Community acquisitions of goods within the territory of the member state for the purposes of an economic activity carried on outside that territory. For "economic activity", see art 9(1).
- A taxable person who receives intermediary services within the territory of the member state in respect of which he is liable to pay VAT in accordance with art 196.
- A taxable person established within the territory of the member state who supplies intermediary services within the territory of another member state in respect of which the recipient is liable to pay VAT in accordance with art 196.

For the "territory of the member state", see art 5(2).

Allocation of an individual number constitutes a formal requirement for the purposes of verification. It is not a measure giving rise to the right of deduction: that right arises under art 168. It follows that someone who is a taxable person for VAT purposes cannot be prevented from exercising his right of deduction on the ground that he had not been identified as a taxable person for those purposes before using the goods in the context of his taxed activity: see *Nidera Handelscompagnie BV v Valstybiné mokesčiu inspekcija prie Lietuvos Respublikos finansu ministerijos* (case C-385/09) [2010] ECR I–0000 at [50], [51].

Article 215
(ex art 22(1)(d))

Individual identification numbers must have a prefix identifying the member state of issue. Prefixes must conform to ISO code 3166 alpha 2. However, Greece is authorised to use the prefix "EL".

Article 216
(ex art 22(1)(e))

Member states must take the necessary measures to:

- Ensure that their identification systems distinguish the taxable persons referred to in art 214.
- Apply the transitional arrangements for the taxation of intra-Community transactions referred to in art 402.

CHAPTER 3—INVOICING

SECTION 1—DEFINITION

Article 217*
(ex art 22(3)(e) (first para))

The term "electronic invoice" is defined

SECTION 2—CONCEPT OF INVOICE

Article 218
(ex art 22(3)(e) (second para))

Member states must accept documents or messages on paper or in electronic form as invoices if they meet the conditions laid down in arts 215–240.

Article 219
(ex art 22(3)(a) (fifth para, first sentence))

A document or message is treated as an invoice if it amends the initial invoice and refers specifically and unambiguously to it.

SECTION 3—ISSUE OF INVOICES

Article 219a*

In principle, invoicing is subject to the rules applying in the member state in which the supply of goods or services is deemed to be made. For the place of supply, see Title V. However, a special rule applies in the following circumstances:

(a) The supplier is not established in the member state in which the supply of goods or services is deemed to be made and the person liable for payment of the VAT is the person to whom the goods or services are supplied. The place where the supplier is established is determined in accordance with Title V. The general rule applies if the customer uses self-billing (ie he issues the invoice).

(b) The supplier has an establishment in the member state in which the supply of goods or services is deemed to be made, that establishment does not intervene in the supply and the person liable for payment of the VAT is the person to whom the goods or services are supplied. Whether an establishment intervenes in a supply is determined in accordance with art 192a. The general rule applies if the customer uses self-billing (ie he issues the invoice).

(c) The supply of goods or services is deemed to be made in a third country in accordance with Title V.

Under the special rule, invoicing is subject to the rules applying in the member state in which: (1) the supplier has established his business; (2) the member state in which the supplier has a fixed establishment from which the supply is made; or (3) (in the absence of a place of establishment or fixed establishment) the member state where the supplier has his permanent address or usually resides.

For "permanent address", see Regulation (EU) No 282/2011 art 12. For the place where a person usually resides, see Regulation (EU) No 282/2011 art 13.

Article 220

1. A taxable person must ensure that an invoice is issued in respect of:

(1) A supply of goods or services made by him to another taxable person or to a non-taxable person.

(2) A supply of the goods made by him where the goods are despatched or transported from one member state to another by him or on his behalf.

(3) A supply of goods made by him which is carried out in accordance with the conditions specified in art 138 (exemptions for intra-Community transactions).

(4) Any advance payment made to him in respect of a supply of goods in point (2).

(5) Any advance payment made to him by another taxable person or non-taxable legal person in respect of a supply of services.

The invoice must be issued by: (1) the taxable person himself, (2) his customer, or (3) by a third party in the name, and on behalf of, the taxable person.

For additional circumstances in which taxable persons may be required to issue an invoice, see art 221(1) and (2). For circumstances in which taxable persons may be released from the obligation to issue an invoice, see art 221(3).

Part I VAT

2. In principle, it is not necessary to issue an invoice in respect of a supply of services exempted under art 135(1)(a)–(g). For an exception, see art 221(2).

Article 220a*

1. Member states must allow taxable persons to issue a simplified invoice in either of the following circumstances:

(a) The amount invoiced is not more than EUR 100 (or the equivalent in national currency).

(b) The invoice issued comprises a document or message treated as an invoice in accordance with art 219.

2. Member states must not allow taxable persons to issue a simplified invoice in any of the following circumstances:

(a) An invoice is required to be issued in accordance with art 220(1) points (2) or (3).

(b) The taxable supply of goods or services meets the following conditions: (1) the supply is made by a taxable person; (2) the taxable person is not established in the member state in which the VAT is due; and (3) the person liable for payment of VAT is the person to whom the goods or services are supplied.

(c) The taxable supply of goods or services meets the following conditions: (1) the supply is made by a taxable person; (2) the taxable person does not intervene in the supply; (3) the taxable person's establishment is in the member state in which the tax is due; and (4) the person liable for payment of VAT is the person to whom the goods or services are supplied. For the circumstances in which an establishment intervenes in a supply, see art 192a.

For circumstances in which a taxable person may be released from the obligation to issue an invoice or simplified invoice, see art 221(3).

Article 221*

1. Member states may require a taxable person to issue an invoice showing specified information in respect of supplies of goods or services (other than those specified in art 220(1)). For the information to be shown on the invoice, see arts 226 (general rule) and 226b (simplified invoice).

2. A member state (X) may require a taxable person to issue an invoice showing specified information if:

(a) The taxable person has either established his business in the territory of member state X or has a fixed establishment in the territory of member state X from which the supply was made.

(b) The taxable person makes a supply of services.

(c) The services are supplied in the territory of member state X or in a third country.

(d) The services are exempt from VAT under art 135(1)(a)–(g).

For the information to be shown on the invoice, see arts 226 (general rule) and 226b (simplified invoice).

3. In principle, an invoice (see art 220(1)) or simplified invoice (see art 220a) must be issued in respect of a supply of goods or services. A member state may waive this requirement if: (1) the supply is made in the territory of that member state; and (2) the goods or services are exempted, or exempted with refund, under arts 110, 111, 125(1), 127, 128(1), 132, 135(1)(h)–(l), 136, 371, 375, 376, 377, 378(2) or 379(2). Articles 380–390b do not apply to the UK.

Article 222*

An invoice in respect of the following supplies must be issued no later than the fifteenth day of the month following that in which the chargeable event occurred:

(a) A supply of goods carried out in accordance with the conditions specified in art 138 so as to be exempt from VAT under that provision.

(b) A supply of services in respect of which the customer is required to pay the VAT in accordance with art 196.

As regards other supplies of goods or services, member states may impose time limits for the issue of invoices.

Article 223*

A summary invoice is an invoice recording two or more separate supplies of goods or services. Member states must allow taxable persons to issue summary invoices. The VAT on each recorded supply must be chargeable in the same calendar month or in such longer period as the member state may allow.

Article 224*

The invoice in respect of a supply of goods or services made by a taxable person may be drawn up by the customer in accordance with a prior agreement between the parties. Invoices must be accepted or rejected by the taxable person in accordance with a procedure laid down in the agreement or in some other manner. Member states may require the invoices to be issued in the name, and on behalf, of the taxable person.

Article 225*

A customer or thid party who issues invoices may be established in a country which is not bound by mutual assistance provisions similar in scope to those provided by Directive 2010/24/EU (which repeals and replaces Directive 2008/55/EC with effect from 1 January 2012) and Regulation (EU) No 1798/2003 (which is repealed and replaced with effect from 1 January 2012 by Regulation (EU) No 904/2010). Where this is so, member states may impose specific conditions on taxable persons.

SECTION 4—CONTENT OF INVOICES

Article 226*
(ex art 22(3)(b) (first para))

The information to be shown on invoices issued in accordance with arts 220 and 221 is listed. For additional information which may be required by member states, see art 227.

The following table lists the information specific to certain types of transaction:

	Transaction		*Information to be shown*
(1)	The customer is liable to pay the tax (points 4, 11a)	(1)	The VAT identification number under which the customer received the goods or services; and (2) a reference to "reverse charge"
(2)	VAT becomes chargeable or deductible when payment is received or made (point 7a)		A reference to "cash accounting".
(3)	The customer issues the invoice (point 10a)		A reference to "self-billing"
(4)	The goods or services are exempt from tax (point 11)		A reference to: (1) the appropriate provision in this directive, (2) the corresponding national provision, or (3) an indication that the supply is exempt
(5)	An intra-Community supply of new means of transport (point 12)		The characteristics specified in art 2(2)(*b*) identifying the means of transport as new
(6)	The margin scheme for travel agents is applied (point 13)		A reference to "margin scheme – travel agents"

	Transaction	*Information to be shown*
(7)	The margin scheme for second-hand goods, works of art, collectors' items and antiques is applied (point 14)	A reference to: (1) "margin scheme – second-hand goods", (2) "margin scheme – works of art", or (3) "margin scheme – collectors' items and antiques". See also art 325 regarding non-disclosure of the VAT chargeable
(8)	A tax representative (see art 204) is liable to pay the tax (point 15)	The tax representative's full name, address and VAT identification number (see art 214)

For the "taxable amount" and "price exclusive of VAT" (point (8)) in relation to the special scheme for travel agents, see art 308. For taxable persons making a supply of goods or services to a customer liable for payment of the VAT, see art 226a.

Article 226a*

A taxable person making a supply of goods or services to a customer who is liable for payment of VAT may omit the details in art 226(8), (9) and (10) from his invoice iin either of the following circumstances:

(a) He is not established in the member state where the tax is due.

(b) His establishment in the member state where the tax is due does not intervene in the supply. For the circumstances in which an establishment intervenes in a supply, see art 192a.

If he does so, he must instead indicate the taxable amount of the goods or services by reference to: (1) their quantity or extent; and (2) their nature.

Article 226b*

Member states must require the following information to be shown on simplified invoices:

(a) The date of issue.

(b) The identity of the taxable person supplying the goods or services.

(c) The type of goods or services supplied.

(d) The amount of VAT payable or the information needed to calculate it.

(e) (As regards a document or message treated as an invoice in accordance with art 219) specific and unambiguous reference to the document or message and the specific details which are being amended.

Member states may require additional information to be shown. This information must fall within one or more of the descriptions in arts 226, 227 and 230.

Article 227
(ex art 22(3)(b) (second para))

As regards the information to be shown on an invoice specified in art 226(4), member states may require taxable persons established in their territory to indicate the customer's VAT identification number in circumstances other than those specified in that provision.

Article 228*
(ex art 22(3)(a) (fifth para, second sentence))

[Repealed.]

Article 229
(ex art 22(3)(b) (third para))

There is no obligation for invoices to be signed.

Article 230*

Amounts shown on an invoice may be expressed in any currency. However, the VAT payable or to be adjusted must be expressed in the national currency of the member state. The conversion mechanism laid down in art 91 must be used.

Article 231*
(ex art 22(3)(b) (fifth para))

[Repealed.]

SECTION 5—PAPER INVOICES AND ELECTRONIC INVOICES

Article 232*
An electronic invoice (see art 217) may be sent if the recipient so agrees.

Article 233*

1. It is necessary to safeguard: (1) the "authenticity of the origin" (as defined) of an invoice; (2) the "integrity of its content" (as defined); and (3) its legibility. This requirement applies from the time when the invoice is issued to the end of the period for which it is required to be stored. The requirement applies to both paper invoices and electronic invoices. For electronic invoices, see art 217.

A taxable person must decide how to achieve this. He may use any business control which creates a reliable audit trail between a supply of goods or services and the invoice issued in respect of it.

As regards electronic invoices, authenticity of origin and integrity of content my be achieved, for example, by the following technologies:

(a) An advanced electronic signature (as defined in Directive 1999/93/EC art 2(2)). This is based on a qualified certificate and be created by a secure-signature-creation device (as defined in art 2(6), (10) of the 1999 Directive).

(b) Electronic data interchange (see Recommendation 1994/820/EC Annex I, art 2). Here, the agreement relating to the exchange must provide for the use of procedures guaranteeing the authenticity of the origin and integrity of the data.

Article 234*
(ex art 22(3)(c) (fourth para))
[Repealed.]

Article 235*
Member states may lay down specific conditions for electronic invoices (see art 217) issued in respect of goods or services supplied in their territory from a country with which there are no mutual assistance arrangements similar in scope to those laid down by Directive 2010/24/EU and Regulation (EC) No 1798/2003. The 2003 Regulation is repealed and replaced (subject to transitional provisions) by Regulation (EU) No 904/2010 with effect from 1 January 2012.

Article 236*
Batches of electronic invoices (see art 217) may be sent, or made available, to the same recipient. Where this is so, details common to the individual invoices may be mentioned only once if, for each invoice, all the information is accessible.

Article 237*
The Commission is required to present a report on the impact of the electronic invoicing rules applicable from 1 January 2013. The report must be presented to the European Parliament and Council no later than 31 December 2016.

SECTION 4—SIMPLIFICATION MEASURES

Article 238*
(ex art 22(9)(d))

A simplified invoice sets out the information listed in art 226b. It may be issued in the circumstances described in art 220a. A taxable person who is not be entitled to issue a simplified invoice in respect of a supply of goods or services may nevertheless be entitled to issue a similar invoice under the "simplified arrangements" described below.

1. Member states may introduce simplified invoicing arrangements in respect of supplies of goods or services meeting any of the following conditions:

- The amount of the invoice is more than EUR 100 but not higher than EUR 400 (or the equivalents in national currency).
- Commercial or administrative practice makes it difficult to comply with the obligations in arts 226 or 230.
- The technical conditions under which the invoices are issued make it difficult to comply with the obligations in arts 226 or 230.

Member states must consult the VAT Committee (see art 398) before introducing simplified invoicing arrangements. They may lay down conditions for using the arrangements..

2. [Repealed.]

3. The simplified arrangements must not be used in any of the following circumstances:

- An invoice is required to be issued in accordance with art 200(1) points (2) and (3).
- The taxable supply of goods or services is carried out by a taxable person who is not established in the member state in which the VAT is due, and the customer is liable for payment of the VAT due on the supply.
- The taxable supply of goods or services is carried out by a taxable person whose establishment in the member state does not intervene in the supply, and the customer is liable for payment of the VAT due on the supply. For the circumstances in which an establishment intervenes in a supply, see art 192a.

Article 239
(ex art 22(9)(e) (first para))

Member states exercising the option under art 272(1)(*b*) may dispense with VAT identification numbers for taxable persons who do not make any of the transactions referred to in arts 20–22, 33, 36, 138 or 141. If they do so, member states allocate an alternative identification number (known as a "tax reference number") in accordance with national provisions. Accordingly, the requirement to show the supplier's, or customer's, VAT identification number tax on an invoice is met by showing his tax reference number.

Article 240
(ex art 22(9)(e) (second para))

Member states exercising the option under art 272(1)(*b*) may allocate VAT identification numbers to taxable persons who do not make any of the transactions referred to in arts 20–22, 33, 36, 138 or 141. If they do so, they may also require invoices to show:

- As regards supplies of services within arts 44, 47, 50, 53–55: both the supplier's VAT identification number and his tax reference number.
- As regards supplies of goods within arts 138, 141: both the supplier's VAT identification number and his tax reference number.
- As regards other supplies of goods and services: either the supplier's VAT identification number or his tax reference number.

For tax reference numbers, see art 239.

CHAPTER 4—ACCOUNTING

SECTION 1—DEFINITION

Article 241
(ex art 22(3)(e) (first para))

The term "storage of an invoice by electronic means" is defined.

SECTION 2—GENERAL OBLIGATIONS

Article 242
(ex art 22(2)(a))

Every taxable person must keep accounts in sufficient detail for VAT to be applied and for the application of VAT to be checked by the tax authority.

For supervision of the right to deduct input tax, see the commentary to art 273.

Article 243*

1. Every taxable person must keep a register of the goods despatched or transported by him, or on his behalf, to a destination outside the territory of the member state (see art 5(2)) but within the territory of Community (see art 5(1)) for the purposes of:

- Valuation of those goods.
- Work on those goods.
- A supply of services performed for the taxable person (as to which see art 17(2)(f)).
- Temporary use of the goods for the purposes of a supply of services by the taxable person (as to which see art 17(2)(g)).
- Temporary use for a period not exceeding 24 months (as to which see art 17(2)(h)).

2. Every taxable person must keep accounts identifying the goods despatched to him from another member state in the following circumstances:

- The goods were despatched to him by or on behalf of a taxable person.
- The taxable person is identified for VAT purposes in the member state from which the goods were despatched.
- The goods are used for services consisting of valuing the goods or carrying out work on them.

For requirements in respect of specific goods and services, see arts 324 (second-hand goods, works of art, collectors' items and antiques), 356 (gold) and 369 (electronic services supplied under the special scheme).

SECTION 3—SPECIFIC OBLIGATIONS RELATING TO THE STORAGE OF ALL INVOICES

Article 244
(ex art 22(3)(d) (first para))

A taxable person must keep:

- Copies of invoices prepared by himself, his customers and third parties in relation to supplies made by him.
- All the invoices he has received.

Article 245
(ex art 22(3)(d) (second para))

1. A taxable person may decide where to store invoices. He must make the invoices, or the information stored there, available to the competent authorities on request without undue delay.

2. Member states may impose the following requirements on taxable persons:

- The duty to notify a place of storage outside the territory of the member state (see art 5(2)).
- (If invoices are not stored by electronic means guaranteeing full on-line access to the data concerned) the duty to store invoices within the member state.

Article 246*
(ex art 22(3)(d) (third para))

[Repealed.]

Article 247*
(ex art 22(3)(d) (fourth, fifth and sixth paras))

1. The period for which invoices must be stored is determined by member states.

2. In order to ensure that the conditions in art 233 are met, member states may require paper invoices and electronic invoices to be stored in the original form in which they were sent or made available. As regards invoices stored by electronic means, member states may also require data guaranteeing the authenticity of origin of the invoices, and the integrity of their content, to be stored by electronic means. For "authenticity of origin" and "integrity of content", see art 233(1).

3. Member states may impose conditions prohibiting or restricting the storage of invoices in a country in either of the following circumstances:

- The country does not have mutual assistance arrangements similar in scope to those laid down by Directive 2010/24/EU and Regulation (EC) No 1798/2003. The 2003 Regulation is repealed and replaced by Regulation (EU) No 904/2010 with effect from 1 January 2012.
- The country does not allow the member state to have electronic access to the invoices, to download them or to use them.

Article 248
(ex art 22(3)(d) (seventh para))

Member states may require non-taxable persons to store the invoices they receive.

Article 248a*

A member state is not permitted to impose a general requirement for invoices to be translated into its official language. However, a member state may require certain taxable persons to prepare a translation, or require a translation to be prepared in certain cases, for control purposes in relation to:

- Invoices relating to goods or services supplied in the territory of the member state.
- Invoices received by a taxable person established in the territory of the member state.

SECTION 4—RIGHT OF ACCESS TO INVOICES STORED BY ELECTRONIC MEANS IN ANOTHER MEMBER STATE

Article 249*

A taxable person storing the invoices he issues or receives may do so by electronic means which guarantee online access to the data concerned. Where this is so, the following authorities are entitled to access, download and use those invoices for control purposes:

- The competent authorities of the member state in which the taxable person is established.
- (If the VAT is due in another member state) the competent authorities of the other member state.

CHAPTER 5—RETURNS

General note For returns submitted by third country traders using the special scheme for electronic services, see arts 364, 365.

Article 250
(ex art 22(4)(a) (fifth sentence) and 22(4)(b))

1. Taxable persons must submit VAT returns. These returns must set out all the information needed to calculate:

- The tax that has become chargeable.

- The deductions to be made.
- (Insofar as necessary establishing the basis of assessment) the total value of the transactions relating to the tax chargeable, the deductions made and the value of any exempt transactions.

For the additional information required, see art 251.

2. Member states must allow VAT returns to be submitted by electronic means. They may require this to be done. The conditions for submitting returns by electronic means are determined by the member states.

Article 251
(ex art 22(4)(c))

The return must also set out the total VAT-exclusive value of the following transactions on which tax has become chargeable during the accounting period:

(a) The intra-Community transactions listed in art 138.

(b) The supplies of goods with transport referred to in arts 33, 36 where:
- The supplies were carried out within the territory of another member state.
- The place of despatch or transport began in the territory of the member state (see art 5(2)) for which the return is made.

(c) The intra-Community acquisitions of goods (or transactions treated as such by virtue of arts 21, 22) made in the member state (see art 5(2)) for which the return is made.

(d) The supplies of goods with transport referred to in arts 33, 36 where:
- The supplies were carried out within the territory of for which the return is made.
- The place of despatch or transport began in the territory of another member state (see art 5(2)).

(e) Supplies of goods made within the territory of the member state (see art 5(2)) for which the return is made and in respect of which the taxable person is liable for the payment of the VAT in accordance with art 197.

Article 252
(ex art 22(4)(a) (first to fourth sentences))

1. Returns must be submitted by a deadline determined by the member states. This must be no later than two months after the end of each tax period.

2. In principle, member states must fix tax periods of one, two or three months. However, member states may fix different periods. If they do so, the periods must not exceed one year.

Article 253
(ex Fourth Accession Treaty (1994), Annex XV (IX) point 3(x))

[Applies to Sweden.]

Article 254
(ex art 22(6)(d))

As regards new means of transport supplied in the following circumstances, member states must take the measures necessary to ensure that the vendor communicates all the information necessary for VAT to be applied, and its application to be checked by the tax authority. The circumstances are:

- The supply is carried out in accordance with the conditions specified in art 138(2)(*a*).
- The supply is made by either: (1) a taxable person identified for VAT purposes to a customer who is not so identified; or (2) a person making occasional supplies of new means of transport who is treated as a taxable person by virtue of art 9(2).

Article 255
(ex art 26bF (second sentence))

As regards gold material, semi-manufactured products or investment gold (as defined in art 344(1)), member states must take the measures necessary to ensure that the vendor communicates all the information needed for VAT to be applied, and its application to be checked by the tax authorities, where the customer is designated as the person liable for payment of VAT in accordance with art 198(1) or (2).

Article 256
(ex art 22(7) (part))

As regards persons who, in accordance with arts 194–197 and 204, are regarded as liable for payment of VAT in place of a taxable person not established within the territory of a member state, that member state must take the measures necessary to ensure that those persons comply with the obligation to submit VAT returns set out in arts 250–261.

Article 257
(ex 22(10))

As regards non-taxable legal persons who are liable for payment of VAT due in respect of intra-Community acquisitions of goods, member states must take the measures necessary to ensure that those persons comply with the obligation to submit VAT returns set out in arts 250–261. For the charge to VAT on intra-Community acquisitions of goods, see art 2(1)(*b*)(i).

Article 258
(ex art 22(11))

Member states must lay down detailed rules for the submission of VAT returns in respect of the following intra-Community acquisitions of goods:

- New means of transport covered by art 2(1)(*b*)(ii).
- Products subject to excise duty referred to in art 2(1)(*b*)(iii).

Article 259
(ex art 22(6)(e) (second para))

As regards intra-Community acquisitions of new means of transport (see art 2(1)(*b*)(ii)), member states may require persons submitting VAT returns to provide all the information needed for VAT to be applied and for its application to be checked by the tax authorities.

Article 260
(ex art 23 (first para))

Member states must lay down detailed rules for the submission of VAT returns in respect of imported goods.

Member states can prescribe different accounting periods in respect of: (1) VAT on imported goods; and (2) VAT arising under the internal system: *Dansk Denkavit Aps v Ministeriet for Skatter og Afgifter* (case 42/83) [1984] ECR 2649, [1985] 3 CMLR 729.

Article 261
(ex 22(6)(a))

1. Member states may require taxable persons to submit a return in respect of all transactions carried out in the preceding year. This return shows:

- All the particulars specified in arts 250, 251.
- All the information necessary for any adjustments.

2. Member states must allow, and may require, taxable persons to make these returns by electronic means in accordance with national rules.

CHAPTER 6—RECAPITULATIVE STATEMENTS

Article 262

A taxable person identified for VAT purposes must submit a recapitulative statement of:

- The acquirers identified for VAT purposes to whom he has supplied goods in accordance with the conditions specified in art 138(1), (2)(*c*).
- (As regards an intra-Community acquisition of goods acquired for the purposes of an onward supply meeting the conditions in art 42) the persons identified for VAT purposes to whom the onward supply of goods was made.
- The taxable persons and non-taxable legal persons identified for VAT purposes to whom he has supplied taxable services for which the recipient is liable to pay the tax in accordance with art 196.

For the circumstances in which a customer is, or is not, required to notify his VAT identification number to the supplier, see Regulation (EU) No 282/2011 art 55.

Article 263

1. Recapitulative statements must be drawn up for each calendar month. This is done in accordance with procedures determined by the member states. Recapulative statements must be submitted no later than the last day of the following month.

Directive 2008/117/EC art 2 requires the Commission to present a report assessing whether this provision assists member states fight VAT fraud connected with intra-Community supplies of goods and services. This must be done no later than 30 June 2011.

1a. Member states may allow taxable persons to submit recapitulative statements for each calendar quarter if the VAT exclusive total of supplies of the goods specified in arts 264(1)(d) and 265(1)(c) does not exceed either of the following limits:

- EUR 50,000 (or its equivalent in national currency) for the quarter concerned.
- EUR 50,000 (or its equivalent in national currency) for the previous four quarters.

The procedures are determined by the member states. The recapulative statements must be submitted no later than one month from the end of the quarter.

The VAT exclusive total of supplies may exceed EUR 50,000 (or its equivalent in national currency) in a subsequent quarter. If so, the option to submit quarterly statements is withdrawn and separate monthly statements must be submitted for each calendar month falling within the quarter. These statements must be submitted within one month.

Directive 2008/117/EC art 2 requires the Commission to present a report assessing the usefulness of the foregoing options. This must be done no later than 30 June 2011.

1b. Member states may apply a quarterly limit of EUR 100,000 (or its equivalent in national currency) for the purposes of para 1a until 31 December 2011.

1c. Member states may allow taxable persons to submit recapitulative statements on a quarterly basis in respect of goods specified in art 264(1)(d). If so, they must: (1) prescribe conditions and limits; and (2) provide that statements are to be submitted no later than one month after the end of the quarter. Member states may require the taxable person to submit statements in accordance with the deadlines specified in paras 1, 1a and 1b above.

2.Member states must allow, and may require, taxable persons to make recapitulative statements by electronic means in accordance with national rules.

Article 264
(ex art 22(6)(b) (third and fourth paras))

As regards goods supplied in accordance with the conditions specified in art 138(1), recapitulative statements must set out:

- The VAT identification number under which the taxable person supplied the goods.
- For each person acquiring goods: (1) the VAT identification number under which he acquired the goods; and (2) the total value of goods supplied to him. The value in (2) is declared for the period of submission (see art 263(1)–(1b)) in which the VAT became chargeable.

Part I VAT

- The amount by which the taxable amount of the supplies has been reduced in accordance with art 90. Amounts are declared for the period of submission (see art 263(1)–(1b)) in which the person acquiring the goods was notified of the adjustment.

As regards transfers of goods to another member state in accordance with art 138(2)(*c*), recapitulative statements must set out:

- The VAT identification number under which the taxable person carried out the transfer.
- The taxable person's VAT identification number in the member state where the despatch or transport ended.
- The total value of the supplies. This value is determined in accordance with art 76.

As regards taxable services supplied in accordance with the conditions specified in art 44, recapitulative statements must set out:

- The VAT identification number under which the taxable person supplied the services.
- For each person acquiring services: (1) the VAT identification number under which the person acquired the services; and (2) the total value of services supplied to him. The value in (2) is declared for the period of submission (see art 263(1), (1c)) in which the VAT became chargeable.
- The amount by which the taxable amount of the supplies has been reduced in accordance with art 90. Amounts are declared for the period of submission (see art 263(1), (1c)) in which the person acquiring the services was notified of the adjustment.

Article 265
(ex art 22(6)(b) (fifth para))

As regards the intra-Community acquisitions of goods specified in art 42, recapitulative statements must set out:

- The VAT identification number under which the taxable person made the acquisition and subsequent supply of the goods.
- The VAT identification number of the person to whom the subsequent supply was made. This is the person's identification number in the member state in which the despatch or transport ended.
- For each person to whom a subsequent supply was made, the VAT-exclusive value of the supplies made by the taxable person in the member state in which despatch or transport of the goods ended. This value is declared for the period of submission (see art 263(1)–(1b)) in which VAT become chargeable.

Article 266
(ex art 22(6)(c) (second indent))

Member states may derogate from arts 264, 265 so as to require additional information to be given in recapitulative statements.

Article 267
(ex art 22(7) (part))

Certain persons liable for payment of VAT in place of a taxable person who is not established in the territory of the member state (see art 5(2)): see arts 194, 204. Member states must take the measures necessary to ensure that those persons comply with the obligation to submit recapitulative statements.

Article 268
(ex art 22(6)(e) (first para))

A taxable person making intra-Community acquisitions of goods (or transactions treated as such in accordance with arts 21, 22) in the territory of a member state may be required to submit statements giving details of those acquisitions. The minimum period covered by these statements is one month.

Article 269
(ex art 22(12) (introductory sentence))

The Council may authorise a member state to introduce the special measures in arts 270, 271 in order to simplify the obligation to submit recapitulative statements. These measures must not jeopardise the proper monitoring of intra-Community transactions.

Article 270
(ex art 22(12)(a))

A member state may, if authorised under art 269, permit taxable persons to file one-year recapitulative statements showing the VAT identification numbers of the persons to whom they have supplied goods in accordance with the conditions laid down in art 138(1), (2)(*c*). A taxable person must meet the following conditions:

- The total VAT-exclusive annual value of his supplies of goods and services must not exceed the aggregate of: (1) the registration limit (if any) applicable in the member state by virtue of arts 282–292; and (2) EUR 35,000.
- The total VAT-exclusive annual value of goods supplied in accordance with art 138 does not exceed EUR 15,000.
- None of the goods supplied in accordance with art 138 comprise new means of transport.

Decision 93/609/EEC authorises the UK to introduce a particular measure to simplify the obligations regarding recapitulative statements.

Article 271
(ex art 22(12)(b))

A member state prescribing a VAT return period exceeding three months may, if authorised under art 269, permit taxable persons to submit recapitulative statements for VAT return period. A taxable person must meet the following conditions:

- The total VAT-exclusive annual value of his supplies of goods and services does not exceed EUR 200,000.
- The total VAT-exclusive annual value of goods supplied in accordance with art 138 does not exceed EUR 15,000.
- None of the goods supplied in accordance with art 138 comprise new means of transport.

Decision 92/621/EEC authorises the UK to introduce a particular measure to simplify the obligations regarding recapitulative statements.

CHAPTER 7—MISCELLANEOUS PROVISIONS

Article 272*
(ex arts 22(9)(a), (b) and 25(4))

1, 2. Member states may release the following taxable persons from some or all of the oblications referred to in Chapters 2–6 (arts 213–271):

(a) Taxable persons whose intra-Community acquisitions of goods are not subject to VAT.

(b) Taxable persons who do not carry out any of the transactions referred to in arts 20–22, 33, 36, 138 and 141. However, member states exercising this option may not release the taxable persons from the invoicing obligations prescribed in Chapter 3, Sections 3–6 (arts 219a–240) and Chapter 4, Section 2 (arts 244–248a).

(c) Taxable persons whose only supplies of goods and services are exempted from VAT by virtue of any or all of arts 132, 135, 136, 146–149 and 151–153.

(d) Taxable persons covered by the exemption for small enterprises (see arts 282–292).

(e) Taxable persons covered by the common flat-rate scheme for farmers (see arts 295–305). However member states exercising this option must take the measures necessary to ensure that the transitional arrangements for the taxation of intra-Community transactions are correctly applied.

3. As regards other taxable persons, member states may relax the requirement to keep accounts. For the general requirement to keep accounts, see art 242.

Article 273
(ex art 22(8))

Member states can impose other obligations to ensure the correct collection of tax and to prevent evasion. These obligations include administrative penalties: *K-1 sp zoo v Dyrektor Izby Skarbowej w Bydgoszcy* (case C-502/07) [2009] ECR I–161 at [20], [23]. However, any obligations imposed must apply equally to domestic transactions and to transactions carried out between member states by taxable persons. Moreover, the obligations must not give rise to cross-border formalities in trade between member states.

This option does not allow member states to impose obligations in relation to the issue of invoices exceeding those laid down in arts 220–225.

Member states are required to ensure that taxable persons comply with their obligations. They enjoy a measure of latitude in this respect, eg in relation to how they use the means at their disposal. However, this latitude is limited by: (1) the obligation to ensure effective collection of the Community's own resources; and (2) the obligation not to create significant differences in the manner in which taxable persons are treated within a member state or throughout the Community: *Commission v Italy* (case C-132/06) [2008] ECR I–5457 at [38], [39]. For an example of failure to comply with these obligations, see *Commission v Italy* (case C-132/06) [2008] ECR I–5457 (general and indiscriminate waiver of verification of taxable transactions effected in a series of tax years).

National legislation adopted under this provision must go no further than is necessary in order to attain the twin objectives of correct collection of tax and the prevention of avoidance. It follows that national legislation must not be used in a way that would systematically undermine the right to deduct input tax: *Gabalfrisa SL v Agencia Estatal de Administración Tributaria* (joined cases C-110/98 to 147/98) [2000] ECR I–1577, [2002] STC 535 at [52].

This provision (in conjunction with what is now arts 242, 243) gives member states authority to lay down rules regarding the manner in which the right to deduct input tax is supervised and, in particular, the manner in which taxable persons are required to establish that right. As regards invoices, member states may require taxable persons to produce the original invoice. If the taxable person no longer holds the original, member states may allow him to produce cogent evidence that the relevant transaction took place: *Reisdorf v Finanzamt Köln-West* (case C-85/95) [1996] ECR I–6257, [1997] STC 180 at [26]–[31].

This provision does not preclude national measures requiring a person to provide security for the payment of VAT if he is jointly and severally liable for that tax by virtue of national measures adopted on the basis of art 205. This provision does not allow member states to require security from a person in other circumstances: *Customs and Excise Comrs and Attorney General v Federation of Technological Industries and others* (case C-384/04) [2006] ECR I–4191, [2006] STC 1483 at [47], [48].

The obligation to treat domestic and cross-border transactions equally was introduced to regulate trade between member states. It does not preclude the imposition of rules on domestic transactions which are stricted than those applicable to intra-Community trade: *Eismann Alto Adige Srl v Ufficio IVA di Bolzano* (case C-217/94) [1996] ECR I–5287, [1996] STC 1374 at [17]–[20]. For an example of stricter national rules for domestic transactions, see *Eismann Alto Adige Srl v Ufficio IVA di Bolzano* (case C-217/94) [1996] ECR I–5287, [1996] STC 1374 (requirement for accompanying documents to be drawn up in respect of goods transported within the confines of a member state).

The situation can arise where a trader invoices his customer for an amount of VAT that is not due. He may do so by mistake, eg by charging tax on a supply which is exempt from tax (so that none of the VAT is properly chargeable) or by charging VAT at the standard rate instead of the reduced rate (so that part of the VAT is not properly chargeable). A trader may also issue an invoice showing VAT in respect of a taxable supply that does not take place, a situation which may or may not involve fraud. The directive does not make any specific provision for the correction of invoices in these situations. It appears, however, that this provision provides the legal basis for national legislation dealing with this situation.

It is for member states to lay down the conditions in which improperly invoiced VAT may be adjusted. They may provide that the adjustment takes place: (1) as part of the procedure for determining the tax payable; or (2) in the course of a subsequent procedure, so that the tax authorities can verify whether any risk of loss of revenue has been eliminated. However, the adjustment cannot be dependent upon the discretion of the tax authorities where the risk to the revenue has been eliminated. The principle of neutrality requires that the amount properly invoiced can be adjusted where the issuer of the invoice has, in sufficient time, wholly eliminated the risk of any loss to the revenue, eg by retrieving and destroying the invoice before the recipient makes an input tax deduction in respect of the incorrect amount of VAT shown, or by accounting to the tax authorities for the incorrect amount of tax shown. The adjustment is made whether or not the issuer acted in good faith. By contrast, where the risk of any loss of revenue has not been wholly eliminated, member states may provide that adjustment is conditional upon the issuer having acted in good faith. Community law does not prevent member states treating the issuing of bogus invoices improperly mentioning VAT as attempted tax evasion and imposing penalties accordingly: *Schmeink & Cofreth AG & Co KG v Finanzamt Borken; Strobel v Finanzamt Esslingen* (case C-454/98) [2000] ECR I–6973, [2000] STC 810 at [57]–[70]. For the adjustment of input tax deductions, see art 184.

Chapter 8—Obligations relating to certain importations and exportations

Section 1—Importation

Article 274–277
(ex art 33a(1))

The following provisions apply to goods entering the Community (ie the territories of member states excluding the territories listed in art 6(1)) in free circulation from a third territory (ie one of the territories listed art 6(1)). The territories listed in art 6(1) are: (1) the Åland Islands, (2) the French overseas departments, (3) Mount Athos, (4) the Canary Islands and (5) the Channel Islands. Although forming part of the Community customs territory, these territories do not form part of the Community for VAT purposes.

	Circumstance	*Consequence*
(1)	The goods enter the Community (as defined above) from a third territory (as defined above)	The goods are subject to the same Community customs formalities as goods imported into the customs territory of the Community
(2)	Goods (which were declared for the internal Community transit procedure when they entered the Community) are despatched or transported from the member state where they enter the Community to another member state	The goods circulate in the Community under the internal Community transit procedure
(3)	The goods would (if they had been imported within the meaning of art 30) qualify for either: (1) an arrangement referred to in art 156, or (2) a temporary arrangement with full exemption from import duties	Member states must take measures ensuring that the goods remain in the Community under the conditions applicable to the relevant arrangement

SECTION 2—EXPORTATION

Articles 278–280
(ex art 33a(2))

The following provisions apply to an exportation of goods in free circulation where the goods are despatched or transported from a member state (in this context, being a part of the territory of a member state which does not comprise a third territory as listed in art 6(1), see art 5(2)) to a third territory (ie one of the territories listed art 6(1)). The territories listed in art 6(1) are: (1) the Åland Islands, (2) the French overseas departments, (3) Mount Athos, (4) the Canary Islands and (5) the Channel Islands. Although forming part of the Community customs territory, these territories do not form part of the Community for VAT purposes.

	Circumstance	*Consequence*
(1)	The goods are despatched or transported from a member state to a third territory	The goods are subject to the same Community customs formalities as goods exported outside the customs territory of the Community
(2)	The goods are temporarily exported from a member state to a third territory for subsequent reimportation	Member states must take measures ensuring that, on reimportation into the Community, the goods are treated in the same manner as goods that have been temporarily exported outside the Community customs territory

TITLE XII—SPECIAL SCHEMES

CHAPTER 1—SPECIAL SCHEME FOR SMALL ENTERPRISES

SECTION 1—SIMPLIFIED PROCEDURES FOR CHARGING AND COLLECTION

Article 281
(ex art 24(1))

Member states have the option of applying simplified procedures (eg flat-rate schemes for charging and collecting tax) under such conditions and within such limits as they may be set. They may exercise this option after consulting the VAT Committee (see art 398) if:

- They might encounter difficulties in applying the normal tax scheme to small undertakings by reason of their activities or structures.
- The simplified procedures do not lead to a reduction of tax.

This option constitutes an exemption to the normal rules of the directive. It must be construed strictly. A simplified scheme must be applied only to the extent necessary to achieve its objective, ie to simplify charging procedures: *Commission v Austria* (case C-128/05) [2006] ECR I–9265, [2008] STC 2610 at [22], [25], [26]. For an example of a scheme that did not meet this test, see *Commission v Austria* (case C-128/05) [2006] ECR I–9265, [2008] STC 2610 (scheme exempting undertakings from declaring and paying VAT).

For exemptions and graduated tax relief in relation to small enterprises, see art 282.

SECTION 2—EXEMPTIONS OR GRADUATED RELIEF

Article 282
(ex art 24(3) (first para))

The exemptions and graduated tax relief conferred by arts 283–292 apply to goods and services supplied by small enterprises.

Article 283
(ex art 24(3) (second and third paras))

Exemption from tax and graduated tax relief do not apply to:

- The transactions in art 12 carried out on an occasional basis.
- Supplies of new means of transport made under the conditions specified in art 138(1) and (2)(*a*).
- Supplies of goods and services made by a taxable person who is not established in the member state in which the tax is due. This provision does not contravene TFEU art 56 (freedom to provide services): see *Ingrid Schmelz v Finanzamt Waldviertel* (case C-97/09) [2010] ECR I–0000, [2011] STC 88.
- Other transactions excluded by member states.

Article 284
(ex art 24(2)(a))

1. Directive 67/228/EEC art 14 (repealed) (the Second Directive) permitted member states to introduce exemptions and graduated relief. Member states which did so may retain them, and the arrangements for applying them, if they comply with the VAT rules.

2. A member state may, at 17 May 1977, have exempted taxable persons whose annual turnover was less than the national currency equivalent of EUR 5,000. If so, it may increase that ceiling to an amount not exceeding EUR 5,000. "Annual turnover" for the foregoing purposes is turnover generated by an undertaking in one year in the member state in which it is established: see *Ingrid Schmelz v Finanzamt Waldviertel* (case C-97/09) [2010] ECR I–0000, [2011] STC 88. For "turnover", see art 288.

A member state may have applied graduated relief. If so, it may neither raise the ceiling for relief nor relax the conditions for granting it.

Article 285
(ex art 24(2)(b))

A member state may not have exercised the option under Directive 67/228/EEC art 14 (repealed) (see the commentary to art 284). If so, it may exempt taxable persons whose annual turnover does not exceed EUR 5,000 or the national currency equivalent. It may also grant graduated tax relief to taxable persons whose annual turnover exceeds the national ceiling fixed for its application. "Annual turnover" for the foregoing purposes is turnover generated by an undertaking in one year in the member state in which it is established: see *Ingrid Schmelz v Finanzamt Waldviertel* (case C-97/09) [2010] ECR I–0000, [2011] STC 88. For "turnover", see art 288.

Article 286
(ex art 24(2)(c))

A member state may, at 17 May 1977, have exempted taxable persons whose annual turnover was equal to, or higher than, the national currency equivalent of EUR 5,000. If so, it may increase that ceiling in order to maintain the value of the exemption in real terms. "Annual turnover" for the foregoing purposes is turnover generated by an undertaking in one year in the member state in which it is established: see *Ingrid Schmelz v Finanzamt Waldviertel* (case C-97/09) [2010] ECR I–0000, [2011] STC 88. For "turnover", see art 288.

Article 287
(ex art 24a; Act of Accession (1979), Annex VIII(II) point 1; Act of Accession (1985), Annex XXXII((v) points 2, 3; Act of Accession (1994), Annex XV(IX) point 2(c), (j), (x))

[Applies to Austria, Bulgaria, Cyprus, Czech Republic, Estonia, Finland, Greece, Hungary, Latvia, Lithuania, Malta, Poland, Portugal, Romania, Slovakia, Slovenia, Spain and Sweden.]

Article 288
(ex art 24(4))

For the purposes of applying exemption and graduated tax relief, turnover comprises the following VAT-exclusive amounts:

- The value of supplies of goods and services chargeable to tax.
- The value of transactions subject to exemption with refund in accordance with any of arts 110, 111, 125(1), 127 or 128(1).
- The value of transactions exempt from tax in accordance with any of arts 146–149 and 151–153.
- The value of real property transactions, in so far as they are not ancillary transactions.
- The value of financial transactions exempt from tax under art 135(1)(*b*)–(*g*), in so far as they are not ancillary transactions.
- The value of insurance services, in so far as they are not ancillary transactions.

However, disposals of tangible or intangible capital assets are not taken into account for the purposes of calculating turnover.

Article 289
(ex art 24(5))

Taxable persons exempt from VAT are not entitled to:

- Deduct input tax in accordance with arts 167–171 and 173–177.
- Show VAT on their invoices.

Article 290
(ex art 24(6))

Taxable persons eligible for exemption from VAT may opt to apply either the normal VAT arrangements or the simplified procedures provided for in art 281. In this case, they are entitled to any graduated tax relief conferred by national legislation.

Article 291
(ex art 24(7))

Taxable persons enjoying graduated tax relief are treated as taxable persons subject to the normal VAT arrangements.

Article 292
(ex art 24(2) (introductory para))

The arrangements in arts 282–291 apply until a date to be fixed by the Council in accordance with EC Treaty art 93 (now TFEU art 113). This may not be later than the date on which the definitive arrangements (see art 402) enter into force.

SECTION 3—REPORTING AND REVIEW

Article 293
(ex art 24(8))

The Commission must submit reports to the Council at four-yearly intervals on the application of Chapter 2 and, where appropriate, make proposals for:

(1) improving the special scheme for small enterprises.
(2) adapting national systems regarding exemptions and graduated tax relief.
(3) adapting the ceilings prescribed in arts 284–287.

Article 294
(ex art 24(9))

The Council is required to decide whether a special scheme for small enterprises is necessary under the definitive arrangements. For the definitive arrangements, see art 402.

Derogations granted to the UK

- For a simplification measure retained by the UK granting exemption from registration to traders making zero-rated supplies, see Appendix 1.

CHAPTER 2—COMMON FLAT-RATE SCHEME FOR FARMERS

Article 295
(ex art 25(2), Annex A (Part V), Annex B (introductory sentence))

1. Various words and phrases are defined. For "agricultural services", see Annexs VII, VIII; *Finanzamt Rendsburg v Harbs* (case C-321/02) [2004] ECR I–7101, [2006] STC 340 (farmer letting material assets of his farming business); *Finanzamt Arnsberg v Stadt Sundern* (case C-43/04) [2005] ECR I–4491 (grant of hunting licences); and para 2.

2. A farmer may process products, which are essentially derived from his agricultural production, using means normally employed in an agricultural, forestry or fisheries undertaking. Where this is so, the processing activities are treated as an agricultural production activity for the purposes of Annex VII.

Article 296
(ex art 25(1), 25(9) (first para) and 25(10))

1. Member states may apply a flat-rate scheme for farmers if the normal VAT arrangements, or the special scheme for small enterprises (see arts 281–292), gives rise to difficulties when applied to farmers. The scheme must tend to offset input tax incurred by them.

The flat-rate scheme constitutes an exemption to the normal rules of the directive. It is therefore construed strictly. The scheme must be applied only to the extent necessary to achieve its objective: *Finanzamt Rendsburg v Harbs* (case C-321/02) [2004] ECR I–7101, [2006] STC 340 at [27].

2. Member states may exclude the following farmers from the flat-rate scheme:

- Certain categories of farmers. By implication, these categories are determined by the member states.
- Farmers for whom the application of the normal VAT scheme would not give rise to administrative difficulties.
- Farmers for whom the special scheme for small enterprises would not give rise to administrative difficulties.

3. Flat-rate farmers may opt to apply the normal VAT scheme or the special scheme for small enterprises. This option is exercised in accordance with rules and conditions laid down by the member states.

Article 297
(ex art 25(3) (first para, first sentence) and 25(3) (second para))

Member states must fix flat-rate compensation percentages. Varying percentages may be fixed for forestry, for different sub-divisions of agriculture, and for fisheries. Having fixed the percentages, member states must notify them to the Commission before applying them.

Article 298
(ex art 25(3) (first para, second and fourth sentences))

Flat-rate compensation percentages are calculated on the basis of macro-economic statistics relating solely to flat-rate farmers.

The "macro-economic statistics" comprise inputs (intermediate consumption and gross fixed asset formation) and outputs (final production, including own consumption), together with the total amount of taxes relating to inputs. The flat-rate compensation percentages are obtained by dividing the latter amount by outputs: *Commission v Italy* (case 3/86) [1988] ECR 3369, [1989] 3 CMLR 748 at [8].

Member states may:

- Round flat-rate compensation percentages to the nearest half point.
- Reduce flat-rate compensation percentages to a nil rate.

Part I VAT

Article 299
(ex art 25(3) (first para, third sentence))

Flat-rate compensation percentages must not enable flat-rate farmers to obtain refunds exceeding the input VAT charged (as defined in art 295(6)).

Article 300
(ex art 25(5) (first para))

Flat-rate compensation percentages are applied to the VAT-exclusive prices of the following supplies made by flat-rate farmers:

(1) Agricultural products (as defined in art 295(4)) supplied to taxable persons who are not covered by the flat-rate scheme in the member state concerned.

(2) Agricultural products supplied in accordance with the conditions laid down in art 138 to non-taxable legal persons whose intra-Community acquisitions are charged to VAT in the member state of arrival.

(3) Agricultural services (as defined in art 295(5)) supplied to taxable persons who are not covered by the flat-rate scheme in the member state concerned.

Article 301
(ex art 25(6)(a) (first para, first sentence), 25(6)(b), 25(8))

1. Member states must provide for the payment of flat-rate compensation on the supplies of agricultural products and agricultural services referred to in art 300. They may choose one or other of the following methods:

- Payment by the customer. Here, the customer is reimbursed by way of deduction or refund.
- Payment by the public authorities.

2. Flat-rate compensation is deemed to be paid by the purchaser or customer in respect of agricultural products and agricultural services other than those specified in art 300.

Article 302
(ex art 25(5) (second para))

A flat-rate farmer entitled to flat-rate compensation is not entitled to deduction of VAT in respect of the activities covered by the flat-rate scheme.

Article 303
(ex art 25(6)(a) (first para, second sentence), 25(6)(a) (second and third paras))

1. A taxable customer is entitled to deduct the flat-rate compensation paid to flat-rate farmers. The deduction is made in accordance with arts 167–169, 173–177 and procedures laid down by the member states. Refunds are made in accordance with the method determined by member states. In particular, they may apply Directives 79/0172/EEC (refunds to EC traders) and 86/560/EEC (refunds to third country traders).

2. Flat-rate compensation paid by a customer in respect of the following transactions must be refunded to him by the relevant member state:

- Supplies of agricultural products to: (1) taxable persons, or (2) non-taxable legal persons acting as such in another member state where their intra-Community acquisitions are charged to VAT.
- Supplies of agricultural products to taxable customers established outside the Community. The supplies must be made under the conditions laid down in arts 146–148, 156, 157(1)(*b*), 158, 160 and 161. The products must be used by the purchasers for the purposes of: (1) the transactions referred to in art 169(*a*) or (*b*); or (2) services deemed to take place in the territory of the member state in which the customer is established and in respect of which VAT is payable solely by the customers under art 196.

- Supplies of agricultural services to taxable customers established within the Community but in another member state. The services must be used by the customer for the purposes of: (1) the transactions referred to in art 169(*a*) or (*b*); or (2) services deemed to take place in the territory of the member state in which the customer is established and in respect of which VAT is payable solely by the customers under art 196.
- Supplies of agricultural services to taxable customers established outside the Community. The services must be used by the customers for the purposes of: (1) the transactions referred to in art 169(*a*) or (*b*); or (2) services deemed to take place in the territory of the member state in which the customer is established and in respect of which VAT is payable solely by the customers under art 196.

3. Member states must determine how to make the refunds in para 2. In particular, they may apply the provisions of Directive 2008/9/EC (formerly Directive 79/1072/EEC) (refunds to EC traders) and Directive 86/560/EEC (refunds to third country traders).

Article 304
(ex art 25(7))

Member states must take steps to ensure that flat-rate compensation is correctly paid to flat-rate farmers.

Article 305
(ex art 25(9) (second para))

Member states applying the flat-rate scheme must ensure that intra-Community supplies of agricultural products by flat-rate farmers and other taxable persons are taxed in the same way.

CHAPTER 3—SPECIAL SCHEME FOR TRAVEL AGENTS

General note This scheme was introduced to resolve problems arising in connection with travel services which include elements in more than one member state. However, the scheme also applies to supplies of services within a single member state: *Customs and Excise Comrs v Madgett and Baldwin (trading as Howden Court Hotel)* (cases C-308/96 and C-94/97) [1998] ECR I–6229, [1998] STC 1189 at [19].

Article 306
(ex art 26(1))

1. This Chapter applies to the operations of a travel agent (see art 306(3) who meets the following conditions:

- He deals with customers in his own name.

  It is for the national court to determine whether a travel agent acts in his own name. In doing so, national courts must have regard to all the circumstances of the case and, in particular, the nature of the travel agent's contractual obligations towards the traveller: *Beheersmaatschappij Van Ginkel Waddinxveen BV v Inspecteur der Omzetbelasting, Utrecht* (case C-163/91) [1992] ECR I–5723, [1996] STC 825 at [21].
- He uses the supplies and services of other taxable persons to provide travel facilities.

  A travel agent's services must relate to a journey. He appears to provide travel facilities if his services comprise (or include) accommodation, transport or both: see *Minerva Kulturreisen GmbH v Finanzamt Freital* (case C-31/10) [2010] ECR I–0000, [2011] STC 532 at [15], [19]–[22]. For an example of services which amount to the provision of travel facilities, see *Beheersmaatschappij Van Ginkel Waddinxveen BV v Inspecteur der Omzetbelasting, Utrecht* (case C-163/91) [1992] ECR I–5723, [1996] STC 825 (provision of holiday accommodation without arranging the traveller's transport to and from the accommodation). For an example of services which do not, see *Minerva Kulturreisen GmbH v Finanzamt Freital* (case C-31/10) [2010] ECR I–0000, [2011] STC 532 (sale of opera tickets in isolation without the provision of a travel service).

Where the overall package price consists partly of in-house services and partly of bought-in services, the special scheme is confined to the bought-in services: *Customs and Excise Comrs v Madgett and Baldwin* (*trading as Howden Court Hotel*) (cases C-308/96 and C-94/97) [1998] ECR I–6229, [1998] STC 1189 at [32]–[35].

2. This article does not apply to travel agents who act only as an intermediary and who account for tax in accordance with the disbursement arrangements in art 79(*c*).

3. For the purposes of this Chapter, the term "travel agents" includes tour operators.

The term also includes traders who, although not a travel agent or tour operator within the normal meaning of those terms, effect identical transactions in the context of another activity, eg that of hotelier: *Customs and Excise Comrs v Madgett and Baldwin* (*trading as Howden Court Hotel*) (cases C-308/96 and C-94/97) [1998] ECR I–6229, [1998] STC 1189 at [20]–[23]. For examples, see: (1) *Customs and Excise Comrs v Madgett and Baldwin* (*trading as Howden Court Hotel*) (cases C-308/96 and C-94/97) [1998] ECR I–6229, [1998] STC 1189 (hotelier providing travel to the hotel from distant pick-up points); (2) *Finanzamt Heidelberg v iSt Internationale Sprach- und Studienreisen GmbH* (case C-200/04) [2005] ECR I–8691, [2006] STC 52 (educational package including return flight, board and lodging with host family, classes, support while overseas and travel cancellation insurance).

Traders supplying services usually associated with travel may find it necessary to use travel supplies acquired from third parties which, in comparison with the principal service supplied, make up only a small proportion of the package price. The bought-in supplies represent a better means of enjoying the principal service rather than an aim it themselves. They are ancillary to the in-house service and are not taxed under the special scheme. However, travel services habitually offered to customers in addition to the principal service are not ancillary services if they have a substantial effect on the package price charged: *Finanzamt Heidelberg v iSt Internationale Sprach- und Studienreisen GmbH* (case C-200/04) [2005] ECR I–8691, [2006] STC 52 at [26]–[28].

Article 307
(ex art 26(2) (first and second sentences))

All transactions performed by travel agents in respect of a journey (see art 306(1)) are treated as a single service supplied by them to the traveller.

This service is taxable in either:

- The member state in which the travel agent has established his business.
- (If the services are provided from a fixed establishment) the member state in which the fixed establishment is located.

A tour operator may have established his business in member state X but supply services from a fixed establishment in member state Y. If so, the services are taxable in member state Y. The tour operator may trade in member state Y through a subsidiary, which acts as agent for the tour operator. In determining whether, in these circumstances, the tour operator has a fixed establishment in member state Y, it is necessary to ascertain first, whether the subsidiary is independent of the tour operator, and secondly, whether the fixed establishment in member state Y has the requisite minimum size in terms of necessary human and technical resources: *Customs and Excise Comrs v DFDS A/S* (case C-260/95) [1997] ECR I–1005, [1997] STC 384 at [24]–[29].

Article 308
(ex art 26(2) (third sentence))

The taxable amount of the service is the travel agent's margin. This is the difference between:

- The total amount to be paid by the traveller, exclusive of VAT.
- The actual cost to the travel agent of supplies and services for the direct benefit of the traveller provided by other taxable persons.

The "travel facilities" supplied to a traveller may consist partly of in-house services and partly of bought-in services. If so, the overall price charged must be apportioned in order to ascertain "the total amount to be paid by the traveller" in respect of the "supplies and services . . . provided by other taxable persons". The overall price is apportioned by reference to: (1) the cost of bought-in services; and (2) either the cost or market value of the in-house services: *Customs and Excise Comrs v Madgett and Baldwin* (*trading as Howden Court Hotel*) (cases C-308/96 and C-94/97) [1998] ECR I–6229, [1998] STC 1189 at [39]–[42].

A travel agent is not required to use the cost method if he can identify the market value of similar services: *Customs and Excise Comrs v Madgett and Baldwin* (*trading as Howden Court Hotel*) (cases C-308/96 and C-94/97) [1998] ECR I–6229, [1998] STC 1189 at [46]. On the other hand, he does not have an unfettered discretion to use the market value method. He can use the cost method if he can prove that, for the tax period under consideration, the cost method accurately reflects the actual structure of the package. He must use the market value method in other circumstances. If it is necessary to use the market value method, but a market value can be established for only some of the in-house services (eg because the taxable person does not sell the other services on a non-package basis), the market value method is used in relation to those services and the cost method in relation to the remainder: *My Travel plc v Customs and Excise Comrs* (case C-291/03) [2005] ECR I–8477, [2005] STC 1617 at [31], [34], [35], [38]–[40]. A travel agent must clearly use the cost method is he is unable to identify the market value of similar services.

Use of the market value method is not subject to a condition that it is simpler to apply than the cost method, or that it produces a similar VAT liability to the cost method: *My Travel plc v Customs and Excise Comrs* (case C-291/03) [2005] ECR I–8477, [2005] STC 1617 at [23], [26].

It is for the national court to establish market value. This is done in the light of the circumstances of the case. Market value may be established on the basis of average values. As regards in-house flights, the price at which seats are sold to other tour operators may constitute the most appropriate market: *My Travel plc v Customs and Excise Comrs* (case C-291/03) [2005] ECR I–8477, [2005] STC 1617 at [44], [45].

The agency agreement between a tour operator ("X") and travel agent ("Y") may allow Y to fix the price charge to his customer ("Z") in respect of a holiday. It may nevertheless provide that Y must account to X for the full brochure price (eg £1,000) and that his commission (eg 10%) is determined by reference to that price. Suppose that the price agreed between Y and Z is (say) £950. Y is required to account to X for £900, representing the brochure price (ie £1,000) less commission of £100 (ie 10% of £1,000). The net amount actually retained by Y is £50, representing the difference between the amount paid by Z (ie £950) and the net amount accounted for to X (ie £900). The question arises whether the margin for the purposes of the scheme is £100 (the commission) or £50 (Y's profit on the transaction). The consideration for the supply made by X to Z (ie the holiday) is determined in accordance with art 11A(1)(*a*), ie everything obtained by the supplier from the customer or a third party. X receives £1,000 (representing £950 received by Y from Z plus £50 which Y has effectively contributed from his own resources). This is the consideration for the supply made by him. Y receives £100 (the commission due under the agreement between X and Y and received by deduction from the brochure price accounted for to X). This is the consideration for the supply made by him. See *First Choice Holidays plc v Customs and Excise Comrs* (case C-149/01) [2003] ECR I–6289, [2003] STC 934.

Article 309
(ex art 26(3))

A travel agent's service is treated as an intermediary activity for the purposes of exemption under art 153 if:

- The travel agent has entrusted transactions to other taxable persons.
- The taxable persons perform those transactions outside the Community.

If the transactions are performed both inside and outside the Community (see art 5(1)), exemption is confined to that part of the travel agent's service relating to transactions outside the Community.

For exemption during the transitional period, see art 371 and Annex X Part B; *Commission v Germany* (case C-74/91) [1992] ECR I–5437.

Article 310
(ex art 26(4))

VAT incurred by a travel agent is not eligible for deduction or refund in any member state if it arises in respect of transactions for the direct benefit of a traveller.

CHAPTER 4—SPECIAL ARRANGEMENTS FOR SECOND-HAND GOODS, WORKS OF ART, COLLECTORS' ITEMS AND ANTIQUES

SECTION 1—DEFINITIONS

Article 311
(ex art 26aA)

The terms "works of art", "collectors' items" and "antiques" are defined in Annex IX. Pictures, engravings and sculptures within Annex IX Part A points 5–7 are not regarded as works of art if member states so decide.

The term "second-hand goods" is defined. Live animals fall with this definition: *Förvaltnings AB Stenholmen v Riksskatteverket* (case C-320/02) [2004] ECR I–3509, [2004] STC 1041.

The term "taxable dealer" is defined. For the scope of this term, see *Jyske Finans A/S v Skatteministeriet* (case C-280/04) [2005] ECR I–10683, [2006] STC 1744 (sale and leaseback).

The terms "organiser of a sale by public auction" and "principal of an organiser of a sale by public auction" are defined.

SECTION 2—SPECIAL ARRANGEMENTS FOR TAXABLE DEALERS

Subsection 1—Margin scheme

Article 312
(ex art 26aB(3) (second para))

The terms "selling price" and "purchase price" are defined.

Article 313
(ex arts 26aB(1), 26aD(a))

1. Member states must apply special arrangements (referred to as "the margin scheme") for taxing the profit margin on supplies of second-hand goods (as defined in art 313(1)), works of art (as defined in art 313(2)), collectors' items (as defined in art 313(3)) and antiques (as defined in art 313(4)) made by taxable dealers (as defined in art 313(5)).

2. New means of transport are excluded from the margin scheme if the conditions in art 138(1), (2)(*a*) are met.

Article 314
(ex art 26aB(2))

The margin scheme applies to supplies of the goods in art 313(1) by a taxable dealer who purchased them within the Community from one of the following persons:

	Person from whom the goods were purchased	Circumstances in which the goods were purchased
(*a*)	A non-taxable person	No tax was charged (ie because the supply was not made by a taxable person)
(*b*)	Another taxable person	The supply was exempt from tax in accordance with art 136
(*c*)	Another taxable person	1. The goods are capital assets 2. The supply is covered by the exemption for small enterprises (see arts 282–292)
(*d*)	Another taxable dealer	VAT was charged under the margin scheme

The margin scheme does not apply to goods imported into the EU under the normal VAT scheme by a taxable dealer: see *Direktsia "Obzhalvane I upravlenie na izpalnenieto" – Varna v Auto Nikolovi OOD* (case C-203/10) [2011] ECR I–0000, [2011] STC 1294.

This provision has direct effect: see *Direktsia "Obzhalvane I upravlenie na izpalnenieto" – Varna v Auto Nikolovi OOD* (case C-203/10) [2011] ECR I–0000, [2011] STC 1294.

Article 315
(ex art 26aB(3) (first para))

The taxable amount of the supply made by the taxable dealer is his profit margin (exclusive of the VAT included therein). The "profit margin" for this purpose is the difference between: (1) his selling price (as defined art 312(1)), and (2) the purchase price (as defined in arts 312(2) (general rule) and 317 (option made in respect of the goods in art 316(1)(*a*)).

Article 316
(ex art 26aB(4) (first and second paras))

1. A taxable dealer is entitled to opt for the margin scheme to apply to supplies of the following goods:

(a) A work of art, collectors' item or antique which he imported himself.
(b) A work of art purchased from its creator or his successor in title.
(c) A work of art purchased from a taxable person (who is not a taxable dealer) who charged tax at the reduced rate in accordance with art 103.

2. The detailed rules for exercising this option are fixed by the member states. The option must apply for a minimum period of two calendar years.

Article 317
(ex art 26aB(4) (third para))

If a taxable dealer exercises the option in art 316, the taxable amount is determined in accordance with art 315.

As regards the goods in art 316(1)(*a*), the purchase price is the aggregate of: (1) the taxable amount on importation (see arts 85–89); and (2) the VAT due or paid on importation.

Article 318
(ex art 26aB(10))

1, 2. Member states may simplify the collection of VAT by providing that the taxable amount is determined by reference to a tax period (as to which, see art 250)). This procedure may be applied to certain transactions or by certain categories of taxable dealer.

The taxable amount of goods chargeable to tax at the same rate is the total margin made by the taxable dealer (excluding VAT). The "total margin" for this purpose is the difference between:

- The total selling price of all supplies made by the taxable dealer under the simplification measure during the tax period.
- The total purchase price of goods purchased by the taxable dealer during the tax period.

Member states must consult the VAT Committee (see art 398) before introducing simplification measures.

3. Member states must ensure that taxable persons neither enjoy an unjustified advantage nor sustain an unjustified loss by using the simplification measure.

Article 319
(ex art 26aB(11) (first para))

A taxable dealer may apply the normal VAT arrangements to any supply covered by the margin scheme.

Article 320
(ex art 26aB(11) (second and third paras))

1. A taxable dealer is entitled to deduct the VAT incurred on the importation of a work of art, collectors' item or antique if he accounts for VAT on his onward supply under the normal arrangements. This provision has direct effect: see *Direktsia "Obzhalvane I upravlenie na izpalnenieto" – Varna v Auto Nikolovi OOD* (case C-203/10) [2011] ECR I–0000, [2011] STC 1294.

A taxable dealer is entitled to deduct the VAT incurred on his puirchase of a work of art if he accounts for VAT on his onward supply under the normal arrangements. The work of art must have been purchased from one of the following persons:

- Its creator.
- The creator's successors in title.
- A taxable person who is not a taxable dealer.

2. The right to deduct arises at the time when VAT becomes chargeable on the taxable dealer's onward supply. This provision is confined to works of art, collectors' items and antiques: see *Direktsia "Obzhalvane I upravlenie na izpalnenieto" – Varna v Auto Nikolovi OOD* (case C-203/10) [2011] ECR I–0000, [2011] STC 1294.

This provision has direct effect: see *Direktsia "Obzhalvane I upravlenie na izpalnenieto" – Varna v Auto Nikolovi OOD* (case C-203/10) [2011] ECR I–0000, [2011] STC 1294.

Article 321
(ex art 26aB(5))

A work of art, collectors' item or antique supplied under the margin scheme is exempt if it meets the conditions specified in arts 146–148 or 151.

Article 322
(ex art 26aB(7))

VAT incurred in the following circumstances is not deductible by a taxable dealer if his onward supply of the goods takes place under the margin scheme:

	Circumstances	***Non-deductible input tax***
(*a*)	Works of art, collectors' item or antique imported by the taxable dealer himself	VAT due or paid on the importation
(*b*)	Work of art purchased from the creator or his successors in title	VAT due or paid on the purchase
(*c*)	Work of art supplied to him by a taxable person who is not a taxable dealer	VAT due or paid on the purchase

Article 323
(ex art 26aB(6))

A taxable person is not entitled to deduct the VAT incurred in respect of any goods purchased from a taxable dealer under the margin scheme.

Article 324
(ex art 26aB(8))

A taxable dealer must keep separate accounts for: (1) goods supplied under the margin scheme, and (2) goods supplied under the normal arrangements. The accounting rules are laid down by the member states.

Article 325
(ex art 26aB(9))

A taxable dealer must not show VAT on an invoice issued by him in respect of goods supplied under the margin scheme.

Subsection 2—Transitional arrangements for second-hand means of transport

Articles 326–332
(ex art 28o(1)(a)–(f) and 28o(2))

Member states are entitled to retain any national tax arrangements in force at 31 December 1992 in relation to supplies of second-hand means of transport in so far as those arrangements comply with, or are amended to comply with, the conditions set out in arts 327–332.

Denmark is authorised to introduce such arrangements.

SECTION 3—SPECIAL ARRANGEMENTS FOR SALES BY PUBLIC AUCTION

Article 333
(ex arts 26aC(1) (introductory sentence), 26aD(a))

1. Member states may apply special arrangements for taxing the profit margin on supplies of second-hand goods, works of art, collectors' items or antiques made by an organiser of sales by public auction (as defined in art 311(6)) ("an auctioneer") acting in his own name for the persons listed in art 334 pursuant to a contract under which commission is payable on the sale of those goods by public auction.

2. New means of transport are excluded from the special arrangements if the conditions in art 138(1), (2)(*a*) are met.

Article 334
(ex art 26aC(1) (first to fourth indents))

The special arrangements in art 334 apply to supplies on behalf of the following persons in the circumstances stated:

	Person for whom the organiser acts	*Circumstances*
(*a*)	A non-taxable person	None specified
(*b*)	Another taxable person	The taxable person's supply is exempt under art 136
(*c*)	Another taxable person	**1.** The goods are capital assets **2.** The taxable person's supply is covered by the exemption for small enterprises (see arts 282–292)

	Person for whom the organiser acts	*Circumstances*
(*d*)	A taxable dealer	The taxable dealer's supply is charged to VAT under the margin scheme

Article 335
(ex art 26aC(7))

The supply of goods to an auctioneer takes place when the goods are sold by public auction.

Article 336
(ex art 26aC(2))

The taxable amount in respect of each supply of goods is the total amount invoiced to the purchaser by the auctioneer, less: (1) the net amount paid by the auctioneer to his principal (see art 337); and (2) the VAT payable by the auctioneer in respect of his supply.

Article 337
(ex art 26aC(3) (first and second indents))

The net amount paid by the auctioneer to his principal is the difference between: (1) the auction price of the goods; and (2) the auctioneer's commission.

Article 338
(ex art 26aC(6))

An auctioneer must account for the following amounts in a suspense account: (1) the amount due from the purchaser of the goods; and (2) the amounts to be reimbursed to the vendor.

Article 339
(ex art 26aC(4))

The auctioneer must issue an invoice itemising:

- The auction price of the goods.
- Taxes, dues, levies and charges.
- Incidental expenses (eg commission, packing, transport and insurance costs) charged to the purchaser by the organiser.

Article 340
(ex art 26aC(5))

The auctioneer must issue a statement to his principal. This statement must specify the amount of the transaction (ie the auction price less commission due from the auctioneer's principal).

Article 341
(ex art 28o(3))

Member states making special arrangements for the goods in art 33(1) must also apply those arrangements to supplies of second-hand means of transport (as defined in art 327(3)) on behalf of a taxable dealer whose supply would be charged to VAT in accordance with the transitional arrangements for second-hand means of transport (see arts 326–332).

SECTION 4—MEASURES TO PREVENT DISTORTION OF COMPETITION AND TAX EVASION

Article 342
(ex Directive 94/5/EC art 2)

Member states must ensure that taxable dealers neither enjoy an unjustified advantage nor sustain unjustified harm.

Article 343
(ex Directive 94/5/EC art 3)

The Council may authorise any member state to introduce special measures to combat tax evasion. The VAT due under the margin scheme may not be less than the VAT which would be due if the profit margin were equal to a percentage of the selling price fixed by reference to the normal profit margins made by traders in the sector concerned.

Chapter 5—Special scheme for investment gold

Section 1—General provisions

Article 344
(ex art 26bA (first and second paras))

The term "investment gold" is defined by reference to: (1) gold in bar or wafer form; and (2) gold coins. For "weights accepted by the bullion markets", "price" and "open market value" for the purposes of that definition, see Regulation (EU) No 282/2011 arts 56 and 57.

A comprehensive list of the gold coins is published annually in the *Official Journal of the European Communities*. Gold coins published in the list are deemed to fulfil the stated criteria for the whole year for which the list is published. For the list in force for the calendar year 2011, see OJ C322/13, 27.11.10.

Article 345
(ex art 26bA (third para))

Member states must identify the coins meeting the criteria in art 344(1) point 2 traded within their territory and inform the Commission accordingly.

Section 2—Exemption from VAT

Article 346
(ex art 26bB (first para))

Member states must exempt supplies, intra-Community acquisitions and importations of investment gold (as defined in art 345). This includes:

- Investment gold represented by certificates for allocated or unallocated gold.
- Gold traded on gold accounts.
- Gold loans and swaps involving a right of ownership or claim in respect of investment gold.
- Transactions concerning investment gold involving futures and forward contracts leading to a transfer of right of ownership or claim in respect of investment gold.

For exemption with refund, see art 354, 355.

Article 347
(ex art 26bB (second para))

Member states must exempt the services of agents who act in the name, and for the account, of another person when they take part in the supply of investment gold for their principal.

Section 3—Taxation option

Article 348
(ex art 26bC (first para))

Member states must allow taxable persons the right to opt for the taxation of investment gold supplied to another taxable person if:

- The supplier either produces gold or transforms gold into investment gold.
- The supplies would otherwise be exempt from tax under art 346.

Article 349
(ex art 26bC (second para))

1. Member states may allow taxable persons the right to opt for the taxation of gold bars or wafers supplied to another taxable person if:

Part I VAT

- The supplier normally supplies gold for industrial purposes.
- The supply would otherwise be exempt from tax under art 346.

2. Member states may restrict the scope of the option.

Article 350
(ex art 26bC (third para))

Where a supplier has exercised the right of option under arts 348 or 349, member states must allow his agent to opt for taxation of the services specified in art 347.

Article 351
(ex art 26bC (fourth para))

Member states must: (1) lay down detailed rules for exercising the options in arts 348–350; and (2) inform the Commission accordingly.

SECTION 4—TRANSACTIONS ON A REGULATED GOLD BULLION MARKET

Article 352
(ex art 26bG(1))

A member state may, after consulting the VAT Committee (see art 398), apply VAT to the following transactions relating to investment gold taking place in its territory:

- Specific transactions between taxable persons who are members of a bullion market regulated by the member state. For simplification provisions, see art 253.
- Specific transactions between: (1) a taxable person who is a member of a bullion market regulated by the member state, and (2) another taxable person who is not a member of that market.

This option is confined to transactions taking place in that member state. It does not apply to: (1) intra-Community supplies exempted under art 138; or (2) exports.

Article 353
(ex art 26bG(2)(a))

Member states taxing transactions between members of a regulated gold market under art 352 must: (1) suspend collection of the tax due; and (2) dispense with accounting requirements in respect of VAT.

SECTION 5—SPECIAL RIGHTS AND OBLIGATIONS FOR TRADERS IN INVESTMENT GOLD

Article 354
(ex art 26bD(1))

A taxable person is entitled to deduct the VAT due or paid by him in respect of the following transactions if his subsequent supply of the gold concerned is exempt from tax under art 346:

- Investment gold supplied to him by a person who has exercised the right of option in arts 348, 349.
- Investment gold supplied to him under a transaction excluded from exemption in accordance with art 352.
- Gold (other than investment gold) which he purchases, acquires or imports and subsequently transforms into investment gold.
- Services supplied to him in respect of a change to the form, weight or purity of any gold.

Article 355
(ex art 26bD(2))

A taxable person is entitled to deduct VAT due or paid by him in respect of goods and services linked to the production or transformation of gold if: (1) he produces investment gold, or (2) he transforms gold into investment gold. His subsequent supply of the investment gold produced or resulting from the transformation is deemed to be a taxable supply for this purpose.

Article 356
(ex art 26bE)

1. Member states must ensure that traders in investment gold:

- Keep accounts of all substantial transactions in respect of investment gold. These accounts must be retained for at least five years.
- Retain documents in respect of investment gold transactions that enable the customer to be identified. These documents must be retained for at least five years.

2. Member states may accept equivalent EC obligations in lieu of these requirements, eg those in relation to money laundering in Directive 2005/60/EC.

3. Member states may impose more stringent obligations, eg in relation to special records or special accounting requirements.

CHAPTER 6—SPECIAL SCHEME FOR NON-ESTABLISHED TAXABLE PERSONS SUPPLYING ELECTRONIC SERVICES TO NON-TAXABLE PERSONS

SECTION 1—GENERAL PROVISIONS

Article 357
(ex Directive 2002/38/EC art 4, as substituted by Directive 2006/58/EC art 1)

Chapter 6 (arts 357–369) applies until 31 December 2014.

Article 358
(ex art 26cA)

The terms "non-established taxable person", "electronic services", "electronically supplied services", "member state of identification", "member state of consumption", and "VAT return" are defined. For "electronically supplied services", see also Regulation (EU) No 282/2011 art 7.

SECTION 2—SPECIAL SCHEME FOR ELECTRONICALLY SUPPLIED SERVICES

Article 359
(ex art 26cB(1))

1. Member states must permit a non-established taxable person (as defined in art 358(1)) to use the special scheme if:

- He supplies electronic services to a non-taxable person.
- The non-taxable person is established, has his permanent address or usually resides in a member state.

The special scheme must be used for all electronic services supplied in the Community. For electronically supplied services, see the commentary to art 358.

For "permanent address", see Regulation (EU) No 282/2011 art 12. For the place where a person usually resides, see Regulation (EU) No 282/2011 art 13.

Article 360
(ex art 26cB(2) (first para))

A non-established taxable person using the scheme must notify the member state of identification (as defined in art 358(3)) when his activity as a taxable person:

- Commences.

- Ceases.
- Changes so that he no longer qualifies for the special scheme.

Notifications must be given electronically.

Article 361
(ex art 26cB(2) (second para))

1. The information to be given in a notification of commencement (see art 360) is specified.

2. A non-established taxable person using the scheme must notify the member state of identification (see art 358(3)) of any changes in the information provided.

Article 362
(ex art 26cB(3))

The member state of identification (see art 358(3)) must allocate an identification number to a non-established taxable person using the scheme and notify it to him electronically. A member state of consumption (see art 358(4)) may have recourse to its own identification systems.

Article 363
(ex art 26cB(4))

A non-established taxable person using the scheme is removed from the identification register in any of the following circumstances:

(a) He notifies the member state of identification (see art 358(3)) that he no longer supplies electronic services.
(b) It can otherwise be assumed that his taxable activities have ceased.
(c) He ceases to be eligible to use the special scheme.
(d) He persistently fails to comply with the rules of the special scheme.

For the time from which the person may be excluded and his duty to make a return for the quarter in which his exclusion takes effect, see Regulation (EU) No 282/2011 art 58.

Article 364
(ex art 26cB(5) (first para))

A non-established taxable person using the scheme must submit a VAT return (as defined in art 358(5)) for each calendar quarter. This applies whether or not any electronic services have been supplied. The return must be submitted electronically to the member state of identification (see art 358(3)) within 20 days after the end of the tax period covered by the return. Each calendar quarter is regarded as a separate return period: see Regulation (EU) No 282/2011 art 59.

Article 365
(ex art 26cB(5) (second para))

The information to be shown on a VAT return (see art 358(5)) is specified.

For exact accounting, correction of errors and repayent of VAT overstated in a return, see Regulation (EU) No 282/2011 arts 60–63.

Article 366
(ex art 26cB(6) (first para))

VAT returns are completed in the currency of the member state of identification (ie the euro or a national currency). Thus, VAT returns made to the UK are completed in sterling.

If supplies have been made in other currencies, the relevant amounts are converted into euros (or the national currency of the member state of identification) using the rate of exchange published by the European Central Bank in respect of the last day of the reporting period or (if no rate is published in respect of that day) the next day of publication.

Article 367
(ex art 26cB(7))

VAT must be paid when the VAT return is submitted. Payment must be made to a bank account (denominated in euros or the national currency) designated by the member state of identification.

Article 368
(ex art 26cB(8))

A non-established taxable person using the special scheme does not deduct input tax. Instead, he is entitled to a refund in accordance with Directive 86/560/EEC (the Thirteenth Directive).

As regards refunds, this entitlement derogates from art 1(1) of the Thirteenth Directive (which provides that a refund is denied to taxable persons making supplies in the member state) and arts 2(2), 2(3) and 4(2) of that directive do not apply.

Article 369
(ex art 26cB(9))

A non-established taxable person must keep records of transactions covered by the special scheme. He must do so in sufficient detail to enable the accuracy of his VAT return to be verified by the tax administration of the member state of consumption (see art 358(4)). These records must be made available electronically to the member state of identification (see art 358(3)) and member state of consumption. They must be kept for ten years, counted from the end of the year in which the transaction was carried out.

TITLE XIII—DEROGATIONS

CHAPTER 1—DEROGATIONS APPLYING UNTIL THE ADOPTION OF DEFINITIVE ARRANGEMENTS

SECTION 1—DEROGATIONS FOR STATES WHICH WERE MEMBERS OF THE COMMUNITY ON 1 JANUARY 1978

Article 370
(ex art 28(3)(a))

Member states which taxed the transactions listed in Annex X Part A at 1 January 1978 may continue to tax those transactions.

This provision authorises member states to retain certain provisions of their national legislation which predate this directive and which would, without authorisation, be incompatible with it. The taxation allowed by this provision is not harmonised taxation forming an integral part of the VAT regime for certain activities in the public interest; it is taxation authorised only for a transitional period. This provision must be strictly interpreted. It cannot be applied by member states which have exempted the activities in the public interest listed in art 132. Having introduced exemption for the relevant transactions, a member state cannot introduce or reintroduce a taxation scheme for them. On the other hand, if a member state applies taxation under this provision, there is nothing to prevent it from changing to exemption: *Administration de l'enregistrement et des domaines v Eurodental Sàrl* (case C-240/05) [2006] ECR I–11479, [2007] STC 275 at [51]–[56].

Article 371
(ex art 28(3)(b))

Member states which exempted the transactions listed in Annex X Part B at 1 January 1978 may continue to exempt those transactions. Exemption applies under the conditions in force in the relevant member state on that date.

This provision authorises member states to retain certain national exemptions predating this directive which would otherwise have become incompatible with the directive following its entry into force. It does not permit member states to introduce new exemptions, or extend the scope of existing exemptions, after the directive came into force. A member state may abolish some or all of the exemptions it has retained. To the extent that exemptions are retained, member states do not transpose this directive and do not, therefore, infringe either the directive or the principle of equal treatment: *Idéal Tourisme SA v Belgian State* (case C-36/99) [2000] ECR I–6049, [2001] STC 1386 at [32], [38].

For examples of exemptions validly retained, see: (1) *Norbury Developments Ltd v Customs and Excise Comrs* (case C-136/97) [1999] ECR I–2491, [1999] STC 511; (2) *Idéal Tourisme SA v Belgian State* (case C-36/99) [2000] ECR I–6049, [2001] STC 1386. For examples of situations where Annex X did not apply, see: (1) *Commission v Spain* (case C-35/90) [1991] ECR I–5073; (2) *Commission v Federal Republic of Germany* (case C-74/91) [1992] ECR I–5437, [1996] STC 843; (3) *Commission v Spain* (case C-414/97) [1999] ECR I–5585; (4) *Commission v Republic of Finland* (case C-169/00) [2002] ECR I–2433.

Article 372
(ex art 28(3)(d))

Member states which, at 1 January 1978, applied provisions derogating from the principle of immediate deduction (see art 179 (first para)) may continue to apply those provisions.

Having continued to apply national derogating measures in accordance with this provision, a member state may enact new legislation reducing the scope of those measures. It does not infringe arts 167 and 183 by so doing. It is for the national court to verify that, in its application to the case before it, the new legislation reduces the effects of the national derogating measures: *Cedilac SA v Ministère de l'Économie, des Finances et de l'Industrie* (case C-368/06) [2007] ECR I–12327, [2008] SWTI 21 at [36], [43].

Article 373
(ex art 28(3)(e))

Member states which, at 1 January 1978, applied provisions derogating from arts 28 or 79(*a*) may continue to apply provisions.

Article 374 (ex art 28(3)(g))

Member states which, at 1 January 1978, exempted the following services without deduction of VAT paid at the preceding stage may continue to exempt those services:

- The services of travel agents referred to in art 309.
- The services of travel agents acting in the name and on the account of the traveller.

SECTION 2—DEROGATIONS FOR STATES WHICH ACCEDED TO THE COMMUNITY AFTER 1 JANUARY 1978

Article 375
(ex Act of Accession (1979), Annex VIII(II) point 2(b))

[Applies to Greece.]

Article 376
(ex art 28(3a))

[Applies to Spain.]

Article 377
(ex Act of Accession (1985), Annex XV(IX) point 3(i))

[Applies to Portugal.]

Article 378
(ex Act of Accession (1994), Annex XV(IX) point 2(j))

[Applies to Austria.]

Article 379
(ex Act of Accession (1994), Annex XV(IX) point 2(m), (n))

[Applies to Finland.]

Article 380
(ex Act of Accession (1994), Annex XV(IX) point 2(aa))

[Applies to Sweden.]

Article 381
(ex Act of Accession (2003), Annex V(5) point 1(b))

[Applies to the Czech Republic.]

Article 382
(ex Act of Accession (2003), Annex VI(7) point 1(b))

[Applies to Estonia.]

Article 383
(ex Act of Accession (2003), Annex VII(7) point 1)

[Applies to Cyprus.]

Article 384
(ex Act of Accession (2003), Annex VIII(7) point 1)

[Applies to Latvia.]

Article 385
(ex Act of Accession (2003), Annex IX(8) point 1)

[Applies to Lithuania.]

Article 386
(ex Act of Accession (2003), Annex X(7) point 1(c))

[Applies to Hungary.]

Article 387
(ex Act of Accession (2003), Annex XI(7) point 2)

[Applies to Malta.]

Article 388
(ex Act of Accession (2003), Annex XII(9) point 2)

[Applies to Poland.]

Article 389
(ex Act of Accession (2003), Annex XIII(9) point 1(b))

[Applies to Slovenia.]

Article 390
(ex Act of Accession (2003), Annex XIV(7))

[Applies to Slovakia.]

Article 390a

[Applies to Bulgaria.]

Article 390b

[Applies to Romania.]

SECTION 3—PROVISIONS COMMON TO SECTIONS 1 AND 2

Article 391
(ex art 28(3)(c) and Annex G)

Member states exempting the transactions listed in Annex X Part B after 31 December 1977 in accordance with art 371 may allow taxpayers to opt for taxation of those transactions.

Similar provisions in arts 375, 376, 377, 378(2), 379(2) and 380–390b do not apply to the UK.

Article 392
(ex art 28(3)(f))

Member states may provide that the taxable amount of buildings and building land is the difference between the selling price and the purchase price if:

- The land or buildings were purchased for resale.
- The taxable person was not entitled to deduct input tax in respect of the purchase.

Article 393
(ex art 28(4), (5))

1. The Council must review the derogations in arts 370–390 and decide whether any or all of them should be abolished.

2. Under the definitive arrangements (see art 402), passenger transport will (in so far as it relates to that part of a journey taking place within the Community) be taxed in the country of departure. The detailed rules will be laid down by the Council.

CHAPTER 2—DEROGATIONS SUBJECT TO AUTHORISATION

SECTION 1—SIMPLIFICATION MEASURES AND MEASURES TO PREVENT TAX EVASION OR AVOIDANCE

Article 394
(ex art 27(5))

Member states may retain special measures if:

- They were applied to simplify the procedure for collecting VAT or to prevent certain forms of tax evasion or avoidance. Cf *Commission v Kingdom of Belgium* (case 324/82) [1984] ECR 1861, [1985] 1 CMLR 364 at [29].
  For an example of measures within this description, see *Heintz Landewyck SARL v Staatssecretaris van Financiën* (case C-494/04) [2006] ECR I–5381 (collection of VAT by means of tax stamps). For an example of provisions that were not, see *Commission v Kingdom of Belgium* (case 324/82) [1984] ECR 1861, [1985] 1 CMLR 364 (measures disproportionate to the aim of preventing tax evasion or avoidance by departing from rules regarding the taxable amount in a general and systematic way).
- They were applied on 1 January 1997.
- They were notified to the Commission before 1 January 1998.
  Failure to observe the period for notification does not constitute a material procedural defect capable of rendering inapplicable a derogating measure which was notified late: *Heintz Landewyck SARL v Staatssecretaris van Financiën* (case C-494/04) [2006] ECR I–5381at [50], [51].
  For the special measures notified by the UK, see Appendix 1
- (In the case of simplification measures) they have no more than a negligible effect on the overall amount of tax revenue collected at the final consumption stage.

An authorisation cannot extend beyond the purpose of the basis on which it was requested: *British American Tobacco International Ltd and another v Belgian State* (case C-435/03)

[2005] ECR I–7077, [2006] STC 158 at [44]. Thus, for example, an authorisation to apply measures facilitating monitoring of the charging of VAT does not provide a legal basis for national legislation subjecting the theft of manufactured tobacco to VAT: *British American Tobacco International Ltd and another v Belgian State* (case C-435/03) [2005] ECR I–7077, [2006] STC 158 at [48], [49].

In principle, a special measure retained under this provision ceases to be effective if it is replaced by a new measure. However, this is not so if it is shown that the new provision is substantially the same as the previous one: *Direct Cosmetics Ltd v Customs and Excise Comrs* (case 5/84) [1985] ECR 617, [1985] STC 479 at [25]. For an example of a national measure ceasing to be effective, see *Direct Cosmetics Ltd v Customs and Excise Comrs* (case 5/84) [1985] ECR 617, [1985] STC 479 (deletion of "protection of the revenue" from Finance Act 1977 Sch 3 para 3).

Article 395
(ex art 27(1)–(4))

1. The Council may authorise any member state to introduce special measures derogating from the provisions of this directive in order to:

- Simplify the procedure for charging tax. A special measure may not affect the overall amount of tax revenue collected by the member state at the final consumption stage by more than a negligible extent.
  For examples of national measures that do not exceed what is necessary for the simplification of the procedure for charging tax, see *Heintz Landewyck SARL v Staatssecretaris van Financiën* (case C-494/04) [2006] ECR I–5381 and *Vandoorne NV v Belgian State* (case C-489/09) [2011] ECR I–0000 (collecting VAT by means of tax stamps).
- Prevent certain types of tax evasion or avoidance.
  An essential element of "evasion" is intention on the part of the taxpayer: *Direct Cosmetics Ltd v Customs and Excise Comrs; Laughtons Photographs Ltd v Customs and Excise Comrs* (joined cases 138/86 and 139/86) [1988] ECR 3937, [1988] STC 540 at [20], [21].
  "Tax avoidance" is a concept of Community law. Thus, the definition of that term is not left to the discretion of member states. "Tax avoidance" represents a purely objective phenomenon. Intention is not a requirement for the existence of avoidance. A special measure may be authorised even where the taxable person carried on a business for commercial reasons without any intention of obtaining a tax advantage: *Direct Cosmetics Ltd v Customs and Excise Comrs; Laughtons Photographs Ltd v Customs and Excise Comrs* (joined cases 138/86 and 139/86) [1988] ECR 3937, [1988] STC 540 at [20]–[24].
  A special measure intended to prevent certain types of tax evasion or avoidance may derogate from the relevant provision of this directive only to the extent necessary to prevent evasion or avoidance. It must not affect the overall amount of tax revenue collected by the member state at the final consumption stage by more than a negligible extent: *Direct Cosmetics Ltd v Customs and Excise Comrs; Laughtons Photographs Ltd v Customs and Excise Comrs* (joined cases 138/86 and 139/86) [1988] ECR 3937, [1988] STC 540 at [52].

A strict approach is required in deciding whether a special measure is compatible with the foregoing purposes: *Finanzamt Sulingen v Sudholz* (case C-17/01) [2004] ECR I–4243, [2005] STC 747 at [45]. In relation to evasion or avoidance, see *Finanzamt Bergisch Gladbach v Skripalle* (case C-63/96) [1997] ECR I–2847, [1997] STC 1035 at [24].

Member states cannot rely on a national measure to the detriment of a taxable person if: (1) it derogates from the scheme of the directive; and (2) it has neither been notified to the Commission under art 394 nor authorised by the Council under para 1: see *Direct Cosmetics Ltd v Customs and Excise Comrs* (case 5/84) [1985] ECR 617, [1985] STC 479 at [37]; *Lennartz v Finanzamt München III* (case C-97/90) [[1991] ECR I–3795, [1995]

Part I VAT

STC 514 at [33], [34]. For a recent example, see *Campsa Estàciones de Servicio SA v Administración del Estado* (case C-285/10) [2011] ECR I–0000 (events taking place prior to request for authorisation).

An authorisation does not appear to be invalid merely because the application was made after enactment of the relevant national legislation. However, an authorisation granted with retrospective effect is invalid if it infringes the legitimate expectations of those concerned: *Finanzamt Sulingen v Sudholz* (case C-17/01) [2004] ECR I–4243, [2005] STC 747 at [21], [31], [40], [41].

An authorisation must be compatible with the principle of proportionality. Thus, it must be necessary for the attainment of the specific objective it pursues. It must also have the least possible effect on the objectives and principles of this directive: *Amparfrance SA v Directeur des Services Fiscaux de Maine-et-Loire; Sanofi Synthelabo (formerly Sanofi Winthrop SA) v Directeur des Services Fiscaux du Val-de-Marne* (joined cases C-177/99 and C-181/99) [2000] ECR I–7013 at [60].

For examples of derogations meeting these requirements, see: (1) *Direct Cosmetics Ltd v Customs and Excise Comrs; Laughtons Photographs Ltd v Customs and Excise Comrs* (joined cases 138/86 and 139/86) [1988] ECR 3937, [1988] STC 540 (measure applicable only to certain taxable persons amongst those selling goods to non-taxable resellers, where the resultant difference in treatment was justified by objective circumstances and the measure was not disproportionate to the aim pursued); (2) *Finanzamt Sulingen v Sudholz* (case C-17/01) [2004] ECR I–4243, [2005] STC 747 (flat-rate input tax deduction for vehicles used for both business and private purposes).

For examples of authorisations which did not meet these requirements, see: (1) *Finanzamt Bergisch Gladbach v Skripalle* (case C-63/96) [1997] ECR I–2847, [1997] STC 1035 (national rules not confined to introducing derogations strictly necessary to deal with the risk of tax evasion or avoidance); (2) *Amparfrance SA v Directeur des Services Fiscaux de Maine-et-Loire; Sanofi Synthelabo (formerly Sanofi Winthrop SA) v Directeur des Services Fiscaux du Val-de-Marne* (joined cases C-177/99 and C-181/99) [2000] ECR I–7013 (appropriate means less detrimental to the right to deduct can be contemplated or already exist in the national legal order).

For examples of situations where it was unnecessary to seek an authorisation, see: (1) *GIL Insurance Ltd v Customs and Excise Comrs* (case C-308/01) [2004] ECR I–4777, [2004] STC 961 (insurance premium tax not a measure derogating from art 13B(*a*)); (2) *K-1 sp zoo v Dyrektor Izby Skarbowej w Bydgoszcy* (case C-502/07) [2009] ECR I–161 (imposition of administrative penalties).

For the measures currently authorised under this provision in relation to the UK, see Decisions 89/466/EEC, 89/534/EEC, 2006/659/EC, 2007/250/EC, 2007/884/EC, 2009/938 and the Authorisation of 10 December 1986.

2, 3. The following procedure is adopted when a member state wishes to introduce a special measure under para 1:

- The member state sends an application to the Commission and provides it with all necessary information.
- The Commission contacts the member state if it considers that it has insufficient information. It must do so within two months of receiving the application.
- The Commission notifies the requesting member state once the necessary information has been received. It must do so within one month.
- The Commission transmits the request to the other member states in its original language.
- The Commission must present to the Council either an appropriate proposal or a communication setting out its objections. It must do so within three months.

For examples of national measures introduced by member states without authorisation under the procedure laid down in paras 2 and 3 as originally enacted, see: (1) *Direct Cosmetics Ltd v Customs and Excise Comrs* (case 5/84) [1985] ECR 617, [1985] STC 479 (measure authorised under para 5 replaced by new measure); (2) *BP Supergas Anonimos Etairia Geniki Emporiki-Viomichaniki kai Antiprossopeion v Greece* (case C-62/93) [1995] ECR I–1883, [1995] STC 805 (failure to inform Commission of special measure). For procedural defects under those provisions, see *Direct Cosmetics Ltd v Customs and Excise Comrs; Laughtons Photographs Ltd v Customs and Excise Comrs* (joined cases 138/86 and 139/86) [1988] ECR 3937, [1988] STC 540 (no defects of kind affecting the validity of the Council's tacit decision authorising the derogating measure). For an authorisation granted after a member state had enacted the special measure, see *Finanzamt Sulingen v Sudholz* (case C-17/01) [2004] ECR I–4243, [2005] STC 747 (Council's decision not thereby invalidated).

4. The procedure in paras 2, 3 must be completed within eight months. Time runs from the day when the Commission receives the application.

SECTION 2—INTERNATIONAL AGREEMENTS

Article 396
(ex art 30)

1. The Council may authorise a member state to conclude an agreement with a third country or international organisation derogating from this directive.

2, 3. The following procedure applies when a member state wishes to conclude such an agreement:

- The member state sends an application to the Commission and provides it with all necessary information.
- The Commission contacts the member state if it considers that it has insufficient information. It must do so within two months of receiving the application.
- The Commission notifies the requesting member state once the necessary information has been received. It must do so within one month.
- The Commission transmits the request to the other member states in its original language.
- The Commission must present to the Council either an appropriate proposal or a communication setting out its objections. It must do so within three months.

4. The foregoing procedure must be completed within eight months. Time runs from the day when the Commission receives the application.

TITLE XIV—MISCELLANEOUS

CHAPTER 1—IMPLEMENTING MEASURES

Article 397
(ex art 29a)

The Council must adopt the measures necessary to implement this directive. In doing so, it acts unanimously on a proposal from the Commission.

CHAPTER 2—VAT COMMITTEE

Article 398
(ex art 29)

1. This article establishes an advisory committee on VAT called "the VAT Committee".

2. The VAT Committee consists of representatives of the Commission and the member states. The chairman is a representative of the Commission. The Commission provides secretarial services.

3. The VAT Committee adopts its own rules of procedure.

4. The VAT Committee examines:

- Points subject to the consultation procedure. For matters on which member states are required to consult the VAT Committee, see arts 11, 27, 164, 177, 191 and 281.
- Questions raised by the Chairman relating to the application of Community VAT provisions.

In its advisory capacity, the Committee adopts guidelines on questions raised by the member states or the Commission. As the Commission has pointed out, these guidelines "have no legal status and are not published". In consequence: (1) member states are not obliged to implement them, (2) the parties to litigation cannot rely on them, and (3) they do not form part of the accession agreements for new member states. See COM (97) 325 p 2.

CHAPTER 3—CONVERSION RATES

Article 399
(ex art 28m)

National currency equivalents of amounts specified in euro are determined on the basis of the euro conversion rate applicable on:

- 1 January 1999 (as regards Austria, Belgium, Denmark, Finland, France, Germany, Greece, Ireland, Italy, Luxembourg, the Netherlands, Portugal, Spain, Sweden and the UK).
- 1 May 2004 (as regards Cyprus, the Czech Republic, Estonia, Hungary, Latvia, Lithuania, Malta, Poland, Slovakia and Slovenia).
- 1 January 2007 (as regards Bulgaria and Romania).

Article 400
(ex art 31(2))

When converting euro into national currency eqivalents (see art 399), member states may round the resulting amount by up to 10% either way.

CHAPTER 4—OTHER TAXES, DUTIES AND CHARGES

Article 401
(ex art 33(1))

This Directive does not prevent member states from maintaining or introducing: (1) taxes on insurance contracts, (2) taxes on betting and gambling, (3) excise duties, (4) stamp duties, and (5) taxes, duties or charges which cannot be characterised as turnover taxes. However, any taxes, duties or charges maintained or introduced must not give rise to frontier formalities in trade between member states.

In order to decide whether a tax can be characterised as a turnover tax, it it necessary, in particular, to determine whether it has the effect of compromising the functioning of the common system of VAT by levying a charge on the movement of goods and services, and on commercial transactions, in a way comparable to VAT: *Bergandi v Directeur Général des Impôts* (case 252/86) [1988] ECR 1343, [1991] STC 529 at [14].

A tax is levied in a way comparable to VAT if it exhibits the essential characteristics of VAT. Those characteristics are: (1) it applies generally to transactions relating to goods or services, (2) it is proportional to the price paid charged for the supply of those goods or services, (3) it is charged at each stage of the production and distribution process, including that of retail sale, irrespective of the number of transactions that have previously taken place, and (4) the amounts paid during the preceding stages of the process are deducted from the tax payable by a taxable person, with the result that the tax applies, at any given stage, only to the valued added at that stage, and (5) the final burden of the tax rests ultimately on the consumer: *Erna*

Peizi and others v Steiemärkische Landesregierung and other cases (joined cases C-338/97, C-344/97, C-390/97) [1999] ECR I–3319 at [21]. The relevant national legislation need not expressly provide that the tax may be passed on to the consumer. It is not necessary for the passing on to be recorded in an invoice or similar document: *Careda SA and others v Adminisstración General del Estado* (case C-370/95) [1997] ECR I–3721 at [15], [18].

It is for the national court to establish whether the tax at issue is capable of being charged on the movement of goods and services in a manner comparable to VAT: *Careda SA and others v Adminisstración General del Estado* (case C-370/95) [1997] ECR I–3721 at [25].

For an example of a tax characterised as a turnover tax, see *Dansk Denkavit ApS and Poulsen Trading ApS v Skatteministeriet* (case C-200/90) [1992] ECR I–2217, [1994] STC 482 and *Commission v Kingdom of Denmark* (case C-234/91) [1993] ECR I–6273, [1997] STC 721 (Danish employment market contribution).

For examples of taxes which cannot be characterised as a turnover tax, see: (1) *Rosseau-Wilmot SA v Caisse de Compensation de l'Organisation Autonome Nationale de l'Industrie et du Commerce* (*Organic*) (case 295/84) [1985] ECR 3759, [1986] 3 CMLR 677 (charge of a non-fiscal nature to finance social security schemes calculated on the basis of annual turnover); (2) *Bergandi v Directeur Général des Impôts* (case 252/86) [1988] ECR 1343, [1991] STC 529 and *Lambert v Directeur des Services Fiscaux de l'Orne* (joined cases 317/86; 48, 49, 285, 363–367/87; and 65, 78–80/88) [1989] ECR 787 (tax on automatic machines providing an entertainment, game or amusement); (3) *Wisselink en Co BV v Staatssecretaris van Financiën* (joined cases 93/88 and 94/88) [1989] ECR 2671 (special consumption tax on passenger cars); (4) *Giant NV v Commune of Overijse* (case C-109/90) [1991] ECR I–1385, [1993] STC 651 (special tax on performances and entertainments); (5) *Aldo Bozzi v Cassa Nazionale di Previdenza ed Assistenza* (case C-347/90) [1992] ECR I–2947, [1996] STC 1193 (supplementary contribution to the Lawyers' National Provident Fund); (6) *Beaulande v Direcueur des Services Fiscaux, Nantes* (case C-208/91) [1992] ECR I–6709, [1996] STC 1111 (stamp duty on the full value of real estate); (7) *Fazenda Pública v Fricarnes SA* (case C-28/96) [1997] ECR I–4939, [1997] STC 1348n (meat marketing charges); (8) *Fazenda Pública v Solisnor-Estaleiros Navais SA* (case C-130/96) [1997] ECR I–5053, [1998] STC 191 (stamp duty); (9) *Fazenda Pública v União das Cooperativas Abastecedoras de Leite de Lisboa, UCRL* (case C-347/95) [1997] ECR I–4911, [1997] STC 1333 (charge onmarketing of dairy products); (10) *Spar Österreichische Warenhandles AG v Finanzlanddesdirektion für Salzburg* (case C-318/96) [1998] ECR I–785, [1998] STC 960 (levy to finance chambers of commerce); (11) *Erna Peizi and others v Steiemärkische Landesregierung and other cases* (joined cases C-338/97, C-344/97, C-390/97) [1999] ECR I–3319 (charges to promote tourism); (12) *Evangelischer Krankenhausverein Wien v Abgabenberufungskommission and related case* (case C-437/97) [2000] ECR I–1157 (beverage duty); (13) *GIL Insurance Ltd v Customs and Excise Comrs* (case C-308/01) [2004] ECR I–4777, [2004] STC 961 (insurance premium tax); (14) *Banca Popolare di Cremona Soc Coop arl v Agenzia Entrate Ufficio Cremona* (case C-475/03) [2006] ECR I–9373 (regional tax on productive activities); (15) *Kögáz rt and others v Zala Megyei Közigazgatási Hivatal Vezetõje; OTP Garancia Biztosító rt v Vas Megyei Közigazgatási Hivatal* (joined cases C-283/06 and C-312/06) [2007] ECR I–8463, [2008] STC 2367 (local business tax); (16) *Commission v Poland* (case C-49/09) [2010] ECR I–0000 (turnover tax applicable in Poland at 1 January 1991).

Community law does not prevent the same transaction being charged to both VAT and a tax that cannot be characterised as a turnover tax: *Kerrutt v Finanzamt Mönchengladback-Mitte* (case 73/85) [1986] ECR 2219, [1987] 2 CMLR 221.

Part I VAT

TITLE XV—FINAL PROVISIONS

CHAPTER 1—TRANSITIONAL ARRANGEMENTS FOR THE TAXATION OF TRADE BETWEEN MEMBER STATES

Article 402
(ex art 28l (second and third paras))

1. The arrangements for the taxation of trade between member states in this directive are transitional. They will be replaced by definitive arrangements based on the principle (known as the "origin principle") that goods and services should be taxed in the member state where the goods or services are supplied.

2. The Council must adopt the necessary legislation to bring the definitive arrangements into force. It will act in accordance with EC Treaty art 93 (now TFEU art 113) in so doing.

Article 403
(ex art 35)

The Council is required to adopt further directives supplementing the common system of VAT. In particular, derogation from the common system should be progressively restricted or abolished.

Article 404
(ex art 34)

The Commission is required to report to the Council every fourth year on the operation of the common system of VAT in the member states.

CHAPTER 2—TRANSITIONAL MEASURES IN THE CONTEXT OF ACCESSION TO THE EUROPEAN UNION

Articles 405–410 (ex art 28p)

This Chapter sets out transitional provisions for goods in transit, goods in free circulation, goods subject to a tax suspension regime, and like matters at 31 December 1994 (accession of Austria, Finland and Sweden), 30 April 2004 (accession of Cyprus, the Czech Republic, Estonia, Hungary, Latvia, Lithuania, Malta, Poland, Slovenia and Slovakia) and 31 December 2006 (accession of Bulgaria and Romania).

CHAPTER 3—TRANSPOSITION AND ENTRY INTO FORCE

Article 411
(new)

1. Directives 67/388/EEC (the First Directive), 77/388/EEC (the Sixth Directive) and the directives amending them are repealed. For a list of the repealed directives, see Annex XI Part A.

2. References to the First and Sixth Directives are construed as references to this directive. They are read in accordance with the correlation table in Annex XII.

Article 412
(new)

Member states must implement arts 2(3), 44, 59(1), 399 and Annex III point 18 with effect from 1 January 2008.

Article 413
(new)

This Directive enters into force on 1 January 2007.

Article 414
(ex art 38)
This Directive is addressed to the member states.

ANNEXES

Annex I—List of activities
(ex Annex D)

This is the list referred to in art 13(1) third para. Bodies governed by public law are treated as a taxable person in relation to a listed activity if they carry it on to a material extent.

Laying a mains connection forms part of a "supply of water" for the purposes of point 2: *Finanzamt Oschatz v Zweckverband zur Trinkwasserversorgung und Abwasserbeseitgung Torgau-Westelbien* (case C-442/05) [2008] ECR I–1817, [2009] STC 1.

For an example of a body which is not an "agricultural intervention agency" within point 7, see *Landesanstalt für Landwirtschaft v Franz Götz* (case C-408/06) [2007] ECR I–11295 (milk quota sales point).

For an example of a body which is not a "staff shop" within point 12, see *Landesanstalt für Landwirtschaft v Franz Götz* (case C-408/06) [2007] ECR I–11295 (milk quota sales point).

Annex II—Indicative list of the electronically supplied services referred to in article 58 and point (k) of the first paragraph of article 59
(ex Annex L)

This is the list of services relevant to the meaning of "electronically supplied services" referred to in arts 58 and 59(*k*). See also Regulation (EU) No 282/2011 art 7.

Annex III—List of supplies of goods and services to which the reduced rates may be applied
(ex Annex H)

This is the list referred to in art 98(2). It lists the goods and services which may be taxed at the reduced rates.

For category 1 (foodstuffs, live animals, seeds, plants and ingredients), see *Commission v Netherlands* (case C-41/09) [2011] ECR I–0000 (horses); *Finanzamt Burgdorf v Manfred Bog; CinemaxX Entertainment GmbH & Co KG v Finanzamt Hamburg-Barmbek-Uhlenhorst; Lothar Lohmeyer v Finanzamt Minden; Fleischerei Nier GmbH & Co KG v Finanzamt Detmold* (joined cases C-497/09 C-499/09 C-501/09 C-502/09) [2011] ECR I–0000, [2011] STC 1221 (food and meals prepared for immediate consumption by boiling, grilling, roasting, baking or other means).

For Category 2 (water), see *Finanzamt Oschatz v Zweckverband zur Trinkwasserversorgung und Abwasserbeseitgung Torgau-Westelbien* (case C-442/05) [2008] ECR I–1817, [2009] STC 1 (specific aspects of water supplies).

For Category 5 (transport of passengers and their accompanying baggage), see *Commission v Kingdom of Spain* (case C-83/99) [2001] ECR I–445 at [20], [21]; *Commission v French Republic* (case C-94/09) [2010] ECR I– 0000 (transport of body by undertakers).

For category 7 (admission to shows, theatres, circuses, fairs, amusement parks, concerts, museums, zoos, cinemas, exhibitions and similar cultural events and facilities), see *Erotic Center BVBA v Belgian State* (case C-3/09) [2010] ECR I–0000, [2010] STC 1018 (provision of cubicles in which people could watch films on a television screen).

For Category 8 (writers, composers and performing artists), see *Commission v Germany* (case C-109/02) [2003] ECR I–12691, [2006] STC 1587 (musicians).

For caterory 12 (accommodation), see Regulation (EU) No 282/2011 art 43.

For category 15 (goods and services supplied by organisations recognised as being devoted to social wellbeing by member states and engaged in taxable welfare or social security work) see *Commission v French Republic* (case C-492/08) [2010] ECR I– 0000 (services of lawyers under legal aid scheme).

For category 16 (services of undertakers and cremation services) see *Commission v French Republic* (case C-94/09) [2010] ECR I– 0000 (transport of body).

Annex IV—List of services
(ex Annex K)

[Repealed.]

Annex V—Categories of goods covered by warehousing arrangements other than customs warehousing
(ex Annex J)

This is the list referred to in art 160(2). In effect, services carried out on warehoused goods included in the list must be treated equally for the purposes of exemption whether the relevant warehouse is a customs warehouse or another class of warehouse.

Annex VI—List of supplies of goods and services
(ex Annex M)

This is the list of goods and services referred to in art 199(1)(*d*). Member states may provide that the recipient of the supply is the person liable to pay the tax chargeable thereon.

Annex VII—List of agricultural production activities
(ex Annex A Parts I–IV)

This is the list referred to in the definitions of "agricultural, forestry or fisheries undertakings" and "agricultural products" in arts 295(1)(2), 295(1)(4) and 295(2).

Annex VIII—Indicative list of agricultural services
(ex Annex B first to ninth indents)

This is the list of services referred to in the definition of "agricultural services" in art 295(1)(4). See *Finanzamt Rendsburg v Harbs* (case C-321/02) [2004] ECR I-7101, [2006] STC 340.

Annex IX—Works of art, collectors' items and antiques
(ex Annex I)

This Annex lists the objects relevant to the definitions of "work of art", "collectors' items" and "antiques" in art 311.

Annex X—List of transactions covered by the derogations referred to in articles 370 and 371 and articles 375 to 390b
(ex Annex E, F; Directive 67/288/EEC Annex B)

Part A is the list referred to in arts 370. It lists certain goods and services exempted from tax. Notwithstanding this exemption, certain member states may continue to tax transactions in these goods and services during the transitional period. For the transitional period, see art 402(1).

For Part A point 1, see *Administration de l'enregistrement et des domaines v Eurodental Sàrl* (case C-240/05) [2006] ECR I–11479, [2007] STC 275.

Part B is the list referred to in art 371. It lists certain goods and services chargeable to VAT. Certain member states may continue to exempt transactions in these goods and services during the transitional period. For the transitional period, see art 402(1). Exemption applies under conditions existing in the member state concerned. For the option to tax in respect of these goods and services, see art 391.

The exemptions in Part B must be interpreted strictly: *Commission v Republic of Finland* (case C-169/00) [2002] ECR I–2433 at [33], [34].

For Part B point 2, see: (1) *Commission v Spain* (case C-35/90) [1991] ECR I–5073; (2) *Commission v Republic of Finland* (case C-169/00) [2002] ECR I–2433; (3) *Urbing (née Adam) v Administration de l'Enregistrement et des Domaines* (case C-267/99) [2001] ECR I–7467.

The "liberal professions" mentioned in Part B point 2 are activities which, inter alia, are of a marked intellectual character, require a high-level qualification and are usually subject to clear and strict professional regulation. In the exercise of such an activity, the personal element is of special importance and such exercise always involves a large measure of independence in the accomplishment of the professional activities. It is for the national court to decide, having regard to those criteria, whether an activity is regarded as a liberal profession: *Urbing (née Adam) v Administration de l'Enregistrement et des Domaines* (case C-267/99) [2001] ECR I–7467 at [39], [40].

The concept of "services supplied by artists" in Part B point 2 does not cover the supply of works of art, even in cases where the supply is made by the artist or his agent. Such a supply constitutes a non-exempt supply of goods: *Commission v Republic of Finland* (case C-169/00) [2002] ECR I–2433 at [35].

As regards the option to tax in relation to Part B point 9, the right of option relates inseparably to buildings (or parts of buildings) and the land on which they stand: *Finanzamt Goslar v Breitsohl* (case C-400/98) [2000] ECR I–4321, [2001] STC 355. For examples, see: (1) *Kerrutt v Finanzamt Mönchengladback-Mitte* (case 73/85) [1986] ECR 2219, [1987] 2 CMLR 221; (2) *Finanzamt Goslar v Breitsohl* (case C-400/98) [2000] ECR I–4321, [2001] STC 355; (3) *Norbury Developments Ltd v Customs and Excise Comrs* (case C-136/97) [1999] ECR I–2491, [1999] STC 511.

For Part B point 10, see: (1) *Commission v Federal Republic of Germany* (case C-74/91) [1992] ECR I–5437, [1996] STC 843; (2) *Idéal Tourisme SA v Belgian State* (case C-36/99) [2000] ECR I–6049, [2001] STC 1386.

Annex XI—Repealed directives with their successive amendments

Part A lists the directives repealed by art 411. Part B lists the time limits for implementing those directives.

Annex XII—Correlation table

This is a destination table. It shows where provisions of the repealed directives have been incorporated in this directive.

DIRECTIVE 2007/74/EC
EXEMPTION OF GOODS IMPORTED BY PERSONS TRAVELLING FROM THIRD COUNTRIES

General note This directive repealed and replaced Directive 69/169/EEC with effect from 1 December 2008. It applies to both VAT and excise duties. Excise duties are outside the scope of this work and no further reference is made to them.

CHAPTER 1—SUBJECT MATTER AND DEFINITIONS

Article 1

This directive lays down rules for exemption in relation to goods imported in the personal luggage of a person travelling from: (1) a third country (as defined in art 3(1)); or (2) a territory where the Community VAT provisions do not apply (as defined in art 3(2)).

Article 2

A journey may: (1) involve transit through the territory of a third country (as defined in art 3(1)); or (2) begin in a territory where the Community VAT provisions do not apply (as defined in art 3(2)). Where this is so, this directive applies as if the traveller is unable to establish that the goods transported in his luggage have been acquired subject to the general conditions governing taxation on the domestic market of a member state and do not qualify for any refund of VAT.

Overflying without landing is not regarded as transit.

Article 3

Various words and phrases are defined.

CHAPTER II—EXEMPTIONS

SECTION 1—COMMON PROVISIONS

Article 4

Member states must exempt goods from VAT if: (1) they are imported in the personal luggage (see art 5) of a traveller; and (2) the goods are of a non-commercial character (see art 6). Member states may apply exemption on the basis of either: (1) monetary thresholds; or (2) quantitative limits.

Article 5

For the purposes of exemption (see art 4), personal luggage comprises: (1) the luggage presented to the customs authorities on arrival; and (2) luggage presented to the same authorities at a later time. In the latter case, the traveller must provide proof that the luggage was registered as accompanied baggage with the carrier at the time of his departure.

Fuel can be regarded as accompanied baggage only if it meets the conditions for exemption in art 11.

Article 6

Goods have a non-commercial character only if they are imported only occasionally. They must be imported exclusively for the traveller's personal or family use or be intended as presents. The nature or quantity of the goods must not indicate that they are being imported for commercial reasons.

SECTION 2—MONETARY THRESHOLDS

Article 7

A person is entitled to exemption (see art 4) if the total value of the goods he imports does not exceed 430 euro (in the case of air and sea travellers) or 300 euro (in other cases). Member states may apply a lower monetary value (minimum 150 euro) for travellers aged under 15 years. The value of an individual item may not be split for the purpose of applying these monetary limits. The value of goods exempted by arts 8, 9, 11 is disregarded for the purposes of applying the foregoing thresholds: see art 12.

The following items are excluded in determining the total value of the goods imported by a person: (1) goods which are not personal luggage; (2) goods having a commercial character; (3) goods temporarily imported; (4) goods re-imported following temporary export; and (5) medicinal products required to meet the personal needs of the traveller.

SECTION 3—QUANTITIVE LIMITS

Article 8

Member states must exempt the following classes of tobacco products. They must apply quantitative limits within the range indicated.

Tobacco product	***Minimum quantity***	***Maximum quantity***
Cigarettes	40	200
Cigarillos (ie cigars having a maximum weight of 3 grammes)	20	100
Cigars	10	50
Smoking tobacco	50 grams	250 grams

Exemption may be confined to tobacco products in one class or to a combination of classes. In the latter case, the quantitative limits are reduced proportionately. Different quantitative limits may be applied to air travellers and other travellers.

For travellers under 17 years of age, see art 10.

Article 9

As regards alcohol or alcoholic beverages other than still wine and beer, member states must exempt:

- a total of 1 litre of either: (1) alcohol or alcoholic beverages with an alcoholic strength exceeding 22% vol; or (2) undenatured ethyl alcohol of 80% vol or over; or
- a total of 2 litres of alcohol and alcoholic beverages of an alcoholic strength not exceeding 22% vol.

Exemption may be confined to alcohol or alcoholic beverages in one class or to a combination of classes. In the latter case, the quantitative limits are reduced proportionately.

Member states must also exempt a total of 4 litres of still wine and 16 litres of beer.

For travellers under 17 years of age, see art 10.

Article 10

The exemptions in arts 8 and 9 do not apply to travellers under 17 years of age.

Article 11

As regards any one means of motor transport, member states must exempt:

- the fuel contained in the standard fuel tank; and
- fuel (maximum 10 litres) contained in a portable container.

Article 12

The value of goods exempted by arts 8, 9, 11 is disregarded for the purposes of the exemption conferred by art 7(1).

CHAPTER III—SPECIAL CASES

Article 13

Reduced monetary thresholds (see art 7) and/or quantitative limits (see arts 8–12) may be applied to: (1) persons resident in a frontier zone; (2) frontier-zone workers; and (3) the crew of a means of transport used on a journey from a third country (as defined in art 3(1)) or from a place in a member state which does not form part of the VAT territory of the Community (see art 3(2)). The reductions apply to goods imported by persons in heads (2) and (3) when travelling in the course of their work. They do not apply to travellers in heads (1)–(3) who produce evidence that (1) they are going beyond the frontier zone; or (2) they are not returning from the frontier zone of the neighbouring third country.

CHAPTER IV—GENERAL AND FINAL PROVISIONS

Article 14

Member states may waive payment if the VAT due does not exceed EUR 10.

Article 15

The national currency equivalents of values expressed in euro are fixed annually by reference to the rates of exchange applicable on the first working day of October. They apply during the following calendar year. Rounding-off is permitted, but it must not exceed EUR 5. Revalorisation is not required if the movement in exchange rates is less than 5 per cent.

For exchange rates on 1 October 2007, see OJ C230/2, 2.10.07.

Article 16

Every fourth year the Commission must prepare a report on the implementation of this directive. The first report is due in 2012.

Article 17

[Applies to Finland.]

Article 18

This directive repeals and replaces Directive 69/169/EC with effect from 1 December 2008.

References to the 1969 Directive are construed as references to this directive. These references are read in accordance with the correlation table in the Annex.

Article 19

Member states are required to take the necessary measures to bring arts 1–15 into force with effect from 1 December 2008.

Article 20

This directive came into force on 29 December 2007. It applies with effect from 1 December 2008.

Article 21

This directive is addressed to the member states.

ANNEX—CORRELATION TABLE

This is the destination table referred to in art 18. It shows how the provisions of Directive 69/169/EEC have been transposed in this directive.

DIRECTIVE 2008/8/EC
THE PLACE OF SUPPLY OF SERVICES (AMENDING DIRECTIVE 2006/112/EC)

General note This directive prospectively amends Directive 2006/112/EC from various dates between 1 January 2009 and 1 January 2015. It gradually brings about the changes to the place of supply of services outlined in Commission Communications COM (2003) 822 (Brussels, 23 December 2003) and COM (2005) 334 (Brussels, 20 July 2005).

Article 1

This article amends Directive 2006/112/EC with effect from 1 January 2009. These amendments are reflected in the commentary to the 2006 Directive.

Article 2

This article amends Directive 2006/112/EC with effect from 1 January 2010. These amendments are reflected in the commentary to the 2006 Directive.

Article 3

This article replaces Directive 2006/112/EC with effect from 1 January 2011. These amendments are reflected in the commentary to the 2006 Directive.

Article 4

This article amends Directive 2006/112/EC arts 56 with effect from 1 January 2013.

Article 5

This article inserts Directive 2006/112/EC arts 358a and 369a–369k; replaces arts 58, 59a, 358, 359–365, 367, 368; amends arts 59, 204, 366, 369; and deletes arts 59b, 357. These changes have effect from 1 January 2015.

Article 6

The Commission is required to submit a report on: (1) the feasibility of applying the rule laid down in art 5 to the supply of telecommunications services, radio and television broadcasting services and electronically supplied services to non-taxable persons; and (2) whether that rule still corresponds to the general policy at that time concerning the place of supply of services. The report must be submitted by 31 December 2014.

Article 7

Member states are required to take the necessary measures to bring arts 1–5 into force from the dates specified therein.

Article 8

This directive came into force on 20 February 2008.

Article 9

This directive is addressed to the member states.

DIRECTIVE 2008/9/EC
DETAILED RULES FOR THE REFUND OF VAT TO TAXABLE PERSONS NOT ESTABLISHED IN THE MEMBER STATE OF REFUND BUT ESTABLISHED IN ANOTHER MEMBER STATE

General note This directive replaces Directive 79/1072/EEC (the Eighth Directive) as regards refund applications submitted after 31 December 2009 (see art 28(1)). For the continued effect of the 1979 Directive in relation to refund applications submitted before 1 January 2010, see art 28(2) first para.

Article 1

This directive lays down the detailed rules for the refund of VAT to "taxable persons who are not established in the member state of refund" (see art 2(1)) who meet the conditions in art 3.

Article 2

1. A person is a "taxable person not established in the member state of refund" if:

- He is a taxable person (see Directive 2006/112/EC art 9(1)).
- He is established in the territory of another member state.
- He is not established in the member state of refund.

2. The "member state of refund" is the member state in which VAT was charged in respect of either:

- a supply of goods or services made by a taxable person in that member state; or
- an importation of goods into that member state.

3. A "refund period" is the period covered by a refund application. For the length of a refund period, see art 16.

4. A "refund application" is an application for refund of VAT arising in the following circumstances:

- It was charged in the member state of refund (see art 2(2)).
- It was charged to a taxable person not established in the member state of refund (see art 2(1)).
- It was charged in respect of either: (1) a supply of goods or services made by a taxable person in the member state of refund; or (2) an importation of goods into the member state of refund.

Article 3

A "taxable person not established in the member state of refund" (see art 2(1)) does *not* meet "the conditions laid down in Article 3" (see art 1) in a refund period (see art 2(3)) if he falls within any of the following descriptions:

- The seat of his economic activity is in the member state of refund.
- He has a fixed establishment in the member state of refund from which business transactions were effected.
- (In the absence of such a seat or fixed establishment) his domicile or normal place of residence is in the member state of refund.
- (If he has supplied any goods or services in the refund period) any of those goods or services were deemed to have been supplied in the member state of refund. Supplies are disregarded for this purpose if: (1) the supply comprises transport services or services ancillary thereto exempted in accordance with Directive

2006/112/EC arts 144, 146, 148, 149, 151, 153, 159 or 160; or (2) Directive 2006/112/EC arts 194–197 or 199 provide that the person liable for payment of VAT is the person to whom the goods or services were supplied.

It follows that a taxable person meets "the conditions laid down in Article 3" in a refund period in other circumstances.

Article 4

No refund is made in respect of an amount of VAT shown on an invoice if:

(a) the VAT has been incorrectly invoiced. Whether or not VAT has been incorrectly invoiced is determined in accordance with the legislation of the member state of refund; or

(b) the relevant supply is a supply of goods which is, or may be, exempt by virtue of Directive 2006/112/EC art 138 or 146(1)(*b*).

Article 5

VAT is eligible for refund if, or to the extent that, the goods or services for the purposes of any of the following transactions:

- The transactions referred to in Directive 2006/112/EEC art 169(*a*) (transactions relating to economic activities carried out in another country if the VAT would be deductible had the activities been performed in the territory of the country).
- The transactions referred to in Directive 2006/112/EEC art 169(*b*) (specified exempt transactions).
- Transactions where VAT is payable by the recipient of the supply in accordance with national legislation giving effect to Directive 2006/112/EEC arts 194–197 or 199. The relevant national legislation is that of the member state of refund.

For the purposes of this directive, entitlement to an input tax refund is determined in accordance with national legislation of the member state of refund giving effect to Directive 2006/112/EC. For an exception, see art 6.

Article 6

A taxable person not established in the member state of refund is eligible for a refund in the member state of refund only if, in his member state of establishment, he carries out transactions giving rise to a right of deduction. If he carries out there both transactions giving rise to a right of deduction and transactions not giving rise to a right of deduction, the refund to which he is entitled is the proportion of VAT attributable to the former transactions. This proportion is determined in accordance with national legislation of the member state of establishment giving effect to Directive 2006/112/EC art 173.

Article 7

A taxable person not established in the member state of refund obtains a refund by submitting an electronic refund application to the member state of refund via the electronic portal set up by the member state of establishment. The application is addressed to the member state of refund.

Article 8

1. The information to be provided in a refund application (see art 7) is listed. For descriptions of the applicant's business activity, see art 11.

2. The additional information to be provided in respect of each invoice or import document is listed. If applications are addressed to more than one member state, a separate list must be prepared in respect of each member state.

Article 9

This article prescribes the codes used to designate the nature of goods and services for the purposes of art 8(2)(*h*). The member state of refund may require the applicant to provide additional electronic coded information in prescribed circumstances.

Article 10

The member state of refund may require a copy of an invoice or importation document to be submitted if the taxable amount shown thereon equals or exceeds the following amounts or their equivalent in foreign currency: EUR 250 (in the case of fuel) or EUR 1,000 (in other cases). The copy must be submitted by electronic means with the refund application.

Article 11

The member state of refund may require the applicant to describe his business activity (see art 8(1)(*c*)) by reference to harmonised codes. For the codes, see Regulation (EC) No 1798/2003 art 34a(3) (second para).

Article 12

The member state of refund may specify the language in which a refund application must be completed.

Article 13

The deductible proportion used in a refund application (see arts 6 and 8(2)(*g*)) may subsequently be adjusted in accordance with Directive 2006/112/EC art 175. If so, the applicant must correct the amount claimed or refunded. The correction is made in a refund application submitted in the next calendar year or (if no such application is made) by submitting a separate declaration via the electronic portal established by the member state of establishment.

Article 14

A refund application is made in respect of:

- Purchases of goods or services which were invoiced during the refund period. The VAT must have become chargeable at, or before, the time of invoicing.
- Purchases of goods or services in respect of which the VAT became chargeable during the refund period. The purchase must have been invoiced before the VAT became chargeable.
- Goods imported during the refund period.
- Invoices or import documents not covered by previous refund applications for the same calendar year. The invoices or import documents must relate to transactions completed during that year.

Article 15

A refund application for a refund period ending in one calendar year must be submitted no later than 30 September in the following calendar year. An application is not "submitted" for this purpose if any of the information specified in arts 8, 9 or 11 has been omitted.

The application is submitted to the member state of establishment (see art 7). The member state of establishment is required to confirm receipt without delay. This is done electronically.

Refund applications for periods in 2009 must be submitted to the member state of establishment no later than 31 March 2011.

Article 16

A refund period comprises all or part of a calendar year. It must normally comprise three or more months. A shorter period is permissible only if it relates to the remainder of a calendar year. For example, if one or more applications have been made for the period 1 January to 31 October, the next application for the calendar year must relate to the period 1 November to 31 December.

Article 17

The minimum amount for which a refund application may be made is set out in the following table:

Refund period	***Minimum amount of the claim***
The calendar year	EUR 50 or the equivalent in national currency
The remainder of a calendar year	EUR 50 or the equivalent in national currency
Any other period	EUR 400 or the equivalent in national currency

Article 18

The member state of establishment must *not* forward a refund application to the member state of refund if any of the following circumstances apply to the applicant in the member state of establishment:

(a) The applicant is not a taxable person for VAT purposes.

(b) All of the supplies made by the applicant are exempt without deduction of the VAT paid at the preceding stage. As regards the UK, the relevant exemptions are conferred by Directive 2006/112/EC arts 132, 135, 136, 371 and 374.

(c) The applicant is covered by the exemption for small enterprises. As regards the UK, the relevant exemption is conferred by Directive 2006/112/EC art 286.

(d) The applicant is covered by the common flat-rate scheme for farmers. For the flat-rate scheme, see Directive 2006/112/EC arts 296–305.

The member state of establishment must notify the applicant accordingly. The member state does so electronically.

Article 19

1. The member state of refund must notify the applicant of the date on which it received the application. The member state must do so electronically and without delay.

2. The member state of refund must notify the applicant of its decision to approve or refuse the refund. It must do so within four months of receiving the application. This period is modified if a request for additional information is made: see art 21. For requests for additional information, see art 20.

Article 20

1. The member state of refund may request additional information from the applicant, the competent authorities of the member state of establishment or some other person. It may do so if it considers that it does not have all the relevant information on which to make a decision in respect of all or part of the refund application.

If the member state of refund has reasonable doubts regarding the validity or accuracy of a particular claim, the information requested may include submission of the original invoice or importation document, or a copy thereof.

The request must be made electronically within four months of receiving the application. A request to the applicant or the competent authorities of the member state of establishment must be made electronically. A request to any other person is made electronically only if those means are available to him. The member state of refund may make more than one request to the same person.

2. The applicant, competent authority or other person must provide the requested information within one month of receiving the request.

Article 21

The time limit for notifying acceptance or rejection of a refund application (see art 19(2)) is modified if the member state of refund makes a request for additional information in accordance with art 20. If the requested information is received, the member state of refund must notify the applicant of its decision to approve or refuse the refund within the later of: (1) two months of receiving the requested information; and (2) six months of receiving the application. If no reply is received to its request, the member state of refund must notify approval or refusal within the later of: (1) three months of the date on which the request reached the person to whom it was addressed; and (2) six months of receiving the application.

Article 22

1. If a refund application is approved, the member state of refund must pay the approved amount. This must be done no later than 10 working days after the member state of refund has notified the applicant of its decision to approve his application. For the date of notification, see arts 19(2) and 21.

2. The refund is paid in the member state of refund. However, the applicant may request the refund to be paid in another member state. If he does so, the amount paid to him is the approved amount less any bank charges incurred by the member state of refund in respect of the transfer.

Article 23

1. If all or part of the refund application is refused, the notification of this decision must set out the grounds for the refusal. For notifications, see arts 19(2) and 21.

2. The applicant has a right of appeal against the decision. The appeal is made to the competent authorities of the member state of refund. The appeal is made in the same manner, and within the same time limits, as an appeal against the refusal of a refund application made by a person established in the member state of refund.

The law of the member state of refund may provide that failure to take a decision on a refund application within the prescribed time limits (see arts 19–21) is treated as neither an approval nor a refusal. If so, any administrative or judicial procedures available in these circumstances must apply to the applicant in the same manner as they apply to taxable persons established in the member state of refund. If not, the failure to take a decision is treated as a rejection of the application.

Article 24

1. A refund may be obtained in a fraudulent way or otherwise incorrectly. Where this is so, the competent authority of the member state of refund must take immediate steps to recover amounts wrongly paid and any penalties or interest imposed under national law. The competent authority applies the remedies available under national law in so doing. However, the competent authority may also have recourse to EU provisions on mutual assistance for the recovery of VAT, as to which see Directive 2008/55/EC (the principal directive) and Regulation (EC) No 1179/2008 (formerly Directive 2002/94/EC) (detailed rules).

2. The member state of refund may suspend further refunds if interest or administrative penalties have not been paid. The amount suspended may not exceed the amount unpaid.

Article 25

The amount of a refund is increased or decreased by the amount of any correction to a previous refund application. For corrections to previous applications, see art 13. A separate payment or recovery is made if a separate declaration is submitted.

Article 26

The applicant is entitled to interest if the amount due to him is not paid by the last date for payment prescribed in art 22(1). However, no entitlement to interest arises if the applicant is late in submitting any further information, or any additional further information, requested by the member state of refund. For requests for further information or additional further information, see art 20.

If the member state of refund requires the applicant to submit a copy of an invoice or importation document, the entitlement to interest does not apply until the documents have been received. For the requirement to submit these documents, see art 10.

Article 27

1. Interest runs from the day following the last day for payment of a refund (see art 22(1)) to the day on which the refund is actually paid.

2. If the national law of the member state of refund makes provision for the payment of interest on refunds of VAT made to taxable persons established in that member state, the same rate is applied to interest arising under art 26. In other cases, the rate is determined by reference to the rate charged on late payments of VAT by the member state of refund.

Article 28

1. This directive applies to refund applications submitted after 31 December 2009.

2. Directive 79/1072/EEC (the Eighth Directive) is repealed with effect from 1 January 2010. However, it continues to apply to refund applications submitted before that date.

As regards refund applications submitted after 31 December 2009, references to Directive 79/1072/EEC are construed as references to this directive.

Article 29

Member states are required to take the necessary measures to comply with this directive with effect from 1 January 2010.

Article 30

This directive came into force on 20 February 2008.

Article 31

This directive is addressed to the member states.

DIRECTIVE 2008/55/EC
MUTUAL ASSISTANCE FOR THE RECOVERY OF CLAIMS TO CERTAIN LEVIES, DUTIES, TAXES AND OTHER MEASURES

General note This directive repealed and replaced Directive 76/308/EEC with effect from 30 June 2008 (see arts 25, 26). It sets out rules enabling claims in respect of the levies, duties, taxes and other measures arising in one member state to be recovered in another member state. These measures include VAT (see art 2(*e*)).

This directive is repealed with effect from 1 January 2012 by Directive 2010/24/EU art 29. It is replaced by the 2010 Directive. Although the 2010 Directive came into force on 20 April 2010 (see art 29 of the 2010 Directive), member states are required to apply its provisions from 1 January 2012 (see art 28(1) of the 2010 Directive).

Detailed rules for implementing arts 4(2), 4(4), 5(2), 5(3), 7–9, 11, 12(1), 12(2), 14, 18(3) and 24 of this directive are set out in Regulation (EC) No 1179/2008. The 2008 Regulation is repealed and replaced with effect from 1 January 2012 by Regulation (EU) 904/2010. For transitional provisions, see the commentary to art 62 of the 2008 Regulation.

DIRECTIVE 2009/47/EC
REDUCED RATES OF VAT (AMENDING DIRECTIVE 2006/112/EC)

General note This directive amended Directive 2006/112/EC with effect from 1 June 2009 and 1 January 2011. These amendments are reflected in the commentary to the 2006 Directive.

DIRECTIVE 2009/69/EC
TAX EVASION LINKED TO IMPORTS (AMENDING DIRECTIVE 2006/112/EC)

General note This directive came into force on 24 July 2009. It amends Directive 2006/112/EC. Member states were required to enact implementing legislation taking effect from 1 January 2011. The amendments made by this directive are reflected in the commentary to the 2006 Directive.

DIRECTIVE 2009/132/EC
EXEMPTION FROM VALUE ADDED TAX ON THE FINAL IMPORTATION OF CERTAIN GOODS

General note This directive codifies Directive 83/181/EEC, which is accordingly repealed.

TITLE I—SCOPE AND DEFINITIONS

Article 1

This directive defines the scope of the exemptions from VAT referred to in Directive 2006/112/EC art 143(b) and (c). It also defines the rules for implementation referred to in art 145 of the 2006 Directive. Member states must fix the conditions for applying the exemptions laid down in this directive. These conditions must: (1) ensure that the exemptions are correctly and simply applied, and (2) prevent any evasion, avoidance or abuse.

Article 2

The terms "imports", "personal property", "household effects", "alcoholic products" and "Community" are defined.

TITLE II—IMPORTATION OF PERSONAL PROPERTY BELONGING TO INDIVIDUALS COMING FROM THIRD COUNTRIES OR THIRD TERRITORIES

CHAPTER 1—PERSONAL PROPERTY OF NATURAL PERSONS TRANSFERRING THEIR NORMAL PLACE OF RESIDENCE TO THE COMMUNITY

Articles 3–11

Personal property (see art 2(1)(b) and (2)) is exempt from VAT if it is imported by a natural person transferring his normal place of residence from a place outside the Community (see art 2(1)(*e*)) to a member state of the Community.

The conditions for exemption are set out in arts 4–10. For the power to derogate from these conditions, see art 11. For persons leaving a place outside the Community without establishing a normal place of residence in the member state, see art 10.

CHAPTER 2—GOODS IMPORTED ON THE OCCASION OF A MARRIAGE

Articles 12–16

The following are exempt from VAT:

- Trousseaux and household effects (see art 2(1)(*c*)) belonging to a person transferring his or her normal place of residence to the territory of the Community (see art 2(1)(*e*)) on the occasion of marriage.
- Presents customarily given on the occasion of a marriage. Their value must not exceed specified limits.

The conditions for exemption are set out in arts 12(2) and 13–16.

CHAPTER 3—PERSONAL PROPERTY ACQUIRED BY INHERITANCE

Articles 17–20

Personal property (see art 2(1)(*b*)) is exempt from VAT if it is acquired, by inheritance, by one of the following persons:

- A natural person having his normal place of residence in the territory of the Community (art 17).
- A legal person who is: (1) engaged in a non-profit-making activity, and (2) established in the territory of the Community (art 20).

The conditions for exemption are set out in arts 18 and 19.

TITLE III—IMPORTATION OF SCHOOL OUTFITS, EDUCATIONAL MATERIALS AND RELATED HOUSEHOLD EFFECTS

Articles 21, 22

Exemption is granted in respect of outfits (as defined in art 21(2)(*b*)), educational materials (as defined in art 21(2)(*c*)) and household effects (as defined in art 2(1)(*c*)) representing the usual furnishings for a student's room. The following conditions apply:

- The goods must belong to a pupil or student (as defined in art 21(2)(*a*)) coming to stay in the Community for the purpose of studying there.
- The goods are intended for the personal use of the pupil or student during the period of his studies.

Exemption must be granted at least once per school year.

TITLE IV—IMPORTS OF NEGLIGIBLE VALUE

Articles 23, 24

Goods are exempt on admission if:

- The value of the goods does not exceed EUR 10. Member states may opt to apply a limit that does not exceed EUR 22. For the exchange value of euro in national currency, see art 92.
- The goods comprise something other than alcoholic products (as defined in art 2(1)(*d*)), perfume, toilet water, tobacco, tobacco products or (at the option of member states) goods imported on mail order.

TITLE V—CAPITAL GOODS AND OTHER EQUIPMENT IMPORTED ON THE TRANSFER OF ACTIVITIES

Articles 25–29

Member states may allow exemption for imports (as defined in art 2(1)(*a*)) of capital goods, other equipment and (in the case of an agricultural holding) livestock belonging to the undertaking (as defined in art 25(2)(b)) if:

- The undertaking definitely ceases its activity in the country of departure in order to carry on a similar activity (as defined in art 25(2)(a) in the member state into which the goods are imported.
- The undertaking has given advance notice of the commencement of this activity in accordance with Directive 2006/112/EC art 213(1).

For exceptions and limitations, see arts 26–29.

TITLE VI—IMPORTATION OF CERTAIN AGRICULTURAL PRODUCTS AND PRODUCTS INTENDED FOR AGRICULTURAL USE

Chapter 1—Products Obtained by Community Farmers on Properties Located in a State Other than the State of Importation

Articles 30–33

The following are exempt on admission:

- Agricultural, stock-farming, bee keeping, horticultural and forestry products from properties located in a third country or third territory adjoining the territory of the Community. An agricultural producer must operate the properties. The producer's principal undertaking must be located in the member state adjacent to the third country or third territory.
- The products of fishing or fish-farming activities. The activities must be carried out in lakes or waterways bordering the territory of the Community. The fishermen must be established in the Community.
- The products of hunting activities. The activities must be carried out in lakes or waterways bordering the territory of the Community. The sportsmen must be established in the Community.

The conditions for exemption are set out in arts 30(1) (second para), 30(2), 31 and 32.

Chapter 2—Seeds, Fertilisers and Products for the Treatment of Soil and Crops

Articles 34, 35

Seeds, fertilisers and products for the treatment of soil and crops are exempt on admission if:

- The goods are intended for use on a property located in a member state adjoining a third country or third territory.
- The property is operated by an agricultural producer.
- The producer has his principal undertaking in the adjacent third country or third territory.

The conditions for exemption are set out in art 35.

TITLE VII—IMPORTATION OF THERAPEUTIC SUBSTANCES, MEDICINES, LABORATORY ANIMALS AND BIOLOGICAL OR CHEMICAL SUBSTANCES

CHAPTER 1—LABORATORY ANIMALS AND BIOLOGICAL OR CHEMICAL SUBSTANCES INTENDED FOR RESEARCH

Article 36

The following are exempt on admission:

- Animals specially prepared and sent free of charge for laboratory use.
- Biological or chemical substances meeting the conditions in art 36(1)(*b*). From 1 January 2010, the reference to Regulation (EEC) No 918/83 art 60 is construed as a reference to Regulation (EC) No 1186/2009 art 53: see art 133 of the 2009 Regulation.

The conditions for exemption are set out in art 36(2).

CHAPTER 2—THERAPEUTIC SUBSTANCES OF HUMAN ORIGIN AND BLOOD-GROUPING AND TISSUE-TYPING REAGENTS

Articles 37–39

The following are exempted:

- Therapeutic substances (as defined in art 37(2)(a)) of human origin.
- Blood-grouping reagents (as defined in art 37(2)(b)).
- Issue-typing reagents (as defined in art 37(2)(c)).
- Special packaging essential for the transport of the foregoing goods.
- Any solvents and accessories which are needed for the use of the foregoing goods and which are included in the consignments.

The conditions for exemption are set out in art 38.

CHAPTER 3—REFERENCE SUBSTANCES FOR THE QUALITY CONTROL OF MEDICAL PRODUCTS

Article 40

Consignments containing samples of reference substances are exempt on admission if:

- The reference substances are approved by the World Health Organisation for the quality control of materials used in the manufacture of medicinal products.
- The consignments are addressed to consignees authorised to receive such consignments free of tax. Consignees are so authorised by the competent authorities of the member states.

CHAPTER 4—PHARMACEUTICAL PRODUCTS USED AT INTERNATIONAL SPORTS EVENTS

Article 41

Pharmaceutical products are exempt on admission if:

- The products are for human or veterinary medical use by persons or animals participating in an international sports event.
- The quantities are necessary to meet the requirements of the persons or animals during their stay in the Community.

TITLE VIII—GOODS FOR CHARITABLE OR PHILANTHROPIC ORGANISATIONS

CHAPTER 1—GENERAL PROVISION

Article 42

Member states may impose quantity or value limits on the goods exempted under Chapters 2–4 of this Title. They may do so to remedy any abuse and to combat major distortions of competition.

CHAPTER 2—GOODS IMPORTED FOR GENERAL PURPOSES

Articles 43–47

The following are exempt on admission:

- Basic necessities (as defined in art 43(2)) obtained free of charge for distribution free of charge to needy persons. The goods must be imported by: (1) a state organisation; or (2) an approved charitable or philanthropic organisation.
- Any goods for use for fund-raising at occasional charity events for the benefit of needy persons. The goods must be sent free of charge by a person or organisation established outside the Community. They must be sent to: (1) a state organisation; or (2) an approved charitable or philanthropic organisation. They must be sent without any commercial intent on the part of the sender.
- Equipment and office materials sent free of charge by a person or organisation established outside the Community. For exceptions, see art 44. The goods must be sent to an approved charitable or philanthropic organisation. They must be sent without any commercial intent on the part of the sender. They must be sent for use solely for the purposes of: (1) meeting the organisation's operating needs; or (2) carrying out their stated charitable or philanthropic aims.

For the conditions to be met by recipient organisations see art 45. For the consequences of ceasing to fulfil them, see art 47. For excepted goods and restrictions on use, see arts 44, 46.

CHAPTER 3—ARTICLES IMPORTED FOR THE BENEFIT OF HANDICAPPED PERSONS

Articles 48–50

The following goods are exempt on admission:

- Articles designed for the education, employment or social advancement of blind or other physically or mentally handicapped persons.
- Specific spare parts, components or accessories specifically for the articles in question.
- Tools to be used for the maintenance, checking, calibration and repair of the articles.

The conditions for exemption are set out in art 48(2), (3). For the charge to tax if the goods are lent, hired out or transferred in certain circumstances, see art 49. For the consequences of ceasing to fulfil the conditions for exemption, see art 50.

CHAPTER 4—GOODS IMPORTED FOR THE BENEFIT OF DISASTER VICTIMS

Articles 41–57

The following goods are exempt on admission:

- Goods for distribution free of charge to victims of a disaster affecting the territory of one or more member states.
- Goods to be loaned free of charge to the victims of a disaster affecting the territory of one or more member states.
- Goods imported by disaster-relief agencies in order to meet their needs during the period of their activity

The conditions for exemption are set out in arts 52–54. For restrictions on the loan, hire or transfer of the goods, see arts 55–57. For organisations ceasing to fulfil the conditions for exemption, see art 57.

TITLE IX—IMPORTATION IN THE CONTEXT OF CERTAIN ASPECTS OF INTERNATIONAL RELATIONS

CHAPTER 1—HONORARY DECORATIONS OR AWARDS

Article 58

Exemption is granted in respect of:

- Decorations conferred by the government of a third country on a person whose normal place of residence is in the Community.
- Cups, medals and similar articles of an essentially symbolic nature awarded: (1) as a tribute to the recipient's activities in fields such as the arts, the sciences, sport or the public service, or (2) in recognition of merit at a particular event. The article must have been awarded in a third country to a person having his normal place of residence in the member state of importation.
- Cups, medals and similar articles of an essentially symbolic nature for presentation in the territory of the Community: (1) as a tribute to the recipient's activities in fields such as the arts, the sciences, sport or the public service, or (2) in recognition of merit at a particular event. The article must have been given by an authority or person established in a third country.
- Awards, trophies and souvenirs of an essentially symbolic nature intended for distribution free of charge to persons normally resident in a third country or third territory at a business conference or similar international event. The goods must be of limited value. Exemption does not apply if the nature, unitary value and other features indicate that the goods are intended for commercial purposes.

CHAPTER 2—PRESENTS RECEIVED IN THE CONTEXT OF INTERNATIONAL RELATIONS

Articles 59–61

Exemption is granted in respect of:

- Goods imported by a person who received them as a gift from the host authorities on the occasion of an official visit to a third country or third territory.
- Goods imported by a person coming to pay an official visit in the Community. The person must intend to offer the goods on that occasion as a gift to the host authorities.
- Goods sent as gifts in token of friendship or goodwill by: (1) an official body, (2) a public authority, or (3) a group carrying on an activity in the public interest. The body, authority or group must be located in a third country or third territory. The gift must be for presentation to a like body, authority or group which is located in the member state of importation and approved by the competent body to receive such goods exempt from tax.

The conditions for exemption are set out in arts 60 and 61.

CHAPTER 3—GOODS TO BE USED BY MONARCHS OR HEADS OF STATE

Article 62

Exemption is granted in respect of:

- Gifts to a reigning monarch or head of state.
- Goods to be used or consumed by the reigning monarch, or head of state, of a third country during his official stay in the Community.
- Goods to be used or consumed by the official representative of the reigning monarch, or head of state, of a third country during his official stay in the Community.

TITLE X—IMPORTATION OF GOODS FOR THE PROMOTION OF TRADE

CHAPTER 1—SAMPLES OF NEGLIGIBLE VALUE

Article 63

Samples of goods (as defined in art 63(3)) are exempt on admission if:

- They are of negligible value.
- They can be used only to solicit orders for goods of the type they represent.

The conditions for exemption are set out in art 63(2).

CHAPTER 2—PRINTED MATTER AND ADVERTISING MATERIAL

Articles 64–66

The following goods are exempt on admission:

- Printed advertising matter relating to goods for sale or hire by a person established outside the Community.
- Printed advertising matter relating to transport, commercial insurance or banking services offered by a person established outside the Community.
- Articles for advertising purposes sent free of charge by suppliers to their customers. The articles must have no intrinsic commercial value. They must be incapable of use for anything other than their advertising function.

For examples of printed advertising matter, see art 64. For the conditions to be met in respect of it, see art 65.

CHAPTER 3—GOODS USED OR CONSUMED AT A TRADE FAIR OR SIMILAR EVENT

Articles 67–71

The following goods are exempt on admission:

- Small representative samples of goods intended for a trade fair or similar event. For limitations, see arts 68 and 71.
- Goods imported solely in order to be demonstrated at a trade fair or similar event. For limitations, see arts 69 and 71.
- Goods imported solely in order to demonstrate machines and apparatus displayed at a trade fair or similar event. For limitations, see arts 69 and 71.
- Materials (eg paints, varnishes and wallpaper) of little value which are to be used in building, fitting out or decorating temporary stands at a trade fair or similar event. The goods must be destroyed by being used.
- Articles supplied free of charge in order to advertise goods displayed at a trade fair or similar event. For examples, see art 67(1)(d). For limitations, see art 70.

For "trade fair or similar event", see art 67(2).

TITLE XI—GOODS IMPORTED FOR EXAMINATION, ANALYSIS OR TEST PURPOSES

Articles 72–78

Goods are exempt on admission if they are to undergo examination, analysis or tests in order to determine their composition, quality or other technical characteristics for purposes of: (1) information; or (2) industrial or commercial research.

The conditions for exemption are set out in arts 73–76 and 78. For the charge to tax on products remaining at the end of the examination, analysis or test, see art 77.

TITLE XII—MISCELLANEOUS EXEMPTIONS

CHAPTER 1—CONSIGNMENTS SENT TO ORGANISATIONS PROTECTING COPYRIGHTS OR INDUSTRIAL AND COMMERCIAL PATENT RIGHTS

Article 79

The following are exempt on admission:

- Trademarks, patterns or designs and their supporting documents.
- Applications for patents for invention or the like.

The goods must be imported in order to be submitted to the bodies competent to deal with the protection of copyright or the protection of industrial or commercial patent rights.

CHAPTER 2—TOURIST INFORMATION LITERATURE

Article 80

The following are exempt on admission:

- Documentation intended for distribution free of charge.
- Foreign hotel lists and yearbooks intended for distribution free of charge. The lists and yearbooks must be published by, or under the auspices of, an official tourist agency.
- Timetables intended for distribution free of charge. The timetables must relate to foreign transport services.
- Reference material supplied to accredited representatives or correspondents appointed by official national tourist agencies and not intended for distribution.

CHAPTER 3—MISCELLANEOUS DOCUMENTS AND ARTICLES

Article 81

This article lists the documents and articles exempt on admission. For articles produced by the United Nations (arts 81(1)(r)), see art 81(2) and Annex I.

CHAPTER 4—ANCILLARY MATERIALS FOR THE STOWAGE AND PROTECTION OF GOODS DURING THEIR TRANSPORT

Article 82

Various materials (eg rope, straw, cloth, paper and cardboard, wood and plastics) are exempt on admission if:

- They are used for the stowage and protection of goods during their transport to the territory of the Community.
- They are not normally re-usable.

- The consideration paid for them forms part of the taxable amount on importation (as defined in Directive 2006/112/EC arts 85–89).

CHAPTER 5—LITTER, FODDER AND FEEDING STUFFS FOR ANIMALS DURING THEIR TRANSPORT

Article 83

Litter, fodder and feeding stuffs of any description are exempt on admission if:

- They are put on board the means of transport used to convey animals to the territory of the Community.
- They are intended to be distributed to those animals during the journey.

CHAPTER 6—FUEL AND LUBRICANTS PRESENT IN LAND MOTOR VEHICLES AND SPECIAL CONTAINERS

Articles 84–88

The following are exempt on admission:

- Fuel contained in the standard tanks (as defined in art 84 first para, point (2)(*c*) and second para) of a commercial motor vehicle (as defined in art 84 first para, point (2)(*a*)), private motor vehicle (as defined in art 84 first para, point (2)(*b*)), motorcycle or special container (as defined in art 84 first para, point (2)(*d*)).
- Fuel contained in portable tanks carried by a private motor vehicle or motorcycle.
- Lubricants carried in a motor vehicle. The lubricants must be required for the normal operation of the motor vehicle during the journey in question.

The conditions for exemption are set out in arts 85–87. For the charge to tax if fuel exempt on admission is misused, see art 87(2)).

CHAPTER 7—GOODS FOR THE CONSTRUCTION, UPKEEP OR ORNAMENTATION OF MEMORIALS TO, OR CEMETERIES FOR, WAR VICTIMS

Article 89

The following goods are exempt on admission:

- Goods for use in the construction, upkeep or ornamentation of the cemeteries or tombs of third country war victims who have been buried in the Community.
- Goods for use in the construction, upkeep or ornamentation of memorials for third country war victims who have been buried in the Community.

The goods must be imported by organisations authorised by the competent authorities to receive goods free of tax.

CHAPTER 8—COFFINS, FUNERARY URNS AND ORNAMENTAL FUNERARY ARTICLES

Article 90

The following are exempt on admission:

- Coffins containing the bodies of deceased persons.
- Urns containing the ashes of deceased persons.
- Flowers, funeral wreaths and other ornamental objects normally accompanying coffins and urns.
- Flowers, funeral wreaths and other ornamental objects imported by a person attending a funeral, or coming to decorate a grave, in the territory of the Community. The person must be resident outside the Community.

TITLE XIII—GENERAL AND FINAL PROVISIONS

Article 91

The relevant person must furnish proof that any conditions for exemption have been met.

Article 92

The rate of exchange for converting national currency into euro is fixed annually by reference to the rate ruling on the first working day in October. This rate applies for the following calendar year.

Article 93

Member states may maintain:

- The privileges and immunities granted by them under cultural, scientific or technical co-operation agreements concluded with third countries.
- The special exemptions granted by them under frontier agreements with third countries. The exemptions must be justified by the nature of the frontier traffic.
- Exemptions granted under reciprocal arrangements with third countries. These countries must be contracting parties to the Convention on International Civil Aviation (Chicago, 1944). The exemptions must implement Recommended Practices 4.42 and 4.44 in Annex 9 of the Convention.

Article 94

Member states may retain exemptions granted to:

- Merchant navy seamen.
- Workers returning to their country of origin following a work-related residence of six months or more in a third country.

Article 95

Member states must inform the Commission of the measures they have adopted to give effect to this directive.

Article 96

Directive 83/181/EEC and the amending directives listed in Annex II are repealed. References to the 1983 Directive are construed as references to this directive in accordance with the correlation table in Annex III.

Article 97

This directive entered into force on 30 November 2009.

Article 98

This directive is addressed to the member states.

Annex I—Visual and Auditory Materials of an Educational, Scientific or Cultural Character

This lists the materials referred to in art 81(1)(q).

Annex II—Repealed Directive with the List of its Successive Amendments

This lists the directives repealed by art 96.

Annex III—Correlation Table

This is the correlation table referred to in art 96.

DIRECTIVE 2009/162/EU
THE COMMON SYSTEM OF VALUE ADDED TAX (AMENDING DIRECTIVE 2006/112/EC)

General note This directive amends Directive 2006/112/EC. It came into force on 15 January 2010. Member states were required to enact implementing legislation taking effect on 1 January 2011. The amendments made by this directive are reflected in the commentary to the 2006 directive.

DIRECTIVE 2010/23/EU
THE COMMON SYSTEM OF VALUE ADDED TAX (AMENDING DIRECTIVE 2006/112/EC)

General note This directive entered into force on 9 April 2010. It amends Directive 2006/112/EC by temporarily inserting a new art 199a. This directive (and therefore the new art 199a) expires on 30 June 2015. This amendment is reflected in the commentary.

DIRECTIVE 2010/24/EU
MUTUAL ASSISTANCE FOR THE RECOVERY OF CLAIMS RELATING TO TAXES, DUTIES AND OTHER MEASURES

General note This directive sets out rules enabling taxes, duties and other charges (as defined in art 2) arising in one member state to be recovered in another member state. The taxes concerned include VAT (see art 2(1)(a)).

This directive entered into force on 20 April 2010 (see art 30). Member states are required to implement it with effect from 1 January 2012 (see art 28(1)).

This directive replaces Directive 2008/55/EC, which is accordingly repealed with effect from 1 January 2012 (see art 29).

The Commission is required to adopt detailed rules for implementing arts 4(2)–(4), 5(1), 8, 10, 12(1), 13(2)–(5), 15, 16(1) and 21(1) (see art 26). No rules have been made to date.

DIRECTIVE 2010/45/EU
THE RULES ON INVOICING (AMENDING DIRECTIVE 2006/112/EC)

General note

This directive entered into force on 11 August 2010. It amends Directive 2006/112/EC as follows:

- The following provisions are inserted: arts 167a, 219a, 220a, 226(7a), 226(10a), 226(11a), 226a, 226b, 248a.
- The following provisions are replaced: arts 17(2)(f), 64(2), 66 (first para, point (c)), 66 (second para), 67, 69, 91(2) (second para), 178(a), 178(c), 181,197(1)(c), 217, 220, 221, 222, 223, 224, 225, 226(11), 226(13), 226(14), 230, 232, 233, 235, 236, 237, 238(1), 238(3), 243, 247(2), 247(3), 249, 272(1) (second para) and the heading to Title XI, Chapter 3, Section 5.
- The following provisions are deleted: arts 228, 231, 234, 238(2), 246.

The amendments made by this directive are reflected in the commentary to the 2006 Directive. Member states are required to enact implementing legislation by 31 December 2012 and apply it from 1 January 2013.

DIRECTIVE 2010/66/EU REFUND OF VAT TO TAXABLE PERSONS NOT ESTABLISHED IN THE MEMBER STATE OF REFUND BUT ESTABLISHED IN ANOTHER MEMBER STATE (AMENDING DIRECTIVE 2008/9/EC)

General note

This directive amends Directive 2008/9/EC. It entered into force on 21 October 2010. It applies from 1 October 2010. The amendments made by this directive are reflected in the commentary to the 2008 Directive. Member states are required to enact implementing legislation having effect from 1 October 2010.

DIRECTIVE 2010/88/EU THE STANDARD RATE OF VAT (AMENDING DIRECTIVE 2006/112/EC)

General note

This directive amends Directive 2006/112/EC. It entered into force on 11 December 2010. The amendments made by this directive are reflected in the commentary to the 2006 Directive. Member states are required to enact implementing legislation having effect from 1 January 2011.

8. EU Decisions

Contents

AUTHORISATION (10 DECEMBER 1986) DEROGATION REQUESTED BY THE GOVERNMENT OF THE UNITED KINGDOM

The UK is authorised to derogate from Directive 77/388/EEC (repealed), now Directive 2006/112/EC, in relation hotel accommodation occupied by individuals on a long-term basis. In effect, the taxable amount (as to which see Directive 2006/112/EC arts 73, 78, 79) is apportioned between:

- a letting of immoveable property (which is exempted from tax by Directive 2006/112/EC art 1335(1)(*l*)); and
- other services.

The taxable amount of the letting is assessed on a flat-rate basis.

This authorisation replaces a simplification measure retained by the UK in accordance with what is now Directive 2006/112/EC art 394 (see Appendix 1). The Council is deemed to have adopted a decision authorising this derogation on 10 December 1986. For the measures introduced by the UK, see VATA 1994 Sch 6 para 10.

DECISION 89/466/EEC AUTHORISING THE UNITED KINGDOM TO APPLY A MEASURE DEROGATING FROM ARTICLE 11A(1)(B) OF THE SIXTH DIRECTIVE

As regards applications of goods for non-business purposes treated as a supply of goods for consideration in accordance with Directive 77/388/EEC art 5(7)(*a*), (*b*) (repealed), now Directive 2006/112 art 18(*b*), the UK is authorised to derogate from Directive 77/388/EEC art 11A(1)(*b*), now Directive 2006/112/EC art 74, by using open market value as the taxable amount for a supply of buildings or parts of buildings before first occupation of the land on which they stand.

This decision is addressed to the UK. It is granted pending the deletion of Directive 77/388/EEC Annex F point 16, now Directive 2006/112/EC Annex X Part B point 9. For the measures introduced by the UK, see VAT (Self-supply of Construction Services) Order 1989, SI 1989/472.

DECISION 89/534/EEC AUTHORISING THE UNITED KINGDOM TO APPLY A MEASURE DEROGATING FROM ARTICLE 11A(1)(A) OF THE SIXTH DIRECTIVE IN RESPECT OF CERTAIN SUPPLIES TO UNREGISTERED RESELLERS

The UK is authorised to derogate from Directive 77/388/EEC art 11A(1)(*a*) (repealed), now Directive 2006/112/EC art 73, by prescribing that the taxable amount for supplies to non-taxable persons is to be the open market value for the goods as determined at the final stage of consumption. The UK may do so in cases where a marketing structure based on the supply of goods through non-taxable persons results in non-taxation at the stage of final consumption.

This decision is addressed to the UK. For the measures introduced by the UK, see VATA 1994 Sch 6 para 2.

DECISION 2006/659/EC AUTHORISING THE UNITED KINGDOM TO INTRODUCE A SPECIAL MEASURE DEROGATING FROM ARTICLES 5(6) AND 11A(1)(B) OF THE SIXTH DIRECTIVE

This decision repeals and replaces Decision 86/356/EEC. It authorises the UK to derogate from Directive 77/388/EEC arts 5(6) and 11A(1)(*b*) (repealed), now Directive 2006/112/EC arts 16, 74. The UK is authorised to fix, on a flat-rate basis, the proportion of VAT relating to expenditure on fuel used for private purposes in business cars. This proportion is expressed in fixed amounts determined by reference to the CO2 emissions of particular vehicles. It must reflect fuel consumption. Fixed amounts must be adjusted annually to reflect changes in the average cost of fuel. Taxable persons must be allowed to choose whether or not to apply the flat-rate system.

This decision is addressed to the UK. It applies between 1 May 2007 and 31 December 2015. For the measures introduced by the UK, see VATA 1994 s 57, which came into force in its amended form on 22 March 2007 (see F(No 2)A 2005 s 2; Finance (No 2) Act 2005, Section 2(7), (Appointed Day) Order 2007, SI 2007/946).

DECISION 2006/774/EC AUTHORISING CERTAIN MEMBER STATES TO APPLY A REDUCED RATE OF VAT TO CERTAIN LABOUR-INTENSIVE SERVICES IN ACCORDANCE WITH THE PROCEDURE PROVIDED FOR IN ARTICLE 28(6) OF THE SIXTH DIRECTIVE

This decision expired on 31 December 2010.

DECISION 2007/250/EC AUTHORISING THE UNITED KINGDOM TO INTRODUCE A SPECIAL MEASURE DEROGATING FROM ARTICLE 193 OF DIRECTIVE 2006/112/EC

This decision (as amended by Decisions 2009/439/EC and 2010/710/EU) authorises the UK to derogate from Directive 2006/112/EC art 193 by designating, as the persons liable to pay VAT, the taxable persons to whom the following goods are supplied:

- Mobile telephones.
- Integrated circuit devices.

This derogation applies to supplies of goods with a taxable amount of £5,000 or more. The UK is required to introduce appropriate and effective control and reporting obligations on taxable persons making such supplies. The UK is required to evaluate the operation and effectiveness of the measures taken and submit a report to the Commission.

This decision is addressed to the UK. It expires on the earlier of: (1) the entry into force of EU rules allowing all member states to adopt similar measures; and (2) 31 December 2013.

For the measures introduced by the UK, see VATA 1994 s 55A, which came into force on 1 June 2007 (see FA 2006 s 19; Finance Act 2006, section 19, (Appointed Day) Order 2007, SI 2007/1419).

DECISION 2007/884/EC AUTHORISING THE UNITED KINGDOM TO CONTINUE TO APPLY A MEASURE DEROGATING FROM ARTICLES 26(1)(A), 168 AND 169 OF DIRECTIVE 2006/112/EC

This decision (as amended by Decision 2011/37/EU) replaces Decision 98/198/EC (as amended by Decisions 2003/909/EC and 2004/855/EC), which expired on 31 December 2007. From 1 January 2008, the UK is authorised to:

- Derogate from Directive 2006/112/EC arts 168, 169, by restricting the right to deduct VAT on the cost of hiring or leasing a motor car used for private purposes. The hirer or lessee's deduction is restricted to 50% of the VAT concerned.
- Derogate from Directive 2006/112/EC art 26(1)(*a*), by providing that the private use of a business car hired or leased by a taxable person is not treated as a supply of services for consideration.

This decision is addressed to the UK. It expires on the earlier of: (1) 31 December 2013; and (2) the date when Community rules enter into force regarding expenditure ineligible for deduction of tax in respect of motorised road vehicles.

For the measures introduced by the UK, see VAT (Input Tax) Order 1992, SI 1992/3222 art 7(2H). Cf VAT (Supply of Services) Order 1993, SI 1993/1507 art 6A.

DECISION 2009/938/EU AUTHORISING SWEDEN AND THE UNITED KINGDOM TO APPLY A MEASURE DEROGATING FROM ARTICLE 167 OF DIRECTIVE 2006/112/EC

This decision authorises the UK to derogate from Directive 2006/112/EC art 167 by postponing the right of a taxable person to deduct input tax until such time as he has paid the person who supplied the goods or services. The following conditions must be met:

- The taxable person must have opted for a scheme whereby VAT on his supplies of goods and services becomes chargeable on receipt of the payment.
- His annual turnover does not exceed £1,500,000.

This decision expires when a directive introducing a cash accounting scheme enters into force, or on 31 December 2012 at the latest.

This decision is addressed to Sweden and the UK. As regards the UK, it replaces Decision 2007/133/EC, which expired on 31 December 2009.

All member state have the option to introduce a cash accounting scheme from 1 January 2013 in accordance with Directive 2006/112/EC art 167a (as inserted by Directive 2010/45/EU art 1(7)). The 2010 Directive came into force on 11 August 2010 (see art 3 of the 2010 Directive).

For the cash accounting scheme currently applied by the UK in accordance with this decision, see VAT Regulations 1995, SI 1995/2518 regs 56–65. From 1 January 2013, the scheme is required to be applied in accordance with Directive 2006/112/EC art 167a.

DECISION 2010/710/EU AUTHORISING GERMANY, ITALY AND AUSTRIA TO INTRODUCE A SPECIAL MEASURE DEROGATING FROM ARTICLE 193 OF DIRECTIVE 2006/112/EC AND AMENDING DECISION 2007/250/EC TO EXTEND THE PERIOD OF VALIDITY OF THE AUTHORISATION GRANTED TO THE UNITED KINGDOM

This decision extends the expiry date of Directive 2007/250/EC.

DECISION 2011/37/EU AMENDING DECISION 2007/884/EC AUTHORISING THE UNITED KINGDOM TO CONTINUE TO APPLY A MEASURE DEROGATING FROM ARTICLES 26(1)(A), 168 AND 169 OF DIRECTIVE 2006/112/EC ON THE COMMON SYSTEM OF VALUE ADDED TAX

As regards the UK, this decision extends the expiry date of Directive 2007/884/EC.

9. Appendices

Contents

APPENDIX 1.

SPECIAL MEASURES APPLIED IN THE UK ON 1 JANUARY 1977

Directive 77/388/EEC art 27(5) (the Sixth Directive) allows member states to retain the special measures they applied on 1 January 1977 if:

- They notified the Commission of them before 31 December 1978.
- The special measures simplify the procedures for charging tax or prevent certain types of tax evasion or avoidance.
- (In so far as the measures are designed to simplify the procedure for charging tax) they have no more than a negligible effect on the amount of tax due at the final consumption stage.

The special measures applied by the UK were notified to the Commission in a letter dated 28 December 1977 from HM Customs and Excise and described in the Annexes thereto. An edited text of the Annexes is set out below.

ANNEX 1: SPECIAL VAT SCHEMES FOR RETAILERS

. . . [R]etailers may choose any scheme or combination of schemes for which their business is eligible, under the rules set out in [notices published by HM Customs and Excise]. The Notices were given vires under the Finance Act 1972 s 30(3).

The purpose of the United Kingdom's special value added tax schemes for retailers is to simplify the calculation of output tax by retailers, in that they do not have to record full details and calculate tax on each transaction. It is considered that the special schemes do not in principle derogate from the provisions of the Sixth Directive, but only apply a totality of the considerations received or receivable in determining the tax due at different rates.

Some minor changes . . . will be introduced on 1 January 1978, but these do not alter the basic framework of the schemes in use on 1 January 1977.

[FA 1972 s 30(3) has now been consolidated as VATA 1994 Sch 11 para 2(6). For the notices currently in force, see Notice Nos 727, 727/2, 727/3, 727/4 and 727/5.]

ANNEX 2: TRADING STAMPS

[This measure no longer applies. VAT (Treatment of Transactions) (No 1) Order 1973, SI 1973/325, and VAT Regulations 1995, SI 1995/2518, regs 76–80, were revoked with effect from 1 June 1996. Trading stamps are now treated in the same manner as other discount vouchers.]

ANNEX 3: EXEMPTION FROM REGISTRATION

Under the Finance Act 1972 Sch 1 para 11(*a*) the Commissioners of Customs and Excise have discretion to treat as exempt from registration any person who, although the value of his taxable supplies exceeds the exemption limits for registration, satisfies them that all these supplies are or would be zero-rated if he were a taxable person. Traders seeking such exemption are generally in a fairly small way of business, eg small service traders in the construction and transport industries and food retailers, and prefer to bear the tax on their inputs rather than come under control as registered taxable persons and claim refunds of input tax.

Arrangements are in hand to take account of the activities of these traders in calculating the United Kingdom "own resources" contribution.

[For exemption from registration, see now VATA 1994 Sch 1 para 14. This provision sets out conditions that were absent from the 1972 provision.]

ANNEX 4: VALUATION

[This measure no longer applies. The relevant UK legislation was FA 1972 Sch 3 para 2. A new Sch 3 para 2 was substituted by FA 1981 s 14(1) and consolidated as VATA 1983 Sch 4 para 3. The substituted provision was held to be a special measure that required authorisation under art 27(1) of the Sixth Directive: see *Direct Cosmetics Ltd v C & E Comrs* (case C-5/84) [1985] ECR 617, [1985] STC 479, 1 CEV 85. For the authorisation currently in force under art 27(1) of the Sixth Directive, see Decision 89/534/EEC.]

ANNEX 5: OPERATION OF UK TERMINAL MARKETS

(1) There are in the United Kingdom a number of commodity markets. These are centres of much international merchanting trade. Some are solely "physical" markets dealing in consignments of goods, usually on [cost, insurance and freight] terms, for either immediate or forward delivery, eg the London Tea Market and the Liverpool Cotton Exchange. The normal value added tax rules are applied to transactions on these markets and are operated without distortion of competition. The application of normal value added tax rules to all transactions on the "futures" market, however, would have had damaging consequences. The eleven "futures" markets in the United Kingdom provide growers, merchants and manufacturers with the facility of buying and selling "futures" contracts in certain commodities to protect themselves against loss of their real trading operations through changes in price. "Futures" trading on each of the markets is generally confined to small groups of "ring-dealing" members. In most cases these members deal as principals on their own account; in other cases members may act as agents on behalf of outside clients. A "futures" contract is normally drawn up so as to require the eventual delivery of goods and a small percentage of contracts in fact run to maturity. This helps to maintain a close relationship between "futures" prices and "physical" prices. However, most dealings in "futures" are of the nature of financing or insurance and are not performed with the intention of acquiring goods.

(2) If value added tax had been applied without relief to all "futures" transactions, this would have distorted United Kingdom market prices which presently command international acceptance. This could have led to the loss of much of the international "futures" trade to countries outside the Community. Further, there is a very substantial volume of business on the "futures" markets which is often conducted in very short periods of the day and application of the full system of value added tax would have imposed considerable administrative burdens on the markets which it would not have been easy for them to sustain, and the pattern of trading could have been seriously disrupted. Additionally, it would have been difficult to institute effective verification of the complete chain of transactions of each "futures" market. It was decided, therefore, that a scheme of relief was necessary for these markets. The scheme provides a simplified system of control and reduces the administrative burdens on the market without a substantial loss of revenue at the final consumption stage.

(3) In broad terms, the scheme provides that transactions on the eleven "futures" markets involving defined market members are traded free of valued added tax and of the recording requirements of value added tax. The markets involved and the extent of zero-rating of those transactions are defined in the terms of regulations made under the Finance Act 1972 s 26 [now VATA 1994 s 59]. These are the VAT (Terminal Markets) Order 1973, SI 1973/173, and the VAT (Terminal Markets) (Amendment) Order 1975, SI 1975/383. . . . The exception to the normal requirement of keeping valued added tax records of these zero-rated transactions is made under the "care and management" provisions vested in the Commissioners of Customs and Excise. The zero-rating extends only to "futures" transactions in a commodity which involves a member of the relevant market and agency charges by market members in connection with these transactions. Brokerage charges are normally levied at certain specific rates and usually as part of the contract price. It is difficult to distinguish it as the services of an agent distinct from the market in which he operates. If a "futures" contract runs to maturity and delivery of the goods takes place where a non-market member is involved, the supply of both the goods and any agency service by a market member is not relieved by the Orders and normal value added tax rules apply. The orders do not allow users of these commodities to acquire them free of tax in the United Kingdom, although it is important to bear in mind that many commodities may of course still be zero-rated

under the Finance Act 1972 Sch 4 [now VATA 1994 Sch 8] and agency services by market members to overseas customers may also be zero-rated as an export of services.

ANNEX 6: LONG STAYS IN HOTELS

[This measure no longer applies. For the substituted special measure authorised under art 27(1) of the Sixth Directive, see Authorisation (10 December 1986).]

ANNEX 7: GOODS IN WAREHOUSE—ARTICLE 16

[This measure no longer applies in relation to the postponed accounting provisions. VAT (General) Regulations 1975, SI 1975/2204, regs 33, 34, subsequently consolidated as VAT (General) Regulations 1980, SI 1980/1536, regs 33, 34, were revoked from 1 October 1984 by VAT (General) (No 2) Regulations 1984, SI 1984/929.]

Imports

. . . Article 16(1)(C) . . . covers our practice of disregarding all supplies in warehouse before duty is paid. . . .

Excise goods

In equity we allow excise goods the same treatment as customs goods. If excise goods are required to be warehoused for security of duty then we disregard supplies before duty payment . . . .

This would seem to be adequately covered by the interplay of art 16(1)(A)(*e*)—which implicitly refers to excise warehouses—and art 16(1)(C), which refers to supplies within them.

Similar facilities are granted in respect of home produced excisable goods and in cases where imported goods and home produced goods are mixed in warehouses, eg the fortifying of wine with British spirits. . . .

APPENDIX 2. TERRITORIAL EXTENT OF THE EUROPEAN UNION

The territorial scope of the Treaty on European Union ("the EU Treaty") and the Treaty on the Functioning of the European Union ("the Functioning Treaty") (collectively, "the founding treaties") is determined in accordance with EU Treaty art 52 (formerly EC Treaty art 299(1)) (which lists the states to which the founding treaties apply) and Functioning Treaty art 355 (formerly EC Treaty art 299(2)–(6)) (which lists specific territories to which the founding treaties do, or do not, apply).

This definition of territorial extent does not apply for all purposes. Thus, for example, the relevant territories for VAT and customs purposes differ from both themselves and from the territory to which the founding treaties apply.

The VAT territory of the EU is defined in Directive 2006/112/EC arts 5–8 by reference to the territory of the member states to which the founding treaties apply, which is modified by the inclusion, or exclusion, of specified countries and territories.

The customs territory of the EU is defined in Regulation (EEC) No 2913/92 art 3 (the Community Customs Code) without reference to any other legislation.

The foregoing provisions are defined in deceptively simple terms. In practice, it is necessary to refer to a variety of documents in order to ascertain the position of a particular territory and to draw inferences where the position is left unstated. The following tables summarise the VAT and customs territories of the EU in so far as they can be gathered from the available documents. The Court of Auditors Special Report No 2/93 (OJ C347/1, 27.12.93) has been a particularly useful source. For a more recent treatment, see Fiona Murray *EU and Member State Territories: The Special Relationship under Community Law* (Palladian Law Publishing, 2004).

Table 1 lists the member states and indicates the regions to which special provisions apply. Table 2 lists the territories having a special link with the member states indicated. Table 3 lists the independent countries having special arrangements with the EU, or with an individual member state, in relation to VAT and customs matters.

TABLE 1—MEMBER STATES AT 1 JANUARY 2007

Country	*Founding treaties apply*[1]	*VAT territory*[2]	*Customs territory*[3]
Austria	Yes	Yes	Yes
• Jungholz[4]	Yes	Yes	Yes[5]
• Mittleberg (Kleines Walsertal)[6]	Yes	Yes	Yes[7]
Belgium	Yes	Yes	Yes
Bulgaria	Yes	Yes	Yes
Cyprus [8]	Yes[9]	Yes	Yes
Czech Republic	Yes	Yes	Yes
Denmark	Yes	Yes	Yes
• Faeroe Islands[10]	No[11]	No	No[12]
• Greenland[13]	Partial[14]	No[15]	No[16]
Estonia	Yes	Yes	Yes
Finland	Yes	Yes	Yes
• Aland Islands[17]	Partial[18]	No[19]	Yes[20]
France	Yes	Yes	Yes
• Overseas departments[21]	Yes[22]	No[23]	Yes[24]

Country	*Founding treaties apply*	*VAT territory*[2]	*Customs territory*[3]
Germany	Yes	Yes	Yes
• Heligoland[25]	Yes	No[26]	No[27]
• Büsingen[28]	Yes[29]	No[30]	No[31]
Greece	Yes	Yes	Yes
• Mount Athos[32]	Yes	No[33]	Yes[34]
Hungary	Yes	Yes	Yes
Ireland	Yes	Yes	Yes
Italy	Yes	Yes	Yes
• Livigno[35]	Yes	No[36]	No[37]
• Campione d'Italia[38]	Yes	No[39]	No[40]
• Italian waters of Lake Lugano	Yes	No[41]	No[42]
Latvia	Yes	Yes	Yes
Lithuania	Yes	Yes	Yes
Luxembourg	Yes	Yes	Yes
Malta	Yes	Yes	Yes
Netherlands	Yes	Yes	Yes
Poland	Yes	Yes	Yes
Portugal	Yes	Yes	Yes
• Madeira and the Azores[43]	Yes[44]	Yes	Yes[45]
Romania	Yes	Yes	Yes
Slovakia	Yes	Yes	Yes
Slovenia	Yes	Yes	Yes
Spain	Yes	Yes	Yes
• Ceuta[46] and Melilla[47]	Partial[48]	No[49]	No[50]
• Canary Islands[51]	Yes[52]	No[53]	Yes[54]
Sweden	Yes	Yes	Yes
United Kingdom[55]	Yes	Yes	Yes

Notes

1 The member states listed in EU Treaty art 52 (formerly EC Treaty art 299(1)) are shown in bold. The territories indicated by bullet points form part of the national territories of those states and are treated as such for the purposes of Functioning Treaty art 355 (formerly EC Treaty art 299(2)—(6)) unless otherwise indicated.

2 The VAT territory of the Community comprises the territories of the member states to which the EU Treaty applies, as defined in EU Treaty art 52 and Functioning Treaty art 355 (formerly EC Treaty art 299), other than the territories listed in Directive 2006/112/EC art 6: see Directive 2006/112/EC art 5(1), (2).

3 The customs territory of the Community comprises the territory of the member states: see Regulation (EEC) No 2913/92 art 3(1). Specific modifications to this principle are indicated.

4 The commune of Jungholz is situated between Füssen and Sonthofen and is virtually surrounded by German territory. It was placed within the German customs territory under the Customs Union Treaty of 3 May 1868 between Austria-Hungary and Bavaria.

5 This commune is part of "the territory of the Republic of Austria".

6 The commune of Mittelberg (Kleines Walsertal) is situated south-west of Oberstdorf in a valley

accessible only from Bavaria. It became affiliated to the customs union of the German Reich by the German-Austrian Treaty of 2 December 1890.

7 This commune is part of "the territory of the Republic of Austria".

8 The territory of the Republic of Cyprus comprises some 95 per cent of the island of Cyprus. The remainder comprises the UK Sovereign Base Areas of Akrotiri and Dhekelia, as to which see Table 2.

9 The government of the Republic of Cyprus does not currently exercise effective control of the northern (Turkish) part of the island forming some 37 per cent of its territory. The Community acquis is currently suspended in relation to this territory: see Protocol No 10 art 1 to the Act of Accession (2003).

10 The 18 islands of the Faeroe Islands are situated in the north-east Atlantic Ocean some 300 kilometres north-west of Scotland. They are a self-governing community within the Kingdom of Denmark: see Murray, op cit, pp 61, 62.

11 Functioning Treaty art 355(5)(a) (formerly EC Treaty art 299(6)(*a*)).

12 Regulation (EEC) No 2193/92 art 3(1).

13 Greenland was originally a Danish colony. It became part of Denmark in 1953 and acquired the status of a separate community in 1979: see Murray, op cit, p 10.

14 Greenland withdrew from what was then the EC by Treaty with effect from 1 February 1985. The special arrangements for association set out in Part Four of the Functioning Treaty (formerly Part Four of the EC Treaty) apply: see Functioning Treaty art 355(2) and Annex II (formerly EC Treaty art 299(3) and Annex II).

15 The founding treaties do not apply to Greenland.

16 Regulation (EEC) No 2193/92 art 3(1).

17 The Aland islands comprise some 6,000 islands to the north-east of Stockholm at the mouth of the Gulf of Bothnia. Some 200 islands are inhabited. The islands make up the autonomous province of Aland. This is governed under a system devised by the League of Nations in the 1920s.

18 The founding treaties apply to the Aland islands subject to derogations set out in Protocol No 2 to the Act of Accession (1994): see Functioning Treaty art 355(4) (formerly EC Treaty art 299(5)).

19 Directive 2006/112/EC art 6(1)(*d*). Protocol No 2 to the Act of Accession (1994), art 2(*a*) provides that the territory of the Aland islands "shall be excluded from the territorial application of the EC provisions in the fields of harmonisation of the laws of the Member States on turnover taxes . . . ".

20 The Aland islands form part of the territory of Finland. They are not specifically mentioned in Regulation (EEC) No 2913/92 art 3(1).

21 Guadeloupe (which includes Saint-Martin (a dependency) and Saint-Barthélemy (a sub-prefect)), French Guiana, Martinique and Reunion. Saint-Barthélemy is excluded from this list after 31 December 2011: see Decision 2010/718/EU art 2.

22 Functioning Treaty art 355(1) (formerly EC Treaty art 299(2)).

23 Directive 2006/112/EC art 6(1)(*c*).

24 According to the Court of Auditors, the French overseas departments ("DOM") are "an integral part of the Community, and are part of the customs territory of the Community, and all the customs rules of the Community apply": Special Report No 2/93 para 6.4. However, the DOM are not specifically referred to in Regulation (EEC) 2913/92, art 3(1).

25 The UK transferred possession of the island to Germany under an Anglo-German colonial agreement of 1 July 1890. The "duty free" status gained under this agreement has been acknowledged by EU law.

26 Directive 2006/112/EC art 6(2)(*a*).

27 Regulation (EEC) No 2193/92 art 3(1).

28 The Büsingen enclave is part of Germany although it is geographically situated in Switzerland. Arrangements for Büsingen were agreed under the Treaty of 23 November 1964 between Germany and Switzerland. Büsingen is part of Swiss customs territory.

29 Büsingen is part of German national territory.

30 Directive 2006/112/EC art 6(2)(*b*).

31 Regulation (EEC) No 2193/92 art 3(1).

32 Mount Athos is an administratively autonomous part of Greece. Since 1926 it has the status of a "Theocratic Republic" ruled by a Holy Community under the supervision of a Greek governor and a small Greek police force. All monks must adopt Greek citizenship. The special status of Mount Athos is guaranteed by art 105 of the Hellenic constitution and the Joint Declaration concerning Mount Athos annexed to the Act of Accession (1979). It is taken into account in applying EU law relating to, inter alia, customs franchise privileges and tax exemptions.

33 Directive 2006/112/EC art 6(1)(*a*).

34 Mount Athos forms part of the territory of Greece.

35 The Municipality of Livigno is situated at the most northern part of the province of Sondrio. It has a long border with Switzerland. Livigno has direct links to Switzerland through the Forcola di Livigno and the Passo del Gallo. Its only direct link with the rest of Italy is via the Passo del Foscag. History and geography have given rise to a privileged position under Italian customs law that is recognised by Community law.

36 Directive 2006/112/EC art 6(2)(*e*).

37 Regulation (EEC) No 2193/92 art 3(1).

38 The commune of Campione d'Italia is situated on the shore of Lago di Luga. It is completely surrounded by Swiss territory. It has an area of 2.6 sq km. On the basis of a modus vivendi agreement between Italy and Switzerland, it is regarded as part of Switzerland for customs purposes.

39 Directive 2006/112/EC art 6(2)(*f*).

40 Regulation (EEC) No 2193/92 art 3(1).

41 Directive 2006/112/EC art 6(2)(*g*).

42 Regulation (EEC) No 2193/92 art 3(1).

43 Madeira and the Azores are autonomous regions of Portugal.

44 Functioning Treaty art 355(1) (formerly EC Treaty art 299(2)). A joint declaration annexed to the Accession Treaty (1985) called upon the Community institutions to devote special attention to the development policies of the two archipelagos. On the setting up of a programme of options specific to the remote and insular nature of the two regions, see Decision 91/315/EEC (OJ L171/10, 29.6.91).

45 The preamble to Decision 91/315/EEC states that "the autonomous regions of the Azores and Maderia belong politically and economically to the Community by virtue of the Act of Accession". As such, they appear to be part of "the territory of the Portuguese Republic" for the purposes of Regulation (EEC) No 2193/92 art 3(1). Free zones are established in both territories: see the preamble to Regulation (EC) No 1482/97.

46 Ceuta is a city of some 20 square kilometres situated on the Mediterranean coast of Morocco. It is a Spanish territory governed as part of the province of Cadiz: see Murray, op cit, pp 78–80.

47 Melilla is a town of some 12 square kilometres situated on the Mediterranean coast of Morocco. It is a Spanish territory governed as part of the province of Malaga: see Murray, op cit, pp 78–80.

48 The founding treaties apply to Ceuta and Melilla subject to the derogations set out in Accession Treaty (1985) art 25 and Protocol No 2.

49 Directive 2006/112/EC art 6(2)(*c*), (*d*).

50 Accession Treaty (1985) Protocol No 2 art 1(3); Regulation (EEC) No 2193/92 art 3(1).

51 The Canary Islands form one of the 17 Autonomous Spanish Communities established by the 1978 Spanish Constitution: see Murray, op cit, p 20.

52 Functioning Treaty art 355(1) (formerly EC Treaty art 299(2)).

53 Directive 2006/112/EC art 6(1)(*b*).

54 Accession Treaty (1985) Protocol No 2 art 1(3) provides that the customs territory of the Community does not include the Canary Islands. However, the Council may, at Spain's request, decide to include the Canary Islands in the customs territory of the Community: Act of Accession (1985) art 25(4) (first para). Spain made such a request on 7 March 1990. Regulation (EEC) 1911/91 art 6 provides for the Common Customs Tariff to be progressively introduced during a transitional period ending on 31 December 2000. See also Regulation (EEC) No 2193/92 art 3(1), which does not make any specific provision regarding the Canary Islands.

55 The UK comprises England, Scotland and Wales (which together comprise "Great Britain") and Northern Ireland: see Interpretation Act 1978 ss 5, 22(1) and Sch 1. The Channel Islands and the

Isle of Man do not form part of the UK. For the position of these territories, see Table 2.

TABLE 2—TERRITORIES ASSOCIATED WITH MEMBER STATES

Country	*Founding treaties apply*	*VAT territory*[1]	*Customs territory*[2]
France			
• Overseas territories[3]	Partial[4]	No	No[5]
• Territorial collectivities[6]	Partial[7]	No	No[8]
Netherlands			
• Aruba and the Netherlands Antilles[9]	Partial[10]	No[11]	No[12]
United Kingdom			
• Channel Islands[13]	Partial[14]	No[15]	Yes[16]
• Isle of Man[17]	Partial[18]	Yes[19]	Yes[20]
• Gibraltar[21]	Partial[22]	No[23]	No[24]
• Sovereign Base Areas in Cyprus	Partial[25]	Yes[26]	Yes[27]
• Overseas territories[28]	Partial[29]	No	No

1 In the absence of express reference, the general provisions of the founding treaties do not apply to the overseas countries and territories to which Functioning Treaty Part Four (formerly EC Treaty Part Four) applies: see *Bernard Leplat v Territory of French Polynesia* (case C-260/90) [1992] ECR I–643 at [10]. Thus, negative answers are assumed in the absence of any specific provision.

2 In the absence of specific provisions, negative answers are assumed by virtue of the fact the territories do not form part of the territory of the member states concerned.

3 New Caledonia and Dependencies, Wallis and Futuna Islands, French Polynesia, and French Southern and Antarctic Territories.

4 The special arrangements for association set out in Part Four of the Functioning Treaty (formerly Part Four of the EC Treaty) apply: Functioning Treaty art 355(2) and Annex II (formerly EC Treaty art 299(3) and Annex II).

5 Regulation (EEC) No 2193/92 art 3(1).

6 Mayotte and St Pierre et Miquelon.

7 The special arrangements for association set out in Part Four of the Functioning Treaty (formerly Part Four of the EC Treaty) apply: Functioning Treaty art 355(2) and Annex II (formerly EC Treaty art 299(3) and Annex II).

8 Regulation (EEC) No 2193/92 art 3(1).

9 Bonaire, Curaçao, Sint Maarten, Saba, and Sint Eustatius.

10 The special arrangements for association set out in Part Four of the Functioning Treaty (formerly Part Four of the EC Treaty) apply: Functioning Treaty art 355(2) and Annex II (formerly EC Treaty art 299(3) and Annex II).

11 As regards goods entering the territory of a member state from the Netherlands Antilles, see *A J van der Kooy v Staatssecretaris van Financiën* (case C-181/97) [1999] ECR I–483.

12 Only the territory of the Netherlands "in Europe" forms part of the customs territory of the Community: see Regulation (EEC) 2193/92 art 3(1).

13 Comprising: (1) the Bailiwick of Jersey (including the islets and reefs of Les Minquiers and Les Ecrétios), and (2) the Bailiwick of Guernsey (including the island of Herm and the islets of Jethou and Lihou), Alderney and Sark. The Channel Islands are dependent territories of the British Crown. They were part of Normandy when William the Conqueror acquired the English Crown in 1066. They have an area of 194 sq km.

14 The founding treaties apply to the Channel Islands only to the extent necessary to ensure the implementation of the arrangements for them set out in the Accession Treaty (1972): see Functioning Treaty art 355(5)(c) (formerly EC Treaty art 299(6)(*c*)). For the arrangements

concerned, see Protocol No 3 to the Act of Accession (1972).

15 Directive 2006/112/EC art 6(1)(*e*).

16 The Act of Accession (1972) Protocol No 3 art 1 provides that Community rules on customs matters and quantitative restrictions apply to the Channel Islands. The Channel Islands are specifically included in the customs territory of the Community by Regulation (EEC) No 2193/92 art 3(1).

17 The Isle of Man is an independent territory of the Crown and is not part of the UK. However, the UK and the Isle of Man have been in customs union since 1765. For the current agreement, see Customs and Excise Agreement (1979) (Cmnd 7747).

18 The founding treaties apply to the Isle of Man only to the extent necessary to ensure the implementation of the arrangements set out in the Accession Treaty (1972): see Functioning Treaty art 355(5)(c) (formerly EC Treaty art 299(6)(*c*)). For the arrangements concerned, see Protocol No 3 to the Act of Accession (1972).

19 The Isle of Man is not treated as a third country for VAT purposes: see Directive 2006/112/EC art 7(1).

20 The Act of Accession (1972) Protocol No 3 art 1 provides that Community rules on customs matters and quantitative restrictions apply to the Isle of Man. The Isle of Man is specifically included in the customs territory of the Community by Regulation (EEC) No 2193/92 art 3(1).

21 Spain ceded Gibraltar to Britain under the Treaty of Utrecht 1713. It has had the status of a UK Crown colony since 1830.

22 The founding treaties apply because Gibraltar is a European territory for whose external affairs the UK is responsible: see Functioning Treaty art 355(3) (formerly EC Treaty art 299(4)). However, Community acts relating to agricultural policy and the harmonisation of turnover taxes do not apply: see Act of Accession (1972) art 28.

23 Acts of the institutions on the harmonisation of legislation of the Member States concerning turnover taxes do not apply to Gibraltar: see Act of Accession (1972) art 28. However, for the application of the mutual assistance provisions prior to 1 January 2004, see Directive 77/799/EEC; *Commission v United Kingdom* (case C-349/03) [2005] STC 1944. For administrative cooperation in relation to VAT from 1 January 2004, see Regulation (EC) No 1798/2003 as implemented by Regulation (EC) No 1925/2004.

24 As a Crown Colony, Gibraltar does not form part of "the territory of the United Kingdom of Great Britain and Northern Ireland" and, unlike the Channel Islands and the Isle of Man, it is not separately specified as part of the Community customs territory in Regulation (EEC) No 2913/92 art 3(1). According to the Court of Auditors, exclusion from the customs territory of the Community appears to conflict with Functioning Treaty art 355 (formerly EC Treaty art 299): see Special Report No 2/93 para 6.14.

25 The EC Treaty (now the Functioning Treaty) applies only to the extent necessary to ensure implementation of the arrangements set out in Protocol No 3 to the Act of Accession (2003): see Functioning Treaty art 355(5)(b) (formerly EC Treaty art 299(6)(*b*)).

26 The UK Sovereign Base Areas are not treated as a third country. Transactions originating in, or intended for, the UK Sovereign Base Areas are treated as transactions originating in, or intended for, the Republic of Cyprus: see Directive 2006/112/EC art 7(1).

27 The UK Sovereign Base Areas form part of the Community customs territory: see Regulation (EEC) No 2913/92 art 3(2)(*b*); Protocol No 3 art 2 to the Act of Accession (2003).

28 Anguilla, Cayman Islands, Falkland Islands, South Georgia and the Sandwich Islands, Montserrat, Pitcairn, Saint Helena and Dependencies, British Antarctica Territory, British Indian Ocean Territory, Turks and Caicos Islands, British Virgin Islands, and Bermuda.

29 The special arrangements for association set out in Part Four of the Functioning Treaty (formerly Part Four of the EC Treaty) apply: see Functioning Treaty art 355(2) and Annex II (formerly EC Treaty art 299(3) and Annex II). The founding treaties do not apply to other overseas countries and territories having special relations with the UK: see Functioning Treaty art 355(2) (now EC Treaty art 299(3)).

TABLE 3—ANDORRA, MONACO, SAN MARINO AND THE VATICAN

Andorra[1], Monaco[2], San Marino[3] and the Vatican are sovereign states. They are not member states of the Community.

As regards VAT, Monaco is not treated as a third country. Transactions originating in or intended for Monaco are treated as transactions originating in or intended for France.[4]

As regards customs duties:

(1) Andorra does not form part of the customs territory of the Community. However, an agreement for a customs union between Andorra and the Community has been in operation since 1 July 1991.[5]

(2) Monaco is considered to be part of the customs territory of the Community.[6]

(3) San Marino does not form part of the customs territory of the Community. However, an agreement for a customs union between San Marino and the Community has been in operation since 1 December 1992.[7]

(4) The Vatican is not part of the customs territory of the Community. Customs status is governed by the Italian-Vatican customs agreement of 30 June 1930, which came into force on 1 August 1931.[8]

---

1 The fief of Andorra is an independent principality dating from 1278. It is situated in the Pyrenees and has landlocked boundaries with France and Spain. It has an area of 495 sq km.

2 The Principality of Monaco is not part of the Community. For a history of the Principality, see www.monaco-consulate.com/about_history.htm.

3 San Marino is an independent republic dating back to the twelfth century. It is situated in the Apennines. It has an area of 61 sq km. It is not part of the Community.

4 Directive 2006/112/EC art 7(1).

5 See Decision 90/680/EEC of 26 November 1990 on the conclusion of an agreement in the form of an exchange of letters between the parties (OJ L374/13, 31.12.90). For mutual assistance in the recovery of duties, see EC-Andorra Joint Committee Decision No 1/2003, Title 1 Chapter 2 and Annex 1.

6 Regulation (EEC) 2913/92 art 3(2). The legal basis for this position is the customs convention of 18 May 1963 between France and Monaco.

7 See Decision 92/561/EEC of 27 November 1992 on the conclusion of an interim agreement between the parties (OJ L359, 9.12.92). This agreement was replaced from 1 April 2002 by the Agreement on Cooperation and Customs Union (see OJ L84/43, 28.3.02). For implementing measures, see "Omnibus" Decision No 1/2010 of the EU-San Marino Cooperation Committee (OJ L156/13, 23.6.10). San Marino was originally treated as part of the customs territory of the Community: see Regulation (EEC) No 2151/84 art 2 and Annex, point 3 (repealed). The legal basis for this position was the customs union between San Marino and Italy established by a Convention of 31 March 1939 under which San Marino became part of the Italian customs territory. San Marino is not mentioned in Regulation (EEC) No 2913/92 art 3.

8 For information regarding the arrangements, see the Court of Auditors Special Report 2/93 paras 6.19–6.23.

Part II Stamp Taxes

Contents

1. Statutes

[*NB 1* Following a lengthy consultation process, which started with the publication in April 2002 of a consultation document entitled "Modernising Stamp Duty on Land and Buildings in the UK", FA 2003:

(1) introduced a new tax called "stamp duty land tax" for land transactions (FA 1993 s 42); and

(2) abolished stamp duty on all property other than stock and marketable securities in relation to instruments effecting transactions where executed on or after 1 December 2003 (FA 2003 s 125(5)(*b*) and Sch 19 para 2(2)(*b*)). However, it remains necessary to include the earlier stamp duty legislation in this volume (even where it appears to relate only to transactions in land) because of the potential application of those provisions in cases where, under the transitional rules, the completion of a contract entered into before 11 July 2003 would still be subject to stamp duty and not to SDLT.]

[*NB 2* In relation to the proposed abolitions of all stamp duty charges on transactions in shares, bearer instruments and units under trust schemes and of stamp duty reserve tax, see Revenue Press Releases of 20 March 1990, 19 March 1991 and 19 December 1991, and the commentary on FA 1990 and FA 1991. Following the decision by the Stock Exchange in March 1993 to abandon "TAURUS", the system for paperless trading, the Chancellor of the Exchequer announced in the March 1993 Budget Speech that stamp duty on securities and property other than land and buildings would remain, at least for 1993–94. In the absence of any reference to the proposed abolitions of charges in or at the time of the Revenue Press Release of 28 November 1995 announcing stamp duty and stamp duty reserve tax amendments on the introduction of "CREST" (the replacement for "TAURUS"), it would appear that the proposed abolitions have been shelved for the foreseeable future. However, a number of recent statutes, up to and including FA 2002, contain prospective repeals of some of their own provisions, effective from the "abolition date".]

Contents

Finance Act 1971
Finance Act 1973
Friendly Societies Act 1974
Finance Act 1976
Finance Act 1980
Finance Act 1981
British Telecommunications Act 1981
Finance Act 1982
Finance Act 1983
Finance (No 2) Act 1983
Finance Act 1984
Finance Act 1985
Finance Act 1986
Insolvency Act 1986
Building Societies Act 1986
Finance Act 1987
Finance Act 1988
Finance Act 1989
Electricity Act 1989
Property Services Agency and Crown Suppliers Act 1990
National Health Service and Community Care Act 1990
Finance Act 1990
Finance Act 1991
Stamp Duty (Temporary Provisions) Act 1992
Social Security Administration Act 1992
Further and Higher Education Act 1992
Parliamentary Corporate Bodies Act 1992
Friendly Societies Act 1992
Museums and Galleries Act 1992
Finance (No 2) Act 1992
Finance Act 1993
Education Act 1993
Finance Act 1994
Coal Industry Act 1994
Finance Act 1995
Health Authorities Act 1995
Merchant Shipping Act 1995
Environment Act 1995
Atomic Energy Authority Act 1995
Finance Act 1996
Finance Act 1997
Finance Act 1999
Limited Liability Partnerships Act 2000
Finance Act 2000
Transport Act 2000
Finance Act 2001
Finance Act 2002
Finance Act 2003
Finance Act 2004
Finance Act 2007
Finance Act 2008
Finance Act 2009

Pensions and Yeomanry Pay Act 1884

47 & 48 Vict c 55

Exemption from stamp duty

5. (See the notes printed at the end of the contents list to Part II Stamp Taxes.)

This provision was extended to the Air Force (SR & O 1918/548) and was amended by FA 1949 s 52 and Sch 11 Pt V, and by FA 1970 s 36 (8) and Sch 8 Pt IV.

Stamp Duties Management Act 1891

54 & 55 Vict c 38

Note: *A number of provisions are repealed by FA 1999, with effect from 1 October 1999. These repeals are made either on the basis that the provisions were obsolete or that they relate to administrative fines, which were themselves abolished by FA 1999 and replaced by penalties under a regime now mainly set out in FA 1999 Sch 17. See commentary on that Schedule for the new system and see earlier editions of this work in relation to the provisions which have now been repealed.*

APPLICATION OF ACT

Act to apply to all stamp duties

1. (See the notes printed at the end of the contents list to Part II Stamp Taxes.)

Responsibility is conferred on the Commissioners of Inland Revenue (the Commissioners) for administrating the collection of all fees and duties which as a matter of law are chargeable as stamp duties, ie which are collected or received by means of adhesive or impressed stamps, which may include, for example, the payment of Class 2 or Class 3 national insurance contributions (which may be by means of adhesive stamps if the Secretary of State so provides pursuant to the Social Security Act 1975 Sch 1 para 6 (2) and (3)).

Certain provisions of the Acts also apply to national savings stamps (by virtue of the National Savings Stamps Regulations 1969, SI 1969/1343), savings certificates (see the Savings Certificates Regulations, SI 1972/641) and to national savings stocks (see the National Savings Stock Register Regulations 1976, SI 1976/2012).

The Inland Revenue Regulation Act 1890 sets out the general powers of the Commissioners of Inland Revenue with regard to the relevant duties.

Since 1974, the administration of stamp duty payable in Northern Ireland has also been the responsibility of the Commissioners of Inland Revenue in the United Kingdom (see the Northern Ireland Constitution Act 1973, and the Northern Ireland (Modification of Enactments—No 1) Order 1973, SI 1973/2163, made thereunder). The Stamp Office in Belfast continues in full operation under the functional control of the Stamp Office in London.

MODE OF RECOVERING MONEY RECEIVED FOR DUTY

Moneys received for duty and not appropriated to be recoverable in High Court

2. (See the notes printed at the end of the contents list to Part II Stamp Taxes.)

The Commissioners are able to recover from any person who has received any sum of money in respect of stamp duty payable to the Commissioners that sum of money if it is improperly withheld or detained by that person. It should be noted that, whilst an amount of actual stamp duty is almost invariably a "voluntary" payment which is not enforceable by legal process, an amount which is improperly detained in the circumstances described under this section is treated as a "debt" and is "recoverable as such"—ie by legal proceedings on the part of the Commissioners.

The legislation originally prescribed a writ of summons as the means of enforcing the Commissioners' claim but this procedure had become obsolete and that part of the section has been repealed by FA 1999 with effect from 1 October 1999. Proceedings are taken in the High Court by originating motion or originating summons.

Under the Crown Proceedings Act 1947 s 14 (1), the Commissioners can now take summary proceedings to recover money withheld.

In the case of *Lord Advocate v Gordon* (1901) 8 SLT 439, it was held that a solicitor was accountable to the Crown under s 2 (1) when he deducted, from moneys payable to a client, an amount for stamp duty and subsequently withheld payment to the Revenue for more than three years.

Compliance with any order of the Court may be enforced by attachment (see *Re Coulson* (1894), cited in *Highmore's Stamp Laws* (4th edn), p 17 and *Halsbury's Laws of England* (4th edn), Vol 44 para 605 note 3).

ALLOWANCE FOR SPOILED STAMPS

9. Procedure for obtaining allowance

(See the notes printed at the end of the contents list to Part II Stamp Taxes.)

Subject to certain conditions, stamp duty can be recovered where it is paid on an instrument which is ineffective or useless, so that the duty would be wasted. Examples include cases where an instrument is prepared on stamped paper and never used, or where errors are made in preparing an instrument so that it cannot be used, or where an instrument turns out to be completely void. Application must be made within two years of the fixing of the stamp and it can only be made in a fairly restricted class of cases, for example where the instrument is void ab initio or is never executed by a required party, or is inadvertently spoiled. The duty cannot be recovered in cases where an instrument fails through non-fulfilment of a condition precedent, or where a voidable instrument is avoided or rescinded by some party entitled to do so. It is also not possible to recover the duty where legal proceedings have been commenced in which the instrument would or could have been given in evidence. By contrast, what was formerly SA 1891 s 59 (now FA 1999 Sch 13 Part I para 7) contained a much less restrictive provision in relation to the stamp duty charged under that paragraph on certain contracts which are chargeable as conveyances on sale. Under what was formerly s 59 (6), and is now FA 1999 Sch 13 Part I para 9, if the contracts is rescinded or annulled or not substantially performed, then any ad valorem duty paid to the Commissioners must be returned (now with interest, following the enactment of FA 1999 s 98). The para 9 procedure has the additional advantages that, first, there is no time limit for reclaiming duty and, secondly, there is no requirement that the instrument in question shall not have been admitted or admissible in evidence.

The Stamp Office might, of course, be prepared to make ex gratia repayments of duty outside the strict time limits in certain situations. They have recently indicated their willingness to do this in relation to what they now seem to accept as overpayments of duty on lease rentals where the Stamp Office has misapplied the decision in *LM Tenancies 1 plc v IRC* [1998] STC 326 in calculating the duty. See commentary on FA 1999 Sch 13 Part II and the article by Patrick Cannon in the *Tax Journal* dated 7 June 1999.

By virtue of the provisions of FA 1966 s 46 (4), any reference in s 9, and in s 10, to any stamp is deemed to include (unless the context otherwise requires) a reference to any indication of the payment and the amount of stamp duty referred to in FA 1966 s 46 (1) (*b*).

Allowances for spoiled stamps are made by the issue of fresh stamps in lieu, by a cash payment or by the issue of a payable order as arranged at the time the claim is made. A cash refund will only be made where the amount of the claim does not exceed £20. It is a condition precedent to allowances being made that the spoiled instrument be surrendered for destruction, and only in very exceptional circumstances will this condition be waived.

Furthermore, spoiled instruments must be presented in a complete state without mutilation—no allowances will be made where stamps have been removed from documents. Claims have to be made in writing by the owner of the stamps (ie the person for whose use and business they were purchased) or by his agent or employee authorised by him in writing. Claims are made on Form 52 (Stamps).

For other provisions in relation to the repayment of stamp duty, see FA 1965 s 90 (2) and (5). As to lost or spoiled instruments see SDMA 1891 s 12A.

10. Allowance for misused stamps

(See the notes printed at the end of the contents list to Part II Stamp Taxes.)

The Commissioners are empowered to treat as spoiled any stamp used which was of greater value than required or was inadvertently used on an instrument not liable to any duty, provided that application is made within two years after the date of the instrument (or, if it is not dated, within two years after execution) and the instrument, if liable for duty, is stamped with the proper duty.

11. Allowance how to be made

(See the notes printed at the end of the contents list to Part II Stamp Taxes.)

The Commissioners may make allowances for spoiled or misused stamps by giving other stamps in lieu or, at their discretion, stamps of any other denomination to the same amount in value, or cash.

12A. Lost or spoiled instruments

(See the notes printed at the end of the contents list to Part II Stamp Taxes.)

Where a duly stamped instrument has been accidentally lost or spoiled a replica may be executed and stamped free of charge. This relief is available on application to the Commissioners (in the case of a spoiled instrument within two years after the execution of the spoiled instrument). No relief is available where legal proceedings have been commenced in which the instrument has been or could or would have been given in evidence. This section enacts Extra-statutory concessions G1, G2 which previously covered this situation.

OFFENCES RELATING TO STAMPS

13. Offences in relation to dies and stamps

(See the notes printed at the end of the contents list to Part II Stamp Taxes.)

As the Forgery Act 1913 did not extend to Scotland, the repeals made by that Act of the words in s 13 (1) ("forges a die or stamp") s 13 (2) ("prints or makes an impression upon any material with a forged die") s 13 (8) ("any forged stamp, or") and s 13 (9) ("any forged die or stamp or") do not apply as regards Scotland and the words are still in force there.

By virtue of the Post Office Act 1969 s 118, this section also applies to offences in relation to postage stamps.

The wording of this section was modernised by FA 1999 so as to remove any references to the now redundant distinction between felonies and misdemeanours, and also to replace references to penal servitude and hard labour with references to terms of imprisonment. The maximum prison sentence has been reduced from 14 years to 10 years.

For the purposes of this section, the expression "forged stamp" is deemed to include a stamp bearing a cancellation mark as well as an unused stamp (see *R v Lowden* [1914] 1 KB 144). Lack of knowledge that a stamp was forged has been held not to be a lawful excuse for possession unless the stamp was acquired lawfully, eg at a post office (see *Winkle v Wiltshire* [1951] 1 KB 684, a decision on the interpretation of the Post Office Act 1953 s 63 (1) (*b*)). It has also been held that a die for making a false stamp which was in the defendant's possession for a purely innocent purpose was still possession without lawful excuse within the meaning of the Post Office (Protection) Act 1884 s 7 (*c*), the provision repealed and replaced by the Post Office Act 1953 s 63 (1) (*b*) (see *Dickins v Gill* [1896] 2 QB 310).

21. Penalty for frauds in relation to duties

(See the notes printed at the end of the contents list to Part II Stamp Taxes.)

Any person who commits an act with intent to defraud the Government is liable to a penalty not exceeding £3,000.

MISCELLANEOUS

22. As to discontinuance of dies

(See the notes printed at the end of the contents list to Part II Stamp Taxes.)

The Commissioners can discontinue the use of any die used for the impression of stamps and replace it with a new die, and the change takes effect on the day specified in public notices to be given in the London, Edinburgh, Dublin and (by virtue of the Government of Ireland (Adaptation of the Taxing Acts) Order 1922 Pt IV para 17 (*d*) (SR & O 1922/80)) Belfast Gazettes. Any instrument first executed by any person after that date, or dated after that date, and stamped with a discontinued die will be deemed not to be properly stamped, except as provided in sub-paragraphs (*a*) and (*b*). Sub-paragraph (*a*) relates to instruments executed outside the UK and provides that any such instrument which is stamped with a discontinued die can be produced to the Commissioners within 14 days of its arrival in the UK for the discontinued stamp to be cancelled and the instrument to be stamped with the new die. Sub-paragraph (*b*) allows any person in the possession of an instrument rendered useless by virtue of the fact that it has been stamped with a discontinued die to produce it to the Commissioners within six months of the adoption of the new die to enable the old stamp to be cancelled and the instrument to be stamped with the new die.

23. Application of Act to excise labels

(See the notes printed at the end of the contents list to Part II Stamp Taxes.)

The provisions in relation to offences in connection with stamps apply to labels used for the purposes of excise duties.

24. Declarations, how to be made

(See the notes printed at the end of the contents list to Part II Stamp Taxes.)

Any statutory declaration required for the purposes of the Act is to be made before the Commissioners themselves, or any person authorised by them, or before any Commissioner for Oaths, Justice of the Peace or Notary Public in the United Kingdom, or in any place outside the United Kingdom before any person duly authorised to administer oaths there.

This section also applies to affidavits and oaths (Revenue Act 1898 s 7 (6)). See also the Solicitors Act 1974 s 81, whereby solicitors are generally empowered to administer oaths. Similarly, see also the Solicitors (Northern Ireland) Order 1976 art 78.

REPEAL, SHORT TITLE

30. Short title

Stamp Act 1891

54 & 55 Vict c 39

Note: *The main charging provisions which were formerly contained in this Act have been transferred to FA 1999 Schs 13 and 15. Reference should now be made to the commentary on FA 1999 s 112 for the principal discussion on the scope and nature of the charges to stamp duty. It should also be noted that, in principle, there was only one charging provision under the old rules (namely, SA 1891 s 1) and that instruments then fell to be charged under various "heads of charge", as set out in SA 1891 Sch 1. There is something of a conceptual shift in the drafting of the FA 1999 Sch 13 provisions, since the various types of stampable instrument are each now governed by separate, and apparently free-standing, charging provisions. Since all the charges are set out in Schedules, the new charging provisions are, strictly speaking, FA 1999 ss 112 and 113. However, rather than expressly imposing any charge to duty, those sections simply state that Schs 13 and 15 "have effect". See also the notes printed at the end of the contents list to Part II Stamp Taxes*

PART 1 REGULATIONS APPLICABLE TO INSTRUMENTS GENERALLY

CHARGE OF DUTY UPON INSTRUMENTS

2. All duties to be paid according to regulations of Act

(See the notes printed at the end of the contents list to Part II Stamp Taxes.)

As regards the words "except where express provision is made to the contrary", provision was in fact made to the contrary in several cases, but the instruments concerned have now all been removed from the charge to duty.

3. How instruments are to be written and stamped

(See the notes printed at the end of the contents list to Part II Stamp Taxes.)

The application of this section was reviewed in *Prudential Assurance Co Ltd v IR Comrs* [1935] 1 KB 101, which held that it applied to enable a memorandum endorsed on a life insurance policy, increasing the sum assured, to be regarded as a separate policy stampable ad valorem on the amount of the increase. See now FA 1989, in relation to the abolition of life insurance policy duty.

This section does not apply in relation to any bearer instrument issued on or after 9 December 1987 which represents shares in the UK company or the foreign company transferable only as part of paired-share units, or rights to allotment of or subscription for such shares; see FA 1988 s 143 (1).

4. Instruments to be separately charged with duty in certain cases

(See the notes printed at the end of the contents list to Part II Stamp Taxes.)

Subsection (a)

Following the case of *Limmer Asphalte Paving Co v IR Comrs* (1872) LR 7 Exch 211, it has been a well settled principle in relation to stamp duty that an instrument is only stampable for its leading and principal object, and that the relevant stamp covers everything accessory to that object. The corollary to this is that an instrument which is exempt from duty by reason of its leading and principal object will not be rendered liable to duty by any provision which is merely accessory to that object. Thus, historically, only one stamp was payable on the conveyance of land on sale, and no further duty was payable because the conveyance contained covenants on the part of the vendor. Similarly, the ad valorem duty chargeable on

Part II ST

a lease would normally have covered a provision contained in the lease guaranteeing the rent. The difficulty lies in determining what is the leading and principal object and what is merely ancillary. In *General Accident Assurance Corpn v IR Comrs* (1906) 8 F (Ct of Sess) 477, a leading Scottish case, Lord President Dunedin stated (at p 482) "I cannot think of any better test than to take the second so-called contract and see if it would stand alone; and that is to say, to use the current expression, whether it would stand on its own feet".

The general principle applies where there is only one leading and principal object of an instrument, and one or more ancillary matters. It does not apply where an instrument relates to several distinct matters each of which is separately chargeable to stamp duty, as if contained in a separate instrument pursuant to s 4 (*a*). The difficulty in construing s 4 (*a*) lies in the definition of the word "matters". Arguably, the "matters" referred to are the various heads of charge listed in Sch 1 (see *Reversionary Interest Society Ltd v IR Comrs* (1906) 22 TLR 740). The distinction between one matter and several is not, however, easy to draw. See the examples of separate stamps being required, and of separate stamps not being required, cited in the notes to SA 1891 s 4 in *Sergeant and Sims on Stamp Duties*.

Where several parties join in one instrument to effect the same transaction, it has been held that only a single stamp is payable where there is a community of interest between the parties, or the transactions are effected with a common purpose. See for example *Allen v Morrison* (1828) 8 B&C 565 (a case involving a power of attorney executed by all the members of a mutual insurance club authorising named persons to sign the club policies). However, if the conditions relating to community of interest or common purpose are not satisfied, two duties must be paid. For example, where executors used one instrument to convey assets, part of residue, to four residuary legatees, it was held that four stamps could be levied (*Freeman v IR Comrs* (1871) LR 6 Ex 101).

Where an instrument effects two transactions between different parties separate stamps will clearly be required.

Subsection (b)

The type of situation where this subsection used to apply was where, for example, a lease (of land, rather than moveable assets) provided both for an ascertainable rent and also an unascertainable fixed royalty. In such case, the lease would formerly have been charged to ad valorem duty on the fixed rent and to the fixed duty of £2 (as the relevant duty was before all fixed duties became £5, as a result of the changes in FA 1999) in respect of the unascertainable royalty.

A historical example of this section in operation is to be found in *Hadgett v IRC* (1877) 3 Ex D 46 (which was actually decided under a similar provision in the Stamp Act 1870). It is important to remember that this kind of situation can still arise in principle although it is less likely to do so in practice now that the stamp duty legislation no longer consists of numerous separate "heads of charge".

In the *Hadgett* case, an instrument was held to have been properly charged to two different duties as both an instrument of appointment of new trustees (which no longer attracts a charge, as such) and what is now chargeable under FA 1999 Sch 13 Part III para 1 as a "conveyance or transfer otherwise than on sale". One of the two charging provisions in issue in the *Hadgett* case stated that the charge to duty was not to exceed 10 shillings in the case of an instrument of appointment of a new trustee and yet the court held that the instrument had been properly adjudicated to both that charge and a further charge to another 10 shillings as a "conveyance". This was because, purely in its capacity as an appointment of a trustee, the instrument had *not* been charged to more than 10 shillings and the fact that the instrument also vested property in that trustee was a quite separate matter, justifying a further charge to duty.

It should be understood that when FA 1971 abolished stamp duty charges on mortgages, debentures and certain other debt instruments, the provision abolishing the specific heads of charge for such instruments specifically stated that such instruments were not to be charged with duty under any other heads of charge in what was then SA 1891 Sch 1 (now recast as FA 1999 Schs 13 and 15). However, the abolition provisions also contained a specific saving in respect of s 4 so that any document embodying any exempt mortgage, debenture, etc is exempt from all stamp duties but *only* in its character as such an exempt mortgage, debenture, etc. The instrument itself remains stampable to the extent that it could be stamped on any other basis (ie if it has any other or further character beyond that of an exempt debt instrument; for example, if it were also a "conveyance on sale" of something other than the exempt mortgage, debenture, etc).

5. Facts and circumstances affecting duty to be set forth in instruments

(See the notes printed at the end of the contents list to Part II Stamp Taxes.)

Any person who submits an instrument for stamping may be required by the Commissioners to provide such evidence as they may consider necessary to show that the facts and circumstances affecting the amount of duty are "fully and truly set forth" in the instrument (see eg *R v IR Comrs, ex parte Evill* [1951] 2 TLR 857). However, no penalty will be payable as long as the full facts are disclosed at the time of stamping, whether in the document itself or by another means, eg a covering letter. See also s 12 (2) and s 14 (4) where the implications of *Parinv (Hatfield) Ltd v IR Comrs* [1996] STC 933 are discussed. Following the *Parinv* case [1998] STC 305 (CA), the Revenue stated that they regard a failure to declare that a party is seeking to rely upon an unstamped document, held offshore, as a breach of s 5.

Note that, because of the Revenue view (see Press Releases of 22 July and 12 September 1991 and SP 11/91) with regard to the interaction between stamp duty and the VAT payable in respect of commercial buildings (discussed in relation to ss 55, 56 and what is now FA 1999 Sch 13 Part III para 5, and the "Lease" head of charge in what is now FA 1999 Sch 13 Part II), supported by the decision in *Glenrothes Development Corporation v IR Comrs* [1994] STC 74, it would be unwise in the light of s 5 to omit from the face of a document submitted for stamping a reference to any VAT that is payable on the consideration expressed in the document.

Reference should also be made to any VAT which *might* be payable and to the circumstances giving rise to this possibility, such as the fact that rent under a lease could be increased if currently exempt land were ever subsequently "opted" (see commentary on what is now FA 1999 Sch 13 Part II) or that a particular transaction is thought to qualify as a "transfer of a business as a going concern" for VAT purposes (see commentary on what is now FA 1999 Sch 13 Part I).

A failure to comply with s 5 does not lead to the document being a nullity (see *Nisbet v Shepherd* [1994] 1 BCLC 300 and, obiter, in *Re Brown & Root McDermott Fabricators Limited's Application* [1996] STC 483).

6. Mode of calculating ad valorem duty in certain cases

(See the notes printed at the end of the contents list to Part II Stamp Taxes.)

This section provides a method of calculating ad valorem duty in cases where the consideration consists of stock or securities, or foreign or colonial currency. The duty is calculated on the value, on the date of the instrument, of the money in British currency according to the rate of exchange prevailing on that date, or of the stock or security according to the average price thereof (when there is one).

The Board adopts the CGT basis for valuing shares and securities listed on The Stock Exchange for the purposes of stamp duty, in accordance with the provisions of TCGA 1992 s 272 (ie the lower of one quarter of the difference between the lower and higher closing prices added to the lower price (one quarter up) or mid-way between the highest and lowest prices at which the bargains were marked). When no average price can be quoted, by reason of there having been no dealings at the relevant date of the stock or marketable security, reasonable evidence of value must be furnished. For valuation of shares generally, and in particular valuation of shares in private companies.

In *Crane Fruehauf Ltd v IR Comrs* [1975] 1 All ER 429, CA, it was held that "the date of the instrument", being an instrument of transfer signed under hand conditionally on the issue of the consideration shares, was the date on which the condition was satisfied so that the consideration shares fell to be valued at that date. For the rules relating to the date of a deed, see the commentary on SA 1891 s 122(1A).

USE OF ADHESIVE STAMPS

9. Penalty for frauds in relation to adhesive stamps

(See the notes printed at the end of the contents list to Part II Stamp Taxes.)

Any person who fraudulently removes or causes to be removed an adhesive stamp from any instrument, or uses that stamp again for any purpose, or sells it or offers it for sale, or alters any other instrument with that stamp affixed (knowing it to have been removed from the original instrument), is liable to a penalty not exceeding £3,000.

The expression "instrument" in this section has been extended to include postal packets within the meaning of the Post Office Protection Act 1884 (see the Revenue Act 1898 s 7) and the expression "stamp" has been extended to insurance stamps (see the Social Security Contributions and Benefits Act 1992 Sch 1 para 8 (3)).

APPROPRIATED STAMPS AND DENOTING STAMPS

11. Denoting stamps

(See the notes printed at the end of the contents list to Part II Stamp Taxes.)

Denoting stamps are most commonly used:

(a) on duplicates or counterparts of stamped instruments (in relation to which the Revenue issued a notice concerning the use of denoting stamps in the *Law Society's Gazette*, 7 July 1976 p 564);

(b) on conveyances on sale following contracts of sale bearing ad valorem duty under what is now FA 1999 Sch 13 Part I paras 7 and 8;

(c) on conveyances, transfers, leases or tacks where there is a conveyance or transfer of land subject to an agreement for a lease for a term exceeding 35 years or a grant of a lease or tack subject to such a term, the ad valorem duty having been paid on the agreement or lease under FA 1984 s 111 (1); and

(d) on substituted bearer instruments.

A denoting stamp is not a guarantee that the stamp denoted on the original instrument is sufficient. Such guarantee can be obtained only by the process of adjudication under the provisions of s 12.

Where a document is required to be denoted under s 11, the Board normally requires the original of the principal document, on which the ad valorem duty was paid, to be produced to them for that purpose, except where the original is filed with the Land Registry (in which case a Land Registry Office copy will be accepted for denoting purposes—provided the amount of duty paid is clear from the copy).

ADJUDICATION STAMPS

12. Assessment of duty by Commissioners

(See the notes printed at the end of the contents list to Part II Stamp Taxes.)

The Commissioners may be required, by any person, to express their opinion as to whether an executed instrument is chargeable with any duty, and if so the amount of duty. In the new version of this section (inserted by FA 1999) the Commissioners may also be required to state whether any penalty (and, if so, what) is payable in respect of late stamping. When required to make an adjudication, the Commissioners are entitled to require such information to be provided to them as they consider necessary to enable them to make an assessment—*R v IR Comrs ex parte Evill* [1951] 2 TLR 857).

The wording of subs (2) has changed somewhat in the new version of this section although no change of substance appears to have been introduced as a result. It seems that the Stamp Office sometimes tried to use that subsection as a means of obtaining possession of other stampable documents in order to levy duty on those further documents. However, it was strongly arguable in relation to the old wording—and it appears at least equally strongly arguable in relation to the new wording introduced by the FA 1999 amendments—that the purpose of the provision was confined to that of enabling the Stamp Office to ensure that it had in its custody all information relevant to the calculation of duty on the document submitted for adjudication. It may well be that the Stamp Office is abusing its powers if it rejects secondary evidence of facts and circumstances merely so as to force a party to submit alternative evidence in the form of documents which are themselves stampable.

It should be noted that the opinion of the Commissioners can only be "required" to express their opinion in relation to an "executed instrument", so that the Stamp Office cannot be compelled to give a ruling in advance upon a draft instrument or upon a preliminary description of a proposed instrument. The decision in *R v IRC, ex parte Bishopp* [1999] STC 531 suggests that the courts would not readily support any attempt by a taxpayer to force the Revenue to carry their administrative functions in a way which involved the answering of hypothetical questions or the giving of advance rulings on tax matters in circumstances where Parliament has not provided a specific mechanism enabling or requiring the Revenue to do this.

The procedure on application for adjudication of stamp duty varies somewhat between England and Wales, Scotland and Northern Ireland. For a detailed description of the procedure, together with a description of the information required with certain classes of application, and copies of relevant forms, see Division F of *Sergeant and Sims on Stamp Duties*.

Adjudication is obligatory for certain claims to exemption from stamp duty. It must be appreciated that transactions falling within most of the categories set out below have ceased to be subject to stamp duty, either because the relevant transactions are now outside the scope of stamp tax altogether or because the relevant tax is now SDLT rather than stamp duty. However, if a late claim is to be made for exemption in relation to an instrument executed but not adjudicated at the relevant time, the obligation to adjudication remains:

(a) in the case of conveyances claimed to be exempt from duty under the provisions of FA 1930 s 42, relating to certain transfers from one associated body corporate to another and FA 1995 s 151, relating to certain leases and agreements for lease or letting between associated bodies corporate;

(b) in the case of conveyances or transfers where property is conveyed or transferred to any person in contemplation of a sale of that property under FA 1965 s 90 (3);

(c) in claims for exemption for maintenance and funds for historic buildings under FA 1980 s 98;

(d) for relief on conveyances in consideration of a debt under FA 1980 s 102;

(e) in claims for exemption for conveyances, transfers and leases to charities (FA 1982 s 129);

(f) in claims for exemption for instruments executed for the purposes of or in connection with acquisitions of the whole or any part of a company's undertaking or share capital, pursuant to FA 1986 ss 75, 76 or 77;

(g) in claims for exemption for instruments executed in connection with mergers of authorised unit trusts pursuant to FA 1997 s 95;

(h) in claims for exemption for instruments executed in connection with demutualisation of an insurance company pursuant to FA 1997 s 96;

(i) in claims for exemption for sales of stock to intermediaries pursuant to FA 1986 s 80A;

(j) in claims for exemption for arrangements involving stock lending in accordance with FA 1986 s 80C;
(k) in claims for exemption for the instrument transferring property on the conversion of an authorised unit trust to an open ended investment company (OEIC) in the circumstances described in the Stamp Duty and SDRT (OEIC) Regulations 1997, SI 1997/1156, reg 7;
(l) in claims for exemption for the instrument transferring property on the amalgamation of an authorised unit trust with an OEIC in the circumstances described in the Stamp Duty and SDRT (OEIC) Regulations 1997, SI 1997/1156, reg 9; and
(m) in claims for exemption for an instrument transferring property to a newly-formed limited liability partnership in accordance with the Limited Liability Partnership Act 2001 s 12.

Adjudication was formerly required:
(i) under FA 1985 s 82 (5), in respect of any conveyance or transfer operating as a voluntary disposition inter vivos, within the meaning of F(1909–10)A 1910 s 74, provided that it did not attract stamp duty under what was then the "conveyance or transfer on sale" head of charge in SA 1891 Sch 1; and
(ii) under FA 1985 s 84, in respect of certain variations made in dispositions out of the estate of a deceased person by the persons who benefit or would benefit under the dispositions, and in respect of certain appropriations made by the personal representatives of a deceased person to satisfy dispositions out of his or her estate.

By virtue of the Stamp Duty (Exempt Instruments) Regulations 1987, made pursuant to FA 1985 s 87 (2), adjudication is no longer a requirement in respect of such instruments: they will be deemed to be duly stamped if certified in the manner specified in the Regulations. However, whilst adjudication is no longer a requirement, it may still be sought under SA 1891 s 12 and in view of the complexity of the law, particularly in relation to voluntary dispositions inter vivos, parties who are unwilling to give the certificate envisaged by the Regulations may nevertheless still prefer to seek adjudication. See further the commentaries on FA 1985 ss 82, 84 and 87.

Except as mentioned below, adjudication stamps are conclusive and preclude any question raised as to the sufficiency of the stamp. Adjudication will not, however, prejudice rights that have already been asserted and relied on before adjudication (*Marx v Estates and General Investments Ltd* [1975] 3 All ER 1064).

Adjudication will not conclusively render a document duly stamped:
(a) in the case of a transfer on sale of the fee simple of land, or the grant of a lease of land for a term of seven years or more, or a transfer on sale of any such lease, where the relevant document does not also bear a "produced stamp" under FA 1931 s 28 and Sch 2;
(b) where a single document is chargeable in respect of several distinct matters, and therefore requires more than one stamp under s 4, but it has only been adjudicated in respect of one or some of those matters;
(c) where a bearer instrument to which what is now FA 1999 Sch 15 para 1 applies does not also bear a "denoting stamp" under what is now FA 1999 Sch 15 para 21 (2) (*b*); or
(d) where the adjudication was obtained by misrepresentation or without a full disclosure of all material facts.

Court orders, etc

It should be noted that the definition of "transfer on sale", in what is now FA 1999 Sch 13 Part I para 1, specifically states that the concept of "transfer on sale" extends, for stamp duty purposes, to court orders which transfer or vest property to or in a person.

As regards orders made under the CA 2006 s 900, the solicitors having the conduct of the proceedings will be required, on the settling of the order, to give a written undertaking to the court to submit the order (or a duplicate thereof) for the assessment of stamp duty under SA

1891 ss 12 and 13, and to pay the duty so assessed. Similarly, office copies of orders involving schemes of arrangement cannot be lodged at the Companies Registry as required by the CA 2006 s 900 without their having first been seen by HMRC, which has to determine the stamp duty position before the matter can be dealt with at the Companies Registry. In *Sun Alliance Insurance Ltd v IR Comrs* [1971] 1 All ER 135, it was held, in connection with a scheme of arrangement under what was then the Companies Act 1948 s 206, involving a transfer of the whole of the issued share capital of a company, that the court order sanctioning the scheme was a conveyance or transfer on sale and was liable to ad valorem stamp duty.

12A. Adjudication: supplementary provisions

(See the notes printed at the end of the contents list to Part II Stamp Taxes.)

This section was inserted by FA 1999 with effect from 1 October 1999. The section imposes a penalty, of an amount not exceeding £300, for not stamping a document in accordance with an adjudication. Note that this penalty is *not* added to the duty on a document but is imposed independently upon "the person by whom the adjudication was required". There may sometimes be doubt as to the identity of that "person" and it would seem prudent for professional advisers to ensure in future that their dealings with their clients and with the Stamp Office are conducted on the basis that the client is held out at all times as the "person" who "requires" the adjudication.

It is not entirely clear how this penalty is to be enforced since, although it appears to be within the scope of the new rules relating to the imposition of penalties *other than* for late stamping (see FA 1999 Sch 17), those rules only allow penalty proceedings to be commenced against a person where liability to a penalty "arises by reason of his fraud or the fraud of another person". The mere non-payment of duty, even after requesting an adjudication, has never been regarded as fraudulent. It has always been the case that (except in those rare cases where payment of duty is or was enforceable by legal process—see, for example, FA 1895 s 12, where the duty gives rise to a "debt") the taxpayer had an unfettered right to withdraw a document from adjudication or to decline to pay the duty which had been adjudicated as payable, provided that he was prepared to accept the indirect civil sanctions that accompany non-payment (the most obvious being the inability to adduce the document in evidence in civil proceedings in the UK). However, the new rules do allow regulations to be made, under which the collection and recovery provisions of the Taxes Management Act 1970 may be applied to stamp duty penalties. It may be that this power will be used in relation to s 12A.

Although there are now potentially more onerous sanctions for non-payment of duty (see commentaries on ss 15A and 15B below), there is still a genuinely free choice as to whether duty is paid or not, and this section seems to be something of an aberration in this respect. The principle that stamp duty is a "voluntary tax" still seems to be respected fully in the other new provisions, since the new rules relating to appeals to the High Court state that the court may make such order as it thinks fit with regard to the *repayment* of any duty, and there does not appear to be any scope for the court ordering a greater amount of duty to be paid than was determined by the adjudication under appeal. See commentary on s 13B below.

13. Appeal against Commissioners' decision on adjudication

(See the notes printed at the end of the contents list to Part II Stamp Taxes.)

Any person dissatisfied with an adjudication may appeal to the High Court (or, where relevant, the First-tier Tribunal), provided that he has paid the duty before doing so (plus any penalty imposed, and interest accumulated to the date of the appeal).

It should be noted that, before an appeal may be brought, there is a requirement to pay "any penalty" that has been imposed as well as the duty which has been adjudicated as payable. However, this is only a reference to late stamping penalties (and not also to, for example, the non-payment penalty under s 12A) because the wording cross-refers to s 12 and the only decision as to penalties which may be given under *that* section is as to the question "whether any penalty is payable under section 15B" (a section which relates only to late stamping, any decision on any other penalty being under the authority of FA 1999 Sch 17 Part II).

Appeals (unless they relate only to penalties for late stamping and so are taken before the First-tier Tribunal rather than the High Court) are by way of case stated, and the Commissioners are responsible for stating the case (although in practice they usually submit it in draft form to the appellant and agree it with him). This state of affairs, in which one of the parties to the dispute has an official monopoly on determining the scope and direction of the proceedings for resolving the dispute, is widely regarded as unacceptable; it is to be hoped that provision will one day be made for an independent tribunal of fact to make the preliminary investigation of stamp duty disputes.

At the hearing the court may hear oral evidence to supplement the facts in the stated case (as was done in *Speyer Brothers Ltd v IR Comrs* [1906] 1 KB 318). Subject to rules of the court, there may then be a further appeal by either party to the Court of Appeal and thereafter to the House of Lords. Leave has always been required to appeal to the House of Lords but, with effect from 1 January 1999, leave is also generally now required to appeal to the Court of Appeal (for the original source of the new practice see *Practice Direction (Court of Appeal: Leave to Appeal and Skeleton Arguments)* [1999] 1 WLR 2 which was then replaced by an updated version as *Practice Direction* [1999] 1 WLR 1027, and see also *Nascimento v Kerrigan* [1999] The Times, 23 June, on the validity of the new practice, under either version of the Practice Direction). An appeal which relates only to the imposition of a penalty may be brought before the First-tier Tribunal—see s 13A below.

The wording of sub-ss (4) and (5) suggests that the High Court and First-tier Tribunal have concurrent jurisdiction in relation to penalty proceedings and it is understood that this is the way the Stamp Office intend the appeals legislation to operate. In other words, a person who wishes to appeal against both a substantive point of law in relation to the charge to duty and also wishes to appeal against the imposition of a penalty can take both claims directly to the High Court and is not required to take any separate proceedings before the First-tier Tribunal, either before or at the same time as the main proceedings, simply to dispose of the claim relating to the penalty.

It should be noted that s 13 does not necessarily provide the only basis for commencing court actions in relation to stamp duty disputes. For example, *M&G Securities Ltd v IR Comrs* [1999] STC 315 was a case which was commenced by originating motion. This was because the point at issue there was not as to the amount of duty payable on a document but whether that duty was repayable in the circumstances which had arisen, in accordance with the refund provisions relating to unit trusts in FA 1946. The particular provisions under consideration in that case have now been repealed but a similar situation could arise in relation to, for example, a refund dispute under FA 1999 Sch 13 Part I para 9 (formerly SA 1891 s 59 (6)) where a contract is chargeable as a conveyance but the contract becomes incapable of performance after duty has been paid. Any dispute about the entitlement to such a refund would appear to be outside the scope of this section because the subject matter of the dispute would not be "an adjudication under section 12". There would also appear to be a lacuna where a person has paid an excessive amount of stamp duty which has been impressed on the relevant instrument. In such a case, no statutory procedure exists to facilitate the recovery of the excess and the Stamp Office has been known to deny the existence of any remedy in such a case. It would appear (although the matter remains to be determined) that the remedy in such a case lies in an action for money paid under a mistake, with the relevant forum depending on the amount of duty overpaid – the County Court or the High Court, as the case may be.

13A. Appeal to the First-tier Tribunal

(See the notes printed at the end of the contents list to Part II Stamp Taxes.)

Where there is to be an appeal to the First-tier Tribunal, it is made by notice of appeal, not (as in s 13 above and s 13B below) by case stated. The First-tier Tribunal has power to increase or decrease the amount of the penalty appealed against, or to confirm it or to set it aside altogether. Interestingly, the High Court, on appeal from any such decision, is stated to have the same powers as the First-tier Tribunal, which appears to mean that, although it is thought that the courts have never previously had an inherent power to make an order increasing the amount of duty payable, they can now increase the amount of a penalty payable in respect of the late payment of any such duty. If the First-tier Tribunal confirms the penalty in some amount, the person liable to the penalty has the right not only to appeal the decision on a point of law but, the amount of the penalty held to be payable. As with all appeals from the First-tier Tribunal since 1 April 2009, such an appeal is to the Upper Tribunal and not to the High Court and is subject to permission from one or other Tribunal.

13B. Appeal to the High Court

(See the notes printed at the end of the contents list to Part II Stamp Taxes.)

As noted above, it has always been thought that, since stamp duty is a "voluntary tax", the courts have no power to make an order increasing the amount of duty payable beyond the amount determined in the adjudication which is appealed against. The wording of subs (4) appears to confirm this, since the court's role is limited to giving such directions as it thinks fit "with respect to the repayment of any duty or penalty". That suggests that the most it could do is to order no repayment at all.

Somewhat oddly, however, the court's power appears to be similarly confined in relation to penalties *if* the appellant takes the case directly to the High Court in respect of both the underlying duty and a penalty which has been imposed. This contrasts with the situation under s 13A above where, on appeal from the First-tier Tribunal, the Upper Tribunal has "the same powers as are conferred on the First-tier Tribunal" and so could increase a penalty as well as reduce it. Query whether an appeal against a large penalty ought to be taken directly to the High Court, in order to limit the powers which the court would otherwise be able to exercise in the event of a subsequent appeal from an initial decision of the First-tier Tribunal respecting that penalty.

PRODUCTION OF INSTRUMENTS IN EVIDENCE

14. Terms upon which instruments not duly stamped may be received in evidence

(See the notes printed at the end of the contents list to Part II Stamp Taxes.)

The general rule, set out in s 14 (4), is that an instrument executed in the UK or relating (wherever executed) to any property situated or to any matter or thing done or to be done in any part of the UK shall not (except in criminal proceedings) be given in evidence or be available for any purpose whatever unless it is duly stamped in accordance with the law in force at the time when it was executed.

Judges, arbitrators and referees may not admit in evidence in proceedings before them any stampable document which is unstamped or insufficiently stamped. This duty exists whether or not any objection is raised as to the admissibility of a document.

However, in *Don Francesco v De Meo*, 1908 SC 7, it was stated that a court is only bound to intervene to protect the Revenue where there is good reason to believe that an instrument produced in evidence has not been duly stamped, and need not raise test cases or spend time trying dubious questions of stamp duty law which are not germane to the main issue before it.

It is not permissible even to give secondary evidence of an instrument which has not been duly stamped, and a court, arbitrator or referee cannot, even with the consent of the parties, make any ruling on an insufficiently stamped document (*Re Brown & Root McDermott Fabricators Limited's Application* [1996] STC 483 and *Parinv (Hatfield) Ltd v IR Comrs* [1996] STC 933). See also *Delta Finance Newco v Inland Revenue Commissioners* [2002] STC (SCD) 274 where the Special Commissioners found that an unstamped Bill of Sale for plant and machinery could not be relied on in establishing that the plant and machinery belonged to the purchaser who wished to claim capital allowances on the plant and machinery. The purchaser could not convince the Special Commissioners of its entitlement to specific performance of the sale contract and was therefore treated as not owning the assets. It is unclear why title was not passed by delivery in the usual way for moveables. This aspect of the Special Commissioners' decision was approved by the High Court in *BMBF (No 24) Ltd v Inland Revenue Commissioners* [2002] STC 1450, 1499, but the Court found (at 1501) that equitable title in the goods had passed having regard to the intention of the parties, which the court was able to derive from the terms of the contact, the conduct of the parties and all the circumstances of the case without needing to rely on the Bill of Sale.

In relation to documents which are insufficiently stamped, but which can still be stamped at the time they are tendered in evidence, the procedure laid down by s 14 (1), involving the payment of the relevant amount of duty, the full penalty, and a further penalty of £1, is rarely followed. It is the normal practice of the court to allow an unstamped document to be used upon the personal undertaking of the solicitor acting for the party tendering the document to have the document stamped and pay every appropriate penalty—see *Re Coolgardie Goldfields Ltd* [1900] 1 Ch 475 at p 477, and *Parkfield Trust v Dent* [1931] 2 KB 579. The Bar Council has abandoned its ruling that, except in Revenue cases, it is unprofessional conduct for counsel to object that a document is not properly stamped unless the judge specifically raises the issue, or unless the insufficiency of stamping affects the validity of the document.

It used to be stated specifically in the rules of court that the decision of a judge that a document is properly stamped, or does not require a stamp, is final and cannot be challenged (RSC Ord 59 Rule 11 (5)) but no equivalent provision exists in the new Civil Procedure Rules. It is possible to appeal against the decision to reject a document produced in evidence on the grounds that it is not properly stamped (provided that in this case counsel formally tenders the duty). However, it was held in *Routledge v McKay* [1954] 1 All ER 855 that if a lower court overlooks a stamp duty point, it may be taken by the Court on appeal.

"The United Kingdom" means England, Scotland, Wales and Northern Ireland, but it does not include the Channel Islands or the Isle of Man. Under the first limb of s 14 (4), an instrument executed in the UK is stampable whatever it relates to, eg a conveyance on sale of land in Australia between two Australians for Australian dollars (*Wright v IR Comrs* (1855) 11 Exch 458). The cautious view is that an instrument will be regarded as executed in the UK if any party to it executes it in the UK although, arguably, execution by one or more parties in the UK would not fall foul of this provision if one or more further signatures were required to make the document effective and these further signatures were appended to the document at a place outside the UK. (The provision used to refer to a document being "first executed", as did the old version of s 15, which has been replaced by a new version as a result of the provisions in FA 1999. It was suggested in a previous edition of this work that references to a document being "first executed" abroad ought to be read as meaning "originally executed", rather than as a reference to the appending of only the first of a total of two or more signatures, seals or marks. It is submitted that this is confirmed by the FA 1999 amendments and that "execution" means the whole process of execution by all those persons whose signatures, seals or marks are necessary in order to render the document effective.)

The second limb of s 14 (4) is concerned with instruments "relating to any property situate, or to any matter or thing done or to be done in any part of the United Kingdom" and is thus extremely wide.

The leading case concerning the construction of these words is *IR Comrs v Maple & Co (Paris) Ltd* [1908] AC 22, involving the transfer by one English company to another English company of property situated in France by means of an instrument expressed to be governed by French law and in the normal French legal form, the consideration for which was, however, the issue of shares in the transferee company. The instrument was held to be dutiable because it related to property situated in the UK (the shares in the transferee company to be issued as consideration) and to a thing to be done in the UK (the issue and registration of those shares). In a more recent case (*Faber v IR Comrs* (1936) 155 LT 228) an engineer who worked in the UK executed a deed of covenant in Canada to pay a specified proportion of the income he received from his job in the UK to a Canadian company, in consideration of the issue to him of shares and debentures of that company, and it was held that the deed was dutiable because it related to something "done or to be done in any part of the United Kingdom", namely the carrying on of the engineer's job.

The words "duly stamped in accordance with the law in force at the time when it was first executed" in s 14 (4) have been taken in practice to mean the time when the relevant instrument first becomes an effective instrument, and not necessarily when the first person to sign does so. In *Clarke v Roche* (1877) 3 QBD 170) it was held that, where an instrument appeared to be sufficiently stamped according to the law in force on the day that it was dated, but it subsequently transpired that the instrument was executed some years before the date, when the stamp duty was different, the instrument was inadmissible. In *Crane Fruehauf Ltd v IR Comrs* [1974] 1 All ER 811, instruments of transfer signed conditionally upon the issue by the acquiring company of the consideration shares were held to take effect upon satisfaction of the condition and to be stampable by reference to the then value of the consideration shares. Similarly, an instrument delivered in escrow does not attract stamp duty until the condition subject to which it was delivered has been performed (*Terrapin International Ltd v IR Comrs* [1976] 2 All ER 461). However, the decision of Walton J in *Terrapin* was not applied by the Court of Appeal in *Alan Estates Ltd v WG Stores Ltd* [1982] 1 Ch 511 in a case involving litigation between the two parties to the deed – and where it was decided that if the condition under the escrow were satisfied the deed related back for such purposes as were necessary to give effect to the deed to its date of delivery – at least as far as the parties to the deed were concerned. The interaction of the two cases is, it is fair to say, less than wholly clear.

Insufficiently stamped documents are not to "be given in evidence or be available for any purpose whatever", but unstamped instruments have been admitted to refresh a witness's memory (*Birchall v Bullough* [1896] 1 QB 325), to prove fraud (*Re Shaw* (1920) 90 LJKB 204) or an act of bankruptcy (*Re Gunsbourg* (1919) 88 LJKB 562). In an action to set aside an agreement and to restrain the defendant from carrying it into effect the plaintiff was not compelled to stamp it when, if his claim succeeded, the agreement would be void (*Mason v Motor Traction Company* [1905] 1 Ch 419).

In the case of an instrument that has been lost or destroyed, it is presumed that the instrument was properly stamped and it is for the party taking the objection to prove that it was unstamped. If the party taking the objection can show that some time after execution the instrument was unstamped, then this presumption will be rebutted unless it is revived by the other party proving facts which imply that the document was properly stamped. See, eg *Marine Investment Company v Haviside* (1872) LR 5 HL 624 and *Henty and Constable (Brewers) Ltd v IR Comrs* [1961] 3 All ER 1146, CA.

The case of *Re Brown & Root McDermott Fabricators Limited's Application* [1996] STC 483 concerned the validity of the registration of a patent which had allegedly been infringed. The plaintiff had entered into a contract to purchase global intellectual property rights which it initially completed by an assignment (which contained no apportionment of the consideration) and which the Patent Office returned because it was unstamped. Rather than amend the initial assignment, the parties executed another purported assignment (in which the consideration was this time apportioned) which was stamped and accepted by the Patent Office which registered it. Subsequently, a third party (the defendant) argued that it had not infringed the patent because the first assignment was effective; the second assignment therefore passed no title and was a nullity and its registration was invalid. However, the High Court held that the first assignment, being unstamped, could not be produced in evidence to prove that the second assignment was a nullity. The judge, however, acknowledged that this did not mean that the first document was ineffective in law for all purposes (it is undoubtedly effective if registered, even if unstamped—see *Nisbet v Shepherd* [1994] 1 BCLC 300), despite the words "shall not be . . . available for any purpose whatever" in s 14 (4).

The scope of s 14 (4) was later examined in *Parinv (Hatfield) Ltd v IR Comrs* [1996] STC 933 (affirmed [1998] STC 305), in particular its interaction with s 5 (facts and circumstances affecting duty to be set forth in instruments) and s 12 (2) (information the Stamp Office may require to assess whether s 5 has been complied with). The High Court held that information about the existence of an offshore contract, obtained under ss 5 and 12 (2), entitled the Stamp Office to conclude that an onshore Land Registry transfer was a transfer of the legal and equitable interest in land for sale and the Stamp Office were not required by s 14 (4) to ignore this information (as secondary evidence of an unstamped document). However, the Stamp Office were entitled to rely on s 14 (4) to ignore the existence of an unstamped offshore declaration of trust which completed the contract because, not being duly stamped, it was not available for any purpose. The judge said that s 14 (4) was not to be construed literally. In *Marx and Others v Estates and General Investments Ltd* [1975] STC 671 at 678 Brightman J had said that the reference in s 14 (4) to an instrument not duly stamped being "available for any purpose whatsoever" meant that one person could not compel another person to rely on and accept an instrument which was not at the time of presentation duly stamped.

Lindsay J in *Parinv* held that a further relaxation of s 14 (4) was justified in the context of the stamping of documents by the Stamp Office: "the Revenue makes a case, in effect, for a further relaxation of the literal meaning of s 14 (4) being compelled by the Act itself. It is this: the taxpayer is obliged by s 5 of the 1891 Act to set out in the instrument concerned all facts and circumstances affecting its liability to duty or the amount with which it is chargeable. The Revenue is also able to require that it be furnished with such evidence as it may deem necessary for the purposes of its adjudication or assessment under s 12 (2). The disclosure of the existence and terms of the declaration of trust was plainly necessary under s 5 and a copy of it was produced by Parinv in or towards satisfaction (consciously or not) of the duty upon it under s 5. Later a copy of the agreement was produced in intended satisfaction of s 12 (2). It cannot be, says Mr Furness, and as I accept, that the taxpayer can, in respect of the same information, produce it to satisfy a statutory obligation and in relation to a statutory purpose—assessment of duty—and yet require that it necessarily be put out of mind by the Revenue in the course of that statutory purpose. It is hardly likely that Parliament would have imposed a fine in relation to the fraudulent non-disclosure of material which, were it to be produced, would then have to be ignored. I thus have no difficulty in letting the Revenue take account, for the purpose of its assessment of duty, of the information supplied to it, namely that there was here a sale of the equitable interest in the property and one at £37,223,000 and for its conclusion that ad valorem duty was payable and that it came out, therefore, at £372,230. To that extent there is, by reference to s 5 and s 12, a limited further relaxation of the rigours of a literal reading of s 14 (4) which those sections compel." The Stamp Office would therefore now appear to be entitled, in assessing the duty on a document, to pick and choose to a certain extent whether to take account of other unstamped documents in order to change the legal effect (and therefore stampability) of the document presented to them. The implications of this have yet to be fully explored. This case is also discussed in relation to s 54.

The meaning of the words in s 14 (4) "duly stamped in accordance with the law in force at the time it was executed" was also examined in the *Parinv* case. Lindsay J held that a stampable instrument executed and retained offshore (such as the offshore contract and the declaration of trust) was not "duly stamped" until it had actually been stamped. The old version of s 15 (before it was replaced by the provision described below, inserted by FA 1999) provided periods of grace during which a document could be stamped without penalty but did not mean that the document was "duly stamped" during that period; the cases which allowed effect to be given to documents which later required to be stamped, referred to in *Re Brown & Root McDermott Fabricators Limited's Application* [1996] STC 483 (see above) and *Re English Scottish and Australian Chartered Bank* [1892] 3 Ch 385, were distinguished.

The view that a document, even while held offshore, is not duly stamped until actually stamped appears to be reinforced by the new provisions relating to interest (inserted into SA 1891 by FA 1999), under which interest begins to run on amounts of unpaid duty from 30 days after execution even where the document in question is originally executed, and thereafter remains physically located, outside the UK. The old version of s 15 provided periods of grace in relation to both interest and penalties in such a situation but the new s 15A imposes an interest charge from 30 days after execution, whether or not the document in question is in the UK (although the imposition of penalties is still geared to the location of the document).

The Bar Council has now ruled that it is no longer against the rules of etiquette to take stamp objections to the other side's documents in litigation. This ruling has far reaching implications. Not only do professional advisors have to assess stamp duty risks when preparing for litigation, but it also raises the question of who, following the renewal of the list identifying those people liable to penalties for documents executed after October 1999, is accountable for a penalty incurred due to late stamping. It is quite likely that the person who presents the document, although not a party to it, may be liable to the penalty. A further question is raised in relation to whether a vendor, who wishes to rely on a document that has not been properly stamped, can stamp the document themselves, and whether the vendor can claim the amount of the stamp duty from the purchaser.

The transfer of shares in an English or Scottish company registered in an "overseas branch register" (see the Companies Act 2006 ss 129–135) is deemed to be a transfer of property situated outside the UK and will not be liable to duty unless executed in the UK. This does not apply in the case of overseas branch registers kept in Northern Ireland. HMRC has recently accepted that where a company buys back its own shares held on an overseas branch register, the return that the company is required to send to Companies House is relieved from stamp duty by CA 2006 s 133 (previously CA 1985 Sch 14 para 8) unless the return is executed in the United Kingdom. This reverses their prior view that such a return was always dutiable at 0.5%: HMRC Press Release 8 September 2009.

For an interesting case in which an unstamped agreement was admitted in evidence in criminal proceedings, despite an objection from counsel for the defendant, see the unreported decision in *Abdel-Rahim v DPP* (1989) QBD CO/1796/87.

Stamping of Instruments after Execution

15. Penalty upon stamping instruments after execution

(See the notes printed at the end of the contents list to Part II Stamp Taxes.)

The general principle under the stamp duty legislation was that instruments executed in the UK must be stamped before execution (which is the implication given by the provisions relating to stamping after execution, although there is no express provision to that effect), but this general principle is subject to a number of general qualifications and special exemptions in respect of particular instruments. Following FA 2002 s 114, a penalty for late stamping will apply if an instrument relates to land in the UK and is not presented for stamping within 30 days after execution of the instrument, irrespective of whether the instrument was executed inside or outside the UK. See the commentary on s 15B below. Certain instruments may, without any penalty, be stamped after their execution.

However, interest and/or a penalty may then be payable in accordance with the provisions of ss 15A and 15B below. These provisions set out a new regime for interest and penalties, taking effect from 1 October 1999, in which there is something of a shift of emphasis in the penalty provisions. In the old form of s 15, interest and penalties were closely allied with each other but in the new legislation (inserted into this Act by FA 1999) the interest rules focus upon the mere non-payment of duty, whereas the penalty provisions focus upon the fact of presentation of a document for adjudication. See the commentary on each of ss 15A and 15B below.

15A. Late stamping: interest

(See the notes printed at the end of the contents list to Part II Stamp Taxes.)

As a result of the insertion of this section (by FA 1999, with effect from 1 October 1999), interest will now run on unpaid duty from 30 days after execution of a stampable document, even if execution takes place outside the UK. Until this section was introduced, the execution of a document outside the UK effectively placed the entire stamp duty legislation in suspension in relation to that document until it was first brought into the UK (although it remained stampable and the fact of being unstamped while held abroad meant, according to the *Parinv* case [1998] STC 305, that it was not "duly stamped" during that period).

Interest will now be levied at a rate set by the Treasury from time to time (see SI 1989/1297), instead of the former fixed rate of 5% per annum which used to be stated in s 15 (in the pre-1999 version of that provision). There is a possible exception in the case of instruments chargeable under FA 1895 s 12, since that Act itself provides for interest to be charged at 5% and it is not clear whether s 15A overrides this. The rate set by the Treasury is penal (ie above prevailing commercial rates of interest).

It should be noted that, whereas the old interest rules capped the total amount of interest payable at an amount equal to the amount of unpaid duty, there appears to be no such limitation contained in the new interest rules. This would accord with the Commissioners' view that interest is no more than commercial restitution for the Treasury having been kept out of money due.

It should also be noted that it is necessary actually to *pay* stamp duty within 30 days in order to prevent interest running. Specific provision is now made in the legislation for amounts to be lodged with HMRC on an estimated basis so as to prevent interest running on the amount lodged. One cannot simply *submit* documents for adjudication within 30 days and thereafter pursue arguments about the nature and scope of the charge, even if there is genuine doubts about the amount of duty payable, without suffering an interest charge for late payment (although, strictly speaking, this was already the correct legal position because the old version of s 15 only suspended the penalty provisions, not the interest provisions, where a document was submitted for adjudication before the initial 30 day stamping "window" had expired).

It is not specifically stated in the new legislation that the lodgment of money on account itself needs to be made within 30 days of execution of the document to which that lodgment relates. However, to hold that it could be paid after more than 30 days would appear completely to frustrate the operation of the new rules and it is to be presumed, whether or not we are moving towards a general principle of purposive statutory interpretation (see commentary on FA 1999 s 112), that a court would read in the requirement to lodge a payment on account within the 30 day period allowed for the payment of duty free of interest and/or penalties.

Since a payment on account is not actually a payment of stamp duty, it will presumably not be treated as discharging any underlying stamp duty reserve tax liability (or, at least, will not be so treated as at the time at which the payment is initially made). In practice, this ought not to matter because no consequences tend to flow from technical breaches of the stamp duty reserve tax legislation provided that the correct amount of stamp duty is eventually paid. However, it should be borne in mind that the mere lodgment of money on account of a stamp duty liability is probably not sufficient to prevent there being a technical breach of the stamp duty reserve tax legislation, at least until the stamp duty position is finalised. For further details, see the article by Mark Sheiham in the edition of the *Tax Journal* dated 19 July 1999.

Since the whole subject of dates and timing issues may now become more significant in the light of the more onerous interest provisions, it should be noted that FA 1999 Sch 18 Part I para 2 specifically states that a payment by cheque is to be treated as made on the day on which the cheque was first received by the Commissioners (presuming that the cheque is paid "on its first presentation"), it seems that the new repayment interest will be available in respect of such an amount (but subject to conditions—see commentary on FA 1999 s 110).

In view of the fact that the interest provisions have now become rather more onerous than they used to be, a correspondingly broader and more generous regime has been introduced in relation to repayment interest (see commentary on FA 1999 s 110) although, as is usual with tax adjustment provisions, the rate of interest for repayments by the tax authorities will generally be a little lower than the rate charged to taxpayers for any late payment of duty by them. Although an amount lodged *on account of* stamp duty is not itself, strictly speaking, a payment of stamp duty, the repayment provisions do relate to such amounts as well as to actual stamp duty—again, see the commentary on FA 1999 s 110.

In the context of the new interest charge on documents held offshore, it should be remembered that there is no legislative basis for apportioning duty on an actual instrument of conveyance (as opposed to a contract which is chargeable as a conveyance under what used to be s 59, now FA 1999 Sch 13 Part I para 7) so that a conveyance of foreign property which includes a very small UK component is potentially stampable on the *entire* consideration stated therein. This appears to mean that, since interest now runs on documents even while they are held offshore, if what was essentially regarded by the parties as a foreign document (and so deliberately left unstamped) was ever subsequently needed in the UK to enforce rights in respect of the small UK component of the subject matter, a considerable interest charge would arise in respect of the *whole* transaction value for the whole of the period (less 30 days) since the date of execution of that document. Consideration should therefore be given to the use of split documents in such a situation, so as to avoid the incurring of unnecessary interest charges on parts of the transaction value which are attributable solely to non-UK elements of the underlying subject matter.

Essentially the same interest regime also applies to bearer instruments as from 1 October 1999, although the legislation on bearer instruments identifies specific persons who are liable (jointly and severally, if more than one in number) to pay both the duty and any interest on unpaid duty—see commentary on FA 1999 Sch 15 para 23 (4). Given the manner in which the bearer instrument legislation is drafted, it is not entirely clear whether the basic obligation to pay interest is still derived from this section in such cases or whether an interest charge is imposed independently in such cases by FA 1999 Sch 15.

It should also be noted that the special timing rule in FA 1994 for agreements for leases (under which, broadly speaking, an agreement for lease would never suffer interest or penalties for late presentation if it was presented for stamping at the same time as the actual lease to which it gave effect) has been carried over, although in a reworded provision, as part of the 1999 reforms. Therefore, the interest charges if any, on an agreement for lease is calculated on the assumption that the agreement for lease was executed at the same time as the lease.

However, it must be remembered that FA 1994 s 240 (in either its pre-1999 or its post-1999 form) only applies to a situation where an agreement for lease and the actual lease are presented *together* for stamping. There would seem to be no protection at all from the full rigours of the new interest rules in any situation where an agreement for lease is presented for stamping without an accompanying lease.

This new interest regime does *not* apply to unit trust transactions in the transition period between the introduction of this regime on 1 October 1999 and the abolition of stamp duty on unit trust transfers on 6 February 2000—see FA 1999 s 122 (1).

15B. Late stamping: penalties

(See the notes printed at the end of the contents list to Part II Stamp Taxes.)

As a result of this section, inserted by FA 1999 and amended by FA 2002 s 114, the penalty regime has been altered substantially. With effect from 1 October 1999, the maximum penalty payable is (i) the lesser of £300 or the amount of duty, for stamping within one year after the normal 30 day period, or (ii) the *greater* of £300 or the amount of duty for stamping after one year has elapsed.

As under the old law on penalties (ie SA 1891 s 15, before that and the accompanying provisions were recast by FA 1999), the imposition of penalties is subject to discretionary mitigation and penalties are still only charged by reference to the date of an instrument first entering the UK providing (since FA 2002) that it does not relate to land in the UK. FA 2002 s 114 amends this section to state that even where an instrument is executed outside the UK, if it relates to land in the UK, penalties may be charged from 30 days after the execution rather than the first entry into the UK. Subsection (1A) states that an instrument relating to land in the UK includes every instrument that (whether or not it also relates to any other transaction) relates to a transaction which involves land in the UK to any extent. As to HMRC's practice regarding mitigation see Stamp Taxes customer leaflet SO10. In addition to the general power to mitigate, it is also specifically provided that no penalty is payable "if there is a reasonable excuse for the delay" although no guidance is given in the legislation itself as to the possible ambit of this phrase.

The penalty provisions have been generalised in that the new wording simply refers to a penalty being imposed on "an instrument" on which duty has not been paid, whereas the old version of s 15 listed specific instruments and so, by implication, exempted other instruments from the late stamping penalties. The most significant practical effect of this generalisation of the application of the penalties would appear to be that the new legislation draws no distinction between an actual "conveyance or transfer on sale" and a contract which falls to be stamped (under what is now FA 1999 Sch 13 Part I para 7, formerly SA 1891 s 59) as though it were such a "conveyance or transfer".

The penalty provisions have also been assimilated to the general charge to duty in that the penalty is simply imposed on the instrument but no particular person is now made liable to discharge the penalty. The former version of s 15 contained a table in which designated persons were stated to be liable for the penalty on specified instruments. The responsibility for paying the penalty would now seem to rest with any person who has a need to stamp the document.

It should also be noted that, whilst the new interest rules in s 15A above are specifically stated to apply only to an instrument which is "chargeable with ad valorem duty", this section simply refers to the late stamping of "an instrument". This suggests that the failure to stamp an instrument within 30 days if it is chargeable with a fixed duty of £5 (as all fixed duties will now be, as from 1 October 1999) could ultimately result in such an instrument having to bear duty of £305, being a fixed duty plus a £300 late stamping penalty. Such a delay could prove embarrassingly expensive if, for example, a large number of different share portfolios (or a large number of freehold or leasehold interests in land) were all being transferred to a nominee under separate instruments, each of which ought to have been stamped with a fixed duty.

For the purposes of the special timing rule for agreements for leases (see FA 1994 s 240, as substituted by FA 1999) the time *and place* of execution of an agreement for lease is treated as being the same time and place as that of the actual lease to which it gives effect. In other words, no late stamping penalties can arise on an agreement for lease independently of any such penalty chargeable on the actual lease. However, this will only be the case if the agreement and the actual lease are presented *together* for stamping because s 240 (in either its pre-1999 or its post-1999 form) has no application to a situation where an agreement for lease is presented for stamping without an accompanying lease.

ENTRIES UPON ROLLS, BOOKS, ETC

16. Rolls, books, etc, to be open to inspection

(See the notes printed at the end of the contents list to Part II Stamp Taxes.)

A "public officer" has been defined as a person "who is appointed to discharge a public duty and receives a compensation in whatever shape, whether from the Crown or otherwise" (Best CJ in *Henly v Lyme Corpn* (1829) 5 Bing 91 at 107).

It also formerly included the trustees and managers of a unit trust scheme (and their agents, servants, or officers) but such persons have been removed from the scope of the section (by the repeal, in FA 1999 of FA 1946 s 56) now that stamp duty charges on dealings in the units of a unit trust have been abolished.

It should be noted that the former fine of £10 for breach of this provision has been replaced, with effect from 1 October 1999, by a penalty not exceeding £300.

17. Penalty for enrolling, etc, instrument not duly stamped

(See the notes printed at the end of the contents list to Part II Stamp Taxes.)

This section renders liable to a penalty not exceeding £300 any person whose office it is to enrol, register, or enter in or upon any rolls, books, or records any stampable document who does so in relation to a document which is not duly stamped. The most important practical effect of this is that the secretary of a company presented with a share transfer for registration should not register it unless he is satisfied that the correct amount of stamp duty has been paid. The section also prevents the Registrar of Companies from accepting for filing such documents as contracts or particulars of contracts relating to the issue of shares for a non-cash consideration unless he is satisfied that they have been duly stamped.

In determining whether an instrument is duly stamped, the person concerned is entitled to go behind what appears on the face of the document (see *Maynard v Consolidated Kent Collieries Ltd* [1903] 2 KB 121, CA, followed in *Conybear v British Briquettes Ltd* [1937] 4 All ER 191). Any person who objects to the refusal of the relevant officer to enrol, register or enter any instrument must present the instrument to HMRC for adjudication, and if necessary appeal, and not apply for a court order compelling enrolment or registration, etc.

The correct view today seems to be that a title resting on registration would apparently not be adversely affected merely because registration was procured by the use of an unstamped instrument (see *Lap Shun Textiles Industrial Company Ltd v Collector of Stamp Revenue* [1976] AC 530, [1976] 1 All ER 833, PC).

Thus, registration of a transfer of shares while inadequately stamped nevertheless will operate as a legal transfer of the shares into the name of the transferee.

In the case of the purchase by a company of its own shares pursuant to the Companies Act 2006 s 690, the return required to be delivered to the Registrar of Companies is to be charged with stamp duty, and treated for all purposes of SA 1891 as if it were an instrument transferring the shares on sale to the company in pursuance of the contract (or contracts) of purchase concerned: FA 1986 s 66 (2). The Registrar of Companies will not therefore register the return unless he has been satisfied that the return has been duly stamped.

The Land Registration Act 1925 s 14 (3), provided that the Land Registrar had to be satisfied, before registering any person who has not previously acquired the estate intended to be registered, that all ad valorem stamp duty (if any) which, if the estate had been acquired by him, would have been payable in respect of the instrument vesting that estate in him, has been discharged. See also the Land Registration Rules 1925 rr 94 and 95 with regard to the procedures to be adopted in relation to registered instruments. The 1925 Act has now been replaced by the Land Registration Act 2002; and the corresponding obligations of the Land Registrar in relation to Stamp Duty Land Tax are to be found in FA 2003 s 79.

PART 2 REGULATIONS APPLICABLE TO PARTICULAR INSTRUMENTS

Bills of Sale

41. Bills of sale

(See the notes printed at the end of the contents list to Part II Stamp Taxes.)

This section expressly prohibits the registration of insufficiently stamped bills of sale.

TRANSFERS ON SALE

55. How ad valorem duty to be calculated in respect of stock and securities

(See the notes printed at the end of the contents list to Part II Stamp Taxes.)

The value of stock or marketable securities is to be ascertained in the manner set out in s 6 in every case where there is an "average price" on The Stock Exchange. Where there is no such average price, the Commissioners must reach their own conclusions as to the value of the shares or stock. There seems to be some justification in the relevant body of case law for arriving at the value of the consideration by reference to the value of the property conveyed or transferred (see eg *John Foster & Sons v IR Comrs* [1894] 1 QB 516, CA, *Faber v IR Comrs* (1936) 155 LT 228 and *Carlyon Estate Ltd v IRC* 46 TC 413). The analysis which supports this view is that, by the time the relevant property is conveyed or transferred to the company, the assets of the company include the right of the company to have the assets transferred to it for no consideration other than the issue of the relevant shares. The shares are thus valuable assets in their own right. This analysis used to be the basis of a stamp duty avoidance scheme by which assets could be incorporated for little stamp duty if, first, there was an issue of a substantial number of low-denomination shares (to the incorporating owner of the assets) at par, followed by an agreement for the sale of the assets to the company for a modest number of additional shares). A conveyance is treated as a sale if the consideration consists of stock or marketable securities (*a*) whether or not they have been or are to be issued at the time of execution of the conveyance on sale and (*b*) where the stock or marketable securities is still to be issued, irrespective of (1) when it is or is to be issued and (2) whether the issue is certain or contingent. It had previously been considered, despite suggestions to the contrary from the Stamp Office, that a right to receive shares or securities in the future is not dutiable consideration (being different from the actual shares or securities).

56. How consideration consisting of periodical payments to be charged

(See the notes printed at the end of the contents list to Part II Stamp Taxes.)

This section applies where purchase consideration is payable by instalments or where additional periodical payments (whether contingent or not) are to be payable after completion. It does not apply in respect of periodical payments which are inherently incidental to the property sold (eg the rent in the case of leasehold property).

In a case where a company agreed to sell its business to a new company in consideration of money and shares, and it was agreed in addition that the original company would be paid a proportion of the profits of the new company, it was held that the further consideration, though payable contingently, was "money payable periodically in perpetuity or for an indefinite period not terminable with life" within the meaning of s 56 (2) (*Underground Electric Railways Company of London Limited v IR Comrs* [1906] AC 21).

A provision in a sale and purchase agreement, allowing for the purchase price to be payable in fixed annual instalments for a period of 125 years, to the effect that the whole of the instalments would become immediately payable in the event of a default in payment of any one instalment will not entitle the Commissioners to avoid s 56 (2) and claim ad valorem duty on the whole of the purchase price (*Western United Investment Company Limited v IR Comrs* [1958] 1 All ER 257).

The Court of Appeal re-examined s 56 (2) in two cases, heard together, involving the assessment of stamp duty payable on the grant of leases (*Blendett v IR Comrs* and *Quietlece v IR Comrs* [1984] STC 95, CA). In the first case, B Ltd was granted a long underlease of certain property at a peppercorn rent in consideration of a premium of £240,500 payable as to £50,000 on the execution of the lease and as to the balance on the 23rd anniversary of the lease. In the second case, Q Ltd was granted a long lease on similar terms save that the premium of £370,900 was payable as to £50,000 on the execution of the lease and as to the balance in three yearly instalments of £106,966 commencing on the 23rd anniversary of the lease. The companies paid ad valorem stamp duty on the instruments amounting to 2% of the initial payment of £50,000 on the basis that the premiums consisted of "money payable periodically for a period exceeding 20 years" within s 56 (2), and accordingly that stamp duty was payable only on so much of the consideration as would be paid within 20 years from the dates of the leases.

It was held by both Vinelott J and the Court of Appeal that s 56 (2) applied to neither of the two leases. In relation to the *Blendett* case, Vinelott J held that money could not be said to be payable "periodically" unless a payment fell to be made between the payment which marked the beginning and the payment which marked the end of the period; the Court of Appeal held that there could not be said to be "periodical payments" when there were only two payments which were to be made over 20 years apart. In the *Quietlece* case, Vinelott J held that the phrase "payable periodically for a definite period" envisaged the payment of instalments more than one of which would occur during the 20 years following the date of the instrument, but the Court of Appeal held, to the contrary, that the three instalments did constitute money payable periodically but since the duration of that period did not exceed 20 years s 56 (2) did not apply.

As will be seen from the commentary on the "Lease" head of charge in what is now FA 1999 Sch 13 Part II, the view of a number of practitioners is that VAT on rent payable in respect of commercial buildings cannot itself constitute "rent" and be dutiable as such under that head of charge. Whether or not that is correct, the VAT element is regarded by HMRC as dutiable on the basis that, if the VAT is treated under the lease as part of the "rent" it will be dutiable as such but, if it is not, it will constitute some other form of consideration or premium for the grant of the lease, payable periodically and therefore dutiable under this section. See the Revenue Press Releases of 22 July and 12 September 1991 and SP 11/91. See also the correspondence between the Law Society's revenue law committee and the Revenue as published in the *Law Society's Gazette* of 4 March 1992 p 16 (reproduced in Appendix 4) and the decision in *Glenrothes Development Corporation v IR Comrs* [1994] STC 74.

57. How conveyance in consideration of a debt, etc, to be charged
(See the notes printed at the end of the contents list to Part II Stamp Taxes.)

Where property is conveyed either in satisfaction of a debt or subject either certainly or contingently to the payment or transfer of any money or stock, duty is payable on the amount of the debt or money or the value of the stock. Thus, if mortgaged property is sold, duty is paid on the purchase price together with the amount outstanding on the mortgage, whether the purchaser assumes personal liability for the debt or not (*IR Comrs v City of Glasgow Bank Liquidators*, 1881 8 R (Ct of Sess) 389). Where a creditor takes over the property of his debtor in consideration of the release of his debt, the transaction is also a sale and dutiable under this section (*IR Comrs v North British Railway Company*, 1901 4 F(Ct of Sess) 27). Similarly, where a business is purchased, the purchaser undertaking to discharge the business debts of the vendor, the amount of these debts will be added to the consideration (*E Gomme Ltd v IR Comrs* [1964] 3 All ER 497).

In the case of *Huntington v IR Comrs* [1896] 1 QB 422 it was held that a conveyance to an equitable mortgagee in pursuance of an order for foreclosure was liable to ad valorem duty under this section, but it was also suggested that the "amount or value of the consideration" on which the duty was to be assessed should not exceed the value of the property notwithstanding that the amount of the debt exceeded the value of the property. This suggestion received statutory effect in FA 1980 s 102.

Where, on the sale of a business, "net assets" are purchased at their valuation, it is important to note that stamp duty will be payable on a gross basis—ie on the gross value of the fixed and current assets (including book debts) acquired *plus* the amount of the liabilities assumed. Where, therefore, the purchaser of a business undertakes to discharge the business debts of the vendor, it is common to avoid the additional stamp duty which would then be payable by a clause in the sale and purchase agreement to the effect that the purchaser will collect the book debts of the business as agent for the vendor and apply them in discharging the debts of the vendor, the purchaser keeping the balance (if any). This is effective, but it should be noted that if the purchaser also undertakes to make good any deficiency then this may amount to a contingent liability to discharge all the debts and therefore give rise to a claim for duty accordingly.

This section involves a trap for the unwary donor and donee in respect of a gift of property subject to a mortgage. Notwithstanding the abolition of ad valorem stamp duty on voluntary dispositions inter vivos, where gifted property is subject to a mortgage which the donee undertakes to discharge the conveyance or transfer of the property will be stampable ad valorem, as a conveyance or transfer on sale, on the amount of the liability assumed. There will, of course, be no stamp duty if the donor retains liability for the mortgage after making the gift. (See SP 6/90.)

As with s 56, liabilities which are an integral part of the property conveyed (eg the rent payable in respect of leasehold property or liabilities of a company on the transfer of its shares) are disregarded; see *Swayne v IRC* [1900] 1 QB 172, CA.

Notwithstanding this section, the practice of the Commissioners was not to claim, in respect of transfers on sale of partly paid shares, that the contingent liability for further calls is part of the consideration for the sale. It is not known whether this practice is still current.

58. Direction as to duty in certain cases

(See the notes printed at the end of the contents list to Part II Stamp Taxes.)

Subsections (1), (2) and (3) provide for the separate stamping of the several instruments involved where property contracted to be sold to a single purchaser for a single consideration is conveyed to that purchaser in separate parts or parcels by different instruments, or where property is contracted to be sold to two or more purchasers for a single consideration, and is conveyed in parts or parcels by separate instruments to the individual purchasers, or where there are several instruments of conveyance necessary to complete the purchaser's title to property sold. See the commentary on FA 1991 in relation to the interpretation of sub ss (1) and (2) as a result of the prospective abolitions referred to in the note at the beginning of the commentary on SA 1891 s 1.

Subsections (4) and (5) are, subject to the exceptions, relieving provisions to prevent two amounts of stamp duty being payable where an immediate sub-sale (or on-sale) is effected by a purchaser of property and the two transactions are both completed by a single instrument of conveyance. In the absence of such relief, that conveyance would generally be required to bear the duty attributable to the two (or possibly—see further below—more than two) transactions of which it was the instrument of completion.

Subsection (4) appears to be drafted to cover situations where there are *precisely* two transactions, although it seems generally to be assumed in practice that a chain of more than two transactions qualifies, in principle, for the relief and this seems to be borne out by the provisions relating to FA 2002 s 115. Where, for example, A agrees to sell property to B who agrees to sell it to C who agrees to sell it to D, all three agreements being completed by an instrument of conveyance from A direct to D, there is a single charge to duty on that instrument (provided that the appropriate conditions are satisfied, eg as to the level of consideration provided for in the agreement between C and D). As stated, it is generally assumed that chains of more than two transactions qualify although it is perhaps open to question who is meant to be covered by the term "the sub-purchaser" in such a case. If chains of more than two transactions do not qualify—the point does not appear to have been considered by the courts even though such situations must arise fairly frequently in practice—it is also open to question whether any part, or parts, of a chain qualify individually or whether every stage of the chain then attracts duty as if it were an independent transaction (in which case there could also be a question as to whether this amounted to a "series of transactions" for the purposes of what are now FA 1999 Sch 13 Part I paras 4 and 6).

There are also certain unanswered questions as to the application, if any, of this relief in cases now covered by the market value rules for land transactions, in FA 1994 ss 241 and 242 (see commentary on those sections).

The exceptions in subsection (4) were inserted by FA 1984 s 112 to counter a tax avoidance device involving a sub-sale of land by the real purchaser to a third party for a nominal sum and an agreement by the third party to grant the purchaser a long lease, followed by a direct conveyance from the original vendor to the third party and a subsequent reconveyance to the original purchaser. It would appear that relief was unavailable wherever the ultimate purchaser to whom the property was to be transferred was liable to stamp duty on an amount of consideration less than the market value of the property at the time of the contract with him: *Keston v IR Comrs* [2004] EWHC 59 (Ch), [2004] STC 902. In the *Keston* case there was a sub-sale to a connected company, in circumstances where the consideration was payable by small periodical payments over 20 years, followed by a later balloon payment which would fall outside the scope of the charge to stamp duty: see SA 1891 s 56. It was held that section 58(4) relief was unavailable, so that the transfer was charged both with the consideration from the intermediate purchaser and on the chargeable consideration passing from the sub-purchaser.

FA 1984 s 112 also inserted subsection (7) for the purposes of construing the exceptions inserted in subs ss (4) and (5). It was amended by FA 1985 s 82 in consequence of the abolition of voluntary disposition duty.

Where the provisions of subs ss (4) and (5) apply, the conveyance or transfer giving effect to the sub-sale is stampable on the basis of the consideration paid by the sub-purchaser, whether that consideration is greater or less than the consideration paid by the original purchaser. The potential problems arising out of the drafting of the two subsections were given detailed consideration in *Fitch Lovell Ltd v IR Comrs* [1962] 3 All ER 685, [1962] 1 WLR 1325 at 1341–1344. The general principle that can be extracted from that case is that the sub-sale relief will not be available in any of the following circumstances:

(a) where the original purchaser takes a conveyance or transfer before entering into the sub-sale agreement (see *Peter Bone Ltd v IR Comrs* [1995] STC 921 for a case where a purported contract was held to constitute either an actual conveyance of an equitable interest or an agreement to convey an equitable interest within the first limb of SA 1891 s 59 (1) and which indicates—correctly, it is submitted—that a declaration of a trust prior to a sub-sale is sufficient to prevent s 58 (4) applying);

(b) where the original purchaser so alters the nature of the property conveyed or transferred that it is not "the same" (although, given the style in which the provision is drafted, it would seem more natural to read the words "the same" as meaning "that which has already been mentioned before", rather than "that which is identical"); or

(c) possibly where the original purchaser enters into the sub-sale agreement before the main purchase agreement; or

(d) where the consideration provided by the sub-purchaser does not consist solely of cash, stock, etc equal to the market value of the property conveyed or transferred.

As regards (*c*) above, the wording of the legislation appears to require the agreements to be entered into in the correct chronological order. The Revenue argued this point in the *Fitch Lovell* case but Wilberforce J expressed no final view there on whether this was actually necessary. If this is a requirement for sub-sale relief, care should be taken if a contract is expressed to be "conditional". The word "conditional" has a number of meanings in contract law but if, in the circumstances of a particular transaction, it is being used to mean that no binding legal agreement exists at all until the condition is fulfilled, sub-sale relief would not appear to be available if the first contractual document was initially executed (ie conditionally) before the sub-sale was executed but only became unconditional after the sub-sale agreement was executed (or after the sub-sale itself became unconditional, if that was also initially a conditional agreement).

Where sub-sale relief is not available, two amounts of stamp duty will be payable on the instrument of transfer (one on the consideration moving from the original purchaser and one on the consideration moving from the sub-purchaser) or (on the assumption that multiple transactions fall within the subsection at all) more than two amounts if there are more than two transactions completed by a single instrument (one lot per transaction): *Keston v IR Comrs* [2004] EWHC 59 (Ch), [2004] STC 902.

This section does not seem to provide for what is to happen where, in the case of property contracted to be sold to a single purchaser for a single consideration, it is conveyed in separate parts or parcels at the direction of the purchaser, some to the purchaser himself and some to sub-purchasers. It has been suggested that the transfer of the property direct to the purchaser should be assessed on the basis of the appropriate proportion of the original purchase consideration, ie not including any pro rata share of the profit the purchaser may have made in respect of any sub-sales. This would seem to be the most logical application of this section and is supported by the decision in *Maples v IR Comrs* [1914] 3 KB 303.

In principle, subsection (4) can be used to mitigate stamp duty charges on the transfer of property of any kind. However, any attempt to use sub-sale relief for multiple sales of shares in UK companies (or any other form of property falling within the definition of "chargeable securities" in FA 1986 s 99) would give rise to at least one, and possibly more than one, charge to stamp duty reserve tax. Broadly speaking (but see FA 1986 ss 87–99 for fuller discussion of the subject) stamp duty reserve tax is chargeable on agreements to sell UK shares and other "chargeable securities" (as defined) unless stamp duty is paid on an instrument of completion, such as a stock transfer form. For example, if A agreed to sell UK shares to B, who agreed to sell the same shares to C, a direct conveyance of the shares from A to C would mean that no instrument of completion could be stamped to complete the agreement between A and B. Arguably, there would also be a liability to stamp duty reserve tax on the agreement between B and C since the stock transfer form executed by A in favour of C might not be regarded as being executed, as required by FA 1986 s 92 (1A), "in pursuance of" the agreement between B and C.

It should be noted that, in order to obtain the relief, the intermediate purchaser must make an onward disposition before "having obtained a conveyance". It is an open question whether the reference at that particular point in the legislation to "a conveyance" is a reference to a conveyance in the narrow, technical sense (ie an instrument which effects the formal transfer of legal title to a transferee) or whether it is a reference to a conveyance in the broader and vaguer sense in which that word is commonly used in the context of stamp duty legislation (ie as defined in what is now FA 1999 Sch 13 Part I para 1 (2), formerly SA 1891 s 54).

This could be of some significance because certain instruments might be provided to an intermediate purchaser which could qualify as "a conveyance" in the broader sense and so, contrary to the parties' subjective understanding and belief as to the effect of what they were doing, prevent subsale relief being claimed, on the basis that (without realising or intending it) an intermediate purchaser had "taken a conveyance" before entering into a further contract of sale.

In practice, the most likely instrument to cause such a problem is probably a power of attorney (a type of instrument which it is often said is *capable of* constituting a "conveyance" for stamp duty purposes—see *Diplock v Hammond* (1854) 5 DeGM&G 320—although the particular circumstances of the case should always be borne in mind when deciding whether such an instrument does in fact have the necessary characteristics). However, it should always be borne in mind (and see commentary on FA 1999 Sch 13 for a fuller discussion of the subject) that there is no limit to the range of instruments which are capable, in principle, of constituting a "conveyance" for stamp duty purposes.

As stated above, it is not entirely clear whether the reference to "conveyance" in this section is to be read as a reference to this broad concept but it is reasonable to suppose that it *is* to be so read. First, in terms of normal principles of statutory interpretation, it is reasonable to presume that a term which has been specifically defined somewhere in the relevant body of legislation, is always to be read in the light of that definition in that particular body of legislation unless the legislation itself specifically states otherwise. Nothing in this section specifically states that "conveyance" is not to be regarded as having its defined meaning (which, although now to be found in FA 1999 Sch 13, is still notionally located in the original legislation since the stamp duty sections in FA 1999 are required to be "read as one" with SA 1891). Secondly, although subsale relief is almost always applied to land sales in practice, there is no restriction, as a matter of principle, to the range of subject matter to which the section may apply (including company shares, despite the potentially unpleasant stamp duty reserve tax consequences, referred to above) and so no obvious reason why the concept of "conveyance" should be confined to its technical meaning in the sphere of land law.

59. Certain contracts to be chargeable as conveyances on sale

(See the notes printed at the end of the contents list to Part II Stamp Taxes.)

This section has been repealed and its substance reproduced as FA 1999 Sch 13 Part I paras 7–9. See commentary on FA 1999 Sch 13.

60. As to sale of an annuity or right not before in existence

(See the notes printed at the end of the contents list to Part II Stamp Taxes.)

The scope of this section was considered in *Great Northern Railway Company v IR Comrs* [1901] 1 KB 416, in which it was held that it does not apply to every contract whereby a right is acquired in consideration of a money payment, but that the transaction must be one of sale. Collins LJ stated (at p 426) that "to bring an instrument within this section, there must be (*a*) a sale of an annuity or other right, (*b*) that right must not be an already existing right, but must take its origin from the transaction of sale itself, (*c*) the right must be one, the sale of which is capable of being completed by grant or conveyance". See also the discussion of s 60 by Pennycuick J in *George Wimpey & Co Ltd v Inland Revenue Commissioners* [1975] STC 248.

Contrast *Cormack's Trustees v IRC* 1924 SC 819 (where an instrument securing an annuity agreed to be paid in consideration of a transfer of property was held not be an instrument given on the "sale" of an annuity) and *Faber v IR Comrs* (1936) 155 LT 228 (where a covenant by an engineer to pay an annuity to a company in return for the issue and allotment to him of shares and debentures of the company was held to be chargeable as a conveyance on sale under this section).

For an interesting scheme involving the sale of an annuity to a charitable company for tax avoidance purposes, which has now been held to be a fiscal nullity on the basis of the principles enunciated in the House of Lords decision in *W T Ramsay Ltd v IR Comrs* [1981] STC 174 and the cases that followed that decision (further described in the commentary on what is now FA 1999 Sch 13 Part I para 1), see the decision in *Moodie v IR Comrs and Sinnett (Inspector of Taxes); Sotnick v IR Comrs and Edwards (Inspector of Taxes)* [1990] STC 475.

61. Principal instrument, how to be ascertained

(See the notes printed at the end of the contents list to Part II Stamp Taxes.)

In all cases (except one) the parties to a transaction may determine for themselves which of several instruments is to be deemed the principal instrument chargeable to ad valorem stamp duty. The exception is where in Scotland there is a disposition or assignation executed by a vendor, and another instrument is executed for completing the title, in which case the disposition or assignation is to be regarded as the principal instrument.

Effectively, following the Court of Appeal's decision in the *Parinv* case [1998] STC 305, this section may only be used to choose between two (or more) documents where both (or all) such instruments are actually presented for stamping—ie, it is not permissible to present an unstamped original document in a UK court on the basis that the person presenting it has elected to treat another stampable document as the document which will bear duty but which is retained offshore to avoid actual payment of that duty.

77. Directions as to duty in certain cases

(See the notes printed at the end of the contents list to Part II Stamp Taxes.)

An additional rent which becomes payable if and when a lessee commits a breach of the covenants in the lease is a "penal rent", and no additional duty will be payable in respect of that rent. However, if the lessee has the option either of performing or abstaining from some action or of paying an increased rent, the increased rent will not be a penal rent, and additional duty will be payable accordingly.

No additional duty is to be charged where part of the consideration for the grant of a lease consists either of a covenant by the lessee to make any substantial improvement or addition to the property, or of his having previously done so, or any other covenant relating to the subject matter of the lease. Under the Revenue Act 1909 s 8, the exemption does not apply in respect of any further consideration in the lease consisting of a covenant which if it were contained in a separate deed would be chargeable with ad valorem stamp duty, and accordingly the lease should in any such case be charged with duty in respect of any such further consideration under s 4.

Subsection (5), concerning instruments which increase the rent under existing leases, has been repealed and replaced by FA 1999 Sch 13 Part III para 20. See commentary on that Schedule.

A deed of variation increasing the rent reserved by a lease, but leaving the original lease in existence, prima facie attracts "bond, covenant" duty, but this duty is relieved by s 77 (5) and is chargeable on the additional rent as if it were a lease or tack (see *Gable Construction Co Ltd v IR Comrs* [1968] 2 All ER 968).

83. Penalty on issuing, etc, foreign, etc, security not duly stamped.

(See the notes printed at the end of the contents list to Part II Stamp Taxes.)

Any person who, in the UK, assigns, transfers or negotiates a foreign security or a Commonwealth government security that is not duly stamped is liable to a penalty not exceeding £300.

STOCK CERTIFICATES TO BEARER

109. Penalty for issuing stock certificate unstamped

(See the notes printed at the end of the contents list to Part II Stamp Taxes.)

This section has been extended to cover instruments to bearer issued by or on behalf of companies or bodies of persons formed or established in the UK In addition, the provision for cancellation of stock certificates to bearer in certain cases is extended to certificates to bearer in respect of a unit under a unit trust scheme when the owner of that unit is registered on any register kept under the scheme.

PART 3 SUPPLEMENTAL

MISCELLANEOUS

117. Conditions and agreements as to stamp duty void

(See the notes printed at the end of the contents list to Part II Stamp Taxes.)

A purchaser is entitled to have every deed forming a link in the vendor's title duly stamped (*Whiting to Loomes* (1881) 17 Ch D 10, CA).

The second half of the section is somewhat obscure but appears to prevent a party from enforcing an obligation imposed on another party to pay any interest and penalties which arise as a consequence of late stamping. The words "liability on account of absence or insufficiency of stamp" suggest that the prohibition only applies to interest and penalties and not to the principal amount of duty payable immediately upon execution of a stampable instrument. However, it should be remembered that under the old system of penalties (contained in the version of s 15 which has been replaced by the new interest and penalty provisions inserted by FA 1999, with effect from 1 October 1999) a specific legal obligation to discharge the penalty was imposed on a designated person (eg on the transferee, where the document was a transfer on sale).

It seems to be the case that this provision against indemnities was based upon the fact that it was regarded as contrary to public policy to allow a person to indemnify himself in respect of a "wager" on the possibility that he would never have to pay duty at all. If that is correct, it seems questionable whether the same policy considerations can apply now that no identifiable person is charged specifically with any legal duty in relation to the discharge of the obligation to pay a penalty for late stamping.

This section might now assume greater practical importance, given the more onerous interest and penalty provisions which have been introduced by FA 1999 s 109. Quite apart from the fact that the provisions have become more onerous in general, it should also be noted that the application of these provisions has become more *uniformly* onerous. This is because the new penalty rules, in the reworded s 15, simply refer to "an instrument" on which duty has not been paid, whereas the old version of s 15 listed specific instruments.

In particular, the old rules imposed late stamping penalties on an actual "conveyance on sale" but apparently not on a contract which fell to be charged as though it were such a conveyance by virtue of what was then s 59 and is now FA 1999 Sch 13 Part 1 para 7. Even though the old s 59 appeared to treat such contracts as conveyances for *all* stamp duty purposes, the Stamp Office's own explanatory leaflets indicated that the reference to "conveyance" in the penalty provisions contained in the old version of s 15 did not extend to contracts which were treated as conveyances (some support for this being obtained from the fact that agreements for leases were specifically listed in the old s 15 even though such an agreement was, and still is, effectively stamped as a deemed lease and not under a separate head of charge—see now FA 1999 Sch 13 Part 2 para 14).

It seems that any such distinction has now been removed by virtue of the adoption of much more general wording in the penalty provisions. This, in turn, appears to have increased the range of documents in relation to which a person may in future need to rely upon indemnities and contractual undertakings to pay stamp duty (always presuming that such indemnities and undertakings are not rendered void ab initio by virtue of this section).

However, it is possible that the generalisation of the wording in the penalty provisions has created a new anomaly. This is because the new charging provision for contracts (now found in FA 1999 Sch 13 Part I para 7) carries over from the old version in SA 1891 s 59 the wording which specifically imposes liability on the purchaser to pay the duty on such a contract. It is an open question whether this obligation extends also to the payment of any interest and penalty that might have to be paid. It would be rather ironic if, in the course of removing any specific obligation to pay the penalty in the case of actual conveyances, the legislation inadvertently imposed such a specific obligation in the case of contracts.

It might be argued that the word "duty" in what is now Sch 13 Part I para 7 means only the basic duty and not also any interest or penalties that might be payable in the particular circumstances of the case. It is certainly the case that a clear distinction of this kind is maintained in some of the provisions of SA 1891 but this is largely because the provisions in question are specifically concerned with the imposition of interest and or penalties on the underlying basic duty. It is arguable that a reference to "duty" in a statutory provision which is *not* specifically concerned with interest and penalties bears the more general meaning of "anything which has to be paid in order to render the instrument duly stamped", in which case it would include any interest and/or penalties that were appropriate in the circumstances.

119. Instruments relating to crown property

(See the notes printed at the end of the contents list to Part II Stamp Taxes.)

Crown property is chargeable.

121. Recovery of penalties

(See the notes printed at the end of the contents list to Part II Stamp Taxes.)

Administrative fines are replaced by penalties under the provisions in FA 1999 Sch 17 Part I, and this section is therefore repealed, with effect from 1 October 1999.

122. Definitions

(See the notes printed at the end of the contents list to Part II Stamp Taxes.)

Note the definition of "stock" and "marketable security" becomes of even greater significance following the abolition of stamp duty on other forms of property. The definition of "marketable security" has been considered by the courts on a number of occasions. It appears that a security can be "marketable" whether or not it is actually dealt in on any stock exchange, so long as it is capable of being so dealt—see *Texas Land and Cattle Co v IR Comrs* 1888 16 R (Ct of Sess) 69, per Lord Shand. Thus, promissory notes of a type dealt in on The Stock Exchange have been held to be marketable securities (*Brown Shipley & Co v IR Comrs* [1895] 2 QB 598, 601, and *Speyer Brothers v IR Comrs* [1907] 1 KB 246, 259, [1908] AC 92). In addition, although HMRC do not in practice treat them as such, in theory the debentures of a private company containing no provision objectionable to The Stock Exchange, such as a restriction on transfer or possibly a prohibition against Stock Exchange dealings, are marketable securities (see *Deddington Steamship Co v IR Comrs* [1911] 1 KB 1078).

By virtue of FA 1946 s 54 (1), the expression "stock" also includes units under a unit trust scheme (although the stamp duty charge on a transfer of units was abolished by FA 1999, with effect from 6 February 2000, and replaced by stamp duty reserve tax—see commentary on FA 1999 ss 122 and Sch 19) and, by virtue of FA 1996 Sch 40, includes a strip of a gilt-edged security (as defined in FA 1942 s 47).

See also the commentary on FA 1994 s 239 in relation to the definitions of "executed" and "execution".

REPEAL; COMMENCEMENT; SHORT TITLE

124. Commencement

125. Short title

Finance Act 1895

58 & 59 Vict c 16

PART II STAMPS

12. Collection of stamp duty in cases of property vested by act or purchased under statutory power

(See the notes printed at the end of the contents list to Part II Stamp Taxes.)

Where, by virtue of any Act of Parliament, either (*a*) stock or marketable securities are vested by way of sale in any person, or (*b*) any person is authorised to purchase such property, then that person must, within three months after the passing of the relevant Act of Parliament, or the date of vesting (whichever is the later), or after the completion of the purchase, as the case may be, produce to the Commissioners a Queen's Printer's copy of the statute or some instrument relating to the vesting in the first case, and an instrument of transfer in the second case, duly stamped with the ad valorem stamp duty payable on a transfer on sale of the property.

Any transfer required to be produced need not at present include any goods, wares or merchandise forming part of the property, and if the property consists wholly of goods, wares or merchandise no conveyance need be produced (FA 1949 s 36 (4)). When the prospective abolitions (referred to in the note at the beginning of the commentary on SA 1891 s 1) come into effect, the exclusion in relation to "goods, wares and merchandise" will be extended to all "exempt property" (see the commentary on FA 1991).

In default of production, the duty and interest at the rate of 5% from the date of vesting or the completion of the purchase of the property, as the case may be, become a debt due to the Crown from the person in default.

It seems that the wording of this statute has not been modified as part of the general process, in FA 1999, of modernising the interest regime in relation to stamp duty and it is not clear how, if at all, the reference in this section to a fixed 5% rate of interest interacts with the apparently general wording of SA 1891 s 15A. The contents of SA 1891 s 15A notionally predate the enactment of this section (although s 15A has, of course, only just been enacted, as part of the reforms contained in FA 1999) and it should be observed that nothing in FA 1895 expressly requires that Act to be "read as one" with SA 1891 or indeed with any other stamp duty legislation.

The leading cases in relation to this section are:

(a) *A-G v Eastbourne Corporation* [1902] 1 KB 403 at 408, 409, CA; affirmed sub nom *Eastbourne Corporation v A-G* [1904] AC 155 at 158 (but overruled in relation to the definition of "property" by FA 1949 s 36 (4));

(b) *A-G v Felixstowe Gas Light Co* [1907] 2 KB 904 (in which it was held that it is not necessary, for this section to apply, that there should be a contract of sale between the parties—the terms of the sale may be imposed by Act of Parliament without a contract);

(c) *Lord Advocate v Caledonian Railway Co* 1908 SC 566 (in which it was held that a purchase of property by a railway company in pursuance of compulsory powers contained in the relevant special Act fell within this section, and that the date of "completion of the purchase" for the purposes of the section is the date of the final payment of the price to the seller).

There are numerous statutory exclusions from these provisions, mostly in relation to the nationalisation of industries and the setting up of statutory bodies. See for example the Aircraft and Shipbuilding Industries Act 1977 Schs 3 and 4.

There may, of course, also be a specific provision in the Act itself (ie the Act which would otherwise constitute the "transfer" for stamp duty purposes) which exempts it from any charge to stamp duty.

See further, in relation to nationalisation schemes, FA 1946 s 52.

PART IV MISCELLANEOUS

20. Short title

Finance Act 1898

61 & 62 Vict c 10

PART II STAMPS

6. Removal of doubt as to 54 & 55 Vict c 39 ss 54, 57, so far as regards foreclosure decrees

(See the notes printed at the end of the contents list to Part II Stamp Taxes.)

The definition of “transfer on sale” in what is now FA 1999 Sch 13 Part I para 1 (2) includes a foreclosure decree or order. The maximum amount of ad valorem stamp duty payable on any such decree or order is on a sum equal to the value of the property to which the decree or order relates. Any conveyance following upon such decree or order is exempt from ad valorem stamp duty.

Revenue Act 1898

61 & 62 Vict c 46

PART II STAMPS

7. Amendments of 54 & 55 Vict c 39

(See the notes printed at the end of the contents list to Part II Stamp Taxes.)

Postal packets are within the definition of the word "instrument" in SA 1891 s 9. SDMA 1891 s 24 applies to affidavits and oaths as well as to statutory declarations.

10. Amendment of 54 & 55 Vict c 38 s 22

(See the notes printed at the end of the contents list to Part II Stamp Taxes.)

After the discontinuance of the use of particular stamp duty office dies, documents stamped with discontinued dies are not duly stamped.

12. Extension of certain sections of 54 & 55 Vict c 36, to paper used for excise licences

(See the notes printed at the end of the contents list to Part II Stamp Taxes.)

Paper used for excise licences is within SDMA 1891 ss 14, 15 and 16 in relation to frauds in connection with the manufacture of paper provided by the Inland Revenue for receiving the impression of a stamp duty office die.

Finance Act 1899

62 & 63 Vict c 9

PART II STAMPS

5. Extension of stamp duty on share warrants and stock certificates to bearer

(See the notes printed at the end of the contents list to Part II Stamp Taxes.)

SA 1891 s 109 is extended to provide for a penalty for the issue of unstamped stock certificates to bearer by "companies or bodies of persons".

Finance Act 1900

63 & 64 Vict c 7

PART II STAMPS

10. Conveyances on sale

(See the notes printed at the end of the contents list to Part II Stamp Taxes.)

Where further consideration is expressed, in a dutiable conveyance on sale, as consisting of a convenant by the purchaser to make, or of his having made, any substantial improvement of or addition to the property, or as consisting of any covenant relating to the subject matter of the conveyance, such further consideration does not attract additional ad valorem stamp duty.

This section has been considered by the courts in detail in relation to the problems which arise in connection with conveyances on sale of building plots where at the date of the contract for sale no building has been erected, or a building has been partly erected, on the site which constitutes or is included in the subject matter of the sale, and where at the date of the conveyance a building has been wholly or partly erected on the site. The leading cases are *M'Innes v IR Comrs* 1934 SC 424, *Kimbers & Co v IR Comrs* [1936] 1 KB 132, and the three cases, heard together, of *Paul v IR Comrs*, *Span v IR Comrs*, and *Blair v IR Comrs* 1936 SC 443. (For a discussion of these cases, see the judgment of the Vice-Chancellor in *The Prudential Assurance Co Limited v IR Comrs* [1992] STC 863.) From these cases, the generally accepted principle appears to be that where the vendor and the contractor responsible for erecting the building are one and the same person, and the building contract is expressed to be conditional on the completion of the purchase of the site, then by virtue of this section the consideration paid for the building (as distinct from the consideration paid for the site) does not attract duty, even where the builder may have begun to build before completion. Where, however, there is in substance a contract to purchase a plot of land with a completed building on it, even where the contract is constituted by separate documents, then the consideration for the building will attract ad valorem stamp duty and s 10 will not apply. If the builder is not also the vendor, then the consideration paid for the building will not attract ad valorem conveyance on sale duty even where the landowner and the builder habitually act together.

See, further, FA 1999 Sch 13 Part I para 6 and SP 8/93.

Finance Act 1902

2 Edw 7 c 7

PART II STAMPS

9. Amendment of 54 & 55 Vict c 39 s 62

This provision extended SA 1891 s 62 (under which the duty charged on an instrument vesting property in trustees was limited to 50p) to cases where a trustee retired without a new appointment being made. This section, together with SA 1891 s 62, are repealed by FA 1999. Instruments which would have been protected by this section would now appear to be exempt from duty (including fixed duty) by virtue of SI 1987/516, such instruments falling within category "A" of the documents described in the Schedule to that enactment.

Finance Act 1930

20 & 21 Geo 5 c 28

PART IV STAMPS

42. Relief from transfer stamp duty in case of transfer of property as between associated companies

(See the notes printed at the end of the contents list to Part II Stamp Taxes.)

The general rule is that, subject to the anti-avoidance provisions contained in FA 1967 s 27 (3), discussed below, stamp duty under what is now FA 1999 Sch 13 Part I (ie conveyances or transfers on sale, and any contracts chargeable on the same basis) is not to be charged on any instrument if it is shown to the satisfaction of the Commissioners that the effect of the instrument is to transfer a beneficial interest in property from one body corporate to another and the bodies in question are "associated" at the time the instrument is executed. See also SP3/98 below (Appendix 2). Readers are also referred to FA 2002 s 111 under which group relief for transfers of land in the UK may be withdrawn if the transferee leaves the group within 2 years.

The relief applies only to stamp duty charged on a conveyance or transfer on sale under what is now FA 1999 Sch 13 Part I and not, for example, to a conveyance or transfer otherwise than on sale under Part III of the same Schedule. It might be thought that there would, in any case, be little point going to the time and trouble of preparing a claim for relief in respect of the fixed duties under Part III and this will generally be the case. However, situations can sometimes arise where a large number of instruments, perhaps several hundred, fall to be executed at the same time in respect of transfers from one nominee to another. The stamp duty consequences of such an undertaking would be not inconsiderable in their own right now that (as from 1 October 1999) all fixed duties are set at £5 (representing a tenfold increase, in most cases, over the old rates of fixed duty). There is no equivalent relief for stamp duty reserve tax so parties should beware of resting on contract or of sub-sales within a group as the stamp duty reserve tax charge on the contract will be extinguished only by a properly adjudicated conveyance or transfer. However, for a case where execution of an instrument of transfer of chargeable securities exempt from stamp duty under FA 1930 s 42 does not cancel the stamp duty reserve tax charge, see the commentary on FA 1986 s 88 (1B). For a case where FA 1930 s 42 is disapplied see SI 1997/1156 reg 11 in the context of open ended investment companies. For the application of similar group relief to stamp duty charged on leases and agreements for leases, see the discussion in relation to FA 1995 s 151.

Exceptionally, this relief is applied to stamp duty reserve tax in the context of the new rules on unit trusts in FA 1999 Sch 19—see paragraph 6 (4) of that Schedule and also the amendment made thereby to FA 1986 s 90. This is presumably because no meaningful adjudication of a stampable document could be sought in such a case, the charge to stamp duty on transfers of units in a unit trust having been abolished with effect from 6 February 2000.

The effect of the instrument must be to transfer a beneficial interest in property. There is no problem in the simplest case, where the transferor company is the beneficial owner of the property at the time the instrument is executed and the instrument in question causes the beneficial ownership to pass to or vest in the transferee company. However, it is fatal to the relief if the beneficial interest was not previously vested in the transferor body corporate but in an unassociated person or body corporate, or the beneficial interest does not as a result of the transfer vest in an associated body corporate. The most commonly encountered issues in this respect are as follows:

(a) usually the formal instrument of transfer follows a prior sale and purchase agreement between the two companies by virtue of which the beneficial interest will already have passed to the transferee before the formal instrument is executed.

In these circumstances, it was held in *Escoigne Properties Ltd v IR Comrs* [1958] ACT 549 that the formal instrument qualifies for relief because it would otherwise be stampable in respect of the value of the beneficial interest which passed by virtue of the prior agreement.

(b) A problem arises where the transferor company is in liquidation. A company ceases to be the beneficial owner of its property when it goes into liquidation: *Ayerst v C and K (Construction) Ltd* [1976] AC 167 (though not when an administration order is made in respect of the company under the Insolvency Act 1986: see ICAEW TR 799 "Tax aspects of the Insolvency Act 1986", June 1990 para 9 (*c*) *Simon's Tax Intelligence* 1990 p 631). Accordingly the transfer of assets by a company in liquidation to an associated body corporate would vest beneficial ownership in the transferee, but that beneficial ownership would not pass from the transferor company itself, and relief is therefore denied in these circumstances: *Holmleigh (Holdings) Ltd v IR Comrs* (1958) 46 TC 435 at 453. The effect, however, of the House of Lords decision in *Escoigne Properties Ltd v IR Comrs* as mentioned above, is that, where one associated body corporate goes into liquidation between (i) the date of a contract of sale entered into with another associated body corporate and (ii) the date of execution of the formal conveyance or transfer, relief cannot be refused. The company which goes into liquidation must not be the one which is required to be the beneficial owner of 75% of the ordinary share capital of the other body or bodies corporate.

(c) Relief is also denied if the transferor body corporate or, more commonly, the transferee body corporate, has entered into an unconditional contract to sell an asset to an outsider which is the subject of the intra-group transfer or has otherwise divested itself of beneficial ownership of the asset. Particular care is needed, for example, when it is intended that a parent will transfer an asset to a subsidiary, and then the subsidiary will sell it in order to crystallise the gain or loss in the subsidiary. FA 1967 s 27 (3) (*a*) is also likely to be an issue. Although it would not appear strictly necessary on the wording of the legislation, where beneficial ownership passes before the conveyance the Stamp Office's view is that beneficial ownership must still be held by the transferee at the time of the conveyance to it.

(d) Relief may also be denied if the transferee body corporate is in liquidation, as the beneficial interest will not vest in the body corporate if it is in liquidation.

(e) The fact that the relevant asset is subject to a mortgage, or that there is an arrangement in place whereby a charge will be created when the asset is received by the transferee, does not of itself mean that beneficial ownership is not held by the transferor or vested in the transferee, although FA 1967 s 27 (3) (*a*) is likely to be an issue (at least, in any situation where there is doubt as to whether the mortgagee's involvement goes beyond that of a normal third party lender).

(f) Where a company purchases its own shares from a 75% parent, relief should not in theory be available, because beneficial ownership of the shares does not vest in the transferor: the shares are treated as cancelled on purchase under the Companies Act 2006 s 688. In practice, however, the Stamp Office grant relief.

The reason for allowing relief in such a situation might simply be one of policy, although there is possibly also a technical justification, since FA 1986 s 66 states that the form of return required for such a transaction "shall be treated for all the purposes of the Stamp Act 1891 . . . as if it were an instrument transferring the shares on sale to the company". It is arguable that that phrase ("for *all* the purposes of the Stamp Act . . . ") deems a company to become beneficial owner of its own shares, purely for the purposes of analysing the stamp duty consequences of the transaction. This would be on the basis that analysing the possible entitlement to intra-group relief was one of the "purposes of the Stamp Act" for which the transaction was deemed to be a sale (since the stamp duty provisions of FA 1930, as with most post-1891 provisions relating to stamp duty, are to be "read as one" with SA 1891).

The transferor and transferee must each be a body corporate. This term is not defined but it is suggested that the entity should have its own separate legal personality and be capable of perpetual succession. The bodies may be incorporated anywhere in the world (*Canada*

Safeway Ltd v IR Comrs [1973] Ch 371). However, it appears that intra-group relief may now be extended in certain circumstances to entities which are partnerships consisting of corporate partners (even though such entities would not seem, at least under English law, to be "bodies corporate" in their own right) or where relevant group relationships fall to be traced through such partnerships (see the notes to FA 1930 s 42 in *Sergeant and Sims on Stamp Duties*). The Commissioners have stated that "body corporate" includes companies with limited or unlimited liability, companies limited by guarantee, charter companies and bodies created by statute. They also indicated that relief may be available where a local authority, being a body corporate, is a party to a document and the other party has a share capital which is beneficially owned by the authority: Stamp Taxes Manual 6.123.

In October 2010 the Commissioners published a change in their view of the scope of the phrase "body corporate": they now accept and assert that limited liability partnerships are bodies corporate for group relief purposes. This has two effects: first, an LLP may be the parent company of a group of companies, so that a transfer between two sister subsidiaries may qualify for group relief. Second, an LLP is treated as opaque, so that a subsidiary of the LLP cannot be grouped with corporate members of the LLP. Contrast this with the position which obtains where a general partnership or a limited partnership sits between its corporate members and a subsidiary owned by the partnership. In such a case a transfer of land from the corporate members to the partnership's subsidiary may be treated as a transfer between group members since the partnership is treated as transparent. Scottish partnerships require separate consideration: as both Scottish limited and general partnerships have legal personalities but are not bodies corporate, the Commissioners treat them as opaque but not as companies. Where therefore a Scottish partnership owns a number of companies, those companies cannot rely on the partnership to establish a group for group relief purposes.

The Commissioners have indicated that they will not seek to revisit earlier claims for group relief which would be disallowed following their change in practice.

The two bodies corporate must be associated at the time the instrument is executed. For those purposes two bodies corporate are associated if either one body corporate is the beneficial owner of not less than 75% of the ordinary share capital of the other, or a third body corporate is the beneficial owner of not less than 75% of the ordinary share capital of both bodies corporate. Such ownership may be either direct or through another body corporate or other bodies corporate, or partly direct and partly through another body corporate or other bodies corporate, in each case in accordance with the rules for determining chains of ownership as set out in FA 1938 Sch 4 Pt I. Until the enactment of FA 1995 s 149, the measure of association used to be 90% of the issued share capital.

Ordinary share capital has the same meaning for the definition of associated bodies corporate as for the definition of subsidiary for corporation tax. It means all the issued share capital (by whatever name known) of the body corporate, other than capital the holders of which have a right to a dividend at a fixed rate but have no other right to share in the profits of the body corporate. Shares are issued when registered: *National Westminster Bank v IR Comrs* [1994] STC 580. The test of association now requires 75% ownership not only of ordinary share capital (as defined in s 42(4)), but also entitlement to not less than 75% of any profit available for distribution to equityholders and of any assets available for distribution to its equityholders on a winding-up. The two bodies corporate will not be treated as associated if arrangements are in existence by virtue of which another person or persons together has or could obtain control of the transferee but not of the transferor. The definition of control is borrowed from TA 1988 s 840.

In relation to beneficial ownership and whether two bodies corporate are associated, the following issues are commonly encountered:

(a) Relief is denied if the parent, or any other company by or through whom the parent derives beneficial ownership of the transferor or transferee, is in liquidation. For this purpose it does not matter if the transferee itself is a subsidiary and is in liquidation, as its shares are still owned by the parent, but it is relevant to whether beneficial ownership of the relevant asset is vested in the transferee (see above).

(b) Relief is also denied if, at the time the relevant instrument is executed, there is an unconditional agreement to sell ownership (or other arrangement which has resulted in beneficial ownership being divested) of the transferee, or any other company by or through whom the parent derives beneficial ownership of the transferee.

(c) The transfer of an asset between unassociated parties for an issue of shares which will make the seller the parent of the buyer will not qualify for relief. This would seem to be on the basis that the critical moment when the parties must be associated is immediately *before* the relevant instrument is executed.

The concept of beneficial ownership and when it is lost is relevant to two aspects of relief under the section: (1) it determines whether beneficial ownership of the relevant asset is transferred and (2) whether the transferor and transferee are associated. But it can be a difficult question of law to determine at what stage beneficial ownership is lost. Beneficial ownership is transferred immediately upon entry into an unconditional contract of sale, but the analysis is more difficult in the case of a contract subject to a condition precedent or a condition subsequent, a call option, or informal arrangements not constituting a binding agreement which once begun are likely to be continued to their conclusion. The principal cases are *Leigh Spinners Ltd v IR Comrs* (1956) 46 TC 425, *Holmleigh Holdings Ltd v IR Comrs* (1958) 46 TC 435, *Baytrust Holdings Ltd v IR Comrs; Thomas Firth and John Brown (Investments) Ltd v IR Comrs* [1971] 3 All ER 76, *Brooklands Selangor Holdings Ltd v IR Comrs* [1970] 2 All ER 76, *Wood Preservation Ltd v Prior* (1968) 45 TC 112 and *Times Newspapers Ltd v IR Comrs* [1973] Ch 155. The decision of the House of Lords in *Furniss v Dawson* is also relevant. The leading case is *J Sainsbury plc v O'Connor* [1991] 1 WLR 936, where the Court of Appeal held that the mere existence of a call option granted to a third party by a parent company over shares in its subsidiary did not deprive the parent company of the beneficial ownership of those shares. The courts appear to be moving towards a position where beneficial ownership is not lost until specific performance is available, but this has not yet been stated as a principle or established as the ratio decidendi of any judgment.

In an answer to a question put at the 2009 Stamp Taxes Practitioners' Group Conference the Commissioners confirmed that the appointment of an administrator over a company or a receiver over the assets of a company did not, in itself, trigger a claw-back of any SDLT relief previously claimed or prevent the availability of SDLT group relief on a future intra-group transfer. This was because, in such circumstances, the company retained control of its assets, its shareholders did not change, so that control remained the same as well. The Commissioners also observed that such events did not usually, or in and of themselves, constitute an arrangement for someone to gain control of the purchaser but not of the vendor within paragraph 2(1). It would seem reasonable to assume that the same approach will be applied to stamp duty group relief.

In any claim for exemption under this section, the onus of proof is on the person claiming the relief. Section 42 (1) states that an instrument to which this section applies is only duly stamped if it has received an adjudication stamp. The Stamp Office have issued guidance notes for applications for adjudication. Broadly, the notes require the claimant to submit a sworn statutory declaration setting out the group structure and the circumstances surrounding the transaction. A change of practice was announced in the March 2000 Budget enabling group relief claims to be made without a formal statutory declaration.

PART VI MISCELLANEOUS AND GENERAL

53. Construction, short title, application and repeal

Finance Act 1931

21 & 22 Geo 5 c 28

PART III LAND VALUE TAX

28. Production to Commissioners of instruments transferring land

(See the notes printed at the end of the contents list to Part II Stamp Taxes.)

Upon the transfer on sale of the fee simple of land, the grant of a lease of land for a term of seven or more years, or the transfer on sale of any such lease, the transferee, lessee or proposed lessee must produce to the Commissioners the instrument of transfer, or lease, together with the required "Particulars Delivered Form" giving the information set out in Sch 2. The document is then stamped with a "produced stamp", in addition to any ad valorem duty stamp, and without the produced stamp the document is not duly stamped.

The procedure does not apply to any transaction within the scope of SDLT (see the SDLT (Consequential Amendment of Enactments) Regulations 2003, SI 2003/2867.

This procedure has been substantially amended by virtue of FA 1985 s 89 and the Stamp Duty (Exempt Instrument) Regulations 1985, SI 1985/1688.

See also the Land Registry Press Release of 5 April 1994 (Appendix 4).

To the extent that an agreement for lease (as opposed to an actual lease) has to be produced under this section, it appears that the more generous timing rule under FA 1994, s 240 applies if the agreement is presented at the same time as an actual lease—see paragraph 28 of the Revenue's guidance notes on FA 1994 (IR Tax Bulletin August 1995), reproduced at Appendix 6.

SCHEDULES

SCHEDULE 2 REQUIREMENTS IN CONNECTION WITH PRODUCTION OF INSTRUMENTS OF TRANSFER (SECTION 28)

(See the notes printed at the end of the contents list to Part II Stamp Taxes.)

This sets out the information to be provided on the "Particulars Delivered Form" to be furnished to the Commissioners.

Finance Act 1938

1 & 2 Geo 6 c 46

PART V NATIONAL DEFENCE CONTRIBUTION

42. Further provisions as to subsidiary companies

(See the notes printed at the end of the contents list to Part II Stamp Taxes.)

Section 42 (2) and Sch 4 Pt I are relevant for FA 1930 s 42 and FA 1967 s 27.

SCHEDULES

SCHEDULE 4 PROVISIONS RELATING TO SUBSIDIARY COMPANIES FOR PURPOSE OF NATIONAL DEFENCE CONTRIBUTION (SECTION 42)

PART I PROVISIONS FOR DETERMINING AMOUNT OF CAPITAL HELD THROUGH OTHER BODIES CORPORATE

These provisions are best illustrated by examples, as set out below.

(1) Where A owns 100% of B and B owns 100% of C, then A is also deemed to own 100% of C.

(2) Where A owns 100% of B, B owns 100% of C and C owns 100% of D, then A is also deemed to own 100% of both C and D and B is also deemed to own 100% of D.

(3) Where A owns 75% of B, B owns 80% of C and C owns 100% of D, then A is also deemed to own 60% (ie 75% of 80%) of C and D and B is also deemed to own 80% of D.

(4) Where A owns 75% of B, B owns 80% of C and C owns 55% of D, then A is also deemed to own 60% of C and 33% of D and B is also deemed to own 45% of D.

(5) Where A owns 75% of B and also 10% of C directly, B owns 80% of C and C owns 60% of D, then A is also deemed to own 70% of C and 42% of D and B is also deemed to own 48% of D.

(6) Where A owns 75% of B and also 10% of C directly, B owns 80% of C and also 5% of D directly and C owns 60% of D, then A is also deemed to own 70% of C and 45.75% of D and B is also deemed to own 53% of D.

Finance Act 1946

9 & 10 Geo 6 c 64

PART VII STAMP DUTY

52. Exemption from stamp duty of documents connected with nationalisation schemes

It is intended that this exemption should be repealed in the Finance Act 2012 with effect from 6th April 2013.

Transfers of property by Act of Parliament to bodies running nationalised undertakings are exempt from the duty which would otherwise be payable.

67. Short title, construction, extent and repeals

Finance Act 1949

12, 13 & 14 Geo 6 c 47

PART IV STAMP DUTIES

35. Abolition of and exemptions from other duties

36. Amendments as to conveyances on sale

(See the notes printed at the end of the contents list to Part II Stamp Taxes.)

Under FA 1895 s 12, where an Act of Parliament vests property by way of sale in any person, or authorises any person to purchase property, either the Act (in the first case) or the instrument of conveyance (in the second case) must be produced to the Commissioners duly stamped. It was held in *Eastbourne Corpn v A-G* [1904] AC 155 that the expression "property" included goods and other property not normally transferred by conveyance. That decision is nullified by this section and there is no need for a conveyance on sale of "goods, wares or merchandise" to be produced under FA 1895 s 12. If the prospective abolitions (referred to in the general note at the end of the contents list to Part II Stamp Duty and Stamp Duty Reserve Tax) come into effect, the exclusion in relation to "goods, wares or merchandise" will be extended to all "exempt property" (see the commentary on FA 1991).

However, it should be noted that this section only restricts the application of the rules in FA 1895 relating to property transferred by or by virtue of Acts of Parliament. It does *not* lay down any general rule to the effect that written transfers of moveable property are not stampable. Although such instruments are not generally required as a matter of law (except under FA 1895 s 12, hence the amendment in this Act to disapply that rule insofar as it extends to goods) such instruments are still stampable if the parties choose to create them. This is made clear by the wording of what is now FA 1999 Sch 13 Part I para 6 (2) (*a*): although the presence of "goods, wares or merchandise" in a mixed package of transferred property can generally be ignored when assessing the duty on documents connected with such a transfer, para 6 (2) (*a*) specifically states that this exclusion does not apply to "an actual conveyance or transfer of the goods, wares or merchandise (with or without other property)".

Finance Act 1958

6 & 7 Eliz 2 c 56

PART VI STAMP DUTIES

This Act formerly contained the provisions relating to certificates of value which, in conjunction with the provisions formerly contained in FA 1963, determined the rates at which duty was chargeable on any given set of facts. The subject of certification is now dealt with in FA 1999 Sch 13 Part I para 6—see commentary on that section.

Finance Act 1960

8 & 9 Eliz 2 c 44

PART V MISCELLANEOUS

74. Visiting forces and allied headquarters (stamp duty exemptions)

The Government intends to include provisions in Finance Bill 2012 to repeal this relief with effect from 6 April 2013.

Exemption from stamp duty is conferred on visiting forces and allied headquarters; this corresponds to the exemption granted to HM Forces. For a list of the countries and allied headquarters designated for this purpose, see the notes to FA 1960 s 74 in *Sergeant and Sims on Stamp Duties*.

Stock Transfer Act 1963

1963 Chapter 18

1. Simplified transfer of securities

(See the notes printed at the end of the contents list to Part II Stamp Taxes.)

This Act introduced a new system simplifying the means by which registered securities can be transferred. An instrument of transfer can be under hand in the form set out in Sch 1, executed by the transferor only and not also the transferee, and specifying particulars of the consideration, the description and number or amount of securities, the person by whom the transfer is made, and the full name and address of the transferee, and the execution of the form does not need to be witnessed.

A "brokers' transfer form" could be used in connection with the stock transfer form where a holding of shares sold on the Stock Exchange was to be transferred to more than one purchaser. The brokers' transfer form was superseded under the new system for Stock Exchange transactions introduced by the Stock Exchange (Completion of Bargains) Act 1976.

Section 1 (4) (f) has been substituted to read:

"(*f*) shares issued by an open-ended investment company within the meaning of the Open-Ended Investment Companies Regulations 2002"

by the Open-Ended Investment Companies Regulations, SI 2001/1228 reg 84, Sch 7 para 2.

See also the commentary on FA 1989 and the Uncertificated Securities Regulations 1992 (SI 1992/225); Inland Revenue Press Release, 14 March 1989 (Appendix 4); and DTI Consultative Paper: Dematerialisation of share certificates and share transfers (Appendix 9 of the 1990–91 edition of this Guide).

2. Supplementary provisions as to simplified transfer

(See the notes printed at the end of the contents list to Part II Stamp Taxes.)

The simplified system of transferring securities is not to affect any right of the directors of a company to refuse to register a transfer on grounds other than in relation to the form of transfer, or any law regulating the execution of documents by companies or other bodies corporate, or any Articles of Association or other instrument regulating the execution of documents by a particular company or body corporate. The result of this is that, although s 1 provides for the execution of instruments of transfer under hand, execution by a body corporate having a common seal must still be under seal.

See also the commentary on FA 1989 and the Uncertificated Securities Regulations 1992 (SI 1992/225); Inland Revenue Press Release, 14 March 1989 (Appendix 4); and DTI Consultative Paper: Dematerialisation of share certificates and share transfers (Appendix 9 of the 1990–91 edition of this Guide).

3. Additional provisions as to transfer forms

(See the notes printed at the end of the contents list to Part II Stamp Taxes.)

The Treasury is given power to amend the forms set out in Schs 1 and 2, or to substitute new forms in their place, by means of statutory instrument. The brokers' transfer form set out in Sch 2 was superseded under the new system introduced by the Stock Exchange (Completion of Bargains) Act 1976.

See also the commentary on FA 1989 and the Uncertificated Securities Regulations 1992 (SI 1992/225); Inland Revenue Press Release, 14 March 1989 (Appendix 4); and DTI Consultative Paper: Dematerialisation of share certificates and share transfers (*Moores Rowland's Orange Tax Guide* 1990–91 Appendix 9).

4. Interpretation

5. Application to Northern Ireland

Part II ST

Finance Act 1963

1963 Chapter 25

PART IV STAMP DUTIES

Note: This Act formerly contained the provisions setting out the rates of duty, and it also contained most of the key provisions relating to stamp duty charges on bearer instruments. The rates of duty are now set out in FA 1999 Sch 13 Part I paras 3 and 4 (or Part II, in the case of leases and agreements for lease). The main provisions relating to bearer instruments are now set out in FA 1999 Sch 15. See commentary on those provisions for further details.

MISCELLANEOUS

65. Miscellaneous exemptions

(See the notes printed at the end of the contents list to Part II Stamp Taxes.)

Applications for legal aid, and legal aid certificates, are not chargeable.

67. Prohibition on circulation of blank transfers

(See the notes printed at the end of the contents list to Part II Stamp Taxes.)

A penalty not exceeding £300 may be imposed on any person who completes a “transfer in blank” (ie, a transfer in which the name of the transferee has not been inserted) delivered to him pursuant to a sale of the stock to which it relates and who then parts with possession of it or removes it or causes or permits it to be removed from Great Britain. The maximum fine is £50 plus an amount equal to the stamp duty chargeable in respect of the transfer.

A transfer will be regarded as duly completed only when the name of the transferee has been inserted, that being either the purchaser or a mortgagee of the stock, a nominee of any such person, or an agent of the purchaser.

This does not apply to instruments chargeable under the “bearer instrument” head of charge, or which are exempt by virtue of Exemption 3 to that head of charge.

References to the purchaser of the stock are deemed to include references to any person to whom the rights of the purchaser are transmitted by operation of law. In the case of sub-sales to which SA 1891 s 58 (4) or (5) apply, references to the purchaser and the sale are to be construed as references to the sub-purchaser and the sub-sale.

PART V MISCELLANEOUS

73. Short title, commencement, construction, extent, amendments and repeals

Finance Act 1965

1965 Chapter 25

PART V MISCELLANEOUS AND GENERAL

90. Stamp duty: conveyances and transfers

(See the notes printed at the end of the contents list to Part II Stamp Taxes.)

The section nullifies *William Cory & Sons Ltd v IR Comrs* [1965] 1 All ER 917, where the owners of the issued share capital of the company entered into an agreement pursuant to which they granted an option to purchase their shares. They agreed that "with a view to protecting [the purchasing company's] rights arising out of the grant of the option" they would execute transfers of the shares in favour of the intending purchasers. The intending purchasers agreed that such transfers would not pass any beneficial interest in the shares, that they would hold the shares in trust for the vendors, and that if the option lapsed as a result of its non-exercise the shares would be re-transferred to the vendors. Transfers were accordingly executed and registered and almost immediately afterwards the intending purchasers orally exercised their option (as they were entitled to do). It was held that ad valorem stamp duty was not chargeable on the transfers as "conveyances on sale" because the liability of the transfers to stamp duty had to be determined at the time when they were executed, and at the time there was no sale but only an option, with the consequence that the transfers were not transfers "on sale".

Now any instrument whereby property is conveyed or transferred to any person "in contemplation of a sale of that property" is to be treated for stamp duty purposes as a conveyance or transfer on sale for a consideration equal to the value of the property.

Although this section is designed primarily to reverse the decision in the *William Cory* case, it can potentially affect transactions which are *not* deliberately structured as stamp duty avoidance schemes. In particular, it should be noted that the section does not require the contemplated sale to be to the same person as to that to whom the conveyance is made. There is a risk, in relation to transactions involving any property which constitutes "chargeable securities" for the purposes of FA 1986 ss 87–99, that execution of a stock transfer form in favour of a broker, as part of the arrangements for selling the chargeable securities to another party, could create an ad valorem stamp duty charge under this section which is *not* capable of "franking" the charge to stamp duty reserve tax on the underlying agreement. The wording of the stamp duty reserve tax legislation appears to require the stampable instrument which "franks" the stamp duty reserve tax charge to be created on or after the "relevant day" (ie the time when the agreement is entered into or when a conditional agreement becomes unconditional) in order to prevent a stamp duty reserve tax charge arising. Subject to extensions of the general principle of purposive interpretation (see commentary on what is now FA 1999 Sch 13 Part I para 1), there is no rule of law to prevent both a stamp duty charge and a stamp duty reserve tax charge on what is essentially the same subject matter.

This section also has had to be taken into account in relation to structures which have become relatively prevalent in relation to land sales, where legal title to property is transferred to a nominee company and a contract for the sale of the property is then entered into but left uncompleted (for instance because the contract is outside the FA 1999 Sch 13 para 7 charge on contracts), often accompanied by a transfer of the nominee company to the purchaser. The Revenue published a customer newsletter entitled "Split title schemes and section 90 FA 1965" giving guidance/warning in this area. It is thought that this section does not apply to lease grants.

The whole or part of the duty charged will be returned if, not later than two years after the making or execution of the instrument, it is shown to the satisfaction of the Commissioners either that the sale has not taken place and the property has been re-conveyed or that the sale has been completed but for a consideration lower than the value on which duty was originally paid. There is a view that the use of the words "the sale" in subsection (2) (*a*) means that s 90 is only applicable where a specific sale to a specific person is in contemplation.

Any instrument chargeable to duty under subsection (1) is to be adjudicated under SA 1891 s 12.

This section applies whether or not the relevant instrument conveys or transfers other property in addition to the property in contemplation of the sale of which it is made or executed, but this section is not to affect any stamp duty chargeable in respect of the other property.

To nullify the stamp duty avoidance schemes invented as a result of the House of Lords decision in *Stanyforth v IR Comrs* [1930] AC 339, in assessing the value of property for the purposes of a charge no account is to be taken of any power (whether or not contained in the instrument) of the person by whom the property was conveyed or transferred to have that property re-conveyed or re-transferred back to him, or any annuity reserved out of the property, or any life or other interest so reserved, being an interest which is subject to forfeiture. However, if any such power of revocation is exercised and the property is re-conveyed, then a claim may be made to the Commissioners not later than two years after the making or execution of the instrument for the duty or excess duty to be repaid.

97. Short title, construction, extent and repeal

Finance Act 1967

1967 Chapter 54

PART V STAMP DUTIES

27. Conveyances and transfers on sale: reduction of duty, and amendment of provisions for exemption

(See the notes printed at the end of the contents list to Part II Stamp Taxes.)

This section substantially amends FA 1930 s 42 which exempts from duty conveyances and transfers between associated bodies corporate, where one owns 75 per cent of the ordinary share capital of the other or a third body corporate owns 75 per cent of the ordinary share capital of each ("ordinary share capital" being defined for these purposes by FA 1930 s 42 (4)).

Subsection (3) and its predecessor, FA 1938 s 50, were introduced to counteract stamp duty avoidance schemes which had been developed in reliance on the reliefs available pursuant to FA 1930 s 42. The following cases illustrate the two principal types of scheme developed:

(1) *Shop and Store Developments Ltd v IR Comrs* [1967] 1 AC 472, the facts of which were summarised by Lord Reid as follows: " . . . a family who owned the shares of two companies, referred to as the clothing company and the property company, wished to turn the property company into a public company, to issue a number of shares for sale to the public, to obtain a Stock Exchange quotation and to get out of the proceeds a sum of over £250,000. An elaborate scheme was put into operation to achieve this. The only parts of it which I need to set out were first a sale of certain property by the clothing company (the transferor) to the property company (the transferee) for which the transferee gave to the transferor allotment letters for 2,920,000 new shares of the transferee, and secondly a sale by the transferor of allotment letters for 1,200,000 of those shares to underwriters . . . for £385,000. So as a result of carrying out the arrangement the transferor company had parted with the property and had acquired 1,720,000 shares of the transferee and £385,000." Relief was granted under FA 1930 s 42 on the transfer of the property by the transferor to the transferee, notwithstanding that the transferor had effectively received £385,000 in cash from a third party as part of the arrangements. As a result of this, it became possible wherever a vendor wished to sell property to a purchaser for the vendor to form a company as a wholly owned subsidiary and sell property to the company in return for shares which it could then renounce in favour of the purchaser for a cash payment.

(2) *Escoigne Properties Ltd v IR Comrs* [1958] AC 549, in which Lord Denning explained the "dummy bridge company" device as follows: "They took advantage of s 42 by forming a small company which was a puppet in their hands. It was done in this way: if Company A wished to sell property to Company B for £100,000 and avoid stamp duty, Company A would form a small "bridge" company of 100 £1 shares in which it held all the shares. Company A would convey the property to the "bridge" company for £100,000 but the price would be left owing. By reason of s 42 that conveyance would be exempt from stamp duty. Then Company A would sell the 100 shares in the "bridge" company to Company B for £100 and stamp duty of a trivial amount would be paid on the transfer. The "bridge" company would then convey the property to Company B for £100,000 on the terms that the £100,000 should be paid direct to Company A. By reason of s 42 no stamp duty would be payable on that conveyance. So the sale from Company A to Company B was completed without paying any stamp duty on the £100,000." See also, with similar facts, *Curzon Offices Ltd v IR Comrs* [1944] 1 All ER 606, and *Times Newspapers Ltd v IR Comrs* [1973] Ch 155.

Part II ST

The second of the above devices had been stopped by FA 1938 s 50; both were stopped by FA 1967 s 27 (3) which superseded s 50.

The Stamp Office have recently released a new Statement of Practice setting out their views as to the ambit of this section—see SP 3/98, dated 13 October 1998 (reproduced in Appendix 2). Whilst this is not a definitive statement of law, and is open to challenge in the courts like any other non-judicial expression of opinion, it is clearly prudent to pay close attention to the wording of this document when considering entering into a transaction for which it is desired to claim relief. (For criticisms of the Stamp Office's views in SP 3/98, see the article by Nock at [1999] BTR 21.)

For the relief to be obtained it must be shown to the satisfaction of the Commissioners not only that the effect of the instrument is to transfer the beneficial interest in property from one associated body corporate to another (as laid down in FA 1930 s 42) but also that the transfer was not effected in pursuance of any arrangement under which:

(a) the consideration or any part of the consideration for the conveyance or transfer was to be provided or received, directly or indirectly, by a person other than a body corporate associated with either the transferor or the transferee; or

(b) the beneficial interest in the property conveyed or transferred was previously conveyed or transferred by a person other than a body corporate associated with either the transferor or the transferee; or

(c) the transferor and the transferee were to cease to be associated by reason of the transferor or a third body corporate ceasing to be the transferee's parent (within the meaning of FA 1930 s 42).

The following types of situation commonly fall foul of paragraph (*a*): where the consideration for the intra-group transfer is left outstanding and a third party guarantees it or otherwise arranges to provide for it to be paid; where the consideration is left outstanding and is financed by an on-sale of the relevant assets to a third party; it is probably safer for the transferee to finance the purchase by way of a simple bank overdraft or pre-existing facility (see *Curzon Offices Ltd v IR Comrs* [1994] 1 All ER 163 and *Times Newspapers Ltd v IR Comrs* [1973] Ch 153 where this point was not taken by the Stamp Office) but a specific borrowing, particularly if secured over the relevant assets, taken out to finance the purchase may be caught (see also the debates in standing committee on the Finance Act 1995 amendments); where the consideration for the intra-group transfer takes the form of assets, as opposed to cash, and there is an arrangement to sell those assets; where land is transferred intra-group and the transferee grants a long lease of the property to finance the purchase; where, on the transfer of a trade, the outstanding liabilities are assumed by the purchaser and the creditor has joined in the sale; where the consideration takes the form of shares which as part of an arrangement are to be sold to a third party so the consideration is received by the third party.

As regards secured, or other transaction-specific borrowings, the Stamp Office may now be taking a somewhat more generous line than in the past. They specifically state in SP 3/98 that taking out specific borrowings and/or securing a loan on the assets being transferred does not in itself disentitle an applicant from claiming group relief. This would appear to be correct because the debates (referred to above) on what became FA 1995 suggest that the real concern was not in itself the provision or receipt of consideration by a non-associated third party (where that party was a professional lender and its participation was confined to the undertaking of bona fide commercial lending) but the possibility that an outright transfer of property to a third party could be effected in the form of what appeared, superficially, to be a lending transaction. In very broad terms, it appears that there is no objection, as such, to participation by a third party in a group transaction provided that the net result is not to leave the third party with a substantial interest in property which he has acquired from within the group without paying more or less the amount of stamp duty that would be paid on a conventional transfer of such property.

Circumstance (*b*) prevents the sale of property under a contract between unassociated companies being implemented with the benefit of relief by a conveyance or transfer at a time when they have become associated so that s 42 relief applies. Circumstance (*b*) will therefore prevent s 42 relief applying to the second sale in the "dummy bridge company" device and circumstances (*a*) and (*c*) will apply to the first sale.

As noted above, circumstance (*c*) prevents the hive-down of assets to a new company where there is an arrangement to sell the new company, thus preventing the repackaging of assets stampable at the rate of 1, 3 or 4 per cent in a company the shares of which are stampable at the rate of 0.5 per cent and also preventing the "dummy bridge company" device explained above. The receiver of a company contemplating a hive-down often has to time the hive-down so that it takes place before any arrangements are in place. As regards timing generally, if it is known that there is some reasonable likelihood of a transaction with a third party occurring some time after an intra-group transaction relating to the same property, the longer the interval of time between the two transactions, the easier it will be to demonstrate that the two transactions are not part of a single "arrangement". However, the Revenue specifically state in SP 3/98 that a long interval of time is not in itself conclusive as to the absence of an offending arrangement. Indeed, they specifically mention in SP 3/98 that, on the facts of the *Escoigne* case (see above), there was an interval of *four years* between two steps in a transaction. Care is also needed that there is no arrangement for the parent or any company through which the parent owns its shares in the transferee to be put into liquidation. An arrangement at the time of the intra-group transfer for a transfer of the *transferor* out of the group will not be caught as a third body corporate will remain the transferee's parent.

For the above purposes the expression "arrangement" does not imply that the parties are contractually bound to carry out all the steps forming part of the "arrangement", nor is it necessary that every step should have been determined by the parties before implementing the scheme. Thus a transfer of assets by the receiver of a company to a newly incorporated subsidiary with a view to selling that subsidiary would qualify for relief provided that the receiver at the time of transfer had no prospective purchaser in mind. The position would be more difficult where negotiations were in progress at the time of the transfer.

For many years the scope of "arrangements" has been based on *Times Newspapers Ltd v IR Comrs* [1973] Ch 155 when the judge said: "If I may refer again to the wording of the section it speaks of 'an arrangement where under . . . the consideration for the transfer or conveyance was to be provided directly or indirectly' by a person other than an associated company. The words quoted must, in my judgement, mean that the arrangement contemplated is one necessarily involving the provision of the consideration or some part of it by the person in question, and it is not enough for the Crown to say that it may or will probably do so". Relying on this the general view of tax practitioners had been that there were no "arrangements" where there were substantial commercial risks that the transaction may not proceed, because for example agreement might not be reached on price or some other commercial point. However, there have been indications that the Stamp Office since 1995 have been looking at applications for relief more critically and taking a somewhat tougher view of the meaning of "arrangements", particularly where the Stamp Office regard the transaction as taking unacceptable advantage of FA 1930 s 42 relief. In this respect, see para 20 of SP 3/98. The Stamp Office do not regard it as sufficient to argue that an arrangement will not exist because the overall plan "may possibly be frustrated by unforeseen events or unlikely occurrences".

It should be noted that there does not appear to be any scope for revising an initial adjudication where, the Stamp Office having originally refused relief on the basis that an offending "arrangement" existed, no transaction ever in fact proceeded in the manner contemplated by that arrangement. The Stamp Office are quite firm about this point in SP 3/98.

PART VI MISCELLANEOUS

45. Citation, interpretation, construction, extent and repeals

Provisional Collection of Taxes Act 1968

1968 Chapter 2

1. Temporary statutory effect of House of Commons resolutions affecting . . . , stamp duty reserve tax . . .

Changes in relation to stamp duty reserve tax and stamp duty land tax can take effect provisionally from the date of the Budget.

Where any resolution is passed by the House of Commons providing for the renewal for a further period of any tax in force or imposed during the previous financial year, or for the variation or abolition of any existing tax, and that resolution contains a declaration that it is expedient in the public interest that the resolution should have statutory effect under the provisions of this Act, then the resolution is to have statutory effect as if contained in an Act of Parliament.

The maximum period during which such a resolution can have effect is a period expiring (in the case of a resolution passed in November or December in any year) on 5 May in the next calendar year, and (in the case of any other resolution) at the end of four months after the date on which it is expressed to take effect or, if no such date is expressed, after the date on which it is passed. Any such resolution is to cease to have statutory effect, even if the period specified above has not expired, if within 30 days of House of Commons sittings after the passing of the resolution a new Bill giving effect to the resolution is not introduced, or an existing Bill is not amended so as to do so.

A resolution also ceases to have statutory effect if the provisions giving effect to it are rejected during the passage of the relevant Bill, or any Act comes into force replacing the resolution, or Parliament is dissolved or prorogued.

If a resolution ceases to have statutory effect or the period specified above expires before an Act comes into force replacing the resolution, then any money paid in pursuance of the resolution is to be repaid and any deduction made pursuant to the resolution is to be deemed to have been an unauthorised deduction. Similar provisions apply for the repayment of excess moneys paid, or excess deductions made, if the Act which eventually comes into force is not identical to the resolution.

A resolution with statutory effect under this section cannot be reintroduced during the same session of Parliament.

This section applies only to stamp duty reserve tax and stamp duty land tax. Similar provisions in relation to stamp duty, but with important differences, are made in FA 1973 s 50. Stamp duty, stamp duty reserve tax and stamp duty land tax are completely separate taxes and the provisions in FA 1986 and FA 2003 respectively introducing the latter are not construed as one with SA 1891.

Taxes Management Act 1970

1970 Chapter 9

Note: *The following modified provisions of TMA 1970 are applied by the Stamp Duty Reserve Tax Regulations 1986, SI 1986/1711, reg 20 as amended by the Stamp Duty Reserve Tax (Amendment) Regulations 1993, SI 1993/3110 and the Transfer of Tribunal Functions and Revenue and Customs Appeals Order 2009, SI 2009/56 art 3 and Sch 2 paras 2 and 19.*

PART III OTHER RETURNS AND INFORMATION

23. Power to obtain copies of registers of securities

HMRC may request a copy of the whole or part of a register of chargeable securities and must pay for it at the rate of 25p per hundred entries.

25. Issuing houses, stockbrokers, etc

An issuing house or person acting as such may be required to give particulars of the names and addresses of allottees and the number of shares issued to them.

A stockbroker may be required to give particulars of the parties to a stock exchange deal including the number and value of the securities dealt in. Similar information may be required of a person acting as an agent or broker. There is no obligation to return particulars of transactions effected more than three years before service of the notice.

26. Nominee shareholders

A nominee shareholder may be required to supply the name and address of the beneficial shareholder.

PART V APPEALS AND OTHER PROCEEDINGS

47C. Meaning of Tribunal

Following the introduction of the new unified Tribunal system, the historic system of appeals to the General and Special Commissioners has been replaced by an entirely new appeal system to the First-Tier Tribunal and the Upper Tribunal. The system came into effect on 1 April 2009. The rules for appeals in this Part V of the TMA 1970 apply to appeals against a notice of determination served by the Commissioners under reg 6 of the SDRT Regulations 1986. SDLT appeals are governed by their own separate procedure afforded by FA 2003 Sch 10.

49A. Appeal: HMRC review or determination by tribunal

The procedure will begin by the Commissioners serving a person (generally the accountable person: see reg 2 of the SDRT Regulations 1986) with a notice of determination stating that the person is liable for SDRT. Then, in accordance with reg 8 of the 1986 rules, the person in question may within 30 days appeal by notice given to HMRC. If notice of appeal is given, the appellant may then take one of two courses. Either he may notify the First-tier Tribunal of the appeal (see section 49D) or he may proceed by way of the review procedure (as to which see sections 49B and 49C). In line with the procedure adopted under the new tribunal rules, if notice of appeal is given to the Commissioners, the appellant may notify the Commissioners that he requires them to review the matter under appeal, or the Commissioners may notify the appellant of their offer to review it. Alternatively, the appeal may proceed direct to the tribunal. The review procedure is a potentially important stage in proceedings, since it reflects the philosophy that the parties should be encouraged to resolve their differences, if at all possible, outside of the confines of the tribunal. In order to fit this review procedure into the new framework, it will be understood that the legislation now contemplates two separate notifications of an appeal: the first, the *notice* of appeal, is given to HMRC by the taxpayer under reg 8 of the SDRT Regulations 1986; the second, the *notification* of the appeal, is given to the tribunal under TMA 1970 s 49D. The review procedure, if it is to take place, occurs between those two events.

49B. Appellant requires review by HMRC

In the event that the Appellant requires a review, the Commissioners are obliged to review the matter. However, as a preliminary element of the review process, HMRC are required to notify the Appellant of their 'view of the matter' (a phrase which recurs throughout this part of the TMA 1970) within 30 days of the receipt of the notice requiring the review to be undertaken. The time limit of 30 days is not, in fact, absolute. The legislation specifies 30 days 'or such longer period as is reasonable', which clearly will depend on the complexity of the case and (perhaps) how much work has been done on the case before the assessment was raised.

Section 49E prescribes the manner in which the review is to be carried out.

If, though, the appellant notifies the tribunal of the appeal in accordance with s 49D, this terminates the review procedure; it is no longer open to the appellant to require a review nor to the Commissioners to offer one; and if the appellant begins by requiring a review but then notifies the tribunal of the appeal, HMRC's obligation to complete the review process falls away.

49C. HMRC offer review

If HMRC offer a review, the procedure starts with the Commissioners notifying the appellant both of their offer to review the matter and of their 'view of the matter'. In every case it is important for the appellant to know at the outset what the Commissioners' views are as, although the expectation is that the review will be carried out by a different officer from the one whose decision or assessment has been appealed, the process is best served if the appellant is able to make considered representations as to why the Commissioners' views are wrong. In addition, and significantly, the appellant's notification of the Commissioners' view of the matter determines the provision which applies when notifying the tribunal of the appeal (as to which see ss 49D, 49G and 49H) and thus the time limit within which the appellant must notify the tribunal of his appeal.

Once the offer to review has been made, the appellant can either accept the offer – in which case he must notify HMRC of his acceptance within 30 days of the date of the offer letter – or he must proceed to notify the tribunal of the appeal in accordance with s 49H (rather than, it should be noted, in accordance with s 49D).

The importance attached to the review process is emphasised by sub-section (4): if HMRC offers to review the matter and the appellant does not accept the offer within the specified period, the Commissioners' view is taken to be conclusive of the matter. Since this will necessarily occur on the termination of the acceptance period (see above), the appellant will require the tribunal's permission under s 49H(3) in order to notify (and thus continue) his appeal.

It should be noted that there appears to be no s 49C(5). It would seem that the omission (while ineptly effected) is deliberate, being of a provision which would have prevented the appellant from withdrawing from an agreement with the Commissioners settling the appeal: cf FA 2003 Sch 10 paras 36C(5) and 37 and TMA 1970 ss 49C and 54 (as it applies to taxes other than SDRT). However, Part V of the TMA 1970 (as it applies for SDRT purposes) contains no equivalent to FA 2003 Sch 10 para 37 or TMA 1970 s 54 (as it generally applies), so that the provision which would have been s 49C(5) was considered superfluous and omitted.

49D. Notifying appeal to the tribunal

This section applies where the review process has not proceeded to the stage of the Commissioners giving the appellant their view of the matter, either because the appellant notifies the tribunal before requiring or being offered a review, or because, having required a review, he changes his mind and notifies the tribunal before the Commissioners have taken the preliminary step in the process. In such a case there are no restrictions on the appellant notifying the tribunal of the appeal. By contrast, if the Commissioners have given their view of the matter, the appellant's rights of appeal are somewhat more circumscribed (see ss 49G and 49H).

49E. Nature of review

Once the appellant has committed himself to the review process, either by requiring or by accepting an offer of a review, the nature and extent of the review are left at the discretion of the Commissioners themselves (sub-section (2)). The section does require that in determining what is appropriate the Commissioners must have regard to the steps taken before the beginning of the review both by HMRC themselves in deciding the matter in issue and by anyone else in seeking to resolve the disagreement over that matter. Presumably this means that if there has been an exhaustive dialogue between the parties as to the legal and factual aspects of the disputed matter, there is little need for the Commissioners to do much more than to submit the issue to a different officer for reconsideration. By contrast, if the notice of determination was issued in haste, it would be appropriate for the review to be conducted at greater length. In any case, the reviewing officer is obliged to take account of representations made by the appellant – provided that the Commissioners 'have a reasonable opportunity to consider them' (sub-section (4)). The circumstances in which HMRC might not have such a reasonable opportunity are, it is assumed, where the appellant both fails to offer any assistance until the statutory period of 45 days (see below) is almost exhausted before submitting his representations and refuses to agree an extension of the period for review. Other cases will ordinarily be resolved by the amicable agreement of the parties to take advantage of the liberty given to them by sub-section 6(*b*) to extend the period within which the Commissioners must notify the appellant of the outcome of the review.

The Commissioners have, as a general rule, 45 days within which to notify the appellant of the outcome of the review and their reasoning. This time limit may be extended by agreement. More importantly, time only starts running from the 'relevant day'. In the case where the review was required by the appellant under s 49B, the relevant day is the day when HMRC notified the appellant of their view of the matter; and under s 49B the Commissioners have 30 days from receiving notification that the Appellant requires a review before they are obliged to provide him with that initial view. In the case where HMRC offered the appellant the review (and where they were therefore obliged to give him their view at the same time as they offered the review), time runs from the date on which they received notification of the appellant's acceptance of the offer.

The possible outcomes of a review are indicated by sub-section (5); it may conclude that HMRC's view of the matter is upheld, varied or cancelled. Depending on whether the outcome is favourable to the appellant or not (or, if unfavourable, on the appellant's enthusiasm for further proceedings), the notification will lead either to the appellant pressing on with his appeal (as to which see s 49G) or to the conclusion of the appeal in accordance with the procedure set out in s 49F.

Provision is made for the case where the Commissioners fail to notify the appellant of the conclusions of the review within the prescribed period (sub-section (8)); the review is assumed to have upheld HMRC's view of the matter. In such a case, sub-section (9) requires the Commissioners to notify the appellant of the conclusions which the review is treated as having reached. Oddly, no time limit is prescribed within which the Commissioners must serve the appellant with this notification.

49F. Effect of conclusions of review

If the Commissioners give notice of the conclusions of the review, those conclusions are deemed to be conclusive of the appeal. Thereafter the appellant cannot deny his liability to pay the tax, save by notifying the tribunal of the appeal in accordance with s 49G.

49G. Notifying appeal to tribunal after review completed

As will have been seen in the commentary to s 49E, the review can be concluded either by the Commissioners complying with their statutory obligation to notify the appellant of their conclusions within the prescribed period (s 49E(6)); or by their failing to do so – in which latter case they are still obliged to serve him with a notification of what their conclusions are deemed to be (s 49E(9)). In either case, the appellant is permitted to move the appeal process to the tribunal by notifying the tribunal of the appeal. The period within which the appellant may notify his appeal is called the 'post-review period' and differs according to whether or not the Commissioners satisfied s 49E(6). If they did so, the appellant has 30 days from the date of the notice of their conclusions – not, it will be observed, from the date on which that notice was received by the appellant. If they did not, the post-review period begins on the day after that on which the notification period under s 49E(6) expired (ie 45 days after the beginning of the relevant period for s 49E) and ending 30 days after the date of the document in which the Commissioners gave the appellant notice of the conclusions which the review is deemed to have reached under s 49E(9).

Provided that the appellant notifies the tribunal of the appeal within the post-review period, the tribunal is required to determine the matter in issue (sub-section (3)).

49H. Notifying appeal to tribunal after review offered but not accepted

In a case where the Commissioners have offered to review the matter in question under s 49C and that offer has not been accepted, the appellant has until the end of the acceptance period in which to notify the tribunal of his appeal (sub-section (2)). That is to say, he must notify the tribunal within 30 days of the date of the document which offered the review (s 49C(8)). If he fails to do so, he must seek permission from the tribunal for late notification: sub-section (3).

Provided that the appellant notifies the tribunal of the appeal within the post-review period, the tribunal is required to determine the matter in issue (sub-section (4)).

PART VI COLLECTION AND RECOVERY

60. Issue of demand notes and receipts

Collectors of taxes must issue a formal demand to the taxpayer's last known abode and must, if requested, issue a receipt. Overseas tax is not collectable in the United Kingdom courts (*London & South American Investment Trust Ltd* v *British Tobacco Co (Australia) Ltd* (1946) 5 ATC 633, *In re Delhi Electric Supply & Traction Co Ltd; Government of India* v *Taylor* (1955) 34 ATC 10; *United States Government* v *Brokaw Shaheen and Seabrain United Kingdom Ltd* (1971) 50 ATC 95).

DISTRAINT AND POINDING

61. Distraint by collectors

A collector may distrain on taxpayer's goods and chattels for the payment of tax. The goods would be kept for five days and, if not redeemed plus costs, would be auctioned. A JP's warrant is needed for a collector to break into premises.

63. Recovery in Scotland

The rules as to distraint are adapted to Scottish law. Amended by Abolition of Poindings and Warrant Sales Act 2001 s 3(1).

63A. Sheriff officer's fees and outlays

A sheriff officer's costs in executing a warrant are chargeable to the debtor. Amended by Abolition of Poindings and Warrant Sales Act 2001 s 3(1).

COURT PROCEEDINGS

65. Magistrates' courts

Tax due of less than £1,000 may be recovered by summary proceedings as a civil debt by proceedings commenced in the name of a collector in a magistrate's court.

66. County courts

The collector may proceed in the county court for outstanding tax of up to any amount in England and Wales from 1 July 1991; in Northern Ireland there is still a limit.

67. Inferior courts in Scotland

The provisions relating to recovery in a magistrates' court or county courts do not apply to Scotland, but a debt within the sheriff's court limits (£250) may be sued for by the collector.

68. High Court, etc

The collector can sue for greater sums in the High Court or in Scotland in the Court of Session.

SUPPLEMENTAL

69. Interest on tax

Interest on tax may be collected as if it were outstanding tax; as to interest see TMA 1970 s 86.

PART VII PERSONS CHARGEABLE IN A REPRESENTATIVE CAPACITY ETC

INCOME TAX

71. Bodies of persons

The treasurer is responsible for making the tax returns and any officer is entitled to retain sufficient to pay any tax due out of monies coming into his hands.

72. Trustees, guardians, etc of incapacitated persons

A trustee or guardian of an incapacitated person is accountable or liable to the tax which that person would be accountable or liable for were he not incapacitated. The trustee may retain sufficient funds to meet the tax liability.

73. Further provisions as to infants

An infant's parent or guardian is liable to pay the tax in default of payment by the infant and may be proceeded against as if the infant's tax liability were his own.

74. Personal Representatives

Personal representatives are responsible for settling the deceased's tax liabilities subject to the sufficiency of the deceased's estate.

PART VIII CHARGES ON NON-RESIDENTS

78. Method of charging non-residents

A non-resident who has a trustee, guardian etc or branch or agency in the UK is liable to tax as if he were resident in the UK.

83. Responsibilities and indemnification of persons in whose name a non-resident person is chargeable

An agent etc of a non-resident is responsible for payment of the tax and may retain sufficient to pay this when accounting to his principal.

PART IX INTEREST ON OVERDUE TAX

86. Interest on overdue tax

Interest at the rate applicable under FA 1989 s 178, and the Taxes (Interest Rate) Regulations 1989, SI 1989/1297, runs from the accountable date (even if not a business day) until the date of payment.

90. Disallowance of relief for interest on tax

No income tax relief is available in respect of interest on unpaid tax.

PART X PENALTIES, ETC

93. Failure to give notice for stamp duty reserve tax

The basic penalty for failing to deliver a notice required under regulations 4, 4A or 4B of the SDRT Regulations 1986 is £100. If, though, the taxpayer's failure continues for a year or more after the last date on which the notice should have been given, the penalty which may be imposed is a sum not exceeding the tax which should have been paid. As to the possible defence of reasonable excuse see TMA 1970, s 118 (2).

Penalties should not be levied until any appeals have been heard, *A-G for Irish Free State* v *White* (1931) 38 TC 666. The Commissioners should be presented with the full facts in assessing penalties (*Stableford* v *Liverpool General Comrs and Others* [1983] STC 162).

Other cases on penalties include *Wells v Croydon Comrs* (1968) 47 ATC 356, *Taylor v Bethnal Green Comrs and IR Comrs* (1976), [1977] STC 44, *Willey v IR Comrs & East Dereham Comrs* [1985] STC 5695. Incorrect notice etc for stamp duty reserve tax

Where tax has been lost through the taxpayer's fraud or negligence the penalty is a sum not exceeding the difference between the tax due and the tax which would have been payable had his return been correct. The penalty is in addition to making good the tax lost. These are the maximum penalties unless HMRC institute criminal proceedings for fraud or perjury. In most cases settlements are arrived at to include a mitigated penalty. See TMA 1970 s 102.

97. Incorrect notice; supplemental

If an innocent mistake in any notice is not put right without unreasonable delay the mistake is deemed to have been caused by negligence and the penalty provisions of TMA 1970 s 95 apply.

98. Special returns, etc

If the taxpayer fails to comply with a notice under a provision in column 1 or to supply anything required under a provision in column 2 of the Table he is liable to a penalty of up to £300, plus up to £60 per day if the failure continues after the initial penalty has been imposed. A false return gives rise to a further penalty of up to £3,000 for negligence or fraud. No penalty is incurred if the taxpayer takes remedial action.

98C. Notification under Part 7 of FA 2004

A person who fails to make disclosure of a tax scheme, as required by the DOTAS rules, is liable to a substantially greater penalty than is generally imposed outside the class of tax-geared penalties. The standard penalty is up to £5,000, together with further penalties not exceeding £600 for each day for which the failure continues after that on which the initial penalty was set.

99. Assisting in giving incorrect notice, etc

There is a penalty of up to £3,000 for assisting in the production of an incorrect notice under regs 4, 4A or 4B of the SDRT Regulations 1986 or under FA 2008 Sch 36 (Information and Inspection Powers).

100. Determination of penalties by officer of board

In the normal case penalties are imposed by an officer issuing a determination. The determination must state the date of issue and date by which any appeal must be made. A further determination may be made if the officer discovers that the original one is insufficient.

In practice it is usual to agree a penalty with the officer which is then confirmed to him in writing in the form of an offer in respect of tax, interest and penalties to the Board, the consideration for the offer being their agreement not to institute or continue proceedings for the recovery of these items. Most offers will in practice be accepted at officer level with only larger cases and substandard offers being submitted to the Board.

100A. Provisions supplementary to section 100

Personal representatives are liable for penalties which could have been imposed on the deceased.

Penalties are due and payable 30 days after the notice of determination. A penalty is treated for all purposes as though it were tax due and payable.

100B. Appeals against penalty determinations

Appeals are made to the First-Tier Tribunal against penalty determinations as though they were notices of determination of an amount of SDRT. The First-Tier Tribunal may set the determination aside or confirm, or increase or reduce it. Appeal from the First-Tier Tribunal is to the Upper Tribunal, not only on a point of law but also against the amount of the penalty.

100C. Penalty proceedings before First-Tier Tribunal

Provision is made for proceedings before the First-Tier Tribunal for initial (capped) penalties for failing to give notice as required by regs 4, 4A or 4B, SDRT Regulations 1986, or to deliver documents or provide information under FA 2008 Sch 36. In other cases s 100 permits the officer to determine the penalty. In these cases, the Tribunal determines the penalty.

100D. Penalty proceedings before court

Proceedings for penalties in cases of suspected fraud may be taken in the High Court, which may determine a penalty whether or not fraud is proved.

101. Evidence for purposes of preceding provisions of Part X

A final notice may be treated as evidence of the matters specified.

102. Mitigation of penalties

The Board have power to mitigate penalties.

103. Time limit for penalties

Penalty proceedings may be commenced within six years from the date on which the penalty was incurred or at any later time within three years after the final determination of the amount of the tax.

104. Saving for criminal proceedings

The power of HMRC to institute criminal proceedings, usually for fraud or perjury, is reserved and remains unaffected by any settlement of the tax liabilities and penalties (*R* v *Hudson* (1956) 36 TC 561; *R* v *Patel* (1973) 48 TC 647).

105. Evidence in cases of fraud or wilful default

It is HMRC practice to inform the taxpayer at the beginning of an investigation that provided he gives full co-operation to HMRC the Board will usually accept a negotiated settlement.

Such an inducement towards co-operation does not serve to make any evidence provided by the taxpayer inadmissible for the purpose of criminal or penalty proceedings.

On 18 October 1990, [Vol 177 col 882] the Chancellor of the Exchequer gave the following written answer, replacing that of 5 October 1944:

> "The practice of the Board of Inland Revenue in cases of tax fraud is as follows:
>
> (1) The Board may accept a money settlement instead of instituting criminal proceedings in respect of fraud alleged to have been committed by a taxpayer.
>
> (2) They can give no undertaking that they will accept a money settlement and refrain from instituting criminal proceedings even if the case is one in which the taxpayer has made full confession and has given full facilities for investigation of the facts. They reserve to themselves full discretion in all cases as to the course they pursue.
>
> (3) But in considering whether to accept a money settlement or to institute criminal proceedings, it is their practice to be influenced by the fact that the taxpayer has made a full confession and has given full facilities for investigation into his affairs and for examination of such books, papers, documents or information as the Board may consider necessary."

The matter was further revised in 2002 in a response to a Parliamentary Question to the Chancellor:

> "Further to the statement made on 18th October 1990 at column 882 by the then Chancellor, the Rt. Hon. John Major, the practice of the Board of Inland Revenue in cases of suspected serious tax fraud is as follows:-
>
> The Board reserves complete discretion to pursue prosecutions in the circumstances it considers appropriate.
>
> Where serious tax fraud has been committed, the Board may accept a money settlement instead of pursuing a criminal prosecution.
>
> The Board will accept a money settlement and will not pursue a criminal prosecution, if the taxpayer, in response to being given a copy of this Statement by an authorised officer, makes a full and complete confession of all tax irregularities".

Subsequent to this the Commissioners stated (in Tax Bulletin 62):

> "The significant points to note are that a taxpayer making a full confession under this procedure may now be assured that the Inland Revenue will not pursue a criminal prosecution. The term "pursue" is used because the Revenue is a prosecuting body in its own right only in England and Wales. In Scotland and in Northern Ireland it refers cases to the Procurator Fiscal and the Director of Public Prosecutions, respectively, for their consideration.
>
> The revised text refers to a copy of the Statement being given by an authorised officer. For these purposes, an authorised officer is a current serving member of the Inland Revenue Special Compliance Office. A copy of the Hansard Statement will normally be given at the first meeting with the taxpayer after the case has been taken up for investigation under Code of Practice 9."

COP 9 (Civil Investigation of Fraud) (which sets out this policy in greater detail) has been revised to take account of the new penalty rules which came into effect for stamp taxes purposes on 1 April 2010.

PART XI MISCELLANEOUS AND SUPPLEMENTAL

COMPANIES

108. Responsibility of company officers

The proper officer of a company on whom documents etc should be served is the secretary unless the company is in liquidation in which case it is the liquidator. For a club the proper officer is the treasurer.

VALUATION

111. Valuation of assets: power to inspect

The Board have power to inspect assets for valuation purposes.

DOCUMENTS

114. Want of form or errors not to invalidate notice of determination, etc

Minor defects in an assessment or determination do not invalidate it provided the recipient is not misled (*Martin* v *IR Comrs* (1938) 22 TC 330 and *Baylis* v *Gregory* [1986] STC 22).

INTERPRETATION

118. Interpretation

Various terms are defined. It should be noted that failure to comply with a time limit is not enforced where the Commissioners grant further time within which the required action is completed, nor while there is reasonable excuse for not doing it (*Thorne* v *General Comrs for Sevenoaks* [1989] STC 560).

Finance Act 1970

1970 Chapter 24

PART III STAMP DUTIES

MISCELLANEOUS

33. Composition by stock exchanges in respect of transfer duty

The Commissioners may enter into an agreement with, or with persons acting on behalf of, any recognised investment exchange or recognised clearing house for the composition of the stamp duty chargeable in respect of a "conveyance or transfer on sale" or a "conveyance or transfer otherwise than on sale" in what is now FA 1999 Sch 13 Part I para 1 or Part III para 1, as the case may be, on such instruments as may be specified in the agreement. For that purpose the expressions "recognised investment exchange" and "recognised clearing house" have the same meaning as in the Financial Services Act 1986.

Such an agreement must provide for every instrument to bear on its face an indication of the stamp duty chargeable thereon, and for the issue in respect of every such instrument by or on behalf of the relevant investment exchange or clearing house of a certificate to the effect that stamp duty to the amount so indicated has been or will be accounted for to the Commissioners. It must also provide for the delivery to the Commissioners by or on behalf of the relevant investment exchange or clearing house of periodical accounts in respect of instruments to which the agreement relates, and for the payment to the Commissioners by or on behalf of the relevant investment exchange or clearing house (on the delivery of any such account) of the aggregate amount of the stamp duty chargeable on the instruments to which the agreement relates during the period to which the account relates.

A fine is payable by any investment exchange or clearing house which is a party to such an agreement and which is in default in delivering any accounts required by the agreement, or in paying any amounts due, and amounts due bear interest from the due date for delivery of the relevant account to the date of actual payment.

36. Citation, interpretation, construction, extent and repeals

Finance Act 1971

1971 Chapter 68

PART V MISCELLANEOUS

64. Stamp duty—abolition of duty on bonds, mortgages etc

(See the notes printed at the end of the contents list to Part II Stamp Taxes.)

This provision has been repealed and replaced by FA 1999 Sch 13 Part IV para 2 (*a*). See commentary on that section.

Finance Act 1973

1973 Chapter 51

PART V STAMP DUTY

50. Temporary statutory effect of House of Commons resolution affecting stamp duties

This section applies to stamp duty similar provisions as are applied to income tax by virtue of PCTA 1968 s 1. There are, however, important differences. Income tax is directly enforceable by assessment, so that if a resolution lapses any tax paid while it was in force can easily be repaid to the taxpayer. Stamp duty, on the other hand, is a tax on instruments and the lapse of a resolution cannot affect anything done while it was in force.

If the House of Commons passes a resolution providing for the variation or abolition of an existing stamp duty, and the resolution is expressed to have effect for a certain period and contains a declaration that it is expedient in the public interest that the resolution should have statutory effect, then (subject as mentioned below) the resolution has statutory effect for the period so stated as if it were contained in an Act of Parliament.

The maximum period which can be stated in such a resolution is the period beginning on a date stated in the resolution and ending on (or up to 31 days after) the earliest of:

(a) the 30th day of House of Commons sittings without a Bill containing provisions to the same effect as the resolution being read for a second time, or without a Bill being amended so as to include similar provisions;
(b) the rejection of the provisions during the passage through the House of Commons of a Bill containing them;
(c) the dissolution or prorogation of Parliament; and
(d) the expiration of six months from the date on which the resolution takes effect.

A resolution also ceases to have statutory effect if an Act of Parliament varying or abolishing the relevant duty comes into force.

The ending of the period for which a resolution has statutory effect under these provisions does not affect the validity of anything done while it is in force.

PART VI MISCELLANEOUS AND GENERAL

54. Amendments consequential on establishment of the Stock Exchange

Various amendments were made as a consequence of the establishment of The Stock Exchange.

59. Citation, interpretation, construction, extent and repeals

Friendly Societies Act 1974

1974 Chapter 46

105A. Exemption from stamp duty land tax

Exemption from stamp duty land tax is granted in respect of a land transaction effected:

(a) where two or more registered societies amalgamated; and

(b) where there is a transfer of engagements under FSA 1974 s 82.

The exemption is to be claimed in the appropriate land transaction return.

Finance Act 1976

1976 Chapter 40

PART V MISCELLANEOUS AND SUPPLEMENTARY

127. Stamp duty: stock exchange transfers

This section prepared the way for the introduction by The Stock Exchange of the TALISMAN system, its computerised settlement and stock transfer system, TALISMAN being a contraction of the words "Transfer Accounting, Lodgement for Investors and Stock Management for jobbers". In relation to any transfer giving effect to a transaction carried out on or after 27 October 1986 (ie, the date on which the Stock Exchange rule prohibiting a person from carrying on business as both a broker and jobber was abolished or, more commonly, "Big Bang") stamp duty is not to be chargeable on any transfer to a "Stock Exchange nominee", meaning "any person designated for the purposes of this section as a nominee of The Stock Exchange by an order made by the Secretary of State".

131. Inter-American Development Bank

This confers exemption from stamp duty under the "bearer instrument" head of charge in what is now FA 1999 Sch 15 in relation to any instrument issued by the Inter-American Development Bank.

Finance Act 1980

1980 Chapter 48

PART V STAMP DUTY

97. Shared ownership transactions

The Government intends to include provisions in the Finance Act 2012 to repeal this relief with effect from 6 April 2013.

Local authorities, housing associations and housing action trusts have introduced shared ownership or equity sharing schemes to enable those people who could not afford to buy their council houses in the normal way to do so in stages, whereby they would purchase part of the house and then pay rental on the balance, with an option to acquire the entire reversion. To avoid such persons paying more stamp duty than they would otherwise have had to if they had bought the whole house, they can elect to pay "conveyance or transfer on sale" duty on the market value of the house, instead of both lease duty on the grant of the lease and conveyance duty on the purchase of the reversion. A private landlord who has taken over a public housing estate can similarly elect as regards leases granted on or after 1 August 1987.

The provisions only apply where a lease is granted for the exclusive use of the lessee or joint lessees, partly in consideration of the rent and partly in consideration of a premium calculated by reference to the market value or a sum calculated by reference to that value (ie, whether at market value, or at either a premium or discount to market value). The lease must provide for the lessee to acquire the reversion and contain a statement of the market value and a statement to the effect that the parties intend duty to be charged in accordance with these provisions. In addition, the lease must be granted by one of the specified bodies. No duty will be payable upon the sale of the reversion provided that the conveyance of the reversion includes a statement that it has been executed pursuant to a lease stamped in accordance with these provisions.

98. Maintenance funds for historic buildings

(See the notes printed at the end of the contents list to Part II Stamp Taxes.)

No stamp duty is chargeable on any instrument whereby property ceases to be comprised in a settlement, if as a result of the property or part of it becoming comprised in another settlement (other than by the instrument itself) there is by virtue of IHTA 1984 Sch 4 para 9 (1) or 17 (1) no IHT charge in respect of it, or by virtue of para 9 (4) or 17 (4) only a reduced charge. The provisions are those relating to exemptions for transfers of property into settlements for the maintenance of historic buildings. Where only part of the property becomes comprised in the other settlement referred to, liability to stamp duty in relation to the rest is not affected, provided that the relevant instrument is adjudicated under SA 1891 s 12.

102. Conveyance in consideration of debt

(See the notes printed at the end of the contents list to Part II Stamp Taxes.)

Under SA 1891 s 57, where property is conveyed in consideration wholly or in part of any debt due, the debt is to be deemed to form the whole or part, as the case may be, of the consideration in respect of which the conveyance is chargeable with ad valorem duty. As a result of a number of cases concerning s 57 (eg, *IR Comrs v North British Railway Company* 1901 4 F (Ct of Sess) 389; *Huntington v IR Comrs* [1896] 1 QB 422; and *IR Comrs v City of Glasgow Bank Liquidators* 1981 8 R (Ct of Sess) 389) it became increasingly uncertain as to the correct treatment of cases where the value of the property transferred was less than the amount of the indebtedness agreed to be discharged.

The Revenue attempted to clarify the position by the issue on 8 November 1978 of Statement of Practice SP 5/78 to the effect that duty would in such circumstances be charged on the amount of the indebtedness agreed to be discharged.

It was generally thought that this practice was unfair and, in an attempt to mitigate its results, it is provided that where the property is conveyed wholly or in part in consideration of a debt due to *the transferee*, then the duty chargeable is limited by reference to the value of the property conveyed if this is less than the amount of the debt, provided that the conveyance is adjudicated under SA 1891 s 12.

The relief only applies where a conveyance is made to a creditor in discharge of a debt due to him.

Finance Act 1981

1981 Chapter 35

PART VI STAMP DUTY

107. Sale of houses at discount by local authorities etc

(See the notes printed at the end of the contents list to Part II Stamp Taxes.)

Where there has been a sale of a dwelling house (including the grant of a lease) by any of the bodies specified, and such sale has been at a discount, the conveyance or transfer on sale to give effect to it is liable to stamp duty ad valorem (if any) on the post-discount price actually paid. No account is to be taken of any discount that might have to be repaid in certain circumstances, eg, if the property is resold.

See also the Local Government Reorganisation (Preservation of Right to Buy) Order 1986, SI 1986/2092, para 12.

108. Shared ownership transactions

This provision will be repealed, together with the principal section Finance Act 1980 s 97, with effect from 6 April 2013 by Finance Act 2012.

FA 1980 s 97 is amended in relation to stamp duty in "shared ownership transactions", so as to ensure that that section applies to sales at a discount price. The earlier provisions are extended to some leasehold cases that were not previously covered. A private landlord who has taken over a public housing estate is covered as regards leases granted on or after 1 August 1987.

110. Pooled pension funds

In the legislation governing the position of unit trusts for stamp duty purposes, references to unit trust schemes do not include references to common investment arrangements made by the trustees of exempt approved schemes (within the meaning of TA 1988 s 592 (1)) solely for the purposes of the schemes.

PART X MISCELLANEOUS AND SUPPLEMENTARY

139. Short title, interpretation, construction and repeals

British Telecommunications Act 1981

1981 Chapter 38

81. Stamp duty

(See the notes printed at the end of the contents list to Part II Stamp Taxes.)

Stamp duty is not chargeable on any instrument certified to the Commissioners by the Corporation, the Post Office, or by any wholly-owned subsidiary of either of them, as having being made or executed in pursuance of s 10 or Sch 2, provided that such instrument is adjudicated under SA 1891 s 12.

Finance Act 1982

1982 Chapter 39

PART V STAMP DUTY

129. Exemption from duty on grants, transfers to charities, etc

(See the notes printed at the end of the contents list to Part II Stamp Taxes.)

Where any conveyance, transfer or lease is made or agreed to be made to a body of persons established for charitable purposes only or to the trustees of a trust so established or to the Trustees of the National Heritage Memorial Fund, no stamp duty is chargeable on any conveyance or lease by virtue of what is now FA 1999 Sch 13 Parts I and II, provided that the instrument in question is adjudicated under SA 1891 s 12.

Finance Act 1983

1983 Chapter 28

PART IV MISCELLANEOUS AND SUPPLEMENTARY

MISCELLANEOUS

46. Historic Buildings and Monuments Commission for England

For the purposes of FA 1982 s 129, the Historic Buildings and Monuments Commission for England is to be treated as a body of persons established for charitable purposes only.

Finance (No 2) Act 1983

1983 Chapter 49

PART III MISCELLANEOUS AND SUPPLEMENTARY

15. Relief from Stamp duty for local constituency associations of political parties on reorganisation of constituencies

(See the notes printed at the end of the contents list to Part II Stamp Taxes.)

An existing constituency association may dispose of land either (*a*) to a new constituency association which is a successor to the existing constituency association (which it will be if any part of the existing association's area is comprised in the new association's area), or (*b*) to a body (whether corporate or unincorporate) which is an organ of the political party concerned and, as soon as practicable thereafter, that body disposes of the land to a new constituency association which is a successor to the existing constituency association. In such cases SA 1891 s 57 (conveyances in consideration of a debt to be charged with ad valorem duty as if the debt forms the whole or part of the consideration for the conveyance) do not apply in relation to conveyances or transfers giving effect to any such disposal.

Finance Act 1984

1984 Chapter 43

PART IV STAMP DUTY

110. Extension of stamp duty relief on sales at discount

(See the notes printed at the end of the contents list to Part II Stamp Taxes.)

In relation to the sale of dwelling houses by certain public sector bodies at a discounted price subject to a condition that the discount should be paid in the event of the purchaser re-selling the property within a specified period, stamp duty is payable by reference to the price after deduction of the discount notwithstanding the possibility that the discount may subsequently become payable by the purchaser.

The UK Atomic Energy Authority is also added to the list of bodies to which the provisions apply, and the Treasury is empowered by statutory instrument to prescribe other bodies at a later date.

The relevant provisions are also extended to apply where the transfer in question is in relation to a sub-sale at a discount price by a housing association.

See also the Local Government Reorganisation (Preservation of Right to Buy) Order 1986, SI 1986/2092, para 12 and FA 1988 s 142.

111. Agreements for leases

(See the notes printed at the end of the contents list to Part II Stamp Taxes.)

Where an interest in land is conveyed or transferred, or a lease is granted, subject to an agreement for a lease exceeding 35 years, the conveyance transfer or lease must bear a denoting stamp to the effect that duty has been paid upon the agreement for lease. However, this applies only where the agreement for lease is directly enforceable against the interest in the land which is conveyed or transferred, or out of which a new lease is granted, and not where the agreement for lease is enforceable against some other interest to which the interest conveyed or transferred, or the lease granted, is superior.

See also now the provisions of FA 1994.

PART VI MISCELLANEOUS AND SUPPLEMENTARY

MISCELLANEOUS

126. Tax exemptions in relation to designated international organisations

(See the notes printed at the end of the contents list to Part II Stamp Taxes.)

There is complete exemption from stamp duty in relation to the issue of any instrument by, or the transfer of the stock constituted by or transferable by means of any instrument issued by, certain international organisations of which the UK or any EC country is a member, provided that the relevant membership agreement provides for the relevant organisation to be granted this type of exemption, and provided the Treasury designates the organisation by statutory instrument.

Similarly, there is an exemption from the stamp duty reserve tax that would otherwise be chargeable under FA 1986 ss 93 or 94, on securities issued on a UK register by any such organisation to a nominee for either a depositary bank or a clearance service (as to which, see

Revenue Press Release, 14 June 1990, the commentary on FA 1990, and SI 1991/1202—The International Organisations (Tax Exempt Securities) Order 1991).

128. Short title, interpretation, construction and repeals

Finance Act 1985

1985 Chapter 54

PART III STAMP DUTY

81. Renounceable letters of allotment etc

The background to this section is described in the commentary on the "bearer instrument" head of charge in what is now FA 1999 Sch 15.

Where there is an arrangement pursuant to which rights to shares in a company are renounced in favour of a person who (together with persons connected with him) has control of that company, or will have such control in consequence of the arrangement, the instrument is not to be exempt from stamp duty as a "transfer on sale" under FA 1999 Sch 13, by virtue of para 24(*d*) of that Schedule.

The provisions also apply where the rights renounced are rights to convertible loan capital and excessive return capital, to which FA 1976 s 116(1) does not apply by virtue of FA 1976 s 126(2) or (3). The word "shares" includes stock.

A person has control of a company if he has power to control that company's affairs by virtue of holding shares in, or possessing voting power in relation to, that company, or any other body corporate.

"Connected person" has the meaning in TCGA 1992.

The provisions apply to instruments where the rights are renounced under them on or after 1 August 1985, except where the renunciation results from an offer which had become unconditional as to acceptances on or before 27 June 1985.

82. Gifts inter vivos

By virtue of F(1909–10)A 1910 s 74, any conveyance or transfer operating as a "voluntary disposition inter vivos" was formerly chargeable as a conveyance or transfer on sale for a consideration equal to the value of the property conveyed or transferred. A "voluntary disposition inter vivos" was defined as "any conveyance or transfer (not being a disposition made in favour of a purchaser or incumbrancer or other person in good faith and for valuable consideration)". For that purpose, the consideration was deemed not to be "valuable" where the Commissioners were of the opinion "that by reason of the inadequacy of the sum paid as consideration or other circumstances the conveyance or transfer confers a substantial benefit on the person to whom the property is conveyed or transferred", except where the consideration was marriage. F(1909–10)A 1910 s 74 did not apply in certain circumstances, for example where the conveyance or transfer was for a nominal consideration to secure a loan or where the conveyance or transfer did not pass the beneficial interest in the property. However, all such conveyances or transfers were required to be adjudicated under SA 1891 s 12 and the body of case law regarding the interpretation of s 74, and the valuation of property for the purpose of s 74, is voluminous.

For a detailed discussion of this topic see *Sergeant & Sims on Stamp Duties* (8th edn), pp 202–214.

F(1909–10)A 1910 s 74, and the ad valorem stamp duty charged thereunder on conveyances or transfers operating as voluntary dispositions inter vivos, was abolished by this section.

Notwithstanding the abolition, certain instruments which would have been chargeable under the abolished provisions had still to be adjudicated under SA 1891 s 12. The effect was to require the adjudication of any conveyance or transfer operating as a voluntary disposition inter vivos, within the meaning of the abolished provisions, provided that it did not attract

Part II ST

stamp duty under what was then the "conveyance or transfer on sale" head of charge in SA 1891 Sch 1 (now FA 1999 Sch 13 Part I para 1). This meant that where a transaction was one of sale the conveyance or transfer did not need to be adjudicated, whether or not the sale was at an undervalue, but where the transaction was not one of sale the conveyance or transfer of the property did need to be adjudicated if it fell within the definition of a "voluntary disposition inter vivos" under the abolished provisions. The most obvious example of this was in the case of a transfer of property by way of gift, but there are a large number of other transactions which as a matter of law are deemed to involve "conveyances or transfers" and because the consideration is other than cash, stock (including shares and units under a unit trust scheme), marketable or other securities, or debts, they are not "on sale" for the purposes of SA 1891 (see the cases cited in *Sergeant & Sims on Stamp Duties* (8th edn), pp 202–214, and in Monroe and Nock, *The Law of Stamp Duties* (6th edn), pp 93–96 inclusive). It was therefore sensible in order to avoid adjudication problems in cases of doubt, wherever a "conveyance or transfer" of property (whether by way of gift or otherwise) was contemplated, for the transaction to be effected for a cash or debt consideration. As long as such a consideration was given, the transaction would for stamp duty purposes have been regarded as a "sale" (even if at an undervalue) and the need for adjudication would have been avoided. If consideration was given in the form of stocks or marketable or other securities, although the transaction would then have been one of sale, adjudication would still have been required in order to value the consideration.

However, as part of a policy of reducing the administrative burden on business, FA 2008 s 99 and Sch 32 abolished the fixed duty chargeable on certain instruments by FA 1999. In support of this objective FA 2008 s 100 has also removed the obligation which previously existed to have some such instruments submitted for adjudication by the Commissioners. This provision does not, however, apply to land transactions which, by reason of the transitional provisions in FA 2003 Sch 19 para 125 remain liable to stamp duty rather than SDLT.

83. Transfers in connection with divorce, dissolution of civil partnership etc

An instrument transferring stock or marketable securities does not attract ad valorem duty as a "transfer on sale" under what is now FA 1999 Sch 13 Part I para 1, if it involves the conveyance or transfer of property from one party to a marriage (which it is presumed also included a former marriage) to the other and the instrument:

(a) is executed in pursuance of an order of a court made on granting in respect of the parties a decree of divorce, nullity of marriage or judicial separation; or

(b) is executed in pursuance of an order of a court made in connection with the dissolution or annulment of the marriage or the parties' judicial separation and was made at any time after the granting of such a decree; or

(c) is executed at any time in pursuance of an agreement of the parties made in contemplation of or otherwise in connection with the dissolution or annulment of the marriage or their judicial separation.

Most transfers of property on the break-up of a marriage will be by the way of a gift and therefore exempt from stamp duty under s 82 (gifts inter vivos) and the provisions of SI 1987/516 relevant to s 82. However, not all transfers of property from one spouse to another will inevitably escape duty under these provisions. Transfers involving actual consideration, equivalent to cash for stamp duty purposes, will be dutiable as transfers on sale. Thus in the rare case where the stamp duty rules still apply to a land transfer (ie where the parties agreed to a transfer before the introduction of FA 2003 but only belatedly completed the land transaction by a formal transfer) a transfer of property subject to a mortgage which the transferee agrees to discharge will be stampable under what is now FA 1999 Sch 13 Part I by virtue of SA 1891 s 57. (See SP 6/90.) Even property adjustments involving, for example, an exchange of property between the spouses or former spouses may constitute a transaction for valuable consideration stampable as a conveyance on sale (see eg, *Re Abbott* [1983] Ch 45) and therefore not exempt from ad valorem duty under s 82.

The further exemptions given by this section and the relevant provisions of SI 1987/516 were designed to remove the above uncertainties. They do, however, have limitations. In particular, the further exemptions apply only to transfers between the parties to the marriage, and not also, for example, to transfers made by one spouse to trustees for the benefit of the children of the marriage.

A similar exemption from stamp duty is available in the case of transfers on the break-up of a civil partnership. Section 83(1A) provides that stamp duty is not to be chargeable on an instrument by which property is conveyed from one party to a civil partnership to the other in circumstances which mirror those mentioned above in the case of divorce or judicial separation.

84. Death: varying dispositions, and appropriations

Where, within two years after a person's death, any of the dispositions (whether effected by will, under the laws relating to intestacy or otherwise) of the property of which he was competent to dispose are varied by an instrument executed by the person or any of the persons who benefit or would benefit under the relevant disposition, stamp duty under what is now FA 1999 Sch 13 Part I is not chargeable on the instrument.

The exemption applies whether or not the administration of the estate is complete or the property has been distributed in accordance with the original disposition, but it does not apply where the variation is made for any consideration in money or money's worth other than consideration consisting of the making of a variation in respect of another of the original dispositions.

Where property is appropriated by a personal representative in or towards satisfaction of a general legacy of money, stamp duty under the "conveyance or transfer on sale" head of charge is not chargeable on the instrument giving effect to the appropriation.

Where on an intestacy property is appropriated by a personal representative in or towards satisfaction of any interest of a surviving spouse or civil partner in the intestate's estate (including the capital value of life interests redeemed under the Intestates' Estates Act 1952), then stamp duty is not chargeable on an instrument giving effect to the appropriation.

Again, a deed of family arrangement will normally be exempt from stamp duty by virtue of the repeal of F(1909–10)A 1910 s 74 (gifts inter vivos) and the provisions of SI 1987/516 relevant to documents formerly chargeable under the abolished provisions. However, it is possible for a family arrangement to amount to a sale, and this section and the relevant provisions of SI 1987/516 provide specific exemptions to cover any such circumstances.

85. Repeal of certain fixed duties

This section, coupled with Sch 24, abolished a large number of fixed duties chargeable under various heads of charge in SA 1891 Sch 1 (itself now repealed and replaced by FA 1999 Schs 13 and 15), most of which were obsolete and had ceased to be of any practical effect.

87. Certificates

This section provides for the introduction, by way of regulations to be issued by the Commissioners from time to time, of a system of certification rendering adjudication unnecessary. The regulations may provide that as regards instruments of a specified kind, which will normally attract the fixed duty, the inclusion of an appropriate certificate signed by appropriate parties shall be sufficient to render that instrument as being duly stamped.

The Treasury, in exercise of the powers conferred on them by this section, have made the Stamp Duty (Exempt Instruments) Regulations 1987 (SI 1987/516) which came into force on 1 May 1987; see commentary under Statutory Instruments.

It seems that, in the context of the *Parinv* case [1998] STC 305, HMRC take the same view of instruments certified exempt as they do of instruments stamped with the fixed duty of 50p (or £5, as it would be in any such situation arising on or after 1 October 1999)—ie failure to disclose that the parties to a transaction were attempting to rely on a further instrument, held offshore and unstamped, in order to effect a transaction by means of a certified instrument would constitute a breach of SA 1891 s 5.

88. Exchange rates

Where the amount on which stamp duty is payable is expressed in a foreign currency, SA 1891 s 6 provided that the amount was to be converted into sterling at the rate applying on the date of the document. This section removes the exception made by FA 1899 s 12 which provided for certain specified currencies to be converted at rates published by the Board of Inland Revenue; all foreign currency amounts are converted at the rate applying on the date of the document.

89. Exemption from section 28 of Finance Act 1931

This section is effectively obsolete, although it is possible that it, and the regulations made under it, could apply in a case where the transitional rules in FA 2003 Sch 19 were to operate. Under FA 1931 s 28 it was obligatory for the transferee of a freehold interest or a lessee under or purchaser of a lease for seven years or more to produce the instrument in question to the Commissioners (the particulars delivered, or PD, form). This section made provision for regulations, the Stamp Duty (Exempt Instruments) Regulations 1985, SI 1985/1688, exempting certain low-value instruments from the PD procedure. However, since section 28 is inapplicable to SDLT transactions, both the PD procedure and the need for an exemption have ceased to be of relevance.

FA 1931 s 28, requires any transfer on the sale of the fee simple of land, any lease on land granted for a term of seven years or more, and any transfer on sale of any lease for a term of seven years or more, to be produced to the Stamp Office, whether or not duty is payable, together with the PD form summarising the details of the transaction. In addition to any ad valorem duty stamp, the document is then stamped with a "produced stamp", without which it is not deemed to have been duly stamped.

See also the Land Registry Press Release of 5 April 1994 (in Appendix 4).

PART V MISCELLANEOUS AND SUPPLEMENTARY

96. European Communities and Investment Bank: exemptions
98. Short title, interpretation, construction and repeals

Finance Act 1986

1986 Chapter 41

Note: *In relation to the proposed abolitions of all stamp duty charges on property other than land and buildings (including all charges on transactions in shares and bearer instruments) and of stamp duty reserve tax, see note 2 at the end of the contents list to Part II Stamp Duty, Stamp Duty Reserve Tax and Stamp Duty Land Tax.*

PART 3 STAMP DUTY

SECURITIES

66. Company's purchase of own shares

Shares in a company which are purchased by that company pursuant to the Companies Act 2006 s 690, can be surrendered and delivered to the company by the relevant shareholder without any instrument of transfer, but pursuant to the Companies Act 2006 s 707, within a period of 28 days from the date on which the shares are purchased the company must deliver to the Registrar of Companies a return giving certain prescribed particulars, together with (where a contract is entered into between the company and the relevant shareholder) a copy of the contract if it is in writing or, if it is oral, a memorandum of its terms.

With effect from 27 October 1986 the 0.5 per cent rate of duty applies to a purchase by a company of its own shares, and the statutory return required under s 169 is to be treated as an instrument transferring the shares on sale and liable for stamp duty accordingly. It seems to be accepted that, in appropriate circumstances, intra-group relief is available for such a transaction under FA 1930 s 42 although it is perhaps questionable whether beneficial ownership of the shares can ever vest in the company which issued them. (For a possible explanation of the reason for allowing relief in this situation, see the commentary on FA 1930 s 42). On the other hand, the Stamp Office seems to accept that an agreement by a company for the purchase of its own shares is not an agreement falling within s 87(1), so that no charge to stamp duty reserve tax will arise in relation to any such agreement.

The Commissioners have recently changed their practice and now consider that a company's purchase of its own shares held on an overseas branch register is relieved from Stamp Duty by Companies Act 2006 s 133 (formerly Companies Act 1985 Sch 14 para 8) unless the return which relates to the shares bought back and which is to be delivered to Companies House (currently, form SH03) is executed in the UK.

[*Note:* See note at commencement of commentary on this Act.]

DEPOSITARY RECEIPTS

67. Depositary receipts

This section must now be read in light of the decisions of the European Court of Justice in *Commission v Kingdom of Belgium* Case C-415/02 (15 July 2004) and *HSBC Holdings plc v Revenue & Customs Commissioners*, Case C-569/07 [2010] STC 58 (1 October 2009). In *Commission v Belgium* the Court of Justice held that by imposing stamp duty on stock exchange transactions on applications for new securities, or the physical delivery of newly-issued bearer securities, on the formation of a company or following the completion of an increase in capital or as part of a loan issue, Belgium was in breach of its obligations under Art 11 of the Capital Duties Directive (Council Directive 69/355/EEC of 17 July 1969 concerning indirect taxes on the raising of capital as amended). Article 11 prevents a member state from levying any tax other than capital duty on, inter alia, the creation, issue admission

Part II ST

to quotation on a stock exchange, making available on the market or dealing in shares, etc, by whomsoever issued, subject only (Art 12) to specified exceptions, including taxation on the *transfer* of securities. The court held that "transfer" was to be interpreted strictly and could not include either the issue of the securities or their initial physical delivery. It will be appreciated that this calls into question the whole basis of the charges levied by the UK on the introduction of newly-issued securities into a depositary receipt system or into a clearance system or under FA 1999 Sch 15. In *HSBC Holdings plc v Revenue and Customs Comrs* the Court of Justice held that Article 11 of the Capital Duties Directive prohibited the imposition of a duty on the transfer or issue of shares into a clearance service as part of an offer for the acquisition of the entire issued share capital of another company. A similar question necessarily arose (although the question for reference did not relate to such a case) in relation to transfers into a depositary receipt scheme.

Following the decision of the Court of Justice, the Commissioners issued a press release stating that with immediate effect HMRC would not seek to apply a 1.5% charge to SDRT on the issue of shares to a clearance system within the European Community but that legislation would be passed to secure that a subsequent transfer of those securities into another clearance service or a depositary receipts scheme would not benefit from the exemptions designed to prevent a double charge to tax. In January 2010 HMRC invited statutory claims under reg 14 of the SDRT Regulations 1986 from persons who had paid SDRT under FA 1986 s 93 or s 96 pursuant to the issue of shares in a UK incorporated company either to a depositary receipts issuer or to a clearance service located within the European Union. Nothing was said in that press release as to the position of persons who had paid stamp duty under s 67, although there had been an indication in the Pre-Budget Report Note of 9 December 2009, PBRN 17, that the same rules applied to s 67. What is clear is that the Commissioners have decided that the Capital Duties Directive (now Council Directive 2008/7/EC of 12 February 2008 concerning indirect taxes on the raising of capital) is only effective as regards the issue or transfer of shares within the European Union. This is a matter of great difficulty and the question will no doubt be the subject of future litigation.

At the time of publication a Group Litigation Order (GLO) has been issued for persons wishing to make claims to recover overpaid tax in consequence of the *HSBC* decision.

Before the enactment of this section, ad valorem stamp duty at the normal rate was payable on transfers of shares to a person (usually a bank) who issued depositary receipts in respect of them, or to a person (usually known as the custodian) who was to hold them as nominee for such issuer. Duty was payable either because the transfers themselves amounted to "conveyances on sale" or (where the depositary receipts were initially issued to the transferor, so that there was initially no change in beneficial ownership) because they were treated as transfers "in contemplation of a sale" under FA 1965 s 90. However, transfers of the depositary receipts subsequently issued (unlike transfers of the underlying shares) seldom attract ad valorem stamp duty because the receipts are usually in registered form, with the register of holders being situated overseas, and transfers are normally executed overseas and not brought into the UK (as, for example, is the case with the most common variety—American Depositary Receipts, or "ADRs"). The section was enacted to compensate for the fact that (as stated in the Revenue's Press Release of 18 March 1986) "a substantial slice of the market in certain UK shares has been diverted to the market in American Depositary Receipts in New York"; it effectively renders transfers to depositary receipt issuers or their nominees liable to triple the normal amount of ad valorem duty.

Section 67 applies to "transfers" (ie, not direct allotments, deliveries of bearer securities, or renunciations of renounceable letters of allotment, although in certain circumstances an equivalent charge to stamp duty reserve tax will apply) of "relevant securities" (defined in s 69(3)) of a company incorporated in the United Kingdom, to a person who at the time of the transfer is:

(a) a person whose business is exclusively that of holding relevant securities as nominee or agent for a person whose business is or includes issuing "depositary receipts" (defined in s 69(1)) for relevant securities, where the transfer is for the purpose of the issue of depositary receipts; or

(b) a person whose business is or includes issuing depositary receipts for relevant securities who is specified for the purposes of these provisions by the Treasury by statutory instrument; or

(c) a person who is specified for the purposes of these provisions by the Treasury by statutory instrument whose business is not exclusively that of a nominee (as described in (*a*) above) but whose business includes holding relevant securities as nominee or agent for a person whose business is or includes issuing depositary receipts for relevant securities, and he holds the relevant securities as nominee or agent for such person for the purpose of the issue of depositary receipts.

If the relevant instrument of transfer is chargeable as a "conveyance or transfer on sale" under what is now FA 1999 Sch 13 Part I para 1(1), it is dutiable at the rate of 1.5 per cent of the amount or value of the consideration for the sale to which the instrument gives effect. If, for some reason, a written instrument is used to transfer a bearer instrument, provision is made by s 67(1) for the transfer to be excluded from charge, no doubt on the basis that the bearer instrument will, on issue, have been subjected to the 1.5% "season-ticket charge" by FA 1999 Sch 15 para 4.

Where the transaction is not one of sale, and the relevant instrument of transfer is chargeable as what is now called a "transfer otherwise than on sale" under FA 1999 Sch 13 Part III para 16(1) then, although the rate of duty is the same as that mentioned above (ie, 1.5 per cent), it is in this case charged on the *market value* of the securities on the date of execution of the instrument and not on the amount or value of the consideration for the sale.

The repeal of the reduced rate for qualified dealers will result in transfers into a depositary scheme effected through a qualified dealer who is not an "intermediary" for the purposes of the new relief in s 80A suffering an effective 2 per cent charge.

Where securities are issued or transferred for a consideration to be paid in instalments, and the securities are initially held by a person who holds them until the last instalment has been paid and then transfers them into a depositary scheme by means of an instrument of transfer which would previously have been charged with fixed duty as a "transfer otherwise than on sale", the instrument of transfer is chargeable under sub-s (3) on the total of the instalments payable on the shares less those paid before the instrument of transfer is executed, rather than on the value of the shares at the date of the transfer. These provisions are designed to take account of arrangements made in connection with the Government's privatisation schemes, where shares subscribed are frequently payable in instalments (as, for example, in the case of British Gas plc).

When an instrument transfers relevant securities of a company incorporated in the UK from one company to another, both of whose businesses are exclusively those of holding relevant securities as nominee or agent for a depositary (as described in sub-para (*a*) above), then, as from 1 October 1999, stamp duty is not chargeable on that instrument. Nothing appears to limit such transfers to those between two persons acting as nominees or agents for the same depositary. However, it will be noted that the legislation requires each person concerned to conduct a business which consists exclusively of acting as nominee for a clearance service operator. Somewhat oddly, this requirement of exclusivity is removed, by FA 1999, from the similar provisions relating to stamp duty reserve tax but not those relating to stamp duty (see s 90(5), (6), as amended). This appears to add to the list of situations where the rules affecting the two different taxes fail, apparently in a completely arbitrary manner, to harmonise with one another.

[*Note:* See note at commencement of commentary on this Act.]

68. Depositary receipts: notification

Any person whose business is or includes issuing depositary receipts for relevant securities of a company incorporated in the UK is required to notify the Commissioners of that fact within one month of the date on which he first issues such depositary receipts. Any person whose business includes (but does not exclusively consist of) holding relevant securities of a company incorporated in the UK as nominee or agent for a person whose business is or includes issuing depositary receipts, and for the purposes of issuing depositary receipts, is also required to notify the Commissioners of that fact within one month of the date on which he first holds such securities as such nominee or agent and for such purpose. Failure to notify in either case renders the relevant person liable to a penalty of up to £1,000.

A company incorporated in the UK which becomes aware that any of its shares are held by a person who is required to notify the Commissioners within the above provisions is itself required to notify the Commissioners of that fact within one month of becoming aware of the holding, and failure to do so renders it liable to a penalty of up to £100.

[*Note:* See note at commencement of commentary on this Act.]

69. Depositary receipts: supplementary

"Depositary receipt for relevant securities" means an instrument acknowledging that a person holds the relevant securities, or evidence of the right to receive them, and that another person is entitled to rights, whether expressed as units or otherwise, in or in relation to relevant securities of the same kind, including the right to receive such securities (or the evidence of the right to receive them) from the person who holds the securities or evidence of the right to receive them. Basically, this effectively means that a depositary receipt is a document entitling the holder or bearer to rights in shares which are held by the receipt issuer or his nominee.

There is an express exclusion for instruments acknowledging rights in or in relation to securities issued or sold on terms providing for payment in instalments and for the issue of the instrument as evidence that an instalment has been paid; as in s 67, this is designed to take account of arrangements made in connection with the Government's privatisation schemes.

The Treasury can change the definition of "depositary receipt" for the purposes of ss 67 and 68.

"Relevant securities" means shares or stock or marketable securities of any company which (unless otherwise stated) need not be incorporated in the UK.

For the purposes of s 67(3) the value of securities at the date the instrument is executed is to be taken as the price they might reasonably be expected to fetch on a sale at that time in the open market.

Before FA 1987 it was arguable that where a depositary scheme involved the depositary holding a "pool" of underlying securities in which the receipt holders had a proportionate interest, rather than an interest attaching to specific shares in the pool, the scheme fell within the definition of "unit trust scheme" contained in FA 1946 s 57(1). This would have meant that any deed setting up the scheme and relating to its overall operation would have been regarded as a unit trust instrument liable to unit trust instrument duty (since abolished by FA 1988 s 140) at the rate of 25p for every £100 or part of £100 of the amount or value of the shares comprised in the scheme or added thereto from time to time, unless the scheme could be shown to be in the nature of a contract rather than a trust. Any such charge might have been avoided if there was no instrument setting up the scheme or relating to its overall operation and the terms and conditions were contained in the receipts themselves. However, FA 1987 s 48 amended FA 1946 s 57(1) by importing the definition of "unit trust scheme" in the Financial Services Act 1986 s 75 and s 75(6)(*h*) seems to exclude arrangements of the kind involved in depositary schemes.

The provisions of ss 67, 68 and 69 apply only to the transfer of the underlying securities into a depositary scheme. The depositary receipts themselves will be stampable either (*a*) on transfer as a "conveyance or transfer on sale" (if they are in registered form) or (*b*) under the bearer instrument provisions (if, as they normally will be, they are in bearer form) on issue (if they are issued in the UK or by or on behalf of a UK company) or on their first transfer in the UK (if they are not chargeable on issue). In determining whether a depositary receipt in bearer form is issued on behalf of a UK company, the key factor is the place of formation or establishment of the depositary itself and not that of the company or other body whose shares are represented by the depositary receipts. (Note that in FA 1999 s 119 power is granted in relation to stamp duty reserve tax—but *not* stamp duty—to exempt UK depositary receipts for foreign securities from tax).

[*Note:* See note at commencement of commentary on this Act.]

CLEARANCE SERVICES

70. Clearance services

This section must now be read in light of the decision of the European Court of Justice in *Commission v Kingdom of Belgium* Case C-415/02 (15 July 2004) and *HSBC Holdings plc v Revenue & Customs Commissioners*, Case C-569/07 [2010] STC 58 (1 October 2009). In *Commission v Belgium* the Court of Justice held that by imposing stamp duty on stock exchange transactions on applications for new securities, or the physical delivery of newly-issued bearer securities, on the formation of a company or following the completion of an increase in capital or as part of a loan issue, Belgium was in breach of its obligations under Art 11 of the Capital Duties Directive (Council Directive 69/355/EEC of 17 July 1969 concerning indirect taxes on the raising of capital as amended). Article 11 prevented a member state from levying any tax other than capital duty on, inter alia, the creation, issue admission to quotation on a stock exchange, making available on the market or dealing in shares, etc, by whomsoever issued, subject only (Art 12) to specified exceptions, including taxation on the *transfer* of securities. The court held that "transfer" was to be interpreted strictly and could not include either the issue of the securities or their initial physical delivery. (It should be noted that a replacement and somewhat more restrictive directive on capital duty, Council Directive 2008/7/EC of 12 February 2008 concerning indirect taxes on the raising of capital, took effect as from 1 January 2009). It will be appreciated that this judgment calls into question the whole basis of the charges levied by the UK on the introduction of newly-issued securities into a depositary receipt system or into a clearance system or under FA 1999 Sch 15. In *HSBC Holdings plc v Revenue and Customs Comrs* the Court of Justice held that art 11 of the Capital Duties Directive prohibited the imposition of a duty on the transfer or issue of shares into a clearance service as part of an offer for the acquisition of the entire issued share capital of another company. In the course of his Opinion, Mr Advocate-General Mengozzi ranged further than the eventual decision of the Court of Justice (which, as is usual, confined itself more closely to the questions referred to it). It is nevertheless interesting to observe the views of the Advocate-General. His objections to the United Kingdom's regime for charging issues of shares into a clearance service were wide-ranging, beginning from the position that it was wrong that the person who should bear the tax was (in practice) the issuer of the shares; and dismissing the United Kingdom's contention that the 1.5% charge was an acceptable pre-payment of the estimated tax on future transactions within the clearance service, partly because it was paid by the wrong person and partly because there was no evidence that it was an accurate pre-estimate of future charges, or indeed more than an arbitrary amount; and concluding that such a charge was in breach of Art 11 of the Directive. He further considered that the charge was incompatible with one of the fundamental freedoms of Community law, as it constituted a restriction on the free movement of capital, was thus prohibited by Article 56 EC and could not be justified by a need to ensure effective fiscal supervision as the United Kingdom had failed to establish why such a drastic measure was the only way of ensuring the effective payment of taxes due, or why no other less onerous mechanism was considered capable of achieving the same objectives. The Court of Justice considered it unnecessary to deal with the question whether the United Kingdom was in breach of the fundamental freedoms since the Directive required complete harmonisation of the cases in which capital duty could be levied. It therefore followed that the court was restricted to the interpretation of the Directive and the national measure had to be measured in the light of the Directive and not in the context of the EC Treaty.

Following the decision of the Court of Justice, the Commissioners issued a press release stating that with immediate effect HMRC would not seek to apply a 1.5% charge to SDRT on the issue of shares to a clearance system within the European Community but that legislation would be passed to secure that a subsequent transfer of those securities into another clearance service or a depositary receipts scheme would not benefit from the exemptions designed to prevent a double charge to tax. In January 2010 HMRC invited statutory claims under reg 14 of the SDRT Regulations 1986 from persons who had paid SDRT under FA 1986 s 93 or s 96 pursuant to the issue of shares in a United Kingdom incorporated company either to a depositary receipts issuer or to a clearance service located within the European Union. Nothing was said in that press release as to the position of persons who had paid stamp duty under section 70, although there had been an indication in the Pre-Budget Report Note of 9 December 2009, PBRN 17, that the same rules applied to s 70. What is clear is that the Commissioners have decided that the Capital Duties Directive (now Council Directive 2008/7/EC of 12 February 2008 concerning indirect taxes on the raising of capital) is only effective as regards the issue or transfer of shares within the European Union. This is a matter of great difficulty and the question will no doubt be the subject of future litigation.

At the time of publication of this volume a GLO (Group Litigation Order) had been issued for persons wishing to make High Court claims to recover overpaid tax in consequence of the *HSBC* decision.

The provisions of this section in relation to clearance services were introduced in the light of the existence of computerised settlement systems (such as Euroclear) which enable UK shares to be held indefinitely by a clearance service operator or its nominee and rights bought and sold by book entry transfer, thus without payment of stamp duty, and are almost identical to the provisions of s 67 in relation to depositary receipts. With effect from 1 July 1996 this section does not apply where the clearance service operator so elects under FA 1986 s 97A. Subject to that, the section applies where an instrument "transfers" (ie, unlike stamp duty reserve tax excluding direct allotments, deliveries of bearer securities and renunciations of renounceable letters of allotment) "relevant securities" of a company incorporated in the UK to a person (resident in the UK or not) who at the time of the transfer is:

(a) a person whose business is exclusively that of holding shares, stock or other marketable securities (whether relevant securities or not) as nominee or agent for a person whose business is or includes the provision of clearance services for the purchase and sale of such securities, and the transfer is for the purpose of the provision of such services; or

(b) a person who is specified for the purposes of these provisions by the Treasury and whose business is or includes the provision of clearance services for the purchase and sale of relevant securities; or

(c) a person who is specified for the purposes of these provisions by the Treasury whose business is not exclusively that of holding relevant securities as nominee (as described in sub-paragraph (*a*) above) but whose business includes holding relevant securities as nominee or agent for a person whose business is or includes the provision of clearance services for the purchase and sale of relevant securities at the time of transfer, and holds relevant securities as nominee or agent for such person for the purposes of the provision of such services.

If stamp duty is chargeable on the relevant instrument by reference to the "conveyance or transfer on sale" provisions in what is now FA 1999 Sch 13 Part I, the rate at which the duty is charged is 1.5 per cent of the amount or value of the consideration for the sale. But if, for some reason, a written instrument is used to transfer a bearer instrument into a clearance service, provision is made by s 70(1) for the transfer to be excluded from charge, no doubt on the basis that the bearer instrument will, on issue, have been subjected to the 1.5% "season-ticket charge" by FA 1999 Sch 15 para 4.

If stamp duty is chargeable on the instrument by reference to the "conveyance or transfer otherwise than on sale" provisions in what is now FA 1999 Sch 13 Part III, the rate at which the duty is charged is 1.5 per cent of the value of the securities at the date the instrument is executed rather than the value of the consideration for the instrument.

The repeal of the former reduced rate for qualified dealers results in transfers into a clearance service effected through a qualified dealer who is not an "intermediary" for the purposes of the relief in s 80A suffering an effective 2 per cent charge.

Sub-section (5) is identical to s 67(5), and deals with any case where securities are issued or transferred on sale, upon terms that (in either case) they are to be paid for in instalments, to a person who holds them until the last instalment is paid and then transfers them into a clearance system by means of an instrument chargeable as a conveyance or transfer otherwise than on sale. The duty chargeable under subs (3) is on the total of the instalments payable less those paid before the instrument of transfer is executed, rather than on the value of the shares at the date of the transfer.

Where an instrument transfers relevant securities of a company incorporated in the UK from one nominee of a provider of clearance services to another such nominee, then, as is the case with s 67(9) in relation to transfers between nominees for persons who issue depositary receipts, there is no charge to stamp duty. As in s 67 above, nothing appears to require these two persons to be acting for the same principal.

[*Note:* See note at commencement of commentary on this Act.]

71. Clearance services: notification

A person whose business is or includes the provision of clearance services for the purchase and sale of relevant securities of a company incorporated in the UK is required to notify the Commissioners of this fact within one month of commencing to provide such services. A person whose business includes (but does not exclusively consist of) holding relevant securities of a company incorporated in the UK as nominee or agent for a person whose business is or includes the provision of clearance services, and for the purpose of such business, must notify the Commissioners of that fact within one month of the date on which he first holds such relevant securities as such nominee or agent and for such purpose. Any person who fails to make the appropriate notification in accordance with these provisions is liable to a penalty of up to £1,000.

A company incorporated in the UK which becomes aware that any of its shares are held by persons who are required to notify the Commissioners in accordance with the above provisions must itself notify the Commissioners of that fact within one month of the date on which it becomes aware of it, and failure to do so renders the company liable to a penalty of up to £100.

[*Note:* See note at commencement of commentary on this Act.]

72. Clearance services: supplementary

"Relevant securities" means shares in or stock or marketable securities of any company which (unless otherwise stated) need not be incorporated in the UK

For the purpose of s 70(3) the value of securities at the date of execution of an instrument is to be deemed to be the price they might reasonably be expected to fetch on a sale in the open market on that date.

The penalties of s 15(2) apply to instruments chargeable under these provisions under the heading "conveyance or transfer of any kind not hereinbefore described". The penalties already apply to instruments chargeable under these provisions under the heading "conveyance or transfer on sale".

As with depositary schemes, under the definition of "unit trust scheme" which for stamp duty purposes applied before FA 1987, it was possible that any document setting up and governing the overall operation of a clearance system might have been chargeable to the now abolished unit trust instrument duty as a unit trust instrument if the provider of the services held a "pool" of securities in which the members had proportionate rather than specific interests. However, clearance systems seem to be specifically excluded from the definition of "unit trust schemes" by virtue of the Financial Services Act 1986 s 75(6)(*i*).

The expression "clearance services" is not defined. Concern has been expressed that the provision of any nominee services to facilitate dealings in securities could be within its meaning. HMRC have indicated that this is not the intention, and that their policy is to construe the expression so as to include only arrangements which are expressly marketed as "clearance services". In cases of doubt, HMRC's guidance should be sought. The absence of a definition of clearance service was specifically noted by the 2007 Solutions Report of the European Commission's Fiscal Compliance Experts' Group ("FISCO"), which observed that "the definition of a clearing system is unclear in relation to Stamp Duty Reserve Tax (SDRT) purposes, which may prevent a level playing-field between settlement service providers that are considered a clearing service (such as CSDs) and those who are not". In *HSBC Holdings plc v HMRC* [2010] STC 58, Mr Advocate-General Mengozzi attempted a definition, or at least a description of the activity, of a clearance service: "Clearance services play a role which may be defined as the holding of shares. In particular, they keep a record of the owners of the shares, and of transfers of shares, although, at all times, the bearer certificates are held by the clearance service concerned. In other words, clearance services make the acquisition and disposal of shares simpler, quicker and more secure."

Concern has also apparently been expressed over the possibility that, by virtue of the forms of settlement process adopted on such exchanges, applying for listing of UK shares on some foreign stock exchanges would arguably amount (albeit unintentionally) to the act of "entering a clearance system", with the result that the listing attracted a 1.5 per cent charge to stamp duty reserve tax on the price or value of the UK shares so listed. Again, HMRC should be approached for advice in such cases.

[*Note:* See note at commencement of commentary on this Act.]

72A. Transfers between depositary receipt system and clearance system

This section ensures that no stamp duty (rather than the s 67 depositary receipt charges or s 70 clearance service charges) is chargeable on instruments transferring relevant securities between a depositary receipt system and a clearance system provided, in the case of a transfer from a clearance system, the transfer is not covered by a s 97A election for alternative system of charge.

Reconstructions and Acquisitions

75. Acquisitions: reliefs

(See the notes printed at the end of the contents list to Part II Stamp Duty, Stamp Duty Reserve Tax and Stamp Duty Land Tax.)

This section applies where a company (the "acquiring company") acquires the whole or part of the undertaking of another company (the "target company") in pursuance of a scheme for the reconstruction of the target company. It replaces the reliefs formerly available under FA 1927 s 55 and FA 1985 ss 78, 79, and 80. This section does not apply to open-ended investment companies (see SI 1997/1156 reg 12).

The reliefs formerly available under FA 1927 s 55 were available for both reconstructions and amalgamations, which were technically very different. The fact that the new provisions do not refer to "amalgamations" means that the relief will only be available for "reconstructions", so that many forms of corporate reorganisation in respect of which relief was formerly available will not now qualify for exemption from stamp duty. An analysis of the technical construction of both the term "reconstruction" and the term "amalgamation" is required to determine what does qualify and what does not.

For the purposes of FA 1927 s 55, a scheme for the reconstruction of a company comprised a transfer of the undertaking, or part of the undertaking, of an existing company to a new company, the new company having substantially the same members as had the existing company and carrying on substantially the same business as the business transferred to it (see generally the cases of *Hooper v Western Counties and South Wales Telephone Co Ltd* [1892] 68 LT 78; *Re South African Supply and Cold Storage Co* [1904] 2 Ch 268; *Brooklands Selangor Holdings Ltd v IR Comrs* [1970] 2 All ER 76; *Baytrust Holdings Ltd v IR Comrs* [1971] 3 All ER 76).

The meaning of the words "scheme for the amalgamation of any companies" for the purpose of FA 1927 s 55 was considered by the Court of Appeal in *Crane Fruehauf Limited v IR Comrs* [1975] 1 All ER 429. In that case it was held that an amalgamation consists of the combining of the businesses of more than one company in such a way that the businesses remain in substance owned by the same persons, which result could be achieved in one of two ways:

(a) by a transaction involving the business of an existing company (the transferor company) being acquired by another company (the transferee company) in return for an issue of shares in the transferee company to the transferor company or to the shareholders of the transferor company; or

(b) by a transaction involving the acquisition by the transferee company of shares of the transferor company in exchange for shares in the transferee company being issued to the shareholders of the transferor company.

It was also held in *Crane Fruehauf Ltd v IR Comrs* that a scheme for reconstruction or amalgamation does not lose its character as such if it forms part of a larger scheme involving other transactions, so that in that case a scheme involving an acquisition of shares in return for shares plus cash was held to be a scheme for amalgamation and to retain its character as such notwithstanding that the vendor shareholders were obliged under the overall scheme to sell one third of the consideration shares issued to them.

It was not essential for the purposes of FA 1927 s 55 that the company whose undertaking was being acquired, or which was being absorbed on amalgamation, should be put into liquidation (see the cases of *Re Walker' Settlement* [1935] Ch 567, per Romer LJ at 583 and 585, and per Maugham J at 589; *Lever Brothers Ltd v IR Comrs* [1938] 2 KB 518 at 524 per Greene MR; and *Nestle Company Ltd v IR Comrs* [1935] Ch 395 at 403, per Evershed MR). It was, however, essential that, for there to be a scheme of reconstruction, there should after completion of the transaction be no change in the real ownership of the undertaking transferred (*Brooklands Selangor Holdings Ltd v IR Comrs* [1970] 2 All ER 76 applying dicta of Lord Hanworth MR in the case of *Oswald Tillotson Ltd v IR Comrs* [1933] 1 KB 134 at 155). As a result, a partition, ie, the division of a company into two separate parts, the different parts going to different shareholders, is not a reconstruction. It was also essential that a reconstruction should involve the transfer of a *business*, or part of a business, which could be carried on as a genuinely independent trading activity, as a going concern, by the transferee company in the same way as it was carried on by the transferor (*Baytrust Holdings Ltd v IR Comrs* [1971] 3 All ER 76) so that a mere distribution of assets not required by a company for the purposes of its business will not be within the definition.

The respective meanings of "reconstruction" and "amalgamation" in the context of FA 1927 s 55 were more recently analysed by Ferris J, in the case of *Swithland Investments Ltd v IR Comrs* [1990] STC 469 in relation to a cleverly designed scheme to effect the sale by an existing company of part of its business and to accommodate the different future requirements of its shareholders by a series of transactions some of which were intended to fall within the section. It was held by the judge (applying the principles laid down in the *Baytrust* and *South African Supply and Cold Storage* cases) that the overall scheme actually involved a partition rather than a reconstruction or amalgamation (or a series of reconstructions or amalgamations) and relief was therefore denied.

Under the new s 75, stamp duty under the "transfer on sale" provisions in what is now FA 1999 Sch 13 Part I will not be chargeable on any instrument executed for the purposes of or

Part II ST

in connection with the transfer of an undertaking (or part thereof) as part of a scheme of reconstruction, provided that two conditions are satisfied.

The first condition specified is that the consideration for the acquisition:

(a) consists of or includes the issue of non-redeemable shares in the acquiring company to all the shareholders of the target company; and

(b) includes nothing else (if anything) but the assumption or discharge by the acquiring company of liabilities of the target company.

The second condition is that:

(a) the acquisition is effected for bona fide commercial reasons and does not form part of a scheme or arrangement of which the main purposes, or one of the main purposes, is avoidance of liability to stamp duty, income tax, corporation tax or capital gains tax; and

(b) after the acquisition has been made, each shareholder of each of the companies will be a shareholder of the other; and

(c) after the acquisition has been made, the proportion of shares of one of the companies held by any shareholder is the same or as nearly as may be the same as the proportion of shares of the other company held by that shareholder.

If these conditions are satisfied the exemption from stamp duty will be available, provided the relevant instruments are adjudicated under SA 1891 s 12. The requirement that the consideration must consist of or include the issue of non-redeemable shares in the acquiring company to *all* the shareholders of the target company is a departure from the traditional ideas of a "scheme of reconstruction" for which relief was formerly available under FA 1927 s 55. Previously, it was only necessary to show that the new company had *substantially* the same members as the existing company (see for example *Brooklands Selangor Holdings Ltd v IR Comrs* [1970] 2 All ER 76). The exemption will not be available under the new provisions if the holder of even a single share in the existing company does not receive a share or shares in the new company. This will have particular relevance in relation to a scheme of reconstruction where there may be dissentient shareholders under Insolvency Act 1986 s 111, but it will also make it essential to ensure that any nominee shareholders in the existing company also receive shares in the new company, and that no new nominees receive shares in the new company.

In addition, the consideration must consist *only* of non-redeemable shares or the assumption or discharge by the new company of liabilities of the existing company or both. Under FA 1927 s 55 it was only necessary for 90 per cent of the consideration to consist of shares or the discharge of liabilities or both, which made it possible for cash to be paid or loan stock to be issued for up to 10 per cent of the existing company.

No relief is available if the requiring company issues any redeemable shares to the shareholders of the target company. This is because the intention of one of the conditions is that cash does not constitute a significant part of any consideration given for shares being issued under the reorganisation. Redeemable shares were being issued, and redeemed shortly after acquisition, so virtually providing a cash consideration.

The second condition to the exemption involves inter alia a requirement that each shareholder of the new company ends up with exactly the same proportion of the issued share capital of the new company as he held in the issued share capital of the existing company, so that the consideration shares in the new company must be issued *exactly* pro rata to the shareholders of the existing company.

Provision is made for cases where either the target company or the acquiring company holds any of its own shares in treasury. Such shares would, without more, prevent the requisite matching being achieved between the two companies. To that end, sub-section (5A) treats the treasury shares as having been cancelled before the acquisition takes place, enabling them to be ignored and the company to be treated as if it were not a shareholder in itself.

The meaning of the words "the consideration for the acquisition" has been judicially reviewed on a number of occasions in connection with the relief formerly available under FA

1927 s 55. In the case of *Central and District Properties Ltd v IR Comrs* [1966] 2 All ER 433 the majority view of the Court of Appeal and the House of Lords seemed to have been that consideration provided by an independent third party could be ignored, provided that the transferee company was not under any contractual obligation to procure that third party to make the consideration available. In that case the appellant company was a subsidiary of U Ltd, 98 per cent of whose ordinary share capital was held by two directors. The appellant company had a stock exchange quotation, but the parent company, U Ltd, whose shares were very valuable, had not. In order to render U Ltd's shares more marketable the two directors took steps to enable the whole of the shares of U Ltd to be acquired by the appellant company, of which they were also directors but of which they did not have shareholding control, with a view to a "merger" of the companies. Ordinary shares of the appellant company were accordingly sold by U Ltd to L Ltd, an issuing house unconnected by shareholding either with U Ltd or the appellant company, so that the appellant company would cease to be a subsidiary of U Ltd (a subsidiary company being debarred by the Companies Act 1948 s 27 (now Companies Act 2006 s 136), from acquiring shares in its parent company). In order to induce 90 per cent of the preference shareholders of U Ltd to exchange their preference shares for preference shares of the appellant company, U Ltd's preference shareholders were offered, in the event of the exchange offer becoming unconditional, transferable low priced options over certain ordinary shares of the appellant company. These ordinary shares were provided in part by U Ltd selling to L Ltd more shares in the appellant company, and as to the rest were to be provided by the two directors transferring shares to L Ltd Under FA 1927 s 55(1)(*c*) there would be exemption from ad valorem stamp duty on the transfers of shares involved in the "merger" if the "consideration for the acquisition" consisted as to not less than 90 per cent thereof in the issue of shares by way of exchange. If the value of the option rights was part of the consideration, then less than 90 per cent of the consideration would consist in the issue of shares by way of exchange, and the ad valorem stamp duty exemption would not apply. The inducement put forward to preference shareholders of U Ltd was in a circular accompanying an elaborate document entitled "merger proposals" (both documents being dated 25 June 1958) and addressed by the board of U Ltd and the appellant company to the shareholders of both companies. The circular stated that if the offers became unconditional L Ltd would in due course offer stock units of the appellant company to the preference shareholders of U Ltd by way of negotiable letters of entitlement, and that the rights under these could be sold. Accompanying the merger proposals were also the formal offers and other documents. In due course the offers became unconditional. The Commissioners assessed ad valorem stamp duty of £109,098 on the transaction on the basis that the condition of exemption provided by FA 1927 s 55(1) was not satisfied.

It was held that, taking the transaction as a whole, the appellant company had made itself legally responsible to ensure (or had warranted) that L Ltd would carry out the options offers. Accordingly the value of the options was part of the consideration for the acquisition of the preference shares in U Ltd, the condition of FA 1927 s 55(1)(*c*) was not satisfied, and exemption from ad valorem stamp duty under s 55(1) was not established. The majority of the House of Lords, obiter, expressed the view that for the purposes of s 55(1) the natural meaning of the words "consideration for the acquisition" is the quid pro quo provided by, or moving from, the acquiring company. Consequently, a truly independent additional inducement from an independent source, at any rate if not devised as part of the scheme of reconstruction or amalgamation, will not be part of the "consideration for the acquisition".

If the transferee company by its contract with the shareholders of the existing company imposes a condition that in certain circumstances those shareholders on-sell a proportion of their consideration shares to a third party, then the consideration for the acquisition comprises the consideration shares which the vendor shareholders retain plus the cash, in the event, they receive for the sale to the third party: *Crane Fruehauf Ltd v IR Comrs* [1975] 1 All ER 429.

For an issue of shares to form part of "the consideration for the acquisition", the shares must be issued to the recipients as beneficial owners, and where the recipients of the shares were not free to deal with them because they were bound by an agreement to transfer them to a third party, the shares were not issued to the recipients as beneficial owners and therefore did not form part of the consideration (see *Baytrust Holdings Ltd v IR Comrs* [1971] 3 All ER 76; *Thomas Firth and John Brown (Investments) Ltd v IR Comrs*). The word "issue" in the context of consideration shares for an acquisition means that the relevant shareholders must be registered in the register of members of the new company, so that the giving of renounceable letters of allotment will not suffice, and the consideration shares cannot be issued in the names of nominees for the persons entitled to them (see *Crane Fruehauf Ltd v IR Comrs* and *Oswald Tillotson Ltd v IR Comrs* cited above, and also *Brotex Cellulose Fibres v IR Comrs* [1933] 1 KB 158 and *Murex v IR Comrs* [1933] 1 KB 173).

The above principles were reaffirmed, and the decisions in *Central and District Properties Ltd v IR Comrs, Crane Fruehauf Ltd v IR Comrs*, and *Baytrust Holdings Ltd v IR Comrs* applied, in *IR Comrs v Kent Process Control Ltd* [1989] STC 245.

In *IR Comrs v Kent Process Control Ltd* the taxpayer company, Introl Ltd (Introl) and BBK Investments Ltd (BBK) were each wholly-owned subsidiaries of Brown Boveri Kent plc (the holding company). In 1979, under a scheme for the internal reorganisation of the companies, Introl and BBK agreed to transfer their undertakings, property and assets to the taxpayer company in return for the issue to them of new shares in the taxpayer company as equalled the net asset value of their undertakings and the discharge of their debts and liabilities. In July 1980 the taxpayer company resolved to increase its share capital by the creation of some 5,002,325 shares of £1 each and to allocate such new shares as to 2,765,952 to Introl and 2,236,373 to BBK. On 15 December 1980 Introl and BBK transferred their newly acquired shares to the holding company for a monetary consideration.

In respect of the taxpayer company's application for relief under FA 1927 s 55 from stamp duty on the transfers to it of the undertakings of Introl and BBK, the Revenue claimed that (*a*) there had been no issue of shares by the taxpayer company to Introl and BBK within s 55(1)(*c*), and (*b*) even if there was such an issue "the consideration for the acquisition" by the taxpayer company of the undertakings of Introl and BBK did not "consist as to 90 per cent thereof in the issue of shares" since it also included a monetary consideration to be provided by the holding company.

As to the first contention the Revenue submitted that Introl's and BBK's transfer of the shares in the taxpayer company to the holding company was one which the holding company could compel in spite of the absence of any formal agreement to that effect and that Introl and BBK were therefore never able to deal with those shares as they wished and accordingly never took them as beneficial owners. It was held as follows:

(1) To prevent Introl and BBK from holding the shares, allocated to them by the taxpayer company, as beneficial owners, the limitation on dealing with the shares must have been imposed by the taxpayer company as part of the consideration for the acquisition of the undertakings of Introl and BBK. Although the holding company could compel Introl and BBK, as its wholly owned subsidiaries, to transfer to it the new shares acquired by them from the taxpayer company, any such obligation to pass on those shares was not part of the consideration moving from the taxpayer company. Accordingly the shares had been issued to Introl and BBK within the meaning of FA 1927 s 55(1)(*c*)(i).

(2) The monetary consideration provided by the holding company for the transfer to it of the new shares did not emanate from the taxpayer company and accordingly was not part of the consideration for the acquisition by the taxpayer company of the undertakings of Introl and BBK. As the consideration for the acquisition consisted of 90 per cent in the issue of the shares the conditions specified in s 55(1) had been fulfilled.

(3) The taxpayer company was therefore entitled to relief from stamp duty and the Revenue's claim failed.

The Stamp Office have indicated that they will regard the requirement that the reconstruction be effected for bona fide commercial reasons (and not as part of a scheme or arrangement which has as its main purpose or one of its main purposes the avoidance of liability for stamp duty, income tax, corporation tax or capital gains tax) as being satisfied where clearance has been granted under TCGA 1992 s 138 or TA 1970 s 267(3A).

The procedure for claims under ss 75 to 77 is as follows:

(a) A statutory declaration is not required. A claim should be made in a letter signed by a responsible officer of the acquiring company (eg, the secretary or a director) or the company's professional advisers.

(b) The letter should include the following information and be accompanied by:
   (i) the name, registered number and authorised and issued capital of the acquiring company at the relevant date;
   (ii) the name, registered number and authorised and issued capital of the acquired company at the relevant date;
   (iii) details of and the reason for the reconstruction;
   (iv) details of the consideration paid and how it was satisfied;
   (v) whether an application for clearance under TCGA 1992 s 138, or TA 1970 s 267(3A) has been made to HMRC, and a copy of any application for clearance together with copies of any correspondence with HMRC;
   (vi) confirmation that the shares in the acquiring company have been issued to the registered shareholders of the acquired company and that their names have been entered on the register of members of the acquiring company;
   (vii) a copy of the certificate of incorporation of all relevant companies and all changes of names;
   (viii) particulars of the register of members of the acquired company immediately prior to the transaction;
   (ix) particulars of the register of members of the acquiring company immediately after the transaction for which relief is claimed;
   (x) a copy of the agreement or offer document; and
   (xi) a copy of the instruments of transfer.

(c) A completed Adjudication Application Form Adj 467, stating any related adjudication references known should be sent with the claim to: The Stamp Office, Adjudication Section, Ridgeworth House, Liverpool Gardens, Worthing, West Sussex, BN11 1XP.

The Stamp Office has issued explanatory notes and a set of precedent letters for use in England and Wales.

[*Note:* See note at commencement of commentary on this Act.]

76. Acquisitions: further provisions about reliefs

The Government intends to introduce provisions in the Finance Act 2012 to repeal this relief with effect from 6 April 2013.

For transactions involving the acquisition of the whole or part of a company's undertaking, the rate of duty under the heading "transfer on sale" which would otherwise be payable in respect of the relevant instruments of transfer is reduced to 0.5 per cent from (depending on the amount or value of the consideration, and the entitlement to use a certificate of value) 1, 3 or 4 per cent. Clearly, the potential value of this relief has increased in the recent past; a couple of years ago, it had the effect of halving the duty otherwise payable and it now reduces the duty to up to one eighth of that otherwise payable.

This section does not require that there must be a scheme of reconstruction or amalgamation, and there is therefore no requirement that the beneficial ownership of the business must remain substantially the same.

Where a company (the "acquiring company") acquires the whole or part of the undertaking of another company (the "target company"), any instrument executed for the purposes of or in connection with the transfer of the undertaking, or part thereof, or the assignment to the acquiring company by a creditor of the target company of any "relevant debts" (secured or unsecured) owed by the target company, is chargeable to stamp duty under the "transfer on sale" provisions of what is now FA 1999 Sch 13 Part I at the rate of 0.5 per cent of the amount or value of the consideration for the sale to which the instrument gives effect, provided that the first and second conditions specified are satisfied.

The first condition is that the consideration for the acquisition consists of or includes the issue of non-redeemable shares in the acquiring company to the target company, or to all or any of its shareholders, and nothing else (if anything) except cash amounting to 10 per cent of the nominal value of the consideration shares, or the assumption or discharge by the acquiring company of liabilities of the target company, or both.

The second condition (introduced by FA 2002 s 112 with effect for instruments executed after 23 April 2002), which only applies in relation to an instrument transferring land in the UK, is that the acquiring company is not associated with another company that is a party to arrangements with the target company relating to shares of the acquiring company issued in connection with the transfer of the undertaking or part. This condition is aimed at schemes which became relatively prevalent in the pre-FA 2002 period under which a company could sell land and pay duty on the s 76 transfer then sell the acquiring company's shares and pay duty on that transfer, but the overall duty was less than on a straight transfer of the land. Companies are "associated" if one has control (TA 1989 s 416) of the other or both are controlled by the same person or persons, and "arrangements" includes any scheme, agreement or understanding, whether or not legally enforceable. Where an instrument transfers land in the UK together with other property, it is treated as if it were two instruments, one relating to the land and one to the other property.

Note the provisions contained in FA 2002 s 113 relating to the withdrawal of s 76 relief where relief is claimed in relation to a transfer of land and the acquiring company leaves the group within 2 years.

The expression "relevant debt" is defined as any debt in the case of which the assignor is a bank or trade creditor, and any other debt incurred not less than two years before the date on which the instrument is executed.

Any instrument claimed to be eligible for the reduced rate of duty under these provisions must be adjudicated under SA 1891 s 12. The provisions apply to all instruments executed on or after 27 October 1986.

As to problems which have arisen in interpreting the word "undertaking" and the expression "the consideration for the acquisition", see the notes to s 75.

The ability to ignore liabilities assumed or discharged by the acquiring company, for the purpose of determining whether or not the reduced rate is available, does not affect the application of SA 1891 s 57 by virtue of which the amount on which the duty is chargeable is the value of the consideration shares together with the amount of cash paid and the amount of the liabilities taken over or discharged.

Under this section (unlike s 75) the consideration shares can be issued to the target company or to all or any of its shareholders. The requirement is still, however, that the consideration shares be "issued" to such persons, ie, that such persons be registered in the register of members.

This section does not apply to open-ended investment companies (see SI 1997/1156 reg 12).

As to the procedure for claims, see the notes to s 75.

77. Acquisition of target company's share capital

There is a complete exemption from stamp duty under the "transfer on sale" provisions of what is now FA 1999 Sch 13 Part I in relation to any instrument transferring shares in one company (the "target company") to another company (the "acquiring company") if certain conditions are satisfied and the instrument is adjudicated under SA 1891 s 12.

The conditions are that:

(a) . . .

(b) the transfer forms part of an arrangement (ie, one single transaction) by which the acquiring company acquires the whole of the issued share capital of the target company (ie, the exemption will not be available where the acquiring company already holds shares in the target company before the "arrangement"); and

(c) the acquisition is effected for bona fide commercial reasons and does not form part of a scheme or arrangement of which the main purpose, or one of the main purposes, is avoidance of liability to stamp duty, stamp duty reserve tax, income tax, corporation tax or capital gains tax; and

(d) the consideration for the acquisition consists only of the issue of shares in the acquiring company to the shareholders of the target company; and

(e) after the acquisition has been made, each person who immediately before it was made was a shareholder of the target company is a shareholder of the acquiring company; and

(f) after the acquisition has been made, the shares in the acquiring company are of the same classes as were the shares in the target company immediately before the acquisition is made (it is not clear whether the references to "same classes" simply means the same number and type of classes or whether, for example, the issue of new £1 ordinary shares as consideration for the acquisition of existing 50p ordinary shares would fail to satisfy the test on the basis that shares of differing nominal values in the two companies were not shares "of the same classes"); and

(g) after the acquisition has been made, the number of shares of any particular class in the acquiring company bear to all the shares in that company the same proportion or as nearly as may be the same proportion as the number of shares of that class in the target company bore to all the shares in that company immediately before the acquisition was made; and

(h) after the acquisition has been made, the proportion of shares of any particular class in the acquiring company held by any particular shareholder is the same or as nearly as may be the same as the proportion of shares of that class in the target company held by him immediately before the acquisition was made.

Provision is made for cases where either the target company or the acquiring company holds any of its own shares in treasury. Such shares would, without more, prevent the requisite matching being achieved between the two companies. To that end, sub-section (3A) treats the treasury shares as having been cancelled before the acquisition takes place, enabling them to be ignored and the company to be treated as if it were not a shareholder in itself.

Note that, unlike in ss 75 and 76, it is not possible to ignore liabilities assumed or discharged by the acquiring company. The consideration for the acquisition must consist *solely* of the issue of shares and the word "issue", as before, means that the target company or its shareholders must be entered on the register of members of the acquiring company, so that the giving of renounceable letters of allotment or the registration of nominees will cause the exemption to be lost.

The Commissioners have indicated that a clearance obtained under what is now either s 138 or 139 of the Taxation of Chargeable Gains Act 1992 (formerly CGTA 1979 s 88 or TA 1970 s 267(3A)) will satisfy them in relation to the requirement that the acquisition is effected for bona fide commercial reasons.

It is generally thought that the severity of the restrictions will limit the availability of this relief to situations where a new company is formed specifically to acquire the whole of the issued share capital of an existing company, where the new company and the existing company have identical share capitals. It seems unlikely that the relief will ever be available where two existing companies merge, either by the formation of a new holding company over both of them or where one takes over the other.

This section does not apply to open-ended investment companies (see SI 1997/1156 reg 12).

As to the procedure for claims, see the notes to s 75.

[*Note:* See note at commencement of commentary on this Act.]

LOAN CAPITAL, LETTERS OF ALLOTMENT, ETC

78. Loan capital

The existence of this section is due to a change of mind by the Chancellor of the Exchequer between his Budget speech on 18 March 1986 and the enactment of FA 1986 on 25 July 1986.

The Budget speech announced that the exemption from stamp duty on transfers of most forms of loan stock was to be withdrawn, and a charge at 0·5 per cent imposed. This announcement was given effect to by a Budget Resolution (No 33) passed on 24 March 1986 pursuant to FA 1973 s 50 which enables temporary statutory effect to be given to Budget proposals by way of "Budget Resolution".

Because of a subsequent change of mind by the Government, Resolution 33 was withdrawn with effect from 7 July 1986 and the previous exemption was reinstated. Section 78 contains the text of Resolution 33 and is included only to impose the charge for the interim period.

However, sub-ss (7), (9), (10) and (14) have a continuing relevance because they were imported into s 79, which contains the new exemptions.

"Loan capital" means:

(a) any debenture stock, corporation stock, or funded debt by whatever name known issued by a body corporate or other body of persons (which here includes a local authority and any body whether formed or established in the UK or elsewhere);

(b) any capital raised by such a body if the capital is borrowed or has the character of borrowed money, and whether it is in the form of stock or any other form;

(c) stock or marketable securities issued by the government of any country or territory outside the UK; or

(d) capital raised in the form of alternative finance investment bonds under FA 2005 s 48A.

This definition is very similar to the definition applicable to the former duty on loan capital under FA 1899 s 8(5). The decisions in relation to the repealed provisions are therefore still relevant in interpreting the new definition. The principal cases are:

(1) *A-G v South Wales Electrical Power Distribution Co* [1920] 1 KB 552, CA, which held that it is essential that there is some sort of issue or raising of "capital", so that "deferred warrants" issued by a company in respect of interest it was unable to pay on its debenture stock were not within the definition.

(2) *A-G v Regent's Canal and Dock Co* [1904] 1 KB 263, which held that an issue by a company of a new series of debenture stock to the holders of its existing debenture stock, which was then extinguished, was within the definition even though no further funds were borrowed.

(3) *Reed International Ltd v IR Comrs* [1975] 3 All ER 218, HL, which held that a debt was a "funded debt" if it had some degree of permanence or long-term character and other features which would be expected by a creditor whose debt will not be repaid for some time, including the payment of a stipulated rate of interest and various other provisions, and that it was not necessary for the debt to be supported by some fund or to be transferable in separate amounts, or that it should have been created by the conversion of an existing short-term debt.

It has been suggested that short-term borrowing may also be within the definition, if it is of a capital nature (see, eg Monroe and Nock, *The Law of Stamp Duties*, (6th edn)) and it is thought that this must be right in view of the inclusion in (*b*) of "any capital raised . . . if the capital is borrowed or has the character of borrowed money, and whether it is in the form of stock or any other form" (ie, with no indication of a minimum required period for the loan).

"Designated international organisation" means an international organisation which has been designated by an Order made under FA 1984 s 126.

The effect of s 78 (and s 79) is to be ignored in construing FA 1985 s 81(3).

References in s 78 (and s 79) to FA 1963 s 60 include FA (Northern Ireland) 1963 s 9(1).

[*Note:* See note at commencement of commentary on this Act.]

79. Loan capital: new provisions

There is a complete exemption from stamp duty under the provisions relating to bearer instrument duty in what is now FA 1999 Sch 15 in respect of the issue of an instrument which relates to loan capital (as defined in s 78(7)) or on the transfer of loan capital constituted by, or transferable by means of, such instrument: (2). This exemption is not subject to the provisos in sub-ss (5) and (6) restricting the exemption from conveyance on sale stamp duty of instruments which transfer loan capital, but such instruments issued on or after 26 November 1996 are likely to be subject to stamp duty reserve tax on transfer under FA 1986 s 90(3E).

There is also an exemption from duty under the "transfer on sale" provisions in what is now FA 1999 Sch 13 Part I on an instrument which transfers loan capital issued or raised by the OECD, the Inter-American Development bank, or any organisation designated under FA 1984 s 126, or any other loan capital except as mentioned below: (3), (4).

The above exemption does not apply to an instrument transferring any loan capital which, at the time the instrument was executed, carries a right (exercisable then or later) of conversion into shares or other securities, or to the acquisition of shares or other securities, including loan capital of the same description: (5). (See also Statement of Practice 3/84 in Appendices in relation to FA 1976 s 126 2), the precursor of sub-section (J).)

The exemption also does not apply to any instrument transferring loan capital which, at the time the instrument is executed or at any earlier time, carries or has carried:

(a) a right to interest the amount of which exceeds a reasonable commercial return on the nominal amount of the capital; or
(b) a right to interest the amount of which falls or has fallen to be determined to any extent by reference to results of, or of any part of, a business or to the value of any property; or
(c) a right on repayment to an amount which exceeds the nominal amount of the capital and is not reasonably comparable with what is generally repayable (in respect of a similar nominal amount of capital) under the terms of issue of loan capital listed in the Official List of The Stock Exchange: (6).

The fact that any interest or premium on loan capital is index-linked or interest varies in inverse proportion to the success of the business does not, however, of itself, prevent the exemption from applying: (7), (7A). Similarly, the fact that the loan capital had to be issued on limited recourse terms will not necessarily preclude a subsequent transfer of that debt being exempt from stamp duty. Loan capital that carries a right to a return that is calculated by reference to the results of a business is not prevented from obtaining the benefit of the exemption if the issuer is a debtor in a capital market arrangement and issuer of a capital market investment and the loan capital is issued on limited recourse terms.

Special treatment is afforded to alternative finance investment bonds taking the sukuk form (see FA 2005 s 48A), which might well fail the conditions imposed by sub-s (6) on conventional debt instruments. Such bonds will generally not carry a conventional right to interest but will require the debtor to acquire assets from which an income return will be generated and which will be used to compensate the lender for being kept out of the funds lent. In the case of such bonds, condition (*a*) is omitted and for condition (*c*) is substituted a requirement that the sum payable at the end of the term must not exceed the aggregate of the amount paid for the issue of the bond and a sum that (taken with sums received during the period) would represent a reasonable commercial return over the bond period. The effect of the amendments is to invite a comparison between the interest payable on an ordinary bond and the "right to additional payments" carried by the alternative finance investment bond.

Where loan capital falls under any of the headings in respect of which the exemption is not available, then stamp duty under the "conveyance or transfer on sale" provisions in what is now FA 1999 Sch 13 Part I is chargeable at a reduced rate of 0.5 per cent of the amount or value of the consideration for the sale to which the relevant instrument of transfer gives effect. The new provisions apply to inland bearer instruments issued, and overseas bearer instruments transferred, after 31 July 1986, and to transfer instruments executed after 31 July 1986.

It is interesting to note that the various changes of mind by the Chancellor of the Exchequer, and the timing difference between the withdrawal of Resolution 33 and the introduction of the new provisions, meant that non-exempt transfers of loan capital paid duty of 0·5 per cent between 25 March and 6 July 1986, 1·0 per cent between 7 July and 31 July 1986, and 0·5 per cent again from 1 August 1986.

It should be noted that, although certain types of loan capital might be exempt from stamp duty, dispositions of individual rights relating thereto will not necessarily be exempt. For example, the transfer of a right to a specific proportion of the total interest payable under a debenture (eg a "coupon strip") would not in itself appear to qualify for any loan capital exemption so that a written transfer of such a right would be stampable as a conveyance or transfer on sale, and an agreement to make such a transfer would be stampable under what is now FA 1999 Sch 13 Part I para 7 as an agreement to transfer intangible property. (Compare the position to stamp duty reserve tax, where, if any loan capital fell outside the definition of "chargeable securities", any rights in or over such loan capital would themselves also fall outside the scope of the charge.)

[*Note:* See note at commencement of commentary on this Act.]

80A. Sales to intermediaries

This section provides relief from Stamp Duty on instruments which transfer stock to intermediaries and their nominees. The objective of this section is to encourage liquidity by enabling intermediaries in the stock and stock options markets to buy stock without incurring stamp duty. Significant amendments have been made to this section to coincide with the implementation of the Market in Financial Instruments Directive (2004/39/EC) ("MiFID") on 1 November 2007. Effectively these remove the requirement that the intermediary must be a member of the relevant exchange and substitute a requirement that the stock in question be regularly traded on the exchange.

Provided that the relevant instrument is denoted as not stampable with any duty (see sub-s (7)), stamp duty is not chargeable (subject to what is said in relation to s 80B below) on any instrument:

- (a) executed on or after 20 October 1997;
- (b) transferring stock (defined in s 80B(7)) by way of transfer on sale;
- (c) which is:
  - (i) effected (defined in sub-section (6)) on a prescribed multilateral trading facility ("MTF") (as defined in MiFID) or on a recognised foreign exchange, provided in each case that it is one on which stock of that kind is regularly traded; or
  - (ii) is stock of that kind which is regularly traded on a regulated market (as defined by MiFID); and
- (d) which is sold:
  - (i) to an intermediary (defined in sub-section (4)(*a*), subject to s 80B(7)) (or his nominee) who is a member of the MTF, market or exchange and who is recognised as an intermediary by the facility or exchange in accordance with arrangements approved by the Commissioners; or
  - (ii) to an intermediary who is approved for the purposes of section 80A by the Commissioners (or to his nominee).

AIM, OFEX and POSIT (a market operated by Investment Technology Group Ltd) have been prescribed as MTFs by the Stamp Duty and Stamp Duty Reserve Tax (Extension of Exceptions Relating to Recognised Exchanges) Regulations 2005, SI 2005/1990.

Subject to similar conditions, an instrument transferring stock to an options intermediary (defined in sub-s (4)(*b*)) is also exempt. The stock must (*a*) be of a kind that is regularly traded on the facility or exchange, and (*b*) be stock in which options to buy or sell stock of that kind are both regularly traded and listed or quoted on that facillity or exchange.

The "intermediary" or "options intermediary" must satisfy a regulatory test (be a member of the relevant exchange or be approved by the Commissioners) and satisfy the definition in sub-ss (4) and (5). This definition requires the intermediary to carry on a bona fide stock dealing business (or, in the case of an options intermediary, a bona fide business in dealing in quoted or listed options). It should be noted that nothing specifically requires a particular transaction to be carried out in the course of such a business, provided that the transaction is carried out on the facility or exchange and that the intermediary or options intermediary concerned does not carry on an "excluded business". The following types of business are excluded: making or managing investments, providing services to connected persons (borrowing the TA 1988 s 839 definition of "connected"), insurance business, pension scheme trusteeship or management, and fund management. The Commissioners are restricted in their approval of intermediaries who are not themselves members of a facility or exchange: (6A). They may only approve persons who are authorised under the law of an EEA State to provide investment services and activities as defined in Sections A2 and A3 Annex 1 to MiFID (ie execution of order on behalf of clients or dealings on own account).

80B. Intermediaries: supplementary

This section supplements s 80A. It defines "connected", "collective investment scheme", "EEA State", "insurance business", "quoted or listed options", "stock", "trustees" and "the operator" in relation to a collective investment scheme, "recognised foreign exchange", "recognised foreign options exchange".

Instruments are not exempt under this section if executed in pursuance of certain kinds of agreement specified by Treasury regulation. Other instruments described by Treasury regulation may be chargeable at the reduced rate of up to 0.1 per cent of the consideration for the sale.

[*Note:* See note at commencement of commentary on this Act.]

80C. Repurchases and stock lending

This section exempts from stamp duty the transfers and re-transfers on sale of stock under "repo" and stock lending arrangements but this relief is governed by the status of the transaction rather than by the status of the parties thereto. Certain transfers may be relieved both under this section and s 80A. Most repos and stock loans relating to UK securities are in practice settled through the CREST paperless settlement system so that stamp duty is not an issue. However, this section must also be read in conjunction with the corresponding relief from SDRT which is to be found in s 89AB below. One matter of particular importance is that the relief is given on the basis that both purchase and repurchase will take place as arranged. If this proves not to be the case then an SDRT charge will be imposed: see s 88(1C), (1D). This is to prevent a sale of stock being disguised as a repo in order to secure exemption from stamp duty and SDRT in circumstances where the repurchase is never intended to take place.

The relief is subject to the following conditions:

(a) the transfer and re-transfer must be made under and in accordance with the same arrangement (usually one of the industry's standard master agreements): (1), (2);

(b) either the transferor or transferee is authorised under the law of an EEA State to provide relevant investment services as defined in Section A2 or A3 of Annex 1 to MiFID: (2A);

(c) the arrangement must be effected on a prescribed MTF, regulated market or recognised foreign exchange (see s 80A above) on which stock of the kind concerned is regularly traded: (3);

(d) the arrangement must be on arm's length terms: (4)(*a*);

Part II ST

(e) the interim owner must not be given any "economic rights" in the stock during the period of the repo or stock loan: (4)(*b*). This probably means, in practice, that the interim owner must pass on any dividends or interest to the original owner and the repurchase price should not differ from the sale price except to reflect fees, financing costs or compensation for interim dividends or receipts.

An instrument of transfer qualifying for relief under this section is not to be treated as duly stamped unless stamped with a stamp denoting that no duty is payable; adjudication is not necessary.

The Treasury powers to substitute a lower rate of stamp duty or amend the conditions of the exemption are the same as under s 80B but such powers may be exercised independently in relation to each of ss 80A and 80C (ie in relation to one but not the other, or differently in relation to each).

This section applies to instruments executed (or if conditional when the condition is satisfied) on or after 20 October 1997. The main difference from the old rules is that the relief covers repos and chains with more than one intermediate "stock borrower".

For stamp duty reserve tax on repos and stock lending generally see s 89AA. An instrument stamped not chargeable with any duty under sub-s (5) remains exempt from stamp duty, even if it transpires that s 80C(1)(*b*) was not satisfied or that the relief was disapplied under s 80C(4)(*a*) or (*b*), but stamp duty reserve tax is payable instead (s 88(1C), (1D)).

[*Note:* See note at commencement of commentary on this Act.]

80D. Repurchases and stock lending: replacement stock on insolvency

This section affords relief in circumstances where a stock lending arrangement has been entered into between unconnected persons that falls within the scope of s 80C but, after the stock has been lent, one or other party to the arrangement becomes insolvent in circumstances where it is apparent that, as a result of the insolvency, the transaction will not be unwound by the re-transfer of the stock to the lender.

The relief is designed to secure that the stock lender is not disadvantaged by having to go into the market to buy replacement securities for those which ought to have been returned to it without a stamp duty charge. The thrust of the legislation is that the stock lender must first make use of the collateral with which it may have been provided to acquire the replacement securities; and may only look to other funds once the collateral has been disposed of. If this were not the case, the lender would be placed in a more advantageous position, since it would have acquired collateral without a stamp duty charge in addition to the further relief given by s 80D.

Accordingly, if within 30 days of the insolvency, the solvent party (or its nominee) acquires replacement stock (ie stock of the same kind as the stock which is not to be re-transferred), stamp duty is not chargeable on the instrument transferring the replacement stock to the solvent party or his nominee. Section 80D(3) affords relief where the solvent party was provided with collateral under the arrangement and uses that collateral (directly or indirectly) to acquire the replacement stock. If the collateral is insufficient to meet the whole of the cost of acquiring the replacement stock, s 80D(3)(*b*) affords relief where other funds are used to meet the residue of the cost. Section 80D(4) affords relief where there was no collateral provided under the arrangements and the solvent party uses other funds to acquire the replacement stock. In each case, relief from duty is limited to the amount of stock lent which will not be transferred as a result of the insolvency (s 80D(6)). The instrument (or instruments) which are relieved from duty require a denoting stamp in order to qualify as 'duly stamped' (s 80D(7)). For the requirement to be duly stamped in order to be received in evidence, see the commentary on SA 1891 s 14 above.

A corresponding relief from SDRT is afforded by FA 1986 s 89AB.

The provision applies where the insolvency occurs on or after 1 September 2008 (FA 2009 s 82(2))

CHANGES IN FINANCIAL INSTITUTIONS

81. Sales to market makers

This section was repealed by FA 1997 s 97(2) with effect from 20 October 1997 in relation to instruments executed on or after that date. The new provisions are in ss 80A, 80B.

[*Note:* See note at commencement of commentary on this Act.]

82. Borrowing of stock by market makers

This section was repealed by FA 1997 s 98(2) in relation to instruments executed on or after 20 October 1997. The new provisions are in s 80C.

[*Note:* See note at commencement of commentary on this Act.]

83. Composition agreements

Under FA 1970 s 33, HMRC has the power to enter into composition arrangements with The Stock Exchange for the payment of stamp duty. Similar arrangements can be made with any "recognised investment exchange" or "recognised clearing house" under the Financial Services Act 1986.

84. Miscellaneous exemptions

Transfers of stock to a recognised clearing house or its nominee, or to a recognised investment exchange or its nominee, which has entered into a composition agreement for the payment of stamp duty, are not chargeable with stamp duty.

[*Note:* See note at commencement of commentary on this Act.]

PART 4 STAMP DUTY RESERVE TAX

INTRODUCTION

86. The tax: introduction and territoriality

This section introduces "stamp duty reserve tax". This is a misleading name because it is a completely separate tax and the provisions in Pt IV (ss 86 to 99) are not to be construed as one with SA 1891. Stamp duty reserve tax is directly enforceable by assessment and, unlike stamp duty, not by means of stamping documents. Appeals against assessment lie to the Special Commissioners under the TMA 1970, and not by way of adjudication and case stated under SA 1891 ss 12 and 13.

Stamp duty reserve tax was introduced to apply in circumstances where shares are sold but stamp duty is not payable because there is no instrument of transfer chargeable to duty. Contracts for the sale of a legal interest in stock and marketable securities are not chargeable to stamp duty by virtue of what is now FA 1999 Sch 13 Part I para 7 and it is therefore possible to avoid stamp duty in respect of a sale where no instrument of transfer is taken and the registered holder of the shares remains the same. Accordingly, stamp duty is not payable on sales of listed securities during a Stock Exchange account period (which are all contractual, transfers being made only to the purchaser entitled at the end of the account period), purchases of shares where the shares are registered in the name of a nominee who acts both for the seller and the purchaser, or transfers of letters of allotment. Stamp duty reserve tax was therefore introduced to render such transactions chargeable. Transactions in securities in relation to depositary and clearance schemes are the subject of stamp duty reserve tax provisions which create, in effect, separate regimes from the principal charge (see ss 93–97A). The principal charge relates only to *transfers* of shares and similar instruments, whereas the charges for depositary schemes and clearance services sometimes arise on the *issue* of new instruments. Stamp duty reserve tax can also be charged in relation to other "one-off" situations, such as on the transfer of certain inland bearer instruments under FA 1986 s 90.

Part II ST

The introduction of the CREST paperless share transfer system (which became operational on 15 July 1996) has increased the significance of stamp duty reserve tax because most shares listed on the London Stock Exchange are subject to stamp duty reserve tax settled through CREST.

Because stamp duty reserve tax is an entirely separate tax from stamp duty, transactions which are exempt from stamp duty by virtue of specific statutory provisions are not automatically exempt from the new tax. For example, in the case of internal group re-organisations which are exempt from stamp duty by virtue of FA 1930 s 42, there is no automatic exemption from stamp duty reserve tax. However, where instruments of transfer are executed for such purposes, and are adjudged as not chargeable to any duty by virtue of the exemption, this enables stamp duty reserve tax to be avoided or reclaimed (see s 92).

Exceptionally, however, FA 1930 does apply automatically to stamp duty reserve tax (ie without the taxpayer having first to create a physical document and then have it adjudicated as exempt from stamp duty) in the context of the new stamp duty reserve tax regime for unit trusts transactions, set out in FA 1999 Sch 19—see para 6(4) of that Schedule and also the amendment made thereby to FA 1986 s 90. This is presumably because no meaningful stamp duty adjudication of a stampable document could be sought, the charge to stamp duty having been abolished.

The tax is under the care and management of HMRC. PCTA 1968 s 1 applies to the tax.

Until 1 July 1996 the only express rule on the territoriality of stamp duty reserve tax was that it applied only to "chargeable securities" (defined in FA 1986 s 99(4)) which confined it mainly to United Kingdom securities. In practice, an agreement to purchase securities made overseas between non-residents was regarded by the tax authority as outside the scope of stamp duty reserve tax (see paragraph 2.10 of the Stamp Duty Reserve Tax Notes). This concession effectively introduced some additional territorial limit to the scope of stamp duty reserve tax by reference to residence of the parties and the place where the agreement to purchase was made. From 1 July 1996 this concession is reversed by statute so that, for example, stamp duty reserve tax applies to an agreement to transfer UK securities made outside the UK between non-resident parties. No doubt the charge will be difficult to enforce against non-residents unless the transfer is settled through CREST or another clearance service with responsibility for collecting the charge.

[*Note:* See note at commencement of commentary on this Act.]

THE PRINCIPAL CHARGE

87. The principal charge

Stamp duty reserve tax is charged in any case where one person (A) agrees with another (B) to transfer chargeable securities (whether or not to B) for consideration in money or money's worth. The charge arises on the date of the agreement or, where it is conditional, the date on which the conditions are satisfied. The concept of "conditionality", which is also used in a similar manner in the field of capital gains tax, has sometimes given rise to problems. Most of the cases on the subject of conditional contracts, which are not themselves necessarily anything to do with tax issues, concern sales of land although the principles would appear to be equally applicable in other contexts, including that of dealings in "chargeable securities". It is submitted that the reference to a "conditional" contract in this section is a reference to a contract the performance of which is subject to the satisfaction of a condition lying wholly (or, at least, partly) outside the control of the actual parties to the contract, and that where relevant acts, approvals, consents or preliminary matters lie entirely within the discretion or competence of one or more of the parties themselves, the mere fact that performance is subject to some kind of precondition does not mean that the contract is "conditional"—see the discussion of this subject in *Michaels v Harley House (Marylebone) Ltd* [1997] 3 All ER 446 (reversed, for reasons which do not affect this analysis, at [1999] 1 All ER 356). The charge is cancelled if an instrument executed in pursuance of the agreement is duly stamped within six years (see s 92) but the introduction of the CREST system for paperless share transfers will make this less common in relation to listed securities. A charge to the tax is assessed at the rate of 0·5 per cent of the amount or value of the consideration agreed to be given for the chargeable securities. "Chargeable securities" is defined in s 99.

It should be noted that this charge is geared to the agreement to transfer chargeable securities, and not the actual transfer of those securities (compare the provisions relating to the higher rate charge on depositary receipts and clearance services in ss 93 and 96 below and the new charge on surrenders of units in a unit trust, in FA 1999 Sch 19). Care should be taken to ensure that, to the extent that it remains feasible to do this, any possible stamp duty mitigation techniques are not rendered futile on the facts of the case by paying insufficient attention to the timing aspects of the steps in a transaction. For example, it might be possible in some situations to avoid or reduce a stamp duty charge on the sale of shares by means of a scheme of arrangement, approved by the courts. However, if it is sought to add such a scheme as an "afterthought" to a share sale that has already been agreed upon, there will be a grave risk of having already incurred a charge to stamp duty reserve tax before the scheme of arrangement is ever implemented, on the basis that there already existed an unconditional and fully executed agreement to transfer the shares in question. No subsequent events, such as a court-approved cancellation of those shares, would serve to cancel or rescind the tax charge already incurred on the initial agreement.

In relation to the liability to pay the charge where it is not practically possible to duly stamp an instrument before liability to pay the charge arises see the 16 January 1997 letter to the *Tax Journal* (reproduced in Appendix 4), although it should be remembered that the Revenue's comments there reflect time limits for the payment of stamp duty reserve tax which have subsequently been shortened (see the commentary to reg 2 of the Stamp Duty Reserve Tax Regulations 1986, as amended). It is understood that HMRC has relaxed this practice and does not now insist on payment of the charge unless difficulties are encountered in getting the stock transfer form stamped.

An instrument which is stampable but does not attract any duty (provided that, where required, it is adjudicated) is sufficient to relieve a stamp duty reserve tax liability. It also seems to be sufficient if an instrument is executed which is not required to be stamped or adjudicated in any way. There need not be a stamped instrument but only an instrument which, if it needs to be stamped, is stamped.

The agreement may be written or oral, express or implied, and it does not make any difference whether or not the governing law of the contract is English, whether the agreement is made in the UK, or whether either or both of the parties to the agreement is or are resident, incorporated or established in the UK. The agreement must, however, be an agreement *"to transfer"* securities. An agreement for the issue of shares, where no transfer is involved, will clearly not be caught.

An example of a situation where an "agreement to transfer" for the purposes of this section was not deemed to have taken place, is found in *Save & Prosper Securities Limited v IRC* [2000] STC (SCD) 408. This involved an amalgamation of two unit trust schemes that shared the same trustee (and hence legal ownership of the underlying scheme property never altered). The manager of the discontinuing scheme wrote to the discontinuing scheme unitholders proposing a scheme of amalgamation under which, on the effective date, the trustee would hold the property of the discontinuing scheme as an accretion to the property of the continuing scheme; the units in the continuing scheme remained; the units in the discontinued scheme were cancelled; new units in the continuing scheme were then to be issued pro rata. The change of equitable ownership in the underlying scheme property fell within s 87(1), and hence SDRT would be charged if the discontinuing scheme unitholders agreed to transfer their equitable interests in the underlying property of the discontinuing scheme. The Commissioners held that there was no agreement within s 87(1) between, as the Revenue argued, the discontinuing scheme unitholders and the manager, nor could such an agreement be identified as one element in the whole transaction. The amalgamation took place by operation of law under the Financial Services (Regulated Schemes) Regulations 1991 and was best characterised as a "scheme of arrangement" involving a multiplicity of parties with interlocking and interdependent rights and obligations. The essential ingredient in the scheme of amalgamation was the vote of the requisite number of unitholders in the discontinuing scheme following which the parties were under a statutory obligation to implement the scheme. Although the finding that there was no agreement was sufficient to decide the case the Commissioners went on to find that there was no transfer from the unitholders of the discontinuing scheme to the unitholders of the continuing scheme. Rather, the unitholders in both schemes surrendered their equitable interests in their separate schemes and received in return new equitable interests in the enlarged scheme.

However, in the context of the CREST system, it is important to ensure, if new shares are to be issued in de-materialised form via a broker, that the intended beneficial owner of the new shares is capable of being identified by the time the shares are "enabled" within the broker's CREST account. Since a person cannot act as agent for a "principal" who has not yet been identified (meaning a case where the contractual counterparty has not actually been selected, not merely a situation where the identity of a specific person has not yet been revealed) the conclusion in such a case would have to be that new shares had been issued to the broker as beneficial owner and not as nominee for another person (ie the "real" subscriber). Any further disposition by the broker in favour of that other person would then involve a transfer of beneficial ownership in the new shares, giving rise to a stamp duty reserve tax charge on the underlying agreement. In such cases, brokers will presumably adopt a practice of requiring an indemnity from the "real" subscriber to cover cases where, by that person's failure to lodge appropriate contractual documentation on time, the broker discovers that shares have been issued to it as beneficial owner rather than as nominee for a third party subscriber.

In addition, the Stamp Office has indicated that it does not consider either an agreement by a company to purchase its own shares or the grant of an option to purchase shares as falling within s 87(1). In the case of a grant of an option to purchase shares, HMRC's view does not appear to accord with stamp duty case law (which admittedly does not automatically apply for the purposes of stamp duty reserve tax) concerning options. It was held in *George Wimpey Ltd v IR Comrs* [1975] STC 248 that the grant of an option to purchase property effectively amounted to a conveyance on sale of property (the option itself) liable to ad valorem stamp duty. It is therefore arguable that (if the stamp duty cases are held to apply) whilst the grant of an option to purchase shares is clearly not of itself an agreement to transfer those shares, it may be an agreement to transfer the option itself, and (since an option to acquire shares falls within the definition of "chargeable securities" in s 99, discussed below) give rise to a charge to stamp duty reserve tax on the consideration for the grant. However, it is submitted that, despite the resulting inconsistency between the application of stamp duty and stamp duty reserve tax (which would be by no means unique) it is correct to regard the grant of an option as outside the scope of stamp duty reserve tax. This is because the latter tax is only stated to apply to an agreement to "transfer" property whereas a "conveyance or transfer" is defined for stamp duty purposes (in what is now FA 1999 Sch 13 Part I para 1(2)) so as to cover cases where property is "transferred to or vested in" a purchaser. The trial judge and all three members of the Court of Appeal in the *Wimpey* case appear to have proceeded on the basis that a grant of an option could only be dutiable as a sale by virtue of vesting property in a party, rather than transferring it to them.

A possible example of the reverse situation—where a mismatch of terminology possibly makes the stamp duty regime less onerous than the stamp duty reserve tax regime—is a transfer of shares as security for a loan; whereas a transfer by way of security is clearly not a "sale" (and therefore not dutiable under that heading), it *is* equally clearly a "transfer" and might be a transfer for "money's worth" and so liable to tax on the value of the consideration). The same argument will not apply to the grant of an option to sell shares (ie, a "put option") because only an option to *acquire* shares falls within the definition of "chargeable securities".

The value of any consideration which does not consist of money is to be taken to be the price it might reasonably be expected to fetch on a sale in the open market at the time the agreement is made. It might generally be assumed that stamp duty reserve tax is more onerous than stamp duty because there is no group relief from stamp duty reserve tax and the chargeable consideration is not confined to the categories of "sale" consideration in stamp duty law but extends to any "money's worth". However, it should be remembered that there is no statutory or judicial authority for applying the stamp duty "contingency principle" to stamp duty reserve tax. This means that, depending upon the precise circumstances of the case, it might sometimes be cheaper to pay stamp duty reserve tax than stamp duty.

For example, if variable consideration is to be subject to an upper "cap", that maximum amount is likely to provide the value by which to charge stamp duty whether or not consideration of that amount is ever actually received. However, it is arguable that the appropriate way to value the transaction for stamp duty reserve tax purposes is to seek the market value of the right to receive the variable consideration. Specific support for this approach is provided in the words of subs (7). That kind of valuation is highly likely to produce some kind of discount from the value which would otherwise be used for calculating stamp duty on the same transaction and the greater the degree of uncertainty as to the receipt, length of time over which it falls to be received, etc, the larger the element of discount from the "cap" there ought to be.

"The enactments relating to stamp duty" mean SA 1891 and any enactment which amends or is required to be construed together with that Act.

The duly stamped instrument or instruments of transfer which avoid the tax being paid or allow it to be repaid must be in favour of the purchaser under the agreement, ie, B, or his nominee or a person who takes the transfer by way of security for a loan to B. Accordingly, where there is a sub-sale to another person a charge will arise, notwithstanding that stamp duty is paid on a transfer of the securities from the original seller to the sub-purchaser. In that case, the charge will be on the consideration paid by B. The agreement by the sub-purchaser to purchase the securities from B may not be liable for stamp duty reserve tax although, on a strict reading of the legislation, it is perhaps questionable whether a single instrument of transfer, completing two successive sales of "chargeable securities", is actually effective to cancel the charge to stamp duty reserve tax on either of the underlying agreements.

Before the insertion of s 87(7A), one problem was that in order to give relief from a charge to stamp duty reserve tax, the relevant instrument or instruments of transfer had to be in respect of *all* the chargeable securities to which the agreement related. The effect of this was that if even a single share covered by the agreement was either not the subject of a duly stamped instrument of transfer within the two month period (as the law then allowed), or was transferred directly to a sub-purchaser, then the original purchaser, ie, B, was liable to stamp duty reserve tax on *all* the chargeable securities covered by the relevant agreement, in addition to the stamp duty he would have paid on the securities actually transferred to him by duly stamped instruments of transfer. Under s 87(7A), however, stamp duty reserve tax is only chargeable on the agreement between the vendor and the original purchaser in respect of the chargeable securities which are transferred direct to the sub-purchaser rather than to the original purchaser.

Under s 87(7A) the section takes effect as if there were separate agreements in relation to each parcel of shares—ie, one or more agreements covering the shares transferred to B or his nominee, and one or more separate agreements covering the shares either not transferred at all or sub-sold to one or more third parties. This effectively means that the stamp duty reserve tax will only be paid in respect of the shares which are not actually transferred to B or his nominee. The Revenue Press Release of 8 April 1987 gave the following example to show how this provision would operate:

A sells to B 1,000 shares in X plc for £1,500.

B resells 750 of the shares to C.

A transfers 750 shares to C and 250 shares to B.

The agreement between A and B is deemed to be two separate agreements, one in respect of 750 shares and one in respect of 250 shares, with the result that B incurs a stamp duty reserve tax liability on the agreement to purchase 750 shares, ie, on £1,125 (75 per cent of £1,500). The ad valorem stamp duty on the transfer to B of the 250 shares relieves, or "franks", the stamp duty reserve tax liability on that agreement.

The position would be the same even if no sub-sale was involved. If, in the above example, B did not resell any of the shares he agreed to purchase from A, but simply took a transfer of 250 shares (which was duly stamped) and left the remaining shares registered in A's name, A then acting as his nominee, the same result would follow—ie, there would be deemed to be two agreements and the stamp duty reserve tax would only be payable in respect of the 750 shares not transferred to B.

HMRC historically have regarded only the principals to an agreement to transfer chargeable securities as falling within the definition of A and B for the purposes of s 87, and not also their respective agents, (even if any such agent is himself liable as a principal on the contract eg, where acting for an undisclosed principal). HMRC took the view that only the agreement between the principals themselves would be chargeable with stamp duty reserve tax, and not also the agreement (if any) between the agent and his named principal. This seemed to flow from the fact that s 87 refers to an agreement *to transfer* rather than an agreement *relating to* a transfer. This analysis may not be correct, despite HMRC's assurances, if the principal is obliged by the terms of his agreement with his agent to effect the eventual transfer; in that case there is an agreement by which the principal (A) agrees with his agent (B) to transfer chargeable securities, even if not to the agent, which would appear to be caught by the precise wording of s 87(1). Since this alternative analysis would involve a double charge, one on the agency agreement and one on the agreement with the actual purchaser, HMRC accepted that agency agreements would not give rise to a stamp duty reserve tax liability.

A specific issue has now arisen in relation to investors in collective investment schemes which has been addressed by HMRC in SDRT Customer Newsletter Issue 10 "Collective investment schemes—Net dealing by intermediaries". Such investors often make their investment through an intermediary. Intermediaries may deal with underlying fund managers by sending aggregated sell and aggregated buy instructions separately (known as "gross dealing"); or intermediaries may net off buy and sell instructions for each fund and thus send only one net buy or sell instruction to each underlying fund manager (known as "net dealing"). The question that arises in relation to such transactions is whether SDRT should be charged on the net transaction or on the gross dealing. So far as the charge to SDRT under section 87 is concerned, the view of HMRC, adopted with effect from 14 July 2009, is that net dealing will generally (depending on the facts of each case) give rise to two principal SDRT charges in respect of the transactions which have been netted off —one on the intermediary and one on the ultimate purchaser of the investment, but further announced that HMRC would not pursue any such charges that arose on or before the date of this announcement. However, at the same time and by the same newsletter HMRC announced an amelioration of the position for the underlying fund managers (as to which see the commentary to FA 1999 Sch 19). It is assumed (although this has not been confirmed) that the specific change in policy adopted by HMRC as regards collective investment schemes has not affected their general policy as set out above in relation to transactions between principals and their agents.

[*Note:* See note at commencement of commentary on this Act.]

88. Special cases

Sub-section (1)

An instrument which is not chargeable to stamp duty by virtue of FA 1976 s 127(1) (transfer to The Stock Exchange nominee) or FA 1986 s 84(2) and (3) (transfers to recognised investment exchanges and clearing houses, and their respective nominees) is disregarded in construing s 92(1A), (1B). This means that the execution of such an instrument does not exclude liability for stamp duty reserve tax. Any transfer by such a person to a purchaser or sub-purchaser, if duly stamped, relieves the purchaser or sub-purchaser, but not the original vendor, from liability to stamp duty reserve tax.

An agreement to transfer a renounceable letter of allotment (or similar instrument) with a life of up to six months (which is exempt from stamp duty under what is now FA 1999 Sch 15 para 16 is subject to stamp duty reserve tax on the date of the agreement (or, with a conditional agreement, on the date it becomes unconditional).

The most important consequence of the application of a charge to stamp duty reserve tax on agreements to transfer renounceable letters of allotment and similar instruments (including the renounceable letters of acceptance commonly used, for example, in offers for sale) with a life of less than six months, is its impact (subject to the exemptions provided by s 89A) on the structuring of the various forms of domestic corporate finance transactions, for example offers for sale or subscription, bonus or rights issues and vendor placings.

The following brief analysis may help in understanding the issues involved.

(1) In an *offer for sale of new shares*, the company allots the new shares to its merchant bank on a nil paid renounceable letter of allotment; this is deemed to be fully paid when the admission of the company's shares to the Official List of The Stock Exchange becomes effective. The merchant bank issues renounceable letters of acceptance to successful applicants, evidencing the allocation made to them and enabling dealings to commence immediately so that an orderly market may be preserved. Following the last day for renunciation of the letters of acceptance the merchant bank renounces its renounceable letter of allotment in favour of the final renouncees of the renounceable letters of acceptance. The agreement to allot the shares to the bank (on the nil paid letter) does not attract a charge because it is an agreement to allot rather than transfer shares; and the initial issue by the bank of a renounceable letter of acceptance to a successful applicant, although constituting an agreement between the bank and that applicant to transfer the right to be allotted the shares, will clearly be within the exemptions provided by s 89A and so not attract a charge. Each subsequent renunciation of the letter of acceptance will attract a charge. The final renunciation by the bank of its letter of allotment in favour of the ultimate renouncees does not attract a charge, because it does not itself involve an agreement to transfer, or a transfer of, chargeable securities.

(2) In an *offer for subscription of new shares*, the company allots fully paid renounceable letters of allotment to successful applicants and subsequently issues definitive share certificates in favour of the ultimate renouncees. The issue of the letters of allotment does not attract a charge, as the letters are agreements to allot rather than transfer chargeable securities, and nor does the issue of the definitive certificates, but each intermediate renunciation attracts a charge.

(3) In a *bonus issue* or a *rights issue*, the company allots the new shares to existing holders on fully paid renounceable letters of allotment or nil paid provisional renounceable letters of allotment and (following, in the latter case, a period for splitting nil-paid and fully-paid rights) issues definitive share certificates to the ultimate renouncees. In either case the issues of the letters of allotment and the definitive share certificates do not attract a charge, but each intermediate renunciation does (on the consideration paid by the renouncees, ie, only on the premium in the case of a renunciation of nil-paid rights).

(4) An *offer for sale by existing shareholders* will usually involve a bonus issue to the existing shareholders on renounceable letters of allotment. The shareholders will agree with their merchant bank to sell the new shares to it, for which purpose they will renounce the letters of allotment in blank and execute powers of attorney in favour of a third party authorising him to complete the registration application forms in favour of such persons as the bank may nominate (upon receipt of the net proceeds of sale). The merchant bank, having purchased the letters of allotment,

Part II ST

will then offer the new shares for sale, as *principal*, and issue renounceable letters of acceptance to successful applicants. The bank will subsequently direct the completion of registration application forms in respect of the letters of allotment (received from the existing shareholders) in favour of the ultimate renouncees of the letters of acceptance. The issue of the letters of allotment to the existing shareholders by the company and the final registration of the ultimate renouncees of the letters of acceptance will not attract a charge, because they do not constitute agreements to *transfer* chargeable securities. The sale by the existing shareholders to the merchant bank (involving the renunciation by the existing shareholders in blank and the execution of powers of attorney) will not attract a charge, because it is clearly within the exemptions provided by s 89A. However, whether or not the issue of the letters of acceptance by the bank attracts a charge will depend upon whether the bonus shares fall within the definition of "newly subscribed securities" for the purposes of s 89A(2), as to which, see below. Each intermediate renunciation of the letters of acceptance will attract a charge. Before the enactment of s 89A both the sale of the new shares by the existing shareholders to their merchant bank and the issue by the bank of renounceable letters of acceptance would certainly have attracted a charge and banks had therefore developed the practice of offering the new shares for sale as *agent* for the existing shareholders, in which case the first charge was avoided because the existing shareholders would renounce their letters of allotment directly in favour of the ultimate renouncees of the letters of acceptance (which the bank issued on their behalf) without there first being a sale to the bank.

Commonly, an offer for sale by existing shareholders will also involve a sale of existing shares already registered in the names of the shareholders, instead of or in addition to new shares created by means of a bonus issue. In that case, the shareholders will again agree to sell the shares to the merchant bank and execute powers of attorney to transfer the shares to such persons as the bank chooses, against payment of the offer for sale price. The bank will then again offer the shares for sale, as *principal*, issue renounceable letters of acceptance to successful applicants, and subsequently deliver share transfers (executed under the aforesaid powers of attorney) in favour of the ultimate renouncees of the letters of acceptance. The agreement between the existing shareholders and the bank and the issue by the bank of the letters of acceptance will clearly be within the exemptions provided by s 89A(1) and (3) respectively and therefore not attract a charge to stamp duty reserve tax, but each intermediate renunciation of the letters of acceptance will attract a charge. Again, before the enactment of s 89A the charge which would then have arisen on the initial agreement to sell the shares to the bank was avoided by the bank acting as *agent* rather than as principal in the offer for sale.

It is understood that HMRC view the problem of a double charge sympathetically but the problem of how best to provide relief is rendered difficult by the fact that offers for sale usually involve sales of both existing registered shares and new bonus issue shares represented by renounceable letters of allotment. It would be difficult to tell which ultimate renouncees had acquired rights to registered shares (where the double charge would arise) and which had acquired shares represented by letters of allotment (where there would be no double charge, because there would be no stamp duty on the eventual *issue* of the shares concerned).

(5) A *vendor consideration placing* involves the acquisition by a company of assets (other than shares in a listed company pursuant to a public takeover bid, as to which see below) in consideration of an issue of fully paid shares in the company which the vendors wish to sell, to realise cash. The company issues either definitive share certificates (where stamp duty relief on the transfers of the assets is to be sought under FA 1986 s 76) or renounceable letters of allotment (where s 76 relief is not available) to the vendors, who then agree to sell the shares to the merchant bank, who in turn on-sell them (as principal) to the placees. If definitive

share certificates are used, transfers are executed by the vendors in favour of the placees. Stamp duty on the transfers to the placees will prevent a charge to stamp duty reserve tax arising on the agreement between the bank and the placees, provided they are stamped within six months. If renounceable letters of allotment are used, stamp duty is avoided but stamp duty reserve tax is payable on any renunciations by the placees before definitive share certificates are issued.

In either case, the stamp duty reserve tax position in relation to the other elements of the transaction will depend on whether the exemptions provided by s 89A apply. If definitive share certificates are used stamp duty reserve tax will be payable on the agreement between the vendors and the bank, and if renounceable letters of allotment are used stamp duty reserve tax will be payable on the renunciation by the vendors to the bank and on the renunciation by the bank to the placees, unless in either case the bank's offer to the chosen placees can be said to be an offer to "the public", which (by analogy with the repealed provisions of the Companies Act 1985) seems unlikely. Alternatively, to avoid any possible stamp duty reserve tax charge the bank could agree with the vendors to place the shares as their agent.

(6) Where shares to be issued in consideration for an acquisition exceed certain proportions of the acquiring company's existing issued share capital, it is a requirement of the Stock Exchange that the consideration shares allotted to the vendors be offered back to the shareholders of the acquiring company. This is achieved either by means of a *vendor rights offer* (which may take the form of an *open offer*) or by means of a *vendor rights issue*.

The former method involves a vendor consideration placing with a so-called "claw-back", whereby the acquiring company's merchant bank invites the acquiring company's existing shareholders to apply for a pro-rata proportion of the consideration shares and, to the extent insufficient applications are received, either (in the case of an *open offer*) gives existing shareholders an opportunity to apply for a proportion of the balance or (in the more common case) places the balance with pre-arranged placees.

In the case of a *vendor rights issue*, the merchant bank, as principal, will first purchase or agree to purchase the consideration shares from the vendors and then offer them on a pro rata basis to the acquiring company's existing shareholders. The offer is made by means of a nil-paid renounceable letter of rights which can be dealt in the market, and at the acceptance and payment day for the offer the shares are either purchased by the offeree shareholders (or their renouncees) or, if a premium over the net issue price and expenses of sale can be obtained, sold in the market for the benefit of the shareholders originally entitled thereto, or, if this is not possible, sold by the merchant bank to sub-underwriters. The persons accepting the offer have their nil-paid renounceable letters of rights endorsed as fully paid upon payment.

The stamp duty reserve tax implications for the agreement between the vendors and the bank and the offers by the bank will again depend upon whether the offer by the bank can be said to be an offer "to the public". If the analogy with the repealed provisions of the Companies Act 1985 is valid (see s 89A) a carefully drafted letter of rights will evidence an invitation "calculated to result, directly or indirectly, in the shares . . . becoming available for . . . purchase by persons other than those receiving the offer . . ." and therefore constitute an offer to the public. In that case, the stamp duty reserve tax implications for these transactions will be similar to those relating to an *offer for sale by existing shareholders*, as described in paragraph 3 above. The purchase of the consideration shares by the bank from the vendors and the issue by the bank of renounceable documents will be within the s 89A exemptions and therefore not attract a charge, but each intermediate renunciation will attract a charge. The bank could still avoid any uncertainty caused by the lack of a definition of "offer to the public" for the purposes of s 89A by offering the shares for sale as agent for the vendors.

(7) In a *public takeover bid* involving an exchange of shares, the acquiring company often wishes to offer a *cash alternative*, without having to raise the money to fund the payment, and this is usually structured by means of an offer by the bidder's merchant bank to purchase for cash any of the shares in the bidder which the shareholders of the target company do not wish to keep (the bank usually mitigating its contingent liability to buy the shares by inviting institutions to "sub-underwrite" its purchase). In such cases, either the consideration shares will be registered in the names of the vendors and definitive certificates of title will be issued at the outset, or renounceable documents of title will initially be issued. Until the enactment of FA 1988 s 142 the former would normally be the preferred course of action in order that capital duty relief could be obtained on the issue of the consideration shares.

If the bank acts as principal in purchasing the relevant shares from acceptors of the cash alternative and selling them to the sub-underwriters, then if definitive certificates are used at the outset there will be a charge to stamp duty reserve tax on acceptances of the bank's offer which is not recoverable by stamped transfers to sub-underwriters, those transfers only relieving the stamp duty reserve tax liability on the agreements between the bank and the sub-underwriters. If renounceable documents of title are used there will be no double charge, since stamp duty reserve tax will be payable on the renunciations to the bank and sub-underwriters but no stamp duty will be payable.

(8) In all the above examples, extra care will need to be taken in relation to any *underwriting* and *sub-underwriting arrangements*, to ensure that they do not give rise to an "agreement to transfer" the underwritten securities, or rights to them, resulting in an additional charge to stamp duty reserve tax. However, provided that the main underwriting agreement is structured so that it imposes on the lead underwriter an obligation to subscribe or purchase, *or procure* subscribers or purchasers for, shares *which are not otherwise taken up* by existing shareholders (eg, in a rights issue) or members of the public (eg, in an offer for sale) it is probable that no "agreement to transfer" securities, or rights to them, and hence no charge to stamp duty reserve tax, arises at the time the agreement is entered into. Until it is known exactly how many shares, if any, are not taken up by shareholders or members of the public, underwriting and sub-underwriting agreements cannot "crystallise" as agreements to transfer chargeable securities. Moreover, the company or vendors will not, by virtue of an underwriting agreement, have an unconditional obligation to the lead underwriters to issue or sell to them all of the shares which are the subject of the agreement. The company or vendors have not *agreed* to issue or sell, but have merely imposed on the lead underwriters (who in turn have imposed on sub-underwriters) a commitment to subscribe or purchase, *if* called on. In theory, the company or vendors could choose *not* to call on the underwriters but to dispose of the unwanted shares elsewhere.

If and when the underwriters are in fact called on, then an agreement (binding on the company or vendors) to issue or transfer the unwanted shares arises directly with the lead underwriters. At that point there will also be sub-underwriting agreements in place which will enable the lead underwriters to discharge their liability (in whole or in part) to the company or vendors by procuring the sub-underwriters to comply with their obligations under the sub-underwriting agreements, the sub-underwriters at that stage becoming contractually bound direct to the company or vendors.

Accordingly, an underwriting and sub-underwriting structure involves, on creation, merely a series of conditional agreements relating to an unknown number of shares, and does not involve any agreement to transfer an interest in securities between any members of the underwriting group (lead underwriters and sub-underwriters). On crystallisation, there comes into effect a number of parallel agreements between the company or vendors on the one hand and each member of the underwriting and sub-underwriting groups on the other, not a series of sub-sales within the group. Only at that point is there a liability to stamp duty reserve tax in the case of existing shares which are transferred (which is relieved to the extent that the underwriters or sub-underwriters take duly stamped transfers).

(9) A further problem may arise as a result of the inter-action between FA 1985 s 81 and FA 1986 s 88. Where an offer for sale involves more new shares than the company has existing shares, this is done by an issue of bonus shares on renounceable letters of allotment which are then renounced for sale by the merchant bank as principal. Since FA 1985 s 81 that renunciation theoretically, giving as it does control of the company to the merchant bank, gives rise to stamp duty. As the agreement between the vendors and the bank also falls within s 88, this results in a double charge, as the s 88 charge cannot be relieved by the stamp duty.

The whole mechanics of corporate finance have now become a good deal more complicated, and great care at each stage will need to be taken by a company and its professional advisers.

Sub-section (1A)

Any instrument effecting the transfer of securities to a member of CREST (or any other paperless dealing system approved under the Treasury regulations made under Companies Act 2006 s 785) is exempt from stamp duty by virtue of FA 1996 s 186. Normally such an instrument would, by virtue of FA 1986 s 92, cancel any stamp duty reserve tax liability. Where an instrument of transfer exempted from stamp duty under FA 1996 s 186 is executed after 1 July 1996 in pursuance of an agreement to transfer securities, the stamp duty reserve tax charge on the agreement is not cancelled under FA 1986 s 92 unless the transfer is made by a "stock exchange nominee" (as defined in FA 1976 s 127(5)) and the transfer is not on sale.

Sub-section (1B)

An anti-avoidance provision applies to corporate groups with a fellow market making or broker dealer member or fellow intermediary or options intermediary member. Until 4 January 1996 such groups had been able to avoid stamp duty and stamp duty reserve tax on the acquisition of securities by purchasing them through the market maker (taking advantage of the market maker exemptions) and then transferring them intra-group (taking advantage of FA 1930 s 42 relief).

Sub-section (1B) applies where a company enters into an agreement to acquire securities from an associated company (being a market maker or broker dealer in the securities which, as such, obtained exemption from stamp duty and stamp duty reserve tax on its acquisition of the securities) and an instrument of transfer of those securities or those and other securities is executed within two years which is exempt from stamp duty by virtue of FA 1930 s 42. In those circumstances, stamp duty reserve tax is chargeable on the transfer between the associated companies (there is no equivalent in stamp duty reserve tax to the FA 1930 s 42 stamp duty relief) and execution of an instrument of transfer exempt from stamp duty under s 42 will not cancel the stamp duty reserve tax charge in the normal way. Adjudication of an instrument of transfer under s 42 still appears to cancel the stamp duty reserve tax charge if the parties wait for more than two years after the initial acquisition by the market maker, broker dealer, intermediary or options intermediary before executing the intra-group instrument of transfer.

Sub-section (1B) applies where the instrument qualifying for exemption from stamp duty under s 42 is executed on or after 4 January 1996 unless it is made in pursuance of an earlier agreement.

Sub-sections (4) and (5) determine whether the instrument of transfer relates to securities acquired (when the old reliefs applied) from a group market maker, broker dealer or (since the introduction of the new reliefs on 20 October 1997) an intermediary or options intermediary. Where the securities the subject of an instrument of transfer cannot be identified

Part II ST

(eg a holding of shares is made up of a number of shares in the same company acquired on different occasions), all securities of the kind to which the instrument of transfer relates acquired in the two years preceding execution of the instrument are identified (whether acquired from the group market maker or broker dealer or not). The instrument of transfer is taken to relate to those securities acquired later in priority to those acquired earlier: (4). Where stamp duty reserve tax applies to an agreement to transfer securities intra-group by virtue of sub-s (1B) and some of the securities transferred were not acquired from a market maker, broker dealer, intermediary or options intermediary, the agreement is treated as if split into two agreements, one relating to securities acquired from a market maker, broker dealer, intermediary or options intermediary on which stamp duty reserve tax applies and the other relating to securities not acquired from a market maker, broker dealer, intermediary or options intermediary exemption on which the stamp duty reserve tax charge should be cancelled in the normal way by a formal transfer adjudicated exempt under FA 1930 s 42.

The date of the agreement to acquire securities is taken to be the date of the agreement (or, if the agreement is conditional, the date when the condition is satisfied): (6).

The sub-s (1B) stamp duty reserve tax charge on certain intra-group agreements to transfer securities is extended to agreements to transfer securities intra-group where the formal transfer completing such agreement is executed on or after 4 January 1997 and the initial transfer of the securities into the group was effected pursuant to an agreement (whenever made) exempt from the principal stamp duty reserve tax charge by virtue of the exemption for repurchases and stock lending under either s 89B(1)(*a*) or, from 20 October 1997, under s 89AA (1) (*a*), (2).

Sub-sections (1C) and (1D)

The practical effect of these sub-sections is to impose a charge to stamp duty reserve tax where an unstamped transfer of securities has been registered and it subsequently becomes apparent that the conditions for exemption of repos and stock loans relied upon will not be satisfied.

Under sub-s (1C), if the instrument of transfer in relation to the transfer by the original owner to the interim owner is exempt pursuant to the s 80C(2) repurchase and stock lending exemption and it becomes apparent that the s 80C(1)(*b*) condition relating to the re-transfer will not be satisfied, that instrument of transfer will be disregarded so that the stamp duty reserve tax on the initial transfer leg of a repo or stock loan will not be cancelled or repaid under s 92. It would appear that a double charge could conceivably arise as even the subsequent stamping of the transfer would appear not to eliminate the sub-s (1C) charge.

Under sub-s (1D) a similar stamp duty reserve tax charge arises if an instrument is stamped on an exempt basis under the s 80C(5) stamp duty relief for repurchases and stock lending but the anti-avoidance provisions in s 80C(4) apply. No double charge arises as the stamped instrument of transfer is deemed to be duly stamped.

These sub-ss apply to instruments executed on or after 20 October 1997.

[*Note:* See note at commencement of commentary on this Act.]

88A. Section 87: exceptions for intermediaries

Subject to conditions identical to those which apply to the exemption from stamp duty of transfers under s 80A, agreements made (or, if conditional, where the condition is satisfied) on or after 20 October 1997 to transfer securities to certain intermediaries are exempt from the principal stamp duty reserve tax charge (but subject to the power, mentioned in relation to s 88B below, to introduce a charge at a reduced rate under Treasury regulations). The old regime is in s 89.

In accordance with the differences in wording between stamp duty and stamp duty reserve tax legislation generally, s 80A defines "intermediaries" and "options intermediaries" in terms of dealings in "stock", whereas s 88A defines them in terms of dealings in "chargeable securities".

[*Note:* See note at commencement of commentary on this Act.]

88B. Intermediaries: supplementary

The definitions of terms used in s 88A are the same as those given for the stamp duty exemption under s 80B. Section 88A may not apply to certain kinds of agreement specified by Treasury regulation. There is power to introduce by regulations a charge to stamp duty reserve tax at a rate not exceeding 0.1 per cent in respect of certain types of agreement falling within s 88A above. The Treasury may also change the meaning of "intermediary" or "options intermediary".

[*Note:* See note at commencement of commentary on this Act.]

89. Section 87: exceptions for market makers etc

This section was repealed by FA 1997 s 102(2) in relation to agreements made (or, if conditional, when the condition is satisfied) on or after 20 October 1997. The new provisions are in s 88A.

[*Note:* See note at commencement of commentary on this Act.]

89A. Section 87: exceptions for public issues

Until F(No 2)A 1987 inserted this section, merchant banks were compelled to act as agents (for the company or the vendor shareholders) rather than as principals in order to avoid the incidence of a stamp duty reserve tax liability on as many as possible of the individual stages in domestic corporate finance transactions, described in more detail in the notes to s 88. This was on the basis that (as noted under s 87) the Revenue regarded only the principals in a given transaction, and not their respective agents, as falling within the definition of A or B for the purposes of a stamp duty reserve tax charge. For a number of reasons, it was generally recognised that this was an unfortunate side-effect of the new tax.

In an offer for sale involving both existing and new shares the public must be confident that none of the shares being offered are in any way more of a risk than the others as a result of potential problems with bad title or default in delivery because of subsequent bankruptcy, death or other reasons. Any uncertainty in respect of particular shares would undermine the marketability of all the shares being offered because applicants for them would not know the source of any individual share which they might receive should their application be successful. If the merchant banks in such cases act as principal, they take on any risk there might be of bad title or failure to deliver and they offer the public a single root of title which the public can confidently accept. They also give successful applicants for the shares a single vendor to sue, should the need ever arise. The potential problems of bad title and default are resurrected by any structure which involves the merchant bank acting as agent.

To meet these arguments the section provides that s 87 does not apply:

(1) as regards an agreement to transfer securities other than units under a unit trust scheme to B or B's nominee if:
  (a) the agreement is part of an arrangement, entered into by B in the ordinary course of B's business as an issuing house, under which B, as principal, is to offer the securities for sale to the public, and
  (b) the agreement is conditional upon the admission of the securities to the Official List of The Stock Exchange, and
  (c) the consideration under the agreement for each security is the same as the price at which B is to offer the security for sale, and
  (d) B sells the securities in accordance with the agreement referred to in (*a*) above;

(2) as regards an agreement if the securities to which the agreement relates are newly subscribed securities other than units under a unit trust scheme and:
  (a) the agreement is made in pursuance of an offer to the public made by A as principal under an arrangement entered into in the ordinary course of A's business as an issuing house, and

(b) a right of allotment in respect of, or to subscribe for, the securities has been acquired by A under an agreement which is part of the arrangement, and

(c) both those agreements are conditional upon the admission of the securities to the Official List of The Stock Exchange, and

(d) the consideration for each security is the same under both agreements,

for which purposes "newly subscribed securities" are securities which, in pursuance of the arrangement referred to in (*a*) above, are issued wholly for new consideration; and

(3) as regards an agreement if the securities to which the agreement relates are registered securities other than units under a unit trust scheme and:

(a) the agreement is made in pursuance of an offer to the public made by A, and

(b) the agreement is conditional upon the admission of the securities to the Official List of The Stock Exchange, and

(c) under the agreement A issues to B or his nominee a renounceable letter of acceptance, or similar instrument, in respect of the securities.

The above changes apply to all agreements to transfer securities made on or after 8 May 1987, and the Treasury are empowered by statutory instrument to amend para (1) (*b*), para (2) (*c*), and para (3) (*b*).

Thus, where there is an offer to the public and the relevant shares are to be listed, then provided that the consideration for the relevant transactions matches the public offer price, there will be no stamp duty reserve tax liability in respect of (1) the purchase by an issuing house of any securities other than units under a unit trust scheme (whether held by vendors in registered form, or in respect of which vendors hold renounceable letters of allotment, eg, as with bonus shares in an offer for sale by existing shareholders) provided that the issuing house actually goes on to sell the shares as arranged, or (2) the sale by an issuing house of newly-issued shares to which it has acquired the rights, or (3) the sale by any person (whether or not an issuing house) of existing registered shares, where the sale is effected by the issue of renounceable letters of acceptance. This, HMRC hope, will achieve the object desired by corporate finance practitioners, that the interposition of an issuing house as principal should not lead to a stamp duty reserve tax liability which would not arise if the issuing house acted as agent.

Unfortunately s 89A as drafted has a number of problems.

First, in each case the relevant agreement must be made in connection with an "offer to the public". That expression is not defined. However, the Commissioners' view (see para 12.45 of the Stamp Taxes Manual) is that the meaning of "offer to the public" is that founded on case law – i.e. an invitation to the public in general, and not restricted to a limited class. Thus, a placing of shares to (for example) 75 financial institutions, they suggest, is not an issue to the public at large in the ordinary sense. Nevertheless, the Commissioners consider that it may still be possible for such an offer to fall within the definition of "offer to the public" by considering whether or not the offer is calculated to result, directly or indirectly, in the shares becoming available for subscription or purchase by persons other than those receiving the offer or invitation.

It is far from clear whether this view is valid after the incorporation into UK law of Council Directive 2003/71/EC, the Prospectus Directive (implemented in the UK by Part VI of the Financial Services and Markets Act 2000 as amended by the Prospectus Regulations 2005, SI 2005/1433, and to section 102B of FSMA as amended), where "an offer of securities to the public" is defined as a "communication to persons in any form and by any means, presenting sufficient information on the terms of the offer and the securities to be offered, so as to enable an investor to decide to purchase or subscribe to these securities", including the placing of securities through financial intermediaries. Clearly, this is much wider than the Commissioners' view

Rights issues of public companies are prima facie "offers to the public". There is an exemption where the number of shares issued over a 12 month period does not exceed 10%

of the same class already admitted to trading on the regulated market, as well as an exemption for bonus issues; but these apart, all such issues would appear to be offers to the public, and even in those cases where the exemption is available, the effect is simply to except the offer from the requirement to issue a prospectus and not to exclude it from the category of public offers.

It is by no means certain that the courts will construe s 89A by analogy with the Prospectus Directive, but in the absence of any other guidance it is difficult to see how else s 89A can be construed. If the courts do adopt such an interpretation, the new provisions will not avoid completely a double charge to stamp duty reserve tax in every situation where a merchant bank acts as principal rather than as agent in corporate finance transactions. The exemptions will apply in offers for sale (either of new shares or by existing shareholders) on an initial flotation, and possibly in vendor rights offers and vendor rights issues (ie, vendor consideration placings with "claw-back"), but they will not apply to private placings, including the traditional forms of vendor consideration placing (ie, without "claw-back"), or any other capital raising exercises involving a limited number of investors and the interposition of a merchant bank.

The same difficulty of construction arises in relation to TMA 1970 s 25(2), which applies (with modifications) to stamp duty reserve tax by virtue of the Stamp Duty Reserve Tax Regulations 1986, reg 20. HMRC can, under s 25(2), require issuing houses and others to make a return of all public issues or placings of shares or securities in any company effected by them during a specified period, giving certain particulars. Questions of construction will for this purpose be rather less of a problem because any issue of shares involving a merchant bank will almost always be a placing if it is not a public issue, although rights issues which do not constitute public offers (if the arguments set out above are correct) may not be placings either, and therefore could conceivably be excluded altogether.

One other definitional problem is the use of the expression "issuing house" in s 89A(1) and (2). Although the expression is generally recognised by corporate finance practitioners, it is not an expression which has a very precise meaning. TMA 1970 s 25(2), as mentioned above, contains provisions empowering the HMRC to require particular returns to be made by certain persons and includes (by association) "issuing houses" as within the category of persons "carrying on a business of effecting public issues of shares or securities in any company, or placings of shares or securities in any company, either on behalf of the company, or on behalf of holders of blocks of shares or securities which have not previously been the subject of a public issue or placing". Presumably that is the way in which the term "issuing house" will be construed for the purposes of s 89A, although it again gives rise to the same questions regarding the definition of a "public" issue.

Agreements relating to units under unit trust schemes, and any agreement which is not conditional upon the admission of the relevant securities to the Official List of The Stock Exchange, are specifically excluded. Also, in the case of agreements within s 89A(1) and (2) (transfers of securities to issuing houses, and the sale by issuing houses of newly-subscribed securities), the price at which the securities are sold to the public by the issuing house must be the same as the price which the issuing house paid for them. In the case of agreements to which s 89A(1) relates (purchases by an issuing house) it is of course a condition that the issuing house actually on-sells the securities in accordance with the relevant arrangements.

The requirement of s 89A(2) that "newly-subscribed securities" must be securities issued "wholly for new consideration" is somewhat confusing. On one analysis, this could be construed as meaning that the consideration for the issue of the shares must be a fresh injection of cash or assets into the company, so that the exemption would apply to offers of shares issued for cash or in consideration for acquisitions of assets (in vendor consideration placings) but not offers of shares issued by way of capitalisation of reserves (in a bonus issue) to existing shareholders immediately prior to an offer for sale. The only statutory usage of the term "new consideration" is in TA 1988 s 254. For the purpose of determining the tax treatment of company distributions, the word "distribution" includes not only a cash dividend but also any other distribution out of the assets of a company *except* (amongst other things)

Part II ST

a distribution equal in amount or value to any "new consideration" received by the company for the distribution. In this connection only, "new consideration" is deemed to mean consideration not provided directly or indirectly out of the assets of the company, and in particular is deemed not to include amounts retained by the company by way of capitalising a distribution, unless by way of capitalisation of share premium account where the capitalised premium was itself created by the company receiving new consideration. Bonus issues, other than by way of capitalisation of share premium account, are therefore (for these purposes only) not treated as distributions for "new consideration". However, for the purposes of company law the consideration for an issue of shares by way of bonus is no less valuable than the consideration for an issue of shares in return for cash or assets. Bonus shares are not a gift from the company, ie, issued for no consideration at all, but are paid up in full or part by the capitalisation of profits or reserves which could otherwise have been distributed to the shareholders as a cash dividend, or (in the case of unrealised profits) retained as a reserve. For company law purposes an issue of bonus shares is treated as an issue for a consideration otherwise than in cash, and an appropriate return has to be delivered to the Registrar of Companies under the Companies Act 2006 s 555.

Irrespective of whether or not an offer for sale of existing registered shares involves the interposition of a merchant bank, either as principal or agent s 89A(3) is drafted in such a way as to relieve one of the two potential double charges to stamp duty and stamp duty reserve tax which would otherwise arise as a result of the use of renounceable letters of acceptance. Although the matter was not entirely free from doubt, it was generally believed that, where renounceable letters of acceptance were issued in respect of existing registered shares, which at the end of the renunciation period were transferred to the new holders, stamp duty reserve tax was payable both on the issue of the renounceable letters of acceptance to successful applicants and on each subsequent purchase of a renounceable document in the market, and that stamp duty was payable on the transfer of the underlying securities to the ultimate renouncee. Before the enactment of s 89A(3), it seems that, in the case of applicants who did not renounce letters of acceptance issued to them, payment of the stamp duty on the transfers of the underlying securities to them would have relieved them from the stamp duty reserve tax payable in respect of the original issue of the letters of acceptance. However, in the case of letters of acceptance which were renounced, the stamp duty on the ultimate transfers of the underlying securities would not have relieved the stamp duty reserve tax payable either by the original successful applicants (because the shares were not ultimately transferred to them in accordance with s 89(4)) or by the ultimate renouncees (because the shares were represented by renounceable documents of title so that s 88(2) and (3) prevented the stamp duty reserve tax from being relieved by the stamp duty). Under s 89A(3) a stamp duty reserve tax liability cannot arise on the issue of renounceable letters of acceptance to successful applicants for existing registered shares (whether those letters of acceptance are subsequently renounced or not) but it neither relieves the stamp duty reserve tax payable by ultimate renouncees nor allows the stamp duty paid on the share transfers in their favour to "frank" that liability. Ultimate renouncees of letters of acceptance evidencing rights to existing registered shares remain liable for stamp duty reserve tax on the renunciation in their favour notwithstanding the delivery to them of a duly stamped instrument of transfer.

Section 89A(3)(*a*) does not require A to be an issuing house entering into the agreement in the ordinary course of its business, and it therefore applies wherever renounceable letters of acceptance are issued in respect of existing registered shares offered to the public, whether or not a merchant bank is involved.

[*Note:* See note at commencement of commentary on this Act.]

89AA. Section 87: exception for repurchases and stock lending

This section exempts from the principal charge to stamp duty reserve tax agreements to transfer and re-transfer chargeable securities under "repo" and stock lending arrangements. Certain agreements to transfer may be exempt either under this section or s 88A.

The conditions for the relief to apply are the same as for stamp duty relief under s 80C (except that the one is drafted in terms of transactions in "stock", and the other in terms of "chargeable securities") with the additional condition that the agreement must be completed by an actual transfer and re-transfer of the chargeable securities.

The section appears to cover transfers and re-transfers of collateral securities although these are not specifically referred to.

The same Treasury powers apply to introduce a charge to stamp duty reserve tax at a rate not exceeding 0.1 per cent and to modify the conditions under which the section is to apply, as in relation to stamp duty under s 80C.

This regime applies to agreements made (or, if conditional, where the condition is satisfied) on or after 20 October 1997 (replacing the former regime in s 89B, which is repealed with effect from that date).

See also s 88(1C), (1D).

89AB. Section 87: exception for repurchases and stock lending in the case of insolvency

This section affords two reliefs where a stock lending arrangement has been entered into between unconnected persons that falls within the scope of s 89AA(1) but, after the stock has been lent, the condition in that section requiring chargeable securities of the same kind and amount to be transferred back is not satisfied because one or other party to the arrangement becomes insolvent in circumstances where it is apparent that, as a result of the insolvency, the transaction will not be unwound.

First, section 89AB(3) removes the SDRT charge that would otherwise arise under FA 1986 s 87 in relation to the original stock lending arrangements which would have been triggered by the failure to comply with the condition in s 89AA(3)(*c*) that the chargeable securities (or their equivalent) must be returned to the lender on the unwinding of the arrangements.

The second relief is designed to secure that the stock lender is not disadvantaged by having to go into the market to buy replacement securities for those which ought to have been returned to it without an SDRT charge. If, within 30 days of the insolvency, the solvent party (or its nominee) acquires replacement securities (ie stock of the same kind as the chargeable securities which are not to be re-transferred), FA 1986 s 87 is not to apply to the agreement to transfer the replacement stock to the solvent party or his nominee. The thrust of the legislation is that the stock lender must first make use of the collateral with which it may have been provided to acquire the replacement securities; and may only look to other funds once the collateral has been disposed of. If this were not the case, the lender would be placed in a more advantageous position, since it would have acquired collateral without an SDRT charge in addition to the further relief given by s 89AB. Accordingly, s 89AB(5) affords relief where the solvent party was provided with collateral under the arrangement and uses that collateral (directly or indirectly) to acquire the replacement chargeable securities. If the collateral is insufficient to meet the whole of the cost of acquiring the replacement stock, s 89AB(5)(*b*) affords relief where other funds are used to meet the residue of the cost. Section 89AB(6) affords relief where there was no collateral provided under the arrangements and the solvent party uses other funds to acquire the replacement stock. In each case, relief from the charge is limited to the amount of chargeable securities lent which will not be transferred as a result of the insolvency (s 89AB(8)).

The provision applies where the insolvency occurs on or after 1 September 2008 (FA 2009 s 82(2)).

89B. Section 87: exceptions for stock lending and collateral security arrangements

This section was repealed by FA 1997 s 103(5) in relation to agreements made (or, if conditional, when the condition is satisfied) on or after 20 October 1997. The new provisions are in s 89AA.

90. Section 87: other exceptions

No liability arises to stamp duty reserve tax in relation to an agreement to transfer a unit under a unit trust scheme if the transfer is in favour of the managers of the scheme, or if (at the time the agreement is made) the trustees under the scheme are resident outside the UK and the unit being transferred is not registered in a register kept in the UK by or on behalf of the trustees. However, it should be noted that, whilst an agreement to transfer units is exempt, the actual transfer of a unit to the managers will now be charged to stamp duty reserve tax (with effect from 6 February 2000) under the rules set out in FA 1999 Sch 19.

No liability to SDLT arises in the case of an agreement to transfer a unit under a unit trust scheme if the group relief exemption in FA 1930 s 42 or the demutualisation exemption for insurance companies in FA 1997 s 96 would apply if the units were actually transferred under an instrument executed at the time of the agreement.

No liability to stamp duty reserve tax arises in respect of an agreement to transfer securities constituted by, or transferable by means of, either (*a*) an overseas bearer instrument, or (*b*) an inland bearer instrument (unless the inland bearer instrument is in one of the three categories identified in s 90(3B), (3C) and (3E) which are exempt from stamp duty on issue). Categories in s 90(3C) and (3E) apply only to instruments issued on or after 26 November 1996 (unless the relevant instrument was issued pursuant to a pre-26 November 1996 unconditional agreement).

Section 90(3B)–(3F) were enacted to prevent the exempt inland bearer instrument scheme being used to sell UK companies substantially free of stamp duty and stamp duty reserve tax. The essence of the scheme was:

(i) that the target company's share capital would be reorganised by the issue of new foreign currency-denominated inland bearer shares, foreign currency-denominated bearer shares warrants, or bearer securities (whether or not foreign currency-denominated) convertible into ordinary shares to the selling shareholders (free of bearer instrument stamp duty by virtue of FA 1967 s 30 or, in the case of sterling denominated securities, FA 1980 s 79(2), and free of stamp duty reserve tax, which does not generally apply on the issue of securities); and

(ii) the conversion of their existing shares into worthless deferred shares; the bearer shares, bearer share warrants or bearer convertible securities could be transferred to the purchaser (free of stamp duty provided they were transferred by delivery, or in the case of sterling denominated bearer convertible securities by virtue of FA 1986 s 79(2), and free of stamp duty reserve tax by virtue of FA 1986 s 90(3) in its previous form); the deferred shares would generally be transferred for a nominal consideration attracting minimal stamp duty or stamp duty reserve tax.

However, the new charges introduced by s 90(3B)–(3F) appear to be wider in application than merely countering the established avoidance scheme, since bearer instruments of a kind which (prior to the amendment of this section) would not have had the effect of producing a "takeover" (as defined below) will now be caught by s 87 unless they not only fail to produce a takeover but are also listed on a recognised exchange. This requirement appears to go beyond what was strictly required to terminate the former avoidance scheme.

The first category of inland bearer instrument within the s 87 charge is renounceable letters of allotment where the rights are renounceable no later than six months after the issue of the relevant instrument: (3B).

The second category is foreign currency-denominated bearer instruments (other than bearer instruments relating to loan capital) issued by companies incorporated in the UK, unless the instrument in question (or a depositary for it) is listed on a recognised stock exchange and the transfer is not made in contemplation of, or as part of an arrangement for, a "takeover" of the issuer.

The third category comprises bearer instruments (whether denominated in sterling or a foreign currency) which:

(i) are issued by a body corporate incorporated in the UK;

(ii) relate to loan capital;

(iii) would be subject to stamp duty on transfer if they were in registered form (see s 79(5), (6)); and

(iv) are not "exempt".

An instrument is exempt for this purpose if:

(a) the loan capital in question is listed on a recognised stock exchange or represented by a depositary receipt listed on a recognised stock exchange;

(b) the agreement to transfer the loan capital is not made in contemplation of, or as part of an arrangement for, a takeover of the issuer (note that the agreement need not specifically be part of an "arrangement", provided that it is "in contemplation of" a takeover); and

(c) the loan capital does not carry any right of conversion into, or right to the acquisition of, securities not listed on a recognised stock exchange.

The legislation specifies that, for this purpose, "there is a takeover of the body corporate if a person, on his own or together with connected persons, loses or acquires control of it" and that "control" is to be construed in accordance with TA 1988 s 416.

The definition of "control" in s 416 is so widely drawn that subscribers for bearer bonds or foreign currency-denominated bearer instruments need to be careful that the rights attached to their bearer instruments do not give them control of the issuer.

An issuer of bearer loan capital within s 90(3E) might consider using a non-UK subsidiary to issue the loan capital, or issue the loan capital directly into a clearing system so as to qualify for relief under FA 1986 s 97(3) (provided that the operator of the clearance system has not made this impossible by electing for the alternative taxation treatment now available on transactions within the system in lieu of an increased charge on entry to the system—see s 97A below).

Where a company is an SE (a Societas Europaea, a new European company created by Council Regulation (EC) No 2157/2001 of 8 October 2001), which has its registered office outside the United Kingdom following a transfer in accordance with Article 8 of the 2001 Regulation, it is treated as no longer being a body corporate incorporated in the United Kingdom, so that neither of the exclusions from the exemption for bearer instruments issued by such a company apply. What is less clear is whether the exemption is then available for instruments issued before the company transferred its registered office outside the United Kingdom, although the better view (having regard to the terms of s 99(4A)(*b*)) is that the exemption is available.

There are specific exclusions in relation to agreements forming part of arrangements for depositary schemes and schemes for the provision of clearance services, which are subject to the special provisions set out in ss 93–97.

The exemption provided in s 90(5) and (6) as substituted is wider than the exemption originally granted. The exemption from the principal charge on securities which are held by a nominee for a clearance service was widened, with retrospective effect, by the removal of references to "chargeable securities" (defined in FA 1986 s 99(3) as including units in a unit trust scheme) and the substitution of references to "shares, stock or marketable securities", whether or not "chargeable securities". Consequently, the stamp duty definition of "marketable securities" contained in SA 1891 s 122(1) was imported. Previously, the exemption would only have been available if all the securities held by the nominee were chargeable securities.

However, the wording of s 90(6) remains slightly curious. This is because each of the special charges for depositary schemes and clearance services (see ss 93–97 below) appear to be based on the theory that (subject to the possibility of making an election for an alternative treatment in the case of clearance services—see s 97A) a higher rate of stamp duty reserve tax is paid on entry to the system but all subsequent dealings within the system are free of any further tax charges. The essence of the transaction giving rise to the entry charge in each case is a transfer or issue of certain securities to the operator of the system or their nominee. However, although each set of rules appears to contemplate an issue or transfer of securities to either a nominee of the operator or the operator itself, there would not appear to be any exemption from tax on further dealings within the system in the case of clearance services (but not depositary schemes) unless a nominee is used. Whereas exemption in the case of depositary schemes is obtained by specifically excluding the traded depositary receipts from the definition of "chargeable securities" in s 99 (so that, in principle, the identity of the holder of the deposited securities, represented by that receipt, is irrelevant), exemption is only obtained in the case of clearance services by defining the circumstances of each transaction in s 90(6). That sub-s only refers to securities being held by a nominee of a clearance service operator, not by the operator itself.

The wording of s 90(5) and (6) is made more curious by an amendment inserted by FA 1999 which removes, with effect from 9 March 1999, the requirement of exclusivity in order for transfers within the clearance system itself to be free of SDRT. It was formerly the case that the nominee referred to in these sub-ss acted exclusively as a nominee for a clearance service operator, but this is no longer the case.

However, it is questionable whether the removal of this restriction will be particularly useful in practice. This is because, whilst a "non-exclusive" nominee can now be used by the operator without prejudicing the general operation of the clearance system (in terms of exposure to possible charges within the system under s 87 above), it appears that the operator will never be able to change from that nominee to another nominee (whether or not the second nominee is intended to act exclusively in such a capacity) without incurring a stamp duty reserve tax charge (or, alternatively, a stamp duty charge) on that transfer. This is because the exemption in s 97(1) for transfers between nominees simply cross-refers to the description of a clearance service nominee as set out for stamp duty purposes in s 70(6). That provision still contains a requirement of exclusivity on the part of both the transferor and the transferee (ie the outgoing and the incoming nominees). By definition, at least one of the two nominees will not satisfy this requirement if advantage has been taken of the liberalised nominee regime under the amended s 90(5) and (6).

No liability to stamp duty reserve tax arises in respect of an agreement to transfer securities to a charitable body or trust, to the Trustees of the National Heritage Memorial Fund, or to the Historic Buildings and Monuments Commission for England.

[*Note:* See note at commencement of commentary on this Act.]

91. Liability to tax

Pursuant to this section, as amended by F(No2)A 1987, the person liable to pay the stamp duty reserve tax is the person who agrees to purchase the shares, ie, B.

However, B is not necessarily the person with responsibility for reporting the transaction to HMRC and actually paying over to HMRC the amount of the tax. Originally, this was the role of the "accountable person", which might ultimately be B but would more usually be some kind of broker or dealer in chargeable securities. The identity of the "accountable person" is determined in accordance with reg 2 of the Stamp Duty Reserve Tax Regulations 1986 (see commentary on the regulations). However, with effect from 20 October 1997, these regulations have been amended by the insertion of a new reg 4A. This adapts the regulations to accommodate the introduction of CREST (and the possibility of further electronic trading systems also being recognised for stamp duty reserve tax purposes) by providing that, in effect, the primary liabilities to report and account for transactions are usually with the operator of CREST (or any other electronic system to which the regulations may be applied). Where a transaction takes place outside CREST, the accountable person continues to be primarily liable to report the transaction and account for tax, although it is, and has always been, possible to substitute another person by agreement with HMRC (a "regulation 4 agreement"). The definition of "accountable person" has itself been amended by the replacement of terminology such as "broker dealer" with updated terminology in accordance with the new intermediary reliefs for both stamp duty and stamp duty reserve tax in ss 80A and 88A.

[*Note:* See note at commencement of commentary on this Act.]

92. Repayment or cancellation of tax

If, within a period of six years from the date beginning on the date of the agreement (or, if the agreement is conditional, the date it became unconditional), the conditions for relief are satisfied (ie, an instrument or instruments transferring all the chargeable securities to B or his nominee has or have been executed and duly stamped) then the stamp duty reserve tax, if paid, is refundable or, if not paid, ceases to be payable. Refunds of £25 or more carry interest at the rate applicable under FA 1989 s 178, and the Taxes (Interest Rate) Regulations 1989, SI 1989/1297. It should be noted that, strictly speaking, the mere payment of stamp duty is not enough to cancel the charge to stamp duty reserve tax. There must be a duly stamped "instrument of transfer" (not, for example, a stamped contract pursuant to what is now FA 1999 Sch 13 Part I para 7) which must be executed on or after the "relevant day" (so that a conveyance in contemplation of a sale could not qualify even though that would itself be chargeable to ad valorem stamp duty—see the commentary on FA 1965 s 90).

All interest paid on repayments of stamp duty reserve tax is exempt from income tax. This brings the stamp duty reserve tax repayment provisions into line with similar provisions for other taxes.

A liability to stamp duty reserve tax is relieved by sub-s (7) if the seller transfers securities, not to the buyer or his nominee, but to a person who has agreed to take the securities as security for a loan to the seller. This clarifies the position where there is a transfer of securities to a person, such as a bank, who is providing a loan for the purchase of the securities (or, indeed, any other purpose it would seem) and who is to hold the securities as security for the loan. It should be remembered that the "principal charge" to stamp duty reserve tax simply relates to a "transfer" and not (as with the principal stamp duty charge) a "sale".

[*Note:* See note at commencement of commentary on this Act.]

Other Charges

93. Depositary receipts

This section and those following it must now be read in light of the decisions of the European Court of Justice in *Commission v Kingdom of Belgium* Case C-415/02 (15 July 2004) and *HSBC Holdings plc v Revenue & Customs Commissioners*, Case C-569/07 [2010] STC 58 (1 October 2009). In *Commission v Belgium* the Court of Justice held that, by imposing stamp duty on stock exchange transactions on applications for new securities, or the physical delivery of newly-issued bearer securities, on the formation of a company or following the completion of an increase in capital or as part of a loan issue, Belgium was in breach of its obligations under Art 11 of the Capital Duties Directive (Council Directive 69/355/EEC of 17 July 1969 concerning indirect taxes on the raising of capital as amended). Article 11 prevents a member state from levying any tax other than capital duty on, inter alia, the creation, issue admission to quotation on a stock exchange, making available on the market or dealing in shares, etc, by whomsoever issued, subject only (Art 12) to specified exceptions, including taxation on the *transfer* of securities. The court held that "transfer" was to be interpreted strictly and could not include either the issue of the securities or their initial physical delivery. It will be appreciated that this calls into question the whole basis of the charges levied by the UK on the introduction of newly-issued securities into a depositary receipt system or into a clearance system or under FA 1999 Sch 15. In *HSBC Holdings plc v Revenue and Customs Comrs* the Court of Justice held that Article 11 of the Capital Duties Directive prohibited the imposition of a duty on the transfer or issue of shares into a clearance service as part of an offer for the acquisition of the entire issued share capital of another company. A similar question necessarily arose (although the question for reference did not relate to such a case) in relation to transfers into a depositary receipt scheme.

Following the decision of the Court of Justice, the Commissioners issued a press release stating that with immediate effect HMRC would not seek to apply a 1.5% charge to SDRT

Part II ST

on the issue of shares to a *clearance system* within the European Community, but that legislation would be passed to secure that a subsequent transfer of those securities into another clearance service or a depositary receipts scheme would not benefit from the exemptions designed to prevent a double charge to tax. In January 2010 HMRC invited statutory claims under reg 14 of the SDRT Regulations 1986 from persons who had paid SDRT under FA 1986 s 93 or s 96 pursuant to the issue of shares in a United Kingdom incorporated company either to a depositary receipts issuer or to a clearance service located within the European Union. Nothing was said in that press release as to the position of persons who had paid stamp duty under section 67. What is clear is that the Commissioners have decided that the Capital Duties Directive (now Council Directive 2008/7/EC of 12 February 2008 concerning indirect taxes on the raising of capital) is only effective as regards the issue or transfer of shares within the European Union. This is a matter of great difficulty and the question will no doubt be the subject of future litigation.

At the time of publication a GLO has been issued for persons wishing to make claims to recover overpaid tax in consequence of the *HSBC* decision.

Depositary receipts for stocks and shares are not included in the definition of "chargeable securities" for the purposes of a charge to stamp duty reserve tax, and special provisions make them subject to the tax in appropriate circumstances.

There is a charge to stamp duty reserve tax where, in pursuance of an arrangement, a person (whose business is or includes that of issuing depositary receipts for chargeable securities) has issued or is to issue a depositary receipt for chargeable securities, and chargeable securities of the same kind and amount are transferred or issued to him or to his nominee or agent, or appropriated by his nominee or agent towards the eventual satisfaction of the entitlement of the receipt-holder to receive chargeable securities.

The expression "depositary receipt for chargeable securities" is defined in s 94 and "chargeable securities" in s 99.

The basic rate of stamp duty reserve tax in these circumstances is 1·5 per cent of the following:

(a) in a case where the securities are issued, their price when issued;
(b) in a case where the securities are transferred for a consideration in money or money's worth, the amount or value or the consideration; and
(c) in any other case, the value of the securities.

As to the meaning of the word "value", either of the consideration or (as the case may be) the securities, see s 94.

Where the securities are transferred by means of an instrument on which stamp duty is chargeable under what is now FA 1999 Sch 13 Part III para 16 (ie a transfer otherwise than on sale), the rate is reduced to 1 per cent provided that:

(a) at the time of the transfer the transferor is a qualified dealer in securities of the kind concerned or a nominee of such a qualified dealer; and
(b) the transfer is made for the purposes of the dealer's business; and
(c) at the time of transfer the dealer is not a market maker in securities of the kind concerned; and
(d) the relevant instrument contains a statement that these conditions have been fulfilled; and
(e) the securities are transferred before the relief for sales to intermediaries under s 88A comes into effect and replace the market maker and broker dealer relief, unless the securities were acquired by the transferor before that day.

As to determining when a person is a qualified dealer or market maker in securities of a particular kind, see s 94. The repeal of the reduced rate for qualified dealers results in transfers into a depositary scheme, effected through a qualified dealer who is not an intermediary for the purposes of s 80A, suffering an effective 2 per cent charge.

Stamp duty reserve tax is calculated by reference to the total of the instalments payable less those already paid where:

(a) securities are issued or transferred upon terms that (in either case) they are to be paid for in instalments; and
(b) the person to whom they are issued or transferred holds them and transfers them to another person when the last instalment is paid; and
(c) stamp duty reserve tax on the latter transfer is calculated on the basis of the value of the securities; and
(d) before the execution of the final transfer an instrument is received by a person whose business is or includes holding chargeable securities as nominee or agent for a depositary; and
(e) that instrument evidences the rights vested in the shares; and
(f) the final transfer contains a statement that the above conditions have been fulfilled.

Unlike in the normal case, where the payment of stamp duty on an appropriate instrument relieves from any liability for stamp duty reserve tax, in the case of a transfer into a depositary scheme where the ad valorem stamp duty is less than the stamp duty reserve tax, the stamp duty reserve tax is only relieved to the extent of the stamp duty and the excess is chargeable. If the ad valorem stamp duty equals or exceeds the stamp duty reserve tax, then no stamp duty reserve tax is payable, but neither is any excess stamp duty repayable. Effectively, therefore, in the case of transfers into a depositary scheme, the charge is the higher of the ad valorem stamp duty and the stamp duty reserve tax.

The person liable for stamp duty reserve tax is the person who has issued or is to issue the depositary receipt, but where such person is not resident in the UK and does not have a branch or agency in the UK, the person liable for the tax is the person to whom the transfer was made.

Where chargeable securities are issued or transferred on sale on terms providing for payment by instalments and for an issue of other chargeable securities, and stamp duty reserve tax would normally be payable in respect of the issue, then no stamp duty reserve tax is payable unless any of the instalments becomes payable by a person whose business is or includes issuing depositary receipts for chargeable securities, or by his nominee or agent, in which case tax becomes payable when an instalment is payable, at the rate of 1·5 per cent of the instalment payable. The person liable to pay the instalment is in these circumstances the person liable for the stamp duty reserve tax.

There is a complete exemption from any charge that would otherwise arise under this section on securities issued by certain international organisations of which the UK or any EC country is a member (see FA 1984 s 126).

[*Note:* See note at commencement of commentary on this Act.]

94. Depositary receipts: supplementary

A depositary receipt for chargeable securities is an instrument acknowledging that a person holds chargeable securities, or evidence of the right to receive them, and that another person is entitled to rights, whether expressed as units or otherwise, in or in relation to chargeable securities of the same kind, including the right to receive such securities (or evidence of the right to receive them) from the person holding such securities or evidence. It does not include an instrument acknowledging rights in or in relation to securities if they are issued or sold on terms providing for payment in instalments and for the issue of the instrument as evidence that an instalment has been paid. The Treasury are given power by statutory instrument to amend this definition.

It should be noted that, since the current definition states that a depositary receipt is an "instrument", any dematerialised equivalent (eg within CREST) does not fall outside the definition of "chargeable securities" and so is not subject to the 1.5 per cent charge on creation but is subject to the 0.5 per cent charge on every transfer within the system (subject to the availability of intermediary relief, repo relief, etc, in any particular case). This also means that a dematerialised depositary receipt for foreign securities is likely to give rise to a tax charge which would not otherwise have existed, since foreign securities themselves generally fall outside the definition of "chargeable securities"—see s 99(4).

In this respect, it should be noted that power is given in FA 1999 s 119 to enable stamp duty reserve tax legislation to be amended in such a manner as to ensure that a UK depositary interest for foreign securities does not create a tax charge that would not have existed in respect of the underlying securities themselves. It is understood that the Stamp Office's view is that any depositary interest which is purely in the nature of a UK-oriented administrative "wrapper", designed to facilitate dealings in foreign property ought, by virtue of regulations under s 119, to be treated as outside the scope of stamp duty reserve tax.

The value of any consideration not consisting of money is taken to be the price it might reasonably expect to fetch on a sale in the open market at the time the securities are transferred. The value of any securities is taken to be the price they might reasonably be expected to fetch on a sale in the open market at the time they are transferred or appropriated (as the case may be).

A person is a qualified dealer in securities of a particular kind if he deals in securities of that kind and is a member of a recognised stock exchange (within the meaning given by TA 1988 s 841), or is designated a qualified dealer by the Treasury by statutory instrument.

A person is a market maker in securities of a particular kind if he holds himself out at all normal times in compliance with the rules of The Stock Exchange as willing to buy and sell securities of that kind at a price specified by him, and is recognised as so doing by the Council of The Stock Exchange. This definition is the same as that contained in FA 1986 ss 69 (stamp duty provisions relating to depositary receipts) and 82 (borrowing of stock by market makers) and is to be contrasted with the definitions in ss 81(3) and 89(3) (stamp duty and stamp duty reserve tax exemptions in relation to sales to market makers) which, as amended, extend to transactions in unlisted securities by authorised persons under the Financial Services Act 1986. The Treasury has power by statutory instrument to amend the definition. The definitions of qualified dealer and market maker will be repealed at the same time as s 93(4) is repealed.

There is a complete exemption from any charge that would otherwise arise under this section on securities issued by certain international organisations of which the UK or any EC country is a member (see FA 1984 s 126).

[*Note:* See note at commencement of commentary on this Act.]

95. Depositary receipts: exceptions

Subject to the operation of an anti-avoidance provision, FA 1986 s 97C, to which reference should be made, the following transactions are excluded from the charge imposed by s 93:

(a) transfers of securities by a person whose business is exclusively that of holding relevant securities as nominee or agent for a person whose business is or includes issuing depositary receipts for relevant securities, and for the purpose of the issue of depositary receipts, to another such person;

(b) transfers, issues or appropriations of UK bearer instruments (meaning bearer instruments issued by a "UK company", as that term is used in the new bearer instrument provisions—see commentary on FA 1999 Sch 15) other than those within what is now FA 1999 Sch 15 para 16 (such as renounceable letters of allotment where the rights of renunciation do not exceed six months' duration) or those within what is now FA 1999 Sch 15 para 17 but, as regards the latter category, only if they do not "raise new capital" (see further commentary after (*c*) below).

(c) issues by one company (X) of securities in exchange for shares of another company (Y), where either X already has control of Y or X will have control of Y in consequence of the exchange, or in consequence of an offer as a result of which the exchange is made, for which purpose X is deemed to have control of Y if it has power to control Y's affairs by virtue of holding shares in, or possessing voting power in relation to, Y or any other body corporate.

The scope of the exception for issuing or transferring bearer instruments in the context of depositary schemes is altered by means of amendments inserted into this Act by FA 1999 ss 116 and 117.

The change made by FA 1999 s 116 applies to any instrument issued on or after 30 January 1999 unless it relates to a merger or takeover agreement entered into in writing before that date. The effect of the change is that the exception which usually disapplies the special 1.5 per cent charge on depositary schemes where the instrument being issued or transferred is a UK bearer instrument (formerly "inland bearer instrument"—ie an instrument issued by or on behalf of a company *or unincorporated body* formed or established in the UK) cannot now be used as a means of avoiding the stamp duty reserve tax charge that would otherwise arise on the transfer of bearer instruments in circumstances where the anti-avoidance rule in s 90(3C)–(3F), introduced by FA 1997, would apply to a transaction which did not involve a depositary scheme.

In other words, where the real purpose of undertaking a share transaction in bearer form is to avoid a stamp duty charge by relying upon the provisions originally enacted as FA 1967 s 30, and now found in FA 1999 Sch 15 Part II paras 17–19 (which exempt from stamp duty a transfer of, inter alia, bearer shares if those shares are denominated in a foreign currency) a charge to stamp duty reserve tax now arises instead. When this "artificial" use of bearers was first legislated against in FA 1997, it only imposed a stamp duty reserve tax charge under s 87. However, that charge would not apply if a transaction could be structured so as to involve a depositary scheme under s 93 or a clearance scheme under s 96. The new amendments in FA 1999 close that loophole with effect from 30 January 1999 so that the relief available generally for bearer instruments in the context of depositary schemes cannot now be used to avoid this "anti-avoidance" charge.

This restriction is further reinforced by the additional change made by FA 1999 s 117 (which has effect from 9 March 1999, rather than 30 January 1999 as in the above case, except in relation to takeover agreements entered into in writing before 30 January 1999). This restricts the relief from the 1.5 per cent charge to bearer instruments which "raise new capital".

The view of HMRC is that this restriction is justified because the only reason for the original enactment of FA 1967 s 30 was to remove a potential restriction on the ability of UK businesses to raise capital abroad by ensuring that no stamp duty charge arose on dealings in foreign-denominated securities where such dealings had the raising of such capital as their aim. Therefore, in HMRC's view, any use of foreign-denominated bearer instruments for any other purpose (ie for the purpose of avoiding stamp duty on a transaction that, in principle, could equally well have been structured entirely around sterling-denominated and/or registered instruments) is an abuse of the relief offered in FA 1967.

The original draft of this legislation was more restrictive in that it also imposed a requirement for securities to be listed on a recognised stock exchange. Concerns were expressed in the market about the appropriateness of such a restriction and the requirement was removed before the new provisions were enacted.

However, concerns were also expressed about the restriction imposed in relation to the form of consideration (ie that it must consist only of cash). It was felt by some that this could also potentially cause problems because it failed to take account of some forms of transaction which are perfectly common in financial markets (and perfectly genuine, in that their form is governed by actual market conditions, rather than by fiscal planning constraints) such as the issue of "bonus" debt instruments in lieu of interest payable under debt instruments already held.

These additional concerns were not addressed in the revised draft of the legislation save that provisions were added to cover share for share exchanges (of either the more conventional issue-against-transfer variety or the issue-against-cancellation variety).

One can appreciate, at one level of generality, that an instrument could be regarded as failing genuinely to "raise new capital" if the result of issuing that instrument was not to generate a cash sum for the issuer. However, this shows a lack of appreciation of the sophistication of modern financial markets and, in the context of some transactions, it could be virtually impossible to decide whether, or to what extent, the instruments under consideration "raised new capital" in the statutory sense.

[*Note:* See note at commencement of commentary on this Act.]

95A. Depositary receipts: exception for replacement securities

This section is inserted by FA 1999 s 118, with retrospective effect from 1 May 1998. This section prevents any further charge to stamp duty reserve tax where securities which have already been subjected to the higher rate charge on entry to a depositary scheme (see commentary on s 93 above), or which would have been so subjected if the relevant legislation had been in force when the original securities entered the scheme, are replaced by other securities which essentially represent the same interest, right or entitlement as the original securities.

This section appears to be designed to reinforce the general philosophy underlying both stamp duty and stamp duty reserve tax which is that ad valorem tax charges should only be levied on genuine and substantive changes in the beneficial ownership of property, and not on mere administrative or mechanical acts affecting title to any property. On that basis, it is not surprising that subs (3) limits the new relief to the value of the old securities immediately before the replacement occurs. In the absence of such a limitation on the relief, there would clearly be scope for avoiding (or at least reducing) the charge under s 93 above on initial entry to a depositary scheme: the new relief could be used to inject into the depositary scheme securities of a greater value than those which were extracted. A similar relief is also now offered in relation to clearance services—see s 97AA below.

96. Clearance services

This section must now be read in light of the decision of the European Court of Justice in *Commission v Kingdom of Belgium* Case C-415/02 (15 July 2004) and *HSBC Holdings plc v Revenue & Customs Commissioners* Case C-569/07 [2010] STC 58 (1 October 2009). In *Commission v Belgium* the Court of Justice held that, by imposing stamp duty on stock exchange transactions on applications for new securities, or the physical delivery of newly-issued bearer securities, on the formation of a company or following the completion of an increase in capital or as part of a loan issue, Belgium was in breach of its obligations under Art 11 of the Capital Duties Directive (Council Directive 69/355/EEC of 17 July 1969 concerning indirect taxes on the raising of capital, as amended). Article 11 prevented a member state from levying any tax other than capital duty on, inter alia, the creation, issue admission to quotation on a stock exchange, making available on the market or dealing in shares, etc, by whomsoever issued, subject only (Art 12) to specified exceptions, including taxation on the *transfer* of securities. The court held that "transfer" was to be interpreted strictly and could not include either the issue of the securities or their initial physical delivery. (It should be noted that a replacement and somewhat more restrictive directive on capital duty, Council Directive 2008/7/EC of 12 February 2008 concerning indirect taxes on the raising of capital, took effect as from 1 January 2009.) It will be appreciated that this judgment calls into question the whole basis of the charges levied by the United Kingdom on the introduction of newly-issued securities into a depositary receipt system or into a clearance system or under FA 1999 Sch 15. In *HSBC Holdings plc v Revenue and Customs Comrs* the Court of Justice held that Article 11 of the Capital Duties Directive prohibited the imposition of a duty on the transfer or issue of shares into a clearance service as part of an offer for the acquisition of the entire issued share capital of another company. In the course of his Opinion, Mr Advocate-General Mengozzi ranged further than the eventual decision of the Court of Justice (which, as is usual, confined itself more closely to the questions referred to it). It is nevertheless interesting to observe the views of the Advocate-General. His objections to the United Kingdom's regime for charging issues of shares into a clearance service were wide-ranging, beginning from the position that it was wrong that the person who should bear the tax was (in practice) the issuer of the shares; and dismissing the United Kingdom's contention that the 1.5% charge was an acceptable pre-payment of the estimated tax on future transactions within the clearance service, partly because it was paid by the wrong person and partly because there was no evidence that it was an accurate pre-estimate of future charges, or indeed more than an arbitrary amount; and concluding that such a charge was in breach of Art 11 of the Directive. He further considered that the charge was incompatible with one of the fundamental freedoms of Community law, as it constituted a restriction on the free movement of capital, was thus prohibited by Article 56 EC and could not be justified by a need to ensure effective fiscal supervision as the United Kingdom had failed to establish why such a drastic measure was the only way of ensuring the effective payment of taxes due, or why no other less onerous mechanism was considered capable of achieving the same objectives. The Court of Justice considered it unnecessary to deal with the question whether the United Kingdom was in breach of the fundamental freedoms since the Directive required complete harmonisation of the cases in which capital duty could be levied. It therefore followed that the court was restricted to the interpretation of the Directive and the national measure had to be measured in the light of the Directive and not in the context of the EC Treaty.

Following the decision of the Court of Justice, the Commissioners issued a press release stating that with immediate effect HMRC would not seek to apply a 1.5% charge to SDRT on the issue of shares to a clearance system within the European Community, but that legislation would be passed to secure that a subsequent transfer of those securities into another clearance service or a depositary receipts scheme would not benefit from the exemptions designed to prevent a double charge to tax. In January 2010 HMRC invited statutory claims under reg 14 of the SDRT Regulations 1986 from persons who had paid SDRT under FA 1986 s 93 or s 96 pursuant to the issue of shares in a United Kingdom incorporated company either to a depositary receipts issuer or to a clearance service located within the European Union. Nothing was said in that press release as to the position of persons who had paid stamp duty under s 67. What is clear is that the Commissioners have decided that the Capital Duties Directive (now Council Directive 2008/7/EC of 12 February 2008 concerning indirect taxes on the raising of capital) is only effective as regards the issue or transfer of shares within the European Union. This is a matter of great difficulty and the question will no doubt be the subject of future litigation.

At the time of publication of this volume a GLO (Group Litigation Order) had been issued for persons wishing to make High Court claims to recover overpaid tax in consequence of the *HSBC* decision.

This section imposes a charge to stamp duty reserve tax where one person (A), whose business is or includes the provision of clearance services for the purchase and sale of chargeable securities, has entered into an arrangement to provide such clearance services for another person, and in pursuance of the arrangement, chargeable securities are transferred or issued to A or to a person whose business is or includes holding chargeable securities as nominee for A.

The expression "clearance services" is not defined and concern has been expressed that the provision of any nominee services to facilitate dealings in securities could be within its meaning. HMRC have indicated that this is not the intention, and that their policy will be to construe the expression so as to include only arrangements which are expressly marketed as "clearance services". In cases of doubt, HMRC's guidance should be sought. The absence of a definition of clearance service was specifically noted by the 2007 Solutions Report of the European Commission's Fiscal Compliance Experts' Group ("FISCO"), which observed that "the definition of a clearing system is unclear in relation to Stamp Duty Reserve Tax (SDRT) purposes, which may prevent a level playing-field between settlement service providers that are considered a clearing service (such as CSDs) and those who are not". In *HSBC Holdings plc v HMRC* [2010] STC 58, Mr Advocate-General Mengozzi attempted a definition, or at least a description of the activity, of a clearance service: 'Clearance services play a role which may be defined as the holding of shares. In particular, they keep a record of the owners of the shares, and of transfers of shares, although, at all times, the bearer certificates are held by the clearance service concerned. In other words, clearance services make the acquisition and disposal of shares simpler, quicker and more secure.'

Concern has apparently been expressed over the possibility that, by virtue of the forms of settlement process adopted on such exchanges, applying for listing of UK shares on some foreign stock exchanges would arguably amount (albeit unintentionally) to the act of "entering a clearance system", with the result that the listing attracted a 1.5 per cent charge to stamp duty reserve tax on the price or value of the UK shares so listed.

Although there would appear to be a difference of some kind between clearance services and "mere" nomineeship, it is suggested (and the Stamp Office appear to agree) that an essential element of clearance services is the holding as nominee, or the appointing of another person to hold as nominee, of the *legal* title to shares or other "chargeable securities". This is important because it seems that in practice, "chains" of beneficial ownership develop in relation to securities within a clearance system, such that the beneficial ownership in securities enjoyed by the participators in the system is itself often held in trust for another person—ie the participator is itself a nominee for one of its clients. Since that client may well be a bank or other financial institution, the client may itself be a nominee for a further party. Furthermore it seems that some of the intermediate links in such a chain may be persons who are themselves operators of clearance services. Whilst it would seem to be contrary to the underlying philosophy of the increased charge applicable under s 96, it is not beyond doubt on the strict wording of s 96(1) (if read in isolation and without any purposive gloss—see commentary on what is now FA 1999 Sch 13 Part I para 1) that a further charge arises in such circumstances (since an interest in "chargeable securities" itself constitutes "chargeable securities"). However, as stated above, the Stamp Office do not appear to regard this as an appropriate interpretation of s 96(1) and it is suggested that they are correct in holding that opinion on the basis that the holding on trust of a mere beneficial interest in securities for another does not amount to the provision of "clearance services".

The rate payable is 1.5 per cent of the following:

(a) in a case where the securities are issued, their price when issued;
(b) in a case where the securities are transferred for consideration in money or money's worth, the amount or value of the consideration; and
(c) in any other case, the value of the securities.

The value of any consideration which does not consist of money is taken to be the price it might reasonably be expected to fetch on a sale on the open market at the time the securities are transferred, and the value of securities is taken to be the price they might reasonably be expected to fetch on a sale in the open market at the time they are transferred.

The duty is reduced to 1 per cent where:

(a) the securities are transferred by an instrument on which stamp duty is chargeable on what is now called a "conveyance or transfer otherwise than on sale" under FA 1999 Sch 13 Part III para 16; and
(b) at the time of transfer the transferor is a qualified dealer in securities of the kind concerned or a nominee of such qualified dealer; and
(c) the transfer is made for the purposes of the dealer's business; and
(d) at the time of the transfer the dealer is not a market maker in securities of the kind concerned; and
(e) the instrument contains a statement that conditions (*b*) to (*d*) are fulfilled; and
(f) the securities are transferred before the relief for sales to intermediaries under s 88A comes into effect and replaces the market maker and broker dealer relief, unless the securities were acquired by the transferor before that day.

"Qualified dealer" and "market maker" mean the same as they do for the purposes of s 93 in connection with depositary schemes. The repeal of the reduced rate for qualified dealers results in transfers into a clearance service, effected through a qualified dealer who is not an intermediary for the purposes of s 80A, suffering an effective 2 per cent charge.

As with depositary schemes, the stamp duty reserve tax is chargeable by reference to the total of the instalments payable, less those paid before the transfer to the other person is effected in any case where:

(a) securities are issued or transferred on sale upon terms (in either case) that they are to be paid for in instalments; and
(b) the person to whom they are issued or transferred holds onto them and transfers them to another person when the last instalment is paid; and

(c) the latter transfer would attract stamp duty reserve tax on the value of the securities transferred; and
(d) before the making of the latter transfer an instrument is received by A or a person whose business is or includes holding chargeable securities as nominee for A; and
(e) that instrument evidences all the rights vested in the securities; and
(f) the transfer to the other person contains a statement to the effect that the above conditions are fulfilled.

Where chargeable securities are issued or transferred on sale upon terms providing for payment in instalments and for an issue of other chargeable securities, no stamp duty reserve tax is chargeable notwithstanding any other provisions of this section unless any instalment becomes payable by A or his nominee, in which event tax is payable at the rate of 1·5 per cent of the instalment payable.

As is the case with depositary schemes, unlike the usual rule that a payment of stamp duty relieves from any liability for stamp duty reserve tax, in the case of clearance services where ad valorem stamp duty paid on a transfer of securities is less than the stamp duty reserve tax, the stamp duty reserve tax is only relieved to the extent of the ad valorem stamp duty and tax will be payable on the excess. In any case where the ad valorem stamp duty equals or exceeds the stamp duty reserve tax, there is no stamp duty reserve tax, but neither is there a corresponding provision that the excess stamp duty be repaid, so that effectively the charge is the higher of the ad valorem stamp duty and the stamp duty reserve tax.

In the case of clearance services, stamp duty reserve tax is payable by the person who provides the services, ie, A, unless at the time of the transfer such person is not resident in the UK and has no branch or agency in the UK, in which case the transferee is liable for the tax. The only exception to this is where stamp duty reserve tax becomes payable on payment of an instalment, in which case the person liable to pay the instalment is liable for the tax.

The expression "chargeable securities" is defined in s 99.

[*Note:* See note at commencement of commentary on this Act.]

97. Clearance services: exceptions

Subject to the operation of an anti-avoidance provision, FA 1986 s 97C, to which reference should be made, no charge to stamp duty reserve tax under s 96 in relation to clearance services arises in any of the following cases:

(a) Where securities are transferred by one company whose business is exclusively that of holding securities as nominee for a person providing clearance services to another such company, (nothing in the legislation specifically requires the transferor and transferee to be nominees of the same clearance service operator; this seems strange, considering that—and see also commentary on s 90(6) above—no such relief covers transfers between an actual clearance service operator and its own nominee).
(b) Where a transfer is effected by an instrument on which stamp duty is not chargeable by virtue of FA 1976 s 127(1) (transfer to The Stock Exchange nominee) or FA 1986 s 84(2) or (3) (transfer to a recognised investment exchange or a recognised clearing house, or their respective nominees).
(c) In a case of a transfer or issue of a UK bearer instrument (meaning bearer instruments issued by a "UK company", as that term is used in the new bearer instrument provisions—see commentary on FA 1999 Sch 15) other than those within what is now FA 1999 Sch 15 para 16 (such as renounceable letters of allotment where the rights of renunciation do not exceed six months' duration) or those within what is now FA 1999 Sch 15 para 17 but, as regards the latter category, only if they do not "raise new capital" (see further commentary after (*d*) below).
(d) In respect of an issue by one company (X) of securities in exchange for shares in another company (Y) where X already has control of Y, or will have control in consequence of the exchange or in consequence of an offer as a result of which the

exchange is made, for which purpose X is deemed to have control of Y if X has power to control Y's affairs by virtue of holding shares in, or possessing voting power in relation to, Y or any other body corporate.

As regards case (*c*) above, changes are introduced by FA 1999 ss 116 and 117, which restrict the extent to which the relief for UK bearer instruments is available after 30 January 1999. The relief is further restricted with effect from 9 March 1999. See commentary on s 95 above, in relation to which changes have been made which are identical in substance to those made here.

[*Note:* See note at commencement of commentary on this Act.]

97AA. Clearance services: further exception

This section is inserted by FA 1999 with retrospective effect from 1 May 1998. It provides a relief in relation to clearance services which is identical in substance to that for depositary schemes under s 95A above. See commentary on that section.

97A. Clearance services: election for alternative system of charge

This section provides an alternative to paying stamp duty or stamp duty reserve tax under FA 1986 ss 70 and 96 at the rate of 1·5 per cent on the deposit of UK securities into a clearance service for the purchase and sale of chargeable securities, and then transferring securities free of charge within the service. The alternative system of charge is that the 1·5 per cent upfront charge will not apply and the clearance service operator will have to make arrangements for the collection of stamp duty reserve tax (chargeable at normal rates) on transfers and issues into and transfers within the clearance service.

In *HSBC Holdings plc v Revenue and Customs Comrs* Case C-569/07 [2010] STC 58, the United Kingdom sought to rely on this provision to defend the principal charging section, s 96, from the objection that the 1.5% charge levied on the issue of shares into a clearance service was in breach of the Capital Duties Directive (Council Directive 69/355/EEC of 17 July 1969 concerning indirect taxes on the raising of capital, as amended) on the ground that the taxpayer had a choice – either it could pay the 0.5% charge on each transfer or it could buy a "season ticket"; by paying the 1.5% charge under s 96. The Court of Justice decided that this argument was unsustainable, since neither the tax basis of the tax nor the taxable person was determined by reference to the future transfers, which were, in any event, hypothetical. In other words, a charge of 1.5% could not be imposed on A on the ground that it thereby saved possible future transferees (who would be persons other than A) from smaller charges to tax going forward.

A clearance service operator (such as Euroclear) may, with the approval of the Board, elect that transfers, issues and agreements falling within FA 1986 ss 70(1), 96(1), 90(4) and 90(5) (ie chargeable to stamp duty or stamp duty reserve tax at the rate of 1·5 per cent as transfers or issues into a clearance service) be chargeable as if ss 70, 90(4) and (5) and 96(1) did not apply: (3), (4). This should mean that transfers and agreements to transfer securities to the clearance service operator or his nominee are chargeable to stamp duty or stamp duty reserve tax at the usual rates; usually the consideration for such transfers and agreements is nil so that the charge is generally limited to 50p (or £5, as from 1 October 1999). Issues of securities to the clearance service operator will be outside the scope of stamp duty and stamp duty reserve tax. Agreements to transfer securities within the clearance service are generally subject to stamp duty reserve tax at the usual 0·5 per cent rate—stamp duty should not be in point in relation to transfers within the clearance service assuming that no written instrument is brought into existence.

An operator is a person whose business is or includes the provision of clearance services for the purchase and sale of chargeable securities or relevant securities (defined by reference to FA 1986 s 70).

An election comes into force on the date notified to the operator by the Board in giving its approval: (2). It may be terminated by no less than 30 days' notice given by the operator to the Board or by the Board to the operator, or if there has been a breach of a condition of the approval of the election by notice of the Board with earlier effect: (10).

On termination of an election all chargeable securities held by the operator or his nominee in the clearance system are deemed to be transferred immediately after the termination to the operator or his nominee by a transfer covered by FA 1986 s 96(1) ie chargeable to stamp duty reserve tax at the rate, generally, of 1.5 per cent: (11). Ss 70(9) and 97(1) do not prevent any charge arising: (13).

A transfer by an operator who has made the election (or his nominee) to, or to a nominee of, another operator who has not made an election, is treated as if FA 1986 ss 70 and 96 applied: (5). This would appear to mean that the 1·5 per cent rate of duty will apply except where exemption is available under FA 1986 ss 70(9) and 97(1). Ss 70(9) and 97(1) do not prevent any charge arising: (13).

The Board may require the operator, as a condition of approval of his election, to make arrangements for the collection of stamp duty reserve tax on transfers and issues into and transfers within the clearance system: (6).

Where the operator is not resident in the UK and has no branch or agency in the UK the Board may require him to appoint and maintain a UK based tax representative approved by the Board: (7), (8). The tax representative is entitled to act on the operator's behalf for the purposes of stamp duty and stamp duty reserve tax in connection with the clearance service and is jointly and severally responsible with the operator for the operator's compliance with his obligations: (9).

For the different rules which apply to the Tradepoint system see the Revenue Press Release, 4 August 1995 and SI 1995/2051.

[*Note:* See note at commencement of commentary on this Act.]

97B. Transfer between depositary receipt system and clearance system

This section mirrors the s 72A stamp duty provision and ensures that no charge to stamp duty reserve tax applies (rather than the s 93 depositary receipt charge or s 96 clearance system charge) where securities are transferred between a depositary receipt system and clearance system provided, in the case of a transfer from a clearance system, that the transfer is not covered by a s 97A election for alternative system of charge. The exception is now subject to an anti-avoidance provision: s 97C.

97C. Transfers to non-EU depositary receipt and clearance systems

This section was introduced following the acceptance by the Commissioners that, having regard to the decision of the Court of Justice in *HSBS Holdings plc v HMRC* [2010] STC 58, the UK could no longer justify the continued imposition of SDRT or stamp duty at 1.5% on the issue or transfer of shares into an EU clearance service or depositary receipt scheme. It reflects the current position of the Commissioners (which, it is understood, is itself under challenge) that the decision in *HSBC* does not extend to issues or transfers of shares into clearance services or depositary receipt schemes located outside the European Union. Given the exception from charge generally available where there is a transfer between one clearance service and another, or between a clearance service and a depositary receipt scheme, it was considered that it would be only too easy to avoid a charge to tax by issuing or transferring shares into a European scheme or service and then transferring those securities from the European service or scheme ("an EU system") to one located outside the Union ("a non-EU system").

The effect of the section is to disapply the exceptions from the charges to SDRT imposed by ss 93 and 96 which are afforded by ss 95(1), 97(1) and 97B(1) if the onward transfer is from an EU system to a non-EU system. However, if the securities have previously been the subject of a charge to SDRT on a transfer from one system to another, then the disapplication

Part II ST

does not take effect. In short, the section establishes a new "season ticket" system, albeit one that franks charges on the securities leaving the EU.

It may be observed that there is a dispute as to whether the new section itself is consonant with the Capital Duties Directive (Council Directive 2008/7/EC of 12 February 2008 concerning indirect taxes on the raising of capital) since the Directive itself applies to the share capital of any "capital company", and the definition of a capital company is by reference to its place of incorporation – ie within the European Union. Nothing in the Directive therefore suggests that it is restricted to dealings in the shares of such companies which take place within the EU.

GENERAL

98. Administration etc

The Treasury may make regulations by statutory instrument providing for specific provisions of TMA 1970 to apply in relation to stamp duty reserve tax, with such modifications as the Treasury thinks fit, and making such further provisions with regard to stamp duty reserve tax as the Treasury thinks fit in relation to administration, assessment, collection and recovery. The regulations made are the Stamp Duty Reserve Tax Regulations 1986 (SI 1986/1711 as amended by SI 1988/835, SI 1989/1301, SI 1992/3287 and SI 1994/1813): see commentary under Statutory Instruments.

The *Stamp Duty Reserve Tax—Notes for Guidance* issued by the Stamp Office (see Appendix 7) give, particularly in Chapter 7, a good descriptive guide to the administrative and payment procedures.

[*Note:* See note at commencement of commentary on this Act.]

99. Interpretation

"Chargeable securities" are defined (except for the purposes of ss 93, 94 and 96 in relation to depositary schemes and clearance services) as "stocks, shares, loan capital and units under a unit trust scheme", the words "unit" and "unit trust scheme" being given the same meaning as in FA 1946 Pt VII, save that alternative finance investment bonds taking the sukuk form (as defined by FA 2005 s 48A) are excluded from the definition of "unit trust scheme". This exclusion is intended to secure treatment for such bonds equivalent to that afforded to conventional loan capital: see s 78 above. References to stocks, shares, or loan capital are deemed to include references to any interest in, or in dividends or other rights arising out of, stocks, shares or loan capital (but, interestingly, not interest etc in units in a unit trust scheme), and any right to an allotment of or to subscribe for, or an option to acquire, stocks, shares or loan capital (again, not units in a unit trust scheme).

Stocks, shares and loan capital which are issued or raised by a body corporate not incorporated in the UK (including interests in, rights to an allotment of or to subscribe for, and options to acquire such stocks, shares and loan capital) are excluded unless:

(a) in the case of stocks, shares and loan capital, they are registered in a register kept in the UK by or on behalf of the relevant body corporate; or
(b) in the case of shares, they are paired with shares issued by a body corporate incorporated in the UK; or
(c) in the case of interests, rights or options, the stocks, shares or loan capital to which such interests, rights or options relate are either stocks, shares or loan capital registered in a register kept in the UK or shares paired with shares issued by a body corporate incorporated in the UK.

For the purpose of deciding if an "option to acquire" stocks, shares or loan capital falls within the exclusion in relation to overseas registered securities, the relevant criterion is the place of registration of the securities to which the option related.

Shares issued by a body incorporated outside the UK are deemed to be paired with shares issued by a body incorporated in the UK where the Articles of Association of the UK company and the equivalent instruments governing the foreign company each provide that no share in the company to which they relate may be transferred otherwise than as part of a unit comprising one share in that company and one share in the other and:

(i) such units were offered for sale to the public in the UK and, at the same time and in equal numbers at a broadly equivalent price, in the country in which the foreign company is incorporated (and as to the difficulties of construing what does, and what does not, constitute an "offer to the public", see notes on FA 1986 s 89A); or

(ii) provided there has been an earlier public offering complying with (i) above, such units comprise shares in the UK company and shares in the foreign company which are allotted and issued (as part of such units) as fully or partly paid bonus shares.

In addition, provided that there has been an earlier public offering complying with (i) above, even where paired share units are subsequently issued in *unequal* numbers in the two countries (for example as a pro rata rights issue where, because of trading between the two countries, the units are no longer held equally in the two countries), the new shares in the foreign company are still deemed to be paired with the new shares in the UK company and therefore fall within the definition of "chargeable securities" in sub-s (4).

Units in a unit trust scheme are not chargeable securities if all the trustees are non-resident and the register maintained abroad. There is also an exclusion where the unit trust scheme may only invest in exempt investments. Investments (other than units in a collective investment scheme) are exempt investments if the relevant investments are outside the charge to stamp duty and SDLT. In the case of an investment in a collective investment scheme the scheme must be an authorised unit trust scheme or an OEIC and the assets (a) are so invested that the only tax charge that can arise on the trustees is under Schedule D Case III; and (b) must, as to at least 80% by value, be exempt investments in themselves.

Specific provision is made for securities issued or raised by a Societas Europaea (SE); a new form of European company created by Council Regulation (EC) No 2157/2001 of 8 October 2001. As from 1 April 2005, such securities are chargeable securities if, at the relevant time, the SE has its registered office in the United Kingdom. By contrast, if the registered office of the SE is outside the United Kingdom at the relevant time, securities raised or issued by the SE which are within para (*a*), (*b*) or (*c*) above are nevertheless not chargeable securities for the purposes of SDRT.

Depositary receipts for stocks or shares (but not depositary receipts for loan capital) are excluded from the definition of "chargeable securities". A depositary receipt is taken to be an instrument acknowledging (*a*) that a person holds stocks or shares, or evidence of the right to receive them, and (*b*) that another person is entitled to rights, whether expressed as units or otherwise, in or in relation to stocks or shares of the same kind, including the right to receive such stocks or shares (or evidence of the right to receive them) from the person holding the stocks or shares, or evidence. A depositary receipt does not include an instrument acknowledging rights in or in relation to stocks or shares if they are issued or sold on terms providing for payment in instalments and for the issue of the instrument as evidence that an instalment has been paid (ie, such instruments *are* chargeable securities). The Treasury has the power by statutory instrument to amend the definition of depositary receipts.

The failure to exclude, from the definition of chargeable securities, depositary receipts for loan capital could give rise to a double tax charge. For example, registered depositary receipts for convertible loan stock would be chargeable on issue under s 93 and there would be a further charge under s 87 on each agreement to transfer them.

The most important exclusion from the definition of "chargeable securities" for the purpose of stamp duty reserve tax is "stock or marketable securities the transfer of which is exempt from all stamp duties", (and interests in, rights to and options to acquire stocks, shares or loan capital the transfer of which is exempt from all stamp duties) eg, gilt-edged securities and most forms of non-convertible loan capital (which are exempt by virtue of FA 1986 s 79). For the definition of "stock or marketable securities" see FA 2003 s 125. HMRC has also indicated in the *Notes for Guidance*, (see Appendix 7) that neither options traded on The Stock Exchange nor financial futures traded on the London International Financial Futures Exchange are "chargeable securities".

For the purposes of FA 1986 ss 93, 94 and 96 in connection with depositary schemes and clearance services, the definition of "chargeable securities" includes shares of a foreign company (or interests therein or rights thereto) which are paired with UK shares, even though it does not include for those purposes shares issued by a foreign company which are registered in a register kept in the UK However, where shares of a foreign company (or an interest therein or a right thereto) are transferred into a depositary scheme or clearance service, no stamp duty reserve tax liability arises simply because the shares (or interest or right) are paired with shares in a UK company (or an interest therein or a right thereto) provided that they are "newly subscribed shares", meaning shares issued wholly for new consideration in pursuance of an offer for sale to the public. Again, note the difficulties which might arise in construing this definition discussed in relation to FA 1986 s 89A.

Also, in relation to depositary schemes and clearance services, the effect of s 99(10)(*b*) is that shares are not deemed to be "exempt from all stamp duties", and therefore not subject to stamp duty reserve tax on transfer, simply because they are registered in an overseas branch register under the Companies Act 2006 s 129. Such shares will therefore be chargeable securities, an agreement for the transfer of which would theoretically give rise to a charge to stamp duty reserve tax.

[*Note:* See note at commencement of commentary on this Act.]

PART 7 MISCELLANEOUS AND SUPPLEMENTARY

114. Short title, interpretation, construction and repeals

The stamp duty provisions contained in Part III (ss 64 to 85) are to be construed as one with SA 1891, but the stamp duty reserve tax provisions contained in Part IV (ss 86 to 99) are not to be so construed.

[*Note:* See note at commencement of commentary on this Act.]

Insolvency Act 1986

1986 Chapter 45

190. Documents exempt from stamp duty

(See the notes printed at the end of the contents list to Part II Stamp Taxes.)

In the case of a company registered in England and Wales which is being wound up by a court, or in a creditors' voluntary winding-up, the following documents are exempt from stamp duty: (*a*) every assurance relating solely to freehold or leasehold property, or to any estate right or interest in any real or personal property, which forms part of the company's assets and which, after execution of the assurance, either at law or in equity, is or remains part of those assets, and (*b*) every writ, order, certificate, or other instrument relating solely to the property of any such company, or to any proceeding under the winding up.

Similar provisions are made for companies registered in Scotland.

378. Exemption from stamp duty

(See the notes printed at the end of the contents list to Part II Stamp Taxes.)

This section exempts documents relating to the bankruptcy of an individual which are similar to those contained in s 190 in relation to companies in the course of being wound up by the court, or in a creditors' voluntary winding up.

Building Societies Act 1986

1986 Chapter 53

109A. Exemption from stamp duty land tax

Exemption from stamp duty land tax is given to a land transaction effected:

(a) where two or more building societies amalgamate; and

(b) where there is a transfer of engagements between building societies.

The relief must be claimed in the appropriate land transaction return.

Finance Act 1987

1987 Chapter 16

PART III STAMP DUTY AND STAMP DUTY RESERVE TAX

STAMP DUTY

48. Unit trusts

The definition of "unit trust scheme" in FA 1946 s 57, is replaced by that in the Financial Services Act 1986 s 75 (8), with a consequential amendment to the definition in s 57 of "trust instrument".

In addition, Treasury regulations by statutory instrument may exclude specified schemes from the revised definition of "unit trust scheme" and make supplemental and transitional provisions.

50. Warrants to purchase government stock, etc

Any instrument which vests or transfers an interest in, or a right to be allotted or to subscribe for, or an option to acquire or dispose of, "exempt securities", is exempt from stamp duty under the provisions in what is now FA 1999 Schs 13 and 15 relating to conveyances on sale and bearer instrument duty.

"Exempt securities" means "securities" (ie, stock or marketable securities or loan capital within the meaning of FA 1986 s 78 (7)) the transfer of which is exempt from all stamp duties, or where there is an exemption from the charge to bearer instrument duty by virtue of what is now FA 1999 Sch 15 para 17 (relating to securities not denominated in sterling), or by virtue of FA 1986 s 79 (2) (relating to loan capital constituted by or transferable by means of a bearer instrument).

The definition therefore covers the following types of securities:

(a) gilt-edged securities;
(b) loan capital in bearer form exempt from stamp duty under FA 1986 s 79 (2);
(c) loan capital in registered form exempt from stamp duty under FA 1986 s 79 (4) (loan capital issued by companies and foreign government);
(d) loan capital which falls within the terms of the exemption in FA 1986 s 79 (3) (loan capital issued by certain international bodies); and
(e) bearer securities denominated in a foreign currency exempt from duty under what is now FA 1999 Sch 15 para 17.

52. Clearance services

In FA 1986 s 70 (6) references to shares, stock or other marketable securities replace references to relevant securities (defined in FA 1986 s 72 (1) as shares in or stock or marketable securities of any company).

54. Shared ownership transactions

(See the notes printed at the end of the contents list to Part II Stamp Taxes.)

FA 1980 s 97 and FA 1981 s 108, which limit the duty payable on a shared ownership lease, are amended.

The list of lessees to which FA 1980 s 97 applies includes unregistered as well as registered housing associations because the Housing and Planning Act 1986 brought within the shared ownership scheme leases granted by unregistered housing associations.

The reliefs provided by FA 1980 s 97 and FA 1981 s 108 are extended to leases granted by a private landlord who has taken over a public housing estate. The Housing Act 1985 s 171A, inserted by the Housing and Planning Act 1986, preserves a tenant's right to be granted a shared ownership lease when an estate is privatised.

55. Crown exemption

(See the notes printed at the end of the contents list to Part II Stamp Taxes.)

Exemptions from stamp duties previously granted to the Secretary of State for the Environment and the Secretary of State for Transport (but not other Secretaries of State) are replaced with a general exemption for all Ministers of the Crown and the Treasury Solicitor. No stamp duty is to be charged under the provisions in what is now FA 1999 Schs 13 and 15 relating to conveyances on sale transfers otherwise than on sale, on any instrument effecting a conveyance, transfer or lease to a Minister of the Crown the Treasury Solicitor or to corresponding Ministers and their legal representatives in Wales. "Minister of the Crown" is as defined in the Ministers of the Crown Act 1975.

Finance Act 1988

1988 Chapter 39

PART IV MISCELLANEOUS AND GENERAL

STAMP DUTY AND STAMP DUTY RESERVE TAX

143. Stamp duty: paired shares

Legislative effect is given retrospectively to arrangements announced at the time of the so-called "Equity 3" capital-raising exercise by the Eurotunnel consortium, although ss 143 and 144 are drafted in general terms so as to apply to any similar situation.

Eurotunnel was put together as an Anglo-French partnership comprising two principal holding companies, one (Eurotunnel plc) ("EPLC") incorporated in England and the other (Eurotunnel SA) ("ESA") incorporated in France. The "Equity 3" capital-raising exercise consisted of simultaneous offers for sale to the public in the UK and France of "units", each of which comprised one share with a par value of 40p in EPLC and one share with a nominal value of FFr 10 in ESA, and each of which was issued together with a "New Warrant" which itself comprised the right to subscribe for one-tenth of a share in EPLC and one-tenth of a share in ESA, the warrants being exercisable only in integral multiples of 10.

The shares in EPLC and ESA were therefore effectively "twinned". Under the Articles of Association of EPLC, issues or transfers of shares in that company are not permitted unless they are issued or transferred together with the same number of shares in ESA. The *Statuts* of ESA contain a reciprocal restriction. In addition, the Articles of EPLC and the *Statuts* of ESA provide that shares in EPLC and ESA respectively can only be listed or authorised to be dealt in on any stock exchange in the form of units. Listing was subsequently granted by the London Stock Exchange and the Bourse in Paris for all of the issued shares in EPLC and ESA provided that they are in the form of units.

Without special provision, these arrangements would have given rise to complex liabilities to stamp duty and stamp duty reserve tax; the units could not have been treated in the same way as though each unit were a single share. Although the situation was not free from doubt, it seems that broadly speaking more stamp duty would have become payable than was intended, but less stamp duty reserve tax, and to enable each of these liabilities to be separately assessed the units would have had to have been split into their component shares.

As far as stamp duty is concerned, in addition to the duty which would be (and is) payable in the normal way on transfers of units in the UK, on the whole of the price paid for the units, bearer instrument duty at the rate of 1.5% would also have been payable because shares in EPLC had to be delivered in France (and some other countries) in bearer form to meet the requirements of the local market. It was therefore proposed to relieve the units from bearer instrument duty. For stamp duty reserve tax purposes, shares in EPLC would have been (and are) "chargeable securities" so that agreements to transfer them would give rise to a stamp duty reserve tax liability, but shares in ESA would not necessarily have fallen within the definition because the company is not a UK company, so that there was a possibility that agreements to transfer them would not give rise to a stamp duty reserve tax liability. It was therefore also proposed to change the stamp duty reserve tax legislation so that agreements to transfer units would give rise to a stamp duty reserve tax liability in relation to the whole of the unit and not just its EPLC component part.

This section contains the relieving provision in relation to bearer instrument stamp duty. It applies where the Articles of Association of a UK company and the equivalent instruments relating to a foreign company each provide that no share in the company to which they relate may be transferred except as part of a unit comprising one share in that company and one share in the other, and the units are to be or have been offered for sale to the public in the UK and at the same time in the country in which the foreign company is incorporated. The provision is a little restrictive: units can comprise only one share in each company whereas it is possible to imagine situations where it might be more convenient for a unit to comprise a greater number of shares. The number of units offered in the foreign country is to be exactly equal to the number of units offered in the UK The units must also be offered in the UK and the foreign country "at a broadly equivalent price".

In any such circumstances, no bearer instrument stamp duty is to be chargeable on the issue of any bearer instrument representing shares in the UK company, or a right to an allotment of or to subscribe for such shares, if the purpose of the issue is to make such shares available for sale as part of "twinned" units pursuant to the public offers in the UK or the relevant foreign country, or any other public offer made at the same time and at a broadly equivalent price in a country other than the UK or the relevant foreign country.

On the other hand, bearer instrument stamp duty will be payable on the issue by the foreign company of an instrument which represents shares in that company, or a right to an allotment of or to subscribe for such shares, other than for the purpose of making such shares available for sale as part of units pursuant to the offers for sale in the UK, the relevant foreign country, or any other country as mentioned above. The foreign company is treated as though it were a UK company for these purposes.

The foreign company is also to be treated as though it were a UK company for the purposes of transfers of units into depositary schemes and clearance services.

No stamp duty will generally be payable on the first issue of the units pursuant to the offers for sale notwithstanding that the UK company may as part of the arrangements be issuing bearer instruments to facilitate trading. The issue by the foreign company of bearer instruments will not in any case be chargeable for stamp duty under the existing law. The UK company is accordingly treated as though it were a foreign company for the purpose of bearer instrument duty on the issue of bearer instruments as part of the offers for sale.

Where a transferee (or any other holder) of units in registered form exchanges them for units in bearer form, bearer instrument stamp duty will be payable on the value of the units concerned. In the case of the shares in the UK company comprised in the unit, bearer instrument stamp duty would in any case be payable under the existing law, and the foreign company is treated as though it were a UK company for these purposes.

Similarly the foreign company is treated as though it were a UK company so that transfers of units into a depositary scheme or clearance service will bear the higher rate of duty under the relevant sections of FA 1986.

Bearer instruments representing shares in the UK company or the foreign company, or a right to an allotment of or to subscribe for such shares, are relieved from the requirement of SA 1891 s 3 that every instrument written on the same piece of material as another instrument be separately stamped.

The "equal numbers" test in s 143(1)(*b*) cannot be satisfied where, following a public offering of paired share units, there is a rights issue of such units. When the rights issue is made the original units will be held unequally in the two countries because of trading between the two countries and a pro rata rights issue is bound to be unequal. This section has therefore been amended to enable the new units issued in these circumstances to have the benefit of the exemption from bearer instruments duty without satisfying the equal numbers test. See the Revenue Press Release, 14 June 1990, and the commentary on FA 1990.

Finance Act 1989

1989 Chapter 26

PART III MISCELLANEOUS AND GENERAL

STAMP DUTY ETC

175. Stamp duty: stock exchange nominees

This and the following section confer on the Treasury regulation-making powers to adapt stamp duty and stamp duty reserve tax to the new methods of transferring shares which were being developed, particularly by the Stock Exchange as it attempted to move towards its proposed "dematerialised" (ie paperless) system of share transactions, known as "TAURUS" (a system which was eventually abandoned before implementation and was superseded by "CREST"). A general discussion of paperless systems for transactions in securities is contained in the DTI Consultative Paper, the text of which is set out in Appendix 9 of *Moores Rowlands Orange Tax Guide 1990–91*. Regulation-making powers were needed by the Treasury as an interim measure to ensure that transfers made by these new methods are liable to stamp duty and stamp duty reserve tax on the same basis as ordinary transactions effected by present methods.

In relation to a paperless transaction the charge would be to stamp duty reserve tax, rather than to stamp duty. However, the Revenue believed that there might be circumstances when for example the present rules could:

(a) produce double—or even multiple—charges to stamp duty reserve tax, or a stamp duty liability in addition to a stamp duty reserve tax liability; or
(b) mean a transaction fails to qualify for the stamp duty reserve tax reliefs available to a paper-based transaction; or
(c) impose collection obligations and procedures which do not fit the new arrangements.

The Revenue therefore believed that the present stamp duty reserve tax rules needed to be adapted in one or more ways.

Regulations under this section may be made by the Treasury (by statutory instrument) to treat the stamp duty charge as not arising if there would otherwise be a charge both to stamp duty reserve tax and ad valorem conveyance on sale duty in circumstances to be prescribed by the regulations where a stock exchange nominee is involved.

See also the powers conferred on the Secretary of State by the Companies Act 1989 s 207, and The Uncertificated Securities Regulations 1992, SI 1992/225.

176. Stamp duty reserve tax: stock exchange nominees

For the background to this section, see the commentary on the preceding section, above. Regulations under this section may be made by the Treasury by statutory instrument, where prescribed circumstances exist involving a stock exchange nominee, either:

(a) to treat one of the charges as not arising if there would otherwise be two stamp duty reserve tax charges; or
(b) to treat the stamp duty reserve tax charge as not arising if there would otherwise be a charge both to stamp duty reserve tax and to stamp duty; or
(c) to provide that a statutory provision by virtue of which there is no charge to stamp duty reserve tax shall apply; or
(d) to provide that a statutory provision by virtue of which a lower rate of stamp duty reserve tax is chargeable than would otherwise be the case shall apply.

But note the final paragraph in the commentary on s 175, above.

Part II ST

177. Stamp duty reserve tax: information

This section extends the regulation-making powers conferred on the Treasury by FA 1986 s 98 (1) to enable the Treasury to make regulations entitling the Commissioners to specify the manner or the form in which notices or information are to be given or supplied to them in connection with the routine administration of stamp duty reserve tax.

But note the final paragraph in the commentary on s 175, above.

INTEREST, ETC

178. Setting of rates of interest

Rates of interest on unpaid stamp duty reserve tax (TMA 1970 s 86, by virtue of SI 1986/1711 Sch) and repayments (FA 1986 s 92) are set automatically in accordance with formulae prescribed in regulations made by statutory instrument subject to annulment by a resolution of the House of Commons.

Regulations may, inter alia, provide for a specific rate of interest to be applicable or for the applicable rate to be determined by reference to a given rate or average of rates, for a specific increase or decrease in the applicable rates, or an increase or decrease calculated by reference to given formulae, for a rate calculated by reference to an average to be rounded up or down, and for specified circumstances in which alterations in rates are or are not to take place.

The Board of Inland Revenue is also empowered by order to specify a rate of interest without the need for a statutory instrument where the rate provided for by regulations made under this section is changed and the new rate is not specified in the regulations.

The Regulations made under this section are the Taxes (Interest Rate) Regulations 1989, SI 1989/1297; see commentary under Statutory Instruments.

But note the final paragraph in the commentary on s 175 above.

With effect from 1 October 1999, this section also applies to payments, and/or repayments, of stamp duty (including payments on account of stamp duty under SA 1891 s 15A (2))—see the commentaries on SA 1891 s 15A and FA 1999 s 98.

179. Provisions consequential on section 178

Consequential amendments are made inter alia to FA 1986 s 92 (2).

180. Repayment interest: period of accrual

An amendment is made to FA 1986 s 92 (2) to bring it into line with enactments relating to other taxes and to confirm that interest on overpaid stamp duty reserve tax is calculated up to the day on which the payable order for repayment is issued. (FA 1986 s 92 (4), (5) is repealed as set out in Sch 17 Part XI).

But, again, see above note.

GENERAL

186. Interpretation, etc
187. Repeals
188. Short Title

SCHEDULES

SCHEDULE 17 REPEALS (SECTION 187)

PART IX STAMP DUTY: INSURANCE

Repeals are made in accordance with s 173.

PART X RATES OF INTEREST

Repeals are made in accordance with s 178.

Electricity Act 1989

1989 Chapter 29

103. Stamp duty exemption for certain contracts

(See the notes printed at the end of the contents list to Part II Stamp Taxes.)

Electricity is treated as goods for the purposes of what is now FA 1999 Sch 13 Part I para 7, so that a contract for the sale of electricity is not stampable. See also the similar provision for Northern Ireland made in the Electricity (Northern Ireland Consequential Amendments) Order 1992 (SI 1992/232).

Property Services Agency and Crown Suppliers Act 1990

1990 Chapter 12

SCHEDULE

(See the notes printed at the end of the contents list to Part II Stamp Taxes.)

In respect of a scheme under s 1 of the Act, no scheme document (certified as such by the Secretary of State) transferring property, rights or liabilities to a company which is wholly owned by the Crown will (by virtue of paragraph 3) be chargeable to stamp duty provided that it is adjudicated under SA 1891 s 12.

National Health Service and Community Care Act 1990

1990 Chapter 19

8. Transfer of property, rights and liabilities to NHS trust

(See the notes printed at the end of the contents list to Part II Stamp Taxes.)

Under sub-s (4), no instrument transferring by order of the Secretary of State any property, rights or liabilities from a health authority, or from the Secretary of State, to an NHS trust set up under the Act shall be chargeable to stamp duty.

61. Health service bodies: taxation

(See the notes printed at the end of the contents list to Part II Stamp Taxes.)

Specific exemptions from stamp duty under the "Conveyance or Transfer on Sale", "Conveyance or Transfer of any kind not hereinbefore described" and "Lease or Tack" heads of charge are given by sub-s (3) to any instrument effecting a conveyance, transfer or lease to an NHS trust established under the Act (or its Scottish equivalent), and to any agreement for any such conveyance, transfer or lease.

61A. Health service bodies: SDLT

A land transaction is exempt from SDLT where the purchaser is one of a number of designated health bodies including an NHS trust, a Primary Care Trust and a Local Health Board.

The relief must be claimed on the appropriate land transaction return.

Finance Act 1990

1990 Chapter 29

Note: *In relation to the proposed abolitions of all stamp duty charges on property other than land and buildings (including all charges on transactions in shares and bearer instruments) and of stamp duty reserve tax, see note 2 at the end of the contents list to Part II Stamp Taxes.*

PART III STAMP DUTY AND STAMP DUTY RESERVE TAX

REPEALS

107. Bearers: abolition of stamp duty

Stamp duty under what is now FA 1999 Sch 15 is prospectively abolished. The abolition will have effect in respect of (i) bearer instruments issued on or after the "abolition day" either in or by or on behalf of corporate or unincorporated bodies formed or established in, and (ii) transfers of stock on or after the "abolition day" by means of bearer instruments not issued in or by or on behalf of corporate or unincorporated bodies formed or established in the UK. For these purposes, "abolition day" has the meaning given in FA 1990 s 111.

When originally enacted, this section referred to issues or transfers of bearer instruments in "Great Britain", rather than the UK (and separate rules applied to Northern Ireland, which is not part of Great Britain). The wording was changed by FA 1999 to reflect that the principal provisions on bearer instrument duty, as set out in their recast form in FA 1999 Sch 15, now always refer to events occurring, and/or bodies established, inside or outside the UK, whereas the earlier form of these provisions (in FA 1963 ss 59 and 60) drew a distinction between events occurring, and/or bodies established, inside or outside Great Britain.

108. Transfer of securities: abolition of stamp duty

Stamp duty under FA 1999 Sch 13 (transfer of securities) is prospectively abolished.

The abolition will have effect in respect of instruments executed in pursuance of a contract made on or after the "abolition day" or, in the case of instruments which are not executed in pursuance of a contract or which relate to transfers into depositary receipt schemes or clearance services, executed on or after the "abolition day".

For these purposes "abolition day" has the meaning given in FA 1990 s 111.

109. Stamp duty: other repeals

A number of miscellaneous and consequential provisions are also made.

The fine of £20 (or, from 1 October 1999, the penalty not exceeding £300) payable by any person who in the UK assigns, transfers or negotiates a foreign security or a Commonwealth government security that is not duly stamped will not apply where the assignment, transfer or negotiation is executed or takes place on or after the "abolition day".

The provisions relating to the cancellation of bearer share or stock or unit trust certificates where the holder has been entered on the register are abolished in the case of entries made on or after the "abolition day".

The fine (or, from 1 October 1999, the penalty) payable by a person who completes a blank share transfer delivered to him pursuant to a sale of the shares to which it relates, and then parts with possession of it or removes it offshore, will not apply where the sale takes place on or after the "abolition day".

No notifications to the Commissioners will be required by issuers of depositary receipts or providers of clearance services, or by their respective nominees or agents, where they issue

Part II ST

their first receipts, or provide their first services, or first act as such nominee or agent, on or after the "abolition day", or by companies who first become aware that their shares are held by any such persons on or after that date.

Various ancillary provisions are to cease to have effect as provided by statutory instrument.

For all these purposes, "abolition day" has the meaning given in FA 1990 s 111.

110. Stamp duty reserve tax: abolition

Stamp duty reserve tax is prospectively abolished. The abolition will have effect, so far as the principal charge is concerned, where an unconditional agreement to transfer is made on or after the "abolition day" or where a conditional agreement to transfer becomes unconditional on or after the "abolition day". In so far as arrangements involving depositary receipt schemes and clearance services are concerned, the abolition will have effect where the relevant securities are transferred, issued or appropriated on or after the "abolition day", whenever the arrangements were made.

Similar provisions also apply where there are schemes involving payment for securities by instalments in circumstances where stamp duty reserve tax would be payable; the abolition will have effect where the relevant securities are issued or transferred on sale, pursuant to such schemes, on or after the "abolition day".

Again, for all these purposes "abolition day" has the meaning given in FA 1990 s 111.

111. General

The "abolition day" will be appointed by statutory instrument. It was intended that it should be simultaneous with the Stock Exchange's introduction of its paperless share trading system—TAURUS—but following the decision to abandon TAURUS see the note at the end of the contents list for Part II Stamp Duty and Stamp Duty Reserve Tax. The provisions in relation to the abolitions of stamp duty contained in ss 107 to 109 are to be construed as one with SA 1891.

PAIRED SHARES

112. Stamp duty

This section amends FA 1988 s 143 in relation to "paired share" units offered for sale in the UK, on or after the day on which FA 1990 received the Royal Assent, in circumstances where there has been an earlier offer of "paired share" units in the two companies concerned. As long as in a previous offer equal numbers of units were offered in the relevant countries, units subsequently offered can be offered in unequal numbers in those countries without losing the exemption given by s 143 for bearer instrument duty at the rate of 1.5%.

The rationale behind this section is explained in the Revenue's Press Release of 15 June 1990 [see Appendix 4]. The amendment was made to ensure that rights issues of paired share units receive the same stamp duty treatment as the units of paired shares originally issued, which is consistent with the Government's intention of making it possible for units of paired shares to be traded in the same way as shares in a single company. If the shares comprised in a paired unit are issued in both bearer and registered form, under s 143 as enacted there is an exemption from the bearer instrument duty otherwise chargeable on the issue of the bearer shares in the British company, provided inter alia that the units are issued in equal numbers in both countries. The equal numbers test, however, is one that a rights issue cannot satisfy. When the rights issue is made, the original units will be held unequally in the two countries because of trading between them and a pro rata rights issue is bound to be unequal. This section ensures that rights issues do not have to pass the equal numbers test.

113. Stamp duty reserve tax

Two amendments are made to the definitions of "chargeable securities" for stamp duty reserve tax purposes in FA 1986 s 99.

Again, the rationale for the amendments is explained in the Revenue's Press Release of 15 June 1990 [Appendix 4]. The amendments were made to ensure that rights issues and bonus issues of paired share units receive the same stamp duty reserve tax treatment as the units of paired shares originally issued, which is consistent with the Government's intention of making it possible for units of paired shares to be traded in the same way as shares in a single company.

Under FA 1986 s 99 (as amended by FA 1988 s 144) there is a stamp duty reserve tax charge on the trading of the foreign company's shares as part of the registered units marketed in the UK, provided inter alia that the units are issued in equal numbers in both countries. The equal numbers test, however, is one that a rights issue cannot satisfy. When the rights issue is made, the original units will be held unequally in the two countries because of trading between them and a pro rata rights issue is bound to be unequal. Accordingly, FA 1986 s 99 is amended. Where paired share units of a UK and a foreign company are offered for sale in the UK in circumstances where there has been an earlier offer of such units then, as long as in the earlier offer equal numbers of units were offered in the relevant countries, the units subsequently offered can be offered in unequal numbers in those countries without the shares in the foreign company comprised in the units being excluded from the definition of "chargeable securities" and thereby escaping a stamp duty reserve tax charge on trading.

The inserted FA 1986 s 99 (6B) ensures that bonus issues of paired share units are chargeable securities for stamp duty reserve tax purposes, provided that there has been an earlier offer of such units to which s 99 (6A) applied without the amendment made by subsection (2) of this section (ie the units were offered in equal numbers in the two countries concerned).

INTERNATIONAL ORGANISATIONS

114. International organisations

FA 1984 s 126, enables the Treasury to designate international organisations of which the UK is a member for the purpose of specific exemptions from various taxes. This section amends s 126 to enable such organisations to be given limited exemption from stamp duty reserve tax on the issue of their securities and was enacted as a result of the decision to establish the European Bank for Reconstruction and Development (EBRD) in the UK The Articles of Agreement of the EBRD require exemption from all taxes on the bank's securities which arise solely because they are issued by the bank or because of local factors (ie the place or currency of issue of the securities, or the location of the bank itself). The stamp duty reserve tax charges relieved by this section, which fall within this category, are the higher rate (1.5%) charges which arise on the issue of chargeable securities on a UK register to the nominee for either a depositary bank or a clearance service. The EBRD may decide to make such issues. See also SI 1991/1202—The International Organisations (Tax Exempt Securities) Order 1991.

PART IV MISCELLANEOUS AND GENERAL

GENERAL

131. Interpretation etc

132. Repeals

133. Short title

SCHEDULES

SCHEDULE 19 REPEALS (SECTION 132)

PART VI STAMP DUTY

Repeals are made in accordance with ss 107, 108 and 109.

PART VII STAMP DUTY RESERVE TAX

Repeals are made in accordance with s 110.

Finance Act 1991

1991 Chapter 31

Note: *In relation to the proposed abolitions of all stamp duty charges on property other than land and buildings (including all charges on transactions in shares and bearer instruments) and of stamp duty reserve tax, see note 2 at the end of the contents list to Part II Stamp Taxes.*

110. Stamp duty abolished in certain cases

No stamp duty is to be charged, whether it be ad valorem duty in respect of a "conveyance or transfer on sale" or a fixed duty of 50p (or, with effect from 1 October 1999, £5) in respect of any instrument chargeable to duty under what is now FA 1999 Sch 13 if such instrument is concerned exclusively with property which is "exempt property", meaning property other than land, interests in the proceeds of the sale of land held on trust for sale, and licences to occupy land. Situations where a conveyance or transfer on sale relates partly to "exempt property" and partly to other property are dealt with in the following section.

This section takes effect in respect of all instruments executed on or after the "abolition day" otherwise than pursuant to a contract. In respect of instruments executed pursuant to a contract, the section takes effect where the contract is entered into on or after the "abolition day". The "abolition day" is the day appointed under FA 1990 s 111 (1) for the abolition of stamp duty on transactions in shares, etc. For further details see the commentary on FA 1990 s 111.

111. Stamp duty reduced in certain cases

This section applies if an instrument is chargeable to duty as a "conveyance or transfer on sale" and relates to property part of which is "exempt property" (as defined in the preceding section) and part of which is not. In such cases, the sale consideration is apportioned between the exempt property and the non-exempt property on such basis as is just and reasonable, and the duty is assessed only on that part of the consideration which is apportioned to the non-exempt property. Again, this section applies to instruments executed after the "abolition day" (as defined in the preceding section) or (in the case of instruments executed pursuant to a contract) instruments executed pursuant to a contract entered into on or after the abolition day.

The reduced duty applies only to sale transactions where an instrument is dutiable ad valorem. The fixed duty of 50p (or, as from 1 October 1999, £5) payable on any instrument chargeable under what is now FA 1999 Sch 13 Part III cannot be apportioned where an instrument relates partly to exempt property and partly to non-exempt property. The fixed duty must therefore be paid in full.

112. Apportionment of consideration for stamp duty purposes

SA 1891 s 58 (1) provides that, where property contracted to be sold for a single consideration is conveyed to the purchaser in separate parts by different instruments, the consideration is to be apportioned between the different parts and their respective instruments in such manner as the parties think fit, thus enabling each separate instrument to be assessed with an appropriate amount of ad valorem duty.

The amendments made by this section deal with circumstances where part of the property contracted to be sold consists of "exempt property" (as defined in the preceding section) and part does not. In such cases the consideration is to be apportioned in such manner as is just and reasonable, and not in such manner as the parties think fit.

SA 1891 s 58 (2) provides that, where property is contracted to be purchased for a single consideration by two or more joint purchasers (or persons acting on their behalf) and is conveyed or transferred to the individual purchasers by separate instruments which refer to separate portions of the consideration, then each separate instrument is to be stamped in respect of the separate portions of the consideration specified.

This section amends that provision where part of the property contracted to be purchased consists of "exempt property" (given the same meaning as above) and part does not and the purchasers are all "connected" with one another within the meaning of TA 1988 s 839. In those cases the parties do not have the freedom to determine how much of the consideration is to be apportioned to each separate transfer; the consideration must be apportioned in such manner as is just and reasonable and stamped accordingly. This does not apply where the purchasers are not connected with one another, where the stated consideration can be presumed to have been apportioned on an arm's length basis.

If, despite the above provisions, apportionments of consideration are made in the relevant circumstances which are not just and reasonable, then those apportionments are ignored for stamp duty purposes and stamp duty is charged as if just and reasonable apportionments had been made.

This section applies where the relevant contract is entered into on or after the "abolition day", as defined in the preceding section.

113. Certification of instruments for stamp duty purposes

Under what is now FA 1999 Sch 13 Part I para 4 (formerly FA 1963 s 55), documents may only be charged to duty at less than the highest prevailing rate (which is 4% as from 21 March 2000, subject to certain transitional rules) if they are "certified at" a certain amount. The meaning of this requirement is explained in what is now FA 1999 Sch 13 Part I para 6 (1) (formerly FA 1958 s 34 (4)). Normally, the value of all the property included in one transaction between the same parties has to be taken into account before a certificate of value can be given in relation to the conveyance or transfer of any one item. Previously, however, there was an exception which allowed the value of "goods, wares or merchandise" to be disregarded for the purpose of a certificate of value, except insofar as there was an actual conveyance or transfer of them.

This section prospectively amends what is now FA 1999 Sch 13 Part I para 6 (2) so that it is not just the value of "goods, wares or merchandise" which can be disregarded, but the value of all "exempt property", whether or not there is an actual conveyance or transfer of such property. Again, "exempt property" is given the same meaning as in the preceding sections and this section applies where the relevant instrument is executed on or after the "abolition day", or it is executed in pursuance of a contract and that contract is made on or after the "abolition day".

114. Acquisition under statute: exempt property

This section amends FA 1959 s 36 (4), which itself clarifies FA 1895 s 12. Where an Act of Parliament vests property by way of sale in any person, or authorises any person to purchase property, either the Act (in the first case) or the instrument of conveyance (in the second case) must be produced to the Commissioners duly stamped. FA 1959 s 36 (4) provided that any conveyance required to be produced under this provision need not include any "goods, wares or merchandise" forming part of the relevant property, and if the relevant property consists of "goods, wares or merchandise" no conveyance need be produced.

In respect of any Act passed on or after the "abolition day" (given the same meaning as above) any conveyance required to be produced need not include any "exempt property" (again, given the same meaning as above) forming part of the relevant property, and if the relevant property consists solely of "exempt property" no conveyance need be produced.

116. Investment exchanges and clearing houses: stamp duty

This and the following section conferred on the Treasury regulation-making powers to modify the incidence of stamp duty and stamp duty reserve tax in consequence of the merger between the London Traded Options Market ("LTOM") and the London International Financial Futures Exchange ("LIFFE"), to prevent transactions entered into by market makers in traded options losing exemptions or reliefs which they would otherwise have had but for such merger. The powers were needed since the merger took effect before the proposed introduction by the Stock Exchange of its TAURUS system for paperless share dealing (to be superseded by the CREST system), when the necessary statutory instrument would have been introduced to give effect to the abolition of all stamp duty charges on transactions in shares and of stamp duty reserve tax. Accordingly, The Stamp Duty and Stamp Duty Reserve Tax (Investment Exchanges and Clearing Houses) Regulations 1992 (SI 1992/570) were made pursuant to this section and the next on 9 March 1992 and came into effect on 22 March 1992. See commentary, post. The Stamp Duty Reserve Tax (Tradepoint) Regulations 1995 (SI 1995/2051) were made pursuant to this section and the next and came into effect on 25 August 1995. See SI 1997/2429 and SI 1999/3262. The Stamp Duty and Stamp Duty Reserve Tax (Investment Exchange Clearing Houses) (Jiway Limited) Regulations 2000 (SI 2000/2999) and The Stamp Duty Reserve Tax (Investment Exchanges and Clearing Houses) (The London Stock Exchange) Regulations 2001 (SI 2001/255) were also made pursuant to this section and the next and came into effect on 10 November 2000 and 26 February 2001 respectively. The Stamp Duty and Stamp Duty Reserve Tax (Investment Exchanges and Clearing Houses) (Eurex Clearing AG) Regulations 2007 (SI 2007/1097) were also made under these sections and came into force on 23 April 2007.

Further provision was made by the Stamp Duty and Stamp Duty Reserve Tax (Investment Exchanges and Clearing Houses) Regulations 2004 (SI 2004/3218). See commentary, post.

See also the Revenue Press Releases of 10 July 1991, 18 October 1991, 9 March 1992, 4 August 1995 and 9 November 2000.

The legislation now has a wide effect (in conjunction with a large number of implementing statutory instruments) to prevent charges to SDRT or stamp duty arising where transactions in UK securities are cleared through a central counterparty such as a clearing house. The difficulty can be magnified since the chain of transactions may involve exchange members, their nominees, the clearing house itself and the members and nominees of the clearing house. Each such transaction could give rise to a separate charge to stamp duty or SDRT. In order to obviate such multiple charges, the Treasury is given power to remove all but the last of them: see ss 116(1), 117(1).

In order to remove a doubt which had arisen whether the Treasury had power to include within the scope of the exemption members of the clearing house and nominees of such members (who were not expressly mentioned among the various categories of persons to whom exemption could be afforded by ss 116, 117), the two sections were amended by FA 2010 s 65 to include such persons within the scope of the sections. The amendment (which is wholly ameliorative) is treated as always having had effect.

117. Investment exchanges and clearing houses: SDRT

For the background to this section, see the commentary on the preceding section, above.

Stamp Duty (Temporary Provisions) Act 1992

1992 Chapter 2

This Act is repealed in its entirety by FA 1999 although, in principle, it remains relevant for identifying the threshold for charging duty on documents executed in the period to which the Act related. In the relevant period, duty (other than in relation to "stock") was only charged at 1% under the head "conveyance or transfer on sale" of what was then SA 1891 Sch 1 (now FA 1999 Sch 13 Part I para 1 (1)).

The threshold for the 1% charge was raised from £30,000 to £250,000 in respect of documents executed on or after 21 December 1991 and before 20 August 1992. No duty was payable on the premium for a new lease executed within that period of time if the premium did not exceed £250,000 and the average annual rent was not more than £2,500 (although this did not affect the calculation of any duty which was chargeable by reference to such rent).

Social Security Administration Act 1992

1992 Chapter 5

188. Exemption from stamp duty

(See the notes printed at the end of the contents list to Part II Stamp Taxes.)

Certain documents made pursuant to the Social Security Contributions and Benefits Act 1992 and relating mainly to social security contributions, contributory and non-contributory benefits, and increases for dependants and benefits for industrial injuries, are exempted from stamp duty.

Further and Higher Education Act 1992

1992 Chapter 13

88. Stamp duty

(See the notes printed at the end of the contents list to Part II Stamp Taxes.)

This Act provides for the transfer of sixth form and further education colleges out of local authority control to new further education funding corporations. Certain transfers of properties to those new corporations are exempted from stamp duty.

88A. Stamp duty land tax

This section provides that transactions of the kind exempted from stamp duty by s 88 are correspondingly to be exempted from SDLT. The relief must be claimed on the appropriate land transaction return.

Parliamentary Corporate Bodies Act 1992

1992 Chapter 27

5. Schemes and transfers: supplementary provisions

(See the notes printed at the end of the contents list to Part II Stamp Taxes.)

This Act provides for the establishment of two corporations to hold land and perform other functions for the benefit of the Houses of Parliament. Any transfers of land to such corporations are exempted from stamp duty.

Friendly Societies Act 1992

1992 Chapter 40

105. Exemptions from stamp duty

(See the notes printed at the end of the contents list to Part II Stamp Taxes.)

This Act provides for the cessation of registration under the Friendly Societies Act 1974 and makes provision about disputes involving friendly societies. Any document required or authorised by this Act, the 1974 Act or by the constitution of an incorporated friendly society or of a registered friendly society or registered branch is exempted from stamp duty.

105A. Stamp duty land tax

Land transactions are exempted from SDLT where effected for the purposes of:

(a) an amalgamation of two or more societies; or

(b) a transfer of engagements between two such societies.

The relief must be claimed on the relevant land transaction return.

Museums and Galleries Act 1992

1992 Chapter 44

8. Power to transfer land to governing bodies, and exemption from stamp duty

(See the notes printed at the end of the contents list to Part II Stamp Taxes.)

This Act establishes incorporated Boards of Trustees for certain museums and galleries (for example, the National Gallery and the British Museum). Transfers by the Secretary of State of land vested in him to the newly incorporated Boards of Trustees are exempted from stamp duty.

8A. Stamp duty land tax

A land transaction by which the Secretary of State transfers land to a specified museum or gallery is exempt from SDLT if the land in question is occupied wholly or partly for the purposes of the institution. The relief must be claimed on the relevant land transaction return.

Finance (No 2) Act 1992

1992 Chapter 48

SCHEDULES

SCHEDULE 17 NORTHERN IRELAND ELECTRICITY (SECTION 77)

Stamp duty reserve tax

10.—General exemption from stamp duty reserve tax is given on the transfer of the assets and liabilities of Northern Ireland Electricity to one or more successor companies in preparation for its privatisation.

Finance Act 1993

1993 Chapter 34

PART V STAMP DUTY

202. Rent to mortgage: England and Wales

(See the notes printed at the end of the contents list to Part II Stamp Taxes.)

The Leasehold Reform, Housing and Urban Development Act 1993 added a "rents to mortgages" scheme to the Housing Act 1985 Part V. This gives public sector tenants a new right to buy their homes for an initial payment plus a balance to be met by an interest-free loan from the landlord. That loan is expressed as a percentage of the value of the property, not a cash sum, as the amount needed to redeem it when the purchaser is ready will depend on the value of the property at that time, and on any further discount available. This means that the total purchase price cannot be ascertained at the outset in such a manner as to permit the use of a certificate of value under what is now FA 1999 Sch 13 Part I para 6 (formerly FA 1958 s 34). This in turn would mean, under general principles, that duty would always be payable at the highest prevailing rate even if the actual consideration were ultimately small enough to be charged at a lower rate or to qualify for exemption. (It should also be remembered that this would now place a purchaser in a considerably worse position than he would have faced when this section was originally enacted, since the top rate of duty in 1993 was only 1% but it has since been raised progressively to 4%). Stamp duty will now be charged at the outset on the market value of the property less any discount that may be due.

203. Rent to loan: Scotland

(See the notes printed at the end of the contents list to Part II Stamp Taxes.)

Similar provision to that in s 202 is made in respect of the "rent to loan" scheme in Scotland.

204. Method of denoting stamp duty

Existing legislation requires the use of "impressed" stamps; the Treasury are given power to make regulations governing the method by which the payment of stamp duty is denoted on documents.

Education Act 1993

1993 Chapter 35

299. Stamp duty

(See the notes printed at the end of the contents list to Part II Stamp Taxes.)

This Act provides for the transfer of schools out of local authority control to new incorporated governing bodies thus attaining grant maintained status. Certain transfers of property to those bodies are not chargeable to stamp duty.

Finance Act 1994

1994 Chapter 9

PART VI STAMP DUTY

239. Execution of deeds

Longstanding Stamp Office practice has been that a document in the form of a deed is executed only when it is delivered, ie when the party executing the document considers himself bound by it (or, if delivered subject to conditions, bound by it once those conditions are satisfied). The relevance of the date of execution is that generally duty is determined by reference to the law in force at that date. In Scotland it has been suggested that signature of a deed might constitute execution even if it was never delivered. The change is intended to clarify the position throughout the UK.

The definition of "execution" and "executed" in SA 1891 s 122 (1) is supplemented by providing that a deed is to be treated as executed when delivered or, if later, when the conditions to which it was subject when delivered are satisfied.

The definition of "execution" and "executed", in SDMA 1891 s 27 is replaced with a cross-reference to the amended definition in SA 1891 s 122.

240. Time for presenting agreements for leases

(See the notes printed at the end of the contents list to Part II Stamp Taxes.)

This section has been recast by FA 1999. The original version was designed to ensure that an agreement for lease did not suffer interest and penalties if it had been left unstamped, pending execution of a formal lease, but then had to be presented to the Stamp Office (and so stamped) as part of the process of adjudicating the actual lease granted pursuant to the agreement. (An agreement for lease and an actual lease are both stampable instruments, although any duty paid on the former is credited against any duty payable on the latter—see FA 1999 Sch 13 Part II para 14 (1)–(2), formerly SA 1891 s 75 (1)–(2)—and note that there is no provision for returning any excess if the duty on the agreement exceeds the duty on the lease).

There would often have been good commercial reasons why the process of granting the actual lease took more than 30 days after execution of the initial agreement for lease (ie the period during which the agreement could be stamped after execution without attracting any interest or penalties) and so the agreement would often have been at risk of suffering interest and penalties by the time that the actual lease was presented to the Stamp Office for adjudication. Therefore, this section (in its original form) provided that an agreement for lease was to be treated, for the purposes of stamp duty timing rules, as having been executed at the same time as the lease to which it gave effect.

The new version of this section (as substituted by FA 1999) still provides that relief by treating the agreement as having been executed on the same day as the lease was executed. It also specifically protects an agreement for lease from any penalties, under what is now SA 1891 s 15B, by providing that both the time *and place* of execution of an agreement for lease are to be treated as being the same as those of the actual lease. Therefore, an agreement for lease will now be deemed to be offshore to the extent that any lease to which it gives effect is ever *actually* offshore for any length of time before it is stamped.

However, it should be noted that s 240 (in either its old or its new form) only appears to apply when a lease and an agreement for lease are presented *together* for stamping. If, for example, an agreement for lease was entered into without a formal lease being granted and it was then desired to present the agreement alone for stamping (for instance, pursuant to an attempt to obtain a decree of specific performance against a freeholder who was unwilling to grant a

Part II ST

formal lease), it seems that the ordinary timing rules would apply. In other words, s 240 does not introduce a new *general* timing provision for agreements for leases, merely a special rule where an appropriate pair of documents are presented together.

The new version of this section specifically refers to presentation of the pair of documents "in pursuance of Schedule 13 to the Finance Act 1999". However, in relation to a similarly specific reference in the old version of this section (that reference being to SA 1891 Sch 1, of course) the Stamp Office nonetheless took the view that the special timing rule in this section applied for the purposes of FA 1931 s 28 as well. Presumably, this view will still be maintained.

See also the guidance published in the Tax Bulletin, Issue 18 August 1995, p 234.

240A. Requirements before lease treated as duly stamped

(See the notes printed at the end of the contents list to Part II Stamp Taxes.)

A lease will be duly stamped only if either:

(a) it contains a certificate that there is no antecedent agreement to which it gives effect; or

(b) (i) it has been stamped to the effect that the agreement to which it gives effect is not liable for duty or (ii) the duty paid on the agreementt has been denoted on the lease.

This section was originally an integral part of s 240 above (in the form in which that section existed before the enactment of FA 1999) and reference should be made to the commentary on that section—see above.

241. Exchange, partition, etc

(See the notes printed at the end of the contents list to Part II Stamp Taxes.)

Previously SA 1891 s 73 provided a special regime where one freehold property (or, in Scotland, heritable property) was exchanged for another freehold property. Broadly, ad valorem duty (at the then usual rate of 1%) was payable only on any equality money payable as part of the exchange. Land transactions where the consideration did not take a form liable to conveyance on sale duty by virtue of SA 1891 ss 55–57 (broadly cash, stock or marketable securities, periodical payments or the assumption of a liability) did not attract ad valorem duty.

This section applies when:

(a) the consideration for any transfer or vesting of land consists of any "property" (which need not be land, buildings or other real property), and

(b) no amount or value is attributed to that property on the transfer or vesting of the land.

In the circumstances the consideration, if it consists only of the property, or that part of the consideration, if it comprises other assets as well as the property, for the transfer shall be taken to be the market value of the property—note *not* the market value of the land being transferred or vested—immediately before execution of the stampable document.

As to how HMRC envisage this section operating see their detailed guidance published in Tax Bulletin, Issue 18 August 1995, p 234 (Appendix 6). See also FA 2000 s 118 (Land transferred etc for other property).

It should be noted that this section not only extends the normal notion of "sale" for the purposes of charging duty on a "conveyance or transfer on sale" under what is now FA 1999 Sch 13 Part I but it also provides for duty to be calculated and charged in a similar manner on the grant of a new lease (including an agreement for lease) under what is now FA 1999 Sch 13 Part II.

HMRC's views of the meaning of this section appear in some respects to be too restrictive, reading the legislation in ways which are arguably more generous to the taxpayer than a natural reading would suggest, in isolation. To the extent that the *McGuckian* principle (see commentary on FA 1999 s 112) represents the way forward for interpretation for stamp duty legislation, HMRC's published views are probably correct in the main, since HMRC take the (arguably over-simplistic) view that if, for example, a house could have been sold for £100,000 in money but is instead exchanged for land, goods or valuable rights worth £100,000, s 241 merely "corrects" existing law and ensures that stamp duty is charged on a total of £100,000 worth of consideration.

The market value of property is the price that property might reasonably be expected to fetch on sale at the relevant time in the open market; even though in many cases the transfer or vesting of the land might occur some time after agreement to transfer or vest the land had been reached, at which time the value of the property might have been different. It is an open question whether the hypothetical "open market" involved is one in which it is possible to take account of special purchasers and/or special factors which might increase or depress the price which might otherwise be obtained.

There would appear to be some doubt as to the interface, if any, between SA 1891 s 58 (4) and this section (and/or s 242 below). Suppose, for example, that A agrees to sell freehold land to B for a price in money and B agrees to sell the same freehold to C, the consideration being C's agreement to grant a long lease of the same land to B. Sub-sale relief is not available unless the consideration provided by the sub-purchaser (ie C) is at least equal to "the value of the property immediately before the contract of sale" between the sub-purchaser and the person agreeing to sell to him.

The reference to "the value of the property" is stated, in SA 1891 s 58 (7), to mean the open market value. It is considered that the consideration for the second agreement referred to above will not necessarily be at least the open market value of the freehold transferred. Section 241 (1) provides that where the consideration for the transfer of an interest in land "consists of or includes any property", then the consideration is taken to be the market value of *that* property—ie the new lease, not the freehold to be transferred—if "no amount or value is, apart from this section, attributed to that property".

The problem arises because the property to be valued under s 58 (4) is the freehold being transferred while under FA 1994 s 241 the relevant value is that of the lease being granted. In such a situation, s 58 (4) effectively requires the consideration for a transfer of the freehold to be at least equal to the then market value of a leasehold and a freehold of the same land are ever identical, since the implication of such a conclusion would be that the two estates in the land were identical. Presumably, valuers do not regard such estates as completely identical in practice (even in the case of very long leases) and even if some valuers do take this view, there must be some risk of the Stamp Office challenging such a valuation on the basis that it is conceptually incorrect.

Since s 241 is stated to apply only where "no amount or value is, apart from this section, attributed" to the consideration, it would appear to be open to the parties to attribute their own value to the property in question and so to agree to disapply s 241. Thus, the risk can possibly be avoided, by drafting the consideration clause in such a way that the freehold is stated to be transferred by B to C for a cash price but that such price is to be satisfied by means of the grant of a new lease of the same land to B. However, the Stamp Office maintain (see paragraph 10 of the guidance notes) that part of the consideration—and more than a merely nominal part—must be paid in money for there to be a "sale".

Quite apart from this, however, there appears to be a further risk in terms of the choice of wording for this type of clause. This is because the whole point of such wording is to avoid creating an element of consideration which is "unascertainable" for the purposes of FA 1994 s 242 (1). It is necessary to avoid s 242 because that section would also have the effect of introducing the market value of the new lease as the deemed consideration for transfer of the freehold which, as explained above, is likely to be an insufficient consideration to allow SA 1891 s 58 (4) to be utilised.

It is arguable that an agreement or transfer simply for "open market value" (ie an agreement which actually states those words in the consideration clause) is in itself a sufficient verbal formula to avoid unascertainability since, by definition, open market value is a value that can be "ascertained" by means of a valuation, and is therefore merely *unascertained* before such valuation, rather than unascertainable.

It would perhaps be easier to avoid any taint of unascertainability (and/or introduce greater commercial certainty into the terms of the agreement) if it were possible to use a formula along the lines of "£x+y" where x was a fixed sum and y was such other sum as produced a total price equal to market price at the relevant time. Unfortunately, although this might be more convincing as an "ascertainable" figure (since, by definition, one part of it would already be ascertained), it is also more likely to restrict the availability of sub-sale relief. This is because s 58 (4) refers to the "chargeable consideration" being less than the value of the property to be sold. The phrase "chargeable consideration" is defined in s 58 (7) as "consideration which falls to be brought into account in determining the duty" and is not necessarily the same as the actual consideration.

In the above formula, only x would be "chargeable consideration". This is because, where consideration is stated to be a specified sum which may vary up or down in certain circumstances, stamp duty is charged on the specified figure and the possibility of variations is ignored. This so-called "contingency principle" has not been replaced by the general statutory rule in s 242 (1) since s 242 (3) (*a*) preserves the contingency principle (to some extent at least—see also the commentary on leases in FA 1999 Sch 13 Part II).

Therefore, if a situation arose where x was in fact less than the prevailing market price at the relevant time, the fact that the purchaser of the property ultimately paid more than x would not alter the fact that stamp duty was calculated only by reference to x. Thus the "chargeable consideration" (although not the actual consideration) would be less than "the value" for the purposes of SA 1891 s 58 (4) or (7). This would appear to prevent sub-sale relief being available in such a case.

This provision now needs to be read in conjunction with FA 2000 ss 118 and 121.

242. Where consideration not ascertainable from conveyance or lease

(See the notes printed at the end of the contents list to Part II Stamp Taxes.)

As a general rule ad valorem duty can only be charged if the consideration is ascertained or, if unascertained, capable of ascertainment at the time a document is presented for stamping. However, case law has established that where there is an upper or lower limit on the amount of otherwise unascertainable consideration (or a "basic figure" which might later vary upwards or downwards), duty is to be calculated as if the consideration were equal to that maximum or minimum (or basic) figure—the so-called "contingency principle": see for instance *IRC v Coventry City Council* [1978] STC 151, *L M Tenancies 1 plc v IR Comrs* [1996] STC 880, and the commentaries on FA 1999 Sch 13 Part I para 1 (2) and Part II.

Where the consideration, or any part of the consideration, for the transfer or vesting of any land, or the grant of any lease, is unascertainable at the date of execution of the relevant document the consideration is assumed to be equal to the market value of the land in question or the lease immediately before execution of the document. Similarly, where rent, or any part of the rent, under a lease cannot be ascertained, market rent (as defined below) is substituted. It should be noted, that for rent or for any other consideration covered by s 242, the market value rules *completely* replace the actual rent or consideration where *any part* of the rent or consideration cannot be ascertained.

This provision is likely to result, in practice, in significant compliance costs in relation to genuinely commercial arrangements. For example, where a shop lease has (as many do) a rent including an element based on turnover which is unquantifiable at the outset, market value will have to be determined by a valuer and substituted for the rent to enable it to be duly stamped!

Where the contingency principle would have operated to ascertain the amount on which duty was payable, these provisions do not apply (but query whether the "new" contingency principle would always oust the statutory rules—see commentary on FA 1999 Sch 13 Part II).

The market rent of a lease is the rent which the lease might have been expected to fetch in the open market.

The definition of "market value" in s 241 above applies equally for the purpose of s 242 (1), as do the comments on valuation in s 241.

As to how HMRC envisage this section operating see their detailed guidance published in Tax Bulletin, Issue 18, August 1995, p 234 (Appendix 6).

This provision now needs to be read in conjunction with the numerous provisions requiring transfer duty to be calculated by reference to market value (see FA 1994 s 241; FA 2000 ss 118–121).

243. Agreements to surrender leases

(See the notes printed at the end of the contents list to Part II Stamp Taxes.)

An agreement for surrender, or in Scotland renunciation, is from 7 December 1993 as dutiable as if it were itself a deed, but only if the surrender or renunciation itself is carried out otherwise than by deed.

The Stamp Office Budget Notes state that "the charge will apply to any document evidencing the agreement . . . , whether it is a formal agreement or simply a letter outlining the terms of the procedure to be followed". The latter statement seems of doubtful authority if, for instance, the letter outlines a procedure to be followed *if* agreement is reached where no agreement at that time has been reached. This now appears to be accepted by the Stamp Office: see the guidance published in Tax Bulletin, Issue 18, August 1995, p 234 (Appendix 6).

It should be noted that nothing in the statutory wording specifically requires the agreement in question to be an agreement between either or both of the landlord and tenant of the lease to be surrendered. Also, the section refers only to the surrender of a "lease" and it appears to be an open question whether an agreement (for a sum of money or other relevant consideration) to cancel or surrender a mere *agreement for lease* is stampable ad valorem. The word "lease" is usually used in a stamp duty context only in the strict sense of a formally granted legal estate in land, and not as extending to a mere agreement to make such a grant (such an extended interpretation is generally the result of an express statutory definition—see, for example, the definition sections of the Land Registration Act 1925 and the Capital Allowances Act 1990). It is arguable that an agreement to surrender or cancel an agreement for lease (as opposed to an actual lease) is stampable under what is now FA 1999 Sch 13 Part I para 7 or an agreement for the "sale" of a contractual right and/or sale of a purely equitable interest in land but, on the authority of cases such as *Cormack's Trustees v IRC* 1924 SC 819 it is also arguable that the mere release of rights does not involve a sale or an agreement for sale, if there is nothing in the nature of a disposition of "property". Although contractual rights are capable of constituting "property" for stamp duty purposes (see, for example, *Potter v IRC* (1854) 10 Exch 147) it appears that they are only property in the context of possible marketability or assignability, and that (see commentary on what is now FA 1999 Sch 13 Part I para 1 (2)) the economic and legal value of contractual rights is not "property" as between the contracting parties themselves. On this basis, it is possible that an agreement to surrender the benefit of an earlier agreement is outside the scope of the "conveyance or transfer on sale" head of charge (including the extension thereto in what is now FA 1999 Sch 13 Part I para 7), at least where the surrender agreement is merely between the parties to the lease agreement (the involvement of any other parties might well involve an equitable assignment of contractual rights, which would appear to be dutiable).

Schemes to effect the surrender of leases without creating an agreement to surrender a lease now need to be considered in the light of FA 2000 s 127.

244. Production of documents on transfer of land in Northern Ireland

(See the notes printed at the end of the contents list to Part II Stamp Taxes.)

A version of the particulars delivered arrangements (see FA 1931 s 28) is introduced into Northern Ireland and documents relating to transactions for which the consideration is below the relevant stamp duty threshold can be sent direct to the appropriate registrar. This brings the position in Northern Ireland into line with that already operating in the rest of the UK under FA 1931 s 28, FA 1985 s 89 and SI 1985/1688 whereby appropriate documents can be sent direct to the relevant Land Registry without production to the Stamp Office.

Where there is a transfer on sale of freehold land in Northern Ireland or the grant, or transfer on sale, of a lease over such land—and by virtue of s 245 (5) this extends to agreements for lease of such land—the transferee, lessee or proposed lessee has to produce the relevant instrument to HMRC. The relevant transferee, lessee etc must produce the instrument with a document containing appropriate particulars.

There are criminal penalties for non-production of a document within 30 days of the relevant time.

If an agreement for lease of Northern Ireland land is produced to HMRC, together with the relevant particulars, then the resulting lease or any other further document need not be produced provided that the lease is not "inconsistent" with the agreement. HMRC will, upon request, denote on a "consistent lease" that the agreement has been produced to them.

Only documents which, being required to be produced under s 244, have been denoted with a stamp showing that they have been produced will be deemed to be duly stamped.

245. Production of documents: supplementary

(See the notes printed at the end of the contents list to Part II Stamp Taxes.)

Exemption from the requirements of s 244 is given to certain instruments and may be given in respect of such documents as may be prescribed by statutory instrument: such regulations may contain provisions requiring transfers on sale, leases or agreements for leases of land in Northern Ireland so exempted to be produced to the Commissioner of Valuation for Northern Ireland (see Stamp Duty (Production of Documents) (Northern Ireland) Regulations 1996, SI 1996/2348). It is particularly to be noted that exemption is granted to any instrument relating solely to a SDLT transaction.

HMRC may pass information provided under the PD procedure to the Commissioner.

There is a criminal penalty for any breach of any requirement contained in regulations.

The meaning of "lease" is extended to underleases and other tenancies, and to agreements for leases, underleases etc; consequentially extended definitions apply to "lessee" and "grant"; and mortgages, charges or other liens on property are excluded.

Regulations (which can make different provisions for different cases) are subject to annulment by the House of Commons.

The Treasury shall, by statutory instrument, bring ss 244 and 245 into force from an appointed day.

Coal Industry Act 1994

1994 Chapter 21

SCHEDULES

SCHEDULE 4

PART II STAMP DUTY AND STAMP DUTY RESERVE TAX

Transactions attracting exemptions

26.—This Act provides for a reorganisation of the coal industry and for certain restructuring schemes. Certain transactions whereby property, rights or liabilities are vested in a public-sector body as part of such reorganisation are exempt transactions.

Stamp duty

(See the notes printed at the end of the contents list to Part II Stamp Taxes.)

27.—Exempt transactions which relate to a restructuring scheme do not give rise to any charge to stamp duty. Transfers by the Treasury or the Secretary of State, or any nominee of the Treasury or the Secretary of State of securities from companies owned by the Crown to successor companies are not chargeable to stamp duty.

Stamp duty reserve tax

28.—Certain agreements connected with restructuring schemes and exempt transactions or transfers of securities by the Treasury or the Secretary of State are not chargeable to stamp duty reserve tax.

Finance Act 1995

1995 Chapter 4

PART V STAMP DUTY

149. Transfer: associated bodies

(See the notes printed at the end of the contents list to Part II Stamp Taxes.)

Previously, two bodies corporate had been associated if either one body corporate was the beneficial owner of not less than 90% of the issued share capital of the other, or a third body corporate was the beneficial owner of not less than 90% of the issued share capital of both bodies corporate. This section extended relief under FA 1930 s 42 to 75% groups and subtly restricts the relief by measuring the relationship using ordinary share capital rather than issued share capital. However, it should be noted that "ordinary share capital" is the subject of a special definition for this purpose (see further discussion under FA 1930 s 42) and that certain types of share with rather limited rights could still possibly qualify as "ordinary share capital" for these purposes.

151. Lease or tack: associated bodies

(See the notes printed at the end of the contents list to Part II Stamp Taxes.)

Group relief, which used to be confined to stamp duty on a "conveyance or transfer on sale", is extended by this section to cover a lease, an agreement for lease and an agreement with respect to letting, which would otherwise be chargeable to duty under what is now FA 1999 Sch 13 Part II. In order to qualify for relief the lessor and lessee must be associated bodies corporate at the time the instrument is executed. Unlike FA 1930 s 42, there does not appear to be a requirement that the beneficial ownership of the lease or agreement for lease must pass and vest. In the case of an agreement for a lease or letting, it is the agreement which must be between associated bodies corporate. Under s 151 (2) (*c*) an agreement for lease or letting between associated bodies corporate A and B can still qualify for relief if it includes a term allowing the lease to be granted to body corporate C, provided C was associated to B at the time of execution of the agreement, even if C was not associated to A at that time. It would seem, however, that stamp duty would be payable on the actual lease if granted by A to C and relief under what is now FA 1999 Sch 13 Part II para 14 (2) would not apply.

As in the case of relief under FA 1930 s 42, applying to conveyances and transfers on sale, anti-avoidance rules apply. Thus, relief is denied if the instrument is executed in pursuance of or in connection with an arrangement falling within FA 1995 s 151 (3). The arrangements described in that section correspond with the arrangements provided for in FA 1967 s 27 (3) (*a*) and (*c*) and the same principles should apply. As in s 42 cases, there does not appear to be any mechanism for restoring a right to relief if there is an offending "arrangement" which ultimately fails to result in any kind of prohibited transaction involving an unrelated third party (see discussion under FA 1967 s 27).

The same meaning of "associated bodies corporate" applies for relief under FA 1995 s 151 as for relief under FA 1930 s 42 (see s 149 above).

It is presumed that any change of practice on the part of the Stamp Office in relation to the allowing of intra-group relief under FA 1930 s 42 in the context of corporate partnerships (see commentary on that section) will be equally applicable to the similar relief granted under this section.

A lease, agreement for lease or agreement with respect to letting with regard to which relief is relied upon will not be treated as duly stamped until it has been adjudicated under SA 1891 s 12 and the Stamp Office have issued a pro-forma statutory declaration for this purpose. The instrument should therefore be submitted for adjudication within the usual 30 day time period following execution.

See Statement of Practice SP 3/98 in Appendix 2. Readers are also referred to FA 2002 s 111 under which group relief for transfers of land (including lease grants) in the UK may be withdrawn if the transferee leaves the group within 2 years.

PART VI MISCELLANEOUS AND GENERAL

152. Open-ended investment companies

(See the notes printed at the end of the contents list to Part II Stamp Taxes.)

This section contains power to allow regulations to be made by the Treasury, applying various taxes, including both stamp duty and stamp duty reserve tax, to OEICs. Such regulations have been made in relation to stamp duty and stamp duty reserve tax—see commentary on SI 1997/1156. For a general discussion of the nature of OEICs (which are like ordinary companies in terms of their formal legal mechanics but are more like units trusts in practice), and the stamp duty and stamp duty reserve tax issues arising in relation to such entities, see *Monroe & Nock on the Law of Stamp Duties* (7th edition), paras 10–45 et seq.

Health Authorities Act 1995

1995 Chapter 17

SCHEDULES

SCHEDULE 2 TRANSITIONAL PROVISIONS AND SAVINGS (SECTION 4 (1))

(See the notes printed at the end of the contents list to Part II Stamp Taxes.)

This Act provides for a reorganisation of the Health Service and abolishes Regional Health Authorities, District Health Authorities and Family Health Service Authorities. Certain transfers of property, rights and liabilities from the above bodies to a specified Health Authority, Special Health Authority or NHS trust are not chargeable to stamp duty or stamp duty land tax. Exemption from SDLT must be claimed on the relevant land transaction return.

Merchant Shipping Act 1995

1995 Chapter 21

PART VIII LIGHTHOUSES

221. Exemption from taxes, duties, rates etc

(See the notes printed at the end of the contents list to Part II Stamp Taxes.)

All instruments used by or under any general lighthouse authority in carrying on lighthouse-related services are exempted from stamp duty. All instruments used by or under the directions of the Secretary of State in putting the lighthouse-related provisions in this Act into effect are exempted from stamp duty and stamp duty land tax. Relief from SDLT must be claimed on the appropriate land transaction return.

SCHEDULES

SCHEDULE 9 GENERAL TRANSFER OF LOCAL LIGHTHOUSES TO HARBOUR AUTHORITIES (SECTION 202)

(See the notes printed at the end of the contents list to Part II Stamp Taxes.)

This Schedule provides for the transfer of lighthouses, buoys and beacons from each general lighthouse authority to the relevant harbour authority. Under s 221 (3) stamp duty is not chargeable on the transfers referred to in this Schedule.

Environment Act 1995

1995 Chapter 25

PART V MISCELLANEOUS, GENERAL AND SUPPLEMENTAL PROVISIONS

119. Stamp duty

(See the notes printed at the end of the contents list to Part II Stamp Taxes.)

This Act provides for the establishment of the bodies corporate known as the Environment Agency and the Scottish Environment Protection Agency. Certain transfers of property, rights and liabilities to these bodies and related transfer schemes are not chargeable to stamp duty.

Atomic Energy Authority Act 1995

1995 Chapter 37

SCHEDULE 3 TAXATION PROVISIONS (SECTION 8)

PART III STAMP DUTY AND STAMP DUTY RESERVE TAX

Transactions attracting exemptions

23.—This Act provides for schemes for the transfer of the property, rights and liabilities of the United Kingdom Atomic Energy Authority (the Authority) to a successor company or companies. Certain transactions under the Act whereby property, rights or liabilities are vested in the Authority, its wholly-owned subsidiary or a company wholly-owned by the Crown are exempt transactions.

Stamp duty

(See the notes printed at the end of the contents list to Part II Stamp Taxes.)

24.—An exempt transaction which is a transfer scheme, or is certified to have been made in pursuance of or for the purpose of modifying the effect of a transfer scheme, does not give rise to any charge to stamp duty.

Stamp duty reserve tax

25.—Any agreement which is for purposes connected with giving effect to a transfer scheme relating to any exempt transaction does not give rise to stamp duty reserve tax.

Finance Act 1996

1996 Chapter 8

PART VI STAMP DUTY AND STAMP DUTY RESERVE TAX

STAMP DUTY

186. Transfers of securities to members of electronic transfer systems etc

The introduction of the CREST paperless share transfer system will lead to the transfer of shares to members of CREST to hold in custody. Instruments effecting these transfers would normally be subject to 50p stamp duty (or £5, as from 1 October 1999) in the same way as any other transfer not on sale, but this section exempts such transfers (and transfers into any other paperless system approved under the Treasury regulations) from stamp duty with effect from 1 July 1996. Any charge to stamp duty under FA 1986 s 70 (clearance services) is also removed by virtue of s 186. The section does not give exemption from stamp duty reserve tax and indeed it is specifically stated in FA 1986 s 88(1A) that this exemption is to be disregarded when considering, for the purposes of the conditions under which stamp duty reserve tax is charged, whether a "duly stamped" instrument exists. However, transfers under s 186 would generally be for no consideration so that stamp duty reserve tax will not generally be a significant issue but, in principle, a stamp duty reserve tax charge can apply, for example on a transfer for a consideration or into a clearance service.

PART VII MISCELLANEOUS AND SUPPLEMENTAL

MISCELLANEOUS: OTHER MATTERS

202. Gilt stripping

Treasury regulations as regards government securities may impose a charge to stamp duty or stamp duty reserve tax.

Finance Act 1997

1997 Chapter 16

PART VII STAMP DUTY AND STAMP DUTY RESERVE TAX

STAMP DUTY

95. Mergers of authorised unit trusts

(See the notes printed at the end of the contents list to Part II Stamp Taxes.)

It should be noted that although this section ceases to have effect as from 1 July 1999 with regard to its primary purpose, it remains relevant for an incidental purpose. This is that a similar temporary relief to that described below was introduced by statutory instrument (see commentary on SI 1997/1156) for merger of authorised unit trusts with open-ended investment companies, and this relief has now been extended beyond the deadline of 30 June 1999 originally imposed. No new deadline has been set because the intention is that the current temporary relief will continue to be available until one year after further regulations have been introduced. Therefore, the basic conditions for relief referred to below now continue to be of some relevance for an indeterminate further period. However, it should be noted that, in the press release (issued on 26 May 1999) announcing the extension, the Government stated that it "sees no case for making the exemption permanent".

Mergers are usually documented by a merger agreement pursuant to which the target trust and acquiring trust agree that the target trust will transfer its assets and liabilities to the acquiring trust in consideration of the issue of units by the acquiring trust to the target trust's unitholders. Formal conveyances or transfers are executed of those assets (such as UK land) which require them. An authorised unit trust investing in quoted UK securities will find that most of its underlying assets are transferred in dematerialised form through the CREST paperless share transfer system so that stamp duty reserve tax, rather than stamp duty, will be the concern on a merger (see s 100 below).

Before s 95 came into force the position was that where there was a common trustee for both funds there was no need to transfer legal title to the underlying assets and beneficial ownership would generally pass into the continuing fund without writing by operation of law on the passing of the necessary resolutions to approve the merger so no stamp duty would arise (although the Stamp Office's view was that stamp duty reserve tax would apply where the target trust's assets included chargeable securities). Where there were different trustees the merger agreement would generally be exempt from stamp duty under what is now FA 1999 Sch 13 Part I para 7 but formal transfers of the underlying assets would be subject to stamp duty as conveyances or transfers on sale (ie in consideration of new units).

Under this section there is a two year amnesty providing exemption from all heads of stamp duty (transfer on sale duty being the obvious head) for instruments transferring the underlying assets of an authorised unit trust to another authorised unit trust: (1) executed on or after 19 March 1997 and before 1 July 1999: (6). "Unit" and "unit trust scheme" have the same meaning as in FA 1946 s 57 (see commentary): (4). "Authorised unit trust" means a unit trust scheme designated by order under the Financial Services Act 1986 s 78: (4).

The conditions for the relief to apply are: (2):

(a) that the instrument of transfer is executed pursuant to an arrangement (eg the merger agreement) under which all the underlying assets of the target trust (other than assets retained to meet liabilities of the trustees of the target trust) are transferred to the trustees of the acquiring trust: (4);

(b) under the arrangement all the units in the target trust are extinguished;

Part II ST

(c) the consideration under the arrangement consists of (i) only the issue of units in the acquiring trust to target trust unitholders whose units have been extinguished or (ii) the issue of units together with the assumption or discharge by the trustees of the acquiring trust of liabilities of the trustees of the target trust;
(d) the consideration units issued by the acquiring trust must be issued pro rata to the target trust unitholders' holdings of the extinguished units.

An instrument of transfer of target trust's underlying assets which qualifies for relief under this section is not to be taken as duly stamped unless formally adjudicated not chargeable under SA 1891 s 12: (3).

Each of the parts of an umbrella scheme is regarded as a separate authorised unit trust for the purposes of this section: (5).

96. Demutualisation of insurance companies
(See the notes printed at the end of the contents list to Part II Stamp Taxes.)

This section provides exemption from stamp duty for any instrument of transfer executed on or after 19 March 1997 in connection with the demutualisation of an insurance company when the following conditions are fulfilled:
(a) the transfer is an insurance business transfer scheme to which FSMA 2000 Pt 7 (control of business transfers) applies, or a transfer of the whole or part of the business of a general insurance company which operates through a branch or agency in the UK under an authorisation granted overseas under the relevant provisions of the Life Assurance Consolidation Directive or the Third Non-Life Insurance Directive;
(b) the transfer must be of the whole or any part of the business carried on by a mutual insurance company ("Mutual") (as defined in subsection (8)): subsection (1);
(c) the transferee must be a company which has share capital: subsection (1);
(d) the consideration must take the form of shares in the transferee or its 100% parent: subsections (2), (6);
(e) those shares must be offered to at least 90% (or such lower percentage as is substituted by regulation pursuant to subsection (9)) of the members of the Mutual, thus allowing the offer to exclude certain members, for example on the basis of length of time of membership or size of interest: subsection (3);
(f) the entire share capital of the issuing company in issue immediately after the transfer (except for shares issued or to be issued to the public on a public flotation of the issuing company) must have been offered to members of the Mutual, persons who are entitled to become members of the Mutual, or employees, former employees or pensioners of the Mutual or a wholly owned subsidiary (as defined in subsection (6)) of the Mutual: subsection (4). Employees and pensioners are defined in subsection (8).

The Treasury may by regulations make it possible to adjust the conditions for the relief, if necessary, to cater for cases where a Mutual has more than one class of member and not all classes are to be offered shares on a demutualisation.

By virtue of subsection (5), such an instrument of transfer is not to be taken as duly stamped unless formally adjudicated not chargeable under SA 1891 s 12.

97. Relief for intermediaries

This section introduces a new stamp duty relief for on-exchange transactions in shares by intermediaries on a regulated market in the UK or elsewhere in the European Economic Area (EEA), or a recognised foreign exchange, on which shares of the relevant kind are regularly traded. The new relief replaces the existing relief for market makers with effect from 20 October 1997. See the commentary on FA 1986 ss 80A, 80B.

98. Repurchases and stock lending

This section provides a stamp duty relief on stock borrowing and repo (sale and repurchase agreements), provided (*a*) the arrangements are effected on an exchange in the EEA or a recognised foreign exchange; and (*b*) that the stock is of a kind which is regularly traded on that exchange. This new relief supersedes the more limited stock borrowing relief for market makers. It has effect from 20 October 1997. See the commentary on FA 1986 s 80C.

99. Depositary receipts and clearance services

This section removes provisions setting a 1% rate of duty in certain cases where dealers who are not market makers transfer shares into depository receipt schemes or clearance services. The introduction of the new relief for intermediaries makes these provisions largely unnecessary. The change applies from the same date as the relief for intermediaries, ie 20 October 1997. See the commentary on FA 1986 ss 67, 69, 70.

STAMP DUTY RESERVE TAX

100. Mergers of authorised unit trusts

Under subsection (1) there is a two year amnesty providing exemption from the principal stamp duty reserve tax charge for agreements made (or, if conditional, when the condition is satisfied) on or after 19 March 1997 and before 1 July 1999) to transfer chargeable securities on a merger of authorised unit trusts from the target trust to the acquiring trust where the conditions set out in subsection (2) are fulfilled. Those conditions, broadly, mirror the conditions which apply for stamp duty exemption under FA 1997 s 95. This exemption is relevant only where the target trust owns "chargeable securities" as defined in FA 1986 s 99. It is of limited relevance where the agreement is completed by a transfer, as adjudication of the transfer, as exempt from stamp duty under FA 1997 s 95, would in any case cancel the stamp duty reserve tax liability on the agreement; however, where the transfer of the securities is settled through the CREST paperless settlement system, it will avoid the need to rematerialise the securities in order to obtain adjudication of the transfer under SA 1891 s 12.

If the transfer or agreement to transfer underlying property of the target trust to the acquiring trust pursuant to a merger arrangement is exempt under FA 1997 s 95 (1) or 100 (1), an agreement (or deemed agreement under FA 1986 s 88 (1E)) to transfer a unit in the target trust to the managers of the target trust in order that the unit may be extinguished under the same arrangement is also exempt from the principal charge to stamp duty reserve tax.

101. Direction to hold trust property on other trusts

This section provides a two-year amnesty from the principal charge to stamp duty reserve tax for certain agreements made (or in the case of conditional agreements where the condition is satisfied) on or after 19 March 1997 but before 1 July 1999) effecting the merger of the assets of one trust (the absorbed trust) into the assets of another trust. The exemption is subject to a number of conditions.

Unlike the exemption under FA 1997 ss 95 (1) and 100 (1), the exemption applies not to transfers and agreements to transfer assets from one authorised unit trust to another authorised unit trust, but where there is only one authorised unit trust and the assets of trusts within it are merged. One of the conditions of the exemption is therefore that the trustees of the absorbed trust must be the same persons as the trustees of the continuing trust, in other words legal ownership of the assets subject to both the absorbed and the continuing trusts remains the same.

The exemption only applies if the merger takes a particular form: the agreement to transfer securities must be constituted by a direction of the unitholders in the absorbed trust to the trustees of the continuing trust to hold the whole of the available property of the absorbed trust (as defined in subsection (4)) on the trusts of the continuing trust.

The remaining conditions are identical to those which apply to the exemption under FA 1997 s 100 (1): extinction of units, consideration in the form of units issued pro rata to holdings of extinguished units and, optionally, assumption or discharge of liabilities.

The two year amnesty also extends to an agreement or deemed agreement to transfer a unit to the managers of the absorbed trust which is made in order that the unit may be extinguished: (3).

The FA 1997 s 100 definitions of authorised unit trust and unit are borrowed for the purposes of s 101.

102. Relief for intermediaries

This section introduces a stamp duty reserve tax relief for intermediaries parallel to the stamp duty relief provided by s 97. It replaces the former reliefs for market makers and broker dealers with effect from 20 October 1997. See the commentary on FA 1986 ss 88A, 88B.

103. Repurchases and stock lending

This section provides a relief from stamp duty reserve tax for stock borrowing and repo arrangements, in parallel to the stamp duty relief under s 98. See the commentary on FA 1986 s 89AA.

104. Depositary receipts and clearance services

This section makes parallel amendments to s 97 to the stamp duty reserve tax provisions for depositary receipts and clearance services. See the commentary on FA 1986 ss 93, 94, 96.

Finance Act 1999

1999 Chapter 16

PART 6 STAMP DUTY AND STAMP DUTY RESERVE TAX

109. Interest and penalties in late stamping

(See the notes printed at the end of the contents list to Part II Stamp Taxes.)

This amends the law relating to interest and penalties on late stamping by inserting new ss 15, 15A and 15B into SA 1891 and making consequential amendments. It also gives effect to Sch 12 below in which further amendments are made: see commentaries on SA 1891 ss 12, 12A, 13, 13A and 13B and FA 1994 ss 240 and 240A.

110. Interest on repayment of duty overpaid

(See the notes printed at the end of the contents list to Part II Stamp Taxes.)

It was noted in earlier editions of this work that there was no statutory basis for the payment of interest by HMRC on repayments of overpaid stamp duty, other than in relation to appeals under the old version of SA 1891 s 13. It seems that HMRC did sometimes make *ex gratia* payments in lieu of interest where they had held large sums of money in respect of a claim to duty if such claim was ultimately conceded to be groundless. However, this practice is now given a statutory footing with effect from 1 October 1999. The rate of repayment interest is to be set by the Treasury from time to time under the provisions of FA 1989 s 178 which now apply a common set of interest provisions to most UK taxes.

This section applies not only to payments which are actually payments of stamp duty but also to any amounts which are lodged with the Stamp Office on account of stamp duty under SA 1891 s 15A(2) or FA 1999 s 110(3). However, the new interest rules could also be seen as imposing a further indirect sanction (see SA 1891 s 12A for the main such sanction) on a person who changes his mind about stamping a document, even though the taxpayer has a perfect legal right to decide that he will not pay duty, whether before or after seeking the Stamp Office's opinion as to the duty chargeable upon a document.

The indirect sanction arises because one of the conditions required for obtaining repayment interest under this section is that "the instrument is duly stamped". This seems to mean that a person could only claim statutory interest on the return of a payment on account to the extent, if any, that the payment on account represented an overestimate of the document's actual liability to duty. If a person simply changed his mind and asked for the whole payment on account to be restored (which he must be entitled to do, in principle, because there is no compulsion to pay the duty, and nothing in SA 1891 s 15A indicates that a tender of a payment on account constitutes an irrevocable offer to pay any duty that is held to be due) the repayment would be made in a situation in which the instrument to which it related would not be duly stamped.

Interest on repayments of duty will presumably be a more significant matter in the future given the rather more onerous regime for charging interest on late payments under the newly inserted SA 1891 s 15A, in particular the fact that interest will now be charged on stampable documents which are executed abroad even while they remain abroad.

The new repayment regime relates to repayments of duty and late stamping penalties, including repayments under specified provisions of SDMA 1891 in respect of spoiled or misused stamps. The provisions do not apply to penalties other than late stamping penalties, or to any repayment of less than £25.

It also appears that these provisions are confined to repayments in an administrative (as opposed to judicial) context, since s 98 is stated not to apply in the case of a payment "made

Part II ST

in consequence of an order or judgment of a court having power to allow interest on the payment". It should be noted that all that is required to disapply s 98 is that the court *has power* to allow interest, not that it actually exercises such power in any particular case.

Query also whether the draftsman had any particular technical point in mind when choosing his terminology; for example, was any specific distinction meant to be drawn in referring to "an order or judgment" of a court in this section and "directions" by a court "as . . . to the repayment of any duty" in SA 1891 s 13B(4) (which, although in a different statute, was introduced as part of the same drafting process)?

As usual with interest on repaid tax, the repayment is disregarded when assessing other tax liabilities of the recipient; since the repayment is in the nature of a restitutionary payment, it would clearly be unfair to reduce its effective value to the recipient by subjecting it to income tax or corporation tax in the recipient's hands.

111. Stamp duty on transfer on sale

This section has been superseded by FA 2000 s 114. Refer to the 1999–2000 edition of this work for a commentary on FA 1999 s 111.

112. General amendment of charging provisions

(See the notes printed at the end of the contents list to Part II Stamp Taxes.)

This apparently minor administrative provision is now, strictly speaking, the main charging provision for all stamp duties except bearer instrument duty (as to which, see s 113 below), since it is the provision which gives effect to Sch 13 in which all the stamp duty charges (except those relating to bearer instruments—see Sch 15) are now to be found.

On the basis that the authority to impose duties now derives primarily from this (and, for bearer instruments, the following) section, there is reproduced below a commentary on the general nature of stamp duty which formerly comprised the commentary on the old charging provision, SA 1891 Sch 1 (now repealed).

Stamp duties are payable on written documents and it therefore follows that, if a transaction can be effected orally or by conduct only, there will be no liability to stamp duty because there will be no document to which the stamp can be affixed. This has been reaffirmed many times in a large number of cases since stamp duty was first introduced. See for example Lord Esher MR in *IR Comrs v G Angus & Co* (1889) 23 QBD 579 at 589, CA, and Lord Reid in *William Cory & Son Ltd v IR Comrs* [1965] AC 1088.

The converse is also true, of course, in that any document (presuming it is not a legal nullity) is stampable even if the creation of that document was not strictly necessary. For example, there is no legal obligation to create a written instrument of transfer in relation to a proposed transfer of goods but any written instrument so created will nonetheless be stampable as a "conveyance or transfer on sale" of those goods—see the commentary on FA 1946 s 36. It may well be the case that no party ever needs to rely upon this document but, if they do, it is no defence to a stamping objection to argue that the document would not have been stampable if it had not been created in the first place. Note the *Delta Finance Newco* decision referred to in the commentary on SA 1891 s 14.

Another, but quite different, example of this is provided by *Prudential Assurance Co Ltd v IRC* [1935] 1 KB 101. In that case, a policy of insurance (which was a stampable instrument, as the law then stood) was held to be stampable a second time in respect of a memorandum which was endorsed upon the original policy in order to correct a mistake which necessitated an alteration in the value of the policy. The court accepted, in principle, that the particular mistake concerned could have been corrected by means of the parties simply writing over the old wording and initialling the changes. However, since they had in fact chosen to correct it by drafting what amounted to a further policy of insurance on the same document, that "new" document was stampable.

Many legal transactions can only be effected by a written instrument, for example contracts for the sale and purchase of land (Law of Property (Miscellaneous Provisions) Act 1989 s 2), and some legal transactions can only be effected by deed, for example powers of attorney (Powers of Attorney Act 1971, as amended by Law of Property (Miscellaneous Provisions) Act 1989 s 1(8) and Sch 1). However, where an oral contract is possible, eg where chattels are sold and transferred by delivery, no stamp duty will be payable if the transaction is in fact carried out orally (although it should be noted that a written instrument is in general still stampable if it is created where the transaction could, as a matter of law, have been carried out without such an instrument being created—see also FA 1949 s 36).

The general principle that the charge to stamp duty is a charge on documents rather than on transactions can in certain circumstances cause difficulties, eg where a transaction is effected partly orally and partly in writing. Consider the case of a contract where the offer is in writing and the acceptance is oral, or vice versa: in the former case there is no stamp duty as the offer by itself does not constitute an agreement, but in the latter case, where an offer is made orally and is accepted in writing, the acceptance concludes the contract and is prima facie stampable (*Hegarty v Milne* (1854) 14 CB 627).

Another problem arises when parties enter into a transaction wholly orally and thereafter record or give effect to it in writing. There is no general provision that such a document should bear the same stamp duty as would have been payable had the parties originally entered into the transaction by means of a written instrument. Notwithstanding the lack of statutory provision, however, the courts have in certain circumstances held that duty is in fact payable where the creation of the memorandum or record and the previous oral transaction can in fact be construed as "all one transaction". In *Garnett v IR Comrs* (1899) 81 LT 633, a case concerning a receipt signed for the payment of the purchase price of a share of partnership assets on a dissolution, Channell J said (at p 638) " . . . the question is whether it is one transaction. If there is a clearly independent transaction and it is not all part of one transaction then it would stand on a different footing." This was cited with approval by Finlay J in *Cohen & Moore v IR Comrs* [1933] 2 KB 126 (at pp 137–138), a case involving a deed which purported to be an appointment of new trustees in respect of trusts declared orally some time beforehand, where the deed was held to be chargeable under the heading "Settlement" (repealed by FA 1962 s 34(7)).

It is a general principle of the law relating to stamp duty, and indeed of tax law as a whole, that in determining any liability, regard is to be had to the substance of the transaction rather than to its form (see eg *W T Ramsay Ltd v IR Comrs* [1981] STC 174). This principle is particularly difficult to apply to stamp duty, which is payable on documents rather than transactions. The following propositions have emerged:

(1) It is the true legal effect of a document which determines its stamp duty treatment ie whether it is a conveyance or other document subject to stamp duty. Some of the circumstances where this principle has been enunciated and its implications are set out below.

- (a) What a document calls itself (ie the form of a document) is inconclusive (*British India Steam Navigation v IR Comrs* (1881) 7 QB 165).
- (b) A document will be stamped according to its true legal effect, rather than its purported effect, where it is a "sham". In *Ingram v IR Comrs* [1985] STC 835 Vinelott J said: "It is not clear to me why the Commissioners described the lease agreement as a sham. The Commissioners clearly do not mean that the lease agreement was a sham in the sense in which the word is normally used in a legal context, that is, that it was intended: 'to give to third parties or to the court the appearance of creating between the parties legal rights and obligations different from the actual legal rights and obligations . . . which the parties intend to create'. (See *Snook v London & West Riding Investments Limited* [1967] 2 QB 786 at 802 per Diplock LJ)". It is clear from the *Ingram* case that the presence of a motive to mitigate stamp duty does not, of itself, involve any question of "sham".

(c) Even where a document is not a "sham", it will be stamped on the basis of the true legal nature (sometimes referred to as "legal substance") of the underlying transaction effected by it where that is different from the purported effect of the document. This principle has been applied with various degrees of enthusiasm by the courts.

Examples of the legal substance being fairly actively sought out are in *Wale v IR Comrs* (1879) 4 Ex D 270 where a charge was extinguished and a new charge granted to another person. The instrument was construed as a transfer of a mortgage. In *Eastern National Omnibus Co Ltd v IR Comrs* [1939] 1 KB 161 an agreement by a company to discontinue business in a specified area, assist its successor in obtaining the necessary licences and not to compete, in consideration of a money payment, was held to be an agreement for the sale of goodwill. In *Oughtred v IR Comrs* [1960] AC 206, by a majority, the House of Lords held that a transfer of shares (contemplated by an earlier agreement between a life tenant and the remainderman) was a conveyance on sale for stamp duty purposes notwithstanding that it was a conveyance of the bare legal interest only. In *Great Western Railway v IR Comrs* [1894] 1 QB 507 an amalgamation carried out by means of a statute was held to be "in substance" a "sale", even though there was no preceding agreement for sale. The decision in *Ensign Tankers v Stokes* [1991] 2 WLR 341, although not a case on stamp duty, can be construed as a signal that the courts are prepared to look more vigorously for the substance of a transaction in cases of blatant attempts at tax avoidance (but compare *The Prudential Assurance Co Limited v IR Comrs* [1992] STC 863, *Fitzwilliam v IRC* [1993] STC 502 and *Pigott v Staines Investment Co Limited* [1995] STC 114). The decision in *L M Tenancies 1 plc v IR Comrs* [1996] STC 880 is an indication, however, that the courts may in certain circumstances be prepared to determine stamp duty on the economic, as opposed to legal, substance of a transaction.

There is a strong suggestion in Lord Hoffmann's judgment in *MacNiven (Inspector of Taxes) v Westmoreland Investments Limited* [2001] UKHL 6 that the court will not strain to construe a document which is clearly in legal substance one thing, even if it has no business purpose, as another thing which achieves the same economic effect.

In contrast, there are also a number of cases, many of them involving blatant stamp duty avoidance schemes, where the courts have shown less inclination to look beyond the legal form of transaction. For example, it is clear that resting on contract, even in circumstances where neither party has any intention of completing, is neither a "sham" nor does it require the court to treat the contract as in substance a conveyance (*IR Comrs v Angus* (1889) 23 QBD 579 and *Ingram v IR Comrs* [1985] STC 835). The decision in *Peter Bone Ltd v IR Comrs* [1995] STC 921 emphasises the importance of drafting the relevant instrument as a contract, and not a conveyance or transfer, when it is intended to rest on contract; but it is also an example of the reluctance of the courts to look behind the form of the transaction to the intentions of the parties.

In *Littlewoods Mail Order Stores Ltd v IR Comrs* [1963] AC 135, the owner of freehold property which was subject to a lease in favour of Littlewoods could have sold the freehold to Littlewoods for 22 annual instalments of £42,450 but, in order to minimise stamp duty, entered into a fairly artificial series of deeds producing the same commercial effect culminating in a deed by which a subsidiary of Littlewoods assigned to the owner a 22-year lease at a nominal annual rent (subject to an underlease at a £42,450 annual rent) in exchange for a transfer of the freehold (subject to the leases) to the subsidiary. The House of Lords held that the deed was not an "exchange or excambion" nor in substance or form a "conveyance or transfer on sale" of the freehold.

In *William Cory & Son v IR Comrs* [1965] AC 1088, A agreed to sell C shares to B in principle. A granted an option over the C shares to B and transferred the C shares to B as nominee for a nominal consideration. Seven days later B exercised the option orally and paid a substantial exercise price. The House of Lords held that the liability of an instrument to stamp duty arose at the moment that it was executed, and the character of an instrument of transfer was to be ascertained by what was its legal effect at that date, not by what use was made of it later. Accordingly, there was only an option and no agreement for sale when the share transfers were executed, the option itself was not dutiable as a contract under Stamp Act 1891 s 59 and the share transfers did not constitute conveyances or transfers on sale. It was also said that the court can have regard to what is said and done after the instrument has been executed in order to discover the true position when the instrument was executed, although that was not necessary in the case where the true position at the time of execution was not in doubt.

In *Henty and Constable (Brewers) Ltd v IR Comrs* [1961] 3 All ER 1146, the facts were that A owned company B which owned a substantial property. C was interested in buying the property. A and C agreed to transfer the shares in B to C but did not complete and A agreed to liquidate B and distribute the property in specie. The court held that the transfer of the property by B to C was not a "sham" concealing the transfer of property by A to C and was therefore stampable 50p.

In *The Prudential Assurance Co Limited v IR Comrs* [1992] STC 863, the following transactions were entered into simultaneously: (1) an agreement for the sale of a partly-developed freehold, (2) an agreement to complete the development, and (3) a transfer of the underlying land. The court held that this could not be characterised as a sale of the land with the completed buildings thereon which would have been stampable on the total consideration payable under both agreements. Sir Donald Nicholls V-C stated (at 869): "However, I am unable to characterise the transaction by which that end result was sought to be achieved as a sale of the land with finished buildings thereon. That, manifestly, was not the legal shape of this transaction. The sale agreement was, as the parties intended, completed independently of the carrying out of the building works under the development agreement". It may be significant that this case was decided after *Ensign Tankers* (see above) and *Ingram v IR Comrs* (see below), although those cases were not central to the decision of Sir Donald Nicholls V-C who stated: "I must therefore identify what was the subject matter of the sale. In so doing I must have regard to the commercial substance of the transaction. I must also have regard to the shape, or form, which the parties have chosen for their transaction. A given commercial result can often be reached by more than one route. If the parties have genuinely chosen one route, with the legal incidents and consequences attendant on that route, rather than a different route having different legal incidents and consequences, for better or for worse stamp duty will be assessable accordingly. (I stress the word genuinely because I am leaving on one side transactions into which artificial steps have been inserted for the purpose of avoiding fiscal liabilities. That is not the present case. For the same reason I leave aside sham documents and provisions.)"

The *Duke of Westminster* [1936] AC 1 principles therefore appear to be alive and well and it is still open to parties to structure transactions so as to mitigate stamp duty. Provided each step is genuine and subject to *Furniss v Dawson* which is discussed next, it is not open to HMRC to recharacterise a transaction simply on the basis of its commercial or economic effect or on some sort of moral ground (see *MacNiven v Westmoreland Investments Ltd* [2001] UKHL 6 but compare *L M Tenancies 1 plc v IR Comrs* [1996] STC 880 which may be confined to "contingency principle" situations).

(2) In the context of a multiple-step transaction, where the *Furniss v Dawson* [1984] STC 153 conditions are satisfied, stamp duty can apply as if the true legal effect of the transaction is that it is a single composite transaction.

The *Furniss v Dawson* scheme involved A, who owned shares in company B on which there was an accrued capital gain, transferring the B shares to Offshore Co in exchange for shares in Offshore Co (thus rolling-over the gain on the B shares into the Offshore Co shares, as was then possible). Offshore Co then sold the B shares to C and realised the gain tax-free offshore. A had thus deferred taxation of his gain until he disposed of the Offshore Co shares. The House of Lords decided that the transaction could be collapsed and analysed as a single composite transaction, so that the share for share exchange and subsequent disposal of the B shares by Offshore Co should be ignored and the transaction treated as a sale of the B shares by A. The reasoning ran as follows:

(a) In a pre-planned tax saving scheme, no distinction is to be drawn for fiscal purposes, because none exists in reality, between:
  (i) a series of steps which are followed through by virtue of an arrangement which falls short of a binding contract, and
  (ii) a like series of steps which are followed through because the participants are contractually bound to take each step seriatim.

  Where there is a pre-ordained series of transactions or one single composite transaction, whether or not it includes the achievement of a legitimate commercial (ie business) end, and steps are inserted which have no commercial purposes apart from the avoidance of a liability to tax, the inserted steps are to be disregarded and the end results considered in the light of the relevant taxing statute.

(b) Fears that the Crown's arguments would lead to oppressive double taxation were misconceived. There would be no additional capital gains tax on the steps by which the disposal from A to C was achieved, because the fiscal consequences of the introduction of Offshore Co are to be disregarded. On any subsequent disposal by A of his shares in Offshore Co, the base cost of the Offshore Co shares would be the price which A paid for them, namely the value of the shares in B at the date of the scheme transactions.

After the decision of the House of Lords in *Craven v White* [1988] 3 All ER 495 and subsequent cases it appeared that a narrow interpretation of *Furniss v Dawson* was prevailing. The *Craven v White* scheme was very similar to that in *Furniss v Dawson*. The case settled two important issues. The first was that *Furniss v Dawson* should not be taken as the start of the development of a general anti-tax avoidance jurisprudence. The second issue was what degree of certainty there had to be before the steps could be said to be "pre-ordained". Different law lords gave different formulations. One of the formulations frequently referred to is Lord Oliver's who found that *Furniss v Dawson* only applied where there was no practical likelihood that the pre-planned events would not take place in the order ordained. Lord Oliver also laid down a test which is generally regarded as encapsulating the *Furniss v Dawson* doctrine: "(1) that the series of transactions was, at the time when the intermediate transaction was entered into, pre-ordained in order to produce a given result; (2) that that transaction had no other purpose than tax mitigation; (3) that there was at that time no practical likelihood that the pre-planned events would not take place in the order ordained, so that the intermediate transaction was not even contemplated practically as having an independent life; and (4) that the pre-ordained events did in fact take place. In these circumstances the court can be justified in linking the beginning with the end so as to make a single composite whole to which the fiscal results of the single composite whole are to be applied".

After *Craven v White*, an important subsequent decision was that of the House of Lords in *Fitzwilliam v IR Comrs* [1993] STC 502. Emphasis in that case was placed on the fact that the court has to consider whether it is possible realistically and intellectually to treat the scheme as a whole. If the Crown's case requires the court to pick and choose between different bits of the scheme and treat them in different ways the court cannot realistically or intellectually treat the scheme as a whole and therefore will not do so. There are echoes of this approach in the decision of Knox J in *Piggot v Staines Investment Co Limited* [1995] STC 114 which showed signs that the courts will be slow to disregard transactions which have "enduring effects", although perhaps too much emphasis must not be put on this given that in *Furniss v Dawson* the intermediate share-for-share exchange was ignored.

Because stamp duty is essentially a tax on documents, rather than a tax on transactions, there has been some considerable debate as to whether or not the principles enunciated in the *Ramsay* and *Furniss v Dawson* cases apply to stamp duty. The Commissioners clearly took the view that the principles were applicable to stamp duty and their view received approval from the Chancery Division (Vinelott J) in the case of *Ingram v IR Comrs* [1985] STC 835.

The facts of that case were as follows: The taxpayer negotiated a price of £145,500 for the purchase of an unencumbered freehold property with vacant possession. With a view to reducing the stamp duty payable on the transfer of the property, the following transactions were entered into:

(1) the vendor and the taxpayer made an agreement for the lease of the property for a term of 999 years (then not dutiable) at a premium of £145,000 and an annual rent of £25;

(2) the taxpayer agreed to indemnify the vendor against any liability he might incur which he would not have incurred on a straightforward sale of the property;

(3) H Ltd, owned and controlled by the partners in the taxpayer's firm of solicitors, contracted to buy the freehold of the property for £500;

(4) H Ltd agreed a sub-sale of the property to the taxpayer at a price of £600;

(5) the vendor transferred and H Ltd confirmed to the taxpayer the property subject to and with the benefit of the terms and provisions of the lease.

Thereafter, the taxpayer presented the transfer for adjudication and the Revenue assessed the duty at 1 per cent of £145,600. The taxpayer appealed to the High Court, contending that, stamp duty being chargeable solely on instruments, and SA 1891 s 59 exempting contracts or agreements from the charge to conveyance on sale duty, the transfer, being the conveyance or transfer on sale, was dutiable only in respect of the consideration moving from the sub-purchaser (ie, the £600). The Crown contended that (1) the stamp duty, despite being payable on instruments and not on transactions, was arrived at by reference to the transaction that the instrument was intended to effect, complete or record; (2) that the substance of the matter must be looked at; (3) that the arrangements entered into constituted a single composite transaction, and (4) that, in substance and in reality, the transfer was the completion document of that single composite transaction and was thus chargeable to ad valorem duty on the whole of the consideration. Vinelott J held that, although stamp duty is a tax on instruments, to determine whether an instrument falls within a chargeable category and the duty payable the court must ascertain the substance of the transaction effected by it. The *Ramsay* principle requires that (where the *Furniss v Dawson* conditions are satisfied) a composite transaction or series of transactions be treated as a single transaction achieving the pre-ordained end. Applying that principle, the transfer must be treated as accomplishing the transfer of the unencumbered freehold interest at the agreed price, that being the end pre-ordained when the first step (the lease agreement) was taken. The lease agreement must therefore be disregarded and the two sale agreements be treated as a composite contract for the sale of the property. The stamp duty payable on these instruments would be assessed at £1,456 and the taxpayer's appeal would therefore be dismissed.

Despite the *Ingram* case the scope of the application of the *Furniss v Dawson* principle to stamp duty remains unclear because of the peculiarity of stamp duty and uncertainty over the interpretation of the *Furniss v Dawson* principle itself. The relative incompatibility of stamp duty with the *Furniss v Dawson* principle stems from a number of factors: for instance, stamp duty applies to documents rather than transactions and it is easier to recharacterise a transaction for a transaction-based tax than rewrite a document for a document-based tax; the intentions of the parties are generally not taken into account in assessing whether an instrument is dutiable: see *Peter Bone Ltd v IR Comrs* [1995] STC 921; and there is no independent tribunal for ascertaining the facts and intentions behind any particular instruments.

However, it is possible to see certain guidelines emerging: there are suggestions in Vinelott J's judgment in the *Ingram* case that *Furniss v Dawson* would not have applied to the scheme had the last step not been effected by or recorded in any instrument (eg if the final step had been effected orally), and that *Furniss v Dawson* cannot be used to re-write or "recharacterise" a non-stampable document as a stampable document, or a stampable document as a document stampable under another head of charge. The implication is that the *Littlewoods* and *Cory* cases may not have been decided differently had they been decided after *Furniss v Dawson*. On the other hand, one should note that Vinelott J said that it cannot be the case that the transactions ignored in *Furniss v Dawson* should be treated differently for the

Part II ST

purposes of stamp duty; in other words *Furniss v Dawson* should be applied consistently to all taxes. The *Pigott* and *Fitzwilliam* cases suggest that a step in a multiple-step transaction structured so as to minimise stamp duty cannot be disregarded where it has "enduring legal effects" or to disregard the transaction would lead to a nonsensical "end result". *Furniss v Dawson* does not apply to single-step transactions. Finally, the Stamp Office cannot use *Furniss v Dawson* simply because the parties choose to adopt one set of legal relationships which attract no or a small amount of stamp duty, even though the same economic or commercial result could have been achieved by other legal arrangements attracting a larger liability to stamp duty (see *The Prudential Assurance Co Limited v IR Comrs* [1992] STC 863 and *MacNiven v Westmoreland Investments Ltd* [2001] UKHL 6 but compare *L M Tenancies 1 plc v IR Comrs* [1996] STC 880).

It is submitted that this position has not been altered by the recent decision of Park J in *M&G Securities Ltd v IR Comrs* [1999] STC 315. In that case, the concept of economic equivalence between alternative legal structures *was* emphasised. However, it is submitted that this approach was taken for a specific and (in *that* particular context) entirely justifiable reason. This was because there was specific evidence (in the form of the formal Report which led to the passing of the legislation under consideration in that case) to support the view that the intention behind enacting the legislation in question had been to bring about a greater degree of economic equivalence in the stamp duty treatment of two different forms of transaction (namely dealings in company shares on the one hand and dealings in units of a unit trust on the other). Nothing in the decision in this case suggests any general erosion of the principle evidenced in cases such as *Pigott v Staines Investments Co Ltd* [1995] STC 114 to the effect that tax on transaction will be increased (or indeed reduced) merely because the same ultimate result could have been achieved by means of a transaction in another form.

There is also a separate question as to the duty properly chargeable where, quite apart from any considerations of tax avoidance and recharacterisation, a document is of a kind that could give rise to more than one stamp duty charge. As to possible cumulative charges, see SA 1891 s 4. However, situations may also arise where a document could be charged on more than one basis in respect of a single transaction, act or event.

It seemed for a while that a further element of uncertainty would be created by the decision of the House of Lords in *McGuckian v IR Comrs* [1997] STC 908. However, many commentators soon concluded that this decision was to be seen as some kind of high water mark of purposiveness, and that the tide had rapidly receded. The *McGuckian* case (which entered English law somewhat out of the blue because it was an appeal to the House of Lords from earlier proceedings in the courts of Northern Ireland) seems as though it could have been decided by means of a fairly narrow application of *Furniss v Dawson* principles but in fact it proceeded on what seemed at the time to be a radically different basis. The speeches in the House of Lords suggested that tax statutes (and quite possible non-tax statutes as well) ought now to be read in a spirit of broad purposiveness.

Immediately after *McGuckian*, the superior courts had shown less enthusiasm for developing vague but broad anti-avoidance doctrines. In *Lady Ingram v IR Comrs* [1999] STC 37, the House of Lords effectively declined to deal with general principles of tax avoidance at all, giving a decision, in what was unquestionably a case of structured tax avoidance, that dwelt purely on the technical merits and not on policy. The leading speeches focus squarely upon the extent to which, as a matter of technical property law, the taxpayer's scheme was effective and not upon the extent to which the taxpayer should have been permitted to succeed in her quite blatant attempts to avoid inheritance tax. The only point which might perhaps be made against *Ingram* as evidence of a return to principles of interpretation based upon technical analysis rather than purposiveness, is that it seemed to be beyond dispute that the purpose behind the statutory provision at issue in *Ingram* had never been clear to anyone, despite its having existed in one form or another for roughly 100 years.

Another possible blow against purposiveness seemed to have been struck even more recently than the *Ingram* decision, with the reversal by the Inner House of the Court of Session (at [1999] STC 787) of the decision of the Special Commissioners in the corporation tax case of

Aberdeen Milk Co Ltd v IR Comrs [1998] STC (SCD) 71. At first instance, the kind of broad purposiveness that had been applied in favour of the Revenue in *McGuckian* was applied in favour of the taxpayer. However, the Court of Session not only felt that the Special Commissioners had misconstrued the purpose of the legislation at issue in that case (the Agriculture Act 1993) but, with closing comments highly reminiscent of those made in *Ingram*, showed a general lack of enthusiasm for approaching the case on that basis at all, preferring to treat the taxpayer's claim as standing or falling on its technical merits.

A shift back to a purposive construction of legislation has been caused by the recent decisions of the House of Lords in *Barclays Mercantile Business Finance Ltd v Mawson* [2005] STC 1 and *IRC v Scottish Provident Institution* [2005] STC 15. These cases mark a retreat from Lord Hoffmann's view in *MacNiven v Westmoreland Investments Ltd* [2001] UKHL 6 that a distinction has to be drawn between "commercial concepts" and "legal concepts". Instead, the House has concluded, one is required closely to analyse what, on a purposive construction, the statute actually requires. This, it is said, is no more than the application of the ordinary principles of statutory construction to taxing statutes.

Stamp duty is now expressed in the legislation as a percentage of the consideration, or other relevant value by reference to which any duty is charged, instead of being expressed as an amount of duty per amount of consideration (eg 1 per cent, instead of 50p per £50 of consideration, as in the former charging provisions in SA 1891 Sch 1). This harmonises the format of the charging provisions for stamp duty with those for stamp duty reserve tax, where percentages were adopted in the charging provisions in 1996.

All sums are now to be rounded up or down to multiples of £5.

113. Bearer instruments

As with s 101 above, a provision which at first sight appears to make a series of miscellaneous administrative changes is in fact now the principal charging provision for bearer instrument duties. It gives effect to Schs 15 and 16 in which new provisions are set out, replacing the old bearer instrument law formerly found mainly in FA 1963. By and large, no substantive changes have been made to the bearer instrument legislation but the format has been recast and some of the language has been modernised. See commentary on Sch 15 below.

114. Penalties other than on late stamping

(See the notes printed at the end of the contents list to Part II Stamp Taxes.)

This section gives effect to Sch 17 in which the new regime for administrative penalties is set out. See commentary on Sch 17 below.

115. Minor amendments and repeal of obsolete provisions

This gives effect to Sch 18 in which some miscellaneous amendments are made. See commentary on Sch 18 below.

116. Non-sterling bearer instruments issued in connection with takeover or merger

The scope of the exceptions for bearer instruments, in relation to the 1.5 per cent stamp duty reserve tax charges applicable to depositary receipts and clearance services, is altered by means of amendments inserted into FA 1986 ss 95 and 97. (See also s 117 below)

The change applies to any instrument issued on or after 30 January 1999 unless it relates to a merger or takeover agreement entered into in writing before that date. The effect of the change is that the exception which usually disapplies the special 1.5 per cent charge on depositary or clearance schemes where the instrument being issued or transferred is a bearer instrument, cannot now be used as a means of avoiding the stamp duty reserve tax charge that would otherwise arise on the transfer of bearer instruments in circumstances where the anti-avoidance rule in s 90(3C)–(3F), introduced by FA 1997, would apply to a transaction which did not involve a depositary or clearance scheme.

In other words, where the real purpose of undertaking a share transaction in bearer form is to avoid a stamp duty charge by relying upon the provisions originally set out in FA 1967 s 30 and now re-enacted as FA 1999 Sch 15 Part II paras 17–19 (which exempt from stamp duty a transfer of bearer shares if those shares are denominated in a foreign currency—see commentary on Sch 15 below) a charge to stamp duty reserve tax now arises instead, and the relief available generally for bearer instruments in the context of depositary or clearance schemes cannot now be used to avoid this charge.

117. Scope of exceptions for certain bearer instruments

This section makes an additional change to the scope of the relief available for bearer instruments in relation to the 1.5 per cent stamp duty reserve tax charge on depositary and clearance schemes. However, this provision has effect from 9 March 1999 (rather than 30 January 1999 as in the case of s 116 above) except in relation to takeover agreements entered in writing before 30 January 1999.

This section restricts the relief from the 1.5 per cent charge only to those bearer instruments which "raise new capital". However, the section provides detailed and fairly restrictive guidance as to what constitutes the raising of new capital.

The view of HMRC is that these restrictions are justified because the only reason for the original enactment of FA 1967 s 30 (now FA 1999 Sch 15 Part II paras 17–19) was to remove a potential restriction on the ability of UK businesses to raise capital abroad by ensuring that no stamp duty charge arose on dealings in foreign-denominated securities where such dealings had the raising of such capital as their aim. Therefore, in HMRC's view, any use of foreign-denominated bearer instruments for any other purpose (ie for the purpose of avoiding stamp duty on a transaction that, in principle, could equally well be structured entirely around sterling-denominated and/or registered instruments) is an abuse of the relief offered in FA 1967.

This section also rewords the existing provisions in each of FA 1986 ss 95(6) and 97(7), which make clear that a cancellation of securities in consideration of an issue is equivalent to a transfer in consideration of an issue (there having been some doubt within HMRC, before enactment of these provisions, as to whether a transaction based upon a cancellation of securities was, techincally, an "exchange"). The rewording does not appear to have altered the substance of the provisions.

118. Relief in case of replacement securities

This introduces new provisions into FA 1986, as ss 95A and 97AA of that Act, to prevent a further charge to higher rate stamp duty reserve tax where, broadly speaking, a change of securities in a depositary or clearance scheme is in the nature of a substitution rather than a genuine transfer of property. See commentary on FA 1986 s 95A.

119. Power to exempt UK depositary interests in foreign securities

See commentary on FA 1986 s 94 for background information on the kind of problem that the Treasury seem to have been seeking to alleviate by means of this section. Power is given by means of this section to amend stamp duty reserve tax legislation in such a manner as to ensure that a UK depositary interest for foreign securities does not create a tax charge that would not have existed in respect of the underlying securities themselves. It is understood that the Stamp Office's view is that any depositary interest which is purely in the nature of a UK-oriented administrative "wrapper", designed to facilitate dealings in foreign property ought, by virtue of regulations under s 110, to be treated as outside the scope of stamp duty reserve tax.

120. Minor amendments of exceptions to general charge

This makes minor amendments to the text of FA 1986. See in particular the commentary on FA 1986 s 90(5)–(6).

121. Power to make regulations with respect to administration, etc

(See the notes printed at the end of the contents list to Part II Stamp Taxes.)

This alters the scope of the Treasury's powers to make regulations relating to interest and penalties on late payment of tax and also to the scope of HMRC's information-gathering powers. It also alters the power to alter the range of persons potentially liable to pay the tax. It should be noted that the last-mentioned power shall be deemed always to have existed (ie since the passing of FA 1986, which first introduced stamp duty reserve tax).

122. Stamp duty and stamp duty reserve tax: unit trusts

This section gives effect to Sch 19, which provides for the abolition of stamp duty in relation to unit trust transactions (originally introduced by FA 1946) and sets out the new stamp duty reserve tax regime for unit trusts. The new regime had effect from 6 February 2000. Although this means that stamp duty survived in relation to unit trusts for a few months after the new interest and penalties regime took effect on 1 October 1999, that new regime does *not* apply to unit trust transactions in the period after 1 October 1999 and the abolition of stamp duty on unit trusts on 6 February 2000. The details of the new regime are set out in Sch 19—see commentary on that Schedule.

123. Construction of this Part and other supplementary provisions

(See the notes printed at the end of the contents list to Part II Stamp Taxes.)

The stamp duty provisions are to be read as one with SA 1891 and the stamp duty reserve tax provisions are to be read as one with Part IV of FA 1986. It should be noted (and see also the commentary on Sch 13 below) that the stamp duty provisions are still required to be read as one with SA 1891 even though all the charging provisions are actually now located in *this* Act.

SCHEDULES

SCHEDULE 12 STAMP DUTY: INTEREST AND PENALTIES ON LATE STAMPING (SECTION 109)

This inserts into SA 1891 new ss 12, 12A, 13, 13A and 13B and into FA 1994 new ss 240 and 240A. It also makes certain consequential amendments. See the commentaries on each of those sections for further details.

SCHEDULE 13 STAMP DUTY: INSTRUMENTS CHARGEABLE AND RATES OF DUTY (SECTION 101)

This, together with Sch 15 below, replaces the heads of charge formerly set out in SA 1891 Sch 1. The format of the new schedules is somewhat different to that adopted in the 1891 legislation in that the old heads of charge were set out in the form of an alphabetical list with rates or amounts of duty listed against the various descriptions of instruments. The new provisions tend to adopt more of a "stand alone" format, where the various paragraphs are drafted in a more discursive manner and often consist of free-standing statements of principle or rules of law.

It is not immediately clear why the draftsman chose to make some fundamental changes in the form of amendments to the original provisions in SA 1891 but chose in other cases to insert completely new provisions in the form of schedules to FA 1999. It is also not clear why the draftsman chose to set out in the form of schedules the kind of fundamental material that one would usually expect to find in the main body of a statute, such as the basic charging provisions.

It should be noted that all stamp duty legislation, including the contents of FA 1999, is still notionally located in 1891 since, although only secondary provisions (ie administrative and relieving provisions, as opposed to charging provisions) now remain in SA 1891 itself, the provisions of FA 1999 and other Acts are to be "read as one" with SA 1891. (This may have some unforeseen consequences; for example, it might be the case that the word "land", as used in the 1999 provisions, is not governed by the definition in the Interpretation Act 1978 which is stated to apply to statutes enacted after 1 January 1979. This would be on the basis that the 1999 provisions are still notionally located in 1891, so that any otherwise undefined reference to "land" in the 1999 provisions still falls to be interpreted by reference to the Interpretation Act 1889, which has been repealed but some of the contents of which survive in relation to statutes enacted before 1979—see Sch 2 para 5(*b*) to the Interpretation Act 1978).

In general, the wording of Sch 13 has been incorporated from those parts of SA 1891 which it replaces. The opportunity has been taken to modernise the vocabulary in minor ways (for example, "whereby" becomes "by which") but alterations of vocabulary appear to be confined only to such incidental matters and the opportunity has not been taken to implement any wholesale revision of the text.

PART 1 TRANSFER ON SALE

Charge

(See the notes printed at the end of the contents list to Part II Stamp Taxes.)

1.—(1) Although located in a rather peculiar position, this (together with Part III para 16(1) below) is now the key provision on which modern UK stamp duty law and practice is focused.

(2) This subparagraph contains the definition of "transfer on sale" whose predecessor was SA 1891 s 54. The meaning of "transfer" could be summarised as extending to any document which is the effective cause or means of dealing with the title to, or ownership of, any property whatsoever, whether moveable or immoveable, tangible or intangible, domestic or foreign (but subject to a few specific exemptions, such as ships—see Part IV below).

However, it is important to appreciate that the reference above to an "effective cause or means" does not mean that a document will be a transfer merely because it provides a record of an event or merely because it is evidence of a transaction or event, without itself actually being part of that transaction or event (subject, again, to some specific exceptions, where statute or case law indicates that a document of an "incidental" character is stampable as though it were the actual cause or source of a relevant transaction or event).

The separate elements of the definition are considered in greater detail below but it is important to note at the outset this is not necessarily an exclusive definition ("the expression "transfer on sale" *includes* . . . ") and the Commissioners maintain that a transfer may in fact be chargeable under the head of charge "transfer on sale" even if it does not come within what is now para 1(2) (see *Oughtred v IR Comrs* [1960] AC 206, 222 and 223).

(a) "Every instrument, and every decree or order of a court or commissioners"

The word "instrument" is extremely wide. By virtue of SA 1891 s 122(1) it includes "every written document", and it will not matter whether the document is under seal or under hand. It includes court orders (for example an order sanctioning a scheme of arrangement under the Companies Act 2006 s 895—see *Sun Alliance Insurance Ltd v IR Comrs* [1972] Ch 133 at 148 in relation to a scheme under what was then the Companies Act 1948 s 206). It also includes Acts of Parliament. FA 1895 s 12 provides that where by statute any property is vested by way of sale in any person, or any person is authorised to purchase property, such person must within three months after the passing of the Act or the day of vesting (if later) or after completion of the purchase produce to the Commissioners for stamping an office copy of the Act or the instrument of conveyance of the property. It also includes "the return which relates to the shares purchased and is delivered to the Registrar of Companies" under the Companies Act 2006 s 707 where a company purchases its own shares under the powers conferred by the Companies Act 2006 s 690 (see FA 1986 s 66(2)).

(b) "Any property, or any estate or interest in any property"

Property is "that which belonged to a person exclusive of others, and which could be the subject of bargain and sale to another" (*Potter v IR Comrs* (1854) 10 Ex 147 at 156). The most obvious examples are a legal estate in land (which can only be conveyed or transferred by deed), goods (which are transferable by delivery but dutiable if included in an instrument of transfer in addition to a sale and purchase agreement) and stocks and marketable securities, including most shares, debentures and units under a unit trust scheme (although transfers or surrenders of such units are now specifically exempted from stamp duty, by virtue of FA 1999 s 122 and Sch 19). However, the word "property" has also been held to include the goodwill of a trade or business (*Benjamin Brooke & Co Ltd v IR Comrs* [1896] 2 QB 356, DC; *IR Comrs v Muller & Co's Margarine* [1901] AC 217 at 223, 234, 235, HL), copyrights and trade marks (*Leather Cloth Co v American Leather Cloth Co* (1865) 11 HL Cas 523), secret processes (*Re Keene* [1922] 2 Ch 475), the grant of an exclusive licence to use a UK patent (unless containing a power of revocation), book debts (*Measures Brothers Ltd v IR Comrs* (1900) 82 LT 689, DC), life insurance policies (*Caldwell v Dawson* (1859) 5 Exch 1) and the benefit of contractual rights (*Western Abyssinian Mining Syndicate Ltd v IR Comrs* (1935) 14 ATC 286). Most of this list is now redundant, following the abolition in December 2003 of stamp duty in relation to transfers of any property other than stock or marketable securities (or certain land transactions where the charge to stamp duty was preserved by the transitional provisions): see FA 2003 s 12 and Sch 19.

Almost anything can be the subject of a transfer on sale, and therefore attract stamp duty, but the property or the right being transferred must actually exist. In *Limmer Asphalte Paving Co v IR Comrs* (1872) LR 7 Exch 211 it was held that a deed purporting to grant an exclusive licence to make asphalte paving "within the counties of Lancaster and Chester" was not chargeable as a conveyance on sale on the grounds that the purported licensor did not in fact have any exclusive right to use the asphalte within those counties, so that "if the company had no such property and could not create it, they could not convey or transfer it".

A transfer of property situated abroad is required by s 14(4) to be stamped if it is executed in the UK, or if it relates to any property situated, or thing done or to be done in the UK. For example, a transfer executed in France of property situated in France was nevertheless held to be stampable since the consideration was the issue of shares in an English company (*IR Comrs v Maple & Co (Paris) Ltd* [1908] AC 22).

By virtue of FA 2000 s 128, no stamp duty is chargeable on any instrument for the sale, transfer (including agreement to transfer) or other disposition of intellectual property. Other exemptions (eg for certain types of loan stock, debentures, gilts, ships, etc) are scattered throughout the legislation relating to stamp duty.

By virtue of FA 2003 s 125, stamp duty is now chargeable only on instruments relating to stock or marketable securities. Accordingly, although the definition of "property" is very wide, this is of no relevance to the charge itself. It is lack of Parliamentary time that has caused the retention on the statute book of a significant number of apparently redundant provisions. Their only justification is that there remain transactions (ie those where the parties rested in contact) which, by virtue of FA 2003 s 125 and Sch 19, are outside the scope of SDLT, in the case of which stamp duty would be charged on any instrument of transfer completing the transaction.

(c) "On being sold"

The conveyance or transfer will be a transfer "upon" sale where at the date of the transfer there exists a binding agreement for sale (even if that agreement is conditional—*Ridge Nominees Ltd v IR Comrs* [1962] Ch 376), or where the transfer itself gives rise to the sale, without a pre-existing agreement (eg *Escoigne Properties Ltd v IR Comrs* [1958] AC 549). A transfer made in contemplation of a sale but before the formation of a binding contract (whether conditional or unconditional) is not a transfer on sale (*William Cory & Son Ltd v IR Comrs* [1965] 1 All ER 917) but is nevertheless chargeable with duty at the same rate by reference to the value of the property conveyed (FA 1965 s 90(1)). In that case, a claim for repayment may be made to the Commissioners not later than two years after the making or execution of the instrument charged under s 90(1) and if the Commissioners are satisfied either:

(a) that the sale has not taken place and the property has been re-conveyed or re-transferred to the original transferor or his personal representative or trustee in bankruptcy, or

(b) that the sale has taken place for a consideration less than the value on which duty was paid, then the duty or the excess duty (as the case may be) may be repaid.

Instruments falling within the provisions of s 90(1) must be adjudicated. It has been suggested that the reference in s 90(2) to "the sale in contemplation of which the instrument was made" implies that no duty would be payable in respect of a conveyance in contemplation of sale generally, with no particular purchaser in mind, for example where a person going abroad transfers his portfolio of shares to a stockbroker to enable him to effect any expedient sales during the owner's absence. It is submitted that this is not a correct interpretation of s 90. If a blank share transfer is delivered to a stockbroker in contemplation of a sale and the sale subsequently does in fact take place, then that sale must have been in the "contemplation" of the transferor at the time the transfer was signed, notwithstanding that the identity of the purchaser was not known. Section 90 refers to *the sale* being contemplated, not *the purchaser*. Where a particular purchaser has been found, a blank share transfer will in fact be treated as a conveyance or transfer on sale and stampable as such (*Fitch Lovell Ltd v IR Comrs* [1962] 3 All ER 685).

It is of course of the essence of every sale that there should be a purchase price. For the purpose of SA 1891 and FA 1999, the consideration for a sale may be not only money, but also foreign or colonial currency, stock, including shares and units under a unit trust scheme, marketable and other securities, and debts and transfers either certainly or contingently of any money or stock (see SA 1891 ss 6, 55 and 57, and FA 1999 Sch 19 para 1 s 54(1)). However, there is no general rule that a transfer of property for valuable consideration, such as other property or services, is a sale. For example, in *Littlewoods Mail Order Stores Ltd v IR Comrs* [1962] 2 All ER 279, it was held that an exchange of a freehold reversion in property for the leasehold interests in the same property was not a sale of the freehold property for the rent reserved by the lease. But see now the commentary on FA 1994 in relation to exchanges and partitions in the context of land transactions.

In *Oughtred v IR Comrs* [1960] AC 206, where a settlement entitled a mother to a life interest in 200,000 shares and her son, subject only to his mother's life interest, to the shares in remainder, it was orally agreed between the mother and the son that the son would exchange his reversionary interest in return for certain other shares owned absolutely by the mother in the same company. Completion of that agreement involved the execution of a deed transferring the shares absolutely owned by the mother to the son's nominees, a deed of release releasing and discharging the trustees under the settlement, and a deed transferring the 200,000 shares from the trustees to the mother. It was held that the true nature and intended purpose of the third deed was to complete the oral agreement, so that the third deed was accordingly a transfer "on sale" and assessable to ad valorem duty on the consideration expressed in the deed, which was the agreed value of the shares absolutely owned by the mother which were transferred by her to her son's nominees.

In *Parinv (Hatfield) v IR Comrs* [1996] STC 933 there was clearly a transfer on sale, but the question was whether it was the Land Registry transfer requiring registration (which would have to be stamped before registration) or a declaration of trust executed and retained offshore (on which stamp duty would have been deferred before enactment of SA 1891 s 15A). The case concerned the "offshore declaration of trust trick" which had been used in relation to a number of land transfers over a certain value. The parties in the *Parinv* case entered into a contract to sell UK land which provided that completion would take the form of a declaration of trust stating that the seller held the beneficial interest in the land on trust for the buyer. The contract was therefore a contract for the sale of an equitable interest stampable under what is now FA 1999 Sch 3 Part I para 7 and the declaration of trust was stampable as a transfer on sale: see *Chesterfield Brewery v IR Comrs* and *Peter Bone Limited v IR Comrs* discussed above. Both the contract and declaration of trust were therefore executed and retained offshore. The seller as trustee then executed a Land Registry transfer in favour of the buyer. The buyer contended that the Land Registry transfer was stampable 50p (as the fixed duty then was for what was then called a "Conveyance or Transfer of any kind not hereinbefore described") and not a transfer on sale. The taxpayer conceded from the outset that the Land Registry transfer could pass equitable title.

The High Court held that:

(a) the Stamp Office was entitled to take account of the information obtained under ss 5 and 12(2) concerning the offshore contract in order to conclude that the Land Registry transfer was a transfer on sale of the legal and equitable interest in the land (consistent perhaps with the *Oughtred* case but compare *International Power v IRC* (1933) 12 ATC 413 and *Peter Bone Limited v IR Comrs* [1995] STC 921) and

(b) the declaration of trust, being unstamped,
   (i) could not be adduced in evidence to demonstrate that it, and not the Land Registry transfer, was the stampable transfer on sale and
   (ii) did not exist in law and thus could not be chosen as the stampable document pursuant to ss 58(3) and 61(2).

This case has implications for the scope of SA 1891 ss 5, 12(2) and 14(4) as to which see the commentaries on those sections. It was unfortunate that the case was decided on rather technical evidential grounds (which, nevertheless, one must regard as lying at the heart of the stamp duty enforcement system) and so did not have to consider, assuming all information was admissible, which of the declaration of trust and the Land Registry transfer was stampable ad valorem.

Any transfer which gives effect to an agreement for sale is a transfer on sale, and it is not necessary that the property transferred should be precisely the property sold. On the other hand, it is not sufficient that the property transferred has simply come to represent the property sold, where for example (as in *Henty and Constable (Brewers) Ltd v IR Comrs* [1961] 3 All ER 1146) shares in a company are sold and, the company being wound up, assets are distributed in specie to the purchaser without his having a transfer of the shares to him.

Not only is it the case that the property transferred need not be precisely the property sold, but it also seems to have been held on a number of occasions that the transferor need not be the vendor (*AG v Brown* (1849) 3 Exch 662); that the consideration need not be paid or payable to the vendor (*GHR Co v IR Comrs* [1943] KB 303, where there was a sale by a tenant for life and payment was made to the Settled Land Act trustees); and that the consideration need not be provided by the purchaser or transferee (*Central & District Properties Ltd v IR Comrs* [1966] 2 All ER 433). In addition, the transfer need not necessarily be to the purchaser, but may also be to some person on his behalf or by his direction.

As can be seen, what constitutes a transfer "upon sale" will very much depend upon the nature of the transaction and the documents which are executed. The courts have tried on a number of occasions to state the general principles involved (see eg Lord Denning in *Oughtred v IR Comrs* [1960] AC 206 at 233; Wills J in *Chesterfield Brewery Co v IR Comrs* [1899] 2 QB 7 at 12; Romer LJ and Maugham LJ in *Fleetwood-Hesketh v IR Comrs* [1936] 1 KB 351, at 361 and 364–365 respectively; and Wilberforce J in *Fitch Lovell Ltd v IR Comrs* [1962] 3 All ER 685 at 696). The most succinct statement was made by Lindley LJ in *John Foster & Sons v IR Comrs* [1894] 1 QB 518 at 528, where he said: "I do not know what is necessary to constitute a sale, except a transfer of property from one person to another for money or, for the purposes of the Stamp Act, for stock or marketable securities". In that case, eight partners of a firm executed a deed in favour of a limited company incorporated by them to convey and assign to that company all the property of their partnership; it was held that the deed was a "transfer on sale" because it was a transfer of property from individuals to a corporation in consideration of "stocks or securities", notwithstanding the fact that the eight partners who transferred the property were also the individuals who constituted the company.

In distinguishing between sales which are chargeable and partitions or exchanges which are not chargeable, problems have arisen particularly in two areas: those involving family arrangements and partnerships.

(i) *Family arrangements* Apart from the case of *Oughtred v IR Comrs* mentioned above, there have frequently been cases involving consideration by the courts of whether particular types of family arrangement can be construed as transactions involving chargeable transfers on sale. Usually there is no problem because the arrangement will not involve a consideration in cash or stock or securities—for example in *Cormack's Trustees v IR Comrs* 1924 SC 819 a widow accepted a life annuity in exchange for renunciation of certain legal and equitable rights. There have been cases, however, where family arrangements have been held to be transfers on sale eg in the *Marquess of Bristol v IR Comrs* [1901] 2 KB 336, where a settlor conveyed all his unsettled property to the beneficiary of his settled property, the deeds reciting that the beneficiary had undertaken the payment of the mortgages of the transferor's estates and that the transferor was indebted to the beneficiary for certain sums.

Many of the stamp duty problems relating to family arrangements have now been resolved by FA 1985 s 84 (as to which see below), but this does not apply where, in the case of variations in dispositions of a deceased person's estate (whether by will, under the law relating to intestacy or otherwise), the variation "is made for any consideration in money or money's worth other than consideration consisting of the making of a variation in respect of another of the dispositions".

(ii) *Partnerships* Where one or more partners take a new partner into the business in return for a cash payment, and the incoming partner gets a share of the business, then the deed or instrument of partnership will, as a rule, be construed as a transfer on sale. If, however, the incoming partner merely brings in a capital sum, this will not necessarily be consideration for a sale, unless one or more of the existing partners withdraws capital in consequence of the incoming partner's contribution. A division of assets between partners on the dissolution of the partnership is not a transfer on sale. But where only one partner leaves the partnership in consideration of a sum of money paid to him by the continuing partner or partners, the deed of dissolution constitutes a clear transfer on sale of his share in the partnership to the continuing partners, and is stamped as such.

There is a view (supported by the *Tax Bulletin* Issue 18, August 1995, (Appendix 6)) that a transfer of property expressed as satisfying the price payable on another transfer does not constitute a transfer on sale. This has led to legislation in FA 2000 ss 118–121 deeming certain transfers to be on sale.

An assent or conveyance by a personal representative to give effect to a contract of sale entered into by the deceased vendor was held to operate as a transfer on sale notwithstanding the Administration of Estates Act 1925 s 36(4) in *GHR Co Ltd v IR Comrs* [1943] KB 303. It has also been held that conveyance on sale duty attaches to an assent by personal representatives to give effect to an appropriation made with the beneficiary's consent in satisfaction of the whole or part of a pecuniary legacy (*Dawson v IR Comrs* [1905] 2 IR 69). A similar decision was reached in the case of an appropriation made in satisfaction of a fixed sum payable on an intestacy (*Jopling v IR Comrs* [1940] 3 All ER 279). However, where personal representatives do not need a legatee's consent to appropriate property, either by virtue of a clause in the will or by virtue of the Administration of Estates Act 1925 s 41, then transfer on sale duty will not be chargeable because there is deemed to be no contractual element to the appropriation. The same applies where a legatee is entitled to demand an appropriation in satisfaction whether in whole or in part of a pecuniary legacy. The same applies also to an appropriation in satisfaction of a share of residue notwithstanding dicta supporting the opposite course in *Re Beverly, Watson v Watson* [1901] 1 Ch 681. Where, however, a widow whose interest on intestacy falls short of the value of the matrimonial home pays the difference in value in order that it may be appropriated to her, then the difference will attract conveyance on sale duty.

(d) "Transferred to or vested in the purchaser, or another person on behalf of or at the direction of the purchaser."

Property needs to be vested in the purchaser or someone on his behalf, but it is not necessary for it to be the exact property actually sold nor need it be the vendor that does the vesting. For example, a declaration of trust vesting only the equitable interest may be a transfer on sale, so that where a contract for sale provides expressly that on payment of the purchase price the vendor will hold the property in trust for the purchaser, then the agreement is a transfer on sale: *Chesterfield Brewery Co v IR Comrs* [1899] 2 QB 7; *West London Syndicate Ltd v IR Comrs* [1898] 1 QB 226 at 240, (reversed on another point [1898] 2 QB 507, CA). An instrument of transfer of shares in which the name of the transferee and the amount of the consideration are left blank is a transfer on sale (*Fitch Lovell Ltd v IR Comrs* [1962] 3 All ER 685).

In *Peter Bone Ltd v IR Comrs* [1995] STC 921 a deed of agreement for the sale of a business consisting of land and other assets provided that it was to complete immediately upon its exchange and that the transferor should deliver to the transferee the assets capable of delivery and any documents required to complete title. The transferor did not intend that a transfer be entered into and the deed provided that the transferor was to hold the land as nominee for the transferee and execute such assignments, transfers or conveyances of the property to such persons as the transferee might require. The High Court held that, following completion and delivery of the assets and documents, there was nothing more to be done under the contract and nothing capable of being specifically performed; the transferor held the land for the transferee as bare trustee and not as constructive trustee. In particular, the transferor could transfer the potentially burdensome legal title of the land only to third parties on the instruction of the transferee and could not require the transferee to take a transfer of it. The court held that the deed was not a contract for the sale of the legal and equitable estates in the land (which would not have been a stampable agreement for the purposes of what was then SA 1891 s 59(1)), but did not decide whether the deed was an agreement to transfer an equitable estate (stampable under SA 1891 s 59(1), now para 7 below) or an actual conveyance of the equitable estate (stampable under s 54, now para 1 of this Schedule).

A lease has been held to be a transfer on sale (in *Littlewoods Mail Order Stores Ltd v IR Comrs* [1962] 2 All ER 279), but an instrument which purported to be a conveyance of land, but which could not operate as such since it was not executed under seal, and contained a stipulation not to disturb the party intended to take the premises, was held not to be stampable as a conveyance on sale (*R v Ridgwell Inhabitants* (1827) 6 B & C 665).

A deed effecting a dissolution of partnership reciting that an outgoing partner had no claim to the partnership assets in consideration of a payment of a fixed sum to be made to him was held to be a conveyance on sale of the relevant part of the partnership property (*Garnett v IR Comrs* (1899) 81 LT 633) and a document worded as a receipt for purchase money may in certain circumstances operate as a conveyance or transfer on sale (*Fleetwood-Hesketh v IR Comrs* [1936] 1 KB 351 at 364 CA). An order by a creditor to a debtor for payment to another may constitute an equitable assignment of a debt (see eg *Brice v Bannister* (1878) 3 QBD 569, CA). A letter addressed to a company by a shareholder directing the company to allot certain shares to which he was entitled to certain donees was a valid equitable assignment (*Letts v IR Comrs* [1956] 3 All ER 588).

The grant of an option in consideration of a cash sum has also been held to be a transfer on sale (*George Wimpey & Co Ltd v IR Comrs* [1975] 2 All ER 45) notwithstanding the argument that a document bringing property into existence, ie an option, could not also be treated as having effected a sale of that property. Whilst this does, strictly speaking, fit within the statutory wording, it is doubtful whether the *Wimpey* case should be regarded as establishing a particularly broad principle. By analogy, it would seem that the act of entering into a contract was capable of being a "transfer" of a newly created contractual right to the other party on the basis that executing the contract would "vest" in the counter-party a right to have the contract performed. This in turn would appear to render pointless the distinction recognised in *IRC v G Angus & Co* (1889) 23 QBD 579 between a contract and a transfer because (subject to any questions as to valuation differences, in some circumstances) obtaining the right to receive a thing would then appear to attract the same charge to duty as obtaining the thing itself. Stamp duty law does not appear to have developed on the basis of any such reasoning.

It is probably the case that the *Wimpey* decision only affects the grant of options over land and not, for example, options over shares or other forms of personal and/or intangible property. The *Wimpey* case itself is quite difficult to view in such restrictive terms because the judgments in that case tend to emphasise the generality of the wording in the statutory definition of "conveyance" in SA 1891 (as it then was, now FA 1999). This definition refers to the "vesting" of property as well as the transfer of property in a manner which suggests that the creation of any right is a "sale" of the right to the initial grantee.

It is submitted that that is not correct because the distinction apparently enshrined in the *Angus* case (1889) 23 QBD 579 (see commentary on paras 7–9) between a contract and a conveyance, long regarded as fundamental to the whole operation of the UK stamp duty system, would appear to be utterly meaningless if every act of entering into a contract amounts to the "sale" of the right to have the contract completed by performance.

Although it is not readily gleaned from the *Wimpey* case itself, it is submitted that a reading of the leading non-tax cases on options over land—namely *London and South Western Railway Co v Gomm* (1882) 20 Ch D 562 and *Spiro v Glencrown Properties Ltd* [1991] Ch 537—reveals the true reason for regarding *Wimpey* as correctly decided on its facts but not as laying down any general principle of wide ambit with regard to the vesting of new rights by way of stampable "transfer". In stamp duty terms (and it is emphasised that this explanation is only concerned with the stamp duty aspect of such transactions and is not necessarily an accurate way of describing the technical legal position for purposes other than stamp duty) the grant of an option over land amounts to an agreement to create an express trust of the land, albeit defeasible at the instance of the beneficiary.

The only slight drawback with this analysis is perhaps that, in terms of classifying legal rights, it gives significance to the availability or non-availability of the remedy of specific performance. This approach does find favour in some of the leading cases on property rights—see, for example, *J Sainsbury plc v O'Connor* [1991] STC 318—but it does suggest that, if carried through logically, an option is a "transfer" (for stamp duty purposes) whenever it relates to any type of property in respect of which specific performance of contracts is commonly ordered. This in turn suggests that a difference might exist between options over quoted and unquoted shares (since a court of equity is generally prepared to order specific performance of a contract to sell shares but not if they are readily available in a publicly accessible market).

It is perhaps surprising that this issue has not generated more case law, or other discussion, particularly because there is a further provision (see SA 1891 s 60) which also refers to a charge to duty on a "right not before in existence". However, it should be remembered that the point will only be significant in practice where substantial value is given in respect of the grant of an option, rather than in respect of its subsequent exercise. This may account for the lack of disputes on the point in practice.

Conditional transfers of shares in the context of public takeover bids have also in the past given rise to problems. In the case of *Ridge Nominees Ltd v IR Comrs* [1961] 2 All ER 354, it was held that, where a company makes an offer to shareholders of another company to purchase their shares in that company, the offer being conditional on a specified number of acceptances being received by a certain date, transfers executed by accepting shareholders before the date when the offer becomes unconditional are liable to ad valorem stamp duty as conveyances on sale. An attempt was made by BTR plc, in the context of its takeover bid for Thomas Tilling, to mitigate the effects of this decision by using a scheme involving a reorganisation of the share capital of the target immediately after the bid became unconditional. The attempt, however, failed. The facts of *BTR plc v IR Comrs* [1986] STC 433, were as follows:

On 21 May 1983, a final offer of shares or cash was made by the taxpayer company for the ordinary share capital of T, subject to conditions as to acceptance. In addition the offer provided that if T reorganised its share capital the offer would be adjusted so as to constitute separate offers for the existing ordinary shares and the new ordinary shares allotted pursuant to the reorganisation. The offer was to be conditional on no announcement being made convening a general meeting of T, on or before 21 days after the offer became unconditional, to effect a capital reorganisation. In the event of such an announcement the offer would apply in adjusted terms to both the existing and new shares at no greater cost to the taxpayer company. The offer was declared unconditional on 8 June. On 10 June dealing commenced in the shares issued by the taxpayer company in consideration for the T shares. On the same day T announced that an extraordinary general meeting was to be held on 29 June for the purpose of passing a resolution for a capital reorganisation. At that meeting it was resolved to capitalise reserves and then to issue three new shares for each T share held. On the basis of the cash offer the value of one T share before the reorganisation was 225p; after the reorganisation the value of one T share was 56·25p. The new shares were issued on documents of title renounceable in favour of the taxpayer company. Five block transfers in respect of irrevocable forms of acceptance and transfer received on various dates before 29 June were presented for stamping. Duty was assessed by reference to the value of the shares before the reorganisation on 29 June on the grounds that the offer became unconditional on 8 June and the forms of acceptance and transfer constituted conveyances on sale of the existing shares as from that date. The taxpayer company appealed against the adjudication contending that the shares transferred by forms of acceptance and transfer were dutiable by reference to the value of the new shares because the offer remained conditional until the reorganisation on 29 June.

It was held that irrevocable forms of acceptance and transfer delivered in response to the offer before it became unconditional, ie on 8 June 1983, became effective transfers on that date, and acceptances delivered after that date but before 29 June took effect on delivery. Accordingly there were effective transfers which were conveyances on sale of the shares referred to in the adjudication before 29 June and stamp duty was payable as assessed. The appeal would therefore be dismissed.

As to beneficial ownership, see notes to FA 1930 s 42.

Reliefs from stamp duty are now available in takeover bid situations under FA 1986 ss 75, 76 and 77.

(e) Computation of consideration

Transfer on sale duty is payable on the "amount or value of the consideration for the sale", and not (subject to the rules in FA 1994 and FA 2000 in certain cases involving land and marketable securities) on the value of the property conveyed or transferred, so that any change in the value of the property sold between the agreement and completion will not affect the amount of duty payable. The question how the "amount or value of the consideration for the sale" is arrived at may depend upon the statutory provisions governing the matter, which are contained in SA 1891 ss 55, 56, 57 and 58 (these being sections dealing with particular types of consideration and in particular cases) and FA 1900 s 10. See also the commentary on FA 1994 in relation to exchanges, partitions and cases where the consideration is not ascertainable from the conveyance.

There is no general definition of "consideration" in the stamp duty legislation. One area of uncertainty that the lack of a statutory definition gives rise to relates to the potential interaction between stamp duty and the VAT payable in respect of commercial buildings. The Stamp Office take the view, and it seems difficult to contest, that any VAT payable on the purchase price of land and buildings will form part of the "consideration" and be subject to stamp duty accordingly. This view is taken whether the purchase price in the relevant instrument is expressed as an amount *inclusive* of VAT or an amount *plus* VAT. Arguments by practitioners that HMRC are effectively seeking to impose a "tax upon a tax" have not had a sympathetic hearing from either HMRC or the Treasury. For a more detailed analysis, see for example the articles in *Taxation* by R S Nock on 5 and 12 April 1990 and by P Davis on 29 August 1991. See also Revenue Press Releases of 22 July and 12 September 1991 and SP 11/91. The decision in *Glenrothes Development Corporation v IR Comrs* [1994] STC 74 would seem to have resolved the issue in favour of HMRC.

It is a basic principle that stamp duty is charged by reference to the circumstances which exist at the time the instrument was executed (*William Cory & Son Limited v IR Comrs* [1965] AC 1088) and if the consideration was not ascertainable at that time then, subject to the contingency principle and FA 1994 s 242, no stamp duty can be charged. HMRC are not entitled to "wait and see".

There is a distinction between (*a*) consideration which is incapable of being ascertained at the date of the agreement because, for example, it is based on the future profits of a company being acquired, and (*b*) consideration which is theoretically capable of being ascertained at the date of the agreement, because, for example, it is based on the past profits of a company being acquired, but cannot be so ascertained in fact because the relevant accounts or valuation reports have not been prepared at the date of the agreement. In the latter case HMRC's practice is to require the document to be submitted for stamping and determine the duty when the final consideration is known.

If, in the former case, the consideration is genuinely unascertainable at the date of the agreement, HMRC should at most be able to rely on the "contingency principle". If consideration will become payable on the happening of some future event, that event is treated for stamp duty purposes as though it had occurred at the date of the relevant instrument. The Stamp Office will first determine whether or not there is a maximum (though variable) amount payable on the contingency and assess duty on that amount, even though it is highly unlikely that the maximum will ever be received. If there is a minimum but no maximum amount payable on the contingency, the document will be dutiable on the basis of that minimum. If there is neither a maximum nor minimum but a fixed amount subject to upward or downward adjustment, the duty will be charged on the basis of the fixed amount. However, if the consideration is genuinely unascertainable at the date of the agreement and no definite figure can be determined by applying the above principles, then there is authority for the view that no duty is payable other than (in appropriate cases) the fixed duty of 50p, or £5 as from 1 October 1999 (Scrutton J in *Underground Electric Railways and Glyn Mills & Co v IR Comrs* [1914] 3 KB 210 at 220; *Independent Television Authority v IR Comrs* [1961] AC 427).

However, the decision in *L M Tenancies 1 plc v IR Comrs* [1996] STC 880 appears to have extended the circumstances in which the consideration will be regarded as ascertainable. The facts of the case were that properties were leased to the appellant company by two leases dated 14 August 1993. Each lease provided that the consideration included, inter alia, the payment of a premium calculated in accordance with the formula "a" × "b", where "a" was a specified figure and "b" was the price of 13 ³/₄ per cent Treasury Loan Stock 1993 at the close of business on the 25th business day following the execution of the leases. The Revenue considered that duty was chargeable on both leases by reference to any amount of consideration which was ascertainable from their terms and the circumstances at the execution of the leases, and that the contingency that the closing price of the stock on the 25th business day following the date of execution of the leases might have gone up or down was to be ignored. The Revenue accordingly assessed the premium in each lease to ad valorem duty under SA 1891 Sch 1 as it was then, see now Part II of this Schedule, as a lease or tack by reference to the closing price of the stock, taking the closing price on 13 August 1993 as being that prevailing on the date of execution of the leases, since 14 August was a Saturday when the market was closed. The appellant company appealed against the assessments to the High Court and required the Revenue to state a case pursuant to SA 1891 s 13, contending that the leases were chargeable only with fixed duty of £2 (as it was then in the case of leases) under SA 1891 Sch 1 on the basis that the consideration was not capable of being ascertained at the date of the execution of the lease.

Carnwath J's judgment analysed *Underground Electric Railways Co of London Ltd v IR Comrs* [1906] AC 21 in a novel way as follows: SA 1891 Sch 1 provided for a charge to ad valorem duty in respect of any part of the consideration moving to the lessor which consisted of money. The premium in each of the leases of 14 August 1993 was clearly consideration consisting of money. Stamp duty had, however, to be charged by reference to the circumstances which existed at the time when the instrument was executed (see *Wm Cory & Son Ltd v IRC* [1965] AC 1088 at 1105, 1109 per Lord Reid and Lord Donovan respectively). Accordingly ad valorem stamp duty could not be levied on an instrument by reference to consideration the amount of which was unascertainable at the time when the instrument was executed. The consideration under the leases was not ascertainable at the time they were executed. However, the courts had developed the "contingency principle", under which the money payable was to be ascertained without regard to the fact that the instrument might contain provisions which would in certain circumstances prevent it from being payable at all. The same principle applied where the instrument contained a provision which merely varied the amount to be paid according to specified contingencies. It was immaterial whether the effect of such a provision was that the sum might be increased or reduced. What was necessary was that it should be possible to ascertain from the instrument that there was some "specified sum agreed upon as the subject of payment" which might perhaps fairly be called the prima facie or basic payment (see *Independent Television Authority v IRC* [1961] AC 427 at 443 per Lord Radcliffe).

The appellant company had contended that the leases contained no "specified sum agreed upon as the subject of payment" as at the date of the leases, because the only sum agreed upon was one ascertainable 25 days later, and that to substitute the closing price on the day immediately before the instrument was to rewrite the terms of the leases. The appellant company relied on *Coventry City Council v IRC* [1978] STC 151 at 156–157, where Brightman J had referred to the Crown's submission that, where ad valorem duty was payable on an instrument by reference to a sum payable thereunder, the duty was charged not only by reference to a sum which was unconditionally payable but also by reference to a sum specified in the instruments which was payable contingently. The Crown had, however, conceded in that case that if the form of the instrument had been such that a sum was payable, but the instrument did not name what that sum was, or what it might be, so that the sum could in theory have been any figure, subject to due quantification by reference to some formula, there was nothing by reference to which ad valorem duty could be calculated. Although that case was dealing with rent, it and the other authorities showed that the contingency principle applied to all the various charging heads of SA 1891 (or, as it would now be, all the charging provisions of this Schedule).

The Revenue relied on *Underground Electric Railways Co of London Ltd v IRC* [1906] AC 21 contending that it was indistinguishable from the instant case. It was concerned with the sale of the undertaking of a railway company. Part of the consideration was to be based on the profits of the transferee company. The agreement provided that the profits of the transferee company available for dividend in respect of each year might be applied in paying to the transferor as a further part of the consideration for the sale such sum as should be equal to a dividend of 3 per cent for such year on the amount for the time being paid up on such of the original ordinary share capital of £5m in the transferee company as should for the time being have been issued by the transferee company.

The House of Lords held that the further consideration of 3 per cent, although payable on a contingency (the availability of profits), was "money payable periodically" within the meaning of SA 1891 s 56(2) (which dealt with consideration for a conveyance on sale consisting of periodical payments). The amount of the payment was also dependent on the amount of paid up capital at the time when the payment was due. The amount of paid up capital at the date of the agreement was £1.3m, although that was not stated in the agreement (see [1905] 1 KB 174 at 179 per Collins MR). Lord Lindley (at 22) referred to that part of the consideration which was equal to 3 per cent of the then paid up share capital of the transferee company as a "minimum sum". The "minimum sum" or specified amount was ascertained in that case not simply from the terms of the agreement but by reference to an external factor, namely the amount of capital actually paid up at the date of the instrument. The amount was determined at the date of the agreement, although the contract required the determination to be made, not at that date, but at the later dates when profits from year to year came to be ascertained. The ability to determine a figure at the date of the instrument was accepted as giving the amount sufficient fixity for the purpose of the contingency principle, although it was liable to be increased or reduced before the time when the formula came to be applied under the contract. Although Lord Lindley had referred to it (at 22) as a "minimum sum", he had acknowledged (at 23) that it might have been reduced (on a winding-up or reduction of capital) as well as increased.

The same reasoning applied to the instant case. Although the formula used in the leases could not in terms be applied as at the date of their execution, because the formula referred to a date 25 days thereafter, it was possible to ascertain the price of the Treasury Stock as at that date. It was necessary to ascertain the consideration by reference to the circumstances at the date of the instrument. In the *Underground Railways* case it was accepted that that involved looking at the amount of the issued capital on that date, although the contract itself anticipated calculation by reference to the paid up capital at a later date. In the instant case it was accordingly consistent to take the closing price applicable at the date of the leases, although they specified a later date. Provided that an amount for consideration could be ascertained in the circumstances existing at the date of the instrument, by applying the formula as at that date rather than the date envisaged in the instrument, stamp duty was chargeable on the figure produced.

That conclusion accorded with the language and intention of SA 1891 Sch 1, which was concerned with consideration consisting of money. That wording had to be applied in a context where it was necessary to ascertain the amount at the date of the instrument. Common sense suggested that the substantive question whether there was consideration in money would not be affected by the date at which the formula was to be applied, but that, in calculating the amount, the formula would be applied as at the date of the instrument, if reasonably practicable. That was the result of the Revenue's approach in the instant case.

The appellant company had submitted that there was no closing price of the Treasury Stock applicable at the date of the execution of the leases, which was a Saturday when the market was closed. However, once the conceptual difficulty had been overcome that the contractual formula had to be applied at a different point in time from that envisaged by the leases, there was no practical difficulty in fixing the amount. The appropriate price was that which could fairly be regarded as the "closing price" at the date of the leases, which was the one most recently available. The closing price for the day immediately preceding the leases was to be taken for the purposes of the calculation. The leases were therefore chargeable with ad valorem duty and the duty was to be assessed in accordance with the formula in each lease applying the closing price of the Treasury Stock as at the day before the execution of the leases, ie 13 August 1993.

The two main features of the judgment are:

(a) it confirms that the contingency principle applies to a single sum consideration as well as cash sums of an annual nature; and

(b) it extends the *Independent Television* "fixed amount" principle so that not only is a maximum or minimum sum or sum of money specified in the document variable upwards or downwards to be treated as ascertainable, but so is an amount which the document specifies is to be found by applying a formula to an "external factor" of "sufficient fixity". A consideration to be found by applying a formula to the future value of a gilt allowed an ascertainable "fixed amount" to be determined at the date of the document because the market value of the gilt at the date of the document (or as close to that date as practicable) could be substituted into the formula. It is not certain how this principle will apply to, inter alia, "earn outs", rents which vary in line with RPI, and land sales for a consideration linked to the success of the future development—it may be that the "external factor" will not have "sufficient fixity" to allow the new contingency principle to apply. In relation to rents see the note written by the Secretary to the Law Society's Revenue Law Committee published in the 8 January 1997 issue of the *Law Society Gazette* (see Appendix 4).

In the case of a transfer or vesting of any estate or interest in land, or the grant of any lease or tack, the operation of the contingency principle has been supplemented by statute where the consideration for the transfer, vesting or grant cannot be ascertained at the time the instrument in question is executed: see commentary on FA 1994.

The operation of the contingency principle also gives rise to potentially difficult problems in relation to the interaction between stamp duty and VAT. Assuming the Stamp Office is correct in its view that any VAT payable on the purchase price of land and buildings will form part of the "consideration" and be dutiable as such, which view (as mentioned above) was upheld in the case of *Glenrothes Development Corporation v IR Comrs* [1994] STC 74, the question then arises as to whether a *potential* charge to VAT, either (*a*) upon the deferred or contingent purchase price of non-exempt (ie new commercial) property, or (*b*) upon a future election to standard-rate the purchase price payable on the sale of old commercial property that would otherwise be VAT-exempt, or, even, (*c*) upon a future election to standard-rate the deferred or contingent purchase price of old commercial property that would otherwise be VAT-exempt, will fall within the scope of the contingency principle. See, again, the articles by R S Nock and P Davis referred to above, the Revenue Press Releases of 22 July and 12 September 1991, and SP 11/91. See also the correspondence between the Law Society's revenue law committee and the Revenue as published in the Law Society's Gazette of 4 March 1992 p 16 (reproduced in Appendix 4).

Following the Revenue's victory in the *LM Tenancies* case [1998] STC 326 the Stamp Office tried to apply the contingency principle in a much more expansive manner than they had done in the past. In particular, they seemed to regard that decision as justifying a use of historical data as "best evidence" of future states of affairs, which was, to say the least, a fairly robust deduction of principle from a decision in which the judges simply decided that future states of affairs could be approximated to present (not historical) states of affairs (the only "historical" element being the use of the previous day's stock market prices on the basis that the markets were actually closed on the relevant day). It seems that the Stamp Office now accept that some of their applications of the *LM Tenancies* decision went too far and they issued a press release on 14 May 1999 which indicates that in future they will apply the contingency principle on a much more restrictive basis (see the commentary on leases in Part II below).

However, it should be noted that that press release only applies specifically to the calculation of duty on rent payable under leases (and "leases", in this context, only means leases of land, not leases of chattels, software, etc). It remains to be seen whether any further attempt is made to apply the *LM Tenancies* decision on a "historic" basis where, for example, business assets are sold for a consideration which refers to future profits from that or another business over, say, the three years following the sale. The Stamp Office could argue, in principle, although it is submitted that neither *LM Tenancies* itself nor any other legal authority supports such an argument, that the "best evidence" of those three year's profits was the previous three year's profits. It is submitted that there is a significant difference between, on the one hand, seeking an approximation (as happened on the facts of *LM Tenancies*) of one day's stock values by reference to the preceding day's values, and, on the other hand, seeking an approximation of a lengthy future period of time by reference to an historical period of time of similar duration. It is not unreasonable to say that the value of stock on a non-working day is more or less the same as it was on the most recent working day, whereas the fortunes of a business could fluctuate dramatically over a period of two or three years, so that the last three years could prove to be a wholly unreliable guide to profits in the next three.

It should be noted that the contingency principle is being restricted by a number of provisions which now require stamp duty to be charged by reference to market value, for instance FA 1994 s 241 and FA 2000 ss 118–121.

A further aspect of the interaction of stamp duty and VAT that causes problems is that relating to the VAT rules on the transfer of a business as a going concern ("TOGC"). The Stamp Office have recently changed their practice twice on this point and have now introduced a practice, the lawfulness of which must be open to challenge in the absence of specific statutory authority to implement it, of what is in effect "interim" stamping. Reference should be made to the *Law Society Gazette*, 13 January 1999 (and to the observations thereupon in an article by Paul Giles in the *Tax Journal* for 1 February 1999), for further details. Essentially, however, the Stamp Office now require undertakings to be given when a document is initially presented for stamping in a TOGC situation, to the effect that the same document will be re-presented for further stamping if it later transpires that VAT ought to have been paid on a transaction which was initially treated as a TOGC. (This presumes, of course, that any VAT liability is in fact passed on to the purchaser and so is added to the original consideration for the transaction; no stamp duty issue arises if there is no right to pass on any VAT liability to the purchaser but such a restriction is unusual in practice and there might also be a residual question in such a case as to the validity and/or scope of the agreement not to charge VAT—see *Wynn Realisations Ltd v Vogue Holdings Inc* [1999] STC 524).

In calculating the amount or value of the consideration for the sale, the consideration mentioned in the conveyance is not conclusive. For example, where in *Oughtred v IR Comrs* the life tenant of settled shares agreed orally with the reversioner to exchange other shares owned by her for his reversionary interest in the settled shares, and the transaction so far as it related to the settled shares was completed by a transfer for a nominal consideration, the transfer was held liable to ad valorem duty on the value of the shares received by the reversioner from the life tenant by way of exchange (*Oughtred v IR Comrs* [1960] AC 206).

Following the abolition of the fixed duty of £5 on transfers otherwise than on sale of stock and marketable securities, it is now provided that *ad valorem* duty is not chargeable where the amount or value of the consideration for the transfer of such stock or securities is £1,000 or under and the instrument is certified at £1,000. Previously such a transfer would have attracted duty, at 0.5% at the minimum sum of £5.

Rates of duty

(See the notes printed at the end of the contents list to Part II Stamp Taxes.)

2–4.—These paragraphs set out the rates at which (other than in relation to stock or marketable securities, as to which see para 3 above) ad valorem duty is charged on conveyances or transfers on sale (and by cross-reference—see Sch 13 Part II below—lease premiums). For the different rates which have applied in the recent past, and the periods of time to which those former rates applied, see the commentary on para 6 below.

There is now a significant difference between the potential stamp duty costs of selling, on the one hand, "stock or marketable securities" and, on the other hand, any other form of property. The latter kind of transaction is now chargeable to duty at up to eight times the rate of the former kind, following the most recent rate increases in FA 2000 s 114.

This means that it is important to know whether any particular item of property does in fact qualify as "stock or marketable securities". These terms are both defined to some extent in the legislation (see SA 1891 s 122) but the main problem arises from the fact that the definition of "marketable security" refers to a "security", which is not itself defined in the legislation.

There are some cases which suggest that the word "security" bears a rather more technical and restricted meaning in a stamp duty context than in everyday language. It seems that, in everyday speech, "securities" now possibly connotes anything in the nature of a financial instrument or any investment which is not represented by a physical asset.

The case of *Independent Television Authority v IRC* [1961] AC 427, together with the earlier cases cited therein, suggest that a "security", in the context of stamp duty law, simply means an instrument embodying an enforceable obligation for the payment of money. If correct, that would suggest that an option over shares was not a "security", and so could not be a "marketable security". That in turn would mean that a transfer of an option over shares would be stampable at a rate of up to 4 per cent even though a transfer of the underlying shares themselves would only attract duty at a rate of 0.5 per cent however large the consideration for the transfer (and it should also be remembered that an option over shares might be stampable on its initial *grant* as well as on transfer, since nothing in the case of *George Wimpey & Co Ltd v IR Comrs* [1975] 2 All ER 45 necessarily confines the principles underlying that decision to options over land, even though the case itself concerned land—see commentary on para 1 above—although there may well be technical reasons why an option over shares ought to be treated differently to an option over land).

However, it is quite clear that the judges, both in the *Independent Television* case and in the earlier cases to which reference was made therein, recognised that there might be a difference between the meaning of security "in ordinary parlance" and its meaning for the purposes of what is now FA 1999 Sch 13 Part I.

Furthermore, those cases concern the specific wording of the now repealed "Bond, Covenant, etc" head of charge formerly contained in SA 1891 Sch 1, and it is recognised in some of the judgments that the particular wording of that head of charge forced the judges in the earlier cases to give a somewhat strained meaning to the word "security" in that context. It is therefore suggested that nothing in the cases on the old "Bond, Covenant, etc" head of charge would necessarily prevent the courts giving a broader and more commercial meaning to the word "security" for the purposes of, for example, the conveyance on sale provisions now contained in FA 1999 Sch 13 Part I.

The introduction of differential rates of duty (initially in F(No 2)A 1997, and amended by each of FA 1998, FA 1999 and FA 2000) also increases the potential value of the acquisitions relief in FA 1986 s 76 (see commentary on that section) which, at the time of its introduction, halved the ad valorem duty otherwise payable but could now reduce it by up to seven-eighths.

5.—Note that the rates set out here are subject to any enactment setting a different rate or upper limit on duty. The main provisions under which the ordinary rates of duty are varied are as follows.

(a) FA 1986 s 67(2)—a transfer of relevant securities of a company incorporated in the UK to a person who at the time of the transfer falls within s 67(6), (7) or (8) (depositary receipts);

(b) FA 1986 s 70(2)—a transfer of relevant securities of a company incorporated in the UK to a person who at the time of the transfer falls within s 70(6), (7) or (8) (clearance services);

(c) FA 1986 s 76(2)—a transfer of property, other than shares, by a target company to a company acquiring the whole or any part of the undertaking of the target company for a consideration consisting of or including an issue of shares in the acquiring company to the target company, or to all or any of the target company's shareholders, with no other consideration except cash (not exceeding 10 per cent of the nominal value of the shares to be issued) or the assumption or discharge by the acquiring company of liabilities of the target company, or both;

(d) FA 1986 ss 78(6) and 79(8)—a transfer of loan capital issued after 24 March 1986 except in the case of certain instruments executed in pursuance of a contract made before 19 March 1986.

In addition, there are a number of statutory provisions which provide for reliefs and exemptions from ad valorem "transfer on sale" duty, which are discussed in detail in the commentary following the relevant provisions.

See in particular:

FA 1930 s 42 (stamp duty under this head not chargeable in the case of certain transfers on sale between associated bodies corporate),

FA 1982 s 129 (stamp duty exemption to charities and Trustees of the the National Heritage Memorial Fund),

FA 1985 s 83 (transfer of property in connection with divorce, nullity of marriage or judicial separation—stamp duty exemption under this heading),

FA 1985 s 84 (variations of dispositions by beneficiaries and appropriations of property by personal representatives within two years of death—stamp duty exemption under this heading),

FA 1986 s 75(2), (6) (if certain conditions are satisfied, instruments in respect of business reconstruction schemes are exempt from stamp duty under this heading if executed after 24 March 1986 unless executed in pursuance of an unconditional contract made before 19 March 1986), and

FA 1986 s 77(1) (exemption from stamp duty under this heading for instruments transferring shares in one company to another if specified conditions are satisfied).

Meaning of instrument being certified at an amount

(See the notes printed at the end of the contents list to Part II Stamp Taxes.)

6.—This paragraph explains the basis on which instruments other than those relating to transfers of stock (which are charged at a uniform rate of 0.5 per cent, regardless of the size or value of the consideration involved—see paras 2–4 above) may be charged at one rate of duty rather than another, if they are "certified at a particular amount".

For documents executed after 22 March 2006 the rates are as follows:

(a) nil where the consideration is £125,000 or less and a certificate of value is included;
(b) 1 per cent where the consideration is more than £125,000 but does not exceed £250,000 and a certificate of value is included;
(c) 3 per cent where the consideration is more than £250,000 but does not exceed £500,000 and a certificate of value is included; and
(d) 4 per cent in any other case (including cases where the consideration is less than £500,000 but it is not possible to include a certificate of value).

For documents executed and stamped before 23 March 1993, where the amount or value of the consideration did not exceed £30,000 (or £250,000 for documents executed on or after 20 December 1991 and before 20 August 1992), the applicable rate is reduced from 1 per cent to nil. For documents executed on or after 16 March 1993 and not stamped before 23 March 1993, the applicable rate is reduced from 1 per cent to nil where the amount or value of the consideration does not exceed £60,000.

For documents executed on or after 8 July 1997 (except in pursuance of a contract made on or before 2 July 1997) and before 24 March 1998 (except in pursuance of a contract made on or before 17 March 1998) the rates are as follows:

(a) nil where the consideration is £60,000 or less and a certificate of value is included;
(b) 1 per cent where the consideration is more than £60,000 but does not exceed £250,000 and a certificate of value is included;
(c) 1.5 per cent where the consideration is more than £250,000 but does not exceed £500,000 and a certificate of value is included; and
(d) 2 per cent in any other case (including cases where the consideration is less than £500,000 but it is not possible to include a certificate of value).

For documents executed on or after 24 March 1998 (except in pursuance of a contract made on or before 17 March 1998) the rates are as follows:

(a) nil where the consideration is £60,000 or less and a certificate of value is included;
(b) 1 per cent where the consideration is more than £60,000 but does not exceed £250,000 and a certificate of value is included;
(c) 2 per cent where the consideration is more than £250,000 but does not exceed £500,000 and a certificate of value is included; and
(d) 3 per cent in any other case (including cases where the consideration is less than £500,000 but it is not possible to include a certificate of value).

For documents executed on or after 16 March 1999 (except in pursuance of a contract made on or before 9 March 1999) the rates are as follows:

(a) nil where the consideration is £60,000 or less and a certificate of value is included;
(b) 1 per cent where the consideration is more than £60,000 but does not exceed £250,000 and a certificate of value is included;
(c) 2.5 per cent where the consideration is more than £250,000 but does not exceed £500,000 and a certificate of value is included; and
(d) 3.5 per cent in any other case (including cases where the consideration is less than £500,000 but it is not possible to include a certificate of value).

For documents executed after 27 March 2000 (except in pursuance of a contract made on or before 21 March 2000 unless (1) the instrument is made in consequence of the exercise after 21 March 2000 of any option, right of pre-emption or similar right or (2) the instrument transfers the property to, or vests it in, a person other than the purchaser under the contract (eg where the purchaser under the contract directs the transfer to be to a third party or pursuant to a sub-sale)) the rates are as follows:
(a) nil where the consideration is £60,000 or less and a certificate of value is included;
(b) 1 per cent where the consideration is more than £60,000 but does not exceed £250,000 and a certificate of value is included;
(c) 3 per cent where the consideration is more than £250,000 but does not exceed £500,000 and a certificate of value is included; and
(d) 4 per cent in any other case (including cases where the consideration is less than £500,000 but it is not possible to include a certificate of value).

For documents executed after 16 March 2005 the rates are as follows:
(a) nil where the consideration is £120,000 or less and a certificate of value is included;
(b) 1 per cent where the consideration is more than £120,000 but does not exceed £250,000 and a certificate of value is included;
(c) 3 per cent where the consideration is more than £250,000 but does not exceed £500,000 and a certificate of value is included; and
(d) 4 per cent in any other case (including cases where the consideration is less than £500,000 but it is not possible to include a certificate of value).

The above rules, do, however, apply to grants of new leases to the extent that any part of the consideration consists in a premium (in which case these rules only apply to the premium and not to the rent, if any) but with slight modifications. There is no entitlement to the nil rate of duty on the premium unless the rent (presumably including the VAT element of such rent, where applicable) does not exceed £600 a year. In relation to the earlier time periods specified above, this figure of £600 should be read as £300 for any period in which the nil rate threshold was £30,000 and as £2,500 for the period in which the nil rate threshold was £250,000.

Where the consideration for a transaction is exactly equal to the amount of one of the stated thresholds, care should be taken to check whether VAT is expressed to be payable on that sum as this will take the consideration into a higher rate band. For example, a consideration of exactly £250,000 is now stamped at 1 per cent but such consideration will be taken into the 3 per cent band if it is expressed to be subject to VAT, since the VAT will itself be regarded as part of the consideration to be assessed (possibly even if there is only a contingent right to charge VAT in the future).

It should also be noted that the time limits for the various alterations of the rates, by referring to documents executed pursuant to contracts made before certain specified dates, give the misleading impression that these changes only apply to transfers of land. Despite the drafting of various Budget briefings and media summaries, this is *not* the case and it is sometimes open to question how the transitional provisions, and the consequent time limits for obtaining duty at the old rates, apply to transactions in which unconventional documentation is created.

The "windows" created by the drafting of the transitional provisions in F(No 2)A 1997, FA 1998, FA 1999 and FA 2000 also create the possibility of a total stamp duty charge being spread over separate documents. For example, suppose that an agreement for lease was executed on 4 July 1997 for a lease which included a premium of £300,000, and the actual lease was executed on 4 August 1997. The agreement for lease would be dutiable in respect of the premium at 1 per cent (being executed before 8 July 1997) but the actual lease would be chargeable to duty at 1.5 per cent in respect of the same sum (being executed after 8 July and not in pursuance of a contract executed on or before 2 July). If the agreement was presented alone for stamping before execution of the lease (although there is no legal obligation, as such, to do this in order to comply with the time limits for stamping an agreement for lease, following the amendment introduced by FA 1994 s 240) duty would be charged at 1 per cent. The effect of this, according to what is now FA 1999 Sch 13 Part II para 13, is not to "frank" the subsequent lease but simply to allow credit in respect of that lease for any amount of duty paid upon an earlier agreement from which it derives. Therefore, a further duty of 0.5 per cent (ie 1.5 per cent minus 1 per cent) would be payable upon the lease.

In *Swallow Hotels v IRC* [2000] STC 45, an option was entered into in 1992 entitling the tenant under a lease to call for a binding contract for the landlord to grant the tenant a new lease to come into force. The rate of stamp duty increased from 1 per cent to 2 per cent in respect of documents executed on or after 8 July 1997 (except in pursuance of a contract made on or before 17 March 1998). The tenant exercised its option in September 1997. The High Court held that the contract under which the new lease was created consisted of a combination of the original option provisions and the exercise of the option. Accordingly the rate of duty was 1 per cent. The transitional provisions of FA 2000 have been drafted so as to counteract the *Swallow Hotels* decision.

A document is to be regarded as being "certified at a particular amount" if it "contains a statement certifying that the transaction effected by the instrument does not form part of a larger transaction or series of transactions in respect of which the amount or value, or aggregate amount or value, of the consideration exceeds that amount." Such a statement is commonly known as a "certificate of value".

If a certificate of value is omitted from an instrument where it could appropriately have been given, the traditional practice of the Commissioners has been to allow the certificate to be added subsequently, provided that it is signed by all the persons who are parties to the instrument. However, in view of the increased number of rates, and the consequent increase in the number of cases where a certificate of value will now be required, there is a risk that less leniency might be shown by the Stamp Office in future. The Stamp Office have stated in writing that delays are being caused by the number of uncertified documents they need to return to the senders for inclusion of an appropriate certificate.

The only sanction for giving an incorrect certificate of value (apart from a liability to pay the correct amount of duty together with any interest and/or penalties for late stamping) is imposed by SA 1891 s 5. This provides that every person who, with intent to defraud, executes or prepares any instrument in which all the facts and circumstances affecting the liability of that instrument to duty, or the amount of the duty with which that instrument is chargeable, are not fully and truly set out is liable to a penalty not exceeding £3,000.

Normally, the value of all the property included in one transaction between the same parties should be taken into account before the certificate of value is given in relation to the conveyance or transfer of any one item. There is presently, however, an exception which allows the value of "goods, wares or merchandise" to be disregarded for the purpose of a certificate of value except insofar as there is an actual conveyance or transfer of them. If the prospective abolitions (referred to in the note at the end of the contents list for Part II Stamp Duty and Stamp Duty Reserve Tax) come into effect, there will be an exception allowing the value of all "exempt property" to be so disregarded (see the commentary on FA 1991).

Since the introduction of progressive rates of duty, it should be noted that the applicable rate should be determined, in principle, by the whole amount or value of the consideration for a transaction, or series of transactions, even though the amount of consideration properly chargeable to duty is less than the whole amount. For example, a contract to sell £50,000 of UK debts and £750,000 of foreign debts would only be chargeable to duty in respect of the

£50,000. However, even though £50,000 is within the range of consideration for which the duty is usually nil, the amount of consideration for determining the *rate* of duty would be the total of £800,000 so that the rate of duty on the £50,000 would be 4 per cent. Although, as stated above, there is a specific statutory entitlement to disregard the value of "goods, wares and merchandise", there is no general principle that the value of any item of property outside the scope of a particular charge is disregarded in assessing the rate of duty thereunder.

The question whether or not a transaction does in fact form part of either a larger transaction or a series of transactions can sometimes be quite difficult to determine. The law on this is far from settled, but the question has been judicially considered on a number of occasions in the past. The principal cases are described below.

The purchase at the same auction of a number of different lots does not necessarily constitute a "larger transaction" or a "series of transactions" within the meaning of this paragraph, so that a certificate of value could be given in respect of each lot without reference to the value of the other lots purchased (*A-G v Cohen* [1937] 1 KB 478). This case related solely to public auctions, and HMRC have indicated that in the case of privately negotiated sales, where a number of them take place at the same time, there will be a very strong presumption that the several sales form part of a larger transaction or a series of transactions which the parties will have to produce cogent evidence to rebut.

In *Kimbers & Co v IR Comrs* [1936] 1 KB 132; *Paul v IR Comrs* 1936 SC 443, it was held that where a sale of property (in these cases a sale of land) is linked to a simultaneous related transaction (in these cases an agreement for the vendor of the land to build a house upon it following the sale to the purchaser), then the value of the related transaction is to be disregarded for the purpose of giving a certificate of value in relation to the sale of the property.

In *The Prudential Assurance Co Ltd v IR Comrs* [1992] STC 683, the taxpayer company entered into two separate contracts with developers: one agreeing to buy a freehold property from the developers and the other providing for the development of the property by the developers in return for the payment of building costs by the taxpayer. The two contracts were signed and the freehold land was conveyed, on the same day at a time when a substantial part of the construction work had been completed. The Commissioners assessed stamp duty on the basis of the total amounts payable under both contracts, which they argued amounted to a single agreement, contained in two instruments, for the sale and purchase of the land together with the completed buildings. On appeal to the High Court, it was held that this could not be the correct characterisation of the transaction: the sale agreement was completed independently of the execution of the building works under the development agreement and the sale was of the land and buildings as they were then. The stampable consideration was therefore held to be the price due for the land and for the building works already completed.

The law has been the subject of a number of detailed reviews by the Revenue, first in 1957 and most recently culminating in the issue of a new statement of practice (SP 8/93) issued on 12 July 1993 (reproduced in Appendix 2). See also the Revenue Press Release, 12 July 1993 (reproduced in Appendix 4).

It seems that where in respect of a number of relevant transactions the vendors or the purchasers are not identical or associated, certificates of value may be given in respect of each transaction even if the transactions themselves may be associated. Where, for example, a purchaser sub-sells part of the property purchased by him, a certificate of value in relation to the sub-sale may be given. Also, where there is a single purchaser but a number of different vendors, a certificate of value may be given in respect of each item whether or not each contract is conditional upon completion of the others.

The difficulties arising from the potential interaction between stamp duty and the VAT payable in respect of commercial buildings (discussed in relation to SA 1891 ss 55, 56 and Part II of this Schedule) may also cause difficulties in deciding whether or not an appropriate certificate of value can be given.

See also the Committee debate on FA 1994 (extracts from which are reproduced in Appendix 4) in relation to possible difficulties with certificates of value in exchange transactions.

Contracts or agreements chargeable as conveyances on sale

(See the notes printed at the end of the contents list to Part II Stamp Taxes.)

7.—It was held in the case of *IR Comrs v G Angus & Co*; *IR Comrs v J Lewis & Sons* (1889) 23 QBD 579 that an agreement for the sale of the goodwill of a business was not a conveyance on sale for stamp duty purposes. This case resulted in the Customs and Inland Revenue Act 1889 s 18 and subsequently the Revenue Act 1889 s 15, now reproduced as para 7.

Until the repeals made by FA 1990 and FA 1991 are brought into force, any agreement for the sale of either:

(a) any equitable estate or interest in any property whatever; or
(b) any estate or interest in any property except (i) land, (ii) property locally situated outside the UK, (iii) goods, (iv) stock and marketable securities or (v) ships,

is liable to duty as if it were an actual conveyance on sale.

A transfer in favour of the purchaser pursuant to the contract, or in favour of a sub-purchaser pursuant to a subsequent sub-sale agreement, is not chargeable, or in the case of a sub-sale is chargeable only to the extent of the excess consideration paid by the sub-purchaser, and the transfer has the duty paid on the contract denoted on it or transferred to it.

Where any such contract is not stamped it will nevertheless be treated as sufficiently stamped for all purposes if, within six months or such longer period as the Commissioners may think reasonable, a conveyance in conformity with the contract is presented for stamping and duly stamped.

The duty can be reclaimed from the Commissioners if any such contract is rescinded or annulled or for any other reason, eg by failure of a condition, is not substantially performed.

Although most stamp duty charges are not expressly made the liability of any particular person by statute, it should be noted that para 7 specifically states that the duty arising under this paragraph is to be paid by the purchaser. It is uncertain whether an agreement to vary or indemnify this obligation would be void by virtue of SA 1891 s 117, either in entirety or at least as to the value of any interest and penalties for late stamping. If (as is suggested in *Sergeant & Sims*) the policy of s 117 is simply to encourage prompt stamping of documents, rather than allow parties to take the risk of late stamping, a contractual variation of the statutory rule would not appear to be objectionable to the extent that it relates only to the duty itself and not to any penalties and interest. Any such agreement should, however, be drafted so that, if it covers both the principal duty and interest and penalties, the obligations are treated as severable in the event that one part, but not the other part, is held to be void.

There is a large body of case law in relation to the interpretation of this paragraph (in its SA 1891 form), which in parts has proved to be particularly problematic. The most important of those cases are:

(a) *Farmer & Co v IR Comrs* [1898] 2 QB 141, in which it was held that the words of exception (ie, in (i)–(v) of para (*b*) above) do not qualify the words "equitable estate or interest" (in para (*a*) above) so that, eg, an agreement for the sale of an *equitable* interest (as opposed to a legal interest) in property situated outside the UK will be liable to duty if it falls within s 14(4);
(b) *West London Syndicate v IR Comrs* [1898] 2 QB 507, in which it was held that for an agreement to constitute an agreement for the sale of an equitable interest the vendor must be bound to grant, and the purchaser must be bound to accept, an equitable interest in the property, so that an agreement for the sale of a legal interest in land coupled with an option enabling the purchaser to take a declaration of trust in lieu is not an agreement for the sale of an equitable interest within the meaning of this paragraph;

(c) *Chesterfield Brewery Company v IR Comrs* [1899] 2 QB 7, in which it was held that an agreement to hold property on trust for someone in consideration of the payment of a sum of money, or the transfer of stock or marketable securities, is an agreement for the sale of an equitable interest within this section (see also *Peter Bone Ltd v IR Comrs* [1995] STC 921). It is important to bear in mind that it is possible to adduce extrinsic evidence to establish the true nature of a bargain, which means that a document apparently drafted as an outright transfer of land could be shown, by evidence of a lack of intention to complete a formal legal transfer, to be an agreement to transfer a purely equitable interest in land, and therefore dutiable under para 7 (although, presumably, evidence would have to point to absolute and unequivocal commitment to refrain from completing the title and not the mere absence of any definite intention to complete or not to complete—if a purchaser has a right to call for a conveyance to himself, the mere failure to exercise it is not sufficient to make the underlying contract an agreement to transfer an equitable interest in property);

(d) *Fleetwood-Hesketh v IR Comrs* [1936] 1 KB 351, CA, in which it was held that a memorandum of an agreement within the section requires to be stamped in accordance with it, so that an acknowledgement of receipt of the purchase money for a reversion under a will signed by the reversioner was an agreement for the sale of an equitable interest chargeable under this section;

(e) *William Cory Ltd v IR Comrs* [1965] 1 All ER 917, in which it was held that the grant of an option to purchase property is not a contract to which this section applies;

(f) *George Wimpey & Co Ltd v IR Comrs* [1975] 2 All ER 45, in which it was held that a contract for the sale of an option to purchase a legal interest in land can be a contract for the sale of an equitable interest in land;

(g) *Muller & Co's Margarine Ltd v IR Comrs* [1900] 1 QB 310, CA (affirmed by the House of Lords [1901] AC 217), in which it was held that the goodwill of a business abroad is property locally situated outside the UK within the exemption mentioned in this section and therefore not chargeable; and

(h) *English, Scottish and Australian Bank Ltd v IR Comrs* [1932] AC 238, in which it was held that simple contract debts owed by debtors resident outside the UK constituted "property locally situate out of the United Kingdom", so that a contract for their sale was not stampable under what was then SA 1891 s 59. This case overruled the decision in *Danubian Sugar Factories v IR Comrs* [1901] 1 KB 245, where an agreement for the sale of the benefit of a contract enforceable against a resident of Romania for the transfer of land in Romania was held liable to duty under s 59 as being "an estate or interest in property" not falling within any of the exceptions. An agreement for the sale of the benefit of a contract is now chargeable under para 7 provided it is not enforceable only abroad. The House of Lords in the *English, Scottish and Australian Bank* case decided that, as a matter of "well-settled law", choses in action could have a local situation and therefore in certain circumstances be "property locally situate out of the United Kingdom".

Goodwill is a form of property and an agreement for the sale of goodwill was chargeable under this section until this charge on instruments relating to goodwill was abolished by FA 2002 s 116 and Sch 37 in respect of instruments executed on or after 23 April 2002 (unless the goodwill relates to a business carried on abroad, and so constitutes "property locally situate out of the United Kingdom"). It has been held (for example in *Eastern National Omnibus Co v IR Comrs* [1939] 1 KB 161) that a non-competition undertaking given in return for a monetary consideration was an agreement for the sale of goodwill chargeable under this section.

"Goods, wares or merchandise" form a class of property falling within the exceptions under this section, and an agreement for their sale will not be chargeable. However, problems have arisen in the past as to what exactly is meant by the word "goods". It has been held that an agreement for the sale of tenant's fixtures is neither an agreement for the sale of land nor of goods requiring an agreement in writing under the Statute of Frauds (*Lee v Gaskill* (1876)

Part II ST

1 QBD 700). As a result, the Commissioners claim duty on the apportioned price for tenant's fixtures in the case of an agreement for sale of leasehold property and fixtures, but in the case of freehold property, fixtures form part of the freehold and an agreement for the sale of freehold land and fixtures will therefore fall within the exemption. It has also been held that the owner's interest under hire-purchase agreements of goods (at least in cases where the customer has a purchase option) is not an interest, an agreement for the sale of which is chargeable under what is now para 7 (*Drages Ltd v IR Comrs* (1927) 6 ACT 727). Electricity is treated as "goods" for the purposes of this paragraph, so that contracts for the sale of electricity will not be stampable (see Electricity Act 1989 s 103, a measure introduced in connection with the privatisation of the electricity industry). Some care should be taken, when drafting a written contract for the sale of "goods, wares or merchandise", to avoid creating an instrument which, although intended to be a mere agreement to sell, is actually construed, as a matter of law, as an immediate outright transfer of ownership and so stampable as a "conveyance or transfer on sale". When selling goods, it is usual to make an express statement to the effect that title to the goods is to pass by delivery. Since delivery is, generally speaking, a physical act, no stamp duty can be charged upon the transfer of title as no instrument of transfer is created pursuant to the transaction. Under the Sale of Goods Act 1979 (and under its predecessor of 1893, which itself merely codified the existing common law in this respect) there is no necessity for a conveyance—whether in the form of a document or a physical act—for the transferring of title to goods, and title is capable of passing by mere agreement if the parties expressly or impliedly agree to that. This would appear to create a risk that an ambiguously worded sale agreement could be interpreted as having dispensed with the requirement for any further act or document as a means of passing title. This would seem to be sufficient to make the sale agreement itself a "conveyance" in stamp duty terms (ie an instrument chargeable directly as a "conveyance or transfer on sale" and not under that head only by reference to the terms of para 7) even if it were not technically a conveyance for the purposes of the law of property. The problem would appear to be particularly acute where the relevant document is drafted in a foreign language and/or by reference to a foreign legal system, particularly if the strict English law distinction between contract and conveyance is not regarded as fundamental to property law in that jurisdiction.

Since it is well established that it is permissible to have regard to extrinsic evidence to determine the true nature of a bargain for stamp duty purposes (see, for example, the *West London Syndicate v IRC* [1898] 2 QB 507) there are two further issues to be borne in mind in relation to para 7 and sales of goods.

First, as stated above in relation to land, an agreement will be dutiable if what appeared from the documents alone to be an agreement for the outright transfer of goods was in fact (and in law) shown to be an agreement to create some kind of trust of the goods for the benefit of the "purchaser".

Secondly, it is an open question how an instrument would be interpreted if it purported to provide for title to pass by delivery where the forms of delivery of goods recognised by law appeared to be impossible on the given facts. In particular, where goods are in the possession of a third party, general sale of goods law appears to require some form of written order, warrant or acknowledgement to pass between the possessor and one or other of the parties to the sale. Such a document would appear to be at risk of itself being classified as a "conveyance or transfer" for stamp duty purposes.

An agreement for the sale of book debts was chargeable under this section until 30 November 2003 (see FA 2003 s 125). In *Measures Brothers v IR Comrs* (1900) 82 LT 689, under an agreement for the sale of the entire business of the company including its book debts, the book debts were to be taken as they were at the end of the vendor company's preceding financial year, the vendor company guaranteed their payment in full before the date fixed for completion, and at the date of the agreement only a small part of the debts due at the end of the preceding year were still owing; it was held that ad valorem duty was payable on the consideration apportioned for the book debts as at the end of the financial year, notwithstanding the subsequent repayment.

Cash at a bank represents as a matter of law a debt due from the bank to its customer and, theoretically, when any such cash forms part of the assets of a business agreed to be sold, ad valorem duty should be payable on the consideration for it. In practice, however, the Commissioners do not exact duty in the case of cash on current account, but treat it as falling within the exemption. They do charge cash on deposit account.

Ad valorem duty is also not claimed, in practice, on agreements for the sale of mortgage debts.

Because of the differing treatment of assets and property of different kinds, where there is an agreement for the sale of a business, or a number of different assets, an apportionment of the consideration amongst the various assets involved will be required for the purposes of para 7, and that apportionment must be a bona fide apportionment based on the commercial values of the respective assets. The Stamp Office supplies a form (No 22) for use in connection with apportionments, and will frequently require particulars showing detailed breakdowns of the various items listed (particularly those listed under the general heading of "loose plant and machinery, stock-in-trade, and other chattels"). However, it should be noted that the value of items of property which do not give rise to a stamp duty charge is not necessarily irrelevant in assessing duty (see the commentary on paras 4 and 6 above).

PART 2 LEASE

(See the notes printed at the end of the contents list to Part II Stamp Taxes.)

This contains the provisions for charging stamp duty on the initial grant (as opposed to subsequent transfer) of a lease, and also on the execution of an agreement for lease. The former head of charge in SA 1891 Sch 1 referred to a "lease or tack" but all references to a "tack" have been removed as part of the FA 1999 reforms.

In respect of any new lease (other than certain leases for a fixed term of less than one year) ad valorem duty is charged both on the premium (if any) for the lease, at the rate applicable to a "conveyance or transfer on sale" as specified in Part I para 4 above, and also on the annual rent, or average annual rent, at the appropriate rate set out in the table in paragraph 12(3). The rate varies according to the length of the lease.

To fall within the scope of this charge, the subject matter of the relevant lease must be land, tenements or heritable subjects. The head of charge does not apply to leases or hiring agreements relating to personalty.

Nor does it apply to a mere licence (as distinguished from a lease), which does not now attract any stamp duty. Under FA 1995 s 151, stamp duty under this head is not chargeable in the case of certain leases and agreements for lease or letting between associated bodies corporate. See commentary on that section and also on FA 1930 s 42.

For the purposes of this charge a lease granted for a fixed term and thereafter until determined is to be treated as a lease for a definite term equal to the fixed term together with such further period as must elapse before the earliest date at which the lease can be determined: para 15.

The words "moving either to the lessor or to any other person" in para 12(2) include the common case of a lease to a builder's nominee under a building agreement, where the lease is granted by the ground landlord at the direction of the builder to his nominee and a premium is paid to the builder.

The words "average rate" in para 12(3), referring to the rent, are intended to meet the case of a varying rent over a fixed term.

It would only be possible to calculate the "average rent" if the annual rental for each period of the whole term of the lease were specified in the lease itself. This will quite often not be the case; although rent review procedures will generally be set out in a lease it will almost always be impossible to calculate in advance the annual rental figure which will be produced. If there is a specified rental for the whole term of the lease which may be varied, upwards or

Part II ST

downwards and a percentage or amount as a minimum or maximum increase is also specified, that figure or percentage will be taken into account. It will always be the average of the highest ascertainable rents over the whole period of the lease which will be used as the basis of calculation. This principle ("the contingency principle") was applied in the case of *Coventry City Council v IR Comrs* [1979] Ch 142, [1978] 1 All ER 1107, applying dicta of Collins MR in *Underground Electric Railways Company of London Ltd v IR Comrs* [1905] 1 KB 174 at 182 and of Lord Radcliffe in *Independent Television Authority v IR Comrs* [1960] 2 All ER 481 at 485 and 486 (as to which see above).

In that case, Coventry City Council entered into an arrangement with the Norwich Union Life Insurance Society whereby one of the Council's development projects was financed by the Society by means of a scheme involving a lease and lease back of the relevant site. The Council granted to the Society a lease of the site for 125 years at an annual rental of £17,500, and on the same day the Society granted back to the Council an underlease of the site for 125 years less one day and covenanted to incur certain expenses and reimburse the Council's development costs up to a maximum of £1,300,000, the rent payable under the underlease being a basic rent of £17,500 pa (to match the rent under the headlease) and an annual rent of 8.142 per cent on the total sums incurred or reimbursed by the Society under its covenant not exceeding £1,300,000. It was held that the annual rent reserved was £17,500 plus 8.142 per cent of £1,300,000.

The operation of the contingency principle, in relation (inter alia) to the grant of any lease where the consideration for the grant cannot be ascertained at the time of grant, and to a lease with a rent which (or any part of which) cannot be ascertained at the time of execution, has now been supplemented by statute: see commentary on FA 1994 s 242. The scope of FA 1994 s 242 may have been substantially restricted by the "new" contingency principle enunciated in *L M Tenancies 1 plc v IR Comrs* [1996] STC 880 and affirmed at [1998] STC 326, which has extended the circumstances where consideration will be found to be ascertainable (see commentary on Part I para 1(2) above). However, if there is to be a broader disregarding of possible variations in circumstances, following the *LM Tenancies* case, it is questionable whether some of the factors caught by the "new" contingency principle are actually within the scope of the words in FA 1994 s 242(3)(*a*), a paragraph which is apparently designed to preserve the contingency principle. For example, if the share capital of a company is referred to in an instrument as one of the factors on which a future calculation of consideration is to be based, is the mere possibility that the size of that share capital might increase or decrease in the future caught by the statutory words "any future event mentioned in the instrument"? It would seem not since, if the document simply refers to the share capital as at a future date, the possibility of a variation in that capital is not itself an "event" which is "mentioned in" that document. It remains to be seen whether the *McGuckian* principle, if it becomes well established in the courts, will require such words to be read less literally (see discussion on anti-avoidance principles in the commentary on s 112 above). In relation to leases with provision for future rent to increase in line with RPI see the note written by the Secretary to the Law Society's Revenue Law Committee published in the 8 January 1997 issue of the *Law Society Gazette*.

Following their victory at both High Court and Court of Appeal level in the *LM Tenancies* case [1998] STC 326, the Stamp Office tried to apply the contingency principle in a much more expansive manner than they had done in the past. It seems that the Stamp Office now accept that some of their applications of the *LM Tenancies* decision went too far and they issued a press release on 14 May 1999 which indicates (although in rather delphic language) that in future they will apply the contingency principle on a much more restrictive basis. Reference should be made to the article by Patrick Cannon in the *Tax Journal* for 7 June 1999 for further details but, in essence, it seems that two potentially onerous uses of the contingency principle will *not* now be utilised by the Stamp Office. First, they will *not* seek to use historical data (ie data from periods predating the execution of a lease) as a means of producing forward projections of rent unless the parties to that lease expressly chose a period of time predating the lease as part of the period of time in which to measure RPI changes. Secondly, the Stamp Office will *not* seek to make cumulative, or compound, projections of future rent; for example, if it can be shown that RPI increased by 3 per cent between two given dates, it will be presumed (where, in the light of the first restriction referred to above, those dates are both ones which the Stamp Office feels able to utilise) that the rent will increase by 3 per cent at that next review date but it will *not* also be presumed that the rent will continue to increase by a further 3 per cent for each subsequent rent review date (if several period reviews are provided for). It is presumed that, in this context, any reference on the part of the Stamp Office to a "lease" is also intended, so far as relevant, to be a reference to an agreement for lease.

As far as the length of the lease is concerned, it has been held that a lease for a term of 99 years if A B and C should so long live is a lease for a term exceeding 35 years and not exceeding 100 years and is not a lease for an indefinite term (*Earl Mount-Edgcumbe v IR Comrs* [1911] 2 KB 24). It has also been held that a lease for a stated term of years is a lease for the length of that stated term notwithstanding that it contains a clause providing for the determination of the lease at an earlier date (*Kushner v Law Society* [1952] 1 KB 264).

The term "rent" is not defined and the description of a payment by the parties to an instrument as "rent" is not conclusive (see for example *Donellan v Read* (1832) 3 B&Ad 899). Payments which are not reserved out of the land are not rent (*Hill v Booth* [1930] 1 KB 381). The meaning of the word "rent" and its distinction from other payments such as royalties was considered in detail in *T and E Homes Ltd v Robinson* [1976] STC 462. If periodical payments for services, heating, lighting, cleaning, maintenance, etc are payable under the lease they will not be taken into account in calculating the ad valorem stamp duty payable whether or not they are reserved as rent.

As a matter of strict legal theory, it is debatable whether VAT payable in respect of the rent of non-residential premises can itself be regarded as "rent" and dutiable as such under this head of charge. On the basis of the cases mentioned in the previous paragraph the view of a number of practitioners is that, if "rent" can only include sums reserved out of the land on its demise, and not other sums payable under collateral arrangements, it should exclude any VAT payable. In other words, the VAT should be treated in exactly the same way as a service charge, especially where the lease reserves an amount by way of rent which is exclusive of VAT and makes separate provision for the VAT. Current HMRC practice, however, is to charge stamp duty on VAT on rent whether or not the VAT is actually expressed to form part of the rent (see the Revenue Press Releases of 22 July and 12 September 1991 and SP 11/91). If the lease provides for payment of VAT on the rent otherwise than as rent, duty ought, strictly speaking, to be charged on the VAT element as consideration payable periodically (SA 1891 s 56).

If VAT on rent is itself dutiable as rent, there are further difficulties arising out of the operation of the contingency principle, discussed above. Where for example rent is exempt from VAT at the time the lease is executed, the question arises as to whether the possibility of the landlord in future exercising his option to standard-rate the rent will cause an additional amount of stamp duty to be payable on the VAT which is contingently payable (and, if so, at what rate of VAT). Similarly, there will be difficulties where the lease reserves a rent which is itself contingent. The current HMRC practice in relation to the first of these difficulties is to make use of the contingency principle and assess the amount on which stamp duty is charged on VAT-exempt leases to include the VAT (presumably at the standard rate then in force) that *may* arise later following the exercise of an option to standard rate. See the Revenue Press Releases of 22 July and 12 September 1991 and SP 11/91. For a detailed analysis of these difficulties, see also the articles in *Taxation* by R S Nock on 5 and 12 April 1990 and by P Davis on 29 August 1991, and the correspondence between the Law Society's Revenue Law Committee and the Inland Revenue as published in the *Law Society's Gazette* of 4 March 1992 p 16 (reproduced in Appendix 4). Note also the decision in *Glenrothes Development Corporation v IR Comrs* [1994] STC 74. The decision in *L M Tenancies 1 plc v IR Comrs* [1996] STC 880 provides support for the current HMRC practice.

It is presumably the case that the contingency principle cannot be applied to any situation where a right in principle to add VAT to consideration is expressly precluded in advance.

However, for an example of the fact that attempts to draft contractual VAT restrictions sometimes fail in their intended purpose, see *Wynn Realisations Ltd v Vogue Holdings Inc* [1999] STC 524. (And, for an example of the possibility that failing to reserve a right to charge VAT at all is not necessarily conclusive of a party's inability to charge it, see *Tony Cox (Dismantlers) Ltd v Jim 5 Ltd* (1997) 13 Const LJ 209).

By virtue of para 15, a weekly or monthly tenancy agreement will, for stamp duty purposes, be regarded as a lease for an indefinite term, whereas an agreement for one week or one month certain, and thereafter subject to one week's or one month's notice, will be treated as a lease for a definite term of two weeks or two months, as the case may be.

A lease for a fixed term with an option to renew is regarded as a lease for the fixed term only, and if the option is exercised the instrument exercising it will be liable to stamp duty as for a new lease.

When notice to terminate a tenancy is given, and the notice is afterwards withdrawn by agreement, the withdrawal of the notice will also constitute a new tenancy (see *Freeman v Evans* [1922] 1 Ch 36, CA) and further ad valorem stamp duty will be payable. Since it appears to be well established that a lease cannot be retrospective, so that the commencement of a term cannot be earlier than the date the lease is executed (*Bradshaw v Pawley* [1979] 3 All ER 273), HMRC disregard any period before the date of the lease in calculating the amount of ad valorem stamp duty payable.

The distinction between a lease and a licence was considered in detail by the House of Lords in the case of *Street v Mountford* [1985] 2 All ER 289. The facts of that case were that the landlord had granted to the appellant the right to occupy a furnished room under a written agreement which stated (i) that the appellant had the right to occupy the room "at a licence fee of £37 per week", (ii) that "this personal licence is not assignable", (iii) that the "licence may be terminated by 14 days written notice", and (iv) that the appellant understood and accepted that "a licence in the above form does not and is not intended to give me a tenancy protected under the Rent Act." The appellant had exclusive possession. The House of Lords held that the test as to whether an occupancy of residential accommodation was a tenancy or a licence was whether, on the true construction of the agreement, the occupier had been granted exclusive possession of the accommodation for a fixed or periodic term at a stated rent, and that unless special circumstances existed which negatived the presumption of a tenancy (eg where from the outset there was no intention to create legal relations or where the possession was granted pursuant to a contract of employment) a tenancy arose whenever there was a grant of exclusive possession for a fixed or periodic term at a stated rent—whatever the intention of the parties, as manifested in the agreement. Accordingly, it was held in this case that since the effect of the agreement between the appellant and the landlord was to grant the appellant exclusive possession for a fixed term at a stated rent, and no circumstances existed to negative the presumption of a tenancy, it was clear that the appellant was a tenant. It seems, following the House of Lord's reversal of the majority decision of the Court of Appeal in *Bruton v London and Quadrant Housing Trust* [1993] 3 WLR 150 that this principle even applies where the landlord lacks (and both parties know that he lacks) a title out of which to grant a lease.

No lease will be treated as duly stamped unless it contains a certificate that there is no agreement to which it gives effect, or (if not) it is stamped with a stamp denoting either (i) that there is an agreement to which it gives effect which is not chargeable to duty, or (ii) the duty paid on the agreement to which it gives effect. For this purpose a lease "gives effect" to an agreement if the lease is granted subsequent to the agreement and either is in conformity with the agreement or relates to substantially the same property and term as the agreement (see commentary on FA 1994).

See also *Kildrummy (Jersey) Ltd v IRC* [1990] STC 657, CS.

Where duty is paid on a lease agreement and subsequently a lease is granted which is either in conformity with the agreement or relates to substantially the same property and term as the agreement, then the duty payable on the lease is reduced accordingly. It is important to note that the payment of duty on an agreement for lease merely results in the crediting of that amount against the duty payable upon any subsequent lease to which that agreement gives effect. Payment on the agreement does not "frank" the lease so as to cancel or discharge any numerically greater charge to duty that might otherwise have applied to the actual lease (in the way that, for example, payment of a fixed duty of 50p, or £5 as from 1 October 1999, could "frank" a potentially larger liability to stamp duty reserve tax, calculated as 0.5 per cent of the consideration for the transfer—see FA 1986 s 87 et seq—if stamp duty reserve tax was chargeable in respect of a transaction which was undertaken for valuable consideration but which was not, from a stamp duty perspective, a transfer "on sale").

It should also be noted that the credit mechanism only operates in favour of the lease and not also in favour of the agreement. In other words, if duty is actually paid on the agreement and it later transpires that less duty is properly payable on the lease than on the original agreement, there is no entitlement to any refund of any of the duty previously paid on the agreement. This is not a situation where a stamp could be said to have been "wasted" or "spoiled" for the purposes of any refund provision under SDMA 1891 because, as a matter of law, the correct amount of duty has been paid on the agreement (the agreement for lease being a stampable instrument in its own right).

It is likely that, in most cases, no problems will arise as a result of this one-way credit mechanism. This is because the principal terms of both the agreement and the actual lease will often be the same, with the result that both the method of calculating duty and the mathematical result of the calculation will be the same in each case. However, some situations could arise where the terms differed (but not to the extent that the lease was not treated as one to which the earlier agreement "gave effect") and this could result in duty being calculated on a more onerous basis for one document than for the other.

One possible situation where this might arise is in the context of applications of the contingency principle to "contingent VAT" (as referred to earlier—see the commentary on para 1 above). Where the option to tax is available but has not been exercised, the Stamp Office seem to regard VAT exempt rent as a rent which is subject to the contingency of an option to tax being exercised subsequently, unless this has been made impossible (eg by agreeing a VAT-inclusive rent or by imposing a condition not to opt). If the parties are seeking to prevent any future exercise of the option to tax from increasing the amount of rent, it is therefore prudent to put this matter beyond further question at the agreement stage and not at the lease stage.

This is because, if any doubt remains on the point until the formal lease is granted, there is a risk that the initial agreement for lease will be stampable on a more onerous basis than the actual lease. This is because the duty on the agreement would include an amount in respect of the contingent VAT but (subject to any argument that the drafting of the relevant VAT restriction was defective and so did not preclude the charging of VAT in all possible circumstances) the duty on the actual lease would not. Furthermore, where there is a conveyance or transfer of a freehold or leasehold interest subject to an agreement for a lease for more than 35 years, the conveyance or transfer instrument is not to be taken as duly stamped unless the duty on the agreement is denoted on the conveyance, except where the agreement is directly enforceable against another interest in the land.

See also the commentary on FA 1994 in relation to the time for presenting agreements for leases.

With regard to the interaction between VAT and stamp duty, see also: Revenue Press Releases of 22 July and 12 September 1991; SP 11/91; articles in *Taxation* by R S Nock on 5 and 12 April 1990 and by P Davis on 29 August 1991; and the correspondence between the Law Society's revenue law committee and the Revenue as published in the *Law Society's Gazette* of 4 March 1992 p 16 (reproduced in Appendix 4).

PART 3 OTHER INSTRUMENTS

Conveyance or transfer otherwise than on sale

(See the notes printed at the end of the contents list to Part II Stamp Taxes.)

As part of a policy of reducing the administrative burden on businesses, FA 2008 abolished the provisions within Sch 13 Part 3 for all instruments save for those effecting a land transaction, or for a duplicate or counterpart of such an instrument. The effect of this was to remove the requirement to pay a fixed duty of £5 where a transaction involved stocks or marketable securities but to leave in place the regulatory system required to supervise those remaining land transactions which fall outside the scope of SDLT – ie where the parties to a land transaction "rested in contract" before the introduction of SDLT in late 2003. What follows therefore applies only to those exceptional cases involving an instrument transferring land where the transaction is not an SDLT transaction within the meaning of FA 2003 Sch 19 para 2 or which is excluded from the charge to SDLT by FA 2003 s 125 or Sch 19.

16.—(1) As part of the attempted rationalisation and modernisation of the stamp duty system, all fixed charges (whether or not they have previously been set at 50p) are now raised to £5. Although it is not immediately apparent from the wording of this paragraph, there are a couple of situations where an instrument which transfers property "otherwise than on sale" actually gives rise to an ad valorem charge to stamp duty rather than a fixed charge—see commentary on FA 1986 ss 67(3) and 70(3).

(2) This essentially re-enacts (with slightly modernised wording) the now repealed SA 1891 s 62 which defined "conveyance or transfer" for what was then the head of charge "conveyance or transfer of any kind not hereinbefore described" in SA 1891 Sch 1, now itself re-enacted (with a modernised description) as para 1(1) above.

Declaration of use or trust

(See the notes printed at the end of the contents list to Part II Stamp Taxes.)

17.—A fixed duty of £5 is chargeable upon a declaration of trust. The statutory draftsman has taken the opportunity to harmonise the wording of this provision with the similarly worded provisions relating to releases and surrenders, which are also now set out in this Part of this Schedule. It has long been clear that the fixed charge on a declaration of trust yields to an ad valorem charge where the declaration of trust also constitutes a conveyance or transfer on sale (see *Chesterfield Brewery Co v IRC* [1899] 2 QB 7) but this had not been reflected in the wording of the heads of charge in SA 1891 Sch 1. The opportunity has now been taken to harmonise the wording of these conceptually similar provisions.

18.—[Scotland]

Duplicate or counterpart

(See the notes printed at the end of the contents list to Part II Stamp Taxes.)

19.—The effect of this paragraph is that, in order to be duly stamped, a duplicate or counterpart of a stampable instrument must either bear evidence of the fact that full duty has been paid on the original instrument or it must bear the same duty as the original instrument. If it is shown by means of "some stamp impressed on it" (ie a denoting stamp) that full duty has been paid on the original, then the charge on the duplicate or counterpart is limited to £5. The requirements stated above do not apply to a counterpart lease if the counterpart has not been executed by or on behalf of the lessor or grantor, so that such an instrument is only chargeable to £5 in any case.

Instrument increasing rent

(See the notes printed at the end of the contents list to Part II Stamp Taxes.)

20.—This paragraph substantially re-enacts the now repealed SA 1891 s 77(5). It should be noted that what is chargeable is an instrument "by which" (or "whereby", as it said in the

1891 version) rent is increased. This suggests that the instrument in question must be the operative cause of the rent increase and not merely (but possibly subject to the so-called "memorandum rule") a record or acknowledgment of a certain state of affairs. Accordingly, it is thought that an appropriately drafted memorandum recording a change of rent under a rent review clause will not attract stamp duty.

It was formerly the view of the Stamp Office that where a landlord exercised his option under the relevant VAT legislation to standard-rate a commercial property lease which would otherwise be VAT-exempt, the notification he was required to give to Customs and Excise was an instrument increasing the rent which was dutiable under what was then SA 1891 s 77(5). A number of practitioners regarded this as incorrect: first on the basis that VAT could not itself constitute "rent" (although this is questionable), and secondly because (even if that were not correct) the option to standard-rate the rent is created by the lease itself and this paragraph does not apply to increases of rent arising by reason of the terms of the lease (which is why an appropriately drafted memorandum regarding a change of rent under a rent review clause is not dutiable). For a fuller analysis of these arguments, see the articles in *Taxation* by R S Nock on 12 April 1990 and by P Davis on 29 August 1991.

Now, however, the Stamp Office practice is to make use of the contingency principle and assess the amount on which stamp duty is charged on VAT-exempt leases to include the VAT that *may* arise later following an election to standard-rate, unless the landlord agrees in advance *not* at any time during the term of the lease to exercise his option to levy VAT (in which case, on the basis of the contingency principle, the stamp duty charge would not arise, although see *Wynn Realisations Ltd v Vogue Holdings Inc* [1999] STC 524 for a case where VAT became chargeable even though the parties appeared to have agreed that it would not be charged). They will now *not* treat a notice of election as itself dutiable. Note, however, that a formal deed of variation or similar document varying the terms of a lease so as to provide for payment of VAT by way of additional rent *may* be dutiable under this paragraph. See also the correspondence between the Law Society's revenue law committee and the Revenue as published in the *Law Society's Gazette* of 4 March 1992 p 16 (reproduced in Appendix 4) and the decision in *Glenrothes Development Corporation v IR Comrs* [1994] STC 74.

Partition or division

(See the notes printed at the end of the contents list to Part II Stamp Taxes.)

21.—An instrument effecting a partition or division was normally charged at 50p and, as from 1 October 1999, will be charged with a fixed duty of £5. Where, however, upon the partition or division of any estate or interest in land, any consideration exceeding £100 in amount or value is paid or given, or agreed to be paid or given, for equality, then the instrument effecting the partition or division is charged with the same ad valorem stamp duty as on a conveyance on sale for that consideration and with that duty only. This specific provision is needed to charge ad valorem duty on an instrument effecting a partition because a partition is not a "sale" (see *Henniker v Henniker* (1852) 1 E & B 54) and so the instrument is not otherwise chargeable as a "conveyance or transfer on sale". Where more than one instrument is used for completing the title of either party in such a transaction, only the principal instrument is charged with ad valorem duty; the others are charged in the same manner as in the case of several instruments of conveyance.

Release or renunciation

(See the notes printed at the end of the contents list to Part II Stamp Taxes.)

22.—With the exception of releases or renunciations upon sale, instruments under this head are charged with a fixed duty of 50p (or £5, as from 1 October 1999). As a result of the introduction by F(1909–10)A 1910 s 74, of ad valorem duty on voluntary dispositions, a release or renunciation of any property or interest in property operating as a voluntary disposition inter vivos (for example the voluntary release of a life interest to the remainderman, as in *Platt's Trustees v IR Comrs* (1953) 46 TC 418) was also liable to ad

Part II ST

valorem duty. However, voluntary disposition duty was abolished by FA 1985 s 82 and such releases are chargeable only with 50p (or £5, as from 1 October 1999), and only releases or renunciations in respect of which a consideration is given are chargeable ad valorem as conveyances on sale. However, there must be a release in the nature of an assignment, eg of an interest in property which would, if the property were land, constitute an estate in the land. It has been held that the following were not such releases: the release by a Scottish widow of her claim to jus relictae (*Cormack's Trustees v IR Comrs* 1924 SC 819) and an undertaking not to work coal in a particular area (*Great Northern Railway v IR Comrs* [1901] 1 KB 416).

In this respect, it is interesting to note that the new provision simply refers to a release or renunciation "of property" whereas the old head of charge in SA 1891 Sch 1 referred to a release or renunciation "of any property or of any right or interest in any property". The removal of those words appears to align the scope of the charge with the view already favoured by the courts, namely that the release of a mere contractual (as opposed to proprietary) right was not a "release" for these purposes.

Releases and renunciations are to be distinguished from disclaimers. Releases or renunciations involve dispositions of property whereas disclaimers are simply the rejection of gifts and operate by way of avoidance (*Re Paradise Motor Co* [1968] 2 All ER 625, CA). Accordingly, disclaimers, if in writing, do not attract ad valorem stamp duty under the head "conveyance or transfer".

Surrender

(See the notes printed at the end of the contents list to Part II Stamp Taxes.)

23.—Formerly, surrenders were also treated as conveyances or transfers of property operating as voluntary dispositions inter vivos within the meaning of F(1909–10)A 1910 s 74 and chargeable with ad valorem duty accordingly. See *Platt's Trustees v IR Comrs* (1953) 46 TC 418. Since voluntary disposition duty has now been abolished, surrenders will only be chargeable under this head with a fixed duty of 50p (or £5, as from 1 October 1999) unless a consideration is received for the surrender, in which case they will be stampable as conveyances on sale. For the treatment of surrenders and regrants see the Tax Bulletin, Issue 17, August 1995, p 234 (Appendix 6). See also the commentary on FA 1994 in relation to agreements to surrender leases.

PART 4 GENERAL EXEMPTIONS

(See the notes printed at the end of the contents list to Part II Stamp Taxes.)

There are, in addition to the matters set out in this Part, in addition special exemptions in particular circumstances from the duty under the various heads of charge; eg, exemption from "conveyance or transfer on sale" duty in respect of share for share acquisitions under FA 1986 s 77(1).

In relation to the general exemption contained in para 24(b), there is no general exemption from stamp duty for transfers of aircraft, and a disposition of freight does not appear to be within the exemption in respect of ships or vessels. However, "freight is for many purposes part of the ship inseparably appurtenant thereto"—per Erle CJ in *Willis v Palmer* (1859) 7 CBNS 340 at 358.

The duties chargeable (*a*) under paragraphs (1) and (2) of the heading "Bond, Covenant, or instrument of any kind whatsoever" (except as regards instruments increasing the rent reserved by another instrument), (*b*) under the heading "Bond of any kind whatsoever not specifically charged with any duty", and (*c*) under the heading "Mortgage, Bond, Debenture, Covenant" are abolished.

However, if individual rights are carved out of subject matter which is exempt under these provisions, dealings in those individual rights will not in themselves necessarily be exempt from stamp duty (although they will generally be exempt from stamp duty reserve tax because of the way that the definition of "chargeable securities" is structured for the purposes of that tax). See commentary on FA 1986 s 79.

These abolitions will only relieve an instrument from duty to the extent that any matter covered by that instrument falls within an abolished head of charge. Thus, if the instrument relates to other distinct matters which are chargeable, then the instrument will still be chargeable to duty by virtue of SA 1891 s 4.

This should be compared with the position in relation to stamp duty reserve tax where individual interests in, or subdivisions of, "chargeable securities" will themselves be "chargeable securities" for the purposes of that tax (or, as the case may be, will not be "chargeable securities" if the property as a whole does not constitute chargeable securities). See commentary on FA 1986 ss 87–99. (The stamp duty provisions relating to bearer instruments, now set out in Sch 15 below, do appear to extend to derivative or limited rights in bearer stock, because of the way that the separate definition of "stock" is framed in the bearer instrument provisions, but not to such interests in bearer debt instruments because the exemptions relating to such instruments simply cross-refer to the old FA 1971 exemptions, as now reproduced in this Schedule).

However, although it appears that limited or derivative interests in exempt debt obligations are not themselves exempt from stamp duty, it is submitted that discrete bundles of rights and liabilities subsisting within a greater whole *are* eligible for exemption from duty in their own right. For example, if a syndicated lending arrangement allows for specific tranches, layers or parcels of debt to be transferred (and/ or "sub-participated") without unbundling the entire transaction, it is submitted that if the entire transaction represents exempt debentures or exempt loan capital, then each individual tranche, layer or parcel represents an exempt debenture or other exempt loan instrument in its own right. To the extent that there is any technical objection to this analysis, the point is probably academic because any dealing in a part interest of an exempt debt obligation would itself appear to be exempt, being a transfer of "any money or stock secured by any such instrument" (see the wording of para (4) of the old "Mortgage, Debenture, etc" head of charge in SA 1891 Sch 1).

This is in contrast to a right, for example, merely to obtain a "strip" of interest or other income from an instrument the capital rights of which are (and remain) vested in another person. (It should be borne in mind that a transaction such as those described above might in fact, depending upon the precise terms governing any particular case, constitute a novation rather than an assignment of the rights involved, in which case such a transaction would escape transfer duty for a quite separate reason—namely that there was, by definition, no "transfer" by reference to which to charge duty).

Mortgages

(See the notes printed at the end of the contents list to Part II Stamp Taxes.)

The duties chargeable under this heading have been abolished with regard to instruments executed on or after 1 August 1971 (FA 1971 s 64 Sch 14 Part VI). This abolition is subject to two important qualifications.

First, it is subject to s 4, pursuant to which an instrument containing or relating to several distinct matters is chargeable in respect of each matter so that it will only be relieved from duty by FA 1971 s 64(1) to the extent that any matter falls within an abolished head of charge.

Secondly, FA 1971 s 64(2) expressly provides that "any instrument which, but for subsection (1) above, would be chargeable with duty under a heading mentioned in that subsection shall not be chargeable with any duty under any other heading in the said Schedule." This means that instruments which were chargeable under this heading are not to be chargeable under any of the heads which remain in existence purely because of the abolition of this specific heading. For example, a release of a mortgage which would have been chargeable under para (5) of this heading will not become chargeable under "release . . . in any other case".

It should be noted, however, that a conveyance or transfer of any assets to a lender as security, and a subsequent re-transfer, will each attract duty under the residual head "conveyance or transfer" otherwise than on sale.

SCHEDULE 14 Stamp Duty: Amendments Consequential on Section 112 (Section 112)

This Schedule makes a number of consequential amendments to earlier legislation, to take account of the numerous changes that need to be made to statutory cross-references to the various provisions of SA 1891 which have been repealed and replaced by Sch 13 above.

SCHEDULE 15 Bearer Instruments (Section 113)

This Schedule must now be read in the light of the decision of the European Court of Justice in *Commission v Kingdom of Belgium* (Case C-415/02) [2004] All ER (D) 280 (15 July 2004) in which the Court of Justice held that by imposing stamp duty on the physical delivery of newly-issued bearer securities on the formation of a company or following the completion of an increase in capital or as part of a loan issue, Belgium was in breach of its obligations under Art 11 of the Capital Duties Directive (Council Directive 69/355/EEC of 17 July 1969 concerning indirect taxes on the raising of capital as amended). Article 11 prevents a member state from levying any tax other than capital duty on any of a number of events connected with the raising of capital. These events include: the creation or issue of shares, their issue or admission to quotation on a stock exchange, or their being made available on the market. Article 11 is subject to Art 12, which introduced specific exemptions, including an exception for taxation imposed on the transfer of securities. The court held that "transfer" was to be interpreted strictly and could not include either the issue of the securities or their initial physical delivery. It will be appreciated that this calls into question the whole basis of the charges levied by the UK under Sch 15 as well as those imposed on the introduction of newly-issued securities into a clearance system or a depositary receipt system.

See note at the beginning of Sch 13 above in relation to the format of the new provisions which replace the old heads of charge in SA 1891 Sch 1.

The material now set out in this Schedule reproduces the substance of the rules formerly stated in the "Bearer Instrument" head of charge in SA 1891 Sch 1 and various provisions in FA 1963 and FA 1967. The substance is largely unaltered but four alterations are worthy of note in the form of drafting employed.

First, the charges to duty under the former provisions set out in FA 1963 referred to the issue or transfer of bearer instruments in "Great Britain" but the new provisions, in keeping with most modern fiscal legislation, refer to issues or transfers in the UK (ie England, Wales, Scotland and Northern Ireland).

Secondly, some of the old bearer instrument charges did not explicitly state either a percentage or amount but simply cross-referred in a somewhat oblique manner to the separate heads of charge for non-bearer or registered instruments, which have now been replaced by the provisions of Sch 13 above. The reference in the old provisions to a duty on bearer instruments of "three times the transfer duty" could sometimes leave room for doubt as to the correct underlying rate of duty from which to calculate the bearer instrument duty. It is now explicitly stated that the rate of bearer instrument duty is 1.5 per cent or, in certain specified cases, 0.2 per cent of the instrument's market value (calculated in a manner specified in the legislation—see below). On the assumption that 0.5 per cent was the correct underlying rate of "transfer duty", the new provisions have not altered the rates of ad valorem duty on bearer instruments.

Thirdly, the old legislation divided bearer instruments into "inland" and "overseas" instruments. This terminology has been abandoned in the new provisions although, in reality, the same distinction is maintained in the new legislation by reference to instruments which are issued by, or relate to the stock of, on the one hand, a "UK company" or, on the other hand, a "non-UK company" (both of which expressions, it should be noted, are defined in such a way as to be capable of including *unincorporated* bodies of persons, such as partnerships constituted under English law).

Fourthly, the exemptions from bearer instrument duty are now collected together in one place in paras 13–17. Apart from para 17, the drafting does not make it entirely clear whether the exemptions relate to both transfer and issue but it seems that this is what is intended although, in the case of para 15(*a*) this would seem to follow, even if it was *not* intended in relation to some of the other exemptions now set out here. This is because that particular exemption cross-refers to the now repealed provision of FA 1971, a provision which not only abolished duty on both the issue *and transfer* of mortgages and certain other debt instruments but also provided that such instruments were not to be charged under any other head of charge in what was then SA 1891 Sch 1. At that time, Sch 1 included the head "Bearer Instrument" and so a transfer of anything falling within what is now para 15(*a*) of this Schedule would have been exempt even if the bearer instrument rules did not then (and, hence, does not now) provide any specific exemption—see commentary on what is now Sch 13 Part IV para 25 above. In fact, two of the five exemptions in the new legislation are taken from SA 1891 Sch 1 itself and those exemptions were formerly set out in a manner which drew no specific distinction between charges on issue and charges on transfer (since that distinction emerged from circumstances set out in FA 1963 rather than in SA 1891). Therefore, it seems that all the current exemption provisions for bearer instruments do relate both to issue and transfer. However, if that is correct, it appears that one technical change has been made because nothing in the old legislation specifically exempted a "foreign loan security" (now covered by para 13) from a charge to duty on transfer in the UK (although, given the manner in which such an instrument is defined, query whether there would ever actually be such a transfer).

Essentially, the expression "bearer instrument" is explained by the sweeping-up provision in what is now para 3(*d*) and would seem to mean "any . . . instrument to bearer by means of which stock can be transferred". Since the expression "stock" includes (for the purposes of bearer instrument duty, where it is defined somewhat differently than in SA 1891 s 122) "any interest in, or in any fraction of, stock or in any dividends or other rights arising out of stock and any right to an allotment of or to subscribe for stock", it would include, for example, bearer letters of allotment. The position of renounceable letters of allotment is far from clear: whilst they are quite clearly negotiable instruments transferable by delivery when suitably endorsed, they are not issued "to bearer" and probably fall outside the definition. The question is mostly academic, since there are express exemptions for most forms of renounceable allotment letter, but a useful analysis is contained in Monroe and Nock, *The Law on Stamp Duties*.

Duty on bearer instruments is chargeable either on issue or, in certain circumstances, on transfer, as explained below. Although it is not expressly stated in the legislation, an instrument chargeable on transfer is only chargeable on the occasion of one transfer because, once duty has been paid, such an instrument is "treated as duly stamped for all purposes other than paragraph 25" (ie other than for the purpose of imposing a penalty for making a false statement as to the nature of the instrument).

The one possible exception to this (and this would seem to apply in principle both to instruments chargeable on issue and to those chargeable on transfer, to the extent that it applies at all) is in the case of alteration of the instrument at some point in time after its issue. It may be the case, particularly if the effect of the alteration is to alter the value by which duty ought to be calculated (in accordance with para 7 or 8, as the case may be) that this effectively produces a "new" instrument which needs to be re-stamped—see *Prudential Assurance Co Ltd v IRC* [1935] 1 KB 101 (a case decided primarily upon the basis that an amendment to an insurance policy meant that there were two separate "instruments" on the same "piece of material", for the purposes of SA 1891 s 3(2); the facts of that case seem to support the view that no further duty is chargeable if no further value is added). A limited exception to this was introduced in FA 1970 Sch 7 which has now been reproduced as para 20. It will be noted that the exception only applies to sterling instruments issued by or on behalf of non-UK companies so that it might well be the case that alteration of a non-sterling bearer instrument and/or a bearer instrument issued by or on behalf of a UK company gives rise to a further obligation to pay stamp duty. If, though, a fresh bearer instrument is given in substitution for one which has previously been stamped with *ad valorem* duty, eg in the event of the loss or destruction of the original, the substitute instrument is not itself chargeable with stamp duty; provided that it has been produced to the Commissioners for stamping as duly paid.

Duty is chargeable on issue in the case of a chargeable instrument issued in the UK or by or on behalf of a company or a body of persons corporate or unincorporate formed or established in the UK. It should be noted that a deposit certificate in respect of the stock of a *non-UK company* could fall within the scope of this rule. Although "non-UK company" means a body of persons which is formed or established in a place other than the UK, any deposit certificate in respect of such a body's stock could still itself be a bearer instrument which was issued in the UK, and so would be chargeable to duty on issue. From 1 April 2005, any company that is an SE (a Societas Europaea, a new European company created by Council Regulation (EC) No 2157/2001 of 8 October 2001) which has its registered office outside the United Kingdom following a transfer in accordance with Article 8 of the 2001 Regulation, is also treated as a non-UK company.

Any instrument which is chargeable as a bearer instrument but is not chargeable on issue is to be chargeable on the transfer in the UK of the stock constituted by or transferable by means of the instrument (provided that duty would have been payable under what is now FA 1999 Sch 13 Part I if effected by an instrument of transfer rather than a bearer instrument or that the subject matter consists of units in a unit trust scheme).

Instruments chargeable upon issue are to be produced (before being issued) for endorsement with a "denoting stamp", and within six weeks of the date of issue of the instrument a statement has to be delivered to the Commissioners giving details of the date of issue and such other information as the Commissioners require, whereupon the duty has to be paid on the instrument. Any person who does not deliver an instrument for "denoting" is liable to a penalty of up to the aggregate of £300 and the amount of the duty chargeable, and must pay to the Government both the duty chargeable and interest from the date of default. The interest (as under the old version of SA 1891 s 15) was formerly charged at a fixed rate of 5 per cent but, under the new rules, it is the rate specified under FA 1989 s 178 (the rate also now used for SA 1891 s 15A).

The Commissioners may, in the case of an instrument chargeable on transfer, request from the person presenting it and from the owner of the instrument, "such particulars in writing as they may require for determining the amount of duty chargeable". A penalty of up to £300 plus twice the amount of any unpaid duty is payable by any person who funishes false particulars under this section, wilfully or negligently. Similar penalties are levied on any person who transfers, or is concerned as broker or agent in the transfer of, any stock in default of these provisions.

As to bearer instruments issued in connection with "paired shares" forming part of a joint public offering by a UK company and a foreign company (as, for example, was the case in the Eurotunnel "Equity 3" offerings in 1987) see FA 1988 s 143.

The ad valorem duty chargeable on bearer instruments is calculated on the basis of the "market value" of the underlying stocks or marketable securities in the manner specified in this section.

Where the instrument is chargeable on issue, then in cases where the underlying stock was offered for public subscription (whether in registered or in bearer form) within 12 months before the issue of the instrument the amount subscribed is taken as the market value. In any other case, the value is taken on the first day within one month after the issue of the instrument on which the underlying stock is dealt in on a Stock Exchange in the UK or (if it is not so dealt in) the value of the underlying stock immediately after the issue of the instrument.

Where the instrument is chargeable only on transfer, then in cases where the transfer is pursuant to a contract of sale the value is taken on the date when the contract is entered into, and in any other case the value is taken on the day preceding that on which the instrument is presented to the Commissioners for stamping or (if it is not so presented) on the date of the transfer.

No stamp duty is chargeable under the bearer instrument provisions on the issue of any instrument relating to stock expressed in any currency other than sterling, or in any units of account defined by reference to more than one currency (whether or not including sterling), or the transfer of the stock constituted or transferable thereby.

Where the stock consists of a loan for the repayment of which there is an option between sterling and one or more other currencies, the exemption is only to apply if the option is exercisable only by the holder of the stock.

Where the capital stock of any company or body of persons is not expressed in terms of any currency, it is treated as if expressed in the currency of the territory under the laws of which the company or body was formed or established. Units in a unit trust scheme or shares in a "foreign mutual fund" are treated as capital stock of a company or body incorporated or formed in the territory by whose law the scheme or fund is governed. A foreign mutual fund is a fund administered under arrangements governed by the law of a territory outside the UK whereby subscribers are entitled to participate in profit or income from investments of the fund.

In the case of paired shares (see FA 1988 s 143) this exemption does not apply to any bearer instrument issued after 8 December 1987 which (*a*) represents shares in the paired foreign company, and (*b*) is *not* issued for the purpose of the simultaneous offers of the paired units to the public in the UK and the relevant foreign country. The foreign company is treated as though it were a UK company for these purposes.

Although instruments within para 17 are exempt from stamp duty, the use of such instruments can sometimes give rise to stamp duty reserve tax consequences. The scope of the stamp duty reserve tax charge was amended by FA 1997 and again by FA 1999 with a view to confining the application of the stamp duty exemption in what is now para 17 (formerly FA 1967 s 30) to its originally intended purpose of facilitating overseas borrowing transactions. The aim of the amendments—see commentaries on FA 1986 ss 90, 95 and 97—is to seek to ensure that only genuine loan-raising transactions are exempt from duty and that stamp duty reserve tax is charged on any transaction which is merely designed to avoid the payment of stamp duty on a transfer that (but for the desire to avoid duty) would not have proceeded in bearer form.

SCHEDULE 16 STAMP DUTY: AMENDMENTS CONSEQUENTIAL ON SECTION 113 (SECTION 113)

This Schedule makes a number of consequential amendments to earlier legislation, to take account of the numerous changes that need to be made to statutory cross-references to the various provisions of SA 1891 and FA 1963 which have been repealed and replaced by Sch 15 above.

SCHEDULE 17 STAMP DUTY: PENALTIES OTHER THAN ON LATE STAMPING (SECTION 114)

This Schedule replaces the old system of administrative fines with a new system of penalties. It also raises the maximum amounts of such penalties to more realistic levels. The basic rule is now that the maximum penalty for defaults (other than for late stamping, which is dealt with separately—see SA 1891 s 15B) is either £300 for basic administrative defaults or £3,000 for any matters which are redolent of fraud.

Part 2 introduces a new system for the determination of penalties (other than those imposed under s 15B for late stamping of documents).

Such a penalty is stated to be "due and payable" 30 days after a notice of determination is issued but power to take enforcement proceedings against a person is only provided in cases where liability to a penalty "arises by reason of his fraud or the fraud of another person". However, the new rules in this Schedule do allow regulations to be made, under which the collection and recovery provisions of the Taxes Management Act 1970 may be applied to stamp duty penalties and appropriate regulations have been made (see SI 1999/2537).

SCHEDULE 18 STAMP DUTY: MINOR AMENDMENTS AND REPEAL OF OBSOLETE PROVISIONS (SECTION 115)

This Schedule makes what the legislation itself describes as "minor amendments" although it might be thought that one of these minor amendments looks rather sinister.

Paragraph 2 makes clear the date on which a payment by cheque will be treated as being made, a point which might be of some significance in the light of the apparently more onerous interest and penalty regime introduced into SA 1891 by the newly inserted ss 15A and 15B thereof.

Paragraph 3 appears to provide HMRC with a statutory right to override any attempted "entrapment" defence on the part of a person facing criminal proceedings (or other penalty proceedings or proceedings for the recovery of duty): statements and documents are not to be treated as inadmissible in such proceedings merely because, broadly speaking, anything was done which created the impression that such proceedings would not be pursued if a settlement could be reached in respect of the matter concerned. This would seem to buttress the decision already given in favour of the Revenue and the Crown Prosecution Service by the Court of Appeal in *R v W and another* [1998] STC 550.

Paragraph 4 makes a technical amendment in relation to Scots property law.

SCHEDULE 19 STAMP DUTY AND STAMP DUTY RESERVE TAX: UNIT TRUSTS (SECTION 122)

PART 1 ABOLITION OF STAMP DUTY ON TRANSFERS ETC OF UNITS IN UNIT TRUSTS

1.—Paragraph 1 abolishes the stamp duty charge on unit trusts (other than any charge arising under the separate legislation relating to bearer instruments, formerly contained mainly in FA 1963 and now consolidated in Sch 15 above). This charge is replaced, with effect from 6 February 2000, by a new stamp duty reserve tax regime for dealings in the units of a unit trust—see commentary below. Although transfers of units will now be free of stamp duty, it should be noted (see para 19 below) that a unit will still be within the general stamp duty definition of "stock", for the purposes of determining whether the consideration for a written transfer of any property *other than* units in a unit trust does or does not constitute a "conveyance or transfer on sale" (so as to give rise to an ad valorem stamp duty charge), as opposed to a "conveyance or transfer otherwise than on sale" (attracting only the fixed charge of 50p, or £5 as from 1 October 1999).

It should be noted that, whereas the old stamp duty provisions for unit trusts would, in principle, have applied to either a dealing through the managers of the unit trust scheme or to a direct transaction between two investors, the new stamp duty reserve tax rules will only apply to dealings through the managers of the scheme. However, this does not mean that direct transactions between investors (which are apparently rare in practice) will automatically be tax free. Prior to the enactment of FA 1999, the definition (in FA 1986 s 99) of "chargeable securities" was such that any property which was exempt from all stamp duties on transfer was also outside the scope of the charge to stamp duty reserve tax. However, the definition of chargeable securities has been amended by FA 1999 so that that limitation is disapplied in relation to unit trust transactions—see FA 1986 s 99(5)(*a*), as amended. It should, however, be noted that the definition of chargeable securities has never referred to derivative interests in units (compare the position in relation to shares and loan capital, where rights to subscribe for, or options to acquire, chargeable securities are themselves "chargeable securities"). Query, therefore, whether the example given in HMRC's own guidance notes (that of a transfer of the beneficial interest in units held by a nominee) could be said to fall outside the scope of the general charge to stamp duty reserve tax in FA 1986 s 87 on the basis that—the subject matter of the transfer agreement being an interest in a unit, rather than a unit as such—the transaction simply did not relate to chargeable securities.

PART 2 STAMP DUTY RESERVE TAX ON DEALINGS WITH UNITS IN UNIT TRUSTS

This part introduces a charge to stamp duty reserve tax on the surrender of units in a unit trust to the managers—see also the commentary on FA 1946. It should be noted that, whereas the "principal charge" to stamp duty reserve tax (under FA 1986 S 87) applies to *agreements to transfer* chargeable securities, this new charge applies to the actual surrender of units (or their deemed surrender—see below), and not to any agreement to make such a surrender.

There should be no double charge because, although an agreement to make a surrender would be an agreement to transfer "chargeable securities", an agreement to transfer units to the managers of the scheme is specifically exempted from stamp duty reserve tax under FA 1986 s 90(1). Furthermore, that section has been amended by FA 1999 so that an agreement to transfer units to *or from* the managers of the scheme is now outside the scope of the "principal charge" under s 87.

The concept of a "surrender" for these purposes includes both an actual transfer of units to the managers of the unit trust scheme and also (following the pattern of the now repealed stamp duty provisions on unit trusts, formerly found in FA 1946) the situation where the current unit-holder authorises or requires the trustees or the managers of the scheme to treat him as no longer interested in the units.

Although, in principle, tax is charged on each transaction affecting a particular unit trust, in reality a periodic global charge is imposed on the trustees of that unit trust by reference to the net total of the movement of units between the managers and the totality of unit-holders in a particular scheme during a two week period. (These two week periods are "rolling" periods because they are identified by reference to the date of a particular transaction and not by reference to extraneous matters, such as dates in the calendar.)

The net movement is measured by, broadly speaking, dividing the number of units surrendered into the number of units issued (but disregarding, for the purposes of such calculation, certain transactions which are either specifically exempt from stamp duty reserve tax or which are not specifically exempt but which are undertaken for non-cash consideration).

The theory behind the charge (and see Park J's judgment in *M&G Securities Ltd v IR Comrs* [1999] STC 315 for a lucid explanation of the history of the stamp duty regime for unit trusts, on which these rules are based) is that the process of surrender and (re)issue of a unit is broadly analogous to the transfer of a company share from one shareholder to another. There is no objection as such to the effecting of a transfer of a unit directly from one holder to another but it is usual in practice for transfers of units to be routed via the managers.

Since the aim was to treat these two movements as being, for stamp duty purposes, *one* transfer, a system was adopted under FA 1946 of charging stamp duty on the surrender of a unit to the managers but allowing credit, in the form of a repayment of duty to the managers, if the surrendered unit was not reissued to another investor in the trust within a specified period of time. This was because, by analogy with company shares, only the equivalent of a transfer of rights from one holder to another was thought to be a transaction which ought to be subject to duty. The provisions of FA 1946 were specifically designed to assimilate unit trusts to limited companies for stamp duty purposes and any issue of a unit that had not previously been held by an earlier investor, or any surrender of a unit that was not reissued to a new investor, was analogous to a transaction in company shares that (as the law stood in 1946) would not have attracted ad valorem stamp duty, and so would not have been regarded as suitable for charging under the FA 1946 provisions.

The stamp duty reserve tax regime operates along essentially the same lines as the old stamp duty regime, except that the need to stamp and/or reclaim duty in relation to individual documents and specific transactions is obviated by the process of netting off surrenders and (re)issues over a specified period.

The fraction is calculated by reference to a particular "class" of units. In the first draft of this legislation, it was explicitly stated that "units are of the same class if their nominal value is the same". In the final version of the legislation as enacted, the draftsman has declined to define "class", as such, but has said that any "consolidation or subdivision" is to be disregarded in calculating the percentage change in the size of the total unit-holding.

Having allowed a "proportionate reduction" in respect of possible mismatches between, on the one hand, the number of surrenders and, on the other hand, the number of (re)issues, a further "proportionate reduction" is allowed if a proportion of the trust property subsists in the form of "exempt investments", as defined. Broadly speaking, that means that they are investments which are outside the scope of stamp duty and/or stamp duty reserve tax on transfer.

Two refinements of the basic provisions appear to have been included to reinstate the view of the old law on unit trusts (ie the law regarding stamp duty on unit trusts, repealed by FA 1999 s 122 and this Schedule) which the Revenue unsuccessfully advanced before Park J in the recent case of *M&G Securities Ltd v IRC* [1999] STC 315. In essence, Park J decided in that case that the refund mechanism (now, as noted above, repealed) in FA 1946 s 54(4) applied to *any* act of in specie redemption in relation to any part of the trust property as a means of returning value to a surrendering unit-holder. The Revenue, on the other hand, had argued that the reference in the refund provisions to "a proportionate part of the trust property" being "realised" meant that a refund was only available in the cash of a non-cash distribution to a surrendering unit-holder where an exactly proportionate part of each trust asset was transferred to the out-going unit-holder as a realisation of his "share" of the whole trust. Whilst acknowledging that there was some room for doubt as to the meaning of the FA 1946 provisions, Park J nonetheless gave a total of 15 reasons why he thought the Revenue's view was wrong.

However, the Revenue's view of the old stamp duty exemption is specifically incorporated into the stamp duty reserve tax provisions as para 7. The only concession is that strict proportionality is not insisted upon, in that para 7 permits a transfer of part of each of the trust assets which is "as nearly as practicable proportionate to" the surrendering unit-holder's share in the trust property as a whole.

The argument successfully advanced by the taxpayers in the *M&G Securities* case is now effectively nullified by para 4(5). The effect of this paragraph is that, except in the rather limited circumstances which the Revenue themselves were prepared to accept that an in specie redemption was exempt under the old stamp duty provisions (and which has accordingly, as stated above, been included as a specific exemption to the new stamp duty reserve tax charge, as para (7) a redemption in which a unit-holder's entitlement is realised in any form other than money will not be included in the calculation under which issues and surrenders of different units are netted off, thus reducing the extent to which netting off provisions decrease the overall charge to tax.

(It is interesting to note that in the first draft of FA 1999, in which it was proposed to retain the definitions section of the old stamp duty provisions in FA 1946, rather than to re-enact the relevant definitions in the new legislation, the new legislation would have kept most of the former definitions but would have repealed the definition of the phrase "trust property represented by units" in FA 1946. This definition essentially extended to all property of the trust in question *except* any property which, under the terms of the trust, was required to be distributed to the unit-holders in the form of a dividend or similar disbursement from the trust assets.)

Although HMRC have effectively nullified most of the possible benefits obtained by the taxpayer in the *M&G Securities* case, there are a number of exemptions available from the new charge. The somewhat cryptically worded para 6(1) exempts cases in which a transfer is made for no consideration, and para 6 also exempts transfers to charities and certain designated bodies, and cases in which group relief would be available under FA 1930 s 42 in relation to a stamp duty charge. Generally speaking, no group relief is available in the context of stamp duty reserve tax (other than by going through the formal process of creating a stampable document and then having it adjudicated exempt from stamp duty) but, since the stamp duty charge on unit trusts will have been abolished by the time that this exemption takes effect, it would no longer be possible to obtain the usual adjudication of a stampable instrument in the case of a transfer of units in a unit trust.

What is not entirely clear from this form of drafting is whether the draftsman, in referring to a document that "would be exempt" under FA 1930 s 42 (or the Northern Ireland equivalent of that provision) intends that that provision be considered in isolation or whether it is necessary also to have regard to the anti-avoidance rules in FA 1967 s 27, which qualify and restrict the relief under FA 1930. In other words, has the statutory draftsman exempted all transactions in units which consist of a transfer of beneficial ownership between associated bodies corporate, or has he exempted only transactions of such a kind which do not contain offending "arrangements" of any of the kinds referred to in FA 1967 s 27? Unfortunately, the wording of FA 1930 s 42 does not actually cross-refer to FA 1967 and so there is no express incorporation by cross-reference of FA 1967 in the form of wording adopted in para 6(4), (5). However, if, as appears to be the case, the reason for taking the exceptional step of granting direct intra-group relief from stamp duty reserve tax under this new legislation is that the taxpayer could not follow the usual route of avoiding stamp duty reserve tax indirectly by applying for adjudication of a stampable instrument, then consistency of approach would seem to require a restrictive reading of the words "by virtue of . . . section 42" in para 6 as meaning "by virtue of section 42, as qualified by FA 1967". It remains to be seen whether this point is taken.

Paragraph 6A was inserted by FA 2001 s 93(4). It exempts from SDRT the surrender on or after 6 April 2001 of a unit in a unit trust scheme, if two factors exist. Firstly, the unit must be (or be destined to be) held in an individual pension account immediately prior to surrender. Secondly, the trustee or manager must certify in the monthly tax return that these units in IPAs are readily identifiable, and that IPA holders are not charged SDRT in respect of the surrender of non-IPA units. The exemption takes effect under paragraph 4(6). Note that surrenders of units in unit trusts and shares in open-ended investment companies reserved only for individual pension accounts may also fall within the paragraph 5 SDRT reduction by virtue of FA 1986 s 99(5A)(b) and (5B)(b). Note also the FA 2001 s 94 exemption for the shares in an open-ended investment company (as defined) reserved for individual pension accounts where there are other share classes not so exempt.

It is specifically made clear that there are no territorial limitations, as such, to the scope of this new charge although this would seem to follow in any event from the fact that the new stamp duty reserve tax provisions in FA 1999 are to be "read as one" with Part IV of FA 1986. The fact that stamp duty reserve tax applies, in principle, on a worldwide basis is made clear by FA 1986 s 86 (as amended by FA 1996) and nothing in s 86 indicates that the territorial scope there stated is confined to the "principal charge" set out in s 87 of that Act.

However, although there is no territorial limitation in terms of the residence, nationality, etc, of the parties or the place where the relevant transaction occurs, a connection with the UK is electively imported by means of the amendment inserted by this Schedule—see para 12(3)—into the definition of "chargeable securities" in FA 1986 s 99: no charge arises where all the trustees are resident abroad and the unit is not registered in a register kept in the UK.

It should be noted that the exemption requires *all* the trustees to be resident abroad and there is no scope for partial exemption in a case where a minority of trustees are resident in the UK (compare the regime for unit trusts containing "exempt investments", where partial exemption is effectively provided by means of para 5). It is presumed that the reference to a "register" being "kept" in the UK is a reference to a real register and not merely, for example, a photocopy or duplicate that is kept here for some incidental purpose, not for carrying out the principal administration of the trust from within the UK.

PART 3 MINOR AND CONSEQUENTIAL AMENDMENTS

This makes various amendments to the main stamp duty reserve tax provisions in FA 1986 (ie the main charging section, the main exemption section and the definition of "chargeable securities") so as to facilitate both the new charges and the new exemptions and reliefs described above.

PART 4 GENERAL DEFINITIONS

Note: The original draft of this Schedule was much shorter and cross-referred to earlier legislation but in the final version the draftsman decided to repeal any unit trust related definitions and interpretative provisions in the earlier legislation (FA 1946 and FA 1963) and consolidate all such material in the new legislation. See the commentary on FA 1946 which has been retained in the current edition in view of the continuing validity of the stamp duty provisions until 6 February 2000.

Schemes not treated as unit trust schemes

16.—This section amends FA 1995 s 152 so as to provide the power to alter stamp duty legislation in such a manner as to harmonise the stamp duty treatment of unit trusts and OEICs.

See also the commentary on FA 1946. Regulations were introduced in 1997 under the authority of FA 1995 s 152—see SI 1997/1156—which established a stamp duty regime for OEICs that was closely modelled on the regime formerly applicable to unit trusts by virtue of FA 1946 (since, although their strict legal form is very similar to that of ordinary limited companies, OEICs are, in substance, more like unit trusts than ordinary companies). Stamp duty charges on unit trusts are abolished by s 122 above. They have not been abolished as regards OEICs but this section creates the power under which to do so.

Treatment of umbrella schemes

18.—This confirms that the stamp duty case of *Arbuthnot Financial Services Ltd v IR Comrs* [1985] STC 211 also applies for the purposes of stamp duty reserve tax. In that case, Walton J held that a unit trust scheme consisting of a number of segregated divisions constituted a number of separate unit trust schemes. Even if all the property comprised one trust, it did not comprise one *unit trust* for the purposes of the then current stamp duty law on unit trusts. This means that any transfer of a unit-holder's rights or interest in the unit trust from one subdivision to another will involve that holder in expressly or impliedly authorising the managers of the trust to treat him as no longer interested in the units of the subdivision in which he has initially invested, resulting in a charge to stamp duty reserve tax (unless, of course, the transaction is covered by any of the specific exemptions referred to above).

References to stock in stamp duty enactment include units in unit trust schemes

19.—This preserves the current stamp duty definition of "stock" as including units in a unit trust for the purposes of charging stamp duty on transfers of property other than units in a unit trust—see commentary on para 1 above.

Limited Liability Partnerships Act 2000

2000 Chapter 12

12. Stamp duty

(See the notes printed at the end of the contents list to Part II Stamp Taxes.)

This section exempts from stamp duty an instrument by which property is conveyed or transferred by a person to a limited partnership, in connection with its incorporation, within the period of one year beginning with the date of incorporation. Two conditions must be satisfied.

One of the two limbs to the first condition must be satisfied to qualify for the exemption. The first limb requires that at the relevant time (either immediately before incorporation or, if the property was acquired after incorporation, immediately after the acquisition) the person is a partner in a partnership comprised of all the persons who are or are to be members of the limited liability partnership (and no-one else). The second limb requires that in the alternative the person holds the property conveyed or transferred as nominee or bare trustee for one or more of the partners in a partnership.

The second condition also has two limbs, one of which once again must be satisfied if the exemption is to apply. The first limb requires that the proportions of the property conveyed or transferred, to which the persons mentioned in the first limb of the first condition are entitled immediately after the conveyance or transfer, are the same as those to which they were entitled at the relevant time. The second limb requires that if any differences have arisen, that these were not part of a scheme or arrangement of which the main purpose, or one of the main purposes, is the avoidance of liability to any duty or tax.

Note that although property transferred as described above is free from stamp duty, it will not be taken as duly stamped unless it has (in accordance with Stamp Act 1891 s 12) been stamped with a stamp denoting that it is not chargeable with any duty or that it is duly stamped, or if it is stamped with the duty to which it would be liable apart from this subsection.

Finance Act 2000

2000 Chapter 17

PART IV STAMP DUTY

114. Rates: conveyance as transfer on sale

(See the notes printed at the end of the contents list to Part II Stamp Taxes.)

This section amends the rates of duty on conveyances (other than of stock or marketable securities) so that the former rate of 2.5% (for consideration certified to be more than £250,000 and less than £500,000) becomes 3% and the former rate of 3.5% (for consideration not so certified or of more than £500,000) becomes 4%: (1). The new rates apply only to instruments executed on or after 28 March 2000 except where the instrument question gives effect to a contract made on or before 21 March 2000. Notwithstanding the transitional rule for contracts made on or before 21 March 2000, the new rates will apply if (*a*) the instrument is made in consequence of the exercise after 21 March 2000 of any option, right of pre-emption or similar right; or (*b*) the instrument transfers the property to, or vests it in, a person other than the purchaser under the contract (eg where the purchaser under the contract directs the transfer to be to a third party or pursuant to a sub-sale—this overrules the effect of *Swallow Hotels v IRC* [2000] STC 45: (2), (3)). See the commentary under Sch 13 Part I paras 2–4 and 6.

115. Rates: duty on lease chargeable by reference to rent

(See the notes printed at the end of the contents list to Part II Stamp Taxes.)

The result of this section is that:

(a) in the case of a lease for a definite term less than a year of a furnished dwelling house or apartment the threshold is raised from £500 to £5,000 so that where the rent for the term exceeds £5,000, fixed duty of £5 applies; and

(b) in the case of any lease of land for a definite term less than 7 years or indefinite term in respect of which the consideration or part of the consideration is rent, the threshold is increased from £500 to £5,000 so that if the rate or average rate of rent is £5,000 or less the rate of duty is nil and if such rate of rent is more than £5,000 the rate of duty is 1%.

The new rates apply to leases executed on or after 28 March 2000. No transitional provisions are necessary as an agreement for lease is chargeable as if it were a lease (see FA 1999 Sch 13 Part II para 14). See commentary under FA 1999 Sch 13 Part II.

116. Rate of duty on seven year leases

(See the notes printed at the end of the contents list to Part II Stamp Taxes.)

This section closes a loophole which meant that certain leases and agreements for lease for a fixed term of exactly 7 years were not subject to any charging provision. This section is retrospective to a Revenue Press Release issued on 1 October 1990 announcing the intended rectification of this loophole. See the commentary under FA 2000 Sch 32 for the transitional provisions. See FA 1999 Sch 13 Part II for lease grants generally.

117. Power to vary stamp duties

See commentary under FA 2000 Sch 33.

118. Land transferred etc for other property

(See the notes printed at the end of the contents list to Part II Stamp Taxes.)

This section is an anti-avoidance provision which treats as a conveyance or transfer on sale any instrument transferring land for a consideration which is, or includes any, property. The section is only intended to catch instruments which would not otherwise have been a stampable conveyance or transfer on sale, eg where (*a*) the transfer of the land is expressed to be in satisfaction of the consideration for the transfer of the other property (for example land transferred to satisfy the consideration for the issue of shares or the assignment of exempt property such as loan stock or gilts); or (*b*) the land is exchanged for the other property but that other property does not consist of money, stocks, shares, debt etc. In both examples (*a*) and (*b*) on general principles the transfer is not "on sale" and so is not stampable ad valorem: (1), (2).

The practice, sanctioned by HMRC in *Tax Bulletin* of 18 August 1995 (see Appendix 6), of avoiding a double charge to stamp duty under FA 1994 s 241 by structuring an exchange of land for land as a sale of the more expensive land for a consideration which includes the cheaper land is effectively preserved despite this section, by virtue of sub-s 3: (3).

Where this section applies, the stamp duty is to be charged on the market value of the land immediately before execution of the instrument transferring or vesting it (note not the value of the "other property" consideration) if that market value is less than the actual consideration. Market value is defined in the same way as under FA 1994 s 241(2): (4), (5).

Seemingly for the avoidance of doubt, the charge applies even if the transaction is expressed (*a*) as a transfer or conveyance of the other property for consideration to be satisfied by the transfer or vesting of the land; or (*b*) as an exchange: (6). In case (*b*) there would appear to be an overlap with FA 1994 s 241, but it would seem that s 241 alone would in fact apply as the instrument would fall to be treated as a conveyance or transfer on sale by virtue of s 241 and so outside this section by virtue of s 118(1)(*a*).

Any charge to duty in respect of the conveyance or transfer of the other property (eg exemption for the transfer of loan stock or gilts or transfer on sale duty in the case of a sale of non-exempt property) remains unaffected: (7).

This section is superseded where FA 2000 s 119 (see below) applies: (8). Since s 119 provides that it applies in preference to s 118 only where a greater amount of stamp duty results, the end result is that where ss 119 and 118 overlap whichever produces the greater amount of stamp duty will apply.

Transitional provisions identical to those under FA 2000 s 114 apply.

119. Transfer of land to a connected company

(See the notes printed at the end of the contents list to Part II Stamp Taxes.)

This section applies, broadly speaking, where:

– land or an interest in land;
– is transferred to or vested in;
– a company;
– at an undervalue; and
  (1) either the transferor is connected with the transferee company; or
  (2) some or all of the consideration consists of the issue or transfer of shares (including stock) or securities in a company connected with the transferor (which need not be the transferee); and
– none of the exceptions in s 120 applies.

The effect is that the instrument transferring the land is deemed to be a transfer on sale of the land and stamp duty is chargeable on the market value of the land if that market value is less than the value of the actual consideration. There is deducted from the market value any actual consideration given which is not property (eg cash or services). Thus, if the consideration were the market value fully in cash of the land this section would not bite, and rightly so as normal transfer on sale duty would be due. If the consideration were services, eg the transfer of land in consideration of building services equal in value to the land then no duty would be payable.

This section applies only if it would produce a greater amount of stamp duty than under FA 2000 s 118 (where that also applies) or would otherwise apply.

This section is probably aimed at schemes for the hive-down of land into a subsidiary in a non-stampable way (gift) or in a way which attracts minimal stamp duty followed by sale of the shares in the subsidiary, attracting only a 0.5% rate of duty, (the old "envelope trick"). Although associated companies relief under FA 1942 s 30 may not be available, because of FA 1967 s 27, the charge on the intra-group transfer could be minimised by effecting it for minimal consideration (eg so-called "swamping schemes"). However, considerable care is required as the section appears to catch certain innocent transactions at an undervalue in land (eg gifts and dividends of land in specie—but see FA 2000 s 131) but, for no obvious policy reason, only where the transferee is a company. Whereas ss 118 and 121 are concerned with schemes that exploit the narrow meaning of the conveyance or transfer *on sale*, s 119 is concerned with schemes that manipulate the *value* of the consideration on a transfer.

The section includes provisions defining "market value", "company", "shares" and "connected".

Transitional provisions identical to those under FA 2000 s 114 apply.

120. Exceptions from section 119

The imposition of a charge to ad valorem stamp duty under FA 2000 s 119 (1)(*a*) on instruments transferring or vesting an estate or interest in land to a company at an undervalue does not apply where:

- Case 1: the transferor holds the land as nominee or bare trustee for the corporate transferee;
- Case 2: the corporate transferee holds the land as nominee or bare trustee for the transferor;
- Case 3: the transferor holds the land as nominee or bare trustee for some other person and the corporate transferee is also to hold the land as nominee or bare trustee for that other person;
- Case 4: the transfer/vesting is out of a settlement in or towards satisfaction of a corporate beneficiary's interest (not being an interest acquired for money or money's worth) in accordance with the provisions of the settlement;
- Case 5: the transfer/vesting is to a professional corporate trustee acting as such;
- Case 6: the corporate trustee is to hold the land as trustee and, but for being connected with the transferor under ICTA 1988 s 839(3) would otherwise not be connected with the transferor; or
- Case 7: the transferor is a company which acquired the land by virtue of a duly stamped instrument and transfers/vests it by way of a distribution of assets (eg dividend in specie or on a winding up).

These exceptions were introduced into the Bill at a late stage in its progress but it seems harsh, nevertheless, that the exceptions came into force only from 28 July 2000 whilst the principal provisions came into force from 28 March 2000. These exceptions are therefore extended retrospectively (curiously to 22 rather than 28 March) and if stamp duty has been paid which would have been relieved a refund is available (see FA 2000 s 131).

121. Grant of lease to connected company

(See the notes printed at the end of the contents list to Part II Stamp Taxes.)

This section, broadly speaking, applies the same rules to leases of land for a premium as apply under FA 2000 s 119 to instruments transferring or vesting estates or interests in land.

122. Marketable securities transferred etc for exempt property

(See the notes printed at the end of the contents list to Part II Stamp Taxes.)

This section is basically aimed at sales of exempt gilts and debts for a price to be satisfied wholly or partly in non-exempt shares and securities. The aim of such schemes was for the transfer of the non-exempt shares and securities to escape stamp duty by not being transferred or conveyed *on sale* on the basis (sanctioned in general principle by the *Tax Bulletin* of 18 August 1995 (see Appendix 6)) that the transfer of the non-exempt shares and securities merely discharges the potential obligation to pay the purchase price. The section treats as a conveyance or transfer *on sale* any instrument transferring marketable securities for a consideration which includes "qualifying property" where the instrument would not otherwise be treated as a transfer on sale. Qualifying property means any debt due, stock or securities, to the extent that the debt, stock or securities are not chargeable securities within the meaning of FA 1986 Part IV (eg gilts and certain types of loan stock).

Provisions parallel to those in FA 2000 s 118 substitute market value for actual consideration if market value is greater.

The provisions apply whether or not the marketable securities are expressed as consideration or the transaction is by way of exchange (although an exchange should in any case be stampable on general principles as a transfer on sale).

The duty on the sale of the exempt property is unaffected, ie that sale should remain exempt.

The transitional provisions are the same as for FA 2000 s 114.

123. Transfer of property between associated companies: Great Britain

(See the notes printed at the end of the contents list to Part II Stamp Taxes.)

This section tightens up the 75% ownership test for determining whether two bodies corporate are associated for the purposes of intra-group relief under FA 1930 s 42. The test now borrows the "economic ownership" concept from TA 1988 Sch 18. The test of association now requires 75% ownership not only of ordinary share capital (as defined in s 42(4)), but also entitlement to not less than 75% of any profits available for distribution to equityholders and of any assets available for distribution to its equity holders on a winding-up. The two bodies corporate will not be treated as associated if arrangements are in existence by virtue of which another person or persons together has or could obtain control of the transferee but not of the transferor. The definition of control is borrowed from TA 1988 s 840.

This section applies to instruments executed on or after 28 July 2000.

124. Transfer of property between associated companies: Northern Ireland

Equivalent provisions to those in FA 2000 s 123 apply in relation to stamp duty in Northern Ireland with effect from 28 July 2000

125. Grant of leases etc between associated companies

Equivalent provisions to those in FA 2000 s 123 apply in relation to intra-group relief on leases of land under FA 1995 s 151 with effect from 28 July 2000.

126. Future issues of stock

This section amends SA 1891 s 55 so that a conveyance is treated as a conveyance on sale if the consideration consists of stock or marketable securities (*a*) whether or not they have been or are to be issued at the time of execution of the conveyance on sale; and (*b*) where the stock or marketable securities is still to be issued, irrespective of (1) when it is or is to be issued; and (2) whether the issue is certain or contingent. It had previously been considered, despite suggestions to the contrary from the Stamp Office, that a right to receive shares or securities in the future is not dutiable consideration (being different from the actual shares or securities). This section applies in relation to instruments executed on or after 28 July 2000.

127. Company acquisition reliefs: redeemable shares

This section amends FA 1986 ss 75 (acquisitions: reliefs) and 76 (acquisitions: further provisions about reliefs) (see commentary) so that no relief is available if the acquiring company issues any redeemable shares to the shareholders of the target company (in the case of s 75) and to the target company or its shareholders (in the case of s 76). One of the conditions of these reliefs is that cash does not constitute a significant part of any consideration given for shares being issued under the re-organisation. Redeemable shares were being issued, and redeemed shortly after acquisition, so virtually providing a cash consideration. This section applies to instruments executed on or after 28 July 2000.

128. Surrender of leases

(See the notes printed at the end of the contents list to Part II Stamp Taxes.)

This section is designed to prevent the technique, for avoiding stamp duty on lease surrenders (and agreements for lease surrender—see FA 1994 s 243) for a consideration, of avoiding bringing into existence an agreement to surrender and surrendering the lease by operation of law rather than by means of a deed of surrender. In such cases, registration is commonly achieved by the submission of a statutory declaration to the Land Registry.

This section treats any document evidencing the surrender as if it were a deed of surrender executed at that time: (1). The section provides that such documents will include (*a*) the statutory declaration referred to above; and (*b*) an application for making or removing an entry in a land register (as defined) relating to the lease: (2), (7).

In the case of a surrender and regrant relating to the same subject matter, stamp duty is not chargeable by virtue of this section on the lease (although lease duty in respect of the lease rent may still apply): (3).

Stamp duty is not chargeable by virtue of this section if stamp duty has already been duly paid on another document relating to the same surrender ((4), (5)) or on the lease regrant of the same land (3). Sub-section (6) deals with what evidence of due stamping is necessary before effect is given to a document.

This section applies to documents relating to a surrender on or after 28 July 2000.

129. Abolition of duty on instruments relating to intellectual property

(See the notes printed at the end of the contents list to Part II Stamp Taxes.)

This section introduces a general stamp duty exemption for any instrument for the transfer (and agreement to transfer) or other disposition of intellectual property: (1).

Intellectual property is defined in sub-s (2). It includes patents, trade marks, registered designs and copyright and licences or interests therein. Consideration will need to be given to whether domain names are covered, and whether there may also be a transfer of goodwill with a trademark and whether this is covered by the exemption.

The exemption applies to instruments executed on or after 28 March 2000.

130. Transfers to registered social landlords etc

The Government intends to include provisions in Finance Bill 2012 to repeal this relief with effect from 6 April 2013.

This section extends stamp duty exemption (as transfers to charity can already be adjudicated exempt from duty) to registered social landlords. Sub-section (1) exempts transfers and leases of land to qualifying landlords (defined in sub-s (5)) in certain circumstances from ad valorem transfer duty or lease duty and from duty charged on transfers otherwise then on sale.

There are definitions of "landlord controlled by its tenants", "board member", "company", "qualifying transferor" and "public subsidy".

Transfers are required to be adjudicated free of duty.

Certain instruments are retrospectively exempted by virtue of this section (see FA 2000 s 131).

This section applies to instruments executed after 28 July 2000.

131. Relief for certain instruments executed before this Act has effect

(See the notes printed at the end of the contents list to Part II Stamp Taxes.)

This section retrospectively applies the s 120 exceptions to FA 2000 s 119 and the s 130 (6) (*c*), (*d*), (*e*), (*f*) and (*h*) types of qualifying transferor to instruments executed in the period beginning on 22 March 2000 and ending on the day the FA 2000 was passed (28 July 2000). If an instrument has been stamped during that period which could have been exempt had it been executed after 28 July 2000 then the appropriate person may receive a refund.

132. The Northern Ireland Assembly Commission

(See the notes printed at the end of the contents list to Part II Stamp Taxes.)

This section amends FA 1997 s 55 to enable transfers of assets to the Northern Ireland Assembly Commission to be free of duty. This section applies to instruments executed on or after 28 March 2000.

133. Loan capital where return bears inverse relationship to results

Interest on loans which carry a lower rate of interest when the borrower's business is doing well but carrying higher rates of interest when the business does less well have been treated as potentially falling within the distribution legislation, notwithstanding that the distribution legislation is aimed at loans which carry higher rates of interest or a greater return the better the business was doing. Such loans, if registered, could also attract stamp duty on transfer—see FA 1986 s 79(6)(*b*).

This sub-section amends FA 1986 s 79 by inserting a new sub-s (7A) which clarifies that sub-s (6)(*b*) does not prevent a loan being exempt from transfer duty if the interest varies an inverse proportion to the success of the business. As a consequence, such a loan can now fall outside the definition of chargeable securities for SDRT purposes as a result of FA 1986 s 99(5)(*b*).

For the purposes of stamp duty, this section has effect where the instrument is executed on or after 21 March 2000. For the purposes of SDRT the changes apply to agreements made on or after 21 March 2000 (unless, if conditional, those agreements became unconditional on or after 21 March) and to issues, transfers and appropriations on or after 21 March 2000.

134. Transfers between depositary receipt systems and clearance systems

For transfers between depositary receipt systems and clearance systems see the commentary on FA 1986 s 72A and s 97B.

This section also removes the requirement in FA 1986 ss 67(9), 70(9), 95(1) and 97(1), before £5 fixed duty or stamp duty reserve tax duty applies, for the transferor and transferee to be UK resident.

This section is an anti-avoidance provision which clarifies that certain changes which may arise on termination of an election disapplying the clearance system charge or transfer from an operator of an elected clearance system to a non-elected clearance system are not avoided by reliance on certain other provisions in the clearance system code.

The stamp duty amendments apply to instruments executed after 28 July 2000 and the stamp duty reserve tax amendments apply where the securities are transferred after 28 July 2000.

SCHEDULES

SCHEDULE 8 EMPLOYEE SHARE OWNERSHIP PLANS

A new paragraph 116A was inserted by FA 2001 s 93 with effect from 12 May 2001 so that no stamp duty or SDRT arises when employees buy partnership or dividend shares from an AESOP trust. A stamp duty/SDRT charge may still arise on purchase of the shares by the AESOP trust.

SCHEDULE 32 STAMP DUTY ON 7 YEAR LEASES—TRANSITIONAL PROVISIONS (SECTION 115(2))

Introductory

Paragraph 4 provides that a lease or agreement for lease for 7 years executed after 30 September 1999 and before 28 March 2000 becomes insufficiently stamped with effect from 28 March 2000, even if it was sufficiently stamped by reference to the law in force at the time it was stamped. Accordingly, even if it was originally adjudicated (and so would otherwise be admissible in evidence) it is not admissible, unless any extra duty required to be paid following the changes made by s 115, and interest and or any penalty, are paid in accordance with SA 1891 s 14—see paras 5 and 6.

Paragraph 7 makes consequential alterations to the usual interest and penalty provisions as regards the extra duty payable on such leases or such agreements so that interest and penalties apply only to the extra duty due as a result of s 115.

SCHEDULE 33 POWER TO VARY STAMP DUTIES (SECTION 116)

Paragraph 1 contains an enabling power to introduce regulations to change which documents are liable to duty or the rate or amount of duty applying to particular types of instrument. Paragraph 2 restricts this power, effectively to instruments relating to any extent to land, stock or marketable securities.

Paragraph 3 prevents the power being used to vary ad valorem stamp duty rates, fixed stamp duty rates or thresholds for different rates of duty (subject to the general power in para 1(2)).

Paragraph 4 requires the resolutions to be approved, and if not approved in accordance with para 4, to cease in effect (apparently only at the end of that period without prejudice to their apparent validity during the period ending with non-approval). If regulations are not approved, provision is made in para 5 for repayment claims. Paragraph 6 deals with the admissibility of instruments executed after the regulations came into force and before they were subsequently disapproved.

Paragraph 7 seems to be aiming to impose an 18 month limit on such regulations (presumably during which time the regulations can be incorporated into a Finance Act). However, there does not seem to be any provision preventing a further regulation being made covering substantially the same issue, thus restarting the 18 month period.

SCHEDULE 34 ABOLITION OF STAMP DUTY ON INSTRUMENTS RELATING TO INTELLECTUAL PROPERTY: STATUTORY PROVISIONS (SECTION 127)

Paragraph 2 provides for apportionment of consideration in the case of any transfer dealing with both intellectual property and other property.

Paragraph 3 makes similar apportionment of consideration provision for circumstances covered by SA 1891 s 58(1), (2).

Paragraph 4 enables certificates of value to disregard intellectual property.

SCHEDULE 40 REPEALS

PART III STAMP DUTY

Various enactments are repealed.

Transport Act 2000

2000 Chapter 38

PART V MISCELLANEOUS AND SUPPLEMENTARY

(See the notes printed at the end of the contents list to Part II Stamp Taxes.)

Pursuant to Schedule 7, certain (*a*) relevant transfers, (*b*) certified instruments relating to transfer schemes and (*c*) instruments made under Schedule 6 of the Act are exempt from stamp duty. Agreements relating to (*b*) and (*c*) are also exempt from SDRT.

Schedule 26 makes provisions for further stamp duty, SDLT and SDRT exemptions.

Finance Act 2001

2001 Chapter 9

PART IV OTHER TAXES

92. Stamp duty: exemption for land in disadvantaged areas

The Government intends to repeal this exemption in the Finance Act 2012 with effect from 6 April 2013.

This section as amended by FA 2002 (s 110 (1) and (2)) provides for an exemption from ad valorem stamp duty for transfers and leases of land in the most disadvantaged areas of the UK. It came into force on 30 November 2001 (SI 2001/3748). The areas that will benefit are listed in SI 2001/3747. The instrument will be treated as exempt only if certified by the Commissioners and adjudicated under SA 1891 s 12. Supplementary provisions are given effect in sub-s (6), and are found in Schedule 30.

Schedule 30 para 1 deals with the situation where land is situated partly in a disadvantaged area, and partly outside it. Sub-paragraph (2) states that ad valorem stamp duty will be apportioned to the value of the land outside the area.

Pursuant to s 92A below, variation of Stamp Duties Regulations 2001 (SI 2001/3746) provides that the relief for land in disadvantaged areas, contained in Sch 30 para 1 and s 92, shall not apply to investments where the amount or value of the consideration exceeds £150,000, or the investment could not be certified under FA 1999 Sch 13 para 4 at £150,000 or under if that threshold were specified in the Table in that paragraph.

Regulation 5 of SI 2001/3746 states that where s 92 (1) and Sch 30 para 1 apply to a lease of land, the relief only applies in respect of the amount or value of any qualifying premium and therefore does not affect the amount of duty payable in respect of rent.

Furthermore, reg 6 of SI 2001/3746 states that neither s 92 (1) nor Sch 30 para 1 shall have effect in relation to paragraph 1 (fixed duty on leases of furnished dwelling-houses or apartments where the rent for the term exceeds £5,000, fixed duty on leases not subject to rent duty and fixed duty on conveyances and transfers of property otherwise than on sale) of the Table in FA 1999 Sch 13 Pt 2 paras 11 and 13 and Pt 3 para 16. Under reg 7 of SI 2001/3746 the same principles apply to contracts or agreements chargeable as conveyances on sale, agreements for lease, leases for a fixed term and then until determined, and any other instrument stampable by reference to the conveyance on sale, lease duty and fixed duty for conveyances other than on sale.

Schedule 30 para 2 concerns the apportionment of a single consideration covering property sold by different instruments. Sub-paragraph (1) apportions the consideration between the different instruments, under Stamp Act 1891 s 58(2), in a just and reasonable manner where part of the property is exempted under the section and schedule. Sub-paragraph (2) amends Stamp Act 1891 s 58(2) in cases where part of the property is exempted under the section and schedule, and both or all relevant persons are connected so that the consideration is to be apportioned on a just and reasonable basis.

Schedule 30 para 3 provides that the amount or value of the exempt consideration for land in the relevant disadvantaged area is to be left out of account when determining whether a certificate of value is appropriate in relation to the conveyance, transfer or lease in question (or any larger transaction if it forms part of a larger transaction). This is without prejudice to s 92A(4).

92A. Restriction of exemption in the case of residential property etc

(See the notes printed at the end of the contents list to Part II Stamp Taxes.)

This section provides for Treasury regulations (see SI 2003/1056) to limit the exemption in FA 2001 s 92 and Sch 30 by reference to whether the land in question is residential property as defined in s 92B and/or by reference to the amount or value of the consideration. These regulations may clarify how the legislation applies where land is only partly situated in a disadvantaged area. Where such regulations apply, the certificate under s 92 (2) must contain a statement that the land is not residential property or that the land is not residential to the extent stated and, where the availability of the exemption depends on the value of the consideration not exceeding a specified amount, the instrument in question must certify the relevant amount.

92B. Meaning of "residential property"

This section sets out the definition of "residential property" for the purposes of regulations made under s 92A. Broadly speaking, a "residential property" is a building or part of a building suitable for use as a dwelling (or in the process of being constructed or adapted for such use), plus any garden or grounds of such a building. A number of buildings are specifically listed as being used as a dwelling (subsection (2)) and not being used as a dwelling (subsection (3)). Where a building, not currently in use, can be used for a number of uses found in both subsections (2) and (3), the most suitable use shall be taken to be the use. If no use can be distinguished as the most suitable, the building is treated as suitable for use as a dwelling.

93. SDRT: unit trust schemes and individual pensions accounts

This section exempts surrenders made on or after 6 April 2001 of units in unit trusts held within individual pension accounts (IPAs) from the usual SDRT charge. This exception is available provided that the necessary requirements laid down in the section are complied with. The unit must be (or be destined to be) held in an IPA immediately prior to surrender. Furthermore, the trustee or manager must certify in the monthly tax returns that the units in IPAs were readily identifiable, and that IPA unit holders are not charged SDRT in respect of the surrender of non-IPA units.

The section also inserts a new para 6A into FA 1999 Sch 19. See commentary under FA 1999 Sch 19 for details. See also SI 2001/964 and SI 2000/2549.

94. SDRT: open-ended investment companies and individual pension accounts

This section exempts surrenders of shares in open-ended investment companies (OEICs) from the usual SDRT charge on surrenders where the shares are within a class of shares that are limited to holdings within IPAs and there are other classes of shares not so limited. This section applies to surrenders made on or after 6 April 2001. See also SI 2001/964.

95. Exemptions: in relation to employee share ownership schemes

This section came into force on 12 May 2001 and exempts employees who buy partnership or dividend shares from an AESOP trust (as introduced in FA 2000) from Stamp Duty or SDRT. It amends FA 2000 Sch 8 para 116.

SCHEDULES

SCHEDULE 30 STAMP DUTY: LAND IN DISADVANTAGED AREAS

See commentary on FA 2001 s 92.

Finance Act 2002

2002 Chapter 23

PART 4 OTHER TAXES

110. Land in disadvantaged areas

(See the notes printed at the end of the contents list to Part II Stamp Taxes.)

This section defines "residential property" for the purpose of the stamp duty exemption for land in disadvantaged areas and provides for regulations that limit the exemption by reference to whether the property is "residential property" and to the amount or value of the consideration for the transfer or a new lease. See commentary on FA 2001 ss 92, 92A and 92B.

111. Withdrawal of group relief

(See the notes printed at the end of the contents list to Part II Stamp Taxes.)

This section provides for group relief under FA 1930 s 42 or FA 1995 s 151 or an appropriate proportion to be withdrawn where an instrument which transfers (including grant or surrender) land in the United Kingdom has been stamped on the basis that group relief applies, the transferee company leaves the transferor's group (grouping being defined according to the associated bodies corporate provisions in the relevant group relief provision) within two years of the execution of that instrument and at the time of so leaving the group the transferee still owns the land or an interest in land derived from the land originally transferred to it (otherwise than under a subsequent duly stamped instrument for which group relief was claimed). In such a situation, a charge is imposed equivalent to the amount of stamp duty that would have been paid on the intra-group transfer had group relief not applied and the land had been transferred at market value. The duty is payable within 30 days after the transferee company ceased to be grouped with the transferor company. This section came into force on 24 April 2002 and applies to instruments executed after 23 April 2002. Transitional provisions apply in relation to contracts made on or before 17 April 2002. Supplementary provisions are given effect in subsection (6), and are found in Sch 34.

Schedule 34 paras 2 and 3 provide that group relief will not be withdrawn where the transferee company leaves the group by reason of a transaction relating to shares in, or anything done in, the course of a winding up of the transferor or another company that, as a result of the transaction, ceases to be a member of the same group as the transferee company, eg the transferor company has transferred the land to a sister transferee company, then the transferor company or a company above it leaves the transferee group.

Schedule 34 para 4 deals with sequential FA 1930 s 42 or FA 1995 s 151 intra-group transfers followed by s 75 reconstructions. It provides that group relief will not be withdrawn where the transferee ceases to be a member of the same group as the transferor as a result of a transfer for which relief under FA 1986 s 75 applies and remains within the same group as the parent after the transfer. However, where the transferee then leaves the new group within two years of the original transfer and at the time of so leaving the group the transferee still owns the land or an interest in land derived from the land originally transferred to it (otherwise than under a subsequent duly stamped instrument for which group relief was claimed), group relief is withdrawn in the same way as if the transferee had ceased to be a member of the same group as the transferor.

Schedule 34 para 5 states that interest applies to the amount payable under s 111 (2) (b), and runs from 30 days after the transfer on which group relief is withdrawn.

Schedule 34 para 6 confers a duty on the transferee company to provide notification containing various details specified in para 5 (1) within 30 days of the date on which group relief is withdrawn. A penalty applies if the notification is not made within this period.

Schedule 34 para 7 provides that regulations regarding determination, appeal against determination and the collection and recovery of the duty and interest thereon shall apply as if the amount payable were an amount of stamp duty reserve tax.

Schedule 34 para 8 applies where the whole or part of the amount, determined to be payable by the transferee company under the section, has not been paid within 6 months of the date on which it became payable. In such a situation a notice may be issued by the Commissioners to require any other member of the group which was above the transferee company in the group structure between execution of the original intra-group transfer and the transferee leaving the group, and any person who during such period was a controlling director of the transferee company or of a company which controlled the transferee company at the relevant time, to pay the outstanding amount.

Schedule 34 para 9 states that a notice served under para 8 may require payment within 30 days of that notice. The notice must, however, be served within three years of the issue of the notice of determination to the transferee company, and both the notice and the amount are treated as if it were an amount of SDRT that were due from that person. Paragraph 9 states that any person who pays an amount under it may recover that amount from the transferee company and any payment is not allowed as a tax deduction.

Schedule 34 para 10 provides HMRC with information-gathering powers, subject to legal professional privilege.

112. Restriction of relief for company acquisitions

(See the notes printed at the end of the contents list to Part II Stamp Taxes.)

This section provides for the restriction of relief for company acquisitions of undertakings involving the transfer of land in the UK under FA 1986 s 76. This covers the situation where a company acquires land in the UK, and the acquiring company is associated with another company which has arrangements with the target company relating to the shares of the acquiring company issued in connection with the acquisition. This section takes effect for instruments executed after 23 April 2002 and comes into force on 24 April 2002. See commentary on FA 1986 s 76.

113. Withdrawal of relief for company acquisitions

(See the notes printed at the end of the contents list to Part II Stamp Taxes.)

This section provides for the potential withdrawal of reconstruction relief for acquisitions of undertakings involving land in the UK under FA 1986 s 76. This covers the situation where an instrument, which includes a transfer (including a grant or surrender) of land in the UK to an acquiring company, is stamped on the basis of s 76 relief; control (TA 1988 s 416 definition) of the acquiring company changes within two years of the execution of that instrument and at the time of the change of control the acquiring company still owns the land or an interest in land derived from the land originally transferred to it (otherwise than under a subsequent duly stamped instrument for which s 76 relief was claimed). In such a situation s 76 relief, or an appropriate proportion of it, is withdrawn, and a charge is imposed equivalent to the additional stamp duty which would have been paid on the transfer if s 76 relief had not applied, and the land had been transferred at market value. The charge is payable by the acquiring company within 30 days of the change of control. Supplementary provisions are given effect in subsection (5), and are found in Sch 35. This section comes into force on 24 April 2002 and takes effect for instruments executed after 23 April 2002, subject to transitional provisions for pre-17 April 2002 contracts.

Schedule 35 para 2 provides that s 76 relief will not be withdrawn where control of the acquiring company changes as a result of a transaction listed in the Schedule to the Stamp Duty (Exempt Instrument) Regulations 1987, SI 1987/516.

Schedule 35 para 3 provides that where control of the acquiring company changes as a result of a transfer in relation to which FA 1930 s 42 group relief applies, s 76 relief will not be withdrawn. However, if before the end of two years, beginning with the date of execution of the relevant instrument, the company ("company B") holding shares in the acquiring company to which the intra-group share transfer related, ceases to be a member of the same group as the s 76 target company, and the acquiring company still holds that land or a derivation of it (otherwise than under a subsequent duly stamped instrument for which s 76 relief was claimed), section 76 relief is withdrawn and the additional stamp duty that would have been paid on stamping the relevant instrument, but for the s 76 relief or a proportion of it, is payable by the acquiring company within 30 days of company B ceasing to be a member of the group.

Schedule 35 para 4 provides that s 76 relief will not be withdrawn where control of the acquiring company changes as a result of a transfer of shares to which share acquisition relief applies under FA 1986 s 77. However, if within two years, beginning with the date of the execution of the relevant instrument, the control of the parent company changes (at a time when that company holds any shares transferred to it by the exempt transfer, or any shares derived from shares so transferred, and the acquiring company holds the land or a derivation of the land otherwise than under a subsequent duly stamped instrument for which s 76 relief was claimed), s 76 relief is withdrawn and the additional stamp duty that would have been paid had it not been for the s 76 relief, is payable by the acquiring company within 30 days after control of the parent company changes.

Schedule 35 para 5 provides that s 76 relief will not be withdrawn where control of the acquiring company changes as a result of a loan creditor becoming, or ceasing to be, treated as having control of the acquiring company if the other persons controlling the company continue to do so.

Schedule 35 para 6 states that interest applies to the amount payable, and runs from 30 days after the transfer on which s 76 relief was claimed.

Schedule 35 para 7 confers a duty on the transferee company to provide notification containing various details within 30 days of the date on which group relief is withdrawn. A penalty applies if the notification is not made within this period.

Schedule 35 para 8 provides that regulations regarding determination, appeal against determination and the collection and recovery of the duty and interest thereon shall apply as if the amount payable were an amount of stamp duty reserve tax.

Schedule 35 para 9 applies where the whole or part of the amount, determined to be payable by the transferee company under the section, has not been paid within 6 months of the date on which it became payable. In such a situation a notice may be issued by the Commissioners to require any other member of the group which was above the transferee company in the group structure between execution of the s 76 instrument and change of control, and any person who during such period was a controlling director of the transferee company or of a company which controlled the transferee company, to pay the outstanding amount.

Schedule 35 para 10 states that a notice served under para 8 may require payment within 30 days of that notice. The notice must, however, be served within three years of the issue of the notice of determination to the transferee company, and both the notice and the amount are treated as if it were an amount of SDRT that were due from that person.

Schedule 35 para 11 provides HMRC with information-gathering powers, subject to legal professional privilege.

114. Penalties for late stamping

This section amends SA 1891 s 15B, with effect for instruments executed on or after 24 July 2002.

115. Contracts for sale of an estate or interest in land chargeable and conveyances

(See the notes printed at the end of the contents list to Part II Stamp Taxes.)

This section addresses the avoidance of stamp duty on "large deals" where the parties stop short of executing a formal conveyance of the land, which is the instrument that normally attracts the stamp duty charge, and "rest" on the contract instead. See Stamp Taxes: Customer Newsletter: Contracts for the sale of an estate or interest in UK land—FA 2002 s 115 and Sch 36, for guidance offered by the Stamp Taxes Office.

The section brings certain contracts (including ones which are conditional) executed after 24 July 2002 for the sale of an estate or interest in land in the UK (which would otherwise be exempt under FA 1999 Sch 13 para 7) into the charge to ad valorem stamp duty where (*a*) the amount or value of the consideration exceeds £10 million, or the instrument forms part of a larger transaction or series of transactions in respect of which the amount or value, or aggregate amount or value, exceeds £10 million; and (*b*) a conveyance or transfer made in conformity with the contract is not presented to the Commissioners within 90 days of execution of the contract (or such longer time as the Commissioners may think reasonable in the circumstances of the case). Subsection 3 sets out the circumstances in which the Commissioners may refuse or allow a longer period and the newsletter referred to above goes into the procedure and considerations which they may take into account. The newsletter also offers guidance on apportionment of consideration, the "larger transaction/series of transactions" test, VAT and unascertainable consideration.

Where the section applies, the contract will be chargeable with the same ad valorem duty, to be paid by the purchaser, as if it were an actual conveyance on sale of the estate or interest in land contracted to be sold.

A contract within this section is admissible in evidence and for SA 1891 s 14 (4) purposes up to the end of the 90 day (extended as the case may be) period.

Interest and penalties for late stamping apply as if the contract had been executed at the end of the 90 day period (extended as the case may be).

The ad valorem duty paid upon a contract under this section must be repaid by the Commissioners if the contract is afterwards rescinded or annulled, or is for any reason not satisfactorily performed or carried into effect.

Supplementary provisions are given effect in Sch 36.

Schedule 36 para 2 provides that there is a subsale where (*a*) the purchaser under a contract or agreement for the sale of an estate or interest in land in the UK, or under a subsale of an estate or interest in land in the UK; (*b*) contracts to sell the whole or part of the property (in the case of a subsale the property contracted to be sold by the original sale) to another person; (*c*) without having obtained a conveyance of the property contracted to be sold; (*d*) so as to entitle that person to call for a conveyance from the original seller.

Schedule 36 para 3 imitates the FA 1999 Sch 13 para 7 (2) position for sub-sales where the contract is chargeable by crediting duty paid on earlier contracts against duty payable on later contracts. It provides that where duty has been paid on the original sale or intervening subsale, duty on a subsale, or subsequent subsale, is chargeable only in respect of the amount of the excess by which the latter consideration exceeds the chargeable consideration on the earlier transaction (or a just and reasonable proportion of the consideration if only part sold). Where there is more than one earlier transaction (eg a chain of four where A contracts to sell to B who contracts to sell to C who contracts to sell to D) duty is paid on the excess over the higher or highest amount of chargeable consideration on which duty has been paid—note that in this context there is reference to the duty having been paid whereas no mention is made of this in the case of a chain of three subsale. Where duty on a subsale is chargeable in respect of only part of the consideration for the subsale, it is chargeable at the rate that would be applicable if the whole of the chargeable consideration on the subsale were taken into account.

Schedule 36 para 5 credits s 115 duty against duty on the subsequent conveyance or transfer. This effectively preserves SA 1891 s 58 (4) relief, which prevents the conveyance being

Part II ST

stamped on the aggregate consideration under more than one underlying contract but ensures that the higher or highest consideration applies and imitates FA 1999 Sch 13 para 7 (3) by applying a credit mechanism. It provides that where the original seller conveys the whole of the property contracted to be sold (*a*) to the purchaser; or (*b*) to a sub-purchaser in circumstances where SA 1891 s 58(4) applies, the conveyance or transfer is chargeable with duty only to the extent that the ad valorem duty chargeable on it exceeds the duty paid on the original sale aggregated with the amount of any such duty paid on any intervening subsale. Where the original seller conveys the property contracted to be sold to different sub-purchasers in parts or parcels and SA 1891 s 58 (5) applies, the conveyance or transfer of each part or parcel is chargeable with duty only to the extent that the ad valorem duty chargeable on it exceeds an appropriate proportion of the ad valorem duty paid on the original sale aggregated with the appropriate proportion of the duty paid on any intervening subsale. Any duty paid on a sale or intervening sub-sale is to be denoted on or transferred to the conveyance or transfer.

Schedule 36 para 6 provides that where duty is paid on both the original sale and one or more conveyances or transfers are executed in conformity with the contract or agreement conveying the property to a purchaser or one or more sub-purchasers, and the aggregate amount of duty that would have been paid on these conveyances or transfers but for duty having been previously paid on the original sale, is less than the duty paid on the original sale, the difference will be repaid by the Commissioner to the person who paid the duty on the original sale. Where there have been intervening subsales, the reference to duty having been paid on the original sale includes the payment of duty on the intervening subsale, and the repayment is apportioned among the persons who paid these amounts.

116. Abolition of duty on instruments relating to goodwill

(See the notes printed at the end of the contents list to Part II Stamp Taxes.)

This section abolishes stamp duty on instruments executed after 23 April 2002 for the sale, transfer or other disposition of goodwill.

Supplementary provisions are given effect in sub-section (2), and are found in Sch 37.

Under Sch 37 para 1, the conveyance on sale duty charge on instruments executed on or after 23 April 2002 relating partly to goodwill and partly to other property, is disapplied to the extent of the consideration attributed to the goodwill (on a just and reasonable basis).

Schedule 37 para 2 concerns the apportionment of consideration where property is sold to the same purchaser by different instruments but for one consideration.

Schedule 37 para 3 provides that goodwill be disregarded for the purpose of certificates of value under FA 1999 Sch 13 para 6 (certification of instrument as not forming part of a transaction or series of transactions exceeding a specified amount).

Schedule 37 para 4 provides that FA 1985 s 12 does not require any person who is authorised to purchase any property under statutory powers after 23 April 2002, to include any goodwill in the instrument of conveyance required by that section to be produced to the Commissioner. If the property consists wholly of goodwill, no instrument of conveyance need be produced to the Commissioner under that section.

117. Power to extend exceptions relating to recognised exchanges

This section provides for regulations to extend the exemptions for intermediaries contained in FA 1986 ss 80A and 88A, and the exemptions for repurchases and stock lending contained in FA 1986 ss 80C and 89AA, to any market that is not a recognised exchange but is prescribed by order under Financial Services and Markets Act 2000 s 118(3). Recognition has been extended to the market known as OFEX and to the Alternative Investment Market established under the rules of the London Stock Exchange.

Section 117 is to cease to have effect on 11 August 2005: see The Finance Act 2002, Section 117 (Day Appointed for Cessation of Effect) Order 2005, SI 2005/2007.

SCHEDULES

SCHEDULE 34 STAMP DUTY: WITHDRAWAL OF GROUP RELIEF—SUPPLEMENTARY PROVISIONS

See commentary on FA 2002 s 111.

SCHEDULE 35 STAMP DUTY: WITHDRAWAL OF RELIEF FOR COMPANY ACQUISITIONS—SUPPLEMENTARY PROVISIONS

See commentary on FA 2002 s 113.

SCHEDULE 36 STAMP DUTY: CONTRACTS CHARGEABLE AS CONVEYANCES—SUPPLEMENTARY PROVISIONS

See commentary on FA 2002 s 115.

SCHEDULE 37 STAMP DUTY: ABOLITION OF DUTY ON INSTRUMENTS RELATING TO GOODWILL—SUPPLEMENTARY PROVISIONS

See commentary on FA 2002 s 116.

Finance Act 2003

2003 Chapter 14

PART 4 STAMP DUTY LAND TAX

42. The tax

This section introduces stamp duty land tax ("SDLT") as the replacement for stamp duty on transactions involving land and buildings in the UK. It clarifies that SDLT applies irrespective of whether or not there is an instrument effecting the transaction (and if so, whether or not it is executed in the UK), and whether or not any of the parties are present or resident in the UK. Sub-section (3) establishes that HMRC are responsible for the "care and management" of SDLT.

The then named Inland Revenue issued their consultation document, "Modernising stamp duty on land and buildings in the UK", on Budget Day 2002. The reasons for the reform process cited in the foreword included first and foremost, that it was outdated and no longer reflected "modern commercial practice in the ownership, use and transfer of land and buildings" and was "not suited to the rapidly developing world of e-business and electronic transactions". In addition, however, the government's concern about growing avoidance and their determination to stop such abuse was raised. This determination is duly reflected in the legislative provisions that have been introduced.

The new features of SDLT include that:

- subject to transitional provisions (see Sch 19), it applies;
- it is a charge on transactions (including some uncompleted contracts) and no longer on documents, thus preventing the previous practice of "resting on contract";
- it will be collected by self-assessment and subject to modern enquiry, enforcement and appeal procedures;
- it only applies to UK land;
- it covers certain transactions such as variations of chargeable interests in land which used not to be covered by stamp duty;
- the stamp duty "contingency principle" is replaced by a "reasonable estimate" procedure;
- different rates apply to residential and non-residential property;
- a completely new system of calculating the charge on lease rent applies;
- exchanges can no longer be structured as sales with only one leg of the transaction being stamped;
- as a transaction tax, judicial anti-avoidance principles may be more relevant than in relation to stamp duty (see Lord Hoffmann's judgement in *MacNiven (Inspector of Taxes)* v *Westmoreland Investments Limited* [2001] STC 58);
- consideration now, rather like stamp duty reserve tax, extends generally to "money's worth"; and
- certain Islamic financing transactions will be relieved from multiple tax charges.

43. Land transactions

This section begins by defining "land transaction" as the "acquisition" of a "chargeable interest" (see s 48 below and note that licences and tenancies at will and mortgage interests in land are not chargeable interests). SDLT applies however the acquisition is effected, and thus includes transactions arising from a court order or by operation of law. The section then goes on to analyse the different categories of land transaction involving chargeable interests (namely the creation, surrender or release, and variation of chargeable interests) in terms of disposals by one person (the "vendor") and acquisitions by another (the "purchaser").

Special provision is made for variations of leases; most variations of leases are not to involve the acquisition or disposal of a chargeable interest. The exceptional cases (which are thus to be chargeable) are variations which either take effect in law as the grant of a new lease or which are treated for SDLT purposes as the grant of a new lease, or variations which effect a reduction in the rent reserved by a lease or in the term of the lease. As to when a variation of a lease is treated as the grant of a new lease under general law see *Friends' Provident Life Office* v *British Railways Board* [1996] 1 All ER 336. SDRT treats a variation of a lease so as to increase the amount of the rent as the grant of a new lease for the additional rent: see FA 2003 Sch 5 para 10. As to the charge on the reduction in the rent reserved by, or the term of, a lease see Sch 17A para 15A.

The definition of "purchaser" covers any party to the transaction, even if they have not given consideration for the transaction. Finally, sub-s (6) establishes that the subject matter of a land transaction includes the chargeable interest acquired (defined as "the main subject matter"), together with any interest or right appurtenant or pertaining to it. The intention of this provision is, for example, to prevent the transfer of a freehold and a related right of way from being regarded as separate transactions.

44. Contract and conveyance

The principal purpose of this section is to ensure that in most cases SDLT will arise on completion, but also to prevent avoidance or postponement of SDLT, as was previously the case under the stamp duty regime, by "resting on contract".

If a contract for a land transaction is "substantially performed" before it is formally completed (or is never completed), the "effective date" for the transaction (30 days after which an SDLT return and payment of the SDLT chargeable must be paid) the date of substantial performance. The contract is treated as if it were itself the transaction provided for in the contract. If such a contract is "substantially performed" only at the time it is formally completed, then SDLT is deemed to arise at the time of formal completion. In that case a person is not regarded as entering into a land transaction by entering into the contract but the contract and the transaction effected on completion are treated as parts of a single transaction. Under sub-s (5) substantial performance is deemed to take place either when the purchaser (or someone connected with him) takes possession of the whole or substantially the whole of the subject matter of the transaction, or when a substantial amount of the consideration is paid or provided. Sub-section (6) confirms that possession is taken of a property if, inter alia, the purchaser (or the connected person) receives or is entitled to receive rents and profits—irrespective of whether possession is taken under the contract, or under a licence, or under a lease of a temporary character.

Sub-section (7) sets out the circumstances where a substantial amount of the consideration has been paid or provided. There are four different cases to consider:

- Where none of the consideration is rent. In this case the whole or substantially the whole of the consideration must be paid or provided before there is substantial performance. Although there are no specific percentages provided by the legislation itself, HMRC have indicated (SDLT Manual, para 7950) that, generally speaking, "substantially the whole means an amount equal to or greater than 90 per cent of the total consideration due under the contract unless the circumstances of the transaction are such that in substance the whole of the consideration has been paid or provided". This treatment is not to be afforded in cases where an artificially high consideration is agreed, with less than 90 per cent payable now and the rest payable in, say, 100 years' time.
- Where the purchaser receives or becomes entitled to receive rents and profits. Here one must bear in mind the Standard Conditions of Sale (Third Edition), Condition 5(5)(*e*), which provides that a purchaser permitted to enter into possession is to be entitled to any rents and profits from the land. It is important to exclude the operation of this provision if entry is not to lead automatically to the substantial performance of the contract.
- Where all the consideration is rent. In this case the first payment of any amount of rent constitutes substantial performance.

- Where there is both rent and other consideration to be paid or provided. In this case there will be substantial performance if either 90 per cent or more of the "other consideration" is given or if there is any payment of rent.

Under sub-s (8)(*a*), where a contract is substantially performed before completion, both the contract and any later formal completion of the same land transaction should be notified to HMRC. Under sub-s (8)(*b*), SDLT is chargeable at completion only to the extent (if any) that the amount chargeable on completion exceeds the amount chargeable on the contract. One may thus have two land transactions in relation to the same contract: the first occurs when the contract is substantially performed; the second when the contract is completed.

Where a contract is rescinded, annulled or for any other reason not carried into effect, sub-s (9) provides that all or some of the SDLT paid may be reclaimed from HMRC by amending the land transaction return form made in respect of the contract.

There are special rules for agreements for lease, where FA 2003 Sch 17A para 12A is to apply instead.

Sub-section (10) defines "completion" for the purposes of this section as "the completion of the land transaction proposed, between the same parties, in substantial conformity with the contract. "Contract" is in turn defined as "any agreement". Finally, "conveyance" is defined as "any instrument", which includes leases and is irrespective of whether the instrument is in written or electronic form.

44A. Contract providing for conveyance to third party

This section is intended to counteract what was seen as unacceptable SDLT avoidance by land developers. Historically, such persons have avoided stamp duty by "resting in contract". The developer would exchange contracts with a landowner to buy a parcel of land and would enter on the land and construct dwelling houses. He would then sell the completed houses to consumers and would require the landowner to transfer each house direct to the sub-purchaser. This attracted a single charge to stamp duty in accordance with Stamp Act 1891 s 58(4). This route was effectively blocked by the new substantial performance rules in s 44. In response, developers adjusted their contracts with landowners: instead of contracting to buy the land, they agreed to act as building contractors for the landowner, constructing the same dwelling houses as before and then entering into contracts with consumers to sell the completed houses. The structure generally involved the landowner receiving a fee from the developer in return for granting the developer a licence to go on the land and construct; the developer in turn, by the terms of his agreement with the landowner, would be entitled to retain the full proceeds from the onward sale. Since a licence to use or occupy land was not a chargeable interest in land (FA 2003 s 48(2)(*b*)), the developer acquired nothing in respect of which he could be taxed.

Section 44A seeks to block this route by deeming the developer to enter into a land transaction where there is substantial performance of a contract under which provision is made for the land potentially to be conveyed to a person other than the developer, but at the direction or request of the developer. In such a case where the developer goes onto the land (or substantially performs in some other way), he is treated as acquiring a chargeable interest and thus as entering into a land transaction. The effect is that the developer is obliged to pay SDLT although he never contracts to acquire anything other than a non-exclusive licence to use the land. The section applies to any contract entered into after 17 March 2004.

This section applies where the landowner (A) contracts with another person (B) that a chargeable interest in the land should be conveyed to a person who is not a party to the contract (C) or either to B or C, and that this should be done at the direction or request of B. There is no charge on the exchange of contracts, but a land transaction is taken to occur when substantial performance of the contract takes place. As to the meaning of "substantial performance" see s 44 above.

Where such a contract is entered into and is substantially performed, B is deemed to have acquired a chargeable interest and as having entered into a land transaction. B will therefore be liable to SDLT as purchaser (whether or not he takes a conveyance of the property). No specific provision is made as the consideration on which B is liable to SDLT, so that the usual rules in FA 2003 Sch 4 must be taken to apply. Thus, B is liable for SDLT in respect of the consideration he is to provide to A. The charge arises when substantial performance takes place: sub-s (3).

If B actually directs A to transfer the land to him, provision is made for s 44 to apply to the transfer by A to B, as it would under a contract to be completed by a conveyance to B (sub-s (6)). The effect of this is that B is only liable for additional SDLT on completion to the extent (if any) that the amount chargeable on completion exceeds the amount chargeable on the contract (see s 44(8)).

Section 44A makes clear that C is not affected by the arrangements between A and B; instead, s 44 is to apply to the contract between B and C. C will therefore be liable to SDLT on the consideration he is to provide to B (sub-s (7)).

Where a contract falling within s 44A is rescinded, annulled or for any other reason not carried into effect, sub-s (4) provides that all or some of the SDLT paid may be reclaimed from HMRC.

In debate, the Chief Secretary to the Treasury indicated that s 44A was not intended to apply to an ordinary case of sub-sale. Such transactions are still within ss 44 and 45(1), (3) (Hansard, 28 April 2004, col 916). Nor is the section intended to catch persons acting as estate agents.

45. Contract and conveyance: effect of transfer of rights

This section covers the treatment of subsales and other situations where the purchaser's rights under a contract are transferred to a third party. Sub-section (1) provides that the section applies in cases where the parties enter into a contract for a land transaction to be completed by conveyance and there is a transfer of rights (an assignment, subsale or other transaction which results in a third party being entitled to acquire all or part of the subject matter of the original contract at completion). The transferee is not regarded as entering into a land transaction by reason of the transfer of rights. In accordance with sub-ss (3) and (4), the transfer of rights is to be treated as if it were a separate contract to which s 44 applied, as if the transferee of the rights is the purchaser and the chargeable consideration for the transaction is the amount that remains to be paid under the original contract directly or indirectly by the transferee or a person connected with him and the consideration given for the transfer of rights. Sub-sale relief is given in circumstances where the substantial performance or completion of the original contract takes place at the same time as, and in connection with, the substantial performance or completion of the secondary contract. In such a case, the substantial performance or completion of the original contract is disregarded. By way of exception, the disregard is unavailable if the secondary contract gives rise to a transaction that is exempt under any of section 71A to 73, ie where the financial institution sells or leases the property on to the individual under an Islamic mortgage. Without this exclusion, it would be possible (subject only to section 75A) to avoid SDLT by the use of a transaction in the form of an Islamic funding arrangement.

Sub-sale relief has been the subject of a number of tax-planning devices of a greater or lesser degree of sophistication, and it was the prevalence of such schemes between 2003 and 2006 that led in great part to the inclusion of the anti-avoidance provision, FA 2003 s 75A. Despite the introduction of that section, it is clear that a number of advisers have (rightly or wrongly) continued to market such devices as effective means of mitigating SDLT. On 7 June 2010 the Commissioners published an updated version of their "spotlight" on avoidance schemes which they intend to challenge. Spotlight 10 focuses on schemes "using an intermediate sale introduced into the arrangements with the sole intention of removing the true purchase price from tax". The Commissioners announced that in their view such transactions, including those involving sub-sales, produced a charge to SDLT "on the full amount paid for the property". This, they stated, was the case, in many instances because the transactions failed to achieve what they set out to do, but, in any event, because of the operation of s 75A.

Sub-section (4) confirms that where there are successive transfers of rights, sub-s (3) applies to each transfer. In a similar fashion to sub-s (3), sub-s (4) clarifies that the first secondary contract is to be disregarded when followed by a further transfer of rights.

One uncertainty created by the original form of the legislation was whether the notional contract created by sub-s (3) was between the landowner and the ultimate transferee, or between the intermediate transferor and the ultimate transferee. Sub-section (3) specifically provided that the notional purchaser was the transferee, but was silent as to the identity of the notional vendor. Section 43(4) would suggest that the vendor is the "person disposing of the subject-matter of the land transaction", and the Commissioners' approach has been to assert that the effect of the sub-section is that the original landowner is therefore the vendor for section 44 purposes. On the other hand, various SDLT saving strategies were implemented on the basis that the intermediate transferor was the vendor for the purposes of the notional contract. The schemes operated by that transferor sub-selling to another company within its group, with the result (so it was argued) that the intermediate purchase was disregarded in accordance with sub-s (3); and the final transfer was relieved from SDLT on completion of the notional contract by Sch 7 group relief. To counteract this argument, sub-s (5A) specifies that where there is a sub-s (3) sub-sale, the vendor is to be taken for Sch 7 group relief purposes to be the original vendor and not the intermediate transferor. Accordingly, group relief will be unavailable because the vendor and purchaser will generally not be members of the same group. Other references in the SDLT legislation to the vendor are to be read as referring either to the original vendor or to the intermediate transferor as the context requires.

In *DV3 RS Limited Partnership v HMRC* (TC 1012) the First-Tier Tribunal held that, at least in a case where the property was transferred first to the intermediate purchaser and then to the final purchaser by two TR1s, the effect of section 45(3) was to treat the secondary contract as a tripartite contract between the three parties, and which involved the land being transferred by the intermediate purchaser to the final purchaser. In the circumstances of the case, the Tribunal concluded that the first transaction, between landowner and intermediate purchaser, was excluded from charge by the tailpiece to section 45(3); and the transfer by intermediate purchaser to a partnership of which the purchaser was a partner fell within the special rules for partnerships in Part 3 of Schedule 15 and was to subject to SDLT on the consideration given for the transfer.

The original formulation of s 45 gave rise to another means of avoiding SDLT, where the original purchaser sub-sold a small fraction of the property to a third party and then procured the completion of both the original contract and the sub-sale at the same time and in connection with each other. It would appear that in such cases, SDLT was chargeable only in respect of the small amount of consideration passing on the sub-sale. As sub-s (5) is now drafted, separate charges to SDLT arise on the part sub-sold and the part transferred to the original purchaser, with each transferee paying SDLT by reference to so much of the consideration provided by him as relates to the property transferred to him.

Section 45 does not apply to an assignment of the benefit of an agreement for the grant of a lease, which is covered by FA 2003 Sch 17A para 12B.

45A. Contracts providing for conveyance to third party: effect of transfer of rights

This provision offers the equivalent for s 44A cases of the sub-sale rules in s 45. It deals with cases where B under a s 44A contract (usually a developer) assigns his rights under the contract with A to another person, D (eg a second developer). D is treated as if he himself had entered into a s 44A secondary contract, under which the chargeable consideration for the transaction is the amount that remains to be paid under the original contract directly or indirectly by the transferee (or a person connected with him) plus the consideration given for the transfer of rights. Where the secondary contract is substantially performed or completed, D will be treated as having acquired a chargeable interest under a land transaction (and will be liable to SDLT), but the substantial performance or completion of the earlier contract will be disregarded provided that it takes place at the same time as and in connection with, or indeed after (contrast the wording of s 45(3)), that under the secondary contract. The effect will be to give sub-sale relief to B provided he transfers his rights before he substantially performs the original contract.

There are rules corresponding to those in s 45 relating to (*a*) the charging of SDLT where part only of the rights is assigned; (*b*) successive assignments; and (*c*) preventing the use of Sch 7 group relief where the secondary contract is between group members.

46. Options and rights of pre-emption

Whereas under the stamp duty regime many option agreements were not stamped in practice (and stamp duty could therefore, arguably, be reduced by increasing the option fee and decreasing the price of the land), the intention under the new SDLT regime is to ensure that all the consideration given either for the option or for the transfer of the land comes into charge. Sub-section (1) deals with the SDLT charge on the acquisition of an option or a right of pre-emption over land: that acquisition is to be a land transaction in its own right. Sub-section (1) further provides that where such an option or right is exercised, the consequential transaction that arises is to be regarded as a distinct transaction and is accordingly also chargeable to SDLT. However, the option and the land transaction entered into as a result of the exercise of the option may be linked transactions under s 108. Sub-section (2) confirms that the reference to an option binding the grantor to enter into a land transaction in sub-s (1), includes situations where the grantor can discharge his obligation either by entering into a land transaction or in some other way, for example by "cash settlement".

Under sub-s (3), the effective date of the transaction in relation to options and rights of pre-emption is when they are acquired rather than when they become exercisable. Finally, sub-s (4) provides that if an option or right of pre-emption is already chargeable as part of a wider transaction, then it is dealt with as such, and not in accordance with s 46.

47. Exchanges

This section ensures that where a purchaser enters into a transaction involving the exchange of one interest in land for another, each transaction forming part of the exchange is to be treated as a separate transaction. Accordingly, there will be two charges to SDLT: one on each land transaction. This prevents the stamp duty practice of stamping only the more expensive leg of the transaction as a sale and describing the transfer of the cheaper property as the settlement of the consideration, rather than a sale in its own right or an exchange. In order to prevent an increased charge where the parties to the exchange are connected with each other, provision is made that the two legs of the exchange are not to be treated as linked transactions for the purposes of s 108. In consequence, if A transfers Whiteacre, worth £300,000, to his brother in exchange for Blackacre, worth £200,000, the transfer to B is charged to SDLT at 3% and the transfer by B is charged at 1%, rather than the 4% at which each would otherwise have been charged in consequence of the application of ss 108 and 55(4).

Sub-section (2) confirms that the section equally applies to situations where there is on the face of it a cash sale of land, but the purchaser discharges his obligation to pay cash by entering into another transaction as vendor. With regard to the amount of the chargeable consideration in the case of exchanges and partitions, sub-s (3) refers the reader to the more detailed provisions set out at Sch 4 paras 5 and 6, and in the case of part-exchange of residential property to s 58.

48. Chargeable interests

Under this section, "chargeable interest" is broadly defined as any estate, interest, right or power in or over land in the UK, or the benefit of any obligation, restriction or condition affecting the value of such an estate, interest, right or power. The section removes from the category of "chargeable interest" any "exempt interest". Sub-section (2) goes on to identify what interests are exempt, including security interests, licences to use or occupy land, and, in England and Wales or Northern Ireland, a tenancy at will and advowsons, franchises or manors. "Security interest" is defined at sub-s (3) as an interest or right (other than a rentcharge, and its Scottish equivalent (see sub-s (4)) held to secure the payment of money or the performance of any other obligation (including mortgages). "Franchise" means a grant from the Crown, for example the right to hold a market or fair, or the right to take tolls. See also s 73B by which, in the circumstances specified in that section, interests which do not fall within sub-s (2) are deemed to be exempt interests in the context of alternative finance arrangements.

The section also provides at sub-ss (5) and (6), that the Treasury may, by means of regulations (which may include appropriate supplementary, incidental and transitional provisions) make any other interest or right in relation to land in the UK, an "exempt interest".

This section takes effect subject to specific deeming provisions: (i) s 44A(3) (which deems a chargeable interest to be acquired in the circumstances described in that section, despite the fact that the scheme with which it is concerned is predicated on the basis that the notional purchaser acquires no such interest); and (ii) Sch 17A para 15A, sub-s (7) (which deems a chargeable interest to be acquired where parties agree to reduce the rent reserved by a lease or to reduce the term of a lease).

49. Chargeable transactions

This section defines "chargeable" land transactions as those that are not exempt, and provides for Schedule 3, which sets out the various exempt transactions (see below).

50. Chargeable consideration

This section makes provision for determining the chargeable consideration for a transaction, the details of which are set out in Sch 4 (see below). Under sub-ss (2) and (3), the Treasury reserves the right to amend or repeal SDLT provisions relating to the definition of chargeable consideration and the determination of the amount of chargeable consideration.

51. Contingent, uncertain or unascertained consideration

Sub-section (1) establishes that where any part of the chargeable consideration for a transaction is contingent, the amount of consideration is to be determined for SDLT purposes on the assumption that the contingent amount will be payable, regardless of the outcome of the contingency.

In the case of transactions where some part of the chargeable consideration is uncertain or unascertained, s 51(2) provides that the consideration should be determined on the basis of a "reasonable estimate". Sub-section (3) defines "contingent" and "uncertain" in relation to consideration, and sub-s (4) provides that the section has effect subject to s 80 (adjustment where contingency ceases or consideration is ascertained) and s 90 (application to defer payment in case of contingent or uncertain consideration). It is noteworthy that this is a significant departure from the so-called "contingency principle" which applies to stamp duty. The intention of the legislation (by a combination of ss 51 and 80) is that taxpayers should (eventually) pay SDLT by reference to the consideration actually paid and not by reference to some notional amount which may or may not eventually prove chargeable.

Special rules apply where the relevant consideration consists of rent: the section is only to apply to the extent permitted by Sch 17A para 7 (variable or uncertain rent): sub-s (5).

52. Annuities etc: chargeable consideration limited to twelve years' payments

This section sets out how SDLT is applied where the chargeable consideration for a land transaction is in the form of an annuity payment for life, in perpetuity, for an indefinite period or for a definite period exceeding twelve years. Sub-section (2) confirms that, for the purposes of SDLT, the consideration taken into account is limited to twelve years' annual payments (as defined at sub-s (4)). Under sub-s (3), where the amount payable varies, the twelve highest annual payments will be taken (ignoring RPI adjustments). The use of twelve years in this section follows the application of the old stamp duty regime to annuities terminable on death.

Sub-section (5) confirms that where the amount of any annual payment is contingent, uncertain or unascertained, s 51 applies with regard to determining the amount of the payment but, under sub-s (7), s 80 (adjustment where contingency ceases or consideration is ascertained) does not apply, and no application can be made under s 90 to defer payment. An annuity is defined by sub-s (6) as including any amount of consideration (other than rent) which is to be paid (or provided) periodically.

53. Deemed market value where transaction involves connected company

This section ensures that SDLT is charged at market value when a company purchases land from a vendor with whom the company is connected (sub-s (1)), unless the exceptions set out in s 54 apply (sub-s (5)). The definition of "connected person" at TA 1988 s 839 is used for the purposes of SDLT under sub-s (2). Under sub-s (3) "company" is defined as any body corporate and "shares" are deemed to include stock, as well as securities issued by a company. Sub-section (4) confirms that where this section applies, Sch 3 para 1 (dealing with the exemption of transactions for which there is no chargeable consideration) does not apply. Thus a gift of land to a connected company is chargeable to SDLT by reference to the market value of the land.

54. Exceptions from deemed market value rule

This section sets out the exceptions to the rule set out in s 53, namely where immediately after the transaction the purchaser holds the land as a trustee in the course of a business of trust management ("Case 1"); where immediately after the transaction the purchaser holds land in the capacity of a trustee and is connected with the vendor only because of TA 1988 s 839(3) (where the vendor is the settlor, connected with the settlor or a body corporate connected with the settlement) ("Case 2"); and where the vendor is a company, and the transaction relates to a distribution of the assets of that company, whether or not made in connection with the winding up of a company ("Case 3"). The exception stated in Case 3 does not apply if the vendor has claimed group relief for the land on a transaction that has taken place in the three years prior to the effective date of the transaction. HMRC has announced (Tax Bulletin 71) that it is not their intention that s 54(4) should be prevented from applying where a group relief claim was made by the vendor but recovered under Sch 7 para 3 either at the time of or before the effective date of the transaction.

55. Amount of tax chargeable: general

The section sets out the percentage rates of SDLT chargeable in respect of the chargeable consideration (see s 50) for a chargeable transaction (see s 49) (with the exception of the rental element of a new lease—see s 56). The rates applied to the "relevant consideration" are determined in accordance with a "slab system", as was the case for stamp duty, but the method of calculation under SDLT is different. In accordance with s 55(2), different rates are provided where the "relevant land" is entirely residential property (defined in s 116) (in which case the rates set out in Table A apply) or non-residential property (or mixed residential and non-residential) (in which case Table B applies). "Relevant land" is defined at sub-s (3) as the land an interest in which is the main subject-matter of the transaction, and "relevant consideration" is defined as the total of the chargeable consideration for the transaction.

Sub-section (4) deals with circumstances where a transaction is one of a number of linked transactions (see s 108), and provides that "relevant land" will be all the land comprised in all of the transactions and the "relevant consideration" will be the total of the chargeable consideration for all of the transactions.

Sub-section (5) confirms that the section has effect subject to ss 74 and 75, which provide separate rules for determining the percentage rate to be applied to chargeable consideration in the case of collective enfranchisement by leaseholders and crofting community rights to buy.

Under sub-s (6), the section takes effect subject to s 56 and Sch 5 in situations where the chargeable consideration in relation to the transaction consists wholly or partly of rent.

56. Amount of tax chargeable: rent

This section makes provision for the calculation of the tax chargeable for the grant of a lease (see s 120) on which rent is to be paid, the details of which are set out in Sch 5.

57. Disadvantaged areas relief

The Government intends to include provisions in the Finance Bill 2012 to repeal this relief with effect from 6 April 2013.

This section, together with Sch 6, provides relief from SDLT for low-value residential property in disadvantaged areas in the United Kingdom. For further commentary, see the notes to Sch 6 below. The previous, extremely generous, exemption for non-residential land situate in a disadvantaged area was abolished in relation to any transaction the effective date of which was after 16 March 2005: FA 2005 s 96 and Sch 9 para 4. However, the transitional rules in Sch 9 para 4 secure the continuation of the exemption in respect of any land transaction which is either effected in pursuance of a contract entered into and substantially performed on or before 16 March 2005 or (subject to certain restrictions) effected in pursuance of a contract entered into on or before that date (even though substantial performance had not yet occurred). In this latter case though (ie where there was as at the relevant date no substantial performance) the continuing exclusion is lost if the contract is varied or assigned on or after 16 March 2005, or if the transaction is effected in consequence of the exercise after that date of an option, right of pre-emption or similar right, or if as a result of an assignment, sub-sale or other transaction made after that date, a person other than the purchaser under the contract becomes entitled to call for a conveyance to him.

57A. Relief for sale and leaseback arrangements

Section 57A offers relief from SDRT on the grant of a lease back to a person (A) who has transferred (or granted) a major interest in land to another (B) in circumstances specified by the section. This section recognises that such transactions are undertaken primarily as financing transactions and that it would be unfair if the owner of land were charged SDLT on the effective reacquisition of an interest in land which, immediately before the arrangements in question, had formed part of his estate. The section as it now stands has been extended beyond its original scope, to bring within its ambit sale and leaseback arrangements of residential as well as non-residential property as well as lease and leaseback transactions. It should be noted that although the leaseback element is exempted from SDLT, a charge to SDLT will always be imposed on the sale element of the transaction.

Sub-section (2) defines a "sale and leaseback transaction" as one under which (*a*) A transfers or grants a major interest in land to B (it is this element which is chargeable); and (*b*) out of that interest B grants a lease back to A (it is this element that is exempt). For the meaning of "major interest in land" see FA 2003 s 117.

Sub-section (3) sets out the four conditions which must be satisfied if the exemption is to be available: (*a*) the sale transaction is entered into wholly or partly in consideration of the leaseback transaction being entered into (it would seem that this requires the sale contract expressly to refer to the grant of the lease by the purchaser as being consideration for the sale); (*b*) that the only other consideration given by the purchaser be in cash form, consisting either of the payment of money or in the assumption, satisfaction or release of a debt; (*c*) that the sale is not a transfer of rights under s 45 or 45A (that is to say, the sale is not part of a longer chain of transactions of which A would thus be "the original purchaser" under s 45 or the person entitled to direct or request the current landowner to transfer to a third party under s 45A); and (*d*) that A and B are not members of the same group for the purposes of group relief under Sch 7 para 1.

Conditions (*c*) and (*d*) have been introduced in order to secure that if SDLT is avoided at an earlier stage in the chain (either because s 45(3) requires the intermediate sale to be disregarded or because the transfer from A to B would be exempt under Sch 7 para 1), then relief should not also be available under s 57A. However, it would seem that if A and B are within the same group, it will still be possible for both transactions to be exempted by Sch 7 para 1—although in such a case there will always be a risk of claw-back under para 3 of the Schedule.

57AA. First-time buyers

Section 57AA is introduced by FA 2010 s 6 to provide what is described as an "exemption" from SDLT in certain tightly-prescribed circumstances and where the effective date (as to which see s 119) of the land transaction falls between 25 March 2010 and 24 March 2012. Although described as an exemption, the real effect of the provision is to increase the threshold below which SDLT is not charged from £125,000 to £250,000.

For the exemption to be available:

(a) There must be a relevant acquisition of a major interest in land.
As a general rule, a "major interest in land" as defined by s 117 is taken to include any estate in fee simple absolute or term of years absolute – ie a freehold or leasehold interest of any length. But for the purposes of s 57AA, the exemption is unavailable if the interest is the grant or assignment of a lease with less than 21 years to run. Presumably in determining this, one is to ignore any option to extend the term or, indeed, any right to surrender or determine the lease early. This would accord with the provisions of Sch 17A paras 2 and 3. Interestingly, the explanation for the exclusion of short leases given in the explanatory notes to the Act suggests that the restriction is intended to be helpful. It is stated that 'This ensures that a purchaser will not be denied relief because he or she has previously taken a short lease on a property.' It is certainly true that the restriction will have beneficial effect when determining whether a person is a first-time buyer (as to which see s 57AA(2)); but it has a detrimental effect where a first-time buyer buys a relatively short-term but valuable lease for a price or premium in excess of £125,000.

(b) The land must consist wholly in residential property.
Residential property is defined by s 116, to the commentary on which reference should be made for a fuller explanation.

(c) Each purchaser must intend to occupy the property as his or her only or main residence.
No further explanation is offered as to what constitutes one's "only or main residence". However, one can gain assistance from earlier authorities on the same phrase in different legislation. See, for example, *Frost v Feltham* [1981] STC 115, where Nourse J considered that the phrase referred to what was, or possibly, what the taxpayer saw as, his "principal or more important" property and not necessarily to that in which he spent most of his time. In that case the taxpayer was a publican who lived for most of the year in tied accommodation in Essex and who wished to claim mortgage interest relief (as it then was) for interest paid in respect of a property he had bought in Wales and in which he spent a couple of days each month.

(d) Each purchaser must be a first-time buyer.
This is carefully defined by s 57AA(2) as restricted to persons who have not previously acquired a freehold or long leasehold interest (ie of 21 years or more) either in the United Kingdom or elsewhere and who have not been the counterparty to an alternative financing transaction relating to such an interest. However, a new s 73CA is introduced which affords a similar exemption where the purchase is itself made under an alternative financing transaction.

(e) The transaction must not be one of a number of linked transactions
This condition is included in order to prevent avoidance of tax by "property splitting". However, because the condition could lead to a denial of relief where, for example, a purchaser buys a flat and takes a lease of a parking space elsewhere in the building from the same vendor, s 57AA(4) disapplies this condition where

the linked transactions consist in the acquisition of a building, and of garden or grounds attaching to that building, or of a right over land which benefits that building. For the meaning of 'linked transactions' see the commentary to s 108.

The Commissioners have given an indication in Stamp Taxes Bulletin – June 2010 of their views as to whether a buyer might or might not claim the relief in certain difficult cases. "Approved cases" include those where the purchaser (a) cannot use the property as a residence immediately, but has an ultimate intention to do so as their only or main residence (this can apply even if the property is let in the short term); (b) has held an interest in mixed-use or non-residential property only; (c) has a future right (for example, under the terms of a trust) to acquire an interest in residential property, but has not yet done so; (d) has held legal title as a trustee, but is not a beneficiary of that trust; (e) bought a building plot and constructed a residential property on that plot; or (f) is a director/shareholder or a company which owns an interest in residential property, provided that no direct interest has been held. "Unacceptable cases" include cases where the purchaser: (a) previously had a joint interest in residential property; (b) had previously inherited or been gifted an interest in residential property; (c) previously held an interest in residential property, but not for some considerable time; (d) previously held an interest in residential property, but is regarded as being entitled to first-time buyer rates by a lender; or (e) held an interest in residential property for investment purposes only.

58A. Relief for certain acquisitions of residential property

Section 58A provides for Sch 6A, which introduces a number of related reliefs where an "intermediate purchaser" acquires a dwelling house from an individual in order to facilitate a purchase of another property or a change of residence in the case of the individual's employment being relocated. These reliefs replace those originally afforded by ss 58 (reliefs for certain exchanges of residential property) and 59 (relocation relief), which were repealed and replaced before they came into force.

58B. Relief for new zero-carbon homes

This is an enabling provision, permitting the Treasury to make regulations for granting relief on the first acquisition of a dwelling which is a "zero-carbon home". The relevant regulations are the Stamp Duty Land Tax (Zero-Carbon Home Relief) Regulations 2007 (SI 2007/3437), which are themselves retrospectively to be amended by the Stamp Duty Land Tax (Zero-Carbon Homes Relief) (Amendment) Regulations 2008. The Regulations (commentary on which is to be found elsewhere in this volume) provide for full relief where the consideration (other than rent) does not exceed £500,000 and reduces the SDLT charge by £15,000 where the consideration exceeds that sum. The regulations also define with some precision the parameters for a "zero-carbon home" and make provision for certification by accredited assessors and for reasonable fees to be charged by an assessor for assessing whether a dwelling is entitled to a certificate. For the Commissioners' guidance on the relief see SDLT Technical News 6 (to be found in Appendix 1).

58C. Relief for zero-carbon homes: supplemental

This section makes supplemental provision, prescribing the necessary content of the Treasury regulations to be made under s 58B.

58D Transfers involving multiple dwellings

The section introduces Schedule 6B, which affords a reduction in the rate of SDLT chargeable on the acquisition of a number of dwellings in circumstances where the rate of 5% would otherwise be applicable given the total consideration paid for the linked transactions.

60. Compulsory purchase facilitating development

This section introduces an exemption for the acquisition of land which has been the subject of a compulsory purchase order facilitating development, the aim being to avoid the risk of a double charge to SDLT, ie to both the body acquiring the property under a compulsory purchase order and the developer to whom it is passed on. Sub-section (2) explains when "compulsory purchase to facilitate development" takes place, and also establishes that the purchaser must be the entity that made the compulsory purchase order, and the developer must be "another person". Sub-section (3) confirms that, for the purposes of sub-s (2)(*a*) in relation to England and Scotland (but not Northern Ireland), it is not necessary for the compulsory purchase order to be effected in any particular way. It is only necessary for the order to have been made before the land is acquired under the transaction for the relief to take effect.

61. Compliance with planning obligations

This section introduces an exemption from charge where a land transaction is entered into in order to comply with a "planning obligation" (as defined), provided that the planning obligation is enforceable against the vendor, the purchaser in the transaction falls within the class of public authorities defined at s 61(3), and the transaction takes place within five years from the date on which the planning obligation was entered into or modified. The aim of the section is to prevent a possible double charge to SDLT falling on the developer as a result of complying with such obligations. Sub-section (2) defines "planning obligation" and "modification" in relation to England and Wales, Scotland and Northern Ireland.

62. Group relief and reconstruction or acquisition relief

This section provides for Sch 7 (see below) and that relief must be claimed in a land transaction return or the amendment of such a return.

63. Demutualisation of insurance company

This section carries over to SDLT the stamp duty relief introduced by FA 1997 s 96, relating to land transactions connected with the demutualisation of a mutual insurance company. Sub-section (1) establishes that a land transaction is exempt if it is entered into as part of a "qualifying transfer" of the business of a mutual insurance company to a company with share capital. "Qualifying transfer" is defined at sub-s (2) and includes a transfer of an insurance business under an insurance business transfer scheme, or of a business of a general insurance company carried on through a permanent establishment in the UK and takes place in accordance with authorisation granted outside the UK for the purposes of Article 14 of the Life Assurance Directive or Article 12 of the Third Non-life Assurance Directive. For the above relief to be claimed, the conditions set out in sub-ss (3) and (4) must be fulfilled:

(a) the shares in the issuing company (as defined at sub-s (2)) must be offered to at least 90% of the members of the mutual immediately before the transfer; and

(b) secondly, any shares that have not been offered to the public, must be offered to persons who (at the time of the offer) are members of the mutual, persons entitled to become members of the mutual, or employees or former employees of the mutual (including a wholly owned subsidiary).

Part II ST

In accordance with sub-s (5), the Treasury may make regulations to reduce the percentage set out in sub-s (3) and to provide that members of any particular class are included as members of the mutual. Sub-section (6) defines "wholly owned subsidiary" and sub-s (7) defines a variety of other terms used in the section.

Notably, FA 1997 s 96 will continue to give relief from stamp duty for other matters connected with the demutualisation of insurance companies (see commentary).

64. Demutualisation of building society

This section carries over to SDLT the stamp duty exemption introduced by the Building Societies Act 1986 s 102, relating to land transactions connected with the demutualisation of a building society.

65. Incorporation of limited liability partnership

This section carries over to SDLT the stamp duty relief introduced by the Limited Liability Partnerships Act 2000 s 12 (with some minor amendments), in circumstances where land is transferred to a limited liability partnership in connection with its incorporation. The three conditions set out at sub-ss (2), (3) and (4) must be satisfied, namely:

(a) the effective date of the transaction must be no more than one year after the date of the LLP's incorporation;
(b) the transferor must be a partner in a partnership at the relevant time and the partnership must have the same (and no other) members as the LLP; and
(c) the members of the LLP must acquire the interest in land in the same proportions as it was held by the members of the partnership at the relevant time, or, if this is not the case, none of the differences in those proportions must be for the purpose of any avoidance of liability to any duty or tax.

Sub-section (5) defines "the relevant time" as either immediately after the transferor acquired the interest, in situations where he acquired it after the incorporation of the LLP, or immediately before its incorporation, in all other cases. Sub-section (6) defines LLP with reference to the Limited Liability Partnerships Act 2000 or the Limited Liability (Northern Ireland) Act 2000, as appropriate.

66. Transfers involving public bodies

Where land is transferred from one public body to another under a statutory reorganisation, this section ensures that the transaction is exempt from SDLT. The section also grants the Treasury the power to exempt other land transactions made under statutory authority where either party is a public body by means of an order made under this section. Sub-section (3) defines "reorganisation". Sub-section (4) lists the relevant public bodies for the purpose of the section, sub-s (5) confirms that references to public bodies include companies which are wholly-owned by such a body or a wholly-owned subsidiary of such a company. For the purposes of this section "company" bears its usual meaning under Companies Act 2006 s 1, rather than that given by the definition in FA 2003 s 100.

The section applies in many cases where existing legislation provides stamp duty exemption, and in these cases there is now comparable relief from SDLT.

67. Transfer in consequence of reorganisation of parliamentary constituencies

This section reproduces a relief for stamp duty introduced by F(No 2)A 1983 s 15 (see commentary to that section), exempting transfers of land between Parliamentary constituencies undertaken to give effect to an Order under the Parliamentary Constituencies Act 1986. Sub-sections (1)–(5) provide definitions of the various terms used in the section.

68. Charities relief

Sub-section (1) provides for Sch 8 (see below, which relieves acquisitions by charities), and sub-s (2) states that all claims for relief must be made in a land transaction return form.

69. Acquisition by bodies established for national purposes

This section provides for a relief where the purchaser is one of the bodies established for national purposes listed. The bodies correspond with those set out in TA 1988 s 507.

70. Right to buy transactions, shared ownership leases etc

This section provides for Sch 9 (see below).

71. Certain acquisitions by registered social landlord

This section provides two exemptions from SDLT where the purchaser of the land is a registered provider of social housing. The first relief (in sub-s (A1)) will come into effect once the relevant provisions of the Housing and Regeneration Act 2008 come into force. Those provisions replace the existing class of providers of social housing, RSLs, by a new class of Registered Providers which will be open to profit-making companies. In such cases, land transactions by profit-making registered providers will be exempt from SDLT provided that the transaction is funded with the assistance of a public subsidy. As in the past, there is no need for the provider to demonstrate that the acquisition is wholly funded by the public purse. The second, and existing, relief, will remain in force until the implementation of the relevant provisions of the 2008 Act. This is based on the relief from stamp duty introduced by FA 2000 s 130, providing exemption from SDLT for a range of transactions in which the purchaser is a registered social landlord. In accordance with sub-s (1), the following conditions must be met:

(1) the registered social landlord must be controlled by its tenants;
(2) the vendor must be a qualifying body (as defined at sub-s (3)); or
(3) the transaction must be funded with the assistance of a public subsidy (as defined at sub-s (4)).

The intention of the section is to encourage the provision of social housing and help the voluntary transfer programme. It should be noted that many social landlords are also registered charities, and in these cases, s 68 would also apply (see commentary above).

71A. Alternative property finance: land sold to financial institutions and leased to a person

This section (which applies only to England, Wales and Northern Ireland) is relevant to persons (ie including individuals, companies, clubs and trustees) who enter into arrangements with financial institutions whereby the institution purchases (by transfer or grant of a major interest) a property (not necessarily from the person for whom finance is being provided), lets it to that person over an agreed term (the rent typically repaying the purchase price and an amount equivalent to a financing rate), and grants the individual a right to acquire the property at the end of the term. Relief is similarly made available where the institution and the person in question purchase the interest in land as beneficial tenants in common. In practice, this will principally include Islamic mortgages taking the "ijara" form but will also apply to other forms of financing which are Shari'a compliant. Exemption will also be afforded to any back-to-back ijara financing entered into by the financial institution with another financial institution.

Sub-s (1) describes the type of arrangement that the section applies to, and then sub-ss (2), (3) and (4) set out the circumstances in which the first, second and final stages of the transaction are exempt. The cumulative effect of these exemptions is to balance out the SDLT that arises when purchasing the property under such an arrangement, with the amount due for transactions involving conventional mortgage products. The section also sets out the circumstances in which the section does not apply, and provides definitions for the various terms used. The effect of the section is to impose SDLT on the first transaction (by which the financial institution acquires the major interest in land) except in those cases where it acquires the interest from the person or from another institution; but to exempt acquisitions from the person or such other institution from charge and also to exempt from charge both the lease to the person and the eventual transaction by which the person acquires the interest from the institution.

In order to prevent SDLT being avoided completely on such a financing transaction, relief under section 71A is not available if the first transaction is exempted from SDLT under the group relief provisions in Sch 7: see s 73A.

For the meaning of "financial institution" see section 73BA.

72. Alternative property finance in Scotland: land sold to financial institutions and leased to a person

This section offers the Scottish equivalent of the relief afforded by s 71A and is relevant to persons who enter into arrangements with financial institutions whereby the institution purchases (by transfer or grant of a major interest) a property (not necessarily from the person for whom finance is being provided), lets it to that person over an agreed term (the rent typically repaying the purchase price and an amount equivalent to a financing rate), and grants the person a right to acquire the property at the end of the term. In practice, this will principally include Islamic mortgages taking the "ijara" form. Exemption will also apply to any back-to-back ijara financing entered into by the financial institution with another financial institution.

Sub-s (1) describes the type of arrangement that the section applies to, and then sub-ss (2), (3) and (4) set out the circumstances in which the first, second and final stages of the transaction are exempt. The cumulative effect of these exemptions is to balance out the SDLT that arises when purchasing the property under such an arrangement, with the amount due for transactions involving conventional mortgage products. The section also sets out the circumstances in which the section does not apply, and provides definitions for the various terms used. The effect of the section is to impose SDLT on the first transaction (by which the financial institution acquires the major interest in land) except in those cases where it acquires the interest from the person or from another institution; but to exempt acquisitions from the person in question or such other institution from charge and also to exempt from charge both the lease to the person and the eventual transaction by which the person acquires the interest from the institution.

In order to prevent SDLT being avoided completely on such a financing transaction, relief under s 72 is not available if the first transaction is exempted from SDLT under the group relief provisions in Sch 7: see s 73A.

72A. Alternative property finance in Scotland: land sold to financial institution and individual in common

This section, which applies in relation to land in Scotland, provides further relief for alternative property financing arrangements not falling under s 72 (see above) in cases where the institution and the person purchase the land as owners in common. In such a case, in lieu of a lease, the parties will enter into an agreement by which the person will be given an exclusive right to occupy. In these circumstances, the same exemptions are afforded to the agreement and to any later transaction by which the person acquires the interest from the institution.

73. Alternative property finance: land sold to financial institution and re-sold to a person

Again, this section is most relevant to Islamic mortgages (principally taking the "marabaha" form), and provides a level playing field for arrangements where a financial institution purchases a property (not necessarily from the person for whom finance is being provided) and sells it to a person for a consideration that is paid in instalments. As with s 72, the section sets out exemptions that are relevant to the various stages of the transaction and the circumstances in which the section does not apply.

In order to prevent SDLT being avoided completely on such a financing transaction, relief under section 73 is not available if the first transaction is exempted from SDLT under the group relief provisions in Sch 7: see s 73A.

73A. Sections 71A to 73: supplemental

FA 2006 extended the reliefs under ss 71A–73 from individuals to any person seeking to make use of an Islamic financing arrangement. It was an inevitable consequence of this extension of relief that it would be available to companies who might form an SDLT group for the purposes of Sch 7. Given that the intention of the legislation was to avoid double charges to tax and not to prevent tax arising altogether, s 73A takes the necessary precaution of preventing relief under the alternative finance provisions where the initial transaction was already outside the scope of SDLT under Sch 7.

73AB. Sections 71A to 72A: arrangements to transfer control of financial institution

Following the introduction of s 75A (Anti-avoidance) in December 2006, much consideration was given to the use of s 71A as a means of transferring property without a charge to SDLT.

This was because s 75A(7)(a) precluded the application of the section where the only reason that the amount of SDLT payable under the arrangements was less than it would have been had there been a straightforward transfer from V to P was the operation of ss 71A–73. The legislature recognised that the inevitable consequence of the exemptions and reliefs for alternative finance arrangements was that SDLT would be reduced, thereby satisfying s 75A(1)(c). Accordingly, in order to protect such arrangements from an inappropriate charge to SDLT under s 75A, the anti-avoidance section was disapplied by s 75(7). The inevitable consequence of this protection for alternative property finance was that tax planners focussed on the possibility of structuring purchases to bring them within the scope of s 71A ff. In fact, it would seem that the device has been used less than one might have expected, if only because of the practical difficulty of establishing a purchaser which satisfied the condition of being a "financial institution". One approach has been for a bank to establish a special purpose vehicle to acquire the property in accordance with the requirements of s 71A and for the intended purchaser then to acquire the shares in the SPV. The advantage of this approach was that the definition of "financial institution" included a wholly-owned subsidiary of a bank. There have been some doubts as to the effectiveness of this structure (such as concerns whether the subsequent change of control would itself be a transaction involved in connection with the disposal and acquisition and if, so whether this would enable s 75A to apply; or, again, whether the arrangements for change of control could enable HMRC to argue that the purchaser was not a financial institution at the relevant time); but the legislature considered there to be sufficient doubt to lead to the introduction of provisions to counteract the device. Accordingly, s 73AB provides that the reliefs in ss 71A–73 are not to apply if the arrangements (or any connected arrangements) include arrangements for a person to acquire control of the relevant financial institution, even if such arrangements are conditional on some other event or act. It is far from clear that this legislation will be effective to prevent all forms of s 71A schemes. Despite these restrictions on the operation of the Islamic financing rules, tax planners continued to exploit the provisions, focusing on the fact that "financial institution" included persons with licences under the Consumer Credit Act 1974. To counteract this, section 73BA narrows the meaning of the phrase to exclude such persons from the benefit of the relief.

Part II ST

73B. Exempt interests

This section ensures that where a financial institution has provided an alternative finance product that falls within s 71A, 72 or 72A, any subsequent dealing in the interest held by the institution (or in any interest derived from it) wll also be exempt from SDLT. This is achieved by treating the interest held by the financial institution as an exempt interest and thus as not being a chargeable interest (see s 48(2) for other exempt interests). The interest in question ceases to be an exempt interest when the lease or agreement under which the counterparty to the financial transaction was able to occupy the land comes to an end, or where the counterparty's right to require the transfer of the exempt interest comes to an end or is otherwise restricted. Sub-section (3) precludes the use of the exemption afforded by sub-s (1) where the transaction in question would otherwise obtain group relief under Sch 7. Section 73B is subordinate to the other alternative property finance provisions. If, therefore, a transaction is the "first transaction" within s 71A, 72 or 72A, ie the transaction by which the first financial institution in the financing transaction acquires the interest out of which the counterparty's lease, etc, is then granted, relief must be obtained under those provisions rather than under s 73B. The same is true of transactions flowing from the exercise by the counterparty of the right to call for a transfer of the financial institution's interest – if exemption for this transaction is to be conferred, it must be conferred by the relevant provision in s 71A, 72 or 72A and not by s 73B.

73BA. Meaning of "Financial Institution"

In order to counteract certain aggressive avoidance schemes based on the creation of a purchaser with a Consumer Credit Act licence and which relied on the exemption for land transactions entered into by such persons under an Islamic financing structure, this section redefines the meaning of "financial institution" by reference to Income Tax Act 2007 s 564B but excluding persons holding licences under the Consumer Credit Act 1974 permitting them to carry on consumer credit or consumer hire businesses.

73CA. Sections 71A to 73: first-time buyers

This section allows first-time buyer relief to apply to a purchase under alternative finance arrangements in circumstances where the property is purchased by a financial institution, or jointly by a financial institution and a person, where the person is a first-time buyer. As with s 57AA, the relief is only available if the effective date of the land transaction falls into the period 25 March 2010 to 24 March 2012. The conditions for the exemption to be afforded are similar to those which apply to section 57AA, to the commentary on which the reader is referred. That is to say, the provision exempts the transaction by which the property is acquired by the financial institution if the consideration paid for the relevant interest is no more than £250,000 and the counterparties to the financing arrangements are "first-timer buyers" who are acquiring the property as their only or main residence. As with s 57AA, the exemption is unavailable where the transaction is one of a number of linked transactions, save where the other transactions consist in acquiring garden or grounds or an interest over land which are to be enjoyed with and are connected to the acquisition of the main residence.

The exemption will only be relevant in those cases where the financial institution buys the property from a third party vendor. In cases where the vendor is the counterparty to the finance arrangements, or is another financial institution which itself acquired the property as part of an alternative financing transaction, the more valuable exemptions afforded by ss 71A–73 will instead apply.

74. Collective enfranchisement by leaseholders

This section amends the rate of tax in relation to transactions entered into by a nominee or appointee who acquires the freehold of a block of flats on behalf of leaseholders under a statutory right of leasehold enfranchisement. By virtue of sub-ss (2) and (3), the rate will be determined by reference to a calculated value rather than by reference to the consideration, resulting, in many cases, in SDLT being paid on the transaction at a lower rate than if total consideration were used to determine the rate. The relevant requirements for a leaseholder to buy their freehold by right of collective enfranchisement through a RTE company are set out at Part 1 of the Landlord and Tenant Act 1987, and Chapter 2 of Part 1 of the Leasehold Reform, Housing and Urban Development Act 1993. Originally the relief was available only where the person acquiring the freehold was an RTE company, a definition of which can be found at the Leasehold Reform and Urban Development Act 1993 s 4A. However, it was held that the relief could not be claimed as s 4A of the 1993 Act has not been brought into effect by an appropriate Commencement Order. See *Elizabeth Court (Bournemouth) Ltd v Revenue and Customs Comrs* [2008] STC (SCD) 366, where the taxpayer unsuccessfully sought to argue that the definition of an "RTE company" by reference to s 4A of the 1993 Act did not require the relevant provision to be in force. The Special Commissioner decided that although it would be possible for an Act to define by reference to another statutory provision which was not yet in force, this was not the intention of Parliament when drafting s 74. This problem was overcome by removing the requirement for an RTE company to be involved so that, as Budget Note 46 to the Finance Bill 2009 wryly observed "the relief will operate as originally intended".

The rate is determined by dividing the total amount of consideration for the purchase of the freeholder by the number of flats in respect of which collective enfranchisement is sought. Thus, if the consideration for the acquisition of the freehold reversion were £1 million but the number of flats involved was 10, the rate charged on the total consideration would be the same as would have been charged on a sale for £100,000 – thereby reducing the rate from 4% to 0%.

75. Crofting community right to buy

This section amends the rate of tax in relation to transactions entered into by a crofting community body pursuant to a crofting community right to buy. The rate is determined in a similar fashion to collective enfranchisement transactions, by reference to a calculated value rather than consideration. The relevant requirements for a crofter to buy their croft through a crofting community body are set out under Part 3 of the Land Reform (Scotland) Act 2003.

75A. Anti-avoidance

This is the first of a group of sections which incorporates a general anti-avoidance rule for SDLT. The legislation was first introduced by statutory instrument (the Stamp Duty Land Tax (Variation of the Finance Act 2003) Regs 2006 (SI 2006/3237)) with effect from 6 December 2006. That legislation has been modified and both amended and extended by the provisions in FA 2007, with the result that the transitional arrangements are somewhat more complex than usual; and care must be taken to ensure that the transactions with which the practitioner is concerned do indeed fall within the scope of the new provisions as finally drafted. For the Commissioners' views on the operation of the section, see SDLT Technical News 5 (to be found in Appendix 1).

Although the provisions are entitled "anti-avoidance" one requirement that is wholly absent from the conditions for the application of s 75A is that any party to any of the transactions which make up the scheme transactions has the object of avoiding SDLT. In the course of the Finance Bill Committee debates, Stephen Timms, the Chief Secretary to the Treasury, stated that clause 70 (the incorporating provision) amended FA 2003 "to counter two types of scheme – those that use leaseholds and those that use sub-sales that have been developed specifically to avoid payment of the tax". However, although the section is unusual in identifying particular transactions (see s 75A(3)) that would be included as "scheme transactions", it would be imprudent to assume either that sub-s (3) was exhaustive or that the legislation is intended only to apply to the specific types of scheme to which the Chief Secretary referred. Mr Timms also indicated that the Government was unwilling to introduce a purpose test because it would probably fail in the context of SDLT as the main purpose of the transactions under review was likely to be the commercial one of transferring economic ownership from vendor to purchaser. By way of consolation though, he also indicated that the Commissioners would be willing to use an amending power contained in s 75C(11) retrospectively to disapply the application of the section in specific circumstances, even possibly to the extent of their disapplication in respect of one particular transaction. It remains to be seen whether the Treasury (on whom the s 75C(11) power is conferred) will really be willing to table secondary legislation for the purpose of relieving a particular taxpayer from a s 75A charge.

The effect of this section, where the trigger provisions are satisfied, is to substitute for one or more land transactions which themselves would have been subject to (or possibly exempt from) SDLT a deemed transaction between two persons, the "vendor" and the "purchaser", whose relationship consists in the fact that the purchaser now owns a chargeable interest which is, or which is derived from, a chargeable interest which had previously been disposed of by the vendor; and to identify as the chargeable consideration for that notional land transaction an amount which may be made up of an aggregate sum or value which has been paid or received by any one of the participants in the overall scheme of transactions. The thrust of the legislation is to secure that sums which have been paid, not for the land transaction but for some other service or sale, are brought into charge to SDLT where otherwise they would not have been. The trigger conditions are threefold:

(a) There must be a disposal of a chargeable interest by a person (described as "V") and an acquisition of that chargeable interest (or of an interest deriving from it) by another person (described as "P"). It should be noted that P does not have to acquire the interest directly from V. One of the matters that the section leaves unclear is how one deals with the case where there is a number of "Ps", which is inevitably the case where one P has acquired no more than a chargeable interest derived from the interest of which V disposed; and will also be the case where there is a chain of sub-sales. HMRC has stated that it considers that it is empowered to select which person should be charged as P with SDLT under s 75A(4) on the notional chargeable consideration found by s 75A(5). This is a matter of debate, since it comes close to taxation at the discretion of the taxing authorities: if P1 is selected to pay the tax, then P2 and P3 will be relieved of the tax that otherwise would be due from them.

(b) There must be a number of transactions ("the scheme transactions") (which is to include the disposal and acquisition) which are "involved in connection with" the disposal and acquisition of the chargeable interest. There has been much criticism of the use of the phrase "involved in connection with". However, HMRC have asserted that the phrase bears a readily-understood and limited meaning. Recent authority tends to suggest the opposite: in *Barclays Bank plc and Trustees of the Barclays Bank Pension Fund v HMRC* [2007] EWCA Civ 442, [2007] All ER (D) 183 (May), the meaning of "in connection with past service" was under consideration. The Court of Appeal held that the meaning of the phrase "in connection with" had to be informed by its context and could involve both direct and indirect connections. In some contexts, it could mean nothing more that "having to do with": see McFarlane J in *Re Nanaimo Community Hotel Limited* [1944] 4 DLR 638 and Somervell LJ in *Johnson v Johnson* [1952] P 47, 50–51.

(c) The sum of the amounts of SDLT payable in respect of the scheme transactions must be less than that which would be payable were s 75A to apply. This last condition requires a comparison between the actual SDLT paid on the transactions and that which would be payable if P were to acquire V's chargeable interest on its disposal by V for the consideration prescribed by s 75A(6) (as to which see below).

Section 75A(2) defines "transaction" in the widest possible terms, as including not only transactions which are not land transactions but also "any kind of arrangement whether or not it could be described as a transaction". It is assumed that this is intended to catch cases where circumstances change without the involvement of any outside agency, eg where a leasehold interest expires by effluxion of time or an option ceases to be exercisable on the expiry of the option period. It is important to appreciate that transactions which take place after the date on which P acquires the chargeable interest may also be scheme transactions: s 75A(2)(*d*).

Section 75A(3) specifically describes the kind of case at which the section is aimed. These mainly involved land transactions which were broken down into separate steps, some of which were themselves not land transactions and payment for which was therefore outside the scope of SDLT. Before the introduction of s 75A popular techniques for avoiding SDLT included transactions which involved the manipulation of leases and sub-sales to connected persons for reduced consideration. In Technical Newsletter 4 the Stamp Office gave five examples of the kind of transactions which were the target of s 75A:

"(1) V grants a 999-year lease to N for no premium and a peppercorn rent. V assigns the freehold reversion to P for a nominal sum. P pays N £X in consideration of N's agreement to vary the lease by the insertion of a provision giving the landlord the right to terminate the lease for no payment. P exercises the right to terminate. The notional land transaction is the acquisition of the freehold by P with chargeable consideration of £X.

(2) V grants a 999-year lease to N for no premium and a peppercorn rent. The lease includes a right for the landlord to termnate the lease on payment of £X to the tenant. V assigns the freehold reversion to P for a nominal sum. P exercises the right to terminate and pays N £X.
The notional land transaction is the acquisition of the freehold by P with chargeable consideration of £X.

(3) V grants a 999-year lease to P for no premium and a peppercorn rent. The lease gives the landlord a right to terminate it within 14 days of the date of grant. P offers to pay V £X if V allows the 14 days to elapse without exercising the right to terminate. V does so.
The notional land transaction is the grant of a 999-year lease by V to P with chargeable consideration of £X.

(4) V agrees to sell property to N for £10 million. N agrees to sub-sell the property to P for £5. Both transactions are completed at the same time.
The notional land transaction is the acquisition of the property by P and the chargeable consideration is £10 million (the largest amount received by any person in respect of the scheme transactions).

(5) V agrees to sell property to N Ltd for £10 million. N Ltd declares a dividend in favour of P, its sole shareholder, the dividend to consist of the property and to be paid at the same time as completion of the V–N Ltd contract. The contract is completed and the property transferred to P.
The notional land transaction is the acquisition of the property by P and the chargeable consideration is £10 million (the largest amount received by any person in respect of the scheme transactions)."

Each of these transactions (which HMRC does not admit were successful to avoid SDLT) would now be caught by s 75A.

Sub-sections (4)–(6) are the operative provisions which establish the method of charging SDLT where there are scheme transactions which fall within s 75A(1). Sub-section (4)(*a*) first requires the disregard of any land transaction which is a scheme transaction. Sub-section (4)(*b*) then deems there instead to have been a land transaction which effects the acquisition by P of the chargeable interest disposed of by V. The paragraph (*a*) disregard must be read in conjunction with s 75C(10): any SDLT which has been paid in respect of a disregarded land transaction is treated as having been paid in respect of the notional land transaction under s 75A(4)(*b*). It therefore reduces the amount of SDLT which must be paid to the Commissioners in respect of the notional land transaction. However, since it is a precondition to the operation of s 75A that the SDLT payable on the notional transaction must be greater than that paid on the actual scheme transactions, it does not seem that this could ever trigger a repayment of "overpaid" SDLT. Section 75A(5) prescribes the amount of chargeable consideration deemed to have been paid for the notional land transaction: it is to be the largest amount (or aggregate amount) given by or on behalf of any one person by way of consideration for the scheme transactions, or which is received by or on behalf of V (or someone connected with V), by way of consideration for the scheme transactions. It is assumed that where s 75A(5) refers to the consideration having been given "by way of consideration for the scheme transactions" it in fact means "by way of consideration for all or any of the scheme transactions". HMRC have indicated that where a participant in the scheme transactions both gives and receives amounts (eg because he is the intermediary in a chain of sub-sales) one considers either the sums he has given or the sums he has received, but does not aggregate the two. Section 75C(9) extends the meaning of "sums given" to cover the value of consideration given in the form of money's worth. Section 75C(6) secures that s 53 (market value substitution where transfer to connected company) applies to the notional transaction under s 75A(5). FA 2007 s 71(3) secures that these last two provisions are to apply only to cases where the disposal of V's chargeable interest takes place on or after the passing of FA 2003.

Sub-section (6) establishes the effective date of the notional land transaction: either the date of the last of the scheme transactions or, if earlier, the last date on which a contract in respect of the scheme transactions is substantially performed. Given the open-ended description of scheme transactions in sub-s (2)(*d*), the last transaction may not be easy to establish in every case. However, the alternative also suffers from inadequate drafting: although FA 2003 contains a definition of "substantial performance" in the case of a contract for a land transaction (and which is drafted in land law terms), it is far from clear that the definition is universally applicable: see s 44 of the Act. No specific definition of substantial performance has been provided for the purposes of s 75A.

Sub-section (7) excludes certain types of transaction from the operation of s 75A. The section is not to apply where s 75A(1)(*c*) is satisfied only by reason of ss 71A–73 (alternative finance arrangements) or by reason of a provision of Sch 9 (right to buy and shared ownership leases). In both cases, the relevant provisions offer relief from SDLT provided the transactions in question involve a number of defined steps. Inevitably, those steps would be scheme transactions and their combined effect would be to reduce the SDLT below that which would have been payable had there been an outright sale by V to P.

75B: Anti-avoidance: incidental transactions

This section was introduced to alleviate the problem that the consideration for certain standard transactions which are associated with the sale of land would otherwise be brought into the charge to SDLT by s 75A. Shortly after the passing of the Stamp Duty Land Tax (Variation of the Finance Act 2003) Regs 2006 (SI 2006/3237) concern was expressed in the professional press that s 75A would lead to the consideration for the sale of "fixtures and fittings" and for construction operations in *Prudential* transactions (*Prudential Assurance Co Ltd v IRC* [1992] STC 86) henceforth being within the charge to SDLT. Assurance was given by HMRC that this was not intended and s 75B introduced to give effect to the assurances. Section 75B(1) provides that where a scheme transaction is "merely incidental" to the transfer of the chargeable interest from V to P, the consideration for it is to be ignored in calculating the chargeable consideration for the purposes of s 75A(5). The section then makes further provision both as to what transactions are not to be considered "incidental" and as to those which are or may be. However, s 75B(1) does not prevent the transactions in question being scheme transactions; but by reducing the chargeable consideration for s 75A(5) purposes by the relevant consideration, the effect may be to prevent the transactions falling within s 75A at all. This is because s 75A(5) operates both for the purpose of establishing the notional consideration under s 75A(4) and for the purpose of s 75A(1)(*c*). If the effect of the removal of the additional consideration for the incidental transaction is to secure that the notional chargeable consideration is no greater than the actual chargeable consideration, it is unlikely that s 75A will apply.

Sub-section (2) excludes from the category of "incidental transactions" transactions (*a*) which form part of the process by which the chargeable interest moves from V to P, (*b*) on the completion of which the transfer of the chargeable interest from V to P is conditional, or (*c*) are specifically within the "black list" in s 75A(3). Subject to this (precisely how is determined by sub-s (4)), sub-s (3) makes clear that certain kinds of transaction are specifically intended *not* to trigger the operation of s 75A:

(a) those undertaken for a purpose relating to the construction of a building on the land sold;

(b) the sale or supply of something other than land; and

(c) loans to a purchaser, P, secured by a mortgage on the land, designed to enable P (or another) to pay for the acquisition of the chargeable interest.

Sub-section (5) requires any necessary apportionment of consideration to be effected on a just and reasonable basis.

75C. Anti-avoidance: supplemental

This section draws together a number of disparate rules designed to enable the general anti-avoidance rule in s 75A to operate more fairly.

Sub-section (1) provides for a case where a purchaser buys the shares in a company and thereafter extracts the land from the company. In such a case, the transaction would generally avoid a charge to SDLT: the purchase of the shares would be liable, if at all, to stamp duty or SDRT; and the subsequent removal of the land from the company might, for example, be free from SDLT as a distribution (see FA 2003 s 54(4)). If the share purchase is the first in a series of scheme transactions it is to be ignored. The effect of this is likely to be that s 75A is rendered inapplicable. The position should be contrasted with that which would obtain if steps were taken first to transfer the land into a company and at a later stage the shares were to be sold and the company thereafter wound up. Leaving aside the operation of Sch 7 (Group relief), this case would not be protected from the s 75A charge since the sale of the shares would be the second in the series of scheme transactions.

Sub-section (2) provides that the notional transaction attracts any relief that it would if it were an actual transaction. Thus if, for example, P were a charity, no SDLT would be payable as a result of the application of s 75A. However, the position would potentially be different if the Commissioners were empowered, as they have suggested, to identify who is P in a chain of transactions.

It was appreciated that there might be a difficulty in the application of sub-s (2) where there is a chain of transactions, each of which would attract an SDLT relief, but where the relief would be unavailable if the transaction were deemed to be one direct from V to P. Sub-section (3) provides that if any of the scheme transactions is entered into for the purpose of securing the transfer of an undertaking falling within Sch 7 para 7 or 8, the notional s 75A transaction is also to be treated as entered into for such purposes. The consequence is that reconstruction or acquisition relief, as the case may be, should be available in respect of such s 75A transaction.

Sub-section (4) removes from the computation of the chargeable consideration for the notional land transaction any consideration paid in respect of a transaction to which one or more of a raft of provisions (each of which exempts certain transactions from the charge to SDLT) applies.

Sub-section (5) makes provision for the just and reasonable apportionment for s 75A(5) purposes of consideration given for the acquisition of two chargeable interests of which only one falls within the scope of s 75A. This can be seen as the counterpart to s 75B(3)(*b*) and (5), which deal with the apportionment and exclusion of consideration paid in part for the sale of something other than land.

Sub-section (6) provides for s 53 to apply to the notional land transaction under s 75A. It is assumed that the intention is that where there is a transaction by which land passes indirectly from V to P, in circumstances where P is a company connected with V, and where the chargeable consideration on which SDLT has been paid under the scheme transactions is less than the market value of the property acquired by P, then SDLT shall instead be paid on the market value of the relevant property.

Sub-section (7) applies the exchange rules in Sch 4 para 5 to the notional transaction under s 75A. If, therefore, a chargeable interest passes from V to P and a chargeable interest also passes from P to V in the same series of transactions, it would seem that one brings into charge the market value of each chargeable interest (plus any rent) and disregards the notional consideration found under s 75A(5). An alternative analysis is to assume that where there is an indirect exchange of properties, the rules in Sch 4 para 5 operate to treat the notional consideration as being the market value of the property passing from V to P, whatever may actually have been paid or provided in return. It has to be said, though, that the proper application of s 75C(7) is uncertain.

Sub-section (8) indicates that s 75A is to apply to partnerships. It has two effects: first, to treat an interest in a property-investment partnership as a chargeable interest for the purposes of s 75A. Accordingly, transactions designed to mitigate the charge to SDLT on the sale of a partnership interest are not to escape the operation of s 75A because the interest involved is not generally to be seen as a chargeable interest in land. By contrast, scheme transactions involving the disposal of an interest in a trading partnership (for example) will not fall within s 75A, since they will not involve a chargeable interest. This corresponds to the exclusion of such partnership interests from charges under FA 2003 Sch 15 para 14. The second effect of sub-s (8) is to disapply the rules in Sch 15 Part 3. This latter rule was introduced by the FA 2010 in order to counteract a number of schemes designed to avoid the effect of s 75A by channelling the purchase of an interest in land through a partnership established, in many cases, specifically for the purpose of the relevant land transaction. The schemes operated by the creation of an artificial connection between the vendor and the partnership, the effect of which was to facilitate the reduction in the amount of chargeable consideration on the land sale. However, it has been suggested that the somewhat crude manner in which s 75C(8A) operates causes all land transactions involving a partnership to fall outside the scope of Sch 15 Pt 3 and within s 75A, as all cases in which a partner transfers land to a partnership are likely to involve both the transfer of the land and transactions which are involved in connection with the land transaction. There is considerable merit in the argument, since if, for example, parties agree that they will form a partnership and transfer land to that partnership in order to carry on business, it is hard to see how it can be claimed that the formation of the partnership is not "involved in connection with" the transfer of the land from each partner to the partnership. The effect of this would, of course, be to deny the benefit of the computational provision, Sch 15 para 10 and to require the operation of the charge under s 75A. It remains to be seen what the Commissioners' response will be.

Sub-section (9) secures that s 75A cannot be avoided by transactions being made for consideration in money's worth, rather than cash.

Sub-section (10) confers a credit on P for SDLT previously paid on other land transactions forming part of the series of scheme transactions: any SDLT which has been paid in respect of a disregarded land transaction is treated as having been paid in respect of the notional land transaction under s 75A(4)(*b*). It therefore reduces the amount of SDLT which must be paid to the Commissioners in respect of the notional land transaction. But since it is a precondition to the operation of s 75A that the SDLT payable on the notional transaction must be greater than that paid on the actual scheme transactions, it would not appear that this could ever trigger a repayment of "overpaid" SDLT.

Sub-section (11) confers power on the Treasury to pass secondary legislation which prevents s 75A applying in specified circumstances. This power can be applied with retrospective effect (sub-s (12)). These provisions are intended to enable the s 75A rules to be modified rapidly in the event that it becomes clear that they apply in unintended ways. In the course of the Public Bill Committee debates on the Finance Bill 2007, column 420, the Chief Secretary to the Treasury stated that "if it still proves to be the case that transactions that are not tax avoidance transactions are likely to be caught, we can and will help innocent taxpayers who are inadvertently caught. We can do that by using the power . . . in new section 75C(10), which can disapply the application of new section 75A in specific circumstances. . . . I do not think that it would be usual for the 'specified circumstances' to apply to just one individual transaction, but the wording does not make that impossible."

76. Duty to deliver land transaction return

This section deals with the requirement that in the case of every "notifiable transaction" (see commentary to s 77 below), a land transaction return must be delivered to HMRC within 30 days of the effective date (see s 44) of the transaction. HMRC may, by regulations, shorten the pre-delivery period (and is likely to do so when electronic conveyancing and e-filing is introduced).

77. Notifiable transactions

This section sets out which transactions are notifiable (and therefore subject to the s 76 requirements). An obligation to notify arises in one of four circumstances. First, where the purchaser acquires either a legal or equitable major interest in land, defined by s 117 as a fee simple or a term of years absolute. This rule is subject to and must be read in conjunction with s 77A, which introduces certain exceptions from the obligation to notify. The other three circumstances, which are not subject to s 77A are as follows: where there is an acquisition of a chargeable interest other than a major interest in land and SDLT is chargeable at the rate of 1%, or would be so chargeable but for a relief (other than a relief consisting of one of the exemptions under Sch 3); where there is a deemed land transaction under the anti-avoidance section, s 44A; and where there is a notional land transaction under the anti-avoidance provision, s 75A.

The effect of ss 77 and 77A is that, save where one of the anti-avoidance provisions applies, there is no requirement to report the acquisition of a major interest in land unless the consideration is at least £40,000; and no need to report the acquisition of any other chargeable interest unless the consideration is more than £125,000 (£150,000 in the case of non-residential property). In addition, there is no longer a need to issue a form SDLT 60 certifying that no SDLT is chargeable.

Note that ss 71A(7) and 72A(7) (both of which involve relief for certain Islamic financing transactions) and Sch 15 para 30 (low value partnership transactions) each makes specific provision relieving the purchaser from an obligation to notify under s 77.

77A. Exceptions for certain acquisitions of major interest in land

This section contains a list of transactions which are excepted from the obligation to notify:

(a) Any acquisition which is exempt from charge to SDLT under Sch 3, eg gifts, transactions in connection with a divorce, deeds of variation of an estate of a deceased person and transactions by which personal representatives assent or appropriate property in the estate of a deceased person in satisfaction of the entitlement of a beneficiary.

(b) Any acquisition of a freehold interest where the chargeable consideration is less than £40,000. For this purpose one must take into account any consideration given for a linked transaction, as to which see s 108.

(c) The grant of a lease for a term of seven years or more where the annual rent is less than £1,000 and the premium is £40,000 or less.

(d) The assignment or surrender of a lease originally granted for a term of seven years or more, where the consideration for the transaction is £40,000 or less.

(e) The grant of a lease for less than seven years where the chargeable consideration does not exceed the "zero-rate threshold". According such a lease is only notifiable if SDLT is chargeable at 1% or more on some part of the consideration, or would be were it not for the operation of a relief.

(f) The assignment or surrender of a lease granted originally for less than seven years unless SDLT is chargeable on the consideration at 1% or more, or would be so chargeable but for the operation of a relief.

78. Returns, enquiries, assessments and related matters

This section provides for Sch 10 (see below), and empowers the Treasury to amend its provisions by means of regulations.

78A. Disclosure of information contained in land transaction returns

This section enables the information contained in land transaction returns delivered under s 76 to be made available for the purpose of creating valuation lists for Community Charge purposes as well as to be available as evidence before the Lands Tribunal.

79. Registration of land transactions etc

This section preserves the position set out in Land Registration Act 1925 s 14(3) in respect of ad valorem stamp duty, and also introduces self-certification, previously available in stamp duty (see Stamp Duty (Exempt Instruments) Regulations 1987 (SI 1987/516)), to SDLT. Together with Sch 11, it provides that no document effecting or evidencing a land transaction (see s 43) may be registered, recorded or otherwise reflected in any entry at the various UK land registries without a certificate as to compliance with the requirements of SDLT. This does not apply in cases where an entry is required without receipt of an application (for example certain situations under the commonhold regime) or where the entry relates to an interest or right other than the chargeable interest acquired by the purchaser under the land transaction giving rise to the application.

Sub-section (2) establishes that the section applies to every notifiable land transaction other than transactions *deemed* to take place under a contract substantially performed without having been completed (see s 44(4)), or under a sub-sale contract (see s 45), or under a contract which provides for a conveyance to a third party (see s 44A(3)), or under a secondary contract arising as a result of the assignment of rights under such a contract (see s 45A), or where there is an assignment of an agreement for a lease (see Sch 17A para 12B), or where there is an agreement for lease (see Sch 17A para 12A), or where there is a variation of a lease which increases the rent under the lease (see Sch 17A para 13), or which reduces the rent under the lease, or the term of the lease (see Sch 17A para 15A).

The certificate as to compliance must be issued by HMRC evidencing the submission of a land transaction return. Sub-section (4) establishes that regulations about such certificates may be made by HMRC, and sub-s (5) provides for Sch 11 which makes further provisions as to record-keeing in circumstances where there is no duty to notify (as to which see ss 77 and 77A). Finally, sub-s (6) requires the appropriate land registrar to allow HMRC to inspect certificates in their possession and to enter into arrangements affording HMRC other information and facilities to verify that the requirements under this Part have been complied with.

80. Adjustment where contingency ceases or consideration is ascertained

This section complements s 51, and provides for the amount of SDLT payable to be adjusted when the amount of consideration is determined. Sub-section (1) confirms that the section applies where, in the case of contingent consideration, the contingency either occurs or it becomes clear that it will not, and in the case of uncertain or unascertained consideration, where an amount which is relevant to the calculation of the consideration becomes ascertained. The section also applies to a transaction linked with the transaction in question.

If the outcome of one of the above events is that a transaction becomes notifiable (whether for the first time or because additional tax is payable), sub-s (2) provides that a return is required within 30 days. The return must contain a self-assessment of the SDLT that arises, calculated in accordance with the rates in force at the effective date of the transaction. The tax or additional tax payable must be paid no later than the filing date for the return. Sub-section (3) confirms that Sch 10 also applies to a return under this section.

Alternatively, under sub-s (4), if the outcome of one of the events is that less tax is payable, the purchaser may make an adjustment to his land transaction return if he is within the amendment period (see Sch 10 para 6(3)—generally the period expires 12 months after the filing date) and, after that time, may make a claim to HMRC for repayment (in which case the rules in Sch 11A apply).

A counterpart to the new rules in Sch 17A para 18A (loans or deposits in connection with the grant or assignment of lease) is introduced as s 80(4A). This prevents a claim being made for the repayment of the SDLT attributable to a loan or deposit treated as consideration by para 18A where the loan or deposit itself is repaid. In order to counteract the device of repaying a sum other than the loan or deposit, it is further provided that no such repayment of SDLT is to be made if that refund is made under arrangements made in connection with the loan or deposit and is contingent on the giving up of the lease—eg by its determination or assignment, or by the grant of another chargeable interest out of it. This provision deliberately goes beyond what is necessary to secure an effective charge on such schemes and to impose an effective and absolute penalty on the use of the device. On the face of it, it would have sufficed that the Treasury had the use of the funds paid by way of SDLT during the period of the loan and were obliged to repay the tax, but not the interest earned on the tax, when the loan itself was repaid. See Hansard Standing Committee debates, Thursday, 30 June 2005, Col 295.

81. Further return where relief withdrawn

This section (based on FA 2002 Sch 34 para 6 and Sch 35 para 7) provides that where relief is withdrawn under the "claw-back" avoidance measures set out in Parts 1 and 2 of Sch 7 (group/reconstruction/acquisition reliefs) and Sch 8 (charitable relief), the purchaser must deliver a further return within the 30 day limit. The event in question which triggers a withdrawal of relief is known as "the disqualifying event" (as defined at sub-s (4)). Sub-section (2) deals with the contents of the return, which must include a self-assessment. The tax payable must be paid no later than the filing date for the return. Sub-section (3) confirms that Sch 10 also applies to a return under this section.

81A. Return or further return in consequence of later linked transaction

This section requires a purchaser to deliver a land transaction where the effect of a later land transaction being linked to an earlier transaction is either that the earlier transaction becomes a notifiable transaction or that additional SDLT becomes payable in respect of it. Transactions are linked where they form part of a single scheme or arrangement made between the same persons, or persons connected with them: s 108. One effect of transactions being linked is that the rate of SDLT must be calculated by reference to the aggregate of the consideration payable under all of them: s 55(4). If, therefore, transactions take place at different times (as for example would be the case where an option is granted and subsequently exercised (s 46(1)) the tax chargeable on the earlier transaction may be increased when the later transaction occurs. Similarly, the grant of a lease could become a notifiable transaction as a result of the grant of a further lease of the same premises: Sch 17A para 5. The effect of para 5 is that the series of leases are treated as a single lease for a term equal to the aggregate of the terms of the individual leases. If, therefore, as a result of the application of para 5 the aggregate term exceeded seven years, the grant of the notional lease would become notifiable. In either case, a return would be required by s 81A and the tax or additional tax payable would have to be paid no later than the filing date for the return.

81B. Declaration by a person authorised to act on behalf of an individual

This section enables the declaration required of an individual in a land transaction return made under Sch 10 that the form is, to the best of the declarant's knowledge and belief, correct and complete, to be made by a person authorised to act on the individual's behalf of the individual. The section requires authorisation to be given in the form of a written power of attorney signed by the individual himself.

82. Loss or destruction of, or damage to, return etc

This section covers the position where any returns or documents relating to tax have been lost or destroyed, or so defaced or damaged as to be illegible or useless. By virtue of sub-s (2), rather harshly HMRC is permitted to treat the return of documents as not having been delivered, and to do anything that could be done as if they had never been made or provided. However, if a person is charged with SDLT and successfully proves to the Commissioners that he has already paid SDLT in respect of the relevant transaction, relief may be granted by either reducing the charge or repayment, as appropriate. In *Pariser v HMRC* (TC 725) the Appellant claimed that he had personally sent a land transaction return relating to the acquisition of 14 lots of land acquired at an auction and that he had done within the time prescribed by statute. That return was not received by the Commissioners and the issue was whether a penalty should be levied under Schedule 10 paragraph 3. The Tribunal acknowledged that the burden of proving that the circumstances for the imposition of the penalty were fulfilled lay on the Commissioners. The Tribunal then rejected the Appellant's submission that he had timeously posted the return, indicating that this was "mere assertion". It is to be observed that the Appellant failed to give evidence as to the matter and it may be that a different result would have followed had he submitted himself for cross-examination. In those circumstances, the Commissioners relied on section 82 to demonstrate that the return had not been delivered and, on the strength of that, to discharge the burden of proving that the conditions in Schedule 10 paragraph 3 had been satisfied. Accordingly, the Tribunal held that the penalty had been correctly imposed. It is not clear whether the Tribunal would have decided differently had the Appellant proved that he had sent the letter in time: the Tribunal observed "even if it had been posted it would be necessary for the Appellant to prove reasonable excuse . . . if [there had been some reasonable excuse] it did not exist throughout the relevant period". Sed quare? Compare the position in *Runham and Naramore v HMRC* (TC 933) where the loss of the return was held to be a reasonable excuse.

82A. Claims not included in returns

This section introduces Sch 11A, which makes administrative provision for the making and determination of claims outside of the scope of a land transaction return.

83. Formal requirements as to assessments, penalty determinations etc

This section (based on TMA 1970 s 114) confirms that certain errors made by HMRC do not invalidate assessments, determinations, notices or other documents required. There are two

Part II ST

conditions if a mistake is not to invalidate the relevant document. First, the notice etc must be substantially in conformity with Finance Act 2003 Pt 4. Secondly, the intended effect of the notice must be reasonably ascertainable to the person to whom it is directed.

In *Coolatinney Developments Ltd and others v HMRC* (TC 1116) the Commissioners notified the taxpayers that they intended to enquire into the taxpayers' self-certificate, in a case where the taxpayers had in fact made land transaction returns for the transactions into which the Commissioners intended to enquire. The letters contained copies of letters written to the taxpayers' agents which explained that the Commissioners had issued notices under paragraph 12 of Schedule 10 of their intention to enquire into their land transaction returns. The taxpayers argued that no valid notice had been served on them prior to the expiry of the enquiry window. The First-Tier Tribunal held that the letters to the agents could not of themselves qualify as paragraph 12 notices since they had not been served on the taxpayers as required by the provision. Nevertheless, the Tribunal held that the conditions for the operation of section 83 were satisfied: the bundle of documents provided to the taxpayers between them served notice on them as required by paragraph 12; and, secondly, those documents would have conveyed to the reasonable understanding of the relevant taxpayers the necessary information that the Commissioners were intending to enquire into their land transaction returns. Accordingly, the errors did not invalidate the notice.

84. Delivery and service of documents

This section (based on TMA 1970 s 115) establishes the rules for the delivery and service of notices and other documents for the purposes of SDLT.

85. Liability for tax

This section introduces the concept that the purchaser is liable to pay SDLT in respect of a chargeable transaction. Under the stamp duty regime, whilst it was customary for the purchaser to pay, no liable person was generally actually specified. Sub-section (2) points the reader to other provisions dealing with the liability of certain types of purchaser, namely joint purchasers, partners and trustees.

86. Payment of tax

The basic rule established by this section is that SDLT has to be paid within 30 days of the transaction or assessment. The section also deals with the due date for payment under specific circumstances, including where relief has been withdrawn, where a return has been amended, and where HMRC have completed a determination or assessment. Sub-section (5) provides that s 86(1)–(3) are subject to the s 90 payment deferral rules and paras 39 and 40 of Sch 10 postponement of pending determination of appeal rules.

87. Interest on unpaid tax

This section is also based on provisions introduced by TMA 1970, and deals with the payment of interest on unpaid SDLT, which arises from 30 days (ie usually when SDLT is due) after the relevant dates until the tax has been paid. Sub-section (2) provides for HMRC to make regulations to reduce the time from which the interest can run (for instance as part of a future move to e-filing). Depending on the relevant circumstances, sub-s (3) defines "relevant date" as one of the following:

(a) in the case of an amount payable because relief has been withdrawn under Part 1 or Part 2 of Sch 7 (group/reconstruction/acquisition relief), or Sch 8 (charities relief), the date of the "disqualifying event" (as defined at sub-s (4));

(b) in the case of deferred payment under s 90, the date when the deferred payment is due; or

(c) in any other case, the effective date of the transaction. Sub-section (5) confirms that this sub-s (*c*) applies, in a case within s 51, if payment is not deferred under s 90, with the result that interest on tax that arises under s 80 (adjustment where contingency ceases or consideration ascertained) runs from the effective date of the transaction.

Sub-section (6) provides that if an amount has already been lodged with HMRC then this is taken into account, and sub-s (7) establishes that interest is calculated at the rate prescribed by the Treasury under FA 1989 s 178.

88. Interest on penalties

This section mirrors the provision for income tax and corporation tax set out at TMA 1970 s 103A, and establishes that the interest on unpaid SDLT shall also be at the rate applicable under FA 1989 s 178 (see commentary).

89. Interest on repayment of tax overpaid etc

Repayments for overpaid tax and penalties by HMRC are also made with interest at the rate applicable under FA 1989 s 179. Sub-section (3) confirms that the section also applies to cases where payments are made in advance of the due date, in which case the interest runs from the day of payment to HMRC. The section does not apply however where the repayment is made in consequence of an order or judgment of a court with power to allow interest on payment (sub-s (4)). Sub-section (5) provides that interest paid to any person under s 89 is not income of that person for any tax purposes.

90. Application to defer payment in case of contingent or uncertain consideration

This section provides that a purchaser may apply to HMRC for SDLT to be deferred where the whole or part of the chargeable consideration for a transaction is contingent or uncertain, and may be payable more than six months after the effective date of the transaction. However, sub-s (5) also provides that an application for deferral does not affect the purchaser's obligation to pay SDLT at the normal due date on chargeable consideration which has already been paid or ceased to be contingent and whose amount is ascertained or ascertainable at the time of the application.

HMRC is also empowered under sub-s (2) to make regulations as to the making of such applications to defer payment. The issues such regulations may cover are set out at sub-s (3).

91. Collection and recovery of tax etc

This section provides for Sch 12 (see below) and deals with administrative provisions for the collection of unpaid tax, penalties and interest.

92. Payment by cheque

This section establishes that payment of SDLT by cheque is treated as taking place the day on which HMRC receives the cheque, provided that the cheque is paid on its first presentation to the bank.

93. Information powers

This section provides for Sch 13, which grants HMRC powers to call for documents and information. Sub-sections (3) to (6) also provide penalties for failure to comply with a notice for documents or information under Parts 1, 2 or 3 of Sch 13 (and for each day thereafter), and for fraudulent or negligent submission of incorrect information or an incorrect document.

94. Power to inspect premises

HMRC is empowered under this section to inspect premises for the purpose of ascertaining its market value, or any other matter relevant to SDLT. The penalty for failing to comply, under sub-s (2), is an offence with a penalty on summary conviction of a fine not exceeding level 1 on the standard scale. The powers granted by this section mirror those granted to HMRC in respect of CGT under TMA 1970 s 111.

95. Offence of fraudulent evasion of tax

This section provides that a person commits an offence if he is knowingly concerned in the fraudulent evasion of SDLT. If the person is found guilty, the penalties are, on summary conviction, imprisonment not exceeding six months or a fine not exceeding six months or a fine not exceeding the statutory maximum or both, or on conviction on indictment, imprisonment for a term not exceeding seven years or a fine or both. This mirrors the offence of fraudulent evasion of income tax provided by FA 2000 s 144.

96. Penalty for assisting in preparation of incorrect return etc

This section establishes that HMRC will follow the established procedure set out in TMA 1970 s 99, by penalising any person who assists in the preparation of an incorrect return, information or other document. The maximum penalty under this section is £3,000.

97. Power to allow further time and reasonable excuse for failure

This section provides that in cases where HMRC allows a person further time to do anything, that person shall not be deemed to have failed to have done that thing, provided that it is done within the further time allowed. Sub-section (2) also provides for a person having "a reasonable excuse for not doing anything" not to be deemed to have failed to have done the thing unless he did it without unreasonable delay after the excuse ceased.

The provision of extra time and for the exception of reasonable excuse is designed to allow flexibility in the operation of the fixed penalties, thereby matching that for income tax and corporation tax. If a person appeals against a fixed penalty and the excuse is not accepted as reasonable by HMRC, the matter can be appealed to the First-Tier Tribunal. It has been held (*Browne v HMRC* TC 754) that a reasonable excuse exists where a taxpayer relies on her solicitors to file the land transaction return on her behalf and, for whatever reason, they fail to so. Contrast *Manor House Surgery* (TC 1101) where an error in the agents' computer caused the return not to be filed online and it was held that the solicitors should have checked whether the filing had been successful when a certificate of filing was not immediately issued. The Tribunal thus held that reliance on the solicitors to carry out the filing on the taxpayer's behalf did not amount to a reasonable excuse.

98. Admissibility of evidence not affected by offer of settlement etc

This section is based on TMA 1970 s 105 (as amended by FA 2003 s 203), and deals with the admissibility of statements and documents in any criminal proceedings, and proceedings for the recovery of SDLT and any proceedings for a penalty or related appeal. Sub-section (1) provides that such statements and documents are not inadmissible in court simply because the defendant has been told that the Board will accept a monetary settlement (without pursuing criminal proceedings) if a full confession is made. Similarly, they are not inadmissible on account of being told that the extent to which information is freely disclosed will be taken into account in arriving at the amount of any penalty.

99. General provisions about penalties

This section provides for Sch 14 (see below), which deals with the determination of penalties and related appeals. Sub-section (2) (based on TMA 1970 s 102) empowers HMRC to mitigate penalties under this Part, or to stay or compound any proceedings for the recovery of such a penalty. Sub-section (3) confirms that nothing in Part 4 of the Act will affect criminal proceedings for an offence (based on TMA 1970 s 204). Sub-section (2A) provides for a limitation on penalties where a person is liable for more than one tax-geared penalty in respect of the same land transaction: each penalty other than the first (which presumably is the largest) is reduced to ensure that the aggregate of those additional penalties does not exceed the amount of the largest.

100. Companies

In this section, company is defined for the purposes of SDLT as any body corporate or unincorporated association, but excluding partnerships. The section also establishes at sub-s (2) that it is the company's "proper officer" (as defined at sub-ss (6) and (7)) who is responsible for notifying and paying SDLT (sub-s (2)), and upon whom documents should be served (sub-s (3)). In cases where tax is due from a company that is not a body corporate or is incorporated outside the UK, it may be recovered from the proper officer under sub-s (4). Under sub-s (5), the proper officer may retain company monies in order to satisfy a charge to SDLT, and, where he is not reimbursed, may be indemnified by the company in respect of his liability.

101. Unit trust schemes

This section provides that the trustees of a unit trust scheme (as defined in sub-s (4)), or "umbrella scheme" (as defined at sub-s (3)), are treated as if they were a company, and the rights of unitholders were shares, for the purposes of SDLT. Given that s 100 provides that a "company" means any body corporate or unincorporated association, an unresolved question is whether, by making a unit trust scheme a company, it is also to be assumed that the unit trust scheme is a body corporate. The better view is that there is no justification for the assumption that a unit trust scheme should be treated as being a body corporate since it might equally be assumed to be an unincorporated association. Accordingly, it is recommended that wherever in the Act there is a reference to a "company" (eg s 53: transaction involving a connected company) it must be read as including the trustees of a unit trust scheme; but where the reference is to a "body corporate" (eg Sch 15 para 13: transfer of chargeable interest to a partnership consisting wholly of bodies corporate), that cannot include the trustees of a unit trust scheme. In addition to this general principle, sub-s (7) provides that a unit trust scheme (namely, the trustees of a unit trust scheme) is not to be treated as a company for the purposes of group relief. Accordingly, it is not possible to claim group relief where there is a transfer to or by the trustees of a unit trust scheme from or to a body corporate which is connected with the trust.

In accordance with sub-s (2), each part of an umbrella scheme is regarded for SDLT purposes as a separate unit trust scheme (and thus as a separate company), and accordingly the scheme as a whole is not. Transfers of land between different parts of an umbrella scheme will therefore fall to be treated as chargeable to SDLT as if market value had been paid for the land transaction: see s 53. Under sub-s (5), the Treasury is empowered to make regulations which provides that schemes of certain descriptions are not to be treated as umbrella schemes. Sub-section (6) establishes that TA 1988 s 469A (see commentary to that section) applies for the purposes of SDLT as well, with the substitution of "unit trust scheme" in place of "authorised unit trust".

Issues, surrenders and transfers of units continue to be subject principally to stamp duty reserve tax (see FA 1999 Sch 19 Pt II).

102. Open-ended investment companies

This section provides that the Treasury may make regulations to ensure that SDLT provisions apply to open-ended investment companies in the same way as unit trust schemes. "Open-ended investment company" is given the same meaning as in FSMA 2000 s 236.

103. Joint purchasers

This section deals with situations where a property is purchased jointly by two or more persons (subject to the provisions of Sch 15 relating to partnerships and Sch 16 relating to trustees (see sub-s (8)). The general rules as set out at sub-s (2) are as follows:

(a) any obligation imposed on the purchaser under this Part is imposed on the purchasers jointly but may be discharged by any one of them—one of the aims of the section is to avoid joint purchasers having to make separate returns, and this is confirmed at sub-s (3);

(b) anything required or authorised by this Part to be done in relation to the purchaser must be done in relation to them all—this means, for example, that HMRC determinations or discovery assessments must be made against all of the purchasers (see sub-s (6)), and similarly that HMRC is obliged to keep all purchasers informed about any enquiry into the return (confirmed at sub-s (5)); and

Part II ST

(c) any liability of the purchaser under SDLT is joint and several (eg failure to submit a return and pay SDLT will lead to interest and penalties which can be recovered from all or any of the joint purchasers).

Sub-section (4) states that the declaration required by para 1(1)(*c*) of Sch 10 must be made by all of the partners (see commentary to those paragraphs).

In the case of an appeal, by virtue of sub-s (7), any purchaser is entitled to exercise a right of appeal at any time, but notice must be given to any of them by whom it is not brought. If the appeal is to be settled by agreement, the agreement of all the purchasers is required, but if it is not settled, any of them are entitled to appear and be heard. Finally, the decision made on appeal binds all of the purchasers.

104. Partnerships

This section introduces Sch 15 (see below).

105. Trustees

This section introduces Sch 16 (see below).

106. Persons acting in a representative capacity etc

This section provides for how SDLT applies to a person acting in a representative capacity, ie for an incapacitated person, a minor, a deceased person or a person whose assets are under the direction and control of a receiver appointed by the court. Basically, such a person is responsible for discharging any SDLT obligations. The section follows TMA 1970 ss 72–75.

107. Crown application

This section establishes that SDLT binds the Crown, but exempts transactions where the purchaser is one of the listed Government or Parliamentary bodies. Sub-section (1) notably does not extend to circumstances where SDLT would ultimately be borne by the Crown. By virtue of sub-s (3), HMRC's powers under Sch 13 Pt 7 dealing with entry with warrant to obtain information do not apply to premises occupied for the purposes of the Crown. Sub-section (4) ensures that the Crown is not liable to prosecution for an offence in relation to SDLT.

108. Linked transactions

Sub-section (1) defines "linked transactions" as transactions forming part of a single scheme, arrangement or series of transactions between the same vendor and purchaser or persons connected with them (see s 55(4) with regard to the relevant rate of tax). It also provides that at the option of the purchaser(s), linked transactions with the same effective date can be reported as a single notifiable transaction on a single return (sub-s (3)). Sub-section (4) confirms that where this is done, all the purchasers will be treated as joint purchasers in accordance with s 103. Sub-section (2) defines connected persons with reference to TA 1988 s 839. The section is made subject to the exchange rules in s 47. The effect is to prevent the linked rules operating artificially to increase the rate of SDLT payable where there is an exchange of properties between connected persons.

109. General power to vary this part by regulations

Under this section, the Treasury may make regulations to vary the application of SDLT to any land transaction (subject to s 110 below), thereby providing a mechanism for SDLT avoidance to be countered as it arises, with immediate effect. Sub-section (2) provides that this power allows the alteration of the descriptions of land transactions that are chargeable or notifiable, and in respect of which tax is chargeable at any existing rate or amount. Under sub-s (3), the power may not be used to alter rates or thresholds, other than in relation to alterations made in accordance with sub-s (2). Such regulations are subject to the approval of the House of Commons and will be temporary, with a maximum life of 18 months. Sub-section (6) confirms that the Treasury also has a power to make transitional, supplementary and incidental provisions.

110. Approval of regulations under general power

This section ensures that regulations made under the power established by s 109 must be laid before the House of Commons within 28 days of their introduction. If the regulations are not then approved, they will cease to have effect (without prejudice to anything done in reliance on them).

111. Claim for repayment if regulations under general power not approved

Under this section, where regulations made under s 109 are not approved by the House of Commons, a claim for repayment may, within two years of the effective date of the relevant transaction, be made for the repayment of any tax, interest or penalty which would not have been payable but for the regulations. Under sub-s (4), HMRC may, by means of regulations, vary the time limit for making such a claim or vary any other conditions that must be made before repayment is made.

112. Power to amend certain provisions before implementation

This section empowered the Treasury to introduce a revised structure for lease duty (as set out at Sch 5 and s 55(2)) at any time between Royal Assent (10 July 2003) and 1 December 2003.

113. Functions conferred on "the Inland Revenue"

This section is based on similar provisions in the Taxes Acts and specifies what the functions (and their limits) of HMRC are.

114. Orders and regulations made by the Treasury or the Inland Revenue

This section deals with general provisions for regulatory powers with regard to SDLT, and lists various exceptions.

115. General Commissioners and appeals and other proceedings

This section introduces Sch 17 (see below).

116. Meaning of "residential property"

This section broadly defines "residential property", that is a building or part of a building that is in use or suitable for use as a dwelling, or is in the process of being constructed or adapted for such use. The primary significance of this definition is for establishing the consideration thresholds at which rates change and for the purposes of disadvantaged areas relief. "Residential property" is deemed to include land that is or forms part of the garden and grounds of the building and any outbuildings on such land, or an interest in or right over land that subsists for the benefit of such a building or such land. Sub-sections (2) and (3) list certain types of buildings which are defined as being or not being used as a dwelling respectively. Where it falls within the latter category, sub-s (4) provides that there is no requirement to make an assessment of its suitability for use for any other purpose. Sub-section (5) provides guidance as to how a building is defined when it has not been possible to do so using the preceding sub-sections. Sub-section (7) provides that where six or more separate dwellings are the subject of a single transaction involving the transfer of a major interest in, or the grant of a lease over, them, then the transaction will be treated as one involving non-residential buildings. Under sub-s (8), the Treasury is empowered to amend sub-ss (2) and (3), and amend or repeal sub-s (7).

117. Meaning of "major interest" in land

This section defines "major interest" in land for the purposes of SDLT. In England and Wales, and Northern Ireland, it means any freehold or leasehold estate whether legal or equitable, and in Scotland, it means the interest of an owner of land or the right of a tenant over property subject to a lease.

118. Meaning of "market value"

This section provides a definition for "market value", to be used when valuing chargeable consideration, with reference to TCGA 1992 ss 272–274. The basic rule is that market value is the price which assets might reasonably be expected to fetch on a sale in the open market, with no reduction for flooding the market (see the commentary in the *Chiltern's Yellow Tax Guide*).

119. Meaning of "effective date" of a transaction

This section defines the effective date as the date of completion, subject to ss 44(4), 44A(3), 45A(8) and 46(3) and Sch 17A paras 12A(2), 12B(3) and 19(3). In anticipation of the introduction of e-conveyancing, F(No 2)A 2005 s 4 makes provision for the Commissioners for HMRC by regulation to prescribe an alternative date to completion as the effective date of the land transaction.

120. Further provisions relating to leases

This section introduces Sch 17A (see below).

121. Minor definitions

This section provides definitions of certain miscellaneous terms used in the SDLT regime.

122. Index of defined expressions

This section provides an index of defined expressions used in the SDLT regime.

123. Consequential amendments

This section provides for Sch 18, and also provides the Treasury with the power to make regulations introducing other consequential amendments and repeals. This allows the Treasury to introduce changes to legislation introduced by other Government departments containing references to stamp duty.

124. Commencement and transitional provisions

This section introduces Sch 19, which provides for the commencement of SDLT and transitional provisions (see below).

PART 5 STAMP DUTY

125. Abolition of stamp duty except on instruments relating to stock or marketable securities

This important section abolishes stamp duty on documents transferring property, other than stock or marketable securities and certain partnership transactions.

Accordingly, sub-s (1) confirms that stamp duty is chargeable under FA 1999 Sch 13 (the main stamp duty charging provisions) only on instruments relating to stock or marketable securities, and sub-s (2) confirms that FA 1895 s 12 (collection of stamp duty in cases of property vested by Act or purchased under statutory power) does not apply to property other than stock or marketable securities. Sub-section (3) establishes that the section is to be construed as one with SA 1891 which presumably means, inter alia, that the SA 1891 s 122 definitions of "stock" and "marketable security" apply. Sub-section (4) provides that this section is to be supplemented by Schedule 20 dealing with apportionment of consideration and consequential amendments and repeals.

Sub-section (5) contains the commencement provisions for this section. The abolition of stamp duty on instruments effecting land transactions (as defined in s 43) which are SDLT transactions (as defined in Sch 19), or would be SDLT transactions but for an exemption or relief, is synchronised with the commencement of application of SDLT under Sch 19. Instruments which do not effect a land transaction and do not relate to stock or marketable securities cease to be subject to stamp duty if the instrument is executed after 1 December 2003. Instruments which relate to both a land transaction and a non-land transaction are treated as two separate instruments and sub-s (6) provides for apportionment of the consideration. Sub-section (7) confirms that stamp duty will continue to apply to certain partnership transactions (as set out at Sch 15 para 13(2) and (3)). In each of these cases the rule applies as much to duplicates and counterparts as it does to the instrument itself.

126. Circumstances in which group relief withdrawn

This section applies to instruments executed after 14 April 2003 and amends the anti-avoidance measures set out at FA 2002 s 111 and Sch 34 (see commentary). The major changes are as follows:

(1) Sub-section (2) extends the period in which group relief can be withdrawn from two to three years.

(2) Sub-section (3) seeks to close the loophole whereby it was possible to transfer an interest in land through two subsidiary companies and then transfer the first subsidiary outside the group. The sub-section now specifies that group relief is withdrawn if either the transferee company holds the relevant interest in land or another "relevant associated company" (as defined in sub-s (4A)) holds that interest at the time the transferee company (and in consequence the "relevant associated company") are degrouped.

(3) Group relief is not withdrawn if the relevant interest in land has been transferred at market value between the group relieved transfer and the degrouping by a duly stamped instrument on which ad valorem stamp duty has been paid without group relief being claimed. This seeks to close the loophole whereby land could be transferred outside the group for a nominal sum and then reacquired for the same consideration.

The section also provides definitions for the various terms used, and makes some minor changes to FA 2002 Sch 34 (bringing it in line with FA 2002 Sch 35). Finally, it provides that the section does not apply to an instrument executed after 14 April 2003 that gives effect to a contract made on or before 9 April 2003, unless it results from the exercise of an option, assignment or further contract made after 9 April 2003.

127. Circumstances in which relief for company acquisitions withdrawn

Section 127, in a similar fashion to the previous section, applies to instruments executed after 14 April 2003 (unless pursuant to a pre-10 April 2003 contract) amends anti-avoidance provisions introduced by FA 2002 s 111 and Sch 35.

(1) Sub-section (2) extends the period in which acquisition relief can be withdrawn to three years (sub-s (2)).

(2) Sub-section (3) amends s 113(1)(*a*) so that relief is withdrawn in circumstances where the acquiring company holds the relevant interest in land, or another "relevant associated company" (as defined in new sub-s (3A)) does. In so doing, it closes a loophole whereby it was possible for the acquiring company ("original transferee") to transfer the interest in land to another subsidiary company and then change control of the original transferee which had originally claimed the relief, without withdrawal of acquisition relief as the original transferee no longer held the interest in land.

(3) Sub-section (3)(*c*) amends the final words of s 113(1)(*c*) in order to clarify that re-acquisition of land by a duly stamped instrument within the three year withdrawal period only prevents acquisition relief being withdrawn where ad valorem duty is paid on the market value of the land which is reacquired.

The section also provides for various consequential drafting changes.

128. Exemption of certain leases granted by registered social landlords

It is intended that this exemption should be repealed by the Finance Act 2012 with effect from 6 April 2013.

This section deals with exemptions from stamp duty for leases for an indefinite term, or terminable by notice of one month or less, granted by "registered social landlords" under arrangements with a housing authority to temporarily house the homeless (sub-ss (1) to (3)). This exemption is intended to encourage social landlords to enter into such arrangements. Sub-section (4) provides a definition of "housing authority" in relation to England and Wales, Scotland and Northern Ireland, and sub-ss (5) and (6) deal with administrative procedures with reference to SA 1891.

129. Relief for certain leases granted before section 128 has effect

With reference to s 128, this section allows repayments to be made in respect of stamp duty paid on certain leases executed on or after 1 January 2000 by registered social landlords under agreements to temporarily house the homeless. Sub-section (5) allows the Commissioners to set conditions in relation to the administration of claims. Sub-section (8) confirms that the section applies to housing associations and bodies corporate which are listed on the register maintained by Scottish Homes prior to the enactment of the Housing (Scotland) Act 2001.

SCHEDULES

SCHEDULE 3 STAMP DUTY LAND TAX: TRANSACTIONS EXEMPT FROM CHARGE

This Schedule establishes that there is exemption from SDLT for the following.

(1) Transactions which are not for "chargeable consideration" (as defined at s 50 and Sch 4) eg gifts (para 1).

(2) Certain leases of dwellings granted by registered social landlords under agreements to house the homeless (para 2)—this only applies to arrangements entered into between the registered social landlord and a housing authority, the result of which is that the landlord provides temporary accommodation for individuals nominated by the authority.

(3) Transactions made in connection with the ending of a marriage (para 3).

(3A) Transactions made in connection with the dissolution or annulment of a civil partnership (para 3A).

(4) The acquisition by a person in (or towards) satisfaction of his entitlement under (or in relation to) a will or on intestacy (para 3A). Thus this will apply to cases where, for example, a legatee gives up his or her right to a pecuniary legacy in return for the transfer of a property. The reference to "in relation to" will presumably encompass statutory claims under the Inheritance (Provision for Family and Dependants) Act 1975. However, the exemption will not apply if the property exceeds the value of the entitlement of the beneficiary or claimant, so that he or she is required to provide additional consideration for the acquisition of the property (para 3A(4)). The one exception to this is where the property is taken subject to a mortgage, with the claimant assuming the liability for the debt as part of the arrangement. Where the exemption is unavailable because of the existence of such external consideration, special provision is made to determine the chargeable consideration: see Sch 4 para 8A(1).

(5) Transactions giving effect to certain dispositions following a death, subject to (*a*) the transaction being carried out within the period of two years after a person's death, and (*b*) that no consideration in money or money's worth other than the making of a variation of another such disposition is given for it (para 4). If condition (*b*) is not satisfied, special provision is made to determine the chargeable consideration: see Sch 4 para 8A(2).

Paragraph 5 provides the Treasury with the power to make regulations adding other land transactions to the list above.

SCHEDULE 4 Stamp Duty Land Tax: Chargeable Consideration

Money or money's worth

1.—This Schedule provides details of the rules for determining chargeable consideration for a transaction, which, as set out at para 1, is anything, given directly or indirectly by the purchaser or a connected party, in consideration of the transaction that is money or has money's worth. It is noteworthy that the scope of SDLT, in this context, is wider than stamp duty since it covers money's worth whereas ad valorem stamp duty is restricted by the concept of a conveyance or transfer being "on sale".

Value added tax

2.—This paragraph confirms that any VAT due on the consideration is included as chargeable consideration. However, in cases where the vendor has the option to charge VAT (eg in respect of a supply of land), but has not elected to do so by the effective date of the transaction, then any VAT that becomes payable as a result of a subsequent election is not included.

Postponed consideration

3.—This paragraph ensures that the amount or value of the chargeable consideration for the transaction shall be determined without any discount in cases where some or all of the consideration is to be paid at a later date.

Just and reasonable apportionment

4.—This paragraph confirms that consideration is apportioned on a "just and reasonable basis" between land transactions, or one land transaction and another non-land transaction, or one transaction for which the consideration is chargeable condition and another transaction where it is not, even where the consideration has been split or the transaction split.

Exchanges

5.—This paragraph explains how chargeable consideration is calculated where land transactions are entered into wholly or partly as consideration for each other. Each land transaction is treated as a relevant transaction. The rules differ depending on whether the subject-matter of the relevant transaction is or is not a major interest in land (see s 117). However, paragraph 5 will only apply if the effect of its application is to increase the amount of the consideration.

Subject to that proviso, where the subject matter of any of the relevant transactions is a major interest, whether the purchaser acquires one, two or more chargeable interests, the chargeable consideration is the market value of the subject-matter of each acquisition and, if the acquisition is the grant of a lease at a rent, that rent.

In cases where none of the chargeable interests which are the subject of any of the relevant transactions is a major interest, whether the purchaser acquires one, two or more chargeable interests, the chargeable consideration is the "appropriate proportion" (based on market value) amount or value of any chargeable consideration other than the chargeable interest(s) given for the acquisition(s). In other words, where a minor interest in land and monetary consideration are given in exchange for a minor interest in land, the chargeable consideration is the "equality money" only.

The restriction on the operation of the provision has led to a concern that if, by way of example, A transfers Whiteacre, worth £1 million, to B in return for Blackacre, worth £250,000, plus cash of £750,000, there would be a double charge to SDLT on £1 million – in the case of B, under paragraph 5, because that is the market value of Whiteacre; and, in the case of A, on the aggregate of the value of Blackacre plus the cash. It is understood, though, that the Commissioners consider that in such a case only one-quarter of Whiteacre is given as consideration for the acquisition of Blackacre, with the other three-quarters being given for the cash. Accordingly, paragraph 4 of Schedule 10 is to be applied to effect an appropriate apportionment; and A is then liable to SDLT on the value of Blackacre alone. A similar approach is to be applied where the exchange involves an under-value.

The Commissioners have, until recently, accepted that where the market value rule applies, the market value of the property is determined without regard to the VAT which may be payable by the purchaser. However, they have suggested that it may be that, in determining the chargeable consideration, there was always a need to add VAT where appropriate. This will be the case in future, since it is likely that the competition will be between the market value of the property on the one hand and the consideration given (inclusive of VAT) on the other.

The paragraph is made subject to the s 58 relief for certain exchanges of residential property and to Sch 4 para 6 (partitions). Accordingly, where one or other of those provisions applies, the usual rules on exchanges in para 5 are excluded.

In addition, the paragraph does not apply to certain land exchanges involving sales and leasebacks involving public or educational bodies (as to which see Sch 4 para 17).

Partition etc: disregard of existing interest

6.—Where land is partitioned, the share of the interest held by the purchaser immediately before the partition does not count as chargeable consideration. The effect is that only the party giving "equality consideration" is treated as providing chargeable consideration and only in that amount. "Partition" is not defined.

Valuation of non-monetary consideration

7.—Any non-monetary consideration (ie anything other than money or a debt as defined at para 8) is to be valued at its market value (see s 118) at the effective date of the transaction, unless provided otherwise.

Debt as consideration

8.—This paragraph confirms that the assumption or release of debt by the purchaser counts as chargeable consideration for a transaction, but the amount so chargeable cannot exceed the market value of the subject-matter of the transaction. This protects the lender who accepts a low-value property in satisfaction of a larger debt. "Debt" is deemed not to include any mortgage or similar form of security taken out in order to acquire the property.

In order to counteract the avoidance of SDLT in cases where property charged with debt was transferred temporarily free from the debt and the charge was reimposed immediately after the transfer, it is provided that in such a case, if the rights or liabilities in relation to that debt change as a result of the transaction, the purchaser is to be treated as having assumed the debt, and by doing so is deemed to have given a corresponding amount of chargeable consideration: sub-para (1A).

By way of relaxation of the debt rules, provision is made for cases where the property is owned either before or after the transfer in undivided shares (ie by tenants in common or joint tenants). In such a case, if the purchaser(s) assume debt secured on the property, each is treated as assuming (and each of the vendors is treated as relieved from) a proportion of the debt corresponding to his proportionate share of the property. This is intended to assist in cases where, for example, one owner buys the other out. Take a case where the property was charged with £500,000 debt and one joint tenant bought the other out. Sub-paragraph (1B) ensures that he is treated as giving chargeable consideration of £250,000, rather than £500,000.

Paragraph 8 does not apply in certain cases where the purchaser is the Board of the Pension Protection Fund: see The Pension Protection Fund (Tax) Regulations 2006 (SI 2006/575).

Cases where condition for exemption not fully met

8A.—This paragraph offers limited relief in two cases where an exemption under Sch 3 was unavailable because the transferee gave consideration in a form not permitted by the particular exemption. First, in cases where property charged with debt is assented or appropriated by personal representatives in satisfaction of a claim under the will or intestacy, but the claimant provides additional consideration for the transfer, the chargeable consideration for the transfer is not to include the amount of secured debt assumed by the transferee. Second, in cases where a person receives property under a transaction varying a testamentary disposition (often still referred to as a deed of family arrangement), but exemption is unavailable because the recipient provides "extraneous consideration", the chargeable consideration is to exclude any other variation of the will, etc, which is made by the transferee as part of the arrangements.

Conversion of amounts in foreign currency

9.—Consideration in a foreign currency is to be translated into sterling on the effective date of the transaction by reference to the London closing exchange rate, unless the parties have used a different rate for the purposes of the transaction.

Carrying out of works

10.—The carrying out of works of construction, improvement or repair of a building or other works to enhance the value of the land as consideration in whole or part for the acquisition of a major interest in land counts as chargeable consideration unless:

(a) the works are carried out after the effective date of the transaction;

(b) on land acquired, or to be acquired under the transaction by the purchaser (or on any other land) of the purchaser or any person connected with him; and

(c) it is not a condition of the transaction that the vendor or connected person carries out the works.

In cases where the works do constitute chargeable consideration, the value of that consideration is their open market value.

The legislation is intended to bring into charge consideration in the form of construction works provided by the purchaser on land which he *does not* acquire under the land transaction, whilst excluding from charge construction works on land which he *does* acquire under the transaction. The classic example of this would be the building lease.

It was appreciated that the condition in para (*a*) would lead to unfair charges where the works were carried out by the purchaser on the land he was acquiring after a charge to SDLT had arisen because he had substantially performed the contract but before the land transaction was completed by a conveyance. In such a case, the effect of s 44(8) (for example) is to introduce a second notifiable transaction, in respect of which SDLT is payable to the extent that it exceeds that charged under s 44(4). As originally drafted the exception would not have applied as the works would have been carried out before the second effective date (on completion). Accordingly, sub-s (2A) provides that, in cases where there are two notifiable transactions by reason of the operation of s 44(8), or Sch 17A para 12A (agreement for lease, where the grant of the lease itself triggers a notional surrender and regrant)), or the similar provisions for Scotland (Sch 17A para 19), the para (*a*) condition is satisfied if the works are carried out after the first effective date.

HMRC originally thought that the manner in which the exception was drafted reversed the decision of the High Court in *Prudential Assurance* v *IR Comrs* [1992] STC 863, but Stamp Taxes have subsequently accepted that the case remains good law and that SP 8/93 still applies. Accordingly, if a developer sells and transfers bare land to a purchaser and separately enters into a contract to build on the land then, provided that neither contract is conditional on the other, the purchaser will obtain a completed building having only been obliged to pay SDLT on the purchase price of the bare land. See Revenue Statement of 5 April 2004.

This paragraph does not apply to transactions falling within Sch 4 para 17 (arrangements involving public or educational bodies), a provision which offers significant relief from SDLT in the cases of transactions of a kind generally found in PFI projects.

Provision of services

11.—Where the whole or part of the consideration for the transaction consists of the provision of services by the purchaser (other than works of construction, improvement or repair of a building or other structure—since they are dealt with under para 10), the chargeable consideration is deemed to be the open market value of the services. The provision is subject to the rules in para 17 (relating to arrangements involving public or educational bodies).

Land transaction entered into by reason of employment

12.—This paragraph applies where the transaction is entered into by reason of the purchaser's employment (or that of a connected person). If the transaction is treated as a benefit in kind for income tax purposes under the provision of accommodation provisions, the chargeable consideration for SDLT purposes is the amount treated as the employee's employment related income (unless exempt from income tax under ITEPA 2003 s 99 in which case the consideration is the actual consideration, if any). In any other case, the chargeable consideration is not less than the market value of the subject-matter of the transaction as at the effective date.

Indemnity given by purchaser

16.—Indemnities given by the purchaser to the vendor for any ongoing liabilities to third parties relating to the land (including lease covenants) and payments made under the indemnity do not count as chargeable consideration.

Purchaser bearing inheritance tax liability

16A.—There are many cases in which the donee of a gift will agree to bear the inheritance tax which is or may become due as a result of that gift. This could occur either in the case of a lifetime gift or where a person becomes entitled to assets out of the estate of the deceased (whether under a will or by reason of intestacy). As a matter of strict construction of FA 2003 Sch 4, such an agreement would constitute consideration for SDLT. Paragraph 16A displaces this rule, providing that neither the agreement to pay nor the payment itself is to count as chargeable consideration for SDLT.

Purchaser bearing capital gains tax liability

16B.—This paragraph applies to cases where a liability to capital gains tax arises on a disposal and the disposal is either made otherwise than by way of a bargain at arm's length (ie under TCGA 1992 s 17), or is deemed to be so made (by s 18) being a transaction between connected persons. If the only consideration that is provided by the transferee for the transfer is his undertaking to meet, or his payment of, the capital gains tax liability, then neither the agreement to pay nor the payment of the tax counts as chargeable consideration. The consequence will be that the transaction will be free from SDLT. By contrast, if the transferee gives other consideration than the undertaking to pay the tax, then the relief which would have been afforded by para 16B is unavailable: sub-para (2).

Costs of enfranchisement

16C.—The Leasehold Reform Act 1967 and the Leasehold Reform, Housing and Urban Development Act 1993 make provision for tenants, whether individually or collectively to have the right to acquire the freehold of the properties which they occupy. It is a condition of each Act that the tenants reimburse the landlord certain specified costs incurred in the enfranchisement process. Paragraph 16C secures that the payment of such costs is not to be treated as chargeable consideration for the purposes of SDLT.

For the more general reliefs afforded where a tenant meets the reasonable costs incurred by his landlord in the grant of the lease itself, see Sch 17A para 10(1)(*f*) and (*g*).

Arrangements involving public or educational bodies

17.—This paragraph offers a degree of relief from the double charge which ordinarily arises under Sch 4 para 5 where one chargeable interest in land is exchanged for another. The provision is intended to apply to PFI projects under which a "qualifying body" enters into arrangements with a non-qualifying body. A qualifying body for this purpose includes a public body within FA 2003 s 66 (see above), or an institution within the further or higher education sector, or a local authority further or higher education corporation. The arrangements (which fundamentally offer a definition of a PFI project) must be such that:

(a) There is a sale and leaseback transaction between the parties. This will exist where there is a transfer of land, or the grant of a lease by the qualifying body to the non-qualifying body ("the main transfer"); and in consideration of that, the non-qualifying body grants a lease or under-lease back to the qualifying body. In some PFI projects it will also be part of the deal that the qualifying institution will transfer other land ("surplus land") to the provider.

(b) The non-qualifying body undertakes to carry out works or to provide services to the qualifying body.

(c) The qualifying body gives the non-qualifying body consideration in money for the works or services.

Where these conditions are satisfied, sub-para (3) directs that neither the lease-back, nor the carrying out of building works, nor the provision of other services counts as chargeable consideration for the main transfer; and sub-para (4) provides that neither the main transfer, nor any transfer of surplus land, nor any cash consideration given by the qualifying body for the provision of the building works or other services is to count as chargeable consideration for the lease-back. The non-qualifying body will thus be liable for SDLT to the extent that it provides cash or other property as part of the consideration for the main transfer and the transfer of the surplus land.

The effect is that the only chargeable consideration for either the main transfer, or the transfer of surplus land, or for the lease-back will be any cash consideration which is provided for the transfer or grant (as opposed to for the provision of the services) and any *other* property given by the non-qualifying body to the qualifying body. However, although the effect of sub-paras (3) and (4) is to reduce the amount of chargeable consideration, the transactions will still be notifiable transactions for SDLT: sub-para (4A).

SCHEDULE 5 STAMP DUTY LAND TAX: AMOUNT OF TAX CHARGEABLE: RENT

Introduction

1.—The paragraph introduces the Schedule, and deals with the calculation of tax chargeable for the grant of a lease on which rent is to be paid. The effect of Sch 5 and the net present value calculation is substantially to increase the charge compared to stamp duty (on leases for ten and twenty-five years an increase of four- and eight-fold respectively).

Amounts payable in respect of periods before grant of lease

1A.—This denies the status of rent to any chargeable consideration paid for the grant of a lease that is payable in respect of a period before the lease is granted. Such amounts will be treated as part of the premium paid for the grant of the lease. This is to prevent such amounts being taxed at 1 per cent whilst not being taken into account in determining the annual rent payable under the lease.

Calculation of tax chargeable in respect of rent

2.—Sub-para (1) provides that Sch 5 determines the tax chargeable in respect of rent. The amount of tax is a function of the percentage rate applicable and the net present value of the rent payable over the term of the lease. The charge is 0 per cent, in the case of residential property, where the relevant rental value does not exceed £125,000 and in the case of non-residential or mixed property, where the value does not exceed £150,000. Where, in the case of residential property, the relevant rental value exceeds £125,000, the charge is 0 per cent on the first £125,000 and 1 per cent on the remainder. For non-residential or mixed property, the charge is 1 per cent on so much of the value as exceeds £150,000. Sub-paragraphs (5) and (6) set out how SDLT is charged where the rental lease in question is one of a number of linked transactions.

By way of a temporary relief, SDLT on leases of residential properties has been mitigated for land transactions effected on or after 22 April 2009 and before 1 January 2010: in such cases, the charge is 0% where or to the extent that the relevant rental value does not exceed £175,000 and 1% in respect of so much of the relevant rental value as exceeds that amount.

Net present value of rent payable over term of lease

3.—The formula to be applied in calculating the net present value (v) of the rent is set out in this paragraph, namely:

$$v = \sum_{i=1}^{n} \frac{r^i}{(1+T)^i}$$

where, r_i is the rent payable in respect of year i, i is the first, second, third, etc, year of the term, n is the term of the lease, and T is the temporal discount rate (see para 8). The formula finds the net present value of each future rent payment discounted at the specified discount rate and aggregates them. HMRC have published a calculator on their website.

For this purpose one takes account of the rules in Sch 17A to determine the "amount of rent payable under a lease" (cf para 9 below).

Temporal discount rate

8.—For the purposes of Sch 5, the temporal discount rate is 3.5% or such other rate as may be specified by Treasury regulations. HMRC appear to consider that a "risk-free" discount rate is justified, which therefore bears no relationship to the actual borrowing interest rate of the lessee.

Tax chargeable in respect of consideration other than rent: general

9.—This paragraph, coupled with para 9A, makes provision for the charge where there is chargeable consideration for the grant of a lease other than rent, ie where a premium of some kind is required.

9A.—This paragraph imposes the charge by reference to the nature of the land (ie whether it is wholly or partly residential or non-residential) and by reference to the amount of the "relevant rent". For this purpose the "relevant rent" is the annual rent reserved either by the lease or by any other lease which is a linked transaction.

If the land is entirely non-residential and the relevant rent is at least £1,000, then the 0% band in s 55(2) does not apply in relation to the consideration (other than the rent, which of course, is separately charged under Sch 5 para 3); and SDLT is taxed on this consideration at 1% if otherwise it would have fallen within the 0% band.

If, however, the relevant land is partly residential and partly non-residential, one is required to attribute the relevant rent on a just and reasonable basis between the two. If, on such an apportionment, the relevant rent which is attributable to the non-residential part is at least £1,000, then it becomes necessary to apportion the other consideration between the residential and the non-residential parts of the transaction. The proportion which is attributable to the non-residential part is then charged at 1% rather than 0% if it would otherwise have fallen within the 0% band.

SCHEDULE 6 STAMP DUTY LAND TAX: DISADVANTAGED AREAS RELIEF

PART 1 DISADVANTAGED AREAS

Meaning of "disadvantaged areas"

1.—Defines "disadvantaged area" as an area designated as such by regulations made by the Treasury for any period specified therein. The Treasury may also make regulations making provision for different cases, which may contain incidental, supplementary, consequential or transitional provisions as appropriate. The HMRC website contains an online disadvantaged areas postcode search. SP 1/2004 gives guidance for those claiming exemption from SDLT in respect of transfers of property situated in designated disadvantaged areas.

Continuation of regulations made for purposes of stamp duty

2.—This confirms that any regulations made by the Treasury designating disadvantaged areas which were in force immediately before 1 December 2003 for stamp duty will have effect as if made for the purposes of SDLT.

PART 2 LAND WHOLLY SITUATED IN A DISADVANTAGED AREA

Introduction

3.—This paragraph introduces the provisions which apply to a transaction if the subject-matter is a chargeable interest in relation to land that is wholly situated in a disadvantaged area.

Land all residential

5.—The effect of this paragraph is to raise the 0 per cent threshold for residential land from £125,000 to £150,000 and otherwise to determine the rate of tax as normal. So you have to distinguish between the following situations:

(a) no rent: exemption if the chargeable consideration does not exceed £150,000;
(b) only rent: exemption if the relevant rental value does not exceed £150,000;
(c) where there is both rent and other consideration. In this case, do not take account of the rent if the relevant rental value does not exceed £150,000; and do not take account of the relevant consideration other than rent if that other consideration does not exceed £150,000.

Land partly non-residential and partly residential

6.—Where land is mixed residential and non-residential, consideration is to be attributed on a just and reasonable basis. The consideration that is attributable to non-residential land obtains no relief. In relation to land that is residential property the rules described in para 5 above are effectively replicated to determine whether the £150,000 threshold is available.

Notification of transactions

6A.—This provision ensures that transactions remain notifiable under s 77, even though the effect of Sch 6 is that none of the consideration is chargeable consideration for SDLT purposes.

PART 3 LAND PARTLY SITUATED IN A DISADVANTAGED AREA

Introduction

7.—This part applies to land which is situated partly inside and partly outside a disadvantaged area. The paragraph confirms that consideration (including rent or annual rent) attributable to such land should be attributed on a just and reasonable basis.

Land all non-residential

8.—The effect of paras 8, 9 and 10 is to replicate the rules set out in paras 4, 5 and 6 to the consideration apportioned as per para 7 to the disadvantaged areas. If the disadvantaged area transaction would be exempt or within the 1 per cent threshold on a stand-alone basis, the consideration apportioned to the disadvantaged area transaction will not count as chargeable consideration. The normal SDLT rules are therefore applied to the transaction as a whole but taking no account of this consideration.

Land all residential

9.—See para 8.

Part II ST

Land partly non-residential and partly residential

10.—See para 8.

PART 4 INTERPRETATION

Relevant consideration and relevant rental value

11.—This paragraph provides definitions of "relevant consideration" (see commentary on s 55) and "relevant rental value" (see commentary on para 2 of Sch 5) for the purposes of the Schedule.

Rent and annual rent

12.—For the purposes of the Schedule, "rent" has the same meaning as in Sch 5 and "annual rent" has the same meaning as in para 9A of Sch 5 (see commentary on Sch 5).

SCHEDULE 6A RELIEF FOR CERTAIN ACQUISITIONS OF RESIDENTIAL PROPERTY

Schedule 6A affords relief from SDLT in a number of cases where there is a social need for the interposition of an intermediate purchaser (usually a property trader) who will acquire an individual's private residence in order to facilitate the proper working of the housing market. These cases are:

(1) The acquisition by a house-building company of an individual's old dwelling in consideration (wholly or partly) of the acquisition by that individual of a new dwelling from the house-building company.

(2) The acquisition by a property trader of an individual's old dwelling where that individual acquires a new dwelling from a house-building company, where the property trader is in business to make such acquisitions.

(3) The acquisition by a property trader of property from the personal representatives of a deceased individual, where the property trader is in business to make such acquisitions.

(4) The acquisition by a property trader of an individual's old dwelling where the individual has made arrangements to sell the old dwelling and acquire a new one, and where the arrangements to sell the old dwelling fail, where the property trader is in business to make such acquisitions.

(5) The acquisition by an individual's employer of the individual's dwelling in connection with a change of residence by the individual resulting from relocation of employment.

(6) The acquisition by a property trader of an individual's dwelling in connection with a change of residence by the individual resulting from relocation of employment, where the property trader is in business to make such acquisitions.

It will be seen that for each case there is a limitation on the person who can take advantage of the exemption. In the first case the purchaser must be a "house building company", defined as a company that carries on the business of constructing or adapting buildings or parts of buildings for use as dwellings (para 1(4)). In the fifth case, the purchaser must be the employer of the individual. In all other cases, the purchaser must be a "property trader", defined as a company, a limited liability partnership, or a partnership whose members are either companies or limited liability partnerships (para 8). It is far from clear why the legislation restricts relief in the first case to companies alone.

In each case, the relief is only available if the property satisfies certain tests bearing a strong resemblance to those which apply for the purposes of capital gains tax relief on the disposal of a person's private residence under TCGA 1992 s 222. They are:

(1) that the individual selling the property (or the deceased in the case of purchases from personal representatives) occupied the dwelling as his only or main residence at some time in the period of two years ending with the date of its acquisition by the purchaser (or the date of his death in the case of a sale by personal representatives). "Dwelling", for the purposes of the relief, includes the land occupied and enjoyed with the dwelling as its garden or grounds: para 7(1).

(2) that the area of land acquired from the individual does not exceed the "permitted area", ie land occupied and enjoyed with the dwelling as its garden or grounds that does not exceed ½ hectare or such larger area as is required for the reasonable enjoyment of the dwelling as a dwelling having regard to its size and character: para 7(3). Paragraph 7(4) explains how to identify the part of the property that constitutes the permitted area where the property sold is too large.

If the land sold exceeds the permitted area, the relief is restricted rather than lost completely. It is a peculiar feature of the legislation that the purchaser who must claim the relief must take the risk of the correctness of assurances given to him by the vendor as to the nature of his occupation of the property. Presumably property traders will require appropriate warranties or indemnities from their vendors.

In addition to the requirements above, each relief imposes the following *additional* conditions.

Acquisition by house-building company from individual acquiring new dwelling

1.—Paragraph 1 offers exemption from SDLT for the acquisition by a house building company of a dwelling from an individual, where the individual acquires from the company a new dwelling which he intends to occupy as his only or main residence, and where each acquisition is made in consideration of the other.

If the area of the old dwelling is larger than the "permitted area" (see above), the chargeable consideration for its acquisition is reduced to an amount equal to the market value of the old dwelling *less* the market value of the permitted area: sub-para (3).

A "new dwelling" includes a building or part of a building that has been constructed or adapted for use as a single dwelling and that has not been occupied since its construction or adaptation: para 7(2). Notably, this definition excludes land that was already a single dwelling and has been refurbished.

Acquisitions of dwellings by property traders: introduction

Certain acquisitions of dwellings made by property traders are exempt from SDLT. In each case, the relief is available only if the property in question was the previous owner's only or main residence at some stage in the two years prior to the disposal or his death. The legislation limits what the property trader may do with the property it is to acquire. In each of the cases set out below, the trader must not intend:

(a) to spend more than £10,000 on refurbishment (or, if greater, five per cent of the price of the old dwelling—subject to a maximum of £20,000). Refurbishment is the carrying out of works to enhance the value of the dwelling. However, one disregards the cost of cleaning the dwelling and works required solely for the purpose of ensuring that the building meets safety standards: para 9(1).

(b) to grant leases or licences of the building: the legislation expects the property trade to sell on the interest which it has acquired. However, it is permissible for the trader to grant a lease or licence to the individual for no more than six months.

(c) to permit its directors or employees or (in the case of a partnership, its members) (or persons connected with any of them) to occupy the building.

The relief is withdrawn if the property trader is subsequently in breach of any of these requirements: Sch 6A para 11. In such a case, the trader must deliver a further land transaction return in accordance with FA 2003 s 81 within 30 days of the event which disqualified the transaction from relief (para 11(3)), and at the same time must pay the amount of SDLT that would have been chargeable but for the relief.

Acquisition by a property trader from an individual acquiring a new dwelling

2.—Paragraph 2 exempts from SDLT the acquisition by a property trader from an individual of a dwelling if:

(a) the acquisition is made by the property trader in the course of its business;
(b) the individual acquires a new dwelling from a house building company; and
(c) the individual intends to occupy the new dwelling as his only or main residence.

If the area of the old dwelling is larger than the "permitted area" (see above), the chargeable consideration for its acquisition is reduced to an amount equal to the market value of the old dwelling *less* the market value of the permitted area: sub-para (3).

Acquisition by property trader from personal representatives

3.—Paragraph 3 exempts the acquisition of a dwelling from the personal representatives of a deceased individual if:

(a) the acquisition is made in the course of a business of acquiring such properties; and
(b) the deceased occupied the property as his only or main residence in the two years before his death.

If the area of the old dwelling is larger than the "permitted area" (see above), the chargeable consideration for its acquisition is reduced to an amount equal to the market value of the old dwelling *less* the market value of the permitted area: sub-para (3).

Acquisition by chain-breaking property trader

4.—Paragraph 4 exempts from SDLT the acquisition by a property trader from an individual if the individual has arranged to sell his old dwelling and to buy a new dwelling and the arrangements to sell the old dwelling fall through, provided that the acquisition is made to enable the individual's acquisition of the new dwelling to proceed. The relief is subject to the following conditions:

(a) the acquisition must be made in the course of a business of acquiring such properties; and
(b) the individual must intend to occupy the new dwelling as his only or main residence.

If the area of the old dwelling is larger than the "permitted area" (see above), the chargeable consideration for its acquisition is reduced to an amount equal to the market value of the old dwelling *less* the market value of the permitted area: sub-para (3).

Acquisition by employer in case of relocation of employment

5.—Paragraph 5 provides a similar exemption to that afforded by para 6 (see below) in cases where the individual's employer (rather than a property trader) acquires the dwelling from the relocating employee. In this case, though, the usual restrictions on what the purchaser intends to do with the property do not apply. It suffices to show that the individual occupied the property as his only or main residence at some time in the two years prior to the date of acquisition and that the acquisition is made in connection with a change of residence resulting from relocation of employment. It is a condition of the relief that the employer pays no more than the market value for the property.

"Relocation" involves a change of the individual's place of employment either by reason of a change of employer (the purchaser being the new employer), or a change in the duties of his employment, or a change in the place where the individual normally performs his duties. And it must be shown both that the change of residence is made, wholly or mainly, to allow the individual to have his residence within a reasonable travelling distance of his new place of employment and that the former residence was not within such a distance.

If the area of the old dwelling is larger than the "permitted area" (see above), the chargeable consideration for its acquisition is reduced to an amount equal to the market value of the old dwelling *less* the market value of the permitted area: sub-para (3).

Acquisition by a property trader in case of relocation of employment

6.—Paragraph 6 offers exemption from SDLT where a property trader acquires a dwelling from an individual and the individual is changing his residence resulting from the relocation of his employment. "Relocation" involves a change of the individual's place of employment either by reason of a change of employer; or a change in the duties of the employment; or a change in the place where the individual normally performs his duties. It must be shown both that the change of residence is made, wholly or mainly, to allow the individual to have his residence within a reasonable travelling distance of his new place of employment and that the former residence was not within such a distance.

The relief is conditional on:

(a) the acquisition being made in the course of a business of acquiring such properties; and

(b) the consideration for the acquisition being no more than the market value of the property.

If the area of the old dwelling is larger than the "permitted area" (see above), the chargeable consideration for its acquisition is reduced to an amount equal to the market value of the old dwelling *less* the market value of the permitted area: sub-para (3).

SCHEDULE 6B TRANSFERS INVOLVING MULTIPLE DWELLINGS

This Schedule was introduced in order to afford a reduced rate of tax where a purchaser acquires a number of dwellings at the same time. Although the motivation for the relief might have been assumed to be the introduction of the 5% rate on the acquisition of residential property for £1 million or more, the relief is entirely separate and thus available even where the aggregate consideration does not exceed the £1 million threshold. The relief is also without prejudice to Finance Act 2003 s 116 which defines "residential property" and which excludes from the definition certain categories of building in which people live (e.g. halls of residence), and which provides that a sale of six or more separate dwellings by a single transaction is not to be treated as a sale of residential property. However, section 116 is disregarded for the purposes of determining whether Schedule 6B relief is available, since otherwise it might have prevented the Schedule applying wherever the number of dwellings acquired was six or more. A "dwelling" is widely defined by paragraph 7 to include not only buildings (or parts of buildings) used or suitable for use as a single dwelling but also land occupied with it as its garden or grounds, land subsisting for the benefit of the dwelling and, most importantly, dwellings bought off-plan, where construction or adaption as a dwelling has not commenced at the time when the contract to buy is substantially performed.

Paragraph 2 indicates that relief under Schedule 6B is to be available if certain conditions are satisfied. First, the "main subject-matter of the transaction" must consist of an interest in at least two dwellings. It is of no relevance that it also includes other matters as well. There is no definition of "main subject-matter" in the legislation. The assumption is that the Legislature intended to exclude cases where P buys one dwelling for a sum in excess of £1 million but at the same time acquires a minute interest in another dwelling in order to trigger the relief. In such a case it would reasonably be concluded that the second acquisition was not the main subject-matter of the transaction. As an alternative to this first condition, relief is also available if the transaction consists in the acquisition of an interest in a single dwelling but is a linked transaction, where the other transaction(s) also consist in the acquisition of an interest in one or more other dwellings. The second condition, in either case, is that the transaction already enjoys another relief under section 74 (exercise of collective rights by tenants of flats) or section 75 (crofting community right to buy) or where relief under Schedule 7 (group relief and acquisition relief) or Schedule 8 (charities relief) is available.

Special rules apply to interests which are in reversion: paragraph 2(5), (6). Such an interest is capable of being an interest in one or more dwellings; but only to the extent that the underlying interests are for leases granted for an initial term of 21 years or less. Thus if P buys the freehold reversion in a block of five flats, where four of the flats are held on leases originally granted for more than 21 years, the purchase does not qualify for Schedule 6B relief, as only one flat can be taken into account. If, on the other hand, two of the flats are let on leases of 21 years or less, then P's acquisition is treated as an acquisition of an interest in two dwellings.

Having reached the conclusion that the purchase is within the scope of the relief, the next step involves the apportionment of the consideration. First, the consideration is apportioned between the dwellings and the other property (if any – e.g. flats let on long leases) on a just and reasonable basis: paragraph 4(3). The consideration attributable to the dwellings is then divided by the number of dwellings. One then finds the relevant percentage charge by reference to section 55 (save that the percentage may not be less than 1%) and applies that percentage to the total consideration attributable to the dwellings: paragraph 5.

By way of example: P buys for £2 million a block of 20 flats each of which is let on a short lease. The consideration attributable to the dwellings is the full sum. Divided by the number of dwellings (20) the consideration for each is £100,000. This would normally attract tax at 0%; but since the minimum rate is 1%, the total consideration is £20,000 (as opposed to the £100,000 that would have been charged at the full 5% rate, or the £80,000 that would have been charged had P rellied on section 116 to treat the dwellings as non-residential).

Paragraph 6 provides for adjustment of the relief where there is a change of circumstances which is such that, had the relevant event happened before the claim for relief, the claim would have been disallowed or adjusted. It would seem that the legislation is not concerned with onward sales of the dwellings (ssincethose would collect their own SDLT charges) but with the recombination of the separate dwellings to form fewer dwellings than existed at the time of the claim for relief. Thus if P agreed to buy four flats off-plan, and paid for those flats in full at the time of the contract, then he could claim multiple dwelling relief for that acquisition. If, though, before (or indeed after) completion, he asked the builder to knock the flats into a single, larger, dwelling, that would be an event falling within paragraph 6 in respect of which P would be obliged to make an amending self-assessment return within 30 days of the event.

SCHEDULE 7 Stamp Duty Land Tax: Group Relief and Reconstruction and Acquisition Reliefs

Part 1 Group Relief

This Part is based on the reliefs from stamp duty set out in FA 1930 s 42, and FA (Northern Ireland) 1954 s 11, FA 1967 s 27, FA 1995 s 151 and FA 2002 s 111 and Sch 34 (as amended by s 126 of this Act).

Group relief

1.—This paragraph provides a relief from SDLT for acquisitions of property by companies where the vendor and purchaser are members of the same group as at the effective date of the transaction. Sub-para (2) defines "company" as a "body corporate". This is a departure from the definition of "company in section 100 where it is provided that, save as expressly otherwise provided, "company" means any body corporate or unincorporated association but does not include a partnership. Schedule 7 is thus one of the places where it is expressly otherwise provided. There is no statutory definition of body corporate; but it is generally assumed that the minimum requirements are that the body have a legal personality and be capable of perpetual succession. For stamp duty the Commissioners have stated that "body corporate" includes companies with limited or unlimited liability, companies limited by guarantee, charter companies and bodies created by statute. The also indicated that relief may be available where a local authority, being a body corporate, is a party to a document and the other party has a share capital which is beneficially owned by the authority: Stamp Taxes Manual 6.123, and this definition appears to have been adopted for SDLT purpose: SDLTM 23014.

In October 2010 the Commissioners published a change in their view: they now accept and assert that limited liability partnerships are bodies corporate for group relief purposes. This has two effects: first, an LLP may be the parent company of a group of companies, so that a transfer between two subsidiaries may qualify for group relief. Second, an LLP is treated as opaque, so that a subsidiary of the LLP cannot be grouped with corporate members of the LLP. Contrast this with the position which obtains where a general partnership or a limited partnership sits between its corporate members and a subsidiary owned by the partnership. In such a case a transfer of land from the corporate members to the partnership's subsidiary may be treated as a transfer between group members since the partnership is treated as transparent. Scottish partnerships require separate consideration: as both Scottish limited and general partnerships have legal personalities but are not bodies corporate, the Commissioners treat them as opaque but not as companies. Where therefore a Scottish partnership owns a number of companies, those companies cannot rely on the partnership to establish a group for group relief purposes.

For amendments to the operation of this Schedule where the Board of the Pension Protection Fund is a member of the group see The Pension Protection Fund (Tax) Regulations 2006 (SI 2006/575).

The Commissioners announced that they will not seek to revisit earlier claims for group relief which would be disallowed following their change in practice.

Restrictions on availability of group relief

2.—This paragraph introduces anti-avoidance measures which restrict the availability of group relief, including where different arrangements are entered into relating to the control of the companies (sub-para (1), the provision of consideration from outside the group (sub-para (2)), and where the vendor and purchaser are to cease being members of the same group. The para 2(*a*) and (*b*) restrictions are substantially the same as the FA 1967 s 27(3)(*a*) and (*c*) restrictions (see commentary thereon).

Sub-para (1) introduces a new restriction, which appears to complement and extend the para 2(*b*) de-grouping arrangements restriction. The purpose is clearly to prevent group relief applying where arrangements exist for control of the purchaser to change whilst artificially satisfying the shareholding, economic and Sch 18 tests for the purposes of para (2)(*b*) "75% subsidiary" definition.

"Arrangements" are defined as in sub-para (4) (see commentary on para 3).

As an exception to para 2, sub-para (3A) ensures that where there are arrangements for the transfer of a business on the demutualisation of an insurance company, group relief is to be available provided that the conditions for relief from stamp duty and SDRT under FA 1997 s 96 are met. These conditions are that:

(a) the transfer is an insurance business transfer scheme to which FSMA 2000 Pt 7 (control of business transfers) applies, or a transfer of the whole or part of the business of a general insurance company which operates through a branch or agency in the UK under an authorisation granted overseas under the relevant provisions of the Life Assurance Consolidation Directive or the Third Non-Life Insurance Directive;

(b) the transfer must be of the whole or any part of the business carried on by a mutual insurance company ("the Mutual");

(c) the transferee must be a company that has share capital;

(d) the consideration must take the form of shares in the transferee or its 100 per cent parent;

(e) those shares must be offered to at least 90 per cent (or such lower percentage as is substituted by regulation pursuant to sub-s (9)) of the members of the Mutual, thus allowing the offer to exclude certain members, for example on the basis of length of time of membership or size of interest; and

Part II ST

(f) the entire share capital of the issuing company in issue immediately after the transfer (except for shares issued or to be issued to the public on a public flotation of the issuing company) must have been offered to members of the Mutual, persons who are entitled to become members of the Mutual, or employees, former employees or pensioners of the Mutual or a wholly owned subsidiary (as defined in sub-s (6)) of the Mutual.

By way of a departure from the carefully targeted restrictions on the availability of group relief that have been imposed for many years, a general anti-avoidance restriction was (subject to transitional measures) introduced with effect from 20 July 2005. In future, group relief is only to be available if the transaction (ie the land transaction between the group members) is effected for bona fide commercial reasons and it does not form part of arrangements of which the main purpose, or one of the main purposes, is the avoidance of liability to stamp duty, SDLT, income tax, corporation tax or capital gains tax. It remains a matter of conjecture whether Stamp Taxes are the right department to adjudicate whether a transaction has been carried out for such purposes. A notable feature of the new rules is the absence of any statutory clearance procedure such as that offered in the case of the corresponding provisions, TCGA 1992 s 138 and TA 1988 s 707. However, Stamp Taxes have published a "white list" of transactions which are not considered to fall foul of para 2(4A) and have also indicated their willingness to operate a COP10 ruling procedure where a taxpayer is concerned whether relief might be refused by reason of the possible application of the sub-paragraph.

The list, which is to be found in para 23040 of the SDLT Manual is as follows.

(1) The transfer of a property to a group company having in mind the possibility that shares in that company might be sold more than three years after the date of transfer.

(2) The transfer of a property to a group company having in mind the possibility that shares in that company might be sold within three years of the date of transfer, with a consequent claw-back of group relief, in order that any increase in value of the property after the intra-group transfer might be sheltered from stamp duty land tax.

(3) The transfer of property to a group company having in mind the possibility that either (1) or (2) might occur.

(4) The transfer of a property to a group company prior to the sale of shares in the transferor company, in order that the property should not pass to the purchaser of the shares.

(5) The transfer of property to a group company in order that commercially generated* rental income may be matched with commercially generated losses from a Schedule A business.

(6) The transfer of property to a group company in order that commercially generated* chargeable gains may be matched with commercially generated allowable losses.

(7) The transfer of property to a non-resident group company in the knowledge that future appreciation or depreciation in value will be outside the scope of corporation tax on chargeable gains.

(8) Transactions undertaken as part of a normal commercial securitisation.

(9) The transfer of the freehold reversion in a property to a group lessee in order to merge the freehold and the lease, and thus prevent the lease being subject to the wasting assets rules as respects corporation tax on chargeable gains.

(10) The transfer of property to a group company in order that interest payable on borrowings from a commercial lender on ordinary commercial terms may be set against commercially generated* rental income.

*Including income, gains and losses which are generated intra-group on transactions which would have been commercial had they been entered into by unconnected third parties.

Withdrawal of group relief

3.—Group relief is withdrawn where a successful claim for group relief has been made, and, within three years of the transaction (or under arrangements made within the three year period), the purchaser ceases to be a member of the same group as the vendor. This provision prevents land being transferred to a group company SPC, free of SDLT by virtue of group relief before para 2 "arrangements" exist, followed by a sale of the SPC subject to 0.5% or less duty. There is no motive test. The necessary conditions for withdrawal of group relief are:

(a) there has been a relevant transaction exempt by virtue of group relief;
(b) the purchase has ceased to be a member of the same group within three years after the effective date of the transaction in pursuance of or in connection with arrangements (as defined in sub-para (4)) made within that three year period;
(c) at the time the purchaser ceases to be a member of the same group as the vendor it or a "relevant associated company" (as defined in sub-para (4)) holds a chargeable interest that (i) was acquired by the purchaser under the relevant transaction or is derived from that chargeable interest, and (ii) has not subsequently (presumably since the relevant transaction) been acquired at market value under a chargeable transaction for which group relief was available but was not claimed; and
(d) none of the para 4 or 4ZA cases applies.

The effect of withdrawal of group relief is that the tax (or an appropriate proportion of it if a proportion of the original subject matter remains in the vendor group) that would have been chargeable on the relevant transaction becomes chargeable. The tax is calculated by assuming that the chargeable consideration for the relevant transaction was a sum equal to the market value of the property acquired (and, in addition, the amount of the rent, if the acquisition took the form of a grant of a lease at a rent).

Sub-para (4) defines "arrangements". SP 3/98 sets out HMRC's current practice in relation to a FA 1967 s 27 arrangement and SP 3/93 applies to corporation tax group relief arrangements. HMRC has provided guidance as to their views on the application of group relief for SDLT in Tax Bulletin 70. It is emphasised that although SP 3/98 continues to apply to stamp duty, it is inapplicable to SDLT. However, there is substantial similarity in many important respects between the guidance in SP 3/98 and Tax Bulletin 70. In an answer to a question put at the 2009 Stamp Taxes Practitioners' Group Conference the Commissioners confirmed that the appointment of an administrator over a company or a receiver over the assets of a company did not, in itself, trigger a claw-back of any SDLT relief previously claimed or prevent the availability of SDLT group relief on a future intra-group transfer. This was because, in such circumstances, the company retained control of its assets, its shareholders did not change, so that control remained the same as well. The Commissioners also observed that such events did not usually, or in and of themselves, constitute an arrangement for someone to gain control of the purchaser but not of the vendor within paragraph 2(1).

Cases in which group relief not withdrawn

4.—This sets out exceptions to para 3 withdrawal of group relief, including:

(1) where the purchaser ceases to be a member of the same group by virtue of anything done in the course of winding up the vendor or another company above the vendor in the group; and
(2) where there is an acquisition of shares by another company to which FA 1986 s 75 (stamp duty: acquisition relief) applies and the conditions for relief set out therein are satisfied, and the purchaser who claimed the relief joins the group of the acquirer of shares as a result. This case (3) and case (2) follow the logic that it would not make sense to clawback group relief in respect of a corporate transaction where the transfer of the corporate's underlying assets would normally be transferred free of SDLT. What seems less logical is that, pursuant to sub-para (7), a case (3) transaction should restart a completely new three year clawback period (although the clawback is triggered by the purchaser leaving the share acquirer's group).

Part II ST

A further exception to the withdrawal of group relief under para 3 exists where the transaction by which the relevant company leaves the group is in the course of the demutualisation of an insurance company: sub-para (6A). The conditions for this relief are to be found in FA 1997 s 96: as to these conditions see the commentary to that section and to para 2(3A) above.

4ZA.—This provision is a substitute for an exception previously to be found in para 4 which is reintroduced with additional restrictions designed to counteract what HMRC saw as an avoidance of tax. As before, relief is not withdrawn where the purchaser, who claimed relief, ceases to be a member of the same group as the vendor because the vendor leaves the group. "Leaving the group" has a technical meaning for this purpose: the vendor leaves the group if the vendor and the purchaser cease to be members of the same group of companies by reason of a transaction relating to securities in either the vendor or in another company that is above the vendor in the group structure (eg that is the vendor's parent or grandparent company) and which ceases to be a member of the same group as the purchaser as a result of that transaction. However, it is now provided that if there is a subsequent change of control of the purchaser the claw-back provisions in para 3 are to apply as if the purchaser and the vendor had left the group at the same time. "Change of control" is widely drawn for this purpose: it includes not only a person obtaining control (whether alone or with others) and cases where a person who had control (whether alone or with others) loses control but also cases where the purchaser is wound up. At all times one looks to the senior level of control – a person does not control the purchaser if that person is under the control of one or more others – instead, one looks to the person controlling it. For these purposes, the section adopts the definition of "control" afforded by TA 1988 s 416; but with a limited degree of alleviation: there is no change of control if by reason of refinancing the purchaser otherwise than through a bank, the new lender becomes a loan creditor with control, provided that those who controlled the company before the transaction continue to do so afterwards. Likewise, in Committee the Economic Secretary to the Treasury stated that she would "address the second area of concern, which is that HMRC might construe the meaning of a change of control so widely that the change of one shareholder in a quoted company might result in a change of control and, therefore, trigger the clawback provision. Similar concerns were raised in relation to reconstruction relief. I can confirm that we intend to take the same approach—if control of a publicly owned company changes as a result of an ordinary market transfer of its shares, there will be no recovery, because we do not intend to interpret change of control so widely that simple day-to-day transactions by unconnected minority shareholders in the stock exchange could trigger a clawback. We will issue guidance shortly to confirm that view": Hansard Public Bill Committe Debates, 5 June 2008, col 520.

Withdrawal of group relief in certain cases involving successive transactions

4A.—This provision was introduced to counteract a specific avoidance device known as the "drop and bounce" or "bungee" scheme. The scheme took advantage of a defect in the original drafting of the definition of "relevant associated company", in para 3(4), the effect of which was to restrict the clawback of group relief to cases where either the purchaser held the transferred property or it was held by a company that ceased to be a member of the original group in consequence of the purchaser leaving the group. Accordingly, if the vendor transferred the property to a subsidiary company (the purchaser) and then transferred the purchaser to another subsidiary, clawback would not operate if (*a*) the purchaser then transferred the property to its new parent; and (*b*) the vendor then sold the parent company with both the land and the purchaser inside it. This was because, whilst it could reasonably be said that the purchaser left the group in consequence of its new parent leaving the group, it could not be said that the parent left the group in consequence of the purchaser leaving the group.

Unfortunately, it is possible that the new provision not only successfully defeats its intended target but will also lead to a charge to tax in other wholly innocent cases. The preconditions to the application of the paragraph are: first, that there is a transaction for which group relief is claimed and within three years there is a change of control of the purchaser under that transaction which would not have led to a clawback under para 3; and, second, that within the three years prior to the change of control there was a prior transaction under which group relief (under para 1), or reconstruction relief (under para 7), or acquisition relief (under para 8) was obtained. If the chargeable interest under the later transaction was also transferred under the prior transaction, and there has been no intervening chargeable transaction, then one applies the clawback rules in paras 3 and 4 by treating the vendor under the prior transaction as the vendor. The effect in most cases will be to ensure that the exceptions in para 4 cannot apply, as the transactions will not involve the prior vendor. Thus, taking the example given above in the drop and bounce scheme, the original vendor does not leave the group in any sense so that there will indeed be a clawback under para 3.

If there have been more than two Sch 7 transactions within the three years prior to the change of control of the purchaser, para 4A requires one to treat the vendor under the earliest such transaction as the vendor for the purpose of judging the operation of paras 3, 4 and 4ZA on the purchaser leaving the group.

Last, note should be taken of the wide meaning given to "change of control". A change of control occurs wherever there is a change in those who control the company—so that if one person amongst a group who control the company ceases to do so, even though the company continues to be controlled by the others who previously controlled it, or a further person joins those controlling the company at the relevant time, there is a change. There is also a change of control where the company is wound up. However, there is no change of control for the purposes of the paragraph if the purchaser undertakes a refinancing exercise otherwise than through a bank, in consequence of which the new lender becomes a loan creditor with control, provided that those who controlled the company before the transaction continue to do so afterwards. For the Economic Secretary's explanation both of the anti-avoidance rule and why it should not apply where the change occurs as a result of a refinancing exercise, see Hansard Public Bill Committee Debates, 5 June 2008, cols 520–521.

Recovery of group relief from another group company or controlling director

5.—If the para 3 group relief clawback charge, as finally determined, is not paid within six months after its due date, HMRC is entitled to recover the tax due from the vendor, or another group company higher in the group or a controlling director at the relevant time (being the time between the effective date of the group relieved transaction and the degrouping).

Recovery of group relief: supplementary

6.—HMRC can serve notice on a person within para 5(2) requiring him within 30 days to pay the outstanding amount. The notice must be served within three years of the final determination of the clawback charge. The person paying pursuant to the notice has a right of indemnity against the purchaser.

PART 2 RECONSTRUCTION AND ACQUISITION RELIEFS

This Part is based on the stamp duty reliefs set out at FA 1986 ss 75 and 76 and FA 2002 s 113 and Sch 35 (as amended by s 127 of this Act).

Reconstruction relief

7.—The paragraph provides for exemption for the land transaction element where a company ("the acquiring company") acquires the whole or part of an undertaking (including an interest in land) of another company ("the target company") under a scheme for the reconstruction of the target company. The conditions set out at sub-paras (2), (4) and (5) must also be satisfied. These effectively replicate the conditions relating to FA 1986 s 75 stamp duty acquisition relief (see commentary thereon), with two differences. First, the registered office of the acquiring company need not be in the UK and, secondly, the post-acquisition target company share register need only be "the same, or as nearly as may be the same" rather than identical.

Acquisition relief

8.—By virtue of this paragraph, the rate of tax is reduced to 0.5% in situations where a land transaction is entered into for the purposes of or in connection with a company ("the acquiring company") acquiring an undertaking (or part) of a company ("the target company") in exchange for non-redeemable shares, or non-redeemable shares and cash up to 10 per cent of the nominal value of the shares and/or the assumption or discharge by the acquiring company of liabilities of the target company. The undertaking must primarily comprise the carrying on of a trade other than a trade consisting in dealing in interests in land. In the course of the Standing Committee debates the Government gave an assurance that property developers and house builders who derived most of the profit from their work, rather than from buying and selling, would not be caught by this later condition: Hansard Standing Committe Debates, 30 June 2005, col 292.

Sub-para (4) is an anti-avoidance provision similar in affect to paras 2(1) and 2(2)(*b*) above and substantially the same as FA 1986 s 76(3A) (see commentary thereon).

Withdrawal of reconstruction or acquisition relief

9.—This provides, in similar fashion to para 3 withdrawal of group relief, that relief is withdrawn where control of the acquiring company changes within three years, beginning with the effective date of the transaction, or in pursuance of or in connection with arrangements made before the end of that period. The conditions for withdrawal of reconstruction and acquisition relief are substantially the same as the para 3 conditions on withdrawal of group relief, except that the degrouping is by reference to change of control rather than "ceasing to be a member of the same group", references to group relief are instead to reconstruction and acquisition relief, and "associated company" is defined by reference to control rather than being a member of the same group. Sub-para (6) confirms that the paragraph is subject to para 10.

Cases in which reconstruction or acquisition relief not withdrawn

10.—The five cases in which reconstruction or acquisition relief is not withdrawn under para 9 are as follows:

(1) where control changes as a result of a share transaction which would be an exempt transaction, if a land transaction under para 3 of Sch 3;

(2) where control changes as a result of a share transaction which would be an exempt, if a land transaction under para 4 of Sch 3;

(3) subject to para 11, where control changes as a result of a stamp duty exempt intra-group transfer of shares and "associated" companies relief under FA 1930 s 42 or FA (Northern Ireland) 1954 s 42 applies;

(4) subject to para 11, where control changes as a result of a transfer to another company to which share acquisition stamp duty relief applies under FA 1986 s 77; and

(5) where control changes as a result of a loan creditor becoming or ceasing to be treated as having control and the persons who were previously treated as having control regaining control.

Withdrawal of reconstruction or acquisition relief on subsequent non-exempt transfer

11.—The paragraph sets out anti-avoidance rules for the withdrawal of relief, when there has been no withdrawal of relief because a subsequent transfer is within the exceptions in para 10(4) or (5), and subsequent to that transfer, a corporate shareholder in the original acquiring company ceases to be grouped with under the same control as the original transferor and the original acquiring company or relevant associated company still holds the land in question. Even the Finance Bill 2003 Notes to Clauses are unclear as to what mischief this provision is aimed at, although it must be an ultimate change of control/degrouping of a company whilst holding the land.

Recovery of reconstruction or acquisition relief from another group company or controlling director

12.—This paragraph, broadly speaking, replicates para 5.

Recovery of reconstruction relief or acquisition relief: supplementary

13.—This paragraph, broadly speaking, replicates para 5.

SCHEDULE 8 STAMP DUTY LAND TAX: CHARITIES RELIEF

Charities relief

1.—A transaction is exempt where the purchaser is a charity (as defined in sub-para (4)), provided that the charity in question intends to hold the land for qualifying charitable purposes (as defined in sub-para (2)), and it is not entering into the transaction for the purpose of avoiding SDLT.

Withdrawal of charities relief

2.—Such relief may be withdrawn where a charity which has claimed relief ceases to be a charity or the land is used otherwise than for certain charitable purposes, within three years of the transaction. Similarly, relief may be withdrawn if arrangements are made within the three year period which result in the above occurring at any time. Where relief is withdrawn, the charity becomes liable for the amount that would have arisen but for the relief.

Cases where first condition not fully met

3.—This paragraph offers partial relief in cases where the land is intended partly for charitable use and partly for other purposes (so that the first condition in para 1(2) is not satisfied). Provided the purchaser intends to hold the greater part of the property for qualifying charitable purposes, the entire acquisition will initially be exempt, but there will be a partial withdrawal of the relief if *at any time* the charity disposes of all or part of the property which was not intended for qualifying purposes. There will also be a claw-back of the part intended for charitable use if a disqualifying event happens within the usual period in relation to that part.

Charitable trusts

4.—This paragraph extends the relief under Sch 8 to charitable trusts, ie to trusts or unit trust schemes all the beneficiaries or unit holders of which are charities.

SCHEDULE 9 STAMP DUTY LAND TAX: RIGHT TO BUY, SHARED OWNERSHIP LEASES ETC

Right to buy transactions

1.—This paragraph establishes that in the case of a right to buy transaction (as defined at sub-para (2)), s 51(1) provisions bringing contingent consideration into account do not apply, and also excludes consideration that may become due or becomes due. A "right to buy transaction" is defined at sub-para (2), and a list of the relevant public sector bodies for the purpose of sub-para (2) are set out at sub-para (3). Sub-para (5) excludes from chargeable consideration a grant made under the Housing Act 1996 s 20 or 21 with regard to certain transactions. This paragraph is based on the existing relief set out at FA 1981 s 107 and FA 1984 s 110 (see commentaries).

Shared ownership lease: election for market value treatment

2.—This paragraph allows the purchaser to make an irrevocable election for SDLT to be determined by reference to the market value of the dwelling, where the lease is granted by a qualifying body or under a preserved right to buy (see sub-para (5)) provided that the following conditions are satisfied:

(1) the lease must be a dwelling;

(2) the lease must give the lessee(s) exclusive use;

(3) the lease must provide for the lessee(s) to acquire the reversion;

(4) the lease must be granted partly in consideration of rent and partly in consideration of a premium calculated by reference to the market value of the dwelling or a sum calculated by reference to that value; and

(5) the lease must contain a statement of the market value of the dwelling or the sum calculated by reference to that value, by reference to which the premium is calculated.

Para 2, along with paras 3–5, are based on existing reliefs set out at FA 1980 s 97 and FA 1981 s 108 (see commentaries).

Where a market value election is made, the purchaser pays SDLT at the outset on the stated market value of the dwelling or on the sum which has been used as the basis for calculating the premium which he has paid: sub-para (4). No SDLT is charged, though, on the rent payable by the purchaser under the lease: sub-para (4A).

Transfer of reversion under shared ownership lease where election made for market value treatment

3.—By virtue of this paragraph, the transfer of the reversion to the lessee under the terms of a lease to which para 2 applies where an election was made under that paragraph, and where SDLT was also paid under that paragraph, is exempted.

Shared ownership lease: election where staircasing allowed

4.—This paragraph allows for the purchaser to make an irrevocable election for SDLT to be determined by reference to the minimum rent and the premium obtainable on the open market, where the lease is granted by a qualifying body or under the preserved right to buy, and if certain conditions are satisfied, as follows:

(a) the lease must be a dwelling;
(b) the lease must give the lessee(s) exclusive use;
(c) the lease must provide that the lessee(s) may, on payment of a sum, require the terms of the lease to be altered so that the rent payable under it is reduced;
(d) the lease must be granted partly in consideration of rent and partly in consideration of a premium calculated by reference to the premium obtainable on the open market for the grant of a lease containing the same terms as the lease but with the substitution of the minimum rent for the rent payable under the lease, or a sum calculated by reference to that value; and
(e) the lease must contain a statement of the minimum rent and of the premium obtainable on the open market, or the sum calculated by reference to that premium, by reference to which the premium is calculated.

Shared ownership lease: treatment of staircasing transaction

4A.—This paragraph makes provision for cases where, under a shared ownership lease, the lessees have the right to buy an interest in the dwelling which is in addition to that which they already hold, and on doing so, the rent under their lease is reduced. If the lessees have previously made a market value election under para 2 or 4 (see above), then the acquisition of the interest is exempt from SDLT: sub-para (2). If, on the other hand, the lessees have not made such an election, nevertheless, their acquisition of a further interest is also exempt from SDLT provided that immediately afterwards their total share in the dwelling is not in excess of 80 per cent.

4B.—This paragraph provides for the grant of shared ownership lease (see para 4A) to be treated as not being linked to a subsequent acquisition of a further interest in the building or to a transfer of the reversion to the lease to the lessee. The effect is to prevent a charge to 1% arising where the consideration for the initial interest was below £125,000 (£150,000 in a disadvantaged area) but, when added to the acquisition of a further interest would take the total consideration above the threshold. A charge will, it should be noted, eventually arise if the tenant acquires more than an 80% interest in the property.

Shared ownership leases: meaning of "qualifying body" and "preserved right to buy"

5.—This paragraph defines "qualifying body" and provides the conditions that must be met for a lease to be described as being granted "in pursuance of the preserved right to buy." Essentially, the provider must be a public body or publicly-funded in relation to the particular shared ownership scheme. Thus, a profit-making registered provider of social housing is a qualifying body if the purchase or construction of the premises or their adaption for use as a dwelling has been assisted by public subsidy under the Housing and Regeneration Act 2008. For the connected relief from SDLT for such bodies see the commentary on FA 2003 s 71.

Rent to mortgage or rent to loan: chargeable consideration

6.—This paragraph provides the rules for the determination of the chargeable consideration for a rent to mortgage or rent to loan transaction. This is based on the existing relief contained in FA 1993 ss 202 and 203.

Shared ownership trusts

7.—Paragraphs 7 to 11 extend the SDLT treatment which applies to shared ownership leases (as to which see paras 1 to 6 above) to shared ownership trusts provided by qualifying bodies. A shared ownership trust is a trust of land consisting of a dwelling in England or Wales where one of the beneficiaries is a qualifying body, the "social landlord" (as defined in para 5), and in respect of which a number of conditions is satisfied. The trust must provide for one or more of the individual beneficiaries ("the purchaser") to be entitled to have exclusive rights of occupation of the dwelling, in return for which he or they make an initial payment, and thereafter a number of additional payments, to the social landlord. These additional payments will be of two kinds: rent-equivalent payments, which are compensation for the social landlord being excluded from joint occupation of the property, and equity-acquisition payments, which are made to acquire a further interest in the property. The intention is that the initial ownership rights of the parties will be determined by the amount of the initial payment made as a proportion of the market value of the property as specified by the parties at the time and that, over time, the purchaser's ownership rights will increase and the social landlord's will diminish, as the equity-acquisition payments are made.

Paragraph 8 provides for SDLT to apply as if the purchaser and not the social landlord were the purchaser for SDLT purposes.

Shared ownership trust: election for market value treatment

9.—If the purchaser irrevocably elects for market value treatment, the chargeable consideration on which SDLT is payable is determined by reference to the market value specified by the parties for the purposes of determining the purchaser's initial beneficial interest in the property (see para 7(4)(*f*)). The purchaser is obliged to pay SDLT in accordance with this computation; but, this sum having been paid, the eventual transfer of the property on the termination of the trust (ie after the purchaser has made sufficient additional payments to buy out the social landlord) will be exempt from SDLT. In calculating the SDLT chargeable, the rent-equivalent payments are disregarded.

The election is made in the land transaction return or by an amendment to the land transaction return.

Shared ownership trust: treatment of staircasing transaction

10.—Correspondingly, if a market value election has been made under para 9, para 10 secures that no SDLT is payable as the purchaser's interest in the property increases as he makes equity-acquisition payments.

If, on the other hand, no market value election is made, a different regime applies: no SDLT is charged on increases in the purchaser's interest consequent on equity-acquisition payments unless and until the effect of the payment is to take the purchaser's share above an 80% beneficial interest in the property. Once the 80% threshhold has been breached, though, the purchaser must account for SDLT on the full amount of staircasing payments he has made (other than the initial payment which will have been brought into charge in accordance with para 11 below). Thus if a purchaser originally buys a 25% interest in the property, he will pay SDLT on this amount in accordance with para 11. If he then acquires further interests in the property, in 10% tranches, no further SDLT will be charged until he finally acquires an 85% interest in the property, at which point SDLT will be charged on the aggregate consideration

Part II ST

paid to acquire the further 60%. Further, SDLT will be payable as the purchaser acquires the next 10% and a final sum as he acquires the last 5%. Such transactions are linked transactions: see ss 108 and 55. Accordingly, if the aggregate consideration paid over the period takes the chargeable consideration above the £120,000 or £250,000 or (possibly) £500,000 threshold the SDLT paid to date will be recalculated to take account of the higher rate of duty which has now proved payable,

Shared ownership trust: treatment of additional payments where no election made

11.—Where a purchaser decides not to make a market value election, he pays SDLT on the initial capital as if it were a premium. He is also obliged to pay SDLT by reference to the rent-equivalent payments as if they were rent.

12.—This paragraph provides that the declaration of a shared ownership trust lease (see para 8) is to be treated as not being linked to any later equity-acquisition payment or any consequential increase in the purchaser's beneficial interest in the property. The effect is to prevent a charge to 1% arising where the consideration for the initial interest was below £125,000 (£150,000 in a disadvantaged area) but, when added to the acquisition of a further interest, would take the total consideration above the threshold. A charge will, it should be noted, eventually arise if the tenant acquires more than an 80% interest in the property.

Rent to shared ownership lease

13.—This paragraph is intended to provide simplified SDLT treatment in the case of a shared ownership scheme, called "Rent to HomeBuy", or, in the language of Sch 9, a "rent to shared ownership scheme", which is intended to assist individuals to purchase homes using shared ownership schemes where the qualifying body permits the tenant initially to occupy the property under an assured shorthold tenancy, to allow him to save for a deposit. The scheme itself is targeted at modest-income families where the parties are first-time buyers, public sector tenants, key workers or persons who have separated in circumstances where the individuals concerned cannot afford a deposit. The rate under the assured shorthold tenancy is set at 80% or less of market value for a term of up to five years, during which the tenant has the first option to buy at any time. On exercising the option, the tenant has to find at least 25% of the price, from his own funds or with the assistance of a mortgage.

The paragraph affords two relaxations from the usual SDLT rules. First, in determing the chargeable consideration for SDLT purposes (ie the assured shorthold tenancy and the shared ownership lease) the two leases are treated as if they were neither linked with each other nor with any other land transaction entered into as part of the scheme (eg where, after the first five years tenancy, the landlord has been willing to grant a further tenancy since the tenant still had insufficient funds to meet the requirement to buy a minimum 25% of the value of the property). Secondly, the assured shorthold tenancy is disregarded when determining the effective date of the grant of the shared ownership lease. The effect of the relaxations is to displace the usual SDLT rule, in FA 2003 Sch 17A para 5, which treats such successive leases as a single lease granted at the time of the first lease, for the consideration payable under the aggregate of the leases.

Rent to shared ownership trust: charge to tax

14.—A relief corresponding to that described in para 13 above is afforded in a case where the Rent to Homebuy scheme involves the grant of an assured shorthold tenancy followed by the declaration of a shared ownership trust over the property. For shared ownership trusts see the commentary to para 7 above. In such a case, the paragraph removes the link for SDLT purposes between the grant of the assured shorthold tenancy, the declaration of the shared ownership trust and any other land transaction that forms part of the scheme, and determines the effective date of the grant of the declaration of trust without regard to the prior tenancy (or tenancies). The effect is to displace the linking rules in FA 2003 Sch 17A para 5, which ordinarily would treat such successive transactions as a single lease, granted at the time of the first lease, for the consideration payable under the aggregate of the leases.

First-time buyers

15.—Although the paragraph is less than clearly drafted, its intention is to restrict the availability of first-time buyer relief under ss 57AA and 73CA, in cases falling within Sch 9, to those transactions where the buyer makes a market value election under the relevant paragraph. So, if a buyer makes a market value election in a case where the market value of the property is more than £125,000 but not more than £250,000, first-time buyer relief will be given. If, on the other hand, the purchaser does not make the appropriate election, the relief is not afforded.

SCHEDULE 10 STAMP DUTY LAND TAX: RETURNS, ENQUIRIES, ASSESSMENTS AND APPEALS

PART 1 LAND TRANSACTION RETURNS

Contents of return

1.—This paragraph confirms that a return must be in the form and contain the information prescribed by HMRC regulations and include a declaration by the purchaser (or each of them) that the return is to the best of his knowledge correct and complete. Regulations made by virtue of this paragraph may require the provision of information corresponding to any of the particulars formerly required under Sch 2 of FA 1931 (on the Particulars Delivered Form), or in the case of Northern Ireland, FA 1994 s 244 (see commentary). Provision has been made for the electronic delivery of land transaction returns by the Stamp Duty Land Tax (Electronic Communications) Regulations 2005 (SI 2005/844). The Commissioners have made directions under these Regulations by Notice issued on 13 July 2005, see Appendix 8.

Meaning of filing date and delivery of return

2.—"Filing date" means the last day of the period within which the return must be delivered. The return is deemed delivered when it complies with para (1).

Failure to deliver return: flat-rate penalty

3.—A flat rate penalty is introduced at para 3 where a person fails to deliver a return by the filing date. The penalty is £100 if it is delivered within three months after the filing date, and £200 in any other case. This is based on FA 1998 Sch 18 para 17(1) and (2), and the income tax equivalent set out at TMA 1970 s 93(2), (3). Although the penalty is on its face absolute, it must be read in the context of Finance Act 2003 s 97(2) which deems a person not to have failed to do something required to be done in a limited time if he had a reasonable excuse for not doing it; and provided that he does it without unreasonable depay after the excuse ceases. As to what may or may not constitute a reasonable excuse see *Runham and Naramore v HMRC* (TC 933): land transaction return lost in post when sent in time, loss discovered when Land Registry search made. Held (rejecting view of Commissioners in SDLT Manual 86460 that delay in post does not amount to reasonable excuse) that since the land transaction return was dispatched in time to be received by the Commissioners before the expiry of the 30-day period, there was indeed a reasonable excuse and further that the taxpayer had acted without unreasonable delay once excuse ceased. Cf. *Manor House Surgery v HMRC* (TC 1101): taxpayer's solicitors' computer system in error, causing failure of electronic delivery; prompt action taken once non-receipt of land transaction return discovered by agent. Held, the agents should have checked that the online certificate had immediately been issued and their failure to do so prevented the computer failure constituting a reasonable excuse. However in *Browne v HMRC* (TC 754) the Tribunal held that the taxpayer had reasonably relied on her solicitors to file the return and gave her a reasonable excuse for failing to comply with paragraph 3. The Solicitors' failure to perform their duty was not to be attributed to her. See also *Periclous v HMRC* (TC 930) and *Pariser v HMRC* (TC 725)

Failure to deliver return: tax-related penalty

4.—This paragraph provides for a tax-related penalty (not exceeding the amount of tax chargeable on the transaction), in addition to the flat-rate penalty, where a person who is

Part II ST

required to deliver a return in respect of a chargeable transaction fails to do so within 12 months of the filing date. For the availability of a defence of reasonable excuse see section 97 and the commentary to paragraph 3 above.

Formal notice to deliver return: daily penalty

5.—HMRC may, by virtue of this paragraph, make a request by notice to a person to deliver a return within a given time (not less than 30 days). If the return is still not delivered, HMRC may apply to the Commissioners for the award of a daily penalty of up to £60 per day (based on TMA 1970 s 93(3)). For the availability of a defence of reasonable excuse see section 97 and the commentary to paragraph 3 above.

Amendment of return by purchaser

6.—Purchasers may amend their returns by notice to HMRC within 12 months of the filing date. Relief for overpayments may be claimed by virtue of para 34 (see below).

Correction of return by Revenue

7.—Under this paragraph, HMRC may amend a land transaction return within nine months from the date it is delivered so as to correct obvious errors or omissions (eg errors of principle and arithmetical mistakes). The purchaser may amend the return so as to reject the correction, within three months of the date of issue of the notice of correction. This paragraph is based on FA 1998 Sch 18 para 16. On the introduction of e-conveyancing, provision is to be made for this power to be exercised (in specified circumstances) by the Chief Land Registrar.

PART 2 DUTY TO KEEP AND PRESERVE RECORDS

Duty to keep and preserve records

9.—This deals with the duty of the purchaser to keep and preserve records (including all relevant instruments and financial records relating to a transaction), for the longer of six years from the effective date of the transaction, the end of any enquiry, or the end of the enquiry window.

Preservation of information instead of original records

10.—The duty established at para 9 may be satisfied by the preservation of information contained therein in an alternative form (eg microfiche or electronic facsimile). It also provides that such records may be admissible as evidence before an appeal tribunal.

Penalty for failure to keep and preserve records

11.—Anyone who fails to comply with para 9 is liable to a penalty not exceeding £3,000 subject to the exception set out at sub-para (2), namely that no penalty is incurred if HMRC is satisfied that any facts that they reasonably require to be proved, and that would have been by the records, are proved by other documentary evidence provided to them.

PART 3 ENQUIRY INTO RETURN

Notice of enquiry

12.—This paragraph empowers HMRC to make enquiries into returns, if they give "notice of enquiry" to the purchaser of their intention to do so before the end of the enquiry period. See *Coolatinney Developments Ltd and others v HMRC* (TC 1116): there is no requirement to provide a single document to a taxpayer which may be identified as the notice: it suffices for the taxpayer to be provided with a number of documents from which the notification of the intention to open an enquiry may be discerned.

Scope of enquiry

13.—An enquiry extends to anything contained in the return relating to the question of whether tax is chargeable in respect of the transaction, or to the amount of tax so chargeable.

In cases where an enquiry is made into an amended return after the enquiry period is closed, the enquiries are limited to matters which are amended or affected by the amendment. This is based on FA 1998 Sch 18 para 25, and the equivalent provision for income tax at TMA 1970 s 9(4), (5).

Notice to produce documents etc for purposes of enquiry

14.—This paragraph permits HMRC to issue a notice to produce such documents in his possession or power and such information as they may reasonably require for the purposes of the enquiry. This is based on FA 1998 Sch 18 para 27, and the equivalent provision for income tax at TMA 1970 s 19A.

Appeal against notice to produce documents etc

15.—The purchaser may appeal against a requirement imposed by notice under para 14 to produce documents or information. Notice of appeal must be given in writing, within 30 days after the issue of the notice appealed against, to the officer of the Board by whom the notice was given. The appeal is heard and determined in the same way as an appeal against an assessment. The decision of the Commissioners on an appeal under this paragraph is final. This paragraph is based on FA 1998 Sch 18 para 28, and the equivalent provision for income tax at TMA 1970 s 19A(6).

Penalty for failure to produce documents etc

16.—This paragraph imposes a penalty of £50 for the failure to produce documents required by a notice under para 14. If the failure continues after a penalty is imposed, then further penalties can be determined by HMRC of up to £30 per day and up to £150 if the penalty is determined by the court. This is based on FA 1998 Sch 18 para 29, and the equivalent provision for income tax at TMA 1970 s 97AA.

Amendment of self-assessment during enquiry to prevent loss of tax

17.—This paragraph allows for the amendment of the return by HMRC during the course of enquiry to make good the deficiency and thereby prevent loss of tax. This is based on FA 1998 Sch 18 para 30, and the equivalent provision for income tax at TMA 1970 s 97C.

Amendment of return by taxpayer during enquiry

18.—This paragraph allows the taxpayer to amend his return during the course of an enquiry. This is based on FA 1998 Sch 18 para 17, and the equivalent provision for income tax at TMA 1970 s 97B.

Referral of questions to the tribunal during enquiry

19.—By virtue of this paragraph, HMRC or the person who made the return may refer any question arising in connection with the subject-matter of the enquiry to the First-tier Tribunal (or the Upper Tribunal, as the case may be, in accordance with the Tribunal Procedure Rules) for their determination. This is based on FA 1998 Sch 18 para 31A, and the equivalent provision for income tax at TMA 1970 s 28ZA.

Withdrawal of notice of referral

20.—Under this paragraph, a notice of referral by HMRC or the person who made the return may be withdrawn. Notice of withdrawal must be given in writing to the other party to the referral and to the tribunal before the first hearing by the tribunal in relation to the referral. This is based on FA 1998 Sch 18 para 31B, and the equivalent provision for income tax at TMA 1970 s 28ZB.

Effect of referral on enquiry

21.—This paragraph provides that while proceedings on a referral under para 19 are in progess, no closure notice shall be given in relation to the enquiry and no application may be made for a direction to give such a notice. This is based on FA 1998 Sch 18 para 31C, and the equivalent provision for income tax at TMA 1970 s 28ZD.

Effect of determination

22.—This paragraph confirms that the determination of any question by the tribunal under para 20 is binding on the parties to the same extent as a decision on a preliminary issue in an appeal. This is based on FA 1998 Sch 18 para 31D, and the equivalent provision for income tax at TMA 1970 s 28ZE.

Completion of enquiry

23.—This paragraph provides that an enquiry under para 12 is completed when HMRC informs the purchaser, by means of a "closure notice", that they have completed their enquiries and state their conclusions. This is based on FA 1998 Sch 18 para 32, and the equivalent provision for income tax at TMA 1970 s 28A(1), (3).

Direction to complete enquiry

24.—The purchaser may apply to the tribunal for a direction that HMRC give a closure notice within a specified time. This is based on FA 1998 Sch 18 para 36, and the equivalent provision for income tax at TMA 1970 s 28A(4)–(6).

PART 4 REVENUE DETERMINATION IF NO RETURN DELIVERED

Determination of tax chargeable if no return delivered

25.—Under this paragraph, where no return is delivered by the filing date, HMRC may determine to the best of their information and belief the amount of SDLT chargeable. No determination may be made more than six years after the effective date of the transaction. This is based on FA 1998 Sch 18 para 36, and the equivalent provision for income tax at TMA 1970 s 28C(1), (2) and (5).

Determination to have effect as a self-assessment

26.—A determination under para 25 has effect for enforcement purposes as if it were a self-assessment by the purchaser. This is based on FA 1998 Sch 18 para 39, and the equivalent provision for income tax at TMA 1970 s 28C(3).

Determination superseded by actual self-assessment

27.—Subject to time limits, a self-assessment made by the purchaser after a determination under para 26 supersedes the determination. This is based on FA 1998 Sch 18 para 40, and the equivalent provision for income tax at TMA 1970 s 28C(4), (5).

PART 5 REVENUE ASSESSMENTS

Assessment where loss of tax discovered

28.—This paragraph provides that where information becomes available to HMRC that an amount of tax has not been assessed that ought to have been, an assessment is insufficient, or relief has been given that is excessive, they may make a "discovery assessment". Notably, this can take place after the nine-month time limit for an enquiry has ended (but subject to the restrictions set out at para 30).

Assessment to recover excessive repayment of tax

29.—Where an excessive repayment to a person has taken place, HMRC is permitted under this paragraph to assess the amount in question, and recover as if it were unpaid tax, if necessary. This procedure is subject to the time limits set out at para 31. The paragraph is based on TMA 1970 s 30, and a similar provision with regard to corporation tax at FA 1998 Sch 18 para 52.

Restrictions on assessment where return delivered

30.—This paragraph provides details of the circumstances in which a discovery assessment by HMRC can be made where a purchaser has delivered a return in respect of a transaction. The circumstances are as follows:

(1) where the situation set out at paras 28 or 29 is attributable to fraudulent or negligent conduct on the part of the purchaser, a person acting on behalf of the purchaser or a person who was a partner of the purchaser at the relevant time; and

(2) where HMRC, at the time they ceased to be entitled to give notice of enquiry into the return, or completed their enquiries into the return, could not have been reasonably expected, on the basis of information previously made available to them, to be aware of the situation mentioned in paras 28 or 29.

No assessment may be made if the situation mentioned in paras 28 or 29 is attributable to a computational error in the return and the error was in accordance with general practice at the time.

Time limit for assessment

31.—The general rule as to time limits, as set out in this section, is that no assessment may be made more than six years after the effective date, but in cases of fraud or negligence this is extended to 21 years. Where the purchaser has died, assessments must be made within three years of the date of death and can only cover transactions within the six months prior to death. This is based on FA 1998 Sch 18 para 42, and the equivalent provision for income tax at TMA 1970 s 29(4)–(6).

Assessment procedure

32.—Notice of an assessment must be served on the purchaser and state the tax due, the date on which the notice is issued, and the time within which any appeal against the assessment must be made. This is based on FA 1998 Sch 18 para 47, and the equivalent provision for income tax at TMA 1970 s 30A(3), (4).

PART 6 RELIEF IN CASE OF EXCESSIVE ASSESSMENT

Relief in case of double assessment

33.—This paragraph provides that a purchaser who believes that he has been assessed more than once in respect of the same transaction may claim relief against the double charge. For the procedure for making the claim, see s 80(4) and Sch 11A.

Claim for relief for overpaid tax etc

34.—As from 1 April 2011 changes have been made to the circumstances in which a taxpayer who considers that he has overpaid SDLT may recover that tax from the Commissioners. The general rule is that a taxpayer may amend his self-assessment under his land transaction return within a year of its submission: Schedule 10 paragraph 6. Where this procedure may be adopted, the restrictions in paragraph 34 and the successive paragraphs will not apply. In claims made outside that period, the ability to recover the tax is restricted in seven particular cases.

Subject to those, a taxpayer may make a claim either where he has overpaid tax or where he has been over-assessed to SDLT. In the former case his claim is for the repayment of the tax; in the latter, for the liability to pay tax to be discharged. "Tax" for these purposes includes any sum paid or agreed to be paid under a contract settlement: paragraph 34D.

The new rules were introduced following the decision of the House of Lords in *Deutsche Morgan Grenfell v IRC* [2007] STC 1, which confirmed that a taxpayer could make a common law claim for restitution of tax paid under a mistake of law. Sub-paragraph (6) appears to be designed to preclude such a claim, by relieving the Commissioners from the liability to give relief save under the provisions of Finance Act 2003.

34A.—The cases in which the Commissioners are not liable to give effect to a paragraph 34 claim are:

(a) where the overpayment or over-assessment is attributable to a mistake concerning a claim or election;

(b) where it is possible to take other steps under the SDLT legislation to remedy the overpayment or over-assessment;

(c) where the claimant could have taken other steps under the SDLT legislation when they first knew, or ought reasonably to have known, of the overpayment or over-assessment;

(d) where the grounds of the claim have already been put to the Tribunal or HMRC by the claimant in the course of an appeal;

(e) where the claimant knew or ought reasonably to have known the grounds of the claim at a time when those grounds could have been put forward on an appeal;

(f) where the amount was paid or is liable to be paid following proceedings to enforce payment; and

(g) where the amount was calculated in accordance with the practice generally prevailing at that time.

Thus if a taxpayer becomes aware of the excessive amount of SDLT during the year following the filing date but he fails to amend his return in accordance with Schedule 10 paragraph 6, it is not open to him to make a paragraph 34 claim instead. This would appear to be extremely harsh in a case where the discovery is made just before the amendment period expires; but it is to be hoped that in such a case the Commissioners will exercise their discretion and afford relief. Paragraph 34A merely provides that in the specified circumstances the Commissioners are not liable to give effect to the claim: it does not prevent them doing so.

34B.—A claim must be made within four years of the effective date of the relevant land transaction (not the date of filing). The taxpayer may not use a land transaction return to make the claim: instead the claim is made in accordance with the rules set out in Schedule 11A Finance Act 2003, (the "process now, check later" system used for other SDLT claims) by which payment will be made on receipt of the claim and the claim will become final unless an enquiry is raised within the enquiry window. Schedule 11A also makes provision for the Commissioners to make enquiry and for the claimant to have a right of appeal in the event that the Commissioners amend his claim after enquiry.

34C.—This paragraph sets out the procedure where a claim is made in a case where land was acquired by a partnership. The partnership is required to nominate the person to make the claim on behalf of the partners; and that person must either have been a partner at the time of the relevant land transaction or must be the personal representative of such a partner.

34D.—Where a claim is made under paragraph 34A, the Commissioners are afforded a corresponding right (in appropriate circumstances) to make a discovery assessment on the claimant. They may do so only where the grounds for making the claim also provide grounds for making a discovery assessment. The effect is to permit the Commissioners to make an assessment where one would otherwise have been unavailable either because of the time limits for making a discovery assessment (under paragraph 31 of Schedule 10) or because of the restrictions imposed by paragraph 30 of Schedule 10.

34E.—This paragraph makes appropriate adjustments to the operation of the paragraph 34 process where the claim is for the repayment of a sum paid under a contract settlement. Specific provision is made for the Commissioners to be able to set-off other sums due against the claimed amount and to discharge their obligation to repay by means of such a set-off.

PART 7 REVIEWS AND APPEALS

Right of appeal

35.—An appeal may be brought against the following:

(1) amendments of self-assessment to prevent loss of tax (see para 17);

(2) a conclusion stated or amendment made by a closure notice;

(3) a discovery assessment;
(4) an assessment under para 29 to recover excessive repayment; and
(5) a Revenue determination of the tax under para 25 where no return has been delivered.

This paragraph is based on TMA 1970 s 31(1) and (2).

Notice of appeal

36.—This paragraph confirms that a notice of appeal under para 35 must be given in writing, specifying the grounds of appeal (subject to the sub-para (6) relaxation), within 30 days after the "specified date" to the "relevant officer of the Board" (both terms are defined at sub-paras (2) to (4) in respect of the various different types of appeal). This paragraph is based on TMA 1970 s 31A.

Appeal: HMRC review or determination by tribunal

36A.—In line with the procedure adopted under the new tribunal rules, if notice of appeal is given to the Commissioners, the appellant may notify the Commissioners that he requires them to review the matter under appeal, or the Commissioners may notify the appellant of their offer to review it. Alternatively, the appeal may proceed direct to the tribunal. The review procedure is a potentially important stage in proceedings, since it reflects the philosophy that the parties should be encouraged to resolve their differences, if at all possible, outside of the confines of the tribunal. In order to fit this review procedure into the new framework, the legislation now contemplates two separate notifications of an appeal: the first, the *notice* of appeal, is given to HMRC by the taxpayer under para 36; the second, the *notification* of the appeal, is given to the tribunal under para 36D. The review procedure, if it is to take place, occurs between those two events.

Appellant requires review by HMRC

36B.—In the event that the Appellant requires a review, the Commissioners are obliged to review the matter. However, as a preliminary element of the review process HMRC are required to notify the Appellant of their "view of the matter" (a phrase which recurs throughout this part of Sch 10) within 30 days of the receipt of the notice requiring the review to be undertaken. The time limit of 30 days is not, in fact, absolute. The legislation specifies 30 days "or such longer period as is reasonable", which clearly will depend on the complexity of the case and (perhaps) how much work has been done on the case before the assessment was raised.

Paragraph 37E prescribes the manner in which the review is to be carried out.

If, though, the appellant notifies the tribunal of the appeal in accordance with para 36D, this terminates the review procedure; it is no longer open to the appellant to require a review nor to the Commissioners to offer one; and if the appellant begins by requiring a review but then notifies the tribunal of the appeal, HMRC's obligation to complete the review process falls away.

HMRC offer review

36C.—If HMRC offer a review, the procedure starts with the Commissioners notifying the appellant both of their offer to review the matter and of their "view of the matter". This is likely to be of greater value in the case of a discovery assessment or where there has been an amendment of a self-assessment in order to prevent loss of tax, since if the appeal comes at the end of an enquiry into the appellant's land transaction return, one would anticipate that matters would have been ventilated at some length over a considerable period. But in every case it is important for the appellant to know at the outset what the Commissioners' views are as, although the expectation is that the review will be carried out by a different officer from the one whose decision or assessment has been appealed, the process is best served if the appellant able to make considered representations as to why the Commissioners' views are wrong. In addition, and significantly, the appellant's notification of the Commissioners' view of the matter determines the provision which applies when notifying the tribunal of the appeal (as to which see paras 36G, 36H and 37).

Once the offer to review has been made, the appellant can either accept the offer – in which case he must notify HMRC of his acceptance within 30 days of the date of the offer letter – or he must proceed to notify the tribunal of the appeal in accordance with para 37H (rather than, it should be noted, in accordance with para 36D).

The importance attached to the review process is emphasised by sub-paras (4) and (5); if the HMRC offers to review the matter and the appellant does not accept the offer within the specified period the Commissioners' view is taken to be contained in a binding agreement between the parties that the original decision should be upheld without variation. Since this will necessarily occur on the termination of the acceptance period (see above) the appellant will require the tribunal's permission in order to notify (and thus continue) his appeal.

Notifying appeal to the tribunal

36D.—This paragraph applies where the review process has not proceeded to the stage of the Commissioners giving the appellant their view of the matter, either because the appellant notifies the tribunal before requiring or being offered a review, or because, having required a review, he changes his mind and notifies the tribunal before the Commissioners have taken the preliminary step in the process. In such a case there are no restrictions on the appellant notifying the tribunal of the appeal. By contrast, if the Commissioners have given their view of the matter, the appellant's rights of appeal are somewhat more circumscribed (see paras 36G and 36H).

Nature of review

36E.—Once the appellant has committed himself to the review process, either by requiring or by accepting an offer of a review, the nature and extent of the review are left at the discretion of the Commissioners themselves (sub-para (2)). The para does require that in determining what is appropriate the Commissioners must have regard to the steps taken before the beginning of the review both by HMRC themselves in deciding the matter in issue and by anyone else in seeking to resolve the disagreement over that matter. Presumably this means that if there has been an exhaustive dialogue between the parties as to the legal and factual aspects of the disputed matter, there is little need for the Commissioners to do much more than to submit the issue to a different officer for reconsideration. By contrast, if the assessment or the amendment to the appellant's self-assessment was undertaken with haste, it would be appropriate for the review to be conducted at greater length. In any case the reviewing officer is obliged to take account of representations made by the appellant – provided that the Commissioners "have a reasonable opportunity to consider them" (sub-para (4)). The circumstances in which HMRC might not have such a reasonable opportunity are, it is assumed, where the appellant both fails to offer any assistance until the statutory period of 45 days is almost exhausted before submitting his representations and refuses to agree an extension of the period for review. Other cases will ordinarily be resolved by the amicable agreement of the parties to take advantage of the liberty given to them by sub-para 6(*b*) to extend to the period within which the Commissioners must notify the appellant of the outcome of the review.

The Commissioners have, as a general rule, 45 days within which to notify the appellant of the outcome of the review and their reasoning. This time limit may be extended by agreement. More importantly, time only starts running from the "relevant day". In the case where the review was required by the appellant under para 36B, the relevant day is the day when HMRC notified the appellant of their view of the matter; and under para 36B the Commissioners have 30 days from receiving notification that the Appellant requires a review before they are obliged to provide him with that view. In the case where HMRC offered the appellant the review (and where they were therefore obliged to give him their view at the same time as they offered the review), time runs from the date on which they received notification of the appellant's acceptance of the offer.

The possible outcomes of a review are indicated by sub-para (5); it may conclude that HMRC's view of the matter is upheld, varied or cancelled. Depending on whether the outcome is favourable to the appellant or not, the notification will lead either to the appellant pressing on with his appeal (as to which see para 36G) or to the settlement of the appeal in accordance with the procedure set out in para 37.

Provision is made for the case where the Commissioners fail to notify the appellant of the conclusions of the review within the prescribed period (sub-para (8)); the review is assumed to have upheld HMRC's view of the matter. In such a case sub-para (9) requires the Commissioners to notify the appellant of the conclusions which the review is treated as having reached. Oddly, no time limit is prescribed within which the Commissioners must serve the appellant with this notification.

Effect of conclusions of review

36F.—If the Commissioners give notice of the conclusions of the review, those conclusions are deemed to be an agreement in writing made under para 37 for the settlement of the appeal. The appellant cannot resile from that deemed agreement save by notifying the tribunal of the appeal in accordance with para 36G.

Notifying appeal to tribunal after review completed

36G.—As will have been seen in the commentary to para 36E, the review can be concluded either by the Commissioners complying with their statutory obligation to notify the appellant of their conclusions within the prescribed period (para 36E(6)); or by their failing to do so – in which latter case they are still obliged to serve him with a notification of what their conclusions are deemed to be (para 36E(9)). In either case the appellant is permitted to move the appeal process to the tribunal by notifying the tribunal of the appeal. The period within which the appellant may notify his appeal is called the 'post-review period' and differs according to whether or not the Commissioners satisfied para 36E(6). If they did so, the appellant has 30 days from the date of the notice of their conclusions – not, it will be observed, from the date on which that notice was received by the appellant. If they did not, the post-review period begins on the day after that on which the notification period under para 36E(6) expired (ie 45 days after the beginning of the relevant period for para 36E) and ending 30 days after the date of the document in which the Commissioners gave the appellant notice of the conclusions which the review is deemed to have reached under para 36E(9).

Provided that the appellant notifies the tribunal of the appeal within the post-review period, the tribunal is required to determine the matter in issue (sub-para (3)).

Notifying appeal to tribunal after review offered but not accepted

36H.—In a case where the Commissioners have offered to review the matter in question under para 36C and that offer has not been accepted, the appellant has until the end of the acceptance period in which to notify the tribunal of his appeal (sub-para (2)). That is to say, he must notify the tribunal within 30 days of the date of the document which offered the review (para 36C(8)). If he fails to do so, he must seek permission from the Tribunal for late notification: sub-para (3).

Provided that the appellant notifies the tribunal of the appeal within the post-review period, the tribunal is required to determine the matter in issue (sub-para (4)).

Settling of appeals by agreement

37.—This paragraph permits appeals to be settled by agreement between the appellant and HMRC. It also confirms that such agreements shall have the same force as determinations of appeals by the tribunal. Under sub-para (2), the appellant may give notice in writing to HMRC that he wishes to withdraw from the agreement. Sub-paragraph (3) provides that where the agreement is not in writing, it must be confirmed by notice in writing given by HMRC to the appellant or by the appellant to HMRC. If the appellant notifies HMRC by notice in writing that he wishes to withdraw from the appeal, the decision under appeal is treated as upheld without appeal unless HMRC object within 30 days. Finally, sub-para (5) confirms that the agreement is still binding where it is entered into by a person acting on behalf of the appellant. The paragraph's scope and importance is increased following the introduction of the new review procedure, explained in the commentary to paras 36A to 36H above. In future, if the appellant has required or has been offered a review and the Commissioners have notified him of their view of the matter, his failure fully to participate in the review process will lead to the automatic operation of para 37. In that case, the Commissioners' view of the matter will be treated as if it were contained in the relevant para 37 agreement – with one distinction, namely, that the appellant will not be able to rely on para 37(2) in order to extricate himself from the agreement. In such a case, the appellant must seek to notify his appeal if permitted to do so either para 36G or para 36H, as the case may be.

Recovery of tax not postponed by appeal

38.—This paragraph clarifies that where there is an appeal under para 35, the tax charged by the amendment or assessment in question remains due and payable as if there had been no appeal, subject to para 39 and 40 (see below). The paragraph is based on TMA 1970 s 55(2).

Direction by the tribunal to postpone payment

39.—The appellant is permitted to apply in writing to the Commissioners for a determination that the payment of some or all of the SDLT charged should be postponed pending the determination of the appeal. The notice must be given to the relevant officer of the Board within 30 days after the specified date (unless there is a "change of circumstances" in accordance with sub-para (3)), stating the amount by which the appellant believes himself to be overcharged to tax, together with the grounds for that belief. If the parties cannot agree the amount to be postponed, the appellant is entitled to refer the application to the tribunal within 30 days' of HMRC's decision on the point. Sub-paragraph (5) confirms that an application under this paragraph is heard in the same way as an appeal. The Commissioners (and, if necessary, the tribunal) decide, on the basis of any representations made and evidence adduced, what the reasonable amount to be postponed is. In situations where extra tax is due following such a determination, it is deemed to be due as if it were an assessment on the date of the final determination. Sub-paragraph (8) provides for when tax is due and payable on the determination of the appeal.

Agreement to postpone payment of tax

40.—This paragraph allows applications postponing tax to be settled by agreement between the appellant and the relevant officer of the Board. Any agreement has the same force as if the tribunal had made a direction to the same effect. Sub-paragraph (2) provides that where the agreement is not in writing, it must be confirmed by notice in writing given by HMRC to the appellant or by the appellant to HMRC. Finally, sub-para (3) confirms that the agreement is still binding where it is entered into by a person acting on behalf of the appellant. The paragraph is based on TMA 1970 s 55(3)–(6), (9).

Tribunal determinations

41.—This provision simply affirms the obvious: that the determination of a tribunal in relation to any proceedings relating to SDLT are to be final and conclusive except as is otherwise provided by the relevant provisions of the Tribunals, Courts and Enforcement Act 2007, the Taxes Management Act 1970 and the enactment relating to SDLT. Of these, that with most relevance is the 2007 Act, which makes provision for the new unified tribunal system and which, in ss 9–14 replaces the traditional system of appeals, by which there was an automatic right of appeal from the General or Special Commissioners to the High Court, and thence (with permission) to the Court of Appeal and thence (with leave) to the House of Lords. There is no longer any automatic right of appeal beyond the First-tier Tribunal. If a party is dissatisfied with the decision of the First-tier Tribunal, then permission to appeal to the Upper Tribunal may be sought from the First-tier Tribunal or, if that is refused, from the Upper Tribunal. From the Upper Tribunal (whether sitting as the fact-finding court or on appeal from the First-tier Tribunal) the appeal lies (with the permission of the higher court) direct to the Court of Appeal, and thence, as previously, to the House of Lords (with leave). In future (save for cases heard by the Administrative Court and some historic relics of stamp duty appeals) tax cases will no longer be heard in the High Court. The reader is referred to the relevant section of the Yellow Tax Guide for further information about the new tribunal system.

Assessments and self-assessments

42.—This paragraph sets out the effect of a final and conclusive determination of the tribunal. If the tribunal decides that Appellant has been over-charged either by a self-assessment or by an assessment then the assessment is reduced accordingly; otherwise the assessment stands good (sub-para (2)). This reflects the fact that the burden of proving that an assessment overcharges lies on the appellant; if he fails to discharge that burden, the assessment remains good. By contrast, para 42(3) provides that if it appears to the tribunal that the appellant has been undercharged either by an assessment or by a self-assessment, the assessment is to be increased accordingly,

Payment of SDLT where there is a further appeal

43.—Historically, one way of avoiding paying the tax due was to continue with one's appeal, regardless of its merits: if tax had been postponed at the outset, there was nothing in the legislation that made it payable because the Special Commissioners had found against one. That is no longer the case. If either party to an appeal wishes to pursue the matter further, the SDLT found payable (or repayable) by the tribunal must be paid or repaid in accordance with the tribunal's determination. Then again, on appeal if the Upper Tribunal or the Court of Appeal finds that an excessive amount had been assessed and paid by the purchaser sub-para (2) requires that tax to be refunded with such interest as may be allowed by the Tribunal or the Court.

Provision is also made for the case where too little SDLT had been charged: the sum under-charged is payable within 30 days of HMRC serving the appellant with a notice of the sum due (sub-para (3)).

Late notice of appeal

44.—If the appellant has given a notice of appeal to HMRC but fails to notify the appeal to the tribunal within the time limits laid down, in particular in paras 36D, 36G and 36H, late notice of appeal may be served, either with the consent of the Commissioners or, where HMRC do not agree, with the permssion of the tribunal.

A specific framework of rules is laid down by para 44(3) and (4) which, if satisfied, direct HMRC to agree to late notice being given. There are three conditions all of which must be satisfied if HMRC must agree:

(a) The appellant serves a request in writing on the Commissioners to agree late service.
(b) HMRC are satisfied that there was a reasonable excuse for not giving the notice of appeal within time.
(c) HMRC are satisfied that request was made without unreasonable delay after the reasonable excuse ceased.

The tribunal has power itself to give permission (see sub-para (2)(*b*)), and this is reflected more generally in rule 5(3)(*a*) of the Tribunal Procedure (First-tier) (Tax Chamber) Rules 2009 (as to which see the Yellow Tax Guide). If the appellant wishes to seek an extension of time in which to notify the tribunal of its appeal, rule 20(4)(*a*) of those Rules directs that the notification of appeal is to include a request for an extension of time and the reason why the notice of appeal was not provided in time. If the tribunal refuses to extend time under rule 5(3)(*a*), it cannot entertain the appeal.

Questions to be determined by the relevant tribunal

45.—Paragraph 45 makes provision for the specialist issue of the market value of land to be determined not by the First-tier Tribunal but by the Upper Tribunal. The reason for this is that the Upper Tribunal has a Lands Chambers to which the work will be allocated and which fulfils the function of the old Lands Tribunal. Corresponding provision is made for the relevant adjudication to be made, in the case of land in Scotland or Northern Ireland, by the appropriate Lands Tribunal.

SCHEDULE 11 STAMP DUTY LAND TAX: RECORD-KEEPING WHERE TRANSACTION IS NOT NOTIFIABLE

PART 2 DUTY TO KEEP AND PRESERVE RECORDS

Duty to keep and preserve records

4.—This paragraph provides a duty to keep and preserve records where a transaction is not notifiable, to enable him to demonstrate that the transaction is not notifiable.

Preservation of information instead of original records

5.—This paragraph provides that the above duty may be satisfied by the preservation of the information kept in them, which mirrors the duty introduced by para 11 of Sch 10.

Penalty for failure to keep and preserve records

6.—By virtue of this paragraph, a person who fails to comply with para 4 is liable to a penalty not exceeding £3,000, which mirrors the para 12 of Sch 10 provisions.

SCHEDULE 11A STAMP DUTY LAND TAX: CLAIMS NOT INCLUDED IN RETURN

Introductory

1.—This Schedule makes provision for the administrative rules which apply in the case of claims under the SDLT legislation—other than those which must be made in (or by way of amendment to) a land transaction return.

Making of claims

2.—This paragraph confirms that a claim must be in the form required by HMRC and include a declaration by the claimant that the particulars of the claim are to the best of his information and belief correct. Of particular importance is the requirement that the claimant must hold documentary evidence that the SDLT has been paid before a claim for repayment may be made: sub-para (4).

Duty to keep and preserve records

3.—This deals with the duty of the claimant to keep and preserve such records as are needed to enable him to make a complete and correct claim for the longer of 12 months after the day the claim was made, the end of any enquiry or (where a claim is amended without an enquiry) the end of the enquiry window: sub-paras (1), (2). The duty may be satisfied by the preservation of information contained therein in an alternative form (eg microfiche or electronic facsimile): sub-para (3). It is also provided (sub-para (4)) that such records may be admissible as evidence before an appeal tribunal. Failure to comply with the requirements of the paragraph may be visited by a fine of £3,000: sub-para (5), though it is a defence that the facts in question may by proved by other documentary evidence (sub-para (6)).

Amendment of claim by claimant

4.—The claimant is permitted to amend his claim within 12 months of its making, save that no amendment may be made once HMRC has given notice of an enquiry, until the enquiry window has closed.

Correction of claim by Revenue

5.—Under this paragraph, HMRC may amend a claim within nine months from the date it is made so as to correct obvious errors or omissions (eg errors of principle and arithmetical mistakes). The claimant may give notice of his rejection of the correction within three months of the date of issue of the notice of correction.

Giving effect to claims and amendments

6.—HMRC has a duty to give effect to a claim (or amendment) by discharge or repayment of tax as soon as practicable after the claim has been made (or amended). This duty is suspended during an enquiry, reviving once a closure notice has been given. However, even during an enquiry it is open to HMRC to give effect to the claim on a provisional basis.

Notice of enquiry

7.—This paragraph empowers HMRC to make enquiries into returns, if they give "notice of enquiry" to the purchaser of their intention to do so before the end of the period of nine months after the making of the claim (or amendment).

Notice to produce documents etc for purposes of enquiry

8.—This paragraph permits HMRC to issue a notice in writing to produce such documents as are in the claimant's possession or power and such information as they may reasonably require for the purposes of the enquiry. The claimant must be given a minimum of 30 days in which to produce the documents; and is permitted to produce copies rather than originals. HMRC is then permitted to take copies of the documents produced.

It is a defence to a notice under this paragraph that the documents or information in question relate to the conduct of a pending appeal by the claimant.

Appeal against notice to produce documents etc

9.—The claimant may appeal against a requirement imposed by notice under para 8 to produce documents or information. Notice of appeal must be given in writing, within 30 days after the issue of the notice appealed against, to the officer of the Board by whom the notice was given. The appeal is heard and determined in the same way as an appeal against an assessment. The decision of the Commissioners on an appeal under this paragraph is final.

Penalty for failure to produce documents etc

10.—This paragraph imposes a penalty of £50 for the failure to produce documents required by a notice under para 8. If the failure continues after a penalty is imposed, then further penalties can be determined by HMRC of up to £30 per day for which the failure continues.

Completion of enquiry

11.—This paragraph provides that an enquiry under para 7 is completed when HMRC informs the purchaser, by means of a "closure notice", that they have completed their enquiries and state their conclusions.

Direction to complete enquiry

12.—The purchaser may apply to the General or Special Commissioners for a direction that HMRC give a closure notice within a specified time. The application is considered in the same way as an appeal, but the Commissioners hearing the appeal are required to give the direction to HMRC unless satisfied that HMRC has reasonable grounds for not giving a closure notice.

Giving effect to amendments under paragraph 11

13.—Within 30 days of issuing a closure notice, HMRC is required to give effect to the amendment by making the necessary adjustment, either by assessing the claimant or by discharging or repaying tax.

Appeals against amendments under paragraph 11

14.—The claimant may, within 30 days of the issue of a closure notice, serve notice of appeal against its conclusions on the officer of the Board by whom the closure notice was given. It is a requirement that the notice state the grounds of appeal, although the appeal Commissioners may entertain other grounds of appeal if satisfied that their omission was not deliberate or unreasonable.

Jurisdiction of the Commissioners

15.—The appeal may be to Special Commissioners if the closure notice relates to a claim made to the Board. Otherwise, the appeal is in general made to the General Commissioners.

SCHEDULE 12 STAMP DUTY LAND TAX: COLLECTION AND RECOVERY OF TAX

PART 1 GENERAL

Issue of tax demands and receipts

1.—This paragraph permits a collector to make a demand for the sum of tax charged from the person liable to pay it.

Recovery of tax distraint

2.—This paragraph deals with the recovery of SDLT by distraint in England and Wales, and Northern Ireland. Under sub-para (6), the Treasury may make provision, by means of regulations, with regard to fees and costs. The paragraph is based on TMA 1970 ss 63 and 63A.

Recovery of tax by diligence in Scotland

3.—This paragraph deals with the recovery of tax in Scotland by means of an attachment, an earnings arrestment or an arrestment and action of furthcoming or sale.

PART 2 COURT PROCEEDINGS

Civil proceedings in magistrates' court or court of summary jurisdiction

4.—This paragraph provides for civil proceedings in magistrates' court for the recovery of amounts not exceeding £2,000. This is based on TMA 1970 s 65.

Proceedings in county court or sheriff court

5.—This paragraph provides for recovery proceedings in county courts and sheriffs' courts in Scotland. This is based on TMA 1970 ss 66 and 67.

Proceedings in High Court or Court of Session

6.—This paragraph provides for proceedings in the High Court or, in Scotland, in the Court of Session sitting as the Court of Exchequer.

Evidence of unpaid tax

7.—By virtue of this paragraph, a certificate of an officer of the Board that tax is due and payable, and that to the best of his knowledge and belief payment of the tax has not been made, is sufficient evidence that the tax is outstanding. This paragraph is based on TMA 1970 s 70.

SCHEDULE 13 STAMP DUTY LAND TAX: INFORMATION POWERS

PART 1 POWER OF AUTHORISED OFFICER TO CALL FOR DOCUMENTS OR INFORMATION FROM TAXPAYER

Notice requiring taxpayer to deliver documents or provide information

1.—This paragraph provides the Board with powers to call for documents and information from a taxpayer. Under sub-para (1), the officer of the Board authorised for the purposes of this Part of this Schedule, must do so by notice in writing, requiring the delivery of documents in the person's possession or power which, in the officer's reasonable opinion, contain or may contain relevant information. The taxpayer should first be given a reasonable opportunity to deliver the documents or provide the information. This paragraph is based on TMA 1970 ss 20(1) and 20B(1).

Requirement of consent of General or Special Commissioner

2.—Sub-para (1) confirms that the consent of a General or Special Commissioner is required for the giving of a notice under para 1, and, under sub-para (2), this must not be given unless they are satisfied that in all circumstances the officer is justified. Sub-para (3) establishes that any Commissioner, who has given such consent, may not take part in any proceedings on, or related to, any appeal brought by the relevant taxpayer. This paragraph is based on TMA 1970 s 20(7)(*a*), (*b*), (7AB).

Contents of notice under this part

3.—A notice given under para 1 must comply with the procedural requirements set out in this paragraph. Sub-section (2) provides that the minimum time to comply is 30 days. This is based on TMA 1970 s 20(8D)(*a*).

Summary of reasons to be given

4.—The officer who gives a notice under para 1 must also give to the person to whom it applies a written summary of his reasons for applying for consent to the notice. This does not require disclosure of any information which would or might identify any person providing the information or that the Commissioner giving consent directs need not be disclosed. This paragraph is based on TMA 1970 s 20(8E)(*a*), (8G) and (8H).

Power to take copies of documents etc

5.—This paragraph permits the person to whom the documents are delivered to take copies of the documents, and is based on TMA 1970 s 20(8D)(*b*).

PART 2 POWER OF AUTHORISED OFFICER TO CALL FOR DOCUMENTS FROM THIRD PARTY

Notice requiring documents to be delivered or made available

6.—This paragraph permits an authorised officer of the Board, having given the person reasonable opportunity to comply without a notice, to issue a notice to a third party to deliver documents. It is based on TMA 1970 ss 20(3), (6) and 20B(1).

Requirement of consent of General or Special Commissioner

7.—The consent of a General or Special Commissioner is required before a notice under para 6 can be given. Sub-para (3) confirms that any Commissioner who has given such consent may not take part in any proceedings on, or related to, any appeal brought by the relevant taxpayer. This is based on TMA 1970 s 20(7)(*a*), (*b*), (7AB) and (7AC).

Contents of notice under paragraph 6

8.—A notice given under para 7 must comply with the procedural requirements set out in this paragraph. Sub-section (2) provides that the minimum time to comply is 30 days. This is based on TMA 1970 s 20(8), (8D)(*a*).

Copy of notice to be given to taxpayer

9.—Sub-para (1) provides that a copy of the notice must be given to the person to whom it relates, unless, under sub-para (2), a General or Special Commissioner directs that this does not apply.

Summary of reasons to be given

10.—The officer who gives a notice under para 6 must also give to the person to whom it applies a written summary of his reasons for applying for consent to the notice. This does not require disclosure of any information which would or might identify any person providing the information or that the Commissioner directs need not be disclosed. This paragraph is based on TMA 1970 s 20(8E)(*b*), (8G)(*a*), (*b*), (8H) and (8F).

Power to give notice relating to unnamed taxpayer or taxpayers

11.—This paragraph permits an information notice under para 6 to be given, under strict conditions, without naming the taxpayer or taxpayers to which it relates, provided that it is pursuant to an order of the Board and with the consent of a Special Commissioner. Sub-para (4) provides that the person given the notice may appeal on the grounds that it would be onerous for him to comply with it.

Contents of notice under paragraph 11

12.—A notice given under para 11 must comply with the procedural requirements set out in this paragraph. Sub-section (2) provides that the minimum time to comply is 30 days. This is based on TMA 1970 s 20(8D)(*a*).

Power to take copies of document etc

13.—This paragraph permits the person to whom the documents are delivered to take copies of the documents, and is based on TMA 1970 s 20(8D)(*b*).

PART 3 POWER TO CALL FOR PAPERS OF TAX ACCOUNTANT

Power to call for papers of tax accountant

14.—An authorised officer of the Board is permitted to call for the papers of a tax accountant under this paragraph where the tax accountant is convicted of an offence in relation to tax or has a penalty imposed under s 96. The notice must be in writing and the documents required must be relevant to any tax liability of any client of the tax accountant. Under para 16 (see below) consent is required from the appropriate judicial authority.

When notice may be given

15.—This paragraph confirms at sub-para (1) that no notice under para 14 may be given so long as an appeal is pending against the conviction or penalty, and also, at sub-para (3) that there is a time limit of 12 months from the date of conviction for the power to be exercised. This is based on TMA 1970 s 20A(2), (4).

Requirement of consent of appropriate judicial authority

16.—The consent of a circuit judge in England and Wales, a sheriff in Scotland, or a county court judge in Northern Ireland is required for the giving of notice under para 14.

Contents of notice

17.—A notice given under para 14 must comply with the procedural requirements set out in this paragraph. Sub-section (2) provides that the minimum time to comply is 30 days. This is based on TMA 1970 s 20A(1B) and (1).

Power to take copies of documents etc

18.—This paragraph permits the officer to whom the documents are delivered to take copies of the documents, and is based on TMA 1970 s 20A(2)(*b*).

PART 4 RESTRICTIONS ON POWERS UNDER PARTS 1 TO 3

Introduction

19.—This paragraph introduces this part and confirms that Parts 1–3 of the Schedule are subject to the restrictions set out in Part 4.

Personal records or journalistic material

20.—This paragraph confirms that Parts 1–3 do not apply to documents that are personal records (as defined in PACE 1984 s 12) or journalistic material (as defined PACE 1984 s 13), or to information contained in any personal records or journalistic material. This is based TMA 1970 s 20(8C).

Documents or information relating to pending appeal

21.—This paragraph establishes that a notice under Parts 1–3 does not oblige a person to deliver documents relating to the conduct of a pending appeal relating to tax.

Barristers, advocates and solicitors

22.—Notices under Parts 2 and 3 may not be given to a barrister, advocate or solicitor except by the Board. This is based on TMA 1970 s 20B(3).

Provision of copies instead of original documents

23.—Sub-para (1) permits the delivery of copies of documents, but under sub-para (3), if required the originals must be made available for inspection by a named officer of the Board. This is based on TMA 1970 s 20B(4).

Documents originating more than six years before date of notice

24.—A notice under Part 2 does not oblige a person to deliver documents which originate more than six years before the date of the notice, unless, under sub-para (4), on application the Commissioner giving the notice is satisfied that tax may have been lost by fraud. This paragraph is based on TMA 1970 s 20B(5), (6).

Documents subject to legal privilege

25.—This paragraph confirms that a notice under Part 2 and 3 does not oblige a barrister, advocate or solicitor to deliver or make available, without his client's consent, any document with regard to which legal privilege could be maintained. This is based on TMA 1970 s 20B(8).

Documents belonging to auditor or tax adviser

26.—This paragraph establishes that Part 2 does not apply to certain audit documents and specified communications with a tax advisor, subject to the provisions of para 27. It is based on TMA 1970 s 20B(9), (10).

Documents belonging to auditor or tax advisor: information to be disclosed

27.—This paragraph provides the exceptions to para 26, namely information connected with the preparation of tax returns of any client and, in the case of a notice under para 11, information regarding the identity or address of any taxpayer to whom the notice relates. This paragraph is based on TMA 1970 s 20B(11), (14).

PART 5 POWERS OF BOARD TO CALL FOR DOCUMENTS OR INFORMATION

Notice requiring delivery of documents or provision of information

28.—A notice under this paragraph may only be made in circumstances where the Board has reasonable grounds for believing that the person to whom it relates may fail (or may have already failed) to comply with any provision in this Part of the Act, and that as a result there is (or is likely to be) a serious prejudice to the proper assessment or collection of tax. This paragraph will only be used in serious cases of tax abuse, and is based on TMA 1970 s 20(2), (7A).

Contents of notice

29.—A notice given under para 28 must comply with the procedural requirements set out in this paragraph. It is based on TMA 1970 s 20A(8D).

Power to take copies of documents etc

30.—This paragraph permits the person to whom the documents are delivered to take copies of the documents, and is based on TMA 1970 s 20(8D)(*b*).

Exclusion of personal records or journalistic material

31.—This paragraph confirms that Parts 1 to 3 do not apply to documents that are personal records (as defined in PACE 1984 s 12) or journalistic material (as defined PACE 1984 s 13), or to information contained in any personal records or journalistic material. This is based on TMA 1970 s 20(8C).

PART 6 ORDER OF JUDICIAL AUTHORITY FOR THE DELIVERY OF DOCUMENTS

Order for the delivery of documents

32.—Pursuant to this paragraph, a notice may be issued by a judge or sheriff in cases of serious fraud, having considered information presented on oath by an authorised officer of the Board. By virtue of sub-para (2), the time limit for complying with such a notice is 10 working days or less. This paragraph is based on TMA 1970 Sch 1AA para 2 and s 20BA(1)–(3).

Notice of application for order

33.—Under this paragraph, a person is entitled to notice of intention to apply for an order against him under Part 32, and to appear at the hearing of the application unless the appropriate judicial authority is satisfied that this would seriously prejudice the investigation of the offence in question. It is based on TMA 1970 Sch 1AA para 3.

Obligations of person given notice of application

34.—By virtue of this paragraph, a person who has been given a notice under para 32 must not conceal, destroy, alter or dispose of any document to which the application relates, or disclose any information to other persons. The exceptions to this general rule are set out at sub-paras (2) and (3). If a person fails to comply with the obligations set out in this paragraph, he may be dealt with as if he had failed to comply with an order under para 32. This is based on TMA 1970 Sch 1AA para 4.

Exception of items subject to legal privilege

35.—In accordance with this paragraph, any items which are the subject of legal privilege are excluded from a notice under Part 6. It is based on TMA 1970 Sch 1AA para 5.

Resolution of disputes as to legal privilege

36.—HMRC is empowered to make regulations under this paragraph with regard to the resolution of disputes as to whether a document is or is not subject to legal privilege. This is based on TMA 1970 Sch 1AA para 6.

Complying with an order

37.—HMRC is empowered to make regulations under this paragraph with regard to how an order under para 32 is to be complied with. This is based on TMA 1970 Sch 1AA para 7.

Document not to be retained if photograph or copy of documents delivered

38.—This paragraph provides that where a documents delivered to an officer of the Board is of such a nature that a copy would be sufficient for use as evidence at trial or for forensic examination or investigation, then the original must not be kept by HMRC for longer than is necessary. This is based on TMA 1970 Sch 1A para 8(1) and s 20CC(3).

Access to or supply of photograph or copy of documents delivered

39.—Under this paragraph, an application may be made to the officer in charge of the investigation for permission to be granted for access to documents or copies of documents by a person who had control or custody of them immediately before they were delivered. It is based on TMA 1970 Sch 1AA para 8 and s 20CC(4)–(9).

Sanction for failure to comply with order

40.—This paragraph confirms that a person who fails to comply with an order under this part of this Schedule may be dealt with as if he had committed a contempt of court. It is based on TMA 1970 Sch 1AA para 9.

Notice of order, etc

41.—HMRC is granted the power to make regulations dealing with the circumstances in which a notice of an order under para 32, or a notice for that order, is to be treated. It is based on TMA 1970 Sch 1AA para 10.

General provisions about regulations

42.—This paragraph confirms that regulations under this part of this Schedule may contain such incidental, supplementary and transitional provisions as are appropriate.

PART 7 ENTRY WITH WARRANT TO OBTAIN EVIDENCE OF OFFENCE

Power to issue warrant

43.—Pursuant to this paragraph, an officer of the Board (acting with the approval of the Board) may be granted a warrant to enter and search premises by the appropriate judicial authority, provided that they are satisfied that an offence involving serious fraud is suspected. This is based on TMA 1970 ss 20C(1), (9) and 20D(1).

Meaning of offence involving serious fraud

44.—"Offence involving serious fraud" is defined in this paragraph for the purposes of this Part of this Schedule. It is based on TMA 1970 s 20C(1A).

Approval of application by Board

45.—Under sub-para (1), the Board shall not approve an application for a warrant unless they have reasonable grounds for believing that use of the procedure set out at Part 6 of this Schedule might seriously prejudice the investigation. Sub-para (2) confirms that such approval may not be delegated by disapplying Inland Revenue Regulation Act 1890 s 4A. This paragraph is based on TMA 1970 s 20C(1AA), (2).

Extent of powers conferred by warrant

46.—This paragraph confirms the extent of the powers conferred by a warrant under Part 7, and is based on TMA 1970 s 20C(1B).

Exercise of powers conferred by warrant

47.—Sub-para (1) of this paragraph deals with who the warrant should be served on, and sub-ss (2) and (3) provide for the entering of premises with other persons, seizing and removing items, and searching premises. These provisions are based on TMA 1970 s 20C(3), (3A) and (5).

Items subject to legal privilege

48.—This paragraph prevents warrants under Part 7 from being used to seize items subject to legal privilege, and is based on TMA 1970 s 20C(4)–(4B).

Procedure where documents etc are removed

49.—A record of anything removed by an officer during the course of the exercise of a warrant must be provided on the request of the occupier, or a person having custody or control. It is based on TMA 1970 s 20CC(1), (2).

Document not to be retained if photograph or copy sufficient

50.—This paragraph prevents anything removed by an officer during the course of the exercise of a warrant from being retained if a copy of it can be used as evidence in court. It is based on TMA 1970 s 20CC(3).

Access to or supply of photograph or copy of items removed

51.—Under this paragraph, an application may be made to the officer in charge of the investigation for permission to be granted access to documents or copies of documents by a person who had control or custody of them immediately before they were delivered. It is based on TMA 1970 s 20CC(4)–(6).

Endorsement and custody etc of warrant

52.—In accordance with this paragraph, a list of the things seized must be attached to the warrant and PACE 1984 s 16(1)–(12) apply to a warrant under Part 7, as they apply to a warrant issued to a constable under any other enactment.

PART 8 FALSIFICATION ETC OF DOCUMENTS

Falsification etc of documents

53.—This paragraph provides an offence for the intentional falsification, concealment, destruction or other disposal, of documents required by a notice under Parts 1, 2, 3 or 5 of this Schedule. Causing or permitting the same to happen is also an offence. The exceptions to this general rule are set out at sub-paras (3), (4) and (5). Anyone found guilty of an offence under this paragraph is liable on summary conviction to a fine not exceeding the statutory maximum, or on conviction, to imprisonment for a term not exceeding two years or a fine or both.

SCHEDULE 14 STAMP DUTY LAND TAX: DETERMINATION OF PENALTIES AND RELATED APPEALS

Determination of penalties and appeals

1.—This introductory paragraph confirms that this Schedule applies to SDLT penalties.

Determination of penalty by officer of the board

2.—This paragraph provides that an officer of the Board authorised for the purposes of this paragraph is permitted to make a determination imposing a penalty and setting it at such an amount as, in his opinion, is correct or appropriate. The paragraph also provides that notice of the determination must be served on the person liable, and that it must state the date on which it is issued and the time within which an appeal may be made. Under sub-para (4), the penalty is due and payable within 30 days from the date of issue of the notice. Finally, sub-para (5) provides that various administrative matters regarding penalties may be delegated by the relevant officer of the Board. This paragraph is based on TMA 1970 ss 100, 100A(2) and 113(1D).

Alteration of penalty determination

3.—This paragraph deals with the alteration of a penalty determination after a notice has been served. It allows an "authorised officer" (as defined at sub-para (4)) to make a determination in a further amount where it is discovered that the amount of the penalty is or has become insufficient (sub-para (2)) and to alter a determination where it is deemed insufficient (sub-para (3)). This is based on TMA 1970 s 100(4)–(6).

Liability of personal representatives

4.—This paragraph confirms what the position is as regards the liability of personal representatives where a person who is liable for a penalty has died. It is based on TMA 1970 s 100A(1).

Appeal against penalty determination

5.—Sub-para (1) confirms that an appeal against a determination lies to the General or Special Commissioners. Notice of the appeal must be given in writing to the officer who made the determination within 30 days of the date of issue of the notice (sub-para (2)). An appeal may be brought out of time with the consent of the Board or the Commissioners (sub-para (3)), and, on such an application, the Board shall give their consent if they are satisfied that there was a reasonable excuse for the delay in appealing and, if they are not satisfied, shall refer the matter for determination by the Commissioners (sub-para (4)). Under sub-para (5), the notice of appeal must specify the grounds, but any hearing is not limited to those grounds. Finally, sub-para (6) confirms that the Commissioners may set the determination aside, confirm it or modify it, as appropriate.

Further appeal

6.—Sub-para (1) confirms that TMA 1970 s 56A applies in relation to a decision by the Commissioners under para 5, in other words that a further appeal from decisions of the Commissioners may be made on a point of law. Similarly, by virtue of sub-para (2), an appeal lies against the amount of a penalty determined by the Commissioners under para 5. These provisions are based on TMA 1970 s 100B(3).

Penalty proceedings before the court

7.—This paragraph deals with penalty proceedings before the court, which, under sub-para (1) may only be brought where, in the opinion of the Board, the liability of a person for a penalty arises by reason of fraud.

Time limit for determination of penalties

8.—Subject to the exceptions set out in the paragraph, the general rule (as described at sub-para (2) is that the time limit for the determination of penalties is six years after the date on which the penalty was incurred. In cases where the penalty is tax geared, it is three years after the final determination of the amount of tax (sub-para (3)). A separate rule is provided at sub-para (4) where the liable person has died, and at sub-para (5) for penalties under s 96 (see above). These provisions are based on TMA 1970 s 103.

SCHEDULE 15 STAMP DUTY LAND TAX: PARTNERSHIPS

This schedule, as amended, as from 22 July 2004, brings partnership transactions within the scope of SDLT for the first time. Previously, all partnership transactions had been excluded from SDLT but had remained liable to stamp duty. Contrary to assurances given by the Government when introducing SDLT, the implementation of the new rules has not led to the abolition of stamp duty on partnership transactions: paras 31–33 retain the old rules with certain modifications. The explanation given for this was that to abolish the charge completely would introduce opportunities to avoid stamp duty and SDRT on shares and securities by holding them within a partnership.

PART 1 GENERAL PROVISIONS

Partnerships

1.—This paragraph defines "partnership", "limited partnership" and "limited liability partnership" with reference to the Partnership Act 1890, the Limited Partnerships Act 1907 and the Limited Liability Partnerships Act 2000 (or Limited Liability Partnerships Act (Northern Ireland) 2002) respectively. It also treats as a partnership any firm or entity formed under the law of a country or territory outside the United Kingdom if of a similar character to any of the forms of partnership in the United Kingdom.

Legal personality of partnership disregarded

2.—For the purposes of SDLT, land and interests in land held by or on behalf a partnership are treated as held by the partners and a land transaction entered into for the purposes of a partnership is treated as entered into by the partners, whether or not a partnership has legal personality or is a body corporate.

Continuity of partnership

3.—Where there is a change in the membership of a partnership, the partnership is treated as continuing as long as any one partner who was a member before the change remains one after.

Partnership not to be regarded as unit trust scheme etc

4.—This paragraph confirms that a partnership is not to be regarded as a unit trust scheme or an open-ended investment company for the purposes of SDLT.

PART 2 ORDINARY PARTNERSHIP TRANSACTIONS

Introduction

5.—This paragraph confirms that Part 2 of the Schedule applies to transactions made by or on behalf of the members of a partnership, other than transactions to which Part 3 apply.

Responsibility of partners

6.—Under this paragraph, anything which should be done by the purchaser under a transaction is required to be done by or in relation to all the "responsible partners" (as defined at sub-para (2)).

Joint and several liability of responsible partners

7.—This paragraph confirms that the responsible partners are jointly and severally liable, with regard to making payments or to interest on unpaid tax, making payments in accordance with an assessment under para 29 of Sch 10, or to a penalty under the SDLT regime or to any interest thereon. However, no amount is recoverable under this provision from a partner who did not become a responsible partner until after the effective date of the disputed transaction.

Representative partners

8.—By virtue of this paragraph, a partner who is nominated by a majority of the partners to act as a representative of the partnership may act for and on behalf of the responsible partners.

PART 3 TRANSACTIONS TO WHICH SPECIAL PROVISIONS APPLY

Introduction

9.—The transactions in this Part of Sch 15 apply to certain kinds of transactions in land involving partnerships, namely, transfers of chargeable interests in land to a partnership; transfers of chargeable interests in land from a partnership; and transfers of interests in a partnership (as defined). It is understood that the Commissioners consider that the charges in Part 3 of Sch 15 are self-contained and override the ordinary charges that would arise under the body of the Act. Some support for this is given by para 29, but it is clear that reference has to be made to other parts of the Act for the purpose of defining terms that are not defined by Part 3 itself (eg "consideration").

The paragraph also provides that references to the transfer of a chargeable interest are to be widely defined and to include the grant or creation, the variation, and the surrender or release of such an interest. The reference to "chargeable interest" is intended to limit the scope of the charge to land in the United Kingdom: see s 48(1) for the definition of the phrase. For other interpretation provisions, see Sch 15 paras 34–40.

Transfer of chargeable interest into a partnership: general

10.—This paragraph applies where a person who is not a partner transfers a chargeable interest to a partnership in return for an interest in the partnership. It also applies where a partner, or someone connected with a partner, an incoming partner, transfers such an interest to the partnership. However, it is possible to elect that the paragraph should not apply to a transfer, in which case SDLT is charged on the market value of the chargeable interest: see para 12A.

In *DV3 RS Limited Partnership v HMRC* (TC 1012) the First-Tier Tribunal held that a sub-sale into partnership, by which the landowner contracted to sell to DV3 Ltd, DV3 Ltd contracted to sub-sell to a partnership of which it was a member, and the contracts were completed by two TR1s executed at the same time and in connection with each other at a single completion meeting, fell within the scope of Schedule 15 paragraph 10. The effect was that the first transaction fell to be disregarded under the tailpiece to section 45(3) and the transfer from DV3 Ltd to the partnership fell to be taxed under the then favourable provisions of paragraph 10. The Commissioners argued that paragraph 10 was not engaged because the effect of section 45(3) was to prevent DV3 from acquiring a chargeable interest which it could transfer to the partnership. The Tribunal decided that the nature of the secondary contract prescribed by section 45(3) was, on the facts of the case, a tripartite contract under which DV3 was to transfer the land to the partnership and that section 45 was intended only to affect section 44 and not the whole of the legislation relating to SDLT.

Sub-paragraph (2) establishes the amount of chargeable consideration which is treated as having been given for the transfer. The computation, which has been modified and simplified by FA 2006, is designed to secure that the charge is *not* imposed on that proportion of the value of the land which the transferor(s) (or connected persons) retain in the land in their capacity as partners. For the meaning of a person's partnership share, see Sch 15 para 34(2); and for the meaning of "connected persons" for the purposes of Sch 15, see para 39.

The charge is imposed on the "relevant chargeable proportion" of the market value of the interest transferred. When valuing the "relevant chargeable proportion" (RCP) of the value of the chargeable interest transferred, the RCP is effectively that proportion of the chargeable interest which is attributable to those partners who are not the transferors and who are not connected with the transferors: sub-para (3). The legislation (see para 12) is designed to ensure that a charge arises if the proportionate share of partnership income belonging either to the transferor or to partners connected with him is lower than the transferor's proportionate share in the land before it became partnership property. So, if A, the sole owner of a freehold interest in land, transfers the land to a partnership in which he is entitled to 100 per cent of all capital profits but only 30 per cent of income profits, the RCP will be 70 per cent (being 100-30). If, on the other hand, A (the sole owner of land) transfers the land to a partnership in which he, his wife and his two children have equal 20 per cent shares in income and E (an unconnected third party) also had a 20 per cent income share, SDLT is charged only on the 20 per cent income share that has passed to E. Thus, if the market value of the land is £1m, SDLT is charged on chargeable consideration of £200,000 (£1m × (100 − 80)%).

Paragraph 11 applies to supplement para 10 in cases where the whole or part of the consideration for the transaction is rent. Paragraph 10 is also subject to para 13 (transfer of chargeable interest to a partnership consisting wholly of bodies corporate).

Transfer of chargeable interest to a partnership: chargeable consideration including rent

11.—This paragraph applies where a person transfers a chargeable interest to a partnership in return for an interest in the partnership and part of the consideration for the transaction is rent. It also applies where someone connected with a partner, or an incoming partner, transfers such an interest to the partnership and the whole or part of the consideration for the transaction is rent. That is to say, it applies where a partner or a person connected with a partner grants a lease to a partnership, since in other cases the assignment of a lease generally does not involve the transferee giving consideration to the transferor in the form of the payment of rent. There are certain exceptional cases where an assignment of a lease would be within para 11; those to which Sch 17A para 11 will apply (cases where assignment of a lease treated as grant of lease).

In such a case, Sch 5 (SDLT: amount of tax chargeable: rent) applies as modified by this paragraph: sub-para (2). The paragraph does two things. First, it modifies the operation of Sch 5 para 2 to restrict the chargeable proportion of the net present value of the rent to the relevant chargeable proportion of that sum (sub-para (2A)). Second, sub-para (2C) secures that where there is both a charge to SDLT on the relevant chargeable proportion of the NPV of the rent under Sch 5 and an amount charged to tax under para 10 of Sch 15, both charges are imposed on the grant of the lease into partnership.

For cases where the interest transferred is a market value lease, see Sch 15 para 15.

Taking, then, the RCP of the net present value of the rents, sub-para (2A) effectively establishes this as that proportion of the chargeable interest which is attributable to the partners, other than the transferors and persons connected with the transferors. As with para 10, the legislation treats the RCP as being that proportion (if any) by which the transferors' proportionate interests in partnership income profit is less than their prior proportionate interests in the land: see para 12 (made applicable to para 11 by sub-para (8)). Thus, if the transferors (and those connected with them) were entitled to 90 per cent of the land but are entitled only to 75 per cent of the partnership income, the RCP is 15 per cent. In such a case, 15 per cent of the net present value of the rent reserved by the lease would be charged to SDLT in accordance with Sch 5.Paragraph 11 is subject to para 13 (transfer of chargeable interest to a partnership consisting wholly of bodies corporate).

Transfer of chargeable interest: sum of the lower proportions

12.—This paragraph contains the mechanism for calculating the figure used ("the sum of the lower proportions" or "SLP") for determining the relevant chargeable proportion (the RCP) for the purposes of paras 10 and 11. The paragraph requires one to test whether, in the case of each partner who is either a transferor of the interest transferred or is connected with such a person, his proportionate interest in the relevant chargeable interest immediately before the transaction is larger or smaller than his proportionate share of partnership income profit. In carrying out this exercise, one takes into account any interest in the asset or any share in partnership income profit owned by individuals connected with him. Having carried the exercise out, one takes the lower of the two proportions for all such partners and aggregates them. This is the "SLP". Inevitably, in a case where there is a number of transferors and a number of connected individual partners, there will be various ways in which this calculation can be carried out. The Commissioners accept that a partnership may adopt that method of arriving at SLP that is most favourable to the partnership.For the purposes of this exercise, beneficial joint tenants are treated as owing equal undivided shares in the land.

For the purposes of this exercise, beneficial joint tenants are treated as owing equal undivided shares in the land.

Changes were made to the operation of para 12 with effect from 6 December 2006, in order to prevent advantage being taken of the rules on computing the SDLT on the transfer of property into a partnership which had been introduced by FA 2006. The effect of these changes was to prevent the avoidance of s 53 (charge at market value on transfers to connected companies) by the use of a partnership in which most of the partners were connected companies. The method which had been adopted was to create a partnership in which an "envelope company" was entitled to the majority of the capital and income profit. When land was sold to the partnership, the SDLT charge was low because the SLP was boosted by the profit share held by the envelope company. Once the land had been transferred to the partnership, the vendor then found a purchaser for the shares in the envelope company. The sale of those shares would be outside the scope of SDLT. To counteract this, it is no longer possible to rely on the profit share of a company connected with the vendor. The one exception to this is where the relevant company holds property as trustee and is connected with the relevant owner because of TA 1988 s 839(3). Section 839 treats a person, in his capacity as a trustee of a settlement, as connected with the settlor of the settlement, with any person connected with the settlor and with any body corporate connected with the settlement. Such a corporate trustee is to be treated as an individual for the purpose of computing SLP in para 12.

Provision is made by para 27A for a form of group relief to be afforded under paras 10–12 where a company transfers a chargeable interest to a partnership in which one or more partners are members of a group of which the transferor is a member. In such a case the SDLT charge is reduced to that which it would have been had the relevant companies been corresponding partners of the transferor. The claw-back provisions of Sch 7 (Group relief) are then modified to enable a charge to be imposed on the relevant companies leaving the group within the usual three year period: sub-para (9).

12A.—This paragraph permits the "purchaser" to elect for para 10 not to apply to a transfer of a chargeable interest to a property-investment partnership. This reference to "purchaser" must be read in conjunction with Sch 15 para 6, which provides that anything that is required or authorised to be done by or in relation to the purchaser is required or authorised to be done by or in relation to the "responsible partners", ie those who are partners at the effective date of the transaction. Accordingly, it is the partners at the time of the land transaction who must elect under para 12. The necessary election is to be made either on the land transaction return relating to the acquisition or by means of an amendment of return. In consequence, the election must be made within 12 months of the filing date for the return: Sch 10 para 6 (but see FA 2008 Sch 31 para 11 for an extension of time to make an election where the relevant land transaction preceded the passing of the Act). Once made, the election may not be revoked. No provision has been made for a case where there is no notifiable transaction, so that no return is to be made. It would seem that in such a case no election may be made under para 12A for para 14 purposes.

The effect of an election is that the partnership is treated as acquiring the property for SDLT purposes at its market value and as an ordinary partnership transaction under Sch 15 Part 2. The advantage of this is to enable subsequent dealings in partnership interests to fall outside the scope of the charge under para 14.

If an election is made on the transfer of the chargeable interest to the partnership, para 18 will also be disapplied. It is presumed that the intention of the legislation is that para 18 is disapplied to the extent that the transaction involves the property passing out of one partnership to another, rather than that para 18 is to be disapplied on a future transfer of the property from the partnership to a partner. It must be said, though, that the legislation is wholly ambiguous.

Transfer of interest in property-investment partnership

14.—The Legislature has made a number of attempts to draft para 14 in a manner which gives effect to its purpose without harming commercial dealings in property investment partnerships. Acknowledging that it had been too draconian in its approach in FA 2007, it has sought to rectify the problems thrown up by the previous drafting by amending the paragraph with retrospective effect. The purpose of the amended legislation is to prevent avoidance by the manipulation of property interests in property-investment partnerships without triggering charges to SDLT each time there was a change in the size of a partner's interest in such a partnership. Originally para 14 applied only if there was consideration given for a transfer of an interest in a partnership. This was then amended to restrict the application to cases where the partnership was a property-investment partnership. However, it was easy to avoid the charge under para 14, not because of the terms of the paragraph itself but because of the definition of "transfer of a partnership interest" in Sch 15 para 36. In what might be seen as an excess of caution, FA 2007 amended not only the para 36 definition but also made significant amendments to para 14, in particular removing the requirement that the transfer be made for consideration. The consequence of this was to throw the standard market practice of forming an "open-ended" partnership to acquire a property portfolio and then widening the partnership by seeking further investors who would become partners and make contributions to the partnership (but without others withdrawing any of their funds). The 2008 amendments are designed to alleviate that problem and do so by distinguishing between cases where there is the possibility of avoidance (for example, where the partnership property has passed into the partnership without SDLT being paid on the open market value of the property) and cases where avoidance may be taken not to exist. Paragraph 14 must now be read in conjunction with para 12A, which offers a property-investment partnership that acquires property from a partner the right to elect to pay SDLT on the open market value of the property, rather than at the beneficial rate afforded by paras 10–12.

There are two conditions if this paragraph is to apply: first, there must be a transfer of an interest in a property-investment partnership, and second, the relevant partnership property must include a chargeable interest in land. In such a case, the transfer of the partnership interest is treated as a chargeable land transaction: sub-para (2).

A "property-investment partnership" is given a very wide definition: a partnership whose sole or main activity is investing *or dealing* in property. In this context, unusually, "dealing" is taken to include property development activities. What constitutes the "sole or main activity" of a partnership is not further defined. Similar phrases may be found elsewhere in tax legislation: see, for example VATA 1994 Sch 10 para 3A(7) where the test is one of being in occupation "wholly or mainly for eligible purposes" where HMRC have indicated that the threshold is seen as being 80% or more. It is not clear whether a similar approach would be adopted here, or whether a main activity would exist if more than 51% of the partnership's time was devoted to its property investment activities. Likewise, it is not clear what factors are relevant in determining which activity is predominant: it may be possible and/or necessary to consider profit made, income generated, capital employed, time employed or even the resources applied in each activity. It is to be anticipated that a Court would require all factors to be considered in deciding whether the partnership is a property-investment partnership.

Paragraph 36 defines the circumstances in which a transfer of a partnership interest occurs.

What constitutes "relevant partnership property" depends on whether the transfer of the interest in the property-investment partnership is a "Type A" or a "Type B" transfer. A "Type A" requires that the transfer in question involves either:

(a) consideration being given by or on behalf of the person acquiring the partnership interest (eg A sells his partnership interest to B for a cash sum); or

(b) one person becoming a partner, and an existing partner reducing his partnership interest or ceasing altogether to be a partner *and* the existing partner in question withdrawing money or money's worth from the partnership otherwise than from "resources available to the partnership prior to the transfer". We are not told what resources are to be treated as available to the partnership; but it may be assumed that the intention of the provision (para 14(3B)) is to ignore the withdrawal of funds which belonged to the partnership before the transaction, or which are realised by the disposal of existing partnership assets or which are borrowed by a draw-down on existing loan facilities available to the partnership. What would appear to be the target of the legislation are funds which are withdrawn by the existing partner from funds constituted by the contribution to the partnership of the incoming partner or which are borrowed against the security of that contribution. It is to be borne in mind that such a withdrawal of funds may in certain circumstances itself trigger a charge to SDLT under Sch 15 para 17A.

A "Type B" transfer is any other transfer.

If the transfer is a Type A transfer the "relevant partnership property" extends to every chargeable interest held as partnership property (as to which, see Sch 15 para 34) *other than* chargeable interests transferred to the partnership in connection with the transfer or market rent leases held by the partnership (as to which see Sch 15 para 15). Market rent leases are not treated as susceptible to SDLT charges beyond that imposed on the rent itself when granted. The concept of a chargeable interest transferred to the partnership in connection with the transfer is an interesting one. It clearly extends to land contributed to the partnership by the incoming partner but it could go far further than that. What, for example, of land contributed by one incoming partner which is to be followed, as part of the same arrangements, by further partners making cash contributions? Such a case probably falls within Sch 15 para 17; but it can be imagined that there will be other cases where the subsequent partnership transfer will still be connected with the earlier transfer but not part of the same arrangements.

If, however, the transfer is a "Type B" transfer, there is a wider list of chargeable interests which are excluded from the category of relevant partnership property in addition to those which are excluded for "Type A" transfers. One is to disregard, first, any chargeable interest transferred to the partnership on or before 22 July 2004 (ie before the introduction of Part 3 to Sch 15 in its original form). The expectation is that such transfers will have been subject to stamp duty and not to SDLT, subject only to the application of certain transitional provisions. Next, one disregards any chargeable interest whose transfer did not fall within Sch 15 para 10 – ie any land bought by the partnership from an unconnected third party. Third, one may disregard any chargeable interest "that is not attributable economically to the interest in the partnership that is transferred". It is not entirely clear what is within the scope of this exception, but it is presumed that it covers cases where the partnership interest acquired by the incoming partner has not right to participate in either income or capital profits derived from asset. Last, one disregards any chargeable interest in respect of which an election was made under para 12A. The effect of this is to permit the partnership to elect to pay SDLT on the full market value of the asset when acquired, rather than taking advantage of the reduced rate available under Sch 15 para 10 on a transfer of property to a partnership by a partner or person connected with a partner.

Where a charge arises by reason of this paragraph, it is payable by the incoming partner, or the partner whose share increases as a result of the transfer: sub-para (3). The chargeable consideration is taken to be the appropriate proportion of the market value of the relevant partnership property, that is to say, a proportion corresponding to the incoming partner's partnership share, or the increase in the acquiring partner's partnership share, as the case may be. A partnership share is calculated by reference to the partner's interest in partnership income profit: para 34(2). So, if an incoming partner obtains a 10 per cent share of partnership income profit, he must pay SDLT on an amount equal to 10 per cent of the current market value of the land held by the partnership.

Exclusion of market rent leases

15.—This paragraph provides for the circumstances in which a lease may be left out of the calculation of relevant partnership property for the purposes of para 14 (Transfer of partnership interest: consideration given and chargeable interest held). Four conditions must be met. First, that the lease was granted for no chargeable consideration other than rent and that there are no arrangements for any other such consideration to be given. The reference to "chargeable consideration" is to exclude matters such as covenants to pay service charges or to maintain the premises, etc. Second, the rent payable at the time the lease was granted must have been a market rent (ie such a rent as might be expected to be paid for such a lease in the open market). Third, either the lease must be for five years or less, or there must be provision for rent reviews to market rent at no more than five yearly intervals. And, fourth, there must have been no amendments to the lease which would render the rent less than a market rent.

Partnership interests: application of provisions about exchanges etc

16.—This paragraph is designed to secure the proper application of Sch 4 para 5 (exchanges) where a vendor of land acquires an interest in a partnership in consideration of entering into the land transaction with an existing partner. If the relevant partnership property includes a major interest in land, then the acquisition of the partnership interest is treated as the acquisition of a major interest in land. The effect of this is that the "equality money" rule, which applies where there is an exchange of minor interests in land does not apply, and one brings into charge the market value of the partnership interest. See Sch 4 para 5 for more information on this procedure.

The paragraph also disapplies the similar equality money rule for partitions (Sch 4 para 6) where a vendor of land acquires an interest in a partnership in consideration of entering into the land transaction with an existing partner.

Transfer of partnership interest pursuant to earlier arrangements

17.—This paragraph is an anti-avoidance provision designed to counteract arrangements the effect of which is to artificially increase the partnership share acquired by a transferor in exchange for transferring land into a partnership, where it is intended that there should be an adjustment to the artificial partnership shares. Without para 17, no charge would arise because the transferor's partnership interest would be precisely the same as his interest in the land at the time of transfer: see paras 10 and 11. At a later stage, his interest in partnership income profit sharing ratios would be adjusted downwards in circumstances not falling within para 14 (eg perhaps by an upward adjustment in his partnership capital profit sharing ratio). In this case, para 17 provides that the transfer of the partnership interest, ie the movement in income profit sharing ratios (see para 36), is to be treated as a chargeable land transaction, the purchasers under which are the partners: sub-paras (2) and (3). The transaction is deemed to be made for chargeable consideration equal to the appropriate proportion of the current market value of interest in land which was transferred to the partnership: sub-para (4). That proportion is, in the case where the transferor ceases to be a partner, his partnership share; and in cases where his partnership share reduces, the amount of the reduction.

The partnership transfer and the land transfer are linked transactions: sub-para (6).

Withdrawal of money etc from partnership after transfer of chargeable interest

17A.—This paragraph is designed to counteract a means of transferring land into a partnership and extracting funds without a charge (or significant charge) to SDLT. The preconditions for the operation of the provision are that an interest in land has been transferred into a partnership (either by a partner or in return for a partnership interest) in circumstances such that para 10 has applied to reduce the charge to SDLT and within three years of the transfer a "qualifying event" occurs. The qualifying event is one which involves the withdrawal of funds otherwise than by way of the receipt of monies which are chargeable as income profit. The possible forms of withdrawal are, first, the withdrawal of capital from the transferor's capital account; second, the reduction by the transferor of his partnership interest; and, third, the transferor ceasing to be a partner. In addition, a qualifying event can take place where the transferor has made a loan to the partnership and the partnership repays all or part of the loan (nb: whether or not to the lender), or there is another form of withdrawal of funds by the transferor (otherwise than in a form which counts as his income profit).

Similar rules exist where a person connected with a partner transfers an interest in land to the partnership in circumstances triggering a charge under para 10(1)(*c*). In this case, the qualifying event looks to withdrawals of capital by, or repayments of loans to, either the transferor or to the partner connected with him. In cases where para 17A may be in point it is preferable for the initial transfer to fall within para 10(1)(*a*) or (*b*), rather than para 10(1)(*c*), since withdrawals of capital by connected persons may then be ignored.

The qualifying event is treated as a chargeable land transaction in respect of which the partners are the purchaser (and liable to pay SDLT). The chargeable consideration for this notional land transaction depends on the nature of the qualifying event. In a case involving the withdrawal of capital from the partner's capital account or on the reduction or termination of his partnership interest, the consideration is taken to be equal to the value of the money or money's worth withdrawn. In the case where there is a loan coupled with the repayment of the loan, or a withdrawal of funds related to a loan, the amount repaid or withdrawn is taken to be the chargeable consideration (to the extent that it does not exceed the amount of the loan). In each case there is a further restriction on the amount of chargeable consideration—it must not exceed the market value of the interest in land at the time it was transferred to the partnership, as reduced by any previous amount brought into charge under para 17A.

Presumably the rules for linked transactions under FA 2003 s 108 will apply where funds are withdrawn from the partnership over a period.

Provision is made to prevent a double charge to tax where a qualifying event both gives rise to a charge under para 17A and to a charge under para 14. In such a case sub-para (8) provides that the tax chargeable under para 17A is to be reduced by the tax charged under para 14. In cases where the charge under para 17A would thereby become negative (and thus arguable give rise to a claim for recovery of tax), para 17A(8) reduces the charge to nil, but no further.

Paragraph 17A does not apply if a para 12A election, disapplying para 10, was made in relation to the initial transfer of the chargeable interest to the partnership.

Transfer of chargeable interest from a partnership: general

18.—The paragraph provides that where an interest in land is transferred from a partnership to a partner, or former partner (or, as the case may be, to someone connected with such a person) this is a chargeable transaction. The effect of the provisions is that if the property passes out of the partnership to such a person, that transfer is not brought into the charge to SDLT unless or except to the extent that his proportionate interest outside the partnership is greater than his proportionate interest as a partner. To the extent that the property passes to a person who has no connection with the partnership, it remains chargeable. Thus, if A and B are in 50:50 partnership and land forming part of the assets of the partnership passes out to C and D, in the proportions 25 per cent to C and 75 per cent to D, D being connected with A but C being connected with neither A nor B, the chargeable proportion of the market value of the land would be 50 per cent. 25 per cent would be chargeable because it passes to an unconnected person, C; and 25 per cent would be chargeable because the amount taken by D outside the partnership (75 per cent) exceeded the amount owned (ie notionally owned through A) inside the partnership (50 per cent—which would be the lower proportion for this purpose). If, on the other hand, it had been C and not D who was connected with A, 75 per cent would have come into charge as passing to an unconnected party, with the 25 per cent owned by C being treated as the lower proportion and being left out of account.

The way in which the legislation arrives at this result is the same as paras 10–13, to which reference should be made for further details. Thus para 18(2)–(6) corresponds to para 10(2)–(6).

Paragraph 18 is subject to para 19, which applies whenever the chargeable consideration for the transaction includes rent; and the calculation of the chargeable consideration under para 18(2) is subject to para 24 (transfer of chargeable interest from a partnership consisting wholly of bodies corporate), which itself corresponds to para 13.

Provision is made for para 18 to apply in the case of a partnership dissolution, despite the fact that the partnership comes to an end before the relevant distributions take place. The effect will be that, on property being distributed in the course of a partnership dissolution, no charge to SDLT will occur save to the extent that a partner takes an interest in property larger than his proportionate partnership income profit share. If such adjustments are to be made it might be better if the partners were (if possible) to dissolve and distribute in strict accordance with partnership income profit sharing ratios; and then to partition in accordance with Sch 4 para 6.

Transfer of chargeable interest from a partnership: chargeable consideration including rent

19.—This paragraph supplements para 18 where part of the consideration for the land transaction consists of rent. It thus applies where a new lease is granted by a partnership to a partner or to a person connected with a partner. In cases where the lease is simply assigned, para 18 alone will apply: see the commentary on para 11. Paragraph 19(2)–(8) correspond to para 11(2)–(8) above (in relation to transfers to a partnership) and reference should be made to the commentary on that paragraph for an explanation of the working of the provision.

The calculation of the chargeable consideration under para 19(2) is subject to para 24 (transfer of chargeable interest from a partnership consisting wholly of bodies corporate), which itself corresponds to para 13.

Transfer of chargeable interest from a partnership: sum of lower proportions

20.—This paragraph contains the mechanism for calculating the figure used ("the sum of the lower proportions" or "SLP") for determining the relevant chargeable proportion (the RCP) for the purposes of paras 18 and 19 and corresponds to para 12 above to which reference should be made for an explanation of the working of the provision. There are, though, certain differences between the entrance and exit charges under paras 12 and 20: para 20 affords no form of group relief in circumstances where the transferee is a member of the same group as one or more of the partners; and para 24 provides for a market value exit charge where all the partners are bodies corporate.

Transfer of chargeable interest from a partnership: partnership share attributable to partner

21.—This is a blocking provision, which was introduced to prevent manipulation of partnership interests and partnership property transfers after the proposals for imposing SDLT on partnership transactions were announced on 20 October 2003 (a date falling before the implementation of SDLT). The paragraph makes different provision for cases where the effective date of the transfer of a chargeable interest to a partnership was before 20 October 2003 and cases where the transfer takes place on or after that date. It is concerned with cases where a chargeable interest has at some stage been transferred to a partnership and at some later stage either para 18 or 19 applies on the transfer out of the partnership either of the relevant interest or an interest which is created out of that other interest: sub-para (4). Its effect is to adjust the partnership share attributable to a partner for the purposes of calculating the lower proportion under para 20. It will be remembered that para 20 requires one to test whether, in the case of each relevant partner (or connected person) his proportionate interest in the relevant chargeable interest immediately before the transaction is larger or smaller than his partnership share—ie than his proportionate share of partnership income profit.

In relation to cases where the relevant chargeable interest was transferred to the partnership on or after 20 October 2003, para 21(3) deems the partnership share attributable to the partner to be zero *unless* the land was transferred to the partnership by an instrument duly stamped with ad valorem stamp duty or which was transferred in circumstances such that SDLT was paid. In many instances this will not have been the case, as it will have been possible to contribute the property to the partnership stamp duty and SDLT free by way of a capital contribution. In such cases, as the lower proportion will be 0 per cent, the full market value of the property will be brought into charge under para 18 or 19 (as the case may be) on the eventual transfer of the property out of the partnership in circumstances falling within one of those paragraphs.

In cases where the chargeable interest was transferred to the partnership before 20 October 2003, or the interest was transferred later but under an acceptably taxed transaction, para 22 applies to determine the partnership share attributable to the relevant partner.

22.—The purpose of this paragraph is to identify how much of the partner's share is permitted to be taken into account in determining his lower proportion for the purpose of para 20. If the land in question was transferred to the partnership prior to 20 October 2003, his share is whatever it may have been on 19 October 2003 (assuming him to be a partner on that date) or his initial share on joining the partnership (if he became a partner after that date). To that may be added any increases in his partnership share resulting from a transfer effected by an instrument which was duly stamped, or on which any SDLT due was paid if the transfer took place on or after 22 July 2004. And from that is deducted any decreases in his partnership share which fell within para 18 (transfers of chargeable interest from a partnership).

If, on the other hand, the land was transferred to the partnership after 19 October 2003, one first identified what the partner's partnership share was on the effective date or, if later, on the day he joined the partnership. One then adds to that any increases in his partnership share resulting from a transfer effected by an instrument which was duly stamped, or on which any SDLT due was paid if the transfer took place on or after 22 July 2004, and deducts from the result any decreases in his partnership share which fell within para 18. In each case, the result is the amount of his partnership share which may be taken into account for para 20 purposes. Any negative result is taken to be zero; and in any case where the person left the partnership either before 19 October 2003 or before the land was transferred to the partnership, his partnership share is also taken to be zero. For the effect of the application of these provisions, see paragraph 21 above.

Transfer of chargeable interest from a partnership to a partnership

23.—This paragraph is intended to prevent a double charge where otherwise there would have been a charge both under para 10 (transfer of chargeable interest to a partnership) and under para 18 (transfer of chargeable interest from a partnership). In each case one compares the two possible charges and accepts the higher of them. A corresponding rule applies where there would be charges to rent both under para 11 and under para 19: tax is charged on the greater amount of rent. The provision contemplates that in such a case the disapplication of the nil rate band by Sch 5 para 9(2) might have applied if the provision that does not give the greater amount of chargeable rent had applied. To counteract this possibility, para 23 secures that the nil rate band is disapplied if it would have been disapplied either by para 11(2B) or 19(2B).

Transfer of chargeable interest from a partnership consisting wholly of bodies corporate

24.—This paragraph equates to para 13 above. In each case where either para 18, 19 or 23 applies, and the SLP is 75 or more (as to which see para 20), instead of the complicated rules for determining what the chargeable consideration might be, one assumes the consideration (other than rent) to be equal to the market value of the interest transferred; and charges the consideration in the form of rent in precisely the same way as usual, using the rules in Sch 5 without the amendments made by para 19. However, it may be possible in such a case to rely on the partnership group relief afforded by para 27.

Application of exemptions and reliefs

25.—This paragraph excludes the operation of Sch 3 para 1 (which exempts from SDLT any land transaction for which there is no chargeable consideration) in any case where there is no actual consideration but which otherwise falls within one of the partnership transfer charging provisions, ie para 10, 14, 17 or 18. However, all other exemptions or reliefs from SDLT are available in relation to chargeable partnership transactions, subject only to the limitations imposed in respect of specific reliefs paras 26–28.

Disadvantaged areas relief

26.—Specific provision is made for the application of disadvantaged area relief in the case of a transfer of a partnership interest falling either under para 14 or 17. Such provision is necessary to cater for the fact that the transfer of a partnership interest is not a transfer of land. Accordingly, it is unnecessary to make any particular provision for cases where land in a disadvantaged area is transferred to or from a partnership. Paragraph 26 makes the necessary modifications to Sch 6 (disadvantaged areas relief) so that the relief applies to a transfer of a partnership interest as if it were an interest in land. The result is to secure that so much of the relevant consideration for the transfer of the interest as is attributable to land within a disadvantaged area obtains the appropriate amount of relief.

Application of group relief

27.—This paragraph secures that Pt 1 of Sch 7 (group relief) should apply to transfers from a company to a partnership falling either under para 10 (transfers of chargeable interest to a partnership) or under para 17 (transfer of partnership interest pursuant to earlier arrangements). Provision is made to ensure that a claw-back occurs under Sch 7 para 3 in the event that a partner leaves the partnership at a time when the relevant property is still held by the partnership.

27A—This paragraph introduces a form of group relief for the purposes of the computation of the sum of the lower proportions under para 12. In circumstances where the transferor company is a member of the same group as one or more of the other partners in the partnership, the SDLT chargeable on the transfer of the property to the partnership is reduced to the amount that would have been payable had the connected group partners been "corresponding partners" for the purposes of computing the SLP. The effect is to treat the members of the group as if they were individuals for this purpose. Paragraph 27A(3) makes provision for the modified application of the group relief provisions in Sch 7 to the relief afforded by para 27A(2).

Application of charities relief

28.—This paragraph provides for the application of charities relief under Sch 8 in appropriate circumstances involving the transfer of a partnership interest either falling within para 14 (transfer of partnership interest) or within para 17 (transfer of partnership interest pursuant to earlier arrangements). The transfer will attract charities relief if the transferee is a charity, provided that the partner holds every relevant chargeable interest for qualifying charitable purposes.

Acquisition of interest in a partnership not chargeable except as specially provided

29.—The paragraph confirms that it is only if an acquisition of a partnership interest falls within one of the specific partnership charging provisions, para 10 (transfers of chargeable interest to a partnership), 14 (transfer of partnership interest) or 17 (transfer of partnership interest pursuant to earlier arrangements) that it is liable to SDLT. In any other case, the acquisition is outside the scope of the tax, notwithstanding the fact that the partnership property includes land.

Transactions that are not notifiable

30.—Unless the consideration for a transaction exceeds specified thresholds (the zero rate threshold), the transaction is not notifiable. In each case, whether the consideration is rent or not, the relevant consideration must be such that the rate chargeable is 1 per cent or higher.

Stamp duty on transfers of partnership interests: continued application

31.—This paragraph preserves the charge to stamp duty on the transfer of partnership interests, subject only to certain modifications imposed by paras 32 and 33.

Stamp duty on transfers of partnership interests: modification

32.—Where there is a transfer of an interest in a partnership which attracts stamp duty as a transfer on sale and the relevant partnership property includes a chargeable interest in land (so that there is also a charge to SDLT under the provisions of this Schedule), the consideration for the transaction on which stamp duty is payable is the "reduced amount". This amount is defined as the actual consideration for the transfer less the "excluded amount", which in turn is defined as a proportion of the "net market value of the relevant partnership property immediately after the transfer". That proportion is, where the person acquiring the partnership share was not previously a partner, the partnership share acquired and, where the person was previously a partner, the increase in the partnership share. The "net market value of the relevant partnership property" is the market value of the interest in land at the date of the transfer less the amount of any loan secured solely on the interest in land at that date (where this result is negative it is to be taken as nil). If the excluded amount turns out to be greater than the actual consideration paid, the reduced amount is to be taken to be nil and no stamp duty is therefore chargeable.

There is a requirement that the instrument be produced to the Commissioners in accordance with Stamp Act 1891 s 12 if it is to be duly stamped.

33.—The effect of this paragraph is to restrict the amount of stamp duty payable on the residual charge on the transfer of a partnership interest to the amount which would be paid if the transfer were of the stock and marketable securities which are held as partnership property. The consideration for this transfer is specified to be the net market value of the stock and securities. The "net market value" is the market value of the stock and securities at the date of the transfer *less* the amount of any loan secured solely on the stock or securities at that date (where this result is negative it is to be taken as nil). In cases where the partnership property does not include any stock or marketable securities no stamp duty is payable.

There is a requirement that the instrument be produced to the Commissioners in accordance with Stamp Act 1891 s 12 if it is to be duly stamped.

Interpretation: partnership property and partnership share

34.—"Partnership property" is defined as any interest or right held by or on behalf of a partnership (or the members of the partnership) for the purposes of the partnership business.

Presumably, assets held on the partnership balance sheet but which are not held for the purposes of the partnership business do not constitute partnership property for the purposes of Sch 15.

References to a person's "partnership share" at any time are to the proportion in which he is then entitled to share in the income profits of the partnership: sub-para (2). This definition is central to the operation of Sch 15. It is a peculiarity of the legislation that it is far less concerned with the partner's actual right to participate in the profit (if any) on the sale of partnership capital land than in his right to enjoy the profits from the exploitation of the land during its period of ownership.

Interpretation: transfer of chargeable interest to a partnership

35.—This paragraph prescribes that a transfer of a chargeable interest to a partnership occurs wherever a chargeable interest becomes partnership property. Accordingly, it is irrelevant that an actual transfer occurs, provided that an interest in land which was not partnership property becomes partnership property as a result of a transaction.

Interpretation: transfer of interest in a partnership

36.—This paragraph defines the "transfer of an interest in a partnership" as any occasion on which a person acquires or increases his partnership share. The occasion on which this occurs is treated as one on which there is a transfer from the other partners to the partner of the relevant share in the partnership. Since a person's "partnership share" is itself defined by para 34(2) as the proportion in which he is entitled to share in the income profits of the partnership, it follows that charges to SDLT under para 14 occur only where there are changes in partnership income profit sharing ratios and not where there are changes in partnership capital sharing arrangements.

The above definition was introduced by FA 2007. The Act provides, though, that it is not to apply to a property-investment partnership which was established before the day on which FA 2007 was passed, provided that it has acquired no further chargeable interest from or after that date and that SDLT was paid in respect of each chargeable interest it acquired before that time by reference to an amount not less than the market value of the interest at the relevant time. In such a case, the old definition of a transfer of an interest in a partnership is retained, the effect of which was that there were two methods by which a partnership interest could be transferred. First, where there were arrangements under which an existing partner transferred the whole or part of his partnership interest (nb: *not* his "partnership share", as to which see para 34(2) above) to another person (whether or not that other person was himself a partner at the time). The second was where there were arrangements under which a person became a partner and an existing partner reduced his interest in the partnership (nb: *not* his partnership share—see above) or ceased to be a partner. The significant difference between the old definition and the new is that, under the old definition the mere joinder of a new partner, who made a capital contribution to a partnership, did not constitute a transfer of a partnership interest for the purposes of Sch 15 in the absence of a corresponding and positive withdrawal of partnership capital by another partner: see para 14(4)(*b*) above.

Interpretation: transfer of chargeable interest from a partnership

37.—Two methods of transfer of a chargeable interest from a partnership are defined. First, a transfer of a chargeable interest from a partnership occurs wherever a chargeable interest ceases to be partnership property. Accordingly, it is irrelevant whether an actual transfer occurs, provided that an interest in land which was partnership property ceases to be partnership property as a result of a transaction. Second, where a new chargeable interest is granted or created out of partnership property and the new interest is not partnership property. One obvious example would be the grant of a lease out a freehold interest owned by a partnership.

Interpretation: market value of leases

38.—This paragraph applies to the grant of a lease falling either within para 10 (transfers of chargeable interest to partnership) or 18 (transfer of chargeable interest from partnership). It provides that in valuing the lease, one should take account of tenant obligations only if they are obligations to make payments or they are of a kind within Sch 17A para 10(1) (tenants' obligations that do not count as chargeable consideration).

Interpretation: connected persons

39.—TA 1988 s 839 applies for the purpose of determining whether persons are connected, with the necessary omission of s 839(4), which otherwise would apply to make partners connected persons and with the omission also of s 839(3)(*c*). The latter omission is apparently a response to an SDLT avoidance scheme which was the subject of disclosure under the Tax Avoidance Schemes (Information) Regulations 2004 (SI 2004/1864).

Interpretation: arrangements

40.—For the purpose of the provisions in Sch 15 charging SDLT on partnership transactions (eg see para 36), "arrangements" is defined very widely as including any scheme, agreement or understanding, whether or not legally enforceable.

SCHEDULE 16 STAMP DUTY LAND TAX: TRUSTS AND POWERS

Meaning of "settlement" and "bare trust"

1.—This paragraph provides definitions of "settlement" and "bare trust" (and "nominee").

Interests of beneficiaries under certain trusts

2.—This paragraph provides for beneficiaries in Scotland and other countries or territory outside the UK, to be treated as having an equitable interest in trust property if that would be the result under English law.

Acquisition etc by bare trustee attributed to beneficial owner

3.—Where a person acquires a chargeable interest (other than on the grant of a lease) or an interest in a partnership as a bare trustee, the acquisition is treated as being the acquisition of the person for whom the bare trustee acts. The effect of this is that the interposition of the bare trustee is generally disregarded for SDLT purposes. This led to a possibility that the grant of a lease at a rack rent by the beneficial owner to a person acting for him as bare trustee, or a grant of such a lease by the bare trustee to his beneficial owner, would be a "nothing" for SDLT, since there would be neither vendor nor purchaser, but a person granting an interest in land to himself. The lease could then be assigned for little or no SDLT. To counteract this, it is provided that in such a case, the beneficial owner and the bare trustee are to be treated as vendor and purchaser (or vice versa as the case might be) and that SDLT be chargeable accordingly. There still remains an issue of what the consideration for this transfer might be.

Acquisition by trustees of settlement

4.—This paragraph provides that where trustees acquire a land interest or an interest in a partnership as purchasers, they are treated as acquiring the whole interest (both legal and beneficial). This means that there is no apportionment of consideration, and only a single land transaction, even though other persons will have acquired an equitable interest in the same transaction.

Responsibility of trustees of settlement

5.—By virtue of this paragraph, where the trustees are liable to make a payment of tax or interest on unpaid tax, a payment in accordance with an assessment under para 29 of Sch 10, or to a penalty, or interest on a penalty, under this Part, it may be recovered from one or more of the "responsible trustees" (as defined at sub-para (3)).

Relevant trustees for purposes of return etc

6.—This paragraph sets out the procedure for notification of an enquiry to trustees. Sub-para (1) confirms that a land transaction may be given by any one or more of the responsible trustees in relation to the transaction, and sub-para (2) confirms that the declaration required by para 1(1)(*c*) of Sch 10 must be made by the "relevant trustees." Under sub-para (3), if HMRC give notice of an enquiry, they must give it to each of the relevant trustees. Any of the trustees may apply for a direction that a closure notice be given, which if granted must be given to each of the relevant trustees. In accordance with sub-s (4) a HMRC determination or discovery assessment must be made against all of the relevant trustees, and is not effective against any of them unless it is given to all of the trustees whose identities are known to HMRC. Sub-para (5) sets out the requirements with regard to appeals by trustees.

Consideration for exercise of power of appointment or discretion

7.—In cases where a chargeable interest is acquired by virtue of the exercise of a power of appointment or discretion vested in trustees of a settlement, this paragraph provides that payment in order to become an object of the power or discretion is to be treated as consideration for the acquisition of the interest obtained by the exercise of the power. This is intended to prevent cases where a person who wishes to buy land from a trust instead pays to become an object of a power of appointment conferred on the trustees, and in due course the trustees (as their side of the bargain) exercise the power in favour of the purchaser.

Reallocation of trust property as between beneficiaries

8.—For a long time it was the view of Stamp Taxes that where trustees reallocated land between sub-funds, swapping land within sub-fund A for investments in sub-fund B, such transactions were to be treated as land transactions in respect of which SDLT was chargeable. This untenable view was eventually abandoned by the Commissioners, at least where the trustees were not required to have regard to the wishes of the relevant beneficiaries. Nevertheless, this left the more difficult case of where a beneficiary's consent was required to the changes in investments within the sub-trust. Paragraph 8, which applies from 20 July 2006, provides that, where a beneficiary consents to no longer having an interest in one type of trust property and acquires an interest in other trust property that includes a chargeable interest in land, that consent does not of itself trigger a charge to SDLT; the giving of consent does not constitute chargeable consideration for SDLT purposes. This limitation on the application of SDLT is, it must be observed, without prejudice to other provisions such as Sch 16 para 7: consideration for exercise of power or discretion.

SCHEDULE 17 STAMP DUTY LAND TAX: GENERAL COMMISSIONERS AND APPEALS AND OTHER PROCEEDINGS

General Commissioners: powers conferred by this Part

1.—By virtue of this paragraph, Part 1 of TMA 1970 applies to SDLT, the result of which is that the General and Special Commissioners have jurisdiction in appeals involving SDLT.

Prescribed matters to be determined by Commissioners or Lands Tribunal

2.—The Lord Chancellor may make regulations providing which body of Commissioners, or which relevant Lands Tribunal, is to determine which matter.

General or Special Commissioners: jurisdiction

3.—This paragraph deals with the Lord Chancellor's power to make regulations in order to determine whether the General or the Special Commissioners, or both of them, will deal with a matter. This paragraph also provides for regulations to determine which body of General Commissioners has jurisdiction. The Lord Chancellor may make regulations providing that in certain circumstances the Special Commissioners have jurisdiction and not the General Commissioners and vice versa. It also provides that General Commissioners of one division are to have jurisdiction with regard to a particular matter instead of the General Commissioners for another division.

Proceedings brought out of time

4.—This paragraph deals with the procedure for determining whether a late appeal should be heard.

Quorum etc of the Commissioners

5.—Under this paragraph, the Lord Chancellor may make regulations about the number of General or Special Commissioners required or permitted in relation to a particular matter.

Procedure

6.—The Lord Chancellor may make regulations about the practice and procedure to be followed by the Commissioners.

Consequences of determination by the Commissioners

7.—The Lord Chancellor may make regulations regarding the consequences of any determination by the Commissioners.

Costs

8.—The Lord Chancellor may make regulations dealing with the award of costs at appeal hearings.

Finality of decisions of the Commissioners

9.—The Lord Chancellor may by regulations determine the finality of any matter determined by the Commissioners.

Publication of reports of decisions

10.—The Lord Chancellor may make regulations authorising the Special Commissioners to publish such of their decisions as they consider appropriate.

Supplementary provisions

11.—This paragraph sets out various other provisions with regard to the making of and general administration regarding regulations under this Schedule.

SCHEDULE 17A FURTHER PROVISIONS RELATING TO LEASES

Meaning of "Lease"

1.—This paragraph defines a "lease" for the purposes of SDLT in its application to England and Wales or Northern Ireland. The definition extends (*a*) both to interests in land for a fixed or periodic term and to tenancies at will; and (*b*) to rights over land for a fixed term as well as to any other interest in land which is terminable by notice at any time. It thus appears to extend far beyond the usual meaning of a lease. The Scottish definitions are to be found in Sch 17A para 19.

Leases for a fixed term

2.—This paragraph ensures that for SDLT the length of a lease for a fixed term is to be taken to be the specified term—one ignores contingencies which would trigger the early determination of the lease, and one also ignores the right of either party either to bring the lease to an early end or to extend it. Thus, for example, a lease for a fixed term that includes a break clause exercisable by the tenant at any time is treated as a lease for the fixed term, and the possibility that the break clause might be exercised is disregarded.

Leases that continue after a fixed term

3.—Special rules are laid down for a lease for a fixed term that either specifies that it continues after the term until determined or which may continue beyond the end of the term by operation of law (eg a business tenancy). One begins by treating the lease as having a term equal to the fixed term. Thereafter, if the lease extends beyond the fixed term, it is first of all treated as a lease for the fixed term plus one year. If the lease goes beyond that extended period, it is treated as a lease for a fixed term plus two years. This principle is extended indefinitely, with the term growing on a year by year basis.

However, para 3(2) provides that this rule does not apply for the purposes of ss 77 and 77A (notifiable transactions), which for that purpose remains a lease for the fixed term alone: para 3(5). The effect of these provisions is that if a lease which is not notifiable, because it is for a fixed term of less than seven years, grows under para 3 into a term in excess of seven years, it nevertheless does not *for that reason* become notifiable.

In most cases, the effect of the extension of the lease is that tax (or additional tax) will become payable. Where this is the case, the purchaser must deliver an SDLT return (or a further return) within 30 days of the extension of the period: para 3(3)(*a*). The return will include a self-assessment of the tax (or additional tax) payable (para 3(3)(*b*)) and must be accompanied by the tax (or additional tax) payable: para 3(3)(*d*). Paragraph 3(3)(*c*) provides that the tax chargeable is to be calculated by reference to the rates in force at the effective date of the transaction. Under s 119, the effective date of the transaction would ordinarily be the date the lease was executed. However, para 3(4) provides for the administrative provisions in Sch 10 to apply as they would ordinarily do in relation to the usual SDLT return made under s 76, save that references to the "effective date" are to be read as references to the day on which the lease was extended beyond its previous period. It is far from clear that the effect of this rule applies to the rule in para 3(3)(*c*); but it is equally clear from the draft Lease chapter in HMRC's SDLT Manual that HMRC believes that it does: SDLTM 10620a.

The effect of these provisions is that, on each occasion that a return is made, the taxpayer must account for the difference between the tax as calculated under the longer lease and the tax paid previously.

Treatment of leases for an indefinite period

4.—Similar rules to those in para 3 apply to leases for an indefinite period, save that in the first instance, the initial period is treated as a lease for a fixed term of a year. Once the first year is over, the lease grows to a fixed term of two years and so on: para 4(1).

A lease for an indefinite term is to include periodic tenancies (and other periodic interests or rights) terminable on a period of notice, tenancies at will and other interests and rights terminable by notice at any time: para 4(5). One ignores all statutory rules which prescribe that a lease for an indefinite period is to be treated as a lease for a fixed period: para 4(2). Thus, for instance, one ignores the rule that a lease for life is treated as a lease for 90 years. For SDLT purposes, this is initially treated as a lease for a fixed term of one year; and for s 77 and 77A purposes (notifiable transactions), a lease for an indefinite period is treated as a lease for a term of less than seven years: para 4(4A). Accordingly, even though it may grow into a lease for a term of more than seven years for SDLT purposes generally, it does not, by reason of that extension of its terms alone, become a notifiable transaction.

In most cases, the effect of the extension of the lease is that tax (or additional tax) will become payable. Where this is the case, the purchaser must deliver an SDLT return (or a further return) within 30 days of the extension of the period: para 4(3)(*a*). The return will include a self-assessment of the tax (or additional tax) payable (para 4(3)(*b*)) and must be accompanied by the tax (or additional tax) payable: para 4(3)(*d*). Paragraph 4(3)(*c*) provides that the tax chargeable is to be calculated by reference to the rates in force at the effective date of the transaction. Under s 119, the effective date of the transaction would ordinarily be the date the lease was executed. However, para 4(4) provides for the administrative provisions in Sch 10 to apply as they would ordinarily do in relation to the usual SDLT return made under s 76, save that references to the "effective date" are to be read as references to the day on which the lease was extended beyond its previous period.

The effect of these provisions is that, on each occasion that a return is made, the taxpayer must account for the difference between the tax as calculated under the longer lease and the tax paid previously.

Treatment of successive linked leases

5.—This paragraph is designed to ensure that SDLT is not avoided by the parties granting a series of short leases (whether at the same time or at different times) of the same (or substantially the same) premises. If the grants are linked transactions, ie they form part of a single scheme, arrangement or series of transactions (s 108), the series of leases is treated as a single lease. That lease is taken to have been granted when the first lease was granted, for the aggregate term and for the total rent payable under all the leases.

Since SDLT is charged in full on the first lease, all other leases in the series are disregarded for SDLT purposes. The exception to this rule is that the later leases are not disregarded for the purpose of s 81A (return or further return in consequence of later linked transaction): the grant of the later linked lease imposes an obligation to make a return or further return in respect of the newly "extended" lease, and to pay the SDLT or additional SDLT in accordance with that section.

Note that any leases which were granted during the operation of stamp duty and which are not SDLT transactions are excluded from the application of this provision: Sch 19 para 7(4).

Rent

6.—The general rule is that any sum which is expressed to be payable in respect of rent, or in respect both of rent and other matters (without apportionment) is to be treated as entirely rent, and thus is chargeable to SDLT as such. So, if a single sum is reserved as rent for the occupation of serviced premises, the whole sum is brought into charge. If, on the other hand, a sum is reserved as rent and a further sum is required in respect of the provision of services, the latter sum is not chargeable to SDLT. Where, though, separate sums are reserved in this way, para 6(2) emphasises that Sch 4 para 4 applies (chargeable consideration: just and reasonable apportionment). So it is not possible to reduce the rent reserved by the lease whilst increasing the charge for services supplied beyond what they would reasonably bear.

Variable or uncertain rent

7.—It has proved difficult to strike a balance between the intention of the legislation that all consideration for a land transaction should be brought into charge and the need to ensure that businesses are not overburdened by the requirement to make an SDLT return every time there is an adjustment in the consideration payable under the transaction. This is especially problematical in the case of variable or contingent, uncertain or unascertained rent under a long-term lease. On each occasion that there is a rent review, the consideration reserved by the lease will be adjusted. Should there be a requirement to file an SDLT return after each review? The original rules in the FA 2003 were considered inadequate and were amended before they came into force. They were amended again in 2006.

Paragraph 7 now draws a distinction between rent payable before the end of the fifth year of the term of the lease and that payable after. All adjustments in rent payable during the first five years of the lease are taken into account in the same way as any other land transaction. So, in particular, the rules relating to contingent, uncertain or unascertained consideration contained in s 51(1) and (2) apply during the first five years.

However, a different rule applies to rent payable in any period after the end of the fifth year of the term: the rent payable in such later periods (whether or not that higher rent might be ascertainable from the start) is treated as the same as the highest rent payable in any consecutive twelve month period in the first five years of the term. Paragraph 7(3) provides that if some part of the amount in that twelve month period is uncertain, contingent or unascertained, that must be ascertained in accordance with the usual rules to arrive at the right "highest amount"—even presumably if it is only ascertained after the five year period has elapsed.

Sub-paragraph (4A) requires that where the amount of rent payable under the lease may vary under the provisions of the legislation governing agricultural tenancies (eg agricultural rent reviews under the Agricultural Holdings Act 1986 and the Agricultural Tenancies Act 1995), such variations are treated as the same way for the purposes of paras 7 and 8 as variations for which provision is made by the lease itself.

Adjustments in rent that are determined in line with the retail prices index are always ignored: para 7(5).

When an adjustment is to be made because the rent payable has ceased to be uncertain, the provisions of para 8 apply (see below).

There are special rules which apply where there is an "abnormal increase" in the rent after the fifth year of the lease: see para 14.

First rent review in the final quarter of fifth year

7A.—Paragraph 7A offers a degree of relief from the common situation of a rent review which occurs shortly before the end of the fifth year of the lease. In the case of leases of flats, to avoid a multiplicity of reviews, it is common practice for all rent reviews to occur on the fifth anniversary of a date which is common to all the flats in the block, even though some of the flats may have been let later (so that the fifth year of their term will expire later). Where a lease provides for a rent review five years after a specified date then, provided that that specified date falls within three months before the commencement of the term of the lease, the five year period for SDLT (and especially for para 7) is taken to expire at the review date. The effect of this is, of course, to ignore any increase in rent which occurs by reason of the rent review.

Adjustment where rent ceases to be uncertain

8.—This paragraph establishes when the additional land transaction return must be submitted (and extra tax paid) if a lease falls within para 7 (ie because the rent reserved is variable or uncertain). The rule is that a return is due at the end of the fifth year of the term of the lease or, if earlier, on the date when the rent reserved by the lease becomes certain. So, if the result of para 7 is that the land transaction (ie the grant of the lease) becomes a notifiable transaction, para 8 requires the purchaser to make a return within 30 days of the relevant date, to make the appropriate self-assessment of the tax payable and to pay the tax.

If, on the other hand, the effect of the reconsideration under para 7 is that less tax is due than was previously paid, the purchaser may make a claim to amend his land transaction return, or, if the period for amendment has expired, for the repayment of the excess (plus interest). The administrative provisions in Sch 10 apply as they would ordinarily do in relation to the usual SDLT return made under s 76, save that references to the "effective date" in those provisions are to be read as references to the relevant date under para 8(1), that is to say, the end of the fifth year of the term or the day when the rent became certain.

Rent for overlap period in case of grant of further lease

9.—This is a relieving provision, designed to ensure that SDLT is not paid twice in relation to the same rent. If A surrenders an old lease to B in consideration of B granting A a new lease of substantially the same premises, the rent charged to SDLT on the new lease is reduced by the amount of rent foregone under the old lease for the period from the date of the grant of the new lease to the end of the term of the old lease.

However, the provision does not apply to the early surrender of a lease on which stamp duty rather than SDLT was paid: para 9(4); and the provision does not enable the rent under the new lease to be reduced to a negative sum (presumably preventing a repayment claim from being made where the rent under the new lease is less than the rent reserved under the old): para 9(5).

The Commissioners have given a certain amount of guidance as to the manner in which this provision operates in Stamp Taxes Bulletin – June 2010, in cases where a lease is completed following substantial performance – a case which is treated by Sch 17A para 12A(3) as the surrender of an old lease in consideration of the grant of a new one relating to the same premises. The general rule is, of course, that rent increases in year six of a lease are to be ignored in calculating the NPV of the lease. The question is whether the rent increase in year six can be ignored in the circumstances where the agreement for lease was substantially performed and, nine months later, the lease itself was granted. The Commissioners accept that, where there has been no change in the terms of the lease (eg by a variation of the lease), the increased rent may be considered to have been "taken into account" on substantial performance, for the purposes of para 9 in relation to the grant of the lease. The Commissioners have also indicated that this approach applies to the application of overlap provisions generally (and not only where there has been substantial performance). It must be understood that this policy does not affect the operation of the rules applying where there has been an abnormal increase in the rent after the fifth year.

Backdated lease granted to tenant holding over

9A.—A particular problem of continuing in occupation after a fixed term lease has come to an end but before the terms of the new lease to be granted have been agreed, is the nature of the payments made in the interim period. If the new lease is backdated to the end of the old lease the effect of Sch 5 para 1A is that the rent agreed to be paid for that period is deemed not to be rent but a premium, with the attendant higher charge to SDLT. If on the other hand the old lease continues beyond the contractual termination date by operation of law, the tenant is obliged to make a further SDLT return and account for SDLT on the additional rent thereby falling due: Sch 17A para 3. As a simplification measure para 9A displaces Sch 5 para 1A provided the new lease is of the same or substantially the same premises and the term of the new lease begins on or immediately after the contractual termination date of the old lease. In such a case: (*a*) the lease is taken to begin on the date specified by the new lease; and (*b*) the rent that was charged to SDLT under Sch 17A para 3 is taken to reduce the rent payable under the new lease for the interim period.

Tenants' obligations that do not count as chargeable consideration

10.—This provision excludes certain undertakings and obligations from the class of chargeable consideration. It is necessary because Sch 4 para 11 would otherwise bring all such undertakings into charge as "the provision of services". The paragraph provides that in the case of the grant of a lease, various usual obligations (excluding rent) do not count as chargeable consideration, for example undertakings by the tenant to repair, maintain or insure the premises. Where a lease is assigned or surrendered by either the landlord or the tenant, the assumption or release of any such obligation (eg a rent guarantee) is also excluded. Where a tenant agrees to meet the landlord's reasonable costs of granting a lease, that undertaking is not treated as chargeable consideration for the purposes of SDLT.

Case where assignment of lease is treated as grant of lease

11.—This paragraph was introduced to counteract an SDLT avoidance device which relied on the grant of a lease in certain circumstances being exempt from SDLT. Although there were various different forms of the scheme, one version involved the grant of a rack-rent lease by one group company to another. If the transaction fell within Sch 7 para 1, there would be no charge to SDLT. The lease would then be assigned to a third party purchaser for a nominal consideration (since the lease was valueless, being at a rack-rent). There would thus be no SDLT payable on a transaction which effectively involved the grant of a lease by a vendor to an unconnected purchaser.

Where the grant of the lease is exempt by reason of the application of any of five specified cases, the paragraph requires the first assignment of that lease be treated as the grant of a new lease by the assignor for the residue of the term and for the residue of the rent. Accordingly, SDLT will be payable as if a new lease had been granted between unconnected persons.

There is an exception for cases where the exemption had already been clawed back as a result of a disqualifying event having previously occurred—for example, on the original grantee ceasing to be within the same group as the lessor (see Sch 7 paras 3 and 9) or the lease having ceased to be used for charitable purposes only (see Sch 8 para 2).

A further exception is afforded where the assignment of the lease is within FA 2009 Sch 61 (alternative finance investment bonds). Relief under s 61 is available only where the relevant land transaction takes the form either of a transfer of a freehold interest in land or of an assignment of an existing lease. The effect of the operation of Sch 17A para 11 is to convert what would have been an assignment into a deemed grant, thereby denying relief in circumstances in which Sch 61 is intended to apply. Accordingly, para 11(2A) displaces para 11(1) if the transaction would otherwise be exempt under Sch 61.

Assignment of lease: responsibility of assignee for returns etc

12.—This paragraph shifts to the assignee of a lease continuing responsibilities, which would otherwise have fallen on the original grantee, for adjustments to the original land transaction return (if any). The paragraph applies, for example, where the lease continues beyond its fixed term, or where a contingent event occurs (or fails to happen), or where the amount of rent becomes certain.

Agreement for lease

12A.—The legislation now equates leases and (substantially performed) agreements for leases. An agreement for a lease which is substantially performed is treated as a notional lease separate from the lease which the parties have agreed should be granted by the vendor to the purchaser. So, where a purchaser goes into occupation of the premises under the terms of the agreement (without the lease being granted to him), para 12A(2) treats the agreement as a lease granted on the date of substantial performance. Correspondingly, where the lease itself is eventually granted, it is treated as the surrender of the notional lease and the grant of a new lease in respect of which overlap relief (see para 9) is available: para 12A(3). However, the usual rules for successive linked leases in Sch 17A para 5 do not apply to link the notional old lease with the actual lease. The actual lease is thus to be taken as having been granted for SDLT purposes on the actual date of its grant and not when the agreement for lease was substantially performed; and there is no disregard of the actual lease in favour of the notional lease.

Provision is made for repayment of tax if the agreement is subsequently rescinded or annulled or otherwise not carried into effect: para 12A(4).

It is assumed that the reason for using this device of the notional lease is to secure that all the rules in Sch 17A apply to the agreement for lease as well as to the lease itself.

Assignment of agreement for lease

12B.—Paragraph 12B applies (instead of s 45) where the purchaser under an agreement for lease assigns the benefit of the lease. How the paragraph operates depends on whether the agreement is substantially performed before or after assignment.

If the agreement is assigned *before* substantial performance, then the original purchaser drops out of the equation and s 44 (contract and conveyance) applies as if the agreement were between the vendor and the assignee: sub-para (2). The assignee thus becomes responsible.

If, on the other hand, the agreement is assigned *after* substantial performance, the assignment is treated as a separate land transaction from the agreement for a lease. Thus, in this case a charge to SDLT will have been imposed on the original purchaser on substantial performance and a further charge to SDLT will be imposed on the consideration paid by the assignee for the assignment: sub-para (3). If, though, a lease is then granted to the assignee, he should obtain overlap relief under para 9 (see para 12A(3)), effectively getting credit for the SDLT paid by his predecessor.

Provision is made for these rules to apply where there are successive assignments: para 12B(4).

Increase of rent treated as grant of new lease: variation of lease in first five years

13.—If the parties to a lease agree that the rent should be increased as from a date before the end of the fifth year of the lease, this is treated as the grant of a new lease for the additional rent: sub-para (1). The effect is that SDLT is charged on that extra rent. However, this does not apply if the lease itself makes provision for the potential increase (sub-para (2)), since this will already have been brought into charge as part of the "variable or contingent rent", see para 7. Nor will this provision apply if the lease is reviewed under the legislation governing agricultural tenancies: see Sch 17A para 3. If the rent is increased from a date falling after the first five years of the lease, such an increase will only be chargeable to SDLT if it falls within the provisions for abnormal rent increases in para 14.

Increase of rent treated as grant of new lease: abnormal increase after fifth year

14.—In order to prevent the avoidance of SDLT by leases under which the rent reserved was kept low for the first five years and increased dramatically in year six (which increases would have been outside the scope of the charge under para 7), a special rule exists for leases under which there is an "abnormal increase in the amount of the rent payable" in accordance with the provisions of the lease (eg a rent review) or otherwise (eg by agreement of the parties). Paragraph 15 defines what constitutes an "abnormal increase".

The paragraph requires the increase in rent to be treated as if it were the grant of a new lease for the "excess rent" and SDLT is accordingly payable on that notional additional consideration. The "excess rent" is found by subtracting the rent previously taxed from the "new rent": sub-para (3); and the "rent previously taxed" will generally be the amount which has previously been brought into charge on the application of para 7(3) as payable for years six onwards of the lease: sub-para (4)(*a*). However, in cases where para 13 applied on an increase in the rent during the first five years of the lease, the rent previously taxed is taken to be the rent payable as a result of the variation: sub-para 4(*b*). Note that this will be the whole of the rent so payable and not merely the additional rent which was charged under para 13.

Paragraph 14 can apply on more than one occasion (ie if there is a number of occasions on which an abnormal increase occurs). If this is the case, then account will be taken of the previous charge: sub-para 4(*c*).

Paragraph 14 applies only to leases granted (or treated as granted) after the implementation of the SDLT rules on 1 December 2003: sub-para (7).

Increase of rent after fifth year: whether regarded as abnormal

15.—A complicated set of rules is given to identify whether an increase in rent is "abnormal". The effect of the calculation is, broadly speaking, to treat as abnormal any case where the difference between the old rent and the new rent exceeds a flat-rate annual increase of 20 per cent of the old rent. Thus, if in 2010 there were a review of the rent payable under a lease granted 6½ years previously at an initial rent of £100,000 per annum, the new rent would only be abnormal if it were to exceed £220,000 (£100,000 + (£100,000 × 6/5)).

Examples where the legislation may inadvertently bite are profit rentals, or rents under mineral or forestry leases, where the rent reserved each year is a function of the rate of extraction of the relevant commodity. It is notable that there is no provision for a repayment of SDLT where there is a later "abnormal decrease" in the amount of the rent.

Reduction of rent or term or other variation of lease

15A.—Three new occasions of charge are created by this provision:

(1) If the parties vary the terms of a lease so as to *reduce the rent*, the *lessee* is treated as acquiring a chargeable interest in land. So, if the lessee makes a composition payment to discharge his obligation to pay rent in the future, he will be liable to SDLT as if the payment were consideration for a land transaction (para 15(1)).

(2) If the lessee gives consideration (otherwise than in the form of an increase in rent) for any variation of the lease not involving an adjustment either:

(a) to the rent reserved by the lease (this being dealt with by paragraph 1 above); or

(b) to the term of the lease (which in all likelihood would constitute a surrender and regrant of the lease, with its own SDLT consequences—see para 16 below),

the variation is treated as the acquisition of a chargeable interest by the lessee for the consideration paid (para 15(1A)).

(3) If the parties to a lease agree to *reduce the term* of the lease, the *lessor* is treated as acquiring a chargeable interest in land. So, if the landlord pays the tenant to agree to this, it will be the landlord who must pay SDLT on the transaction (para 15(2)).

These provisions are necessary in light of the amendment to s 43(3) which removes all variations of leases from the class of "acquisitions and disposals of chargeable interests" other than those which take effect as the grant of a new lease. Paragraph 15A(2) thus provides the mirror image to the charge on extensions to the term of a lease (which in English law inevitably involves a surrender and regrant). Paragraph 15A(1) corresponds to the charge on the increase in rent imposed by para 13. Paragraph 15A(1A) was introduced to counteract SDLT planning which involved, for example, the grant of a lease on unfavourable terms (and therefore for a reduced amount of consideration) followed by negotiations between the parties under which a capital sum was paid by the lessee for the removal of the relevant terms.

Surrender of existing lease in return for new lease

16.—In situations where a lease is granted in consideration of the surrender of an existing lease of the same or substantially the same premises, with substantially the same unexpired term, and on the same or substantially the same terms, the grant of the new lease does not count as chargeable consideration for the surrender, and the surrender does not count as chargeable consideration for the grant of the new lease. It should be noted, however, that any additional consideration and rent for the new lease will constitute chargeable consideration. A premium paid by the landlord to the tenant on surrender would also be chargeable, but a reverse premium on the surrender or new lease will not constitute chargeable consideration. It is specifically provided that the surrender and regrant are not to be treated as an exchange of interests in land for the purpose of Sch 4 para 5.

Assignment of lease: assumption of obligations by assignee

17.—This confirms what might have been thought to be obvious, but which was not covered by the original SDLT legislation: the assumption by the assignee of a lease of the various obligations imposed on a tenant by the lease itself, in particular the obligation to pay rent, is not to count as chargeable consideration for SDLT purposes. The obligation to pay such rent in the future will of course already have formed part of the calculation of the SDLT liability of the grantee of the lease. It is to be understood that para 17 does not override paras 7 and 8 (or indeed paras 13 and 14), so that the assignee may yet have responsibilities for SDLT: see para 12.

Reverse premium

18.—A reverse premium does not count as chargeable consideration on the grant, assignment or surrender of a lease. The definition of "land transaction" and "purchaser" might otherwise have included such transactions.

Loan or deposit in connection with grant or assignment of lease

18A.—A scheme was devised to secure a financial advantage for a landowner granting a lease without a charge to SDLT. The lessee would pay a deposit or make a loan (whether or not to the landlord), and the repayment of the loan or deposit was conditional on an act or omission by the lessee, or on the lessee's death. The argument ran that, since the loan or deposit was neither rent nor paid in lieu of rent, it was at best contingent consideration for which an application could be made under FA 2003 s 90 to postpone the payment of the SDLT until the contingency was satisfied. However, the real consideration consisted in the use of the funds and not in the potential right to the funds in the future.

This is counteracted by para 18A. In a case where such arrangements are made in connection with the grant of a lease, the amount of the loan or deposit is treated as a premium given for the grant. And, in the case of the assignment of a lease, where such a sum is paid to another by the assignee, or a person connected with him, the amount of the loan or deposit is taken to be consideration for the assignment.

However, to save ordinary commercial deposit arrangements, these rules do not apply if the sum deposited is no more than twice "the relevant maximum rent". This is taken to be the highest rent payable in any 12 month period in the first five years of the lease, and in the case of assignment the highest rent payable in any 12 month period in the first five years of the unexpired portion of the term.

Provision is made for de minimis adjustments to be ignored in cases where a charge would only arise by reason of the disapplication of the 0 per cent band in cases where the relevant rental figure is not less than £1,000.

Provisions relating to leases in Scotland

19.—This paragraph is designed to secure the corresponding operation of the SDLT legislation for leases under the different legal regime in Scotland.

SCHEDULE 18 STAMP DUTY LAND TAX: CONSEQUENTIAL AMENDMENTS

Provisional Collection of Taxes Act 1968

1.—This paragraph inserts a reference to SDLT into Provisional Collection of Taxes Act 1968 s 1(1) (see commentary).

Inheritance Tax Act 1984

2.—This paragraph inserts a reference to SDLT (after an existing reference to stamp duty) into a IHTA 1984 s 190(4).

Income and Corporation Taxes Act 1988

3.—This paragraph adds references to SDLT to TA 1988 ss 209B(4) (hedging arrangements), 213(11) (exempt distributions), 214(2) (chargeable payments connected with exempt distributions) and 215(2) (advance clearance by Board of distributions and payments), and inserts a new TA 1988 s 827(1F) providing that interest or penalties levied under SDLT legislation are not allowed as a deduction in computing income, profits or losses for tax purposes.

Finance Act 1989

4.—FA 1989 s 178(2) is amended to allow the Treasury to set rates of interest on unpaid tax, penalties and repayments of tax overpaid for SDLT purposes.

Taxation of Chargeable Gains Act 1992

5.—TCGA 1992 s 38(2) (incidental costs of acquisition and disposal) is amended to add a reference to SDLT.

Income Tax (Earnings and Pensions) Act 2003

6.—ITEPA 2003 s 277(3) is amended to add a reference to SDLT.

SCHEDULE 19 STAMP DUTY LAND TAX: COMMENCEMENT AND TRANSITIONAL ARRANGEMENTS

Introduction

1.—By virtue of this paragraph, the provisions relating to SDLT came into force on 10 July 2003 and the paragraphs below have effect to determine what transactions are chargeable/notifiable/subject to the s 79 registration provisions.

The implementation date

2.—This paragraph confirms that a transaction will not be a SDLT transaction unless its effective date (see s 44) is on or after the "implementation date", namely, 1 December 2003.

Contract entered into before first relevant date

3.—A transaction is not an SDLT transaction, whatever its "effective date", if it is effected pursuant to a contract entered into before 11 July 2003. This general rule does not apply if the contract is varied or assigned on or after 11 July 2003, or if the transaction is effected in consequence of the exercise after 11 July 2003 of an option, right of pre-emption or similar right, or if as a result of an assignment, sub-sale or other transaction, made on or after 11 July 2003, a person other than the purchaser under the earlier contract becomes entitled to call for a conveyance to him.

Contract substantially performed before implementation date

4.—The general rule is that a transaction effected in pursuance of a contract entered into (or varied, assigned, etc) on or after 11 July 2003 but before the implementation date (ie 1 December 2003) will be within the SDLT regime if completed after the implementation date, even if the contract was substantially performed before the implementation date (unless the contract was substantially performed before 11 July 2003). However, this rule does not apply to transactions which fall within para 3—which remain stamp duty transactions rather than SDLT transactions. Paragraph 4 thus brings into the class of SDLT transactions: (*a*) all transactions under contracts made *after* 10 July 2003 which are completed on or after 1 December 2003; and (*b*) all transactions under contracts made *before* 11 July 2003 which fall outside para 3 because of an event falling within para 3(3) and which are substantially performed or completed after 1 December 2003.

Contract substantially performed after implementation date

4A.—A transaction effected in pursuance of a contract entered into before 11 July 2003, which is substantially performed (but not completed) only after 1 December 2003, will ordinarily be treated as a stamp duty and not an SDLT transaction: para 3. However, some such transactions will later prove to be SDLT transactions because an event occurs which falls within para 3(3). It is HMRC's view that such a later event may affect the earlier substantial performance of the contract, so that the later event makes the earlier substantial performance the "effective date" of the consequent SDLT transaction in accordance with s 44(4). Whatever the merits of this analysis, since it would be unfair for a taxpayer to be in default of rendering his land transaction return within 30 days of substantial performance, para 4A provides that, in such a case, the effective date of the transaction is delayed until the date of the later para 3(3) event.

Application of provisions in case of transfer of rights

4B.—This paragraph is designed to facilitate the operation of the transitional provisions in paras 3, 4 and 4A, where the original purchaser under the contract has assigned his rights, sub-sold the property or has effected any other transaction as a result of which a person other than that purchaser becomes entitled to call for a conveyance to him (a "transfer of rights" within s 45(1)). In order to prevent the transferee of the rights unfairly being able to claim that he takes under a contract made before 11 July 2003, or 1 December 2003, as the case may be, para 4B treats his secondary contract as made at the date of the relevant assignment or sub-sale and not at the earlier time of the original contract. If, of course, that earlier assignment also took place before 11 July 2003, then he too may be entitled to rely on the transitional provisions.

Credit for ad valorem stamp duty paid

5.—This paragraph confirms that where a transaction is subject to SDLT but the contract has already had ad valorem stamp duty paid on it, the amount of SDLT will be reduced by the

Part II ST

stamp duty paid (but not so as to give rise to a repayment). Under sub-para (2), in cases where the availability of any exemption or relief is dependent on SDLT having been paid or payable on an earlier transaction, that requirement is satisfied if stamp duty was paid or payable.

Effect for stamp duty purposes of stamp duty land tax being paid or chargeable

6.—Sub-paragraphs (2) and (3) extend the exclusion from the claw-back of stamp duty group or acquisition relief under FA 2002 s 111(1)(*c*) or s 113(1)(*c*) respectively, to cases where SDLT has been paid on an intra-group transfer, made at market value, of the estate or interest in land which is held by the company when it leaves the group (or it suffers a change of control) during the three year recovery period.

Earlier related transactions under stamp duty

7.—This paragraph deals with linked transactions where some fall within the old stamp duty regime and some within SDLT and provides that the linked chargeable consideration for SDLT is to be, or include, the stamp duty consideration. Sub-paragraph (2) makes the relief set out at Sch 9 for the transfer of the reversion under a shared ownership lease available where stamp duty was paid on the original lease. Sub-paragraph (3) provides that references to group relief in s 54(4)(*b*) apply to the same relief claimed under the stamp duty legislation before the implementation date. Sub-paragraph (4) excludes from the treatment of successive linked leases under Sch 17A para 5 any transaction that is not an SDLT transaction.

Stamping of contract where transaction on completion subject to stamp duty land tax

7A.—Where a contract was entered into before the implementation date and that contract would have been chargeable with stamp duty by reason only of FA 1999 Sch 13 para 7 (contracts chargeable as conveyances on sale) then, if the transaction effected on completion is an SDLT transaction (or would be if it were not exempted or relieved from SDLT), it may be denoted with the SDLT so paid (or with the fact that it was exempt or relieved from tax). The procedure is for the contract to be presented for stamping together with the relevant HMRC certificate of compliance with the SDLT regime. The contract will then be denoted as explained above and thereupon is deemed to have been duly stamped.

Stamping agreement for lease: lease subject to stamp duty land tax

8.—Where an agreement for lease is entered into before the implementation date and is completed by a lease subject to SDLT (or which is exempt or relieved from SDLT) then, provided the agreement is presented for stamping accompanied by a HMRC certificate that the purchaser has complied with the SDLT requirements on the grant of the lease, the agreement will be denoted with such SDLT paid (or the fact that none was payable) on the grant of the lease, and will be deemed to be duly stamped. The provision thus reverses the position which applied for stamp duty under FA 1994 s 240, under which one stamped the agreement and impressed the denoting stamp on the lease.

Exercise of option or right of pre-emption acquired before implementation date

9.—This provision catches post-17 April 2003 attempts to avoid ad valorem stamp duty by splitting the consideration between the sum paid for the grant of an option and the sum payable for the exercise of the option and not stamping the deed by which the option is granted. Where an option to enter into a land transaction is acquired on or after 17 April 2003 but before 1 December 2003 and is exercised after 1 December, any consideration for the grant is treated as part of the consideration for its exercise and so will be subject to SDLT (with credit for any stamp duty paid on the option grant). Similar provisions apply to rights of pre-emption.

Supplementary

10.—"Contract" is defined as including any agreement.

SCHEDULE 20 STAMP DUTY LAND TAX: RESTRICTION TO INSTRUMENTS RELATING TO STOCK OR MARKETABLE SECURITIES

PART 1 SUPPLEMENTARY PROVISIONS

Reduction of stamp duty where instrument partly relating to stock or marketable securities

1.—This paragraph provides that the consideration contained in an instrument relating partly to the transfer on sale of stock or marketable securities, and partly to other property, is to be apportioned on a just and reasonable basis. Stamp duty is charged on the consideration attributable to the stock or marketable securities.

Apportionment of consideration for stamp duty purposes

2.—This paragraph amends SA 1891 s 58. Sub-section (1) provides that where part of the property referred to in SA 1891 s 58(1) (consideration to be apportioned between different instruments as parties think fit) consists of stock or marketable securities, the consideration is now to be apportioned on a "just and reasonable" basis. Sub-section (2) provides that where property containing stock or marketable instruments is purchased for one consideration by two or more connected persons, and is then conveyed in parts by separate instruments, the consideration is to be apportioned on a just and reasonable basis. The consideration for each part in such cases is to be shown on each instrument and charged to ad valorem stamp duty accordingly. Under sub-para (3), if apportionment under the preceding sub-paragraphs has not been made on a just and reasonable basis, then stamp duty is chargeable as if the consideration had been apportioned on a just and reasonable basis. Sub-para (4) provides a definition of "relevant person" for the purposes of this paragraph, and that whether people are connected with one another or not is to be determined in accordance with TA 1988 s 839.

PART 2 CONSEQUENTIAL AMENDMENTS AND REPEALS

Removal of unnecessary references to "conveyance"

3.—By virtue of this section, references to "conveyance or transfer" are replaced by "transfer" in enactments relating to stamp duty.

Finance Act 1895

4.—This paragraph makes consequential amendments to FA 1895 s 12.

Finance Act 1990

5.—This paragraph makes consequential amendments to FA 1990 s 108.

Finance Act 1999

6.—This paragraph makes consequential amendments to FA 1999 Sch 13 para 1(2).

Power to make further consequential amendments or repeals

7.—The Treasury is empowered to make regulations under this paragraph which amend or repeal stamp duty or stamp duty reserve tax enactments pursuant to the abolition of stamp duty except with regard to instruments relating to stocks or marketable securities.

Finance Act 2004

2004 Chapter 12

PART 7 DISCLOSURE OF TAX AVOIDANCE SCHEMES

306. Meaning of "notifiable arrangements" and "notifiable proposal"

FA 2004 ss 306–319 provide new disclosure obligations on promoters of tax avoidance schemes to provide details of the schemes to HMRC. Taxpayers will be required to provide details of the schemes they have devised in-house or acquired from an overseas promoter who has not made a corresponding disclosure.

Notifiable arrangements means arrangements as described by statutory instrument, which, for SDLT, are The Stamp Duty Land Tax Avoidance Schemes (Prescribed Descriptions of Arrangements) Regulations 2005, SI 2005/1868, which enable any person to obtain a tax advantage and the main benefit or one of the main benefits that might be expected to arise from the arrangements is the obtaining of that advantage. A notifiable proposal means a proposal which if entered into would be notifiable arrangements.

306A. Doubts as to notifiability

There may be a dispute between HMRC and a potential promoter as to whether or not a tax proposal or arrangements fall within the scope of DOTAS. Where this is so, the Commissioners may apply to the First-Tier Tribunal for an order that the proposal or arrangements should be so treated (even though it might not in fact prove on further investigation to be so). The importance of this is that the person in question must then comply with the duties imposed on a promoter (eg disclosing relevant information and notifying his clients of the scheme registration number (SRN)). The section contains safeguards which must be considered by the Tribunal, intended to ensure that HMRC will only obtain an order in cases where they have taken all reasonable steps to establish whether or not the scheme is notifiable and have reasonable grounds for suspecting that it is. When an order is made for a scheme to be treated as notifiable, the Tribunal will specify a date from which the deemed promoter is liable to comply with the statutory requirements for disclosable schemes.

307. Meaning of "promoter"

A promoter is someone who provides taxation services to others in the course of a trade, profession or business or is a bank or securities lease and who is (to any extent) responsible for the design of a notifiable proposal or who designs, organises or manages notifiable arrangements. An exception is made for persons who are taken out of the provisions by statutory instrument, The Tax Avoidance Schemes (Promoters and Prescribed Circumstances) Regulations 2004 SI 2004/1865. Those regulations remove the status of promoter in cases where the person is in the same group of companies as the persons to whom the taxation services are provided; where the potential promoter is an employee of the person to whom the proposal is made available; and, lastly, where the person in question either is not responsible for the design or implementation of the relevant tax advantage or does not give taxation advice in relation to the relevant structure.

The concept of promoter has been extended to include someone who acts in an intermediary capacity, by approaching a client or potential client with a scheme which has been devised by another. The legislation has also been widened to bring in the concept of an 'introducer': someone who markets the notifiable proposals to third parties. Such a person now may be required to provide information as to the name of the promoter and details of the scheme to the Commissioners, in accordance with s 313A–313C. There was a lacuna in the previous form of the legislation which meant that the Commissioners could become aware of a scheme but not who was promoting it; and the intermediary was under no obligation to provide information since he was not himself a promoter for the purposes of the legislation. It is this which the amendment is intended to counteract.

308. Duties of promoter

A promoter must in accordance with regulations, The Tax Avoidance Schemes (Information) Regulations 2004, SI 2004/1864, as amended by The Tax Avoidance Schemes (Information) (Amendment) Regulations 2005, SI 2005/1869, provide HMRC with information relating to any notifiable proposal. Until 2010 the relevant date for the commencement of the prescribed period was the date on which the promoter makes a notifiable proposal available for implementation or becomes aware of any transaction forming part of the proposed arrangements. Although these trigger points still exist, a new event has been added in order to prevent promoters waiting until the last moment before having to submit the necessary scheme information to HMRC. The concern was that, by the promoter delaying the time at which the scheme was made available until very shortly before it was implemented (possibly by a number of clients), HMRC would be unable to counteract the structure until a considerable amount of tax had been lost. Accordingly, the relevant date is now the earliest of the two dates already mentioned and the date on which the promoter first makes a firm approach to a person in relation to a notifiable arrangement. A promoter must give HMRC the required information unless notification has already been made by the promoter or a co-promoter. Where notifiable arrangements are substantially the same only one notification is required. As a general rule, the promoter is obliged to make the disclosure within five days of the relevant date: see reg 4 of The Tax Avoidance Schemes (Information) Regulations 2004.

308A. Supplemental information

In cases where HMRC are not satisfied that the promoter has provided all the information that he is required to provide, the Commissioners may apply to the First-Tier Tribunal for an order that he provide either specified information or further documents relating to the scheme. As usual, safeguards are built in to ensure that the Commissioners may only obtain that which they reasonably suspect is required by statute.

309. Duty of person dealing with promoter outside the UK

Where a client enters into notifiable arrangements with a non-UK resident promoter and there is no UK promoter he must provide HMRC with the required information. A non-UK resident promoter can give information to HMRC on notifiable arrangements, in which case the client is not required to do so.

310. Duty of parties to notifiable arrangements not involving promoter

Where a taxpayer enters into notifiable arrangements and no other UK person is liable to disclose these to HMRC, the taxpayer must provide the required information.

311. Arrangements to be given reference numbers

HMRC may allocate a reference number to any notifiable proposals or arrangements within 30 days and notify the discloser of the reference number.

312. Duty of promoter to notify client of number

Within 30 days of first becoming aware of notifiable arrangements or receipt of a reference number, if later, a promoter must notify the client of that number. Until 2010, the SRN procedure did not apply to SDLT schemes: the DOTAS rules for SDLT obliged promoters to provide HMRC with relevant information about the schemes which were promoted; but there was no requirement that the client be provided with an SRN which he would then have to use in making his own disclosure to the Commissioners that he had implemented the scheme. This is no longer the case: the promoter must obtain an SRN from HMRC and provide it to his client; and the client is then obliged to notify HMRC of his use of the scheme in the usual way. It should be noted, though, that the manner in which the rules have been changed is somewhat unexpected: a wide 'grandfathering rule' has been introduced which exempts from the category of notifiable arrangements any scheme which is the same or substantially the same as an arrangement made available by any person before 1 April 2010. Such a scheme is not disclosable, does not require an SRN and need not be notified to the client under s 312 or by the client under s 313 to HMRC.

312A. Duty of client to notify parties of number

In order to avoid the risk that the promoter might provide an SRN to a client who had transmitted the information relating to the scheme to another who made use of it, this section requires the client to notify the user of the relevant SRN, so that the user may make the appropriate return to the Commissioners.

313. Duty of parties to notifiable arrangements to notify Board of number, etc

As specified in regulations, any party to any notifiable arrangements must, when he obtains or expects to obtain an advantage in relation to tax, notify HMRC of the reference number. Such regulations may require the reference number and other information to be included in any tax return. A failure to provide a reference number does not give rise to a penalty under these rules for incorrect returns or accounts, although penalties may be charged under these provisions in accordance with FA 2004 s 315, inserting TMA 1970 s 98C.

313ZA. Duty to provide details of clients

Any promoter who provides services to clients in connection with notifiable arrangements must provide HMRC with prescribed information as to his clients. This will involve the promoter providing HMRC with a list of his clients' names and addresses from time to time, in a manner to be prescribed by regulations.

313A. Pre-disclosure enquiry

HMRC are given power by this section to serve notice on a potential promoter (or introducer) requiring him to state whether or not a proposal which he is suspected of promoting (or of introducing to third parties) is a notifiable scheme; and if not, why not. The person on whom the notice is served is expected to justify his position in some detail. He may, for example, in the context of SDLT claim that the scheme is 'grandfathered' and thus does not need to be notified. It is to be noted that it is insufficient for the potential promoter to claim that he has received legal advice that the scheme is not notifiable – rather, he must give sufficient information about the scheme to enable HMRC to make their own decision on the matter. No doubt, if the parties disagree, the Commissioners will make use of s 306A; but they will also be able to make use of s 313B, as to which see below.

313B. Reasons for non-disclosure: supporting information

HMRC is empowered to apply to the First-Tier Tribunal for an order requiring a person on whom a pre-disclosure enquiry notice has been served under s 313A to provide either information or documents supporting the reasons the person has given why the proposal under investigation is not a notifiable scheme.

313C. Information provided to introducers

As is mentioned in relation to s 307, HMRC's powers have been extended to enable them to seek information from intermediaries. Regulations are to be made which will prescribe what information is to be obtained in accordance with this section; but the intention is that the intermediary should be obliged to inform HMRC who the promoter of the scheme is, as well as details of the scheme in question. However, an introducer will have no automatic obligation to provide information to HMRC; but will be required to do so if a notice is served on him under this section.

314. Legal professional privilege

Privileged information is not disclosable under these provisions.

315. Penalties.

TMA 1970 s 98C is inserted.

316. Information to be provided in form and manner specified by Board

Information required under FA 2004 ss 300–305 must be provided in a form and manner specified by HMRC.

317. Regulations under Part 7

Regulations under FA 2004 ss 306–319 must be made by statutory instrument and may contain transitional provisions and savings.

318. Interpretation of Part 7

An advantage in relation to tax is defined to include relief from or repayment of tax, the deferral of tax or advancement of any repayment or to avoid withholding taxes. Other terms are defined.

319. Part 7: Commencement and Savings

The disclosure requirements for SDLT came into force on 1 August 2005.

Finance Act 2007

2007 Chapter 11

SCHEDULE 24 PENALTIES FOR ERRORS (SECTION 96)

PART 1 LIABILITY FOR PENALTY

Error in taxpayer's document

1.—A penalty is payable by a person where a document is provided to HMRC and HMRC reasonably believes that there is an understatement of liability to tax, a false or inflated statement of loss or a false or inflated claim for repayment of tax. The documents referred to include returns, accounts, statements or declarations for allowances, deductions or reliefs relating to a host of taxes including SDLT and SDRT, as well as any other document which is likely to be relied upon by HMRC to establish a liability or payment of duties. A table specifying the documents is produced within the Finance Act.

The Schedule was amended to include SDLT and SDRT by FA 2008 Sch 40, which came into force on 1 April 2009: see the FA 2008 Schedule 40 (Appointed Day, Transitional Provisions and Consequential Amendments) Order 2009, SI 2009/571. However, art 3 of the 2009 Order provides that the penalties payable under para 1 of Sch 24 are to have effect in relation to documents which relate to a claim for a repayment of tax which is made on or after 1 April 2010, and, subject to that, in the case of relevant documents which do not relate to a 'tax period' (as is the case for SDRT and SDLT), where the person's liability to pay the relevant tax arises on or after 1 April 2010. This has led to an unresolved debate between HMRC and various organisations representing taxpayers as to whether FA 2003 Sch 10 para 8 (which was repealed by FA 2008 Sch 40 para 21(k) with effect from 1 April 2009 by virtue of SI 2009/571) somehow continued to have effect until the operation of the replacement rules.

Error in taxpayer's document attributable to another person

1A.—A penalty may be charged on a third party where the taxpayer has given HMRC a document which contains a relevant inaccuracy attributable to the third party deliberately supplying false information to the taxpayer whether directly or indirectly or withholding information with the intention that the document would contain the inaccuracy. A relevant inaccuracy for this purpose is one which amounts to or leads to an understatement of a liability to tax, a false or inflated statement of a loss or a false or inflated claim to repayment of tax. The penalty arises whether or not the taxpayer is also penalised for the same inaccuracy. So far as SDLT and SDRT are concerned, this provision has effect in relation to documents which relate to a claim for a repayment of tax which is made on or after 1 April 2010, and, subject to that, where the person's liability to pay the relevant tax arises on or after 1 April 2010.

Under-assessment by HMRC

2.—A penalty is payable by a person where an assessment or determination is issued by HMRC in respect of a relevant tax which understates a person's liability and that person, or a person acting on his behalf, has not taken reasonable steps to notify them within 30 days of the date of assessment or determination that there is an under-statement. HMRC must consider whether the person knew or should have known about the under assessment and what would have been reasonable steps to notify HMRC.

Degrees of culpability

3.—Paragraph 1 defines inaccuracy in a document as restricted to those cases where the error is a result of carelessness (ie failure to take *reasonable* care), or is a deliberate but not concealed error or or a deliberate and concealed error. The distinction between the three categories of error is important in setting the amount of the penalty which may be demanded. A wholly innocent error does not carry a risk of a penalty. It will be appreciated that the new rules move away from the previous classifications of 'fraud or negligence' and the authorities on the meaning of those words thus are unlikely to have any relevance in the interpretation of Sch 24.

Paragraph 2 states an inaccuracy is treated as careless if there was no knowledge of an error at the time a document was submitted but later discovered and reasonable steps were not taken to inform HMRC.

PART 2 AMOUNT OF PENALTY

Standard amount

4.—The penalty payable under para 1 is: for a careless action, 30 per cent; for a deliberate but not concealed error, 70 per cent; and for a deliberate and concealed error, 100 per cent, of the potential revenue lost. For errors treated as careless (para 2) the penalty is 30 per cent of the potential lost revenue. There is no penalty for an innocent error which is corrected as soon as it is discovered.

The penalty payable under para 1A is 100 per cent of the potential lost revenue. There are special rules where the errors relate to 'offshore matters'; but these rules do not apply in the case of SDRT or SDLT.

Potential lost revenue: normal rule

5.—The potential lost revenue is defined as the additional amount due or payable in respect of tax as a result of correcting an inaccuracy, and includes amounts erroneously repaid or that would have been repaid if the inaccuracy had not been corrected. The penalty payable under para 1A is 100 per cent of the potential lost revenue.

Potential lost revenue: multiple errors

6.—Where there are multiple errors and the calculation of potential lost revenue depends on the order of correction, careless inaccuracies are corrected first, followed by deliberate but not concealed inaccuracies and then deliberate and concealed inaccuracies. If one or more understatements in one or more documents for a tax period attract a penalty under para 1, account will be taken of any overstatements of duties payable for the same tax period. There is a particular order for offsetting overstatements of tax payable against understatements, which is: those where the person is not liable to a penalty first, followed by careless understatements, followed by deliberate but not concealed understatements, followed by deliberate and concealed understatements. In the case where another person's overpayment is available to offset against an understatement, it will not be taken into account when calculating the potential revenue lost unless there is an enactment that requires or permits a person's liability to be adjusted in this way.

Potential lost revenue: delayed tax

8.—Where an inaccuracy resulted in an amount of tax being declared later than it should have been, the potential revenue lost is 5 per cent of the delayed tax for each year of the delay or proportion thereof.

Reductions for disclosure

9.—Disclosure is defined as telling HMRC about an inaccuracy or under assessment, giving HMRC reasonable assistance in quantifying the error and allowing access to records for the purpose of ensuring the inaccuracy is fully corrected. The disclosure is regarded as unprompted if the person has no reason to believe that HMRC has discovered or are about to discover the inaccuracy or under assessment. The quality of any disclosure takes into account timing, nature and extent of the disclosure. The supply of false information or withholding information are added to the offences concerning which disclosure may be made under this paragraph.

10.—Where a person would otherwise be liable to a 30 per cent penalty but an unprompted disclosure has been made, HMRC are to reduce the penalty to an amount they think reflects the quality of the disclosure. The penalty can be reduced to nil. If the disclosure was prompted, the penalty can be reduced to an amount they think reflects the quality of the disclosure but not to an amount below 15 per cent.

Where a person would otherwise be liable to a penalty of 70 per cent if the disclosure is unprompted, HMRC are to reduce the penalty to an amount they think reflects the quality of the disclosure, but not below 20 per cent. If the disclosure was prompted, the penalty can be reduced to an amount they think reflects the quality of the disclosure, but not below 35 per cent.

Where a person would otherwise be liable to a penalty of 100 per cent if the disclosure is unprompted, HMRC are to reduce the penalty to an amount they think reflects the quality of the disclosure, but not to an amount below 30 per cent. If the disclosure was prompted, the penalty can be reduced to an amount they think reflects the quality of the disclosure, but not to an amount below 50 per cent.

Special reduction

11.—If HMRC think it right, they may reduce penalties levied under para 1 or 1A. The circumstances for such a reduction specifically excludes a person's ability to pay or the fact that a potential loss from one person is balanced by an overpayment of another. The reduction also applies to staying a penalty or agreeing a compromise in relation to proceedings for a penalty.

Interaction with other penalties and late payment surcharges

12.—Where a penalty under TMA 1970 s 98 (special returns) applies to a document on which HMRC has relied upon to determine a liability or payment of tax (para 1), penalties under these sections do not apply. Where any other penalties have been applied under other sections, any penalties applied under these sections shall be reduced by the amount of the other penalties. Therefore TMA 1970 s 97A, which ensures, in the application of two or more tax-geared penalties, that the total penalty does not exceed the greater penalty, does not apply in these circumstances

Where penalties are levied under both paras 1 and 1A in respect of the same inaccuracy, the total penalty cannot exceed 100 per cent of the potential lost revenue.

PART 3 PROCEDURE

Assessment

13.—Where a person becomes liable to a penalty under para 1 or 2, HMRC will assess the penalty and notify the person and state the tax period to which the notice applies. The assessment is treated for procedural purposes as though it were a tax assessment (except in a matter expressly provided for), and collection may be enforced as if it were tax and it may be combined with an assessment to tax.

An assessment of a penalty under para 1 or 1A must be made within 12 months of the end of the appeal period for the decision correcting an inaccuracy or, where there is no assessment, the date on which the inaccuracy is corrected.

An assessment of a penalty under para 2 must be made within 12 months of the end of the appeal period for the decision correcting the understatement. An appeal period is defined as the period during which an appeal could be brought or an appeal that has been brought has not been determined or withdrawn. Where there is no assessment, FA 2008 Sch 40 provides that the time limit is 12 months from the date on which the understatement is corrected.

FA 2008 Sch 40 provides that a penalty levied under para 1A will be assessed in the same way as a penalty under para 1. Penalties under para 1, 1A or 2 must be paid within 30 days from the date the penalty notice is issued.

A supplementary penalty assessment may be made if HMRC thinks an earlier assessment was insufficient due to an underestimate of potential lost revenue.

Suspension

14.—HMRC may suspend all or part of a penalty for a careless inaccuracy under para 1 if they think that compliance with a condition will help the person avoid becoming liable to further penalties. HMRC must issue a notice to the person, specifying what part of the penalty is suspended, the period of suspension (not exceeding two years) and the conditions to be complied with by the person. A condition may specify an action to be taken and the period in which it must be taken. At the end of the suspension period, if the conditions have been met, the penalty may be cancelled partly or completely, otherwise it becomes payable in part or in full.

Appeal

15.—A person may appeal against the imposition of a penalty, the amount of a penalty or the decision not to suspend a penalty or the conditions set in regard to the suspension of a penalty.

16.—From 1 April 2009, an appeal is to be brought before the First-Tier Tribunal or the Upper Tribunal (Tax Chamber) as the case may be. Except as expressly provided, for procedural purposes an appeal is treated in the same way as an appeal against an assessment.

17.—The tribunal, in relation to the imposition of a penalty, may confirm or cancel HMRC's decision. In regard to the amount of the penalty, the tribunal may confirm HMRC's decision or substitute another decision in accordance with HMRC's powers. The substitute decision can take into account the special circumstances as set out in para 11, including applying the same percentage penalty to a different starting point, or to a different extent if the tribunal thinks HMRC's decision in the application of para 11 was flawed.

If the tribunal thinks HMRC's decision not to suspend a penalty was flawed, they can order HMRC to suspend it and/or order the amendment of the provision of the conditions within the penalty suspension notice.

The definition of "flawed" means flawed when a decision is considered in the light of principles applicable in proceedings for judicial review.

PART 4 MISCELLANEOUS

Agency

18.—A person is liable to a penalty where a document contains a careless inaccuracy, deliberate, unconcealed inaccuracy or deliberate and concealed inaccuracy and is provided to HMRC on his behalf, or there is an under assessment to duties and reasonable steps have not been taken by someone acting on a person's behalf to notify HMRC within 30 days of the date of the assessment. A person would not be liable to a penalty where he can satisfy HMRC that he took reasonable care to avoid inaccuracy or unreasonable failure to notify HMRC of an inaccuracy or understatement.

Companies: officers' liability

19.—Where a penalty under para 1 is payable by a company for a deliberate inaccuracy which HMRC think is attributable to an officer of the company, the officer as well as the company shall be liable to pay the penalty. HMRC may pursue the officer for the proportion of the penalty in accordance with a notice issued to him to a maximum of 100 per cent of the penalty. An officer within a body corporate is defined as meaning a director (including shadow director), manager or secretary. In the case of a limited liability partnership, an officer is taken to mean a person who is a member. In any other case it means director, manager, secretary or any other person managing or purporting to manage any of the company affairs.

It is to be noted that in the context of this paragraph, 'company' includes any body corporate or unincorporated association, but does not include a partnership, a local authority or a local authority association. For partnerships, see para 20 below.

If an officer of a company has been convicted of an offence relating to the same inaccuracy, he cannot be made liable to a penalty under this paragraph as well: para 21.

Partnerships

20.—Where a penalty is imposed under para 1, and the inaccuracy affects the amount payable by a partner of the person, the partner is also liable to a penalty. Paras 4–13 and 19 apply. Para 14 applies jointly to the person's and the partner's penalty. A person may appeal against a partner's penalty in accordance with para 15.

Double jeopardy

21.—A penalty may not be imposed on a person who has been convicted of an offence relating to the same inaccuracy.

Finance Act 2008

2008 Chapter 9

SCHEDULE 36

Note: This Schedule came into force as far as SDRT and SDLT are concerned on 1 April 2010, see s 113(2), (3); the Finance Act 2008, Schedule 36 (Appointed Day and Savings) Order 2009, SI 2009/404, art 2; Finance Act 2009, Section 96 and Schedule 48 (Appointed Day, Savings and Consequential Amendments) Order 2009, SI 2009/3054.

PART 1 POWERS TO OBTAIN INFORMATION AND DOCUMENTS

Power to obtain information and documents from taxpayer

1.—An HMRC officer may require a taxpayer to provide information or produce documents reasonably required to check the taxpayer's tax position (see Sch 36 para 64). This is done by way of a written notice known as a "taxpayer notice" made under Sch 36 para 3.

Power to obtain information and documents from third party

2.—An HMRC officer may require a person to provide information or produce documents reasonably required to check the tax position (see Sch 36 para 64) of another person ("the taxpayer"). This is done by way of a written notice known as a "third party notice". The taxpayer must be named unless the tribunal (see TCEA 2007 s 3) allows otherwise (see Sch 36 para 3(5)).

Approval etc of taxpayer notices and third party notices

3.—A third party notice (see Sch 36 para 2) requires agreement by the taxpayer or approval by the tribunal before it is made. A taxpayer notice appears to require neither agreement nor approval, but an HMRC officer may nevertheless seek approval.

An HMRC officer may ask the tribunal (see TCEA 2007 s 3) to approve a taxpayer notice or third party notice. The application must be made by, or with the agreement of, an authorised HMRC officer (see Sch 36 para 59). The tribunal must be satisfied that the notice is justified by the circumstances.

In principle, the person to whom the notice is to be addressed must be notified of the application made to the tribunal. The tribunal may waive this requirement if it is satisfied that this might prejudice the assessment or collection of tax. In the absence of a waiver, the tribunal may approve an application only if the following conditions have been met:

- the person to whom the notice is to be addressed has been told that the relevant information or documents are required;
- that person has been given reasonable opportunity to make representations to an HMRC officer;
- the tribunal has been given a summary of any representations made; and
- (in relation to a third party notice) the taxpayer has been given a summary of the reasons why an HMRC officer requires the information or documents.

The tribunal may disapply the requirement (see Sch 36 para 2(2)) to name the taxpayer in a third party notice. The tribunal must be satisfied that the officer has reasonable grounds for believing that naming the taxpayer might seriously prejudice the assessment or collection of tax. For "tax", see Sch 36 para 63.

Copying third party notice to taxpayer

4.—In principle, a copy of a third party notice must be given to the taxpayer to whom it relates. However, a tribunal may disapply this requirement in relation to an application for approval (see Sch 36 para 3) made by, or with the approval of, an authorised HMRC officer (see Sch 36 para 59). The tribunal must be satisfied that the officer has reasonable grounds for believing that giving a copy of the notice to the taxpayer might prejudice the assessment or collection of tax. For "tax", see Sch 36 para 63.

Power to obtain information and documents about persons whose identity is not known

5.—An authorised officer may require a person to provide information or produce documents reasonably required to check the UK tax position (see Sch 36 paras 5(5), 63) of an unknown person or class of unknown persons. This is done by way of a written notice approved by the tribunal (see TCEA 2007 s 3).

An application for approval may be made without notifying the person to whom the written notice is to be addressed. The tribunal must be satisfied on the following matters before approving the notice:

- (a) the information or documents are reasonably required for the purpose stated above;
- (b) there are reasonable grounds for believing that the person (or a member of the class of persons) has failed (or may fail) to comply with his UK tax obligations;
- (c) it is likely this failure has seriously prejudiced the assessment or collection of UK tax (see para 5(5)), or may do so; and
- (d) the information or documents are not readily available from another source.

Notices

6.—Notices under Sch 36 paras 1, 2 and 5 are collectively referred to as "information notices". An information notice may specify or describe the information or documents to be provided or produced. An information notice approved by the tribunal must state that approval has been given. A decision given by the tribunal under para 3, 4 or 5 is final.

Complying with notices

7.—An information notice (see Sch 36 para 6(1)) must specify the time limit for compliance and describe the time, means and form (if any) for doing so. These requirements must be reasonable. A person is liable to a penalty if he fails to comply with a notice (see Sch 36 paras 39, 40).

Documents must be produced for inspection at either: (1) a mutually agreed place; or (2) a place (other than a dwelling) reasonably specified by an HMRC officer. Producing a document is not regarded as breaking any lien claimed on it.

Producing copies of documents

8.—A requirement to produce a document is met by producing a copy unless the information notice (or a subsequent written request) specifies the original document. A written request must specify the time limit for compliance and describe the time and means (if any) for doing so. These requirements must be reasonable. The Commissioners may make regulations regarding the production of copies. No regulations have been made to date.

Restrictions and special cases

9.—Parts 4 (restrictions on powers) and 6 (special cases) of this Schedule apply to information notices.

PART 2 POWERS TO INSPECT BUSINESSES ETC

Power to inspect business premises etc

10.—An HMRC officer may enter a person's business premises (see Sch 36 para 10(3)) in order to inspect the premises and any business assets (see para 10(3), (4)) or business documents (see para 10(3)) on the premises. The inspection must be reasonably required to check a person's tax position. The power, it should be observed, is to inspect and not to search. The Commissioners explain this means that they are permitted to look at what they can see; but cannot look for that which is not visible.

This power does not permit the officer to enter or inspect any part of the premises used solely as a dwelling.

For restrictions on the power to inspect business documents, see Sch 36 para 28.

Power to inspect business premises etc of involved third parties

10A.—An HMRC officer may enter business premises of an "involved third party" to inspect the premises as well as business assets and relevant documents on the premises. The inspection must be reasonably required for the purpose of checking the position of any person as regards SDRT. An involved third party is a person who falls within a definition given by Sch 36 para 61A. For SDRT, an involved third party is someone who is an accountable person within the SDRT Regulations 1986; and the relevant information and documents are those which relate to an agreement, transfer, issue, appropriation or surrender of chargeable securities which is or might be subject to SDRT: see box 8 in the Table in para 61A.

This power does not permit the officer to enter or inspect any part of the premises used solely as a dwelling.

For restrictions on the power to inspect business documents, see Sch 36 para 28.

Carrying out inspections under paragraph 10, 10a or 11

12.—An inspection under Sch 36 para 10, 10A or 11 must be carried out at one of the following times:

- a time agreed with the occupier of the premises;
- (if the occupier has been given at least seven days' notice) any reasonable time; or
- (if the inspection is either carried out by an authorised officer or sanctioned by an authorised officer) at any reasonable time. The officer must either: (1) give the occupier (or, in his absence, the person who appears to be in charge of the premises) a written notice stating the possible consequences of obstructing the inspection; or (2) (in other cases) leave such a notice in a prominent place on the premises. A written notice given with the approval of the tribunal (see TCEA 2007 s 3) under para 13 must state that it has been so approved.

Powers to inspect property for valuation etc

12A.—An officer may enter and inspect premises and property on the premises for the purpose of valuing, measuring or determining the character of the premises. However, this power may only be exercised in the context of stamp taxes if the relevant exercise is reasonably required for the purpose of checking someone's position as regards SDLT or SDRT. The officer may bring with him anyone (eg a land valuer) whom he considers needed for the purpose of carrying out the relevant inspection.

Carrying out inspections under paragraph 12a

12B.—Before the officer may exercise the power under para 12A he must have agreed a time to inspect with the occupier (or with the person controlling the premises, in the absence of an occupier). Failing such agreement, the officer must seek the approval of the First-tier Tribunal for the inspection and must give the occupier (or controller) seven days' notice in writing.

Approval of tribunal

13.—An HMRC officer may ask the tribunal to approve an inspection (see Sch 36 paras 12, 12A and 39). The application must be made or sanctioned by an authorised officer. The tribunal must be satisfied that the inspection is justified. In the case of a para 12A inspection, the occupier must have been given the opportunity of making representations to HMRC and the tribunal must be given a summary of those representations to consider. If the tribunal approves, its decision is final.

Restrictions and special cases

14.—Parts 4 (restrictions on powers) and 6 (special cases) of this Schedule apply to inspections. For the power to mark assets and record information, see Sch 36 para 17.

PART 3 FURTHER POWERS

Power to copy documents

15.—An HMRC officer may copy, or make extracts from, the documents to which he is given access.

Power to remove documents

16.—If necessary, an HMRC officer may remove and retain the documents (see Sch 36 para 16(5)) to which he has been given access. Documents may be removed at a reasonable time and retained for a reasonable period. If requested, the officer must give a receipt and provide a copy of the removed documents. The officer does not break a lien by removing documents. If removed documents are lost or damaged, the Commissioners must compensate the owner for any expenses reasonably incurred by him in repairing or replacing them.

Power to mark assets and to record information

17.—The powers conferred by Part 2 of this Schedule include:

- the power to mark business assets (as defined in Sch 36 para 10(3)) to indicate that they have been inspected;
- the power to mark anything containing business assets to indicate that the assets have been inspected;
- the power to obtain and record information relating to the premises, property, goods, assets and documents inspected.

PART 4 RESTRICTIONS ON POWERS

Documents not in person's possession or power

18.—An information notice (see Sch 36 para 6(1)) may require a person to produce a document. He is required to produce the document only if it is in his power or possession.

Types of information

19.—An information notice (see Sch 36 para 6(1)) may require a person to provide or produce information or documents. He is not required to provide or produce the following information or documents:

- information relating to the conduct of a pending appeal;
- any part of a document containing information relating to the conduct of a pending appeal;
- personal records (see below); however, a person may be required to produce that part of a document which does not fall within this description;
- information contained in personal records (see below); however, a person may be required to provide that part of the information which does not fall within this description; or
- journalistic material (see below) or information contained in journalistic material.

"Personal records" are defined by reference to the Police and Criminal Evidence Act 1984 s 12. They comprise documentary or other records concerning an individual (whether living or dead) who can be identified from them, which relate to:

- his physical or mental health;
- spiritual counselling or assistance given, or to be given, to him; or
- counselling or assistance given, or to be given, to him for the purposes of his personal welfare by either: (1) a voluntary organisation; or (2) an individual who (by reason of his office or occupation) has responsibilities for his personal welfare or (by reason of an order of the court) has responsibilities for his supervision.

"Journalistic material" is defined by reference to the Police and Criminal Evidence Act 1984 s 13. It means: (1) material created for the purposes of journalism held by the person who created it; (2) material acquired for the purposes of journalism held by the person who acquired it; and (3) material held by the person who received it from someone who intended that the former would use it for the purposes of journalism.

Old documents

20.—An information notice (see Sch 36 para 6(1)) does not require a person to provide or produce a document wholly originated more than six years before the date of the notice. However, this does not apply if the notice is given by an authorised officer or sanctioned by him.

Taxpayer notices following land transaction return

21A.—If a person has delivered a land transaction return, a taxpayer notice may not be given for the purpose of checking that person's stamp duty land tax position in relation to that transaction. By way of exception to this, a notice is permissible if either there is an enquiry open in relation to that return; or an officer has reason to suspect that an amount of SDLT has not been self-assessed by the taxpayer, or the amount assessed was or has become insufficient; or that an excessive amount of relief has been claimed in respect of the transaction. It is also possible to serve a taxpayer notice where SDLT is not the only tax involved and the notice has also been served in order to obtain a document or information required for investigating his position as regards that other tax.

Deceased persons

22.—An information notice (see Sch 36 para 6(1)) relating to the tax affairs of a deceased person may not be given more than four years after the date of death.

Privileged communications between professional legal advisers and clients

23.—An information notice (see Sch 36 para 6(1)) does not require a person to provide privileged information or produce any part of a document that is privileged. For privileged information and documents, see Sch 36 para 23(2). Disputes as to whether information or documents are privileged are determined by the tribunal (see TCEA 2007 s 3) in accordance with the Information Notice: Resolution of Disputes as to Privileged Communications Regulations 2009, SI 2009/1916.

For the tribunal, see the Tribunals, Courts and Enforcement Act 2007.

Auditors

24.—An information notice (see Sch 36 para 6(1)) does not require an auditor to:

(a) provide information in connection with his statutory functions; or
(b) produce documents created by him (or on his behalf) relating to the performance of his statutory functions.

For the exceptions, see Sch 36 para 26.

Tax advisers

25.—An information notice (see Sch 36 para 6(1)) does not require a tax adviser (see Sch 36 para 25(3)) to:

(a) provide information about relevant communications (see Sch 36 para 25(3)); or

(b) produce documents owned by him and consisting of relevant communications.

For the exceptions, see para 26.

Auditors and tax advisers: supplementary

26.—Although an auditor or tax adviser served with an information notice is exempted from providing certain information and producing certain documents (see Sch 36 paras 24, 25), he is not exempted from providing:

- (as regards any information notice (see Sch 36 para 6(1)) an explanation of any information or document which, in the role as tax adviser, he assisted his client to prepare for HMRC;
- (as regards an information notice under para 5) information regarding the identity or address of the person (or his agent) to whom the notice relates; or
- a document (see Sch 36 para 27) containing the information specified in either of the foregoing heads.

However, he is not required to provide the explanation, information or document if he has already done so.

27.—If an auditor or tax adviser is required to produce a document by virtue of Sch 36 para 26, the information notice requiring this has effect as if it required only the part (or parts) of the document containing the information to be produced.

Corresponding restrictions on inspection of documents

28.—An HMRC officer's powers to inspect documents (see Sch 36 para 10) are aligned with the provisions relating to information notices. If the occupier would not be required to produce documents in accordance with an information notice (see Sch 36 para 6(1)) by virtue of Sch 36 paras 18–27), an officer may not inspect documents of that kind when exercising his power to inspect documents.

PART 5 APPEALS AGAINST INFORMATION NOTICES

Right to appeal against taxpayer notice

29.—A taxpayer may appeal against:

- a taxpayer notice (see Sch 36 para 1) given to him; however, no appeal lies against a notice approved by a Tribunal (see TCEA 2007 s 3) under para 3; or
- any requirement in the notice; however, no appeal lies against a requirement to provide information, or produce documents, forming part of the taxpayer's statutory records.

Right to appeal against third party notice

30.—A taxpayer may appeal (see TCEA 2007 s 3) against:

- a third party notice (see Sch 36 para 2) given to him, on the ground that it would be unduly onerous to comply with the notice; however, no appeal lies against a notice approved by the tribunal under para 3; or
- any requirement in the notice, on the ground that it would be unduly onerous to comply with the requirement; however, no appeal lies against a requirement to provide information, or produce documents, forming part of the taxpayer's statutory records,

Right to appeal against notice given under paragraph 5

31.—A taxpayer may appeal against:

- a notice under Sch 36 para 5 given to him, on the ground that it would be unduly onerous to comply with the notice; or
- any requirement in the notice, on the ground that it would be unduly onerous to comply with the requirement.

Procedure

32.—Notice of appeal under Sch 36 paras 29–31 must be given in writing to the HMRC officer who issued the notice and state the grounds of appeal. This must be done no later than 30 days after the notice was given.

On appeal, the tribunal may confirm, vary or set aside the notice or requirement. The taxpayer must comply with a notice or requirement which is confirmed or varied. He must do so within: (1) the period specified by the tribunal (if the tribunal specifies a period); or (2) the period specified by an HMRC officer in writing following the decision (in other cases). The period specified in the latter case must be reasonable. The tribunal's decision is final.

The appeal is treated as if it were an appeal against an assessment to income tax. TMA 1970 Pt 5 applies accordingly.

Special cases

33.—Part 6 (Sch 36 paras 34–38) applies to appeals against information notices.

PART 6 SPECIAL CASES

Involved third parties

34A.—Sch 36 para 3 permits the Commissioners to serve a third party notice (ie one requiring the third party to provide information or a document as described in para 2) on a person in limited circumstances – either if they have the permission of the taxpayer whose affairs are being checked or if they have obtained the approval of the tribunal. Para 5 makes similar provision where HMRC is checking the tax position of a person or class of persons whose identity is unknown. This paragraph then regulates the operation of the provision of such notices when served on an "involved third party" (as defined by para 61A). Because the person on whom the notice is served has a closer relationship with the transaction or the taxpayers under scrutiny, para 34A affords a corresponding relaxation in the conditions subject to which the notice may be served as regards certain specified categories of documents and information – as far as a notice relating to such items are concerned, the officer need not seek the approval of the taxpayer or the tribunal and need not serve a copy of the third party notice on the taxpayer. However, as a counter-balance the rights of appeal conferred by paras 30 and 31 are extended so that the person served may appeal on any ground and not only because it would be unduly onerous to comply with the notice. Para 61A specifies what documents and information constitute "relevant documents and relevant information" as regards each category of involved third party.

Groups of undertakings

35.—This paragraph modifies the application of Sch 36 paras 2, 3, 4, 5, 21, 21A and 30 in relation to an undertaking (see para 33(7)) which is a parent undertaking (see para 33(7)) in relation to another undertaking (ie a subsidiary undertaking, as to which see para 33(7)). It simplifies the procedure so far as the Commissioners are concerned, not requiring the officer to name each and every subsidiary undertaking which is the subject-matter of the notice; but merely that the notice applies to the parent undertaking and its subsidiaries. Likewise, where the notice is served on the parent undertaking, the need to seek the approval of the taxpayer or the tribunal is removed.

Partnerships

37.—This paragraph modifies the application of the following provisions for the purposes stated:

- Sch 36 paras 2, 3, 4, 21 and 30 in relation to a business carried on by a partnership.
- Sch 36 paras 3, 4 and 30 in relation to a third party notice (see para 2) given to one of the partners for the purpose of checking the tax position of one or more of the other partners in their capacity as such.

- Sch 36 paras 5 and 31 in relation to a notice to provide information or produce documents (see para 5) for the purpose of checking the tax position of one or more of the other partners whose identities are unknown to the officer giving the notice.

Specifically, so far as SDLT is concerned, sub-para (2A) treats para 21A (taxpayer notices following land transaction return) as applying to each and every partner where a land transaction has been entered into by or on behalf of the partnership and one of the partners has made a land transaction return or a claim in relation to that transaction.

Application to the crown

38.—Parts 1–7, 9 and 10 apply to the Crown. However, they do not apply to Her Majesty in Her private capacity (see Crown Proceedings Act 1947 s 38(3)).

PART 7 PENALTIES

Penalties for failure to comply or obstruction

39.—A person is liable to a penalty if:

- he fails to comply with an information notice (see Sch 36 para 6(1)); or
- he deliberately obstructs an HMRC officer in the course of an inspection (see Part 2) which has been approved by the tribunal (see TCEA 2007 s 3).

A person is also liable to a penalty if he breaches the duty to retain documents and keep them available for inspection (see Sch 36 paras 42, 43) by:

- concealing a document;
- destroying or otherwise disposing of a document; or
- arranging the concealment, destruction or disposal of a document.

The prescribed penalty in either case is £300.

For the circumstances in which no liability to a penalty arises, see para 44 (extended time limit for compliance) and para 45 (reasonable excuse).

Daily default penalties for failure to comply or obstruction

40.—A person is liable to a penalty if the failure or obstruction in para 39 continues after the date on which a penalty is imposed under that provision.

The prescribed penalty is a sum not exceeding £60 for each subsequent day on which the conduct continues.

For the circumstances in which no liability to a penalty arises, see Sch 36 para 44 (extended time limit for compliance) and para 45 (reasonable excuse).

Penalties for inaccurate information and documents

40A.—A person may provide inaccurate information, or produce a document containing an inaccuracy, when complying with an information notice (see para 6(1)). He is liable to a penalty if: (1) the inaccuracy is careless (ie it is due to a failure to take reasonable care) or deliberate; or (2) he discovers the inaccuracy some time later and fails to take reasonable steps to inform HMRC.

The prescribed penalty is a sum not exceeding £3,000. If a document contains more than one inaccuracy, the person is liable to a penalty in respect of each inaccuracy.

Power to change amount of penalties

41.—The sums prescribed in Sch 36 paras 39, 40 and 40A may be changed by Treasury regulation. No regulations have been made to date. The new sum does not apply to any conduct which commenced before the date on which the regulations came into force.

Concealing, destroying etc documents following information notice

42.—In principle, a person must not:

- conceal a document subject to an information notice (see Sch 36 para 6(1)) addressed to him;
- destroy or otherwise dispose of the document; or
- arrange for the concealment, destruction or disposal of the document.

However, he may do so once the document has been produced to an HMRC officer unless the officer has given (and not withdrawn) a written notification that the document must continue to be available for inspection. He may also do so if, having complied with the notice by producing a copy of the document (see Sch 36 para 8(1)), he acts more than six months later without the officer having requested the original document (see para 8(2)(b)) during the six months following production of the copy.

Concealing, destroying etc documents following informal notification

43.—In principle, a person must not:

- conceal a document if an HMRC officer has informed him that the document is, or is likely to be, the subject of an information notice (see Sch 36 para 6(1)) addressed to him;
- destroy or otherwise dispose of the document if he has been so informed; or
- arrange for the concealment, destruction or disposal of the document if he has been so informed.

However, the person may do so if at least six months has expired since he was so informed or last so informed. Although the legislation states that he may also do so if an information notice requiring production of the document has been given, the person thereby becomes liable to the duty in Sch 36 para 42.

Failure to comply with time limit

44.—A person's failure to do something within a limited period of time does not give rise to a penalty under Sch 36 para 39 or 40 if the person did it within such further time (if any) as an HMRC officer may have allowed.

Reasonable excuse

45.—A person is not liable to a penalty under Sch 36 para 39 or 40 if he satisfies HMRC or (on appeal) the First-tier Tribunal (see TCEA 2007 s 3) that there is a reasonable excuse for the relevant failure or obstruction of an HMRC officer.

An insufficiency of funds is capable of amounting to a reasonable excuse only if it is attributable to events outside the person's control.

Reliance on another person to do something is capable of amounting to a reasonable excuse only if the taxpayer took reasonable care to avoid the failure or obstruction.

Once a reasonable excuse has ceased, a person is treated as continuing to have a reasonable excuse if the failure is remedied, or the obstruction ceases, without unreasonable delay after the excuse ceased.

Assessment of penalty

46.—A penalty under Sch 36 para 39, 40 or 40A is assessed. HMRC must notify the assessed person. The assessment must be made within twelve months beginning with the date on which the person become liable to a penalty. As regards an information notice against which a person may appeal, this is the later of: (1) the end of the period allowed for appeal; and (2) (if notice of appeal is given) the date on which the appeal is determined or withdrawn. In any other case it is the date on which the person became liable to the penalty.

Right to appeal against penalty

47.—An appeal lies against a decision of an HMRC officer that a penalty is payable under Sch 36 para 39, 40 or 40A or the amount of such a penalty.

Procedure on appeal against penalty

48.—Notice of appeal regarding a penalty under Sch 36 para 39, 40 or 40A must be given to HMRC in writing no later than 30 days after the date on which the assessment (see para 46) was issued. The grounds for appeal must be stated.

As regards a decision that a penalty is payable (see para 47(a)), the tribunal (see TCEA 2007 s 3) may confirm or cancel the decision. As regards a decision relating to the amount of a penalty (see para 47(b)), the tribunal may confirm the decision or substitute another decision that the officer had power to make.

An appeal against a penalty under para 39, 40 or 40A is treated in the same manner as an appeal against an assessment to income tax. TMA 1970 Part 5 applies accordingly, but it is supplemented by Sch 36 paras 48 and 49

Enforcement of penalty

49.—In principle, a penalty under Sch 36 para 39, 40 or 40A must be paid within 30 days, counted from the day on which the notice of assessment is issued. However, if notice of appeal is given (see para 47), the penalty must be paid within 30 days of the day on which the appeal is determined or withdrawn.

A penalty assessment (see para 46) is enforced in the same manner as an income tax assessment. For the enforcement of income tax assessments, see TMA 1970 Part 6.

Tax-related penalty

50.—A failure or obstruction may continue after a penalty has been imposed under Sch 36 para 39. Where this is so, an HMRC officer may apply to the Upper Tribunal (see TCEA 2007 s 3) for an additional penalty to be imposed. He may do so if he has reason to believe that the failure or obstruction has resulted in a significant reduction in the tax paid or payable by the person.

The application must be made no later than twelve months after the relevant date. As regards a failure or obstruction relating to an information notice against which a person may appeal, this is the later of: (1) the end of the period allowed for appeal; and (2) (if notice of appeal is given) the date on which the appeal is determined or withdrawn. In any other case it is the date on which the person became liable to the penalty.

The Upper Tribunal decides whether or not an additional penalty should be imposed and, if imposed, the amount of the penalty. In deciding the amount, the tribunal must have regard to the amount of tax which has not been paid or may not be paid. HMRC must notify the person accordingly.

The penalty is additional to the penalty or penalties imposed under Sch 36 para 39 or 40. It is disregarded for the purposes of TMA 1970 s 97A, FA 2007 Sch 24 para 12(2) and FA 2008 Sch 41 para 15(1).

Enforcement of tax-related penalty

51.—A tax-related penalty (see Sch 36 para 50) must be paid within 30 days of notification (see Sch 36 para 50(4)). The penalty is enforced in the same manner as an income tax assessment. For the enforcement of income tax assessments, see TMA 1970 Part 6.

Double jeopardy

52.—A person is not liable to a penalty under Sch 36 para 39, 40, 40A or 50 if he has been convicted of an offence in respect of the relevant conduct.

PART 8 OFFENCE

Concealing etc documents following information notice

53.—A person required to produce a document in accordance with an information notice (see Sch 36 para 6(1)) approved by the tribunal (see TCEA 2007 s 3) under Sch 36 paras 3, 5 is guilty of an offence if:

- he conceals, destroys or otherwise disposes of the document; or
- he arranges for the concealment, destruction or disposal of the document.

In principle, a person is not guilty of an offence if the relevant conduct takes place after the document has been produced to an HMRC officer. However, the officer may have issued a notification in writing that the document must continue to be available for inspection. If so, the relevant conduct constitutes an offence if it takes place before the notification is withdrawn.

A person may have complied with an information notice by producing a copy of the relevant document (see para 8(1)). In principle, a person is not guilty of an offence if the relevant conduct takes place more than six months after the copy was produced. However, an HMRC officer may have requested the original document during this six-month period (see para 8(2)(b)). If so, relevant conduct in relation to the original document prior to its production constitutes an offence.

For the prescribed penalty, see Sch 36 para 55.

Concealing etc documents following informal notification

54.—A person may be informed in writing by an HMRC officer that a document is, or is likely to be, the subject of an information notice (see Sch 36 para 6(1)) and that the officer intends to seek approval from the tribunal (see TCEA 2007 s 3) for the giving of the information notice (see paras 3, 5). The person is guilty of an offence if he subsequently:

- conceals, destroys or otherwise disposes of the document; or
- arranges the concealment, destruction or disposal of the document.

A person is not guilty of the offence if the relevant conduct takes place more than six months after he was informed, or last informed, by the officer.

A person is not guilty of the offence if the relevant conduct takes place after an information notice has been given to the person. However, the relevant conduct in these circumstances may constitute an offence under Sch 36 para 53.

For the prescribed penalty, see para 55.

Fine or imprisonment

55.—A person guilty of an offence under Sch 36 para 53 or 54 is liable to a penalty as follows:

- on summary conviction (ie by a magistrate in England and Wales): a fine not exceeding the statutory maximum; and
- on indictment (ie by the Crown Court in England and Wales): two years' imprisonment, a fine or both.

As regards England and Wales, the "statutory maximum" is currently £5,000: see Interpretation Act 1979 Sch 1; Magistrates' Courts Act 1980 s 32(9) (as amended by Criminal Justice Act 1991 s 17(2)). In Scotland and Northern Ireland, see Criminal Procedure (Scotland) Act 1995 s 225(8) and Fines and Penalties (Northern Ireland) Order 1984 respectively by virtue of Interpretation Act 1979 Sch 1.

PART 9 MISCELLANEOUS PROVISIONS AND INTERPRETATION

Application of provisions of

56.—TMA 1970 ss 108, 114 and 115 apply for the purposes of this Schedule as they apply for the purposes of the Taxes Acts (as defined in Sch 36 para 58).

Regulations under this sch

57.—Regulations under this Schedule are made by statutory instrument.

General interpretation

58.—Various words and phrases are defined.

Authorised officer of revenue and customs

59.—The term "authorised officer of Revenue and Customs" is defined.

Business

60.—The phrase "carrying on a business" is defined. Regulations may provide that a specified activity, or an activity carried on by a specified class of person, is or is not to be treated as the carrying on of a business. No regulations have been made to date.

Involved third parties

61A.—This paragraph sets out in a Table a number of different cases where a person who is involved in a transaction for tax purposes may be treated as an "involved third party". The effect of this treatment is that the conditions under which a third party notice or a para 5 notice may be served are relaxed, so that it is not necessary for the Commissioners to seek permission for the taxpayer or approval from the tribunal before the relevant notice may be served; and the legislation dispenses with the need to serve a copy of the third party notice on the relevant taxpayer: see para 34A. The relevant category for stamp taxes purposes is category 8, which prescribes that as regards an accountable person in relation to a charge to SDRT in respect of an agreement, transfer, issue, appropriation or surrender of chargeable securities, the person is to be treated as an involved third party as far as information and documents which relate to the relevant agreement, transfer etc.

Statutory records

62.—Information and documents form part of a person's statutory records only if they are required to be kept and preserved by virtue of an enactment relating to a tax (as defined in Sch 36 para 63). They cease to form part of a person's statutory records when the period for preserving them has expired. "Tax" for this purpose includes SDRT and SDLT.

Tax

63.—The term "tax" is defined. It includes SDLT and SDRT.

Tax position

64.—The "tax position" of a person is broadly defined as including not only his liability to tax past, present or future, but also his liability to a penalty, and his position as regards claims and elections in relation to tax.

PART 10 CONSEQUENTIAL PROVISIONS

65–92.—The provisions amended or repealed as a consequence of this Schedule are listed. The provisions repealed in consequence are listed in Sch 36 para 92.

Finance Act 2009

2009 Chapter 10

93. Duties of senior accounting officers of qualifying companies

Schedule 46 is introduced to have effect in relation to financial years beginning on or after the date of royal assent (21 July 2009).

101. Late payment: interest on sums due to HMRC

Section 101 introduces a harmonised interest regime across the spectrum of tax (with the exception of corporation tax and petroleum revenue tax), including SDLT and SDRT. The legislation makes provision for the automatic setting and implementation of interest rate changes and replaces the current range of interest regimes. The measure will provide for interest to be charged from the date the tax was due to be paid to HMRC until the date it is paid. Implementation of interest harmonisation requires changes to HMRC's computer systems and will be staged over a number of years.

102. Repayment interest on sums to be paid by HMRC

This section is intended to introduce a correspondingly harmonised system for taxpayers who receive refunds from HMRC to that which operates under s 101 in favour of the Commissioners.

106. Penalties for failure to make returns etc

Section 106 introduces Schedule 55 which makes provision for the imposition of penalties where a taxpayer fails to make returns or to submit other specified documents.

SCHEDULES

SCHEDULE 46 DUTIES OF SENIOR ACCOUNTING OFFICERS OF QUALIFYING COMPANIES

Note: This Schedule has effect in relation to financial years beginning on or after the day on which this Act was passed (21 July 2009) (see s 92(2)). The Schedule applies, inter alia, to SDRT and SDLT: see para 134(3)(e) and (f). HMRC has published guidance on the application of these rules, to be found at www.hmrc.gov.uk/largecompanies/duties-sen-acc-officer.pdf.

Main duty of senior accounting officer

1.—The senior accounting officer (see para 18) of a qualifying company (see para 17) must take reasonable steps to ensure that the company, and each of its subsidiaries (if any) establishes and maintains appropriate tax accounting arrangements. In particular, he must take reasonable steps to monitor the accounting arrangements and identify any deficiencies in them.

Certificate for Commissioners

2.—The senior accounting officer (see para 16) must provide HMRC with a certificate confirming that the company had appropriate tax accounting arrangements in place throughout the financial year or, if it did not, give an appropriate explanation of their defects. This must be done no later than the end of the period for filing (see para 18) the company's accounts and in the form and manner specified by an HMRC officer. This period may be extended by an HMRC officer. The Commissioners' guidance suggests the certificate should be in the following form:

"I . . . .. as Senior Accounting Officer of the qualifying company /companies listed below, hereby certify that to the best of my knowledge and belief throughout the company's or companies' financial year ended [. . . .] the company/companies had appropriate accounting arrangements or to the extent it/they did not an explanation is provided below."

Notifying Commissioners of name of senior accounting officer

3.—The name of the person (or each of the persons) acting as senior accounting officer at any time during a financial year (see para 18) must be notified to HMRC. This must be done no later than the end of the period for filing (see para 20) the company's accounts and in the form and manner specified by an HMRC officer. This period may be extended by an HMRC officer.

Penalty for failure to comply with main duty

4.—The senior accounting officer is liable to a penalty if he fails to comply with para 1. The prescribed penalty is £5,000. For the person liable to a penalty where there is a change of senior accounting officer during a financial year, see para 8.

Penalties for failure to provide certificate etc

5.—A senior accounting officer is liable to a penalty if he fails to provide a certificate in accordance with para 2. Alternatively, he is liable to a penalty if the certificate provided contains a careless or deliberate inaccuracy. The prescribed penalty in either case is £5,000. For the person liable to a penalty where there is a change of senior accounting officer during a financial year, see para 8.

More than one senior accounting officer

6.—The following consequences follow if the senior accounting officer changes during a financial year:

- as regards the requirement to keep and maintain appropriate tax accounting arrangements, the only person liable to a penalty under para 5 is the latest person in the year to hold that position;
- as regards the requirement to comply with para 2, the person who complied, or purported to comply, with this requirement is the only person liable to a penalty under para 5.

Penalty for failure to notify Commissioners of name of senior accounting officer

7.—A qualifying company (see para 15) is liable to a penalty if it fails to notify HMRC of the name of its senior accounting officer. The prescribed penalty is £5,000. For the requirement to notify, see para 3.

Reasonable excuse

8.—A senior accounting officer of a qualifying company is not liable to a penalty under paras 4–5 if the officer or company satisfies HMRC or, on appeal, the First-tier Tribunal or Upper Tribunal, that there is a reasonable excuse for the failure. For the First-tier Tribunal, see TCEA 2007 s 3. For the chambers into which the tribunals are divided, see TCEA 2007 s 7.

An insufficiency of funds is capable of being a reasonable excuse only if it is attributable to events outside the person's control.

If a person relies on another person to do something, this is capable of being a reasonable excuse only if he took reasonable care to avoid the failure.

A person may have a reasonable excuse for a failure. If the excuse ceases to apply, the person is regarded as continuing to have a reasonable excuse if he remedies the failure without unreasonable delay.

Assessment of penalties

9.—HMRC may assess the penalty to which a senior accounting officer or large company is liable under paras 5–7 or 9. HMRC are not required to do so. Any assessment must be made no later than: (1) six months after the failure or inaccuracy first came to the attention of an HMRC officer; or (2) six years after the end of the period for filing the accounts for the financial year concerned. It must be notified to the person liable to the penalty.

Appeal

10.—A person may appeal against HMRC's decision that a penalty is payable by him. Notice of appeal must be given in writing to HMRC and state the grounds for appeal. This must be done no later than 30 days after the notice of assessment (see para 9) was issued. If an appeal is notified to the tribunal, the tribunal may confirm or cancel HMRC's decision.

TMA 1970 Part 5 (ss 44–58) applies to appeals against HMRC's decision in the same manner as they apply to appeals against an assessment to income tax. This application is subject to the provisions of paras 12(2)–(4) and 13.

Enforcement of penalties

11.—A penalty under paras 5–7 or 9 must be paid within 30 days. The 30-day period is counted from: (1) the date on which the appeal is determined or withdrawn (if notice of appeal has been given); or (2) the date on which the notice of assessment (see para 9) was issued (in other cases).

The penalty may be enforced as if it were income tax charged in an assessment which is due and payable. For recovery of income tax, see TMA 1970 Part 6 (ss 60-–70A).

Power to change amount of penalties

12.—The penalties prescribed in paras 5–7 and 9 may be varied by regulations. No regulations have been made to date.

Application of provisions of TMA 1970

13.—TMA 1970 ss 108, 114 and 115 apply to this Schedule in the same manner as they apply for the purposes of the Taxes Acts (as defined in TMA 1970 s 118(1)).

Meaning of "appropriate tax accounting arrangements"

14.—The terms "appropriate tax accounting arrangements", "accounting arrangements" and "taxes and duties" are defined. Although the Commissioners recognise that what may be "accounting arrangements that enable the company's relevant liabilities to be calculated accurately in all material respects" may vary from case to case, they have suggested that the following elements could form part of such arrangements:

- a process for gathering and recording data in a systematic way;
- an understanding of the key tax compliance risks in the business;
- designing and implementing control activities to mitigate these risks; for example, separation of responsibilities and ensuring that people who undertake delegated activities have the right levels of skill and competency;
- mechanisms for communicating roles and responsibilities; and
- monitoring activities to ensure that controls are operating effectively. The level of monitoring required will vary according to the level of risk present.

The Commissioners have confirmed that the phrase "in all material respects" in the definition of appropriate accounting arrangements places the focus on the significance of the transaction, system or tax and the relative size of these items in terms of the business. HMRC are not, it is said, interested in small or insignificant errors.

One particular area which is fraught with possibility for confrontation under this Schedule is the issue of accounting for cases where there is likely to be a difference of opinion between the company and HMRC as to the proper tax treatment of particular transactions. In such a case, the Commissioners indicate that, although the application of judgement around tax-sensitive decisions is part of "appropriate tax accounting arrangements", their position is that companies are expected to ensure that those making these decisions base them on a reasonable interpretation of accurate information in full knowledge of tax law and having taken appropriate advice. If this is the case, the fact that this judgement may differ from that made by HMRC does not mean that the tax accounting arrangements are inappropriate.

Taxes and duties include SDLT (sub-para (3)(e)) and SDRT (sub-para (3)((f)). In the case of SDRT, although the tax liability may strictly be that of a third party, if the liability is administered by the company by reason of its brokerage activities, the company's SAO must comply with the requirements of the Schedule in respect of such liabilities.

Meaning of "qualifying company"

15.—The term "large company" is defined by reference to CA 2006 ss 383 and 465, ie companies which are not small or medium-sized, ie with either or both of more than £200 million relevant turnover, or more than a £2 billion balance sheet total measured on a group basis. Regulations may provide that companies of a specified description are excluded from this definition. No regulations have been made to date. Because the definition of "company" is taken from the Companies Act, HMRC accepts that the legislation applies only to officers of UK-incorporated companies, including the foreign permanent establishments of such companies; but not non-UK incorporated companies, nor the UK permanent establishments of such companies. UK-incorporated companies which are non-resident are within the legislative scope of this Schedule only if they are trading in, or have some taxable activity within, the UK.

Meaning of "senior accounting officer"

16.—The term "senior accounting officer" is defined as the company or group director or officer who has overall responsibility for the company's financial accounting arrangements.

Regulations

17.—Regulations under this Schedule are made by statutory instrument.

Other definitions

18.—Various words and phrases are defined.

SCHEDULE 55 PENALTY FOR FAILURE TO MAKE RETURN

1.—A penalty is payable when a taxpayer fails to make or deliver a return under Finance Act 2003 ss 76 or 81 of, or paras 3, 4 or 8 of Schedule 17A. Paragraphs 3 and 4 are provisions which require a taxpayer to make a return when a lease continues beyond a fixed term, or where an indefinite lease (which will have been treated originally as a lease for a fixed term of a year) continues for another year, in each requiring the taxpayer to recalculate the amount of SDLT due on the rent. Sections 76 and 81c impose, respectively, a duty to deliver a land transaction return within 30 days of the effective date, and a further return where a relief is withdrawn. Paragraph 8 requires a return where the amount of rent payable under a lease becomes certain, having originally been computed in accordance with section 55 of the Act. A penalty is also due where a taxpayer (P) fails to give notice of charge to SDRT under FA 1986 s 98 and the regulations made thereunder, the Stamp Duty Reserve Tax Regulations 1986, of which the relevant regulation is Regulation 4. It will be apparent that the penalty is for failure to deliver and not for making an incorrect return. The amount of the penalty is £100 (paragraph 3) but there are additional penalties if the failure continues for a lengthy period:

(a) If the failure continues for more than three months beyond the date when the document ought to have been delivered the Commissioners may in their discretion serve notice on P retrospectively specifying a date from which a penalty of £10 per day is payable. The penalty period runs for a maximum of 90 days and may run from the day after the expiry of the three months mentioned above. (paragraph 4).

(b) If the failure continues for more than six months beyond the date when the document ought to have been delivered, P is liable to pay a penalty of 5% of the tax due or, if greater, £300. (paragraph 5).

(c) If the failure continues for more than twelve months beyond the date when the document ought to have been delivered the general rule is that P will be liable to a penalty of 5% of the tax due or, if greater, £300. However, if the effect of failing to make the return P has prevented HMRC from assessing the tax due, or has made it more difficult for HMRC to do so, then a substantially greater penalty is due, depending on P's mens rea. If the withholding of information was deliberate and concealed, the penalty is 100% of the tax due or, if greater, £300. If the withholding of information was deliberate but not concealed, the penalty is 70% of the tax due or, if greater, £300 (paragraph 6). Paragraph 27 defines the difference between "deliberate and concealed" and "deliberate but not concealed". There is concealment if P makes arrangements to conceal the fact that information has been withheld.

The paragraph 6 penalties are the maximum due; and provision is made by paragraphs 14–16 for penalties to be mitigated where P makes disclosure to the Commissioners. The amount of the reduction depends on the quality of the disclosure and the circumstances in which it is made. The legislation draws a distinction between prompted and unprompted disclosure, with greater credit being given for the latter. Disclosure is unprompted only if P makes it at a time when he has no reason to believe that HMRC have or are about to discover the information. Disclosure is given an extended meaning – it covers not only cases where P tells HMRC about the information but also cases where he helps the Commissioners to quantify the tax due or allows HMRC access to his records for the purposes of checking the tax due.

The following table sets out the available reductions:

Standard %	*Minimum % for prompted disclosure*	*Minimum % for un-prompted disclosure*
70	35	20
100	50	30

In addition to the above reductions, the Commissioners, if they think it right to do so because of special circumstances, may reduce or stay (e.g. postpone) a penalty under any of the preceding rules, or may agree a compromise in penalty proceedings: paragraph 16. The Commissioners have not explained what will constitute "special circumstances"; but the paragraph provides that they do not include an inability to pay, or the fact that there has been a potential overpayment elsewhere which balances the underpayment for which a penalty is sought.

Although the penalties under this Schedule and Schedule 56 are cumulative, if P is also liable to tax-geared penalties under other statutory provisions which are calculated by reference to the same liability, the amount of the penalties due under Schedule 55 must be reduced by the amount of the other penalties. In any event, the penalties due under Schedule 55 cannot exceed 100% of the tax due: paragraph 17.

Paragraphs 18 and 19 provide for the penalty to be assessed by HMRC and for its notification to P. P must pay the penalty with 30 days of the date on which the penalty notice was issued. The Commissioners must make their assessment within two years of the filing date or, if later, 12 months after the end of the period in which P could have appealed against the assessment of his liability to the substantive tax. If P appeals the amount of tax, the penalty period is extended until 12 months after the determination or withdrawal of the appeal.

Paragraphs 20 to 22 make provision for an appeal against the imposition of a penalty. The Tribunal has power to affirm or cancel the Commissioners' decision or to substitute their own decision for that of the Commissioners. If the Commissioners have made a special reduction under paragraph 16, the Tribunal may only amend that decision if the Commissioners' decision could have been overturned on an application for judicial review. (i.e. was *Wednesbury* unreasonable – see *Associated Picture Houses v Wednesbury Corporation* [1947] 1 KB 223).

P is not liable to a penalty under Schedule 55 if he has a reasonable excuse for his behaviour: paragraph 23. It should be noted that the test for reasonable excuse in Schedule 55 is more restricted than that in Finance Act 2003 s 97: an insufficiency of funds is not an excuse; and reliance on another is not to be accepted as a reasonable excuse unless P took reasonable care to avoid the failure. Presumably it suffices if P appoints a reputable agent to undertake the filing and provides them with the necessary information and funds to enable them to carry out their duties.

Paragraph 24 permits the Commissioners to assess the penalty to the best of their information and belief in the absence of a return and to reassess once the return has been submitted.

Paragraph 25 establishes the procedure for imposing a penalty on a partnership.

Paragraph 26 affords protection against double jeopardy: if P is convicted of an offence in relation to his conduct, he is not also to be liable to a civil penalty under Schedule 55.

SCHEDULE 56 PENALTY FOR FAILURE TO MAKE PAYMENTS ON TIME

Paragraph 1 imposes an automatic penalty whenever a taxpayer ("P") fails to pay an amount of tax on or before the time specified in the table to the paragraph. The relevant provisions tabled for SDLT and SDRT as as follows:

9	Stamp Duty Land Tax	Amount payable under FA 2003 s 86(1) or (2)	The date falling 30 days after the date specified in FA 2003 s 86(1) or (2) as the date by which the amount must be paid
10	Stamp Duty Reserve Tax	Amount payable under FA 1986 ss 87, 93 or 96 or FA 1999 Sch 19 (except an amount falling within item 17, 23 or 24)	The date falling 30 days after the date determined by or under regulations under FA 1986 s 98 as the date by which the amount must be paid
15	Stamp Duty Land Tax	Amount shown in determination under FA 2003 Sch 10 parag 25 (including that paragraph as applied by section 81(3) of that Act)	The date falling 30 days after the filing date for the return in question

There are corresponding provisions (items 17, 23 and 24) which make similar provision for penalties to be paid where tax is shown to be due in an assessment, or in an amendment or correction of a land transaction return.

In each case P is liable to a penalty of 5% of the unpaid tax once the specified date ("the penalty date") has passed (paragraph 3(1)(*a*), (2)) and to a further penalty of 5% of the amount of any tax remaining unpaid five months after the penalty date (paragraph 3(3)); and to a further 5% of the amount of any tax which remains unpaid 11 months after the penalty date (paragraph 3(4)).

The Commissioners, if they think it right to do so because of special circumstances, may reduce or stay (e.g. postpone) a penalty under any of the preceding rules, or may agree a compromise in penalty proceedings: paragraph 9. The Commissioners have not explained what will constitute "special circumstances"; but the paragraph provides that they do not include an inability to pay, or the fact that there has been a potential overpayment elsewhere which balances the underpayment for which a penalty is sought.

The Commissioners are also given power to suspend a penalty if, on his failing to pay an amount of tax which is due and payable, P asks the Commissioners to defer the payment of the tax and they agree that it may be deferred for a period. Then, provided P does not break the agreement, P is not liable for the penalty under paragraph 3 which would otherwise have been imposed. However, if P breaks the agreement, by failing to pay the tax at the end of the period, or he otherwise fails to comply with a condition imposed as part of the agreement, P will be liable to the relevant penalty: paragraph 10.

Paragraphs 11 and 12 make provision for the penalty to be assessed by HMRC and for its notification to P. P must pay the penalty with 30 days of the date on which the penalty notice was issued. The Commissioners must make their assessment within two years of the filing date or, if later, 12 months after the end of the period in which P could have appealed against the assessment of his liability to the substantive tax. If P appeals the amount of tax, the penalty period is extended until 12 months after the determination or withdrawal of the appeal.

Paragraphs 13 to 15 make provision for an appeal against the imposition of a penalty. The Tribunal has power to affirm or cancel the Commissioners' decision or to substitute their own decision for that of the Commissioners. If the Commissioners have made a special reduction under paragraph 9, the Tribunal may only amend that decision if the Commissioners' decision could have been overturned on an application for judicial review. (i.e. was *Wednesbury* unreasonable – see *Associated Picture Houses v Wednesbury Corporation* [1947] 1 KB 223).

P is not liable to a penalty under Schedule 56 if he has a reasonable excuse for his behaviour: paragraph 16. It should be noted that the test for reasonable excuse in Schedule 56 is more restricted than that in Finance Act 2003 s 97: an insufficiency of funds is not an excuse; and reliance on another is not to be accepted as a reasonable excuse unless P took reasonable care to avoid the failure. Presumably it suffices if P appoints a reputable agent to undertake the filing and provides them with the necessary information and funds to enable them to carry out their duties.

Paragraph 17 affords protection against double jeopardy: if P is convicted of an offence in relation to his conduct, he is not also to be liable to a civil penalty under Schedule 56.

SCHEDULE 61 ALTERNATIVE FINANCE INVESTMENT BONDS (SECTION 122)

As part of the Government's continuing campaign to put alternative finance products on a level footing with standard investment products, s 123 and Sch 61 are designed to remove the SDLT charges that would otherwise arise on the issue of land assets as securities in alternative finance investment bonds. In the absence of specific exemptions, SDLT charges would arise both on the transfer of the land asset to the bond issuer and on the eventual return of the asset to the person seeking to obtain finance. There would also be a potential charge to SDLT arising on bond-holders. In order to secure the necessary exemptions and reliefs, not only from SDLT but also from capital gains tax and to capital allowances, provisions of some complexity have been made. The reader is referred to corresponding passages in the Yellow Tax Guide for commentary on the CGT and capital allowance reliefs available.

So far as SDLT is concerned, the legislation adopts the definition of an alternative finance investment bond in FA 2005 s 48A: essentially, it is an arrangement under which one person ("the bond holder") agrees to pay a capital sum to another, ("the bond issuer"), under arrangements which provide for the bond issuer to acquire a class of assets (here, land assets) from which income and gains will be obtained for a specified term. At the end of the term the bond issuer will dispose of any remaining bond assets and make a repayment of capital, as well as covenanting to make additional payments during the term of the bond whose amount will "not exceed an amount which would be a reasonable commercial return on a loan of the capital".

Schedule 61 para 2 adopts for SDLT purposes the fiction created by FA 2005 s 48B(2) that the bond issuer does not hold the bond assets on trust for the bond holders; and that the bond holders have no equitable interest in the underlying assets. By this means, acquisitions and disposals of bonds or interests in the bonds do not involve land transactions under FA 2003

Part II ST

s 43, with attendant SDLT charges. By way of exception to the general rule, para 3 displaces para 2 if control of the underlying investments is acquired by one or more connected bond holders. "Control" in this context, is defined as the right of management and control of the assets, or sufficient rights to enable the group to exercise the rights of management and control to the exclusion of other bond holders. Presumably, the circumstances in which this will occur will depend on the precise contractual terms of each bond issue. By way of a somewhat unusual exception to the application of para 3, para 4 restores the operation of the general rule in para 2 where control is obtained unwittingly and, as soon as reasonably practicable after discovering the fact, the bond holder takes steps to transfer sufficient rights to divest himself of control. A separate exception exists where the bond holder in question underwrote the public offer of the bonds and refrains from exercising his rights of control and management (para 4).

Paragraph 5 contains seven conditions all of which must be satisfied if the reliefs are to operate. The thrust of the conditions is that a landowner is to enter into a transfer and lease-back transaction with the bond issuer for a term not exceeding ten years and under which the landowner is to make "interest payments" in the shape of the rent due under the lease-back as well as repayments of capital from time to time to reduce the capital by not less than 60% of the market value of the land at the time of the original sale. Furthermore, the land is to remain as a bond asset throughout the term of the bond (though there are provisions for substitution of one piece of land by another) and eventually, within 30 days of the termination of the bond, the land is to be returned to its original owner. In short, the conditions are designed to ensure that the land is transferred as security for the moneys subscribed for the bond issue and not under some arrangement for the avoidance of stamp taxes. To emphasise this, it is a further condition of the relief that the bond issuer grants a legal charge over the land in favour of the Commissioners for the amount not merely of the SDLT that would have been chargeable on a sale by landowner to bond issuer for a sum equal to its initial market value but the interest and penalties that would have been due had the tax not been paid. There is a corresponding obligation to provide HMRC with evidence that the charge has been granted, in the form specified by the Alternative Finance Investment Bonds (SDLT) (Prescribed Evidence) Regulations 2009, SI 2009/2052.

If all these conditions are satisfied, there will be an exemption from SDLT not only on the transfer of the land to the bond issuer but also on the return of the land to the owner. Since, though, it will not be clear at the outset whether all the conditions will be satisfied, the legislation operates by requiring only the first three conditions to be satisfied at the outset (para 6) and withdrawing that relief if either the subsequent conditions are not satisfied or it becomes clear that they cannot or will not be met. In the event that the relief is withdrawn, SDLT is chargeable on the market value of the land at the effective date of its transfer to the bond issuer; and interest is payable as if the tax had been due from the start. Paragraph 7 makes provision for the bond issuer to make the appropriate land transaction return and to pay the tax due within 30 days of the relevant condition being failed, or it becoming clear that a condition will be failed.

Thus, in order to obtain relief on the transfer of the land to the bond issuer, it must be demonstrated that within 30 days of the effective date of the land transaction:

(a) the landowner and the bond issuer have entered into an agreement under which the former transfers his land to the latter and the bond issuer agrees that, on it ceasing to be held as a bond asset, he will return the land to its owner;

(b) the bond issuer enters into an alternative finance investment bond of which the land is a bond asset; and

(c) the bond issuer and the landowner enter into a leaseback agreement for the purpose of generating income or gains for the bond. It is assumed that this transaction will be exempt from SDLT under FA 2003 s 57A ("sale and leaseback arrangements")

Relief for the second land transaction – the return of the land to its owner – is available if all seven conditions have been satisfied (para 8). The final four conditions are:

(a) the issue of the necessary charge in favour of the Commissioners;

(b) the making of repayments of capital amounting in aggregate to not less than 60% of the initial value of the land;
(c) the retention of the land as a bond asset throughout the life of the bond; and
(d) the return of the land to the owner within 30 days of the termination of the bond and no more than ten years after the effective date of the transfer to the bond issuer.

If all these conditions are demonstrated to the satisfaction of the Commissioners, the charge is lifted once the land has been returned (para 9). To this end, the claimant must provide the Commissioners with appropriate evidence, as specified by the Alternative Finance Investment Bonds (SDLT) (Prescribed Evidence) Regulations 2009, SI 2009/2052.

Further provision is made by para 18 for a case where, before the bond terminates, the land is returned by the bond issuer to the landowner and the parties enter into substitute arrangements in relation to replacement land. In this case, the conditions will be treated as satisfied if the relevant conditions are instead satisfied going forward in relation to the replacement land. In such a case, the charge in favour of the Commissioners is removed from the original land and imposed instead on the replacement land. Provision is also made for that land, in turn, to be replaced if necessary by other land on like conditions.

Certain anti-avoidance provisions are built into Sch 61.

Paragraph 20 denies the benefit of the reliefs in paras 6 and 8 where a bond holder (or a group of connected bond holders) obtain control of the underlying land. This is taken to occur (para 20(2)) where the bond holder (or the group) acquire sufficient rights to enable him (or them) to exercise the right of management and control of the asset to the exclusion of the other bond holders. As with para 2, para 21 identifies certain cases where the reliefs are not to be denied, despite the obtaining of control:

(a) where the acquisition of control was inadvertent and the bond holder(s) relinquished control as soon as reasonably practicable by disposing of sufficient rights; or
(b) where the bond holder had underwritten a public issue of the bonds and does not exercise control or management of the relevant assets.

Paragraph 21 also denies relief under paras 6 and 8 if the initial arrangements between the landowner and the bond issuer were not effected for genuine commercial reasons or they formed part of arrangements of which the main purpose, or one of the main purposes, was the avoidance of liability to one of a number of taxes: income tax, corporation tax, capital gains tax, stamp duty or SDLT. The reader is referred to the commentary on FA 2003 Sch 7 para 2(4A) for a similar set of restrictions. However, the "White list" that applies to that provision clearly has no application to para 21; and as yet the Commissioners have given no indication of the circumstances in which they would expect to apply the paragraph.

2. Statutory Instruments

Contents

2004/1864 Tax Avoidance Schemes (Information) Regulations 2004
2004/3218 Stamp Duty and Stamp Duty Reserve Tax (Investment Exchanges and Clearing Houses) Regulations 2004
2005/844 Stamp Duty Land Tax (Electronic Communications) Regulations 2005
2005/1868 Stamp Duty Land Tax Avoidance Schemes (Prescribed Description of Arrangements) Regulations 2005
2005/2462 Taxes (Interest Rate) (Amendment) Regulations 2005
2006/575 Pension Protection Fund (Tax) Regulations 2006
2006/3237 The Stamp Duty Land Tax (Variation of the Finance Act 2003) Regulations 2006
2007/1385 The Finance Act 2003, Section 66 (Prescribed Statutory Provisions) Order 2007
2007/3437 Stamp Duty Land Tax (Zero-carbon Homes Relief) Regulations 2007
2008/710 Stamp Duty Land Tax (Open-ended Investment Companies) Regulations 2008
2009/2052 Alternative Finance Investment Bonds (Stamp Duty Land Tax) (Prescribed Evidence) Regulations 2009
2009/2971 Mutual Societies (Transfers of Business) (Tax) Regulations 2009

SI 1985/1688
THE STAMP DUTY (EXEMPT INSTRUMENTS) REGULATIONS 1985

1. These regulations (made under FA 1985 s 89), came into operation on 1 January 1986. They are effectively obsolete, although it is possible that they could apply in a case where the transitional rules in FA 2003 Sch 19 were to operate. Under FA 1931 s 28 it was obligatory for the transferee of a freehold interest or a lessee under or purchaser of a lease for seven years or more to produce the instrument in question to the Commissioners (the particulars delivered, or PD, Form). FA 1995 s 89 then made provision for regulations exempting certain low-value instruments from the PD procedure. These regulations are made under s 89. However, since s 28 is inapplicable to SDLT transactions, both the PD procedure and the need for an exemption have ceased to be of relevance.

2. Terms are defined by reference to the Land Registration Act 1925 s 126(1).

3. Sale instruments need not be produced to the Stamp Office if they relate to sales of freehold or leasehold property which are below £30,000 for instruments executed and stamped before 23 March 1993 or £60,000 for instruments executed on or after 16 March 1993 and not stamped before 23 March 1993 and they have to be registered with the Land Registry. For instruments executed during the period between 21 December 1991 and 19 August 1992 (inclusive of those dates) the threshold is £250,000—see commentary on the now repealed Stamp Duty (Temporary Provisions) Act 1992.

The arrangements do not apply to sales of property which attract stamp duty, sales which do not have to be registered with the Land Registry, the grant of a new lease, or sales of property in Scotland and Northern Ireland, to which different procedures apply.

4. A "PD form" must be delivered to the Land Registry.

5. The Land Registry must pass the "particulars delivered form" to HMRC.

Part II ST

SI 1986/1711
THE STAMP DUTY RESERVE TAX REGULATIONS 1986

Citation and commencement

1. These regulations (made under FA 1986 s 98), came into operation on 27 October 1986 but were significantly amended with effect from 20 October 1997, primarily to take account of the introduction of the CREST electronic share dealing system, by the Stamp Duty Reserve Tax (Amendment) Regulations 1997 (SI 1997/2430).

Further revisions were made on 6 February 2000 by the Stamp Duty Reserve Tax (Amendment No 2) Regulations 1999 (SI 1999/3264) which introduced stamp duty reserve tax on certain surrenders of units in unit trust schemes and similarly on shares in open-ended investment companies.

Interpretation

2. Various terms are defined.

The definition of "accountable date" has been completely revised. Prior to 20 October 1997, the "accountable date", which is the due date for payment of the tax, meant the last day of the month following that in which the charge arises, except in the case of a charge incurred under the special provisions relating to depositary and clearance schemes, where the time for payment is extended to the last day of the second month following that in which the charge was incurred. As a result of changes taking effect on or after 20 October 1997 and 6 February 2000, the "accountable date" may mean one of four times, as follows:

(a) the seventh day of the month following the month in which the charge to tax arose (ie when the agreement was made, or when a conditional agreement became unconditional);
(b) the fourteenth day following the date of the transaction;
(c) such other date as may be agreed between HMRC and the "operator" (as defined in the recent amendments to the Regulations—see below);
(d) in relation to a charge on the surrender of a unit in a unit trust scheme or share in an open-ended investment company the fourteenth day of the month following the month in which the relevant two-week period (as defined in Schedule 19 FA 1999) occurs.

These four possibilities interact as follows:
(a) applies in all cases unless one of the others applies to any particular transaction;
(b) applies to interest on overdue tax where (broadly speaking) the transaction took place on or through a recognised exchange and/or involved CREST (or another approved electronic trading system) and the transaction was not reported at the correct time;
(c) applies to the principal tax due under a transaction to which (*b*) applies in respect of the interest, where an agreement has been reached to disapply (*b*) to the principal tax. For example, in the case of CREST, it has been agreed that tax will be accounted for on the earlier of (i) ten days after the trade date input into the CREST system and (ii) the date of settlement in relation to a transaction;
(d) applies as detailed in (*d*) above.

The "accountable person" is the person who must give notice of a charge and pay the tax (as opposed to the person who is *liable* for the tax, being the purchaser, or "B", under FA 1986 s 91) and is defined as either the market maker or broker-dealer who purchased the shares or acted as agent for the purchaser, or (if none) the market maker or broker-dealer who sold the shares or acted as agent for the seller, or (if none) the qualified dealer who purchased the shares or acted as agent for the purchaser, or (if none) the qualified dealer who sold the shares or acted as agent for the seller, or (if none) the purchaser himself. Thus, a purchaser who is a private investor (ie, who is not a market maker, broker-dealer or qualified dealer) will only have to *account for* the tax himself (although he is always ultimately *liable* for it) if he buys shares privately without the involvement (in any capacity) of a market maker, broker-dealer or qualified dealer.

From 6 February 2000, "accountable person" also includes (in relation to a charge on the surrender of a unit under FA 1999 Sch 19 para 2(1)) (i) the managers of a unit trust scheme (or failing that) (ii) the trustees of a unit trust scheme; and (in relation to a charge on the surrender of a share in an open-ended investment company under FA 1999 Sch 19(i) para 2(1)) the authorised corporate director of the open-ended investment company (or failing that) (iii) the company.

The definitions "authorised corporate director" and "open-ended investment company" are defined in reg 2 of the Stamp Duty and Stamp Duty Reserve Tax (Open-ended Investment Companies) Regulations 1997—SI 1997/1156 while the definition of "surrender" is the same as that under FA 1999 Sch 2 para 2(1) (added by SI 1999/3264).

The concepts of "broker dealer" and "market maker" have been replaced by terminology which corresponds to the new intermediary reliefs in FA 1986 s 88A. There is a new defined term, the "operator", which means, broadly, the operator of CREST or any other approved electronic trading system, or the operator of a recognised investment exchange or an EEA regulated market (the last two terms being further elaborated in the Financial Services Act 1986).

For guidance on the accountable person and accountable date in relation to securities settled through the CREST paperless settlement system see the June 1995 handbook on using CREST functionality issued by the CREST Project Team at CREST Co and the January 1996 supplement.

2A. Any references made in these Regulations to the provisions of FA 1999 Sch 2 include modifications made to those provisions by SI 1997/1156.

Due date for payment

3. Any tax charged under FA 1986 ss 86–89 and stamp duty reserve tax charged under FA 1999 Sch 19 para 2(1) is due and payable on the accountable date, as defined and revised by SI 1999/3264. See also the 16 January 1997 letter to *The Tax Journal* (reproduced at Appendix 4).

Notice of charge and payment

4. Subject to the new reg 4A, which takes priority, or where reg 4B applies, the accountable person, as defined, unless alternative arrangements are authorised by HMRC, must on or before the accountable date give notice of each charge to tax to HMRC, and pay the tax due. The Board is empowered to prescribe the form of the notice. However, although reg 4A (see below) appears to take priority, it is important to note that the accountable person's liability arises under reg 4 unless the tax "has been" accounted for under reg 4A (ie not merely where that liability "ought to have been" or "could have been" accounted for under reg 4A). In this regard, it is important to appreciate that the CREST software is not sufficiently sophisticated to assess the correct tax due in respect of all the possible transactions which the system is capable of carrying out. There are also some cases where the CREST software is capable of including provision for stamp duty reserve tax liability but where the precise circumstances of the transaction will determine whether the payment of tax takes place inside or outside CREST in relation to a particular transaction of that type. Lucid general explanations of CREST, and the stamp duty reserve tax issues relating thereto, are to be found in articles by Richard Stratton and Jane Tuckley at PLC 1997 8(5) 47–56 and PLC 1997 8(11) 43–48.

Under the definition of "accountable person" before its amendment by FA 1988, the "accountable person" was normally B (the purchaser) unless B was not a member of the Stock Exchange but A (the vendor) was such a member, in which case the tax had to be accounted for (and paid) by A. In the case of flotations or privatisations, therefore, where A was a vendor shareholder, an issuing house, or a Minister of the Crown, and therefore not a member of the Stock Exchange, each applicant for shares was a B and therefore accountable for the tax. Frequent use was therefore made of reg 4, which provides that "where different arrangements are authorised in writing" by HMRC someone else could become the accountable person. Such arrangements were made, for example, in the case of the privatisations of British Gas Plc, British Airways Plc and Rolls Royce Plc, whereby, in order to avoid the private individual investor (who in many cases was a first time share buyer) bearing the administrative burden of accounting for stamp duty reserve tax, it was agreed that the accountable person would be, respectively, the Secretary of State for Energy, the Secretary of State for Transport and the Secretary of State for Trade and Industry.

However, following the changes in the definition of "accountable person" made by FA 1988, such agreements are in most cases not strictly necessary to protect the private individual investor. All issuing houses as members of self-regulating organisations for the purposes of the Financial Services Act 1986 are within the definition of "qualified dealer" and their involvement in an offer for sale either as principal or as agent for the vendor or offerer renders them liable to account for the stamp duty reserve tax where an applicant is a private individual investor. Agreements under reg 4 may, however, still be resorted to in practice, as a matter of administrative convenience to avoid issuing houses being accountable for the tax in respect of some applications but not others (ie where an applicant is a market maker, broker-dealer or qualified dealer).

4A. The operator, as defined, is required to notify HMRC of each charge to tax, and pay the tax due, in respect of any transaction which (broadly speaking) is connected in some way with the electronic system or recognised exchange in respect of which that person falls within the statutory definition of "operator". Given the breadth of the definition of "operator" and the likely increase in electronic trading it would seem that reg 4A will become increasingly more significant than reg 4 in practice. However, it should be noted that, as with reg 4, it is possible to agree with HMRC that a person other than the operator shall discharge the obligations specified under the regulation.

4B. This Regulation applies to surrenders of units in unit trust schemes and similarly surrenders of shares in open-ended investment companies. From 6 February 2000, the "accountable person", as defined, must notify the HMRC of each surrender liable to tax and to pay the tax due on or before the "accountable date", as defined and revised above (added by SI 1999/3264 reg 7).

Notice of determination

6. The Board can issue a "notice of determination" to any person who appears to them to be the accountable person, or the person liable for the tax, or any person who has submitted a claim to them.

Relief from accountability

7. An accountable person or an operator, other than the purchaser, or the principal of a purchaser acting as a nominee or the manager or trustee of a unit trust or authorised corporate director of an open-ended investment company, can be relieved from liability to account for and pay the tax provided that he satisfies the Board that he has taken all reasonable steps to recover the tax from the purchaser.

Appeals against determination

8. An appeal may be made, within 30 days of any notice of determination, to the Special Commissioners, or direct to the High Court if this course of action is agreed between the appellant and the Board, or the High Court itself grants leave. The determination of any question relating to the value of land in the UK on any appeal under this regulation is reserved for the Lands Tribunal. If, before the Special Commissioners, the appellant wants to rely on a ground of appeal not specified in the notice of appeal, the Special Commissioners may allow it if satisfied that the omission was not wilful or unreasonable.

Appeals out of time

9. Leave to appeal after time may be given by the Board or the Special Commissioners if either the Board or the Special Commissioners (as the case may be) are satisfied that there was a reasonable excuse for the appeal not being brought within the time limit and the application has been made promptly thereafter.

Appeals from the Special Commissioners

10. An appeal on a point of law from the Special Commissioners may be made to the High Court. The High Court is given power to hear any question of law arising on the case and reverse, affirm or vary the determination of the Special Commissioners, or remit the matter to the Special Commissioners with the court's opinion on it, or make such other order as it thinks fit. See Schedule 1 to the Civil Procedure Rules, RSC Ord 91 rule 5A.

Interest on overpaid tax

11. Interest on overpaid tax is to be paid at the rate applicable under FA 1989 s 178, and the Taxes (Interest Rate) Regulations 1989 (SI 1989/1297) made under that section. Any such interest is not to constitute income for income tax or corporation tax purposes.

Recovery of tax

12. The Board is not to take proceedings to recover unpaid tax until the amount is agreed or a notice of determination has been issued under reg 6 and any appeal to the Special Commissioners or the High Court under reg 8 (but not any further appeal) has been determined.

Underpayments

13. Underpayments of tax are also to be payable with interest, but no additional tax can become payable more than six years after the date of payment or the relevant accountable date, except in the case of fraudulent or negligent conduct. This period will be reduced to four years with effect from 1 April 2011: see the SDRT (Amendment) Regulations 2010, SI 2010/664, reg 9, at which time the exception for fraudulent or negligent conduct will cease to apply. Instead, from that date, underpayments of SDRT brought about carelessly will be recoverable within six years of the relevant accountable date; and underpayments brought about deliberately will be recoverable within 20 years of that date. Transitional rules apply where the underpayment occurs before 1 April 2011 but the recovery action occurs on or after that date.

Overpayments

14. The Board is relieved from any responsibility to repay over-payments of tax more than six years after the date of the payment or the relevant accountable date. This period will be reduced to four years with effect from 1 April 2011: see the SDRT (Amendment) Regulations 2010, SI 2010/664, reg 9.

Evidence

16. Provisions are made in relation to evidence.

Determination of questions on previous view of the law

17. Liability for the tax is to remain unaltered notwithstanding subsequent legal decisions or changes in the view of the law generally received at the time or adopted in practice.

Recovery of over-repayment of tax, etc

18. Over-repayments of tax and overpayments of interest may be recovered up to six years after the date of the over-repayment or overpayment, as the case may be, except that the time limit does not apply in the case of fraudulent or negligent conduct. This period will be reduced to four years with effect from 1 April 2011: see the SDRT (Amendment) Regulations 2010, SI 2010/664, reg 9, at which time the exception for fraudulent or negligent conduct will cease to apply. Instead, from that date, over-repayments of SDRT brought about carelessly will be recoverable within six years of the date of repayment; and over-repayments brought about deliberately will be recoverable within 20 years of that date. Transitional rules apply where the over-repayment occurs before 1 April 2011 but the recovery action occurs on or after that date.

Service of documents

19. The service of documents is provided for.

Taxes Management Act 1970: provisions to apply

20. Certain provisions of TMA 1970 are applied, with certain modifications, in relation to stamp duty reserve tax. See the commentary on TMA 1970 as so modified and applied.

Inland Revenue Regulation Act 1890: provisions not to apply

21. The Inland Revenue Regulation Act 1890 ss 21, 22 and 35 (containing provisions in relation to proceedings for the recovery of fines, etc) are disapplied.

SCHEDULE (REGULATION 20)

This Schedule specifies, in Pt I, the provisions of TMA 1970 which are to apply and the modifications to such provisions which are to have effect, and sets out, in Pt II, those provisions as so modified. For the commentary thereon, see under TMA 1970.

The Table in Pt I of the Schedule has been amended by substituting the entries relating to TMA 1970 s 86 (amended by the Stamp Duty Reserve Tax (Amendment) Regulations 1999—SI 1999/2536 with effect from 1 October 1999). As a result, the rate of interest applicable under FA 1989 s 178 in respect of overdue stamp duty reserve tax is now the same as that in relation to overdue income tax and capital gains tax.

SI 1987/516
THE STAMP DUTY (EXEMPT INSTRUMENTS) REGULATIONS 1987

1. These regulations made under FA 1985 s 87(2), came into force on 1 May 1987.

1A. The Stamp Duty (Exempt Instruments) (Amendment) Regulations 1999 (SI 1999/2539) adds a new reg 1A to SI 1987/516. Regulation 1A defines "life policy" as any insurance policy on a human life that is payable when the person dies of natural causes, or a grant or contract for the payment of an annuity upon a human life.

2. An instrument which:

(a) is executed on or after 1 May 1987, and

(b) is of a kind specified in the Schedule to the Regulations including declarations in respect of life policies and annuities (included by SI 1999/2539), and

(c) is certified by a certificate which fulfils the conditions set out in the Regulations to be an instrument of that kind,

is to be exempt from duty under what are now FA 1999 Sch 13 Pt III para 16 ("transfer otherwise than on sale"), para 17 ("declaration of use of trust"), para 18 ("dispositions in Scotland") and FA 1985 ss 83(2) and 84(8).

3. The required certificate:

(a) must be in writing and—

  (i) be included as part of the instrument, or

  (ii) be endorsed upon or, where separate, be physically attached to the instrument concerned;

(b) must contain a sufficient description of:

  (i) the instrument concerned where the certificate is separate but physically attached to the instrument, and

  (ii) the category in the Schedule to the Regulations into which the instrument falls; and

(c)

  (i) must be signed by the transferor or grantor or by his solicitor or duly authorised agent, and

  (ii) where it is not signed by the transferor or grantor or by his solicitor, must contain a statement by the signatory of the capacity in which he signs, that he is authorised so to sign and that he gives the certificate from his own knowledge of the facts stated in it.

4. The Schedule is introduced.

5. Any instrument which is certified in accordance with these Regulations is not required under FA 1985 s 82 (5) or s 84 (9) to be adjudicated in accordance with SA 1891 s 12.

The Schedule to the Regulations provides that an instrument which effects any one or more of the following transactions only is an instrument specified for the purposes of the Regulations: see Appendix 1.

With effect from 1 October 1999, a new category has been added to the Schedule to exempt life policies and annuities from duty (included by SI 1999/2539).

In their general notes for guidance issued with the new Regulations (see Appendix 1), the Revenue suggested that an appropriate form of words for the certificate would be as follows:

"I/We hereby certify that this instrument falls within category . . . in the Schedule to the Stamp Duty (Exempt Instruments) Regulations 1987" (the gap to be completed with the letter opposite the category of instrument as listed in the Schedule to the Regulations).

All instruments specified in the Regulations, if duly certified, will be deemed to be duly stamped and need not be produced to, or adjudicated by, the Stamp Office. Once certified, the relevant documents can be sent straight to the registrar or other person who needs to act upon them, if any.

Notwithstanding these Regulations, where there is any doubt as to whether or not a particular instrument can be properly endorsed with the appropriate certificate, it remains possible for that instrument to be submitted to the Stamp Office for adjudication pursuant to SA 1891 s 12. The Stamp Office cannot refuse to adjudicate a document submitted to it simply because on the face of it it appears to come within the list of documents specified in the Schedule to the Regulations. Whilst the new system will undoubtedly reduce the workload of the Stamp Office and generally speed up the completion of transactions of the kind specified in the Regulations, it does transfer the burden of deciding whether or not a document is duly stamped away from the Stamp Office and on to the professional advisers of the parties to a particular transaction. It may be anticipated, therefore, that professional advisers will, in cases of doubt, submit documents for adjudication rather than run the risk of being held to have misinterpreted the Regulations.

The law in relation to a number of the transactions specified in the Schedule to the Regulations is extremely complex, and this is particularly so in relation to category L: "the conveyance or transfer of property operating as a voluntary disposition inter vivos for no consideration in money or money's worth nor any consideration referred to in SA 1891 s 57 (conveyance in consideration of a debt etc)." The requirement that the conveyance or transfer be "for no consideration in money or money's worth", nor any debt consideration, arguably leaves a residual category of transactions falling within the abolished provisions relating to "voluntary dispositions inter vivos" which do still require to be adjudicated.

It will be seen from the commentary in relation to FA 1985 s 82 (5) that any conveyance or transfer operating as a voluntary disposition inter vivos, within the meaning of the abolished provisions, was required to be adjudicated if it was not stampable as a "conveyance or transfer on sale". It was only, therefore, transactions involving a consideration in cash, stock, marketable or other securities, or debts, ie, transactions "on sale" for the purposes of SA 1891, where the need for adjudication was avoided. If there was no such consideration, the instrument had to be adjudicated. Where, therefore, a transaction involves some consideration "in money's worth" which is not cash, stock, marketable or other securities, or debts, then it will not be "on sale", and will not therefore avoid the need for adjudication under s 82 (5), nor will it be within category L of the new Regulations. Whatever the correct interpretation of the Regulations, their very obscurity in such matters may result in the parties to a transaction minimising their own risks by withholding the appropriate certificate and submitting the relevant document for adjudication. The use of the words "inter vivos" suggest that category "L" only applies to dispositions by natural persons (ie individuals) although in practice it seems to be accepted that a company, or other artificial person, is capable of making a disposition of property which is capable of being certified under category "L".

Somewhat surprisingly, the Regulations do not themselves impose any penalties or sanctions in relation to the giving of an improper certificate. Therefore, as is the case with "certificates of value" given pursuant to what is now FA 1999 Sch 13 Part I paras 4 and 6, the only sanction will be imposed by SA 1891 s 5. This imposes (as amended by FA 1999) a penalty not exceeding £3,000 on every person who, with intent to defraud Her Majesty, executes or prepares any instrument in which all the facts and circumstances affecting the liability of that instrument to stamp duty, or the amount of the duty with which it is chargeable, are not fully and truly set forth. However, in the absence of bad faith, ie, where there is no intent to defraud

Her Majesty and an incorrect certificate is given in good faith that it is correct, the sanction will not be available. In the light of that s 5 is unlikely to prove an effective deterrent.

Only the penalties for late stamping which may be imposed in relation to a document (on which a certificate is given) that subsequently proves to have been stampable may prove an effective deterrent, assuming, that is, that the document proves to have been liable to ad valorem duty and not merely the fixed duty of £5. Otherwise the only effective check on the misuse of certificates will be the good faith and professional conduct of the parties and their advisers.

See Statement of Practice SP6/90 in Appendix 2.

SI 1988/268
THE STAMP DUTY AND STAMP DUTY RESERVE TAX (DEFINITIONS OF UNIT TRUST SCHEME) REGULATIONS 1988

Three types of unit trust scheme are excepted from the definition of "unit trust scheme" in FA 1946 s 57(1) and F (No 2) A (NI) 1946 s 28(1). The first is a limited partnership scheme where the scheme property is held on trust for the general partners and the limited partners in a limited partnership under the Limited Partnerships Act 1907. The second is a profit sharing scheme approved under FA 1978 Sch 9 Part I. The third (added pursuant to SI 2000/2549 with effect from 11 October 2000) is an employee share ownership plan approved under FA 2000 Sch 8.

Although stamp duty charges on unit trusts (other than bearer units) have been abolished by FA 1999, the definitions in FA 1946 remain important because (other than in relation to the meaning of "paired shares") the same definitions apply for the purposes of stamp duty reserve tax.

See also SI 2001/964 (unit trusts dedicated to individual pension accounts).

SI 1989/1297
THE TAXES (INTEREST RATE) REGULATIONS 1989

Citation and commencement

1. These regulations, made under FA 1989 s 178, came into force on 18 August 1989.

Interpretation

2. Various terms are defined; in particular;

"established rate" is from 18 August 1989 14% but thereafter is the reference rate on the last reference date:

"operative date" is the 6th of each month; "reference date" is 12 working days before the 6th of the month; for example, if the reference rate changes on 25 September, the next reference date is about 20 October and the new rates automatically apply from the operative date, 6 November.

The reference rate is the average base lending rate of the six banks named, **rounded to the nearest whole number**: one half is rounded down. Thus 6.5% or 5.75% becomes 6%.

Applicable rates of interest on unpaid tax, tax repaid and repayment supplement

3. The rate of interest chargeable on ad valorem stamp duty and unpaid stamp duty reserve tax (see SA 1891 s 15A, SI 1986/1711 Sch, TMA 1970 s 86, FA 1989 s 178) is reference rate (RR) + 2.5.

3AB. With effect from 1 October 1999 the rate of interest payable on repayments of ad valorem stamp duty and stamp duty reserve tax (FA 1986 s 92, FA 1999 s110, FA 1989 s 178 and SI 1986/1711 reg 11) is in line with rates for income tax and capital gains tax.

The rate becomes

$$(RR - 1) \times \frac{100 - \text{lower rate}}{100}$$

If the result is not a multiple of one quarter, it is rounded down to the nearest quarter.

Effect of change in applicable rate

6. If the rate changes it is effective from the 6th of the month.

SI 1992/197
THE STAMP DUTY AND STAMP DUTY RESERVE TAX (DEFINITION OF UNIT TRUST SCHEME) REGULATIONS 1992

There are excluded from the definition of "unit trust scheme" in FA 1946 s 57(1), schemes made by the Lord Chancellor in exercise of the powers conferred on him by the Administration of Justice Act 1982 s 42(1) (schemes establishing common investment funds for the purpose of investing funds in court, and funds held by any other person authorised by the Lord Chancellor, under the management and control of an investment manager appointed by the Lord Chancellor).

SI 1992/232
THE ELECTRICITY (NORTHERN IRELAND CONSEQUENTIAL AMENDMENTS) ORDER 1992

This order makes amendments consequential on the Electricity (Northern Ireland) Order, SI 1992/231. Article 2 provides that electricity is to be treated as goods for the purposes of what is now FA 1999 Sch 13 Part I para 7. Contracts for the sale of electricity are therefore outside the scope of the stamp duty charge imposed by that section. This provision applies to Northern Ireland only (art 1(3)).

SI 1994/1811
THE SPECIAL COMMISSIONERS (JURISDICTION AND PROCEDURE) REGULATIONS 1994

These Regulations, which came into force on 1 September 1994 and apply to appeals where the notice of hearing is issued on or after that date, were made under ss 46A and 56B–56D of the Taxes Management Act 1970. They prescribe new rules for the administration and conduct of appeal hearings before the Special Commissioners. Their aim is to provide a framework of rules for parties to an appeal giving them information about the procedures to be followed and their rights, and also to provide powers to the tribunals to deal with appeals in a systematic and effective way.

The rules contain new powers to enable the Special Commissioners to hear cases in public (unless the taxpayer wants the hearing in private), to publish reports of their decisions and to award costs against any party who acts wholly unreasonably in connection with an appeal. The Special Commissioners are also able to recover (at the special Commissioner's determination) a penalty for failure to comply with a direction or a summons in appeal proceedings relating to stamp duty as though it were a penalty (other than a penalty for late stamping under the Stamp Act 1891 s 15B) (included by the Special Commissioner's (Jurisdiction and Procedure) (Amendment) Regulations 2000—SI 2000/288 with effect from 1 March 2000).

See the notes to these Regulations under Inheritance Tax; see also *Chiltern's Yellow Tax Guide* for a more detailed analysis of the procedural rules.

SI 1995/2051
THE STAMP DUTY RESERVE TAX (SWX EUROPE LIMITED) REGULATIONS 1995

These regulations, which came into force on 25 August 1995, were made under FA 1991 ss 116 and 117 following the recognition of Tradepoint (a new screen-based, order-driven market for dealing in equities) as an investment exchange by the Securities and Investment Board. They were amended by Stamp Duty Reserve Tax (Tradepoint) (Amendment) Regulations 2001 (SI 2001/2267) to reflect the transfer of all the business of Tradepoint Financial Networks plc as a recognised investment exchange, to a wholly owned subsidiary virt-x Exchange Limited (virt-x plc) which came into force on 25 June 2001. In 2008 virt-x Exchange Ltd amended its name to SWX Europe Limited and the regulations were amended accordingly. SWX Europe Limited offers a different trading system to the Stock Exchange as it is order-driven as opposed to quote-driven. Under the order-driven system, brokers' and institutions' buy and sell orders are automatically matched. By contrast, the Stock Exchange currently offers a quote-driven system which requires market-makers to publish prices at which they are prepared to buy and sell. SWX Europe Limited users can deal directly and anonymously with each other rather than being obliged to deal through market makers. The trades are settled through the London Clearing House in its capacity as the clearing house for SWX Europe Limited.

The purpose of the regulations is to prevent, in relation to a single purchase by an SWX Europe Limited client, multiple charges to stamp duty reserve tax or a stamp duty reserve tax liability in addition to a stamp duty liability which could otherwise arise under SWX Europe Limited clearing arrangements. The regulations therefore treat agreements to transfer UK equity securities as exempt from stamp duty reserve tax:

(a)
- (i) where the transfer is between clearing participants, The London Clearing House or their nominees (in each case acting in their capacity as clearing participant or operator); or
- (ii) from a non-clearing participant or a client to a clearing participant or its nominee; or
- (iii) where the transfer is from a non-clearing participant to The London Clearing House or its nominee as a result of a failure by a clearing participant to fulfil his obligations; and

(b) the transferee in each case is required on receipt of the equities to transfer matching equities to another person.

SI 1996/1584
STAMP DUTY AND STAMP DUTY RESERVE TAX (PENSION FUNDS POOLING SCHEMES) REGULATIONS 1996

1. These regulations made under FA 1946 s 57 (1A) and F(No 2)A (NI) 1946 s 28 came into force on 11 July 1996.

2, 3. Certain unauthorised unit trust schemes (pension funds pooling schemes (PFPVs)) are excepted from the definition of unit trust scheme given by FA 1946 s 57. A PFPV is a scheme participation in which is restricted to certain pension schemes or funds and which has the characteristics set out in the Income Tax (Pension Funds Pooling Schemes) Regulations SI 1996/1585. Units in pension fund pooling vehicles (PFPVs) are thus treated as not being stock for the purposes of stamp duty on transfers or as chargeable securities for the purposes of stamp duty reserve tax. So participants in the PFPV are able to transfer assets they own (other than land and buildings—caught by FA 1994 s 241) into the PFPV without incurring a charge to stamp duty or stamp duty reserve tax.

Participation in PFPVs is restricted to exempt approved pension schemes, UK-based superannuation funds used primarily by companies employing British expatriates working overseas, and pension funds schemes established outside the UK which are broadly equivalent to UK-based approved pension schemes.

The provisions supplement FA 1981 s 110.

SI 1996/2348
STAMP DUTY (PRODUCTION OF DOCUMENTS) (NORTHERN IRELAND) REGULATIONS 1996

These regulations, made under FA 1994 ss 244, 245, came into force on 4 November 1996. They:

(a) describe the particulars to be given before a particulars delivered stamp can be denoted on certain documents relating to land in Northern Ireland; and

(b) specify that certain documents, which are exempt from stamp duty by virtue of the value of the consideration not exceeding a certain threshold, need not be produced for denoting with a particulars delivered stamp; but also specify that, in relation to certain documents which are exempt from the particulars delivered stamp, certain specified particulars must be produced to the Register of Titles or Registrar of Deeds.

SI 1997/1156
THE STAMP DUTY AND STAMP DUTY RESERVE TAX (OPEN-ENDED INVESTMENT COMPANIES) REGULATIONS 1997

These Regulations provide a stamp duty and stamp duty reserve tax regime for open-ended investment companies similar to that applicable to authorised unit trusts. These Regulations have been substantially modified by the Stamp Duty and Stamp Duty Reserve Tax (Open-ended Investment Companies) (Amendment No 2) Regulations—SI 1999/3261. The amendments ensure that the enactments relating to stamp duty and stamp duty reserve tax continue to have effect to open-ended investment companies in the same way in which they effect unit trusts following the amendments made in FA 1999. In order to facilitate the electronic trading of shares, stamp duty will not be payable on the transfer of shares in open-ended investment companies however, stamp duty reserve tax of 0.5% is charged on certain dealings of shares as is the equivalent position with units in unit trust schemes.

Citation and commencement

1. These Regulations, which came into force on 28 April 1997, were made under FA 1995 s 152.

Interpretation

2. Various terms are defined.

In relation to the definition of "trust investment", "trust property", "unit", "unit holder" and "unit trust scheme" see FA 1999 Sch 19 paras 14–16. In relation to "authorised unit trust" see the Financial Services Act 1986 s 78.

The definitions for " authorised corporate director", "open-ended investment company", "owner of shares" and "scheme property" have the meanings given by sub-s (10) of s 486 ICTA 1988 to be read with sub-ss (11)–(18) of that section.

The "relevant enactments" relating to stamp duty or stamp duty reserve tax are ss 88(1), 90(1)–(1B), 99(5A) and (5B) FA 1986, and s 122(1) and (2) of paras 1–9, 14 and 17 of Sch 19 FA 1999.

Stamp duty and stamp duty reserve tax treatment of open-ended investment companies

3. This new regulation (inserted by SI 1999/3261) provides, subject to regs 4–4B, that the relevant enactments relating to stamp duty and stamp duty reserve tax apply to open-ended investment companies in the same way as they presently apply to unit trust schemes.

General modifications of the relevant enactments relating to stamp duty or stamp duty reserve tax

4–4B. These new Regulations (inserted by SI 1999/3261) modify the relevant enactments relating to stamp duty and stamp duty reserve tax to ensure that open-ended investment schemes receive similar treatment to that given to unit trust schemes following the FA 1999. From 6 February 2000, under FA 1999 Sch 19, stamp duty is no longer charged on transfers of units under a unit trust but a new charge of stamp duty reserve tax of 0.5% is levied on certain surrenders of units. Regulation 4A modifies Sch 19 so that it applies to the transfer and surrender of shares under open-ended investment companies.

Bearer securities issued by an open-ended investment company in a foreign currency

5. Foreign currency-denominated bearer securities issued by an open-ended investment company are treated as if the securities had been issued in sterling for stamp duty and stamp duty reserve tax purposes. The main effect of this is that what is now FA 1999 Sch 15 para 17 will not apply.

Shares in open-ended investment companies dealing in interest-bearing investments

6. [Revoked by SI 1999/3261 reg 7.]

Conversion of an authorised unit trust to an open-ended investment company—exemptions from stamp duty charge

7. The conversion of authorised unit trusts into open-ended investment companies is facilitated by exempting the transfer of the authorised unit trust's property to the open-ended investment company. Unlike the "amalgamation" relief (see paragraph 9 below), there is no time limit on this exception. A key feature, which distinguishes a conversion from an amalgamation, is that the open-ended investment company must have no other assets before the whole of the available property of the target trust is transferred to it. For a commentary on the other provisions of this regulation see the commentary on FA 1997 s 95.

Conversion of an authorised unit trust to an open-ended investment company—exemption from stamp duty reserve tax charge

8. The conversion of an authorised unit trust to an open-ended investment company is exempted from the FA 1986 s 87 stamp duty reserve tax charge. The conditions for the exemption are substantially identical to the conditions for the stamp duty exemption under reg 7. There is also an exemption from the FA 1986 s 87 stamp duty reserve tax charge on agreements to transfer units to the managers of the target trust made in order that the unit may be extinguished for the purposes of the conversion.

Amalgamation of an authorised unit trust with an open-ended investment company—exemption from stamp duty charge

9. A two-year amnesty from stamp duty is provided for instruments that transfer an authorised unit trust's property to an existing open-ended investment company which already owns property. The conditions for the relief are substantially identical to the conditions which apply to mergers of authorised unit trusts (see FA 1997 s 95).

The stamp duty exemption provided under this paragraph was originally scheduled to expire on 30 June 1999 but the Revenue issued a press release on 26 May 1999 in which they stated that the operation of this exemption was to be extended. The intention is now to retain this exemption until further regulations have been drafted and implemented, permitting the formation of a wider range of OEICs. Once such regulations have come into force, the exemption will then continue in force for one year after that time. It should be noted, however, that the Revenue specifically state in their press release that the Government "sees no case" for making this exemption permanent.

Amalgamation of an authorised unit trust with an open-ended investment company—exemption from stamp duty reserve tax charge

10. A two-year amnesty from the FA 1986 s 87 stamp duty reserve tax charge is provided for agreements to transfer an authorised unit trust's securities to an open-ended investment company. The conditions are substantially identical to the conditions for stamp duty relief contained in reg 9 and this exemption has been similarly extended beyond the originally intended deadline of 30 June 1999. A similar exemption to the reg 8 (3) exemption applies to agreements to transfer units to the managers of the target trust made in order that the unit may be extinguished for the purposes of the conversion.

Disapplication of section 42 of the Finance Act 1930

11. Relief from stamp duty under the "associated company" provision is not available on transfers of property to or from an open-ended investment company.

Disapplication of sections 75 to 77 of the Finance Act 1996

12. Stamp duty relief under FA 1986 ss 75 to 77 does not apply to reconstructions of open-ended investment companies or their amalgamation with other open-ended investment companies or ordinary companies.

SI 1997/2429
STAMP DUTY AND STAMP DUTY RESERVE TAX (INVESTMENT EXCHANGES AND CLEARING HOUSES) REGULATIONS 1997

These regulations came into force on 20 October 1997 and have the same purpose and apply in the same way as SI 1999/3562 save that they apply to LIFFE (A&M) (London International Financial Futures and Options Exchange Administration and Management) and London Clearing House Limited.

SI 1998/3132
THE CIVIL PROCEDURE RULES 1998

See *Chiltern's Yellow Tax Guide*.

SI 1998/3177
EUROPEAN SINGLE CURRENCY (TAXES) REGULATIONS 1998

These regulations prevent stamp duty or stamp duty reserve tax charges arising under FA 1986 s 80 C (repurchases and stock lending) or FA 1986 s 89 AA (section 87: exception for repurchases and stock lending) by virtue of:

— the stock/chargeable securities not being regarded as of the same kind and amount after a euroconversion;

— the interim owner keeping a capital payment of 500 euros or less arising on a euroconversion; or

— euroconversion leading to a renominalisation resulting in a new minimum denomination in which stock/chargeable securities can be held or traded and the interim holder is required to pay the original owner an amount which does not exceed 500 euros.

SI 1999/2383
STAMP DUTY RESERVE TAX (UK DEPOSITARY INTERESTS IN FOREIGN SECURITIES) REGULATIONS 1999

These Regulations (as amended by SI 2001/3779) exempt UK depositary interests in foreign securities from stamp duty reserve tax. To qualify for the exemption the foreign securities underlying the depositary interest must, (i) be shares in a foreign company; (ii) not be held on a UK register; (iii) not be units or shares in a collective investment scheme; and (iv) must be of the same class of shares listed on a stock exchange outside the UK or are of a type that would have been treated as so listed immediately before 28 November 2001 and recognised under TA 1988 s 841. From 7 August 2000 the conditions were relaxed so as to include foreign securities listed on any recognised stock exchange defined under TA 1988 s 841 (refer SI 2000/1871). Under these Regulations operators of electronic trading systems, who are approved under the Uncertified Securities Regulations 1995, are able to provide a settlement service for transactions in foreign shares without purchasers being liable to Stamp Duty Reserve Tax.

Citation and commencement

1. These Regulations (made under FA 1986 s 98 and FA s 119 and 121) came into force on 25 August 1999.

Interpretation

2. Various terms are defined.

"the Board" means the Commissioners of Inland Revenue;

"depositary interest" means a security which—

(a) consists of the rights of a person in or relating to securities of a particular kind which, or entitlements to which, are held on trust for the benefit of that person by another person, and

(b) under the terms of its issue, can only be transferred in accordance with regulations under s 207 of the Companies Act 1989 (transfer of securities without written instrument) or by means of a transfer within s 186(1) of the Finance Act 1996 (transfer of securities to member of electronic transfer system);

"foreign securities" means securities falling within the definition of "securities" in regulation 3(1) of the Uncertificated Securities Regulations 1995 which—

(a) are issued or raised by a body corporate that is not incorporated, and whose central management and control is not exercised in the United Kingdom;
(b) are not registered in a register kept in the United Kingdom by or on behalf of the body corporate by which they are issued or raised;
(c) are not units or shares in, or do not otherwise represent rights relating to, a collective investment scheme; and
(d) are of the same class in the body corporate as securities which—
    (i) are listed on a recognised stock exchange; or
    (ii) are of a type which could have been treated as so listed immediately before 28 November 2001;

"the Management Act" means the Taxes Management Act 1970;

"operator" has the meaning given by regulation 2 of the principal Regulations;

"recognised stock exchange" has the same meaning given by s 841 of the Income and Corporation Taxes Act 1988;

"the principal Regulations" means the Stamp Duty Reserve Tax Regulations 1986;

"relevant day" has the meaning given by s 87(3) of the Finance Act 1986;

"the Schedule" means the Schedule to the principal Regulations;

"UK depositary interest" means a depositary interest which is issued in the United Kingdom or registered on a register kept in the United Kingdom.

Exclusion of a UK depositary interest in foreign securities from the definition of "chargeable securities" securities in Part IV of the Finance Act 1986

3. This paragraph excludes UK depositary interest in foreign securities from the definition of "chargeable securities" in FA 1986 Part IV for the purposes of Stamp Duty Reserve Tax.

Notice relating to UK depositary interest in foreign securities

4. Under reg 4, when a depositary interest in a foreign security is first issued, the operator of the electronic trading system must notify HMRC of the issue date and the depositary interest issued. This notice must be given on or before the fourteenth day following the date of the issue of the depositary interest. HMRC may prescribe the form the notice must take.

Amendments to Part I of the Schedule

5. This Regulation amends the Table in Pt I of the Schedule to the Stamp Duty Reserve Tax Regulations (SI 1986/1711) by adding the words "the Stamp Duty Reserve Tax (UK Depositary Interests in Foreign Securities) Regulations 1999" to the entry relating to TMA 1970 s 98. This addition reflects the obligations on operators of electronic trading systems under Reg 4 of these Regulations.

Amendments to Part II of the Schedule

6. Regulation 6 amends Pt II of the Schedule to SI 1986/1711 by adding the words "the Stamp Duty Reserve Tax (UK Depositary Interests in Foreign Securities) Regulations 1999" to the entry relating to TMA 1970 s 98.

SI 1999/2537
STAMP DUTY (COLLECTION AND RECOVERY OF PENALTIES) REGULATIONS 1999

These Regulations (made under FA 1999 Sch 17 paras 16 and 17) came into force on 1 October 1999. The Regulations provide for the collection and recovery of administrative penalties relating to stamp duty to which FA 1999 Sch 17 Pt II applies other than the penalty on late stamping under the Stamp Act 1891 s 15B. The levels of penalties charged have been brought into line with those with taxes in general. For example, not allowing the HMRC to inspect company records will incur a penalty of up to £300 with the maximum penalty for fraud being increased to £300.

Part I Sch 1 specifies the provisions of the TMA 1970 which are to apply and details the modifications. Part II of Sch 1 sets out the modified provisions.

SI 1999/3262
STAMP DUTY AND STAMP DUTY RESERVE TAX (INVESTMENT EXCHANGES AND CLEARING HOUSES) (OM LONDON EXCHANGE LIMITED) REGULATIONS 1999

These Regulations prevent multiple charges to stamp duty and stamp duty reserve tax when equity securities are transferred by way of the exercise of an option, or under futures contracts. The Regulations apply when OM London Exchange Limited or its clearing members are acting in a clearing capacity.

Citation and commencement

1. These Regulations were made under FA 1991 s 116 and 117 and came into force on 29 December 1999.

Interpretation

2. Various terms are defined.

"clearing member" means a member who is permitted by the rules of OM London Exchange Limited to clear transactions made on that exchange for an equity security;

"equity securities" means stocks and shares which are issued or raised by a company but does not include stocks and shares issued by a company not incorporated in the United Kingdom unless—

- (a) they are registered in a register kept in the United Kingdom by or on behalf of the company, or
- (b) in the case of shares, they are paired, within the meaning of FA 1986 s 99(6A), with shares issued by a company incorporated in the United Kingdom;

"member" means a member of OM London Exchange Limited who is recognised as such by the rules of that exchange;

"non-clearing member" means a member other than a clearing member;

"option" means an option to buy or sell securities which is listed by and traded on OM London Exchange Limited;

"futures contract" means a futures, or a forward, contract conferring rights and obligations to buy or sell securities which is listed by and traded on OM London Exchange Limited.

Prescription of recognised exchange

3. For the purposes of FA 1991 ss 116 and 117, the OM London Exchange Limited is a recognised investment exchange.

Transfers and issues of securities to OM London Exchange Limited—prescribed circumstances

4. Equity security transfers (or agreements to transfer) resulting from the exercise of an option or under a futures contract, to OM London Exchange Limited (or its nominee) in its clearing capacity, are exempt from stamp duty and stamp duty reserve tax.

Transfers of securities to or from members of OM London Exchange Limited—prescribed circumstances

5. This Regulation exempts from stamp duty or stamp duty reserve tax equity security transfers exercised under options or futures contracts in two cases. The first case is between a non-clearing member of OM London Exchange Limited (or its nominee) and an authorised clearing member. The second case is from OM London Exchange Limited, in its clearing capacity, to a clearing member.

SI 1999/3263
DISTRAINT BY COLLECTORS (FEES, COSTS AND CHARGES) (STAMP DUTY PENALTIES) REGULATIONS 1999

These Regulations made under TMA 1970 s 61(6) came into force on 29 December 1999. The Regulations apply to stamp duty penalties by virtue of the Stamp Duty (Collection and Recovery of Penalties) Regulations (SI 1999/2537). The Schedule to the Regulations lists the costs, fees and charges that are levied for non-payment of stamp duty penalties when the Collector of Taxes has to take distraint action. Under reg 5, the District Judge of the county court can tax fees, charges and costs that are disputed.

SI 2000/1871
STAMP DUTY RESERVE TAX (UK DEPOSITARY INTERESTS IN FOREIGN SECURITIES) (AMENDMENT) REGULATIONS 2000

These Regulations amend the definitions of "foreign securities" and "recognised stock exchange" in Stamp Duty Reserve Tax (UK Depositary Interests in Foreign Securities) Regulations, SI 1999/2383.

SI 2000/2549
STAMP DUTY AND STAMP DUTY RESERVE TAX (DEFINITIONS OF UNIT TRUST SCHEME) (AMENDMENT) REGULATIONS 2000

These Regulations amend the Stamp Duty and Stamp Duty Reserve Tax (Definitions of Unit Trust Scheme) (Amendment) Regulations, SI 1988/268. They add a third example of a unit trust that is not treated as such for the purposes of FA 1946 Part VII, or F (No 2) A (Northern Ireland) 1946 Part III. The amendment came into force on 11 October 2000.

SI 2000/2995
STAMP DUTY AND STAMP DUTY RESERVE TAX (INVESTMENT EXCHANGES AND CLEARING HOUSES) (JIWAY LIMITED) REGULATIONS 2000

The Regulations exempt transfers of equity securities, or agreements to transfer equity securities, to Jiway Limited (or its nominee). This applies when Jiway Limited (or its nominee) acts in its capacity as a person providing clearing services in connection with transactions made on the exchange on which it operates.

Citation and commencement

1. These Regulations (made under FA 1991 ss 116, 117) came into force on 10 November 2000.

Interpretation

2. In these Regulations "equity securities" has the same meaning as in the Stamp Duty and Stamp Duty Reserve Tax (Investment Exchanges and Clearing Houses) (OM Exchange Limited) Regulations 1999.

Prescription of recognised investment exchange

3. For the purposes of FA 1991 ss 116 and 117, Jiway Limited is a recognised investment exchange.

Transfers of securities to Jiway Limited—prescribed circumstances

This regulation exempts from stamp duty and stamp duty reserve tax a transaction or transactions made or to be made on the exchange operated by Jiway Limited, under which equity securities are transferred or agreed to be transferred—

(a) to Jiway Limited; or

(b) to a person whose business is or includes holding equity securities as a nominee of Jiway Limited.

SI 2001/255
STAMP DUTY RESERVE TAX (INVESTMENT EXCHANGES AND CLEARING HOUSES) (THE LONDON STOCK EXCHANGE) REGULATIONS 2001

These Regulations (made under FA 1991 ss 116 (3) and (4), and 117) came into force on 26 February 2001. The Regulations exempt certain transfers of equity securities, or agreements to transfer equity securities, to The London Clearing House Limited (or its nominee) or clearing participants (or their nominees) members of The London Clearing House Limited where the transferee is required to transfer equity securities under a matching agreement, from Stamp Duty. Otherwise the regulations are similar to the Stamp Duty and Stamp Duty Reserve Tax (Investment Exchanges and Clearing Houses) (Jiway Limited) Regulations 2000.

SI 2001/964
STAMP DUTY AND STAMP DUTY RESERVE TAX (DEFINITION OF UNIT TRUST SCHEME AND OPEN-ENDED INVESTMENT COMPANY) REGULATIONS 2001

These Regulations (made under FA 1986 s 98, FA 1995 s 152 and FA 1999 s 121, Sch 19 para 17) came into force on 6 April 2001. The Regulations exempt transactions in units of unit trusts, and shares in open-ended investment companies from Stamp Duty and Stamp Duty Reserve Tax, provided that they are holdings within individual pension accounts. These Regulations also amend the Stamp Duty Reserve Tax Regulations 1986, SI 1986/1711, and Stamp Duty and Stamp Duty Reserve Tax (Open-ended Investment Companies) Regulations 1997, SI 1997/1156.

Citation and commencement

1. These Regulations came into force on 6 April 2001.

Interpretation

2. Regulation 2 defines an "individual pension account" (IPA) for the purposes of reg 3. In essence an IPA is an account which satisfies eight conditions. Most importantly, the funds in the account must have been received from and held by the trustees or managers of registered pension funds to be used to provide benefits for individual account holders under such schemes; and the assets in the account must consist only of cash or specified forms of approved investments.

Schemes to be treated as not being unit trust schemes

3. A unit trust scheme the units under which are required by the terms of the trust instrument to be held only within individual pension accounts is treated as not being a unit trust scheme for the purposes of the enactments relating to stamp duty and the enactments relating to stamp duty reserve tax. The effect of this is to remove the charge to SDRT on surrenders of units.

Companies to be treated as not being open-ended investment companies

4. An open-ended investment company the shares in which are required by the terms of the instrument incorporating the company to be held only within individual pension accounts is treated as not being an open-ended investment company for the purposes of the enactments relating to stamp duty and the enactments relating to stamp duty reserve tax. The effect of this is to remove the charge to SDRT on surrenders of shares.

SI 2001/2267
STAMP DUTY RESERVE TAX (TRADEPOINT) (AMENDMENT) REGULATIONS 2001

These Regulations (made under FA 1991 ss 116 (3) and (4) and 117) came into force on 25 June 2001. These Regulations amend the Stamp Duty Reserve Tax (Tradepoint) Regulations, SI 1995/2051. See commentary on SI 1995/2051.

SI 2001/3746
VARIATION OF STAMP DUTIES REGULATIONS 2001

These Regulations (made under FA 2000 Sch 33 para 1) came into force on 28 November 2001. The Regulations provide that certain stamp duty reliefs for land in disadvantaged areas, contained in FA 2001 Sch 30 para 1 and s 92(1), shall not apply to certain instruments and otherwise restrict these reliefs. See commentary on FA 2000 Sch 30 para 1 and s 92(1).

(Note: revoked by Stamp Duty (Disadvantaged Areas) (Application of Exemptions) Regulations 2003, SI 2003/1056.)

SI 2001/3747
STAMP DUTY (DISADVANTAGED AREAS) REGULATIONS 2001

These Regulations (made under FA 2001 ss 92(4) and (9)) came into force on 30 November 2001. These Regulations designate the areas specified in Schs 1–4 as disadvantaged areas for the purposes of FA 2001 Sch 30 and s 92.

SI 2001/3779
STAMP DUTY RESERVE TAX (UK DEPOSITARY INTERESTS IN FOREIGN SECURITIES) (AMENDMENT) REGULATIONS 2001

These Regulations (made under FA 1999 s 119) came into force on 19 December 2001. The Regulations amend the Stamp Duty Reserve Tax (UK Depositary Interests in Foreign Securities) Regulations, SI 1999/2383.

SI 2002/1975
STAMP DUTY AND STAMP DUTY RESERVE TAX (EXTENSION OF EXCEPTIONS RELATING TO RECOGNISED EXCHANGES) REGULATIONS 2002

These Regulations (made under FA 2002 s 117) came into force on 26 July 2002. The Regulations extend the application of the provisions specified in FA 2002 s 117(2) to the market known as OFEX.

SI 2003/1056
STAMP DUTY (DISADVANTAGED AREAS) (APPLICATION OF EXEMPTIONS) REGULATIONS 2003

Citation and commencement

1. These regulations came into force on 10 April 2003.

Interpretation

2. Various terms are defined:

"conveyance of sale" has the same meaning as in FA 1999 Sch 13 Pt 1;

"instrument" and "conveyance" have the meanings given by SA 1891 s 122(1);

"lease of land" has the same meanings as in FA 1999 Sch 13 Pt 2;

"the rate or average rate of rent" means the rate of rent by reference to which stamp duty is determined under FA 1999 Sch 13 Pt 12(3).

"relevant consideration" means (*a*) in the case of a conveyance or transfer on sale, the consideration for the sale; and (*b*) in the case of a lease of land, the consideration in respect of which, under FA 1999 Sch 13 para 12(2) the stamp duty is the same as that on a conveyance on a sale for the same consideration;

"residential property" has the same meaning given by FA 2001 s 92B read together with regulation 7.

Disapplication of exemptions conferred by s 92 or by Sch 30 where all of land is non-residential property

2A. In accordance with the removal by FA 2005 Sch 9 of the SDLT exemption for non-residential property, reg 2A removes the exemptions conferred by FA 2001 s 92 or by Sch 30 where none of the land in question is residential property.

Application of exemptions conferred by s 92 or by Sch 30 where all the land is residential property

3. This regulation specifies cases in which the exemptions are not to apply, including where all the land is residential property and the amount or value of certain consideration is more than £150,000. This restriction of the exemption applies only in relation to the stamp duty chargeable in respect of that consideration.

Leases of Land—further provision as to the application of exemptions conferred by s 92 or by Sch 30

4. Where the instrument in question is a lease of land, the exemptions are not to apply where the rate or average rate of rent is more than £15,000. The restriction of the exemptions applies only in relation to the stamp duty chargeable in respect of the rate or average rate.

Application of exemptions conferred by s 92 or by Sch 30 where land only partly residential property

5. This regulation provides for how the exemptions are to apply where the land in question is only partly residential. Of particular note is the rule that the exemption conferred by s 92 or by Sch 30 does not apply in relation to any duty chargeable in respect of relevant consideration (or the rate or average rate of rent) attributed to the land in question to the extent that it is not residential property.

Determination of consideration for the purposes of regulations 3, 4 and 5—land situated partly in a disadvantaged area and partly outside such an area

6. This regulation provides for how the amount of any consideration is to be determined for the purposes of regs 3, 4 and 5, in particular where land is situated partly in a disadvantaged area and partly outside.

Land comprising or including six or more separate dwellings

7. This regulation confirms that where there is a single contract for the conveyance, transfer or lease of land comprising or including six or more separate dwellings, none of that counts as residential property.

Revocation of the Variation of Stamp Duties Regulations 2001

8. This regulation revokes the Variation of Stamp Duties Regulations 2001, SI 2001/3746.

SI 2003/2837
STAMP DUTY LAND TAX (ADMINISTRATION) REGULATIONS 2003

PART 1 GENERAL

Citation and commencement

1. These regulations came into force on 1 December 2003.

Interpretation

2. Various terms are defined. “Land transaction return” has the meaning given to it in FA 2003 s 76.

PART 2 REVENUE CERTIFICATES AND SELF-CERTIFICATES

Interpretation of Part 2

3. Various terms are given the meaning they bear in FA 2003:

“Revenue certificate” has the meaning given by s 79(3)(*a*);

“Purchaser” the meaning given by s 43(4);

“self-certificate” the meaning given by s 79(3)(*b*);

“Vendor” the meaning given by s 43(4).

Conditions to be met before a Revenue certificate is issued

4. This establishes the conditions which must be met before a Revenue certificate is issued: first, the relevant land transaction return must have been received by HMRC; second, all required returns must have been completed (and must include the purchaser’s declaration that the return is to the best of his knowledge complete and correct; third, the requisite self-assessment must be included with the return and must appear to be correct in the light of the information contained in the return; and last, the return must be accompanied by payment of the tax chargeable.

Form and content of Revenue certificates

5. This regulation sets out the information which HMRC must include in each Revenue certificate.

Duplicate Revenue certificates

6. A duplicate Revenue certificate may be issued if HMRC is satisfied that the original has been lost or destroyed.

Multiple Revenue certificates

7. Even where a land transaction return relates to more than one transaction, the general rule is that HMRC are to issue a single Revenue certificate in respect of the transactions to which the return relates. However, if the purchaser requests *on the return* that separate Revenue certificates be issued, in respect of each transaction, then HMRC *may* provide separate certificates in respect of any of the transactions.

Form and content of self-certificate

8. A self-certificate must be made in writing either on the form prescribed in Sch 1 to these regulations or in a form approved by the Board of Inland Revenue, and in either case must contain all the information required by the Sch 1 form.

PART 3 LAND TRANSACTION RETURNS

Form and content of land transaction return

9. A land transaction return must be made in writing and completed in black ink. It must either be made on the form prescribed by Sch 2 Pt 1 to these regulations (accompanied by such other forms prescribed by Sch 2 Pts 2–4 as may be relevant) or in such other form as may have been approved by the Board of Inland Revenue. In either case, it must contain all the information required by the various forms prescribed by Sch 2.

PART 4 DEFERRED PAYMENTS

Interpretation of Part 4

10. Certain terms are defined:

"Application" means an application under FA 2003 s 90 (ie one to defer payment in the case of contingent or uncertain consideration);

"Relevant events" means the events on the occurrence of which the whole or any part of the consideration will cease to be contingent or uncertain.

When application to be made

11. The application must be made on or before the last day of the period within which the relevant land transaction return must be delivered.

Form and content of application

12. The application must be in writing and must set out all relevant facts and circumstances, including the consideration to which it relates, the respects in which that consideration is contingent or uncertain and the relevant events.

Additional content of application where consideration consists of works or services

13. Where any element of the consideration to which an application relates consists of the carrying out of works of construction, improvement or repair of a building, or other works to enhance the value of land (ie falling within FA 2003 Sch 4 para 10(1)) or the provision of services (ie falling within FA 2003 Sch 4 para 11), the application must contain a scheme for the payment of the tax. This must include a proposal for the payment of the relevant element of the tax within 30 days of the substantial completion of the works or of the provision of the services; and in cases where the works or services will be carried out or provided over a period in excess of six months, must include a proposal for a scheme of payment of tax at intervals of not more than six months.

Provision of information

14. HMRC may by written notice require an applicant to provide such further information as they may reasonably require in order to decide whether to accept the application. The notice is to specify a period (of not less than 30 days) within which compliance is required.

Recovery of tax not postponed by application

15. Where HMRC has yet to accept an application (or when there is an extant appeal against HMRC's refusal of an application) then the tax which is the subject of the application remains due and payable but payment is postponed pending the outcome of HMRC's decision. If the application is refused, then further postponement is available only in accordance with regs 22 and 23. If the application is refused and the applicant fails to appeal, then, for the purpose of determining when the tax postponed is due and payable, that tax is treated as if it were charged by an assessment made by HMRC on the date when the notice of the tax payable was issued.

Notice of decision on an application

16. HMRC are obliged to provide all applicants with written notice of their decision. This regulation specifies what information HMRC must provide in each case.

Grounds on which application may be refused

17. HMRC may refuse an application to postpone for any of the following reasons:

(a) the conditions in FA 2003 s 90 are not satisfied, ie that, at the effective date of the transaction the amount or value of the chargeable consideration is contingent or uncertain, and that the consideration falls to be paid or provided on one or more future dates of which at least one falls, or may fall, more than six months after the effective date of the transaction;

(b) that the application does not comply with the requirements in reg 12 (form and content) or 14 (provision of information) above;

(c) that there are tax avoidance arrangements (defined by reg 18) in relation to the relevant transaction;

(d) that either the application or the information it contains is incorrect; and

(e) that the applicant has failed to provide HMRC with the information requested under reg 14 within the specified period.

Tax avoidance arrangements

18. Tax avoidance arrangements are defined as arrangements whose main object, or one of whose main objects, is either to enable payment of the tax payable to be deferred, or to avoid the determination of the amount or value of the consideration for the purposes of SDLT. "Arrangements" are widely defined as any scheme, agreement or understanding, whether or not legally enforceable.

Right of appeal

19. An appeal lies either to the General or Special Commissioners against the HMRC's refusal of an application.

Notice of appeal

20. Notice of appeal must be given in writing to the officer who gave the notice within 30 days of the issue of the notice of refusal, specifying the grounds of appeal. Liberty is given to the Commissioners hearing the appeal to permit the appellant to advance further grounds of appeal provided they are satisfied that their omission was neither deliberate nor unreasonable.

Settling the appeal by agreement

21. The parties to the appeal may by agreement settle it in advance of the hearing, whether by upholding, or varying, or discharging, or cancelling it, with the same consequences as would have followed had the appeal Commissioners themselves determined the appeal in that way at that time. However, the appellant may resile from the agreement by serving notice in writing that he wishes to do so on HMRC within 30 days. If the parties initially orally agree to settle the appeal, the agreement does not have effect unless within 30 days one side gives the other written confirmation of the agreement and its terms, whereupon the agreement takes effect from the date of the notice. A slightly different approach is adopted where the appellant unilaterally notifies HMRC (whether or not in writing) that he does not wish to proceed with his appeal. In this case, unless the Inland Revenue serves written notice on the appellant within 30 days that they are unwilling for the appeal to be withdrawn, the provisions of reg 21 operate as if the parties had come to an agreement at the time of the appellant's notification to HMRC. The regulation enables an agent to act on behalf of the appellant for the purposes of this provision.

Direction by the Commissioners postponing payment

22. An appellant may, by notice in writing given within 30 days of the issue of the notice of refusal, apply to the General or Special Commissioners for a direction that payment of the tax be postponed pending the determination of the appeal. If, after this application has been determined, there is a change in circumstances, as a result of which either party has grounds for believing that the amount determined has become excessive or insufficient, he may apply to the Commissioners for a further determination of the matter. Any such application is heard and determined in the same way as if it were an appeal; and on hearing the application the Commissioners are to postpone such amount of the tax as appears to them to be appropriate. Any tax which is not postponed is treated as if it were charged by an assessment made by HMRC on the date when the application was determined, for the purpose of determining when the tax postponed is due and payable. Further provision is made for the outcome of the appeal.

Agreement to postpone payment

23. It is open to the appellant and the officer who initially refused the application to postpone subsequently to agree that payment of all or part of the tax should be postponed, in which case the same consequences follow as if the General or Special Commissioners had directed the postponement at the date when agreement was reached. Any agreement which is not in writing must be confirmed in writing by one party to the other, in which case the agreement is treated as made for the purposes of reg 23(1) at the date of the written notice. An agent may act on behalf of the taxpayer in making such an agreement.

Payment and returns

24. This provision regulates the operation of the tax following a successful application.

Where HMRC accepts an application to postpone payment, they must repay any tax previously paid (plus interest).

Once a relevant event occurs, the purchaser must within 30 days make a further return to HMRC; and in cases where the tax has been postponed pending the substantial completion of construction works or the provision of services, the purchaser must make a further return within 30 days of that date, or, if the scheme for payment so requires, at the regular intervals required by the scheme, in each case accompanied by the tax due.

If it proves that tax has been overpaid, the purchaser is entitled to make a claim for repayment (plus interest).

Form and content of returns

25. The return required under reg 24 must be in writing and include a self-assessment and a statement of the tax payable, calculated in accordance with the rates in force at the time of the land transaction.

Adjustment of payments made under section 90(5)

26. Regulations under this SI apply in substitution for FA 2003 s 80 (adjustment where contingency ceases or consideration is ascertained) if there is both a payment of tax in respect of ascertainable consideration and a successful application for postponement of tax in relation to other chargeable consideration.

Returns and payments where consideration consists of works or services

27. This regulation applies to cases where there is to be a series of returns on the basis that the works will last for more than six months and eventually less than six months remain before the works will be complete. In place of the next regular return, agreed as part of the scheme agreed between the parties, the parties may agree that the next return should be made 30 days after the works are substantially completed. However, if the works continue for another six months after the return would have been required under the original scheme, the variation falls and the obligation revives to file returns in accordance with the original scheme.

Applications accepted by the Inland Revenue having no effect

28. If HMRC accepts an application to postpone but it contains false or misleading information, or relevant facts or circumstances are not disclosed, the application is of no effect. Similarly, an application ceases to have any effect if relevant facts and circumstances change materially.

PART 5 DISTRAINT BY COLLECTORS: FEES, COSTS AND CHARGES

Interpretation of Part 5

29. This regulation defines certain terms:

"close possession" means physical possession of distrained goods and chattels by a distrainor or a person acting on his behalf;

"walking possession" means possession in accordance with an agreement between a distrainor and a distrainee, by which, in consideration of the distrainor not remaining in close possession, the distrainee undertakes neither to dispose of any of the distrained items nor to permit their removal from the premises by any unauthorised person.

Ascertainment of fees, costs and charges

30. This regulation introduces Sch 3 to the regulations, which contains certain tables of the fees chargeable and costs and charges recoverable in connection with the levying of distress.

Deduction of fees, costs and charges by the collector

31. Fees, costs and charges recoverable under Sch 3 are to be deducted from the sums received from the execution of distress.

Disputes as to fees, costs and charges

32. This regulation provides that disputes as to the amount of fees, costs and charges shall be resolved by assessment by the district judge of the county court for the district in which distress is levied.

PART 6

Interpretation of Part 6

33. This regulation provides for the definition of certain terms by reference to FA 2003 Sch 13. Thus:

"the appropriate judicial authority" means, in England and Wales, a circuit judge, in Scotland, a sheriff and in Northern Ireland, a county court judge;

"the court" means the court of the appropriate judicial authority;

"items subject to legal privilege" has the usual meaning given to it in the English law of evidence: it includes legal advice privilege and litigation privilege and items enclosed with or referred to in communications themselves covered by either aspect of privilege, other than items held with the intention of furthering a criminal purpose;

"notice of application" means a notice, served on the person against whom the order is sought in accordance with FA 2003 Sch 13 para 33, of intention to apply for an order for the delivery of documents under para 32 sought where there is reasonable ground for suspecting that an offence involving serious fraud in connection with, or in relation to, stamp duty land tax has been or is about to be committed;

"order" means such an order under para 32 itself; and

"working day" means any day of the week other than Saturday, Sunday or a public holiday.

Approval of decision to apply for an order

34. Before the hearing of an application for an order, a senior civil servant (as defined) must give written approval of the decision to seek the order.

Notice of application

35. This regulation specifies the information which the notice of application must contain and directs that the notice must be given to the person entitled to it not less than five working days before the hearing.

Notice of an order, or notice of an application, treated as having been given

36. The regulation establishes that the date of service of the relevant notice is the day of its delivery to the person, or on which it is left at his proper address, unless that was not a working day, in which case it is deemed to be served on the next working day. Provision is made for service by fax or similar means. The regulation also defines the "proper address".

Complying with an order

37. This regulation explains how a person complies with an order. He may do so either by delivering the documents to the officer or by leaving them at an address specified in the order. Provision is also made for deeming service to have been effected two working days after the documents are posted by first class post and four working days after posting using second class post.

Resolution of disputes as to legal privilege

38. If the Board of Inland Revenue and the person against whom an order has been made are in dispute as to whether a document obtains legal privilege, the person may apply to the appropriate judicial authority to resolve the dispute. The regulation provides the necessary procedural rules and in particular (*a*) makes provision for the Board to meet the costs of the application in all cases save those where no document (or part of document) in dispute is found to be subject to legal privilege; and (*b*) secures that a person who has made an application to the appropriate judicial authority is not in contempt of the order made against him until his application has been determined. Provision is also made for the parties themselves to reach agreement resolving the dispute after an application has been made.

SI 2004/1864
THE TAX AVOIDANCE SCHEMES (INFORMATION) REGULATIONS 2004

Citation, commencement and effect

1. These Regulations came into force generally on 1 August 2004 but were not applicable to SDLT schemes until 1 August 2005 (see The Tax Avoidance Schemes (Information) (Amendment) Regulations 2005, SI 2005/1869.

Interpretation

2. Various terms are defined.

Prescribed information in respect of notifiable proposals and arrangements

3. The information to be provided by a promoter to HMRC is sufficient information as might reasonably be expected to enable an officer of the Board to comprehend the manner in which the proposal is intending to operate. It includes the promoter's name and address, details of the provision of the arrangements regulations (in the case of SDLT, the Stamp Duty Land Tax Avoidance Schemes (Prescribed Descriptions of Arrangements) Regulations 2005, SI 2005/1868), a summary of the proposal and the name of the scheme if any, information explaining each element of the proposed arrangements and the way in which they are structured from which the tax advantage expected to be obtained arises and the statutory provisions on which it is based. Broadly similar information is required to be submitted by a client using a scheme provided by a promoter outside the UK or where a promoter is not involved.

Time for providing information under section 308, 209 or 310

4. A promoter must provide HMRC with the proscribed information within five days, beginning with the day on which the promoter makes a notifiable proposal available for implementation or becomes aware of any transaction, forming part of any notifiable arrangements implementing the notifiable proposal. The client using a scheme promoted by a non-UK promoter similarly has five days from entering into the first transaction forming part of notifiable arrangements within which to notify HMRC of the scheme. In the case of an in-house SDLT scheme not involving a promoter, the taxpayer must notify HMRC within 30 days of his entering into the first transaction forming part of the notifiable arrangements. Non-business days are ignored.

Statutory clearances

5. Where the promoter expects to apply for a clearance under TA 1988 s 215, 225 or 707 or TCGA 1992 s 138, 139 or 140, the final date for notification is the date on which the first transaction occurs in pursuance of the arrangement or the promoter ceases to intend to make a clearance application.

Prescribed information under sections 312 and 312A

7. The promoter has to provide the client with the appropriate reference number as well as his name and address and the name or a brief description of the relevant scheme. His client, when obliged to do so in the circumstances specified by FA 2004 s 312A must pass this information on to others, as well as notifying the relevant parties of the date the SRN was sent to him by the promoter.

Time limit for providing information under section 312A

7A. The client is given 30 days in which to comply with his obligations under s 312A, the period running either from the date when he first became aware of a transaction forming part of the notifiable arrangements or, if later, the date when he received the information required under reg 7.

Prescribed information under section 313: timing and manner of delivery

8. Until 1 April 2010 there was no obligation on a party to a notifiable SDLT scheme to provide the Commissioners with the information that he had engaged in a notifiable transaction. Instead, the only obligation was that of the scheme promoter to notify the Commissioners that he had made a scheme available and to provide them with a description of the scheme. In future, though, a corresponding obligation is imposed on a party to a notifiable SDLT scheme to inform HMRC of the following (inter alia):

(a) of the scheme reference number;
(b) the name and address of the purchaser;
(c) the location and title number of the property;
(d) the UTRN of the land transaction;
(e) the market value of the property; and
(f) the effective date of the first land transaction involved in the scheme.

This information has to be provided no later than 30 days after the effective date of the first land transaction involved in the scheme (or, if later, 30 days after the receipt of the SRN).

Exemption from liability for penalty

9. The list of exemptions from penalties for failure to notify a reference number includes that for fraudulently or negligently making an incorrect return in TMA 1970 s 98A(4).

Electronic delivery of information

10. Electronic filing is permitted for notification in a return delivered electronically.

SI 2004/3218
STAMP DUTY AND STAMP DUTY RESERVE TAX (INVESTMENT EXCHANGES AND CLEARING HOUSES) REGULATIONS 2004

These regulations exempt from stamp duty and SDRT certain transfers or issues of equities, or agreements to transfer or issue such equities to LCH.Clearnet Ltd (a recognised clearing house under FSMA 2000). The regulations also exempt from stamp duty and SDRT certain transfers and agreements to transfer equity securities to or from members of EDX London (a recognised investment exchange under FSMA 2000).

Citation and commencement

1. These regulations (made under FA 1991 ss 116, 117) came into force on 1 February 2005.

Prescription of recognised investment exchange

3. Regulation 3 establishes EDX London as a prescribed recognised investment exchange and LCH.Clearnet as a prescribed recognised clearing house for the purposes of FA 1991 ss 116 and 117.

Transfers of securities to LCH.Clearnet—prescribed circumstances

4. Regulation 4 exempts from stamp duty and SDRT transfers of equities and agreements to transfer equities to:

(a) LCH.Clearnet acting in its capacity of a person providing clearance services in relation to transactions on EDX London; or

(b) a person whose business is or includes holding equity securities as a nominee for LCH.Clearnet,

as a result of the exercise of options to buy or sell securities listed or traded on EDX London, or the expiration of a futures contract.

Transfer of securities to or from members of EDX London—prescribed circumstances

5. Regulation 5 exempts from stamp duty and SDRT transfers of equity securities and agreements to transfer equity securities made in order to meet obligations to receive securities resulting from the exercise of options to buy or sell securities listed or traded on EDX London, or the expiration of a futures contract, where the transfers are from:

(a) a non-clearing member of EDX London (or its nominee) to a clearing member of EDX London acting in that capacity (or its nominee); or

(b) LCH.Clearnet (or its nominee) to a clearing member of EDX London acting in that capacity (or its nominee).

SI 2005/844
STAMP DUTY LAND TAX (ELECTRONIC COMMUNICATIONS) REGULATIONS 2005

These regulations are to govern the use of an electronic medium for the delivery of land transaction returns and for the making of payments and repayments of SDLT in connection with such returns. By reg 3, HM Commissioners of Revenue and Customs are only to use an electronic communication method if the recipient has consented to this and has not withdrawn his consent. Correspondingly, a person is only to be permitted to use electronic communications if he uses an approved method, which includes an approved method of authenticating both the sender and the information sent. Further conditions are imposed for the retention of records in approved (physical or electronic) form.

Regulation 5 makes provision for the formulation of rules as to when information is to be treated as delivered. Prominent amongst these is a requirement that information is not to be treated as having been delivered to the Commissioners' computer system unless it has been accepted by the system.

Further provision is made as to the manner in which certain facts (eg the identity of the sender and the content of the communication) are to be proved and as to the circumstances in which certain facts (that information sent on behalf of a person was sent with his consent and that payment has been made or a land transaction return delivered) are presumed to be established (or not established) until the contrary is established.

Finally, it is specifically provided that unauthorised use of electronic communications is conclusively to be presumed *not* to have effected delivery of a land transaction return or the making of a payment.

SI 2005/1868
THE STAMP DUTY LAND TAX AVOIDANCE SCHEMES (PRESCRIBED DESCRIPTION OF ARRANGEMENTS) REGULATIONS 2005

These regulations prescribe descriptions of schemes for the avoidance of SDLT which must be disclosed to HMRC in accorance with FA 2004 Part 7. The manner in which information is to be given to HMRC is dictated by the Tax Avoidance Schemes (Information) Regulations 2004, SI 2004/1864, as amended for SDLT by SI 2005/1869. Stamp Taxes issued guidance notes on 19 July 2005 on the disclosure rules as applicable to SDLT schemes: see Appendix 8.

Citation, commencement and interpretation

1. Regulation 1 cross-refers the definitions of "chargeable interests" and "residential" and "non-residential" back to the principal Act, FA 2003.

Prescribed description of amendments in relation to stamp duty land tax

2. The fundamental statutory rule is that prescribed arrangements are notifiable if they enable or might be expected to enable a person to obtain an advantage in relation to a tax that is prescribed by regulations *and* the arrangements are such that the main benefit or one of the main benefits that might be expected to arise from the arrangements is the obtaining of the tax advantage: FA 2004 s 306. Regulation 2(1) provides that arrangements specified in reg 2(3) are to be prescribed arrangements in relation to SDLT. Unlike the disclosure rules applicable to other taxes, the SDLT disclosure rules contain no general filters of "confidentiality", "premium fee" or in the form of the "off market test". Instead, reg 2(3) prescribes arrangements as those whose subject-matter consists wholly of non-residential property, where the aggregate market value of the chargeable interests involved is at least £5 million; those where the subject-matter consists wholly of residential property, where the applicable value is at least £1 million; and those cases where the subject-matter of the transaction is a mix of residential and non-residential property, and either the applicable value of the residential property is at least £1 million, or the value of the non-residential property is at least £5 million. The collars are removed if a notifiable proposal is made generally available by the promoter and he does not know whether the proposal will be acted upon; and in cases where the applicable value is unknown. Thus, even if the applicable value proves to be less than £5 million (or £1 million, as the case might be), a promoter who failed to notify would be in breach of the rules.

However, there is no obligation to make disclosure in any case where the arrangements falls within the Schedule to the Regulations nor (as from 1 April 2010) where the arrangements are the same, or substantially the same, as arrangements which were first made available for use before that date. It should be understood that this grandfathering provision does not require the promoter to have made the arrangements, or similar arrangements, so available before that date – it is sufficient that someone did so. It may be necessary for the promoter if challenged to provide evidence that the scheme was so available. This might be provided either by the scheme being described in the Commissioners' own manuals or publications extant at that time; or from the practitioner's own records of when they made, or learnt that their competitors were making, such schemes available.

SCHEDULE: EXCLUDED ARRANGEMENTS (REGULATION 2(3)(C))

Of great importance is the Schedule to the Regulations, which sets out those arrangements that are excluded. Unfortunately, the matter is much complicated by the fact that, although there are six steps whose individual inclusion in arrangements does not make the arrangements notifiable, the incorporation of more than one of certain defined combinations of the steps in the relevant arrangements makes the arrangements notifiable.

The steps are:

Step A The acquisition of a chargeable interest in land by a special purpose vehicle (SPV).

Step B A single claim to relief from SDLT under the various provisions in FA 2003 (for example, group relief, reconstruction relief, acquisition relief and charities relief).

Step C The sale of shares in a SPV that holds chargeable interests in land, to a person who is not connected to either the SPV or vendor.

Step D Not electing to waive the exemption from VAT (ie, not "opting to tax").

Step E Structuring a transaction as the transfer of a going concern for VAT purposes.

Step F The creation of a partnership to which a property subject to a land transaction is to be transferred.

The basic rule is that if an arrangement involves one or more of the listed steps and does not include any other step which is necessary for securing the tax advantage, then the arrangements are excluded and notifiable.

The "combination" rule is that if the arrangements involve at least two of steps A, C and D, or more than one instance of step A, C or D, then the arrangements are not excluded and (subject to the standard rules on "main benefit" and market value) will be notifiable. There is no difficulty in combing steps B, D, E and F, unless the arrangements in which these steps are combined breaches the combination rule relating to steps A, C and D.

Thus, if for example an arrangement involves the acquisition of a property in a special purpose vehicle, that would fall within Step A and would be excluded, unless the arrangements involved the sale on of the shares in the SPV.

SI 2005/2462
THE TAXES (INTEREST RATE) (AMENDMENT) REGULATIONS 2005

These Regulations amend the Taxes (Interest Rate) Regulations 1989 to make provision for the setting of the rate of interest on unpaid and late-paid SDLT as well as on SDLT penalties. The Regulations also make provision for the setting of the rate of interest on the repayment of overpaid SDLT. Embarrassingly for the Government, it was discovered that, by oversight, no provision had been made for the amendment of the principal Regulations when SDLT was introduced with effect from 1 December 2003. The amending Regulations rectify the omission but are not retrospective, and interest on late-paid SDLT can thus run from no date earlier than 26 September 2005. By Press Release 27/05 of 6 September 2005 it was announced that no attempt would be made to recover interest already paid on repayments of SDLT, although no assurances were given that persons who later discovered that they had overpaid SDLT would also be compensated for being kept out of their money.

SI 2006/575
THE PENSION PROTECTION FUND (TAX) REGULATIONS 2006

These Regulations have been introduced to make provision for the tax treatment of the Board of the Pension Protection Fund, which has been brought into existence for the purpose of providing compensation to members of pension schemes where there is no solvent sponsoring employer and the scheme is either underfunded or there has been fraud and the misappropriation of scheme assets. The main legislation relating to the Board is to be found in Part 2 of the Pension Act 2004.

Application of the Finance Act 2003: further provisions

43. Regulation 43(1) provides that where the Board of the Pension Protection Fund acquires a chargeable interest as an investment in the course of assuming responsibility for a scheme, FA 2003 Sch 4 para 8 is disapplied. In consequence, no charge to SDLT will arise even though the Board assumes liability for outstanding debts as part of the transaction.

Regulation 43(2) relaxes the group relief rules in FA 2003 Sch 7. In lieu of the usual rule that a group only exists where one company is the beneficial owner of 75 per cent of another, in a case where the Board is a member of the group, relief is to be available where one company is the beneficial owner of 50 per cent of the issued share capital of the other. In addition, the claw-back rules in Sch 7 para 3 do not apply where the vendor is the Board.

SI 2006/3237
THE STAMP DUTY LAND TAX (VARIATION OF THE FINANCE ACT 2003) REGULATIONS 2006

These provisions introduce a general anti-avoidance provision in the form of FA 2003 s 75A, and in addition make significant amendments to FA 2003 Sch 15 Part 3 in order to counteract certain SDLT avoidance schemes which had been disclosed to the Commissioners following the extension of FA 2004 Part 7 (disclosure of tax avoidance schemes) to SDLT by the SDLT Avoidance Schemes (Prescribed Description of Arrangements) Regulations 2005 (SI 2005/1868). The provisions (which took effect as from 2 pm on 6 December 2006, "the relevant time") have been overtaken by the provisions of the FA 2007. Nevertheless, the original regulations remain of importance since they include transitional provisions which continue to have effect despite the replacement of the temporary provisions by those in FA 2007.

The transitional provisions are themselves of some complexity and, it is fair to say, suffer from an unwarranted degree of ambiguity. This commentary deals first with those which apply to the anti-avoidance rules, now to be found as FA 2003 ss 75A–75C. The reader is referred to the commentary to those sections for a full description of their meaning and effect. It is assumed for the purposes of the commentary to these Regulations that the reader is familiar with the principal sections.

There are three transitional rules for s 75A purposes. The first prevents s 75A applying at all. The second and third exclude specific scheme transactions from the operation of s 75A. In these last cases, the effect may be either to prevent 75A applying (because there is then no transaction other than the disposal by V), or, for example, to prevent the consideration paid for that transaction from being used as part of the deemed chargeable consideration paid for the notional transaction.

First, if s 75A is to apply, it is necessary for both the actual disposal of the chargeable interest by V and all of the scheme transactions to have taken place after the relevant time (see above). If, therefore, any of the transactions which may be considered to be scheme transactions took place before that time, the section cannot apply. It is not open to the Commissioners to disregard certain scheme transactions which took place at an earlier date and to rely on the fact that both the disposal and some scheme transactions took place after that time. Given the wide meaning ascribed to scheme transactions (see s 75A(1) and (2)) this may have the effect that transactions of relatively little importance could prevent a transaction falling within the scope of s 75A.

Second, s 75A cannot have effect in relation to a scheme transaction itself effected in pursuance of a contract which was entered into and substantially performed before the relevant time. For this purpose it is assumed that "substantial performance" has the meaning it bears in FA 2003 s 44, although there is nothing in the legislation which warrants the application of s 44 save in relation to contracts for the sale of land: see s 44(1).

Third, s 75A is not to have effect in relation to a scheme transaction which (*a*) is not an "excluded transaction", and (*b*) is effected in pursuance of a contract which was entered into before the relevant time. In this case, it will be observed that it is unnecessary for the relevant contract to have been substantially performed before that time. The Regulation treats transactions as excluded transactions where certain steps have been taken to modify the term's nature or the effect of the original contract to such an extent that it is significantly different from what it previously was.

Regulation 2(8)–(10) make transitional provision for the amendments to Sch 15 Part 3. There are two transitional rules. First, the amendments do not have effect in relation to any land transaction which is effected in pursuance of a contract entered into and substantially performed before the relevant time. Second, the amendments do not have effect where the land transaction was effected in pursuance of a contract entered into (though not substantially performed) before the relevant time, unless the transaction is an "excluded transaction".

The Regulation treats transactions as excluded transactions where certain steps have been taken to modify the term's nature or the effect of the original contract to such an extent that it is significantly different from what it previously was.

Part II ST

SI 2007/1385
THE FINANCE ACT 2003, SECTION 66 (PRESCRIBED STATUTORY PROVISIONS) ORDER 2007

FA 2003 s 66(2) makes provision for land transactions effected under statutory provisions which may from time to time be prescribed by the Treasury to be exempt from SDLT. This Order makes provision for the exemption of land transactions made under School Standards and Framework Act 1998 Sch 22 para A23(2), 4(2), 5(4B) or 8(2)(b) (transfer of land to local education authority) or by virtue of regulations made under Education and Inspections Act 2006 s 27(2)(b) (transfer of land on removal of foundation or reduction in foundation governors. It is a condition of the exemption, as required by section 66, that either the vendor or the purchaser is a public body (as defined by the section).

SI 2007/3437
STAMP DUTY LAND TAX (ZERO-CARBON HOMES RELIEF) REGULATIONS 2007

These regulations make provision for the circumstances in which and the manner by which relief is to be obtained from the charge to SDLT on the *first* acquisition of a dwelling that is a zero-carbon home, in accordance with FA 2003 ss 58B and 58C. The regulations limit the relief according to the value of the property: in a case where the chargeable consideration (other than rent) is £500,000 or less, the transaction is exempt from SDLT, save to the extent of the rent. If, on the other hand the consideration (other than rent) exceeds £500,000 the SDLT chargeable is reduced by £15,000. Thus, in a case where the chargeable consideration is £600,000, the SDLT due is £24,000 – £15,000 = £9,000. The relief must be claimed on a land transaction return or on an amendment to such a return. HMRC are given the power to refuse a claim where they have reasonable grounds to believe that the relevant dwelling is not a zero-carbon home.

The regulations also define in some detail what constitutes a "zero-carbon home" and provide for a certification procedure to be carried out by an assessor accredited under the Buildings Regulations 2000, SI 2000/2531.

SI 2008/710
STAMP DUTY LAND TAX (OPEN-ENDED INVESTMENT COMPANIES) REGULATIONS 2008

These regulations provide a relief from SDLT where a UK authorised unit trust (AUT) converts into an open-ended investment company (OEIC) or merges with an existing OEIC. They apply only in cases where all four of the following conditions are satisfied:

(1) the whole of the AUT's assets becomes the property of the OEIC;
(2) the units in the AUT are extinguished;
(3) shares in the OEIC are issued to the holders of the extinguished units in proportion to their holdings of those units; and
(4) the consideration consists of nothing else, other than the assumption or discharge by the acquiring company of liabilities of the trustees of the target trust.

The regulations follow the similar rules that were introduced in 1997 in relation to stamp duty and SDRT, as to which see the commentary above to the Stamp Duty and Stamp Duty Reserve Tax (Open-ended Investment Companies) Regulations 1997, SI 1997/1156. The reader is also referred to the commentary on FA 1986 ss 75 to 77 for guidance on the manner in which the Courts (and indeed the Commissioners) have interpreted similar rules relating to the acquisition of undertakings for stamp duty and SDRT purposes.

SI 2009/2052
ALTERNATIVE FINANCE INVESTMENT BONDS (STAMP DUTY LAND TAX) (PRESCRIBED EVIDENCE) REGULATIONS 2009

FA 2009 Sch 61 provides relief from SDLT where land is used as security as part of the issue of an alternative finance investment bond. In order to ensure that the exemption is not used as a device for avoiding SDLT on the transfer of ownership of land, various conditions are laid out in the principal legislation, including an obligation to register a legal charge in favour of HMRC at the Land Registry over the relevant land. If in due course the land ceases to be held as a bond asset, and HMRC are provided with the necessary evidence, the Commissioners will remove the charge. These Regulations prescribe the form of the evidence required for the purposes of Sch 61.

SI 2009/2971
MUTUAL SOCIETIES (TRANSFERS OF BUSINESS) (TAX) REGULATIONS 2009

These Regulations are designed to facilitate the transfer of business by mutual societies by removing the fiscal barriers to such transfers, and came into force on 1 December 2009 and are consequential on the Mutual Societies (Transfers) Order 2009, SI 2009/509. They apply where there is an amalgamation of two or more building societies or where a building society transfers the whole or part of its business to another building society or to a commercial company in accordance with s 97 of the Building Societies Act 1986 (reg 3(1)). They also apply to like transfers and amalgamations by Industrial and Provident Societies (reg 3(2)) and by Friendly Societies (reg 3(3)).

The Regulations provide (amongst other things) for various corporation tax losses and allowances which would have been available to the predecessor organisation to carry across to the successor (regulation 4) and for the transfer of the business to take place on a no-gain, no-loss basis for the purposes of corporation tax on chargeable gains.

From a stamp taxes perspective, the relevant provisions are regs 31–33. Reg 31 exempts a land transaction made in connection with the transfer to be exempt from SDLT. Reg 32 provides that an instrument which is executed in order to give effect to a transfer by an industrial and provident society is not to be chargeable to stamp duty. Reg 33 secures that there is to be no clawback of SDLT group relief by reason of the operation of FA 2003 Sch 7 para 3 in a case where there had been a group transfer within the three years prior to the transfer of the business of the society and, as a result of the relevant transfer, the purchaser would be treated as leaving the SDLT group.

3.
Appendices

Contents

APPENDIX 1. SDLT TECHNICAL NEWS

Note: although these technical notes and newsletters are provided in this Appendix as a convenience for readers, HMRC has withdrawn all these bulletins on the ground that the information contained within them is either superseded or is now available in an alternative format on HMRC's website. The reader is referred to Stamp Taxes Bulletin June 2010, which identified three items yet to be published separately relating to scheme transactions under FA 2003 s 75A; consideration and consideration and exchanges, as to which see, at present SDLT Technical News 5 (below).

STAMP DUTY LAND TAX (SDLT) TECHNICAL NEWSLETTER 1

COMPARATIVE SDLT TREATMENT OF LEASE EXTENSIONS AND RENEWALS

This article aims to explain the treatment of the usual methods of extending the term of occupation where occupation is under a lease. This article refers to business leases but the principles are also applicable to residential leases.

The SDLT treatment of these extensions will differ, depending upon whether the initial lease was granted under stamp duty or stamp duty land tax.

1) Most business leases in England and Wales continue irrespective of the term of the lease by operation of law until they are determined (usually by written notice). In Scotland such leases continue one year at a time by virtue of the doctrine of tacit relocation. For SDLT purposes, this period of holding over is initially treated as an extension of the original lease by one year. However, where the original lease was granted on or after 1 December 2003 and was, itself, taxable under SDLT rules, the extended lease is also taxable under these rules. This may make a difference to the tax payable on the rental amount as the Net Present Value of the rent will be increased by the additional year's rent. Where there is such a tax difference, this should be notified to HM Revenue & Customs at the Manchester Complex Transactions Unit, by letter, giving sufficient information to identify the original return, land, parties to the transaction and the additional tax due and how it has been calculated. Where the period of holding over extends into a second or subsequent year, a similar calculation should be made and notification given each year there is more tax due. These are the only times notification of these holding over periods is required.

Where such a period of holding over is followed by the grant of a new lease, it is common for the new lease to have as its start date the express end date of the original lease, thus covering the period of holding over of the original lease. It may also be that a new, increased, rent is payable for this period under the new lease. For the purposes of SDLT, the term of such a renewal lease cannot start before the date it is granted (following the decision in *Bradshaw v Pawley*). For any period that there is an overlap in the tax treatment of the original lease and the renewal lease overlap relief on the rental element of the rent may be claimed. This is despite the fact that the original lease may legally have finished the day before the renewal lease is granted. Where there is an increased rent for the holding over period, if the increased rent during the holding over period is paid for grant of the new lease, it will be treated as a premium for the new lease and taxed as such. If it is paid for occupation under the original lease, it is taxable as rent under the original lease.

Example A

The express term of a business lease came to an end on 30 November 2010 but the tenant continued in occupation whilst negotiating terms for a renewal lease. The original lease had an annual rent of £150,000. The renewal lease is granted on 1 March 2012, having terms from 1 December 2010 and has an increased annual rent of £350,000.

- If the original lease was granted or treated as granted prior to 1 December 2003, the period of holding over, as an extension of the original lease, does not need to be notified at all.
- If the increase in rent during the holding over period (£249,315) is paid for grant of the renewal lease, it will be taxed as a premium for the grant of the renewal lease together with any tax due on the Net Present Value of the renewal lease. Only one return has to be made notifying the grant of the renewal lease (if tax is payable or the term of the renewal lease is 7 years or more).
- If, however, the increased rent during the holding over period is paid for occupation under the original lease, it is not taxed as premium. Instead the new lease will need to be notified and tax paid (if tax is payable or the term of the renewal lease is 7 years or more). Notification will have to be given of the increased rent under the original lease (by virtue of FA 2003 Sch 17A para 13 treating the rent increase as the grant of a lease). As the duration of this deemed lease is known (15 months) the Net Present Value can be calculated to be £239,272 (the total of £200,000 discounted by 3.5% and £49,315 discounted by 3.5% twice). This deemed grant will not be linked with the original grant but will be notifiable with tax due of £892, within 30 days of 1 March 2012 (the effective date of the grant of the renewal lease). As the term end date is one day prior to the effective date, this transaction is to be sent to Manchester Stamp Office. Had there been no tax to pay, it would not be notifiable.
- If the original lease was granted on or after 1 December 2003, the period of holding over, as an extension of the original lease, will need to be notified if the Net Present Value of the rent for each extra year means that more tax is payable. Thus if the lease started on 1 December 2003, the Net Present Value of the original lease would have been £917,181. On 1 December 2010, the lease is treated as extended by one year (to 30 November 2011) and the Net Present Value now becomes £1,031,093. Extra tax is due and notification of this would have to be made by 31 December 2010. On 1 December 2011, the lease is again treated as extended by a further year (to 30 November 2012) resulting in a Net Present Value of £1,141,152. Notification again has to be made as more tax is due.
- If the increased rent during the holding over period (£249,315) is paid for grant of the renewal lease, it will be taxed as a premium for the grant of the renewal lease together with any other premium (if any) and on the Net Present Value of the renewal lease. The rent for the first year of the renewal lease (£350,000) will be reduced by the period of "double counting" of rent (of 275 days from 1 March 2012 to 30 November 2012, commonly known as the overlap period). The reduction will therefore be (£150,000 divided by 365 and multiplied by 275 = £113,013). The amount entered on the NPV calculator for year 1 of the renewal lease will therefore be £236,987 (£350,000 – £113,013). Only one return has to be made notifying the grant of the renewal lease (if tax is payable or the term of the renewal lease is 7 years or more).
- If, however, the increased rent during the holding over period is paid for occupation under the original lease, it is not taxed as premium. Instead the new lease will need to be notified and tax paid (if tax is payable or the term of the renewal lease is 7 years or more). Notification will have to be given of the increased rent under the original lease (by virtue of FA 2003 Sch 17A para 13 treating the rent increase as the grant of a lease). As the duration of this deemed lease is known (15 months) the Net Present Value can be calculated to be £239,272 (the total of £200,000 discounted by 3.5% and £49,315 discounted by 3.5% twice). This deemed grant will not be linked with the original grant but will be notifiable with tax due of £892, within 30 days of 1 March 2012 (the effective date of the grant of the renewal lease). As the term end date is one day prior to the effective date, this transaction is to be sent to Manchester Stamp Office. Had there been no tax to pay, it would not be notifiable.

2) If a lease is specifically extended during its term, this extension is treated as a surrender and regrant. Stamp Duty Land Tax is payable on the Net Present Value of the regranted lease (with the rent element reduced during the overlap period by the rent already taken into account for Stamp Duty Land Tax purposes.

Example B

The express term of a business lease ends on 30 November 2010. In 2008, the tenant negotiates with the landlord to extend the term of the lease by 5 years to 30 November 2015. This new lease is granted on 1 December 2008. The rent remains the same at an annual amount of £200,000.

- If the original lease was granted or treated as granted before 1 December 2003, there is no overlap relief for the rent as it has not been subject to Stamp Duty Land Tax. The new lease (for 7 years) has a Net Present Value of £1,222,908 and should be notified on a return.
- If the original lease was granted on or after 1 December 2003, this is subject to SDLT and the rent used to calculate the Net Present Value of the original lease in the overlap period (1 December 2008 to 30 November 2010) is available for overlap relief. Thus, the rent to take into account for the new lease in the first and second years is zero (as overlap relief is the same as the rent due). The Net Present Value of the rent for this lease is therefore £842,969.

3) It is also possible to enter into a reversionary lease. These are leases which take effect some time in the future when the current lease expires. The SDLT treatment of these leases depends on whether they are actually granted or whether an agreement for such a lease is entered into.

Where such a reversionary lease is granted, notification and any tax is due 30 days after the grant. Thus, where a reversionary lease is granted on 1

December 2005 which has a term from 1 December 2010 to 30 November 2020 at an annual rent of £100,000 the Net Present Value is £831,660. The first years calculation for Net Present Value is £100,000 discounted by 3.5% **not** £100,000 discounted by 3.5% six times. This is because the calculation of the Net Present Value (at Paragraph 3, Schedule 5, Finance Act 2003) only starts at the first year of the **term** of the lease which in the case of a reversionary lease is the date the lease commences (1 December 2010 in the example) and not the date when it is granted.

This compares to the case when an agreement for (reversionary) lease is entered into. The agreement is a contract subject to FA 2003 s 44. Although the tenant may be in occupation of the property, this will be by virtue of the current lease and so does not count as substantial performance of the agreement for lease (as occupation is not by virtue of the agreement). When the current original lease determines, the agreement for lease will be substantially performed (if the reversionary lease has not already been granted as part of the determination of the original lease) and tax will only be payable at that time and the lease (or substantial performance of the agreement) would become notifiable. Thus where an agreement for lease is entered into on 1 December 2005 for a lease to be granted from 1 December 2010 until 30 November 2020 at an annual rent of £100,000, the Net Present Value is again £831,660, but the tax is only payable by 31 December 2010.

Our automated process is unable to deal with reversionary leases, since the correct start date of the lease is in the future. In these cases, the SDLT1 should be completed in the appropriate way and then sent to the Complex Transactions Unit in Manchester with a covering letter.

Deeds of rectification: treatment for SDLT purposes

(1) This note has effect only for land in England & Wales, and Northern Ireland.

(2) For most land transactions there is a contract followed by a deed (for example a transfer or a lease) which gives effect to what the parties agreed in the contract. (Some leases, however, are not preceded by a contract.) It sometimes happens that the deed does not correctly reflect what the parties agreed in the contract. In such cases a further deed will normally be executed which, when read with the original deed, gives effect to what the parties agreed. This process is called "rectification" (sometimes rectification may be effected by Court order rather than by deed).

(3) There are no special Stamp Duty Land Tax rules for deeds (or indeed Court orders) of rectification. Most deeds of rectification will effect a land transaction for Stamp Duty Land Tax purposes. For example the original deed may not have transferred all the freehold land that was agreed. The deed of rectification will effect the

transfer of the land that was left out: this will be a land transaction (the transfer of freehold land). Or the original deed might not have reserved a right of way although the contract provided for this. The deed of rectification will then create a legal right of way: this again is a land transaction.

(4) Most land transactions need to be notified to the Inland Revenue on a Land Transaction Return (form SDLT1). Again there are no special rules for transactions effected by a deed of rectification. So where additional freehold land is transferred by a deed of rectification the transaction must be notified to the Inland Revenue where the transferee gives any consideration for the additional land (unless the transfer is of residential property and the consideration is under £1,000). Where a legal easement such as a right of way, or a restrictive covenant, is created by a deed of rectification the transaction must be notified if there is tax to pay, or a relief to be claimed.

(5) Where a land transaction effected by deed of rectification does not need to be notified to the Inland Revenue, for example because there is no chargeable consideration, a self-certificate (form SDLT60) needs to accompany any application for registration. The self-certificate must be completed to show why no Land Transaction Return is required.

Where the original transaction was the grant of the lease a deed of rectification will normally operate as the variation of the lease. If so the normal Stamp Duty Land Tax rules on variations of leases apply. However where the only effect is to increase the demise (the land which is the subject matter of the lease) the deed of rectification might operate as a supplemental lease.

STAMP DUTY LAND TAX (SDLT) TECHNICAL NEWSLETTER 2

SHARED OWNERSHIP LEASES

It is possible to pay Stamp Duty Land Tax (SDLT) on Shared Ownership leases in two different ways.

HM Revenue and Customs (HMRC) is not in a position to offer advice to purchasers on which election to make although our Help-line 0845 6030135 can help you to calculate how much tax is due under each election to pay. HMRC does suggest that purchasers discuss the options with their solicitor, licensed conveyancer or other adviser as current circumstances and future intentions in respect to staircasing should be considered when deciding which election to make.

Market value election

A purchaser can make an election to pay SDLT by reference to the market value of the property at the time of purchase. The SDLT in this case is intended to be as close as possible to the SDLT due on a more conventional freehold or leasehold purchase.

This is a once and for all payment even if the purchaser staircases to own a greater interest in the property at a later date.

A market value election will normally be beneficial where the initial market value does not exceed £120,000. A market value election is also beneficial for properties entitled to Disadvantaged Areas Relief (DAR) if the initial market value does not exceed £150,000.

How to calculate the tax on a market value election

If your lease gives you the right to acquire the freehold (which will normally be the case for a house) and you make a market value election SDLT will be charged on the market value of the freehold at the time of your initial purchase. This initial market value must be stated in the lease.

If your lease does not give you the right to acquire the freehold (which will normally be the case for a flat) it will instead specify a "minimum rent". In that case if you make a market value election SDLT will be charged on the "open market premium" applicable to the minimum rent. The open market premium must be stated in the lease. In addition there may be a charge on the minimum rent, although this is unlikely for most shared ownership leases. You can find out if there is a charge on the minimum rent by using our online calculator at: http://idcalculator.inlandrevenue.gov.uk/.

Examples of a market value election

1. Miss A buys a 50% interest in a shared ownership house with a right to acquire the freehold. The initial market value of the house is £190,000.

Miss A makes a market value election. The normal rates and threshold apply so SDLT is payable at 1% of £190,000. Stamp Duty Land Tax of £1,900 is due.

2. Mrs B buys a 50% interest in a shared ownership flat with an initial market value of £195,000. When Mrs B has acquired the maximum interest possible under the lease she will pay a peppercorn rent. This is the "minimum rent". The "open market premium" for this rent is £195,000, the market value of the flat. She makes a market value election, SDLT is due at 1% on £195,000 which is £1,950. Mrs B also has to pay SDLT on the net present value of the minimum possible rent in excess of £120,000. The NPV of a peppercorn rent is 0. Total SDLT due is £1,950.

3. Mr. C buys a 50% interest in a shared ownership flat with an initial market value of £200,000. When Mr C has acquired the maximum interest possible under the lease he will still have to pay rent of £50 a month. This is the "minimum rent". The "open market premium" for this rent is £180,000. He makes a market value election.

SDLT is due at 1% on £180,000 which is £1,800. Mr. C also has to pay SDLT on the amount by which the net present value of the minimum rent exceeds £120,000.The net present value of the minimum rent is £16,910. As this is less than £120,000 no SDLT is due on the rental element. Total SDLT due is £1,800.

How to make a market value election

A market value election should be made in your land transaction return (form SDLT1). Note that a market value election cannot be revoked once you have made your return. If, however, you do not make a market value election you can still make one provided you do so within 12 months by amending your return. The procedure for amending your return is explained at: www.hmrc.gov.uk/so/paid-too-much-sdlt.htm

You make a market value election by entering the initial market value, or open market premium in box 22 of your land transaction return and the net present value of the minimum rent, if there is one, in box 23 (a peppercorn rent counts as 0). For example where the lease gives you the right to acquire the freehold the entries on form SDLT1 would be:

- Question 2 = L
- Question 10 = leave blank
- Question 11 = leave blank
- Question 14 = tax assessed at question 24
- Questions 16 to 25, as appropriate but specifically:
  - Question 20 = specified starting rent
  - Question 22 = full market value
  - Question 23 = 0
  - Question 24 = tax due on the full market value
  - Question 25 = 0

Further information about completing the SDLT1 for other types of Shared Ownership transactions is available within the SDLT Manual at www.hmrc.gov.uk/manuals/sdltmanua l/sdltm27080.htm.

Assignment of the lease where a market value election has been made

If you assign a shared ownership lease on which a market value election has been made Stamp Duty Land Tax is payable on the consideration paid by the assignee. There will be no further SDLT payable whether or not the new owner does staircase.

We strongly recommend that the initial purchaser keeps a record of an election for market value having been made so that this can be passed on to the new owner.

What happens in the absence of a market value election

The SDLT due in the absence of a market value election is best considered as having two elements. Firstly, SDLT may be due when the initial purchase is made. Secondly, further SDLT may be due if the purchaser staircases to hold an interest in excess of 80%.

Calculating tax on the initial purchase

In the absence of a market value election you will initially pay; at the rate of 1% on NPV of rent over £120,000.

AND

at the appropriate rate on the initial premium. If the average annual rent is more than £600, any premium falling within the 0% band is chargeable at the rate of 1%

Staircasing up to 80% interest

Once the initial purchase has been made there will be no SDLT to pay when staircasing to hold an interest of 80% or less. For example, if the initial purchase is of 25% of the interest, this will be chargeable as described immediately above. The purchaser can then staircase to 50% and then 80% without incurring any further SDLT.

Staircasing in excess of 80%

Once the interest acquired exceeds 80% SDLT may be due. For example, the purchaser acquires an initial interest of 25%, which will be chargeable. He/she then staircases to 85%, and SDLT will be due on this entire 60% acquisition at a rate determined by the total premiums paid.

If two or more staircasings occur, the first of which takes the interest over 80% then SDLT could be due on both or all these transactions. If the purchaser initially buys 25% and the staircases to 75% this staircasing is exempt. If the purchaser then staircases from 75% to 85% SDLT may be due, and if they then staircase further from 85% to 100% SDLT may again be due.

The charge is on the payment you make for the staircasing. However in order to determine the rate of charge you need to add together all the capital payments you have made. These include the initial premium, all subsequent capital payments, and the one being taxed. This is because these transactions are "linked" for SDLT purposes.

You may also need to revisit the SDLT payable on the initial premium when any staircasing takes place. Again all the capital payments must be added together to determine the rate of charge on the initial premium. This may mean that more SDLT is due on the initial premium. Any additional SDLT is payable 30 days after the later transaction takes place. You should write a letter explaining that additional SDLT is due and send it, with payment, to Manchester Stamp Office. There are more details of this at www.hmrc.gov.uk/so/mctu.htm.

Example

1. Mr and Mrs C buy 50% of a shared ownership lease house for £100,000 (the initial market value of the house being £200,000). They pay an annual rent of £3,000, which is subject to RPI only adjustment. The term of the lease is 125 years.

SDLT is due at 1% of the entire premium as the average annual rent is more than £600. SDLT due on the premium is £1,000. The net present value of the rent is £84,551 so no SDLT is due on the rental element.

Over the next 20 years Mr and Mrs C staircase to hold an 80% interest. As the payments made in each staircasing transaction reflect the market value of the house at the time, Mr and Mrs C gave an additional £90,000 in consideration to acquire the additional 30% interest. No SDLT is due on any of these staircasing transactions. No additional SDLT is due on the initial premium because the total of all capital payments is still in the 1% band.

After 25 years Mr and Mrs C decide to staircase to hold 100% of the interest in their house. For the final 20% Mr and Mrs C pay another £90,000. This again reflects the market value of the house at the time of the final staircasing.

To calculate the SDLT due as a result of the final staircasing the sum of all the transactions is calculated. £100,000 was paid for the initial purchase, £90,000 for the intermediate staircasing transactions, and another £90,000 for the final staircasing. So £280,000 has been paid in total for the property. As £280,000 exceeds £250,000, SDLT is due at 3% on the final staircasing transaction of £90,000. SDLT at 3% of £90,000 is due, which is £2,700. This 3% rate is also applied to the initial premium of £100,000, to create a liability of £3,000. As £1,000 tax has already been paid at the initial purchase, a further £2,000 is due.

Assignment of the lease

If a lease is assigned when a market value election was not made, SDLT will be due on the consideration paid for the assignment. Unlike the market value election, if the new owner undertakes any staircasing that increases their interest in the property to more than 80% SDLT may be due. Only payments made by the new owner are added together to determine the rate of tax unless the old owner was "connected" with the new, for example if they were spouses or brother and sister.

Diagram 1 – SDLT on shared ownership leases

First Stage

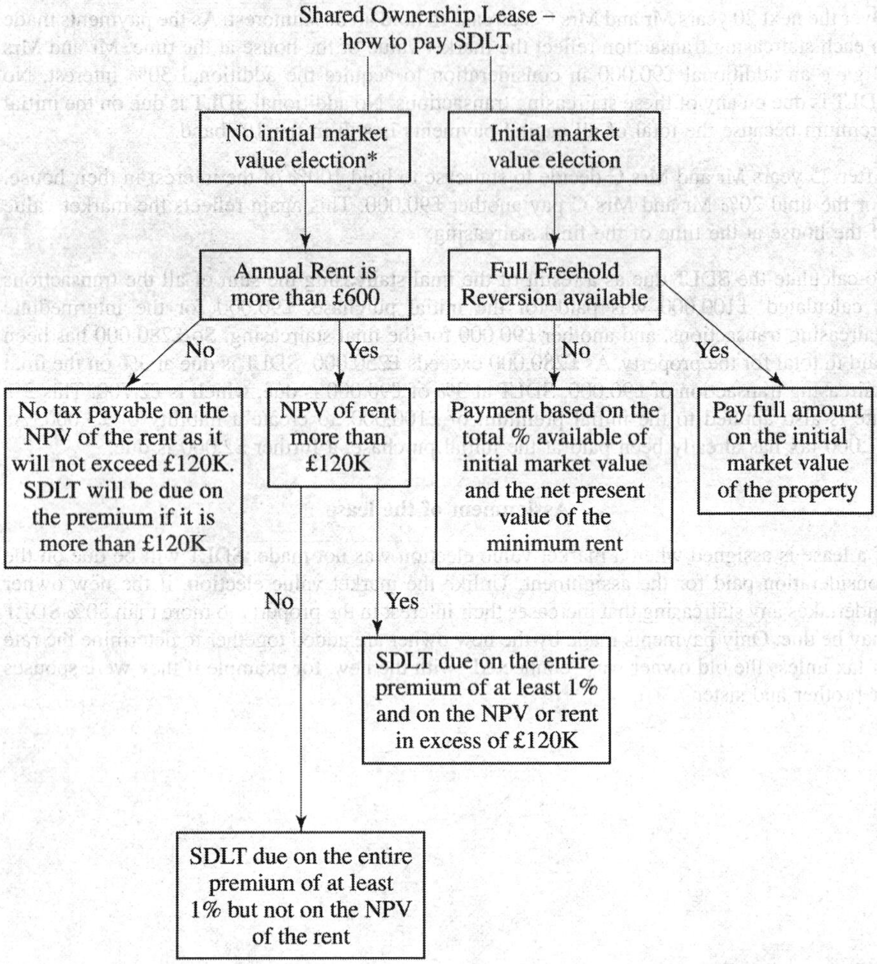

*In the absence of an initial market value election further SDLT may be due.

WORKING ENQUIRY CASES

The purchaser(s) in a land transaction has/have a responsibility for ensuring that the contents of a land transaction return are correct and complete.

HMRC has the power to enquire into land transaction returns, to ensure that the correct amount of stamp duty land tax has been paid, and into self-certificates.

If we wish to enquire into a return we must open the enquiry within 9 months of the filing date (or within 9 months of the return being delivered if it is delivered late). If we wish to enquire into the amendment of a return we must do so within 9 months of the amendment being made. If we wish to enquire into a self-certificate we must do so within 9 months of it being produced.

Stamp Taxes undertake a programme of enquiry work into transactions where it is considered that tax may be at risk and also into "random" cases. There is no requirement for HMRC to explain to either a purchaser or their agent why an enquiry has been opened.

Enquiry officers will approach their work in a neutral manner, they do not start from the premise that the land transaction return or self-certificate is incorrect. Rather they seek documentary evidence and other information that they need to satisfy themselves that the self-assessment is correct.

A purchaser's rights and obligations once an enquiry has been opened are set out in our Codes of Practice COP24 (www.hmrc.gov.uk/pdfs/cop24.pdf) and COP25 (www.hmrc.gov.uk/pdfs/cop25.pdf), one of which is always issued to the purchaser at the start of the enquiry.

Each enquiry is worked on a case-by-case basis. It follows therefore that the general advice that follows may not apply in some circumstances.

If a purchaser has told us that their agent is authorised to handle correspondence on their behalf (normally by marking box 59 of form SDLT1) we will make our initial request for documentation and information to the agent, but we will tell the purchaser that we have done so.

Information requested in our opening letter may include items such as

- The contract or agreement relating to the transaction and any side letters or correspondence exchanged between the parties.
- The completion documentation, TR1, lease etc.
- The completion statement provided by the agent for the purchaser. This should show what monies were paid by the purchaser and to what they related.
- Copies of any valuation reports obtained by the purchaser in respect of the transaction.
- Copies of any advertising material provided by the vendor or their agents.
- A detailed explanation of the circumstances surrounding the transaction.
- Other information that may be relevant to claims for relief etc.

If an agent or purchaser feels that our request for information is

- unreasonable, or
- perhaps that more time than the usual 30 days is necessary to reply, or
- they simply feel that discussion of the case with the enquiry officer would be helpful.

The enquiry officer's contact details, including a direct phone number and file reference, will be shown on all correspondence relating to the enquiry. A phone call to discuss the perceived difficulties may be of help to the agent or purchaser and the enquiry officer.

A purchaser cannot appeal against our decision to open an enquiry. They may however apply at any time to the Commissioners (an independent tribunal) for a direction that HMRC should bring the enquiry to an end. We may oppose such an application if we consider we do not have enough information to decide whether the correct amount of tax has been paid.

The enquiry should progress as quickly as possible. If a reply to a letter hasn't been received by HMRC after approximately a month the enquiry officer may phone and ask if there is a problem for the agent or purchaser in providing the information requested.

If after another month a full response hasn't been received the enquiry officer will consider using formal statutory powers to obtain the information required. A formal notice requiring information will be sent directly to the purchaser, a copy is also sent to the agent if appropriate. Failure to comply with such a notice may result in the imposition of penalties.

The purchaser may appeal to the Commissioners against the formal notice if they consider the request for information is unnecessary or onerous.

Quite often a telephone discussion about a transaction with an agent or purchaser can clarify details that sometimes are not clear in documentation held on file. Sometimes a meeting between the enquiry officer, the purchaser and their agent may be helpful. The meeting could take place at the agent's offices, the purchaser's premises or at the enquiry officer's workplace.

At the end of an enquiry the enquiry officer will consider whether additional tax may be due and will inform the purchaser of their conclusions. If additional tax is due then there may also be a liability to penalties if the return (or an amendment to the return) was incorrect because of the purchaser's fraudulent or negligent conduct. Such penalties can be as much as the additional tax due. In addition interest is chargeable as from the filing date on any additional tax due or from 26 September 2005, whichever is the later.

The purchaser can appeal to the Commissioners against our conclusion that additional tax is due, and against the imposition of any penalty.

There is further comprehensive guidance on how Stamp Taxes will seek to open, work and conclude an enquiry in the stamp duty land tax Manual at SDLTM80800 onwards at www.hmrc.gov.uk/manuals/sdltmanual/SDLTM80800.htm.

The applicable Legislation is at FA 2003 Schs 10 and 11. It can be found at www.opsi.gov.uk/acts/acts2003/30014-z.htm#sch10pt3.

The Department for Constitutional Affairs has published a booklet on Tax Appeals, explaining in particular the role of the Commissioners. This can be found at www.hmrc.gov.uk/leaflets/tax-appeals.pdf.

Our booklet SD8 "How settlements are negotiated" is available at www.hmrc.gov.uk/leaflets/sd8.pdf.

FIXTURES & CHATTELS

We have been asked about the distinction between "fixtures" and "chattels"; and about the significance of the distinction for SDLT purposes. "Fixtures" are things in which in law are part of the land, just as buildings are in law part of the land. "Chattels" ("moveables" in Scotland) are things which in law are separate from the land. Anything paid for fixtures is part of the purchase price of the land for the purposes of SDLT. By contrast the sale of chattels is not subject to SDLT. However where a transaction includes the sale both of land (including buildings and fixtures) and of chattels there must be a fair apportionment of the total price paid in order to arrive at the purchase price of the land for the purposes of SDLT. The purchaser is responsible for the accuracy of this apportionment.

Although we cannot give an exhaustive list of what is a fixture and what is a chattel there is a list of some common examples at www.hmrc.gov.uk/manuals/sdltmanual/SDLTM04010.htm

GOODWILL (INHERENT & FREE)

SDLT is a charge on transactions in "land". Thus the subject matter of the charge includes anything forming part of the land as a matter of law, such as buildings and structures forming part of the land, and fixtures.

There is no specific exemption for goodwill. The subject matter of the charge also includes goodwill that is attached to and inseparable from the land and therefore any amount that is 'attributed' to such goodwill is within the charge to Stamp Duty Land Tax. This is often described as inherent goodwill because it is inherent in the land.

In other cases goodwill, sometimes called free goodwill, is separate from the land.

Free goodwill will only be present on the sale of a business or part of a business, but not necessarily even then.

Issues relating to the categorisation of goodwill, or the valuation of free goodwill where an apportionment is required should be referred to the Valuation Office Agency.

Information on goodwill is available within the SDLT Manual at www.hmrc.gov.uk/manuals/sdltmanual/SDLTM04005.htm.

EXCHANGES

An exchange of land occurs where a land transaction is entered into by the purchaser (alone or jointly) wholly or partly in consideration of another land transaction being entered into by them (alone or jointly) as vendor, and applies in relation to each transaction as if each were distinct and separate from the other.

The words 'in consideration of' do not mean that one land transaction has to be entered into as (part) payment for another land transaction. In other words one land transaction does not have to be entered into as consideration for another land transaction. Rather, "in consideration of" means that the fact that a second transaction will occur has been taken into account in making the decision to enter into the first transaction.

Thus, a sale and leaseback scheme is an exchange as the sale has been entered into in the knowledge that the leaseback will occur (and vice versa – the leaseback is entered into in the knowledge that the sale has occurred). A purchase and onward lease (B purchases from A and onward leases to C) may be an exchange within the meaning of the legislation if the onward lease is undertaken in consideration of the purchase. This will frequently occur where A and C are connected persons. Circular transactions are also within this provision where A purchases from B, who purchases from C who purchases from A, if the purchases are entered into in the expectation that the corresponding sale will occur.

If there is an exchange of land, where at least one of the interests in land is a major interest, there are two transactions and two "purchasers". Each purchaser must complete a separate SDLT1 for each transaction. The chargeable consideration for each transaction is the open market value of the interest in land that each purchaser receives as a result of the exchange.

An exchange of land will comprise linked transactions only if between connected persons.

Further guidance and examples are shown on our website at www.hmrc.gov.uk/manuals/sdltmanual/SDLTM04020.htm.

LAND TRANSACTIONS: THE COMMONHOLD AND LEASEHOLD REFORM ACT 2002

Background

Commonhold is a new way of owning freehold properties which have communal facilities, such as a block of flats. A commonhold consists of individual "units" such as flats, together with common parts such as lobbies and staircases. Each "unit-holder" owns the freehold interest in his or her unit and is a member of the "commonhold association" which owns the freehold interest in, and manages, the common parts. The intention is to provide an alternative to the long-established practice whereby individual flats in a block are held on long leases granted by the freeholder (either a third party or a company controlled by the flat-owners), and the freeholder manages the common parts. Commonhold applies only in England & Wales.

Commonhold was created by the Commonhold and Leasehold Reform Act 2002 ("CLRA"). CLRA was brought fully into force on 27 September 2004.

Commonhold interests have to be registered at the Land Registry. There are more details of commonhold, and of the registration procedure, in Land Registry Practice Guide 60, which can be found at www.landregistry.gov.uk/publications/?pubtype=35.

There are two ways in which commonhold land can be created. Registration with unit-holders occurs when an existing freehold and/or leasehold development (for example, an owner-occupied block of flats) is converted to commonhold. The individual owners or lessees will

Part II ST

become unit-holders and will each own a freehold interest in their own unit (and any leases under which they formerly held will come to an end). Each unit-holder will become a member of the commonhold association, which will take over ownership and management of the common parts.

Registration without unit-holders is designed for a new development. The property is registered as commonhold but the developer continues to be the registered proprietor until the first unit is sold. At that point the unit that is sold is registered in the name of the unit-holder and the common parts are registered in the name of the commonhold association. Further unit-holders are registered as further units are sold.

The stamp duty land tax treatment of commonhold

The registration of the common parts in the name of the commonhold association and the registration of a unit in the name of a unit-holder are all land transactions (the acquisition of a chargeable interest by operation of law). However there will generally be no chargeable consideration for any of these land transactions. The exception (which might apply in particular to the acquisition of the common parts by the commonhold association) is where the transferee is a company or other body corporate "connected with" the transferor. In that case FA 2003 s 53 deems the consideration to be the market value of the interest transferred. We accept, however, that the market value of the common parts held by the commonhold association is negligible as the commonhold association is not able to deal in or profit from the common parts and is under an obligation to maintain and insure them.

Registration without unit-holders is not in itself a land transaction, and neither is it a land transaction when land registered as commonhold without unit-holders ceases to be so registered before any units are sold.

In order for registration with unit-holders to take place the consent of all the unit holders and the landlord, if there is one, is needed. A payment made to obtain consent is not chargeable consideration for a land transaction.

The extinguishment of a unit-holder's lease when the unit is registered in his or her name is not an exchange because the lease is extinguished by operation of law. The extinguishment is not consideration for the registration.

"LINKED TRANSACTIONS"

What is the significance of "linked" transactions?

"Linked" transactions are significant in determining the rate of SDLT to be used in calculating the tax. For example, the rate of SDLT on a transaction where the consideration is £200,000 would normally be 1%. However, if it is "linked" with a transaction where the consideration is £100,000 the rate becomes 3% (rate applicable to the aggregate consideration of £300,000). The rate applicable to the other transaction, which would normally be 0%, also becomes 3%. If the transactions are "linked" with a third transaction where the consideration is £250,000 then the rate applicable to each of them will be 4% (rate applicable to the aggregate consideration of 4%).

The principle is the same when calculating the Net Present Value (NPV) charge on the grant of 'linked' leases but the detailed calculation is different. Where leases are granted on different properties the NPVs are added together to arrive at an aggregate NPV, tax is charged at 1% of the excess of the NPV over £150,000 (£120,000 for residential leases) and the tax is apportioned between the "linked" leases, calculated pro-rata to the respective NPV's. Where, however, successive "linked" leases are granted in respect of a single property they are treated as a single lease.

When are transactions "linked"?

Transactions A and B are "linked" if:

- they form part of a "single scheme, arrangement or series" of transactions, and

- the purchaser in transaction A is the same as, or is connected with, the purchaser in transaction B, and
- the vendor in transaction A is the same as, or is connected with, the vendor in transaction B.

"Connected with" is defined in TA 1988 s 839, as supplemented by SI 3229/2005. It includes spouses and linear relatives, the owner of a company and companies controlled by the same people.

What is a "single scheme, arrangement or series"?

This phrase is not defined but is potentially quite wide. However we accept that transactions do not form a "series" just because one takes place after another. There must be some connection, though not necessarily interdependence, between the transactions. In particular we accept that transaction A is not linked to transaction B where the terms of transaction A (not limited to price and including the availability of the transaction in the first place) are in all respects identical to what they would have been had transaction B not existed.

Can land transactions be linked with non-land transactions?

Only land transactions and other land transactions can be linked. So the purchase of land cannot be linked with the purchase of chattels so as to affect the rate at which SDLT is charged on the land transaction (although there must be a just and reasonable apportionment of the total consideration in order to arrive at the chargeable consideration for SDLT purposes). Land transactions cannot be linked with share transactions.

Are land transactions in a chain linked?

Despite the use of the word 'linked' the concept of linking has nothing to do with the common conveyancing "chain", where A agrees to buy B's home and B agrees to buy C's home. There will be no linking here (unless A and C are the same person or connected with each other). "Linked transaction" relates to land transactions where the purchaser in each transaction is the same (or the purchaser in one is connected with the purchaser in the other) and the vendor in each transaction is the same (or the vendor in one is connected with the vendor in the other).

Disclosure of stamp duty land schemes

This article is about the new rules requiring certain persons to give HMRC information about certain tax planning arrangements, or proposals for those arrangements, relating to SDLT. The new rules ("the disclosure rules") came into force, as regards SDLT, on 1 August 2005.

This article is only a brief, non-technical, summary of the disclosure rules. Full guidance can be found on HMRC's website at: www.hmrc.gov.uk/aiu/ and anyone who is in doubt whether the disclosure rules apply to them should consult this guidance.

Broadly speaking the disclosure rules apply to

- any arrangements, or proposals for arrangements (a "scheme")
- which might be expected to result in an SDLT advantage for any person
- where that advantage is the main benefit, or a main benefit, of the scheme.

However the disclosure rules do not apply where

- the scheme will be used only for residential transactions, or
- the aggregate market value of all the property for which the scheme is expected to be used does not exceed £5 million.

There is also a list of some schemes where disclosure is not required.

The primary duty to disclose rests with "promoters", that is, those who make schemes available to others. However in certain circumstances (for example, where the promoter is off-shore) users of schemes are under a duty to disclose.

Part II ST

Where a promoter is under a duty to disclose a disclosure must be made within five days of the scheme being made available. Where a user is under a duty to disclose because the promoter is off-shore the time limit is again five days from the date of the first land transaction where he or she uses the scheme. In other circumstances where the user is under a duty to disclose the time limit is 30 days from the date of the first land transaction where he or she uses the scheme. The guidance explains how a disclosure should be made and what it needs to contain, and also gives contact details for any enquiries.

STAMP DUTY LAND TAX (SDLT) TECHNICAL NEWS 3

BUDGET 2006 AND FINANCE ACT 2006 CHANGES

This article summarises the changes made to SDLT legislation by The Stamp Duty Land Tax (Amendment to the Finance Act 2003) Regulations 2006 (SI 2006/875) ("the Treasury Regulations on consideration") and by Finance Act 2006.

The Treasury regulations on consideration

The Treasury Regulations took effect on 12 April 2006, but the treatment for which they provide will in practice be applied for earlier transactions (see below).

The main provisions on what is and what is not chargeable consideration are in FA 2003 Sch 4. The Treasury Regulations amend Schedule 4 to provide that certain amounts do not count as chargeable consideration as follows:

(a) The payment by a tenant of a landlord's reasonable costs on, or incidental to, the grant of a lease, or an obligation to pay such costs, does not count as chargeable consideration. Note that this will cover the reasonable costs of an extension to the lease since this is treated in law as the grant of a new lease.

(b) The payment by a tenant of a landlord's costs under the statutory provisions governing the enfranchisement or extension of leases of flats and long leases of houses, or an obligation to pay such costs, does not count as chargeable consideration.

(c) Where there is a "transfer of value" for inheritance tax purposes (including a potentially exempt transfer) or a person becomes entitled to property under a will or intestacy, then any liability or potential liability of the donee or beneficiary for inheritance tax relating to the transfer, and any payment of such inheritance tax by the donee or beneficiary or agreement by them to pay such tax, does not count as chargeable consideration.

(d) Where there is a disposal for the purposes of capital gains tax which is otherwise than by way of a bargain made at arm's length (for example, a gift), or is treated as such because it is between connected persons, then any liability or potential liability of the transferee for capital gains tax on the disposal, and any payment of such tax by the donee or agreement by them to pay such tax, does not count as chargeable consideration, provided there is no other chargeable consideration for the transaction.

(e) An obligation on an agricultural tenant to surrender his or her entitlement to Single Farm Payment to the landlord on termination of the lease does not count as chargeable consideration.

Note that the exemption in (*a*) does not apply where a purchaser pays or agrees to pay vendor's costs on the transfer of a freehold (except on the statutory enfranchisement of a lease).

As all these areas were ones where the treatment before the Regulations was in doubt HM Revenue & Customs (HMRC) will accept that the treatment in the Regulations should be applied for all transactions since the introduction of SDLT.

Finance Act 2006 measures

(1) Leases

(*a*) Variations of leases to increase the rent

By virtue of FA 2003 Sch 17A para 13 the variation of a lease to increase the rent is treated as the grant of a new lease in consideration of the increase in rent.

Finance Act 2006 restricts paragraph 13 so that unless the increase is an "abnormal" increase (see below) there is a charge only if the variation takes place before the end of year 5 of the lease. This means in particular that where a lease was subject to stamp duty (not SDLT) when originally granted there will never be an SDLT charge if the lease is varied to increase the rent (but not varied in any other way) after the end of year 5. This change applies where the variation is on or after 19 July 2006.

Finance Act 2006 also puts it beyond doubt that statutory rent reviews under the legislation governing agricultural tenancies are not variations of the lease.

It follows that when calculating the net present value of the rent under such tenancies a reasonable estimate must initially be made of the rent for the first five years, with that estimate being revised by a further return after five years or once the rent for the first five years becomes certain (see SDLTM12200–12202 (page 17 of the Leases chapter)

(*b*) "Abnormal" increases in rent

FA 2003 Sch 17A paras 14 and 15 provide for a charge on "abnormal" increases in rent following the end of year 5. As a result of Finance Act 2006 the "abnormal" increase provisions apply whether the increase is provided for in the lease or is a variation of the lease.

The Act also simplifies the definition of what constitutes an "abnormal" increase. In practice only very large increases in rent (at least doubling) can possibly be 'abnormal'. The "abnormal" increase provisions apply only to leases which were subject to SDLT when originally granted.

(*c*) "Backdating" a renewal lease

It often happens that on the expiry of a lease the tenant remains in occupation while negotiations for a new lease take place and then after a time a new lease is granted.
The term of this new lease is sometimes expressed to commence from the day after the expiry of the old lease. The normal rule in England & Wales in Northern Ireland is that the term of a lease cannot commence earlier than the date the lease is granted.
Finance Act 2006 disapplies this rule where the "backdating" described above takes place so that for SDLT purposes the term of the new lease commences on the date stated in the new lease. This treatment applies only where the old lease was subject to SDLT when originally granted. This change applies where the new lease is granted on or after 19 July 2006.

(*d*) Agreement for lease followed by the grant of the lease

FA 2003 Sch 17A para 5 provides for special treatment where leases of the same premises are granted (whether at the same time or not) to take effect one after the other and the grants are "linked transactions".

Finance Act 2006 makes it clear that this treatment does not apply where an agreement for lease (including, in Scotland, missives of let which do not themselves constitute a lease) is "substantially performed" (and so is treated as a lease) and subsequently a lease is granted in pursuance of the agreement.

This change applies where substantial performance of the agreement takes place on or after 19 July 2006.

(2) Partnerships

(*a*) Limitation of the charge on transfers of a partnership interest

FA 2003 Sch 15 para 14 provides for an SDLT charge on the transfer of a partnership interest where the partnership property consists of or includes land.

The charge is based on the market value of the land and the proportionate interest transferred. Finance Act 2006 restricts this charge to partnerships whose sole or main activity is investing in or dealing in land. There will no longer be an SDLT charge on transfers of partnership interests in other partnerships such as professional partnerships, farming partnerships or partnerships carrying on a trade which is not land-related.

For partnerships which are still subject to an SDLT charge on the transfer of a partnership interest Finance Act 2006 removes a potential double charge where a transfer of a partnership interest is accompanied by the extraction of money by a partner.

These changes apply to all transfers on or after 19 July 2006.

(*b*) Removal of "actual consideration"

Under the provisions of FA 203 Sch 15 there is a charge where property is transferred into a partnership by a partner (or someone connected with them) or is transferred by a partnership to a partner or an ex-partner (or someone connected with them).

The charge was partly based on a proportion of the market value of the land and partly based on "actual consideration" given by the transferee. In practice it was not always clear what constituted "actual consideration".

Finance Act 2006 removes the references to "actual consideration" so that (except for some transfers where all the partners are bodies corporate) the charge is based solely on a proportion of market value.

This change applies to all transactions where the effective date is on or after 19 July 2006.

(3) Reallocation of property in a settlement

It is possible for a settlement to be made up of "sub-funds", each sub-fund having particular beneficiaries. Concern has been expressed that the reallocation of property between sub-funds, which trustees may undertake from time to time to balance the interests of beneficiaries, may give rise to an SDLT charge.

We are satisfied that there is no SDLT charge where the beneficiaries are purely passive and play no part in the reallocation. Finance Act 2006 also makes it clear that a mere requirement that beneficiaries should consent to the reallocation does not of itself give rise to an SDLT charge. HMRC will apply this treatment to all reallocations since the introduction of SDLT.

(4) Alternative property finance

The reliefs for alternative property finance in FA 2003 ss 71A to 73 which formerly applied only to transactions between a financial institution and one or more individuals, have been extended (with effect from 19 July 2006) to transactions between a financial institution and any person(s), individual or corporate.

COMPARATIVE SDLT TREATMENT OF LEASE EXTENSIONS AND RENEWALS

An article on this subject was included within issue 1.

Practitioners should now read the revised SDLT lease manual (which will be available shortly on our website) to obtain more up-to-date information.

CONSIDERATION

The amount of consideration that should be shown at question 10 on the SDLT1 land transaction return is the consideration given for the subject-matter of the transaction. In most cases this will be the amount shown on the transfer form (TR1) or lease, as the case may be, although this may require adjustment:

- if the figure does not include the price paid for fixtures,
- or if the amount paid for chattels does not represent a just and reasonable apportionment,
- or if the buyer has paid seller's costs (other than landlord's reasonable costs on the grant or enfranchisement of a lease).

If the amount actually paid on completion is less than the amount shown on the transfer document (TR1) or lease this would not normally affect the SDLT payable, since the figure entered on the transfer document (TR1) or lease, to the extent it is not paid on completion, is acknowledgement of a debt. In addition if this is the figure stated in the contract there is a contractual promise to pay this figure.

SDLT IMPLICATIONS OF SOME COMMON LAND TRANSACTIONS ASSOCIATED WITH MARRIAGE, DIVORCE AND CIVIL PARTNERSHIP

We have recently received several enquiries on the SDLT implications of property transfers on marriage, divorce and civil partnerships.

Where a couple are getting married/entering into a civil partnership/setting up home together and want to transfer one partner's property into their joint names

There is no SDLT relief for transactions in connection with marriage or entering into a civil partnership.

SDLT is charged where an interest in land is transferred for consideration. Consideration will include:

- any cash payment and
- any assumption of liability to pay a mortgage. The liability assumed is taken to be a proportion of the outstanding mortgage corresponding to the proportion of the share of the property which is acquired.

Example

A house is valued at £180,000. The transferring partner has equity of £90,000 and there is an outstanding mortgage of £90,000.

The transferee partner pays a cash sum equivalent to half the equity and acquires a 50% share in the property.

The consideration in this case will be the cash payment (£45,000) plus 50% of the outstanding mortgage (£45,000) = £90,000. As this is below the stamp duty land tax threshold of £125,000 there will be no tax to pay.

Although there is no tax to pay, details of the transaction must be returned in a land transaction return.

(Note: for this purpose joint tenants are treated as each owning a 50% share in the property.)

Where a couple are divorcing/dissolving a civil partnership/splitting up and want to transfer a property from their joint names into the sole ownership of one partner

A transaction of this kind will be exempt from SDLT if it is effected in pursuance of a court order or an agreement between the parties in connection with divorce, nullity of marriage or judicial separation, or the dissolution of a civil partnership (FA 2003 Sch 3).

In this case the transaction can be self-certified to the Land Registry using form SDLT 60 and no land transaction return is needed.

Otherwise, SDLT will be charged, based on the consideration given for the transfer including:

- any cash payment and
- any assumption of liability to pay a mortgage. The liability assumed is taken to be a proportion of the outstanding mortgage corresponding to the proportion of the share of the property which is acquired.

Example

A house is valued at £350,000. The partners have equity of £250,000 and there is an outstanding mortgage of £100,000.

The transferee partner pays a cash sum equivalent to 50% of the equity and acquires sole ownership of the property.

The consideration in this case will be the cash payment (£125,000) plus 50% of the outstanding mortgage (£50,000) = £175,000. This is above the stamp duty land tax threshold of £125,000 and the tax due on the consideration at 1% will be £1,750.

Details of the transaction must be returned in a land transaction return in the usual way.

GOODWILL

Our helpline continue to receive many queries about goodwill, which they are unable to answer.

As mentioned in the previous edition, issues relating to the categorisation of goodwill, or the valuation of free goodwill where an apportionment is required require specialist advice and should be referred to the Valuation Office Agency (VOA).

For example the VOA rather than staff on our Helpline have the expertise to decide how much of a hotel's goodwill is due to its location (inherent goodwill, part of the land) and how much is due to its reputation (something else).

They can also offer advice on such questions as to whether the reputation of a hotel can be transferred (involving the personality and skills of staff) and is that chargeable and whether the expertise of a chef connected to a restaurant is chargeable.

SDLT: GUIDANCE ON PARAGRAPH 2(4A) OF SCHEDULE 7, FINANCE (NO 2) ACT 2003

Practitioners should note that Paragraph 2(4A) of Schedule 7 Finance Act 2003, inserted by paragraph 19 of Schedule 10, Finance (No 2) Act 2005, introduces new restrictions on the availability of SDLT group relief under Schedule 7, F.A. 2003. Further details are on our website at Stamp Duty Land Tax: Guidance on Paragraph 2(4a) of Schedule 7, Finance (No 2) Act 2003.

STAMP DUTY LAND TAX (SDLT) TECHNICAL NEWS 4

SDLT CHANGES INCLUDED IN THE PRE-BUDGET REPORT

As part of the Pre-Budget Report published on 6 December 2006 the Government has announced measures to counter schemes designed to avoid stamp duty land tax. The measures are contained in Regulations made by the Treasury, which have effect (subject to transitional provisions) for transactions taking place on or after 6 December 2006.

The Stamp Duty Land Tax (Variation of the Finance Act 2003) Regulations 2006

1. The Regulations were made by HM Treasury under powers contained in FA 2003 s 109. They have immediate effect but will cease to have effect after 18 months and accordingly they will be replaced by permanent provisions in Finance Bill 2007.

2. The substantive part of the Regulations is the Schedule. The Schedule consists of two paragraphs. Paragraph 1 inserts a new section 75A into Finance Act 2003. Paragraph 2 amends the provisions in Part 3 of FA 2003 Sch 15 Part 3 dealing with certain partnership transactions. Note that paragraph 2 is an anti-avoidance provision even though it is not explicitly described as such.

3. Statutory references are to Finance Act 2003 unless otherwise specified.

New section 75A

4. New section 75A applies where

- one person disposes of a chargeable interest and another person acquires that interest, or a chargeable interest derived from it, and
- a number of transactions ("scheme transactions") are involved in connection with the disposal and acquisition, and
- the total SDLT payable in respect of all the scheme transactions is less than the amount that would be payable on a notional land transaction effecting the acquisition (the "tax saving" test).

5. "Chargeable interest" is defined in section 48. The chargeable consideration for the notional land transaction that is taken into account for the tax saving test is discussed below.

6. The phrase "involved in connection with" implies that there must be some connection between the disposal and acquisition on the one hand and the transactions on the other which goes beyond the fact that a number of transactions happen in chronological order. However it is not necessary that the transactions should be interdependent.

Example

V sells two properties at arm's length to third party purchasers N1 and N2. At some later stage, and in transactions which are not connected in any way with the purchases by N1 and N2, P buys both properties at arm's length. These transactions would not be within section 75A.

7. Where section 75A applies the individual scheme transactions are disregarded for SDLT purposes and SDLT is instead charged on the notional land transaction.

8. The chargeable consideration for the notional land transaction (and for the tax saving test) is the largest amount (or aggregate amount) given or received by any person in respect of the scheme transactions.

9. In determining what is a scheme transaction "transaction" includes any land transaction but is not limited to land transactions. New section 75A gives examples of what might be scheme transactions but the list is not exhaustive. In particular a scheme transaction includes any kind of arrangement whether it could otherwise be described as a transaction.

10. The effective date of the notional land transaction is the last date of completion of the scheme transactions or, if earlier, the last date on which a contract in respect of the scheme transactions is substantially performed.

11. For the purposes of section 75A an interest in a partnership is treated as a chargeable interest so far as it concerns land owned by the partnership.

12. The notional land transaction attracts any relief which it would attract if it were an actual land transaction.

13. Some reliefs involve a number of transactions where the tax saving test may be satisfied. Accordingly section 75A does not apply where the tax saving test is satisfied by reason only of sections 71A to 73 (alternative property finance) or a provision in Schedule 9 (right to buy, shared ownership leases, etc).

Examples

14. The following examples illustrate the application of section 75A on the assumption that the tax saving test is satisfied. **HM Revenue & Customs does not accept that the tax saving test is necessarily satisfied in any of these examples.**

Part II ST

(1) V grants a 999-year lease to N for no premium and a peppercorn rent. V assigns the freehold reversion to P for a nominal sum. P pays N £X in consideration of N's agreement to vary the lease by the insertion of a provision giving the landlord the right to terminate the lease for no payment. P exercises the right to terminate.

The notional land transaction is the acquisition of the freehold by P with chargeable consideration of £X.

(2) V grants a 999-year lease to N for no premium and a peppercorn rent. The lease includes a right for the landlord to terminate the lease on payment of £X to the tenant. V assigns the freehold reversion to P for a nominal sum. P exercises the right to terminate and pays N £X. The notional land transaction is the acquisition of the freehold by P with chargeable consideration of £X.

(3) V grants a 999-year lease to P for no premium and a peppercorn rent. The lease gives the landlord a right to terminate it within 14 days of the date of grant. P offers to pay V £X if V allows the 14 days to elapse without exercising the right to terminate. V does so.

The notional land transaction is the grant of a 999-year lease by V to P with chargeable consideration of £X.

(4) V agrees to sell property to N for £10 million. N agrees to sub-sell the property to P for £5. Both transactions are completed at the same time.

The notional land transaction is the acquisition of the property by P and the chargeable consideration is £10 million (the largest amount received by any person in respect of the scheme transactions).

(5) V agrees to sell property to N Ltd for £10 million. N Ltd declares a dividend in favour of P, its sole shareholder, the dividend to consist of the property and to be paid at the same time as completion of the V–N Ltd contract. The contract is completed and the property transferred to P.

The notional land transaction is the acquisition of the property by P and the chargeable consideration is £10 million (the largest amount received by any person in respect of the scheme transactions).

Amendments to the partnership provisions

15. There are amendments to

- the charge on transfers into partnerships set out in paragraphs 10–12 of Schedule 15
- the charge on transfers out of partnerships set out in paragraphs 18–20 of Schedule 15
- the charge on transfers of an interest in a property-investment partnership set out in paragraph 14 of Schedule 15.

16. The amendments to paragraphs 10–12 of Schedule 15 concern the calculation of the "sum of the lower proportions" ("SLP"). Before amendment the calculation provided for the interest of partners connected with a transferor to be included in the calculation of SLP. The amendments restrict this so that interest of a partner connected with a transferor is included in the calculation of SLP only if that partner is an individual.

17. However where a partner is a member of the same group as a transferor the amendments provide for relief, so that the charge is reduced to what it would have been if the interest of that partner had been included in the computation of SLP. This relief is governed by the same provisions that apply to group relief, with minor modifications.

Example

A Ltd, B Ltd, C Ltd and D are partners, sharing profits 40:35:15:10. A Ltd and B Ltd are members of the same group, owned by Mr X. C Ltd is also owned by Mr X, but is not a member of the same group as A Ltd and B Ltd. D is unconnected.

A Ltd transfers property into the partnership. Before the amendments SLP would have been 90, so there would have been a charge on 10 per cent of the market value of the property. Following the amendments SLP is 40 because the interests of companies connected with the transferor are not included. So there is a charge on 60 per cent of the market value of the property. However relief is available in respect of B Ltd's 35 per cent interest to reduce the charge to 25 per cent of the market value. This relief will be withdrawn if (for example) B Ltd ceases to be a member of the same group as A Ltd while the partnership still owns the property.

18. The amendments to paragraphs 18–20 of Schedule 15 concern the calculation of the "'sum of the lower proportions" ("SLP"). Before amendment the calculation provided for the interest of partners connected with a transferor to be included in the calculation of SLP. The amendments restrict this so that interest of a partner connected with a transferor is included in the calculation of SLP only if that partner is an individual.

19. For paragraphs 18-20 there is no relief similar to that described in paragraph 19 above.

20. The amendments to paragraph 14 of Schedule 15 make two changes. First they provide that where there is a transfer of a partnership interest, and the transferee is a person connected with the transferor who is not an individual, there is no requirement (as there currently is in paragraph 14(1)(*b*)) for consideration to be given.

21. Second they clarify existing legislation to put it beyond doubt that the provisions for recovery of group relief apply where group relief is claimed on the transfer of a partnership interest.

22. Enquiries as to the application of these provisions to specific transactions should be made to the Birmingham Stamp Office.

Stamp Duty Land Tax on new zero carbon homes

In support of the target that by 2017 all new homes will be required to reach the zero carbon standard, this Pre-Budget report announces that a stamp duty land tax relief for the majority of new homes that meet the zero carbon standard will be introduced in 2007. The relief will be time limited but will help kick start demand for zero carbon homes through an incentive to homebuyers, and recognises that in order to raise energy efficiency standards significantly beyond where they are now the industry will have to modernise production methods and innovate through employment of new materials and technologies. Full details will be published at the time of the Budget 2007.

Part II ST

THE STAMP DUTY LAND TAX (VARIATION OF THE FINANCE ACT 2003) REGULATIONS 2006: INTERIM GUIDANCE ON SECTION 75A FINANCE ACT 2003

1. This article provides guidance on new section 75A Finance Act 2003, inserted by paragraph 1 of the Schedule to The Stamp Duty Land Tax (Variation of the Finance Act 2003) Regulations 2006 (SI 2006/3237). It supplements the Technical Note issued by HM Revenue & Customs on 6 December 2006.

2. The guidance in this article has been produced in response to enquiries and representations, as an interim measure to assist taxpayers and their advisers. It should not be taken as representing HM Revenue & Customs' settled view, nor as being of general application. The guidance has effect only for transactions to which the Regulations apply and not for transactions to which any provisions of Finance Act 2007 will apply. Revised guidance will be published for transactions to which any similar provisions of Finance Act 2007 might apply.

3. HM Revenue & Customs will accept that the 2006 Regulations may be applied subject to the following guidance:

- A construction contract is not a scheme transaction in relation to a land transaction where the circumstances are such that, by virtue of the decision in *Prudential*

Assurance Co Ltd v IRC [1992] STC 863 (see SDLTM04015), the consideration properly attributable to the construction contract is not part of the chargeable consideration for the land transaction
- The carrying out of works of construction, improvement or repair of a building or other works to enhance the value of land is not a scheme transaction in relation to the purchase of the land provided that the works are not carried out by the vendor or a person connected with the vendor.
- The purchase of assets other than land is not a scheme transaction in relation to a land transaction where the provisions of FA 2003 Sch 4 para 4 apply to the apportionment of consideration between the purchase of assets and the land transaction.
- A transfer of shares in a company or units in a unit trust which is not preceded by any land transaction in relation to which it might be a scheme transaction is not a scheme transaction in relation to any subsequent land transaction.
- A loan from a person who is not a party to, or connected with a party to, any other scheme transaction to fund the purchase of property is not a scheme transaction in relation to the purchase of the property.
- Where a land transaction qualifies for reconstruction relief or acquisition relief the issue of shares under FA 2003 Sch 7 para 7(2) or 8(2) is not a scheme transaction in relation to that land transaction.
- Where the only transactions are the transfer of a number of properties into a partnership by partners none of the transfers is a scheme transaction in relation to any of the other transfers.
- Where the only transactions are the purchase of land and a lease (or leases) of all or part of the land to a person not connected with the purchaser of the land the purchase is not a scheme transaction in relation to the lease(s) and vice versa.
- Land transactions involving separate parcels of land are not scheme transactions in relation to each other.

We have been asked about the availability of group relief in relation to transactions carried out in preparation for an acquisition to which FA 1986 s 75(acquisition relief) will apply. In particular concern has been expressed that because the transactions are carried out in preparation for the acquisition there may be "arrangements" which deny the availability of group relief under FA 2006 Sch 7 para 2.

There are two relevant types of arrangements:
- Arrangements whereby someone could obtain control of the transferee but not of the transferor ("control" arrangements) (paragraph 2(1) of Schedule 7).
- Arrangements whereby transferor and transferee will cease to be members of the same group by reason of the transferee ceasing to be a 75% subsidiary of the transferor or of a third company' ('de-grouping' arrangements) (paragraph 2(2)(*b*) of Schedule 7).

In many acquisitions to which section 75 Finance Act 1986 will apply both a change of control and a de-grouping will occur.

Paragraph 2(1) ends with a proviso to the effect that arrangements entered into with a view to an acquisition to which FA 1986 s 75 applies are not "control" arrangements denying group relief. Paragraph 2(2)(b) does not include a similar proviso. However in our view paragraph 2 must be read as a whole and the proviso must apply also to paragraph 2(2)(*b*), otherwise it would in practice be of no effect. In other words we accept that arrangements entered into with a view to an acquisition to which FA 1986 s 75 applies are not "de-grouping" arrangements denying group relief.

This guidance will be incorporated in the SDLT Manual in due course.

GROUP RELIEF "ARRANGEMENTS"

We have been asked about the availability of group relief in relation to transactions carried out in preparation for an acquisition to which FA 1986 s 75 (acquisition relief) will apply. In particular concern has been expressed that because the transactions are carried out in preparation for the acquisition there may be "arrangements" which deny the availability of group relief under FA 2006 Sch 7 para 2.

There are two relevant types of arrangements:

- Arrangements whereby someone could obtain control of the transferee but not of the transferor ("control" arrangements) (paragraph 2(1) of Schedule 7).
- Arrangements whereby transferor and transferee will cease to be members of the same group by reason of the transferee ceasing to be a 75% subsidiary of the transferor or of a third company ("de-grouping" arrangements) (paragraph 2(2)(*b*) of Schedule 7).

In many acquisitions to which FA 1986 s 75 will apply both a change of control and a de-grouping will occur.

Paragraph 2(1) ends with a proviso to the effect that arrangements entered into with a view to an acquisition to which FA 1986 s 75 applies are not "control" arrangements denying group relief. Paragraph 2(2)(*b*) does not include a similar proviso. However in our view paragraph 2 must be read as a whole and the proviso must apply also to paragraph 2(2)(*b*), otherwise it would in practice be of no effect. In other words we accept that arrangements entered into with a view to an acquisition to which FA 1986 s 75 applies are not "de-grouping" arrangements denying group relief.

This guidance will be incorporated in the SDLT Manual in due course.

STAMP DUTY LAND TAX: FINALITY AND "DISCOVERY"

1. After a land transaction return has been filed or amended HM Revenue & Customs (HMRC) may decide to open an enquiry into the return so that we can be satisfied that the correct amount of SDLT has been paid. Such an enquiry must be opened within a certain time period. For example, where a return is filed on time and no later amendment is made HMRC must open an enquiry within nine months of the filing date (the filing date is the date by which the return must be filed to avoid a penalty and in normal circumstances is 30 days after the effective date of the transaction). At the conclusion of the enquiry HMRC will decide whether the right amount of SDLT has (in our opinion) been paid. If we think the right amount of SDLT has not been paid we can amend the return in order to assess the right amount of tax. There is the right of appeal to an independent tax tribunal.

2. However in some circumstances HMRC can make an assessment even where an enquiry has not been opened during the nine-month period. Such as assessment is referred to as a "discovery" assessment (because we "discover" that not enough SDLT has been paid). In most cases a discovery assessment is made because we consider that tax has been underpaid because of the fraudulent or negligent conduct of the purchaser, a person acting on behalf of the purchaser or a business partner of the purchaser. This article is not concerned with fraudulent or negligent conduct and nothing in this article affects our approach where we consider there has been fraudulent or negligent conduct.

3. But a discovery assessment can also be made where, at the time the nine-month enquiry period came to an end or (if later) the time HMRC completed their enquiries, we could not reasonably have been expected, on the basis of the information available to us before that time, to have been aware that insufficient tax had been paid.

4. This provision is similar to an income tax provision, which was considered by the Court of Appeal in the case of Langham v Veltema [2004] STC 544. This case gave rise to some uncertainty among taxpayers, first, as regards the lack of finality for the taxpayer at the close of the enquiry window and second, as regards the inherent difficulty of complying with the law as expounded in the Court of Appeal.

5. For this reason we issued a Statement of Practice, SP1/06, in 2006 (Statements of Practice explain how we intend to apply the law in cases of uncertainty). This explained what taxpayers had to do to guard against the possibility of a subsequent discovery assessment.

6. We intend to apply the Statement of Practice to SDLT. However it would be very unusual for purchasers to have to make a disclosure in ordinary residential or small commercial transactions. For example it is very common in such transactions to apportion part of the purchase price to chattels. There is no need to disclose to us that you have done so. Similarly, on the sale of a business, there is no need to provide us with any information additional to that in box 1 of form SDLT4.

7. If purchasers or their advisers do feel that they need to protect themselves from discovery by making a disclosure in relation to a land transaction they should do so by writing to the Complex Transactions Unit in Manchester, quoting the UTRN, at or before the time they submit the land transaction return for that land transaction. Information disclosed in this way will be treated, for the purposes of FA 2003 Sch 10 para 30(4)(*a*), as if it had been contained in the land transaction return for that land transaction. Please do not send disclosures to the Rapid Data Capture Centre at Netherton, or put them in the same envelope as land transaction returns, as this causes difficulty for the automated processing system.

LEGISLATION GOVERNING PAYMENT OF SDLT

We have recently received queries concerning the statutory authority to send payment of any SDLT due in respect of a transaction.

The legislation (FA 2003 s 76(3)(*b*)) does not allow 30 days for payment following the "effective date" of the transaction but says that the return must be "accompanied" by payment of the total amount of tax due. In other words the legislation requires payment to be made at the same time as the return is delivered, whether that is 1 day or 29 days after the effective date.

This is obviously not practicable where the return has been delivered using the Stamp Taxes Online service, so it makes sense to allow an interval for payment after the return has been successfully filed online. This stands at 12 days, which we consider to be an appropriate interval. Payment should be received by us within 30 days of the "effective date" or 12 days of filing the return online, whichever is earlier. Interest only runs from the end of 30 days.

The issue of the SDLT5 certificate is dependant on the receipt of a correct and full return and as long as all of the information is entered on the return then a certificate can be issued before we receive the monies due.

Inevitably there will be delays when payment is sent by cheque and we recommend that if you are submitting your SDLT tax returns online then you should also pay electronically. Electronic payments are generally more efficient and secure than payment by post. Practitioners can pay electronically by BACS Direct Credit, Internet or Telephone banking, CHAPS or by Debit Card over the Internet.

Users of the Stamp Taxes Online Service or a third party product which generates the UTRN from the application itself, under which circumstances an SDLT payslip is not required, should always ensure that whichever payment method they choose, the Unique Transaction Reference Number (UTRN) is included on the electronic feed for the bank or written on the back of the cheque if sending payment by post.

WHEN AN SDLT1 NEEDS TO BE SUBMITTED WHERE AN AGREEMENT OR CONTRACT PREVIOUSLY NOTIFIED BECAUSE OF "SUBSTANTIAL PERFORMANCE" NEEDS TO BE NOTIFIED AGAIN ON "COMPLETION"

An article on this subject was included within Issue 1.

A substantially performed agreement for lease (SPAL) is treated as a lease. The grant of a lease is then for SDLT purposes another lease, which is linked for threshold purposes (but not for the purposes of paragraph 5 of Schedule 17A). So for SDLT purposes we have two leases, each of which needs an SDLT1 and SDLT4 (unless the actual lease can be self-certified). The actual lease benefits from a relief (paragraph 9 overlap relief) which reduces the rent, and it is the reduced figure that is used in the NPV calculation for the actual lease. Note that paragraph 9 relief works by reducing the rent on the new (or in this case actual) lease, not by giving credit for SDLT previously paid.

The only complication is if the threshold linkage gives rise to further tax on the SPAL, in which case a further return must be made to the Birmingham Stamp Office, in the form of a covering letter until forms are produced for further returns.

Within the 3rd paragraph of the article in issue 1, the phrase "completely separate" should read "separate (but almost certainly linked)".

LEASE TRANSACTIONS FOR SEVEN YEARS OR MORE WITH NO CHARGEABLE CONSIDERATION

A lease for seven years or more can be self-certified provided there is no premium and no rent of any monetary value (section 77(2A) FA 2003 as substituted by section 164(1) FA 2006). A peppercorn rent is of no monetary value. In practice we accept that rent of less than £1 p.a. is of no monetary value as the SDLT forms do not take account of pence.

In some circumstances there is no chargeable consideration on the grant of a lease even though the lease provides for rent. An example of this type of transaction is where there has been the grant of a lease in respect of which the entire rent has been fully taxed on substantial performance of an agreement for lease, perhaps from entry into occupation under licence. Overlap "relief" actually works by reducing the chargeable rent on the actual lease, normally to nil. Supposing that there is no premium, the actual lease appears not to be notifiable even though it reserves rent and may be for seven years plus.

If this is the case the lease can be self-certified but we would expect practitioners to explain the circumstances to the appropriate Land Registry in a covering letter.

. . .

STAMP DUTY LAND TAX (SDLT) TECHNICAL NEWS 5

CONTENTS

- SDLT Finance Act changes 2007
  The main SDLT changes included in the 2007 Finance Act (which received Royal Assent on 19 July 2007) as announced in Budget 2007 on 21 March 2007.
- Finance Act 2007 measure in relation to form SDLT 60
  Finance Act 2007 does not allow agents to sign the SDLT 60 self-certificate on clients' behalf or, in particular, to amend the existing paper form for this purpose.
- Section 75A Finance Act 2003
  Guidance on FA 2003 s 75A, which is intended to counter certain schemes which have the effect of reducing SDLT liability.
- Partnership property
  This article supersedes the guidance in draft SDLTM35100 as to when a chargeable interest is partnership property for SDLT purposes.
- SDLT Code of Practice 10 extension
  The extension of existing clearances so that as normal business practice, HMRC will provide businesses with their view of the tax consequences of significant commercial issues whenever there is uncertainty as included in proposals from the HMRC review of links with Large Business review as announced in Budget 2007.
- SDLT1 question 9 (are you claiming relief?)—the charities registration number that should be entered
  The charities registration number entered at question 9 should be that of the person which is the purchaser for SDLT purposes.
- SDLT6 Guidance Notes—guidance on completing SDLT1 question 12
  For transactions where SDLT is chargeable on the market value of the property acquired rather than the actual consideration paid, code 34 should be used unless it is an exchange in which case code 37 applies; the completion of the question is non-mandatory when the answer to question 2 is L.
- Stamp taxes online service—linked freehold transfer and grant of new lease
  Users can notify online a deal involving purchase of a freehold plus the grant of a lease (same parties).

- Consideration and exchanges
  The meaning of "in consideration of" within the provision charging SDLT by reference to the market value of the chargeable interest acquired which imposes a market value charge where one land transaction takes place wholly or partly in consideration of another land transaction.
- Section 77
  Clarification of issues under section 77.
- Transfer of property on winding up—loan from shareowners
  SDLT would not be chargeable in a situation where, for example a purchaser has not assumed any liability or given any other form of consideration.

SDLT FINANCE ACT CHANGES 2007

The main SDLT changes contained in the Finance Act 2007, which received Royal Assent on 19 July 2007 are:

- SDLT rates and thresholds remain unchanged by Budget 2007.
  For transactions with an effective date on or after 22 March 2007:
- Reliefs for alternative property finance will be extended, to allow dealings in the interest held by the financial institution to take place free of SDLT. Further details about this measure are published in [the] Technical Note[at] www.hmrc.gov.uk/so/further-provisions.htm.

Apart from the extension of reliefs for "alternative property finance" there were no changes which took effect before Royal Assent to the Finance Bill.

From Royal Assent to the Finance Bill:

- The relief from SDLT offered to shared-ownership leases will be replicated for shared ownership trusts (a new way of providing affordable housing).
- The exchange of property between connected persons will no longer be treated as a linked transaction for the purposes of SDLT.
- Existing stamp duty and SDLT reliefs for certain transfers of surplus school land under provisions in the School Standards and Framework Act 1998 will be repealed. These provisions are amended by the Education and Inspections Act 2006 and Regulations will be introduced to bring transactions under the amended provisions within the general SDLT relief for statutory transfers involving public bodies.
- The Government will make two minor changes to SDLT legislation which will facilitate development of electronic conveyancing and registration systems.
- There will be permanent provision to counter SDLT avoidance schemes, replacing the Regulations made on 6 December 2006. These provisions, in particular, increase the number of circumstances in which a charge on a partner in property investment partnership can arise, for example, where there are new properties added into the investment portfolio on or after Royal Assent and where there are changes to profit sharing ratios.
- For those of you who read documents placed on the HMRC website following Budget 2007, we regret that there was a slight discrepancy between what paragraph 3 of Budget Note 22 says about the effective date of the anti-avoidance measures and what was in the Finance Bill. **The Budget Note stated "This change will have effect for any transaction the effective date of which is on or after the date on which Finance Bill 2007 receives Royal Assent."** At the time of the Budget this was what we were planning to do but following further discussion of our draft legislation our intentions changed.
- **We would therefore like to clarify that as Clause 71 was enacted in its current form by the Finance Act 2007, the version of section 75A contained in the Act (and not that in the Regulations) will apply to any transaction on or after 6 December 2006, subject to the transitional provisions.**
- Changes will be made to the stamp duty and stamp duty land tax acquisition reliefs. A company that has purchased its own shares will no longer be regarded as a shareholder of itself for the purpose of the reliefs.

From 1 October 2007:

A time limited relief from SDLT for most zero-carbon homes on first acquisition will be introduced to help kick start the market for new technologies and techniques that will be needed to support the Government's ambition that all new homes be zero carbon by 2016. The relief will be available on the first sale of new zero-carbon homes from 1 October 2007. Please see more details [at] www.hmrc.gov.uk/budget2007/bn26.htm.

More detail on specific measures can be found on the Budget 2007 [at] www.hmrc.gov.uk/budget2007/index.htm page.

FINANCE ACT 2007 MEASURE IN RELATION TO FORM SDLT 60

Section 81 of the Finance Act 2007 which inserts a new FA 2003 Sch 11 para 2A only allows agents to sign an SDLT 60 self-certificate where this is in a form specified by HMRC for this purpose. This measure is intended to allow electronic submission of self-certificates to Registers of Scotland via the ARTL (Automated Registration of Title to Land) system and in due course to the Land Registry via the forthcoming e-Conveyancing system.

Although we had not intended to extend this facility to the paper SDLT 60 we will consider whether there is any merit to doing such. Meanwhile agents should not amend the form in order to sign it on their clients' behalf; it will not be accepted by the land registries.

SECTION 75A FINANCE ACT 2003

1. FA 2003 s 75A is intended to counter certain schemes which have the effect of reducing stamp duty land tax (SDLT) liability. Section 75A exists in two versions. The first was introduced by The Stamp Duty Land Tax (Variation of the Finance Act 2003) Regulations 2006 (SI 2006 No 3237) ("the Regulations"). The Regulations were made on 6 December 2006. The second was introduced by section 71 FA 2007 (which also introduces supplementary provision in sections 75B and 75C).

Commencement

2. The FA provisions have effect (replacing the provisions in Regulations) in respect of disposals and acquisitions if:
- the disposal (see below) takes place after 2 pm on 6 December 2006, and
- all the scheme transactions (see below) take place after that time.

3. However section 75C does not have effect where a disposal takes place before 19 July 2007 (the date of Royal Assent to FA 2007) and the effect of section 75C would be to impose a higher tax charge than that provided for in the Regulations.

4. The transitional provisions are set out in paragraphs 35–37 below.

General application of section 75A

5. Section 75A applies where:
- one person ("V") disposes of a chargeable interest,
- another person ("P") acquires that interest, or a chargeable interest derived from it, and
- a number of transactions ("scheme transactions"), including the disposal and acquisition, are involved in connection with the disposal and acquisition, and
- the total SDLT payable in respect of all the scheme transactions is less than the amount that would be payable on a notional land transaction effecting the acquisition (the "tax saving" test).

6. "Chargeable interest" is as defined in section 48. "Disposal" and "acquisition" have the extended meanings set out in section 43.

Scheme transactions

7. The term "transaction" includes in particular:
- a transaction which is not a land transaction;
- an agreement, offer or undertaking not to take specified action;
- any kind of arrangement whether or not it could otherwise be described as a transaction;

Part II ST

- a transaction which takes place after the acquisition by P of the chargeable interest.

8. Section 75A(3) gives examples of what may be scheme transactions:

- the acquisition by P of a lease deriving from a freehold owned or formerly owned by V;
- a sub-sale to a third person;
- the grant of a lease to a third person subject to a right to terminate;
- the exercise of a right to terminate a lease or to take some other action;
- an agreement not to exercise a right to terminate a lease or to take some other action;
- the variation of a right to terminate a lease or to take some other action.

Scheme transactions "involved in connection with" a disposal and acquisition

9. The first three bullet points in paragraph 5 above must be read together. Thus the first step is to identify a disposal and the relevant V, the second step is to identify an acquisition and the relevant P and the third step is to consider whether a number of transactions are "involved in connection with" the disposal and acquisition. In a complex scenario this process may need to be repeated with different identifications of V and P, possibly with different results.

10. The phrase "involved in connection with" implies that there must be some connection between the disposal and acquisition on the one hand and the transactions on the other which goes beyond the fact that a number of transactions happen in chronological order, and that they affect the same property.

11. In particular it is unlikely that (except on a transfer of rights, see below) section 75A can apply to a disposal by V and an acquisition by P where:

- neither P nor his associates nor his advisers have had any involvement in or any connection with transactions other than the one by which P acquired the property, and
- neither P nor his associates obtains any SDLT benefit from the way in which the acquisition is effected.

12. However section 75A will apply where the acquisition by P is effected by a "transfer of rights" within the meaning of section 45, for example a sub-sale. So if V agrees to sell to X and X agrees to sell on to P section 75A applies to the disposal by V and the acquisition by P whether or not P or his associates or his advisers had any involvement in or connection with the V-X contract.

13. Section 75A(1)(b) refers to the scheme transactions as being "involved in connection with" the disposal and acquisition. Thus scheme transactions need not necessarily be connected with each other. For example, if V agrees to sell to X and X agrees to sell to P the two transactions are "involved in connection with" the disposal by V and the acquisition by P even if V is unaware of the sale on by X.

14. There follow some examples where section 75A does not apply to a disposal by V and an acquisition by P because there are not a number of transactions involved in connection with the disposal and acquisition.

Examples

- V sells two properties at arm's length to third party purchasers N1 and N2. At some later stage, and in transactions which are not connected in any way with the purchases by N1 and N2, P buys both properties at arm's length. Section 75A does not apply as regards the disposal by V and the acquisition by P.
- V grants a long lease to X. At a later stage, and in a transaction which is not connected in any way with the grant of the lease, X assigns the lease to an unconnected third party P. P exercises a statutory right of enfranchisement. Section 75A does not apply as regards the disposal by V and the acquisition by P.
- V grants an option to purchase land to X. At a later stage, and in a transaction which is not connected in any way with the grant of the option, X assigns the benefit of the option to an unconnected third party P. P exercises the option. Section 75A does not apply as regards the disposal by V and the acquisition by P.
- V agrees to sell land to H. H agrees to sell on to his spouse W. These transactions are completed at the same time. At a later stage W sells on to an unconnected third

party P. Section 75A does not apply as regards the disposal by V and the acquisition by P (although section 75A will apply as regards the disposal by V and the acquisition by W).

- V agrees to sell land to P. P agrees to sell on to C. The transactions are completed at the same time. Section 75A does not apply as regards the disposal by V and the acquisition by P (although section 75A will apply as regards the disposal by V and the acquisition by C). The sale on to C is not "involved in connection with" the disposal by V and the acquisition by P because it does not in any way affect the nature of the interest acquired by P.
- There follow some examples where a number of transactions are involved in connection with a disposal by V and an acquisition by P.

Examples

(1) V grants a 999-year lease to N for no premium and a peppercorn rent. V assigns the freehold reversion to P for a nominal sum. P pays N £X in consideration of N's agreement to vary the lease by the insertion of a provision giving the landlord the right to terminate the lease for no payment. P exercises the right to terminate.

(2) V grants a 999-year lease to N for no premium and a peppercorn rent. The lease includes a right for the landlord to terminate the lease on payment of £X to the tenant. V assigns the freehold reversion to P for a nominal sum. P exercises the right to terminate and pays N £X.

(3) V grants a 999-year lease to P for no premium and a peppercorn rent. The lease gives the landlord a right to terminate it within 14 days of the date of grant. P offers to pay V £X if V allows the 14 days to elapse without exercising the right to terminate. V does so (an example of a scheme transaction which occurs after the acquisition of the chargeable interest by P).

(4) V agrees to sell property to N for £10 million. N agrees to sub-sell the property to P. Both transactions are completed at the same time. (See the note above on the application of section 75A where an acquisition is effected by means of a "transfer of rights").

(5) V agrees to sell property to N Ltd for £10 million. N Ltd declares a dividend in favour of P, its sole shareholder, the dividend to consist of the property and to be paid at the same time as completion of the V-N Ltd contract. The contract is completed and the property transferred to P.

The tax-saving test and notional consideration

15. If there is a disposal and acquisition, and a number of transactions are involved in connection with the disposal and acquisition, the final step is to consider the tax saving test. For this purpose it is necessary to identify the "amount that would be payable on a notional land transaction" and compare the SDLT payable on that amount with the sum of the amounts of SDLT payable in respect of the scheme transactions.

16. The amount that would be payable on a notional land transaction (referred to in this guidance as the "notional consideration") is specified in section 75A(5). It is the largest amount (or aggregate amount):

- given by or on behalf of any one person by way of consideration for the scheme transactions, or
- received by or on behalf of V (or a person connected with V) by way of consideration for the scheme transactions.

17. "Connected with" has the same meaning as in TA 1988 s 839.

18. The following show how the notional consideration is calculated.

Examples

HM Revenue & Customs does not accept that the tax saving test is necessarily satisfied in any of these examples.

- V grants a 999-year lease to N for no premium and a peppercorn rent. V assigns the freehold reversion to P for a nominal sum. P pays N £X in consideration of N's agreement to vary the lease by the insertion of a provision giving the landlord the right to terminate the lease for no payment. P exercises the right to terminate.

- The notional consideration is £X, the amount given by P and received by N.
- V grants a 999-year lease to N for no premium and a peppercorn rent. The lease includes a right for the landlord to terminate the lease on payment of £X to the tenant. V assigns the freehold reversion to P for a nominal sum. P exercises the right to terminate and pays N £X.
- The notional consideration is £X, the amount paid by P and received by N.
- V grants a 999-year lease to P for no premium and a peppercorn rent. The lease gives the landlord a right to terminate it within 14 days of the date of grant. P offers to pay V £X if V allows the 14 days to elapse without exercising the right to terminate. V does so (an example of a scheme transaction which occurs after the acquisition of the chargeable interest by P).
- The notional consideration is £X, the amount paid by P and received by V.
- V agrees to sell property to N for £10 million. N agrees to sub-sell the property to P for £5. Both transactions are completed at the same time.
- The notional consideration is £10 million, the amount received by V.
- V agrees to sell property to N Ltd for £10 million. N Ltd declares a dividend in favour of P, its sole shareholder, the dividend to consist of the property and to be paid at the same time as completion of the V-N Ltd contract. The contract is completed and the property transferred to P.

The notional consideration is £10 million, the amount received by V.

Incidental transactions

19. In calculating the notional consideration the consideration properly attributable to "incidental" transactions (on a just and reasonable apportionment) is disregarded. Incidental transactions are those that are **merely incidental** to the disposal by V and the acquisition by P.

20. Examples of incidental transactions are:
- the sale or supply of anything other than land (for example, the sale of chattels or moveables);
- the construction of a building on the subject matter of the disposal and acquisition;
- a loan to P secured by a mortgage, to enable P to pay for all or part of the chargeable interest he acquires.

21. However a transaction is not incidental if:
- it forms part of a process, or series of transactions, by which the disposal and acquisition are effected, or
- it is one of the examples of scheme transactions in section 75A(3) (paragraph 8 above), or
- (except in the case of the sale or supply of anything other than land) the disposal and acquisition is conditional on the completion of the transaction.

The effect of section 75A

22. Where section 75A applies:
- the individual scheme transactions are disregarded for SDLT purposes;
- there is instead a notional transaction effecting the acquisition of V's chargeable interest (that is the chargeable interest which was the subject matter of the disposal by V) by P;
- the chargeable consideration for the notional transaction is the notional consideration (see above).

23. Thus in the Examples in paragraph 19 above the notional transaction is as follows (assuming again that the tax saving test is satisfied) and the chargeable consideration is the notional consideration as stated above:
- The acquisition of the freehold by P.
- The acquisition of the freehold by P.
- The grant by V of a 999-year lease to P.
- The acquisition of the property by P.
- The acquisition of the property by P

24. The effective date of the notional transaction is the last date of completion of the scheme transactions or, if earlier, the last date on which a contract in respect of the scheme transactions is substantially performed.

25. Stamp duty land tax paid in respect of a land transaction which is disregarded because of the application of section 75A is treated as having been paid in respect of the notional transaction.

Other provisions

26. A transfer of shares or securities (or units in a unit trust scheme) is ignored for the purposes of section 75A if it would otherwise be the first of a series of scheme transactions (and several such transfers are likewise ignored if they all precede any other scheme transaction).

27. The notional transaction attracts any relief which it would attract if it were an actual land transaction. In addition the consideration attributable to any scheme transaction which would qualify for relief under section 60, 61, 63, 64, 65, 66, 67, 69, 71, 74 or 75, or Schedules 6A or 8, is disregarded in calculating the notional consideration.

28. Some reliefs involve a number of transactions where the tax saving test will almost certainly be satisfied. Accordingly, section 75A does not apply where the tax saving test is satisfied by reason only of sections 71A to 73 (alternative property finance) or a provision in Schedule 9 (right to buy, shared ownership leases, &c).

29. If any of the scheme transactions is entered into for the purposes of or in connection with the transfer of an undertaking or part of an undertaking for the purposes of paragraphs 7 or 8 of Schedule 7 (reconstruction and acquisition relief) then the notional transaction is also deemed to be entered into for such purposes or in such connection. This enables the notional transaction to qualify for reconstruction or acquisition relief if the other conditions for relief are satisfied.

30. The notional transaction will be subject to the market value rule in section 53 if P is a company connected with V.

31. If part of the consideration for the notional transaction is a land transaction entered into by V as purchaser, or by P as vendor, then the market value rules in paragraph 5 of Schedule 4 will apply.

32. An interest in a property investment partnership is treated as a chargeable interest for the purposes of section 75A.

33. Where V or P is a partnership the provisions in Part 3 of Schedule 15 apply as they would to the transfer of a chargeable interest into or out of a partnership.

Transitional provisions

34. Section 75A, and the Regulations, do not have effect in relation to:

- any scheme transaction which is effected in pursuance of a contract entered into and substantially performed before 2 pm on 6 December 2006 (the "relevant time");
- any other scheme transaction which is effected in pursuance of a contract entered into before the relevant time and which is not an "excluded transaction".

35. For this purpose, a scheme transaction effected in pursuance of a contract is an excluded transaction if:

- at or after the relevant time the contract is varied in a way that significantly affects the scheme transaction,
- the subject-matter of the scheme transaction is not identified in the contract in a way that would have enabled its acquisition before the relevant time,
- rights under the contract are assigned at or after the relevant time,
- the scheme transaction is effected in consequence of the exercise, at or after the relevant time, of any option, right of pre-emption or similar right, or
- at or after the relevant time there is an assignment, sub-sale or other transaction (relating to the whole or part of the contract's subject-matter) as a result of which a person other than the purchaser under the contract becomes entitled to call for a conveyance to him.

36. A contract is varied in a way that significantly affects the scheme transaction if (and only if):

- it is varied so as to substitute a different purchaser in relation to the scheme transaction,
- it is varied so as to alter the subject-matter of the scheme transaction, or
- it is varied so as to alter the consideration for the scheme transaction.

PARTNERSHIP PROPERTY

A chargeable interest is partnership property for SDLT purposes if:

- it is held by or on behalf of the partnership, or by all the members of the partnership, and
- it is held for the purposes of the partnership business.

(FA 2003 Sch 15 para 34.)

These two tests must both be satisfied in order for a chargeable interest to be partnership property. Each is a question of fact. Often there will be an agreement between the partners which will be determinative as to the facts in the particular case.

In practice whether a chargeable interest is or is not partnership property for SDLT purposes will be decided in similar manner as whether or not it is partnership property by virtue of section 20 of the Partnership Act 1890. So a chargeable interest acquired, whether by purchase or otherwise, on account of the firm, or for the purposes and in the course of the partnership business, will be partnership property for SDLT purposes.

The mere fact that a business is carried on in property belonging to one or more partners does not make that partner's chargeable interest partnership property. Where a chargeable interest is owned by all the partners then whether it is partnership property will depend upon the basis on which it is held by the co-owners.

It is unlikely (in England & Wales and Northern Ireland) that a chargeable interest in which the equitable interests were subject to an express declaration of joint tenancy on acquisition is partnership property unless there is clear evidence of a change of intention to bring the chargeable interest in as an asset of the partnership business.

There is further guidance on the definition of partnership property at BIM72058 (www.hmrc.gov.uk/manuals/bimmanual/BIM72058.htm). This article supersedes the guidance in draft SDLTM35100 (www.hmrc.gov.uk/so/pftmanual.htm#20).

SDLT CODE OF PRACTICE 10 EXTENSION

At Budget 2007, HM Revenue & Customs (HMRC) announced that it would take forward the proposals in the Review of Links with Large Business (www.hmrc.gov.uk/large-business/review-report.pdf) (published in November 2006). The second proposal was:

> "The extension of existing clearances so that as normal business practice, HMRC will provide businesses with their view of the tax consequences of significant commercial issues whenever there is uncertainty."

Code of Practice 10 (COP 10) (Information and Advice), the guidance on clearances, says that where there is genuine uncertainty about the meaning of the law HMRC will advise upon their interpretation of legislation passed in the last four Finance Acts. The proposal from the Review of Links with Large Business means that, by Budget 2008, regardless of when legislation was enacted, HMRC will provide advice on the tax consequences of genuine significant commercial issues.

Also announced at Budget 2007 (www.hmrc.gov.uk/large-business/review-2007.htm), was that during 2007/08, there would be an early extension of clearance work where there is genuine uncertainty regarding the interpretation of tax legislation (without time limit) in two particular areas of tax law:

- Stamp duty land tax from Royal Assent of Finance Act 2007; and
- Substantial Shareholding Exemption (SSE) from 01 June 2007

The Code of Practice 10 facility for the purpose of the Substantial Shareholding Exemption was reinstated on 1 June 2007 (www.hmrc.gov.uk/briefs/company-tax/brief4107.htm). Foll owing the Royal Assent of Finance Act 2007 on 19 July 2007 HMRC will now, in line with the commitment made at Budget 2007, be extending the application of the Code of Practice 10 for all businesses to areas of genuine uncertainty regarding stamp duty land tax without a time limit. This means that the Code of Practice facility will cover all stamp duty land tax legislation going back to its introduction in Finance Act 2003.

Clearance requests under Code of Practice 10 on stamp duty land tax matters should be submitted to: HM Revenue & Customs, Birmingham Stamp Office (COP 10), 9th Floor, City Centre House, 30 Union Street, Birmingham B2 4AR.

SDLT1 QUESTION 9 (ARE YOU CLAIMING RELIEF?)—THE CHARITIES REGISTRATION NUMBER THAT SHOULD BE ENTERED

It is not uncommon for a corporate trustee—for example a charity in its own right—to be trustee of charitable trusts that are not separate persons but have their own charity numbers.

The charities registration number entered at question 9 on the SDLT1 Return should be that of the person which is the purchaser for SDLT purposes, as this is also the claimant of the relief. Where the legal purchaser purchases as a bare trustee, the purchaser for SDLT purposes will be the beneficial owner.

SDLT6 GUIDANCE NOTES—GUIDANCE ON COMPLETING SDLT1 QUESTION 12

What form does the consideration take?—code 34 or 37?

For transactions where SDLT is chargeable on the **market value** of the property acquired rather than the actual consideration paid (for example, an exchange of properties where at least one of the interests is a major interest), **code 34** should be used at question 12 unless it is an exchange in which case code 37 applies. See the guidance below contained within the SDLT6 Guidance Notes for using codes 34 and 37.

Other (such as an annuity)—Code 34

Please see SDLTM06010 www.hmrc.gov.uk/manuals/sdltmanual/SDLTM06010.htm.

Any other consideration, in money's worth, not otherwise listed here, or, as noted above, the market value of the interest in land acquired should be notified using code 34 except for exchanges where code 37 should be used.

Within this section of the guidance, the reference to the market value of land under Code 34 is intended to refer back to the note about market value and Code 34 on the preceding page. However we agree that the reference in the guidance notes could be made clearer and will consider dividing the Code 34 guidance into two bullets; one for annuities, and one for market value cases.

The completion of question 12 is non-mandatory when the answer to question 2 is L.

The guidance within the SDLT6 Guidance Notes was changed in March 2007. Previously the guidance stated that SDLT1 question 12 was mandatory. However, following representations from users of the online service, we agreed to a change to the current version of the notes. Customers may now ignore question 12 if they have entered L at question 2.

STAMP TAXES ONLINE SERVICE—LINKED FREEHOLD TRANSFER AND GRANT OF NEW LEASE

Users can notify online a deal involving purchase of a freehold plus the grant of a lease (same parties). However as these are two different interests, the transactions have to be completed and submitted as separate transactions, as would be the case if completing on paper.

Each transaction should be marked as linked at 13.1 and the total consideration entered in 13.2. In question 10 the "total consideration" should be apportioned to each interest.

We have now taken steps to make our guidance (www.hmrc.gov.uk/so/online/completion.htm) on this clearer.

CONSIDERATION AND EXCHANGES

FA 2003 Sch 4 para 5 charges SDLT by reference to the market value of the chargeable interest acquired when

- one or more land transactions is entered into by a person (alone or jointly) as purchaser;
- wholly or partly in consideration of;
- one or more other land transactions being entered into by him (alone or jointly) as vendor;
- and the subject matter of any of the relevant transactions is a major interest (for example, the transaction is the transfer of a freehold, the grant of a lease or the assignment of a lease).

Put simply the provision imposes a market value charge where one land transaction takes place wholly or partly in consideration of another land transaction.

We have been asked about the meaning of "in consideration of" in this provision. This article replaces paragraphs 2 and 3 of the article in Technical Newsletter 2 (www.hmrc.gov.uk/so/tech-newsletter2.pdf). The contents of this article will be incorporated in the Manual in due course.

In many cases a contract will provide expressly that land transaction 1 is wholly or partly in consideration of land transaction 2 and vice versa. If so paragraph 5 of Schedule 4 clearly applies.

If there is no such express reference then it is in our view a question of fact whether land transaction 1 is in consideration of land transaction 2.

In our view it is the element of "reciprocity and mutuality", or "quid pro quo", or "give and take" that is crucial. Although land transactions are often preceded by a formal contract we do not consider that the existence of a prior contract is necessary in order for one land transaction to be in consideration of another. A contract that refers to both transactions will often be evidence that each is in consideration of the other but even in the absence of such a contract it might be clear from the circumstances that as far as the parties were concerned each transaction was in return for the other.

So if land transaction 1 is as a matter of fact in whole or part a quid pro quo for land transaction 2 then each is in consideration of the other.

Often an A to B land transaction takes place at the same time as one from B to A or to a person connected with A. In the absence of proof to the contrary, it would be inferred that land transaction 2 was a benefit in return for land transaction 1, and so each is in consideration of the other.

On the other hand, if land transaction 1 from A to B takes place at the same time as one from B to C (not connected to A), perhaps a lease of the land acquired by B, then in the absence of some linked benefit for A or a person connected with A, or some linked benefit from land transaction 1 for C or a person connected to C, then land transaction 1 would not be in consideration of land transaction 2. Such benefit might arise from an associated land transaction 3 from C to A.

Mere incidental benefit to A or a person connected with A which happens to arise from land transaction 2 would not be sufficient to make it be in consideration of land transaction 1.

Completion of the land transactions need not be at the same time. Land transaction 1 from A to B may be in consideration of an agreement by B to make land transaction 2 to A at a later date. Whether there is such an agreement would be a matter of fact and inference from fact. If land transaction 2 is soon after land transaction 1 then it is likely to have been agreed at the time of land transaction 1, but it would be possible to show that it arose because of some unexpected change of circumstance in the intervening period.

Nature of consideration

As regards the test for what is consideration we will be guided by the comments of the Court of Session in *Glenrothes Development Corporation v IRC* [1994] STC 74 (although this case concerned stamp duty the meaning of consideration is in our view the same for SDLT as it was for stamp duty, subject to any express provision to the contrary).

The Court indicated that "consideration" must be construed according to its ordinary meaning and not by reference to any technicalities peculiar either to English or to Scottish law. Thus for SDLT purposes "consideration" does not in our view have the technical meaning peculiar to the law of contract.

The judges made a number of comments about the nature of consideration for stamp duty purposes:

- "closely linked in its ordinary meaning to the principle of mutuality of contractual obligations" (the Lord President at page 80);
- "what the purchaser had to do in order to compel implementation by the seller of his obligations" (same page);
- "the ordinary meaning of the word involves the element of reciprocity or mutuality between the obligation to provide it and that or those in respect of which it is given" (Lord Morison at page 82);
- "something given or promised in return for something else" (Lord Mayfield at page 83);
- "the element of reciprocity or mutuality" (Lord Mayfield at page 84);
- "what the purchasers paid in exchange for implement of the seller's obligations to provide title" (Lord Mayfield at page 85).

SECTION 77

We are conscious that section 77 presents us with opportunities for simplification and deregulation and it is an area we shall continue to keep under review. For example, certain practitioners have suggested to us that it seems odd that they do not need to complete an SDLT1 Return for assignment (whole or part) of a short lease for small consideration but they do need to complete it for a surrender.

"Major interests"

In particular, we have recently received queries concerning "major interests" as described in section 77. For example, section 117 refers to fee simple or term of years, however there has been a difference in whether or not practitioners consider that granting a freehold right of way for say £100k is "major", and therefore use form SDLT60 to notify the transaction instead of an SDLT1 Return.

Our view is that the definition is, as the wording suggests, intended to mirror the wording of LPA 1925 s 1(1). The words "in equity" are intended to extend the scope of "major interest" to equitable interests which are equivalent to an estate capable of subsisting at law. So interests which are within section 1(2), such as those mentioned in section 1(2)(a), and their equitable equivalents, are not major interests.

In addition, we would not wish to argue that an undivided share was a major interest.

Freehold easements and easements for a term of years are not major interests.

A minor can be the purchaser of a chargeable interest

There is no reason why a minor should not be the purchaser of a chargeable interest for SDLT purposes. This would normally be by operation of paragraph 3 of Schedule 16.

TRANSFER OF PROPERTY ON WINDING UP—LOAN FROM SHAREOWNERS

We would not seek to argue that the dividend in specie should bear SDLT in a situation for example where A owns the shares of B Ltd. A lends money to the company to buy property, the loan being secured by mortgage on the property.

Later B Ltd is wound up and there is a transfer to A as beneficial owner of the equity. That is the reason for the Transfer. The loan is not released etc but obviously the mortgage will be taken off as the lender also owns the property because of the liquidation.

Clearly in this scenario A has not assumed any liability or given any other form of consideration.

STAMP DUTY LAND TAX (SDLT) TECHNICAL NEWS 6

CONTENTS

- Announcements made relating to SDLT in the Pre-Budget Report (October 2007)
  The announcements made relating to stamp duty land tax on 9 October 2007.
- HMT consultation on use of SPVs to avoid payment of SDLT and on extending the SDLT disclosure rules to residential property
  A consultation on these two subjects was issued by HM Treasury on 17 December. The closing date for comments is 25 January 2008.
- SDLT relief for zero-carbon homes
  Relief from SDLT for zero-carbon homes was introduced on 1 October 2007.
- 75A notional land transactions
  Advice on how 75A notional land transactions (either real or follow-ups), which have already been filed electronically should be filled (whether another electronic return should be filed or a paper version).
- Code of Practice 10 (COP 10) requests
  Code of Practice 10 (COP 10) requests for information and advice should always be sent to Birmingham Stamp Office.
- Surrender of a lease for little or no consideration
  What practitioners should do if the freeholder insists on a separate surrender deed.
- Provisions for relief from forfeiture of a lease
  The position where for example a mortgagee is seeking to obtain relief from forfeiture.

ANNOUNCEMENTS MADE RELATING TO SDLT IN THE PRE-BUDGET REPORT (OCTOBER 2007)

- Change in notification thresholds for land transactions (www.hmrc.gov.uk/pbr2007/pbrn21.pdf).

Please note that for leases the wording of the PBR Note at the end of paragraph 4 should have stated that:

"Leases will have to be notified when the lease is for a term of seven years or more and where any chargeable consideration is more than £40,000 or the annual rent is more than £1,000". (the relevant amendment is underlined).

- Changes to 2007 anti-avoidance legislation on partnerships (www.hmrc.gov.uk/pbr2007/pbrn22.pdf).
- Consultation on the use of special purpose vehicles to reduce SDLT liability on high value residential property transactions.

The Government has now issued a consultation document about the use of special purpose vehicles (SPVs) in the purchase of high value residential property. SPVs are increasingly being used to avoid payment of SDLT on high value residential property transactions. The consultation sets out how the Government intends to address the issue and explores the practicalities of introducing a charge on the use of SPVs. The consultation also proposes an extension of the disclosure rules to residential property worth £1 million or more. The document will be available on the Treasury website [www.hm-treasury.gov.uk/]. Any comments should be sent to: Property Tax Team, HM Treasury, 1 Horse Guards Road, London SW1A 2HQ.

STAMP DUTY LAND TAX: ENSURING FAIRNESS FOR ALL—A CONSULTATION DOCUMENT

In the recent PBR the Government announced that it would seek to explore the practicalities of introducing a charge on the use of special purpose vehicles on high value residential property and on extending the SDLT disclosure rules to residential property. On 17 December 2007 the Government published a consultation document seeking views on its proposals. More details about this consultation can be found on the HM Treasury website [www.hm-treasury.gov.uk/].

SDLT RELIEF FOR ZERO-CARBON HOMES

Budget 2007 announced that relief from SDLT for zero-carbon homes would be introduced from 1 October 2007.

Q. What is the definition of a zero-carbon home?

A. Homes must be "zero-carbon" over the course of the year. They can be connected to mains electricity and gas but will have to come with sufficient additional renewable power to cover the average consumption of a home over a year.

This means that the fabric of the building will have to be insulated and built to very high standards (triple glazing windows and air-tight walls, for example.) And will need to incorporate renewable energy technologies.

Q. How does the relief work?

A. New homes that meet the Treasury criteria for zero-carbon will be eligible to qualify only on the first sale. The relief will provide complete removal of SDLT liabilities for all homes up to a purchase price of £500,000.

In cases where the purchase price of a new home exceeds £500,000, the SDLT liability will be reduced by £15,000 and SDLT will be charged on the balance of the purchase price of the home above £500,000.

Q. What standard do homes have to meet to get the relief?

A. Houses must meet all of the following three tests:

Aspects of energy efficiency	*Evidence*
Heat loss parameter ("HLP")	The HLP of the dwelling calculated in accordance with the approved methodology must be no more than 0.8 Watts per square metre Kelvin (W/m^2K)
Dwelling CO2 emission rate ("DER")	The DER over the course of a year calculated in accordance with the approved methodology must be no more than zero kilograms per square metre ($kg/m^2/year$)
Net CO2 emissions	The net CO2 emissions from the dwelling over the course of a year calculated in accordance with the approved methodology must be no more than zero kilograms per square metre ($kg/m^2/year$)

Please see further details about these tests [www.hmrc.gov.uk/so/zero-carbon.htm].

Q. When can people start claiming?

A. The relief applies retrospectively to 1 October 2007.

Part II ST

Q. How do you claim the relief?

A. The relief is just like any other SDLT relief and can be claimed simply by ticking the appropriate box on the return confirming that you are entitled to it. You should use relief code 30 when claiming. This code will be available to online filers from the end of October 2007.

Q. Who does the test to verify entitlement to the relief?

A. An accredited assessor. The certification process is overseen by:

- In England and Wales:
  - Department for Communities and Local Government (DCLG)
- In Northern Ireland:
  - Department of Finance and Personnel (DFPNI)
  - Department for Social Development (DSDNI).

Q. Who pays for the test?

A. This is not the HMRC's responsibility but often developers will have had these tests done before they offer houses for sale and will give the certificate to the purchaser. If the developer has not had a test done then the onus is on the person claiming the relief (ie the purchaser) to show that a test has been done and the house is eligible for the relief. This includes the purchaser paying for any test.

Q. What if I have no certificate?

A. The onus is on the claimant to prove that the house entitles the relief to be claimed. The certification process for verifying whether a house meets the Treasury's zero-carbon standard is set out in legislation (The Stamp Duty Land Tax (Zero-Carbon Homes Relief) Regulations 2007).

Q. What does a certificate look like?

A. There is no set form for a certificate however it has to contain the following information:

- The address of the building, including postcode;
- Confirmation that the dwelling qualifies as a zero-carbon home;
- For dwellings in England and Wales only, the unique identifying number from the energy performance certificate if an energy performance certificate has been produced;
- The accredited assessor's full name;
- The name and address of the accredited assessor's employer, or if he is self-employed, the name under which he trades and his address; and
- In relation to dwellings in England and Wales only, the accreditation scheme, if any, to which the accredited assessor belongs;
- The date on which it was issued.

Q. Do flats qualify?

A. No—there were problems with incorporating flats into the test due to shared walls, communal space and heating facilities. The SDLT relief is currently restricted to the sale of new homes defined in primary legislation as a "building which has been constructed for use as a single dwelling, and has not been previously occupied". This definition is designed to capture most new homes—including terraced homes, semi-detached homes and bungalows—but it excludes new flats. The Government is considering whether to extend the relief to new flats.

Q. Can I claim a relief for [a] house that is not new?

A. No. The relief is for new build houses.

Q. Can I claim on the second or subsequent sale?

A. No. The relief is restricted to the 'first point of sale' of a new zero-carbon home. This fits in with the key objective of the measure, which is to kick-start the building of ZCHs by stimulating consumer demand. Once these homes are built we expect the benefit in terms of energy savings (reductions in carbon dioxide emissions) to remain in the home for many years. There would be no value to the taxpayer to extend the relief to second and subsequent sales.

Q. Why is the relief time limited?

A. To encourage the development of these houses now. It's intended that all new houses are built to a zero-carbon standard will be mandatory by 2016, so a relief beyond this point would not represent value for money to the taxpayer. The exemption is time limited for 5 years until 30 September 2012 but before the end of the time limit the Government will review the effectiveness of the relief and consider the case for an extension.

Q. What about linked transactions?

A. If the relief is claimed for one home in series of transactions the relief will only apply to that one house which is zero-carbon eg linked transaction involving 10 homes worth total of £1m, relief is allowed only on the zero-carbon home—related to what its value is.

- Please see further details [www.hmrc.gov.uk/so/zero-carbon.htm].

75A NOTIONAL LAND TRANSACTIONS

Some have asked about how notional land transactions affected by the anti-avoidance legislation introduced at Finance Act 2007 should be notified to HMRC. HMRC wish to avoid any confusion that could arise if practitioners try to file an electronic return or a paper version in respect of 75A notional land transactions in addition to a return for the real transaction. Practitioners are therefore advised that they should notify details of the notional transaction separately and by letter to the Birmingham Stamp Office. The letter should set out the relevant details about the notional transaction.

CODE OF PRACTICE 10 (COP 10) REQUESTS

Code of Practice 10 (COP 10) requests for information and advice should only be sent to Birmingham Stamp Office and not directed to the Stamp Taxes Policy Team in London. Our customer service standards require us to provide a 28-day turnaround on these. We are unable to promise early responses, although we will do our best to do so.

SURRENDER OF A LEASE FOR LITTLE OR NO CONSIDERATION

Where a lease is surrendered by operation of law no chargeable consideration is normally paid for the surrender. If the surrendered lease is registered, the Land Registry will need an SDLT60 self certificate in respect of the surrender except where a new lease of the same property has been granted—either expressly or by a deed of variation that takes effect as an implied surrender and regrant. Land Registry Practice Guide 26 (para 5.2) confirms that no SDLT60 is required in those circumstances.

If there is an express deed of surrender the Land Registry will always require an SDLT60.

Although as a matter of law a surrender of a lease is not an assignment of it, for SDLT purposes the surrender of a chargeable interest is treated as a disposal and acquisition of it under FA 2003 s 43(3)(b), in other words it is treated as an assignment. HMRC therefore suggest that surrenders of leases are notified in exactly the same way as assignments of leases under s 77(2A).

PROVISIONS FOR RELIEF FROM FORFEITURE OF A LEASE

Q. What is the position where for example a mortgagee is seeking to obtain relief from forfeiture of a lease?

Various types of breach of leasehold covenants are within section 146 of the Law of Property Act 1925. It has provisions for relief from forfeiture of a lease in certain circumstances. It defines lessee and underlessee to include persons deriving title under them, such as a mortgagee.

Section 146(2) is one route available to a mortgagee. It retrospectively restores the lease (hence a mortgagee who has meanwhile been in possession could not be liable for mesne profits). One view. (Fisher & Lightwood, Law of Mortgage, 12th edition) is that the lease is restored for the lessee (but so that the mortgagee can sell it) in which case the mortgagee would not have personal liability to the lessor under the lease.

That subsection does not apply, for example, to forfeiture for non-payment of rent. The lessee or a person deriving title under it might apply for relief under some relevant other provision—Supreme Court Act 1981 s 38, County Courts Act 1984 s 138(9A)–(9C), Common Law Procedure Act 1852 ss 210 and 212.

If the lease is vested in the mortgagee (without a new lease) under such a provision it would be do so by way of security and so the vesting is exempt from SDLT (the lease does not become beneficially owned by the mortgagee, in satisfaction of the debt).

The other route is under section 146(4) of the Law of Property Act 1925. An underlessee can be granted relief by way of a new lease (not retrospective). If the old lease had been within SDLT there could be overlap relief for the SDLT on the new lease to the underlessee. That relief could also apply to a negotiated new lease taken by an underlessee or one which the lessee guarantor is required to take or is entitled to take in pursuance of the guarantee—in that case the lease to the guarantor does not have to replace the lessee's lease and I suppose that it might include an overriding lease taken by virtue of an authorised guarantee agreement under the Landlord and Tenant (Covenants) Act 1995.

Section 146(4) also applies to vest a new lease in a mortgagee. Overlap relief is not relevant but the vesting is exempt from SDLT as it is by way of substituted security and so subject to a proviso for redemption etc (not acquired beneficially in satisfaction of the debt).

None of these situations should trigger a charge to SDLT

APPENDIX 2. STATEMENTS OF PRACTICE

Contents

SP 3/84 (13 MARCH 1984)
STAMP DUTY: CONVERTIBLE LOAN STOCK

Transfers of certain loan capital are exempted from stamp duty by FA 1986 s 79. [Subsection (5)] provides that the exemption is not available where the loan capital carries an unexpired right of conversion into shares or other securities or to the acquisition of shares or other securities, including loan capital of the same description. The Board of Inland Revenue are advised that [subsection (5)] does not exclude from the exemption loan capital which carries an unexpired right of conversion into or acquisition of loan capital which itself comes within terms of the exemption.

NOTE

This Statement was revised in Booklet IR131 Supp (November 2000), and is printed here as revised.

Part II ST

SP 6/90 (27 APRIL 1990)
CONVEYANCES AND TRANSFERS OF PROPERTY SUBJECT TO A DEBT: SA 1891 S 57

INTRODUCTION

1. Since the abolition of the duty on voluntary dispositions in 1985, many enquiries have been received about the stamp duty chargeable on conveyances etc subject to a debt where *no* chargeable consideration (*eg* money or stock) unrelated to the debt is given by the transferee. This Statement of Practice sets out the Board's view of the correct stamp duty treatment of such conveyances.

2. For the sake of completeness it should be noted that where chargeable consideration unrelated to debt *is* given by the transferee, s 57 renders the conveyance liable to ad valorem duty on the aggregate of that consideration and the debt whether the transferee assumes liability for the debt or not (*IRC v City of Glasgow Bank* (1881) 8 R (Ct of Sess) 389, 18 SLR 242).

SA 1891 S 57

3. The most commonly misunderstood applications of s 57 arise where:

— a mortgaged property held in the name of one spouse is transferred into the joint names of both spouses;
— a mortgaged property held in the name of one spouse or in their joint names is transferred into the sole name of the other;
— a mortgaged business property, frequently farmland, is conveyed from a sole proprietor to a family partnership or from a family partnership to a fresh partnership bringing in other members of the family.

4. The critical question is whether the transaction to which the conveyance gives effect is or is not a sale. If it is, s 57 will apply and the conveyance will be chargeable to ad valorem duty on the amount of the debt assumed. If it is not, then s 57 will not apply and ad valorem duty will not be payable.

EXPRESS COVENANTS

5. Where property is transferred subject to a debt, the transferee may covenant, either in the instrument or by means of a separate written undertaking, to pay the debt or indemnify the transferor against his personal liability to the lender. Such a covenant or undertaking constitutes valuable consideration and, in view of s 57, establishes the transaction as a sale for stamp duty purposes.

6. Where the transferor covenants to pay the debt and the transferee does not assume any liability for it, no chargeable consideration has been given and there is no sale. The transfer would then be a voluntary disposition—ie an unencumbered gift capable of being certified as Category L under the Stamp Duty (Exempt Instruments) Regulations 1987 (SI 1987/516)—and so exempt from the 50p charge that would otherwise arise.

IMPLIED COVENANTS

7. Where no express covenant or undertaking is given by the transferee, the Board are advised that, except in Scotland, a covenant by the transferee may be implied. That makes the transaction a sale, as in para 4 above.

8. Such an implied covenant may be negated if there is evidence that it was the intention of the parties at the time of the transfer that the transferor should continue to be liable for the whole of the mortgage debt. Where evidence of such a contrary intention exists, the transfer would again be treated for stamp duty purposes as a voluntary disposition.

9. Where property in joint names subject to a debt is transferred to one of the joint holders (though with no cash passing), a covenant by the transferee to indemnify the transferor may be implied even where both parties were jointly liable on the mortgage.

AMOUNT CHARGEABLE

10. Where a conveyance of property subject to a debt is chargeable to ad valorem duty and the express or implied covenant by the transferee relates only to part of the debt, only the amount of that part is treated as chargeable consideration within s 57. A certificate of value under [FA 1999 Sch 13 para 6] may, where appropriate, be included in the conveyance where the relevant amount of the debt does not exceed the amount certified.

OTHER PROVISIONS

11. The foregoing does not affect any statutory exemption from duty that may apply, *eg* that for transfers to a charity (FA 1982 s 129) and that available for certain transfers of property from one party to a marriage to the other in connection with their divorce or separation (FA 1985 s 83(1) and Stamp Duty (Exempt Instruments) Regulations 1987, Category H).

PROCEDURE

12. Where the applicant is satisfied that the conveyance or transfer is made on sale, it may be sent or taken for stamping with a remittance for the duty payable. If the transfer contains an appropriate certificate of value—see para 10 above—it may be sent direct to the Land Registry in the usual way if appropriate. In either case, if the amount of the debt outstanding is not given in the conveyance or transfer the amount should be stated in a covering letter.

13. Where the conveyance or transfer contains a covenant by the transferor to pay the debt (see para 6) and is certified as within the Stamp Duty (Exempt Instruments) Regulations 1987, Category L it should also be sent direct to the Land Registry if appropriate.

14. In any other case where the applicant believes that the conveyance or transfer effects a voluntary disposition—see para 8 above—it should be presented for adjudication accompanied by a statement of the facts and any supporting evidence.

NOTE

This Statement was revised in Booklet IR131 Supp (November 2000), and is printed here as revised.

SP 11/91 (12 SEPTEMBER 1991)
STAMP DUTY AND VAT: INTERACTION

1. This statement is a revised version of the statement about stamp duty and VAT issued on 22 July 1991, SP 6/91, and replaces it.

INTRODUCTION

2. To comply with a judgment of the European Court of Justice in June 1988, standard rate UK VAT has been applied to non-residential construction with effect from 1 April 1989 (FA 1989 s 18). VAT is compulsory on sales of buildings treated as new for this purpose, which are mainly buildings under three years old that have been completed after March 1989. And owners of non-residential property were given the option from 1 August 1989 of charging VAT on sales of old buildings and on leases.

3. These new charges have prompted a number of enquiries about the relationship between stamp duty and VAT where both taxes arise on a sale or lease of commercial property or, occasionally, other assets.

SALES OF NEW NON-DOMESTIC BUILDINGS

4. The Board are advised that for stamp duty purposes the amount or value of the consideration for a sale is the gross amount inclusive of VAT. Therefore where VAT is payable on the sale of new non-residential property, stamp duty is calculated on the VAT-inclusive consideration.

OTHER NON-DOMESTIC TRANSACTIONS

5 Transactions in non-residential property other than sales of new buildings are exempt from VAT. These include—

— sales of old buildings

— the assignment of existing leases, or the creation of new leases, in old or new property.

However, the vendor or lessor can elect to waive the exemption.

6. The Board have received legal advice that—

— where the election has already been exercised at the time of the transaction, stamp duty is chargeable on the purchase price, premium or rent including VAT;

— where the election has not been exercised at that time, VAT should similarly be included in any payments to which an election could still apply (which will depend on the facts of each case).

7. The Board propose to follow this advice, which will result in a change of practice: in the past, the Stamp Office did not seek to include the VAT element in the stamp duty

Part II ST

charge in cases where an election to waive the exemption from VAT had not yet been exercised. The new practice applies to documents executed on or after 1 August 1991.

8. Neither a formal notice of election made to HM Customs & Excise, nor any notification to the purchaser or lessee that such an election has been made, will attract stamp duty.

RENT

9. Where VAT is charged on the rent under a lease, and is itself treated as rent under the lease, stamp duty at the appropriate rate according to the length of the term will be charged on the VAT-inclusive figure. If the lease provides for payment of VAT on the rent otherwise than as rent, duty will be charged on the VAT element as consideration payable periodically (Stamp Act 1891 s 56). In either case the rate of VAT in force at the date of execution of the lease will be used in the calculation.

10. In the case of a formal Deed of Variation or similar document varying the terms of the original lease so as to provide for payment of VAT by way of additional rent, further stamp duty may be payable (Stamp Act 1891 s 77(5)).

AGREEMENTS FOR LEASES

11. Paragraphs 5 to 10 above also apply to an agreement for lease if that is the instrument to be stamped [FA 1999 Sch 13 para 14].

PROCEDURE

12. Applicants for stamping are requested to make clear, either in the conveyance or lease document itself, or in a covering letter to the Stamp Office, whether the property is commercial or residential.

13. Deeds of Variation etc (para 10 above) should be presented for adjudication together with a copy of the original lease.

NO VAT ON STAMP DUTY

14. It is sometimes suggested that stamp duty might itself attract a charge to VAT. This is not the case. The value for VAT depends on the amount (consideration) obtained by the supplier from the purchaser, less the included VAT itself. Stamp duty is paid by the purchaser/lessee of property direct to the Inland Revenue and not to the supplier; it does not therefore form part of the consideration for VAT purposes.

NOTE

This Statement was revised by Booklet IR131 Supp (November 2000), and is printed here as revised.

SP 8/93 (12 JULY 1993)
STAMP DUTY: NEW BUILDINGS

This statement sets out the practice the Commissioners for HMRC will apply in relation to the stamp duty chargeable in certain circumstances on the conveyance or lease of a new or partly constructed building. It affects transactions where, at the date of the contract for sale or lease of a building plot, building work has not commenced or has been only partially completed on that site but where that work has started or has been completed at the time the conveyance or lease is executed.

This statement reflects the advice the Commissioners for HMRC have received on this subject in the light of the decision in the case of *Prudential Assurance Company Ltd v IRC* ([1992] STC 863; [1993] 1 WLR 211). The statement does not apply to the common situation where the parties have entered into a contract for the sale of a new house and that contract is implemented by a conveyance of the whole property. This statement replaces the statements of practice issued in 1957 and 1987 (SP 10/87) on this subject which are now withdrawn.

The Commissioners for HMRC are advised that, whilst each case will clearly depend on its own facts, the law is as follows—

1 TWO TRANSACTIONS/TWO CONTRACTS

Where the purchaser or lessee is entitled under the terms of a contract to a conveyance or lease of land alone in consideration of the purchase price or rent of the site and a second genuine contract for building works is entered into as a separate transaction, the ad valorem duty on the conveyance or lease will be determined by the amount of the purchase price or rent which the purchaser or lessee is obliged to pay under the terms of the first contract. In these circumstances it does not matter whether any building work has commenced at the date of the conveyance or lease. The consideration chargeable to ad valorem duty will still be only that passing for the land.

2 ONE TRANSACTION/TWO CONTRACTS

Where there is one transaction between the parties but this is implemented by two contracts, one for the sale or lease of the building plot and one for the building works themselves, the amount of ad valorem duty charged on the instrument will depend on the amount of the consideration, which in turn will depend on whether those contracts can be shown to be genuinely independent of each other.

(i) if the two contracts are so interlocked that they cannot be said to be genuinely capable of independent completion (and in particular where if default occurs on either contract, the other is then not enforceable) ad valorem duty will be charged on the total consideration for the land and buildings, whether completed or not, as if the parties had entered into only one contract.

(ii) if the two contracts are shown to be genuinely independent of each other, ad valorem duty will be charged by reference to the consideration paid or payable for the land and any building works on that land at the date of execution of the instrument. It follows that, where the instrument is executed after the building works are completed, ad valorem duty will be charged on the consideration for the land and the completed building(s).

3 SHAM OR ARTIFICIAL TRANSACTIONS

This statement does not apply to cases where the transaction concerned, or any part of it, involves a sham or artificial transaction.

CONTRACTS ALREADY ENTERED INTO

Where unconditional contracts have been entered into before or within 28 days of the date of this Statement and the duty payable on the resulting conveyance or lease would have been less under the earlier Statements of Practice, the Stamp Office will accept duty in the lesser amount. In such cases the instrument should be submitted together with all the evidence to support the claim that unconditional contracts were entered into within this transitional period.

PROCEDURE FOR SUBMITTING DOCUMENTS

Where a person accepts that a conveyance or lease of a building plot is chargeable on the total price paid or payable for the land and the completed building, it should be submitted for stamping in the usual way together with a covering letter giving the aggregate price and a payment for the duty appropriate to that price.

Where the total price does not exceed the amount up to which the instrument is liable to nil duty (currently £60,000) and a certificate of value is included in the instrument, a conveyance may be sent direct to the Land Registry in England and Wales or, in Scotland, to the Keeper of the Registers of Scotland. A lease will need to be stamped in respect of the rent.

Where the total price exceeds the threshold at which duty becomes payable but the taxpayer takes the view that duty is payable on some smaller sum, the instrument should be submitted to the Stamp Office. This applies even where the taxpayer believes that the amount potentially chargeable to ad valorem duty is below the threshold and a certificate of value is included in the instrument. The instrument should be accompanied by a copy of the agreement(s) for sale etc and a letter stating the amount which the taxpayer regards as chargeable consideration, identifying separately any amount attributable to building work. Details of any contractual arrangements not covered by the agreement(s) should also be given in the covering letter.

NOTE

This Statement was revised in Booklet IR131 (August 2002), and is printed here as revised.

SP 3/98 (13 OCTOBER 1998)
STAMP DUTY: GROUP RELIEF

1. FA 1930 s 42 gives relief from stamp duty for transfers of property between members of the same group of companies. FA 1995 s 151 similarly gives relief from duty on the grant of a lease between members of the same group.

2. FA 1967 s 27 (3) and FA 1995 s 151 (3) are designed to prevent the use of group relief to avoid stamp duty when property, or an economic interest in it, passes out of the group.

3. This statement sets out the Stamp Office's current general practice in order to assist practitioners in determining whether claims to relief might qualify. The treatment of a particular case will of course depend on the precise facts. This statement is for general guidance only; and the facts of a particular transaction may, exceptionally, place it outside the guidelines. It applies also to the equivalent Northern Ireland legislation.

GENERAL

4. Broadly, s 27 (3) and the corresponding provisions in s 151, provide that relief is not to be given if the transfer was made in pursuance of, or in connection with, an arrangement under which—

(a) all or part of the consideration for the transfer was to be provided or received, directly or indirectly, by a person outside the group; or

(b) the interest being transferred was previously transferred by a person outside the group; or

(c) the transferor and transferee were no longer to be part of the same group.

5. The person claiming the relief when the relevant instrument is adjudicated has the onus of satisfying the Stamp Office that the intra-group transaction is not carried out in pursuance of, or in connection with, an arrangement of a kind which disqualifies the transaction from relief—*Escoigne Properties Ltd v IRC* [1958] AC 549, 564.

"ARRANGEMENT"

6. In this context, arrangement means the plan or scheme in pursuance of which the things identified in ss 27(3), 151(3) have been or are to be done—*Shop and Store Developments Ltd v IRC* [1967] 1 AC 472, 493, 494. The arrangement need not be based in contract. it is sufficient if the intra-group transaction is made in connection with that plan or scheme. The intra-group transaction may be the first bi-lateral step by which legal rights and obligations are created in pursuance of the arrangement. If there is an expectation that a disqualifying event will happen in accordance with the arrangement and no likelihood in practice that it will not, relief will be refused.

7. The words "in connection with" are very broad. In *Escoigne*, there was a gap of four years between the two steps in issue.

PROVISION OR RECEIPT OF CONSIDERATION BY A PERSON OUTSIDE THE GROUP—FA 1967 S 27 (3)(A); FA 1995 S 151 (3)(A), (4)

8. Section 27(3)(*a*) denies relief where the instrument was executed in pursuance of or in connection with an arrangement under which any of the consideration is to be provided or received, directly or indirectly, by a person outside the group. It also denies relief if the arrangement is one under which the transferor or transferee (or a member of the same group as either of them) is to be enabled to provide any of the consideration, or is to part with it, in consequence of a transaction involving a payment or other disposition by a person outside the group. Section 151 lays down similar rules for leases.

9. In some cases, the question arises whether loan finance for the purchase or lease will disqualify an intra-group transaction from relief. It is necessary to look at all the facts of the individual case, but the Stamp Office will interpret the provisions in the light of their general purpose of denying relief where the intra-group transaction is a means of saving stamp duty when the property, or an interest in it, moves out of the group. Accordingly, the Stamp Office are likely to be satisfied that relief is due if the intra-group transaction is not to be followed by a sale of the property transferred, or an underlease, to a person outside the group. If the intra-group transaction is to be followed by a sale or underlease to a person outside the group, but the claimant can demonstrate that stamp duty will be paid in respect of that transaction in approximately the same amount as would have been payable if the intra-group transferor or lessor had itself sold the property or granted title underlease, the Stamp Office are likely to be satisfied that the intra-group transaction and the transfer or lease out are independent for stamp duty purposes and grant the relief sought.

10. A transaction is not disqualified merely because the transferee within the group obtains a specific loan for the purchase of the asset; or the loan is secured on the asset; or arrangements are made to replace or novate an existing charge on the property transferred. It will be necessary to consider the facts as a whole, especially if the loan finance is not straightforward finance on ordinary commercial terms.

11. Intra-group transactions will be very carefully scrutinised, and relief may be refused, where, for example, the intra-group transaction involves or is to be followed by—

- the creation or transfer of loan stock or equity capital;
- a capital reorganisation of the transferee;
- a guarantee by a third party not associated with the group;
- the creation of a new charge or financial arrangement whereby title to the property is, or may be, vested in the lender otherwise than in satisfaction of all or part of the debt; or
- the assignment of the freehold reversion or the intra-group lease to a person outside the group.

12. Similarly transactions will be very carefully scrutinised where—

- all or part of the consideration for the transaction is to remain outstanding or is represented by intra-group debt, (as the aim and effect may be to reduce the value of the transferee company on a possible future sale outside the group); or
- the existing shareholders of the transferee include shareholders outside the group and the transaction is to be followed by the declaration of a dividend in *specie*, or by the liquidation of the transferee.

13. Further assurances by way of statutory declaration—the document in which the claim is made to the Stamp Office—will be required in any case in which the property transferred or vested intra-group is the only, or only substantial, asset of the transferee. Information to that effect should be provided in the statutory declaration submitted with the documents.

14. Where group member A has granted a lease to a person outside the group, and subsequently grants an underlease to its fellow group member B, so that the rent already payable by the lessee becomes payable to B rather than A, relief is likely to be given for the intra-group underlease, provided there are no other factors which suggest that relief should be denied.

PROPERTY PREVIOUSLY CONVEYED BY A PERSON OUTSIDE THE GROUP—FA 1967 S 27(3)(B)

15. Section 27(3)(*b*) was intended to prevent the avoidance of duty on the transfer of property into a group by means of a sub-sale, so as to take advantage of the Stamp Act 1891 s 58 (4). For example, suppose the property is sold to a group member by a vendor outside the group, but the sale rests in contract without a transfer of the legal title. The group member then sells the property to another member omits own group, and directs the vendor to transfer the legal title to that other member. In accordance with s 58 (4) the transfer completing the sale and the sub-sale is chargeable to duty only in relation to the sub-sale (thus relieving the effect of s 4 of the Stamp Act). However, s 27(3)(*b*) would deny group relief for that transfer.

16. The Stamp Office will continue to apply s 27(3)(*b*) to schemes of this type and to any other scheme where an attempt has been made to avoid the duty payable on the acquisition by the group. However, where an outside vendor sells a property to a member of the group, the sale is completed by a transfer and stamp duty is paid on that transfer, the Stamp Office will normally regard any subsequent intra-group transfer as independent, and grant relief for the transfer within the purchaser's group.

DISSOCIATION OR DEMERGER OF TRANSFEREE—FA 1967 S 27 (3)(C): FA 1995 S 151 (3)(B)

17. Before the introduction of s 27 (3), almost all the avoidance devices encountered in this area involved the transfer of property to a subsidiary, often created solely as a vehicle for that property, followed by the transfer of the shares in the subsidiary out of the group. Compared with a transfer of the property out of the group, a substantial amount of duty could be avoided even where the subsidiary paid for the property from its own resources. If the consideration for the intra-group transaction remained outstanding or was represented by debt, duty could be reduced further by reducing the value of the shares—hence s 27(3)(*a*).

18. Section 27(3)(*c*) was introduced to counter this avoidance in relation to conveyances and transfers on sale. Section 151(3)(*b*) deals with leases on similar lines.

19. In cases of this kind, the Stamp Office will need to be satisfied that the intra-group transfer or lease is not a step in pursuance of an arrangement to demerge the transferee. The existence of such an arrangement may be apparent from company documents, correspondence and other dealings between members of the group and professional advisers, or from discussions or negotiations with the potential purchasers, underwriters or minority shareholders.

20. In practice, the Stamp Office will apply these provisions so as to preclude group relief if there is evidence of a plan or scheme to dispose of the subsidiary and there is no practical likelihood that the scheme will not be carried through. It will not be regarded as sufficient for the claimant to contend that such an arrangement which is less than contractual may possibly be frustrated by unforeseen events or unlikely occurrences. Even a contract may be frustrated.

21. As the liability of the relevant instrument must, as a matter of general principle, be determined as at the date of the instrument, the question whether an arrangement of the relevant kind exists must also be determined at that time, although the Stamp Office may have regard to what is said and done thereafter to establish the true position (*Wm Cory and Son Ltd v IRC* [1965] AC 1088). For the purposes of stamp duty, it is therefore the existence of the scheme or plan to which these provisions direct attention, not the ultimate outcome of steps which may be taken to implement that scheme. Accordingly, statements of practice in relation to other taxes have no application in this context.

SP 1/03 (APRIL 2003)
STAMP DUTY: DISADVANTAGED AREAS RELIEF

This Statement of Practice is intended as guidance for those claiming exemption from stamp duty in respect of transfers of property situated in designated areas ("Disadvantaged Areas

Relief") and explains how Inland Revenue Stamp Taxes will interpret the extension to the relief introduced with effect from 10 April 2003.

The relief is one of a number of measures set out in the Government's Urban White Paper "Our towns and cities—the future—delivering an urban renaissance" published in November 2000. The measure is designed to stimulate the physical, economic and social regeneration of the UK's most disadvantaged areas by attracting development and by encouraging the purchase of residential and commercial property by individuals and businesses. The areas eligible for relief were designated "Enterprise Areas" by the Chancellor in his 2002 pre-Budget report. In addition to the relief, a range of other Government policies designed to support enterprise and economic regeneration, including the Community Investment Tax Relief, will benefit these areas, helping to support the development of new and existing businesses.

INTRODUCTION

1. Disadvantaged Areas Relief (provided for by FA 2001 Sch 30 [and] s 92) was introduced on 30 November 2001 and was initially only available for conveyances or transfers on sale (of both residential and commercial property) for which the consideration did not exceed £150,000. Stamp duty in respect of conveyances or transfers of commercial property in disadvantaged areas was abolished in consequence of the Stamp Duty (Disadvantaged Areas) (Application of Exemptions) Regulations 2003 [(SI 2003/1056)] ("the Regulations"), which have effect in relation to instruments executed on or after 10 April 2003. Thereafter the £150,000 limit applies only in relation to residential property.

2. FA 2002 inserted the following provisions in FA 2001 to distinguish residential from other property and to provide for differing stamp duty exemptions:

- FA 2001 s 92A which enables stamp duty relief in designated disadvantaged areas in respect of all properties to be varied depending on whether or not the property is "residential";
- FA 2001 s 92B which defines "residential property" for the purposes of the relief. Non-residential property, in respect of which unlimited relief is available, is therefore defined in the Act by exclusion. The section also sets out particular building uses that are specifically included within, or specifically excluded from, the definition.

3. In most cases there will be no difficulty in practice in establishing whether or not a property is "residential". This statement sets out in more detail the Stamp Office's approach to borderline cases and gives guidance on the practical application of the legislation. The annexed flowchart provides a quick guide for simpler cases as to whether property constitutes "residential property".

CERTIFICATION

4. Claims for unlimited relief must be accompanied by a certificate stating either that none of the land in question is residential property or, if part is residential, the proportion that is non-residential (together with the usual certificate of value for the remainder).

- Residential property—FA 2001 s 92A(4), together with the Regulations, provides that the exemption will only apply if the document is certified to the effect that the amount or value of the consideration does not exceed £150,000.
- Non-residential property—FA 2001 s 92(2) provides that the exemption will only apply if the document is certified to the Commissioners as being an instrument on which stamp duty is not chargeable by virtue of subsection (1) of that section.

5. The following are suggested forms of words for particular certificates:

- Residential Property—"I/We hereby certify that the transaction effected by this instrument does not form part of a larger transaction or series of transactions in respect of which the amount or value of the consideration exceeds £150,000 and that stamp duty is not chargeable thereon by virtue of the provisions of sections 92 and 92A of the Finance Act 2001."
- Non-residential Property—"I/We hereby certify that this is an instrument in respect of non-residential property on which stamp duty is not chargeable by virtue of the provisions of section 92 of the Finance Act 2001."

- Mixed Use Property—"I/We hereby certify that the transaction effected by this instrument is in respect of property part of which is residential property, and which does not form part of a larger transaction or series of transactions in respect of which the amount or value of the consideration relating to the residential part exceeds £150,000 so that stamp duty is not chargeable by virtue of sections 92 and 92A of the Finance Act 2001, and part of which is non-residential property on which stamp duty is not chargeable by virtue of the provisions of section 92 of the Finance Act 2001. The basis upon which the allocation between residential and non-residential parts has been made is as follows— . . . "

6. While the legislation does not specifically require the certificate to be included as part of the document, it is suggested that it should be so included. If the person submitting the document for stamping does not provide a certificate, either in the document or separately in writing, exemption will not be granted.

7. Appropriate contemporaneous evidence should be retained to support any certificate provided. Estate agents' specifications, site plans, planning practical application of the legislation. The annexed flowchart provides a quick guide for simpler cases as to whether property constitutes "residential property".

8. Anyone falsely certifying a document with a view to obtaining relief that is not due will be committing a stamp duty fraud.

THE MEANING OF RESIDENTIAL PROPERTY

9. Section 92B defines "residential property" as a building which:

- is used as a dwelling, or
- is suitable for use as a dwelling, or
- is in the process of being constructed or adapted for such use.

If a property meets any one of these separate tests it will be treated as residential property and be subject to the £150,000 limit for relief, as will any garden or grounds belonging to it or any interests or rights attaching to it. Each element of the definition is considered in turn below. The question of whether and to what extent a building and grounds are defined as residential property for stamp duty purposes may also have implications for its treatment for capital gains tax and local authority rates.

USE AS A DWELLING

10. Where a building is in use at the date of execution of the relevant instrument, it will be a question of fact whether and to what extent it is used as a dwelling. Use at the date the instrument is executed overrides any past or intended future uses for this purpose.

11. Where the property in question is in use as a dwelling at the date of execution, it is residential property for the purposes of the relief unless it is part of a multiple transaction qualifying for relief under the Regulations (see paragraphs 35 to 39 below).

12. For the treatment of buildings put to both residential and non-residential use, see paragraphs 17 and 18 below.

SUITABLE FOR USE AS A DWELLING

13. The suitability test applies to the state of the building at the time the instrument is executed, having regard to the facilities available and any history of use. For example, the Inland Revenue will not regard an office block as "suitable for use as a dwelling" but a house which has been used as an office without particular adaptation may well be so.

14. If a building is not in use at the date of execution but its last use was as a dwelling, it will be taken to be "suitable for use as a dwelling" and treated as residential property for the purposes of the relief, unless evidence is produced to the contrary (see paragraph 15).

15. Whether a building is suitable for use as a dwelling will depend upon the precise facts and circumstances. The simple removal of, for example, a bathroom suite or

kitchen facilities will not be regarded as rendering a building unsuitable for use as a dwelling. Where it is claimed that a previously residential property is no longer suitable for use as a dwelling, perhaps because it is derelict or has been substantially altered, the claimant will need to provide evidence that this is the case. See also paragraph 29.

16. Where a building has been used partly for residential purposes and partly for another purpose, its overall suitability for use as a dwelling will be judged from the facilities available at the date of execution of the relevant document. For example, if two rooms of a house were in use as a dentist's surgery and waiting room at the date of execution, the Inland Revenue would nevertheless normally consider this property suitable for use as a dwelling unless the claimant provided evidence to the contrary. In other words, the interaction of the Regulations with s 92B(1) enables a building that is used only partly as a dwelling to be nevertheless suitable for use wholly as a dwelling, with the effect that the £150,000 limit applies to the whole of the consideration. Where only a distinct part of the building is used and suitable for use as a dwelling, that part will be residential property for the purposes of the relief and the mixed use provisions will apply (paragraphs 17 and 18 below).

MIXED USE

17. Where only part of a building (and land or interest relating to it) is "residential property" within s 92B(1), the consideration "shall be apportioned on such basis as is just and reasonable" between the residential and non-residential elements. The £150,000 limit is then applied only to the residential portion, in accordance with the appropriate certification (regulation 5 of the Regulations). For example:

A property situated wholly within a disadvantaged area is bought for:

(a) £200,000.
(b) £400,000.

50% of the property is "residential property" on the basis of a just and reasonable apportionment.

Relief is conferred by FA 2001 s 92, applied in conjunction with reg 5 of the Regulations. Paragraph (3) of reg 5 calls for an apportionment of the total consideration between residential and non-residential elements. Paragraph (4) confirms that relief applies to the residential property element only where the consideration attributed to it does not exceed £150,000. In these examples:

(a) £100,000 is attributed to the residential property element, so relief is due. The part of the land that is not residential property is also exempt under the normal operation of FA 2001 s 92. So no duty is payable.
(b) The £200,000 attributed to the residential property element is not exempt, because of regulation 5(4), but attracts duty at the rate of 1% (stamp duty payable £2,000). The non-residential property element is exempt as above.

18. The "just and reasonable" test is necessarily subjective, and each case will be considered on its merits. Apportionment might be on the basis of the percentage areas quoted in planning applications, where appropriate, or alternatively of floor space relating to the respective uses. Other methods of apportionment will be considered as part of a claim.

SPECIFIC CASES

19. Some types of communal or institutional building are used neither as dwellings nor for commercial purposes. The legislation therefore outlines how these are classified for the purposes of relief, specifically including some such buildings within the definition of "dwelling" (s 92B(2)) and specifically excluding others (s 92B(3)). If they do not fall within any of the specific categories of s 92B(3), most residential institutions will come within s 92B(2)(*d*) and will be treated as dwellings by default.

20. Categories of building use specifically included within the definition of "use as a dwelling" (so that transfers of such buildings only qualify for relief if the consideration does not exceed £150,000) (s 92B(2)) are:

(a) residential accommodation for school pupils, for example accommodation blocks in boarding schools;

(b) residential accommodation for students, other than that within s 92B(3)(*b*). Student accommodation provided by private landlords is "a dwelling", as is accommodation leased to students by universities or colleges in flats or houses rather than in halls of residence (see s 92B(3)(*b*));
(c) residential accommodation for members of any of the armed forces, including accommodation for their families (s 92B(2)(*c*));
(d) an institution that is the sole or main residence of at least 90% of its residents and does not fall within any of the categories referred to in s 92B(3) (see s 92B(2)(*d*) and also paragraph 21 below).
This would include, for example:
- sheltered accommodation for the elderly where no nursing or personal care is provided
- accommodation for religious communities (subject to the rules regarding mixed use; see paragraphs 17 and 18).

21. Categories of building use specifically excluded from the definition of "use as a dwelling" (so that transfers of such buildings in a disadvantaged area will qualify for unlimited relief) (s 92B(3)) are:
(a) a home or other institution providing residential accommodation for children;
(b) a hall of residence for students in further or higher education. This is not defined in the legislation but in practice property provided by a university or similar establishment will be judged on the facts (number of inhabitants, type of facilities, availability of communal areas);
(c) a home or other institution providing residential accommodation with personal care for persons in need of personal care by reason of old age, disablement, past or present dependence on alcohol or drugs or past or present mental disorder;
(d) a hospital or hospice;
(e) a prison or similar establishment; or
(f) a hotel or inn or similar establishment.

22. The specific inclusions and exclusions set out in paragraphs 20 and 21 above apply not only to a building's actual use at the date of the transfer, but to the uses for which it is suitable at that date. Where, however, a building is being put to one of the non-residential uses specified in s 92B(3), this overrides any suitability for another use (s 92B(4)). For example, a building used as a children's home may also be suitable for use as a school boarding house, but this will not preclude a claim to unlimited relief.

23. Where a vacant building is suitable for at least one of the uses specified in s 92B(2) and at least one specified in s 92B(3), the tiebreaker in s 92B(5) determines, for the purposes of the relief, the use for which it is "most suitable". Whether or not a vacant building has one or more uses for which it is most suitable is a question of fact. Evidence supporting such uses should be provided with the claim for relief.

24. Where there is a single use for which a building is most suitable, the fact that it is also suitable for another use will be discounted.

25. If there are a number of uses for which a building is most suitable and they all come within either of the two subsections, any other use for which the building is suitable will be discounted.

26. Where no most suitable use can be shown, the default will be to classify the building as residential property and apply the £150,000 limit.

27. Land and buildings that are not suitable for any use at the date of execution will be treated as residential property if they are "in the process of being constructed or adapted for such use"—see paragraphs 28 and 29 below.

PROCESS OF BEING CONSTRUCTED OR ADAPTED FOR USE AS A DWELLING

28. Undeveloped land is in essence non-residential, but land may be "residential property" for the purposes of disadvantaged areas relief if a residential building is being built on it at the date the instrument is executed. The process of construction is taken as commencing when the builders first start work. A development of six or more dwellings is deemed to be non-residential under reg 6 of the Regulations, even if in the process of construction at the date of the instrument (see paragraph 35 below).

29. Where (at the date the relevant instrument is executed) an existing building is being adapted for, or restored to, domestic use, it is "residential property" for the purposes of the relief. This may apply, for example, where a derelict building is being made fit for habitation, or where a previously non-residential building is being converted to a dwelling. Again, the process is taken as commencing when the builders start work.

THE GARDEN OR GROUNDS OF A BUILDING USED ETC AS A DWELLING

30. Section 92B(1)(*b*) includes within the definition of residential property "land that is or forms part of the garden or grounds of a building within paragraph (*a*) (including any building or structure on such land)". The test the Inland Revenue will apply is similar to that applied for the purposes of the capital gains tax relief for main residences (TCGA 1992 s 222(3)). The land will include that which is needed for the reasonable enjoyment of the dwelling having regard to the size and nature of the dwelling.

31. A caravan or houseboat is not a "building" for this purpose.

32. Commercial farmland is not within the definition of residential property. A farmhouse situated on agricultural land would be dealt with under the mixed use provisions (paragraphs 17 and 18 above).

33. Outhouses on land within the s 92B(1)(*b*) definition will also be "residential property" unless it can be demonstrated that they have a specific non-residential purpose. Where a distinct non-residential use can be demonstrated, the mixed use provisions will apply.

INTEREST IN OR RIGHTS OVER RESIDENTIAL PROPERTY

34. The treatment of interests in, or rights over, land or buildings for the purposes of disadvantaged areas relief will follow that of the land or buildings to which they relate.

SIX OR MORE SEPARATE DWELLINGS TRANSFERRED BY SINGLE CONTRACT

35. The Regulations provide that "where there is a single contract for the conveyance, transfer or lease of land comprising or including six or more separate dwellings, none of that land counts as residential property . . . " Accordingly the transaction will qualify for unlimited relief. This recognises that commercial developers and institutional landlords, for example, frequently deal in numerous properties at one time. The fact that those properties may individually be "residential property" does not detract from the inherently commercial nature of the transaction itself.

36. To qualify as "separate", the dwellings must be self-contained. So for example, flats within a block, sharing some common areas but each with their own amenities, will qualify as separate dwellings. Rooms let within a house will not constitute separate dwellings if tenants share amenities such as a kitchen and bathroom.

37. A transaction in respect of six or more such dwellings must be carried out by means of a single contract in order to qualify for relief. Several instruments may however be presented for stamping if the properties are held under separate title.

38. Qualifying multiple transactions will be treated as non-residential property for the purposes of relief, even where the proportionate consideration for individual dwellings exceeds the £150,000 limit for residential property. It is not a condition of relief that multiple transactions comprise only dwellings.

39. The fact that some of the six or more dwellings within the single contract are outside a designated disadvantaged area will not prevent them from constituting a non-residential transaction. However relief will only be available for the portion of the land situated within the disadvantaged area.

PROPERTY ONLY PARTLY WITHIN A DISADVANTAGED AREA

40. FA 2001 Sch 30, together with the Regulations, determines how property situated partly within and partly outside a designated disadvantaged area is to be treated for the purposes of the relief. Such cases are relatively rare in practice. Queries may be referred to Inland Revenue (Stamp Taxes) for guidance.

LEASE DUTY

41. Relief is also available from duty on the rental element of new leases executed on or after 10 April 2003. Rental leases of residential property shall be eligible for relief where the average annual rent is no more than £15,000 and/or where any premium does not exceed £150,000. For non-residential property, full relief is available for the rental element of leases as well as for any premium.

OTHER ISSUES

42. The extended relief applies to documents executed on or after 10 April 2003, irrespective of whether the contract was entered into before or after that date. There is no scope to reclaim stamp duty already paid in respect of transfers executed on or before 9 April 2003.

FLOWCHART TO DETERMINE WHETHER PROPERTY IS OR IS NOT "RESIDENTIAL PROPERTY"

Is the subject of the conveyance/transfer/lease . . .

(A)

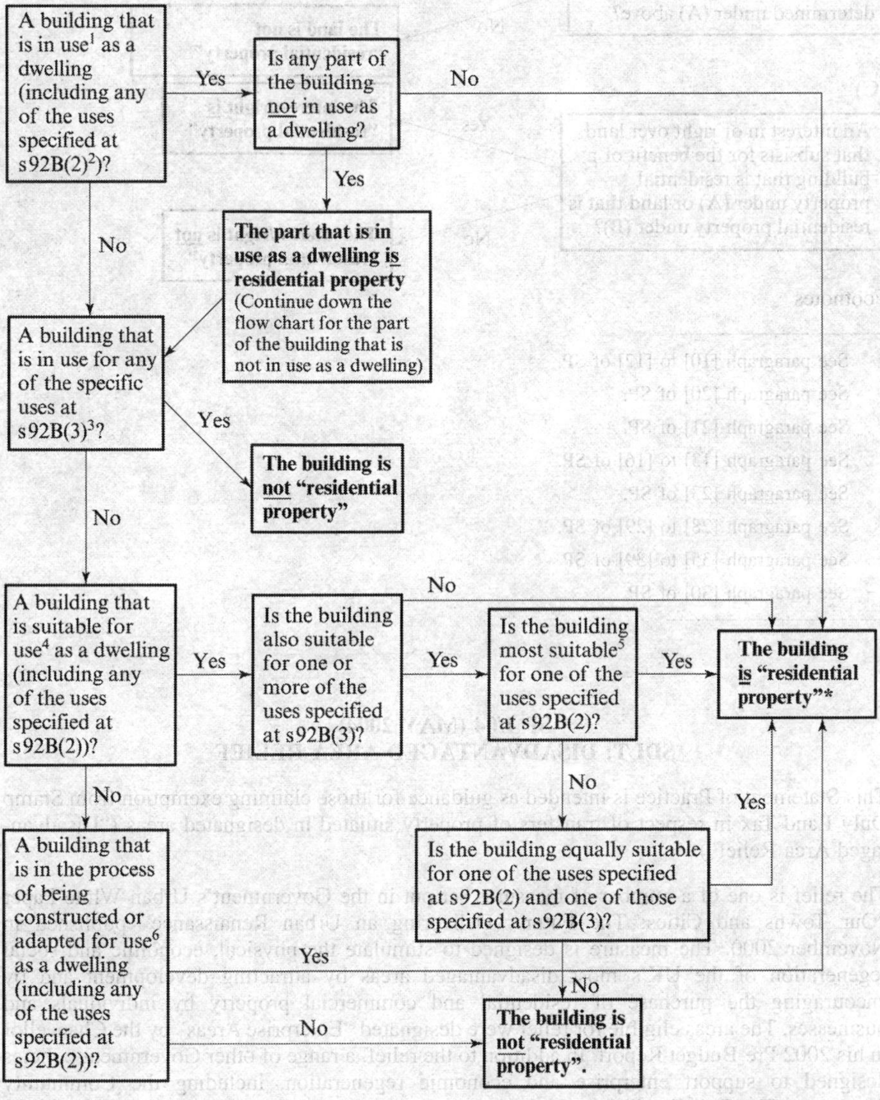

*unless the conveyance, transfer or lease comprises or includes six or more separate dwellings[7] made pursuant to a single contract, in which circumstances none of the land will be "residential property".

Is the subject of the conveyance/transfer/lease . . .

(B)

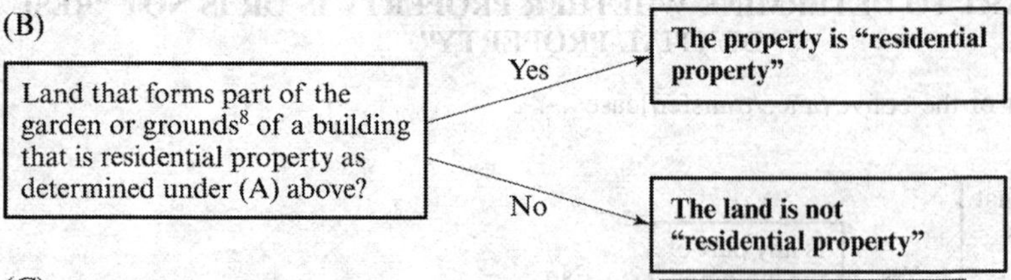

(C)

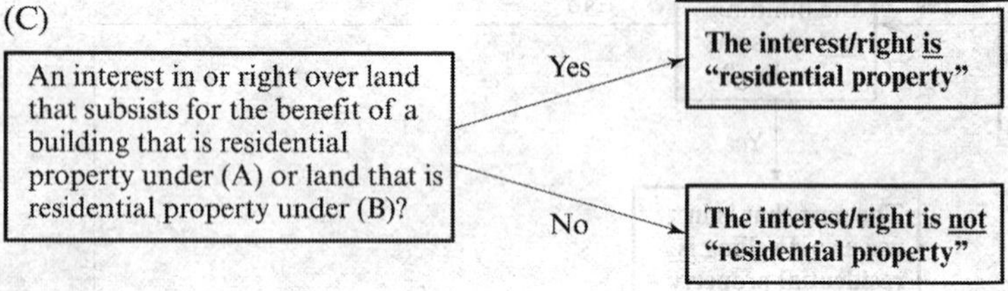

Footnotes

---

1 See paragraph [10] to [12] of SP.

2 See paragraph [20] of SP.

3 See paragraph [21] of SP.

4 See paragraph [13] to [16] of SP.

5 See paragraph [23] of SP.

6 See paragraph [28] to [29] of SP.

7 See paragraph [35] to [39] of SP.

8 See paragraph [30] of SP.

SP 1/04 (MAY 2004)
SDLT: DISADVANTAGED AREA RELIEF

This Statement of Practice is intended as guidance for those claiming exemption from Stamp Duty Land Tax in respect of transfers of property situated in designated areas ("Disadvantaged Area Relief").

The relief is one of a number of measures set out in the Government's Urban White Paper "Our Towns and Cities: The Future: Delivering an Urban Renaissance" published in November 2000. The measure is designed to stimulate the physical, economic and social regeneration of the UK's most disadvantaged areas by attracting development and by encouraging the purchase of residential and commercial property by individuals and businesses. The areas eligible for relief were designated "Enterprise Areas" by the Chancellor in his 2002 Pre-Budget Report. In addition to the relief, a range of other Government policies designed to support enterprise and economic regeneration, including the Community Investment Tax Relief, will benefit these areas, helping to support the development of new and existing businesses

BACKGROUND

1. Disadvantaged Area Relief (provided for by FA 2001 s 92 and Sch 30) was introduced on 30 November 2001 and was initially available for conveyances or transfers on sale (of both residential and commercial property) for which the consideration did not exceed £150,000. Stamp duty in respect of conveyances or transfers of commercial property in disadvantaged areas was abolished in consequence of the Stamp Duty (Disadvantaged Areas) (Application of Exemptions) Regulations

2003 ("the Regulations"), which have effect in relation to instruments executed on or after 10 April 2003. Thereafter the £150,000 limit applies only in relation to residential property.

2. FA 2002 inserted the following provisions in FA 2001 to distinguish residential from other property and to provide for differing Stamp Duty Land Tax exemptions:

- FA 2001 s 92A which enables stamp duty relief in designated disadvantaged areas in respect of all properties to be varied depending on whether or not the property is "residential".

DISADVANTAGED AREA RELIEF UNDER STAMP DUTY LAND TAX

3. FA 2003 s 57 and Sch 6 provides for Disadvantaged Area Relief under Stamp Duty Land Tax.

4. The definition of residential property under Stamp Duty Land Tax is provided at FA 2003 s 116. Non-residential property is therefore defined in the Act by exclusion. Section 116 also sets out particular building uses that are specifically included within, or specifically excluded from, the definition.

5. In most cases there will be no difficulty in practice in establishing whether or not a property is "residential". This statement sets out in more detail the Stamp Office's approach to borderline cases and gives guidance on the practical application of the legislation. The annexed flowchart provides a quick guide for simpler cases as to whether property constitutes "residential property".

CLAIMING THE RELIEF

6. The way in which relief is claimed is different under Stamp Duty Land Tax.

FA 2003 s 76 requires that most land transactions, including those that qualify for Disadvantaged Area Relief, must be notified to the Inland Revenue on a Land Transaction Return Form (SDLT 1).

7. Relief is claimed by simply completing a box within this form. Certificates of Value are no longer required and no supporting evidence or documentation is required at this point. Once the return has been submitted and we are satisfied with the information provided, the purchaser is issued with a certificate which they must present with documents when applying for registration of title at Land Registry, Registers of Scotland or Land Registry of Northern Ireland.

8. FA 2003 Sch 10 Pt 3 gives the Inland Revenue the power to enquire into a Land Transaction Return. These provisions permit the Inland Revenue to open an enquiry into any aspect of a Land Transaction Return, including claims to reliefs.

Appropriate contemporaneous evidence should be retained to support any claim to the relief. There is no need to create records that would otherwise not be available. Estate agents' specifications, site plans, planning applications or permissions, marketing material, photographs and print outs of an internet post code search may all provide relevant information should there be an enquiry into a land tax return.

9. As with all claims the onus is on the purchaser to check whether or not the relief is due.

THE MEANING OF RESIDENTIAL PROPERTY

10. FA 2003 s 116(1) defines "residential property" as a building which:

- is used as a dwelling,
- or is suitable for use as a dwelling,
- or is in the process of being constructed or adapted for such use.

If a property meets any one of these separate tests it will be treated as residential property and be subject to the £150,000 limit for relief, as will any garden or grounds belonging to it or any interests or rights attaching to it. Each element of the definition is considered in turn

Part II ST

below. The question of whether and to what extent a building and grounds are defined as residential property for stamp duty purposes may also have implications for its treatment for capital gains tax and local authority rates.

USE AS A DWELLING

11. Where a building is in use at the effective date of the transaction it will be a question of fact whether and to what extent it is used as a dwelling.

Use at the effective date overrides any past or intended future uses for this purpose. For example, a purchaser is buying a house with the intention to refurbish it to create, in its place, an alternative therapy treatment centre. For the purposes of the relief the house in considered to be a dwelling because it was suitable for that use at the effective date of the transaction. (For another example see paragraph 34.)

12. Where the property in question is in use as a dwelling at the effective date of the transaction, it is residential property for the purposes of the relief unless it is part of a multiple transaction qualifying for relief under FA 2003 s 116(7) (see paragraphs 40 to 44 below).

13. There is no motive test applicable to the usage of land or buildings, so where a residential property is purchased with the owner intending to use it as a non-residential business the building is considered residential, under the suitability test, for the purposes of the relief.

14. For the treatment of buildings put to both residential and non-residential use, see paragraphs 19 and 20 below.

SUITABLE FOR USE AS A DWELLING

15. The suitability test applies to the state of the building at the effective date of the transaction, having regard to the facilities available and any history of use. For example, the Inland Revenue will not regard an office block as "suitable for use as a dwelling", but a house which has been used as an office without particular adaptation may well be so.

16. If a building is not in use at the effective date of the transaction but its last use was as a dwelling, it will be taken to be "suitable for use as a dwelling" and treated as residential property for the purposes of the relief, unless evidence is produced to the contrary (see paragraph 17).

17. Whether a building is suitable for use as a dwelling will depend upon the precise facts and circumstances. The simple removal of, for example, a bathroom suite or kitchen facilities will not be regarded as rendering a building unsuitable for use as a dwelling. Where it is claimed that a previously residential property is no longer suitable for use as a dwelling, perhaps because it is derelict or has been substantially altered, the claimant will need to provide evidence that this is the case. See also paragraph 34.

18. Where a building has been used partly for residential purposes and partly for another purpose, its overall suitability for use as a dwelling will be judged from the facilities available at the effective date of the transaction. For example, if two rooms of a house were in use as a dentist's surgery and waiting room at the effective date of the transaction, the Inland Revenue would nevertheless normally consider this property suitable for use as a dwelling unless the claimant provided evidence to the contrary. A building that is used only partly as a dwelling may nevertheless be suitable for use wholly as a dwelling, with the effect that the £150,000 limit applies to the whole of the consideration. Where only a distinct part of the building is used and suitable for use as a dwelling, that part will be residential property for the purposes of the relief and the mixed use provisions will apply (See paragraphs 19 and 20 below).

MIXED USE

19. Where only part of a building (and land or interest relating to it) is "residential property" within s 116(1), the consideration "shall be apportioned on such basis as is just and reasonable" between the residential and non-residential elements. The £150,000 limit is then applied only to the residential portion (FA 2003 Sch 6). For example:

A property situated wholly within a disadvantaged area is bought for

(a) £200,000
(b) £400,000

50% of the property is "residential property" on the basis of a just and reasonable apportionment.

In these examples:

(a) £100,000 is attributed to the residential property element, so relief is due. The part of the land that is not residential property is also exempt. So no duty is payable.
(b) the £200,000 attributed to the residential property element is not exempt, because of Sch 6 para 6, but attracts duty at the rate of 1% (Stamp Duty Land Tax payable £2,000). The non-residential property element is exempt as above.

Where a transaction involves six or more mixed use properties, under FA 2003 s 116(7), providing certain conditions are met, the residential element is exempt and no Stamp Duty Land Tax is payable. See paragraphs 40 to 44.

20. The "just and reasonable" test is necessarily subjective, and each case will be considered on its merits. Apportionment might be on the basis of the percentage areas quoted in planning applications, where appropriate, or alternatively of floor space relating to the respective uses. Other methods of apportionment will be considered as part of a claim.

SPECIFIC CASES

21. Some types of communal or institutional building are used neither as dwellings nor for commercial purposes. The legislation therefore outlines how these are classified for the purposes of relief, specifically including some such buildings within the definition of "dwelling" (s 116(2)) and specifically excluding others (s 116(3)). If they do not fall within any of the specific categories of s 116(3), most residential institutions will come within s 116(2)(*d*) and will be treated as dwellings by default.

22. Categories of building use specifically included within the definition of "use as a dwelling" (so that transfers of such buildings only qualify for relief if the consideration does not exceed £150,000) (s 116(2)) are:

(a) residential accommodation for school pupils, for example accommodation blocks in boarding schools;
(b) residential accommodation for students, other than that within s 116(3)(*b*). Student accommodation provided by private landlords is "a dwelling", as is accommodation leased to students by universities or colleges in flats or houses rather than in halls of residence (see s 116(3)(*b*));
(c) residential accommodation for members of any of the armed forces, including accommodation for their families (s 116(2)(*c*));
(d) an institution that is the sole or main residence of at least 90% of its residents and does not fall within any of the categories referred to in s 116(3) (see s 116(2)(*d*) and also paragraph 23 below).

This would include, for example,

- sheltered accommodation for the elderly where no nursing or personal care is provided. An example of this would be where an elderly person purchases a home on a warden-assisted housing development.
- accommodation for religious communities (subject to the rules regarding mixed use; see paragraphs 19 and 20).

23. Categories of building use specifically excluded from the definition of "use as a dwelling" (so that transfers of such buildings in a disadvantaged area will qualify for unlimited relief) (s 116(3)) are:

(a) a home or other institution providing residential accommodation for children;
(b) a hall of residence for students in further or higher education. This is not defined in the legislation but in practice property provided by a university or similar establishment will be judged on the facts (number of inhabitants, type of facilities, availability of communal areas);

(c) a home or other institution providing residential accommodation with personal care for persons in need of personal care by reason of old age, disablement, past or present dependence on alcohol or drugs or past or present mental disorder (for example, an institution that provides accommodation as part of a wider care service such as residential care homes or residential drug treatment centres);
(d) a hospital or hospice;
(e) a prison or similar establishment, or
(f) a hotel or inn or similar establishment.

BED AND BREAKFASTS/GUEST HOUSES

24. Each case will be taken on its merits, however, paragraph 25 below provides general examples of the treatment of B&Bs/guest houses.

25. A property providing a Bed and Breakfast (B&B) service, which has amenities installed in each room such as bathing facilities, telephone lines etc and is available all year round as the rooms do not need any further adaptation, would be considered non residential for the purposes of the relief.

EXAMPLE

Mr and Mrs Boyd run a bed and breakfast in a disadvantaged area of Blackpool. They live on the premises and it is open all year round but trade declines during the winter months.

Under FA 2003 s 116(3), the Boyd's B&B is a "hotel or inn or similar establishment" and is therefore not used as a dwelling.

Mrs Leaver lives in Southwest London and lets out two spare rooms on a B&B basis during the fortnight of the Wimbledon tennis tournament. She doesn't make any adaptations to the rooms other than the removal of some of her personal items.

For the purposes of the relief Mrs Leaver's property is, at all times, considered to be in use as and suitable for use as a dwelling.

26. Buy-to-let properties suitable for use as a dwelling are residential unless they are a development of six or more dwellings whereby they would be non-residential under s 116(7).

27. The specific inclusions and exclusions set out in paragraphs 22 and 23 above apply not only to a building's actual use at the effective date of the transaction, but to the uses for which it is suitable at that date. Where, however, a building is being put to one of the non-residential uses specified in s 116(3), this overrides any suitability for another use (s 116(4)). For example, a building used as a children's home may also be suitable for use as a school boarding house, but this will not preclude a claim to unlimited relief.

28. Where a vacant building is suitable for at least one of the uses specified in s 116(2) and at least one specified in s 116(3), s 116(5) determines, for the purposes of the relief, the use for which it is "most suitable". Whether or not a vacant building has one or more uses for which it is most suitable is a question of fact. Evidence supporting such uses should be retained.

29. Where there is a single use for which a building is most suitable, the fact that it is also suitable for another use will be discounted.

30. If there are a number of uses for which a building is most suitable and they all come within either of the two subsections, any other use for which the building is suitable will be discounted.

31. Where no most suitable use can be shown, the default will be to classify the building as residential property and apply the £150,000 limit.

32. Land and buildings that are not suitable for any use at the effective date of the transaction will be treated as residential property if they are "in the process of being constructed or adapted for such use"—see paragraphs 33 and 34 below.

PROCESS OF BEING CONSTRUCTED OR ADAPTED FOR USE AS A DWELLING

33. Undeveloped land is in essence non-residential, but land may be "residential property" for the purposes of Disadvantaged Area Relief if a residential building is being built on it at the effective date of the transaction. A development of six or more dwellings is deemed to be non-residential under s 116(7), even if the process of construction or marketing has begun at the effective date of the transaction (see paragraph 40).

34. Where (at the effective date of the transaction) an existing building is being adapted for, marketed for, or restored to, domestic use, it is residential for the purposes of the relief. The process is taken as commencing when the developer begins marketing the properties for sale or starts physical work on the site which ever is earlier.

This may apply, for example, where a derelict building is being made fit for habitation, or where a previously non-residential building is being converted to a dwelling. For example:

(a) Kristian is buying an apartment, in what will be a converted church, off-plan. The sale is completed on 15th March 2004, the properties were marketed for sale on 3 January 2004 and work on converting the church commenced on 2nd February 2004. For the purposes of this transaction the church is considered to be a dwelling, even though it has yet to be fully converted, from 3rd January. If the consideration is greater than £150,000 Kristian will have to pay the appropriate rate of Stamp Duty Land Tax.

In the above example the developer that initially purchased the church will have bought it as a non-residential property regardless of the intention to turn the building into residential units.

THE GARDEN OR GROUNDS OF A BUILDING USED ETC. AS A DWELLING

35. Section 116(1)(*b*) includes within the definition of residential property "land that is or forms part of the garden or grounds of a building within paragraph (*a*) (including any building or structure on such land)". The test the Inland Revenue will apply is similar to that applied for the purposes of the capital gains tax relief for main residences (TCGA 1992 s 222(3)). The land will include that which is needed for the reasonable enjoyment of the dwelling having regard to the size and nature of the dwelling.

36. A caravan or houseboat is not a "building" for this purpose.

37. Commercial farmland is not within the definition of residential property. A farmhouse situated on agricultural land would be dealt with under the mixed use provisions (paragraphs 19 and 20 above).

It may often be the case that farmhouses will occupy only a small fraction of the total land and will therefore, when apportioned, fall below the £150,000 consideration limit thus attracting the residential relief.

38. Outhouses on land within the s 116(1)(*b*) definition will also be "residential property" unless it can be demonstrated that they have a specific non-residential purpose. Where a distinct non-residential use can be demonstrated, the mixed use provisions will apply.

INTEREST IN OR RIGHTS OVER RESIDENTIAL PROPERTY

39. The treatment of interests in, or rights over, land or buildings for the purposes of Disadvantaged Area Relief will follow that of the land or buildings to which they relate.

SIX OR MORE SEPARATE DWELLINGS TRANSFERRED BY A SINGLE TRANSACTION

40. FA 2003 s 116(7) provides that "where six or more separate dwellings are the subject of a single transaction involving the transfer of a major interest in, or the grant of a lease over, them, then . . . those dwellings are treated as not being residential property". This recognises that commercial developers and institutional landlords, for example, frequently deal in numerous properties at one time. The fact that those properties may individually be "residential property" does not detract from the inherently commercial nature of the transaction itself.

41. To qualify as "separate", the dwellings must be self-contained. So for example, flats within a block, sharing some common areas but each with their own amenities will qualify as separate dwellings. Rooms let within a house will not constitute separate dwellings if tenants share amenities such as a kitchen and bathroom.

42. A transaction in respect of six or more such dwellings must be carried out by means of a single transaction in order to qualify for relief.

43. Qualifying multiple transactions will be treated as non-residential property for the purposes of relief, even where the proportionate consideration for individual dwellings exceeds the £150,000 limit for residential property. It is not a condition of relief that multiple transactions comprise only dwellings. One example of this would be where a purchaser is buying eight houses and four shops. Mixed use properties, such as pubs with self-contained residential accommodation, are also treated as non-residential.

44. The fact that some of the six or more dwellings within the single transaction are outside a designated disadvantaged area will not prevent them from constituting a non-residential transaction. However relief will only be available for the portion of the land situated within the disadvantaged area.

PROPERTY ONLY PARTLY WITHIN A DISADVANTAGED AREA

45. FA 2003 Sch 6 Pt 3 determines how property situated partly within and partly outside a designated disadvantaged area is to be treated for the purposes of the relief. Such cases are relatively rare in practice. Queries may be referred to Inland Revenue (Stamp Taxes) for guidance.

GRANTS OF NEW LEASES

46. FA 2003 Sch 6 Pt 2 deals with the charge to Stamp Duty Land Tax on the grant of a new lease.

Land all non-residential

47. If all of the land is non-residential it is exempt from any charge to Stamp Duty Land Tax.

Land all residential

48. The general rule is that:

(a) if the premium (and any other consideration than rent) does not exceed £150,000 then this is exempt from Stamp Duty Land Tax, and

(b) if the "net present value" of the rental payments does not exceed £150,000 then this is exempt from Stamp Duty Land Tax.

"Net present value" is, broadly speaking, the total rental payments due under the lease, discounted to reflect the fact that future rental payments are of less value than current rental payments. There is a tool for calculating net present value on the Inland Revenue website.

There is a special rule where the average annual rent exceeds £600. In such a case there is no relief or exemption for any premium. Any premium, however small, will be charged at 1% (or at higher rates if it exceeds £250,000).

49. Where there is mixed use apportionment is applied. The non-residential portion is exempt from lease duty.

If the consideration includes rent and the relevant rental value does not exceed £150,000, the rent does not count as chargeable consideration.

50. If the consideration includes consideration other than rent then:

(a) If the annual rent does not exceed £600 and the relevant consideration does not exceed £150,000, the consideration other than rent does not count as chargeable consideration
(b) If the annual rent exceeds £600, the consideration other than rent is counted as chargeable consideration

The "annual rent" is the average annual rent over the term of the lease.

FURTHER RESOURCES

Information can be found on our website, which also contains:

- a postcode search tool [www.hmrc.gov.uk/so/dar/dar-search.htm] to help identify whether a property falls within a disadvantaged area, and
- an intelligent decision-maker [www.hmrc.gov.uk/so/decisionmaker2.pdf] to help you decide whether a property is residential or non-residential.
- a lease duty calculator [www.ldcalculator.inlandrevenue.gov.uk/] which provides the amount of Stamp Duty Land Tax payable on a lease transaction

FLOWCHART TO DETERMINE WHETHER PROPERTY IS OR IS NOT "RESIDENTIAL PROPERTY"

Is the subject of the conveyance/transfer/lease . . .

(A)

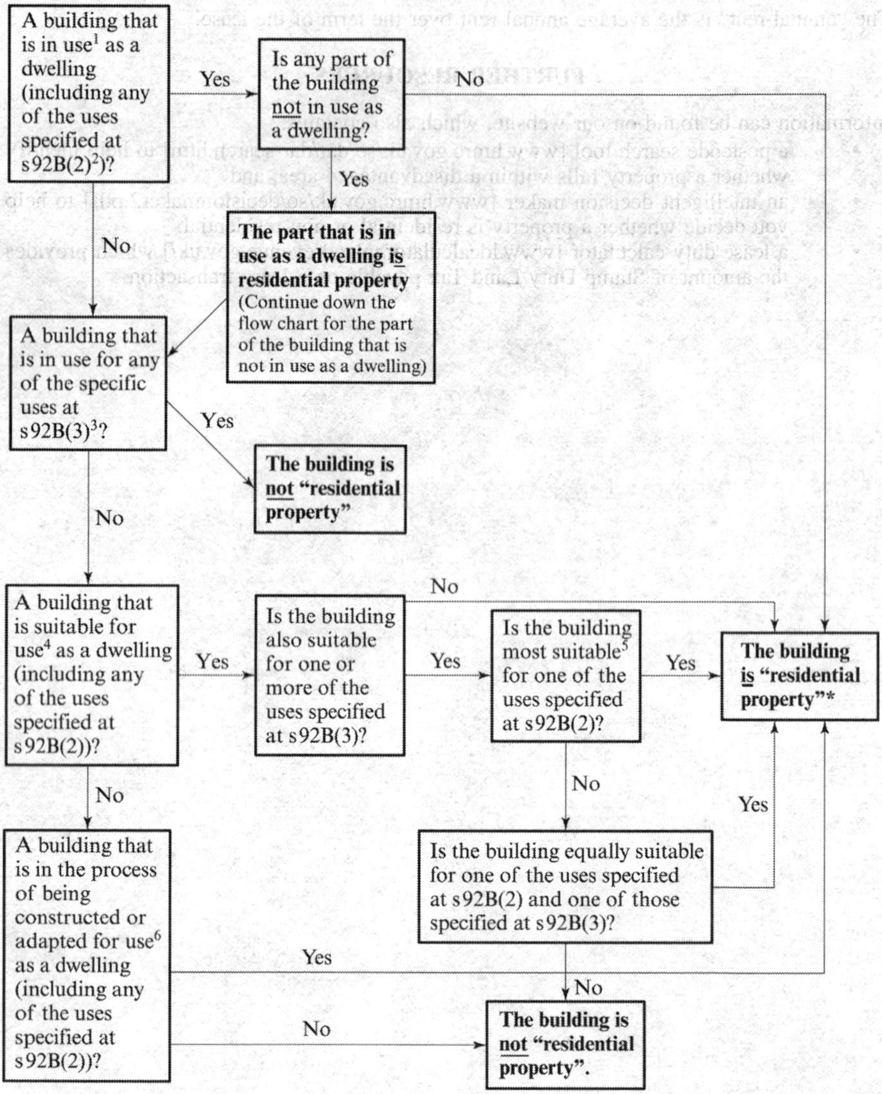

*unless the conveyance, transfer or lease comprises or includes six or more separate dwellings[7] made pursuant to a single contract, in which circumstances none of the land will be "residential property".

Is the subject of the conveyance/transfer/lease . . .

(B)

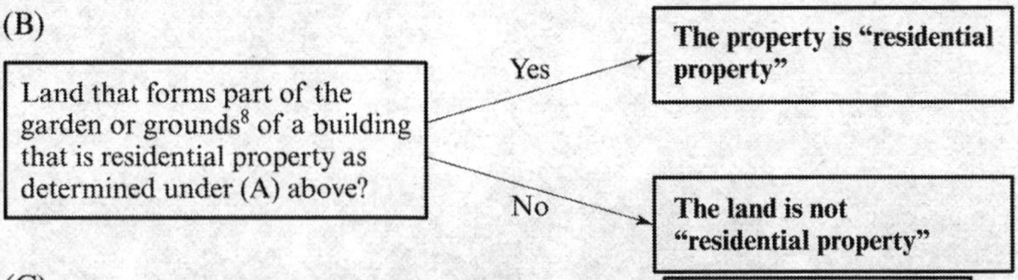

(C)

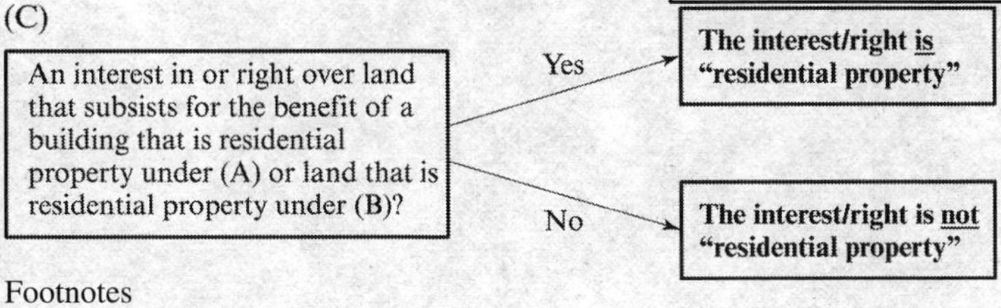

Footnotes

[1] See paragraph [11] to [14] of SP.

[2] See paragraph [22] of SP.

[3] See paragraph [23] of SP.

[4] See paragraph [15] to [18] of SP.

[5] See paragraph [29] of SP.

[6] See paragraph [33] to [34] of SP.

[7] See paragraph [40] to [44] of SP.

[8] See paragraph [35] of SP.

APPENDIX 3. EXTRA-STATUTORY CONCESSIONS

Contents

Concessions

G Concessions Relating to Stamp Duties

G1. STAMP ALLOWANCE ON LOST DOCUMENTS

Obsolete. See now SDMA 1891 s 12A.

G2. STAMPING OF REPLICAS OF DOCUMENTS WHICH HAVE BEEN SPOILT OR LOST

Obsolete. See now SDMA 1891 s 12A.

G3. GROUP LIFE AND PENSION POLICIES

Obsolete. See FA 1989 s 173.

G4. REPAYMENT OF DUTY ON CANCELLED POLICIES OF INSURANCE

Obsolete. See FA 1989 s 173.

G5. TRANSFER OF STOCK FROM PERSONS TO THEMSELVES OPERATING AS AN EXECUTORS' ASSENT

Stamp duty is not claimed on transfer of stock in a company registered in England, Wales or Northern Ireland from a person to himself (or from two or more persons to themselves) which operates as an executors' assent. The point does not arise in relation to companies registered in Scotland.

G6. TRANSFERS OF ASSETS BETWEEN NON-PROFIT MAKING BODIES WITH SIMILAR OBJECTS

When the reconstruction of a non-profit making body with objects in a field of public interest such as education, community work or scientific research, or the amalgamation of two or more such bodies involves a transfer to the successor body of assets for which there passes no consideration in money or money's worth, the instruments of transfer are treated as exempt from ad valorem stamp duty and charged to £5 fixed duty only. There must be sufficient identity between the members of the transferor and transferee bodies and the rules of both must prohibit the distribution of assets to members and provide that on a winding-up the assets can only be transferred to a similar body subject to like restrictions.

G7. TRANSFERS OF STOCK INTO SEPON

Replaced by FA 1996 s 191.

G8. STOCK LOAN RETURNS

Replaced by FA 1996 s 191.

G9. TRANSFERS OF COLLATERAL

Replaced by FA 1996 s 191.

APPENDIX 4. PRESS RELEASES, ETC

2 JANUARY 1963. CONTROLLER OF STAMPS STAMP DUTY ON LEASES

THE BASIS OF ASSESSMENT

The Revenue have recently given consideration to the basis of assessment of duty on leases which contain one or more of the following provisions:

(a) a known rent not exceeding £100 pa and a further unascertainable rent;
(b) a term commencing from a date prior to the date of execution;
(c) a rent or rents fixed for part only of the term, the rent for the remainder of the term to be agreed subsequently.

The question under consideration in regard to leases of type (*a*) . . .

[NB This question was rendered obsolete by FA 1963, which repealed FA 1947 s 54 (2).]

In regard to leases of type (*b*) the Board's view is that, in computing the length of the term, any period prior to the date of the lease is to be left out of account on the authority of *Shaw v Kay* (1847) 1 Ex 412, *Cadogan v Guiness* (1936) Ch 515, and *Colton v Becollda Property Investments Ltd* [1950] 1 KB 216. These cases do not, however, provide any authority as to the treatment of rent payable in respect of a period prior to the date of the lease: for the sake of consistency and simplicity, the Board have decided that such rent shall be left out of account, so that the treatment approved by the courts in relation to the term will in practice also be applied to the rent. This means, in effect, a continuation of existing practice, although this practice may not have been applied consistently in individual cases in the past.

Leases of type (*c*) . . .

[NB The treatment of leases of type (*c*) no longer applies: see IR Tax Bulletin, Issue 18, August 1995, p 234.]

28 FEBRUARY 1978. PRACTICE DIRECTION OF THE PRINCIPAL REGISTRY OF THE FAMILY DIVISION GRANTS OF REPRESENTATION

1. Where, for the purposes of applying for a grant of representation, it is necessary for the applicant to produce to the Principal or a District Probate Registry an original deed or other instrument, it is the practice of the Registry to examine the instrument to ensure that it has been properly executed and duly stamped under SA 1891 before proceeding with the application. Where there is any doubt whether the instrument is duly stamped, the applicant will be asked to present the instrument to the Controller of Stamps (Inland Revenue) for adjudication before the issue of the grant.

2. To avoid delay in the issue of the grant in such cases, the Commissioners of Inland Revenue have agreed that the applicant may, if so desired, submit the original instrument to the Adjudication Section of the Office of the Controller of Stamps for preliminary noting, endorsement and return, providing that a written undertaking is at the same time given to the Controller by the solicitor applying for the grant of representation that he will, on or immediately after the issue of the grant, re-submit the original instrument to the Controller for formal adjudication and pay the stamp duty (if any) to which the instrument is adjudged liable.

3. In every case on the application for a grant, the original instrument (after inspection) will be returned as soon as practicable to the applicant, or his solicitor, by the probate registry. Practitioners are reminded, however, that where the application is for a grant to an assignee or assignees under the Non-Contentious Probate Rules 1954, Rule 22, a copy of the original instrument of assignment must be lodged in the registry (see Rule 22 (3)).

1 MAY 1984. INLAND REVENUE
STAMP DUTY: PURCHASE BY A COMPANY OF ITS OWN SHARES

In reply to a Parliamentary Question the Financial Secretary to the Treasury gave the following Written Answer yesterday:

> "The Companies Act 1981 enables companies to purchase their own shares. A specific exemption from ad valorem stamp duty was not provided although it was intended that s 52 of the Act (Disclosure of Particulars of Purchase and Authorised Contracts) should effectively provide for this. Doubts have arisen as to whether s 52 achieved this objective.
>
> Ad valorem duty is payable on any conveyance or transfer on sale and SA 1891 s 54, provides that the expression 'conveyance on sale' includes every instrument whereby any property sold is transferred or vested in the purchaser. The Revenue are advised that although the matter is not free from doubt there are grounds for holding that this section does not apply when a company purchases its own shares. This is the view that the Board proposes to adopt. A Secretary or Registrar of a company may accordingly amend the register without requiring that any delivery statement is stamped with ad valorem duty.
>
> The Companies Act 1981 provides an exemption from capital duty for future re-issues of the repurchased shares."

NOTE

The Financial Secretary has clarified the stamp duty treatment on the purchase by a company of its own shares.

The Companies Act 1981 enabled companies to purchase their own shares. An exemption from capital duty was provided to cover any future issues of the cancelled shares but nothing was said in the Act about transfer duty. The Bill however was amended to remove the need for a document which would attract stamp duty. Doubts have arisen as to whether the amendments achieved their objective. The Financial Secretary has informed the House that the Revenue has been advised that although the position is not free from doubt there are grounds for holding that ad valorem duty is not payable. This is the view that the Revenue proposes to adopt.

[NB The successor to the Companies Act 1981 s 52 is now to be found as Companies Act 2006 s 69. Note FA 1986 s 66 effects charge to stamp duty on such purchases by the imposition of ad valorem stamp duty on the return (Form SH03) made to the registrar of companies in accordance with Companies Act 2006 s 707.]

20 MARCH 1990. INLAND REVENUE
STAMP DUTY ON SHARES TO BE ABOLISHED

The Chancellor proposes in his Budget to abolish all stamp duties on transactions in shares from a date late in 1991–92 [but see the Revenue Press Release of 19 December 1991] to coincide as far as possible with the introduction of paperless dealing under the Stock Exchange's new share transfer system ("TAURUS").

Abolition of these duties will also:

(a) enhance London's competitiveness as an international centre for equity trading;
(b) boost wider share ownership by reducing transaction costs and benefit savers.

This is the sixth major tax to be abolished since 1983. It makes a significant contribution to the overall simplification of the tax system and the reduction of compliance burdens on taxpayers.

DETAILS

Stamp duties on shares: main duties

1. The main duties to be abolished are:
   (a) stamp duty on individual share transfers, which is levied on UK securities at a rate since 1986 of, broadly, 0·5% of the price paid;
   (b) stamp duty of 1·5%, which is payable where UK shares are converted into depositary receipts ("ADRs") or transferred into clearance services;
   (c) stamp duty reserve tax, which applies, at the same rates as stamp duty, to some share transactions which are outside the stamp duty net.

Stamp duties on shares: associated charges

2. Also to be abolished are:
   (a) the stamp duty charges on bearer shares;
   (b) the 50p fixed duty on share transfers other than sales;
   (c) stamp duty on all transfers of units under a unit trust scheme.

Timing

3. Legislation to abolish these duties will be in the 1990 Finance Bill. The Chancellor proposes that abolition should be triggered by Treasury Order in due course. He has indicated that this Order will broadly coincide with the start of paperless trading under the Stock Exchange's planned TAURUS system—ie towards the end of 1991–92 on the current timetable [but see above note]. Until then, duty continues to apply at the existing rates.

Effects of abolition

4. The Government believes abolition of these taxes will:
   (a) smooth the path for cheaper and more efficient paperless share dealing, by removing the need for the systems involved to take account of stamp duty;
   (b) increase the liquidity and efficiency of the London equity market, and maintain its competitiveness in the face of planned tax reductions in other financial centres;
   (c) encourage investment in UK equities and so foster wider share ownership;
   (d) benefit savers, including beneficiaries of pension funds and life policies;
   (e) further simplify the tax system and ease the compliance burden on individual shareholders, the equity market and company registrars.

Cost

5. The timing means that no cost will arise until late in 1991–92. The cost that year will depend on precisely when the duty is abolished; a 1 January 1992 start would for example produce a 1991–92 cost of £120 million. The full year cost will be around £800 million.

Stamp duty on property

6. The Chancellor is not proposing to make any changes to the stamp duty on the transfer of land and property (including houses).

NOTES

Abolition of duties

1. This Government has already abolished
   (a) Investment income surcharge (1984);

Part II ST

(b) National insurance surcharge (1984);
(c) Development land tax (1985);
(d) the tax on lifetime gifts (1986);
(e) capital duty and the associated unit trust instrument duty (1988)

as well as a number of minor duties. Abolition of stamp duty on shares carries this process forward, making a significant contribution to the overall simplification of the tax system.

Stamp duty on shares

2. The ad valorem stamp duty on individual transfers of UK companies' shares is currently charged at 50p per £100 or part thereof, ie broadly at 0·5%. There are exemptions for purchases by market-makers and charities. Government stock and most commercial loan capital are outside the scope of the charge.

3. Conversion of UK shares into depositary receipts ("ADRs") or their transfer into a clearance service attracts a 1·5% "season ticket" charge—see para 8 below.

4. Bearer instruments are normally charged at 1·5% on a once-and-for-all basis, either on issue (for instruments issued in the UK) or on their first transfer in Great Britain.

5. Certain transfers of shares otherwise than on sale can give rise to a fixed 50p charge—for example transfers where there is no change of beneficial ownership.

Stamp duty reserve tax

6. This tax was introduced in 1986 in order to broaden the base of stamp duty on shares, by charging a wider range of transactions. Stamp duty is a tax on *documents*, but stamp duty reserve tax applies to most *agreements* to sell UK securities. It therefore brings within the scope of the charge:
(a) the purchase and resale of a security within the same Stock Exchange account;
(b) the purchase of renounceable letters of allotment or acceptance;
(c) the purchase of shares registered in the name of a nominee acting for seller and purchaser;
(d) the purchase of shares which are resold before they are taken into the purchaser's name.

7. Stamp duty reserve tax on individual share transfers is charged at the same rate, 0·5%, as stamp duty on shares. For conversion into ADR form etc there is again a 1·5% charge to parallel the higher rate of stamp duty—see 8 below.

Depositary receipts and clearance services—the higher rate charges

8. Where shares are transferred into depositary receipt form or into a clearance service, the higher rate of 1·5% stamp duty or stamp duty reserve tax applies on the initial transfer. This charge is in the nature of a "season ticket"—subsequent transfers of depositary receipts, or of shares within a clearance service, then take place free of stamp duty or stamp duty reserve tax.

Unit trusts

9. Stamp duty arises on the purchase of units by one unit holder from another, and in the more common situation of a surrender for cash of units to the managers. The rates are broadly the same as the ad valorem charge on shares, but special reliefs apply.

[*Note:* See note printed at the end of the contents list to Part II Stamp Duty, Stamp Duty Reserve Tax and Stamp Duty Land Tax.]

18 JULY 1990. THE LAW SOCIETY
STAMP DUTY ADJUDICATION

The Stamp Office has announced a change in its adjudication procedures. Following examination of an instrument for adjudication, the Stamp Office's practice is to notify the applicant of the amount of duty estimated to be payable.

It will continue to allow 28 days for applicants to respond to estimates of duty payable. If no response has been received after the 28 days, only one reminder will be issued. The office will consider the request for adjudication as having been withdrawn once a further 14 days have elapsed after the issue of the reminder, and will then return the instrument unstamped to the applicant.

This will not prevent the applicant from re-presenting the instrument for adjudication. However, SA 1891 ss 14 (4) (instrument not duly stamped not to be given in evidence), 15 (penalty upon stamping instruments after execution) might apply in the event of delay [*Law Society's Gazette*, 18 July 1990, p 13].

19 MARCH 1991. INLAND REVENUE STAMP DUTY: CHARGES TO BE ABOLISHED

The Chancellor proposes in his Budget to abolish stamp duty charges on property other than land and buildings. The intention is to abolish these charges at the same time as the duty on shares (likely to be late in 1991–92).

The stamp duty on Northern Ireland bank notes will be abolished from 1 January 1992.

Abolition of these charges will:

(a) relieve from stamp duty a variety of types of property, such as patents, goodwill and debt, including sovereign debt;

(b) further simplify the tax system, and reduce the compliance burden on taxpayers.

DETAILS

1. At present stamp duty is charged on transactions in various types of property. FA 1990 included provisions abolishing all the stamp duty charges (including stamp duty reserve tax) on transactions in shares, from a date to be fixed by Treasury order. The date will be fixed to coincide as closely as possible with the introduction of paperless share dealing under the Stock Exchange's automated share transfer system ("TAURUS").

2. The new proposals will remove the 1% and fixed (mainly 50p) stamp duty charges on documents relating to all other types of property except land and buildings (including houses).

3. The only charges that will remain are the 1% sale duty on land and buildings, and the associated fixed charges; and the charge on the premium and rent of new leases, known as lease duty. The Chancellor is not proposing changes to these duties.

4. The Government intend to introduce the legislation at the Committee Stage of the Finance Bill.

5. The full-year cost will be £15 million.

Part II ST

NOTES

Existing stamp duties

1. Stamp duty is a tax on documents. There are a number of separate duties, under different heads of charge.

2. The main stamp duty is a charge at 1% of the price paid on a conveyance or transfer of property by means of a document. In addition, fixed (generally 50p) duties arise on certain deeds where no money usually changes hands—for example, declarations of trust and exchanges.

Stamp duty reforms

3. In addition to the FA 1990 provisions to abolish the duties on shares, this Government has already abolished:

— stamp duty on gifts (1985);
— capital duty (1988);
— unit trust instrument duty (1988);
— life assurance policy duty (1989);

and a number of the fixed duties have been removed.

4. Since 1979 the rate of duty on land and buildings has been reduced, and the threshold below which no stamp duty is payable on land and buildings raised three times. The current threshold is £30,000.

Stamp duty on Northern Ireland bank notes

5. Northern Ireland bank notes, unlike those issued in Great Britain, attract stamp duty under the "Bank Note" head of charge in SA 1891 Sch 1. The duty is charged, at 50p per £100, on the average value of notes in circulation each half year. The duty on bank notes in Great Britain was abolished in 1972.

[*Note:* see note to the Revenue Press Release of 20 March 1990.]

29 MAY 1991. THE LAW SOCIETY
STAMP DUTY—MITIGATION OF PENALTIES

A letter from the Inland Revenue Stamp Office (published in the *Law Society's Gazette*, 29 May 1991) sets out the Revenue practice as regards mitigation of the statutory penalties (SA 1891 s 15(2)(*c*)) for late presentation of documents liable to stamp duty as follows:

"In addition to the duty payable, the price to be paid for late stamping is—

— £10 (SA 1891 s 15 (1)), plus
— interest at 5% per annum on the duty outstanding where this is more than £10 (SA 1891 s 15 (1)), plus
— a sum equal to the amount of duty outstanding (SA 1891 s 15 (2) (*c*)).

In all but those cases of deliberate withholding of duty, avoidance or extreme delay (over one year late), this could be said to be a disproportionately high price to pay. We would not dissent from this view and our practice will be to invoke the authority provided by SA 1891 s 15 (3) (*b*) and mitigate the penalty. The degree of mitigation will be influenced by the reasons for and length of delay. However the minimum level to which a penalty can be expected to be mitigated will reflect interest rates prevailing during the period of delay.

Our offices are instructed in general to mitigate penalties to a level equivalent to an interest rate charge of 12% to 15% per annum for a delay of up to three months, 15% to 20% per annum for three to six months delay, and 20% to 25% for six to 12 months."

[See further the letter published in the *Law Society's Gazette* on 9 June 1993, referred to below.]

14 JUNE 1991. INLAND REVENUE
FINANCE BILL: STAMP DUTY: ABOLITION OF CHARGES

The Government has tabled six new clauses to the Finance Bill containing its proposals for abolishing stamp duty charges on all property other than land and buildings, as announced in the Chancellor's Budget.

DETAILS

1. Under the new proposals all stamp duty charges will be abolished except where the property being transferred is:

(a) land;
(b) an interest in the proceeds of sale of land held on trust for sale; or
(c) a licence to occupy land.

2. "Land" includes buildings.

3. The property to be exempted includes goodwill, patents and debt, including sovereign debt. The charges to be abolished are the 1% duty on sales of such property, and the fixed (mainly 50p) charges on certain other transactions where none of the property being transferred is land.

4. No change is proposed to the duties on land. So the 1% sale duty on houses and land where the price is above £30,000 [but see FA 1963 s 55, and the Stamp Duty (Temporary Provisions) Act 1992], and the charges on the premium and rent of new leases, remain the same.

5. The rules for cases where property is transferred subject to a debt, or in consideration of a debt, will also remain unchanged.

6. The new clauses provide that, where land and exempt property are transferred together, the purchase price is to be apportioned fairly between them. For example, a business may be transferred at a price which includes both the business premises and goodwill. The provisions will ensure that the chargeable property does not attract either too much or too little stamp duty.

7. With one exception the changes will come into effect at the same time as the abolition of stamp duties on shares, which will be fixed to coincide as closely as possible with the introduction of paperless share dealing ("TAURUS"). The exception is the duty on Northern Ireland banknotes, which will be abolished from 1 January 1992. The TAURUS system is expected to be introduced in May 1992.

NOTES

1. The Chancellor's Budget proposals for stamp duty were set out in a press release "Stamp duty: Charges to be abolished" issued on Budget Day, 19 March 1991.

2. Under FA 1990, the abolition date of stamp duties on shares is to be fixed by Treasury Order.

[*Note:* see note to the Revenue Press Release of 20 March 1990.]

18 OCTOBER 1991. INLAND REVENUE PROPOSED MERGER OF LIFFE AND LTOM: NEW TAX RULES

The Financial Secretary to the Treasury, Francis Maude, announced yesterday proposed new tax and stamp duty rules for the new market formed from the merger of the London International Financial Futures Exchange (LIFFE) and the London Traded Options Market (LTOM).

In a written reply to a Parliamentary Question (HC Written Answer, 17 October 1991, Vol 196, col 214), the Financial Secretary said—

"The rules for certain tax reliefs which are available at present to market-makers in traded options assume that the London Traded Options Market is part of the Stock Exchange. When the proposed merger of the London Traded Options Market with the London International Financial Futures Exchange takes place, this will no longer be so. New regulations will be made to adapt the present reliefs accordingly, and to widen them in some respects to take account of the structure of the new market, once the arrangements for the merger have been finalised.

The new regulations will provide stamp duty and stamp duty reserve tax reliefs for members of the new merged market acting as principal traders in equity options. The reliefs will apply, within certain prescribed limits, to transactions in equities which are necessary to hedge positions in options to buy or sell securities which members enter into on their own account and not on behalf of clients.

Stock lending reliefs, and exemption in certain circumstances from the anti-bond-washing legislation, will also apply to such transactions and to transactions where stock is borrowed or purchased to meet a delivery obligation arising from the exercise or assignment of an option, again within certain prescribed limits.

For members of the merged market acting as principal traders in option contracts, regulations will be made to place them on a comparable basis to Stock Exchange market-makers when required to manufacture a dividend."

DETAILS

Stamp duty/SDRT

1. Currently, market-makers in options to buy or sell securities get relief from stamp duty reserve tax (SDRT) on agreements to purchase securities in the ordinary course of their market-making business, provided the options—

(a) are quoted on the Stock Exchange; and

(b) relate to the same securities as the securities purchased.

This relief—which does not extend to other options dealers—mirrors the SDRT relief for market-makers in shares quoted on the Stock Exchange.

2. The merger of the markets will mean that the traded options market will no longer be part of the Stock Exchange. The regulations will adapt the current stamp duty and SDRT provisions to cater for the merged market. By giving a relief to principal traders on the new market (subject to a more restrictive limitation than market-makers) they will broaden the scope of the present exemption.

3. The regulations will make other provisions about stamp duty and SDRT arising out of the merger. For example, they will ensure that the stamp duty relief for stock-borrowing transactions is extended to members of the merged market subject to the relevant limits; and that delivery of stock on the exercise of an option under the new arrangements does not lead to multiple charges to SDRT.

Stock lending

4. Stock lending is a long established practice that enables securities dealers, in return for a fee, to "borrow" securities (including shares) from institutions such as insurance companies or pension funds when they need them in order to deliver on sales. The dealer undertakes to replace the borrowed stock at a later date with securities of the same kind and amount.

5. Although termed "stock lending" the process involves the transfer of ownership of the securities. Under present law, if securities are borrowed under an approved stock lending arrangement by a market-maker in those securities, both borrower and lender are exempt from tax charges which would otherwise arise when the securities were transferred. These exemptions currently apply only where the borrower is a market maker. This is because such market-makers provide liquidity, and so assist the efficiency of the market, by taking on an obligation to deal at all times at the prices they quote. This may involve selling securities which they do not have, so they may need to borrow securities to enable them to meet their obligations to deliver on the sale.

6. Traded options dealers, whether or not they are market-makers, may be faced with an obligation to deliver securities on which they have entered into options contracts. In the new traded options market it is envisaged that dealers who are not market-makers will play an important role in providing liquidity. The Government has therefore decided to allow tax relief on stock borrowed to hedge positions they have taken in options. Limitations will be prescribed to ensure that the reliefs are restricted to genuine hedging transactions or transactions entered into to enable a delivery obligation to be fulfilled. These limitations will be more restricted for non-market-making principal traders (who can choose whether or not to deal in a particular option) than for market-makers (who have to deal and who therefore require a more flexible regime). Nevertheless the limitations will in each case recognise the need to hedge, and to maintain a hedge, against options positions.

Manufactured dividends

7. Where stock is lent, payments made by the borrower to the lender to compensate the lender for the dividends that would have been received had the securities not been lent are known as "manufactured dividends". The rules for accounting for tax on manufactured dividends include provisions to prevent relief for the tax in respect of manufactured dividends paid outside approved procedures. These rules will apply to members of the new merged market who borrow stock in the same way as they currently apply to equivalent market makers on the Stock Exchange.

Bond-washing

8. Bond-washing is the practice whereby shares are sold with an accrued dividend and bought back immediately after the shares have gone ex dividend so that the payment for the accrued dividend is treated as a capital gain rather than as income and so receives more favourable tax treatment. TA 1988 s 732 discourages securities dealers from entering into such transactions by reducing the amount which they can deduct for tax purposes in respect of the accrued dividend.

9. At present market-makers in securities are exempted from the anti-bond-washing provisions of TA 1988 s 732. This is because a market-maker's business involves buying and selling securities at all times, regardless of whether they are cum or ex dividend.

10. The exemption for market-makers reflects the existing market structure of the Stock Exchange (of which LTOM is presently part). The options and futures market to be formed from the merger of LIFFE and LTOM, however, will rely for its liquidity on a wider category of principal traders than just market-makers, and it has therefore been decided that they too should benefit from the exemption. As with the stock lending reliefs, there will be prescribed limitations to restrict the exemption to hedging transactions, and transactions entered into, to enable a delivery obligation to be fulfilled.

NOTES

Stamp duty/SDRT

1. The regulations will be made under the powers in FA 1991 ss 116, 117.

2. The existing exemption from SDRT for market-makers in options is in FA 1986 s 89 (1A).

3. Stamp duty on shares and SDRT are due to be abolished under legislation in FA 1990. The abolition date will be fixed by Treasury Order.

Stock lending

4. The regulations will be made under the powers contained in TA 1988 s 129 (4).

5. The existing arrangements for the approval of stock lending arrangements are set out in TA 1988 s 129 and SI 1989/1299 [see *Simon's Tax Intelligence* 1989, p 662] (as amended by SI 1990/2552 [see *Simon's Tax Intelligence* 1990, p 53]).

Manufactured dividends

6. The regulations will be made under the powers contained in TA 1988 Sch 23A.

Bond-washing

7. The regulations will be made under TA 1988 s 732 as amended by FA 1991 s 56.

4 MARCH 1992. LAW SOCIETY STAMP DUTY AND VAT

Following the publication of Statement of Practice SP 11/91 on the interaction between stamp duty and VAT (see *Simon's Tax Intelligence* 1991, p 818), the Law Society's revenue law committee raised a number of points of uncertainty in correspondence with the Inland Revenue. The Revenue's views on the points raised are noted below.

[AMOUNT ON WHICH STAMP DUTY IS PAYABLE]

It has emerged from [the correspondence that the Revenue's] view, as a result of the legal advice it has received, and in the light of which SP 11/91 was published, is first that the contingency principle will apply to any transaction in respect of a property which could be affected by an election to waive exemption from VAT, where the election has not been exercised by a landlord at the time that a lease is entered into (and there is no contemporaneous or binding agreement between the parties to the lease that the election will not be exercised). Accordingly in calculating the duty payable VAT should therefore in the Revenue's view be added to any payments to be made by the purchaser or lessee to which an election could still apply.

Secondly, in the cases which deal with the so-called contingency principle it was held that stamp duty is chargeable on a *prima facie* sum regardless of whether that sum might increase or decrease depending on the occurrence of some contingency.

The Revenue considers that the calculation should be based on current rates of VAT, notwithstanding that there may be a fluctuation in the rate of VAT in the period which elapses between the date when the lease is granted and when any election is made.

Apart from the correspondence on the quantum of duty [the Law Society's revenue law committee reports that the correspondence to date has also established the Revenue's views on the following points].

[AGREEMENT BY LESSOR NOT TO ELECT TO WAIVE EXEMPTION]

If, having entered into an agreement for a lease which made no reference to the intending lessor making an election to waive exemption from VAT, the intending lessor subsequently agreed that he or she would not make the election, on what basis would the agreement for lease be stamped, ie what would be the value of the consideration?

[Revenue view] A binding undertaking by a lessor, after an agreement for lease is entered into but before it is stamped, not to exercise an option to charge VAT, would be effective to exclude any stamp duty on VAT that might otherwise be charged on that agreement.

[TRANSFER OF BUSINESS AS A GOING CONCERN]

[The revenue law committee] assume that where the transferor has elected to charge VAT in relation to land (so it will be necessary for the transferee to make a similar election), if the transfer is to be treated as a supply of neither goods nor services for VAT purposes, then conveyances or transfers will be stamped as if no VAT is due, provided the agreement itself or any covering letter to the local stamp office makes it clear that the parties expect such treatment to be available or can confirm that Customs & Excise will apply the transfers of going concerns provisions to the transaction. This would save having to delay submission of documents until it is clear (or has been confirmed post-transfer) that such treatment will apply. Could the Stamp Office confirm that this procedure would be adopted?

[Revenue view] Yes. Such documents can be dealt with at any stamp office and do not need to be sent for adjudication on those grounds alone.

[GROUPS OF COMPANIES]

Where a lease is made between two companies in a VAT group registration (and so the supply is to be ignored for VAT purposes) will the possibility of an election being made at a later date be ignored?

[Revenue view] Yes.

[SUB-SALES]

With sub-sales, is the additional amount that would be payable, had an election to charge VAT been made prior to A agreeing to transfer land to B, ignored in determining whether the consideration provided by C to B upon a sub-sale of the property was less than its value (Stamp Act 1891 s 58 (4) (*a*), (7))?

[Revenue view] Yes.

Law Society's Gazette, 4 March 1992, p 16.

9 JUNE 1993. LAW SOCIETY STAMP DUTY—MITIGATION OF PENALTIES

[The following statutory penalties may be imposed for the late presentation of documents liable to stamp duty—

— £10 (Stamp Act 1891 s 15 (1)), plus
— interest at 5% per annum on the duty outstanding where this is more than £10 (Stamp Act 1891 s 15 (1)), plus
— a sum equal to the amount of duty outstanding (Stamp Act 1891 s 15 (2) (*c*)).

In practice, except in cases of deliberate withholding of duty, avoidance or delays exceeding one year, the Revenue exercises its authority to mitigate penalties (Stamp Act 1891 s 15 (3) (*b*)).]

In the *Law Society's Gazette* of 29 May 1991, a letter from the Controller of Stamps, Keith Hodgson, was published, which gave details of the scale of charges which the Stamp Office would apply where instruments were not presented for stamping at the proper time.

Since then, there has been a reduction in the level of interest charged, to reflect the general reduction in interest rates, and Stamp Offices are now instructed to mitigate penalties to a level equivalent to an interest rate charge of around 10% per annum for delays of up to three months, and 10% to 15% for three to 12 months: *Law Society's Gazette*, 9 June 1993, p 32.

12 JULY 1993. INLAND REVENUE STAMP DUTY—NEW BUILDINGS

The Inland Revenue have today published a statement of practice (SP 8/93) setting out their view of how the law on stamp duty applies to certain transactions involving new buildings. The transactions concerned are where there purport to be separate contracts for the construction of the buildings and the purchase of the land on which they are to stand. The statement does not affect the common situation where a contract for the sale of a new house on a plot of land is subsequently given effect by a conveyance of the whole property, in the same way as most ordinary sales of new houses. A copy of the statement is [reproduced in Appendix 2].

The statement reflects legal advice given to the Board following the High Court decision in the case of the *Prudential Assurance Company Ltd v IR Comrs* ([1992] STC 863; [1993] 1 WLR 211). It replaces previous statements on this subject published in 1957 and 1987 (SP 10/87).

DETAILS

1. The statement applies only where—

— there is a contract for the sale or lease of a building plot and the builder or developer is to construct buildings on the site for the purchaser; and

— at the date of the contract, building work on the plot has either not been started or is incomplete; and
— at the time the conveyance or lease is executed, building work on the plot has begun (and perhaps been completed).

2. The statement sets out the stamp duty consequences of a number of different arrangements. The stamp duty treatment in a particular case will depend on the precise facts of the case. But in broad terms—

(i) where there is a contract for a conveyance or lease of land and, as a separate transaction, a further contract for building works, stamp duty on the conveyance or lease will be calculated without regard to the further contract.

(ii) where within a single transaction there are separate contracts for the sale or lease of a building plot, and for building works on that plot, the stamp duty charge depends on whether the contracts are genuinely independent. If the contracts are independent, duty will be charged on the price paid or payable for both the land itself and for any building that is on the land at the time the instrument is executed, including partly completed buildings. If the contracts are not independent, stamp duty will be charged on the total price for the land and completed buildings.

3. The statement does not apply where there is evidence of a sham or artificial transaction.

Transitional arrangements

4. Stamp duty can be paid on the basis which applied before this Statement, where that is more beneficial, if unconditional contracts have been entered into either before the Statement or within 28 days after it.

Procedure

5. If stamp duty is offered on the total price paid for a building plot and the completed building, the documents should be submitted to the Stamp Office in the usual way.

6. If the total price does not exceed the stamp duty threshold (£60,000 for documents executed on or after 16 March) the documents (except for new leases) can be submitted direct to the Land Registry (in Scotland, the Keeper of the Registers) provided the usual certificate can be included. New leases will need to be stamped in respect of the rent.

7. If the total price paid exceeds the threshold but duty is offered on a lesser amount, the documents should be sent to the Stamp Office together with a full explanation.

17 MARCH 1994. HANSARD
STAMP DUTY (CLAUSE 226)

Mr Andrew Smith: Would not it have been better if the Government had structured the law so that there was equity between the different ways of organising transactions, rather than leaving it to members of the public to organise their affairs so that they can structure the transaction in a way that takes advantage of the ambiguous position of that important aspect of the law?

. . .

Mr Nelson: I think and hope that the Government have got it right, but to be fair to the hon Gentleman, I asked the same question when I examined the original proposals. The answer is that stamp duty is a tax on documents, and it is important to consider the substance of the documents involved. Of course, one seeks and hopes for clarity in the imposition of tax so that those who construct documents know exactly what their liabilities are. One cannot, however, avoid considering the nature of the document to ascertain whether duty will arise.

To clarify matters for my hon Friend the Member for Slough, under the new rules, where a property worth £100,000 is exchanged for another worth £70,000 plus £30,000 cash, it is true that stamp duty will fall on the full £100,000 value on both sides of that exchange. There is no need, however, for that to happen where a cash equality sum is involved, and it can be obviated in two ways. One way is that the exchange contract should have a clause apportioning an amount of £70,000, as in the example, which relates to the value. So it could be said that in exchange for a property worth £100,000, the other party will hand over another which is assumed to have a notional value of £70,000 of the total. Where the value of the property is apportioned in that exchange, I understand that that is the only amount that is liable to stamp duty.

That is not necessarily the only way of getting round a problem that might arise where there is a cash equality sum and stamp duty might otherwise be liable. The better way is for there to be a contract of sale. There is little difference between the effect of a contract of exchange and a contract of sale, but the latter would essentially say, "I sell to you this property worth £100,000 and you will pay me a property worth £70,000 and cash of £30,000." Where it is a sale document, the stamp duty will apply on only one side of that and it would not be necessary to pay full stamp duty the other way round.

House developers and others who take properties in part exchange will be able to do that, only with the imposition of the nominal 50p stamp duty, and then they can sell them. When a part exchange property was sold, its purchaser would have to pay stamp duty in the normal way. That is what would happen if it involved three parties instead of two.

. . .

Mr Nelson: . . . The stamp duty office is willing to advise practitioners, or others who are in doubt, about how to structure a contract to ensure that it is effective and that people do not have to pay stamp duty on a value over and above that of the property which is being transferred. That is the right way to proceed.

. . .

Mr Butterfill: Does my hon Friend agree that it is almost inconceivable that a house builder of any substance who was operating a part-exchange scheme would fail to point out to a purchaser the way in which the matter should be structured so as to minimise the liability?

Mr Nelson: My hon Friend is right. I can tell him and the hon Member for Christchurch (Mrs Maddock), who rightly referred to the propensity of people to part exchange their properties, that the House Builders Federation made representations and explained its concern about the impact that the measure would have on its marketing and on the form of part-exchange deals that are such an essential part of the marketplace. The Government clarified that that would be permitted. I believe that that was broadly welcome by the House Builders Federation.

Mr Andrew Smith: I beg to move amendment No 361, in page 194, line 40 [clause 226 (5)], at end insert—

> "(5A) For the purposes of section 34 (4) of the Finance Act 1958 (certificates of value) a transaction shall not be regarded as forming part of a larger transaction solely because it is or comprises part of the consideration for the transfer or vesting of another estate or interest in land or the grant of any lease or tack.".

The amendment would make it clear that the £60,000 threshold below which duty is payable applies to both legs of the transaction or exchange. I understand that once again conflicting advice has been issued by different stamp offices on the application of the threshold to exchange transactions following the Budget. Some have said that the threshold will apply to the combined value of the two properties, others that it will apply to each property individually.

. . .

The treatment of a particular case will depend on all the facts, but where one property is exchanged for another, the stamp office would apply the thresholds to each separately. For

Part II ST

example, if a property worth £50,000 was being exchanged for a house worth £50,000, the threshold would apply separately to each property and neither would be liable for duty. Therefore, the amendment is unnecessary.

Mr Smith: I am grateful to the Minister for clarifying that he understands that that is the case. Would any compensation be payable to people who have been advised differently by the Stamp Office on that matter?

. . .

Mr Nelson: . . . People can claim repayment if the stamp office has charged them incorrectly. I hope and believe that they have not.

HC Official Report, Standing Committee A (Thirteenth Sitting), cols 714, 715, 718–722.

[NB Superseded: see IR Tax Bulletin, Issue 18, August 1995, p 234.]

5 APRIL 1994. HM LAND REGISTRY
LAND REGISTRY ANNOUNCES CHANGE IN STAMP DUTY ADJUDICATION PROCEDURES

As a means of improving customer service and after discussion with the Stamp Office, the Chief Land Registrar has decided to revise the practice under which an original instrument requiring adjudication must, to gain priority, be lodged at the Land Registry prior to its submission to the Stamp Office.

With effect from 5 April 1994, it will no longer be a requirement for an applicant to lodge the original instrument with an application for registration when that instrument requires adjudication by the Stamp Office.

Instead, a certified copy of the instrument may be lodged with the application, together with a letter to the Land Registry explaining the position and confirming that the original instrument will be lodged with the Land Registry promptly on its return from the Stamp Office.

When the original instrument has been stamped, it must be sent without delay to the district land registry where the application was lodged, with a covering letter of explanation.

18 APRIL 1994. INLAND REVENUE
STAMP DUTY—PROPERTY TRANSACTIONS

This Press Release gives guidance, in response to enquiries and representations, about some aspects of the stamp duty changes introduced by the 1994 Finance Bill [clauses 237–243 of the 1994 Finance Bill as amended]. They are—

(a) the calculation of duty on an exchange of properties, particularly where the properties are of unequal value and a payment of money (known as equality money) is also made;

(b) the application of the £60,000 threshold to exchanges;

(c) the treatment of sales where one property is sold and another property is given in part payment of the sale price. The guidance makes clear that in these circumstances duty at 1% is charged (subject to the threshold) on the consideration for the property being sold; the transfer of the other property which is given in part payment is liable only to the fixed duty of 50p.

DETAILS

Exchanges

1. Clause 239 of the 1994 Finance Bill [as amended] (originally clause 226) introduces new rules for stamp duty on exchanges of interests in land or buildings.

Under the new rules duty is charged on each transfer. The duty in each case is calculated by reference to the "consideration" (ie the value) given for the transfer; where the consideration consists of property, its open market value will be taken. For example, if one house worth £100,000 is exchanged for another house worth £100,000, duty of £1,000 (1% of £100,000) is charged on each transfer. The £60,000 threshold is applied separately to each side of the exchange. For example, if there is a straightforward exchange of one house worth £50,000 for another worth £50,000, both transfers are within the threshold and so no duty would be payable on either (see para 10 below).

2. Where the market values of the two properties being exchanged are not equal, a payment of money (or some other consideration) may often be given with the lower value property, so as to equalise the bargain. The treatment of such cases for stamp duty purposes will depend on the facts and the effect of the relevant documents.

Examples

3. For example, where one house worth £100,000 is exchanged for another worth £80,000 plus £20,000 money, the conveyance for the transfer of the £100,000 house will normally say that the consideration for the transfer consists of the £80,000 house and the £20,000 money; and the conveyance will be stamped accordingly with duty on £100,000.

4. On the conveyance of the £80,000 house, the Stamp Office have charged duty under the new rules by reference to the consideration expressed in the conveyance—

(a) where the conveyance provides that the consideration for the transfer of the cheaper property is the appropriate proportion of the value of the more expensive property, stamp duty is applied accordingly. Thus if the conveyance provides that the consideration for the £80,000 house is the appropriate proportion of the £100,000 house, the amount charged to duty on the transfer of the £80,000 house is limited to £80,000;

(b) more commonly the conveyance may say simply that the consideration for the transfer of the £80,000 house consists of the £100,000 house. In these circumstances, the Stamp Office will have charged duty by reference to the value of the £100,000 house.

Representations

5. Representations have been made that in many cases the wording of the conveyance of the cheaper property may not fully reflect the consideration expressed in the initial contract or agreement. It has been suggested that where the contract provides for an exchange and also provides for money to be paid as equality money by one party to the other, the equality money should be taken into account in deciding how much of the more expensive property is regarded as consideration for the cheaper property (even though the equality money has not been mentioned in the conveyance of the cheaper property).

Revised practice

6. The Revenue have taken legal advice on this. The conclusion is that where it is clear from the contract that the intention of the parties to the transaction is that the cheaper property should be transferred for the more expensive property *less* the equality money the Stamp Office will limit the charge to duty accordingly. For example, if the initial contract provided for an £80,000 house to be exchanged for a £100,000 house, and for £20,000 to be paid as equality money, the amount charged to duty on the transfer of the £80,000 property would be limited to £80,000. The result in an individual case will depend on the facts of the case and the relevant documents. The Stamp Office will need to see the relevant contract with the conveyance which is to be stamped.

7. Where there is a multiple exchange of properties, an apportionment on similar lines may be made to determine how much of the consideration is attributable to each of the transfers. For example, two or more properties may be exchanged for one larger property, with or without a payment of equality money. Here again, the precise result will depend on the facts of the case.

Past cases

8. Where the transfer of a cheaper property has already been stamped by reference to the full value of a more expensive property, but the person who has paid the duty thinks that the duty would be reduced on the basis explained in paras 6 or 7 above, the Stamp Office will be prepared to review the case. Applicants should resubmit the relevant conveyance, and the contract (or a certified copy of the contract). (If it is not possible to obtain the original stamped document from the relevant Registrar, the Stamp Office should be consulted about alternative arrangements.) Where appropriate, excess duty will be repaid provided the claim is made within the two-year time limit laid down by the Stamp Duties Management Act 1891 s 10.

9. Claims for repayment should be made to the Stamp Office at Worthing (for England, Wales and Northern Ireland), or Edinburgh (for Scotland).

Application of £60,000 threshold

10. Sales of property (other than shares) for a price not exceeding the £60,000 threshold are exempted from duty, provided that a "certificate of value" is given stating that the transfer is not part of a larger transaction, or a series of transactions, for a total price of more than £60,000. The threshold is applied separately to each side of an exchange of properties. If in a particular case the threshold has not been applied separately to each side of an exchange (or to two sales where the purchase prices have been set off against each other), and the person who paid the duty believes that too much duty was paid, the documents (with the certificate of value) may be returned for reconsideration to the Stamp Office on the same basis as in paras 8 and 9 above.

11. Where there is a multiple exchange—for example, properties A and B are exchanged for property C—the transfers of properties A and B would be regarded as parts of a larger transaction, and the threshold would not apply to either of them if the total consideration for both was more than £60,000. The threshold would be applied separately to the transfer of property C.

Sales

12. In many cases, transactions which in the past have been structured and documented as exchanges could equally well be carried out as sales for a price which may be partly satisfied in kind. For example, when a builder offers a property for sale, he may receive the price from the buyer in the form either of money, or partly of money and partly of the buyer's old house. Such a transaction can be carried out and documented (commencing with the initial contract) as a sale. Stamp duty is charged on the consideration for the sale. So if, for example, the buyer is buying a new house for £100,000, and pays for it with £30,000 in cash plus his old house worth £70,000, duty of £1,000 (1% of £100,000) would be charged on the transfer of the £100,000 house. The house which the builder accepts as part payment for the sale would not be regarded as a separate sale for stamp duty purposes. It would be charged only to the fixed duty of 50p. The threshold would not be of relevance to this transfer as it is not a conveyance on sale.

General

13. In cases of doubt about how a particular document of the types mentioned above would be treated by the Stamp Office for stamp duty purposes, the Technical Section, The Stamp Office, Ridgeworth House, Liverpool Gardens, Worthing BN11 1XP, will be willing to help.

[NB Superseded: see IR Tax Bulletin, Issue 18, August 1995, p 234.]

29 NOVEMBER 1994. INLAND REVENUE STAMP DUTY: GROUP RELIEF

The Chancellor proposes in his Budget to make two changes to the stamp duty relief for transfers between companies in the same group. Under these measures,

— companies within a group will, subject to conditions, be able to grant new leases to each other free from stamp duty;
— the test for group membership for the purpose of the relief will be changed from 90% ownership of issued share capital to 75% ownership of ordinary share capital.

The changes will apply to documents executed on or after the day on which the Finance Bill receives Royal Assent.

The Chancellor's intention is to extend stamp duty group relief to new leases, in line with representations; and to bring the group control test for this relief closer to the test for corporation tax purposes.

DETAILS

New leases

1. Sales of land or shares by one company to another company in the same group are exempt from stamp duty, subject to anti-avoidance provisions designed to discourage exploitation of the relief. Assignments of existing leases are similarly exempt. But grants of new leases are outside the scope of these provisions. A number of representations have been received for the relief to be extended to grants of new leases.

2. Under the new rules, new leases will qualify for group relief in the same way as sales and assignments of existing leases. Agreements for lease will similarly qualify (provided they are executed on or after the date of Royal Assent).

Test for group membership

3. Under the present rules, companies are associated for the purpose of the stamp duty group relief if either one company owns 90% of the other, or both are 90% owned by a third company. Ownership is measured by reference to issued share capital.

4. The new rules will be different in two respects. The requirement of 90% ownership will be changed to 75% ownership; and only ordinary shares will be taken into account, instead of the whole of the issued share capital.

5. These changes will broadly align the group control test for stamp duty with that for corporation tax. More transfers between companies will be exempt from stamp duty. In a few cases, the new rules will preclude relief where it would currently be available.

4 AUGUST 1995. INLAND REVENUE
TRADEPOINT—TAX AND STAMP DUTY RESERVE TAX RELIEFS

Regulations have been laid today to remove the tax obstacles which might otherwise have prevented effective trading by Tradepoint (a new screen-based market for dealing in equities).

DETAILS

1. These regulations are the Income Tax (Dealers in Securities) (Tradepoint) Regulations 1995, the Income Tax (Manufactured Dividends) (Tradepoint) Regulations 1995 and the Stamp Duty Reserve Tax (Tradepoint) Regulations 1995. They will allow the London Clearing House in its capacity as the clearing house for Tradepoint to be exempt from Stamp Duty Reserve Tax (SDRT) and the anti-bondwashing legislation. They will also allow favourable treatment in respect of manufactured dividends. These three benefits will also apply to certain members of Tradepoint in particular circumstances. Copies of the regulations will be available shortly from Her Majesty's Stationery Office.

2. Bond washing is a device for turning income into capital gains and so, in certain cases, avoiding tax. This is countered by legislation which does not apply to Stock Exchange market makers acting in the ordinary course of market making business. It would also be inappropriate for it to apply to the London Clearing House and to certain members of Tradepoint where they are taking no proprietary interest in Tradepoint transactions but are simply involved as part of Tradepoint's clearing process. These regulations ensure this.

3. Manufactured dividends are paid to compensate recipients for real dividends that are not received. They can be paid when stock is lent over a period which straddles a dividend date or where sales of cum-dividend stock are satisfied by delivery of ex-dividend stock. Unless such payments are approved, the payer is penalised for tax purposes. When made by Stock Exchange market makers such payments are normally treated as approved. These regulations will ensure that the same applies for the London Clearing House and for members of Tradepoint when they are involved only as part of Tradepoint's clearing process.

4. SDRT is a tax on certain agreement to transfer securities, which supplements the stamp duty on shares. Stamp duty applies only where there is a transfer document. Without these regulations, Tradepoint's clearing arrangements could result in more than one charge to stamp duty/SDRT for a single purchase by a Tradepoint client. The regulations ensure that extra charges to SDRT under such arrangements will not arise. In line with transactions on other exchanges, a single charge to stamp duty or SDRT will occur on the transfer of the shares to the purchaser.

NOTE

Tradepoint received recognition as an investment exchange from the Securities and Investments Board on 7 June 1995.

2 OCTOBER 1995. INLAND REVENUE
STOCK LENDING—STAMP DUTY RESERVE TAX

The Inland Revenue have today published three extra-statutory concessions giving relief from stamp duty reserve tax on certain stock lending transactions.

The text of the concessions is [printed in Appendix 3].

DETAILS

1. In the ordinary course of their business Stock Exchange market makers borrow shares from institutions for the purpose of their market making operations. In return, the lender is given security. These transactions are carried out under standard agreements substantially in a form approved by The Stock Exchange and the Inland Revenue.

2. The Stock Exchange propose to introduce a new Dematerialised Stock Lending Service on 2 October. Stock lenders will be permitted to hold their stock in SEPON (the Stock Exchange's nominee company), so that stock loans (and returns of borrowed stock) can be carried out by electronic transfer within SEPON rather than by paper transfers. Under the new service, the Stock Exchange will collect stamp duty reserve tax (SDRT) on transfers within SEPON where appropriate.

3. The first two concessions relate to the SDRT treatment of the new service.

4. The first concession is concerned with the transfers of stock by lenders into SEPON for the purpose of the new service. Under present legislation transfers into SEPON are exempt from stamp duty but are liable to SDRT at 0·5%, unless they qualify for a specific exemption. Thus if a lender transferred his existing holding of shares into SEPON, the transfer would be liable to 0·5% SDRT. The concession will reduce the SDRT in those circumstances to 50p (in line with the stamp duty charge on a transfer to a nominee in similar circumstances).

5. The second concession is concerned with the return of stock from the market maker to the lender at the end of the loan. Present legislation limits the stamp duty charge on the transfer to 50p. But under the dematerialised service, the return will no longer be a paper transfer. It would therefore be liable to SDRT rather than stamp duty,

but there is at present no corresponding SDRT relief limiting the charge to 50p. The concession will limit the SDRT charge to 50p in circumstances where stamp duty would have been limited to 50p if there had been a paper transfer.

6. The third concession stems from changes made in December 1990 to the terms of the standard stock lending agreements to strengthen the security given to stock lenders. These were technical changes but would strictly result in a liability to SDRT in certain circumstances where no stamp duty or SDRT was charged under the previous agreements. The concession, which is already in operation, gives relief from these extra charges.

NOTES

1. An extra-statutory concession is a relaxation which gives taxpayers a reduction in tax liability to which they would not be entitled under the strict letter of the law. Most concessions are made to deal with what are, on the whole, minor or transitory anomalies under the legislation and to meet cases of hardship at the margins of the code where a statutory remedy would be difficult to devise or would run to a length out of proportion to the intrinsic importance of the matter.

2. Inland Revenue extra-statutory concessions are of general application, but in a particular case there may be special circumstances which must be taken into account in considering the application of a concession. A concession will not be given in any case where an attempt is made to use it for tax avoidance.

3. Inland Revenue concessions are published in a free booklet IR1 available from any Tax Enquiry Centre or Tax Office. If anyone has difficulty in getting copies locally they are also available from the Inland Revenue Public Enquiry Room, West Wing, Somerset House, London WC2R 1LB. The concessions published today will be included in a later edition of the booklet.

[*Note:* the concessions will be superseded when the FA 1997 reform of the repurchase and stock lending regime is brought into effect (expected to be in September 1997).]

Part II ST

28 NOVEMBER 1995. INLAND REVENUE STAMP DUTY ON SHARES

Changes to the present rules for stamp duty on shares and stamp duty reserve tax (SDRT) were announced by the Chancellor today. Under the proposals:

— the present rules will be adapted to cater for the introduction of paperless share transfers under the CREST system, due to start in July 1996;
— an optional alternative to the present regime for clearance services will be provided.

The changes will apply from 1 July 1996.

DETAILS

1. Stamp duty is charged on documents transferring shares. A company registrar cannot register the transfer of ownership unless the transfer document has been stamped with the appropriate duty (or has been certified as exempt from duty). The Stock Exchange collect duty on transactions involving Stock Exchange members. SDRT is charged on certain agreements to transfer securities, where there is no transfer document and so no liability to stamp duty.

2. The Treasury have laid draft regulations before Parliament to amend company law to permit shares to be held in uncertificated form and to be transferred through an approved paperless transfer system. The proposed CREST system for paperless share transfers is expected to start in July 1996. Paperless transfers will be liable to SDRT rather than stamp duty, and the present stamp duty and SDRT rules need some amendment to cater for them.

CREST (and any other system approved under the Treasury regulations) will be required by the tax rules to collect SDRT on relevant transactions settled within the system or reported through it for regulatory purposes.

3. Legislation will be included in the Finance Bill to make a number of changes:

(i) as the law stands, a transfer which is not on sale is liable to 50p stamp duty. There is no corresponding 50p rate of SDRT, and a 50p rate is not being introduced. Deposits of certificated shares into CREST will be exempted from the 50p stamp duty charge. They will not be liable to SDRT unless the 0·5% or 1·5% SDRT charge applies—for example because they are transfers for consideration in money or money's worth;

(ii) at present, a charge to SDRT does not arise until two months after the agreement to transfer the shares. This allows time for a transfer document to be produced and stamped, as will normally happen under the present system. The stamp duty then franks the SDRT liability. With paperless transfers, there will generally be no stamped document, and the two-month delay will no longer be appropriate. The two-month gap will be removed to avoid a cash-flow loss to the Exchequer. Where there is still a stamped transfer document, the stamp duty paid on it will cancel the SDRT charge;

(iii) at present, the rates of SDRT round the tax up to the next 50p—eg 50p per £100 or part of £100. To simplify the calculations, the rates will be changed to a flat percentage—eg 0·5% (The stamp duty rates will however remain unchanged; the machines used to stamp documents are designed to cater for the present form of rates);

(iv) the territorial scope of SDRT will be clarified. The practice up to now has been to regard agreements made overseas between persons not resident in the United Kingdom (UK) as outside the scope of the tax. Recent legal advice, however, suggests that these agreements are chargeable to SDRT. The legislation will be amended to confirm that. Thus, transfers between non-residents which are settled through CREST will be liable to SDRT (just as they are liable to stamp duty at present where there is a paper transfer). The present practice will however continue to be operated in relation to unconditional agreements which are made before 1 July 1996;

(v) where stock is borrowed by a Stock Exchange market-maker, the stamp duty charge on a transfer of borrowed stock back to the lender is limited to 50p (FA 1986 s 82). In the case of dematerialised stock lending, the SDRT charge on the return of stock to the lender is limited to 50p by extra-statutory concession (Inland Revenue Press Release, 2 October). These stock loan returns will be exempted from SDRT from 1 July 1996. The legislation will also provide in statutory form the SDRT relief given at present by extra-statutory concession for transfers of collateral under stock lending arrangements;

(vi) stamp duty and SDRT are charged at 1·5% on transfers of shares into "clearance services"—ie broadly, systems where the shares are held indefinitely by a nominee and rights are bought and sold by book entry transfer without a transfer of the shares themselves. An option will be introduced to enable clearance services to opt for the normal SDRT charges to apply to transactions within the service, instead of the 1·5% charge on transfers into the service. It will be a condition of the option that satisfactory arrangements are made by the clearance service operator for the collection of SDRT and for compliance with the requirements of the SDRT legislation. Where the clearance service has no UK presence, the appointment of a UK tax representative may be required as a condition of the option, unless satisfactory alternative arrangements are made;

(vii) the present rules for the 1·5% SDRT charge on transfers of shares into depositary receipt schemes assume that the shares will be held by a nominee rather than by the issuer of depositary receipts. The legislation will be amended so as to apply also where the shares are held by the *issuer* of the depositary receipts itself.

4. CREST (and any other paperless system approved under the Treasury regulations) will have a statutory obligation to *collect SDRT* on relevant transactions carried out within its system or reported through it for regulatory purposes. Firms which are market-makers, brokers and dealers or "qualified dealers" for the purpose of the SDRT regulations—ie broadly firms which are regulated—will be able to obtain any reliefs to which they (of their clients) are entitled, by identifying the relevant transactions in CREST rather than by claiming repayment from the Stamp Office. The present regulations governing the assessment and collection of SDRT are being reviewed and will be amended in due course to make any changes needed to take account of the introduction of paperless share transfers.

DECEMBER 1995. THE STAMP OFFICE CUSTOMER NEWSLETTER A NEW COMPREHENSIVE STAMP DUTY SERVICE

NEW ARRANGEMENTS

Following a major review of our organisation, the Stamp Office has made changes to the way we deliver our services and we aim to provide, by 1 April 1996, a comprehensive stamp duty service to customers in each Stamp Office.

Customers will then be able to send *all documents*, including applications for adjudication to any Stamp Office, a service which was previously only available in Worthing.

In order to achieve this aim it has been necessary to re-structure the Stamp Office. This has resulted in the closure of two offices in Cardiff and Liverpool, the transfer of the London postal work to Worthing and an extension of the services available in Bristol, Birmingham, Manchester and Newcastle.

WHERE SHOULD YOU SEND YOUR DOCUMENTS FOR STAMPING?

Please continue to use your current office.

However, customers who are used to posting documents to London Stamp Office should note that the postal section in London has now closed and arrangements have already been made for you to send your documents to Worthing.

WHAT IF YOU REQUIRE ADJUDICATION?

This service is now available in Bristol and Newcastle as well as Edinburgh and Worthing. Plans are underway to introduce this service in Birmingham and Manchester by 1 April 1996.

In the meantime customers in Birmingham and Manchester should continue to send their applications for adjudication to Worthing.

TELEPHONE ADVICE

In order to provide you with information on specialist stamp duty matters we have appointed additional Technical Services Managers in the following offices:

Birmingham	Lindsay Murphy	0121 200 2616 Ext 219
Bristol	Paul Needham	0117 9456939
Manchester	Phil Holmden	0161 833 0413 Ext 200
Newcastle	Doug Robson	0191 2015504

WHO SHOULD USE THE WORTHING ENQUIRY LINE?

Calls should only be made to Worthing Stamp Office if you are a customer of that office, or the enquiry relates to an existing adjudication case.

QUESTIONS OR COMMENTS ABOUT THESE NEW ARRANGEMENTS

We will make every effort to maintain the highest level of service to customers, nonetheless we realise that there may be some disruption for which we apologise. If you have any questions or comments about these new arrangements please contact your local Stamp Office.

Alternatively you can write to, or telephone Alan Bush, our Customer Service Manager at:

The Stamp Office
Room 0.66A. FitzRoy House
PO Box 46
Castle Meadow Road
Nottingham. NG2 1BD

Part II ST

Tel: 0115 974 1833
Fax: 0115 974 1831

9 DECEMBER 1995. WORTHING STAMP OFFICE CUSTOMER NOTICE

CHANGE OF ADDRESS

Please note that the Worthing Stamp Office will be moving from Ridgeworth House, Liverpool Gardens, Worthing, West Sussex BN11 1XP to a new address on 9 December 1995.

NEW ADDRESS

From *8 December 1995* will you please send all your post (Royal Mail or DX) to:

Worthing Stamp Office
Ground Floor
South Wing
Durrington Bridge House
Barrington Road
Worthing
West Sussex BN12 4SE
DX 3799 Worthing 1
New tel no will be 01903 701280

QUESTIONS AND COMMENTS

Please direct these to Jim Simpson (Worthing Customer Service Manager) on 01903 288835.

9 MAY 1996. INLAND REVENUE OPEN-ENDED INVESTMENT COMPANIES AND AUTHORISED UNIT TRUSTS—STAMP DUTY

The Economic Secretary to the Treasury, Mrs Angela Knight MP, today announced proposals to relax the stamp duty and stamp duty reserve tax rules for authorised unit trusts converting into open-ended investment companies, and for mergers between authorised unit trusts. The proposals will facilitate the introduction of OEICs and at the same time will provide a window of opportunity for rationalisation in the unit trust industry. In reply to a Parliamentary Question, she said:

> "In response to the consultative document which the Treasury published last year with draft regulations to permit the creation of open-ended investment companies (OEICs), the Treasury have received a number of representations that conversions of authorised unit trusts into OEICs should be exempted from stamp duty and stamp duty reserve tax (SDRT), including conversions of two or more trusts into a single OEIC.
>
> When regulations are made to deal with the stamp duty and SDRT treatment of OEICs, I intend to include in them an exemption for conversions of an authorised unit trust into an OEIC or a single sub-fund of an umbrella OEIC. The regulations will also contain an exemption from stamp duty and SDRT, for a period of some two years, for conversions which involve a merger (such as the conversion of two or more authorised unit trusts into a single OEIC or subfund, or the merger of an authorised unit trust with an OEIC).
>
> We also intend to introduce legislation in the next Finance Bill to exempt mergers between authorised unit trusts from stamp duty and SDRT if the merger is carried out after the Bill becomes law and within a period of some two years thereafter.

These measures will give unit trust groups a unique opportunity to rationalise their range of authorised unit trusts, and to convert some or all of them into OEICs if they wish. At the same time the introduction of OEICs will continue to widen the opportunities for share ownership for the investing public."

DETAILS

1. Open-ended investment companies (OEICs) cannot currently be formed under UK company law. Last year the Treasury issued for consultation a draft of regulations which would permit OEICs to be set up, and the Securities and Investments Board issued draft product regulations for consultation. FA 1995 included powers to make regulations for the tax treatment of OEICs.

2. When an authorised unit trust (AUT) is converted into an OEIC, the transfer of the trust's investments to the OEIC would, as the law stands, generally be liable to stamp duty or stamp duty reserve tax (SDRT). When regulations are made later this year, they will include an exemption from stamp duty and SDRT for the conversion of an AUT into an OEIC, or into a sub-fund of an umbrella OEIC. They will also include an exemption, for a period of some two years, for a merger of two or more AUTs into an OEIC (or a sub-fund of an umbrella OEIC).

3. The Chancellor also proposes to introduce legislation in the next Finance Bill to exempt mergers between authorised unit trusts from stamp duty and SDRT if the merger is carried out after the Bill becomes law and within a period of some two years thereafter.

NOTES

Open-ended investment companies are open-ended in the sense that their shares will be continually created or redeemed depending on the net demand by investors to acquire shares or to redeem their existing holdings. As with existing authorised unit trusts, these transactions will be undertaken at a price derived from the net asset value of the OEIC's underlying investments. An OEIC may take "umbrella" form, ie incorporating a number of subfunds in which shareholders can invest separately.

26 NOVEMBER 1996. INLAND REVENUE
STAMP DUTY—UNIT TRUSTS AND OPEN-ENDED INVESTMENT COMPANIES

The temporary stamp duty exemption announced in May for mergers between authorised unit trusts, and mergers of authorised unit trusts into open-ended investment companies (OEICs), is to run until 30 June 1999, under the Chancellor's proposals today. The Government also wishes to simplify the present stamp duty regime for repurchases of units by unit trust managers.

DETAILS

Conversions and mergers

1. The Economic Secretary to the Treasury, Angela Knight MP, announced in May that:

— when regulations were made in due course to deal with the stamp duty and stamp duty reserve tax (SDRT) treatment of OEICs, she intended to include in them an exemption for conversions of an authorised unit trust into an OEIC (or a single sub-fund of an umbrella OEIC);

— the regulations would also provide an exemption, for a period of some two years, for conversions which involve a merger (such as a conversion of two or more authorised unit trusts into a single OEIC);

— legislation would be introduced in the next Finance Bill to exempt mergers between authorised unit trusts if the merger was carried out after the bill became law and within a period of some two years thereafter (Inland Revenue Press Release, 9 May 1996 [see *Simon's Weekly Tax Intelligence* 1996, p 839]).

2. The two temporary exemptions will run until 30 June 1999. This will help to facilitate the introduction of OEICs, and will also provide an opportunity for rationalisation in the unit trust industry.

Repurchase of units

3. Under the present stamp duty rules for unit trusts, there is a 0·5% charge on the repurchase of units by the manager from investors, but the duty can be repaid if the units are cancelled within the next two months and the underlying investments are sold. This is, however, complex to operate, and is unlikely to fit easily with single pricing of units. It may be uncertain at the time of the repurchase whether the units will in due course be cancelled and the duty repaid.

4. The Government therefore intends to introduce a simpler regime which will apply both for units in unit trusts (whether authorised or unauthorised) and for shares in OEICs. They have in mind to replace the present rule by a lower charge on repurchases, but with no repayment when units (or shares in OEICs) are cancelled. The details are under discussion with representatives of the industry, and a further announcement will be made in the near future.

NOTES

1. Open-ended investment companies are open-ended in the sense that their shares can be continually created or redeemed depending on the net demand by investors to acquire shares or to redeem their existing holdings. As with authorised unit trusts, these transactions will be undertaken at a price derived from the net asset value of the OEIC's underlying investments. An OEIC may take "umbrella" form, with a number of sub-funds with different investment objectives.

2. OEICs cannot currently be formed under UK company law, but the Treasury have made regulations to permit OEICs to be set up (The Open-Ended Investment Companies (Investment Companies with Variable Capital) Regulations 1996, SI 1996/2827). The regulations will come into effect on 6 January 1997. The Securities and Investments Board have issued a final draft of product regulations for OEICs. These are also expected to take effect in January 1997. Regulations for the tax treatment of OEICs will keep in step with that timetable.

3. When an authorised unit trust is converted into an OEIC, the transfer of the trust's investments to the OEIC, would, as the law stands, generally be liable to stamp duty or SDRT. Similarly there would be a stamp duty or SDRT liability when unit trusts merge with each other.

8 JANUARY 1997. LAW SOCIETY'S GAZETTE
STAMP DUTY ON LEASES

A change in practice by the Stamp Office in its approach to calculation of stamp duty on new leases which contain provision for future rent increases in line with RPI (retail prices index) changes has resulted in the Law Society's revenue law committee receiving a number of inquiries from solicitors.

The Stamp Office is relying upon the decision in *LM Tenancies plc v IR Comrs* [1996] STC 880 to apply the contingency principle to rent reserved under a lease so that stamp duty is calculated by reference to RPI changes in the year ending with the date of execution of the lease. This approach has led to some excessive estimates of liability.

The revenue law committee has taken up the issue with the Stamp Office and has made two main points. Firstly, it does not consider that the new approach is justified. *LM Tenancies* was concerned with stamp duty avoidance; to apply the decision in that case across the board to any lease with a rent review clause linked to the RPI is unjustified. Secondly, this is an extremely important change in practice which the Stamp Office has not apparently published effectively.

In response, the Stamp Office has assured the committee that it will examine the facts of each case and give careful consideration to the application of the *LM Tenancies* decision.

The Stamp Office points out that a public announcement of the new practice was made in *Hansard* in a reply given by the Economic Secretary to the Treasury to a parliamentary written question asked by a Conservative MP. It followed representations from the House Builders Federation, the Manufacturing and Construction Industries Alliance and individual property owners.

This reply states:

> "Stamp duty is charged on the grant of a new lease of property by reference to the premium paid for the lease and the average annual rent. Duty on the premium is charged at 1% but there is no charge on the premium where the premium is £60,000 or less and the average annual rent is £6,000 or less. Duty is charged on the average annual rent by reference to a sliding scale of rates which depend on the length of the lease. For example, for a lease of over 100 years, the rate is 24% (£12 per £50 or part of £50 of the average annual rent).
>
> Where an existing lease is sold by the leaseholder to someone else, duty is charged at 1% on the price paid, in the same way as with the sale of a freehold. No duty is charged on the rent. I have received representations from the House Builders Federation, the Manufacturing and Construction Industries Alliance, and McCarthy and Stone about the treatment of a grant of a new lease under which the rent is to be adjusted in future in line with RPI changes.
>
> Where the terms of a lease lay down specific figures for future rent payments, or provide for the rent to be increased by a fixed percentage each year, there is no difficulty in calculating what the average annual rent is for the purpose of the stamp duty charge. The calculation is more difficult where the rent is to depend on the future movement of an index such as the RPI. Decisions of the courts, including the recent case *LM Tenancies plc v IR Comrs*, have given some guidance on the calculation of the charge to duty where an element is not ascertainable at the outset.
>
> The Inland Revenue has reviewed its practice on the stamp duty treatment of leases of this type in the light of representations that have been made. It accepts that in some cases the calculations made by Stamp Offices produce too high a figure. In the *LM Tenancies* case, the premium paid for a lease was to be calculated by reference to the market price of a Treasury loan stock 25 days after the execution of the lease. The Court decided that duty should be calculated by reference to the value of the stock at the date of execution of the lease.
>
> The Inland Revenue's view, in the light of the court's decision in *LM Tenancies*, is that where the rent under a lease is to be adjusted by reference to RPI changes the duty should be calculated by reference to the change in the year ending with the date of execution of the lease. The precise method of adjustment may depend on the terms of the lease and on the way they provide for the calculation to be made. For example, whether the rent is to be increased annually or only at longer intervals. Generally, where the adjustment is to be made by comparing the value of the RPI at different dates, the difference between the two values over the latest year will be used to measure the rent increase for stamp duty purposes.
>
> For example, if the initial rent is £300 a year and is to be adjusted annually, and the RPI has gone up from 150 to 153, equivalent to 2% over the relevant 12-month period, it would be assumed that the rent would go up by £6 (2% of £300) each year. Thus, the rent

Part II ST

would be taken as £306 in the second year, £312 in the third year, and so on, in order to calculate the average annual rent under the lease.

The Inland Revenue is issuing instructions to Stamp Offices accordingly, to ensure that individual cases are dealt with on a consistent basis. A taxpayer who disagrees with the Stamp Office's calculation of the duty in a particular case will, of course, have the normal rights of appeal."

One firm of solicitors has already obtained counsel's opinion on this issue, to the effect that the Stamp Office's approach is "not sustainable". If there are any changes in this area the revenue law committee will ensure they are reported as soon as possible.

This note was written by Jill Hallpike, the secretary to the Law Society's revenue law committee.

[Now see IR Press Release 14 May 1999.]

21 MARCH 1997. HANSARD FINANCE ACT 1997

Mr Matthew Banks asked the Chancellor of the Exchequer if he will make a statement about the operation of FA 1997 ss 97, 102.

Mrs Angela Knight: The definition of "intermediary" for the purposes of the new relief aims broadly to distinguish between dealers and end-investors, on the lines recommended by the Securities and Investments Board in its report to the Chancellor in July 1996.

FA 1997 ss 97, 102 define "intermediary" as a person who carries on a bona fide business of dealing in stock or securities, and who does not also carry on business which the sections describe as an "excluded business". It will depend on the facts of the particular case whether a dealer is also carrying on an "excluded business".

One category of "excluded business" is a business which consists wholly or mainly in making or managing investments. Thus if the dealing firm also carries on a separate business of making and managing investments in exchange-traded chargeable securities or stock on its own behalf, that would be an excluded business and the dealer would not qualify as an intermediary. But if the dealer is holding such investments merely as an incidental part of a dealing activity taxable under Schedule D Case 1, and not as a separate business, that would not disqualify the firm from being an intermediary. For example, if the dealer buys and holds shares merely to hedge derivative contracts which it has made, that would not be regarded as a business of making investments for the purpose of the excluded business test.

Similarly, the Inland Revenue would not regard a dealer as disqualified merely because the firm also makes and manages investments for clients, if the investments are not beneficially owned by the dealer. By contrast, if the dealer purchases investments for clients and the clients hold something short of beneficial ownership in those investments—as would happen, for example, under the American arrangements known as prime brokerage—that would be regarded as a business of making or managing investments for the purpose of the excluded business test.

A firm may also be excluded from relief if it carries on a business which consists wholly or mainly of providing services to persons with which the firm is connected, such as members of the same group of companies. For example, if the dealer carries on a business of taking positions in equities as a service to connected persons who would not themselves qualify for relief as intermediaries, the sections would exclude the firm from relief. The Inland Revenue would not however regard the dealer as disqualified if business with connected persons is merely an incidental part of the firm's business with third parties, or if the services the firm provides are not related to handling securities within the scope of stamp duty and stamp duty reserve tax—such as research, secretarial or cleaning services. If the dealing firm buys

4. In future where rent reviews are to be based on an external index such as the RPI only any change in the RPI up to the date of the execution of the lease will be taken into account for Stamp Duty.

5. In most cases this will result in the average rent being little more than the initial rent.

6. Under Stamp Duty law, repayments of excess duty are made by adjusting the stamps impressed on the document, so as to reflect the correct amount due.

7. Applicants for repayments should contact the Stamp Office at the following address:

Stamp Allowance Claims Section
Manchester Stamp Office
Alexandra House
Parsonage
Manchester M60 9BT
DX 14430 Manchester 2

1. Applications should where possible be accompanied by the original stamped document. If that is not in the applicant's possession, for example because it is held by a solicitor, building society or land registry, the Stamp Office should be consulted as to alternative arrangements. Duplicate and copy documents are not acceptable.

2. Information and advice are also available by telephoning the Stamp Office Helpline: 0845 6030135. (All calls to this number are charged at local rates.)

8 NOVEMBER 2000. INLAND REVENUE MODERNISING STAMP DUTY

The new system for electronic conveyancing came one step closer today as the Government announced the introduction of legislation in the next Finance Bill to modernise the stamp duty rules to deal with electronic transfers of land and buildings.

The Electronic Communications Act, which came into force earlier this year, will remove the need for transactions in land and buildings to be on paper.

The change will help to modernise the tax system and underlines the Government's firm commitment to removing legislative barriers to electronic dealings with government.

DETAILS

The stamp duty charge on land transactions currently depends on the existence of paper documents. Under the Electronic Communications Act, the legal requirement for certain transactions to be on paper will be removed. In parallel with developments by the Land Registries of England, Scotland and Northern Ireland, this means that it will be possible for land to be transferred electronically.

Stamp duty reserve tax, which applies to shares, is already accounted for and collected electronically and provides a recent precedent for modernising stamp duty on land and buildings.

As part of the design process for the modernised legislation the Inland Revenue intends to set up a technical advisory group (TAG). The TAG will consist of representatives from the Revenue, other government departments and external organisations. With the assistance of the TAG it is intended that draft clauses will be published before Budget 2001 to allow time for detailed comment before the Finance Bill.

NOTES

The Electronic Communications Act came into force on 25 May 2000.

Stamp duty reserve tax was introduced in 1986 to deal with the electronic trading and settling of shares. It replaces stamp duty where the transfer is completed electronically.

16 APRIL 2003. INLAND REVENUE
FINANCE BILL 2003: STAMP DUTY ON UK LAND AND BUILDINGS

The Finance Bill, published today, sets out the framework for stamp duty land tax, which will be introduced on 1 December 2003 to replace the existing stamp duty regime on UK land and buildings. [See FA 2003 Pt 4 Stamp Duty Land Tax and Schedules 3–20].

Reform paves the way for the introduction of e-conveyancing systems which will allow purchases of property to be effected or registered electronically, making the acquisition of property faster and more efficient.

The reform builds on measures introduced in FA 2002 to tackle avoidance of stamp duty on certain property transactions, and modernises the compliance regime for stamp duty by bringing it into line with other taxes and incorporating appropriate enforcement powers. There will be new processes for reporting the details of land transactions and for paying any tax due.

The full reform package will be implemented on 1 December 2003 for all land transactions completed on or after that date, unless they relate to certain contracts entered into before Royal Assent.

In addition to the legislation published today, prior to implementation there will be regulations made to cover administrative issues, such as the content of the land transaction return form.

The Government has also announced that consultation will continue on certain key aspects of the regime. These are the transfer of land into and out of a partnership by a partner, and the transfer of interests in partnerships that hold UK land, the approach to large developments, including the treatment of subsales and successive transfers, sale and leaseback deals and securitisation of land. Any changes arising from the consultation may be enacted either on implementation of the new regime or in FA 2004. There will also be the opportunity for further dialogue on the proposed changes to lease duty, which will only proceed if a suitable alternative is not identified.

DETAILS

Outline of the modernised regime

For the vast majority of individual house-buyers and their agents, transactions which are liable to stamp duty land tax should be reported and duty paid as now, within 30 days of completion.

From 1 December 2003, when the new system starts, customers will no longer need to submit documents to the Inland Revenue for stamping. Instead they will have to notify liability to tax using the new land transaction return. Payment should be sent at the same time as the return, as now, to our central processing centre in Netherton. Any stamp office will be able to forward returns and payments to Netherton on behalf of customers, but customers will benefit from a quicker service if they make their returns direct to Netherton.

In future, customers will receive a stamp duty land tax certificate which they or their agents will need to submit to land registries in order to register ownership of land or to record a deed, as appropriate.

Under this "process now, check later" system, the Inland Revenue will issue certificates from the central processing centre. From the filing date of the return, there will be an "enquiry window" (the period during which the Inland Revenue can open an enquiry or a customer can request that an enquiry be opened into a transaction). This will be a period of nine months for all transactions.

In the longer term, the introduction of electronic systems for conveyancing and registration by the land registries should allow stamp duty to be processed simultaneously with registration.

There will be cases where no tax is due, for instance where a relief can be claimed or where the transaction is below the zero rate band threshold. It is proposed the threshold will be £60,000 for residential property and £150,000 in other cases.

In these cases purchasers may still have to make a return to the Inland Revenue or, in certain cases, provide a self-certificate to the land registries (which includes any register maintained by the Keeper of Registers of Scotland and, in Northern Ireland, the Land Register of Northern Ireland and the Registry of Deeds).

Summary of Finance Bill legislation published today

The main features of the legislation published today are:

- Broadly, the scope of stamp duty land tax will cover transactions involving any estate, interest, right or power in or over land in the UK. There are then a number of exclusions, including:
  - — mortgages and similar security interests,
  - — licences to use or occupy land, and
  - — transactions for no chargeable consideration.
- The charge will include:
  - — completions of transfers of freehold property and leases,
  - — grants of leases (including, in Scotland, missives of let),
  - — contracts for land transactions which are substantially performed before completion,
  - — transfers of such contracts, and
  - — options and rights of pre-emption in respect of land transactions.
- Tax is due (on the due date) 30 days after the effective date of the transaction. The effective date is normally the date of completion or the date substantial performance occurs, if before completion.
- The purchaser, who is the person acquiring the interest in land, is liable pay any tax due by the due date and to send in the return.
- The rate of charge for all transactions other than the grant of leases depends on the amount paid for the transaction (this includes any payment or "consideration" for linked transactions). It is proposed that the rate of charge for the rental element of new leases is determined by the net present value of the rental payments due to be made under the lease. Consultation, however, is continuing on this proposal and it will only be introduced if an acceptable alternative is not identified. Premiums for new leases, as now, will generally be charged at the main rates.
- Stamp duty rates for 2003–04 were set out in the Budget Day press notice PN 08. Broadly, the existing regime will continue with current rates and thresholds until the modernised regime is implemented. At that point the following changes are proposed, subject to further consultation:
  - — lease duty is charged on the net present value of the rental stream of the lease, at a rate of 1% where that net present value exceeds the zero rate band upper threshold, and
  - — the zero rate band upper threshold is increased to £150,000 for all wholly or partly non-residential transactions (for new leases and conveyances and transfers).
- Some transactions are relieved from charge, even though they still need to be reported to the Inland Revenue. Reliefs that have been carried forward from the existing regime include:
  - — acquisitions by a charity,
  - — transfers between group companies,
  - — transfers arising from company reconstructions,
  - — certain purchases by registered social landlords,
  - — acquisitions of land in disadvantaged areas, and
  - — crown exemption.
- New reliefs for the modernised regime include:
  - — acquisitions of dwellings by house-building companies in part-exchange for the sale of a new home,

Part II ST

- acquisition of dwellings by relocation companies,
- acquisitions by local authorities or other public bodies under compulsory purchase orders, and
- acquisitions by local authorities or other public bodies under the terms of planning arrangements.

- Some transactions qualify for special rules. They include:
  - transfers between companies and connected parties,
  - collective enfranchisement by leaseholders and crofting community right to buy schemes,
  - alternative property financing arrangements for individuals (which can be used, for instance, to provide "Islamic mortgages"),
  - acquisitions of dwellings under shared ownership schemes, and
  - right to buy and rent to mortgage transactions.
- Chargeable consideration is, broadly, money or money's worth. Where a single bargain includes more than one interest in land, or an interest in land and another interest or asset, the amount paid should be apportioned between the interests. Anything paid for goodwill that cannot be sold separately from the land is part of chargeable consideration.
- VAT is included as chargeable consideration only where it is paid as part of the transaction, or where a landlord has elected on or before the grant of a new lease to charge VAT on the rents under that lease.
- Broadly, land transaction returns should be submitted to the Inland Revenue for the following transactions:
  - any transfer of a freehold or assignment or assignation of a lease for consideration, whether or not giving rise to a charge,
  - any transaction for which a relief is being claimed,
  - the grant of a lease for a contractual term of seven years or more or which gives rise to a charge, and
  - any other transaction giving rise to a charge.
- Where a complete land transaction return is received, and any payment of tax due as stated in the return, the Inland Revenue will issue a certificate. This certificate should be included with documents submitted to the land registries when applying for registration of title.
- In some other cases the land registries will require a self-certificate to say that a land transaction return is not needed. These will mainly be required for freehold conveyances and assignments or assignations of leases.
- Arrangements for certain transactions may provide for consideration to be paid in one or more instalments after the effective date of the transaction. Where:
  - there is uncertainty about whether anything more will be paid, and/or about the amount of additional consideration due, and
  - at least one instalment might be more than 18 months after the effective date it will be possible to apply to the Inland Revenue to defer payment of tax until the amounts to be paid are determined. If there is no application to the Inland Revenue for deferred payment, or an application is refused, payment should be made by the due date based on an estimate of the consideration that will be paid. This amount may then be adjusted once the final amount to be paid is confirmed.
- These arrangements do not apply when consideration is paid by annuity. In this case payment should be made at the due date based on 12 years' annual payments. No further adjustment will be made.
- Returns submitted after the due date, or containing incorrect information or omissions may be subject to penalties. Late payment of tax is subject to interest. The penalty and interest regimes are similar to those for other Inland Revenue taxes, and may be subject to mitigation.
- The Inland Revenue have nine months from the due date (or actual filing date, or date of amendment, if later) to start an enquiry into a return or amended return. After that, if new information comes to light under-reported tax can still be recovered. Self-certificates will be audited for validity and, if necessary, enquiries started. Persons knowingly concerned in fraud relating to tax will be liable to prosecution under a provision similar to that for income tax.
- Purchasers are obliged to keep suitable records for six years from the effective date.

- The purchaser has full appeal rights to the General or Special Commissioners, which are independent tax tribunals.

Transitional arrangements

The new regime will apply to all land transactions completed on or after 1 December 2003 except those:

- enacting contracts or agreements (excluding options and rights of pre-emption) made on or before the date the 2003 Finance Bill becomes law, and
- arising from options and rights of pre-emption made on or before today (16 April).

Stamp duty under the current regime may have been paid on documents in respect of some transactions within the new regime. In this case, any ad valorem stamp duty paid under the current regime may be set against the amount of stamp duty land tax due under the new regime.

The existing stamp duty regime will continue to apply to stocks, marketable securities and bearer instruments, and transfers of land into or out of partnerships by partners or former partners, and acquisitions of an interest in a partnership. It may also apply to transactions completed and leases granted on or after 1 December 2003 where those conveyances and leases fulfil contracts or agreements entered into on or before the Finance Bill becomes law (provided they have not been varied after the Finance Bill becomes law).

Stamp duty will cease to apply to transfers of other property for contracts entered into on or after 1 December 2003.

11 JULY 2003. INLAND REVENUE STAMP DUTY LAND TAX—FLOWCHART

Inland Revenue Stamp Taxes has published the following flowchart, to help determine whether a transaction would be liable to Stamp Duty Land Tax (SDLT) by reference to Royal Assent to the Finance Act (10 July 2003) and the proposed implementation date of SDLT on 1 December 2003.

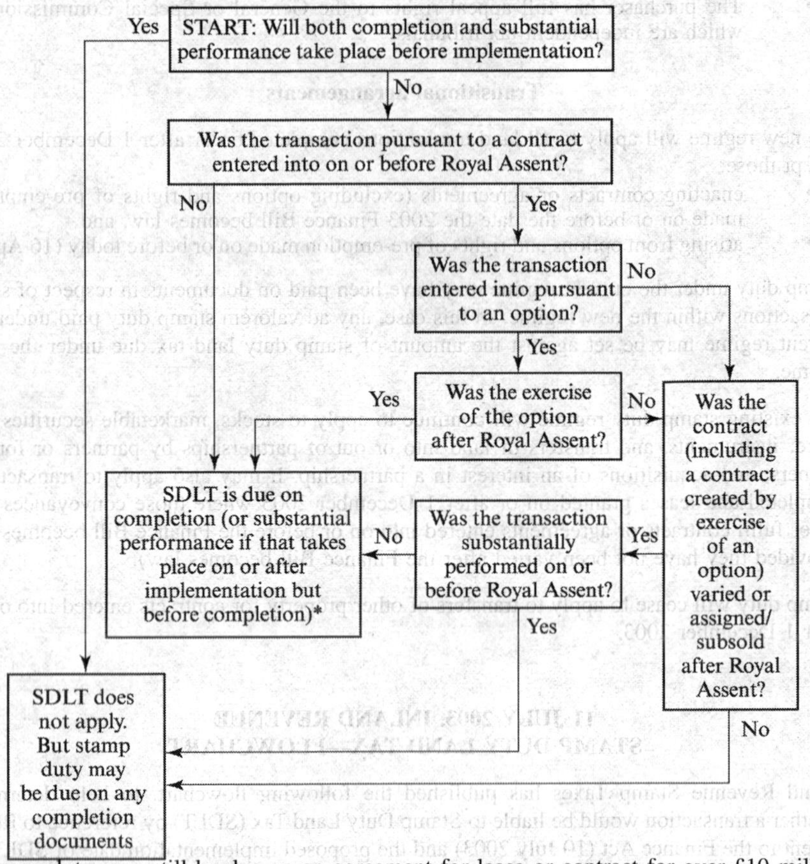

* Stamp duty may still be due on an agreement for lease or contract for over £10 million entered into before implementation. Credit is available against the SDLT due on subsequent completion or substantial performance.

20 OCTOBER 2003. INLAND REVENUE MODERNISING STAMP DUTY ON LAND TRANSACTIONS

The Government today announced the next steps in the process of modernising stamp duty on land transactions, following the announcement of the main proposals in Budget 2003.

These include—

- A significant change to the proposed charge on the rental element when a new lease is granted ("lease duty"), reducing tax bills by £1500 per lease on commercial transactions (£600 per lease on residential transactions), which will be of special benefit to smaller businesses.
- A new relief for businesses raising finance through the sale and leaseback of their land and buildings and relief for "chain-breaking" and similar companies which help to ensure an active housing market.
- Further consultation on how the new regime might apply to partnerships. The announcement follows extensive consultation on the process throughout the earlier part of this year.

Ruth Kelly MP, Financial Secretary to the Treasury, said—

"Stamp Duty Land Tax is on course for implementation on 1 December 2003. The proposals announced today, along with those announced in Budget 2003, will help to achieve the Government's aim of a modern, efficient, system of taxing land transactions which promotes fairness between taxpayers, reduces distortions and prevents avoidance. I am also pleased that our proposals, which follow extensive and valuable consultation with interested parties, will be of particular help to small and medium-sized enterprises and business start-ups."

The Government will shortly be laying regulations before the House of Commons to give effect to the changes to lease duty, sale and leaseback, chain-breaking and other reliefs. The regulations will also make some technical corrections and clarifications which are set out in the attached Technical Note. The Government has today published draft clauses for consultation on partnerships.

DETAILS

The story so far

1. In his Budget Statement on 9 April 2003 the Chancellor of the Exchequer announced that a modernised system of stamp duty, renamed "Stamp Duty Land Tax", would apply to most land transactions on or after 1 December 2003. This system will replace the current archaic system of impressing a physical stamp on documents with a regime in line with that for other taxes. People acquiring interests in land will be required to submit a "Land Transaction Return" to the Inland Revenue along with payment of the duty. This will substantially reduce the scope for avoidance since liability will depend on the nature of the transaction and not on the technicality of which particular document was used.

2. The Chancellor also announced that on or after 1 December 2003 the threshold below which no stamp duty is payable would be raised, for commercial transactions, to £150,000 from the current £60,000. Furthermore, as an aid to regeneration, commercial transactions in designated disadvantaged areas would be entirely exempt from stamp duty.

3. Stamp Duty Land Tax is on course for implementation on 1 December 2003. The Inland Revenue has launched a substantial customer education programme aimed at ensuring in particular that solicitors, licensed conveyancers and other professional advisers are aware of the significance of the change for their practices.

4. The announcements made today cover Stamp Duty Land Tax on the rental element of newly granted leases ("lease duty"), further reliefs for particular commercial transactions and Stamp Duty Land Tax on partnership transactions.

Lease duty

5. In his Budget Statement the Chancellor announced his decision that a new structure for lease duty should come into force on 1 December. The current structure, with its arbitrary "cliff edges" and reliance on average annual rent, created distortions, encouraged decisions which were tax-driven rather than business-driven, and gave opportunities for avoidance.

6. The Government is keen that any new structure should—
- minimise potential scope for avoidance;
- reduce the distortions inherent in the current system to achieve greater fairness in the treatment of different transactions;
- better reflect modern commercial practice;
- be based on clear economic principles and in line with modern valuation and accounting principles; and
- be more in line with the charge on freehold transfers (transfers of ownership).

7. A structure which in the Government's view achieves these aims was accordingly included in FA 2003. However the Chancellor made it clear that consultation on a new structure would continue and that changes might be made before implementation of the new structure on 1 December 2003.

8. The Government is extremely grateful to all who participated in the consultation process. A good deal of valuable information and data was provided by participants

and some important work was done in partnership. Throughout the consultation process the Government has been particularly keen to have regard to the effect of any new structure on small and medium-sized enterprises and business start-ups.

9. Having considered all the contributions made the Government now proposes to modify the structure contained in FA 2003 as follows—

- The Finance Act charges Stamp Duty Land Tax on the "Net Present Value" ("NPV") of rent payable under a lease. NPV sums the discounted values of the rents. This discount recognises that future rent payments will be of less value. The Government believes that NPV represents a fair way of assessing the amount on which Stamp Duty Land Tax should be charged and proposes to retain it.
- The Finance Act sets a threshold of £150,000 for commercial leases, £60,000 for residential leases. If the NPV does not exceed the threshold no Stamp Duty Land Tax is charged on the rental element. These thresholds mean that 60% of commercial leases and 93% of residential leases will pay no Stamp Duty Land Tax on the rental element. The Government believes these thresholds are fair and intend to retain them.
- The Finance Act provides that once the threshold is exceeded Stamp Duty Land Tax is charged at 1% of the full amount of the NPV. The Government proposes to modify this so that Stamp Duty Land Tax is charged at 1% of the excess over the threshold. This means that on any commercial lease chargeable to Stamp Duty Land Tax the tax payable on the rental element will be £1,500 less than under the Finance Act provisions. Similarly for residential leases, the Stamp Duty Land Tax payable on the rental element will be £600 less.

EXAMPLE

"A lease of commercial property for 18 years at an annual rent of £15,000 will have an NPV of £197,845. Under the Finance Act provisions Stamp Duty Land Tax of £1,978 would be payable. Under the Government's proposals only £478 will be payable."

1.0. The Government also proposes to clarify the Stamp Duty Land Tax treatment of leases with uncertain rents, so as to avoid an undue compliance burden on tenants, and to provide that rent increases more than five years after the start of a lease are ignored (subject to anti-avoidance provisions). Details are set out in the attached Technical Note.

1.1. The changes to lease duty are estimated to reduce the expected yield from Stamp Duty Land Tax by £20 million in a full year.

Other reliefs

1.2. The Finance Act already provides for many reliefs from Stamp Duty Land Tax, for example for property acquired by charities or let by Registered Social Landlords. There are reliefs for house-builders who take houses in part exchange (which benefits in particular those providing retirement homes) and companies which assist in employee relocation.

1.3. The Government proposes, in line with commitments given by the Chief Secretary to the Treasury, the right Hon. Paul Boateng MP, during the passage of Finance Bill 2003 through Parliament, to widen these reliefs to include companies who help to ensure an active housing market, by "chain-breaking" (buying property when a prospective sale falls through) and by buying houses from the personal representatives of people who have died. Details are set out in the attached Technical Note.

1.4. The Government also proposes to give relief for sale and lease-back transactions (where a company raises finance by selling a property for a capital sum and leasing it back at an annual rent). Provided certain conditions are met the "lease-back" leg of the transaction will not be charged to Stamp Duty Land Tax.

1.5. The cost of and yield from these reliefs is expected to be negligible.

1.6. Technical corrections and clarifications

1.7. The attached Technical Note sets out a number of technical corrections and clarifications. The Government is grateful to all those who made representations on these issues. The cost of and yield from these changes is expected to be negligible.

Partnerships

1.8. In his Budget statement the Chancellor announced that certain transactions involving partnerships would remain within the existing stamp duty regime until at least 2004 to give time for further consultation. These are: transactions between a partnership and a partner or an incoming partner, changes in partnership interests and transactions between a partnership and a departing partner.

1.9. The Government is today publishing draft clauses which bring these transactions, so far as they involve dealings in land, within the scope of Stamp Duty Land Tax. As with the Government's other proposals the aim is to give fairness between taxpayers, reduce distortions and prevent avoidance.

2.0. The Government will be meeting interested parties to discuss these proposals but would welcome comments from others. The Government's intention is that the clauses will be included in Finance Bill 2004 and will take effect from the date of Royal Assent to Finance Bill 2004.

NOTES

1. Stamp Duty Land Tax applies (subject to some transitional provisions) to all "land transactions" completed on or after 1 December 2003. "Land transaction" includes the conveyance or transfer of a freehold (in Scotland, transfer of ownership), the assignment or assignation of an existing lease and the grant of a new lease. It replaces stamp duty, which is abolished except for instruments relating to stock and marketable securities, and for instruments relating to some partnership transactions.

2. Where a land transaction takes place the purchaser (including a new tenant) must submit a "Land Transaction Return" to the Inland Revenue (there are exceptions for some transactions which do not have to be notified, for example where there is no consideration in any form chargeable to tax). This replaces the current procedure whereby documents are presented to the Inland Revenue for stamping.

3. The rates and thresholds for Stamp Duty Land Tax are the same as they currently are under stamp duty, except that—

(a) Under stamp duty the rate is nil for land transactions where the purchase price does not exceed £60,000. For non-residential transactions this threshold will be raised to £150,000 under Stamp Duty Land Tax.

(b) There will be a new regime for charging Stamp Duty Land Tax on the rental element of new leases ("lease duty") as described above.

4. The current rates of lease duty under stamp duty are based on Average Annual Rent ("AAR") and on the term of the lease. They are—

- Term not more than seven years (including indefinite leases and periodic tenancies);
  - (a) if the rent is £5,000 or less Nil
  - (b) if the rent is more than £5,0001%
- Term more than seven years but not more than 35 years 2%;
- Term more than 35 years but not more than 100 years 12%;
- Term more than 100 years 24%.

STAMP DUTY LAND TAX: TECHNICAL NOTE

1. This Note supplements the News Release of 15 October 2003. It gives further details of—

- The technical changes to Stamp Duty Land Tax on the rental element of leases ("lease duty");
- The reliefs being given for sale and lease-back transactions and acquisitions by "chain-breaking" and similar companies;
- Other technical corrections and clarifications.

2. These changes will be effected by way of regulations made under FA 2003 s 109. The regulations require approval by the House of Commons.

Stamp duty land tax on leases

3. The News Release gives details of the main change proposed for the charging structure. The changes set out below supplement this in order to—

Part II ST

- remove uncertainty in the treatment of some leases;
- keep the compliance burden to a minimum; and
- ensure that taxpayers know what duty they will have to pay.

4. The amendments are as follows.

Post five year rent changes

5. Currently, where rent changes are known and included in the terms of a lease from the outset, they are fully taken into account in calculating the Net Present Value ("NPV") of the lease (unless they are increases only to reflect RPI). However, where rent changes are made, after two years, to reflect market rents, these changes are ignored for the purposes of calculating the NPV.

6. The proposed changes remove this disparity of treatment. They provide that all rent changes after five years are ignored for the purposes of the NPV calculation and, for rental due after 5 years, the highest rent paid in any previous period of 12 months is substituted and used in the calculation. This will provide comparability of treatment for these types of lease.

Leases with uncertain rent

7. Where rent is expressed as relating to turnover, or where there are rent sharing or similar measures in place, the lessee is required to make a reasonable estimate of the rent due and include this estimate in their land transaction return. When any part of this estimated rent is determined, they must make an amended return including that part of the rent which is now determined. Representations have been received that this could place a severe compliance burden on many small businesses whose rent is determined by monthly turnover.

8. To simplify this area, it is proposed to amend FA 2003 so that, where a lease has a rent which is still uncertain after five years (eg a turnover based lease for 15 years), one and only one additional return is required at the five year point. This return will base the NPV on the actual rent paid in the first five years and (for any post five year rent due) will apply the amendment at para 6 above ie the highest rent paid in any 12 month period over the previous five years will be used in the NPV calculation.

9. Where all the uncertainty in the rental of a lease is determined before five years, one and only one additionally return is required at that point.

1.0. These measures will provide certainty and substantially reduce the compliance burden for small businesses.

Contingencies

1.1. Amendments will be made to clarify that break and forfeiture clauses in a lease do not operate to artificially shorten the term of a lease in the NPV calculation. Similarly, options to renew, contained in the lease, will not be treated as a contingency extending the term of a lease.

Extensions to leases during their term

1.2. An amendment will be introduced so that where a lease is extended during the currency of its term, this extension is treated as the grant of a new lease for the period by which the term of the lease is extended. This will be treated as a transaction linked with the original grant and, if not already notifiable, should the total term then extend to seven or more years, the whole transaction will be notifiable.

Continuation of leases and leases for an indefinite term

1.3. Currently, where there is a lease for a fixed term and thereafter, this term is defined as the term plus such further period as must elapse before the earliest date at which the lease can be determined. This will be amended so that the term is defined as the term specified in the lease.

1.4. Where a lease comes to the end of its term but the landlord does not require possession of the property, this extension is treated, in England and Wales, as a periodic tenancy which extends the term of the lease. In Scotland, there is a similar treatment called tacit relocation. Currently, the treatment of this extension is unclear and an amendment will be introduced to clarify the situation. Where a lease continues after the end of its term, this extension will be deemed to be the grant of a new lease for the period of 12 months (or the original term of the previous lease if shorter). Should this continue past this period, it will be deemed to be another lease of similar length and so on. These leases will be linked transactions. This will also apply in Scotland, where the lease is for an unspecified period at the outset. The original period of such a lease will be deemed to be 12 months.

1.5. Where a lease is granted for an indefinite term, for example if it is for life of until repayment of a debt, the term of these leases will be deemed to be for a period of 12 months. As above, should the lease continue after this period, the continuation will be deemed as the grant of another lease for 12 months and so on with each deemed grant being treated as a linked transaction with those previously.

1.6. For all these leases and deemed leases, treated as linked transactions, there will be notification requirements, so that, whenever the total NPV of the rents means that Stamp Duty Land Tax is due or where the total term of the leases is seven years or more, the series of deemed leases will be notifiable transactions.

Anti-avoidance

1.7. To prevent avoidance of Stamp Duty Land Tax using these amendments, it is proposed that, after the five year point when rent changes are not taken into account in the NPV, if the rent rises by more than 5% + RPI annually, this rent increase is deemed to be the grant of a new lease in a similar way to the way Sch 5 para 10 already treats rent increases not included in the terms of a lease.

1.8. Currently, assignments or assignations of leases where the payment of a premium is not involved are Stamp Duty Land Tax transactions but the assumption of the obligation to pay rent is not treated as consideration. Therefore, no duty is paid on these type of assignments or assignations. It is proposed to change this treatment in a limited variety of circumstances. Where the lease, at the previous transaction, benefited from a relief, so that the duty payable was reduced or eliminated, assignment or assignation of such a lease will be deemed to be the grant of a lease by the assignor to the assignee. This will prevent the use of reliefs to avoid Stamp Duty Land Tax.

Other reliefs

1.9. In accordance with commitments made by the Chief Secretary to the Treasury during Standing Committee debates on Finance Bill 2003, the Government has consulted with interested parties with a view to widening the scope of the relief package to include full or partial reliefs from stamp duty land tax for sale and leaseback transactions, certain types of exchange transactions involving house-building companies and for purchases of residential property by "chain-breaking" companies. The following additional reliefs are now proposed:

Sales and leasebacks

2.0. Partial relief will be given for the leaseback element of a sale and leaseback of commercial property. These transactions take the form of a sale of premises (or the assignment or assignation of an existing lease of premises) followed by a leaseback of those premises by the purchaser to the vendor. They are commonly entered into as a means of raising finance by companies or other commercial entities. The leaseback element of the transaction will be relieved from a charge to Stamp Duty Land Tax, provided that certain conditions are met. These are that the sale and leaseback arrangement does not involve residential property, that the leaseback is of the same premises that were the subject of the sale or assignment (or assignation) and that the consideration for the sale or assignment (or assignation) element of the transaction consists only of cash or the release or assumption of a liability.

Part II ST

Exchange transactions involving house-building companies

2.1. FA 2003 s 58 provides for relief where a house-building company acquires a dwelling from individuals in consideration of their agreeing to purchase a new dwelling from the house-building company. However, if the house- building company uses an unconnected company to acquire the individuals' former dwelling, no relief from Stamp Duty Land Tax exists in respect of that acquisition. Such an arrangement may commonly occur where the selling individuals are seeking to move to a retirement home. Relief will be introduced in these circumstances where the unconnected company acquires the individuals' former dwelling in the course of carrying on a trade as a property trader, does not spend more than a permitted amount on refurbishments, does not grant a lease or licence over the acquired property and does not permit any officer or employee to occupy the property. If these conditions are met, it is right that the role of the property trading company in providing liquidity to the housing market should not suffer a charge to Stamp Duty Land Tax. A charge to tax as provided for under Stamp Duty Land Tax legislation enacted in FA 2003 will arise when the property trading company on-sells the property.

2.2. A similar relief will be provided for companies who specialise in purchasing residential properties from personal representatives of deceased individuals and then on-sell the property. These companies provide liquidity to the residential housing market and, subject to conditions, relief from Stamp Duty Land Tax will be given on the acquisition.

Chain-breaking companies

2.3. Relief from Stamp Duty Land Tax will be introduced for companies part or all of whose trade consists of buying residential property in order to keep a chain of residential transactions from failing. Individuals looking to move house are often dependent on selling their own house before buying their target home. If their prospective purchaser pulls out, then their own purchase cannot go ahead. In these circumstances, a chain-breaking company would acquire the individuals' current property so that the move can still take place. The chain-breaking company purchases the property and then sells on in a short space of time. The purchase by the chain-breaking company will [be] relieved from Stamp Duty Land Tax, provided that it is acting in the course of a trade of buying properties in these circumstances, does not spend more than a permitted amount on refurbishments, does not grant a lease or licence over the acquired property and does not permit any officer or employee to occupy the property. Stamp Duty Land Tax will be paid on the eventual sale by the chain-breaking company.

Surrenders and regrants

2.4. The law will be clarified so that the surrender of any lease will not be consideration for the grant of another and the grant will not be consideration for the surrender. When a new lease is granted the charge to Stamp Duty Land Tax will be on the premium and rent due and not on the value of any interest surrendered. Where a lease is surrendered to the landlord, then as long as the surrendered lease is for a fixed rent credit will be given in computing the Stamp Duty Land Tax due on the new lease for the amount of rent that was due for the surrendered years. This will help many commercial arrangements for surrenders and regrants.

EXAMPLE

"A commercial lease ('lease 1') is granted for 10 years, rent £100,000 per year. The NPV is £831,660 so Stamp Duty Land Tax of £6,816 is chargeable. After 5 years it is surrendered and a new lease ('lease 2') of 10 years with rent of £150,000 per year is granted. Without any relief the NPV of lease 2 would be £1,247,490 and so Stamp Duty Land Tax of £10,794 would be chargeable. The relief recognises that rent paid for the first five years of lease 2 has already been partially taken into account in taxing lease 1. So the rent payable under lease 2 is taken to be £50,000 per year for the first five years and

£150,000 per year thereafter. This reduces the NPV to £795,985 and the Stamp Duty Land Tax chargeable to £6,459."

Technical corrections and clarifications

2.5. These are—

(a) Clarification of the interpretation of "taking possession" in s 44, and provision that this includes possession by a person connected with the purchaser;

(b) Clarification that fixed duty is abolished on duplicates and counterparts of instruments that effect a land transaction which is an Stamp Duty Land Tax transaction;

(c) Clarification as to the operation of the transitional provisions where a contract is entered into on or before 10 July 2003 in two respects—

— Where a contract is entered into on or before 10 July 2003 but the contracting purchaser sub-sells or assigns his rights after that date the proposed changes make it clear that the sub-sale or assignment (or assignation), if completed or substantially performed on or after 1 December 2003, is an Stamp Duty Land Tax transaction.

— Where the transaction provided for in the contract becomes an Stamp Duty Land Tax transaction by virtue of FA 2003 Sch 19 para 3(3) the "effective date" is the date of that event if it is later than the date the contract is substantially performed. There are examples of the operation of the transitional provisions at the end of this Note.

(d) Confirmation that the holder of a Power of Attorney can sign a land transaction return

(e) Clarification of the obligation to submit a further land transaction return when Stamp Duty Land Tax becomes chargeable, or chargeable at a higher rate, as a result of a later "linked transaction". The purchaser will need to submit a further land transaction return in respect of the earlier transaction(s) and for this purpose the "effective date" will be the date of the later transaction.

(f) Clarification that Stamp Duty Land Tax applies to the Crown in the same way as stamp duty does, but subject to the specific exemptions for Government departments and similar bodies (s 107(2)) and for certain transactions by other public bodies (s 66).

(g) A change to the way in which agreements for leases entered into before 1 December 2003 are dealt with for stamp duty purposes if the execution of the lease is an Stamp Duty Land Tax transaction. Sch19 para 8 provides that the agreement for lease can be presented for stamping and the stamp duty is then credited against Stamp Duty Land Tax due on the execution of the lease. It has been pointed out to us that this causes delay in being able to deliver the land transaction return. We propose to reverse the procedure so that the Stamp Duty Land Tax is paid first and the agreement for lease can then be stamped with a "denoted" stamp.

Transitional provisions—examples

Examples 1–5 show the current operation of the transitional provisions and no change is proposed. Example 6 relates to the proposed new provision.

1. A enters into a contract with B on 1 January 2003. The contract is completed on 1 January 2004 without any para 3(3) event having occurred. This is not an Stamp Duty Land Tax transaction and the conveyance is chargeable to stamp duty.

2. A enters into a contract with B on 1 January 2003. The contract is varied on 1 September 2003 and completed on 1 January 2004 without having first been substantially performed. The variation is a para 3(3) event and accordingly this is an Stamp Duty Land Tax transaction. The effective date is the date of completion.

3. A enters into a contract with B on 1 January 2003. The contract is varied on 1 September 2003, substantially performed on 1 October 2003 and completed on 1 January 2004. The variation is a para 3(3) event and accordingly this is an Stamp

Duty Land Tax transaction. The effective date is the date of completion because substantial performance pre-implementation is disregarded (Sch 19 para 4(3)).

4. A enters into a contract with B on 1 January 2003. The contract is varied on 1 September 2003, substantially performed on 1 January 2004 and completed on 1 February 2004. The variation is a para 3(3) event and accordingly this is an Stamp Duty Land Tax transaction. The effective date is the date of substantial performance (s 44(4)).

5. A enters into a contract with B on 1 January 2003. The contract is substantially performed on 1 November 2003, varied on 1 July 2004 and completed on 1 December 2004. The variation is a para 3(3) event and accordingly this is an Stamp Duty Land Tax transaction. The effective date is the date of completion because substantial performance pre- implementation is disregarded (Sch 19 para 4(3)).

6. A enters into a contract with B on 1 January 2003. The contract is substantially performed on 1 January 2004, varied on 1 July 2004 and completed on 1 December 2004. The variation is a para 3(3) event and accordingly this is an Stamp Duty Land Tax transaction. By virtue of the changes now being proposed the effective date will be 1 July 2004.

19 DECEMBER 2003. INLAND REVENUE STAMP DUTY LAND TAX—TREATMENT OF PRIVATE FINANCE INITIATIVE PROJECTS

The Government has today made Regulations clarifying the Stamp Duty Land Tax treatment of land transactions forming part of a Private Finance Initiative ("PFI") project. These Regulations will take effect from 19 December 2003. Ruth Kelly MP, Financial Secretary to the Treasury, said—

> "The Government recognises the importance of PFI transactions and the economic benefits which they bring. Having consulted at length with interested parties, our proposals will ensure that the treatment of these transactions under current stamp duty will be continued for the present under stamp duty land tax".

DETAILS

1. The Regulations are Stamp Duty Land Tax (Amendment of Schedule 4 to the Finance Act 2003) Regulations, SI 2003/3923.

2. The Regulations clarify the Stamp Duty Land Tax treatment of certain land transactions in PFI projects. The Regulations apply to "qualifying transactions", defined as transactions between certain public and educational bodies ("qualifying bodies") and a private sector supplier under a global agreement which provides for—

- the provision of services or the carrying out of works by the private sector supplier;
- payment for those services by the qualifying body;
- the transfer of land or the grant (or assignment) of a lease by the qualifying body;
- the grant of a lease back to the qualifying body; and
- in some cases, the transfer of land (sometimes termed "Surplus Land") by the qualifying body.

3. The Regulations provide that where a transaction is a qualifying transaction—

- neither the lease back to the public body nor the carrying out of works nor the provision of services is chargeable consideration for the transfer or grant of the lease by the qualifying body, or for the transfer of the Surplus Land (in other words tax will generally be charged only on any cash premium or rent paid by the private sector supplier);
- there is no chargeable consideration for the lease back (in other words there is no charge on the qualifying body); and

- the Stamp Duty Land Tax provisions relating to exchanges (which normally charge tax on the market value of the property) do not apply to qualifying transactions.

NOTES

1. Stamp Duty Land Tax applies (subject to some transitional provisions) to all "land transactions" completed on or after 1 December 2003. "Land transaction" includes the conveyance or transfer of a freehold (in Scotland, transfer of ownership), the assignment or assignation of an existing lease and the grant of a new lease. It replaces stamp duty, which is abolished except for instruments relating to stock and marketable securities, and for instruments relating to some partnership transactions.

2. Stamp Duty Land Tax is charged on the "chargeable consideration" given for the transaction. It does not matter whether the consideration is in the form of money or some other form.

3. A PFI transaction is an agreement under which a private sector supplier performs services for a public sector or educational body such as—
(i) the design and construction of a building or complex of buildings (eg a hospital, school, university accommodation, army garrison, bus station, leisure centre, care homes and other buildings or facilities that may be publicly owned);
(ii) the financing of the design and construction of the buildings in (*a*) above;
(iii) the management and delivery of various services within or related to the buildings constructed at (*a*) above on a continuous basis.

4. The treatment of PFI transactions under the old stamp duty regime was set out in Tax Bulletin 43C (parts 1–6) published by the Inland Revenue in October 1999.

17 MARCH 2004. INLAND REVENUE BN15
STAMP DUTY TAX—PARTNERSHIP TRANSACTIONS

WHO WILL BE AFFECTED?

1. Potentially all partnerships owning property, but primarily partnerships involved in property investment.

GENERAL DESCRIPTION OF THE MEASURES

2. Stamp duty land tax was introduced from 1 December, largely replacing stamp duty on land transactions. A number of changes were made in December 2003 to clarify points of uncertainty; counter avoidance and extend some reliefs. These new measures will apply SDLT to certain partnership transactions which involve an interest in land, and which are currently excluded from the scope of the tax.

OPERATIVE DATE

3. From Royal Assent.

CURRENT LAW AND PROPOSED REVISIONS

4. Currently, SDLT applies to most acquisitions of an interest in land situated in the UK. However, the transfer of an interest in land into a partnership, the acquisition of an interest in a partnership (where the partnership property includes an interest in land) and the transfer of an interest in land out of a partnership, were excluded from SDLT. Draft legislation was published on 20 October 2003 and following consultation, these transactions will be brought within the scope of SDLT from Royal Assent.

5. SDLT will now be charged on the following transactions—
- where an interest in land is transferred into a partnership, either by an existing partner or by a person in exchange for an interest in that partnership. SDLT will be chargeable, at the appropriate rate, on a proportion of the market value of that

land interest. The proportion will be equal to the proportion of the land interest transferred to the other partners as measured by their partnership;
- where partnership property includes an interest in land and arrangements are in place so that either—
  - existing partner transfers all or part of their partnership interest, to a person who is or becomes a partner, for money or money's worth; or
  - person becomes a partner and an existing partner reduces their partnership share (or ceases to be a partner) and withdraws money or money's worth from the partnership; then

  SDLT will be chargeable, at the appropriate rate, on the person acquiring the interest or increased interest, on a proportion of the market value of the land interest so transferred. The proportion will be equal to the increased (or new) partnership share held by the acquiring partner; and
- where a partnership transfers an interest in land to a partner or former partner. SDLT will be chargeable, at the appropriate rate, on the person acquiring the interest, on the proportion of the market value of the land interest transferred on which tax (which includes ad valorem stamp duty or, for transactions executed before 20 October 2003, fixed duty) has not previously been paid.

8. The changes will charge only the proportion of the property being transferred into a partnership. This recognises concerns raised, that charging the whole value of the land meant that the part of the land retained (through their partnership share) by the person transferring it, was being brought into the charge to tax unfairly.

Further advice

If you have any questions about these changes please contact the Stamp Taxes Enquiry Line on 0845 603 0135.

17 MARCH 2004. INLAND REVENUE BN37
STAMP DUTY LAND TAX—TECHNICAL CLARIFICATIONS

WHO IS LIKELY TO BE AFFECTED?

1. Purchasers and lessees/tenants of land, especially those engaging in more complex commercial transactions. Residential purchasers and tenants are unlikely to be affected.

GENERAL DESCRIPTION OF THE MEASURE

2. Stamp duty land tax (SDLT) was introduced from 1 December, largely replacing stamp duty on land transactions. A number of changes were made in December 2003 to clarify points of uncertainty; counter avoidance and extend some reliefs. These new measures make further changes in these areas.

OPERATIVE DATE

3. The majority of measures apply from Budget Day. Those in paragraphs 15, 16 and 18 below apply from Royal Assent. The measure in paragraph 17 applies with effect from 1 December 2003.

CURRENT LAW AND PROPOSED REVISIONS

Anti-avoidance

4. Changes will clarify the provision for sub-sales (where a contracting purchaser sells on without taking title) where part only of the property is sub-sold.

5. Potential avoidance opportunities exploiting the interaction between the provisions on sub-sales and those on group relief and sale-and-leaseback will be closed.

6. Changes will be made so that the transitional provisions apply as the Government intended on contracts entered into pre-implementation, where there is a sub-sale post-implementation.

7. Changes to the relief for Private Finance Initiative (PFI) projects will ensure that such transactions are always notifiable.

Clarifications

8. Currently SDLT is charged on uncompleted contracts which are "substantially performed" when the purchaser either pays or takes possession. Changes will make explicit how the charge works for agreements where the contracting purchaser has a right to direct a conveyance to a third party. Such agreements are common where land is to be developed and sold.

9. Under certain conditions, works carried out on land after it is purchased do not count as consideration. Changes will ensure that an unintended charge does not arise when a contract is later completed by conveyance.

1.0. "Agreements for lease" are an important part of conveyancing in England, Wales and Northern Ireland. These look like contracts to grant a lease but in practice are often treated as equivalent to leases. There will be clarification on the treatment of agreements for leases which are "substantially performed" so that for most purposes, and in particular when they are assigned, they are treated as leases. This will apply to all agreements for lease whenever they were entered into.

1.1. Similar changes will be made as regards "missives of let" in Scotland. Missives of let are in essence agreements under which a lease is to be executed

1.2. To provide certainty, all variations that extend a lease or increase the rent will be treated as the grant of a new lease. All other variations will be disregarded. This will apply to all leases whether the original grant of the lease was within the scope of SDLT or not.

1.3. Minor amendments will be made to the rules on leases—

- to ensure the rules on surrenders and regrants work as intended;
- to clarify that where a lease ends part-way through a year only the rent actually paid is taken into account;
- to reduce the compliance burden where there is a rent review just before the end of the fifth year because a lease is expressed to commence from a date earlier than the date it is granted
- to provide that "rent" for a period before a lease is granted is taxed as a premium and not as rent.

1.4. Changes will ensure shared ownership leases are treated in a way similar to their treatment under the old stamp duty regime.

Extensions of reliefs

1.5. Current rules provide relief for "chain-breaking", relocation and similar transactions when people move house. However, the rules do not permit relief when people buy a new house but cannot move into it immediately and stay on in their old house. Changes will extend this relief provided people do not stay on in their old home for more than six months

1.6. Currently relief for "sale and leaseback" transactions is restricted to commercial property. This restriction will be removed to help people entering into "home reversion plans" to raise capital from their homes. The relief will also be extended to include "lease and leaseback" transactions and transactions where part only of the property is leased back.

1.7. Changes will put it beyond doubt that when property passes to a beneficiary under or in satisfaction of an entitlement under a will, or on an intestacy, there is no charge to SDLT. This change, which reflects the law under the old stamp duty regime, will apply to all such transmissions of property since 1 December 2003.

Reduced compliance burden

1.8. To help reduce the burden on purchasers there will be changes to the administrative and compliance provisions with effect from Royal Assent of Finance Bill 2004—

- At present all acquisitions of a freehold interest have to be notified to the Inland Revenue where there is chargeable consideration, however small. This includes for example the purchase by a lessee of a residential property of the freehold reversion for a few hundred pounds. In future there will be no requirement to notify where the transaction is the acquisition of a freehold (or other "major interest in land") where the consideration is less than £1000. Instead such transactions may be self-certified;
- The grant of a lease for seven years or less (a "short lease") only has to be notified to the Inland Revenue if there is tax to pay, or a relief to be claimed. But all assignments of such leases by tenants have to be notified, whether or not there is tax to pay. In future a short lease is assigned this will only have to be notified to the Inland Revenue if there is tax to pay, or a relief to be claimed. Other assignments of short leases may be self-certified;
- Changes will make clear that the Inland Revenue will not charge two tax-geared penalties on the same amount of tax. This is the same as the rule for income tax;
- Current procedures for claiming relief do not cover all kinds of claim. There will be comprehensive rules similar to those for income tax; and
- Changes will ensure that the acquisition of "community interests in land" will not have to be notified to the Inland Revenue when these interests are created in Scotland later this year.

FURTHER ADVICE

1.9. Further guidance on the provisions taking effect on Budget Day is on the Inland Revenue web-site at www.inlandrevenue.gov.uk/so. If you have any questions about these changes please contact the Stamp Taxes Enquiry Line on 0845 603 0135.

17 MARCH 2004. BUDGET SUMMARY. INLAND REVENUE STAMP DUTY LAND TAX

PARTNERSHIP TRANSACTIONS

On the introduction of stamp duty land tax (SDLT) with effect from 1 December 2003, certain partnership transactions which involve an interest in land were excluded and remained within the scope of stamp duty. Such transactions are to be brought within the charge to SDLT with effect from the date of Royal Assent to the Finance Act. The transactions involved are where—

- an interest in land is transferred into a partnership either by an existing partner or in exchange for an interest in the partnership;
- arrangements are in place for the transfer by an existing partner of all or part of their partnership interest for money or money's worth to a person who is or becomes a partner, and the partnership property includes an interest in land;
- arrangements are in place so that a person becomes a partner and an existing partner reduces his partnership share (or ceases to be a partner) and withdraws money or money's worth from the partnership, and the partnership property includes an interest in land; and
- a partnership transfers an interest in land to a partner or former partner.

There are detailed rules determining the amount chargeable to SDLT in each case.

TECHNICAL CLARIFICATIONS

A number of changes are to be made to the stamp duty land tax (SDLT) regime. Except where indicated below, they apply with effect from 17 March 2004.

There will be anti-avoidance legislation to clarify the provisions for sub-sales where only part of the property is sub-sold. Legislation will also close loopholes that exploit the interaction between the provisions on sub-sales and those on group relief and sale-and-leaseback. The provisions relating to PFI projects will be amended to ensure that all such transactions are notifiable transactions. Changes to the legislation will ensure that the transitional provisions apply as intended to contracts entered into before the implementation date (1 December 2003) where there is a sub-sale post implementation.

There will also be clarification as to how the "substantial performance" principle applies where the purchaser has a right to direct a conveyance to a third party.

Although in certain circumstances, works carried out on land after it has been purchased do not constitute chargeable consideration, an unintended SDLT charge may occur when a contract is later completed by conveyance. Changes will be made to prevent this.

An agreement for a lease which has been "substantially performed" will be treated as a lease for most purposes. The Revenue intend this change to apply to all agreements for lease, regardless of when they were entered into. This also applies to missives of let in Scotland.

A variation that increases the term of a lease or the rent will be treated as the grant of a new lease. This applies to all leases irrespective of whether the original grant was within the scope of SDLT. All other variations will be disregarded.

Minor amendments will be made to the rules on surrenders and regrants of leases. Also, where a lease ends partway through the year, only the rent actually paid will be taken into account. Any rent for a period before the grant of a lease will be taxed as a premium.

There will be changes to ensure that shared ownership leases are treated in a similar way as under stamp duty.

There is no SDLT charge when property passes to a beneficiary under (or in satisfaction of an entitlement under) a will or intestacy. The legislation will be amended to put this beyond doubt. The amendment has effect for all transmissions of property since 1 December 2003.

The following provisions apply with effect from Royal Assent to the Finance Act 2004.

- The relief for "chain-breaking", relocation and similar transactions will be extended to cases where the purchaser of a new house cannot move into it immediately, and stays on in his old house. The relief will be granted on condition that the purchaser does not stay in the old house for more than six months.
- The relief for sale-and-leaseback transactions will be extended to residential property. The relief will also be extended to include lease-and-leaseback transactions, and those where only part of the property is leased back.
- The acquisition of a freehold (or other major interest in land) where the consideration is less than £1,000 will cease to be a notifiable transaction. This also applies to the assignment of a short lease where there is no tax to pay, or no relief to be claimed. Such transactions may instead be self-certified. Furthermore, the acquisition of 'community interests in land' in Scotland will not be a notifiable transaction.
- Minor amendments to the legislation will ease the compliance burden in certain circumstances. There will also be comprehensive rules for claiming relief. Also, the legislation will be amended to provide that the Revenue will not charge two tax-geared penalties on the same amount of tax.

5 APRIL 2004. INLAND REVENUE SDLT—SALE OF LAND WITH ASSOCIATED CONSTRUCTION, &C, CONTRACT

We have been asked how to determine the chargeable consideration for stamp duty land tax purposes where V agrees to sell land to P and V also agrees to carry out work (commonly works of construction, improvement or repair) on the land sold. Our view is that the decision in *Prudential Assurance Co Ltd v IRC* [1992] STC 863 applies for the purposes of stamp duty land tax as it does for stamp duty. This is because the basis of the decision was the identification of the subject matter of the transaction and this is as relevant for stamp duty land tax as it is for stamp duty.

It follows that SP 8/93 will be applied for stamp duty land tax as it was for stamp duty. The paragraphs on "contracts already entered into" and "procedure for submitting documents" are, however, not relevant to stamp duty land tax.

Where, however, the sale of land and the construction, &c, contract are in substance one bargain (as they were in the *Prudential* case) there must be a just and reasonable apportionment of the total consideration given for all elements of the bargain in order to arrive at the chargeable consideration for stamp duty land tax purposes.

The SDLT Manual will be amended in due course to reflect this.

12 NOVEMBER 2004. INLAND REVENUE GUIDANCE NOTE STAMP DUTY LAND TAX AND NIL-RATE BAND DISCRETIONARY TRUSTS

1. We have received a number of enquiries about the interaction between Stamp Duty Land Tax and "nil-rate band discretionary trusts" ("NRB Trusts"). This note should enable taxpayers and their advisers to decide on the Stamp Duty Land Tax consequences of transactions with NRB Trusts. This note does not cover any taxes other than Stamp Duty Land Tax. Neither does it cover the powers or fiduciary responsibilities of trustees of NRB Trusts, or of personal representatives, under general law. Trustees and personal representatives may wish to take independent legal advice on those aspects.

2. An NRB Trust is commonly established under the Will of a deceased person. The typical form is a pecuniary legacy, not exceeding the nil-rate band for inheritance tax, to be held by the trustees of the NRB Trust ("the NRB trustees") on discretionary trusts for a specified class of beneficiaries. The residue of the estate, often including the matrimonial home, commonly passes to the surviving spouse, although it may pass to residuary trustees.

3. Where the personal representatives discharge the pecuniary legacy by payment of the specified sum to the trustees no Stamp Duty Land Tax issue arises. However in many cases the personal representatives satisfy the legacy otherwise than by payment of the specified sum. It is in these cases that a Stamp Duty Land Tax liability may arise on the transfer of the matrimonial home or other land to the surviving spouse or residuary trustees.

4. The transfer of an interest in land, whether to a residuary beneficiary or to any other person, and whether in satisfaction of an entitlement under a Will or not, is a land transaction for Stamp Duty Land Tax purposes. The question is whether the transferee gives any chargeable consideration for the transfer. Very often a beneficiary gives no chargeable consideration for the transfer of land under a Will. However transactions in connection with NRB Trusts may result in the beneficiary giving chargeable consideration.

5. The commonest examples of such transactions, and their Stamp Duty Land Tax consequences, are as follows:

- The NRB trustees accept the surviving spouse's promise to pay in satisfaction of the pecuniary legacy and in consideration of that promise land is transferred to the surviving spouse. The promise to pay is chargeable consideration for Stamp Duty Land Tax purposes.
- The NRB trustees accept the personal representatives' promise to pay in satisfaction of the pecuniary legacy and land is transferred to the surviving spouse in consideration of the spouse accepting liability for the promise. The acceptance of liability for the promise is chargeable consideration for Stamp Duty Land Tax purposes. The amount of chargeable consideration is the amount promised (not exceeding the market value of the land transferred).
- Land is transferred to the surviving spouse and the spouse charges the property with payment of the amount of the pecuniary legacy. The NRB trustees accept this charge in satisfaction of the pecuniary legacy. The charge is money's worth and so is chargeable consideration for Stamp Duty Land Tax purposes.
- The personal representatives charge land with the payment of the pecuniary legacy. The personal representatives and NRB trustees also agree that the trustees have no right to enforce payment of the amount of the legacy personally against the owner of the land for the time being. The NRB trustees accept this charge in satisfaction of the legacy. The property is transferred to the surviving spouse subject to the charge. There is no chargeable consideration for Stamp Duty Land

Tax purpose provided that there is no change in the rights or liabilities of any person in relation to the debt secured by the charge.

6. We have also been asked about the consequences for Stamp Duty Land Tax purposes of a Deed of Variation made by beneficiaries after the death of the deceased person. A Deed of Variation may effect a land transaction if it alters the beneficial interests in land, for example by settling land in trust. However, placing a charge on land is not in itself a land transaction. In addition FA 2003 Sch 3 para 4 provides that under certain conditions a land transaction effected by a Deed of Variation is exempt from charge.

13 APRIL 2005. INLAND REVENUE
BUDGET 2005 PROVISIONS ON STAMP DUTY LAND TAX

1. A number of Stamp Duty Land Tax measures were announced on Budget Day, 16 March 2005. This note summarises the effect that subsequent developments have had on these measures. In particular it explains that in some circumstances a repayment may be due to purchasers who have paid tax on the basis of measures announced in the Budget (see paragraph 8 below).

2. All the Budget measures were included in the Finance Bill published on 22 March 2005. However, that Bill has now been withdrawn. Instead the Finance (No 2) Bill, containing some but not all of the provisions in the original Finance Bill, was passed by the House of Commons on 6 April and received Royal Assent as Finance Act 2005 on 7 April 2005.

INCREASE IN THE THRESHOLD FOR RESIDENTIAL TRANSACTIONS FROM £60,000 TO £120,000

3. This measure has been included in Finance Act 2005 (as section 95) and will have effect as announced, that is, for land transactions the effective date of which was on or after 17 March 2005.

WITHDRAWAL OF DISADVANTAGED AREAS RELIEF ON NON-RESIDENTIAL TRANSACTIONS

4. This measure has been included in Finance Act 2005 (as section 96 and Schedule 9) and will have effect as announced, that is, for land transactions the effective date of which was on or after 17 March 2005, subject to transitional provisions for some contracts entered into on or before 16 March 2005.

EXTENSION OF RELIEFS FOR ALTERNATIVE PROPERTY FINANCE

5. This measure has been included in Finance Act 2005 (as section 94 and Schedule 8) and will have effect for land transactions where the effective date of the "first transaction" is on or after 7 April 2005.

MISCELLANEOUS AMENDMENTS

6. Budget Resolution 46 gave provisional statutory effect under the Provisional Collection of Taxes Act 1968 ("the 1968 Act") to a number of miscellaneous amendments to the legislation governing Stamp Duty Land Tax. These amendments were summarised in a Technical Note published by the Inland Revenue on 16 March 2005. Broadly speaking the Resolution had effect for transactions the effective date of which was on or after 17 March 2005.

7. Provisions giving effect to Budget Resolution 46 were included (as Part 1 of Schedule 17) in the original Finance Bill, now withdrawn. However Finance Act 2005 does not contain any provisions giving effect to Budget Resolution 46. It follows that by virtue of section 1(5) of the 1968 Act the Resolution ceased to have statutory effect when Parliament was prorogued on 7 April 2005.

8. If you have paid tax which would not have been payable but for the provisional statutory effect of Budget Resolution 46 a repayment is due to you. Any requests for

Part II ST

repayment should be sent, along with an explanation of why you think a repayment is due to you, to: Complex Transactions Unit, Manchester Stamp Office, Upper 5th Floor, Royal Exchange, Exchange Street, Manchester M2 7EB.

If you are in doubt as to whether a repayment is due please contact the Complex Transactions Unit with an explanation of the circumstances.

11 JULY 2005. HMRC
DISCLOSURE OF TAX AVOIDANCE SCHEMES—STAMP DUTY LAND TAX

The Government has today introduced legislation to extend the direct tax scheme disclosure rules to stamp duty land tax with effect from 1 August 2005.

The Paymaster General, Dawn Primarolo said:

> "The disclosure rules have proved a valuable tool in tackling tax avoidance. They provide HMRC with earlier information about tax avoidance schemes, enabling the Government to make a faster and better-targeted response. Extending the rules to include stamp duty land tax will allow HMRC to stop more abusive schemes used by those who seek to avoid tax at the expense of the vast majority who pay their fair share."

A full Regulatory Impact Assessment (RIA) of the legislation has been published and can be found on the HMRC website.

The Stamp Duty Land Tax Avoidance Schemes (Prescribed Descriptions of Arrangements) Regulations 2005 (SI 2005/1868) describe the arrangements for stamp duty land tax that must be disclosed. These are where there is a substantial risk of tax avoidance.

The Tax Avoidance Schemes (Information) (Amendment) Regulations 2005 (SI 2005/1869) amend the existing regulations that specify what information must be provided, and the time limits for providing it.

NOTES FOR EDITORS

1. Finance Act 2004 included new rules requiring promoters and users of certain direct tax schemes to disclose details of those schemes to the Inland Revenue. The rules came into effect on 1 August 2004.

2. The Government announced in Budget 2005 that the rules would be extended to stamp duty land tax schemes for non-residential property with a value of at least £5 million. Draft regulations were published, with a partial RIA, for comment on 24 March. The proposed commencement date was 1 July 2005.

3. Following the General Election, HMRC discussed with representative bodies and tax advisers how these rules would work in practice. The Government revised the commencement date to 1 August to accommodate these discussions and the regulations introduced represents the Government's response to the issues raised.

3 OCTOBER 2006. HMRC
STAMP DUTY: "WAIT & SEE" CASES—WRITTEN UNDERTAKINGS

We were recently asked whether we have changed our practice on acceptance of written undertakings in Stamp Duty "wait and see" cases. (Where the amount of consideration is subject to variation, pending completion accounts.)

We can confirm that there has been no change and that the position remains as set out in the guidance at 4.317 of the Stamp Taxes Manual, which is:

Documents can be provisionally stamped, using the initial consideration (or your estimate of the consideration), provided we receive an undertaking to resubmit the documents, with any additional duty and interest, when the final figure is known.

- If you are a practitioner submitting the application for provisional stamping on behalf of your client, the undertaking must come from you.
- If you are the client submitting the application for provisional stamping, the undertaking must come from you—but it is acceptable for the cheque to be drawn on the practitioners' client account.

14 DECEMBER 2007. HMRC GUIDANCE NOTE INTERMEDIARY AND STOCK LENDING RELIEFS—FA 2007, SCH 21

Transaction reporting to a Multilateral Trading Facility, Recognised Foreign Exchange or Recognised Foreign Options Exchange.

HM Revenue and Customs (HMRC) has been asked to clarify the operation of the stamp duty and stamp duty reserve tax rules for intermediary and stock lending relief, as amended with effect from 1 November 2007, in respect of transactions involving stocks other than those that are regularly traded on a regulated market.

The intermediary relief legislation covering stocks regularly traded on a multilateral trading facility (MTF), recognised foreign exchange (RFE) or recognised foreign options exchange (RFOE) provides that relief is only available where the transaction is subject to the rules of the particular MTF/exchange and is reported to the MTF/exchange in accordance with those rules (see FA 1986 ss 80A(6) and 88A(6)). The stock lending relief provisions contain a similar requirement (see FA 1986 ss 80C(6) and 89AA(5)).

HMRC understands that the rules of some MTFs/exchanges may, following the implementation of the Directive on Markets in Financial Instruments (MiFID), no longer contain a requirement to report a transaction to the MTF/exchange. This means that members of those organisations are strictly unable to fulfil the requirement in the legislation that transactions must be reported to the MTF/exchange.

HMRC recognises that a strict reading of the legislation would result in intermediary or stock lending relief not being granted. It therefore intends to amend the legislation to address this at the earliest opportunity. In the meantime, HMRC will not refuse relief where the rules of an MTF/exchange are either silent about the need to report transactions or specifically state that a report is not required. Nor will stock lending relief be denied if the stock loan is reported to CREST for settlement and the Trade System of Origin (TSO) field completed in accordance with the rules of the market/MTF/exchange.

For trading transactions on the Alternative Investment Market (AIM) of the London Stock Exchange (LSE), the trade report that AIM members are required to make to the LSE will be regarded as satisfying the reporting condition for the purposes of ss 80A(6) and 88A(6).

31 MARCH 2008. HMRC INFORMATION SHEET STAMP DUTY ON SHARED OWNERSHIP HOMES

BACKGROUND

Shared ownership purchasers acquire a lease, for which they pay a premium representing a percentage of the market value of the property, and rent in respect of the remainder. They may be able to make further capital payments (which will increase their share and reduce the rent payable) and ultimately to acquire the freehold. This is known as "staircasing".

SDLT AND SHARED OWNERSHIP

- Shared ownership purchasers can elect to pay SDLT at the outset on the market value of the property. In this case there will be no further SDLT charges at any stage.
- If no election is made, SDLT will be charged on the initial purchase in the normal way — that is, on the premium and the net present value of the rent payable under the lease. (In practice it is very unlikely that any tax will be due on the rent.)

Part II ST

- There is then a special SDLT relief which means staircasing payments are not charged to SDLT until an 80 percent share of the property is reached.
- Any further 'staircasing' payments which take the purchaser above this level—including the acquisition of the freehold, will attract SDLT

BUDGET MEASURE

- The measure announced in the Budget abolishes, from Budget Day, the so called "£600 rule" for residential leases. This rule meant that, where the annual rent under the lease (not the NPV) exceeded £600, SDLT applied at 1 per cent on the premium even where this was below the SDLT threshold (£125,000, or £150,000 in a disadvantaged area).
- The special rules for shared ownership purchasers have not changed, but in practice these purchasers were often hit by the £600 rule because their initial payment was below the threshold but their annual rent was more than £600.

EFFECT OF THE MEASURE FOR SHARED OWNERSHIP PURCHASERS

- Where a market value election is not made, no SDLT will be payable on the premium where this does not exceed the SDLT threshold (£125,000, or £150,000 in a disadvantaged area), whatever the annual rent paid. If the premium is more than this, SDLT will still be charged on the whole premium at 1 per cent (and at higher rates in the unlikely event that the premium exceeds £250,000).
- No tax will be payable on "staircasing" payments which do not take the purchaser above an 80 per cent share of the property.
- Any further "staircasing" payments which take the purchaser above this level—including the acquisition of the freehold, will attract SDLT. Tax will be payable on the amount actually paid at the appropriate rate in force at the time the payment is made.
- The rate of tax charged on these further "staircasing" payments will be based on the total capital payments made to date—that is, on the initial premium and all "staircasing" payments, regardless of whether any tax has previously been paid on them. This is because the various payments are treated as "linked transactions" for SDLT purposes.

EXAMPLE 1

Market value of the property is £220,000.

Initial lease premium is £110,000, representing a 50 per cent share of the property. SDLT payable is nil (because this amount is below the SDLT threshold).

First "staircasing" payment is £55,000, taking the purchaser's share to 75 per cent. SDLT payable is nil (this payment attracts relief as it doesn't take the purchaser's share over 80 per cent).

Final "staircasing" payment is £55,000, taking the purchaser's share to 100 per cent including acquisition of the freehold. SDLT is payable at 1 per cent on £55,000 (because the rate of SDLT is determined by the total of all payments made, that is £220,000).

EXAMPLE 2

Market value of the property is £220,000.

Initial lease premium is £165,000, representing a 75 per cent share of the property. SDLT is payable at 1 per cent on £165,000 (because this amount is above the SDLT threshold).

Final staircasing payment is £55,000, taking the purchaser's share to 100 per cent including acquisition of the freehold. SDLT is payable at 1 per cent on £55,000 (because the rate of SDLT is determined by the total of all payments made, that is £220,000).

17 APRIL 2008. HMRC NOTICE
SDLT—BUDGET CHANGES TO NOTIFICATION REQUIREMENTS

Following on from the announcement of changes in the Stamp Duty Land Tax (SDLT) notification thresholds in Budget 2008 [BN57 and Finance Bill clause 91], the various Land Registries and HM Revenue & Customs (HMRC) have agreed to produce this note which conveyancers and others involved in land transactions may find helpful in explaining how these changes will work in practice.

As you know, Budget 2008 announced changes in requirements for notification of land transactions to HMRC. These changes will have effect for transactions with an effective date on and after 12 March 2008.

The changes raise the threshold for notification of non-leasehold transactions involving major interests in land from a chargeable consideration of £1,000 to £40,000. The changes also affect transactions involving leases for a term of seven years or more, which will now only have to be notified where any chargeable consideration other than rent is equal to or more than £40,000 or where any rent is equal to or more than £1,000.

As a result of these changes it will no longer be necessary to complete either form SDLT 1 Land Transaction Return or form SDLT 60 Self certificate if the transaction is below the new notification threshold.

The new notification system is we hope, much simpler and easier to understand for customers.

Some people have asked whether there are any circumstances in which a certificate that no SDLT is due (form SDLT 60) is now required. We are happy to confirm that there are now no circumstances in which an SDLT 60 is required in order for documents to be registered. Indeed, the current Finance Bill legislates to remove all reference to this form. Subject to Parliamentary approval, these consequential amendments will become law when the Bill receives Royal assent later this summer.

It may also help to mention that the acquisition of a chargeable interest other than a major interest in land remains notifiable only where there is chargeable consideration for which SDLT is due at a rate of 1 per cent or more. The acquisition of an easement, for example, is an acquisition of a chargeable interest other than a major interest in land. So, if the chargeable consideration on it was at the rate of 1 per cent or higher, the transaction would be notifiable.

It will be noted that the new notification threshold differs in two major respects from the previous rules. First, the threshold for notification in relation to major interests in residential property has risen from £1,000 to £40,000. Second, there is now a threshold for mixed and non-residential property, where none previously existed.

HMRC and the land registries will be working together over the coming months to update published guidance and will be happy to advise on any queries you might have.

25 JUNE 2008. HMRC
GUIDANCE NOTE ON THE STAMP DUTY LAND TAX (OPEN-ENDED INVESTMENT COMPANIES) REGULATIONS 2008 (SI 2008 NO 710)

GENERAL OVERVIEW

The Stamp Duty Land Tax (Open-ended Investment Companies) Regulations 2008 (SI 2008/710) provide relief from SDLT for land transactions which transfer property from an authorised unit trust (AUT) to an open-ended investment company (OEIC), as part of an arrangement for the conversion of the AUT into an OEIC, or the amalgamation of the AUT with an existing OEIC.

This relief must be claimed in a land transaction return or an amendment to such a return. Enter the “other” relief code (28) at question 9 of the return.

CONDITIONS FOR THE RELIEF

Vendor and purchaser

- The vendor must be a UK-authorised unit trust in respect of which an authorisation order made by the Financial Services Authority under Financial Services and Markets Act 2000 s 243 is in force. For this purpose each part of an umbrella scheme is treated as a separate AUT.
- The purchaser must be an open-ended investment company incorporated in the UK, which satisfies the conditions set out in Financial Services and Markets Act 2000 s 236.

The property

The subject-matter of the transaction must be property which is subject to the trusts of the AUT at the time of the transaction.

The transfer

The transfer must form part of an arrangement under which:

- the AUT converts into, or amalgamates with, the OEIC;
- the whole of the property of the AUT (that is, not just property which constitutes chargeable interests for SDLT purposes) becomes the property of the OEIC, except for any property retained in order to discharge the trustees' liabilities;
- all the units in the AUT are extinguished;
- the consideration for the transfer consists of, or includes, the issue of shares in the OEIC to the holders of the extinguished units, in proportion to their holdings of those units and
- there is no other consideration for the transfer, except for the assumption or discharge by the OEIC of liabilities of the trustees of the AUT.

26 NOVEMBER 2008. HMRC
STAMP DUTY LAND TAX: GROUP RELIEF—PARAGRAPH 4ZA OF SCHEDULE 7 FA 2003

INTRODUCTION

1. This article gives practical and technical guidance following the introduction of paragraph 4ZA of Schedule 7 to the FA 2003 in Budget 2008. HM Revenue & Customs (HMRC) will be monitoring this legislation and if necessary, further guidance will be published to assist customers.

2. This article also sets out how HMRC will interpret paragraph 4(4) of Schedule 7 to the Finance Act 2003.

3. The guidance provided in this note will apply in normal commercial situations. But where it appears that the guidance is being used for avoidance purposes the circumstances may warrant strict application of the group relief legislation.

BACKGROUND

4. Paragraph 1 of Schedule 7 to FA 2003 provides for relief from stamp duty land tax where land and buildings are transferred between companies, (or other bodies corporate), and, at the effective date of the transaction, the companies are members of the same group. The exemption extends to the grant of leases between group companies.

5. Paragraph 2 of Schedule 7 to FA 2003 restricts the availability of group relief if certain events occur. See SDLTM 23030+ (www.hmrc.gov.uk/manuals/sdltmanual/sdltm23030.htm).

6. Paragraph 3 of Schedule 7 provides that relief may be withdrawn if certain events occur within 3 years of the effective date of the transaction. See SDLTM 23070+ (www.hmrc.gov.uk/manuals/sdltmanual/sdltm23070.htm).

7. Paragraph 4 of Schedule 7 provides that certain events will not result in group relief being withdrawn.

8. The first case is where the purchaser ceases to be a member of the same group as the vendor because the vendor leaves the group. This was previously dealt with in the now repealed sub-paragraphs 4(2) and 4(3).

9. The vendor is regarded as leaving the group where the purchaser and vendor cease to be members of the same group by reason of a transaction relating to shares in the vendor or another company that, as a result of the transaction, ceases to be a member of the same group as the purchaser.

10. It was acknowledged by the Economic Secretary to the Treasury when the legislation was introduced that there was scope for avoidance schemes to be constructed using this legislation.

11. HMRC Stamp Taxes was asked to monitor carefully the use of this relief. We have done so and found an increasing number of schemes which are structured so that the vendor leaves the group first, meaning that the subsequent sale of the purchaser will not trigger the withdrawal of the original relief.

12. Paragraph 4ZA has been introduced to counter such schemes, replacing paragraph 4(2) and 4(3) of schedule 7 to FA 2003. This legislation will also apply to those situations where, although no avoidance motive is present, the same sequence of events has occurred.

13. Further information concerning the other circumstances in which group relief will not be withdrawn is available at SDLTM 23080 (www.hmrc.gov.uk/manuals/sdltmanual/sdltm23080.htm).

PARAGRAPH 4ZA OF SCHEDULE 7 FA 2003

14. This provision applies to all group relief claims for transactions where the effective date is on or after 13 March 2008.

15. Sub-paragraph 4ZA(1) of Schedule 7 ensures that a vendor can still leave a group without triggering withdrawal of group relief, thus preserving the intention of the original legislation.

16. Sub-paragraph 4ZA(4) however, provides that it will no longer be possible to avoid the withdrawal of group relief where there is a subsequent change in control of the purchaser within three years of the effective date of the group-relieved intra group transfer, or at any time in the pursuance of or in connection with arrangements made before the end of that period.

17. For example, in the group of H (parent), P (purchaser) and V (vendor), V transfers a property intra group to P and group relief is claimed (the qualifying conditions are met). V then leaves the group. Although P is no longer part of the same group as V, group relief is not withdrawn at this stage. This maintains the position pre FA 2008.

18. Two years after the purchase by P, H sells its shares in P to an unconnected third party. This change in control of P will now trigger withdrawal of the original group relief.

19. Withdrawal of group relief will similarly be triggered if there is a change in the control of H as this effectively changes the control of P.

CHANGE IN CONTROL

20. This section considers certain situations involving a change in control which may lead to a withdrawal of group relief. The guidance sets out HMRC's general approach to these, but should be read in conjunction with the comments at paragraph 3.

Sub-paragraph 4ZA (5) of Schedule 7 states that there is a change in control of the purchaser if:

(a) a person who controls the purchaser (alone or with others) ceases to do so,

Part II ST

(b) a person obtains control of the purchaser (alone or with others) or,
(c) the purchaser is wound up

21. Sub-paragraph 4ZA(8) of Schedule 7 provides that any references to control are to be interpreted in accordance with section 416 of the Taxes Act 1988.

This defines control as:

- control over the affairs of the company
- control through voting power
- control through share capital or through issued share capital
- control over income of the company
- control over the assets of the company

22. Further information concerning control is available at CTM60200+ (www.hmrc.gov.uk/manuals/ctmanual/ctm60200.htm)

CIRCUMSTANCES WHERE HMRC CONSIDERS THERE HAS NOT BEEN A CHANGE IN CONTROL

Liquidation

23. The appointment of a liquidator and any subsequent liquidation results in a company losing its beneficial interest in its assets, including any shares it owns in other companies (*Ayerst v C&K Construction Ltd* 50 TC 651).

24. Without special provision, the commencement of a winding up of a holding company within a group would result in the breaking up of a group. This may present difficulties for groups undertaking genuine reorganisations.

25. To address these concerns HMRC will no longer view the appointment of a liquidator as resulting in a change of control of a company for the purposes of sub-paragraph 4ZA(5)(*b*), provided that the liquidation can be shown to be part of a scheme of reconstruction which involves a successful claim to reconstruction or group relief or where the economic ownership of the relevant assets remains within the group. Similarly the eventual liquidation of that company will not be regarded as giving rise to a change in control of its subsidiaries (if any) where the transfer of those shares on the liquidation involves a successful claim to relief from stamp duty or where the economic ownership of those shares remains within the group.

New intermediate holding company

26. Sub-paragraph 4ZA(6) provides that a change in control does not arise where a new holding company is inserted either between the original ultimate parent company and its shareholders, or between the purchaser and the parent company with no change in overall economic ownership of the group. This is because HMRC will look at the ultimate shareholding in order to establish whether there has been a change of control.

Loan creditors

27. Sub-paragraph 4ZA(7) provides that, where there is change in control of the purchaser because of a loan creditor, group relief will not be withdrawn if the persons (other than loan creditors) who controlled the purchaser before that change continue to do so. This ensures that difficulties will not arise in relation to the introduction of loan creditors, which may otherwise have impacted on the ability of a group to organise its financing in a commercial manner.

Share transactions in quoted companies

28. The Economic Secretary to the Treasury made the following comments during a debate in Parliament in response to concerns that HMRC might construe the meaning of change in control so widely that the change in one shareholder in a quoted company might be seen as a change in control.

> "Similar concerns were raised in relation to reconstruction relief. I can confirm that we intend to take the same approach that – if control of a publicly owned company changes

as a result of an ordinary market transfer of its shares there will be no recovery, because we do not intend to interpret change of control so widely that simple day to day transactions between unconnected minority shareholders in the stock exchange could trigger a claw back." (see Hansard 6 June 2008, column 521)

Partnerships

29. Where the purchaser group's majority shareholder is a partnership a withdrawal of group relief would arise if a partner leaves the partnership or a new partner joins, however small the relevant partnership interest involved. This is due to the wording in section 416(6) which, coupled with the provisions of TA 1988 s 417(3)(*a*), means that each individual partner controls the group in its own right for [section] 416 purposes, since the rights of all partners are attributed to each other.

30. For the purposes of this legislation, however, the rights or powers held by partners will not be attributed. In addition any changes in the general partner will also be disregarded for the purposes of establishing whether there has been a change in control.

CIRCUMSTANCES WHERE HMRC CONSIDERS THERE HAS BEEN A CHANGE IN CONTROL BUT MAY NOT SEEK TO WITHDRAW RELIEF

31. It is recognised that in certain situations strict application of the legislation will result in changes of control which do not reflect an actual change in the economic ownership of the asset. In order to ensure that group relief is not withdrawn in such circumstances a "minimum" controlling combinations test will be applied in order to establish whether there has been "actual" change in ownership of the asset.

Example of minimum controlling combination test

32. If three persons, A, B and C, each hold one third of the shares in a company, and are not connected in any way which would allow the rights and powers of one to be attributed to another, then control is held by A and B, B and C, or A and C but not A, B and C together. This is because for the purposes of the 'minimum' controlling combinations, you disregard combinations containing superfluous members

33. If A leaves then the "minimum controlling combination" test ensures that a change in control will not be triggered. This reflects the fact that B and C "control" the company before and after A's departure.

34. If, however, both A and B leave and are replaced by new shareholders D and E then the "minimum" controlling combination test is no longer satisfied. In this situation a change in control has occurred.

35. Further information regarding minimum controlling combinations is available at CTM60250 (www.hmrc.gov.uk/manuals/ctmanual/ctm60250.htm). The minimum cont rolling combination test will be applied for SDLT purposes in this matter.

Application of minimum controlling combinations

Share options

36. It is possible for an option over shares to result in two unrelated parties both being treated as having control of a company. This is because, under TA 1988 section 416(2), a person is taken to have control of a company if he exercises or is entitled to acquire direct or indirect control over the company's affairs.

37. An option over shares will not be taken into account in determining whether there has been a change in control of the purchaser. HMRC regards the grant or entitlement date to the shares to be the point at which an "inalienable" right to the shares is triggered. This is the point at which any conditions attaching to share options are considered to be satisfied and it is at this point that a change in control of the purchaser may occur.

38. If the application of a minimum controlling combinations test at this point does not result in a change in control, then group relief will not be withdrawn.

39. However, if a change in control does occur as a result of the granting of the shares then group relief will be withdrawn.

Control established through different tests

40. It is possible for more than one person or one group of persons to "control" a company. For example, one person may have a greater part of the voting power, while two people hold the greater part of the assets on winding up. All three combinations of people can be taken to have control of the company at the same time.

41. If there was a change in one of these three combinations, then a change in control would be triggered, which could result in relief being withdrawn.

42. In this situation there will not be a withdrawal of relief if one of the minimum controlling combinations established under the tests for control is present following the sale or transfer of shares.

CIRCUMSTANCES IN WHICH HMRC CONSIDERS THERE HAS BEEN A CHANGE IN CONTROL

Group takeover

43. Where this is a sale of an entire group and this has occurred within three years of the transaction, a withdrawal of group relief will be triggered as there has been a change in control of the purchasing company.

PARAGRAPH 4(4) OF SCHEDULE 7 FA 2003

44. Paragraph 4(4) of Schedule 7 of Finance Act 2003 provides that group relief is not withdrawn where the purchaser ceases to be a member of the same group as the vendor because of anything done for the purposes of, or in the course of, winding up the vendor or another company that is above the vendor in the group structure.

45. A company is above the vendor in the group structure if the vendor (or another company above the vendor in the group structure) is a 75 per cent subsidiary of the company.

46. This provision has not altered following the introduction of paragraph 4ZA. However, our approach has. A company above the vendor in the group structure can be the purchaser.

47. If paragraph 4(4) applies the provisions of paragraph 4ZA will not normally apply.

CONTACTS

Customers seeking further guidance on the application of this legislation can apply for a non-statutory business clearance.

A non-statutory clearance is a written confirmation of our view of the application of tax law to a specific transaction or event that you can rely on in most circumstances, as our view of the tax consequences of your transaction.

We will aim to send you our view within 28 calendar days, though in complex cases this may take longer.

Clearances will be provided where you have demonstrated that:

- there is a material uncertainty; and/or
- that the issue is commercially significant.

We will provide non-statutory clearances both pre transaction where evidence is supplied that the transaction is genuinely contemplated post transaction

Please see "Clearance service for businesses – how to get certainty on significant business tax issues".

Clearance application requests should be made to: Birmingham Stamp Taxes (www.hmrc.gov.uk/so/contact/royal-mail.htm).

Any queries about this article should be addressed to: Yasmin Ali, Policy Adviser, Stamp Taxes, 1/38, 100 Parliament Street, London SW1A 2BQ.

30 JANUARY 2009. HMRC
GOODWILL IN TRADE RELATED PROPERTIES BACKGROUND NOTE

In the past HM Revenue & Customs (HMRC) have taken the view that it was unlikely that there would be "free goodwill" of any significant value in businesses carried out from trade related properties (for example public houses, hotels, petrol filling stations, cinemas, restaurants, care homes etc) because the occupation and use of the particular, specially adapted, premises was usually essential and integral to the generation of the business income.

However, it is now acknowledged that when a business is sold as a going concern the sale price will reflect the combined value of the tangible assets together with the benefit of other business assets such as any contracts with customers, staff and suppliers, records of previous customers etc. Substantial value can be realised by combining the tangible and other business assets together for sale as a going concern but this enhanced value may be reduced if the assets are split and sold separately.

In the unusual event of this type of business being transferred without some form of property interest, it would be highly likely that the value otherwise achieved, would be substantially diminished or removed. This is why such businesses are rarely, if ever, transferred without any form of property rights.

It remains important to recognise this distinction from most other businesses where there is no such reliance on a specific property interest and business goodwill can be readily sold and will be of value irrespective of the actual premises. Recently published articles in the professional press do not fully address this important distinction and appear to misinterpret some fundamental valuation issues.

There are a host of real and practical reasons why the assets in such premises cannot be actually separated without depreciating their combined value but HMRC now accept that for taxation purposes HMRC need to recognise the contribution that each asset makes to the combined value.

The attached Practice Note explains the issues in more detail and sets out how HMRC and the Valuation Office Agency (VOA) consider one should go about apportioning the price paid for a business as a going concern between goodwill and other assets included in the sale. The Practice Note reflects the VOA view that the appropriate method of valuing this type of property is by reference to the profit making potential of the premises. The VOA are currently discussing this valuation approach with the Royal Institution of Chartered Surveyors.

PRACTICE NOTE: APPORTIONING THE PRICE PAID FOR A BUSINESS TRANSFERRED AS A GOING CONCERN

Index

Part II ST

(8) Valuing the tangible assets—valuation approach
(9) Valuations of the "operational entity" (RICS Red Book GN1)
(10) Apportionment approach—CGT and SDLT cases
(11) Apportionment approach—Schedule 29 FA 2002 cases
(12) Leasehold interests

Appendix A: RICS Guidance to Members—July 2006

1. Background

1.1 An apportionment of the price paid for a business as a going concern between the underlying assets may be required for tax purposes in a number of instances, for example:

a. For the purpose of calculating the capital gains arising on the disposal of the separate assets in accordance with the TCGA 1992.

b. On an acquisition for the purpose of calculating the SDLT due on the interest in the land and buildings only.

c. On an acquisition for the purpose of calculating the allowances available against Corporation Tax for Capital Allowances, such as Machinery and Plant Allowances (see Section 3), or for purchased goodwill (Schedule 29, FA 2002).

1.2 The price paid for a business sold as a going concern may include any or all of the following assets:

a. The land and buildings including landlord's fixtures ("the property").

b. The trade fixtures, fittings, furniture, furnishings and equipment ("the chattels").

c. Any transferable licences.

d. Goodwill.

e. Other separately identifiable intangible assets (eg. registered trade marks).

The purchaser may also separately acquire consumables and stock but these are usually valued separately and will not normally be included in the sale price to be apportioned.

1.3 Some of the principles set out in this Practice Note are applicable to apportionments for all types of businesses but the note deals mainly with the particular issues that have arisen where the property is a "trade related property" valued using a profits approach (eg. public houses, hotels, petrol filling stations, cinemas, restaurants, care homes etc). In these cases there can be particular difficulties in identifying the sum attributable to "goodwill" and this is fundamental to the apportionment.

2. The statutory provisions

2.1 For the purposes of calculating a capital gain TCGA 1992 s 52 provides that any apportionment shall be on a "just and reasonable" basis.

2.2 For the purposes of calculating any SDLT due FA 2003 Sch 4 para 4 similarly provides that any apportionment shall be on a "just and reasonable" basis.

2.3 For the purposes of calculating any Capital Allowances claimed CAA 2001 s 562 similarly provides that any apportionment should be on a just and reasonable basis.

2.4 For the purpose of calculating the cost of purchased goodwill FA 2002 Sch 29 para 4 provides that "goodwill" has the meaning it has for accounting purposes. Accounting guidance (FRS10) provides that "goodwill" should be taken to be the "difference between the cost of an acquired entity and the aggregate of the fair values of that entity's identifiable assets and liabilities" (see paragraph 11 below).

2.5 The various statutory provisions do not define the method of arriving at a "just and reasonable" apportionment but any apportionment should generally seek to apportion the price paid between the underlying assets included in the sale on the basis of their relative values and the contribution they make to the price that is being apportioned.

3. Legal definitions of goodwill

3.1 Halsbury's Laws of England, 4th edition, Vol. 35 at page 1206 states that:

> "The goodwill of a business is the whole advantage of the reputation and connection with customers together with the circumstances whether of habit or otherwise, which tend to make that connection permanent. It represents in connection with any business or business product the value of the attraction to the customers which the name and reputation possesses."

3.2 The definition contained in the Shorter Oxford Dictionary is:

> "Goodwill is the privilege granted by the seller of a business to a purchaser of trading as his recognised successor; the possession of a ready-formed connection with customers considered as a separate element in the saleable value of a business."

3.3 The leading legal authority on the meaning of goodwill is found in *IRC v Muller & Co Margarine Limited* [1901] AC 217. In answer to the question "what is goodwill?" Lord Macnaghten said:

> "It is a thing very easy to describe, very difficult to define. It is the benefit and advantage of the good name, reputation and connection of a business. It is the attractive force which brings in custom. It is the one thing which distinguishes an old-established business from a new business at its first stage."

Lord Macnaghten went on to say that:

> "Goodwill is composed of a variety of elements. It differs in its composition in different trades and in different businesses in the same trade. One element may preponderate here; and another there."

3.4 In the decision of the Special Commissioners in *Balloon Promotions Ltd v Wilson* SpC 524 [2006] STC (SCD) 167, goodwill for CG purposes was construed in accordance with legal rather than accountancy principles.

3.5 Traditionally goodwill has been subdivided into different types such as "inherent goodwill", "adherent goodwill" and "free goodwill". These subdivisions are no longer considered helpful as they tend to cause confusion. "Inherent" and "adherent" goodwill are not really goodwill at all as they form part of the value of the property asset.

Part II ST

4. Accountancy and international valutaion standards council definitions

4.1 International Financial Reporting Standards (IFRS 3, 2008 revised version, Appendix A) defines goodwill as;

> "An asset representing the future economic benefits arising from assets acquired in a business combination that are not individually identified and separately recognised".

Intangible Assets are defined by IVSC as;

> "Assets that manifest themselves by their economic properties. They do not have physical substance; they grant rights and privileges to their owner and usually generate income for their owner".

4.2 IVG Note 4 defines a subset of Intangible Assets as Grouped Intangibles;

> "The residual intangible asset value left after all identifiable Intangible Assets have been valued and deducted from total Intangible Asset value. Alternative concepts include

patronage, excess earnings and residual value. Grouped Intangibles are often called Goodwill. Goodwill has, at various times, been said to be the tendency for customers to return to a place of business, the extra income generated by a business over and above a fair return to the identified assets, and/or the extra value of the entity as a whole over and above the aggregate value of its constituent identifiable assets".

5. Goodwill in trade related properties

5.1 It has in the past been argued that because the business in trade related properties is usually largely or wholly incapable of being sold separately from the property there is little or no goodwill (see the Lands Tribunal decision in *Coles Executors v IRC* (1973) concerning the valuation of a public house for Estate Duty). On the sale of a business operated from such properties, unless there were other separately identifiable intangible assets included in the sale, the whole of the purchase price would normally be apportioned to the property and chattels, it being argued that there was no goodwill.

5.2 The above view was often put forward by taxpayers seeking to claim Capital Allowances on fixtures which formed part of the property. However, since the introduction of SDLT and the provisions in FA 2002 Sch 29 this view has been challenged by taxpayers seeking to maximise the amount apportioned to goodwill in order to maximise their claim under FA 2002 Sch 29 and minimise the amount of SDLT payable.

5.3 The view now is that if a business is sold as a going concern then the sale must include some element of goodwill. The question to be answered is not whether goodwill exists but what is the value of that goodwill? That question has to be decided on the facts of each individual case. In some cases the value of the goodwill may be nominal but in some it may be substantial.

6. Valuing goodwill and other intangible assets

6.1 There is a broad consensus across the valuation, accountancy and legal professions that the value of goodwill and any other separately identifiable intangible assets (eg. registered trade marks) is represented by the difference between the value of a business as a going concern and the value of the tangible assets included in the sale.

6.2 The value of a business as a going concern will usually be represented by the actual sale price achieved in the open market. However, if it is necessary to value a business as a going concern, because the sale price was not at arm's length, then this is the responsibility of HMRC (SAV).

6.3 Similarly, if it is necessary to apportion the excess value between the goodwill and any other intangible assets this is the responsibility of HMRC (SAV).

6.4 However, the difficulties in arriving at the value of the goodwill usually relate to the assumptions and approach to be adopted when arriving at a valuation of the tangible assets. This is addressed in the paragraphs below.

7. Valuing the tangible assets—assumptions

7.1 Difficulties relating to the assumptions to be adopted when valuing the tangible assets often arise in cases involving trade related properties. Some of the reasons for this relate to the fact that:

a. The established approach to valuation of this type of property typically relies on the profits method and in determining the income and trading potential there can be confusion with valuation of the operator's business. The profits approach remains an appropriate property valuation basis where it is based on expected fair maintainable levels of income that are expected to be achieved from use of the property and other tangible assets by a reasonably competent operator. This is distinct from any valuation of the actual operators own business.

b. The value of such properties is often significantly reduced if the property ceases to be occupied for any length of time because customers go elsewhere and the level of trade has to be built up again by the purchaser. (The enhanced value that arises as a result of the property being occupied by the vendor and any predecessors for the particular use is part of what in the past has been described as "adherent" goodwill but is properly part of the property value).

c. The value is often significantly reduced if the property is stripped of chattels because the purchaser has to re-fit the premises and cannot re-open until the property has been fully fitted out and is ready to trade.

d. If licences are lost there may sometimes be difficulties in obtaining new licences.

If it were to be assumed for the purposes of valuation that the property has lost any licences, been stripped of chattels and left vacant for a period of time then the value will be significantly reduced and the value of goodwill in the final apportionment, arrived at by deduction, would be inflated.

7.2 When valuing goodwill using the approach outlined in paragraph 6 above it will usually be appropriate to value all the tangible assets together for sale as an operational entity so that a purchaser can if they wish trade from the day of purchase. It is critical that this availability is reflected to ensure a fair apportionment of the sale price (and any premium arising from a sale of combined assets) between the tangible and intangible elements and avoid any over or understatement.

7.3 Another area of difficulty regarding the assumptions to be made relates to the benefit of contracts entered into by the vendor with customers, staff and suppliers. In reality, if the business is sold as a going concern, any benefit attached to these contracts will normally pass to the purchaser and will be reflected in the price paid for the business as a going concern. However, these contracts do not form part of the tangible assets so, if they add any value, the added value should not be reflected in the valuation of the tangible assets.

7.4 When valuing goodwill using the approach outlined in paragraph 6 above it is considered appropriate to assume that the benefit of any contracts with customers, staff and suppliers would either have to be acquired separately from the vendor or the purchaser would have to make their own arrangements.

7.5 Applying the assumptions in paragraph 7.4 will have different effects depending on the facts of the particular case in question. For example:

a. A small public house to be run by the purchaser with help from part-time bar staff. The purchaser has acquired the business as a going concern but there are no contracts with customers and the purchaser wishes to enter their own contracts with suppliers and employ their own staff. In such a case there may be no identifiable difference between the price paid for the business as a going concern and the price that a purchaser would pay to acquire all the tangible assets. In such a case the value of the goodwill may be nominal.

b. A nursing home, offering an element of specialist care, that is fully occupied by residents and to be run by the purchaser with the help of full-time medically qualified staff. In such a case (depending on the degree of difficulty the purchaser may face in finding any new residents and staff) there may be a significant difference between the price paid for the business as a going concern and the price a purchaser would pay to acquire all the tangible assets. In such a case the value of the goodwill may be more substantial.

7.6 When purchasing such a business as a going concern the purchaser will often have obtained a valuation of the tangible assets as an "operational entity" in accordance with the RICS Red Book GN1. An alternative valuation of the property based on special assumptions (eg. vacant following a failure of the business, no accounts providing evidence of trade, stripped of chattels and licences lost) may also be obtained for bank lending purposes. For the purposes of valuing goodwill it would not be appropriate to deduct a valuation based on such special assumptions that do not reflect the actual circumstances prevailing at the valuation date. The question of the assumptions underlying a valuation of the "operational entity" and how they may differ from a valuation in accordance with paragraphs 7.2 and 7.4 above is considered in paragraph 10 below.

8. Valuing the tangible assets—valuation approach

8.1 Having decided on the appropriate assumptions (paragraphs 7.2 and 7.4 above) it is then necessary to consider the most appropriate method of valuation. For trade related properties that are valued on a profits basis two alternatives need to be considered, these are a capitalised EBITDA/fair maintainable trade (FMT) approach and a rental value/investment based approach. The aim should be to arrive at a capital value that fairly represents the price that an owner-occupier purchaser would be prepared to pay to acquire all the tangible assets, having regard to the circumstances existing at the valuation date.

8.2 The advantages of a capitalised EBITDA/FMT approach are as follows:

a. This is the method that is used in the market to arrive at both going concern values and valuations of the tangible assets as an operational entity under the RICS Red Book GN1.

b. The valuation represents the value to an owner-occupier purchaser.

c. The purchase price paid for the going concern and any GN1 valuation of the tangible assets as an operational entity can be analysed to provide evidence of the FMT and a multiplier for the actual subject property at the valuation date.

d. It produces a value for all the tangible assets to be valued together as a single operational entity.

The difficulty with this approach is that in cases where the contracts with customers, staff and suppliers are of some value it is necessary to reflect this in the valuation. However, it is considered that in most cases this approach will nevertheless give a reliable valuation in most cases.

EXAMPLE

A simple example may be a nursing home like the one described in paragraph 7.5(*b*) above:

Say the business had been sold as a going concern for £2m and an analysis of this sale price was say FMT £250k pa x 8YP.

If it was estimated that it would take a purchaser of the tangible assets 1 year to get the property staffed, fully occupied and trading at FMT level again a valuation using this approach may be:

£250k x 8YP	=	£2,000,000
Defer for 1 year @ 10%	=	0.909
		£1,818,000

The value of the goodwill (and any other intangible assets) would be £2m – £1.818m = £182k.

8.3 A rental value/investment based approach may be useful in some cases but as a primary method of valuation the difficulties and flaws of this approach are as follows:

a. In order to arrive at a capital value the method involves making difficult judgements not only about the FMT but the percentage of profits to adopt as the rental value and the appropriate investment yield, both of which can only be derived from comparison with lettings and sales of other properties at different dates, which significantly increase the scope for disputes over the analysis and comparability of the evidence.

b. Much of the available comparable rental evidence will relate to new lettings of properties that are either new or have previously been vacant or rent reviews/renewals that disregard the occupation of the property by the tenant and predecessors in title in accordance with LTA 1954 s 34.

c. Much of the comparable rental evidence will relate to lettings where the tenant has had to provide the chattels and the return on this capital and risk is reflected in the rents paid.

d. The valuation using this approach represents the value of the property to an investor not an owner-occupier.

e. The valuation produces a valuation of the property only to which it is then necessary to add a valuation of the chattels. It will not include the premium value to an occupier of acquiring the tangible assets together as a package with the enhanced trading potential due to the established trading history and the ability to continue trading from day 1. Isolating the bare property asset may unfairly apportion any premium or share of marriage value away and overstate the intangible elements.

However, in cases where there are particular difficulties in arriving at a valuation using the capitalised EBITDA/FMT approach the rental value/investment approach may provide a guide as to the minimum value of the property to an incoming purchaser.

EXAMPLE

A simple example of the problems with the rental approach may be illustrated by considering a small public house like the one described in paragraph 7.5(*a*) above:

Say the property was trading at FMT level, it had been sold as a going concern for £1m and an analysis of this sale price was say FMT £125k pa x 8YP.

For illustration purposes, the rental value on a new letting without chattels may be say £62,500 and an investment yield may be say 8%. This would give a capital value of £781,250 leaving a balance of £281,750. If the in situ value of the chattels was say £50,000 this would leave a sum of £231,750 being attributed to the goodwill when in reality most valuers would agree that the purchaser had acquired nothing of any value beyond the value of the tangible assets. The excess is artificially created because the valuation of the property reflects its notional investment value whereas, just as with some other classes of property, the owner-occupier market is influenced by different factors and the price an owner-occupier may pay is not always the same as an investor.

9. RICS Red Book GN1—Valuations of the "Operational Entity"

9.1 The question of the assumptions underlying a valuation of an "operational entity" in accordance with the Red Book GN1 and how those assumptions may differ from the valuation required to arrive at the value of goodwill in accordance with paragraphs 7.2 and 7.4 above is a matter of some debate amongst valuers. The RICS issued some helpful guidance on this in July 2006 and a copy of this is attached as Appendix A.

9.2 The following reasons are put forward by some valuers as the justification for not adopting a GN1 valuation of the operational entity as representing the value of the tangible assets:

a. A valuation of the operational entity will include "transferable goodwill" and this includes all goodwill which is capable of being transferred.

Comment

"Transferable goodwill" is defined in GN1 as "That intangible asset that arises as a result of **property-specific name and reputation, customer patronage, location and similar factors**, which generate economic benefits. **It is inherent to the specialized trading property** and will transfer to a new owner on sale". GN1 goes on to say "In previous RICS guidance **transferable goodwill has also been referred to as inherent goodwill. In the valuation context these terms are identical**". The use of the word "intangible" in the definition causes some confusion but from the description of the trading potential included (in bold above) it seems clear that the only goodwill that should be included in a GN1 valuation

Part II ST

is inherent goodwill which forms part of the value of the property. As advised at paragraph 3.5 above, inherent and adherent "goodwill" are not strictly goodwill but form part of the property asset value.

b. A GN1 valuation of the operational entity is a notional value because in practice it is always based on an assumption that the property is trading at FMT level even when in reality it is not.

Comment

The GN1 valuation is supposed to represent the "market value" of the property and other tangible assets (ie. what a willing purchaser would actually pay in the open market). GN1 does not require valuers to assume FMT is achievable from day 1 but they may choose to do so because in reality the period to build up the trade is negligible. Alternatively valuers may choose to reflect some element of deferment in the YP adopted when capitalising the FMT.

c. A GN1 valuation is a valuation of the actual business and usually the same as the going concern value.

Comment

GN1 makes it clear that the valuation "should only reflect the transferable goodwill that relates to the trading potential of the property" (GN1, para. 4.4), not the trading potential of the particular business. GN1 paragraph 6 also makes it clear that a GN1 valuation of the operational entity is not the same as the going concern value of the business.

d. A GN1 valuation is based on a capitalisation of the EBITDA/FMT and this includes the occupier's share of the profit. This element of occupier's or tenant's profit needs to be excluded and the way to do this is to adopt the rental/investment value approach described above.

Comment

Valuers may well capitalise the total EBITDA/FMT but the fact that this is a "gross" figure is reflected in the YP. If the element of occupier's profit were deducted from the EBITDA/FMT figure then the yield would have to be increased to reflect this (ie. valuers would have to analyse sales on a similar basis and then value on the same basis as they devalue). The tenant's share of the profit on taking a new lease is supposed to represent a fair reward for running the business and the risks involved but this potential share of the income on its own would not be expected to have a capital value (ie. one would not expect a tenant to pay a premium for the right to receive this income alone.) This is illustrated by the fact this income of course exists from day 1 when a new business takes a new lease but tenants do not generally pay landlords a premium to receive it. If they did then it would simply represent a premium for the property, it could not possibly represent goodwill because a new business does not have any goodwill, goodwill is something that grows over time.

e. A GN1 valuation assumes that the purchaser receives the benefit of any contracts with customers, staff and suppliers (as they do in reality when they acquire the business as a going concern) so the valuation includes or reflects an element of value that is not automatically available to a purchaser of just the tangible assets.

Comment

The assumptions that should be made by valuers regarding such contracts is not set out in GN1 and actual practice seems to vary. In some cases the valuer may have taken the view that the contracts in the particular case in question add little or no value but in others they may have assumed that any benefits automatically pass to the purchaser of the tangible assets. Some argue that a GN1 valuation should assume that such contracts are available but that they are not cost free (ie. if they are of value to the purchaser the purchaser would have to pay the vendor an additional sum to acquire the benefits). If in a particular case the contracts do add value then one would expect a GN1 valuation on this basis to be less than the sale price of the business as a going concern. Until such time as this area of confusion is clarified, caseworkers should value on the basis set out in paragraph 7.4 above – and in some cases there may therefore be a difference with a GN1 valuation of the operational entity.

10. Apportionment approach—CGT and SDLT cases

10.1 In CGT and SDLT cases the apportionment of the sale price paid for a business as a going concern should be approached by first identifying the value of any goodwill (and other separately identifiable intangibles assets) along the lines described above. After deducting this from the total sale price, the in-situ value of the chattels may then be deducted to leave the value of the property.

10.2 In practice, for trade related properties, the approach outlined in paragraph 10.1 above will involve the following steps:

Step 1 – Estimate the market value of all the tangible assets together as an operational entity having regard to the special assumptions in paragraphs 7.2 and 7.4 above. (See paragraphs 10.3 and 10.4 below.)

Step 2 – Identify the sum attributable to goodwill and any other intangible assets included in the sale by deducting the value of the property, licences and chattels (Step 1 value) from the sale price (or market value) of the business as a going concern. (See paragraph 10.5 below.)

Step 3 – Identify the sum attributable to the chattels by estimating their "in-situ" value (ie. the value to an incoming purchaser. (See paragraph 10.6 below).

Step 4 – Identify the sum attributable to the property by deducting the value of the chattels (Step 3 value) from the Step 1 value. (See paragraph 10.7 below).

Step 5 – Stand back and consider whether the answer produced is reasonable in the particular circumstances of the case (see paragraphs 2.11–2.12 below).

10.3 Step 1

The market value of the tangible assets should be assessed as at the date of disposal/sale on the basis defined in UKGN3 (Valuations for CGT, IHT and SDLT), subject to the special assumptions in paragraphs 7.2 and 7.4 above and the following:

a. The valuation should reflect the market's perception of the trading potential of the property excluding Goodwill.

b. The valuation should reflect the benefit of any transferable licences, consents and certificates. (If any of the licences [Licences are a separate asset for CGT purposes.] etc have been lost or are in jeopardy at the valuation date that fact should be reflected in the valuation).

c. The valuation should have regard to all the facts pertaining at the valuation date.

d. The valuation should assume that any accounts available to the purchaser are available at the valuation date to inform judgments as to reasonable future trading potential.

e. The valuation should assume that the purchaser may either bring in their own staff or seek to re-employ some of the existing staff.

f. The valuation should assume that the purchaser will take into account the likelihood of any future bookings sticking with the property if they choose to run the business in the same manner as the vendor.

g. The valuation should assume that the purchaser will take into account the likelihood of any existing care home residents opting to stay with the property if they choose to run the business in the same manner as the vendor.

10.4 The market value should reflect only that trade that can reasonably be expected to be maintained by a reasonably efficient operator purchasing the property and chattels. "Reasonably efficient operator" has the same meaning as that used in the RICS Red Book GN1, paragraph 2.4:

A market-based concept whereby a potential purchaser, and thus the valuer, estimates the maintainable level of trade and future profitability that can be achieved by a competent operator of a business conducted on the premises, acting in an efficient manner. The concept involves the trading potential rather than the actual level of trade under the existing ownership so it excludes *personal goodwill*. ((c) IVSC GN 12, para 3.4.)

The market value of the property interest should capture the true value of the property asset reflecting any enhancement from the established generic use at the valuation date but ignoring any additional value of the actual business carried on in the premises at that date. The aim is to establish the value that an incoming purchaser would bid for the property based on their views as to what might reasonably be achieved in terms of trading potential as distinct from the actual trade achieved by the current business.

10.5 Step 2

The sum attributable to goodwill and any other intangible assets included in the sale should be arrived at by deducting the value of the tangible assets (from Step 1 above) from the sale price (or market value) of the business.

10.6 Step 3

The sum attributable to any chattels included in the sale should be arrived at by estimating the value of the chattels to an incoming purchaser. The value of the chattels to an incoming purchaser will normally be based on their depreciated replacement cost but in some cases they may be of no value, for example, if the purchaser intends to refit the premises.

10.7 Step 4

The sum attributable to the property should be arrived at by deducting the value of the chattels (the Step 3 value) from the value of the tangible assets (the Step 1 value).

10.8 Step 5

Caseworkers should always stand back and consider whether the answer produced by the above approach is reasonable in the particular circumstances of the case. For instance, if a business is sold in an arm's length transaction at a price that is significantly in excess of the market value of the business as a going concern it may be appropriate to firstly value the business and then apportion the excess sale price on a pro-rata basis.

EXAMPLE

Sale price	=	£600,000
Market value of business	=	£500,000
Property	=	£450,000
Chattels	=	£20,000
Goodwill	=	£30,000 (ie. £500,000 – (£450,000 + £20,000))

Pro-rata apportionment:

Property	=	450/500 × £600,000	=	£540,000
Chattels	=	20/500 × £600,000	=	£24,000
Goodwill	=	30/500 × £600,000	=	£36,000

10.9 A criticism of the above approach may be that it adopts a deduction approach and such an approach was criticised by the High Court in the case of *Bostock v Totham (HMIT)*. However, the above approach does not just consider the value of one element, as was the taxpayer's approach which was criticised in the Bostock case, it considers the value of all elements on a basis that reflects the contribution of the various elements to the price being apportioned. If one were to value all of the elements in strict isolation then the apportionment may become artificially distorted to the extent that the answer may not be just and reasonable. For instance, the property value in isolation may be less than when it is lotted with the other tangible assets, the value of the chattels if not sold in-situ with the property may be little more than scrap value and any goodwill may be of nominal value if the business is not sold with the property as a going concern.

10.10 Taxpayers may also challenge the above approach based on the Special Commissioner's decision in the case of *Balloon Promotions Limited v Wilson (Insp of Taxes)* in which it was suggested that goodwill should be looked at as a whole and that the value of adherent goodwill was not automatically subsumed in the property value. The decision of the Special Commissioner in the Balloon case concerned appeals against a refusal to grant rollover relief under s 152 of the Taxation of Chargeable Gains Act 1992 in respect of chargeable gains following the sale of the Company's franchised Pizza Express restaurants to the franchisor. Whilst the decision includes discussion of existing legal authorities dealing with goodwill the conclusions reflect the individual circumstances of the case. It is worth noting that in this case the values of the property interests submitted by the taxpayers were not challenged and there was no evidence to demonstrate whether or not those values included adherent goodwill. As mentioned above, the subdivisions of goodwill that were previously used are no longer considered helpful as they tend to cause confusion. The view now is that what used to be referred to as "inherent" and "adherent" goodwill are, in reality, attributes which add value to the property in which a business is carried on and that they do not represent goodwill at all.

11. Apportionment approach—Schedule 29 FA 2002 cases

11.1 As noted above, for the purpose of calculating the cost of purchased goodwill FA 2002 Sch 29 para 4 provides that "goodwill" has the meaning it has for accounting purposes. Accounting guidance (FRS10) provides that "goodwill" should be taken to be the "difference between the cost of an acquired entity and the aggregate of the fair values of that entity's identifiable assets and liabilities".

11.2 FRS 15 sets out the principles for calculating the "fair value" of tangible fixed assets and provides that non-specialised properties should be valued on the basis of existing use value (EUV) (FRS15, para.53).

FRS15, para. 56 states:

> "Certain types of non-specialised properties are bought and sold 'and therefore valued' as businesses. The EUV of a property valued as an operational entity is determined by having regard to trading potential, but excludes personal goodwill that has been created in the business by the present owner or management and is not expected to remain with the business in the event of the property being sold"

FRS 15, para. 85 states:

> "It would not be appropriate, however, to treat the trading potential associated with a property that is valued as an operational entity, such as a public house or hotel, as a separate component where the value and life of its trading potential is inherently inseparable from that of the property".

The above guidance on the value to be deducted appears to accord with a valuation of the operational entity in accordance with GN1. Accordingly it would not be acceptable in a Schedule 29 case for a taxpayer to put forward a value different from their valuation in accordance with GN1.

12. Leasehold interests

12.1 In some cases it will be necessary to apportion the price paid for a leasehold interest but the same principles apply. The valuations and apportionment should be approached using the same assumptions and approach described above.

12.2 It should be borne in mind that for trade related properties it is quite common for leasehold interests to be sold for substantial premiums even when the rent has recently been reviewed. The premium in such cases may be attributable to any or all of the following:

a. The reviewed rent may not reflect the full rental value because it may disregard the enhanced trading potential attributable to the occupation of the property by the tenant and predecessors (in accordance with LTA 1954 s 34).

b. The reviewed rent may not reflect the value of improvements carried out by the tenant or predecessors when fitting out the property (in some cases the rent may only represent a shell rent).

c. The value of the chattels and fittings belonging to the tenant.

d. The premium value to an occupier of offering the tangible assets together as a package with the enhanced trading potential due to the established trading history and the ability to continue trading from day 1.

e. There may be some element of goodwill, particularly if the business is trading at above FMT level and contracts of some value are included in the sale.

f. There may be other separately identifiable intangible assets included in the sale (eg. registered trade marks).

g. Market perception and prevailing conditions whereby it is expected there will be some "key money" or premium to acquire the interest in order to move in to this market sector.

12.3 The value of any goodwill and other intangible assets included in the sale should be determined by adopting the same valuation assumptions and approach outlined in paragraphs 7 and 8 above.

Appendix A: RICS Guidance to Members—17 July 2006

Valuation for tax purposes of Specialised Trading Property—goodwill

This note provides the context within which goodwill is to be considered by RICS members when valuing trade related properties; and in particular the issues arising in the UK when valuing goodwill for tax purposes.

The usual basis of valuation for a property valuation is Market Value. This is defined in the Red Book, PS 3.2. The commentary to PS 3.2 recognises that certain categories of property change hands in the open market as fully operational business units for specific uses at prices based upon their trading potential.

Such properties are known as "Specialised Trading Properties". Guidance on the valuation of Specialised Trading Properties is contained within GN1. Further information on the approach is contained in Valuation Information Paper No 2.

Some RICS members may also be asked to value the goodwill of a going concern business. The Red Book guidance relates to the valuation of tangible assets only; being the real property and other fixed assets.

Confusion may arise between the valuation of a going concern and the valuation of fixed assets because the profits method of valuing the property includes a requirement for the valuer to assess the fair maintainable level of trade and future profitability that could be achieved by a Reasonably Efficient Operator, usually including consideration of the occupier's actual accounts.

Care has to be taken not to include in the assessment any element of value that includes any personal goodwill to the present owner or operator which might pass to a purchaser of the going concern business but which is not inherent in the property by virtue of the fair maintainable level of trade.

The revision of VIP2 issued in early 2006 includes new guidance on this distinction.

The Red Book does not contain any guidance on the assessment of goodwill separate from the value of the property asset or the valuation of going concern businesses as a whole.

For these purposes the valuer is directed to the International Valuation Standard GN6 which specifically relates to Business Valuation, usually as a going concern.

Both the RICS and IVS identify just two forms of goodwill; either inherent to the property and transferable as such, or else personal to the individual, partnership, company or other entity running the business, which may or may not be transferable as part of a going concern, but which does not attach to the property.

Whenever possible, RICS guidance follows the international IVS Guidance in relation to the valuation of real property assets, avoiding the creation of specific standards applying only to the UK.

UK tax legislation provides that the basis of value for tax computations shall be an open market price; whether for tangible property assets or for intangibles such as personal goodwill.

Although the statutory definitions and interpretation by the courts generally follow the Red Book definition of Market Value for tangible property, there are differences.

UKGN3 provides a commentary on the basis of value for tax purposes in the UK. Where the property being considered is a specialised trading property GN1 will be relevant, but subject to UKGN3.

For some tax purposes, where a transaction relates to the transfer of a going concern business, it may be necessary to apportion the consideration into its various elements and it will be seen that the extent to which the transaction included either or both types of goodwill may affect the tax burden.

It is this apportionment issue which is to be discussed in the context of UK tax assessments.

17 AUGUST 2009. HMRC
STAMP DUTY AND STAMP DUTY RESERVE TAX: STOCK LENDING AND REPURCHASES IN CASES OF INSOLVENCY

FA 2009 s 83 and Sch 37 provide relief from Stamp Duty and Stamp Duty Reserve Tax (SDRT) where one of the parties to a stock lending or sale and repurchase (repo) arrangement becomes insolvent before the arrangement is completed by the return of the securities originally lent or sold. Relief is available where the insolvency occurred on or after 1 September 2008.

Normally, the non-return of securities under a stock lending or repo arrangement triggers an SDRT charge on the party that borrowed or bought them. FA 2009 modifies this rule so that, where the non-return of the securities is attributable to one of the parties to the arrangement having become insolvent:

- no SDRT charge arises on the recipient of the securities (the relief also covers any securities provided as collateral that are retained by the lender under a stock loan arrangement)
- purchases of securities by the solvent party to replace those that are not returned by the insolvent party will not incur a Stamp Duty or SDRT charge

Relief is conditional upon the parties to the arrangement not being connected persons within the meaning of TA 1988 s 839.

Because the new rules have effect for insolvencies occurring on or after 1 September 2008, anyone who has subsequently paid Stamp Duty or SDRT in either of the circumstances set out above is entitled to repayment.

HOW TO CLAIM A REPAYMENT

Send your claim headed "Stock Lending – Insolvency" to: Birmingham Stamp Office, 9th Floor, City Centre House, 30 Union Street, Birmingham B2 4AS.

Your claim must include the information set out below.

1. Repayment of SDRT – original stock loan or sale

- the name of the insolvent party and the date of insolvency
- the CREST ID for the original stock loan or sale transaction (or a copy of the stock transfer form if the original transfer was effected by a written instrument)
- the amount and type of stock originally lent or sold
- the amount of SDRT paid that is being reclaimed

You should send your reclaim in the format detailed in Stamp Duty Reserve Tax newsletter – issue1

Stamp Duty Reserve Tax newsletter – issue 1 [www.hmrc.gov.uk/so/sdrt/sdrt_news1.htm].

2. Claims for relief for purchase of replacement securities

SDRT

- the CREST transaction ID for the replacement purchase
- the trade date (**NB** the replacement purchase(s) must be made within a period of 30 days from the date of insolvency)
- the name of the insolvent party and the date of insolvency
- the CREST ID for the original stock loan or sale transaction
- the amount and type of stock originally lent or sold
- the amount of that stock that was replaced
- the amount of SDRT paid on the replacement purchase
- confirmation that any collateral provided by the insolvent party, or realised proceeds from its sale, has been utilised in making the replacement purchase
- the information and format required for claims is set out at Annex A of this document

Stamp Duty

- the name of the insolvent party
- the amount and type of stock originally lent or sold
- the date(s) the replacement securities were acquired (**NB** the replacement purchase(s) must be made within a period of 30 days from the date of insolvency)
- the amount of that stock that was replaced
- the original instrument(s) of transfer showing the duty stamps (required so that the duty stamps can be blocked out)
- the information and format required for claims is set out at Annex B of this document

Repayment is available for purchases of replacement securities up to but not exceeding the amount originally lent or sold. To assist HMRC in processing claims, if the replacement purchase was effected by more than one transaction in the market, please provide the relevant information for all transactions in a single letter of claim.

General information about submitting SDRT repayment [is available at www.hmrc.gov.uk/so/sdrt/sdrt_news1.htm].

If you have any questions about the reclaim process please contact Adam Shooter, Birmingham Stamp Office at the address above or on Tel 0121 616 4588.

ANNEX A: SDRT – CLAIMS FOR RELIEF FOR PURCHASE OF REPLACEMENT SECURITIES

Please provide information in the format outlined below:

Original CREST Transaction ID – XX123456

Number of Shares on that Transaction – 500

Number of Shares on Reclaimed Transaction – 500

Reclaim CREST Transaction ID – ZZ123456

SDRT to be reclaimed – £2500.05

Trade Date – 18/09/08

Reclaim Reason Code – 5

ANNEX B: STAMP DUTY – CLAIMS FOR RELIEF FOR PURCHASE OF REPLACEMENT SECURITIES

Please provide information in the format outlined below:

Number of Shares on Original Transaction – 500

Trade Date of Original Transaction – 01/09/2008

Customer or reference of Original Transaction – XR14

Number of Shares on Reclaimed Transaction – 500

SD to be reclaimed – £2600.25

Date of Instrument of Transfer – 30/09/2008

9 APRIL 2010. HMRC
DISCLOSURE OF STAMP DUTY LAND TAX AVOIDANCE SCHEME – FORM AAG4 (SDLT)

From 1 April 2010 the disclosure regime will be further extended to include certain arrangements relating to Stamp Duty Land Tax where the subject matter involves residential property.

BACKGROUND

Details of certain Stamp Duty Land Tax avoidance schemes must be notified to HM Revenue & Customs (HMRC), usually by the scheme promoter. The user of the scheme must make the notification where the scheme is devised 'in-house', where the promoter is outside the UK and no promoter notifies, or where the information is to be covered by legal professional privilege.

When a scheme is notified, HMRC may issue an eight-digit Scheme Reference Number (SRN) to the person making the notification. A promoter to whom an SRN is issued must provide it to each client who implements the scheme. If there are other users of the scheme the client must provide the SRN to them.

WHO SHOULD USE THIS FORM?

If you have received an SRN, whether from HMRC, the scheme promoter, or a client of the promoter, you are required to declare the use of the scheme to HMRC each time you use the scheme or arrangement. This is done by entering the SRN and certain other information on this form. A user of a Stamp Duty Land Tax scheme cannot make a valid notification of their use of the scheme on any other form. Entering the Scheme Reference Number on a Stamp Duty Land Tax or other return is not a valid notification of the use of the scheme.

This form is not used for Income Tax, Capital Gains Tax, Corporation Tax and National Insurance contributions schemes. See notes on the use of form AAG 4 for full information. (www.hmrc.gov.uk/aiu/form-aag4.htm)

WHEN TO SEND IN THE FORM?

You should submit form AAG4 (SDLT) within 30 days of entering into the first land transaction in connection with the scheme.

Please follow the link below to make an online notification on form AAG4 (SDLT).

Disclosure Of Avoidance Scheme - Form AAG4 (SDLT) - https://online.hmrc.gov.uk/shortforms/form/AAG4_N?dept-name=&location=35&origin=http://www.hmrc.gov.uk

APPENDIX 5. TAX BULLETINS: EXTRACTS

Please note that Tax Bulletins are no longer being published by HMRC. They have been replaced by Revenue and Customs Briefs.

ISSUE 18. AUGUST 1995.

PAGE 234. STAMP DUTY

Finance Act 1994

1. We have received a number of enquiries about the stamp duty provisions in FA 1994 ss 240–243. This article aims to give some general guidance on these points. The precise treatment of a particular document will, of course, depend on all the facts of the case and the legal effect of the document.

Exchanges etc—FA 1994 s 241

2. Section 241 introduced new rules of stamp duty on exchanges of interest in land or buildings. Section 241 operates in a similar manner to SA 1891 ss 6, 55 and 57. These provisions impose a charge on instruments which implement transactions which would not be characterised as a sale at common law because the consideration is something other than a price in money paid or promised. Pursuant to these provisions, certain kinds of consideration are to be treated for the purposes of the charge as equivalent to a money price, the charge being imposed by reference to the value of the consideration to be given. (In relation to s 57, Statement of Practice SP 6/90 remains effective).

3. For the purposes of the charge to duty under the "conveyance or transfer on sale" heading in SA 1891 s 241(1) attributes a value to the consideration and states that "the instrument shall be charged with ad valorem duty under that heading" where a charge is not imposed in respect of that consideration by virtue of any other provision.

4. As stamp duty is charged on instruments, rather than transactions s 241(1) falls to be applied to each instrument which satisfies the terms of the provision. Accordingly, if, for example, the consideration for the transfer of an interest in land is the transfer of an interest in land, each transfer is chargeable by reference to the market value of the interest transferred by the other.

The £60,000 threshold

5. The £60,000 threshold is applied separately to each side of the exchange. For example, if there is a straightforward exchange of one house worth £50,000 for another worth £50,000, both transfers are within the threshold and no duty would be payable on either provided each is certified in accordance with FA 1958 s 34(4).

6. Where there is a multiple exchange—for example, properties A and B are exchanged for property C—the transfers of properties A and B would be regarded as parts of a larger transaction (under FA 1958 s 34(4)). The threshold would not apply to either of them if the total consideration for both was more than £60,000, but would be applied separately to the transfer of property C.

Equality money

7. Where the market values of two properties being exchanged are not equal, a payment of money (or some other consideration) is often given with the lower value property, so as to

Part II ST

equalise the bargain. In many cases the wording of the conveyance of the lower value property may not fully reflect the consideration expressed in the original contract or agreement. Where it is clear from the contract that the lower value property has been transferred for the higher value property less the equality money, the Stamp Office will limit the charge to duty accordingly. For example, if the initial contract provided for an £80,000 house to be exchanged for a £100,000 house, and for £20,000 to be paid as equality money, the amount charged to duty on the transfer of the £80,000 house would be limited to £80,000. In these cases the Stamp Office needs to see the relevant contract as well as the conveyance.

8. Where there is a multiple exchange of properties, an apportionment on similar lines may be made to determine how much of the consideration is attributable to each of the transfers. For example, two or more properties may be exchanged for one larger property, with or without a payment of equality money.

Sales

9. In many cases, transactions which in the past have been structured and documented as an exchange could equally well be carried out as a sale for a price which may be partly satisfied in kind. For example, when a person offers a property for sale, he may receive the price from the buyer in the form either of money, or partly of money and partly of the buyer's existing house. Such a transaction can be carried out and documented (commencing with the initial contract) as a sale. Section 241 does not apply where duty is already imposed under the conveyance on sale head of charge. Accordingly, if the transaction is within the common law concept of "sale" s 241 is excluded and duty is simply charged by reference to the price of the sale.

10. Although a sale ordinarily involves a price in money paid or promised (*Littlewoods Mail Order Stores Limited v IR Comrs* [1963] AC 135 at page 152), the Courts have held that the transaction is still a "sale" if property is taken in satisfaction of part of the purchase price: *Simpson v Connolly* [1953] 2 All ER 474, p 477; *Connell Estate Agents v Begej* [1993] 2 EGLR 35. In the Connell case, the purchaser had agreed to purchase land for £109,000. In satisfaction of this price the vendor was "to receive ownership of 10 Milner Road, Finedon, plus balance of £53,000". The Court of Appeal held that the transaction was a sale of the more valuable property for the price of £109,000 and that the purchaser's property was part of that price. The Court confirmed however, that a transaction cannot be characterised as a sale unless some money is paid by the purchaser to the vendor and the cash element is more than merely nominal. So if, for example, the buyer is buying a house for £100,000, and pays for it with £30,000 in cash plus his existing house worth £70,000, duty of £1,000 (1% of £100,000) would be charged on the transfer of the £100,000 house.

11. The house which the vendor accepts as part payment for the sale would not be regarded as a separate sale for stamp duty purposes. The consideration for the purchaser's property is not the vendor's property but merely the discharge of a potential obligation to pay part of the purchase price on completion. Accordingly s 241 does not apply to the transfer of the purchaser's property. SA 1891 s 57 does not apply to the transfer of the purchaser's property because the purchaser's property is not conveyed to the vendor in consideration, wholly or in part, of any "debt due" to the vendor. The word "due" when used in relation to a debt means due and payable (*Re European Life Assurance* [1869] LR 9 Eq 122, and the other cases cited in *Stroud's Judicial Dictionary* 5th Edn Vol 2 pp 781–783). As the purchase price is not payable until completion, a transfer of property by the purchaser on or before completion cannot be said to be in consideration of a debt due. Ordinarily, on completion, the transfer of the purchaser's property will be handed to the vendor's solicitor, together with a cheque or other means of payment, at the same time as the vendor's solicitor hands over the transfer of the vendor's property. For there to be a debt due to the vendor, the purchaser would have to be put in the position of having taken a transfer of the vendor's property without having paid for it.

12. On the basis that there is a sale for cash to be satisfied in part by the transfer of another property, ad valorem stamp duty is charged on the consideration for the sale, but not on the transfer of the other property. That transfer would only be charged to the fixed duty of 50p. The threshold would not be relevant to this transfer as it is not a conveyance on sale.

Surrender and regrant of leases

Where a lease is granted in consideration only of the surrender or abandonment of an existing lease of the same property, SA 1891 s 77(1) provides exemption from duty. If the new lease is granted in consideration of a premium and/or rent as well as the surrender of the existing lease, there is a grant of a lease which is partly exempt (the surrender) and partly chargeable to duty (the premium and/or rent). The Stamp Office would not seek to refuse exemption under SA 1891 s 77 (1) merely on the grounds that there were some minor changes in the property subject to the lease, provided that these could be regarded as de minimis. The same treatment would apply where a variation of a lease takes effect in law as a surrender and regrant.

14. Where the lease on one property is being replaced by a lease on another property, the stamp duty treatment will depend on the facts of the case and the effect of the document. But if, for example, the document granted a new lease on one property and the consideration was the surrender of a lease on another property, duty would be charged on the grant of the new lease, by reference to the market value of the lease surrendered (as premium/consideration) and any other payment by way of premium or rent.

15. The stamp duty treatment of the surrender of the old lease will similarly depend on the facts and the documents. In most cases where there is a surrender and regrant, the Stamp Office's experience is that no deed of surrender is submitted for stamping, either because the new lease simply supersedes the old one by operation of law and there is no surrender document, or possibly because any surrender document is not submitted for stamping.

Sale and leaseback

16. Where there is a sale and leaseback, the Stamp Office normally sees a contract of sale for a price, and an agreement for lease (followed by the grant of a lease), rather than an exchange of one for the other. In that case, the sale would be liable to duty in the normal way by reference to the price and the agreement for lease would be charged by reference to any premium and rent.

17. If, however, the property is transferred in consideration of a leaseback of the same property, alone or together with a sum of money, duty would be assessed on the transfer by reference to the value (if any) of the lease plus any cash element. Duty would also be assessed on the lease by reference to any amount by which the value of the property transferred exceeded the cash consideration.

Unascertainable consideration—FA 1994 s 242

18. Section 242 deals with sales of land or buildings where the price is not ascertainable at the time the relevant document is executed. In these circumstances, the open market value of the property is to be taken as the consideration for stamp duty purposes. Similarly, where the rent under a new lease is not ascertainable the open market rent is to be taken.

19. That rule does not, however, apply where the amount of the consideration can already be determined by reference to the "contingency principle"—s 242 (3) (*a*). Under this principle, if the consideration agreed between the parties and specified in the instrument is subject to possible future variation, the specified figure would be taken for stamp duty purposes (*Independent Television Authority v IR Comrs* [1961] AC 427, 443). thus if the consideration is 25% of profits over five years, but not to be less than £100,000, the consideration for stamp duty purposes would be £100,000. The existence of additional but unascertainable consideration would bring the transaction within s 242.

20. The ascertainable figure produced by the contingency principle may be a maximum or minimum, or a basic sum which is subject to future variation. But a minimum figure which

Part II ST

was merely a nominal figure inserted in a lease to avoid s 242, or which did not represent the agreed consideration or rent, would not satisfy s 242 (3) (*a*) as it would not be a minimum rent for the purpose of the contingency principle as formulated by Lord Radcliffe in the Independent Television Authority case. We consider that for this purpose a minimum rent must be an amount genuinely agreed between the parties as such, ie, as an amount which is contemplated by the parties and accepted by the landlord as compensation for the use and occupation of the premises by the tenant(s). It is therefore necessary to consider all the facts in order to ascertain the true nature and intended purpose of the instrument (*Oughtred v IR Comrs* [1958] Ch 678, 688; [1960] AC 206).

21. The market value rule applies where part of the consideration or rent is unascertainable. Duty would then be charged on the market value or rent (but not the market value or rent plus the ascertainable consideration). Where the rent under a lease is unascertainable for only part of the term, the market rent will be taken for the whole term in order to calculate the average annual rent. In establishing the market rent, all the terms and conditions of the actual lease will be taken into account under normal valuation principles; s 242 (3) (*b*). It is the market rent for the particular lease and not merely the market rent for the land at a particular time which must be established for the purposes of s 242 (2).

22. It has been suggested to us that s 242 is ineffective on the grounds that if there is a valid contract, the consideration will be ascertainable, even though it may not be immediately quantifiable. For a contract to be valid, it is sufficient that the consideration is ascertainable either at the time of the contract or subsequently. Section 242 by contrast applies where the consideration is not ascertainable at the time the document is executed. The section has to be read in conjunction with FA 1963 s 55, which refers to the amount or value of the consideration, and the words "cannot . . . be ascertained" clearly mean "cannot be ascertained for the purpose of the charge", rather than "cannot be ascertained as a matter of contract law". Our view is that the wording of s 242 (1) is apt to cover the case where the amount or value of the consideration cannot be ascertained at the relevant time for the purposes of stamp duty chargeable under the conveyance on sale head of charge.

23. It has also been suggested that some transactions could come within both s 241 and s 242, on the grounds that where the amount or value of the consideration is not ascertainable, the right to it might be "property" within s 241 (1). In general, the two sections deal with distinct types of cases. There may be some cases which could fall within both sections, but the precise treatment will depend on the facts of the case. In practice, where the transfer is for full value, it should make little or no difference to the amount of duty whether s 241 or s 242 applies. Where there is a difference, duty would be charged under the provision which produces the higher amount of duty (following the principle in *Speyer Bros v IR Comrs* [1908] AC 92).

24. The treatment of split-term leases set out in our letter of 2 January 1963 to the Law Society's Gazette (where they are described as leases of type (*c*)) no longer applies. The annex on page 237 reproduces the relevant part of the 1963 letter.

Surrenders—FA 1994 s 243

25. Section 243 provides that where, in pursuance of an agreement, a lease is surrendered or renounced without a deed of surrender, the agreement is liable to duty as if it were a deed.

We have been asked what particular types of document would be regarded as an "agreement". In an individual case, it would of course be necessary to consider the facts and the terms of the relevant document. The case of *Fleetwood-Hesketh v IR Comrs* [1936] 1 KB 351 shows that a document recording or implementing an agreement may itself be treated as an agreement for stamp duty purposes where there is a previous oral agreement or an oral agreement contemporaneous with the written agreement. Where such a document satisfies the requirements of the Law of Property (Miscellaneous Provisions) Act 1989 s 2 it will be an agreement within s 243.

Valuations

27. Although the stamp duty legislation does not provide for appeals on valuation to go to the Lands Tribunal, a reference by consent could be made to the Tribunal under the Lands Tribunal Act 1949 s 1 (5) on a question of land valuation. We would normally consent. However, where questions of both law and valuation arise in relation to an appeal relating to liability and quantum respectively, we would wish to resolve the legal issue in the High Court prior to any determination of value by the Lands Tribunal. In contrast, a valuation issue would after appeal go to the Lands Tribunal.

Agreement for lease FA 1994 s 240

28. Section 240 provides that if an agreement for lease and the lease which gives effect to the agreement, are presented for stamping at the same time, and any duty chargeable on the agreement is paid, the agreement shall be treated as having been executed at the same time as the lease for the purposes of the provisions relating to penalties for late stamping. We have been asked whether FA 1931 s 28 means that the agreement must nevertheless be produced to the Stamp Office with 30 days of execution. Presentation of the agreement with the lease, within 30 days after the execution of the lease, will be accepted as satisfying the requirement under s 28 to produce the agreement.

General

29. This article supersedes the relevant parts of the Press Releases of 30 November 1993 and 18 April 1994 and the Stamp Office guidance notes issued in December 1993.

Extract from the Controller of Stamps' letter of 2 January 1963 to the Law Society's Gazette

"The Board of Inland Revenue have recently given consideration to the basis of assessment of duty on leases which contain one or more of the following provisions:

(*c*) a rent or rents fixed for part only of the term, the rent for the remainder of the term to be agreed subsequently.

Leases of type (*c*) present great difficulty and the Board are advised that in the absence of authority, it cannot be said with certainty how the provisions of the lease head of charge should properly be applied. In the absence of such authority and with the object of securing a consistent practice, hitherto lacking, and to bring the assessment of duty as far as possible into line with the facts, the Board have decided that such leases shall be assessed by treating separately the part of the term in respect of which the rent is known from that in respect of which it is unknown; ad valorem duty under 'Lease (3)' will be assessed in respect of the former part as if it were a lease at the known rate or average rate of rent for a term of that length, and fixed duty under 'Lease (4)' will be assessed in respect of the latter part.

The practice explained above in relation to leases of type (*c*) will not affect the basis of assessment of leases where there is a rent of one description (eg a ground rent) of known amount for the whole of the term and a further rent of another description (eg a service rent) ascertainable for part only of the term. In such cases the basis of assessment will continue to be ad valorem duty under 'Lease (3)' on the average ascertainable annual rent payable throughout the term and fixed duty under 'Lease (4)' on the further uncertain rent."

INLAND REVENUE TAX BULLETIN ISSUE 50. DECEMBER 2000.

PAGE 801. LIMITED LIABILITY PARTNERSHIPS

Transfer of Property to a LLP

Section 12 of LLPA 2000 requires that for the stamp duty exemption to apply the proportions of property conveyed or transferred into a LLP must either be unchanged "before" and "after" the transfer, or the proportions must not have been changed for tax avoidance reasons. Strictly under property law the partners' interest in the LLP will replace their interests in the old partnership's assets. In determining whether the stamp duty exemption applies the Revenue will not, however, take this point.

The Revenue will accept that any property transferred to the LLP within one year of its incorporation will qualify for relief from stamp duty under LLPA 2000 s 12, provided that the conditions for that relief are met.

Section 12(2) of LLPA 2000 prevents stamp duty exemption being available if property is transferred at the time of the LLP's incorporation and also there are retirements of former partners and/or admission of new partners to the LLP.

Provided that all the other conditions for the exemption are met the Revenue accepts that this charge can be averted by arranging matters so that the change of partners takes place the instant before or after incorporation. To confirm that matters were organised in this way the Stamp Office will need to see all associated documents effecting any change in the membership of the old partnership and of the LLP prior to and/or after incorporation, as well as evidence that any stamp duty appropriate to those documents has been paid. It may be necessary to call for further information once these documents have been reviewed.

Transfers of interests in a LLP

An interest in a LLP is not a chargeable security for Stamp Duty purposes. So if stamp duty is due on the transfer of such an interest it will be payable at the 1%, 3% or 4% rate, as appropriate, rather than the 0.5% rate applicable to shares. This is in line with the intention behind the LLP Act that the treatment of LLPs should be the same as for partnerships. Since the sale of an interest in any other type of partnership bears duty at the property rates, the sale of an interest in a LLP will be charged in the same way.

General

As with all transactions potentially liable to stamp duty, the Technical Services Unit Manager at any Stamp Office will be happy to assist customers in connection with any enquiries regarding the operation of the stamp duty relief in the Act.

STAMP TAXES BULLETIN ISSUE 1. AUGUST 2001.

PAGE 2. HELPING US TO HELP YOU—A REMINDER ABOUT ADJUDICATION PROCEDURES

For many years we have asked customers to provide a copy of the document when lodging an application for formal adjudication under the provisions of section 12 of the Stamp Act 1891. This copy is retained by Stamp Taxes after completion of the adjudication. There are recent instances where this has been overlooked by some customers.

Can we remind you, please, to send us a photocopy of all documents requiring adjudication. This will enable us to process adjudication applications swiftly.

Documents sent for straightforward stamping, without adjudication, need not be accompanied by a copy.

Remember you can send your adjudication documents to any of our local offices the addresses are listed below.

PAGE 2. SETTING STANDARDS IN CUSTOMER SERVICE

Stamp Taxes sets itself demanding targets which reflect the high standards of service our customers expect. Last year we were proud to receive our third Charter Mark Award, which puts us among the top organisations in the country for service excellence and "going the extra mile" to help our customers.

We measure our performance in terms of the service the customers actually receive, including the length of time we take to deal with your documents. Provided that you send us the right amount of duty and we have all the information we need, we aim to process and return your documents within 5 working days.

We have continued to deliver responsive services to meet your needs. Last year we extended the availability of our telephone Helpline service which you can ring between 8.30 am and 5 pm on weekdays.

The number to remember for all general enquiries is 0845 6030135.

We also gave our customers the opportunity to discuss current issues directly with us, by setting up User Groups at each of our locations. If you would like to get involved in these meetings please contact the local Customer Service manager at the address shown below.

Despite a fire at our Newcastle office and the relocation of our offices in Manchester and Edinburgh, we managed to return 96% of all documents in five working days. We aim to improve on this still further in the coming year.

We try to keep to a minimum our costs in administering the duty and your costs in complying with the legislation. In 2000/01 the cost of collecting stamp duty was the lowest ever, at just 12p to collect every £100 of duty.

Overall the volume of documents processed is showing a decline and this is due to the growth in electronic trading as we move to the paperless dealing system for CREST transactions on the stock market.

Our Achievements . . .

STAMP DUTY	2000/01		2001/02
	Forecast	*Result*	*Forecast*
Documents processed (millions)	2.70	2.12	1.98
Duty collected (£ millions)	3,951	4,375	4,271
Documents processed in 5 days	99.1%	96.5%	99.1%
Cost of collecting £100 of duty	13 pence	12 pence	15 pence

SDRT	2000/01		2001/02
	Forecast	*Result*	*Forecast*
Tax Collected (£ millions)	3,255.40	3,884.20	3,750
Cost of collecting £100 of tax	2 pence	2 pence	2 pence

PAGE 3. WHEN IS A FIXTURE NOT A FIXTURE?

Deductions for Chattels (or Moveables in Scotland)

Where the consideration for the conveyance or transfer on sale of a property includes an amount attributed by the parties to chattels (or moveables in Scotland), that amount will not normally be charged to stamp duty provided the chattels pass by delivery and are not conveyed in the document.

Case law provides that where assets of different character are agreed to be sold for one consideration for the whole, an apportionment between the chargeable and non-chargeable property must be a bona fide one. This is taken to mean that it must be based on the commercial value of the property concerned. A contract for sale based on a false apportionment may be unenforceable because of its improper intent and can therefore have more far-reaching consequences.

Over the last year or so, Stamp Taxes has seen a steady increase in the number of cases where the amount of consideration attributed to items claimed to be chattels is more than a small percentage of the total consideration. This is especially the case where this brings the chargeable amount just below the £250,000 or £500,000 thresholds.

Customers should note that in cases where it appears that an excessive amount of the consideration has been artificially attributed to non-chargeable items a full inventory and breakdown of the consideration will be requested by Stamp Taxes. This is to ensure that all the items claimed as chattels are properly within that description and that the allocation of the consideration is bona fide and not in breach of Stamp Act 1891 s 5.

Stamp Taxes does not provide a comprehensive list of items which are accepted as chattels or moveables since many cases need to be considered on their own merits and case law is evolving in this area all the time. However, items which will generally be accepted as chattels or moveables include—carpets, curtains, light shades, pot plants, free-standing kitchen white goods and portable electric or gas fires.

Items which are generally unacceptable as chattels are—fitted kitchen cabinets and cupboards, fitted kitchen white goods, fitted bathroom sanitary ware, central heating systems, plants growing in the soil, central heating systems and gas fires connected to a piped gas supply.

Loose Plant and Machinery

Plant and machinery may in certain circumstances be treated as "goods, wares and merchandise" and will then fall within the exception to the charge to stamp duty under FA 1999 Sch 13 para 7.

The requirement for plant and machinery to be in an actual state of severance at the date of the agreement for sale for it to fall within the "goods, wares and merchandise" description is an historical one. It stems from case law based on circumstances involving mortgagees in possession. The two main tests as to whether plant and machinery constitutes goods, wares and merchandise are essentially the same as for chattels, namely (1) the degree of annexation to the building or land and (2) the purpose or object of annexation. Stamp Taxes has for many years required customers to certify that plant and machinery claimed as loose plant must be in an actual state of severance if it is to be considered as goods and therefore outside the charge to duty on an agreement for sale. We will no longer insist upon this certification being given.

Where it would be possible for plant and machinery to be relatively easily severed from the property to which it is fixed, say for example by the simple expedient of removing some bolts securing it to the floor or walls, we will no longer insist that this is actually done before it will be considered to be "loose plant and machinery".

The position in law has not changed nor does this mean that all plant and machinery suddenly falls within the exception. As in the past, the consideration attributed to fixed plant will be chargeable to stamp duty on the agreement for sale document. Heavy plant and machinery which is integral to a building and plant where its removal would damage the building or land will still be considered fixed plant. This will be particularly relevant in respect of plant such as, for example, escalators and elevators, boilers, furnaces, walk-in refrigerators and restaurant cooking stations, none of which would be likely to be classed as loose plant for stamp duty purposes. Each case will be considered on its own merits. The Stamp Taxes form Stamps 22 will be amended to reflect this new treatment. The equivalent forms used in Scotland and Northern Ireland do not require amendment since they did not previously include the certification requirement.

Archie Brown—Technical Adviser

PAGE 4. STAMP DUTY ON GOODWILL AND INTELLECTUAL PROPERTY

With the rapidly changing face of today's business world and the growth of new technology, there are now many different types of assets relating to the trade of a company.

We are receiving an increasing number of enquiries about certain types of "intellectual property" relating to computer applications.

This is a brief outline of what is and isn't chargeable.

Intellectual property including:

- Domain names
- Databases
- Software applications

All these are not chargeable.

- Goodwill—traditionally this refers to the rights associated with carrying on the business, the "good name" and established reputation which brings with it the promise of trade.

Business goodwill is chargeable with stamp duty.

However, if the goodwill is derived from intellectual property, for instance, it is associated with a trademark, then it is exempt from duty under FA 2000 s 129 (2).

- "Know-how" is not chargeable with stamp duty.

PAGE 4. HOW TO MAKE THE MOST OF YOUR STAMP OFFICE

A Guide To Services

We have offices in 8 locations throughout the UK in Belfast, Birmingham, Bristol, Edinburgh, London, Manchester, Newcastle and Worthing.

All of our offices offer a comprehensive range of services including the facility for dealing with adjudication matters, such as charity exemptions and inter-company relief.

You can send your documents, including those requiring formal adjudication to any of our local offices. The addresses are printed below.

Our London office provides a counter-only service for personal callers. Any postal applications should therefore be sent to one of our other offices.

Don't adjudication documents have to be sent to Worthing?

No You can send adjudication applications to any office.

Although in the past, Worthing was our main adjudication centre, where claims for exemption and special relief had to be sent. For some time now this service has been available in local Stamp Offices throughout the country and you should send adjudication documents to the office that you normally use for all your general stamp duty applications.

What if I need help on a technical point?

We have technical advisers in each of our offices, who can provide you with information and guidance on more complex issues and explain the procedures for making an exemption claim.

On more general matters, our Helpline operators are available to assist you in answering your basic stamp duty enquiries from 8.30 am to 5 pm on weekdays.

The Helpline number is 0845 6030135.

All calls are charged at local rate to keep your costs to a minimum.

Where do I find out more?

If you want to know more about a specific subject, we publish a range of leaflets covering different topics. These are available free of charge from any of our offices. They can also be found on the Internet.

To find out what's new and all the latest developments visit our website at www.inlandrevenue.gov.uk/so.

PAGE 5. IN YOUR INTEREST

News About Recent Interest Rate Changes

In line with other taxes, we charge interest on late payments of stamp duty. This is aimed at making sure the tax operates fairly for all our customers by encouraging everyone to pay us the right amount of duty on time.

We also pay you interest in certain circumstances. If you pay more duty than is due and your document is over-stamped we will add interest to the repayment amount. The interest charged on late paid tax is higher than that added to repayments.

The interest rates for stamp duty, like those for other taxes are set by reference to changes in the base rate.

New rates of interest came into effect from 6 May 2001.

This table gives you a quick guide to recent changes in the rates of interest.

	Late paid duty	***Repayments***
1/10/99	7.5%	3%
6/2/00	8.5%	4%
6/5/01	7.5%	3.5%

If the delay crosses over periods where different interest rates apply, we will charge interest at the old rate for any period prior to the rate change, and at the current rate for any subsequent period.

PAGE 5. CASTING THE NET WIDER . . .

Developments In E-Business

More than 25% of our customers regularly access our web-site to find out all the latest information and news about stamp duty changes.

We receive a number of suggestions from customers about the things they would like to see on the web. In particular, our Northern Ireland users said they would like an electronic version of the form PD1 to be available on-line.

We responded by including this on our web-site.

We are also working hard to make sure that every contact with our customers counts, enabling them to understand and meet their obligations in paying the right amount of duty.

To help customers find their way around our forms, we have recently incorporated a "help" feature on our form Stamps 61 on the web-site. This guides the reader through the various sections, telling them what information to include. We are intending to extend this facility to all our forms in time, and we are currently working on a "help" index for our form LA451 to give guidance in completing the information. This will replace the printed information on completing our forms, which was available in the SO5 leaflet.

STAMP OFFICE ADDRESSES

Belfast Stamp Office
Ground Floor
Dorchester House
52–58 Great Victoria Street
Belfast BT2 7QE
028 90 505127
DX: 2003 Belfast 2

Birmingham Stamp Office
5th Floor
Norfolk House
Smallbrook Queensway
Birmingham B5 4LA
0121 633 3313
DX: 15001 Birmingham 1

Bristol Stamp Office
The Pithay
All Saints Street
Bristol BS1 2NY
0117 927 2022
DX 7899 Bristol 1

Edinburgh Stamp Office
Grayfield House
Spur X
4 Bankhead Avenue
Edinburgh EH11 4AE
0131 442 3161
Dx: ED 543303 Edinburgh 33

London Stamp Office (Personal callers only)
South West Wing
Bush House
Strand
London WC2B 4QN
020 7 438 7252/7452

Worthing Stamp Office (Postal applications only)
Room 35
East Block
Barrington Road
Worthing BN12 4XJ
01903 508962
DX: 3799 Worthing 1

Manchester Stamp Office
Upper Fifth Floor
Royal Exchange
Exchange Street
Manchester M2 7EB
0161 834 8020
DX: 14430 Manchester 2

Newcastle Stamp Office (Temporary relocation following a fire)
4th Floor
Weardale House
Washington
Tyne & Wear NE37 1LW
0191 261 1199
DX: 61021 Newcastle upon Tyne 1

SDRT (Operations)
Customer Service Unit
Room 5
East Block
Barington Road
Worthing BN12 4XJ

STAMP TAXES BULLETIN ISSUE 2. FEBRUARY 2002.

PAGE 2. DISADVANTAGED AREAS—STAMP DUTY EXEMPTION

On 30 November 2001, the Government introduced the first phase of a stamp duty exemption for property transactions in designated disadvantaged areas. The exemption applies to all transfers, conveyances and leases of land, or interests in land, executed on or after 30 November 2001, where the consideration or premium does not exceed £150,000.

Background

In the Pre-Budget Report in November 2000 the Chancellor announced that a stamp duty exemption for land transactions in disadvantaged areas would form part of a fiscal package, worth £1 billion over five years, designed to encourage investment and stimulate regeneration in deprived areas. The primary legislation to implement this relief was enacted as FA 2001 s 92 and Sch 30. The effect of this legislation was restricted to transactions up to £150,000 by regulations made on 28 November (SI 2001/3746), immediately following the 2001

Pre-Budget Report. The regulations to specify the qualifying areas (SI 2001/3747) and to confirm the date of commencement of the relief (SI 2001/3748) were made on 29 November 2001. This package of regulations reflects the fact that the relief is being implemented in two stages. The next phase, which is subject to approval as state aid by the European Union, is to increase substantially or remove the limit for non-residential property transactions. Before this can be done it is necessary to introduce a definition of residential property in the next Finance Bill.

The Qualifying Areas: Where Are They and How Were They Selected?

The areas that qualify for the relief are the most deprived, as determined by the indices of deprivation in each of the four nations that comprise the United Kingdom. In England and Scotland the poorest 15% of wards and postcodes qualify. In Wales and Northern Ireland the poorest 42% of wards are designated as disadvantaged.

In England, Wales and Northern Ireland, the indices refer to electoral wards or divisions. In Scotland the index uses postcode areas. The regulations use wards and postcode areas accordingly.

We have published the qualifying wards and postcode areas in Scotland on our website at www.inlandrevenue.gov.uk/so. In total there are nearly 2,000 qualifying areas.

What Happens If the Electoral Ward or Postcode Area Has Been Abolished or Changed?

From time to time, reorganisations of local government can result in changes to ward boundaries. Postcode areas can also be subject to revision. The ward and postcode areas specified in the regulations match the ward boundaries and postcodes used in each country's most recent index of deprivation. In England and Wales the indices were compiled in 1998, using the wards and electoral divisions that existed at that time. In Northern Ireland the index of deprivation was compiled in 2001, using the electoral boundaries that existed in 1991.

The Scottish index was updated in 1998, using 1991 postcodes. The question of whether a particular property falls within an area that qualifies for relief therefore depends on whether the property is situated in a qualifying area as determined by boundaries current at:

— 7 May 1998 for England.
— 1 April 1998 for Wales.
— 21 April 1991 for Scotland and Northern Ireland.

How Should Claims For the Relief Be Made?

When you are satisfied that a property falls within an area that qualifies for relief from Stamp Duty, you should submit a claim to one of our offices. The London office offers a counter service for personal callers and cannot accept postal applications. The exemption is an adjudicated relief and documents on which the relief is claimed must be presented for formal adjudication. To assist us in dealing with claims it would help if the following are provided at the time the document is presented for stamping:

- a certificate confirming that it is a document on which duty is not chargeable by virtue of FA 2001 s 92.

The certificate may be within the document itself or in an accompanying letter. FA 2002 s 92 (2) provides that the exemption will only apply if the document is so certified.

- the full postcode for the property on which the relief is claimed.

Reference to the postcode is the quickest way for us to confirm that the property is in a qualifying area. The Royal Mail Postcode Enquiry Line 08457 111 222 will supply the postcode for any postal address. For properties that are newly constructed, or for land on

Part II ST

which no buildings have been erected, there will be a recently allocated postcode or no postcode at all. We will not in these circumstances, be able to confirm that the property is in a qualifying area. Claims for relief in such cases should be made naming the ward in which the property was located at the qualifying date. A map showing the location of the property and the ward boundaries should be supplied. If this is not possible we will accept a map showing the location of the property in relation to established adjacent properties. The status of the surrounding properties will enable us to confirm that the property, on which relief is claimed, falls within a qualifying area.

- a completed form L(A)451;
- a photocopy of the document;
- a copy of the relevant contract;
- a certificate of value for £250,000 (not £150,000).

It was not possible to use the regulations that limit the effect of FA 2001 s 92 (SI 2001/3746) to alter the various levels of certificates of value, as set out in FA 1999. Instead the regulations provide that relief only applies if the document could have included a £150,000 certificate of value if that had been one of the levels of certificate in the FA 1999. Thus the requirement to provide a certificate of value for £250,000 still holds good.

- the duty payable on the rental element, if the document is a lease and/or agreement for lease.

The exemption applies only to lease premiums up to £150,000 and duty is payable on ground rents at usual rates.

- a note of whether the property is residential or non-residential.

We need this for statistical and evaluation purposes.

You are reminded that if an examination of your claim results in a decision that relief under FA 2001 s 92 is not due, and as a consequence, stamp duty is paid after the due date for payment, an interest charge may be incurred.

What Is Happening About the Next Phase?

The Government announced an intention to raise significantly, or abolish entirely, the £150,000 limit for transactions in "non-residential" property, probably during this year, subject to approval from the European Union as state aid. The current limit will remain in force for "residential" properties.

Before this second phase can be implemented it is necessary to distinguish "residential" and "non-residential" property in the statute.

On 21 December 2001 we issued a consultation document setting out a draft clause for inclusion in the Finance Bill 2002 to define "residential property" for the purposes of the second phase of the Stamp Duty exemption for land transactions in disadvantaged areas. Comments on the draft clause are invited by 22 February 2002.

Copies of the press release and consultation document are available in paper form from the Visitor Centre, South West Wing, Bush House, Strand, London WC2B 4QN. An electronic version of the consultation document can be obtained at our web site: www.inlandrevenue.gov.uk/so.

Further Information

If any further information is needed we have published a detailed customer newsletter, which is available from any of our offices. If your question has not been answered in this article, nor in the newsletter, a member of our telephone helpline staff on 0845 603 0135 (Monday to Friday 08.30–17.00) will be pleased to assist you.

PAGE 5. IN YOUR INTEREST

News About Recent Interest Rate Changes

Since the last edition of the Tax Bulletin there has been a change to the rates of interest we charge on late payment of duty and on certain repayments.

The new rates of interest, which came into effect from 6 November 2001 are included in the table below:

	Duty Paid Late	*Repayments*
1/10/99	7.5%	3%
6/2/00	8.5%	4%
6/5/01	7.5%	3.5%
6/11/01	6.5%	2.5%

Interest will be charged on duty that is paid late at previous levels for any period prior to the rate change and at the current rate for the subsequent period.

Provisional/Informal Advice—A Timely Reminder

In Stamp Taxes we do our best to keep you informed of any changes in legislation and/or practice to enable you to calculate your stamp duty liability to ensure compliance.

Under the provisions of Stamp Act 1891 s 12 you can ask for a binding opinion of the duty payable on a document if you provide us with the original executed instrument and tell us all the relevant facts or circumstances surrounding the transaction.

However, there may be occasions when you will only be able to send us a draft or copy documents or an outline of a proposed transaction. This may be a request made in writing or orally by telephone or in person at one of our public counters.

In these circumstances we will help you as far as reasonably possible but customers are reminded that any opinion that we give should be regarded as provisional and does not bind us to assess the duly executed document to the duty stated in the opinion.

Furthermore FA 1999 divided the compliance regime for stamp duty into two parts: presentation and payment.

The onus was firmly placed on the person responsible for the payment of stamp duty to both ensure that the document was presented to a stamp office and that an appropriate payment was paid within thirty days of the date of execution of the document.

A failure to present a document incurs a penalty and a failure to make a payment incurs interest under the provisions of Stamp Act 1891 s 15 as amended by FA 1999 s 109.

We would like to take this opportunity to remind customers that interest charges are a mandatory charge. There is no right of appeal and IR Stamp Taxes has no authority to waive or mitigate any interest that is due.

Further Advice and Information

- Stamp Taxes Customer Newsletter—Interest and Penalties—May 2001
- Stamp Taxes Customer Newsletter—Penalties and Interest—further guidance
- Stamp Taxes leaflet SO10—Interest and Penalties
- Stamp Taxes Manual—Chapter 3—Stamp Duty Compliance

PAGE 6. PAYMENT IN EUROS

The euro was introduced in a non-cash form in January 1999 by 11 EU countries. The countries involved are: Austria, Belgium, Finland, France, Ireland, Italy, Germany, Luxembourg, Netherlands, Portugal and Spain. These countries were later joined by Greece in January 2001 to make up the 12 countries who introduced euro notes and coins on 1 January 2002. The euro cash is replacing existing national currencies (legacy), which will be withdrawn from circulation and cease to be legal tender by no later than 28 February 2002.

Following the impetus of these recent changes, we have received a few enquiries with regard to processing euro payments.

For transactions undertaken in the UK, the euro is classed as a foreign currency and as such the procedures for accepting euro payments are the same as those for any other foreign currency. Stamp Offices can accept foreign payments but they are unable to stamp a document until they are notified of the £ sterling value received. Our local banking procedures do not cater for exchanging foreign currencies so these payments have to be referred by us to the Inland Revenue's central Financial Accounting Office.

There is a lead-time between presenting a foreign payment and receiving notification of its sterling value. This may result in a different exchange rate being used at the time of conversion. If this occurs and the amount received is insufficient to enable us to stamp the document(s) with the duty assessed, then customers will have to pay the shortfall before the document can be stamped. Interest will be chargeable on any shortfall until the date received. If, however, the amount received is greater than the amount required then we will refund the balance.

Customers considering making a payment in euros are encouraged to exchange currency at a local Post Office or make a CHAPs payment direct to the Inland Revenue. This will benefit customers as you will not be affected by exchange rate fluctuations that may occur in the time it takes for our banking procedures to process payments.

For further details on the bank account details to be used for CHAPs payments or any payments in a foreign currency, or any other information in relation to the euro, please contact Robert Duncan on: 01903 509599.

More information is available on the Inland Revenue web site at: www.inlandrevenue.gov.uk/euro/.

PAGE 7. COMPLAINTS: A REVISED CODE OF PRACTICE

The Inland Revenue introduced a new Code of Practice (COP1) "Putting things right when we make mistakes" on 31 October 2001, which is available under "forms and leaflets" on the Inland Revenue web site.

The Revised COP1:

- introduces important changes to our redress policy;
- stresses the importance of working with customers to resolve problems as quickly as possible;
- explains how customers can help us provide a good service;
- provides answers to commonly asked question about complaints and redress.

Following the introduction of the COP1, IR Stamp Taxes is reviewing the way in which we handle customers' complaints to ensure a consistent approach, part of the review will include updating our procedures for handling complaints and our leaflet "If Things go Wrong . . . . Complaints and Lost Documents" (SO3), available on our web site.

In IR Stamp Taxes we take any expression of dissatisfaction in the service we provide seriously and our aim is to identify what has gone wrong and put things right as quickly and effectively as possible, with the minimum of cost and inconvenience to the customer.

Although we hope that you don't have to pay any extra costs as a result of our mistake or unreasonable delay, there will be times when this happens. If this is the case you can claim any reasonable costs which you have had to pay as a direct result.

However, as we do not want to put you to extra time and expense, when things go wrong or there is any problem with the way we are dealing with matters please tell us. You may address any complaint in the first instance to the Office Manager, who will try to settle matters quickly and fairly.

Alternatively you may contact Judith Baydoun, the Customer Service Manager direct on: 0117 927 3742. (Contact details including the Office Managers are shown below.)

PAGE 7. BETTER QUALITY SERVICES

Better Quality Service (BQS) reviews are a central part of the Inland Revenue's response to the Modernising Government White Paper that says that all Government Departments must examine all their activities over the next five years particularly focusing on customers' needs.

IR Stamp Taxes is currently undergoing such a review, which gives us the opportunity to take a structured look at how we provide services to meet the needs of our customers both now and in the future. We are also identifying better ways of carrying out our business.

Over the last couple of months we have consulted widely with customers and various representative bodies and we have built up a picture of the service we deliver now and will need to deliver in the future particularly in the area of electronic business.

Thank you to all our customers who have contributed to this review either through face to face interviews or the recent telephone surveys. We are always interested in hearing your views about the service we deliver and how it can be improved.

If you have any comments please contact Judith Baydoun, Bristol Stamp Office, The Pithay, All Saints Street, Bristol BS1 2NY.

PAGE 9. IR STAMP TAXES—NETWORK OFFICES

Belfast Stamp Office
Ground Floor
Dorchester House
52–58 Great Victoria Street
Belfast BT2 7QE
029 90 505127

DX:2003 Belfast 2
Manager: Martine MacLaughlin

Birmingham Stamp Office
5th Floor
Norfolk House
Smallbrook Queensway
Birmingham B5 4LA
0121 633 3313

DX:15001 Birmingham 1
Office Manager: June Checketts

Bristol Stamp Office
1st Floor
The Pithay
All Saints Street
Bristol BS1 2NY
0117 927 2022

DX:7899 Bristol 1
Office Manager: Judith Baydoun

Edinburgh Stamp Office
Grayfield House
Spur X
4 Bankhead Avenue
Edinburgh EH11 4AE
0131 442 3161

DX ED: 543303 Edinburgh 33
Office Manager: David Hunter

London Stamp Office
(Public Counter service only)
South West Wing
Bush House
Strand
London WC2B 4QN
0207 438 7252/7452

Office Manager: Trevor England

Worthing Stamp Office
(Postal service only)
Room 35
East Block
Barrington Road
Worthing BN12 4XJ
01903 508962

DX: 3799 Worthing 1
Office Manager: Jan Betteridge

Manchester Stamp Office
Upper Fifth Floor
Royal Exchange
Exchange Street
Manchester M2 7EB
0161 834 8020

DX:14430 Manchester 2
Office Manager: Les Shiell

Newcastle Stamp Office
(Temporary location)
4th Floor
Weardale House
Washington
Tyne & Wear NE37 1LW

DX: 61021 Newcastle upon Tyne 1
Office Manager: Tony Stoker

SDRT (Operations)
Customer Service Unit
Room 5
East Block
Barrington Road
Worthing BN12 4XJ
01903 509471

Office Manager: Robert Duncan

STAMP TAXES BULLETIN ISSUE 3. OCTOBER 2002.

PAGE 2. MODERNISING STAMP DUTY

A package of proposals to modernise stamp duty was set out in a consultative document earlier this year. We have since been considering responses to that consultation as we develop those proposals to include legislation in Finance Bill 2003.

When Will Modernising Stamp Duty Be Implemented?

Following legislation in Finance Bill 2003, the modernising regime will be implemented towards the end of that year.

What Will the Changes Mean For Customers?

Our aim is to minimise the impact of change for the majority of our customers, particularly individual home-buyers and their agents. For these customers, the main changes in practice will be in the way in which stamp duty is paid. We will no longer need to see documents related to transfers and we will no longer impress stamps on those documents to confirm payment of stamp duty. Instead, transactions which are within the scope of stamp duty will have to be notified to Inland Revenue Stamp Taxes using a standard notification form. This form will supersede the existing particulars delivered (LA 451) form and for this reason some transactions which are not currently notified to Inland Revenue will be subject to the notification requirements.

If Stamped Impressions on Documents Are to Be Discontinued, How Can I Prove to Land RegistriesThat I Have Paid Stamp Duty?

We are exploring a range of options, including the production of a stamp duty certificate which can be attached to the documents which are presented for registration.

Will the Scope of the Charge Change?

The revised charge will apply to all transactions in respect of interest in and rights over UK land and buildings. This will include transactions in indirect holdings of UK land and

Part II ST

buildings and the charge will apply regardless of whether transactions are effected inside or outside the UK. The Government is also reviewing the charge on the grant of new leases.

The revised regime will not apply [to:]

- Transfers of, and agreements to transfer, goodwill. These are already exempted from stamp duty (with effect from 23 April 2002).
- Transfers of debts. In order to make it easier for businesses to raise finance through debt factoring and the issue of bonds secured on debt portfolios, these will be removed from the scope of the modernised stamp duty regime.

How Will Stamp Duty on Shares be Affected?

Most transfers of shares and securities are charged to stamp duty reserve tax (SDRT).

The modernisation of stamp duty on UK land and buildings will not affect the scope and impact of the main SDRT charge and of stamp duty as it applies to share transfers.

For more information on modernising stamp duty, visit our website at: www.inlandrevenue.gov.uk/so or contact our helpline on 0845 6030135.

Inland Revenue Press Office

Press enquiries: 020 7438 6692/6706/7327, (out of hours): 07860 359544, non-media enquiries: 020 7944 3000 (office hours only).

PAGE 3. OPTIONS—A RESPONSE TO PRESS ARTICLES

Stamp Offices have received a significant number of telephone enquiries following the publication of certain newspaper articles that promoted the use of options as a stamp duty saving scheme. Callers have been asking us to confirm that the scheme works in the manner described in the articles.

The Inland Revenue considers that these articles contain serious errors in stamp duty law. We are therefore publishing this item to clarify the issues.

The articles suggested that stamp duty on a purchase of a property at a price of £700,000 could be reduced by structuring the transaction so that the purchaser paid a price of £210,000 for an option to acquire the property at a price of £490,000. It was suggested that by doing so the duty of £28,000 that would apply to a purchase at £700,000 would be reduced to £14,700 (ie duty at 3% on the consideration of £490,000 only).

Under Stamp Act 1891 s 5, all relevant facts and circumstances affecting the liability of an instrument to duty or the amount of that duty must be "fully and truly set forth in the instrument". To comply with section 5 it would therefore be necessary when presenting a transfer document reciting a purchase price of £490,000, to produce the Option Agreement for stamping. An Agreement granting an option to purchase property made for consideration, is a document liable to ad valorem conveyance on sale duty (*George Wimpey & Co Ltd v IRC* [1975] 2 All ER 45).

The transfer of the property at a price of £490,000 would not be stampable at the 3% rate as suggested in the press articles. Since it stems from the Option Agreement, it forms part of a larger series of transactions at an aggregate value exceeding £500,000. A certificate of value for £500,000 could not be validly inserted in the transfer document and duty would, accordingly, be payable at 4%.

The question also arises as to the rate of duty that should apply to the stamping of the option agreement. In any transaction structured in the manner set out in the articles the Stamp Office will require full disclosure of all correspondence surrounding the negotiations and the manner in which the purchase money or monies was paid. Each case will be treated on its merits, but it should be borne in mind that, in some cases, the Stamp Office are likely to contend that the Option Agreement is itself part of a series of transactions, so that any certificate of value to be included in it must take into account the price to be paid upon exercise of the option.

PAGE 4. DISADVANTAGED AREAS—POSTCODES ARE NOW AVAILABLE ON OUR WEBSITE

In IR Stamp Taxes we are continually looking for ways of improving the service that we provide customers to help you when dealing with any stamp duty matters.

In the last edition of Stamp Taxes Bulletin we told you about designated disadvantaged areas and the exemption from stamp duty available on properties where the consideration or premium does not exceed £150,000 as provided by FA 2001 s 92.

With the exception of Scotland, where it is postcode areas, qualifying areas for this relief are based on electoral wards as determined by boundaries current at:

- 7 May 1998 for England.
- 1 April 1998 for Wales.
- 21 April 1991 for Scotland and Northern Ireland.

However, as it is usually quicker and easier to confirm whether a property falls within a qualifying area by reference to the postcode, you can now go online to check if a postcode falls within a qualifying area to be eligible for the relief from stamp duty.

Access to the postcode search tool is straightforward and enables you to carry out checks as quickly and efficiently as possible.

If you are unsure of the postcode you can find it at: www.consignia-online.com or telephone the Royal Mail Enquiry Line at: 08457 111 222.

To perform a search:

- Go to our website at: www.inlandrevenue.gov/so to take you to our front page.
- Click on Disadvantaged Areas Relief: new postcode search.
  This will take you to the search tool where you will be asked to enter the postcode in the two boxes on the page.
- Enter the postcode—the postcode must be entered in the correct format.
  In the first box enter the first part of the postcode which must contain either 1–2 letters followed by 1–2 digits or letters—eg NE99 or a letter, a number and another letter such as W2B.
  In the second box enter 1 digit followed by 2 letters eg 1ZZ.
- When you have entered the postcode click on search.
  The result of your search will give a positive or negative return.
- A positive result will return:
  The postcode (TF1 2NL) has been identified as being situated in a qualifying area.
  Please see '"Stamp Taxes Bulletin Issue 2" for additional information.
  Search performed 01/07/2002 14.57.
- A negative result will return
  This postcode (TF1 2NL) has not been identified as being situated in a qualifying area.
  If you still believe this postcode falls within a disadvantaged ward eg property is a new build or there have been ward boundary changes.
  Please see "Stamp Taxes Bulletin Issue 2".
  Search performed 01/07/2000 14:57.

Depending on the result of your search the hyperlink to the Tax Bulletin will provide you with guidance on what you should now do to complete the transaction.

As we are continually reviewing the information that we provide customers we are always interested in any comments/suggestions that you as user may have to improve the service that we offer. Please contact Judith Baydoun on: 0117 927 3742 with any comments.

PAGE 5 IR STAMP TAXES—CONTRACTS UNIT AT MANCHESTER

A specially dedicated unit has been established in Manchester with effect from 1 July 2002 to exclusively deal with all aspects of the general application of the legislation at FA 2002 s 115 and Sch 36.

That legislation brings within the charge to stamp duty contracts for the sale of interests in UK land where the purchase consideration in respect of that land exceeds £10 million. Duty is chargeable on such contracts as though they were conveyances.

The administration of the legislation, including stamping of contracts within the scope of section 115, the processing of applications to extend the 90-day time limit, and the granting of the benefit of sub-sale relief are all matters that will be **exclusively** dealt with by the Contracts Unit.

Please do not refer any matters relating to section 115 to other Stamp Offices.

The Contracts Unit will be happy to deal with any enquiries as to whether a particular contract is, or will be, within the scope of [a] section 115 charge and you may contact the Contract Unit at: Stamp Taxes Contracts Unit, Manchester Stamp Office, Upper Fifth Floor, Royal Exchange, Exchange Street, Manchester M2 7EB; tel: 0161 839 6260, fax: 0161 834 3350.

For more information about the legislation and its application please refer to our Customer Newsletter Issue 3 *Contracts for the sale of an estate or interest in UK land—Section 115 and Schedule 36 Finance Act 2002* which is available under Newsletters on our website: www.inlandrevenue.gov.uk/so.

PAGE 6. NOTICE BOARD

This section tells you about the latest Stamp Taxes publications and highlights recent information. All can be accessed via our website at: www.inlandrevenue.gov.uk/so.

- Modernising Stamp Duty-Consultation document.
- Budget and Finance Bill 2002—summary.
- Customer Newsletters issued in July 2002.
  - Split Title Schemes and Section 90 Finance Act 1965 Issue 4.
  - Contracts for the sale of an estate or interest in UK land—section 115 and Schedule 36 Finance Act 2002 Issue 3.
  - SDRT Issue No 1.
  - SDRT Issue No 2.
- Customer Newsletter Special Edition Belfast Stamp Office.
  (Please note Belfast Stamp Office's new telephone number is: 02890 505312/4/6.)

The content of Stamp Taxes Bulletin gives the view of our technical specialists on particular issues. The information published is reported because it may be of interest to tax practitioners. Publication will be twice a year.

- You can expect that the interpretations of the law contained in the Bulletin will normally be applied in relevant cases, but this is subject to a number of qualifications.
- Particular cases may turn on their own facts, or context, and because every possible situation cannot be covered, there may be circumstances in which the interpretation given here will not apply.
- There may also be circumstances in which the Board would find it necessary to argue for a different interpretation in appeal proceedings.
- The Bulletin does not replace formal Statements of Practice.
- The Board's view of the law may change in the future. Readers will be notified of any changes in future editions.

Nothing contained in this Stamp Taxes bulletin affects a taxpayer's right of appeal on any point.

PAGE 7. IR STAMP TAXES—NETWORK OFFICES

Belfast Stamp Office
Third Floor
Dorchester House
52–58 Great Victoria Street
Belfast BT2 7QE
Tel: 02890 505312/4/6

DX: 2003 Belfast 2
Manager: Martine MacLaughlin

Birmingham Stamp Office
5th Floor
Norfolk House
Smallbrook Queensway
Birmingham B5 4LA
Tel: 0121 633 3313

DX: 15001 Birmingham 1
Office Manager: June Checketts

Bristol Stamp Office
1st Floor
The Pithay
All Saints Street
Bristol BS1 2NY
Tel: 0117 927 2022

DX: 7899 Bristol 1
Office Manager: Judith Baydoun

Edinburgh Stamp Office
Grayfield House
Spur X
4 Bankhead Avenue
Edinburgh EH11 4AE
Tel: 0131 442 3161

DX ED: 543303 Edinburgh 33
Office Manager: David Hunter

London Stamp Office
South West Wing
Bush House
Strand
London WC2B 4QN
Tel: 0207 438 7252/7452

DX: 146766 London (Somerset House)
Office Manager: Trevor England

Worthing Stamp Office
(Postal service only)
Room 35, East Block
Barrington Road
Worthing BN12 4XJ
Tel: 01903 508962

DX: 3799 Worthing 1
Office Manager: Paul Cox

Manchester Stamp Office
Upper Fifth Floor
Royal Exchange
Exchange Street
Manchester M2 7EB
Tel: 0161 834 8020

DX: 14430 Manchester 2
Office Manager: Les Shiell

Newcastle Stamp Office
(Temporary location)
4th Floor, Weardale House
Washington
Tyne & Wear NE37 1LW
Tel: 0191 201 7402

DX: 61021 Newcastle upon Tyne 1
Office Manager: Tony Stoker

Stamp Taxes Contracts Unit
Manchester Stamp Office
Upper Fifth Floor
Royal Exchange
Exchange Street
Manchester M2 7EB
Tel: 0161 839 6260

Fax: 0161 834 3350

SDRT (Operations)
Customer Service Unit
Room 5
East Block
Barrington Road
Worthing BN12 4XJ
Tel: 01903 509471

Office Manager: Penny Darburn

General Enquiries Helpline: 0845 603 0135.

STAMP TAXES BULLETIN ISSUE 4. MARCH 2003.

PAGE 2. MODERNISING STAMP DUTY

As part of our preparation for modernising stamp duty we have decided to make some changes to the service that we currently offer you.

The purpose of this article is to explain the changes we have made in relation to two particular areas of our work and what we would like you to do in future.

The areas of work affected are:

- Share/stock transfer forms;
- Telephone Enquiry Line—postcode checks.

Share/Stock Transfer Forms

At the end of this year as part of the modernisation programme we will no longer have the facilities to stamp documents at all our local offices. For this reason we have started to centralise some areas of our work and this includes stock transfer forms. All stock transfers currently stamped at local stamp offices, including those presented at the public counters are to be processed at a single location—London Stamp Office.

We have selected the London office as it already handles a high proportion of this kind of work and it is now able to receive postal applications.

With immediate effect we would ask you to send all stock transfer forms **except** those that require formal adjudication direct to the London Stamp Office for stamping.

Where stock transfers require formal adjudication please continue to use your local stamp office.

The postal address for London Stamp Office is: London Stamp Office, Ground Floor, Bush House, The Strand, London WC2B 4QN. Or by DX to: London Stamp Office, DX: 146766 London (Somerset House), Telephone Enquiry Line: 0845 6030135.

From 17 March 2003 we will be centralising all postcode telephone enquiries.

If you do not have access to the Internet and you would like a postcode check to be carried out please will you contact our Enquiry Line where we have a team dedicated to handling these enquiries. All calls to this number are charged at a local rate to keep your costs to a minimum.

The Enquiry Line is open from Monday to Friday from 0830–1700 to deal with your calls, please ring: 0845 6030135.

We would like to remind customers that the postcode search tool is available for your use on our website at: www.inlandrevenue.gov.uk/so—click on Disadvantaged Areas: postcode search tool.

PAGE 3. DISADVANTAGED AREAS—SECTION 92 FINANCE ACT 2001

Since the postcode search tool has been available on our website we have received a number of follow up telephone calls from customers seeking further advice about this exemption.

In response to this we have compiled a list of frequently asked questions (FAQs) and the answers to these questions that we hope you find helpful.

Q: Do I Have to Claim This Relief From Stamp Duty?

A: Yes as an adjudicated relief the onus is on the customer to make a claim for exemption from stamp duty.

Part II ST

Once you are satisfied that you meet all the qualifying criteria you should submit all the relevant information and documentation to your local stamp office. You should not submit any payments.

Q: What Happens If I Make a Claim For Relief and It Fails?

A: In the event that you fail to meet all the qualifying criteria your claim for exemption will fail and we will request payment of the stamp duty together with any interest that may be due.

Q: What Happens If I Have Paid the Stamp Duty and Later Find Out That the Property Qualifies For Exemption From Stamp Duty?

A: Providing that you find this out within two years from the date of the document you will be able to claim back any stamp duty paid in error. If we agree with your claim we will add interest to any monies that we repay. You should in the first instance contact the office that dealt with the stamping of your document.

Q: What Happens If the Result of My Postcode Search Is Negative and the Message Says that the Postcode Has Not Been "Found"?

A: The result of your postcode search may be negative because your property/land:

- is part of a new development and/or has been allocated a postcode recently which does not appear on our postcode database yet;
- has yet to be allocated a postcode.

In cases such as this if you are claiming exemption from stamp duty you should tell us that the postcode has not been found or no postcode is available.

You should name the ward in which the property was located as at the qualifying date.

A map showing the location of the property and the ward boundaries should be supplied. If this is not possible we will accept a map showing the location of the property, in relation to established adjacent properties. The status of the surrounding properties will enable us to confirm that the property, on which relief is claimed, falls within a qualifying area.

A list of the qualifying wards (postcode areas in Scotland) as at the qualifying dates is available on our website).

Q: What Are the Current Rates of Interest?

A: The current rates of interest which came into effect from 6 November 2001 are 6.5% on duty that has been paid late and 2.5% on any monies that is due for repayment.

PAGE 4. NOTICE BOARD

- Budget Statement—Wednesday, 9 April 2003.

For more information about articles covered in this Bulletin and other stamp duty matters visit our website at: www.inlandrevenue.gov.uk/so.

The content of Stamp Taxes Bulletin gives the view of our technical specialists on particular issues. The information is published is reported as it may be of interest to tax practitioners. We aim to issue a publication twice a year.

- You can expect that the interpretations of the law contained in the Bulletin will normally be applied in relevant cases, but this is subject to a number of qualifications.
- Particular cases may turn on their own facts, or context, and because every possible situation cannot be covered, there may be circumstances in which the interpretation given here will not apply.

- There may also be circumstances in which the Board would find it necessary to argue for a different interpretation in appeal proceedings.
- The Bulletin does not replace formal Statements of Practice.
- The Board's view of the law may change in the future. Readers will be notified of any changes in future editions.

PAGE 5. IR STAMP TAXES—NETWORK OFFICES

Belfast Stamp Office
Third Floor
Dorchester House
52–58 Great Victoria Street
Belfast BT2 7QE
Tel: 02890 505312/4/6

DX: 2003 Belfast 2
Manager: Martine MacLaughlin

Birmingham Stamp Office
5th Floor
Norfolk House
Smallbrook Queensway
Birmingham B5 4LA
Tel: 0121 633 3313

DX: 15001 Birmingham 1
Office Manager: Claire Fell

Bristol Stamp Office
1st Floor
The Pithay
All Saints Street
Bristol BS1 2NY
Tel: 0117 927 2022

DX: 7899 Bristol 1
Office Manager: Judith Baydoun

Edinburgh Stamp Office
Grayfield House
Spur X
4 Bankhead Avenue
Edinburgh EH11 4AE
Tel: 0131 442 3161

DX ED: 543303 Edinburgh 33
Office Manager: David Hunter

London Stamp Office
South West Wing
Bush House
Strand
London WC2B 4QN
Tel: 0207 438 7252/7452

DX: 146766 London (Somerset House)
Office Manager: Trevor England

Worthing Stamp Office
(Postal service only)
Room 35, East Block
Barrington Road
Worthing BN12 4XJ
Tel: 01903 508962

DX: 3799 Worthing 1
Office Manager: Paul Cox

Manchester Stamp Office
Upper Fifth Floor
Royal Exchange
Exchange Street
Manchester M2 7EB
Tel: 0161 834 8020

DX: 14430 Manchester 2
Office Manager: Les Shiell

Newcastle Stamp Office
(Temporary location)
4th Floor, Weardale House
Washington
Tyne & Wear NE37 1LW
Tel: 0191 201 7402

DX: 61021 Newcastle upon Tyne 1
Office Manager: Tony Stoker

Stamp Taxes Contracts Unit
Manchester Stamp Office
Upper Fifth Floor
Royal Exchange
Exchange Street
Manchester M2 7EB
Tel: 0161 839 6260

Fax: 0161 834 3350

SDRT (Operations)
Customer Service Unit
Room 5
East Block
Barrington Road
Worthing BN12 4XJ
Tel: 01903 509471

Office Manager: Penny Darburn
Stamp Taxes Enquiry Line: 0845 603 0135.
Website address: www.inlandrevenue.gov.uk/so.

STAMP DUTY INFORMATION BULLETIN ISSUE 4. SEPTEMBER 2003.

THE NEW PROCESS FROM 1 DECEMBER 2003

Stamp Duty Land Tax is a tax on transactions, not documents. For transactions in land and buildings in the UK, completed on or after 1 December 2003 you will no longer need to send in documents for stamping but will be required instead to complete and send in a land transaction return to our data capture centre. The land transaction return should be submitted to notify

- any transfer of a freehold or assignment or assignation of a lease for consideration, whether or not giving rise to a charge;
- any transaction for which relief is being claimed;
- the grant of a lease for a contractual term of 7 years or more or which gives rise to a charge;
- any other transaction giving rise to a charge.

N.B. Transactions where the rate is 0% will be notifiable, under Stamp Duty Land Tax, from 1 December **and a land transaction return will need to be completed for these transactions**. The 0% upper threshold remains at £60,000 for residential transactions but rises to £150,000 for non residential transactions. A list of the circumstances in which no land transaction return is required but where a self certificate will be required by HM Land Registry, Registers of Scotland or Land Registry Northern Ireland for registration of title, is detailed at the end of this note. For example, when there is a transaction in connection of a divorce.

The land transaction return replaces the Particulars Delivered forms. Documents and forms received with (or without in Scotland) PD forms for transactions completed on or after the 1 December will not be accepted.

For the vast majority of straightforward conveyances, the completion of the land transaction return and its submission to us along with the correct payment will be all that will be required of you.

Where additional information is required supplementary returns are required as follows:

SDLT2 – where there are more than two vendors (sellers) and/or two purchasers (buyers)

SDLT3 – where land is involved and further space is required in addition to the space provided on SDLT1

SDLT4 – for complex commercial transactions and leases.

You will be able to obtain land transaction returns, supplementary forms and guidance notes on how to complete the forms, from the IR Orderline by telephoning **0845 302 1472** from the end of **October/early November**. To assist this changeover, Stamp Offices will be forwarding blank land transaction returns when returning documents to you during November, for your use from 1 December for transactions within the scope of Stamp Duty Land Tax.

Part II ST

Submission of Plans

Accurate identification of property is of vital importance. If you are able to find out the National Land and Property Gazetteer Unique Property Reference Number (box 31 on the land transaction return), you should enter it on the return, as this will assist greatly in ensuring the correct identification of the property.

However, a plan submitted with the return can also be of great help in the identifcation process for certain types of property. Plans are required for development land, agricultural land and small "garden" plots. You do not need to submit plans for domestic property—this includes new housing developments where properties are often referred to by plot numbers.

Completing and Signing the Land Transaction Return

The detailed guidance notes should be used when completing the form which must be completed in **black ink**. The completed land transaction return **must legally be signed by the purchaser (buyer). If there is more than one purchaser it must be signed by all purchasers**. The return **may not** be signed by the purchaser's solicitor or agent.

It is the purchaser's responsibility to ensure that the information contained in the land transaction return is correct and complete.

The purchaser may request that their agent be authorised to handle correspondence on their behalf, by completing box 59 of the land transaction return, however the purchaser remains responsible for the return and the payment of the Stamp Duty Land Tax.

Each form has a unique reference number, so photocopies may not be used.

Where to Send the Land Transaction Return

The land transaction return must be sent to the Inland Revenue's rapid data capture centre within 30 days of the effective date of the transaction.

The full address is: Inland Revenue, Stamp Taxes, Comben House, Farriers Way, Netherton, Merseyside L30 4RN.

It is important not to send the returns to local Stamp Offices as this will delay the issue of a certificate. Local offices will not be able to process land transaction returns and will re-direct them to the data capture centre. You should send payment of Stamp Duty Land Tax at the same time as you submit the land transaction return. Payment may be made by

- cheque, enclosed with the return;
- electronic payment (BACS, CHAPS etc);
- at your bank, Post Office or by Alliance and Leicester/Giro account using the payslip.

The certificate will be based solely on information contained on the land transaction return (and where appropriate supplementary forms). Any additional information provided by way of covering letter or documents will not be considered. Therefore no covering letter, other information or documents should be submitted with the return unless you are submitting a plan because the land is for development, is agricultural or is a small "garden" plot.

Envelopes will be available, via the Orderline, with the Netherton DX (Document exchange) number provided for those firms that have this postal service.

What Happens At the Rapid Data Capture Centre

The completed land transaction return is scanned and the data optically-captured. The return will only be processed if it contains:

- a unique reference number;
- the liable person's name and address (the liable person is generally the purchaser);
- a signed declaration, signed by all purchasers;

- the effective date of the transaction (an explanation of what is an effective date is described in the frequently asked questions).

Land transaction returns that do not meet these basic requirements cannot be processed and so will be returned to customers. If other areas of the form are not completed, although we may be able to accept the form for processing we will seek that additional information through a follow up letter. To assist us in providing you with a quality service, we would urge you to complete the return as fully as possible to avoid delays.

Land Transaction Return Certificate

A certificate will be issued once the land transaction return has been processed at our data capture centre if

- all relevant information is provided;
- our own system check verifies the calculation of Stamp Duty Land Tax due;
- payment is enclosed.

The certificate replaces the impressed stamp and provides you with valid proof that Stamp Duty Land Tax has been paid. The certificate must be presented to HM Land Registry, Registers of Scotland or Land Registry Northern Ireland when applying for registration of title.

Late Returns

The Finance Act 2003 introduced a penalty for late notification and payment of Stamp Duty Land Tax. Where the land transaction return and/or payment is not received within 30 days of the effective date of the transaction (the filing date) but within three months of the 30 day limit, a penalty of £100 will be charged automatically. A penalty of £200 will be automatically charged in all other cases. Any late payment will also give rise to an interest charge.

Amended Returns

Where customers wish to query or amend information captured, they should write to a local Stamp Office who will have a facility to amend the original notification. An amendment may not be made more than 12 months after the filing date.

Circumstances When No Land Transaction Return Is Required

The following transactions do not need to be notified for Stamp Duty Land Tax purposes. However, you will need to certify that the transaction is exempt and submit, as now, that self-certificate to HM Land Registry, Registers of Scotland or Land Registry Northern Ireland when applying for registration of title. We have provided a special form for this purpose which is available from the Orderline.

(1) Transfer or conveyance of a freehold interest in land (in Scotland, ownership of land or the interest of the proprietor of the *dominium utile* of land) for no chargeable consideration.

(2) Transfer or assignment of a leasehold interest in land (in Scotland, assignation of a tenant's interest under a lease of land) for no chargeable consideration.

(3) Grant of lease (in Scotland, exchange of missives of let) where all the following are satisfied.
   - The term of the lease is less than seven years.
   - The amount of any premium is not such as to attract a charge to Stamp Duty Land Tax at a rate of 1% or more (ignoring the availability of any relief).
   - The amount of any rent is not such as to attract a charge to Stamp Duty Land Tax at a rate of 1% or higher (ignoring the availability of any relief).

(4) Other land transaction (for example, the grant of an easement or servitude) where the chargeable consideration is not such as to attract a charge to Stamp Duty Land Tax at a rate of 1% or higher (ignoring the availability of any relief).

(5) Land transaction exempt from Stamp Duty Land Tax under FA 2003 Sch 3 para 3 (transactions in connection with divorce).

(6) Land transaction exempt from Stamp Duty Land Tax under FA 2003 Sch 3 para 4 (variation of testamentary dispositions).

Self-certificate forms will be available from the IR Orderline and HM Land Registry, Registers of Scotland and Land Registry of Northern Ireland from 1 December. You can use photocopies of this form.

FREQUENTLY ASKED QUESTIONS

1. Why Do I Have To Send the Form To Netherton?

The Inland Revenue's rapid data capture centre in Netherton, near Liverpool, is one of the sites used for scanning a variety of Inland Revenue forms. This is where completed land transaction returns will be scanned in order to produce a Stamp Duty Land Tax certificate, the equivalent of the stamping process undertaken now. This certificate is the document you submit to HM Land Registry, the Registers of Scotland or the Land Registers of Northern Ireland in order to apply for registration of title.

Centralising and automating the process in this way will streamline the capture of your property information data and the production of the certificate with the aim of providing rapid and consistent turnaround times for you throughout the year. It is worth noting that our local Stamp Offices will not have this scanning facility so will be unable to offer an alternative service to that provided by the Netherton centre.

2. Why Does the Form Need To Be Signed By the Purchaser(s)?

Unlike the current stamp duty regime, Stamp duty Land Tax introduces a clearly identifiable liable person—usually the purchaser or lessee. This person is legally responsible, for notification and payment of Stamp Duty Land Tax. They will also be liable to pay any additional tax, interest or penalties arising as a result of a formal enquiry into the return. It is therefore important that the liable person satisfies him/herself that the information being provided on the land transaction return is complete and correct to the best of their knowledge. Following precedents in other taxes where there is a liable person, the best way for a liable person to confirm to Inland Revenue that they are satisfied with the information being provided is by way of signature on the return. This is a statutory requirement under Stamp Duty Land Tax and returns which are not signed will not be accepted.

3. Why Is the Land Transaction Return (SDLT1) Longer Than the LA451 ("Particulars Delivered")?

The new form replaces the information included on the LA451 and the supporting documents provided with it, which can be scrutinised by the Stamp Office. Although there are six pages to the new form, for most straightforward transactions (eg simple residential conveyances), less than half the boxes will need to be completed. The information requested is necessary for the correct liability to be established and for the tax to be properly and fairly administered. Comprehensive and accurate data supplied to us will be invaluable in building up a detailed picture of the property market and will help inform possible future policy and operational decisions on Stamp duty Land Tax.

4. Why Do I Have To Supply National Insurance Numbers?

The purchaser's National Insurance number is only required where the purchaser, or one of the purchaser's, is an individual. The Inland Revenue's main record system uses National Insurance numbers and as part of our modernisation programme we are linking into this system. This will allow Stamp Duty Land Tax to be administered more efficiently and fairly in line with our other mainstream taxes. We do however appreciate that not all individual purchasers may have a National Insurance number for example if the purchaser is a non-UK national. Our guidance notes to the form cover what you need to do in these circumstances.

5. Why Can't I Send In Documents As Previously?

In the vast majority of cases all the necessary data will have been provided on the form so it will no longer be necessary to send in documents as well. This will reduce the amount of paper to be sent through the post to us and should avoid any chance of valuable original documents going astray. The new process also represents a first step towards more streamlined ways of submitting data to us and helps prepare the way for possible future changes, such as the plans for an electronic conveyancing system to co-ordinate the electronic delivery of various aspects of the conveyancing process.

6. Can I Complete the Form Electronically?

We are currently looking at a number of ways to allow the form to be completed on-screen and are working closely with representative bodies and others. We'll keep you informed of our progress as we appreciate that many of you would welcome the opportunity to complete the form this way. Please look out for information about this in future bulletins and on our website.

7. What Are the Transitional Provisions For Land & Property Transactions That Take Place Around the December 2003 Changeover Date?

The transitional provisions are contained in FA 2003 Sch 19. This Schedule provides the rules for determining whether a transaction, entered into prior to 1 December 2003 which is completed after 1 December, is chargeable to Stamp Duty or Stamp Duty Land Tax. A flowchart is available to help you decide if the transaction is subject to Stamp Duty Land Tax on our website at: www.inlandrevenue.gov.uk/so/sdlt_flowchart.pdf.

Also, information and examples our provided in our Customer Newsletter Issue 3 available at www.inlandrevenue.gov.uk/so/newsletter3.pdf.

8. What Is the Effective Date Of a Transaction?

For the majority of transactions the effective date is the date of completion of the transaction, whether or not this is evidenced by a document. However if a contract is substantially performed before completion, the date on which substantial performance takes place is the effective date. Broadly substantial performance is the point at which

- Payment of a substantial amount of the consideration (generally 90% of the total amount) is made.
- The purchaser is entitled to possession of the property.
- The first payment of rent is made.
- Option or right of pre-emption—is when the option or right is acquired.

9. What Records Covering Transactions Need To Be Retained and For How Long?

The new arrangements for Stamp Duty land Tax are built on the basis of a "process now—check later" system. This is again in line with the way that the Inland Revenue administers other taxes. In order to undertake the "check later" part of this, we will select a small number of transactions for enquiry. In those cases we will ask for supporting evidence concerning the particular property transaction. All records supporting transactions should be kept for six financial years. It is the responsibility of the purchaser to ensure records are kept.

Examples of the types of records that need to be retained are detailed below but the list is not exhaustive:

– A contract/agreement for sale and any related papers.
– Professional valuations of both the land and any apportionments of fixed fixtures and loose fittings, if such valuations were obtained at the time.

Part II ST

– Relevant instruments relating to the transaction, in particular any contract or conveyance, and any supporting maps, plans or similar documents.

10. How Do I Find Out If the Property Is In a Disadvantaged Area and Qualifies For Relief?

There is an on-line "postcode tool" on our website at: http://home.inrev.gov.uk/inlandrevenue/so/pcode_search.htm.

This will enable you to determine whether a property is in a disadvantaged area from the postcode.. Where exceptionally the answer cannot be found, for example for a new property that has only just received a postcode, you can gain further guidance from our Enquiry Line by telephoning 0845 603 0135.

We are looking at other ways of improving how this information is provided to you. Full details will be provided on our website.

We would also like to clarify a point arising from an overview of the changes that we made in issue 3.

In the previous bulletin where an overview of some of the changes to Stamp Duty was provided including the point that for transactions completed on or after 1 December 2003, legal practitioners will no longer need to submit documents, on behalf of purchasers, to the Inland Revenue for stamping. Instead they will have to notify liability to tax using the new land transaction return. Payment should be sent at the same time as the return to the Inland Revenue processing centre in Netherton. Provided information and payment are submitted in full, the Inland Revenue will issue a stamp duty land certificate which they or their agents will need to submit to land registries in order to register ownership of land or to record a deed, as appropriate. The certificate replaces the current stamped impressions, which are made onto documents.

We would like to clarify that this is subject to transitional provisions under which certain transactions effected in pursuance of contracts entered into on or before Royal Assent of the Finance Act (10 July 2003) remain subject to Stamp Duty.

INLAND REVENUE TAX BULLETIN ISSUE 67. OCTOBER 2003.

PAGE 1059. CHANGES TO STAMP DUTY

Introduction

The Finance Act 2003 sets out the framework for stamp duty land tax, which will be introduced on 1 December 2003 to replace the existing stamp duty regime on UK land and buildings for all transactions completed on or after that date. Stamp duty in its current form will therefore cease to apply to transfers of other property for contracts entered into on or after 1 December 2003.

Reform of the stamp duty regime paves the way for the introduction of e-conveyancing systems which will allow purchases of property to be effected or registered electronically, making the acquisition of property faster and more efficient.

The vast majority of individuals buying or renting residential property will see no immediate changes under the new regime, though there will be some administrative changes of which practitioners need to be aware. In most residential purchase cases liability to stamp duty land tax should be reported and duty paid, as now, within 30 days of completion.

The reform builds on measures introduced in Finance Act 2002 to tackle avoidance of stamp duty on certain property transactions, and modernises the compliance regime for stamp duty by bringing it into line with other taxes and incorporating appropriate enforcement powers. There will be new processes for reporting the details of land transactions and for paying any tax due.

Scope of Stamp Duty Land Tax

Broadly the scope of stamp duty land tax will cover all transactions involving land in the UK. There are a number of exclusions, including mortgages and similar security interests, licences to use or occupy land and transactions for no chargeable consideration. The charge will include transfers of freehold property and assignments and assignations of leases, grants of leases (including in Scotland, exchange of missives of let), and options and rights of pre-emption in respect of land transactions.

There will also be a charge on contracts for land transactions which are "substantially performed" either by the payment of rent, or by the payment of substantially the whole (normally at least 90%) of the purchase price or because the contracting purchaser takes possession.

The new regime will expand a range of anti-avoidance powers to discourage the transfer of properties into companies (sometimes called special purpose vehicles) in certain circumstances. A number of changes to the group and acquisition relief clawback provisions will be introduced with immediate effect, including extending the period in which these clawbacks can be withdrawn to three years.

It will also see the abolition of stamp duty on transactions involving property other than land, shares and interests in partnerships. This de-regulation will take many transactions out of stamp duty altogether, including transfers of book debts and other receivables.

The existing stamp duty regime will continue to apply to stocks, marketable securities and bearer instruments, and transfers of land into or out of partnerships by partners or former partners, and acquisitions of an interest in a partnership. It may also apply to transactions completed and leases granted on or after 1 December 2003 where those conveyances and leases fulfil contracts or agreements entered into on or before Royal Assent of the Finance Act 2003 on 10 July 2003.

Stamp duty land tax will also introduce the concept of a '"liable person" for the purposes of the tax. In most cases this will be the purchaser or lessee—whoever is acquiring the benefit of the property.

Further Consultation

Consultation will continue on certain key aspects of the regime. These include the transfer of land into and out of a partnership by a partner, and the transfer of interests in partnerships that hold UK land, the approach to large developments, sale and leaseback deals and securitisation of land. Any changes arising from the consultation may be enacted either on implementation of the new regime or in Finance Act 2004.

Administration of Stamp Duty Land Tax—What Practitioners Will Need To Do

When the new system is implemented for transactions completed on or after 1 December 2003, practitioners will no longer need to submit documents, on behalf of purchasers, to the Inland Revenue for stamping. Instead they will have to notify liability to tax using the new land transaction return. Payment should be sent at the same time as the return to the Inland Revenue processing centre in Netherton. Any Inland Revenue stamp office will be able to forward returns and payments to Netherton on behalf of individuals, but customers will benefit from a quicker service if they make their returns direct to Netherton. Provided information and payment are submitted in full, the Inland Revenue will issue a stamp duty land tax certificate which purchasers or their advisers will need to submit to land registries in order to register ownership of land or to record a deed, as appropriate. The certificate replaces the current stamped impressions, which are made onto documents.

In broad terms, land transaction returns should be submitted to the Inland Revenue for transactions that cover any transfer of a freehold, assignment or assignation of a lease for consideration, whether or not giving rise to a charge, and any transaction for which a relief is being claimed. They should also be submitted for the grant of a lease for a contractual term of seven years or more or which gives rise to a charge, and any other transaction giving rise to a charge.

In line with other taxes administered by the Inland Revenue, stamp duty land tax will be administered under a "process now, check later" system. From the filing date of the return, there will be an "enquiry window" (the period during which the Inland Revenue can open an enquiry or an individual can request that an enquiry be opened into a transaction). This will be a period of nine months for all transactions. Purchasers must keep suitable records for six years from the effective date.

Rates and Thresholds

For freehold transfers and assignments or assignations of leases, and for the premium element of new leases, the rates and thresholds will be the same as at present, except that for non-residential property the nil-rate limit is increased from £60,000 to £150,000.

There will be a new structure for charging the rental element on the grant of a new lease. The charge will be based on the "net present value" of the rentals payable under the lease. We shall give more details of the charge on the rental element of new leases shortly.

Under the new regime, there will be cases where no tax is due, for instance where a relief can be claimed or where the transaction is below the nil-rate band threshold. The threshold will be £60,000 for residential property and £150,000 in other cases.

In these cases purchasers may still have to make a return to the Inland Revenue or, in certain cases, provide a self-certificate to the land registries (which includes any register maintained by the Keeper of Registers of Scotland and, in Northern Ireland, the Land Register of Northern Ireland and the Registry of Deeds).

Reliefs

Reliefs that have been carried forward from the existing regime include transfers between group companies, transfers arising from company reconstructions and certain purchases and leases by registered social landlords. In addition, there will also be new reliefs for the modernised regime. These include acquisitions of dwellings by house-building companies in part-exchange for the sale of a new home, acquisition of dwellings by relocation companies, and acquisitions by local authorities or public bodies under compulsory purchase orders or under the terms of planning arrangements.

Since 10 April 2003, stamp duty has not been due on certain non-residential property transactions in designated disadvantaged areas. This builds on the existing exemption from stamp duty on all property in disadvantaged areas where the consideration does not exceed £150,000. A full list of qualifying areas is available on the Inland Revenue website at www.inlandrevenue.gov.uk/so. Customers who do not have access to the Internet can also receive advice on this and other stamp duty issues from the Stamp Taxes Enquiry Line on 0845 6030135.

Special rules will apply to certain transactions. They include transfers between companies and connected parties, collective enfranchisement by leaseholders and crofting community right to buy schemes, alternative property financing arrangements for individuals (which can be used, for instance, to provide "Islamic mortgages"). Also included will be acquisitions of dwellings under shared ownership schemes, and right to buy and rent to mortgage transactions.

Developing a Compliance Regime

The modernised regime will bring a modern, comprehensive compliance framework to stamp duty for the first time. An enquiry regime will be implemented which will mirror provisions already in place for other taxes administered by the Inland Revenue such as Income Tax and Corporation Tax. The main enquiry regime will be underpinned by a risk assessment process. A random enquiry programme will be implemented to enable us to measure the effectiveness of our compliance approach.

We are also taking forward work related to the practicalities of the enquiry regime, including a Code of Practice covering how those enquiries are to be handled and an appeals process.

We will also develop a compliance regime around exempt instrument transactions and stamp duty certificates.

Further Information

Further details are available in the Inland Revenue's Finance Bill 2003 press notice (REV 55) and Budget day press notice, PN05: Modernising the Taxation of Property. Both of these can be found on the Stamp Taxes' website at www.inlandrevenue.gov.uk/so/news.htm. Customers who do not have access to the Internet can also call the Stamp Taxes Enquiry Line on 0845 6030135. For more information on the further consultation we are undertaking on certain policy measures, contact Des Newman, Stamp Taxes Policy team at msd.stampscondoc@ir.gsi.gov.uk.

A draft of the Stamp Duty Land Tax manual which will only be available electronically was published on the Internet at www.inlandrevenue.gov.uk/so/ during the week commencing 22 September 2003. We would welcome constructive feedback. Please forward your responses to Viv Scrimshire by e mail or post to the following address: Room 116, 3rd Floor New Wing, Somerset House, Strand, London WC2R 1LB, E mail: Vivienne.Scrimshire@ir.gsi.gov.uk.

Information Bulletins and SDLT Customer Newsletters

The first issues in a series of Information Bulletins have been produced and mailed to around 10,000 firms of solicitors who have had contact with our Stamp Offices in the past. These bulletins will continue to be produced in the run up to the commencement of the changes. The aim of the bulletins is to keep customers informed of developments on an ongoing basis. They will be produced every 4 to 6 weeks.

We have also recently begun to publish SDLT Customer Newsletters. The newsletters will provide more detailed information relating to specific areas of the changes and how they will affect our customers. These will also be published every 4 to 6 weeks.

Both of these publications are available from the eight Stamp Offices across the country and on our website at www.inlandrevenue.gov.uk/so/land_tax_changes.htm.

STAMP DUTY INFORMATION BULLETIN ISSUE 5. NOVEMBER 2003.

In presenting his 2003 Budget, the Chancellor promised that further consultation with interested parties would continue in connection with the Stamp Duty Land Tax charge on leases. Following this consultation, an announcement has been made about the changes to be implemented to FA 2003 Sch 5 (which deals with the Stamp Duty Land Tax treatment of leases) for 1 December 2003.

This issue will primarily cover the technical changes to Stamp Duty Land Tax on the rental element of leases ("lease duty") that are proposed and which will be debated before implementation. These will have the effect of

- removing uncertainty in the treatment of some leases,
- keeping the compliance burden to a minimum, and
- ensuring that taxpayers know what duty they will have to pay.

The amendments are:

1) POST 5 YEAR RENT CHANGES

Currently, where rent changes are known and included in the terms of a lease from the outset, they are fully taken into account in calculating the Net Present Value (NPV) of the lease (unless they are increases only to reflect the Retail Price Index (RPI)). However, where rent changes are made, after two years, to reflect market rents, these changes are ignored for the purposes of calculating the NPV.

The proposals wish to remove this disparity of treatment. Therefore, it is proposed that **all** rent changes after 5 years are ignored for the purposes of the NPV calculation and, for rental due after 5 years, the highest rent paid in any previous period of 12 months is substituted and used in the calculation. This will provide comparability of treatment for these types of lease.

2) LEASES WITH UNCERTAIN RENT

Where rent is expressed as relating to turnover, or where there are rent sharing or similar measures in place, the lessee is required to make a reasonable estimate of the rent due and include this estimate in their land transaction return. When any part of this estimated rent is determined, they must make an amended return including that part of the rent which is now determined. Representations have been received that this could place a severe compliance burden on many small businesses whose rent is determined by monthly turnover.

To simplify this area, it is proposed to amend Finance Act 2003 so that, where a lease has a rent which is still uncertain after five years (eg a turnover based lease for 15 years), **one and only one** additional return is required at the five year point.

This return will base the NPV on the actual rent paid in the first five years and (for any post five year rent due) will apply the amendment at (1) above ie the highest rent paid in any 12 month period over the previous five years will be used in the NPV calculation.

Where all the uncertainty in the rental of a lease is determined before five years, **one and only one** additional return is required at that point.

These measures will provide certainty and substantially reduce the compliance burden for small businesses.

3) CONTINGENCIES

Amendments will be made to clarify that break and forfeiture clauses in a lease do not operate to artificially shorten the term of a lease in the NPV calculation. Similarly, options to renew, contained in the lease, will not be treated as a contingency extending the term of a lease.

4) EXTENSIONS TO LEASES DURING THEIR TERM

An amendment will be introduced so that where a lease is extended during the currency of its term, this extension is treated as the grant of a new lease for the period by which the term of the lease is extended. This will be treated as a transaction linked with the original grant and, if not already notifiable, should the total term then extend to seven or more years, the whole transaction will be notifiable.

5) CONTINUATION OF LEASES AND LEASES FOR AN INDEFINITE TERM

Currently, where there is a lease for a fixed term and thereafter, this term is defined as the term plus such further period as must elapse before the earliest date at which the lease can be determined. This will be amended so that the term is defined as the term specified in the lease.

Where a lease comes to the end of its term but the landlord does not require possession of the property, this extension is treated, in England and Wales, as a periodic tenancy which extends the term of the lease. In Scotland, there is a similar treatment called tacit relocation. Currently, the treatment of this extension is unclear and an amendment will be introduced to clarify the situation. Where a lease continues after the end of its term, this extension will be deemed to be the grant of a new lease for the period of 12 months (or the original term of the previous lease) if shorter. Should this continue past this period, it will be deemed to be another lease of similar length and so on. These leases will be linked transactions and similar notification requirements will apply should the total period of these leases extend to seven years or more (if they are not already notifiable). This will also apply in Scotland, where the lease is for an unspecified term at the outset.

ANTI AVOIDANCE

To prevent avoidance of Stamp Duty Land Tax using these amendments, it is proposed that, after the five year point when rent changes are not taken into account in the NPV, if the rent rises by more than 5% + RPI annually, this rent increase is deemed to be the grant of a new lease in a similar way to the way Paragraph 10 Schedule 5 already treats rent increases not included in the terms of a lease.

Currently, assignments of leases where the payment of a premium is **not** involved are Stamp Duty Land Tax transactions but the assumption of the obligation to pay rent is not treated as consideration. Therefore, no duty is paid on these type assignments. It is proposed to change this treatment in a limited variety of circumstances. Where the lease, at the previous transaction, benefited from a relief, so that the duty payable was reduced or eliminated, assignment of such a lease will be deemed to be the grant of a lease by the assignor to the assignee. This will prevent the use of reliefs to avoid Stamp Duty Land Tax.

FURTHER CONSULTATION ON THE TREATMENT OF PARTNERSHIPS UNDER STAMP DUTY LAND TAX

Consultation will continue on the transfer of land into and out of a partnership by a partner, and the transfer of interests in partnerships that hold UK land. Any changes arising from the consultation may be enacted either on implementation of the new regime or in Finance Act 2004.

The draft partnership legislation is on the website at www.inlandrevenue.gov.uk/so/. Contri butions should be made to John Neale, e mail address; John.Neale@ir.gsi.gov.uk.

NEW STAMP DUTY LAND TAX RETURN FORMS

The new returns are currently being printed and will be available from the Inland Revenue orderline 0845 3021472 from 17 November.

STARTER PACKS

To provide extra help for you at the start of Stamp Duty Land Tax, we shall be sending each of you a "starter pack" containing a small initial supply of returns as follows:

SDLT 1

SDLT 2, 3 & 4's

SDLT 6

Example—of a correctly completed residential return (further explanations of the use of each return is given below). This pack will be issued to all Solicitors who are detailed on our customer database. Licensed Conveyancers will receive their packs through the Council for Licensed Conveyancers.

This initial supply should reach you by 24 November and is aimed at ensuring that everyone who needs forms will have an initial working supply for the start of Stamp Duty Land Tax. Quite separately, you should also order your bulk supply through the orderline.

Given that demand is likely to be high, the order line will be very busy, but everyone who places an order will receive their bulk supplies. In the meantime, you may find the starter pack ensures you have an initial supply to be getting on with.

Local Stamp Offices will also receive small stocks of the returns at this time. So if for any reason you find yourself without returns and need some urgently, you can collect them from local offices. Whilst they will be pleased to supply returns to personal callers, please note they will not have sufficient stock nor the facilities to mail the returns to you.

RETURNS AND GUIDANCE NOTE ON THE WEBSITE

In the meantime the following samples can be viewed on our website at www.inlandrevenue.gov.uk/so/sdlt_website.htm to enable you to view and become more familiar with the new returns.

The SDLT1 is the main Land Transaction Return which must be completed for all transactions. We expect this form to cover the vast majority of residential transactions.

In a minority of more complex cases the following supplementary returns may also need to be completed.

SDLT2 must be completed only where there are more than two vendors and/or purchasers.

SDLT3 must be completed only where additional information is required to identify the property or the transaction involves more than one property.

SDLT4 must be completed only where additional information is required about the transaction, for example when the purchaser is a company, where land is part of a business sale agreement, some leases.

SDLT6 is the guidance notes for the completion of the Land Transaction Return. We will be unable to accept photocopies of the SDLT1 as each return has a unique reference number printed on the return. You should therefore ensure that you maintain a sufficient supply of the return since we will reject photocopied versions of SDLT1. [You may, however, use photocopies of SDLT2, 3 and 4.]

It is our intention to open up an electronic channel to enable customers to submit returns via the Inland Revenue Web-site. This will not be available until the summer of 2004, but in the meantime interim arrangements are being set up to provide alternative channels of submission, both which enable on-screen completion of the forms.

SUBSTITUTE RETURNS

We have been working closely with providers of legal software and electronic forms to enable them to add the Stamp Duty Land Tax returns to their products. These include Oyez, Laserforms, Peapod and other providers. However, you will need to check with your provider about their plans and any timetable for providing Stamp Duty Land Tax returns.

We are looking at other ways to enable customers to complete approved forms on screen and on-line. Further information about filing options will be given in due course.

You will be able to order a bulk supply of payslips and each will have a unique identifier printed on them which will need to be entered onto the substitute form to make it a valid return and enable us to link payments with the completed return.

THE ENQUIRY REGIME
PROCESS NOW—CHECK LATER

Stamp Duty Land Tax is a tax on transactions, not documents. For transactions in land and buildings in the UK, completed on or after 1 December 2003 customers will no longer need to send in documents for stamping but will be required instead to complete and send in a land transaction return to our data capture centre in Netherton.

The enquiry regime to be implemented will mirror provisions already in place for other taxes administered by the Inland Revenue.

In line with other taxes Stamp Duty Land Tax will introduce the concept of "process now, check later". This will also apply to reliefs where you need to complete the land transaction return and relevant box to claim the relief. The obligation to retain the records remains with the client as the liable person.

We want everyone to pay the right amount of Stamp Duty Land Tax; no more, no less. We also want people to feel confident that:

- Other taxpayers are paying what they should.
- We operate the tax system fairly.

In order to do this, we will enquire into some land transaction returns. This means that we will ask for further information to help us to understand the amount of Stamp Duty Land Tax paid or to confirm that a relief is due and to check that it is right. We want to make sure you do not pay too much Stamp Duty Land Tax or too little. Either way, we will tell you if we find something wrong.

RANDOM AND RISK BASED ENQUIRIES

A small selection of returns will be selected for review. Some enquiries will be selected at random and others will be selected on a risk basis. The overwhelming majority of transactions will be accepted and certificates issued without an enquiry.

ENQUIRY WINDOW

We will have a fixed time that we can start an enquiry—this is known as the enquiry window and is a period of 9 months:

- After the filing date, if the return was delivered on or before that date.
- After the date on which the return was delivered, if the return was delivered after the filing date.
- After the date on which the amendment was made.

Enquiries will also be conducted into self-certificates given to the land registries.

Any enquiry will start with a letter to the purchaser with a copy sent to their professional adviser, if they have completed the correspondence box on the land transaction return (SDLT1). At the end of the enquiry a letter closing the enquiry will be issued to your client and copied to yourselves, again where the correspondence box has been completed (question 59 page 5 of SDLT1).

RETENTION OF RECORDS

In line with other taxes, records supporting transactions must be retained for six years. However, we are not expecting professional advisers to keep any additional records than the records that you already retain.

An example of the types of records include the following, however this list is not exhaustive:

- A contract/agreement for sale and any related side papers.
- Details of any apportionment of consideration between the land transaction and other transactions (eg purchase of chattels/moveables).
- Any professional valuations that have been obtained.
- Relevant instruments relating to the transaction, in particular any contract or conveyance, and any supporting maps, plans or similar documents.
- Partnership agreements.
- Completion documents.
- Records of relevant payments, receipts and financial arrangements.
- Deed of attorney, where you have the power of attorney in particular cases.

INTEREST AND PENALTIES

As well as the penalties and interest mentioned earlier for submitting the land transaction return late, a penalty and interest may be due if we find something wrong with a return. We can only seek penalties for incorrect returns if tax is underpaid and the error was due to negligence or fraud.

When calculating any penalty we will take into account:

– The extent to which you voluntarily disclosed anything that was wrong,
– Your help in concluding our enquiries, and
– The seriousness of the errors or omissions.

APPEALS

At present a stamp duty payer can only appeal against an adjudication directly to the High Court. Under Stamp Duty Land Tax there will be a range of appeals to both the General and Special Commissioners in line with other taxes with disputes about valuation being referred to the appropriate valuation tribunal.

The normal time limit for making appeals is 30 days.

FURTHER INFORMATION

We are currently producing Code of Practice leaflets and enquiries, appeals and penalties leaflets specifically relating to Stamp Duty Land Tax and these will be available from the date of implementation. Details will be available on our website at www.inlandrevenue.gov.uk/so/.

CONFIRMATION THAT THE HOLDER OF A POWER OF ATTORNEY CAN SIGN A STAMP DUTY

Land Tax Land Transaction Return

Further to the previous bulletin which included details on completing and signing the new land transaction return, it should be noted that although the return **may not** be signed by the purchaser's solicitor or agent, the holder of a Power of Attorney may sign. The holder of a Power of Attorney must indicate they are signing in that capacity within the space provided in box 71. Also they need to write "Power of Attorney" underneath the signature. The deed of attorney itself does not need to be submitted with the return.

We would also like to clarify a point arising from the last issue. Under the heading "Where to send the land transaction return" it was stated that the certificate will be based solely on information contained on the land transaction return (and where appropriate supplementary forms) and that any additional information provided by way of covering letter or documents will not be considered by us. This is incorrect and we would like to confirm that we will consider any additional information that is provided in a covering letter or document.

UPDATING OUR MAILING LISTS FOR THESE LEAFLETS

If you want to receive additional copies of this leaflet, are aware of a colleague who would like to be added to it or alternatively be removed from our mailing list, please contact Vanessa Jenkins on msd.stampscondoc@ir.gsi.gov.uk.

INLAND REVENUE TAX BULLETIN ISSUE 70. APRIL 2004.

PAGE 1099. STAMP DUTY LAND TAX: GROUP RELIEF

1. This article gives practical and technical guidance on claims for group relief in Stamp Duty Land Tax under Schedule 7 to the Finance Act 2003. It deals with material which was previously covered by the Statement of Practice issued for stamp duty group relief, SP3/98 published on 13 October 1998. That Statement does not apply to Stamp Duty Land Tax but will continue to apply to stamp duty.

How To Claim Group Relief In Stamp Duty Land Tax

2. In contrast to stamp duty, documents must not be submitted with a claim. The claim should be made on form SDLT1 by putting a cross at box 9 and inserting code 12.

3. Following procedures for other returns within Stamp Duty Land Tax, the certificate that enables title to be registered will be issued provided that the return is complete. Certificates will not be delayed simply because the Inland Revenue may wish to enquire into particular aspects of the return including a claim to group relief.

[**4.** The relief is self-assessed and will be dealt with on a "process now/check later" basis along with all other Stamp Duty Land Tax matters. Under Stamp Duty Land Tax the Inland Revenue does not require the preparation and submission of the letter of claim covered in (see paragraph 6.163 of the Inland Revenue Stamp Taxes manual). [*Note*: this para is printed here as amended by Tax Bulletin Issue 73.]]

5. This means that companies must judge the admissibility of the claim themselves. Under Stamp Duty Land Tax the Inland Revenue has the power to assess and collect under-declared tax and seek penalties in cases where errors in returns (including errors in group relief claims) are the result of negligence or fraud.

Enquiries Involving Group Relief Claims

6. If the decision is taken to enquire into a return where the transaction is subject to a group relief claim, the Inland Revenue will open an enquiry under FA 2003 Sch 10 para 12. The enquiry must be made within 9 months of the filing date. Enquiries may cover all aspects of the return and will not necessarily be limited to the group relief claim itself.

7. The decision to enquire into a transaction will be made after the certificate (form SDLT5) is issued and will not therefore delay registration of title. But the issue of the certificate should not be taken as an indication that the Inland Revenue either accepts the validity of a group relief claim or has chosen not to enquire into that return.

8. Enquiries will consider all aspects of the transaction, including the group relief claim. Documents may be called for and these may include the instruments of transfer and related documents. The Inland Revenue may also ask for more information about the claim. In particular, evidence may be sought to show that the tests in paragraphs 1 and 2 of Schedule 7 were met.

9. If the evidence presented does not support the claim the self assessment will be amended to remove the relief.

Paragraph 1 of Schedule 7

10. Paragraph 1 of Schedule 7 to FA 2003 provides exemption from Stamp Duty Land Tax where, at the effective date of the transaction, the companies are members of the same group. Exemption extends to the grant of leases between group companies.

Meaning of Company

11. Relief is extended to any "body corporate" through the definition of "company" in FA 2003 s 100(1). To determine whether an entity qualifies as a body corporate the Inland Revenue will follow the guidelines for stamp duty set out at paragraph 6.124 of the Stamp Taxes Manual.

Meaning of subsidiary

12. Paragraph 1(2)(*b*) requires that the companies claiming relief must be 75% subsidiaries of one another or 75% subsidiaries of a third company.

13. Paragraph 1(3) provides that for a company (A) to be a 75% subsidiary of another company (B) if:

- company B is the beneficial owner of at least 75% of the ordinary share capital of company A;

- it is beneficially entitled to not less than 75% of profits available for distribution to equity holders; and
- it would be entitled to not less than 75% of any assets of A available for distribution to equity holders on winding up.

14. Paragraph 1(4) provides that "ownership" for these purposes is either directly or indirectly through another company or group of companies. The rules in TA 1988 s 838(5)–(10) apply to determine the amount of ordinary share capital. Paragraph 1(5) defines "ordinary share capital".

15. TA 1988 Sch 18 para 1(6) which defines "equity holder".

16. The meaning of subsidiary is also relevant to the arrangements test in paragraph 2(2)(*b*) of Schedule 7 (see 19 below).

17. The tests in paragraph 1 of Schedule 7 apply independently of the tests in paragraph 2 and claims are not allowable if these tests are not met.

Paragraph 2 of Schedule 7

18. Paragraph 2 provides anti-avoidance rules which restrict the availability of group relief. It will prevent relief being allowable in circumstances where certain "arrangements" are in place.

Meaning of Arrangements

19. "Arrangements is defined generally for the purposes of paragraph 2 in paragraph 2(5) to include any scheme, arrangement or understanding, whether or not legally enforceable". This definition is used in FA 1986 s 76(6A)(*b*) (inserted by FA 2002 s 112(6)) but "arrangements" was not defined for the equivalent stamp duty provisions in FA 1930 s 42(2) or FA 1967 s 27(2). Under this new definition, "arrangements" will include schemes, arrangements or understandings not in writing and the existence of arrangements in a particular claim will depend on a consideration of all of the facts relating to the claim and the surrounding circumstances.

20. In considering whether arrangements exist that might disqualify the claim, the Inland Revenue will seek to establish whether there was any scheme arrangement or understanding.

Paragraph 2(1): Arrangements For Change of Control of Purchaser

21. Paragraph 2(1) prevents a claim to group relief if arrangements are in existence at the time of the claim for a person (or persons together) to obtain control of the purchaser but not the vendor. Arrangements under paragraph 2(1) have to be in existence at the effective date of the transaction.

22. Where there is a change of control, paragraph 2(1) is intended to prevent avoidance of Stamp Duty Land Tax by passing property, or an economic interest in it, out of the group.

23. The statements of the Economic Secretary during debate in Parliament on the equivalent stamp duty provision in Finance Act 2000 are still relevant. The Economic Secretary said:

> "I have received representations expressing concern about the blocking of relief for transfers from the company about to leave the group to another group member—in other words, when the company leaving the group is the transferor. I am persuaded that there are commercial situations in which an asset is transferred to another group company after arrangements are in place for the transferor company to leave the group. In a sense, therefore, the asset never leaves the original group. I am willing to make a concession for such cases, which will be useful to businesses, as their legal advisers have suggested.
>
> I have some worry that it might be possible to construct avoidance devices from the concession, so I have asked the Stamp Office to monitor carefully the use of the relief. If the concession is abused, the Government will not hesitate to act swiftly."

(see Hansard 18 July 2000, column 253)

24. The Inland Revenue will not argue that paragraph 2(1) denies group relief in cases where the transferor is to leave the group having transferred the land to other group members.

25. Furthermore, paragraph 2(1) does not apply if the arrangements that are in place are those for the acquisition of shares by a company under a reconstruction as long as the conditions in paragraph 2(1)(*a*), (*b*) and (*c*) are met. These are:

- that FA 1986 s 75 will apply to the acquisition and the conditions for relief under that section will be met;
- that after the acquisition the purchaser will be a member of the same group as the acquiring company.

Paragraph 2(2) of Schedule 7

26. Paragraph 2(2)(*a*) denies relief where there are arrangements under which consideration is to be provided or received (directly or indirectly) by a person other than a group company.

27. Where group relief is claimed the Inland Revenue will consider all of the facts and interpret paragraph 2(2)(*a*) as not denying relief unless the loan finance is provided as part of a scheme to save Stamp Duty Land Tax when the property or an interest in it leaves the group.

28. For example, it is unlikely that there will be arrangements within paragraph 2(2)(*a*) if:

- the claim is not to be followed by a sale or underlease outside the group; or
- the claim is followed by a sale or underlease outside the group but Stamp Duty Land Tax is to be paid by the purchaser outside the group on consideration close to market value (or is deemed to be a grant of a lease under FA 2003 Sch 17A para 11), then again it is unlikely that relief will be prevented by paragraph 2(2)(*a*).

29. Loans from commercial lenders on ordinary commercial terms to facilitate the transfer between group members will also not normally disqualify a claim for the purposes of the arrangements test in paragraph 2(2)(*a*). For example, a claim can be accepted if:

- a specific loan is taken for the purchase of the asset; or
- the loan is secured on the asset; or
- arrangements are made to replace or novate an existing charge on the property transferred.

30. Paragraphs 27 to 29 above are limited to paragraph 2(2)(*a*) of Schedule 7. They do not mean that if other tests in paragraphs 1 and 2 of Schedule 7 are not met the claim is acceptable.

31. When an enquiry is opened the case will be considered on their particular facts. Some examples of the type of circumstances which the Inland Revenue might want to examine in more detail during an enquiry are where the claim is part of (or is to be followed by):

- the creation or transfer of loan stock or equity capital;
- a capital reorganisation of the transferee;
- a guarantee by a third party not associated with the group;
- the creation of a new charge or financial arrangement whereby title to the property is, or may be, vested in the lender otherwise than in satisfaction of all or part of the debt; or
- the assignment of the freehold reversion or the intra-group lease to a person outside the group.

32. Other circumstances which can indicate that the claim is not admissible include where:

- all or part of the consideration for the transaction is to remain outstanding or is represented by intra-group debt, (as the aim and effect may be to reduce the value of the transferee company on a possible future sale outside the group); or
- the existing shareholders of the transferee include shareholders outside the group and the transaction is to be followed by the declaration of a dividend in specie, or by the liquidation of the transferee.

Subsales and Group Relief In Stamp Duty Land Tax

33. Paragraph 2(2) provides rules for Stamp Duty Land Tax based on those for stamp duty in FA 1967 s 27(3). FA 1967 s 27(3)(*b*) (intended to prevent acquisitions of land from outside the group without stamp duty being paid) is not included in Schedule 7 and this is because the problem it seeks to address, resting on contracts, is not relevant to Stamp Duty Land Tax. It is not possible to "rest on contract" to avoid Stamp Duty Land Tax because of the "substantial" performance rule in FA 2003 s 44.

Paragraph 2(2)(b): Arrangements For the Purchaser To Cease To Be a Member of the Same Group

34. A claim for relief is not appropriate if there are arrangements for the purchaser to cease to be a 75% subsidiary of the vendor or a third company. In deciding whether there are any such arrangements, the practical likelihood of the scheme being carried through is not in itself relevant.

35. But the Inland Revenue will not take the view that just because land is transferred to a group company which does nothing other than hold property it follows that there are arrangements for the purchaser to leave the group. We recognise that there are many commercial reasons why groups may transfer property internally. It is necessary to consider the full circumstances of the case to decide whether such arrangements are in place.

36. Whether such arrangements were or were not in place must be decided at the time of the return and Inland Revenue enquiries will seek to establish the facts at the effective date of the transaction.

Relevance of Arrangements Under Paragraph 2 To a Recovery of Tax Under Paragraph 3 ("Clawback")

37. Paragraph 3 of Schedule 7 is independent of paragraph 2. When an enquiry is made into a claim the question will be the admissibility of the claim itself in accordance with the statutory provisions. The fact that the arrangements, if carried out as planned, could lead to a recovery or will be exempt from a recovery will not mean that claim itself is allowable except as provided in paragraph 2.

Paragraph 3(1)(a)(ii): Arrangements During the Three Year Recovery Period

38. Paragraph 3 imposes a requirement to make a return (under FA 2003 s 81) for the withdrawal of relief when the purchaser ceases to be a member of the same group within three years of the effective date of the transaction.

39. Paragraph 3(1)(*a*) deals with the recovery period. Paragraph 3(1)(*a*)(ii) provides that group relief will be recovered if the transfer outside the group after the end of the period is under arrangements made before the end of the period.

40. "Arrangements" is defined in paragraph 3(4) with the same definition as in paragraph 2.

41. When there is a transfer outside the group, companies will need to decide whether to make a return under section 81. If the transfer outside the group is after the end of the three year period, companies will still need to consider whether there were arrangements in place for the transfer during the three year period. To make this decision a proper consideration of all of the circumstances will be required.

42. The Inland Revenue will not assume that just because a company is transferred outside the group shortly after the end of the three year period it will be in accordance with arrangements made within the three year period. We will only seek to argue that there should have been a recovery return if the facts of the case point to there having been such arrangements.

Section 54(4) FA 2003: Exception From the Connected Company Charge on a Winding Up

[**43.** FA 2003 s 54(4) provides the third case of exception from the deemed market value rule in FA 2003 s 53. The exception applies to the distribution of assets on the winding up of a company, as long as the subject matter of the transaction or an interest from which that interest is derived, has not been the subject of a transaction in respect of which a claim to group relief was made by the vendor. But it is not the Inland Revenue's intention that section 54(4) should be prevented from applying where a group relief claim was made by the vendor but recovered under paragraph 3 of Schedule 7 either at the time of or before the effective date of the transaction. [*Note*: this paragraph is printed as amended by Tax Bulletins 71 and 74.]]

INLAND REVENUE TAX BULLETIN ISSUE 71. JUNE 2004.

PAGE 1115. COMPLIANCE UNDER STAMP DUTY LAND TAX (SDLT)

In an earlier issue we gave you a basic understanding of the new Stamp Duty Land Tax (SDLT). This is a brief guide to the new Compliance regime that is built into SDLT, highlighting the changes in procedures and policies.

Previously stamp duty was a charge on documents and there was no legal obligation to have documents stamped. However, if they were not, they could not be used in a variety of situations such as registration of title to land and civil court action.

In practice, stamp duty was "voluntary" and the compliance regime that existed comprised of the ability to refuse to stamp documents in certain circumstances.

SDLT introduced on 1 December 2003 is a "process now, check later" system, requiring the completion and submission of a land transaction return (and payment) to our data capture centre in Netherton, for transactions in land and buildings in the UK, completed on or after 1 December 2003.

SDLT has brought a modern, comprehensive compliance framework to stamp duty, for the first time mirroring enquiry provisions already in place for other taxes administered by the Inland Revenue. In common with those other taxes the responsibility for completing the form correctly lies with the purchaser. Practitioners may need to draw their clients' attention to this and to the part of the form where the purchaser can indicate that they want their agent copied in on any subsequent correspondence from us.

Random and Risk Based Enquiries

A small selection of SDLT returns are selected for review. Some enquiries will be selected at random and others will be selected on a risk basis. The overwhelming majority of transactions are accepted and certificates issued without an enquiry.

Enquiry Window

We have a fixed time that we can start an enquiry—this is known as the enquiry window and is a period of 9 months:

- after the filing date (the date on which the return is due), if the return was delivered on or before that date;
- after the date on which the return was delivered, if the return was delivered after the filing date;
- after the date on which any amendment was made by the purchaser.

Enquiries will also be conducted into self-certificates given to the land registries.

Any enquiry will start with a letter to the purchaser, with a copy sent to their professional adviser if they have completed the correspondence box on the return (SDLT 1). At the end of the enquiry a letter closing the enquiry will be issued to the purchaser and copied to their professional adviser, again where the correspondence box has been completed (question 59 on page 5 of the SDLT 1).

Interest and Penalties For Late Delivery/Incorrect Completion of Returns

SDLT returns are due within 30 days of the effective date of the transaction. For the majority of transactions the effective date is the date of completion of the transaction, whether or not this is evidenced by a document. However if a contract is substantially performed before completion, the date on which substantial performance takes place is the effective date. Broadly substantial performance is the point at which:

- payment of the whole, or substantially the whole, of consideration other than rent (in practice, and unless the circumstances are unusual, we will accept that "substantially the whole" means not less than 90%); or
- the purchaser is entitled to possession of the property; or
- the first payment of rent is made.

If the filing date is missed a penalty or penalties will be imposed.

If the SDLT owed is paid late, interest will also be charged.

When Penalties Are Imposed, How Much Are They?

Fixed penalties

If we don't receive the SDLT return or any payment of the SDLT due within 30 days of the effective date of the transaction (the filing date) but within three months of the filing date, a £100 penalty will automatically be levied. In all other cases, a £200 penalty will be automatically charged.

NB. Under the special arrangements that currently apply, we will forego late filing penalties for SDLT returns and any payment of the SDLT due that have been submitted more than 30 days but not more than 40 days after the effective date of the transaction. More details of these arrangements can be found on our website at www.inlandrevenue.gov.uk/so/sdlt-admin.pdf.

If we find something wrong with an SDLT return during an enquiry

As well as imposing penalties for the late submission of a SDLT return, a penalty may be due if we find something wrong with an SDLT return.

We can only seek penalties for incorrect SDLT returns if SDLT is understated and the error was due to negligence or fraud.

When calculating any penalty we will take into account:

- the extent to which anything that was wrong was voluntarily disclosed;
- the help we receive in concluding our enquiries; and
- the seriousness of the errors or omissions.

We should be informed about any relevant matters when we work out what penalty to charge.

General

We will try to agree a settlement by contract on the amounts of tax, interest and penalties that are due. If agreement cannot be reached, we may formally determine the penalty we think is appropriate.

If an SDLT return is more than a year late we can impose a tax-based penalty of up to the total amount of tax due on the SDLT return.

When a Penalty Has Been Imposed

If a penalty is imposed we will send out a formal notice.

The penalty is due for payment at the end of the period of 30 days beginning with the date of the notice. Interest is charged on penalties paid late.

When a Penalty Notice Is Received

If not already done so, we advise that customers should do what is necessary to send in their SDLT return as soon as they can, to avoid further possible penalties. They should also pay the penalty on time, to avoid an interest charge.

Appeals Against Penalties For Late Returns

The main ground of appeal is where customers think they have a good reason why they did not send back their SDLT return in time. The law says that the only good reason is that a customer had or there is a "reasonable excuse" for not meeting the deadline and that after the reasonable excuse ceased, the customer sent back the SDLT return "without unreasonable delay". Appeals are made to the General or Special Commissioners, who are independent tribunals. The procedure requires a notice of appeal to be sent to us. This enables us to consider whether we agree there is a reasonable excuse. If we do, there is no need for the Commissioners to consider the appeal.

If a customer intends to appeal we must be given a notice of appeal, in writing, within 30 days of the date of the penalty notice. Appeals can be made in the form of a letter or using the form we send with each penalty notice.

Payment of Penalty If an Appeal Is Being Made

To avoid any interest charge, we advise that customers may want to pay the penalty even if they are appealing against it. If the penalty is paid and the appeal succeeds, we will repay the penalty and pay interest for the period from when the penalty was paid until we repay it.

If the Appeal Succeeds

If the appeal succeeds so that the customer does not have to pay the penalty, then obviously no interest is payable on the penalty that was determined in the notice, because the penalty itself is treated as if it were never determined.

If the Appeal Does Not Succeed

If the appeal does not succeed and the penalty has not been paid while the appeal was being considered, interest will be charged from after the end of the period of 30 days, beginning with the date of the notice, until the day the interest is paid.

Discovery Enquiries

We also have the opportunity to go back to a transaction that is outside the 9-month enquiry window. This is known as a "discovery" enquiry. A discovery enquiry happens when it becomes clear, (through third party information or otherwise), that not enough SDLT has been paid on a land transaction and, broadly, the reason for that is either that the customer (or certain people connected with him) has acted negligently or fraudulently, or that we did not have enough information before the end of the enquiry window to know that the customer ought to have paid more SDLT.

Further Information

Further information on any of the points raised above can be obtained on the Stamp Taxes website at www.inlandrevenue.gov.uk/so or by telephoning the Stamp Taxes Enquiry Line on 0845 6030135. The Enquiry Line is open between the hours of 8.30am to 5pm (Monday to Friday). Calls are charged at the local rate.

Shortly, a leaflet on penalties for the late submission of SDLT returns will be available.

Other leaflets we produce that customers might find useful are:

- COP 1 Putting things right—how to complain
- COP24 Stamp Duty Land Tax enquiries
- COP25 Stamp Duty Land Tax—enquiries into companies and partnerships
- SD1 Enquiries into land transaction returns.

PAGE 1123. CORRECTION TO PARAGRAPH 43 OF THE STAMP DUTY LAND TAX—GROUP RELIEF ARTICLE IN TAX BULLETIN 70

Section 54(4) FA 2003: Exception From the Connected Company Charge on a Winding Up

43. FA 2003 s 54(4) provides the third case of exception from the deemed market value rule in FA 2003 s 53. The exception applies to the distribution of assets on the winding up of a company, as long as the subject matter of the transaction or an interest from which that interest is derived, has been the subject of a transaction in respect of which a claim to group relief was made by the vendor. It is not the Inland Revenue's intention that section 54(4) should be prevented from applying where a group relief claim was made by the vendor but recovered under paragraph 3 of Schedule 7 either at the time of or before the effective date of the transaction.

INLAND REVENUE TAX BULLETIN ISSUE 73. OCTOBER 2004.

PAGE 1158. CORRECTION TO PARAGRAPH 4 OF THE STAMP DUTY LAND TAX—GROUP RELIEF ARTICLE IN TAX BULLETIN 70

This should read:

> "The relief is self-assessed and will be dealt with on a 'process now/check later' basis along with all other Stamp Duty Land Tax matters. Under Stamp Duty Land Tax the Inland Revenue does not require the preparation and submission of the letter of claim required by paragraph 6.163 of the Inland Revenue Stamp Taxes manual."

INLAND REVENUE TAX BULLETIN ISSUE 74. DECEMBER 2004.

PAGE 1171. TAX BULLETIN 70: STAMP DUTY LAND TAX: GROUP RELIEF: CORRECTION

Tax Bulletin 71 (June 2004) contained a corrected version of paragraph 43 of the article on Stamp Duty Land Tax: Group Relief (Tax Bulletin 70, April 2004, page 1107). We are sorry that another misprint was not corrected. Paragraph 43 should read:

43. FA 2003 s 54(4) provides the third case of exception from the deemed market value rule in FA 2003 s 53. The exception applies to the distribution of assets on the winding up of a company, as long as the subject matter of the transaction or an interest from which that interest is derived, has not been the subject of a transaction in respect of which a claim to group relief was made by the vendor. But it is not the Inland Revenue's intention that section 54(4) should be prevented from applying where a group relief claim was made by the vendor but recovered under paragraph 3 of Schedule 7 either at the time of or before the effective date of the transaction.

INLAND REVENUE TAX BULLETIN ISSUE 75. FEBRUARY 2005.

PAGE 1175. USE OF THE SDLT CD-ROM

In December 2004, Stamp Taxes issued a CD-ROM version of the Stamp Duty Land Tax returns. The CD-ROM also includes interactive help in completing the returns and validation to help ensure that the returns are correctly completed. This article sets out the benefits of using the CD-ROM version of the returns and Stamp Taxes' views on how it should be used.

The CD-ROM is a non-network product designed for use on Windows PCs with hard drives and was developed to provide practitioners who do not use commercial Case Software Management (CSM) products a means of generating self-validating SDLT1s. There is a training function to help users gain familiarity with the on screen use of the product. Further supplies of the CD-ROM envelopes and payslips may be obtained from the IR Orderline (0845 302 1472).

We see use of the CD-ROM as having a number of strong advantages over completing paper returns. It incorporates:

- interactive help updating and clarifying our current guidance;
- "validation" using many of the rules that the Inland Revenue IT system applies to check that returns are acceptable;
- 2D-barcode technology to capture the information from the return without reliance on the very exacting optical character recognition parameters associated with scanning technology;
- drop-down menu boxes from which to select the answers to certain questions and free-flow fields into which others may be keyed. Although users will find that they are limited to the same number of characters as on the paper form, this means that poor handwriting or difficulty in inserting written characters within the small boxes provided by the paper form will not delay the issue of a land transaction certificate;
- a facility which enables the purchaser to opt to confirm that information on the SDLT1 is correct and complete apart from the effective date. The purchaser then authorises the agent to insert the effective date when known, to sign the full return and to submit it to the Inland Revenue.

The combination of these features means that, if used correctly, the CD-ROM will provide greater certainty that we will be able to process the return first time, resulting in a certificate being issued quickly and without the need to ask for additional information.

Special Features

The CD-ROM:

- enables up to six of each supplementary form SDLT2, 3 and 4 to be printed for manual completion and submission with the SDLT1;
- provides for agent's details to be prepopulated on successive SDLT1 returns.

Please note that it is expected that Case Software Management providers and legal forms suppliers will shortly be updating their products to incorporate 2D-barcode technology. Practitioners who already use these products or who are looking for additional features not found on this CD-ROM should keep our website under review. Names of commercial providers and suppliers will be published as their 2D barcoded products receive Inland Revenue recognition.

User Trial CD-ROM

Last year a previous version of the CD-ROM was issued to selected practitioners in south west England. We are extremely grateful to all those who installed and used it and who reported to us difficulties and drawbacks in its application as well as advantages. We have worked hard in conjunction with our IT contractors to eliminate those difficulties and believe that this product which is distributed throughout the United Kingdom will prove a robust and practical tool especially for smaller firms and individuals.

Correct Use of the CD-ROM

Included with the CD-ROM is a booklet advising on the key aspects. Further information on use of the CD-ROM is also available on our website at www.inlandrevenue.gov.uk/so/sdlt_index.htm. If users are still unable to find an answer to their query, Stamp Taxes Enquiry line is available on 0845 6030135.

The CD-ROM will not allow the printing of a final 2D barcoded return until the relevant validation rules have been satisfied. So for example, a final return cannot be printed until the "effective date" question has been completed. This is because the Inland Revenue system will collect the data from the barcodes, not from the completed question fields. The software in the CD-ROM will automatically convert the data from the return fields into the barcode before printing. But a facility has been added to allow an "agent's copy" to be printed without a barcode and without an effective date having been entered. This is for the purchaser to sign and the agent to retain.

We recognise that, in practice, many practitioners send the SDLT returns to their clients to complete the statutory declaration before the transaction has completed and before the "effective date" is known. We also recognise that not allowing the final return to be printed and sent to the client until after the effective date eats into the 30 day filing period. Regulations have been introduced to allow some, very limited, flexibility in how the statutory declaration may be completed.

New Regulations

Where the CD-ROM or other 2D barcoded methods of completing form SDLT1 are used, new regulations give practitioners the option of sending to their clients a copy of the form for signature prior to confirmation of the effective date. This copy is for retention by the practitioner, who can send us a fully completed return including a declaration that the effective date is correct and that the property purchaser has signified that all other information is correct.

The agent's declaration option is only available where a method of completing form SDLT1 employs the 2D barcode. The technology allows the form to be printed for signature by the purchaser when **all** relevant information has been entered **except** question 4, the effective date of the transaction. But this form, signed by the purchaser does not itself carry a barcode. **It must not be submitted to the Inland Revenue** and is intended for retention by the agent.

Only when the agent accesses on his computer the saved details of the return and completes the form by entering the effective date, will the technology permit the printing of a 2D barcoded return for signature and submission to the Inland Revenue. At that point the agent is able to choose if the final full return is to be signed by:

- the purchaser;
- the agent (having received the purchaser's signature confirming all the information on the return except question 4, and the purchaser's authority to confirm question 4 by signing and submitting the return to the Inland Revenue).

A Land Transaction Return comprises form SDLT1 together with such supplementary forms SDLT2, 3 or 4 and schedules as may be required to make a full return. It is therefore essential that a purchaser when signing an SDLT1, either the full final barcoded form, or the "agent's copy" (with question 4 blank) reads, understands and confirms as correct, all the information to be submitted in that Land Transaction Return.

The new form of declaration uses the term "agent" as an "agent" is somebody authorised by the purchaser(s) to act on their behalf. In practice we would normally expect this to be the solicitor, licensed conveyancer or other practitioner acting in respect of the property transaction, but anyone may be authorised to act as an agent. This authorisation is specific to the transaction being notified.

Why Are We Doing This?

The most common reason why we are unable to process SDLT returns is because the effective date has not been completed. To help ensure that property purchasers get a land transaction certificate as quickly as possible, a final 2D barcoded return is not printable until all relevant information has been included in the return. But we also want purchasers, who are the persons liable to penalties for late filing, to have as long as possible to get the completed returns to us.

It is our view that the use of this option has no bearing on the person who is liable to tax, interest and penalties. This remains the purchaser as defined in FA 2003 s 43(4). Where the agent's declaration is used, we would expect the practitioner to have evidence that the purchaser has confirmed that the information in the return is correct. This would normally consist of a copy signed by the purchaser. Where we take up cases for enquiry, we would still normally expect to seek any additional tax, interest or penalties which may result, from the purchaser.

There is no obligation on practitioners to use the agent's declaration. The CD-ROM works perfectly well when it is not chosen. However Stamp Office believes it is an additional option, which will allow users to get maximum benefit from the advantages offered by the CD-ROM.

Other Things to Consider

Correcting errors

An SDLT return for sending to the IR can only be printed if all necessary information has been completed **on screen**. If any manual amendments are made to the information, our capture process will not identify that change. So if for example the effective date is changed, our processes will calculate interest and late filing penalties by reference to the original effective date. Errors found on saved or open returns may be corrected on screen, but if an error is spotted after the form has been printed, that print must be destroyed. Reopen that return on screen, make the necessary corrections and print the corrected version for signature and submission.

Printing

The 2D barcode which appears on each page of the SDLT1 form for submission has to be a complex pattern in order to reflect all the information that has been entered on that page. The detail of that complexity must be picked up when the barcode is "read" in an automatic process. It is therefore important that the printing of the form in your office is of a good standard.

Generally we have found that a well maintained laser printer, not low on toner, gives the best results. But a good quality inkjet printer can be successful provided that it has an adequate supply of ink which is allowed to dry without any contact resulting in smudging.

Part II ST

Supplementary Form SDLT4

The CD-ROM features a revised version of supplementary form SDLT4.form SDLT4. Guidance notes for this new version are available on our website at www.inlandrevenue.gov.uk/so/sdlt_index.htm. Until the end of March it is permissible to use either this new form or the current version which may still be downloaded from our website at www.inlandrevenue.gov.uk/so/sdlt_website.htm.

Submitting the Final Return

Before you send the completed 2D barcoded copy of the return to our processing centre at Netherton, you must ensure that:

- the return is signed, and there are no manual amendments as this information will not be incorporated in the barcode and will consequently be ignored,
- you provide the payment due or make direct payment using the Internet, telephone, BACS Direct Credit or CHAPS. Further details about payment methods can be found at www.inlandrevenue.gov.uk/so/.

- any forms printed from the CD-ROM are stapled in the top left hand corner,
- all forms are placed in the envelope unfolded.

Any SDLT1s completed using this product will need a Unique Transaction Reference Number (UTRN) that can be found on the paying-in book payslip.

There is no in-built calculator on the CD-ROM, so we've provided a link to SDLT and Lease calculators on the Stamp Taxes website at www.inlandrevenue.gov.uk/so/.

Feedback on the CD-ROM

We are very interested in receiving feedback from those using the CD-ROM. We should be grateful if all comments are forwarded by e mail to Mark Appelby at msd.stampscondoc@ ir.gsi.gov.uk.

But for any problems, either with the CD-ROM or with how the return should be completed, in the first instance, please refer firstly to our website or thereafter telephone the Stamp Taxes Enquiry line.

SDLT: FINANCE ACT 2003, S 75A — NEW GUIDANCE
LNB News 01/03/2011 53

Published Date

1 March 2011

Issue Date

1 March 2011

Issuing Department

HM Revenue and Customs (HMRC)

Jurisdiction

England;Scotland;Northern Ireland;Wales

Abstract

HMRC has published new guidance on the stamp duty land tax anti-avoidance provision contained in Finance Act 2003, 75A.

FULL TEXT

Finance Act (FA) 2003 s 75A is an anti-avoidance provision that is intended to counter certain schemes which have the effect of reducing Stamp Duty Land Tax liability.

COMMENCEMENT

S 75A has effect in respect of disposals and acquisitions, and all related scheme transactions, which take place after 2.00 pm. on 6 December 2006.

OVERALL APPROACH

Section 75A is an anti-avoidance provision. HM Revenue & Customs (HMRC) therefore takes the view that it applies only where there is avoidance of tax. On that basis, HMRC will not seek to apply s 75A where it considers transactions have already been taxed appropriately.

Section 75A applies where:

- One person ('V') disposes of a chargeable interest, and another person ('P') acquires, that interest, or a chargeable interest derived from it (s 75A (1) (a)).

- A number of transactions ('scheme transactions'), including the disposal and acquisition, are involved in connection with the disposal and acquisition (s 75A (1) (b)).
- The total Stamp Duty Land Tax payable in respect of all the scheme transactions is less than the amount that would be payable on a notional land transaction effecting the acquisition (s 75A (1) (c)).

All of the above must be read together.

Where it applies, the effect of S 75A is as follows:

- The individual scheme transactions are disregarded for Stamp Duty Land Tax purposes.
- There is instead a notional transaction effecting the acquisition of V's chargeable interest (that is the chargeable interest which was the subject matter of the disposal by V) by P.
- The chargeable consideration on the notional transaction is referred to as the 'notional consideration'.
- The effective date of the notional transaction is the last date of completion of the scheme transactions or, if earlier, the last date on which a contract in respect of the scheme transactions is substantially performed.

SCHEME TRANSACTIONS

The term 'transaction' includes:

- a transaction which is not a land transaction
- an agreement, offer or undertaking not to take specified action
- any kind of arrangement whether or not it could otherwise be described as a transaction
- a transaction which takes place after the acquisition by P of the chargeable interest

Section **75A** (3) gives some examples of what may be considered a scheme transaction:

- the acquisition by P of a lease deriving from a freehold owned or formerly owned by V
- a sub-sale to a third person
- the grant of a lease to a third person subject to a right to terminate
- the exercise of a right to terminate a lease or to take some other action
- an agreement not to exercise a right to terminate a lease or to take some other action
- the variation of a right to terminate a lease or to take some other action

This is not an exhaustive list of transactions to which s 75A applies.

APPLICATION OF S 75A

There are three steps to consider when contemplating the application of s 75A:

- firstly identify a disposal and the relevant person who is V
- secondly identify an acquisition and the relevant person who is P
- thirdly consider whether a number of transactions are 'involved in connection with' the disposal and acquisition

In a complex scenario this process may need to be repeated with different parties being identified as V and P, possibly with different results.

The meaning of the phrase 'involved in connection with' has not yet been tested in the courts and, therefore, the dictionary definition of 'connection' should be applied. In HMRC's view to be 'involved in connection with' each other the disposal, acquisition and other related transactions would normally involve more than one transaction in sequence relating to the same property. For example, related transactions would be considered to be 'in connection with' a disposal and acquisition ('the composite transaction') if the intended outcome of the composite transaction cannot be achieved in the form envisaged without those transactions taking place.S 75A will apply whether or not V, P or their associates or advisers have had any involvement with, or knowledge of, each other.

SITUATIONS WHERE HMRC ACCEPT THAT S 75A IS UNLIKELY TO APPLY

In deciding whether s75A applies to a set of transactions, it is necessary to look at the arrangements as a whole rather than simply at each individual step in isolation. Even the transactions below could be part of a scheme that purports to mitigate Stamp Duty Land Tax. But in general HMRC accepts that, to the extent that the situations below genuinely stand alone, the transactions will be taxed appropriately under the normal Stamp Duty Land Tax rules and so s 75A will not be triggered.

1. X, Y and Z are individuals who decide to establish a partnership to manage their investment portfolio. They transfer investment property and cash into that partnership at value. HMRC considers this to be a straightforward establishment of and transfer of property into a partnership.

2. X, Y and Z are the partners of a partnership. The purpose of the partnership is to acquire and develop a large residential property into 6 flats. When the development is complete they disagree as to how to manage the completed development so the partnership is dissolved and the partnership property (the flats and any partnership monies) is divided among the partners. It is assumed here that the agreements and documents relating to creation of the partnership demonstrate that the intention was for the partnership to manage the property after development and that the dissolution of the partnership arises from an unforeseen disagreement. HMRC would not seek to apply s 75A to this situation as long as the general Stamp Duty Land Tax legislation has been applied to the creation and dissolution of the partnership.

3. A property investment business is carried on by a company owned in equal shares by four family members. The company is to be sold to an unconnected third party. The four individuals establish a partnership to hold the properties that were held by the company but that aren't included in the sale. There is a clear commercial reason for the properties to be transferred out of the company that is to be sold to the unconnected third party.

4. A property lettings business is carried on by three individuals X, Y and Z through a partnership. X, Y and Z consider that, commercially, the best way to continue to carry on their business is through a company. They therefore decide to incorporate the business. X, Y and Z subscribe for shares in a new company in the same proportion as their respective partnership holdings. The properties are transferred to the company.

5. X and Y are corporate partners in a joint property-letting venture. They are unconnected except through their shares in the partnership. The partnership owns one property. Y's shareholders have accepted an offer from a third party, Z, to acquire all of its share capital. Z does not wish to continue to operate the business with X so the decision is taken to distribute the property to Y. There is a clear commercial reason for the transactions. The normal Stamp Duty Land Tax rules applied to the original acquisition of the property by the company.

6. V sells land to X and at the same time X sells the land to P. P pays Stamp Duty Land Tax based on the full amount of consideration received by V.

7. V sells land to X and at the same time X sells the land to P. P pays Stamp Duty Land Tax based on the full amount of consideration received by V. At a later date P sells the land to Y and Y pays the full amount of Stamp Duty Land Tax that arises from the consideration that P received.

8. V sells two properties at arm's length to third party purchasers N1 and N2. Subsequently, and in transactions which are not connected in any way with the purchases by N1 and N2, P buys both properties at arm's length. It is assumed that there is no connection between the sale by V and the purchase by P.

9. V grants a long lease to X. At a later stage, and in a transaction which is not connected in any way with the grant of the long lease, X assigns the lease to an unconnected third party P. P exercises a statutory right of enfranchisement. S 75A does not apply as regards to disposal by V and the acquisition by P because it is taxed appropriately under the normal Stamp Duty Land Tax rules.

10. V grants an option to X to purchase land. Subsequently, and in a transaction which is not connected in any way with the grant of the option, X assigns the benefit of the option to an unconnected third party P. P exercises the option. There is no connection between the transactions.

SITUATIONS WHERE HMRC CONSIDERS THAT S75A APPLIES

1. V agrees to sell land to X, and X agrees to sell the same land to P which is a partnership where the partners are X and persons connected to him. At the same time as the completion of the V-X contract, the X-P contract completes, this acquisition is effected by means of a 'transfer of rights'. X argues that no Stamp Duty Land Tax is due as his contract is disregarded by s.45, whilst P argues that no Stamp Duty Land Tax is due per Schedule 15 of FA 2003 given its connection with X. Section 75A applies because HMRC considers that the conditions of s75A 1(a) — (c) are met and that the notional transaction V-P could have been achieved in a more straight forward manner that would not have satisfied s75A(1)(c); Stamp Duty Land Tax is due on the notional consideration which is the full amount of consideration received by V.

2. V grants a 999-year lease to Nominee for no premium and a peppercorn rent. V assigns the freehold reversion to P for a nominal sum. P pays Nominee £x in consideration of Nominee's agreement to vary the lease by the insertion of a provision giving the landlord the right to terminate the lease for no payment. P exercises the right to terminate. Under s 75A, the notional transaction is the acquisition of the unencumbered freehold by P and the notional consideration chargeable is £x given by P to Nominee.

3. V grants a 999-year lease to Nominee for no premium and a peppercorn rent. The lease includes a right for the landlord to terminate the lease on payment of £x to the tenant. V assigns the freehold reversion to P for a nominal sum. P exercises the right to terminate and pays Nominee £x. Under s 75A, the notional transaction is the acquisition of the unencumbered freehold by P from V, and the notional consideration chargeable is £x given by P to Nominee.

4. V grants a 999-year lease to P for no premium and a peppercorn rent. The lease gives the landlord a right to terminate it within 14 days of the date of grant. P offers to pay V £x if V allows the 14 days to elapse without exercising the right to terminate. V does so. Under s 75A, the notional transaction is the grant by V of a 999-year lease to P and the notional consideration, which is the chargeable consideration, is £x, the amount paid by P and received by V.

5. V agrees to sell property to X Ltd for £10 million. X Ltd declares a dividend in favour of P, the dividend to consist of the property and to be paid at the same time as completion of the V-X Ltd contract. The contract is completed and the property transferred to P. X argues that the £10 million is not chargeable to Stamp Duty Land Tax as his contract is disregarded under s.45. P argues that there is no Stamp Duty Land Tax charge on the transfer of the property to him because a dividend in specie is a transaction that does not constitute consideration for the purposes of the Stamp Duty Land Tax legislation. Under s 75A, the notional transaction is the acquisition of the property by P, and the notional consideration, which is the chargeable consideration, is £10 million, the amount received by V.

6. V agrees to sell land to X, and X agrees to sell the same land to P which is a partnership where the partners are X, X1 Ltd. and X2 Ltd. companies connected to X which manage a trust for which X is the beneficiary. V and X enter an arrangement where V settles a nominal amount into X's trust, thereby creating a connection between V and X as per s.839 of ICTA 1988. The V-X contract completes and at the same time and simultaneously the X-P contract completes. X claims that no Stamp Duty Land Tax is due as his contract is disregarded by s.45 of FA 2003, whilst P claims that no Stamp Duty Land Tax is due per Schedule 15 of FA 2003 given its connection with X. Section 75A applies and the notional transaction involved is V-P Stamp Duty Land Tax is due on the notional consideration which is the full amount of consideration received by V.

OTHER PROVISIONS

A transfer of shares or securities — or units in a unit trust scheme — is ignored for the purposes of s 75A if it would otherwise be the first of a series of scheme transactions (and several such transfers are likewise ignored if they all precede any other scheme transaction).

The notional transaction attracts any relief which it would attract if it were an actual land transaction.

EXAMPLES:

(1) V sells land to X and at the same time and simultaneously X sells to P. V, X and P are all companies within the same group. The notional transaction involved is V-P but, provided the conditions for group relief at Schedule 7 of FA 2003 are met, Group Relief will apply to the notional transaction.

(2) V sells land to X and at the same time and simultaneously X sells to P, which is a registered charity. The notional transaction involved is V-P; but, provided the conditions for Charities relief at Schedule 8 of FA 2003 are met, P can claim Charities relief which will apply to the notional transaction and no Stamp Duty Land Tax will be due.

(3) Section 75A does not apply where the relief is available only by reason of sections 71A to 73 (alternative property finance) or a provision in Schedule 9 (right to buy, shared ownership leases, etc.)

(4) If any of the scheme transactions is entered into for the purposes of, or in connection with, the transfer of an undertaking or part of an undertaking for the purposes of paragraphs 7 or 8 of Schedule 7 (reconstruction and acquisition relief) then the notional transaction is also deemed to be entered into for such purposes or in such connection. This enables the notional transaction to qualify for reconstruction or acquisition relief if the other conditions for relief are satisfied.

(5) The notional transaction will be subject to the market value rule in s53 if P is a company connected with V.

(6) Where applicable s 75A will charge consideration to tax regardless of the s45 position including any amount paid as a deposit.

(7) If part of the consideration for the notional transaction is a land transaction entered into by V as purchaser, or by P as vendor, then the market value rules in paragraph 5 of Schedule 4 will apply.

(8) An interest in a property investment partnership is treated as a chargeable interest for the purposes of s 75A.

(9) Where V or P is a partnership the provisions in Part 3 of Schedule 15 apply as they would to the transfer of a chargeable interest into or out of a partnership for all transactions with an effective date before 24 March 2010.

(10) But for transactions where the effective date is 24 March 2010 or later, S.75C(8)(b) no longer applies to treat the notional transaction between V and P as a transaction involving a partnership under Schedule 15. The normal rules under s75A will apply to ascertain the chargeable consideration on such transactions.

STAMP DUTY LAND TAX: RELIEF FOR TRANSFERS INVOLVING MULTIPLE DWELLINGS — DRAFT GUIDANCE

Published Date

20 May 2011

Issue Date

19 May 2011

Issuing Department

HM Revenue and Customs (HMRC)

Jurisdiction

England;Scotland;Northern Ireland;Wales

Abstract

Draft guidance on the measure announced at Budget 2011, under which the rate of SDLT is determined by reference to the amount of consideration, divided by the number of dwellings, subject to a minimum rate of 1%. The relief is available on transactions where the effective date is on or after the date of Royal Assent to the Finance Bill.

FULL TEXT

Finance Bill 2011 clause 83/Schedule 22

OVERVIEW

This is a relief for transactions which include the acquisition of interests in more than one dwelling. The relief must be claimed in a Land Transaction Return.

The relief was announced at Budget 2011 and applies to transactions where the effective date is on or after the date of Royal Assent to the Finance Bill. The Finance Bill introduces new FA03/S58D and FA03/SCH6B.

Where the relief is claimed, the rate of Stamp Duty Land Tax (SDLT) which applies to the consideration attributable to interests in dwellings is determined by reference to the amount of this consideration, divided by the number of dwellings, ie the mean consideration attributable to the dwellings. This is subject to a minimum rate of 1%.
The rate of SDLT which applies to the consideration attributable to interests in land other than dwellings, if any, is the rate which would apply in the absence of the relief.

Superior freehold or leasehold interests in dwellings subject to leases granted for an initial period of 21 years or more are not eligible for relief unless those leases are also transferred.

The relief includes provision for 'off-plan' purchases where construction or adaptation of the property for residential use may not have commenced by the effective date of the transaction. It also provides for the tax calculation to be adjusted if the number of dwellings involved is reduced within three years of the effective date of the transaction.

THE RELIEF

1. The relief is available for transactions the effective date of which is on or after [the date of Royal Assent to the Finance Bill 2011] and which is not linked with any transaction with an effective date before that date except:

- an option binding the grantor to enter into the later transaction or
- a right of pre-emption restricting the right of the grantor to enter into the later transaction.

2. The relief must be claimed in a Land Transaction Return or an amendment to a return, using relief code 33.

RELEVANT TRANSACTIONS FA03/SCH6B/PARA2

3. The relief may be claimed in respect of a transaction which is a "relevant transaction". A relevant transaction is either of the following:

- a transaction, the main subject-matter of which includes interests in more than one dwelling
- a transaction which is one of a number of linked transactions, the main subject-matter of which includes interests in at least one dwelling and where one or more transactions linked to it includes interests in at least one other dwelling.

4. In either case, the main subject-matter of the transaction may include interests in land other than dwellings.

EXCLUSIONS

5. A transaction cannot be a relevant transaction if relief under FA03/S74 (Exercise of collective rights by tenants of flats) or FA03/S75 (Crofting community right to buy) applies to it.

6. A transaction cannot be a relevant transaction if relief under FA03/SCH7 (Group relief, reconstruction relief and acquisition relief) or FA03/SCH8 (Charities relief) is available for it, would be available on the making of a claim or has been withdrawn from it.

SUPERIOR INTERESTS

7. For the purpose of determining whether a transaction is a relevant transaction, a superior interest (freehold or headlease) over property which includes dwellings is treated as if it were an interest in those dwellings.

Part II ST

If for example, a purchaser acquires the freehold of a new block of four flats which are untenanted. The transaction is a relevant transaction.

8. However, such a superior interest cannot be taken into account for this purpose to the extent that it is a superior interest in relation to a lease over a dwelling which was granted for an initial term of 21 years or more.

EXAMPLE

A purchaser acquires the freehold of a block of four flats. The transaction is not linked with any other transaction.

- Where two of the four flats are tenanted under long leases, the transaction is a relevant transaction, the main subject-matter of which includes two dwellings, i.e. the two flats not tenanted under long leases.
- If three of the four flats are tenanted under long leases, the transaction is not a relevant transaction, because only one flat can be taken into account, ie that which is not tenanted.

THE TAX CALCULATION — FA03/SCH22/PARA4

9. The chargeable consideration for a relevant transaction is apportioned between:
- the consideration attributable to interests in dwellings and
- the remaining consideration, if any.

The consideration must be so apportioned on a 'just and reasonable' basis.

10. The percentage rates of tax which apply, firstly to the consideration attributable to interests in dwellings and secondly to the remaining consideration, are then calculated separately.

CONSIDERATION ATTRIBUTABLE TO INTERESTS IN DWELLINGS — FA03/SCH22/PARA5(1)-(6)

11. The relevant consideration for the purposes of FA03/S55 is the aggregate consideration:
- for this transaction and any transactions linked to it (whether relevant transactions or not),
- which is attributable to dwellings, interests in which are included in this and any relevant transactions linked to it,

divided by the number of such dwellings.

12. The rate of tax that applies is set by Table A of FA03/S55, except that the minimum rate is 1% — FA03/SCH22/PARA5(2).

13. FA03/S116(7) (six or more dwellings treated as non-residential property) does not apply.

THE REMAINING CONSIDERATION — FA03/SCH22/PARA5(7)

14. The relevant consideration for the purposes of FA03/S55 is the aggregate consideration for the transaction and all transactions which are linked to it (whether relevant transactions or not). In most cases Table B of FA03/S55 will apply, but Table A may apply in some circumstances where the transaction or transactions consist wholly of property comprising five or fewer dwellings.

15. The rate of tax that applies is the rate that would apply by virtue of FA03/S55 in the absence of the relief.

TAX DUE ON CONSIDERATION IN THE FORM OF RENT — FA03/SCH22/PARA4(5)

16. Where the chargeable consideration for a relevant transaction includes rent, the normal provisions of FA03/SCH5 apply to determine the amount of tax chargeable on the rent.

MEANING OF 'DWELLING' — FA03/SCH22/PARA7

17. For the purposes of the relief a 'dwelling' means a building or part of a building which is suitable for use as a single dwelling or is in the process of being constructed or adapted for such use.

18. Land that is, or is to be, occupied or enjoyed with the dwelling such as a garden or grounds (including any building or structure on such land) and land that subsists, or is to subsist, for the benefit of the dwelling, is taken to be part of the dwelling.

19. Land within paragraph 17 above includes land which is needed for the reasonable enjoyment of the dwelling, having regard to the size and nature of the dwelling. HMRC will apply a similar test to that applied for the capital gains tax relief for main residences — TCGA92/S222(3).

20. FA03/S116(2)-(5) apply to determine whether certain types of property are or are not dwellings.

'OFF PLAN' TRANSACTIONS

21. Where:

- there is a contract to purchase a building, or part of a building, which is to be constructed or adapted under the contract for use as a dwelling or dwellings,
- the contract is substantially performed before construction of the building, or part of the building, concerned has commenced and
- the effective date of the transaction is deemed to be the date of substantial performance by virtue of FA03/S44/44A/45/45A or FA03/SCH17A/PARA12A or 19(3)

then, for the purposes of the relief, the main subject-matter of the transaction will be taken to consist of or include an interest in a dwelling.

22. For this purpose a contract includes any agreement including, in Scotland, missives of let not constituting a lease.

FURTHER RETURN WHERE NUMBER OF DWELLINGS IS REDUCED — FA03/SCH22/PARA6

23. Where:

- relief is claimed under FA03/SCH6B for a relevant transaction,
- during a period following the effective date of the transaction(s) an event occurs and
- if that event had occurred, immediately before the effective date, either the transaction would not have been a relevant transaction or the rate of tax charged on dwellings would have been higher

then the event is deemed to have taken place immediately prior to the effective date of the transaction.

24. For this purpose, "event" includes any change of circumstance or change of plan.

25. This provision may be triggered where

- the subject-matter of the transaction ceases to include dwellings (so that the transaction ceases to be a relevant transaction), or
- where the number of dwellings included in the subject-matter of the transaction is reduced and the rate of tax charged on the consideration attributable to dwellings would increase as a result.

26. The period concerned is:

- the period ending three years after the effective date of the transaction or, if earlier,
- the date on which the purchaser disposes of the interest in the building to a person who is not connected with him.

27. In the case of a transaction substantially performed before completion, the 3-year period runs from the date of substantial performance.

28. In these circumstances, the purchaser must make a further return and pay any additional tax due within 30 days of the event.

29. Further returns should be made by letter to the Birmingham Stamp Office

30. References in FA03/SCH10 to the effective date of the transaction are to be read as references to the date of the event. The tax chargeable is calculated by reference to the rates in force at the effective date of the transaction.

STAMP TAXES BULLETIN — JULY 2011

LNB News 07/07/2011 44

Published Date

7 July 2011

Issue Date

7 July 2011

Issuing Department

HM Revenue and Customs (HMRC)

Jurisdiction

England;Scotland;Northern Ireland;Wales

Abstract

This edition includes articles on the the new SDLT online system; introduction of the 5 per cent rate for residential property for transactions where the effective date is on or after 6 April 2011; a relief for purchasers of residential property who acquire interests in more than one dwelling; and revised guidance on the treatment of certificates of value regarding partnership interests.

FULL TEXT

We usually aim to publish the Stamp Taxes Bulletin three times a year. Each bulletin is withdrawn when the guidance in it has been updated. The next issue is planned to follow Royal Assent to the Finance Bill 2011.

Feedback on this bulletin or any other topic is welcomed, as are suggestions for areas that could be covered in future.

CONTENTS

Land

- New SDLT online system
- Introduction of the 5 per cent rate for residential property
- Overpayments of tax due to a mistake in the return
- First-time buyers
- Multiple dwellings acquisitions
- Preventing avoidance

Shares

- Partnership interests

LAND

New SDLT online system

The current SDLT online system is changing as part of a cross-department project to rationalise IT systems. There is a new field to complete when a National Insurance number is given for the first purchaser. The date of birth will also be required.

The paper forms have changed too two questions about companies have moved from the SDLT4 to the SDLT1. The SDLT3 now has a box that can be marked to show whether it is a continuation of the address from the SDLT1. These changes will be less obvious online but, if you select the option to show the box numbers relating to the paper form, the references will change.

Paper filing

The new forms SDLT1, 3 and 4 are now available from the HM Revenue & Customs Orderline, as is updated guidance booklet SDLT6. Businesses which still file using a paper form have been contacted and provided with a small supply of the new forms and an explanatory letter. Although you can still use the paper forms until the end of June, we would encourage all paper filers to order new stocks and dispose of any existing stocks, as any of the old style forms received after the end of June will be rejected.

Online filing

The online system will not change until the beginning of July. During the switchover, online filing will not be available for a number of days, but it is planned to be up and running on 4 July.

Any returns that are partly completed and saved, but not submitted before the system is taken down, will be affected by the changes. When you access those returns again after the changes, click 'check this return' to find any validation errors.

Further information

For the most up to date information check the Stamp Taxes news page.

INTRODUCTION OF THE 5 PER CENT RATE FOR RESIDENTIAL PROPERTY

The draft guidance for this is given below

SDLTMxxxxx — 5 per cent rate for chargeable consideration over £1 million — residential property.

This rate applies for transactions where the effective date is on or after 6 April 2011. It is added to Table A within S55(2)/FA03. If the transaction completes an unamended contract made before 25 March 2010, or was substantially performed before 6 April 2011, then the previous 4 per cent rate will apply.

- FA03/S116 sets out the statutory definition of residential property for SDLT purposes. Residential property is (FA03/S116(1)(a)) a building or (FA03/S116(6)) part of a building that, at the date of the relevant transaction, is one of the following:
- used as a dwelling
- suitable for use as a dwelling
- in the process of being constructed or adapted for such use

The definition includes (FA03/S116(1)(b)) land that is or forms part of the garden or grounds of a such building (including any building or structure on such land) and (FA03/S116(1)(c)) an interest in or right over land that subsists for the benefit of a building within (FA03/S116(1)(a)) or of land within (FA03/S116(1)(b)).

In most cases, the use of a room or area within a residence as an office will not cause it to fall into the mixed use category, as the room or area would still be suitable for use as a dwelling. Similarly, any indoor pool, gymnasium or similar feature, or an interest in a garage in a separate block, would still be residential as it contributes to the enjoyment of the residential premises. In all such cases the 5 per cent rate would apply for a chargeable consideration in excess of £1 million.

FA03/S116(2) specifies that buildings used for the following purposes are residential property:

- residential accommodation for school pupils
- residential accommodation for students — other than a hall of residence
- residential accommodation for members of the armed forces,
- an institution which is the sole or main residence of at least 90 per cent of its residents and is not excluded by FA03/S116(3)

If a building meets any one of these separate tests it will be treated as residential property, as will any garden or grounds belonging to it or any interests or rights attaching to it.

Where (FA03/S116(7)) six or more separate dwellings are the subject of a single transaction involving the transfer of a major interest in, or the grant of a lease over, them, those dwellings are not treated as residential property.

'Garden or grounds' includes land which is needed for the reasonable enjoyment of the dwelling, having regard to the size and nature of the dwelling..This will usually be a question of fact depending on the individual circumstances of each case

It should be noted that a single land transaction is either within Table A or Table B. There is no apportionment between the two tables.

EXAMPLE

P is buying a house for £2 million. One room is used as an office, but there have been no alterations made which would make it unsuitable for use as part of a residence.

Because that room is suitable for use as a dwelling (S116(1)(a)/FA03) the whole property is residential. Table A applies so the rate of tax is 5 per cent.

EXAMPLE

P is buying an estate for £3 million. The estate contains a sawmill and wood yard which is run as a business. Because the property is not wholly residential, Table B applies and the rate of tax is 4 per cent.

EXAMPLE

P buys a large property which is in multiple occupation by students. He pays £1.2 million. By virtue of S116(2)(b) this is residential property so Table A applies and the rate of tax is 5 per cent.

EXAMPLE

P buys a hotel for £3 million. It had previously been a single dwelling and P intends to restore it as a family home.

Table B applies and the rate is 4 per cent. S116(4) says that any building listed in S116(3) is not residential even if it is suitable for residential use. S116(3) includes 'hotel or inn or similar establishment'.

OVERPAYMENTS OF TAX DUE TO A MISTAKE IN THE RETURN

Draft guidance for the new regime following changes in legislation.

SDLTM54000 — Procedure
Overpayment relief: commencement and time limits

From 1 April 2011 a person may claim overpayment relief to recover overpaid SDLT or to reduce an excessive assessment.

The time limit for a claim to relief is four years after the effective date of the transaction.

SDLTM54010 — Procedure
Overpayment relief: Legislation
Section 28 and Schedule 12 Finance (No.3) Act 2010 From 1 April 2011 introduce new legislation for claiming overpayment relief.

Paragraph 34 Schedule 10 Finance Act 2003 is amended alongside new paragraphs 34A-E.

SDLTM54100 — Procedure
Overpayment relief: Exclusions

Overpayment relief is not available if one of the exclusions listed in the legislation applies. The exclusions are called cases.

Case A is where the amount in the overpayment relief claim arises from a mistake concerning a claim or election SDLTM 54110

Case B is where the person can correct the overpayment or over-assessment by other means, SDLTM54120

Case C is where the person could have obtained relief by other means when they first knew, or ought reasonably to have known, that the relief was available, see SDLTM54130

Case D is where a court or tribunal has already considered the grounds on which the overpayment relief claim is made. It also covers the situation where HMRC has considered the grounds and settled the appeal by agreement, see SDLTM54140

Case E is where the person knew, or ought reasonably to have known, the grounds for the overpayment relief claim at a time when they could have put them forward on an appeal to a court or tribunal, see SDLTM54150

Case F is where HMRC has taken proceedings to enforce payment of the amount in the overpayment relief claim, see SDLTM54160

Case G deals with amounts that were understood to be due under the practice generally prevailing at the time the liability was calculated, see SDLTM54170.

SDLTM54110 — Procedure
Overpayment relief: Exclusions: Case A mistake concerning a relief or election

Overpayment relief is not due where the amount paid, or due, is excessive because of a mistake

- in any other formal claim or election
- in making any other claim or election, or failing to do so, or
- If a person has overpaid or been overcharged tax due to a mistake in any other claim whether in a return or otherwise or because they failed to make any other claim or election.

HM Revenue & Customs (HMRC) may in limited circumstances accept a late claim or election, see SACM 10035.

SDLTM54120 — Procedure
Overpayment relief: Exclusions: Case B mistake concerning a relief or election

If there are any other formal means of recovering an overpayment of tax or reducing an excessive assessment, such as by amending a transaction return, the person must use that instead of overpayment relief.

SDLTM54130 — Procedure
Overpayment relief: Exclusions: Case C other relief out of time

SDLTM54140 explains that if there is another formal means of correcting a tax liability, the person must use this instead of claiming overpayment relief.

If a person knew, or ought reasonably to have known, that they had some other means of correcting an overpayment or over-assessment, they cannot claim overpayment relief if they failed to use those other means within the relevant time limit.

You must judge on a case by case basis whether a person ought reasonably to have known that they

Part II ST

- had made a mistake, and
- could obtain a repayment or correct an excessive assessment.

You should not necessarily refuse overpayment relief merely because the person could have realised that they should do something about the matter sooner. You should consider whether, taking into account their ability and circumstances, the person

- took reasonable care to ensure they paid the right amount of tax, and
- had any reason to suppose that they might have overpaid.

Persons are not required to take advice on every aspect of their tax affairs, nor can we expect them to avoid every possible mistake. However, they should take care with their tax affairs, try to be sure of the facts and seek HMRC or independent professional advice if they have any significant uncertainty.

If a person realises that they have overpaid or that an assessment is excessive but they are uncertain what they might do about the mistake, we would normally expect them to seek advice.

We do expect a person to take note of any advice or guidance that we or their advisors have given them.

SDLTM54140 — Procedure
Overpayment relief: Exclusions: Case D grounds of claim considered on appeal

If an assessment has been determined on appeal by the tribunal, overpayment relief is not available if the overpayment relief claim is on the same basis as the appeal.

The tribunal's determination of the point is final.

Similarly, if the appeal was determined by agreement or by a deemed agreement under para 37 Sch 10 FA 2003 (see ARTG2720-50), that determination is also final.

SDLTM54150 — Procedure
Overpayment relief: Exclusions: Case E grounds of claim not considered on appeal

Overpayment relief is not available if the grounds on which the person is claiming relief could have been put to a tribunal or court on an appeal relating to the amount paid or due.

Overpayment relief is not due if the person knew, or ought reasonably to have known, of the grounds for the claim before

- the end of the period in which the person could have made an appeal, or
- the date the appeal was determined by a court or tribunal, or
- the date the appeal was determined under para 37 Sch 10 FA 2003, or
- the date on which the person withdrew the appeal.

If more than one of these events has happened we look at what the person knew, or ought reasonably to have known, before the latest of them.

See SDLTM54130 or guidance on what a person ought reasonably to have known.

An appellant is expected to consider and put forward all the grounds of appeal that they might rely on.

See ARTG2240 (http://www.hmrc.gov.uk/manuals/artgmanual/ARTG2240.htm) if the person wishes to make a late appeal.

SDLTM54160 — Procedure
Overpayment relief: Exclusions: Case F HMRC proceedings

A person cannot claim overpayment relief if HMRC has already taken court action to recover amounts due under an assessment or determination. This is the same as the restriction on income tax overpayment relief.

The Exchequer Secretary to the Treasury gave the following response to a point raised during Public Bill Committee consideration of income tax overpayment relief in the 2009 Finance Bill

> "In order to be able to enforce a tax debt HMRC must have an assessment or other determination of the amount due. Taxpayers will already have had an opportunity to self-assess or to appeal an HMRC assessment. Before HMRC commence proceedings for recovery, they will at least have attempted to contact the taxpayer to obtain payment of the outstanding amounts. At this point and at any time before judgment is given or the taxpayer reaches an agreement with HMRC to settle the proceedings, they will be able to make a claim under this legislation, providing that the other conditions for making the claim are met in particular, that the four year time limit has not already passed. If HMRC has been forced to take legal proceedings to recover a debt any amount determined by the Court or by agreement between HMRC and the taxpayer should remain final."

Written answer to Jim Hood MP and Peter Atkinson MP, 1 July 2009

SDLTM54170 — Procedure
Overpayment relief: Exclusions: Case G practice generally prevailing

Overpayment relief is not due if the claim relates to a mistake in an SA return or other tax calculation and the tax liability was calculated in accordance with the practice generally prevailing, see below, at that time, except where the claim relates to PAYE income.

PRACTICE GENERALLY PREVAILING

Whether there was a 'practice generally prevailing' is a question of fact (Rose Smith 17 TC 586).
In HMRC v Household Estate Agents Ltd Henderson J. stated

> 'Without attempting to give an exhaustive definition, it seems to me that a practice may be so described only if it is relatively long-established, readily ascertainable by interested parties, and accepted by HMRC and taxpayers' advisers alike: compare the decision of the Special Commissioners (Dr A N Brice and Mr John Walters QC) in Rafferty v HMRC.'

In relation to overpayment relief, the onus is on HMRC in any appeal hearing to demonstrate that there was a practice generally prevailing. You may need to refer, among other things, to our published guidance, advice from HMRC technical specialists, reported cases and external comment as evidence of a practice generally prevailing.

A practice need not have been universally followed. But where a tribunal or court decides that a practice is wrong you should take it to have ceased to be a generally prevailing practice at that point even if the decision is subject to appeal.

SDLTM54180 — Procedure
Overpayment relief: Claims

The person applying for overpayment relief must make a claim to HMRC for repayment or discharge of the amount of tax which they believe they should not have paid, or should not be due.

Claims must be in writing and should be sent to:

Birmingham Stamp Office
9th floor, City Centre House
30 Union Street
Birmingham B2 4AR

A person cannot make an overpayment relief claim by including it in a land transaction return.

Part II ST

Overpayment relief claims must be made by the person who is due the relief except for overpayment relief claims arising from mistakes in partnership returns — see SACM12045 (http://www.hmrc.gov.uk/manuals/sacmanual/SACM12045.htm).

An overpayment relief claim must

- state that the person is making a claim for overpayment relief under paragraph 34 Schedule 10 FA 2003
- identify the land transaction in respect of which the tax was paid
- state the grounds on which the person considers that the overpayment or excessive assessment has occurred
- state whether the person has previously made an appeal in connection with the payment or the assessment
- include a declaration signed by the claimant stating that the particulars given in the claim are correct and complete to the best of their knowledge and belief.

SDLTM54190 — Procedure
Overpayment relief: Partnerships

If an overpayment relief claim relates to a land transaction entered in to by a partnership all the relevant partners must agree to the claim.

A relevant partner is anyone who was a member of the partnership during the period to which the incorrect partnership return relates. If that person has died it includes their personal representative.

The relevant partners must nominate one of themselves to make the overpayment relief claim. This does not need to be the partner for whom the relief is claimed but all of the partners must agree to the nomination.

SDLTM54200 — Procedure
Overpayment relief: Discovery assessments

If the grounds for an overpayment relief claim also give us grounds for believing that the person has paid less tax than was due in respect of another land transaction, we may be able to make a discovery assessment to recover that amount.

If we make a discovery assessment, determination or amendment as a result of the overpayment relief claim, some of the normal rules that restrict our ability to make a discovery assessment do not apply in that we do not have to show that the conditions of paragraph 30 are met if the person has made a return, see SDLTM84210.

The assessment, determination or amendment will be in time if it is made before the overpayment relief claim is finally determined. This is when the overpayment relief claim, or the amount to which it relates, can no longer be varied, including on appeal.

SDLTM84280 — Compliance: Assessments and Revenue determinations
Relief in case of double assessment FA03/SCH10/PARA33

If a purchaser is assessed twice in error in respect of the same transaction, they can claim a refund under this paragraph.

The claim has to be made in writing and the decision then has to be made whether the claim can be accepted. If it is, then the assessment should be duly amended and relief given by either discharging or repaying the tax to resolve the double assessment. In practice, this is unlikely to happen as the tax will usually only be collected as a result of the submission of a land transaction return.

The purchaser can appeal against any decision made.

First-time buyers

First-time buyers relief under the provisions of Section 57AA Finance Act 2003 was introduced by the Finance Act 2010. The relief is due to expire for transactions with an effective date on or after 25 March 2012. The Government is currently reviewing this provision and will announce the outcome of the review in the autumn.

Multiple dwellings acquisitions

Legislation was introduced in Finance Bill 2011 to provide a relief for purchasers of residential property who acquire interests in more than one dwelling. The purpose of the relief is to reduce the rate of Stamp Duty Land Tax on the purchase of more than one dwelling closer to the rate that would apply if the dwellings were purchased independently.

The measure will have effect from Royal Assent to the Finance Bill. As previously mentioned, our intention is to produce a further Bulletin, which will include that guidance, if not previously published, following Royal Assent.

Preventing avoidance

HM Revenue & Customs is aware of avoidance schemes which attempt to exploit the following three areas:

sub-sales;

Alternative Finance reliefs;

exchanges.

Measures were introduced in the Finance Bill 2011, effective on and after 24 March 2011, to put beyond doubt that the schemes do not work to avoid Stamp Duty Land Tax.

An explanatory note, together with a Tax Information and Impact note, is available on HM Treasury website.

Further guidance will be made available following Royal Assent.

SHARES

Partnership Interests

It has been drawn to our attention that existing guidance at SDLTM34610 is incorrect in its treatment of certificates of value. Revised guidance is given below.

SDLTM34610 — Special provisions relating to partnerships: Stamp Duty implications of Schedule15 — Examples

EXAMPLE 1

A of A and B has with relevant partnership property including a commercial unit and various shareholdings in several companies. The commercial unit has a market value of £1.5 million, subject to an outstanding mortgage debt of £500,000, and the shares have a market value of £580,000.

C joins the partnership paying £400,000 for a 25 per cent share. The provisions of para14 would be considered when establishing any SDLT liability but as the relevant partnership property includes shares we also need to consider any SD liability under Paras31-33.

Para 32 states that the SD liability will be based on the consideration given less the excluded amount.

Firstly we need to establish the net market value of the chargeable interest in accordance with Para 32(6):

MV – SL

MV = £1.5 million

SL = £500,000

Net market value equals £1 million.

Part II ST

We now need to establish the appropriate proportion.

As C was not a partner before the transfer this will be equal to the partnership he acquired — i.e. 25 per cent

The excluded amount is therefore
25% x £1 million = £250,000

To establish consideration for SD purposes we look at the consideration passing less the excluded amount:
£400,000 — £250,000 = £150,000.

This is the consideration for SD purposes. The rates of duty are as laid down in Para4/Sch13/FA99, but the instrument of transfer can benefit from a certificate of value in the form set down at Para6/Sch13/FA99. If the instrument contains a £250,000 certificate, the appropriate rate of duty is 1 per cent. The duty on £150,000 is thus £1,500.

However, Para33/Sch15/FA03 tells us that the duty payable shall not exceed that which would be payable on an equivalent transfer of those particular stocks and marketable securities.

In the first instance, it is necessary to look at the nature of the assets in the form of stocks and marketable securities. Any that would be exempt from charge on a transfer of same, such as some forms of loan stock or bearer shares, are disregarded. (But note that there is no territorial scope. If the assets include, say, common stock in a US company, these are not disregarded but attract Stamp Duty under this legislation.) In this example, all of the assets held in stocks or marketable securities would be chargeable if transferred separately.

We therefore need to calculate the appropriate proportion of the net market value of the shares:

The net market value is £580,000 as there was no loan secured on the shares.

The proportion of the partnership acquired by C is 25 per cent

The net market value of the assets in the form of stocks and market chargeable is therefore 25% x £580,000 = £145,000. Duty on this sum at the 0.5 per cent rate is £725.

As this is less than the sum arrived at under para32 the original SD liability of £1,500 is limited to £725.

EXAMPLE 2

A partnership of A and B has relevant partnership property including a commercial unit and various shareholdings in several companies. The commercial unit has a market value of £1.5 million subject to an outstanding mortgage debt of £500,000 and the shares have a market value of £180,000.

C joins the partnership paying £300,000 for a 25 per cent share. The provisions of para14 would be considered when establishing any SDLT liability but as the relevant partnership property includes shares we also need to consider any SD liability under Paras31-33.

Para 32 states that the liability will be based on the consideration given less the excluded amount.

Firstly we need to establish the net market value of the chargeable interest in accordance with Para 32(6):
MV – SL

MV = £1.5 million
SL = £500,000
Net market value equals £1 million.

We now need to establish the appropriate proportion.

As C was not a partner before the transfer this will be equal to the partnership share he acquired — i.e. 25 per cent

The excluded amount is therefore
25% x £1m = £250,000
To establish consideration for SD purposes we look at the consideration passing less the excluded amount:
£300,000 — £250,000 = £50,000.
This will be the consideration for SD purposes.

As the SD consideration is less than the 0 per cent threshold, if a certificate of value at £125,000 is included in the instrument, the SD liability is nil, so there is no need to consider Para 33.

APPENDIX 6. STAMP DUTY RESERVE TAX: NOTES FOR GUIDANCE

FEBRUARY 1990. OFFICE OF THE CONTROLLER OF STAMPS

 They provide guidance to the Stamp Duty Reserve Tax provisions in FA 1986 and to the Stamp Duty Reserve Tax Regulations 1986, as subsequently amended. They are intended primarily for brokers, dealers and others concerned with accounting for the tax. They have no binding force and do not affect taxpayers' rights of appeal on points concerning their own liability to the tax. The 1986 edition of these notes is withdrawn.

NB: In relation to the prospective abolitions of all stamp duty charges on property other than land and buildings (including all charges on transactions in shares, bearer instruments and units under trust schemes) and of stamp duty reserve tax, see the Revenue Press Releases of 20 March 1990 and 19 March 1991, the commentaries on FA 1990 and FA 1991 and the notes on the end of the contents list for Part III Stamp Duty and Stamp Duty Reserve Tax.

NB: The introduction of the CREST paperless settlement system and changes made in FA 1996 and FA 1997 mean that many parts of these Notes are out of date.]

Contents

CHAPTER 1 GENERAL DESCRIPTION

1.1 FA 1986 Pt IV provides for a tax, known as the stamp duty reserve tax, to be charged on certain agreements to transfer securities. Most of the provisions relating to the collection and recovery of the tax are contained in The Stamp Duty Reserve Tax Regulations 1986 (SI 1986/1711). Except where otherwise indicated, all section references in these notes are to FA 1986 and Regulation references are to SI 1986/1711.

1.2 The tax applies principally to certain purchases of securities on or after 27 October 1986. It also applies, however, to transactions after 18 March 1986 involving the "conversion" of securities into depositary receipts (see Chapter 5) and the transfer or issue of securities into clearance systems (see Chapter 6).

1.3 Stamp duty reserve tax is administered from the Controller of Stamps Office, Bush House, London and by the stamp duty reserve tax unit at Worthing.

Principal charge

1.4 The tax applies where there is an agreement to transfer "chargeable securities" (see Chapter 3) for money or money's worth, unless there is an instrument of transfer and either:

(a) stamp duty is paid; or
(b) the instrument is exempt from stamp duty.

1.5 The situations in which stamp duty reserve tax liability will most frequently arise will be where a person:

(a) buys a security and resells it within the same Stock Exchange account;
(b) buys renounceable letters of allotment or acceptance;
(c) buys shares which are registered in the name of a nominee who acts both for the seller and the purchaser;
(d) buys shares which are resold before being transferred into his name;
(e) bed and breakfast transactions.

Stamp duty would not normally be paid in any of these circumstances. This list is, however, by no means exhaustive. In any transaction involving chargeable securities where stamp duty is *not* paid you should consider whether stamp duty reserve tax *has* therefore to be paid.

Exemptions

1.6 The principal charge does not apply to:

(a) Government securities ie gilt-edged stocks (see **3.5**);
(b) non-convertible loan stocks (see **3.5**);
(c) foreign securities or interests in foreign securities, unless they are registered on a register kept in the UK (see **3.2–3.4**);
(d) purchases by a charity (see **2.20**);
(e) certain transactions involving units in a unit trust scheme (see **3.6** and **3.7**);
(f) deals on The Stock Exchange's Traded Options Market or the London International FinancialFutures Exchange (see **3.10**);
(g) bearer securities (other than certain renounceable letters of allotment etc) (see **3.8**);
(h) the issue of new securities unless to a depository or clearance service nominee.

1.7 There are in addition special exemptions for Stock Exchange market makers (see 2.13–2.15) and for Stock Exchange broker-dealers where the shares bought are resold within seven calendar days (see **2.16–2.21**) and for certain purchases and sales of shares by issuing houses under public offers for sale.

Rate of tax and chargeable amount

1.8 Tax is chargeable at the rate of 50p for every £100 or part of £100 of the amount or value of the consideration for the sale ie, at the same rate as applies for stamp duty to purchases of shares.

Payment arrangements

1.9 Where securities are bought on The Stock Exchange the buying broker is responsible for collecting the tax from his client and accounting for it to the Inland Revenue. Where under Stock Exchange rules an investor buys securities direct from a Stock Exchange member firm, that firm is responsible.

1.10 Where a Stock Exchange firm is not involved in a transaction the responsibility for accounting for the tax is that of any qualified dealer who is party to the transaction either as a principal or as an agent for someone other than a qualified dealer. If qualified dealers are involved on both sides of the transaction it is the dealer who is buying or acting for the buyer who is the accountable person. Where a qualified dealer buys from a Stock Exchange member firm, the Stock Exchange member firm must account for the tax.

1.11 In other circumstances, the responsibility for paying the tax rests with the buyer, who will need to write to the Controller of Stamps giving details of the transaction and enclosing the tax. Buyers will not need to do this when on an offer for sale the seller has agreed to pay the tax. The prospectus will make this clear.

When the tax has to be paid

1.12 The charge in respect of registered shares arises two months after the date of the agreement for the sale. The tax is due on the last day of the month following the month in which the charge arises (the accountable date). Thus an agreement in respect of registered shares made on 5 January gives rise to a charge to stamp duty reserve tax on 5 March (assuming that the agreement is not concluded before then by a duly stamped instrument of transfer). The accountable date for this transaction, and for all agreements during the month of January relating to registered shares is 30 April. For Renounceable Letters of Allotment the charge arises immediately and the tax is due on the last day of the following month. Thus an agreement made on 5 March gives rise to a charge to stamp duty reserve tax on 5 March and the accountable date for this transaction, and for all agreements relating to Renounceable Letters of Allotment effected during March, is 30 April. Interest is charged on tax paid late (see Chapter 7).

Other charges

1.13 Stamp duty reserve tax is charged at a special rate where shares are "deposited" with a bank for conversion into depositary receipts (see Chapter 5) and where shares are put into a clearance system (see Chapter 6).

CHAPTER 2 THE PRINCIPAL CHARGE

2.1 Stamp duty reserve tax applies where one person (A) agrees with another person (B) to transfer chargeable securities for money or money's worth. It applies to agreements made on or after 27 October 1986.

Definition of chargeable securities

2.2 The expression chargeable securities is explained in Chapter 3. Chargeable securities include stocks, shares and rights to stocks and shares in a UK company or in those shares of a foreign company which are kept on a register in the UK. Most categories of loan stock are not chargeable securities.

When a charge arises

2.3 A charge arises when there is an agreement to transfer chargeable securities for money or money's worth unless the securities are transferred to the original purchaser and:

(a) stamp duty is paid on the transfer; or
(b) the transfer is exempt from stamp duty.

2.4 To allow time for an instrument of transfer to be produced s 87 provides for the charge to arise two months after the date of the agreement, unless in the meantime a duly stamped instrument of transfer has been executed (normally this would be a stock transfer form or, in the case of most Stock Exchange transactions, a TALISMAN bought transfer) transferring the securities either to the person described in **2.1** as B or to B's nominee. Where in the case of a transaction carried out on The Stock Exchange the agreement is concluded between a member firm selling as a principal and a broker-dealer acting as an agent, this condition is regarded as satisfied if within the two month period a duly stamped instrument of transfer is executed transferring the securities to which the agreement relates to the broker-dealer's principal. Where the transaction involves the sale of a renounceable letter of allotment then with effect from 1 August 1987 the charge arises on the date of sale (s 88 (3)).

Sub-sales

2.5 If the securities to which the agreement relates are not transferred directly to the purchaser (B) or his nominee but to another person (eg, a sub-purchaser), a charge arises notwithstanding that stamp duty is paid on the transfer of the securities from the original seller to the other person (see the example at **4.5–4.6**).

Conditional agreements

2.6 If the agreement to transfer securities is conditional, the charge does not arise until two months after the condition is satisfied (s 87 (3)) and, if more than one condition, when the final condition is satisfied.

Rate of tax

2.7 Stamp duty reserve tax is charged at 50p for every £100 or part of £100 of the price paid for the securities. Where payment is made other than in money—eg, by way of shares—tax is calculated on the market value of the consideration at the time the agreement was made (s 87 (7)).

Accountable persons

2.8 The rules governing the payment of the tax are set out in Chapter 7. In most cases the buying broker (or if no broker is acting the dealer who sells the securities) will be responsible for collecting the tax and paying it to the Stamp Office.

2.9 Where a person who is not resident in the UK buys chargeable securities from a dealer (ie, a Stock Exchange market maker or a broker-dealer or a qualified dealer as defined in Regulation 2) the dealer will be accountable for the tax (see **7.3** and **7.5**). When a non-resident with a branch or agent in the UK buys securities through the branch or agent, other than from a dealer as above, the non-resident is the accountable person through the branch or agent. (TMA 1970 s 78, as applied). An agent would only be liable if he acted in relation to the particular transaction.

Purchases from a non-resident

2.10 A charge is not regarded as arising where a non-resident buys chargeable securities from another non-resident and the agreement to transfer is made abroad. Where a person who is resident in the UK buys chargeable securities from a non-resident the buyer will be accountable for the tax in the normal way (see **7.6**).

Documents stamped more than two months after the agreement

2.11 Where stamp duty is paid on an instrument transferring securities to which the charge relates more than two months after the date of the agreement, any stamp duty reserve tax paid will be repaid. If the repayment is £25 or more interest will be paid. If stamp duty reserve tax has not been paid the charge is cancelled though any interest or penalties which have arisen may still be chargeable. A claim for a repayment or cancellation must be made within six years of the date of the agreement. If the agreement is conditional, the claim must be made within six years of the condition being satisfied (see also **7.12**).

Exemption for market makers

2.12 Section 89 (1) provides an exemption from stamp duty reserve tax where securities are bought by a market maker. The exemption applies if the purchaser is recognised by The Stock Exchange as a market maker in the kind of securities bought, and the securities are bought in the course of his ordinary business as a market maker in securities of that kind. Where a broker-dealer is recognised by The Stock Exchange as a market maker in some securities but not others, the exemption is limited to purchases of securities in which he is so recognised. An exemption from stamp duty reserve tax where securities are bought by a market maker in traded or traditional options is provided in s 89 (1A). The market maker must be recognised by the Stock Exchange as a market maker in options to buy or sell securities of the kind transferred and the securities must be bought in the ordinary course of his business as a market maker in those options. There are rules to ensure that purchases excess to hedging requirements are charged to stamp duty reserve tax in the normal way.

2.13 There are enabling powers for the definition of a market maker to be amended. These have been used to provide that the exemption applies also to certain purchases of securities which are not dealt in on The Stock Exchange. The purchaser must be an "authorised person" under the Financial Services Act 1986 and the securities must be bought as a principal in the ordinary course of his business as a dealer in investments. Purchases made in the course of managing assets belonging to another person or operating a collective investments scheme do not qualify for the exemption. The market maker definition was extended by the FA 1986 (Stamp Duty and Stamp Duty Reserve Tax) (Amendment) Regulations 1988, (SI 1988/654) which are available from Her Majesty's Stationery Office.

Exemption for broker-dealers

2.14 Section 89 (2) provides an exemption from stamp duty reserve tax for broker-dealers in respect of securities resold by them within seven days of purchase. To qualify for the exemption:

(a) the broker-dealer must be a member of The Stock Exchange who carries on his business in the UK and is not a market maker in the kind of securities bought;

(b) there must be an agreement to transfer the securities to the broker-dealer or his nominee;

(c) the agreement must be made by the broker-dealer acting as principal in the ordinary course of his business as a broker-dealer in the kind of securities bought; and

(d) the broker-dealer must, within seven days of making the agreement to buy the securities, have made an unconditional agreement to sell the securities to another person. Where the agreement to buy the securities is conditional, the seven days start to run from the day on which the condition is satisfied.

2.15 There is an identification rule for determining whether securities bought by a broker-dealer have been sold within seven days. Where the securities sold cannot otherwise be identified, they are to be identified with any securities acquired in the seven days ending with the day of sale. Within this period securities acquired earlier are taken before those acquired later (ie on a FIFO—first in first out—basis) (s 89 (7)).

How the special rule works

2.16 A sale of securities will be matched with the earliest acquisition of securities of the same kind within the preceding seven days ending with the day of sale for which relief has not already been given against an earlier sale. If there is no such acquisition, relief will not be available.

2.17 For the purposes of this rule, securities are acquired on the day the broker-dealer enters into an agreement for them to be transferred to him or his nominee; or, where the agreement to buy is conditional, the day on which the condition is satisfied. The securities are sold on the day the broker-dealer enters into an unconditional agreement to sell them.

Example

Day	1	B-d agrees to buy 300 Xplc
Day	11	B-d agrees to buy 100 Xplc
Day	12	B-d agrees to buy 200 Xplc
Day	13	B-d agrees to buy 200 Xplc
Day	12	B-d agrees to sell 100 Xplc
Day	13	B-d agrees to sell 300 Xplc
Day	19	B-d agrees to sell 50 Xplc
Day	12	Sale is set against Day 11 purchase

Part II ST

Day 13 Sale is set against Day 12 purchase and against 100 shares of Day 13 purchase. Day 19 sale is set against 50 of the remaining 100 shares of the Day 13 purchase.

Stamp duty reserve tax is paid on the remaining balance of 50 of the Day 13 purchase.

As no securities of the same kind were sold by Day seven stamp duty reserve tax is also charged on the agreement to buy 300 shares on Day one.

2.18 There are enabling powers for the definition of a broker-dealer to be extended to broker-dealers on other recognised exchanges.

2.19 Individual claims will not normally be necessary. The Stock Exchange will be dealing with this on behalf of its members.

Charities, etc

2.20 Section 90 (7) provides an exemption for purchases by:
- (a) a body of persons established for charitable purposes only, or
- (b) the trustees of a trust so established, or
- (c) the trustees of the National Heritage Memorial Fund, or
- (d) the Historic Buildings and Monument Commission for England.

Issuing houses

2.21 Section 89A provides various reliefs for purchases and sales by issuing houses sponsoring offers for sale or placings. These are further explained in **4.8** et seq.

Taurus exemptions

2.22 There are enabling powers to adapt stamp duty reserve tax and stamp duty to paperless share transactions and other new methods of share dealing such as The Stock Exchange's proposed TAURUS system (FA 1989 s 176). Regulations may be introduced to provide that in prescribed circumstances involving a Stock Exchange nominee a stamp duty reserve tax charge may be cancelled where there is also a stamp duty charge or where more than one stamp duty reserve tax charge arises on a single transaction. As yet no Regulations have been made under these powers.

CHAPTER 3 CHARGEABLE SECURITIES

3.1 As a broad generalisation, securities are chargeable securities for stamp duty reserve tax if transfers of them would normally attract stamp duty. There are some important exceptions; eg, although a sale of renounceable letters of allotment or acceptance would not normally be stamped, renounceable letters are chargeable securities for stamp duty reserve tax purposes.

Definition of chargeable securities

3.2 Section 99 defines "chargeable securities" to include:
- (a) stocks, shares and loan capital issued or raised by bodies incorporated in the UK;
- (b) stocks, shares and loan capital issued or raised by bodies not incorporated in the UK if:
  - (i) the stocks etc are registered in a register in the UK, or
  - (ii) in the case of stocks or shares, they are paired with shares issued by a body corporate incorporated in the UK
- (c) rights to securities within (*a*) and (*b*) above;
- (d) units under a unit trust scheme (but see **3.6** and **3.7**).

3.3 Rights included within the definition of chargeable securities are:
- (a) an interest in stocks, shares or loan capital or an interest in dividends or other rights arising out of stocks, shares etc,
- (b) rights to an allotment of or to subscribe for stocks, shares or loan capital; and

(c) an option to acquire stocks, shares or loan capital.

Exclusions

3.4 The definition of chargeable securities excludes the following:

(a) stocks, shares or loan capital the transfer of which is exempt from all stamp duties;
(b) an interest in, or in dividends or other rights arising from, stocks, shares or loan capital the transfer of which is exempt from all stamp duties;
(c) a right to an allotment of, or to subscribe for, or an option to acquire stocks, shares or loan capital the transfer of which is exempt from all stamp duties;
(d) an interest in a depositary receipt;
(e) foreign shares not on a UK register unless they are paired with the shares of a UK company.

Loan capital

3.5 Most non-convertible loan capital is exempt from stamp duty on transfer (ss 78 and 79) and is not therefore a chargeable security. The expression loan capital is regarded as covering short term loans eg, loans for five years or less. Thus if an investor buys a security, eg, a gilt edged security—which is exempt from stamp duty no stamp duty reserve tax arises. Similarly, if an investor buys an allotment letter which gives rights to a security—eg registered loan capital which is exempt from duty—no stamp duty reserve tax arises on the purchase of the allotment letter.

Other exclusions

Unit trusts

3.6 Although units in a unit trust are chargeable securities s 90 (1) excludes from the charge to stamp duty reserve tax transfers of units under a unit trust scheme to the managers of the scheme. Other transfers of units themselves are generally liable to stamp duty and hence stamp duty reserve tax will not normally have to be paid. The issue of new units by a fund manager is not a transfer of securities. Particular care is needed where either mergers or takeovers of unit trusts occur. Depending on the circumstances a variety of stamp duty and stamp duty reserve tax consequences can arise and you should seek specific advice. (Similar difficulties can be met where pension funds merge).

3.7 Transfers of units in a foreign unit trust are excluded from stamp duty reserve tax. A foreign unit trust is one where all the trustees are resident abroad and the units are not registered in a register kept in the UK by or on behalf of the trustees (90 (2)).

Bearer instruments

3.8 Bearer instruments liable to bearer instrument duty are excluded from the charge to stamp duty reserve tax (90 (3)). Renounceable letters of allotment and acceptance, which are exempt from bearer instrument duty, are however liable to stamp duty reserve tax (see 3.12).

Depositary receipts and clearance services

3.9 Agreements to transfer securities which are liable to either the depositary receipt charge (see Chapter 5) of the clearance service charge (see Chapter 6) are excluded from the principal charge. Purchases of depositary receipts and of securities held within a clearance system by a nominee whose business is exclusively that of holding securities for a person providing a clearance service are also excluded from the principal charge (ss 90, 99).

Traded options and futures

3.10 Stamp duty reserve tax does not in practice arise on options dealt in on The Stock Exchange Traded Options Market where dealing takes the form of writing put or call options. The writing or grant of an option does not constitute a transfer. The exercise of an option may give rise to stamp duty reserve tax if there is no stamped share transfer. The futures dealt in on the London International Financial Futures market are not stocks and shares or interests in them and are not therefore chargeable securities.

Special cases

Charities

3.11 No charge arises on purchases of chargeable securities by a body of persons established for charitable purposes only or by the trustees of a trust so established.

Renounceable letters of allotment etc

3.12 Agreements to buy renounceable letters of allotment, acceptance etc (RLAs) are chargeable to stamp duty reserve tax notwithstanding the stamp exemptions in FA 1963 ss 59, 65.

Transfers to The Stock Exchange's nominee

3.13 Although transfers to The Stock Exchange's nominees SEPON LTD are exempt from stamp duty (FA 1976 s 127 (1) and s 84 (1)) this exemption does not by itself preclude a charge to stamp duty reserve tax on a purchase of the securities transferred (s 88 (1)). Other exemptions eg, for market makers (see **2.13–2.15**) and broker-dealers (see **2.16–2.19**) may however apply.

3.14 The same position will arise on transfers to other recognised clearing houses, recognised investment exchanges or their nominees to which the exemption from stamp duty in s 84 is extended under the Financial Services Act regime.

CHAPTER 4 THE PRINCIPAL CHARGE: SOME PRACTICAL APPLICATIONS

4.1 Stamp duty reserve tax will apply to certain transactions which do not attract stamp duty. The situations in which stamp duty reserve tax will most frequently arise are set out in **1.5**. This Chapter describes how the charge will operate in those cases. It is assumed in each case that the purchaser is not entitled to any special exemptions.

Stock Exchange: intra account transactions

4.2 Where an investor contracts to buy securities and to sell them on within the same Stock Exchange account, the purchaser does not take delivery of the shares and so no stamp duty is paid. The purchase contract gives rise to a charge to stamp duty reserve tax. A charge also arises where an investor contracts to buy securities which he has previously contracted to sell (s 87).

4.3 Where the number of shares a person contracts to buy exceeds the number of shares he sells, the unsold shares will be delivered to him and stamp duty will be paid on them. In these circumstances the stamp duty reserve tax is chargeable only on the consideration for the shares sold on (s 87 (7A)).

4.4 The following examples show how stamp duty reserve tax will be charged in intra-account transactions.

Example 1

Securities purchased	100	for £1,500
Securities sold	100	
Securities transferred to original purchaser	nil	

£7.50 stamp duty reserve tax is payable on £1,500, the consideration for the purchase.

Example 2

Securities purchased	100	for £1,500
Securities sold	75	
Securities transferred to original purchaser	25	for £375
		(25% of £1,500)

£2 stamp duty is payable on £375, the consideration for the securities transferred to the original purchaser.

£6 stamp duty reserve tax is payable on £1,125, the consideration for the purchase of the 75 shares sold on (75% of £1,500).

Example 3

Securities purchased	100	for £1,500
Securities sold	150	
Securities to be delivered by purchaser	50	

£7.50 stamp duty reserve tax will be payable on £1,500, the consideration for the purchase.

Off-market transactions: sub-sales

4.5 Similar dealing sequences can arise with off-market transactions, in particular where a bank or a dealer is acting as principal. FA 1963 s 67 prohibits circulation of blank stock transfer forms (ie, forms which do not show the name of the transferee). Where however a purchaser sells securities before the delivery of the stock transfer form, the securities transferred can be delivered direct from the original vendor to the sub-purchaser. In these circumstances stamp duty is payable only on the consideration paid by the sub-purchaser.

4.6 The purchase by the original buyer will give rise to a charge to stamp duty reserve tax. The sale to the sub-purchaser will only give rise to a stamp duty reserve tax charge if stamp duty is not paid within two months of the agreement.

Example

X agrees to sell N securities to Y for £100

Y agrees to sell N securities to Z for £120

N securities are transferred from X to Z by stock transfer form and stamp duty is paid on £120.

See **4.8** et seq (Offers for Sale).

Part II ST

Renounceable documents

4.7 Rights to and interests in securities which are themselves chargeable securities are also chargeable securities for stamp duty reserve tax (see Chapter 3). Renounceable letters of allotment and renounceable letters of acceptance are the commonest examples of these securities.

Offers for sale

4.8 These paragraphs deal with stamp duty reserve tax charges and reliefs in respect of offers for sale to the public. These offers for sale could include any combination of the following:

(a) new shares issued by the company for sale to the public;
(b) bonus shares issued by the company to its shareholders and renounced by them for sale to the public; and
(c) registered shares sold by the company's shareholders to the public.

4.9 These sales are usually sponsored by issuing houses acting either as agents for the issuing company and its shareholders or as principals. If the sponsor acts as agent then the sale of bonus and registered shares are chargeable transactions, being sales of chargeable securities by the vendor shareholders to the public. The issue of new shares is not an agreement to transfer securities and is, accordingly, not chargeable.

4.10 If the sponsor acts as principal then its purchase of bonus and registered shares and its sale of new, bonus and registered shares will all be chargeable transactions. With effect from 8 May 1987 s 89A provides exemption for such purchases and sales where the shares are to be admitted to the Official List of the Stock Exchange, to enable issuing houses to act as principals without incurring the additional stamp duty reserve tax charges.

4.11 Section 89A (1) exempts purchases of securities (other than unit trust units) by issuing houses and s 89A (2) exempts the subsequent sale by them of *newly subscribed* securities where:

(a) the securities are bought by the issuing house and sold on under the same arrangements to the public;
(b) the sale is subject to an Official Listing on the Stock Exchange; and
(c) the securities are bought and sold on at the same price.

4.12 It is usual with such offers for sale for the sponsor to pay stamp duty reserve tax on behalf of the company or the vendors under an arrangement with the Revenue (see **7.9**) and accounted for in the normal way.

Subsequent to the offer for sale, the sale of securities in renounceable form is liable and this is explained in **4.15** et seq.

4.13 When registered shares are offered for sale on renounceable letters of acceptance, at the end of the renunciation period a transfer of shares is executed by the vendor shareholders in favour of the persons who then hold renounceable letters of acceptance, renounced or otherwise. The transfer will be impressed with stamp duty, usually paid by the vendors or sponsor. If the original purchaser does not renounce the letter the stamp duty reserve tax charge arising on the purchase will be cancelled by the stamp duty on the transfer. If the letter of acceptance is renounced the stamp duty reserve tax falling on the original purchase remains in place, as do the charges on subsequent purchases of the renounced letter. The stamp duty payable on the eventual transfer will not cancel any stamp duty reserve tax charges arising in respect of such renounced letters of acceptance (s 88 (3)).

4.14 However, with effect from 8 May 1987 s 89A (3) provides an exemption for sales of registered shares to the public (or placees) where the sale is effected by the issue of renounceable letters of acceptance (or similar documents) and the sale is conditional upon an Official Listing on the Stock Exchange. The stamp duty reserve tax charges on the subsequent renunciations remain in place as does the stamp duty charge on the eventual transfer document.

Renounceable letters of allotment

4.15 Where a company issues *new* shares (whether in connection with a rights issue or a bonus issue) existing shareholders will normally receive a renounceable letter of allotment. A renounceable letter of allotment is exempt from stamp duties provided its life does not exceed six months. It is, however, a chargeable security for stamp duty reserve tax purposes (**3.12**).

4.16 The *issue* of a renounceable letter does not give rise to the charge to stamp duty reserve tax as there is no agreement to *transfer* securities. The purchase of a renounced letter (including a split letter) however does give rise to a charge to stamp duty reserve tax on the consideration paid. The purchaser is liable for the tax but his broker is normally accountable for it (**7.3–7.8**).

4.17 The issue of a share certificate at the end of the renunciation period to the person surrendering the allotment letter is not chargeable to stamp duty reserve tax.

Renounceable letters of acceptance

4.18 The issue of a renounceable letter of acceptance, under an offer for sale of shares, can give rise to a charge to stamp duty reserve tax unless the conditions in s 89A(3) have been met (see **4.14**). The purchase of a renounced letter (including a split letter) also gives rise to a charge to stamp duty reserve tax. The purchase is liable for the tax but his broker is normally accountable for it.

Instalment arrangements

4.19 Where shares sold are to be paid for over a period of time, special provision may be made to enable the purchasers to sell freely without prejudicing the interest of the seller. An arrangement of this kind typically involves an agreement between the seller and a custodian bank to which the purchaser is also a party. Under the terms of the agreement the shares concerned will be registered in the name of and retained by the custodian bank until the instalments have been paid. A purchaser's rights and obligations in relation to the shares (ie, his interim rights) are evidenced by letters of acceptance (which are renounceable for a limited period) and interim certificates issued by the custodian bank.

4.20 Where these circumstances apply, the agreement between the vendor and the purchaser gives rise to a stamp duty reserve tax charge. In practice this charge is often borne by the vendor. Sales of the letter of acceptance, during the renunciation period, also give rise to a stamp duty reserve tax charge (see **4.13**). Where after the renunciation period, the letters of acceptance become registered documents and the shares are transferred by a stock transfer form, stamp duty reserve tax will only arise if stamp duty is not paid within two months of the agreement to buy the letter.

4.21 The *issue* of interim certificates (when the acceptance letters are surrendered) does not give rise to stamp duty reserve tax (but see Chapters 5 and 6 as regards Depositary receipts and Clearance system charges). When interim certificates are transferred by stock transfer form, a charge to stamp duty reserve tax arises only if stamp duty is not paid within two months of the agreement.

4.22 When the final instalment is paid, the shares are transferred from the custodian bank to the shareholder and a charge to stamp duty of 50p arises on each transfer. There is no charge to stamp duty reserve tax.

Underwriting

4.23 Where shares are offered for sale to the public or placees it is customary for the company or vendor shareholders to enter into an agreement with a financial institution whereby the latter agrees to purchase shares not taken up by the public. This underwriting function can in fact be performed by the issuing house sponsoring the offer for sale by agreeing to procure purchasers and to purchase shares for which purchasers cannot be procured. When that condition is satisfied and the number of shares to be taken up by the underwriter is known, the agreement is liable to stamp duty reserve tax in respect of the shares so purchased.

4.24 It is also customary for underwriters to agree with sub-underwriters (sometimes a "chain" of sub-underwriters) to the effect that the latter will take up part of the underwriter's liability to purchase shares not accepted by the public. No chargeable transaction exists at this stage but when unsold shares have to be taken up by the underwriters and sub-underwriters, then any shares taken up by sub-underwriters would result from a chargeable agreement between the issuing company or vendor shareholders and the sub-underwriters and not a sub-sale of shares purchased by underwriters for sale on to sub-underwriters.

4.25 If registered shares are delivered to underwriters or sub-underwriters, the stamp duty paid on the transfer document will cancel the stamp duty reserve tax charge. If bonus shares are issued stamp duty reserve tax will be payable but the issue of new shares will not be an agreement to transfer securities and accordingly will not attract stamp duty reserve tax. If an underwriter or sub-underwriter sells shares taken up then that sale will attract stamp duty reserve tax in addition to the charge on the underwriter's or sub-underwriter's purchase.

Nominee acting for seller and buyer

4.26 Where securities are registered in the name of a nominee and the beneficial interest is sold to a person using the same nominee so that the legal title remains unchanged, a charge to stamp duty reserve tax arises unless the written instructions from the vendor to nominee instructing him to hold the shares as nominee for the purchaser has been duly stamped as a letter of request. This situation arises frequently within the discretionary nominees operated by many qualified brokers and qualified dealers. They will be accountable for the stamp duty reserve tax arising within those nominees, where letters of request are not stamped.

Bed and breakfast transactions

4.27 Where such transactions are carried out, two charges to stamp duty reserve tax arise, one on the sale to the broker or dealer and one on the repurchase. (Since the stock does not move it is unlikely that stamp duty will be paid.) If the transaction is carried out through a Stock Exchange Member Firm, they will be accountable for *both* transactions. Otherwise the qualified dealer who arranges the transactions is accountable. (Again for both transactions.)

CHAPTER 5 DEPOSITARY RECEIPTS

5.1 United Kingdom shares are traded on a number of foreign stock exchanges in depositary receipt form. The depositary receipt (see **5.27**) is in effect a substitute for the UK share certificate. A stamp duty reserve tax charge at a special rate (depositary receipt charge) is imposed when UK shares are "deposited for conversion" into depositary receipts (s 93). The rate is normally one and a half%. The charge complements the similar one and a half% stamp duty charge that applies to the transfer of shares to certain nominee holding companies (s 67). Unlike the stamp duty charge the stamp duty reserve tax charge applied from 19 March 1986. There are provisions to ensure that both the one and a half% stamp duty and the one and a half% stamp duty reserve tax charges will not both arise on the same transaction, and that the principal charge does not arise if there is a depositary receipt charge (s 90 (4)). There is no stamp duty reserve tax charge when a depositary receipt changes hands. (s 99 (6)).

Main Rules

When the charge arises

5.2 Depositary banks issue receipts against the deposit of securities with a nominee. A depositary receipt charge (see **5.3**) arises where (i) chargeable securities are "deposited" with a nominee of a person whose business is or includes the issuing of depositary receipts and (ii) a receipt is issued. It is assumed for the purpose of these explanatory notes that the person concerned will be a bank. If exceptionally the person concerned is not a bank the notes should be read accordingly.

5.3 The Finance Act does not define a "deposit"; instead it specified (s 93 (1)) three separate occasions of charge:

(a) the transfer of the chargeable securities to the bank's nominee;
(b) the issue of chargeable securities to such a nominee;
(c) the appropriation by the bank's nominee of chargeable securities it already holds against the issue of a depositary receipt.

5.4 The charge arises if the securities are transferred, issued or appropriated on or after 19 March 1986. The charge does not, however, apply to certain transactions which straddled 18 March ie, transfers of securities after 18 March where the commitment to deposit them was entered into before that date. It has to be shown that the securities transferred were bought or appropriated for deposit before 19 March but the depositary receipt can have been issued on or after that date (s 93 (12)).

5.5 The issue of bonus shares to the nominee of the bank issuing the receipt (where there is no consideration) does not give rise to a charge (see **5.6**). The issue of shares for a scrip dividend can however result in a charge, as a right to cash has been exchanged for shares.

Rate of tax and chargeable amount

5.6 Tax is chargeable at the rate of £1.50 per £100 or part of £100, as follows:
(a) where the securities are transferred for consideration, on the amount of value of the consideration;
(b) where the securities are issued, on their price when issued;
(c) in other cases, on the open market value of the securities at the time of the transfer or appropriation.

5.7 A special rate of duty may apply on transfers by a qualified dealer (see **5.19–5.25**) (s 93 (5)).

Credit for stamp duty

5.8 Section 67 provides for *stamp duty* at £1.50 per £100 to be charged in the case of transfers (on sale or otherwise) of securities in UK companies to:
(a) a person whose business is exclusively that of holding as nominee or agent securities for a bank's depositary business; or
(b) to certain other persons specified by Treasury Order.

This provision applied to transfers executed on or after 27 October 1986.

5.9 Where both a stamp duty reserve tax depositary receipt charge and ad valorem stamp duty are payable in respect of a transfer of securities, the stamp duty reserve tax charge is reduced by the amount of the stamp duty paid. Where the stamp duty equals or exceeds the amount of stamp duty reserve tax charge, no tax will be payable. This credit is not available where a fixed duty of 50p has been paid on the transfer (s 93 (7)).

5.10 The effect of these rules, therefore, is as follows. A transfer on sale of securities to a depositary bank's nominee company to which the stamp duty charge applies between 19 March and 26 October 1986, will have been stamped (if the consideration was over £500) at the rate of £1 for every £100 or part £100 of the consideration. Because stamp duty has been paid, the stamp duty reserve tax charge in this instance is limited to 50p per £100 or part £100 of the consideration. However, for a transfer on or after 27 October 1986, which is liable to stamp duty at the rate of £1.50 for every £100 of the consideration, or in the case of a transfer other than on sale the value of the securities, the stamp duty charge will in effect cancel out the stamp duty reserve tax charge.

Exemptions

5.11 Since the stamp duty reserve tax charge applies in respect of transactions involving "chargeable securities" as defined for the purpose of the principal charge to stamp duty reserve tax (see Chapter 3), it does not arise where the transaction involves most categories of loan capital (s 99 (5)) or stocks and shares of companies incorporated outside the UK (s 99 (10)). Exceptionally, the charge does extend to any such shares if they are paired with shares in a UK company unless the transaction involves the issue of the paired shares direct to the bank as part of an offer for sale to the public.

5.12 Nor does the charge apply to inland bearer instruments within the meaning of the heading "bearer instrument" in SA 1891 Sch 1 (s 95 (2)) other than renounceable letters of acceptance or allotment etc which are exempt from stamp duties. Where, therefore, applicants allocated shares under the terms of an offer for sale are sent a renounceable letter of acceptance in respect of those shares, a depositary receipt charge will arise if the letter of acceptance is "deposited" (see **5.3**) with a depositary bank in connection with the issue of a depositary receipt. No charge arises when shares are issued to a depositary bank which holds letters of acceptance or allotment. See **5.16–5.18** as regards letters of acceptance issued in connection with certain instalment arrangements.

5.13 An exemption is provided for certain "share for share" exchanges in connection with a takeover, where an acquiring company (company X) issue securities in exchange for shares in another company (company Y). To qualify for the exemption, company X must either have control of company Y, or obtain control as a consequence of the exchange or of an offer as a result of which the exchange is made. Company X is taken to have control of company Y if it has (direct or indirect) voting control of that company (s 95 (3) and (4)).

5.14 There is also an exemption for transfers of securities between depositaries. There is no charge in respect of transfers between one nominee company whose business consists exclusively of holding securities in connection with a bank's depositary receipt business and another such company, provided both companies are resident in the UK (s 95 (1)). If either company's business does not meet this requirement the exemption does not apply. Segregation of securities held for depositary receipt business by the use of designated accounts is not enough to bring a company within the scope of the exemption. A company can, however, hold foreign shares provided these are held in connection with the issue of a depositary receipt.

5.15 The position is similar for transfers between nominees for companies operating clearance services (see **6.9**). An exemption is not available for transfers between a depositary receipt nominee and a clearance service operator's nominee, even if both nominees only hold securities for the principal's depositary receipt issuing business or the principal's clearance service business, as the case may be.

Special Cases

Instalment arrangements

5.16 The following paragraphs set out the implications of the depositary receipt charge where shares are sold under an instalment arrangement of the kind described in **4.19**.

5.17 Where letters of acceptance are issued by a custodian bank to a nominee for a depositary, and either the depositary or the nominee is liable to pay the first of the instalments, the usual depositary receipt charge will not apply. Instead, when the depositary or its nominee makes payment of each of the instalments for which it is liable, there is a special charge at the rate of £1.50 for every £100 or part of £100 of the instalment payable (s 93 (10)). The normal depositary receipt charge will, however, apply where letters of acceptance or interim certificates are transferred to (or appropriated by) the depositary's nominee. The special charge applies to any instalment for which the depositary or its nominee is liable, whether or not letters of acceptance were issued to it.

5.18 There is neither a stamp duty reserve tax depositary receipt charge nor a s 67 stamp duty charge when, after payment of all the instalments, the custodian bank transfers the underlying securities to the depositary's nominee (ss 67 (5), 93 (6)) provided that the transfer instrument is certified to the effect that:

(a) the securities transferred are the subject of an instalment arrangement;
(b) the transferor is acting as a custodian bank; and
(c) the interim certificate held by the depositary bank's nominee evidences all the rights which under the terms of sale subsist at the time of the receipt in the securities sold.

The certificate can be in terms that s 93 (6) applies.

Qualified dealers

5.19 Relief is available where a qualified dealer transfers to a depositary bank's nominee, securities the dealer previously bought and registered in his own name (or that of his own nominee) (s 93 (5)). This is designed to ensure that a dealer who buys shares to transfer against the issue of depositary receipts pays no more than one and a half% on the transaction. "Qualified dealer" has a different meaning in this context from the term used in the accountable person rules in Regulation 2 (see **5.22** and **7.8**).

5.20 Where the relief applied in respect of securities transferred to a depositary bank's nominee before 27 October 1986, the stamp duty reserve tax charge will be 50p per £100. For transfers on or after 27 October the charge, either to stamp duty under s 67 (3) or to stamp duty reserve tax under s 93 (5), will be £1 per £100. Where a dealer bought shares before 27 October 1986 and paid stamp duty at £1 per £100, there will be a reserve tax charge of £1 per £100 on transferring stock to the depositary bank's nominee company on or after that date.

5.21 For the stamp duty reserve tax relief to apply the following conditions must be met:
- (a) the transfer to the depositary bank's nominee must be effected by a transfer made otherwise than on sale;
- (b) the transferor must be a qualified dealer (or his nominee) in securities of the kind concerned;
- (c) the transfer must be made for the purposes of the transferor's business;
- (d) at the time of the transfer the dealer must not be a market maker in securities of the kind concerned, and
- (e) the transfer must be certified to the effect that the above conditions are fulfilled.

5.22 A dealer in securities is a "qualified dealer" if he is either:
- (a) a member of a recognised stock exchange within the meaning of TA 1970 s 535 [TA 1988 s 841] or
- (b) designated a qualified dealer by order made by the Treasury.

5.23 No orders by the Treasury have yet been made. Appendix 1 lists the stock exchanges recognised under TA 1970 s 535 [TA 1988 s 841]. It should be noted that the s 535 [s. 841] applies to "Any exchange registered with the Securities and Exchange Commission of the United States as a *national* securities exchange". It does not apply to any local exchanges registered with the SEC.

5.24 A market maker in securities of a particular kind is a firm recognised by the Council of the Stock Exchange as a market maker in those securities (s 94 (6)).

5.25 For the purpose of **5.21**, the transfer may be certified in the following terms:

> "I/We hereby certify that I/we am/are [a nominee of] a qualified dealer in securities of the kind hereby transferred (within the meaning of s 94 (5) Finance Act 1986) and that the conditions in s 93 (5) (*c*) and (*d*) Finance Act 1986 are fulfilled."

Where the transfer has already taken place and all the conditions are met except the certification condition, the relief will be given if it is confirmed that the transfer otherwise qualifies.

Payment arrangements

5.26 The depositary bank will normally be the person accountable and liable for the tax (s 93 (8)). The exceptions are where the bank is not resident in the UK and has no branch or agent here, when the bank's nominee is liable, and where the charge arises under the special provisions dealing with instalment arrangements, when the person liable to pay the instalment is liable for the tax. Where the responsibility for accounting for the tax falls on the nominee, despositary banks may make arrangements to account for the tax themselves.

Definition of depositary receipt

5.27 A depositary receipt is defined for the purposes of the charge as an instrument acknowledging that a person holds stocks or shares (or evidence of the right to receive them) and that another person is entitled to rights in relation to stocks or shares of the same kind including the right to receive such securities (s 94 (1)). This definition reflects the legal rights and obligations contained in depositary receipts currently traded. These receipts acknowledge that:

(a) the issuing bank holds (ie, has deposited with it) securities (often described as deposited shares) or rights to receive them;
(b) the owner of the receipt is entitled to rights in or over the deposited shares (eg, to dividends); and
(c) the owner of the receipt is entitled on surrender of the receipt to a specific number of deposited shares or rights to receive them.

5.28 An interim certificate issued in connection with sales of shares where the purchase price is paid by instalments (see **5.16–5.18**) is not a "depositary receipt".

CHAPTER 6 CLEARANCE SERVICES

6.1 There is a stamp duty reserve tax charge when UK securities of the type to which the depositary receipt charge applies (Chapter 5) are transferred or issued to a person providing clearance services or its nominee (clearance service charge). The charge is at the special one and a half% rate and, like the depositary receipt charge, it complements a one and a half% stamp duty charge (570). The rules that govern the clearance service charge are similar to those that apply to the depositary receipt charge.

6.2 The charge applies from 19 March 1986. There are provisions to ensure that both the one and a half% stamp duty charge and the one and a half% stamp duty reserve tax charge do not arise on the same transaction and that the principal charge does not arise if there is a clearance service charge (s 90 (4)). There is an exemption for transfers of securities between clearance systems. The nominee company that holds the securities must, however, meet certain conditions (see **6.9**).

Main Rules

When the charge arises

6.3 A clearance service is an arrangement for settling (ie, clearing) transactions in securities, which may be held indefinitely on the system, despite changes in ownership. Securities within the system are held in the name of the company operating the clearance system or its nominee. The shares concerned can be traded without the need to produce transfer documents though, sometimes, documents akin to depositary receipts are issued to evidence title. The clearance service charge arises where chargeable securities are either transferred or issued to either:

(a) the clearance service operator; or
(b) its nominee.

6.4 The charge applies to securities transferred or issued on or after 19 March 1986 (s 96 (13)). The charge does not, however, apply to certain transactions which straddled 18 March (s 96 (14)). This transitional exemption applies where the following conditions are satisfied:

(a) the transferor (or, where the transferor acts as agent, the principal) agreed on or before 18 March 1986 to sell securities of the same kind and amount to a person other than the clearance service operator; and
(b) the transfer is effected in pursuance of that agreement.

6.5 The issue of bonus shares to the clearance service operator or its nominee does not give rise to a charge. The issue of shares for a scrip dividend can however result in a charge, as a right to cash has been exchanged for shares.

Rate of tax and chargeable amount

6.6 Tax is charged at the rate of £1.50 for every £100 or part of £100 as follows:

(a) where securities are transferred for consideration, on the amount or value of the consideration;
(b) where securities are issued, on their price when issued;

(c) in any other case, the open market value of the securities at the time of transfer.

A special rate may apply on transfers by a qualified dealer, on terms similar to those that apply to the relief from the depositary receipt charge provided for qualified dealers (see paragraphs 5.19–5.25) (s 96 (3)).

Credit for stamp duty

6.7 Section 70 provides for *stamp duty* at £1.50 per £100 to be charged in the case of transfers (on sale or otherwise) of securities in UK companies to:

(a) a person whose business is exclusively that of holding as nominee securities for a clearance service system; or

(b) certain other persons specified by Treasury Order.

This provision applies to transfers executed on or after 27 October 1986.

6.8 Where both a stamp duty reserve tax clearance service charge and ad valorem stamp duty are payable in respect of a particular transfer of securities, the stamp duty reserve tax charge is reduced by the amount of stamp duty paid. Where the stamp duty equals or exceeds the amount of the stamp duty reserve tax charge, no tax will be payable. This credit is not available where a fixed duty of 50p has been paid on the transfer (s 96 (5)).

Exemptions

6.9 There is an exemption for transfers between clearance systems. The securities concerned must, however, be held by and transferred to a UK resident company which acts only as a nominee or agent of a clearance service operator and who holds relevant securities only in connection with the provision of the clearance service (s 97 (1)).

6.10 An exemption is not available for transfers between a depositary receipt nominee and a clearance service operator's nominee, even if both nominees hold securities only for the principal's depositary receipt issuing business or the principal's clearance service business, as the case may be.

6.11 Section 97 (2) exempts from the charge transactions involving instruments of transfer to The Stock Exchange's nominee company or to any other nominee company of any other investment exchange which enters into an agreement with the Revenue for the composition of stamp duty.

6.12 There are exemptions relating to loan stocks, securities of non-UK companies, inland bearer instruments and takeovers similar to the exemption from the depositary receipt charge (see **5.11–5.13**).

Special Cases

Instalment arrangements

6.13 There are special rules relating to instalment arrangements which mirror those which apply under the depositary receipt charge (see **5.17–5.18**).

Qualified dealers

6.14 As in the case of the depositary receipt charge, relief is available under similar conditions (see **5.19–5.25**) where a qualified dealer transfers to a clearance service operator (or its nominee) securities which the dealer had previously bought and registered in his own name (or that of his own nominee) (s 96 (3)).

6.15 Transfers qualifying for the relief may be certified in the following terms:

> "I/We hereby certify that I/we am/are [the nominee of] a qualified dealer in securities of the kind hereby transferred (within the meaning of Section 94 (5) Finance Act 1986) and that the conditions in Section 96 (3) (*c*) and (*d*) Finance Act 1986 are fulfilled."

Payment arrangements

6.16 The clearance service operator will normally be the person accountable and liable for the tax (s 96 (6)). The exceptions are where the operator is not resident in the UK and has no branch or agent here, when the operator's nominee (if it has one) is liable; and where the charge arises under the special provisions dealing with instalment arrangements, when the person liable to pay the instalment is liable for the tax. Where the responsibility for accounting for the tax falls on the nominee, clearance service operators may make arrangements to account for the tax themselves.

CHAPTER 7 ADMINISTRATION AND PAYMENT

7.1 Stamp duty reserve tax is to be administered centrally from the Controller of Stamps Office, Bush House (South West Wing), Strand, London WC2B 4QN (tel 071–438 7039/7048). Enquiries should be addressed there. Notification and payments should be made to the stamp duty reserve tax unit, TOBI, South Block, Barrington Road, Worthing BN12 4SF. Other stamp offices will not handle stamp duty reserve tax. Taxpayers in Scotland may address general enquiries about the tax to the Controller (Scotland), 16 Picardy Place, Edinburgh EH3 1NF.

7.2 The responsibility for collecting the tax from the purchaser and paying the tax to the Revenue will normally rest with the purchaser's broker. Ordinary investors will have to account to the Revenue for the tax themselves when buying shares privately ie not through a market maker, broker-dealer or qualified dealer by notifying the stamp duty reserve tax unit. Special rules apply in the case of the depositary receipt and clearance services. Most of the provisions relating to collection and recovery of the tax are contained in the Stamp Duty Reserve Tax Regulations 1986, SI 1986/1711 [see after FA 1990]. These Regulations were amended by the Stamp Duty Reserve Tax (Amendment) Regulations 1988, SI 1988/835.

The Principal Charge

Responsibility for payment

7.3 Responsibility for payment depends on whether or not securities are bought on The Stock Exchange. Where securities are bought on The Stock Exchange via a broker acting as agent, the buying broker will normally be the person responsible for accounting for it to the Revenue though his client will be liable. The contractual arrangement between the broker and his client does not constitute a *separate* chargeable agreement. Where an investor buys securities direct from a Stock Exchange member firm (ie, where the firm is selling as a principal) the person ultimately liable in law for the tax will be the investor; but under the Regulations the Stock Exchange firm will be responsible for notifying the Revenue of the charge and accounting for the tax.

7.4 Arrangements are being made with The Stock Exchange for certain stamp duty reserve tax obligations of member firms to be dealt with centrally. Individual member firms will not therefore be required to notify the Revenue of these transactions or account for the tax. They are required to account for the tax to The Stock Exchange, and notify the Revenue about client transactions that are not reported to The Stock Exchange. There are still, however, a range of transactions for which central accounting via the Stock Exchange is not possible. The one most commonly met is in connection with Stock Situations arising in connection with takeovers. (Though deals in Residual Securities can also give rise to problems.)

It often happens that, before settlement of a deal in the target company's shares can take place, the offer becomes unconditional. The deal is then settled in accordance with the acquiring company's offer. Where this involves settlement by shares and cash, cash, renounceables, loan stock or foreign securities the stamp duty arising on the original deal will not be, or not fully, paid. Thus stamp duty reserve tax arises and had to be accounted for direct by the Member Firm.

7.5 Where a Stock Exchange firm is not involved in a transaction the purchaser will be liable for the tax. However, he will be responsible for accounting for it only if a qualified dealer is not involved in the transaction. If a qualified dealer buys securities as a principal or as an agent for someone other than a qualified dealer he will be the accountable person. If the buyer or the buyer's agent is not a qualified dealer but a qualified dealer is selling securities as a principal or as an agent for someone other than a qualified dealer that dealer is required by the Regulations to account for the tax.

7.6 In other circumstances, the purchaser will be both liable for the tax and responsible for accounting to the Revenue. He will need to write to the Controller of Stamps, Stamp Duty Reserve Tax Unit giving details of the transaction and enclosing the tax (see **7.10–7.11**).

7.7 An accountable person can be relieved of his obligations where the Revenue are satisfied that he has, without success, taken all reasonable steps to recover the tax from the liable person (reg 7). Where the acountable person is relieved of his obligations the person liable for the tax (the purchaser) is required to pay it.

7.8 A "qualified dealer" for the accountable person rules is a dealer who is not a member of The Stock Exchange but who is a member of a self-regulatory organisation or a person otherwise authorised under the Financial Services Act 1986 Part I Chapter III or a person treated as authorised under that Act's transitional provisions.

Offers for sale

7.9 Generally, a public offer of shares will be made by a seller who is not either a market maker, nor a broker-dealer nor a qualified dealer. In law, the person liable for the tax will then be the purchaser under the Offer and there will be no market maker, broker-dealer or qualified dealer to account for the tax. Where, however, the vendor undertakes to meet any liability and enters into an arrangement with the Revenue to do so, the investor will not need to concern himself with it. Where the Revenue makes such an agreement with the vendor, there will be a statement to that effect in the Prospectus or Offer document. Vendors wishing to do this must obtain the Revenue's agreement beforehand (reg 4).

What the accountable person has to do

7.10 The principal charge arises in law two months after the "relevant day" (s 87 (3)). In most cases the relevant day will be the date shown on the contract note. The accountable person has both to notify the Revenue of the charge and to pay the tax before the "accountable date" (reg 4). The "accountable date" is the last day of the month following that in which the charge arises. Thus, an agreement made on 5 January would give rise to a charge on 5 March (assuming that the agreement is not concluded with a duly stamped instrument of transfer). The accountable date for this transaction (and for all agreements made during January) would be 30 April (but see **1.12** for the payment date where RLAs are involved in the transaction).

7.11 Regulation 4 provides for notices to be in such form as the Board may prescribe or authorise and to contain such information as they may reasonably require for the purposes of the Act. FA 1989 s 177 provides that Regulations may also be introduced to prescribe the manner or form in which information is provided, (eg in a particular computer format where relevant). As yet a form of notice has not been prescribed. Notice can be given either by letter or a computer print-out containing the following information:

(a) date of the agreement;
(b) names of the parties;
(c) the description and number of securities;
(d) consideration paid;
(e) the stamp duty reserve tax payable.

Cheques should be made payable to the Inland Revenue and should accompany the notification. Both should be sent to the Stamp Duty Reserve Tax Unit, TOBI, South Block, Barrington Road, Worthing BN12 4SF (Tel. 0903 509782).

Repayments where instruments stamped after the two month period

7.12 The principal charge arises where an agreement is not followed within two months by an instrument of transfer which is duly stamped (or exempt from stamp

Part II ST

duty) (see **2.4**). If such an instrument is executed and stamped after the end of the two month period but before the tax has been paid, a charge to tax arises, but accountable persons are not required to pay the tax in these circumstances. Details of the transaction should, however, be notified along with other chargeable transactions. Where the instrument is executed and stamped after the accountable date (**2.11**) but within six years of the date of the agreement giving rise to the charge, repayment of the reserve tax can be claimed. Where the tax is not less than £25 it will be repaid with interest (s 92).

Other repayments

7.13 Where it is proved that too much tax has been paid in respect of a particular transaction, the tax will be repaid with interest at the rate mentioned (regs 11 and 14). A claim has to be made to the Controller of Stamps within six years of the date of payment or the accountable date, whichever is the later.

Underpayments and overdue tax

7.14 Regulation 13 provides for tax underpaid to be paid with interest. The time limit for recovery of tax underpaid is six years from the date of payment or the accountable date, whichever is the later. In the case of fraud, wilful default or neglect the period of six years runs from the discovery by the Revenue of the fraud etc

Determination of liability

7.15 Where it is necessary to determine formally various matters relating to a chargeable transaction, eg, the occurrence of charge, or the liable person, the Revenue may give notice in writing to the person concerned stating that they have determined the matter specified in the notice (reg 6).

Appeals

7.16 The Regulations give anyone served with a notice of determination the right of appeal. An appeal against a notice of determination should be made within 30 days of the service of the notice (reg 8). In general, appeals lie to the Special Commissioners. Appeals may be brought out of time, with the consent of the Revenue or the Special Commissioners (reg 9). Any party to an appeal may question the determination of the appeal by the Special Commissioners on a point of law by requiring the Commissioners to state a case for the opinion of the High Court (in Scotland the Court of Session and in Northern Ireland the Court of Appeal in Northern Ireland). There are provisions to enable appeals to go direct to the High Court, either where this is agreed between the appellant and the Board, or where the High Court, on an application made by the appellant, agrees (reg 8). Appeals in relation to the value of land lie to the Lands Tribunal.

Recovery of tax

7.17 The Revenue may not recover tax or interest unless the amount has been agreed in writing or determined by a notice of determination (reg 12). If an appeal has been lodged against a notice, legal proceedings can be taken only for such amounts as have been agreed or formally determined by further notice (which itself is subject to appeal) as not being in dispute. But proceedings may be taken for the tax due in accordance with the decision of the first tribunal or Court to hear the appeal, even though a further appeal has been made against that decision.

Information

7.18 The Revenue may by written notice require any person to furnish them with information needed for the purposes of the tax. Communications between solicitors and barristers and their clients are in general privileged (reg 5). Accountable persons may be required to make available their records for inspection (reg 15). The Board is also entitled to obtain information from company registrars, issuing houses, brokers and dealers on the Stock Exchange and nominees (TMA 1970 ss 23, 25, 26).

7.19 The Taxes Management Act provides for penalties to be charged where there is a failure to give notice of charge, or incorrect notice of statement or claims or furnish information. Penalties can also arise on a failure to notify the Revenue that securities are held for the purpose of issuing depositary receipts or providing clearance services (ss 68 and 71).

Depositary receipt and clearance service charges

7.20 In the case of a depositary receipt charge or a clearance service charge, the "accountable date" is the last day of the second month following that in which the charge arises. Thus where the charge arises during January, the accountable date is 31 March. In the case of transactions that took place between 19 March and 30 September 1986, the accountable date is 28 November 1986.

7.21 Where the charge arises under s 93 (1) to (7) (the main depositary receipt charge) the depositary bank is both accountable and liable for the tax (s 93 (8) and reg 2). Where the bank is not resident in the UK and has no branch or agency in the UK, the person liable and accountable is its nominee. Similar rules also apply to charges under s 96 clearance services charge (s 96 (6) and (7) and reg 2).

7.22 Where shares are sold under an instalment arrangement and the charge arises either under s 93 (10) (depositary receipt) or s 96 (8) (clearance services), the person accountable and liable is the person liable to pay the instalment (ss 93 (10 (*c*) and 96 (8) (*c*) and reg 2).

7.23 Where the person otherwise accountable is the nominee, the Board will, if it is more convenient, be prepared to accept notifications and payments from the depositary bank or the person providing the clearance services, as the case may be.

APPENDIX 1 TA 1988 S 841: RECOGNISED STOCK EXCHANGES

The following list gives the stock exchanges recognised for the purposes of "qualified dealer" relief (see **5.23**).

Australia	The Australian Stock Exchange and any of its stock exchange subsidiaries;
Austria	Any stock exchange in Austria which is a stock exchange within the meaning of the Austrian law relating to stock exchanges;
Belgium	Any stock exchange in Belgium which is a stock exchange within the meaning of the Belgian law relating to stock exchanges;
Brazil	The Rio de Janeiro and São Paulo Stock Exchanges;
Canada	Any stock exchange prescribed for the purposes of the Canadian Income Tax Act;
Denmark	The Copenhagen Stock Exchange;
Finland	The Helsinki Stock Exchange;
France	Any stock exchange set up in France in accordance with the French legislation;
Germany	Any stock exchange approved under the laws relating to stock exchanges in the Federal Republic of Germany;
Greece	The Athens Stock Exchange;
Hong Kong	Any stock exchange in Hong Kong which is recognised under s 2A(1) of the Hong Kong Companies Ordinance;
Ireland	Any stock exchange in the Republic of Ireland which is a stock exchange within the meaning of the law of the Republic of Ireland relating to stock exchanges. (On 25 March 1973 these stock exchanges became part of The Stock Exchange; now the International Stock Exchange of the United Kingdom and the Republic of Ireland.)
Italy	Any stock exchange in Italy which is a stock exchange within the meaning of the Italian law relating to stock exchanges;

Japan	Any stock exchange in Japan which is a stock exchange within the meaning of Japanese law relating to stock exchanges;
Korea	The Korea Stock Exchange;
Luxembourg	Any stock exchange in Luxembourg which is a stock exchange within the meaning of the Luxembourg law relating to stock exchanges;
Malaysia	The Kuala Lumpur Stock Exchange;
Mexico	The Mexico Stock Exchange;
Netherlands	Any stock exchange in the Netherlands which is a stock exchange within the meaning of the Netherlands law relating to stock exchanges;
New Zealand	The New Zealand Stock Exchange;
Norway	Any stock exchange in Norway which is a stock exchange within the meaning of the Norwegian law relating to stock exchanges;
Portugal	Any stock exchange in Portugal which is a stock exchange within the meaning of the Portuguese law relating to stock exchanges;
Singapore	The Singapore Stock Exchange;
South Africa	The Johannesburg Stock Exchange;
Spain	Any stock exchange in Spain which is a stock exchange within the meaning of the Spanish law relating to stock exchanges;
Sri Lanka	The Colombo Stock Exchange;
Sweden	The Stockholm Stock Exchange;
Switzerland	The Basle Stock Exchange;
	The Geneva Stock Exchange;
	The Zurich Stock Exchange;
Thailand	The Stock Exchange of Thailand;
United Kingdom	The London Stock Exchange;
United States	Any exchange registered with the Securities and Exchange Commission of the United States as a national securities exchange;
	The Nasdaq Stock Market.

APPENDIX 7. CUSTOMER NEWSLETTERS

DECEMBER 1995. THE STAMP OFFICE CUSTOMER NEWSLETTER A NEW COMPREHENSIVE STAMP DUTY SERVICE

NEW ARRANGEMENTS

Following a major review of our organisation, the Stamp Office has made changes to the way we deliver our services and we aim to provide, by 1 April 1996, a comprehensive stamp duty service to customers in each Stamp Office.

Customers will then be able to send *all documents*, including applications for adjudication to any Stamp Office, a service which was previously only available in Worthing.

In order to achieve this aim it has been necessary to re-structure the Stamp Office. This has resulted in the closure of two offices in Cardiff and Liverpool, the transfer of the London postal work to Worthing and an extension of the services available in Bristol, Birmingham, Manchester and Newcastle.

Where Should You Send Your Documents for Stamping?

Please continue to use your current office.

However, customers who are used to posting documents to London Stamp Office should note that the postal section in London has now closed and arrangements have already been made for you to send your documents to Worthing.

What If You Require Adjudication?

This service is now available in Bristol and Newcastle as well as Edinburgh and Worthing. Plans are underway to introduce this service in Birmingham and Manchester by 1 April 1996.

In the meantime customers in Birmingham and Manchester should continue to send their applications for adjudication to Worthing.

Telephone Advice

In order to provide you with information on specialist stamp duty matters we have appointed additional Technical Services Managers in the following offices:

Birmingham	Lindsay Murphy	0121 200 2616 Ext 219
Bristol	Paul Needham	0117 9456939
Manchester	Phil Holmden	0161 833 0413 Ext 200
Newcastle	Doug Robson	0191 2015504

Who Should Use the Worthing Enquiry Line?

Calls should only be made to Worthing Stamp Office if you are a customer of that office, or the enquiry relates to an existing adjudication case.

Questions or Comments about These New Arrangements

We will make every effort to maintain the highest level of service to customers, nonetheless we realise that there may be some disruption for which we apologise. If you have any questions or comments about these new arrangements please contact your local Stamp Office.

Part II ST

Alternatively you can write to, or telephone Alan Bush, our Customer Service Manager at:

The Stamp Office
Room 0.66A. FitzRoy House
PO Box 46
Castle Meadow Road
Nottingham. NG2 1BD
Tel: 0115 974 1833
Fax: 0115 974 1831

9 DECEMBER 1995. WORTHING STAMP OFFICE CUSTOMER NOTICE

CHANGE OF ADDRESS

Please note that the Worthing Stamp Office will be moving from Ridgeworth House, Liverpool Gardens, Worthing, West Sussex BN11 1XP to a new address on 9 December 1995.

NEW ADDRESS

From *8 December 1995* will you please send all your post (Royal Mail or DX) to:

Worthing Stamp Office
Ground Floor
South Wing
Durrington Bridge House
Barrington Road
Worthing
West Sussex BN12 4SE
DX 3799 Worthing 1
New tel no will be 01903 701280.

QUESTIONS AND COMMENTS

Please direct these to Jim Simpson (Worthing Customer Service Manager) on 01903 288835.

MAY 1999. THE NEWCASTLE STAMP OFFICE CUSTOMER NEWSLETTER A REVISED APPROACH TO "RPI" LEASES

BACKGROUND

Some leases define the amount of rent as an initial sum to be adjusted periodically by reference to changes in the Retail Price Index (RPI).

In November 1997 the Stamp Office issued a Newsletter explaining the method we use for calculating duty in such cases.

NEW ARRANGEMENTS

In the light of recent legal advice given to the Inland Revenue, the treatment of these leases for stamp duty is to be changed.

In future, where there is a formula expressed in the lease for rent reviews based on the RPI, only the change in the RPI between the date the lease begins and the date it is executed will be taken into account in working out the duty.

These changes will only be relevant where the base date specified in the rent review clause is before the date of execution. In these circumstances we will take account of the change in the RPI between the base date and the date the lease is executed.

If the first rent review is after the date of execution we will apply these known changes in RPI in working out the average annual rent for the remainder of the term.

If the base date is on or after the date of the document we will ignore any changes in RPI in calculating the rent.

Will this mean that duty will now be calculated differently?

Yes. We will no longer be using the current rate of change in RPI as a basis for projecting future rent rises. Generally, this will mean that the starting level for the rent will be used in the stamp duty calculation.

In most cases this should result in less duty being payable. This also means that many people have paid too much stamp duty in the past.

If I paid too much duty am I entitled to claim my money back?

Yes. We will make repayments of excess stamp duty to those affected, provided that the claim is made within 2 years of the date of execution of the lease. You are also entitled to claim if you lodged an appeal against the assessment on your lease. Exceptionally, on this occasion we will also consider claims on similar leases dating back to 25 February 1995.

How do I make a claim?

If you think you are entitled to a repayment, or you act for a client who is entitled to a repayment, you should make your claim to:

Stamp Allowance Claims Section
Manchester Stamp Office
Alexandra House
Parsonage
Manchester M60 9BT
DX: 14430 Manchester 2

Information and advice is also available by telephoning our Claims Helpline on: 0845 6030135.

To keep your costs to a minimum, all calls will be charged at local rate.

What documents do I need to provide?

To enable us to deal with your claim please send your original stamped document to the address above. We cannot accept duplicate or copy documents, as we need to make an adjustment to the stamps on the document itself.

What if I no longer have the document?

If you no longer have the document in your possession because it is held by a Solicitor, Building Society or Land Registry, please contact our Claims Section about alternative arrangements.

Further information and advice

We will make every effort to deal with your enquiries and claims as quickly as possible. Although we aim to keep delays to a minimum, some customers may find that it takes us a little longer to process claims initially because of the high volume we are expecting.

Further details about these changes can be obtained from our Helpline. Information is also available on the Internet: www.inlandrevenue.gov.uk.

SEPTEMBER 1999. THE NEWCASTLE STAMP OFFICE CUSTOMER NEWSLE TTER NEW WAYS OF CALCULATING STAMP DUTY

BACKGROUND

Many of the methods of charging stamp duty were established in the last century. Changes in the FA 1999 will bring stamp duty up to date, by raising fixed duties to more realistic modern levels and simplifying the way stamp duty is worked out.

NEW ARRANGEMENTS

From 1 October 1999 the stamp duty you pay will be calculated differently.

The changes will mean:

- An increase in the minimum level of duty to £5.
- A new method of charging so that the amount payable is rounded up to a multiple of £5.

What Documents Will the New Minimum Rate Apply to?

This will affect:

- documents which have previously been subject to a 50p charge, ie lease counterparts, declarations of trust and transfers to a nominee;
- documents which were previously chargeable with amounts of less than 50p ie leases and their counterparts with very low rents;
- fixed duties over 50p ie furnished letting agreements for a term of less than 1 year, which up until now have been £1.

The duty on all these documents is set to rise to £5 from 1 October this year.

How will the new "rounding" work?

In the past stamp duty has always been expressed as a ratio. ie £1 per £100 or £12 per £50. From 1 October we will apply percentages in working out your duty and round this figure up to the next multiple of £5.

For instance, if the purchase price of a house is £67,295, we will work out duty at 1%, ie £672.95 which will then be rounded up to £675.

What about leases?

Duty on both the rental and the premium elements of leases will be expressed as percentages.

If duty is payable on both the rent and the premium under a lease, we will work out the duty separately on these 2 elements. These 2 amounts will then be added together, and the total rounded up to the next multiple of £5.

Further information and advice

We have produced a new leaflet SO99, which gives you more detailed information about the changes introduced in the FA 1999. This leaflet is available free of charge from any Stamp Office.

Alternatively, you can obtain further details about these changes by telephoning our Helpline on: 0845 6030135.

Information is also available on the Internet: www.inlandrevenue.gov.uk.

SEPTEMBER 1999. THE NEWCASTLE STAMP OFFICE CUSTOMER NEWSLETTER NEW INTEREST AND PENALTY ARRANGEMENTS

BACKGROUND

New measures in the FA 1999 aim to make stamp duty fairer by encouraging everyone to pay us the right amount of duty on time.

These changes will bring stamp duty in line with other taxes by raising penalties to more realistic levels and introducing a new interest charge to discourage late payments.

NEW ARRANGEMENTS

There is a 30-day time limit for getting documents stamped.

As from 1 October 1999 you should expect to pay interest and a penalty if you do not present your document to us on time with the correct amount of duty.

HOW WILL THE CHANGES AFFECT ME?

If you send us your document at the appropriate time with the correct amount of duty you will not be affected.

If you present your document outside of the 30-day time limit you will be charged a penalty.

Interest will be charged if you do not pay us the full amount of duty on time.

WHAT ABOUT DOCUMENTS EXECUTED ABROAD?

If you do not pay us on time you will be charged interest, even if the document was executed abroad.

A document which is executed abroad and brought into the UK for stamping at a later date will attract an interest charge, which will run from the 30-day limit.

Penalties will only be charged on documents executed abroad if they are not presented for stamping within 30 days of first being brought into the UK.

HOW WILL INTEREST BE CALCULATED?

The amount of interest you pay depends on the duty and the length of the delay in making the payment. A standard rate of interest is applied in working out the charge.

The changes will also mean that we will repay interest on certain types of documents. If you pay more duty than is due and your document is overstamped, we will then add interest to the repayment amount.

The rate of interest charged on late paid tax will be higher than that added to repayments.

Interest rates on stamp duty, like other taxes will be set by reference to the base rate level. Our interest rates will be in line with Income Tax—the rates for which are currently:

- 7.5% on late payments and
- 3% on repayments.

FURTHER INFORMATION AND ADVICE

Further information about these changes is contained in our leaflet SO1099, which is available free of charge from any Stamp Office.

Alternatively, you can telephone our Helpline on: 0845 6030135.

Information is also available on the Internet: www.inlandrevenue.gov.uk.

24 NOVEMBER 1999. THE NEWCASTLE STAMP OFFICE CUSTOMER NEWSL ETTER STAMP DUTY RESERVE TAX REGIME FOR UNIT TRUSTS AND OPEN-E NDED INVESTMENT COMPANIES

SDRT Operations Unit
Room 5
East Block
Barrington Road
Worthing
West Sussex BN12 4SE

The new stamp duty reserve tax regime for Unit Trusts and Open Ended Investment Companies comes into force on 6 February 2000. This newsletter is aimed at smoothing the transition to SDRT and complements the Guidance notes, issued on the 1 September 1999.

GENERAL STRUCTURE OF THE NEW REGIME

The information below is intended as a brief outline of the regime and does not cover all the points that can arise. For further details please refer to the Guidance Notes.

SDRT is charged at 0.5% on the value of surrendered units of a Unit Trust or shares in an OEIC, and this figure can be reduced by two ratios.

Firstly if more units are surrendered than issued during the relevant two week period then the liability is reduced by multiplying the value of the surrenders in the first week by the ratio I/S. This is where I and S are the numbers of units issued and surrendered in the relevant two week period.

Secondly if a fund has investments in exempt assets, the liability is further reduced by multiplying it by the ratio N/(N + E). This is where N and E are the average market values of the non-exempt and exempt assets of the fund over the two-week period.

It is not our intention to lay down a single rule for averaging values. However whether you take

(1) an average over all the valuation points falling within the two week period, or
(2) an average from a valuation point at an equivalent time in each of the two weeks concerned, or
(3) an average from the values on the last business day of month one and month two, or
(4) another specifically agreed valuation method

we will expect to be informed of the selected approach chosen and for it to remain consistent. Should you need to change the way in which the valuation is done the reason must be given on the first return following the change.

Third party transfers registered with the fund manager or authorised corporate director generally fall within the scope of this regime but exemptions are available in some cases; in particular the categories which can be certified as exempt or attracting fixed duty on the reverse of a stock transfer form, eg change of nominee, gifts, death etc. Fuller details can be found in FA 1999 Sch 19 and the Guidance Notes.

RETURNS

A monthly return will be required on or before the "accountable date". The accountable date is the 14th day of the month, following the month in which the relevant two week period ends. Hence a return for periods which end during the month of April should be accounted for by the 14 May at the latest. The liability for the tax lies with the Trustee of a Unit Trust or with the Company for an OEIC but the regulations define the accountable person as the fund manager, in the case of a unit trust, or the authorised corporate director, in the case of an OEIC.

A return will cover a month, during which 4 or 5 two week periods will end. Hence the return will consist of 4 or 5 subsidiary calculations. Attached is a spreadsheet which sets out the information required and the calculations needed to arrive at an SDRT figure for the month. Where returns are submitted after the accountable date, or if they prove to be incorrect, then they will be subject to an interest charge and penalty.

The return must also contain a declaration relating to the number of units for Pro-rata in-specie Redemptions and exempt transactions, although these do not form part of the calculation for SDRT purposes. Where relevant the certification on the reverse of a stock transfer form will be deemed as acceptable evidence of the exemption from SDRT by The Stamp Office. We recognise that accurate records may not be readily available in the early months of the new regime but we will accept best estimates during that period with the expectation that full details will be provided in subsequent returns.

We will issue a receipt to acknowledge payment, which should be kept as it may be needed as proof of payment to us. Cheques should be made payable to "The Inland Revenue" but should you wish to pay by CHAPS the account name and number are as follows: National Westminster Bank PLC, Worthing, West Sussex, Commissioners of Inland Revenue – Stamp Office Shares Unit No 2 a/c, 60-24-31 74636758

If you choose to pay by CHAPS we will need a separate notification of the payment made along with the monthly return showing the individual calculations. Also, the paying bank must be instructed to quote the fund's unique reference number when executing the transfer to our account.

Enquiries about the operation of the new regime should be directed to Sue Steward at the address above.

ANNEX "A"

Data Required for Monthly SDRT Computation

	WEEK (w) 1		2		3		4		5	
	Number of Units	Value (£)	Number of Units	Value (£)	Number of Units	Value (£)	Number of Units	Value (£)	Number of Units	Value (£)
Issues (incl. 3rd party transfers liable for SDRT)										
Week w	330,000		110,000		400,000		200,000		600,000	
Week w + 1	110,000		400,000		200,000		600,000		80,000	
(I)	440,000		510,000		600,000		800,000		680,000	
Surrenders (incl 3rd party transfers liable for SDRT)										
Week w	500,000	160,000	30,000	9,600	100,000	32,000	650,000	208,000	150,000	48,000
Week w + 1	30,000		100,000		650,000		150,000		950,000	
(S)	530,000		130,000		750,000		800,000		1,100,000	
Para 4 Calculation (only if S>I)										
I/S × value of week w surrenders =		132,830		n/a		25,600		n/a		29,673
plus										

Week w non pro-rata in-specie redemptions	5,000	1,600	3,750	1,200	0	0	0	0	1,500	480
Sub-Total "A"		134,430		10,800		25,600		208,000		30,153
Para 5 Calculation (where applicable)										
(N) Value of Non-Exempt assets		1,500,000		1,500,500		1,500,250		1,500,600		1,400,000
(E) Value of Exempt assets		500,000		501,000		500,500		500,600		450,000
Sub-Total 'B' (ie (N/N + E) × Sub-Total "A")		100,823		8,097		19,196		155,969		22,818
SDRT Due		504.12		40.49		95.98		779.85		114.09
(Sub-total "B" × 0.5% to nearest penny)								Total SDRT for Month =1534.53		
DECLARATION										
Week w Pro-rata In-Specie Redemptions	10,000		0		3,300		0		1,200	
Week w Exempt 3rd Party Transfers	600		1,000		2,000		600		4,500	

ANNEX "B"

In order to assist our planning for the transition of Unit Trusts and OEICs to the SDRT environment it would be helpful if you would annotate your list of funds to show into which of the following categories each fund falls. Note that this information is requested only for planning purposes and does not constitute a formal claim that a particular fund is exempt or otherwise.

Category	*Description of Fund*
A	A fund which is deemed not to be a Unit Trust for the purposes of stamp duty and SDRT (see FA 1999 Sch 19 paras 15–17).
B	A fund which does not fall into category A but nevertheless is wholly exempt from SDRT by virtue of having incorporated into the fund's particulars or trust deed a condition that the fund can only invest in exempt assets (see para 39 of the 1 September Guidance Note).
C	A fund which does not qualify as wholly exempt but habitually invests only in assets which are "exempt investments" for the purposes of FA 1999 Sch 19 para 5 (3). In other words this is a fund whose liability to SDRT, for the foreseeable future, will be nil after applying the fraction N/N + E.
D	All funds which are • not wholly exempt, and • contain some non-exempt investments.
E	A fund which is not considered to fall into any of the above categories. Please separately state the reason(s) why this should be so.

9 DECEMBER 1999. THE STAMP OFFICE NEWSLETTER UNIT TRUSTS: PRO RATA IN SPECIAL REDEMPTION OF UNITS

BACKGROUND

On the 21 January 1999 in the Chancery Division of the high court, Mr Justice Park gave judgement in the cases of *M & G Securities Ltd v IRC* and *Schroder Unit Trusts Ltd v IRC* in favour of the plaintiffs. The Inland Revenue has decided not to pursue its appeal, and so these cases are now final.

The cases concerned the situation where a unit is redeemed in specie, for a pro rata share of assets in the trust. The Inland Revenue's view was that stamp duty paid in respect of such redemption was not eligible for repayment under the provisions of FA 1946 s 54 (4). The decision means that such repayments can be allowed.

Cases in which the Stamp Office has refused a claim for repayment will, of course, now be reconsidered on request.

CURRENT POSITION

The position now, in relation to pro rata in specie cases in the period up to 6 February 2000 (when the provisions of FA 1999 Sch 19 take over from the legislation in FA 1946) is that:

- the notional reclaim procedure will be available (so that stamp duty need not be paid and then reclaimed on the redemption of units involved), and
- securities being transferred from the unit trust to the unit holder concerned will, as before, attract only fixed duty (and if they are being transferred in Crest TSS flag 5 may be used to ensure that no SDRT is deducted).

CHANGES FROM 6 FEBRUARY 2000

From 6 February 2000 the new SDRT regime for unit trust will apply, which contains an exemption for pro rata in specie redemption. The details are that:

- Sch 19 para 7 exempts surrenders from the new SDRT charge if they are made in return for pro rata in specie distribution of assets, and
- FA 1986 s 90 (IB) makes it clear that there is no SDRT charge on the distribution of assets to the unit holder (and Crest TSS flag 5 can still be used).

FURTHER ADVICE AND INFORMATION

Guidance on the new SDRT regime for unit trusts and OEICs issued on 1 September.

A customer newsletter about the implementation of the new regime issued on the 24 November 1999.

MARCH 2000. THE NEWCASTLE STAMP OFFICE CUSTOMER NEWSLETTER NEW RATES OF STAMP DUTY

BUDGET CHANGES

The Budget announcement will mean increases in the rates of stamp duty on transfers of property over £250,000.

What Are the New Rates?

Where the consideration exceeds £60,000 but does not exceed £250,000 the current rate of 1% is unchanged.

Where the consideration exceeds £250,000 but does not exceed £500,000 the rate will increase to 3%.

Where the consideration exceeds £500,000 the rate will increase to 4%.

When Do the Changes Take Effect?

The new rates will generally apply to documents executed on or after 28 March. But the old rates will apply where the document gives effect to a contract made on or before 21 March, unless the document results from the exercise of an option, an assignment, or further contract made after 21 March.

Are the Levels for Certificates of Value Affected by the Budget?

No The 3 existing levels for certificates of value of £60,000, £250,000 and £500,000 are unchanged. The certificate you need will depend on the consideration paid as follows:

To qualify for the nil rate of duty . . .

If the consideration is £60,000 or less and the transaction is not part of a larger transaction or series of transactions, a certificate of value for £60,000 should be included. No duty will then be payable.

To qualify for the rate of 1%

If the consideration is £250,000 or less, but more than £60,000, a certificate of value for £250,000 should be included. Duty will be payable at the rate of 1%.

To qualify for the rate of 3%

If the consideration is £500,000 or less, but more than £250,000, a certificate of value for £500,000 should be included. Duty will then be payable at the rate of 3%.

No certificate of value is appropriate where the consideration exceeds £500,000. Duty will be payable at the rate of 4%.

Unless a document contains the appropriate certificate of value, it will be liable to duty at the rate of 4%.

Do the New Rates of Duty Apply to Leases with a Premium?

Yes. Duty on any premium paid for a lease is charged at the same rate as a conveyance on sale. A certificate of value cannot however be included in a lease with a premium of £60,000 or less if the annual rent exceeds £600 per annum. Such a lease may however contain a £250,000 certificate of value if appropriate.

The threshold for the stamp duty charge on the annual rent for new leases of up to seven years (or of indefinite term) is increased from £500 to £5,000. The new threshold also applies to furnished lettings.

Are Any Other Documents Affected by the Changes?

Yes. The new rates of duty apply to all transfers of property (except shares). This will include business sale agreements and assignments of leasehold property.

Share transfers will still be charged at ½%

OTHER CHANGES

Intellectual Property

Transactions in intellectual property will be exempted from Stamp Duty. This will exempt transfers of patents, trade marks, registered designs, copyrights, plant breeders' rights, and licences in respect of them.

The exemption will apply to instruments executed on or after 28 March.

Where an agreement for sale relates partly to intellectual property and partly to other chargeable property, an apportionment of the sale price will be made to determine the amount chargeable to duty.

Statutory Declarations Supporting Claims to Group Relief

The procedure for making a claim to group relief has been simplified. Companies making group relief claims no longer need to produce a formal statutory declaration when the claim for relief is made.

How should a claim be made?

The claim should be made in an ordinary letter, and include all the information and supporting evidence, for example extracts from the company share registers, which would formerly have been contained in the Declaration. Guidance on the form of the claim can be obtained from your usual Stamp Office.

When does the change take effect?

The change takes effect immediately.

Stamp Taxes Manual

The Stamp Taxes Manual was published through Croner CCH Editions Ltd on 14 March. It will be updated to reflect the Budget changes later in the year.

How to Find Out More . . .

If you want further details about the Budget changes described in this Newsletter you can telephone our Helpline on: 0845 603 0135 (Office hours only).

Information (including the Stamp Taxes Manual) is also available on the Internet—www.in landrevenue.gov.uk/so.

Enquiries which relate exclusively to the contents of the Manual to: 0191 261 1301 (Office hours only).

The Press Release describing all the Budget changes to Stamp Duty, including new reliefs for Registered Social Landlords and a number of anti-avoidance measures, is available from your usual Stamp Office and on the Internet.

SEPTEMBER 2000. THE NEWCASTLE STAMP OFFICE CUSTOMER NEWSLETTER

In the early hours of Tuesday 5 September 2000 our building, Cale Cross House in Newcastle, was seriously damaged by a fire on the second floor. Although there is some serious smoke damage on our floor, the flames did not reach our office. No documents have been destroyed.

The Health & Safety Executive examined the building and have decided that the premises are not fit for occupation on any floor for the time being. It is expected to be at least three months before the premises are habitable again and we can move back in. As a consequence of this, Newcastle Stamp Office has had to be relocated to temporary premises in Washington, Tyne & Wear.

We are doing everything we can to ensure that the disruption to our customers is kept to an absolute minimum and we are now once again able to stamp documents, at the Washington site. We have arranged for all mail which is sent to our usual DX box number, DX 61021 Newcastle-upon-Tyne, via the Document Exchange Service, to be redirected to our temporary premises in Washington.

The Royal Mail address of our temporary premises is The Stamp Office, 4th Floor, Weardale House, Washington, Tyne & Wear NE37 1LW. Our current telephone number at our temporary office is 0191 201 7413. The fax number is 0191 201 7392.

Unfortunately we are unable to offer a counter service for the immediate stamping of documents for Newcastle-based customers. We are exploring the possibility of providing an alternative counter service and I will let you know more as soon as I can.

We were unable to gain access to some documents held in Cale Cross House on the night of the fire until now. If you sent a document to Newcastle Stamp Office shortly before 5 September and have not yet had it returned to you please allow a few more days before you contact us. We will return your document as soon as we can. Some work for the period following 5 September has been redirected to Edinburgh Stamp Office and you may receive your document back from that office.

I will write to you again on 20 September to keep you informed of developments. If you have any queries about the arrangements please do not hesitate to contact me on 0191 201 7393.

Tony Stoker, Assistant Director

SEPTEMBER 2000. THE NEWCASTLE STAMP OFFICE CUSTOMER NEWSLETTER
FURTHER INFORMATION

The Stamp Office
4th Floor
Weardale House
Washington
Tyne & Wear NE37 1LW
DX 61021 Newcastle-upon-Tyne

NEWCASTLE STAMP OFFICE: CUSTOMER UPDATE

The previous Newsletter informed you of immediate developments following the fire at Cale Cross House on 5 September. Our temporary relocation to Weardale House is likely to last until January 2001. We are now fully operational on the Washington site and able to offer a normal service, with the exception of a counter service for the immediate stamping of documents.

Turning specifically to our Newcastle based customers, it does not seem likely that an immediate counter stamping facility will be available in Newcastle for the period of our temporary relocation. Other options are being considered and I will be contacting Newcastle based customers when an alternative service is available. In the meantime would you please use the DX or Royal Mail route.

Postal Arrangements

We have arranged for the mail which is sent to our usual DX number, DX 61021 Newcastle-upon-Tyne, via the Document Exchange service to be re-directed to our Washington site.

Any mail sent to Cale Cross House via the Royal Mail will also be re-directed to our Washington site.

Telephone Numbers

Our telephone numbers are 0191 201 7408 to 7417. Our fax number is 0191 201 7392.

Documents

All documents which were in Cale Cross House at the time of the fire have been retrieved. The documents sent to us on 30 and 31 August and 1 and 4 September are currently being actioned. We anticipate our work on those documents will be finalised by 28 September. If you sent us a document for stamping immediately prior to 30 August please bear with us until 28 September.

Some of the mail we received between 6 and 13 September has been redirected to Bristol and Edinburgh Stamp Offices. You may therefore receive your stamped document back from one of those offices instead of Newcastle.

Tony Stoker, Assistant Director

JANUARY 2001. THE NEWCASTLE STAMP OFFICE CUSTOMER NEWSLETTER FURTHER INFORMATION

The Stamp Office
4th Floor
Weardale House
Washington
Tyne & Wear NE37 1LW
DX 61021 Newcastle-upon-Tyne

NEWCASTLE STAMP OFFICE: CUSTOMER UPDATE

In my previous Newsletter I explained the situation following the fire at our Newcastle premises, Cale Cross House on 5 September 2000.

We had originally hoped to return to Cale Cross House by the end of January 2001. But it has become far clearer over the intervening period that the refurbishment works required are substantial and no completion date for that work has yet been given by the owners of the building. It seems likely that we will remain at our temporary base at Weardale House, Washington until May 2001 at least.

Whilst we are fully operational at our temporary base we are unable to provide a counter service for the immediate stamping of documents and this will continue to be the case during our period of relocation. This is disappointing news but please be assured that we are working closely with the landlords to ensure that any delay in our return to Cale Cross House is kept to a minimum. Please accept my apologies for any inconvenience caused.

We were able to update some of you at our local user group forum held at Newcastle in December 2000. We intend to run a further forum during the first week in March 2001; if you are interested in attending will you please contact my Customer Service Manager, Paul Dinsley on 0191 201 7408.

Postal Arrangements

We continue to arrange for the mail which is sent to our usual DX number, DX61021 Newcastle Upon Tyne, via the Document Exchange Service to be re-directed to our Washington site.

Any mail sent to Cale Cross House via the Royal Mail will also be re-directed to our Washington site.

Telephone Numbers

Our telephone numbers continue to be 0191 2017408 to 7417. The fax number is 0191 2017392.

Further Update

A further update will be provided at the end of March 2001, although, of course, I will let you have any news on a return date should I have that any earlier.

If there are any questions concerning this newsletter please contact me on 0191 2017393.

Tony Stoker, Assistant Director

Part II ST

FEBRUARY 2001. THE STAMP OFFICE CUSTOMER NEWSLETTER PENALTIES AND INTEREST

BACKGROUND

FA 1999 introduced measures to make stamp duty fairer by encouraging everyone to pay the right amount of duty on time.

If you do not present your documents within the 30-day time limit you should expect to pay a penalty.

Interest will also be charged if you delay in paying us some or all of the money.

Full information about penalty and interest charges is contained in our leaflet SO10, available free of charge from any Stamp Office.

Latest Information

When the new arrangements were introduced we explained that certain cases would be subject to individual review. We are now receiving enquiries about the basis for charging penalties where the delay is longer than a year. These further guidelines explain how penalties will be worked out in these cases to ensure fairness and consistency for all our customers.

Delays of More Than a Year

In cases over 1 year late, the legislation gives us authority to charge a maximum amount equivalent to the duty or £300—whichever is higher.

However, this maximum is only charged where there is a substantial delay and we would normally mitigate the penalty to a lower amount. If the duty payable on your document is £5,000 or less then the penalty rates in our leaflet SO10 will apply.

For cases where the duty exceeds £5,000 the following table shows how your penalty will be worked out.

Duty over £5,000

Months late	*% of duty*
Under 15	20%
Under 18	40%
Under 21	60%
Under 24	80%
24 and over	100%

Documents over 2 years late: no mitigation is appropriate where a document is more than 2 years late, and we will charge an amount equivalent to the duty, subject to an overriding minimum of £300.

Fixed Duty Cases

You will not normally be charged a penalty on fixed duty cases which are less than 1 year late. If there is substantial delay the following rates will usually apply:

- £10 for cases over 12 months late but not over 24 months late.
- £25 for cases over 24 months late.

We will still charge a penalty of £300 if people try to avoid paying duty or repeatedly fail to get documents stamped.

Explaining the Delay . . .

So that we can decide if the penalty can be mitigated, you need to tell us of any factors you consider relevant to the delay when sending your documents to us.

There is no mitigation of interest charges and the full amount will always be payable. The rate of interest we charge on late paid duty is currently 8.5%.

Further Information and Advice

These guidelines supplement the information contained in our leaflet SO10 which explains our penalty and interest charges more fully.

If you want advice you can telephone our Helpline on: 0845 6030135. Our operators are available to take your calls from 8.30 am to 5 pm. on weekdays.

MAY 2001. THE NEWCASTLE STAMP OFFICE CUSTOMER NEWSLETTER

Following a fire at Cale Cross House our Newcastle Stamp Office has temporarily relocated to:

4th Floor
Weardale House
Washington
Tyne & Wear NE37 1LW
DX 61021 Newcastle-Upon-Tynes
Tel: 0191 261 1199
Fax: 0191 201 7392

The extensive damage to the building means that the move back to our permanent base in the City Centre will be delayed until August 2001 at least, and the office will remain at the temporary location in Weardale House until this time.

We aim to provide customers with the same level of postal service at the temporary base, although, unfortunately we are unable to provide a Counter Service for the immediate stamping of documents. In order to minimise the disruption for our customers in Newcastle city centre who wish to deliver documents by hand, we have a limited service available for dropping off and collecting documents at:

The Inland Revenue Enquiry Centre
Newcastle 1
Aidan House
All Saints Office Centre
Newcastle-Upon-Tyne NE1 2TT

Opening hours: 8.30 am to 4.30 pm Monday–Friday.

Tony Stoker, Assistant Director

15 MAY 2001. THE STAMP OFFICE CUSTOMER NEWSLETTER STAMP DUTY RESERVE TAX AND INDIVIDUAL PENSION ACCOUNTS (IPAS) UNIT TRUSTS AND OPEN-ENDED INVESTMENT COMPANIES (OEICS)

The Finance Act together with regulations published on 14 March contain the new SDRT exemption for units in unit trusts and shares in OEICs held within IPAs. The exemption came into effect from 6 April 2001. A Budget Press Release dated 7 March 2001 (REV BN8) explains the three methods (*a*), (*b*) or (*c*) Investment Fund Managers have in order to operate the new exemption.

Part II ST

Investment Fund Managers wishing to undertake this type of business and claim the new exemption will need to ensure their systems enable them to identify units held within IPAs and provide the Stamp Office SDRT Operations Unit with relevant details.

Method (*a*) applies if a unit trust instrument requires that all units be held in IPAs (or in the case of an OEIC the instrument of incorporation requires that all the shares must be held within IPAs). In such a unit trust or OEIC all transfers of units or shares will be exempt and no monthly return to the SDRT Operations Unit will be necessary.

Method (*b*) applies to OEICs that have one or more share classes that the company's instrument of incorporation restricts to holding in IPAs, and the OEIC also has at least one other class of shares which is not restricted in this way. Surrenders of shares in IPA share classes are exempt from SDRT and are left out of account for the purpose of calculating tax payable under FA 1999 Sch 19.

We suggest that an additional "exempt" category be added to the monthly SDRT Return in which you state the number of shares in the IPA class (or classes) that have been surrendered. No return will be necessary where there is no charge to SDRT for a particular month (for example, if all surrenders were of shares in the IPA classes).

Method (*c*) is only available to a unit trust that has in place systems that enable the person making the return to provide a certificate in or with the return in the following terms:

(a) that at all times in the period to which the Return relates, the trustees or managers were able to identify which of the units under the scheme were held within individual pension accounts, and

(b) that at no time in that period have the trustees or managers imposed any charge on, or recovered any amount from, an IPA unit holder which included an amount directly or indirectly attributable to tax payable by the trustees under FA 1999 Sch 19 Pt II.

In a qualifying unit trust, surrenders of units held in IPAs are exempt from SDRT and are left out of account for the purpose of calculating tax payable under FA 1999 Sch 19.

If exemption is claimed, we suggest that an additional "exempt" category be added to the monthly SDRT return in which you state the number of exempt units that have been surrendered. No return will be necessary where there is no charge to SDRT for a particular month (for example, if all surrenders were of units held within IPAs).

Any enquiries relating to the above can be made to SDRT Operations staff, David Why 01903 509752 or Ian Timms 01903 508793.

MAY 2001. THE STAMP OFFICE CUSTOMER NEWSLETTER INTEREST AND PENALTIES—INTEREST RATE CHANGE

BACKGROUND

Measures introduced in the FA 1999 aim to make stamp duty fairer by encouraging everyone to pay us the right amount of duty on time.

These changes brought stamp duty in line with other taxes by raising penalties to more realistic levels and introducing an interest charge to discourage late payments.

Penalty and Interest Arrangements

There is a 30-day time limit for getting documents stamped.

If you do not present your documents to the Stamp Office within the time limit allowed, you can expect to pay a penalty. You should also expect to pay interest if there is a delay in paying us some or all of the money.

How Will This Affect Me?

If you send us your document with the correct amount of duty within the 30-day time limit, you will not be affected.

If you present your document late you will be charged a penalty.

Interest will be charged if you do not pay us the full amount of duty on time.

What About Documents Executed Abroad?

If you do not pay us on time you will be charged interest, even if the document was executed abroad.

A document which is executed abroad and brought into the UK for stamping at a later date will attract an interest charge, which will run from the 30-day limit.

Penalties will only be charged on documents executed abroad if they are not presented for stamping within 30 days of first being brought into the UK.

How Will Interest Be Calculated?

The amount of interest you pay depends on the duty and the length of the delay in making the payment. A standard rate of interest is applied in working out the charge.

The changes will also mean that we will pay interest on certain types of documents. If you pay more duty than is due and your document is overstamped, we will then add interest to the repayment amount. No interest will be added where the duty repaid is less than £25.

The rate of interest charged on late paid duty will be higher than that added to repayments.

Interest rates on stamp duty, like other taxes are set by reference to the base rate level. New rates will become effective from 6 May 2001.

Previous rate changes are as follows:

	Late paid duty	*Repayments*
1/10/99	7.5%	3%
6/2/00	8.5%	4%
6/5/01	7.5%	3.5%

Interest will be charged on late paid duty at previous levels for any period prior to the rate change and at the current rate for the subsequent period.

Further Information & Advice

Further information about penalties and interest charges is contained in our leaflet SO10, which is available free of charge from any Stamp Office.

Alternatively, you can telephone our Helpline on: 0845 6030135.

Information is also available on the Internet: www.inlandrevenue.gov.uk/so.

DECEMBER 2001. THE STAMP TAXES CUSTOMER NEWSLETTER DISADVANTAGED AREAS STAMP DUTY EXEMPTION

In his Pre-Budget Report of 27 November the Chancellor of the Exchequer announced his Government's intention to implement the first phase of the stamp duty exemption relating to the purchase of property in certain designated disadvantaged areas of the UK, which will apply where the consideration, or premium for a lease, does not exceed £150,000. Relief will be available with effect from 30 November 2001.

This newsletter has been designed to help you make an application for the exemption and sets out the information that we need from you in order to deal with your document promptly. If

Part II ST

you have any questions about the exemption which are not answered in this newsletter please telephone the Stamp Taxes Helpline on 0845 603 0135 (office hours only) where one of our staff will be pleased to assist you.

. . .

WHAT DOCUMENTS ARE COVERED BY THE EXEMPTION?

The exemption applies to all conveyances and transfers of land or an interest in land, and to all leases of an interest in land, executed on or after 30 November 2001, where the land falls wholly or partly within one of the disadvantaged areas designated under the Variation of Stamp Duties Regulations 2001 and the consideration for the transfer or the premium for the lease is more than £60,000 but not more than £150,000.

IF A LEASE HAS A PREMIUM OF £150,000 OR LESS BUT ALSO HAS A RENT, IS IT EXEMPT FROM STAMP DUTY UNDER THIS RELIEF IN RESPECT OF THE RENT?

No The rent will be liable to duty even though the premium may be exempt from duty under this relief.

IF VAT HAS BEEN PAID BY THE PURCHASER, IN ADDITION TO THE CONSIDERATION OR PREMIUM FOR THE TRANSFER OR LEASE, DOES THE £150,000 LIMIT APPLY TO THE GROSS OR NET FIGURE?

Stamp duty applies to the VAT-inclusive consideration or premium. If the VAT, when added to the consideration or premium, brings the total amount above the £150,000 limit the exemption will not apply.

ARE CONVEYANCES, TRANSFERS AND LEASES PREVIOUSLY LIABLE TO £5 FIXED STAMP DUTY WITHIN THE NEW EXEMPTION?

No The exemption does not currently apply to documents liable to fixed duty which must continue to be stamped. The exception is for duplicate documents that do not attract stamp duty in excess of that paid on the original document. If the original is exempt from duty under the disadvantaged areas provisions the duplicate will not bear any duty either but must be sent to us to be denoted as a duplicate document.

WHERE CAN I FIND OUT WHETHER THE PROPERTY I AM BUYING, OR DEALING WITH ON BEHALF OF MY CLIENT, IS WITHIN ONE OF THE DESIGNATED AREAS?

A list of the designated areas has been published on our website and can be viewed here. The list has been drawn up on the basis of electoral wards, except in Scotland where it is based on postcodes.

WILL I NEED TO KNOW THE POSTCODE FOR THE PROPERTY?

Yes. We need everyone who claims this exemption to let us know the postcode for the property so that we can confirm that it is within a designated disadvantaged area. See Stop Press—Disadvantaged Areas Stamp Duty Exemption.

WHERE CAN I FIND THE POSTCODE FOR A PROPERTY IF I DO NOT ALREADY KNOW IT?

Postcode information is readily available for any given postal address from the Postcode Enquiry Line on 08457 111 222 or via the internet at www.royalmail.co.uk/quick_tools/postcodes/ . . . If you enter the above URL in an internet browser yourself, please note that there is an underscore "_" between the words "quick" and "tools" which must be shown or the URL will not work.

WHAT HAPPENS IF THE PROPERTY I AM BUYING IS A PIECE OF LAND WITH NO BUILDINGS AND IT HAS NO POSTCODE DESIGNATED?

If you are claiming the exemption on the document relating to such a piece of land you should tell us in your application letter that no postcode is available. You should include a map of the property with sufficient detail to pinpoint the location of the property and tell us which ward on the list of designated areas it falls within. If you know where the ward boundary lies you should indicate it on the map. We will check this information. Cases such as these are likely to take longer to process than those where a postcode is known.

WHAT HAPPENS IF THE POSTCODE FOR THE PROPERTY COVERS A NUMBER OF PROPERTIES, SOME OF WHICH ARE INSIDE ONE OF THE QUALIFYING AREAS AND SOME OF WHICH ARE OUTSIDE THE AREA?

The legislation provides that where a single postcode straddles the boundary of a ward all properties covered by that one postcode will be considered to fall within the ward and will qualify for the exemption. If all the properties covered by one postcode are outside the ward boundary the exemption will not apply to any of those properties.

DOES ANY CERTIFICATE HAVE TO BE INCLUDED IN THE DOCUMENT?

FA 2001 s 92(2) provides that the exemption will only apply if the document is certified to the Commissioners as being an instrument on which stamp duty is not chargeable by virtue of subsection (1). It is suggested that an appropriate wording for the certificate is as follows:

> "I/We hereby certify that this is an instrument on which stamp duty is not chargeable by virtue of the provisions of Section 92 of the Finance Act 2001"

While the legislation does not specifically require the certificate to be included as part of the document we suggest that it should be included in it. If the position is not certified to us, either in the document or separately in writing by the person submitting the document for stamping, exemption will not be granted.

Anyone falsely certifying a document with a view to obtaining relief that is not due will be committing a stamp duty fraud.

DO I HAVE TO SEND THE DOCUMENT FOR STAMPING EVEN THOUGH IT IS EXEMPT FROM DUTY UNDER SECTION 92?

Yes. Like most stamp duty exemptions the legislation requires the document to be lodged for formal adjudication if the exemption is to be granted.

DO I STILL NEED TO SUPPLY A COMPLETED PARTICULARS DELIVERED FORM WITH THE DOCUMENT EVEN THOUGH I AM CLAIMING EXEMPTION FROM DUTY?

Yes. If you would normally have had to provide a PD form with the document in the past you will still need to do so. Even though the document may be exempt from stamp duty there will still be valuable information which the Valuation Office Agency need which they glean from these forms.

WHEN I CLAIM EXEMPTION DO I NEED TO INCLUDE A DUPLICATE OF THE DOCUMENT?

Yes. As required by the legislation in all adjudication claims, you need to let us have a photocopy of the document on which the exemption is claimed. We will retain that copy for our records.

WHAT IS THE POSITION WHERE THE LAND CONCERNED IS ON THE BOUNDARY OF A DESIGNATED DISADVANTAGED AREA AND SOME OF THE PROPERTY IS WITHIN THE AREA AND SOME IS OUTSIDE IT?

The legislation in FA 2001 Sch 30 para 1 provides that in this scenario the full consideration is to be apportioned between the part inside and the part outside the disadvantaged area on a just and reasonable basis. Only the consideration in respect of the part outside the disadvantaged area is to be charged to stamp duty.

You must draw this to our attention when claiming partial exemption from duty and you must explain the basis on which you consider the apportionment of the consideration, including any VAT paid in addition to the consideration, to be a just and reasonable one.

DOES THE DOCUMENT NEED TO INCLUDE A £250,000 CERTIFICATE OF VALUE WHERE THE CONSIDERATION IS £150,000 OR LESS AND I AM CLAIMING THE EXEMPTION?

Yes. The certificate proves that the document is not part of any larger or series of transactions which would mean the relief was not appropriate.

DOES THE DOCUMENT NEED TO INCLUDE A £150,000 CERTIFICATE OF VALUE WHERE THE CONSIDERATION IS £150,000 OR LESS AND I AM CLAIMING THE EXEMPTION?

No The legislation does not require there to be a £150,000 certificate in the document. However, it is important to remember that the legislation does provide that if a £150,000 certificate could not properly be included in the document, if that were one of the levels of certificate mentioned in FA 1999, the exemption is not appropriate.

In other words, where the document shows a consideration of £150,000 or less it can only qualify for exemption if it does not form part of a larger transaction or a series of transactions in respect of which the amount or value, or the aggregate amount or value, of the consideration exceeds £150,000.

WHAT ABOUT PHASE TWO?

Under phase two, which is expected to start in 2002, the Government intends to significantly raise the level of stamp duty exemption, or abolish it entirely, in the designated areas but only in respect of non-residential property.

SUMMARY CHECKLIST—DISADVANTAGED AREAS STAMP DUTY RELIEF—FA 2001 S 92

All instruments in respect of which relief is claimed must be formally adjudicated. To prevent delay in processing claims it will greatly assist if all the following information is supplied at the time the instrument is presented for stamping.

The document contains a certificate confirming it is within the provisions of FA 2001 s 92.

The full postcode for the property being transferred is supplied.

The relevant PD form is enclosed, if appropriate.

A full photocopy of the transfer document is provided.

A copy of the contract or sale agreement is provided

The document contains a £250,000 certificate of value.

If the document is a lease, a payment in respect of the rent element is enclosed.

Provision of all the information above when the document is presented for stamping should enable claims to be processed without further correspondence.

You are reminded that if examination of the claim results in a decision that relief under FA 2001 s 92 is not due, and, as a consequence, payment of stamp duty is made after the proper time, a charge to interest may be incurred.

Wards qualifying for the stamp duty relief for Disadvantaged Areas are shown [at www.inlandrevenue.gov.uk/so/england.pdf, www.inlandrevenue.gov.uk/so/nireland.pdf, www.inlandrevenue.gov.uk/so/scotland.pdf and www.inlandrevenue.gov.uk/so/wales.pdf].

To view these documents you need to use a PDF file viewer such as Acrobat Reader.

If you have trouble viewing, downloading or printing PDF files with Acrobat Reader then visit Adobe's online technical guides.

JULY 2002. THE STAMP TAXES CUSTOMER NEWSLETTER STAMP DUTY RESERVE TAX (SDRT)—ISSUE 1

BACKGROUND

Inland Revenue Stamp Taxes have been reviewing its procedures with regard to the way it administers the SDRT environment. As a consequence of the review, they will be introducing changes within the repayments process as well as implementing new assurance procedures.

REPAYMENTS

In the past, CREST participants have been aware that detailed checks have been undertaken by SDRT Operations Unit on all repayment claims submitted to check the validity of the claim. Whilst the new procedures will include verification of all transactions it will only include a detailed post-payment check on a sample of the claims received. This will mean that all valid transaction IDs will be repaid immediately upon receipt, on a without prejudice basis. SDRT Operations Unit does, however, reserve the right to contact customers at a later date (usually within 60 days of the claim date) to request additional supporting material where necessary.

Where a CREST participant "input" error has led to an erroneous SDRT charge, customers are requested to submit the following information to SDRT Operations Unit (Worthing) for reclaim purposes:

- Crest Transaction ID (not the STP transaction ID)
- Individual SDRT claim amounts.
- Trade Date.
- Repayment Code 1–11 (as per listing attached).

If multiple transactions are in point, the above information should be supplied on a disk (in excel format).

The provision of this information will allow SDRT Operations Unit to check payment details against CREST data held and create a database of circumstances that cause repayments to arise. The Unit will then seek to identify solutions to reduce common recurrent error types.

ASSURANCE TESTING

CREST participants are aware that the SDRT Assurance Team undertakes periodic audit visits to review a sample of transactions back to source data. SDRT Operations Unit will in future supplement the work carried out by Assurance and begin to undertake small sample checks on various transactions input to CREST. These will include SDRT exemption categories to ensure that adequate documentary evidence is being maintained. It is appreciated that this may cause additional work to participants, but this will be kept to a minimum.

CHEQUE AND CHAPS PAYMENTS RECEIVED IN SDRT OPERATIONS UNIT

With immediate effect, SDRT Operations Unit will be requesting customers provide full information pertaining to their cheque or CHAPS payment. This will include the following:

- Trade Date.
- Names of the parties concerned.
- Description and number of securities.
- Consideration paid.
- SDRT due.

The full facts and circumstances/reasons as to why the tax has been accounted for in cheque/CHAPS form as opposed to being settled through CREST.

The provision of this information will allow SDRT Operations Unit to check payment details and create a database of circumstances that cause payments to be made. The Unit will then seek to identify solutions to reduce common recurrent error types.

All enquiries surrounding the content of this Newsletter are to be addressed to:

Inland Revenue Stamp Taxes
SDRT Operations Unit
Room 5, East Block
Barrington Road
Worthing
West Sussex
BN12 4SE
Telephone: 01903 509928 or 01903 509469

REPAYMENT CODES

Code		*Explanation*
Exemption Applicable		
	1	NCBO
	2	Charity
	3	Intermediary Relief (Principal purchase)
CREST inputs incorrect or missing		
	4	TSS flag (identify flag applicable)
	5	TSO/Stock Lending Relief
	6	Market Sale/ADR conversion back to underlying shares
	7	Stampable consideration
	8	Agent indicator
Double SDRT payments made		
	9	Cancelled/Rebooked or duplicated trades
	10	Bulk/Splits, paid both in and outside of CREST, paid by both parties
Others		
	11	Other reasons not listed

JULY 2002. THE STAMP TAXES CUSTOMER NEWSLETTER STAMP DUTY RESERVE TAX (SDRT)—ISSUE 2

BACKGROUND

Inland Revenue Stamp Taxes has been reviewing its procedures with regard to the way SDRT is administered in relation to the Unit Trust and OEIC Monthly Returns (FA 1999 Sch 19).

As a consequence of the review, we will be introducing changes to the way in which Monthly Returns are processed within SDRT Operations Unit (Worthing).

NEW PROCEDURES

In the past, Fund Managers/Trustees have been aware that detailed checks have been undertaken by SDRT Operations Unit on all Unit Trust/OEIC returns submitted to ensure validity. The new procedures will provide for additional assurance checks against a "sample" of the returns received. Fund Managers/Trustees will, upon request, be required to provide supporting material (on a small random selection of funds) as a means of substantiating the figures recorded on the Monthly Return. These checks will also include SDRT exemption categories such as exempt 3rd party transfers and pro rata in-specie redemptions.

It is appreciated that this may cause additional work to Fund Managers/Trustees, but we will endeavour to keep this to a minimum.

All enquiries surrounding the content of this Newsletter are to be addressed to: Inland Revenue Stamp Taxes, SDRT Operations Unit, Room 5, East Block, Barrington Road, Worthing, West Sussex BN12 4SE, telephone: 01903 509928 or 509469.

JULY 2002. THE STAMP TAXES CUSTOMER NEWSLETTER CONTRACTS FOR THE SALE OF AN ESTATE OR INTEREST IN UK LAND—FA 2002 S 115 AND SCH 36

1. GENERAL

1.1 This Newsletter provides guidance on the general application of the legislation at FA 2002 s 115 and Sch 36. That legislation brings within the charge to stamp duty contracts for the sale of interests in UK land where the purchase consideration in respect of that land exceeds £10 million. Duty is chargeable on such contracts as though they were conveyances.

1.2 The Newsletter also outlines

- the procedures for making applications to extend the 90-day time limit under FA 2002 s 115 (2) to the newly-established Stamp Taxes Contracts Unit located in Manchester, and
- the Inland Revenue's view of the application of the new legislation in a number of specific circumstances.

1.3 The administration of the legislation, including stamping of contracts within the scope of section 115, the processing of applications to extend the 90-day time limit, and the granting of the benefit of sub-sale relief are all matters that will be exclusively dealt with by the Stamp Taxes Contracts Unit in Manchester (see Appendix B). It follows that such matters should not be referred to other Stamp Offices.

2. BACKGROUND

2.1 In his Budget on 17 April 2002, the Chancellor announced a package of measures intended to counter avoidance of stamp duty on property transactions. These measures are intended to discourage a range of techniques currently used to avoid stamp duty on high-value property deals.

2.2 Under FA 2002 s 115, certain contracts or agreements for the sale of land situated in the UK are brought within the charge to ad valorem stamp duty. This addresses the avoidance of stamp duty on large deals where the parties stop short of executing a formal conveyance of the land, which is the instrument that normally attracts the stamp duty charge, and "rest" on the contract instead.

2.3 The contracts within the scope of section 115 are those where the amount or value of the consideration given for an estate or interest in land in the UK exceeds £10 million, or where the instrument forms part of a larger transaction or series of transactions relating to UK land in respect of which the amount or value, or aggregate amount or value, of the consideration exceeds £10 million.

2.4 Such contracts will be stampable with ad valorem duty as if they were conveyances on sale, if, upon the expiry of a 90-day period from the date that the contract, including one that is conditional, is entered into, a conveyance or transfer has not been presented for stamping.

2.5 The legislation has effect in respect of contracts or agreements executed after 24 July 2002.

2.6 Where it is envisaged that completion of a transaction by the execution of a formal conveyance of the land will not happen within the 90 day period, the legislation provides for an application to be made to the Commissioners of Inland Revenue to extend this period. The procedure and conditions for such applications are set out at 4 below.

2.7 References in this Newsletter to contracts and conveyances include, for transactions in Scotland, the conclusion of missives and dispositions respectively.

3. THE STAMP TAXES CONTRACTS UNIT

3.1 A specially dedicated unit has been established in Manchester to deal with all aspects of the operation of the new legislation, including formal applications for extending the 90 day period. Communications should be addressed to: Stamp Taxes Contracts Unit, Manchester Stamp Office, Upper Fifth Floor, Royal Exchange, Exchange Street, Manchester M2 7EB, Telephone: 0161 839 6260, Fax: 0161 834 3350.

3.2 A contract that is chargeable under section 115 must be presented for stamping to the Contracts Unit in Manchester only. The Unit will also be solely responsible for processing applications for extending the 90-day time limit. It follows that the benefit of relief in respect of sub-sales, including, where appropriate, any repayment of duty paid on the original sale or an earlier sub-sale (see Appendix A of this Newsletter) will also be dealt with by the Unit in Manchester and not by any other Stamp Office.

3.3 The Contracts Unit will be happy to deal with enquiries as to whether a particular contract is, or will be, within the scope of the section 115 charge.

4. APPLICATIONS TO EXTEND THE 90-DAY PERIOD

4.1 FA 2002 s 115 (2)(b) provides that the Commissioners of Inland Revenue may grant an extension to the 90-day period allowed for presentation of a conveyance for stamping where completion of a transaction is not anticipated within that period.

4.2 Applications for an extension should be made in writing, to the Stamp Taxes Contracts Unit, by a responsible officer of the transferee company, which may include a solicitor or accountant acting on behalf of the company and who is aware of the full circumstances of the application, or, where the transferee is not a company, an authorised representative of the transferee, and must contain all of the following:

(a) the full postal address of the land contracted to be sold;
(b) the date of the contract;
(c) the full names and addresses of the vendor and purchaser (if a company, the registered office address and the name of the ultimate parent company are also required);
(d) the amount of the purchase consideration, specifying amounts already paid and any further amounts that will or may become payable by the purchaser;
(e) any apportionment of value between land and buildings, on the one hand, and other assets;
(f) a description of the nature of the transaction, including details of any sub-sales or part sub-sales already in contemplation;
(g) the anticipated completion date and a full explanation of the reason for requesting an extension;
(h) where the contract or agreement forms part of a larger transaction or series of transactions in respect of which the amount or value, or aggregate amount or value, of the consideration attributable to land in the UK exceeds £10 million, details of all relevant transactions;

(i) details of any stamp duty reliefs (eg group relief) to be claimed in respect of the transaction.

Note that it is not necessary to provide a copy of the contract with the application, although this may be requested later.

5. TREATMENT OF APPLICATIONS TO EXTEND THE 90-DAY PERIOD.

5.1 The Stamp Taxes Contracts Unit will consider all applications to extend the 90-day period, and may seek additional information and documentation before granting an extension.

5.2 The length of the extension granted is a matter for the Unit's discretion having regard to all the facts and circumstances of the case under consideration, and compliance with any conditions that it sees fit to impose (section 115 (3)(b)).

5.3 The Unit may, on behalf of the Commissioners of Inland Revenue, refuse to extend the period in any case unless full documentation, including, where requested, a copy of the contract, is provided (section 115(3)(a)). An extension will also be denied if "the whole, or substantially the whole, of the intended consideration" has changed hands (section 115 (3)(c)). 90% or more of the consideration will usually be regarded as "substantially the whole" for this purpose.

5.4 Applications for an extension should be submitted to the Stamp Taxes Contracts Unit as soon as it is appears likely that a conveyance will not be produced within the 90-day time limit. The Unit will endeavour to process applications within thirty days of receipt. To be certain of knowing the outcome of an application by the 90-day point, an application for extension should be lodged with the Contracts Unit no later than 60 days after the contract is entered into. Where applications are made later than that, if an extension is not agreed by the 90-day point, there may be a short period where the contract is technically in charge because an extension has still to be approved. If, however, an extension is subsequently approved, the contract will again be protected from coming into charge until the extension expires (see section 115 (2)(b)).

5.5 Where an extension has been granted, the Contracts Unit will be prepared to consider one or more further applications for extension of the period allowed under section 115 (2)(b). When considering such applications, the Unit may request further information and documentation. If a further extension is not granted, the contract will become chargeable to ad valorem duty on the date upon which the existing extension expires.

5.6 When, in due course, legislation is introduced to modernise the stamp duty regime, further guidance will be provided as necessary concerning the transitional treatment of extensions granted under section 115 (2)(b) that remain outstanding at the date of implementation of the new legislation.

6. CONSIDERATION ISSUES

6.1 The figure of £10 million that appears in section 115 (1) relates to the amount or value of the consideration given for the sale of an estate or interest in UK land. So a contract for the sale of UK land and other assets for £12 million, only £8 million of which is attributable to the UK land will be outside the scope of section 115.

6.2 The apportionment between UK land and other assets must be made on a just and reasonable basis.

6.3 Where the contract forms part of a larger transaction or series of transactions the aggregate value of which exceeds £10 million attributable to UK land, section 115 will apply. For example, four connected and inter-linked contracts for £3 million each will be within the scope of the provision. The £10 million is a VAT inclusive figure. So where the consideration is £9 million plus VAT of £1.575 million, the contract is within section 115.

6.5 Where, when the contract is made, all or part of the consideration is unascertainable, but a maximum, minimum or basic amount can be ascertained, construction of the new legislation as one with the Stamp Act 1891 (Sch 36 para 10) means that the contingency principle applies. So a contract showing consideration of £8 million with a further £4 million contingent upon the happening of some event, will be treated as a contract for £12 million and within the scope of the provision. Where the consideration cannot be ascertained under the contingency principle, FA 1994 s 242 applies (see paragraphs 18–22 of the August 1995 Tax Bulletin article).

7. SUBSEQUENT CONVEYANCE

7.1 Where stamp duty is paid upon a contract under the provisions of section 115 and subsequently a conveyance is presented for stamping, the conveyance is only chargeable with duty if the duty chargeable on it exceeds the duty paid on the contract (Sch 36 para 5 (1)(a)). In this circumstance only the excess duty is payable on the conveyance. The duty paid on the contract will be either denoted on, or transferred to, the conveyance (Sch 36 para 5(4)).

8. USE OF CONTRACT IN COURT PROCEEDINGS

8.1 Where a contract within section 115 remains unstamped, it will nevertheless be admissible as evidence in Court proceedings until the expiry of the 90-day or extended period granted by the Contracts Unit (section 115 (5)(a)).

9. INTEREST AND PENALTIES

9.1 A contract that is chargeable with duty under section 115 is treated, for the purposes of the late stamping interest and penalty provisions (Stamp Act 1891 ss 15A and 15B) as if it had been executed at the end of the 90-day or extended period allowed by the Inland Revenue. Thereafter the normal 30-day limit for presenting a document which has been executed applies before interest and penalties become exigible.

10. SUB-SALES

10.1 FA 2002 Sch 36 para 115 introduce a new form of sub-sale relief for contracts that are chargeable under section 115. The relief is similar to the existing relief in FA 1999 Sch 13 para 7 (2) for property sold under an agreement which is sold on before the original purchaser takes a conveyance. The existing scheme of sub-sale relief under Stamp Act 1891 s 58 (4) and (5) is preserved unaltered for contracts that are not chargeable under FA 2002 s 115.

10.2 The broad scheme of the new relief is that any duty paid on the original sale contract and any intervening sub-sale contracts is credited against duty payable upon the conveyance. Where the duty paid on the contract(s) exceeds that due in respect of the conveyance(s), repayment of the excess will be made.

10.3 Full details of how the relief operates in conjunction with section 115, together with a series of examples, is set out in Appendix A. The examples do not cover every possible situation that might arise in practice, but the Contracts Unit will be pleased to advise on the application of the law to particular circumstances that are not specifically covered in the Appendix.

APPENDIX A

Sub-Sale Relief

Section 115 (2) provides for sub-sale relief where duty has not been paid on contracts under section 115. Schedule 36 deals with sub-sale relief where duty has been paid on contracts within section 115. "Sub-sale" is defined as the situation where a purchaser, or sub-purchaser, under a contract, without having obtained a conveyance of the property contracted to be sold, contracts to sell the whole or part of the property to another person, putting that person in the position to call for a conveyance from the original seller (Sch 36 para 2). In these circumstances there will be more than one contract potentially chargeable under section 115. For example, suppose A contracts to sell UK land to B for £11 million, and, before completing the transaction, B contracts to sell the land to C for £12 million, with the land being conveyed by A directly to C. Both the A-B and B-C contracts are within the scope of section 115 (although duty would not, of course, be payable on the B-C contract if completion took place within 90 days). The examples below illustrate how section 115 (2) and Sch 36 deal with this situation.

Sub-sale relief will be administered only by the Stamp Taxes Contract Unit in Manchester, to which all sub-sale contracts and final conveyances should therefore be sent.

(1) Sub-sale where no duty paid on the contracts followed by a subsequent conveyance.
In the above example the conveyance from A to C is regarded as made in conformity with both the A-B and the B-C contracts and duty will be payable upon the conveyance for £12 million (section 115 (2)).

(2) Sub-sale where duty paid on the contract followed by a subsequent conveyance.
A contracts to sell UK land to B for £11 million, and B pays stamp duty on the contract of £440,000 (£11m × 4%). B then contracts to sell the land to C for £12 million and A conveys the land directly to C.
The conveyance to C for £12 million is only chargeable with duty if the duty chargeable on it (£480,000) exceeds the duty paid on the contract (£440,000)—Sch 36 para 5(1)(a). As £480,000 exceeds £440,000, duty of £40,000 must be paid on the A-C conveyance.
In the event that the consideration for the conveyance from A-C is less than the consideration on which B paid stamp duty on the A-B contract, Sch 36 para 6 provides for repayment. So if B paid duty on £11 million (£440,000) and the conveyance from A-C was for £9 million (£360,000), para 6(1) applies and B, as the person who paid the duty on the original sale, will be entitled to a repayment of £440,000 – £360,000 = £80,000. This assumes that the £9 million is not less than the value of the property immediately prior to the sub-sale (see FA 1984 s 112).

(3) Sub-sale contract for part followed by conveyance where additional duty payable.
A contracts to sell UK land to B for £30 million and B pays stamp duty on the contract. Before taking a conveyance, however, B contracts to sell one-third of the land to C for £12 million and A conveys one-third of the land directly to C.
The sub-sale to C is in respect of part only of the property that was the subject of the original sale. Duty on the A-C conveyance is chargeable in respect of the amount by which the ad valorem duty chargeable on it exceeds an "appropriate proportion" of the ad valorem duty paid on the original sale (Sch 36 para 5(2)). The appropriate proportion is determined on a just and reasonable basis having regard to the ad valorem duty paid on the original sale together with any intervening subsale. In this example, B paid duty on the original sale of £1.2 million. B has sold 1/3 of the land to C. So the appropriate proportion of duty to be credited on the A-C conveyance might, depending upon the circumstances, be £1.2 million × 1/3 = £400,000. Duty on the A-C conveyance is therefore £12 million × 4% = £480,000 – £400,000 = £80,000.

(4) Sub-sale contract for part followed by conveyance where duty repayable.
Once the whole of a property contracted to be sold in parts has been conveyed, and the aggregate duty chargeable on the conveyances is less than the duty paid on the original sale and the intervening sub-sales, then a repayment is due under Sch 36 para 6.
For example—A contracts to sell UK land to B for £11 million. B pays duty of £440,000 on the contract. B then parcels the land into 60 parts and contracts to sell them for £200,000 each. Once the final part has been conveyed from A to the 60th purchaser, if the duty chargeable on the conveyances is less than £440,000, a repayment will be due.
The duty on each conveyance is £200,000 × 1% = £2,000. £2,000 × 60 conveyances = £120,000. Therefore a repayment of duty is due to B in the sum of £440,000 – £120,000 = £320,000.

(5) Where whole property sold and duty previously paid on original sale (or an earlier sub-sale).

Suppose that A contracts to sell land to B for £11 million but, before taking a conveyance, B contracts to sell the land on to C for £12 million. B pays duty on £11 million, but the conveyance from A to C does not take place. Duty on the B-C contract is chargeable only in respect of the excess of the chargeable consideration on that contract over the chargeable consideration on the A-B contract. So C would pay duty on £1m (£12m – £11m) @ 4% = £40,000 (Sch 36 para 3 (1)).

If, in turn, C, having paid duty on the B-C contract, contracts to sell the whole property on to D for £15million, D will be liable for duty calculated by reference to the excess of £15 million over the higher amount of chargeable consideration on which duty has been paid on an earlier transaction. The higher amount of chargeable consideration in this case is the £12 million on the B-C contract, and so D will pay duty on £3m (£15m – £12m) @ 4% = £120,000 (Sch 36 para 3(2)).

(6) Where part only of property sold and duty previously paid on original sale or earlier sub-sale.

Suppose A contracts to sell UK land to B for £30 million. Before taking a conveyance B contracts to sell one-third of the land to C for £12 million, and subsequently contracts with D to sell the remaining two-thirds of the land for £25 million. B pays duty on the £30 million consideration for the A-B contract. The sub-sale to C is in respect of part only of the property that was the subject of the original sale. Duty on the B-C contract is chargeable in respect of the amount by which the consideration of £12 million exceeds an "appropriate proportion" of the consideration on the earlier transaction (Sch 36 para 3 (3)). The appropriate proportion is determined on a just and reasonable basis having regard to the subject matter of the sub-sale and the earlier transaction (para 3 (4)). In this case C would pay duty on £12m less £10m (£30m × ⅓) = £2m @ 4% = £80,000.

If D paid the duty but did not take a conveyance from A, but instead sold the whole of his two-thirds of the original property on to E for £27 million, E would be required to pay duty on the amount by which the chargeable consideration on the D-E contract exceeds the higher amount of chargeable consideration on an earlier sale or sub-sale of that property. In this example, the chargeable consideration on which duty was paid by D was £25 million, so E pays duty on £2m (£27m – £25m) = £2m @ 4% = £80,000.

If D only sold on to E half of the property he bought from B, for £15 million, then the calculation of duty payable by E would need to take into account the higher of the "appropriate proportion" of the chargeable consideration on the original sale (A-B) and the "appropriate proportion" of the chargeable consideration on the intervening sub-sale (B-D), as follows:

B's chargeable consideration £30m.

Appropriate proportion thereof (30m × ⅔ × ½) £10m. (X)

D's chargeable consideration £25m.

Appropriate proportion thereof (25m × ½) £12.5m. (Y)

(Y) is greater than (X), so E pays duty on £15m – £12.5m = £2.5m @ 4% = £100,000

(Sch 36 para 3 (1)–(5)).

(7) Where part sub-sold and part retained by original purchaser, and duty paid on original contract.

Suppose A contracts to sell UK land to B for £15 million. Before taking a conveyance, B agrees to sell one third of the land to C for £7 million and a further third of the land to D, also for £7 million. B pays duty on the £15 million consideration for the A-B contract. Following the principle in 5 above, both C and D would pay duty on £7m less £5m (£15m × ⅓) = £2m @ 4% = £80,000. The conveyance from A to B of the land not agreed to be sub-sold is liable to duty, not on a consideration of £1m, but following the decision in *Maples v IRC* [1914] 3 KB 303, on £5m, which represents the proportionate value of the land in relation to the original contract price. The conveyance is therefore liable to duty of £200,000 (£5m @ 4%). As the original contract was stamped with £600,000 duty, and £400,000 has been credited against the stamping of the conveyances to C and D, the balance is available to satisfy the liability on the conveyance from A-B.

(8) Rate of duty.

Where duty is chargeable on a contract within Sch 36 para 3, duty on a sub-sale is chargeable in respect of part only of the consideration for the sub-sale, the rate of duty chargeable on the sub-sale is the rate that would be applicable if the whole of the chargeable consideration on the sub-sale were taken into account.

A contracts to sell UK land to B for £30 million. B pays stamp duty at 4% on the contract. B then contracts to sell the land to C for £30.1 million. Duty is payable by C on the additional £100,000 consideration at 4% under Sch 36 para 3(6).

APPENDIX B

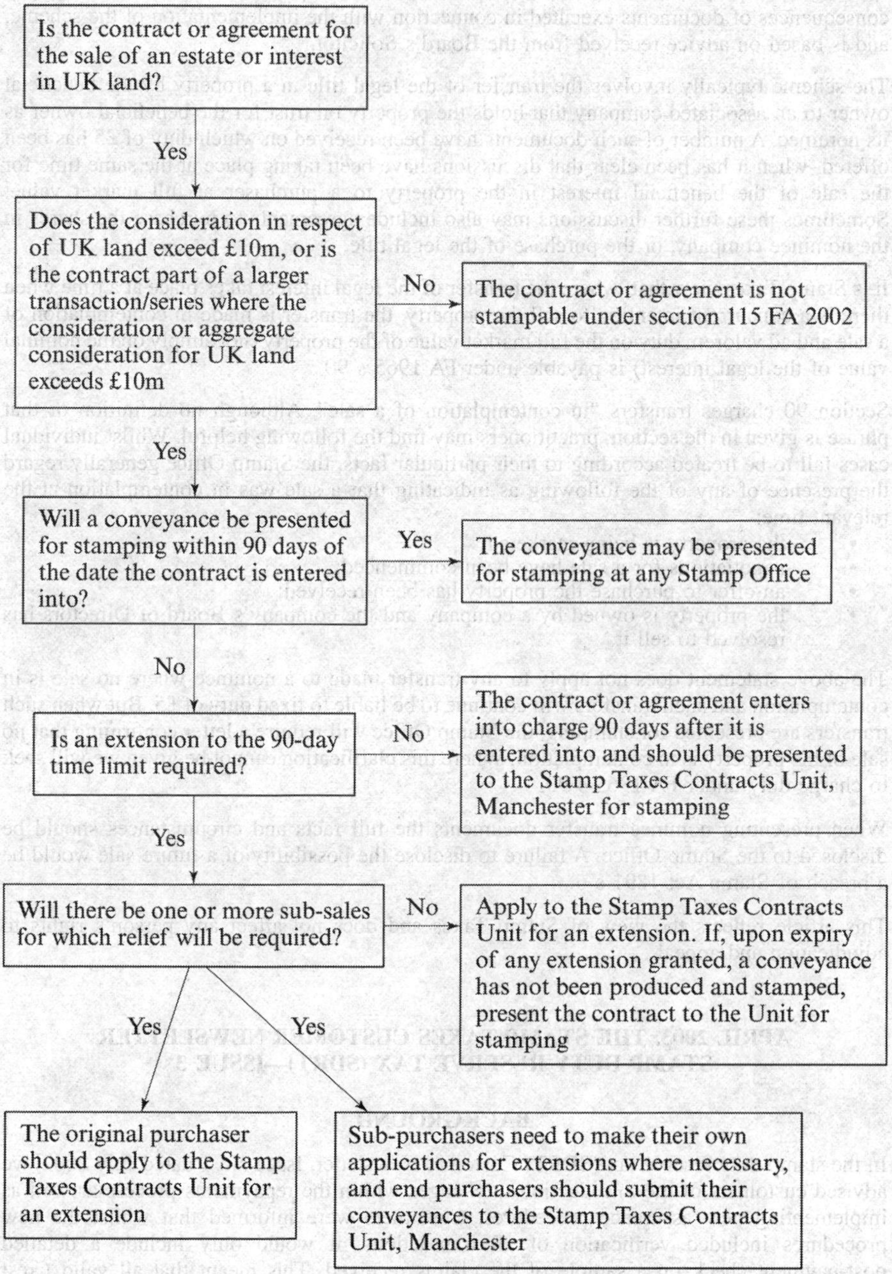

JULY 2002. THE STAMP TAXES CUSTOMER NEWSLETTER SPLIT TITLE SCHEMES AND FA 1965 S 90

In recent months Stamp Offices have received a significant number of documents and enquiries in connection with a perceived stamp duty avoidance scheme known as "title splitting". The purpose of this article is to publicise the Stamp Taxes' view of the stamp duty consequences of documents executed in connection with the implementation of the scheme, and is based on advice received from the Board's Solicitor.

The scheme typically involves the transfer of the legal title in a property by the beneficial owner to an associated company that holds the property on trust for the beneficial owner as its nominee. A number of such documents have been received on which duty of £5 has been offered, when it has been clear that discussions have been taking place at the same time for the sale of the beneficial interest in the property to a purchaser at full market value. Sometimes these further discussions may also include agreements to purchase the shares in the nominee company, or the purchase of the legal title.

It is Stamp Taxes view that, where the transfer of the legal interest takes place at a time when there is a concurrent intention to sell the property, the transfer is made in contemplation of a sale and ad valorem duty on the full market value of the property (not simply on the nominal value of the legal interest) is payable under FA 1965 s 90.

Section 90 charges transfers "in contemplation of a sale". Although no definition of that phrase is given in the section, practitioners may find the following helpful. Whilst individual cases fall to be treated according to their particular facts, the Stamp Office generally regard the presence of any of the following as indicating that a sale was in contemplation at the relevant time:

- the property is being marketed;
- negotiations for a sale have been commenced;
- an offer to purchase the property has been received;
- the property is owned by a company and the company's Board of Directors has resolved to sell it.

The above statement does not apply to any transfer made to a nominee where no sale is in contemplation and such transfers will continue to be liable to fixed duty of £5. But when such transfers are presented for stamping, the Stamp Office will require a letter confirming that no sale of the property is in contemplation. Where this clarification cannot be given we will seek to charge duty under FA 1965 s 90.

When presenting nominee transfer documents the full facts and circumstances should be disclosed to the Stamp Office. A failure to disclose the possibility of a future sale would be a breach of Stamp Act 1891 s 5.

This article reflects the view of Stamp Taxes and does not affect any person's rights to adjudication and appeal.

APRIL 2003. THE STAMP TAXES CUSTOMER NEWSLETTER STAMP DUTY RESERVE TAX (SDRT)—ISSUE 3

BACKGROUND

In the stamp duty reserve tax (SDRT) Customer Newsletter, Issue No 1 dated July 2002, we advised customers of the introduction to changes within the repayments process as well as implementing new assurance procedures. Customers were informed that whilst the new procedures included verification of all transactions, it would only include a detailed post-payment check on a sample of the claims received. This meant that all valid Crest Transaction IDs would be repaid immediately upon receipt, on a without prejudice basis, but SDRT Operations Unit reserved the right to contact customers at a later date (usually within 60 days of the claim date) to request additional supporting material where necessary.

Customers were asked to submit certain information when presenting a reclaim, and if multiple transactions were in point, the information was to be supplied on a disk.

REPAYMENTS

IR Stamp Taxes (SDRT) is committed to providing a high standard of customer service and always looking for continuous improvement in order to achieve that standard. SDRT reclaims have now been processed in line with the new repayment procedures for nine months or so, and the way in which customers submit their claims has accordingly been reviewed. As a result, and in order to provide a faster and more effective service, it is suggested that claims be submitted in the following format as per the diagram below:

Crest Trans ID	*Claim*	*Date*	*Repayment Code*
ABC0225466	£33.22	12/02/03	1
ABC0525498	£504.36	12/02/03	1
ABC0525467	£1.32	04/09/02	2
ABC0625330	£5,601	14/07/02	8
BC056989910102	£1,036.89	30/08/01	4
BC00605484	£784.63	01/01/03	2
MM36599845	£3.35	14/05/00	5
LP22144546	£6.92	09/10/99	1
FG10569881	£69,188.22	03/11/00	8
FG10569882	£12.54	03/11/00	10
FG10569833	£222.30	04/11/00	10
FG10569884	£45.71	28/06/00	1
FG10569880	£0.45	29/06/01	10
FG1056988402	£1.87	13/12/01	11
ADC0562337	£2,120.33	04/11/00	8

- **Crest Transaction ID (not the STP transaction ID)** This is the transaction ID upon which a reclaim of SDRT is being sought.
- **Individual SDRT claim amounts** This is the individual amount of tax applied against a relevant Crest Transaction ID (not the total STP amount).
- **Trade Date** This is the trade date of the agreement.
- **Repayment Code 1–11** Please **ensure** a repayment code is applied against each reclaim.

Failure to submit the above information may result in reclaims being returned with a request for further details. Customers are reminded to include their reference number on any covering letter when submitting a reclaim, and that if multiple transactions of 15 or more are in point, a disk (in Excel format) should be supplied.

If the total reclaim amount is £150,000 or more and payment is required by CHAPS, please remember to send bank details together with the reclaim information.

It is hoped that this newsletter will not only enable SDRT Operations Unit to provide customers with a better quality service, but also to encourage customers to ensure that all reclaim details are submitted in full.

All enquiries surrounding the content of this Newsletter should be addressed to: Inland Revenue Stamp Taxes, SDRT Operations Unit, Room 5, East Block, Barrington Road, Worthing, West Sussex BN12 4SE, tel: 01903 509471 or 01903 509469.

REPAYMENT CODES

Code	*Explanation*
Exemption applicable	
1	NCBO
2	Charity
3	Intermediary Relief (Principal purchase)
CREST inputs incorrect or missing	
4	TSS flag (identify flag applicable)
5	TSO/Stock Lending Relief
6	Market Sale/ADR conversion back to underlying shares
7	Stampable consideration
8	Agent indicator
Double SDRT payments made	
9	Cancelled/Rebooked or duplicated trades
10	Bulk/Splits, paid both in and outside of CREST, paid by both parties
Others	
11	Other reasons not listed

DECEMBER 2003. THE STAMP TAXES CUSTOMER NEWSLETTER STAMP DUTY RESERVE TAX (SDRT)—ISSUE 4

CHARITY REFERENCES (CHARITY ID FIELD: CHID-IRLST)

Inland Revenue Stamp Taxes has recently received a number of enquiries from CREST members seeking clarification on the inputting of charity references (as detailed on page 13 of "CREST Stamp Duty Reserve Tax—A Guide to Market Practice September 1999", otherwise known as the "blue book").

The purchase of UK registered securities by UK charities is exempt from SDRT, and where exchange members or qualified dealers deliver securities to a counterparty custodian whose underlying client is a charity, the exchange member or qualified dealer (as the "accountable person" for SDRT purposes), is responsible for completing the CREST Transaction Stamp Status (TSS) value with an "S" and an Inland Revenue FICO or Charity Commissioners reference number in the Charity ID field.

There is, however, one exception to this general rule. Where the exchange member's or qualified dealer's counterparty custodian or fund manager enters into specific arrangements with Inland Revenue Stamp Taxes and agrees to supply the charity details on his side of the matching CREST instruction (and to retain those details), the delivering exchange member or qualified dealer is required to complete the Transaction Stamp Status value with "S", as above, and enter "CHID-IRLST" in the Charity ID field to indicate that his counterparty will be inputting the relevant charity reference number.

Custodians and Fund Managers wishing to input the charity reference numbers must initially apply in writing to Inland Revenue Stamp Taxes SDRT Operations Unit, seeking approval to the arrangement and for inclusion on a Published List of custodians and fund managers. Once approval has been granted, it will be the custodians' responsibility to input the charity number in the CREST Charity ID field.

Details of Custodians and Fund Managers approved by Stamp Taxes are listed on the Excel spreadsheet which accompanies this bulletin—this information can also be accessed on the Inland Revenue website www.inlandrevenue.gov.uk (Stamp Taxes area). Any requests by firms to be added to or deleted from the Published List (or for details currently held to be amended) are to be forwarded to Inland Revenue Stamp Taxes, SDRT Operations Unit, Room 5 East Block, Barrington Road, Worthing, West Sussex BN12 4SE. Telephone 01903 509928 or 01903 509469

DECEMBER 2003. THE STAMP TAXES CUSTOMER NEWSLETTER STAMP DUTY LAND TAX (SDLT)—ISSUE 1

THE SWITCH TO "STAMP DUTY LAND TAX" PLANNED TO TAKE PLACE ON 1 DECEMBER 2003

Welcome to the first of a series of newsletters designed to provide guidance on the introduction of stamp duty land tax later this year.

Background

In Budget 2002, the Government announced its intention to modernise the stamp duty charge on UK land and buildings. Current legislation was considered outdated, incompatible with modern commercial practice and the move to e-business. A modernised regime is needed to support the automated electronic systems that the land registries intend to introduce in the next 3–8 years. There has also been increasing evidence of widespread avoidance of duty in large commercial transactions.

In April 2002 a consultative document was published outlining proposals of how the duty might be modernised. A number of consultative committees were established and met regularly through the summer and autumn of last year. The responses to the Consultative Document and the contributions of the various committees informed the next stage of the modernisation project. In November 2002 we published draft legislation to stimulate further debate.

Following from this, the publication of the Finance Bill 2003, on 16 April sets out the statutory framework for the modernised tax, which the Chancellor has announced is planned for introduction from 1 December 2003.

Not all aspects of the tax have been finalised and there is to be a further round of consultation about how it will apply in a number of complex commercial areas. But the basic fundamentals that will apply to the vast majority of transactions are set out in the primary legislation. This newsletter provides information about them and how the changes will affect our customers.

The Key Changes

Stamp duty has always been a tax on documents. But stamp duty land tax will be a tax on transactions involving interests in land in the UK. The tax will not be triggered by the execution of a document. Instead, tax will become payable automatically on the due date, which will be 30 days after the effective date of the transaction. The effective date is generally the date that the purchaser acquires the subject matter of the transaction, which may be in advance of legal completion of the transfer.

Another major change is that the tax will become mandatory. Stamp duty has sometimes been regarded as a "voluntary tax" because it was not directly enforceable against any person and the Stamp Office could not compel payment of it. Payment of duty has traditionally been made as a result of the pressures that stem from having an unstamped document, the chief ones being the inadmissibility of such documents in court in civil proceedings and the fact that registrars, particularly the land registries, cannot register stampable documents that have not been stamped. The legislation introducing the tax will provide that the Purchaser, or

Part II ST

person acquiring the subject-matter of the transaction must notify the Stamp Office of the transaction by making a land transaction return together with a self-assessment of the tax due. For this purpose "purchaser" includes a lessee where the transaction in question is the grant or assignment of a lease.

How Will the Process Work in Practice?

There are specific transitional rules that will apply to contracts entered into prior to the implementation date but which are completed after it. These will be covered in a separate newsletter. But generally from 1 December 2003, the purchaser will be required to deliver a land transaction return, giving particulars of the transaction and paying the tax that is due. The Land Transaction Return and payment should be sent to our Processing Centre at Netherton. It will not be necessary to send any supporting documentation such as the contract or the actual transfer. The return can also be submitted to local stamp offices, but this will result in a slower service, as the return has to be processed in the central location. The Processing Centre will process the return and issue a stamp duty land tax certificate. The certificate will be required by the land registries before they will accept documents as evidencing a change of ownership. In effect therefore, the certificate replaces the traditional duty stamps that are currently impressed on documents.

The issuing of the stamp duty land tax certificate does not necessarily mean that the matter is finalised. We will be operating a "process now, check later system". We can open an enquiry into a transaction notified to us at any time within 9 months of the date that the return is due, or is actually notified to us, if later (the "filing date").

As now, some transactions will not be liable to the tax either because they are below the threshold or because the transaction qualifies for a relief. These will still have to be notified to us on a land transaction return if chargeable consideration has been provided and the transaction is the transfer of a freehold, the assignment or transfer of an existing lease or the grant of a new lease for a term of 7 years or more. By contrast, certain transactions will not require notification and documents can be self certified as being exempt from the tax and sent direct to the land registries. These will be subject to audits and the same enquiry process. Further guidance will be issued on this in a later newsletter.

Eventually we plan to streamline the system further. The introduction of electronic conveyancing and land registration systems should allow the tax to be paid at the time of registration.

Are There Any Changes to the Rates of Duty?

For conveyances and transfers of land, tax will continue to be charged as a percentage of the "chargeable consideration". The definition of chargeable consideration has been widened so that it is now defined as "money or money's worth". The present rates of stamp duty will continue to apply to purchases of residential property and the threshold remains at £60,000. But for transactions in non-residential and mixed- use properties the threshold will be increased to £150,000 from the implementation of stamp duty land tax.

For leases, tax on premiums will be calculated in exactly the same way as now, that is as a percentage of the amount paid. Again the threshold for non–residential and mixed-use properties will be increased to £150,000. But the Finance Bill includes legislation that provides for an entirely different method of calculating tax on new lease rents. The new charge will be levied at 1% of the net present value of rental payments payable under the terms of the lease. However, the Government has stated that it will consult further on this proposal and will not implement it if an acceptable alternative basis can be found.

Late Notification of Transactions and Late Payment of Tax

A land transaction return must be delivered and payment of the tax must be made within 30 days of the effective date of the transaction. Penalties are payable if the transaction is notified late and interest is payable on tax paid late.

Further Information

More information will be provided in later customer newsletters. We recognise that the changes represent a major reform of part of the conveyancing system and that our customers need to be fully informed. For this reason we have developed a customer education programme that was launched in Somerset House on 16 May. We will follow this up with further customer newsletters, information bulletins and articles in Solicitors' and Conveyancers' journals and magazines. We will be enhancing our Internet site and publishing revised leaflets.

In addition, we are planning a series of regional training events for the legal profession in partnership with the Law Societies of England & Wales, Scotland and Northern Ireland.

In the meantime, you may like to consult our website at www.inlandrevenue.gov.uk/so/index.htm for the details published on Budget Day and when the Finance Bill was issued.

Transactions in Shares

It is stressed that the information in this leaflet applies only to interests in UK land. Transactions in shares are not affected by the changes and they will continue to be liable to stamp duty or stamp duty reserve tax exactly as they are now.

DECEMBER 2003. THE STAMP TAXES CUSTOMER NEWSLETTER STAMP DUTY LAND TAX (SDLT)—ISSUE 2

THE SWITCH TO "STAMP DUTY LAND TAX" PLANNED TO TAKE PLACE ON 1 DECEMBER 2003

Welcome to the second of our newsletters designed to provide guidance on the introduction of stamp duty land tax later this year. This issue focuses on customer awareness and customer education issues.

We are committed to helping to make the changeover as smooth as possible. We will be keeping our customers informed of developments throughout the next few months using a variety of methods, which will be explained later in this newsletter.

What Can You Do Now?

It is important that our customers are prepared for the changes. Practitioners can do this by ensuring that they consider the legal and practical implications for both themselves and their clients.

Current Awareness of Modernisation of Stamp Duty

We recently commissioned a study conducted by the British Market Research Bureau to ascertain current awareness levels of the modernisation of stamp duty. 1,100 telephone interviews were conducted with a range of solicitors and Licensed Conveyancers from both large and small firms.

The overall level of awareness was 45% but a more detailed breakdown showed that London practitioners were slightly more aware of the changes than those elsewhere—49% compared to 44%. And the more employees in the firm, the greater the level of awareness.

The 493 respondents who were aware of the changes, were asked how they became aware of modernisation. The main sources were the law societies and industry journals at 44% and 42% respectively.

Respondents were then asked whether they felt they had received enough information and a fairly significant 72% said that they hadn't.

In order to assist in the development of an awareness campaign, respondents were asked about their preferred method of receiving information. Leaflets came out well on top at 53%.

How We Will Help You Prepare For the Changes

On 16 May we hosted an open morning for solicitors, accountants and representatives from various groups affected by the changes to mark the launch of our customer education campaign. The event featured an overview of the new processes and their impact on customers together with a presentation on preparing customers for the changes. The event was very well attended and well received. We intend to hold similar presentations over the next few months. Details and invitations will appear on our website.

The first two issues in a series of **Information Bulletins** have been produced and mailed to around 10,000 firms of solicitors who have had contact with us in the past. These bulletins will continue to be produced in the run up to the commencement of the changes. If people want to be added to the list they should contact Des Newman on 020 7438 7762. The aim of these bulletins is to keep customers informed of developments on an ongoing basis. They will be produced every 4 to 6 weeks.

This series of **Customer Newsletters** will contain more detailed information about technical changes. Again they will be produced every 4 to 6 weeks and will be enclosed when documents are returned from Stamp Offices to Conveyancers.

Eight weeks prior to implementation of the changes, **flyers** will be enclosed with all returned documents reminding Conveyancers about what they need to do from 1 December. This message will focus on a different issue each week.

The above documents will also be available on the Stamp Taxes website.

The market research demonstrated that **industry journals** were one of the key ways in which people obtained information and therefore we will be proactively contacting various magazines and journals with a view to having articles placed.

An exhibition stand has been produced which we are willing to take to any relevant exhibitions and events.

Training

Actual training for solicitors will be delivered by ourselves working in partnership with the three law societies (England & Wales, Scotland and Northern Ireland). Training will be rolled out from September onwards and dates and venues are available from the respective law societies.

The events will be organised by the law societies who will be responsible for the administration and advertising. The actual training material will be produced by us and we will provide the speakers at the sessions which will last around 2 hours.

The training will cover:

- an overview of the main legislative changes
- details of the enquiry process from opening through to closure
- completion of the new Land Transaction Return
- the various ways in which customers can obtain advice and guidance.

Customer Assistance

Customers will be helped with their obligations both before and after [the legislation] go[es] live in a variety of ways.

The existing stamp duty **leaflets** are being reviewed and it is likely that there will be one main SDLT leaflet covering all aspects which will be available only on the Internet. There will then be a simple quick reference guide to SDLT aimed at the public but this will be available in hard copy as well.

In line with other taxes, there will be a **Code of Practice** to support the enquiry process. This will automatically be enclosed when a letter is issued to notify the customer that an enquiry is to take place.

A number of **calculation tools for the Internet** are being developed. An SDLT calculator will allow users to input the price, the date of their purchase in order to obtain the amount of SDLT due (including SDLT on leases). In addition a digital mapping tool for disadvantaged areas is being developed which will allow users to search for, and identify, land and property that qualifies for disadvantaged area relief.

The introduction of SDLT will bring with it a requirement for new **guidance** and an SDLT Manual will be produced covering three areas: technical, procedural and compliance. In accordance with the Code of Practice on Access to Government information the manual will be published on the Internet.

Where Can I Find Further Information?

The **Enquiry Line** has already been expanded and there is the capacity to add additional resources should they be required. The Enquiry Line is open from Monday to Friday from 8.30am to 5pm and the number is 0845 6030135. All calls are charged at local rates.

Further information can be found on the Stamp Taxes website.

Additional details are available in the Finance Bill 2003 press notice (REV 55) and the budget day press notice, PN05: Modernising the taxation of property. These can also be found on our website.

DECEMBER 2003. THE STAMP TAXES CUSTOMER NEWSLETTER STAMP DUTY LAND TAX (SDLT)—ISSUE 3

THE SWITCH TO STAMP DUTY LAND TAX PLANNED TO TAKE PLACE ON 1 DECEMBER 2003

Commencement and Transitional Provisions

This issue of the Newsletter is concerned with the introduction of stamp duty land tax on 1 December 2003. It provides guidance on whether transactions that may have been entered into prior to that date but which are completed at a later date are within the existing stamp duty regime, or come within the scope of stamp duty land tax.

In this article we focus on general principles and the main points that are likely to arise. It is not possible to cover every possible scenario. We have already published on our web site a flow chart that can be used to determine whether or not a transaction is a stamp duty or stamp duty land tax matter. More detailed guidance will be available in the new stamp duty land tax manual that will be published in electronic form. A draft version of the manual will be published on the Internet in the beginning of October 2003. We would welcome comments on the content of the manual. Please send comments by post to: Vivienne Scrimshire, Room 116, New Wing, Somerset House, London WC2B 1 LR, or alternatively these may be e-mailed to: Vivienne. Scrimshire @ir.gsi.gov.uk.

The legislation dealing with the commencement and transitional provisions is contained in FA 2003 Sch 19. FA 2003 received Royal Assent on 10 July 2003 and this is an important date in considering whether or not a transaction is to be subject to stamp duty or stamp duty land tax.

The Basic Charge to Stamp Duty Land Tax

As a general rule, a land transaction falls within the scope of stamp duty land tax if the "effective date" of the transaction is on or after "implementation date". The "effective date"

Part II ST

of a transaction is the earlier of the transaction being completed by a conveyance, or the date that the contract is "substantially performed." Substantial performance of a contract occurs when

- the purchaser (which includes a lessee under the terms of a lease) has paid any rent, or
- the purchaser has paid the whole or substantially the whole (not normally less than 90%) of any consideration other than rent, or
- the purchaser has taken possession, or become entitled to possession of the property. This includes receipt of, or entitlement to receipt of, rents and profits. Implementation date means 1 December 2003.

Example 1

A contracts to sell a property to B on 15 December 2003. The transaction is completed by the purchase price being paid in full on 15 January 2004 and a transfer is executed the same day. This is a stamp duty land tax transaction as the effective date of the transaction is after "implementation date", 1 December 2003. Accordingly the transaction will be notifiable as a stamp duty land tax transaction on a Land Transaction Return. (For guidance on this please refer to Customer Newsletter 1, which is available on our web site.)

In example 1 both the contract and the effective date of the transaction were after implementation date. It is not necessary however for the contract to have been entered into after 1 December 2003 for a transaction to be subject to stamp duty land tax. Contracts entered into prior to 1 December 2003 may give rise to a stamp duty land tax charge (see example 2).

Example 2

A contracts to sell a property to B on 18 September 2003. The transaction is completed by the purchase price being paid on 7 December 2003 and a transfer is executed the same day. As the effective date of the transaction is after "implementation date", the transaction is a stamp duty land tax transaction.

Contracts Entered Into On or Before 10 July 2003

There are however, special rules that apply for land transactions that implement contracts entered into on or before 10 July 2003. The key points are as follows

- Contracts that are substantially performed on or before 10 July 2003 are not stamp duty land tax transactions (see example 3).
- Contracts that are not substantially performed on or before 10 July 2003 are not stamp duty land tax transactions (see example 4) unless,
  - (a) there is any variation of the contract or assignment of rights under the contract after 10 July 2003; or
  - (b) the transaction is effected in consequence of the exercise after 10 July 2003 of any option, right of pre-emption or similar right; or
  - (c) the purchaser under the transaction is a person other than the purchaser under the contract because of a further contract (for example a sub-sale contract) made after 10 July 2003.

A variation of a contract under (*a*) does not include minor matters peripheral to the contract such as changes to colour schemes or pets being permitted on premises. It does however, include any changes to the following; the parties to the transaction, the subject matter of the sale, the contractual consideration or in an agreement for lease, the length of the term.

Example 3

On 1 May 2003, A contracted to sell a property to B. On 1 June 2003, B paid the purchase price in full (an act of substantial performance). The contract is completed by a conveyance dated 1 March 2004. This is not a stamp duty land tax transaction because it was substantially performed on or before 10 July 2003. The conveyance is liable to Stamp Duty.

Example 4

A contracts to sell a property to B on 1 July 2003. The contract is not substantially performed in advance of completion and none of the exceptions listed at (*a*) to (*c*) above apply. A conveyance of the property is made to the contracting purchaser, B, on 7 March 2004. This is not a stamp duty land tax transaction but the conveyance is liable to Stamp Duty.

Variations and Contracts Entered Into On or After 10 July 2003.

FA 2003 Sch 19 para 4(3) makes special provisions for contracts entered into prior to implementation date. These include a contract made on or before 10 July 2003 which has not been substantially performed before 10 July 2003, a similar contract that has been varied after that date, or where the contracting purchaser has sub-sold or transferred his rights after that date. It also makes provision for contracts entered into in the period between 10 July 2003 and 1 December 2003. The substantial performance of such contracts before implementation is disregarded. Consequently a charge to stamp duty land tax can only arise on completion. The following examples illustrate this.

Example 5

A contracts to sell a property to B on 1 October 2003. Substantial performance of the contract takes place on 20 November 2003 when B pays the purchase price in full. The contract is completed by the conveyance of the property to B on 1 July 2006. A charge to stamp duty land tax arises on 1 July 2006.

Example 6

A contracts to sell a property to B on 1 September 2003 and substantial performance occurs on 15 October 2003 when B pays the purchase price in full. On 1 November 2003 B contracts to sell the property to C. The contract is completed on 1 February 2004, when A transfers the property direct to C. There is no charge to Stamp Duty Land tax on B because the conveyance to the ultimate purchaser does not trigger a stamp duty land tax charge. C incurs a stamp duty land tax liability on 1 February 2004.

In the example above, B has been able to benefit from the availability of a modified form of sub-sale relief. But it should be borne in mind that this relief was available only because substantial performance of the A-B contract occurred before 1 December 2003. Sub-sale relief will only be available in respect of contracts entered into after 10 July 2003 in very limited circumstances. More guidance on sub-sales will be provided in a later Newsletter.

Example 7

A contracts to sell a property to B on 1 November 2003, which is substantially performed (for the first time) on 1 March 2004 in advance of completion when B pays the purchase price. As substantial performance occurred after 1 December 2003 a stamp duty land tax charge arises on B, on 1 March 2004.

Stamp Duty Credit Available to Offset Against Stamp Duty Land Tax Charge

Where a stamp duty land tax transaction is effected pursuant to a contract entered into before 1 December 2003 any ad valorem stamp duty paid on the contract is available for crediting against the stamp duty land tax liability that arises when the transaction is substantially performed or completed. There is however, no entitlement to a refund if it transpires that the stamp duty liability exceeds the stamp duty land tax charge. Examples of contracts liable to ad valorem stamp duty are pre implementation date:

- Agreements for Lease, and
- Contracts for sale chargeable under FA 2002 s 115 (consideration exceeding £10 million).

Stamp Duty Provisions Affecting Land Transactions

- An instrument effecting a land transaction is not subject to stamp duty if the transaction is a stamp duty land tax transaction (FA 2003 s 125(5)(*a*))—see example 2 above.
- If a conveyance is within the charge to stamp duty there is no charge to stamp duty land tax—see example 4 above.
- Schedule 19 para 8 makes special provisions that broadly replicate the provisions of FA 1994 s 240 as amended, relating to Agreements for Lease and leases. The following is an example of this.

Example 8

An agreement for lease is entered into on 1 October 2003, which is completed when the lease is executed on 1 March 2004. The Agreement for Lease is a stamp duty transaction because at the time that it was executed it did not effect a stamp duty land tax transaction. It is liable to stamp duty under FA 1999 Sch 13 para 14. Under the provisions of FA 1994 s 240 as amended, stamping of the Agreement can be deferred until 30 days after the execution of the lease without the penalty or interest provisions applying. In these circumstances the delivery of a stamp duty land tax Return, the Agreement for Lease and payment within 30 days of 1 March 2004 will not give rise to the Agreement incurring a stamp duty penalty or interest charge. Procedural guidance will be issued at a later date regarding the manner that the Return and the Agreement should be presented to Stamp Taxes.

If the Agreement for Lease had been stamped prior to the lease being granted, the duty paid on the Agreement would be credited against the stamp duty land tax charge. Again further guidance will be provided at a later date regarding the procedural arrangements.

An important point to note is that the timing differences of the Agreement for Lease and lease, which straddle the "implementation date," means that an entirely different basis of calculation is used to determine the amount of stamp duty payable on the Agreement, and the amount of stamp duty land tax payable when the lease is granted. This is because lease rents are charged to stamp duty on the average annual rent, whereas stamp duty land tax calculates tax on the net present value of the lease rents over the term. Additional information will be provided on how stamp duty land tax on lease rents is calculated in a later Newsletter.

Additional Miscellaneous Provisions

In this Newsletter we have attempted to concentrate on the main issues that are likely to arise on the more routine transactions. It is not proposed to comment in greater detail on the following, which are, nevertheless, listed for information.

- Contracts liable to stamp duty under FA 1999 Sch 13 para 7 (equitable interests) are deemed to have been duly stamped if they are completed by a stamp duty land tax transaction (FA 2003 Sch 19 para 6(1)).
- Transitional provisions that apply in relation to group relief and acquisition relief are provided at FA 2003 Sch 19 paras 6(2) and 6(3).
- FA 2003 Sch 19 para 7 makes provisions for transactions which are not themselves stamp duty land tax transactions but are "linked" to stamp duty land tax transactions.
- FA 2003 Sch 19 para 9 makes provisions for options and rights of pre-emption acquired before implementation date but exercised on or after implementation date.

In addition to the further Newsletters that will be published in the run up to implementation further guidance will be given at a number of regional training events. For further information on these please refer to Newsletter issue 2, which is available on our web site.

DECEMBER 2003. THE STAMP TAXES CUSTOMER NEWSLETTER STAMP DUTY LAND TAX (SDLT)—ISSUE 4

Welcome to the fourth of our newsletters designed to provide guidance on the introduction of stamp duty land tax on 1 December 2003. This issue focuses on the new lease duty provisions. Further newsletters will follow on other aspects of the changes.

TECHNICAL NOTE ON AMENDMENTS TO STAMP DUTY LAND TAX AS APPLIED TO LEASES

In presenting his 2003 Budget, the Chancellor promised that further consultation with interested parties would continue in connection with the stamp duty land tax charge on leases. Following this consultation, an announcement has been made about the changes to be implemented to FA 2003 Sch 5 (which deals with the stamp duty land tax treatment of leases) for 1 December 2003.

This note gives further detail about the technical amendments which are proposed and which will be debated before implementation. These will have the effect of

- removing uncertainty in the treatment of some leases
- keeping the compliance burden to a minimum and
- ensuring that taxpayers know what duty they will have to pay.

The amendments are:

(1) Post 5 year rent changes

Currently, where rent changes are known and included in the terms of a lease from the outset, they are fully taken into account in calculating the Net Present Value (NPV) of the lease (unless they are increases only to reflect RPI). However, where rent changes are made, after two years, to reflect market rents, these changes are ignored for the purposes of calculating the NPV.

The proposals wish to remove this disparity of treatment. Therefore, it is proposed that **all** rent changes after 5 years are ignored for the purposes of the NPV calculation and, for rental due after 5 years, the highest rent paid in any previous period of 12 months is substituted and used in the calculation. This will provide comparability of treatment for these types of lease.

(2) Leases with uncertain rent

Where rent is expressed as relating to turnover, or where there are rent sharing or similar measures in place, the lessee is required to make a reasonable estimate of the rent due and include this estimate in their land transaction return. When any part of this estimated rent is determined, they must make an amended return including that part of the rent which is now determined. Representations have been received that this could place a severe compliance burden on many small businesses whose rent is determined by monthly turnover.

To simplify this area, it is proposed to amend FA 2003 so that, where a lease has a rent which is still uncertain after five years (e.g. a turnover based lease for 15 years), **one and only one** additional return is required at the five year point. This return will base the NPV on the actual rent paid in the first five years and (for any post five year rent due) will apply the amendment at (1) above i.e. the highest rent paid in any 12 month period over the previous five years will be used in the NPV calculation.

Where all the uncertainty in the rental of a lease is determined before five years, **one and only one** additionally return is required at that point.

These measures will provide certainty and substantially reduce the compliance burden for small businesses.

Part II ST

(3) Contingencies

Amendments will be made to clarify that break and forfeiture clauses in a lease do not operate to artificially shorten the term of a lease in the NPV calculation. Similarly, options to renew, contained in the lease, will not be treated as a contingency extending the term of a lease.

(4) Extensions to leases during their term

An amendment will be introduced so that where a lease is extended during the currency of its term, this extension is treated as the grant of a new lease for the period by which the term of the lease is extended. This will be treated as a transaction linked with the original grant and, if not already notifiable, should the total term then extend to seven or more years, the whole transaction will be notifiable.

(5) Continuation of leases and leases for an indefinite term

Currently, where there is a lease for a fixed term and thereafter, this term is defined as the term plus such further period as must elapse before the earliest date at which the lease can be determined. This will be amended so that the term is defined as the term specified in the lease.

Where a lease comes to the end of its term but the landlord does not require possession of the property, this extension is treated, in England and Wales, as a periodic tenancy which extends the term of the lease. In Scotland, there is a similar treatment called tacit relocation. Currently, the treatment of this extension is unclear and an amendment will be introduced to clarify the situation. Where a lease continues after the end of its term, this extension will be deemed to be the grant of a new lease for the period of 12 months (or the original term of the previous lease) if shorter. Should this continue past this period, it will be deemed to be another lease of similar length and so on. These leases will be linked transactions and similar notification requirements will apply should the total period of these leases extend to seven years or more (if they are not already notifiable). This will also apply in Scotland, where the lease is for an unspecified term at the outset.

Anti avoidance

To prevent avoidance of stamp duty land tax using these amendments, it is proposed that, after the five year point when rent changes are not taken into account in the NPV, if the rent rises by more than 5% + RPI annually, this rent increase is deemed to be the grant of a new lease in a similar way to the way Sch 5 para 10 already treats rent increases not included in the terms of a lease. Currently, assignments of leases where the payment of a premium is **not** involved are stamp duty land tax transactions but the assumption of the obligation to pay rent is not treated as consideration. Therefore, no duty is paid on these type assignments. It is proposed to change this treatment in a limited variety of circumstances. Where the lease, at the previous transaction, benefited from a relief, so that the duty payable was reduced or eliminated, assignment of such a lease will be deemed to be the grant of a lease by the assignor to the assignee. This will prevent the use of reliefs to avoid stamp duty land tax.

NEW STAMP DUTY LAND TAX RETURN FORMS

The new returns are currently being printed and will be available from the Inland Revenue orderline 0845 3021472 from 17 November.

Starter packs

To provide extra help for you at the start of stamp duty land tax, we shall be sending a "starter pack" to all Solicitors who are currently detailed on our customer database. These packs will contain a small initial supply of returns as follows:

- SDLT 1
- SDLT 2, 3 & 4's

- SDLT 6
- Examples—of a correctly completed residential and non-residential return (further details regarding the returns are detailed below) Licensed Conveyancers will receive their packs through the Council for Licensed Conveyancers.

This initial supply should reach recipients by 24 November and is aimed at ensuring that everyone who needs forms will have an initial working supply for the start of stamp duty land tax. Quite separately, you should also order your bulk supply through the orderline.

Given that demand is likely to be high, the orderline will be very busy, but everyone who places an order will receive their bulk supplies. In the meantime, you may find the starter pack ensures you have an initial supply to be getting on with. Local Stamp Offices will also receive small stocks of the returns at this time. So if for any reason you find yourself without returns and need some urgently, you can collect them from local offices. Whilst they will be pleased to supply returns to personal callers, please note they will not have sufficient stock nor the facilities to mail the returns to you.

VIEW THE RETURNS AND GUIDANCE NOTES ON OUR WEBSITE

In the meantime the returns and guidance notes can be viewed on our website at www.inlandrevenue.gov.uk/so/sdlt_website.htm to enable you to view and become more familiar with the new returns.

The SDLT 1 is the main Land Transaction Return which must be completed for all transactions. We expect this form to cover the vast majority of residential transactions.

In a minority of more complex cases the following supplementary returns may also need to be completed.

SDLT 2 must be completed only where there are more than two vendors and/or purchasers.

SDLT 3 must be completed only where additional information is required to identify the property or the transaction involves more than one property.

SDLT 4 must be completed only where additional information is required about the transaction, for example when the purchaser is a company, where land is part of a business sale agreement, some leases.

SDLT 6 is the guidance notes for the completion of the Land Transaction Return. We will be unable to accept photocopies of the SDLT 1 as each return has a unique reference number printed on the return. You should therefore ensure that you maintain a sufficient supply of the return since we will reject photocopied versions of SDLT 1.

[You may, however, use photocopies of SDLT 2, 3 and 4.]

It is our intention to open up an electronic channel to enable customers to submit returns via the Inland Revenue Web-site. This will not be available until the summer of 2004, but in the meantime interim arrangements are being set up to provide alternative channels of submission, both which enable on-screen completion of the forms.

SUBSTITUTE RETURNS

We are looking at other ways to enable customers to complete approved forms on screen and on-line. Further information about filing options will be given in due course.

You will be able to order a bulk supply of payslips and each will have a unique identifier printed on them which will need to be entered onto the substitute form to make it a valid return and enable us to link payments with the completed return.

FURTHER INFORMATION

Further information on the introduction of stamp duty land tax can be found on our website at www.inlandrevenue.gov.uk/so/.

FEBRUARY 2004. THE STAMP TAXES CUSTOMER NEWSLETTER STAMP DUTY RESERVE TAX (SDRT)—ISSUE 5

UNIT TRUST/OEIC MONTHLY NOTICES

Background

Inland Revenue Stamp Taxes, SDRT Operations has recently reviewed its procedures with regard to the processing of Unit Trust & Open Ended Investment Company (OEIC) monthly notices (FA 1999 Sch 19) for the purpose of SDRT payment. As a result of this review, we will be introducing procedural changes to the way in which we deal with the monthly notices.

New Procedures

In the past, Fund Managers/Trustees have been aware that the figures included in all their monthly notices have been recorded and scrutinised to ensure the accuracy of the calculations undertaken. New procedures to be introduced by SDRT Operations will include detailed assurance checks that will involve a review of a random selection of notices received. Fund Managers will, upon request, be required to provide necessary supporting material, to verify the figures and SDRT exempt declarations recorded on their monthly notices.

In relation to a charge to SDRT on the surrender of a unit or an OEIC share under FA 1999 Sch 19 para 2(1), the provisions of Regulation 2(*f*) and (*g*) of The Stamp Duty Reserve Tax Regulations 1986 (SI 1986/1711) define the unit trust manager (or trustee) or the authorised corporate director of an OEIC as the "accountable person" for forwarding notice and payment of SDRT due to the Inland Revenue. In undertaking our assurance reviews, whilst it is appreciated that some Fund Managers and ACD's outsource their work to third party Administrators, who retain much of the required material, our requests for additional information or clarification will initially be directed to the SDRT "accountable person".

Wherever possible we will endeavour to keep our requests for further supporting material to a minimum.

Additional Issues

To enable us to maintain accurate assurance records, it would be appreciated if monthly notices were forwarded for all existing funds, including funds where no charge to SDRT arises, although it is acknowledged that this may result in many "Nil" notices being submitted.

Please note that for future payments of SDRT, we will issue a Receipt to the party forwarding the SDRT payment i.e. if the Trustee has forwarded payment, then it will be the Trustee who will receive the Receipt from our office.

NB Please ensure that all CHAPS payments include your unique Inland Revenue "3 alpha" reference to enable us to match the payment to the relevant monthly notice(s).

To assist with the information required from Fund Managers, we are happy to accept details on Disk (Floppy or CD). At the present time however, we are unable to accept information via e-mail.

All enquiries regarding the content of this Newsletter should be forwarded to: Inland Revenue Stamp Taxes, SDRT Operations Unit, Room 5, East Block, Barrington Road, Worthing, West Sussex BN12 4SE. Telephone: 01903-509583 or 01903-509465. Fax: 01903-509462.

FEBRUARY 2004. THE STAMP TAXES CUSTOMER NEWSLETTER STAMP DUTY RESERVE TAX (SDRT)—ISSUE 6

UNIT TRUST/OEIC MONTHLY NOTICES—NEGATIVE ISSUE/SURRENDER VALUES

Subject: Cancelled/Altered Deals Resulting in a Negative Quantity of Issues and/or Surrenders

Background

On 1 September 1999, Stamp Taxes published initial guidance material in relation to the stamp duty reserve tax regime for surrenders of units in unit trust schemes and shares in open-ended investment companies (OEICs). Paragraphs 23 and 24 of the guidance afforded unit trust managers/OEIC Authorised Corporate Directors two methods of accounting for cancelled/altered deals, as follows:

(a) cancelled and altered deals may be included as amendments to issues and surrenders—whichever is applicable—in the charging period and relevant two-week period in which they occur, provided this is done on a consistent basis;

(b) alternatively, a full re-computation can be carried out, again provided this is done on a consistent basis.

The internal systems operated by some funds employ a third method whereby a cancelled issue or surrender is reported by inputting a contra transaction to reverse the trade, for example a cancelled issue is reversed by inputting a surrender in a later period. This method does not give rise to the particular difficulties that the rest of this Newsletter seeks to address.

Where, however, a fund accounts for cancelled or altered deals in accordance with option (*a*) above, it can happen that a negative figure for issues and/or surrenders results. The application of the I/S formula may, as a consequence, sometimes produce a negative "SDRT due" figure. Fund managers have been treating this outcome in different ways. Some have simply set the negative amount off against SDRT liability arising in another week. Others have made a claim for repayment, sometimes even in circumstances where SDRT has not been paid in the first place.

In order to eliminate this uncertainty and ensure consistent treatment, Stamp Taxes now issues the following guidance to customers who choose option (*a*):

(i) where, by including cancelled and altered deals in the period in which they occur, a cumulative negative figure representing issues or surrenders in the charging period and relevant two-week period results, the cumulative net negative figure should be treated as zero;

(ii) excess cancelled/altered issues over the actual number of issues in the charging period are to be carried forward and offset against the number of actual issues in the next charging period;

(iii) similarly, where a cumulative positive figure of surrenders in the charging period and relevant two-week period results, but the value of surrenders in the charging period itself is negative, the negative value should be treated as nil for the purposes of the SDRT calculation;

(iv) excess cancelled/altered surrenders over the actual number of surrenders in the charging period are to be carried forward and offset against the number of actual surrenders in the next charging period;

As an alternative, a fund may, of course, still choose option (*b*) and carry out a full re-computation—provided this is done on a consistent basis.

Where option (*a*) is chosen, it will therefore be necessary for monthly notices to include additional information to show the net cumulative quantity of excess issues or surrenders brought and carried forward. Annexes A and B provide examples of net negative excess calculations. Both assume that all fund assets are non-exempt investments with no pro-rata or non-pro rata redemptions in specie or exempt third party declarations.

This practice will take effect for all notices still open at 14 February 2004 and to all those newly submitted after that date. All enquiries about this Newsletter should be addressed to: Inland Revenue Stamp Taxes, SDRT Operations Unit, Room 5, East Block, Barrington Road, Worthing, West Sussex BN12 4SE. Telephone: 01903 509469 or 01903 509471.

Annex A
Data Required for Monthly SDRT Computation

	Week 1		*Week 2*		*Week 3*		*Week 4*		*Week 5*	
	No of units	*Value £*	*No of units*	*Value £*	*No of units*	*Value £*	*No of units*	*Value £*	*No of units*	*Value £*
Issues										
W	400,000		100,000		30,000		45,000		5	
B/f net negative excess	0		0		0		0		0	
W + 1	100,000		30,000		45,000		5		0	
C/f net negative excess	0		0		0		0		0	
Total (I)	500,000		130,000		75,000		45,005		5	
Surrenders										
W	0		10,000	10,000	100,000	100,000	–20,000	0	–100,000	0
B/f net negative excess	0		0		0		0		–20,000	
W + 1	10,000		100,000		–20,000		–100,000		0	
C/f net negative excess	0		0		0		20,000		120,000	
Total (S)	10,000		110,000		80,000		0		0	
If S>I										
I/S × value of W surrenders		0		0		93,750		0		0
SDRT due at 0.5%		0.00		50.00		468.75		0.00		0.00

Total SDRT for Month = £518.75

Annex B

	Week 6		Week 7		Week 8		Week 9		Week 10	
	No of units	*Value £*	*No of units*	*Value £*	*No of units*	*Value £*	*No of units*	*Value £*	*No of units*	*Value £*
Issues										
W	0		100,000		–150,000		250,000		50,000	
B/f net negative excess	0		0		0		–150,000		0	
W + 1	100,000		–150,000		250,000		50,000		100,000	
C/f net negative excess	0		0		150,000		0		0	
Total (I)	100,000		0		100,000		150,000		150,000	
Surrenders										
W	0	0	75,000	0(1)	75,000	30,000(2)	50,000	50,000	15,000	15,000
B/f net negative excess	–120,000		–120,000		–45,000		0		0	
w + 1	75,000		75,000		50,000		15,000		35,000	
C/f net negative excess	120,000		45,000		0		0		0	
Total (S)	75,000		30,000		80,000		65,000		50,000	
If S>I		0		0		18,750		0		0
I/S × value of w surrenders										
SDRT due at 0.5%		0.00		0.00		150.00		250.00		75.00

Total SDRT for month = £475.00

Notes

(1) The value of surrenders in charging period week 7 is reduced from £75,000 to nil as the figure of excess surrenders brought forward is set against the figure of actual surrenders in that week.

(2) The value of surrenders in charging period week 8 is reduced from £75,000 to £30,000 as the figure of excess surrenders brought forward is set against the figure of actual surrenders in that week.

OCTOBER 2004. THE STAMP TAXES CUSTOMER NEWSLETTER STAMP DUTY RESERVE TAX (SDRT)—ISSUE 7

STAMP DUTY RESERVE TAX AND STAMP DUTY: AMALGAMATIONS AND MERGERS OF UNIT TRUSTS AND OPEN-ENDED INVESTMENT COMPANIES: EFFECT OF SAVE & PROSPER SECURITIES LTD V CIR (SPC 251)

Background

Since August 2000, the Inland Revenue has, on a number of occasions, been asked to consider whether the scope of the Special Commissioners' decision in *Save & Prosper Ltd v CIR* extends to situations other than that with which that case was immediately concerned (namely, the amalgamation of two authorised unit trusts with a common trustee and manager).

This newsletter sets out the Revenue's view, following the Special Commissioners' decision, of the stamp duty and stamp duty reserve tax (SDRT) implications of various other mergers and reconstructions involving UK authorised unit trusts and open-ended investment companies.

The Save & Prosper Case

Save & Prosper Income Units and Save & Prosper UK Equity Income Fund (both authorised unit trusts with a common trustee and manager) amalgamated on 13 December 1996.

The Inland Revenue argued that a stamp duty reserve tax (SDRT) charge had arisen under FA 1986 s 87. This section applies where one person agrees with another to transfer chargeable securities for money or money's worth. In this case the Revenue argued that an agreement had been made between the unit holders of the discontinuing scheme and the Appellant (the trustee and fund manager of the continuing scheme) to transfer chargeable securities (the discontinuing scheme investments) in consideration of the issue of units in the amalgamated scheme.

The Special Commissioner (Dr A N Brice) held that:

- no "agreement" was made between the unit holders of the discontinuing scheme and the Appellant. The amalgamation was a scheme of arrangement which took effect by operation of law, under the terms of the trust deed of the discontinuing scheme, the Financial Services Act 1986 and the Financial Services (Regulated Schemes) Regulations 1991. Accordingly, the amalgamation did not take effect as an agreement between the parties.
- there was no "transfer" of units in the discontinuing scheme to the unit holders of the enlarged scheme. The units in the discontinuing scheme were surrendered in return for new units in the (enlarged) continuing scheme.

Wider Implications

The Inland Revenue accepts, following the Special Commissioner's decision in *Save & Prosper*, that in the following circumstances FA 1986 s 87 will not normally impose a charge to SDRT, provided that the transaction in question takes place under a scheme of arrangement which has effect by virtue of Financial Services and Markets Act 2000 s 251 or regulation 21

Part II ST

of the Open-ended Investment Companies Regulations 2001 (SI 2001/1228), and the appropriate section of the Financial Services Authority Handbook (which for this purpose has replaced the Financial Services (Regulated Schemes) Regulations 1991).

Authorised Unit Trusts (AUTs)

- Where an AUT amalgamates with another AUT. This is the case whether the two AUTs share the same manager or trustee, or they have separate managers or trustees.

Sub-funds of AUTs

- Where two sub-funds of a common AUT merge.
- Where one or more sub-funds of one unit trust merge with a sub-fund of a different unit trust with the same manager or trustee.
- Where one or more sub-funds of one unit trust merge with a sub-fund of a different unit trust with a different manager or trustee.

Partitions

- Where part of the investments of an AUT or a sub-fund of an AUT are merged with the investments of another AUT or a sub-fund of that AUT.

Open-ended Investment Companies (OEICs)

- Where an OEIC merges with another OEIC. This is the case whether they have the same manager or depository, or different managers or depositories.

Sub-funds of OEICs

- Where two or more sub-funds of a common OEIC merge.
- Where one or more sub-funds of one OEIC merge with a sub-fund of a different OEIC with the same manager or depository.
- Where one or more sub-funds of one OEIC merge with a sub-fund of a different OEIC with a different manager or depository.

Partitions

- Where part of the investments of an OEIC or a sub-fund of an OEIC are merged with the investments of another OEIC or a sub-fund of that OEIC.

Reconstructions

- Where a sub-fund of an AUT or OEIC is reconstructed as a separate AUT or OEIC with the same manager, trustee or depository or different managers, trustees or depositories.
- Where a sub-fund of an AUT or OEIC is reconstructed as a sub-fund of a separate AUT or OEIC with the same manager, trustee or depository or different managers, trustees or depositories.
- Where the investments of an AUT or OEIC, or a sub-fund of an AUT or OEIC, are split between separate AUTs or OEICs, or separate sub-funds of an AUT or OEIC, with the same manager, trustee or depository or different managers, trustees or depositories.

Any transactions other than those listed above will continue to be dealt with on a case-by-case basis.

SDRT: FA 1999 Sch 19

FA 1999 Sch 19 para 2 imposes an SDRT charge where a person surrenders units in a unit trust scheme to the manager of that scheme or requires the manager to treat him as no longer interested in units. Schedule 19 para 18 treats each part of an umbrella scheme as a unit trust scheme. Regulations 4 and 4A of The Stamp Duty and Stamp Duty Reserve Tax (Open-ended Investment Companies) Regulations 1997 (SI 1997/1156), as amended, apply these provisions to shares in OEICs in the same way as to units in a unit trust scheme.

We accept that a charge to SDRT under Sch 19 para 2 does not arise in the case of conversions, amalgamations, partitions, or reconstructions of AUTs or OEICs where units or shares in the discontinuing scheme are cancelled and extinguished by the manager to allow the scheme assets to be transferred to the continuing scheme in accordance with the terms of a scheme of arrangement. In this case the unit or shareholders in the discontinuing scheme do not authorise or require the trustee or manager of that scheme to treat them as no longer interested in the units or shares.

Similarly, the issue of units or OEIC shares by the continuing scheme in accordance with the terms of a scheme of arrangement is not regarded as being an issue for the purposes of FA 1999 Sch 19.

Stamp Duty

FA 1999 Sch 19 para 1 disapplies a stamp duty charge on a transfer or other instrument relating to a unit under a unit trust scheme. However, units in a unit trust are "stock" for stamp duty purposes and, by virtue of para 1(2), where they form the whole or part of the consideration for a transfer on sale of property other than units under a unit trust scheme, an ad valorem stamp duty charge may still apply. Regulation 4 of SI 1997/1156 applies these provisions to shares in an OEIC.

Following the principles established in *Save & Prosper*, we accept that an amalgamation, partition or reconstruction of AUTs or OEICs under a scheme of arrangement in the situations set out above will not normally give rise to a transfer on sale and so will not normally attract ad valorem stamp duty. Nor, by virtue of Sch 19 para 1(1), will a fixed £5 stamp duty charge apply to any instrument of title.

Statutory Reliefs: SI 1997/1156

Regulations 7–10 of SI 1997/1156 provide statutory reliefs from stamp duty and SDRT on a transfer of fund investments where an authorised unit trust converts to an OEIC, or merges with an existing OEIC.

We accept that units or OEIC shares held as an investment by an AUT or OEIC are "property" or "securities" for this purpose and that the reliefs apply where the transferring fund's investments include such units or OEIC shares.

CREST Transaction Stamp Status

Where a transfer of securities is undertaken in CREST in consequence of any of the specific transactions referred to above, in accordance with the terms of a scheme of arrangement, CREST TSS value 6 can be used when reporting the transaction. Use of this value will be subject to periodic compliance checks and reviews.

Further Enquiries

Requests for advice about cases other than those identified above may be addressed in writing to Inland Revenue Stamp Taxes, Room 131 New Wing, Somerset House, London WC2R 1LB. Please include full details of the transaction concerned.

Note

The appropriate section means section 11.5 of the Collective Investment Schemes Sourcebook (CIS) or section 7.6 of the New Collective Investment Schemes Sourcebook (COLL) introduced by the New Collective Investment Schemes Sourcebook Instrument 2004 (FSA 2004/33).

AUGUST 2005. THE STAMP TAXES CUSTOMER NEWSLETTER STAMP DUTY RESERVE TAX (SDRT)—ISSUE 8

STAMP DUTY RESERVE TAX (SDRT) REGIME FOR UNIT TRUST AND OEIC MONTHLY NOTICES EXEMPT INVESTMENTS

BACKGROUND

On 1 September 1999, Stamp Taxes published initial guidance in relation to the Stamp Duty Reserve Tax regime for surrenders of units in unit trust schemes and shares in open-ended investment companies (OEICs). Paragraphs 32 to 38 of the guidance provided unit trust managers/OEIC Authorised Corporate Directors with assistance in determining whether an investment held by the fund should be classified as an "exempt investment" for the purposes of applying the formula in FA 1999 Sch 19 para 5. That paragraph provides a proportionate reduction of the SDRT charge by reference to the nature of the assets held by the fund.

Further clarification on the classification of investments has been requested by fund managers in respect of various types of investment held by a fund, and this Newsletter sets out HM Revenue and Customs' view as to whether these are to be regarded as exempt or non-exempt investments

FA 1986 ss 99(5A)(b) and 99(5B) provide rules for determining when an investment is regarded as exempt and differ for:

- investments that are holdings in other collective investment schemes (such as unit trusts or OEICs), and
- direct investments held other than in unit trusts and OEICs.

Investment Holdings in Other Collective Investment Schemes

An investment in a collective investment scheme such as a unit trust and OEIC is to be regarded as an exempt investment if, and only if, all of the following conditions apply:

- The underlying collective investment scheme is itself an authorised unit trust scheme or a UK-incorporated OEIC; and
- that scheme does not permit investment that allows income to arise to the trustees or the company that will be chargeable to tax in their hands otherwise than under Case III of Schedule D.

For example, where the terms of the underlying collective investment scheme only allow investment in UK or non-UK bonds and/or gilts, any interest or investment held in that scheme can be regarded as being an exempt investment. But, where the terms of the underlying scheme permit investment in, say, UK or non-UK registered stocks and shares, or a mixture of bonds, gilts and UK/non-UK registered stocks and shares, an interest in the scheme is regarded as being a non-exempt investment, and

- the terms of the scheme permit only investment in assets the transfer of which would not be chargeable to ad valorem stamp duty and which do not represent chargeable securities for the purposes of SDRT.

For example, transfers of gilts, bonds and most forms of loan capital as defined in FA 1986 s 78(7), are not chargeable to ad valorem stamp duty. Similarly the provisions of FA 1986 s 99(5) preclude a charge to SDRT on transfers of securities that are exempt from all stamp duty. But, the stamp duty and SDRT exemption does not apply to transfers of loan capital which:

- at the time the instrument is executed, carries a right (exercisable then or later) of conversion into shares or other securities, or to the acquisition of shares or other securities including loan capital of the same description, or
- at the time the instrument is executed or any earlier time, carries or has carried a right to interest or repayment as defined under FA1986 s 79(6).

All of the above conditions must be fulfilled for an investment to be considered an "exempt investment".

Direct Investments Held by a Fund Other Than Interests in Collective Investment Schemes

Investments in convertible loan capital

Whereas transfers of most forms of loan capital, as defined in FA 1986 s 78(7), are exempt from stamp duty and SDRT, the exemption does not apply to an instrument transferring loan capital which:

- at the time the instrument is executed, carries a right (exercisable then or later) of conversion into shares or other securities, or to the acquisition of shares or other securities including loan capital of the same description, or
- at the time the instrument is executed or any earlier time, carries or has carried a right to interest or repayment as defined under FA 1986 s 79(6).

In this situation, the holding of any UK registered convertible loan capital that fits the above description is to be classified as a non-exempt investment.

Investments in depositary interests

Depositary Interests are UK registered securities that enable trading in non-UK incorporated and registered company shares to be undertaken and settled within the UK in electronic/paperless form (such as CREST). A UK depositary interest in foreign securities is a chargeable security for the purposes of a charge to SDRT. The Stamp Duty Reserve Tax (UK Depositary Interests in Foreign Securities) Regulations 1999 (FA 1999 s 119and SI 1999/2383 (as amended by SI 2000/1871 and SI 2001/3779)) however, afford relief from SDRT if, and only if, all of the qualifying conditions detailed in the regulations are fulfilled.

Provided that all of the qualifying relief conditions are met, the holding of a depositary interest can be classified as an exempt investment.

Shares in a non-UK incorporated and registered company and depositary interests of the same class of security in the underlying company are generally identified by a common ISIN (International Securities Identification Number), so care is required to ensure that holdings are correctly classified.

Investment in non-UK incorporated companies with a UK register

Securities issued or raised by a company incorporated outside of the UK that are registered in a register that is kept in the UK by the company are "chargeable securities" for SDRT purposes. Accordingly, interests in, or other rights in, such an investment held by a fund rank as non-exempt investments for the purposes of FA 1999 Sch 19.

Investments in derivatives including options

The SDRT charge arising on the value of surrendered units and OEIC shares to the fund manager or trustees can be reduced if, in the relevant two-week period, the fund property is invested in both exempt and non-exempt investments by applying the fraction N/(N+E).

Where a fund's investments include derivative holdings ie options, futures, forward contracts etc, each individual derivative, for the purpose of the SDRT monthly notice, is to be valued by reference to the open market value or price rather than on any other valuation basis. Derivatives that are not attractive to potential purchasers, being of no intrinsic value or of negative worth, will have no market value and therefore a zero value for SDRT.

Where call (buy) and put (sell) options relating to the same underlying property are held as investments of the fund, each should be valued in their own right (with no netting value recorded) as they can be traded independently.

. . .

Please note: Any enquiries about this Newsletter should now be sent to: Birmingham Stamp Office, SDRT Team, 9th Floor, City Centre House, 30 Union Street, Birmingham B2 4AR; Tel: 0845 603 0135; Fax: 0121 633 3921.

DECEMBER 2008. THE STAMP TAXES CUSTOMER NEWSLETTER STAMP DUTY RESERVE TAX (SDRT)—ISSUE 9

STAMP DUTY RESERVE TAX – EXEMPTION FOR CHARITIES

HM Revenue & Customs (HMRC) Stamp Taxes has recently received a number of enquiries from clients of Euroclear UK & Ireland seeking clarification of guidance in the Euroclear UK & Ireland publication "Stamp Duty Reserve Tax – a guide to market practice", concerning the evidence that is required to be retained in support of a claim to exemption from Stamp Duty Reserve Tax (SDRT) where the underlying purchaser is a charity. Following consultation with various financial representative organisations, HMRC will be revising its current practice in terms of assurance testing and issues the following guidance, which includes new arrangements whereby fund/investment managers may assume responsibility for retaining evidence to support claims for SDRT charity exemption.

This guidance note will take effect from 1 April 2009 to allow fund/investment managers to forward a prior application seeking an approved arrangement with HMRC Stamp Taxes and be allocated a unique HMRC reference number, as outlined in this note.

Background

Where a charity buys chargeable securities, exemption from SDRT can be claimed. In practice, the exemption is secured by the exchange member or qualified dealer (as the "accountable person" for SDRT purposes) who is purchasing the shares either directly on behalf of the charity, or on instructions from a fund/investment manager with an underlying client (or clients) who is a charity, and who would otherwise be accountable for the tax. When reporting the transaction to CREST, the exchange member or qualified dealer inputs the CREST Transaction Stamp Status (TSS) value "S" and enters the HMRC Charities (formerly Inland Revenue FICO) or Charity Commissioners' reference number in the Charity ID field.

HMRC needs to be able to verify that the exemption claimed in this way is properly due and will want to be satisfied on two matters. An accountable person must be able to demonstrate that:

(1) instructions to purchase shares have been received from a client that is a bona fide charity, or from a client acting for and on behalf of an underlying client that is a bona fide charity; and

(2) checks have been undertaken to verify that the charity is, and continues to be, a registered charity and eligible for exemption from SDRT

The above two obligations placed upon an accountable person typically arise in the following scenarios:

a. An accountable person with a direct contractual relationship with a charity client

On a first claim to exemption, the accountable person must obtain a copy of the certificate issued by the Charity Commissioners or HMRC Charities. Where, however, an original Charity Commissioners' certificate has been lost or is unobtainable, HMRC will accept a letter on headed notepaper from the charity to the accountable person, giving the instruction to act and purchase the shares on its behalf, as satisfying this obligation.

The letter should also include the address and reference number of the charity. A letter of instruction from a charity registered outside England and Wales must, in addition, include the date of charity registration. The website of the Office of Scottish Charities Regulator does not provide this information for Scottish charities and as yet there is no governing body for charities established in Northern Ireland. The date of registration of these charities will therefore need to be provided to the accountable person by the charities themselves.

On subsequent occasions an accountable person must obtain, and keep on file, a print-out from the Charity Commissioners' website showing that the charity is still registered, and therefore eligible for SDRT exemption, at the time the securities are agreed to be transferred. Where the Charity Commissioners are not responsible for the charity, an accountable person is obliged to satisfy himself of his client's eligibility to tax exemption by obtaining, and keeping on file, a copy of the HMRC Charities letter from the client confirming charity status.

In strictness, an accountable person should ensure that a print-out from the Charity Commissioners website is obtained every time instructions to purchase securities for and on behalf of the same charity client are received. Where, however, an accountable person regularly buys shares for the same charity, it will be sufficient to obtain print-outs from the Charity Commissioners' website to check the charity's status periodically (but at least once every six months). An accountable person will need to be able to demonstrate to HMRC, upon enquiry, that a charity's status is being regularly checked in order to ensure that it remains eligible for exemption from SDRT.

When reporting a share purchase transaction undertaken on behalf of a recognised charity to Euroclear UK & Ireland, the exchange member or qualified dealer inputs the CREST Transaction Stamp Status (TSS) value "S" and enters the HMRC Charities (formerly Inland Revenue FICO) or Charity Commissioners' reference number in the Charity ID field.

Where an accountable person is not in a position to satisfy himself that the instruction to purchase shares is undertaken on behalf of a bona fide charity client or charity clients, an accountable person must not allow a transaction with a charity "S" exemption value to match and settle in the CREST system. In this situation, the accountable person must input into the CREST system, the standard rate Transaction Stamp Status "P".

Multiple charities

In the CREST Charity ID field, an accountable person must quote the Charity Commissioners' or HMRC Charities reference for all the charities. Where there is insufficient space in the field for all the references, at least one reference must be quoted, followed by the symbols "++" to indicate that more references are appropriate. In any enquiry by HMRC these will all need to be quoted.

b. An accountable person with a direct contractual relationship with a fund/investment manager acting on behalf of charity clients

Where an accountable person's client is a fund/investment manager (acting for and on behalf of a single (or multiple) charity client), circumstances can arise where the fund/investment manager may not be willing for client confidentiality, or other commercial, reasons to provide evidence to the accountable person that his underlying client is a bona fide charity that is eligible for SDRT exemption.

In these situations and with effect from 1 April 2009, a fund/investment manager may enter into specific prior arrangements with HMRC Stamp Taxes whereby the fund/investment manager, rather than the accountable person, agrees to retain and, upon any HMRC enquiry, make available records regarding the charity client and the instructions to purchase for and on behalf of the charity client.

After clearly establishing with the fund/investment manager that they have entered into such an arrangement with HMRC, the delivering accountable person must populate the Charity ID field of his Euroclear UK & Ireland instruction by inserting the fund/investment manager's unique HMRC reference, and complete the Transaction Stamp Status value with "S" before the purchase transaction is allowed to be matched and settled in the CREST system.

In these circumstances, HMRC will expect to see evidence from the delivering accountable person that the fund/investment manager has agreed to this arrangement. This may be in the form of a letter or other similar instruction received from the fund manager advising of his/her unique HMRC approved reference and that the fund manager agrees to retain records regarding the charity client and the purchase undertaken for, and on behalf of, the charity client. Where the fund/investment manager's HMRC reference number is not input, the accountable person will be required to retain evidence on file to clearly demonstrate that the purchasing charity is eligible for exemption from SDRT.

HMRC Stamp Taxes will publish & maintain on its website a list of fund and investment managers along with their respective HMRC reference numbers falling within this arrangement.

View [a] list of fund and investment managers [at www.hmrc.gov.uk/so/sdrt/charity-list1.htm].

HMRC STAMP TAXES APPROVED ARRANGEMENTS WITH A FUND/INVESTMENT MANAGER

A fund/investment manager's application seeking an approved arrangement with HMRC must be headed "Application for a HMRC Stamp Taxes fund manager reference in support of charity exemption", and include the full address and postcode of the fund/investment manager, contact name and telephone number. The application is to be sent to HMRC Stamp Taxes, SDRT Operations, 9th Floor, City Centre House, 30 Union Street, Birmingham B2 4AR. On approval, HMRC will allocate a unique reference number prefixed "IMxxxx" to each fund or investment manager which must be quoted to an "accountable person" whenever a charity exemption is claimed on a purchase transaction to be settled in the CREST system.

Fund and investment managers who have approved arrangements with HMRC are subject to the same requirements as an accountable person in that they have to satisfy themselves of the charitable status of their client. In the event of an HMRC enquiry, a fund manager must be able to demonstrate that the status of the underlying client who has purchased shares is that of a bona fide charity, and that the charity is, and continues to be, eligible for exemption from SDRT, by providing similar evidence to that outlined in a) above.

Failure by a fund/investment manager, upon HMRC enquiry, to provide information regarding a share purchase undertaken for, and on behalf of charity client[s], or failure to notify HMRC of any changes to the fund/investment manager's business activities as it affects charity clients, may lead to termination of the HMRC approved arrangement.

The accountable person will be accountable for payment of SDRT where a fund/investment manager has not retained evidence (or is unable) to verify the client's status or has failed to provide information upon any HMRC enquiry.

A fund/investment manager not electing to make an application to HMRC will need to provide the accountable person with similar evidence to that outlined in a) above. Where, on a claim to exemption, a fund manager is unable to provide an accountable person with an original Charity Commissioners certificate or HMRC Charities reference because it has been lost or is unobtainable, HMRC will accept a letter on headed notepaper from the charity to the fund manager which gives the instruction to act and purchase the shares on its behalf, being provided to the accountable person as satisfying this obligation. The letter however should also include the address and reference number of the charity along with the date of charity registration. Where a fund/investment manager is unable to provide evidence to demonstrate that the instruction to purchase shares is undertaken on behalf of a bona fide charity client or clients and no Charity Commissioners or HMRC Charities reference is provided to the accountable person, an accountable person must not allow a transaction with a charity "S" exemption value to match and settle in the CREST system. In this situation, the accountable person must input into the CREST system, the standard rate Transaction Stamp Status "P".

CHIDIRLST PROCEDURE

With the introduction of the arrangement enabling a fund/investment manager to seek HMRC approval and be allocated a unique reference number that can be quoted to an accountable person when claiming exemption from SDRT in respect of a charity purchase, the current

HMRC "CHIDIRLST" procedure that is available and used by some fund managers and custodians is to be withdrawn with effect from 1 April 2009.

All current HMRC approved "CHIDIRLST" users will need therefore to reapply to HMRC for a unique fund/investment manager reference number that must be quoted (instead of "CHIDIRLST") to an "accountable person" whenever a charity exemption is claimed on and after 1 April 2009.

Information and guidance on "market norms" in processing charity purchase transactions as outlined in the October 2007 Euroclear UK & Ireland publication "Stamp Duty Reserve Tax in CREST: a guide to market practice" will be revised to take account of the above HMRC guidance with effect from 1 April 2009.

All enquiries regarding this HMRC Guidance Note should be sent to the SDRT team at the Birmingham Stamp Office [www.hmrc.gov.uk/so/contact/aboutsdrt.htm].

JULY 2009. THE STAMP TAXES CUSTOMER NEWSLETTER STAMP DUTY RESERVE TAX (SDRT)—ISSUE 10

STAMP DUTY RESERVE TAX (SDRT) ON COLLECTIVE INVESTMENT SCHE MES—NET DEALING BY INTERMEDIARIES

[HMRC has changed its position the on the SDRT liability of net dealing in relation to FA 1999 Sch 19 and FA 1986 s 87 from 14 July 2009.]

["Intermediaries" here is used in its everyday sense and not in the technical sense set out in the Stamp Duty and SDRT legislation providing relief for intermediaries.]

Investors in collective investment schemes often make their investment through an intermediary. Intermediaries may deal with underlying fund managers by sending aggregated sell and aggregated buy instructions separately (known as "gross dealing"); or, intermediaries may net off buy and sell instructions for each fund and thus send only one net buy or sell instruction to each underlying fund manager (known as "net dealing").

HM Revenue & Customs (HMRC) has historically taken the view that where net dealing occurs, the underlying fund managers should obtain gross transaction information from the intermediary and include that information in calculating their SDRT liability under FA 1999 Sch 19 ("Schedule 19").

Following representations, HMRC has taken legal advice and, as a result, announces a change of view with effect from 14 July 2009. In future, underlying fund managers should only include in their Schedule 19 calculations transactions for which they have received instructions.

Furthermore, HMRC previously took the view that net dealing would not generally give rise to any principal SDRT charges under FA 1986 s 87. HMRC also announce a change in this position. HMRC advice is that net dealing will generally, depending on the facts of each case, give rise to two principal SDRT charges in respect of the transactions which have been netted off – one on the intermediary and one on the ultimate purchaser of the investment. HMRC will not pursue any such charges that arose on or before the date of this announcement.

HMRC accepts that it could take several weeks for firms to adjust to this revised approach. So long as steps are taken to make any adjustments as quickly as reasonably possible (and in any event by 22 September 2009), and provided there is no suggestion that the handling of the change is being exploited to minimise tax, HMRC will not seek to challenge the transitional arrangements adopted.

HMRC will monitor the situation following this announcement to ensure that the rules apply fairly and will take action against any attempt to exploit this change of view to minimise tax liabilities artificially.

HMRC understands that some fund managers have entered into arrangements with clearance services. Under these arrangements, fund managers may be accounting, through their Schedule 19 calculation, for SDRT which is strictly a liability of the clearance service. HMRC considers that these arrangements are unaffected by this announcement.

Any queries relating to this announcement should be made to the HMRC Stamp Taxes policy/technical team (telephone: 020 7147 2788, email: Jeremy Schryber).

APPENDIX 8. MISCELLANEOUS

This Appendix contains the following miscellaneous information.

8 JANUARY 1997. LAW SOCIETY'S GAZETTE STAMP DUTY ON LEASES

A change in practice by the Stamp Office in its approach to calculation of stamp duty on new leases which contain provision for future rent increases in line with RPI (retail prices index) changes has resulted in the Law Society's revenue law committee receiving a number of inquiries from solicitors.

The Stamp Office is relying upon the decision in *LM Tenancies plc v IR Comrs* [1996] STC 880 to apply the contingency principle to rent reserved under a lease so that stamp duty is calculated by reference to RPI changes in the year ending with the date of execution of the lease. This approach has led to some excessive estimates of liability.

The revenue law committee has taken up the issue with the Stamp Office and has made two main points. Firstly, it does not consider that the new approach is justified. *LM Tenancies* was concerned with stamp duty avoidance; to apply the decision in that case across the board to any lease with a rent review clause linked to the RPI is unjustified. Secondly, this is an extremely important change in practice which the Stamp Office has not apparently published effectively.

In response, the Stamp Office has assured the committee that it will examine the facts of each case and give careful consideration to the application of the *LM Tenancies* decision.

The Stamp Office points out that a public announcement of the new practice was made in *Hansard* in a reply given by the Economic Secretary to the Treasury to a parliamentary written question asked by a Conservative MP. It followed representations from the House Builders Federation, the Manufacturing and Construction Industries Alliance and individual property owners.

This reply states:

> "Stamp duty is charged on the grant of a new lease of property by reference to the premium paid for the lease and the average annual rent. Duty on the premium is charged at 1% but there is no charge on the premium where the premium is £60,000 or less and the average annual rent is £6,000 or less. Duty is charged on the average annual rent by reference to a sliding scale of rates which depend on the length of the lease. For example, for a lease of over 100 years, the rate is 24% (£12 per £50 or part of £50 of the average annual rent).

Where an existing lease is sold by the leaseholder to someone else, duty is charged at 1% on the price paid, in the same way as with the sale of a freehold. No duty is charged on the rent. I have received representations from the House Builders Federation, the Manufacturing and Construction Industries Alliance, and McCarthy and Stone about the treatment of a grant of a new lease under which the rent is to be adjusted in future in line with RPI changes.

Where the terms of a lease lay down specific figures for future rent payments, or provide for the rent to be increased by a fixed percentage each year, there is no difficulty in calculating what the average annual rent is for the purpose of the stamp duty charge. The calculation is more difficult where the rent is to depend on the future movement of an index such as the RPI. Decisions of the courts, including the recent case *LM Tenancies plc v IR Comrs*, have given some guidance on the calculation of the charge to duty where an element is not ascertainable at the outset.

The Inland Revenue has reviewed its practice on the stamp duty treatment of leases of this type in the light of representations that have been made. It accepts that in some cases the calculations made by Stamp Offices produce too high a figure. In the *LM Tenancies* case, the premium paid for a lease was to be calculated by reference to the market price of a Treasury loan stock 25 days after the execution of the lease. The Court decided that duty should be calculated by reference to the value of the stock at the date of execution of the lease.

The Inland Revenue's view, in the light of the court's decision in *LM Tenancies*, is that where the rent under a lease is to be adjusted by reference to RPI changes the duty should be calculated by reference to the change in the year ending with the date of execution of the lease. The precise method of adjustment may depend on the terms of the lease and on the way they provide for the calculation to be made. For example, whether the rent is to be increased annually or only at longer intervals. Generally, where the adjustment is to be made by comparing the value of the RPI at different dates, the difference between the two values over the latest year will be used to measure the rent increase for stamp duty purposes.

For example, if the initial rent is £300 a year and is to be adjusted annually, and the RPI has gone up from 150 to 153, equivalent to 2% over the relevant 12-month period, it would be assumed that the rent would go up by £6 (2% of £300) each year. Thus, the rent would be taken as £306 in the second year, £312 in the third year, and so on, in order to calculate the average annual rent under the lease.

The Inland Revenue is issuing instructions to Stamp Offices accordingly, to ensure that individual cases are dealt with on a consistent basis. A taxpayer who disagrees with the Stamp Office's calculation of the duty in a particular case will, of course, have the normal rights of appeal."

One firm of solicitors has already obtained counsel's opinion on this issue, to the effect that the Stamp Office's approach is "not sustainable". If there are any changes in this area the revenue law committee will ensure they are reported as soon as possible.

This note was written by Jill Hallpike, the secretary to the Law Society's revenue law committee.

[Now see IR Press Release 14 May 1999.]

16 JANUARY 1997. TAX JOURNAL. LETTER FROM MACFARLANES WITH EXTRACTS FROM INLAND REVENUE LETTER SDRT ON UK SHARE TRANSFERS

. . . the FA 1996 changes to the stamp duty reserve tax (SDRT) regime. Most of these were designed to deal with the charging and collection of SDRT within CREST. Some of the changes, however, have implications for all transfers of shares in UK companies.

If we ignore, for present purposes, the changes made (in FA 1996 s 187 (1)) to the territorial scope of SDRT, the principal changes are as follows:

- The two month delay before the charge to SDRT arises has been repealed and SDRT charge arises immediately when the agreement to transfer shares is entered into or, in the case of a conditional agreement, when that agreement becomes unconditional (see the amendments made to FA 1986 s 87 (2) by FA 1996 s 188 (1)). The accountable date for SDRT is therefore correspondingly earlier.
- The SDRT charge is not automatically cancelled until a stock transfer form is executed. If the charge is to be cancelled, it must be shown "to the Board's satisfaction" that two conditions have been fulfilled. Those two conditions are (i) that a stock transfer form (or other transfer document) has been executed and (ii) that the stock transfer form has been properly stamped. Until it is so proved, the duty to notify the Inland Revenue of the charge and to pay the SDRT will continue to exist.

Those changes took effect on 1 July 1996.

In correspondence with the Inland Revenue, we have raised the question of how these provisions will affect Stamp Office practice. We referred in particular to cases in which it is not possible to stamp a stock transfer form before the accountable date (and therefore it is not possible to apply for the SDRT charge to be cancelled within that timescale).

This position could, of course, occur in several situations but, in our correspondence, we specifically raised the following circumstances.

The first set of circumstances was where the stock transfer form has been submitted for adjudication and the adjudication has not been completed by the accountable date for SDRT. This might occur (i) where an exemption is being claimed (eg, intra group relief under FA 1930 s 42 or relief for transfers in a reconstruction or amalgamation under FA 1986 s 75) or (ii) where the amount of the consideration is not ascertained or has to be valued (eg, completion accounts being drawn up or the consideration is not in cash).

The accountable date might also be passed without a stampable document being created where completion of the agreement is deferred.

The Inland Revenue's response goes some way to clarifying the practice which the Inland Revenue will adopt in relation to the FA 1996 changes. The Inland Revenue has agreed to the publication of the following extracts from its letter.

> "The revisions introduced by the Finance Act 1996 mean that unless an agreement to transfer chargeable securities for money or money's worth is conditional, the charge to SDRT will arise immediately and will not be cancelled until 'it is proved to the Board's satisfaction' that instruments of transfer have been executed and correctly stamped—FA 1986 s 92 (as amended).
>
> In practice, it is likely that, in most cases, the relevant transfer document will have been stamped before the SDRT accountable date is reached. In these cases, the Inland Revenue will not expect a separate application for cancellation of SDRT to be made and will accept that stamping itself is sufficient to cancel the SDRT charge, although it may be necessary at a later date to check on selected cases to ensure that documents have been correctly stamped.
>
> There are no provisions in the legislation for postponing or waiving the payment of SDRT where documents have not been stamped by the accountable date. Late payments will

Part II ST

incur interest and penalties can be imposed where the tax is over one year late (TMA 1970 ss 86, 93 and 95). The correct procedure is to pay the SDRT by the accountable date. This will be refunded with interest if documents are subsequently stamped. A refund of penalties cannot, however, be guaranteed.

In your letter, you referred to circumstances in which a document cannot be stamped by the accountable date either because it is subject to adjudication or because completion is deferred. The scenarios outlined in your letter fall into two distinct categories:

(i) those where the consideration is not ascertainable by the accountable date or completion will not be possible by this date, although full ad valorem stamp duty will eventually be paid; and

(ii) those where the stamp duty is likely to be nominal or nil (eg, because an exemption is being claimed) but the adjudication process will not be concluded by the accountable date.

In the first scenario, SDRT should be paid on the basis of a reasonable estimate of the likely sum of consideration to be paid; it will not be acceptable to estimate the SDRT as nil simply on the basis that stamp duty will eventually be paid and the SDRT cancelled. Once the consideration has been ascertained and the documents are ready for stamping, provided that the SDRT and accrued interest is not less than the sum required to conclude the stamping process, we would be prepared to transfer the sum paid as SDRT (with interest) to the stamp duty account to facilitate stamping. This will remove the need to pay separately for stamp duty and later claim a refund of SDRT. Please note that once out of the SDRT account, the sum would cease to earn interest. Any overpayment would be refunded by your local stamp office.

Where the sum paid as SDRT and accrued interest is less than the sum required for stamping, there will be no facility for transferring funds internally and accountable persons will be required to produce stamped documents before SDRT can be refunded.

We do not envisage many cases falling into the second scenario because the Stamp Office is usually able to respond quickly to routine applications. If these are made in good time, documents are likely to be stamped before the SDRT accountable date. To the extent that this is not possible, we will be prepared to wait for the documents to be adjudicated on the following conditions:

- The accountable person acknowledges in writing liability for the SDRT due and recognises that the Inland Revenue can pursue him for payment with interest at any time subject to any future production of stamped documents or pending stamping.
- The Shares Unit must be given the adjudication case reference number so that the progress of the case can be monitored.
- If the documents are not stamped within three months of the accountable date, the SDRT should be paid in full with interest.
- If the claim for exemption or nominal stamp fails before the end of three months, SDRT should be paid immediately with any interest due.

The Inland Revenue does not waive its right to impose penalties.

Applications will be considered on a case by case basis and the Inland Revenue reserves the right to exclude any case from the above arrangement.

Subject to agreement with these conditions, SDRT does not need to be paid on the accountable date."

3 MARCH 2003. COMMONS WRITTEN ANSWER (COL 848W) DISADVANTAGED AREAS

Mr John Smith: To ask the Chancellor of the Exchequer what representations he had received about the number of house buyers who have unnecessarily paid stamp duty because of inaccurate information provided by the Inland Revenue relating to post codes; how many people have been affected; and if he will make a statement. [98547]

John Healey: Relief from stamp duty in disadvantaged areas was implemented by this Government on 30 November 2001, exempting from stamp duty all property transactions below £150,000 in around 2,000 of the most deprived areas of the UK. We intend to abolish this cap on non-residential property this year.

Qualifying areas in England, Wales and Northern Ireland are defined in regulations by reference to electoral wards. As with other tax reliefs, the onus is on the customer to claim this relief. To help customers to identify whether they can claim the relief, the Inland Revenue has made available a postcode search facility on its website [www.inlandrevenue.gov.uk/so/pcode_search.htm]. The Inland Revenue is aware that there have been some problems with this tool, particularly where properties straddle ward boundaries or are new developments. As soon as the Inland Revenue has become aware of any shortcomings in the system, they have rectified them and any customer who has paid stamp duty and subsequently discovers relief was due may claim a full repayment of the duty with interest from the Inland Revenue. As an indication of the number of people who have not claimed the relief but have subsequently claimed a repayment, the Inland Revenue currently processes around 300 claims for repayment per month.

6 JUNE 2005. HMRC STAMP TAXES NEWS PENSION SCHEMES—STAMP DUTY, SDRT AND SDLT

Q: Do SDRT, stamp duty or SDLT arise on the transfer of assets and liabilities between pension schemes where the only consideration is the assumption by the receiving scheme of the obligation to pay pension benefits?

A: Where, on the merger of pension schemes or on other transfers of assets between such schemes, the only consideration for the transfer of assets from the transferring scheme to the receiving scheme is the assumption by the receiving scheme of the obligation to pay pension benefits (and any other benefits permitted to be provided by Inland Revenue approved pension schemes) to the former members of the transferring scheme:

(1) No charge to SDRT will arise. This will be the case whether or not the assets of the transferring scheme consist of or include units or shares in a UK unit trust or open-ended investment company. There is no consideration in money or money's worth for SDRT purposes and therefore no charge arises under FA 1986 s 87 or FA 1999 Sch 19.
Notwithstanding the absence of a Schedule 19 charge to SDRT, where units or shares in a UK unit trust or open-ended investment company are transferred in such a way that a change of ownership needs to be recorded in the unit or share register, the fund manager will need to report as a third party exemption the number of units or shares surrendered on his monthly SDRT Notice. The fund manager will also need to retain sufficient evidence to support the third party exemption in the event of an inspection by the Inland Revenue.

(2) No ad valorem stamp duty will arise in respect of the agreement for the transfer of assets from the transferring scheme to the receiving scheme because the assumption of the liability by the trustee of the receiving scheme to provide pension benefits to members of the transferring scheme is not chargeable consideration for stamp duty purposes. However, all transfer documents or other instruments that give effect to the transfer of stock or marketable securities from the transferring scheme to the receiving scheme are liable to a fixed stamp of £5.

(3) No charge to SDLT will arise on any transfers of land from the transferring scheme to the receiving scheme because there is no agreement to transfer land for consideration in money or money's worth.

1 JULY 2005. HMRC STAMP TAXES NEWS DEEDS OF RECTIFICATION: TREATMENT FOR STAMP DUTY LAND TAX PURPOSES

1. This note has effect only for land in England & Wales, and Northern Ireland.

2. For most land transactions there is a contract followed by a deed (for example a transfer or a lease) which gives effect to what the parties agreed in the contract (some leases, however, are not preceded by a contract). It sometimes happens that the deed does not correctly reflect what the parties agreed in the contract. In such cases a further deed will normally be executed which, when read with the original deed, gives effect to what the parties agreed. This process is called "rectification" (sometimes rectification may be effected by Court order rather than by deed).

3. There are no special stamp duty land tax rules for deeds (or indeed Court orders) of rectification. Most deeds of rectification will effect a land transaction for stamp duty land tax purposes. For example the original deed may not have transferred all the freehold land that was agreed. The deed of rectification will effect the transfer of the land that was left out: this will be a land transaction (the transfer of freehold land). Or the original deed might not have reserved a right of way although the contract provided for this. The deed of rectification will then create a legal right of way: this again is a land transaction.

4. Most land transactions need to be notified to HM Revenue & Customs on a Land Transaction Return (form SDLT1). Again there are no special rules for transactions effected by a deed of rectification. So where additional freehold land is transferred by a deed of rectification the transaction must be notified to HM Revenue & Customs where the transferee gives any consideration for the additional land (unless the transfer is of residential property and the consideration is under £1000). Where a legal easement such as a right of way, or a restrictive covenant, is created by a deed of rectification the transaction must be notified if there is tax to pay, or a relief to be claimed.

5. Where a land transaction effected by deed of rectification does not need to be notified to HM Revenue & Customs, for example because there is no chargeable consideration, a self-certificate (form SDLT60) needs to accompany any application for registration. The self-certificate must be completed to show why no Land Transaction Return is required.

6. Where the original transaction was the grant of the lease a deed of rectification will normally operate as the variation of the lease. If so the normal stamp duty land tax rules on variations of leases apply. However where the only effect is to increase the demise (the land which is the subject matter of the lease) the deed of rectification might operate as a supplemental lease for stamp duty land tax purposes.

13 JULY 2005. ELECTRONIC BUSINESS: INLAND REVENUE BOARD DIRECTIONS

DIRECTIONS UNDER REGULATION 3 OF THE STAMP DUTY LAND TAX (ELECTRONIC COMMUNICATIONS) REGULATIONS 2005

RETURNS UNDER PART 1 OF SCHEDULE 10 TO THE FINANCE ACT 2003

The Commissioners for Her Majesty's Revenue and Customs ("the Commissioners") direct that, on and after 13 July 2005, a person who is required to deliver a land transaction return under Part 1 of Schedule 10 to the Finance Act 2003 ("the relevant information") is authorised to do so over the Internet.

The Commissioners further direct that—

(a) the methods approved by them for—
  (i) authenticating the identity of the person sending the relevant information;
  (ii) delivery of the relevant information; and
  (iii) authenticating the relevant information; and

(b) the form approved by them in which the relevant information is to be delivered;

are the methods and form set out, at the time of, and for the purposes of, the delivery of the relevant information, in the terms and conditions for use of the Stamp Taxes Online Land Transaction Return on the website of Her Majesty's Revenue and Customs (www.hmrc.gov.uk).

AGENTS ACTING ON BEHALF OF PURCHASERS—RETURNS UNDER PART 1 OF SCHEDULE 10 TO THE FINANCE ACT 2003

The Commissioners for Her Majesty's Revenue and Customs further direct that, on and after 13 July 2005, an agent who delivers information on behalf of a person who is required to deliver the relevant information is authorised to do so over the Internet provided that the following conditions are met.

The first condition is that—

(a) the agent makes a copy of the relevant information before it is sent; and
(b) the person, who is required to deliver the land transaction return, makes a declaration to the agent, before the return is sent, that either
  (i) the relevant information contained is correct to the best of his knowledge and belief; or
  (ii) the relevant information, with the exception of the effective date, is correct to the best of his knowledge and belief.

The second condition is that the agent completes the appropriate declaration within the Stamp Taxes Online computer application.

The Commissioners further direct that—

(a) the methods approved by them for—
  (i) authenticating the identity of the person sending the relevant information;
  (ii) delivery of the relevant information; and
  (iii) authenticating the relevant information; and
(b) the form approved by them in which the relevant information is to be delivered; are the methods and form set out, at the time of, and for the purposes of, the delivery of the relevant information, in the terms and conditions for use of the Stamp Taxes Online Land Transaction Return on the Inland Revenue website (www.hmrc.gov.uk).

David Varney

Helen Ghosh

Two of the Commissioners for Her Majesty's Revenue and Customs.

11th July 2005.

APPENDIX 9. CHANCERY GUIDE EXTRACT

The following extract is taken from the *The Chancery Guide 2005*, produced by the Court Service and available to view on the Internet at: www.hmcourts-service.gov.uk/cms/1231.htm.

STAMP DUTY

An undertaking by solicitors with regard to stamping is not required to be included in an order under the Variation of Trusts Act 1958 whether made by a Judge or Master.

The Commissioners of Inland Revenue consider that the stamp duty position of duplicate orders is as follows:

(1) Orders confined to the lifting of protective trusts. These orders are not liable for duty at all and should not be presented to a stamp office.

(2) Orders effecting voluntary dispositions inter vivos. These orders may be certified under the Stamp Duty (Exempt Instruments) Regulations 1987 (SI 1987/516), as within category L in the schedule to those regulations, in which case they should not be presented to a stamp office. Without such a certificate they attract 50p duty under the head "Conveyance or transfer of any kind not hereinbefore described."

(3) Orders outside those described at paragraphs (1) and (2) above that contain declarations of the trust, i.e. that effect no disposition of trust property. These orders attract 50p fixed duty under the head "Declaration of trust." They may be presented for stamping at any stamp office in the usual way, or sent for adjudication if preferred.

APPENDIX 10. LIST OF HMRC LEAFLETS AND BOOKLETS

Most leaflets and booklets can be ordered online from HMRC. They can also be ordered from HMRC orderlines: tel: 0845 9000 404, fax: 0845 9000 604 or online at www.hmrc.gov.uk/contactus/staustellform.htm.

Many withdrawn leaflets have been replaced by guidance that is available online. A list of withdrawn leaflets and their replacements is available at www.hmrc.gov.uk/leaflets/obsolete.htm.

The Stamp Office

Leaflet/Booklet	*Description*
SD 7 (2004)	Penalties for late land transaction returns This leaflet is aimed at property buyers and explains about penalties if you do not complete and send HMRC your land transaction return and any SDLT you owe on time. It explains what the penalties are, how to avoid them and how to appeal to Appeal Commissioners.
SD 8 (2004)	Enquiries under SDLT. How settlements are negotiated This leaflet explains what happens at the end of an enquiry into land transaction returns for SDLT. It tells customers how penalties are worked out, how to negotiate an offer and how to appeal against the conclusions, amendments and penalties made by the Stamp Office.
COP 10 (2009)	Information and advice This Code of Practice tells you about the different way that HMRC will give you information and advice.
COP 24 (2003)	SDLT enquiries This leaflet tells you how HMRC Stamp Offices will carry out enquiries into SDLT land transaction returns. (See Appendix 11.)
COP 25 (2004)	SDLT: enquiries into companies and partnerships This leaflet explains how HMRC Stamp Offices carry out enquiries into company and partnership land transaction returns. (See Appendix 12.)
Tax Appeals (2008)	Tax appeals A guide to appealing against decisions of HMRC on tax and other matters. There are references to SDLT on pages 2, 6 and 7.

APPENDIX 10 LIST OF HMRC LEAFLETS AND BOOKLETS

Most leaflets and booklets can be ordered online from HMRC. They can also be ordered from HMRC orderline: tel: 0845 9000 404, fax: 0845 9000 604 or online at www.hmrc.gov.uk/contactus/staustelforms.htm.

Many withdrawn leaflets have been replaced by guidance that is available online. A list of withdrawn leaflets and their replacements is available at www.hmrc.gov.uk/leaflets/obsolete.htm.

The Stamp Office

Leaflet/Booklet	*Description*
SD 7 (2004)	Penalties for late land transaction returns This leaflet is aimed at property buyers and explains about penalties if you do not complete and send HMRC your land transaction return and any SDLT you owe on time. It explains what the penalties are, how to avoid them and how to appeal to Appeal Commissioners.
SD 8 (2004)	Enquiries under SDLT. How settlements are negotiated This leaflet explains what happens at the end of an enquiry into land transaction returns for SDLT. It tells customers how penalties are worked out, how to negotiate an offer and how to appeal against the conclusions, amendments and penalties made by the Stamp Office.
COP 10 (2009)	Information and advice This Code of Practice tells you about the different way that HMRC will give you information and advice.
COP 24 (2003)	SDLT enquiries This leaflet tells you how HMRC Stamp Offices will carry out enquiries into SDLT land transaction returns. (See Appendix 11.)
COP 25 (2004)	SDLT enquiries into companies and partnerships This leaflet explains how HMRC Stamp Offices carry out enquiries into company and partnership land transaction returns. (See Appendix 12.)
Tax Appeals (2008)	Tax appeals A guide to appealing against decisions of HMRC on tax and other matters. There are references to SDLT on pages 2, 6 and 7.

APPENDIX 11.

CODE OF PRACTICE 24: SDLT ENQUIRIES

[Note page references in this appendix are to the leaflet containing the code of practice.]

COP 24 Contents

Part II ST

INTRODUCTION

This Code of Practice promises you fair treatment under the law and in accordance with Our Service Commitment to you. There is a copy of the service commitment at the back of this leaflet, which explains the rules that we will follow and your rights and responsibilities in particular situations.

We want you to pay the right amount of Stamp Duty Land Tax (SDLT): no more, no less.

We also want you to feel confident that

- other taxpayers are paying what they should, and
- we operate the SDLT system fairly.

In order to do this, we enquire into some land transaction returns.

We ask for further information to help us understand the amount of SDLT you have paid and to check that it is right. We want to make sure you do not pay too much tax or too little. Either way, we will tell you if we find something wrong.

To encourage compliance with SDLT obligations and make sure the whole system is operating fairly, we will select some land transaction returns for enquiry at random. We can then check if anything is wrong which may not be apparent at first glance.

This Code of Practice tells you how our Stamp Offices will carry out enquiries into land transaction returns.

What happens when you receive my land transaction return?

We use the information that you give us to work out if the SDLT you have paid is correct.

If we find any obvious mistakes, for example, in the rate of SDLT you have applied to the transaction, we may contact you to get clarification without enquiring into the transaction.

If your land transaction return shows that you have paid too much SDLT, we will normally repay the excess to you. But, if we have already started enquiries into your land transaction return we will usually hold on to the repayment until we are sure the land transaction return is correct. However, if it is clear from the facts that some repayment will be due whatever the outcome of our enquiries, we will repay that amount before final settlement of your SDLT liability.

We carry out a full programme of checks, including
- looking at information on the land transaction return, and
- comparing it with information from other sources.

After these checks, if we think that your land transaction return may be incorrect, or if we think something needs a fuller explanation, we will start enquiries.

Why are you starting an enquiry?

We are checking whether your land transaction return is correct.

We can enquire into any land transaction return, and may do so at random. Therefore, if we do make enquiries into your land transaction return it does not mean that we think it is incorrect.

When we ask questions or need information we will not tell you whether we have selected your land transaction return at random or as a result of our checks. This is because it does not alter the way in which we carry out our enquiry.

Once we start an enquiry, our only purpose is to make sure the land transaction return is correct. However, the initial request may identify particular areas to focus our enquiries on.

Can I change the land transaction return?

Yes, but there is a time limit.

When you have sent in your land transaction return, you should tell us at once about anything that
- you discover is wrong, or
- should have been included but has been left out.

You can amend your land transacttion return, as long as we receive your amendment **within 12 months** of the filing date (that is, 30 days after the "effective date" of the transaction). The effective date is generally the completion date of the transaction, whether or not this is shown in a document.

However, if a contract is substantially performed before completion, the date that "substantial performance" takes place is the effective date. Broadly, substantial performance is when
- a substantial amount of the consideration (generally 90% of the total amount) is paid
- the purchaser is entitled to possession of the property
- the first amount of rent is paid, or
- option or right of pre-emption is acquired.

You cannot amend your land transaction return after this time.

But if you discover later that you made a mistake, you may claim "mistake relief".

If you make an amendment during an enquiry, we can check it as part of that enquiry. This Code will then apply to the amendment as well as to the land transaction return that we were already enquiring into. If we enquire into the amendment as well, it will not take effect until we finish the enquiry.

If you believe you have underpaid tax because of your amendment, we recommend that you make a payment towards any additional amount because interest will run from the date that the SDLT should have been paid. See *Do I have to pay interest?* on page 16.

Part II ST

Do I have to co-operate with your enquiry?

We would welcome your co-operation with our enquiry and in establishing the correct Stamp Duty Land Tax. How much you co-operate with us and provide us with information is entirely up to you. However, in making your decision, you may wish to get help from a professional adviser. If you do, your adviser can

- accompany you to any meetings held with us, and
- correspond with us on your behalf.

We will make notes of any meetings and copies of these notes will be given to you or your adviser if you ask for them.

Our enquiry may show that an offence has been commited for which you may have to pay a penalty, which is worked out as a percentage of the SDLT underpaid or paid late.

When working out the amount of the penalty, we will take into account

- how helpful you have been, and
- how freely and fully you volunteered any information, which was omitted or understated.

There is more information about penalties on page 16 (see *Do I have to pay penalties?*).

What do I do about any subsequent land transaction returns?

You should not let our enquiries into one land transaction return delay the submission of any subsequent land transaction returns.

THE ENQUIRY

When do you start an enquiry?

After we receive the land transaction return, we normally have nine months from the fixed filing date (that is, 30 days after the effective date of transaction) to tell you that we intend to start enquiries.

If you send in your land transaction return late, we will have nine months from the date we received the land transaction return. We have the same time to open an enquiry into any amendment that you make to your land transaction return after the fixed filing date.

Example

If the effective date of the transaction is 2 April 2004 and we receive your land transaction return on 15 April 2004 we can start an enquiry at any time up to 3 January 2005.

If you then amend the land transaction return on 25 April 2004 we can start an enquiry at any time up to 26 January 2005. But if the enquiry time limit for the land transaction return has closed, we can only enquire into the amendment.

A the end of that time, if we have not started any enquiries, your land transaction return will normally be accepted as the final version.

After the time for starting an enquiry

We cannot start an enquiry after the times given above. But we can still assess and collect from you any extra SDLT we later find that you owe. We can only make an assessment after the time for starting an enquiry if we discover

- an error that we could not reasonably have been expected to know about from the information that you gave on your land transaction return (We can make an assessment at any time up to six years after the effective date of the transaction.), or

- your land transaction return was incorrect because of negligent or fraudulent conduct. (We can make an assessment at any time up to 21 years after the effective date of the transaction.)

If we discover an error after the time for starting an enquiry we might ask you for further information to make sure that we assess the right amount of SDLT. We will behave towards you in the same way as we set out in this leaflet but the legal rules for enquiries will not apply. This means we do not

- issue the formal opening and closing letters that we do in an enquiry. In particular, the section How do you start your enquiries? below and any references to a "closure notice" will not apply
- have the same formal powers, but we do have some different ones to help us get the information we need.

If we discover an error after the time for starting an enquiry we will write to tell you what we are doing and why. This may be referred to as an "investigation" rather than an "enquiry". We will try to agree the final position with you.

If we discover that you do owe us extra SDLT we can settle the matter by making assessments for the SDLT you owe us. You can appeal against any assessment (see the sections *Can I appeal?* and *What happens after I've appealed?* on page 15).

How do you start your enquiries?

We will tell you (and your professional adviser if you have one) in writing

- that we intend to start enquiries, and
- your rights and responsibilities.

We will also tell you what information we need from you.

Exceptionally, we may not be able to do this, but we will always explain why and say when we expect to be able to do so.

In our letter we will tell you when we expect you to reply and send us any information we have asked for.

Can I have professional representation?

You can, at any time

- choose to be professionally represented, for example, by an accountant, tax adviser or solicitor
- change or stop using a professional adviser.

If you want us to deal with your professional adviser you need to complete box 59 on the land transaction return. This lets us know that your professional adviser has the authority to act on your behalf.

We will deal with any professional adviser you have appointed, unless you ask us not to. If there is little progress in settling matters, we will tell you and may then deal with you direct (or with any other professional adviser that you appoint).

Make sure your professional adviser has all the facts. **You** are personally responsible for your own SDLT affairs and for the accuracy of all the information given to us, even if you have a professional adviser.

What do I have to do if you ask for information?

When we ask for information you should reply as quickly as you can.
This will help to keep your time and costs, and ours, to a minimum.

You must keep the records supporting the transaction and any other records you have used to fill in your land transaction return.

We can charge a penalty if you do not keep all your records. In particular, once we start an enquiry you must keep all records that are relevant throughout the whole enquiry.

We will ask questions and explain what further information we need as clearly and simply as possible. We will only ask for information relevant to anything that is in, or should be in, your land transaction return.

If we ask to see the documents and records that your land transaction return was based on, you should be able to provide these quickly and easily, as they should already be in your professional adviser's possession. If we decide we need other information, we will tell you why.

We will try to

- take up as little of your time as possible by asking early on in our enquiries for everything we need to know
- avoid asking for information in a piecemeal way, but this is not always possible as one question may lead to another.

It may help if you tell us about any special features of your transaction, which you think may be relevant to any questions we have asked.

Occasionally, we may need to get information from other people if we cannot get it directly from you or we need to check something.

We will

- keep your affairs confidential
- not tell other people that we are enquiring into your land transaction return.

Time limits

We will give you a reasonable amount of time to provide any information that we need, normally 30 days, but we will be flexible about this. We can agree a time limit if we realise it may take longer than normal for you to get the information we have asked for.

If you think that we have not given you enough time you should tell us how much more time you need, and why. We will let you have more time if this seems reasonable. If we cannot agree, we will tell you why.

You should tell us straightaway if

- you have difficulty getting the information we have asked for and we will discuss with you how you might get it
- you think it is not relevant to our enquiries.

We will consider your reasons carefully and if we think we still need the information we will tell you why.

Formal powers

If you do not give us the information we have asked for and we have to use our legal powers to get it from you we will

- explain our legal powers to you
- advise you of any penalties that might arise if you do not co-operate, and
- tell you about your right to appeal to independent Appeal Commissioners.

Place

If you are in business you can ask us to examine the records at your business premises. We will usually be able to do this. Sometimes we may suggest this ourselves. This will save you sending them to us and can often be more convenient for everyone. The length of our visit will depend on the amount and complexity of the records we need to examine.

You can also ask us to examine your records at the premises of your professional adviser or we can take records to our office to examine them.

Returning records

We will try to return your records as soon as possible. If you need them in the meantime, you can ask us to return any records that we hold. You should tell us what you need, and when you expect to be able to send them back. We will either

- send them to you if we can. You should take care of these records so that you can send them back to us complete and in their original condition, or
- give you copies, if we need to keep them. We will do this free of charge, and within seven days of receiving your request if possible.

What about meetings?

Sometimes, we will ask to meet you to discuss aspects of your transaction of which only you have first hand knowledge or because a meeting may be the quickest way of discussing a large amount of information you have sent us. We will tell you in advance, in an agenda, which aspects we will want to discuss.

If you do not have a professional adviser you can ask a friend or relative to come with you. Just let us know. We have a duty to keep your tax affairs confidential and will ask you during the meeting whether you mind discussing matters in front of your companion.

You do not have to attend any meeting, but we will expect you to give us quickly any information we consider essential to our enquiries. Meetings allow you to

- clarify and explain any points you think we may not have understood, and
- ask questions as well.

If we believe that a meeting would be more beneficial than correspondence, we will make this clear to you.

Place and time

We may ask you to have a meeting at

- our offices
- your business premises
- your home, or
- your professional adviser's premises.

You should tell us if it is not convenient for you to have the meeting where we suggest. We are usually able to meet you wherever is most convenient to you.

Meetings will usually be in office hours but if this is difficult for you it may be possible to meet at other times.

Answering questions

You should make sure the answers you give us at meetings are correct. If you are not sure about an answer you should say so. It is better to say you don't know, or can't remember, rather than worry that you may have given the wrong answer.

If, after a meeting, you realise something you said may have been wrong, you should tell us straightaway.

Bringing documents

You and your professional adviser should bring to the meeting any documents relating to the land transaction return under enquiry, which you think may help you answer questions or support points about the transaction.

If you are not sure what you will need you can ask us.

Taking notes

We will take notes in any meeting we have with you and you can ask for a copy.

We may ask you to sign a copy of our notes to show that they record the main points of what was said. You can comment on these notes and tell us about anything you disagree with. You do not have to sign them or comment on them, but a signed record could be useful to both of us if we cannot reach agreement and have to ask the Appeal Commissioners to resolve matters.

You or your professional adviser can also take notes during the meeting.

Can I stop your enquiry?

You can ask us why we are continuing our enquiries, if you believe

- you have given us all the information and explanations that we need to check your land transaction return, and
- we have had enough time to consider the information and explanations.

We will reconsider the matter to see whether we can agree or explain what further information we need to check your land transaction return.

If you think we don't have any grounds for continuing our enquiry, you can ask the Appeal Commissioners to consider whether the enquiry should be closed. For example, if you believe

- you have given us all the information that we need to determine the accuracy or completeness of the land transaction return, or
- we are prolonging the enquiry unnecessarily.

If you want to apply for the enquiry to be closed you should tell us your reasons in writing. You can send your application to the officer dealing with your enquiry to pass on to the local Commissioners, or you can send your application directly to the Clerk to the Commissioners.

IF NOTHING IS WRONG

What happens if you find nothing wrong during your enquiry?

If we find nothing wrong, we will tell you and let you know that our enquiries have finished.

We will send you a letter called a "closure notice" (see *Closure notices* overleaf). You have the right to appeal against our conclusions in the closure notice. If we have found nothing wrong we will not change anything in your land transaction return.

You can appeal if you feel that our enquiries showed you had paid too much SDLT but we did not reduce the amount you paid.

If you amended your land transaction return during our enquiries, the closure notice will show your amendment. This may mean that you owe us more SDLT. Interest is charged on any SDLT paid late.

If you have paid too much SDLT you may be due interest from us.

IF SOMETHING IS WRONG

What happens if I have paid too much Stamp Duty Land Tax?

During our enquiry we may find that you do not owe us as much Stamp Duty Land Tax (SDLT) as you have paid. We will correct any mistakes whether they lower the amount of SDLT you should have paid or mean you owe more.

A the end of our enquiry if we decide that the amount of SDLT you paid was too high, we will repay the overpaid tax to you.

If we owe you money because you paid too much, we will pay you interest from the date of your payment up to the day we repay you.

The rate of interest we pay is lower than the rate of interest we charge.

What happens if you find something wrong?

If we find something wrong in your land transaction return we will

- suggest changes we believe are reasonable in the light of all the information we have
- try to agree with you any changes that are needed to your own figures, and
- explain how we arrived at the figures we put forward. If you do not understand them, you should let us know.

If you make an amendment to your land transaction return during an enquiry, it will not take effect until we have finished the enquiry.

We have a separate right to enquire into the amendment, but will normally look at it as part of the enquiry we have already started.

Our conclusions and amendments will then be about both the original land transaction return and your amendment.

Closure notices

When we have finished our enquiries, we will normally (but see *Contracts* below) tell you in writing

- that the enquiry has finished
- what our conclusions are, and
- what amendments we are making.

This is called a "closure notice".

You have the right to appeal against our conclusions or amendments; the closure notice will explain this.

Contracts

If our enquiry ends with penalties being charged (see *Do I have to pay penalties?* on page 16) we will try to settle matters through a contract settlement between us.

We will talk to you and your professional adviser about this.

What happens if we cannot agree?

If we cannot agree a contract or any amendments or assessments, we may use the information or documents you gave us during the enquiry in any appeal proceedings to decide the SDLT, interest and penalties which you owe.

Can I appeal?

You can appeal to independent Appeal Commissioners **within 30 days** of the issue date against

- our conclusions or any amendment we make to your land transaction return, or
- any other assessment we make that you do not think is correct.

You can find out how to make an appeal by reading the notes with the amendment or assessment, or by asking us to explain the process to you.

What happens after I've appealed?

We will try, wherever possible, to reach an agreement with you about your SDLT without a formal appeal hearing.

If we cannot reach an agreement, you have the right to ask for any appeals to be heard by the Commissioners. We will arrange for this to be done or, if you prefer, you can contact the Clerk to the Commissioners yourself. We will give you the Clerk's address if you ask for it.

If you ask for an appeal hearing and we think we will need more time for our enquiries, we will ask the Commissioners to adjourn the hearing to a later date. Likewise, if we ask for an appeal hearing and you need more time to provide information, you can ask the Commissioners to adjourn the hearing to a later date. In both cases, the Commissioners will decide whether to accept the request for an adjournment.

If there is little or no progress being made towards settling your appeal by agreement we may ask the Commissioners to hear it.

We will

- tell you if we intend to ask the Commissioners to settle your appeal, and
- explain the figures we propose to put forward at least 14 days before the hearing date, unless there are exceptional circumstances. The figures we put forward may differ from those we suggested to you during our negotiations.

You have the right to

- put your case to the Commissioners and to tell them the figures you believe are correct, and
- choose whether or not to have your case presented for you by a professional adviser, or by any other person, providing the Commissioners do not object.

After listening to both parties and considering all the evidence, the Commissioners will decide whether the amendment or assessment should

- remain unchanged
- be increased, or
- be reduced.

If there is anything that you do not understand or feel you need to know about the appeal procedure, you can ask us or, if you prefer, the Clerk to the Commissioners.

What do I do about paying Stamp Duty Land Tax after the enquiry?

We will ask you to pay any Stamp Duty Land Tax (SDLT) due on an amendment to your land transaction return **within 30 days** of receiving the closure notice for the amendment. You should pay the tax as soon as possible.

Do I have to pay interest?

Interest is payable whenever amounts are paid late.

Do I have to pay penalties?

You may have to pay a penalty if

- you send in your land transaction return late
- we find something wrong with your land transaction return during our enquiry.

If we don't receive the land transaction return or any payment **within 30 days** of the effective date of the transaction (the filing date) but within three months of the 30-day limit, you will automatically get a £100 penalty. In all other cases, you will automatically get a £200 penalty. If you pay late, you will also get an interest charge.

We can only seek penalties for incorrect land transaction returns if SDLT is understated and the error was due to negligence or fraud.

When working out any penalty, we will take into account

- how much you voluntarily disclosed anything that was wrong
- your help in concluding our enquiries, and
- the seriousness of your errors or omissions.

For example, if we ask you to come to a meeting but you choose not to and, as a result, the enquiry took longer to settle than was necessary, we may then take the delay into account when working out the level of penalty that is due.

You should tell us about any matters you think are relevant when we are working out what penalty to charge.

We will try to agree a settlement by contract on the amounts of tax, interest and penalties that are due from you. If we cannot reach an agreement, we may formally determine the penalty we think is appropriate.

You have the right to ask the Appeal Commissioners to hear an appeal against any penalty determination.

If you do not understand how we have worked out interest or penalties, or why they are due, you should ask your professional adviser or us.

What happens at the end of your enquiries?

If our enquiries show that something is wrong we will

- explain what it is
- tell you how to get things right in the future.

If you are still not sure about the records you need to keep in the future, or the amount of detail required, ask your professional adviser or us to help you.

If our enquiries show that your land transaction return was incorrect we may ask you to sign a Certificate of Disclosure, confirming that you have now declared all the transaction details.

We will not do so if our enquiries have shown that your land transacttion return was correct.

We will take a very serious view if you sign a Certificate of Disclosure you know to be false, so you should consider it carefully before signing.

YOUR RIGHTS UNDER OUR SERVICE COMMITMENT TO YOU

During our enquiries

We will always be courteous, fair and professional.

We will normally deal with letters from you or your professional adviser **within 15 working days**. If we cannot reply quickly, for instance, because of the amount or complexity of the material you have sent us, we will let you know the reason for the delay.

Keeping you informed

Although we will not give reasons for making enquiries, we will explain your legal rights and the reasons for any actions we take as our enquiries proceed. We will tell you, for example, why we

- need a meeting with you
- are not satisfied with an explanation you may have given
- are amending your land transaction return
- need to use our legal powers to get information or documents.

You can ask us at any time to

- explain your rights
- tell you why we have taken a particular action, or
- explain what you must to do under the law.

You can ask for these explanations even if we have already given them to your professional adviser.

You can also ask for any of our information leaflets, some of which are listed on page 20. These have been written to help you. We have leaflets in other languages, Braille, large print or audio, just ask about them at your local Inland Revenue office or Enquiry Centre.

Copies of our leaflets are on our website at www.inlandrevenue.gov.uk.

Confidentiality

You have the right to the same high degree of confidentiality that all taxpayers receive.

We may ask you to discuss your personal tax affairs in front of other people, such as, your business partners, your spouse or domestic partner. This can speed up our enquiries, and help to keep costs down. But, we will ask for your agreement beforehand.

You do not have to discuss your personal tax affairs in front of other people. If there is anything you do not wish to discuss with others present, please tell us.

We will only disclose information to people without your authority in the limited circumstances allowed by law, such as, at Appeal Commissioners' hearings.

Your costs

We know that dealing with our questions may cost you time and money, so we will only ask for information that we need to check that your land transaction return is correct.

We will end our enquiries as soon as possible. That is, when we are confident your land transacttion return is correct, or that any mistakes or omissions involving more than a trivial amount of SDLT have been identified and put right.

Complaints

Our leaflet COP1 "Putting things right. How to complain" explains when we will give financial redress for mistakes we make.

Please tell us if you believe

- you have been denied your rights
- we have made a mistake
- you have been treated badly during our enquiries
- we have not acted in accordance with this Code of Practice.

To help you to do this and to avoid further inconvenience we have a straightforward and easy complaints procedure.

You can complain in writing or by phone or fax. We will try to settle your complaint as quickly as possible.

FURTHER INFORMATION

We produce a wide range of leaflets. Some we have mentioned which you might find useful are

COP1 Putting things right. How to complain.

Our leaflets are available at www.inlandrevenue.gov.uk and from any Inland Revenue office or Enquiry Centre. Most offices are open to the public from 8. 30am to 5. 00pm, Monday to Friday. Addresses are in your local phone book under "Inland Revenue" and at [www.hmrc.gov.uk/local].

You can get most of our leaflets from our Orderline, seven days a week (except Christmas Day, Boxing Day and New Year 's Day) by

- phone or textphone (for Minicom users)on **0845 9000 404** between 8.00am and 10.00pm

- fax on **0845 9000 604**
- e-mail at saorderline.ir@gtnet.gov.uk
- writing to: PO Box 37, St Austell, Cornwall PL25 5YN.

Orderline calls are charged at local rates.

Your library or Citizens Advice Bureau may also have copies of some of our leaflets, but may not have them all.

We have a full range of services for people with disabilities, including leaflets in Braille, audio and large print. For details, please ask your local Inland Revenue office or Enquiry Centre.

OUR SERVICE COMMITMENT TO YOU

The Inland Revenue and Customs and Excise are committed to giving you the best service we can by acting fairly and impartially.

We
- treat your affairs in strict confidence, within the law
- want you to pay or receive only the right amount due.

Communicating effectively with you

We aim to provide
- clear and simple forms and guidance
- accurate and complete information.

Providing good quality service

We aim to
- handle your affairs promptly and accurately
- be accessible
- keep your costs to the minimum
- help customers with special needs
- be courteous and professional.

Taking responsibility for our service

We
- publish our customer service aims and achievements annually
- want to hear from you if you wish to comment, or complain, so we can improve our service. We advise you how to do this.

We can provide better service if you help us by
- keeping accurate and up-to-date records
- letting us know if your personal or business circumstances change
- giving us correct and complete information
- paying on time.

Further information on customer service is available at Inland Revenue and Customs and Excise local offices, set out in our Charters, complaint leaflets and Codes of Practice.

APPENDIX 12.

CODE OF PRACTICE 25: ENQUIRIES INTO COMPANIES AND PARTNERSHIPS

[Note page references in this appendix are to the leaflet containing the code of practice.]

COP 25 Contents

Part II ST

This Code of Practice tells you how our Stamp Offices will carry out enquiries into company and partnership land transaction returns.

INTRODUCTION

This Code of Practice promises companies and partnerships fair treatment under the law and in accordance with Our Service Commitment to you. There is a copy of the service commitment at the back of this leaflet, which explains the rules that we will follow and your rights and responsibilities in particular situations.

We want companies and partnerships to pay the right amount of Stamp Duty Land Tax (SDLT): no more, no less.

We will be pleased to help if you

- have any queries after reading this leaflet, or
- need more information on completing a company or partnership land transaction return.

Enquiries into company and partnership land transaction returns

We want you to feel confident that

- other taxpayers are paying what they should, and
- we operate the SDLT system fairly.

In order to do this, we enquire into some land transaction returns. We ask for information to help us understand the amount of SDLT the company (or partnership) has paid and to check that it is right. We want to make sure you do not pay too much tax or too little. Either way, we will tell you if we find something wrong.

To encourage compliance with SDLT obligations and make sure the whole system is operating fairly, we will select some land transaction returns for enquiry at random. We can then check if anything is wrong which may not be apparent at first glance.

When the company (or partnership) has sent in the land transaction return, you should tell us at once about anything that

- you discover is wrong, or
- should have been included but has been left out.

Can we amend the land transaction return?

You can amend the company's (or partnership's) land transaction return, as long as we receive your amendment **within 12 months** of the filing date (that is, 30 days after the "effective date" of the transaction). The effective date is generally the completion date of the transaction, whether or not this is shown in a document.

However if a contract is substantially performed before completion, the date that "substantial performance" takes place is the effective date. Broadly, substantial performance is when

- a substantial amount of the consideration (generally 90% of the total amount) is paid
- the purchaser is entitled to possession of the property
- the first amount of rent is paid, or
- option or right of pre-emption is acquired.

You cannot amend the land transaction return after this time, but if you discover later that you made a mistake, you may claim "mistake relief".

If you make an amendment during an enquiry, we can check it as part of that enquiry. This Code will then apply to the amendment as well as to the land transaction return that we were already enquiring into. If we enquire into the amendment as well, it will not take effect until we finish the enquiry.

If you believe the company (or partnership) has underpaid tax because of your amendment, we recommend that you make a payment towards any additional amount because interest will run from the date that the SDLT should have been paid. See Interest and penalties.

What happens when you receive a land transaction return?

We use the information that you give us to work out if the SDLT the company (or partnership) has paid is correct.

If we find any obvious mistakes, for example, in the rate of SDLT the company (or partnership) has applied to the transaction, we may contact you to get clarification without making an enquiry into the transaction.

If the land transaction return shows that you have paid too much SDLT, we will normally repay the excess. But, if we have already started enquiries into the land transaction return we will usually hold on to the repayment until we are sure the land transaction return is correct. However, if it is clear from the facts that some repayment will be due whatever the outcome of our enquiries, we will repay that amount before final settlement of your SDLT liability.

We carry out a full programme of checks, including

- looking at information in the company's (or partnership's) land transaction return, and
- comparing it with information from other sources.

After these checks, if we think that the land transaction return may be incorrect, or if we think something needs a fuller explanation, we will start enquiries.

We can enquire into any land transaction return, and may do so at random. Therefore, if we do make enquiries into the company's (or partnership's) land transaction return it does not mean that we think it is incorrect.

When we ask questions or need information we will not tell you whether we have selected the land transaction return at random or as a result of our checks. This is because it does not make any difference to how we carry out our enquiry.

Once we start an enquiry, our only purpose is to make sure the land transaction return is correct. However, the initial request may identify particular areas to focus our enquiries on.

THE ENQUIRY

Starting enquiries

We start an enquiry to check whether the company's (or partnership's) land transaction return is correct.

We will tell you (and your professional adviser if you have one) in writing
- that we intend to start enquiries, and
- explain your rights and responsibilities.

We will also tell you what information we need from you. Exceptionally, we may not be able to do this, but we will always explain why and say when we expect to be able to do so.

In our letter we will tell you when we expect you to reply and send us any information we have asked for.

After we receive the land transaction return, we normally have nine months from the fixed filing date (that is, 30 days after the effective date of transaction) to tell you that we intend to start enquiries.

If you send in the company's (or partnership's) land transaction return late we will have nine months from the date we received the land transaction return. We have the same time to open an enquiry Into any amendment that you make to your land transaction return after the fixed filing date.

Example

If the effective date of the transaction is 2 March 2004 and we receive the land transaction return on 15 April 2004 we can start an enquiry at any time up to 3 January 2005.

If you then amend the land transaction return on 25 April 2004 we can start an enquiry at any time up to 26 January 2005. But if after the enquiry time limit for the land transaction return has closed, we can only enquire into the amendment.

At the end of that time, if we have not started any enquiries, the land transaction return will normally be accepted as the final version.

After the time for starting enquiries

We cannot start an enquiry after the times above. But we can still assess and collect from you any extra SDLT we later find that the company (or partnership) owes. We can only make an assessment after the time for starting an enquiry if we discover
- an error that we could not reasonably have been expected to know about from the information that you gave on your land transaction return (We can make an assessment at any time up to six years after the effective date of the transaction.), or
- the land transaction return was incorrect because of negligent or fraudulent conduct. (We can make an assessment at any time up to twenty one years after the effective date of the transaction.)

If we discover an error after the time for starting an enquiry we might ask you for further information to make sure that we assess the right amount of SDLT. We will behave towards you in the same way as we set out in this leaflet but the legal rules for enquiries will not apply. This means we do not
- issue the formal opening and closing letters that we do in an enquiry. In particular, the section on Starting enquiries and any references to a "closure notice" will not apply
- have the same formal powers, but we do have some different ones to help us get the information we need.

If we discover an error after the time for starting an enquiry we will write to tell you what we are doing and why. This may be referred to as an "investigation" rather than an "enquiry". We will try to agree the final position with you.

If we discover that the company (or partnership) owes us extra SDLT we can settle the matter by making assessments for the SDLT you owe us. You can appeal against any assessment (see the section on Appeals).

Do we have to co-operate with your enquiry?

We would welcome your co-operation with our enquiry and in establishing the correct Stamp Duty Land Tax. How much you co-operate with us and provide us with information is entirely up to you. However, in making your decision, you may wish to get help from a professional adviser. If you do, your adviser can

- accompany you to any meetings held with us, and
- correspond with us on your behalf.

We will make notes of any meetings and copies of these notes will be given to you or your adviser if you ask for them.

Our enquiry may show that an offence has been committed for which the company (or partnership) may have to pay a penalty. This is worked out as a percentage of the SDLT underpaid or paid late.

When working out the amount of the penalty, we will take into account

- how helpful you have been, and
- how freely and fully you volunteered any information, which was omitted or understated.

There is more information about penalties, see Interest and penalties.

Professional representation

The company (or partnership) can, at any time

- choose to be professionally represented, for example, by an accountant, tax adviser or solicitor
- change or stop using a professional adviser.

If you want us to deal with your professional adviser you need to complete box 59 on the land transaction return. This lets us know that your professional adviser has the authority to act on your behalf.

We will deal with any professional adviser the company (or partnership) appoints, unless you ask us not to. If there is little progress in settling matters, we will tell you and may then deal with you direct (or with any other professional adviser that you appoint).

Make sure the professional adviser has all the facts. **You** are responsible for the company's (or partnership's) SDLT affairs and for the accuracy of all the information given to us, even if you have a professional adviser.

Providing information

When we ask for information you should reply as quickly as you can. This will help to keep the company's (or partnership's) time and costs, and ours, to a minimum.

You must keep the records supporting the transaction and any other records you have used to fill in the land transaction return. We can charge a penalty if you do not keep all the records. In particular, once we start an enquiry you must keep all records that are relevant throughout the whole enquiry.

We will ask questions and explain what further information we need as clearly and simply as possible. We will only ask for information relevant to anything that is in, or should be in, your land transaction return.

If we ask to see the documents and records that the land transaction return was based on, you should be able to provide these quickly and easily, as they should already be in your professional adviser's possession. If we decide we need other information, we will tell you why.

We will try to

- take up as little of your time as possible by asking early on in our enquiries for everything we need to know
- avoid asking for information in a piecemeal way, but this is not always possible as one question may lead to another.

It may help if you tell us about any special features of the company's (or partnership's) transaction, which you think may be relevant to any questions we have asked.

Occasionally, we may need to get information from other people if we cannot get it directly from you or we need to check something. We will

- keep the company's (or partnership's) affairs confidential
- not tell other people that we are enquiring into the land transaction return.

Time limits

We will give you a reasonable amount of time to provide any information that we need, normally 30 days, but we will be flexible about this. We can agree a time limit if we realise it may take longer than normal for you to get the information we have asked for.

If you think that we have not given you enough time you should tell us how much more time you need, and why. We will let you have more time if this seems reasonable. If we cannot agree, we will tell you why.

You should tell us straightaway if

- you have difficulty getting the information we have asked for and we will discuss with you how you might get it
- you think it is not relevant to our enquiries.

We will consider your reasons carefully and if we think we still need the information we will tell you why.

Formal powers

If you do not give us the information we have asked for and we have to use our legal powers to get it from you we will

- explain our legal powers to you
- advise you of any penalties that might arise if the company (or partnership) does not co-operate, and
- tell you about your right to appeal to independent Appeal Commissioners.

Place

You can ask us to examine the company (or partnership) records at your business premises. We will usually be able to do this. Sometimes we may suggest this ourselves. This will save you sending them to us and can often be more convenient for everyone. The length of our visit will depend on the amount and complexity of the records we need to examine.

You can also ask us to examine the company's (or partnership's) records at the premises of your professional adviser or we can take records to our office to examine them.

Returning records

We will try to return company (or partnership) records as soon as possible. If you need them in the meantime, you can ask us to return any records that we hold. You should tell us what you need, and when you expect to be able to send them back. We will either

- send them to you if we can. You should take care of these records so that you can send them back to us complete and in their original condition, or
- give you copies, if we need to keep them. We will do this free of charge, and within seven days of receiving your request if possible.

Submitting any subsequent land transaction returns

You should not let our enquiries into one land transaction return delay the submission of any subsequent land transaction returns.

Stopping the enquiry

You can ask us why we are continuing our enquiries, if you believe

- you have given us all the information and explanations that we need to check your land transaction return, and
- we have had enough time to consider the information and explanations.

We will reconsider the matter to see whether we can agree or explain what further information we need to check your land transaction return.

If you think we don't have any grounds for continuing our enquiry, you can ask the Appeal Commissioners to consider whether the enquiry should be closed. For example, if you believe

- you have given us all the information that we need to determine the accuracy or completeness of the land transaction return, or
- we are prolonging the enquiry unnecessarily.

If you want to apply for the enquiry to be closed you should tell us your reasons in writing. You can send your application to the officer dealing with your enquiry to pass on to the local Commissioners, or you can send your application directly to the Commissioners.

What about meetings?

Sometimes, we will ask to meet you and other officers (or partners) of the company (or partnership) to discuss aspects of your transaction of which only you have first hand knowledge or because a meeting may be the quickest way of discussing a large amount of information you have sent us. We will tell you, in advance, in an agenda, which aspects we will want to discuss.

You can ask the company's (or partnership's) professional adviser, if it has one, to attend any meeting we have with you.

You or other officers or employees of the company (or partnership) do not have to come to any meeting, but we will expect you to give us quickly any information we consider essential to our enquiries. Meetings allow you to

- clarify and explain any points you think we may not have understood, and
- ask questions as well.

If we believe that a meeting would be more beneficial than correspondence, we will make this clear to you.

Place and time

We may ask you to have a meeting at

- our offices, or
- the company's (or partnership's) business premises.

You should tell us if it is not convenient for you to have the meeting where we suggest. We are usually able to meet you wherever is most convenient to you.

Meetings will usually be in office hours but if this is difficult for you it may be possible to meet at other times.

Answering questions

You should make sure the answers you give us at meetings are correct. If you are not sure about an answer you should say so. It is better to say you don't know, or can't remember, rather than worry that you may have given the wrong answer.

If, after a meeting, you realise something you said may have been wrong, you should tell us straightaway.

Bringing documents

You and your professional adviser should bring any documents relating to the land transaction return under enquiry, which you think may help you answer questions or support points about the transaction.

If you are not sure what you will need, you can ask us.

Taking notes

We will take notes in any meeting we have with you and you can ask for a copy.

We may ask you to sign a copy of our notes to show that they record the main points of what was said. You can comment on these notes and to tell us about anything you disagree with. You do not have to sign them or comment on them, but a signed record could be useful to both of us if we cannot reach agreement and have to ask the Appeal Commissioners to revolve matters.

You or your professional adviser can also take notes during the meeting.

IF NOTHING IS WRONG

If we find nothing wrong, we will tell you and let you know that our enquiries have finished.

We will send you a letter called a "closure notice" (see Closure notices). You have the right to appeal against our conclusions in the closure notice. If we have found nothing wrong we will not change anything in the company's (or partnership's) land transaction return.

You can appeal if you feel that our enquiries showed the company (or partnership) had paid too much SDLT but we did not reduce the amount you paid.

If you amended the company's/partnership's land transaction return during our enquiries the closure notice will show your amendment. This may mean that you owe us more SDLT. Interest is charged on any SDLT paid late. See Interest and penalties.

If the company (or partnership) has paid too much SDLT you may be due interest from us.

IF SOMETHING IS WRONG

If we find something wrong in the company's (or partnership's) land transaction return we will

- suggest changes we believe are reasonable in the light of all the information we have
- try to agree with you any changes that are needed to your own figures, and
- explain how we arrived at the figures we put forward. If you do not understand them, you should let us know.

If you make an amendment to the company's (or partnership's) land transaction return during an enquiry, it will not take effect until we have finished the enquiry. We have a separate right to enquire into the amendment, but will normally look at it as part of the enquiry we have already started. Our conclusions and amendments will then be about both the original land transaction return and your amendment.

What if the company (or partnership) has paid too much Stamp Duty Land Tax?

During our enquiry we may find that the company (or partnership) does not owe us as much Stamp Duty Land Tax (SDLT) as you have paid. We will check any mistakes whether they lower the amount of SDLT the company (or partnership) should have paid or mean you owe more.

At the end of our enquiry if we decide that the amount of SDLT the company (or partnership) paid was too high, we will repay the overpaid tax to you.

If we owe you money because the company (or partnership) paid too much, we will pay you interest from the date of your payment up to the day we repay you.

The rate of interest we pay is lower than the rate of interest we charge.

Closure notices

When we have finished our enquiries, we will normally (but see Contracts below) tell you in writing

- that the enquiry has finished
- what our conclusions are, and
- what amendments we are making.

This is called a "closure notice".

You have the right to appeal against our conclusions or amendments; the closure notice will explain this.

Contracts

If our enquiry ends with penalties being charged (see Interest and penalties) we will try to settle matters through a contract between us.

We will talk to you and the company's (or partnership's) professional adviser about this.

What if we cannot agree?

If we cannot agree a contract or any amendments or assessments, we may use the information or documents you gave us during the enquiry in any appeal proceedings to decide the SDLT, interest and penalties which the company (or partnership) owes.

Paying Stamp Duty Land Tax after the enquiry

We will ask you to pay any Stamp Duty Land Tax (SDLT) due on an amendment to your land transaction return **within 30 days** of receiving the closure notice for the amendment. The company (or partnership) should pay the tax as soon as possible.

Appeals

You can appeal to independent Appeal Commissioners **within 30 days** of the issue date against

- our conclusions or any amendment we make to the company's (or partnership's) land transaction return, or
- any other assessment we make that you do not think is correct.

You can find out how to make an appeal by reading the notes with the amendment or assessment, or by asking us to explain the process to you.

What happens next?

We will try, wherever possible, to reach an agreement with you about your SDLT liability without a formal appeal hearing.

If we cannot reach an agreement, the company (or partnership) has the right to ask for any appeals to be heard by the Commissioners. We will arrange for this to be done or, if you prefer, you can contact the Clerk to the Commissioners yourself. We will give you the Clerk's address if you ask for it.

If you ask for an appeal hearing and we think we will need more time for our enquiries, we will ask the Commissioners to adjourn the hearing to a later date. Likewise, if we ask for an appeal hearing and you need more time to provide information, you can ask the Commissioners to adjourn the hearing to a later date. In both cases, the Commissioners will decide whether to accept the request for an adjournment.

If there is little or no progress being made towards settling the appeal by agreement we may ask the Commissioners to hear it.

We will

- tell you if we intend to ask the Commissioners to settle the appeal, and
- explain the figures we propose to put forward at least 14 days before the hearing date, unless there are exceptional circumstances. The figures we put forward may differ from those we suggested to you during our negotiations.

You have the right to

- put the case to the Commissioners and to tell them the figures you believe are correct
- choose whether or not to have the case presented for you by a professional adviser, or by any other person, providing the Commissioners do not object.

After listening to both parties and considering all the evidence, the Commissioners will decide whether the amendment or assessment should

- remain unchanged
- be increased, or
- be reduced.

If there is anything that you do not understand or feel you need to know about the appeal procedure, you can ask us or, if you prefer, the Clerk to the Commissioners.

Interest and penalties

Interest is payable whenever amounts are paid late.

The company (or partnership) may have to pay a penalty if

- you send in the land transaction return late
- we find something wrong with the land transaction return during our enquiry.

If we don't receive the land transaction return or any payment **within 30 days** of the effective date of the transaction (the filing date) but within three months of the 30-day limit, the company (or partnership) will automatically get a £100 penalty. In all other cases, the company (or partnership) will automatically get a £200 penalty. Any late payment will also receive an interest charge.

We can only seek penalties for incorrect land transaction returns if SDLT is understated and the error was due to negligence or fraud.

When working out any penalty, we will take into account

- how much you voluntarily disclosed anything that was wrong
- your help in concluding our enquiries, and
- the seriousness of your errors or omissions.

For example, if we ask you to come to a meeting but you choose not to and, as a result, the enquiry took longer to settle than was necessary, we may then take the delay into account when working out the level of penalty that is due.

You should tell us about any matters you think are relevant when we are working out what penalty to charge.

We will try to agree a settlement by contract on the amounts of tax, interest and penalties that are due from the company (or partnership). If we cannot reach an agreement, we may formally determine the penalty we think is appropriate.

You have the right to ask the Appeal Commissioners to hear an appeal against any penalty determination.

If you do not understand how we have worked out interest or penalties, or why they are due, you should ask your professional adviser or us.

What happens at the end of the enquiry?

If our enquiries show that something is wrong we will

- explain what it is
- tell you how to get things right in the future.

If you are still not sure about the records the company (or partnership) needs to keep in the future, or the amount of detail required, ask the company's (or partnership's) professional adviser or us to help you.

If our enquiries show that the land transaction return was incorrect we may ask you to sign a Certificate of Disclosure, confirming that you have now declared all the transaction details. We will not do so if our enquiries have shown that the land transaction return was correct. We will take a very serious view if you sign a Certificate of Disclosure you know to be false, so you should consider it carefully before signing.

YOUR RIGHTS UNDER OUR SERVICE COMMITMENT TO YOU

During enquiries

We will always be courteous, fair and professional.

We will normally deal with letters from you or the company's (or partnership's) professional adviser **within 15 working days**. If we cannot reply quickly, for instance, because of the amount or complexity of the material you have sent us, we will let you know the reason for the delay.

Keeping you informed

Although we will not give reasons for making enquiries, we will explain the company's (or partnership's) legal rights and the reasons for any actions we take as our enquiries proceed. We will tell you, for example, why we

- need a meeting with you
- are not satisfied with an explanation you may have given
- are amending the land transaction return
- need to use our legal powers to get information or documents.

You can ask us at any time to

- explain the company's (or partnership's) rights
- tell you why we have taken a particular action, or
- explain what you must to do under the law.

You can ask for these explanations even if we have already given them to your professional adviser.

You can also ask for any of our information leaflets. These have been written to help you. We have leaflets in other languages, Braille, large print or audio, just ask about them at your local Inland Revenue office or Enquiry Centre.

Copies of our leaflets are on our website at [www.hmrc.gov.uk].

Confidentiality

The company (and its directors and shareholders) or partnership (and its partners) has the right to the same high degree of confidentiality that all taxpayers receive.

You do not have to discuss the company's (or partnership's) tax affairs in front of other people. If there is anything you do not wish to discuss with others present, please tell us.

We will only disclose information to people without your authority in the limited circumstances allowed by law, such as, at Appeal Commissioners' hearings.

Costs

We know that dealing with our questions may cost the company (or partnership) time and money, so we will only ask for information that we need to check that the land transaction return is correct.

We will end our enquiries as soon as possible. That is, when we are confident the land transaction return is correct, or that any mistakes or omissions involving more than a trivial amount of SDLT have been identified and put right.

Complaints

Our leaflet COP1 "Putting things right. How to complain" explains when we will give financial redress for mistakes we make.

Please tell us if you believe

- you have been denied your rights
- we have made a mistake
- you have been treated badly during our enquiries
- we have not acted in accordance with this Code of Practice.

To help you to do this and to avoid further inconvenience we have a straightforward and easy complaints procedure.

You can complain in writing or by phone or fax. We will try to settle your complaint as quickly as possible.

Help us to improve our service

We welcome any general comments you may have on how to improve our service to all our customers.

If you would like to suggest any changes to the way we do things or if you have any comments about this Code of Practice, please write to us at: Inland Revenue, Stamp Taxes Policy Team, Room 116, New Wing, Somerset House, Strand, London WC2R 1LB.

FURTHER INFORMATION

We produce a wide range of leaflets. Some we have mentioned which you might find useful are

COP1 Putting things right. How to complain.

Our leaflets are available at www.inlandrevenue.gov.uk and from any Inland Revenue office or Enquiry Centre. Most offices are open to the public from 8.30am to 5.00pm, Monday to Friday. Addresses are in your local phone book under "Inland Revenue" and at [www.hmrc.gov.uk/local].

You can get most of our leaflets from our Orderline, seven days a week (except Christmas Day, Boxing Day and New Year's Day) by

- phone or textphone (for Minicom users) on **0845 9000 404** between 8.00am and 10.00pm
- fax on **0845 9000 604**
- e-mail at saorderline.ir@gtnet.gov.uk
- writing to: PO Box 37, St Austell, Cornwall PL25 5YN.

Orderline calls are charged at local rates.

Your library or Citizens Advice Bureau may also have copies of some of our leaflets, but may not have them all.

We have a full range of services for people with disabilities, including leaflets in Braille, audio and large print. For details, please ask your local Inland Revenue office or Enquiry Centre.

Our Service Commitment to you

The Inland Revenue and Customs and Excise are committed to giving you the best service we can by acting fairly and impartially

We

- treat your affairs in strict confidence, within the law
- want you to pay or receive only the right amount due.

Communicating effectively with you

We aim to provide

- clear and simple forms and guidance
- accurate and complete information.

Providing good quality service

We aim to

- handle your affairs promptly and accurately
- be accessible
- keep your costs to the minimum
- help customers with special needs
- be courteous and professional.

Taking responsibility for our service

We

- publish our customer service aims and achievements annually
- want to hear from you if you wish to comment, or complain, so we can improve our service. We advise you how to do this.

We can provide better service if you help us by

- keeping accurate and up-to-date records
- letting us know if your personal or business circumstances change
- giving us correct and complete information
- paying on time.

Further information on customer service is available at Inland Revenue and Customs and Excise local offices, set out in our Charters, complaint leaflets and Codes of Practice.

APPENDIX 13.

DISCLOSURE OF TAX AVOIDANCE SCHEMES—GUIDANCE

[This guidance sets out the disclosure rules on tax arrangements relating to income tax, corporation tax, capital gains tax and stamp duty land tax. This version of the guidance was published by HMRC in February 2010.]

Contents

. . .

1. INTRODUCTION

1.1 What is this guidance about?

This guidance is about what to do if you promote or use arrangements (including any scheme, transaction or series of transactions) that will or are intended to provide the user with a tax and/or National Insurance contribution advantage when compared to adopting a different course of action. It includes advice on:

- deciding if arrangements relating to income tax, corporation tax, capital gains tax, National Insurance contributions and stamp duty land tax are required to be disclosed to HMRC;
- how to make a disclosure (section 11);
- the systems we expect users of tax arrangements to have in place to monitor for arrangements that they, rather than the promoter, may need to disclose to HMRC (see paras 3.7 to 3.9 and 10.4 to 10.7); and
- how to notify HMRC that you are using a disclosed arrangement.

It does not include advice on revoked, repealed or superseded legislation.

1.2 The status of this guidance

The parts of this guidance (detailed in paragraph 1.5.3 below) that specify the form and manner for providing specified information have the force of law.

The remainder of this guidance is not a substitute for the relevant legislation. Whilst you can rely on this guidance as an accurate explanation of how HMRC will apply the legislation, it does not cover every possible issue that may arise.

1.3 Effective date and superseded guidance

This guidance replaces and supersedes all previous guidance with effect from 1 April 2010, including:

- the guidance "Disclosure of tax avoidance schemes (Income Tax, Corporation tax, Capital Gains tax and Stamp Duty Land Tax)" dated June 2006 (including Update 1 of July 2006);
- "Disclosure of National Insurance avoidance schemes" dated March 2007;
- "Revenue & Customs Brief 57/07 – Disclosure of avoidance schemes: New Information powers";
- "Disclosure of Tax and National Insurance Avoidance Schemes (Income Tax, Corporation Tax, Stamp Duty Land Tax and National Insurance Contributions" (November 2008);
- "Disclosure of Tax Avoidance Schemes, Income Tax, Corporation Tax and Capital Gains Tax, National Insurance Contributions and Stamp Duty Land Tax" (Update August 2009 (effective 1 September 2009)) – Pensions Tax Relief;
- "Disclosure of Tax and National Insurance Avoidance Schemes (Income Tax, Corporation Tax, Stamp Duty Land Tax and National Insurance Contributions)" (Update 1 — March 2009) – for changes to the Scheme Reference Number (SRN) procedures to come into effect on 1 April 2009 (Non-consolidated).

1.4 What's changed?

This notice has been rewritten to reflect changes in legislation and to clarify those areas where previous advice may have been unclear.

The main changes in content are as detailed below:

- Commentary on revised rules for stamp duty land tax which take effect from 1 April 2010 extending disclosure to schemes related to residential property over £1 million and requiring the provision of Scheme Reference Numbers by promoters etc to users.
- Commentary on revised rules, which took effect from 1 September 2009, on a new hallmark for pensions tax relief (consolidated from separate guidance).
- Commentary on revised rules, which take effect from 1 April 2009, on how scheme reference numbers and associated information is reported (consolidated from separate guidance).

1.5 What law does this guidance cover?

The main legislation covered by this guidance is detailed below.

1.5.1 Primary legislation

- The Finance Act 2004, Part 7 (s 306 to s 319) (as amended by FA 2007, s 108 and FA 2008, s 116 and Sch.38);
- The Social Security Administration Act 1992, s 132A; and
- The Taxes Management Act 1970, s 98C.

1.5.2 Secondary legislation

- The Tax Avoidance Schemes (Information) Regulations 2004 (SI 2004/1864, as amended by SI 2004/2613, SI 2005/1869, SI 2006/1544, SI 2007/2153, SI 2007/3103, SI 2008/1947 and SI 2009/611);
- The Tax Avoidance Schemes (Promoters and Prescribed Circumstances) Regulations 2004 (SI 2004/1865, as amended by SI 2004/2613);
- The Stamp Duty Land Tax Avoidance Schemes (Prescribed Descriptions of Arrangements) Regulations 2005 (SI 2005/1868);
- The Tax Avoidance Schemes (Prescribed Descriptions of Arrangements) Regulations 2006 (SI 2006/1543, as amended by SI 2007/2484 and by SI 2009/2033);
- The National Insurance Contributions (Application of Part 7 of the Finance Act 2004) Regulations 2007 (SI 2007/785, as amended by SI 2008/2678 and SI 2009/612);
- The Tax Avoidance Schemes (Penalty) Regulations 2007 (SI 2007/3104).
- The Stamp Duty Land Tax Avoidance Schemes (Prescribed Descriptions of Arrangements) (Amendment) Regulations 2010 (SI 2010/407).
- Stamp Duty Land Tax The Tax Avoidance Schemes (Information) (Amendment) Regulations 2010 (SI 2010/410).

1.5.3 Tertiary legislation (FA 2004, s 316; and SI 2007/785, reg 13)

The Commissioners for Her Majesty's Revenue and Customs hereby specify that the information required under the provisions described below (including, for National Insurance purposes, the appropriate corresponding provision (see paragraph 1.6)) must be provided in the following form and manner:

- Finance Act 2004, section 308(1) and (3) – on forms AAG 1 and AAG 5
- Finance Act 2004, section 309(1) – on forms AAG 2 and AAG 5
- Finance Act 2004, section 310 – on forms AAG 3 and AAG 5
- Finance Act 2004, section 312(2) – on form AAG 6
- Finance Act 2004, section 312A(2) – on form AAG 6
- Finance Act 2004, section 313(1) and (3)(a) – in the boxes provided for this purpose on the return
- Finance Act 2004, section 313(1) and (3)(b) – on form AAG 4 and AAG4 (SDLT)

The address for, and means of, delivering forms AAG 1 to AAG 3 and AAG 5 is that detailed at paragraph 11.2.

The address for, and means of, delivering form AAG 4 is that detailed at paragraph 12.5.

The address for, and means of, delivering form AAG 4 (SDLT) is that detailed at paragraph 13.5.

Warning: The above specified form and manner for providing required information has the force of law and there are penalties for not complying with this – see section 15.

1.6 Use of legal references

Selected legal references and extracts from the legislation are provided in the headings to, and reproduced in the text of, this guidance to act as a quick reference and to aid understanding.

The National Insurance related provisions are, in the main, not referred to or reproduced as they are intended to mirror, with some minor differences explained at the relevant paragraphs of this guidance, those found in the Finance Act 2004 and other legislation. The table below, however, details the main corresponding or modifying provisions:

Tax provision	*Corresponding or modifying provision*
TMA 1970, section 98C	SI 2007/785, regulations 14 and 15
FA 2004, section 306	SI 2007/785, regulation 5
FA 2004, section 306A	SI 2007/785, regulation 5A
FA 2004, section 307	SI 2007/785, regulation 6
FA 2004, section 308	SI 2007/785, regulation 7
FA 2004, section 308A	SI 2007/785, regulation 7A
FA 2004, section 309	SI 2007/785, regulation 8
FA 2004, section 310	SI 2007/785, regulation 9
FA 2004, section 311	SI 2007/785, regulation 10
FA 2004, section 312	SI 2007/785, regulation 11
FA 2004, section 312A	SI 2007/785, regulation 11A
FA 2004, section 313	SI 2007/785, regulation 12
FA 2004, section 313A	SI 2007/785, regulation 12A
FA 2004, section 313B	SI 2007/785, regulation 12B
FA 2004, section 314	SSA 1992, section 132A(6)
FA 2004, section 314A	SI 2007/785, regulation 12C
FA 2004, section 316	SI 2007/785, regulation 13
SI 2004/1864	SI 2007/785, regulation 17
SI 2004/1865	SI 2007/785, regulation 18
SI 2006/1543	SI 2007/785, regulation 16
SI 2007/3104	SI 2007/785, regulation 19

1.7 Terminology

Arrangement: This includes any scheme, transaction or series of transactions.

Disclosable: The requirement to provide prescribed information to HMRC.

Hallmarks: The descriptions prescribed for the purpose of FA 2004, s 306(1)(a) and (b); or SI 2007/785, regulation 4(1) as appropriate.

Hallmarked NI contribution scheme: An arrangement in relation to National Insurance contributions that meets all of the tests at section 5.

Hallmarked scheme: A "tax arrangement" in relation to income tax, corporation tax or capital gains tax that meets all of the tests at section 4.

Scheme: With the exception of paragraph 6.2.1 (where the normal meaning applies), the term "scheme" is used in subsequent sections as an alternative to or shorthand for "arrangement", "tax arrangement", "hallmarked scheme", "hallmarked NI contribution scheme" or "stamp duty land tax scheme" as context dictates.

Stamp duty land tax scheme: A "tax arrangement" (q.v.) in relation to stamp duty land tax that meets all of the tests at section 8.

Tax arrangement: Any arrangement that will, or is expected to, provide the user with a tax advantage when compared with adopting a different course of action.

1.8 Help and advice

If you are concerned about any arrangement being marketed to you, or you would like to discuss any aspect of these guidance notes, you can contact us by post at the following address: Anti-Avoidance Group (Intelligence), HM Revenue & Customs, 1st Floor, 22 Kingsway, London WC2B 6NR.

Alternatively you can:

- telephone us on 020 7438 6733, or
- email us at aag@hmrc.gov.uk

2. AN OVERVIEW OF THE DISCLOSURE RULES

2.1 Objectives

The objectives of the disclosure rules are to obtain:

- early information about tax arrangements and how they work; and
- information about who has used them.

2.2 The effect of disclosure

On its own the disclosure of a tax arrangement has no effect on the tax position of any person who uses it. However, a disclosed tax arrangement may be rendered ineffective by Parliament, possibly with retrospective effect.

2.3 Scope and summary of the disclosure rules

2.3.1 Scope

Currently, disclosure covers certain tax arrangements relating to:

- income tax, corporation tax and capital gains tax – the detailed rules are in sections 4, 6 and 7;
- National Insurance contributions – the detailed rules are in sections 5 to 7; and
- stamp duty land tax – the detailed rules are in sections 8 and 9.

. . .

2.3.4 Summary: Stamp duty land tax

From 1 April 2010 the rules for stamp duty land tax became more closely aligned with the rules for the main regime. From that date stamp duty land tax uses a system of Scheme Reference Numbers which have to be passed on by promoters to users in the same way as those for the main regime including the rules for co-promoters and intermediaries.

The disclosure regime includes tax arrangements relating to stamp duty land tax where the subject matter of the arrangements is non-residential property with a market value of at least £5 million, residential property with a market value of at least £1 million, or mixed property with a total market value of at least £5 million or which includes residential property with a market value of at least £1 million (see sections 8 and 9).

The main differences compared to the disclosure regime for income tax, corporation tax and capital gains tax are:

- the hallmarks are not applied to limit what is required to be disclosed, however there is a "white list" of arrangements that are not required to be disclosed (paragraph 9.7.1);

- promoters are not obliged to provide reference numbers to scheme users; and
- some minor differences in the time limits for making disclosure.

3. WHO DISCLOSES?

3.1 General

The duty to disclose normally falls on the scheme promoter, however special rules apply when:

- a non-UK based promoter does not disclose a scheme – here the client of the promoter is required to disclose the scheme (see paragraph 3.7).
- the promoter is a lawyer and legal professional privilege prevents him from providing all or part of the prescribed information to HMRC – here the lawyer's client must disclose the scheme (see paragraph 3.8).
- there is no promoter (i.e. the scheme is devised "in-house" for use within that entity or a corporate group to which it belongs) – here the scheme is disclosed by the scheme user (see paragraph 3.9).

Warning:

Penalties can apply if a scheme is not disclosed accurately and at the right time (see section 15).

The Anti-Avoidance Group in HMRC works closely with compliance teams to ensure that schemes discovered by them have been disclosed properly. Anyone likely to have a liability to disclose a scheme should ensure that effective identification and reporting arrangements exist.

3.2 Who is a promoter? (FA 2004, s 307)

You may be a promoter if, in the course of providing services relating to taxation (or, where applicable, National Insurance contributions), or if you are a bank or securities house, you:

- are to any extent responsible for the design of a scheme;
- make a scheme available for implementation by others; or
- organise or manage the implementation of a scheme.

Both UK and non-UK based promoters are subject to the disclosure rules but they only apply to the extent that the scheme enables or is expected to enable a UK tax advantage to be obtained.

3.3 Scheme designers

A person who is only involved in the design of a scheme, and does not make the scheme available for implementation by others or organise or manage it, is not a promoter if any one of three tests is passed. These are:

- the benign test (see paragraph 3.3.1);
- the non-advisor test (see paragraph 3.3.2); and
- the ignorance test (see paragraph 3.3.3).

3.3.1 The benign test (SI 2004/1865, reg 4(1) and (2))

The benign test applies where, in the course of providing tax (or National Insurance contributions) advice, the person is not responsible for the design of any element of the arrangement or proposal (including the way in which it is structured). For example, a promoter marketing or designing a scheme may consult a second firm to provide advice in relation to a particular element of it. This second firm will not be a promoter, despite being involved in the design of the overall scheme, so long as any tax (or National Insurance contributions) advice does not contribute to the tax (or National Insurance contributions) advantage element of it.

For example, a promoter may seek advice from an accounting or law firm on whether two companies are "connected" for any purpose of the Taxes Acts. Provided the advice goes no further than explaining the interpretation of words used in tax legislation, it would be benign; as would advice on general compliance requirements and so on.

On the other hand, if the advice given seeks to highlight opportunities to exploit the relevant provisions then it is not benign advice.

Where the advice recommends some alteration to "a taxpayer's affairs", then whether the advice is benign will depend on the expected tax outcomes of any transactions entered into as a result of the advice.

3.3.2 The non-adviser test (SI 2004/1865, reg 4(1) and (3))

The non-adviser test applies where a person who, although involved in the design of a scheme, does not contribute any tax advice. This test does not apply to a bank or securities house.

This might typically happen where:

- a promoter consults a law firm (which has a business that includes giving tax advice) in relation to company law. The law firm will not become a promoter as long as it provides no tax advice (other than benign advice) in the course of carrying out its responsibilities; or
- a promoter consults an accounting firm in relation to accounting aspects of a scheme. The firm is not a promoter so long as it provides no tax advice in the course of carrying out its responsibilities.

3.3.3 The ignorance test (SI 2004/1865, reg 4(1) and (4))

The ignorance test applies when a person could not reasonably be expected to have either:

- sufficient information to enable them to know whether or not the arrangements are disclosable schemes; or
- sufficient information so as to enable that person to comply.

This test might apply where, for example, a person has insufficient knowledge of the overall arrangements to know whether the "benign" or "non-adviser" tests are failed; or has only a partial understanding of the scheme so that they would be unable to comply with the disclosure requirements.

Where having the relevant "information" depends not merely upon factual knowledge, but upon the application of some particular expertise, persons will not normally be expected to have such an expertise if it falls outside their own area of professional expertise (unless the matters in question can reasonably be said to be common knowledge amongst business and professional persons generally).

3.4 Who makes a scheme available for implementation by others?

A scheme can be made available by more than one person such as by the scheme designer or those who provide the scheme under a licensing agreement with the designer. Each such person may be a promoter for disclosure purposes and have obligations as described in this guidance. Paragraphs 10.2.2 and 10.2.3 describe when a co-promoter is exempt from making disclosure, however co-promoters are not exempt from other obligations, such as providing their client with the relevant scheme reference number (see paragraph 12.2).

A person who acts solely as an introducer or intermediary between the scheme provider and potential scheme user is not regarded as making the scheme available for implementation by others for disclosure purposes and so is not a promoter under this test. For stamp duty land tax schemes, a person providing the usual services of a conveyancer will typically be either an introducer or an intermediary.

Paragraph 10.3 provides information on when a scheme is "made available for implementation by others".

3.5 Scheme organisers and managers (SI 2004/1865, reg 5)

A person who organises or manages a scheme that they did not design or make available for implementation is not regarded as a promoter if he is unconnected with a person who has marketed or designed it or similar schemes.

If the person who organises or manages the scheme is connected with a person who has designed or made it or similar schemes available for implementation, the need for both persons to make a disclosure will not arise when the co-promoter rule applies (see paragraph 10.2.2 and 10.2.3).

Section 839 of ICTA 1988 applies to determine whether a person is connected with another.

3.6 Corporate groups (SI 2004/1865, reg 2)

A group company that provides tax services to other companies within the same group is not a promoter. This ensures that disclosable schemes devised within a group for its own use are disclosed in the same way as those devised by a single company "in-house" for its own use – see paragraph 3.9.

For the purpose of these rules a company is a group company where it is a member of a group under any of the existing provisions of the Taxes Acts, for example group relief and/or capital gains, but as modified by SI 2004/7865, reg 2.

3.7 Schemes marketed by offshore promoters (FA 2004, s 309)

The obligations on promoters to disclose schemes they market and/or design apply to both UK and non-UK based promoters. Where a non-UK based promoter fails to disclose a scheme when required to do so, the user must make the disclosure. The time limits are explained at paragraph 10.4.

A non-UK based promoter who has disclosed a scheme will be able to provide his or her clients with the 8-digit reference number issued by the Anti-Avoidance Group in HMRC.

If you are a user of such a scheme please contact the Anti-Avoidance Group for advice if you are unsure whether these rules apply to you – see paragraph 1.8.

3.8 Schemes promoted by lawyers (FA 2004, s 310 and SI 2004/1865, reg 6)

Schemes promoted by lawyers are within the scope of the disclosure rules in the same way as for other promoters.

However, where an adviser who would ordinarily be a promoter is prevented by reason of legal professional privilege from providing any of the information needed to make a full disclosure, that adviser has no obligation to make a disclosure. Unless there is another promoter who has an obligation to disclose the scheme, it must be disclosed by any person in the UK who enters into any transaction forming part of it. But the client of the lawyer has the option of waiving any right to legal privilege. If legal privilege is waived the lawyer is required to disclose.

The following important points should be noted in relation to waiver of legal privilege:

- any waiver must be made within sufficient time to enable the lawyer to disclose within 5 days of the scheme being made available (see paragraph 10.2), otherwise the client must make the disclosure within 5 or 30 days, as applicable, of the first transaction (see paragraph 10.5); and
- any waiver can be limited by the client so as to apply only to the extent necessary to enable the lawyer to comply with the disclosure obligation and to have no relevance for any other purpose.

Your lawyer or tax adviser will be able to help you but you can also contact the Anti-Avoidance Group in HMRC if you are in doubt – see paragraph 1.8.

Where a lawyer is "marketing" a scheme, as described at paragraph 10.3.2, the lawyer cannot assert legal privilege. This means that such marketing is subject to the disclosure obligation and the lawyer should disclose the scheme (providing the other conditions are met) to the Anti-Avoidance Group in the normal way.

3.9 Schemes with no promoter, including "in-house" schemes (FA 2004, s 310)

Where there is no person who is a "promoter" in respect of a scheme, it must be disclosed by any person in the UK who enters into any transaction forming part of it. Whilst these rules can apply to an individual, partnership, trust or company, we expect them to be of most relevance to those companies with their own in-house tax departments.

Hallmarked schemes and hallmarked NI contribution schemes are only required to be disclosed where the advantage is intended to be obtained by a business that is not a small or medium enterprise (see paragraph 6.6).

For stamp duty land tax schemes, any in-house user has to disclose but only if the scheme is in relation to residential property with a market value of at least £1 million, non-residential property with a market value of at least £5 million, or mixed property with a total market value of at least £5 million or which includes residential property with a market value of at least £1 million (see sections 8 and 9).

In both cases, disclosure only applies to schemes that have been implemented; there is no requirement to disclose mere plans and ideas.

. . .

8. DETERMINING A STAMP DUTY LAND TAX SCHEME – FLOW CHART

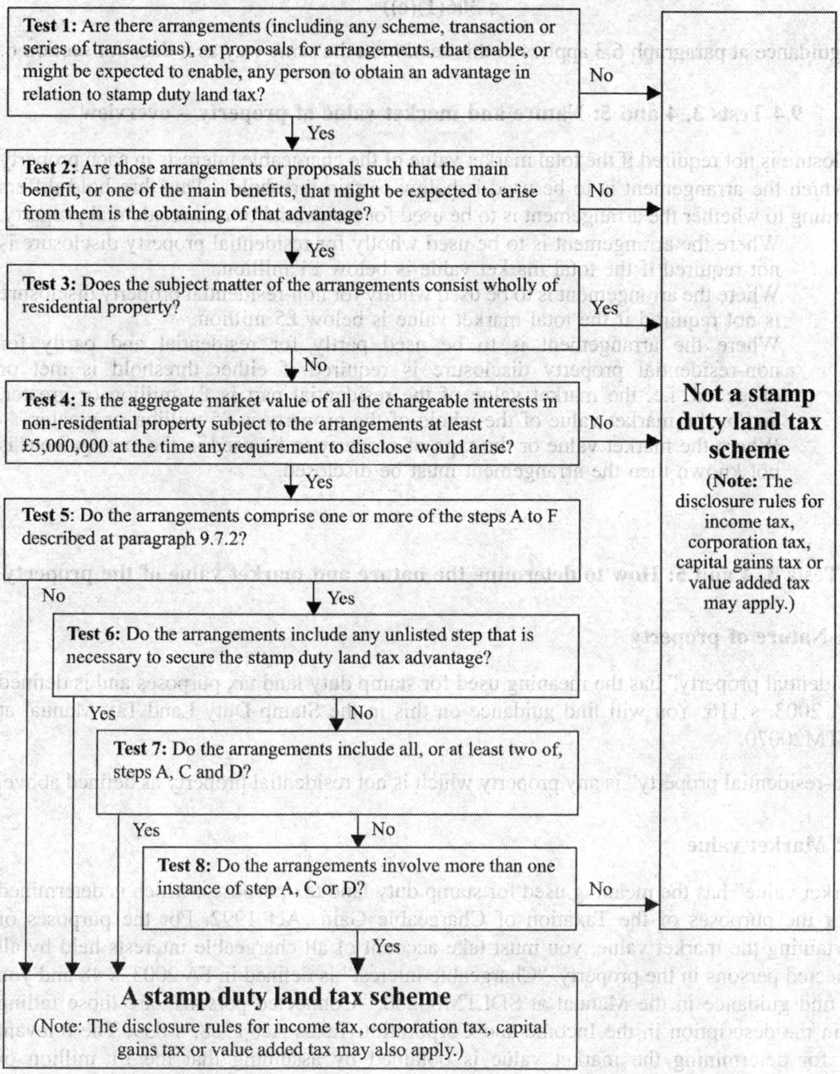

9. DETERMINING A STAMP DUTY LAND TAX SCHEME – THE TESTS

9.1 General

The hallmarks at section 7, including the "confidentiality", "premium fee" and "off market test" hallmarks do not apply to this section.

9.2 Test 1: Are there arrangements that enable an SDLT advantage be obtained? (FA 2004, s 306(1)(a) and (b) and s 318)

The guidance at paragraph 6.2 applies to this section in the same way as it does for section 6.

Note: The definition of "arrangements" used for disclosure purposes is wider than the concept of "linked transactions" used for stamp duty land tax purposes (FA 2003, s 108).

9.3 Test 2: Is the advantage a main benefit of the arrangements? (FA 2004, s 306(1)(c))

The guidance at paragraph 6.3 applies to this section in the same way as it does for section 6.

9.4 Tests 3, 4 and 5: Nature and market value of property – overview

Disclosure is not required if the total market value of the chargeable interests in each property for which the arrangement is to be used is below certain thresholds. This threshold differs according to whether the arrangement is to be used for residential or non-residential property.

- Where the arrangement is to be used wholly for residential property disclosure is not required if the total market value is below £1 million.
- Where the arrangement is to be used wholly for non-residential property disclosure is not required if the total market value is below £5 million.
- Where the arrangement is to be used partly for residential and partly for non-residential property disclosure is required if either threshold is met or exceeded, i.e. the market value of the residential part is £1 million or greater, and/or the market value of the whole of the property is £5 million or greater.
- Where the market value or the type of property to be used in the arrangement is not known then the arrangement must be disclosed.

.

9.5 Tests 3, 4 and 5: How to determine the nature and market value of the property

9.5.1 Nature of property

"Residential property" has the meaning used for stamp duty land tax purposes and is defined at FA 2003, s 116. You will find guidance on this in the Stamp Duty Land Tax Manual at SDLTM20070.

"Non-residential property" is any property which is not residential property as defined above.

9.5.2 Market value

"Market value" has the meaning used for stamp duty land tax purposes, which is determined as for the purposes of the Taxation of Chargeable Gains Act 1992. For the purposes of ascertaining the market value, you must take account of all chargeable interests held by all connected persons in the property. "Chargeable interest" is defined in FA 2003, s 48 and you will find guidance in the Manual at SDLTM00280. "Connected persons" are those falling within the description in the Income and Corporation Taxes Act 1988, s 839. The relevant time for determining the market value is obtained by assuming that the £1 million or £5 million threshold has been reached and using the rules on when to disclose a scheme detailed at section 10 below.

9.6 Tests 3, 4 and 5: Nature or market value of property unknown or uncertain

A common question asked by professional advisers is "how will I know what the arrangement is to be used for and what its market value is? I won't know if the property will be residential, non-residential or a combination of the two and I won't know what its market value will be as any arrangement could theoretically be used for property of any description or value?" The rule of thumb is that if the nature or type of property is not known then the arrangement must be disclosed but more detail as to how to determine this is given below.

The starting point is that the tests apply at the time of the event that triggers the potential requirement to disclose a scheme. There are two possible "triggers", depending upon the type of scheme.

9.6.1 Marketed arrangements

For marketed arrangements the trigger is making proposals available for implementation by any person – see paragraph 10.3.2. We expect that in most cases the scheme will be made available to specific users. In that case, the promoter should apply the test:

- Will the arrangements be used, at least in part, for residential property with a value of £1 million or more or for any property with a value of £5 million or more in respect of the persons to whom the scheme has been made available?

If the answer is "I don't know", the promoter must notify the scheme.

In some cases, the scheme may be made available at a time when no specific users have been identified. For example, the promoter may communicate proposals at arm's length via a distributor (see paragraph 10.3.5). In such cases, the promoter cannot know the details of the property for which the arrangements are to be used and must notify the scheme.

9.6.2 Bespoke arrangements

For bespoke arrangements, the trigger is that the promoter becomes aware that a transaction forming part of the arrangements has taken place – see paragraph 10.3.3. In such cases the promoter should apply the test:

- Will the arrangements be used, at least in part, for residential property with a value of £1 million or more or for any property with a value of £5 million or more to the property which is the subject of the transactions that have triggered the potential disclosure?

If the answer to either test is "I don't know", the promoter must notify the scheme.

9.6.3 In-house arrangements

Where users are required to disclose an arrangement, we expect that they will always know the details, including the market value, of the property for which the scheme is to be used. Consequently, we expect they will know, at the time that disclosure would normally be required, whether or not the transaction(s) forming part of the arrangements that triggers the disclosure requirement relates, at least in part, to residential property with a value of £1 million or more, or to any property with a value of £5 million or more. . If it does – or if the user does not know the answer – the user must notify the scheme.

Part II ST

9.6.4 Using the same arrangements with future unknown properties

In the circumstances described in paragraphs 9.6.1 and 9.6.2 there will usually be a theoretical possibility that the same arrangements could be used in the future for other properties and the value of those properties is inevitably unknown. This situation alone does not require the arrangements to be notified. If and when either proposals are made available to further clients, or the promoter becomes aware of further transactions involving different clients or property, then the promoter should apply the tests again in relation to the new circumstances.

9.7 Test 6: Grandfathering

One of the aims of the extension of the disclosure rules for stamp duty land tax is to restrict disclosure to those schemes which are new or innovative. This is achieved by exempting from disclosure those schemes which are the same or substantially the same as arrangements made available by any person before 1st April 2010. This is known as "grandfathering".

See paragraph 10.2.5 below for the meaning of "substantially the same". It is irrelevant whether a given legal entity made the arrangements available prior to 1st April 2010; what is important is whether any person made them available prior to this date.

It is a matter of fact whether an arrangement is "grandfathered". Evidence of grandfathering would include:

- the existence and substance of the arrangement being clearly described in tax manuals or publications;
- a practitioner's own record as to when they made, or learnt that competitors were making, an arrangement available.

"Makes available for implementation" takes the meaning at S308(2) Finance Act 2004 and detailed guidance as to its meaning is given at paragraph 10.3 below.

9.7.1 List of grandfathered schemes

A list of schemes which HMRC regards as being "grandfathered" may be found below. This list is purely illustrative and should not be regarded as being exhaustive. If there is any doubt as to whether a scheme ought to be disclosed then a disclosure should be made. The use of the six steps in Tests 7 to 10 below will also remove the need to notify HMRC of schemes of which it is already aware.

The fact that any particular scheme is exempted from disclosure by the application of test 6 should not be taken as an indication that HMRC either finds the scheme acceptable, or that we accept that it works under current law. It merely signifies that we are already aware of it.

(a) those that satisfy the requirements at Steps 7–10 as described in Section 9.8 of the DOTAS Guidance April 2010, and

(b) those which are of the same, or substantially the same, description as arrangements which were first made available for implementation before 1st April 2010.

(2) The arrangements referred to in paragraph (1)(b) include (although this is not an exhaustive list) —

(a) arrangements which rely on the completion of the original contract being disregarded under S45 FA 2003;

(b) arrangements that rely upon the interaction between the definition of a connected person at S993 ITA 2007 and the computational rules for partnerships at Schedule 15 FA 2003.

9.8 Tests 7 to 10: Introduction to steps A to F

9.8.1 General

The Schedule to the regulations contains a list of six "steps" (A to F). You are **not** required to notify schemes that comprise one or more of those steps (test 7). However, this is subject to:

- an overarching rule that **any** arrangement that contains an unlisted step – where that unlisted step is necessary for securing the stamp duty land tax advantage – is not exempted from disclosure (test 8); and
- certain restrictions on using combinations of steps or multiples of the same step (tests 9 and 10 – see paragraph 9.10 below).

The purpose of tests 7 to 10 is to remove the need to notify certain tax arrangements that HMRC is already fully aware of (in terms of content and extent), so that disclosure would serve no purpose.

The steps A to F have been described to us as "existing toolkit". We believe a better term would be "existing building blocks". For stamp duty land tax purposes, we are not interested in the existing building blocks in themselves. But we are interested in the ways in which the building blocks are put together to form more complex products. Hence the limits on the ways in which steps A to F can be used in combination.

The fact that any particular scheme is exempted from disclosure by the application of tests 5 to 8 should not be taken as an indication that HMRC either finds the scheme acceptable, or that we accept that it works under current law. It merely signifies that we already know about it.

9.8.2 The six steps – A summary

The six listed steps are:

- **Step A** – The acquisition of a chargeable interest in land by a special purpose vehicle (SPV);
- **Step B** – Claims to certain reliefs (see paragraph 9.8.3 below)
- **Step C** – The sale of shares in a SPV which holds chargeable interests in land, to a person who is not connected to either the SPV or the vendor;
- **Step D** – Not electing to waive the exemption from VAT (i.e. not "opting to tax");
- **Step E** – Structuring a transaction as the transfer of a going concern for VAT purposes; and
- **Step F** – The creation of a partnership to which a property subject to a land transaction is to be transferred.

9.8.3 The six steps – The legislation

The six steps are listed in the Schedule to The Stamp Duty Land Tax Avoidance Schemes (Prescribed Descriptions of Arrangements) Regulations 2005 (SI 2005/1868):

The steps are as follows.

Step A: Acquisition of a chargeable interest by special purpose vehicle

The acquisition of a chargeable interest in land by a company created for that purpose ("a special purpose vehicle").

Step B: Claims to relief

Making—

(a) a single claim to relief under any of the following provisions of the Finance Act 2003—
  (i) section 57A (sale and leaseback arrangements);
  (ii) section 60 (compulsory purchase facilitating development);
  (iii) section 61 (compliance with planning obligation);
  (iv) section 64 (demutualisation of building society);
  (v) section 64A (initial transfer of assets to trustees of unit trust scheme);
  (vi) section 65 (incorporation of limited liability partnership);
  (vii) section 66 (transfers involving public bodies);
  (viii) section 67 (transfer in consequence of reorganisation of parliamentary constituencies);
  (ix) section 69 (acquisition by bodies established for national purposes);
  (x) section 71 (certain acquisitions by registered social landlords);
  (xi) section 74 (collective enfranchisement by leaseholders);
  (xii) section 75 (crofting community right to buy);
  (xiii) Schedule 6 (disadvantaged areas relief);
  (xiv) Schedule 6A (relief for certain acquisitions of residential property);
  (xv) Schedule 7 (group relief and reconstruction acquisition reliefs);
  (xvi) Schedule 8 (charities relief); or
  (xvii) Schedule 9 (right to buy, shared ownership leases etc.);

(b) one or more claims to relief under any one of the following provisions of the Finance Act 2003—
  (i) section 71A (alternative property finance: land sold to financial institution and leased to individual);
  (ii) section 72 (alternative property finance in Scotland: land sold to financial institution and leased to individual);
  (iii) section 72A (alternative property finance in Scotland: land sold to financial institution and individual in common); or
  (iv) section 73 (alternative property finance: land sold to financial institution and resold to individual).

Step C: Sale of shares in special purpose vehicle

The sale of shares in a special purpose vehicle, which holds a chargeable interest in land, to a person with whom neither the special purpose vehicle, nor the vendor, is connected.

Step D: Not exercising election to waive exemption from VAT

No election is made to waive exemption from value added tax contained in paragraph 2 of Schedule 10 to the Value Added Tax Act (treatment of buildings and land for value added tax purposes).

Step E: Transfer of a business as a going concern

Arranging the transfer of a business, connected with the land which is the subject of the arrangements, in such a way that it is treated for the purposes of value added tax as the transfer of a going concern.

Step F: Undertaking a joint venture

The creation of a partnership (within the meaning of paragraph 1 of Schedule 15 to the Finance Act 2003) to which the property subject to a land transaction is to be transferred.

9.9 Approach to tests 7 to 10

The way to approach the steps is as follows:

- Identify all the single listed steps comprised in the arrangement. Paragraph 9.9.1 provides guidance on what constitutes a single step B.
- Identify any unlisted steps in the arrangement that are necessary to secure the expected stamp duty land tax advantage (if there are any such steps, the scheme is not exempted from disclosure – see paragraph 9.8.1 above).
- If the arrangement involves a combination of steps, or more than one instance of the same step, refer to tests 9 to 10 (paragraph 9.10 below) to see if that combination or multiple falls within the arrangements exempted from disclosure.

9.8.1 Single step B

A single instance of step B consists of either:

- a single claim to one of the reliefs listed under step B(a)(i) to (a)(xvii) in the Schedule (see paragraph 9.8.3); or
- one or more claims to one the reliefs listed under step B(b)(i) to (b)(iv) in the Schedule (see paragraph 9.8.3).

Note: For this purpose a claim can still be a "single claim" even if it is one of a number of identical claims being made in respect of separate and distinct properties. So, for example, where two properties are transferred from group company A to group company B, each of the two claims to group relief is a "single claim" for this purpose.

Examples of single step B:

- A single claim to charities relief is one step B (single use of a relief in group (a)); and
- Two claims to alternative property finance: land sold to a financial institution and leased to an individual constitutes one step B (multiple use of a relief in group (b)).

We will accept that a single step B(a)(xv) includes actions taken or not taken with the intention of ensuring that, within the context of the withdrawal of group, reconstruction or acquisition relief:

- the purchaser ceases to a member of the same group as the vendor; or
- control of the acquiring company changes; or
- arrangements for either of the above events are entered into;

on or after the end of the period of three years beginning with the effective date of the relief, rather than before the end of that period.

A "single claim" to a relief means step B does not include any arrangement that comprises more than one claim to the same listed relief within group (a) of the Schedule. Nor do such schemes constitute multiples of step B. They are not within step B at all. For example:

- Two claims to group relief fall outside step B (two claims to the same listed relief); and
- A claim to group relief and a claim to reconstruction relief also fall outside step B (two claims to the same listed relief – although these are separate reliefs, they are listed together in group (a)(xv)).

Any such arrangement is not excepted from disclosure.

An arrangement that comprises the use of two or more different listed reliefs will amount to two or more separate instances of step B. For example:

- A claim to charities relief and a claim to group relief constitute two separate steps B (use of two separately listed reliefs);
- A claim to group relief and a claim to alternative property finance: land sold to financial institution and leased to individual constitute two separate steps B (use of two separately listed reliefs).

In such cases, you should refer to paragraph 9.10 to see whether the combination is excepted from disclosure.

9.10 Tests 9 and 10: Combination steps

Rules 1 and 2 of the schedule to The Stamp Duty Land Tax Avoidance Schemes (Prescribed Descriptions of Arrangements) Regulations 2005 (SI 2005/1868) specify which combinations of steps, or multiples of the same step, can be used as part of the excepted arrangements. These two rules are separate (i.e. they are not two legs of a single rule in which Rule 2 is merely an extension of Rule 1). It is necessary to consider Rule 2 even where Rule 1 is not in point.

9.10.1 SI 2005/1868: Rule 1 to the schedule

This rule merely confirms that arrangements exempted from disclosure can include any combination of steps B, D, E and F, including multiple uses of the same step.

9.10.2 Tests 9 and 10 (SI 2005/1868, Rule 2 to the schedule)

These tests provide that arrangements are not excluded from disclosure if they:

- include any combination of steps A, C and D; or
- involve a multiple use of any of steps A, C or D.

9.10.3 Examples of arrangements exempted from disclosure

Examples of arrangements exempted from disclosure include schemes that consist of:

- two steps B;
- two steps B and a single step A; and
- two Steps B and two steps F.

9.10.4 Examples of arrangements not exempted from disclosure

Examples of arrangements that are not exempted from disclosure include schemes that consist of:

- two claims to group relief (double use of the same relief does not fall within step B at all – see paragraph 9.9.1 above);
- two steps A only;
- two steps B and single steps A and D; and
- two steps B and two steps A.

10. WHEN TO DISCLOSE A SCHEME

10.1 General

Section 3 explains who is required to disclose a notifiable scheme. In general, it is the scheme promoter who has to disclose. However, the user may have to disclose where an offshore promoter or lawyer markets the scheme, or it is devised for use "in house".

A scheme may have been first made available to clients before an obligation to disclose it arises, such as prior to the introduction of the disclosure rules. In such cases the scheme is to be disclosed once it has been made available on or after the obligation to disclose has arisen.

10.2 Schemes where the promoter must disclose

10.2.1 Time limits (FA 2004, s 308(1) and (3), and SI 2004/1864, reg 4(2), (3) and (6))

Where a promoter is required to disclose he must do so within 5 days of the earlier of the date on which he:

- makes the scheme available for implementation by another person – see paragraph 10.3; or
- becomes aware of a transaction forming part of the scheme.

For marketed schemes, the first of these tests is likely to be met before the second. So the time for disclosure would normally be by reference to that earlier date.

However, where the activity of the promoter is restricted to the creation of bespoke schemes, the disclosure requirement arises only when he becomes aware that a transaction forming part of the scheme has taken place (see also paragraph 10.3.3). This ensures that where the bespoke planning goes through a number of iterations each of the iterations need not be disclosed.

In practice, there may only be a minimal timing difference between the time a bespoke scheme is disclosed compared to a marketed scheme.

Weekends, Bank Holidays, Good Friday and Christmas Day are ignored for the purposes of determining the due date.

. . .

10.2.3 Stamp Duty Land Tax schemes – Co-promoter rule

From 1 April 2010 the co-promoter rule at paragraph 10.2.2 applies equally to Stamp Duty Land Tax schemes as it does to Income Tax, Corporation Tax, Capital Gains Tax and National Insurance Contributions schemes.

10.2.4 Stamp Duty Land Tax schemes – Legal, professional privilege

Where disclosure has to be made by a client or purchaser in respect of a stamp duty land tax scheme because the promoter is subject to legal, professional privilege the time limit for disclosure is within 5 days of the date on which he enters into the first transaction becoming part of the notifiable arrangements.

10.2.5 Exemption for substantially the same scheme (FA 2004, s 308(5))

A promoter is required to disclose the same scheme only once. Minor changes, for example to suit the requirements of different clients, need not be separately disclosed providing the revised proposal remains substantially the same.

What constitutes a change in a scheme or arrangement so that it is no longer substantially the same is a matter which will need to be considered on each occasion.

In our view a scheme is no longer substantially the same if the effect of any change would be to make any previous disclosure misleading in relation to the second (or subsequent) client.

In general provided the tax analysis is substantially the same we will regard schemes as "substantially the same" where the only change is a different client including a different company in the same group.

We will not regard schemes as substantially the same where there are changes to deal with changes in the law or accounting treatment, changes in the tax attributes e.g. schemes creating income losses instead of capital losses or other legal and commercial issues.

However, special care must be taken where an existing tax product is used as part of an otherwise bespoke scheme. This has been described to us as "the use of existing toolkit".

Where a piece of "existing toolkit" is used as part of a separate scheme for the same or different client then it may be that the resulting scheme is so different from the earlier planning idea that the disclosure position needs to be considered afresh. In some situations this might involve the client being given two or more numbers, for example where the scheme involves a combination of ideas that were themselves disclosed and allocated a number.

10.2.6 Timing when clearance application made (SI 2004/1864, para 5)

There are special rules to avoid duplication of information where the arrangement includes transactions for which a statutory clearance exists. In practice, to date these rules have been used very little.

They apply for the purposes of:

- ICTA 1988, s 215 (Purchase of own shares by an unquoted company)
- ICTA 1988, s 225 (Company demergers)
- ICTA 1988, s 444A (Transfer of business)
- ICTA 1988, s 707 (Transactions in securities)
- TCGA 1992, s 138, 139, 140B or 140D (Reconstruction of company or trade).

Where a company or other person able to apply for statutory clearance has a reasonable intention of submitting a clearance application in respect of a transaction that forms part of a scheme made available for implementation by a promoter, both the promoter disclosure and the clearance application can be made at the same time.

Where the user of the scheme decides not to make a clearance request then the promoter must make the disclosure no later than 5 working days following the day on which reasonable expectation to make a clearance application ceased or the normal "relevant date" if this is later.

In any case where a transaction occurs prior to the submission of a clearance application then the disclosure must be made within 5 working days of any transaction that is part of the scheme occurring.

Clearance applications will be considered in the usual way and clearance will not be refused merely on the grounds that some part of the proposed transaction involves a disclosable scheme.

Disclosures made in this way should be sent with the clearance application.

It should be noted that combining the clearance with disclosure is optional and promoters can if they wish disclose in the usual way. However any clearance given may be void if the existence of a scheme within the transaction for which clearance is requested is not mentioned in the application. For example, where a number has been issued by the Anti-Avoidance Group this information should be included as part of the clearance application.

10.3 The "made available for implementation by another person" test

10.3.1 General

A scheme is regarded as being made available for implementation by another person when it:

(a) has been developed to such a stage that the promoter has a high degree of confidence in the tax analysis applying to it; and

(b) is communicated to a potential user in sufficient detail that he could be expected to:

- understand the expected tax advantages; and
- decide whether or not to enter into it.

10.3.2 Marketed schemes

By marketed schemes we mean schemes planned with no specific client in mind or possibly marketed to a class of user, for example wealthy individuals, large companies or employers. The promoter may actively seek the potential user or make the product available in response to a general request for tax efficient ideas.

Such products may require some alteration to suit specific clients but the way in which the tax advantage is expected to be achieved remains as originally planned or pre-packaged and can be applied almost irrespective of the characteristics of the user.

A marketed scheme will typically be "made available for implementation by another person" when the promoter:

- communicates what is essentially a fully formed proposal to existing or potential clients, or
- provides an existing proposal to a client in respect of arrangements that would otherwise comprise a bespoke scheme (see below).

That a marketed scheme is tailored to the particular user does not affect the time limit for making disclosure. Similarly the proposal need not be marketed to the user or potential user in written form but could be by way of oral presentation of the proposal.

Where two or more schemes are made available to a client or potential client who later chooses to proceed with only one of them, both of the schemes must be disclosed.

10.3.3 Bespoke schemes

By bespoke schemes we mean a tax arrangement designed in response to a client's specific tax management issue.

A promoter who designs such a scheme is not normally regarded as "making it available for implementation by another person", with the relevant date being determined only by reference to when the first scheme transaction takes place – see paragraph 10.2.1.

10.3.4 Internal approval processes

Most promoters have internal approval processes for new products. Schemes are accepted as being "made available for implementation by another person" when they are first put to a client after receiving approval.

This will not apply in any situation where the user has entered into any part of the scheme before the promoter's approval process has been completed.

10.3.5 Communications to non-users

Where the promoter communicates a scheme to a second person that acts as a distributor to potential users we will regard both parties as making the scheme available for implementation. However, the co-promoter rule allows that only one of the parties need make a disclosure (see paragraphs 10.2.2 and 10.2.3). Regardless of who makes the disclosure, we would expect the scheme reference number to be provided to the scheme user.

However, where a promoter communicates an idea to another person for incorporation into their own scheme, only the second party is regarded as making a scheme available for implementation. The resulting scheme will need to be disclosed in the normal way unless it is substantially the same as one that they have previously disclosed – see paragraph 10.2.5.

10.4 Schemes marketed by offshore promoters (FA 2004, s 309 and SI 2004/1864, reg 4(4) and (6))

Where a non-UK based promoter fails to comply with any disclosure obligation, the user must disclose (see paragraph 3.7). He must do so within 5 days of entering into the first transaction forming part of the scheme (see paragraph 10.7). Weekends, Bank Holidays, Good Friday and Christmas Day are ignored for the purposes of determining the due date.

We will not seek to penalise users who have relied upon written assurances given to them by non-UK based promoters that either the disclosure obligation has been complied with or does not arise, providing it was reasonable in the circumstances to rely upon the assurance given. Where disclosure has been made, the scheme reference number allocated to it by the Anti-Avoidance Group in HMRC should be provided to the user. The Anti-Avoidance Group can confirm whether a genuine reference number has been provided. Contact details are at paragraph 1.8.

10.5 Schemes marketed by lawyers (FA 2004, s 310 and SI 2004/1864, regs. 4(5), (5ZA), (5A) and (6))

Where a promoter is a lawyer and legal professional privilege prevents him from providing all or part of the prescribed information to HMRC the user must disclose (see paragraph 3.8). Disclosure must normally be made within 5 days of entering into the first transaction forming part of the scheme (see paragraph 10.7). However, the time period is 30 days where the scheme is a stamp duty land tax scheme. Weekends, bank holidays, Good Friday and Christmas Day are ignored for the purposes of determining the due date.

10.6 Schemes with no promoter, including "in-house" schemes (FA 2004, s 310 and SI 2004/1864, reg 4(5), (5ZA) and (6))

Where there is no promoter the user must disclose (see paragraphs 3.6 and 3.9). He must do so within 30 days of entering into the first transaction forming part of the scheme (see paragraph 10.7). Weekends, Bank Holidays, Good Friday and Christmas Day are ignored for the purposes of determining the due date.

10.7 The "first transaction" test

The due date for making a disclosure, where the user is required to make the disclosure, is by reference to the first transaction forming part of the scheme.

In the majority of cases where disclosure is required, it is likely that the tax department or individual is fully aware that the scheme is to be implemented and can monitor as to when the first transaction takes place.

In other cases, especially in larger organisations, systems should be put in place to identify and report disclosable schemes within the relevant time limit. What those systems are depends on individual circumstances. However they should be reasonable and proportionate to the risk.

In general, we expect the adopted system to involve the people who have the ability and authority to purchase, design or implement the sorts of schemes that are disclosable. These will normally be people within the tax department itself. Such people should be identified and be made sufficiently aware of the adopted system in order that disclosure can be made on time. The system should be reviewed periodically, at least once a year.

It is, however, accepted that there may be exceptional circumstances where a disclosable scheme is not captured by the adopted system in sufficient time for the disclosure to be made within the relevant time limit. In some cases the scheme may not be discovered until the end of year audit and tax computation. Concerns have arisen, in particular, over a UK tax advantage arising as a main benefit following:

- a controlled foreign company entering into local tax planning arrangements;
- unusual accountancy treatment;
- commercial transactions being carried out by non-tax specialists without the knowledge of the tax department; or
- the size of the tax benefit being too small for the tax department to be aware of it.

You should make disclosure of the scheme as soon as you are aware that it is late with an explanation as to why. If you have a reasonable excuse for not disclosing earlier you will not be liable to a penalty (see section 15).

. . .

11. HOW TO MAKE A DISCLOSURE

11.1 The forms to complete (s 316)

There are four different forms available for use in the following circumstances:

- AAG 1 – Notification of scheme by promoter
- AAG 2 – Notification by scheme user where offshore promoter does not notify
- AAG 3 – Notification by scheme user where no promoter, or promoted by lawyer unable to make full notification
- AAG 5 – Continuation sheet

Use of these forms is a legal requirement (see paragraphs 1.2 and 1.5.3).

11.2 How to obtain and submit the forms

You can make an online disclosure by clicking the relevant links on the Anti-Avoidance Group website at www.hmrc.gov.uk/aiu/index.htm.

You can obtain PDF and WORD versions of the forms by clicking the relevant links on the same web page, or by contacting the Anti-Avoidance Group (Intelligence) within HMRC at the address shown at paragraph 1.8. Alternatively, paper copies can be obtained from the order line by telephoning 08459 000404 or by faxing on 08459 000604. The completed forms should then be sent by either post or e-mail to the Anti-Avoidance Group (Intelligence) at the address shown at paragraph 1.8.

11.3 The information to be provided

11.3.1 General (SI 2004/1864, reg 3)

Briefly, the regulations prescribe that the following information must be provided:

- Your name and address if you are a promoter making the disclosure, a client making a disclosure where the promoter is a lawyer, or making an "in-house" disclosure where there is no promoter.
- Your and the promoter's name and address if you are disclosing as the client of an off-shore promoter.
- Details of the provision, in the Prescribed Descriptions of Arrangements Regulations that makes the scheme disclosable – see paragraph 11.3.3.
- A summary of the proposal/arrangements and the name by which it/they are known – see paragraph 11.3.4.
- Information explaining the elements and how the expected tax advantage arises – see paragraph 11.3.4.
- The statutory provisions on which that tax advantage is based – see paragraph 11.3.4.

11.3.2 Legal advice (FA 2004, s 314)

Legal professional privilege may apply to certain advice given by lawyers to their clients. Such information need not be disclosed.

11.3.3 The prescribed arrangement(s)

The relevant forms have a list of the relevant provisions.

For hallmarked schemes, the relevant hallmark (see section 7) should be indicated. For some schemes, more than one hallmark may apply. Here you need only indicate one hallmark. However, in order to allow HMRC to monitor the value of the hallmarks, we would prefer you to indicate the main applicable hallmark.

For stamp duty land tax schemes there are three options to indicate the type and market value of the property for which the arrangement is to be used. One box only should be ticked. Further guidance to help you determine the appropriate property type and market value is provided at paragraphs 9.4 to 9.6 above.

.

11.3.4 Explaining the scheme

Sufficient information is required to be provided such that an Officer of the Board of HMRC is able to understand how the expected tax advantage is intended to arise. The explanation should be in straightforward terms and should identify the steps involved and the relevant UK tax law. Common technical or legal terms and concepts need not be explained in depth.

If the scheme is complex then copies of any prospectus or scheme diagrams will help us understand what is proposed but even where you send such documents you must still use form AAG 1. Where such documents are supplied there is no objection to these documents excluding information that would identify a client.

11.4 Notification of co-promoters (s 308(4A)(a) and (4C)(a))

When you make your disclosure, you may also provide HMRC with details of any other promoter of the same or substantially the same scheme. You are not required to provide their details to HMRC but if you do so and provide the promoter with the information at 11.3 above he will be exempt from making his own disclosure of the scheme (see paragraph 10.2.3).

The details to be provided are the co-promoter's name and address. Where the co-promoter is a company, it is the company's name and address that is to be provided not that of an individual.

The details should be sent to the mail, or email, address at paragraph 1.8 and accompany the disclosure.

If you have already made a disclosure of the scheme and hold the scheme reference number allocated by HMRC, and your co-promoter seeks exemption from making his own disclosure, his details need not be provided to HMRC if rule (b) at paragraph 10.2.3 is followed.

. . .

13. WHAT TO DO IF YOU RECEIVE A SCHEME REFERENCE NUMBER RELATING TO A STAMP DUTY LAND TAX SCHEME

13.1 Outline of the scheme reference number system

The scheme reference number system is a means of identifying the users of disclosed schemes, allowing HMRC to prioritise and co-ordinate enquiries into users' returns. The scheme reference number system applies to stamp duty land tax schemes and arrangements which became notifiable on or after 1 April 2010. Prior to 1 April 2010 numbers relating to notifiable schemes and arrangements were given to promoters etc but these were not Scheme Reference Numbers within the meaning of the legislation and there was no obligation either to pass the number to users etc or for the users to notify the number to HMRC. The remainder of the guidance in section 13 relates solely to stamp duty land tax schemes and arrangements which became notifiable on or after 1 April 2010. If you are in doubt as to whether a reference

Part II ST

number you have received should be passed on or notified to HMRC you should contact Anti-Avoidance group using the contact details at paragraph 1.8.

The scheme reference number system works by scheme users reporting an 8-digit scheme reference number to HMRC. For stamp duty land tax schemes the scheme reference number has to be reported on a specified HMRC form.

This reference number is allocated by HMRC at the time the scheme is disclosed and is given to the person or persons who disclosed the scheme. They then in turn pass it to the scheme user, sometimes via a third party client, in accordance with the rules explained below. Where a scheme user is the person required to disclose the scheme, HMRC will provide the number directly to him, who nevertheless must report the number on the specified form.

The allocation or notification of a scheme reference number does not indicate that HMRC accept that the scheme achieves or is capable of achieving any purported tax advantage.

Warning: You may incur a penalty if you fail to comply with the rules outlined in this section (see section 15).

.

13.2 Promoters must provide scheme reference number to clients

As the promoter of a stamp duty land tax you will have been provided with a reference number by HMRC because you disclosed a stamp duty land tax scheme.

You must:

- provide it to any other person (your "client") to whom you provide, or have provided, services in connection with the disclosed scheme or any scheme that is substantially the same. Your client may be the person who is intended to obtain the tax advantage or he may be a third party (ie a person who does not himself enter into the scheme and/or expect to obtain a tax advantage);
- do so using form AAG 6 available by clicking the relevant links on the Anti-Avoidance Group website at www.hmrc.gov.uk/aiu/index.htm; and
- do so within 30 days of either being provided with the scheme reference number or becoming aware of any transaction that forms part of the scheme, whichever is later.

While there is no obligation to do so, you may find it more convenient to provide the number to a client when you make the scheme available rather than wait until it has been implemented. If, but only if, you do so using the form AAG 6, you need not re-notify the number to your client when you become aware of a transaction forming part of the scheme.

If you have been provided with more than one scheme reference number in relation to any given scheme, you only need provide one of those numbers to your client.

13.3 Clients must provide scheme reference number to parties to the scheme

As explained at paragraph 13.2 above, if a promoter provides, or has provided, you with services in connection with a disclosable scheme, he may also provide you with a scheme reference number. This should be given to you on an HMRC form AAG6 (SDLT) containing guidance about when and how to report the reference number to HMRC or provide it to other parties.

When you have been provided with a scheme reference number, by whatever route, you must:

- provide it to any other person who you might reasonably expect to be a party to, and whom might reasonably be expected to gain a tax advantage from, the scheme;
- do so using form AAG 6 available by clicking the relevant links on the Anti-Avoidance Group website at www.hmrc.gov.uk/aiu/index.htm; and
- do so within 30 days of either being provided with the scheme reference number by the promoter or becoming aware of any transaction that forms part of the scheme, whichever is the later.

13.3.1 Reasonable expectation

Your obligation, as the client of a promoter, to pass a scheme reference number to third parties only applies when you have sufficient commercial connection with that party to have a reasonable expectation that they will gain a tax advantage from the scheme. As examples:

- You are a parent company which purchases a scheme and makes it available for subsidiary companies to use but without yourself becoming a party to the arrangements that make up the scheme. You must provide the scheme reference number to those subsidiaries that are expected to gain a tax advantage from the scheme.
- You are a property developer which purchases a scheme and makes it available to property purchasers but without yourself becoming a party to the arrangements that make up the scheme. You must provide the scheme reference number to those purchasers that are expected to gain a tax advantage from the scheme.

You are not required to provide a number to a person simply because, for example, you learn about their use of a scheme through hearsay, reading about it in the press or a Tribunal decision, etc.

13.4 Purchaser receiving a stamp duty land tax advantage must include the scheme reference number and other information on form AAG 4 (SDLT)

As explained at paragraphs 13.2 and 13.3, if you expect to obtain a tax advantage from a tax avoidance scheme, the promoter of the scheme or his client may provide you with a scheme reference number. This should be provided to you on an HMRC form AAG6 (SDLT), which contains guidance about when and how to report the reference number to HMRC. In some cases you may receive the number directly from HMRC as a result of disclosing the scheme yourself (see paragraphs 3.7 to 3.9).

The scheme reference number and additional information specified at paragraph 13.4.2 must be entered on form AAG 4 (SDLT). This is the only means by which HMRC may be notified of a stamp duty land tax scheme. The Scheme reference number for stamp duty land tax schemes should never be entered on either an SDLT 1 return or the user's tax return. Such an entry will not discharge a scheme user's obligations under DOTAS.

If you are a purchaser for stamp duty land tax purposes (see SDLTM07200 for definition) and expect to receive a stamp duty land tax advantage you must within the time limit detailed at 13.4.1:

- include the number on form AAG 4 (SDLT) and
- provide the information specified in paragraph 13.4.2

The purchaser is limited to a person who is either a party to the transaction or has provided consideration for that transaction. The term purchaser is defined as the person who acquires the subject matter of a land transaction and includes a tenant if the interest in land is a grant of a lease (S43 9780754542087).

When stamp duty land tax group relief is withdrawn, group relief may be recovered from a person other than the purchaser (Schedule 7, Para 5, Finance Act 2003, SDLTM 23100). The obligation to disclose a Scheme Reference Number falls only on the purchaser. Any other person from whom Group Relief may be recovered [is concerned] . . . whilst they may be in receipt of a stamp duty land tax advantage, they are not obliged to be passed a Scheme Reference Number nor to disclose that to HMRC.

13.4.1 When to enter information on form AAG 4 (SDLT)

The information detailed at paragraph 13.4.2 must be entered on form AAG 4 when you receive the number or you enter into the first land transaction in connection with the arrangements, whichever is later.

You must continue to do this for each subsequent transaction in which you expect to obtain a stamp duty land tax advantage from the scheme.

Form AAG 4 (SDLT) should be sent to the Anti-Avoidance Group (Intelligence) within HMRC (the address can be found at paragraph 1.8) in sufficient time for it to be received within 30 days of the later of the following two events:

- receiving a scheme reference number from the promoter or another party to the scheme;
- the effective date of the first land transaction which forms part of the scheme

The effective date takes its normal meaning for stamp duty land tax purposes (S119 Finance Act 2003). The general rule is when the land transaction is completed but there are exceptions and further guidance may be found in the Stamp Duty Land Tax Manual at SDLTM 7600.

13.4.2 What to enter on form AAG 4 (SDLT)

- the scheme reference number;
- the name and address of the person providing the scheme reference number (the person who is expecting to obtain a stamp duty land tax advantage);
- the address of the property forming the subject of the arrangements (see 13.4.3);
- the title number (or numbers) of the property (see 13.4.4);
- the unique transaction reference number which is found, for a paper return, in the 'Reference' box attached to the payslip on the Land Transaction Return (Form SDLT 1) or, for an electronic return, on the electronic SDLT submission receipt.
- the market value of the property (see 13.4.5);
- the effective date (see 13.4.1) of the first land transaction which forms part of the arrangement;
- the name of the person providing the declaration as to the accuracy and completeness of the notification (see 13.4.6); and
- the capacity in which that person is acting (for example purchaser, company secretary etc).

Regardless of who has provided the information the signatory should be that of the purchaser.

13.4.3 Address of property

Give the full address including the postcode if there is one. If the property does not have a postcode or a building number then you must provide sufficient information of the nature and location of the property to enable it to be accurately identified.

13.4.4 Title number

If the property or properties that is/are the subject(s) of the arrangements is/are registered give the title number for the property. If no title number has been allocated then this information need not be provided.

13.4.5 Market value

The figure to be entered for the market value is the Open Market Value of all the property on which a stamp duty land tax advantage is to be obtained assuming it has been purchased without the benefit of the stamp duty land tax arrangements. Market value takes the statutory definition for stamp duty land tax purposes at S118 Finance Act 2003. This in turn is tied to Sections 272 to 274 of the Taxation of Capital Gains Tax Act 1992.

The market value of an asset is the price which that asset might reasonably be expected to fetch on a sale in the open market. In a normal land transaction such a value will normally have been arrived at by an independent valuer before the transaction has been entered into and so should be readily available.

If, exceptionally, such a value has not been obtained then a reasoned estimate is acceptable bearing in mind that HMRC requires the information in order to assess the likely tax at risk. Submission of the AAG4 (SDLT) should not be held up because a valuation has not been obtained nor should the market value be omitted. Either of these courses of action could render the user liable to a penalty.

13.4.6 Declaration as to accuracy and completeness.

The person obtaining the stamp duty land tax advantage from the arrangements should sign the declaration. This will usually be the purchaser. Whilst in the majority of cases the return is likely to be drafted and submitted by a solicitor, licensed conveyancer, legal executive or accountant, it is the responsibility of the person obtaining the advantage to ensure that the information given on the AAG 4 (SDLT) is complete and correct and sign the declaration accordingly.

13.4.7 Expectation of obtaining a tax advantage

If you are a party to a scheme, have been provided with a scheme reference number, but do not expect to obtain a tax advantage (for example, because the advantage is expected to be obtained by another person or you have not yet decided to implement the scheme), you need not include the number on form AAG 4 (SDLT) unless and until such time as your expectation changes.

13.4.8 Partnerships Finance Act 2003, Schedule 15, Part 3

Where the arrangements involve a partnership all of the partners have joint and several liability for any stamp duty land tax subject to special provisions. Further guidance may be found at www.hmrc.gov.uk/so/pftmanual.htm. Whilst more than one partner might therefore be expected to receive a stamp duty land tax advantage, HMRC will accept a single joint notification, signed by the representative partner on behalf of all of the liable partners, rather than each making their own notification.

13.5 How to obtain and submit form AAG 4 (SDLT)

You can obtain and submit form AAG 4 (SDLT) online by clicking the relevant links on the Anti-Avoidance Group website at www.hmrc.gov.uk/aiu/index.htm. You can obtain PDF and WORD versions of the forms by clicking the relevant links on the same web page, or by contacting the Anti-Avoidance Group (Intelligence) within HMRC at the address shown at paragraph 1.8. Alternatively, paper copies can be obtained from the order line by telephoning 08459 000404 or by faxing on 08459 000604. The completed forms should be sent by either post or e-mail to the Anti-Avoidance Group (Intelligence) at the address shown at paragraph 1.8.

Part II ST

14. INFORMATION POWERS

14.1 Summary

Information powers introduced in 2007 enable HMRC to:

- enquire into the reasons why a promoter has not disclosed a scheme;
- enforce disclosure in appropriate cases; and
- call for more information where a disclosure is incomplete.

These provisions are mostly exercisable through the Tribunal (see paragraph 14.6 below) and provide a mechanism for resolving disagreements as to whether a scheme is required to be disclosed.

14.2 Enquiries into non-disclosure of a scheme

14.2.1 Explaining why a scheme has not been disclosed (FA 2004, s 313A and SI 2004/1864, reg 8A(1))

HMRC can, by written notice, require a person suspected of being the promoter of a notifiable scheme to state whether, in his opinion, he is required to disclose the scheme. The notice will specify the scheme in relation to which the promoter's opinion and reasons are sought.

If the person does not consider there to be a disclosure obligation he must provide a full explanation as to why this is the case. In doing so it is insufficient for the reply to simply refer to the fact that a lawyer or other professional has given an opinion to that effect. Instead it must engage with the relevant legal tests. For example, where it is asserted that the obtaining of a tax (or National Insurance contribution) advantage is not a "main benefit" of a scheme, the response must include an identification of the various benefits and how they had been measured relative to the advantage.

Where it is asserted that the scheme does not fall within any of the hallmarks, sufficient information must be provided to enable HMRC to confirm the assertion.

The opinion and reasons must be provided by the 10th day after the date of the notice or any longer period directed by HMRC. Failure to do so may result in a penalty (see section 15).

14.2.2 Orders for supplementary information or documents (FA 2004, s 313B and SI 2004/1864, reg 8A(2))

HMRC may apply to the Special Commissioners for an order that a person provide specified information or documents in support of his stated reasons as to why a scheme is not disclosable, whether or not the reasons were given in response to a notice under s 313A (see paragraph 14.2.1 above).

The information must be provided by the 14th day after the date of the order or any longer period directed by HMRC. Failure to do so may result in a penalty (see section 15.1).

14.3 Enforcing disclosure

14.3.1 Orders stating a scheme is disclosable (FA 2004, s 314A; TMA 1970, s 98C(2E))

HMRC may, in relation to a specified promoter, apply to a Tribunal for an order stating that a scheme is disclosable.

The Tribunal can only make an order if they are satisfied on the evidence that the scheme is indeed disclosable.

As an order has the effect of confirming that a scheme is, and was always, disclosable under s 308, HMRC may, subject to "reasonable excuse" considerations, seek a late notification penalty of up to £5,000 under the existing penalty regime – see paragraphs 15.1 and 15.3.

Once a late disclosure penalty is awarded, should non-disclosure continue after the tenth day from when the order is made, the maximum daily penalty rate will increase. The increased daily maximum will be £5,000. After the tenth day the specified promoter cannot, in respect of any time after then, rely on doubt as to notifiability as a reasonable excuse for failing to disclose.

14.3.2 Orders deeming a scheme to be disclosable (FA 2004, s 306A)

HMRC may, in relation to a specified promoter, apply to the Tribunal for an order that a scheme is to be treated as disclosable.

The Tribunal can only make an order if they are satisfied that HMRC have reasonable grounds for suspecting that the scheme is disclosable and have taken all reasonable steps to establish whether it is.

Grounds for suspicion may include:

- the fact that the arrangements fall with any "hallmark" prescribed in the relevant regulations;
- an attempt to avoid or delay complying with s 313A or s 313B; or
- a failure to comply with s 313A or s 313B in relation to another scheme.

The effect of an order is that a scheme is deemed to be disclosable under s 308 and must be disclosed. The disclosure must be made by the 10th day after the date of the order. Failure to do so may result in HMRC applying to the Special Commissioners for a late notification penalty under the existing penalty regime in section 98C of the Taxes Management Act 1970. If the failure continues after the initial penalty has been imposed, an additional penalty of up to £5,000 per day may be imposed.

However, even if disclosure is made within the time period described above, if HMRC can nevertheless demonstrate the information was always disclosable and has been provided later than the normal disclosure due date, an application to the Tribunal for a late notification penalty may still be made.

14.4 Incomplete disclosures (FA 2004, s 308A)

If HMRC believe that a promoter has not provided all the prescribed information in relation to a disclosure, they may apply to the Tribunal for an order that the promoter provide specified information and/or related documents.

The Tribunal can make an order only if they are satisfied that HMRC have reasonable grounds for suspecting that the specified information or documents form part of, or will support or explain, the prescribed information.

The effect of an order is that the specified information and/or documents must be provided to HMRC in the same way as if it were prescribed information. This must be done by the 10th day after the date of the order. Failure to do so may result in HMRC applying to the Tribunal for a late notification penalty. If the failure continues after the initial penalty has been imposed an additional penalty of up to £600 per day may be imposed.

If the information or documentation is provided within the time period described above but HMRC nevertheless believe the information was always disclosable as prescribed information, and has been provided later than the normal disclosure due date, an application to the Tribunal for a late notification penalty may still be made.

14.5 Invoking the powers

In order to use the powers described above, HMRC must have reasonable grounds to suspect that the promoter has been non-compliant in relation to a particular scheme. In the majority of cases, HMRC expect to be able to resolve the issue in an informal way, with use of the powers limited to those occasions where a promoter does not provide sufficient information to resolve the issue or where there is a genuine dispute as to notifiability which can only be resolved before the Tribunal.

The powers will be exercised only by officers within HMRC's Anti-Avoidance Group.

14.6 Application hearings

The majority of the powers described above are dependant upon the Tribunal making a relevant order following an application from HMRC. The precise procedure is a matter for the Tribunal. However, when making an application, HMRC will notify the potentially affected promoter at the same time.

15. PENALTIES

15.1 Penalties for non-compliance by scheme promoters (TMA 1970, s 98C(1))

A promoter is liable to a penalty if he fails to comply with his obligations. A penalty may be charged where, without reasonable excuse, he fails to:

- make a disclosure to the Anti-Avoidance Group in HMRC when required to do so (see paragraph 3.1);
- make the disclosure in the prescribed form and manner (see paragraph 1.5.3);

- provide his client with the scheme reference number, when required to do so – the number may have been obtained from either HMRC or (other than for stamp duty land tax schemes) from a co-promoter who has disclosed the scheme (see paragraphs 10.2.2, 12.1 and 12.2);
- provide the reference number using the specified HMRC form AAG 6 (see paragraphs 12.1 and 12.3); or
- respond to enquiries (see paragraph 14.2).

There is an initial penalty and a daily penalty. The maximum initial penalty is £5,000 for each failure. If the failure continues after the initial penalty has been imposed then an additional penalty of up to £600 per day can be imposed.

The Tribunal are responsible for imposing any initial penalty and there is a right of appeal.

Failures to disclose after the making of an order from the Tribunal that a scheme is, or is to be treated as, disclosable can be subject to increased daily penalties (see paragraph 14.3).

15.2 Penalties for non-compliance by client of promoter or parties to the scheme (TMA 1970, s 98C(1) and (3))

A client of a promoter or a party to a scheme is liable to a penalty if he fails to comply with his obligations. A penalty may be charged where, without reasonable excuse, he fails to:

- disclose a scheme when required to do so (the obligation may arise as a result of the promoter being offshore or a lawyer who is unable to make a full disclosure, or when the scheme is devised "in-house" – see paragraphs 3.1 and 3.7 to 3.9);
- make the disclosure in the prescribed form and manner (see paragraph 1.5.3);
- where he is a client of the promoter, provide the scheme reference number to any other person whom he might reasonably expect to be a party to, and who might reasonably be expected to gain a tax advantage from, the scheme, when required to do so (see paragraphs 12.1 and 12.3);
- where he is a client of the promoter, provide the reference number to another person using the specified HMRC form AAG 6 (see paragraphs 12.1 and 12.3); or
- where he is a party to the scheme, enter on his tax return or form AAG4 (as appropriate) the scheme reference number and the last day of the year of assessment, tax year, accounting period or earnings period (as the case may be) in which, or the date on which, he expects the advantage to be obtained (see paragraph 12.4).

15.2.1 Failure to disclose a scheme or pass on number, etc.

The penalty is the same as for promoters – i.e. an initial penalty of £5,000 and daily penalties of up to £600 per day for continued failure.

15.2.2 Failure to enter the scheme reference number on return, etc. The penalty will increase for each failure as follows:

- 1st failure penalty £100
- 2nd failure penalty £500
- 3rd and subsequent failure penalty £1000

There is a right of appeal against the penalty to the Tribunal and onwards to the High Court on a point of law.

It is important to note that the penalty is per failure per scheme and not per year.

15.2.3 Stamp duty land tax schemes

Stamp duty land tax schemes are always notified on form AAG4 (SDLT) so there is no requirement to enter a scheme reference number on a stamp duty land tax return. HMRC will only require one AAG 4 (SDLT) from a partnership in respect of each notifiable arrangement, regardless of the number of partners. All partners are jointly and severally liable for any penalties arising from any non-compliance as detailed at 15.2 above.

15.3 Reasonable excuse (TMA 1970, s 118(2))

No penalty is due where the promoter, client or party to a scheme (as applicable) has a reasonable excuse and the failure to comply is remedied within a reasonable time after the excuse ceased. Consideration of reasonable excuse will include whether the person has clearly followed current guidance or has otherwise made a reasonable judgement in determining whether or not a disclosure is required.

. . .

APPENDIX 14.

SD7: PENALTIES FOR LATE LAND TRANSACTION RETURNS AND INTEREST CHARGES FOR LATE PAYMENTS OF STAMP DUTY LAND TAX (SDLT)

Contents

INTRODUCTION

This publication tells you about additional charges that you may incur if you do not complete and send your land transaction return or payments on time. It also explains how to avoid these charges and what you can do to appeal against penalties and get help with your return if you need it.

PENALTIES AND INTEREST SUMMARY

Penalties

Penalties are a fixed charge imposed when an SDLT 1 form is received at HMRC after the filing date. These are automatically generated when the form has not been submitted by the filing date.

Penalties are charged at set rates depending on the date the return is received.

For example, if the SDLT 1 is returned after the filing date but within the next 90 days, there is a £100 fixed penalty charge. If it is returned over 120 days later than the effective date, a £200 penalty is charged.

In addition, should it be over 12 months late, a tax-based penalty is due (up to 100 per cent of the tax).

You may appeal against a penalty charge if you believe you have sufficient reason for the return being late.

Interest

Interest is [a] separate charge to penalties that will be applied when we have not received a payment of SDLT on time. For the purposes of interest calculations, please note that interest will begin to accrue from and [includes] the day after [the] filing date.

Interest is a legislative charge designed to recompense the Chancellor of the Exchequer for money it was legally entitled to, but which it was denied the benefits of.

As such it is not a penalty.

Because this is a mandatory charge, there is no appeal process for interest.

Part II ST

When should a land transaction return be delivered?

A land transaction return should be delivered so that we receive it by the "filing date". This is **30 days** after the effective date of the transaction. The effective date is normally the completion date of the transaction, whether or not a document shows this.

However, if a contract is substantially performed before completion, the date that "substantial performance" takes place is the effective date. Broadly, substantial performance is when:

- payment of a substantial amount of the consideration (generally 90 per cent of the total amount) is made;
- the purchaser takes possession of the property;
- the first payment of rent is made;
- option or right of pre-emption is acquired.

What happens if my land transaction return is late?

If you miss the filing date, you will be charged a penalty.

WHEN PENALTIES OCCUR

Fixed penalties

If we do not receive the return within 30 days of the effective date but within three months of the 30-day limit, you will be charged a £100 penalty. If your return is more than three months late you will be charged a penalty of £200. If you pay the tax late, you will also be charged interest.

Tax-based penalties

If your return is more than a year late, you may be liable to a tax-based penalty, which can be up to 100 per cent of the amount of SDLT due on the return.

How will I know if I have been charged a penalty?

If you are charged a penalty, we will send you a formal notice. The penalty is due for payment 30 days after the date of the notice. We may charge interest on any penalties paid late.

What if I receive a penalty notice?

If you have not already done so, you should:

- do what is necessary to send in your return as soon as you can, to avoid further possible penalties;
- pay the penalty on time, to avoid any interest charge.

Checking your notice for a tax-based penalty

Check that you agree the calculation shown on the notice. Where a tax-based penalty is imposed, we will normally have written to you (or your tax adviser, if you have one) about it and shown how it has been calculated.

What if the taxpayer has died?

If you are acting on behalf of a taxpayer who has died since submitting a return for which we have charged a penalty, please tell us the date of death and give your details.

APPEALS AND COMMISSIONERS

Can I appeal?

You can appeal against a penalty if you think you have "exceptional circumstances" for not sending your return on time.

You should read the guidelines on what we agree are exceptional circumstances before you make an appeal.

You may want to appeal if you think that the calculation of a tax-based penalty is wrong.

You should make your appeal to the Commissioners, although you should send your application to appeal against the penalty determination (form SDLT46) to us. This enables us to consider whether we agree you have exceptional circumstances. If we do, there is no need for the Commissioners to consider your appeal. If we do not, we will arrange for the Commissioners to hear your appeal.

How do I appeal?

You can appeal in writing or by completing the form we send with each penalty notice within 30 days of the date of the penalty notice.

Appealing because you have exceptional circumstances

If you appeal because you think you have exceptional circumstances for not sending your return by the deadline, you need to give us full details of your excuse, including dates of when events happened. When the situation causing the exceptional circumstances ends we expect the land transaction to be sent to us immediately, but normally we will make reasonable adjustments on a case by case basis.

Do I need to pay the penalty if I am appealing?

To avoid any interest which may be charged on the late payment of a penalty you should pay the penalty even if you are appealing against it. If you pay it and your appeal succeeds, we will repay the penalty with interest.

If your appeal succeeds and you have not paid the penalty, no interest charge arises. But, if your appeal does not succeed and you have not paid the penalty, you may be charged interest from 30 days after the date of the penalty notice until the day you pay it.

If we agree you have exceptional circumstances

If we agree that your circumstances are exceptional, we will write to tell you and cancel the penalty.

If we do not agree you have exceptional circumstances

If we do not agree that your circumstances are exceptional, we will explain why and ask if you accept this. If you still think you have a good reason, the Commissioners, who are an independent tribunal, will consider your appeal at an appeal hearing. They listen to the arguments of both sides and decide if you have exceptional circumstances.

We usually arrange the hearing, but you can do it yourself if you wish.

Commissioners

There are two bodies of Commissioners, General and Special, and both are independent of the HM Revenue & Customs (HMRC). It is possible for you to elect the General or Special Commissioners hear your appeal. Unless you or HMRC request otherwise, your appeal will normally be heard by the General Commissioners. If your case is unusually complicated, technical or lengthy, or if either you or HMRC so choose, it will normally be heard by the Special Commissioners.

The General Commissioners are appointed by the Lord Chancellor—rather like local magistrates—to deal with cases arising in a particular area, or Division. They are assisted by a Clerk who is often a solicitor or accountant.

Normally, the General Commissioners consider appeals. When you appeal, you must choose whether you want the General Commissioners for:

- the area where the property (which is the subject matter of the land transaction return) is situated;
- where you live;
- where your business is.

They usually hold their proceedings in public, but they can suggest that all or part of a hearing should be in private if justice so requires. Likewise, if you want your hearing to be in private, you should ask the Clerk to the Commissioners who will hear your appeal.

Alternatively, you can choose to have your appeal considered by the Special Commissioners.

The Special Commissioners are a special tribunal with full-time members. Their meetings are normally public and held in London, Manchester, Belfast or Edinburgh. If you need more details about the Commissioners, you can get the Department for Constitutional Affairs leaflet "Tax Appeals. A guide to appealing against decisions of the HM Revenue & Customs on tax and other matters" from any HMRC Enquiry Centre.

REASONS FOR NOT MEETING THE DEADLINE

What are exceptional circumstances?

We consider each case on its own merits.

In our view, you only have a reasonable excuse where some exceptional event, beyond your control, has prevented you:

- sending your completed return to us;
- making other arrangements to do this by the deadline.

If you disagree with our view of what are exceptional circumstances then you can appeal to the independent Commissioners.

Examples of what we may agree as exceptional circumstances

Lost or delayed in the post

You should allow sufficient time for your return to reach us by the due date. However, where it was posted in good time, we would agree as a reasonable excuse an unforeseen event, which disrupted the normal postal service and led to the loss or delay of your return. For example:

- fire or flood at the Post Office where the return was handled;
- prolonged industrial action within the Post Office or other document carrier, which occurred after the return had been posted to us or delivered to the document carrier to send to us.

Serious illness of your adviser

We would agree that serious acute illness, such as a heart attack, stroke, or other life threatening condition that prevented your adviser from controlling his or her business and private affairs are exceptional circumstances.

Death of your adviser

We would agree that the death of the adviser dealing with your return is an exceptional circumstance.

When the circumstances causing the exception cease the position must be remedied immediately.

What are not exceptional circumstances?

It is your responsibility to gather all the necessary information to ensure that your return is completed and sent by the deadline.

We are unlikely to agree you were prevented from sending in your return if you were able to manage the rest of your private or business affairs during the period which you claim to be covered by exceptional circumstances.

Examples of what we would not agree as exceptional circumstances

Land transaction return is too difficult

We would not agree as exceptional circumstances your opinion that the return is too difficult to complete. If you have difficulties, you should ask for help as early as possible from

- the stamp taxes helpline on 0845 6030135;
- a tax adviser.

Pressure of work

We would not agree that pressures of work are exceptional circumstances.

Adviser is waiting for payment

We would not agree as exceptional circumstances that the reason for not submitting your return on time is because your adviser is waiting for payment or the SDLT is being paid by another firm of advisers.

Waiting for a valuation

We would not agree that waiting for a valuation are exceptional circumstances for not sending your return on time. You should submit one with a best estimate of the valuation.

Delay caused by vendor's adviser

If the delay is due to the vendor's adviser, and this means that your adviser is unable to submit the return within 30 days, we would not accept this as exceptional circumstances.

Return cannot be signed as you are abroad

We expect you to submit the return within the deadline. Although your adviser cannot sign the return, your Power of Attorney can. They must indicate they are signing in that capacity within box 71, by writing "Power of Attorney" underneath their signature. (The Deed of Attorney does not need to be submitted with the return.)

APPENDIX 15. REVENUE AND CUSTOMS BRIEFS

REVENUE & CUSTOMS BRIEF 44/07
LITIGATION AND SETTLEMENTS STRATEGY (LSS)

The Litigation and Settlements Strategy (LSS) [available at www.hmrc.gov.uk/practitioners/lss.pdf] is relevant to all aspects of how HMRC enters into, handles and settles disputes about any of our taxes, duties or credits. It sets out principles for bringing tax disputes to a conclusion, whether by agreement with the taxpayer, or by litigation, i.e statutory appeal to an independent body, including the General or Special Commissioners, the VAT Tribunal, or the courts.

The aim of the LSS is to ensure that we conduct disputes in a way that is professional, effective and that supports HMRC's objectives to close the tax gap and provide customers with a clear understanding of the law.

The central themes of the LSS are:

- Seek non-confrontational solutions where possible.
- Focus on issues that will best serve HMRC's goal of tax gap reduction.
- Choose cases for their wider impact, as well as for their own value.
- Where we have a strong case we should seek full value from settlement, or take the matter to litigation.
- Do not pursue weak arguments.
- Team-work cases with colleagues, including those in other parts of HMRC.

CONTACT INFORMATION

Andrew Page (HMRC Central Compliance) [andrew.page@hmrc.gsi.gov.uk].

Issued 11 June 2007.

REVENUE & CUSTOMS BRIEF 10/09
TRIBUNALS REFORM – CHANGES TO THE TAX APPEALS SYSTEM AND NEW INTERNAL REVIEW PROCESS

SUMMARY

This Revenue & Customs Brief outlines the new tax appeals system and HMRC's new internal review process, due to be implemented from 1 April 2009.

INTRODUCTION

From 1 April 2009 there will be a major change to the current system of tax tribunals. To coincide with this, HMRC is changing the way it handles disagreements about tax. The new review process will help provide a more consistent approach to the way we seek to resolve disputes with those who disagree with appealable tax decisions made by HMRC.

At the moment, there are three main tribunals which deal with appeals against HMRC decisions. From April, these tribunals will be abolished and replaced by a single Tax Chamber in the First-tier Tribunal which will consider all disputes and hear appeals in relation to both direct and indirect tax.

NEW TRIBUNAL

The Tribunals, Courts and Enforcement Act 2007 introduced two new bodies, the First-tier Tribunal and the Upper Tribunal. Over time most existing tribunal jurisdictions including the

Part II ST

tax tribunals will be transferring into the new bodies. The new system went live on 3 November 2008 when appeals formerly heard by the Social Security Appeals Tribunal successfully transferred to the First-tier Social Entitlement Chamber. These new statutory bodies are administered by the Tribunals Service which is part of the Ministry of Justice.

Both First-tier and Upper Tribunals are divided into "chambers" where similar types of appeal are heard.

Tax appeals will transfer to a new First-tier Chamber, to be known as the Tax Chamber, on 1 April. A right of appeal against decisions of the First-tier Tax Chamber will also be created to a new chamber in the Upper Tribunal to be known as the Finance and Tax Chamber.

Tax appeals will transfer to a new First-tier Chamber, to be known as the Tax Chamber, on 1 April. A right of appeal against decisions of the First-tier Tax Chamber will also be created to a new chamber in the Upper Tribunal to be known as the Finance and Tax Chamber.

The First-tier Tribunal will deal with the vast majority of appeals, apart from a very small number of the most complex appeals that will transfer to the Upper Tribunal at first instance. The Upper Tribunal will mainly deal with appeals against decisions of the First-tier Tribunal. Work within each tier of the tribunal will be organised into specialist chambers, one of which will deal with tax.

The reforms will affect everyone who disagrees with one of our tax decisions and may wish to have it reviewed, or to make an appeal. As part of the reforms, the General Commissioners and Special Commissioners of Income Tax, the Section 706/704 Tribunal and the VAT & Duties Tribunals will be abolished after 31 March 2009 and their existing functions will transfer into the new First-tier Tax Chamber.

Some straightforward appeals will in future usually be dealt with on paper without the need for HMRC or customers to attend a hearing.

Where a hearing is needed the Tribunals Service will arrange this. Most appeals will be heard at one of a national network of tribunal hearing centres.

INTERNAL REVIEW

To coincide with tribunal reform, our customers will be entitled to request an internal review of appealable tax decisions. This new legal right to a review will replace reconsiderations and mandatory reviews in indirect taxes (mandatory reviews will remain for decisions about the restoration of seized goods).

Reviews will be optional and will be done by a trained review officer, who has not previously been involved with that decision, who will be able to offer a balanced and objective view. In the vast majority of cases the review officer will be outside the immediate line management chain of the decision maker.

We must complete reviews within 45 days (unless another period is agreed with the customer). If customers do not want a review, or if they do not agree with the result of the review, they can appeal to the tribunal for a decision.

FURTHER INFORMATION

You can find out more about tribunals reform and internal reviews from the Tribunals Reform Project web pages [at www.hmrc.gov.uk/about/tribunals-reform.htm] and more about changes to the tax tribunals from the Tribunals Service website [at www.financeandtaxtribunals.gov.uk/taxAppealsModernisation.htm].

Index

VALUE ADDED TAX: PART 1A UK LEGISLATION

C

G

H

T

Index

VALUE ADDED TAX: PART 1B EU LEGISLATION

Index

STAMP DUTY, SDRT AND SDLT

A

E

F

G

H

I

T

U

V

W